Hargus Taylor
1-20-58

Encyclopedia of SOUTHERN BAPTISTS

Encyclopedia of SOUTHERN BAPTISTS

II

Ker - Yu

BROADMAN PRESS
Nashville, Tennessee

Library of Congress Catalog Card Number: 58-5417
Printed in the United States of America
7.5057K.S.P.

KERFOOT, FRANKLIN HOWARD (b. Llewellyn, Clark County, Va., Aug. 29, 1847; d. Atlanta, Ga., June 22, 1901). Minister, theological professor, mission secretary. After receiving elementary education Kerfoot enlisted in the Confederate Army at 18, serving only a brief period, and in 1866 he entered Columbian College in Washington, D. C., where he completed six years' work in three years and earned M.S. and LL.B. degrees. Kerfoot attended Southern Baptist Theological Seminary, Greenville, S. C., for more than a year, after which he rested a year because of failing health; he then entered Crozer Seminary in 1871 and graduated at the end of one session. As agent for Southern Seminary, he traveled in Texas and Missouri. In 1874, after a visit to Egypt and the Holy Land, Kerfoot studied at the University of Leipzig, and when he returned to America the following year, he was ordained by the church at Midway, Ky. He served pastorates at Midway and Forks of Elkhorn churches in Kentucky (1875–77), Eutaw Place Baptist Church, Baltimore, Md. (1877–83), and Strong Place Baptist Church, Brooklyn, N. Y. (1883–86), where he was forced to resign because of an injury which occurred when a platform on which he was seated collapsed. Entering Southern Seminary again in 1886, Kerfoot attended one session, at the end of which he was elected co-professor of systematic theology. In 1889 he became full professor, succeeding James Petigru Boyce (*q.v.*) in the Chair of Systematic Theology and also as treasurer, because of his financial ability. Kerfoot resigned after 10 years to become corresponding secretary of the Home Mission Board, Atlanta, Ga., where he remained from 1899 until his death. When Kerfoot left Kentucky he was moderator of the General Convention of Baptists in the state. Kerfoot's published works include several of his addresses; *Parliamentary Law* (1897); and a revision of James Petigru Boyce's *Abstract of Systematic Theology* (1899). LEO T. CRISMON

KERR, JOHN (b. Caswell County, N. C., Aug. 14, 1782; d. Danville, Va., Sept. 29, 1842). Evangelist and pastor. Licensed to preach in 1801, Kerr became a traveling evangelist in South Carolina, Georgia, and Virginia. In 1805, after marrying in Halifax County, Va., he settled there and continued his ministry. He served two terms in the national Congress (1813–17), then returned to Halifax County and preached at Arbor and Miry Creek Baptist churches until 1825, when he became pastor of the First Baptist Church of Richmond, Va.

Under his ministry the Richmond church had large congregations and stirring revivals. In 1831 the church reported 555 baptisms. During the winter of 1829–30 Alexander Campbell, a member of the State Constitutional Convention then meeting in the First Baptist Church, preached many times for the church at Kerr's invitation. The church experienced a schism over his views. Later, Kerr was chairman of the committee that drafted the "Dover Decrees" against Campbellism, and shortly thereafter, 1833, he resigned to engage in evangelistic work. After moving to Danville, Va., he became co-pastor of the church there. Kerr was the first president of the Virginia Baptist Education Society. He served as president of the Baptist General Association of Virginia 1827–34 (except 1830). BEN LYNES

KERSEY CHILDREN'S HOME, OGBOMOSHO. See NIGERIA, MISSION IN.

KESLER, MARTIN LUTHER (b. Iredell County, N. C., Aug. 25, 1858; d. Thomasville, N. C., Aug. 19, 1932). Superintendent of orphanage. Son of Charles Washington and Elizabeth Keziah (Lazenby) Kesler, he attended Cool Springs and Moravian Falls academies, Wake Forest College (A.B., 1888; D.D., 1916), and Southern Baptist Theological Seminary (Th.M., 1891). Kesler held pastorates at Laurinburg and Spring Hill, 1891–96; Red Springs, 1893–96; High Point, 1896–98; Scotland Neck, 1898–1903; and Morganton, 1903–05. He was general manager of Thomasville Baptist Orphanage (cf. Mills Home) from Sept. 1, 1905, until his death nearly 27 years later. He served as member of the State Board of Public Welfare, president of the Tri-State Orphanage Conference, director of the Child Welfare League of America, and leader in organization and president of the Southern Baptist Social Service Association. He was recognized for his contribution to orphanages of the state and the nation. He was trustee of Wake Forest and Meredith colleges and member of the following boards: Missions and Sunday Schools of the North Carolina Baptist State Convention, Baptist Hospital, Southern Baptist Assembly, State School for the Blind, and Davidson County School Board. Kesler married Ethel Browne, and they had three children. I. G. GREER

KIAMICHI ASSEMBLY. Located three miles north of Talihina, Okla., developed from the pastors and laymen's retreat and Y.W.A. and G.A. camps held at Robbers Cave State Park, 1938–41. It was incorporated July 22, 1941, and held its first meeting beginning July 22, 1942. The original 85 acres with 13 modern cabins cost $5,000. The 1955 value of the property, 225 acres and 65 buildings, was $75,000. Lease holders constitute the assembly board which meets annually at the time the assembly is in session in July. Interim business is directed by an executive committee of seven men.

HERBERT M. PIERCE

KILPATRICK, JAMES HALL TANNER (b. Iredell County, N. C., July 24, 1788; d. Hephzibah, Ga., Jan. 9, 1869). Minister. He studied at various academies, and lastly under the famous Moses Waddel in South Carolina.

He taught at various places in Louisiana and fought in the 1815 Battle of New Orleans. In 1816 he was married to Sarah Adeline Tanner and had one son. Though born a Presbyterian, he restudied the matter of baptism and in 1817 joined a Baptist church, and soon afterward was licensed to preach. In 1820 his wife died and he left to visit his native home, but he was persuaded to preach a year at Robertville, S. C. Attending a meeting at Big Buckhead, Burke County, Ga., in 1822, he met and married Harriet Eliza Jones and settled there. Five children were born to them, including Washington Lafayette Kilpatrick (*q.v.*) and James Hines Kilpatrick (*q.v.*).

The Hephzibah Association in 1822 was bitterly antimissionary, but in 13 years, mainly through the efforts of Kilpatrick and Joshua Key, the association joined the Georgia Baptist convention and made definite commitment to missions.

Kilpatrick wrote effectively on baptism and preached strongly against Alexander Campbell's view of communion. He helped to match the Penfield legacy, from which Mercer University eventually came, and was on its first board of trustees. When he died, the association reported: "In his death is extinguished the brightest intellectual life which it has ever been our pride to honor." W. H. KILPATRICK

KILPATRICK, JAMES HINES (b. Burke [now Jenkins] County, Ga., Oct. 18, 1833; d. White Plains, Ga., Mar. 27, 1908). Minister. He received his A.B. degree from Mercer University in 1853, sharing first honor; and his D.D. degree from the same institution in 1882. After teaching a year at White Plains, he was called to the pastorate there Dec. 7, 1854, and was ordained at Hopeful Church (Burke County). The presbytery consisted of Elisha Perryman, Joseph Polhill, and James Hall Tanner Kilpatrick (*q.v.*), his father. He served the White Plains church continuously until his death, meanwhile serving other churches.

On May 9, 1856, he married Cornelia Hall (1837–70) of Greene County, Ga. Five children reached maturity. On Dec. 20, 1870, he married Edna Perrin Heard (1843–1925) of Augusta, Ga. Four children reached maturity.

Active in all Baptist affairs, he served as moderator of Georgia Association, 1871–73, 1888–1907; as president of Georgia Baptist Convention, 1890–95; as trustee of Mercer University, 1891–93, 1896–1908; as trustee of the Southern Baptist Theological Seminary, 1885–1908; as vice-president of the Foreign Mission Board of the Southern Baptist Convention, 1900–03; and as chairman of the order of business committee of the Georgia Baptist Convention, 1900–06.

He published articles on Baptist doctrines. A selection of these was published in 1911 by Georgia Association with a biographic introduction by Lansing Burrows (*q.v.*). W. H. KILPATRICK

KILPATRICK, WASHINGTON LAFAYETTE (b. Burke [now Jenkins] County, Ga., Oct. 18, 1829; d. Hephzibah, Ga., Aug. 3, 1896). Minister. He received the A.B. degree with first honor from Mercer University in 1850 and his D.D. degree from the same institution in 1882. Licensed to preach, 1850, by Penfield Church, he was ordained at Hopeful Church (Burke County) in 1852. The presbytery consisted of James Hall Tanner Kilpatrick (*q.v.*), Joseph Polhill, and Joshua Key. He served several churches, mostly in the Hephzibah Association. He helped to organize the Hephzibah High School and was principal in 1866–77. He was clerk of Hephzibah Association for seven years, moderator for 13 years, and wrote its centennial history in 1894. He was trustee of Mercer University from 1869 to his death and president of the board of trustees from 1887 to his death.

A strong advocate of temperance, he encouraged the passage of the Georgia law forbidding the sale of liquor (outside of incorporated towns) within three miles of a school or church. In 1868 he helped to organize the Walker Association of Negro Churches, whose members, prior to emancipation, had belonged to the Hephzibah Association. In 1878 he organized the Georgia Baptist Historical Society and became its secretary. He married Sarah E. Shick on Apr. 28, 1854, and five of their children reached maturity; on July 24, 1873, he married Emma J. Hudson, and four of their children reached maturity. He was buried at Hephzibah. The Hephzibah church said of him: "It may well be said that he advanced whatever he touched." W. H. KILPATRICK

KIND WORDS SERIES. This designation was originally given to the line of Sunday school periodicals published by the Home Mission Board beginning in 1887 and later taken over by the present Sunday School Board. The name was derived from the Sunday school paper known as *Kind Words,* founded in Greenville, S. C., in 1866, by the first Sunday School Board of the Southern Baptist Convention.

Under the leadership of Basil Manly, Jr. (*q.v.*), and John Albert Broadus (*q.v.*), president and corresponding secretary of that board, *Kind Words* began as a small monthly paper for Sunday school children. In 1868 the board moved to Memphis, and *Kind Words* was issued from there until 1873 when the board was dissolved. The Convention then turned the paper over to the Home Mission Board (at that time called the Board of Domestic Missions), located at Marion, Ala. In 1882 when this board moved to Atlanta, it carried *Kind Words* to Macon, Ga.

In 1886 the Convention voted permission for the Home Mission Board to publish "a full line of graded Sunday school periodicals" with *Kind Words* as the basis. The series was called Kind Words Series of Sunday School Periodicals and consisted of two weeklies (*Kind Words* and *The Child's Gem*), one monthly (*Kind Words Teacher*), and three lesson quarterlies (Advanced, Intermediate, and Primary).

In 1891, when the present Sunday School Board was created by the Convention, the entire Kind Words Series was transferred to the new board, and the name of the series was changed to Convention Series of Sunday School Helps. The first issues from Nashville appeared Jan., 1892, and consisted of *Kind Words, The Child's Gem, Advanced Quarterly, Intermediate Quarterly,* and *Primary Quarterly.*

Of *Kind Words* James Marion Frost (*q.v.*) in 1914 wrote as follows: "This paper may be traced like a golden thread through the annals of the Southern Baptist Convention, and is the connecting link between the past and present. . . . It is in great sense the basis of all we have today in Sunday school life and literature." Samuel Boykin (*q.v.*) became its editor at Memphis, and continued with it through all the years until his death at Nashville in 1899.

Kind Words came to the end of its career in Sept., 1929. In October of that year the board began to publish five instead of four illustrated weeklies, all designated as The Kind Words Series of Illustrated Weeklies. At present the board publishes three such weeklies, *Storytime, The Sentinel,* and *Upward,* all lineal descendants of *Kind Words* and carrying the designation Kind Words Series. The various Sunday school lesson helps being published by the board in 1956 are together known as the Southern Baptist Convention Series.

HOWARD P. COLSON

KING, SPENCER BIDWELL, SR. (b. Rome, Ga., Jan. 2, 1880; d. Americus, Ga., Nov. 30, 1954). Minister, denominational officer. His formal schooling was limited to the elementary grades in Rome and two years at Hearn Academy, Cave Spring. He served in the Spanish-American War, and was ordained to the ministry, Mar. 10, 1907. New Prospect (Floyd County) was his first church; and he was the first pastor of the Maple Street (now Second Avenue) Church in Rome. Other pastorates in that vicinity include Friendship, Oostanaula, and Sugar Valley. As clerk of Floyd County Association, he produced minutes which attracted the attention of Hugh Robertson Bernard (*q.v.*), auditor of the state mission board, who brought him to Atlanta in 1912 as office secretary. He held the position of secretary of the committee on co-operation from 1914 to 1919. During this period he was pastor at Jonesboro-Hampton and Capital View, Atlanta. After a two-year pastorate at Fayette, Ala., he served the Blakely and Pelham churches (1921–26); then he returned to Atlanta to accept the position of superintendent of state missions. He resigned this office in 1931 to serve again at Blakely until declining health caused his retirement in 1945. The Georgia Baptist Convention honored him by electing him as its treasurer (1932–44); and the executive committee of the convention made him recording secretary (1933–44). In addition to many tracts and his contributions to *The Christian Index,* he wrote *Georgia: A Mission Field* (1928). His burial place is at Oak Grove Cemetery, Americus, Ga.

B. C. SMITH

KINGDOM OF GOD. The rule of God over his people, especially the justification of his people in glory at the consummation of history. The kingdom is the spiritual condition of a life when the will of God as revealed in Christ is in complete control. The kingdom was established when Christ came to earth. Mark describes the beginning of our Lord's ministry thus: "Jesus came into Galilee, preaching the gospel of God, and saying, 'The time is fulfilled, and the kingdom of God is at hand; repent, and believe in the gospel'" (Mark 1:14–15 RSV). The purpose of Christ's preaching was to announce the kingdom of God, and many Scripture messages speak of the coming of Christ as the coming of the kingdom (Mark 1:15; Matt. 10:7; Luke 10:9, 11; Matt. 12:28). The Scriptures point to the progressive coming of the kingdom of God on earth (Mark 4:26–29). The kingdom is also represented as the consummation of the divine reign (Matt. 25:34; 16:28; 13:24 ff., 47 ff.).

Indicating the importance of the concept of the kingdom, John Bright has written, "To grasp what is meant by the Kingdom of God is to come very close to the heart of the Bible's Gospel of salvation." From the time of Abraham, who set out to seek "a city . . . whose builder and maker is God" (Heb. 11:10; Gen. 12:1 ff.), until the New Testament closes with "the holy city, new Jerusalem, coming down from God out of heaven" (Rev. 21:2), the concept of the kingdom of God permeates all Scripture. Human redemption, the theme of the Bible, is described in terms of a chosen people who are called to live under the rule of God and to share the hope of a kingdom of righteousness which will ultimately triumph over all evil.

Wherever Jesus taught and preached, he spoke of the kingdom of God. He likened it to a sower who goes forth to sow, to a costly pearl, and to a mustard seed. To enter the kingdom, one must become as a little child. So important is it for man to enter the kingdom that it would be better for him to mutilate himself and enter maimed than not to enter at all. The kingdom of God is so paramount in the teachings of Christ that we cannot understand him at all without some grasp of its meaning. As frequently as Christ mentioned the kingdom, he never once sought to define it. He spoke as if he were perfectly convinced that those who heard him understood what he meant by the term. Strange as it may seem, the "kingdom" was in the vocabulary of every Jew. What the term meant to Christ and to those to whom he spoke must therefore be ascertained. The expression "kingdom of God" does not occur very frequently in the New Testament and is never mentioned in the Old Testament at all. The idea of the kingdom, however, is much broader than the term, and it is not difficult to trace the idea even when the term is absent.

The roots of the meaning of the kingdom lie in the Jewish concept of the Messiah. The Jews' paramount hope was for a Redeemer who would establish the kingdom of God. Many elements in Israel's history entered into the formation of the messianic hope. The revelation of God made its way through the tragic experiences of Israel. For example, before a Messiah could be born of David's line, there had to be a David. Therefore, it was inevitable that Israel's estimation of her Messiah was colored by what she thought of David. Consequently, her estimation of the kingdom of God was colored by what she thought of the kingdom of David. Israel's faith was not created by the reign of David; it was solidified long before David was born; however, it was inevitable for her faith to be expressed in terms of the best Israel had known as a nation during the golden age of David.

Proper perspective of Israel's religious faith in the kingdom of God makes it necessary to remember that she was a covenant people. Throughout her history Israel believed that she was the chosen of God. Beginning with Abraham, God had elected Israel to be his own people. However, it was in the Exodus that God demonstrated most dramatically his intervention to solidify her into a nation. With the strong conviction that God had spoken to him, Moses endeavored to lead the oppressed Israelite slaves into a land of promise. With the enormous confidence that God had promised them the land of Canaan, Israel arose to take it. God had intervened in a definite time in history to make Israel his own. It was the memory of this intervention that pervaded the national consciousness throughout Israel's history. The prophets continually referred to it as the unforgettable example of the power and grace of God (Amos 2:9–11; Micah 6:2–5; Ezek. 20:5–7). In the Exodus God carried the infant Israel as a little child (Hos. 11:1); Israel was married in a covenant ceremony which demanded her loyalty forever (Hos. 2; Jer. 2:23). Israel, permeated with the conviction that she was God's chosen people, found it extremely difficult to believe the prophets who foretold her doom. This conviction became an invulnerable conceit which no prophet could penetrate.

Israel's birth as a nation in a narrow land of Palestine would have been utterly irrelevant in history had it not been that with her birth there was born a religion which represented an unprecedented and rationally unexplainable break with ancient paganism. Her religion completely transcended every other religion known to man. Moses, her great religious leader, relentlessly insisted that there is but one God and sternly forbade the Israelites to worship any other. No group of gods surrounds Israel's God; no consort shares his honors. The Hebrew vocabulary does not even have a word for "goddess." The very name of Israel's God claims that he created all things. Israel's God is not only the ruler of nature but also of history, especially the history of Israel. God did not choose to rule over Israel because of any merit she possessed. On the contrary, the Exodus narratives carefully depict the cowardly, ungrateful, and utterly unworthy acts of Israel. God's covenant with Israel was, therefore, a covenant of pure grace. With this concept of a chosen people, called to live under the rule of God, the idea of the kingdom of God began. At her best Israel could never take her relationship as God's chosen people for granted, for the covenant was morally conditioned. The best prophetic preaching was based upon Israel's covenant: "Now therefore, if ye will obey my voice indeed, and keep my covenant, then ye shall be a peculiar treasure unto me above all people" (Exod. 19:5). This pronouncement clearly prepared the way for the prophetic preaching of the doom of a disobedient Israel and also for the proclamation of faithful Israel's hope at the end of the age.

Israel's concept of herself as a covenant-people created in her a strong sense of destiny and an unswerving confidence that her destiny was being guided by God. The Israelites probably gathered about their nomadic campfires talking about the good land "flowing with milk and honey" which God had promised them (Exod. 3:8, 17). God would one day make of Israel a mighty nation (Gen. 12:2), defend her from her foes (Num. 23:21–24; 24:8–9), and make her great (Num. 23:9–10; 24:5–7). God would provide indescribable peace and plenty (Gen. 49:25–26; Deut. 33:12–17) and would send a leader whom all the nations would serve (Gen. 49:10; Num. 24:17–19). God had called Israel to serve his purpose in the world (Gen. 12:3; 18:18; 22:18). Israel's robust confidence saw her through rugged battles and brought her at last into the Land of Promise. God had guided Israel through dreadful ordeals and had kindled within her a blaze of hope which would never die. Israel never doubted that one day God would bring his chosen people to a glorious kingdom.

God's dealings with the leaders of Israel further reflect the tenacious confidence of the Israelites in the coming of the kingdom of God. In the 13th century B.C. Israel was a loose federation of clans with no organized central authority. The shrine of the ark of the covenant, which was moved from place to place and finally was located at Shiloh (I Sam. 1–4), provided the gathering place where the clans came on feast days to renew their allegiance to God. There was no supreme political leader. Rather, when danger arose, a hero appeared upon whom the Spirit of Yahweh rushed (Judg. 3:10; 14:6), a hero called a *shophet,* a judge. The *shophet* united the clans and repelled the foe with victories which gave him enormous prestige, but he was never regarded as a king. His authority came solely through the fact that the Spirit of the Lord had come upon him. He was only God's representative; it was God who ruled his people. Thus Gideon, spurning a crown, said: "I will not rule over you, neither shall my son rule over you: the Lord shall rule over you" (Judg. 8:23). When the Philistine menace brought about a need for closer unity in

Israel, Saul was anointed king; yet he also was regarded as God's instrument upon whom the Spirit of Yahweh rushed (I Sam. 11:6–7). Saul did not endeavor to create a state or establish an administrative organization. When he died a suicide on Gilboa (I Sam. 31), all for which he had labored was lost, and the Philistines re-established their garrisons in the land (II Sam. 23:14).

The most dramatic reversal of Israel's fortunes came under David. At Saul's death, with the consent of the Philistines, David ascended to the throne of Judah in Hebron (II Sam. 5:1–5). Even before Saul's death the people realized that the Spirit had passed from Saul to David. Early Israel recognized and followed only the representative of God; thus David could never have become king if the people had not regarded him as the man of God. The case of Ish-baal (II Sam. 2–4) indicates that heredity could not make a man king of Israel. Ish-baal's uncle, Abner, acclaimed him king, but the people would not follow him. David subdued the Philistines, seized Jerusalem, and made it his new capital (II Sam. 5:6–10); he conquered the Moabite, Ammonite, and Edomite kingdoms of Transjordan and made them tributary; he subdued the Aramean states of Syria. These conquests gave him an empire ranging from the Gulf of Aqabah in the south to Central Syria in the far north and made Israel the chief nation of Palestine and Syria.

With David's military victories came unparalleled economic prosperity, for Israel held the trade routes from Egypt to the north, from the Phoenician plain to the hinterland, and from Damascus through Transjordan to the Hedjaz. Solomon expanded the economic prosperity of Israel, a feat which was reflected in biblical accounts of the magnificence of his court (I Kings 10:11–29). The transition from David to Solomon, however, showed a radical change in Israel's method of selecting a king. So firmly established was David's glory, so personally his was the state, that the people knew only an heir of David could hold the nation together. Thus the question became which one of David's sons would succeed him. Solomon came to the throne of Israel by palace plot, not by the appointment of the Spirit of Yahweh.

In the days of Israel's decline from glory, the nostalgic yearning for the golden days of David grew stronger. Evil in David's personal life and reign was forgotten. He was remembered as the man after God's own heart whose house should rule forever (II Sam. 7:16; 23:5). So strongly imbedded in the national consciousness was the longing for the return of the glory and prosperity which the nation knew under David that it was natural for a man of Judah to think of the coming Messiah in terms of the days when the favor of heaven was so abundantly upon Israel. Israel's great danger lay in thinking that in the Davidic state the kingdom of God had fully come. To prevent this, the kingdom of Israel came under God's judgment, and the kingdom was divided. Amos pointed out how far short Israel had fallen from the kingdom of God; he pronounced doom upon her and declared that God would no longer defend her. The messianic hope was transferred from the nation to a remnant (Isa. 9:1–7; 11:1–5; 53:2). Jeremiah prophesied that the broken covenant would be replaced by a universal inward covenant (Jer. 31:31–34); he totally rejected the Israelite state as the vehicle of the kingdom of God and declared that God would not defend a disobedient nation.

When the kingdom of Judah fell, never to rise again, the hope of God's re-establishing the people under his rule had to be reinterpreted. With the captivity all popular political ideas of the kingdom of God withered; the messianic hope was refined in the fire, and the pure light of God began to burn brightly. Now Israel was seen as the servant of God who, through missionary labor and great sacrifice, would be the instrument for bringing people of all nations into the kingdom of God (Isa. 44:1; 51:1, 7). Through the remnant the Redeemer would come to fulfil the mission of the Suffering Servant (Luke 4:21; Isa. 61:1–2), taking on himself the form of a servant (Phil. 2:7). With the coming of Christ, the kingdom of God was declared to be at hand. The establishment of the rule of God in man who believed was being fulfilled. Christ's miracles were demonstrations that the power of the kingdom of God was present in him and that a new age had dawned.

The kingdom of God is not a kingdom of this world (John 18:36), although this world provides the sphere of its operation (Matt. 6:10). The kingdom means the will of the Father in heaven being done on earth (Matt. 6:9–10). In that sense, as the modern mind would understand the term, it is more a family than a kingdom concept. To be in the kingdom means to be a child of God. The same power which binds the kingdom together binds the family together, namely, love.

Augustine, in *The City of God*, presents the kingdom of God as the kingdom of grace engaged in constant warfare with and destined to triumph over the kingdom of sin, Satan, and death. Underlying the theology of the Council of Trent is the concept that the kingdom of God is the instrument of divine revelation and grace in this present world; that it will one day take the place of this world when the church militant and the church triumphant merge. Albrecht Ritschl depicted the kingdom of God as the consummation of human history, a concept which permeated the science and philosophy of the 19th century; it held that the kingdom of God is "the one far-off divine event toward which the whole creation moves." An element of this concept seems to appear in Paul's view (Col. 1:9–20). Others have interpreted the kingdom of God as a sublime social hope or as an ideal world of peace and material plenty.

The "kingdom of heaven" is a synonym for

the kingdom of God, evidenced by Matthew's use of "kingdom of heaven" in the precise sayings of Christ in which Mark uses "kingdom of God" (Matt. 13:31; Mark 4:30–31). Matthew alone uses the phrase "kingdom of heaven," and he uses it 30 times. Only four times (Matt. 6:33; 12:28; 21:31, 43) does he use "kingdom of God." Although no other New Testament writer uses the phrase "kingdom of heaven," Matthew's preference for the term can probably be traced to his Jewish background. His Gospel presents the Christian faith as it was proclaimed by the church centered in Jerusalem, many of whose members were also priests of the Temple (Acts 6:7). The priests regarded the name of God as a part of God himself; therefore they revered it as they revered God. It was vastly more than a mere name. The Third Commandment expressly forbade profaning the name of God (Exod. 20:7; Lev. 18:21; 19:12; 21:6; 22:2, 32), and since perhaps the best way to avoid profaning it was to refrain from using it, synonyms were introduced, such as "the Blessed One," "the Holy One," "the High and Lofty One," "the Almighty" (used in Job more than 30 times). One of these synonyms was the word "heaven" (Matt. 5:34). Some scholars, however, insist that Matthew used the phrase "kingdom of heaven" to emphasize the origin or the source of the kingdom (Matt. 7:21). Christ taught that the kingdom is never the creation of man nor does it come from below; it is a gift of God from above.

BIBLIOGRAPHY: J. Bright, *The Kingdom of God* (1953). W. T. Conner, *The Faith of the New Testament* (1940). CHARLES A. TRENTHAM

KING'S CREEK ACADEMY. A school at King's Creek, N. C., under Baptist control in 1895. Caldwell Association endorsed it.

D. L. SMILEY

KIRTLEY, JAMES ADDISON (b. May 12, 1820; d. Feb. 13, 1904). Minister. Son of the pioneer Baptist preacher, Robert Kirtley, he was converted while still a boy during a revival in the Bullitsburg, Ky., Baptist Church, with which he was connected for most of his life. In Apr., 1842, he was licensed to preach; in Oct., 1844, he was ordained to the ministry to serve as assistant pastor of the Bullitsburg church. Leaving Bullitsburg in 1847, he served as pastor in Madison, Ind., and Louisville, Ky., until the summer of 1851, when he returned to the North Bend Association as a missionary within the boundaries of the association. In 1856 he was again the assistant at Bullitsburg and assumed the full pastoral responsibility in 1859, succeeding his father. For the remainder of his active life, he was pastor at Bullitsburg and at Big Bone Church. From 1865 to 1895, he was moderator of the North Bend Association. He wrote several apologetic and polemic works including *Cody's Theology Examined* and *The Design of Baptism Viewed in Its Doctrinal Relations.* He also wrote a history of the Bullitsburg church.

BIBLIOGRAPHY: J. A. Kirtley, "History of Bullitsburg Baptist Church" (1872). F. M. Masters, *A History of Baptists in Kentucky* (1953).

W. C. SMITH, JR.

KNIGHT, WILLIAM HENRY (b. Pine, La., Aug. 22, 1888; d. Alexandria, La., Dec. 13, 1951). Teacher, pastor, evangelist, and denominational leader. He was converted in 1907 and began to preach in 1909. He was educated at Louisiana College (A.B., 1914; D.D., 1929), and at Southwestern Baptist Theological Seminary (Th.M., 1917; Th.D., 1919). At the seminary he was professor of missions from 1918 to 1923, and professor of evangelism, 1929–32.

His pastorates included Tabernacle Baptist Church, Atlanta, Ga. (1932–38), which for three years during his tenure led the nation in additions; First Church, Baton Rouge, La.; First Church, El Dorado, Ark.; First Church, Pineville, La. As an evangelist he led campaigns in some of the South's leading cities.

Knight became secretary-treasurer of the Louisiana Baptist Convention in 1941 and continued in that position until his death. This period was marked by growth and expansion. The annual budget of the convention rose from $150,000.00 to $858,040.44, a debt of $200,000 was liquidated, and missions were extended to every parish in the state. During this period these new departments were added to the executive board: rural evangelism, Baptist Student Union, church music, and Baptist foundation.

C. W. AVERETT

KNOWLEDGE OF GOD. Knowledge of God comes through revelation, which includes facts about God but is essentially God's personal encounter with the soul through Christ. To know Christ is life eternal because through union with him he brings the eternity of God into human souls. Paul speaks of being in union with Christ as sharing the mind of Christ (Phil. 2:5). To know God is not to stand apart and speculate about him, for God is not interested in satisfying man's speculative curiosity but in building His kingdom. He reveals himself to the obedient.

Men do not believe in God because they can prove him. Rather, they seek to prove him because they already believe in him. Theistic proofs (cosmological, teleological, ontological, etc.) have value chiefly for those who already believe. Kant contended that man can never by the world prove a god greater than the world. Neither can man with his human mind prove a god greater than that mind. The chasm between the phenomenal and noumenal worlds can only be spanned by faith. God speaks through nature and reason, although he is above them both (Isa. 55:8–9). Man knows God solely because God takes the initiative in making himself known through his Word, the living voice of God made real and relevant through the Holy Spirit.

See also REVELATION and THEISM.

BIBLIOGRAPHY: J. Baillie, *Our Knowledge of God* (1939). E. P. Dickie, *God Is Light* (1954).

CHARLES A. TRENTHAM

KOKERNOT, HERBERT LEE (b. Gonzales County, Tex., 1868; d. San Antonio, Tex., Apr. 14, 1949). Business executive, benefactor of Baptist institutions. Organizer and director of the First National Bank of Alpine, Tex., and National Finance Credit Corporation, Fort Worth, Kokernot was a member of the Budget Control Committee which recommended forming the Baptist Foundation, and he served as its director and president for 18 years until his death. Kokernot, a cattleman and operator of a 260,000-acre ranch, established Corpus Christi properties, a trust of $1,500,000 as endowment for Baylor University, Mary Hardin–Baylor College, and Southwestern Baptist Theological Seminary. He helped organize Paisano Encampment and was its largest supporter. His pastor at First Baptist Church, San Antonio, said of Kokernot, who was chairman of the deacons, "In addition to his continuous and munificent financial gifts, he has contributed a generous spirit, an unselfish devotion and a pure heart."

A. B. CULBERTSON

KOREA, MISSION IN. The first Southern Baptist missionaries to Korea, John and Jewell (Leonard) Abernathy, arrived in Feb., 1950, at the request of Baptists of the country. Independent missionaries from Boston had begun work in Korea, but their support had failed and the mission had dwindled away. Abernathy was unable to visit churches in Communist-dominated North Korea, but had visited churches throughout South Korea when the outbreak of the Korean war forced him to leave after only four months.

Returning in the spring of 1951, Abernathy found most of the 40 South Korean churches partially or wholly destroyed, their members scattered and 61 of them martyred.

With headquarters in Pusan, the missionaries began relief work among refugees and later opened a clinic, which led to construction of the William L. Wallace (*q.v.*) Memorial Hospital, dedicated Nov., 1955. Rex Ray joined the Abernathys to help with relief work and Nelson A. Bryan and Alfred W. Yocum to give medical aid. By Jan. 1, 1956, Baptist missionaries in South Korea numbered 19 in three centers—Seoul, Pusan, and Taejon. A seminary campus was purchased in 1955 at Taejon. The mission was officially organized in July, 1954.

GENEVIEVE GREER

KOREAN BAPTIST CONVENTION. Organized in May, 1946, when Koreans, following their release from 35 years of Japanese domination, asked Southern Baptists to send missionaries; two were stationed briefly in Seoul before the Korean war. Since early in 1951, 19 missionaries have gone to Korea, engaging in evangelism, relief work, medical service, and theological training.

Under Japanese occupation, Baptist churches in Korea called themselves the Church of East Asia. Baptist work began in 1895 when Boston's Clarendon Street Church sent missionaries, but their sponsor died and mission interest faded. Prior to 1950 no Baptist missionaries had worked in Korea for several years. Korean Baptists themselves had sent missionaries to Siberia, Manchuria, and Mongolia. At first, Communist domination in the north permitted Baptist missionaries to work only with the 40 churches in South Korea. By 1955, 146 churches reported 5,489 members, with Sunday schools, youth groups, and women's organizations.

GENEVIEVE GREER

KOREAN SEMINARY, TAEJON. See KOREA, MISSION IN.

KU KLUX KLAN. The original Ku Klux Klan was a secret organization which originated in the Southern states of the United States in the days of reconstruction following the Civil War, particularly in the period from 1867 to 1870. Its purpose was to protect against the conquering attitude of the National Government and to frighten the Negro freedmen from participation in public or private affairs. Political appointees from the North and their Southern assistants placed Negro freedmen in positions of domination over the white citizens and organized them into secret organizations to terrorize Southern citizens into submission to the politicians' exploitation of political power. This created an atmosphere conducive to some sort of guerrilla protest.

One such protest grew out of a harmless social club organized in Pulaski, Tenn., in 1866 by a group of young Confederate soldiers. This secret society was called by the Greek name *Kuklos* which means "circle." It was an easy transition to Ku Klux Klan—"the circle clan." This was not the only society of its kind, but it came to be the most widespread and best known, having at one time a membership of 550,000.

The mask worn by the Klan was intended to produce panic and fear, but it proved to be a disguise used unofficially for all kinds of immoral and criminal acts against the Negro and anyone else who might fall under the displeasure of men with evil intent. Klan terrorism resulted in a congressional investigation, which helped to bring a moderation of previous political methods and a realization of the unwisdom of continuing to treat the South as a conquered territory. As the National Government gradually improved its administration in keeping with these findings of Congress, the Klan was not needed and soon disappeared.

What might be called the modern Klan was originated in 1915 in Atlanta, Ga., by William J. Simmons. It was used as an instrument of racial and religious strife. Its acts of violence and of political corruption brought down upon it a congressional investigation resulting in a split in its ranks. Control passed from Simmons to Hiram Wesley Evans, a dentist of Dallas, Tex.

The new regime discouraged violence and

moved toward the acquisition of political power. Its political influence was an issue in many states. In the Democratic Convention of 1924 and the election of 1928 the anti-alien and the anti-Catholic aspects of the Klan's platform were a strong factor.

Southern Baptists in their 1923 Convention had this to say: "In the recent months mob violence has become active and menacing perhaps more than at any time previous. . . . As if to make their crime all the more cowardly and diabolical in many cases the mobs have concealed their identity by wearing masks. It goes without saying that no true, intelligent, patriotic American can or will give support or approval to mob violence whether the mob be masked or unmasked, much less can our Baptist people and preachers think of so doing."

A. C. MILLER

KUTTAWA CAMP. Located at Kuttawa, Ky., and owned by a group of citizens in Lyon County with no religious connections. The facilities of the camp were rented jointly each year by both the southwestern region Woman's Missionary Union and the western region Woman's Missionary Union from 1939 to 1950 for Royal Ambassador, Girl's Auxiliary, and Young Woman's Auxiliary camps. Southwestern region Woman's Missionary Union rented the facilities during 1951–52. The Kuttawa Camp facilities are no longer used by any Baptist group.

ELDRED M. TAYLOR

KYLE BAPTIST SEMINARY. A coeducational school, established at Kyle, Hays County, Tex., by San Marcos Baptist Association. Aided by citizens of Kyle in 1884, the school continued until 1890.

RUPERT N. RICHARDSON

L

LACKEY, MARGARET McRAE (b. Copiah County, Miss., Oct. 24, 1858; d. Jackson, Miss., June 5, 1948). Woman's Missionary Union leader. The first employed corresponding secretary of Mississippi Baptist Woman's Missionary Union. Elected Apr. 1, 1912, she served until the end of 1930 with a vision of what might be accomplished through better organized efforts of women in the country churches. In Feb., 1931, she became hostess at the Baptist hospital in Jackson, Miss., and served in that position several years. The Mississippi state mission week of prayer offering was named "Margaret Lackey Offering" in 1938.

Bibliography: "Hearts the Lord Opened," *The History of Mississippi Woman's Missionary Union* (1954). *The Baptist Record* (June 10, 1948).

C. B. HAMLET III

LADONIA MALE AND FEMALE INSTITUTE. Established at Ladonia, Tex., by Sister Grove Association in 1860 with trustees elected by the association. The school was moved to Sandy Creek in 1863, and activity was suspended 1865–67. In 1867 the Institute was reopened in Ladonia and maintained until 1873.

RUPERT N. RICHARDSON

LAFAYETTE ACADEMY (1825–30). Known also as Lafayette Baptist High School, located at LaGrange, in Chambers County, Ala. Founded by D. P. Bestor and named after the French General Lafayette, who visited Alabama in that year, it was one of the first institutions of learning in Alabama.

JAMES E. DAVIDSON

LAFAYETTE FEMALE COLLEGE (1850–84). A school for girls, formerly known as Lafayette Female Academy, founded by the East Liberty Baptist Association at Lafayette, in Chambers County, Ala., with T. G. Freeman as first president. The school was closed in 1884 and the properties given to the Lafayette Baptist Church.

JAMES E. DAVIDSON

LAKE BROWNWOOD BAPTIST ENCAMPMENT. One of four Texas encampments organized in 1946. The Brotherhood of District 16 took the camp as a project and successfully established it on Lake Brownwood near Brownwood, Tex.

J. E. ROTH

LAKE LAVON DISTRICT 13 ENCAMPMENT. A Texas Baptist encampment organized in 1953. It is located on Lake Lavon in Collin County.

J. E. ROTH

LAKE SALLATEESKA BAPTIST ASSEMBLY, ILLINOIS. In Apr., 1941, the Illinois Baptist State Association purchased 40 acres known as Hiller's Lake, near Pinckneyville, and an additional 40 acres in June, 1956. The first Woman's Missionary Union youth camps were held at Hiller's Lake in 1928, and until the property was purchased it was used for assemblies on a rental basis. Now known as Lake Sallateeska, the assembly is used annually by the various departments of Baptist work in the state. Assembly buildings include 24 cabins, a tabernacle, dining hall and kitchen, and superintendent's residence. Total property value is estimated at $32,000. WILLIAM J. PURDUE

LANDMARK BANNER AND CHEROKEE BAPTIST, THE. A newspaper which first appeared Oct. 5, 1859, supporting the interests of the Cherokee (Landmark) Baptist Convention in north Georgia. It was published first in Rome, Ga., by Jesse M. Wood, and then moved to Atlanta in July, 1860, with H. C. Hornady assisting in the editing. The paper prospered for a time as a Landmark organ but did not long survive the dissolution of the Cherokee convention, which failed to function after the Civil War. JOHN J. HURT, JR.

LANDMARK BAPTIST. Established in 1901 by W. A. Clark and other anti-convention individuals after the state convention renounced as state paper the *Arkansas Baptist,* of which Clark was editor. Clark and those allied with him withdrew from the convention and continued to publish their paper, naming it the *Landmark Baptist.* B. H. DUNCAN

LANDMARKISM. A term used to denominate a Baptist party which developed considerable strength and influence in the 19th century, under the dynamic leadership of James Robinson Graves (*q.v.*), from 1846 editor of *The Tennessee Baptist.* The name came from a tract written by James Madison Pendleton (*q.v.*) answering the question "Ought Baptists to invite pedobaptists to preach in their pulpits?" which Graves entitled "An Old Landmark Reset." A third figure prominently involved in the movement was Amos Cooper Dayton (*q.v.*), who wrote *Theodosia Ernest,* a religious novel elucidating what he regarded as Baptist teachings, from which Graves took some ideas.

The Landmark controversy apparently was precipitated by John Lightfoot Waller's editorial in the *Western Baptist Review.* Answering a query regarding a baptism administered upon a profession of faith in Christ by a pedobaptist minister, Waller asserted its validity. Graves responded immediately by taking the opposing position. In 1851, meeting in Cotton Grove, Tenn., Graves' followers issued a statement which repudiated the authority of non-Baptist churches, ministers, and ordinances.

During the following years, Graves, through his paper and books as well as by preaching and debate, persuasively and energetically expounded Landmark doctrines. Although many Baptists refused to accept his position, a great number did, making the new Southwest a stronghold of Landmarkism. By 1880 Graves could boast that a majority of denominational papers had endorsed Landmarkism.

The distinctive tenets of this movement fall into the category of ecclesiology, fitting into a very logical system centered around the primacy of the local church. Since a valid church is an assembly of baptized (immersed) believers, then pedobaptist organizations cannot be recognized as true churches, but only as religious societies. Such groups cannot give authority to preach, and therefore their ministers should not be recognized as regular gospel ministers. Upon this follows a rejection of their ordinances. Even an occasional immersion must be designated alien and nugatory, since it lacks proper authority.

Graves also advanced the "church-kingdom" idea. Christ established a visible kingdom and guaranteed its perpetuity. This kingdom is composed of all true (Baptist) churches, which, therefore, have had a continuous existence. Dissenting sects, such as the Montanists, Paulicians, Waldenses, *et al.,* are marshaled to provide the needed continuity.

Close communion, another distinctive, allowed only members of a local Baptist church to participate in the Lord's Supper. Landmarkism held that in its administration the Supper should not extend beyond discipline. Obviously, a church could discipline only its own members. There was also a general opposition to boards as extra-biblical organizations and to the plan of convention membership.

Despite the extremists of Landmarkism, the heat of debates it generated, and the wide divergences from other Baptists, complete separation did not occur until 1905, when, led by Ben M. Bogard and others, the General Association of Landmark Baptists was organized at Texarkana, Ark. In 1924 it took the name American Baptist Association.

See also AMERICAN BAPTIST ASSOCIATION, NORTH AMERICAN BAPTIST ASSOCIATION.

BIBLIOGRAPHY: A. H. Autry, *Grapeshot and Canister* (1911). W. W. Barnes, *The Southern Baptist Convention 1845–1953* (1954). A. C. Dayton, *Theodosia Ernest* (*c.* 1855). J. R. Graves, *Old Landmarkism: What Is It?* (1880). O. L. Hailey, *J. R. Graves, Life, Times and Teachings* (1929). D. O. Moore, "The Landmark Baptists and Their Attack Upon the Southern Baptist Convention Historically Analyzed" (1949). J. M. Pendleton, *An Old Landmark Reset* (1854).

W. MORGAN PATTERSON

LANDRUM, SYLVANUS (b. Oglethorpe County, Ga., Oct. 3, 1820; d. Brunswick, Ga., Nov. 16, 1886). Pastor. The son of William and Jane Landrum, he was educated at Meson Academy, Lexington, Ga., and Mercer University, where he graduated in 1846. An occasional preacher while in college, he was ordained on Oct. 23, 1846, at Salem, Ga. He began serving pastorates in Lexington and Athens in Jan., 1847, where he remained until called, in Dec., 1849, to the First Baptist Church, Macon, serving there for 10 years. Called to the First Baptist Church of Savannah in Dec., 1859, Landrum continued courageously during the difficult war years. One biographer states that his was "perhaps the only white church on the coast, from Baltimore to Galveston, Texas, that did not close during the war." He left Savannah in Oct.,

1871 for the Central Baptist Church, Memphis, Tenn. While there, the Landrum family lost two promising sons in a Tennessee yellow fever epidemic. On Sept. 1, 1879, Landrum returned to the First Baptist Church, Savannah. In 1881 he resigned his pastorate to become an agent for Mercer University and to lecture to ministerial students. Leaving this position after six months, Landrum accepted a call to the Coliseum Place Baptist Church in New Orleans. Despite failing health, Landrum led the Coliseum Place church out of debt, the mortgage being cancelled in 1883. Urged to take a vacation, Landrum went to St. Paul, Minn., in the summer of 1886. Learning that he was a victim of Bright's disease, he began the arduous journey to the home of his son-in-law, B. W. Bussey, in Brunswick, Ga., where he died.

A denominational leader, Landrum was president of the Tennessee Baptist Convention for a term. A member of the board of trustees at Mercer University for 15 years, he was one of the leaders in having the Mercer campus moved from Penfield to Macon. Two colleges conferred honorary degrees upon him: Georgetown College in Kentucky, and Columbian College in Washington, D. C. He was twice married: to Naomi Lumpkin in 1846, and to Eliza Jane Warren in 1852. Two children survived to adulthood, one of whom was William Warren Landrum (*q.v.*). BENJAMIN W. GRIFFITH, JR.

LANDRUM, WILLIAM WARREN (b. Macon, Ga., Jan. 18, 1853; d. Russellville, Ky., Jan. 24, 1926). Pulpiteer, pastor, parliamentarian, teacher. Landrum's family moved from Macon to Savannah, Ga., where his father, Sylvanus Landrum, became pastor in 1859. Landrum was converted there and baptized Mar. 25, 1866, at the age of 13.

First attending Mercer University, Landrum graduated *magna cum laude* from Brown University in 1872 when he was 19 and from Southern Baptist Theological Seminary in 1874. Brown and Washington and Lee universities both conferred upon him the honorary D.D. degree, and the University of Georgia, the LL.D. degree. Late in life, through the influence of James Henry Rushbrooke, then secretary general of the Baptist World Alliance, Landrum was made a Fellow in the Royal Society of Arts, London.

Licensed to preach in Aug., 1870, by the First Baptist Church, Savannah, Landrum was ordained in May, 1874, in Jefferson, Tex., where the Southern Baptist Convention was meeting that year. The council for his examination included John A. Broadus (*q.v.*), Henry Allen Tupper, Sr. (*q.v.*), William Williams (*q.v.*), William Carey Crane (*q.v.*), and his own father, Sylvanus Landrum. After his ordination he went into his first pastorate, First Baptist Church, Shreveport, La., where he served two years, 1874–76. Other pastorates were First Baptist Church, Augusta, Ga., 1876–82; Second Baptist Church, Richmond, Va., 1882–96; First Baptist Church, Atlanta, Ga., 1896–1909; Broadway Baptist Church, Louisville, Ky., 1909–19; and First Baptist Church, Russellville, Ky., 1919–26. During his pastorate at Russellville, Landrum was also professor of philosophy, ethics, and church history in Bethel College.

Twice elected vice-president of the Southern Baptist Convention, once in 1917 and again in 1920, Landrum was a trustee of many denominational agencies and institutions. Elected on three different occasions to the presidency of Baptist educational institutions, he declined each time, preferring to remain a pastor. About 1895 Landrum championed from his pulpit in Richmond the idea of an international group of Baptists on a world-wide scale. By the time the first Baptist World Congress was held in 1905, he had moved to Atlanta. He attended the London congress and served on the American and executive committees.

Landrum served on the Committee on Unification in 1913–14 for the General Association of Baptists in Kentucky, out of which developed the system of contributing to a group of causes percentage-wise through a single gift. This system, adopted within a few years by the Southern Baptist Convention, became the Cooperative Program.

Landrum's literary interest led to his organization of the Ten Club in Atlanta; he belonged to the Filson Club in Louisville. In Russellville he organized the Rotary Club, and so appreciative were the Rotarians of his leadership as their first president that they purchased a black riding mount for him which he rode for the last years of his life as long as his health permitted. Author of *History, Gospel and Prophecy* and *Our Baptist Message—Its Use and Abuse,* an 11-page tract, Landrum's published book of sermons is entitled *Settled in the Sanctuary.* GEORGE RALEIGH JEWELL

LANE, TIDENCE (b. near Baltimore, Md., Aug. 31, 1724; d. near Whitesburg, Tenn., Jan. 30, 1806). He was the son of Richard and Sarah Lane and an older brother of Dutton Lane, a pioneer preacher in Virginia—"a minister of prominence and influence." The parents of Tidence Lane moved from Maryland to Virginia, then to North Carolina where young Lane "grew to manhood, and where he married Esther Bibbin [or Bibber], May 9, 1743. To this union were born . . . seven sons and two daughters." About the time of his marriage, young Lane was convicted and converted under the famous preacher, Shubal Stearns (*q.v.*). Soon after this he surrendered to preach.

He has the distinction of being "the first pastor of the first permanent church organization of any denomination in the state of Tennessee, Buffalo Ridge, in Washington County, constituted in 1779." He has also the distinction of being "the first Moderator of the first association of any denomination in the state, the old Holston, organized at 'Cherokee meeting-house,' in Washington County, on Saturday before the fourth Sunday in October, 1786, ten years before Tennessee was admitted into the Union." Lane moved west in about six years into what is now Hamblen County and, with William Murphy, constituted the Bent Creek Church (now Whitesburg), the second Sunday in June, 1785. Lane became pastor of this church and continued until his death. Lane was blessed with good organizing and good preaching ability. Benedict describes him as a preacher "of reputation and success." W. LEONARD STIGLER

LANGUAGE GROUPS, NEW MEXICO, MISSIONS TO. See VELARDE DAY SCHOOL and TWO GRAY HILLS DAY SCHOOL.

LATHAM SPRINGS BAPTIST ENCAMPMENT. A Texas encampment organized in 1923 by Hill County Baptists, located on the Brazos River between Waco and Hillsboro in District 14. In 1949 Latham Springs became the first encampment in Texas to employ a full-time executive secretary. Although 12 Texas encampments carry insurance on all campers, Latham Springs is the only one which has its own insurance company; it collected $1,567 in fees and paid out $59 in claims in 1955.
J. E. ROTH

LATIN AMERICA, MISSIONS IN. See ARGENTINA, MISSION IN; THE BAHAMAS, MISSION IN; BRAZIL, MISSION IN; CHILE, MISSION IN; COLOMBIA, MISSION IN; COSTA RICA, MISSION IN; ECUADOR, MISSION IN; GUATEMALA-HONDURAS, MISSION IN; JAMAICA, MISSION IN; MEXICO, MISSION IN; PARAGUAY, MISSION IN; PERU, MISSION IN; SPANISH BAPTIST PUBLISHING HOUSE, EL PASO, TEX.; URUGUAY, MISSION IN; and VENEZUELA, MISSION IN.

LATTIMORE, OFFA SHIVERS (b. Marion, Ala., Jan. 10, 1865; d. Austin, Tex., Oct. 27, 1937). Attorney, Texas Baptist leader. Educated at Baylor University, where he received the A.B. degree in 1889, Lattimore was an attorney in Fort Worth, Tex. He helped organize College Avenue Church in Fort Worth, where he was deacon and Sunday school superintendent. Vice-president of the Southern Baptist Convention, and president of the Baptist General Convention of Texas from 1923 to 1925, Lattimore helped establish Southwestern Baptist Theological Seminary and was chairman of its board for many years. After being elected to the Court of Criminal Appeals in 1918, he served until his death. A. B. CULBERTSON

LATVIA, BAPTISTS IN. The Latvians, a predominantly Lutheran people, speak a language much like Sanskrit. Latvian Baptists began under the influence of Baptists in Memel (Lithuania), and sought to obtain baptism from them. In spite of the many dangers involved in crossing the frontier, seven men and one woman made the journey in a cart and were baptized in Memel in 1860. Those who had been baptized, baptized others. After World War I there was freedom in Latvia. The work grew, and a seminary was opened in Riga under the leadership of J. A. Frey, who was followed by J. Riess. W. O. LEWIS

LAUREL BAPTIST SEMINARY. A coeducational secondary school at London, Ky., which was initiated largely by the labors of W. B. McGarity under the auspices of the Laurel River Baptist Association in 1901. The school reached an enrolment of 157, but closed after two years of operation because of inadequate facilities. GLYNN R. FORD

LAUREL SPRINGS SCHOOL. A school at Laurel Springs, N. C., operated temporarily under J. E. Alderman in 1904. The school was under supervision of the committees on education of Ashe and Allegheny and Grayson associations. D. L. SMILEY

LAW. Generally speaking, law is the will of an authority. Since God is the creator and sustainer of all things, he is the ultimate authority. Hence, his law is supreme and at the same time the expression of his will.

The law of God has two forms—elemental law and positive enactment. Elemental law refers to the principles woven into his creation, both rational and irrational, which are designed to produce harmony between the Creator and his work. Positive enactment is the partial disclosure of elemental law in published ordinances—the Ten Commandments, the ceremonial requirements, the ethical teachings of the New Testament.

BIBLIOGRAPHY: E. Y. Mullins, *The Christian Religion In Its Doctrinal Expression* (1917). A. H. Strong, *Systematic Theology* (1907). N. W. CARPENTER, JR.

LAWS AFFECTING BAPTISTS. In spite of the basic separation of church and state provided for in the United States Constitution, the civil authority and religious bodies are related at various points. The first and most important area of civil jurisdiction is in matters of property, which, even when owned by a church, is a creature of the law and therefore subject to civil regulation. This subject is treated more fully in the monograph CHURCH PROPERTY AND THE LAW OF TRUSTS. Concern over the proper definition of the church as property-holder has led to various provisions for incorporation or other means whereby a church can be recognized as a legal individual. Other laws regulate marriage, which has a civil as well as a religious aspect. Still others, designed more for the maintenance of the peace than for the protection of the mores of any sect, protect church property, church assemblies, and the days or hours of church worship from interference by liquor, vandalism, or the competition of commercial activity. From state to state, these laws differ, usually in minor points but sometimes markedly. A treatment of the specific laws affecting religious bodies, particularly as applied to Baptists, in the various states comprising the territory of the Southern Baptist Convention, follows.

Alabama. *Organization.*—An unincorporated Baptist church is without capacity to acquire or hold title to realty in Alabama. However, realty may be conveyed to individuals as trustees for such an unincorporated church, and this results in a transfer of legal title to the trustees, with the church as beneficiary. In the event the church subsequently incorporates, it succeeds to all the rights of the unincorporated church, including the benefits of such a trust, and it is likely that title under the trust would vest in the corporation at that time. Incorporation of the church prior to an attempted conveyance of land to it by deed or will is probably the safer course.

The incorporation of a church relates only to the properties or temporalities of the church and does not affect the church as a spiritual organization. Alabama courts generally decline to hear and determine any controversy pertaining purely to the spiritual phase of an incorporated religious body but will exercise jurisdiction to protect the temporalities thereof. It necessarily follows that incorporation is not necessary to the existence of a local church, although statutes governing the method of incorporation have been included in Alabama law since the earliest time and have continued without substantial change until the present. Churches and conferences of churches may incorporate by adopting a resolution of intent and electing not less than three, nor more than 24, trustees. The trustees must, within 30 days after election, file in the office of the judge of probate a certificate stating the corporate name, the names of the trustees, the length of time for which they were elected; this certificate must be subscribed by the trustees and recorded. The members of such church, and their successors, are incorporated from that time. The method of incorporation approximates that provided by statute for private corporations; the primary distinguishing feature is that there is no requirement that a religious corporation have any assets. No capital stock is issued. The religious corporation remains substantially free from governmental control, while the operations of private corporations are ever more closely scrutinized and regulated.

Church property.—Once incorporated, the church may acquire and hold realty and personalty, may receive property by gift, will, or devise, holding it in conformity with all lawful conditions imposed by the donor, and may exercise such other powers as are incident to private corporations. These powers may be exercised in its own right, as trustee, or as personal representative. Unless clearly stated in the instrument by which the church derives title to property, or unless afterward approved by a majority of the adult members of the congregation at a meeting held after announcement from the pulpit at least seven days after the date of announcement, any church corporation heretofore or hereafter existing shall remain a distinct and independent church corporation, free from the control of any higher church body with which it is affiliated, insofar as the management, control, disposition, or alienation of its real property is concerned.

Trustees of an incorporated church may convey all or such part of its realty or personalty as they may be authorized to do by resolution of the church assembled at a regular or special meeting. If this is done in special meeting, notice of the time, place, and object must be given at least 10 days prior thereto by posting at the place of regular meeting. A majority of the trustees or authorized agents of the church may authorize the borrowing of money, and may by mortgage or deed of trust convey all or any of the realty or personalty owned by the church to secure the payment of any debt which the trustees contract. Before the mortgage can be executed, a majority of the trustees shall have authorized incurring the debt and executing the mortgage, this authorization being made at a meeting of the trustees called specifically for that purpose. The church may authorize its trustees to mortgage property. There is no limitation concerning the kind or amount of property which a local Baptist church may hold.

Taxation of church property.—All real and personal property used exclusively for religious worship is exempt from ad valorem taxes. However, church property rented or used for business purposes is not exempt from taxation, notwithstanding the income from the property may be used exclusively for religious purposes. Further, the only constitutional prohibition against ad valorem taxation of property used exclusively for religious worship guarantees the exemption to one lot in a city, one acre within one mile of a city, and five acres outside this one-mile limit. The exemption applies only to the land and the improvements thereon. The legislature is free to enlarge the exemption, as it has done, but cannot diminish it. In any event the exemption is dependent upon the use rather than the ownership of the property. Religious corporations shall not be required to pay a franchise tax. The exemptions from taxation granted do not extend to exemption from liability for municipal improvements. Churches are not liable for income tax or unemployment compensation tax.

Powers of general bodies.—Alabama law now recognizes the right of state conventions or associations of congregational churches, heretofore incorporated under any general or special law, and hereafter incorporated, to act by trustees in the intervals between state conventions, and recognizes the power of the convention to confer upon the trustees the power to do all acts which the convention itself might perform. Such conventions may acquire property as incorporated churches may, and such property is specifically exempted from all state, county, municipal, and other taxes as long as it is exclusively devoted to religious, educational, and charitable purposes. Such conventions, as well as sectional or national conventions incorporated under the laws of any state, are authorized to establish schools, hospitals, colleges, orphanages, and other institutions, which shall always be under the complete control and ownership of said conventions or of boards of trustees appointed by such conventions.

Other provisions.—Church property is protected by all state laws relating to private property in Alabama. There are very few special statutes dealing with the specific protection of church property, but the general law of the state, as well as many local laws and ordinances, deal with the restriction and prohibition of certain commercial and recreational activities on Sundays. It is a misdemeanor to disturb any assemblage of people met for religious worship by any act, at or near the place of worship, and in Jefferson County it is made a misdemeanor to be guilty of a disturbance of the peace on church grounds.

Licensed ministers, as well as circuit, appellate, and probate judges and justices of the peace, may perform marriage ceremonies. Marriages may also be solemnized by the pastor of any religious society according to the rules ordained or custom established by such society. In no event is a marriage to be solemnized without a license. The libraries of ministers are exempt from ad valorem taxation. A minister of a condemned prisoner is among the few individuals who are allowed to visit him and to witness his execution.

No religion may be established by law, and no preference may be given by law to any religious denomination or mode of worship. No one shall be compelled by law to attend any place of worship nor to pay any tithe or other rate for building or repairing any place of worship or maintaining any minister or ministry. No religious test shall be required as a qualification to any public office, and the civil rights, privileges, and capacities of any citizen shall not be in any manner affected by his religious principles. The Supreme Court of Alabama has stated that "all religions, save such as shock the public morals, or offend our statutes, are alike tolerated and protected by . . . our republican policy." There are no special restrictions on meetings of religious bodies, although these meetings would be subject to the same restrictions to which other lawful assemblies would be subject. Likewise, no specific restrictions on practices of religious bodies are contained in the statutes, but no general immunity from the operation of our laws regulating public morals and prohibiting breaches of the peace and similar offenses is granted to religious bodies. A statute prohibiting the handling of poisonous snakes in such a manner as to endanger the life or health of any person has been held to authorize the conviction of a member of a church who handled snakes during a meeting of his congregation and as a part of the service. It was held that the legislature retains the power to restrain acts prejudicial to the public welfare and productive of social injury, and this statute was found to be a valid exercise of the police power, not violative of the constitutional guarantee of religious freedom.

There are no statutory requirements or restrictions relating to the religious beliefs of teachers in the public schools. Courses in Bible and religion may be taught, as electives, in the public schools, provided they do not stress any particular creed or denomination but are taught from a historical, biographical, or literary standpoint. No money raised for the support of the public schools shall be appropriated to or used for the support of any sectarian or denominational school. Free textbooks are supplied only in the public schools, by statute. All public schools must have Bible readings once every day, and the students must receive temperance instruction.

The Supreme Court of Alabama has recognized the following concerning local Baptist churches:

> The Baptist Church is congregational in its policy. It is democratic in its organization. It is the right of each congregation to rule itself in accordance with the law of the church. The will of the majority having been expressed, it becomes the minority to submit. By the law of the church, we take it to be the law made by that congregation, either in terms or in practice.

DREW REDDEN

Arizona. *Organization.*—A church or religious association may exist as an unincorporated association or may be incorporated as a religious, nonprofit corporation. It must be incorporated in order to constitute a legal entity. To incorporate, it will follow procedures set forth in the Arizona code.

Membership and discipline.—A church may, within reason and when not contrary to law, adopt bylaws and regulations in regard to its membership and discipline thereof. If incorporated, it may have not less than three or more than 25 directors. Courts have held that even a majority of a local church, abandoning the old faith by becoming independent or uniting with another denomination, cannot take with them the trust property of the church, but that the right to use such property remains in adherents to the original doctrines, even though they constitute a minority.

Property.—The church may hold property in its own name if incorporated. If it is not incorporated, the legal title to property is to be taken in the name of individuals as trustees for the church; but in such cases the individuals do not own the property but hold same in trust for the church. In case of a change of trustees, the title to the property passes to the successor trustees. In case of the death of a trustee, the property is not inherited by the heirs of the deceased trustee but passes to the successor or subsequent trustees. The statutes of Arizona provide that religious, charitable, and scientific corporations shall not own or hold more real property than is reasonably necessary for the objects of the corporation, except that any corporation may hold for 10 years any real property required in payment of a debt or by gift or demise and real estate exchanged therefor.

Miscellaneous.—The courts have held that one who joins a religious sect holding the community theory of ownership of property and contributes his property to the community, but later withdraws from the society, cannot recover the value of his property in the absence of any such agreement. Educational associations may hold the real property necessary to carry out their purposes or for establishment and endowment of institutions of learning connected therewith. Religious corporations are exempt from the annual registration and report fees. Church property used for public worship or religious worship is exempt from taxes, provided rent is not paid therefor and the same is not used or held for profit. Communication of members to clergymen of confidential matters of confessions is privileged and not to be testified to in court. Every person who wilfully disturbs any assemblage of people met for religious worship by profanity, rude or indecent behavior, or any unnecessary noise is guilty of a misdemeanor. Churches are to withhold state income tax from the salaries of its employees and pastors. MILBURN N. COOPER

Arkansas. *Incorporation of religious bodies.*—Churches and religious organizations (except institutions of learning) are generally incorporated as benevolent associations by the circuit court of the county in which the organization is located. Not less than three persons may file petition seeking incorporation in said court, having first filed with the clerk of the court their constitution and bylaws and a list of petitioning members. After incorporation any amendments to the bylaws must be filed with the clerk within 60 days after passage. Such a corporation has power to borrow money for accomplishment of the purposes of the corporation; to execute promissory notes, bonds, and other negotiable and non-negotiable instruments and evidences of indebtedness; to purchase property or to receive same as gift; to mortgage, lease, or sell property; or to sue and be sued.

Incorporation of colleges, or other institutions of learning, is governed by separate act. A charter for same is granted by the state board of education if found to be in accordance with the laws of the state and is filed with the secretary of state. CARLETON HARRIS

Property of religious bodies.—Under Arkansas law religious bodies may own, control, and dispose of property, real and personal, acquired to promote the purposes for which the body was instituted. Property may be acquired by purchase, devise, gift, and adverse possession. A religious body owning property may control and use such property for the purposes its governing body, whatever that may be, shall, under its constitution and rules, determine; provided such use is consistent with the purposes for which such body was instituted, and provided the instrument conveying title to the organization imposes no limitation upon the uses to which such property shall be devoted. If a specific trust is attached, such property must be used only for purposes consistent therewith and may not be diverted to any inconsistent use.

When a church, strictly congregational or independent in its organization, is governed solely within itself by a majority of its membership and holds property with no other trust attached than that it is for the use of the church, the numerical majority of the church membership may ordinarily control the right to the use and title of such property. Civil courts steadily refuse to determine any controversy in a church, except to protect the temporalities of such bodies and to determine property rights. But courts may properly assume jurisdiction of a dispute between factions of a church organization where property rights are involved.

Where the congregation is the governing body of an individual church, the majority, if they adhere to the organization and to the doctrines of the church, are entitled to the control of the church property. The principle of majority control is, however, limited to independent or congregational religious bodies and is not to be extended to bodies belonging to an ecclesiastical system.

A statute enacted in 1923 provides, "Except where otherwise provided for in the charter, constitution, or by-laws of any church . . . the trustee, deacons, or other governing body shall have the right and authority to . . . execute . . . oil, gas, and mining leases and mineral deeds upon lands owned by such institutions."

Houses used exclusively for public worship and the grounds attached to such buildings necessary for the proper occupancy, use, and enjoyment and not leased or otherwise used for profit are exempt from taxation. Parsonages owned by churches and used as homes for pastors are exempt from taxes, except improvement district taxes.

Other provisions.—The Arkansas state constitution guarantees that no preference shall be given by law to any religious establishment or denomination and directs the state legislature to enact laws to protect every religious denomination in its mode of worship. The right to organize voluntary religious societies to promote the expression and dissemination of any religious doctrine is unquestioned. Religious bodies have power to decide the status of individual members. In a church having a congregational form of government, the majority, if they adhere to the organization and doctrines, represent the church. Religious bodies have inherent power to unite with other religious bodies without statutory sanction.

Religious bodies may establish and maintain

institutions of learning. Such institutions are authorized to acquire property by purchase, gift, or devise, and, if incorporated as colleges or universities, may confer customary degrees and grant diplomas as conferred by reputable institutions of like grade.

Regularly ordained ministers or priests of any denomination may solemnize marriages. Such marriage ceremonies shall be according to the forms and customs of the church to which the officiating minister belongs. If a religious body rejects formal marriage ceremonies, its members may be united in marriage according to the customs of such religious body.

E. L. COMPERE

Florida. *Organization.*—A local Baptist church may be an unincorporated or a corporate body. If unincorporated, the church has no legal existence and cannot contract, sue, or be sued in its own name. If a church is unincorporated, the members own the property of the church individually, and conveyances to an unincorporated church should be to the individuals by name or to several, as trustees for the church. Five or more persons wishing to form a church may become incorporated by presenting to the judge of the circuit court for the proper county a proposed charter subscribed by the intended incorporators. A local church may purchase, accept, own, sell, or mortgage property like any other unincorporated association or, if incorporated, like any other private corporation.

Church property.—There is no limitation on the amount of property a Baptist church may own, but if it is incorporated, its charter must state the value of the real estate which it may hold. This provision is subject to approval of the circuit judge. An incorporated church may not at any time incur an indebtedness or liability greater than two thirds of the value of the property of the corporation. A person may leave property by will to a church, but if such person dies leaving issue of his body, an adopted child, the lineal descendants of either, or a spouse, the bequest is invalid if the will was executed within six months prior to the death of the person.

Property held by a church used exclusively for religious, educational, or charitable purposes is exempt from ad valorem taxation. Paving and sidewalk assessments do not come within this exemption and must be paid by the church.

Other provisions.—Church property is protected by the law applying to all private property in the state. In addition there are special laws further protecting church property. No advertising, advertising sign, or advertising structure shall be constructed, erected, used, maintained, or operated within 100 feet of any church outside the limits of any incorporated city or town. No license to sell alcoholic liquors shall be granted outside the limits of an incorporated city or town to a vendor whose place of business is within 2,500 feet of an established church. No permit to operate a *fronton* (*jai alai*) within 1,000 feet of any existing church may be issued. Anyone wantonly and maliciously destroying, defacing, marring, or injuring a church or any outbuilding, fences, walls, or furniture or apparatus used in connection with such church shall be guilty of a felony.

Privileges of ministers.—Clergymen have all the privileges and immunities of any other citizen of the state. In addition clergymen are exempt from payment of tolls on state bridges and ferries and may be granted free or reduced rates while traveling on a common carrier. They are exempt from jury duty. Such clergymen as a condemned criminal may desire may attend the execution of such criminal.

Any regularly ordained minister of the gospel in communion with some church may perform the marriage ceremony, but before marrying anyone he should require of the parties a marriage license issued according to law, and within 10 days after performing the marriage he must make a certificate thereof and transmit it to the office of the county judge from which the license was issued. It is unlawful for a minister wilfully and knowingly to perform a ceremony of marriage between a white person and a Negro person.

MARION W. GOODING

Georgia. *Constitutional provisions.*—All men are guaranteed freedom of conscience and an inalienable right to worship God in their own way. Religious opinion may not prevent one from holding public office; but the right of liberty of conscience shall not excuse acts of licentiousness or justify practices inconsistent with the peace and safety of the state. No public money shall ever be used directly or indirectly in aid of any church. The Georgia general assembly is given the power to exempt from taxation places of religious worship, burial, property used solely for residential purposes, and certain income from property used exclusively for religious purposes. Ministers, like other citizens, must reside in the state one year and in the county six months next preceding the election in order to be eligible to vote.

Taxation of church property.—Places of religious worship and burial and all property owned by the church used only for single family residences and from which no income is derived; all institutions of purely public charity; intangible personal property held in trust for the exclusive benefit of religious institutions; endowment not invested in real property, and buildings used for the operation of the church, but not rented for income, are exempt from taxation. Church property is not exempt from paving assessment. A church is subject to sale-and-use taxes. Long-term notes (in which a part of the principal falls due more than three years from the date made) secured by real estate held by a church are not exempt from payment of the state intangible property tax. Intangible personal property owned by a church is exempt from state intangible property tax.

The church is not subject to income tax, although a minister is treated like any other citizen.

The church entity.—The church is an assembly of persons united by the profession of the same Christian faith, met together for religious worship. The courts do not concern themselves with the internal management of the church, but they will intervene if property rights are involved; therefore, the supreme court of Georgia has said, "The church is a building consecrated to the honor of God and religion, with its members united in the profession of the same Christian faith." A majority of those who adhere to its organization and doctrines represent the church. In absence of other property, the church edifice and site are liable to sale for payment of a valid debt incurred by the congregation. A church, not qualifying for corporate rights and liabilities, may not be sued or sue as an entity, but the members thereof are liable on its contracts as joint promissors or partners. An unincorporated church is controlled by the majority of its members, and they have the right to devote its funds to any purpose calculated to promote the objects of the church; but they do not have the right to apply them to other uses, except with the unanimous consent of the members. A Baptist church is one with a congregational form of government. The church itself, by and through a majority of its members, is the highest tribunal with jurisdiction to pass upon and determine all differences between its members upon questions of doctrine, discipline, ecclesiastical law, rule, custom, church government, faith and practice of the church. Where church property is devoted to a specific doctrine, the courts may prevent it from being diverted from such use. Jurisdiction to determine who are the duly constituted trustees of the church rests with the church and not with a court of equity. Trustees of churches are proper parties to bring suit or to defend them or to serve with process of papers in a proper proceeding involving trust property. Deeds of conveyance of property may be made to trustees of an unincorporated church, and they and their successors will hold title for the use of the church, and they may sue and be sued in their representative capacity to subject the trust property to a church debt. A church may incorporate under the laws of Georgia as any other corporation, by securing a charter for a maximum of 35 years and filing annual returns with the secretary of state. Three or more persons must obtain the charter from the superior court of the county where the church is to be located. Incorporators must first obtain a certificate from the secretary of state that the name of the proposed church is not the name of any other existing corporation registered in his office. Besides attorney's fees, the cost is 15 cents per 100 words for recording the charter and $5 for other services of the clerk of the court. The charter must be published in a newspaper once a week for four weeks, the cost of publishing being borne by the incorporators. A church corporation enjoys the same powers as business corporations and may sue and be sued in the corporate name. A church corporation is authorized, in addition to the propagation of the gospel, to conduct schools, printing plants, publishing houses, hospitals, nurses' homes, orphanages, old people's homes, and to have other necessary powers incident to the attainment of its objects.

Legal protections of the church.—One may not camp on a camp ground used for religious purposes and place an animal in any booth, tent, or arbor on such camp ground without consent. One may not vend within one mile of the place of worship in the camp ground. This regulation does not apply to established businesses. One may not disturb a Sunday school. One may not interfere with divine services by cursing, using profane or obscene language, being intoxicated, or acting indecently. Talking or whispering so as to disturb a congregation is "indecently acting." One may not pursue business or work of his ordinary calling on the Lord's Day, works of necessity or charity being excepted. One may not hunt with a gun or dogs on Sunday. Wilfully using a gun or pistol on Sunday, not in defense of person or property, is illegal. Fishing on Sunday is illegal. Dancing or permitting dancing on Sunday at any public place is illegal. Twenty-five per cent of the registered voters of a city or county can require an election once each year to determine whether operation of motion picture theaters and holding of athletic events, games, and contests on Sunday may be permitted or prohibited. Auto racing on Sunday is a game or contest. No liquor store shall be operated within 100 yards of any church. No alcoholic beverages of any kind shall be sold upon any church ground or within 100 yards of such ground. No person shall carry intoxicating drink to a place of divine worship. It is unlawful to appear at any church under influence of liquor or to use liquor at any church or other place of divine worship. Wines for sacramental purposes are excepted from these provisions.

Liability of the church for its torts.—Ordinarily a church is not liable for the negligence of its officers and employees unless it fails to exercise ordinary care in their selection or fails to exercise such care in retaining them. Statutes and regulations requiring public buildings to be constructed to meet state fire and safety regulations apply to churches.

Other provisions.—At least one chapter of the Bible must be read in all public schools each day, although a parent may request a child to be excused from hearing the reading of the Bible. No student may be excluded from the University of Georgia because of religious affiliation. Nothing is deemed religious which affirms doctrines of licentiousness or which is inconsistent with the peace and safety of the state. A Baptist minister may perform the marriage ceremony. A minister engaged regularly in discharge of ministerial duties is exempt from jury duty upon his request. When the congregation of a Baptist church terminates an indefinite call to a pastorate, such action is binding, and a court of equity will enforce such action. No person having a wife or child shall by will devise more than one third of his estate to the church to the exclusion of wife or child; and in all cases the will containing such devise must be executed at least 90 days before the death of testator, or devise is void. Provided, if the estate exceeds $200,000 in value, these restrictions shall not apply to such excesses.

CECIL A. BALDWIN

Illinois. *Church organization.*—A local Baptist church may be either an association or a corporation. As an organized association of individuals without a charter, its members are jointly and severally liable for the debts of the church. Grants or conveyances to the church should be to "A, B, and C, as trustees, and their successors in office."

A church may become a religious corporation in one of two ways. First "by electing or appointing, according to its usages or customs, at any meeting held for that purpose, two or more of its members as trustees; and may adopt a corporate name; and upon the filing of an affidavit, as provided, it shall be and remain a body politic and corporate, by the name so adopted." In such case the corporation does not have a seal or charter, but all property, real and personal, of the organization vests in the corporation. Such corporation may lay out and maintain a burying ground. Not more than 10 acres of land shall be exempt from taxes. Second, a church may become a corporation organized under the General Not For Profit Corporation Act. It receives a charter from the secretary of state and is required to make an annual report to the secretary of state.

A church desiring to incorporate under the General Not For Profit Corporation Act must apply to the secretary of state on forms furnished by the secretary of state. Three or more persons who are citizens of the United States, 21 years of age or more, may act as incorporators. The filing fee for a Not For Profit Corporation is $10. If incorporated under the Not For Profit Corporation Act, the corporation may not have shares of stock or pay dividends. It may issue bonds or mortgages, pledge or dispose of assets.

Church property.—A church organized under either of the above provisions may purchase, take, receive, lease, mortgage, take by gift, devise or bequest, or otherwise acquire, hold, use, deal in and with real or personal property, or interest therein, situated in or out of the state of Illinois. It may sue, be sued, invest funds, make contracts, and exercise all powers necessary or convenient to effect any or all of the purposes for which the corporation is organized.

There is no limitation on the amount of property a local church may own. However, only the land and premises actually used by a church for religious purposes, or for orphanages, and not leased or otherwise used with a view to profit, are exempt from ad valorem property tax. Property owned by the church and used by its pastor as residence, not for profit, is taxable.

Legal protection of the church.—Church property in Illinois is protected by the same state laws which are applied to all private property in the state. In addition there are special laws further protecting the existence and use of church property. A tavern may not operate within 100 feet of church or school. Whoever by menace, profane swearing, vulgar language, or any disorderly or unusual conduct interrupts or disturbs any assembly of people met for the worship of God, shall be fined not more than $100. No one may hawk or peddle goods or establish a place for vending goods within one mile of a camp or field meeting for religious purposes, without permission of the authorities having charge of such meeting. Any person wilfully injuring church property shall be guilty of a misdemeanor and fined not more than $500, or confined in the county jail not over one year. Corporations and organizations operated exclusively for religious and charitable purposes are exempt from the unemployment compensation act and the tax imposed thereby.

Other provisions.—A minister of the gospel in regular standing in the church or society to which he belongs may perform the marriage ceremony. Marriage must take place in the county where the license was obtained. Ministers are exempt from jury service. On request of a condemned person, a minister may witness the execution.

Ministers, like other voters, are required to live in the state of Illinois one year, in the county 90 days, and in the precinct 30 days, be citizens of the United States, and be 21 years of age before they are qualified to vote in all elections. They have all the other privileges and immunities of any other citizen of the state.

Adoptive parents shall, whenever possible, be of same religious faith as that of the child. Denial of petition for adoption where petitioner and child to be adopted are of different faiths is within sound discretion of the court. A city may as a valid exercise of its police power prohibit certain business activity on Sunday. No public funds may be paid in aid of any church or sectarian purpose or to help support or sustain any school, academy, seminary, college, university, or other literary or scientific institution controlled by any church or sectarian denomination whatever. The free exercise and enjoyment of religious profession and worship, without discrimination, shall forever be granted; and no person shall be denied any civil or political right on account of his religious opinion.

A. R. CAGLE

Kentucky. *Church property.*—A local Baptist church may hold real estate up to 50 acres of ground. There is no limitation upon the use of this property, as the statute is now worded, but the statute is an outgrowth of Section 319, Carroll's Kentucky Statute, 1930, which provided that the ground must be used for the purpose of erecting thereon houses of public worship, public instruction, parsonages, or graveyards. This statute has been held to be violated where a testator devised 500 acres to a church in trust for the maintenance of a church house on the assumption that the house would remain forever a memorial to the testator's wife. However, the will provided that, if the church board decreed otherwise, the land was to go to the synod in fee simple. The ultimate devise to the synod violated this section prohibiting churches and societies from holding legal or equitable title to more than 50 acres of land. However, the Kentucky court of appeals has also held that the division of land to a trustee for the purpose of paying the income therefrom to a certain church for a period of 99 years for the purpose of supplementing the pastor's salary and maintaining and insuring the church property does not come within this particular statute.

"Places actually used for religious worship, with grounds attached thereto and used and appurtenant to the house of worship, not exceeding ½ acres in cities or towns, and not exceeding two acres in the country" are exempt from taxation. In addition all parsonages or residences owned by any religious society, occupied as a home and for no other purpose by the minister of any religion, with not exceeding one-half acre of ground in towns and cities and two acres of ground in the country appurtenant thereto, are also exempt from taxation.

The Kentucky constitution also provides that burial places not held for private or corporate profit shall not be taxable. In addition, the same constitution provides that institutions of education as well as institutions of purely public charity, not used or employed for gain by any person or corporation, the income of which is devoted solely to the cause of education, shall not be taxed. Thus, clearly, property owned by a church for purposes other than worship and parsonages that are rented out are subject to taxation. Especially is this true when buildings have been built upon land leased under a 99-year lease from a charitable, educational, or religious institution. Improvements on real estate made by a tenant may be assessed separately from that of the owner of the land. Baptist schools, including the Southern Baptist Theological Seminary, children's homes, and hospitals are exempt from taxation under Section 170 of the Kentucky constitution.

With regard to property rights in a church, it is provided that "in case a schism or division shall take place in a society, the trustees shall permit each party to use the church and appurtenances for divine worship a part of the time, proportioned to the members of each party. The excommunication of one party by the other shall not impair such right, except it be one on the grounds of immorality." This statute was amended in 1940, and the word "schism" was dropped from the statute. Thus, this section may now come into play when there is any division in the church, even though there is no schism involved.

In the event it becomes necessary to sell charitable property, it is necessary in Kentucky to have a suit by means of a petition in equity stating the necessity of such action, that it will not violate any reservation or limitation, and the court may direct the sale of the property to reinvest the proceeds in the same county and for the same general purpose.

The law requiring that in case of a division, the trustees allocate the use of the church building by both factions in proportion to the number of their members does not apply where the congregation obtained its own property, and no trust is created. Thus, in a controversy between opposing factions of a Baptist church where the congregation obtained its own property, the trustees of the church had no authority under the statute to allot the time each faction should use the church. The "division" contemplated by the statute imports no more than a separation of the society into two parts without any change of faith. Those who dissolve their connection with the society of which they are members and unite with another and distinct organization are not entitled to the use of the church property. However, where a division arises in a Baptist church which is self-governing, but neither faction has withdrawn but each claims control, the trustees must apportion the use if the property was not purchased by the corporate body.

In Kentucky the court of appeals has declared the law to be that a Baptist church is supreme as to all ecclesiastical affairs, including church government, membership, and discipline, and the court will not intervene therein unless civil or property rights are involved. A Baptist church is a "pure democracy," and there can be no permanent division or schism therein as long as it maintains its organization under rules and regulations. Acts of the majority of the membership present will be valid and binding. However, under the congregational form of government, the voice of the majority is supreme so long as there is no departure from the doctrines of the church. Thus, the Kentucky court will exercise its powers to protect a minority in a Baptist church, no matter how regular the action or procedure may be, against a diversion of the property of the church to another denomination or to a group supporting doctrines radically and fundamentally opposed to the characteristic doctrine of the society. It will also support the minority when the majority disclaims the fundamental practices and doctrines, even though the property is not subject to an express trust.

This has long been the law in Kentucky as to all denominations, in that the title to the property of a divided congregation is in that part of the congregation which is acting in harmony with its own fundamental laws and doctrines. A majority of the congregational church cannot divert the property to a use inconsistent with the purposes of the church by employment of a pastor whose teachings are inconsistent with those fundamental doctrines of the founders of the church. The same case also determined that, where the founders of the church accepted the New Testament without specific interpretation, but the majority faction was opposed to the use of instrumental music in the church, support of missionary organizations, activity of women in church, and use of literature in the Sunday school, the courts of Kentucky would protect the minority and would not support as the true church trustees elected by a majority. Of course, the basis is that the new majority had departed from the fundamental doctrines of the original organization and the faith of the founders.

The majority of a Baptist church in Kentucky is determined by its members in good standing, and it does not matter if some of the voters are minors because there is no restriction on voting age.

The rule in Kentucky may be very well summarized that, in regard to the holding of church property, the majority is usually recognized as having the right. Where no basic doctrines are involved, but where factions are caused by the clash of personalities, the majority rule is recognized in any grouping of the churches for fraternal or co-operative efforts, as an association of Baptists. However, it is clear that where there is a division of a Baptist church, the moderator and any group of ministers in a local association gathered together do not have a right to determine the possession or title to the congregation's property. Associations, however, have generally followed the courts and as an example, the division in the First Baptist Church of Danville from 1925 to 1927 may be cited. Here the Southern District Association decided in favor of the majority following a decision of the Kentucky court of appeals as follows:

> A Baptist church is a pure democracy, and in all matters relating to its government, the election of its officers, its articles of faith, and in the management of its affairs the local congregation is supreme and a majority of the congregation present and voting on any question decides the question finally until the decision is likewise revoked by the congregation. . . . The congregation is supreme and there is no appeal to any ecclesiastical or civil authority from the judgment of the majority. . . .

However, there is no doubt that the association might also be influenced by an opinion of the court of appeals that a majority is not the true church in the same manner.

Constitutional protections.—Under the constitution of Kentucky adopted in 1891 it is stated,

> All men are, by nature, free and equal, and have certain inherent and inalienable rights, among which may be reckoned . . . the right of worshipping Almighty God according to the dictates of their consciences.

The same constitution also provides in Section 5 as follows:

> No preference shall ever be given by law to any religious sect, society or denomination; nor to any particular creed, mode of worship or system of ecclesiastical polity; nor shall any person be compelled to attend any place of worship, to contribute to the erection or maintenance of any such place, or to the salary or support of any minister of religion; nor shall any man be compelled to send his child to any school to which he may be conscientiously opposed; and the civil rights, privileges or capacities of no person shall be taken away, or in any wise diminished or enlarged, on account of his belief or disbelief of any religious tenet, dogma or teaching. No human authority shall, in any case whatever, control or interfere with the rights of conscience.

Other protections.—Church property is protected by the same laws as private property, and it is protected further from trespass, robbery, arson, and the sale of intoxicating liquors within 200 feet from the church. A minister of religion may not be arrested while he is publicly preaching or performing religious worship in any religious assembly.

In Kentucky any person who handles, displays, or uses any kind of reptile in connection with any religious service or gathering shall be fined not less than $50 nor more than $100. Any person who wilfully interrupts or disturbs a congregation assembled for or engaged in worshiping God, or any school, seminary, or college, is subject to a fine of not less than $20 nor more than $50, or imprisoned for not more than 20 days, or both. A minister of the gospel is also protected from anyone who interrupts him, while speaking, by the use of insulting or offensive language or opprobrious epithets, or who attempts to interrupt or injure the speaker by throwing missiles of any kind at him. Such a person shall be fined not less than $50 nor more than $500, or imprisoned for not less than one nor more than six months, or both.

In Kentucky there is a special provision concerning association, camp, or arbor meetings. Any person who, while present at an association, camp, or arbor meeting, engages in the business of erecting or running any place where soft drinks, tobacco, cigars, or refreshments of any kind are offered for sale, within one and one-half miles of the grounds on which the meeting is being held, shall be fined not less than $10 nor more than $100. However, this section does not apply to meetings in cities.

As to the advertisement of malt beverages by trade name or trademark, no licensee shall so advertise within 100 feet of the property line of any school or church. This distance shall be by straight line.

A minister of the gospel in regular communion with any religious society may solemnize marriages. However, it is necessary for him to

> obtain a license therefor from the county court of the county in which he resides, upon satisfying the court that he is a man of good moral character and in regular communion with his religious society, and upon giving covenant to the Commonwealth, with good surety, not to violate the law of this state concerning marriage. Any such license may be annulled by any county court, after notice to the person holding the license.

This provision for the annulment of licenses has been held constitutional. Soliciting marriages is a ground for revoking the license. No marriage may be solemnized without a license, and in Kentucky there is a three-day waiting period. It is unlawful to solicit persons to be married before a particular individual, and it is unlawful for any pastor to divide or share his fee with another person for solemnizing a marriage. A medical examination is required in Kentucky prior to the time the license is issued. Kentucky also has a prescribed form that must be filled out by the minister performing the marriage ceremony concerning the time and place therein. This is to be recorded upon the marriage license. It is the duty of the person solemnizing the marriage to return the license and the certificate to the clerk of the county court in which it was issued within three months after the marriage. It is unlawful in Kentucky to marry a white person and a Negro or a mulatto, or to marry a feeble-minded person as well as an idiot or lunatic.

In Kentucky ministers because of their position are not exempt from jury duty. Only those who, in sound discretion of the Court, are entitled to exemption shall be exempt from service on any grand or petit jury. However, it is customary in Kentucky to release ministers from jury duty if they so request.

Incorporation of churches.—Under Kentucky law Baptist churches may be organized into nonprofit corporations. The articles must be filed with the secretary of state and in the office of the county clerk where the principal place of business of the church is located. The trustees and managers of the corporation may adopt rules for its government and operation. The charter or articles of the corporation may be amended upon the vote of two thirds of the directors, managers, or trustees. In Kentucky there is also an additional provision concerning nonstock and nonprofit corporations for religious, educational, or charitable purposes whereby any three or more persons may form such a corporation. The statute also provides what the articles of a corporation shall contain and that the corporation shall come into existence upon the filing of the necessary articles with the secretary of state and the county court. It is specifically provided that, in this type of corporation, the members are not liable for the debts of the corporation solely by reason of being members. It further provides that all corporations that were in existence prior to the date of the enactment of this new statute on June 17, 1948, for a charitable and religious purpose shall be deemed to be incorporated under its provisions, with the exception that religious, charitable, or educational corporations shall continue to be governed under the provisions of K.R.S. 273.010 to K.R.S. 273.050.

Any religious society, whether a corporation or a voluntary association, may by a majority vote appoint one to three trustees in whom legal or equitable title to the society's property shall be vested to the use of the society. These appointments shall be entered upon the record book of the society and any vacancies shall be filled in the same manner. If any religious society holding land dissolves, the title shall vest in the trustees of the county seminary in which the land lies for the use of that seminary; and if there is no such seminary, then in the county court, for the benefit of common schools in the county. This section has no application to the case where the property reverts to the original owners in case the property is not used for religious purposes.

JOHN P. SANDIDGE

Louisiana. *Incorporation of religious bodies.*—A religious body may obtain a charter by following the procedures set forth in the nonprofit corporation statute, enacted as Act 455 of 1948. The requirements are the same as for any other nonprofit corporation not involving pecuniary profit or gain to its members. Three or more natural persons of full age, or fully emancipated, may form a religious corporation.

Articles of incorporation shall be executed by authentic act signed by each of the incorporators or by his agent duly authorized in writing. The articles of incorporation must state in the English language, among other things: the purpose or purposes for which the corporation is formed; the fact that it is a nonprofit corporation; the term for which it is to exist; the location and address of its registered office; and the full name and post office address of each of its incorporators and directors. A religious corporation must be organized on a nonstock basis.

The articles of incorporation must be filed in the office of the recorder of mortgages for the parish in which the registered officer of the corporation is situated. A multiple original or a certified copy of the articles bearing the certificate of the proper recorder of mortgages, showing the date and hour when the articles were filed for record in his office, shall be delivered to the secretary of state. The certificate of incorporation shall show, according to the certificate of the recorder of mortgages, the date and hour when the original articles were filed for record, which the secretary of state shall certify to be the date and hour when corporate existence began.

Prior to 1948 the method for incorporating a religious body was the same as for other "non-trading corporations." All nonprofit corporations, such as a church, that were organized and incorporated previously under any special or general act were not required to reorganize but are considered to exist under and be governed by the provisions of this act.

The courts have been liberal in upholding action taken by a Baptist church to validate its failure to meet every legal requirement when originally incorporated.

A religious corporation has power to make contracts, borrow money, acquire and dispose of real estate, remove directors, and expel members. A religious corporation is subject to judicial supervision with regard to property rights, but the courts will not deal with spiritual organizations or ecclesiastical matters. Neither will civil courts interfere in church government in ecclesiastical relation with their members.

Property of religious bodies.—The common law rule, that a voluntary unincorporated association has no legal existence and is unable to hold title to real property, does not prevail in Louisiana. When an unincorporated Baptist body acquires and possesses estates, the individual members have common interests as well as individual liabilities. An incorporated Baptist church may acquire, own, sell, and convey property like any other nonprofit corporation. However, mere incorporation by a religious society does not vest in it possession and rights to premises possessed and acquired by the society before incorporation.

Places of religious worship and rectories and parsonages belonging to religious denominations and used as places of residence for ministers are exempt from taxation. However, only the property used exclusively for church purposes is exempt from ad valorem taxes. The exemption does not apply to property owned by a church but leased for profit or income. Paving assessments are not exempt and must also be paid by the church.

There is no limitation as to the kind or amount of property a local Baptist church may own. However, if incorporated, it may take and hold property in trust only for the purpose or purposes set forth in its articles.

Church property in Louisiana is protected by state laws applying to all private property in the state. It is unlawful to do violence against church buildings and property. Violators are subject to fines and/or imprisonment varying with the offenses.

Laws affecting public health and safety apply to church property. Spitting on the floor or walls of a church house is punishable by a fine of not less than $5 nor more than $25, and if default of payment is made, the violator shall be imprisoned for not more than 10 days.

The mayor and aldermen of cities and towns have power to regulate the entrances to church buildings and the way of ingress and egress from same. Churches erecting buildings are subject to building, health, and sanitary codes and ordinances of local boards of health. In addition the State Board of Health and local boards of health have authority to rectify or abate any conditions on private (such as church property) premises, which are prejudicial to the public health.

Other provisions.—A minister of the gospel, in order to be authorized to perform marriage ceremonies in the state, must first register with the clerk of the district court for the parishes in which he is officiating. To perform marriages in the Parish of Orleans, a minister must register with the City of New Orleans Health Department. A minister empowered by law to perform marriage ceremonies must be sure that 72 hours have elapsed between the time of the issuance of the license and the proposed ceremony, except when waiver is granted by proper civil authority. Violation of this requirement shall result in the revoking of the authority of any minister to perform marriages for one year. Conviction of a minister of the gospel of having performed a marriage ceremony of persons under legal minimum age shall forever deprive him of the right of celebrating marriage.

The rental value of a dwelling house furnished to a minister of the gospel as a part of his compensation shall not be included in gross income and is exempt from taxation. Ministers are exempt from paying an occupational tax. They are excused from tutorship and civil jury service. No alcoholic beverage tax is imposed upon any priest, minister, rabbi, or other clergyman possessing or using wines for religious or sacramental purposes in the regular course of his religious duties.

A clergyman who is the spiritual adviser to a convict may visit him while he is being held in solitary confinement prior to execution. He may witness the execution of a criminal only if the convict so requests.

A minister of the gospel is denied the right to take by donation *mortis causa* from a person with whom he has no tie of consanguinity and whom he attends, in his ministerial capacity, during a sickness of which such person dies, under a will made during such sickness.

No tax is imposed on a gift made exclusively to a religious organization provided no part of the net earnings of such organization inures to the benefit of any private individual. All legacies and donations to a church body located within the state are exempt from inheritance tax. In general a bequest to a religious corporation fails if the legatee is not capacitated to take at the testator's death.

A religious corporation cannot take a larger bequest than allowed by its charter, though the restriction be removed by a legislative act before the bequest, payable a certain time after the testator's death, became due.

A religious corporation not operating for profit is exempt from the corporation franchise tax.

State laws have been passed for the protection of morals and public worship, and freedom of religion is guaranteed. No preference shall be given to, nor any discrimination made against, any church or any form of religious faith or worship.

The state Sunday law has been declared constitutional. Police juries have power to regulate the sale of liquors and totally to prohibit the same on Sunday. Alcoholic beverages are prohibited from being sold within 300 feet of the nearest property line of a church.

Expenditure of public funds for the aid of any church, minister, or teacher thereof is prohibited. The use of public funds for the support of any private or sectarian schools is prohibited, and all agreements, tacitly or expressly, directly or indirectly, for combining of public and parochial schools are forbidden. Nevertheless, the furnishing of free school books, free lunches, and free transportation to children attending private and parochial schools has been declared legal. There are no laws as such relating to nuns or priests teaching in public schools. However, school boards are prohibited from paying a teacher to teach certain high school subjects in a parochial school. Religious teaching, or reading of the Bible, is not permitted in public schools.

HERSCHEL C. PETTUS

Mississippi. *Incorporation of religious bodies.*—There are three classes of Baptist churches: religious societies or associations, organized bodies, and corporations. Churches may own at any one place, without limit on the value, a building for worship, a Sunday school house or houses, and a residence for the pastor, with reasonable ground annexed to all of such buildings. The said buildings and land and all personal property are exempt from ad valorem taxes. Conveyances of property to churches as religious societies or associations should be in the names of the officers or trustees and not in the name of the church, as they would be void. Members of said churches approving liabilities are jointly and severally liable. Members are liable for contracts and for torts. Moreover, the officers or trustees acting for such churches are liable for both contracts and torts.

Churches may be organized under the statute and, as an organized body, may sue and be sued without liability against individual members. Baptist churches may be incorporated with no individual liability of the members and with the powers and privileges of corporations for a period not to exceed 99 years.

WILL M. WHITTINGTON

Property of religious bodies.—Any religious body may hold and own, at any one place, real and personal property, necessary for its purposes, without limit as to value; if used exclusively for its own purposes, not for profit, it is exempt from taxation; the church may sell or mortgage it in the manner provided by statute. Any person, not having a spouse or child or descendant of a child, may devise any or all of his property to a religious body at any time; but if a person has a spouse or child or descendant of a child, he may devise to a religious body not exceeding one third of his estate, by will executed at least 90 days before his death. In either case the religious body may only hold the land devised for a period of 10 years after the devise becomes effective. It may sell and convey the land or any part thereof and pass the title held by the testator, at any time within the 10-year period; but if it fails to do so, the land will revert to the testator's heirs or devisees at the end of the 10-year period. This 10-year restriction does not apply to personal property devised.

A. S. BOZEMAN

Other provisions.—Religious liberty, separation of church and state, and freedom of worship without molestation or disturbance are guaranteed in Mississippi. Freedom of speech and of the press shall be held sacred. Freedom of religion does not justify acts of licentiousness, injurious to morals or dangerous to the peace and safety of the state, and does not exclude the holy Bible from use in any public school of the state. No donation or gratuity of public funds may be made to a sectarian or church purpose or use. An ordained minister of the gospel, in good standing, among others, may perform marriage ceremonies. Church property is exempt from ad valorem taxation so long as it is used for church purposes and not for profit. Only certain necessary businesses can be conducted on Sunday; a number of recreations are prohibited; and certain others are permitted only during nonchurch hours.

J. P. COLEMAN

Missouri. The fundamental law of Missouri affecting Baptists, as well as other religious groups, is found in the constitution of the state of Missouri. Various statutes implementing these basic provisions have been enacted by the legislature from time to time; these, in common with the law in general, fall into both civil and criminal classifications.

Missouri recognizes that all men have a right to worship God according to the dictates of their consciences. A minor may not be placed in the guardianship of a person having a religious persuasion different from that of the parents or surviving parent of the minor, if another suitable person can be procured, unless the minor, being of proper age, shall so choose, or unless no suitable person of the same faith can be found. Likewise, the juvenile court, in committing children to other than public institutions, should consider the religious background of the child. However, a guardian may not be removed simply because he is of a different religious faith from that of his ward or his ward's parents.

No person is ineligible for any public office of trust or profit because of his religious beliefs, nor is any person disqualified from testifying or serving as a juror because of his religious beliefs. Persons believing in other than the Christian religion shall be sworn according to the peculiar ceremonies of their religion, if there are such ceremonies. Neither can any person be molested in his person or estate because of his religious beliefs. However, religious liberty is not an excuse by which licentiousness or practices inconsistent with good order, peace, or safety of the state or the rights of others is sanctioned.

By statute unnecessary labor and the sale of merchandise, including fermented or distilled liquor, is prohibited on Sunday; but these statutes have been held to be civil, not religious, regulations to protect health, peace, and good order by requiring a periodical day of rest.

Freedom of worship and the separation of church and state are further safeguarded by the constitutional provisions that no person can be compelled to erect, support, or attend any place or system of worship or to maintain or support any priest, minister, preacher, or teacher of any sect, church, creed, or denomination of religion; that no money shall ever be taken from the public treasury, directly or indirectly, in support of any religious group or in aid of any priest, preacher, minister, or teacher thereof as such; and that no preference shall be given to, or discrimination made against, any religious group or form of religious faith. These provisions are mandatory and must be obeyed—long acquiescence by the public in contrary practices does not make a contrary practice proper. However, a contract made by an individual for the support of a religious group is enforcible.

In general, property belonging to religious groups is exempt from taxation, but the exemption is lost if part of the real estate is rented out to others. However, church property is subject to the payment of special tax bills for public improvements, and a tax which is a lien at the time of purchase by a church must be paid in full. There is no restriction on the amount of property which may be held by a religious group. Baptist churches are considered to be of the congregational type, so that control over the church property is vested in the local church and is subject only to the will of a majority of those members who attend a regular or stated meeting. Baptist churches may be incorporated, and title to church property may be held by the corporation or by trustees.

Churches may be incorporated upon the application of any number of persons, not less than three, who have associated themselves together by articles of agreement in writing, made to the circuit court. Upon the approval of the court, the articles of agreement must be recorded with the recorder of deeds of the county and filed with the secretary of state of Missouri, who is required to issue a certificate of incorporation. Thereupon, the petitioners, their associates, and successors are created a body corporate and politic, by the name designated in the application and charter. The method of incorporation has not been changed since 1879, and the general plan is substantially the same as that originally formulated in 1851.

Religious groups and their property are also protected by a number of statutes designed to protect the quiet enjoyment of religious rights. Carrying a concealed weapon into a church, wilfully setting fire to a church or meeting-house, breaking into or entering a church or building used for church purposes, embezzlement of church funds, and operating a bawdy house within 100 yards of a church are felonies. Trespassing upon, injuring, defacing, or destroying church property is a misdemeanor. Discharging firearms within 200 yards of a church, disturbing a group assembled for religious worship, entering, in an intoxicated condition, a church where there is an assemblage of people met for a lawful purpose, are also misdemeanors. Intoxicating liquor cannot be sold within 100 feet of a church without the consent of the church, and any city is empowered to forbid such sale within 300 feet of a church. Protection similar to that given by state statute may also be given by city ordinance.

In addition to the exemption from property taxation, churches are also exempt from the payment of state income tax, state sales tax, state inheritance tax, and motor vehicle use tax. Contributions made to churches are deductible from gross income in determining taxable income for state income tax purposes.

Churches are subject to regulation with respect to their construction for the protection of the public. JOSEPH J. RUSSELL

New Mexico. Laws respecting New Mexico religious groups do not differ vitally from other areas, except in their enforcement. Ownership, incorporation, taxation, bequests, marriages, and liberty are the natural points of concern. Encroachments are common.

Ownership of property.—A Baptist church may purchase, accept, own, sell, or convey as an individual or corporation. There are no limitations on the amount.

Incorporation.—Any five or more persons, a majority of whom shall be citizens of the United States and residents of New Mexico, may organize a corporation for religious, benevolent, and charitable purposes, filing articles of incorporation with the state corporation commission. Such corporation may, by purchase, gift, devise, or bequest, acquire property and use same. The power to sell, exchange, transfer, convey, lease, mortgage, or otherwise encumber is all within the authority of the charter itself.

Taxation.—While the state constitution provides that "all church property is exempt from taxation," in actuality courts have held that this exemption is confined to restricted classifications only, and that property used for profit, even though the profit may be channeled into religious use, is subject to taxation. Anything rented for income is taxed. Paving assessments must be paid.

Bequests.—The New Mexico statutes specifically state that an incorporated church may receive anything within the scope of its charter powers. There is silence regarding the unincorporated church, but in practice the same rule applies.

Marriage.—Union, contemplated by the law as a civil contract, may be solemnized by any ordained clergyman, or by any civil magistrate, with the provision that the male must be 21 and the female 18 or older. With consent of parents or guardians, the minimum ages may be lowered two years. In all cases, certification of marriage must be reported for recording in the county where the license is issued. Health certification is not required; neither is the minister required to register. In New Mexico there are notable laxities and exceptions in the case of the Indians, particularly in open reservations, where multiple common-law wives are frequent.

Religious liberty.—It has been only within 15 years that evangelical groups have equaled in number the majority religious order, aggressive over a period of four centuries. Even today the long-time minority is still subjected to encroachments and persecutions by the nonevangelicals who have no scruples on separation of church and state. Although the state constitution guarantees freedom for worship according to dictates of conscience, and specifically states that no person will ever be denied civil rights because of his religious opinion and mode of worship, or required to attend any worship or support any religious sect, nor shall any preference be given to any order; actually on every count, violations occur, and Baptists have been required to stand for the preservation of this heritage through four court actions within 10 years (1945–53).

Since no qualification is required for public school teaching, except professional fitness, there is nothing to prevent ministers, nuns, brothers, or priests from teaching. In certain counties, nuns and priests have been employed, selected by a religious order from members of the order, and the salaries have been paid from tax money direct to the order itself. Religious emblems have been hung on classroom walls, pupils have been required to know the catechism before graduation, to kiss the symbolic ring and reverence appropriately placed imagery—all without respect to the faith of those involved. Twenty-two major violations were recounted in the Dixon Free School Case, carried through district and state supreme courts with the county and state boards of education, the bishop of the diocese, and 143 members of the order as defendants. The judgment was handed down Mar. 12, 1949, banning 143 nuns from ever teaching in New Mexico public schools again, and pronouncing in favor of the plaintiffs on 21 other counts, among them those concerning free textbooks and transportation to parochial schools. Even so, the contest was not over. A state attorney general, a member of the violating sect, ruled that parochial pupils could be issued textbooks, tax-purchased on the basis of a certified list from the pupils.

There are areas in the state in which there is not the slightest semblance of liberty. Two Indians of the Zia Pueblo, after embracing Christianity, were, with their families, banished from their tribe and their allotted lands confiscated. When the case was carried to the courts, the judgment was lost and they went without redress.

Another case, similar in aspects, in the Jemez Suit, brought by an evangelical group to force their pueblo council to allow Protestant services to be conducted inside the village and to make a religious choice without the denial of their tribal burial ground. Here again, court action ran into complications embracing treaty rights which transcend constitutional provisions and which limit an action against a ward rather than a citizen of the government. This case was dismissed.

Two other matters, more damaging to religious liberty than all else, are: (1) The clause in the state constitution, written at the time of statehood, 1912, which guaranteed tax support for 12 institutions, owned and controlled by a religious order. Provision was made that there should be a biennial appropriation to these schools and hospitals out of public funds. Succeeding legislatures have continued to make this appropriation, and advocates of liberty have been unable to make an effective protest. (2) The enactment of a pupil transportation law by the legislature of 1955 providing, in the face of court decisions to the contrary, that parochial schools could, on certification of county commissions, receive tax aid for transportation.

Baptists of the state have stood in the forefront in defense of the liberty principle.

HARRY L. CARTER and LEWIS A. MYERS

North Carolina. *Church property.*—There is no limitation as to the kind or amount of property which a church or religious body may hold in North Carolina. Ownership can be acquired either by deed or will. By statute both real and personal property may be acquired, held, and conveyed by unincorporated associations in their common names if such associations or societies are organized for charitable, fraternal, religious or patriotic purposes. The property of a religious body or association can be aliened by grant or mortgage by valid conveyance when the conveyance is authorized by resolution of the body duly constituted and held, by a deed signed by its chairman or president and its secretary or treasurer, or such officer as is the custodian of the common seal which must be affixed to the deed. The association or religious society can sue or be sued in its common name with reference to matters concerning its property.

Property, both real and personal, may also

be held for a church or religious body in the names of trustees appointed by the church or religious body. The property may be acquired and held by the trustees for the uses and purposes of a particular church or religious association according to the instrument by which the property is acquired or according to the constitution and bylaws of such church or association.

The trustees who hold title to church property may be removed by the body appointing them and are accountable to the church society, congregation, or denomination for the use and management of such property. The trustees of any religious body may mortgage or sell and convey in fee simple any real or personal property owned by such body when so directed by such congregation, society, or denomination for which title is held, or its committee, board, or body having charge of its finances, as designated by its constitution or bylaws, and all such conveyances are valid for the purpose of passing title to a purchaser or to a mortgagee for purposes expressed. The trustees who hold property for a religious society or church may sue or be sued with reference to such property.

If property is held by a Baptist church either in its common name as an unincorporated association or in the names of its trustees duly appointed, the control and supervision of the church property is vested in a majority of the membership of said church, each Baptist church being a self-governing unit. Notwithstanding that a Baptist church is a self-governing unit, however, the majority of its membership is supreme and is entitled to control the church property only so long as the majority remains true to the fundamental usages, customs, and practices of the particular church, as accepted by both the majority and minority of the members before any dissension or schism has arisen. If a minority of members of a church adhere to the faith of the church, its usages, customs, and practices, and a majority of the membership makes a material departure from the fundamental usages, customs, doctrines, and practices of the church as they existed before dissension, then the minority shall control.

Buildings owned and held by churches and religious bodies and the land upon which they are situated are exempt from taxation if used exclusively for religious worship or as a residence of the minister of any such church or religious body. Any additional lands necessary for the convenient use of any such building are also tax exempt. Buildings and real property owned by religious bodies for educational or seminary purposes are also exempt from taxation. If real property of churches is not used for purposes of religious worship, the minister's residence, or for educational or seminary purposes, such real property is taxable. Personal property such as furniture and furnishings of church buildings used in connection with religious worship, for the church minister's residence, or for educational or seminary purposes is exempt from taxation. All property held or used for investment, speculation, or rent by a religious society or church, shall not be exempt from taxation unless said rent, or the interest or income from such investment, shall be used exclusively for religious, charitable, educational, or benevolent purposes or in payment of the interest upon the bonded indebtedness of the said religious, charitable, or benevolent institution.

Inheritance taxes in North Carolina are inapplicable to property passing to religious, charitable, or educational institutions such as churches, hospitals, orphan asylums, public libraries. Inheritance taxes are likewise inapplicable to property passing to any trustee or trustees for religious, benevolent, or charitable purposes within the state.

The minister and marriage.—A minister in North Carolina is authorized to perform a marriage ceremony if ordained by any religious denomination or if authorized by his church to perform marriage ceremonies.

No minister or officer shall perform a ceremony of marriage between any two persons, or shall declare them to be husband and wife, until there is delivered to him a license for the marriage of the said persons, signed by the register of deeds of the county in which the marriage is intended to take place, or by his lawful deputy. Every minister or officer who marries any couple without a license being first delivered to him, as required by law, or after the expiration of such license, or who fails to return such license to the register of deeds within two months after any marriage celebrated by virtue thereof, with the certificate appended thereto duly filled out and signed, shall forfeit and pay $200 to any person who sued therefor, and he shall also be guilty of a misdemeanor.

JAMES A. WEBSTER, JR.

Oklahoma. *Organization of religious bodies.*—Persons associated together for religious purposes may incorporate, as any other corporation. Such corporations may hold title to property and transact business relative thereto, but may not hold or own more property than is reasonably necessary for the business and objectives of the corporation. Any such corporation may sell, exchange, or mortgage any or all of its property. The members of any church or religious society, not less than three, who do not wish to incorporate may organize and become corporate, capable of suing; of being sued; and of holding, purchasing, or receiving real property. It must adopt and sign articles containing the name of the body, its plan of operation, its general purpose and place of location, the terms of admission and qualification of membership and selection of officers, and the manner in which it is to be governed. Such articles must be recorded in the office of the secretary of state and the office of the register of deeds in the county in which the body is located.

The officers of religious associations and societies, whether incorporated or not, are subject to control by mandamus. Where persons voluntarily form and organize an association or church upon specific terms and conditions agreed upon by persons forming such association or church, the members thereof will be bound by the terms and conditions of their compact. Where a church is organized upon the express condition that a majority of its members shall rule in church affairs, the will of the majority must prevail. The courts will inquire into proceedings of ecclesiastical bodies when property rights are involved but in no other instance.

Property of religious bodies.—All grants conveying real property in Oklahoma to any officer or officers of any church in trust for the use of such organization of which they are officers shall be vested in their successors in office.

There is no limitation on the amount of property a local church may own. However, only the property used exclusively for religious purposes is exempt from taxation. A religious institution is allowed an exempted valuation of $2,500 on property not used exclusively or directly for religious purposes. In ascertaining whether church property is exempt from taxation, the purpose for which it is used, not its ownership or presence or absence of pecuniary profit to the owner or user thereof, is the determinative factor. Religious corporations and associations are benefited by other statutes which permit personal gifts or bequests to religious institutions deducted from the individual's gross estate in determining estate taxes, and which exempt religious corporations from the state sales tax on dues and gross receipts, and from the state income tax.

Legal protections.—Church property is protected by state laws applying to all private property in the state. In addition, there are special laws further protecting the existence and use of church property. It is a felony wilfully to break, deface, or otherwise injure any house of worship, or any part thereof, or any appurtenance thereto, or any book, furniture, ornament, musical instrument, article of silver or plated ware, or other chattel kept therein for use in connection with religious worship. It is a misdemeanor to utter any profane discourse; to commit any rude or indecent act; to make any unnecessary noise, either within the place of worship or so near as to disturb the order and solemnity thereof; to exhibit within one mile any shows or plays without a license by the proper authority; to engage in, aid, or promote within one mile of any place of worship any racing of animals or gaming of any description; to obstruct in any manner without authority of law, within one mile of a place of worship, the free passage along any highway to the place of such worship. It is unlawful for any person, except a peace officer, to carry into a church any firearm. It is unlawful to hunt or pursue game or to use firearms near any church or other assemblage so as to disturb such assemblage. It is also unlawful for any person to be intoxicated in or near a church, but the provisions which prohibit the manufacture, sale, or barter of intoxicating liquor do not apply to manufacturing and furnishing wine for sacrament purposes in religious bodies.

The state under its general police power has a right and duty to protect the health, welfare, and morals of its citizens. Under this power the following acts are forbidden to be done on the first day of the week and are described as sabbath-breaking: servile labor, except works of necessity or charity; trading, manufacturing, and employing; all shooting, horse racing, or gaming; and all manner of public selling, or the offering or exposing for sale publicly, of any commodities except meats, bread, fish, and all other foods, which may be sold at any time. Food and drink may be sold to be eaten and drunk upon the premises where sold; and drugs, medicines, milk, ice, surgical appliances, burial appliances, and all other necessities may be sold at any time of the day.

Any wilful attempt, by means of threats or violence, to compel any person to adopt, practice, or profess any particular form of religious belief is a misdemeanor. Toleration of religious sentiment shall be secured, and no inhabitant of this state shall ever be molested in person or property on account of his or her mode of religious worship; and no religious test shall be required for the exercise of civil or political rights. Polygamous or plural marriages are forever prohibited. No sectarian or religious doctrine shall be taught in any of the public schools, but this does not prohibit the reading of the holy Scripture. No public money or property shall ever be appropriated, for the use, benefit, or support of any sect, church, denomination, or system of religion, as such, but churches may purchase brick, tile, and furniture made with convict labor from the state penitentiary.

Copies of the register of marriages, births, baptisms, and deaths kept by a church are admissible into evidence in court actions when certified to by the pastor, clerk, or other keeper of the records.

Privileges of ministers.—Any preacher, minister of the gospel, or other ecclesiastical dignitary of any denomination who has been duly ordained and authorized by his church to preach the gospel and who has filed in the office of the judge of the county court a copy of his credentials from his church authorizing him to perform marriages, may solemnize marriages. In addition to performing marriages, ministers have other privileges. They are exempt from jury service and may witness executions of criminals; the library and office equipment of a minister who is actively engaged in ministerial work is exempt from taxation. They have all the privileges and immunities of any other citizen of the state. LAVERN FISHEL

South Carolina. *Church property.*—A local Baptist church may purchase, accept, own, sell, and convey property as any other unincorporated association, or, if incorporated, as any other private corporation. If the church is unincorporated, the members own the property individually, and there is no real difference between a grant to X, Y, and Z as trustees for a church and a grant directly to a church. The debts of an unincorporated church are joint and several against the individual members, each member being jointly and severally liable for the payment of such debts or any resulting judgment.

There is no limitation on the amount of property a local Baptist church may own. However, only the land and premises actually used by a church are exempt from ad valorem property taxes. This exemption does not apply to holdings exceeding two acres in any single case, or to any land or building from which income is derived. Paving assessments do not come within this exemption and must be paid by the church.

Legal protection.—Church property in South Carolina is protected by the state laws applying to all private property in the state. In addition there are special laws further protecting the existence and use of church property. It is unlawful to operate a dance hall within one-fourth mile of a rural church or cemetery, and the operation of a dance hall is prohibited entirely on Sundays. Any person using obscene or profane language within hearing of a church shall be guilty of a misdemeanor. It is unlawful for a hawker or peddler to carry on his business or camp within one-half mile of any church in Greenwood County. It is unlawful to operate a filling station within 100 feet of any church in Union County. Any person who burns, or causes to be burned, or advises another to burn any church shall be guilty of felony. Any member or officer of an incorporated church wilfully injuring church property shall be guilty of a misdemeanor.

Incorporation of churches.—Any church holding or desiring to hold property in common may incorporate. Such church must apply to the secretary of state by means of a declaration of charter containing the names of the petitioners, name of proposed corporation, headquarters or location, purpose of the corporation, and the names of the officers or trustees of the proposed corporation. The total fee for a corporate charter for a church may not exceed $3. There need be no capital stock of such corporation. Such corporation has power to make contracts, loan and borrow money, expel or suspend members, and enforce collection of dues by appropriate bylaws. The requirements and conditions for incorporation of religious bodies have remained substantially unchanged for over 50 years.

Other provisions.—The South Carolina general assembly shall make no law respecting an establishment of religion or prohibiting the free exercise thereof. This does not mean that the state may not in any respect restrict the exercise of religious beliefs. Where such practices violate the public morals or conscience, the state may restrict them; but the state and a municipality may not wholly prevent the preaching or disseminating of any religious views. The state under its general police power has a right and duty to protect the health, welfare, and morals of its citizens. Under this power the state may prohibit a practice of polygamy and the use of dangerous animals or reptiles.

The property of the state, its credit or monies, cannot be used to aid in the operation or maintenance of any institution which is under the direction or control of a church or religious organization in whole or in part. This excludes the extension of any financial assistance to church schools in any manner or degree. The directors of an eleemosynary institution, operated without profit, as a home for orphans or needy children, may have a school established at such institution by the state.

Church corporations are exempt from income tax, and the rental of a house furnished a minister is also exempt from income tax. Religious organizations are not subject to employment compensation taxes.

Privileges of ministers.—Only ministers of the gospel, Jewish rabbis, and officers authorized to administer oaths may perform marriage ceremonies in this state. In addition to performing marriages, ministers have other statutory privileges in this state. Ministers are exempt from payment of road taxes and business or professional license taxes, as well as tolls at bridges, ferries, and turnpikes. Ministers are exempt from jury duty, and may witness executions of criminals. Ministers in charge of congregations are required to live in the state only six months prior to registering and voting in all elections. They have all the privileges and immunities of any other citizens of the state.

EUGENE BRYANT

Tennessee. *Organization of churches.*—A local church may be organized either as a general welfare corporation or a voluntary association. The organization of a corporation requires compliance with prescribed statutory procedures. The organization of a voluntary association is consummated by the church members associating themselves together for a common purpose.

A general welfare corporation acts in its corporate name through its directors who are elected and controlled by a majority vote of its members. It has continuous existence and powers necessary to its function. It may not engage in a commercial enterprise for profit, may not pay dividends, and all income must be devoted to its religious purposes. Neither directors nor members are personally liable for its debts.

A voluntary association acts through trustees who are elected and controlled by a majority vote of its members. It has powers necessary to its function. Individual members are liable for debts authorized or assented to by them.

The constitution, charter, bylaws, or statutes

may require more than a simple majority for the exercise of some powers by either an association or corporation.

Courts have no control over the internal affairs of a church or of ecclesiastical matters unless incident to determination of some property right. General welfare corporation charters are available for schools, associations, boards, or agencies. Such corporations possess the powers necessary to their function, and their trustees or directors may be elected by an unincorporated convention. In general they enjoy the same exemptions and are subject to the same limitations as affect churches.

No person can be compelled to attend or support any place of worship or minister against his consent, and no preference shall be given by law to any religious establishment or mode of worship.

Ownership of property.—Any religious denomination, society, or church, whether incorporated or not, may take and hold by deed, will, or otherwise any amount of land for use as a church, parsonage, or burial ground.

In Tennessee clauses in the charter, will, or deed are enforceable which provide that title is conveyed "for the use and benefit of those of the membership, even though they be a minority, who adhere to, maintain and propagate the doctrine, faith and practices of missionary Baptists in churches and who co-operate with local, Tennessee and Southern Baptist Conventions."

An association may receive gifts and bequests of money or other personal property for use in carrying out its religious purposes, but bequests of money to be held and invested must be made through trustees. A corporation is not so limited.

The property of a church which is used solely for religious purposes may not be taken to pay judgments against it for negligence. Income-producing property may be sold to pay such judgments. Church property is subject to the payment of church debts.

Taxation of churches.—Real or personal property owned by a church and used for religious purposes is exempt from property taxes. Real property which is held for producing income is subject to taxation. Income from stocks and bonds owned by a church is exempt from income taxes. Gifts to a church for religious purposes are not subject to gift or inheritance taxation. Churches are exempt from sales and use taxes.

Laws affecting marriages.—All regular ministers of the gospel over 18 years of age are empowered to perform marriage ceremonies when presented with a license issued by the county court clerk of the county in which the marriage is to be performed to which is attached a physician's certificate of freedom from disease. The marriage must be solemnized in the county where the license is issued. The officiating minister must return the license to the county court clerk who issued it within 30 days after the date of the marriage. No particular form need be observed. It is sufficient for the parties respectively to declare, in the minister's presence, that they accept each other as husband and wife.

Miscellaneous provisions.—Ministers are exempt from jury duty and are not eligible to be members of the legislature.

It is a misdemeanor to disturb assemblies of worship by noise, rude or indecent behavior at or near place of meeting; to move into tent or building belonging to religious assembly without permission; to expose for sale or gift articles within one mile of worship place, and not at usual place of business; and to sell or offer to sell any articles within one mile of assembly in such manner as to disturb same; and to handle or use poisonous or dangerous snakes or reptiles so as to endanger life or health of any person. ANDREW TANNER

Texas. *Organization of religious bodies.*—A religious society is a voluntary association of individuals or families united for the purpose of having a common place of worship and providing a proper teacher to instruct them in religious doctrines and duties and to administer the various ordinances of religion. Where rules and regulations are made by the proper functionaries, and they are authorized by the society, they will be enforced by the courts, if not in conflict with some law on the subject. The right of a church to decide for itself whom it may admit into fellowship, or who shall be expelled or excluded from its fold, cannot be questioned by the courts when no civil or property rights are involved. There is no such thing as a general Baptist church, but each local church is supreme in control of its own affairs and bound only by the action of a majority of its members.

An unincorporated religious society is not an entity in law and cannot sue or be sued in its association name and cannot be held generally for a personal debt, but its property may be sold to enforce a lien. Nor can the trustees be sued in their capacity as such so as to bind the church unless enforcement of property rights or lien is involved. But the members and managing committees who incur the liability, assent to it, or subsequently ratify it, become personally liable. The civil courts can determine only questions affecting property rights, and ecclesiastical and doctrinal questions will be examined only to determine property rights.

Any religious society may, by the consent of a majority of its members, become a body corporate, electing directors or trustees, and performing such other things as are directed in the case of other corporations; and when so organized it shall have all the powers and privileges, and be subject to all the restrictions in this title contained, for the objects named in the charter, and shall have the same power to make bylaws for the regulation of their affairs as other corporations.

The secular affairs of a religious corporation

shall be under the control of a board of trustees, to be elected by the members of such corporation; and the title to all property of any such corporation shall vest in such trustees. This has been the rule since 1899. Charters for such corporations are acknowledged by three or more members and filed in the office of secretary of state.

Ownership and taxation of property.—Any religious corporation organized under the laws of the state may acquire, own, hold, mortgage, and dispose of and invest its funds in real and personal property in this state for the use and benefit, and under the direction of, and in trust for, such electing, controlling, and parent body in furtherance of the purposes of the organization of the member institution, but not for profit.

A Baptist church corporation holds legal title to the church's physical property, but equitable title is in the church and subject to control of its members.

It is as liable for its debts created in the furtherance of its lawful purposes as corporations created for any other purpose. A receiver may be appointed for any defunct or disorganized church or congregation when the fact of such condition is brought to the attention of any district court or other court having jurisdiction by an application for the appointment or a receiver or receivers for such defunct or disorganized church or congregation.

When a church divides, the majority rules, and if no restrictions are imposed in the title to the property, a minority cannot obtain possession by showing that the majority has departed from the articles of faith adopted when the property was acquired.

The following property shall be exempt from taxation: actual places of religious worship, also any property owned by a church or by a strictly religious society, for the exclusive use as a dwelling place for the ministers of such church or religious society, the books and furniture therein, and the grounds attached to such buildings necessary for the proper occupancy, use, and enjoyment of the same, and which yields no revenue whatever to such church or religious society; provided that such exemption as to the dwelling place for the ministers shall not extend to more property than is reasonably necessary for a dwelling place and in no event more than one acre of land. Controversies exist with taxing authorities regarding the status of ministers of education and music, not ordained, as to whether or not they are included within the exemption of ministers under the constitution and statutes.

Other provisions.—A city may not zone an area so as to exclude churches from it, but may provide reasonable rules for health and public safety under its police powers.

No witness shall be disqualified for his religious convictions or lack of religious convictions. The people are given complete freedom of worship. No religious test shall ever be required as a qualification to any office or public trust in this state; nor shall anyone be excluded from holding office because of his religious sentiments, provided he acknowledges the existence of a Supreme Being. Eligibility may not be made to depend on religious views.

Ministers may be allowed free passes in intrastate travel in the state if principal occupation is minister of religion. They are exempt from jury duty and service in the militia, road duty, and work on town or village streets. All licensed ordained ministers of the gospel, rabbis, judges of district and county courts, and justices of the peace may perform marriages. The basic science law shall not affect or limit in any way the application or uses of the principles, tenets, or teachings of any church in the ministration to the sick or suffering by prayer, without the use of any drug or material remedy, provided sanitary and quarantine laws and regulations are complied with; provided, however, that the provisions of Art. 742-b shall not apply to a member of any religious faith in administering the last rites of his faith; and provided further that all those so ministering or offering to minister to the sick or suffering by prayer shall refrain from maintaining offices, except for the purpose of exercising the principles, tenets, or teachings of the church of which they are bona fide members.

Securities issued by a church are exempt from registration under the Securities Act.

All men have a natural and indefeasible right to worship Almighty God according to the dictates of their own consciences. No man shall be compelled to attend, erect, or support any place of worship, or to maintain any ministry against his consent. No human authority ought, in any case whatever, to control or interfere with the rights of conscience in matters of religion, and no preference shall ever be given by law to any religious society or mode of worship. But it shall be the duty of the state legislature to pass such laws as may be necessary to protect equally every religious denomination in the peaceable enjoyment of its own mode of public worship.

No money shall be appropriated, or drawn from the state treasury for the benefit of any sect, or religious society, theological or religious seminary; nor shall property belonging to the state be appropriated for any such purposes.

The Texas constitutional provision guaranteeing freedom of religion and proscribing the establishing of any religion was in part declaratory of the earlier experiences of America, but in part it also reflected an immediate experience in religious intolerance suffered by the Texas settlers prior to their separation from the Mexican Republic.

Generally it is not for the judiciary to strike down bequests for religious uses, since to do so would necessarily infringe on the constitutional guaranty of perfect freedom and equality in all religions. Sunday laws are constitutional as within the police power of the state.

An ordinance of the city of Houston, which made the sale on Sunday of spirituous, vinous, or malt liquors a misdeameanor, punishable by fine, was held to be constitutional.

An ordinance denying pupils the right to attend school unless vaccinated for smallpox was held not to interfere with any rights of conscience in matters of religion.

Religious instruction of a sectarian character may not be offered in the public schools during school hours, and the noon hour is considered part of the school day.

A board of trustees of an independent school district may for a reasonable consideration lease school property for sectarian purposes, provided such lease in no way interferes with use of such property for school purposes and "reasonable consideration" for such lease shall be determined by the board of trustees.

Any person who shall labor, or compel, force, or oblige his employees, workmen, or apprentices to labor on Sunday, or any person who shall hunt game of any kind whatsoever on Sunday within one-half mile of any church, schoolhouse, or private residence, shall be fined not less than $10 nor more than $50.

The commissioners court of any county in the territory thereof outside incorporated cities and towns and the governing authorities of any city or town within the corporate limits of any such city or town may prohibit the sale of alcoholic beverages by any dealer where the place of business of any such dealer is within 300 feet of any church, public school, or public hospital, the measurements to be along the property lines of the street fronts and from front door to front door and in direct line across intersections where they occur.

Whoever shall wilfully or maliciously throw a stone or other missile, or fire any gun or pistol at, against, or into any church house, shall be fined not less than $5 nor more than $1,000 or be confined in jail not less than 10 days nor more than two years.

Any person who, by loud or vociferous talking or swearing, or by any other noise, or in any other manner, wilfully disturbs any congregation or part of a congregation assembled for religious worship and conducting themselves in a lawful manner, or who wilfully disturbs in any manner any congregation assembled for the purpose of conducting or participating in a Sunday school, or to transact any business related to or in the interest of religious worship or a Sunday school, and conducting themselves in a lawful manner, shall be fined not less than $25 nor more than $100.

Any person who shall run or be engaged in running any horse race, or who shall permit or allow the use of any ninepin or tenpin alley, or who shall be engaged in match shooting or any species of gaming for money or other consideration, within the limits of any city or town on Sunday, shall be fined not less than $20 nor more than $50.

Any merchant, grocer, or dealer in wares or merchandise, or trader in any business whatsoever, or the proprietor of any place of public amusement, or the agent or employee of any such person, who shall sell, barter, or permit his place of business or place of public amusement to be open for the purpose of traffic or public amusement on Sunday, shall be fined not less than $20 nor more than $50. The term "place of public amusement" shall be construed to mean circuses, theaters, variety theaters, and such other amusements as are exhibited and for which an admission fee is charged; and shall also include dances at disorderly houses, low dives, and places of like character, with or without fees for admission. A. B. CULBERTSON

Virginia. From this state comes the statute for religious freedom. Its principles are found in the constitution of Virginia, and in the constitutions of many other states and of the United States. The Virginia general assembly has since reaffirmed the principle of freedom of religion. Because of the doctrine of separation of church and state, the Virginia constitution provides that the general assembly shall not grant a charter of incorporation to any church or religious denomination.

Church property.—A local Baptist church may acquire real property by conveyance, devise, or dedication, provided it is to be used as a place of public worship, burial place, parsonage, meeting place for societies or committees, or residence of the sexton located adjacent to or near the house of worship. Land can be held for no other purposes. If a devise does not specify the purpose, it shall be deemed to be for one of the above purposes.

Title to real property is held by trustees nominated by the church and appointed by the court. The trustees need not be members of the church. They merely hold legal title to the real property and have no power over its management, control, or acquisition of their own volition.

The quantity of land the trustees may take or hold at any one time for the benefit of the church is limited to four acres in a city or town or 75 acres outside of a city or town. If the church is in a city, however, the city, by ordinance, may authorize the trustees to take and hold land in such city not exceeding 10 acres at any one time if such acreage is devoted exclusively to a church building, chapel, administrative offices, Sunday school building and playgrounds therefor, and parking lots for the convenience of those attending any of the foregoing. Real estate owned by a church may not be sold or encumbered except by a proceeding in court, but this does not apply to encumbrances created by law, such as mechanics' liens. The proceeding may be instituted by the congregation or by the trustees. When the church has become extinct or has ceased to occupy the property as a place of worship, so that it may be regarded as abandoned property, the petition for authority to sell may be filed by the surviving trustee or trustees, should there be any, or by one or more members of the church, should there be any, or by the denomination to which the church belongs. The statute also provides for the determination of property rights on division of a church.

A local Baptist church may acquire and own books and furniture to be used on land owned and used by the church for public worship or at the residence of the minister. There is no legal limitation on the quantity of books and furniture a church may own. Legal title to books and furniture is held by the trustees for the benefit of the church under the same conditions as legal title to land is held for its benefit.

Personal property may be acquired by a local Baptist church by gift, grant, or bequest to the church or to its trustees for its benefit. Thus, any interest in personal property, legal or equitable, may be acquired by any mode of transfer, *inter vivos* or testamentary. Ordinarily, legal title to personal property is held by the church trustees, but one who creates a trust for the benefit of a church may designate other individual or corporate trustees to administer the trust for its benefit. A church may not take or hold at any one time money, securities, or other personal estate, exclusive of books and furniture, the total value of which exceeds two million dollars. Included in this limitation is the corpus of trust funds in the hands of trustees other than the church trustees. The rule against perpetuities does not apply to churches.

The Virginia constitution provides that the following property, *inter alia,* shall be exempt from state and local taxation, including inheritance taxes:

> Buildings with land they actually occupy, and the furniture and furnishings therein and endowment funds lawfully owned and held by churches or religious bodies, and wholly and exclusively used for religious worship, or for the residence of the minister of any such church or religious body, together with the additional adjacent land reasonably necessary for the convenient use of any such building.

However, when any such building or land, or any part thereof, shall be leased or shall otherwise be a source of revenue or profit, all such buildings and land shall be liable to taxation. Also, *inter vivos* and testamentary gifts to churches are not subject to gift and inheritance taxes. Churches are likewise exempt from taxes for recordation of deeds, deeds of trust, and mortgages.

Organization, rights, and obligations.—A Baptist church, as any other unincorporated association, may sue and be sued in the name by which it is commonly known, and judgments and executions against the church are binding on its real and personal property in like manner as if it were incorporated. Service of process may be had on any officer or trustee of the church. The trustees, in their own names, may sue for and recover any real or personal property held by them as trustees of the church, or for damages on account of injury thereto. They may also be sued, in their own names, in relation to the property so held. If a trustee fails to perform his duty, a class suit in equity may be brought by any one or more members of the church on its behalf to compel him to use the property he holds for church purposes.

Local churches may contract and be contracted with as any other unincorporated association. They are subject to liability for breach of contract. There is doubt in Virginia as to the personal liability of individual members of the church for breach of a contract made in the name of the church. Trustees and others who sign contracts on behalf of a church may be personally liable thereon. This is especially true when the contract is signed without proper authority from the church, and even though they sign in their representative capacities as agents or trustees of the church. Personal liability also exists when the trustees, board, or others sign contracts on behalf of the church with proper authorization of the church unless they sign in such a manner as to expressly negative personal liability, or the contract expressly so provides. This rule, however, has been modified in Virginia insofar as negotiable instruments are concerned. The statute provides:

> When the [negotiable] instrument contains, or a person adds to his signature, words indicating that he signs for or on behalf of a principal, or in a representative capacity, he is not liable on the instrument if he was duly authorized; but the mere addition of words describing him as an agent, or as filling a representative character, without disclosing his principal, does not exempt him from personal liability.

Also, members of boards and committees who authorize others to execute contracts on behalf of the church are subject to personal liability on such contracts.

It seems that a church may be subject to liability for injuries caused to persons by defective premises.

Legal protections.—Church property is protected by Virginia law applying to property generally. In addition there are special laws giving further protection to the existence and use of church property. It is a misdemeanor to wilfully and maliciously break any window or door of a church, injure or deface a church building, or destroy or carry away any furniture belonging to a church or in its building. It is unlawful for any person, without consent of an authorized person, to go upon or enter, in the nighttime, the premises or property of a church for any purpose other than to attend a meeting or service held in such church. Any person who maliciously burns, or by the use of an explosive maliciously destroys or damages, or causes to be burned or destroyed, or aids, counsels, or procures the burning or destroying of a church building, or sets fire to anything, or causes to be set on fire, or aids, counsels, or procures the setting on fire of anything, by the burning whereof any church shall be burned is guilty of a felony. It is a misdemeanor for any person who knows himself to be infected with a dangerous, contagious, or infectious disease, or recently had such a disease and has not since cleansed himself and his clothes so as to be free from the infection, to go into any church or other house used for public worship. It is unlawful to carry a dangerous weapon to a place of worship while a meeting for religious purposes is being held at such place, or to carry such a weapon without good and sufficient cause, at any place other than his own premises. It is also a misdemeanor to expectorate or deposit any sputum, saliva, or mucus upon any part of a church. Any person who displays, exhibits, handles, or uses any poisonous or dangerous snake or reptile in such a manner as to endanger the life or health of another is guilty of a misdemeanor. It is a crime to wilfully, or while intoxicated, interrupt or disturb any assembly met for the worship of God. The worship service need not be in progress at the time of the disturbance. Virginia prohibits or limits working and the transaction of business on Sunday.

There are some miscellaneous provisions affecting churches. Motion picture films for religious purposes need not be examined by the Division of Motion Picture Censorship provided the application for the required permit contains, *inter alia,* a sworn statement that the film is to be exhibited only for religious purposes. Participation in a prize fight is a felony in Virginia, but it is not unlawful for a religious association to conduct amateur boxing or sparring matches or exhibitions. It is unlawful to manufacture, sell, or otherwise distribute ice cream and other frozen products without a state permit which is issued only if the product meets certain standards of purity and quality and certain standards of sanitation as to handlers, buildings, equipment, etc. Churches are, however, required to comply with the standards of purity and quality of the product only.

Marriage and ministerial privileges.—Only such persons as are authorized by the court may celebrate the rites of marriage in this state. An ordained minister of any religious denomination who is in regular communion with the religious society of which he is a reputed member may be so authorized upon the execution of a bond, with surety, conditioned according to law. For failure to return, within five days after the marriage has been celebrated, the license and certificates of the clerk, together with his own certificates of the time and place at which the marriage was celebrated, to the clerk who issued the license, the bond will be thereby forfeited and the minister shall also be guilty of a misdemeanor. The husband shall pay a fee of $1 to the minister for performing the marriage ceremony. Any person exacting a greater fee shall forfeit to the party aggrieved $50. It is a misdemeanor to perform the ceremony without a license, or without having been authorized by law to do so. It is also a misdemeanor knowingly to perform a marriage ceremony between persons either of whom is an habitual criminal, idiot, imbecile, hereditary epileptic, or insane person, unless it be that the female is over the age of 45 years. If anyone performs the ceremony of marriage between a white person and a Negro, he shall be subject to a forfeiture of $200. Ministers have the same rights and duties generally as other persons. They are, however, exempt from jury service.

WILLIAM T. MUSE

LAWTON, JOSEPH JAMES (b. Allendale, S. C., Apr. 18, 1861; d. Hartsville, S. C., June 13, 1941). Businessman, college trustee, South Carolina Baptist leader. Son of Benjamin William and Josephine (Polhill) Lawton, he attended Richmond Academy, Augusta, Ga., and was a student at Furman University, 1877–79. After moving to Hartsville, Jan. 1, 1883, he became associated with James Lide Coker as a member of the firm of J. L. Coker and Co.; and in 1900 he organized Hartsville Oil Mill, became president and treasurer, and began his rise to national prominence in the oil industry. Lawton was one of the founders of Coker College and served as treasurer, 1908–38, and as president of the board, 1918–41. He was a member of the board of trustees of Furman University, 1893–1941, serving as president of the board, 1916–39. A deacon of the Hartsville Baptist Church, 1887–1941, and superintendent of the Sunday school, 1888–1924, Lawton was honored by the church in 1938 when the new Sunday school building was named for him. Lawton served as moderator of Welsh Neck Association, 1916–37; president, South Carolina Baptist Convention, 1920–22; member of the convention's general board, 1925–28 and 1930–33; and trustee of Southern Baptist Theological Seminary, 1914–27. Furman University granted him the Ph.B. degree of the class of 1880 in 1936. He was an ardent advocate of temperance. On Oct. 3, 1883, he married the daughter of J. L. Coker, Margaret, who died in 1912.

BIBLIOGRAPHY: *The National Cyclopedia of American Biography,* XXX (1943). *Who's Who in the South* (1927). *Baptist Courier* (June 26, 1941).

MRS. GEORGE J. WILDS, JR.

LAWTON, WESLEY WILLINGHAM (b. Allendale, S. C., Oct. 31, 1869; d. Asheville, N. C., Mar. 3, 1943). Missionary to China. Son of Thomas Oregon and Mary (Willingham) Lawton, he graduated from Furman University and Southern Baptist Theological Seminary and served as a missionary to China under the Southern Baptist Foreign Mission Board, 1894–1939. His evangelizing and church-building work centered in Chinkiang in Central China and Kaifeng in Interior China. With W. Eugene Sallee (*q.v.*) he pioneered in opening Southern Baptists' Interior China Mission. Lawton married Ida Deaver (1869–1954) Oct. 14, 1897, and five of their six children returned to China as missionaries, three of them later being transferred to other Asiatic fields. B. L. NICHOLS

LAYMEN'S MOVEMENT. See Brotherhood, Baptist.

LEA FEMALE COLLEGE. Established in 1877 by C. H. Otkin at Summit, Pike County, Miss., where two women in the Lea family contributed $1,750 for the purchase of the old academy property. Backed by Baptists of the area, the school enrolled 120 in 1885 and 142 in 1894, after which it was moved to McComb, continuing as McComb Female Institute. It is now extinct. J. L. BOYD

LEACHMAN, EMMA (b. Beechland, Washington County, Ky., July 6, 1868; d. Louisville, Ky., Aug. 5, 1952). Worker in Hope Rescue Mission, city missionary, director of practical missions in Woman's Missionary Union Training School, and a Good Will Center in Louisville, Ky. She came to Louisville after attending Central Teachers College in Indiana. In 1921 she was appointed by the Home Mission Board to help establish Good Will centers and to enlist Baptist churches in the activities of the Home Mission Board. She traveled throughout the South speaking to Woman's Missionary Union leaders, to city, associational, and state missionaries, and to city and country churches, emphasizing home mission needs and opportunities. She was speaker at the W.M.U. Training School, Louisville, at commencement in 1944, and on Founders' Day, 1947. She retired in 1938. Her last years were spent in Morton Home, Louisville, Ky. E. C. ROUTH

LEADERSHIP TRAINING, THE LOCAL CHURCH PROGRAM OF. The classes and other activities by means of which a church prepares as many of its members as can be enlisted to share in the administration and execution of the church's program of activities. Through the use of trained laymen in various positions of responsibility, the church multiplies the usefulness of its vocational ministers, who are thus given the help which frees them from much detail and allows them time for creative planning and leadership. Volunteer lay leaders supervise and lead in the various activities of the church and its organizations, depending on their vocational ministers for co-ordination, direction, and counsel as needed.

A person who accepts a position of leadership in the church may better equip himself by participating in the church's program of leadership training. This program includes many opportunities, both formal and informal, such as the study course or training school, group study plans, individual study, correspondence courses, prospective workers' classes, weekly officers' and teachers' meetings and other business meetings, officers' clinics, committee work, substitute teaching or leading, personal conferences, work under supervision, observation, associational or community schools and workshops, and the training programs of state and Southern Baptist agencies, including summer assemblies. In many churches the minister of education or another designated worker serves as co-ordinator of the training activities.

Bibliography: M. W. Connor, *Leadership in Religious Education* (1947). *Correlated Church Study Course* (annually, 1950–). G. S. Dobbins, *The Churchbook* (1951); *For You and Your Church* (1950). G. L. Freeman and E. K. Taylor, *How to Pick Leaders* (1950). N. C. Harner, *The Educational Work of a Church* (1939). F. L. Knapp, *Leadership Education in the Church* (1933). M. H. Leiffer, *The Effective City Church* (1949). H. C. Mayer, *Young People in Your Church* (1943). F. M. McKibben, *Guiding Workers in Christian Education* (1953). P. W. Milhouse, *Enlisting and Developing Church Leaders* (1947). M. F. J. Preston, *Christian Leadership* (1934). O. Tead, *The Art of Leadership* (1935). C. H. Titus, *The Processes of Leadership* (1950). JOHN K. DURST

LEAKSVILLE-SPRAY INSTITUTE. A Baptist school at Leaksville, Rockingham County, N. C., founded in 1905 by citizens of Leaksville. It was the associational school of Pilot Mountain Association and was opened in Sept., 1905, with J. A. Beam as principal. The school had high school, normal, commercial, and post-high school departments and offered courses in music, art, voice, and expression. Leaksville-Spray Institute was closed after the war of 1917–18. D. L. SMILEY

LEAVELL, FRANK HARTWELL (b. Oxford, Miss., Mar. 11, 1884; d. Nashville, Tenn., Dec. 7, 1949). Pioneer leader of organized student work in the Southern Baptist Convention and secretary of the Department of Student Work of the Sunday School Board from 1928 until his death. He was the son of George Washington and Corra Alice (Berry) Leavell. He received the B.S. degree from the University of Mississippi in 1909, the M.A. degree from Columbia University in 1925, the LL.D. degree from Mississippi College in 1935, and the L.H.D. degree from Baylor University in 1945. He married Martha Maria Boone on Apr. 15, 1917. They had three children—Eddie Belle, Mary Martha, and Frank Hartwell, Jr. Leavell went to California in 1909 to engage in real estate business. Later he was for nine years the Baptist Young People's Union secretary of Georgia. He left that work in 1922 to become the executive secretary of the Inter-Board Commission of the Southern Baptist Convention, which position he held for six years. On Oct. 1, 1928, the Inter-Board Commission became the Department of Student Work of the Baptist Sunday School Board. His influence was a major factor in the development of a program of Baptist student work by state conventions. Under his direction the Baptist Student Union became a significant Christian force on the college and university campuses throughout the territory of the Southern Baptist Convention. Leavell's influence in his denomination was early recognized by selection for important responsibilities. He was treasurer of the Education Commission, 1928–29, and a member of its promotional agency, 1928–30. He served as lecturer at the Baptist Bible

Institute, New Orleans, La., in 1930. He was a member of the executive committee of the Baptist World Alliance, 1934–49, and secretary of its Youth Committee from 1931 to 1949. In this capacity he made a visit to London in 1949, at great hazard to his life because of a heart ailment, in order to insure the election of a world secretary for Baptist young people. This he considered one of his major achievements.

Leavell was a world traveler, having made research tours to Europe, Asia, China, Japan, Hawaii, the Near East, and South America. He initiated the annual Student Retreat at Ridgecrest Baptist Assembly in 1926. Also, he organized and promoted the Southern Baptist student conferences of 1926, 1930, 1934, and 1938. He was the editor of *The Baptist Student* (1922–49), *Christ, Master of My Generation* (1927), *Christ My Only Necessity* (1931), *Making Christ My Master* (1935), and *My Maximum for Christ* (1939). He was the author of *Training in Stewardship* (1920), *The Baptist Student Union* (1927), *The Layman Measures the Minister* (1930), *Baptist Student Union Methods* (1935), *Christian Witnessing* (1942), *The Master's Minority* (1949). His body was buried in the Leavell family plot in Oxford, Miss. WILLIAM HALL PRESTON

LEAVELL, GEORGE WASHINGTON (b. Cherry Creek, Pontotoc County, Miss., Jan. 29, 1844; d. Oxford, Miss., Sept. 7, 1905). Consecrated Baptist layman. Leavell made an outstanding contribution to Christian causes and the Baptist denomination through his wife, Corra Alice Berry (1851–1913), and their nine sons. Their oldest son, Landrum Pinson (*q.v.*), became a Sunday school and Baptist Young People's Union worker; Arnaud Bruce was a dentist; and James Berry, a bank cashier, pastor, and evangelist. George Walne, the Leavell's fourth son, served as a medical missionary in China 23 years, while Frank Hartwell (*q.v.*), originally a businessman, became state secretary of the Baptist Young People's Union and Southwide secretary of Baptist Student Union. The sixth son, Leonard O., was a businessman, state Sunday school secretary, and pastor; and the next son, Clarence Stanley, also state Sunday school secretary, was an educational director. Roland Quinche, a pastor, served as Southwide secretary of evangelism and became president of New Orleans Baptist Theological Seminary. The ninth son, Ullin Whitney, became an educational missionary in China.

BIBLIOGRAPHY: "George W. Leavell: A Tribute," *The Baptist Record* (Sept. 28, 1905). R. Q. Leavell, *Corra Berry Leavell, A Christian Mother* (1952).

C. B. HAMLET III

LEAVELL, LANDRUM PINSON (b. near Cherry Creek, Miss., May 10, 1874; d. Hot Springs, Ark., June 4, 1929). B.Y.P.U. leader and second field secretary of the Sunday School Board. The son of George Washington and Corra Alice (Berry) Leavell, he was educated in the public school of Oxford, Miss., the University of Mississippi, and the Southern Baptist Theological Seminary, and was awarded the D.D. degree by Mississippi College in 1921. For three years he taught at Jefferson Military College, Washington, Miss. While thus engaged, he was elected the first Sunday school secretary of the Mississippi Baptist Convention. In 1903 he began his work as field secretary of the Sunday School Board.

With his first headquarters established in Oxford, Miss., he traveled extensively over the territory of the Southern Baptist Convention, teaching in institutes and promoting efficiency in Sunday school work. His major interest in those early years was grading and departmentalization, with special concern for the understanding of pupil life. In 1907 the board appointed him its first B.Y.P.U. secretary, and he led in formulating and in popularizing B.Y.P.U. methods. He was the first secretary and editor of the B.Y.P.U. Department, created by the Sunday School Board in 1918. An effective speaker, he helped churches to visualize the possibilities of a progressive program of teaching and training, and he inspired large numbers of young people and mature laymen to dedicate their talents to Christian service, both in their churches and through denominational channels. The strength of his personality was illustrated by the influence he exerted over his eight younger brothers. His brother, Roland Quinche Leavell, called him "the pivotal person in his family." In addition to his duties at the Sunday School Board, for six years (1915–20) he taught Sunday school pedagogy at the Southern Baptist Theological Seminary, Louisville, Ky. He was the author of *The B.Y.P.U. Manual* (1907), "The Pupil and His Needs," Second Division of the *Convention Normal Manual for Sunday School Workers* (1909), *The Intermediate Department of the Sunday School* (1917), *Training in Christian Service* (1917), *Pupil Life* (1919), *Pilgrim's Progress for the B.Y.P.U.* (1922). He married Vara Pulliam on July 23, 1903. His children were Marian Frost and Frances Louise (Mrs. Claude Bowen). He was buried in Oxford, Miss.

C. AUBREY HEARN

LEBANON, MISSION IN. Baptist work in Lebanon was begun by Said M. Jureidini, a young Lebanese photographer who was converted during a visit to the United States in 1893. A church was organized in Beirut in 1895 with Jureidini as pastor, and another in Rasheiya in 1904 with Joseph K. David (and later his brother Najeeb) as pastor. Their work was supported for a time by some Illinois churches.

At the London Conference of 1920 the Southern Baptist Convention accepted responsibility for Baptist missions in Palestine and Syria. Missionaries in Palestine made periodic visits to Lebanon (then a part of Syria), but it was not until late in 1948 that two Southern Baptist missionaries, Finlay Morrison and Julia Saccar (Hagood) Graham, went to Lebanon to live. They were followed in 1949 by Mabel Miller Summers, in 1952 by Mary Virginia Cobb, in 1954 by James Keith and Leola (Kelley) Ragland, and in 1955 by John William and Mozelle (Hodge) Turner.

The Lebanese Baptist Association includes four churches with a combined membership of 125. There are five additional preaching stations. Baptist schools are located in Beirut and Kefr Mishky. FINLAY M. GRAHAM

LELA INDIAN BAPTIST ASSEMBLY. Sponsored by the Oklahoma Indian Baptist Association, it is located on 30 acres of land seven miles west of Pawnee, Okla. Founded at Fairfax, Okla., in June, 1933, the assembly met at various places for 17 years. The present site was purchased in 1951 by the Home Mission Board of the Southern Baptist Convention for $1,500 and was developed at an additional cost of $6,000. The assembly is financed by registration fees and gifts from churches in the sponsoring association. J. M. GASKIN

LELAND, JOHN (b. Grafton, Mass., May 14, 1754; d. Cheshire, Mass., Jan. 14, 1841). Known widely as a shrewd, witty, and somewhat eccentric man, he was a resourceful champion of the rights of conscience, an able interpreter of Jeffersonian political thought to the masses, and a warm evangelical preacher. He married Sallie Devine, Sept. 30, 1776, and was the father of eight children. Though lacking in formal education, he was throughout his life an avid reader—having learned to read the Bible at the age of five years—and was regarded as one of the most learned preachers of his day. He was ordained, without the customary laying on of hands by a presbytery, to become pastor of the Mount Poney Baptist Church, Culpeper County, Va., in Aug., 1777. Since this departure from traditional practice constituted a barrier to fellowship in many Virginia churches, he received ordination "with the laying on of hands" in June, 1787.

Unsuited by temperament for the life of a pastor, he was one of the most widely traveled preachers of his day. His frequent and extended preaching tours through the territory from Virginia to Massachusetts took him a total distance equal to three times around the world. During the 15 years of his ministry in Virginia, he preached 3,009 sermons and during his total ministry personally baptized 1,278 persons. Once he was about to baptize a woman when word came that her husband, who was bitterly opposed to religion in any form, had stated his intention to murder Leland and was on his way with a gun. The resourceful preacher quickly sent a detachment of the congregation to detain the irate husband, while he baptized the woman. He moved from Virginia to Cheshire, Mass., in 1792.

Having grown up amid the restlessness which brought on the Revolution, he developed an instinctive hostility toward all forms of civil and ecclesiastical oppression. He was interested keenly in politics and in Baptist history and became a zealous interpreter of the religious and humanitarian aspects of slavery and manumission. He agitated unrelentingly for the repeal of the act respecting the incorporation of the Protestant Episcopal Church in Virginia, and was a member of a delegation from the Baptist general committee which presented a memorial in this connection to the general assembly in 1787. His interest in Baptist history led him to collect a considerable body of materials which were later used by others in compiling a history of Baptists in Virginia. He was a prolific writer of hymns. Burrage lists 21, the best known being "The Day Is Past and Gone." The election of James Madison to the Virginia Convention to ratify the federal Constitution is attributed directly to the efforts of Leland, and his influence was clearly behind Madison's introduction of the First Amendment to the Constitution, which guaranteed the separation of church and state. The inscription on the marker over his grave in Cheshire, Mass., characterized him as a man who "labored 67 years to promote piety and vindicate the civil and religious rights of all men."

BIBLIOGRAPHY: L. H. Butterfield, *Elder John Leland, Jeffersonian Itinerant* (1953). W. Cathcart, *The Baptist Encyclopedia* (1881). L. F. Greene, *The Writings of the Late Elder John Leland, Including Some Events in His Life* (1845). J. Leland, *Some Events in the Life of John Leland* (1836); *An Elective Judiciary, with other things, recommended in a speech, pronounced at Cheshire, July 4, 1805* (1805). JACK MANLY

LEMEN, JAMES, SR. (b. Nov. 20, 1760; d. Jan. 8, 1823). Soldier, statesman, pioneer settler, and preacher. With him begins Illinois Baptist history. He served two years in the Revolutionary army. He married Catherine Ogle in 1782. They left Virginia in the spring of 1786 with two small sons, Robert and Joseph, traveling to Illinois on a flatboat down the Ohio River. They lost all their possessions in the river and barely escaped death but finally arrived at their settlement in Illinois, named New Design because of the antislavery principles on which it was founded, on July 10, 1786. Lemen had moved from Virginia to get away from slavery, and his influence was probably instrumental in making Illinois a free state. He died a year before the famous election of 1824 settled the slavery matter forever. "The very summer of their arrival, Mrs. Lemen's sister and her husband, James Andrews, were murdered by the Indians and their two daughters carried away as captives. One died and the other was recovered by French traders and adopted into the family of James Lemen."

Neither Lemen nor his wife were Christians when they arrived in Illinois, but both read the Bible, and their home was the place of religious gatherings. In 1787 James Smith, a Baptist preacher from Kentucky, visited New Design. He was the first preacher of any denomination to enter Illinois. He held a series of meetings in which the Ogles and Lemens were converted. Smith returned in 1790 and conducted another series of meetings, and many others were converted. Perhaps a church would have been organized at this time, but Smith was captured by the Indians. Because they had seen him on his knees praying, and because of their superstition, the Indians did not kill Smith.

In 1791 Lemen and seven others engaged in a pitched battle with a band of Indian horse thieves and killed five of them.

Lemen and his wife and several others were baptized in Fountain Creek in Feb., 1796, by Josiah Dodge from Kentucky. They still did not organize into a church. On May 28, 15 new converts were baptized and 13 came by letter; a church was organized in New Design. This was the first Baptist church in Illinois.

Although not ordained until 1810, Lemen was prominent in the organization of many of the first Baptist churches of Illinois, the organization of the first association in the state, Illinois Association, and conducted many successful revival meetings in the state. Lemen, an ardent opponent of slavery, withdrew from the New Design church in 1807 and joined Richland Creek, probably because of the warmer antislavery sentiment of that body. He preached against slavery and by 1809 had come to the front as the leader of the antislavery movement. The question of slavery resulted in a split in the Illinois Association in 1809. Lemen had no intention of leaving the denomination, but he and a group of his followers withdrew from the association and organized an independent Baptist church, the Cantine Baptized Church of Christ, Friends to Humanity. The church's convenant denied "union and communion with all persons holding the doctrine of perpetual, hereditary and involuntary slavery." Thus began a movement that, though small in its beginning, eventually figured prominently in Illinois' remaining a free state.

Lemen for many years served as justice of the peace and also as county judge. Four of his sons became influential Baptist preachers in Illinois: James, Jr., Joseph, Josiah, and Moses.

ARCHIE E. BROWN

LENOIR ACADEMY. A Baptist school at Lenoir, N. C., founded in 1898 with J. A. White as principal. It was the associational school of Caldwell Association and was one of the Baptist academies organized into a system by Albert Erskine Brown (*q.v.*) of Asheville. In 1905 indebtedness had been removed and the association's title to the property had become clear. Plans were made to enlarge the building, and the Home Mission Board offered $750 toward that project. Two years later White, the principal, moved away, and the trustees were unable to secure a replacement. In 1908 the school was officially closed because of competition from public graded schools.

D. L. SMILEY

LEUNG KWONG HOSPITAL, CANTON. See China, Mission in.

LEVERING, EUGENE, JR. (b. Baltimore, Md., Sept. 12, 1845; d. Baltimore, Md., Aug. 2, 1928). Baptist layman, philanthropist. The son of Eugene Levering, Sr. (*q.v.*), and twin brother of Joshua Levering (*q.v.*), Levering was baptized into the fellowship of the Seventh Baptist Church, Baltimore, *c.* 1857. Continuing in his father's coffee importing firm until the business was closed out, he in 1878 became president of the National Bank of Commerce in Baltimore, holding that office 43 years. After the institution's merger with the Merchant's National Bank, he continued as chairman of the board. Later he presided over a further merger which established the First National Bank, one of the great financial institutions of the South, retiring only a month before his death. Levering founded the Workingmen's Residential Club in downtown Baltimore as a refuge for the down-and-out, gave the money for the original YMCA building on the Johns Hopkins campus, and was a large contributor toward the present Levering Hall for the "Y" on the new Homewood campus. A deacon and Sunday school teacher for 50 years at Eutaw Place Baptist Church, he helped found the Baptist Church Extension Society in Baltimore. His first wife, Mary Armstrong, was the sister of Annie W. Armstrong (*q.v.*), home missions leader. His second wife was Harriet Ellis Levering (*q.v.*), who left funds which made possible the founding of the Maryland Woman's Missionary Union camp, Wo-Me-To, in Harford County.

ROY L. SWIFT

LEVERING, JOSHUA (b. Baltimore, Md., Sept. 12, 1845; d. Baltimore, Md., Oct. 5, 1935). Baptist layman, civic leader, denominational leader, philanthropist. The son of Eugene Levering, Sr. (*q.v.*), and twin brother of Eugene Levering, Jr. (*q.v.*), Levering was baptized into the fellowship of the Seventh Baptist Church, Baltimore, *c.* 1857. After the dissolution of the family firm, Levering devoted himself to philanthropic, religious, and civic affairs. Engaged in the Prohibition cause, he served as candidate for governor of Maryland on the Prohibition ticket in 1896. As the party's candidate for President in 1896, he polled one of the largest votes ever tendered a candidate on that platform. In 1880 he was named a trustee of the Southern Baptist Theological Seminary in Louisville and served as president of the board for 40 years (1895–1935). For 48 years he was the Maryland representative on the Foreign Mission Board, making two trips to foreign fields (1903–04, 1907–08). For 65 years he held membership on the Maryland state mission board.

He helped found the Baptist Laymen's Missionary Movement (now the Brotherhood), with headquarters at first located in Baltimore, and in 1906 in New York he helped launch the Interdenominational Laymen's Missionary Movement. At Hot Springs, Ark., in 1908 he became president of the Southern Baptist Convention, an office held by few laymen, and was re-elected the following two years at Louisville and Baltimore. A leader at the Eutaw Place Baptist Church, which sponsored several other Baptist churches in Baltimore, Levering in 1917, at the age of 72, led in founding the University Baptist Church, adjacent to the Johns Hopkins University. Thrice married, Levering was the father of seven children, one of whom served with her husband, Philip S. Evans, Jr. (*q.v.*), as a Southern Baptist missionary to China for 40 years. ROY L. SWIFT

LEVERING FUND (HOME MISSION BOARD). Mrs. Harriett S. Levering, widow of the late Eugene Levering, of Baltimore, bequeathed to the Home Mission Board 20.27 per cent of her residuary estate, stipulating that the funds accruing to the board thereunder be invested and the income therefrom used in the discretion of the board for Indian work throughout the western states. Following Mrs. Levering's death on Feb. 20, 1950, the board received $41,507.14 through the First National Bank of Baltimore, Md., executor of her estate, to be administered in accordance with the provisions of her will. G. FRANK GARRISON

LEXINGTON BAPTIST FEMALE COLLEGE. A private secondary school for girls, established in 1868 at Lexington, Ky., under the patronage of the Elkhorn Baptist Association. Its presidents included A. S. Worrell, 1868–71; Robert Ryland, 1871–77; and W. S. Ryland, 1877–80. The school was discontinued in 1880. GLYNN R. FORD

LIBERIA, MISSION IN. When a company of freed slaves emigrated to what is now Liberia in 1821, Lott Cary and Colin Teague, sent by the Richmond Foreign Mission Society, went with them. Before leaving they organized a church of seven members, which became the first Baptist church in Monrovia, Liberia.

The Triennial Convention took over the mission, and after Southern Baptists separated from the convention it became a joint project of the two until 1856, when Northern Baptists withdrew. John Day and A. L. Jones, residents of Liberia, were among the first appointees of the Foreign Mission Board in 1846.

During the Civil War in America mission work in Liberia was suspended. Although some aid was given between 1871 and 1875, the mission never fully revived. When William Joshua David (*q.v.*) went to reopen work in Africa in 1875, he was instructed to work in Liberia only if unable to enter Nigeria. He entered Nigeria and thus closed the mission in Liberia. GENEVIEVE GREER

LIBERALISM. This term refers to a theological movement in Europe, England, and especially in America during the 19th and early 20th centuries, which broke away from the conservative theology of Reformation orthodoxy, rejecting the authority of the Bible and the concept of revelation. It was deeply tinged with humanism, Darwinian evolution, and a rigorous rationalism which set reason against faith.

Liberalism in American Protestantism has come to stand for the effort to give a reasonable account of Christianity in harmony with modern science and the historical criticism of the Bible, at the expense (more or less) of biblical supernaturalism. Modernism, insofar as it should be distinguished from liberalism, is the extreme expression, e.g., religious humanism and theistic naturalism. Within Roman Catholicism modernism refers to a movement condemned by Pius X (1835–1914). Flowering in America in the 20th century, liberalism tended to confuse the historical process with a theoretical evolutionary progress and held to a perfectionist view of the possibilities of life here and now. It emerged dominant from the liberal-fundamentalist controversy (1920–30), but the depression of the mid-thirties and the threat of a second global war gave rise under Reinhold Niebuhr to "realistic theology," a new school of chastened liberals who made greater allowance for the sinfulness of man, the transcendence of God, and the need for divine revelation. At the mid-20th century, a neo-liberalism, less repentant and voicing more of the older optimism, is increasingly vocal.

In Germany liberalism developed out of the Renaissance emphasis upon man as the measure of all things, received its philosophical creed from the rationalistic idealism of Kant and Hegel, found its theological innovation in the man-centered theology of Schleiermacher, and in the mid-19th century reached its most radical expression in the critical work of Strauss and Baur. In England the empirical philosophy of Hume, 18th-century Deism, and the writings of Coleridge issued in a liberal or "Broad Church" party, with strong emphasis upon the social implications of Christianity. Against the doctrine of the Fall, English liberalism urged a recognition of the divine capacity of man; against the doctrinal divisions of Christendom, it emphasized the great unity of Christians upon the affirmatives of their faith.

Under the impact of German and British liberalism, American liberalism became a humanitarian and anti-authoritarian reaction against Calvinism and Old World orthodoxy. Closely connected with Unitarianism in New England because the liberals could not accept the Trinitarian definitions of orthodoxy, American liberalism adopted the doctrine of universal salvation, holding that the concept of hell was inhuman and immoral. With this movement must be connected the names of the great Unitarians, James Freeman, Henry Ware, and

William Ellery Channing, and such transcendentalists as Ralph Waldo Emerson and Theodore Parker. In recent years the term "liberalism" has become a theological title intended to characterize a thinker of unorthodox bent who emphasizes free-thinking with regard to the classic doctrinal statements of the Christian faith. Such thinking is usually marked by philosophical and religious idealism, a rejection of the authority of the Scriptures in Christian faith and practice, an interpretation of creation in terms of Darwinian evolutionary pantheism, an emphasis upon the role of Christ as ethical teacher rather than as divine Redeemer and Lord, a superficial view of the seriousness of sin, and a strong repugnance toward the doctrine of eternal punishment for the unrepentant.

BIBLIOGRAPHY: J. Dillenberger and C. Welch, *Protestant Christianity* (1954). C. F. H. Henry, *Fifty Years of Protestant Theology* (1950). D. E. Roberts and H. P. Van Dusen, eds., *Liberal Theology* (1942). Mary Frances Thelen, *Man as Sinner* (1946).

WAYNE E. WARD and W. BOYD HUNT

LIBERTY COLLEGE. A school operated at Glasgow, Ky., from 1875 to 1913, and sponsored by the Liberty Baptist Association. The founder, N. G. Terry, was possibly motivated by the impending demise of his own school in the same town, Allen Lodge Female College. Among the promoters of the school was Basil Manly, Jr. (*q.v.*), at that time president of Georgetown College, who drafted the charter and used his influence to secure the approval of the Kentucky legislature in 1873. The debt on the building was paid by 1881.

Among the administrators of the school were John Phelps Fruit, a co-president at Liberty College and later a professor of English at William Jewell College for nearly 50 years; T. S. McCall, later president of Bethel Female College at Hopkinsville, Ky.; and J. M. Bruce, a pastor of the Glasgow Baptist Church, who led the institution through a financial crisis and left it solvent in 1895.

Liberty was originally a school for girls, but was coeducational from 1893 to 1902. In 1913 the regents, pressed by debt, sold the institution to the public school system for $19,400.

GEORGE RALEIGH JEWELL

LIBERTY-PIEDMONT INSTITUTE. A Baptist school at Wallburg, Davidson County, N. C., established in 1903 by the Liberty Association. In 1907 Piedmont Association joined in support of the school, and the name was changed to reflect the new patronage. In Jan., 1908, the building was destroyed by fire, but a better one was soon erected, because of which the school incurred a heavy debt. In 1911 South Yadkin Association adopted the school and promised to support it. The following year the Home Mission Board promised $750 a year to the school if its debt were removed, but this was not done. The school had Primary, Intermediate, and high school departments and offered courses in music, Bible, and elocution. By 1920 the school was in serious need of equipment and support, but received neither. The following year a final, failing effort was made to save the institute.

D. L. SMILEY

LIBRARY, CHURCH. A collection of books through which a church attempts to serve the reading needs of its constituency. These needs vary in relation to the total resources of the community, but usually require books in some or all of the following categories: biblical interpretation, primarily for the pastor and teachers; background materials for the educational organizations; devotional reading for all age levels; standard reference materials and books of reference in religious areas; recreational reading for all age levels, particularly for juvenile readers. Church libraries have two primary values: accessibility and selectivity. Open whenever church members assemble, they seek to provide helpful and trustworthy books for all groups.

As early as 1890, the Southern Baptist Convention expressed interest in libraries, which were then considered a part of the Sunday school rather than the church program. The newly created Sunday School Board was instructed to work in this field in 1892. In 1902 Bernard Washington Spilman (*q.v.*) wrote, "There should be a library. . . . The Sunday school should help to direct the reading in the right direction." As Sunday school libraries, however, little progress was made toward stabilizing this endeavor.

In 1927 Arthur Flake (*q.v.*) initiated a promotional program for establishing and maintaining libraries through the board's Department of Sunday School Administration. The emphasis was changed from Sunday school to church libraries. In 1934 a full-time worker, Leona Lavender, was placed in the field for promotion. She prepared a textbook, *The Church Library Manual,* which was approved for publication in July, 1934. In Nov., 1943, the library promotion was placed under the newly established Church Library Service authorized by the board. A secretary, Florida Waite, was elected to direct the promotional program. The 1,500 libraries established from 1927 to 1944 grew to 5,798 in the next 12 years. By this time various promotional materials were being regularly published: an eight-page monthly bulletin for church librarians, a monthly bulletin for association library council officers, a revised edition of the manual, a book list of over 2,500 titles, and a number of free leaflets. The office staff had been increased from one to include a technical adviser, an editorial assistant, field consultants both in the office and in Baptist Book Stores, a bibliography specialist, and stenographers. Two schools for church librarians were conducted annually. State library conventions and conferences were held to assist in the training of librarians. The correlation of library promotion with the church program is emphasized. Church control and support of the library are promoted. FLORIDA WAITE

LIMESTONE COLLEGE. One of the four oldest colleges for women in the South, established Nov. 6, 1845, at Limestone Springs, now part of Gaffney, S. C., Limestone has sought throughout its history to combine the finest traditions of Christian religion, liberal education, and Southern culture. Thomas Curtis, eminent Oxford scholar and Baptist minister, was founder and first president of Limestone. He was assisted by his son, William Curtis, also a Baptist minister, who became the second president. The Curtises opened the school with seven faculty members and 67 students, many of whom came from some of the most aristocratic and influential families in the South. In 1878 Peter Cooper, noted New York philanthropist, became interested in developing the college. Along with the Bomar family of Spartanburg, S. C., part owners, Cooper, in 1880, donated the Limestone property to the Spartanburg Baptist Association, after which Harrison Patillo Griffith and Robert Oswald Sams helped direct the college for several years.

In 1921 Limestone College was placed under control of the Baptist state convention of South Carolina, but upon request of Limestone authorities in 1941, the convention returned the charter to a self-perpetuating board of trustees. Since 1941 Baptist influences have continued to be strong, and the present charter stipulates that both the president of the college and the professor of religion shall be Baptists. Lee Davis Lodge, Limestone president from 1899 to 1923, and Robert Colley Granberry, president from 1923 to 1951, have been the predominant leaders in the school's development during the past 50 years. Andrew Jackson Eastwood, elected president in 1953, has continued their tradition.

Physical properties of Limestone College, valued in excess of $1,000,000, include 14 well-furnished buildings, located on a 50-acre tract of land. On May 31, 1955, endowment was $820,498.56. The annual operating budget, which was $251,955.27 in the 1954–55 session, is drawn from endowment earnings, donations, foundation grants, and student fees. Recognized as a four-year liberal arts college by state, regional, and national accrediting agencies, Limestone had an enrolment of 300 in the 1955–56 session. A total of 9,378 students have attended the college from its founding through 1955.

BIBLIOGRAPHY: H. P. Griffith, *Life of John Gill Landrum* (1885). J. B. O. Landrum, *History of Spartanburg County, South Carolina* (1900). R. W. Sanders, "The Life and Labors of Dr. Thomas Curtis" (n.d.). W. C. Taylor, *History of Limestone College* (1937). E. J. TRUEBLOOD

LING TONG AND HAKKA CONVENTIONS, SOUTH CHINA. These two conventions in Kwangtung province, South China, are the administrative bodies for the Hakkas of the highlands and the Tie Chiu or Swatow-speaking Chinese near the coast. Work was opened among the Tie Chiu in 1836 and among the Hakkas in 1880. The Ling Tong Convention of the Tie Chiu was organized in 1925. During wartime, internment or evacuation of missionaries of the American Baptist foreign mission societies and the two conventions, with their respective home mission societies, have been responsible for administration of the evangelistic program, hospitals, and schools. Such emergencies occurred during the political uprising in 1925–27, the occupation of Manchuria by the Japanese in 1931–32, the Sino-Japanese War in 1937–45, and the conquest of the entire country by Russian Communists leading to formation of the People's Republic of China in 1949. In 1953 after China came under Communist domination, the last missionaries were "deported," terminating their imprisonment in solitary confinement for 21 months. Thousands of Chinese in Kwantung province fled to Hong Kong, where American Baptist missionaries and Chinese workers carry on a relief and spiritual ministry among the refugees. Four churches have been organized, and there are several smaller congregations.

Baptist work in Kwangtung province was opened in 1836 by missionaries from Siam who previously had been carrying on work in Hong Kong as an interim station. In 1837 at Macao, John Lewis Shuck (b. 1812; d. 1863) baptized the first Baptist convert in China. The Opium War of 1842 opened five "treaty ports" to the West, and Shuck, William Dean (b. 1807; d. 1895), and I. J. Roberts (b. 1802; d. 1866) moved to Hong Kong. Here Dean, on May 28, 1843, organized the first church on the mainland among the Tie Chiu, although work among them had gone on for 30 years, largely in Siam. Workers related to the American Baptist foreign mission societies have been largely responsible for work among the Tie Chiu ever since.

DATA

	1934	*1949* *
Baptisms	665	—
Churches	117	117
Church members	6,284	9,709
Missionaries	41	11
Chinese workers	452	394
Students	6,523	6,728
Schools	112	67
Patients	67,577	18,813
Hospitals & Dispensaries	14	8
Field contributions	$19,149	—

* Latest figures incomplete.

ADA STEARNS

LINK, JOHN BODKIN (b. Rockbridge County, Va., May 7, 1828; d. Austin, Tex., Jan. 10, 1894). Editor, historian, denominational statesman. Converted in Oct., 1840, and baptized at Natural Bridge, Va., in 1841, Link was ordained at Mount Pleasant, Jessamine County, Ky., in 1852. After graduating from Georgetown College in 1853 and from Rochester Theological Seminary in 1855, he was pastor of churches at Paris, Ky., and Liberty, Mo. As agent for William Jewell College, he raised $20,000 for the institution. Link entered the Confederate army and spent most of his time as a chaplain. In 1865 he went to Texas as a missionary of the Southern Baptist Board of Domestic Missions and established the *Texas Baptist Herald,* a denominational newspaper, in December of that year. As owner, editor, and promoter, he gave Texas Baptists a newspaper to support and promote all the interests of state work. Link and William Carey Crane (*q.v.*) championed the cause of women's societies when they were just beginning. In 1886 Link contributed to the unification of Texas Baptist bodies and institutions, and in 1891–92 he published two volumes of his *Texas Historical and Biographical Magazine,* which contained biographical sketches of most of the Texas Baptists who had attained distinction up to that time and the history of certain churches and associations. W. M. SHAMBURGER

LIPSEY, PLAUTUS IBERUS (b. Independence, Miss., July 5, 1865; d. Jackson, Miss., July 16, 1947). Minister, editor, founder of Baptist institutions. Lipsey, who was taught Greek at the age of 12 by his "preacher-teacher" father, was always an avid student of classical languages and became known for his expository preaching because of his knowledge of Greek and Hebrew. He attended Union University, graduated from the University of Mississippi in 1886, and obtained his Th.M. degree from Southern Baptist Theological Seminary in 1889. On Nov. 21 of that year he married Julia Toy Johnson, daughter of John Lipscomb Johnson, Sr., and wife (Mrs. J. L. Johnson, *q.v.*). Pastor successively in Columbus, Ind.; Vicksburg, Miss.; Murfreesboro, Tenn.; Guthrie and Adairville, Ky.; Greenwood and Clinton, Miss., Lipsey assumed editorship of the Mississippi convention paper, *The Baptist Record,* in Feb., 1912, which position he held for nearly 30 years. As editor he pioneered in suggesting that Southern Baptists establish Baptist Bible Institute in New Orleans and was one of its trustees for many years. He was a founder and trustee of the Southern Baptist Hospital in New Orleans and Mississippi Baptist Hospital in Jackson. Lipsey wrote two books, *Tests of Faith: An Exposition of the Book of James* and *Revelation: An Interpretation.*

BIBLIOGRAPHY: P. I. Lipsey, *Memories of His Early Life, 1865–88* (1949). *The Baptist Record* (July 24, 1947). *Who's Who in America, 1946–47.*

C. B. HAMLET III

LITERARY CRITICISM, THE BIBLE. The critical study of the Bible falls naturally into two divisions, the Old and the New Testament phases. These areas must be examined individually as to the results of investigation, but a common approach to the study of the Scriptures is at once apparent in both: The Bible must be allowed to speak for itself; the Holy Spirit must interpret the Word, apart from preconceived views, to the mind of each age; and each generation must be free to read, listen, and speak.

This critical evaluation of the Bible is often mistrusted by devoted Christians because of the radical views of many pioneers of critical thought. Yet erroneous ideas concerning the Word of God cannot be denied by dogmatic preachments, but by more thorough and consecrated scholarship. Growing uncertainty about the human authors of some biblical books has resulted in the renewed conviction that it is not the human but the divine origin of the Scriptures that gives them true meaning.

Literary study of the Old Testament has centered upon four critical areas: the Pentateuch, the Psalms, Isaiah, and Daniel. At the turn of the 20th century, it was commonly believed that the Pentateuch was composed of four basic documents, all dated after the age of Moses. These were denoted J, E, D, and P. The J writer preferred Jehovah (Yahweh) as the name for God, and the E document favored Elohim. D stood for the type of literature found in Deuteronomy, and P designated the priestly sources to be detected by the careful scholar. This naive concept of great literary artists sitting down to write original treatises giving their concepts of Jewish history has been thoroughly contradicted by recent scholarship. The Pentateuch today is still viewed as having four basic sources, but these are no longer looked upon as documents. Rather they are groupings of tradition, some oral and some written, some going back to Moses or even before and some coming later, but altogether furnishing a trustworthy account of Israel's beginnings. A similar pattern is followed in the study of the Psalms. It was once quite common to deny David's authorship of any psalms. Today scholars are becoming more convinced that many psalms owe their origin to David. However, the book of Psalms itself is regarded as a collection of devotional literature from the entire history of Israel. Many scholars find three basic divisions in the book of Isaiah. The original work, eighth century B.C. in date, comprises most of chapters 1–39. Chapters 40–55 apparently were written about 150 years later, and chapters 56–66 are to be dated in the age of Ezra-Nehemiah. The book of Daniel, regarded by many as Maccabean in origin (*c.* 167 B.C.), was probably written to encourage the faithful during the persecution of Antiochus Epiphanes.

New Testament investigation has been concentrated upon the Gospels and the letters of Paul. The most convincing result of the study of the Gospels has been the assurance that Jesus commonly spoke in Aramaic. Form criticism, the investigation of the literary shape taken by the oral traditions of the Christian community, held the day for a time. Although scholarship generally has been compelled to acknowledge the phenomenon of tradition, the usual conclusions of the form critics have been roundly criticized. More generally acceptable to scholars is the source theory concerning the Synoptic Gospels. Four distinct sources are recognized: Mark (material peculiar to Mark), Q (material common to Matthew and Luke), M (material peculiar to Matthew), and L (one of Luke's sources). The Gospel of John, once viewed by scholars as a theological rather than a historical work, is now regarded as being amazingly accurate. In recent years students of the New Testament are taking more seriously the words of the apostle Paul. The letters traditionally ascribed to him are now safely back in the fold, with the exception of Ephesians, Hebrews, and the Pastoral Epistles (Timothy, Titus, Philemon). Many scholars continue to defend ably the Pauline authorship of Ephesians and the Pastorals.

It can be readily seen, therefore, that recent biblical scholarship has been characterized by two trends: the re-examination of both the traditional and the critical views concerning the human authors of biblical books; the other is renewed insistence upon the reliability of the claims of the Bible concerning itself, that it is the result of the revelation of God, delivered by Spirit-inspired men.

BIBLIOGRAPHY: A. Bentzen, *Introduction to the Old Testament* (1948). E. Hoskyns, *The Fourth Gospel* (1940). A. M. Hunter, *Interpreting the New Testament, 1900–1950* (1951). T. W. Manson, *The Teaching of Jesus* (1931). R. H. Pfeiffer, *Introduction to the Old Testament* (1941). H. H. Rowley, *The Old Testament and Modern Study* (1951). B. H. Streeter, *Four Gospels* (1924). M. F. Unger, *Introductory Guide to the Old Testament* (1951).

CLYDE T. FRANCISCO

LITHUANIA, BAPTISTS IN. The Lithuanians, who speak a language much like Sanskrit, are dominantly Roman Catholic. Baptist ideas spread in the area from the city of Klaipeda (Memel), an important commercial center which Baptist businessmen from America, Germany, and England visited. Johann Gerhard Oncken (*q.v.*) founded a Baptist church there in 1841. Before 1939 there were groups of Lithuanian-speaking Baptists in Kaunas (Kovno), Siauliai (Shavli), and Vilnus (Vilno), the ancient capital of the country. W. O. LEWIS

LITTLE MISSIONARY. A monthly paper for Negro Baptists, published at Guthrie, Okla., first issued Sept. 15, 1905, with 18 four-column pages, size $14 \times 10\frac{1}{2}$ inches. Solomon S. Jones was editor and publisher. The second issue, Oct. 15, 1905, carried as a motto, "How Shall They Hear Without a Preacher?" The paper is now extinct. J. M. GASKIN

LITTLETON HIGH SCHOOL. A school at Littleton, N. C., under Baptist control in the 1890's. It was endorsed by Tar River Association and was operated by L. W. Bagley. In addition to the preparatory department, the school had a business institute with courses in commercial sciences. D. L. SMILEY

LIU, HERMAN CHAN-EN (b. near Hankow, China, 1896; d. Shanghai, China, Apr., 1938). Chinese Baptist leader. Educated at Soochow (China) University (B.A. degree), Chicago University (M.A. degree), and Columbia University (Ph.D. degree). Liu served as educational secretary of the National Committee, Chinese Y.M.C.A., 1922–27. He was the first Chinese president of the University of Shanghai (Shanghai Baptist College and Seminary), 1928–38. Contributing to Christian educational, philanthropic, and patriotic causes, including the executive committee of the National Christian Council and the executive committee of Higher Education of Christian Colleges, Liu was a member of the International Red Cross and a delegate to the Banff Conference of Pacific Relations in 1933. He was assassinated during the Sino-Japanese War. J. B. HIPPS

LOCKETT, BASIL LEE (b. Hartsville, Tenn., Oct. 6, 1879; d. Oklahoma City, Okla., Nov. 13, 1933). Southern Baptist medical missionary to Nigeria, Lockett served at Abeokuta, Oyo, and Ogbomosho. He was distinguished for his work in mission schools, in training national leaders, in clinics and hospitals, and in a leper colony. His first wife, Josie Still, a classmate at Baylor University, died in 1911, less than a year after their arrival in Africa, and in 1915 he married Elkin Lightfoot. While studying at Baylor, Lockett was one of six founders of a foreign mission band, the Covenanters, out of which later grew the Baptist Student Union movement.

JOSEPH MARTIN DAWSON

LOCUST GROVE SCHOOL. Began under sponsorship of Flint River Association in Henry County, Ga., in 1894. In the summer of that year B. J. W. Graham, pastor of the Locust Grove Baptist Church, called a community mass meeting to discuss the establishment of a school. At a second meeting, Sept. 19, the citizens agreed to offer a site and $2,000 for a Baptist high school; and on Sept. 24 the proposition was taken to Flint River Association which approved and provided an additional $2,000. Other associations, each electing two trustees, joined Flint in supporting the school, which was coeducational from the beginning. The school opened Nov. 1, 1894, with 13 pupils, Y. E. Bargeron, principal, and Graham, financial agent. When Bargeron resigned after three years, 156 students were enrolled, and Claude Gray (*q.v.*), his successor, headed the school for 31 years. Locust Grove was fully integrated with Georgia Baptist educational purposes and co-operative with Mercer, becoming a member of the Mercer system in 1920.

Courses of study included primary and secondary grade subjects to college sophomore level. In 1906 a stock company was formed to finance two new dormitories, and in 1909, $14,000 was raised for the school. Property was transferred to the Georgia Baptist convention in 1917. Locust Grove was one of the first preparatory schools in Georgia to be accredited by the Southern Association of Schools and Colleges. In 1928, however, the school was sold to a corporation headed by W. W. Williams. The growth of public schools and weak financial support contributed to the school's closing. ARTHUR JACKSON

LOFTON, GEORGE AUGUSTUS (b. Panola County, Miss., Dec. 25, 1839; d. Nashville, Tenn., Dec. 11, 1914). Minister. Although his early intentions were to be a Methodist minister, in 1859, as a result of studying Greek New Testament, Lofton became convinced that the Baptist views are scriptural; he then united, by immersion, with the Second Baptist Church, Atlanta, Ga. He entered the Baptist ministry in Americus, Ga., in 1868 and later served as pastor at Dalton, Ga.; First Baptist Church, Memphis, Tenn.; and Third Baptist Church, St. Louis, Mo. Lofton attended Mercer University (1859–60) and was awarded the D.D. degree by Denison University of Ohio (1865). Regarded as an accomplished debater, he wrote many articles and sermons for the periodical press. For two years he was president of the Southern Baptist Publication Society, Memphis, Tenn. In 1875 he led in the Centennial effort to endow Southwestern Baptist University, Jackson, Tenn. HAROLD STEPHENS

LOLLARDS. Followers of John Wycliffe (*c.* 1320–84), English ecclesiastical reformer and writer, who attacked church endowments, emphasized the authority of the Scriptures and translated them into the vernacular, proclaimed Christ as the spiritual head of the church, attacked the monastic orders of the church, protested the worship of saints, and eventually denied the mediating power of the priests and the doctrine of transubstantiation. He retained belief in the real presence of Christ in the Eucharist and belief in purgatory. Wycliffe sent out itinerant preachers, who proclaimed his doctrines to the masses. The movement gained numerous adherents in England and spread into Bohemia. Though severely persecuted, the sect persisted in secret until the Reformation. LYNN E. MAY, JR.

LONDON CONFERENCE OF 1920. The first general conference of European Baptists after World War I, called by the executive committee of the Baptist World Alliance in co-operation with the unions, boards, and conventions in America and Europe to meet in London, July 19–23, 1920. Represented at the conference were the United States, Canada, Great Britain, Austria, Belgium, Czechoslovakia, Denmark, Estonia, Finland, France, Germany, Holland, Hungary, Italy, Latvia, Norway, Poland, Romania, Spain, and Sweden.

One of the most important questions considered at the conference was the need of relief on the Continent. In some cases Baptists were neglected by larger organizations because they were a minority. James Henry Rushbrooke of England was appointed to serve as European commissioner for a period of three years. It was his duty to protest against the persecution of Baptists in Romania and elsewhere and to administer the relief program.

At the time of the conference it was thought that Russia might need help, although it was not anticipated, of course, that as the result of a drought in the Volga region in 1921 millions would starve. Herbert Hoover's American Relief Administration and the Nansen Committee fed millions. Baptists contributed thousands of dollars' worth of food through these organizations to help Baptists and others.

The conference recommended the founding of new theological seminaries and urged stronger Baptist bodies to help weaker unions. Southern Baptists were asked to take the responsibility of helping Baptist groups in Spain, Yugoslavia, Romania, Hungary, Russia, Palestine, and Syria. W. O. LEWIS

LONDON CONFERENCE OF 1948. Widespread feeling prevailed after the close of World War II in favor of another conference like the London Conference of 1920, but representing more of the nations in the Baptist World Alliance. A meeting in Amsterdam in 1948 of the constituent assembly of the World Council of Churches made it seem appropriate to call a conference of Baptist leaders that year, since Baptists would come from America to the Amsterdam meeting. Thus the Executive Committee of the Baptist World Alliance scheduled a general conference in London, Aug. 15–17, 1948.

Almost the entire executive committee was either present or represented by proxy. Canada and the United States had full delegations, and 14 European nations had representatives present. Czechoslovakia sent H. Prochazka and J. Ricar, although soon afterward it became practically impossible for Baptists to go in or out of Czechoslovakia.

Decisions made at the conference included abolition of the so-called "mandate system," according to which a country outside Europe made itself responsible for aiding one country in Europe. Henceforth any country could extend help wherever it chose. Steps were taken to form a European organization for women. Hope was expressed for establishment of seminaries in Holland and in Helsinki; and the Southern Baptist proposal to found an international seminary in Zurich was approved. Plans were made for aiding Baptist displaced persons on the Continent. W. O. LEWIS

LONG, NIMROD (b. Logan County, Ky., July 31, 1814; d. Russellville, Ky., Apr. 24, 1887). Banker, merchant, philanthropist. He received a public school education and, at 14, became a clerk in a dry goods store in Russellville. Three years later, he became a partner in the store. After some years, Long resigned from this business to become a commission merchant. He later established the banking house of N. Long and Company, and in 1870 built the largest flour mill in the state. Long's bank in Russellville at one time was robbed of $9,000 by the James boys, at which time he was shot and badly beaten. Jesse James's father had been educated by Long and George W. Norton I.

Long united with the Baptist church in Russellville at an early age, and he used his business talents and his fortune to the advancement of the cause of Christ. He was ordained a deacon in the Russellville church in 1832 and served as treasurer for about 45 years. He was the first financial agent of the board of trustees of Bethel High School (later Bethel College) at Russellville. After contributing generously to the erection of the buildings on the college campus, he endowed the chair of English, known as the N. Long Professorship. In 1876 he caused the erection of a dormitory for 100 young men, and it was named in his honor.

Long was married three times: in 1833 to Elizabeth W. Curd; after her death, to Angelina Nantz; and finally, to Mrs. Mary A. Smedley. He had five children from these marriages.

LEO T. CRISMON

LONG CREEK ACADEMY. Located in the mountains of Oconee County, 15 miles northwest of Westminster, S. C., the school was organized in 1913 by Beaverdam Baptist Association and the Southern Baptist Home Mission Board. Paul L. Sullivan and John Dean Crain, who raised the money for the first building, were largely responsible for the establishment of this Christian high school for worthy boys and girls. The first building was dedicated Sept. 17, 1914, and Grover C. Mangum, principal for two years, was succeeded by Luther Henry Raines who has been in charge since 1916.

Until 1923 the school was in the system of mountain mission schools of the Home Mission Board. By action of the Baptist state convention Dec. 6, 1922, the general secretary-treasurer of the general board was directed to take over the school as soon as arrangements could be made. Until 1931 the school was under the general board when the convention directed the executive committee of the general board to dispose of the property. Raines then organized the school as a private corporation, and the state of South Carolina helped to pay the teachers until May, 1952. Since then the school, distinctly Baptist throughout its existence, has operated on faith. Plans are now being made for a self-perpetuating board of trustees.

LUTHER HENRY RAINES

LONGFELLOW, PERRY WILSON (b. Grape Grove, Green County, Ohio, Jan. 20, 1854; d. Albuquerque, N. Mex., June 13, 1915). Singing schoolteacher, editor, historian, and pastor. The son of Nathan Morris and Mary Caroline (Creamer) Longfellow, he was converted at 14 and soon after felt called to the ministry. His father was a farmer-teacher, but Longfellow himself had a talent for music and taught several singing classes. Educated at William Jewell College, Denison University, and Union Theological Seminary, he held pastorates at Grand Forks, N. Dak.; Eau Claire, Wis.; Urbana, Ohio; Roswell and Albuquerque, N. Mex. Longfellow served as corresponding secretary of the New Mexico Baptist Convention from 1907 to 1912, during which time he edited *The Baptist Bulletin* for two years. His work, "Baptist Beginnings and Progress in New Mexico," a historical treatise, was published in the *Baptist New Mexican* in 14 installments, Feb., 1913, to May, 1914. His four-page tract by the same name had been printed in Roswell in 1909. Few men were so closely identified as Longfellow with the Baptist cause in New Mexico or understood it so well.

THELMA MARDIS

LORD'S DAY. Seems to have been the commonly accepted designation for the day of Christian worship at the close of the first century (Rev. 1:10). The resurrection of Christ occurred on the first day of the week (Luke 24:1), and the day became a fitting symbol of this central truth of the Christian message. The Saviour's first appearance to the group of disciples was on the evening of the resurrection (John 20:19). The church was baptized with the Holy Spirit and began its worldwide mission on the seventh "first day" after the Passover (Acts 2). At Troas the apostle Paul worshiped on the first day of the week (Acts 20:7). He urged the Corinthian Christians to bring their offerings when they assembled for worship on the first day of the week (I Cor. 16:2). Though perhaps alone, John was in the spirit of worship on "the Lord's Day" (Rev. 1:10), and on this occasion the marvelous revelation described in the last book of the New Testament was given him. The Old Testament sabbath was a "shadow" (Col. 2:16–17) of the rest to be realized in the redemptive work of Christ. The believer has entered the rest of a continuous sabbath life (Heb. 4:1–9).

No instructions for the observance of the Lord's Day are found in the New Testament. We do have, however, the example of how the early Christians on that day fellowshiped with Christ (John 20:19–29), witnessed for Christ (Acts 2), observed the Lord's Supper (Acts 20:7), brought their offerings (I Cor. 16:2), and received special revelation and assurance (Rev. 1:20 ff.). It is unthinkable for the Lord's Day to be observed with less devotion than was the Jewish sabbath. William Owen Carver (*q.v.*) has correctly said that "the individual who sanctifies in his heart Christ as Lord (I Peter 3:15) will rejoice in the Lord's Day for its liberating fellowship, for its opportunity to reorient his life and redirect and reintegrate his aims and activities."

EUGENE T. PRATT

LORD'S SUPPER. This symbol of the Christian faith, known to Baptists as the Lord's Supper, has been given a variety of names, e.g., eucharist, communion, or holy communion. Actually no specific name is given to this symbol in the New Testament. The term "eucharist" comes from the Greek word *eucharistein* in the record of the Last Supper given in the Synoptic Gospels and in I Corinthians (11:23–24). In Matthew and Mark *eucharistein,* meaning to give thanks, is used with the cup, but *eulogein,* meaning to bless, is used with the bread. The term "Lord's Supper" is used in recognition that Jesus is Lord and is host at the supper. It is possible, however, to interpret Paul's use of this term (I Cor. 11:20) as simply saying that the purpose of the coming together of the Corinthian Christians was not to eat a "lordly" meal such as was had by the mystery cults, because this supper is altogether different from a "lordly" meal. The word that approximates a technical term for the supper is the word "communion," used by Paul (I Cor. 10:16–17) in the sense of fellowship. However, this great symbol of Christian fellowship has become a root of bitterness and division among the followers of Christ, largely because dogmatic conceptions of the meaning of the supper are allowed to prevail over the New Testament statements.

The institution of the supper.—The fact that Jesus on the evening before his death ate a farewell meal with his disciples is historically attested by the Gospel writers and the apostle Paul, although John's Gospel does not give statements made over a cup and bread. Certain difficulties emerge, however, concerning the occasion of the supper, what Jesus did and said, and what meaning he attached to the supper. The earliest written account of Jesus' last meal with his disciples is given by Paul in I Corinthians 11:23–26. In the Gospels the institution of the Lord's Supper is recorded in Mark 14:22–25; Matthew 26:26–29; Luke 22:14–20. These passages may be divided into two groups. Luke and Paul, with minor variations, are in agreement; Matthew and Mark are agreed, with the exception of a few words. Luke and Paul indicate that the supper is to be repeated and present the covenant as a "new" covenant. Paul adds a reference to the second coming by quoting the words of Jesus at the supper, "For as often as ye eat this bread, and drink the cup, ye proclaim the Lord's death till he come" (I Cor. 11:26 ASV). In Matthew, Mark, and Luke also, there is an eschatological note: In Luke this statement is placed before the institution of the Lord's Supper, and in Matthew and Mark it is placed after the supper. A few minor differences in the four accounts may be noted; therefore, it is extremely difficult to determine the exact words of Jesus at the original supper. The disciples, however, were not concerned with verbal literalness in repeating these words at their observances of the supper. Since these differences in the presentation of the account are not contradictory, we may be able, after a study of all four accounts, to arrive at a clear meaning of the supper in its historical setting.

Some difficulty in interpretation has arisen, however, because of a seeming discrepancy in the date of Jesus' death. The Synoptic Gospels are in agreement in placing the death of Jesus on the 15th day of Nisan, but the evidence in John's Gospel has been interpreted to make it the 14th day of Nisan. No problem is presented with respect to the day of the week, because both regard Friday as the day of crucifixion. The matter of chronology is significant, however, because it is tied in with the original meaning of the last meal of Jesus with his disciples. If the 15th day of Nisan is correct, the last meal was a Passover meal, and the Lord's Supper should be interpreted in the light of such a meal. If the 14th day of Nisan is correct, the last meal could not have been the Passover meal because Jesus died on the cross a few hours before the Jews partook of the Paschal lamb. A variety of interpretations have been given to relieve this difficulty. Whether Jesus ate the Passover meal, we are unable to affirm, but the Paschal interpretation was prevalent in the early Christian community (I Cor. 5:7; I Peter 1:19; Rev. 5:6, 9, 12; 12:11). Therefore, this last meal must have had some connection with the Paschal supper.

The Lord's Supper and its relation to the Passover.—The Feast of the Passover in the day of Jesus caused the people to look both backward and forward. They remembered the immunity God afforded their fathers' houses which were sprinkled with the blood of lambs at the first Passover, and they remembered the delivering act of God in bringing them out of Egypt. They also looked for a coming deliverance, which was symbolized by the deliverance from Egypt. In later rabbinical literature some of the rabbis believed that this deliverance was to be in the month of Nisan, probably connecting the hope with the Passover feast. When Jesus and his disciples ate the Paschal lamb and drank the red wine, they remembered God's deliverance in the past and they also renewed allegiance to the God of the covenant by binding themselves more closely in bonds of common brotherhood. Since Peter's confession at Caesarea-Philippi, Jesus had been preparing his disciples for his immediate death (Mark 8:31; 10:45; 14:3–9). After the meal Jesus took bread and wine and, in a dramatic parable, prepared his disciples for his death which was to take place on the following day. Jesus viewed his forthcoming death not as fate but as a freely given sacrifice which would effect final deliverance for the whole world. As deliverance came to the Israelites in Egypt through the act of God, so now God would act again in Christ, who is the Passover lamb of the new age. The disciples, by partaking of the bread and wine which were symbols of the giving of his body and blood, received the blessing of that love depicted by Christ and joined themselves to the delivering act of God.

Jesus did not make a statement about the bread and wine before the disciples received them; after they had received these elements, he explained the meaning. This is a clear indication that the whole procedure is symbolic, and that the bread and wine are in no way transformed.

According to New Testament evidence, the Lord's Supper is not a repetition of the sacrifice of Christ, as the Roman Catholics believe, but is rather a commemoration of the sacrifice made by Christ. The bread and wine are symbols of the body and the blood of Christ and not the actual body and blood of Christ. If the disciples had thought that Jesus spoke realistically about the wine actually being blood, their Jewish sensitiveness would have compelled them to forsake him on the spot.

The Lord's Supper as a ratification of a new covenant.—Although the analogy of the Passover seems to have been uppermost in the mind of Jesus at this last meal with his disciples, the analogy does not fully explain the supper which he instituted. All four accounts refer to "covenant," and both Paul and Luke wrote of the "new covenant." After the law was given at Mount Sinai, the Israelites entered into a covenant relation with God, pledging their allegiance to him to walk in his ways as set forth in the law (Exod. 24:3–8). This covenant was ratified with the blood of animals. Jesus must have had in mind the old covenant at Mount Sinai. He also must have remembered the statements of the prophets, who had spoken of a covenant or peace which God had reserved for the future (Jer. 32:40; Ezek. 34:25; 37:26; Isa. 55:3). Jeremiah spoke of a new covenant that God would make with his people (Jer. 31:31–33). Therefore, in Jewish thought there was an old covenant and a new covenant reserved for the future. Jesus then looked upon himself as effecting a new covenant. Through Jesus' crucifixion God would deliver the people from their sins, and they would be joined in a new covenant relation with him. Although the Lord's Supper is not mentioned by name in the Epistle to the Hebrews, the analogy between the covenant at Mount Sinai and the new covenant proclaimed by Jeremiah in the Old Testament and the new covenant in the blood of Christ is worked out in detail in this epistle. The high-priestly action of Jesus in giving himself as an offering which was superior to the sacrifices offered by the Aaronic line of priests denotes that his blood became the means for ratification of a new covenant, as the blood of animals had been a means for ratification of the old covenant relation between Israel and God.

The Lord's Supper as a memorial.—As the Israelites were commanded to keep the Feast of Passover as a remembrance of their deliverance from Egypt (Exod. 12:14), so the disciples were instructed by Jesus to continue the Lord's Supper as a remembrance of him. The Greek word *anamnēsis,* meaning a memorial or a remembrance, includes the thought of a memorial before God, although the idea of a reminder to man is not excluded. The word *anamnēsis* occurs five times in the Septuagint, and in four of these references it signifies a memorial before God. In addition to its use in I Corinthians 11:24–25 and Luke 22:19, this word occurs in Hebrews 10:3, where it denotes a remembrance of sins in the Jewish sacrifices. This memorial was designed to serve the same purpose for the Christian community as the Passover had served for the Jews. This supper is a reminder of the suffering of Christ in our behalf and of our deliverance, now in operation, because of his death. However, the remembrance is more than just the proclamation of the beginning of deliverance. It also looks toward the consummation of deliverance with the coming of Christ.

The meaning of the supper necessary for observance.—In I Corinthians there are three allusions and one specific reference to the Lord's Supper (I Cor. 10:1–13; 10:14–21; 12:13; 11:17–34). In I Corinthians 10:14–21 Paul warned the Christians in Corinth to flee from idolatry. Some of the Christians had been eating at the pagan sacrificial feasts, and Paul objected to their action, because it meant they were actually having communion with the god of the cult. He then reminded them that they could not have communion with demons and also have communion with Christ. In I Corinthians 11:17–34 Paul, having received information concerning the terrible abuses in the church with respect to the observance of the Lord's Supper, upbraided the congregation for profaning the observance of the supper by their misunderstanding of its purpose. Instead of being a common meal exhibiting Christ's great sacrifice of love, they had made it an occasion where people demonstrated selfishness and greed. According to Paul, an understanding of the full significance of the supper is prerequisite to its observance. If the democratic principle does not prevail, the meaning of the supper is lost.

The administration of the Lord's Supper.—The New Testament has nothing to say with respect to the administrant of this symbol of our Christian faith. In I Corinthians 11:17–34 Paul made no appeal to a particular individual whom he could hold responsible for the behavior at Corinth; he addressed all the members. In the Pastoral Epistles, where the duties of elders and bishops are set forth, there is nothing said with respect to the administration of the supper as one of their duties. The practice of a president presiding appears in the second century in the writings of Justin Martyr.

Bibliography: D. G. Dix, *The Shape of the Liturgy* (1945). F. Gavin, *The Jewish Antecedents of the Christian Sacraments* (1928). A. J. B. Higgins, *The Lord's Supper in the New Testament* (1952). J. Jeremias, *The Eucharistic Words of Jesus* (1955). J. C. Lambert, *The Sacraments in the New Testament* (1903).

T. C. SMITH

LORD'S SUPPER, ADMINISTRATION OF. The administration of the Lord's Supper in Baptist churches varies according to the customs and traditions of the congregation, the conception of its meaning in the mind of the pastor, and the rule or custom of the church as to who is eligible to partake of the Supper. Custom and tradition determine its frequency; in some localities it is observed monthly; in many states, quarterly; and in some rural areas, annually or semiannually. Variety is also found in administration because of the influence of various conceptions of the meaning of the elements. Some consider the elements mere symbols, and believe that the service does not involve much corporate experience; others consider the celebration a means of grace equal at least to that of the reading of the holy Scriptures or the preaching of a gospel sermon; and there are various interpretations between these two views. Other variations in administration are based on different customs with regard to eligibility of persons to partake of the elements. Churches may admit to the ordinance only an immersed member of that local congregation, an immersed member of any church of like faith and order, or a self-examined disciple of Jesus of any Christian fold. The administrator, in his introductory remarks preceding the service as a whole or just prior to the distribution of elements (or by saying nothing at all), indicates the practice followed by his particular congregation.

In their administration of the ordinance, most Baptist churches use unfermented grape juice rather than wine; cubicled light bread, instead of the traditional "unleavened bread," is considered acceptable. The minister presides at the table as the servant of the congregation (although it seldom happens, any member may be asked by the church so to serve); the deacons gather about the table and serve the people; the bread and the cup are "blessed" (by prayers which are really for the people); individual glasses are used; the elements are received by each member of the congregation from his neighbor in the pew whom he may not even know; a collection for the indigent is taken; a concluding hymn (usually "Blest Be the Tie") is sung. The service most frequently comes at the Sunday morning hour of worship.

More significant practices include the careful effort to preserve the scriptural symbolism of the New Testament in action and in words, the emphasis upon the priesthood of all believers (in permitting layman to administrate and in taking the elements from another layman), the fellowship of a Christian democracy (all eating or drinking together), the confession of sins, and the expression in song, anthem, and prayer of grateful joy for the sacrifice made once for all.

An increasing number of pastors are making every effort to obtain a more meaningful observance by rediscovering for themselves and their people the New Testament truths concerning the memorial. Deacons, choir members, and ushers are instructed in worshipful procedures and are led to make a more prayerful and careful preparation of themselves and all they say and do in order to obey faithfully and well the Master's injunction concerning the ordinance. As a result, there are fewer churches which go for months without observing the ordinance and fewer who do so as an apparent afterthought.

BIBLIOGRAPHY: W. T. Conner, *Christian Doctrine* (1949). H. Cook, *What Baptists Stand For* (1953). G. S. Dobbins, *The Churchbook* (1955). J. R. Hobbs, *The Pastor's Manual* (1948). G. W. McDaniel, *The People Called Baptists* (1919). W. J. McGlothlin, *Baptist Confessions of Faith* (1911). E. A. Payne, *The Fellowship of Believers* (1953). H. W. Robinson, *The Life and Faith of Baptists* (1946). G. W. Truett, *The Supper of Our Lord* (1951). JOHN T. WAYLAND

LORD'S SUPPER, REQUISITES TO. The majority of Baptists today are in accord with other Christians in the basic principles governing the observance of the Lord's Supper. All denominations agree that the supper should be restricted to those who have made a Christian profession. They further agree that only properly baptized church members should be admitted to the Lord's table. Most Baptists, however, while agreeing with the basic principles, differ from other denominations and even differ among themselves on the second factor; that is, with regard to what constitutes a properly baptized church member. Baptists historically have insisted that the New Testament teaches that the *subject* of baptism must be a believer (not an infant or anyone incapable of voluntary choice), and that the *form* of baptism should be immersion, not sprinkling or pouring. It follows, then, that Baptists holding to restricted communion adhere to the same standards for admission to the Lord's table as do all Christians, but believe that the second requisite for admission consists only of baptism by immersion upon confession of faith in Jesus Christ. Therefore, the restrictions which most Baptists have placed on admission to the supper root basically in their conception of baptism. In addition most Baptists have held firmly to the conception that both baptism and the Lord's Supper are ordinances of the local congregation, so that authorization for baptism and the invitation to participate in the observance of the supper are the prerogatives of each Baptist congregation, not of an episcopal officer.

Baptists have not agreed among themselves concerning the practical operation of these principles. Generally speaking, there have been three points of view relative to communion, sometimes referred to as open communion, closed intercommunion, and closed intracommunion.

Open communion.—Many Baptists have developed historically as a minority group in the midst of other denominations. While not agreeing that other forms of baptism are scripturally proper, these Baptists have been willing to waive the requirement of baptism by immersion for admission to the Lord's table, partly, perhaps, because of the feeling that the most important requisite is the Christian profession and partly from a desire to maintain mutual respect and fellowship with denominations whose congregations are recognized as churches of Jesus Christ. This general point of view is quite prevalent in groups other than Southern Baptists.

Closed intercommunion.—Under this view communion is restricted in the sense that immersion by the authority of a Baptist church after profession of faith in Jesus Christ is always demanded before participation in the supper is permitted. However, those holding this view believe that membership in any Baptist church qualifies a person to participate in the Supper in any other Baptist church.

Closed intracommunion.—The most restricted view of communion among Baptists is that which demands that one must be immersed by the authority of a Baptist church upon profession of faith and in addition limits his participation in the Lord's Supper to those occasions when it is served in the church where he is a member. He is not qualified to participate in the observance of the supper in any other Baptist church. This position stems in part from the feeling that the supper is related to church discipline, and that no one should be permitted to partake of the supper in a congregation unless his membership is there, i.e., he is subject to their discipline.

It is impossible to estimate what proportion of Southern Baptists holds to each of these general views or to some similar position. The number of churches officially practicing open communion is not proportionately large. However, it is the practice in a great number of churches, when the Lord's Supper is to be served, to make no statement as to the essential qualifications for participation. No general invitation is given, but the elements are passed to all who are present, and each person is left to be the judge of his own personal qualifications to partake. Doubtless in sentiment, at least, the majority of Southern Baptists are closed intercommunionists. Closed intracommunionists follow the pattern set by James Robinson Graves (*q.v.*) and his Landmark associates. ROBERT A. BAKER

LOTT CARY BAPTIST FOREIGN MISSION CONVENTION. Organized in the Shiloh Baptist Church, Washington, D. C., Dec., 1897. Since its inception it has carried on a continuous missionary and educational enterprise in foreign areas, with headquarters in Washington. The convention's name is in memory of Lott Cary, former slave of Richmond, Va., who bought his freedom and sailed to West Africa as a missionary in 1821, thereby becoming the first American missionary to Africa. Upon his arrival on the coast of West Africa, he organized and erected the Providence Baptist Church, Monrovia, Liberia, West Africa. The original church edifice stands in Liberia today.

The program of the Lott Cary Baptist Foreign Convention, restricted to foreign missions, supports currently 88 full-time missionaries, with major fields of operation in Liberia, India, and Haiti. "Building a Better World Through Christian Missions" is the convention's motto. Constituents of the convention come from Negro Baptist churches in 16 states, chiefly along the Atlantic Seaboard and the District of Columbia.

The convention has had eight presidents; J. Vance McIver, Orange, N. J., holds this position at present. W. L. Ransome is chairman of the executive board, and Wendell C. Somerville has served as executive secretary since 1940. The convention is an affiliate of the Baptist World Alliance, the International Missionary Council, and the Division of Foreign Missions of the National Council of Churches of Christ in the U. S. A. Operating on an annual budget of $140,000, it expended 12 per cent of the total receipts for current operating expenses and 88 per cent for missions in 1954–55.

WENDELL C. SOMERVILLE

LOTTIE MOON CHRISTMAS OFFERING. See WOMAN'S MISSIONARY UNION.

LOUISIANA ASSOCIATIONS.

ACADIA. Organized in 1918 by representatives from 15 churches from Carey Association. It is located in the southwestern part of Louisiana and includes Acadia Parish and portions of St. Landry and Evangeline parishes. In 1954, 19 churches and 9 missions reported 343 baptisms, 4,632 members, $234,394 total gifts, $60,073 mission gifts, $796,314 property value, and $36,065 church debt. W. F. TOWN, JR.

ADOLPH STAGG. Organized by messengers from seven churches belonging to Judson, New Orleans, and Evangeline associations, meeting at the First Baptist Church of Houma, Oct. 2, 1942. In 1954, 11 churches and 13 missions reported 172 baptisms, 1,931 members, $149,750 total gifts, $12,794 mission gifts, $358,450 property value, and $19,758 church debt.

MACK STEWART

AMITE RIVER. Formed by the combination of the Mississippi and Tangipahoa associations, meeting with the Macedonia Church in Livingston Parish on Oct. 22, 1910. Thirteen churches were represented. This association covers St. Helena Parish and parts of Livingston. In 1954, 22 churches reported 234 baptisms, 4,556 members, $96,406 total gifts, $6,127 mission gifts, $129,147 property value, and $23,760 church debt. J. W. STARKEY

ASCENSION PARISH. Organized at Oak Grove Church on Nov. 3, 1923, by 22 messengers from six churches, all from Eastern Louisiana Association. R. P. Mahon and E. F. Haight from the Baptist Bible institute (now New Orleans Baptist Theological Seminary) assisted in the organization. Articles of faith were adopted. In 1954, 8 churches reported 41 baptisms, 1,533 members, $54,339 total gifts, $6,628 mission gifts, $174,007 property value, and $17,651 church debt. T. W. GAYER

ATCHAFALAYA. Organized at Plaquemine, Sept. 27, 1947, by representatives of 10 churches from the Judson Association. Articles of faith adopted were taken from the New Hampshire Confession of Faith. In 1954, 13 churches reported 72 baptisms, 1,507 members, $66,898 total gifts, $9,500 mission gifts, $170,200 property value, and $8,198 church debt. D. H. ROCKETT

BAYOU MACON. Organized Nov. 29, 1855, by messengers from six churches which had a total membership of 184. The territory was the northeastern section of the state. It has divided several times; in 1914 Deer Creek was organized; in 1924 Morehouse-Ouachita was formed; in 1948 Madison was organized. In 1954, 24 churches and 2 missions reported 303 baptisms, 6,718 members, $179,445 total gifts, $19,254 mission gifts, $734,200 property value, $33,831 church debt. J. D. CHEATHAM

BEAUREGARD. Organized in 1860 as the Calcasieu Association by churches and ministers connected with the Sabine and Louisiana associations. At its meeting in 1922 held at Ragley the name was changed to Beauregard. In 1954, 41 churches and 1 mission reported 378 baptisms, 7,259 members, $228,221.94 total gifts, $31,672.85 mission gifts, $779,663.95 property value, and $26,995.00 church debt. JAMES F. COLE

BETHLEHEM. Organized in 1878 by 22 churches. The first annual session was held with Pleasant Hill Church in 1879 with William Brice as moderator and G. L. Wild as clerk. Most of the churches have united with other associations. Its territory is now restricted to the western part of Lincoln Parish. In 1954, 8 churches reported 24 baptisms, 1,179 members, $26,967 total gifts, $2,066 mission gifts, $120,495 property value, and $3,000 church debt. T. W. GAYER

BIENVILLE. Organized by messengers from 12 churches in Bienville Parish Nov. 29, 1925. It adopted the constitution, by-laws, and abstract of faith of the Red River Association, most of the churches having come out of that association. At the first annual session the association had 22 churches and 4,156 members. In 1954, 25 churches reported 203 baptisms, 5,319 members, $144,744 total gifts, $28,978 mission gifts, $543,526 property value, and $9,817 church debt. E. D. GIDDENS

BIG CREEK. Organized on Dec. 29, 1871, by messengers from churches located in Grant, Avoyelles, and Rapides parishes. The meeting was held in Big Creek Church and the association was named Big Creek. It adopted the articles of faith of Ouachita Association. In 1947 it divided on territorial grounds. Those in Grant Parish retained the name Big Creek. Those located in Rapides Parish organized North Rapides Association. In 1954, 27 churches reported 162 baptisms, 5,061 members, $124,645 total gifts, $14,127 mission gifts, $385,500 property value, $32,145 church debt. M. E. MERCER

BOSSIER. Organized in 1923 by representatives from eight churches in the northwestern part of Louisiana. It is bordered on the west by Caddo Parish and on the south by Red River Association. In 1954, 13 churches and 1 mission reported 297 baptisms, 5,884 members, $296,132 total gifts, $57,179 mission gifts, $817,347 property value, and $186,477 church debt. W. L. SEWELL

CADDO. Organized at Walnut Hill Church on Oct. 22, 1892. The churches which formed this association came out of Grand Cane Association. Until 1948 it covered Caddo Parish. It now covers the southern half of Caddo and includes the city of Shreveport. In 1954, 33 churches reported 1,333 baptisms, 26,654 members, $1,682,808 total gifts, $375,963 mission gifts, $6,059,316 property value, and $918,674 church debt. E. E. FIELDS

CALDWELL. Organized in 1927 at Mt. Pleasant Church by churches in Caldwell Parish which had belonged to Ouachita Association. In 1954, 16 churches and 1 mission reported 106 baptisms, 2,823 members, $62,146 total gifts, $10,378 mission gifts, $214,200 property value, and $3,950 church debt. GEORGE M. JENKINS

CAREY. Organized in 1860 under the name Calcasieu by churches from Louisiana and Sabine associations. It adopted the New Hampshire Confession of Faith. On Nov. 11, 1892, the name was changed to Carey. In 1918, 15 churches withdrew and formed Luther Rice Association. In 1954 the churches were all located in the southwestern corner of Louisiana. In 1954, 33 churches and 3 missions reported 810 baptisms, 14,605 members, $918,597 total gifts, $131,599 mission gifts, $2,654,800 property value, $309,616 church debt. L. A. STAGG

CENTRAL LOUISIANA. Formed by a division of Louisiana Association on Oct. 15, 1946, at Woodworth. The 14 churches in the northern part of the area, including Alexandria, went into the new organization. When organized the churches had 8,048 members. In 1954, 20 churches and 1 mission reported 256 baptisms, 8,741 members, $348,556 total gifts, $70,479 mission gifts, $1,443,499 property value, and $215,091 church debt. TROY V. WHEELER

CONCORD. The second oldest association in Louisiana, organized by representatives from four churches Nov. 3, 1832, at Black Lake Church, near Minden. Before this time Louisiana Association had extended to the Arkansas line. From 1832 until 1844, when Ouachita Association was organized, Concord covered all north Louisiana. The articles of faith adopted were taken from the Philadelphia Confession. It recognized baptism, the Lord's Supper, and "Feet-Washing . . . as ordinances of the Gospel." Feet-washing was soon discarded, and the word "Missionary" was dropped from the name of the association as being "unnecessary." The men who led in the organization of the Louisiana Baptist Convention in 1848 were for the most part leaders in Concord. In 1954, 30 churches reported 282 baptisms, 9,769 members, $382,524 total gifts, $75,066 mission gifts, $1,230,953 property value, and $35,478 church debt. T. W. GAYER

DEER CREEK. Organized at Mangham, La., Sept. 30, 1914, by messengers from 19 churches in Franklin and Richland parishes (coming from Bayou Macon Association). In 1954, 35 churches reported 460 baptisms, 8,692 members, $205,285 total gifts, $24,312 mission gifts, $967,309 property value, and $191,339 church debt. A missionary is employed jointly with Richland Association. C. B. HALL

DELTA. Organized on Feb. 8, 1944, at St. Joseph, by messengers from six churches which had withdrawn from Deer Creek. First annual session was held at Newellton on Oct. 20, 1944. Two churches were added. The territory covered Tensas Parish and a part of Concordia Parish. In 1954, 26 churches reported 171 baptisms, 2,860 members, $93,911 total gifts, $12,570 mission gifts, $430,000 property value, and $28,626 church debt. SHIRLEY BRIGGS

DESOTO PARISH. Organized at Summer Grove on Dec. 21, 1849, as Grand Cane Association by five churches from Caddo and DeSoto parishes. In 1915 the Caddo churches withdrew and united with Caddo Association. In 1945 the name was changed to DeSoto Parish Association. When organized the association adopted the New Hampshire Confession of Faith. In 1954, 26 churches reported 188 baptisms, 5,129 members, $292,369 total gifts, $38,698 mission gifts, $691,600 property value, and $64,795 church debt. GEORGE A. RITCHEY

EASTERN LOUISIANA. Originally a part of the Mississippi River Association, organized at Beulah Church, Washington Parish, on Saturday, Nov. 19, 1842. Earlier in the year several churches had petitioned their Mississippi Association for the privilege of forming a new association. To fulfil the purpose of organizing the churches in the eastern part of the Florida parishes, 22 churches with a membership of 699 formed the Eastern Louisiana Baptist Association. Five resolutions relating to the program of work were adopted, which indicated the harmony of its beginning. In 1954, 23 churches reported 237 baptisms, 2,717 members, $242,997 total gifts, $53,512 mission gifts, $781,850 property value, and $82,500 church debt. In co-operation with the other associations in District 11, a missionary is employed. D. LEWIS WHITE

EVANGELINE. Organized at Abbeville on Aug. 15, 1939. Acadia Association had granted letters to the following churches to form a new association: Abbeville, Avery Island, Franklin, Jeanerette, Lafayette, Morgan City, New Iberia, and Nunez. The churches of this association organized French radio broadcasts. They have also sponsored the student center and student work at Southwestern Louisiana Institute at Lafayette. Emmanuel Church, Lafayette, and Trinity at New Iberia, have been organized since the association was formed. In 1954, 14 churches reported 191 baptisms, 3,650 members, $185,649 total gifts, $35,830 mission gifts, $718,000 property value, and $114,410 church debt. R. L. HOLMES

JACKSON. Organized in 1924 by representatives from 19 churches located in Jackson Parish. In 1954, 22 churches reported 209 baptisms, 4,182 members, $132,146 total gifts, $93,743 mission gifts, $530,542 property value, and $95,476 church debt. J. E. CALLOWAY

JUDSON. Organized in 1890 by Baptist churches in southcentral Louisiana, bordered largely on the west by the Mississippi River and on the east by East Louisiana Association, including the city of Baton Rouge. In 1954, 30 churches reported 995 baptisms, 17,674 members, $2,066,908 total gifts, $185,725 mission gifts, $4,744,679 property value, and $1,040,035 church debt. R. P. BUTLER

LA SALLE. Organized by messengers from eight churches in La Salle Parish, meeting in Jena, Nov. 26, 1944. In 1954, 28 churches and 2 missions reported 299 baptisms, 6,047 members, $244,566 total gifts, $32,341 mission gifts, $734,350 property value, and $60,000 church debt. O. M. CORLEY

LIBERTY. Located in north Louisiana, organized in 1895 in the First Church of Homer. As originally constituted, it had 17 reporting churches, 11 of which came from North Louisiana Association, 3 from Red River Association, and 3 from Concord Association. In 1954, 15 churches reported 171 baptisms, 4,454 members, $191,908 total gifts, $37,983 mission gifts, $700,500 property value, and $34,906 church debt. EUGENE L. SKELTON

LOUISIANA. The oldest association in the state, organized at Cheneyville on Oct. 31, 1818, by 11 messengers from five churches—Calvary, Debourn, Vermillion, Plaquemine, and Beulah. Ezekiel O'Quin was moderator and J. T. H. Kilpatrick, clerk. By 1848 there were 714 members in the association. The last of many divisions came in 1947 when the churches in Rapides Parish west of Red River withdrew to form Central Association. When the association organized, the articles of faith of the Mississippi Association were adopted. In 1954 nearly all 26 churches were located in Avoyelles Parish. These churches reported 183 baptisms, 4,237 members, $145,158 total gifts, $21,730 mission gifts, $587,100 property value, and $76,455 church debt. R. H. WHITTINGTON

LUTHER RICE. Organized at Welsh on Feb. 9, 1951, by representatives from 10 churches from Carey Association. The territory covered by this association is in southwest Louisiana. It is touched by Carey, Mt. Olive, Acadia, and Beauregard associations. W. H. Knight and Edgar Godbold assisted in its organization. At the first annual session, held at Elton, Oct. 26, 1951, 10 churches reported 183 baptisms, 2,250 members, and full-time preaching at every church. In 1954, 10 churches and 2 missions reported 137 baptisms, 2,521 members, $140,158 total gifts, $26,351 mission gifts, $629,000 property value, and $74,747 church debt. E. N. WEAVER

MADISON. Organized Oct. 16, 1952, by representatives from nine churches from Richland-Madison Association. The territory covered is Madison Parish. In 1954, 9 churches reported 104 baptisms, 1,991 members, $58,530 total gifts,

$7,911 mission gifts, $242,000 property value, and $47,438 church debt. IRVIN CHENEY, JR.

MOREHOUSE. Organized early in 1925 in a meeting in the First Baptist Church, Monroe, under the name Morehouse-Ouachita. Later in that same year some of the churches withdrew and formed Ouachita Parish Association. In 1950 the name was changed to Morehouse Association and its territory confined to Morehouse Parish. In 1954, 22 churches reported 293 baptisms, 5,367 members, $287,219 total gifts, $36,182 mission gifts, $504,125 property value, and $38,388 total church debt. A. E. PRINCE

MOUNT OLIVE. Organized Mar. 27, 1885, at Amiable Church by representatives from nine churches. At the first annual session, held at New Hope, Oct. 22–23, 1885, the New Hampshire Confession of Faith and Kerfoot's rules of order were adopted. At the 1886 session the committee on foreign missions stated that while they realized the importance of foreign missions, not a single dollar had been contributed to that cause. In 1954, 36 churches reported 405 baptisms, 7,376 members, $198,713 total gifts, $27,098 mission gifts, $611,189 property value, and $60,793 church debt. H. T. SULLIVAN

NATCHITOCHES. Organized in the First Baptist Church, Natchitoches, Nov. 6, 1912. In 1954, 33 churches reported 194 baptisms, 6,254 members, $166,963 total gifts, $25,030 mission gifts, $840,807 property value, and $63,169 church debt. PERRY F. WEBB, JR.

NEW ORLEANS. Organized on Apr. 30, 1906, at St. Charles Avenue Church by representatives from five New Orleans churches and two St. Tammany Parish churches. Representatives from these same churches had met at Coliseum Place Church on Mar. 12, 1906, but failed to effect an organization. The first annual meeting was held at Slidell on Oct. 17, 1906. New Orleans and St. Tammany associations combined in 1914, and remained joined until 1924, when it was decided to divide into two associations as before. The New Orleans group then re-organized at Grace Church on Oct. 13, 1925. In 1954, 52 churches and 25 missions reported 1,359 baptisms, 22,988 members, $1,242,115 total gifts, $161,221 mission gifts, $5,491,594 property value, and $1,642,098 church debt. W. R. FUSSELL

NORTH CADDO. Organized at Vivian in Jan., 1948, by messengers from 17 churches from Caddo Association, and in the northern part of Caddo Parish. It adopted the articles of faith of the mother association. In 1954, 17 churches reported 160 baptisms, 3,538 members, $104,671 total gifts, $12,779 mission gifts, $338,249 property value, and $10,865 church debt. E. E. FIELDS

NORTH RAPIDES. Organized Oct. 28, 1947, at Philadelphia Church by messengers from 20 churches with 5,600 members. Formerly affiliated with the Big Creek Association, the churches north of Red River in Rapides Parish withdrew to form the new organization because the parent association had grown too large. Among the denominational leaders produced by this association are Greene W. Strother, R. Houston Smith, and A. L. Smith. In 1954, 26 churches reported 316 baptisms, 8,315 members, $291,621 total gifts, $58,805 mission gifts, $1,117,209 property value, and $176,279 church debt. W. A. BROWN

NORTH SABINE. Organized in 1896 by a group of churches from Sabine Association, all located in the northern part of Sabine Parish. In 1947 the churches of Sabine and North Sabine united under the name Sabine Association. In 1953 the churches of the northern part of the parish again withdrew and organized North Sabine Association. A line drawn from east to west and passing through the town of Many divides the parish into two equal parts. The churches north of this line belong to North Sabine Association, and the churches south of this line belong to Sabine Association. In 1954, 24 churches reported 183 baptisms, 3,973 members, $98,925 total gifts, $19,658 mission gifts, $338,560 property value, and $6,770 church debt. J. C. SALLEY

OUACHITA. Organized in 1844 out of churches from Concord Association. It included the parishes of Ouachita, Caldwell, Catahoula, and Franklin. It adopted Calvinistic articles. The 1846 session requested the churches to send funds to evangelize the territory. This request aroused such a protest from the antimission brethren that the next session withdrew the request. In 1850 a group of churches withdrew and formed an anti-missionary association. The 1853 session reported a marked improvement in the missionary cause. In 1867 a Negro church was received into the association. The 1868 session adopted the New Hampshire Confession. In 1954 it included Catahoula Parish and part of Concordia; 25 churches reported 242 baptisms, 3,706 members, $135,537 total gifts, $11,949 mission gifts, $384,946 property value, and $13,755 church debt. T. W. GAYER

OUACHITA PARISH. Organized Nov. 1, 1945, by messengers from 19 churches from Morehouse-Ouachita Association, which had voted on Oct. 12, 1945, to divide. The name was Ouachita Valley until 1948. In 1953 the association again divided; the 18 churches west of the Ouachita River withdrew to form Trenton Association, the 18 churches east of the Ouachita, including the churches of Monroe, remained in Ouachita Parish Association. In 1954, 18 churches and 2 missions reported 508 baptisms, 10,014 members, $45,151 total gifts, $95,314 mission gifts, $1,542,863 property value, and $278,658 church debt. W. L. IVEY

RED RIVER. Organized at Mt. Zion Church in Bossier Parish, Nov. 24, 1848, by 11 churches with 307 members; included Bienville, Bossier, Claiborne, Jackson, Red River, and Webster parishes. In 1851 the association recommended that the churches unite with the Louisiana Baptist Convention. Before that time they had done missionary work in the territory of their association. In 1954, 17 churches reported 132 baptisms, 4,660 members, $115,506.25 total gifts, $17,374.28 mission gifts, $401,000.00 property value, and $15,272.00 church debt. JACK SHAW

RICHLAND. Organized Oct. 29, 1951, by 26 churches in Richland Parish which came out of Richland-Madison Association. In 1954, 27 churches and 2 missions reported 307 baptisms, 6,629 members, $208,011 total gifts, $32,497 mission gifts, $802,830 property value, and $53,177 church debt. C. W. JONES

SABINE. Organized Oct. 22, 1847, by representatives from nine churches with a total membership of 129. William Cook of Mississippi had moved into what is now Sabine Parish in 1824. He preached the first Baptist sermon in that area and did much to establish the Baptist cause.

In 1853 the association, being "fully convinced of the moral and religious influence of Sabbath schools," resolved to encourage every church to establish such schools. B. H. Bray was appointed "general agent for Sabbath schools for the association." In that same year "the Abstract of Faith known as Union Articles" was adopted. In 1954 a resolution was passed to "eliminate from the annual minutes the 'Gospel Order' and 'Articles of Faith' because the Sabine Missionary Baptist Association claims the New Testament as its creed." In 1954, 26 churches reported 149 baptisms, 4,285 members, $106,141 total gifts, $19,905 mission gifts, $283,600 property value, and $2,900 church debt.

T. W. GAYER

SHADY GROVE. Organized in 1885 by representatives from eight churches located in the eastern half of Winn Parish. In 1954, 16 churches reported 74 baptisms, 2,010 members, $31,448 total gifts, $2,004 mission gifts, $77,950 property value, and $5,401 church debt.

J. E. CALLOWAY

ST. TAMMANY. Organized in 1924 by representatives from 13 churches which came out of Orleans–St. Tammany and West Pearl River associations. Its location is St. Tammany Parish. In 1954, 17 churches and 4 missions reported 173 baptisms, 3,669 members, $98,449 total gifts, $6,425 mission gifts, $347,700 property value, and $16,128 church debt.

M. H. FIELDS

TANGIPAHOA. Organized Jan. 4, 1905, in Tangipahoa Parish. The first annual session was held Nov., 1905, at Hammond with seven churches represented. In 1954, 25 churches reported 321 baptisms, 7,831 members, $241,471 total gifts, $36,693 mission gifts, $881,823 property value, and $18,096 church debt.

RAY P. RUST

TRENTON. Organized in West Monroe by messengers from 17 churches on Jan. 26, 1953. W. L. Sewell, president of Louisiana Baptist Convention, delivered the organizational sermon. The first regular session was held with the Calhoun Church on Oct. 15–16, 1953. Its territory is Ouachita Parish west of Ouachita River. In 1954, 20 churches reported 421 baptisms, 9,935 members, $509,801 total gifts, $60,720 mission gifts, 2,025 tithers, $1,613,000 property value, and $124,715 debt. H. L. DRISKELL

UNION. Organized in 1890 and called Everett Association. The first annual meeting was held in 1891 with the Oakland Church. In doctrine and fellowship Everett and Concord associations were similar. In 1893 Everett was composed of 16 churches. Until 1909 Everett supported Everett Institute at Spearsville, a Baptist preparatory school. In that year the school was donated to the Spearsville Public School District. In 1946, in an effort to unite all the churches in Union Parish into one association, the name was changed to Union Association. In 1954, 27 churches reported 147 baptisms, 3,680 members, $81,166 total gifts, $9,177 mission gifts, $205,000 property value, and $4,250 church debt. T. W. GAYER

VERNON. Organized at Castor on Oct. 15, 1872, by representatives from nine churches, all having letters of dismission from Sabine Association. Churches entering the organization were Castor, Anacoco, Walnut Hill, Mount Vernon, Comrade, Clementine, Elim, Pleasant Grove, and Smyrna; they had a total membership of 288. In 1954, 39 churches reported 216 baptisms, 6,184 members, $152,327 total gifts, $19,098 mission gifts, $522,495 property value, and $50,000 church debt. R. S. CRAWFORD

WASHINGTON PARISH. Organized at Mt. Hermon on Nov. 16, 1894, by messengers from seven churches. It adopted the "Rules of Decorum, Articles of Faith, Gospel Order, and Objects and Powers" of the Magee's Creek Association, and was called Union Association. Edwin Oswald Ware (*q.v.*) was present. In 1906 it changed its name to Washington Parish. Half Moon Bluff, the first Baptist church organized in Louisiana, had existed in the territory of Washington Parish. Baptist leaders coming from this association include William Henry Knight (*q.v.*), W. A. Corkern, T. W. Gayer, T. J. Delaughter, W. R. Fussell, and Alma Graves. In 1954, 26 churches reported 321 baptisms, 10,026 members, $373,730 total gifts, $61,942 mission gifts, $1,358,900 property value, and total church debt of $75,956.

T. W. GAYER

WEBSTER PARISH. Organized at Minden on Oct. 17, 1922. In 1954, 20 churches and 1 mission reported 395 baptisms, 9,114 members, $402,499 total gifts, $90,658 mission gifts, $1,477,400 property value, and $228,570 church debt. TRUMAN ALDREDGE

WILLIAM WALLACE. Organized on Oct. 16, 1953, in the First Baptist Church of Jackson by representatives of 10 churches from Judson Association and four from Eastern Louisiana Association. The churches are located in East Baton Rouge, East and West Feliciana parishes. These are small town and rural churches. In 1954, 14 churches reported 186 baptisms, 4,011 members, $629,400 property value, $183,373 total gifts, $21,455 mission gifts, and $79,429 church debt. J. H. PENNEBAKER

WINN PARISH. Organized as Central Association, Oct. 29, 1859, at Mars Hill Church in Winn Parish. The session in 1861 had 20 churches from Winn, Grant, Natchitoches, Jackson, Bienville, and Caldwell parishes. The large territory covered by the association made it necessary to organize new units. The session in 1926 held at Zion Hill Church changed the name to Winn Parish and limited its territory to the parish. In 1954, 23 churches reported 153 baptisms, 4,503 members, $133,909 total gifts, $20,763 mission gifts, $567,665 property value, and $47,250 church debt.

W. L. HOLCOMB

LOUISIANA BAPTIST. A weekly, established at Mt. Lebanon, La., in 1855. Hanson Lee edited the paper with such ability that it soon ranked among the ablest religious papers in the South. The paper was published throughout the Civil War. The circulation was sold to J. R. Graves (*q.v.*) of *The Baptist* (Memphis) in 1869. F. W. TINNIN, SR.

LOUISIANA BAPTIST CHILDREN'S HOME. The Louisiana Baptist Convention in 1899 appointed a committee to establish an orphanage. For a short time a few children were placed in a Protestant orphanage in Baton Rouge. Then a dormitory at Keachie College was used. The institution was called the Louisiana Baptist Orphanage. In 1903 it was moved to Lake Charles, where it soon outgrew its quarters. In 1925 it was moved to its present location, five miles east of Monroe, where a 430-acre farm had been purchased; and the name was changed to Louisiana Baptist Children's Home.

In 1954 the home served 207 children; the total budget for the year was $152,442.63; the property consisted of 660 acres of land with 38 buildings valued at $721,691.37. Up to 1955 support came from individuals and churches. The children were clothed by missionary societies. Beginning with 1955, the home has been supported by the Cooperative Program. The home has no debt.

By 1955 a total of 1,807 children had been served by the home. The children attend the public schools of Monroe until they finish high school. Those who qualify are sent to college; others are given special training.

BIBLIOGRAPHY: J. T. Christian, *A History of the Baptists of Louisiana* (1923). C. P. St. Amant, *A Short History of Louisiana Baptists* (1948).

T. W. GAYER

LOUISIANA BAPTIST CONVENTION.

I. Baptist Beginnings. Although individual Baptists probably moved into Louisiana from the Natchez country of Mississippi as early as 1780, the first Baptists of whom there is a documented record, to enter the state were Bailey E. Chaney (*q.v.*) and his family, who came into East Feliciana Parish in 1798. This heroic man, defying the regulation which forbade all except Roman Catholic priests to preach in Louisiana, was "taken prisoner by the Catholic authorities." They released him shortly thereafter but refused to let him "establish a church in Louisiana, which was a cherished object with him."

First Louisiana Baptist churches.—The first Baptist church established in Louisiana was the Half Moon Bluff Baptist Church, organized Oct. 12, 1812, near the Bogue Chitto River, between the present towns of Franklinton and Clifton. Knowledge of who organized this church is uncertain, though Joseph Lewis and Joseph Irwin, the first "delegates" from the church to the Mississippi Association, probably share this honor with Ezra Courtney, the only preacher in east Louisiana at that time. This historic church ceased to function about 1870, and "Hay's Creek Church was later organized" from it, according to John T. Christian. Half Moon Bluff and four other churches—Mt. Nebo, 1813; Peniel, 1813; Hepzibah, 1814; Sharon, 1818—formed the nucleus of Baptist work in the Florida parishes.

The Calvary Baptist Church in Evangeline Parish near Bayou Chicot, organized on Nov. 13, 1812, became the second Baptist church in Louisiana, the first west of the Mississippi River, and the oldest in the state with a continuous history. Joseph Willis (*q.v.*) organized this church and, assisted by Ezekiel O'Quin, led a vigorous missionary campaign in the southwestern and central sections of the state for 50 years.

New Orleans.—Samuel Mills, a Congregational missionary who visited New Orleans in 1813, stated that he found one Baptist minister, who expected to leave soon. But other Baptist preachers later visited the city. James A. Ranaldson came in Dec., 1816, and preached in the house of Cornelius Paulding. W. B. Johnson of South Carolina, later president of the Triennial Convention, visited the city in 1817 and found "a regular weekly prayer meeting . . . of different denominations." He also spoke in behalf of the Poydras Orphans Asylum to "hundreds" in the (Roman Catholic) St. Louis Cathedral! Benjamin Davis, a missionary from the Mississippi Baptist Society of Missions, constituted a Baptist church on Aug. 13, 1818, with 32 members, 8 white and 24 Negro. This church, however, and several later ones eventually ceased to exist, and it was not until Dec. 28, 1843, that the church now known as the First Baptist Church was organized. Two years later, this body joined the Mississippi River Association, which had been formed in 1842 by churches in southern Mississippi and the Florida parishes in Louisiana. The eastern Louisiana Association was also formed in 1842 to unify the churches in the eastern part of the Florida parishes. Coliseum Place Baptist Church in New Orleans was organized in 1854.

First associations.—On Oct. 13, 1818, the first Baptist association in Louisiana was organized at Cheneyville in the Beulah Baptist Church, which had been formed in 1816. This initial effort beyond the level of local churches to unify Baptist work in the state was appropriately named the Louisiana Association. The five churches constituting the association at its inception, all of which Willis had been instrumental in founding, were Calvary, Beulah, Debourn, Vermillion, and Plaquemine, with a combined membership of 86. O'Quin, pastor of Beulah Church, preached the sermon and was elected moderator. The organization of the Concord Association, formed on Nov. 3, 1832, in the Black Lake Baptist Church with 15 members from four churches, was almost fatal to the Louisiana Association. The Red River Association, an offshoot of the Concord Association, was organized at the Saline Baptist Church in Bienville Parish in Oct., 1848. Other associations formed in Louisiana prior to the organization of the convention in 1848 were Ouachita in 1844, Grand Cane in 1845, and Sabine in 1847.

North Louisiana.—The first Baptist preacher to settle in north Louisiana was probably James Brinson, who came from Tennessee in 1820. He and the group with whom he came organized the Pine Hills Church, which joined the Louisiana Association in 1822. Brinson and others extended their labors westward into what was then the northern part of Natchitoches Parish. A church near what is now Minden, called Black Lake, was organized in 1823. Henry Humble emigrated from Mississippi in 1822 and settled on the Ouachita River near Harrisonburg. Despite his advanced age this hardy frontiersman in 1826 organized the Catahoula Baptist Church, the source of most of the churches of that region. Asa Mercer, Humble's successor, was later assisted by Thomas Meredith, the eventual leader of an antimission movement which threatened the unity of Louisiana Baptists.

One of the most notable of the early Louisiana Baptist communities was established at Mt. Lebanon in 1837. A group of Baptists, who had come almost as a single group from the Edgefield district of South Carolina, organized the historic Mt. Lebanon Baptist Church on July 8 of that year, and chose Henry Adams, a freeborn mulatto, as the first pastor. George Washington Baines (*q.v.*), who became pastor of the church in 1845, William Edwards Paxton (*q.v.*), and J. T. Burnett laid the foundations of many churches in the parishes of Bienville, Jackson, Claiborne, Bossier, and Natchitoches. Mt. Lebanon became the center of Louisiana Baptist work in the mid-19th century. It was here the Louisiana Baptist Convention was organized in 1848, a college was started in 1856, and many distinguished Baptists lived.

John Bryce, who came to Shreveport when there was no other Baptist preacher west of the Red River, organized the First Baptist Church of Shreveport on Feb. 14, 1845. The Grand Cane Association, organized on Dec. 21, 1845, was made up of five northwest Louisiana churches with 195 members.

Preconvention difficulties.—Prior to the organization of the state convention in 1848, there was no unifying factor among the few scattered Baptists in Louisiana, who faced considerable hostility from the Roman Catholic Church in the southern part of the state. Even now, the average parish priest in south Louisiana looks upon the Baptist preacher as an invader and purveyor of strange doctrines. Baptist leadership was zealous but, with several notable exceptions, poorly educated. The population of north Louisiana was widely scattered, and Roman Catholicism predominated south Louisiana. Baptists west of the Mississippi River had little contact with those in the Florida parishes. The rise of associations brought churches in various sections together but contributed little, and may have militated against the larger unity of Louisiana Baptists. There was no common means for the exchange of ideas. *The Southwestern Baptist Chronicle,* begun in 1847 in New Orleans, was hardly a statewide paper and by no means a denominational organ. It was "devoted to religion, science, literature, commerce, and general intelligence."

The antimission movement among the Baptists presented a severe problem. Antimissionism was the outgrowth of an undue emphasis upon the Calvinistic theology, stressing God's sovereignty and divine election to salvation, which was carried to extremes by a few dissatisfied Baptist leaders. Thomas Meredith (*q.v.*), often the author of the doctrinal letter in the minutes of the Louisiana Association, became the antimission leader in the state. John Hill, a former missionary of the Ouachita Association, joined him in opposing missions. The movement reached its climax in 1850 and quickly declined.

Another difficulty for Louisiana Baptists was the "Campbellite" movement. A participant of this disruptive cause in Louisiana seems to have been James A. Raynaldson, who was excluded from the Mississippi Association in 1835 because of "heretical views," though the exact nature of his theological outlook is not known. The Campbellites received added prestige when President Shannon of the state university accepted their tenets, but the movement rapidly declined after the turn of the century.

Louisiana Baptists had reached a critical point. They could either continue to dissipate their energies and leadership in sectional concerns and local controversies or unite around common tasks. They chose the latter course and in 1848 organized the Louisiana Baptist Convention. C. PENROSE ST. AMANT

II. History of Convention. Two futile attempts to unite the Baptists of the state preceded the formation of the Louisiana Baptist Convention. A group within the Louisiana Association advocated without success a strict-communion convention. A second effort to create a convention was made in an informal unrecorded meeting held at Mt. Lebanon in 1847.

Inception of the convention.—The impulse which resulted in the formation of the convention in the Rehoboth Baptist Church at Mt. Lebanon on Dec. 2, 1848, came not from the associations but from individuals who desired a unified effort to promote missions and education. In the beginning it was intended that the convention should comprise only one section of the state, for the founders of the initial organization named it "The Baptist State Convention of North Louisiana." The word "North" was dropped in 1853, and the body was called The Louisiana Baptist State Convention. However, the Baptists in south Louisiana east of the Mississippi River did not come completely into the convention until late in the 19th century. The First Baptist Church of New Orleans in 1860 sent to the convention a letter which was "laid on the table, there being present neither delegates nor friends from that body." In 1880 there was only one self-supporting Baptist church "along the line of the Mississippi River from Memphis to the Gulf of Mexico." Added evidence for the sectional character of the convention is the fact that its first meeting in south Louisiana did not occur until 1889. The body adopted the present official title, The Louisiana Baptist Convention, in 1886.

The convention was organized by a group of 13 men: James Scarborough, Obadiah Dodson (*q.v.*), J. Q. Burnette, W. W. Crawford, Mathias Ardis, George Washington Baines, Sr. (*q.v.*), James Canfield, W. Edins, Eldred Hardy, T. B. Pitts, W. B. Prothro, R. H. Burnette, and Bartholomew Egan (*q.v.*). The body elected Scarborough president, Dodson and Burnette vice-presidents. The constitution of the convention demonstrated its missionary and educational purposes, which provided growing bonds of unity for the approximately 2,000 Baptists in Louisiana in 1848.

Executive board.—An executive board, appointed by the convention, met on Dec. 8, 1848, and made plans to raise funds to support the activities of the convention. The means of support were set forth in the second article of the constitution, which stated that "each Baptist Church or Association and Baptist Auxiliary Society shall be entitled to one delegate for every five dollars contributed annually for the funds of the Convention." Individual membership cost $2.50 per year, and life membership, $50. In 1879 the numerical basis replaced the financial, an arrangement which has lasted to the present.

The constitution indicates that "the Executive Board shall transact all business during the recess of the Convention." At first the board was concerned chiefly with implementing the missionary purpose of the convention by appointing and financing the work of missionaries in the state. Three boards, Domestic, Education, and Sunday School, in 1871 supplanted the single board. A Foreign Board, added in 1881, made a total of four, each having its own officers and managing its own affairs between the meetings of the state convention. The convention in 1885 merged the four boards into a single board, whose members were drawn from the associations, each of which was entitled to one member, and from a group residing near the headquarters of the board. This made the executive board a truly representative body, both as to responsibilities and membership, and provided a framework for administering Louisiana Baptist affairs which continues effectively today.

Growing unity.—Charles William Tompkies (*q.v.*) was the first state secretary under the unified plan of administration. This unity was strengthened in 1886 by the establishment of a state paper, *The Baptist Chronicle,* which, though privately owned, supported and was given full support by the convention. Greater geographic cohesion among Louisiana Baptists resulted when the churches east of the Mississippi River gradually entered convention activities in the closing decades of the 19th century.

Edwin Oswald Ware (*q.v.*), who became state secretary in 1892, established a method of "systematic beneficence" and sought to unify Louisiana Baptists, with particular emphasis upon state missions. He served until 1906 and again from 1910 to 1912. George Harvey Crutcher (*q.v.*), who succeeded Ware, was state director of the 75 Million Campaign until 1920, when Edgar Godbold (*q.v.*) assumed the secretaryship and also leadership of the campaign. The total amount pledged in Louisiana in the campaign was $3,002,067.00, of which less than one half was actually paid, a total of $1,416,385.06. E. D. Solomon succeeded Godbold and led in developing a "cooperative program," which quickly became the accepted method of financing denominational work. F. J. Katz became state secretary in 1931 and guided Louisiana Baptists through the economic depression. By 1933 "there were not sufficient funds to pay interest on the debts of Louisiana Baptists, to say nothing of retiring principal." The low point in the depression was reached in 1933, when Louisiana Baptists contributed $85,558.26. But total contributions climbed to $136,361.22 by 1935. The financial efficiency of the convention was increased in 1937 by the appointment of a budget control committee. Under the leadership of William Henry Knight (*q.v.*), the convention recorded a total of $1,331,585.38 in receipts in 1947, the same year the headquarters of the executive board were moved from Shreveport to Alexandria. Floyd Chaffin succeeded Knight as secretary in 1952, and total gifts reached more than $2,000,000 in 1954.

Early schools.—Interest in education did not yield immediate results because Louisiana Baptists were limited in resources and widely scattered. Agitation for a denominational college first appeared in 1847, but no action was taken until the meeting of the convention in 1852, when the committee on education recommended the establishment of a college "with a theological department" at Mt. Lebanon. "The preparatory department" of the school opened in 1853, and Mt. Lebanon University secured a charter the following year. By 1857 the school, under the leadership of Jesse Hartwell, was "no longer an experiment." This institution and Mt. Lebanon Female College, which was opened in 1855, prospered until the outbreak of the Civil War which closed both schools. The Keatchi Female College, chartered by the Grand Cane Association in 1857, also closed.

In 1871 Mt. Lebanon "University" became a high school. Keatchi Female College was revived, and "growing interest" in it was reported. Shreveport University opened in 1871 under local Baptist auspices but lasted only three years, due to a yellow fever epidemic in 1873 and the money panic in 1874. Concord Institute at Shiloh, under the patronage of Concord Association, was organized in 1877 but was permanently closed seven years later. This left two Baptist schools in the state, at Mt. Lebanon and Keatchi, neither of which was owned by the convention but both of which co-operated with it. These institutions persisted, sometimes precariously, until 1912, when they were permanently closed.

Louisiana College.—At the 1902 convention the committee on education, realizing that "a crisis" in the history of Mt. Lebanon College had been reached, made it known that Louisiana Baptists would establish a new institution at "any place" where an attractive campus might be provided, plus $30,000 in cash. A site in Pineville, across the Red River from Alexandria, was selected, and the school opened Oct. 3, 1906, with W. E. Taylor as chairman of the faculty. After the brief administrations of Edwin Oswald Ware (*q.v.*) and W. C. Friley, Claybrook Cottingham (*q.v.*) became the third president in 1910. He led the college brilliantly until his resignation in 1941 and was an active participant in Louisiana Baptist affairs, serving three successive years as president of the convention. Edgar Godbold succeeded Cottingham in 1942 and served through the difficult days of World War II. In 1951 G. Earl Guinn became the fifth president. The school has been strengthened academically and financially under his leadership.

With the closing of Dodd College in Shreveport in 1941, after 14 years of service as a Baptist girls' school, Louisiana College became, and is now, the only college owned and operated by the Louisiana Baptist Convention. Acadia Baptist Academy, near Eunice, is a high school which the convention has owned since 1919.

State papers.—*The Louisiana Baptist,* started in 1855 at Mt. Lebanon by Hanson Lee, was considered one of the best religious papers in the South. *The New Orleans Baptist Chronicle* was discontinued in 1857 after several years of publication. The editors of the *Louisiana Baptist,* Franklin Courtney and William Edwards Paxton (*q.v.*), in 1869 sold their subscription list to James Robinson Graves (*q.v.*), editor of *The Baptist* of Tennessee, in which he opened a Louisiana department. In 1877 *The Baptist Record* of Mississippi became the official organ of Louisiana Baptists, and in 1882 it absorbed the *Baptist Messenger,* a short-lived Louisiana Baptist publication. Thus the Baptists of Louisiana, unable to sustain a paper, used the publications of other states.

A special committee reported to the convention in 1885 that a state paper was "indispensable." Consequently *The Baptist Chronicle* was launched under the editorship and ownership of W. C. Friley. The executive board reported in 1887 that this publication was "a potent auxiliary in eliciting, combining, and directing the energies of the Baptist hosts of the State." R. M. Boone assumed direction of the paper in 1888 and edited it until 1903. Though privately owned, it served as a medium of communication for the denomination, carrying the annual proceedings of the state convention and emphasizing denominational matters. Boone sold the paper, and Bruce Benton became editor in 1903. *The Chronicle* struggled along with varying success under several editors until 1912, when the convention resolved to buy it. This plan failed to materialize, however, and Ware relinquished the state secretaryship to George Harvey Crutcher (*q.v.*), purchased the paper, and became its publisher. Seven years later the convention purchased it from Ware for $8,000, changed the name to *The Baptist Message,* and elected W. H. Barton as editor. Finley Watson Tinnin has served as editor of the paper since 1920.

State missions.—Following the Civil War the Board of Domestic Missions, called the State Mission Board in 1875, faced financial difficulties which seriously curtailed its work. W. C. Friley was engaged as the first "state evangelist" in 1878. Two years later the board contributed $100 "to help the church constituted at Lake Charles to erect a house of worship in that growing city." The convention in 1883 reported six state missionaries. Particular attention was devoted to south Louisiana, concerning which Secretary Tompkies commented at the 1886 convention: "There is no grander field for the accomplishment of good than that which now presents itself to us among the French population of 250,000." This region, where Roman Catholicism was once absolutely dominant, is now covered with Baptist churches and mission stations. The work of state missionaries in this area has been supplemented by the missionary endeavors of students from the New Orleans Baptist Theological Seminary, who are sent on mission trips in busses, and the steady support of this enterprise by the Louisiana Baptist Woman's Missionary Union. In recent years Baptist work has been solidly established in the deep Delta country below New Orleans. By 1954 the state mission program was thoroughly organized under the direction of district missionaries.

Women's work.—The first missionary society sponsored by women in Louisiana was organized in 1874 in the home of Mrs. H. E. Ardis at Mt. Lebanon. Ladies' Aid societies, which sought to aid the unfortunate, sprang up over the state and were gradually merged with the missionary societies. A statewide organization of these societies, formed at Alexandria on July 14, 1899, with Mrs. Charles Ammen as president, is regarded as the initial annual meeting of the Woman's Missionary Union of Louisiana. The first mention of this organization as an auxiliary to the Louisiana Baptist Convention appears in the 1905 minutes of the convention. Georgia Barnette was chiefly responsible for laying the foundation of the women's work in the state. She was succeeded as executive secretary in 1930 by Hannah Reynolds, who served through 1954 and was followed by Kathryn Carpenter.

Brotherhood.—A statewide "ministers' and deacons' meeting" occurred in connection with the convention in 1910. This was the forerunner of the Laymen's Movement, then the Laymen's Brotherhood, and finally the Brotherhood. The first committee on laymen's work was appointed at the 1912 convention, and two years later the initial statewide meeting was held in Alexandria. R. C. Holcomb in 1927 became the first state Brotherhood secretary. He was succeeded in 1929 by Dudley R. Isom, who wrote *The Baptist Brotherhood Manual,* which had a Convention-wide circulation. He reported 100 local organizations in 1930. This number had doubled by 1936. L. Mark Roberts, Shirley Briggs, Ira C. Prosser, and A. S. Newman have served as Brotherhood secretaries. The 1945 report of the department to the state convention stated that "the Brotherhood is not merely an organization, it is a plan of work, a program of definite objectives striving to enlist the activities of our men and inform them along lines of evangelism, stewardship, missions, and whole-hearted support of our denominational program."

Children's Home.—The first reference to an "orphanage" occurred in the convention minutes of 1898. Temporary quarters were secured for a few children at the "Female College" at Keatchi until 1903, when they were moved into new facilities secured by the convention at Lake Charles. Frank C. Flowers, who became superintendent in 1918, envisaged a plan of housing the children in cottages rather than in dormitories. His dream became a reality in 1925 when the children were moved from Lake Charles to Monroe into new quarters on 430 acres of excellent property. The convention in 1926 wisely changed the name of the institution to the Louisiana Baptist Children's Home. When Theodore Wilmot Gayer became superintendent in 1941, the home reported 125 children. A campaign projected in that same year eventuated in 1942 in the completion of "Daddy Flowers Memorial Chapel." D. C. Black is the present superintendent.

Hospitals.—The first official consideration of a state Baptist hospital occurred at the 1906 convention. A committee was appointed, but it never reported. Ten years later, the trustees of the Alexandria Sanitarium offered the institution to the convention on the condition that it would be operated as "a general hospital," and that it would be expanded to meet the hospital needs of the area. Louisiana Baptists accepted the offer and thus entered the hospital field. Called The Louisiana Baptist Hospital in 1921, the institution showed steady progress until the economic depression came in 1929. At this time a home for nurses was left half finished. The total indebtedness of the institution amounted to $80,000 by 1930. Two years later, the condition of the hospital was said to be "greatly improved," and recent progress was described as "encouraging." H. O. Barker, who became superintendent in 1943, led the hospital into a program of expansion and financial stability. The net operating profit of the institution in 1944 amounted to $134,715.36. The hospital has continued to grow and occupies a secure and useful place in Louisiana Baptist life.

Baton Rouge General Hospital was offered to the convention in 1944 on condition that Louisiana Baptists participate in a campaign for funds to erect a new plant and agree to operate the institution for the general welfare. Louisiana Baptists accepted the offer and soon constructed a completely modern 250-bed hospital. This institution, the one at Alexandria, and the Beauregard Memorial Baptist Hospital at DeRidder, a recent acquisition, are the hospitals owned and operated by the Louisiana Baptist Convention. C. PENROSE ST. AMANT

III. Program of Work of Louisiana Baptists. *Executive board.*—The administrative work of the convention is carried out by an executive board elected at the annual session of the convention. Membership in this body includes the president of the convention, together with one representative from each association co-operating with the convention, one additional representative from each association having as many as 10,000 members, and one additional representative for each 5,000 members. One third of the membership is elected annually, each member to serve three years and not more than two three-year terms consecutively. The present membership totals 63. It is the function and duty of the board to promote and give direction to the work of the convention in keeping with its constitution and bylaws and to "serve as the Convention ad interim." The object of the convention, and consequently of its board, is to foster missions at home and abroad and to support Christian education and benevolence through institutions and service departments necessary to the promotion of missions. It further promotes "harmony of feeling and concert of action in adopting and carrying into operation such measures as may promote the Redeemer's Kingdom in Louisiana and in regions beyond."

Officers are a president, a vice-president, a recording secretary, and an executive secretary-treasurer, each elected by the board with the exception that the convention in session may elect the executive secretary-treasurer when it deems wise. In addition to his duties as treasurer of convention funds, the executive secretary is the chief promotional officer of the executive board.

The board holds an annual meeting within 30 days following the convention session, at which time officers are elected. Other regular meetings are held in September and immediately preceding the annual meeting of the convention. Special meetings may be called by the president and/or the executive secretary.

Work done by the board, its departments, and institutions must be reported in full to the convention each year, together with a recapitulation of the total indebtedness of the Executive Board and its institutions. The board supervises all departments, institutions, and properties owned by the convention. It does much of its work through committees and determines when special committees should be named. Standing committees include the following:

The executive committee consists of the board president plus eight members geographically representative of the state, whose duty is to review and study the work and problems of this board, its departments and institutions, and from time to time make recommendations concerning needs, changes, and improvements.

The budget control committee, composed of five members, is charged with the responsibility of conferring with various boards, departments, and institutions of the convention relative to proposed expenditures and anticipated receipts for the forthcoming year, and then recommending to the executive board the budget and its divisions.

The nominating committee, which consists of five members, brings recommendations to the board when and if a vacancy occurs in any of the following departments: Sunday School, Training Union, Brotherhood, Baptist Student Union, Evangelism, *Baptist Message,* Woman's Missionary Union, and Music; it also nominates members of the executive committee, the budget control committee, and the *Baptist Message* operating committee. It also nominates individuals to fill all vacancies in board membership during the year.

The missions committee is responsible for the convention's program of direct missions and for recommending to the board the apportionment of state missions funds to supplement the salaries of mission pastors and general missionaries within the state.

In its capacity as treasurer of gifts received from most of 1,146 churches in the convention, the board handled $2,034,481.33 during the convention year ending in 1954.

Missions.—Three types of missions promotion are used in Louisiana, viz., general, educational and benevolent, and direct state missions. The executive board promotes general missions by lending assistance to the churches through the nine departments of service and the Baptist Foundation. Through its educational and benevolent work, the convention supports Louisiana College in Pineville, Acadia Academy (high school) at Eunice, the Baptist Children's Home in Monroe, and four hospitals, including Baptist Hospital, Alexandria; Baton Rouge General, Baton Rouge; Beauregard Memorial, DeRidder; and Homer Memorial, Homer. Through its program of direct missions the convention supplements salaries of mission pastors, implements associational programs and churches through large salary supplements to district missionaries, reaches language groups through evangelistic radio broadcasts, and partially supports a hospital chaplain ministry. There are now 15 men in 13 districts giving counsel and help, especially to weaker churches and missions. The missionary is selected by and under the authority of his district, although the state convention supports the program with $5,100 to each district. The city missions programs in New Orleans and Baton Rouge are under the direction of district missionaries. Work with rural churches is emphasized in 10 of the 13 districts. The efforts of district missionaries, pastors, and associational leaders are co-ordinated to help the churches. Objectives are determined by the total Southern Baptist principles of church development. Through the office of promotion and missions, salary supplements were paid in 1954 to 66 mission pastors, mainly in south Louisiana, which is notably French, five mission teachers at mission teaching stations in remote southern areas, four general missionaries with minority groups, four hospital chaplains, two in Charity Hospital, New Orleans, and the 15 district missionaries.

W. R. Grigg was emlpoyed, in co-operation with the Home Mission Board, as director of Negro work beginning Jan. 1, 1954. He supervises the program of teaching and training. Efforts to reach the French, largely a Roman Catholic population, have been supplemented by the Home Mission Board and its south Louisiana program of direct missions. French radio broadcasts sponsored by the Louisiana Baptist Convention are presented in the French language over 11 stations in 30-minute programs two days a week. Follow-up visiting is done by missionaries and pastors in those areas.

Educational ministry.—Departments include the Administrative, Sunday School, Training Union, Woman's Missionary Union, Brotherhood, Evangelism, *Baptist Message,* Music, and Student, each of which is directed by a secretary. J. L. Pollard assumed his duties as secretary of the Sunday School Department in 1953. During 1954 new work included three Cradle Roll departments, 36 Extension departments, 22 mission Sunday schools, and 30 churches which developed from class to department Sunday schools. Training awards totaled 25,355 in the 1,139 Sunday schools of the state. Vacation Bible schools reached a total of 621. In 1954 the Training Union Department reported a total enrolment of 102,990 in 945 churches. Planning meetings for associational officers were held in four sections with 35 associations represented. The Training Union Convention was attended by 2,700, and 11,763 attended "M" Night in December. The present secretary, Jimmy Crowe, succeeded A. L. Russell in Dec., 1956. The Woman's Missionary Union reported 844 Woman's Missionary Societies and 2,309 young people's organizations in 1954. This organization has purchased a new site for a camp near Alexandria and has inaugurated long-range plans for its use. On Jan. 1, 1955, Hannah Reynolds, executive secretary for 25 years, resigned, and Kathryn Carpenter was elected as her successor. The Brotherhood Department reported 555 active church Brotherhood organizations in 1954. It also conducted 10 "Man and Boy" rallies during the year, and a statewide Labor Day Rally, held at the Children's Home in Monroe. Fred Forester, the present Brotherhood secretary, succeeded A. S. Newman, who resigned in 1954. The 1954 program of the Evangelism Department featured a statewide evangelistic conference and eight regional evangelistic conferences. The department also made plans to support a nation-wide simultaneous evangelistic crusade in 1955. The *Baptist Message* reported a circulation of over 50,000 and set a new goal to reach 5,000 additional subscribers. Budgets of 453 churches include the *Baptist Message,* and 437 churches have club plans. Finley W. Tinnin has been editor and manager of the paper since 1920. The Music Department sponsored music festivals during 1954 with 8,065 in attendance. It also conducted a pastor-music director conference, a statewide church music leadership school that enrolled 130, and an initial state youth music week with 101 youth attending. In 51 music schools 2,200 church music training awards were issued. The music secretary, L. C. Alexander, assumed his duties in 1947. The Baptist Student Department in 1954 reported 21 Baptist Student Unions with 12 campus directors, who ministered to 10,000 students. A new student center was completed adjoining each of two schools, McNeese in Lake Charles and Northeast in Monroe. Udell Smith, secretary of this department, began his work in 1949.

Louisiana Baptists operate five encampments. Dry Creek Encampment at Dry Creek, La., was the site of a Preachers' School and Pastors' Retreat, conducted in 1954 to stimulate Bible study and Christian fellowship. Clara Springs, near Pleasant Hill, La., is the site of the District Eight Encampment, the facilities of which were donated in 1953. Acadia Encampment, which began in 1948, is held annually on the campus of Acadia Baptist Academy near Eunice. S. G. Rogers, pastor in New Iberia, was president of the encampment in 1954. North Louisiana Encampment, located near Olla, meets annually under the direction of a local committee. For many years Mandeville served as the site of the state encampment, but in 1954 the convention voted to lease the grounds to an incorporated operating board elected by Districts 11, 12, and 13. Receipts from the five encampments with which the programs respectively were carried out during the year 1954 totaled $18,866.89.

Since the organization of the Louisiana Baptist Historical Society in 1907 at Homer, La., the convention has gathered a collection of annuals and associational minutes that now exceeds 30,000 volumes. The larger part of the collection is located at New Orleans Baptist Theological Seminary, though some volumes are housed in the Louisiana College library.

Promotional work.—The convention established the office of promotion and missions and called Robert L. Lee in June, 1953, to become assistant executive secretary. Tracts on stewardship, soul-winning, doctrines, social problems, and publicity materials are issued upon request from this office. Pastors and workers annually receive the Baptist diary, calendar of activities, maps, church promotion suggestions, and other Southern Baptist materials. In addition to missions publicity and promotion through the *Baptist Message,* and through missionaries and mission pastors over the state, a fall stewardship campaign was launched in the fall of 1954 with the assistance of T. W. Gayer. It was designed to stimulate adequate church budgets, regular percentage giving to the Co-operative Program, and individual giving of tithes and offerings. Visual aids on missions and stewardship are distributed periodically. In 1956, following the resignation of Floyd Chaffin, Robert L. Lee was elected executive secretary.

Co-operative work.—The state convention does not contribute as a body to the American Bible Society but requests the church and people to make contributions to the work of this society. It also resolved in 1954 that faith and confidence be expressed in the leaders of the Louisiana Moral and Civic Foundation as they continue the fight against evils in the state.

BIBLIOGRAPHY: T. M. Bond, *A Republication of the Minutes of the Mississippi Association from its Organization to the Present Time* (1849). J. T. Christian, *A History of the Baptists of Louisiana* (1923). L. G. Cleverdon, "A History of Early Louisiana Baptists" (MS, 1922). F. Courtney, *The Relation of Mt. Lebanon College to the Baptists of Louisiana* (1887). E. F. Haight, "The Beginnings of the Baptist Denomination in New Orleans" (MS, 1946). W. W. Hamilton, Jr., "The Raynaldson Legend" (MS, 1948). M. L. Jenkins, *Around the World in Louisiana* (1937). A. T. Pate, *The Incense Road: A History of*

IV. LOUISIANA STATISTICAL SUMMARY

Year	Associations	Churches	Church Membership	Baptisms	S. S. Enrolment	V.B.S. Enrolment	T. U. Enrolment	W.M.U. Enrolment	Brotherhood Enrolment	Mission Gifts	Total Gifts	Value Church Property	State Capital Worth
1830													(Explanation: This column includes total value of Schools, Children's Homes, Hospitals, Foundation, Buildings, etc.)
1840													
1850													
1860													
1870													
1880													
1890	21	423	22,633	1,816	....	....	....	....	....	....	$ 24,447	....	
1900	29	....	....	....	....	....	....	....	....	....		....	
1905	30	589	44,870	3,492	9,918	....	....	....	....	$ 14,218	73,637	$ 530,850]	
1910	32	658	57,593	3,639	22,497	....	....	....	....	18,312	137,573	874,639	
1915	31	688	66,880	....	....	....	....	....	....	33,280	124,730	850,500	....
1920	33	776	88,327	5,716	39,311	....	6,092	....	....	....	1,055,521	2,122,235	....
1925	35	801	118,634	9,159	60,497	....	9,766	....	....	309,048	1,016,160	4,310,380	....
1930	37	817	131,159	7,123	84,751	....	23,668	....	....	326,559	1,218,205	5,629,002	....
1931	37	828	136,695	7,490	79,246	....	16,622	....	....	480,206	1,265,474	5,505,020	....
1932	37	848	136,982	7,866	86,368	....	24,666	....	....	175,806	....	5,446,566	....
1933	37	847	167,551	9,150	88,521	....	26,501	....	....	189,445	753,396	5,334,331	....
1934	37	832	145,380	8,544	89,068	....	22,307	....	....	176,871	847,194	5,322,688	$ 1,214,162.12
1935	37	837	155,760	7,812	91,262	....	23,979	....	2,154	249,321	803.616	5,254,058	....
1936	37	835	159,944	8,352	91,835	....	23,014	....	2,066	298,328	1,120,292	4,951,850	....
1937	37	847	163,224	7,651	92,279	....	21,743	17,293	2,346	291,941	1,253,625	5,416,204	....
1938	37	861	172,190	10,389	101,244	....	25,815	20,832	3,353	247,396	1,311,304	6,012,126	....
1939	38	866	180,393	10,568	104,473	....	28,450	20,084	3,642	252,972	1,775,276	6,170,263	....
1940	38	892	189,861	9,910	115,502	....	31,972	24,327	4,348	289,119	1,629,269	4,144,574	....
1941	38	879	197,951	8,756	109,659	....	31,845	25,951	3,931	331,803	1,807,034	5,183,550	....
1942	39	883	202,603	9,093	103,315	....	29,224	26,960	3,721	418,359	1,260,177	8,023,964	....
1943	39	910	215,737	8,623	110,413	....	30,692	31,545	3,834	577,707	2,919,731	7,578,375	....
1944	40	932	221,146	8,986	113,569	....	35,682	20,558	4,669	701,070	3,431,380	10,523,724	2,256,550.79
1945	42	963	234,663	11,514	118,334	....	39,383	24,705	5,012	1,467,473	4,804,770	8,870,735	....
1946	41	958	232,929	10,334	122,804	....	45,464	25,754	6,338	1,554,895	5,656,322	10,098,263	....
1947	42	986	253,793	12,143	144,852	36,830	52,932	29,368	7,837	1,074,587	7,065,641	13,433,892	....
1948	45	1,001	263,207	12,146	155,587	40,751	57,985	32,039	7,757	1,202,040	8,040,485	17,189,329	....
1949	45	1,019	276,971	12,886	169,461	45,670	67,895	36,027	9,846	1,318,145	9,599,910	21,345,751	....
1950	45	1,053	292,405	16,782	187,991	47,411	82,218	41,218	11,998	1,380,248	8,584,282	26,155,963	....
1951	46	1,060	299,800	14,854	196,837	62,547	88,444	43,019	11,437	1,526,202	10,451,799	31,965,880	....
1952	47	1,088	314,775	14,656	206,381	70,746	95,078	45,659	13,324	1,895,342	11,168,402	37,171,549	....
1953	49	1,123	323,158	13,428	215,094	79,130	101,990	47,290	13,527	1,992,080	12,670,001	43,015,327	....
1954	50	1,146	333,256	15,094	234,692	97,492	117,811	51,338	14,061	2,343,710	13,964,929	50,336,933	10,509,351.98

MELBA B. VODA

Louisiana Woman's Missionary Union (1939). W. E. Paxton, *A History of the Baptists of Louisiana from the Earliest Times to the Present* (1888). C. P. St. Amant, *A Short History of Louisiana Baptists* (1948). I. M. Wise, *Footsteps of the Flock: or Origins of Louisiana Baptists* (1910). ROBERT L. LEE

LOUISIANA BAPTIST ENCAMPMENT. Encampments in Louisiana began early in the twentieth century. First written reference says: "As to our young people's assembly . . . we are pleased to report that two beautiful sites have been offered . . . one of which may soon be selected as a permanent meeting place." A 1906 recommendation asked "that we encourage the establishment of a permanent B.Y.P.U. Encampment." Mandeville, on Lake Pontchartrain, was selected as the site. In 1907 C. V. Edwards, of the First Baptist Church of New Orleans, rented 20 tents for use at Mandeville. It was at this meeting that W. H. Knight (*q.v.*) surrendered to preach. No meeting was held in the summer of 1910, and the convention in November of that year authorized a committee to help reinvigorate B.Y.P.U. work and make "permanent one or two more encampments."

In 1915 a committee recommended that a Sunday school encampment be held simultaneously with the B.Y.P.U. meeting. Committees in 1916 and 1917 made similar suggestions. In 1918 the convention accepted the encampment as "a self-perpetuating auxiliary." By 1922, 36 acres of property were purchased at Mandeville for $25,000. A 1923 report says: "The encampment is one of our greatest recruiting stations for the ministry and other special callings." In 1930 the convention began appointing trustees annually. The 1945 trustees asked long-range plans for a greater Mandeville. Such plans were favorably received in 1946 but not put into action. The 1948 convention approved the district plan for encampments. In 1954 the Mandeville property was leased to Districts XI, XII, and XIII, provided they assumed the financial obligations and made the grounds available to any group in the state. G. AVERY LEE

LOUISIANA BAPTIST FOUNDATION. Established by the Louisiana Baptist Convention meeting in Shreveport on Nov. 27, 1941. At the convention meeting in West Monroe in 1939, A. E. Prince ". . . moved that the President appoint a committee to go into the matter of a Baptist Foundation for Louisiana." The committee was appointed and made reports to the conventions in 1940 and in 1941. The foundation was created to encourage giving to causes fostered by the Baptist denomination in Louisiana; to provide a sound financial agency to administer and invest funds entrusted to it; and to assist, found, or maintain other Baptist institutions thereafter created. The charter of incorporation was granted by the state of Louisiana on June 8, 1944. The first executive officer of the foundation, W. E. B. Lockridge, began work Aug. 1, 1944. He was succeeded by John Caylor on Nov. 5, 1945. Others who followed, with dates of their election, were C. W. Culp, Dec., 1945; Richard W. Moseley, Jan., 1947; and Herschel C. Pettus, Apr., 1948.

The convention controls the foundation by electing three trustees of the corporation at each annual session and by supervising its operating budget. The foundation must operate in harmony with the constitution of the Louisiana Baptist Convention and must submit annual reports. Total assets of the foundation increased from $190,590.53 at the end of the first year of operation to $1,534,736.03 at the end of 1954. Of this amount, $426,790.24 represented deposits by institutions. The remaining $1,107,954.79 was received from churches and individuals through the program promoted by the convention and the foundation. Income from all investments was $75,970.68 in 1954. Receipts for capital assets were $62,093.64. The operating budget for the foundation is supplied by the convention from the Cooperative Program. For the year 1954, it was $14,350.23.

BIBLIOGRAPHY: H. C. Pettus, "Our First Decade," *Louisiana Baptist Foundation Report* (1954).
H. C. PETTUS

LOUISIANA BAPTIST MESSENGER. Established by S. C. Lee in 1879. For a while published at Farmerville, later at Arcadia, on the Vicksburg, Shreveport and Texas Railroad, it soon became popular. For a time J. D. Head was publisher and D. F. Head associate editor. It was the organ of the Louisiana convention for three and one-half years; then the list of subscribers was turned over to the *Baptist Record.* T. W. GAYER

LOUISIANA COLLEGE. A four-year liberal arts college operated by the Louisiana Baptist Convention at Pineville, Rapides Parish, La., since Oct. 3, 1906. The college was established as a result of the work of a committee appointed by the Louisiana convention in July, 1904. The committee was authorized to consider the location of a Baptist college at some accessible point, and, in order to avoid delay, was given full power to decide upon a location and to receive bids from any suitable city that would offer an ample site and a bonus of $30,000. The committee was also instructed to arrange for the erection of the necessary buildings. The following men were appointed: G. W. Bolton, chairman, W. A. West, J. L. Love, Manly Enos Weaver, Ben Stagg, L. E. Thomas, A. L. Ponder, M. A. Price, P. B. Wright, E. O. Ware, W. H. Dodson, J. R. Edwards, F. J. Madison, W. C. Beall, and J. W. Bolin. These men are generally regarded as the founders of the school.

The committee followed the instructions of the convention, advertising for and receiving bids from several interested cities. One of the three sites offered by the city of Alexandria was selected. It was a 40-acre tract on the north

FIRST BAPTIST CHURCH, Roanoke Va. Organized 1875; 1956 membership, 2,430. Auditorium of Romanesque architecture built 1929, seats 1,450, Sunday school accommodates 1,250. Property worth $1,250,000.

FIRST BAPTIST CHURCH, Oklahoma City, Okla. Founded 1889, present Gothic buildings begun 1912. Membership 1956 was 5,885, property evaluation $2,750,000. Auditorium serves 1,500, Sunday school 3,600.

side of Red River in the village of Pineville and is two miles from Alexandria, state convention headquarters since 1947.

The $30,000 was raised by private subscription from the citizens of Alexandria and Pineville. The money was used to erect some temporary buildings needed for the opening of the fall term and to construct the first permanent building. This building, called Ware Hall, has three stories and is now used as a girls' dormitory. The college was administered by an educational commission made up of members of Baptist churches in Louisiana chosen by the Louisiana Baptist Convention in annual session. Seven of the 21 members were chosen for a term of three years, seven for two years, and seven for one year. In 1921 a new charter was obtained. By it the education commission was replaced by a board of trustees chosen by the convention in the same manner as before. Members of the commission whose terms had not expired served on the new board of trustees until their terms were finished.

The first administrative head of Louisiana College was W. E. Taylor, with the title of chairman of faculty. He served from Oct. 3, 1906, until June, 1908, when he resigned. E. O. Ware, the man who was most instrumental in founding Louisiana College, was its first president. He served for nearly a year after June 4, 1908. C. W. Friley then served from Apr. 15, 1909, to Apr. 26, 1910. Claybrook Cottingham was elected president June 10, 1910, served a total of 31 years, and resigned Apr. 1, 1941. Edgar Godbold served for the next 10 years and was succeeded on July 26, 1951, by G. Earl Guinn.

Louisiana College began as a school for men but was made coeducational in 1909. The institution has been a liberal arts college since its founding. It was admitted to membership in the Southern Association of Colleges and Secondary Schools in 1922 and has been a member continuously since that date. Degrees of Bachelor of Arts or Bachelor of Science may be earned in 19 major departments. In addition to the baccalaureate curriculum, special courses are offered in prelaw, premedicine, pre-engineering, and medical technology.

The enrolment was 19 in 1906, 385 in 1936, and 676 in 1956. A total of 2,362 students have been graduated from Louisiana College. Three men made up the faculty in 1906. They were W. E. Taylor, Claybrook Cottingham, and Bruce Benton. In 1936 there were 23 members of the faculty and 45 in 1956. The original campus of 40 acres has been increased to 81. There are 17 buildings, 12 of which are constructed of pressed brick. The property and equipment are valued at $2,460,947.99. Louisiana College has an endowment of $1,376,477.54. The budget for 1955 was $568,032. The sources of income are from the Louisiana Baptist Convention, interest on endowment, gifts, tuition, fees, rents, and incidentals.

LELA BEALL COSTELLO

LOUISVILLE BAPTIST ORPHANS' HOME. See SPRING MEADOWS CHILDREN'S HOME.

LOVE. See VIRTUE, CHRISTIAN.

LOVE, JAMES FRANKLIN (b. Elizabeth City, N. C., July 14, 1859; d. Richmond, Va., May 3, 1928). Foreign mission leader. After attending Wake Forest College, Love received D.D. degrees from Wake Forest and Baylor University. He married Caroline Gregory, Aug. 14, 1894, and held pastorates at Bayboro, Rocky Mount, and Wadesboro, N. C.; Suffolk, Va.; and First Church, Baltimore, Md., where he was associate pastor with J. W. M. Williams. Love served as state secretary of missions in Arkansas, assistant corresponding secretary of the Home Mission Board for eight years, home secretary and later executive secretary of the Foreign Mission Board, May 1, 1914, to May 3, 1928. The 14 years of Love's service with the Foreign Mission Board, among the most difficult in the board's history, covered the period of World War I, reconstruction, inflation, and depression. The 75 Million Campaign for mission funds, which promised to exceed the goal, fell short by approximately $15,000,000, burdening boards, institutions, and churches with heavy debts. Commitments based on anticipated income from pledges which were not paid entailed terrific liabilities. At one time the Foreign Mission Board, confident of meeting its obligations and sending eager volunteers to foreign fields, owed more than $1,000,000.

Love warned Southern Baptists of the perils of the Interchurch World Movement and related programs, which eventually resulted in interdenominational collapse. He urged loyalty to Baptist principles and policy. Love's published works include *Today's Supreme Challenge to America, The Mission of Our Nation, The Union Movement,* and *The Unique Message and Universal Mission of Christianity.* During his service with the Foreign Mission Board, he visited mission fields in the Orient, South America, and Europe.

BIBLIOGRAPHY: *Southern Baptist Handbook* (1945), pp. 10–25. G. B. Taylor, *Virginia Baptist Ministers,* 6th series (1935).

E. C. ROUTH

LOWE, JOHN WILLIAM (b. St. Joseph, Mo., Oct. 2, 1868; d. Richmond, Va., May 6, 1948). Clergyman and foreign missionary. From his home in Daviess County, Mo., Lowe traveled in a covered wagon to William Jewell College, in Liberty, from which he later received his A.B. degree. He received the Th.M. degree from Southern Baptist Theological Seminary and also studied medicine at the Kentucky School of Medicine in Louisville. In 1898 he was appointed by the Foreign Mission Board as a missionary to China. Lowe's first three years in China were spent as a medical dispensary worker; later he did pioneer mission work in Shantung Province. From his headquarters in Laichowfu, his influence spread to many places in the North China mission. Lowe was engaged in relief work in three great famines in China: Central China (1907), North China (1922), and Shantung Province (1932). He served as professor of Old Testament in Bush Theological Seminary in Hwanghsien, and promoted many Bible conferences in China. In 1919 he was recalled by the Foreign Mission Board to help in the promotion of the 75 Million Campaign. He spent five years in this endeavor, constantly making appeals by letters, circulars, and telephone calls for the relief of suffering in China. Lowe always sent personal messages to the annual meetings of the Missouri Baptist General Association. Much of his furlough time was spent in schools of missions and speaking on college campuses to stimulate interest in foreign missions.

BIBLIOGRAPHY: *Catalogue of the Officers and Students of William Jewell College, 1892–93* (1893). *Catalogue of the Officers and Students of William Jewell College, 1893–94* (1894). J. C. Maple, *Missouri Baptist Centennial 1906* (1907). J. S. Ramond, *Among Southern Baptists* (1936). M. T. Rankin, "In Memoriam," *The Commission* (July, 1948). *The Word and Way* (May 24, 1928; May 20, 1948; Feb. 9, 1928; Jan. 30, 1919). W. C. LINK, JR.

LOWE, SAMUEL FRANKLIN (b. Houston County, Ga., June 6, 1890; d. Atlanta, Ga., Oct. 4, 1952). When still a boy, he was left the responsibility of helping to support a large family. He was graduated from Locust Grove Institute in 1911, Mercer University in 1914, and Southern Baptist Theological Seminary in 1917. The D.D. degree was conferred upon him by Mercer University in 1940. He served as pastor of a number of churches from 1918 to 1944, including Tennile, Dawson, and Atlanta, Ga.; Enterprise, Ala.; and Meridian, Miss. In 1938, while pastor of Atlanta's Inman Park Baptist Church and vice-president of the Southern Baptist Home Mission Board, he conceived the idea of a radio ministry for Southern Baptists. He became chairman of the Convention's first Radio Committee in 1938 and was the director of the Radio Commission from 1944 until his death. In 14 years he overcame almost impossible obstacles and succeeded in gaining for his denomination a creditable radio ministry and a beginning for Baptists in television. His written works include *Successful Religious Broadcasting* (1945). CLARENCE DUNCAN

LOWNDES, ELIZABETH CHASE CHAPMAN (b. Baltimore, Md., Nov. 4, 1858; d. Mar. 5, 1936). Woman's Missionary Union treasurer. Daughter of Allen and Mary (Chase) Chapman, she was one of 15 children, all of whom were educated in liberal arts and music. Elizabeth, who attended Mount Vernon Institute, one of the best private schools of that day, in Baltimore, was always at the head of her class, and at one time she tutored a number of pupils in Latin, French, and mathematics. She married William Chapman Lowndes Nov. 17, 1880, and they had three sons. One of them, a banker, expressed the wish that he might have inherited more of his mother's ease in solving financial and investment problems. Elected treasurer of Woman's Missionary Union in 1895, Mrs. Lowndes asked to be relieved in 1904, after which she was made treasurer emeritus. However, in 1906 she was re-elected treasurer, and she continued in that position until 1934, serving 14 years without salary. No officer of Woman's Missionary Union has had a longer record of service than Mrs. Lowndes. Member of the Woman's Missionary Union executive committee from 1895 until her death, she served even after her retirement in 1934, when the union elected her an honorary member of the committee. An avid reader, Mrs. Lowndes knew the works of Dickens well and frequently alluded to his characters in her conversation. She taught a Sunday school class of about 50 women at Seventh Baptist Church in Baltimore.

The Elizabeth Lowndes Memorial Scholarship was established in her honor in 1934, with $7,000 from the 1933 interest on the Margaret Fund endowment, the cash balance of Woman's Missionary Union, and voluntary contributions. It is a coveted $200 scholarship awarded annually to the senior Margaret Fund student of the year superior in scholarship, character, and campus leadership. JULIETTE MATHER

LOWREY, MARK PERRIN (b. McNairy County, Tenn., Dec. 30, 1828; d. Middleton, Tenn., Feb. 26, 1885). Confederate general, associational missionary, college founder. The ninth of 11 children, Lowrey lost his father when he was only four. He joined the Baptist church at Farmington, Miss., at 17. After serving as a volunteer in the Mexican War in 1847, Lowrey married Sarah Holmes when he returned in 1849 and became a farmer and brickmason. Although he had no formal education, Lowrey took advantage of every opportunity to study and at 24 entered the Baptist ministry. He served four years as a missionary in the Chickasaw Association and organized the church at Corinth. Elected captain by a company of Confederate 60-day troops, Lowery soon became a colonel and, after distinguished action in the battle of Chickamauga, was promoted to brigadier-general. At the close of the Civil War, he returned to Tippah County, Miss., and refused several large pastorates and denominational and public positions to fulfil his life's dream of founding Blue Mountain Female Institute (later Blue Mountain College). From 1868 he served 10 consecutive years as president of the Mississippi Baptist Convention, was a trustee of the University of Mississippi and also of Mississippi College. Lowrey died suddenly in the railroad station at Middleton, Tenn.

BIBLIOGRAPHY: J. L. Boyd, *A Popular History of Baptists in Mississippi* (1930). *Dictionary of American Biography* (1933). L. S. Foster, *Mississippi Baptist Preachers* (1895). "Lowrey and Berry," *Goodspeed's Biographical and Historical Memoirs of Mississippi* (1891). R. S. Sumrall, *A Light on a Hill* (1947).

C. B. HAMLET III

LOWREY, WILLIAM TYNDALE (b. near Booneville, Miss., Mar. 3, 1858; d. Waco, Tex., May 28, 1944; buried Clinton, Miss.). Preacher, college president and teacher, denominational leader. The eldest son of M. P. Lowrey (*q.v.*), W. T. Lowrey entered Blue Mountain Male Academy at the age of 16 and was graduated from Mississippi College with distinction in 1881. Upon the sudden death of his father, he was called home from Southern Baptist Theological Seminary to become president of Blue Mountain College, Mar. 3, 1885. His first administration of this college (1885–98) was a period of expansion and growth. In 1898 he was elected president of Mississippi College, and the following year he was able to bring to the state convention a proposition which assured Mississippi Baptists of legal claim to the college. Mississippi College increased its endowment, gained better financial support, and added buildings during his administration (1898–1911). Upon the resignation of his brother, B. G. Lowrey, in 1911, he was again made president of Blue Mountain College and set himself to the task of standardization, improvement of curriculum, and enlargement of facilities. The college was taken over by the state convention in 1919, but the trustees in their first meeting at Winona, Dec. 11, 1919, unanimously elected Lowrey president, a position be held until 1925. In addition to serving as president of Mississippi College and Blue Mountain College, he was president of Hillman College, Clinton; Gulf Coast Military Academy, Gulfport; and Clarke College, Newton. He taught during most of the time he was president of the various schools and served as head of the department of ancient languages at State Teachers College (now Mississippi Southern), Hattiesburg (1927–29). Lowrey was one of the sponsors of the Baptist Memorial Hospital in Memphis and served as president of the board of trustees from the beginning until he was made president emeritus, Jan. 13, 1944. Although his educational and administrative ability overshadowed his preaching, he was also an effective minister.

BIBLIOGRAPHY: J. L. Boyd, *A Popular History of the Baptists in Mississippi* (1930). L. S. Foster, *Mississippi Baptist Preachers* (1895). R. N. Sumrall, *A Light on a Hill* (1947). *The Baptist Record* (June 1, 1944).

C. B. HAMLET III

LUCAS, WILLIAM GILBERT (b. Lawrence County, Ala., Mar. 14, 1874; d. Howe, Okla., Aug. 7, 1947). Oklahoma pioneer missionary and rural pastor. Lucas was ordained in Aug., 1900, and spent 15 years as missionary for the Short Mountain and LeFlore associations. He was pastor of rural churches in the same area for 32 years. Widely acclaimed as a denominational leader, he was reported an exponent of homespun philosophy and quaint wit and humor. He led in founding Kiamichi Baptist Assembly at Talihina, Okla., was its first president, and guided its affairs until his death. He is buried at Mount View, near Wister, Okla.

BIBLIOGRAPHY: J. M. Gaskin, *The Sage of the Hills* (1949).

J. M. GASKIN

LUEDERS BAPTIST ENCAMPMENT. A Texas encampment organized in the summer of 1922. Located one mile east of Lueders on the banks of the Clear Fork of the Brazos, the camp is 14 miles east of Stamford. The property consists of 62 acres of land with a tabernacle, a dining room, and buildings providing sleeping accommodations for 600 people.

J. E. ROTH

LUMBLEY, CARIE GREEN (b. London, England, Dec. 20, 1869; d. Bournemouth, England, May 24, 1947). A missionary to Nigeria, Africa, she resigned when her husband died in 1906 but two years later was reappointed by the Foreign Mission Board and returned to Nigeria with Mr. and Mrs. S. G. Pinnock, English missionaries for Southern Baptists. (The board had never before sent a widow or unmarried woman to West Africa.) Pioneer in the Christian education of girls in West Africa, Mrs. Lumbley founded the Girls' School (*Idi Aba*) at Abeokuta. In 1928 the king of England conferred on her the title "Member of the British Empire."

BIBLIOGRAPHY: S. Anderson, *So This Is Africa* (1943). C. E. Maddry, *Day Dawn in Yoruba Land* (1939). S. G. Pinnock, *Romance of Missions in Nigeria* (1918). G. W. Sadler, *A Century in Nigeria* (1950).

E. C. ROUTH

LUNSFORD, LEWIS (b. Stafford County, Va., *c.* 1753; d. Essex County, Va., Oct. 26, 1793). He was largely "the founder of the Baptist denomination in the Northern Neck of Virginia," an evangelist, an appealing orator, an advocate of freeing slaves, a student of medicine, and an organizer of churches.

He was born in Stafford County, Va., about 1753 and grew up under the hardships and limitations of poverty. His educational opportunities were few, but he often spent "a large portion of the night in reading by firelight." While still a lad he was baptized by William Fristoe (*q.v.*) and joined Potomac Baptist Church.

Before he was 18 years old he began to preach, "and large crowds flocked to hear 'the Wonderful Boy,' so remarkable were his talents and eloquence."

In 1775, while on his first preaching tour in the Northern Neck of Virginia, he was arrested in Richmond County but was released after giving security that he would not preach again without obtaining the necessary license. This he was not able to secure, and he regretted that he had not accepted the sentence of a year in jail.

In less than a year he returned to Richmond and carried on his ministry there and in Westmoreland, Lancaster, and Northumberland counties. His preaching was often interrupted by violence and legal technicalities. Once in Lancaster 65 men destroyed the outdoor stage from which he was speaking. On another occasion a constable, sent with a warrant to arrest him, was so fascinated by his preaching that he became a convert.

Among the churches he organized, Nomini, Moratico, and Wicomico were outstanding. He became pastor of Moratico when it was constituted in 1778 and served it until his death. There were two great revivals in this church during his pastorate. Many people of wealth and high social rank became Baptists under his ministry. Among them was "Councillor" Robert Carter, a wealthy man widely esteemed for his social station and public services, and his wife, the daughter of Governor Tasker of Maryland. They gave great support to Lunsford's work.

His evangelistic tours spread as far as Kentucky on three occasions. His powers of oratory were much esteemed, and he was called "an ambassador of the skies, sent down to command all men everywhere to repent."

Due to his reading in medicine, he was often called to serve as a physician. "It is highly probable no man was more beloved by a people when living, or more lamented when dead."

He was twice married, and four children survived him. Years after his death his body was moved from his burial place in Essex County to be interred in the cemetery of Moratico Baptist Church. CLAYTON PITTS

LUNSFORD, WILLIAM (b. Roanoke County, Va., May 22, 1859; d. Dallas, Tex., May 24, 1927). First executive secretary of the Relief and Annuity Board. The son of Charles and Julia Ann (Preston) Lunsford, he was educated in the public and private schools of Roanoke County and was graduated in law from the University of Virginia.

Lunsford taught school for several years, and afterward practiced law in Roanoke. It was during this time, at the age of 38, that he felt his call to the ministry. When finally assured of the Lord's will, he was ordained at Vinton, Va., Mar. 18, 1897. Lunsford began his ministry in a small mission church on Jefferson Street in Roanoke in 1897–98. Feeling the need for further education, he enrolled in Southern Baptist Theological Seminary. Later he served as pastor at First Baptist Church, Bowling Green, Ky. (1898–1903); First Baptist Church, Waco, Tex. (1903–04); and First Baptist Church, Asheville, N. C. (1908–09). His longest pastorate was with Edgefield Church, Nashville, Tenn. (1909–18), a portion of which time he was president of the Sunday School Board.

In June, 1917, having led in creating interest in ministerial relief, he was made secretary of a commission of 12 appointed by the Southern Baptist Convention to work out a plan for ministerial relief. He spent most of that summer in the North among actuarial experts and secretaries of other denominational boards. The plan he presented in a special report to the commission was adopted and later accepted by the Convention. In July, 1918, he was made corresponding secretary of the newly created Board of Ministerial Relief and Annuities, a position he held until his death in 1927.

The D.D. degree was conferred by Wake Forest College in 1906. He was married to Nannie Pettie Preston of Roanoke County, Dec. 31, 1885. They had six children: W. Bruce, Charles Julian, Preston, Gordon, Campbell, and Julia. RETTA O'BANNON

LUTHERAN CHURCH. A major Protestant denomination which emerged under the leadership of Martin Luther (1483–1546) in Germany early in the Reformation era. Luther was an Augustinian monk, a professor of theology, and a dynamic preacher whose 95 theses led to the great 16th-century schism of the Roman Catholic Church. Cardinal doctrines emphasized by Luther included justification by faith alone, the supremacy of the Scriptures, the priesthood of all believers, and the "invisible church" composed of all true believers. Politically, he represented German nationalism, and by his appeal to the upper and middle classes, he was able to survive the violent ecclesiastical opposition to his person and views. Later reformers like Zwingli, Hubmaier, Calvin, Knox, and Cranmer were greatly influenced by Luther and his voluminous writings.

Nine separate creeds form the basis of Lutheran theology today, of which four are universally accepted by Lutherans. These are the ancient Apostles', Nicene, and Athanasian creeds, and the Augsburg Confession (1530). Luther's two catechisms are also widely adopted.

Perhaps largely because of its insistence upon the priesthood of all believers, Lutheranism has been rent by numerous schisms. The Antinomian controversy (1537–60), the Arminian dispute (1550–80), and the serious debates with regard to the atonement and the presence of Christ in the sacraments, led to prolonged dissensions and in some cases to denominational divisions. European emigration has carried all the major groups and nationalities of Lutherans throughout the world, chiefly to North America. Lutherans are the predominant religious groups today in Germany, Sweden, Norway, Denmark, Finland, and Russian-occupied Estonia and Latvia. They are also numerous in Czechoslovakia, Poland, Hungary, the Netherlands, the United States, and Canada.

Lutheranism in the United States is theologically conservative in varying degrees. The five groups in the Synodical Conference retain the most conservative position. In 1955 there were 17 bodies of Lutherans in the United States, with 7,372,938 members organized into 17,398 churches. The United Lutheran Church in America is largest, having (1955) 4,383 congregations and 2,270,702 members. The Lutheran Church—Missouri Synod has (1955) 5,123 congregations and 2,076,379 members. The Lutheran Church is the third largest Protestant denomination in the United States and Canada.

In 1923 Lutherans of 22 countries formed in

Germany a co-operative association called the Lutheran World Convention, which in 1947 was transformed into a Lutheran World Federation. The estimated 75 million Lutherans comprise the world's largest Protestant body.

BIBLIOGRAPHY: R. H. Bainton, *Here I Stand—A Life of Martin Luther* (1950). H. J. Grimm, *The Reformation Era, 1500–1650* (1954). T. Harnack, *Luther's Theology,* 2 vols. (1862–67). H. E. Jacobs, *Martin Luther, The Hero of the Reformation* (1898); ed., *The Works of Martin Luther,* 6 vols. (1915–32). J. Kostlin, *Life of Luther* (1913); *Luther's Theology* (1897). T. M. Lindsay, *A History of the Reformation,* 2 vols. (1906–07); *Martin Luther and the German Reformation* (1900). E. L. Lueker, ed., *Lutheran Cyclopedia* (1954). A. C. McGiffert, *Martin Luther* (1911). P. Smith, *The Age of the Reformation* (1920); *The Life and Letters of Martin Luther* (1911). A. R. Wentz, *A Basic History of Lutheranism in America* (1955).

ROBERT H. SPIRO, JR.

LYERLY HIGH SCHOOL. Founded by Chatooga Association in 1894 at Lyerly, Ga. Due to indebtedness the property was sold in 1897.

ARTHUR JACKSON

LYNCH, JAMES WILLIAM (b. Henry County, Va., Jan. 20, 1865; d. Wake Forest, N. C., May 23, 1940). Teacher. Son of John William and Mary Catherine (Pratt) Lynch. Wake Forest College awarded him the M.A. degree in 1888; the D.D. degree in 1902. He studied at Southern Baptist Theological Seminary, Louisville, Ky., 1888–89. Ordained in 1889, he served as pastor of First Baptist Church, Danville, Ky., 1888–99; Wake Forest Baptist Church and chaplain of Wake Forest College, 1899–1901; 1902–09; Calvary Baptist Church, Roanoke, Va., 1901–02; First Baptist Church, Durham, N. C., 1909–11; First Baptist Church, Athens, Ga., 1911–20. Lynch served as trustee and confidential financial adviser of Wake Forest and was professor of Bible there, 1923–38; he was professor emeritus of Bible until his death in 1940. Lynch married Rebecca Aldene Pope, July 20, 1899, and they had two children.

GARLAND A. HENDRICKS

LYNCHING. The term usually refers to the killing of a person by a mob without a legal trial for the victim. In some states the lynch laws include any assault or injury inflicted by a mob, such as tarring and feathering. The term is believed to have originated in the 1700's when Charles Lynch, a Virginia planter, punished lawbreakers very cruelly.

It is usually assumed that lynching is a form of mob violence used against the Negro in the South. But by no means are the victims always Negroes. There were many lynchings in the United States during the opening of the West. According to statistics compiled by Tuskegee Institute, there were 4,589 persons lynched between 1882 and 1931; 3,307 of them were Negroes and 1,282 were whites. Only the six New England states were free from lynchings during this period.

It is generally agreed that all legislative measures can at best be of incidental and supplementary effect unless they are accompanied by changes in the racial attitudes, economic conditions, and moral standards which give rise to lynching, and until the practice is outlawed by public opinion. It is in the forming of public opinion that the churches have rendered their greatest service in meeting this social evil of lynching.

The Southern Baptist Convention has consistently expressed its opposition to all forms of mob violence. Its condemnation of lynching came in 1906 in a paper on "Crimes and Lynching." No further reference condemning lynching is found until 1933, following which nine successive annual reports of the Social Service Commission strongly condemned this form of mob violence. The 1936 report recommended "that our pastors be urged to preach from time to time upon the sanctity of human life and of civil rights under orderly government to the end that a wholesome respect for law and order may be created and maintained." Another recommendation in the same report reads: "That as a people we stand firmly for the orderly processes of justice in all cases and give to all officers of the law our support and commendation in the performance of their duties." The last recommendation in this report says: "We shall not be satisfied or content until lynchings shall cease and mob violence shall be completely banished."

The report of 1940 recommended that "we will continue to exercise all diligence and to urge upon our entire Baptist constituency and upon the citizenry at large the constant exercise of all diligence that this form of barbarism may be entirely banished."

A. C. MILLER

LYNNLAND INSTITUTE. A school offering work on all levels through college, operated under various names at Glendale, Ky., from 1866 to 1913. It was twice chartered—in 1867 and in 1887. Backed by a stock company of farmers who had secured a 100-acre tract on the Louisville and Nashville Railroad, the school opened with G. A. Coulson as principal. It was nominally sponsored by the Salem Baptist Association, but soon drew students from far beyond its own local area. Coulson, however, became involved in doctrinal difficulties, split a church, and was succeeded as principal of the institute by W. R. Perry. Under him the school had in its curriculum primary, preparatory, academic, and collegiate departments, and awarded bachelor's degrees. Enrolment reached 160. But academic standards were too high for income, and the school went into receivership in 1879. The property was for two years a residence, then was purchased by E. W. Elroy and E. W. White, formerly heads of Liberty College at Glasgow, Ky. They reopened the school as Lynnland Female Institute and enjoyed a period of prosperity until the panic of 1893. After a financial struggle, they gave up in 1895 and joined the teaching staff of Georgetown College. W. B. Gwynn purchased the school that year and resumed work on a coeducational basis. In 1905 Severns Valley Baptist Association gained control and operated the school through their education society until 1914, when the property was sold to the trustees of the Kentucky Baptist Children's Home (now Glen Dale Children's Home).

GEORGE RALEIGH JEWELL

M

MACAO. See HONG KONG–MACAO, MISSION IN.

MACON FEMALE SEMINARY. Established about 1865 at Macon, Miss., with Jesse H. Buck principal. The seminary, flourishing in the 1880's, was recognized as a Baptist school in 1890. It is now extinct. J. L. BOYD

MACON HIGH SCHOOL. Associational school of Macon County Association, located at Franklin, N. C., founded in 1903. In 1905 the association adopted the school and undertook to "build up, encourage and support" it. In 1907, when the citizens of Franklin voted to establish a graded public school in the town, the association decided to move Macon High School. After some indecision about a new location, the association voted in 1910 to abandon the school and to assist the Tuckaseige Association in supporting Sylva Collegiate Institute. D. L. SMILEY

MADISON COLLEGE. A school at Spring Creek, Tenn., begun in 1852 with three students, chartered in 1854 as West Tennessee Baptist Male Institute with Duncan H. Selph as principal. By 1858 the school had both preparatory and college departments with an enrolment of 96 and property valued at $15,000. Suspended during the Civil War, it was reopened in 1867 with W. T. Bennett as president and an enrolment of 88. Heavy indebtedness and lack of support resulted in its dissolution in 1868.

LYNN E. MAY, JR.

MAGOFFIN BAPTIST INSTITUTE. An accredited grammar and high school, offering work in grades one through twelve, and located at Mountain Valley, Ky. It was founded in 1905 at Salyersville, Ky., by the Home Mission Board of the Southern Baptist Convention for the purpose of providing mountain children with education "for time and eternity." When the mountain school system of the board was discontinued, Magoffin continued to operate with support from individuals and churches, and later, from the General Association of Baptists in Kentucky. It is one of two home mission mountain schools to survive. In 1940 the school moved to its present location, and after enlargement of activities in 1950, it maintained a year-round program of mission service. A farm is operated in connection with the school. Enrolment in the fall of 1956 was 65. In 1955–56 the school's property was worth $193,862. There was no endowment. Accreditation was by the Kentucky State Department of Education. ERWIN L. MC DONALD

MALAYA, MISSION IN. The Malaya Baptist Mission was organized in Singapore, Malaya, Jan. 7, 1952, by missionaries Lora Clement, Jessie L. Green, and Eugene L. and Louise (Heirich) Hill. Singapore and Kuala Lumpur were the first designated stations of the mission, and work was begun immediately in the two cities. In time, other stations were established in Alor Star (1952), Penang (1953), and Ipoh (1954). Since its organization, the mission has initiated a program of (1) medical missions and established a clinic at Petaling Jaya, Selangor; (2) educational missions and established a Baptist kindergarten (the Phil Dawson Gadsden Memorial Kindergarten) and a theological seminary (Malaya Baptist Theological Seminary) in Penang, in co-operation with the Malaya Baptist Convention, and has operated children's day classes in all the chapels; (3) evangelistic missions through 14 chapels, 16 other preaching points, and many open-air meetings. Beginning with Lora Clement in 1950, 12 missionaries who formerly served in China transferred to Malaya before 1955. Six new missionaries have been appointed for Malaya, making a total of 18 on the mission staff. The missionaries have ministered among the 3,000,000 Chinese in Malaya, primarily, but the education and medical programs have served some Indians, Europeans, and a few Malays. EUGENE L. HILL

MALAYA BAPTIST CONVENTION. Organized in Penang Aug. 16, 1953, by 16 messengers from the Swatow and Cantonese Baptist churches in Singapore, the Swatow Baptist Church in Alor Star, and Baptist churches in Kuala Lumpur, Penang, and Sungei Patani, to promote fellowship and co-operation between the churches and to project a Baptist program in Malaya. A constitution was adopted, and officers were elected. On Aug. 19, 1953, the convention's executive committee met with the executive committee of the Malaya Baptist Mission, and the two committees set themselves up as the Malaya Baptist General Board to represent their constituent bodies in planning and executing a Baptist mission program in Malaya. The Malaya Baptist Theological Seminary was established at Penang, an evangelistic program was projected, and Sunday school, Training Union, and women's work were planned and promoted. Since organization, the Malaya Baptist Convention, through its varied ministries, has continued to promote a full denominational program in Malaya. EUGENE L. HILL

MALAYA BAPTIST THEOLOGICAL SEMINARY, PENANG. See MALAYA, MISSION IN.

MALLARY, CHARLES DUTTON (b. West Poultney, Rutland County, Vt., Jan. 23, 1801; d. Albany, Ga., July 31, 1864). He graduated from Middlesbury College in 1821 with first honors and received the D.D. degree from Columbian College. In 1822 he went to South Carolina and two years later was ordained to the Baptist ministry. He served the church in Columbia, S. C., for two years and the Beulah and Congaree churches at Fork, S. C., for two years. Georgia pastorates were at Augusta, 1830–34; at Milledgeville, 1834–36; at La Grange, 1848–52; and at Jeffersonville, Macon, and Forsyth briefly. From 1837–40 he was financial agent for Mercer University. He was a trustee of Mercer from its founding until his death in 1864. He married Susan Mary Evans, Georgetown, S. C., in 1825 and Mrs. Mary E. Welch, Jeffersonville, Ga., in 1862. He wrote *Life of Botsford, Memoirs of Mercer, Soul-Prosperity, Sanctification, Simple Rhymes for Children, The Alphabetical Dinner,* and *Prince Alcohol.* Bartow Davis Ragsdale says that "he helped in a large way to develop and shape the life and institutions of Georgia Baptists." LESLIE S. WILLIAMS

MALLERY, MRS. JESSIE SYMONDS (b. London, England, Oct. 20, 1871; d. Corning, Calif., Oct. 4, 1950). Woman's Missionary Union leader. Daughter of John L. and Emma Symonds, she was converted at an early age and baptized into a Baptist church. She married Nellis P. Mallery Sept. 1, 1908, and moved with him to Albuquerque, N. Mex., in 1919.

Mrs. Mallery, who worked in the 75 Million Campaign, became recording secretary of the New Mexico Woman's Missionary Union in 1921, serving in this capacity for 23 years until she resigned in 1944. For several years she was treasurer at Inlow Youth Camp. Mrs. Mallery's name appears as an elected messenger to annual meetings of Central Association and the New Mexico State Convention from 1919 until 1946. She lived in California during her last years. MRS. RICHARD THOMAS BAKER, SR.

MALLORY, HUGH SHEPHERD DARBY (b. Talladega County, Ala., Feb. 6, 1848; d. Selma, Ala., Mar. 10, 1920). He was the son of James and Anna Marie (Darby) Mallory. After finishing the Talladega Male Academy he attended the University of Alabama and the University of Virginia, where he received the Bachelor of Laws degree in 1868. He established his law practice in Selma in 1869 and was active in the civic and cultural life of the city, serving on the Board of Education; in 1885 he was elected mayor of the city. In 1899 he was elected president of the Alabama Baptist State Convention and served for five terms. In 1911 Howard College conferred upon him the honorary LL.D. degree. He served as president of the Alabama State Sunday School Convention and as a trustee of the Southern Baptist Theological Seminary. He was a staunch leader for the cause of prohibition and because of his stand on this question was defeated in his race for governor in 1910. His wife was Jacqueline Louisa Moore of Summerfield, where they were married on Oct. 15, 1872. They were the parents of Kathleen Moore Mallory (*q.v.*), an executive secretary of the Southern Baptist Woman's Missionary Union. DAVIS WOOLLEY

MALLORY, KATHLEEN MOORE (b. Summerfield, Dallas County, Ala., Jan. 24, 1879; d. Selma, Ala., June 17, 1954). Woman's Missionary Union leader. She was the daughter of Hugh Shepherd Darby and Jacqueline Louisa (Moore) Mallory, "distinguished citizens of Selma whose home was a center for culture and Christian living." Her father was prominent in the state, both as a lawyer and as a Baptist layman, "his fine judgment molding many policies of the Alabama Baptist Convention." After joining the church at the age of 10, Kathleen Mallory graduated with first honors from Dallas Academy in 1898 and attended Goucher College (then Woman's College of Baltimore) from 1898 to 1902, receiving the A.B. degree.

During her senior year at Goucher, she became engaged to Edward Janney Sidwell Lupton, medical student at Johns Hopkins. While waiting for him to finish his internship before marriage, she taught the fourth and fifth grades in Demopolis, Ala., and spent the following winter with her parents in Selma. She was one of the founders of the local Parent-Teacher Association and served in her church as leader of a Sunbeam Band and the young women's missionary organization. Her engagement to Lupton was terminated by his death following a long illness.

In 1907 Kathleen Mallory became superintendent of Woman's Missionary Union work in the Selma Association, and in 1909, corresponding secretary for the Alabama Woman's Missionary Union, a position in which she served for three years. Elected corresponding secretary of Woman's Missionary Union, auxiliary to the Southern Baptist Convention, in

1912, she served in Baltimore, Md., until the fall of 1921, when the offices were moved to Birmingham. Her title was changed to executive secretary in 1937.

Promoting the growth of Woman's Missionary Union on foreign fields, she twice visited foreign mission fields at her own expense—spending six months in the Orient in 1923–24, and a summer in South America in 1930. In 1917 Miss Mallory wrote the manual of Woman's Missionary Union methods on which subsequent method books have been based. After serving six years as assistant editor of *Royal Service,* she became editor in chief in 1920. Subscriptions increased from 11,000 to 181,000 under Miss Mallory, who also edited the annual Woman's Missionary Union *Year Book.*

Miss Mallory served through the period of World War I, the 75 Million Campaign, and World War II, also the period in which the Woman's Missionary Union's Ruby, Golden, and Sixtieth Anniversaries were celebrated. "Under her long administration Woman's Missionary Union became the important auxiliary, the vital missionary ally to the denomination which it is today."

Miss Mallory's 36 years of service paralleled the extraordinary growth of the union.

When she became secretary there were 6,654 Woman's Missionary Societies and 3,909 young people's organizations. The Lottie Moon Christmas Offering was $28,943.21 and the Annie Armstrong Offering, $19,180.72, though neither then bore the memorial names. Miss Mallory led Woman's Missionary Union so ably and so co-operatively that when she retired in 1948 there were 14,043 Woman's Missionary Societies and 32,679 young people's organizations. The Lottie Moon Christmas Offering had reached $1,472,411.04 and the Annie Armstrong Offering was $654,432.75 at her retirement.

Louisiana College, Pineville, La., awarded to her an honorary doctorate, and Selma University, a Negro institution, conferred on her a similar degree in recognition of her work in promoting better racial relationships through mission institutes.

Memorials established to perpetuate Kathleen Mallory's name include Kathleen Mallory Hospital in Laichowfu, China, erected by Alabama Baptists just after her resignation as state secretary; Woman's Missionary Union building in Birmingham, in recognition of her services as executive secretary, toward which state women's unions gave $100,000; Mallory Hall, the administration chapel building, to be erected from Lottie Moon Christmas Offering funds on the campus of Seinan Jo Gakuin in Kokura, Japan; and a new Good Will Center building in Baltimore, for which the Home Mission Board allocated $100,000 of the Annie Armstrong Offering. ANNIE WRIGHT USSERY

MALONE, HERMIONE BROWN (MRS. D. M.) (b. Thomaston, Ala., Oct. 24, 1864; d. Thomaston, Ala., Nov. 29, 1942). One of the first delegates from Alabama to the Southern Baptist Woman's Missionary Union annual meeting in Fort Worth, Tex., in 1890, she carried and gave the first report. She was the first state corresponding secretary for Woman's Missionary Union, 1897–1909; vice-president of Southern Baptist Woman's Missionary Union, 1909–10; state personnel service chairman, 1912–16; district vice-president, 1909–18; Bethel Association superintendent, 1914–22; and member of state Woman's Missionary Union executive board, 1923–29. She was the daughter of Mr. and Mrs. I. C. Brown of East Lake, Birmingham, Ala. MRS. HENRY LYON

MAN. *The image of God.*—Genesis 1:26 declares that man was made in the image of God. Thus man's differentiation from the beasts does not lie in the fact that he is a reasoning animal or a social creature, but rather in the fact that he alone of all creation is able to respond freely to God's gracious demand in humble obedience and loving trust. This, the true meaning of man's freedom, implies that he is not free to do as he likes. His true freedom consists in choosing God and fulfilling God's will. The biblical revelation that man was made in God's image implies also that man is not an automaton but a moral agent. Nature does God's will because no other choice is before it. Man may refuse to do God's will and thus fall below nature; at the same time he can rise far above the glory of nature when he commits himself to God in humble faith and allows the grace of God to shine through his life. Man's distinctive mark is that he is created to reflect back to God in trustful obedience and total commitment the will and glory of his Creator.

The unity of man.—The image of God is seen not only in man's inmost spiritual nature but also in his outward physical organism. The Bible regards man as a unity of inner life and outer manifestation, of body and spirit. Man's body indicates the state of his spirit; his face reflects the condition of his soul. Man's body is distinctively fitted to express his fellowship with and service to God. When that divine fellowship is absent, man's true unity is partially dissolved, and bodily disharmony matches the disharmony of the spirit. Because man is a part of sinful humanity and affected by the sins of his fellows as well as by his own sinful rebellion, even the redeemed man in Christ carries in his body the marks of the sinful rebellion of his race. Because he is in process of redemption, his body as much as his spirit is still infected by the old Adam. Yet man was meant to be perfectly fitted in body and mind for fellowship with God, and the doctrine of the resurrection of the body points to the truth that beyond death, in a "body of glory," the redeemed man will enjoy God's grace and reflect his glory.

The unity of the race.—The image of God is seen in man's social relationships. These relationships are a part of man's innermost nature. Man is born with them. Significantly, the author of Genesis 1 declares that God made "man and woman" in his image, suggesting that the image is seen in the two together. They are complementary at the human level. God created man in his image, male and female. The most intimate of human relationships is thus a means of reflecting back God's glory. Just as God in his innermost nature as the Trinity is a holy communion of love, the Father loving the Son and the Son the Father in the Holy Spirit, so man in his most intimate relationship with woman (and thus in all other human relationships) is created to reflect in the created order the communion of love. He is made to follow God's will in serving and loving his fellows. Even in his sin and rebellion this responsibility is not lost. In spite of division and strife, men are still bound to one another, morally obligated to one another, and compelled to live together and serve their fellows by the created conditions of existence.

Fallen man.—Biblical revelation makes it clear that man is not what he ought to be. Having mishandled his freedom, he lives in contradiction with his true destiny. The story of the garden makes it quite clear that all men have rebelled against God, choosing themselves and their own satisfaction instead of him and his will. As a result, the human race is a race in bondage and, in the racial solidarity of Adam, is unable to lift itself by its own efforts back into its true destiny. In this situation, only the grace of God in Christ suffices.

The new man in Christ.—In Christ, the incarnate Son of God, men see themselves as they ought to be. The image of God is evident in the midst of history. The old man is defeated, and man in God's image shines clear. The utter surrender of Christ's will to that of the Father, the communion of prayer in the Spirit, the self-sacrifice of perfect love, as seen in the life of Christ, are a perpetual judgment on man's sinful nature, a reminder of his true destiny. Christ came, not only to exemplify man as man ought to be, living in God's image, but also to give man the power to live in God's world. In Christ, by the surrender of faith, man, though unworthy, may be reconciled to God and live in his fellowship. Just as Christ is the perfect image of God, the very essence of God himself expressed through human life, Christ, in reconciling man to God, imparts to man the power to reflect his glory.

See also Fall of Man and Innocence.

Bibliography: D. Cairns, *The Image of God in Man* (1953). E. C. RUST

MANAGAN, WILLIAM HENRY (b. Covington, Pa., Sept. 22, 1864; d. Lake Charles, La., May 20, 1934). Pioneer Baptist layman and denominational leader. He was converted in Williamsport, Pa., in 1887 and united with First Baptist Church, Covington, Pa. He began in the lumber business in 1888 in Orange, Tex., and remained in this business until his death. In 1889 he moved to Lake Charles, La. He married Martha Matilda East, who became a leader of the women of her church and state. Managan was an officer in his church in Westlake, La., from the day the church was formed until his death. During his active life he served in many positions: president of the Louisiana Baptist Convention (1910–11); president of the executive board; trustee of the Louisiana Children's Home; president of the board of trustees of Louisiana College; trustee of Southern Baptist Theological Seminary; trustee of New Orleans Seminary; and a member of the Lake Charles Rotary Club. A building at New Orleans Seminary is named in his honor. He was buried in the Magnolia Cemetery, Westlake, La. T. W. GAYER

MANCHURIA, MISSION IN. The migration of Chinese to Manchuria because of China's famines and overtaxation led to the opening of Southern Baptist missionary work in Manchuria. Charles Alexander and Evelyn (Corbitt) Leonard and Carmen Easley and Eula C. (Pearson) James began work in Harbin in northern Manchuria in 1924. Wayne Womack and Floy (White) Adams went to Dairen in southern Manchuria in 1925. Victor and Aurora L. (Hargrove) Koon located in Harbin in 1935; Reba Cloud Stewart, in 1936. At first the work in Manchuria was a part of the China Mission (North). The missionaries in Dairen continued that relationship. Missionaries in northern Manchuria formed a separate mission in 1937.

By 1940 intimidation of Christians and hindrances to mission work by the Japanese military force caused missionaries to comply with the request of the United States government that they leave Manchuria. During 16 years of service missionaries reported progress at both the Dairen and Harbin stations; opening of work in Yingkow, Mukden, and Hsinking; 35 centers of worship with two-thirds providing their own meeting places; baptism of 4,000 people by the churches; and the opening of a Bible school in Harbin.

Reports from Communist Manchuria indicate continuation of Baptist work, some of it openly, although with much persecution and some death. CHARLES A. LEONARD

MANLY, BASIL, JR. (b. Edgefield County, S. C., Dec. 19, 1825; d. Louisville, Ky., Jan. 31, 1892). Minister, seminary professor, hymn writer, Sunday School Board leader. Son of Basil (*q.v.*) and Sarah Murray (Rudulph) Manly, he spent his early boyhood years in Charleston, S. C., where his father was pastor of First Baptist Church. In 1837, when his father was elected president of the University of Alabama, Manly moved with his family to Tuscaloosa. He entered the university in 1840 at the age of 14 and graduated four years later at the head of his class. After uniting with the Baptist church of Tuscaloosa in 1840, Manly was licensed to preach May 13, 1844, and began theological studies at Newton Theological Institution, Newton Centre, Mass., that year. When the North-South division of Baptists occurred, Manly left

Newton and entered Princeton Theological Seminary, where he received his diploma in 1847.

He was ordained by the Tuscaloosa church Jan. 30, 1848, after accepting a call to Providence Baptist Church in Sumter County, Ala., which required only two services a month, thus making it possible for Manly to serve two other churches at the same time: Sumterville Church in Sumter County, Ala., and Shiloh Church in Noxubee County, Miss. Broken in health, he retired from the active pastorate at the end of 1848 in order to regain his strength. During 1849–50 Manly was the stated supply of First Baptist Church, Tuscaloosa, but in Sept., 1850, he resumed active service, accepting a call to First Baptist Church, Richmond, Va., at that time the largest white church of the denomination and in many respects the most influential. Manly, who for breadth of general culture and educational background had few peers among the Baptist ministers of his day, held this strategic pastorate until Oct. 1, 1854, when he became president of Richmond Female Institute, which he had been instrumental in establishing. He served three Sundays each month at Walnut Grove Church in Hanover County.

When the Southern Baptist Theological Seminary was founded, Manly was chosen to draw up articles of faith or an "Abstract of Principles" which each future professor was to be required to sign at his inauguration. Divergent trends in the doctrinal position of the Convention demanded a broad platform upon which all Baptists could unite, and significantly, during the interval since Manly's "Abstract of Principles" was drafted, no serious controversy has centered around it. With the opening of the seminary at Greenville, S. C., in 1859, Manly was elected professor of biblical introduction and Old Testament interpretation. In addition, he preached at Damascus, Fellowship, Siloam, and Clear Springs churches. Although the seminary opened with marked success, the Civil War soon forced it to close, but in 1865 Manly and his colleagues immediately returned to the task of rehabilitation. Manly evidently became disheartened by 1871, when he accepted the presidency of Georgetown College, Kentucky, but six years later, when the seminary moved to Louisville, Manly was re-elected to the faculty as professor of Old Testament, and he devoted the remainder of his life to ministerial education. He was treasurer of a fund for needy students for many years, a fund raised through the personal efforts of Manly and John Albert Broadus (*q.v.*).

Author of more than 20 hymns, Manly, in collaboration with his father, compiled the *Baptist Psalmody,* published in Charleston in 1850, and it contained nine of his original hymns. He also compiled and published *Baptist Chorals,* Richmond, 1859; and *Manly's Choice,* 1891. Manly wrote his hymn, beginning "Soldiers of Christ in truth arrayed," for the first commencement of Southern Seminary in 1860, and it has been sung at every succeeding commencement of the seminary. Manly's only major literary contribution, *The Bible Doctrine of Inspiration,* was published in 1888. An apologetic treatise following the Toy controversy, it provided a comprehensive, though not exhaustive, treatment of the doctrine of inspiration.

Under Manly's leadership the Sunday School Board of the Southern Baptist Convention was established in 1863. Under the direction of Manly, who was elected president, and John A. Broadus, secretary, the periodical *Kind Words* was established and it continued as an important Sunday school publication for many years. Broadus (*q.v.*) observed that Manly was the most versatile man he ever met. His ability to engage in many tasks gave the denomination, and especially the seminary, an individual who could be relied upon to see a task through to completion. Manly's versatility proved a virtue in the sense that it was particularly valuable at a time when few trained men could be found to administer the affairs of the denomination, but it also proved a weakness in that it prevented him from attaining great distinction in any one field of endeavor.

BIBLIOGRAPHY: J. P. Cox, "A Study of the Life and Work of Basil Manly, Jr." (1954).

JOSEPH POWHATAN COX

MANLY, BASIL, SR. (b. Pittsborough, Chatham County, N. C., Jan. 29, 1798; d. Greenville, S. C., Dec. 21, 1868). Patriot, educator, and preacher. Without question, he was one of the outstanding men of his day. He became president of the University of Alabama in 1837 and served for 18 years. He was a promoter of the Insane Hospital at Tuscaloosa, and cofounder of Southern Baptist Theological Seminary and of the Alabama Historical Society. He was a champion of Southern rights, and he supported the secession movement. As early as 1844, he was the inspiration and author of the resolutions, adopted by the Alabama State Baptist Convention at Marion. These resolutions concerning the relations between Baptists of the North and South led to the formation of the Southern Baptist Convention at Augusta, Ga., in 1845—a denominational cleavage 15 years before the political. During his ministry in South Carolina, he was largely influential in securing the establishment of the institution of learning for the special training of young men for the gospel ministry. That institution, after several changes of name and location, became Furman University. The son of Basil and Elizabeth (Maultsby) Manly, he was married Dec. 23, 1824, to Sarah Murray Rudulf. They had five children, including Basil Manly, Jr. (*q.v.*), and Charles Manly (*q.v.*).

MRS. HENRY LYON

MANLY, BASIL, CHAIR OF RELIGIOUS EDUCATION AND CHURCH ADMINISTRATION. Endowed as a chair of Southern Baptist Theological Seminary by the Baptist Sunday School Board in 1909 in recognition of the services Basil Manly, Jr. (*q.v.*), rendered to the Sunday school cause in the early 1860's by his leadership and management of the first Sunday School Board of the Southern Baptist Convention. The board proposed to raise the endowment through gifts from Sunday schools throughout the South, donating $1,000 to the endowment for every $2,000 contributed by the Sunday schools, up to $20,000. The proposal for the endowment came in connection with the celebration of the jubilee year of the seminary, when the board made an initial gift of $5,000. By Apr., 1922, amounts contributed from the Sunday schools supplemented by gifts from the Sunday School Board totaled $73,766.01. James Marion Frost (*q.v.*), secretary of the Sunday School Board, stated in the letter of transmittal, "What we say about the naming of the Chair is only a suggestion and not a condition." Accordingly, with the change of the term "Sunday School Pedagogy," the original designation of the chair, to "Religious Education and Church Administration," the chair assumed its present name. Occupants of the chair have included Byron Hoover DeMent (*q.v.*), Landrum Pinson Leavell (*q.v.*), Gaines Stanley Dobbins, and Findley Bartow Edge.

GAINES S. DOBBINS

MANLY, CHARLES (b. Charleston, S. C., May 28, 1837; d. Gaffney, S. C., May 1, 1924). Pastor, school administrator. Manly was the son of Basil Manly (*q.v.*) and the brother of Basil Manly, Jr. (*q.v.*). He was reared in Alabama, entered the University of Alabama when only 14, and graduated in 1855. He graduated from Princeton Theological Seminary four years later and became pastor of the Baptist church in Tuscaloosa, Ala., where he remained until 1871. Twice during this pastorate he was co-president of Alabama Central Female College, where he met Mary Esther Hellen Matthews, whom he married on Nov. 16, 1864. They had nine children, three boys and six girls.

From 1871 to 1873, Manly was president of Union University in Murfreesboro, Tenn., and also pastor of the Baptist church there. Later, after serving as pastor in Staunton, Va., from 1873 to 1880, he accepted the pastorate of First Baptist Church, Greenville, S. C., in 1880. Manly became president of Furman University in 1881, when the school was in financial distress and its future was doubtful. His distinguished administration (1871–97) improved the financial situation and laid the foundation for future growth. While at Furman, Manly continued to serve as a rural pastor. He returned to full-time pastoral work in 1897 and served churches in Lexington, Mo., and Lexington, Va., until 1914. He loved to laugh and used many homely anecdotes in his sermons. Manly died at the home of a daughter in Gaffney, S. C., and was buried in Springwood Cemetery, Greenville.

BIBLIOGRAPHY: *Baptist Courier* (May 8, 15, 22, 1924). *Furman Hornet* (May 23, 1924). L. Manly, *The Manly Family* (1930). *Annual of the State Convention of the Baptist Denomination in South Carolina* (1925). *The National Cyclopedia of American Biography* (1935). *Who's Who in America* (1943).

J. DAN WILLIAMS

MANUAL LABOR INSTITUTE (1833–37). Known also as the Alabama Institute of Literature and Industry, located on a 355-acre farm at Greensboro, Ala., with W. L. Williford, president. Founded by the Alabama Baptist State Convention in its 10th annual session, for the purpose of "the improvement of the ministry of our denomination," this school marked the beginning of Christian education under the auspices of the Baptists in Alabama. Financial difficulties, disturbances in the faculty, and mismanagement led to its dissolution in 1837. The property was sold, and the net proceeds of $2,000 were given to ministerial education.

JAMES E. DAVIDSON

MAPLE, JOSEPH C. (b. Guernsey County, Ohio, Nov. 18, 1833; d. Springfield, Mo., Oct. 20, 1917). Clergyman, writer, educator, denominational leader. At the age of four he moved from Ohio to Peoria County, Ill. He was converted Jan. 18, 1849, and joined a Baptist church; he was educated at Shurtleff College. As a minister he held the following pastorates: Cape Girardeau, Mo.; Owensboro, Ky.; First Baptist Church of Kansas City, Mo.; Chillicothe, Mo.; Springfield, Mo.; a second pastorate at Cape Girardeau; Mexico, Mo.; Marshall, Mo.; Keokuk, Iowa; Trenton, Mo.; and Armstrong, Mo. Maple was a prolific writer of biography. Upon the authorization of the Missouri Baptist General Association, he wrote, with the assistance of R. P. Rider, the four-volume work, *Missouri Baptist Biography*. His writing also included letters on travel; articles on the history of Baptist effort in Missouri; and *Memoirs of W. Pope Yeaman,* written by an agreement between the two men that the survivor should write the biography of the deceased. In 1861, with the assistance of his wife, he opened the Jackson Academy in Jackson, Mo. In 1878 he was appointed by J. S. Phelps, governor of Missouri, to represent Missouri at the World Exposition, Paris, France. A member of the state mission board (1877–86), he served as its president (1878–86). He received an honorary master's degree from Shurtleff College, and D.D. degrees from William Jewell College and Baylor University. He was one of the curators of Stephens College and a member of the board of trustees of William Jewell College. He was also a member of the Board of Home and Foreign Missions. He gave a historic address of the early Baptist work in the Cape Girardeau district to the 1875 session of the Missouri Baptist General Association in St. Joseph and, symbolic of his interest in Missouri Baptist history, presented to that body a gavel made from the wood of one of the sills of old Bethel Baptist Church, the first permanent Baptist church organized in Missouri.

BIBLIOGRAPHY: R. S. Douglass, *History of Missouri Baptists* (1934). R. S. Duncan, *History of the Baptists in Missouri* (1882). J. C. Maple, *Memoirs of William Pope Yeaman* (1906). J. C. Maple and R. P. Rider, *Baptist Biography,* Vol. III (1914). W. P. Yeaman, *A History of the Missouri Baptist General Association* (1899). W. C. LINK, JR.

MARGARET FUND. A memorial fund of Woman's Missionary Union used to furnish scholarships for sons and daughters of regular missionaries of the Foreign and Home Mission boards of the Southern Baptist Convention. The amount needed, now $52,000 a year, has been allocated from the Lottie Moon and Annie Armstrong offerings since Dec., 1937, and Mar., 1938. The original gift of $10,000 was made in 1904 by Mrs. Frank Chambers of New York, formerly of Alabama. The sum was used to purchase a home in Greenville, S. C. The Margaret Home, named by Mrs. Chambers for her grandmother, mother, and daughter, provided a home for missionaries' children while at school in the homeland and also a resting place for missionaries when on furlough. Because of changing conditions on mission fields, the home was sold in 1914, and the amount from the sale was invested in an educational fund which better meets the needs of the missionaries.

The amount for regular Margaret Fund scholarships is $500 for the scholastic year, but arrangements vary according to the kind of training, purposes of graduate study, and other special conditions. From 1916 to 1956, 777 students received Margaret Fund scholarships totaling $857,279.43. In 1955 funds amounting to $49,612.50, an average of $410.02 per student, were distributed among 121 recipients. Several particularized scholarships have been provided within the Margaret Fund, e.g., a medical mission scholarship in memory of Mrs. H. M. Rhodes, Margaret Fund chairman from 1938 to 1941. The tendency of some groups to shower miscellaneous presents on individuals has been somewhat controlled by the Burney Gifts, which provide stated gifts equally to all Margaret Fund scholarship students for their personal use. This fund was named in tribute to Mrs. Frank S. Burney, Margaret Fund chairman from 1922 to 1938. JULIETTE MATHER

MARION FEMALE SEMINARY (1836–39). A girls' school located at Marion, Ala., founded by leading Baptists of that city, including Gen. E. D. King. The Baptists withdrew their support from the school in 1839 due to a course of events that had deprived them of proper representation on the faculty. In 1839 they founded another school which later was known as Judson College. JAMES E. DAVIDSON

MARITIME PROVINCES, UNITED BAPTIST CONVENTION OF THE (CANADA). A body including Baptists, except a few splinter groups, of Nova Scotia, New Brunswick, and Prince Edward Island. In 1955 a Baptist church organized in Newfoundland was admitted to the convention.

Baptist origins in this area resulted partly from the influence on the denomination of the Great Awakening in New England. In addition the Nova Scotia Legislature granted equal rights to all Protestant bodies in 1759, which encouraged migration of Baptists and others from New England who had suffered restraints. Among the immigrants were two Baptist ministers from Massachusetts, Ebenezer Moulton and Nathan Mason. Moulton came to Nova Scotia in 1760 and founded at least two churches; Mason came to New Brunswick with a group from his church at Swansea, where he established a church in 1763. Although these churches ceased to exist when their founders returned home, they created an interest in the Baptist faith.

The interest was greatly augmented in 1776–83 by the vigorous itinerant ministry of Henry Alline, a New Light evangelist produced by the Great Awakening. Although Alline was not a Baptist, his converts readily identified themselves with the Baptists in the Maritime area. Since many of the New Lights were indifferent to the mode of baptism, some of the first Baptist churches included both immersed and unimmersed members, continuing this practice until 1800 when the formation of an all-Baptist association prescribed admitting only immersed persons to church membership. The association churches were strongly Calvinistic.

Baptist origins in Prince Edward Island date from 1806 when a Scottish layman, John Scott, began preaching there. Scott and Alexander Crawford, a fellow countryman who soon came to assist him, were rigidly Calvinistic and exercised strict discipline over the churches they founded, even forbidding believers to marry unbelievers.

David George, an escaped slave from Virginia, began an itinerant ministry among the Negroes of the Maritimes in 1783; the first Negro church was organized in 1832. The African Baptist Association, organized in 1854, now includes nine pastorates with 22 churches.

Nine associations have evolved from the all-Baptist association founded in 1800—five in Nova Scotia, three in New Brunswick, and one in Prince Edward Island. The churches in these associations formed a convention in 1846 to support phases of the work at home and abroad previously undertaken by the separate associations with varying degrees of co-operation.

A Free Will Baptist denomination, less Calvinistic in doctrine, developed during this period in the convention area. Also owing their origin to visiting New England preachers, the Free Will Baptists were organized in two conferences, one for New Brunswick in 1832, the other for Nova Scotia in 1837.

Since Calvinistic and Free Will Baptists carried on similar activities, some persons on both sides long regarded a merger of the two bodies the most logical step. As the hard lines of their respective doctrinal positions softened, negotiations toward a union were carried out, resulting in the formation of the present United Baptist Convention of the Maritime Provinces in 1905.

The convention maintains a liberal arts college, Acadia University, Wolfville, Nova Scotia. Founded in 1838, the college provides training in theology in addition to the liberal arts. The Home Mission Board, organized in 1919, brought home mission work, which dates back to 1814, under central direction. As a constituent member of the Canadian Baptist Foreign Mission Board (formed in 1911), the convention helps maintain overseas mission service with 25 missionaries in India, four in Bolivia, and two in Portuguese West Africa. In 1954 the convention contributed $123,408 for missions, as compared with $53,000 in 1934. The convention publishes a weekly journal, *The Maritime Baptist;* United Baptist Women's Missionary Union publishes *Tidings,* a monthly. Boards have been established for social service, Christian education, evangelism, annuity provision for retired ministers, the collection of historical materials concerning the denomination within the convention, stewardship, and ministerial education.

While the convention has continued to maintain its own identity, it became part of the Baptist Federation of Canada in 1944. The Federation Publications Committee supervises the preparation of literature for the Baptist Sunday schools of Canada.

In 1954 the convention included 653 churches arranged in 261 pastorates, with a membership (resident and nonresident) of 66,413, and Sunday school enrolment, 37,047. The churches reported 2,119 baptisms and $28.87 per capita gifts.

BIBLIOGRAPHY: I. E. Bill, *Fifty Years with the Baptist Ministers and Churches of the Maritime Provinces of Canada* (1880). G. E. Levy, *The Baptists of the Maritime Provinces* (1946). R. S. Longley, *Acadia University, 1838–1938* (1938). I. F. MacKinnon, *Settlements and Churches in Nova Scotia, 1749–1776* (1930). E. M. Saunders, *History of the Baptists of the Maritime Provinces* (1902). GEORGE E. LEVY

MARKS, LUTHER WHITFIELD (b. Benjamin, Mo., Feb. 1, 1862; d. Edmond, Okla., Jan. 10, 1943). Writer, pastor; a graduate of William Jewell College and Southern Baptist Theological Seminary. He held pastorates at Shelbyville, Meadville, Wyaconda, and Lamar, Mo.; Jeffersonville, Ind.; and Edmond, Okla. A number of years prior to establishment of the *Baptist Messenger,* he represented the *Word and Way* in Oklahoma, and edited a column in that paper on Oklahoma work, entitled "Marks' Remarks." He was the first historical secretary of the Baptist General Convention of Oklahoma. His written works include *L. L. Smith of Oklahoma,* and "The Story of Oklahoma Baptists" an unpublished manuscript now in Oklahoma Baptist University Library, Shawnee. M. E. RAMAY

MARRIAGE AND THE FAMILY. Prevalence of divorce, broken homes, marital infidelity, and juvenile delinquency give evidence of marked deterioration of marriage and family relationships, and graphically portray the need for an understanding and application of the plan and purpose of God for this basic institution and these basic relationships. Contemporary conditions are evidence of the failure of both the church and the home to teach young people concerning the relationship which is second only to relationship with Christ. The intent of God as the proper pattern for all relationships in the home has not been adequately accepted. Real reform can only be based on the ethic of the Bible, proclaimed from the pulpit, taught in the churches, and demonstrated in the home.

In marriage is found God's provision for the basic needs of man and for the propagation of the human race. "And Jehovah God said, It is not good that the man should be alone; I will make him a help meet for him" (Gen. 2:18 ASV). Because of his nature it was not good for man to be alone, and God created woman as an answer to man's need for love, companionship, understanding, and sympathy. Man and woman find the answer to their deepest needs in one another as they are totally and truly united in marriage. God created humanity in two halves, the male and the female, ordaining that they should be united by pairs into a single organism, being joined together by the Lord himself in such a total and essential way as to make them one flesh. God commanded the couple so united to cleave to one another as though welded into one, warning that no man should seek to sever or cut asunder this "one flesh" (Gen. 1:26–27; 2:24; Matt. 193–6). It is the plan of God that the marriage relationship shall be permanent, being severed only by death (Rom. 7:1–2; I Cor. 7:38–39). Man may put it asunder by infidelity to the marriage vows, but only in violation of the will of God. After consummation of the marriage, the relationship between husband and wife is determined by divine law, and they have a natural obligation to fulfil their mutual and individual duties.

Beyond the mutual fulfilment of husband and wife, the most fundamental purpose of marriage is the propagation and perpetuation of the human race. "And God said unto them, Be fruitful, and multiply, and replenish the earth" (Gen. 1:28 ASV). It is the intent of God that marriage carry with it the responsibility of parenthood, and the marriage union which wilfully does not assume this responsibility violates a fundamental law of marriage and forfeits the possibility of receiving the full benefit from the marriage union which God intended. Since marriage is a part of the natural order, disregard of the intent of God on the part of any will bring evil consequences.

The home should be the nearest approximation of heaven possible on earth, and it will be if relations within it are in accordance with God's will. The Christian ethic for these relations is not an ethic of claim or demand, but one which speaks to every individual and to every institution concerning how others should be treated. Never does it speak of anything that should be demanded of another, whether it be in family relations or in any other social relations. The intent of God is that each member shall voluntarily accept certain duties and responsibilities in the family relationship. The husband is to love his wife with an unselfish, sacrificial love "even as Christ also loved the church, and gave himself up for it" (Eph. 5:25 ASV). He is to serve voluntarily as head of the family, "as Christ also is the head of the church" (Eph. 5:23 ASV). Likewise, the wife is to love her husband and hold him in such respect that she voluntarily subjects herself to him. "As the church is subject to Christ, so let the wives also be to their husbands in everything" (Eph. 5:24 ASV). It is not the duty of the husband to bring the wife under subjugation. It is the duty of voluntary self-subjection or self-subordination which is here laid upon the wife. If the husband has voluntarily assumed his responsibilities according to the intent of God, the wife need not fear this submission any more than the Christian fears submitting himself to Christ.

Parents are to love their children and "nurture them in the chastening and admonition of the Lord" (Eph. 6:4 ASV). They are to rear their children in such a way as to provide instruction, training, discipline, and counsel, toward the end that this rearing shall be a purifying or refining process through which the child passes, being freed as much as possible from fault as he grows to adulthood. Parents should exercise the authority and control necessary to carry out this responsibility toward their children. Failure to correct, reprove, and punish children when needed indicates a lack of proper love for the children; for the parent who truly loves his child will correct him early (cf. Prov. 13:24). It is the intent of God that children be willing to heed counsel and set the course of their lives under the guidance of the mature minds of their parents. Unless children honor their father and mother, they will hardly accept their counsel and take their advice.

The marriage relationship should never be established until both man and woman understand the intent of God for marriage and home relations and are willing to accept the responsibilities peculiar to their place in the family relationship. The nearer marriages and homes approximate the intent of God, the more blessed they will be, and the more blessed will be all relationships in the human community.

See also Mixed Marriages.

Bibliography: T. F. Adams, *Making Your Marriage Succeed* (1953). T. A. Lacey, *Marriage in Church and State* (revised by R. C. Mortimer, 1947). A. L. Murray, *Youth's Marriage Problems* (1947). J. A. Pike, *If You Marry Outside Your Faith* (1954). E. and P. Trueblood, *The Recovery of Family Life* (1953). C. W. SCUDDER

MARRIAGE CEREMONIES AND CUSTOMS. For Baptists, marriage is both a civil and a divine contract. Since it is civil, the minister cannot perform the marriage ceremony unless he is legally qualified and has the license in his possession. Since it is divine, it is the minister's prerogative and responsibility to decide on the eligibility of the couple for this sacred relationship in the light of his interpretation of the New Testament teachings. Baptist ministers generally refuse to marry couples who do not qualify by New Testament standards. Three policies are followed regarding the interpretation of who is eligible to be married. Many ministers refuse to marry couples when one or both of them have a living mate, regardless of the reason for divorce. Some ministers will perform the ceremony for a couple, one or both of whom are divorced, if the reason for the divorce (whether legal or moral) was sexual immorality. This group feels that the innocent party has a right to remarry. Some ministers will remarry divorced people who were faced with an intolerable situation in the first marriage. These ministers would consider "intolerable" any marriage broken by extreme alcoholism, homosexuality, some types of insanity, desertion, irresponsibility, extreme cruelty, and the like.

Some Baptist ministers consider themselves only as officers of the law and will, therefore, marry all who come to them requesting a ceremony. They are a minority. Baptist churches usually exercise no control over the individual minister in these matters except that of social disapproval. Generally these matters are influenced or determined by counsel, by resolutions at conventions and associations, by conversation within groups, etc.

The practice of premarital counseling is growing among Baptists. One or many interviews may be held to help in determining eligibility for marriage. Emotional and social factors which make for success in marriage may be analyzed. The minister may give advice on private and religious practices in the home and on other matters, sometimes with the help of results from psychological testing. Sex information generally is omitted or dealt with incidentally. If one or both of the persons to be married are not Christians, the minister frequently looks upon premarital interviews as an evangelistic opportunity.

The marriage ceremony proper is usually performed in the minister's home or study, in the bride's home, in the church parlor or chapel, or in the church sanctuary, customarily in the afternoon or evening. No prescribed ceremony is recognized as official or authorized by Baptists. The *Church Manual* by James Madison Pendleton (*q.v.*) gives a short marriage ceremony which, no doubt, has been of wide influence. The greatest single influence on Baptists, especially Southern Baptists, has been *The Pastor's Manual* by James Randolph Hobbs, published first in 1924. It contains a section entitled "Notes on Ministerial Conduct at Weddings" and several typical marriage ceremonies, including the Presbyterian and Episcopal.

The marriage ceremony, as conducted by Baptists, is generally simple and fairly brief. It may be composed by the individual minister or adapted from traditional forms and may occasionally involve elements of improvisation.

No fees are required by Baptist ministers for performing a marriage ceremony. It is customary for the groom to give the minister an honorarium. Many ministers give this to their wives; some ministers give the fee to the bride as a wedding gift, especially if one or both of the contracting parties are members of the officiating minister's church. A very few refuse fees altogether.

BIBLIOGRAPHY: J. R. Hobbs, *The Pastor's Manual* (1934). R. LOFTON HUDSON

MARS HILL COLLEGE. The first educational institution established by Baptists of North Carolina west of the Blue Ridge Mountains and now the oldest college in the western part of the state. Located in a picturesque village which bears its name, Mars Hill has been called a "gem in the emerald ring of the hills." The school opened in 1856 as the French Broad Baptist Institute, named for the association which at one time included all of North Carolina west of the Blue Ridge Mountains. Three years later it was chartered as Mars Hill College, with the "power of conferring all such degrees or marks of literary distinction as are usually conferred by colleges and seminaries of learning."

At first the college consisted of only one two-story brick building on a four-acre tract, donated by Edward Carter. Made of handmade brick and hand-hewn timbers, the building was erected by a small group of mountain farmers and entrepreneurs who wanted a school in which they could educate their children according to the tenets of their faith. The modest financial undertaking was such, however, that a slave, owned by J. W. Anderson, secretary of the board of trustees, was levied on as security for the debt due the contractors. The college flourished until forced to close due to the Civil War, 1863–65. While troops were quartered on the campus, two wooden buildings were burned and the original building was badly damaged. The college reopened amid the bitterness, wrack, and gloom immediately following the war, and for three decades until Robert Lee Moore (*q.v.*) became president in 1897, the college was maintained by a few loyal families of limited means.

The first president of the college was W. A. G. Brown, pioneer educator of East Tennessee and Western North Carolina, who served until 1858. John B. Marsh, of Binghamton, N. Y., succeeded Brown and served until 1861, when the outbreak of the Civil War made his position untenable. For two years during the war Pinkney Rollins was president, and then from 1866 to 1897, 13 different men occupied the presidency. During Moore's 41-year administration, beginning in 1897, largely due to his personality and ability as an educator and inspirer of youth, the college gradually developed, multiplied its assets, and assumed its distinctive character. Following Moore in 1938, Hoyt Blackwell, formerly a faculty member, was chosen president. Under his administration the same high moral and academic standards have been maintained, curriculum has been expanded, and physical assets have been increased. Seven modern buildings have been added, and property is now valued at $5,000,000, endowment at $500,000.

At present the campus includes 120 acres with 18 buildings for administration and residence and 16 cottages and faculty homes. Faculty and administrative staff total more than 100, and enrolment in 1955 was 1,035 from 80 North Carolina counties, 21 states, and nine other countries. Alumni files contain the names of 16,534 former students, a large number of which are serving in church-related vocations, as ministers, education or music directors, or missionaries. Forty former students are now listed among the foreign missionaries serving under the Southern Baptist Foreign Mission Board.

Mars Hill is recognized for thorough scholarship and is fully accredited by every agency which accredits a junior college in the area, including the Southern Association of Colleges and Secondary Schools and the National Association of Schools of Music. About 90 per cent of the graduates continue their education in senior colleges, universities, and professional schools and consistently rank high in these institutions. Mars Hill is primarily a residence college, with most of the students living on the campus, where they may study in a wholesome and stimulating environment surrounded by an atmosphere of friendliness and Christian culture. A full program of student activities includes sports, literary societies, choral clubs, band, orchestra, dramatic groups, forensics, journalism, photography, and religious organizations. As stated in the catalogue, "The constant aim of the college is the development of character through knowledge and training that give emphasis to spiritual values. The college seeks to prepare young men and women for victorious personal living, for successful attainments in further study, for sympathetic and responsive social relationships, according to the moral imperatives of Christ."

BIBLIOGRAPHY: E. J. Carter, "A History of Mars Hill College" (1940). J. A. McLeod, *From These Stones, Mars Hill College the First Hundred Years* (1955). J. A. MCLEOD

MARSH, ROBERT HENRY (b. Ore Hill, Chatham County, N. C., Nov. 8, 1837; d. Oxford, N. C., Oct. 6, 1924). Vice-president of the Southern Baptist Convention, 1897 and 1902, and president of the North Carolina Baptist State Convention for 14 years, 1891–1905. He was baptized at Chapel Hill in 1856. After graduation from the University of North Carolina in 1858, he became tutor of ancient languages at Wake Forest College, then professor at Oxford Female College, 1862–63. He was ordained to the Baptist ministry at Raleigh, Sept. 1, 1861. His first charge as a minister was with the 26th Regiment of North Carolina troops in the Civil War. He was pastor at Henderson, N. C., 1878–81. As a pastor and preacher he had few equals. For 50 years he was pastor in Flat River Association, serving for some years as moderator. He served Hester Church 48 years; Enon, 31 years; and Tally Ho, 23 years. On retirement in 1916 he was made pastor emeritus by Hester and Enon churches. He was a member of the board of trustees of Wake Forest College (1870–1916) and president (1890–93); was a member (1896–1912) of the board of trustees of Southern Baptist Seminary, which he had attended two years at Greenville, S. C. He left his personal library to Wake Forest College.

S. L. MORGAN

MARSHALL, ABRAHAM (b. Windsor, Conn., Apr. 23, 1745; d. Columbia County, Ga., Aug. 15, 1819). Georgia Baptist preacher. Converted and baptized about 1770, Abraham Marshall came with his father, Daniel Marshall (*q.v.*), to Georgia and was ordained in 1775. Succeeding his father in the Kiokee pastorate, he served there until his death. Noted primarily as an itinerant preacher, however, Marshall preached along the Atlantic seaboard from Georgia to Connecticut. After serving in the Revolution as a soldier and chaplain, he devoted the remainder of his life to Baptist work. As moderator of the Georgia Baptist Association, he was instrumental in constituting many new Baptist churches, among them the first Negro church in Georgia at Savannah. He was a trustee of the University of Georgia and a member of the Georgia Constitutional Convention of 1789.

MALCOLM LESTER

MARSHALL, DANIEL (b. Windsor, Conn., 1706; d. Columbia County, Ga., Nov. 2, 1784). Preacher, Georgia Baptist leader. Born in New England of English ancestry, Marshall was converted about 1726 and early in life became a deacon in the Congregational church. Stirred by the preaching of George Whitefield, whom he first heard about 1744, Marshall left Windsor in 1751 or 1752 to serve as a missionary to the Mohawk Indians at the headwaters of the Susquehanna River in New York and Pennsylvania. Because of Indian troubles antecedent to the French and Indian War, Marshall in 1754 moved southward to Winchester, Va., where he was baptized into the fellowship of the Millcreek Baptist Church in the Philadelphia Association. After being licensed to preach by that church, he continued southward and settled at Sandy Creek in Guilford County, N. C., in 1755. While engaged in the itinerant ministry in eastern Carolina and Virginia, Marshall was ordained by the Abbott's Creek Church in 1757. Moving southward again in 1760, Marshall established himself on Beaver Creek in South Carolina. In 1762 he went to Stephen's Creek, 10 miles north of Augusta, Ga. During the 1760's Daniel Marshall continued his ministry of evangelizing the lost and constituting new churches throughout the region of northern South Carolina. Crossing the Savannah River, Marshall began the Baptist witness in Georgia about 1770. While preaching in St. Paul's Parish, Marshall was arrested for preaching the gospel contrary to the Anglican form and was forbidden to preach. Ignoring the order, he continued to preach and defend the cause of religious liberty without further molestation. In 1771 he moved his family to Georgia and settled in what is now Columbia County. The following year Daniel Marshall constituted the Kiokee Church, the first regularly constituted Baptist church in Georgia, which he served as pastor until his death in 1784.

During the American Revolution, Marshall was the only minister of any denomination who continued his ministry in Georgia. Serving as a chaplain to the Revolutionary forces, he was once imprisoned by the Tories because of his rebel sympathies. As a result of Marshall's labors, the Baptists of Georgia increased in number even during the troublous times of the Revolution, and by 1784, the last year of Marshall's life, they were sufficiently numerous to organize the Georgia Baptist Association. Jesse Mercer (*q.v.*) described Daniel Marshall as being "neither profoundly learned, nor very eloquent as a preacher, yet, he was," according to Mercer, "fervent in spirit, and indefatigable in labors."

BIBLIOGRAPHY: S. Boykin, *History of the Baptist Denomination in Georgia with Biographical Compendium* (1881). J. H. Campbell, *Georgia Baptists, Historical and Biographical* (1874). J. Mercer, *A History of the Georgia Baptist Association* (1838). J. D. Mosteller, *A History of the Kiokee Church* (1952). B. D. Ragsdale, *Story of Georgia Baptists* (1938). R. C. Strickland, *Religion and the State in Georgia in the Eighteenth Century* (1939).

MALCOLM LESTER

MARSHALL, JABEZ PLEIADES (b. Kiokee, Ga., *c.* 1794; d. Kiokee, Ga., Mar. 29, 1832; buried at Kiokee Church). Georgia Baptist preacher. Educated at the University of Georgia, Jabez Marshall succeeded his father, Abraham Marshall (*q.v.*), as pastor of the Kiokee Church. From 1820 until his death, he was clerk of the Georgia Baptist Association. He also served as clerk of the first and second sessions of the Georgia Baptist Convention (1822–23). His death in 1832 brought to a close the 60-year pastorate of father, son, and grandson at Kiokee, the mother church of Georgia Baptists.

MALCOLM LESTER

MARSHALL COLLEGE. Opened in Griffin, Ga., in Aug., 1853, chartered in December.

Jesse H. Campbell (*q.v.*) was one of its founders; and Flint River Association was its chief sponsor, although Presbyterians and Methodists were also actively interested in it. The school was suspended in 1862, and the building, used for a time as a hospital during the war, was destroyed by fire during Sherman's campaign in Georgia. ARTHUR JACKSON

MARTIN, MATTHEW THOMAS (b. Smith County, Miss., Aug. 6, 1842; d. near St. Louis, Mo., Oct. 24, 1898). Minister, professor, college financial agent. Professor of mathematics in Mississippi College for nine years, Martin was responsible for saving the college from financial ruin after the Civil War. Serving as financial agent, he redeemed the property of the college from mortgage, added $50,000 to the endowment, and secured relinquishment of $42,000 of outstanding scholarships. From 1877 to 1881, Martin personally assumed the financial and business management of the new convention-sponsored newspaper, the *Baptist Record*. Licensed to preach in 1877, Martin became a successful evangelist and returned from Texas and Georgia in 1892 to the pastorate in Gloster, Miss., where he caused division in the fellowship of Mississippi Association and the state convention over the doctrinal position of "Martinism." The report on obituaries in the *Mississippi Baptist Convention Annual* for 1899 described Martin as "the dauntless logician, a man of great power, great mind, and great toil."

See also MARTINISM.

BIBLIOGRAPHY: J. L. Boyd, *A Popular History of Baptists in Mississippi* (1930). W. Cathcart, *The Baptist Encyclopedia* (1880). L. S. Foster, *Mississippi Baptist Preachers* (1895). T. C. Schilling, *Abstract History of the Mississippi Baptist Association for One Hundred Years, 1806–1906.* C. B. HAMLET III

MARTIN, THOMAS THEODORE (b. Smith County, Miss., Apr. 26, 1862; d. Jackson, Miss., May 23, 1939). Evangelist, teacher, and writer. The son of Matthew Thomas Martin (*q.v.*), he graduated from Mississippi College in 1886, taught mathematics and the natural sciences in Baylor Female College, Belton, Tex., from 1886 to 1888, and was ordained by the First Baptist Church in Belton on May 27, 1888. He entered Southern Baptist Theological Seminary, Louisville, Ky., in 1888. His first pastorate was at Glenview, Ky., in 1890; he was pastor at Leadville, Colo., 1891–93, and at Canon City, Colo., 1894. He returned to Glenview, 1895–96, and was at Beattyville, Ky., in 1896 when he received his Th.M. degree from Southern Seminary. While awaiting assignment to a foreign mission field, he was stricken with an almost fatal attack of food poisoning and was advised to return to Colorado for recovery. He was pastor of Cripple Creek from 1897 to 1900, when he entered full-time evangelistic work. His preaching in the open air to the miners had prepared him for his effective ministry in large auditoriums and tents. He organized into teams a corps of gospel singers and evangelists known as the Blue Mountain Evangelists, which he booked throughout the country. His preaching was the happy combination of teacher, expositor, and debater. It was concerned chiefly with the theme of salvation by faith through the grace of God and was addressed to the lost both within and without the church. His writings include *God's Plan with Men* (1912), *Redemption and the New Birth* (1913), *The New Testament Church* (1917), *Heaven, Hell and Other Sermons* (1923), and *Hell in the High Schools* (1923).

BIBLIOGRAPHY: L. S. Foster, *Mississippi Baptist Preachers* (1895). A. D. Muse, *Viewing Life's Sunset* (n.d.). C. B. HAMLET III

MARTINISM. A controversy which arose about 1893 within the bounds of the Mississippi Baptist Association over the doctrinal views of Matthew Thomas Martin (*q.v.*), then pastor of the Galilee church and associational evangelist. Briefly, his views were: (1) Men are dead in trespasses and sins and "made alive" by the Holy Spirit, which process is *generation.* (2) Under proper conditions the sinner is enabled by the Spirit to repent and believe (simultaneously) and is then "regenerated" by the "engrafted Word of God," which process is *regeneration.* (3) Thus being *completely* saved by grace through faith by a complete Saviour from all sins—past, present, and future—the believer is to submit to Christian (believer's) baptism. (4) The Christian has within himself the witness of full assurance, which depends *not* on feeling *or* obedience to duty but on dependence on God to keep his word. (5) The true Christian never doubts his assurance of full and eternal salvation. (6) If a professed Christian has doubts that his experience of grace was real, he is still in the bonds of sin. (7) If under favorable conditions the professed Christian has a blessed experience, accompanied by the joys of salvation, this is to be regarded as a genuine experience of grace (that is, *regeneration*), and the individual should submit to believer's baptism.

Under Martin's powerful preaching and irresistible appeals, scores of church members were "converted" and requested "rebaptism." However, due to the confusion in churches of the Mississippi Association and outside of it, the association passed a resolution in 1895 protesting the practice of rebaptism "to an unlimited extent, unwarranted by the Scriptures" in the Galilee church. Galilee called a council of all the pastors in the association and one deacon from each church to "test the orthodoxy of Bro. Martin," using her own articles of faith as a criterion. The council recommended that the church accept Martin's proffered resignation and that "each shall pledge himself before God never to refer to these troubles again, in the spirit of strife."

The Zion Hill Church, also in Mississippi Association, called Martin as pastor, and a year later the association resolved to "withdraw the hand of fellowship from the said church and its pastor" and urged all affiliating churches not to recognize Martin "as a Baptist preacher." A resolution was presented favoring a free and full discussion of his doctrinal views and practices but was "laid on the table as out of the purview and authority of the Association." When the resolution was tabled, J. R. Sample, physician from Summit, proposed that the association request the editor of the *Baptist Record* to permit Martin the use of its columns to present his views. Robert Abram Venable (*q.v.*) was importuned to answer and agreed to the requests, but later he declined.

In 1897 repeated efforts by preamble and resolution were made by the association to have the doctrinal views and practices of Martin considered before the Mississippi Baptist Convention, but these were voted down on the ground that it was not "within the purview of that body to pass upon." However, the association resolved finally by a vote of 101 to 16 "that this Convention does not indorse, but condemns, the doctrinal views of Prof. M. T. Martin, as these views are set forth by himself and published over his own name in his pamphlet entitled 'The Doctrinal Views of M. T. Martin.'" Efforts were made later by individuals and the convention to reconcile the parties directly involved in the controversy.

Bibliography: J. L. Boyd, *A Popular History of the Baptists in Mississippi* (1930). L. S. Foster, *Mississippi Baptist Preachers* (1895). T. C. Schilling, *Abstract History of the Mississippi Baptist Association* (1908).

J. L. BOYD

MARY AND MARIOLATRY. The biblical data about the mother of Jesus are set forth in several episodes. The most detailed episode is the birth and infancy narratives of Matthew (1:18 to 2:12) and Luke (1:26–56; 2:1–40). Both describe a virgin birth. Matthew's account is objective, revealing the suspicion which fell upon Mary and her vindication; Luke's is subjective, describing her maidenly feelings, her submission to God, her grateful and reverent joy. Mary appears in both accounts as a devout, obedient Jewish maiden. On the assumption that Luke gives Mary's genealogy (3:23–38), and in the light of her kinship to Elisabeth, it is likely that Mary was descended from both the royal family of David and the priestly tribe of Levi. At Cana (John 2:1–11) Mary sought and obtained the aid of her son in supplying wine for a wedding feast. Undisturbed by Jesus' apparently abrupt reply, she gave effective orders to the servants. Her action was that of a resourceful, efficient matron. In the one recorded incident in which Mary was related to the public ministry of Jesus (Matt. 12:46–50; Mark 3:31–35; Luke 8:19–21), she was evidently prompted by loving solicitude. She and "his brethren" were unsuccessful in inducing him to retire for a time, as Jesus affirmed his committal to doing the Father's will. The last picture of Mary in the Gospels (John 19:25–27) portrays the filial devotion of Jesus, as from the cross he committed her to the apostle John, who "took her unto his own home." The reference in Acts (1:14) places her in the fellowship of Jesus' disciples while they prayerfully awaited the day of Pentecost.

Legend and Roman Catholic dogma have interpreted and supplemented this data and given rise to Mariolatry, "the act or practice of worshiping the Virgin Mary." This term is usually used opprobriously. However, Roman Catholics distinguish between worship, accorded only to God, and veneration, which is shown Mary "as the most highly favored of God's creatures." The unique place of Mary in Catholic devotion is the result of several historical developments which led to the veneration of Mary. As early as *c.* 185, Ireneus called Mary the second Eve. His contemporaries, Tertullian and Clement of Alexandria, asserted her perpetual virginity. The apocryphal *Protevangelium of James* exalted her. The Council of Chalcedon in 451 condemned Nestorius because he rejected the designation of Mary as the "Mother of God," and it adopted the expression as an essential part of Catholic doctrine. The immaculate conception of the virgin, i.e., the view that Mary shared in no taint of original sin, became a necessary dogma of faith in 1854. The climax in the developing exaltation of Mary came in 1950, when Pius XII declared the dogma of the assumption of Mary, i.e., that Mary did not die but was taken, body and soul, into heaven.

Bibliography: Anselm, *Cur deus homo*. Aquinas, *Summa theologica*. Ayer, *A Sourcebook of Ancient Church History* (1926). Ireneus, *Adv. haer.* Pius IX, The Bull *Ineffabilis Deus* (1854). Pius XII, The Bull *Munidicentissimus Deus* (1950). E. F. HAIGHT

MARY HARDIN–BAYLOR COLLEGE. The oldest college for women west of the Mississippi and Texas Baptists' only woman's college, Mary Hardin–Baylor is a four-year fully accredited liberal arts college owned and operated by the Baptist General Convention of Texas. Founded in 1845 at Independence and still operating under principles of the original charter granted by the Ninth Congress of the Republic of Texas, Mary Hardin–Baylor in 1956 had an enrolment of 623, including a full academic branch which opened with the spring semester, 1956, at Fort Hood, Tex.

Early history of the college coincides with that of Baylor University, whose charter provided for "a primary and a female department." The separate department for young women was organized sometime prior to June 13, 1851, when the records suggested that "Elder Horace Clark (*q.v.*) and his lady be requested to take charge of the Female Department of Baylor University." The first diploma was granted to Mary Gentry Kavanaugh on Dec. 20, 1855. The female branch was named Baylor Female College in 1866.

Clark was succeeded in 1871 by J. L. Graves,

who served one year, followed by W. W. Fontaine, who served until 1875. William Royall then headed the school until 1878, when John Hill Luther became the last president at Independence and the first at Belton. At a meeting of the general convention in Lampassas, Tex., in 1885, it was decided to move both schools from Independence. When bonus bids for locations for the schools were opened, Belton had subscribed $32,000, and Baylor Female College was thus moved to Belton, retaining its original charter granted by the Republic of Texas in 1845. The cornerstone of the first building, Luther Hall, on the new 75-acre campus was laid Apr. 12, 1886.

With the coming of John C. Hardy (*q.v.*) as president in 1912, a new era was inaugurated. His administration of 25 years was marked by a notable increase in enrolment and the addition of several new buildings, as well as strengthening of the faculty and development of the curriculum. At the end of Hardy's presidency the college plant included Wilson Administration Building, with Alma Reeves Chapel; Presser Hall, which houses music, art, and speech departments; Wells Science Hall; three dormitories; and Hardy Hall, with the college dining room and parlors. In 1926 Mary Hardin–Baylor was approved for membership in the Southern Association of Colleges and Secondary Schools. Material investments during Hardy's administration increased from $250,000 to $1,000,000.

In 1934 the name of the institution was changed to Mary Hardin–Baylor College in honor of Mrs. Mary Hardin, who with her husband, John G. Hardin of Burkburnett, set up a $900,000 trust fund, from which Mary Hardin–Baylor received one fourth of the income. Gordon G. Singleton served as president from 1937–52, when Albert C. Gettys was called from retirement to serve as acting president until Arthur K. Tyson assumed the presidency in Sept., 1954.

Under Tyson's administration a $500,000 campaign, begun in 1953, was completed; and trustees voted in Feb., 1956, to launch a $1,000,000 drive to meet the growth and development of the school in its present needs. A $250,000 gymnasium to be known as the Goodman Building, commemorating a grant of M. T. Goodman, Port Isabel, in 1954, will be completed this year (1956). A new building to house the college library of 34,094 volumes is planned for the immediate future. The college endowment fund reached $2,095,801.09 in 1955.

The first woman missionary to Brazil, Annie Luther Bagby (*q.v.*), was a graduate of the college at Independence in 1879. Fannie Breedlove Davis, former student at Independence, was the organizer and first president of Texas Woman's Missionary Union and a member of the committee which organized the Southwide Woman's Missionary Union. One of the early Baptist student unions in Texas was organized at Mary Hardin–Baylor, Oct. 8, 1920. In addition to hundreds of ministers' wives, missionaries, and Baptist laywomen, Mary Hardin–Baylor can add other "firsts" from her former students and graduates, including Oveta Culp Hobby, director of the first Women's Army Auxiliary Corps and Women's Army Corps and second woman to be appointed to the cabinet of the President of the United States; and Mary McClellan O'Hair, the first woman appointed to Board of Regents of the University of Texas. Many others of the 35,000 graduates and former students have proved that Mary Hardin–Baylor "daughters may be as cornerstones polished after the similitude of a palace," as inscribed on the cornerstone of Wilson Administration Building.

BIBLIOGRAPHY: D. L. Gingrich, *By Their Fruits Ye Shall Know Them* (1944). E. M. Townsend, ed., *After Seventy-five Years* (1920). FAIR BROWN

MARY P. WILLINGHAM SCHOOL FOR GIRLS. Founded by the Georgia Baptist Woman's Missionary Union in 1915 at Blue Ridge, Ga., in connection with the Georgia Baptist Assembly. The Georgia Baptist Convention had authorized the school in 1908. A member of the Mercer system, the school closed in 1930.

ARTHUR JACKSON

MARY SHARP COLLEGE. A school at Winchester, Tenn., chartered in 1848 as Tennessee Female Institute. It opened in 1850 with Zuinglius Calvin Graves as president, eight instructors, and 110 students. The property was valued at $16,000. Graves continued for 40 years as president.

The annual catalog of 1893 lists a preparatory department and a collegiate department. The collegiate department had its curriculum divided into eight schools—philosophy, English, history, mathematics, natural sciences, ancient and modern languages, art, and music. Mary Sharp College claimed to be the oldest college for women in America where Latin and Greek were required for graduation. Though thought by some "extravagant," it enjoyed a wide and favorable reputation and by 1861 was enrolling over 300 students from 12 states. Graves maintained a high scholastic standing for the institution, which was almost unique among women's schools in America.

In 1889 John L. Johnson succeeded Graves as president. O. M. Sutton served as president from 1891 to 1892, when the school was forced to close because of inadequate support. Graves returned and reopened the college in 1893, but by June, 1896, the school had ceased to exist because of the financial stringency of the times.

HARLEY FITE

MARY WASHINGTON FEMALE COLLEGE. Established at Pontotoc, Miss., and chartered in 1852 by Aberdeen, Chickasaw, Choctaw, and Columbus associations. With William L. Slack principal, the school had an enrolment of 94 in 1854 but closed four years later. J. L. BOYD

MARYLAND, BAPTIST HOME OF (FOR AGED). An institution located at 1615 Park Ave., Baltimore, Md., that provides for aged persons a comfortable residence with board, clothing, and medical care. Willoughby M. McCormick and other benevolent-minded Baptists on Nov. 17, 1915, formed a corporation and on July 25, 1916, elected a board of trustees for the establishment of a home for the aged. The home, originally located at 2301 N. Charles St., opened Sept. 1, 1917, with five guests. Others became interested in this first benevolent institution among Maryland Baptists and joined the corporation by paying an annual membership fee of $5 or $200 for life membership. At the present time (1956) the Maryland Baptist Convention elects the members of the corporation from among the churches that contribute specified amounts to the Cooperative Program. The corporation elects the trustees, who regulate and administer the affairs of the home. This institution now occupies two buildings, which accommodate 21 guests and are valued at $93,000. It operates on an annual budget of approximately $23,000. The home's $509,000 endowment in 1955 produced an income of $24,500, while contributions from the Cooperative Program reached a total of $5,500. The institution supplies complete facilities for its guests, including clothing, spending money, medical service, and burial. WILLIAM PITT

MARYLAND ASSOCIATIONS.

BALTIMORE. Organized 1929, and composed of those Baptist churches situated within the area of greater Baltimore. The first moderator was Russell Bradley Jones; the recording secretary, Benjamin F. Richards; and the treasurer, W. T. Hall. In 1954, 39 churches and 7 missions reported 980 baptisms, 16,142 members, $1,172,205 total gifts, $187,206 mission gifts, and $5,032,550 property value.

BLUE RIDGE. Organized May 20, 1954, at Weverton Church, Knoxville, by messengers from five churches in Frederick and Washington counties. Formerly part of the Seneca Baptist Association of Maryland, this association was formed of churches having a total membership of 2,473. In 1954 eight churches reported 170 baptisms, 2,545 members, $143,337 total gifts, $26,126 mission gifts, $566,100 property value, and $27,688 church debt.

EASTERN. Organized 1871, and one of the first three district associations formed in Maryland. It was composed of all Baptist churches on the Eastern Shore of Maryland, plus a few of the Baltimore churches. Since 1929, when the Baltimore Association was organized, only Eastern Shore churches have composed the association. In 1954, 20 churches and 3 missions reported 372 baptisms, 3,856 members, $291,698 total gifts, $53,972 mission gifts, $1,221,828 property value, and $32,803 church debt.

NORTHERN. Organized June 7, 1934, at Oak Grove Church, with A. H. Goering as moderator. In 1954, 22 churches and 1 mission reported 469 baptisms, 4,026 members, $227,721 total gifts, $28,493 mission gifts, $701,595 property value, and $99,329 church debt.

SENECA. Organized in the First Baptist Church of Frederick on June 7, 1935, and composed of those churches in Washington, Frederick, and Montgomery counties which were formerly affiliated with Western District Association. The first regular meeting of the association was held at the First Baptist Church of Rockville, May 21–22, 1936. In 1954, 10 churches reported 476 baptisms, 2,524 members, $204,005 total gifts, $22,040 mission gifts, $645,000 property value, and $114,823 church debt.

SOUTHERN. Organized as result of unanimous action taken at a meeting of Middle District Association in 1933, and composed of Baptist churches in Anne Arundel, Charles, Prince George's, and Carroll counties. In 1954, 19 churches and 9 missions reported 714 baptisms, 5,425 members, $405,723 total gifts, $61,405 mission gifts, $1,358,200 property value, and $329,937 church debt.

WESTERN. Organized in 1871 with 12 churches, at Rockville, with S. R. White, moderator, and S. C. Jones, clerk. In 1954, 11 churches and 2 missions reported 169 baptisms, 2,710 members, $108,428 total gifts, $15,975 mission gifts, $576,500 property value, and $50,812 church debt. ELMER F. RUARK

MARYLAND BAPTIST, THE. A 16-page Baptist state paper. It was first published as the *Maryland Baptist Church Life* on Feb. 1, 1917, by a group of young people from the state B.Y.P.U. organization under the leadership of Kingman A. Handy, at that time Sunday school and B.Y.P.U. secretary for Maryland. Norman R. McVeigh was editor, and associated with him were J. Walter Gressitt and Irvin R. Gorman. It was a monthly, printed on high-grade paper, and priced at 50 cents a year. From the start no salaries were paid; all work was on a volunteer basis. By Apr., 1918, all of the staff were in war service. P. Roland Wagner was editor from Apr., 1918, to Mar. 1, 1919, when McVeigh returned. He was succeeded by John Kastandike in May, 1919, followed by Robert L. Bausum in June, 1920, and J. F. Apsey, Jr., in July, 1921. From Apr. 1, 1922, until the present time, Francis A. Davis has served as editor. From 1920 to 1933, the state mission board sent the paper free to all Baptists in Maryland (about 6,000 copies per year). The paper suspended from Feb., 1933, to June, 1933, due to the closing of the banks. When it resumed publication on Oct. 1, 1934, the name was changed to *Maryland Baptist.* It is now a 16-page paper with 10,432 subscriptions, most of which are on a church budget basis of 75 cents per year. Regular subscriptions are $1 per year. It is issued from the state office, Baptist Building, St. Paul and 23rd Streets, Baltimore 18, Md. FRANCIS A. DAVIS

MARYLAND BAPTIST SUMMER ASSEMBLY. Founded in 1918 at Braddock Heights,

Md., in connection with the second annual Western Maryland Educational Conference. William Carson Royal, pastor of the First Baptist Church, Frederick, Md., was the founder and the president until 1952. In 1921 the Maryland Baptist Union Association formally adopted the assembly as a statewide enterprise. Begun as a Chautauqua-type conference, it soon developed along lines of other state summer assemblies. Since 1948 the assembly has been held on the campus of Hood College, Frederick, Md.

ROBERT F. WOODWARD

MARYLAND BAPTIST UNION ASSOCIATION.

I. Baptist Beginnings. The history of Baptists in Maryland, prior to the organization of the Maryland Baptist Union Association in 1836, may be divided roughly into three periods: the colonial period (1634–1781), the period of growth and expansion (1782–1820), and the period of antimissionary controversy (1821–36). Cecil Calvert, second Lord Baltimore, was determined to establish a colony, not only as a refuge for persecuted Roman Catholics, but also as a place where the rights, franchises, and liberties of all Englishmen, and liberty of conscience should be secured and guaranteed. Three Roman Catholic priests sailed with the first colonists, although Catholics were greatly outnumbered by Protestants and by those who professed no religious convictions. In 1649 the colonial assembly, urged by the Lord Proprietor, passed an act of religious toleration, motivated by self-interest on the part of both Lord Baltimore and the colonists, and not so liberal as the religious freedom of Rhode Island, but still allowing a good measure of liberty. Only denying the doctrine of the Trinity and speaking against the virgin Mary were subject to penalty of the law. During this period a few churches were constituted, and missionary work was carried on. During the second period new churches sprang up with the growth of missionary societies, the formation of associations, the beginning of Sunday schools, and the foundation of a tract society which later became the Baptist Publication Society. In the third period came the rise of antimissionary sentiment leading to the Black Rock controversy, the division of the (Old) Baltimore Association, and the formation of the Maryland Baptist Union Association.

Early Baptist life.—When the first Baptist church was planted, Maryland was a Roman Catholic colony, but Baptists were not persecuted in the proper sense of the word. In 1742 Henry Sater (*q.v.*) invited itinerant Baptist preachers to conduct preaching services in his home on Chestnut Ridge, near Baltimore Towne. Some of these visiting preachers were George Eglesfield, from Pennsylvania, Paul Palmer (*q.v.*), who later ministered in North Carolina, Henry Loveall, and probably others. On Nov. 16, 1742, Sater deeded an acre of land to Henry Loveall, first pastor of the Chestnut Ridge congregation, for use as a church site, a church having been organized in Sater's home. There were 57 members in this Chestnut Ridge Church, later known as Sater's Baptist Church. In 1754 a church was organized by Benjamin Griffith and Peter Patterson Van Horn at Winter Run, afterward called Harford Church. Harford was received into the Philadelphia Association, Oct. 7, 1755, under the name of Baltimore and bears that name in the minutes until 1774. The name of the first pastor at Winter Run is unknown, but in 1756 John Davis, a Virginian, became its pastor. Davis, with the aid of Abraham Butler, was instrumental in the founding of First Baptist Church, Baltimore, in 1785, and the churches at Taneytown, Gunpowder, and probably Frederick Town, also. In 1773 some Baptist laymen, Messrs. Griffith, Shields, Lemmon, Presstman, McKim, and Cox, purchased a lot and erected a church structure where the Shot Tower now stands. It was here, in 1782, that John Davis, pastor of Harford Church, assisted in the organization of First Baptist Church, Baltimore.

The origin of Second Baptist Church, Baltimore, is somewhat unique. John Healey emigrated to Baltimore from Leicister, England, bringing with him his wife and 17 others. Meeting first in a sail loft on Fells Point, they afterward removed to another location and were constituted as a Baptist church in 1797, with John Healey as pastor.

Forming of associations.—The first meeting of the Baltimore Baptist Association was held at Frederick Town, Aug. 10–12, 1793, with messengers present from six churches: Harford, Frederick, Hammond's Branch, Taneytown, Seneca, and Huntington, Pa. Elijah Baker and Phillip Hughes began preaching on the eastern shore of the Chesapeake in 1776. In 1782, when, due to their missionary and evangelistic zeal, a number of churches had been organized on "the shore," the Salisbury Association was formed on the eastern shore of Maryland and Virginia. This association continued thus until 1808 when the Virginia churches were dismissed to form the Accomac Association of Virginia. In the years following, churches were planted at Nanjemoy, Rockville, Good Hope, Pikesville, and on High Street in Baltimore.

Tract societies and Sunday schools.—Some of the most zealous advocates of missions sprang from Maryland churches. Among these was Noah Davis, of Salisbury, the real founder of the American Baptist Pulication Society, which began its organized life in Washington, D. C., Feb. 25, 1824. With Davis as its first president, it was known at its inception as the Baptist General Tract Society. At the solicitation of Davis, the tract society was moved from Washington to Philadelphia in Dec., 1826. Baptists were the first to organize Sunday schools in Maryland, beginning with the one organized in Second Baptist Church, Baltimore, July 17, 1797. This was distinctly a Bible school served by voluntary teachers who gave religious instruction only. This school was not only the first Sunday Bible school on the American continent, but it was the first to introduce volunteer teachers in the Sunday school.

The antimissionary controversy.—The minutes of the (Old) Baltimore Association show that the association, from 1793 to 1835, was favorable to the missionary enterprise. In 1818 resolutions were passed favoring the Baptist Board of Foreign Missions (Triennial Convention). In 1794 there were 23 churches, numbering 1,200 to 1,400 members, co-operating with the Baltimore and Salisbury associations. Antimissionary sentiment began creeping into both associations in the 1820's, but it was in the Baltimore Association that the controversy raged at white heat in the 1830's. In 1832, following the annual association meeting, the messengers came together in special meeting to consider the evils of missionary, Bible, and tract societies, Sunday schools, and other "inventions of men." On May 12, 1836, the Baltimore Baptist Association met at Black Rock Church, in Baltimore County, attended by only 28 persons, seven of whom were not properly authorized messengers, and the one elected as moderator was not a member of the body. The antimissionary members forced the adoption of a resolution that issued in division. The messengers of seven churches withdrew, viz., Rockville, Pleasant Valley, Linganore, Second of Baltimore, Mt. Zion, and Frederick. Gunpowder later joined the delegations which met in Second Baptist Church, Baltimore, to form another association. They adopted the old name, Baltimore Baptist Association, which resulted in two associations, holding the same name but differing in their attitude toward missions and evangelism. These held together for but a brief period, being too weak to last long. The Second Church, Baltimore, and the Gunpowder and Rockville churches, uniting with several churches from Washington, D. C., joined the Maryland Baptist Union, which was organized about the same time. The schism caused by the antimissionary sentiment was fatal to many of the churches in Maryland. LAURENCE A. FREE

II. History of Union Association. *Organization.*—The fervor of opposition to the antimissionary, antitract, anti-Sunday school, anti-Bible society, etc., views held by a small group of Old School Baptists served to weld more firmly together those who formed and organized the Maryland Baptist Union Association in 1836. This association included the state of Maryland and that part of the District of Columbia situated north of the Potomac River. Sixteen persons were present, representing six churches, at the first meeting of the new association, held in the First Baptist Church, Baltimore, on Oct. 27, 1836. The first officers were James Wilson, president; George F. Adams, corresponding secretary; William Crane, treasurer. Members of the first executive board, in addition to the officers named, were Thomas Leaman, Joseph Mettam, Peter Levering, James Carnighan, Thomas Mayberry, R. P. Anderson, and Jacob Correll.

The first circular letter was prepared and read by Stephen P. Hill. It served to lay the spiritual foundation and to set forth the Christian attitude of the new organization. In such a time there was great feeling and chagrin over the actions of the Baltimore Association, in making it impossible for the progressive churches to continue in its fellowship. For such a time Hill's words were remarkably temperate and constructive. He said, in part:

> The objects of the Association are not to wage war on any existing body; nor it is [*sic*] our object to associate for the purpose of discussing matters of faith or questions of discipline, or anything that engenders strife. Any questions about the propriety and expediency of measures we deem equally irrelevant. Positively we wish to combine our energies to do good. We are come kindly to improve the vantage ground of our geographical position, and to show an unbroken chain of communications throughout the Atlantic states; the promotion of brotherly love and devotional fervor. The means of accomplishing these objects are simple and obvious—and require only the warm heart and the open hand of charity to be rendered efficacious, the high motive of it all being to listen to the command and promises of God.

The minutes of 1837 show that Gunpowder Church joined the association. This brought the total number of churches to seven with a combined membership of 535, a gain of 51 members. The other churches were First, Baltimore; Taneytown; Nanjemoy; Second, Washington; Calvert Street, and Pikesville. They were the beginning of an aggressive and continuously missionary group.

In 1870 an effort was made to redistribute the churches of Maryland and the District of Columbia, looking toward making four district associations. The next year, there were reports and letters from three districts in Maryland. In 1872 a committee was proposed by resolution to "consider the desirability of dividing the Association." It would appear that the District of Columbia churches had not complied with the suggestion to organize a fourth district association.

Later, the District of Columbia churches were lettered out of the Maryland Baptist Union Association on their own request so that they could form the Columbia Association, under which the churches in that city have grown to large proportions. In 1878 five of the colored Baptist churches of the District of Columbia were still connected with the Maryland Association, but by 1880 they had connected themselves with the Columbia Association.

The Maryland Baptist Union Association was the only co-operative body until 1877, when the churches of the District of Columbia were lettered out to organize the Columbia Association. The co-operation of district associations with the Maryland Baptist Union Association and the Southern Baptist Convention is purely voluntary.

Constitution and bylaws.—Article III of the

constitution gives the requirements for membership as follows:

This Association shall be composed of members of regular Baptist churches only, in the following manner: any church of thirty members or less, that shall contribute to the funds of this body, shall be entitled to send two delegates, and for every additional thirty members, one additional delegate. Any missionary society, or individual, may have one such representative in this body, for every ten dollars they may annually contribute to its funds.

Article VIII pledges the association not to interfere with the internal affairs of the member churches and refers directly to Article II, in which the objects of the association are clearly defined:

. . . to advance the cause of true religion in Maryland, and that part of the District of Columbia north of the Potomac; by efforts to aid feeble churches, and supply destitute neighborhoods with preaching; to encourage the more general diffusion and reading of the sacred Scriptures, and evangelical books and tracts; to promote fraternal intercourse among the churches, and to afford opportunity, during the sessions, of preaching, exhortation, and other devotional exercises.

At the session in 1845, a constitutional change was proposed calling for a preamble stating the fundamental doctrines held by Baptists. However, at the next session, in 1846, it was resolved: "That in rejecting the declaration of faith in the proposed amendment to the constitution, the Association does not disavow the views therein stated, but we regard the adoption of such a declaration as foreign to the objects for which the Association was organized, as specified in Article II of the constitution." This action settled the matter in Maryland permanently.

In 1853, rather than enter into a local dispute, the association unanimously adopted a report recommending ". . . that the name of Bethel church be stricken from our list." Article VIII was adopted by the session of 1858, providing as follows: "But in case of any church violating the faith and order under which it was received into the body, the Association shall withdraw fellowship from that church." That provision still stands. The sessions of 1861 and 1862 proposed to amend the constitution by including in Article II the words "to promote foreign missions," this being the first time that definite attention to foreign missions was proposed constitutionally. No action was recorded as taken until 1872 on foreign missions and 1892 on home missions. In 1862 the constitution was amended to provide "that no missionary of the Board was to be elected a member thereof." That has been the practice ever since.

In 1879 in Baltimore, the constitution was amended to provide that the association be composed of regular Baptist churches in the state of Maryland. In explanation the association adopted the following resolution:

That in adopting the amendment to Article II of the constitution, limiting membership in the Association, to Baptists in the state of Maryland, we make not the slightest reflection on the character and standing of the colored churches in the District of Columbia; but as they are in a territory occupied by another association, we simply express our belief that it will be better for them, as well as ourselves, to be united in an association with which they can be more closely and actively identified; and we hereby assure them of our cordial fellowship, and bid them Godspeed in all their efforts to extend the Redeemer's Kingdom.

From 1836 to 1894, the association had a standing committee on Negroes and reported its activities with and for them annually to the association. In 1894 the Lott Cary Convention was organized but remained organically related to the white Maryland association. In 1902 it merged with the Colored Baptist Convention to form the independent Cooperative Convention.

No executive of the state mission board has ever undertaken to exercise authority over the churches. He has, however, had great influence with the churches and with the Church Extension Society and has been quite helpful in assisting the churches in their decisions regarding the ministers they were considering calling to the charges within the state.

Institutions.—"Seldom, perhaps never, has the college had a more flourishing prospect of permanent usefulness and success" is the first of a vast number of references to the Columbian College (later called Columbian University; still later, George Washington University), in the reports to the association. From time to time, generous contributions were made to its endowment fund. In 1868 a report quoted:

A Methodist paper says, "Columbian College has checked in a great measure the proselytism of the Roman Catholic Church here (Washington). . . . Being the only Protestant institution of high grade, it has furnished teachers for our public schools, as well as private schools, and today, as in times past, every Protestant school in the district is controlled by members of Baptist churches."

The first reference to the Southern Baptist Theological Seminary is found in records of 1860, when a resolution was adopted: "That we highly approve the Baptist Theological Seminary, at Greenville, S. C., and commend it to the attention and liberality of our churches."

A Chinese Sunday school, the only Chinese work conducted in Maryland by the association, was recorded as being conducted at the Eutaw Place Church, Baltimore, by Mrs. William Clark and other Baptist women; James Pollard was superintendent. Miss Minnie Hoffman, reporting on the school in 1908, said: "Dr. Willingham informs us that while he was visiting in China he learned of an aged father and his family who had been brought to Christ through the Christian influence of a son who is a scholar in our school. Three of the scholars have returned from China to the school. . . ."

The University of Richmond, while located in Virginia, is a beneficiary of the Maryland Baptists in a large way. Maryland Hall, opened in 1933, is one of several projects of Maryland Baptists. Reports from the university expressed gratitude for the co-operation and gifts of Maryland Baptists. Said President Modlin in 1947: "Maryland Baptists have supported the University of Richmond as their own institution, and the University has looked upon Maryland as part of its denominational constituency."

The Maryland Baptist Children's Aid Society, organized in 1920 as the Baptist Children's Home of Maryland, was able to care for only 9 children in 1921, while in 1922 there were 35 under its care. In 1939 there were 70 children receiving aid from the society, and, as late as 1952, there were 66 being cared for by the society.

The Baptist Home of Maryland, Inc., had 5 guests when it opened its doors in 1917 and in 1933 was caring for 19. *The Evening Sun* of Baltimore commended the Baptists for this work in an editorial.

Co-operation with the Southern Baptist Convention.—In Apr., 1841, the General Missionary Convention of the Baptist Denomination in the United States of America for Foreign Missions (Triennial Convention) met in the First Baptist Meeting House, Baltimore. It was the last of the national conventions to meet in the South, since 1845 saw the organization of the Southern Baptist Convention. From that time on, the Maryland association has co-operated in every way possible with the Southern Baptist Convention. Special collections for home missions and foreign missions have been taken and have proved very helpful. During the Civil War, when the Foreign Mission Board was cut off from its mission fields, the contributions of Maryland Baptists saved the work from total extinction.

Austin Crouch, long-time executive secretary of the Convention's Executive Committee, commended "the excellent record of Maryland Baptists," whose per capita gifts for all purposes averaged $14.53, as compared with the average for all Southern Baptists in the entire Convention territory of $5.75. "The average per capita gifts of all Southern Baptists to missions and other benevolences was 99⅖¢, while in Maryland the per capita was $2.54." The Maryland state mission board also agreed in 1934 that Convention wide funds should be sent to Nashville for allocation according to the percentages agreed upon by the Southern Baptist Convention. This became the consistent practice of the association.

Missionary outreach.—In 1934 the report of the state mission board said in its introduction:

> We have grown from 6 churches in 1836 with 478 members to 100 churches, with a net membership of 19,238. Four other churches are affiliated with the Columbia Association, although in Maryland, and one church cooperates with a Pennsylvania Association. It should also be borne in mind that our colored brethren during the past fifty years registered a marvelous growth numbering now at least 80,000 in 125 churches, so that the Baptists of Maryland now occupy fourth place as to membership among the evangelical denominations.

In 1851 N. C. Collins of Wheeling, W. Va., was employed by the board as a missionary to the Negroes of Maryland. In his report he stated: "The field is very destitute and very difficult to cultivate, owing principally to the strong prejudice against the Baptists, and in many cases against vital piety." The First Baptist Church (Negro) was constituted in 1836 with 10 members, under the pastoral care of Moses Clayton who came from Virginia. Prior to this the few Negro Baptists in Baltimore held their membership in the white churches.

The Russian work on Spring Street in Baltimore reported through the board that "one brother, baptized here, has himself baptized 1,325 persons since his return to Poland, and three others, baptized here, have baptized more than 1,500 persons since their return to Poland." Said the report: "The Board is therefore doing foreign mission work through Brother Diachenko and his helpers." Thus the Maryland association demonstrated the extent of its missionary mindedness. GEORGE E. THEISZ

III. Program of Work of Maryland Baptists. *State mission board.*—The administrative board of the Maryland Baptist Union Association is called the state mission board. It is composed of 89 members, 36 from the Baltimore Association, six from each of the other six district associations in the state, 12 appointed by the president of the Maryland Baptist Union Association, and five appointed by the president of the state mission board, if he so desires. The term of office of the appointees is one year. The other members are elected by the Maryland Baptist Union Association for terms of three years so arranged that about one third of the terms expire each year. Employees or missionaries of the state mission board are ineligible to serve on the board. The state body grants to this board full powers to collect and disburse all funds, to employ missionaries and agents, to accomplish the purposes of the association, and to supervise the total program of work in the interim of annual sessions. The board reports to the association annually. Meetings of the state board are held four times a year, or more often as the president of the board may direct. Fifteen members constitute a quorum. The board elects its own president and recording secretary. There are regularly two committees appointed by the president, the investments committee and the advisory committee. The latter consists of 12 members with all district associations represented. The advisory committee elects its own chairman. To this committee broad powers are given by the board, including the authority to act for the board between its sessions. Usually, the advisory committee functions through recommendations of the board. The state mission board elects a general secretary and any other persons as the needs of the state work may require, including a treasurer.

The general secretary is elected annually by the state mission board at its meeting in December and is the chief executive officer for the program of work in the state. He is charged with the promotion, administration, and supervision of all state mission activities, serving specifically as superintendent of missions and evangelism. He is also responsible for editing the state paper, *The Maryland Baptist*. He approves all bills of the state mission board and countersigns all checks drawn by the treasurer. Clifton C. Thomas, the present general secretary of the state mission board of the Maryland Baptist Union Association, came to the office on Apr. 1, 1949.

Missions.—The state mission program is carried on through the district associations by agents of the state mission board and through direct work of the Home Mission Board of the Southern Baptist Convention. In 1955 the salaries of 31 pastors were supplemented by the state board in the amount of $21,419.93. Two district associational missionaries are employed with their expenses and salaries shared by the district association, the state board, and the Home Mission Board. Work among migrants on the eastern shore is conducted each summer by missionaries of the Home Mission Board, usually for a period of about 10 weeks. Churches in Baltimore sponsor a ministry to the special needs of minority and language groups. The Baltimore Baptist Church Extension Society of Maryland operates throughout the state in aid of churches needing funds for expansion. The society is chartered separately, elects its own trustees, but receives money from the state mission board and regularly reports to the association in its annual session. The program of evangelism is administered by the general secretary and is promoted through conferences on the district association level and an annual conference of three days' duration on a state basis.

In 1955 there were seven associations in the state, which reported a total of 136 churches and 30 missions. Total church membership was 40,922; total baptisms were 3,202; total contributions to all causes were $2,338,358, and to the Cooperative Program, $256,390. The state mission budget for 1955–56 was $166,188.

Educational ministry.—Sunday school, Training Union, Baptist Student Union, and Vacation Bible school activities are within the Department of Religious Education of the state mission board. L. J. Newton has been secretary of this department since Sept., 1951. In early 1955 he was given an assistant, Jimmie J. Hartfield, who has special responsibilities for Training Union work. In 1955 the Sunday school enrolment was 42,399, a net gain of 1,041 over the previous year. There were 2,637 awards. The Training Union enrolment in 1955 was 9,582, a net gain of 1,011 over the previous year. There were 4,122 awards. During 1955 a Baptist Student Union was organized at Towson State Teachers College, and a city-wide union was formed for college students in Baltimore. Organization was completed for the Baptist Student Union at Western Maryland College, and plans were begun for a union at Frostburg State Teachers College. Vacation Bible school in the summer of 1955 enrolled 17,462 in 140 schools. Woman's Missionary Union of Maryland, an auxiliary to the Maryland Baptist Union Association, reported in 1955 a total of 516 organizations, including children's groups, in 133 churches throughout the state. Josephine Norwood, the executive secretary, came to that office in 1954. Erleen Gaskin was elected secretary of youth work in 1955.

Institutes for pastors are conducted twice a year, at the time of the annual meeting of the association and at the summer assembly of the association. These programs are under the auspices of the Maryland Baptist Pastors' Conference with the co-operation of the general secretary of the state mission board. The summer assembly of Maryland Baptists is held each July for one week at Hood College in Frederick, Md. The programs are designed to offer guidance in every aspect of the work in a Baptist church. Specialists in the various fields are brought from every area of the nation. The first secretary of the Baptist Brotherhood of Maryland, J. Allen Beck, was elected by the state mission board in 1955 to undertake the work Jan. 1, 1956, along with assisting the general secretary in business affairs. Previously, the Brotherhood activities had been promoted by a committee of the association. In 1955, 1,804 men were enrolled in 67 organizations. Radio and television promotion is assigned to a committee of the association which encourages the use of these media in the proclamation of the gospel, assists in arrangements with stations, and cooperates with the Radio and Television Commission of the Southern Baptist Convention in securing outlets for "The Baptist Hour" and other productions of this organization. The state mission board published in Apr., 1953, *The Rise and Progress of Maryland Baptists*, by Joseph T. Watts, general secretary emeritus.

Institutions.—The office of the state mission board and those of related organizations are in the Baptist Building, 100 E. 73rd Street, Baltimore, purchased by the board in 1952 at a cost of $60,000. The care of children deprived of home and parents is vested in the Baptist Children's Aid Society, which has a separate charter and board. The society receives funds from the state mission board, works closely with its officers, and reports regularly to the association. In 1955 the society worked with 93 children, representing 29 families. Ministerial relief is administered in co-operation with the Relief and Annuity Board of the Southern Baptist Convention. The endowment funds of the state mission board are administered by the investments committee of the board and expended as the board directs. In 1955 the endowment amounted to $274,609.00. In the year ending Sept. 30, 1955, the income was $13,831.03. The Baptist Home,

IV. MARYLAND STATISTICAL SUMMARY

Year	Associa-tions	Churches	Church Member-ship	Baptisms	S. S. Enrol-ment	V.B.S. Enrol-ment	T. U. Enrol-ment	W.M.U. Enrol-ment	Brother-hood En-rolment	Mission Gifts	Total Gifts	Value Church Property	State Capital Worth
1837	1	7	535	58	339	....	....	....	....	....	....	....	(Explanation:
1840	1	7	1,183	655	745	....	....	....	....	....	....	....	This column
1850	1	26	2,034	95	1,480	....	....	....	....	$ 1,014.58	....	....	includes total
1860	1	37	4,275	265	2,462	....	....	....	....	2,436.21	....	....	value of Schools,
1870	1	38	5,544	664	4,682	....	....	....	....	....	....	....	Children's Homes,
1880	1	45	5,130	393	5,045	....	....	....	....	8,607.00	$ 52,233.00	....	Hospitals,
1890	3	54	7,693	626	9,053	....	....	900	....	12,521.00	139,311.00	....	Foundation,
1900	3	59	10,408	584	9,823	....	....	....	....	16,465.00	102,368.00	$ 730,350.00	Buildings, etc.)
1905	3	59	10,534	457	11,158	....	....	....	....	21,542.00	149,459.00	836,100.00	....
1910	3	70	12,018	578	13,189	....	....	1,135	....	36,180.00	160,877.00	882,600.00	....
1915	3	78	13,697	1,385	16,467	....	....	....	....	39,627.00	188,403.00	255,600.00	....
1920	3	84	15,984	909	11,536	....	....	....	....	204,201.00	452,061.00	1,794,200.00	....
1925	3	95	17,884	890	18,238	....	....	....	....	103,005.00	456,085.00	2,829,000.00	....
1930	3	97	17,561	699	14,507	....	2,325	4,921	....	14,446.00	139,152.00	3,120,150.00	....
1931	4	88	18,012	839	17,062	....	2,301	4,586	....	5,445.00	28,870.00	1,973,700.00	Baptist Head-
1932	4	97	18,462	896	18,503	....	2,476	4,650	....	7,389.00	25,527.00	2,733,275.00	quarters in
1933	4	99	19,012	864	19,042	....	2,594	5,203	....	49,840.00	275,466.00	2,836,500.00	Maryland
1934	5	100	19,288	789	19,231	....	2,724	4,789	....	49,251.00	280,429.00	2,780,300.00	$80,000
1935	6	100	20,203	770	19,085	....	2,276	4,899	....	48,340.00	285,105.00	3,270,900.00	(Baptist Building)
1936	6	99	20,267	882	19,373	....	3,260	4,992	....	47,557.00	284,701.00	3,199,800.00	....
1937	6	99	20,689	817	19,753	....	2,917	5,063	....	49,793.00	219,211.00	3,217,425.00	....
1938	6	99	21,195	1,025	22,085	....	3,263	4,862	....	52,784.00	325,586.00	3,290,350.00	....
1939	6	97	21,012	1,084	21,497	....	3,489	4,899	....	50,991.00	314,962.00	3,143,235.00	....
1940	6	96	22,604	779	21,704	....	3,519	4,487	....	55,082.00	333,307.00	3,256,387.00	....
1941	6	96	23,085	738	22,497	....	3,501	4,383	....	60,121.00	355,758.00	3,290,950.00	....
1942	6	96	23,567	808	22,713	....	3,121	4,355	....	54,006.00	414,332.00	3,248,500.00	....
1943	6	96	24,272	749	22,904	....	2,792	4,140	....	65,579.00	518,494.00	3,323,918.00	....
1944	6	98	25,046	912	23,428	....	3,095	3,685	....	77,979.00	662,131.00	3,497,228.00	....
1945	6	102	26,102	1,264	23,591	....	3,316	4,565	....	86,556.00	650,882.00	3,642,500.00	....
1946	6	104	26,778	1,034	24,004	....	3,894	4,377	....	87,184.00	735,303.00	3,936,250.00	....
1947	6	104	27,367	1,132	24,532	....	4,138	4,552	....	93,370.00	790,657.00	3,917,750.00	....
1948	6	106	28,555	1,365	25,553	....	4,407	4,886	....	106,648.00	882,555.00	4,716,150.00	....
1949	6	107	29,235	1,263	25,553	8,800	4,432	5,461	158	104,854.00	1,057,910.00	5,392,570.00	....
1950	6	110	29,498	1,457	26,835	8,528	5,088	6,473	210	120,886.00	994,012.00	5,466,650.00	....
1951	6	114	31,020	1,733	29,023	9,228	5,425	6,821	415	144,079.00	1,199,957.00	6,241,450.00	....
1952	6	116	32,849	2,038	30,695	10,404	6,511	7,452	588	162,448.00	1,344,970.00	7,702,400.00	....
1953	6	118	34,771	2,108	33,754	11,894	7,077	7,397	745	178,444.00	1,516,693.00	6,837,700.00	....
1954	6	127	37,201	2,242	41,358	14,638	8,571	7,494	1,063	332,078.00	2,597,177.00	9,165,327.00	....

MRS. ETHEL AIREY

located at 1615 Park Avenue, is maintained for the care of aged Baptist women of the state. It has a capacity of 21. Its supervision is vested in a separate board of directors under its own charter. The board of directors of the home reports to the association at its annual meeting. The Woman's Missionary Union of Maryland owns and operates Camp Wo-Me-To at Rocks, Md., consisting of 150 acres valued at $200,000 (with improvements). The state mission board in 1955 erected and provided the funds for the Baylor-Watts Chapel and Educational Building, costing $30,000, named in honor of two former general secretaries of the board.

Promotional work.—The state paper, entitled *The Maryland Baptist,* supported by the state mission board, had a circulation in 1955 of 10,-432. It was sent by 84 churches to each family in their membership. The contents of *The Maryland Baptist,* as well as the contents of other promotional literature, is under the supervision of the general secretary.

Co-operative work.—The Maryland Baptist Union Association maintains a co-operative relationship with the American Bible Society and transmits to that organization funds received through the churches and designated to that work. The program of social work of the association is assigned to a committee called the Christian Life Commission. LAURENCE A. FREE

BIBLIOGRAPHY: T. Armitage, *A History of the Baptists* (*c.* 1886). D. Benedict, *A General History of the Baptist Denomination* (1813). J. H. Jones, *A History of the Baltimore Baptist Association* (1872). I. W. Maclay, *Henry Sater* (1897). Maryland Historical Society, *Proceedings and Acts of the General Assembly of Maryland, Jan. 1637/8–Sept. 1664* (1883). R. B. Semple, *Rise and Progress of Virginia Baptists* (1894). H. C. Vedder, *History of the Baptists in the Middle States* (1898). J. T. Watts, *The Rise and Progress of Maryland Baptists* (1953). J. F. Weishample, Jr., ed., *History of the Baptist Churches in Maryland* (*c.* 1885).

MARYLAND ENDOWMENT FUND. This fund amounts to approximately $400,000 at current prices. The Mercantile-Safe Deposit Company of Baltimore is custodian of the fund and collects all income and remits to the state board monthly. A committee of three appointed by the state association supervises all investments. For the fiscal year ending Sept. 30, 1956, the income was $16,496.06, which was divided according to the terms of the donors as follows:

State Board	$10,527.86
Ministers' Education	1,126.36
Building and Loan Fund	77.35
Baptist Home	843.14
Baptist Childrens Aid Society	512.70
Church Extension Society	2,385.34
Foreign Mission Board	553.35
Home Mission Board	469.96

FRANCIS A. DAVIS

MASS AND TRANSUBSTANTIATION. The Code of Canon Law of the Roman Catholic Church describes the sacrament of the Holy Eucharist as a rite in which "Christ the Lord Himself is contained, offered, and received under the species of bread and wine." James J. Graham, a Roman Catholic theologian, says, "Insofar as Christ is *contained* and *received* in the Eucharist," what is involved is "holy communion"; and, "insofar as Christ is *offered* in the Eucharist," what occurs is "the sacrifice of the mass." The term "eucharist" is derived from the Greek *eu;* meaning "good," and *charis,* meaning "thanks." The historical reason for this designation is that Christ offered a prayer of thanks when he instituted the rite (Luke 22:19); the practical reason is that it "affords a *good thanksgiving* for benefits received." The sacrament of the Holy Eucharist differs from the other sacraments in that it is not only a channel of grace but is considered to contain Christ, the giver of grace, and in that it exists not merely at the moment of reception but also "before and after reception as long as the appearances remain intact."

The alleged change in the bread and wine, called transubstantiation, became a dogma in 1215 at the Fourth Lateran Council, which decreed that "the bread [is] . . . transubstantiated into the body and the wine into the blood by the power of God. . . ." The "substance" (*substantia*) of the elements—what makes them really what they are—becomes the substance of the body and blood of Christ when the priest pronounces the words spoken by Jesus, "This is my body," "This is my blood." The "accidents" (*accidentia*) of the elements—their sensory qualities, sometimes called "appearances"—undergo no change. The word "transubstantiation" is derived from the Latin *trans,* meaning "across," and *substantia,* meaning "substance." The reason this word is used is because it means literally "a going over from one substance to another." Transubstantiation describes the change in the substance believed to transpire during the observance of the sacrament so that the "real presence of Christ's body and blood, His soul and divinity," is realized on the altar, and the "mass" is an "unbloody sacrifice" of Christ repeated at each celebration of the rite. However, the "mass" includes the consecration and communion as well as the offering of what is consecrated, "since all three have a more or less direct contact with sacrifice." Charles G. Herzog, a Roman Catholic apologist, holds that "the sacrifice takes place in the act of consecrating the body and blood of Christ."

The name "mass" probably comes from the Latin *missio,* meaning "sending," and *dismissio,* meaning "dismissal." These words were used in dismissing the catacumens before the celebration of the Eucharist—a practice no longer followed—and in releasing the "faithful" after the completion of the rite. This latter dismissal is still made with the words, *"Ite, missa est"* (Go, it is the dismissal).

According to most Roman Catholic theologians, participation in the mass does not free one from the guilt of sin—this comes through the sacrament of penance—but does remit the penalty of sin remaining after absolution in proportion to the devotion of the participant. Thus the mass is an act of satisfaction received by God as compensation for the penalty of sin remaining after confession. It also increases grace in the soul and strengthens against temptation. The mass "is rightly offered . . . not only for . . . the faithful living but also for the dead in Christ whose purification is not yet accomplished" in purgatory.

BIBLIOGRAPHY: H. Bettenson, ed., *Documents of the Christian Church* (1947), especially pp. 209–213. H. Denzinger, ed., *Enchiridion symbolorum, definitionum et declarationum, etc.* (1922), especially section on Council of Trent. L. Duchesne, *Christian Worship: Its Origin and Evolution,* translated by M. L. McClure (1903). A. Fortesque, "Liturgy of the Mass," *The Catholic Encyclopedia,* ed. by C. G. Herbermann *et. al.* (1913), Vol. IX. J. J. Graham, *Faith for Life* (1939), Chapters XXII–XXIII. C. G. Herzog, *Channels of Redemption* (1931), Chapters IV–V. J. D. Mansi, ed., *Sacrorum Conciliorum Nova et amplessima collectio* (1759). J. Pohle, "Eucharist," *The Catholic Encyclopedia,* ed. by C. G. Herbermann *et al.* (1913), Vol. V. S. I. Stuber, *Primer on Roman Catholicism for Protestants* (1953).

C. PENROSE ST. AMANT

MASS EVANGELISM. See EVANGELISM.

MASTERS, VICTOR IRVINE, SR. (b. Anderson County, S. C., Mar. 4, 1867; d. Avon Park, near De Soto City, Fla., June 30, 1954). Minister and writer with a prolific output. A son of Priestly A. and Martha Amelia (Burris) Masters, he grew up in Anderson, S. C. He received from Furman University the A.B. degree in 1888, the A.M. degree the following year, and an honorary D.D. degree in 1913. The Southern Baptist Theological Seminary conferred on him a Th.M. degree in 1893. He was ordained to the Baptist ministry by Yorkshire (S. C.) Church in 1889. During 1890–94 he was pastor of churches in Rock Hill and Yorkshire, S. C., and Pocahontas, Va., 1894–96. He was associate editor of *The Baptist Courier,* Greenville, S. C., from 1896 to 1905. He was editor and owner of *The Baptist Press,* South Carolina, 1905–07; and associate editor of the *Religious Herald,* Richmond, Va., 1905–07. During 1909–21 the Home Mission Board, Atlanta, Ga., employed him as its superintendent of publicity. His duties included editing *The Home Field,* 1909–17, and writing books on home missions, as well as pamphlets and articles and stories for the denominational press. In 1921 he became editor of *The Western Recorder* and continued until his retirement Oct. 1, 1942. He married Lois Eunice Wickliffe, Anderson, S. C., July 19, 1893, and they had two sons, William Wickliffe and Victor Irvine, Jr. Masters was author of: *The Home Mission Task* (1912), *Baptist Home Missions* (1914), *Baptist Missions in the South* (1915), *Country Church in the South* (1916), *Call of the South* (1918), and *Making America Christian* (1921). He edited *Re-Thinking Baptist Doctrines* (1937). LEO T. CRISMON

MAT SERVICE, SOUTHERN BAPTIST CONVENTION. A service owned and operated by the Executive Committee for distributing publicity printing mats to churches, established in 1947 under the leadership of Duke K. McCall and C. E. Bryant. In 1955 the Stencil Service was added, in which the same material furnished in mat form was provided through die-impressed stencils. In 1956, 300 churches used the mat service, and 500 churches used the stencil service. Mailing address is S.B.C. Mat Service, 127 Ninth Avenue, North, Nashville, Tenn.

ALBERT MC CLELLAN

MATERIALISM. Originally the affirmation that matter alone is real and that the universe, and even man with his religious consciousness and moral idealisms, are the results of an accidental collocation of material atoms. The new scientific emphasis on physical energy, which may take the form of matter or radiation, has led to a revision of this materialistic creed. This revision has actually outmoded materialism, and many physicists have moved to a more spiritual philosophy.

In practice, materialism is almost the same as secularism—a concern for material things as the chief ends of human existence. In theory, materialism is found in two guises. The first guise is that of naturalism which calls us to concentrate on what can be observed by the methods of science and to avoid any speculation as to what may lie beyond. In the hands of Herbert Spencer, this meant agnosticism as far as ultimate reality is concerned. Dewey regarded human experience as the upper limit for our understanding of reality and preached a practical naturalism, which concentrated upon adjusting man to his natural environment and avoided all efforts to speculate upon the existence, if any, and nature of a spiritual order. He held that man's values were grounded in nature and concerned with his adjustment to nature. The idea of a spiritual order was eliminated from practical consideration and theoretical speculation. The higher was explained in terms of the lower. This point of view is prominent in our educational system.

A much more significant development of materialism lies in communism, which emphasizes materialism from the dynamic aspect. So far as the natural order is concerned, physical energy is the all-embracing and determinate ground. Life and mind are simply higher organizations which have emerged in the process of evolution, and the key to their understanding lies in these higher organizations of which energy is capable and not in any spiritual order which creates, sustains, and directs the process. At the human level man's ethical ideals and religious aspirations are grounded in this material process and not in any spiritual order. They are economically determined and arise out of man's economic needs and hungers. Freedom fundamentally means the urge for economic freedom, and religion is an escape mechanism by which men seek to compensate for material bondage and oppression by postulating a spiritual order in which such bondage does not exist.

BIBLIOGRAPHY: J. Bennett, *Christianity and Communism* (1948). F. A. Lange, *History of Materialism* (1950). E. C. RUST

MATHIAS, JOSEPH DODGE (b. Morganfield, Ky., Aug. 10, 1869, d. Los Angeles, Calif., Nov. 30, 1935). Children's home superintendent, Illinois Baptist leader. His mother died when he was only one year old, and his father deserted him when he was four. Mathias joined Mt. Olive Baptist Church in Union County, Ky., when he was 19. He married Cecelia Matilda Klein, Apr. 8, 1891, at Spring Grove, Ky. In 1919, while living in Broughton, Ill., Mathias was appointed to visit churches and individuals to raise money for the new administration building at Carmi Baptist Orphanage. At a meeting of the benevolence committee of the Illinois Baptist State Association held in West Frankfort Nov. 3, 1920, he was made assistant superintendent and farm manager of the Carmi Children's Home. When G. W. Danbury (*q.v.*) retired as superintendent of the orphanage in 1920, Mathias was elected to succeed him. He served in this capacity until Nov. 30, 1935, at which time he took a 90-day leave of absence due to ill health. He died during his absence, however, and his body was returned to Carmi and buried in Maple Ridge Cemetery. Chairman of the board of trustees for the Carmi Township High School for three years and chairman of the Fairfield Baptist Association for 22 years, Mathias was for a long time a member of the board of directors of the state association. ARCHIE E. BROWN

MATTHEWS, CHARLES EVERETT (b. Gasconade County, Mo., Mar. 23, 1887; d. Marshall, Tex., Oct. 5, 1956). Businessman, pastor, evangelist, denominational leader, and author. Orphaned by his father's death when he was 11 months old and his mother's death when he was 16 years old, Matthews attended rural schools and Tipton High School in Missouri and was graduated from Hill's Business College in St. Louis. For 15 years he was employed by Simmons Hardware Co. and Swift and Co. Converted at the age of 27 in the First Baptist Church of Fort Worth, Tex., Matthews later served that church as financial secretary and educational director. Ordained to the ministry on Sept. 28, 1921, at the age of 34, he served as pastor of Birdville and Hurst Baptist churches one year each and Travis Avenue Baptist Church, Fort Worth, 1922–46. During this last pastorate the membership of the church increased from 200 to 6,034.

Matthews received his theological education at Southwestern Baptist Seminary, where he studied for three semesters. Later he served as a trustee of that institution for 16 years, serving 10 years as vice-president of the board and two years as president. In 1947 he was awarded the LL.D. degree by Baylor University. For one year Matthews served as secretary of evangelism for Texas Baptists and for nine years as secretary of evangelism of the Home Mission Board of the Southern Baptist Convention. In addition to his work in conducting revivals, Matthews promoted the election of a secretary of evangelism in all state conventions, the election of a chairman of evangelism in each association, and the plan for annual associational simultaneous revivals. He was the author of several books, including *Life's Supreme Decision* (1941), *The Southern Baptist Program of Evangelism* (1949), *Every Christian's Job* (1951), and *A Church Revival* (1955). C. E. WILBANKS

MAXCY, JONATHAN (b. Attleborough, Mass., Sept. 2, 1768; d. Columbia, S. C., June 4, 1820). Preacher and college president. The son of Levi and Ruth (Newell) Maxcy, he attended Wrentham Academy and Rhode Island College (now Brown University), 1783–87. After becoming a Baptist in 1789, Maxcy was licensed to preach on Apr. 1, 1790, and was ordained on Sept. 8, 1791. He served as pastor of the First Baptist Church of Providence, R. I., 1791–92. Maxcy served Rhode Island College as a tutor and librarian (1787–91), professor of divinity (1791–1802), president *pro tempore* (1792–97), and president (1797–1802). Later he served as president of Union College, Schenectady, N. Y. (1802–04). Having been recommended by Richard Furman, Maxcy became the first president of South Carolina College, serving from 1805 until his death in 1820. He established the college on a sound footing, expanding the curriculum from that of a classical college to include chemistry, mineralogy, political economy, law, and natural philosophy. Charitable in religion, energetic, eloquent, and learned, Maxcy commanded respect and gave the college a tone of distinction. He stimulated among the students a love of practical Christian virtues and a hatred of bigotry. *Literary Remains of the Rev. Jonathan Maxcy, D.D.,* edited by Romeo Elton (1844), is a collection of sermons and lectures originally published as pamphlets.

BIBLIOGRAPHY: W. C. Bronson, *The History of Brown University* (1914). J. Daggett, *A Sketch of the History of Attleborough* (1894). R. Elton, ed., *The Literary Remains of the Rev. Jonathan Maxcy, D.D. . . . With a Memoir of His Life* (1844). E. L. Green, *A History of the University of South Carolina* (1916). R. Henry, *Eulogy on Jonathan Maxcy* (1822). J. C. Hungerpiller, "A Sketch of the Life and Character of Jonathan Maxcy, D.D.," *Bulletin of the University of South Carolina* (1917). M. LaBorde, *History of South Carolina College* (1859). S. C. Mitchell, "Jonathan Maxcy," *Dictionary of American Biography* (1933). W. B. Sprague, *Annals of the American Pulpit,* Vol. VI (1860). D. D. Wallace, *History of South Carolina,* Vol. III (1934). ALBERT NEELY SANDERS

MAYNARD ACADEMY. Founded in 1899 by Current River and State Line associations, co-sponsored by Ouachita College until 1911. The Arkansas Baptist State Mission Board operated it in 1915; then as a mission school, with aid of the Home Mission Board, from 1916 until it closed in 1927. The school had two buildings and an average enrolment of 77. H. D. MORTON

MAYSVILLE LITERARY INSTITUTE. A secondary school for girls, established by the Bracken Association of United Baptists in 1855 at Maysville, Ky., under the name Maysville Female Institute. The name was changed when boys were admitted in 1859. The female department was discontinued in 1872 when Miss Jane R. Parks, principal from its beginning, withdrew to form her own school. The institute was replaced by public schools in 1886.

GLYNN R. FORD

McCALL, MOSES NATHANAEL (b. Screven County, Ga., Dec. 15, 1874; d. Jacksonville, Fla., Mar. 8, 1947). Pastor, missionary. Born into a family of preachers, McCall was educated in Mercer University, Denison University, and the Southern Baptist Theological Seminary, and was awarded the D.D. degree by Mississippi College. After pastoral experience in Georgia, he went to Cuba in Feb., 1905, under the Home Mission Board of the Southern Baptist Convention. At that time internal dissension and war conditions had demoralized the results of two decades of Baptist work in Cuba. McCall found one church and two missions in Havana and one church in Piñar del Río, with a total of about 50 church members. Studying the language and the condition and needs, McCall laid long-range plans to develop in Cuba a self-governing, self-propagating Baptist denominational life. A seminary to train native pastors was begun in 1906. That same year, to foster fellowship among the churches, a convention was organized. Sunday schools were strengthened, and missionary unions and Brotherhoods were organized for the women and men. A denominational paper was established and, ultimately, provision was made to care for orphans and the aged. As a result of McCall's service, a well-organized denomination was developed. The Convention of Western Cuba has foreign and home mission boards. Converts have migrated to various nations of Latin America, and some have gone to the mother land, Spain.

McCall's Christian character and his high standard for himself helped to establish a high standard for the church members in a land whose religion through four centuries had failed to develop a high level of Christian living. The Cuban government, recognizing his contribution to the well-being of the nation, conferred upon McCall, Mar. 28, 1945, the highest civilian honor one of her own citizens can receive—the Order of Carlos Manuel de Cespedes. At the time of his death in 1947, there were in Cuba 67 Baptist churches, 50 pastors, and 5,721 members.

BIBLIOGRAPHY: M. N. McCall, *Baptist Generation in Cuba* (1942). A. L. Munoz, *Apostol Bautista en la Perla Antillana* (1943). L. D. Newton, *Amazing Grace* (1948). W. W. BARNES

McCALL FOUNDATION. Established May 15, 1954, by the family of Lizette Kimbrough McCall in her honor. Income from the invested corpus of the foundation is to be used to promote world evangelism through lectures, sermons, and other special exercises for the entire student body of Southern Baptist Theological Seminary. Choice of speakers and the type of services used are decided upon by the president and the faculty of the seminary. H. Guy Moore delivered the inaugural series of foundation lectures Nov. 8–11, 1955. The initial gift to establish the foundation was $9,494.93, and additional gifts have been made by members of the family.

DUKE K. MCCALL

McCARTY, V. V. (d. Feb., 1886). Pioneer Indian Territory preacher, resided at Brokin, near Canadian, Indian Territory, 1881–83 and 1885; at Oklahoma, Indian Territory, 1886. He became the first moderator of Short Mountain Association organized Oct. 24, 1884, the oldest white Baptist association in Oklahoma with a continuous history. This body re-elected him moderator in 1885. McCarty and W. M. Holland organized an un-named Baptist church with 10 members in the western part of Sugar Loaf County, Indian Territory, in 1884. As pastor of the Canadian church, McCarty attended and reported statistics to the Choctaw-Chickasaw (Indian) Baptist Association up to the time of his death. Mormons harassed him at Briartown, but he prevailed over them. His death in 1886, caused by a fall from a wagon, which broke his back, ended a ministry in Indian Territory of about 10 years. HERBERT M. PIERCE

McCOLLUM, JOHN WILLIAM (b. Dallas County, Ala., June 5, 1864; d. Seattle, Wash., Jan. 23, 1910). Missionary to Japan. Graduate of Howard College in 1886 (A.B., 1886, D.D., 1901) and Southern Baptist Theological Seminary in 1889, McCollum married Dru Collins, Sept. 11, 1889. Appointed as missionary to Japan, May 3, 1889, he spent a year at Kobe, after which he was located at Osaka, 1891; Moji, 1893; and Fukuoka, 1895. To the Japanese slogan "Japan for the Japanese," he added, "but both Japan and the Japanese for Christ." McCollum was a teacher in the theological seminary insituted at Fukuoka in 1907 and was chosen by Japanese Baptists as one of the preachers at the National Exposition in Osaka during Baptist Week, part of an evangelistic campaign of 1902–03.

BIBLIOGRAPHY: W. T. Clark, *Outriders for the King* (1931). T. B. Ray, *Southern Baptist Foreign Missions* (1910).

E. C. ROUTH

McCOMBS, WILLIAM (b. near Ft. Gibson, Creek Nation, Indian Territory, July 22, 1844;

d. Eufaula, Okla., Jan. 30, 1930). Baptist preacher, Confederate soldier, language interpreter. His father was a white man and his mother one-half Creek. Educated in government schools, he was a proficient linguist skilled in the use of both English and Creek, which made him valuable as an interpreter while a soldier in the Confederate army during the Civil War. Later he served as interpreter for white missionaries and later in many tribal affairs, including personal interpreter six years for Pleasant Porter, governor of the Creek Nation. He was for 30 years moderator of the Creek Baptist Association, a tribal councilman, and interpreter and assistant to Henry Frieland Buckner (*q.v.*). Reared a Methodist, he united with the Baptist church in 1867. In many ways he impressed his influence on tribal politics, religion, and education. In 1865 he settled on a farm nine miles west of Eufaula, Okla., where he lived 65 years. GLEWNOOD BUZBEE

McCONNELL, FERNANDO COELLO (b. Clay County, N. C., Aug. 2, 1856; d. Atlanta, Ga., Jan. 12, 1929). Minister and denominational leader. Converted at 11, he united with Macedonia Baptist Church near Hiawassee, Ga., where his parents had located soon after his birth. He married Emma England and entered mercantile business at Mt. Airy, Ga. Although successful in business, he became convinced that he should enter the ministry. Selling his store, he entered the high school in Hayesville, N. C., and in 1880 he was ordained. The presbytery was composed of three mountain preachers of note, Alfred Corn, Elisha Hedden, and Elijah Kimsey. He entered the Southern Baptist Theological Seminary, where he studied under James Petigru Boyce (*q.v.*), John Albert Broadus (*q.v.*), Basil Manly, Jr. (*q.v.*), and William Williams (*q.v.*). Returning to Georgia, he served as a missionary in the mountain areas for two years. In 1884 he addressed the Georgia Baptist Convention so effectively that the leaders who heard him urged him to enter Mercer University. He did so and graduated in 1888. During his stay at Mercer, he served as pastor at Jeffersonville, Byron, Eatonton, and Harmony. During this period of study at Mercer, he went into the mountains during the summer of 1886 and founded Hiawassee High School, naming George Washington Truett (*q.v.*) of Hayesville as principal.

Upon graduation from Mercer, McConnell became pastor of the First Baptist Church, Gainesville, Ga. After five years at Gainesville, he was elected assistant secretary of the Home Mission Board. In 1894 he accepted the call to the First Baptist Church, Lynchburg, Va. Upon the death of Secretary Franklin Howard Kerfoot (*q.v.*), 1901, McConnell was elected secretary of the Home Mission Board. In 1903 he became pastor of Calvary Baptist Church, Kansas City, Mo., serving on the board of William Jewell College. In 1909 he accepted the call to the First Baptist Church, Waco, Tex., succeeding Benajah Harvey Carroll (*q.v.*). On Jan. 1, 1915, he began the pastorate of a church then unconstituted, the Druid Hills Baptist Church, Atlanta, which was constituted on July 1, 1915. Many regard this pastorate as the high point in his career. McConnell served as trustee of Mercer University, member of the executive committee of the Georgia Baptist Convention, chairman of the board of directors of *The Christian Index*, and several other state and Southwide boards. He preached the sermon at the Southern Baptist Convention in 1902. One of his sons, F. C. McConnell, Jr., served as pastor at Tifton, Ga., First Church, Jacksonville, Fla., and First Church, Anderson, S. C. LOUIE DEVOTIE NEWTON

McCONNELL, FRANZ MARSHALL (b. Buffalo, Mo., Oct. 6, 1862; d. Sept. 1, 1947). Denominational leader. McConnell, a graduate of Clark's Academy, Berryville, Ark., taught school in Arkansas, New Mexico, and Indian Territory, and practiced law for a short time in New Mexico. Converted in 1879, he was ordained to the ministry at Kaufman, Tex., in 1886. After serving as pastor for a few years, he entered the evangelistic ministry in 1902; after eight years in this work, he was elected corresponding secretary of the Baptist General Convention of Texas, 1910. In 1914 he became superintendent of evangelism at Southwestern Baptist Theological Seminary. From 1916 to 1922, he served as corresponding secretary for the Baptist General Convention of Oklahoma. He was president of Burleson College, 1922–24. Later he served as pastor of First Baptist Church, Bonham, Tex.; secretary of Baylor Medical College; and pastor of Calvary Church, San Antonio, Tex. He became editor of the *Baptist Standard* in 1928, serving until 1944. He is the author of *Winning Souls and Strengthening Churches, The Deacon's Daughter* (1918), *Baptist Church Manual* (1926), *After the Feast,* and *The Rights and Obligations of Labor.* J. PAUL CARLETON and J. M. GASKIN

McCONNICO, GARNER (b. Lunenburg County, Va., 1771; d. Williamson County, Tenn., 1833). Pioneer preacher in Middle Tennessee. Born into an aristocratic home in Virginia, he received religious instruction from his mother that led to his conversion and union with a church at an early age. His church later licensed him to preach and prior to his 28th birthday ordained him to the ministry. The attractive prospects for settlement in the Cumberland Valley caused him in 1798 to move to Williamson County, Tenn., where he secured a large, rich tract of land that enabled him soon to become a prosperous settler. Upon his arrival in Williamson County, he began to preach to the settlers in the surrounding area. In 1800 McConnico, with 19 others, organized Big Harpeth Church and became its first pastor. Three years later he helped organize the Cumberland Association and more than once served as its moderator.

By 1813 his church had grown to be the second largest in the association with a membership of 256. During his 33-year pastorate he led Big Harpeth to send out from its membership numerous ministers and to establish at least five churches in the surrounding area. In addition to his regular pastorate, he served seven near-by churches as supply pastor, itinerated through much of Middle Tennessee, won many converts, and organized them into churches. During the great revival of the early 1800's unusual gesticulations sometimes appeared among the worshipers. On one such occasion a "jerker" began his motions in one of McConnico's meetings. Benedict, the historian, in relating the incident in 1813 stated, "the preacher suddenly made a pause, and with a loud and solemn tone exclaimed, 'In the name of the Lord, I command all unclean spirits to leave this place.' The jerker immediately became still, and the report was spread abroad that McConnico cast out devils." Death came suddenly for the popular preacher in 1833, thus ending a fruitful ministry of 35 years. JAMES BREWER and LYNN E. MAY, JR.

McCOY, ISAAC (b. Fayette County, Pa., June 15, 1784; d. Louisville, Ky., June 21, 1846). Missionary to the Indians. When he was six years old his family moved to Kentucky, and at the age of 17 he united with the Buck Creek Baptist Church. In 1810, after moving to Clark County, Ind., he was ordained a Baptist minister. In 1817 the board of the Triennial Convention appointed him a missionary to the Indians of Indiana and Illinois for one year. His work among Indians, however, covered 29 years. In 1822 he established the Carey Mission near the present Niles, Mich., and in 1825 he preached the first sermon in English ever preached in the Chicago area.

In 1826 he resigned as superintendent of the Carey Mission in order to work for the creation of a territory in which the tribes of Indians could be colonized. On horseback he made 10 trips to Washington, D. C., to perfect his territorial plans. The final decision, however, was not wholly in accord with McCoy's plans, and the course of history has brought about great changes which have practically eliminated his plan. McCoy sought to engage the board of the general convention in a larger work among the Indians; but failing in this objective, he led in organizing the American Indian Mission Association (1842), hoping to make it the western subsidiary of the general convention. Although the project was not opposed in the East, it did not succeed as McCoy had hoped. Since the association was Southern in its location (Louisville, Ky.) and its officers and support came largely from Baptists in the South, in 1855 its work and assets were combined with the Board of Domestic Missions of the Southern Baptist Convention, thus beginning the permanent work among the Indians by the Southern Baptist Convention through its Home (Domestic) Mission Board. McCoy served as executive officer until his death in 1846.

BIBLIOGRAPHY: *Baptist Banner and Western Pioneer* (June 23 and Nov. 3, 1842). E. J. Lyons, *Isaac McCoy: His plan of and Work for Indian Colonization* (1945). I. McCoy, *History of Baptist Indian Missions* (1840). *The Baptist* (Aug. 15, 1846). W. W. BARNES

McCURRY, JOHN GORDON (b. Hart County, Ga., Apr. 26, 1821; d. Hart County, Ga., Dec. 4, 1886). Singing-school teacher, tune composer, and compiler of the *Social Harp*. He married Rachel S. Brown in 1842. They had no children. In addition to his music activities, he was a farmer and a tailor. He was a missionary Baptist and the "mud sill" of the Baptist church at Bio. He is buried in the churchyard of this church. He compiled and published the *Social Harp* (1855, later edition 1859). Forty-nine tunes in this collection are believed to be original compositions by McCurry. In this tune book he shows a particular liking for lively tunes and included many camp meeting songs. The unusually large number of indigenous tunes in this book are predominantly of the five-tone-scale type. Because of the influence of the Southern folk idiom, *Social Harp*, more than any other shaped-note book, "grew out of its native soil."

WILLIAM J. REYNOLDS

McDANIEL, GEORGE WHITE (b. Grimes County, Tex., Nov. 30, 1875; d. Richmond, Va., Aug. 12, 1927). Pastor, Southern Baptist Convention leader. Educated in the public schools of Navasota, Tex., McDaniel was converted and baptized into Navasota Baptist Church in 1892. He continued his education at Hills' Business College, Waco; Male Academy, Belton; Baylor University, Waco; and Southern Baptist Theological Seminary, Louisville, Ky. He was ordained to the ministry Sept. 13, 1899, by First Baptist Church, Waco, and held pastorates at Central City Baptist Church, Kentucky; Temple Baptist Church, Texas, 1900–02; Gaston Avenue Baptist Church, Dallas, 1902–05; First Baptist Church, Richmond, Va., 1902–27. A member of the Virginia Baptist Board of Missions and Education, Southern Baptist Foreign Mission Board, and Virginia Baptist Historical Society, McDaniel was a trustee of Richmond College (later University of Richmond) and Southern Baptist Theological Seminary, and member and president of the boards of trustees of Virginia Baptist Orphanage and Virginia Home and Industrial School for Girls. He was president of the Baptist General Association of Virginia and the Southern Baptist Convention.

A consistent champion of Baptist principles, McDaniel represented Baptist associations of Virginia and the Baptist General Association in presenting to the General Assembly of Virginia a protest against a proposed law for making Bible reading in public schools compulsory. The law was not passed. While the president of

FIRST BAPTIST CHURCH, Lancaster, S. C. Founded 1871, air conditioned building in modified Colonial design completed 1954 for $300,000, serves 1,000.

FIRST BAPTIST CHURCH, Smithville, Tenn. Organized 1844, Colonial architecture includes auditorium seating 450, Sunday school facilities for 450. Membership 1956 was 350, property valued at $95,000.

Southern Baptist Convention in 1926 when the theory of evolution was a burning issue, McDaniel made a pronouncement which rejected the theory of evolution in any form and affirmed that man was a special creation of God. The Convention adopted this pronouncement. McDaniel was a leader in First Baptist Church, Richmond, throughout Virginia and the South, in promoting successfully the 75 Million Campaign. He was the author of *Our Boys in France; Seeing the Best; The Supernatural Jesus;* and *The Churches of the New Testament.* McDaniel was married to Martha Douglass Scarborough.

SOLON B. COUSINS

MacDONALD, WILLIAM DAVID THOMPSON (b. Edinburgh, Scotland, Aug. 8, 1851; d. Temuco, Chile, Dec. 18, 1939). Missionary to Chile. MacDonald accepted the Baptist faith after studying the Bible and church history. He married Janet MacLeod (d. 1923) and, after preaching several years in Scotland, came to the United States, preaching in the South and the West. Returning to Scotland for his family, he was led to Chile rather than to North America. As a result of his teachings, the Baptist Union of Chile was founded in 1909. In 1917 the first North American missionaries to Chile were sent by Southern Baptists, and in 1919, after 32 years in Chile, MacDonald and his wife became missionaries of the Foreign Mission Board.

BIBLIOGRAPHY: A. Graham, *Pioneering with Christ in Chile* (1942). E. C. Pacheco, *The Apostle of the Chilean Frontier* (1945).

E. C. ROUTH

McDOWELL, ARCHIBALD (b. Kershaw District, S. C., Apr. 10, 1818; d. Murfreesboro, N. C., May 27, 1881). Son of Archibald and Mary (Drakeford) McDowell, spending his youth on a farm, where he acquired habits of industry that characterized his life. He traveled by muleback to Wake Forest College, N. C., graduated in 1847 with the A.B. degree, and was given the D.D. degree by that college. He wished to accompany Matthew T. Yates (*q.v.*) to China but was turned down by the Foreign Mission Board on account of a weak throat. Thwarted in that desire, he chose Christian education as his field, and on Oct. 11, 1848, opened the Chowan Baptist Institute, the first institution of learning for young women established by the Baptists of North Carolina. He served as its first president and, although he twice resigned, was called back to remain until his death. His influence helped stamp a fine culture upon the coastal plains of eastern North Carolina and southeastern Virginia. On June 15, 1847, he married the brilliant Mary Hayes Owen. Their children were Fannie Garland, William Owen, Sallie Emma, Mary Henderson, Rebecca Ruth, Eunice, and Archibald.

MRS. W. H. MCDOWELL

McGLOTHLIN, JAMES THOMAS (b. Portland, Tenn., June 26, 1875; d. Nashville, Tenn., June 9, 1934). Baptist minister and denominational worker. He was educated in Bethel College (B.A., 1897), Russellville, Ky., and the Southern Baptist Theological Seminary (Th.M., 1921), Louisville, Ky. On Dec. 19, 1901, he married Bessie June Williams of Springs Station, Woodford County, Ky. McGlothlin served as pastor of the following churches: Midway Baptist, Midway, Ky., 1901–03; Franklin Baptist, Franklin, Ky., 1903–12; First Baptist, Hampton, Va., 1912–15; First Baptist, Frankfort, Ky., 1915–21; Parker Memorial Baptist, Anniston, Ala., 1921–32. In 1924 he was elected by the Southern Baptist Convention to the Sunday School Board and continued on the board until 1932. After serving with distinction as chairman of a survey committee of the board, he was elected business manager of the board Aug. 1, 1932. In evaluation of his activity in this position, Prince Emmanuel Burroughs (*q.v.*) said: "McGlothlin served with much prudence and a growing mastery of business details, and rendered a most distinct and valuable service. . . . He was just reaching the period of greatest usefulness when his sudden death ended his career."

NORRIS GILLIAM

McGLOTHLIN, WILLIAM JOSEPH (b. near Gallatin, Tenn., Nov. 29, 1867; d. May 28, 1933). Professor, college administrator, Baptist historian. McGlothlin received B.A. and A.M. degrees from Bethel College, Kentucky, in 1889 and 1891; the Th.M. degree from Southern Baptist Theological Seminary in 1894; and the Ph.D. degree from the University of Berlin in 1901. He married May Belle Williams, June 8, 1897 (d. 1926), by whom he had five children; later he married Mrs. Mary Louise Bates, Dec. 28, 1929.

After teaching in Tennessee public schools, at Bethel College, and Bardstown (Ky.) Male and Female Institute, McGlothlin became professor of church history at Southern Baptist Theological Seminary, 1894–1919. Following that professorship he became president of Furman University, where he served until his death. Active in denominational affairs, McGlothlin was president of the Southern Baptist Convention, 1930–33; trustee of Southern Baptist Theological Seminary, 1932; and representative of Southern Baptists in the Federal Food Administration in Washington, 1917. During his presidency at Furman, the physical plant was expanded; scholastic standing was advanced, with admission to the Southern Association of Colleges in 1924, and to the approved list of the Association of American Universities in 1929; sounder financial basis was achieved through Baptist support and inclusion in the Duke Endowment in 1924; and plans were formulated for the co-ordination of Furman and Greenville Woman's College.

His published works include *History of Glen's Creek Baptist Church* (1900); *Die Bernische Wiedeltaufer* (1902); *A Guide to the Study of Church History* (1908); *Kentucky Baptists, the Seminary, and Alien Immersion* (1908); *Baptist Confessions of Faith* (1910); *A Vital Ministry* (1913); *Infant Baptism in History* (1915); *The*

Course of Christian History (1917); and *Baptist Beginnings in Education, A History of Furman University* (1926).

BIBLIOGRAPHY: *Baptist Courier* (Jan. 2, 1930). J. M. Cattell, ed., *Leaders in Education* (1932). *Who Was Who in America,* Vol. 1 (1897–42), *Who's Who in the South* (1927). KATHRYN MC GLOTHLIN ODELL

McINTOSH, JOHN (b. Creek Nation, Indian Territory, Aug. 11, 1833; d. Creek Nation, Indian Territory, Dec. 25, 1906). Creek Indian, Baptist preacher, and tribal leader. A descendant of General William McIntosh of Georgia fame, he grew to manhood in the wild Creek country of pioneer days where "horse racing, card gambling and shooting it out was the law of the land." As a young man he took part in these activities and joined with the Creek council in persecuting Christian Indians and Negro slaves. Converted in 1866, he was ordained to the Baptist ministry in 1868. He served 38 years as a tribal judge and was the first Baptist missionary to the Plains Indians. About 1876 he made his pioneer visit to the Wichita Agency near the present city of Anadarko, Okla. This and subsequent visits resulted in the organization of the Rock Springs Baptist Church, the first Baptist church among the Plains Indians. His grave is near his home church, Big Arbor, near Eufaula, Okla. GLENWOOD BUZBEE

McKENZIE, WALTER HALE (b. Erath County, Tex., Sept. 17, 1885; d. Dallas, Tex., June 13, 1952). Pastor, denominational and prohibition leader. McKenzie attended Carlton Grammar School, Hico High School, Baylor University, and Southwestern Baptist Theological Seminary. After serving as associational missionary in Montague County, McKenzie held pastorates at the First Baptist churches of Nocona, Grand Prairie, and Waxahachie, Tex. He also served as pastor of University Baptist Church, Austin, and Ervay Street Baptist Church, Dallas, Tex. He was professor of Bible at Goodnight Baptist College for three years.

Strongly identified with the fight against the sale of alcoholic beverages, McKenzie resigned his pastorate at University Baptist Church, Austin, in Oct., 1943, to accept the leadership of the United Texas Drys. Of his service to this cause, *The Christian Crusader* said:

> For the past nine years the people of Texas have been led and inspired by the unceasing labours of Dr. Walter H. McKenzie in the fight against the legalized liquor industry. Under his leadership the organization, bankrupt at the time of his coming, has made steady gain until now the organization has a staff of nine full-time workers, a comfortable financial reserve, and a backlog of confidence and good will upon which to build the future.

McKenzie, president of the executive board of the Baptist General Convention of Texas for one term, preached the annual state convention sermon in 1946 at Mineral Wells, Tex. GLEN NORMAN

McKIE, KATE STITELER (b. Savannah, Ga., July 29, 1856; d. Dallas, Tex., Mar. 26, 1936). Pioneer mother of marked devotion, culture, and refinement; Christian philanthropist; missionary advocate; and promoter of education. She was the daughter of Jacob and Martha Matilda (Halbert) Stiteler. Her father was a pioneer Texas Baptist preacher, pastor of First Baptist Church, Galveston, Tex., and teacher at Baylor University. She attended public schools, then Baylor University (1872–75), which institution granted her the degree of LL.D. in 1932. She married William J. McKie, distinguished attorney; they had six children: William J., Jr.; Blanche; Evalyn; Ben; Francis; and Kate. Beyond her immediate family, her lifelong interest was in her church and the cause of Christ; she became a generous benefactor of various causes and institutions, principally foreign missions, Buckner Orphans Home, and Baylor University. She challenged the women of Texas to complete payment on the Woman's Missionary Union memorial dormitory at Baylor University by giving more than $125,000. She left in trust additional funds for her church and denomination, indicating the breadth of her interest by stipulating that her gifts should support all causes fostered by the Baptist General Convention of Texas. She died in Dallas while on a visit but was buried in her home city, Corsicana, Tex. J. HOWARD WILLIAMS

McKINNEY, BAYLUS BENJAMIN (b. Heflin, La., July 22, 1886; d. Bryson City, N. C., Sept. 7, 1952). Gospel song writer, evangelistic singer, teacher, and music editor. He was educated at Mt. Lebanon Academy, Louisiana; Louisiana College, Pineville, La.; Southwestern Baptist Theological Seminary, Fort Worth, Tex.; Siegel-Myers School of Music, Chicago, Ill. (B.M., 1922); Bush Conservatory of Music, Chicago, Ill. Oklahoma Baptist University, Shawnee, Okla., awarded him the honorary Doctor of Music degree, 1942. He served in the United States Army in 1918. On June 11, 1918, he married Leila Irene Routh, to whom were born two sons, Baylus Benjamin, Jr., and Eugene Calvin. McKinney was music editor for Robert Henry Coleman (*q.v.*), songbook publisher of Dallas, Tex., 1918–35. From 1919 to 1931, he taught in the School of Sacred Music at Southwestern Baptist Theological Seminary, serving as assistant director of the school and professor of voice, harmony, and composition. He was assistant pastor of Travis Avenue Baptist Church, Fort Worth, Tex., from 1931 to 1935. In 1935 he became music editor of the Baptist Sunday School Board and became secretary of the newly created Department of Church Music in 1941. Under his leadership the board inaugurated an annual Church Music Week at the Ridgecrest Baptist Assembly (1940), fostered the practice of having a secretary of music employed by each state Baptist convention (1944), developed the Church Music Training Course (1946), and began the publication of the *Church Musician* (1950). Throughout his career McKinney led the music in revivals and assemblies and taught in schools of church music conducted by local churches. He was the author of the words and music of 149 gospel hymns and songs, and he composed the music for 114 texts by other authors. Some of his best-loved songs are "The Nail-Scarred Hand" (1924), "Let Others See Jesus in You" (1924), "Satisfied with Jesus" (1926), "Speak to My Heart" (1927), " 'Neath the Old Olive Trees" (1934), "Breathe on Me" (1937), and "Wherever He Leads I'll Go" (1937).

JOSEPHINE PILE

McKINNEY, EDMUND JAMES ARCHIBALD (b. Etowah County, Ala., Nov. 11, 1869; d. Little Rock, Ark., July 6, 1936). Editor and historian. He was the son of John and Elizabeth (Coffey) McKinney. On Oct. 22, 1895, he married Rebecca Hinton. He received the B.A. degree from Ouachita College in 1894. He was pastor, editor, enlistment secretary in Arkansas for the Home Mission Board and statistical secretary of the Arkansas Baptist Convention from 1901 to 1935. In 1905, urged by James Phillip Eagle (*q.v.*), he sacrificed his seminary education to pioneer the building of a denominational newspaper into a power for unifying Baptist work in Arkansas. He founded the Baptist Book Store in the office of the *Baptist Advance* in 1917. He was a strict Baptist and a contender for orthodoxy. He was a competent statistician and historian and, shortly before his death, was commissioned to write a history of Arkansas Baptists.

MRS. PATTON BODIE

MACLAREN, ALEXANDER (b. Glasgow, Scotland, Feb. 11, 1826; d. Edinburgh, Scotland, May 5, 1910).* Minister, expositor, and author. The youngest of six children of David and Mary (Wingate) McLaren, Maclaren as a growing boy was influenced by puritanical upbringing and his parents' deep piety and reverence for the Bible. During his early years his father was pastor of Scotch Baptist Church, Glasgow. In his 14th year he had a profound conversion experience and was baptized in the Hope Street Baptist Church, Glasgow. In his home he early received the impression that he was destined for the Christian ministry. Following the impression without hesitation, as a youth he came to believe that the chief end of life was to glorify God. With this sense of mission directing his native talents, he early became a diligent and thorough student. After his high school course and a year at Glasgow University, his family moved to London and he entered Stepney College, where he completed his formal training for the ministry. There, under the influence of the eminent Hebrew scholar, Benjamin Davies, he developed the lifelong habit of patient, minute study of the Bible in the original languages. In 1846 he received his B.A. degree from London University. The same year he became pastor of Portland Baptist Chapel, Southampton, where he remained until 1858; when he was called to Union Chapel, Manchester. Making his ministry primarily one of exposition of the Scriptures, Maclaren served in Manchester for more than 40 years. During that time large congregations, including all classes and creeds, were drawn by his powerful preaching of the Bible. With the publication of his sermons and expositions, he became widely known and greatly respected. He retired at Union Chapel in June, 1903.

A zealous promoter of missions and education, Maclaren was twice elected president of the British Baptist Union, first in 1875 and again in 1900. The University of Edinburgh in 1877 conferred upon him the D.D. degree, and in 1907 the University of Glasgow gave him the same degree. He received the Doctor of Letters degree from the University of Manchester in 1902. In 1905, climaxing a 60-year ministry, he served as president at the meeting of the Baptist World Alliance in London. Beginning in 1862 with *Sermons Preached in Manchester*, some 21 volumes of his sermons were published during his active ministry. He wrote the lessons for the *American Sunday School Times* for a period of 20 years, and he contributed numerous articles to the religious press. He did the exposition of *Psalms, Colossians*, and *Philemon* for *The Expositor's Bible.* His last years were spent in the editing of his life's work, *Exposition of Holy Scripture*, sermons he preached to his own congregation arranged in the order of the Bible.

BIBLIOGRAPHY: *Baptist Times and Freeman* (May 13, 1910). W. Cathcart, *The Baptist Encyclopedia* (1883). E. T. McLaren, *Dr. McLaren of Manchester* (1912). *Review and Expositor* (Jan., 1911). *Scottish Baptist Magazine* (June, 1910).

C. ARTHUR INSKO

* *The family name "McLaren" was spelled "Maclaren" in his published works.*

McLURE, MAUD REYNOLDS (b. Talladega County, Ala., Apr. 25, 1863; d. Columbus, Ga., Apr. 8, 1938). Educator, Woman's Missionary Union leader, social worker, missionary advocate, first principal of Woman's Missionary Union Training School.

Born at "Mount Ida," the plantation of her parents, Walker and Hannah Elizabeth (Welch) Reynolds, she was reared in a Christian home with her four older sisters and one older brother. She was baptized at the age of eight into the membership of the near-by Baptist church at Alpine, Ala., where her maternal grandfather, Oliver Welch, was pastor.

She was educated by private instructors in her home, at Judson College, and at a finishing school in Baltimore, Md. On Jan. 20, 1886, she was married to Thomas E. McLure, a lawyer, and went to live in Chester, S. C. Her husband died Apr. 27, 1889, and she was left with their only child, John Thomas, then a year old. For the next six years she continued to live in Chester, and then she went to make her home with a sister, Jane Pinckard (Reynolds) Crook, in Jacksonville, Ala.

Later she moved to Columbus, Ga., to establish herself as a musician, for which she was both trained and accomplished. In 1904 she went to Cox College, College Park, Ga., as teacher of voice. From here she was called by Woman's Missionary Union in 1907 to become the first principal of the Woman's Missionary Union Training School. For 16 years she gave distinguished leadership to the school as it grew and developed. She "came to the Training School in its formative period and impressed upon it a character which it has not lost."

She pioneered in social service work among Southern Baptists in the establishment in 1912 of the Training School Settlement (later known as Good Will Center) in Louisville, Ky., as a laboratory for the training of students, as well as a practical ministry of the school. Prior to the opening of the settlement, she spent the summer in New York City studying at the School of Social Work and observing in leading social and church settlements of the city. At Good Will Center she introduced various avenues of service including the Vacation Bible school. As early as 1914, the Vacation Bible school at the center enrolled 105 pupils.

At the Asheville, N. C., meeting of the Southern Baptist Convention in 1916, she gave a report concerning the school's enlargement program, and thus with Kathleen Moore Mallory (*q.v.*) she was one of the first two women to address the Convention.

For the academic year 1918–19 she was granted a year's leave from the school to work with the Young Men's Christian Association in its program of services in military training camps. In Sept., 1919, she returned to the school and continued the direction of its growing ministry to the end of the academic year in 1923, when she resigned as principal that she might be free to make a home for her unmarried son.

Upon her retirement from the principalship of the school, the local board in Louisville adopted resolutions stating that because of her leadership for 16 years the school "is in a very real sense what she has made it," that she was a "wise counsellor and beloved guide to our students," and that the Good Will Center under her had become "the pioneer and exemplar of the personal service work of Woman's Missionary Union." Her active service to Woman's Missionary Union continued to the end of her life. She was editor of the "Calendar of Prayer" 1929–38.

Her son died on Mar. 24, 1931, and a few months thereafter she went to make her home for the remainder of her life with a niece, Hannah Crook. Her death at this home in Columbus, Ga., Apr. 8, 1938, followed a prolonged illness and operation.

A new home at 2801 Lexington Rd., Louisville, Ky., was erected in 1940 for the W.M.U. Training School, which became in 1953 the Carver School of Missions and Social Work. Beneath her portrait in this building the inscription reads: "As a Memorial to Mrs. Maud Reynolds McLure/ First Principal of W.M.U. Training School/ in Loving Appreciation of Her Service/ Woman's Missionary Union/ Auxiliary to S.B.C./ Gave Toward the Erection of This Building/ One Hundred and Eleven Thousand Dollars." GEORGE A. CARVER

MEDICAL MISSIONS. The term "medical missions" includes hospitals, nursing schools, dispensaries, clinics, and the missionary personnel connected with them.

The Foreign Mission Board appointed its first medical missionary, J. Sexton James, in 1846, but he was lost at sea before reaching China. In 1851 a second doctor, George Washington Burton, was appointed for China, but he resigned after a few years. Following the loss of James and Burton, "Southern Baptists seem to have become discouraged over the work of medical missions, and for thirty years had no medical missionary."

There were apparently three reasons for the loss of interest in medical missions: financial conditions following the Civil War, the desire to use available funds for direct evangelism, and the difficulty of securing medical volunteers. A new beginning in medical missions came with the turn of the century. The following action was taken by the Southern Baptist Convention in 1901:

> We approve the action of the [Foreign Mission] Board in sending out medical missionaries who, while they are ministering to the multitudes of suffering natives, will also render professional service to our own missionaries. We commend the policy of the Board in sending as medical missionaries those who, in addition to their professional work, will render distinctly missionary service in presenting the truths of the gospel.

The Foreign Mission Board undertook the work of medical missions for five main reasons:

1. The understanding of medical missions as being in accord with the command of Jesus to heal the sick. Thomas Willburn Ayers (*q.v.*), medical missionary to North China, states that his call came as a result of his study of the healing work of Jesus: "In the light of the vision which I had caught of the Master in His ministry of healing, . . . I saw that He wanted His followers to demonstrate their compassion for the sick and suffering by putting love into action in healing their diseases." In 1927 T. Bronson Ray (*q.v.*), educational secretary for the Foreign Mission Board, wrote:

> Upon the threshold of our study must be noted the absorbing interest our Saviour exhibited in the physical suffering of our fellow-creatures. . . . Nine times it is recorded in the Gospels that "He was moved with compassion," for the bodily infirmities of men. . . . Twenty-three of the forty recorded miracles were miracles of healing. . . . Our Lord and Master was compassionate over the sick because He is who He is, and we, as far as our ability will allow,

should strive to relieve the suffering because we have caught His spirit and are like Him in compassion.

2. The example of the early apostles in healing. Ray continues his exposition of the biblical basis for medical missions with a reference to the healing activities of the apostles, as recorded in the book of Acts. Rosewell Hobart Graves (*q.v.*), after reference to the same activities, mentions Paul's inclusion of healing as one of the gifts of the Spirit and asks, "May we not infer from this that the healing of the sick should occupy the first place among the helps to the preaching of the word, as being the only one of these subsidiary agencies mentioned in the Scripture?"

3. The need for medical work. The first medical missionaries were appalled at the stupendous need for medical care which met them on every side. Graves gives a detailed description of the people and the lack of trained doctors. Deaths of children were estimated by Ray in 1925 to be 48 per cent in China and 60 per cent in Africa, while in the villages of India, 98 per cent died without attention from an educated physician.

4. The belief that medical work was an effective means of opening new fields to evangelization. This was the experience of early missionaries in China, among the Mohammedans, and in country districts of many lands. In Africa the medical missionary was not only a doctor but also "pastor, evangelist, general referee, and arbitrator in every dispute . . . between native brethren." In 1941 E. C. Routh wrote that "medical missions have had a big part in opening mission fields to the gospel message."

5. The necessity for doctors to help preserve the health of other missionaries. In the early years of mission work, mortality in missionary families was distressingly high. It was the appeal of two missionaries in North China, C. W. and Anna (Seward) Pruitt, who had lost two children for lack of medical care, that caused Baptist women of Georgia and Robert Josiah Willingham (*q.v.*), then secretary of the Foreign Mission Board, to unite in prayer that God would "thrust out a doctor who would make the sacrifice to go in answer to this appealing need." From the standpoint of the board, Ayers was the answer to that prayer. The need for medical care for missionaries was particularly acute in Africa, and it was not until the arrival of George Green, the first medical missionary to that land, in 1906 that the loss of missionaries through sickness was halted. Routh states that Green's service to the missionaries in this respect was "worth a thousandfold more than the Board has ever expended for his support. . . ."

Medical missions is considered an indispensable part of the foreign mission program today.

J. B. HIPPS

MELL, JOHN DAGG (b. Athens, Clarke County, Ga., Feb. 25, 1865; d. Athens, Ga., May 31, 1952). Minister, denominational officer. He was the son of Patrick Hues Mell (*q.v.*) and Elizabeth Eliza (Cooper) Mell. He attended the University of Georgia and received his B.A. degree with honors in 1884, his M.A. degree in 1885, and his LL.B. degree in 1886. Mercer University conferred upon him the D.D. degree in 1909. He was solicitor of the Athens city court for a number of years and taught parliamentary law in the University of Georgia. For 40 years he was president of the Athens Board of Education. Mell left the career of lawyer to become a minister. For nearly half a century he devoted his life to country churches. Notable pastorates include Antioch, Sardis, Bairdstown, Cloud's Creek, Danielsville, and Crawford. He was moderator of Sarepta Association from 1901 to 1940 and president of the Georgia Baptist Convention from 1912 to 1928. He served on every major Baptist board in the state and on many Southwide boards. Like his father, he was one of the great authorities of his day in parliamentary law. He married Helen Carlton of Athens and had by her four children. His body was buried in Oconee Cemetery, Athens. HOWARD P. GIDDENS

MELL, PATRICK HUES (b. Liberty County, Ga., July 19, 1814; d. Athens, Ga., Jan. 26, 1888). Parliamentarian, educator, and minister. His father was Benjamin Mell and his mother Cynthia (Sumner) Mell. Patrick Hues Mell was only 14 years of age when his father died and only 16 or 17 at the time of his mother's death. As the eldest son in the family, he had to provide means of support for himself and for his dependent brothers and sisters. His desire to obtain an education was so great that he borrowed money and entered Amherst College in Massachusetts where he was a student from 1833 to 1835. Furman University conferred upon him the D.D. degree in 1858 and Howard College, the LL.D. degree in 1869. He was professor of ancient languages at Mercer University, 1841–55, and at the University of Georgia, 1856; vice chancellor of the University of Georgia, 1860–72; and chancellor, 1878–88. He was ordained to the ministry Nov. 19, 1842, at Penfield, Ga. Among the Georgia churches he served were Greensboro, Bairdstown, and Antioch. He was president of the Southern Baptist Convention, 1863–71 and 1880–87, president of the Georgia Baptist Convention, 1857–64, moderator of the Georgia Baptist Association for 31 years, and an able writer on educational and religious topics. Among his books are *Baptism in Its Mode and Subjects* (Charleston, S. C., 1854); *Corrective Church Discipline* (Charleston, S. C., 1860); *The Doctrine of Prayer* (N. Y., *c.* 1876); and *A Manual of Parliamentary Practice* (N. Y., *c.* 1867), which was widely adopted and followed. He also published small works on slavery, predestination, Calvinism, God's providential government, and the philosophy of prayer. At the time of his death he was working on several articles and on what perhaps would have been his most useful book, a volume on Baptist church polity.

Mell was married twice. His first wife was Lurene Howard Cooper, a resident of Montgomery County, Ga., by whom he had nine children, five sons and four daughters. His second wife was Elizabeth Eliza Cooper, and four sons and two daughters were born of this union. Educator, author, and teacher, a soldier during the Civil War, a preacher who devoted himself and his ministry to country churches in a territory which was called Mell's kingdom, he was a master of assemblies and was known as the prince of parliamentarians. HOWARD P. GIDDENS

MEMBERSHIP, BAPTIST WORLD. See BAPTIST WORLD ALLIANCE.

MEMORIAL HOSPITAL, BAPTIST, BIRMINGHAM. Located in Gadsden, Ala., formerly known as Forrest General Hospital, it became a Baptist institution on July 17, 1944, and was owned and operated by Etowah Baptist Association. From 1944 through 1954, it served 57,468 patients. Total patient income was $3,635,342.39. Designated gift income was $10,697.65. Four buildings compose the plant. Value of land, buildings, and equipment in 1954 was $304,951.07. In 1954 the hospital had 97 beds and served 9,299 patients of all races. It has no school of nursing, is not approved for internship, and is only conditionally accredited. Annual patient income for 1954 was $628,694.73. Designated gift income was $858.29. Charity work totaled $52,304.10. JOHN W. GIBBS

MEMORIAL HOSPITAL, BAPTIST, MEMPHIS. A corporation chartered Apr. 8, 1907, by the state of Tennessee, established by the Baptists of Arkansas, Mississippi, and Tennessee, located in Memphis, Tenn. The only records available indicate that the first public suggestion that a Baptist hospital be established in Memphis was made at an all-day meeting of the Shelby County Baptist Association at Central Baptist Church, Memphis, in July, 1906. During the day's activities H. P. Hurt, pastor of Bellevue Baptist Church, pointed out the need for an additional general hospital in the community and offered a resolution asking the denomination to sponsor such an institution. His plea was seconded by Thomas S. Potts, pastor of the host church, and by A. U. Boone, pastor of First Baptist Church, Memphis. That day those three leaders were appointed as a committee to visit the Baptist conventions of Arkansas, Mississippi, and Tennessee and appeal to them to support the building of a Baptist hospital in Memphis. They found support in the mid-South area; and Apr. 8, 1907, a charter was signed for the proposed hospital. All members of missionary Baptist churches in the three states were eligible for membership in this corporate body with the payment of one dollar as annual dues. A governing board of 18 directors was to be elected annually by the membership.

In 1908 arrangements were completed with the near-by University of Tennessee College of Medicine whereby the university was to deed a lot on Madison Avenue for the new hospital building and provide instructors for student nurses in return for clinical privileges with charity patients for teaching purposes. A building fund was soon raised through contributions and loans, and in 1910 ground was broken for the new hospital. The 150-bed hospital, which was valued at $250,000, was formally opened to patients July 20, 1912.

In the beginning the new hospital prospered, but by 1915 it faced financial difficulty, and the board of directors discussed selling the institution. At that time A. E. Jennings offered to assume the large indebtedness of the hospital and to become responsible for its operation. He remained as chairman of the executive committee until his retirement in 1946.

In 1924 a new charter was procured, vesting control and ownership in the Baptist conventions of Arkansas, Mississippi, and Tennessee. The hospital was duly incorporated as a nonprofit organization under the laws of Tennessee; and provisions for a 27-man governing board were made, with nine trustees to be elected from each of the three states. Buildings and equipment were valued at $1,500,000.

Baptist Memorial is located in the heart of the Memphis Medical Center. Additions have been made periodically as the need for hospital facilities in the mid-South community increased. The hospital was first enlarged in 1918 with the erection of a 100-bed wing. Another wing was added in 1920, the same year that construction began on a nurses' dormitory. The Physicians and Surgeons Building, housing offices for doctors, a drugstore, a restaurant, patient rooms, and hotel rooms for families of the sick, was completed in 1929. Another section was added to the hospital in 1938, providing an additional 100 beds. In 1941 the nurses' dormitory was enlarged and classrooms and recreational facilities added. The largest expansion program in the hospital's history was undertaken in 1953 and completed with the opening of the 13-story Madison-East wing in Dec., 1955. Gifts from Memphians and mid-Southerners were instrumental in the completion of this giant addition, as they had been in previous building programs.

Baptist Memorial Hospital has received full approval from the Joint Committee on Accreditation, standard accreditation agency. It provides approved training in six hospital-related professions.

It is approved by the Council on Medical Education and Hospitals of the American Medical Association for 28 internships and residencies in nine specialties. Its medical teaching program is affiliated with the University of Tennessee, and all staff members directly charged with teaching are members of the University faculty. The school of nursing is fully approved by the National Nursing Accreditation Service and is affiliated with Memphis State College, where student nurses take their first six months of instruction. The hospital also maintains an approved school for medical technologists and another for medical record librarians. Baptist Memorial offers advanced training in hospital administration and dietetics and has approved clinical programs for practical nurse students and surgical technicians. The hospital is a member of the American Hospital Association, the Tennessee Hospital Association, the American Protestant Hospital Association, and the Southwide Baptist Hospital Association.

Recent expansion of facilities has included the addition of a radioisotope laboratory, a psychiatric unit, a program of domiciliary care, the establishment of an aorta bank, and the installation of specially designed equipment using cobalt for deep therapy of malignancies.

In all, the hospital has cared for 649,330 patients, and 1,909 students have graduated from the Baptist Memorial Hospital School of Nursing since its establishment in 1912.

During 1955 charity service to those unable to pay for their care totaled $474,427. The hospital employs a full-time chaplain to minister to the spiritual needs of patients, and student nurses receive special religious guidance by a trained counselor. Gross income from patients during 1955 was $4,580,427. A total of 26,285 patients were admitted. The hospital received $53,317 from the denomination. Total operating receipts were $6,580,427.

In 1955 hospital property included, in addition to the hospital proper, the student dormitory, parking lots, a garage, and several frame dwellings intended for use in future expansion. Replacement value of property and equipment was approximately $19,256,000. With completion of the Madison-East addition the indebtedness totaled $3,500,000. Capacity of Baptist Memorial was 800 beds. A scheduled remodeling program in a portion of the original building was expected to increase the bed capacity to approximately 920 by 1957. JOYE PATTERSON

MEMORIAL HOSPITAL, BAPTIST, OKLAHOMA CITY. Plans were given some consideration for the erection of a Baptist hospital in Oklahoma City for several years, prior to Nov. 9, 1952, when the Oklahoma convention approved a recommendation from its hospital committee to engage a professional firm to conduct a survey to determine the hospital needs and initiate a financial campaign to establish a centrally located hospital and school of nursing. This proposal was renewed Nov. 10, 1954, with the added agreement that the convention would provide an equal amount up to $1,000,000 to funds raised by citizens of Oklahoma City. This campaign was conducted in April and May, 1955, and the incomplete report June 3, 1955, showed total cash and pledges were $930,146. Architects were selected in 1955, a site was selected, plans were drawn, and groundbreaking ceremonies were held May 17, 1956, for the first 200-bed unit of Baptist Memorial Hospital at Northwest Highway and Grand Boulevard, Oklahoma City.

TOM E. CARTER

MEMORIAL HOSPITAL, BAPTIST, SAN ANTONIO. A 282-bed general hospital owned and operated by the Baptist General Convention of Texas. Originally organized as a small clinic in 1926 by a group of physicians, it was soon enlarged into the Medical and Surgical Hospital and later merged with another group on adjacent property operating as the Physicians and Surgeons Hospital. In 1934 a nonprofit charter was secured and a board of trustees created. Although progress was made in the years which followed, the board in 1948, sensing a precarious financial situation and the need for financial support not entirely dependent upon pay patients, offered the entire plant as a gift to the Southern Baptist Convention providing it would maintain and operate the hospital and add a 100-bed unit. The proposition was accepted, the property deeded to the Baptists, and a new wing erected at a cost of approximately $1,400,000. Financial changes prompted Southern Baptists to relinquish control, which was assumed by the Baptist General Convention of Texas in Mar., 1952.

The physical plant now consists of six buildings valued at $2,500,000 with an outstanding indebtedness of $858,683.09. The hospital is accredited and is approved for internships and residencies. The school of nursing had an enrolment of 112 in 1955, from which was graduated the largest class of nurses in Texas that year.

In 1954, 15,471 patients were admitted, of which 964 were charity cases treated at a cost of $83,815.76. Total income from patients was $2,181,158.87; from the Cooperative Program, $73,374.64; from designated gifts, $28,871.59.

During the entire period of Baptist control (1948–55) a total of 122,722 patients of all races have been admitted; patient income totals $12,612,126.90; denominational income, $191,944.10; designated gift income, $54,708.27.

F. R. HIGGENBOTHAM

MEMORIAL HOSPITAL, HOUSTON. Founded in Aug., 1907, the second hospital in the nation under Baptist control, owned by the Baptist General Convention of Texas with its board of trustees elected annually by the convention.

The 17-bed institution was first known as the Ida J. Rudisell Sanitarium, but when it was taken over by the holding committee of the Baptist denomination, it continued after Sept. 1, 1907, under the name Baptist Sanitarium. The sanitarium became the property of the Baptist General Convention of Texas in 1910; a new charter was procured and the name changed to Baptist Sanitarium and Hospital. In 1932 the name was changed again, to Memorial Hospital.

From the original 17 beds, Memorial Hospital enlarged to 50 beds in 1911, 130 in 1915, 300 in 1942, 485 beds and 60 bassinets in 1955. In 1955 John Gant Dudley was hospital administrator, having held that position since 1946.

The school of nursing was opened in 1907, and through 1954 it had graduated 1,171 nurses. It is now named the Lillie Jolly School of Nursing of Memorial Hospital. A full-time chaplain and a student secretary serve in the department of religion, which includes a clinical training program in pastoral care.

Memorial Hospital admits all types of patients and offers special facilities such as electrocardiograms, electroencephalograms, laboratories, radiology, radioisotopes, 13 operating rooms, a blood bank, a pharmacy, and emergency rooms.

The hospital is a member of Blue Cross, Houston Area Hospital Council, Texas Hospital Association, National League for Nursing, American Hospital Association, American Protestant Hospital Association, and Southwide Baptist Hospital Association. It is accredited by the Joint Commission on Accreditation of Hospitals and National League for Nursing.

Hugh Roy and Lilly Cullen made a gift of $2,000,000 for Cullen Nurses Building; Mrs. J. W. (Elizabeth Mitchell) Neal established two endowments through the hospital, the Jolly Robert Neal Fund for treatment of cancer and the Margaret Ophelia Neal Fund for children.

From 1907 through Aug. 31, 1955, the hospital served 364,599 patients. In 1955 the land, the three buildings, equipment, and other assets were valued at $6,975,657.03; indebtedness in Sept., 1955, was $2,208,333.45. The school of nursing had 130 students, and 19,245 patients were admitted during the year ending Aug., 1955.

Serving all races, the hospital had in 1955 an annual income from patients of $2,936,941.64. Income from the Baptist Cooperative Program in 1954 was $76,024.26; Mother's Day designated gifts were $12,046.32. The value of charity work in 1954–55 was $37,655.43. JOE F. LUCK

MEMPHIS MEDICAL COLLEGE. A medical college operated in Memphis under the charter of Southwestern Baptist University at Jackson (later Union University) for some 10 years after 1879. The medical college was announced in the university catalogue as the medical department of the university. The faculty was listed in the Southwestern Baptist University catalogue, and the requirements for graduation were included. The university received an annual report from the medical college but claimed no further responsibility for it.

HARLEY FITE

MENNONITES. A group of Anabaptist bodies named for the former Dutch priest, Menno Simons. The Mennonites derive from the Swiss Brethren, who in early 1525 began a separate existence after being in the Zwingli circle in Zurich. Led for a time by Grebel, Manz, Blaurock, Sattler, Marbeck (and in a sense by Hubmaier), the movement became chiefly centered in Holland and was led by Menno Simons and Dirk Philips. Despite persecution the movement spread all over Europe and came also to the United States and Canada. There are now more than 200,000 members in North America.

In the left-wing tradition of the Reformation movement, two tendencies appeared regarding the understanding of the church: the Spiritualist (led by Schwenckfeld, Frank, etc.), which played down or rejected the organizational side of the Christian community; and the Free Churchmen, who stressed the formation of a church on the basis of believers' baptism and a separation from the world and to God, maintained by nurture and discipline. The Mennonites belong to this latter tradition.

See also ANABAPTISTS.

BIBLIOGRAPHY: H. S. Bender (ed.), *Mennonite Encyclopedia* (1955–56). *New Schaff-Herzog Encyclopedia of Religious Knowledge,* Vol. VII (1950). *Twentieth Century Encyclopedia of Religious Knowledge,* Vol. II (1955). J. C. Wenger, *Separated Unto God* (1951).

T. D. PRICE

MERCER, JESSE (b. Halifax County, N. C., Dec. 16, 1769; d. Butts County, Ga., Sept. 6, 1841). Son of Silas Mercer, able pioneer minister and the eldest of eight children, five boys and three girls. His formal education was obtained under the tuition of John Springer, a Presbyterian minister and Princeton graduate who lived near Washington, Ga., and embraced some knowledge of learned languages. He had an additional year of study under a man named Armor in Salem Academy, a school maintained by his father, the first private Baptist school in Georgia.

Although reared an Episcopalian, Silas Mercer became a Baptist from conviction. He baptized his 17-year-old son Jesse into the membership of the historic Kiokee church. At the age of 20, Jesse Mercer was ordained as a minister, and in 1789 he began his first pastorate at Hutton's Fork (now Sardis) which had been established by his father. Following the death of his father in 1796, he moved back to the old family home in Wilkes County to administer the estate. He became principal of Salem Academy which his father had founded, continued to serve as pastor of Sardis, and accepted calls to the other three of his father's churches, Phillips' Mill, Wheatley's Mill (later Bethesda), and Powelton, and served them for 39, 32, and 28 years respectively. One of these, Powelton Church, was one of the chief rallying points of Georgia Baptists.

It was in the Powelton conference in 1801 that the foundation was laid for the missionary work of the Georgia Association, especially to the Creek Indians. In the Powelton conferences in 1802 and 1803, the general committee of Georgia Baptists for itinerant preaching and missionary work was formed. In 1822 the General Association of Georgia Baptists (changed, in 1827, to Georgia Baptist Convention) was organized. It held its first meeting in Powelton in 1823, and during the first eleven years of its history it met seven times in churches of which Jesse Mercer was or had been pastor.

At the age of 19 Jesse Mercer married Sabrina Chivers, who was his wife for nearly 40 years. Throughout his ministry he was an itinerant volunteer missionary and preached to many congregations in various localities in the belief that only through itinerant preaching would the gospel be carried to needy people in sparsely settled areas. On his trips he carried the tracts and books of the American Tract Society for gift and sale and also gave his support to mission work among the slaves. He was an ardent supporter of missions, Sunday schools, and temperance and financed the *Temperance Banner,* the first temperance paper in the South. He was a successful businessman as well as a preacher and philanthropist of his day.

For many years Jesse Mercer was the recognized leader of the Georgia Baptist Association and in the Georgia Baptist Convention. He served as clerk of the association for 21 years, as moderator for 23 years, and as writer of its history. He was president of the Georgia Baptist Convention for 19 years, from its founding in 1822 until 1841, when feeble health made his attendance impossible. He was a trustee of Columbian College in Washington, D. C., and the first president of the board of trustees of Mercer University, which bears his name. He was an able advocate and a liberal patron of education, particularly ministerial education, as indicated in his conducting Salem Academy for two years following his father's death, in his gift of $2,000 for the first missionary to Texas, William Melton Tryon (*q.v.*), and in his support of Mount Enon Academy, Columbian College, and Mercer University.

He attended four meetings of the Triennial Convention and preached the convention sermon in 1826. While returning from this meeting and en route home through South Carolina, Mrs. Mercer became seriously ill, passed away, and was buried at Andersonville, S. C. Soon Mercer's own failing strength led him to lighten his work. He moved to Washington, Ga., where he founded the First Baptist Church in 1827, became its pastor, and served until his death 14 years later in 1841.

In Dec., 1827, he married Mrs. Nancy Simons of Wilkes County, the Gentile widow of a wealthy Jew, Captain Abraham Simons. She shared wholeheartedly in all Mercer's plans and benefactions. They agreed that their possessions should go to religious causes. He outlived her by four months and carried out their agreement in bequests in his will to the Baptist Convention in the United States for Foreign Missions, the American Baptist Home Mission Society, the American Baptist Publication Society, the American Tract Society, the American and Foreign Bible Society, Columbian College, and Mercer University.

Aside from his father, the one who most influenced his interest in missions and Christian education was Luther Rice (*q.v.*), whose service to missions and Christian education was nationwide. Jesse Mercer had the qualities of statesmanship in a high degree. He played the leading role in the organization of the Georgia Baptist Convention for collective counsel and co-operation, in the founding of Mercer University for the training of ministerial and lay leadership, and in the purchase and gift to Georgia Baptists of the *Christian Index* for publicity and promotion, which he published for seven years. His *Cluster of Spiritual Songs,* many of which were produced by him, went through several editions and was a worthy contribution to American hymnology. He also wrote *A History of the Georgia Baptist Association* (Washington, 1838).

The D.D. degree was conferred upon him by the board of fellows of Brown University in 1835. In deference to his wishes the title was used but little, and his host of friends continued to address him in the endearing terms of "Father" and "Brother." He devoted his best energies to Mercer University, giving large sums of money for its support while he lived and making it the principal legatee of his estate when he died. SPRIGHT DOWELL

MERCER ACADEMY. A preparatory school in Penfield, Ga., established in 1839 as a result of Mercer Institute's elevation to the university level. In 1841 the academy became separate from the college, with two or more professors composing its faculty. ARTHUR JACKSON

MERCER INSTITUTE. A Baptist manual labor school established at Penfield, Ga., in 1833. Adiel Sherwood (*q.v.*), who had set up a manual labor school at Eatonton in 1832, closed his school and worked with Jesse Mercer (*q.v.*) and others to bring Mercer Institute into existence. The school had as its primary purpose the training of "pious young men for the gospel ministry," as Josiah Penfield (*q.v.*), deacon in Henry Holcombe's (*q.v.*) church in Savannah, had specified in his will, bequeathing $2,500 for such a school. The institute became Mercer University in 1839. ARTHUR JACKSON

MERCER UNIVERSITY. A coeducational institution offering liberal arts, graduate, and professional training, supported and controlled by the Baptist Convention of the State of Georgia. It is located in Macon, Ga., and was founded on Jan. 14, 1833, when a manual labor school was opened near Greensboro, Ga., in accordance with a resolution adopted by the Georgia convention in 1831. This school, named Mercer Institute in honor of Jesse Mercer (*q.v.*), was the culmination of a long period of Georgia Baptist interest in education and denominational work. The private school conducted by Silas Mercer in his home at Salem from 1793 to his death in 1796; the Powelton Conferences in the early years of the 19th century; the opening of Mount Enon Academy in 1807 with Henry Holcombe, Savannah pastor, as founder and chief supporter; and the stimulating visits of Luther Rice beginning in 1813 were stages in the development of Jesse Mercer's zeal for missions and Christian education and were evidences of a growing denominational consciousness in Georgia. In 1822 was formed the General Association of Georgia Baptists, which by 1828 became the Georgia Baptist Convention. In 1829 this body turned to education.

At the annual meeting of the convention that year in Milledgeville the will of the late Josiah Penfield (*q.v.*) of Savannah was read. It provided a legacy of $2,500 for the "education of pious young men for the gospel Ministry," conditioned upon the provision of a like amount by the convention. Thus encouraged, the convention acted.

A plantation in Greene County six miles north of Greensboro, consisting of 450 acres, and an adjoining 12½ acres were purchased, and plans were begun for establishing Mercer Institute and the village of Penfield. The village was named in honor of a deacon of Savannah who, as a jeweler and silversmith, had profited enough to enable him to become the first benefactor of the projected school.

Along with Jesse Mercer and Josiah Penfield, these were instrumental in the founding of the school: Adiel Sherwood (*q.v.*), the "spiritual father"; Thomas Stocks, Christian statesman and philanthropist; Absalom Janes, trustee and financier; and Billington McCarty Sanders (*q.v.*), first president both of Mercer Institute and Mercer University. Mercer was the first agency established by the Georgia Baptist Convention in accordance with the educational objectives set out in the original constitution of that body.

At the meeting of the convention in 1833, Adiel Sherwood, treasurer, reported a total investment of $1,935. Of this amount $1,465 had been given for a "Plantation Fund" with which the 462½ acres had been purchased. The remainder was used for deepening the well and for erecting two log cabins. Before the end of the first term, a larger building, two stories high, was erected at the cost of $1,500, two thirds of which was given by Jesse Mercer, and an adjacent tract of 500 acres was purchased for $1,500, one third of which was given by Mercer. This brought the land and buildings to an evaluation of $6,500. In 1838 the total value of the property had increased to about $30,000.

In the meantime, the convention at a meeting in Talbotton (1836) approved the idea of a Southern Baptist college. A board of trustees was elected, and a campaign to raise $100,000 was launched. The money was pledged, and bids for the location of the college were received and considered, but the whole subject was referred to the executive committee of the convention with power to act. This committee promptly decided to elevate Mercer Institute to Mercer University, transfer all subscriptions to the institution, and go forward with the work of organization and promotion in accordance with a charter granted in Dec., 1837.

The first president of Mercer Institute and of Mercer University was Billington McCarty Sanders. With the assistance of his wife, Cynthia (Holliday) Sanders, he laid the foundation of Mercer as a Christian school.

With reference to the opening, Sanders wrote: "With accommodations limited to two log cabins and with one assistant I opened the institution in January, 1833, with 39 students, having 26 of them to board in my own family. Among them were seven young men preparing for the ministry. . . . While living as in a camp in their midst, and burdened with the charge and responsibility of the literary, theological, laboring and boarding departments, I found no little support in all my cares and labors from witnessing that while they lived upon the cheapest fare, had no place for study but the common schoolroom, no place to retire to for rest but a garret without a fire in the coldest weather, and labored three hours diligently every day, no complaint was heard, but that the most entire cheerfulness ran through all their words and activities."

The number of students increased to 90 in the next four years. There were never more than nine ministerial students in any one year during this period. Three students composed the first graduating class in 1841. Upon recommendation of the Georgia Baptist Convention's committee on education, the manual labor plan was discontinued in 1844, and the preparatory department was detached from the college in 1847. Agitation for the removal of the institution and the establishment of the Cherokee Baptist College at Cassville and Marshall College at Griffin resulted in a drop in enrolment, and in the years 1861–72 the college faced the additional and greatly increased difficulties growing out of the Civil War. Service was reduced to a voluntary and unofficial basis, no catalogues were published for some four or five years, and student enrolment dwindled. The decline continued until 1871 when the institution was removed to Macon.

Another serious agitation had its beginning at the convention in Elberton in 1910 with the introduction of a resolution for the removal of Mercer University to Atlanta. Feelings waxed warm, and Macon countered with the proposed removal of the state capital from Atlanta to Macon. At their meeting in June, 1912, the board of trustees expressed their disapproval of the agitation for removal and its harmful effect upon the college. At the convention in 1912, the committee on removal presented a conciliatory report deploring the confusion and ending the controversy with news of the pledge of additional support by the citizens of Macon.

Throughout its entire history Mercer University has adhered faithfully to the policy of maintaining a high-grade college of liberal arts. From time to time programs of expansion in theological, pre-professional, and business administration departments were undertaken which required more funds than were available. The most ambitious undertaking was during the administration of President Rufus Washington Weaver who served from 1917 to 1927. It was during this period that the Debt-paying and 75 Million campaigns were conducted, and funds were made available in unprecedented amount. Efforts were made to secure the approval and support of the Southern Baptist Convention in raising Mercer to the rank of a Southern Baptist university or in enlarging the theology department to make it a Southern Baptist theological seminary. These plans could not be carried out for lack of the necessary approval and financial support, and, following an official educational survey in 1927, the institution limited its scope to include only a college of liberal arts and school of law.

During the administration of President Spright Dowell, which was the longest in the history of the school (1928–53), a comprehensive program of expansion was planned and carried out. As a basis for sound growth, the curriculum was studied and revised to provide an optimum balance between social studies, the humanities, and the natural and physical sciences. Improvement and expansion of buildings and grounds began in 1933, with the celebration of the centenary of the school, and continued under one long-range plan for the next five years. A subsequent five-year plan emphasized endowment. Other campaigns were carried out for the specific endowment of the Columbus Roberts School of Christianity, the Walter F. George School of Law, and the Spright Dowell School of Education. As a result Mercer's physical properties were nearly doubled in value, the endowment was increased more than fourfold, and scholastic standards were raised to the standard necessary for approval by the Association of American Universities.

During the 122 years of its history, Mercer University has served slightly more than 20,000 students, including those in attendance during the summer quarters as well as during the regular college years. Of this number 7,821 have completed requirements for graduation. Graduates of Mercer have achieved distinction in every field. Representative of them are the following men: Louie Devotie Newton, Georgia pastor, denominational leader, and member of the executive committee of the Baptist World Alliance; Solon Bolivar Cousins, head of the religion department at the University of Richmond and member of the Southern Baptist Foreign Mission Board; Walter Pope Binns, president of William Jewell College; Rufus Carrolton Harris, president of Tulane University; William Heard Kilpatrick, teacher at Columbia University; William Fielding Ogburn, teacher at the University of Chicago; Walter F. George and Carl Vinson, United States congressmen; R. C. Bell, past chief justice of the Georgia Supreme Court; Lee B. Wyatt, presiding justice of the Georgia Supreme Court and a member of the military tribunal which tried major war criminals at Nuremberg, Germany; the late J. Edgar Paullin and Hal M. Davison, doctors; Eugene W. Stetson, chairman of the board of the Guaranty Trust Company of New York; Hamond Burke Nicholson, chairman of the board of the Coca-Cola Company; Mark F. Etheridge, publisher of the *Louisville Times* and the *Courier Journal;* and Malcolm M. Johnson, Pulitzer Prize-winning reporter for the *New York Sun.*

In 1955 Mercer was a small university with a college of liberal arts, and schools of law, education, and Christianity. A strong department of business administration had not attained the status of a separate school, due to lack of adequate endowment. The law school, founded in 1873, became an integral part of the university in 1920 and was named for the senator, Walter F. George, in 1947. Allowing for some breaks in continuity, the school of Christianity can be traced to a beginning in 1839, when Adiel Sherwood became head of Mercer's theology department. In 1945 this school was named for Columbus Roberts, Mercer's most substantial benefactor. A special feature is the extension department of Christian education, organized in 1948 for the special training of ministers who lack college and seminary training. In 1955, 43 training centers were in operation throughout the state of Georgia. The school of education, named for President Spright Dowell, was established in 1952 with a faculty of six.

In 1955 the school property was valued at $2,791,236. Equipment included the Hardman Library with more than 80,000 volumes and the law library with more than 25,000 volumes, together valued at $750,000. The endowment for maintenance and support is $4,438,308.30, of which three fourths is for the University proper and one fourth for the Walter F. George School of Law. The regular enrolment in 1955–56 was 1,843, and the total enrolment was 2,141. An additional 1,500 were enrolled in evening and Saturday classes and in extension courses. Mercer is on the approved list of the Association of American Universities, the Southern Association of Schools and Colleges, the Association of American Law Schools, and the American Bar Association, and is also a member of the American Council on Education and of the Association of American Colleges.

The budget for 1955–56 amounted to $640,166 and was provided from incomes from the following sources: Georgia Baptist Convention, 11 per cent; endowment, 20 per cent; tuition and fees, 65 per cent; and auxiliaries, 4 per cent. In addition, gifts for endowment, maintenance, campus improvements, and special objects are received from year to year in varying but substantial amounts. Among the many benefactors of the university the name of Jesse Mercer stands first of all for the first century of the institution's history with respect to both liberality and leadership. For the second century the name of Columbus Roberts leads the list with gifts of more than a million dollars to Christian education. The major portion of this amount is for the endowment of the school of Christianity which bears his name.

PRESIDENTS OF MERCER

1833–39	Billington McCarty Sanders, A.B.
1840–44	Otis Smith, A.B.
1844–54	John Lindley Dagg, D.D.
1854–65	Nathaniel Macon Crawford, D.D.
1866–71	Henry Holcombe Tucker, D.D., LL.D.
1871–72	Joseph Edgerton Willet, M.D. (Acting)
1872–89	Archibald John Battle, D.D., LL.D.
1889–93	Gustavus Alonzo Nunnally, D.D.
1893–96	James Bruton Gambrell, D.D., LL.D.
1896–1904	Pinckney Daniel Pollock, A.M., LL.D.
1904–05	William Heard Kilpatrick, A.M., Ph.D. (Acting)
1905–06	Charles Lee Smith, Ph.D.
1906–13	Samuel Young Jameson, D.D.
1913–14	James Freeman Sellers, LL.D. (Acting)
1914–18	William Lowndes Pickard, D.D.
1918–27	Rufus Washington Weaver, D.D., LL.D.
1927–28	Andrew Philip Montague, Ph.D. (Acting)
1928–53	Spright Dowell, A.M., LL.D.
1953–	George Boyce Connell, A.M., LL.D.

SPRIGHT DOWELL

MERCER'S CLUSTER. A hymnbook compiled by Jesse Mercer (*q.v.*), the most widely known and influential minister in Georgia in his day. Mercer spent the year 1799 preaching in South Carolina, North Carolina, and Virginia. Because of their respect for his reputation and character, large congregations attended his meetings. He usually carried with him and distributed an assortment of select pamphlets and books. Faced with the lack of hymnbooks in the new and growing churches, he collected and compiled a volume under the title, *The Cluster of Spiritual Songs, Divine Hymns, and Sacred Poems; Being Chiefly a Collection.*

To meet the popular demand, seven editions were printed. The first was unbound and was printed in Augusta, Ga., in 1813. This was followed in the same city by a bound and enlarged edition in 1815 and again in 1816. In 1817 while attending the Triennial Convention in Philadelphia he published a revised edition. The use was widespread, and other editions followed in 1820, 1826, and 1835. The 1835 edition was the fifth to be copyrighted. Thomas, Cowperthwaite, and Company published it in Philadelphia; and Collins and Brother, in New York. Two copies of this edition are deposited in the Mercer Library.

Among the more than 300 hymns in *Mercer's Cluster,* a few of which Jesse Mercer himself composed, are such ageless songs as "Rock of Ages"; "Amazing Grace"; "Am I a Soldier of the Cross?"; "Come, Thou Fount"; "Jesus, Lover of My Soul"; "Guide Me, O Thou Great Jehovah"; "From Greenland's Icy Mountains"; "On Jordan's Stormy Banks I Stand"; "Come Ye Sinners, Poor and Wretched"; and "How Firm a Foundation."

The Columbian Star, established in 1821 under the influence of Luther Rice (*q.v.*) to furnish a medium of communication for missions, published in Philadelphia, carried the following in 1829:

> As an evidence of its uncommon success and popularity we state upon undoubted authority that thirty-three thousand copies of the Mercer Cluster have been provided in this city. An edition lately completed amounts to ten thousand. . . . The good which has already been effected by this publication cannot be measured in the estimates of time. A great proportion of the hymns are of standard character, and such as occur in our judicious selection, while many others come under the description of Spiritual Songs, and are adapted to society meetings and to the private circles.

This hymnbook has been permanently memorialized in *The Mercer Cluster,* the student weekly at Mercer University since 1920.

SPRIGHT DOWELL

MERCY. See GOD.

MEREDITH, THOMAS (b. Bucks County, Pa., July 7, 1795; d. Philadelphia, Pa., Nov. 13, 1850). Son of John Meredith, a farmer, and Charlotte (Hough) Meredith. He graduated from the University of Pennsylvania (A.B., 1816; A.M., 1819), and in 1818 went to North Carolina. In 1819 he was married to Georgia Sears, and to them 11 children were born—Laura, Claudia, Marcus, Bettie, Cordelia, Cornelia, John, Luther, and three who died in infancy. From 1819 to 1837 Thomas Meredith held pastorates successively in New Bern and Edenton, N. C., in Savannah, Ga., and again in New Bern. One of the 14 founders of the North Carolina Baptist State Convention, organized in 1830, he drew up the constitution of that body, serving at various times as secretary, vice-president, and president. In 1835 he established the *Biblical Recorder* as the organ of the state convention, continuing as its editor until his death. In 1834 Meredith was offered the chair of mathematics and moral philosophy in Wake Forest Institute and was for several years trustee of that school. In 1838 he offered to the state convention a resolution urging the establishment of "a female seminary of high order." It was in recognition of his interest in the education of women and of his leadership in the denomination that the Baptist University for Women was in 1909 renamed Meredith College.

BIBLIOGRAPHY: *Baptist Interpreter. Biblical Recorder* (1833–1850; Jan. 2, 1935). N. C. Baptist State Convention, *Minutes* (1838–1850). Trustees of Meredith College, *Minutes* (1909). G. W. Paschal, *History of Wake Forest College* (1935). W. B. Sprague, *Annals of the American Pulpit* (1860).

MARY LYNCH JOHNSON

MEREDITH COLLEGE. A four-year college for women in Raleigh, N. C., chartered in 1891 as Baptist Female University, it first opened its doors to students in 1899. Meredith was founded by the North Carolina Baptist state convention and has always been under its control. James Carter Blasingame, first president of the institution, served with a faculty and staff of 18. Richard Tilman Vann (*q.v.*) succeeded Blasingame as president in 1900 and served until 1915, a period which saw a $43,000 debt paid, $127,000 endowment accumulated, and property value increased from $75,000 to $280,000. During this same period enrolment rose from 220 to 383 in spite of the discontinuance of business and elocution departments and nine years' preparatory work. In 1900 the school offered only a little more than a year of real college work, estimated by requirements of the Southern Association of Colleges and Secondary Schools; in 1915 a study of the catalogue indicated that four years of standard college work were offered. The school's name was changed May 24, 1909, to Meredith College in honor of Thomas Meredith (*q.v.*), one of the 14 founders of the North Carolina Baptist state convention and founder of the *Biblical Recorder,* who urged the convention in 1838 to establish "a female seminary of high order to be modeled and conducted on strictly religious principles but . . . as far as possible free from sectarian influences."

During the administration of Charles Edward Brewer (*q.v.*), 1915–39, Meredith was moved from a single city square one block northeast of the North Carolina Capitol to a 170-acre campus on Hillsboro Street three miles west of the Capitol, where erection of six brick and three temporary wooden buildings was financed by the sale of property in town and the issuing of bonds. In the new location libraries, churches, and lectures, concerts, and plays in Raleigh are still accessible to the students, as well as schools and institutions for supervised teaching and social work.

Although a nation-wide financial depression occurred during Brewer's administration, endowment increased from $127,000.00 to $531,162.44; property value from $289,050.00 to $1,430,568.94; enrolment from 383 to 583; and faculty and staff from 30 to 64. In 1921 Meredith was admitted to membership in the Association of Southern Colleges and Secondary Schools; in 1924 graduates were admitted to membership in the American Association of University Women; and in 1928 Meredith was placed on the list of colleges approved by the Association of American Universities.

Under Carlyle Campbell, who became president in 1939, an enlarged building program was undertaken. A $500,000 auditorium was completed in 1949 followed by a classroom building under construction in 1956, with a science building, library, and gymnasium planned for the near future. Toward this expansion program the state convention was making appropriations over a nine-year period, which in 1954–55 amounted to $64,488.51. The annual convention appropriation for current expenses, far exceeding annual interest on college endowment, was $94,140 in 1954–55. Total cost of room, board, and tuition for the nine-month session is $790.

Meredith offers two degrees, Bachelor of Arts and Bachelor of Music, and candidates for the Bachelor of Music degree must have been granted an A.B. degree. Degree requirements are based on the general principle of a broad distribution of studies among representative fields of human culture and concentration within a special field.

With the number of resident students limited to about 500, Meredith has for its aim the development in its students of the Christian attitude toward life and preparation for intelligent citizenship, homemaking, graduate work, professional, and other fields of service. Since Meredith stresses liberal arts, no distinctly preprofessional programs are offered. Enrolment in 1954–55 was 674. A total of 3,530 students have received degrees or diplomas from the institution, and 4,900 have been students who did not receive degrees. MARY LYNCH JOHNSON

MERIDIAN FEMALE COLLEGE. Established at Meridian, Miss., in 1865 and chartered two years later. The school continued operation under J. B. Hamberlin, president, until 1882.

J. L. BOYD

MESSIAH. This term is derived from the Hebrew word *Mashiach,* and the Aramaic word *Meshicha,* meaning Anointed. The Greek *Christos,* Christ, is the exact equivalent. As a proper name the word Messiah does not appear in the Old Testament; its first appearance is in apocalyptic literature (Enoch 48:10; 52:4). It was the custom of the Hebrews to anoint a person set apart for a high office, especially as a priest or a king, by pouring oil upon his head. The New Testament presents Christ as the Messiah who fulfilled the hopes of the prophets for one who should redeem his people (Mark 1:11; Matt. 4:1–11; Luke 4:16–21; Mark 3:22–27; Luke 7:18–23; Matt. 16:15–17).

See also JESUS CHRIST.

BIBLIOGRAPHY: J. W. Bowman, *The Intention of Jesus* (1943). H. R. Mackintosh, *The Doctrine of the Person of Jesus Christ* (1921).

CHARLES A. TRENTHAM

METHODIST CHURCH. The religious movement which traces its origin principally to John Wesley (1703–91) and, to a lesser degree, to his brother, Charles (1707–88), and George Whitefield (*q.v.*) (1714–70). Susannah (Annesley) Wesley, mother of John and Charles, must share largely in the foundation of the movement to the extent that she influenced their early lives. The name Methodists, according to John Wesley, was given by way of reproach to several young men at Oxford in 1729 or shortly thereafter because of the exact regularity of their lives as well as studies. In 1738 the name was applied to the Holy Club, a group of popular preachers which included the Wesleys and Whitefield.

May 24, 1738, the date of John Wesley's "conversion" experience, marks the beginning of Methodism as a distinct and enthusiastic evangelistic movement. Wesley entertained no thought of separation from the established Church of England and, indeed, fought separation, but it finally came. Officially, the separation occurred in America in 1784 with the organization of the Methodist Episcopal Church. Following John Wesley's death in 1791 and the adoption of a compromise plan in 1795, separation gained ascendancy in the Methodist Societies of England.

During John Wesley's lifetime the movement was dominated by his strong personality—his organizing genius, militant and evangelistic field preaching, ardent zeal, and strict discipline. Opposition and persecution were often encountered. Following Wesley's death the same crusading evangelism persisted, extending into a worldwide missionary activity. Francis Asbury became well known as the outstanding "circuit riding" propagator of Methodism in America. Schisms arose, but in recent years the marked tendency has been toward reunion. In 1925 the Methodist Church of Canada united with the Congregational churches, the Presbyterian Church, and the local Union churches in western Canada to form the United Church of Canada. In 1932 a reunion occurred in British Methodism. In 1939 the Methodist Episcopal Church, the Methodist Episcopal Church, South, and the Methodist Protestant Church in America became reunited.

Methodism is largely episcopal in polity. The three orders of the American ministry are bishop, pastor, and district superintendent. The close co-ordination of these gives a high degree of unity to the church. The function of the bishop of Methodism is that of "office" and not of "order." Little emphasis is given to apostolic succession, as the validity of the ministry is based on efficiency. Governing bodies of the Methodist Church consist of an ascending scale of Conferences—Quarterly, District, Annual, Jurisdictional—and on the foreign field, Central and General. Laymen are represented in all of these. Bishops, elected by the Jurisdictional and Central conferences, form the Council of Bishops, which meets at least once a year. Bishops supervise their areas and are responsible for making annual appointment of pastors to the churches. The district superintendent, between bishops and pastors, is in effect a subbishop.

Methodist theology has been fundamentally Arminian and of the mediating type. Following John Wesley's example great latitude has been allowed in theological opinion. Borden P. Bowne (1847–1910), a philosophical theologian, has probably influenced Methodist theology more than any other man since Wesley. Today there are well over 15 million Methodists in the world.

BIBLIOGRAPHY: N. Curnock, ed., Wesley's *Journal* (1909–16). Luccock, Hutchinson, and Goodloe, *The Story of Methodism* (1949). F. J. McConnell, *John Wesley* (1939). A. Stevens, *History of Methodism* (1858); *History of Methodist Episcopal Church* (1864). E. H. Sugden, ed., Wesley's *Sermons* (1922). W. W. Sweet, *Religion on the American Frontier, the Methodists* (1946). J. Telford, ed., *Wesley's Letters* (1931).

JOE KING

MEXICAN BAPTIST CONVENTION. Organized Baptist churches have existed in Mexico since 1864. The Mexican Baptist Convention met for its 50th anniversary in 1953 with the First Baptist Church of Mexico City, the church in which it was organized in 1903. The convention's program includes organized work in missions, Christian education, stewardship, and evangelism.

The Baptist constituency in the country is readily assuming the missionary task. Stewardship has been an emphasis in recent years. Much of the missionary work of the convention is carried on among the Indians, many of whom speak only their native dialects. A Revolving Chapel and Ministers' Fund provides loans for new Mexican churches; church members who are committed to tithing make it possible for loans to be founded on the principle of self-support. Twenty graduates of the 10-year-old seminary are serving Baptist churches in Mexico. Seminary enrolment in 1955 was 19. Pastors' conferences and strong women's and young people's organizations help present a world outlook to Mexican Baptists.

Sponsored by the American Baptist Home Mission Societies of the American Baptist Convention, the Mexican Baptist Convention in 1955 consisted of 32 active churches, 93 missions and outstations, 5,469 church members. In a Baptist constituency of 15,300 there were 25 ordained ministers. Twenty-nine teachers in day schools worked with 388 children in primary and secondary schools and 20 in high school. Total gifts by Mexican Baptists in 1955–56 amounted to $22,895.

MRS. MILO E. WENGER

MEXICAN BAPTIST CONVENTION OF TEXAS, THE. Organized May 25, 1910, upon recommendation of a special committee of the Baptist General Convention of Texas, appointed one year earlier. While the committee advised organization of the convention, it specified that this body did not constitute a separation from the Baptist General Convention of Texas. The principal reason for the formation of the new body was that the Mexican people spoke only Spanish and therefore could receive little benefit from attending meetings where only English was spoken. The convention soon saw the need for publicity and sought to establish a periodical. At last *El Bautista Mexicano,* published by the Home Mission Board of the Southern Baptist Convention, became the official organ.

Statistical reports are so fragmentary that they present no true picture of the activities of the convention. The convention held in July, 1918, reported 18 churches with 191 baptisms and a membership of 1,069. In 1921 it reported 31 churches, 237 baptisms, and 1,280 members. The Home Mission Board report of 1927 listed 65 churches, 68 missions, and 6,000 Mexican Baptists; the same year, however, the Mexican convention held in Laredo registered only 66 messengers representing 26 churches, of which only 17 sent statistical reports. Of 87 churches mentioned in the 1930 minutes, only 36 reported to the convention. J. L. Moye, for seven years superintendent of Mexican missions for the Home Mission Board, laid foundations for much of the work.

At present the Mexican convention is in a period of transition. All except a few of its member churches are also affiliated with local English-speaking associations and with the Baptist General Convention of Texas. Messengers from missions participate in the Mexican convention on an equal basis with messengers from churches, and the missions are "arms" of churches co-operating with the general convention. As this dual relationship continues, there is a growing consciousness among Mexican Baptists of their unity with the Baptist General Convention of Texas and with its program of world missions.

The Mexican convention is autonomous despite the fact that it is composed largely of messengers from congregations affiliated with the Baptist General Convention of Texas. It serves as a medium of fellowship, inspiration, and information for the total program of Texas Baptists. The language barrier necessitates continuation of this body, but for the most part Mexican Baptists are Southern Baptists both by conviction and by practice. Eventually the Mexican Baptist Convention will probably become an official part of the Baptist General Convention of Texas, although continuing to meet separately due to the problem of language.

Nearly all of the Spanish-speaking churches in Texas receive financial aid from the Baptist General Convention of Texas, and almost all of them in return contribute to the work of Texas and Southern Baptists through the Cooperative Program with some degree of regularity. It appears that this interest will grow.

BIBLIOGRAPHY: W. B. Miller, "Texas Mexican Baptist History" (1931). L. D. WOOD

MEXICAN BAPTIST ORPHANS HOME. Chartered June 2, 1944, and located on a 122-acre site 10 miles west of Bexar County Courthouse, San Antonio, Tex., center of Latin American population. Faced with urgent appeals, San Antonio Baptist Association began movement which resulted in the purchase of property, organization, and subsequent presentation of the home to the Mexican Baptist Convention of Texas and the Baptist General Convention of Texas in 1944, obtaining endorsement of both, which elected seven and eight members of a board of directors respectively. Construction of the home began in Jan., 1946, and by the end of 1955, 10 cottages for children, four dwellings for employees, a personnel building, administration-assembly-hospital building, garage and workshops, warehouses and dairy barns, light, water, gas, and sewer systems were in operation, all valued at $534,637.26. A total of more than $1,150,000 has been received from voluntary contributions of individuals and churches. Gifts of clothing, food, and live animals; products from the home dairy, beef, and pork program; and vegetables from truck gardens help supply daily needs.

Only destitute children of Latin American descent, ages 3 through 12, are received, but they may remain through high school, all attending public schools of San Antonio. A home program of physical, mental, social, and religious development is maintained with trained staff, modern cottages and furnishings. All children attend services of Spanish-speaking Baptist churches in the city, but the home provides Training Union and mid-week services on the premises. The Baptist Memorial Hospital of San Antonio and some physicians give their services free of charge to the children. Associated with similar institutions in Texas, the Southwest, and the Southern Baptist Convention territory, the home, when it reaches maximum growth, will have capacity for 360 children and will rank among the larger denominational homes for children. E. J. Gregory has been superintendent of the home since its founding. E. J. GREGORY

MEXICAN BAPTIST THEOLOGICAL SEMINARY, Torreón. See MEXICO, MISSION IN.

MEXICO, MISSION IN. Missionary work in Mexico was begun in 1880, when the Foreign Mission Board accepted T. M. Westrup of Mexico as its missionary and assumed responsibility for the work he had already begun in the states of Coahuila and Nuevo León. This work was supported jointly by the Foreign Mission Board and the state Baptist convention of Texas. In 1882 the board appointed Mr. and Mrs. W. M. Flournoy. In spite of the serious setbacks occasioned by the Mexican Revolution of 1910–20, the religious conflict of 1926–35 in Mexico, and the depression which ravaged our own country following the stock market crash of 1929, Southern Baptist mission work in Mexico has prospered. Today (1956) the Mexican mission maintains work in 15 of the republic's 29 states and in the Federal District, ministering to 61 per cent of the total territory of the country and to 52 per cent of its 29,675,000 inhabitants. Thirty missionaries are under appointment, serving from six stations: Hermosillo, Sonora; Chihuahua, Chihuahua; and Torreón, Coahuila, in the north and Guadalajara, Jalisco; Morelia, Michoacán; and México, Federal District, in the south.

Because Mexican law precludes any foreign-born person's serving as pastor of a church, the work of the Mexican mission is limited to three broad categories. The first is popularly known as "field work," with a "field" comprising a single city (e.g., Guadalajara, Jalisco, and Mexico City) or from one of three states. In the latter case it generally coincides with the limits of some Baptist association. The field missionary endeavors to promote evangelism and Christian education in the territory for which he is responsible, working in close cooperation with the local pastors. His work includes preaching and helping to develop national leadership through such media as local study courses, pastor's institutes, and encampments. The second category is the educational work. The mission maintains four student homes (at Chihuahua, Chihuahua, Guadalajara, Jalisco, Iguala, Guerrero, and México, Federal District). These are not schools as such, but rather boarding houses providing the atmosphere, discipline, and orientation of a consecrated Christian home for the young people who live in them and attend the public schools. For ministerial and missionary training the Mexican Baptist Theological Seminary is maintained at Torreón, Coahuila. A coeducational institution, it possesses a splendidly equipped plant with a maximum capacity for 150 students. The curriculum includes an adequate and practical course of study in the fields of theology, Christian education, and music. The third and newest phase of the mission's work is the medical, centered in Guadalajara, Jalisco, the country's second largest city. A 50-bed Baptist hospital is currently under construction.

In the area served by the Mexican mission the following statistics obtained for the fiscal year ending Mar. 31, 1956:

Number of churches	65	
Number self-supporting churches	15	(23%)
Number preaching stations	218	
Number church members	5,418	
Number of baptisms	589	
Number ordained pastors	34	
Number unordained workers	84	

See also STUDENT HOMES, CHIHUAHUA AND GUADALAJARA. JAMES D. CRANE

MEYER, FREDERICK BROTHERTON (b. London, England, Apr. 8, 1847; d. London, England, Jan. 28, 1929). English Baptist preacher, known best for devotional expositions of the Scriptures and emphasis upon the Holy Spirit. He was born into a wealthy Christian home of Baptist parents. Converted at seven, he decided to preach at the age of 16. He was active as a preacher for 63 years, beginning in 1866. He attained prominence as a pastor, Bible and devotional lecturer, and writer. After schooling by private tutors and in private schools, Meyer studied two years at Regent's Park, Oxford, completing his B.A. degree at London University in 1869. He was given a D.D. degree in 1911 by McMaster University of Canada.

He was pastor of five Baptist and two independent churches, doing his most outstanding work at Christ Church, London, in his latter years. The last 41 years of his ministry centered in London. Men who had marked influence on Meyer by close ties of friendship included Dwight L. Moody, Archibald Thomas Robertson (*q.v.*), J. Wilbur Chapman, R. A. Torrey, G. Campbell Morgan, and many others of the evangelical and conservative group.

Meyer lectured in many parts of the world, making several trips around the world and at least 13 tours of America, beginning in 1891, when Moody invited him to speak at his Northfield Conference. He became well known for his discourses on the inner life, reflecting his own personal piety and the high regard he held for the work of the Holy Spirit in the life of a Christian. Meyer spoke at the first meeting of the Baptist World Alliance in 1905. He frequently addressed the Keswick Convention, a seven-day annual meeting in England on the Spirit-filled life. He enjoyed traveling and was much in demand as a speaker.

A prolific writer, Meyer produced over 80 books and about 50 pamphlets. Many were brief devotional treatments dealing with the theme of consecration. His most substantial work is represented by his biblical biographies and devotional expositions, such as: *Exodus* (2 vols.); *Christ in Isaiah; Elijah and the Secret of His Power; Gospel of John; John the Baptist; Joseph, Beloved, Hated, Exalted; Joshua and the Land of Promise; Moses, the Servant of God; Our Daily Homily* (5 vols.); *The Way into the Holiest; Tried by Fire;* and many others.

Prominent positions held by Meyer include president of the Free Church Council, 1904; president of the Baptist Union (of England), 1907–09; president of the National Sunday School Council, 1902; and president of the World Sunday School Convention, 1907.

He married Miss J. E. Jones in 1871. She preceded him in death by only six weeks. Their only child was a daughter.

BIBLIOGRAPHY: W. Y. Fullerton, *F. B. Meyer, A Biography* (1929). A. Gamie, *Preachers I Have Heard* (1945). A. C. Mann, *F. B. Meyer* (1929). R. E. Nielson, "An Appraisal of F. B. Meyer as a Preacher" (MS, 1955). R. ELMER NIELSON

MIAMI BAPTIST HOSPITAL (Okla.). At the meeting of the Oklahoma convention's board of directors in June, 1917, an offer was presented to build a hospital in Miami, to be under the control of the convention. It opened July 1, 1919. This 60-bed institution has cared for over 40,000 patients in 35 years of operation. In 1954 its plant was valued at $223,482 with total assets of $228,750 and a total indebtedness of $22,689. TOM E. CARTER

MIDDLETON, EDWIN LEE (b. near Warsaw, Duplin County, N. C., Sept. 10, 1866;

d. Winston-Salem, N. C., Feb. 14, 1928). Sunday school leader. He was the son of David John and Lucy Jane (Nicholson) Middleton. Educated in the best local schools, he studied at Wake Forest College, 1884–88. After graduation Middleton taught in schools at Wilson, Durham, and Cary. On June 1, 1908, he became Sunday school secretary, North Carolina Baptist Convention. Middleton distinguished himself for his leadership in the organization of Sunday schools, especially in rural areas; for his emphasis on teacher training; and for his interest in church architecture, helping 670 churches in North Carolina in their building programs. He wrote *Building a Country Sunday School* (1923), recognized for its mastery of the principles of organization and promotion of Sunday schools. Middleton married Mary Eva Rigsbee and to them were born six children.

BIBLIOGRAPHY: J. L. W. Moose, "Sunday School Work as Promoted by the Baptist State Convention, 1830–1930" (1950). B. W. Spilman, "Edwin Lee Middleton," *Baptist Leaders in Religious Education*, ed., J. M. Price (1943). C. SYLVESTER GREEN

MIDDLETON LITERARY AND THEOLOGICAL INSTITUTE. Established in 1839 by Baptists of Middleton, Carroll County, Miss., with S. S. Lattimore principal. The school merged with Judson Institute in 1840.

J. L. BOYD

MID-MISSIONS (General Council of Cooperating Baptist Missions of North America). Independent faith mission loosely related to ("approved by") General Association of Regular Baptists, founded in 1920 at Elyria, Ohio, by William Clarence Haas and others. It is not affiliated with Southern Baptist Convention. Haas had gone to Africa under the Africa Inland Mission in 1912. After working in the Belgian Congo, he broke with the Africa Inland Mission, was related briefly to the Heart of Africa Mission, then went independently to French Congo. On furlough in 1920, he led in founding this society; later he took back a party to establish missions in French Equatorial Africa. At first known as the General Council of Co-operating Baptist Missions of North America, the society adopted the shorter name Mid-Africa Missions. When work was extended to fields outside of Africa, the name became Mid-Missions. Since 1953 the longer official name has been rarely used.

French Equatorial Africa, the first field, has continued to be the chief area of activity, with 126 missionaries in 1955. However, work has been extended to many other countries, and as of Apr., 1955, Mid-Missions reported over 500 missionaries in 23 different lands, including nearly 100 in home missions in the United States. Fields in 1955 were French Equatorial Africa, Belgian Congo, Gold Coast, Liberia, India (Assam), Indonesia, Japan, Honduras, France, Germany, Italy, Netherlands, British West Indies, Dominican Republic, Haiti, Alaska, Canada, Hawaii, Brazil, British Guiana, Peru, Venezuela, and the United States. The home office is located at 1120 Chester Avenue, Cleveland 14, Ohio. H. C. GOERNER

MILLENNIUM. The term applies to that doctrine which constitutes an interpretation of the "thousand years" mentioned six times in Revelation 20:2–7. The term itself is derived from the Latin, *mille anni*, "thousand years," a translation of the Greek, *chilia etē*. Biblically, the concept is rooted in intertestamental apocalyptic literature, and historically, it has had various interpretations.

Premillennialism, early expounded by certain early Christian fathers, teaches that Christ's second advent will precede a reign by Christ upon the earth for one thousand years, together with two or more resurrections and two or more judgments. Pretribulational dispensational premillennialism, such as that taught by the Plymouth Brethren and appearing in the Scofield Reference Bible, differs from historic premillennialism in its doctrine of two comings, in the first of which Christ is to deliver Christians by the "rapture" from the "tribulation period"; it differs also in its seven-period interpretation of history and stress upon the postponement of the kingdom. Postmillennialism, which is somewhat similar to the Medieval pure church expectation of Joachim of Floris and the Franciscan Spirituals and was first articulated by Daniel Whitby (1638–1726), teaches that a thousand years of peace and righteousness on the earth, inaugurated by the power of the gospel, will be followed by Christ's second advent, one general resurrection, one general judgment, and the eternal order.

Still another interpretation is amillennialism teaching that the "thousand years" is not a future era of earthly history and that Christ's second advent, the resurrection, and the judgment will terminate history and inaugurate eternity. Amillennialism consists of at least two types, the Augustinian view, which interprets the millennium as the interadventual or Christian era, and the view of Theodor Friedrich Dethlof Kliefoth (1810–95), that it is the eternal, heavenly state itself.

Not until the 20th century has millennial doctrine become a major issue among Baptists. Certain English Baptists participated in the Fifth Monarchy Movement (*c.* 1649–61), and a few American Baptists became followers of William Miller's Adventism. Major Baptist confessions prior to this century did not define or articulate the doctrine. Baptists in the contemporary period tend principally toward premillennialism or amillennialism.

BIBLIOGRAPHY: O. T. Allis, *Prophecy and the Church* (1954). B. H. Carroll, "Revelation," *An Interpretation of the English Bible* (1913). L. S. Chafer, *Systematic Theology*, vol. 4 (1948). R. H. Charles, *A Critical History of the Doctrine of a Future Life* (1913). R. B. Jones, *The Things That Shall Be Hereafter* (1947). D. H. Kromminga, *The*

Millennium in the Church (1945); *Scofield Reference Bible* (1909). G. E. Ladd, *Crucial Questions About the Kingdom of God* (1952). E. A. McDowell, *The Meaning and Message of Revelation* (1951). W. H. Rutgers, *Premillennialism in America* (1930). R. Summers, *Worthy Is the Lamb* (1951). JAMES LEO GARRETT

MILLERITE MOVEMENT. A chiliastic phenomenon of the 1830–40's centering about William Miller (1782–1849), a farmer and Baptist preacher, who initiated the movement in New York by predicting that the Second Advent would occur about the year 1843. Accelerated by extremist revivals, the movement expanded to New England and reached a climax in 1843–44, attracting national attention and some fanatics. Despite implementation by numerous publications, adherents drawn from leading revivalistic denominations, principally Baptists, and revised calculations, the movement eventually suffered from disillusionment and recrimination. Denominations evolved from the movement include the Advent Christian Association, Seventh Day Adventists, influenced by association with Seventh Day Baptists, and the Church of God.

See also ADVENTISTS and ESCHATOLOGY.

BIBLIOGRAPHY: W. R. Cross, *The Burned-over District, The Social and Intellectual History of Enthusiastic Religion in Western New York, 1800–1850* (1950). F. D. Nichol, *The Midnight Cry* (1944).
GLEN LEE GREENE

MILLS, JOHN HAYMES (b. Halifax County, Va., July 9, 1831; d. near Thomasville, N. C., Dec. 15, 1898). Founder of orphanages. Mills was the son of John Garland and Martha Williams (Haymes) Mills. He was an honor student at Wake Forest College, graduating in 1854. Mills taught in Milton, N. C., 1854, and was professor of mathematics at Oxford Female Seminary, 1855–58; president, 1858–67. He sold the property and for one year conducted his school in the building of St. John's College, which had been supported for a while by the Masons but had been abandoned. From 1863 to 1873, Mills was owner and editor of the *Biblical Recorder*.

Stirred by the need for orphanages in his state, Mills gave up the Baptist paper and started the Masonic Orphanage at Oxford, 1873, and struggled for 11 years against poverty, indifference, and sometimes hostility. In 1884 he moved to a farm three miles west of Thomasville. When the Baptists, after heated discussion, decided to establish an orphanage at Thomasville, Mills was chosen manager and served from 1885 to 1895. His zeal, love for children, and ability to win the confidence of the denomination helped secure hearty support for the Baptist Orphanage of North Carolina. He founded the orphanage paper *Charity and Children* in 1887. Mills introduced the cottage unit system at the orphanage and established the orphanage school and the church. In 1895 he retired to farm near Thomasville. Mills married Elizabeth Williams, a teacher at the Oxford Female Seminary, in 1856. They had one child.

I. G. GREER

MILLS HOME. Founded as the Thomasville Baptist Orphanage Nov. 11, 1885, at Thomasville, N. C., and now owned by the Baptist State Convention of North Carolina. Ten-year-old Mary Presson from Hertford County was the orphanage's first child, received by the institution's founder and first general manager, John Haymes Mills (*q.v.*), who served in that capacity until 1895. The North Carolina Baptist Orphanage Association, the first organization devoted to child care work among Baptists in the state, was formed in Raleigh on Nov. 15, 1884; but although the Thomasville Orphanage opened the following year, its charter was not ratified by the North Carolina General Assembly until Mar. 11, 1889. The name of the child care organization was changed in 1928 to the Baptist Orphanage of North Carolina, Inc., with the Thomasville Orphanage named Mills Home in memory of its founder.

On a 500-acre site within the city limits of Thomasville, Mills Home consists of 34 buildings, which include 18 cottages for children, church, library, infirmary, print shop, recreation building, kindergarten building, freezer locker, administration building, maintenance shop, 12 residences for staff members, and several smaller auxiliary buildings. Livestock, poultry, dairy, and truck farms are maintained by the home, which also owns and operates a farm at Wallburg, 10 miles from Thomasville. Assets of the Baptist Orphanage of North Carolina, Inc., on Dec. 31, 1954, were $3,843,-885.27, including land, buildings, and general endowment funds of $743,684.65. With income in 1954 of $690,340.26, the orphanage cared for a total of 713 children. The home went into the Cooperative Program on Jan. 1, 1955, "for that part of the support not otherwise provided." The staff of 100 people who direct the work includes nine trained social workers in the social service department. The entire program of child care, including Kennedy Memorial Home, is under general direction of an 18-member board of trustees, named by the state convention.

Mills Home serves dependent children from all sections of North Carolina. In addition to 340 children who live at the home, 84 are supported in foster homes and 51 assisted through Mother's Aid. A full-time pastor serves in the campus church. After children attend Thomasville city schools, from the first grade through high school, the home assists them in finding employment or in enrolling in colleges or vocational schools. Limited scholarship loans are available. J. MARSE GRANT

MILTON BAPTIST FEMALE INSTITUTE. A school at Milton, N. C., the first Baptist preparatory school in the state, chartered Dec. 24, 1844, and opened in Jan., 1845. Milton Institute received support from Beulah and Flat River associations in North Carolina and Roanoke and Dan River associations in Virginia. On Jan. 29, 1849, its charter was amended to enable the trustees to operate Beulah Male Institute. Both schools are now extinct. D. L. SMILEY

MINISTER, THE SOUTHERN BAPTIST. In the Greek New Testament there are at least 15 words and phrases which refer directly to the pastoral office. The first of these is "apostle." The apostles were the first ministers. The modern preacher follows in their train, not because of apostolic succession but because he is (1) one who has experienced Christ and can bear testimony to that experience and (2) one who has received a personal commission from Christ.

The New Testament minister was called a "prophet," meaning not so much one who foretells the future as one who interprets the present. A prophet is one endowed to teach divine truth in times of ignorance, to give divine light to those in darkness. The word "evangelist," although used only three times in the New Testament (Acts 21:8; II Tim. 4:5; Eph. 4:11), is important. The evangelist is the bearer of good news, glad tidings. The word "pastor" has lost much of its old significance. It is correctly translated "one who feeds his flock." It deals with the tender relations of the pastor to the people, his spiritual rather than official relationship to them. He is a shepherd charged with the direction, affection, and protection of his flock. The preacher is also the "teacher" of spiritual truth. The preacher in his role as a teacher has the responsibility of helping his people "know," as well as "feel." The words "elder" or presiding officer of an assembly, "bishop" or overseer of a local congregation, "ambassador" or messenger, and "steward" are all used of the pastoral office.

No individual can fully measure up to the New Testament ideal. Although the Southern Baptist preacher should aspire to do so, he does not measure up to the highest standard. There is no "typical" Southern Baptist preacher. Wide variations occur. However, from observations and surveys a certain composite picture can emerge.

A sense of mission is the most uniform characteristic of the preacher in a Southern Baptist church. The "call to the ministry" and the ministry as a calling have remained unchanged although educational attainment, pastoral and preaching emphases, and even the conceptions of the church have varied and do vary.

The average Southern Baptist minister is about 43 years old and was born either in the country or a small town. He was converted before the age of 16 and began preaching around the age of 24. He has held five pastorates of an average of four years each. He probably attended a Baptist college in his home state. He has three children, belongs to a civic club, and has led at least one church in a building program. He holds one and sometimes two revivals in his church each year, and his favorite invitation hymn is "Just as I Am." The formal educational level of the Southern Baptist preacher is increasing. Approximately 80 per cent of all ministers have a high school education, 62 per cent have finished college, and 60 per cent have attended a seminary, the vast majority attending one of the five Southern Baptist seminaries. This picture is improved by the thousands who add to their education through extension and correspondence courses offered by Baptist colleges and seminaries.

The average age of the active minister has been lowered largely by more adequate retirement programs, giving rise to a modern phenomenon of great value—the interim pastor. Numerous retired preachers render inestimable service in giving stability and counsel to churches between regular pastors.

Most preachers carry on the same general organizational program which has been developed by the denomination from local needs and then handed back down by the agencies involved. This program is inapplicable to some local situations but is a pretty accurate average of the answer to general needs. The greatest frustration of the minister comes from the conflict of his desire to be a prophet and preacher and his necessity to be a promoter and an "oiler of wheels" to keep the machinery going.

Most Southern Baptist preachers were reared in Christian homes, homes in which well-nigh all parents approved the decision to enter the ministry. Their own homes rank high in the realm of character, good literature, fine opportunities. They rank low on the number of things the family does together. Too often it is true that the preacher is pastor to all except his own family. The preacher's family is not only in the public eye but is also susceptible to all kinds of criticism. His wife is subject to many different kinds of pressure. She is expected to do more than she is physically able to do.

The typical service as conducted by the Southern Baptist preacher is austerely simple. Three hymns, interspersed with prayer and scripture and followed by the offering, mark the early parts of the service. If there is a choir, an anthem or hymn is sung before the sermon. The sermon is 30 to 35 minutes in length, but growing shorter all the time. The sermon generally is closed with an appeal to commitment and church membership. During the singing of a hymn of invitation, those responding make their way to the front where they are received for church membership. The sermons preached are characterized by emotional zeal. They are essentially evangelistic, aiming always at a commitment. There is one sermon a year on the resurrection—at Easter, one on the incarnation—at Christmas, and few on Christian growth. The favorite text is John 3:16.

By virtue of his office, the preacher is accepted in the community, but not always in the way he would wish. He is alternately lis-

Distribution of Pastors' Salaries, S.B.C., 1955

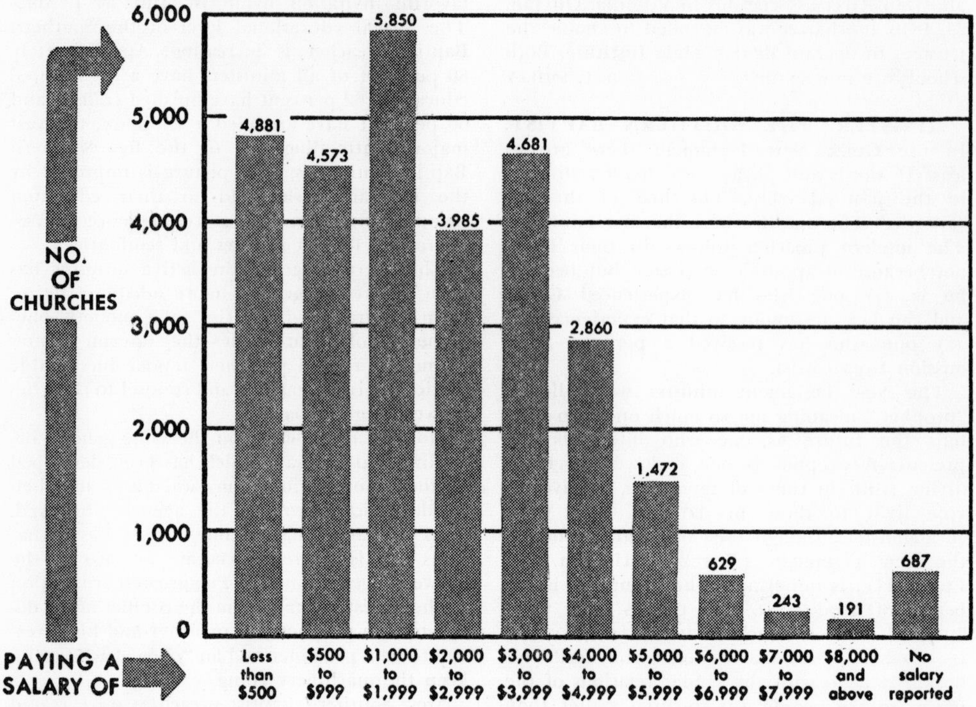

tened to and bypassed. His help is sought, but sometimes his advice is shunned.

The average Southern Baptist preacher lives in a home owned by the church, although a large number (21 per cent) now own their own homes, which are about on the level of the community or above. Most of them are used by both pastor and people, and although he may protest, the preacher likes it and his wife endures it. The preacher's income has increased rather rapidly, although still small on the average. In 1955, 15,304 preachers in the Southern Baptist Convention received less than $2,000 in salary; 14,041 received more than $2,000. For full-time pastors the average salaries run from $2,242 in churches under 399 members to $9,452 in churches above 3,000 members.

Some Baptists are noncreedal in belief and nonconformist in practice, and variations from the norm are to be expected in the ministry. For example more emphasis is laid on the dignity and value of worship in the Southeast, while in the Southwest informality is the rule and practice. Young churches tend toward informality, while older churches give more emphasis to the stately order of service. Seminary education gives the preacher more tools with which to vary the service, but he does not always use them.

It is to be understood that the term "Southern Baptist preacher" includes the pastor of a quarter-time church as well as the pastor of a church with a staff of 25 and a membership of thousands. In one church one person may be expected to be preacher, counselor, administrator, pastor, and evangelist; in another there may be full-time staff members who specialize in one or another of these ministries.

Nearly all preachers manifest an evangelistic zeal, sometimes characterized by more heat than light, but always demonstratively warm. There are those who emphasize expansion more than growth. There are others whose determination to foster Christian growth makes them seem circumscribed in outreach. All are interested, however, in making more Christians and better Christians. The Southern Baptist preacher—called of God, depending on the Holy Spirit, seeking always new light, ever an evangelist, continually a promoter of the program—is sometimes frustrated by the size of his task, yet generally is determined to do it to the best of his ability. DOTSON M. NELSON, JR.

MINISTERIAL EDUCATION, MISSISSIPPI BOARD OF. In 1837 the Mississippi Baptist Education Society was commended by the Education Committee of the Mississippi Baptist Convention for its work in aiding ministerial students to attend out-of-state Baptist schools, since there were no Baptist schools in the state. By 1849 the society became an auxiliary of the convention, and in 1870 the Ministerial Education Board was created as an agency of the state convention. First chartered in 1889 under the laws of Mississippi as the Board of Ministerial Education of the Baptist Denomination of Mississippi, the board apparently now operates under a charter granted in 1920. The purpose of the board is to aid ministerial students at all four state Baptist colleges in securing a college education. Students qualifying for aid may be provided with low-rental or no-rental housing, occasional cash grants, and emergency loans, according to individual need. The board owns 30 apartments at Clarke College and 31 at Mississippi College, valued at $200,000. The board's operating receipts for the year ending Aug. 31, 1955, were $30,407.42, of which $29,002.42 was received from the Cooperative Program. W. E. STRANGE

MINISTERIAL RELIEF AND RETIREMENT, ALABAMA. In 1878 the Alabama Baptist State Convention took definite action to help provide for its aged and infirm ministers and their dependents. In 1880 it appointed a standing central committee to receive and disburse its Aged and Infirm Ministers Fund with headquarters at Selma. In 1908 The Aged and Infirm Ministers Endowment Fund was started. The Board of Aged and Infirm Ministers Fund was created in 1909 to handle both the Endowment Fund and the current fund with headquarters in Birmingham. Various methods of supporting this cause have been used, such as, individual gifts, Sunday school offerings, free-will offering on the first Sunday in December, and Mother's Day offering. In 1919 the state board turned over its funds and functions to the Relief and Annuity Board, Southern Baptist Convention. DAVIS COOPER

MINISTERIAL RELIEF AND RETIREMENT, NORTH CAROLINA. Following action of the Baptist state convention in 1889, the Ministers' Relief Board was organized Feb. 1, 1890, and continued its existence until 1921. After the Southern Baptist Convention organized the present Relief and Annuity Board in Sept., 1918, the work of providing relief for aged ministers became, by the following year, a function of the Southern Baptist Convention with the states co-operating. In 1921 the North Carolina convention voted to turn over all relief funds in hand to the North Carolina Baptist Foundation for investment, with the understanding that the annual interest be paid to the Southern Baptist Relief and Annuity Board in Dallas, Tex. By 1922, 73 beneficiaries residing in North Carolina were receiving relief funds from the Convention-wide board.

During the 75 Million Campaign which began in 1919, the North Carolina relief board inaugurated a plan whereby a minister could take out a certificate of membership, make regular annual payments, and receive at 68 years of age an annuity of $500 annually. The board was in a position to guarantee this amount after Jan. 1, 1924. Then from 1938 to 1940, the board inaugurated new plans for retirement annuities, in which the minister paid an amount and churches and conventions paid a stated amount, in order to build up a retirement annuity of $2,000 annually.

M. A. HUGGINS

MINISTERIAL RELIEF AND RETIREMENT, OKLAHOMA. The Ministers' Retirement Plan was inaugurated in Oklahoma on July 1, 1939, with 255 ministers and 274 churches participating during the first year. Prior to that time no retirement plan had been in effect in Oklahoma, although the Old Annuity Fund, inaugurated by the Relief and Annuity Board of the Southern Baptist Convention, theoretically included every pastor in the Southern Baptist Convention. In 1955 Oklahoma had 432 active members in the Ministers' Retirement Plan and 137 in the Southern Baptist Protection Plan, making a total of 569 members, serving 822 Oklahoma churches, participating in the two state unit plans. The same year the board paid annuitants of the Ministers' Retirement Plan in Oklahoma the total annual sum of approximately $45,910, and Oklahoma's 21 ministers and 34 widows on the board's Relief Roll received grants totaling $8,502 per year.

J. C. SEGLER

MINISTERS' AID SOCIETY OF KENTUCKY, BAPTIST. In 1870 a committee was appointed by the general association of Kentucky Baptists to study the problem of relief for indigent ministers, but it never reported. In 1887 the general association created the Baptist Ministers Aid Society of Kentucky, and Owensboro was chosen for the headquarters location. The society was incorporated under the laws of Kentucky in 1890.

Reference to the annual reports of the Ministers Aid Society show that in 1889 the endowment fund was $1,647. By 1893 it had risen to $16,916. Ten years later it had more than doubled with $34,187. By 1925 the number of beneficiaries had reached 100 for the first time and continues to increase.

From the time of its organization, the trustees of the Baptist Ministers Aid Society were elected by and responsible to the General Association of Baptists in Kentucky and reported to it. In 1918 when the Relief and Annuity Board of the Southern Baptist Convention was organized, it became necessary to correlate the work of these two agencies. After some difficulties, the work proceeded harmoniously on a co-operative basis. The society has acted on applications for relief benefits and made recommendations to the Relief and Annuity Board. Both agencies contributed to the welfare of the beneficiaries.

In 1948 the society's assets, amounting to $65,515, were transferred to the Kentucky Baptist Foundation. Subsequent bequests have increased this to $72,606. Investment earnings on this fund since 1948 have amounted to $19,500. These earnings are remitted quarterly to the Relief and Annuity Board, where they continue to provide relief benefits for aged Kentucky ministers. BAYNARD F. FOX

MINISTERS' RELIEF FUND, VIRGINIA BAPTIST. The Baptist General Association of Virginia in 1871 adopted a plan for the relief of needy Baptist ministers and their dependents. A committee was instructed to seek incorporation, and in 1872 a charter was granted to the Trustees of the Baptist Ministers' Relief Fund of Virginia. Charles L. Cocke was chosen president of the board.

When the plan became more widely understood and the need more fully recognized, collections were taken in the churches as for other causes sponsored by the denomination; also special gifts and bequests were made from which the income was used along with current contributions.

When the Convention's Relief and Annuity Board at Dallas was organized and the Cooperative Program was inaugurated, the Virginia Baptist Ministers' Relief Fund ceased to receive regular contributions from the churches. Its income now consists in earnings from invested funds, individual gifts, and occasional legacies. Since resources have thus been curtailed and major responsibility for ministers' relief has been assumed by the Dallas board, the trustees have restricted their donations to the Baptist Ministers' Relief Fund of Virginia emergency cases, such as hospitalization without insurance and occasional supplements of the meager funds of superannuated ministers and widows.

Members of the board are elected by the board for indefinite terms from lists approved by the general association. The audited report to the association in 1954 showed assets of $94,-594.32 and gross income of $4,078.01. Approximately 20 persons are helped per year in amounts from $100 to $300. R. E. LOVING

MINORITIES, DEFENSE OF. In 1845 the Southern Baptist Convention adopted a constitution that contained in its preamble this significant statement, "a plan for eliciting, combining and directing the energies of the whole denomination in one sacred effort, for the propagation of the gospel."

In 1908 the Committee on Civic Righteousness said "that this Convention holds that . . . every wrong, public and private, political and social, retards the consummation of the commission of our King." Defense of minorities and propagation of the gospel were made inseparable.

Concerning our treatment of the Indians, the Convention stated in 1883, "the repeated removals of Indian tribes and nations from established homes to new reservations . . . effectively [bars] the progress of Christianity."

The Convention of 1893 resolved "That this Convention hereby expresses its sympathies with the Chinese people resident among us in their efforts to obtain justice and protection at the hands of our national government." The Convention 30 years later referred to "a great wrong done many years ago to the subjects of a nation friendly to our own." The report continues, "The details of this persecution, in the harsh and rigid enforcement of the Chinese Exclusion Laws are shocking to the conscience of humanity."

It was a similar concern that prompted the 1924 Convention to appoint a committee on Modification of Chinese Exclusion Laws. They expressed concern about immigration laws having to do with the Japanese.

In 1925 the committee appointed the previous year reported to the Convention, "We have the satisfaction of knowing that Southern Baptists have gone on record protesting against inhuman treatment and injustice inflicted upon innocent people."

Southern Baptists at their Convention of 1896 said "that we deeply sympathize with the persecuted Christians in Armenia."

The beginnings of Southern Baptist interest in Cuba are found in their defense of a minority people there. In 1896 they said "that we . . . earnestly protest against the banishment of our missionaries from Cuba." Then in 1898 a resolution by William Jonathan Northen (*q.v.*) of Georgia was adopted, "that in the adjustment of the political affairs of the island of Cuba they use every proper endeavor to secure equality of religious right to every inhabitant of that island."

In 1904 the Convention resolved "that it is the belief of this convention, representing the Baptists, that our government . . . do all it can . . . to free native peoples from the tyranny and oppression of the government of King Leopold."

The atrocities practiced by the government of King Leopold upon the inhabitants of the Belgian Congo were sturdily resisted by the Southern Baptist Convention. In 1906 Edgar Young Mullins (*q.v.*) offered a resolution which was adopted urging that Congress take all possible steps to halt these outrages. Another resolution read, "*Resolved,* That we express our horror of the atrocious cruelty practiced by Leopold . . . upon the . . . Congo country."

In 1923, 1924, 1927, 1936, and 1939, the Convention repeatedly protested the persecution of Baptist peoples in Rumania. In 1923 George Washington Truett (*q.v.*) introduced a resolution which was adopted and about which he said, "the convention notes with astonishment and indignation that many acts of persecution have been directed against Baptists in Rumania during the past year." The 1924 minutes listed the abuses of minorities in that country.

In 1936 the Convention took note of "wrongs suffered by the members of the Baptist churches in Italy."

In the years following World War II, Southern Baptists took notice of the plight of displaced persons in the countries of Europe, and in 1949 concern was expressed for them.

Southern Baptist defense of minorities is reflected in a statement of 1948 adopted by the Convention which had been offered by W. R. White of Texas, "that Communism, Fascism, political ecclesiasticism and anti-Semitism are utterly contrary to the genius of the Baptist concept of freedom and spiritual values."

See also RACE RELATIONS. ROBERT E. NAYLOR

MIN-TOM CHILDREN'S HOME. A charitable institution in Chattanooga, Tenn., for the care of dependent Negro children, founded by Mrs. C. M. Deakins, and under the control of the Baptist denomination since 1952. In that year the home came under the control of the Hamilton County Baptist Association. The building burned Mar. 9, 1953, and on Aug. 24, 1954, a contract was let for a new building, costing $58,670. Faced with a shortage of funds, the association transferred the home to the Tennessee Baptist Convention, which assumed control in 1954, "with the understanding that when the colored Baptists are in a position to adequately operate the Home they will be asked to assume that responsibility." Since that time it has been operated under the board of the Tennessee Baptist Children's Homes, Inc. Its statistics are not reported separately.

JUDSON BOYCE ALLEN

MIRACLES. The Scriptures contain a religion supernatural in character from Genesis through Revelation. God, free to act as he wishes, has power to perform what he wills; the Bible consistently affirms that God has freely exercised his power supernaturally. The presupposition of this divine action is human sin. The miracle, related to sin in two ways, is first of all part of the pattern of redemption. It is one of the means by which God breaks through man's ignorance and indifference, awakening his mind to spiritual reality, revealing divine power and will to overcome the effects of sin. Second, the miracle is God's indication that the prophet and apostle are speaking God's truth (cf. Heb. 2:3–4). Both prophet and apostle, at God's direction, performed miraculous deeds as a proof that their message came from God. With the cessation of divine revelation, the need for this type of miracle ceased. Unusual means now employed by God to assist mankind are under the jurisdiction of his providence.

Since critics of the miraculous attempt to base their argument on a prejudiced definition, a miracle must be defined with care. Any definition viewing a miracle as an "intrusion" or "interruption" of nature (as if the miraculous bursts in upon nature like an uninvited guest) is not true to the biblical concept of miracle. The real issue in the validity of the miracle-accounts is the truth of the entire Christian faith.

God's miraculous action is varied. It includes foreknowledge (as in fulfilled prophecy) and omnipotence (power over nature, over a wide variety of diseases and deformities, over evil spirits, and over death itself). The supreme miracle of the entire Scripture is the resurrection of Christ, his personal victory over the two great enemies of man, sin and death.

The modern mind, to a great extent, has not accepted the supernatural religion of the Bible and has therefore placed the miraculous under heavy fire. Denials have come from philosophers (Hume *et al.*), from theologians (the religious liberals), and from New Testament critics. With due regard for the arguments of the critics, Machen's question is a pointed one: Christianity may be more acceptable in our times if pruned of the supernatural, but then, would it be worth believing? BERNARD RAMM

MIRACULOUS CONCEPTION. This term is a synonym for virgin birth. Both terms indicate that Christ is a direct gift of God. By using the term "miraculous conception," proper significance is placed upon *conception* in the womb of the virgin Mary nine months before Christ was born, the crucial point in which the supernatural broke into the natural process. The term is deficient in its failure to distinguish sufficiently between the wonder births of the sons of promise (e.g., Isaac and John the Baptist) and the birth of Christ. It is also easily confused with the Roman Catholic doctrine of immaculate conception.

See also VIRGIN BIRTH. CHARLES R. TUCKER

MISSIONARY. Published at Oklahoma City, Okla., each week with W. N. Nichols, editor. A four-page paper, 17 x 22 inches, it sold for $1 per year. The Baptist Publishing Company published the paper and 575 copies were circulated. In 1894 its size changed to 15 x 22 inches. It is now extinct. J. M. GASKIN

MISSIONARY EDUCATION COUNCIL. An organization of representatives of Southern Baptist agencies which are responsible for the production and utilization of missionary education materials. The council had its inception in a meeting of the executives of the Home Mission Board, Foreign Mission Board, Sunday School Board, Woman's Missionary Union, and Brotherhood Commission in Nashville, Tenn., in Sept., 1945. They authorized a meeting of representatives of the respective agencies in Richmond, Va., Jan. 9–10, 1946, when the council became an organized body. The chairman for the first year was Joe Wright Burton, whose leadership was a strong factor in perfecting the organization. The full name agreed on was The Missionary Education Council of Southern Baptist Agencies. The purpose was stated: "This shall be a co-operative council of Southern Baptist agencies for consultation on the production and utilization of missionary materials." The membership of the council was to be composed of representatives of the agencies named above, together with a representative of the Southern Baptist Press Association, the state convention secretaries, and each of the Southern Baptist seminaries. Provision was made for co-opted members to be named by the officers of the council and to be chosen annually from qualified persons living in the city in which the council would meet. The council meets annually. It conceives its function to be consultation regarding the whole area of missionary education—needs, objectives, materials, techniques, and promotion. The council's chief concern is the improvement of the program of missionary education in Southern Baptist churches. Attention is given in the annual meetings to such matters as annual themes for the Home and Foreign Mission boards' graded series of mission books, textbook ideas and evaluation, periodical evaluation, book needs, audio-visual aids, promotional materials, the correlation of missionary emphases, and the means for implementing creative concepts of Christian world missions. Recommendations are made to the co-operating agencies, it being understood that each agency will act in keeping with its own functional responsibility. CLIFTON J. ALLEN

MISSIONARY JOURNALS, EXTINCT. When the Southern Baptist Convention was formed (1845–46) and the two mission boards, foreign and domestic, were set up, it was realized at once that some medium of publicity was absolutely necessary for the work of each board. At the annual meeting of the Board of Foreign Missions at Savannah, Ga., May 14, 1847, a committee on the organ of publication, *Southern Baptist Missionary Journal,* reported as follows:

> We are of opinion . . . in view of the great lack of missionary information in the churches—the necessity of enlightened views of Christian obligation to the successful prosecution of our enterprise—and the desirableness of keeping the denomination constantly apprised of the operations of its Boards of Missions—that a greatly increased number of the organs of the Convention should be circulated.
>
> Soon after the adjournment of the Convention in June last, an arrangement was entered into, by which the Journal became the joint organ of the Boards of Foreign and Domestic Missions.

Another journal was begun, entitled *The Commission.* The purpose of the *Missionary Journal* was to furnish detailed information of the work of the missionaries in both the domestic and foreign fields, and other details that would indicate the progress of the work. The purpose of *The Commission* was primarily to make appeals on the basis of the information otherwise furnished, to churches and friends of missions.

The Domestic Mission Board expressed some dissatisfaction concerning the arrangement. In 1851 the Foreign Mission Board reported: "The Board have, however, determined to discontinue both the *Journal* and *Commission,* and to issue in their place, in connection with the Domestic Board, a monthly paper, to be called, *The Home and Foreign Journal.*" This continued to be the organ of the two boards until the outbreak of the Civil War. The Foreign Mission Board resumed publication of *The Commission* in Apr., 1856. However, because of war conditions, the publication of both *The Commission* and *The Home and Foreign Journal* was suspended.

In 1867 the two boards raised the question of resuming publication of an organ of the boards and the Convention. The Foreign Mission Board reported in 1868: "The three Boards of the Convention have agreed to send out the first number in time for the meeting." There was at this time a Sunday School Board that joined the other two boards in resuming publication of *The Home and Foreign Journal.*

In 1873 the Home Mission Board raised a question as to the utility of such publication. The next year the Convention instructed the Foreign Mission Board to continue publication of the *Journal.* In 1875 the Home Mission Board retired from the publication venture.

For 10 years the Home Mission Board had no medium of publicity except the Baptist papers in the several states. In 1888 it began the publication of *Our Home Field.* The title was changed to *The Home Field* in 1909. This was the organ of the board until 1916.

However, for a year and a half the two mission journals were again combined into one, *The Mission Journal,* in 1896, but the venture did not succeed. In 1897 the Foreign Mission Board reported that it had resumed publication of the *Foreign Mission Journal.* In 1898 the Home Mission Board reported that it had resumed publication of *Our Home Journal.*

In 1915 the Convention recommended that the boards of the Convention, the Woman's Missionary Union, and the Laymen's Movement confer with reference to publishing one Journal to serve all these interests. In Nov., 1916, the *Home and Foreign Fields* was published. This continued until Dec., 1937.

The Home Mission Board began publishing a quarterly bulletin, *Southern Baptist Home Missions,* in 1930. In June, 1938, the quarterly became a monthly. It was published under this title until 1955, when the name was changed to *Home Missions.* In addition to *Home Missions,* the Home Mission Board has published a number of magazines. *Southern Baptist Home Missions* was the title of *Home Missions* from 1930 to 1954. *Home and Foreign Fields* was a publication of the Sunday School Board, edited by John L. Hill, which absorbed the *Foreign Mission Journal* and *The Home Field* in a joint publication. From 1919 until 1932, *Home and Foreign Fields* was edited by Gaines S. Dobbins, of Louisville, Ky. The Sunday School Board published the magazine under the editorship of Dobbins on a volunteer basis. In 1932 Hill was given the assignment of editing the publication. He continued as editor until Dec., 1937, when the publication was discontinued.

JOHN CAYLOR

MISSIONARY MAGAZINES, BAPTIST. Baptist journalism owes its birth to the Christian world mission enterprise. The need for disseminating information about the work of missionaries and stimulating adequate support in prayer and money inspired the publication of quarterlies, monthlies, and weeklies.

The first denominational periodical on record was published in London from 1790 to 1802 by John Rippon (1775–1836), pastor at Carter Lane Baptist Church. It was entitled *"The Baptist Annual Register, Including Sketches of the State of Religion Among Different Denominations at Home and Abroad."* This annual was dedicated to "all the baptized ministers and people in America, England, Ireland, Scotland, Wales, the United Netherlands, France, Switzerland, Poland, Prussia, Russia, and Elsewhere." If the title and the dedication are not sufficient proof of the fact that this was a missionary magazine, the content is: It published foreign news and missionaries' letters.

The Baptist Missionary Society, William Carey's sponsoring organization, began publishing a monthly entitled *Missionary Herald* in Jan., 1819. It took the place of "Periodical Accounts," the reports published by the society from the date of its founding, 1792. The *Missionary Herald* at first formed an integral part of *The Baptist Magazine,* but it was also issued for sale separately, with occasional slight alterations, and continued independently after *The Baptist Magazine* ceased publication in 1904. In 1956 the *Missionary Herald* was still being published by the society from 93 Gloucester Place, London W. 1, and the circulation was 28,000.

The first American Baptist missionary publication appeared in 1803. It claims to be the oldest church paper in the United States. Appearing first under the title *The Massachusetts Baptist Missionary Magazine,* a quarterly in pamphlet format with 32 pages, it was "published for the benefit of the [Missionary] Society." The editor, Thomas Baldwin, pastor of the Second Baptist Church of Boston, was "one of the most eminent Baptist ministers of the time." The hero of the magazine was Adoniram Judson (*q.v.*) of Burma. Extracts of letters from William Carey (*q.v.*) and other missionaries and editorials on missionary effort were its chief contents.

The Triennial Convention adopted this publication in 1817 as its official organ, and the name was changed to the *American Baptist Magazine.* A bimonthly until 1825, it then became a monthly. In 1836 the name was changed to *The Baptist Missionary Magazine,* and again in 1910, when it combined with *The Home Missions Monthly,* it chose the title *Missions.* Some time later it added a subtitle: "an International Baptist Magazine." Its circulation in 1955 was 50,000.

In 1816, as a result of a suggestion by Luther Rice (*q.v.*) that a quarterly be published by the Foreign Mission Society, *The Latter Day Luminary* appeared in Philadelphia under the auspices of a committee of "the Baptist Board of Foreign Missions for the United States, Price, $3.00." It was transferred in 1821 to Washington, became a monthly, and lasted until 1826.

A weekly religious newspaper was started by Rice in Jan., 1922, entitled *The Columbian Star.* "From the first the interests of missions were given a large place in its columns," according to Dobbins. It was moved from Washington to Philadelphia in 1828, and in 1833 to Georgia as *The Christian Index,* to become the official organ of Georgia Baptists.

Between 1820 and 1845 Baptist periodicals were produced "in bewildering abundance," according to Frank Luther Mott, but controversy rather than missionary fervor spawned them.

When the Southern Baptist Convention was organized in 1845, it launched two mission boards. The Foreign Mission Board immediately laid plans for a publication, and the *Southern Baptist Missionary Journal* appeared in 1846. The Board of Domestic Missions of Marion, Ala., accepted the offer "to occupy" eight pages in each issue.

The Foreign Mission Board soon began to issue a monthly news sheet captioned "The Commission" to supplement the more formal publication. The *Journal* "gives instruction," and "The Commission makes the practical application," the board reported in May, 1849. The two mission boards conferred in 1853 and decided to discontinue both and to issue instead a monthly called *The Home and Foreign Journal.*

For the next 85 years Southern Baptists had alternately a single denominational missions periodical and two missions periodicals. The final effort to win support for one missionary publication for overseas and domestic missions was authorized by the Convention in 1916, and the Sunday School Board became the publisher. This publication, entitled *The Home and Foreign Fields,* was ably edited by Gaines S. Dobbins in Nashville, Tenn., with a steady flow of copy from the mission boards situated in Richmond, Va., and Atlanta, Ga. It lasted 20 years but never gained adequate support. Its circulation the final year was 12,184, about one fourth of the combined circulation of the two independent mission journals when they merged.

Immediately after *The Home and Foreign Fields* suspended publication, the Foreign Mission Board launched a new monthly under the title of the old news sheet, *The Commission,* and the Home Mission Board began regular publication of *Southern Baptist Home Missions,* which had appeared spasmodically since 1929 as a 20-page bulletin. By the Convention's centennial *The Commission* had a circulation of 65,000; and by 1956, 119,000. The Home Mission Board monthly changed its four-word title in Sept., 1954, to *Home Missions,* and in 1955 it reported a circulation of 122,000. A special offer of a year's subscription to both missionary monthlies for $1 boosted the circulation in schools of missions.

Baptist women entered wholeheartedly into the world missionary movement. As early as 1868, small groups gathered to hear missionary letters read and to pray. A publication was needed to connect these scattered groups. The first appeared sometime between 1876 and 1885, entitled *The Heathen Helper,* in Louisville, Ky., with Agnes Osborne and the secretaries of the 11 Central Committees as editors. It was described by Foreign Mission Board secretary Henry Allen Tupper (*q.v.*) as a "bright, eight-page sheet, handsomely illustrated, and filled with reports, letters, and pithy editorials."

The Young Missionary appeared in Mississippi in 1882 as a periodical for young Christians; *Missionary Talk,* in 1887 in North Carolina; *The Baptist Basket,* in 1888 in Kentucky, dedicated to tithing and missionary giving; *The Missionary Worker,* in 1888 in Texas; and *The Missionary Helper,* in 1893 in Georgia. These were a few of several short-lived publications which served to weld the women and young people of the Convention together as a mission force.

Small wonder that Frank Luther Mott declared:

> The Baptists [of the United States] had more periodicals in the postbellum period than any other denomination. . . . With their traditional activity in missions, the Baptists maintained several monthlies devoted to that interest, most of them being veterans. . . . When we turn to the Southern Convention, we find that the torrent has become a flood.

It became apparent soon after the women formed their Convention-wide organization in 1888 that one women's magazine would best serve the new union. In 1906 *Our Mission Fields,* a quarterly, was launched with Fannie E. S. Heck (*q.v.*) as editor. In 1914 it became a monthly with a new name, *Royal Service.* By 1920 it had reached financial independence, and Kathleen Moore Mallory (*q.v.*) became editor as well as corresponding secretary of Woman's Missionary Union, to serve until retirement in 1948. In its 50th year of publication, the circulation of *Royal Service* had reached 260,000, at a price of $1.50 a year.

Missionary literature for young people was also provided by the women's organization. *World Comrades* began in 1922 as a quarterly, to become a monthly two years later. It ceased publication in May, 1953, when graded periodicals took its place.

The need for program materials and home reading suggested publications for the individual missionary organizations. *The Window of Y.W.A.,* monthly for young women, appeared in 1929. In 1944 a monthly magazine for boys was launched with the title *Ambassador Life.* This was followed in 1951 by a monthly for girls, entitled *Tell.* For the youngest missionary organization a quarterly entitled *Sunbeam Activities* was provided in 1953. The combined circulation of the five periodicals in 1955 was 465,000.

Of significance in missionary journalism is the international Baptist paper inaugurated in Jan., 1954, by the Baptist World Alliance at its headquarters in Washington, D. C. The title chosen for the official Alliance publication was first used by J. N. Prestridge, founder and editor of a paper which appeared in Louisville, Ky., in 1897 under the title *The Baptist Argus.* To dramatize the broadened scope of his paper, the editor renamed it in 1908 *The Baptist World.* "He made Baptists catch a vision of a world mission as they had not seen it," said his friend Archibald Thomas Robertson (*q.v.*). The editor died in 1913, and his paper was soon suspended, but he anticipated a growing Baptist world fellowship. The modest, four-page paper produced by the Alliance became eight pages in 1956 and announced plans for larger development in 1957.

BIBLIOGRAPHY: W. W. Barnes, *The Southern Baptist Convention, 1945–1953* (1954). F. A. Cox, *History of Baptist Missionary Society, London, from 1792 to 1842* (1842). F. L. Mott, *A History of American Magazines* (1938). A. H. Newman, *A History of the Baptist Churches in the United States* (1915). E. C. Routh, *Adventures in Christian Journalism* (1954).

MARJORIE MOORE ARMSTRONG

MISSIONARY SOCIETIES, KENTUCKY. The subject of foreign missions was first introduced in Kentucky in 1814, the year in which the General Convention of the Baptist Denomination in the United States for Foreign Missions was formed. The following year Luther Rice (*q.v.*) visited most of the district associations in Kentucky, and many missionary societies were organized, e.g., Green River Country Society, Mt. Sterling Society, Shelbyville Society, Washington Missionary Society, Henderson Foreign Mission Society, Louisville Missionary Association, Bardstown Missionary Society, the Kentucky Baptist Society for Propagation of the Gospel, Owensboro Female Home Missionary Society, Spottsville Female Home Missionary Society, Henderson Female Missionary Society, and Louisville Female Missionary Association. These societies functioned successfully for a time but dissolved during the Campbellism schism.

The Roberts Fund and China Missionary Society, with headquarters in Louisville, was organized about 1838. On Oct. 14, 1842, the name was changed to the China Missionary Society of Kentucky, Auxiliary to the American Baptist Foreign Mission Board of Boston. The following year the name was shortened to China Missionary Society of Kentucky. In 1845 the society withdrew from the American Baptist Board of Foreign Missions and became associated with the Foreign Mission Board of the Southern Baptist Convention. In 1848 the name was changed to the Kentucky Foreign Mission Society. On Oct. 20, 1851, this society and the Kentucky Baptist Society for Propagation of the Gospel united with the General Association of Baptists in Kentucky. MRS. GEORGE R. FERGUSON

MISSIONARY WORKER. A paper edited by James Bruton Gambrell (*q.v.*) while he was corresponding secretary of the Baptist General Convention of Texas, 1897–1909. E. C. ROUTH

MISSIONS. The noun form of the Latin verb *mittere* (to send), meaning the sent, the send-ers, and the sending. Christian missions is the giving of the gospel to all men everywhere as commanded by Christ. Missions is a kingdom movement with a twofold plan: the making of disciples and the development of Christians. Missions introduces the kingdom of heaven, while other work deepens and develops it in the extent and power of its influence in the whole life of man. As distinguished from evangelism, missions is the proclamation of the good news of the kingdom where it is news, while evangelization and ministration make manifest the goodness of the news, emphasizing and applying it in the various relations of life. In one sense every act of the Christian which is aimed at the conversion of sinners or the growth and development of Christians is a missionary effort, but in terms of promotion and avenues of service, missions must be differentiated from evangelism, Christian education, and benevolences.

The authority for missions is in the power of Christ and the commission he gave to his disciples. While the field is the world, for the sake of understanding and promotion, missions is divided into foreign, home, state, and associational missions.

Foreign missions is the term used for missionary endeavor in lands afar. For Southern Baptists the agency for administration and promotion is the Foreign Mission Board of the Southern Baptist Convention, Richmond, Va. The activities of the agency must include the securing of financial support, the commitment of missionaries, the survey of fields, the supervision and protection of missionaries, and the promotion at home and abroad of the work related to foreign missions.

Home missions among Baptists was begun by Luther Rice (*q.v.*) when he returned from the foreign mission field in order to stir up Baptists to be missionary so as to support foreign missions. Rice organized associations and conventions, established schools, and promoted benevolences. Home missions offers a ministry to the underprivileged and overprivileged, the handicapped, language groups, and racial groups, and aids in the co-ordination of services in which all the people in the Southern Baptist Convention can unite in making disciples of those who are not the sole responsibility of any state convention.

State missions offers a full ministry of the whole denominational program within the limits of a state. This ministry includes benevolences, evangelism, and education as well as those functions commonly designated as missions.

Associational missions is both described and limited by the district association, which may include a county, a portion of a county, or one or more counties or portions of counties. The associational unit is made up of co-operating churches uniting their efforts in promoting missions. The ministry serves all functional and organizational expressions of missions, evangelism, organizational activities, and extension of the message and ministry of the gospel.

JOHN CAYLOR

I. The biblical basis of missions. Missions is the central theme of the Bible. It proclaims a personal God of love and mercy who has made provision for the salvation of the fallen human race and indicates that all who know him are responsible for giving his message of salvation to all peoples.

The Bible assuringly proclaims that God exists. It assumes that all recognize his being. God is described as perfect in character and therefore the pattern of what we should be (Matt. 5:48). He is holy in nature, and in order to have communion with him man must be holy (Lev. 19:2; Heb. 12:14). He is compassionate in his love toward mankind and his desire for fellowship with men (John 3:16; Rom. 5:6–8).

The Bible, furthermore, pictures man, whom God made in his own image, thus being free and able to choose, as fallen and ruined because of his rebellion against God (Rom. 3:10–20; 5:12). But the Lord, who is perfect in wisdom, provided the plan of salvation whereby the sinner could be saved (Rom. 5:6–21). The whole program of salvation is God's provision (Eph. 2:8–9). It is measureless in its wisdom, grace, and glory (Rom. 11:33–36). It is precious in its cost and provisions (I Peter 1:4, 18–21). It is limitless in its possibilities and endurance (John 10:28–29; I Cor. 2:9–10). It is beyond the human mind to grasp in its full significance, yet this is the good news that has come from the gracious God to the fallen, destitute human race (Luke 2:6–14). Since that first resurrection morning the story has ever been: "Come, see"—"Go, tell" (Matt. 28:6–7).

The Bible is also a record of God's patient revelation of himself and his salvation to individuals and nations in order to save them and use them in bearing his message to other members of the human race (Gal. 3:3–8). God's one supreme desire is for this glorious message of salvation to be known by every human being in all the world (John 17:23). Thus he has ordained that all who come to know him shall become missionaries sent by him to the rest of the human race with his message of good news (Luke 24:47–48). God chose Abraham not only in order to save him from the idols of his forefathers but in order to bless all the nations of the earth through him (Gen. 12:1–3). In like manner the Lord chose the shepherd boy David, and through long years of training by suffering and by revelation prepared him to be king of Israel; through His Son, the Christ, God brought salvation to all the world. The Lord called Jonah to go to the wicked city of Nineveh with his message of warning. Jonah tried to escape the responsibility, but God effectively constrained him to do his will (John 1:2; 3:4). God saved Isaiah from his sins and called him to go to a sinful people with a message of salvation (Isa. 6:5–8). The Old Testament is full of instances of God's call and commission of the prophets to take his message to others. When they were faithful to this charge, they pleased the Lord; but when they failed, they were held accountable (Ezek. 33: 7–10).

In the New Testament we find much evidence of the responsibility of those who know the Lord to take his message to others. The Lord himself emphasized this procedure when he called the 12 (Mark 3:14) and sent them out (Luke 9), and also when he commissioned the 70 (Luke 10). He told Andrew and Peter that he would make them fishers of men (Mark 1:16–17), and later he used the example of the draught of fishes to emphasize his meaning (Luke 5:5–10). Jesus taught by his parables that the kingdom was to spread from one believer to another (Matt. 13:33; 22:1–13). He used figures of speech such as "ye are the salt of the earth" and "ye are the light of the world" (Matt. 5:13–16) to emphasize the responsibility for missions. Finally, Jesus explicitly commanded his disciples to take his message into all the world. He implied no alternative and left the full responsibility squarely upon the individual disciple and upon the body of believers. We find the early disciples following these instructions and taking up their task in earnest. Especially did Paul feel his responsibility for the propagation of the gospel (I Cor. 9:16–17, 27; II Cor. 5:19–20). We also find the early churches fulfilling their obligation to preach (Phil. 1:5; I Thess. 1:7–8).

God's missionary message of redemption from sin through the atoning work of Jesus Christ (Matt. 20:28; II Cor. 5:19) is for all peoples. Although he did call Abraham to leave his country and go to the Promised Land, and although God made of him His chosen nation, Israel (Gen. 12:1–3), he did not confine himself to Abraham's seed alone. We see God permitting Joseph to take a wife from among the Egyptians (Gen. 41:45, 50), whose two sons were among the 12 tribes (Gen. 48:15–20). Moses also took a wife from the Midianites, and her children were counted among the Israelites (Exod. 18:1–4). God also made provision for the strangers among his people (Exod. 12:49; 22:21; Lev. 24:22); for Rahab the Canaanitess (Josh. 6:22–23); for the Gibeonites (Josh. 9); for Ruth the Moabitess (Ruth); and for Bathsheba the Hittitess (II Sam. 11–12).

The New Testament shows that Jesus came to save the Gentiles as well as the Jews. He saved the woman of Sychar and her fellow townsmen (John 4). He rejoiced over the faith of the Syrophenician woman (Mark 7:26) and the centurion (Matt. 8:8). He ministered to the Pereans (John 10:39–42). Jesus said he was the Good Shepherd (of the fold of Israel), and that he had other sheep (the Gentiles) who were not of Israel whom he must bring into the one fold (the church)—John 10:11–16. His outlook was worldwide. He said, "God so loved the world" (John 3:16); again, "The field is the world" (Matt. 13:38). Jesus prayed that the Christians who are in the "world" might be united that the "world" might know and believe that the Father had sent him and had loved him (John 17:11–23). He said, "As the Father hath sent me [into the world], even so send I you" (into the world). Jesus said, "For this cause came I into the world, that I should bear witness unto the truth" (John 18:37); and again, "For the Son of man is come to seek and to save that which was lost" (Luke 19:10). The writers of the Epistles understood Christ's commission to mean that the message was for all peoples.

CHARLES L. CULPEPPER

II. The teaching of missions. The first course in missions offered in a Southern Baptist institution was introduced in 1895 at Southern Baptist Theological Seminary by H. H. Harris. Not in the regular curriculum, it was an elective listed under "special studies." In 1897 this course was taught by William Owen Carver (*q.v.*), who also taught New Testament and homiletics. In 1899 a course in missions was introduced into the regular curriculum by Carver, and the following year the department of comparative religion and missions was officially established.

When the Southwestern Baptist Theological Seminary was founded in 1907, a course in missions was included in the department of practical theology. A separate department of missions was instituted in 1914. Baptist Bible Institute (later New Orleans Baptist Theological Seminary) provided a missions course in the department of church history in its first year, 1917, and established a separate department with a full-time professor in 1925. Golden Gate Baptist Theological Seminary established a chair of missions from its foundation in 1944, and a full professorship was provided in 1950. In 1951 the Southeastern Baptist Theological Seminary opened, with a professor of missions among its first faculty.

A second full-time instructor in missions was added to the department at Southern Seminary in 1935, at New Orleans in 1954, at Southwestern and Southeastern seminaries in 1956. Seminaries typically provide courses in the biblical basis of missions, history of Christian missions, theory and methods of missions, Baptist missions, comparative religion, and modern cults.

The Woman's Missionary Union Training School, from its founding in 1907, placed emphasis upon missions, comparative religion, and missionary education. In 1952 the name of this institution was changed to Carver School of Missions and Social Work, and its curriculum was reorganized so that it became more distinctively a vocational training school for missionaries and social workers, both at home and abroad, both men and women. Practical courses not ordinarily included in seminary curricula were provided, such as phonetics, literacy education, teaching English as a foreign language, and medical information.

In 1954 all but three of the 29 Southern Baptist senior colleges offered at least one course in missions and/or comparative religion. Such courses were usually listed in the department of Bible or religious education. Two of the 21 Southern Baptist junior colleges offered missions courses. H. G. GOERNER

III. The history of missions. On the basis of the locale, major group being reached, and outstanding features, the history of Christian missions is most accurately outlined according to the following periods:

- I. Winning the Roman Empire, A.D. 29 (Pentecost) to 500
  - 1. Expansion before Emperor Constantine, A.D. 29–325
    - a. Predominantly among Jews, Jewish proselytes, and Gentiles familiar with and sympathetic to Judaism, A.D. 29–100
    - b. Transition to an almost entirely Gentile faith, A.D. 100–180 (death of Emperor Marcus Aurelius)
    - c. Expansion under social turmoil and religious persecution, A.D. 180–325
  - 2. Expansion from Constantine's sole imperial authority to fall of Roman Empire, A.D. 325–500
- II. Winning the Barbarians of Europe, A.D. 500–1500
- III. Expansion of European Christianity into All the World, A.D. 1500–1910
  - 1. Roman Catholic era, A.D. 1500–1800
  - 2. The "Protestant century," A.D. 1800–1910
- IV. Rise of the Younger Churches and of Ecumenical Christianity; Revival of Roman Catholic Endeavor, A.D. 1910–

Outside the New Testament record, which makes no claim to historical completeness even for the apostolic era, there is little literary evidence to describe the spread of Christianity during the first three centuries. At best we can only observe that the gospel expanded from Palestine through Asia Minor into the Aegean world, the Balkans, Greece, Italy, Spain, Gaul (France), Britain, Egypt, North Africa, and Ethiopia, as well as into the Tigris-Euphrates Valley to the east of the Roman Empire. Few personal names are known; in fact, the most significant characteristic of this period is the absence of vocational missionaries and the spreading of the gospel by the laity wherever Christians went. Nonetheless, by A.D. 325 Christianity had won probably one-tenth of an estimated empire population of 100,000,000; had cut across all racial, cultural, social, and economic lines; had challenged the keenest minds of the age; and had effected, in the church, the strongest social institution within the empire aside from the state itself.

The Rescript of Constantine and Licinius (A.D. 313) gave legality to Christianity; this act resulted in preferential treatment and equality and finally in the status of official state religion (in A.D. 395 under Emperor Theodosius I, "the Great"). This greatly accelerated the expansion of Christianity until it was the nominal religion of practically the entire population of the empire by A.D. 500. Among the very few historical personages known for this period are Gregory Thaumaturgos in Pontus, Gregory the Illuminator in Armenia, Bardaisan of Edessa ("Father of Syrian Christianity"), and Martin of Tours (Gaul). Prior to Constantine the spread was largely by the witness of hosts of ordinary Christian individuals; after Constantine it was due largely to the social privileges accompanying the esteemed position accorded Christianity by the state.

Among the earliest of the barbarian peoples to infringe upon the Roman Empire were the Goths. As early as the third century, some of these people became Christians, apparently through Christians whom they took as captives on raids into the empire. The great majority of the Gothic Christians were Arians; this circumstance was probably the result of the work of "one of the most prominent figures in the roster of Christian missionaries, Ulfilas." This man, who gave about 40 years of service along the Danube, dying in A.D. 380 or 381, has the distinction of being probably the first missionary to reduce a language to writing in order to translate the Scriptures into it. Not until the close of the sixth century did the last of the Goths turn from Arian to Catholic Christianity. The gospel won the tribal peoples of Ireland largely through the work of the colorful Patrick, born in Roman Britain around A.D. 389. Though he was probably not the only missionary working in Ireland in the fifth century, overwhelming credit is due this one man for the conversion of that land.

Events of the era marking the fall of the Roman Empire also mark the new directional advance for Christianity. By A.D. 476 the imperial provinces in Europe were almost wholly occupied by Teutonic peoples. Clovis, founder of the Frankish Empire, "successor to Rome," turned from paganism and was baptized a Catholic (rather than an Arian) in A.D. 496. In 529 Benedict of Nursia founded, at Monte Cassino, a new order that was not only to bear his name but to become a major instrument for winning barbarian peoples; in that same year Justinian I, ruler of the Eastern Empire, closed the last of the avowedly non-Christian Greek philosophical schools without raising any protest. There followed a millennium of very slow and uncertain spread of Christianity, mainly on the soil of Europe and amid the various waves of invaders who were gradually settling down and becoming amalgamated into nations. This "missionary advance" was intimately associated with political personages; for the tribe or nation, almost without exception, received the Christian religion either by voluntarily following the example of its chief, prince, or king, or more often as a result of such a leader's active effort. This spread was marked frequently by coercion and sometimes by extreme violence. Consequently, it was usually of a mass movement character, associated with nationalism, and suffered many reverses at the hands of paganism. At best it was merely a veneer over the old tribal beliefs and practices. At the same time this spread was marked by one of the noblest evangelical outreaches of Christian history, by the amazing establishment of the Roman Church on all this territory, as Romanism time after time reaped the fruit of the evangelical efforts of Celtic Christianity, and by a large number of missionary personalities without superior in any age.

Ireland, cut off from any extensive contact with the Roman Empire, developed a distinctive Christian faith. Celtic Christianity was Nicene in theology but was grounded in the Bible (result of Patrick's work) and partook of a unique monastery-centered rather than diocesan form of ecclesiastical organization. This indigenous, biblically oriented Christianity was dynamically missionary in character, so that among the many movements of peoples in the Western world throughout the sixth and seventh centuries, this was the only instance of a movement for purely religious reasons. These Irish people wandered far and wide over the British Isles and Europe, singly and in groups of 12 (after the number of Jesus' disciples), for no other reason, on their own declaration, than "for the love of the name of Christ." The most famous of these wandering Irish monks was Columban. Born in the second quarter of the sixth century, trained at the noted monastery at Bangor in Ulster, Columban led a band of 12 missionaries into the Frankish domains of Europe. He set about a program of preaching to win nominal Christians to an earnest Christian life and to win pagans to an initial conversion experience. The response was so great that he founded three monasteries in the Vosges mountain range to provide the base for his missionary work. Luxeuil, an abandoned fort, became the headquarters of this endeavor. Neither the full extent nor the significance of this man's labors and influence in southern Europe can be measured, but they were profound and far-reaching.

A contemporary of his, with a very similar name, was still more significant for the history of missions. This was Columba (Columcille), born in Donegal, Ireland, probably in 521. He became a missionary at 42, establishing headquarters on a small island named Iona just off the coast of Scotland. Here he founded the first specifically missionary training school in Christian history. Its influence continued for centuries, and from this community went forth most of the best trained of the Celtic missionaries. In some instances these missionaries founded similar monastic communities as missionary bases; the most important of such was Lindisfarne off the coast of Northumbria, from which most of Britain was rewon. Britain also furnishes the clearest example of the process referred to above. Gregory I, "the Great," was the first pope of the Roman Church to send out missionaries directly. He sent a band, headed by Augustine, which launched a Roman Catholic work in Kent in 597. In the early years of the seventh century, Britain was being won by these two sources simultaneously, but the close-knit ecclesiastical organization of the Roman Church gained the ascendancy over the Celtic work, and the Synod of Whitby, 664, gave the victory to Rome, which then held Britain until the English Reformation.

Not always was the process of Romanization one of conflict. Willibrord, "Apostle to the Netherlands," was born in England in 657, trained in Ireland under the evangelical Celtic tradition, and went voluntarily to Rome to secure the backing of the pope to aid his missionary work in the Low Countries. Laboring for four and a half decades, he brought the southern half of the Netherlands into the Christian faith and into loyalty to Rome. Similarly, Winfrith, one of the greatest missionaries of all time, was born about 672 and trained in England but spent some time in Rome, where he became completely imbued with Roman ecclesiology and principles, indicated by the new name, Boniface, with which Gregory II consecrated him. Throughout a long life Boniface labored in central Europe, where he was remarkably effective in three regards: extending Christianity into areas still pagan; inculcating an experientially spiritual and moral quality into nominally Christian people; and establishing everywhere such a strong hierarchical system in full loyalty to Rome that to Boniface is given credit for the fact that eight centuries later, the territory where he labored was hardly affected by the Protestant Reformation. He died a martyr's death in 754.

Also in the spiritual succession of Columban and Irish monastic Christianity was Anskar, pioneer missionary to the Scandinavians. Born in northwest France in 801, he was trained at the monastery of Corbey (founded by monks from Luxeuil). His commission from Pope Gregory IV was as "Legate to the Swedes, Danes, Slavs, and all other Peoples at the North." Because of the fierceness of the Northern peoples, Anskar adopted a technique of bringing promising Scandinavian and Slavic boys to a school in Hamburg, where he trained them to be Christian missionaries to their own people. Anskar, however, typifies what was almost the universal situation in winning the European barbarians; for despite the work of missionaries, the task was usually accomplished only in conjunction with the use of political pressure or force. Men like Anskar laid the groundwork, and large numbers of other missionaries came in to build on the foundations after the people were coerced into turning to Christianity.

In eastern Europe the competition to win peoples to Christianity lay between Rome and the Eastern Orthodox Church. The struggle was keen in the Balkan area, usually with results similar to the struggle between the Celtic missionaries and Rome. However, some of the Balkan countries established Eastern Orthodoxy as their faith and have retained it to the present. Illustrative of the interaction are two other noted missionaries, the brothers Constantine and Methodius, appointed as missionaries to the Slavs by Photius, Patriarch of Constantinople and ablest churchman of the ninth century. Conflict arose between them and German missionaries over certain techniques which Constantine and Methodius were using, notably putting the Scriptures and liturgy into the language of the people. This resulted in a trip to Rome by these missionaries, where they came into such agreement with the Roman Church (except upon use of the native language) that Constantine took a Latin name, Cyril. Moravia was won largely as a result of the work of these two brothers, and when that land was devastated by barbarian invaders, the Moravians scattered far and wide throughout eastern Europe, spreading their faith wherever they went. The winning of Russia was the greatest missionary achievement of the Eastern Orthodox Church. This was accomplished by the close of the 10th century, and the Russian Orthodox Church became one of the most powerful wings of Christianity, with Moscow known as the "third Rome" (after Rome and Constantinople).

Nestorian missionaries carried Christianity to the Far East in this second major period (A.D. 500–1500). Alopen, the first known missionary to China, arrived in 635, probably coming from Syria. This was an era of general cultural activity in China, and Christianity enjoyed some success until 845, when the emperor issued a rigid proscription against all foreign religions. However, the Chinese had responded hardly at all, and converts to Christianity were confined to foreigners living in China. The first Roman Catholic missionary to China was the Franciscan, John of Montecorvino, who reached Cambaluc in 1294. He had considerable success among the Mongol conquerors of China, but in less than a century (1362), many martyrdoms closed the endeavor to plant Christianity in China during the medieval period.

Except for the Jews, who remained unmovable, by 1500 all of the peoples of Europe were at least nominally Christian, as were those of Russia and the territory of the Eastern or Byzantine Empire. The gospel had gone as far as China and had expanded in India. On the other hand, Christianity had suffered its first two major recessions. The first and greatest recession was from 500 to 950 and was due to the decline of the Roman Empire, the barbarian invasions, and the rise and spread of a militant new religion, Islam. The second recession, 1350–1500, was also largely due to an onslaught from Islam. The earlier advance of Islam accompanied the creation of an Arab empire; the later advance was an adjunct of Mongol and Turkish conquests. The losses to Islam were not in the "fringe" areas but in the oldest and most advanced centers of Christianity: Palestine, Asia Minor, North Africa, Egypt, Syria, Constantinople, the Nestorian communities of the Euphrates Valley and eastward, the Balkans and southern Russia, and the Iberian Peninsula. These advances were stopped only by military activity, in the form of both political warfare and the Crusades. From 1500 until near the middle of the 20th century, with rare and insignificant exceptions, neither Christianity nor Islam won territory or adherents from the other, despite rather extensive missionary efforts among the Moslems in the 13th, 14th, and 15th centuries by monks of the Franciscan and Dominican orders and by the Jesuits later, and despite such notable personalities as Ramon Lull, the Catholic "Apostle to Islam" in the 13th century, and Samuel M. Zwemer, the Protestant of the 20th century worthy of the same title.

While the third main period of the history of missions, A.D. 1500–1910, is divided into the Roman Catholic era (1500–1800) and the Protestant century (1800–1910), this does not mean that Protestants were doing no missionary work during the first three centuries of their history, nor that the Catholics did nothing in the 19th century. Gustav Warneck undertook to explain why evangelicals were so long delayed in assuming the missionary obligation. Six explanations may be advanced: 1. Protestantism was so engrossed in establishing itself, both against Roman Catholicism and internally as to ecclesiology and theology, that it had neither time nor thought for a proclamation of the faith among non-Christian peoples. 2. Hampering theological beliefs were held by the leading reformers, such as the idea that the Great Commission was binding only on the original disciples, the expectation of the imminent return of Christ in person, and the predestinarian views of the Calvinists. 3. The political ramifications of the Reformation and the establishment of the "territorial church" principle limited missionary activity. 4. Difference in attitude on the part of governments—the great political powers of the era were Spain, Portugal, and France, all staunchly Roman Catholic nations whose rulers considered the spread of the faith a part of their responsibility, whereas Protestant countries were small and weak and without much sense of missionary obligation. 5. Protestants lacked both the agencies and the experience for missionary work; the monastic orders had provided these for the Roman Church, and Protestantism everywhere abolished monasticism. 6. The Protestants had virtually no contact with non-Christian peoples, and knowledge, at least, of such peoples is necessary for missionary motivation.

While most of the orders participated in the great Roman Catholic missionary outreach after 1500, the Society of Jesus (Jesuits), organized by Ignatius Loyola in 1540 for the express purpose of missions, and the general energizing of the Counter-Reformation were the factors most responsible. Spain brought most of Central and South America, as well as the Philippine Islands, under the domain of the Roman Church, while Portugal won Brazil, and the French fixed Romanism upon much of Canada. The most notable Catholic missionary in the New World was Bartholomé de Las Casas (1474–1566), who labored incessantly in behalf of the Indians and the imported Negroes. Catholicism also spread throughout Asia, Francis Xavier (1506–52) being more responsible than any other one person. A charter member of the Society of Jesus, though almost having become a Protestant at the University of Paris, Xavier ranged over all of South India from 1541 to 1545, when he went to Malacca and from there in 1549 to Japan. He died en route to China to reintroduce Christianity there. Other outstanding Catholics were Robert de Nobili (1577–1656) in India and Matteo Ricci (1552–1610) in China. The Portuguese established the Catholic faith in their colonies on the west and east coasts of Africa.

By the close of the 16th century, there were missionary stirrings among Protestants, but contact with Indians in the New World and the Pietist-Halle-Moravian movement on the European continent really led to the evangelical endeavor. Notable among the pioneer missionaries to the Amerinds were John Eliot, whose work led to the formation of the first missionary society ("the President and Society for the Propagation of the Gospel in New England," incorporated by the Long Parliament in 1649), Thomas Mayhew, David Brainerd, and David Zeisberger. Philip Jacob Spener (1635–1705), father of the Pietist movement, became deeply concerned that the Protestants had left the spread of Christianity almost entirely to the Catholics. His successor, August Hermann Francke (1663–1727), made the University of Halle a great center of missionary interest and training. Count Nicholaus Ludwig von Zinzendorf (1700–60), trained at Halle, became head of the Unitas Fratrum (Moravian Brethren) community at Herrnhut. This group became something unique in Christian history: an entire community devoted utterly to the single objective of spreading the gospel. Before the close of the 18th century, this community had mission work established in Russia, India, Ceylon and the Nicobar Islands, Danish and British West Indies, North and Central America, Gold Coast and South Africa, Greenland, and Labrador, and among the Lapps. The Moravian missions furnished Carey with much of both his inspiration for missions and his techniques. The Danish-Halle Mission, initiated in Tranquebar, southern India, in 1706 by Bartholomaus Ziengenbalg and carried forward by Christian Friedrich Schwartz, is the outstanding Protestant work prior to Carey.

William Carey is rightly known as the founder of the modern evangelical effort because (1) the Baptist Missionary Society was the first with the avowed purpose of carrying the gospel *to the whole world,* (2) its organization stimulated the formation of mission agencies throughout the Protestant world, and (3) it established the means of support and conduct of missionary work that has largely prevailed to the present. The Baptist society was organized in 1792; the London Missionary Society (interdenominational), in 1795; and the Church Missionary Society (Anglican), in 1799. The first two decades of the 19th century witnessed the formation of denominational societies throughout the Anglo-Saxon world and of regional societies in Europe. In the United States the first society was the American Board of Commissioners for Foreign Missions (1810), resulting from the famous Haystack Prayer Meeting on the campus of Williams College, led by Samuel John Mills. When two of the American Board's first missionaries, Adoniram Judson and Luther Rice, became Baptists, this occurrence led to the formation in 1814 of the General Missionary Convention of the Baptist Denomination in the United States for Foreign Missions (Triennial Convention). Notable among other agencies in behalf of missions were the rise of the tract and Bible societies (Religious Tract Society, 1799; British and Foreign Bible Society, 1804; American Bible Society, 1816; etc.), the rise of home missions in the United States (United Domestic Missionary Society [Presbyterian], 1822; American Home Missionary Society [interdenominational], 1826; American Baptist Home Mission Society, 1832), and the rise of the student Christian movements, notably the Student Volunteer Movement for Foreign Missions founded in 1888 by Robert P. Wilder and John R. Mott. These agencies were the means by which thousands of missionaries were recruited, sent forth, guided, and aided in the great Protestant advance of the 19th century. Among the outstanding pioneer missionaries were William Carey, Henry Martyn, John Scudder, Alexander Duff, John E. Clough, Robert Morrison, J. Hudson Taylor, G. F. Verbeck, H. N. Allen, Lott Carey, Robert Moffat, David Livingstone, H. B. Pratt, and J. G. Oncken.

The fourth and contemporary period in mission history was inaugurated by the new kind of "total revolution" that began in Mexico in 1910 and has since become the major feature of the 20th century, by the rise of competent, trained, consecrated Christian nationals who are taking over the leadership of the church in all the "mission fields" and placing the younger churches on a par with the older churches of the sending countries, and by the World Missionary Conference held in Edinburgh, Scotland, in 1910. The latter resulted in worldwide, interdenominational co-operation in missions, expressed organizationally in the International Missionary Council, founded in 1921, and in the ecumenical movement, expressed organiza-

FIRST BAPTIST CHURCH, Dallas, Tex. Organized 1868, membership 1956 over 11,000. Americanized Gothic auditorium accommodates 3,000, Sunday school 4,000. Building at right houses recreation facilities. Total property worth $7,000,000.

FIRST BAPTIST CHURCH, Hattiesburg, Miss. Founded 1884, membership 1956 was 1860. Colonial style auditorium serving 1,400 completed 1953, educational unit serves 1,200, property worth $1,000,000.

tionally in the World Council of Churches, constituted in Amsterdam in 1948. The 19th-century achievements of Protestant missions also found a reflex action in a revived Roman Catholic missionary endeavor, which is still on the increase. In the rise and spread of communism, Christianity has suffered its greatest setback since the onslaughts of Islam. The resurgence of the great non-Christian cultural religions, in conjunction with the virulent nationalism abroad today, presents tremendous barriers to the further spread of Christianity.

Today Christians and the church are found in every country of the world except possibly one (Outer Mongolia). Following is a summary of the Christian population by areas of the world:

	Population	*Protestant Community*	*Roman Catholic Community*	*Orthodox Community*	*No. Christians per 100 Population*
Europe	574,973,785	97,028,051	164,792,662	35,179,899	52
Near East and North Africa	129,743,000	233,186	3,359,485	1,883,586	4
Africa	146,686,655	9,355,044	10,166,451	4,592,879	16
Australia and New Zealand	10,370,863	8,585,018	1,609,812	17,012	99
Southern Asia	450,783,165	4,864,000	5,456,000	757,000	2
Southeast Asia	173,793,000	4,122,000	17,222,000	1,573,793	13
East Asia	585,570,174	3,168,031	3,633,326	233,122	1
Pacific Islands	1,368,804	894,501	280,590	—	86
Mexico and Middle America	37,442,000	530,465	30,252,263	—	82
The Caribbean	17,045,057	2,261,718	11,737,274	—	82
South America	117,223,506	2,498,862	93,866,400	38,000	82
North America	174,659,000	82,059,563	37,559,757	2,638,359	70
WORLD TOTALS	2,419,659,009	215,600,439	379,936,020	46,893,650	27

BIBLIOGRAPHY: J. Aberly, *An Outline of Missions* (1945). L. C. Barnes, *Two Thousand Years of Missions Before Carey* (1902). E. J. Bingle and K. G. Grubb (eds.), *World Christian Handbook, 1952* (1952). W. O. Carver, *The Course of Christian Missions* (1939). V. R. Edman, *The Light in Dark Ages* (1949). R. H. Glover, *The Progress of World-Wide Missions* (1939). A. Harnack, *The Mission and Expansion of Christianity in the First Three Centuries* (trans. by J. Moffatt) (1908). *Interpretative Statistical Survey of the World Missions of the Christian Church* (1938). K. S. Latourette, *A History of the Expansion of Christianity,* 7 vols. (1937–45); *Anno Domini* (1940); *The Christian World Mission in Our Day* (1954); *The Unquenchable Light* (1941). G. F. Maclear, *History of Christian Missions in the Middle Ages* (1863). B. Mathews, *Forward Through the Ages* (1951). C. H. Robinson, *The Conversion of Europe* (1917). J. Schmidlin, *Catholic Mission History* (trans. by M. Braun) (1933). G. Warneck, *Outline of a History of Protestant Missions* (trans. by G. Robson) (1901). HERBERT C. JACKSON

MISSIONS, SCHOOLS OF. A church school of missions is a program in which the church, led by the pastor and his cabinet, studies missions in age-graded classes on week nights and hears visiting missionaries at an assembly following the classes and on Sunday. In the Simultaneous Associational Program, all the churches conduct their schools the same week. By a rotation schedule each guest missionary speaks at a different church each succeeding service.

Following World War I schools of missions were promoted by several denominations. The earliest reference to Baptist schools of missions was in the 1924 Foreign Mission Board report. Reports appear almost every year since. The Home and Foreign Mission boards have produced literature and jointly promoted such schools since 1932. Early simultaneous programs were conducted in several states about the same time.

Specific Convention-wide promotion of simultaneous programs by the Home Mission Board began in 1932. Jan. 1, 1943, a Schools of Missions Department with Lewis W. Martin as secretary was established. Since 1944 the Foreign Mission Board has shared in the joint promotion. The first Church Schools of Missions Manual appeared in 1944 and was revised in 1947, 1950, and 1956.

From 1944 through 1955, 1,987 associational simultaneous programs, participated in by 28,380 churches in 25 states, reported a grand total attendance of 9,580,108. Each year, 1,500 missionary addresses were delivered, and more than 1,200 young people volunteered for special service.

Because the number of missionaries available for this service is limited, the boards restrict their missionary commitment services to 150 associational programs per year. Local schools and simultaneous programs with inspirational messages brought by other than guest missionaries are increasing in number.

LEWIS W. MARTIN

MISSISSIPPI ASSOCIATIONS.

I. Extant. ALCORN. Organized in 1920 by 15 churches of the Tishomingo Baptist Association. Articles of faith appear in the 1922 minutes. Since 1950 it has been served by a missions superintendent. In 1954, 27 churches reported 213 baptisms, 6,577 members, $148,020 total gifts, $16,102.83 mission gifts, and $779,000 property value. RUSSELL M. MCINTIRE

ATTALA. Organized in 1860 as the Kosciusko Baptist Association. In 1869 it constituted 26 churches located in central section of the state in Attala and contiguous counties. An abstract of faith appeared in the 1881 minutes. The name was changed in 1940 to Attala County Baptist Association. Since 1949 it has been served by a missions superintendent. In 1954, 31 churches reported 261 baptisms, 5,940 members, $154,627 total gifts, $7,893 mission gifts, $718,968 property value, and $82,880 church debt.

J. L. BOYD

BENTON. Organized in Oct., 1922, by 12 churches in Benton County, northern part of the state, who came from the Tippah Baptist Association. An abstract of faith appears in the 1922 records. In 1954, 13 churches reported 71 baptisms, 2,232 members, $37,320.00 total gifts, $2,237.26 mission gifts, $114,529.00 property value, and $7,358.00 church debt.

BOLIVAR. Organized in 1923 in Bolivar County by 13 churches. Since 1941 it has been served by an associational superintendent of missions. In 1954, 22 churches reported 226 baptisms, 5,678 members, $196,813.00 total gifts, $33,585.01 mission gifts, and $875,000.00 property value.

CALHOUN. Organized in Sept., 1875, by a group of churches from the Yalobusha and the Chickasaw Baptist associations. In 1877, 23 churches reported 1,147 members. Articles of faith were adopted in 1882. In 1921 the name was changed to the Calhoun County Baptist Association. Since 1946 it has been served by a missions superintendent. In 1954, 49 churches reported 263 baptisms, 8,944 members, $126,753 total gifts, $21,652 mission gifts, and $626,300 property value.

CARROLL. Organized in Oct., 1920, by 18 churches from the Yazoo Baptist Association. Since 1950 it has been served by a missions superintendent. In 1954, 19 churches reported 82 baptisms, 2,381 members, $43,422.50 total gifts, $3,798.42 mission gifts, and $125,900 property value.

CHICKASAW. Organized in 1919 by 18 churches from Aberdeen Baptist Association. In 1954, 19 churches reported 123 baptisms, 3,558 members, $87,527 total gifts, $12,262.38 mission gifts, and $321,800 property value.

CHOCTAW. Organized in Oct., 1920 by 23 churches from Chester Baptist Association. Since 1954 it has been served by a missions superintendent. In 1954, 27 churches reported 153 baptisms, 3,641 members, $52,788 total gifts, $7,713.50 mission gifts, and $196,450 property value.

CLARKE. Organized in 1918 by six churches, located on the eastern side of the state, from the Chickasahay Baptist Association. Articles of faith were adopted in 1919. In 1954, 27 churches reported 178 baptisms, 4,862 members, $116,567.00 total gifts, $19,594.38 mission gifts, $437,350.00 property value, and $1,878.00 church debt.

CLAY. Organized in 1928. At its 12th annual session eight churches reported. In 1954, 11 churches reported 177 baptisms, 3,083 members, $103,348 total gifts, $18,299.39 mission gifts, and $357,600 property value.

COPIAH. Organized in 1887 by four churches from Central, Strong River, and Union associations. It adopted articles of faith in 1887. In 1954, 29 churches reported 167 baptisms, 8,049 members, $210,993 total gifts, $42,305.43 mission gifts, and $885,800 property value.

RUSSELL M. MCINTIRE

COVINGTON. Organized as Pearl-Leaf Baptist Association in 1884 by 6 churches from Covington, Lawrence, Marion, and Perry counties. The articles of faith were adopted at organization. From it a group of churches withdrew to join in forming Greene County Baptist Association. Name was changed to Covington County Baptist Association in 1919. In 1954, 18 churches reported 159 baptisms, 4,370 members, $123,408 total gifts, $11,639 mission gifts, $501,500 property value, and $31,869 church debt. J. L. BOYD

DE SOTO. Organized as North Mississippi Baptist Association in 1841 by six churches in De Soto and Marshall counties. At its first annual session in 1842 the name was changed to Coldwater Baptist Association. Articles of faith were adopted at organization. In 1920 it voted to grant letters of dismission to any churches "desiring to go into county organizations." The name changed again in 1938 to De Soto County Baptist Association. In 1954, 14 churches reported 95 baptisms, 2,373 members, $65,427 total gifts, $8,213.25 mission gifts, and $235,500 property value, and $15,875 church debt.

FRANKLIN. Organized in 1919 by churches from Lincoln and Union Baptist associations. In 1943 the name was changed to Adams-Franklin, but the original name was restored in 1950. Articles of faith were adopted. In 1954, 23 churches reported 130 baptisms, 3,421 members, $95,543 total gifts, $9,886 mission gifts, $413,950 property value, and $2,000 church debt.

GEORGE. Organized in 1920 by five churches in George County. Articles of faith were adopted in 1920. Since 1953 it has been served by an area missions superintendent. In 1954 five churches reported 86 baptisms, 2,448 members, $77,783.90 total gifts, $10,980.48 mission gifts, $387,000 property value, and $30,000 church debt.

GREENE. Organized in 1920 by 19 churches in Greene County out of the Leaf River Baptist Association. Articles of faith were adopted in 1920. It has been served by a missions superintendent since 1953. In 1954, 18 churches reported 107 baptisms, 2,350 members, $61,200 total gifts, $6,073.46 mission gifts, and $145,700 property value.

GRENADA. Organized in 1920 by 10 churches in Grenada County. In 1954 nine churches reported 153 baptisms, 2,862 members, $155,061.00 total gifts, $25,826.53 mission gifts, $634,974.00 property value, and $88,346.22 church debt.

W. HENRY CROUCH

GULF COAST. Organized May 26, 1877, at the dissolution of the Providence Baptist Association, by 16 churches along the Gulf Coast from New Orleans, La., to Mobile, Ala. In 1924 when the territory had narrowed to Hancock, Harrison, Jackson, and Stone, the body voted to organize by counties, with the exception that churches in Stone County remain affiliated with those of Harrison. They formed the Harrison County Baptist Association, which chose to be the "Successor to Old Gulf Coast Association." In 1933 the Hancock Association dissolved, the churches returning to the mother association (Harrison); and a Tri-County Baptist Association was formed which in 1936 voted to reclaim the original name, Gulf Coast Baptist Association, and established the broken line of the number series. (Hence, the records of the churches of Hancock County, during the time they operated as a separate association, are integrated into the files of the Gulf Coast Baptist Association.) Since 1946 it has been served by a missions superintendent. In 1954, 31 churches reported 555 baptisms, 9,788 members, $418,788 total gifts, $70,441 mission gifts, $1,625,-425 property value, and $163,219 church debt.

J. L. BOYD

HINDS. Organized in 1947 by 33 churches in Hinds County from Hinds Warren Association. Articles of faith were adopted in 1947. A full-time superintendent of missions was employed Oct. 25, 1951. In 1954, 41 churches reported 948 baptisms, 29,462 members, $1,575,246.00 total gifts, $250,018.29 mission gifts, $7,528,843.00 property value, and $1,861,202.00 church debt.

HOLMES. Organized in 1920 by 21 churches in Holmes County from the Yazoo Baptist Association. In 1954, 19 churches reported 133 baptisms, 3,207 members, $121,953.00 total gifts, $16,760.15 mission gifts, $524,000.00 property value, and $2,220.00 church debt.

HUMPHREYS. Organized in 1877 as Brooksfield Baptist Association upon the division of the Sunflower Baptist Association. Its churches were distributed along the course of Deer Creek, and the name was changed in 1881 to Deer Creek Baptist Association. In 1920 the Deer Creek and Sunflower associations were divided into four bodies nearly equal in size: Riverside (Tunica, Bolivar and Coahoma counties), Tallahatchie (Leflore, Quitman and part of Tallahatchie counties), Sunflower (Sunflower County), and Deer Creek (Washington, Humphreys, Sharkey, Issaquena counties). In 1950 Deer Creek gave 10 churches letters to organize Sharkey-Issaquena Baptist Association. In 1952 nine churches were given letters to form the Washington County Baptist Association. Since 1944 it has been served by a missions superintendent. In 1953 the name was changed to Humphreys County Baptist Association. In 1954 seven churches reported 71 baptisms, 1,766 members, $49,276 total gifts, $9,689.08 mission gifts, and a total property value of $147,500.

W. HENRY CROUCH

ITAWAMBA. Organized in 1883 as the Tombigbee Baptist Association by churches in northeastern area of state. In 1891 there were 16 churches in Mississippi and one in Alabama. Articles of faith were adopted at organization. The name was changed in 1921 to Itawamba County Baptist Association. Since 1945 it has been served by a missions superintendent. In 1954, 14 churches reported 45 baptisms, 1,561 members, $14,703 total gifts, $635.64 mission gifts, and $58,000 property value.

JACKSON. Organized in 1924 by churches from the Gulf Coast Baptist Association. At its 1927 session it had 13 churches with 1,073 members. A missions superintendent is employed. In 1954, 21 churches reported 434 baptisms, 6,239 members, $311,018 total gifts, $46,754 mission gifts, $972,150 property value, and $159,563 church debt.

J. L. BOYD

JASPER. Organized in 1904 as Bay Springs Baptist Association by 18 churches located in Jasper and nearby counties. Articles of faith and gospel order were adopted. The name was changed to Jasper County Baptist Association in 1926. Since 1949 it has been served by a missions superintendent. In 1954, 19 churches reported 105 baptisms, 2,902 members, $100,-922 total gifts, $9,640.88 mission gifts, $310,000 property value, and $23,659 church debt.

JEFFERSON DAVIS. Organized in 1913 by 13 churches in Jefferson Davis County. In 1954, 16 churches reported 89 baptisms, 3,815 members, $128,277.00 total gifts, $14,950.12 mission gifts, $501,845.00 property value, and $33,198.00 church debt.

JONES. Organized in 1916. The 1917 minutes reported 30 churches. A full-time associational missionary was employed in 1945. In 1954, 43 churches reported 617 baptisms, 13,648 members, $491,657 total gifts, $50,807 mission gifts, $1,882,-035 property value, and $282,653 church debt.

KEMPER. Organized Oct. 23, 1920, by 11 churches. Articles of faith were adopted at that time. In 1954, 15 churches reported 73 baptisms, 1,578 members, $29,831.00 total gifts, $3,295.47 mission gifts, $123,300.00 property value, and $276 church debt.

LAFAYETTE. Organized in 1870 as the Oxford Association by 13 churches. The name was changed to Lafayette County Association in 1920. In 1948 it employed a missions superintendent. In 1954, 22 churches reported 208 baptisms, 4,720 members, $95,098 total gifts, $11,125.03 mission gifts, $460,773 property value, and $13,600 church debt.

LAMAR. Organized July 3, 1949, by eight churches in Lamar County. In 1954 nine churches reported 119 baptisms, 2,085 members, $55,029.00 total gifts, $2,850.79 mission gifts, $157,500.00 property value, and $2,155.00 church debt.

W. HENRY CROUCH

LAUDERDALE. Organized June, 1902, by 13 churches in Lauderdale County. The articles of faith were adopted in 1902. In 1954, 42 churches reported 483 baptisms, 13,757 members, $602,518.00 total gifts, $114,271.72 mission gifts, $2,715,550.00 property value, and $372,-295.00 church debt.

LAWRENCE. Organized Mar., 1901, by 15 churches. Articles of faith were adopted in 1901. In 1954, 22 churches reported 155 baptisms, 4,899 members, $99,280.00 total gifts, $13,840.53 mission gifts, $443,500.00 property value, and $3,414.00 church debt.

LEAKE COUNTY. Organized as Harmony Baptist Association in 1849 by churches in the central area of the state located in Leake, Madison, Neshoba, Rankin, and Scott counties. In 1852, 24 churches reported 1,163 members. The declaration of faith and gospel order appeared in the 1857 minutes. The name was changed to Leake County Baptist Association in 1920. In 1954, 31 churches reported 135 baptisms, 4,335 members, $117,739 total gifts, $16,020.95 mission gifts, and $357,001 property value.

LEBANON. Organized Nov., 1894, by 12 churches in the southeastern area of the state. Articles of faith were adopted in 1894. From it churches have withdrawn to join in forming three other associations: Jones County (1915), George County (1920), and Lamar County (1949). In 1954, 35 churches reported 568 baptisms, 15,845 members, $573,848 total gifts, $85,-136.01 mission gifts, and $2,561,943 property value.

LEE. Organized Sept., 1920, by 24 churches in Lee County. In 1954, 34 churches reported 437 baptisms, 11,190 members, $364,651 total gifts, $56,480.97 mission gifts, and $1,397,645 property value.

LEFLORE. Organized Oct., 1926, by eight churches in Leflore County. In 1954, 12 churches reported 255 baptisms, 5,527 members, $193,-107 total gifts, $30,775.26 mission gifts, $715,300 property value, and $23,419 church debt.

ROBERT W. MARTIN, JR.

LINCOLN. Organized in 1872 as Fair River Baptist Association by 10 churches in Copiah, Lawrence, and Lincoln counties. The articles of faith were adopted at organization. The name was changed in 1903 to Lincoln County Baptist Association. In 1954, 35 churches reported 290 baptisms, 10,959 members, $433,006.32 total gifts, $55,667.19 mission gifts, $1,225,736.00 property value, and $107,817.00 church debt.

LOWNDES. Organized in 1837 as Columbus Baptist Association by churches in Lowndes and nearby counties. At the fourth annual session nine churches were located in Mississippi and six in Alabama. Articles of faith appeared in 1844. From it groups of churches have withdrawn to join in forming other associations: Oktibbeha (1920), Noxubee (1922), Clay (1928). Since 1946 it has been served by an associational missions superintendent. The name was changed in 1950 to Lowndes County Baptist Association. In 1954, 18 churches reported 269 baptisms, 6,300 members, $225,479 total gifts, $49,340.39 mission gifts, and $1,096,100 property value.

J. L. BOYD

MADISON. Organized Oct., 1921, by eight churches in Madison County. The constitution and bylaws were adopted in 1953. In 1954, 12 churches reported 235 baptisms, 3,121 members, $137,164 total gifts, $26,707.78 mission gifts, $729,-800 property value, and $50,720 church debt.

ROBERT W. MARTIN, JR.

MARION. Organized in 1820 as Pearl River Baptist Association by 10 churches in the southern section of the state embracing five counties and east Louisiana. Articles of faith were adopted at organization. From it groups of churches have withdrawn to join in forming other associations: Lawrence (1901), Jefferson Davis (1912), Lamar (1949). The name was changed in 1920 to Marion County Baptist Association. Since 1950 it has been served by an associational missions superintendent, for whom a home was provided in 1953. In 1954, 21 churches reported 232 baptisms, 6,613 members, $209,704 total gifts, $39,604 mission gifts, $658,-500 property value, and $18,971 church debt.

J. L. BOYD

MARSHALL. Organized Sept., 1921, by 12 churches in Marshall County. Since 1948 it has been served by an associational missions superintendent. In 1954, 16 churches reported 149 baptisms, 3,172 members, $60,976 total gifts, $16,-611.48 mission gifts, and $207,100 property value.

ROBERT W. MARTIN, JR.

MISSISSIPPI. Organized in 1806 by six churches in the southwestern section of the state. Articles of faith and gospel order were adopted at the time of organization. In 1820 groups of churches withdrew to form the Pearl River and Union Baptist associations. Since 1950 it has been served by a missions superintendent. In 1954, 26 churches reported 204 baptisms, 5,058 members, $172,047.00 total gifts, $25,797.95 mission gifts, $699,600.00 property value, and $68,151 church debt.

J. L. BOYD

MONROE. Organized Oct., 1907, by 14 churches in Monroe County subsequent to the dissolution of Sipsey Association. Articles of faith were adopted in 1907. In 1954, 20 churches reported 162 baptisms, 4,227 members, $75,678 total gifts, $13,668.92 mission gifts, and $370,300 property value.

ROBERT W. MARTIN, JR.

MONTGOMERY. Organized in 1915 by churches in Montgomery and Carroll counties. In 1918 there were 20 churches; in 1919 churches in Carroll County formed the Carroll Association. There was a county missionary in 1921. Since 1950 it has been served together with Carroll Association by a missions superintendent. In 1954, 22 churches reported 110 baptisms, 3,643 members, $70,152.00 total gifts, $10,094.70 mission gifts, and $255,600.00 property value.

C. B. HAMLET III

NESHOBA. Organized Oct., 1920, by five churches in Neshoba County. Articles of faith were adopted in 1920. In 1944 it employed a superintendent of missions. In 1954, 27 churches reported 206 baptisms, 4,970 members, $109,007 total gifts, $16,467.17 mission gifts, $584,800 property value, and $28,543 church debt.

NEW CHOCTAW. Organized in 1910 by seven churches in four counties in center of state. Articles of faith were adopted in 1910. In 1954, 11 churches reported 48 baptisms, 806 members, $2,872 total gifts, $346.76 mission gifts, and $37,047 property value.

NEWTON. Organized in May, 1921, by 13 churches in Newton County. Articles of faith were adopted. Since 1944 it has been served by a missions superintendent. In 1954, 31 churches reported 140 baptisms, 5,924 members, $151,368 total gifts, $20,283 mission gifts, $577,607 property value, and $43,000 church debt (1952).

NOXUBEE. Organized in Dec., 1922, by nine churches in Noxubee County. Articles of faith were first recorded in 1927. In 1954, 12 churches reported 27 baptisms, 1,577 members, $56,347.00 total gifts, $4,845.92 mission gifts, $220,700.00 property value, and $10,000.00 church debt.

OKTIBBEHA. Organized in Oct., 1921, by 18 churches in Oktibbeha County. In 1954, 16 churches reported 252 baptisms, 4,168 members, $105,930.00 total gifts, $15,602.58 mission gifts, $394,750.00 property value, and $9,418.00 church debt.

PANOLA. Organized in Nov., 1920, by 18 churches in Panola County. Since 1947 it has been served by a missions superintendent. In 1954, 24 churches reported 220 baptisms, 4,389 members, $130,084.00 total gifts, $21,728.76 mission gifts, $499,230.00 property value, and $14,284.00 church debt. CAREY COX

PEARL RIVER COUNTY. Organized as the Hobola Chitto Baptist Association in 1856 by churches in Pearl River and adjoining counties. At the fourth session there were eight churches with 264 members. Articles of faith and gospel order were adopted in 1866. The name was changed in 1920 to Pearl River County Baptist Association, and the articles of faith were continued with a few changes. In 1954, 30 churches reported 386 baptisms, 7,756 members, $287,742.00 total gifts, $437,992.24 mission gifts, and $1,101,578.00 property value. J. L. BOYD

PERRY. Organized in 1911 by 13 churches in Perry County. Articles of faith were adopted in 1911. It has been served since 1953 by a missions superintendent. In 1954, 17 churches reported 125 baptisms, 2,931 members, $67,291 total gifts, $5,999.32 mission gifts, and $289,700 property value. CAREY COX

PIKE COUNTY. Formerly the Bogue Chitto Association, organized in 1870 by 16 churches in the southern section of the state and east Louisiana. Articles of faith and gospel order were adopted at time of organization. The name was changed at the request of the convention board to the Pike County Baptist Association following county lines. In 1954, 29 churches reported 333 baptisms, 11,050 members, $388,077 total gifts, $70,438.39 mission gifts, and $1,465,000 property value. J. L. BOYD

PONTOTOC. Organized in 1918 by 31 churches in Pontotoc County. Since 1944 it has been served by a missions superintendent, and it has owned a home for its missionary since 1948. In 1954, 41 churches reported 260 baptisms, 8,092 members, $155,938.00 total gifts, $19,437.99 mission gifts, $457,319.00 property value, and $17,691.00 church debt.

PRENTISS. Organized in 1920 by 13 churches in Prentiss County. Articles of faith were adopted in 1921. Since 1945 it has been served by a missions superintendent, and it has owned a home for its missionary since 1948. In 1954, 17 churches reported 157 baptisms, 4,784 members, $87,404.00 total gifts, $10,841.77 mission gifts, $448,200.00 property value, and $7,075 church debt.

RANKIN. Organized in Oct., 1893, by 14 churches in Rankin County. Articles of faith were adopted. In 1954, 37 churches reported 215 baptisms, 7,330 members, $238,923 total gifts, $26,056 mission gifts, $921,247 property value, and $91,524 church debt. CAREY COX

RIVERSIDE. Organized in 1920 by churches in the northwestern section of the state, in Coahoma, Quitman, and Tunica counties. By the sixth annual session the churches numbered 12 with 571 members. Since 1942 it has been served by a missions superintendent. In 1954, 23 churches reported 507 baptisms, 7,485 members, $292,688 total gifts, $33,562 mission gifts, $1,291,235 property value, and $230,421 church debt.

SCOTT. Organized in 1900 as the Hopewell Association by uniting the Old Scott County Baptist Association and the Old Springfield Baptist Association. Articles of faith appear in the 1905 minutes, the first ones in the historical files and in which 19 churches reported 1,175 members. In 1920 the name was changed to Scott County Baptist Association, to conform to county lines. Articles of faith recur in 1953. Since 1949 it has been served by a missions superintendent. In 1954, 31 churches reported 198 baptisms, 5,401 members, $147,346.00 total gifts, $18,506.91 mission gifts, $730,725.00 property value, and $59,344.00 church debt.

SHARKEY-ISSAQUENA. Organized in 1950 by 10 churches from the Deer Creek Baptist Association in the Delta section of the state. In 1954, 10 churches reported 67 baptisms, 1,867 members, $65,845 total gifts, $6,054 mission gifts, $217,850 property value, and $11,416 church debt.

SIMPSON COUNTY. Organized as Strong River Association in 1853 by 16 churches out of the Pearl River Association located in Copiah, Lawrence, Rankin, and Simpson counties. Articles of faith were adopted when organized. In 1892 letters were granted to groups of churches to join in formation of Rankin County Association and others in 1905. The name was changed to Simpson County Baptist Association in 1920. The body voted in 1926 to build a preacher's cottage at Clarke Memorial College, and in 1927 commissioned a history. In 1954, 40 churches reported 247 baptisms, 9,289 members, $197,743 total gifts, $16,362.69 mission gifts, and $869,250 property value.

SMITH COUNTY. Organized in 1888 as New Liberty Baptist Association by churches in central Mississippi. An abstract of faith and gospel order was adopted in 1889. In 1902, 50 churches in Covington, Jasper, Jones, Simpson, and Smith counties reported 3,921 members. The name was changed in 1919 to Smith County Baptist Association. In 1954, 38 churches reported 160 baptisms, 6,469 members, $108,096.00 total gifts, $7,344.68 mission gifts, $379,200.00 property value, and $3,682.00 church debt.

SUNFLOWER. Organized in 1870 as Sunflower Baptist Association. In 1879 it had six churches located in Bolivar, Coahoma, Sunflower, and adjoining counties. Articles of faith were adopted in 1884. In 1920, on recommendation of the pastors, Deer Creek and Sunflower Association split up, and the Delta territory was divided into four sections containing about an equal number of churches who were asked to form four associations. The 21 churches in Sunflower County were accorded the privilege of retaining the historical sequence of the old Sunflower by the new name of Sunflower County Baptist Association. In 1954, 18 churches reported 340 baptisms, 6,402 members, $298,224 total gifts, $33,-820 mission gifts, $986,000 property value, and $103,986 church debt.

TALLAHATCHIE. Organized Oct., 1920, by 12 churches, several of which came from the hill section of Tallahatchie County and Yalobusha Baptist Association to make it a county unit. Since 1953 it has been served by a missions superintendent, for whom a home has been provided. In 1954, 19 churches reported 190 baptisms, 4,218 members, $169,814.04 total gifts, $22,-166.66 mission gifts, $465,000.00 property value, and $43,252.00 church debt.

TATE. Organized in 1920 by churches in the north central section of the state. At its sixth annual session it numbered 12 churches with 1,662 members. In 1954, 16 churches reported 118 baptisms, 2,973 members, $97,514 total gifts, $8,416 mission gifts, $583,000 property value, and $1,775 church debt.

TIPPAH. Organized in 1921 by 19 churches in Tippah County out of Tippah Baptist Association. Articles of faith were adopted the following year. Since 1953 it has been served by a missions superintendent. In 1953, 29 churches reported 184 baptisms, 5,561 members, $64,-954.18 total gifts, $14,966.66 mission gifts, $252,-200.00 property value, and $6,950.00 church debt.

TISHOMINGO. Organized as Tishomingo Baptist Association in 1860 by 19 churches in the northern section of the state. Articles of faith appear in 1887. The name changed in 1931 to Tishomingo County Baptist Association. Since 1946 it has been served by a missions superintendent. In 1954, 21 churches reported 72 baptisms, 3,068 members, $62,158 total gifts, $4,787 mission gifts, $221,400 property value, and $24,-150 church debt.

UNION. Organized Sept. 18, 1820, by eight churches from the Mississippi Baptist Association, located north of the Himochitto River. Its 1825 minutes (first in the files) listed 12 churches in Adams, Claiborne, Franklin, Jefferson, and Warren counties. Articles of faith were adopted. Groups of churches were lettered to form other associations: Central Baptist Association in the northern section in 1845, and Franklin County Baptist Association in 1919. Since 1949 it has been served by a missions superintendent. In 1954, 25 churches reported 405 baptisms, 5,634 members, $243,672.00 total gifts, $25,111.80 mission gifts, $784,500.00 property value, and $69,038 church debt.

UNION COUNTY. Organized Sept., 1919, by 28 churches in Union County, which formerly belonged to the Chickasaw and West Judson Baptist associations. Articles of faith were adopted at the time of organization. Since 1945 it has been served by a missions superintendent. In 1954, 33 churches reported 289 baptisms, 8,635 members, $162,198.00 total gifts, $24,832.06 mission gifts, $695,100.00 property value, and $4,319.00 church debt. J. L. BOYD

WALTHALL. Organized Nov. 26, 1914, by nine churches in Walthall County. Articles of faith were adopted at the organizational meeting. In 1954, 12 churches reported 139 baptisms, 4,345 members, $115,794.00 total gifts, $16,491.60 mission gifts, $412,253.00 property value, and $964.00 church debt.

WARREN. Organized Nov. 9, 1947, by eight churches in Warren County, the Hinds-Warren Association having voted Oct. 16, 1947, to form two associations. Since 1947 it has been served by a missions superintendent. In 1954, 11 churches reported 183 baptisms, 4,529 members, $198,261.00 total gifts, $26,824.57 mission gifts, $553,500.00 property value, and $26,045.00 church debt.

WASHINGTON. Organized Oct. 26, 1952, by 12 churches in Washington County. In 1954, 15 churches reported 378 baptisms, 7,685 members, $355,604.00 total gifts, $35,385.59 mission gifts, $1,509,250.00 property value, and $462,154.00 church debt.

WAYNE. Organized in 1919. In 1921 there were 18 churches in the county. Articles of faith appear in 1921. Since 1954 it has been served by an associational missions superintendent. In 1954, 23 churches reported 168 baptisms, 3,521 members, $96,594 total gifts, $9,245.78 mission gifts, and $356,600 property value. C. B. HAMLET III

WINSTON. Organized in 1838 as the Louisville Baptist Association by 10 churches out of the Choctaw Confederation. In the 1852 minutes there were reported 39 churches in Attala, Choctaw, Neshoba, Oktibbeha, and Winston counties. An abstract of faith appears in 1853. In 1892, 16 churches were granted letters to organize Chester Baptist Association. In 1920 the clerk was authorized to furnish letters of dismission to all churches desiring to unite with churches in forming associations along county lines. In 1921 the name was changed to Winston County Baptist Association. Since 1944 it has been served by an associational missions superintendent. In 1954, 29 churches reported 227 baptisms, 5,206 members, $162,953 total gifts, $10,905.46 mission gifts, and $729,990 property value. J. L. BOYD

YALOBUSHA. Organized Oct. 7, 1920, by six churches, but had 20 churches in the first annual session in Sept., 1921. Articles of faith were published in 1923. From July, 1947, to Oct., 1952, an associational missions superintendent was employed with Panola County Association. In 1954, 20 churches reported 132 baptisms, 3,631 members, $59,925 total gifts, $9,285.34 mission gifts, and $199,000 property value.

YAZOO. Organized Oct., 1920, by 16 churches in the county. Since 1954 it and Madison County

Association have been served by an associational missions superintendent. In 1954, 22 churches reported 178 baptisms, 5,052 members, $191,239 total gifts, $26,505.55 mission gifts, and $602,000 property value.

ZION. Organized in 1836 by churches in nine counties in north central part of the state. Abstract of faith was published in 1858, and 24 churches reported that year. In 1920 it was composed primarily of churches in Webster County, but voted down a motion to dissolve. Since 1954 it has been served by an associational missions superintendent. In 1954, 31 churches reported 184 baptisms, 5,027 members, $78,920 total gifts, $10,709.14 mission gifts, and $279,475 property value. C. B. HAMLET III

II. Extinct. ABERDEEN. Organized as Aberdeen Baptist Association in 1843 by churches in the northern section of the state. It contained 33 churches by 1854. The articles of faith appeared in 1874. In 1919 it dissolved to organize on a county basis. LEWIS RHODES

BETHLEHEM. Organized in 1852 by churches from Choctaw Baptist Association located in Clarke and Lauderdale counties. Articles of faith were adopted at organization. The peak years were in the 1870's. In 1902, 18 churches reported 1,181 members.

BILOXI. Organized in 1849 by churches on the Gulf Coast. In 1852 only four churches reported. It dissolved in 1854. J. L. BOYD

BUTTYHATCHY. Organized in May, 1836, by churches in Lowndes and Monroe counties. The records in one book are written in longhand, pen and ink. The last minutes preserved are Aug. 25, 1883. It probably dissolved or died soon thereafter. LEWIS RHODES

CAREY. Organized in 1884 as Carey Baptist Association by 12 churches in the southwestern part of the state and east Louisiana. Articles of faith and gospel order appear in 1885. In 1889, 27 churches reported 1,400 members. It dissolved in 1920 to organize along county lines. J. L. BOYD

CENTRAL. Organized as Central Baptist Association in 1845 by 24 churches located in central Mississippi. Articles of faith were adopted at the time of organization. It established Central Baptist Female Institute (later Hillman College) at Clinton in 1853. It dissolved in 1920 to reorganize Hinds-Warren (now Hinds), Madison, and Yazoo County associations along county lines.

CHESTER. Organized in 1892 by churches in Choctaw and adjoining counties, embracing 28 churches in 1893 with 2,018 members. The articles of faith were adopted in 1893. It dissolved in 1920 to organize on county lines.

CHICKASAHAY. Organized Dec., 1876, by churches in the eastern section of the state. It adopted articles of faith. It dissolved in 1918 and reorganized into Clarke and Wayne County associations.

CHICKASAW. Organized in 1837 by churches in Monroe and adjacent counties. In 1844, 34 churches reported 1,664 members. An abstract of principles appeared in 1848. It dissolved in 1919 to organize along county lines.

CHOCTAW. Organized in 1834 by churches in Kemper and adjoining counties. In 1837, 39 churches reported 1,008 members. The association reorganized in 1838 and the articles of faith appeared in 1869. It dissolved in 1922 to organize on county lines. LEWIS RHODES

DELTA. Organized as Delta Baptist Association in 1920 by 16 churches in Leflore and Quitman counties. Minutes of 1921 to 1925 are preserved. It was displaced by Leflore in 1926.

EBENEZER. Organized in 1846 by eight churches out of the Leaf River Association, some in Alabama. Articles of faith appear in 1869. Its best years were in the 1880's, with 29 churches reporting 1,312 members. It affiliated with the General Association of Southeast Mississippi. It declined by 1937, when it had six churches and 231 members, and soon dissolved. J. L. BOYD

HINDS. Organized Oct. 8, 1920, by 10 churches out of Central Baptist Association. The churches of Warren County, not numerous enough to maintain a separate body, joined; and the name was changed in 1927 to Hinds-Warren Baptist Association. It dissolved in 1947 to organize along county lines.

JUDSON. Organized in 1853 by five churches in Pontotoc and adjoining counties. It adopted an abstract of principles in 1870. The minutes of the 71st annual session in 1923 are the last on record.

LEAF RIVER. Organized in 1829 by 11 churches in the southeastern section of the state and a few in Alabama. Antimission spirit grew, and those favoring withdrew *c.* 1845 to form the Ebenezer Baptist Association. It soon disappeared.

LEAF RIVER. Organized in 1890 by churches in the southeastern area of the state. At the 1896 session 14 churches reported 554 members. The articles of faith and gospel order appeared in 1896. A group of churches withdrew in 1912 to join in the organization of Perry County Baptist Association. It dissolved *c.* 1920.

LIBERTY. Organized in 1837 by churches in the eastern section of the state and west Alabama. In 1888, 17 churches (5 in Alabama) reported 976 members. The articles of faith appeared in 1888. It dissolved in recent years. LEWIS RHODES

MAGEE'S CREEK. Organized as Magee's Creek Baptist Association in 1880 by four churches in the southern part of Mississippi and east Louisiana. Articles of faith were adopted at organization. The next year seven churches joined from the Bogue Chitto Association. Time of dissolution is unknown.

MISSISSIPPI RIVER. Organized as Mississippi Baptist Association in 1843 by seven churches in southwestern area of state and east Louisiana along the Mississippi River. The articles of faith and gospel order were adopted in 1846. By 1904 the four Mississippi churches had rejoined the Mississippi Baptist Association and the remaining 16 became affiliated with the Louisiana Baptist Convention. J. L. BOYD

OKTIBBEHA. Organized in 1879 by churches in Leake and near-by counties. In 1882, 14 churches reported 718 members. The abstract of faith and gospel order appeared in 1883. In 1949, 16 churches reported 2,132 members affiliating with the General Association of Regular Baptists.

LEWIS RHODES

OLD SCOTT COUNTY. Organized in 1894. By 1898 churches of other counties had joined to make the name a misnomer, and the body sought to unite with the Springfield to form in 1900 Hopewell Baptist Association. J. L. BOYD

OXFORD. Organized in 1870 by 13 churches in Lafayette and near-by counties. A declaration of faith was adopted. It dissolved in 1920 to organize along county lines. LEWIS RHODES

PROVIDENCE. Organized as Providence Baptist Association in Jackson County in 1855 with most of the churches in Alabama. It dissolved in 1877 to give place to the organization of Gulf Coast Baptist Association. It thus was the link between the Biloxi and Gulf Coast.

SOUTH MISSISSIPPI. Organized as South Mississippi Baptist Association in 1896 by five churches in Amite and Pike counties. In 1900, four churches reported 318 members.

SPRINGFIELD. Organized as Springfield Baptist Association in 1873 by 14 churches in Leake, Rankin, Scott, and Smith counties. In 1875, 20 churches reported 978 members. The articles of faith and gospel order were adopted 1884. Its peak years were in the 1880's with 40 churches. In 1900 it united with Old Scott County Association to form the Hopewell Baptist Association.

J. L. BOYD

TIPPAH. Organized in 1862 by churches in the northern section of the state and south Tennessee. In 1869, 25 churches (9 from Tennessee) reported 1,811 members. The abstract of faith appeared in 1869. The association dissolved in 1921 to organize on county lines.

WEST JUDSON. Organized in 1884, having in 1886, 18 churches with 1,643 members located in Pontotoc and near-by counties. Abstracts of principles appeared in 1886. It dissolved in 1919 to organize Lee County and Union County Baptist associations.

YALOBUSHA. Organized in 1836. In 1841 it constituted 12 churches located in Carroll, Lafayette, and Yalobusha counties. A declaration of faith appeared in 1872. The name changed in 1883 to Yalobusha-Oxford Baptist Association as the Oxford, Miss., Baptist Church joined its fellowship. Name changed back to its original in 1890, the Oxford church disappearing from list of churches. Articles of faith appeared in 1879. It established the Yalobusha Baptist Female Institute at Grenada in 1851. It dissolved in 1920 to organize along county lines.

YAZOO. Organized in 1851. In 1854, 18 churches reported 1,808 members. The articles of faith appeared in 1854. It dissolved in 1920 to organize along county lines. LEWIS RHODES

III. Non-co-operative. In their articles of faith, these associations conform, in the main, to co-operative associations, except with reference to foot washing. But their constitutions and rules of decorum are peculiar to themselves.

AMITE. Organized in 1857 by churches in Amite and adjoining counties. It was in existence in 1904.

BETHANY. Organized in 1842. In 1902 it had 19 churches in Attala, Clarke, Leake, Neshoba, Newton, and Scott counties. In 1936, 14 churches reported 469 members.

BETHEL. Organized *c.* 1835 by churches in Hinds, Holmes, Rankin, Madison, and adjoining counties. It figured largely in the organization of the Convention and its progress. In 1836 it began to exchange correspondence with the Mississippi Baptist Association. In 1837 six churches reported about 300 members. It existed only a short time.

BETHEL. Organized in 1886 by churches in the southern area of the state out of Red Creek Baptist Association. In 1891 half the churches rejoined the Red Creek. In 1903 nine churches reported 556 members.

FIRST ENTERPRISE. Organized in 1871 by churches in Clarke and near-by counties, adopting articles of faith at organization, and having 70 churches in 1912.

GOOD HOPE. Organized in 1889 by churches in Jasper, Scott, Simpson, and Smith counties. The articles of faith were adopted in 1892. In 1948, 14 churches reported 709 members.

HOPEWELL. Organized in 1865 by churches in Pontotoc County and near-by churches. In 1896 it included 10 churches in Calhoun, Lafayette, Montgomery, Pontotoc, and Yalobusha counties.

LITTLE BLACK. Organized *c.* 1902 by churches in Attala, Choctaw, and Winston counties. In 1937 nine churches reported 540 members.

LITTLE VINE. Organization date not known. In 1904 it was almost non-existent.

LITTLE ZION. Organized in 1884 by churches in Green, Jones, Marion, and Wayne counties, Miss., and Mobile County, Ala. In 1902 eight churches reported 133 members.

LOOCASOONA. Organized in 1839 by four churches out of Yalobusha Baptist Association. In 1843 four churches reported 137 members. The association was dissolved in 1863.

MOUNT OLIVE. Organized in 1874 by nine churches in Leake, Madison, Rankin, and Scott counties. It adopted articles of faith in 1877. In 1930, 10 churches reported.

NEW HOPE. Organized in 1842. The articles of faith were adopted in 1877. In 1902, 10 churches reported 332 members in Alcorn, Prentiss, Tishomingo, and Union counties. In 1939 it had 12 churches.

NEW LIBERTY. Organized in 1887 and adopted articles of faith in 1889. In 1917 it had 22 churches.

PEARL VALLEY. Organized in 1886 by seven churches in Attala, Leake, Neshoba, and Winston counties. In 1898, 15 churches reported 539 members. The articles of faith and gospel order appeared in 1909.

PRIMITIVE. Organized in 1839 by four churches in Carroll, Holmes, and Yazoo counties. In 1846 nine churches reported 523 members, and in 1900 it was active.

RED CREEK. Organized in 1880 by churches out of the Hobola Chitto Baptist Association in the southern area of the state. The articles of faith and gospel order appeared in 1887. In 1901, 23 churches reported 1,235 members. In 1927 there were 22 churches.

REGULAR BAPTIST. Date of organization not known, but slightly active in 1902.

SALEM. Organized in 1860 by churches in Clarke, Covington, Green, Simpson, and Smith counties; in 1869, 30 churches reported 1,232 members. In 1884, 33 churches reported 1,460 members.

SIPSEY. Organized in 1887 by five churches out of Aberdeen and Judson associations. The articles of faith were adopted at organization. In 1900 seven churches reported 327 members.

TALLAHALA. Organized in 1885. In 1887 seven churches in Jones County reported 165 members. The articles of faith and gospel order appeared that year. In 1910, 32 churches reported 1,946 members.

TALLAHATCHIE. Organized in 1841 by churches in the northern part of the state. In 1844, 15 churches located in De Soto, Lafayette, Marshall, and Tippah counties and one in Tennessee reported 394 members. An abstract of faith appeared in 1844. In 1939 four churches reported 187 members.

TOMBIGBEE. Organized in 1845 as a Primitive association. In 1916 nine churches reported 294 members, in Lee, Monroe, and adjoining counties. The articles of faith appeared in 1916 records.

TRINITY. Organized in 1895 by churches in Chickasaw, Clay, and Webster counties. In 1900, 20 churches reported 1,321 members. By 1925 it constituted only six churches with 622 members.

YAZOO. Organized in 1833 by churches in Yazoo and adjoining counties. In 1834 the Mississippi Baptist Association began correspondence with it. Yazoo made favorable response and sustained correspondence through 1837, but never affiliated with the Mississippi Baptist Convention. It later merged with the Primitive Baptist Association.

ZION'S REST. Organized in 1838 by churches in Kemper and Neshoba counties. These churches were originally in the Old Choctaw Confederation. In 1843, 18 churches reported 585 members. It was still in existence in 1902.

J. L. BOYD

MISSISSIPPI BAPTIST. A Baptist newspaper established in 1846 with William H. Taylor as editor, but which temporarily ceased operations between 1849 and 1856. The Mississippi Baptist Convention sponsored this privately owned paper from 1857, when it had a circulation of 3,000, to 1862, when the Civil War forced the paper to suspend publication. Among its editors were William Carey Crane (*q.v.*), J. B. Hiteler, J. T. Freeman, and Aaron Jones, Jr.

A. L. GOODRICH

MISSISSIPPI BAPTIST CONVENTION.

I. Baptist Beginnings. The history of Mississippi Baptists prior to the organization of the general convention in 1836 may be roughly divided into four periods: the period of settlement and persecution, the period of rapid early growth, the period of dissension and strife, and the period of expansion. During the first period (1780–98) the population of the land which was to become Mississippi consisted almost entirely of Indians—mainly Choctaw, Chickasaw, Natchez and Pascagoula—except for a sparsely settled portion in the extreme south, where Spanish and French explorers had infiltrated. This region was called the Natchez Country, or the Great Southwest, the white population being almost entirely Roman Catholic. During this period only two evangelical churches were constituted, a Congregational church in 1772 on the Homochitto River, which disbanded in the 1780's because of persecutions and Indian molestations; and a Baptist church, organized in 1791 on Cole's Creek, which suffered many privations and hardships, yet survived the bitter opposition of the Catholic clergy until the newly constituted government of the United States gained possession in 1798.

The second period (1798–1824) was marked by a great increase in population, due to the Choctaw land treaties of 1805, 1816, and 1820. Among the newcomers were a host of Baptists who constituted churches in rapid succession and organized associations, beginning with the Mississippi Baptist Association in 1806. Mutually helpful fraternal correspondence was established with like bodies on the Atlantic seaboard. Missionary societies were organized, and a plan of education was laid out as early as 1817. As early as 1815, the Baptists of the Mississippi Territory began to share in the support of the cause of foreign missions through the Foreign Mission Board of the Triennial Convention. To implement these progressive moves, the first state Baptist convention was organized in 1824. The third period (1824–29) was marked by dissension and strife, which was engendered by ill feeling growing out of bitter controversies with interlopers of various religious sects, resulting in the convention's being dissolved in 1829.

The fourth period (1829–36) saw a recovery from the reverses of the previous period through an added interest in, and emphasis on, a cooperative effort on the associational level. Additional land treaties with the Choctaw Indians in 1830 and the Chickasaws in 1832 opened to white settlers the whole of Mississippi to the Tennessee line. As the Indians were conducted on the "Trail of Tears" to reservations west of the Mississippi River, wave after wave of immigrants moved in, new Baptist churches sprang up as if by magic, and associations were formed. By 1836 the Baptist constituency in the state numbered almost 5,000, in 128 churches and 9 associations, served by 92 ministers.

Early religious life.—The first Baptists arriving in the Natchez Country came from the Great Pee Dee Valley of South Carolina in 1780, bringing their church letters with them. (John Jones had in his wallet, also, his discharge papers from the Continental army, containing favorable recommendations from his commanding officer and signed by other members of his company.) The group traveled overland and down the Holston, Tennessee, Ohio, and Mississippi rivers on flatboats and settled about 20 miles northeast of Natchez on Cole's Creek, forming the Stampley Settlement. The leader of the group was Richard Curtis, whose son, Richard Curtis, Jr. (*q.v.*), a licensed preacher, became the spiritual head of the community. Private meetings were held in the homes from the first, though quietly and unmolested, till after the Salem or Cole's Creek Baptist Church was organized with 11 members in Oct., 1791, in the home of Margaret Stampley. Young Curtis was the first pastor, William Thompson, recording clerk, and William Chaney, the first known deacon. The church was strongly Calvinistic in doctrine.

After the church was constituted, and Curtis began by invitation to visit other settlements to hold "private meetings," make converts, and baptize them in secret (by authority of the Salem Church), the Catholic clergy was aroused and incited the Spanish Commandant to warn Curtis for doing what "was violative of the laws of the Province and against the peace and safety of the country." For his disregard of the warning, Curtis was arrested, brought before the court, and threatened with a life at hard labor in the silver mines of Mexico if he did not desist. He promised with reservations to refrain from disobeying the laws of the land; but he yielded to the clamor for "private meetings" for prayer and meditation. Two prominent citizens, William Hamberlin and Stephen De Alvo, who had married an American, applied for membership by baptism into the Salem church and were baptized. He officiated secretly in the marriage of his niece, Phoeba Jones, to David Greenleaf. Greenleaf was a machinist and later probably served a term in the territorial house of representatives.

Enraged by the rumors of these unlawful acts, the Catholic authorities ordered that Curtis, Hamberlin, and De Alvo be arrested and brought to trial. After a prolonged and fruitless search by the authorities and the spectacular exploit of Chloe Holt in supplying the fugitives with horses and provisions for the journey, Curtis and his companions made their escape to South Carolina in 1795 to await a change in the civil rule of the province. In the absence of the pastor, Salem Church showed sufficient signs of life to build a rude house of worship of logs in the Stampley Settlement with primitive furnishings hewn from trees of the forest, against the day of their pastor's return. The United States government obtained possession by treaty in Mar., 1798, and the American flag was hoisted over the ramparts of Fort Rosalie in the midst of great rejoicing by the throng who had assembled for the ceremonies. Bailey Chaney (*q.v.*) was present; by request he mounted an improvised platform and preached a gospel sermon, to the discomfort of the opposers of religious liberty. (An opportunist, Bailey was also the first to preach a gospel [Baptist] sermon on Louisiana soil. He later served three terms in the house of representatives of the Mississippi Territory.)

While in South Carolina, Curtis was ordained; on his return to the Natchez District, he led his congregation in the summer of 1798 to put official sanction "in due and ancient form" on what they had done in 1791. A petition came shortly from a group of Baptists in Bayou Pierre community, near Port Gibson, asking that Salem send a delegation to organize them into a church in the fork of Bayou Pierre. Pastor Curtis, William Thompson, and others were authorized "to attend at the home of Thomas Hubbard on Friday before the third Sunday in August" when the Bayou Pierre Church was constituted. This church was the first known to sponsor an African Baptist Church in the Mississippi Territory. In the following order, other churches were constituted: New Hope, Amite County, 1800; Bethel, Wilkinson County, *c.* 1800; New Providence, Amite County, 1805, with 12 members; Ebenezer, Amite County, 1806, with 11 members. Thomas Mercer, the revivalist of the day, was a member of the presbyteries at the organizations of most of these early Baptist churches. He came from Georgia around 1800, and made a great contribution to the beginnings of Baptists in the state.

There were also other leaders who figured largely in Baptist life in this early period. David Cooper, who appeared in 1802, combined the profession of the physician with the calling of preacher; David Snodgrass, arriving about 1802, was an influential pastor; Ezra Courtney, who came from South Carolina about 1802, was an aggressive leader, esteemed in later years "as one of the patriarchs." Moses Hadley came about 1805 and was the most dearly beloved of all the pastors; John Stampley was an outstanding leader in the association and the president of the legislative council of the Mississippi Territory, 1801–02.

The six churches thus far constituted united in the organization of the Mississippi Baptist Association in the meetinghouse of Salem Church in Sept., 1806. The Preamble and Constitution, Articles of Faith, Gospel Order (Covenant), Rules of Decorum, and Powers of the Association adopted at the first annual session in 1807 bear evidence of having been written by Courtney. Two delegates from each church up to 100 members, and one for each additional 50, were to constitute the association. An emphasis was placed on the article: "This Association shall have no power to lord it over God's heritage, nor infringe upon any of the internal rights of the churches." Significant features of the 1807 session were these: (1) The first two days were given to public worship, concluding with the observance of the Lord's Supper. (2) A committee was appointed, Thomas Mercer, chairman, to examine a young man with a view to ordination to the gospel ministry at the next session.

Domestic and foreign missions promoted.—The Mississippi proved a mother association to Baptist organizational life, even beyond the bounds of the Mississippi Territory, particularly in Louisiana. The association sent Cooper and Mercer to assist the brethren along the Bogue Chitto River in east Louisiana in organizing the Half Moon Bluff Church in Washington Parish on Oct. 12, 1812, the first on Louisiana soil. In response to a petition from brethren in the Opelousas, west of the Mississippi River, the Mississippi Association delegated Cooper and L. Scarborough to go and ordain Joseph Willis and constitute the Calvary Baptist Church in St. Landry Parish on Nov. 13, 1812, the first in Louisiana west of the river. Both these became affiliated with the Mississippi Association. In 1818, upon request from Willis and his group of five churches in the Opelousas area, Cooper, Courtney, and John Smith were sent to direct in the organization of the Louisiana Baptist Association on Oct. 13, 1818, which was said to be "the legitimate daughter" of the Mississippi Association. The Baptists of Mississippi regarded south Louisiana, including New Orleans, as their home mission field even up to 1881.

One year after the Triennial Convention was organized, the Mississippi Association voted to support foreign missions through that convention, appointing William Snodgrass to receive and forward all funds designated for the purpose to the board's treasurer. The pastors were urged to present the cause of missions to the churches and receive contributions "from such persons as may be disposed to favor this great and blessed work." The sum of $20 was voted from the treasury to be sent without delay, together with any other monies received at this meeting "after paying for printing of the Minutes." One year hence, Snodgrass reported $83.93 as having been forwarded to the New York board for foreign missions. (Snodgrass was an outstanding layman in Baptist circles with considerable business interests in Natchez, including a book store, "perhaps the first in the State [which] contributed largely to the dissemination of religious literature in the country, especially of the Calvinistic caste." He was a member of the territorial house of representatives for four years and speaker of that body one session.)

Growing out of the relation with the national body, the Mississippi Society for Baptist Missions, Foreign and Domestic, was organized in 1817 with Benjamin Davis as president and Snodgrass as secretary. Its aims were "to promote missions in all the world, but more especially . . . to supply the very destitute parts of Mississippi Territory and the State of Louisiana east of the Mississippi River . . . to aid all who are destitute of the precious Word of life." Steps were taken immediately to send, under the auspices of the society, Davis and Mercer among the Creek Indians to inquire concerning the feasibility of establishing schools and preaching the gospel among them. Mercer died of exposure on this trip and was buried among strangers. Davis returned to his work among the Negroes in New Orleans as a missionary of the American Baptist Home Mission Society. James A. Raynaldson was serving as general missionary in the city under the same society in 1816. His financial support was assumed by the Mississippi society in 1817. He held services in the "Paulding Long Room" and organized a Baptist church in 1818, which joined the Mississippi Association. The churches were urged by the association to have a sermon preached each year on missions, to take a collection for the support of foreign and domestic missions, and to set aside a special fund in each church for the aid of traveling preachers. The pastors were asked to practice itinerant preaching, particularly in the destitute settlements of west Florida and the African Church in the Bayou Pierre community.

Plans for ministerial education.—The Mississippi Association formulated plans in 1817 for the education of young preachers. A committee of three—Cooper, Davis, and Raynaldson—was named to draw up the plan, which was adopted. The three also prepared an address to be published in the minutes to acquaint the churches of the plan and to appeal for their co-operation. A larger committee was created—namely, Cooper, Raynaldson, Courtney, Davis, Snodgrass, Scarborough, and G. W. King, "to manage the affairs of education." The next year a Mississippi Baptist Education Society was organized, with Cooper as president, Raynaldson as secretary, and Bartlett Collins as treasurer, to screen the list of potential beneficiaries and assist those deemed worthy in securing an education in institutions of learning in the older states of the Union.

Mississippi Association divided.—Baptist churches increased rapidly in Mississippi following the War of 1812—six new ones in 1815, five in 1816, seven in 1817, eight in 1818—numbering in 1819, 41 churches in the one association with 1,125 in total membership, covering the territory from Port Gibson south to New Orleans, and from the Mississippi to beyond the Pearl River. In 1819 two groups of churches presented petitions for letters of dismission to form new bodies—8 north of the Homochitto River and 14 along the Pearl River. Both petitions were granted, and the Union Baptist Association was organized, probably in Oct., 1820. The Pearl River Baptist Association was constituted in Nov., 1820.

The mother association, feeling somewhat bereft, passed resolutions in the 1820 session recommending to the Pearl River and Union associations that they three send delegates annually to get together at the time and place of the annual meeting of the Mississippi Missionary Society, to elicit "the energies of the whole . . . unite and concentrate the whole in the best and most efficient endeavors to propagate the gospel at home and abroad." The suggestions were agreeable to the daughter associations, and such a fraternal gathering was held each year until the time of the organization of the first Mississippi Baptist Convention in 1824.

First state convention organized.—The number of co-operating Baptist churches in the state had increased by 1823 to 61, with a total membership of 2,301; 16 affiliated with the Mississippi Association, having 495 members; 32 with the Pearl River, having 1,181 members; 13 with the Union, having 625 members. (A second African church was listed with the Pearl River, having 30 members, with Ben belonging to Sellers and Bob belonging to McGraw as delegates to the association. Their regular meeting day was the third Sunday.)

The three associations declared in 1823 in favor of a state body, the Pearl River taking the lead. The Mississippi, coming last in October, "*Resolved, unanimously* that we concur with the Pearl River and the Union Associations, in appointing faithful brethren to assist in forming a constitution, for the more systematic and efficient appropriation of your talents in the great concerns of religion . . . and . . . our delegates, to meet those of the other Associations at Bogue Chitto church, Pike county, on Saturday before the third Lord's day in February, 1824." A tentative organization was set up, and a constitution was adopted to be presented to the churches for their approval, accompanied by a request that they express their views through their delegates to the annual meetings of the associations in the fall. The constitution was adopted by each association by large majorities, the Mississippi taking an advanced step in voting to "loan the Convention all their unappropriated funds for the promotion of Domestic Missions." (This association was the most liberal to the convention in later years, giving $90 in 1825 and $110.75 in 1826.) The convention was organized in Nov., 1824, convening each year following the associations. In 1827 it met at Mars Hill Church, Amite County, when David Cooper was president; Jacob Creath, recording secretary; and Davis Collins, corresponding secretary. Five missionaries—Cooper, J. P. Martin, Norvell Robertson, Sr., Charles Felder, and Andrew Mercer—made encouraging reports. They shared in the fund designated for domestic missions, totaling $569.80. The treasurer's report in 1828 (only published record extant of the convention available) shows total receipts $576.36½, with a balance of $284.36½. Cooper was treasurer, and the report was audited by Raynaldson and Moses Robinson. Men most frequently chosen as delegates to the convention were: William Balfour, Ezra Courtney, James A. Raynaldson, Charles Felder, James Crain from the Mississippi; Chadrach Coker, Davis Collins, Jesse Crawford, J. P. Martin, Norvell Robertson, Sr., James Thigpen from the Pearl River; John Burch, Elliott Estes, Elisha Flowers, Nathaniel Perkins, John Richards from the Union.

From its beginning the state body was opposed by those who opposed Sunday schools, mission societies, temperance societies, and instrumental music in the churches. Some of the most outstanding pastors were adversely affected. Finally the convention in its 1828 session "resolved . . . that it would be more to the glory of God . . . that the said Convention be dissolved." It was formally dissolved at the Jerusalem Church, Amite County, in Sept., 1829. Funds remaining in the treasury were directed to be equally divided "between the Pearl River and Mississippi Associations." The share of each was $72.12½, and the Pearl River donated its share to the Mississippi Baptist Evangelistic Society.

Baptists on the defensive.—Following the dissolution of the state body, the three associations, together with the Leaf River Baptist Association, then recently organized, entered upon an intensive effort to hold the churches together in the several associations and to establish them in the faith. Committees of pastors were appointed to visit all the churches in a given association "to inquire into their state" and report their findings at the next meeting. Accounts of the actions of corresponding bodies of other states were published in their association minutes, telling of churches and associations being "cut off" for "embracing or countenancing" the teachings of Alexander Campbell; and the recent translation of the New Testament edited by him was cited as "well calculated to mislead . . . spread the leaven of heresy, sow the seed of discord and thus mar the peace of the Churches." Appeals were made in an effort to discourage the use of the new translation of the New Testament "in our pulpits and families." A supply of a standard Baptist confession of faith was purchased ($150 worth) and distributed among the churches of the Pearl River Association. A concordance of the Scriptures bearing on distinctive doctrines of Baptists was prepared and published in the associational minutes. *The Baptist Chronicle* was strongly recommended as "a religious work of high merit and an able defender of our faith and order." The Mississippi Association eventually withdrew fellowship from the Natalbany church, Louisiana, for "having imbibed a heresy very injurious to the cause of God." James A. Raynaldson was publicized as "one no longer [to] be considered as one of our order," he having embraced views "contrary to those held by us."

Mississippi Baptists on the march.—Beginning in 1834, there was a new spirit and outlook, and the scene was dominated by a new personality. Ashley Vaughn (*q.v.*) appeared at Natchez in 1833 from New York state as a missionary of the American Baptist Home Mission Society and on a quest for a climate favorable to the recovery of his health. A spirit of optimism is noted in the proceedings of the annual meeting of the Mississippi Association in 1834 in a recommendation "to take into view the blessing of God, on foreign and home missionary labours; that each individual should instruct himself, by a liberal and prayerful zeal, to send the gospel to every human being; for it is god's [*sic*] method by which he will give to his son the heathen for his inheritance . . . and the remotest parts of the earth for his portion." A year later all the missionary money in the treasury of the association ($201.43) was ordered to be sent to the missionary society.

A Mississippi Baptist Education Society was organized Mar. 14, 1835, with L. B. Holloway president and T. S. N. King secretary to establish a school for young men, particularly those called to preach the gospel. Vaughn was an enthusiastic supporter of the movement, becoming a member of the board of directors of the society and a member of the board of trustees of Judson Institute. Having joined by letter the Clear Creek Baptist Church, Washington, Adams County, in Dec., 1835, Vaughn began the publication in Sept., 1836, of a Baptist paper in Natchez, *The South-Western Religious Luminary*. He was also Mississippi vice-president of the American Baptist Home Mission Society and thus was interested in the formation of a Baptist state convention. His paper was given largely to the promotion of these two objects during its first year of publication.

In the fall of 1836, Vaughn attended two meetings of the board of directors of the education society, at which plans were perfected for the opening of Judson Institute with L. B. Holloway as president and S. S. Lattimore as teacher of Greek and Latin and financial agent. On horseback he extended his travels, covering 400 or 500 miles, attending the meetings of the Bethel, Pearl River, and Mississippi associations. Resolutions were passed at each meeting favoring the organization of a Mississippi Baptist convention. Being assured of the co-operation of a majority of the Baptist leaders in such a venture, Vaughn issued a call in the October number of his paper, "respectfully and earnestly requesting" that churches, associations, and missionary societies favoring the movement send delegates to a meeting to be held with the Clear Creek Church "on Friday before the 4th Lord's day in December, next, to take into consideration the propriety of forming a Convention." Those opposed to the proposition were also invited to attend the meeting. For said he,

> Let it be remembered that it is a meeting to *consider the propriety of forming a Convention, therefore, let those who are opposed to as well as those in favor of* the project, attend. If there are *valid* objections to such an organization as is contemplated, they ought to be known; the safety of the Denomination depends on it; but if they are *invalid* they ought to be removed.

In preparation for this meeting, Vaughn wrote lengthy editorials in the *Luminary* setting forth proposed objects and some distinct advantages of a convention. J. L. BOYD

II. History of Convention. *Organization.*—On Dec. 23, 1836, delegates from several Baptist churches met in the Clear Creek Baptist Church of Washington, Miss., to form a state organization of Mississippi Baptists. Ashley Vaughn (*q.v.*), sometimes called the "father of the Baptist convention," was responsible for calling this meeting.

The body of Baptists formed a temporary organization with R. G. Green, of Lexington, chairman; and L. B. Holloway, of the Bethel Association, as secretary. Vaughn submitted the following resolution: "Resolved, That we deem it expedient to form a Convention of the Baptist Denomination in the State of Mississippi, for Missionary purposes, and other objects connected with the Redeemer's Kingdom on Earth —Particularly in the State of Mississippi." Reconvening the next day, Dec. 24, the resolution was adopted unanimously. The chairman appointed two committees, one to draft a constitution, and another to nominate officers. The members present adopted the constitution and approved the following officers: president, Ashley Vaughn; vice-presidents, Charles Felder, N. R. Granberry, Benjamin Whitfield, R. G. Green, Norvell Robertson, Jr. (*q.v.*), and Joseph Morris; corresponding secretary, S. S. Lattimore; recording secretary, Stephen Dodge; treasurer, T. S. N. King. In addition, 30 directors were chosen.

The first article of the constitution listed the name of the body of Baptists as "The Convention of the Baptist Denomination of the State of Mississippi." The second article gave as the object of the convention the promotion of religious education. Any person contributing $10 annually could be a member; $30 purchased a life membership; and $100 contribution made any person a director for life. All members, however, had to be regular Baptists in good standing.

Following the organization the convention met in a brief session. Several resolutions were adopted. One requested the convention to appoint delegates to the Triennial Convention, meeting in Philadelphia in Apr., 1837. Another concerned the choosing of a general agent for the convention. Before adjourning the convention addressed a statement to the ministers of the Baptist churches of the state explaining the action taken at the meeting and asked co-operation "in an undertaking, which we believe, if prosecuted with pure motives, with united hearts, and with holy hands, cannot fail to have a salutary and beneficial influence upon the interests of our denomination." At this time Mississippi Baptists had 9 associations and 122 churches, with 4,287 members.

The convention met for its first annual session in May, 1837. In the brief period since organization, the board of directors had been unable to find a general agent or to set up its missionary activities. In accordance with the instructions of the organizational meeting, the board did make arrangements for the publication of the *South-Western Religious Luminary,* allowing Ashley Vaughn, the editor, $500 annually for his services.

At the time the Mississippi Baptist Convention was organized, an antimissionary element in the state opposed its formation. This element feared that the new body would exert too much authority over the local churches. To quiet this feeling, the board explained in its first report that the convention "forever disclaimed all right to exercise any authority whatever, over any church or association, or any other body, or man, or set of men. . . ."

In 1837 the first convention reported 10 associations, 155 churches, and 4,668 members. The official census for the state of Mississippi reported 144,351 white inhabitants and 164,393 slaves. The largest incorporated town was Natchez, with a population of 3,731; Vicksburg was second, with 2,796; then Columbus, with 1,448. Jackson in 1837 had only 520 inhabitants, and Clinton had 613.

Growth to 1866.—The major problems facing the Baptists of Mississippi from the period of organization to 1866 concerned education, the state of missions, especially home missions, the formation of the Southern Baptist Convention, and the Civil War. From its beginning the state convention expressed an interest in education as a missionary endeavor of vital importance to the growth of the Baptist denomination. Judson Institute, located near Clinton, received the commendation of the convention. As early as 1839, the convention sought a suitable location for a college which would be under its control. A committee decided on Judson Institute, but efforts to bring it under the legal control of the convention failed, and the school soon collapsed for lack of financial support.

Fifteen or more Baptist schools were established under private control in the period prior to the Civil War, but it was not until 1850 that the convention acquired a college. In that year the city of Clinton, Hinds County, transferred the control of Mississippi College to the Baptist denomination.

Education, however, was a corollary to the major purpose for the establishment of the convention. That major purpose was missions. Dividing the mission work into two parts, the Baptists of Mississippi gave emphasis to both foreign and home missions. In the field of foreign missions, Mississippi Baptists co-operated with the Baptist Board of Foreign Missions of the Triennial Convention in its efforts to send missionaries to needed points overseas and urged its members to give financial support to this cause.

Having no missionary body, the convention looked with pride to the Home Mission Society of the Mississippi Association and two others existing within the bounds of the Union Association and the Pearl River Association. The board of directors noted this progress but lamented the existence of many other locations where churches could be constituted if ministers could be found.

The Baptists of Mississippi, unable to supply their local mission needs, looked to the American Baptist Home Mission Society for help. When this organization failed to send needed missionaries into the field in 1838, they looked to other sources for a solution. The committee on home missions of the Mississippi convention recommended co-operation with the Southwestern Baptist Home Mission Society, recently formed at Columbus under the leadership of R. T. Daniel of North Carolina. However, it lapsed after three years. In 1842 the convention adopted a resolution making itself an auxiliary of the American Baptist Home Mission Society with the hope that more aid would be received for the work.

The numerous protests lodged with the American Baptist Home Mission Society for failure to send more missionaries into Southern states were not wholly justified. The society tried but had difficulty finding qualified men willing to go into the needy areas of the South. Nevertheless, the feeling of neglect remained and soon became intermingled with growing resentment of the antislavery movement. Gradually a schism came between Northern and Southern Baptists. In 1845 the state executive board reported on the action of the American Baptist Home Mission Society in refusing to appoint slaveholders as missionaries or agents.

The board recommended "that the connection existing between the convention and the American Baptist Home Mission Society be dissolved. . . . We would further recommend that the convention become auxiliary to the Southern Baptist Convention, so that all funds contributed for foreign missions may be sent to the board of foreign missions located at Richmond, Virginia."

The expansion of the convention throughout the state created a transportation problem. Inadequate facilities presented difficulties in reaching one statewide convention. In 1842 the convention considered dividing the state into three parts, with the middle portion of the state embracing the principal body. The division was not considered further, but the convention board was for a few years divided into a Northern board and a Southern board, which apparently functioned independently.

The membership of the convention was increasing rapidly. In 1843 the denomination showed gains with 20 associations, 288 churches, and a total Baptist population of 14,382. In 1844 the membership had increased to 17,366. Within the next five years the churches of Mississippi had 35,000 members.

Mississippi Baptists continued to develop their organization with expanding needs. As early as 1838, the convention recognized the need for "Sabbath School instruction." The Sunday school movement was recognized from this time on. The Mississippi Baptist State Bible and Colportage Society was organized in 1859.

Minority groups also received attention from the convention. Work among the Negro slaves and the Indians found sympathetic favor. The committee on the colored population believed "that it is the imperative duty of masters to provide for the spiritual improvement of their servants."

From the year 1846, when Mississippi Baptists affiliated with the Southern Baptist Convention, until the final break between the Northern and Southern states, the Mississippi Baptist Convention devoted a large part of its attention to missionary efforts, co-operating with the agencies of the Southern Baptist Convention. However, when the political relations between the two sections reached a critical point, the state convention felt compelled to take a stand on the matter. The committee on the state of the country reported:

> Your committee on the State of the Country finds that the Southern Baptist Convention, which recently convened in Savannah, Georgia, unanimously adopted a report on this subject, drawn up by a committee of able and discreet brethren, which, in matter and spirit, so exactly meets the exigencies of the case, that we recommend its adoption as fully expressive of the views and feelings of this Convention.

The report as quoted in full stated that the convention could not be silent on the issues and was in full accord with the Confederate States of America.

The war years practically stopped the work of the convention. No meetings were held during the years of 1862–63. Meetings of the convention were held at Crawfordsville, Oct., 1864, and at Meridian in May, 1865, but no minutes were published. Though the convention was inactive during most of the war, Baptist ministers were not. At Hillsboro, Dec. 4, 1863, messengers from a number of churches and associations met for a meeting of the Mississippi Baptist Bible and Colportage Society. On assembling, the body voted unanimously to adjourn and at once organized the Soldiers' Bible and Missionary Association. The object of this association was to co-operate with the churches in furnishing missionaries and religious literature to the Confederate army. Two meetings were held in 1864, one in April at Brandon, and another in October at Fannin.

Reconstruction and development to 1900.— During the next 35 years, the convention made several changes in its constitution, developed new agencies, and worked toward a more perfect organization. In 1866 the convention assembled at the First Baptist Church, Jackson, and was called to order by Daniel Perrin Bestor (*q.v.*), president. The work of reconstruction of the activities of the convention began. One of the first activities undertaken after the war was the establishment of an orphanage for the homeless children of Confederate dead. The Orphans' Home of the State of Mississippi, conceived at Crawfordsville in 1864, opened its doors in Oct., 1866, at Lauderdale Springs with S. S. Granberry the first superintendent and T. C. Teasdale, financial agent. The institution had remarkable success for a few years but then struggled for existence until 1875, when a tornado destroyed much of the property, and the trustees suspended operations.

A constitutional amendment designed to eliminate the troublesome individual membership in the convention was recommended in 1866 and adopted in the next session. In 1879 the name of the convention was changed to Mississippi Baptist State Convention. Another amendement in 1881 changed the composition of membership in the convention to one delegate for each 100 members in each association and one from every church in the territory desiring representation.

Home missions still remained one of the great concerns of the convention. In the years following the Civil War, old mission fields needed reorganizing, and new fields needed opening. The convention believed that the Home Mission Board of the Southern Baptist Convention was the best agent through which to accomplish this purpose. By 1867, 11 missionaries were working in Mississippi under appointment and support of the Home Mission Board. In the following years, however, financial difficulties reduced its efforts in Mississippi. In an effort to correct the conditions within the work of domestic missions, the convention created the state mission board, composed of 15 members with headquarters at Hazlehurst. The new board was directed to take charge of the domestic mission work within the convention and to employ a corresponding secretary. The board chose J. A. Hackett as its first president and Thomas Jefferson Walne (*q.v.*) as its first secretary, a position he held until 1884.

The state mission board progressed under the leadership of Walne but found mission work difficult because of the great extent of the territory covered. It encompassed the state of Mississippi and all of Louisiana east of the Mississippi River, including New Orleans, where Baptist work hardly existed. However, in 1888 Baptist forces in Louisiana unified under the Louisiana Baptist State Convention, thus relieving the Mississippi Baptist Convention of the mission work in the area east of the Mississippi River. Nevertheless, not all the New Orleans or Louisiana churches severed connections with the Mississippi associations until the 1890's.

State missions continued to be a problem for Mississippi Baptists. In fact the administration of all the work of the convention had proved none too satisfactory. An evolutionary process took place. As early as 1871, the convention created five boards, each with its own headquarters: board of foreign missions, Canton; board of domestic missions, Ripley; Sunday school board, West Point; board of Bible and colportage, Meridian; and board of ministerial education, Clinton. Even the reorganization in 1873 did not solve the administrative problems.

In 1883 a move toward the solution of the benevolent agencies came when James Bruton Gambrell (*q.v.*) reported on recommendations for a better organization. The suggestions in the report were so radical that a motion was carried to postpone the report indefinitely. However, in the next session William Harris Hardy (*q.v.*), president of the convention, urged reorganization of all the agencies. A new committee was appointed to bring a report to the next session. In 1885 the reorganization came. A convention board was created composed of 15 members from different sections of the state. and was given general control of all the work of the convention concerning education, state missions, home missions, and foreign missions. Gambrell, who had submitted the first report on a better organization in 1883, was asked to become the first secretary of the convention board.

Other auxiliary agencies continued to appear. At Meridian on June 8, 1868, the Baptists formed a Sunday school convention. The state convention gave official sanction to the women's missionary organizations in 1875. Three years later the committee on women's mission work recommended that the convention name a state central committee of women, as suggested by the Southern Baptist Convention, to encourage the formation of women's missionary societies in all the churches of Mississippi. To further Baptist work through the state, the convention arranged with the editor of *The Baptist* (Memphis, Tenn.) in 1870 for one page of that paper to present Mississippi convention news.

Other developments included the creation of the Mississippi Baptist state historical society in 1888, with L. S. Foster as its first corresponding secretary. Another development was the establishment of an orphanage. Since the Lauderdale Springs Orphans' Home had closed in 1875, the convention remained without an orphanage until 1897, when the Baptist Orphanage opened its doors in Jackson, under the superintendency of L. S. Foster.

As evidence of the growth of the state convention, the membership increased 50 per cent in the last decade of the century, showing in 1900 a membership of 100,406, largely rural, while the population of the state increased only 20 per cent during the same period. A picture of the rural nature of the Baptist denomination is shown in a report of the frequency of church meetings in 1891. Of the 957 churches in the convention at the time, only 24 were full-time, having preaching every Sunday, while 30 had preaching two Sundays out of the month. There were 14 associations, of a total 38 in the state, in which no church had preaching more than once a month.

The 20th century.—The new century opened with much optimism, but before the year 1900 was over, there was much reason for pessimism. Excessive rainfall brought ruin to the crops and as a result lowered the collections for mission work and the other activities of the convention. At that time the policy was to have separate collections for each cause at different times of the year. The disastrous financial year caused the board to urge a plan by which the churches over the state would bring in collections each month for distribution to the various causes of the convention.

Despite the pessimism over finances, the new century brought remarkable growth in the membership of the convention. In 1905 the total was 109,294 white Baptists in the state. Five years later the membership had reached 142,-191. With this growth came increased activities, the most significant being in the fields of education and hospital work. To take care of the additional load placed on the convention board, its membership was increased to 27 members in 1911, with no change in its duties.

In 1907 Mississippi Baptists entered a new field of endeavor when they accepted an offer looking toward the establishment of the Tri-State Memorial Hospital in Memphis, Tenn., jointly with the Baptists of Arkansas and Tennessee. The committee, however, recommended "that it shall be definitely agreed by this convention that this institution shall not be understood as finally taking the place of a Mississippi Sanitorium, but rather as preparing the way for it." Before the Memphis hospital was completed, Mississippi Baptists did have a hospital exclusively theirs. At the 1911 session it was reported that the first year of the Mississippi Baptist Hospital at Jackson had just been completed. The hospital was an eight-room building given to the Baptists by two Jackson physicians.

In the field of education, the convention also expanded. The board of trustees of Mississippi Woman's College, Hattiesburg, Miss., offered the school to the Baptist convention in 1911. In 1912 the convention created an education commission with W. M. Whittington as chairman and P. I. Lipsey (*q.v.*) as secretary. In its first report to the convention in 1913, the commission recommended the acceptance of the college, and a board of trustees was appointed by the convention during the same session.

In 1907 another move was made toward a greater expansion of publicity for mission work. The convention expressed its readiness to affiliate with the Layman's Missionary Movement of the Southern Baptist Convention, the name of which was changed in 1926 to the Baptist Brotherhood of the South.

In 1916 the membership of the convention board was increased to include one member from each association co-operating with the convention. The board now had direct charge of the work of state missions, Christian education, and ministerial relief, and indirectly fostered ministerial education, the orphanage, hospitals, colleges, schools, and all other interests fostered by the Baptists of the state. Also, it became responsible for the promotion, in co-operation with their respective boards, of home and foreign missions.

The convention took another agency under direct control in 1918 by purchasing *The Baptist Record* and the Baptist Record Book Store from the Mississippi Baptist Publishing Company. P. I. Lipsey was retained as editor, a position he had held since 1912, and in which he continued to serve until 1941.

In an effort to standardize the financial contributions to the denomination and pay off all outstanding debts of its institutions, the convention in 1916 adopted the five-year program, a six-point program looking toward paying off debts, increasing subscriptions to *The Baptist Record,* increasing contributions to the three mission activities, perfecting the organization of the Sunday school, Baptist Young People's Union, and the Woman's Missionary Union, and advancing spiritually through evangelism and Christian living. The adoption of the budget system was suggested as the best method to accomplish the financial portion of the program. The next year the convention board recommended that the churches adopt a budget, that they follow faithfully the custom of monthly remittances of all denominational funds to the board office, and that the churches adopt the One Treasury Single Budget Envelope System. The convention board employed N. T. Tull to promote the budget plan. In 1918 the board announced that the budget had been completed and apportioned to the associations and churches. State, home, and foreign missions received 64 per cent of the budget, and the balance of 36 per cent was distributed to the other objects in the budget.

Before the five-year program was completed, Mississippi Baptists became involved in the 75 Million Campaign organized by Southern Baptists. Mississippi Baptists were asked to raise $3,-500,000 as their part in this campaign. The convention board prorated the money among the various objects to be benefited by the receipts. When the campaign came to an end in 1924, Mississippi Baptists had contributed a total of $2,475,600.45 through their corresponding secretary.

The convention continued its emphasis on education. A fourth college was added in 1920 when the Lowrey and Berry families gave Blue Mountain College to the convention. In 1930 two special sessions of the convention were held, the only time in its history. Both meetings involved one of its colleges. The first, in Jackson on Apr. 24, 1930, considered the closing of Clarke College, which had been acquired in Apr., 1914, and the removal of the Mississippi Baptist Orphanage from Jackson to Newton. The second, in Newton, desired to consummate a sale of the Clarke College property to the orphanage. Both actions were approved. The regular session, meeting in Nov., 1930, rescinded the actions of the special sessions. At the same session, however, the education commission recommended the closing of Clarke College and received the approval of the convention. A group of Baptist men leased the college property, continuing to operate the school under private control.

In 1932 the convention ordered the education commission dissolved, and in 1933 the executive committee of the convention took over its duties, maintaining the education commission in name only for legal reasons. Another curtailment in education came in 1940 when the Mississippi Woman's College was closed for financial reasons.

A trend toward expansion of educational facilities started in 1942, when Mississippi College absorbed Hillman College, a woman's school in Clinton, and became coeducational. With the close of World War II, Clarke College was taken back under the control of the convention as a junior college, and Mississippi Woman's College began operating again in Sept., 1947. The latest educational development came in 1953, when the convention voted to change Mississippi Woman's College to a coeducational senior college. The name was changed to William Carey College the next year.

In 1921, while changes were being made in the educational field, other developments were in process. The convention adopted the recommendations of the committee on work and program calling for the classification of the work of the convention under the headings of missions, education, and social service. All mission activities were included in the report of the state convention board; all state and Convention-wide educational interests, in the report of the education commission; and all social service work, state and Convention-wide, under a general report presented by a standing committee created by the convention.

Constitutional changes were made. In 1923 a committee was appointed to bring the constitution up to date. In 1937 the convention changed its name to the Mississippi Baptist Convention, dropping the word "State." Under the leadership of W. M. Whittington, the convention received and adopted in 1940 a new constitution and bylaws. The latest major constitutional change came in 1953. A constitutional document, presented in 1952, had three parts: the Constitution proper, having basic and fundamental articles; the Plan of Organization and Action, a collection of provisions dealing with the permanent and continuing organization and work of the convention; and the By-Laws, a body of rules considered less permanent than the other two parts. After some changes the convention adopted the new document in 1953.

As the regular activities of the convention advanced, new ones developed. Baptist Student Unions were organized in the state-controlled colleges. In 1925 the first student secretary was located at Mississippi State College for Women. The work progressed until a state student secretary was needed. In 1955 the Baptist Student Union work included student unions on 26 campuses and at the Baptist Hospital, with 19 Baptist student directors. The Mississippi Baptist Historical Society, organized in 1937, became an agency of the convention in 1950. Mississippi Baptists began participation in the Ministers' Retirement Plan of the Relief and Annuity Board of the Southern Baptist Convention in 1940. In 1943 the convention approved the establishment of the Mississippi Baptist Foundation, an organization designed to secure and hold endowment securities of the institutions and agencies of the convention for safekeeping and investment, but only at their request.

The Mississippi Baptist Convention has had a remarkable growth since its meager beginning in 1836. In 1955 the convention embraced 75 associations, 1,734 churches, and a membership of 430,134. In that year Owen Cooper of Yazoo City was president of the convention, and Chester L. Quarles, executive secretary-treasurer.

JACK W. GUNN

III. Program of Work of Mississippi Baptists. *Administration.*—The administrative body of the Mississippi Baptist Convention is the Mississippi Baptist Convention Board, composed of 75 members, one from each co-operating Baptist district association in the state. The association nominates, but the convention elects. Members are elected for three-year terms, one-third being elected at each annual meeting of the convention. Board membership is limited to two consecutive terms of three years each. Persons become eligible for re-election after one year. Paid workers of the convention's agencies are ineligible for board membership.

The convention grants to the board the authority to supervise the general work of the convention. This embodies all business and the work of missions, education, social service, and benevolences in the interim between annual sessions of the convention. The board meets three times annually or upon call. It elects annually its own officers, standing committees, and an executive committee of nine members. Officers of the board are president, vice-president, recording secretary, executive secretary and treasurer. There are standing committees for each phase of the general work of the board.

The executive committee meets quarterly or upon call. This committee is empowered to carry on the work of the convention as directed by the convention board. It is also trustee of all convention funds. The executive committee has three committees: personnel, policy, and business advisory. The Cooperative Program budget, including allocations to all convention boards, agencies, and institutions, is recommended by the convention board to the convention for adoption. Ex officio members of the executive committee include the convention president and executive secretary of the convention board.

Currently, one man serves as the convention board executive secretary and as treasurer. As executive secretary, he is chief executive, administrative, and promotional agent of the convention and the convention board. As treasurer, he is in charge of all properties and funds of the convention under supervision of the convention board, keeps a record of receipts and disbursements, and makes a written report annually to the convention board and the convention. Chester L. Quarles, in 1957 the executive secretary-treasurer, came to this work in 1950.

The general work of stewardship, evangelism, and missions is promoted by the associate executive secretary. Working closely with the executive secretary-treasurer, he and his assistants prepare and distribute stewardship and Co-operative Program promotional materials, promote annual Christian Stewardship Week and annual district world mission conferences. He also leads in the promotion of the Southern Baptist program of evangelism in the state. A state evangelistic conference each year is a main feature.

The home of the convention board is the Baptist Building in Jackson, a two-story and basement building purchased in 1945 at a cost of $110,000.

The Baptist Record.—This paper is the official journal of the convention and the convention board. The *Record* is under supervision of the convention board, which annually elects all its regular personnel, including the editor. It is published weekly, its purpose being to publish religious news and Baptist doctrines, promote the work of the convention and convention board, and create good will. Beginning in 1956, the work of press relations was added to its duties.

The major item of promotion charged to the convention board is state missions. This includes 27 different items, with a budget of $236,000 for 1955–56. The major items follow:

The Baptist Training Union Department.—This department employs a secretary, three associates, one office secretary, and one part-time office secretary. There are two approved workers who work on call for small honorariums. The department works through the 75 associations, seeking to lead all of them to organize and promote active associational meetings and activities. It promotes numerous meetings as follows: state convention; three full weeks of assemblies at Kittiwake; state nursery, beginner, and primary leadership clinics; three regional associational officers' planning meetings; 16 district conventions; and associational "M" Night. Special emphasis is given to promotion of study courses, Youth Week, Youth Night, Ridgecrest and Glorieta assemblies, the Junior memory work drill, Intermediate Sword Drill, Young People's speakers' tournament, and Adult mission story feature. The department annually conducts two to three central associational leadership schools and simultaneous enlargement campaigns. In the student summer service programs, about 25 college young people go into churches and conduct study courses. The department emphasizes standard organization, both in the churches and associations.

The Sunday School Department.—The staff

includes a secretary, three associates, and one office secretary. The department utilizes meetings for promotion as follows: three regional state conventions, a state assembly, 20 district conferences, and a statewide Vacation Bible school clinic. The department annually conducts central associational leadership schools and simultaneous enlargement campaigns. It annually increases its emphasis on standard organizations, with a current high number of 600 standard units in the state, including schools, departments, classes, and groups. The promotion of training awards and the promotion of better church buildings are other features of the work. The department continually promotes associational work, including good organizations, meetings, and activities.

The Brotherhood Department.—This department employs a secretary, an associate, a Royal Ambassador counselor, and two office secretaries. It is responsible for Brotherhood work, Royal Ambassador promotion, and the management of Kittiwake Baptist Assembly. The department sponsors a state Brotherhood rally annually, the day prior to the state Baptist convention, and a two-day statewide Brotherhood and R.A. Encampment at Kittiwake. It emphasizes associational promotion, having been instrumental in developing associational Brotherhood organizations (now more than 50). Series of associational clinics and district rallies are sponsored annually. The department promotes annual Layman's Day as well as all other Convention-wide Brotherhood events. Two twin-state R.A. Congresses are sponsored annually as well as five one-week R.A. camps and two boys' camps each summer.

The Student Department.—This staff is composed of a secretary and an office secretary, who work with the Baptist churches in college communities, seeking to tie the students to the local churches. The department annually promotes a state convention, a state retreat for local officers, a state preschool retreat, a seminar for B.S.U. directors, and a state assembly at Kittiwake. There are 26 local student organizations through which the department works. Twenty-one of these have local B.S.U. directors, most of whom are full-time. The expenses of six to eight student missionaries are paid as they serve a home mission field somewhere in the United States. There are 30,000 college students in the state, 9,000 of whom are Baptist.

The Music Department.—This department has a secretary and an office secretary. Annually it promotes a three-week state assembly, a state festival, a series of district festivals, a state music leaders' laboratory, and a state associational directors' planning meeting. The department conducts a number of associational and local church music schools and serves as the clearing house for a group of from 30 to 40 approved music school teachers who serve the churches regularly. The department promotes music study courses, the Hymn of the Month program, associational hymn sings, and Christmas carol sings. Thousands of pamphlets are sent annually to the churches. The department perennially emphasizes associational promotion, seeking to establish in every association a functioning organization.

The Department of Rural Church Work.—This department employs a secretary and an office secretary and seeks to offer special assistance to the more than 1,100 open-country churches in the state. Its program includes schools of missions, the Church Survey program, the Progress Chart program, and rural church clinics. It serves as the co-ordinating agency for the approximately 30 associational superintendents of missions. One feature of this work is the annual state associational missionaries' institute held in connection with the Pastors' Assembly. It also works closely with the state executive secretary-treasurer and the associate secretary in the promotion of the entire state mission program.

The Negro Work Department.—This staff has a secretary and an office secretary. Its primary program is offering assistance to the Mississippi Baptist Seminary System (for Negroes) with a central center in Jackson and more than 20 extension centers over the state. In 1955 there were 1,555 students enrolled, 400 of whom were ministerial students. The department also sponsors annually a series of stewardship conferences, student work of four college campuses, a youth Christian training program, and a Vacation Bible school promotional program. A state assembly, the Sophia Sutton Begley assembly near Prentiss, has been acquired, and a program has been begun. One phase of the department's work has been the inauguration of a program to place 100,000 Bibles in homes without Bibles throughout the state. The World Home Bible League, Chicago, and the state Woman's Missionary Union have co-operated.

The Woman's Missionary Union.—Auxiliary to the Mississippi Baptist Convention, it has a state organization which maintains a department of work along with the other departments. Its staff includes a secretary, executive assistant, young people's secretary, mailing superintendent, and two office secretaries. It sponsors annually a state convention, a state Business Woman's Circle Federation banquet, a series of district rallies, and a W.M.U. officers' clinic. It promotes annually three seasons of prayer, with special offerings for foreign missions, home missions, and state missions. The department sponsors Business Woman's Circles, Young Woman's Auxiliaries, Girl's Auxiliaries, and Sunbeam Bands among the churches. Thirteen weekly camps are sponsored each summer for the various organizations at Camp Garaywa, located near Clinton and maintained by the W.M.U.

Other work.—Aid for church building is extended to approximately 30 churches each year. The Choctaw Indians of the state are aided through an allocation to this work, which is sponsored by the Home Mission Board. The money goes for church building aid, pastoral aid, and educational work and is expended by the various departments. The Rural Church Department gives general supervision to these budgetary amounts. Pastoral aid is given to approximately 17 pastors each year, based on need and mission opportunity. The convention board pays a part of the cost of about 30 associational and two area mission programs. The remainder of the cost of the associational programs is paid by the participating associations. The convention board shares with the Home Mission Board in underwriting the area mission programs: the northeast, Monroe and Ittawamba counties; the southwest, Green, George, and Perry counties. The 1955–56 allocation for both was $35,500. The Mississippi Baptist Historical Society serves the history interests of the Baptists of the state. Its main feature is a collection of historical materials in the library of Mississippi College, Clinton. The society receives an allocation from the convention board, which in 1955–56 amounted to $750. Sanatorium evangelism is sponsored through an allocation to the pastor of the Baptist church at Magee, near the state tubercular sanatorium, who gives part of his time to this work. For 1955–56, $900 was allocated. The State Religious Education Association, composed of religious education workers of the churches, receives an allocation to promote its work, with $250 provided for 1955–56. The Mississippi Church Council for Alcohol Education is supported by the Convention Board, which gave $10,000 in 1955–56, and ten other groups in the state.

The convention co-operates with the American Bible Society by publicizing its work and by urging churches to contribute to its program. It provides a place for the society in the state convention program. The convention co-operates with the work of the Southern Baptist Relief and Annuity Board through the office of the executive secretary-treasurer of the convention board, which assists in processing applications for entrance and benefits of the various plans of the board, and annually promotes an offering for ministerial relief. For 1955–56 there were 448 persons active in the various plans with 967 churches enrolled.

Kittiwake Baptist Assembly.—The state's assembly was purchased in 1955 for the state convention by the convention board and is operated by the assembly committee of the board. The assembly is located at Pass Christian and faces the Gulf Coast shore line for 487 feet. It contains 14 acres, and its properties include 10 cabins, a swimming pool, two tennis courts, an eight-unit faculty house, manager's cabin, caretaker's cabin, and central lodge, which contains the auditorium, dining room, kitchen, classrooms, and Baptist Book Store exhibit. Its first summer of operation began in 1956, covering 12 full weeks of camps and assemblies, with a total attendance of 1,979.

Colleges.—The convention owns and maintains four colleges, each operated by a separate board of trustees, as follows:

Mississippi College has a property valuation of $2,351,171, an endowment of $1,121,751.56, a 1955–56 budget of $563,000, a library of 52,000 volumes, a student enrolment of 1,785, and a faculty of 72.

William Carey College has property valued at $1,048,788.01, an endowment of $457,276.95, a student enrolment of 403, a budget of $199,600, and a 40-acre campus.

Blue Mountain College has a plant replacement value of $1,460,000, an endowment of $529,400, a budget of $238,280, and an enrolment of 341. It is the only Baptist girls' college in Mississippi.

Clarke Memorial College, the only Baptist junior college, has a student enrolment of 452 and propery valuation of $403,329.26.

Agencies, institutions, commissions, and committees.—The convention maintains one other board, one agency, and two other institutions, each under a separate board of trustees, as follows:

The Board of Ministerial Education aids ministerial students in the four colleges. It owns 61 apartments, valued at $200,000, and had operation receipts in 1954–55 of $30,407.42.

The Mississippi Baptist Foundation has as its purpose the raising and administering of endowment and trust funds for the convention's causes and institutions. Assets in 1954–55 were $924,958.96.

The Mississippi Baptist Orphanage in 1954–55 cared for 260 children and had a property valuation of $1,000,000 and a budget of $184,500.

The Mississippi Baptist Hospital is a 350-bed institution, which in 1954–55 had property valuation and other assets of $2,252,410 and gave free service valued at $120,000. The hospital maintains a school of nursing and operates a Medical Arts Building near by.

The Baptist Memorial Hospital, Memphis, Tenn., is owned and operated jointly by the Mississippi, Arkansas, and Tennessee Baptist conventions. Each body elects nine of the 27-member board of trustees, and each contributes annually to the support of the hospital. The Mississippi convention contributed $20,000 for 1955–56, for both capital needs and operating expenses.

The convention has two commissions as follows:

The Education Commission, composed of 12 members, elected annually, has general oversight of the convention's program of Christian education. It receives and evaluates the reports and audits of the four colleges and the Board of Ministerial Education and makes its reports, including any recommendations, to the convention through the convention board. The commission's membership includes six active pastors, three educators, not connected in any way with the convention's educational institutions, and three businessmen.

IV. MISSISSIPPI STATISTICAL SUMMARY

Year	Associa-tions	Churches	Church Member-ship	Baptisms	S. S. Enrol-ment	V.B.S. Enrol-ment	T. U. Enrol-ment	W.M.U. Enrol-ment	Brother-hood En-rolment	Mission Gifts	Total Gifts	Value Church Property	State Capital Worth
1830													(Explanation: This column includes total value of Schools, Children's Homes, Hos-pitals, Foundation, Buildings, etc.)
1840													
1850													
1860													
1870	12	305	18,378	1,983	....	....	....	....	....	....	....	....	
1880	37	910	56,630	4,832	....	....	....	....	....	....	....	....	
1890	37	1,166	80,807	4,768	....	....	....	....	....	$ 8,682.71	....	....	
1900	55	1,562	100,406	3,907	....	....	....	....	....	15,810.00	....	$ 836,860.00	
1905	52	1,306	109,236	7,667	32,588	....	....	....	....	44,901.26	....	1,158,725.00	
1910	52	....	....	....	....	....	....	....	....	70,332.20	....	....	
1915	53	1,362	....	....	....	....	....	....	....	100,470.93	....	....	....
1920	72	....	....	....	....	....	....	....	....	699,994.91	....	....	....
1925	71	....	....	12,266	....	....	....	....	....	362,407.34	....	....	....
1930	75	1,504	228,422	11,740	131,649	....	34,613	....	....	314,782.28	$ 1,845,763.66	9,180,176.00	....
1931	..	....	....	10,231	....	....	....	....	....	260,487.46	....	....	....
1932	74	1,476	236,124	10,334	137,981	....	32,729	....	....	181,984.44	1,111,111.69	9,946,301.00	....
1933	75	1,491	242,919	9,921	136,799	....	35,612	....	....	100,259.48	962,052.00	8,911,136.00	....
1934	75	1,489	247,599	9,776	131,910	....	35,708	....	....	157,801.93	1,032,537.51	8,493,720.00	....
1935	75	1,512	252,586	10,367	135,248	....	38,092	....	....	182,178.58	1,168,587.74	8,616,905.00	....
1936	..	....	....	10,375	....	....	....	....	....	202,614.98	....	....	....
1937	75	1,540	265,812	10,128	136,781	....	43,854	123,225	....	205,206.80	1,368,464.55	8,794,988.00	....
1938	75	1,552	272,281	13,393	143,761	....	43,411	....	....	194,754.45	1,484,803.95	8,821,347.00	$ 1,921,432.88
1939	75	1,550	279,772	12,882	148,303	....	44,133	....	....	220,389.92	1,926,315.76	8,911,350.00	2,054,932.70
1940	..	....	287,885	13,367	150,133	....	47,104	....	....	278,069.93	1,644,442.93	9,191,977.00	1,550,591.77
1941	72	....	292,803	11,232	148,445	....	49,104	....	....	354,315.98	1,936,122.98	9,303,583.00	2,078,068.12
1942	80	....	300,638	11,893	142,221	....	41,665	....	....	493,526.49	2,214,721.49	9,948,723.00	2,832,588.46
1943	74	....	307,817	11,693	140,298	....	39,069	....	....	1,014,542.15	3,299,893.15	10,421,123.00	2,152,906.29
1944	73	1,566	315,817	12,189	144,185	....	39,864	....	....	880,758.30	3,536,432.30	11,088,352.00	1,245,561.08
1945	74	1,566	324,194	13,249	149,235	41,265	39,767	38,146	918	1,404,326.47	4,831,290.47	11,829,121.00	2,100,886.87
1946	74	1,577	335,274	13,043	164,267	50,814	49,103	38,256	2,609	1,810,615.56	6,137,479.56	14,262,990.00	1,636,410.17
1947	..	1,592	349,314	14,605	179,286	....	55,206	....	....	1,627,666.74	....	17,449,812.00	7,269,634.02
1948	75	....	....	....	....	....	....	....	....	....	....	....	....
1949	..	....	....	....	....	....	....	....	....	....	....	....	....
1950	75	1,554	388,426	17,091	214,611	79,448	89,965	48,252	8,108	1,278,946.26	6,540,408.74	23,633,308.55	....
1951	74	1,645	399,519	17,527	235,025	90,609	98,328	51,359	8,214	1,567,756.00	7,459,525.33	34,948,892.00	6,944,662.68
1952	74	1,599	407,443	16,611	243,016	101,164	103,273	51,792	8,788	1,848,196.00	10,770,899.00	33,310,481.55	6,841,537.61
1953	75	1,696	413,514	16,280	255,349	100,000	112,070	55,422	10,509	1,964,980.00	12,589,148.00	46,311,313.00	8,453,734.21
1954	75	1,715	421,917	16,448	277,838	125,000	122,126	59,656	11,395	2,164,840.00	13,367,132.00	54,796,408.00	8,693,302.29

JOE ABRAMS

The Social Service Commission of nine members, elected annually, studies social trends, observes the convention's social service institutions, and makes recommendations regarding them to the convention.

Members of the convention's boards, agencies, institutions, and commissions are elected for a term of three years, not to exceed two terms. Vacancies may be temporarily filled by the convention board. Officers or paid workers of the above group are not eligible for membership thereon with the exception of the Board of Ministerial Education. A person may not be a member of more than one group at the same time.

The Cooperative Program is the convention's principal plan of financing its organized work. Participating churches of the convention are asked to contribute to it, and the convention, upon recommendation of the convention board, determines the proportionate amount each cause will receive. The right to designate funds to a specific cause, however, is recognized.

The convention annually has four standing committees, as follows: Order of Business, Nominations, Constitution and Bylaws, and *Baptist Record* Advisory. At the close of each annual session, the president appoints a committee on committees, which in turn appoints the committees which serve during the interim and through the next session. Two other committees, Resolution and Time, Place and Preacher, are appointed at each session to serve during the session. JOE ABRAMS

Departmental Expense, Mississippi Baptist Convention Board Year Ended Nov. 2, 1955

Executive Secretary's office	$ 41,135.00
Treasurer's office	26,220.00
Director of Evangelism	2,942.55
Director of Promotion	5,307.50
Woman's Missionary Union	33,670.00
Relief and Annuity	77,943.36
Overexpended departmental appropriations, year ended Nov. 2, 1954	4,635.24
Baptist Student Union	16,057.50
Sunday School	35,849.37
Training Union	35,426.16
Brotherhood	23,859.20
Rural Church	12,794.92
Church Music	13,245.88
Negro Work	17,117.62
Miscellaneous	2,000.00
Week of Prayer Campaign	1,396.09
Baptist Record	100,570.02
TOTAL	$450,170.41

BIBLIOGRAPHY: W. W. Barnes, *The Southern Baptist Convention 1845–1953* (1954). T. M. Bond, *A Republication of the Minutes of the Mississippi Baptist Association, 1806–1849* (1949). J. L. Boyd, *A Popular History of the Baptists in Mississippi* (1930). W. Cathcart, *The Baptist Encyclopedia* (1883). L. S. Foster, *Mississippi Baptist Preachers* (1895). J. G. Jones, *A Concise History of the Introduction of Protestantism into Mississippi and the Southwest* (1866). Z. T. Leavell and T. J. Bailey, *A Complete History of Mississippi Baptists* (1904). H. L. Moorehouse, *Baptist Home Missions in North America* (1883). A. H. Newman, *A History of the Baptist Churches in the United States* (1915). W. E. Paxton, *A History of the Baptists of Louisiana* (1888). D. Roland, *History of Mississippi, the Heart of the South* (1925). C. P. St. Amant, *A Short History of Louisiana Baptists* (1948). R. G. Torbet, *A History of the Baptists* (1950).

MISSISSIPPI BAPTIST FEMALE COLLEGE. Established in 1851 by Baptists of Hernando, Miss., and chartered with William Carey Crane (*q.v.*) president. The school had eight teachers in 1856 but declined during the Civil War and ceased operation in 1874. J. L. BOYD

MISSISSIPPI BAPTIST FOUNDATION. An agency of the Mississippi Baptist Convention, established and chartered Dec. 13, 1943, under the laws of the state of Mississippi for the purpose of raising and administering endowment and trust funds for the institutions and causes of the convention. The first step toward its establishment was a resolution presented to the convention in Meridian Nov. 11–13, 1941, which resulted in the appointment of a committee for the purpose of bringing recommendations the following year. The report of the special committee, presented to the convention Nov. 17–19, 1942, recommended establishment of a foundation. Due to some opposition, a motion carried to defer action until the following year and to continue the committee. In 1943 a report similar to that of the previous year was made by the special committee and was adopted, including a charter for the foundation and election of charter trustees. The first report of the foundation showed total assets of $13,035.80, and on Sept. 30, 1955, assets totaled $924,958.96. HARRY LEE SPENCER

MISSISSIPPI BAPTIST HISTORICAL SOCIETY. Organized July 18, 1888, with 23 members enrolled on a basis of $1 each per year, the society's constitution stipulated that its purpose was "to collect and preserve a library . . . pertaining to the history of Christianity in general and Baptists of the State in particular." The society's charter, granted in July, 1888, authorized a board of directors, and L. S. Foster served as corresponding secretary for most of the society's duration. He collected historical materials which were preserved in Clinton, where Mrs. Adelia Hillman served as librarian. The society became extinct in the early 1900's.

In 1926 the Mississippi Baptist Convention created a committee "for the preservation and compilation" of Baptist historical data, with Plautus Iberus Lipsey (*q.v.*) as chairman and Jesse Laney Boyd, secretary and custodian. Growing out of this committee, a second historical society was organized in 1937 with its constitution providing for voluntary membership as before. Lipsey continued to serve as president of the society and Boyd as secretary-treasurer and custodian.

Hoping to secure enlarged membership and

to create a widening interest and participation in reaching the objectives of the historical society, the convention unanimously adopted a resolution in 1950 which created a Mississippi Baptist Historical Society as an auxiliary and agency of the state convention, a society of which associational clerks were to serve as ex-officio members with no financial basis for their membership. The society's constituency is thus perpetuated in a similar way to that of the convention board, with clerks elected in affiliating associations regarded as nominees for election by the convention to full membership in the society. Subservient to the convention and dependent on the parent body for financial support, the society holds its annual meeting during the hour immediately preceding the opening of the first session of the convention.

J. L. BOYD

MISSISSIPPI BAPTIST HOSPITAL. Located in Jackson, Miss., the hospital was founded as a private institution by two physicians in 1909. Two years later it was given to the Mississippi Baptist Convention and was incorporated Jan. 11, 1912. The original nine-room ante-bellum house was replaced about 1915 by a 15-bed capacity brick structure which is still in use. Two additions, completed between 1915 and 1935, increased total bed capacity to 170. In 1946 the Hederman addition added 80 beds, and the opening of a portion of the new Simmons addition in 1953 increased bed capacity to the present total of 350. Three dormitories were constructed for student nurses between 1925 and 1954, and a fourth dormitory and a large educational building were acquired by purchase. The rapid growth of Jackson and its increasing prominence as a medical center in Mississippi has placed tremendous demands upon the hospital, evidenced by the fact that 40 per cent of the patients admitted in 1954 came from outside Hinds County.

The hospital is fully accredited by the Joint Commission on Accreditation and has approved training programs for interns and X-ray and laboratory technicians. Land, buildings, equipment, and other assets, valued at $2,924,050.68, are free of mortgaged indebtedness. Patient income in 1954 was $2,013,725, while Cooperative Program gifts totaled $33,888, and designated gifts, $5,601. The value of charity work in 1954 was $120,000.

Mississippi Baptist Hospital is the only hospital maintained by Mississippi Baptists, except for their one-third interest in the Tri-State Memorial Hospital in Memphis, Tenn.

J. B. PARKER

MISSISSIPPI BAPTIST HOSPITAL SCHOOL OF NURSING. Since accepting its first student for training Jan. 16, 1912, the school has graduated 631 young nurses, 577 white and 54 Negro. Four large dormitories and a classroom building now comprise the school, which has as its goal the admission of 100 students each year. Each class elects its own officers, and every student nurse is encouraged to join a local church and to participate actively. The school has vesper services, a Young Woman's Auxiliary, a Baptist Student Union secretary, and two chaplains to work with the nurses. Total operating expense for the year, including instructors' salaries, supplies, utilities, upkeep of dormitories, meals for students, etc., amounts to $163,937.

J. B. PARKER

MISSISSIPPI BAPTIST ORPHANAGE. Chartered July 18, 1894, under the leadership of L. S. Foster, first superintendent. Earlier, Mississippi Baptists had sponsored an orphans' home from 1864 to 1875 in Lauderdale Springs, Miss. For the new Mississippi Baptist Orphanage 112 acres of land were purchased in Jan., 1896, and they comprise the present site of the orphanage in Jackson. Reception and care of children began in a rented cottage on West Capitol Street May 12, 1897, pending erection of a building on the orphanage property. The first building, occupied in Mar., 1898, was named in honor of Mrs. Lou H. Moore, who had contributed the first dollar for the orphanage. The home survived a scourge of yellow fever in 1898, and two years later a school was established on the campus. After six years J. R. Carter succeeded Foster as superintendent of the home, and under Carter's 24-year tenure many buildings were completed. In 1954, when the orphanage served 260 children, the total budget was $104,500. Property consisted of 110 acres of land and 17 buildings, valued at $1,000,-000. Support for the orphanage, which has no debt, is derived from a Cooperative Program allotment, annual Thanksgiving offerings, and designated gifts. Children attend school on the campus through the eighth grade, after which they attend junior and senior high schools in the Jackson city system. College opportunities are provided for those who qualify.

W. C. CATHEY

MISSISSIPPI BAPTIST SEMINARY. An interracial co-operative mission effort, which seeks to provide for Negroes of the area training in theology, Christian citizenship, and Christian leadership. It was founded in 1942, under the leadership of Herbert L. Lang. Chartered Mar. 15, 1944, as Mississippi Union Theological Seminary, it was located at Prentiss. The charter was amended May 7, 1948, the name was changed to Mississippi Baptist Seminary, and the institution was moved to Jackson. The seminary receives financial assistance from the Mississippi Baptist Convention board through its Negro Work Department, and from all the seven Negro Baptist conventions of the state. In 1955 it was reported that the seminary, with 22 extensions, had a total enrolment of 1,555, 400 being ministers.

W. P. DAVIS

MISSISSIPPI COLLEGE. Located in Clinton, Miss.; the oldest institution of higher learning in the state and one of the oldest and largest Baptist colleges in the United States. Chartered by the state legislature in 1826 as Hampstead Academy and renamed Mississippi Academy in 1827, the institution was named Mississippi College in 1830 and authorized "to confer . . . such degrees in the arts, sciences and languages as are usually conferred in the most respectable colleges in the United States. . . ." A private institution, the college was for many years coeducational and was perhaps the first such college in the United States to grant a degree to a woman (1831). The female department was discontinued, however, in 1851. So far as is known, the first male graduate was John P. Mapes (1843).

Few details are known of the development of the college prior to 1850. F. G. Hopkins was principal of the academy in 1827, and E. N. Elliott, of Bloomington College, was apparently the first president, elected in 1836. The college was transferred to the Clinton Presbytery in 1842, and presidents during the following eight years were all Presbyterian ministers. Various difficulties caused the Presbyterians to return the college to private control, however, on July 27, 1850. Later that same year (Nov. 12), the Mississippi Baptist Convention accepted tender of the school and its properties, valued at $11,000.

The college experienced unparalleled growth during the first decade of Baptist control. Beginning with "one teacher and fourteen small boys" in Oct., 1851, there were eight instructors and 228 students in 1860–61, making Mississippi College the largest such institution in the state and third among Baptist colleges in the South. An endowment campaign, authorized by the convention in 1851, secured more than $100,000 in subscriptions by 1858. Two years later a $25,000 brick chapel was completed.

The coming of the Civil War caused drastic changes. Mississippi seceded in Jan., 1861, and most of the faculty, students, and trustees went to war. More than 100 students joined three faculty members in forming the Mississippi College Rifles, commanded by J. W. Welborn, a trustee. Only President Urner remained as caretaker of the property and instructor of the students who applied; attendance during the four years averaged "about thirty students," who were either in preparatory grades or too young for the army.

Although hostile troops camped "repeatedly, for days and weeks at a time, on the college grounds," and the new chapel was used as a hospital for the wounded of the Federal armies, the trustees reported in 1866 that "the college buildings, libraries and apparatus escaped from the war without any material injury. For this preservation we are indebted to the active and successful efforts of Brother Urner." However, marks of hard usage were left on the new chapel and other buildings. Due to the distressful conditions caused by four years of war, the college stood on the brink of ruin, with endowment swept away, Confederate currency worthless, and a debt of "about eight thousand dollars," including $6,881.65 for salary past due to Urner, which he demanded to be paid before stepping aside.

For assistance the trustees turned to Walter Hillman, president of Central Female Institute (Hillman College) in Clinton. He consented to assume the presidency, dividing his time between the college and the institute. His wife, Adelia Hillman, was sent North, where she obtained a temporary loan and cash gifts from James B. and Samuel Colgate and others sufficient to pay off indebtedness and make necessary repairs on the buildings. By 1872, through the heroic efforts of M. Thomas Martin (*q.v.*), Mississippi Baptists had repaid the loan, and the following year Hillman relinquished the presidency of the college. He had reopened the college in Oct., 1867, with one instructor, two freshman students, and nine students in the preparatory department. When he resigned in 1873, the faculty numbered 10 and student enrolment totaled 190.

Warren Sheldon Webb, a native of New York and a graduate of Madison (now Colgate) University, was serving as instructor of theology in the college and pastor of Clinton Baptist Church when elected to succeed Hillman in 1873. Leading the college in slow but steady growth, he served until 1891 when endowment had grown to $44,544.31 and enrolment to 250. Robert Abram Venable (*q.v.*), Webb's son-in-law, succeeded him in the presidency. The first alumnus (1876) to serve as president, he became involved in an effort in 1893 to move the college to Meridian and resigned in 1896. John William Provine (*q.v.*), a chemistry professor in the college, was elected president the following year. In 1898, however, he resigned to devote his full attention to the science department of the college.

The trustees elected William Tyndale Lowrey (*q.v.*), president of Blue Mountain College, to succeed Provine. Attendance had declined to 115 in the "yellow fever year" of 1897–98, but by 1902–03 enrolment had climbed to 302 and endowment to $130,000. When Lowrey resigned in 1911, Provine was re-elected president, serving until his retirement in 1932. Lowrey, Ratliff, Chrestman, and Alumni halls, and Farr-Hall Hospital were erected during his administration, and endowment was increased to $632,734.

Dotson McGinnis Nelson, an alumnus and professor of physics, was elected president of Mississippi College in 1932. A rigorous financial administrator, he led in payment of a $491,000 debt. Since 1932 the college has never had an annual deficit. When Hillman College properties were leased in 1942, the college again became coeducational. Hillman's properties were deeded to the college in 1945. Buildings constructed recently include Nelson Hall; Hederman, Gunter, and Senior residence halls for women; Whittington Student Center; a library annex; and a band building. Ratliff Hall was enlarged and remodeled in 1953–54, and the Aven and Provine residence was acquired. Currently the campus embraces about 200 acres, on which are located more than 30 buildings. Enrolment has increased from 360 in 1932–33 to 1,785 in 1955–56, the faculty from 20 to 72.

Value of college properties totals $2,351,171, and endowment, $1,121,751.56. The 1955–56 budget provided for an expenditure of $563,300. Anticipated income was $573,100, derived as follows: endowment, $50,600; tuition fees, $331,000; dormitory rentals, $75,000; Cooperative Program, $100,000; and auxiliary enterprise, $17,500. The college library, begun as separate collections by the Philomathean and Hermenian Literary Societies four generations ago, contains 52,000 volumes. The library subscribes to 430 periodicals and 10 newspapers.

Mississippi College offers four undergraduate degrees, B.A., B.S., B.S. in Ed., and B.M., and also the M.Ed. It holds membership in the Mississippi Association of Colleges, the Southern Association of Colleges and Secondary Schools, the American Association of Colleges, the American Council on Education, the National Commission on Accrediting, the American Association of University Women, and the National Association of Business Teacher Training Institutions. The total number of graduates since 1850 is 5,556, including 398 who were graduated in 1956. The college is owned by the Mississippi Baptist Convention and operated through a 15-member board of trustees.

BIBLIOGRAPHY: J. L. Boyd, *A Popular History of the Baptists in Mississippi* (1930). C. H. Brough, "Historic Clinton," *Publications of the Mississippi Historical Society,* VII (1903). J. T. Buck, *History of Mississippi Baptist State Convention* (1883). Z. T. Leavell and T. J. Bailey, *A Complete History of Mississippi Baptists, From the Earliest Times* (1904). E. Mayes, *History of Education in Mississippi* (1899). W. H. Weathersby, *A History of Educational Legislation in Mississippi from 1798 to 1860* (1921).

ROBERT H. SPIRO, JR.

MISSISSIPPI HEIGHTS MALE ACADEMY. Established in 1904 with J. E. Brown principal. It had its peak year in 1920 with an enrolment of 207, but ceased to exist in 1943 when there were 109 students, 10 graduates. J. L. BOYD

MISSISSIPPI WOMAN'S COLLEGE. See WILLIAM CAREY COLLEGE.

MISSOURI AND ILLINOIS BAPTIST. A bimonthly paper established in Aug., 1843, and published in St. Louis, Mo., in co-operation with the Baptist convention of Illinois at a subscription rate of $1 per year. Due to lack of financial backing the paper was published only one year. J. R. BLACK

MISSOURI ASSOCIATIONS. The only machinery of organization which Missouri Baptists knew, prior to the organization of the Missouri Baptist General Association in 1834, was first the churches, and then the district associations. Bethel, organized in 1816, was the first association to be formed in Missouri. Then followed the Missouri (1817), Mount Pleasant (1818), Salt River (1823), Little Piney (1833), and Bethel (Northeast) (1834). By the time the Missouri Baptist General Association was organized in Aug., 1834, 13 associations had been formed. Following the organization of the Missouri Baptist General Association, new associations were organized as the population in a given area increased and as churches were formed. In some instances existing associations began work in adjoining territory and then divided and produced a new association for convenience of organization and meetings.

It is a matter of deep concern and a commentary on the practicality of the New Testament plan of kingdom expansion that the churches and associations which have become antimissionary have either ceased to exist or have become weak and anemic bodies, while those which have been missionary at heart have grown to be the burden bearers of the kingdom. Most of the associations in existence at the time of the Civil War found the strife a detriment to their work and fellowship so that most of them did not meet during the war years.

In 1875 the executive board of the Missouri Baptist General Association recommended a division of the churches into district associations to conform with county-line boundaries. This plan of districting the state into associations was not brought to eventual completion until the second decade of the 20th century and is currently largely followed.

In the early life an association often had several approved workers or missionaries in the field. The method of supporting associational missionaries has varied from the early period. In the beginning of the employment of the associational organized work, the missionaries, whose work was evangelistic, either went without any remuneration from the association or received an insignificant amount. Often food supplies were given in lieu of the small salary. By the middle of the 19th century the associations began to develop plans to give definite financial support to associational missionaries. About the turn of the century (1889 to 1916) the missionaries became a joint agent of the district association and the Missouri Baptist General Association. A departure from the usual plan of work with one missionary in each association came in 1922 when the St. Joseph Association, in co-operation with three neighboring associations, formed a federation to do mission work in northwest Missouri. This plan was successful and was soon recommended by the state organization. The state organization then joined with the co-operating district associations to support more adequately the enlistment evangelist whose work, in addition to being evangelistic, became administrative in all departments and phases of denominational work. This plan has been followed by many areas in the state. It is a matter of record that weaker associations can do more effective work when linked with stronger associations which have a missionary spirit.

The associational missions superintendent, successor to the associational missionary, has become a combined denominational administrator and a servant of the churches in the geographic area in which he works. As a representative of all phases of denominational life, a promotional secretary, a pastor at large, an associate to pastors, and a pastor of pastors in the area in which he works, he co-ordinates the work among the churches. The advance in the developing program of the churches, the total enlistment of the members of the churches, and the effective co-operation between the churches is due largely to the work of the missions superintendent who is employed by an individual association or in the co-operation of two or more associations.

I. Extant. Audrain. Organized at First Baptist Church of Mexico, Oct. 15, 1884, by 15 churches from Audrain County. Articles of faith were adopted. A missions superintendent is employed in co-operation with Callaway and Little Bonne Femme associations. In 1954, 17 churches reported 153 baptisms, 4,020 members, $148,000 total gifts, $19,935 mission gifts, $392,747 property value, and $20,636 church debt.

Barry County. Organized from Shoal Creek Association, Nov. 22, 1884, at Friendship Church by 21 churches from Barry County. Articles of faith were adopted. A missions superintendent is employed. In 1954, 29 churches reported 156 baptisms, 4,430 members, $98,966 total gifts, $16,011 mission gifts, $288,705 property value, and $15,190 church debt.

Barton County. Organized at Forrest Grove Church, Lamar, Barton County, Oct. 11, 1889, by eight churches from Barton County. A missions superintendent is employed in co-operation with Dade County Association. In 1954, 11 churches reported 73 baptisms, 1,321 members, $38,455 total gifts, $7,667 mission gifts, $97,200 property value, and $33,500 church debt.

Bear Creek. Organized May 18, 1854, at Zion Church in Montgomery County. Nine churches from Warren, St. Charles, Montgomery, Pike, and Lincoln counties sent letters and messengers to the "convention" called for the purpose of forming the new organization. These churches were Union, which had been dismissed from the Little Bonne Femme Association, and the following eight churches which had been affiliated with the Salt River Association: Mt. Pleasant, Zion, Mt. Hope, Sulphur Lick, Bethlehem, Indian Creek, Cotton Wood, and Middleton. A missions superintendent is employed in co-operation with Salt River and Cuivre associations. In 1954, 13 churches reported 81 baptisms, 1,608 members, $55,611 total gifts, $10,197 mission gifts, $110,600 property value, and $8,200 church debt.

Benton County. Organized at Warsaw on Oct. 20, 1892, by eight churches from Benton County. A missions superintendent is employed in co-operation with Osage Pomme de Terre Association. In 1954, 10 churches reported 42 baptisms, 1,030 members, $41,427 total gifts, $5,263 mission gifts, $78,500 property value, and $2,300 church debt.

Bethel. Organized Sept. 25, 1835, at Providence Church in Marion County by 17 churches. A missions superintendent is employed in co-operation with Wyaconda Association. In 1954, 29 churches reported 232 baptisms, 6,360 members, $215,170.00 total gifts, $3,217.00 mission gifts, $583,897.00 property value, and $30,968.67 church debt.

Black River. Organized Nov. 14, 1835, by six churches from Cape Girardeau and has included churches in Wayne, Stoddard, Dunklin, New Madrid, Madison, and Pemiscott counties. From its inception it has been aggressive and missionary. From its original territory were organized St. Francois Association (1850) with 12 churches, Cane Creek Association (1857) with five churches, and Stoddard County Association (1894). In 1954, 37 churches reported 577 baptisms, 8,593 members, $316,494 total gifts, $40,854 mission gifts, and $916,525 property value. A missions superintendent is employed.

Blue River. Organized at the Little Sni-a-Bar meetinghouse in Lafayette County on Oct. 11, 1843 by 10 churches formerly belonging to Fishing River Association and located south of the Missouri River in the present counties of Lafayette, Jackson, Cass, Johnson, and parts of Bates and Henry. In 1841 an antimission element consisting of four churches and the majority of two other churches withdrew to form the Mount Zion Regular Baptist Association. In 1855, the association dismissed 11 churches to form the Tebo Association. The association continued meeting with interruptions until 1860 when 38 churches reported 305 baptisms. The attendance in 1861 was small and the association did not meet again until 1866 when 27 churches sent messengers. Western Missouri Baptist Association, now Butler, was formed Oct. 17, 1867, by five churches in Bates and Cass counties which were dismissed for the purpose by Blue River. In 1874, when 49 of 51 churches were represented, the association had become too large for convenience and 18 churches of Lafayette and Johnson counties were dismissed to form the Lafayette and Johnson Association. The association's continually strong missionary interest is indicated by the organization of the Women's Missionary Society of Blue River Association at the session of 1885, by the encouragement given to the organization of new churches in the rapidly growing metropolis of Kansas City, and by the organization of the Kansas City Baptist Union in 1882 to promote a more perfect union among the churches in Kansas City, to secure the utmost harmony in denominational councils and "to buy, receive, hold, and sell property for denominational purposes, to assist feeble churches and to direct mission work in Kansas City, Missouri." At the 1925 session a division was agreed upon which resulted in the formation of the Kansas City Association, which left 33 churches with 5,316 members in the Blue River Association. In 1954, 38 churches with one mission reported 676 baptisms, 11,528 members, $535,168 total gifts, $87,986 mission gifts, and $1,383,150 property value. An associational missions superintendent is employed.

BOURBOIS. Organized in 1851. The second annual meeting was held with Mt. Pleasant Church and six churches from Gasconade and Maries counties reported. By this time an abstract of faith had been agreed upon. In the 1865 sessions a resolution was adopted which recommended feet-washing as an ordinance among the churches. In 1867 it adopted the name Bourbois United Baptist Association. In 1954 eight churches reported 46 baptisms, 824 members, $16,671 total gifts, $2,003 mission gifts, and $30,500 property value. A missions superintendent is employed in co-operation with Dixon Association.

BUTLER. Organized at Austin, Cass County, Oct. 17, 1867, by five churches in Cass and Bates counties. The name was changed on Sept. 1, 1871, from Western Missouri Baptist Association. A missions superintendent is employed. In 1954, 20 churches reported 137 baptisms, 2,989 members, $101,499 total gifts, $6,399 mission gifts, $288,500 property value, and $25,335 church debt.

CALDWELL-RAY. Organized in 1904 by churches from Caldwell and Ray counties. They had been in North Liberty Baptist Association. Hamilton, Polo, Cowgill, and Hopewell asked for letters of dismission from that association in Aug., 1904. The organizational meeting was held at Hamilton, Oct. 29, 1904, with 15 messengers present from the four churches above and Morris Hill which was still a member of the mother association. At the 1905 meeting at Cowgill, 19 churches were represented. A superintendent of missions is employed in co-operation with Clinton Association. In 1954, 22 churches and one mission reported 239 baptisms, 4,476 members, $148,050.81 total gifts, $18,889.59 mission gifts, $326,000.00 property value, and $5,000.00 church debt.

CALLAWAY. Organized Aug. 24, 1922, at Providence Church of New Bloomfield, by 19 churches from Callaway County and 2 churches from Montgomery County, all of which had been dismissed from Little Bonne Femme Association. A missions superintendent is employed in co-operation with Audrain and Little Bonne Femme associations. In 1954, 20 churches reported 132 baptisms, 3,224 members, $163,108 total gifts, $19,785 mission gifts, $314,000 property value, and $12,642 church debt.

CAMDEN COUNTY. Organized in 1889. In 1893, 17 churches located in Camden County reported 648 members. In 1954, 18 churches reported 85 baptisms, 3,009 members, $95,596 total gifts, $4,618 mission gifts, and $143,122 property value.

CANE CREEK. Organized with five churches from Black River Association dismissed in 1857 to form a new association. In 1867 there were 14 churches in Butler and Ripley counties and some in Arkansas. From its inception the association was strongly missionary. In 1954, 28 churches located in Butler and part of Ripley and Carter counties reported 280 baptisms, 4,576 members, $147,045 total gifts, $25,150 mission gifts, $416,750 property value, and $7,214 church debt. An associational missions superintendent is employed.

CAPE GIRARDEAU. Organized June 12, 1824, at the Hebron Church, near Jackson, by 10 churches from Cape Girardeau and Perry counties. A missions superintendent is employed. In 1954, 24 churches reported 315 baptisms, 5,969 members, $194,909 total gifts, $33,355 mission gifts, $634,667 property value, and $32,497 church debt.

CARROLL COUNTY. Organized at Carrollton on Oct. 8, 1890, as the Missouri Valley Association by 10 churches located in Carroll County and part of Livingston County which were formerly associated in the North Grand River Association. The name was changed to Carroll County Association at the 1955 meeting. A missions superintendent is employed in co-operation with the Saline Association. In 1954, 19 churches reported 144 baptisms, 3,343 members, $91,917 total gifts, $19,003 mission gifts, and $268,400 property value.

CHARLESTON. Organized in 1876 at Morley by four churches in Scott County, dismissed for the purpose from Cape Girardeau Association, and with other churches from Mississippi and New Madrid counties. Articles of faith were adopted in 1879. A superintendent of missions is employed. In 1954, 31 churches reported 490 baptisms, 8,093 members, $288,171.25 total gifts, $39,108.98 mission gifts, $835,816.45 property value, and $63,671 church debt.

CHRISTIAN COUNTY. Formerly the Southwest Bethel Association, its name was changed to Christian County at its 13th annual session in 1889 when there were 23 churches with 1,395 members. The association co-operates with Stone County in the employment of a full-time superintendent of missions. In 1954, 23 churches reported 75 baptisms, 3,703 church members, $72,919 total gifts, $11,430 mission gifts, and $181,750 property value.

CLAY-PLATTE. Organized Sept., 1938 by the merging of Clay and Platte Associations and with a combined list of 27 churches. In 1954, 26 churches reported 324 baptisms, 6,914 members, $306,738 total gifts, $55,658 mission gifts, and $1,132,650 property value. A missions superintendent is employed.

CLINTON COUNTY. Organized Sept. 26, 1922, by nine churches of Clinton County withdrawing from North Liberty Association. A full-time superintendent of missions is employed in co-operation with Caldwell-Ray Association. In 1954 eight churches reported 68 baptisms, 1,650 members, $42,664 total gifts, $10,007 mission gifts, $171,000 property value.

CONCORD. Organized in 1823 at Nebo Meetinghouse in Cooper County with eight churches from Mount Pleasant Association located on the south side of the Missouri River; articles of faith were adopted at the organization meeting. Its churches are located in Cole, Moniteau, and part of Cooper counties. A full-time superintendent of missions is employed in co-operation with Lamine Association. In 1954, 30 churches reported 285 baptisms, 8,270 members, $324,715.00 total gifts, $60,822.00 mission gifts, $801,900.00 property value, and $70,882.98 church debt.

CUIVRE. Organized in 1822 by eight churches, formerly belonging to the Missouri Association, and situated north of the Missouri River in the counties of St. Charles, Warren, and Lincoln. By 1882 this association was extremely Calvinistic in doctrine and opposed to missions in practice. Evidently this association became extinct, and its successor by the same name was organized Sept. 18, 1891, at Corner Stone Baptist Church, near Whiteside, Mo., with eight churches from the area of the former association and formerly associated with Salt River Association. Articles of faith were adopted at the first meeting. In 1954, 16 churches reported 110 baptisms, 2,266 members, $79,935 total gifts, $22,934 mission gifts, $247,830 property value, and $800 church debt. An associational missions superintendent is employed in co-operation with Bear Creek and Salt River associations.

DADE COUNTY. Organized as Rock Prairie Association of United Baptists, 1867, by six churches from Dade County. By 1877 the name was changed to Dade County Baptist Association. In 1954, 13 churches reported 82 baptisms, 1,763 members, $44,337 total gifts, $6,606 mission gifts, $160,800 property value, and $1,569 church debt.

DALLAS COUNTY. Organized at Mission Chapel in Polk County in 1889 by 19 churches from parts of Polk and Dallas counties. Articles of faith were adopted from the New Hampshire Confession at the meeting in 1891. A missions superintendent is employed in co-operation with Polk County Association. In 1954, 16 churches reported 98 baptisms, 2,280 members, $36,989 total gifts, $4,711 mission gifts, $107,160 property value, and $1,850 church debt.

DAVIESS. Organized Oct. 9, 1901, by churches from Daviess County. A superintendent of missions is employed in co-operation with Harrison County Association. In 1954, 13 churches reported 67 baptisms, 1,704 members, $41,219 total gifts, $6,618 mission gifts, and $112,800 property value.

DENT COUNTY. Organized as Dry Fork in 1877 at Carney Schoolhouse. Twelve churches from Dent and sections of Texas, Phelps, Shannon, and Crawford counties had been received by 1879. At a meeting in 1929, the name was changed to Dent County Baptist Association. A missions superintendent is employed. In 1954, 17 churches reported 114 baptisms, 2,835 members, $60,913 total gifts, $7,736 mission gifts, $229,150 property value, and $8,000 church debt.

DIXON. Organized Nov. 6, 1871, by "Churches located in the vicinity of the Atlantic and Pacific railroad in southwestern Missouri" (located in Phelps, Pulaski, and adjacent counties). A missions superintendent is employed in co-operation with Bourbois Association. In 1954, 15 churches reported 155 baptisms, 2,569 members, $85,651.00 total gifts, $15,835.00 mission gifts, $226,000.00 property value, and $22,051.51 church debt.

DOUGLAS-OZARK. One of the newest associations in Missouri, organized as Douglas Missionary Baptist Association Nov. 24, 1946, at the Ava church by Bruce Maples and Arch Bolerjack with five churches from Douglas and Ozark counties. At the annual meeting at Ava Sept. 26, 1952, the name was changed to Douglas-Ozark Baptist Association. Articles of faith similar to the Philadelphia Confession were adopted at the first meeting. A missions superintendent is employed in co-operation with Wright County Baptist Association. In 1954 nine churches reported 80 baptisms, 706 members, $21,200 total gifts, $3,144 mission gifts, $49,050 property value, and $2,932 total church debt.

ELEVEN POINTS RIVER. Organized in Sept., 1888, at Many Springs under the leadership of the State Line Association by 20 churches from Oregon and adjoining counties, including Fremont Church in Carter County. A missions superintendent is employed. In 1954, 14 churches reported 26 baptisms, 679 members, $13,707 total gifts, $1,866 mission gifts, and $214,000 property value.

FRANKLIN. Decidedly missionary in purpose, the third association to be formed in southeast Missouri was organized in 1832, at the home of J. C. Duckworth. The first annual meeting was at Meramec Church, Sept. 14–17, 1832, with the record showing 10 churches, 10 ministers, 82 baptisms, 374 members. The association included Franklin and Washington counties and parts of Jefferson, St. Francois, Gasconade, and Crawford. A missions superintendent is employed. In 1954, 35 churches reported 565 baptisms, 9,865 members, $330,597 total gifts, $57,818 mission gifts, $1,147,800 property value, and $161,050 church debt.

FRANKLIN COUNTY. Organized at Sullivan in Oct., 1890, by seven churches from the Jefferson County Association and three from the Meramec Association. The organization was completed Nov. 15, 1890, at a meeting at Pleasant Hill Church when 11 churches were represented. A missions superintendent is employed. In 1954, 22 churches reported 225 baptisms, 2,876 members, $130,749 total gifts, $24,447 mission gifts, $412,300 property value, and $65,620 church debt.

GENTRY. Organized in 1856 by three churches dismissed from the West Fork Association. It did not survive the Civil War. An organization by the same name and located in the area occupied by its predecessor (Gentry and Worth counties) was organized in 1864. In 1868 the association contained 17 churches. In 1954, 14 churches reported 52 baptisms, 1,984 members, $35,478 total gifts, $4,365 mission gifts, and $121,100 property value. A missions superintendent is employed in co-operation with Northwest Association.

Greene County. Organized in 1873 at Friendship Church with six churches located mostly in Greene County. It was the successor to Union Association (organized 1855) which was the name of the consolidated Liberty (organized May 5, 1840) and Sac River (organized 1842). In 1954, 50 churches reported 804 baptisms, 19,439 members, $676,655 total gifts, $96,490 mission gifts, and $2,518,368 property value. A missions superintendent is employed.

Harmony. Organized on Jan. 6, 1866, as the Sedalia Baptist Association at the First Baptist Church of Sedalia with eight churches from Pettis County represented. The name was changed to Central at the 1872 meeting in the hope that certain prejudices that existed against the association might be allayed. In 1879 a new association was formed by six churches, leaving only nine churches in Central Association. Harmony Association was formed in 1881 by most of the churches in Pettis County and its existence finally brought peace to the churches which were not harmoniously related in any of the three preceding associational organizations. Positive action was taken by Harmony Association early in its history on the subject of missions and temperance, and the association has continued to maintain this position. In 1954, 22 churches reported 215 baptisms, 5,105 members, $146,283 total gifts, $24,896 mission gifts, and $413,100 property value. An associational missions superintendent is employed.

Harrison County. Organized Oct. 31, 1947, at First Baptist Church of Bethany by 12 churches which withdrew for the purpose from other associations as follows: seven from West Fork, one from North Grand River, two from Daviess, and two from Gentry. The New Hampshire Confession of Faith was adopted. In 1954, 10 churches reported 105 baptisms, 1,758 members, $37,035 total gifts, $4,028 mission gifts, and $86,500 property value. An associational missions superintendent is employed in co-operation with Daviess and Mount Moriah associations.

Howell County. Organized as Union Association in 1865 by churches formerly in Richland and Hutton Valley associations. In 1873 five churches were dismissed to form the now extinct State Line Association. The date of the change of name to Howell County is not definite. In 1954, 23 churches reported 189 baptisms, 3,523 members, $101,592 total gifts, $15,782 mission gifts, and $317,800 property value. An associational missions superintendent is employed.

Jefferson County. Organized Oct. 8, 1853, at Sandy Church by 12 messengers representing nine churches from Jefferson County. Following the organization of the association the county was swept with a revival spirit which resulted in the formation of churches whose pastors and messengers were present at the second annual meeting. The association adopted articles of faith from the Philadelphia Confession; it employs a full-time superintendent of missions. In 1954, 23 churches reported 326 baptisms, 5,571 members, $267,979 total gifts, $36,922 mission gifts, $592,286 property value, and $69,493 church debt.

Johnson County. Organized Sept. 11, 1912, by 12 churches from Johnson County, formerly associated in the Lafayette and Johnson Baptist Association which was dissolved by mutual agreement for the purpose of forming associations in each of the two counties. The minutes of the 1913 meeting show 25 churches. A superintendent of missions is employed in co-operation with Lafayette and Tebo associations. In 1954, 19 churches reported 146 baptisms, 3,852 members, $152,772 total gifts, $27,150 mission gifts, and $356,250 property value.

Kansas City. Organized Sept. 21, 1926, at Calvary Branch Church by 32 churches dismissed from Blue River Association, in order to meet the peculiar needs of a great city. The Kansas City Baptist Union, an auxiliary to the Blue River Association, had been organized in 1882 "to promote a more perfect union among the churches in Kansas City, to secure the utmost harmony in our denominational councils: to buy, receive, hold, and sell property for denominational purposes, to assist feeble churches and to direct mission work in Kansas City, Missouri." The Kansas City Baptist Union keeping the above purpose has continued as the incorporated body of the Kansas City Association. The association subscribes to the New Hampshire Confession of Faith. In 1954, 47 churches with 12 missions reported 1,872 baptisms, 31,365 members, $2,303,219 total gifts, $436,036 mission gifts, and $6,642,261 property value. An office is maintained in the building owned by the Sunday School Board of the Southern Baptist Convention, which houses the Baptist Book Store. A missions superintendent and his staff of workers administer the work of the association.

Laclede. Organized in 1855 as the Zion Association of United Baptists by churches located in Laclede and Camden counties and formerly in the area of the Gasconade River Association. Missionaries for the association were elected in 1868 but by 1873 the association could agree only that mission work should be no bar to fellowship. In 1879 eight churches were dropped because they had become disorganized, leaving 14 churches with 498 members in the organization. In 1895 the name was changed to Laclede County Association of United Baptist Churches. The articles of faith are adapted from the Philadelphia Confession. In 1954, 21 churches reported 204 baptisms, 3,966 members, $130,205 total gifts, $35,009 mission gifts, and $302,300 total property value. An associational missions superintendent is employed.

Lafayette County. Organized at Elm Springs Church in Johnson County on Sept. 11, 1912, at a unique meeting of the Lafayette and Johnson County Association when it was resolved to divide the association along the line between the two counties. The messengers of the two counties met in separate meetings. At the first annual meeting, Oct. 15–16, 1913, 17 churches reported. A missions superintendent is employed in co-operation with Johnson and Tebo associations. In 1954, 14 churches reported 205 baptisms, 3,587 members, $138,915 total gifts, $27,964 mission gifts, $355,100 property value, and $13,650 church debt.

LAMINE. Organized Sept. 20, 1872, at Freedom Church in Morgan County by 13 churches dismissed from Concord Association. In 1954, 17 churches located in Cooper and Morgan counties reported 78 baptisms, 2,975 members, $99,326 total gifts, $14,700 mission gifts, and $397,900 property value. An associational missions superintendent is employed in co-operation with Concord Association.

LAWRENCE COUNTY. Formerly associated in Southwest Bethel Association, this association was organized as the James River Association of Baptists on Sept. 11, 1871, at Mount Pizgah Church, north of Mount Vernon in Lawrence County, by messengers from 11 churches located in Lawrence and Stone counties. At a meeting at Mount Olivet, Sept. 26, 1873, with 15 churches represented, the name was changed to Lawrence County Association. In 1923 the churches in Stone County were dismissed to form the Stone County Association. A missions superintendent is employed. In 1954, 23 churches reported 243 baptisms, 5,259 members, $148,190 total gifts, $25,786 mission gifts, $495,900 property value, and $16,600 church debt.

LINN COUNTY. Organized at Linneus, Nov. 2, 1872, by seven churches dismissed from the North Grand River Association. The New Hampshire Confession of Faith was adopted. A superintendent of missions is employed in co-operation with Livingston County Association. In 1954, 17 churches reported 130 baptisms, 3,572 members, $138,782 total gifts, $17,529 mission gifts, $507,400 property value, and $68,766 church debt.

LITTLE BONNE FEMME. Organized in 1839 at Providence Church in Callaway County by nine churches, four of which had withdrawn from Salem Association because of antimissionary action by that association. In 1922 there were 21 churches dismissed to form the Callaway County Association. In 1954, 17 churches reported 240 baptisms, 5,268 members, $166,851 total gifts, $25,073 mission gifts, and $555,607 property value. A missions superintendent is employed in co-operation with Callaway and Audrain associations.

LIVINGSTON. Organized Dec. 5, 1872, at Chillicothe, by five churches located in Livingston County which had been dismissed from the North Grand River Association for that purpose. A missions superintendent is employed in co-operation with Linn County Association. In 1954, 14 churches reported 116 baptisms, 2,348 members, $82,755 total gifts, $10,882 mission gifts, $200,900 property value, and $10,367 church debt.

MACON. Organized as Mount Tabor Association in 1843 by four churches which withdrew from Mount Pleasant Association for this purpose. The name became Middle Fork in 1846 and Macon in 1956. In 1954, 22 churches reported 242 baptisms, 4,335 members, $147,059 total gifts, $19,670 mission gifts, $609,000 property value, and $85,000 church debt. An associational missions superintendent is employed in co-operation with North Central and North Missouri associations.

MERAMEC. Organized in 1870 by six churches located in Washington County and dismissed from Franklin Association. In 1954, 15 churches reported 160 baptisms, 1,962 members, $75,683 total gifts, $8,146 mission gifts, $221,800 property value, and $21,880 church debt. An associational missions superintendent is employed.

MILLER COUNTY. Organized as Osage River Association in 1844, at Gilgal Church near Bagnell, by churches which were formerly in the Concord Association and which were located in Camden, Pulaski, Miller, and Morgan counties. It was "resolved that the cause of missions shall not be a bar to fellowship and that the subject be not stirred any more in any church nor brought upon the association hereafter and that each individual be left to act and think in the matter as he pleases. . . ." At the 1891 meeting the name was changed to Miller County Association. The Philadelphia Confession of Faith was adopted at the meeting in 1845. A superintendent of missions is employed. In 1954, 22 churches reported 162 baptisms, 3,471 members, $105,219 total gifts, $19,730 mission gifts, $222,500 property value, and $17,800 church debt.

MONROE. Organized Oct. 13, 1904, by 13 churches from Monroe County. In 1954, 12 churches reported 26 baptisms, 1,443 members, $28,266 total gifts, $5,759 mission gifts, and $111,050 property value. An associational missions superintendent is employed in co-operation with Mt. Pleasant Association.

MOUNT MORIAH. Begun in Aug., 1869, at the session of North Liberty Association at New Salem Church, Daviess County; organized at Zoar Church in Oct., 1869, by 12 churches in Andrew, Daviess, Gentry, and DeKalb counties. In 1870 the old London Confession of Faith was adopted. In 1954, nine churches located in parts of DeKalb and Gentry counties reported 46 baptisms, 1,280 members, $24,177 total gifts, $2,425 mission gifts, and $55,450 property value.

MOUNT PLEASANT. The third association to be formed in Missouri Territory, was organized July 25, 1818, at Mount Pleasant Church by five churches which had not previously been in any association. Mount Pleasant, "the mother of associations," has accounted directly for the formation of Fishing River (1823) with seven churches, Concord (1823) with eight churches, Salem (1827) with 13 churches, Old School Mount Pleasant (1837) from antimissionary division, Mount Tabor (1843) with four churches, Macon (1843), North Union [in Adair, Schuyler, and part of Macon counties] (1843), and Mount Zion (1880) with 13 churches. This association indirectly has accounted for the beginning of work in the areas now served by other associations by aggressively sending out itinerant preachers. From its inception Mt. Pleasant was plagued by an antimissionary spirit over which she triumphed. In 1954, 21 churches reported 290 baptisms, 5,899 members, $180,409 total gifts, $37,752 mission gifts, $692,250 property value, and $69,879 church debt. The association subscribes to the Philadelphia Confession of Faith. An associational missions superintendent is employed in co-operation with Monroe Association.

MOUNT SALEM. Organized at Mount Salem Church in Knox County Oct. 19, 1878, by seven churches located in Knox, Lewis, and Shelby counties which had been dismissed from Bethel Association. The Philadelphia Confession of Faith was adopted. In 1954 nine churches reported 26 baptisms, 540 members, $11,958 total gifts, $1,153 mission gifts, and $21,000 property value.

MOUNT ZION. Organized Oct. 5, 1880, at Mount Zion Church in Howard County by 13 churches which had been dismissed from Mount Pleasant Association for the purpose. It adopted the Philadelphia Confession of Faith. An associational missions superintendent is employed. In 1954, 19 churches reported 70 baptisms, 2,007 members, $58,327 total gifts, $8,564 mission gifts, $150,700 property value, and $2,200 church debt.

NEVADA. Organized in 1867 by 12 churches located in Barton, Cedar, and Vernon counties. In 1889 eight churches formed the Barton County Association. In 1947 the territory was extended to include Cedar County and three churches formerly listed with the Cedar County Association were listed in Nevada Association. In 1954, 23 churches reported 167 baptisms, 3,436 members, $123,450 total gifts, $20,962 mission gifts, and $410,900 property value. A full-time associational missions superintendent is employed.

NEW MADRID. Organized in 1882. The earliest minutes on file are for the year 1884 which report six churches in New Madrid and Pemiscot counties. In 1954, 25 churches reported 469 baptisms, 7,098 members, $212,720 total gifts, $28,085 mission gifts, $728,150 property value, and $25,934 church debt. An associational missions superintendent is employed.

NORTH CENTRAL. This association, located in Sullivan and Putnam counties, was organized at Unionville, Sept. 1, 1865, by messengers from six churches who adopted the Philadelphia Confession of Faith in the constitution. A missions superintendent is employed in co-operation with Macon and North Missouri associations. In 1954, 14 churches reported 135 baptisms, 1,297 members, $25,188 total gifts, $3,860 mission gifts, $47,600 property value, and $100 church debt.

NORTH GRAND RIVER. Organized in Feb., 1841, at the house of William Mabley in Livingston County, by representatives of three churches (Carrollton, Locust Creek, and Salt Creek) with a combined membership of 100. This association has included a part or all of the territory of Carroll, Livingston, Linn, Chariton, Putnam, Sullivan, Mercer, Daviess, and Harrison counties and a part of the state of Iowa. North Grand River has been prolific, having contributed to the formation of five other associations: West Fork (1845), Missouri Valley (1860), Locust Fork (organization date unknown), Livingston (1872), and Linn (1872) associations. A missions superintendent is employed. In 1954, 30 churches reported 223 baptisms, 4,315 members, $119,203 total gifts, $21,371 mission gifts, $236,300 property value, and $8,500 church debt.

NORTH MISSOURI. Organized as North Union in Oct., 1843, by churches in Adair, Schuyler, and part of Macon counties dismissed for the purpose by Mount Pleasant Association at its 1843 meeting. Evidently in the confusion of the Civil War the association became disorganized because the association is not mentioned in the period following the war. On Sept. 4, 1868, the North Missouri Association was organized at Fabius Church by messengers from four churches, mainly of Schuyler County, all of which had been members of the North Union Association (which name is not to be confused with the association by the same name in the northwest section of the state). In 1954, eight churches reported 82 baptisms, 1,002 members, $32,453 total gifts, $3,756 mission gifts, $120,300 property value, and $800 church debt.

NORTHWEST. Organized in the area of the prewar West Union Association on Aug. 2, 1867, by five churches of Atchison, Holt, and Nodaway counties, which having become disorganized during the war were reorganized through the efforts of J. H. Best, of the Platte River Association, and G. W. Huntley, of the American Baptist Home Mission Society. At its organization meeting the association took a collection for the American Baptist Home Mission Society and appointed delegates to the Missouri Baptist State Convention. After the dissolution of the Missouri Baptist State Convention, the association joined in the support of the Missouri Baptist General Association. In 1954, 11 churches reported 154 baptisms, 1,764 members, $77,948 total gifts, $8,098 mission gifts, $192,300 property value, and $18,725 church debt.

OLD PATH. Organized by 11 churches Oct. 25, 1867, at Hopewell Church in Polk County. Eight of the constituting churches had withdrawn from Freedom Association because of an amendment in 1866 to its confession of faith. The obnoxious item declared: "Non-fellowship for those who had been in rebellion against the government of the United States, without evidence of gospel repentance." This provision was removed in 1868, but it came after the formation of Old Path. Three churches withdrew in 1950 to co-operate with nine churches from the St. Clair Association to form the Osage–Pomme de Terre Association. The association subscribes to the Philadelphia Confession of Faith. In 1954, 13 churches, all located in Hickory County, reported 30 baptisms, 1,664 members, $8,436 total gifts, $470 mission gifts, none of which were for the Cooperative Program or for foreign missions, and $29,500 property value.

Osage–Pomme de Terre. Organized in Oct., 1950, by 13 churches located in St. Clair and Hickory counties, nine of which were formerly in St. Clair County and three in Old Path associations, which were seeking a positive, aggressive and co-operative missionary fellowship. In 1954, 10 churches reported 68 baptisms, 1,666 members, $42,326 total gifts, $8,945 mission gifts, and $86,300 property value. An associational missions superintendent is employed in co-operation with Benton County Association.

Phelps County. Organized Oct. 26, 1907, by seven churches formerly in Dixon Association. A peculiar statement in the constitution that the association was composed of churches holding strictly to Baptist principles gives some color to the inference that there had been some doctrinal differences. A mission superintendent is employed. In 1954, 12 churches reported 156 baptisms, 3,016 members, $96,770 total gifts, $15,003 mission gifts, $258,637 property value, and $22,855 church debt.

Pleasant Grove. Organized Sept. 21, 1877, by nine churches in Scotland County dismissed for the purpose by the Wyaconda Association. Two more churches were admitted at the first meeting. In 1954, 19 churches reported 102 baptisms, 1,701 members, $41,696 total gifts, $7,084 mission gifts, $194,200 property value, and $3,071 church debt. An associational missions superintendent is employed.

Polk County. Organized Sept. 18, 1889, when Freedom Association dismissed nine churches in Dallas County to form the Dallas County Association, and the remaining 27 churches located in Polk County took the name of Polk County Association. In the 1950 annual meeting 22 of the 36 churches were dropped from the associational roll for non-co-operation. A missions superintendent is employed in co-operation with the Dallas County Association. In 1954, 12 churches reported 52 baptisms, 2,242 members, $74,550 total gifts, $13,790 mission gifts, $254,050 property value, and $14,295 church debt.

Pulaski County. Organized as the Smith Valley Association in 1870 by several churches in Pulaski County and one in Phelps County. By 1874 there were 14 churches. On Aug. 21, 1890, at which time there were 13 co-operating churches, the name was changed to Pulaski County Association. A missions superintendent is employed. In 1954, 23 churches reported 173 baptisms, 4,173 members, $122,716 total gifts, $22,979 mission gifts, $517,000 property value, and $11,331 church debt.

Reynolds County. Organized at O'Dell schoolhouse in the southern part of Reynolds County on Oct. 1, 1892. By the next annual meeting eight churches reported. A missions superintendent is employed. In 1954, 21 churches reported 89 baptisms, 2,342 members, $56,347 total gifts, $11,749 mission gifts, $173,500 property value, and $3,670 church debt.

St. Francois. Organized in Oct., 1850, by 12 churches scattered over Wayne, Madison, and Bollinger counties and dismissed for the purpose from Black River Association and taking the name St. Francois Association of United Baptists, "devoted to benevolent purposes." The mission spirit was strong, the number of churches and members increased, with the exception of the period of the Civil War, until 1876 when 10 or more churches were dismissed to form Wayne County Association. This left 18 churches in St. Francois. In 1954, 20 churches reported 97 baptisms, 2,790 members, $73,797 total gifts, $19,354 mission gifts, $226,664 property value, and $7,050 church debt. An associational missions superintendent is employed.

St. Joseph. Organized Dec. 30, 1871, at Bethel Baptist Church, Andrew County, with 33 messengers from 16 churches. The first meeting was the outgrowth of a previous meeting where a group of brethren from Buchanan County, Platte River, and Mount Moriah associations met to discuss the possibility of merging the three associations into one. This informal meeting was held at Easton, Mo., Nov. 4, 1871. The association employs a full-time superintendent of missions. In 1954, 34 churches and 4 missions reported 649 baptisms, 10,235 members, $404,-244.16 total gifts, $81,585.16 mission gifts, $1,-381,470.00 property value, and $162,725.00 church debt.

St. Louis. The second oldest association in Missouri, organized Nov. 7, 1817, at the home of Thomas R. Musick in St. Louis, Missouri Territory, ten years after the organization of Fee Fee, the first Baptist church to be organized in the area. The seven constituting churches were located in the area which later became St. Louis, Lincoln, St. Charles, and Franklin counties. Sometime prior to 1840 the name was changed from Missouri to Missouri United Baptist Association. At a meeting at Concord Church in 1853 the name was changed to St. Louis Baptist Association. In 1882 the churches north of the Missouri River were dismissed to form a new association called Cuivre. In 1832 three churches were dismissed to join in the formation of the Franklin Association. The St. Louis Baptist Mission Board, which is the incorporated agency of the association, employs an associational missions superintendent and about six other workers, and has a church building loan fund totaling $230,000. In 1954, 60 churches reported 2,702 baptisms, 45,689 members, $2,879,275 total gifts, $549,641 mission gifts, $9,364,695 property value, and $1,398,556 church debt.

Saline. Organized Oct. 3, 1842, Mount Gilead meetinghouse in Cole County by eight churches dismissed for the purpose from Concord Asso-

DAUPHIN WAY BAPTIST CHURCH, Mobile, Ala. Organized 1904, now Alabama's largest with membership over 6,000. Property worth $2,500,000 includes educational unit for 3,000 and auditorium of Romanesque design seating 1,650.

FIRST BAPTIST CHURCH, New Orleans, La. Organized 1843, property today worth $1,650,000. Auditorium of contemporary design seats 1,800, educational unit accommodates 2,000, both air conditioned. Membership in 1956 was 3,345.

ciation. After organizing the new association received one new church. The nine churches were located in Saline, Cooper, and Pettis counties. The newly constituted association accepted the New Hampshire Confession of Faith. In 1954, 18 churches, all located in Saline County, reported 196 baptisms, 3,971 members, $148,552 total gifts, $23,220 mission gifts, $409,550 property value, and $17,620 church debt. An associational missions superintendent is employed in co-operation with Carroll County Association.

SALT RIVER. Organized Aug. 23, 1823 at the Baptist church in Peno, Pike County, by eight churches. Because the association was so large 14 churches were dismissed in 1834 to form Bethel Association. In 1840 three antimissionary churches withdrew. In 1853 nine churches withdrew to form Bear Creek Association. Salt River was one of the few associations that held meetings during the entire Civil War period. Louisiana College, afterward called McCune College, was fostered by this association. In 1954, 23 churches reported 128 baptisms, 3,255 members, $98,925 total gifts, $22,063 mission gifts, and $324,200 property value.

SHANNON COUNTY. Organized Oct. 20, 1899, at the Amity Baptist Church, Ink, Mo., by eight churches dismissed for the purpose from Texas County Association. In 1954 six churches reported 38 baptisms, 697 members, $16,963 total gifts, $2,572 mission gifts, and $21,000 property value. A missions superintendent is employed.

SHOAL CREEK. Organized in 1871 by 22 churches from Spring River Association and located in McDonald, Barry, and Newton counties. There were no meetings during the Civil War. Shoal Creek co-operated with Lawrence and Greene County associations to organize the Pierce City Baptist College in 1877. In 1884 the 21 churches in Barry County formed the Barry County Association. The association has conformed to principles of the Philadelphia Confession of Faith. In 1954, 30 churches reported 289 baptisms, 5,671 members, $151,374 total gifts, $24,321 mission gifts, and $478,660 property value. A missions superintendent is employed.

SPRING RIVER. Organized July 11, 1840, 10 years after the first white man, Lunsford Oliver, settled in this part of the state. The association was composed of five churches having a total of 91 members and scattered over much of southwest Missouri. An antimission spirit brought a resolution in the organization meeting providing that the cause of missions would not be a bar to fellowship and that the subject not be mentioned in the association. Each church was to deal with missions as they chose. This resolution was rescinded in 1848. In 1871 the association divided, with churches in the section south of the Atlantic and Pacific Railroad choosing the name of Shoal Creek. The articles of faith adopted at the 1840 meeting are adapted from the Philadelphia Confession of Faith. In 1954, 46 churches reported 645 baptisms, 13,171 members, $508,528 total gifts, $86,669 mission gifts, $1,259,065 property value, and $107,666 church debt. An associational missions superintendent is employed.

STODDARD COUNTY. Organized on Sept. 20, 1894, by 16 churches located in Stoddard County. It was the outgrowth of Bloomfield Association, formed from a division of Black River Association. In 1954, 10 churches reported 126 baptisms, 1,951 members, $90,536 total gifts, $11,821 mission gifts, and $224,000 property value. An associational missions superintendent is employed.

STONE COUNTY. Organized Aug. 22, 1923, at Crane, Mo., by seven churches in Stone County belonging to Lawrence County Association. The area was formerly served by the Bethel (1853–69), by the Southwest Bethel (1869–71), by the James River (1871–73), and by the Lawrence County (1873–1923) associations. A missions superintendent is employed in co-operation with the Christian County Association. In 1954, 13 churches reported 28 baptisms, 1,267 members, $30,934 total gifts, $2,811 mission gifts, $103,500 property value, and $24,228 church debt.

TEBO. Organized Sept. 7, 1855, by 11 churches located in Benton, Henry, and Pettis counties and dismissed for the purpose from the Blue River Association. Tebo became the parent of Benton County Association in 1892 and Sedalia (Pettis County), now Harmony, 1866. The New Hampshire Confession of Faith was adopted at the organization meeting. In 1954, 22 churches reported 120 baptisms, 4,686 members, $112,638 total gifts, $25,850 mission gifts, $414,500 property value, and $50 church debt. An associational missions superintendent is employed in co-operation with Lafayette County and Johnson County associations.

TEXAS COUNTY. Organized as the Gasconade River Association of United Baptists on Sept. 25, 1847, by pastors and messengers from five churches which were widely scattered over Pulaski, Texas, and Wright counties. The area of the association was expanded so as to include Laclede County by 1855 and Dent County by 1857. In 1857 churches in Wright County petitioned the body to divide the association because of the large territory. The division was made on a north and south line along the Roubidoux River with eastern portion keeping the original name. The Gasconade River Association at one time occupied the area now served by the Dent, Laclede, Phelps, Pulaski, Shannon County, and Texas County associations. In 1889 the name was changed to Texas County Baptist Association. The articles of faith are an adaptation of the New Hampshire Confession of Faith. In 1954, 28 churches reported 136 baptisms, 4,665 members, $190,763 total gifts, $15,847 mission gifts, $258,900 property value, and $20,207 church debt. An associational missions superintendent is employed.

WAYNE COUNTY. Organized in Reynolds County in 1876 by 12 churches dismissed for the purpose from Franklin, St. Francois, and Cane

Creek associations. The association subscribes to the New Hampshire Confession of Faith. In 1954, 17 churches reported 40 baptisms, 1,399 members, $28,797 total gifts, $5,611 mission gifts, $73,044 property value, and $1,600 church debt. An associational missions superintendent is employed.

WEBSTER. Organized July 3, 1868, by nine churches located in Webster and parts of Greene, Dallas, Wright, and Douglas counties. The association subscribes to the New Hampshire Confession of Faith. Churches have been dismissed to unite with new associations formed to include them in their geographic limits. In 1954, 20 churches reported 72 baptisms, 2,477 members, $52,780 total gifts, $9,477 mission gifts, $191,700 property value, and $5,580 church debt. An associational missions superintendent is employed.

WRIGHT COUNTY. Organized as the Ozark Baptist Association, Oct. 22, 1870, at the Mount Moriah Church in Wright County, by one church of Douglas County and six churches of Wright County, as the result of opposition to missions in the parent organization, Zion Association. From the beginning of its existence it has been evangelistic and has actively encouraged mission enterprises, Sunday schools, and ministerial education. The name was changed to Wright County Association at the meeting in 1894. In 1954, 21 churches reported 161 baptisms, 3,436 members, $73,335 total gifts, $16,385 missions gifts, and $229,300 property value. An associational missions superintendent is employed.

WYACONDA. Organized in Oct., 1844, at the Wyaconda Church by nine churches, dismissed for the purpose from Bethel Association, and adopting the New Hampshire Confession of Faith. The number of churches was reduced during the Civil War. The association has been consistently missionary in policy and practice. In 1954, 26 churches reported 147 baptisms, 3,861 members, $85,448 total gifts, $17,806 mission gifts, and $285,500 property value. A missions superintendent is employed.

MERLE A. MITCHELL

II. Extinct. ANTIOCH. Organized in 1848 as Cedar Association, in what was Rives County. The name was changed to Cedar County by churches dismissed from Liberty Association. The name was changed to Antioch United Baptist Association at a meeting in 1866, and in 1885 the name was changed to Cedar County Baptist Association. In 1947 Cedar County was included with the Nevada Association.

BETHEL. The first association to be formed in the Territory of Missouri and the first west of the Mississippi River was organized June, 1816, at Bethel Church in Cape Girardeau County by representatives of six churches. Bethel was the only one of the six churches which had previously been in an association, and it had been in the Red River Association of Kentucky. The association was organized on the principles of the United Baptists and was originally missionary. The original Bethel Association became antimissionary and has continued until the present, but has shown very little growth since the division in 1824 when the missionary churches withdrew to form the Cape Girardeau Association.

BETHEL. See MOUNT SALEM.

CEDAR. See ANTIOCH.

CENTRAL MISSOURI. Organized in 1859 when eight churches were dismissed from Bethel, the oldest association in Missouri, to form a new association in Iron County. The articles of faith accepted foot washing as an ordinance. In 1867 seven churches were dismissed to form Concord Association (Southeast). The last report of this association appears in 1883 when nine churches reported 7 ministers, 16 baptisms, 492 members. R. S. Douglass conjectures that it probably disbanded and its churches united with other associations.

CLAY COUNTY. Organized at William Jewell College, 1922, by 14 churches of Liberty and Blue River associations, with "no ill feelings." The Clay and Platte associations merged in Sept., 1938, under the name of Clay-Platte Association.

CONCORD (SOUTHEAST). Organized in 1867 by four churches. In 1869 the association voted to drop correspondence with Franklin Association because Concord declared foot washing to be a gospel ordinance. By 1872 its 16 churches were in Reynolds, Iron, and Shannon counties. Its last report to the general association was in 1887. The churches joined other associations which now occupy that territory.

COUNTY LINE. Organized in 1890 by 11 churches in Ozark, Wright, and Douglas counties. See DOUGLAS-OZARK COUNTY.

DOUGLAS. See DOUGLAS-OZARK.

DRY FORK. See DENT COUNTY.

FISHING RIVER. Organized in 1823 at Fishing River Church in Clay County by seven churches of Clay County and the surrounding territory west of Grand River which had been dismissed for the purpose from Mount Pleasant Association. At the annual meeting the association in 1838 committed itself to the antimissionary position and from that time was identified with the Primitive Baptists. It is reported that the Fishing River Association is still active, but the last minutes for the association in the files of the Missouri Baptist Historical Society are for the 1866 meeting.

FREEDOM. Organized in Oct., 1858, at Zoar Church in Polk County by 26 churches located in Polk, Webster, Dallas, Laclede, Hickory, and Greene counties. The area constituted the eastern section of the Union Association. The very aggressive spirit of evangelism and missions suffered during the Civil War. By 1889 there were 30 churches, most of which united with the Polk County Association, which was organized in that year.

GASCONADE RIVER OF UNITED BAPTISTS. See MISSOURI, Texas County.

James River. See Lawrence.

Locust Fork. This association formerly occupied the territory in which the North Central Association was organized in 1865, but because of dissension, which cannot now be ascertained, it disbanded about 1860 or '61. Some of its churches affiliated with North Union, some with North Grand River Association, and a few dissolved.

Mount Pleasant, Old School. See Mount Pleasant (Extant).

Mount Pleasant. See Mount Zion (Extant).

Mount Tabor. See Macon.

Mount Zion. See Mount Pleasant (Extant).

Mount Zion Regular. Organized Mar. 26, 1842, at Mount Zion Church by four churches and majorities from two others, a minority of Blue River Association. Mount Zion declared nonfellowship for all churches that gave countenance to what they called "benevolent institutions, such as Bible Societies, missionary societies and kindred agencies." One by one, such churches as were in sympathy with the nonaggressive and nonfellowshipping policy united with the association until its rolls at one time showed 18 churches in Johnson, Lafayette, Jackson, Cass, Bates, Benton, and Henry counties. In 1882 the record indicates that Mount Zion Regular Baptist Association had diminished to nine churches.

North Liberty. Organized Apr. 26, 1844, at New Hope Church in Clay County by five churches situated in Clay, Clinton, Platte, and Ray counties, which area was in the territory of the antimissionary Fishing River Association. From its earliest history the North Liberty Association of United Baptists exhibited a genuine spirit of progress. She was depleted by the organization of Northwestern Association in 1852, Mount Moriah in 1869, and by dismissing individual churches to other associations. In 1879 she reported 51 churches in Andrew, Buchanan, Clay, Caldwell, Clinton, Daviess, DeKalb, Platte, and Ray counties. North Liberty became the parent association for Daviess (1901) and Caldwell-Ray (1904). It was decided at the 1922 meeting of North Liberty to disband that great body and to organize smaller associations. Accordingly, Clay County Association was formed (Sept. 17, 1922) with five churches, Clinton County (Sept. 26, 1922) with eight churches, and Platte County (Aug. 23, 1922) with eight churches.

North Missouri. Organized at the New Salem Church in Daviess County, May 25, 1858, by messengers from five churches at a convention called for that purpose. The convention adjourned to meet July 9, 1858, to complete organization and to adopt a constitution. The first meeting was at South Big Creek Church, Daviess County, Oct. 1, 1858. The last meeting was held in 1860 after which the thickening gloom and danger of the war prevented further meetings. "The clerk of the association went South, our records were all lost, and the Association ceased to exist." This association was predecessor to Mount Moriah, but there was not a continuous succession.

North Union. See North Missouri.

Osage Association of Baptists. R. S. Duncan, in *A History of the Baptists in Missouri,* reports the existence of the minutes of such an association for the year 1844 only when it numbered 10 churches, viz., Wablau, Bethel, Tebo, Pleasant Grove, Mt. Vernon, New Hope, Fairfield, Pomme de Terre, North Prairie, and Antioch, located in Polk, Benton, and probably some other adjoining counties. Action at this meeting placed this association with the antimissionary Baptists.

Osage Association of United Baptists. Organized in Sept., 1870, after Tebo Association granted letters of dismission to five churches of St. Clair, Benton, and Henry counties in the Osage River country and south of the Osage River. The association was, in spirit, opposed to missions as was demonstrated in the adoption of an antimissionary resolution in 1872. In 1880 five churches with nine men ordained as ministers were doing comparatively nothing to supply their destitute field. The 1891 minutes were the last to be found in the files of the Missouri Baptist Historical Society.

Osage River. See Miller County.

Ozark. See Douglas-Ozark and Wright County.

Platte County. Organized Sept. 17, 1922, at Pleasant Grove Church near Camden Point by eight churches located in Platte County and formerly in the North Liberty Association. The Clay and Platte associations merged in Sept., 1938, under the name of Clay-Platte Association.

Platte River. Organized in 1842, at Bee Creek meetinghouse, Platte County, by three small churches with 1,251 members. By 1854 it had 26 churches with 1,284 members, but six churches received letters of dismission that year to form the Union Association of United Baptists. The loss of churches to form the St. Joseph Association in 1871 and the Mount Moriah Association *c.* 1871 weakened the association so much that it was dissolved at the 1873 meeting. Letters of dismission were granted to the remaining churches which united with the St. Joseph and Northwest Missouri associations.

Rock Prairie Association of United Baptists. See Dade County Baptist Association.

Salem. Organized Oct. 20, 1827, at Cedar Creek meetinghouse in Callaway County, by 13 churches dismissed for the purpose from Mount Pleasant Association. In 1836 an antimissionary sentiment was aroused, and in 1837 it was recommended that the missionary brethren withdraw from all missionary societies. Four churches withdrew in 1838 to enter into the formation of Little Bonne Femme Association. From this time the Salem Association was antimissionary to all intents and purposes. The last minutes for the association in the files of the Missouri Baptist Historical Society are for the year 1883.

Smith Valley. See Pulaski County.

Southwest Bethel. Organized in Nov., 1853, as the Bethel Association by six churches which were situated in the eastern part of Spring River Association and dismissed for the purpose. The association did not meet during the Civil War. A strong missionary and evangelistic spirit had resulted in the association's reporting 27 churches by the 1867 meeting. The name was changed to Southwest Bethel in the meeting of 1869. Eight churches were dismissed in 1870 to form James River Association, west of the James River. It was later disbanded by its churches going into other near-by associations.

Springfield. See Union.

St. Clair County. Organized in 1883. Ten churches were represented at its second annual meeting. This association became antimissionary and non-co-operative. In 1950 nine churches withdrew because of the antimissionary spirit and united with three churches of the Old Path Association to form the Osage–Pomme de Terre Missionary Baptist Association. No recent minutes of the St. Clair Association are available, but it is reported that a Baptist association continues under that name.

Taney Association of United Baptists. Organized Oct. 8, 1886, at Protem by five churches located in Taney and adjoining counties. Six churches reported in 1920. In 1921 it was merged with the Missouri and Arkansas Association, and it was no longer listed with Missouri associations.

Two River Old School. Organized in Oct., 1838, at North Fork Church in Monroe County by 10 churches. Most of the constituting churches had withdrawn from Salt River Association to enter into an organization rejecting the mission system. This decision meant the eventual disintegration of the body.

Union. Organized in 1855 by the union of the Liberty and Sac River associations, both of which occupied the same territory. At the first annual meeting in 1856 letters and messengers were present from 35 churches scattered over Polk, Greene, Dade, Hickory, Webster, Dallas, Laclede, and Lawrence counties. The association suffered depletion in numerical strength during the Civil War. Other associations were formed within the area so that at the 1869 meeting in Springfield with 10 churches represented the name was changed to Springfield Association because there were at that time three Union associations in Missouri. In 1873 it was "Resolved, That the association grant as many of the churches of this body as wish to do so, the liberty of going into a county association."

West Fork. Organized Sept. 15, 1845, in the area of and with the approval of the North Grand River Association, by messengers from two small churches and with a letter from a third. At one time or another it has served churches in Daviess, DeKalb, Gentry, Grundy, Harrison, Mercer, and Worth counties. West Fork was depleted by the formation of Gentry (1856), Mount Moriah (1869), Daviess (1901), and was finally absorbed when Harrison was organized in 1947.

West Union. Organized as the Union Association, at Nodaway Church in Holt County, by six churches which had been dismissed from Platte River Association. At a meeting at Nishnabotany Church in Atchison County in 1857 the name was changed to West Union Association. Sixteen churches reported in 1861. Because of war trouble, only five churches were represented in 1862 and four churches in 1863. The association did not survive the war.

MERLE A. MITCHELL

MISSOURI BAPTIST. A paper established in Mar., 1860, and published until June 15, 1861. T. W. Ustick was publisher; S. H. Ford, editor.

J. R. BLACK

MISSOURI BAPTIST CHILDREN'S HOME. Founded in 1882, this home for destitute orphans was opened Apr. 1, 1886, by an organized group of Baptists from local churches. First located in St. Louis, the home was moved in 1907 to Pattonville, St. Louis County. The first property, which consisted of one rented dwelling, has been replaced by 10 buildings which provide for 140 children. Four homes are equipped with kitchen and dining room, and six groups use a central dining room. In 1954 the total acreage, including farm, was 85 acres, with property valued at $582,872.32. The budget for the fiscal year 1954–55 was $152,000. Sources of support are Cooperative Program receipts, special promoted offerings, e.g., birthday and Thanksgiving, and individual contributions. Baptist churches in the state sent gifts as early as 1888, and the "home has been under the fostering guidance" of Missouri Baptist General Association since 1891. A total of 7,336 children have been served since the home was established. First known as Baptist Orphans' Home, the home was given its present title in 1941 in keeping with the purpose and service of the institution. The policy of the home is to admit and serve children of any age on the basis of their need, provided the home is equipped to meet that need. Needy Baptist children or children with Baptist background receive preference. From the beginning children have attended public schools. Those who remain in the home through completion of high school attend college, assisted through an interest-free educational loan fund, or receive direction in choosing employment and residence. The home received its first child-placing license from Missouri State Welfare Department Jan., 1951. This license enables the home to maintain foster home care and adoption service. Casework has grown into a department with a child welfare director and six caseworkers. In 1954 there was a total of 339 children in the care of the home.

GERTRUDE LOCKARD

MISSOURI BAPTIST FOUNDATION. Organized on June 28, 1946, the foundation secured its charter of incorporation on Aug. 15,

1946. The report of the foundation to the Missouri Baptist General Association Oct. 29–31, 1946, stated: "Authority will be requested at this session of the General Association for the transfer to this Foundation of the permanent and trust funds now administered by a special committee which has the authority to supervise, control and manage the investment of the permanent funds of the Executive Board." This foundation provides a trustworthy agency to receive money in all recognized legal ways on behalf of the Missouri Baptist General Association and to administer the same in perpetuity for the glory of Christ and to the credit of the Baptists. Money may be left for any institution or interest "fostered by or having the official sanction of the Missouri Baptist General Association," and its accruals will be used as designated, but the principal will be kept forever in the control of the general association. From 1946 to Oct. 1, 1956, over 100 wills were recorded and 28 trust and annuity contracts were executed. Funds in the amount of $568,995.04 have been accumulated. The funds have been left for the support of the cause of Christ through the following Baptist institutions: Hannibal–La Grange College, Southwest Baptist College, William Jewell College, the Children's Home, Home for the Aged, the Missouri Baptist Hospital, and Southwestern Baptist Theological Seminary. The office staff consists of the executive secretary-treasurer and office secretary, whose responsibility it is to secure gifts in wills, trusts, and annuity agreements, to undergird the program of Missouri Baptists and missions around the world.

HARRY L. CAMERON

MISSOURI BAPTIST GENERAL ASSOCIATION.

I. Baptist Beginnings. The history of Missouri Baptist beginnings falls into three periods: the Franco-Spanish period, territorial days, and a period of unorganized growth. During the Franco-Spanish days Missouri was foreign and almost exclusively Catholic territory, where law and circumstances subdued the Baptist voice. But Baptists began to be heard during the days following the Louisiana Purchase. After Missouri became a state, Baptists increased in stature and, although unorganized for several years, were held together by their faith in God, unity of purpose, and some great personalities. A fire in the John Mason Peck home that destroyed this pioneer's great collection of early records and documents and the careless destruction of Peck's journals by a custodian of the Mercantile Library of St. Louis have deprived Missouri Baptists of much valuable source material on their early history.

Franco-Spanish period.—Though geographi-cally Missouri is the central state of the Union, it was once but an outpost frontier and, before that, part of the territory possessed by LaSalle for Louis XIV of France. Some claim that the settlement of Missouri began as early as 1735, but the most widely accepted date is 1763, when settlers selected a site for the village of St. Louis. France ceded Louisiana to Spain in 1762, though the Spanish did not take over St. Louis until 1770. Spain ceded Louisiana back to France in 1780, but before taking possession, France sold the province of Louisiana to the United States in 1803.

During these days of persecution and hardship, it appears that Baptists were the first non-Roman Catholic whites to establish themselves in the forest wilds west of the Mississippi River in upper Louisiana. As early as 1796, Thomas Bull, his wife, and her mother settled south of Jackson in present Cape Girardeau County. Others joined them the following year. These settlers occasionally met for Scripture reading, songs, and prayer in their rude cabins but had no organization. Several Baptist families emigrated to the vicinity of St. Louis in 1797 and lived for several years without church privileges. Among these pioneer Baptists were the Abraham Musick family and others in St. Louis County, and the Boone connections and others, who settled above St. Charles. Colonel Daniel Boone of pioneer and frontier fame was not a member of any church but was "religiously disposed and a Baptist in sentiment," according to John Mason Peck, who preached to and conferred with Boone on several occasions.

John Clark became the first pioneer evangelical preacher of Missouri when he visited the Spanish country west of the Mississippi River in 1798, but he was not then a Baptist except in principle. Later he and Talbot, a dissatisfied Methodist preacher, confessed their faith at a public meeting in Illinois and baptized each other and several others. Later Clark returned to what was by then Missouri Territory and presented himself before Baptists who, satisfying themselves as to his experience, doctrine, and practice, after prayer gave him the right hand to fellowship. This was considered a satisfactory ordination by the churhces to which he ministered the rest of his days.

Thomas Johnson, an aged Baptist missionary among the Cherokee Indians of Georgia, at his own risk and expense in 1799 came into the territory to encourage the faithful. He baptized into Randol Creek Church Mrs. Agnes Ballou, who later became a member of the Bethel Church. This was probably the first New Testament baptism in what is now Missouri.

The reason for the small number of Baptists in upper Louisiana is easy to understand. Non-Catholic activities were forbidden under Spanish and French rule. Sometimes, however, the zeal of the political leaders for Romanism did not match that of the priesthood, and they lightened the harsh restrictions. A commandant at St. Louis, though secretly favorable to an application by a Baptist for permission to have religious services at his residence, publicly rejected the petition thus: "I mean you must not put a bell on your house and call it a church, nor suffer anyone but the parish priest to christen your children, but if any of your friends choose to meet at your house, sing, pray, and talk about religion, you will not be molested, provided you continue, as I believe you to be, good Christians."

Territorial days.—Missouri became United States property in 1803 upon completion of the Louisiana Purchase. With the removal of governmental interference with religious activities, churches soon began to appear. The Tywappity Baptist Church was organized in Scott County in 1805, with 8 or 10 members, but soon became defunct. Reorganized in 1809, it struggled feebly for several years and again died. Bethel Church, though the second organized, is regarded as the first permanent church in Missouri; from it sprang all the churches that composed the first association. Preacher David Green and others organized Bethel on July 19, 1806, and soon erected the first house of worship in Missouri. This building, constructed of very large hewn yellow poplar logs, was located on land about one and one-half miles south of Jackson, now owned by the Missouri Baptist General Association. Bethel was aggressively missionary and extended itself into new churches. Later it became antimissionary and withered and died. Thomas R. Musick in 1801 came from Kentucky to the territory and was the first Baptist preacher permanently to settle in Missouri. He encouraged the believers in and around St. Louis until in 1807 he was able to organize the Fee Fee Church, the oldest Baptist church in Missouri that continues alive and active today. Probably the Baptist population in Missouri at this time numbered about 50.

The Territory of Missouri was organized in 1812, and the next year William Clark of Lewis and Clark Expedition fame, a devout Catholic, was appointed territorial governor, which post he held until Missouri became a state. Though overwhelmingly defeated by popular vote in his attempt to become the first governor of the state, he was then appointed to look after Indian affairs and was stationed at St. Louis. Though Fee Fee Church was near by, and there were about 450 Baptists in the territory, St. Louis in 1817 was a town of about 3,000 population with a few isolated Baptists but no Baptist church. In 1818 James Ely Welch led in organizing the First Baptist Church in St. Louis. He and John Mason Peck, who had just arrived in Missouri as missionaries sent by the Triennial Convention, purchased a lot at Third and Market streets and led the church to construct a brick building at a cost of $6,000. Three years later much of the lot was condemned to widen Market Street, and the building was sold for $1,200. This church never recovered but dwindled and finally dissolved in 1833.

Peck, the leading spirit among Baptists in those days, established Shurtleff College, which still continues at Alton, Ill.; started the St. Charles Academy, which trained several early Baptist leaders; wrote constantly; and preached everywhere. He even found time to publish a paper, *The Western Pioneer and Baptist,* and to write several books. Other Baptist leaders and workers came to Missouri, and still others rose up in those days. Thomas Fristoe in 1817 came from Kentucky to Chariton, in Howard County. David Doyle, also from Kentucky, in 1817 settled in what is now Boone County, where he joined with others in organizing the Little Bonne Femme Church in 1819. Later he helped organize New Salem Baptist Church and served as its pastor 30 years. In 1816 Luke Williams settled in what is now Cooper County, the only ordained Baptist minister in Missouri Territory south of the Missouri River west of St. Louis County. Converted during a revival in the Fee Fee Baptist Church, Lewis Williams, formerly a Universalist, was baptized around 1811 and shortly afterward was ordained by this pioneer church. Seven of his sons and grandsons became preachers.

Period of unorganized growth.—Missouri applied for admission into the Union in 1818, was organized as a state in 1820, and was admitted to the Union in 1821. By this time Baptists in the state numbered approximately 2,000. Already they had constituted several associations: Bethel Association in 1816, Missouri Association (now St. Louis Association) in 1817, and Fishing River Association in Clay County in 1823. However, there was a growing feeling that if Baptists were to fulfill their mission in Missouri and face the growing division of opinion about missions in their own ranks, they must establish a closer co-operative relationship.

Most Missouri Baptists in the early 19th century were best known as United Baptists, a name usually incorporated in early church and associational names and carried on the printed state minutes for several years. However, Baptists were far from united. The antimissionary sentiment of some and missionary zeal of others could not be reconciled. Churches divided, associations deflected, and leaders realized that the Baptist voice would be silenced or its message lose its clear note unless Baptists could speak as a unit and thus be heard by each other and outsiders. Baptists needed to unite and sought a means to make vocal their unity and to give them an avenue of service and co-operation. But many factors combined during the early statehood days of Missouri to impede their progress and hinder their co-operation, such as the antimission controversy, the bitter agitation of the slavery question, the troublesome presence of wandering Indian tribes, the Mormon migration, war, and the terrible cholera epidemic in St. Louis, which created alarm throughout the state. The population of the state at this time was almost a quarter of a million, of whom about 5,000 were Baptists.

Jeremiah Vardeman (the first moderator of the Missouri Baptist General Association), Fielding Wilhite, Thomas Fristoe, William Mansfield, Ebenezer Rodgers, Anderson Woods, James Suggett, and others were boldly holding forth the word of life and working toward a larger and stronger fellowship among Missouri Baptists. In 1833 Fristoe, Wilhite, and Rodgers met in Howard County in an effort to formulate some plan for the evangelization of the state. Travel was difficult, mail infrequent, post offices remote from many homes, and Baptist leaders were scattered. Despite these difficulties and the large personal expense involved, these men traveled throughout the state and then corresponded with those they could not visit in order to enlist the Baptists of Missouri in a larger co-operative relationship. As a result of this concerted effort, 31 messengers convened at Providence Baptist Church in Callaway County, Aug. 29 to Sept. 1, 1834, and laid the groundwork for the present Missouri Baptist General Association. PAUL WEBER

II. History of General Association. *Origin and constitution.*—Pursuant to the call of the preliminary meeting of 1834, messengers gathered in June, 1835, at Little Bonne Femme Baptist Church in Boone County, adopted a previously submitted constitution after making a few minor changes, and formally organized the Baptist Central Society of Missouri. The body changed its name in 1839 to the General Association of United Baptists and finally, in 1875, to the Missouri Baptist General Association.

The original constitution merely required that members of the society be "Baptists . . . in good standing in the churches." Through an amendment of 1852, a payment of dues for individual membership or a contribution from the church sending the individual qualified him for membership. A life membership for members paying a larger sum was also provided, and in 1881 a total of 51 such members attended the annual meeting. However, the concept of messengers from cooperating churches and district associations contributing funds enunciated in 1889 gradually replaced individual membership. The last of such "members at large" were seated in 1944. The requirements of financial contribution were dropped in 1914, and membership was defined as messengers from missionary Baptist churches in sympathy with the objects of the general association and from district associations wishing to co-operate. The general association has never adopted a doctrinal statement or creedal requirement for membership and has been singularly free, even in the North-South dispute, from controversial discussion.

The first stated object of the general association, to promote "the preaching of the gospel . . . within the bounds of the state," was extended a decade later to include "measures as may be calculated to extend the Kingdom of Christ in this State and throughout the world." Because of some opposition to missions, the general association retrenched by refusing to consider work outside the state but eventually committed itself to annual reports on foreign and home missions, to receive "contributions for the spread of the Gospel throughout the earth," and to promote Sunday school work through a standing board.

The earliest interest in incorporation of the state work appeared in 1848. After intermittent study the body, almost 50 years later, decided in 1884 to incorporate its boards, but not the general association itself. The original constitution of the state body established the principle of autonomy with a disclaimer to authority or power over churches or other associations. The 1928 constitutional revision, however, recognized the right of the general association to pass judgment on the character of the churches and district associations from which members come and to limit the number of messengers.

Denominational alignment.—The general association has variably aligned itself with Baptist bodies, both North and South. The close relationship between Missouri Baptists and Northern Baptists through John Mason Peck, pioneer missionary of the American Baptist Home Mission Society, probably had much to do with the 1841 decision of the general association to become auxiliary to the society. A report in 1844 refers to it as the "parent" society. Increasing Southern sentiment, however, led the state body to vote to become auxiliary to the Southern Baptist Convention only eight months after the Convention was chartered in 1845.

The divisive character of the Civil War and the protest by the general association against a loyalty oath for preachers required by a state constitutional amendment resulted in the organization in 1865 of a "loyal" body called the Missouri Baptist State Convention. The new group was auxiliary to the American Baptist Home Mission Society and Northern in sentiment. Largely through the patient statesmanship of Aaron H. Burlingham, the members of the state convention returned after only three annual meetings of their own. To promote harmony, the general association struck from its constitution the words "shall be auxiliary to the Southern Baptist Convention." The spirit of compromise so characterized the body from then on that it paved the way for the Missouri plan for double alignment in 1889. A resolution calling for unification of effort in the state and expressing hope in national unification passed in 1887. This led to the adoption of the above plan, which unified promotion of the work of the five mission boards that had agents in the state at the time. The committee which presented the plan, however, made it clear that a very large majority of members were in sympathy with the Southern Baptist Convention.

Following this movement to combine the state and out-of-state mission work under one board, the sentiment swung strongly toward the Southern Baptist Convention, till in 1919 only 16 churches were totally Northern, 146 were dividing mission offerings, and all the rest were Southern. By this time 61 district associations had taken action favoring single alignment with the Southern Baptist Convention. The vote which established single alignment that year was "with the clear and definite understanding that any individual or church preferring to co-operate with the Northern Baptist Convention is free to do so without hindrance or censure. . . ."

Administration.—The interim body empowered since 1835 to act for the general association between sessions, the executive board, originally consisted of five members at large and four officers of the state body acting ex officio. The board was to meet quarterly and report to the general association annually, practices continued till today. In 1878 this board was consolidated with the board of the State Sunday School Convention. The Missouri plan of double alignment of 1889 set up a separate board charged with raising and forwarding mission monies, but the general association dissolved both boards in 1915 and created a single board for the promotion of all its missionary, educational, and philanthropic work. Incorporated in 1917, this new board had all business and power to hold the property of the general association and its agencies consigned to it. A set of bylaws has governed the work of the board since 1922. Missouri Baptists in 1934 expanded the board to 30 members, limited the membership to one from any one church, and began a plan of rotation election. They increased the number to 51 in 1954.

The executive secretary today is the successor of many servants of the general association and the board who have labored through the years under various titles. The state body in 1836 elected Anderson Woods the first general agent to promote the objects of Missouri Baptists, but when he declined the appointment, they elected Kemp Scott. After the constitution was amended to permit it, and after several years of failure to find a capable person, Nathan Ayers in 1860 became the first corresponding secretary with a salary. Interrupted by the Civil War, the promotion of missions was resumed and co-operation with Southern Baptist agencies renewed in 1866, when Wiley J. Patrick began his work as head of the executive board. When Jehu M. Robinson resigned in 1870, the board elected William R. Rothwell as superintendent of domestic missions. Since that time the board has continued to elect its own head. It called Sylvester W. Marston to the office in 1873. After brief periods of service by several men, including John Decatur Murphy, W. Pope Yeaman, and Joseph C. Maple, Sanford M. Brown served sacrificially as superintendent of state missions almost uninterruptedly from 1887 to 1892. W. T. Campbell succeeded him (1892–97), and T. L. West served from 1897 to 1917.

The general association organized a second board in 1889, the Board of General Home and Foreign Missions, which it charged with soliciting funds for missions and forwarding them to the respective mission boards of Northern and Southern Baptists, in agreement with the newly adopted plan of double alignment. This new board elected two corresponding secretaries: Sam Frank Taylor for home missions and T. M. S. Kenney for foreign missions. W. L. Boyer and B. G. Tutt succeeded them in 1891 and continued five years in office until Manly J. Breaker became sole secretary and served till his death in 1908.

After several proposals for unification of the two boards, a new constitution in 1915 set up one board with a general superintendent of missions who, with other workers, was to promote all interests of the general association. Joe P. Jacobs served as the first secretary of this board until 1919. He was followed by O. L. Wood (1919–24), Arthur J. Barton (*q.v.*) (1924–26), J. B. Lawrence (1926–29), Edgar Godbold (*q.v.*) (1929–42), and T. W. Medearis (1942–54). Earl Harding, serving since 1954, was the first to serve under the present title of executive secretary.

The financial plan of the general association has resulted from considerably development through the years. The first collection for state missions, taken in the meeting of 1836, reached $51. The offerings increased to $303 the next year and to $792, 10 years later. The effects of the Civil War decreased gifts to a mere $124.55 in 1862, but from this low ebb it flowed upward to $2,591.10 in 1866, exclusive of gifts to out-of-state missions and education. The peak of $8,096.44 collected in 1870 resulted in enthusiastic commitments and overspending so that by 1874 a debt of $2,149.88 had accumulated. After this unpleasant experience a special committee in 1883 recommended a systematic plan of weekly giving to the churches' local expenses and four special offerings during the year for missions, one of which was to be for state missions. This emphasis on system resulted in a total gift of $12,491.28 to out-of-state causes, approximately $14,950.00 for district missions and education, and $27,449.07 for state missions and Sunday school work for 1886.

With the adoption of the Missouri Plan in 1889, whereby a board of missions of the general association received and forwarded gifts to home and foreign enterprises, North and South, the board set percentages of distribution for unmarked funds on the basis of previous designated gifts handled, and stimulated total gifts of $122,714.01 to all causes during its first year of operation. Although the next year a statement was made in the general association that "an awful money stringency prevailed in the country," gifts steadily increased for the next five years, thus revealing to Baptists the effectiveness of the plan. Leaders became concerned, however, over the cost of the plan and over the fact that only 16⅓ per cent of the Baptist churches were represented by gifts. But the picture improved steadily so that by 1919, the year of single alignment and the 75 Million Campaign, an estimated 40 per cent of the churches were participating. The budget for 1920, in anticipation of the income from the above campaign, was the first to allocate estimated gifts by percentages. The first unified budget in 1925 set a goal of $750,250, reserved 57.5 per cent for state interests, and forwarded the rest to Convention-wide causes to be distributed according to the Southern Baptist Convention percentages. However, the board actually received that year only $243,776.40 for all purposes. The name Cooperative Program was first used for the Missouri financial plan in 1929.

In the same year the board announced that, for the first time in a number of years, it had no outstanding debt. From then on, the general association intermittently increased the percentage for Convention-wide causes until the 1945 allocations specified 50 per cent each of distributable funds for state and Southern Baptist Convention objects. Missouri Baptists have retained this distribution percentage, while Cooperative Program receipts increased from $432,644.46 in 1945 to $1,682,712.34 in 1955. The general association enlarged its concept of the Cooperative Program by including a capital-needs item of $200,000 in the 1953 allocations to be distributed only after the current budget items were exceeded.

The problems of handling bequests to the general association were solved in the early days by appointing an agent to handle the funds. The 1848 *Minutes* carried on the title page a "form of bequest" to the general association. This body appointed three trustees that year to care for its capital funds. The general association itself disposed of the bequest of Judge Jeremiah H. Neal, the first one received, by voting in 1857 to have it remitted to William Jewell College, although two years later a committee reported that it could not legally be done. This experience and the receipt of a bequest for over $1,000 in 1892, which was to be permanently invested and the interest used for missions, pointed up the need for a more business-like method of handling funds. The single board of 1915 held all property of the general association and entrusted its administration to the association's treasurer until the chartering of the Missouri Baptist Foundation in 1946, when the board turned over the permanent funds to the foundation.

The central office for the work of the general association was for many years in the home town of the executive secretary of the board. Thus the board reported its location as Fayette till 1866, Columbia till 1873, St. Louis till 1878, and Mexico till at least 1898. After the combination of the mission boards, headquarters were established in various rented quarters in Kansas City until they were moved in July, 1949, to the board's own building in Jefferson City.

Methods of work.—The first constitution declared that the object of Missouri Baptists was "to adopt means and execute plans to promote the preaching of the gospel in the destitute churches and settlements within the bounds of the state." To first implement this object, the general association sent men "on horseback to ride each two months in the course of the year" into the vast area of the Missouri Valley to preach. Thirty-one such missionaries were reported in 1842. Empowered that same year by a constitutional amendment, the treasurer received gifts for foreign missions, the American Bible Society, and colportage, and reported them to the next annual session. City mission work began in 1845 when Samuel Howard Ford, whose salary was paid by the American Baptist Home Mission Society, started a work in St. Louis. With the appointment the next year of Noah Flood, a veteran pioneer missionary, to serve the Little Bonne Femme Association, the general association began assisting districts in their mission programs. Further co-operation with the American Indian Mission Association, the German Mission Society, and the Southern Baptist Home Mission Board established a pattern of joint work and outreach to other areas and groups.

The *Word and Way,* official journal of Missouri Baptists, had several privately owned predecessors. Twelve issues of *The Missouri Baptist* appeared in 1843, succeeded by a joint effort, *The Missouri and Illinois Baptist,* which died the following year. *The Western Watchman,* begun in May, 1848, also failed to last a year, but resumed in 1852 and continued publication until the Civil War caused its suspension. Another *Missouri Baptist* came forth in 1860 but lived less than a year and a half. The *Missouri Baptist Journal* and the *Record* were begun in 1866 and consolidated in 1868 under the name *Central Baptist.* The *Word and Way,* launched in 1896 by S. M. Brown and R. K. Maiden, bought out the *Central Baptist* in 1912. The executive board began a promotional monthly organ, the *Missouri Baptist Bulletin,* in Apr., 1917, but discontinued it at the end of 1933 and purchased space in the *Word and Way.* The general association bought the *Word and Way* Jan. 1, 1946, and since 1949 has printed it on the Missouri Baptist Press.

The general association instructed its missionaries in 1855 to give attention to Sunday school work. The growth of the Sunday school movement led to the organization of a Missouri Baptist Sunday School Convention in 1868. The general association elected a Sunday school board to take charge of this work in 1879 and eventually organized a department in this field. J. C. Hockett, Jr., in 1920 became the first secretary with promotional responsibilities for Sunday school and Baptist Young People's Union work. The latter organization had grown out of a meeting of young people at Pertle

Springs in 1891, who sent a delegation that year to the organization meeting of the B.Y.P.U. of America. The interest thus generated resulted in the organization of a state B.Y.P.U. in 1892, which the general association recognized as a valuable auxiliary. J. Marvin Crowe, who first served six years as associate sercetary in the Sunday School and Training Union Department, became the first full-time Training Union secretary in 1942, when the original department was reorganized into two separate departments of work.

The first unified work of Missouri Baptist women began in 1877 at Lexington with the organization of the Missouri Baptist Woman's Foreign Missionary Society, a union of 36 local and regional societies, with Mrs. O. P. Moss as president. This organization in 1885 dropped the word "Foreign" from its name in order to comply with the general association's recommendation that the women extend their efforts to other objects. By 1889 the women's meetings had grown so large that they had to be held in a different place and at a different time from the general association. As a part of the movement for consolidation, the society was dissolved in 1899 and the work continued under a Woman's Central Committee of Missions appointed by the Board of Home and Foreign Missions. Five years later the first full-time salaried secretary, Eleanor Mare, was employed, and the committee was renamed the Woman's Mission Board. In 1915, 10 women members of the executive board were made responsible for directing the women's work. The Missouri Woman's Missionary Union was organized in 1923 as an auxiliary to the general association. This organization met simultaneously with the general association but reported separately from the board for several years. Since 1930, however, the annual meetings have again been held separately from the general association.

The Missouri Baptist Historical Society, organized in 1885, was the second such society in the Southern Baptist Convention. It has served Missouri Baptists by collecting historical materials in the library of William Jewell College, Liberty, by assisting at commemorative services, and by co-operating in publishing historical books.

The board employed W. P. Brooks in 1888 as a full-time missionary among his own Negro people. The work since then has been largely one of co-operation with, and donation to, the Negro Baptists' own program. It was expanded in 1955 to a joint program with the Home Mission Board with a full-time worker, D. B. Hoskins.

The Missouri Baptist Assembly, organized in 1917, grew out of the assemblies which the B.Y.P.U. began to conduct in 1906 at Pertle Springs and continued at Arcadia Heights in 1909. The constitution of the new state assembly called for the approval of its board of managers by the board of the general association. The assembly ceased to operate in 1930 because of insufficient funds. The board purchased the assembly at Hollister in 1945 and has since operated a state assembly under the former name, Missouri Baptist Assembly. Other assemblies organized by regional groups were reported from time to time to the general association: Southwestern Assembly at Ozark and William Jewell Assembly at Liberty no longer exist; Southern (also called Southwest) Assembly at Van Buren and Baptist Hill Assembly (formerly Inter-State) near Mount Vernon still continue service. More recently other regional assemblies have been begun: North Missouri, now Grand Oaks, near Chillicothe; and East Missouri at the Cuiver River State Park near Troy.

The general association has in the present century expanded the scope of its work to include departments of laymen's work, student work, and church music. As early as 1904, a Conference of Baptist Laymen pointed out a need for an organized program of work for laymen. A committee of laymen in 1907 secured the approval of the general association for its recommendation that there be a Laymen's League in each church. After 1927 the state body appointed for the promotion of laymen's work Courts Redford, who served also as a stewardship secretary. The first full-time Brotherhood secretary, Robert J. West, began his work on June 1, 1946. The first student work was done by Jessie V. Roth, employed by the board in 1918 as a "college visitor" to denominational and secular schools. Realizing the need and importance of this work, the board in 1924 proposed a student secretary for Missouri. After several part-time secretaries had paved the way, W. O. Vaught, Jr., began full-time Baptist Student Union work on May 1, 1935. The first church music report was made to the association in 1940, and a decade later James Ferguson came to begin the Department of Church Music.

Institutions.—Missouri Baptists have also developed numerous educational and benevolent institutions. An education society, organized in 1841 to assist young men preparing for the ministry, became in 1858 the Board of Ministerial Education of the general association. It was also a forerunner of special committees and commissions appointed to study the educational institutions operated by Baptists and to make recommendations.

William Jewell College was the first educational institution to be organized and related to the general association. This body appointed a committee in 1843 to study a proposal by William Jewell of Columbia, in which he offered a sum of $10,000 for an institution of learning, provided the Baptists would raise the rest needed. In the general association the offer was debated, declined, restudied, and finally accepted. The committee applied to the state legislature for a charter, which was granted on Feb. 27, 1849. At Boonville on Aug. 21 of the same year, a group of donors voted to locate the college at Liberty and to name it in honor of Jewell. The college began its first session Jan. 1, 1850, and has continued with few interruptions for over 100 years. The trustees reported regularly and directly to the general association and are now elected by it.

By 1948 at least 36 other institutions of learning had been reported to the general association as being operated by Baptists or Baptist groups. A committee in 1883 compiled statistics of 11 schools under Baptist control, disclosing that they held $302,000 in buildings, $176,000 in endowment, employed 81 teachers, and enrolled 1,239 students. Seven of these schools—the Baptist Female College at Lexington, Hardin College at Mexico, McCune College at Louisiana, Grand River College at Edinburg, Monroe Institute at Monroe City, Palmyra Seminary at Palmyra, and Pierce City College at Pierce City—have since ceased to exist. Stephens College for women, chartered in 1856 and adopted by the general association in 1870, was dropped as an affiliated Missouri Baptist institution in 1952. The Will Mayfield College, which grew out of the Mayfield-Smith Academy that was organized in 1878, served the Baptists at Marble Hill before it closed in 1930 because of insufficient funds. Out of the 11 schools of 1883, only William Jewell and two junior colleges, Hannibal-LaGrange and Southwest College, remain as Missouri Baptist institutions.

LaGrange College, sponsored by the Wyaconda Association, opened Sept. 15, 1858, and first reported to the general association the next year. The state body included it in its reports of colleges and since 1926 has elected its board. To enable the college to move to Hannibal, Mo., and merge with Hannibal College, a new charter was secured Sept. 22, 1928, and the two institutions' boards of trustees voted to merge under the present name, Hannibal-LaGrange College.

Southwest Baptist College held its first session in Lebanon, Sept. 17, 1878, with James R. Maupin as president and A. S. Ingman as cofounder. The Southwest Baptist Convention secured a charter for the school on Mar. 19, 1879, and the same year both reported to the general association and moved the college to Bolivar, Mo. The institution's revised charter of 1921 provides that its trustees be elected by the general association.

Under the name Southeast Missouri Baptist Foundation, the Baptists of that area began in 1839 at Cape Girardeau the first chair of Bible in Missouri. The board of the general association organized others at Columbia in 1948, at Warrensburg in 1949, and at Springfield in 1950. After the Cape Girardeau property was transferred to the general association in 1951, these four centers adjacent to state educational institutions continued to offer courses in Bible, seminary extension courses, and Baptist Student Union activities.

The philanthropic work of the general association includes hospitals, a children's home, and a home for aged. The Missouri Baptist Hospital in St. Louis, a continuation of a private institution begun in 1884 by W. H. Mayfield, was incorporated Dec. 16, 1890, and since then has operated under the control of the general association. A movement begun in 1921 to locate a Baptist hospital in Kansas City finally resulted in the incorporation on July 18, 1945, of the Baptist Memorial Hospital. The hospital board offered to affiliate with the general association in 1948 but was censured and repudiated by the general association for accepting Federal funds. However, in 1956 before the hospital was completed and put in operation, differences were resolved, and the board of the general association accepted the property and has since exercised full control of the hospital. The Missouri Baptist Children's Home began its work in 1886 in St. Louis. The home purchased its present site at Pattonville and moved there in 1905. It extended its services to western Missouri in 1953 by opening a Kansas City office. The Home for Aged Baptists at Ironton, the first such institution among Southern Baptists, began service May 6, 1913, purchased its present site in 1919, and was adopted by the general association in 1923. CARL GOODSON

III. Program of Work of Missouri Baptists. ORGANIZATION. *Purpose.*—The purpose of the Missouri Baptist General Association is to provide a convenient means for the co-operation of the churches in their work, and to be an efficient agency for their enlistment in missions, education, and benevolence. The relationship between the general association and the churches is fraternal and co-operative. The state body exercises no authority over the churches and does not interfere with their complete autonomy and independence.

Membership.—Any missionary Baptist church which is in sympathy with the objects of the Missouri Baptist General Association may have one messenger plus one additional messenger for every 100 members or fraction thereof above 100. No church is entitled to more than 15 messengers. Each co-operative district association is entitled to two messengers. The general association has the right to decide whether a person is qualified to be a member and to refuse to seat as a messenger any person whom it deems disqualified for personal reasons or because of the character or attitude of the church or association to which the member belongs.

Officers.—The officers of the general association include the moderator, assistant moderator, recording secretary, and statistical secretary. The latter two may be held by one person if deemed best. These officers serve from the close of the annual meeting during which they are elected until the close of the next annual meeting of the association, or until their successors are elected. The moderator may serve two years and is eligible to serve again after another or others have occupied the same position. The officers of the association are chosen by ballot, each messenger casting one ballot, with a majority of the votes cast necessary for election. In case of only one nomination, the vote may be taken viva voce.

The executive board.—As of 1954 the executive board consists of 51 members. One third of this number are elected each year for a term of three years. No church may have more than one elected member on the board at any one time. Board membership is limited to two consecutive terms. One is eligible for re-election after one year. An unexpired term counts as a whole term. No salaried employee of the board nor any employee of any institution fostered by the board may be a member, nor may a wife or husband of such employee. If a member misses two consecutive meetings without a good and acceptable reason, his position on the board is declared vacant. Vacancies occurring during the year are filled by the board until the next annual meeting of the general association. The board holds four meetings annually, with a majority of the entire membership constituting a quorum. The board elects a chairman, vice-chairman, and recording secretary, who serve without pay. The board also elects a treasurer, who may be the executive secretary, and who shall have custody of all monies coming into possession of the board. The treasurer of the executive board is also the treasurer of the general association. His accounts are to be properly audited, and he must give such bond as the board shall require. The constitution grants the board authority to adopt all necessary regulations for the conduct of its business and to appoint such committees as it may deem wise and requires an annual written report of its proceedings to be made to the general association. The board has full power and authority to act for the general association in the interim of sessions of that body in such matters that may arise affecting the interests fostered by it. This is not to be construed as authorizing the board to reverse any action of the general association or to do anything contrary to the constitution. The executive board is to work in co-operation both with the district associations of the state and with the Southern Baptist Convention. The chairman of the executive board appoints an executive committee which has charge of the business of the board between its quarterly meetings, making reports of its work at each meeting of the board. The executive board has the power to describe the duties and what business may be transacted by the executive committee between the meetings of the board. The executive committee is considered the budget and personnel committee, thus charged with the responsibility of selecting and employing all personnel in all departments of work of the general association. An annual budget, including both state and convention-wide objects, is presented to the general association by the committee. The board has general oversight over all educational and benevolent institutions owned, operated, or maintained in whole or in part by the denomination. It is to keep itself fully informed as to the conditions and needs of these institutions and shall promote said institutions in every way possible.

An executive secretary is elected by the board to superintend the entire work of the executive board in all its departments and to have general charge of the educational, missionary, and benevolent interests of the state. The executive board also has authority to elect such other department heads and workers as it deems necessary to carry on the full program. It is the duty of these department heads and workers to work under the direction of, and in co-operation with, the executive secretary of Missouri Baptists; to aid him in keeping the interests and institutions, both state and convention-wide, before the churches and district associations, and in seeking to enlist them in the active support of all the work.

DEPARTMENTS OF WORK. The work of the Missouri Baptist General Association is a co-operative venture through various departments: Sunday School, Training Union, Brotherhood, Evangelism, Woman's Missionary Union, *Word and Way,* Music, Missouri Baptist Press, Baptist Student Union, Stewardship and Missions.

Department of Sunday School Work.—This department is responsible for helping the churches enrol every member of every family for Bible study, for helping the churches enlist and train workers, and for showing the churches how to use the Sunday school to accomplish the work of a church. The department employs a department secretary, an associate secretary, and an office secretary. It functions in close co-operation with all other departments in the promotion of the total program of Missouri Baptists under the leadership of the state executive secretary.

Department of Training Union Work.—Under the direction of the state secretary, the Training Union Department sponsors and promotes a state Training Union convention. The convention officers help plan the programs and preside at the meetings. When the department was organized in 1921, about 200 churches had probably 287 individual Young People's Unions. As of 1954, 1,185 churches had Training Unions that included all age groups. Some are organized by departments and unions, while others have from one union to a union for each age group. Since 1946 the department has conducted annual Training Union leadership weeks at the Missouri Baptist Assembly, Hollister, Mo. This state department includes the department secretary and an office secretary.

Department of Brotherhood.—A full-time secretary directs the activities of this department, which is designed to organize and promote the work of Baptist laymen in the churches. The department operates on an annual budget. The state executive committee makes the apportionments from funds provided through the state mission budget by the Cooperative Program.

The department co-operates with the Baptist Brotherhood Commission of the Southern Baptist Convention. The state Royal Ambassador secretary is associated with this department and conducts his work in co-operation with it and the Woman's Missionary Union Department.

The Brotherhoods of the state have organized the Missouri Baptist Brotherhood Convention, which meets annually for information, inspiration, and fellowship. It has no legislative powers and exercises no authority over the state department. However, the state convention and the state department work harmoniously in projecting promotional and organizational programs. The personnel consists of a department secretary, a Royal Ambassador secretary, and an office secretary.

Department of Evangelism.—Created in 1947 to promote evangelism in Missouri and to work in full co-operation with the Evangelism Department of the Home Mission Board of the Southern Baptist Convention, this department seeks to promote mass evangelism through a simultaneous crusade in every association each year, to have a revival in each church every year, and to promote a program of personal evangelism. During the period since the organization of the department, 1948–54, the number of baptisms has increased from 16,109 to 19,560.

Department personnel, as of 1956, consists of a secretary and a half-time office secretary. The secretary promotes the statewide evangelistic conference, holds revival meetings, and promotes the Southern Baptist program of evangelism. The program for the future is: (1) To follow the Southern Baptist program of evangelism; (2) To seek to enlist every church in the simultaneous crusade; (3) To seek to have baptisms in every church during the coming year; (4) To intensify Missouri Baptists' program of conservation of results of crusades; (5) To co-operate in the whole program of Missouri Baptists.

Department of Church Music.—Formed to organize and promote work in the church music field throughout the state, the department seeks to provide adequate church music education for leadership as well as for everyone who participates. Emphasis is placed on total participation by the entire congregation. To meet the need for training, church music leadership schools are planned on a statewide basis. Associational and local church music schools are held. Personnel for these events is selected from ministers of music serving Missouri Baptist churches, music teachers, and others who are qualified to teach subjects selected from the Church Music Training Course outlined by the Church Music Department of the Southern Baptist Convention. The department employs a department secretary and an office secretary.

Department of Stewardship and Missions.—Organized on July 12, 1954, by the executive board of the Missouri Baptist General Association, this department co-operates with associational superintendents of missions, offering them whatever assistance possible. It promotes and conducts association-wide mission conferences, schools of missions, stewardship revivals, evangelistic revivals, and local church field surveys. These are also promoted on the individual church level. Another important phase of the work of this department is the reviving of dead churches. Each year a number of these churches have been revived and are now ministering to the needs of their communities. The church finance work of the department has given assistance through the Tithers Enlistment Visitation program, budget making, and budget raising. Loans are also made to churches which are starting new missions. Each year a retreat is held for the associational moderators and missionaries, enabling them to make better plans. In addition rural conferences are held each year in the 10 divisions of the state. The personnel of this department includes a department secretary, an associate secretary, two field representatives, and two office secretaries.

Department of Student Work.—The state student secretary and the local directors of student activity are selected by the executive board of the Missouri Baptist General Association upon recommendation of the personnel committee in consultation with the executive secretary. The Department of Student Work has so progressed through the years that there are now 15 full-time campus directors of student activity, five of whom teach Bible; two part-time associates, a stenographer and a state secretary, who are seeking to minister to more than 8,000 Baptist college students through 28 Baptist Student Union organizations. The goal of the department is to enlist every Baptist college student in the local college Baptist church.

Missions Fund Expenditure for Missouri Baptist General Association for the Year Ending Sept. 30, 1955.

Administrative	$ 67,167.68
Executive Board	4,765.46
General Association	31,216.10
Co-operative Payroll	28,757.36
Co-operative Missions	85,962.95
Department of Bible	41,152.66
Brotherhood Department	10,714.15
Church Music Department	10,365.39
Evangelism Department	10,497.35
Stewardship and Missions Department	35,432.67
Baptist Student Union Department	28,345.70
Sunday School Department	17,472.00
Training Union Department	10,501.66
Woman's Missionary Union Department	32,108.89
Word and Way	9,999.98
Appropriation for Oct., Nov., and Dec., 1954	26,359.66
TOTAL EXPENSES	$ 450,819.66
Total Budget for 1956	$1,850,000.00

FRED E. NEIGER

IV MISSOURI STATISTICAL SUMMARY

Year	*Associations*	*Churches*	*Church Membership*	*Baptisms*	*S. S. Enrolment*	*V.B.S. Enrolment*	*T. U. Enrolment*	*W.M.U. Enrolment*	*Brotherhood Enrolment*	*Mission Gifts*	*Total Gifts*	*Value Church Property*	*State Capital Worth*
1830													(Explanation: This column includes total value of Schools, Children's Homes, Hospitals, Foundation, Buildings, etc.)
1840													
1850													
1860													
1870													
1880	70	1,445	89,915	5,982									
1890	71	1,617	112,296	9,773	52,480					$ 9,815.31	$ 511,608.04	$ 1,841,699.00	
1900	76	1,862	144,561	8,113	97,097					45,999.06	468,000.16	2,118,672.25	
1905	79	1,820	156,014	11,394	90,682					81,786.36	754,946.47	2,716,935.00	
1910	80	1,886	184,999	10,970	101,353					141,488.22	1,042,606.59	4,288,107.00	
1915	81	1,886	193,347	13,878	128,440					151,554.38	940,756.91	5,314,852.00	
1920	81	1,850	196,867	9,545						195,124.39			
1925	86	1,937	226,848	7,155	178,925					233,283.17	3,451,184.16	11,483,812.00	
1930	86	1,786	230,751	11,414	180,587					130,032.47	2,698,466.33	15,442,853.00	
1931	85	1,778	237,096	13,374	184,568					252,505.87	2,394,892.89	15,611,955.00	
1932	85	1,746	240,958	12,813	189,165					228,079.53	1,934,646.85	15,074,137.00	
1933	85	1,741	243,372	12,050	188,692			25,347		175,586.19	1,625,560.52	17,715,195.00	
1934	85	1,728	247,867	12,309	193,543			26,339		93,243.33	1,541,996.21	14,535,818.00	
1935	84	1,701	251,446	11,862	192,474		46,333	27,261		187,157.55	1,652,487.83	13,989,355.00	
1936	84	1,716	256,394	10,890	193,268			25,559		194,398.69	1,781,149.76	15,039,995.00	
1937	84	1,719	257,600	10,565	198,832			34,264		206,657.77	1,858,004.79	14,776,112.00	
1938	84	1,714	263,110	13,251	204,680			39,637		225,827.92	2,071,050.71	14,281,910.00	
1939	84	1,704	270,696	14,633	204,999			42,324		253,219.29	2,091,462.32	14,123,727.00	
1940	83	1,718	277,305	12,445	207,549			43,227		272,273.07	2,340,811.26	14,159,843.00	
1941	83	1,730	284,891	12,079	204,503	42,358		42,599		310,373.90	2,606,984.51	14,822,518.00	
1942	83	1,724	290,863	11,431	194,765	40,753		40,062		372,623.81	3,257,029.80	15,237,527.00	
1943	83	1,726	295,995	9,426	186,872	31,920		38,701		467,886.60	3,337,257.67	15,446,153.00	
1944	83	1,732	302,642	11,376	188,940	39,266				616,247.97	3,980,269.66	16,015,255.00	
1945	83	1,734	309,485	12,683	192,744	51,630	32,822	43,807		722,826.08	4,507,179.76	16,503,700.00	
1946	83	1,740	316,809	12,406	202,621	64,073	34,155	46,644		887,278.85	5,282,215.52	18,097,475.00	
1947	83	1,727	322,559	14,097	198,255	77,191	35,327	46,240		969,775.10	6,892,030.64	18,397,212.00	
1948	83	1,750	339,956	16,109	218,859	87,883	42,272	52,768	9,601	1,525,080.64	7,529,331.23	17,320,829.00	
1949	83	1,750	342,272	16,859	224,283	91,411	50,923	54,927	12,247	1,482,212.11	8,742,000.61	24,023,058.17	$ 8,786,186.54
1950	83	1,786	349,425	21,082	251,183	97,103	58,988	60,311	12,119	1,689,628.38	10,443,666.30	28,153,521.69	9,164,591.40
1951	83	1,713	358,852	16,266	257,958	100,381	63,601	61,610	13,184	1,912,838.15	11,565,957.95	33,465,722.86	9,914,490.49
1952	83	1,724	369,636	18,178	266,436	103,825	66,519	64,911	14,563	2,286,164.78	11,951,763.87	35,741,707.41	10,883,133.38
1953	83	1,740	383,125	18,457	276,218	114,083	72,412	64,412	15,225	2,550,722.00	13,342,433.00	41,561,642.00	11,386,562.76
1954	83	1,727	387,770	19,560	310,163	131,947	82,089	72,639	15,553	2,665,826.00	15,293,702.00	43,868,930.00	12,711,134.15

Bibliography: D. Benedict, *A General History of the Baptist Denomination in America and Other Parts of the World* (1850). W. Cathcart, ed., *The Baptist Encyclopedia* (1880); *The Baptist Encyclopedia* (1883). R. S. Douglass, *History of Missouri Baptists* (1934). J. W. Dowdy, *Fifty-five Years of Missionary Administration in Missouri* (n.d.). R. S. Duncan, *A History of the Baptists in Missouri* (1882). J. C. Maple, *Missouri Baptist Centennial 1906* (1907); *Semi-Centennial Memorial, Missouri Baptist General Association* (1885). J. C. Maple and R. P. Rider, *Missouri Baptist Biography,* Vol. I (1914), Vol. II (1916). E. F. Merriam, *A History of American Baptist Missions* (1913). O. W. Nixon, *Whitman's Ride Through Savage Lands* (1905). A. W. Payne, *What Mean These Stones?* (1934). W. H. Sims, "It's the Team Play That Counts," *The Church Musician* (Nov., 1954); "A Worthy Program of Church Music Education," *The Church Musician* (July, 1956). W. F. Switzler, *Illustrated History of Missouri* (1879). H. E. Truex, *Baptists in Missouri* (1904). E. M. Violette, *A History of Missouri* (1918). W. P. Yeaman, *A History of the Missouri Baptist General Association* (1899).

MISSOURI BAPTIST HISTORICAL SOCIETY. The preliminary meeting which resulted in the organization of the Missouri Baptist Historical Society was held at William Jewell College in Liberty, Mo., on June 10, 1885. Out of this meeting of Baptist leaders, a committee was appointed to draft a proposed constitution and present it at the meeting of the general association in October. The constitution was adopted and a permanent organization was effected on Oct. 24, 1885. The first officers were Professor A. F. Fleet of the University of Missouri, president; J. C. Armstrong, vice-president; J. R. Eaton of William Jewell College, secretary. A board of managers was also named at this meeting. Life memberships were offered at $10 and annual memberships at $1. Chief objectives of this new society were to collect valuable historical materials of all kinds, to stimulate an interest in Missouri Baptist history, and to provide an address on Baptist history at the annual sessions of the general association.

From the very first the society received an encouraging response, especially in the assembling of a valuable collection of Baptist historical materials. These were at first stored in a vault, but after a short while William Jewell College offered to provide space for the collection. Since that time this increasingly valuable collection has been housed in a fireproof building on the campus. This collection, now thoroughly organized and officially catalogued, is regarded as one of the most valuable in the Southern Baptist Convention. The collection contains practically complete collections of the minutes of district associations and of the Missouri general association, volumes of sermons, many manuscripts, church record books, individual church histories, and histories of various associations. It also includes portraits of many Baptist leaders and a collection of historical materials such as gavels, chairs, etc.

A unique service of the society is the publishing of five volumes of biographical sketches of Missouri Baptist leaders. H. I. HESTER

MISSOURI BAPTIST HOSPITAL. Begun in 1884 in the home of Dr. and Mrs. W. H. Mayfield, the hospital was first known as the Mayfield Sanitarium. In 1890 Missouri Baptists joined St. Louis Baptists in the purchase of the hospital, and on Dec. 16, 1890, the Missouri Baptist Sanitarium was incorporated as a self-perpetuating association of 50 Missouri Baptists. The present site of the hospital, 919 North Taylor Avenue, St. Louis 8, was occupied that year; and there was a medical staff of three physicians. The present Missouri Baptist Hospital (name changed in 1929) consists of five adjoining buildings, the first of which was erected in 1892 and the last in 1945. It cares for approximately 13,000 patients annually in the following departments: internal medicine, general surgery, obstetrics, psychiatry, pediatrics, urology, orthopedics, gynecology, otolaryngology, neurosurgery, dermatology, and ophthalmology. The following ancillary services are provided inpatients and outpatients: clinical laboratories, pharmacy, physical medicine and rehabilitation, X-ray, and blood bank. The medical staff is composed of 300 physicians representing all medical and surgical specialties. The school of nursing, now fully accredited and enrolling 200 students, was organized in 1895. There is also a fully accredited School of Medical Technology enrolling seven students annually. C. E. Copeland serves as hospital administrator.

The Missouri Baptist Hospital is an affiliate of the Missouri Baptist General Association. Members of the Missouri Baptist Hospital Association are nominated by a nominating committee of the Missouri Baptist Hospital Association and a nominating committee of the Missouri Baptist General Association; they are then elected by the hospital association in annual session and approved by the general association at its annual convention. All members of this governing body must be Baptists residing in Missouri and active members of Baptist churches co-operating with the general association. The hospital administrator is appointed by the board of managers.

Including houses in which employees live, there are 15 buildings and fixed assets totaling $3,174,998.17. There is no capital indebtedness on hospital property. The bed capacity of the hospital is 525, and the daily patient census is 351. The hospital is fully approved for rotating internship, three years residency in surgery, two years residency in pathology, and one year residencies in internal medicine, obstetrics-gynecology, and urology. The institution is accredited by the Joint Commission on Accreditation of Hospitals. Since there are adequate hospital facilities in St. Louis for Negroes, they are not admitted to this hospital; they are, however, given emergency treatment on an outpatient basis. In 1954 hospital patient income was $2,287,040.35; income from the Cooperative

Program was $33,137.40; designated gifts totaled $80,749.64; and free work totaled $117,695.81.

HELEN V. TREJBAL

MISSOURI BAPTIST INDIAN MISSION ASSOCIATION. Organized, Aug. 31, 1846, auxiliary to the American Indian Mission Association whose headquarters were at Louisville, Ky. The object was the "civilization and evangelization of the aborigines of this country." This was pre-eminently a Missouri institution until 1854, when it withdrew its co-operation with the American Indian Mission Association and became an independent society under the title of the Western Baptist Indian Mission Association.

MERLE A. MITCHELL

MISSOURI BAPTIST JOURNAL. A paper proposed late in 1865 by editor John Hill Luther and his associate R. M. Rhoades, and first issued at Palmyra, Mo., Jan. 8, 1866. Luther and other enthusiastic promoters enlisted 1,000 subscribers for the first edition. Circulation of the paper, which had as its motto "The Faith, the Ordinances, the Life," continued to increase until the middle of the third volume when the *Journal* was consolidated with *The Record*.

J. R. BLACK

MISSOURI BAPTIST MONTHLY, THE. A paper established in 1842 as a result of interest expressed by the Missouri Baptist General Association. Editors Isaac T. Hinton and R. S. Thomas, who issued the first number in Sept., 1842, published 12 numbers in all at a loss of $100.45. Thus in 1843 a plan of co-operation with the Illinois state convention was arranged, which resulted in the *Missouri and Illinois Baptist*.

J. R. BLACK

MISSOURI EXTINCT BAPTIST SCHOOLS. The Baptist education ideal, "education—the high road to missions," was brought to Missouri by missionaries John Mason Peck (*q.v.*) and James E. Welch who, in 1819, opened the first non-Catholic school in Missouri in St. Louis. The purpose of this school, known as the Western Mission School, was to train teachers and preachers. Since this beginning, Missouri Baptists have established three types of schools: those sponsored by associations, those sponsored by smaller organizations of Baptists, and those sponsored by private individuals associated with a Baptist church principle.

Antebellum schools were Bonne Femme Academy, Columbia (1829–45); Pleasant Ridge College, Weston (1850–60); and Bethel Baptist Seminary, Palmyra (1852–60). These were casualties of the Civil War.

Female colleges were organized in Liberty and were operated under several names, e.g., Liberty Female Seminary (1838–54); Clay Seminary (1855–79); and Liberty Female Institute and College (1852–64). Other private institutions for women also failed, but the problem of female education in this area was solved when William Jewell College became coeducational.

Mt. Pleasant College, Huntsville (1839–82), served hundreds of students in the north central area of the state. It was destroyed by fire. Lexington Baptist Female College (1851–1916) produced Missouri's first women missionaries for the foreign fields: Mrs. Anne Luther Bagby (*q.v.*), Miss Sophie Lanneau, Miss Mollie McMinn, and Mrs. Margaret Savage Loe. Grand River College, first located in Edinburg (1850–92), was later moved to Gallatin (1892–1915). This school was merged with William Jewell College, Liberty. Other schools of the middle 19th century period were: Kansas City Seminary, Kansas City (1855–60); Trenton College, Trenton (1858–60); Saline Associational Institute, Miami (1858–60); Chillicothe Seminary, Chillicothe (1858–60); Cooper Institute, Boonville (1850–65); and Monroe Institute, Monroe City (1860–82).

During the Reconstruction era several colleges were organized but were of short duration. These included Alexandria College, Alexandria (1870–81); St. Louis Seminary, St. Louis (1870–74); Clarksburg College, Clarksburg (1877–1907); St. Joseph Female College, St. Joseph (1877–81); Pierce City Baptist College, Pierce City (1877–1903); McCune College (also Louisiana Baptist College and Pardee College), Louisiana (1869–95); Farmington College, Farmington (1886–1902); and Webb City College, Webb City (1894–1903). These colleges succumbed as a result of competition of the high school movement and because of lack of Baptist support.

Hardin College, Mexico (1873–1930), a well-endowed, highly rated scholastic school, and Will Mayfield College, Marble Hill (1878–1925), were lost through failure of the 75 Million Campaign. Stephens College, Columbia (1856–1935), after more than 75 years of operation, passed from denominational control to a private corporation.

Following World War II abortive attempts were made to found two junior colleges: Missouri Baptist College, Poplar Bluff, and Moark College, West Plain.

BIBLIOGRAPHY: R. S. Douglass, *History of the Baptists in Missouri* (1934). R. S. Duncan, *A History of the Baptists in Missouri* (1882). *Semi-centennial Memorial of Missouri Baptist General Association* (1885). F. C. Shoemaker, *A History of Missouri and Missourians* (1927); *Missouri and Missourians, Land of Contrasts and People of Achievements,* 5 vols. (1943). W. Williams, *History of North West Missouri,* 3 vols. (1915); ed., *History of North East Missouri* (1913).

MONTE PETERSON

MISSOURI HOME FOR AGED BAPTISTS. Beginning in Feb., 1913, when a Baptist preacher, Milford Riggs (1866–1947), led in organizing trustees, the Missouri Home for Aged Baptists was chartered in Ironton, Mo., in April of that year. Occupying a rented building and depending on charity, the home received its first guest on May 6; by the end of 1913 the guests numbered 28. The home was adopted by the General Association of Missouri Baptists in

1917, and in 1919 the trustees purchased a scenic site of 175 acres near Ironton. A fireproof four-story red granite building was erected at a cost of $200,000, and in 1923 the home moved to its new location. During the economic depression, however, many pledges were unpaid; and, hopelessly in debt, the home was sold by creditors at the courthouse door, Apr. 20, 1935. In an effort to retain the home, D. J. Scott, a Baptist preacher, led in a campaign to organize the Home for Aged Baptists, which was incorporated June 8, 1935. On June 22, with 70 guests remaining in the home, the property was repurchased, and Scott was elected superintendent. Following Scott's retirement, John H. Burney was elected superintendent on June 9, 1953.

The home is governed by 21 Baptist trustees elected by the general association. Its 100 guests, 60 of whom are wheel-chair patients or bedridden, are dependent upon charity and are received by church application. The annual budget is $900 per capita. Approximately half of the home's support comes through the Cooperative Program and the remainder through gifts, bequests, and an endowment of $500,000. In 1954 property was appraised at $660,000.

JOHN H. BURNEY

MISSOURI UNIVERSITY CHAIR OF BIBLE, Columbia. After a year of research by a special committee, the executive board of the Missouri Baptist General Association in 1947 recommended the establishment of a chair of Bible at the University of Missouri. Strategically located, property was purchased, and Howard P. Colson was employed as professor of Bible. In 1951 the present building was incorporated into a larger and more spacious center at the cost of $145,000. Fred Neiger was professor of Bible in 1956. CLIFFORD INGLE

MITCHELL COLLEGIATE INSTITUTE. Located at Bakersville, N. C. The name was changed in 1909 to Bowman Academy.

D. L. SMILEY

MIXED MARRIAGE. Marriage by a Christian to a person outside his own particular communion, or to a person of a different faith or of no faith. Southern Baptists have warned of the threat to harmony in such marriages through publications, public addresses and forums, and formal resolutions such as that adopted by the Southern Baptist Convention in 1951. While any incompatability of religious experience or viewpoint can be a threat to marriage, even between two of the same religious affiliation, Southern Baptists recognize that the most serious problem is posed by the policy of the Roman Catholic Church in their widely publicized "nuptial vows" requiring the non-Catholic party to a mixed marriage to agree that their children shall be brought up as Catholics. In the 1951 resolution the Convention affirmed "the sacredness of an individual religious faith in which both husband and wife must be equally free," and urged "our young people to refuse to enter upon such agreements."

Southern Baptist policy with regard to mixed marriages operates within the principle of individual soul freedom and on the ground that each person is competent to make his own individual approach to God without going through any intermediary. Thus any alteration or continuation of his religious affiliation should be based on personal conviction and not on ecclesiastical requirement or family expediency. There should of course be sincere concern for the spiritual well-being of the family and for the partner of different or no faith, but this concern should not be based on any legalistic requirement, but should be expressed in humility and hopefulness, consistently but not objectionably. Then any change of religious affiliation will result from personal conviction in the free exercise of soul liberty.

See also MARRIAGE AND THE FAMILY.

JOE W. BURTON

MOBILE MONITOR (1837–40? 1841?). A weekly edited by George Felix Heard, the paper was founded in 1837. It ceased publication in 1840 or the following year when its editor, pastor of the Baptist church, Mobile, Ala., moved to Texas. RAY M. ATCHINSON

MODERNISM. See LIBERALISM.

MONOTHEISM. This term refers to belief in one divine Being, will, and administration. The self-existent and absolute Being is undivided and indivisible, an intelligent, rational, personal Entity who is sovereign over all the universe. His absolute supremacy excludes the existence of any other than dependent creatures and forces.

God, being the creator of all things, is not only in all things but above all things. He is more than the life-producing and life-sustaining Energy of the universe, for he is the Mind that purposes and directs the use of this energy. As supreme authority God exercises ultimate control over all of his creation. All forces represented by nature and man are of God and subordinate to his will.

The Christian belief in the existence of only one God is adequately supported by both the Old and New Testaments. In Deuteronomy 6:4 it is written, "Hear, O Israel: the Lord our God is one Lord." Isaiah 44:6 declares: "Thus saith the Lord the King of Israel, and his redeemer the Lord of Hosts; I am the first, and I am the last; and beside me there is no God." Addressing the Father, Christ said, "And this is life eternal, that they might know thee the only true God" (John 17:3).

See also GOD.

BIBLIOGRAPHY: W. N. Clarke, *The Christian Doctrine of God* (1909). W. T. Conner, *Christian Doctrine* (1937).

N. W. CARPENTER, JR.

MONTAGUE, ANDREW PHILIP (b. Essex County, Va., Sept. 27, 1854; d. Panama City,

Fla., Dec. 3, 1928). College president. He was the son of Howard Williams and Mildred Columbia (Broaddus) Montague. His father and both grandfathers were Baptist ministers.

Following graduation from the University of Virginia in 1875, he joined the faculty of Columbian College (now George Washington University) as a graduate student and instructor in Latin; and served as adjunct professor, 1879–82; professor, 1882–97; principal of the preparatory school, 1884–93; and dean, 1895–97. His other degrees included the M.A., 1879; Ph.D., 1888, Columbian; LL.D., 1896, Richmond College.

On Nov. 3, 1881, Montague married May Christian, who died in 1906. To this union were born Maude Augusta and Howard Christian. A second marriage followed in 1907 to Florence Wood.

He began in 1897 a five-year tenure as president of Furman University. His administration was highlighted by the establishment of the Furman Fitting School and the abolishment of coeducation.

As president of Howard College, 1902–12, Montague "practically made it over" and led a successful endowment campaign culminating in a Rockefeller grant.

Other appointments included the presidency of Columbia College, Lake City, Fla., 1912–19; professor of Latin and public speaking, 1919; dean, 1923; vice-president, 1924; acting president, 1927–28, Mercer University.

In addition to scholarly interests as Latinist and classicist, Montague was licensed to preach by the First Baptist Church, Birmingham, Ala. His edited works include "Selected Letters of Cicero," 1890, and "Selected Works of Pliny," 1893.

BIBLIOGRAPHY: *National Cyclopaedia of American Biography,* Vol. XXV (1936). B. F. Riley, *A Memorial History of the Baptists of Alabama* (1923). *The Baptist Courier* (Dec. 20, 1928). *Who Was Who in America,* 1897–1942. IRA L. BAKER

MONTANISTS. A sect that originated *c.* 156 as a reaction against the growing secular tendencies and worldliness in the church. The founder, Montanus of Phrygia, claimed to be the mouthpiece of the Holy Spirit. He and his two prophetesses, Priscilla and Maximilla, were noted for their "prophetic" outbursts of speaking in tongues. Their followers held these "revelations" to be supplementary, and in a sense superior to the Scriptures. They stressed the immediacy of the Holy Spirit and the speedy return of Christ. Montanists practiced regenerate church membership, immersion, asceticism, fasting, and episcopacy. Though declared heretics, they gained adherents in Asia Minor, North Africa, Spain, and Italy until after the fourth century when they declined rapidly.

LYNN E. MAY, JR.

MONTEZUMA COLLEGE. Established in 1919 with five New Mexico cities, Albuquerque, Artesia, Deming, Las Cruces, and Las Vegas, bidding for the college location. Spurred on by the persistent "need" and supported by the promise for ready cash growing out of the 75 Million Campaign, a favorable vote came for the school's establishment in 1919. The Southwide Education Commission had offered $100,000 on a matching basis, dollar for dollar, and New Mexico Baptists felt they could match the amount over and above the 75 Million quota. Actually, $100,000 was raised, and the offer of the Montezuma Hotel property at Las Vegas, formerly owned by the Santa Fe Railway, was accepted. The property, valued at $350,000, embraced buildings and mountain land, with the main building consisting of 225 rooms. The property was transferred in fee simple with no debts.

Founders had in mind a standard liberal arts college offering the regular Bachelor of Arts degree. J. M. Cook, Rusk College, was first president; Lee A. Wolfard, vice-president. The opening planned for 1920 was delayed until 1922. Meanwhile, Cook resigned, and Layton Maddox became president, offering for the initial year courses in elementary, high school, and college departments. Beginning with freshman work, one additional year was added with the opening of each session, a fact which contradicts charges that the school undertook too much in its beginning. The first year enrolment reached 231; the second, 341. The first graduates received degrees in 1925, by which time the school had secured approval of the educational departments in New Mexico, Texas, Oklahoma, and Arizona, and the property value had risen to $936,350. Montezuma was founded, supported, and controlled by New Mexico Baptists with the co-operation of Southern Baptists.

Three main factors led to the closing of the school in 1937: (1) The school was started in the aftermath of a world war. Its propagation was across a period of a national depression which did not break until the early thirties. (2) Means of student support were inadequate. There were too few churches for the young ministers, and too few industrial jobs to offer supplementary aid. (3) The school was started on a shoe string with no endowment and no immediate prospects for such. By Aug. 1, 1926, a debt of $188,000 had already been contracted. Southern Baptists assisted when possible, particularly with the debts which were not eventually liquidated until the late 1930's. An effort by B. Clarence Evans at private operation, without financial obligation of the convention, proved unsuccessful; after a two-year serious effort, the school was closed for all time, and the property sold in 1937 to a Catholic religious order for $19,537.99. HERBERT E. BERGSTROM

MOODY, JOSEPH BURNLEY (b. Clarksville, Va., June 24, 1838; d. Jacksonville, Fla., Sept. 8, 1931). Pastor, author, editor. The son of William A. and Emily (Royster) Moody, was brought up on a farm and in young manhood engaged in teaching and merchandising. In July, 1855, he professed faith in Christ and was baptized into the membership of Bethel Church, Christian County, Ky. Ordained to the ministry on Sept. 11, 1876, by the Pewee Valley Church, Oldham County, Ky., Moody later served as pastor of the following churches: Pewee Valley, Ky. (1876–80); La Grange, Ky. (1877–80); Harrod's Creek, Ky. (1879–80); Paducah, Ky. (1880–82); Trezevant, Martin, and Round Lick, Tenn. (1883–86); Gilead and Bagdad, Ky. (1889); Overton, Ky. (1890–92); Hot Springs, Ark. (1893–94; 1899–1902); Sunset Church, San Antonio, Tex. (1895–96); and Tampa, Fla. (1897–98). He was educated in Bethel College, Kentucky, which conferred on him the D.D. degree in 1891. He served as editor of the following papers: *Baptist Gleaner* (1882–86), *The Baptist* (1886–89), and *Baptist and Reflector* (1889). He was the author of the following books and tracts: *Nashville Debate, Distinguishing Doctrines of Baptists, The Name Christian, Culpability of Ignorance, Vindication Concerning and Containing the Anderson Letters, The Two Covenants, The Great Salvation, Baptist Authors Vindicated, Church Government,* and others.

BIBLIOGRAPHY: J. H. Grime, *History of Middle Tennessee Baptists* (1902).

LEO T. CRISMON and JAMES BREWER

MOON, EDMONIA HARRIS (b. Albemarle County, Va., 1851; d. Starke, Fla., Nov. 19, 1908). Missionary and younger sister of Charlotte (Lottie) Moon (*q.v.*), a missionary to China. In 1872 she led in the organization of the Baptist Ladies Missionary Association of Richmond, Va., and the Baptist Woman's Missionary Union of Virginia in 1874. She was the youngest of the seven children of Edward Harris and Anna (Barclay) Moon. After her father died, before her first birthday, her name was changed from Robinett B. Moon to Edmonia Harris Moon. She was educated under the tutoring of her sister, Lottie, and at the Richmond Female Institute in Richmond, Va., which she entered in 1866. She was baptized into the membership of Hardware Baptist Church in Albemarle County in the summer of 1867. She spent one winter, 1870–71, as a private teacher in Green County, Ala.

Inspired by the missionary atmosphere of the Gwathmey Memorial Missionary Society of Richmond Female Institute and challenged by correspondence with Mrs. M. F. Crawford, missionary in China, she volunteered as a missionary to China and was appointed by the Southern Baptist Foreign Board, Apr. 9, 1872. Finding the board without funds to support her, she determined to go at her own expense. Women of the five missionary societies of Richmond, Va., responded to an appeal for help from the Foreign Mission Board by organizing the Richmond Female Missionary Society to undertake her support. Two years later an invitation to all "the Baptist ladies of Virginia" to share in this support by building a home in China for the Moon sisters resulted in a state missionary organization for Virginia Baptist women. Her letters greatly impressed her sister, Charlotte, who had felt called to China for a long time, and she followed her there in less than two years.

Edmonia Moon's promising missionary career was cut short by ill health. In 1876 she was brought home by her sister Charlotte and in 1878 resigned her appointment.

She died in Starke, Fla., Nov. 19, 1908.

CLAYTON PITTS

MOON, LOTTIE (CHARLOTTE) (b. Viewmont, Albermarle County, Va., Dec. 12, 1840; d. Kobe, Japan, Dec. 24, 1912). Missionary in Tengchow and Pingtu, China, for nearly 40 years; instrumental in instigating first Christmas offering, 1888. She was educated at Virginia Female Seminary (later known as Hollins) and at Albermarle Female Institute, Charlottesville. She was converted in the spring of 1859 in a meeting by John Albert Broadus (*q.v.*), then pastor at Charlottesville. She taught at Danville, Ky., and Cartersville, Ga. She volunteered for missionary service in Feb., 1873, in response to a sermon on the text, "Lift up your eyes, and look on the fields; for they are white already to harvest," and she was appointed to China, July 7, 1873, by the Foreign Mission Board, Southern Baptist Convention. In 1888 she wrote to the Baptist women of the South, pleading for reinforcements. The first Christmas offering in 1888 provided three additional missionaries. She spent 14 years in China before taking her first regular furlough. Toward the end of her days, she suffered with her Chinese people in the terrible famine. She gave all she had. In the time of deepest trials she wrote, "I hope no missionary will be as lonely as I have been." Literally starving, she grew steadily weaker. Before Christmas, 1912, Cynthia Miller, faithful nurse, started back to America with Lottie Moon; death came to the frail missionary, Christmas Eve, while the ship was at harbor in Kobe, Japan. The present Christmas offering for foreign missions, sponsored by the W.M.U., is named for Lottie Moon.

BIBLIOGRAPHY: F. S. Heck, *In Royal Service* (1913). U. R. Lawrence, *Lottie Moon* (1927). E. C. ROUTH

MOORE, ROBERT LEE (b. Globe, Caldwell County, N. C., Sept. 8, 1870; d. Mars Hill, N. C., Dec. 16, 1949). Served on the Mars Hill College faculty 51 years, 41 years as president. He was the son of Jesse Daniel and Mary Ann (Berry) Moore, and great-grandson of Jesse Moore, first settler of Globe Valley. He was educated at the one-room schoolhouse adjacent to his father's farm, then at Globe Academy and at Wake Forest College (A.B., 1892, D.E., 1927), and did graduate work at the University of North Carolina. Moore was pre-eminently an educator, emphasizing intellectual attainment and Christian character, which he helped stamp upon the students of Mars Hill College throughout half a century. Before going to Mars Hill in 1897, he taught at Globe Academy, at Valle Crucis, and at Amherst Academy, where he was principal for five years. He has been called the second founder of Mars Hill. As an administrator, a teacher, and an inspirer of youth, he attracted and retained a strong faculty and inspired a notable growth and reputation for this widely known junior college. As a loyal Christian layman, he served the Baptist denomination in many other capacities: as deacon, Sunday school teacher, and superintendent in the local church; as clerk, moderator, and historian of the French Broad Association; as trustee of Wake Forest College; as trustee of the North Carolina Baptist Orphanage; as a member of several committees of the state convention. He was the author of numerous articles in denominational journals and publications of the college, but his greatest contribution was made to the lives of the thousands of men and women whom he taught. He was married June 11, 1895, to Edna Corpening, who died Feb. 14, 1950. One daughter, Nona (Mrs. O. E. Roberts), and one son, Ernest Corpening, survived him. J. A. MCLEOD

MOORER, WILLIAM DURANT (b. Orangeburg, S. C., Apr. 13, 1868; d. Shawnee, Okla., May 8, 1922). Pastor, denominational leader, and college professor. Graduate of Furman University (1892) and Southern Baptist Theological Seminary (1894), married Beatrice Graham in 1897 at Kingstree, S. C. After pastorates at Kingstree, Little, and Antreville, S. C., 1894–1902, he served mission pastorates under the Southern Baptist Home Mission Board at Okarche, Okla. (1902–04), and Anadarko, Okla. (1904–06). He was Sunday school secretary for the Baptist General Convention of Oklahoma, 1906–20; librarian and professor of Christianity at Oklahoma Baptist University, 1915–22; cofounder of Falls Creek Assembly, 1917; and author of Bible outlines. He is buried in Fairview Cemetery, Shawnee, Okla.

BIBLIOGRAPHY: J. W. Jent, "The Monumental in the Oklahoma Ministry of William Durant Moorer" (n.d.). C. Redford, "William Durant Moorer" (n.d.).
LEE B. SPENCER

MORAVIAN FALLS ACADEMY. A Baptist school in Wilkes County, N. C., operated in the 1880's and 1890's under A. J. Beach, R. L. Patton, and G. W. Greene. It was endorsed by Ashe and Allegheny, Brier Creek, and Caldwell County associations. D. L. SMILEY

MORGAN HILL ACADEMY. A Baptist school in Buncombe County, N. C., operated in the 1870's and 1880's under J. H. Sams, J. P. Sams, and J. M. Davis. It was endorsed by Buncombe County and French Broad associations.
D. L. SMILEY

MORMONS. Popular synonym for the Church of Jesus Christ of Latter-Day Saints, founded by Joseph Smith (1805–44) at Fayette, N. Y., Apr. 6, 1830. The present headquarters are located in Salt Lake City, Utah.

The Mormons have two authoritative sources of doctrine: the written Word of God and direct revelation from God. Books accepted as Scripture are the Bible; the Book of Mormon; the Doctrine and Covenants; and the Pearl of Great Price. The president of the church is a prophet, a seer, and a revelator.

The doctrines are as follows: (1) The first principle of the gospel is faith in God the Father, in his Son Jesus Christ, and in the Holy Ghost. The Mormons teach that God was once a man, and that man became a God. "The Father is a glorified and perfect person, and Jesus Christ the Son is His express image and likeness. One is an individual as much as the other . . . clothed with a spiritual, yet tangible, immortal body. . . . The Holy Spirit is not a personage of tabernacle, and His influence permeates all things and extends throughout the vast domain of space . . ." and through Him "the Father and the Son are everywhere present." (2) The second principle of the gospel is repentance. (3) The third principle of the gospel is baptism by immersion in water. Remission of sins comes through baptism in a temple. Living persons may be baptized for the dead. (4) The fourth principle of the gospel is the gift of the Holy Spirit, bestowed through laying on of hands.

The government consists of: the first presidency, composed of the president and two counselors, having jurisdiction over the church; the twelve apostles, equal in authority to the presidency, who set in order the affairs of the church in all the world under direction of the first presidency; the seventy, a body of elders who travel under the direction of the apostles, who form the chief missionary corps of the church; and the high priests and elders, local officers for local ministrations, who are called into the mission field when necessary.

There are two orders of priesthood in the Mormon Church. The Melchizedek Priesthood has authority in spiritual affairs, and the Aaronic Priesthood has authority to administer in temporal affairs, such as collecting tithes.

BIBLIOGRAPHY: *Book of Mormon* (1948). *Doctrine and Covenants of the Church of Jesus Christ of Latter-Day Saints* (1949). G. B. Hinckley, *What of the Mormons?* (1947). D. M. McAllister, *Life's Greatest Questions* (n.d.); *Temples of the Church of Jesus Christ of Latter-Day Saints* (n.d.). J. Morgan, *The Plan of Salvation* (n.d.). W. A. Morton, *Why I Believe the Book of Mormon to Be the Word of God* (n.d.). C. W. Penrose, *Baptism for the Dead* (n.d.); *The Book of Mormon* (n.d.); *Divine Authority* (n.d.); *Faith* (n.d.); *The Gift of the Holy Ghost* (n.d.); parts of series, *Rays of Living Light; What the "M" Believe* (n.d.). S. L. Richards, *About Mormonism* (n.d.). B. H. Roberts, *The Second Coming of the Messiah* (n.d.). J. Smith, *J. Smith Tells His Own Story* (n.d.). J. A. Widtsoe, *A God Who Speaks* (n.d.); *Discourses of Brigham Young* (1925); *Universal Salvation* (n.d.).
B. GRAY ALLISON

MORRELL, ZACHARIUS N. (b. South Carolina, Jan. 17, 1803; d. Kyle, Tex., Dec. 19, 1883). Pioneer preacher in Texas. Spending most of his early years in Tennessee, Morrell received little formal education. Because of his fiery temperament, impulsive nature, and courage, he was nicknamed "Wildcat Morrell." He began preaching before he was 20 and served for 14 years in western Tennessee, making long mission tours. For nine years he averaged a sermon a day. Because of lung hemorrhages, he was advised by physicians to stop preaching and seek a drier and warmer climate. Moving to Mississippi in 1835, Morrell nevertheless continued preaching, forming three churches and aiding in the formation of Yalobusha Association. After an exploratory trip to Texas in Dec., 1835, he, with his family, moved to Texas in Apr., 1836. He first settled near the Falls of the Brazos, but because of Indian raids and the disturbed state of the country after the fall of the Alamo and the Goliad Massacre, he found little opportunity for preaching in that area. Moving to Washington-on-the-Brazos, he formed the first missionary Baptist church in Texas in the summer or fall of 1837.

Although a cripple and hampered by ill health, Morrell participated in numerous engagements with the Indians and Mexicans. A staunch advocate of missions, education, Sunday schools, temperance, and other causes, Morrell made significant contributions to the founding and stability of Baptist work in Texas. His frontier ministry consisted in organizing churches and associations, largely in the region between the Trinity and Colorado rivers. Often he did not receive enough remuneration to feed his horse.

Morrell lived to see, however, outstanding growth among Texas Baptists, which in 1835 he estimated to be not more than 50 people of all persuasions. At the time of his death in 1883, there were more than 80,000 white missionary Baptists in 1,500 churches with 60 associations. In 1872 he published *Flowers and Fruits from the Wilderness,* an account of early Texas Baptist history interwoven with his personal experiences. In recognition of his services to Texas, his body was reinterred in the state cemetery in Austin in 1946. His figure is represented on a bas-relief of outstanding Southern Baptists at Southwestern Seminary.

D. D. TIDWELL

MORRISTOWN FEMALE ACADEMY. A school chartered as Baptist at Morristown, Tenn., in 1858; now extinct.

LYNN EDWARD MAY, JR.

MOSELEY, JOSIAH BEE (b. near Raleigh, N. C., May 12, 1875; d. Shreveport, La., Dec. 17, 1934). Consecrated pioneer in the fields of Sunday school and B.Y.P.U. work in Louisiana, and a wise counselor to young and old alike. After completing his early education in the schools of Raleigh, he attended Wake Forest College, Southern Baptist Theological Seminary, Louisville, Ky., and Moody Bible Institute, Chicago, Ill.

Moseley came to Alexandria, La., Emmanuel Baptist Church as the first educational director of any Baptist church in the South. In 1911 he was selected as Louisiana's first Sunday school secretary, and the following year he added thereto the responsibilities of the B.Y.P.U. department. He served continuously in this office until his death, except for five years spent in a similar capacity in Arkansas.

That "Moseley made the difference between the mediocrity which had marked the work for many years and the magnificent growth which was soon manifested" may be seen from the records. In 1911 there were about 300 Sunday schools with a total enrolment of approximately 20,000. In 1933 the report showed 819 Sunday schools with 88,521 enrolled. In like manner, the B.Y.P.U. work grew from 314 unions in the state in 1921 to more than 1,500 in 1934. He always tried to major on work among the rural or small town churches and pastors, with gratifying results.

In a tribute to "Uncle Joe," as he was fondly called, in the *Baptist Message,* Jan. 3, 1935, F. W. Tinnin, editor, wrote: ". . . no other state has made as rapid progress in the Sunday school and B.Y.P.U. work in the past twenty years as has Louisiana. And so far as the human element is concerned, Joe Moseley for the most part was responsible and should be given credit for it."

BIBLIOGRAPHY: J. P. Durham and J. S. Ramond, *Baptist Builders in Louisiana* (1934). C. P. St. Amant, *A Short History of Louisiana Baptists* (1948).

W. A. BROWN

MOULDER, DANIEL WILLIAM (b. Smith County, Miss., Nov. 26, 1867; d. Smith County, Miss., Mar. 24, 1953). Pastor, church organizer. Country preacher and "bishop of five counties," Moulder joined Goodwater Baptist Church in Aug., 1888, and was ordained June 6, 1897. Pastor of 42 churches, Moulder organized 16 of them, baptized 5,156, preached 3,020 funerals, and performed 455 weddings. He was a member of the Mississippi Baptist Convention board for 20 years, trustee of Clarke Memorial College, Newton, and Baptist Hospital, Jackson.

BIBLIOGRAPHY: C. S. Moulder, *Through the Valley* (1954). R. L. Breland, "Veterans of the Cross," *The Baptist Record* (Dec. 23, 1937). "Rev. D. W. Moulder," *The Baptist Record* (Apr. 2, 1953).

C. B. HAMLET III

MOULTON COLLEGE (1849–90). Located at Moulton, in Lawrence County, Ala., also known as Baptist Female Institute and Baptist Male and Female Institute (1888). It was founded as a joint enterprise of the Muscle Shoals, Liberty, and Big Bear Creek associations. Joseph Shakelford was its first principal. The school flourished, with some intermittent lapses, until some time after 1890. JAMES E. DAVIDSON

MT. CALVARY SEMINARY. A school in Dallas County, Tex., taken over by Elm Fork Association in 1870 and continued as Dallas Male and Female College. With never more than 100 pupils, it closed in 1874.

RUPERT N. RICHARDSON

MT. ENON ACADEMY. The only Baptist school established in Georgia before churches organized the state convention in 1822, largely the result of the efforts of Henry Holcombe (*q.v.*), Savannah pastor. In 1804 at a meeting of the general committee at Kiokee a resolution was made for the establishment of a Georgia Baptist College; trustees were chosen, and a meeting held at Mt. Enon, 15 miles southwest of Augusta, in 1806, with Holcombe, Jesse Mercer (*q.v.*), Lewis C. Davis, James Matthews, Abraham Marshall (*q.v.*), Charles O. Screven, Thomas Rhodes, and Benjamin Brooks attending. Holcombe was made president of the board of trustees, and Screven was chosen president of the school. Meeting at Clarks Station in May, 1806, the trustees chose Mt. Enon as the site for the school; Holcombe gave 202 acres of land; a charter was secured in 1807, and Mt. Enon opened in September of that year. Holcombe left Georgia in 1811 to accept a pastorate in Philadelphia, and without his support the school soon died.

ARTHUR JACKSON

MT. IDA ACADEMY. A mission school at Mt. Ida, Ark., founded in 1920 by the Home Mission Board and the Arkansas Baptist State Mission Board. Operated in a leased building, the school had an average enrolment of 153 until it closed in 1929.

H. D. MORTON

MT. LEBANON BAPTIST ENCAMPMENT. One of four Texas encampments organized in 1946. It is located near Cedar Hill in Dallas County, District 13.

J. E. ROTH

MT. LEBANON UNIVERSITY. Located in Mount Lebanon, Bienville Parish, La., and founded in 1852 by the North Louisiana Baptist Convention to train young men for denominational leadership. It was a liberal arts college during most of its existence. It was administered by a board of trustees of 13 members appointed by the convention. A promising beginning was interrupted by the Civil War, when three faculty members and a majority of the students went into the army. During the war the buildings and equipment were used by the state as a medical laboratory, and the physical plant was much damaged. Loss of endowment and scarcity of money for operation prompted the convention to release the school in 1873 to the board of trustees to operate as they thought best. It continued to receive patronage and financial aid from the Baptists of the state, but did not revert to convention control until 1899. Fire destroyed the main buildings in 1886. After rebuilding, the college became coeducational. In the late 1880's it was recognized as one of the leading schools in the state. After the board of trustees returned it to the convention in 1899, it was administered by the Education Commission of the convention until 1906, when it became part of Louisiana College at Pineville.

(MRS.) LELA B. COSTELLO

MT. VERNON INSTITUTE. Organized at Riddleville, Ga., in 1852 by the Riddleville Baptist Church. The school, in which Mt. Vernon Association had an interest, continued until about 1889 when J. J. Hyman, principal and pastor of the church, left Riddleville.

ARTHUR JACKSON

MOUNT VERNON MALE AND FEMALE ACADEMY. See SANDY CREEK BAPTIST ACADEMY.

MOUNTAIN HOME COLLEGE. Founded by White River Association in 1893 at Mountain Home, Ark., with W. S. Johnson first president. One building with a 10-acre campus was financed locally, and 150 students enrolled the first year. After seven years of associational operation the school closed 1901–02; then it operated under the Arkansas Baptist State Convention 1902–06, though the president assumed all expenses. Public and private schools used the building 1906–16, when it was reopened and operated by the Home Mission Board of Southern Baptist Convention and Arkansas Baptist State Convention until 1924. Then properties were deeded to the Arkansas convention.

Enrolment in 1918–19 was 133; in 1926–27, 265. The college was accredited as a two-year teacher training institution by Arkansas, Missouri, and Texas departments of education.

Operating budget 1917–18 was $8,808.50; 1926–27, $35,685.10. Income was from tuition, fees, and appropriations from the Home Mission Board and state executive board 1916–27. In 1927 the Arkansas Baptist State Convention mortgaged the properties for $90,000 to help relieve the indebtedness of its institutions, and discontinued appropriations in 1928. The college closed in 1929, but was reopened by the Arkansas convention in 1930 and operated until permanently closed in 1933.

H. D. MORTON

MOUNTAIN MISSION SCHOOLS. The Home Mission Board through the years has been interested in the highlands of the South and their people. This section includes 203 counties in 10 states with a total area of nearly 100,000 square miles and a population of eight or nine million. West Virginia, parts of Virginia, North Carolina, South Carolina, Georgia, Alabama, Tennessee, and Kentucky in the Southern Appalachians, and parts of Missouri and Arkansas in the Ozarks are included in this territory.

In 1885 Isaac Taylor Tichenor, corresponding secretary of the Home Mission Board, in the annual report to the Convention, stated:

> In co-operation with the [Western North Carolina] Convention . . . the Board has supported twelve missionaries. Our work has been most encouraging. In

no part of our field have the results been greater than in this. The section of the state is rapidly assuming an importance which makes its claim imperative upon the Board. . . . It is filled with Baptists. . . . They have enjoyed slender advantages for either intellectual or spiritual culture. . . . From out of the vastnesses of these mountains will come men who . . . will make the world feel their power and wonder at their strength.

In each succeeding annual report the far-seeing secretary referred to the vast possibilities in the youth of the Southern highlands.

In 1891 the first actual educational work which the Home Mission Board did in this area consisted in paying in part the salary of the principal of Hiawassee Institute in the mountains of Georgia. The board co-operated with the Western North Carolina Convention throughout the 1890's. When this body dissolved and the churches and associations in the area affiliated with the North Carolina state convention (1898), a great opportunity was presented. In 1900 the board announced to the Convention: "North Carolina is now being aroused on the subject. Her State Board has resolved to take up the work of establishing Christian schools for these people in her mountain section, in addition to the work of evangelism, and has earnestly appealed to our Board to co-operate in this work. Shall we do it?" In answer to the question, a committee of seven, of which John Ellington White, corresponding secretary of the North Carolina convention, was chairman, was appointed to give serious study to the proposal and report to the Convention. In a report covering more than three pages, the committee described a detailed study of the situation and concluded: "This committee recommends that this Convention hereby instructs and appeals to the Southern Baptists to enable the Home Mission Board to carry out the provisions of this plan, as far as is possible, during the coming year." Acting under this instruction, the Home Mission Board established a Department of Mountain Mission Schools with missions as the motive and education as the method for evangelization of people of the mountain areas.

First superintendent.—Albert E. Brown was elected to direct the Department of Mountain Mission Schools and continued in full charge of the program until his death on May 30, 1924. He had previously worked in the mountain area of North Carolina in connection with the work of the Western North Carolina Baptist Convention. Being a native of that area, he understood the people, knew their needs, and gave himself wholeheartedly to his task. He was tireless in his efforts and courageously faced the difficulties of travel and the many discomforts connected with the work in the early years of the department. Jesse C. Owen served as associate in the department for seven years, and R. L. Creal for two. J. W. O'Hara began his service in the department in 1923 and was elected as superintendent at the death of Brown.

For three decades the Home Mission Board promoted the program of mountain mission schools. Schools were established or were conducted in association with other Baptist bodies in 47 localities. As these schools served their purpose, they were either discontinued or combined with other institutions. During this period the schools reported a total enrolment of about 125,000 with 10,150 graduates. About 3,000 of the students enrolled were ministerial students. The total number of conversions reported was 6,842, although, during much of this period, no record was kept of the conversions and additions to the churches.

The peak of activity in the Department of Mountain Mission Schools was reached in 1926. At that time there were 30 schools in 9 states reporting an enrolment of 4,808 students; 211 ministerial students; 562 graduates; 405 conversions; 218 volunteers; total income $234,-516.00, of which the Home Mission Board paid $62,679.06; total cost of improvements, $69,-172.00.

The 47 schools supported in some measure by the Home Mission Board between 1900 and 1930 are listed as follows:

SCHOOL	ESTAB-LISHED	HMB AID BEGUN	HMB AID DISCON-TINUED
North Carolina:			
Fruitland Institute	1889	1900	1930
Mars Hill College	1857	1900	1928
Mountain View Institute	1912	1912	1929
Alexander Schools, Inc.	1900	1902	1929
Murphy Institute	1903	1903	1915
Mitchell Institute	1903	1903	1923
Haywood Institute	1893	1900	1927
Yancey Collegiate Institute	1900	1907	1926
Liberty Piedmont Institute	?	*Aid for a brief time*	
Mountain Park Institute	?	*Aid for a brief time*	
South Carolina:			
North Greenville Academy	1893	1905	1929
Six Mile Academy	1912	1912	1928
Sparton Academy	1905	1905	1922
Long Creek Academy	1913	1913	1922
Virginia:			
Lee Baptist Institute	1903	1909	1929
Oak Hill Academy	1911	1911	1922
Alabama:			
Eldridge Academy	1906	1906	1931
Beeson Academy	1908	1908	1921
Gaylesville Academy	1906	1906	1923
Tennessee River Institute	1907	1907	1927
Kentucky:			
Magoffin Institute	1904	1904	1931
Hazard Baptist Institute	1905	1905	1931
Barboursville Baptist Institute	1905	1905	1931
Cumberland College	*H.M.B. assisted for brief period*		
Oneida Institute	1899	1902	1903
Georgia:			
Hiawassee Academy	1887	1891	1930
Blairsville Collegiate Institute	1905	1911	1929

SCHOOL	ESTAB-LISHED	HMB AID BEGUN	HMB AID DISCON-TINUED
Georgia: (Continued)			
Bleckley Memorial Institute	1913	1913	1924
Draketown Institute	1912	1913	1917
North Georgia Baptist Institute	1900	1902	1925
Tennessee:			
Harrison-Chilhowee Institute	1881	1904	1929
Smoky Mountain Academy	?	1920	1929
Cosby Academy	1914	1914	1924
Watauga Academy	1882	1906	1931
Doyle College	1884	1905	1927
Andersonville Institute	1907	1907	1918
Stoctons Valley Academy	1911	1912	1928
Unaka Academy	1911	1912	1915
Carson-Newman College	*H.M.B. aided in support of a Bible teacher for a number of years.*		
Arkansas:			
Mountain Home College	1890	1916	1929
Armo Baptist Academy	1918	1918	1929
Newton County Academy	1920	1920	1929
Maynard Academy	1916	1916	1927
Hagarville Academy	1919	1919	1927
Missouri:			
Southwest Baptist College	1878	1918	1929

Discontinuance of mountain schools.—During the first quarter of the 20th century, the states within which the Southern highland areas are located developed public school systems to meet the general education needs of the people. The need for mission schools in the mountain areas diminished. As the need in a community lessened, the boards of the several Baptist organizations began to reduce the appropriations for schools and to place more emphasis on evangelization. In some localities the property of a discontinued mountain school was sold to the county board of education. At the end of the third decade, the Home Mission Board was struck with a terrible financial situation following the defalcation of a trusted official. In the readjustment of the board's financial program, retrenchment was necessary. Since the demand for mountain mission schools was passing away, the Southern Baptist Convention in session at Birmingham, Ala., May, 1931, passed a resolution providing for the disassociation of the Home Mission Board as the operating agency of those schools, operation being transferred to local boards of trustees. The board expressed its purpose to deed the school property to the local boards of trustees as soon as it could be released from the bond mortgage.

Beginning again in the mountains.—During 1934 the Home Mission Board began in a small way the task of evangelization and spiritual cultivation of areas where little progress in religious life had been made for generations. Louis W. Martin and his wife were elected to serve as missionary evangelists in the Kentucky mountains, and Mr. and Mrs. M. J. Cobble, in the Norris Dam section of Tennessee. For almost 10 years the Martins conducted work under the Home Mission Board, holding revival meetings and Vacation Bible schools and opening new work where there had been no spiritual ministry. During most of this period, Minnie Berry served as a paid worker of the board in the mountain counties of Kentucky.

In 1947 initial steps were taken toward an enlarged program of missions in the mountains. The Home Mission Board and the Kentucky Baptist state mission board agreed to co-operate in the promotion of a special type of mountain mission work. In Nov., 1947, A. B. Cash was elected to direct this program in the mountains of eastern Kentucky. For the next two years the boards co-operated in formulating plans and methods to be used in setting up a program for mission work throughout the highland areas. On the basis of surveys made on progress attained in the mission fields of the Kentucky mountains during this period, the mountain mission program was approved by the Home Mission Board at its annual meeting in Nov., 1949. Using the county as a unit of promotion, this program sets forth five definite objectives: (1) to assist in the establishing of churches in all county-seat towns not now reached by Baptists; (2) to strengthen county-seat churches and other churches already established; (3) to assist mission churches to become self-supporting; (4) to open new fields through mission stations sponsored by local churches; (5) to afford opportunities for further preparation on the part of pastors and other leaders through conferences, fellowship meetings, and institutes.

The mountain mission program provides for the co-ordination and correlation of mission work in the mountain counties through the following co-operative plan: (1) a county missionary employed by the state mission board; (2) a county missionary committee working with the missionary; (3) local missionaries serving as pastors of mission churches; (4) each mission station under the supervision of a local church.

The mountain mission program Is an integral part of the Co-operative Missions Department of the Home Mission Board. The board co-operates with the state mission boards in the promotion of this program on the same basis that it assists in the promotion of other co-operative ministries. In addition to financial assistance, the Home Board provides literature and arranges conferences for the promotion of this work.

BIBLIOGRAPHY: A. B. Cash, *Plan Enlarged Mountain Mission Program* (1953). J. W. O'Hara, *Signal Fires on the Mountain* (1929). W. Weatherford, *Religion in the Appalachian Mountains* (1953). A. B. CASH

MOUNTAIN MISSION SCHOOLS, VIRGINIA. Until relatively recent years and the development of better means of transportation—the automobile and the consequent better roads—public education in the mountainous areas of Virginia was poor and inadequate. This was particularly true on the secondary school level.

To make up for the lack of public high schools and to make possible college education for some of the promising boys and girls of the mountain areas, various religious denominations founded academies.

The first effort of the Virginia Baptists was at Mouth of Wilson in Grayson County where the New River Baptist Association founded an academy, Oak Hill, in 1874. The first principal was W. W. Fuqua. The school was closed as a denominational school about 1883, and from that time until 1911 the buildings were used by the Grayson County school board. When the academy was reopened it was supported by the New River Association of Virginia, by the Ashe and Alleghany associations of North Carolina, and by the Home Mission Board of the Southern Baptist Convention. In 1922 the state mission board of the Baptist General Association of Virginia took over the support and direction.

The Virginia Baptist budget for 1956 allocated 3.27 per cent of the operating budget and 2 per cent of the capital budget for the academy. For the session 1955–56 the school received $27,375 from the denomination. There is no endowment. Enrolment for 1955–56 was 121. The principal since 1948 has been Grover M. Turner.

It is interesting to note that Oak Hill Academy, the first of the Virginia mountain mission schools to be established, is the only one currently in operation.

In 1894 the Clinch Valley Association founded a school at Pennington Gap, in Lee County, known as Curry College. In 1896 the building was transferred to the Powell River Association which opened the school under the name of the Lee Baptist Institute in 1904. Support was given by the education commission of the Virginia general association and by the Home Mission Board. The school was closed in 1930, and the property was sold by the Powell River Association.

The Buchanan Mission School at Council, in Buchanan County, was founded in 1911 and supported by the State Mission Board and the Woman's Missionary Union of Virginia. The school operated for 20 years and was closed in 1931.

In 1916 the Blue Ridge Association established the Blue Ridge Mission School in Patrick County. The state mission board assisted with its support. In 1941 the school was closed and the property sold.

The Piedmont Academy in Nelson County was started by the Piedmont Association with the assistance of the State Mission Board in 1922. After a brief existence of 11 years, it was closed in 1933.

These schools met a real need and made a good contribution to the cause of Christian education. Their closing was due to the improved facilities in public education.

RALPH C. MCDANEL

MOUNTAIN PARK SCHOOL. A Baptist school at Ronda, N. C., operated by Surry Association. In 1912 the association secured 37 acres of land, and interested Baptists donated timber worth $1,300 for the construction of a school. The following year trustees were appointed, and the school was opened with 41 pupils the first year. In 1916–17 the school received financial assistance of $800 each year from the Home Mission Board's program of aid for mountain schools. Despite this assistance, the debt remained high, and in 1921 when an administration building was built, the debt increased still more. The obligation proved too great and the following year a deed of trust was executed on the school property. In 1924 the property was sold to the sheriff of Surry County under an execution, and the management of the school passed to other hands.

D. L. SMILEY

MOUNTAIN VIEW HIGH SCHOOL. Associational school of Stone Mountain, Brushy Mountain, and Elkin associations, located at Hays, Wilkes County, N. C. It was founded in 1913 and was opened on Sept. 2 of that year. Beginning in 1913 the school received financial assistance from the Home Mission Board's program of aid to mountain schools. By 1928 it had received a total of $36,000, including $16,500 for capital improvements. In that year the Home Mission Board withdrew assistance to the school, and Mountain View was forced to close.

D. L. SMILEY

MULKEY, JONATHAN (b. Virginia, Oct. 16, 1752; d. East Tennessee, Sept. 5, 1826). Pioneer preacher. The son of Philip Mulkey, pioneer preacher in Virginia and South Carolina, Jonathan Mulkey was one of the first Baptist preachers to settle in Tennessee, coming with a pioneer party to the westernmost Tennessee settlement in 1775, in Carter's Valley, now known as Hawkins County. He was the second pastor of Buffalo Ridge Church, 1785–1826, the founder, with Isaac Barton, of French Broad Church, now Dandridge Church, Mar. 25, 1786, and probably the founder of Kendrick's Creek Church. He served as pastor of Sinking Creek Church, Carter County (founded by Matthew Talbot, 1775), and of Cherokee and Muddy Creek churches. With Tidence Lane and others, he framed the "declaration called the 'Magna Carta' of Holston Association Churches for 143 years." This was the second article of the plan of association, adopted Oct. 30, 1786: "Not as a legislative body to impose laws or exercise any supremacy, each Church being an independent body." Mulkey was a strong preacher, more inclined to do evangelistic work than to be a pastor. Long a leader in the Holston Association, he was for seven years its moderator. He was buried in Buffalo Ridge Church cemetery.

BIBLIOGRAPHY: D. Benedict, *General History of the Baptist Denomination in American and Other Parts of the World* (1848). J. J. Burnett, *Tennessee*

Pioneer Baptist Preachers (1919). F. Merritt, *Early History of Carter County, 1760-1861* (1950). J. G. M. Ramsey, *Annals of Tennessee* (1853). S. C. Williams and S. W. Tindell, *Baptists of Tennessee* (1930).

FRANCIS MARION WARDEN

MULLINS, DANIEL DAVID (b. Ga., May 17, 1825; d. Marietta, Okla., Jan. 23, 1894). Pioneer missionary and pastor in Indian Territory. He married and began his ministry in Georgia, and migrated to Texas by ox wagon in 1867 or 1868, and was for 14 years active in Hamilton, Erath, and Grayson counties. One of the first pioneer preachers in the Ardmore and Marietta area, Indian Territory, in 1881 or 1882, he conducted revivals, organized churches, and traveled extensively in the area. He organized Enon Association in 1885, embracing the Chickasaw Nation, south central Oklahoma, out of which nine counties were formed, and served as first moderator. Mullins Association, consisting of Stephens and Jefferson counties, was organized out of Enon Association in 1895 and was named for him. He is buried in Gordon Cemetery, near Marietta, Ga. R. L. MC CLUNG

MULLINS, EDGAR YOUNG (b. Franklin County, Miss., Jan. 5, 1860; d. Louisville, Ky., Nov. 23, 1928). Minister, seminary president, and professor. Son of Self Granberry and Cornelia Blair (Tillman) Mullins, he moved with the family to Corsicana, Tex., when he was eight years of age. His minister-teacher father, a Master of Arts graduate of Mississippi College, encouraged each of the nine children to obtain an education. When Mullins was born, following the birth of three daughters, his father and mother dedicated him to God with the prayer that he might become a minister. Helping to pay expenses for his sister's college education, he worked while attending grade and high school and became an expert telegrapher with a man's pay at 15. After obtaining his basic college education at Agricultural and Mechanical College of Texas from 1876 to 1879, Mullins worked as telegraph operator while accumulating funds for his anticipated preparation for the practice of law.

Under the preaching of William Evander Penn (*q.v.*), a notable Baptist evangelist, Mullins was converted in a revival meeting in Dallas, Tex., and was baptized by his father at Corsicana, Nov. 7, 1880. After feeling called to the ministry a few months later, he entered Southern Baptist Theological Seminary in the fall of 1881, and he was elected by the student body as manager of the mess hall at the close of his first year, a position he continued to fill until his graduation in 1885. At his physician's advice, Mullins gave up his commitment to foreign mission service in Brazil and accepted a call to the pastorate of Harrodsburg (Ky.) Baptist Church. Soon after, on June 2, 1886, he married Isla May Hawley of Louisville, by whom he had two sons, both of whom died at an early age. From the Harrodsburg church Mullins was called to the pastorate of Lee Street Baptist Church, Baltimore, Md., in 1888, where he served for seven years. He then accepted the position of associate secretary of the Foreign Mission Board, Richmond, Va., but felt unsuited for the task although deeply devoted to foreign missions, and almost immediately became pastor of the Baptist church at Newton Center, Mass., where he served from 1895 to 1899. This pastorate especially appealed to Mullins, since it was the home of Newton Theological Institution and near Harvard, Wellesley, and Brown. For three years the challenge of this situation prepared Mullins for his call in 1899 to become president of Southern Baptist Theological Seminary.

The election of Mullins to the presidency of the seminary came unexpectedly and without his knowledge or consent. He succeeded William Heth Whitsitt (*q.v.*), president from 1895 to 1899. Whitsitt had resigned under pressure in the midst of a bitter controversy over "a question in Baptist history." Mullins, as the new president, became professor of theology as well as executive head of the institution. His brilliance as teacher and writer, his administrative ability, and his firm but conciliatory attitude soon won the confidence of all and gave him a place of leadership in the denomination. He served as president of the Southern Baptist Convention from 1921 to 1924, and as president of the Baptist World Alliance in 1928.

Under Mullins' guidance, the seminary faculty increased from six to 12 professors, and enrolment from 256 to 501. He increased seminary endowment from $464,428.64 in 1899 to $1,803,768.09 in 1928, and largely through his own efforts made possible the endowment of the James Buchanan Harrison Chair of New Testament Interpretation and the Chair of Sunday School Pedagogy. He organized and promoted a building campaign for the removal of the seminary from its overcrowded downtown site to its present spacious campus of 58 acres known as The Beeches, with its Georgian buildings valued on completion in 1926 at $2,061,118.24.

In addition to numerous articles for the press, Mullins' published works include *Why Is Christianity True?* (1905); *The Axioms of Religion* (1908); *Baptist Beliefs* (1912); *Freedom and Authority in Religion* (1913); *Commentary on Ephesians and Colossians* (1913); *The Life in Christ; The Christian Religion in its Doctrinal Expression; Talks on Soul Winning* (1920); *Spiritualism, A Delusion* (1920); *Christianity at the Crossroads* (1924). GAINES S. DOBBINS

MULLINS LECTURES. In 1935 Mrs. Isla May Mullins (1859–1936) expressed her desire in her last will and testament to add the sum of $3,000 to the $10,000 which she and her husband, Edgar Young Mullins (*q.v.*), had previously given for the purpose of establishing a lectureship fund on "Preaching" at Southern Baptist Theological Seminary. Mrs. Mullins made this bequest in memory of her husband.

The first lectures in the series were delivered in the 1941–42 session by William Lyon Phelps (1865–1943), professor emeritus of Yale University, whose general theme was "The Expression of Christian Religion in Literature." The Mullins lectures have been given each year since that time, except in 1943–44, 1949–50, and 1950–51. The lecturer for the 1955–56 session was Theodore Floyd Adams, pastor of the First Baptist Church, Richmond, Va., on the subject "A Pastor Looks at Preaching." LEO T. CRISMON

MURPHY BAPTIST SCHOOL. Associational school of Liberty and Ducktown Association, located at Murphy, N. C. It was founded in 1901 under A. W. Setzer and B. D. Thames. In 1905 a new structure was erected at a cost of $2,000, half of which amount was donated by M. C. Trent of Washington, Pa. In 1913 the school was also called Cherokee Academy. Beginning with its first year the school received financial assistance from the Home Mission Board's program of aid to mountain schools. By 1914, the last year it received such help, the school had received more than $14,000, including $5,450 for capital improvements. Murphy School was closed after World War I. D. L. SMILEY

MURROW, JOSEPH SAMUEL (b. near Louisville, Richmond County, Ga., June 7, 1835; d. Atoka, Okla., Sept. 8, 1929). Missionary among the American Indians for 72 years. His father, John William Murrow, was a Methodist minister when, in 1821, he was married to Mary Amelia Badger, a teacher in Charleston, S. C. For some reason the elder Murrow was dropped from the list of itinerants and, after failing as a merchant, he became a tenant farmer, finally settling in Georgia.

Joseph Samuel Murrow attended a country school near Whitesville, Ga., until he entered Springfield Academy in 1850. He was converted Oct. 8, 1854, united with the Green Fork Baptist Church in Middle Association, was licensed to preach in the spring of 1855, and entered Mercer University in Jan., 1856. On Sept. 16, 1857, he was ordained by the Rehoboth Association in the First Baptist Church of Macon, Ga., and was appointed a missionary to the Creeks by the Domestic and Indian Mission Board of the Southern Baptist Convention. His salary was paid by the Rehoboth Association. He arrived at Micco, Creek Nation, Nov. 14, the same year, with his bride Nannie Elizabeth (Tatum) Murrow, whom he had married in Fulton, Miss.

He assisted Henry Frieland Buckner (*q.v.*) in his work among the Creeks until Jan., 1860, when he moved 60 miles west and, one month later, organized Ash Creek Church—the first permanent Baptist church among the Seminoles. During the Civil War he served the Confederate government as subsistence agent for some 4,000 refugee Indians, among whom he carried on an intensive missionary work. Following the war he settled among the Choctaws at Atoka, where he organized the Atoka church in 1869, and Choctaw-Chickasaw Association in 1872. He led in organizing the Baptist Missionary and Educational Convention of Indian Territory in 1883 and was one of the founders of Bacone College and Atoka Baptist Academy. Perhaps the crowning work of his life was the founding of the orphanage now called the Murrow Indian Orphans' Home—the only Christian orphanage in existence primarily for Indians.

Due to an unfortunate conflict with Isaac Taylor Tichenor (*q.v.*) of the Home Mission Board, Murrow severed his connection with that agency in 1891 and for the rest of his life was affiliated with the American Baptist Home Mission Society. He was buried at Atoka. Okla.

BIBLIOGRAPHY: W. A. Carleton, *Not Yours But You* (1954). WILLIAM A. CARLETON

MURROW INDIAN ORPHANS' HOME. Named for Joseph Samuel Murrow (*q.v.*), its founder, the only Christian orphanage in existence expressly for Indians. Termed by him "the child of my old age," Murrow in his 67th year became convinced his active work for the Indians was near an end and initiated a meeting Sept. 17, 1902, at South McAlester to organize a governing board for the Indian Orphans' Home which he had envisioned as the crowning work of his life. A board of 20 men and women was elected with Murrow as president, and he was instructed to prepare a charter. He applied for incorporation in the Central District United States Court of Judge W. H. Clayton, and the charter was issued in Nov., 1902. The American Baptist Home Mission Society for $2,500 sold the board its property at Atoka, which had been used by the Atoka Baptist Academy, and the school merged with the home. Murrow willed his estate valued at $10,000 to the orphanage; and other gifts started coming at once, the largest being five sections of surplus tribal land from the Choctaw tribal government. Forty children were received the first year. In 1903 the home moved to Unchuke, 15 miles north of Atoka. Murrow served as superintendent until 1907, when failing strength forced him to seek relief from its responsibilities. He approached the Home Mission Board, Southern Baptist Convention, about assuming its operation and was refused. He then turned to the Home Mission Society, which accepted ownership of the institution in Dec., 1908, and assumed management of it Apr. 1, 1909. In 1910 it was moved to a plat of ground adjoining Bacone College near Muskogee, Okla. In 1956 the home owned 150 acres of land, two large buildings, and had under construction three cottage type structures. A complete shift to the cottage institutional program for the 42 children in the home was under way the same year. J. M. GASKIN

MUSE, THOMAS (b. Middlesex County, Va., Jan. 6, 1810; d. Coleman, Ga., Apr. 19, 1895). Pioneer Baptist preacher of southwest Georgia. Muse settled at Blakely, Ga., in 1836, was licensed to preach in 1837, and ordained in 1840. He spent his entire ministry within the Bethel Association. Among the principal churches he served were Blakely, Cuthbert, and Georgetown. He was moderator of the Bethel Association, 1861–87, and colporteur of the same association, 1886–95. As one of the founders and a benefactor, trustee, and agent of Bethel College (Baptist Female College of Southwestern Georgia) at Cuthbert, he was a loyal supporter of Christian education.

Thomas Muse was twice married: in 1840, to Mrs. Susan Jenkins, who died in 1876; and in 1879, to Mrs. Sara Ellington, who died in 1883.

He was described by Jesse H. Campbell as "that indefatigable worker"; and by E. W. Warren as "the most active and useful preacher in Southwest Georgia." According to Warren, Muse served more churches and baptized more people (an estimated 4,000) than any pastor who ever lived in that part of Georgia. His vigorous advocacy of missions did much to prevent the success of primitive Baptist ideas in his region. He was buried in the Baptist cemetery at Cuthbert, Ga. MALCOLM LESTER

MUSIC, BAPTIST. The history of Baptist music begins with the practices and writings of John Smyth (d. 1612), pastor of the first English Baptist church (in Amsterdam, Holland) of which there is historical record. This church, in its utter reaction against set forms of worship, would not allow the singing of previously prepared texts or music. Even memorization of scriptural psalms could be set form. When singing was a part of worship, both text and music had to come directly from inspiration of the Holy Spirit. The singing was solo in order to be understood unto the edification of the congregation. Singing was not often a part of the service and eventually became disused. Smyth's ideas spread among the General Baptists of England, resulting in churches which opposed congregational singing and instrumental music in public worship.

The Particular Baptists of England, who first appeared in 1638, were less particular about congregational singing and used metrical versions of the psalms in several of their churches. However, instrumental music was not allowed. Benjamin Keach (1640–1704), pastor of the Particular Baptist Church of Horsleydown, Southwark, London, was one of the first in London, if not the first in England, to introduce English hymns into the regular worship of Baptist churches. Keach used a hymn at the end of the Lord's Supper from about 1673. Although meeting great opposition, he patiently but determinedly developed the use of song in his own services and used his influence with other churches to promote what he considered to be a church ordinance.

While the General Baptists were continuing their disuse of music under the leadership of Thomas Grantham (1634–92), the president of the General Association of General Baptists, whose reasonings followed those of John Smyth and who had a strong leaning toward the Quaker doctrine of the Inner Light; a "Controversie of Singing" agitated the Particular Baptists. The basic question was not so much whether to sing the new English hymns, for many were much opposed to these "human composures," but whether to sing congregationally at all, even in the "conjoint" singing of psalms. Both sides based their reasonings on their interpretations of the Scriptures. In the resultant pamphlet war, the writings became so abusive that the 1692 General Assembly of Particular Baptists, for the credit of the denomination, took up the matter. They censured several of the writers and caused the controversy to be held in abeyance for a few years so far as the public press was concerned. As they did not try to settle the matter for the churches, there resulted a struggle which sometimes led to minorities leaving churches which had decided to sing. "Worship by machinery," that is, by the use of instruments, was always disdained.

As the Particular Baptists developed the service of song, choirs were formed to help lead the singing. Although at first completely opposed, instrumental music came into the churches gradually, perhaps in the beginning with the use of a bass viol (violoncello), then a string ensemble, and finally, a miscellaneous band housed in a table-pew or gallery. Reed or pipe organs eventually took the place of the other instruments.

Baptists adopted the psalms and hymns of Isaac Watts (1674–1748) but continued to insist upon hymns of their own composition to emphasize sermon topics and denominational tenets and practices. At first churches had to "line out" their psalms and hymns because of the illiteracy of the people and the absence of songbooks, and this practice lasted in many churches until toward the end of the 18th century.

General Baptists, with but few exceptions, remained opposed to congregational singing until the Wesleyan Revival caused new General Baptist churches to be born. These singing churches formed in 1770 the New Connexion, which ultimately included most General Baptist churches which did not die or become Unitarian. One of the first accomplishments of the New Connexion was the publication of a hymnbook. This provoked the final stage of the "Controversie of Singing." From that time congregational hymn singing was in common practice among most English Baptists. Congregational singing became an important part of public worship, choirs and organs were added, and hymnbooks multiplied.

After the union of General and Particular Baptists in 1891, the united denomination in 1900 published its hymnal, which reflected the current Anglican standard and included hymns, chants, and anthems for both choir and congregation. Baptists had adjusted themselves to, and had become a part of, the contemporary church music life of England. Musically, they were no longer "a peculiar people."

Soon after the Pilgrims and Puritans came to the New World, a Baptist church was organized by Roger Williams (1603?–84) in Providence, R. I. Williams and several others of this small group had come from Salem, Mass., where the Ainsworth version of the psalms was in use for congregational singing in public worship. However, it is not known whether the new church sang. The second American Baptist church (founded between 1640 and 1644), of Newport, R. I., sang from the beginning, although what they sang is not known. Most New England Baptists came from a General Baptist background and did not sing. Probably some of those who did sing lost their ability as a consequence of the hardships of pioneer life.

The Baptists who settled in the Middle Colonies, especially the Welsh Baptists, were more receptive to singing, and when the influential Philadelphia Baptist Association adopted a confession of faith in 1742, an article on the duty of congregational singing in public worship was included.

The revivals of the Great Awakening, which had scattered beginnings in the 1720's and 1730's, were the beginning of Baptist growth and expansion. Regular Baptists had little to do with these revivals, which had congregational hymn singing as a characteristic part. Therefore, Separate Baptist churches had to be created first, and then the theology and spirit of the old churches had to be modified before the evangelical hymns and psalms of Watts could commend themselves. By the beginning of the 19th century nearly all American Baptist churches allowed congregational singing. The change from psalm singing to hymn singing was not the issue it had been in the British Isles or in other American denominations.

Baptists at the end of the 18th century used the hymnody of Watts, the evangelical hymns compiled by John Rippon (1751–1836), an English hymnbook publisher, and their own indigenous spiritual songs. Many of the spiritual songs had been brought over from the British Isles. These, with indigenous American songs, became the song tinder of the camp meetings of the Great Revival at the beginning of the 19th century. The excesses of the Great Revival in rural and frontier areas caused the traditional hymns and folk hymns to be sung to pieces and thereby achieved a final advance to the folk level of song. These songs "of the popular liking" were the forerunners of the revival hymn, the Sunday school song, and the gospel song. This line of development was a part of the evangelical movement which continued to sweep across America and in which American Baptists heartily participated. These successive steps which met the demand for a popular hymnody ran more or less parallel to regular church hymnody and influenced it.

Instrumental music was not considered among the early churches. However, the Newport church created a commotion in the early 19th century by introducing a bass viol into the church service, and the Providence church installed an organ in 1834. In the rural areas and on the frontiers, instrumental music was not allowed in the churches and was not often allowed in the homes.

Early 19th-century singing schools in rural areas taught a four shape method of musical notation, which, when changed to a seven shape system and universally adopted by shape note singers, became a divisive influence between rural and urban music as used in many Southern Baptist churches. Shape note music came under the domination of the gospel song and later degenerated into musical mannerisms of the most trite of secular styles.

Watts' hymns did not dominate the regular hymnody of the Baptist churches, although they became widespread and greatly loved. Baptist insistence upon a denominational hymnody caused a great number of hymnbooks to be published. Several of these were published by the American Baptist Publication Society of Philadelphia and were used by urban churches in both the North and South. After the schism between the Northern and Southern Baptists in 1845, the society continued its publication efforts for both divisions, publishing hymnbooks intended for all American Baptist churches. While these hymnbooks were used gladly in many Southern churches, efforts were made by some Southern Baptists to publish their own books. Representative Baptists of both the North and South tried to create a hymnal for the whole United States in 1883 and the Northern and Southern Baptist conventions tried to do the same thing in 1926. However, the two denominations have gone their own ways, the latest attempt of Northern Baptists being an effort at a closer bond of unity with the Disciples of Christ by the production of a joint hymnal.

Following the Civil War came an era of professional evangelism. Professional singing evangelists developed who were oftentimes very successful congregational song leaders and who organized large mass choirs, teaching them to sing new hymns and new tunes. Many times this stimulated the organization or growth of local church choirs, with local leadership being responsible for the type of choir work done. The new hymns and tunes, called gospel songs, have been and still are greatly used among Southern Baptists. The music and texts so well fitted evangelistic sermons, and both songs and sermons were such effective aids to evangelism that the gospel song became the only music in many Southern Baptist churches, causing generations to grow up largely in ignorance of standard church hymnody.

From 1891 the publications of the Southern Baptist Convention's Sunday School Board intermittently mentioned music and gave some direction to the music efforts in Southern Baptist churches. After the turn of the century the hymns and gospel songs published by Robert Henry Coleman (*q.v.*) were widely used by Southern Baptists. His copyrights were bought by the board in 1945. Interest began to develop in the 1920's for some kind of organized effort to improve music in the churches. A program of study in sacred music was already being offered at Southwestern Baptist Theological Seminary (since 1915) and at the Baptist Bible Institute (since 1919). In 1935 the Sunday School Board appointed Baylus Benjamin McKinney (*q.v.*), a music editor for Coleman, as music editor for its publications. In 1937 the Southern Baptist Convention appointed a committee which was to make a study of the conditions and needs of church music. One of its recommendations was the reiteration of the plea of committee member Isham Emmanuel Reynolds (*q.v.*), director of the school of sacred music at Southwestern Seminary, that a survey be made of music in Southern Baptist churches. This survey was made in 1939 and revealed a great need for an organized effort to improve church worship through music. In 1939 the committee recommended that the Convention urge the state conventions to appoint church music committees for themselves and to work in co-operation with the Convention's committee. Statewide programs began to develop from 1939, and the church music department of the Sunday School Board was established in 1941 under the leadership of McKinney. This department, now under the direction of Walter Hines Sims, has the primary responsibility so far as the Southern Baptist Convention is concerned for the development of a Convention-wide music program for all state conventions, district associations, and local churches.

Church music leadership is developed through the music education programs in the Baptist seminaries (Southern Baptist Theological Seminary [1944] and Golden Gate Baptist Theological Seminary [1948] also offer church music degrees) and in many of the Baptist colleges. The ministry of music is now a recognized function of the church. The minister of music, sometimes ordained for that specific purpose, has developed for himself a place as one of the ministers of the church together with the pastor and the minister of education.

See also HYMNALS, BAPTIST; HYMNWRITERS, BAPTIST; MUSIC EDUCATION, BAPTIST; GOSPEL SONGS, BAPTIST; CHURCH MUSIC EDUCATION, BAPTIST.

BIBLIOGRAPHY: W. T. Whitley (ed.), *The Works of John Smyth* (1915). T. Grantham, *Christianismus Primitivus* (1678). J. J. Goadby, *Bye-Paths in Baptist History* (1871). J. S. Curwen, *Studies in Worship Music* (First Series, 3rd Ed.; 1901). W. T. Whitley, *Congregational Hymn-Singing* (1933). G. P. Jackson, *White Spirituals in the Southern Uplands* (1933). A. A. Reid and G. W. Hughes, "The Tercentenary of Benjamin Keach," *The Chronicle* (Oct., 1940). R. E. Keighton, "Baptist Hymnody," *The Chronicle* (Apr., July, 1947).

FLOYD PATTERSON

MUSIC, CHURCH. Music has always been identified with worship. The first biblical hymn appears in Exodus; the development of choirs, singers, instrumentalists, teachers, directors, composers, and the place of music in worship are emphasized in the Old Testament. The book of Psalms constituted the early hymnbook of the Hebrews; it admonishes the redeemed to praise God with voice and instrument. Encouragement was given to the training of musicians, and attention was called to their appointment to responsibilities and their support.

The New Testament records the song of Mary, the proclamation of the heavenly host, the singing of a hymn following the institution of the Lord's Supper, the singing of Paul and Silas, and the instruction of Paul "to teach and admonish one another in psalms and hymns and spiritual songs," an admonition which constitutes a formula to be followed today.

During and after the transition from the relative democracy of the apostolic age to the hierarchical systems of the Eastern and Western Catholic churches, the music of the church became liturgical and clerical. Worship through singing was taken from the congregation and given to choruses composed of minor clergy. A highly organized body of chant, codified during the papacy of Gregory the Great (590–604), was almost the only worship music of the church for 1,000 years. Hymns, however, continued to be sung by the people for private and social edification.

After the introduction of harmony about the 11th century, the combination of two or more parts being sung simultaneously led to the development of a great school of polyphony which reached its maturity during the last half of the 16th century, exemplified by the music of Palestrina (1525–94).

During this time, however, operatic and instrumental music began a development which ushered in the modern period of music history and resulted in a new type of music in the church: homophony. This new kind of music was not only used by Roman Catholics but was the basis of the music of the churches of the Protestant Reformation. Lutheran church music is primarily based on the congregational hymns which Luther, as Huss before him, encouraged his people to sing in their own language.

Metrical versions of the psalms were used almost exclusively by 17th-century English congregations. Hymn-singing began to be popular and came to be accepted after compilations of Isaac Watts (1674–1748) began to be used. Many English hymn writers, namely, John Wesley (1703–91), Charles Wesley (1708–88), John Newton (1725–1807), William Cowper (1731–1800), John Neale (1818–66), and others, contributed hymns which were successful.

About the middle of the 19th century, the purely American gospel hymn became popular. It arose as the music of the people and is widely used today. Subjective in nature and personal in testimony, its principal contributors have been Fanny J. Crosby (1820–1915), Frances R. Havergal (1836–79), Phillip P. Bliss (1838–76), Ira D. Sankey (1840–1908), Charles H. Gabriel (1856–1932), and Baylus Benjamin McKinney (*q.v.*) (1886–1952).

In Southern Baptist Convention churches there is an emphasis on music for the congregation and for all age groups. The denomination is fostering a church music program designed to develop trained music leadership in the churches, using sound educational principles to encourage congregational singing, graded choirs, classes of instruction, and the quality of music which has superior values for worship and evangelism. As a result, leadership is growing, congregational participation is improving, graded choirs are flourishing, instructional opportunities are being multiplied, and the character and quality of the music are advancing. Periodicals, graded materials, good hymnals, miscellaneous publications, easily accessible practical helps, promotional emphases, improved curricula of colleges and seminaries, and the developing programs of festivals, conferences, and assemblies—all are valuable for the cultivation of higher appreciation and more effective participation. Notable values are anticipated for church music and in the total church life. W. HINES SIMS

MUSIC EDUCATION, BAPTIST. Henry Burrage in his *Baptist Hymn Writers and Their Hymns* gives the first record of Baptists and church music education. He records the writings of some of the Anabaptists who were martyrs to their beliefs, in Switzerland and south Germany, in the 16th century. These hymns, like the hymns of Anabaptists of the Netherlands, show their belief in the "redemption by the blood of Jesus Christ." Burrage further states, "These and the other martyr hymns were the cherished possession in many an Anabaptist home, and next to the Word of God were oftenest on the lips of the scattered members of the Anabaptist host from the Alps to the Baltic and North Sea, and from Bohemia to the borders of France."

The development of music and its use was hindered in England in the first of the 17th century because of disagreement concerning congregational participation. The music mostly used during this period was metrical versions of the psalms set to very simple music. In 1691 Benjamin Keach, pastor, Horsleydown, London, issued a collection of original hymns. His was the first Baptist church to sing hymns as distinct from psalm versions. Toward the end of the century, other Baptist bodies were publishing similar collections; however, they were considered supplementary to the metrical psalms still in use. John Rippon issued a book of hymns in 1787 which, with new editions, appeared up through the middle of the 19th century.

Choirs and orchestras appeared in Baptist churches north of England about 1720. Music developed rapidly in these churches. Singers were furnished the Westminster Abbey Handel Festival of 1784. In the 18th and 19th centuries Baptist musicians came to play a full part in making the church a center of orchestral and choral culture.

Baptist churches were formed in the American colonies before 1640. The music used in these early churches was brought over from England. There was disagreement as to congregational participation, as there was in England.

The earliest advantages in music education offered in America were in singing schools conducted by the churches. The first such school, about 1717 in New England, had the purpose of improving the psalmody of the churches. Although there is no record of such schools having been held in Baptist churches, there was dissatisfaction with, and a desire to improve the hymnbooks, and probably such schools were held in Baptist churches. A group of German Baptists under the leadership of Johann Conrad Beissel settled near Philadelphia in 1735, bringing with them excellent choral music. Beissel, although not born in America, is said to be the first American composer. *Hymns and Spiritual Songs,* the first Baptist hymnbook published in America, came off the press in 1776. This opened the way for the publication of other hymnals for use in Baptist churches.

Brown University, founded in 1764, was the first Baptist college in America. Vassar College, founded by Matthew Vassar, a Baptist, in 1837, was the first college for girls. Judson College in Alabama, founded in 1838, was the first Baptist college for girls in the South. Baptist colleges have increased in numbers until in 1956 Southern Baptists claimed 30 senior colleges, 21 junior colleges, and 5 theological seminaries. Music is given an important place in each of these institutions. In the last decade these schools have given special emphasis to church music, and some are offering degrees in this specialized field. Much progress has been made in music education in the first half of the 20th century.

In 1915 the Southwestern Baptist Theological Seminary, Fort Worth, Tex., established a department of sacred music with courses designed for ministerial students and specialized studies for students choosing sacred music as a vocation. In 1925 this department became the School of Sacred Music, and degrees were offered in this field of study.

The New Orleans Baptist Theological Seminary (formerly Baptist Bible Institute), New Orleans, La., was established in 1918. Its purpose included "the training of gospel singers and directors of music." A department of music was formed at that time, and in 1952 it became the School of Sacred Music with degrees offered in this specialized field.

The Southern Baptist Theological Seminary, Louisville, Ky., added music to its theological course in 1921. The School of Church Music of this seminary was established in 1943 to give professional vocational training.

The Golden Gate Theological Seminary, Berkeley, Calif., was organized in 1944. Courses in music, designed to prepare students for the ministry of music and leading to degrees, were offered from the beginning of the school.

Southeastern Baptist Theological Seminary, Wake Forest, N. C., was opened in 1951. Music was planned for the students in theology and religious education for the 1956–57 session.

In 1925 the Southern Baptist Convention in its annual session was requested by Isham Emmanuel Reynolds (*q.v.*) to appoint a committee of five to investigate the type and character of music used by the average Baptist church and to offer suggestions as to methods of advancement in this matter. The committee appointed, composed of Reynolds, E. C. Dargan (*q.v.*), Charles William Daniel (*q.v.*), Ernest Orlando Sellers (*q.v.*), and J. Fred Scholfield, was asked to report at the 1926 session. At this convention the report requested that the denominational colleges give particular attention to church music in their fine arts departments and also asked that the churches give special emphasis to the first Southern Baptist Music Conference at Ridgecrest, N. C., Aug. 1–12, 1926, under the direction of the Education Board. The Convention was asked to request the Sunday School Board to give consideration to sponsoring a church music department, for the purpose of improving music in church, Sunday school, and B.Y.P.U. This was the first time music education had appeared on the program of the Southern Baptist Convention.

The matter of improving church music was brought to the attention of the Convention again in 1937. The committee recommended that the Sunday School Board assume the responsibility in development of the ideals of worship particularly as they relate to music. The Sunday School Board had already secured Baylus Benjamin McKinney (*q.v.*) as secretary of the music education program, and he began his duties in Dec., 1935. The board organized the Department of Church Music in 1941.

The last committee report on church music was made to the Convention in 1944. The committee was composed of Ellis L. Carnett, chairman, E. Powell Lee, R. Inman Johnson, Joe Canzoneri, and W. Plunkett Martin. This committee reported as follows:

> We urge our Baptist colleges, universities, and seminaries to place in their curriculum a Department of Church Music and that certain definite courses be required of all ministerial students.
>
> We urge states of the Southern Baptist Convention to consider a church music setup equal in scope to the other departments of church activity fostered by our states.
>
> We recommend that the Sunday School Board be instructed to increase the personnel of the Department of Church Music sufficiently to prepare and set going a constructive, educational program of church music among Southern Baptists.

The Sunday School Board now operates a full educational program of church music. State music secretaries work in co-operation with many states, and state programs of music education are in force. State music assemblies, leadership schools, and associational music schools are conducted. Music education has developed greatly in recent years, and the results are seen in all the states. Music weeks at Ridgecrest, N. C., and Glorieta, N. Mex., have become peaks in this program. W. PLUNKETT MARTIN

MUSIC EDUCATION IN INSTITUTIONS. The interest of music within the denomination has been most closely associated with local and denominational needs. Rather than as a result of an established plan, the institutions serving music have been established as an outgrowth of these musical demands.

The colleges.—One of the most powerful forces in popularizing the role of music in the community and church was the growth of the "preacher-singer" combination. In the establishment of colleges and seminaries, the founder or choice for president would, in many cases, be a prominent Baptist minister. Since many of these men were musicians themselves or vitally interested in music due to their church contacts, a number of the early music departments were either established by them or through the adoption of their philosophy. The influence of some of the founders of Baptist colleges (Furman, Mercer) was felt also in early consideration of music in the activities of the school. In the later 19th century hymnology was introduced into the curriculum of Southern Baptist Theological Seminary through the work of Andrew Broaddus (*q.v.*).

Schools which originally offered music study included these courses for cultural purposes or for the benefit of the minister. It is interesting to note that both of the two earliest seminaries were started on college campuses (Southern at Furman, 1859; Southwestern at Baylor, 1908). The early establishment of music as part of the curriculum of seminaries testifies to the influence that the churches, through their ministers and seminary trustees, had in encouraging music as part of the preparation of the minister. As the colleges grew, the music curriculum began to include courses to train music teachers in the public schools. This was an outgrowth of the public school music movement in the eastern section of the country, begun in the middle of the 19th century. Early leadership in college music programs came from former professional musicians, performers, public school music teachers, and the church musician or "singer." The music curricula of Baptist colleges still reflect this major emphasis, first, upon performance and the cultural advantages of music; second, on public school music; and last, in the field of church music. Perhaps the greatest direct influence upon the growth of music within the colleges, so far as an organized demand was concerned, was the need for Christian music teachers in public

FIRST BAPTIST CHURCH, Lubbock, Tex. Established 1891, this Romanesque auditorium seating 2,350 and educational unit serving 3,100 was conceived, erected, and completed without debt during the ten-year ministry of the present pastor. The membership was 7,488 in 1956 and the property value was $2,250,000.

FIRST BAPTIST CHURCH, Richmond, Va. Organized 1780, membership 1956 over 4,000. Modified Doric structure serves 1,675 in auditorium, 2,400 in Sunday school. Property replacement cost estimated at $5,000,000.

schools and communities. In most of the colleges today, this group is still the largest segment of the music student body.

Before the end of the 19th century, music departments had been established in the following schools: Furman, Stetson, Howard Payne, Mary Hardin-Baylor, and Meredith. The early establishment of music in women's colleges seems to indicate the popular persuasion that music was of importance for cultural advantages as well as to train teachers. In the practical utilization of music within the denomination, many orphanages and similar institutions installed music in their curricula on either a formal or an informal basis. Twenty-one junior colleges, which have been founded over the years, also reflect this concern for the performance of music and public school music training for teachers.

The second major growth pattern centered around the need of churches for musicians. As the denomination had placed major emphasis upon congregational singing and the role of the singer as soloist-congregational song leader, this demand seemed to culminate in a need for vocalists rather than instrumental talent. In regard to the source of the college interest in church music, much of this interest reflects the needs of the churches and the success of the seminaries in this area of service. The establishment of denominational and state secretaries in the area of church music further increased the demand for additional college- or seminary-trained church music leadership in the churches. The scope and great demand for church musicians in the Baptist churches of the South and Southwest is a unique musical phenomenon in American college and seminary institutions. In many colleges the church music department is the fastest growing segment of the music student body.

As many of the college music programs expanded and more teachers had diversified backgrounds, education, and training, such degree courses as music theory and composition, music literature, and conducting have taken their place beside the older courses of study. The matter of graduate instruction in music moves rather slowly, basically due to cost and demand, with only two colleges and four seminaries offering master's degrees. One seminary offers the doctorate in sacred music.

There are still many opportunities to be claimed in the field of college music, but these in part must wait for increased financial support for the music departments, enlarged physical facilities, an extensive recruitment program to encourage Baptist musical talent to attend Baptist colleges, and for more music departments to gain national accrediting in the field of music. At the present time only nine of the 30 senior colleges have been accredited by the national music school accrediting body.

In the fall of 1956, a total of approximately 1,750 music majors were enrolled in 30 Baptist senior college music departments or schools.

The seminaries.—The earliest music department in seminary instruction was organized at Southwestern in 1915, with New Orleans, Southern, and Golden Gate music departments or schools being established in that order. The first and still the main objective of seminary music education is to train musicians for the churches. This ministry has been enlarged now to include the training of combination music-religious education directors, denominational workers, and college and seminary teachers.

Although the four seminaries offering degrees in church music had approximately 290 music majors enrolled in the fall of 1956, the demand for seminary graduates far exceeds the supply. Many of the students are working on what is in reality a combination college-seminary Bachelor of Sacred Music degree course of study, which includes a minimum 60 hours of college study and approximately three years of seminary instruction. The major portion of the students pursue a Master of Sacred Music degree, a two-year seminary course of study based upon a college four-year degree. A very limited number have undertaken study toward the Doctor of Sacred Music degree. A diploma course consisting of two to three years of seminary instruction, but with college prerequisites, is available for those qualified to undertake study.

The two major areas of expansion yet to be fully developed in seminary music programs are more extensive enlistment among musically gifted college youth in dedication of life to the ministry of music and the subsequent increased financial support necessary to guarantee the best type of church music instruction.

FORREST H. HEEREN

Baptist Conventions and Assemblies. Music training programs in connection with conventions and assemblies were advocated as early as 1920 by I. E. Reynolds, director of the School of Gospel Music, Southwestern Baptist Theological Seminary, Fort Worth, Tex., and one of the leading contenders for a church music education program. As early as 1920, Reynolds had urged the Baptist Sunday School Board to send music workers to Baptist training schools, institutes, and summer assemblies to instruct and demonstrate what could be done with music in the Sunday schools and Baptist Young People's Unions. In 1929 in his book *The Ministry of Music,* Reynolds suggested assemblies, conventions, and similar meetings as the logical starting point to project a definite plan of music education. He proposed that a church music education program be fostered by churches, cities, or counties, and that it be given a place on the programs of various denominational conferences, conventions, institutes, assemblies, Sunday school and Young People's training schools for lectures and round-table discussions.

Visible signs of improvement continued to be intermittent and sporadic. Of great influence in this movement was Robert Henry Coleman (*q.v.*), compiler and publisher of songbooks and associate of George Washington Truett

SCOPE OF DEGREES AND MAJORS IN MUSIC OFFERED BY SOUTHERN BAPTIST COLLEGES AND SEMINARIES

SCHOOL	B. A.	B. S.	B. M.	M. A.	M. S.	M. M.	B. S. M.	M. S. M.	D. S. M.	Applied Music	Public Sch. Music	Church Mus.	Theory of Composition	Literature	Conducting	General	Piano Ped.
Senior Colleges																	
Baylor Univ.	x	x	x	x	x	x				x	x	x	x	x	x		
Belmont		x									x						
Blue Mountain	x		x							x	x					x	
California Baptist	x	x								x	x	x					
Carson-Newman	x	x								x	x	x					
East Texas Baptist	x	x	x								x						
Furman Univ.	x									x	x	x					x
Georgetown	x		x							x	x		x				
Grand Canyon	x									x			x				
Hardin-Simmons Univ.		x	x		x	x				x	x		x				
Howard	x		x							x	x	x				x	
Howard Payne		x	x							x	x	x	x				
Judson	x									x	x						
Louisiana	x									x	x	x					
Mary Hardin–Baylor	x		x				x			x	x					x	
Mercer Univ.			x									x					
Meredith			x							x							
Mississippi	x	x	x							x	x	x					
Oklahoma Baptist Univ.		x	x							x	x				x		
Ouachita	x		x							x	x	x					
Shorter	x		x							x	x					x	
Stetson	x		x							x	x	x	x				
Tift	x									x							
Union Univ.	x		x							x	x					x	
Univ. of Corpus Christi			x								x						
Univ. of Richmond	x	x									x					x	
Wake Forest	x															x	
Wayland	x									x	x	x	x				
William Carey	x		x							x	x		x				
William Jewell	x									x	x	x					
TOTALS—30 schools	23	10	18	1	2	2	1			24	25	13	8	1	2	7	1
Seminaries																	
Golden Gate							x	x		x		x	x			x	
New Orleans							x	x		x		x	x		x	x	
Southern								x	x	x		x	x	x	x	x	
Southwestern							x	x		x		x	x	x		x	
TOTALS—4 schools							3	4	1	4		4	4	2	2	4	

(*q.v.*), pastor of First Baptist Church, Dallas, Tex. Coleman, Reynolds, B. B. McKinney (*q.v.*), E. O. Sellers (*q.v.*), and others were familiar personalities in various Baptist meetings throughout the Southern Baptist Convention. These men, thoroughly evangelistic and staunch in their Baptist faith, continually emphasized the need for a definite plan of church music education.

They exerted great influence on congregational singing, continually emphasizing the use of hymns and gospel songs that were scripturally true and doctrinally sound. They encouraged participation by all the people in the song services.

Occasional hymn festivals were conducted in various areas. The success of such a festival, held in Broadway Baptist Church, Louisville, Ky., in Mar., 1941, so inspired and encouraged the directors of participating choirs that they proceeded immediately to form a permanent organization known as the Council of Choirs. This council later sponsored a school of music which was attended by 200 people, representing 31 churches and seven denominations. Similar festivals were soon being planned in other sections of the Convention.

In 1941 the Department of Church Music of the Baptist Sunday School Board was created. McKinney, who had been with the board since 1935 as music editor, was elected secretary of the new department.

In stating aims of the newly created department, McKinney emphasized co-operation with the seminaries and denominational universities and colleges in producing better leaders in church music. He further proposed the holding of festivals, institutes, and conferences in these schools, in conventions, summer assemblies, associational meetings, and individual churches throughout the Convention. In announcing the creation of this new department and presenting the secretary to Southern Baptists, T. Luther Holcomb, executive secretary-treasurer of the Sunday School Board, announced that a new manual, *Let Us Sing*, had been prepared. Those studying the book in assemblies and other conferences could receive either Sunday school or Training Union credit. In the manual the author stressed the need of a constructive educational program which would result in developing talents of individual members of each church. He further emphasized the need for trained leaders to achieve their goals. Such a program was suggested in the manual.

The Sunday School Board encouraged and offered financial aid to the various states for the organization of state departments of church music. The state music secretaries would in turn promote a program of music education which would be closely related to the various state conventions and assemblies.

By Dec. 31, 1955, 16 states had music secretaries who were promoting music education programs. Other states anticipated such workers and programs in the immediate future. Each state secretary of music assists with the planning of music for the various state conventions and conferences; he assists with various statewide assemblies, conferences, and conventions, often teaching the classes and leading discussion groups. The promotion of music festivals on a statewide level has become an effective medium of church music education.

The music education program as promoted by the Department of Church Music of the Sunday School Board extends its training emphases through the state secretaries to the various associations with their annual meetings, assemblies, and festivals, on to the local church and the enlistment of the masses of people in music participation.

It is through the state music organizations that music education in conventions, assemblies, and festivals has achieved its greatest benefits. Beginning with Arkansas in 1941, youth choir festivals, youth music camps, and other projects designed to train and educate musicians were promoted. Although no two states have identical programs, there are many similarities. Florida has developed a youth music camp as a part of its training program. Georgia has in its music education program a statewide festival and an annual youth music camp. Illinois has a state choir and hymn playing festival as part of its training program. Louisiana and Mississippi have placed great emphasis on the festival, with both district and state festivals. Missouri established a youth music camp in 1954. New Mexico includes a music festival as a part of the annual Training Union convention. Oklahoma has extended its music education program through the annual Falls Creek Assembly and an annual church music festival for junior and senior high school students. Other states, including Tennessee, Texas, Alabama, Arizona, California, Virginia, and North Carolina, have related their music programs to the assemblies and conventions. Various types of festivals, conferences, camps, and music assemblies are promoted in all of the states.

Each summer the Department of Church Music of the Sunday School Board holds Convention-wide music conferences at Ridgecrest, N. C., and Glorieta, N. Mex. Thousands of church musicians from Baptist churches attend these conferences to continue their studies in various areas of church music education.

LOREN R. WILLIAMS

Music Education in Baptist Churches. Prior to 1939 no definite program of music education existed in Southern Baptist churches. Each church exercised its own resources for its music in the worship services as well as in all church organizations. This usually amounted to no more than one choir and little or no leadership training.

Tremendous progress in the field of music education in the public schools and communities and the miracles of electronics which brought music into every home resulted in a realization that some definite program of music education was needed in the churches. Church members could not be expected to hear good music six days a week and then be subjected to inferior music on Sunday.

Many leaders throughout the Convention realized the great need for a definite and progressive program of music education, denominationally sponsored and encouraged through the various states and associations, which would result in a comprehensive music education program for each church. These leaders brought the matter to the Southern Baptist Convention. Finally in 1937, as a result of a resolution presented by E. O. Sellers, a committee was appointed to make a survey of music needs and bring recommendations to the Convention. Music committees were appointed yearly and presented definite recommendations to the Convention from 1938 to 1944. Their reports urged the denomination to do in the field of music what had been done in the areas of Sunday school and Training Union work, missions, and other activities.

The recommendation adopted by the Convention in Atlanta, Ga., in 1944 set up a definite program to be sponsored by the Convention through assignment to the Sunday School Board. Parts of the recommendation of the committee follow:

> . . . We can't have better church music until we train our people.
>
> . . . We note with satisfaction the growing tendency on the part of states, associations, and churches, to do something definite about church music.
>
> . . . We reaffirm our belief in graded choirs.
>
> . . . We urge our Baptist colleges, universities, and seminaries to place in their curriculum a Department of Church Music and that certain definite courses be required of all ministerial students.
>
> . . . We urge states to consider a church music setup equal in scope to the other departments of church activity fostered by our states.
>
> . . . We feel that Southern Baptists are justified in asking that a considerable amount of the profits received from the sale of songbooks and other music be expended in a worthy Church Music Educational Program. Therefore, realizing the dire need of, and the Macedonian call for, a better Church Music Program for Southern Baptists, we recommend that the Sunday School Board be instructed to increase the personnel of the Department of Church Music sufficiently to prepare and set going a constructive, educational program of church music among Southern Baptists.

Upon assignment to the Sunday School Board, the Department of Church Music under the secretaryship of B. B. McKinney began to project a unified program. First came the book *Let Us Sing,* which was the basis of a graded music education program within the church. The Sunday School Board had previously organized its Church Music Department in 1941 and, after the recommendation of the Convention, added the services of Walter Hines Sims in 1946, Loren R. Williams and Clifford A. Holcomb in 1952, and William J. Reynolds in 1956, to assist in the development of the over-all music education program for the Convention.

In order to implement the program, the Sunday School Board began and continues to do many things which help in the program of the churches. Among these are: (1) financial co-operation with the state mission boards in the development of departments of music in the states; (2) co-operation through the personnel of the music department counseling and advising with state, associational, and church leaders; (3) emphasis upon good music in the publications of the Sunday School Board; (4) the publication of good hymnals, songbooks, choir music, songbooks for children, ensemble music, miscellaneous materials, and supplies which would be of help to a music program; (5) the development of a series of free pamphlets for the churches which presents all areas of church music; (6) a comprehensive church music training course of texts for use in church music training schools in churches, associations, and state leadership schools, camps, and assemblies; (7) the encouragement of a trained music ministry through various emphases which channel talented young people into the field of church music, provide for their training, and assure acceptance and tenure on part of the churches; (8) music weeks at Ridgecrest, N. C., and Glorieta, N. Mex., for the training of music leadership in the churches; (9) the monthly publication of a church music magazine, *The Church Musician,* which supplies helps, materials, plans, programs, graded choir suggestions, as well as music for all age group choirs; and (10) a promotional program which emphasizes September—Church Music Month, hymn sings, carol sings, hymn rehearsals, hymn of the month plan, utilization of specially prepared publications for Baptist churches, and co-operation with associational, state, and Southern Baptist activities.

Through these many emphases and the promotion through the various states and associations, Baptist churches everywhere began the use of uniform methods of promoting music education within the church. The local church program of music utilizes five distinct areas of work, each having its particular emphasis. Great encouragement is given to congregational singing where all of the people participate in the music program of the church. To implement this emphasis, a new hymnal designed for congregational singing, *Baptist Hymnal,* was issued in 1956. Along with the congregational singing, an annual carol sing by the church, quarterly hymn rehearsals scheduled at times best suited to the congregation, and emphasis upon good singing in all of the church departmental organizations which is implemented by able song leaders, accompanists, and special music supplied by the music department of the church are encouraged.

The graded choir program is a second important facet of the music education program. This offers choral participation for Beginners, Primaries, Juniors, Intermediates, Young People, and Adults. Also, choruses of men, women, small ensembles, and speech choirs are being used. Churches having graded Sunday school programs can have a graded choir program. Through the graded choirs the people develop naturally from childhood to adulthood in voice training. Thus the congregational singing improves, and the church grows a singing membership.

The third area is in the field of developing instrumentalists. A program of developing pianists for all of the departments of the church, organists for service, a church orchestra where instrumentalists are available, instrumental ensembles, and instrumental soloists for use within the church in all of its music program is advocated and promoted.

The fourth area is that of regular and progressive training. This involves an annual music school for the church and regular classes in music throughout the year for the purpose of training choir singers to read music, developing song leaders for the agencies of the church, training pianists for the various departments, developing organists, offering to the lay person in the church music courses such as hymnology, music in the Bible, and other subjects which would be of interest. The training program becomes a year-round opportunity.

The fifth area is in that of promotion, wherein the church utilizes the many publications and recommendations prepared by the Department of Church Music of the Sunday School Board; sponsors September as Church Music Month and thereby organizes new choirs, develops future leadership, and schedules the year's program of activities; promotes the hymn of the month plan, which emphasizes a new hymn each month and increases the cycle of hymns sung in the church; uses regular publicity in the church bulletin and other means for keeping the membership informed and for promoting the church music program; participates in church music festivals on the associational and state level so as to encourage the various choirs and enable members to hear other groups sing; and co-operates in the various promotional activities of the association, which includes schools of music, hymn sings, carol sings, festivals, utilization of standard record systems, and the use of publications designed for Baptist churches.

To help implement the programs, the Department of Church Music issues three Standards of Excellence: a Standard of Excellence for a Baptist Church Music Department, an Advanced Standard of Excellence for a Baptist Church Music Department, and an Associational Standard of Excellence. Through these Standards of Excellence the churches and associations are able to produce a balanced program of music which will assist in the training of leadership and develop the entire congregation in a genuine appreciation of music in worship, education, and evangelism. Throughout the entire Convention there now exists a co-operative program of music education that is increasingly meeting the needs of the churches and the people.

See also SINGING SCHOOLS. WALTER HINES SIMS

MYSTICISM. The belief that in religious experience man may enjoy direct, unmediated communion with God. Variations of mystical experience are great, ranging from quiet communion of prayer to ecstasies and trances of famous mystics. Some scholars regard Paul's experience recorded in II Corinthians 12 as manifesting typical mystical traits. Mystics usually prescribe a series of acts which one must faithfully follow to induce the mystical experience. Some scholars believe that there is a genuine Christian mysticism; others feel that Christianity and mysticism are inimical to each other.

BERNARD RAMM

N

NASHVILLE BAPTIST HOSPITAL. An institution operated by Tennessee Baptists for five years after Sept. 22, 1924. The hospital, formerly a private institution called the Women's Hospital of Nashville, was given to the Tennessee convention subject to certain conditions, one of which was that an addition worth $500,-000 was to be added to the hospital within five years after the convention assumed control. When the convention found itself unable to meet this condition, the hospital was returned to its former trustees, in Dec., 1929. D. A. ELLIS

NATIONAL ASSOCIATION OF EVANGELICALS, THE. An interdenominational body composed of representatives of various evangelical denominations, local churches, and church organizations, and maintained for purposes of fellowship, counsel, evangelical testimony, service, and united action. The N.A.E. is not a council of churches and has no authority over the bodies represented within it.

The association was the outcome of a movement seeking inter-church co-operation without compromise of basic Christian doctrine. The movement began in New England (The New England Fellowship). Following representative conferences at the national level in Chicago, Ill., Oct. 27–28, 1941, and in St. Louis, Mo., Apr. 7–9, 1942, a constitutional convention was held in Chicago May 4–7, 1943, at which a statement of faith and a constitution were adopted, and The National Association of Evangelicals was officially organized.

Indicative of its doctrinal viewpoint are the first three items of its seven-point statement:

(1) We believe the Bible to be the inspired, the only infallible, authoritative word of God. (2) We believe that there is one God, eternally existent in three persons, Father, Son, and Holy Ghost. (3) We believe in the deity of our Lord Jesus Christ, in His virgin birth, in His sinless life, in His miracles, in His vicarious and atoning death through His shed blood, in His bodily resurrection, in His ascension to the right hand of the Father, and in His personal return in power and glory.

The activities of the N.A.E. are limited by the expression of counsel and recommendations of its constituent members. It holds an annual delegate convention which has final authority. Its work is carried on by a board of administration, an executive committee, and various commissions and affiliated agencies, which include among their work programs dealing with the following areas: foreign missions, home missions and evangelism, radio and television, public affairs, chaplaincies, welfare and social action, evangelical action, Sunday schools, higher education, Christian day schools, youth, world relief, and international relations. Its official journal is *United Evangelical Action.* In 1956 the N.A.E. had 40 denominations in official membership as well as hundreds of local churches from all evangelical denominations. Its service constituency is officially estimated at 10,000,000. The national headquarters office is at Wheaton, Ill. A world organization, The World Evangelical Fellowship, with which the N.A.E. is affiliated, has headquarters in London and Washington.

JAMES DEFOREST MURCH

NATIONAL BAPTIST CONVENTION, U. S. A., INC. "The older and parent convention of Negro Baptists. This body is to be distinguished from the National Baptist Convention of America, usually referred to as the 'unincorporated' body." It numbers 25,603 co-operating churches, each locally independent, having an aggregate membership of 4,557,416.

J. H. Jackson, pastor of Olivet Baptist Church, Chicago, Ill., was serving his fourth term as president in 1957. The convention's constitution provides for an executive secretary, but none has been called. The strength of the convention lies in the traditional South, with Alabama sending the most representatives to the annual convention meetings. However, population shifts of Negroes from the South have planted co-operating churches in additional states.

The convention operates through boards and commissions. The boards, while incorporated, are under legal control of the convention, which is a "corporation of corporations." Full-time boards include the Sunday School Publishing Board, National B. T. U. Board, Foreign Mission Board, and Home Mission Board. The part-time boards are the Ministerial Benefit Board and the Education Board (which works with convention-related institutions of higher education). The convention maintains a National Baptist Sanitarium-Bath House at Hot Springs, Ark., having a full-time manager. The official convention publication is the *National Baptist Voice,* published monthly at Chester, Pa. The title of the chief executive officer of a particular board is corresponding secretary. There are no limits on the terms of corresponding secretaries. The boards adopt their own budgets, subject to review and approval of the convention. This power to review and approve budgets is not necessarily always exercised. The boards include one member from each state convention co-operating with the Convention. Nine members are chosen for each board from the state in which the board is located, provided there are no more than two members from any one church. The state convention members of the board generally remain the same from year to year. Their election takes place during the state conventions, but they must be confirmed by the Convention.

Commissions of the Convention are the Business Committee, which studies resolutions and other business matters before they go to the floor of the Convention, the Commission on Theological Education, the Commission on International and Inter-Cultural Relations, which deals with cultural exchanges with other nations, Commission on Problems of Labor and Management, Commission on Ecumenical Christianity, which treats the Convention's relationship with other Christian denominations, Commission on Problem of Church-supported Colleges, Commission on Denominational Co-ordination, whose duty it is to report any overlapping and duplication of work by Convention agencies, Rural Life Commission, Commission on Current Civic Issues or Public Affairs Committee, Commission on the United Nations, Public Relations Department, Department of Evangelism, Commission on Race Relations, Commission on Undergraduate Scholarships, Program Committee, which recommends the order of business for the Convention, and Committee on Place, which recommends a meeting place of the Convention up to four years in advance. Various committees are also appointed by the Convention president from time to time.

The Convention meets in annual session, generally in September. It may also hold an adjourned session between the regular sessions. From 4,000 to 5,000 persons register to attend the session, principally ministers from affiliated churches. The Woman's Convention, Auxiliary to the National Baptist Convention, meets simultaneously. The estimated total attendance is 10,000 at all simultaneous meetings. The Convention proper opens on Wednesday, closing the following Sunday.

The officers of this Convention [are] as follows: President, vice-president at large, four vice-presidents, a state vice-president from each of the states and territories having an organization affiliated with this Convention [there are 54 so-called state conventions with many states having more than one], a recording secretary, four assistant secretaries, an executive secretary [an unfilled position], treasurer, statistician, historiographer, attorney, editor, all of whom shall be elected annually by the Convention, and shall hold office until their successors are elected and qualified.

There are three types of membership for the annual convention. Representative membership, as defined in the constitution, is thus:

(a) Churches with 200 to 500 members, $25.00; 500 to 1000 members, $35.00; churches above 1000 members, $50.00; churches with less than 200 members, $10.00. Each church shall be allowed an additional messenger for each $10.00 paid, but no church shall be allowed to exceed (10) ten messengers. (b) State Convention basis of representation, $200.00. The state convention will be allowed an additional messenger for every additional $50.00 paid in as representation, not to exceed two messengers. (c) District State Convention, $50.00. (d) Associations, $35.00.

All of the messengers have voting privileges. Any person in good standing as a member of a co-operating church may become a life member of the Convention upon payment of $200. This also furnishes voting rights. Annual membership may be obtained for the sum of $10, but it does not include the right to vote.

The Convention belongs to the Baptist World Alliance, the National Council of Churches of Christ in the U.S.A., and the World Council of Churches. It also supports the Baptist Joint Committee on Public Affairs.

A board of directors conducts the business of the convention between its sessions. This board consists of the president, vice-president at large, four vice-presidents, 54 vice-presidents (who are the presidents of co-operating local conventions), recording secretary, treasurer, attorney, *National Baptist Voice* editor, historiographer, statistician, executive secretary, assistant secretaries, and nine members at large elected by the Convention. The majority of the board must be present to constitute a quorum. The executive committee of the board of directors is made up of 12 members—the president, secretary, treasurer, and nine others—whose duty it is to look after any unfinished business of the board of directors and to transact any urgent matters of business demanding immediate attention.

"The Cabinet is the workhorse of the Convention, making recommendations to the Board of Directors." The cabinet officers are the Convention's president, vice-president at large, four vice-presidents, recording secretary, corresponding secretary, financial secretary, two assistant secretaries, secretary of publicity, statistician, historiographer, editor of *National Baptist Voice,* treasurer, and attorney.

The Convention, in conjunction with the Southern Baptist Convention, operates a seminary for Negro theological and religious education students known as the American Baptist Theological Seminary, in Nashville, Tenn. It had in 1957 as its acting president Victor T. Glass, the first white man ever to serve as administrative head of the school. The Southern Baptist Convention has a majority of members on the holding board of the seminary. The role of the National Baptist Convention, U.S.A., Inc., in the operation of this seminary was under re-examination in 1957.

Among the other Negro Baptist institutions of higher education, some are affiliated with the American Baptist Convention.

Today there are ten institutions affiliated with the Board of Education of this Convention, namely, Benedict College, Bishop College, Florida Normal and Industrial College, Leland College, Mather School (a secondary school for girls in Beaufort, South Carolina), Morehouse College, Shaw University, Spelman College (for women), Storer College, and Virginia Union University. In most of these schools the (American) Baptists underwrite only a small portion of the annual budgets, but, as stated above, the historical affiliation is strong, and there is mutual satisfaction in the continuing relationships.

There are also schools founded by and still largely controlled by the Negro Baptist state conventions. "The following schools are in this category: Morris College, Selma University, Arkansas Baptist College, Butler College, Virginia Seminary and College, Friendship Junior College, Oklahoma School of Religion, and Western Baptist Seminary." The missionary teacher program of the Home Mission Board of the Southern Baptist Convention operates at several of these institutions.

"The National Baptist Convention has what is called an 'Educational Commission,' but there seems to be no tangible evidence of the accomplishments of this group. It is clear that the Negro Baptists are in a position to do much more for education than is being done at the present time." President Jackson has been advocating the creation of a National Baptist Education Foundation to have a minimum of $10,000,000. The foundation would set the standards for education and help give the schools accreditation and national standing. "Its purpose would be not to create additional schools but to throw weight behind existing institutions." A meeting was held at Morehouse College, in Atlanta, Ga., Nov. 13, 1956, to discuss this proposal.

The president of the National Convention, who is elected annually, has been limited to four successive terms. After that, he must wait one year before being eligible for re-election. Before the adoption of the limit of tenure, one convention president served for 28 years, another for 18 years, and a third for 12 years. However, the convention is debating the abolition of this restriction on the terms of the president.

The financial support of the convention's institutions and over-all program is hard to determine. There appears to be no unified budget or unified channel for distributing funds to objects of convention support. Frequently, the churches take up three or more offerings during a church worship service, each designated for a different purpose. Records of total giving by the denomination's membership for any given period of time are nonexistent. Some boards appear from their financial statements to receive little more than enough money to maintain their administrative functions.

The convention promotes its denomination-wide program by employing special fieldworkers. These fieldworkers serve on a full-time basis for the duration of the cause being promoted and are not permanent employees. Some of the co-operating state conventions have begun to use the same theme in their annual meetings that the Convention chose at its session.

Some of the convention's affiliated churches are also affiliated with the American Baptist Convention. Others are affiliated with associations of churches that co-operate with the Southern Baptist Convention. These churches provide financial support through each of the conventions with which they are affiliated.

There is a likelihood of reunion of the two National Baptist Conventions, incorporated and "unincorporated," at some indefinite future date. They are presently exchanging ministers for revival services. President Jackson of the incorporated body has foreseen the likelihood of a reunion and feels it will come to pass.

A reorganization study of the incorporated convention was proposed by Jackson in his 1956 address to the Convention session.

> The National Baptist Convention is a million-dollar corporation. . . . Therefore I recommend that we select a committee of laymen who are successful businessmen to study, to analyze, and to evaluate the business methods of our Convention and recommend improved techniques that will make our enterprise more efficient and the Convention more self-supporting. This committee should comprise men who will be considered as dollar-a-year men to work for the betterment of our Convention.

There is some relationship implied here between the proposed study and the already existent Commission on Denominational Coordination, but the connection is not clearly defined.

The Convention has under consideration the establishment of a retirement program. This would go beyond the scope of the present Ministerial Benefit Board. The funds contributed to the retirement program might be invested in a revolving church loan fund. Nothing was definite and final in 1957.

The Convention traces its beginnings to the organization of the Foreign Mission Convention, which came into being Nov. 24, 1880, at Montgomery, Ala. There "150 persons, principally ministers and church workers, from eleven states answered the Rev. (W. W.) Colley's call for this noble purpose. . . . The moving spirit of the new movement was the Rev. W. W. Colley, returned missionary of the Southern Baptist Convention." Colley was sent to Africa by the Southern Baptist Convention Foreign Mission Board in 1875 and served until 1879. The name National Baptist Convention was applied to an organization formed Aug. 25, 1886. (However, the Convention has chosen the organization of the Foreign Mission Convention as its own starting. In this connection, the 1955 session of the National Baptist Convention, U.S.A., Inc., was regarded as the 75th anniversary.) The two conventions and the National Educational Convention merged into the National Baptist Convention of the U.S.A. The chief emphasis of the National Educational Convention had been for an educated ministry in the leadership of the churches. The merger came about Sept. 28, 1895, in Atlanta, Ga. The constitution adopted there declared, "This body shall become known and styled, The National Baptist Convention of the United States of America."

The convention divided in 1915 when members differed over the operation of the convention's publishing board in Nashville, Tenn. R. H. Boyd was corresponding secretary of the publishing board. One group felt that the convention directly owned the property and controlled the board; another, and minor, faction asserted that the publishing board was independent of the convention. This apparently generated enough friction to sever fellowship. The courts of Tennessee ruled in a resulting lawsuit that the convention did not control and own the publishing board. The minority group after the division sided with Boyd, who continued as corresponding secretary of the publishing house. This minority became identified as the "unincorporated" group. The majority lost the property and board but established another, the Sunday School Publishing Board, also located in Nashville. They provided that the new board was to be subject to the Convention.

THEO SOMMERKAMP

NATIONAL BAPTIST CONVENTION OF AMERICA. One of the two major Negro Baptist bodies in America that grew out of the 1916 division in the ranks of the original national organization of Negro Baptists. The Baptist Foreign Mission Convention of America, organized in Montgomery, Ala., Nov. 24–26, 1880, by 150 messengers who responded to the call of W. W. Colley, was the first attempt at national coalition. Six years later, on Aug. 25, 1886, 600 delegates representing 17 states met in St. Louis at the call of William J. Simmons and organized the American National Baptist Convention. A third delegation met in 1893 in the District of Columbia and formed the American National Educational Baptist

Convention. These three bodies merged in 1895 at Atlanta, Ga., to form the National Baptist Convention of the United States of America. This body then formed a foreign mission board, home mission board, and education board to promote these phases of its work. E. C. Morris of Arkansas became the first president of the unified convention. Negro Baptists in 1898 established the National Baptist Publishing Board in Nashville, Tenn. This board, now the publication agency accepted by the National Baptist Convention of America, prints a weekly newspaper, *The National Baptist Union Review,* Sunday school periodicals, Baptist Young People's Union literature, commentaries, all types of literature for missionary societies, children's organizations, and church records. Negro Baptists incorporated their national body in 1915, but the following year divided in a dispute over the control of the convention publications, in which the election and tenure of national officers was concerned. Two rival conventions resulted, the National Baptist Convention of the United States of America, Inc., and the National Baptist Convention of America, both of which claim to be a continuation of the parent body. The latter convention claims affiliation with 426 local associations and four auxiliary conventions. It endorses nine of the 31 colleges and seminaries sponsored by these bodies. Although the convention has no national headquarters, it conducts its work through a home mission board, located in Chicago, that assists needy churches and schools; a foreign mission board, which maintains work in Sinoe, West Coast Africa; Jamaica, British West Indies; and in the Bahama Islands; a benevolent board, evangelical board, publishing board, educational board, and a B.Y.P.U. board. The convention in 1954 reported 11,169 churches with 2,658,974 members.
ALBERT MC CLELLAN and LYNN E. MAY, JR.

NATIONAL BAPTIST CONVENTION OF MEXICO, THE. Evangelical Christian work in Mexico was initiated by Baptists. James Thomson, a Baptist preacher and colporteur of the British and Foreign Bible Society, labored in Mexico from 1827 to 1830. The first evangelical church to be organized in Mexico was the Baptist Church of Monterrey, Nuevo León, established Jan. 30, 1864, under the leadership of James Hickey. The National Baptist Convention of Mexico was organized Sept. 14, 1903, in Mexico City, with 43 messengers representing 12 churches and one association. Today 139 churches and 11 associations are affiliated with the convention. The total number of Baptists is listed as 16,125. The convention has no permanent headquarters as such; the address of the annually elected president constitutes the nearest approximation thereto. It promotes its work through five permanent boards respectively entrusted with responsibility for missions, evangelism, stewardship, Christian education, and publications. These boards are elected at the annual meetings of the convention. The official publication is *La Luz,* appearing monthly. The National Baptist Young People's Union and the National Baptist Woman's Missionary Union are auxiliaries of the convention. They publish their own periodicals (*Juventud Bautista* and *La Voz Misionera,* respectively) and carry out promotional and missionary work in co-operation with the general plans of the convention. JAMES D. CRANE

NATIONAL BAPTIST EVANGELICAL LIFE AND SOUL SAVING ASSEMBLY OF THE UNITED STATES OF AMERICA. A relatively new Baptist group, organized in 1921 by A. A. Banks. At first it was not a separate denomination but an evangelical fellowship that worked within the Negro National Baptist Convention (unincorporated). In 1937 it became a separate organization. It emphasizes evangelism and relief and maintains a correspondence course on evangelism, missions, pastoral ministry, the work of deacons, and the work of laymen. Degrees are granted after two, three, and four months of study. In 1951 there were 264 churches with 57,764 members. Headquarters are maintained at 441 Monroe Ave., Detroit 26, Mich. ALBERT MC CLELLAN

NATIONAL BAPTIST FLAG. A Baptist paper (now extinct) founded in Oklahoma City, Okla., in 1896. During 1902–03 it was edited by D. B. Ray and published each Thursday by the Baptist Publishing Company. The 1906 circulation was reported at 5,000, and the next year it was 6,000. The four-column pages were 11 x 14 inches in size, and the price was $1 per year. J. M. GASKIN

NATIONAL COUNCIL OF THE CHURCHES OF CHRIST, U. S. A. The co-operative agency of 30 national church bodies, 25 Protestant and 5 Eastern Orthodox, which have 143,932 local churches and a combined membership of 35,874,601. Through the National Council the constituent bodies carry out together more than 70 different programs ranging from a ministry for migrant farm workers to teaching millions of illiterates around the world to read.

In addition to conducting specific co-operative programs on a year-round basis, the National Council speaks as a united voice on public matters of concern to its constituent churches. Its pronouncements, together with all major policy decisions affecting the life and work of the organization, are made by the National Council's two governing bodies: the 600-member general assembly, which meets every three years, and the 240-member general board, which meets four times yearly. Both bodies are composed of official representatives of the member churches.

The National Council of Churches was formed Nov. 29, 1950, with the merging of 12 formerly separate agencies: The Federal Council of the Churches of Christ in America, Foreign

Missions Conference of North America, Home Missions Conference of North America, International Council of Religious Education, Missionary Education Movement in the United States and Canada, National Protestant Council of Higher Education, United Council of Church Women, United Stewardship Council, Church World Service, Inc., Interseminary Committee, Protestant Film Commission, and Protestant Radio Commission. Since that time the Student Volunteer Movement became the 13th agency to merge.

The work of most of these agencies is now conducted through the National Council's four main divisions: Christian Education, Christian Life and Work, Foreign Missions, and Home Missions. Through two general departments, United Church Women and United Church Men, lay members of the constituent communions carry on interdenominational services. Through the Central Department of Church World Service millions of pounds of food, clothing, and medicines are shipped annually to needy people overseas, and thousands of refugees are aided in resettling in the United States. The divisions and other units have a staff of 702. Members of council committees and commissions total over 4,000 clergy and laity.

The member church bodies of the National Council are: American Baptist Convention; National Baptist Convention of America; National Baptist Convention, U.S.A., Inc.; Seventh Day Baptist, General Conference; Church of the Brethren; General Council of the Congregational Christian Churches; Disciples of Christ, International Convention; Greek Orthodox Church in America; Syrian Antiochan Orthodox Church; Ukrainian Orthodox Church of America; Evangelical United Brethren Church; The Five Years Meeting of Friends; Religious Society of Friends of Philadelphia and Vicinity; Augustana Evangelical Lutheran Church; American Evangelical Lutheran Church; The United Lutheran Church in America; The Methodist Church; African Methodist Episcopal Church; Moravian Church in America; Evangelical Unity of the Czech-Moravian Brethren in North America; Protestant Episcopal Church; Evangelical and Reformed Church; the Reformed Church in America; the Presbyterian Church in the U. S.; the Presbyterian Church in the U. S. A.; and the United Presbyterian Church of North America.

In addition the boards and agencies of 28 other national church bodies co-operate in the work of various units of the National Council, without holding full membership in the council as a whole.

Meeting Nov. 28–Dec. 3, 1954, in Boston, Mass., the general assembly elected Eugene Carson Blake, Stated Clerk of the Presbyterian Church, U. S. A., to serve as council president for the 1955–57 triennium. He succeeded Bishop William C. Martin, Methodist. The first president of the council was Henry Knox Sherrill, Presiding Bishop of the Protestant Episcopal Church.

The council's headquarters are located at 297 Fourth Avenue, New York 10, N. Y. Roy G. Ross is general secretary of the council, and Roswell P. Barnes, associate general secretary.

FLETCHER COATES

NATIONAL FOREIGN MISSION BOARD OF AMERICA. Organized as a result of action taken in 1895, when the Baptist Foreign Mission Convention of America and the National Baptist Convention of America united for the purpose of "doing missionary, educational and all religious work among ourselves and throughout the world." The merged body, subsequently known as the National Baptist Convention of America (not to be confused with the National Baptist Convention, U.S.A., Inc.), established a foreign mission board to act as its planning and executive agency in the area of foreign missions. The missionary activities of the board are centered primarily in Jamaica and Africa.

The modern school built by the board in Jamaica, British West Indies, enrols 90 students; recently construction of a hospital was begun. In Africa the board supports four missionaries and operates two 2,000-acre farms.

GARLAND OFFUTT

NATIONAL PRIMITIVE BAPTIST CONVENTION OF THE U.S.A. Organized in Saint Bartley Primitive Baptist Church, Huntsville, Ala., on July 17, 1907, under the leadership of James H. Carey (first president), C. F. Sams (first secretary), Elias Patton, R. L. Laws, William McCloud, B. F. Lee, W. L. Douglass, Felix Jordan, T. Girley, Ruben Jordan, M. W. Williams, and B. C. Britton. The purpose was to create and perpetuate unanimity of purpose and consolidation of organization of all phases of Primitive Baptist church organization. Its officers and directors were members of the then stated 850 Primitive Baptist churches comprising some 350,000 Primitive Baptists throughout several states of the 48 United States of America. The present headquarters of the convention is in the National Primitive Baptist Publishing House, 834 West Clinton Street, Huntsville, Ala. In 1957 the *Yearbook of American Churches* reported that in 1952 the convention had 1,019 churches, 80,000 members, 600 ministers, and 500 Sunday schools. Principal organizations are the National Primitive Baptist Sunday School and Baptist Training Union Congress, the National Primitive Baptist Women's Congress, and the National Primitive Baptist Young People's Congress. The convention does not maintain a mission program or extensive financial records of gifts to missions and other causes.

ALBERT MC CLELLAN

NATIONAL TEMPERANCE LEAGUE, INC. Formed in 1950 by a merger of the Temperance League of America, successor in Jan., 1948, to the Anti-Saloon League of America, established in 1895, and the National Temperance Movement, Inc., organized in 1943. The National

Temperance League is a federation of state temperance leagues through which church, civic, and social groups can unify their action against the liquor forces, yet maintain their independence in the development of their program and in the enlistment of their people. National Temperance League is governed by a board of directors, elected by the trustees of the several state leagues. Representation is based on the population of the state, but no state has more than five members. The constitution also provides that the national board of directors may elect an additional number of directors-at-large not to exceed 25 per cent of the number of directors elected by the state organizations. The active administration of the league is conducted by an executive director elected at the biennial meeting of the directors. The executive offices and staff are maintained at Washington, D. C., including legal and research departments and an official organ called *The American Issue*. A. C. MILLER

NATIONAL TEMPERANCE SOCIETY AND PUBLICATION HOUSE, THE. This society was organized at the Fifth National Temperance Convention meeting at Saratoga Springs, N. Y., in Aug., 1865. It was attended by 325 delegates from 25 states, representing the churches and various temperance organizations. Its purpose was to promote total abstinence for the individual and total prohibition for the state.

This society filled a large place in temperance reform. It was the creator of modern temperance literature. It held mass meetings, conferences, and conventions in every part of the country; it introduced temperance textbooks into the public schools and scattered literature in prisons, hospitals, shops, and jails; and it sent both missionaries and literature among the freedmen of the South. The only reference we find in the Southern Baptist Convention Annuals to the work of the society is in the *Annual* for 1884, when one of its representatives presented an appeal for the work among the freedmen.

The society contributed much to the development of public opinion which made possible the enactment of the prohibition amendment of 1920. Since that time it has gradually surrendered its place of leadership to a multiplicity of temperance organizations over the land. A. C. MILLER

NATURAL LAW. In sociology, a term that refers to principles which so agree with the nature of man as to be indispensable to the maintaining of society. Protection of offspring is an example. There is such uniformity in human nature that these laws are considered to be universal. Many laws that men enact are based on these laws of human nature.

In natural science and philosophy the term refers to the orderly behavior of the physical world, the sequence of events which seem to be so related as to be expected to occur under given conditions.

BIBLIOGRAPHY: K. Heim, *The Transformation of the Scientific World View* (1953). S. A. NEWMAN

NATURAL REVELATION. See REVELATION.

NATURALISM. The term is opposed to supernaturalism or other-worldliness. Naturalists favor an hypothesis in which the universe is regarded as self-operating, self-directing, and self-explanatory. Nature is the whole of reality according to the naturalist, who holds that the universe is purposeless; it is impossible to conclude that an intelligent mind is behind or within the process of the world. Many different uses of the term "nature" can be found in philosophical discussions. Variation within the term itself is necessary to designate different points of view within the naturalistic movement, such as humanistic, materialistic, spiritualistic, and so on. BOB SOILEAU

NEAR EAST, MISSIONS IN. See ISRAEL, MISSION IN; JORDAN, MISSION IN; LEBANON, MISSION IN; and GAZA, MISSION IN.

NEEL, ISA-BEALL WILLIAMS (b. Cartersville, Ga., June 2, 1860; d. Atlanta, Ga., Aug. 6, 1953). Woman's Missionary Union leader in Georgia. She was graduated from Mary Sharp College in Tennessee and later studied in Germany. She married William Jessie Neel, a lawyer, and made her home in Rome, Ga. Encouraged by her pastor, R. B. Headden, she organized and became the first superintendent of Floyd County Associational W.M.U. The fifth president of the Georgia W.M.U., she served 21 years (1911–32) and upon her resignation was elected president emerita. Active outside her own state, she was asked to plan the Jubilate banquet celebrating the 25th anniversary of Convention-wide W.M.U., to direct W.M.U. in the 75 Million Campaign, and to represent W.M.U. at the Pan-American Conference in Panama. In 1931 Mrs. Neel became the first woman to receive Mercer University's honorary LL.D. degree. The Mrs. W. J. Neel Offering for state missions and the I. Neel prayer room at Camp Pinnacle honor her. She was at one time elected vice-president of the Georgia Baptist Convention. Her interest in youth and Christian education is shown by her having led the Georgia W.M.U. to maintain the Mary P. Willingham School for mountain girls, 1916–31; to make generous gifts toward the endowment of Tift College; and to begin the state G.A. and Y.W.A. house parties. Having unusual strength of body and mind, she attended the executive board meetings of the state W.M.U. regularly until past 90 years of age. She was buried in Oak Hill Cemetery in Cartersville. JANICE SINGLETON

NEFF, PAT MORRIS (b. near McGregor, Tex., Nov. 26, 1871; d. Waco, Tex., Jan. 20, 1952). Lawyer, governor of Texas, university president. He was son of Noah and Isabella

(Sheppard) Neff, who had come to Texas in 1855 and settled at his birthplace. Neff received A.B. and A.M. degrees in 1894 and 1898, both from Baylor University. Between the years when he received these degrees, he taught school in Arkansas and studied law at the University of Texas, where he received the LL.B. degree in 1897.

During nearly 35 years of law practice in Waco, Neff became an outstanding civil lawyer. He was county attorney of McLennan County, Tex., 1906–12, a member of the Texas House of Representatives, 1901–05, and speaker of the house during the last two years, as well as a leader of prohibition forces and state chairman of the League to Enforce Peace. In 1920, after an intense, personal campaign, Neff was elected governor of Texas and served two terms. During his administration the State Parks Board, Board for the Observance of the Texas Centennial, and the State Highway Department were created; the first gasoline tax was levied; the state prison system was reformed and the granting of pardons practically suspended; the position and salary of teachers were raised; and the country schools generally were improved. Neff led in the foundation of both Texas College of Arts and Industries and Texas Technological College, and when trouble occurred in the Texas oil fields, he declared martial law, which he used to suppress lawlessness there and among railroad strikers at Denison, Tex. He kept the legislature in session in Austin until it carried out the long-delayed redistricting of the state.

Returning to Waco following his retirement from the governor's office, Neff resumed his private law practice. In 1932, however, he succeeded Samuel Palmer Brooks as president of Baylor University, after turning down the presidency of the University of Texas. Neff had previously been a member and chairman of board of trustees. During his 15-year presidency, the university became free of debt, enrolment more than doubled, and physical and material assets greatly increased. Neff moved the Baylor College of Medicine from Dallas to Houston, where it was affiliated with the Texas Medical Center and the Anderson Foundation. In addition, he served as president of the Texas Conference for Education in Texas, the Texas Educational Survey Commission, and the Texas Watersheds Association, and chairman of the State Parks Board and the State Draft Appeals Board.

A Baptist, Neff was a member of First Baptist Church, Waco, Tex., and acted as its clerk from 1909 to 1918. He was president of the Texas Baptist General Convention from 1927 to 1929, also president of the Southern Baptist Convention, 1942–46. His published works include *The Battles of Peace; Making Texans,* and *Twenty-three Addresses.* In the last months of his life, Neff gave to Baylor University his collection of papers and association items and aided in integrating them as the Pat Neff Division of the Texas Collection.

Bibliography: P. M. Neff, *The Battles of Peace* (1925). P. M. Neff Papers, Mss, Pat M. Neff Division of Texas Collection. E. M. Shirley, *The Administration of Pat M. Neff, Governor of Texas, 1921–25* (1938). Texas Heritage Foundation, *Hall of Remembrance* (1954). GUY B. HARRISON, JR.

NEGRO MISSIONARIES OF THE FOREIGN MISSION BOARD. Negroes were serving as missionaries to Liberia under the Triennial Convention when the Southern Baptist Convention was organized. All those still in service had come under Southern Baptist auspices by 1856 when the American Baptist Missionary Union transferred all work in Liberia to the Foreign Mission Board. Lewis K. Crocker gave 30 years (1845–75) of splendid service. The first Negro appointees of Southern Baptists (1846) were John Day and Alexander L. Jones, both of Virginia. Day, who served the Triennial Convention from 1830, remained until his death in 1859; he founded a school for African pastors. Jones, a talented and well-educated minister who had spent most of his life in Africa, died before news of his appointment reached him. J. James Cheeseman, son of an American Negro missionary, stands out as "perhaps the most polished and accomplished Colored Missionary who has ever been connected with Baptist African Mission."

In all, 45 Negroes were appointed for Liberia before the mission was thrown on its own resources during the American Civil War and later formally suspended (1875). Assisting William Joshua David (*q.v.*) in re-establishing Yoruba work in 1875 was W. W. Colley, a Virginia Negro, later instrumental in organizing the Negro Baptist Foreign Missionary Convention, Montgomery, Ala. Nine Negro missionaries were appointed for the Yoruba Mission between 1851 and 1883, six of whom were transferees from the Liberia Mission.

Increasingly, Negro missionaries appealed for larger numbers of white missionaries; developing circumstances made the wisdom of this evident to the Foreign Mission Board. Rise of Negro churches in America and their desire for self-expression also made continuance of the co-operative endeavor impractical.

Foreign Mission Board has no stipulations against appointment of Negroes, but Article VIII of the Southern Baptist Convention constitution states that all missionaries must be members of Baptist churches co-operating with the Convention. Apparently this is interpreted more strictly than during the first decades of the Convention, perhaps because the early appointments were made when Negroes were moving from the kind of membership in white Baptist churches which characterized the slavery era to the formation of Negro churches and agencies. HERBERT C. JACKSON

NEGRO THEOLOGICAL EDUCATION. The history of theological education for Negroes in the United States is largely the history of the development of separate colleges for Negroes.

These institutions were organized as soon as the Negro became a distinct group in the national life and was so separated from the usual channels of cultural orientation as to require separate schools. The social and economic effects of slavery, its abolition, and the Civil War produced the conditions and defined the circumstances under which schools for Negroes would be established and maintained.

Before the Civil War sporadic attempts were made to provide higher education for the segment of the Negro population which had been liberated. Avery College in Pittsburgh, 1852; Ashmun (Lincoln), near Philadelphia, 1854; and Wilberforce, near Zenia, Ohio, 1856, are examples.

Following the war scores of schools were organized in the South. Most of them were sponsored by two kinds of organizations. White church groups in the North, less scarred by prejudices growing out of the conflict, founded numerous colleges. By 1870 the American Missionary Association, representing several denominations, had established 21 schools for Negroes. Its activity was typical; many organizations, including the American Baptist Home Mission Society, the Freedman's Aid Society (Methodist), the Board of Missions of Freedmen of the Presbyterian Church, and the Freedman's Bureau, were similarly interested in Negro education.

Many schools were also founded by Negro church groups, several of which were formed prior to 1861. These were principally Methodist and Baptist, for these two denominations then included 95 per cent of all Negro church members.

A survey in 1924 revealed 52 schools devoted to the education of the Negro minister, most of which were colleges with theological departments. They were distributed denominationally as: Methodist, 19; Baptist, 24; Congregational, 1; Lutheran, 1; Presbyterian, 3; Episcopal, 1; undenominational, 2.

By 1951 the number of seminaries and college theological departments had been reduced to 26, 12 of which were Baptist. Although the mortality rate for such Negro schools had been high, this reduction was largely due to the upgrading of the colleges, the integration of the minister's training into the liberal arts program of the schools, and the elimination of separate theological departments.

A list of Baptist schools now in operation indicates that many of them are among the oldest schools for Negroes. It includes Selma University, Selma, Ala., 1878; Arkansas Baptist College, Little Rock, Ark., 1884; Florida Normal and Industrial Memorial College,* St. Augustine, Fla., 1892; Morehouse College,† Atlanta, Ga., 1867; Spelman College,† Atlanta, Ga., 1881; Simmons University, Louisville, Ky., 1873; Leland University, Baker, La., 1870; Natchez Junior College, Natchez, Miss., 1884; Western Baptist Seminary, Kansas City, Mo., 1890; Shaw University,† Raleigh, N. C., 1865; Benedict College,† Columbia, S. C., 1870; Friendship Junior College, Rock Hill, S. C., 1891; Morris College,* Sumter, S. C., 1905; American Baptist Theological Seminary, Nashville, Tenn., 1924; Bishop College,† Marshall, Tex., 1881; Butler College, Tyler, Tex., 1905; Conroe Normal and Industrial College, Conroe, Tex., 1903; Mary Allen College, Crockett, Tex., 1886; Virginia Theological Seminary and College, Lynchburg, Va., 1887; Virginia Union University,† Richmond, Va., 1865; Storer College, Harper's Ferry, W. Va., 1867.

Although recent trends are indicative of a change in his status, the Negro minister has been traditionally the leader of his group. The generally meager education of the Negro minister has been a reflection of the educational deficiencies of his people; there has not been that demand for a highly trained ministry which would help to create a high quality theological school.

One of the chief reasons for the diminishing of the Negro minister's influence among his people, which can be clearly seen at the present, is his loss of status due to an increasingly inferior relative level of education. At a time when more than 70,000 are enrolled each year in the Negro colleges, it is estimated that less than 5 per cent of all Negro Baptist ministers have college and seminary training.

Church-related colleges are not compensating for this decline in the influence of religion. Academically, the Negro Baptist colleges are considerably below the average for Negro schools. A recent list included 118 institutions, 51 of which were listed as nonsectarian. Of the 67 church-related colleges, 21 were Methodist, 24 were Baptist, and 22 were of all other church groups.

Six Baptist schools had an *A* rating by their accrediting agency, two had *B*, and the remainder were not accredited. Two thirds of all Negro colleges in the nation are accredited, and these accredited schools enrol nine tenths of all students who attend Negro schools.

The active interest of Southern Baptists in Negro education has been relatively late. At its original meeting in 1845, the Convention did resolve "that the Board of Domestic Missions be instructed to take all prudent measures for the religious instruction of our colored population."

Again in 1872 they recommended "the establishment of a school as soon as possible" for the education of "colored preachers." Their activities seem to have been limited to occasional assistance to individuals who attended schools that were maintained by others.

In recent years white Baptists of the South have evidenced an increasing interest in the Negro schools. They hold membership on their governing boards and give support to the institutions in their vicinity.

In 1913 a committee was appointed by the Convention to implement its idea of establishing a theological seminary for Negroes. An agreement was made with the National Baptist Convention, and in 1924 the American Baptist Theological Seminary, Nashville, Tenn., was opened under joint control of the two conventions.

The most extensive work of Southern Baptists in the cultivation of the Negro ministry has been done through their Home Mission Board. The support of a teacher-missionary in most of the Negro Baptist colleges has been provided in order to strengthen the departments of religion and improve the training of students for the ministry. Of particular significance has been the in-service training institutes which have brought help to the untrained majority of Negro Baptist church leadership.

Since 1937, largely through the influence of Ryland Knight, Southern Baptist interest in Negro education has been encouraged by a special committee of the Convention. The interests of American Baptists, who own most of the schools, the National Baptists, who patronize the institutions, and Southern Baptists have been correlated by frequent contacts through the committee.

A recent study indicated that the Negro churches in the United States need at least 1,100 trained new ministers each year. Present training facilities are providing, on the average, 100 Negro ministers with the basic equipment of the B.D. degree program of study.

S. A. NEWMAN

---

* Rated class "B" by accrediting agency.
† Fully accredited, four year college.

NEGROES, SOUTHERN BAPTIST RELATIONS TO. The first Negro to join a Baptist church in America found a church home at Newton, R. I., in the atmosphere of religious liberty created by Roger Williams and his co-workers. A Negro slave by the name of Quassey was one of 50 or more members to join the Newton Baptist Church in 1743.

By 1795 there were 17,644 Negro Baptists in the South alone. The Baptist doctrine of civil and religious liberty and the conviction that all men are equal in the sight of God doubtless accounts for the large number of Negroes who became Baptists. Furthermore, the Baptists sought to win the Negroes to the Lord and sought their membership in the white churches. Many of the Southern churches had special "lookout committees" to enlist the Negroes and to "promote love, obedience, and fear" among the Negro members. The consent of the slave master was required for the slave to be admitted to membership. If the master was not a member of the church concerned, he gave his consent in writing. "Dinah is desirous to be received again in your communion, and I know of nothing to forbid it in her conduct, since her former dismission from your church. W. Parker to the Reverend Joshua Lawrence, Pastor of the Baptist Church, Tarboro, North Carolina, Saturday 2 July, 1822."

Early Negro churches.—The first Negro church on this continent of which there is record was constituted in 1773 across the Savannah River from Augusta, Ga., and was known as the Silver Bluff Baptist Church. The First Bryan Baptist Church and the First African Baptist Church, both in Savannah, and the Springfield Baptist Church, Augusta, were founded in 1778 or shortly thereafter. Prior to this time there were some Negro pastors who preached in missions and at other preaching points. Also, in the large Dover Baptist Association in Virginia, there were two Negro pastors who served churches composed of both white and colored members.

The scattered Negro churches remained in association with the white Baptist churches so far as the organized denominational work was concerned. For the most part, they constantly received encouragement and help from their white brethren.

A church composed of Indians and free-born Negroes was organized in Hertford, N. C., in 1850. Until 1883 the pastors were white. In that year C. S. Brown, recently graduated from Shaw University, became pastor. Brown spent his life in Hertford and became a great leader among Negro Baptists.

The religious instruction of their colored members gave the churches much concern. Blanche White, in quoting the minutes of the First Baptist Church of Richmond, Va., for the year 1780, gives the following information:

> Colored deacons were elected whose duty it was to watch over slave and free negro members. According to custom, the church licensed certain colored men who, by consecration and aptitude, seemed best fitted to exercise their spiritual gifts in public. From time to time other colored men were recommended to the church by the colored deacons as candidates for certificates without which they were prohibited from public speaking. In hearing that some of its members were speaking in public without certificates, the church "reproved and silenced" them.

Later, there was the First African Baptist Church, which grew large in size and influence, and which Robert Ryland (*q.v.*) served as pastor from 1841 to 1865, in addition to his duties as president of Richmond College.

The question of slavery.—In the early years Baptists were not agreed in their attitude toward slavery. Some justified slavery as conforming to civil, moral, and scriptural standards, while others definitely opposed it. The great majority sought the course of neutrality, leaving the issue of slavery to civil authorities and seeking the religious welfare of the colored population, whether free or slave.

After Nat Turner, a Negro preacher, incited a slave insurrection in Virginia in 1831, which resulted in the killing of many whites, it became necessary under the civil law for Negro pastors to officiate in church meetings only when a white person was in attendance. When it was first organized, the Triennial Convention admitted slaveholders and nonslaveholders on an equal basis. In fact, three of the first five presidents of the convention were slaveholders, but Francis Wayland, an antislavery man, was president when the division of the convention came in 1844.

When the American Baptist Home Mission Society was formed in 1832 for the purpose of promoting missions among the Indians, foreigners, Negroes, and whites in America, nothing was said about the rights of slaveholders to participate in convention affairs. The records of the society reveal no appointment of either an evangelist or educational missionary to the Negroes during the period before or immediately after the division of the convention. Prior to the organization of the society, there were 14 state conventions, but none carried on any organized work for the Negroes. All that was done for them was done by Christian families and local churches. It was urged that family altars, pastoral visitation, and public worship be used as media for their evangelization and training.

By 1840 the abolition issue had become so sharp that the state convention of Alabama took official notice of it. The response of the board of the General Convention for Foreign Missions satisfied the board of the Alabama convention for the time being.

In Georgia there was suspicion of the American Baptist Home Mission Society. In 1841 the board of the society had declared neutrality on the slavery issue. But in Apr., 1844, the society in annual meeting, after again declaring neutrality, appointed a committee of nine to consider the amicable dissolution of the society. To allay suspicion in Georgia, the executive committee of the Georgia convention requested the executive board of the Home Mission Society to appoint J. E. Reeve, a slaveholder, as missionary to the Indians. Reeve's salary was assured by the Georgia convention and the field of labor indicated. The Georgia executive committee assured the board of the Home Mission Society that such action would allay all suspicion on the part of the churches in Georgia. To the surprise of Georgia Baptist leaders, the board of the society declined to make the appointment. This in turn renewed doubts about the board of the general convention (foreign missions).

During the annual meeting of the Alabama state convention, 1844, an inquiry, presented by Basil Manly (*q.v.*), was received from the church in Tuscaloosa as to the possible attitude of the foreign mission board (Boston). After considering the question, the convention adopted a preamble and six resolutions and submitted them to the board, Daniel Sharp, president. The crux of the matter is found in the second resolution. The Alabama convention demanded "the distinct, explicit avowal that slaveholders are eligible, and entitled, equally with nonslaveholders, to all the privileges and immunities of their several unions; and especially to receive any agency, mission, or other appointment, which may fall within the scope of their operations or duties."

The acting board replied, Dec. 17, 1844, in a lengthy series of paragraphs. The heart of the reply is found in answer to the second of the Alabama resolutions:

> In the thirty years in which the Board has existed, no slaveholder, to our knowledge, has applied to be a missionary. . . . If, however, any one should offer himself as a missionary, having slaves, and should insist on retaining them as his property, we could not appoint him. One thing is certain, we can never be a party to any arrangement which would imply approbation of slavery.

However, the board had been receiving money from the South, the proceeds from slave labor. Furthermore, Henrietta Hall Shuck (*q.v.*), a missionary to China, was the daughter of a Virginia slave-owning planter, Addison Hall, and would have inherited slaves, had she survived her father. E. A. Stevens, son of a slave-owning family of Georgia, remained in Burma under the board after the division in 1845. Mr. and Mrs. Davenport, missionaries of the board in Siam, were slaveholders.

Organization of the Southern Baptist Convention.—The Southerners considered there was nothing for them to do but submit to the ruling of the acting board, although they believed it to be illegal and unfair, or to withdraw from the convention. They chose the latter course. Thus the division in the convention came, not over the advisability of doing work among the slaves or admitting slaves to the white churches or using Negro preachers and missionaries, but over the question of appointing a slaveholder as a missionary. The Virginia Baptist Foreign Mission Society led the way by calling a meeting of Southern messengers to meet in Augusta, Ga., for the purpose of consultation. Three hundred and twenty-seven messengers from the churches in eight states and the District of Columbia gathered in Augusta on May 8, 1845, to form the Southern Baptist Convention. There were 34 multiple representations, leaving a net attendance of 293.

Beginning of Negro work by Southern Baptists.—The new Convention formed two boards for missionary purposes: the Foreign Mission Board and the Board of Domestic Missions. On the last day of the convention, the following resolution relative to Negro work was passed: "Resolved that the Board of Domestic Missions be instructed to take all prudent measures for the religious instruction of our colored population."

At every Convention meeting since its organization, some report on Negro work has been brought. During the first decade little was done other than to encourage the local churches and slaveholders to be faithful in the religious instruction and guidance of the colored brethren and to urge all missionaries to serve the Negro people in every way possible. Year after year, the Committee on Instruction of the Colored Population reported progress attained by the churches and by individual Christians. When the Southern Baptist Convention was organized, there were about 350,000 Baptists in the South. Those among them who were slaveholders owned about 100,000 Negroes. By 1865 the Negro membership in many churches was larger than the white membership. Usually, the slaves did not vote with the whites on the same matters. The colored members voted only on matters having to do with their internal relationship.

During this period many Negro pastors were used in the Christian ministry. The Concord Association (in Tennessee) of United Baptists appointed a committee to raise funds with which to buy a Negro preacher who was to serve the association as a missionary-preacher to the colored population.

The Alabama Association raised funds to buy Caesar Blackmoor in order that he might devote all his time and labor to preaching. Since he could not remain in the state as a freedman, the association assumed the role of master in the eyes of the law. Three trustees, appointed by the association, held the title. Blackmoor occupied a high place in popular estimation as a preacher of the gospel.

Relation of Southern and Northern Baptists in Negro Work.—The pattern of relationship with the Negroes of the South was completely changed by the Civil War. During that conflict most of the Negro slaves remained loyal to their masters, but as the Union armies moved South, the religionists of the North began to turn their attention to the spiritual welfare of the emancipated Negroes. When freed, the colored people found themselves in desperate need of all that makes for human welfare and were eager for any assistance that might be given in religious training and in the establishment of their own churches.

A report of this period was given to the Southern Baptist Convention in the report of the Home Mission Board in 1905 as follows:

> Notwithstanding all that the South had suffered concerning the Negro in that trying day, the South still loved the Negro and the Negro loved the South, and when the work of the Convention was resumed, this was one of the first departments of work taken up by the Convention Board.

However, the board at this time was in no position to give much financial assistance to any phase of mission activity. The people were so impoverished by the war and so harassed by the carpetbaggers that they could scarcely repair their own waste places and carry on their own local church activities. Nevertheless, Baptist leaders of that day in practically every instance voted the Negroes letters of dismissal from the churches in which they as slaves had held membership and gave them encouragement and assistance in the constitution of their own churches. In some instances the white members gave the church building to the Negro members and built another for themselves.

Following the war there were several well-defined stages in the relations between white and Negro Baptists. At first the Negroes hurriedly formed their own churches. Some of their churches came back into associational fellowship, remaining until their own associations were formed. In the Virginia-Portsmouth Association "the following colored churches having formed associations of their own, were dropt: Bute Street, Norfolk; First Colored, Norfolk; Gilfield, African, and Third Colored, Petersburg" in 1868. In associations in North Carolina, South Carolina, Georgia, Alabama, Mississippi, and Texas, comparable situations may be seen. There were no well-defined chronological periods, but rather, stages in development varying in length of time according to local conditions. An incident in the Edgefield Association (S. C.) illustrates the influence of local conditions on relations between white and Negro Baptists. In 1871 a report was made on the religious instruction of the colored people.

> In the first report upon this subject ever presented to the Edgefield Association your Committee would congratulate their body and the churches composing it upon the interest which is hereby manifested in their great work. . . . We thank God that the time has come when the delegates to this body can listen with interest to a paper on the religious improvement of the black man of the South. Not that interest has not been felt before. The existence of thousands of colored Baptists in these Southern states is evidence sufficient that the white Baptists in the South have not neglected to seek the spiritual welfare of the colored man. But heretofore our interests and theirs have been identical. But the change which has come over us has caused this not to be the case; and we are gratified that our people, while recognizing this fact, are yet beginning to realize that their responsibility is not thereby removed. In most of the churches of this body a separation has taken place between the whites and the blacks, generally without any unkind feeling. Many colored Baptists who have thus severed their connection with the white churches are drifting about without anything that deserves to be called an organization. . . . There are in the bounds of this Association ten colored Baptist churches and others about to be organized with seven ordained preachers. . . . The great thing needed by them now is, of course, instruction, and your committees are convinced . . . that where the willingness to impart this is shown by the white people there will be found the corresponding desire on their part to receive it.

The report highly commends Benedict Institute at Columbia, S. C., established by the American Baptist Home Mission Society. The entire report reflects a cordial relationship between the two groups of Baptists, once gathered into the same churches, now separated by the course of events in Southern history.

Two years later, a different picture appears. "Brother L. Broaddus gave notice that Brother George G. Morgan was present as a Messenger from the Storm Branch Association, colored Baptists." The subject was referred to a committee of five.

> Brother J. C. Sheppard submitted the majority report of the committee appointed to consider the mat-

ter of receiving the Messenger from the Colored Association, recommending that he be received.

Brother L. Broaddus submitted the minority report from the same committee.

Pending the discussion of the reports, the Messenger withdrew his credentials. Both reports were then laid on the table.

This attitude may be interpreted from the current situation in lower South Carolina.

The general picture from Virginia to Texas may be seen in records of associations for 25 years following the Civil War. The records of the Tar River Association (N. C.) show the several stages of the relationship between white and Negro Baptists: drawing apart with the first experience of freedom by the Negroes; gradual rapprochement; fellowship of churches, white and black, in the same association; gradual departure of the Negro churches to form associations of their own. In some predominantly white churches a few Negro members remained until their deaths.

During the first years after the war, Negro members withdrew from mixed churches and formed congregations of their own. In 1869

. . . delegates from a colored church in Franklin County were present to ask advice of the Association: Whereupon, on motion, the moderator appointed Elders W. A. Barrett, N. A. Purefoy, J. G. Barkley and Lewis Bartholomew (to which the name of the moderator was later added) as a committee to confer with said delegates, and report to the Association on tomorrow morning.

The Committee appointed to confer with the colored delegates from the Shiloh Church in Franklin County reported . . . that they had discharged that duty, and ascertained that said colored delegates were not petitioning for admission into this body, as regular members thereof, but being sensible of their need of guidance and instruction, and being unwilling to receive the same from foreigners, in whom they have no confidence, they ask only that they be recognized as a regular organized Baptist church, under the care, protection and guidance of this association, in order that they may feel and know that they hereafter may enjoy the right and privilege of applying for instruction, whenever needed, in those among whom they have been raised, and in whom they still confide.

The committee recommended that the petition be granted. A special committee was appointed to study the petition and make recommendation. The committee report is found in Appendix C (1869):

Your Committee on the Baptist Colored Church of Shiloh in Granville (Franklin) County beg leave to report as follows:

Whereas, a letter has been received from Shiloh, in Granville (Franklin) County, a Baptist church composed exclusively of colored members, praying for the establishment of friendly relations with this association in order that they may be in a condition to ask for and receive such advice and instructions as they are now conscious of needing and which advice and instruction they prefer to receive from those whom they know, with whom they have been raised and in whom they confide, rather than strangers whom they know not and trust not in; and whereas, said petitioners expect not, and ask not for the power of any kind in this association, nor for the bestowment of anything implied by the terms civil and social equality, but they pray only to be received under the protection, guidance, and fostering care of this association, and whereas, we, the Tar River Baptist Association, believe that sound policy and Christian duty alike require the establishment and maintenance of friendly relations with the Colored Race in our midst, and to do good as opportunity offers. Therefore:

Resolved: That the petition of the Colored Church of Shiloh be granted, and that said church be henceforth considered as an adjunct, branch or protégé of this association, it being however understood or hereby emphatically declared, that this resolution confers not nor shall be in any way construed to confer upon said Shiloh Church, or any delegation or representative thereof, any social, political, or civil rights whatever, in this association.

Resolved further: That in accordance with the spirit and meaning of the above preamble and resolution, this association does hereby acknowledge and assume the duty of watching over, caring for, aiding and advising the Colored Church of Shiloh at any and all times, as opportunity may offer, and said church is hereby advised and invited at all times as it may feel the need, freely to communicate with this association, or any member hereof, on the terms proposed.

In the years following, delegates from Shiloh are listed with other churches of the Tar River Association. The church is listed in the tables giving the statistics, including the amount of money contributed. In 1874 another Negro church, Hawkins Chapel, was received. After 1889 there is no further reference in the minutes to the Negro churches. They apparently were joining other Negro churches in associations and state conventions.

At the present time (1956), in areas in the South where there are few Negro churches, affiliation of Negro churches in associations of white churches is being revived. In 1955 the Central Association, N. Mex., received a Negro church, and the Austin Association, Tex., received two Negro churches.

Since many of the leaders in the North after the war felt a great responsibility for the slaves now freed and cast out on society without money, without jobs, with no education or institutions of their own, and with no status or prestige, they sought immediately to provide the material and cultural assistance needed. The American Baptist Home Mission Society in 1862 took the following action, looking to a definite ministry to the freedman:

That we recommend the Society to take immediate steps to supply with Christian instruction by means of missionaries and teachers the emancipated slaves whether in the District of Columbia or in other places now held by our forces and also to inaugurate a system of operation for carrying the gospel alike to free and bond throughout the southern section of our country so fast and so far as the progress of our arms and the restoration of order and law shall open the way.

From the beginning, the major emphasis of this group was the training of preachers and church leaders. By 1871 it was reported that 2,768 persons had been given instruction by missionary teachers in weekday schools, and that property value of their schools exceeded $130,000.

In 1865, shortly before the constitutional amendment officially abolishing slavery was ratified, the American Baptist Home Mission Society passed a resolution declaring their intention of prosecuting immediately their proposed effort to help educate the freedman in the South. The resolution further stated,

> The Home Mission Society will expect of all churches and associations connected with it a vigorous and hearty co-operation not only in raising the funds needed in the present emergency but also in commending to the Board for employment such fitting instruments, preachers, colporteurs, and teachers, male and female, as they may know to be qualified and able.

In the early years the teachers from the North sought to give the Negroes the same kind of education as was given white people in the Northern schools. The Negroes were not prepared for such cultural training. Partly because of a conviction on the part of Southern people that the education proffered was not suited to the needs of the Negroes, and partly because the Southerners resented the presence of these Northern schoolmen in their midst, there was in the beginning considerable opposition to the efforts of Northern Baptists to establish schools for the Negroes in the South. No such opposition was expressed by the Southern Baptist Convention or by the Home Mission Board, but it was spoken freely by some of the pastors, the press, and the state conventions.

For example, the editor of *The Christian Index* wrote as follows in 1868:

> The influence of Northern preachers over our colored membership, since the War, with few if any exceptions, has been evil and not good. To the extent of the exposure of these poor people to such influence, they have been fearfully demoralized. . . . The Baptists of the North misrepresented and slandered the Baptists of the South before and during the War, in their pulpits, through their papers, and in their various organizations—and they persist in doing it still.

While there is no record of Baptist workers from the North being denied membership in the white Baptist churches of the South during the Reconstruction period, it appears that the great majority did not seek such affiliation and in many cases despised all efforts of the Southerners to serve their Negro brethren.

For the most part Southern Baptists simply ignored the presence and efforts of Northern Baptists. The feeling of resentment gradually diminished, and the desperate needs of the Southern Negro became a major concern of the white Baptists in both North and South. In 1876 the Northern society sent a resolution to Southern Baptists asking for assistance. It read in part as follows:

> We cordially and urgently invite our brethren of the entire South and particularly the ministers and members of Southern Baptist Churches, to co-operate with our teachers and our Board even more earnestly than ever before in the building up and strengthening of these schools for educating colored preachers and teachers.

The general attitude of the Southern Baptists is well expressed in the Home Mission Board's report to the Southern Baptist Convention in 1900:

> At the close of the War Between the States, Southern Baptists were in such a position they could do little toward helping the Negro in their midst, no matter how kindly they felt or how much disposed they were to help . . . but worse still the Negroes who had been so true and loyal and faithful to the whites during the War, as the effect of their recent emancipation, soon had a great gulf fixed between them and their former owners. . . . This condition made it impossible that the whites should do much for the moral and religious help of the Negro. The Home Mission Society of our northern brethren, however, felt a call, under the condition of affairs, to help the Negroes of the South. Gladly were they hailed by the Negroes. And they were welcomed by the white people of the South also, whenever they showed a proper respect for the existing and ineradicable social conditions. They have contributed thousands of dollars and have done a noble work. The Home Mission Society, however, addressed itself almost entirely to establishing and operating schools in the South. . . . It is questionable if all of the schools that have existed for them since the war have been a compensation for the loss of the religious interest which Southern pastors and Southern Christians took in them before the war.

Indigenous Negro work developed.—When the war closed, only 5 per cent of the Negroes were literate. However, the majority welcomed the opportunities to attend school offered by the religious groups and by the Government. Having now obtained a taste of freedom, they sought places of leadership and became zealous for representation in all phases of organized life. This desire greatly affected their attitude toward the assistance offered by the Home Mission Society. The few Negroes placed on boards of control of institutions were usually selected by the society. Such procedure gave Negro Baptists little opportunity to express their newfound freedom.

Their natural desire for full participation soon led to the organization of Negro Baptist associations and conventions. The first state convention of Negro Baptists was organized in North Carolina in 1866. In 1880 the National Baptist Convention was organized. State conventions and district associations sprang up throughout the South, and because of the thirst for personal power or minor differences among themselves, in many areas these organizations divided so that there were three or four conventions or associations serving in the same territory. In 1915, at the meeting in Chicago, the National Baptist Convention was divided, thus creating two national groups, one known as the National Baptist Convention, U.S.A., Inc., and the other as the National Baptist Convention of America. This division still exists.

The zeal for self-expression and for an indigenous program also led to the establishment of many Negro schools which were sponsored by Negro conventions or associations apart from the educational programs sponsored by white Baptists.

In summarizing this movement Noble Y. Beall aptly points out the problem created for the Home Mission Society.

> Thus we see that the Negroes through their churches and conventions organized and attempted to operate 157 schools in direct competition with and in most cases in opposition to the 14 schools founded by Northern Baptists for the higher education of the race. These were established at a time when the other schools needed most of the full support of the Negroes, both in the giving in funds and furnishing students. This sort of situation made it almost impossible for the "white schools," as they were sometimes called, to survive. . . . That the schools sponsored by white Baptists came through alive was due to the financial support which they received from philanthropists and from Northern Baptists.

This desire to maintain and supervise their own work has persisted and has resulted in their having their own publishing house, their own literature, and their own program of promotion. While they have gladly accepted help from Southern Baptists in the support of evangelism and Baptist Student Union work, they have adapted, rewritten, and published most of the promotional literature which they use in these fields.

In Alaska, where Baptist work among the whites and Negroes was at first integrated, both groups belonging to the same churches, the Negroes have constituted churches composed entirely or primarily of Negro members. The Greater Friendship Baptist Church of Anchorage was organized on June 24, 1951, with a membership of 17. The white Baptist churches of Anchorage helped in the constitution of the church, which, with the other two Negro churches organized in Alaska since that time, hold membership in the Alaska Baptist convention, co-operating in the general program of Alaska Baptists and in the work of the Southern Baptist Convention.

Work begun with Negro Baptist agencies.—As soon as possible after the Civil War, the Home Mission Board began to give some support to a ministry for the freedman. In 1872 assistance was given in establishing institutes for the training of Negro Baptist ministers. One year later, the committee of the board on colored missions reported that "an arrangement has been made by which young men approved by their churches, and endorsed by the intelligent judgment of white brethren, can receive instruction at the Augusta Institute."

The missionaries of the board serving language groups and the missionary pastors were urged to "give special attention to their [Negro] wants, as they had opportunity, as the most speedy and effective way of benefiting them. We would earnestly recommend that Ministers' Institutes be held by our brethren for the instruction of their preachers, wherever, and as often as it is practicable."

As early as 1883, William Hilary McIntosh, former secretary of the Home Mission Board, was employed as "theological instructor of the Colored Pastors." He worked wherever his services appeared to be most profitable.

R. T. Pollard was the first Negro to be employed by the board as a theological professor. He was graduated from Selma University in 1884 and prior to his graduation was appointed by the Home Mission Board under the leadership of I. T. Tichenor.

The New Era Plan.—The New Era Plan, begun in 1895, "embodied the co-operation of the Home Mission Society of New York and different State Mission Boards, both white and Negro, together with this Board." The cost of the program was borne jointly by the Home Mission Society, the Home Mission Board, the respective state conventions, and the Negroes within the state being served. By 1897 the Home Mission Board was co-operating in the New Era Plan in North Carolina, Virginia, Tennessee, Missouri, Georgia, Kentucky, and Alabama, at a total cost to the board of more than $20,000. The missionaries thus employed were expected to preach, aid pastorless churches, promote the Baptist schools and ministerial students, settle difficulties in colored churches, quell strife between churches and associations, and "do all possible to promote the peace, purity and efficiency of the colored population."

The plan was ultimately changed, primarily because of divisions and strife among the various groups of Negro Baptists. Soon the Negroes were failing to provide their share of the support and in some cases were antagonistic to the work because of factional strife and jealousy.

The New Era Plan was modified when B. D. Gray became executive secretary of the Home Mission Board in 1903, and it became known as the Enlarged Plan of Negro Work. At the Southern Baptist Convention in 1904, a definite program of Negro work was adopted, which provided that the National Baptist Convention, Inc., be the Negro agency with which the Home Mission Board would work; that a full-time secretary of negro work should be elected by the board, and in order that "the great cause of Negro self-reliance and progress may be secured, it is proposed that the Home Mission Board will, for the year beginning May 15, 1904, appropriate dollar for dollar, or one-half the amount necessary to execute these propositions up to the amount of $15,000 the first year." A. J. Barton was elected as field secretary at the next meeting of the Home Mission Board and began work June 1, 1904. He served less than two years, after which Gray, the executive secretary, assumed active supervision of the Negro work.

Co-operation with Negro colleges.—The work continued to be promoted vigorously in co-operation with the National Baptist Convention and some of the Negro state conventions, but the divisions within the Negro organizations made the work difficult.

In 1934 four white missionaries were appointed to work among the Negroes. Among them were Rev. and Mrs. Noble Y. Beall. In 1937 Beall was made superintendent of Negro work, and soon thereafter he and J. B. Lawrence, who had succeeded Gray as executive secretary-treasurer of the Home Mission Board, went to New York to confer with the leaders of the National Baptist Convention to determine the type of program that would be most helpful to the Negroes. It was unanimously agreed that help was needed in training Negro leadership. The teacher-missionary program was the outgrowth of this conference. The results of the first year's operation of the program are recorded as follows:

> We are attempting to meet these needs through the men we are supporting in cooperation with the [Negro] schools. In addition to teaching in the schoolroom, . . . one month in the summer [is given] completely to holding institutes for the under-privileged preachers in their respective states. . . . If all of the teachers and students [engaged in these institutes] were congregated in one building or on one campus, it would be the largest training school for Christian workers in the world. But fortunately that is not the case. They are scattered out in eleven states, and are in a position to reach hundreds of thousands of people for Christ.

The American Baptist Theological Seminary.—The Home Mission Board has worked in close co-operation with the American (Negro) Baptist Theological Seminary, located at Nashville, Tenn., since it was opened in 1924. Scholarships have been provided for some of the students, and a teacher-missionary has been employed and supported by the Home Mission Board.

At the request of the seminary, the board made a gift of $60,000 in 1946 for the construction of a classroom building on the campus to be "regarded as a memorial to the Home Mission Board or to its gifted Secretary-Treasurer." By request of the board it was subsequently named the J. B. Lawrence Building.

Negroes in other Southern Baptist seminaries.—Negroes are accepted as students in four of the five seminaries of the Southern Baptist Convention. As early as 1926, Southwestern Baptist Theological Seminary began teaching Bible and theological classes for Negroes in a downtown Negro church. By 1951 all classes were opened to qualified Negroes, but they are not permitted to room in the dormitories.

Negroes were first enrolled in Southern Baptist Theological Seminary through an extension department in 1941. In 1951 they were admitted as regular students without racial distinction.

The New Orleans Baptist Theological Seminary maintained a working relationship with Union Baptist Theological Seminary (Negro) prior to 1951, when graduate work in the seminary was opened to Negroes. In 1952 they were permitted to enrol in any class.

The Golden Gate Baptist Theological Seminary has been open to Negroes since its beginning in 1941.

The Southeastern Baptist Theological Seminary does not at present (1956) admit Negro students.

Extension centers.—Eleven of the Negro colleges in the South now provide extension centers where off-campus work may be taken under the direction and tutelage of carefully chosen instructors. The Home Mission Board first began its co-operation in such work by making an allocation to help Selma University, Alabama, in its extension program in 1952, at which time 11 centers were in operation with an enrolment of more than 500 students.

From 1952 through 1955, Selma University enrolled 2,800 ministers and other Christian leaders in these courses. Many Negro and white leaders have served as teachers with remuneration, and others have served with inadequate pay. In his 1955 report Rev. Guy Bellamy, secretary of the department of Negro work of the Home Mission Board, reported 734 extension classes with a total of 14,213 enrolled, most of whom were preachers.

There are 28 teacher-missionaries, paid in part or in full by the Home Mission Board, serving in 24 colleges or seminaries in 16 states. These missionaries teach Bible or religious education in the colleges during the regular school session and conduct institutes in other areas during the summer. They sponsored 117 such institutes and enrolled more than 8,000 students in 1955.

Co-operation with state conventions.—Most of the state conventions have sought to help and encourage the Negroes in their work since the Southern Baptist Convention was organized in 1845. Some support was given to individual churches, to schools, and to general mission activities among the Negroes, but it was not until 1943, when the Texas Baptist Convention instituted its organized work to serve minority groups, that a department of work was started in any state to help the Negroes.

A. C. Miller began his duties as director of the Department of Interracial Co-operation in Texas on Mar. 15, 1944. The work has been continued since that date, but the name was changed in 1947 to "Ministry with Minorities." It includes not only Negroes but foreign-speaking work, also.

In 1950 the administrative committee of the Alabama Baptist Convention was authorized to "set up at the earliest possible date a department of Negro work as a part of the state mission program and that a full-time white man be employed to serve as secretary and promoter of the department." Collis Cunningham was elected.

In 1953 a Negro work department was established in Mississippi with William A. Keel as secretary.

The Home Mission Board does not share in the salary of any of these first statewide Negro workers, but it has co-operated in the promotion of the work in these respective states.

In 1953 the Survey Committee of the Home Mission Board recommended in its report, adopted by the board in Dec., 1953, that this board co-operate with the respective states in the selection and support of superintendents of Negro missions in those states having a large Negro population. W. R. Grigg, a white pastor of Atlanta, was the first to be so appointed. He was selected jointly by the state mission board of Louisiana and the Home Mission Board. In 1954 Clyde Hart was appointed on a similar basis to serve in Arkansas; in 1955 D. B. Hoskins was selected for Missouri; and in 1956 Durward V. Cason began such work in Georgia.

The Negro Center Program.—During the decade from 1940 to 1950, the population of the whites increased 14.7 per cent, while the Negro population increased 16.3 per cent. The population of whites in cities of more than 50,000 increased 10.4 per cent, while the Negro population increased 49.2 per cent. This shift of Negro population to the cities augmented the need for a plan of work for Negroes in urban centers. The Negro Center Program was inaugurated in 1945 to meet this need. The first report shows the rapid growth of the movement.

> The City Mission Program among Negroes is performing a worthy service in our cities with large population. This program attempts to provide a better ministerial and lay leadership for Negro churches as well as to promote the denominational life of Baptist churches. . . . The worker is employed upon a full-time basis to work with churches and denominational organizations of the city.

The report of the following year indicated the plan of administration. "This program is promoted by a joint committee of white and Negro leaders who serve as a committee of city mission work among Negroes. The work is under the supervision of this joint committee with a well-trained Negro as the worker." The local forces furnish the building and operational expenses, and the Home Mission Board pays the salary of the workers. The program received the name "Negro Center Program" in 1950. In 1955 there were 21 such centers with 23 workers serving in 13 states.

Other ministries.—Negro youth now participate in the student summer mission program on the same basis as other students. There have been 10 or 12 Negroes serving on the home mission fields during the summer months in each of the last four years.

There is only one Good Will Center for Negroes directed by missionaries of the Home Mission Board. Carver Center in New Orleans, La., was dedicated Nov. 18, 1951, for the purpose of reaching and training Negro children and young people on the river front. Many of the other centers give some attention to the Negro population in their midst but are not operated especially for them.

Since 1945 a portion of the Annie Armstrong Offering has been designated to provide limited scholarships for Negro youth who attend colleges or seminaries in preparation for special religious work. Sixty such scholarships were awarded in 1955.

The Home Mission Board report of 1954 records the beginning of the Department of Negro Evangelism as now co-operatively promoted. W. Constello Trotter has been employed as director of evangelism for the National Baptist Convention, Inc. His salary and expenses at the present are paid half from the department of Negro work and half from the Department of Evangelism of the Home Mission Board. He works under the general direction of the secretary of evangelism for the Home Mission Board and in full co-operation with the National Baptist Convention, Inc., and their committee on evangelism. He has an office in Chicago with a full-time secretary. He began work Nov. 1, 1953. Since that time the work has been vigorously promoted on this co-operative basis.

As early as 1939, Noble Y. Beall, then secretary of missionary education of the Home Mission Board, at the request of Frank H. Leavell, secretary of student work for Southern Baptists, made a survey of the 20 schools in which the Home Mission Board had workers, to "determine as far as possible the attitude of their students on Baptist Student Unions. The results were most enlightening, giving us a variety of expressions and opinions. The time does not seem to be here," concluded the report, "for the B.S.U. to function in the Negro colleges."

However, in Apr., 1953, S. E. Grinstead (Negro) began his work as field secretary of Baptist Student Union work among the Negroes, after serving for several years as a part-time worker in the Negro B.S.U. center in Nashville. In 1955 he visited 150 schools and reported 28 active student organizations in schools having a total enrolment of 13,600 students.

Much help has been given by missionaries and by volunteer workers in the promotion of Vacation Bible schools in Negro churches. They have also helped in summer camps, simultaneous revivals, and study classes. Missionary leaders have co-operated in the promotion of leadership and methods conferences. Help has been given in the preparation and distribution of literature. During 1955 the 62 missionaries of the Home Mission Board who were working in the Negro Department reported 2,059 professions of faith and 38,723 leaders trained in classes and institutes.

Correlating agencies.—Ever since the Civil War at least one or more Southern Baptist groups or committees have been studying areas and means of co-operation between white and Negro Baptists. In 1937 a Committee on Negro Ministerial Education was appointed by the Southern Baptist Convention to work with similar committees from the Northern Baptist Convention and from the two Negro conventions "to consider the problem of ministerial education for Negroes and to advise as to how this may be most wisely promoted." From 1938 until 1954, the Committee on Negro Ministerial Education made annual reports to the convention. In 1948 the recommendation was adopted "that this Convention request the Commission of the American Baptist Theological Seminary to co-operate with the Northern Baptist Convention, and the National Baptist Convention, Inc., in a survey of Negro Baptist churches and their leadership."

At the session in 1952, the Joint Survey Commission made its full report to the Convention. The Committee on Negro Ministerial Education was instructed "(1) to disseminate in every way possible the findings of the survey; and (2) to consider ways and means whereby Negro ministerial education may be advanced in the light of the findings of the survey."

The Home Mission Board, at its annual meeting in 1954, passed a resolution asking the Executive Committee of the Southern Baptist Convention to approve the organization of an interagency council of Negro work composed of representatives of those Southern Baptist agencies and institutions interested in such work. The request was approved, and the advisory council was formed at a meeting in Nashville, Tenn., Jan. 13, 1955.

The Advisory Council of Southern Baptists for work with Negroes now meets semiannually and co-operates through its constituent agencies in discovering and meeting the principal needs of Negro Baptists in the realization of worthy goals in kingdom building. A subcommittee confers with a joint committee from other Baptist groups to correlate their common objectives.

Working together.—A summary of this study indicates that there are now many areas in which white Southern Baptists and Negro Baptists are working together. They serve on joint committees to supervise the programs of Negro centers. Both races serve as teachers in Negro centers and in institutes. All the state directors are white and work in close co-operation with the leaders of the various Negro denominational groups.

Both whites and Negroes serve together in Negro Good Will centers, Vacation Bible schools, institutes, and extension classes. In many areas, especially urban centers, the churches plan simultaneous revival services, with Negro and white pastors meeting together for planning meetings and reports.

Negro students receive the same consideration as white students in the student summer mission program and in consideration for scholarships. In many areas joint conferences are held to plan programs of common interest. For years both whites and Negroes have served on joint committees, and there is in prospect the common effort in a nation-wide evangelistic and mission program, when most Baptist forces in America will be working together in the Third Jubilee Program of Advance.

Bibliography: W. W. Barnes, *History of the Southern Baptist Convention, 1845–1953* (1954). N. Y. Beall, "The Northern Baptists and the Higher Education of Southern Negroes During 1865–1875" (n.d.). M. M. Fisher, *A Short History of the Baptist Denomination* (1933). C. S. Johnson, *The Negro in American Civilization* (1930). R. Jones, *History of the Virginia-Portsmouth Baptist Association* (1881). H. L. Morehouse, *Baptist Home Missions in America* (1882). W. W. Sweet, *Religion on the American Frontier. The Baptists* (1911). W. D. Weatherford and C. S. Johnson, *Race Relations* (1934). B. S. White, *First Baptist Church, Richmond 1780–1955* (1955).

COURTS REDFORD

NELSON, ERIK ALFRED (b. Orebro, Sweden, Dec. 17, 1862; d. Manaus, Para, Brazil, June 15, 1939). Missionary to Brazil. Nelson was baptized by his father in a Baptist church in Kansas, Apr. 10, 1877, after the family moved from Sweden. Influenced by a letter from William Buck Bagby (*q.v.*), Nelson went to the Amazon Valley in 1891. After he married Ida Lundburg (1869–1954) Jan. 7, 1893, she joined him in Brazil. He was ordained in 1897, and the next year he and his wife were appointed missionaries by the Southern Baptist Foreign Mission Board. Nelson organized a Baptist church at Belem in Feb., 1897, and led in the organization of a church at Manaus in Oct., 1900. After residence in Santarem and San Luiz, the Nelsons chose Manaus as their location. Mrs. Nelson's health was undermined, forcing her to return home from 1910 until 1928, but Nelson continued his labors. In canoes, launches, and steamers, his travels took him on rivers, tributaries, and lakes in the equatorial region. The Nelsons returned to the States in 1936, but Nelson went back to the Amazon for the last months of his life.

Bibliography: L. M. Bratcher, *The Apostle of the Amazon* (1951). A. R. Crabtree, *Baptists in Brazil* (1953).

E. C. ROUTH

NEO-ORTHODOX THEOLOGY. This school of thought is sometimes called Theology of Crisis, because of the view that man stands under the judgment of the Word of God; Dialectical Theology, because of the use of dialectic; or Realistic Theology, because it attempts to gain a realistic view of man, sin, history. The name neo-orthodoxy is descriptive of the movement because it is a return to the orthodoxy of the Reformation, but it is orthodoxy with a difference. Neo-orthodox theology came out of the parish rather than the classroom, with pastors Karl Barth, Emil Brunner, and Reinhold Niebuhr as leading figures in the school. The movement began in 1919 with the publication of Barth's *Roemerbrief* and broke upon America after Niebuhr published *Moral Man and Immoral Society* in 1932. Neo-orthodoxy is the theologians' reply to the dilemma of liberalism. Although it accepts biblical criticism, neo-orthodoxy is a biblical theology and confronts the world with a new biblical realism. This realism has dispelled the romantic optimism about man and has brought to bear a new emphasis on man as sinner, which is an evidence of Kierkegaardian existentialism.

A second emphasis in neo-orthodox theology is the transcendence of God. Kierkegaard has influenced neo-orthodox theologians in this, as in other matters.

Neo-orthodoxy emphasizes the fact that the transcendent God has revealed himself to sinful man. This revelation, the Word of God, is threefold: Jesus Christ, the "Word made flesh"; the Bible, the words of which bear revelation; and the preaching of the church.

The church has received much attention in recent years by neo-orthodox theologians, most of whom are involved in the ecumenical movement.

The majority of Baptists, little affected by liberalism, have thus paid scant attention to neo-orthodoxy. However, there has been contact between some Baptist theologians and the neo-orthodox group, resulting in the adoption by these Baptists of some of the neo-orthodox insights into the present theological situation. Many Baptists have come to appreciate the contribution of the neo-orthodox theologians in leading American Protestant theology back to a more realistic position.

Bibliography: K. Barth, *The Doctrine of the Word of God* (1936); *Dogmatics in Outline,* translated by G. T. Thomson (1949); *The Epistle to the Romans,* sixth edition, translated by E. C. Hoskins (1950). J. C. Bennett, *Christian Realism* (1947). E. Brunner, *The Christian Doctrine of God,* translated by O. Wyon (1940); *Man in Revolt,* translated by O. Wyon (1937); *The Mediator,* translated by O. Wyon (1947). C. F. H. Henry, *The Protestant Dilemma* (1949). W. M. Horton, *Contemporary Continental Theology* (1938); *Realistic Theology* (1934). E. Lewis, *A Christian Manifesto* (1934). R. Niebuhr, *Beyond Tragedy* (1951); *Faith and History* (1949); *Moral Man and Immoral Society* (1932); *The Nature and Destiny of Man* (1952). "Ten Years That Shook My World," *Christian Century* (Apr. 26, 1939). W. Temple, *Nature, Man, and God* (1949). GRAY ALLISON

NETHERLANDS, BAPTISTS OF THE. English Baptists, led by Smyth and Helwys, had their origin in Amsterdam early in the 17th century, but after Helwys returned to England and Smyth died, there was no survival of Baptist influence in the Netherlands. Dutch Baptist history begins in 1845 with the baptism in Kasselter-Nijveen of a Reformed pastor, Johannes Elias Feisser, and six other persons by Julius Köbner, a Danish fellow worker of the German pioneer, Johann Gerhard Oncken (*q.v.*). Feisser had independently arrived at Baptist views before he met Köbner, and, though German and later British influence was felt in the developing Dutch Baptist work, it was for the most part indigenous. A proposal in 1869 that Danish Baptists adopt the German confession of faith and join the German Baptist Union was not accepted, though some churches joined. In 1881, when there were 608 Baptists in the country, the Union of the Baptist Churches in the Netherlands was established, largely through the influence of H. Z. Kloekers, who had served as a missionary in China with the British Baptist Missionary Society. Ten years later the Dutch union accepted for a while associate membership in the German Baptist Union.

The number of Baptists in the Netherlands has almost trebled since World War I, and encouraging growth has taken place since World War II. Whereas in 1946 there were 38 churches with 5,936 members, a decade later there were 50 churches with 7,150 members. Six additional churches, with 720 members, do not belong to the Baptist union. The great majority of Baptists are in the northern provinces, which are Reformed in religion. Evangelistic work in the Catholic south has been undertaken by the Baptist union.

A Baptist youth movement includes youth fellowships, clubs, and Sunday schools, and operates a conference and camp center. There is an active women's union, which owns a rest home operated by deaconesses. Missionary work is done in the Congo in co-operation with the British Baptist Missionary Society. Ministers have been trained abroad and in Dutch universities, but it has been decided to establish a Dutch Baptist seminary. The official organ of the Baptist union, *De Christen,* appears weekly, and there are also Sunday school, youth, women's, and evangelistic papers. Dutch Baptists participate in the ecumenical movement. Present Dutch Baptist headquarters, with the office of the general secretary, are in Arnhem.

Bibliography: J. D. Franks, ed., *European Baptists Today* (1952). J. H. Rushbrooke, *The Baptist Movement in the Continent of Europe* (1923).

J. D. HUGHEY, JR.

NEW BIRTH. See Conversion and Regeneration.

NEW CENTURY MOVEMENT. A special emphasis planned for the beginning of the 20th century in 1900, involving "a season of thanksgiving for mercies past, and of planning larger things for the glory of God in the century to come." The New Century Movement suggestion was brought to the Southern Baptist Convention in 1898 through the Home Mission Board by a resolution passed by the Baptist convention of Georgia. A committee was appointed in 1898, with Franklin Howard Kerfoot (*q.v.*), of Georgia, as chairman. The committee made a progress report in 1899. By further recommendations adopted in 1900 the Convention decided to

> . . . devote itself for the next two years to the special effort of eliciting and combining the energies of the whole denomination in the sacred effort for the propagation of the gospel; and whatever else may come before it in the meantime, this one thing be allowed all the time and consecration that may be needed;

that it concentrate its thoughts and attention and prayers and effort upon this, saying "this one thing we do."

The primary effort in the campaign had as its purpose the enlistment of the large number of churches not giving anything to state, home, or foreign missions. The committee also called for a "Committee on Co-operation" to plan the project. PORTER ROUTH

NEW CONNEXION BAPTISTS. See GENERAL BAPTISTS.

NEW EBENEEZER COLLEGE. An academy with all elementary grades, founded by P. A. Jessup at Cochran, Ga., in 1887. It existed under its original name until 1902 and is now Middle Georgia College in the University of Georgia system. ARTHUR JACKSON

NEW MEXICO, BAPTIST CONVENTION OF.

I. Baptist Beginnings. Three years after New Mexico became a territory of the United States in 1846, Baptists entered the territory, the first evangelicals to do so. Hiram W. Read, sent West by the American Baptist Home Mission Society of the Northern Baptist Convention, located at Santa Fe in 1849. Two years later, he was joined by Lewis Smith and James Milton Shaw. Samuel Gorman, Fred Tolhurst, and W. J. Kermott came between 1852 and 1864, all except Tolhurst, perhaps, accompanied by their wives, two of whom, Mrs. Gorman and Mrs. Shaw, died on the field. Natives, including Blas Chavez, Jose M. Chavez, Romoldo Chavez, Jose A. Garcia, Jose Senon (an Indian), and Jose Santos Tayes, were employed as assistants to the missionaries after being converted. Read and Shaw traveled and established schools and preaching points wherever they went, while Gorman confined his ministry largely to local fields—Laguna, Santa Fe, and Las Vegas.

The first evangelical church in New Mexico was the Baptist church organized in Albuquerque, Oct. 10, 1852, under the name "Baptist Church of Christ." Minutes of the church, written in longhand by Read, Shaw, and Smith, are still legible and are now on record. One other church was organized during this period at Socorro, Mar. 7, 1857, and buildings for worship were erected at Laguna and Santa Fe in 1853 and 1854. A Baptist convention, organized in 1854, was the last forward step before work was closed in the '60's.

Mission work in New Mexico was hindered from the beginning by the isolation of the territory, the animosity of the Indians, the lack of civilization among many of the Mexicans, and the domination of Roman Catholicism. These factors, particularly the efforts of the Catholics, who appropriated $500,000 in 1867 to extend their influence in New Mexico, forced the Home Mission Society to withdraw support in 1868. According to Shaw in a report to *The Macedonian and Record* in 1867, fear of priests, public opinion, and persecution separated the Spanish population from missionary influence almost entirely. From 1868 to 1880, the society attempted no further work in New Mexico; during this time some of the mission establishments passed over to the Presbyterians, while some, including the churches at Albuquerque and Socorro, disappeared. In 1880 H. N. Wingate was assigned by the society to a combination field, serving half of the time in northern New Mexico and half in southern Colorado, thus reopening the work.

A church was organized in Las Vegas, Jan. 30, 1880, and another in Raton in 1881. The Home Mission Society continued work along the Santa Fe Railroad, south, and at the same time volunteer, self-sustaining laymen and preachers under the leadership of John Hunter, working in Lincoln County, organized Zion Hill Church in 1884. In the same year William Tuck led in founding Elkhorn Church, and a new church in Albuquerque was organized in 1887. Ananias Green and J. Midd Hill organized Lookout and Seven Rivers churches in 1888. A Hopewell church was organized probably also in 1888.

Five of the eight new churches were in the Lincoln area where, at Zion Hill, Sept. 29, 1888, the Lincoln County Missionary Baptist Association became the first organization of its kind with continuous existence. Green was elected moderator and Hill associational missionary "at his own charge." An abbreviated record from 1887 indicates that churches along the Santa Fe Railroad, including Las Vegas, Albuquerque, and El Paso, met at Socorro and organized an association, but the printed record left no name, and whatever was formed has not continued.

Although the chief development of Baptist churches was in the Lincoln County area, other churches were organized, totaling 26 in all of New Mexico between 1880 and 1899. By 1900 two associations had been organized, Lincoln County and Santa Fe, organized May 12, 1900. There were no schools, no hospitals, no assemblies, no home for children. In 1892 Albuquerque's church published a news sheet which received official endorsement of the Lincoln Association and was the nearest approach to a state paper. In 1899 Lincoln Association discussed the possibility of establishing a school and appointed a committee to investigate its cost. All churches, then affiliated, combined to form the first territorial-wide convention in New Mexico in Nov., 1900.

CALOWA WILLIAM STUMPH

II. History of Convention. New Mexico Baptists regard 1912 as the most epochal of their 106 years of history. It marked the beginning of Southern Baptist affiliation and the healing of the rift between Northern and Southern groups. In 1912 two Baptist conventions existed in New Mexico, the New Mexico Baptist Convention (Northern), in its 11th year, and the General Convention of New Mexico (Southern), in its second year. In 1912 the Northern group reported 51 missionaries, 396 churches and stations, 141 baptisms, $1,579 mission gifts, 5,000 members. Comparatively, the Southern group reported 42 missionaries, 88 churches, 255 baptisms, $6,480 mission gifts, 2,672 members. Differences had existed continuously between the two groups. The North had accused the South, "You are rebels and dissenters," and the South had rejoined, "You deny the churches the right of determination, and you have fought them to the bitter end."

Committees of the general bodies, Northern and Southern, met Jan. 24, 1912, to work out a plan of settlement. They subsequently issued a call to the New Mexico groups for state convention meetings in June of that year, which assembled separately in Clovis. Fraternal greetings between the groups were surprisingly warm. Sympathizers with the Home Mission Society wrote, "Our prayer is that this will be the last time that Baptists of New Mexico will meet in separate sessions." Immediately, the Southern group replied, "Our Convention unanimously accepts the fraternal greetings of your body and declares itself ready to effect an organic union with all New Mexico Baptists." Forthwith, June 19, 1912, both groups dissolved their respective bodies, came together and formed the Baptist Convention of New Mexico, with combined strength including 210 churches, 7,672 affiliates, 93 missionaries. The convention elected Elmer B. Atwood, Texas, corresponding secretary.

Headquarters of the convention were moved from Roswell to Albuquerque in 1912, and the *Baptist New Mexican,* official state paper, was established. The mission board headquarters, established at Clovis, moved to Albuquerque within one year. Celebrating the new union, the Woman's Missionary Union staged a jubilant program at Alamogordo in Nov., 1912. The statewide pastors' conference was formed Nov. 6 of that year. The state's mission board, also organized in 1912, had 27 members, rotating over 36 months, and executive, education, and philanthropic committees. The first continuous statewide Training Union organization was established in 1912 when New Mexico Baptists also recognized the need of 145,000 Spanish with only two ministering preachers, and 20,000 Indians with no evangelical assistance.

Annual conventions were held at Tucumcari, 1915; Carlsbad, 1916; Raton, 1917; Albuquerque, 1918; Santa Fe, 1919. Increasing interest in state missions, "evangelism, baptism, enlistment, and development," led to widespread advancement by 1919. A state assembly was established at Cloudcroft, July 3, 1915, under the name "Cloudcroft and El Paso Baptist Bible Assembly." The state paper was enlarged to 16 pages and began weekly publication. The state board personnel was increased to 28 members—21 at large and 7 elected by associations. The convention was incorporated under state laws, and the constitution was consequently changed to require a loyalty committal in conformity with the charter. The period 1915–19 witnessed the organization of churches like Belen and Santa Fe, the organization of the 10th association in the state, Tucumcari, and the reception of 1,430 new church members in one year.

Influenced by the 75 Million Campaign in 1919, "an institutional year," the founding of the children's home at Portales, the beginning of the first hospital at Clovis, and the establishment of Montezuma College at Las Vegas all came about. The convention's quota, spread over five years in the 75 Million drive, was $250,000, and the state board voted to match a $100,000 gift of the Southwide Education Commission, dollar for dollar.

New Mexico, first to go over the top in the 75 Million drive, and with a ratio record in oversubscriptions, became an example for the South. At the opening of victory week, cash and pledges reached $305,000, an excess of $55,000 above her quota to be applied toward matching the educational gift. J. Weston Bruner, Atwood's successor as convention secretary, directed the movement, and Coleman Craig was called from Dallas to edit the state paper, the chief promotional agent. During the five years of the campaign, collections were $50,000, $57,906, $45,000, $32,300, and $38,700 in each of the years respectively. Major beneficiaries of the gifts were state missions, receiving $65,763; the orphanage, $52,253; and Montezuma College, $36,964. For the college, Las Vegas offered in fee simple a $350,000 property in buildings and land. The leadership and Baptist fellowship generally, evidenced their support of the college, stating in pulpit and press, "We cannot afford to start a school and let it die." However, in 1924, with 300 students and others desiring admission, a debt of $130,000 had already been contracted, possibly because of "lack of coordination between a double control—the State Board and the school's trustees." For part of the time, the board had to act as trustees. In the late '20's the college property was finally liquidated for $19,000. The hospital, orphanage, and two state assemblies, however, continued in full operation.

In 1922 Sunday school and Training Union activities were separated; William G. MacArthur became first manager of the Children's Home; H. F. Aulick, first stewardship and enlistment secretary; and Lester Sage, first evangelism secretary. Bruner served as corresponding secretary of the convention until 1923, when he was succeeded by Calowa William Stumph.

Decline in the late '20's and early '30's was due partly to national financial depression. Two years after Montezuma College closed, the property was leased to a private concern headed by B. Clarence Evans; a five-year committee had been set up by the convention to keep school spirit alive. Under private operation, the college enlisted 50 students and reopened the state assembly which had been operated there. In the 1930's a stricter observance of church doctrines was stressed, and a recommendation was approved to the effect that "no church shall authorize its pastor to give the elements of the

Lord's Supper privately or with a committee." Independency was reasserted and its importance reaffirmed even though 25 years had passed since the division in Baptist ranks over "church sovereignty."

In 1932 Baptist student work was first adopted and was placed under the Training Union Department. For the first time, the orphanage was opened to children of Spanish descent, and the convention budget topped $27,000. Under Harry P. Stagg, elected executive secretary of the convention in 1938, a convention program was instituted embracing (1) no debts; (2) operation under a unified plan; (3) erection of a headquarters building; (4) sending more missionaries; and (5) sale of hospital and Montezuma properties.

The Baptist press in New Mexico was founded in 1939, with Horace Burns business manager and then newspaper editor. During the year the Baptist Hospital was sold for $4,000, and co-operative allocations were boosted from 10 to 20 per cent. Total Baptist affiliation in the state reached 20,000. The Bible chair established at Portales secured Charles R. Barrick as teacher. Evangelistic rallies were organized as early as 1939, and every church was asked to promote one or more missions.

In 1942 the constitution was amended to permit indefinite calls to personnel. The '40's witnessed an emphasis on Brotherhoods, the suspension of Ruidoso Assembly, operation of 143 Anglo churches, 14 Spanish churches, 12 Negro churches, and 2 Indian churches—a total of 170—with an unprecedented number of state workers elected.

The period 1945–49 was, for New Mexico Baptists, a time of extraordinary expansion. From the $7,000 budget in 1912, there was an increase to $100,000 by 1945. Church membership increased from 7,672 in 1912 to 40,000 in 1949. Institutional developments were no less striking. In this same five-year period an average of 11 churches were organized annually; a Baptist Foundation was established and incorporated; new buildings at Inlow Youth Camp and at the Children's Home were expanded; Bible chair property was acquired. In 1950 churches totaled 197, with combined membership of 46,304. Circulation of the *Baptist New Mexican,* at 15,000, had reached 95 per cent of the Baptist families of New Mexico through church budgets; Sunday school enrolment totaled 34,745; Training Union, 15,000; Woman's Missionary Union, 6,489; and the Baptist Student Union had activities on six state campuses.

In the period 1950–54, Baptists successfully worked a five-year plan of expansion through a 12 per cent increase with churches and state departments co-operating. The added motivation resulted in the erection of a $275,000 headquarters building, one of the multiple goals in the project. Debts on student buildings were liquidated, and plans were developed for a new center at Western College, Silver City. A medical center was established at Parkview. Added enrolments, study courses, and awards were noted in all working units; the five-year planned budgets were exceeded, with the convention receiving $300,000 in co-operative collections. Total Baptist affiliation was 66,000. A missions and stewardship department, added in 1952, had Jeff Rutherford as secretary. More than 200 pastors were serving 230 churches and missions. Churches in rural areas were reached, and those in populous centers compared favorably with the best in the South. LEWIS A. MYERS

III. Program of Work of New Mexico Baptists. Five divisions constituted the work of the Baptist Convention of New Mexico in 1955: administration, missions, education, institutions, and promotion. The administration of the convention, a striking example of democratic control, is under the direction of the convention president and the 36-member state mission board, an incorporated body under state laws. Election of board members is held annually by the convention, with one third of the members rotating every 12 months. The board, in charge of the convention's work *ad interim,* fills membership vacancies and elects the executive secretary-treasurer and other workers as needed. It meets quarterly, passes upon departmental matters, and, through the executive leader, reports annually to the convention. The executive secretary-treasurer, charged with general administration, cosigns legal documents with the board's president. To insure wide participation, the board breaks into committees which cover all units of state work.

State and associational missions, language groups, and evangelism contribute to the total mission program of New Mexico Baptists, which in 1955 included 69,000 members, 14 associations, 230 churches, 31 missions. Real estate, buildings, and inventories totaled $969,095.79 in value, a net worth of $751,963.97. The Co-operative Program budget of $330,000 was a boost of $30,000 for 1955 alone. Other items, including the Children's Home, over and above the $330,000, raised the total state mission obligation in 1955 to $606,314. Supplementary aid to churches on pastors' salaries was $30,000 and to associational missions, $23,000. The convention has followed the plan of a fall round-up which in 1955 brought in $29,236.36. The 14 associations in the state are fully organized with all departments, with a missionary maintained for each association, directed by a mission committee and supported jointly by churches of the association and by state and home mission funds.

Minority and language groups are largely supported by the Home Mission Board. Under the Home Mission Board and in co-operation with state leadership, a co-ordinator directs work with the three predominant groups, Anglos, Spanish, Indians, and a widely distributed population of Negroes, and unifies it with the local program. He maintains offices in the state headquarters' building, working alongside the state staff. Pastors of the minority groups, along with missionaries—45 for Spanish, 25 for Indians, and 1 for Negro—attend general meetings and have Christian fellowship with the Anglos. Running through the whole program is a spirit of evangelism, the chief concern of a full-time state evangelism secretary, committed to simultaneous as well as personal evangelism. Evangelistic efforts resulted in 4,542 baptisms in 1955. Included in the educational program of the convention are the Sunday school, Training Union, church music, Woman's Missionary Union, Baptist Student Union, the Brotherhood, and miscellaneous agencies. The Sunday School Department, under a full-time secretary, an associate, and an office helper, with a full complement of associational officers, reported a total enrolment of 54,788 in 1955 with 21 per cent of the schools involved attaining standard rating. The Sunday School Department promotes a state convention, clinics, and Vacation Bible schools, which enrolled 26,168 in 284 schools in 1955, reporting 715 professions and $5,291.76 gifts.

The Training Union and church music programs are combined under a full-time secretary, an associate, and an office helper, with associational officers co-operating. The enrolment in this department is 21,819. In 1955, 8,648 training awards were granted, including 390 in the music field. Conventions, clinics, and festivals are promoted.

The state Woman's Missionary Union includes 194 societies, 588 auxiliaries, with total enrolment, 10,386. Annual attendance at associational institutes in 1955 was 4,864. The operation of a youth camp summer program has been particularly successful. In 1955 camps reported 1,888 enrolled, 87 professions, 101 volunteers for mission vocations, and 19 for the ministry.

The Baptist Student Union program is directed by a secretary, an office secretary, two full-time and three part-time secretaries, with work on five state-owned college campuses. Baptists own student buildings adjacent to three of the schools, in which full programs are conducted. Summer student missionaries, promoted by the department, were sent to five states and to Alaska, Hawaii, Cuba, and Jamaica in 1955.

Brotherhood work includes complete associational organization, with the Royal Ambassador program fully under men's supervision. The state is divided into five districts through which rallies are sponsored for instruction and enlistment. Clinics are held in the 14 associations, and special emphasis is placed upon rural and ranch work. The Brotherhood promotes stewardship and laymen's revivals and sponsors an annual statewide conference preceding the convention gathering.

Miscellaneous agencies, educational in function, include a statewide pastors' conference, Inlow Youth Camp and Glenwood Assembly (association-owned and directed, and state-recognized), Glorieta, radio and television (to which assistance is given through local churches), and a state historical society, which has 300 members, voluntarily signed. Much historical material has been microfilmed.

Institutions supported by New Mexico Baptists include a children's home, medical center, three Bible chairs, agencies for ministerial relief and retirement, and an incorporated foundation. The Children's Home, accommodating 74 boys and girls, is supported by personal gifts, birthday offerings from Sunday schools, once-per-month church offerings, and an annual Thanksgiving gift of cash and supplies. The total budget in 1955 was $62,534.23. Part of the farm was sold in 1955 for city development and replaced by an exchange favorable to the convention.

The Medical Center, located at Parkview and designed to serve the whole Chama Valley, has become one of the state's most unusual institutions. A missionary doctor and his wife, former missionaries to China, superintend the work, assisted by one or more nurses and a technician-receptionist. With no drug store and no other laboratory within a 70-mile radius, the center is the only means of medical aid for 10,000 Spanish people. Major service is in the field of obstetrics. Through the medical ministry Christian personnel seek to bring Christ to the patients. A church near the center carries on an active program. The total expense in 1955 was $26,243.41.

Bible chairs at Portales, Las Cruces, and Albuquerque, adjacent to the campuses of state institutions, are maintained with a standard of work comparable to the respective colleges. The teaching is done by convention-employed professors—one full-time and two part-time with additional Baptist Student Union responsibilities. Enrolment in the Bible classes was 459 in 1954–55.

In co-operation with convention-wide agencies, the state mission board provides a program for ministerial relief and retirement. A total of 161 churches and 92 ministers are enrolled with the board. Churches are encouraged to promote at least one annual offering for supplements, and gifts are sent to the convention-wide agency. A program of education to insure maximum participation is carried on constantly.

With assets at $49,402.51, the convention is seeking, through an incorporated foundation, to enlarge its corporate funds by insurance policies, wills, bequests, and annuities. This operation is new, and, thus far, there have been no large endowments. Administration now includes a revolving loan fund to assist projects for mission churches.

Two agencies major in the field of promotion in New Mexico work, the official state paper and the general promotional office. The *Baptist New Mexican,* a 16-page magazine, has a 16,000-family circulation, made possible through the inclusion of the paper in most church budgets. The budget rate is $1 per year, encouraged by a supplement from the state board of 50 cents per family. The paper takes a bold stand on major public issues, promotes local work throughout

IV. NEW MEXICO STATISTICAL SUMMARY

Year	Associa-tions	Churches	Church Member-ship	Baptisms	S. S. Enrol-ment	V.B.S. Enrol-ment	T. U. Enrol-ment	W.M.U. Enrol-ment	Brother-hood En-rolment	Mission Gifts	Total Gifts	Value Church Property	State Capital Worth
1830													
1840													
1850	Work started in 1849, but no statistical records are available.												
1860													
1870													
1880	0	1	....	....	....	....	....	....	....	....	....	....	....
1890	1	8	....	....	....	....	....	....	....	....		....	....
1900	2	17	602	73	836	....	....	....	....	$ 1,121.70	$ 6,445.09	$ 10,500.00 *	....
1905	3	46	1,616	177	1,284 *	....	102 *	54 *	....	2,106.00	14,018.12	43,150.00	....
1910	6	No statistics—year of split in convention alignment											
1915	7	130	5,341	394	4,913	....	864	....	....	7,236.27	41,092.99	171,044.00	....
1920	8	132	6,729	666	5,774	....	....	....	....	49,530.70	125,245.73	317,600.00	....
1925	9	150	10,176	1,057	10,291	....	2,897	....	....	45,070.11	169,870.68	412,450.09	....
1930	8	125	12,209	699	8,507	35	2,145	1,236	....	32,641.90	151,373.46	629,884.16	....
1931	8	124	7,370	408	6,801	201	1,696	1,389	....	22,014.64	113,812.72	510,134.16	....
1932	8	127	10,517	682	10,488	599	2,337	2,391	....	22,832.47	128,772.76	594,839.96	....
1933	8	128	10,218	753	11,154	269	2,510	2,290	....	16,136.24	102,404.65	576,713.16	....
1934	8	127	12,023	910	11,577	207	2,801	2,527	364	19,232.38	117,305.27	542,024.16	$ 53,837.29
1935	8	97	12,474	1,052	12,558	1,132	2,940	2,568	434	23,531.17	148,421.45	597,318.44	....
1936	8	140	14,438	1,092	13,419	2,118	3,272	2,763	474	27,161.31	171,076.40	587,169.86	....
1937	8	126	13,567	827	13,562	3,740	3,713	2,985	316	32,653.02	187,429.48	676,444.75	....
1938	8	126	15,058	1,158	17,652	5,538	3,942	3,531	223	42,203.39	286,575.94	728,645.00	....
1939	8	134	18,580	1,659	19,404	6,926	4,895	3,556	378	39,993.40	231,994.26	810,711.78	....
1940	9	148	22,554	1,751	21,236	9,003	5,720	4,283	453	43,927.05	257,818.96	885,912.00	....
1941	9	150	22,292	1,615	20,564	9,000	5,955	4,022	515	46,157.10	278,362.12	881,464.00	....
1942	10	132	23,005	1,573	20,096	8,569	5,742	3,765	524	65,956.67	344,147.10	1,047,403.11	....
1943	10	146	25,575	1,417	19,526	10,901	5,891	3,243	546	102,675.66	425,242.66	1,048,730.21	....
1944	11	144	26,636	1,451	19,892	12,037	6,326	3,433	689	136,447.30	586,169.53	1,167,910.31	92,770.10
1945	11	147	30,155	1,934	23,832	13,167	7,650	3,938	661	182,141.57	766,729.93	1,255,789.24	....
1946	11	163	32,757	2,065	26,044	13,419	8,011	4,150	904	217,630.83	944,533.02	1,883,823.06	....
1947	10	160	35,799	2,493	28,966	11,995	9,776	4,634	1,532	257,543.49	1,275,374.33	2,230,499.24	....
1948	12	166	38,819	2,610	32,336	13,461	10,817	5,271	1,656	275,076.00	1,543,060.09	3,152,097.83	....
1949	14	172	42,144	2,916	34,984	13,896	12,312	5,870	1,820	301,074.00	2,268,254.00	4,313,911.00	....
1950	14	180	45,497	3,488	37,602	15,622	13,285	6,355	2,091	295,187.00	2,366,718.00	4,975,035.00	....
1951	14	186	49,769	3,876	40,157	16,708	14,353	7,260	2,640	346,998.00	2,672,482.00	6,220,146.00	....
1952	14	196	54,004	3,805	42,848	19,924	16,496	7,639	2,782	361,629.00	2,167,595.00	7,187,295.00	....
1953	14	201	58,452	4,247	50,191	20,595	18,301	8,722	3,131	477,024.00	2,507,270.00	7,733,099.00	....
1954	14	212	62,954	4,419	53,454	21,661	20,539	9,685	3,064	481,836.00	2,836,445.00	9,647,243.00	671,275.66

* Partial report

JESSIE M. KING and THELMA MARDIS

the state, operates on a budget of $25,300, and is printed on a press valued at $50,000.

General promotion is directed by a secretary with assistance from the secretary of missions and stewardship. Promotional emphasis is given to doctrines, evangelism, stewardship, Christian life, and denominational programs, in full coordination with convention-wide movements. Rallies and institutes are held with pastors, with a consistent emphasis on the Cooperative Program and home and foreign missions.

HARRY P. STAGG

NEW MEXICO, TERRITORIAL CONVENTION OF (1900–1911). Baptists of New Mexico territory were widely scattered and numerically weak at the turn of the century, 1900.

However, on Aug. 9, 1900, leaders of the two existing Baptist associations, Lincoln County and Santa Fe, projected the first plans for a territorial convention. By Nov. 16 after all associational churches had been notified, the organizational meeting was held at La Cruces, with two messengers from Lincoln, three from Santa Fe. A constitution was adopted, and articles of cooperation between the convention and the Home Mission Society were approved. Fifteen churches were represented in the organization.

A third association, Portales, was organized Oct. 18, 1903, with 10 new churches. A new chapel was established at Velarde through a gift of the Home Mission Society, New York, and a new Spanish mission was founded at Alcalde, nine miles from Velarde. In Oct., 1903, the New Mexico Woman's Missionary Union came into existence.

Seven new churches were organized in 1905; among them was Monument, which applied immediately to El Paso Association for affiliation but was referred back to New Mexico. Immigrants pouring into eastern New Mexico counties increased the area's challenge for Baptists. As a result, the territorial organization asked for a gift increase of $3,500 from the Home Mission Society.

Churches had multiplied to 105 by 1908, with total membership at 3,000. Thirty-five new churches had been organized during the year, and 62 Sunday schools reported an enrolment of 3,750. The convention of 1909 reported the establishment of Central, Northeastern, Pecos Valley, and Southwestern associations. Meanwhile, alignments, North and South, were shaping up over the question of the "sovereignty of the churches." In the nine years of convention existence, Southern Baptist "infiltration" had been growing, increasing division between the two groups. The state was still Northern Baptist, however, with the Northern interest in the hands of Perry Wilson Longfellow (*q.v.*). The Southern alignment centered around Eugene Perry Alldredge (*q.v.*).

In nine years churches had increased from 29 to 135, and membership had reached 5,000. The Home Mission Society had furnished three-fourths of the finances, and the convention had collected from other sources $165,000, which it spent locally. Southern sympathizers alleged that the society overstepped its bounds of control of missionaries and money.

Culmination of the debate came in 1910 in the annual gathering at Tucumcari when a resolution was presented restricting Northern authority over the churches, affirming that it should be left to the territorial convention. To avoid a rift, representatives appointed a committee to resolve the differences, but the persistence of the Southern group prevented an agreement. Recorders say that arguments on both sides were so vicious that the pastor and deacons of the host church publicly expressed regret for such conduct in their house of worship. Those sponsoring the curtailment of Northern Convention power responded to the invitation of Alldredge and repaired to the Presbyterian church house for a separate meeting. The Alldredge group proceeded to organize on Nov. 12, 1910, the Baptist General Convention of New Mexico.

Work of the two opposing groups continued according to routine through 1911. Meanwhile, efforts in the Northern and Southern Baptist conventions brought the New Mexico camps together at Clovis in 1912 where the reunion was effected, with mission work turned over to Southern Baptists.

HENRY CLAY REAVIS

NEW MEXICO ASSOCIATIONS.

I. Extant. ATOMIC. Organized Jan. 18, 1948, at First Baptist Church, Espanola, with messengers from six churches (Alire, Chama, Espanola, Los Alamos, Santa Fe, and Taos) forming a division of Central Association. Committees were appointed and officers were elected at the organizational meeting. The first annual session was held at First Baptist Church, Espanola, Aug. 16–17, 1948. The association has been served since 1948 by an associational missionary. In 1954, 6 churches reported 129 baptisms, 2,967 members, $95,873 total gifts, $16,669 mission gifts, $288,500 property value, and $113,836 church debt.

CENTRAL. Organized Sept. 10, 1909, at Estancia with ten churches. Churches of the old Lincoln Association divided into three parts in that year: one part retained the historic name Lincoln, another was named Pecos Valley, while the third with part of the dissolving Santa Fe Association formed Central Association, which embraced the churches in the Estancia Valley and all the churches north and west of the valley. It has been served at intervals by an associational missionary since Dec., 1909. In 1954, 28 churches reported 813 baptisms, 11,159 members, $590,480 total gifts, $108,678 mission gifts, $2,078,682 property value, and $582,909 church debt.

ESTANCIA VALLEY. Organized Sept. 17, 1939, at Mountainair with representatives from the churches of Moriarty, Estancia, Ewing, Mountainair, Mesa, and Corona. Because of the inconvenience caused by extraordinary territorial expansion, this association was formed out of Central Association, with its first annual session at Mountainair in Aug., 1940. Within five years Cedarvale, Claunch, Encino, Vaughn, and West Mesa were added to the association. In 1954, 7 churches reported 62 baptisms, 969 members, $28,865 total gifts, $5,232 mission gifts, $99,000 property value, and $13,456 church debt.

LINCOLN. First and oldest association in New Mexico with a continuous record, organized Sept. 29, 1888, at Zion Hill with messengers from five churches: Zion Hill, Seven Rivers, Elkhorn, Lookout, and Hopewell. Lincoln County Association of Missionary Baptists was the complete name. Aug. 11–13, 1892, the association met for its fifth annual session at Elkhorn Church with eight member churches, Eagle Creek, Eddie, Hope, and Roswell having been added. Seven Rivers had dissolved the previous year. During 1892 the name was changed to Lincoln Baptist Association. In 1954, 13 churches reported 147 baptisms, 1,988 members, $95,855 total gifts, $10,562 mission gifts, $280,295 property value, and $67,110 church debt.

MOUNTAIN. Organized Sept. 22, 1948, at Socorro, formed by messengers from Socorro, Magdalena, Pie Town, Mountain View, and Quemado churches. This new association was the 13th to be organized in New Mexico. Coming out of Central Association, these churches were duly dropped from Central's minutes in 1949. Since its organization Mountain has been served by an associational missionary. In 1954, 6 churches reported 56 baptisms, 582 members, $16,431 total gifts, $1,815 mission gifts, $47,000 property value, and $1,700 church debt.

NORTHEASTERN. Organized Sept. 30, 1909, as a result of the division of Portales Association, embracing the territory north of Curry County. Fourteen churches were included in the annual report the first year. The association has been served at intervals by an associational missionary since its beginning. In 1916 Tucumcari Association was formed by a division of Northeastern. In 1954, 20 churches reported 222 baptisms, 2,895 members, $122,979 total gifts, $17,553 mission gifts, $595,500 property value, and $74,104 church debt.

PECOS VALLEY. Organized as far as records are known in August, 1909, at Lake Arthur, resulting from a division of Lincoln Association. Sixteen churches are listed. The association has had an associational mission program at intervals since organization and has owned a residence for the missionary since 1950. In 1954, 28 churches reported 838 baptisms, 11,811 members, $551,868 total gifts, $82,855 mission gifts, $1,679,330 property value, and $281,056 church debt.

PLAINS. Organized July 31, 1941, at the 37th annual session of Portales Association, at Calvary Baptist Church, Portales. The churches in Curry and De Baca counties, the plains region of Quay County, and the panhandle of Roosevelt County formed the new Plains Baptist Association, which was a break from Portales. The first annual meeting was at House, July 28–29, 1942. Plains has shared its missionary with Portales and Tucumcari associations since organization. In 1954, 20 churches reported 290 baptisms, 6,032 members, $220,012 total gifts, $44,568 mission gifts, $1,093,500 property value, and $243,070 church debt.

PORTALES. Organized Sept. 8, 1903, at the "church at Portales, Roosevelt County, New Mexico," with messengers from six small churches, Elida, Lone Star, Portales, Floyd, Lemuel, and Plainview. Almost from the start it grew rapidly because of the great tide of immigrants pouring into the territory from states where Baptists were numerous. For six years the association embraced an area with 70 churches until Sept. 30, 1908, when the association was divided. It has been served by an associational missionary at intervals from its organization. In 1954, 18 churches reported 181 baptisms, 4,691 members, $131,540 total gifts, $25,665 mission gifts, $463,191 property value, and $89,940 church debt.

RIO GRANDE. Organized formerly as Valley Zone of Southwestern Association, Sept. 8, 1943; at Hot Springs, now Truth or Consequences. Mountain Zone retained the name Southwestern, and Rio Grande's first annual session was held at Anthony in 1944. Since 1944 it has been served by an associational missionary. In 1954, 10 churches reported 229 baptisms, 3,442 members, $161,693 total gifts, $35,638 mission gifts, $450,551 property value, and $24,330 church debt.

SAN JUAN. Organized Feb. 21, 1949, at the Farmington Church, embracing Cortez in Colorado, Aztec, Flora Vista, Gallup, and Farmington churches. The first annual session was held at First Baptist Church, Gallup, Aug. 30–31, 1949, with churches reporting 113 baptisms and 1,030 members. At the sixth annual session, Aug. 16–17, 1954, at Grand Junction, Colo., 14 churches, eight of them in Colorado, were included in the association. The 14th association organized in the state, San Juan was formed in an era of rapid expansion of Baptist work. Since 1949 it has been served by an associational missionary. In 1954, 14 churches reported 300 baptisms, 2,885 members, $116,176 total gifts, $19,496 mission gifts, $466,500 property value, and $168,755 church debt.

SOUTHEASTERN. Organized in Apr., 1912, and held its first annual session with the church at King the following September, with 12 churches in the organization. Located in the southeastern corner of the state, the association was organized as a result of the division of Pecos Valley Association. In 1913, 11 churches listed were Eden, King, Knowles, Lovington, Macedonia, McDonald, Midway, Monument, New Life, Pleasant Valley, Ranger Lake. Some of the churches, if not all, were in the organization. The association has been served by an associational missionary at intervals since its organization. In 1954, 21 churches reported 753 baptisms, 9,414 members, $421,065 total gifts, $77,543 mission gifts, $1,213,821 property value, and $192,684 church debt.

SOUTHWESTERN. Organized Aug. 27, 1909, at Lordsburg, by four churches formerly belonging to Santa Fe Association, which dissolved Sept., 1909, by dividing. The association increased to 11 churches by 1942, but diminished to six when the Rio Grande Association was formed Sept. 8, 1943. It is the only one of the 14 associations in the state which owns its own assembly property and promotes an assembly program—Glenwood Assembly at Glenwood, begun in 1947. It has been served by an associational missionary at intervals since 1909. In 1954, 10 churches reported 141 baptisms, 1,892 members, $81,489 total gifts, $18,995 mission gifts, $257,500 property value, and $5,690 church debt.

TUCUMCARI. Organized by 13 churches, Aug. 24, 1916, at Los Tanos. Its first annual session met Sept. 19–20, 1917, at Plain in Quay County. Disbanding in 1946, the association's eight churches presented petitionary letters to the Plains Association at its annual meeting, Sept. 18, 1946, and merged with it. Tucumcari reorganized Nov. 4, 1947. In 1954, 12 churches reported 124 baptisms, 2,817 members, $104,888 total gifts, $18,791 mission gifts, $527,520 property value, and $91,664 church debt.

JOHN RANSDELL

II. Extinct. GAMBRELL MEMORIAL. Organized Oct. 29, 1925, by seven churches: Buckeye, Chandler, Glendale, Pima Mission, First Southern of Phoenix, Prescott, Willcox, all located in Arizona. The churches had first affiliated with Southwestern Association, New Mexico; the new association continued co-operation with the New Mexico convention. However, the association withdrew Sept. 20, 1928, to become the Baptist General Convention of Arizona.

GILA. Organized Sept. 21, 1911, by five churches: Gila, Santa Rita, Hachita, Animas, and Columbus, located in Southwestern Association and formed after a split in the ranks over the Northern and Southern Alignment question. It dissolved in 1912 to become again a part of Southwestern.

SANTA FE. Organized May 12, 1900, by five churches: Dona Ana, Las Cruces, Albuquerque, East Las Vegas, and Deming, located west of the Santa Fe Railroad. It dissolved in Sept., 1909, by division into Central, Southwestern, and Northeastern associations. THELMA MARDIS

NEW MEXICO BAPTIST. The first Baptist paper of official status in the state. It was established at Alamogordo in 1900, at the time of the Baptist territorial organization. Suspended the next year, it was resumed in 1909 as a Southern Baptist paper in competition with the Northern *Baptist Bulletin*. Then affiliated with the Baptist General Convention of New Mexico, it was edited by Eugene Perry Alldredge (*q.v.*) until its discontinuance in 1912.

MRS. RICHARD THOMAS BAKER, SR.

NEW MEXICO BAPTIST CHILDREN'S HOME. Founded by the First Baptist Church, Portales, in 1918, it was transferred to the New Mexico Baptist convention in 1919. The convention, in session at Santa Fe, designated Portales as the permanent location for the home and provided that the corresponding secretary would be ex-officio superintendent with a local manager and matron. Mary E. Joiner was installed first matron, and four years later when William G. MacArthur was called as first manager, it became customary for a man and his wife to serve together as manager and matron. William Callaway Grant was the first to be designated superintendent. The policy of the home has always been "homelike care for homeless children of white parentage."

Beginning with four children, the home's enrolment has reached 85. During its first 35 years of history it reached 525 homeless children. It operates on an annual budget of $65,000. The original property, a gift of one house, was soon increased to 40 acres of land and was later sold for $7,000, when a new location in Portales was secured for $11,200. Embracing 181 acres of land, the Portales property has been enhanced with new buildings through the years, thus being valued in 1954 at $275,103.65.

Grade, high school, and college training are aims for every child. Health care and wholesome recreation go along with vocational training on the farm. The home, governed by a board of trustees, has housemothers for the various buildings and offers separate accommodations for boys and girls. DOYLE WINTERS

NEW MEXICO BAPTIST COLLEGE. Organized as the first Baptist school in New Mexico in 1900 with Lincoln Association providing the funds and sponsoring the movement. C. C. Waller of Texas led in its establishment, with the field of operation at Alamogordo where lots were sold for a college addition. With the first goal at $100,000, enough was raised to erect a two-story brick structure. Waller became the first president, and the first session enlisted 75 pupils.

In 1905, after five years of financial inadequacy, the association offered the school to New Mexico Baptists. With the broader support, churches were still too few and too scattered to give the necessary security; thus after five more years in Dec., 1909, the convention offered the property back to the association. Within one year (1911), the school closed and sold the property for its debts, but the convention urged New Mexico churches to work toward the establishment of another school.

HERBERT E. BERGSTROM

NEW MEXICO BAPTIST HISTORICAL SOCIETY. Under sponsorship of the Public Relations Department of the New Mexico Baptist convention, the state mission board instructed the setting up of a society to affiliate with the Southwide Historical Commission. Organization of the society resulted on May 12, 1954. Active working committees, with chairmen and definite activities, are projects, manuscript preservation, collections and classification, and publication. Although fees are not required for membership in the society, no names are entered except upon application of Baptists in regular standing with the convention. The charter membership reached 140 and later increased to 210 by broadening the appeal to include representatives from all types of convention activity. Calls for mission annuals and minutes of state and associational records have been effective elements of the society's work. Materials related to Baptist work in New Mexico have been classified and microfilmed through the assistance of the Southwide Historical Commission. LEWIS A. MYERS

NEW MEXICO BAPTIST HOSPITAL. Construction of the hospital, under sponsorship of the Clovis church, was completed Oct. 20, 1920, at a cost of $40,000, with a capacity of 23 beds. Although presented that year to the Baptist Convention of New Mexico, acceptance was deferred until indebtedness could be substantially reduced. The church continued operation until Nov. 8, 1923, when the Las Vegas convention authorized the executive board to receive the institution with the recommendation that the remaining $7,000 indebtedness be raised in Clovis. The appraised valuation of the hospital at that time was $50,000. Operational expenses were to be supplied from patient's fees while necessary capital investments were to be supplied by the convention. Reports in 1925–26 indicated operation without indebtedness, with fees of 492 patients amounting to $16,904.67, $1,000 more than cost of operation. During the 1930's records revealed increasing losses, forcing the convention to offer the institution back to Clovis. It was not until 1938, however, that conditions forced the hospital's sale.
DOYLE WINTERS

NEW MEXICO BIBLE CHAIRS. As early as Jan., 1927, New Mexico founded what has been termed the first Baptist Bible chair of the Southwest. It was started at Eastern New Mexico University (then College) at Portales, offering fully accredited courses on the college level, with C. R. Barrick the first director. Gradually, the center came to occupy convention-owned $75,000 brick property with classrooms, assembly halls, recreational lounge, and library. Teachers are now elected by a board of regents on recommendation of the Baptist Mission Board. Courses are open to all students, and teachers must meet all academic requirements of the school. Thirty-four courses are now offered in the fields of Greek and religion, embracing 97 hours.

Other Bible chairs under New Mexico Baptist control are at the State University, Albuquerque, and New Mexico A. & M. College, Las Cruces. Their courses, unlike that at Eastern New Mexico University, are accredited through Hardin-Simmons Baptist University, Abilene, Tex. Classes in the latter centers were started in 1948 and 1949 respectively, and all have been placed in strategic locations adjacent to the campuses. Students enlisted in the three centers totaled 348 in 1953. Baptist student activities are carried out on the college campuses. An effort has been made to reach two remaining schools, Highlands University, Las Vegas, and Western College, Silver City, with plans already drawn for a building at Western.
HERBERT E. BERGSTROM

NEW ORLEANS BAPTIST CHRONICLE. A weekly, launched in 1852 by L. A. Duncan. The new publication built up a sizable circulation in Louisiana, Mississippi, and Alabama. The paper was discontinued after five years.
F. W. TINNIN, SR.

NEW ORLEANS BAPTIST THEOLOGICAL SEMINARY. A coeducational institution of four schools, located at 3939 Gentilly Boulevard, New Orleans 22, La., owned and operated by the Southern Baptist Convention for training in every type of Christian leadership. It was called Baptist Bible Institute from the time it was chartered, Oct. 8, 1917, until 1946. The name was changed to New Orleans Baptist Theological Seminary by the Southern Baptist Convention on May 17, 1946, and the charter was changed on May 27, 1946.

New Orleans, a mission field.—When the institute was chartered, the population of New Orleans was overwhelmingly Roman Catholic, dating back to French and Spanish immigration before the Louisiana Purchase and to migration of Irish laboring people from the Boston area around that date. The population was 387,000, with 130,000 native whites, 37,000 real foreigners, 60,000 French-speaking, 25,000 Italian-speaking, 30,000 Spanish-speaking, 15,000 of other tongues, and 90,000 Negroes. There were approximately 300,000 white population of whom only 29,750 were Protestants, including 1,242 members in six Baptist churches. The first catalogue (1918–19) states:

> The city is one of the strongest Catholic centers in the country, and this presents an unusual opportunity for our students to study this religion at first hand, to do practical work among a Catholic population. We are within easy reach of the Latin-American countries, and New Orleans is the logical point at which to train workers for these as well as other countries.

Of the six Baptist churches, only one was self-supporting, the others being subsidized by mission funds. The Baptist Bible Institute was located in the city, not because of Baptist strength but because of Baptist weakness.

Founding of the Baptist Bible Institute.—Baptists for a century had thought of a training school for ministers in New Orleans. Cornelius Paulding, a New England merchant, in 1817 suggested the idea to a missionary of the Triennial Convention. Such a school was advocated by Basil Manly, Sr. (*q.v.*), in 1849 and by James

FIRST BAPTIST CHURCH, Tulsa, Okla. Organized 1897, membership 1956 approximately 6,000. Modified Gothic auditorium serves almost 2,000, Sunday school 2,500. Property evaluation $3,000,000.

SOUTHERN BAPTIST THEOLOGICAL SEMINARY (*q.v.*), Louisville, Ky. Founded 1859, moved to present site 1926. First seminary established by Southern Baptists, it is valued at more than $12,000,000. Enrolment 1955–56 totaled 1,767.

Bruton Gambrell (*q.v.*) in the 1890's. The idea became permanently alive in 1914 through an editorial by Plautus Iberus Lipsey (*q.v.*) in the Mississippi *Baptist Record*.

Some leaders meeting voluntarily during the Southern Baptist Convention, Houston, Tex., May, 1915, passed a resolution asking the Baptist conventions of Louisiana and Mississippi and the Home Mission Board each to appoint a committee of three to study the feasibility of establishing such a school and to take such action as they deemed fit. George Harvey Crutcher (*q.v.*), representing Louisiana, John Tyler Christian (*q.v.*), representing Mississippi, and Monroe Elmon Dodd (*q.v.*), representing the Home Mission Board, took the request to the three boards. This resulted in appointment of a joint committee, as follows: Baron DeKalb Gray (*q.v.*), C. C. Pugh, and Dodd, from the Home Mission Board; J. B. Lawrence, Lipsey, and Christian, from the Mississippi board; Crutcher, R. P. Mahon, and F. G. Flowers, from the Louisiana board. This committee, meeting in Coliseum Place Baptist Church, New Orleans, Feb., 1916, approved such a school and recommended steps for its immediate establishment. A memorial from this committee, which was endorsed Feb. 23, 1916, in a mass meeting of New Orleans Baptists, was presented by Dodd to the Southern Baptist Convention in New Orleans, May 19, 1917, giving details about purposes, fields of study, relation to other seminaries, finances, and a place for temporary beginnings. It was adopted by the Convention, which instructed the Home Mission Board and the Sunday School Board to co-operate with other interested bodies in establishing and safeguarding a Baptist missionary training school in New Orleans.

Organized by authority of the Southern Baptist Convention.—The Convention's action led to the appointment of three directors by the Mississippi board and six by the Louisiana board, three from New Orleans, and three in the state. The first meeting of the board of directors was held in Coliseum Place Baptist Church, July 10, 1917, the actual birthday of the institution. The following officers were elected: B. P. Robertson, president; A. T. Terry, secretary; Ollie B. Webb, treasurer. They unanimously named the institution the Baptist Bible Institute. Byron Hoover DeMent (*q.v.*), pastor of the First Baptist Church, Greenwood, S. C., was unanimously elected president of the institute on that day and began his duties Oct. 1, 1917. The institute was chartered by the state of Louisiana Oct. 8, 1917. Campaigns for finances, employment of faculty and staff, purchase of Sophie Newcomb College campus on Washington Avenue, planning a curriculum, and recruiting students throughout a year led to opening of classes Oct. 1, 1918. In September Robertson was elected general representative, and Christian succeeded him as president of the board of directors. When Christian joined the faculty in 1919, Lipsey was elected president of the board of directors and served until 1949, when he declined re-election because of failing health.

During the session 1921–22, the board of directors voted to declare their willingness to so amend the charter and by-laws as to provide for complete control, direction, and ownership of the institute by the Southern Baptist Convention, when said Convention should accept it and when agreement was secured from the Louisiana and Mississippi convention boards. The charter was changed on Jan. 20, 1925, and the Southern Baptist Convention thereafter appointed a board of trustees. Lowry B. Eastland of Louisiana served as president of the board of trustees from 1947 until his death in 1950. Owen Cooper of Mississippi was elected in 1951 to succeed Eastland. Trustees are elected by the Southern Baptist Convention for terms of five years, eligible to serve only two such terms successively.

Presidents, faculty members, and student enrolment.—The institution has had four presidents. DeMent served with distinguished success from Oct. 1, 1917, until his resignation Dec. 21, 1927, because of "the infirmities of the flesh and insistence of the physicians." He organized the institute, secured the faculty, developed the curriculum, established the ideals, and won the favor of the Southern Baptist constituency for the institution. After relinquishing the presidency, he retained faculty status as professor of New Testament until his death on Mar. 17, 1933. William Wister Hamilton, Sr., pastor of St. Charles Avenue Baptist Church, New Orleans, was elected president Jan. 25, 1928, and assumed duties Mar. 1. His administration, which lasted until his resignation June 23, 1942, was marked by faith and courage, covering the period of the most serious financial burdens in the school's history. Duke Kimbrough McCall, pastor of Broadway Baptist Church, Louisville, Ky., was elected president on Feb. 17, 1943, assumed his duties in April, and was formally inaugurated Dec. 2. He resigned May 1, 1946, to become executive secretary of the Executive Committee of the Southern Baptist Convention. His three-year administration was marked by internal reorganization, academic strengthening, and paying off all indebtedness for the first time in the institute's history. Roland Quinche Leavell, pastor of First Baptist Church, Tampa, Fla., was elected president on May 14, 1946, assumed duties July 1, and was formally inaugurated Oct. 1. During his administration the Gentilly campus was purchased and buildings constructed, the School of Theology and the School of Religious Education were accredited, the School of Christian Training was organized, the endowment was increased to more than $500,000, and both faculty and student body were trebled in size.

The first faculty under President DeMent was as follows: James Edward Gwatkin (*q.v.*), business manager and professor of biblical introduction; W. E. Denham, Sr., professor of Old Testament exposition; L. O. F. Cotey, professor of French; Mrs. John O. Gough, superintendent of women and teacher of Bible synthesis; Lawrence Zarilli, professor of Italian; Bernard Washington Spilman (*q.v.*) and Margaret Frost of the Sunday School Board, serving part-time as instructors in Sunday school work. During 1918 John T. Christian was made librarian and professor of Christian history; Charles C. Carroll became professor of Christian doctrine. Those who have signed the *Articles of Religious Belief* on attaining faculty status are as follows: Byron H. DeMent, Mrs. John O. Gough, J. E. Gwatkin, W. E. Denham, L. O. F. Cotey, Lawrence Zarilli, Bernard W. Spilman, John T. Christian, Charles C. Carroll, Ernest Orlando Sellers (*q.v.*), R. P. Mahon, George H. Crutcher, M. G. Beckwith, James E. Dean, L. G. Cleverdon, E. F. Haight, L. Bracey Campbell, William Wister Hamilton, Sr., Bessie Welch, B. Locke Davis, Albert E. Tibbs, John Watson Shepard (*q.v.*), J. Washington Watts, Mrs. J. Washington Watts, Mrs. Joseph E. Santo, Park H. Anderson, Sr., William Wister Hamilton, Jr., Hannah Plowden, Charlotte Reed, Ruby Daniel, Ellis L. Carnett, H. Leo Eddleman, W. Plunkett Martin, Duke K. McCall, C. Penrose St. Amant, Frank Stagg, Eugene N. Patterson, Roland Q. Leavell, J. Hardee Kennedy, Roy O. Beaman, Nelle C. Davidson, Mrs. Walter C. Clark, F. C. Schatz, Helen E. Falls, Elliot A. Alexander, H. Clayton Waddell, John M. Price, Jr., Beatrice Collins, Theodore M. Clark, Arthur S. Gillespie, John K. Durst, John P. Newport, Wilbur W. Swartz, Frances Logan Brown, Joseph W. Bartlett, James C. Taylor, Ray F. Robbins, A. Jackson Roddy, J. Kelva Moore, Mrs. George M. Jenkins, Mrs. Warner G. Rutledge, John Olen Strange, B. Gray Allison, V. Wayne Barton, J. B. McMinn, Stanley Jack Watson, Claude H. Rhea, Jr., Genter L. Stephens, Wallace C. McKenzie, T. J. Delaughter, William S. Garmon, W. Morgan Patterson, Margaret Leverett, Mrs. Helon Baldwin Harwell, R. E. Glaze, Jr.

Student enrolment was less than 100 during the first year but has risen steadily. During the 10 years of greatest expansion, the enrolment was as follows:

SESSION	ENROLMENT
1945–46	331
1946–47	378
1947–48	361
1948–49	394
1949–50	543
1950–51	667
1951–52	731
1952–53	728
1953–54	876
1954–55	947
1955–56	972

Articles of religious belief.—Article VIII of the by-laws of the seminary states: "All members of the faculty shall be required to subscribe to the Articles of Faith, or Beliefs, as adopted by the Board, and to publicly sign these articles at the opening of the session at which they enter upon their duties." These articles were composed by DeMent and adopted by the trustees, containing 10 sections on 10 doctrinal points, as follows: (1) sole authority of Scriptures; (2) one triune God, who is Father, Son, and Holy Spirit; (3) Satan and sinful man; (4) Christ, God's way of atonement; (5) Christ the only Saviour from sin, without whom men are condemned; (6) conversion, including repentance, faith, regeneration, and justification; (7) final resurrection of all men; (8) a New Testament church a body of baptized believers, observing ordinances of baptism and Lord's Supper; (9) Lord's Day and Christian support of civil government; (10) Baptist loyalty to distinctive Baptist principles.

Organization and Development of Academic Program.—The 1918–19 catalogue announced eight departments of study, as follows: (1) Old Testament exposition, (2) New Testament exposition, (3) Christian history, (4) Christian doctrine, (5) Christian music, (6) personal work and Christian activities, (7) practical church work, (8) church business. The catalogue of 1919–20 offered a department of evangelism and a department of Spanish, French, and Italian. As the percentage of college graduates in the student body increased, the department of Spanish, French, and Italian became less necessary, and financial strain eventually crowded it out. These various departments evolved through the years into five departments under McCall and were reported in the 1946 *Annual* of the Southern Baptist Convention as follows: (1) Seminary Department, for licensed or ordained men only; (2) Religious Education Department; (3) Music Department; (4) Missionary Education Department; (5) Christian Training Department, awarding certificates to students without college prerequisites. Under Leavell the seminary was organized into four schools with separate faculties, with subject matter classified in fields of study and with a director over three of the schools:

(1) The School of Theology embraces (a) the biblical field, including Greek, survey and intensive courses, archaeology and biblical theology, Old Testament, Hebrew; (b) the theological field, including systematic theology, philosophy of religion, historical theology, and biblical theology; (c) the historical field, including church history, missions, comparative religions, history of preaching, history of Baptists and other denominations, history of biblical criticism; (d) the practical field, including homiletics, speech, social ethics, evangelism, and other subjects elective from music and religious education. The School of Theology awards the degrees of Bachelor of Divinity, Master of Theology, and Doctor of Theology. These degrees are accredited by the American Association of Theological Schools.

(2) The School of Religious Education embraces the fields of (a) psychology and

counseling, (b) education administration, (c) religious arts and crafts, (d) principles of religious education, (e) elementary religious education, (f) social work, (g) church secretarial work, (h) hospital and other clinical work, with elective possibilities and some requirements from the theological and sacred music fields. The School of Religious Education awards the degrees of Bachelor of Religious Education, Master of Religious Education, and Doctor of Religious Education. These degrees are accredited by the American Association of Schools of Religious Education.

(3) The School of Sacred Music embraces the fields of (a) church music education, (b) voice, (c) piano and organ, (d) conducting, (e) theology, (f) choral technique, (g) composition, (h) music history, (i) graded choirs. This school awards the degrees of Bachelor of Sacred Music and Master of Sacred Music.

(4) The School of Christian Training offers a two-year course to students without college or other academic prerequisites, with choice of major studies in theology, religious education, or sacred music. It awards diplomas of graduation without degrees.

The Layne Lectures were established by Mrs. Robert Layne of Shreveport, La., specifying that

> lectures given on this foundation shall be true to the inspiration, authority, and sufficiency of the Holy Scriptures, to the virgin birth, deity, substitutionary death, bodily resurrection and lordship of Jesus Christ, to the doctrine of the salvation of man by grace through faith and to the New Testament churches as self-governing bodies, spiritual in nature, democratic in organization and missionary in spirit and practice.

The James H. Tharp Lectures are given each year by a layman on the general subject, "The Preacher from the Layman's Viewpoint." All lectures may be published at the discretion of the administration.

Financial structure.—From the beginning, students have paid no tuition. At first current operations funds were provided by state appropriations and by campaigns for funds. Since the institute came under Southern Baptist Convention ownership, current operations funds have been provided through the Cooperative Program. Critical financial problems arose during the depression years of 1929–33 because of reduced receipts and heavy interest payments on debts for buildings. The school was dangerously near to foreclosure by creditors. The faculty was reduced to the president and four others, who had no assured salary except board in the dining room for their families and a prorated division of all receipts. Heroic sacrifice saved the school from being closed. The institute became debt-free on Aug. 24, 1943, for the first time in its history. By 1946 the Cooperative Program allocation for current funds had reached $200,000 per year. Capital funds allocations became operative first in 1946.

Presently all current operation funds for Southern Baptist seminaries are divided by a formula based on enrolment, a formula which has been worked out by the seminary presidents. Capital funds allocations each year are made according to needs of each seminary revealed by five-year surveys made by the Executive Committee of the Convention. By 1956 the New Orleans Seminary had built up a reserve fund of $230,000 for emergencies, which may not be used without permission of the Executive Committee of the Convention. Within 10 years the endowment funds have increased from $336.15 to $527,782.67, with additional funds invested in rental property—273 student apartments and 22 faculty residences.

Campus property and building program.—Providentially, the property of Sophie Newcomb College on Washington Avenue in the Garden District of New Orleans became available to the Baptist Bible Institute in 1918 and was purchased. The large square, containing administration building, classrooms, and men's dormitory, plus the women's dormitory across the street, was bought for $100,000 and later the chapel was purchased for $5,000. Transfer was made Aug. 29, 1918, with one fourth paid in cash ($26,250 including $10,000 paid for the option), with the balance to be paid in 15 annual payments of $5,000 each, with 6 per cent interest on unpaid balances. The Sunday School Board paid $10,000 of the purchase price, crediting half of it to the Home Mission Board, and for some succeeding years each board contributed $5,000 annually for the debt and current expenses. Baptists of New Orleans, in a campaign in 1918, subscribed $28,141.25 in cash and pledges. The administration building was named for Monroe Elmon Dodd (*q.v.*), pastor, First Baptist Church, Shreveport, which gave $25,000. The chapel was named for Mr. and Mrs. W. H. Managan, Sr., of Westlake, La., who donated $25,000.

The M. E. Dodd Building was formerly an old mansion built in 1852 at enormous expense by James Robb. The grounds were covered with majestic oaks, camphor trees, and semitropical foliage. The Mirror Room or Pompeiian Room, as it was sometimes called, was exquisitely adorned with Honduras mahogany, five gigantic mirrors with gold-leaf frames, and murals by the famous Italian artist Canova depicting life in ancient Pompeii prior to A.D. 79. (It later became a prayer room for students, dedicated to the deceased Virginia Hamilton, daughter of President and Mrs. Hamilton.) When Robb's finances failed, the fabulous mansion became known as "Robb's Folly" and was sold to a man named Burnside. It passed into the hands of Sophie Newcomb College in 1891. The college added the classroom building, chapel, arts building which was used by the institute as a men's dormitory, women's dormitory, and arcade, all of which came in the purchase by the Baptist Bible Institute.

Year after year, adjacent buildings were purchased by the institute for faculty and student apartments, until the school owned 28 buildings. The central heating plant and Lipsey Hall, a dormitory for men with capacity of 96, costing $177,000, were the only new buildings the institute erected on the Washington Avenue campus. Lipsey Hall was begun under McCall in 1946 and dedicated Jan. 11, 1947, in honor of P. I. Lipsey, president of the trustees. After removal of the seminary to the Gentilly campus, the residences and apartments were sold. Buildings on the central square were demolished and the land subdivided into 17 residential lots. The net sale price of all was $735,615 with Lipsey Hall and two residences yet unsold.

The idea of moving New Orleans Baptist Theological Seminary was first suggested by a survey committee of the Executive Committee of the Southern Baptist Convention, but no desirable property was available at the time. Soon after Leavell assumed his duties as president, 375 acres of highly desirable vacant property on Gentilly Boulevard which had long been in litigation became title clear, kept by providence until the capital funds program of Southern Baptists began in 1946. The Executive Committee of the trustees, Oct. 30, 1946, voted to seek an option. On Dec. 17, the owners agreed to sell 75 acres with 1,000 front feet on Gentilly Boulevard, U. S. Highways 90 and 11, for approximately $3,300 per acre. By authority of the full board of trustees, President Leavell on Dec. 18 paid $25,000 for a 90-day option. The sale was consummated on Feb. 5, 1947, for $247,752, including the option payment. The money was acquired by $209,189.44 from the 1946 capital funds program of the Southern Baptist Convention, some from current operations funds, and the remainder from designated gifts. The property was secured in spite of serious competition from wealthy real estate promoters and an effort by Roman Catholics to purchase it.

Ground was broken on July 1, 1948, for the Christian, Crutcher, Gwatkin, and Managan apartment buildings. Further construction has been continuous since that day. The Eastland-Gray-Willingham apartments and the library were begun in 1950; William Carey residence hall for women, DeMent Administration building, John Bunyan building for the School of Theology, and three faculty residences were begun in 1951; E. O. Sellers building for the School of Sacred Music, cafeteria, children's building, and Spurgeon-Lipsey-Dodd residence hall for men were begun in 1952; the bookstore was begun in 1953; J. H. Martin chapel and J. M. Frost building for the School of Religious Education were begun in 1954; 108 student apartments were begun by Providence Housing Corporation in 1954, and 48 additional ones in 1956. There are 22 faculty residences and other smaller buildings. Definite plans were underway in 1956 for a chapel, gymnasium, building for the School of Christian Training, and additional housing. All building by the seminary has been on a cash basis. The seminary has purchased for cash one third of the assets of the Providence Housing Corporation. The apartments built by this corporation have been financed by a loan of two thirds of the cost price, to be amortized in 20 years, after which the property will accrue to the seminary without cost.

Administrative offices and all classwork were moved to the Gentilly campus in 1953, with formal dedication exercises on Sept. 3. The total expenditure on Gentilly campus through Dec., 1955, was $5,150,000.00 by the seminary and $1,124,457.90 by Providence Housing Corporation apartments, of which the seminary paid $382,000.00. The seminary building funds came from three sources: capital funds of the Cooperative Program of Southern Baptists, sale of the Washington Avenue property, and gifts through bequests and designations.

History and development of the library.—To establish a worthy library was one of the early endeavors of the founders of the Baptist Bible Institute. The first professors made their private libraries available to students. Christian, professor of Christian history and librarian, donated his personal library, said in the 1920–21 catalogue to contain 18,000 volumes valued at $30,000. He traveled extensively at home and abroad collecting valuable and rare volumes. The Christian history collection is especially strong. In Aug., 1944, it became necessary to move the growing library into larger quarters on the top floor of 1220 Washington Avenue. Between 1944 and 1956 the collection grew rapidly as the book budget was increased year after year.

The present library contains many old and rare volumes, some incunabula, manuscripts, Baptist historical documents, polyglot Bibles, facsimiles of Greek Bibles, and a well-balanced, broad, rich field of theological literature. The microfilm collection is extensive. The library's 50,000 volumes are rich in denominational holdings of annuals, minutes, and periodicals, and there are about 14,550 which are not counted among the 50,000 volumes. There are long runs of bound periodicals in which church history material is especially good. At least five eighths of the collection is in the field of theological literature and biography. Philosophy, music, social sciences, and religious arts and crafts make up the remaining part of the collection. Bibliographical materials, encyclopedias, commentaries, dictionaries, lexicons in ancient and modern languages are abundant. The librarian in 1945 began to withdraw all unrelated subject matter and useless duplicates in order to rid the collection of materials too general or too specialized for theological use. Therefore, the collection is basically well sifted and directly pertinent to a growing theological seminary. The seminary budget in 1955–56 for books, periodicals, and microfilm was $12,000, with a total library budget of $28,000.

The first academic structure built on the Gentilly campus was a fireproof library building, erected 1950–51, costing $265,578, with capacity for 100,000 volumes and seating 400 students. Various professors served part-time as librarian until 1944, when Nelle C. Davidson, B.S. in Library Science, was elected full-time librarian. The following have served as librarian of the institution to date: Christian (1919–25), Mrs. Eloise C. Snyder (assistant, 1919–29), E. F. Haight (1926–29), J. E. Dean (1929–30), A. E. Tibbs (1930–35), J. E. Gwatkin (1935–41), D. E. Richardson (1941–44), Nelle C. Davidson (1944–). Mrs. James Peck (1954) and Mrs. John McPherson (1955–) have served as cataloguers.

Contributions to state, home, and foreign missions.—The field mission program of the seminary inevitably has inspired a high percentage of graduates to enter missionary service at home and abroad. Three missionary days each session, given entirely to missionary emphasis, have had far-reaching influence. The six Baptist churches with 1,242 members in 1917 increased in 1956 to 61 churches with approximately 25,000 members, plus 25 mission stations, a large percentage of the increase being due to activities of seminary students in establishing new preaching stations. The River Front Good Will Center mission program, including the Rachel Sims, Toledano, and Carver missions, have long been under the direction of a graduate of the seminary, Gladys Keith, and have been served largely by seminary student leadership. The Rescue Mission and many other institutions under the Home Mission Board and city mission program have used seminary students perennially for every type of service. County, associational, district, and state missionaries have gone from the seminary to every area of the Southern Baptist Convention.

According to tabulations by Helen Falls, professor, 107 graduates or former students have been appointed by the Home Mission Board, 24 of whom were made missionaries during the sessions 1954–55 and 1955–56. One out of every nine graduates since the first class has been appointed by the Foreign Mission Board. A total of 165 have served on foreign mission fields, of whom at various times 56 have been in educational work, 77 in evangelistic work, 2 in agricultural work, 4 in mission business operations, 24 in medical and nursing service, and 2 in music leadership. They have served in 32 countries. Today, 140 of the total 165 are active in foreign service. Z. Paul Freeman, appointed in 1921 as a pioneer missionary to Argentina, was the first graduate of the Baptist Bible Institute to be appointed by the Foreign Mission Board. P. D. Sullivan, appointed to Brazil in 1940, dedicated himself to foreign missions at the first missionary day exercises held in the seminary. Bertie Lee Kendrick, graduate of 1945, was the first missionary appointed by the Foreign Mission Board specifically to Hawaii, the others having been transferred there from other fields. The missionary spirit of the present seminary students is indicated by the fact that 12 graduates were appointed by the Foreign Mission Board in 1954, 10 in 1955, and 8 during the first half of 1956. One fifth of the present students are volunteers for mission service.

See also STUDENT ACTIVITIES, NEW ORLEANS BAPTIST THEOLOGICAL SEMINARY.

ROLAND Q. LEAVELL

NEW TESTAMENT CANON. The books of the New Testament, like those of the Old, were recognized as worthy of being elevated to the rank of Scripture after a long period of time. The Scriptures of Jesus and the apostles were the books of the Old Testament. At what time the actual process of canonizing the apostolic writings began, no one can definitely affirm. There are hints in the Gospels, Acts, and Epistles of a movement in the direction of a new sacred collection, such as the words of Jesus being placed above the words from the Old Testament (Matt. 5:21–48); the appeal of Paul to the words of Jesus for his authority (Acts 20:35; I Thess. 4:15; I Cor. 11:23); the claim of Paul to a revelation not found in the apostolic tradition (I Cor. 7:10); the request of Paul that his epistles be read to the churches (I Thess. 5:27; Col. 4:16); the appearance of written authority for Christians in the pastoral epistles (I Tim. 6:3; II Tim. 1:13–14; II Tim. 4:13); and the statement in II Peter that Paul's epistles had been elevated to a position of authority (II Peter 3:16).

In the middle of the second century, the books of the New Testament were mixed in with a mass of other Christian literature (gospels, apocalypses, sermons, epistles, prophecies, and histories) that was very popular with the majority of Christians. Prior to this time no effort had seemingly been made to sift this material and mark off the boundary between writings accepted as Scripture and those not accepted. According to Eusebius, Papias, bishop of Hierapolis, in A.D. 135 preferred the oral tradition of the words of Jesus to the written documents. Marcion, a native of Sinope in Pontus, went to Rome between A.D. 140 and A.D. 150. Being unable to relate the Old Testament to the Christian faith, he restricted the number of documents that were reliable for Christians. By this action he set forth the first canon of the New Testament. His canon included 10 epistles of Paul (the pastorals excluded) and a mutilated copy of the Gospel of Luke. Marcion was branded as a heretic by Ireneus and Tertullian, but he did focus the attention of Christians on the need for defining the documents which were authoritative.

At the close of the second century, we see in embryo the consciousness of the New Testament canon. Ireneus, who was bishop of Lyons in Gaul and who died between A.D. 190 and A.D. 202, was bitterly opposed to the heretical views of Marcion and the followers of Valentinus. In his opposition he became one of the most interesting witnesses to the canon. Ireneus put little trust in oral tradition and thereby reversed the estimation of Papias. The voice of authority which Ireneus proclaimed was not the voice of Rome but the voice of Asia Minor. He states that there were four Gospels, no more and no less. His proof for this statement rested upon "the four climes of the world," "the four winds of the world," and the four faces of the cherubim (lion, calf, man, and eagle, drawn from Rev. 4:7). The Pastorals, Philemon, Hebrews, James, and Jude were not expressly recognized by Ireneus, but he did ascribe certain passages to Paul which we recognize as coming from I and II Timothy. The standard set forth by Ireneus for including a document as authoritative was that the document must have been written by an apostle. To keep the heretics from defining what documents were reliable, he further affirmed that only those who were the successors to the apostles had such a right.

Tertullian, a presbyter from Carthage in North Africa who died between A.D. 220 and A.D. 240, was in agreement with the standard proposed by Ireneus. We receive information from him that the reason the Epistle to the Hebrews was not accepted was because Barnabas had written it. There is no indication that Tertullian accepted James, II Peter, II and III John. The voice of Rome is first found in the Muratorian Fragment, a document that sets forth a catalogue of Christian Scriptures in use between A.D. 195 and A.D. 210. James, II Peter, and the Epistle to the Hebrews are missing from this collection.

For the support of the 27 books now in the New Testament, we must turn our eyes toward Alexandria, Egypt; but even there discussions over some of the books continued for nearly 200 years. Clement of Alexandria recognized Hebrews, II John, and Jude, but did not include II Peter, James, and III John. Origen, a pupil of Clement, placed II Peter, James, Jude, II and III John in an intermediate position between those books which were recognized everywhere and those books which were rejected. During the time of Athanasius, the archbishop of Alexandria, it was the custom for the archbishop to send out a Festal Epistle to all Christendom to designate the time for the celebration of Easter. This was probably due to the superior astronomical knowledge in Alexandria. In A.D. 367 Athanasius, in his 39th Festal Epistle, gave a catalogue of the books "canonized and handed down and believed to be Divine"; and in the section for the New Testament, the 27 books were set forth without any question. By this time the majority of Christians had come to the conclusion that these and no other books were inspired and should be included in the canon of the New Testament.

The first synodical decision on the canon of the New Testament took place at the Third Council of Carthage in 397, but this council approved of what had already been accepted by the Christians of various areas, with the exception of some in Asia Minor. No book of the New Testament was born with the title "canonical," but all 27 books did originate with qualities which caused them finally to be labelled "canonical."

BIBLIOGRAPHY: G. H. Ferris, *The Formation of the New Testament* (1907). C. R. Gregory, *Canon and Text of the New Testament* (1907). A. Harnack, *The Origin of the New Testament* (1925). J. Knox, *Marcion and the New Testament* (1943). A. Souter, *The Text and Canon of the New Testament* (1925). B. F. Westcott, *On the Canon of the New Testament* (1875).

T. C. SMITH

NEW TESTAMENT LITERATURE.

GOSPELS. Because the four canonical Gospels were written after the Christian message was already being proclaimed in much of the Roman world, they not only contain almost all the existing information about the life of Jesus of Nazareth, but also reflect the importance and meaning of that life to the early Christian congregations. The first three, though differing from each other in purpose and detail, give a common outline of the story of Jesus and, accordingly, since the time of J. J. Griesbach (1774), have come to be called Synoptic Gospels. The Gospel of John gives information which supplements the Synoptics but differs widely from them in style, purpose, and content.

The writers of the Synoptics apparently used both oral and written sources in compiling their narratives. Luke asserts that "many" had already written about Jesus, drawing their information from such as were "eyewitnesses and ministers of the word" (Luke 1:1–4). Close comparison of the first three Gospels has led New Testament scholars to almost universal agreement that Matthew and Luke both used Mark as one of their sources. The majority also agree in assuming the former existence of a document, now called *Logia* or *Q*, which was used by Matthew and Luke. Two reasons are given for this assumption: (1) Besides Markan material, Matthew and Luke have more than 200 other verses in common, often in close agreement. (2) There is relative agreement in the order in which many of these sayings appear. B. H. Streeter has argued that the *Logia* was written about A.D. 50 at Antioch in Syria and was perhaps a translation of an Aramaic work by the apostle Matthew (referred to in the second century by Papias).

The date of writing of such a book as Mark cannot be exactly ascertained. Usually a date between A.D. 60 and 70 is suggested, in conformity with the tradition that the author was John Mark of Jerusalem, the companion of Barnabas and Paul, who is referred to in II Timothy 4:11. Mark is said to have become the interpreter of Simon Peter and after Peter's death to have written down what the apostle had told. The Gospel contains two major sections, with a brief prologue (1:1–13) and a conclusion, the text of which is in question

(16:9–20). About half of the book is devoted to Jesus' ministry and teaching, the opposition aroused, coming to its climax in Peter's confession (1:14 to 9:1); the other half of the story moves toward Jerusalem, the cross, and the resurrection (9:2 to 16:8).

The name of Matthew has long been associated with the first Gospel, although the book itself is anonymous; the tradition is probably accounted for by Papias' reference to a writing by the apostle in Aramaic. The author was a Greek-speaking Jewish Christian whose thesis was that Christianity was no accident but "the consummation of God's saving purpose for His people begun in the Old Testament dispensation." Such usage as "kingdom of heaven" for "kingdom of God" reflects Jewish avoidance of the divine name and supports the hypothesis that the book was originally written with Jewish people in mind.

The author of the third Gospel, according to tradition from the second century, was Luke the physician, companion of Paul. Acts is the sequel to the Gospel and is by the same author (cf. Acts 1:1). Some of the dominant motifs in the book can be seen in such stories as that of Jesus in the synagogue at Nazareth (Luke 4:16–30); the leadership of the Spirit; God's concern for the poor, the outcasts, and the foreigners; and God's rejection of Jewish exclusivism.

When, where, and by whom the Gospel of John was written has been greatly debated by scholars in this century. The traditional view is that it was written in Ephesus by the aged apostle John, about A.D. 90, but the tradition in its oldest form is not clear. The purpose of the book the writer himself states: "These are written, that ye may believe that Jesus is the Christ, the Son of God; and that believing ye may have life in his name" (John 20:31 ASV). John centers his attention on Jerusalem and Judea, in contrast with the other Gospels, in which the ministry in Galilee is dominant. He does not use parables in the manner of the Synoptics, and the miracles recounted are "signs" with spiritual significance, not simply works of compassion. The central ideas of the book are two: (1) The Word became flesh and brought life into the world; and (2) this life became fully available only through his self-sacrifice and death. HENRY TURLINGTON

ACTS AND EPISTLES. Letters, some quite personal, form the earliest writings of the New Testament. These were primary sources of primitive Christianity, emerging from and reflecting much of its life, unposed and unrehearsed. The book of Acts is a historian's interpretation of this same formative period of Christianity.

Thirteen letters bear Paul's name. The Thessalonian letters were written from Corinth shortly after the founding of the work in Thessalonica, clarifying Paul's teaching about last things and calling Gentile converts to moral commitment suited to the Christian life. Galatians, considered by many to be Paul's earliest, was written to meet an emergency in which Gentile believers were being taught that to faith must be added circumcision and possibly other ritual observances. Paul insisted that the issue was between grace and merit, faith and works, with no possible compromise. The Corinthian letters issued from a most critical period for Paul and his readers. Disunity, disorder, incest, litigation, legalism, and license were among the outward problems in Corinth; Paul branded the underlying evil as the "world's wisdom," the disposition to fight for personal advantage. Against this he proclaimed the cross as God's wisdom, and love as the higher way. Romans presents a complexity of ideas built around the theme of God's righteousness revealed in his dealing with Jew and Gentile and in his provision for new status and life for man. Paul's prison epistles (Colossians, Philemon, Ephesians, and Philippians), are traditionally assigned to the Roman imprisonment described in Acts 28:16–31. Colossians interprets the person and work of Christ against a background of influence resembling gnostic thought. Philemon is concerned with problems and ethical values growing out of the escape and conversion of a slave. Ephesians is an exposition of God's purpose to unify humanity in Christ, the church as the body of Christ being its realization, Philippians, concerned with problems of discord involving theological issues, appeals to the self-renunciation of Christ, expressed supremely in the cross but also in such followers as Timothy and Epaphroditus. First and Second Timothy and Titus are known as the pastoral epistles because of their concern with pastoral responsibilities.

The Epistle of James contrasts the true and the false in character, worship, faith, and love. Reflecting primitive Jewish Christianity, it may be the earliest New Testament writing. Two epistles bear the name of Peter, and one bears the name of Jude. These offer encouragement under trial and warning against the corrupting influences of Gnosticism. In Hebrews the anonymous author challenged his readers to move on to a Christian life less limited by the legalism of its Jewish heritage. Three epistles are ascribed to John. The first and longest is a challenge to the common life in Christ, the basic law of which is love.

Acts, volume two of Luke-Acts, traces the growth of the community from Christian Judaism, at home in synagogues and Temple, to a Jewish-Gentile community transcending the limits of nation and race. In this book one sees Christianity making itself at home throughout the Roman world as it presents the good news of God in Christ to all men. FRANK STAGG

THE APOCALYPSE. The book of Revelation is the one book of the New Testament that belongs to the apocalyptic writings, a class of literature that was popular in the last two centuries before Christ and in the first century of the Christian era. It is called "the Apocalypse." (The word is derived from the Greek term *apokalupsis,* meaning "unveiling.") The book of Daniel is the chief representative in the Old Testament of this class of writings. Apocalyptic writings emphasize the deliverance of God's people and their hopes and expectations concerning last things. The messages of these writings are set for the most part in a framework of visions, raptures, and symbols. They devote much attention to prophecy concerning future events.

The consensus of modern scholarship is that the book of Revelation was written about A.D. 95, toward the end of the reign of the Roman Emperor Domitian (A.D. 81–96). It is believed that Christian churches in the Roman Empire, particularly in the province of Asia, were threatened at this time with persecution because of their resistance to the emperor's insistence that he be paid divine honors, that is, that he be worshiped as a god. The persecution described in Revelation had reached into the provinces (2:13) and had resulted in the martyrdom of Christians (6:9; 20:4).

The purpose of Revelation was to encourage the Christians and the churches in their resistance to emperor worship and to assure them of the ultimate triumph of the kingdom of Christ. The ruler of the empire is depicted as a beast whose power is derived from Satan (13:1–8). The officials who carry out his wishes are represented as another beast (13:11–18). The city of Rome is portrayed as "Babylon the Great, the Mother of the Harlots and of the Abominations of the Earth" (17:5 ASV). But Christ is "King of kings, and Lord of lords" (19:16). His complete victory over the evil rulers of the earth is assured (19:19–21). The author goes on to picture the ultimate defeat of Satan himself (20:10) and the final triumph of all the people of God in the unforgettable pictures of the new heaven and the new earth and the new Jerusalem (21:1 to 22:5).

The church fathers—Justin Martyr, Ireneus, Clement of Alexandria, Tertullian, and Origen—identify the author of Revelation as John the apostle. The author identifies himself as John (1:1, 4, 9), but he does not claim to be the apostle. He does represent himself as being a prophet (10:11; 22:9).

EDWARD ALLISON MCDOWELL

BIBLIOGRAPHY: C. H. Allen, *The Message of the Book of Revelation* (1939). E. Andrews, *The Meaning of Christ for Paul* (1949). I. T. Beckwith, *The Apocalypse of John* (1919). W. O. Carver, *The Glory of God in the Christian Calling* (1949). R. H. Charles, *A Critical and Exegetical Commentary on the Revelation of St. John* (1920). J. M. Creed, *Gospel According to Luke* (1950). O. Cullmann, *Peter: Disciple, Apostle, Martyr*, tr., F. V. Filson (1953). H. E. Dana, *The Epistles and Apocalypse of John* (1947). C. H. Dodd, *The Interpretation of the Fourth Gospel* (1953). M. S. Enslin, *Christian Beginnings* (1938). N. Geldenhuys, *Commentary on the Gospel of Luke* (1952). E. J. Goodspeed, *An Introduction to the New Testament* (1937). W. F. Howard, *The Fourth Gospel in Recent Criticism and Interpretation* (1935). F. J. F. Jackson and K. Lake, *The Beginnings of Christianity* (1920–33). E. A. McDowell, *The Meaning and Message of the Book of Revelation* (1951). A. H. McNeile, *An Introduction to the Study of the New Testament* (1953); *Gospel According to Matthew* (1952). J. Moffatt, *An Introduction to the Literature of the New Testament* (1918). A. S. Peake, *The Revelation of John* (n.d.). R. B. Rackham, *The Acts of the Apostles* (1939). W. H. Ramsay, *The Letters to the Seven Churches* (1904). W. D. Richardson, *The Revelation of Jesus Christ* (1939). A. T. Robertson, *A Harmony of the Gospels for Students of the Life of Christ* (1922). E. F. Scott, *The Book of Revelation* (1940); *The Literature of the New Testament* (1936); *The Purpose of the Gospels* (1949). R. D. Shaw, *The Pauline Epistles* (1903). J. W. Shepard, *The Life and Letters of St. Paul* (1950). D. Smith, *The Life and Letters of St. Paul* (1920). F. Stagg, *The Book of Acts, The Early Struggle for an Unhindered Gospel* (1955). J. A. Stewart, *A Man in Christ* (1935). R. H. Strachan, *The Fourth Gospel* (1943). B. H. Streeter, *The Four Gospels* (1951). R. Summers, *Worthy Is the Lamb* (1951). H. B. Swete, *The Apocalypse of St. John* (1906). V. Taylor, *The Formation of the Gospel Tradition* (1949); *The Gospels* (1952); *Gospel According to St. Mark* (1952).

NEW ZEALAND, BAPTIST UNION OF. Organized at Wellington, Oct., 1882, the union comprises in its membership every Baptist church in New Zealand. Charles Dallaston, who "more than any other of God's good men was the father of the Baptist Union," convened a meeting at Oxford Terrace, Christchurch, of representatives from Baptist churches in other parts of the colony at which Josiah T. Hinton made the motion, "It is desirable to form some practical union among the Baptist Churches of New Zealand." At a conference held in Wellington in 1882 Alfred North moved and Dallaston seconded the motion which formally created the Baptist Union of New Zealand.

Charles Carter, a Singhalese scholar, was first president of the union, with W. C. Spencer secretary and Seering H. Matthews treasurer. In addition to them North and Dallaston served on the first executive committee. In 1934 the union, divided into five auxiliaries, comprised 70 churches with a total membership of 8,725; by 1954 the number of churches had increased to 103, and church membership to 11,837. Sunday schools, which include only children from four to 14 years of age, had enrolments of 8,125 in 1934 and 11,234 in 1954. Bible classes attended by youth over 14 had a membership of 1,546 in 1934 and 2,971 in 1954.

The union publishes *The New Zealand Baptist*, with N. R. Wood editor; a Bible class paper, *Contact;* and a Sunday school paper, *Sunday School and Home.* The Bible Class movement publishes a study handbook annually. In 1926 the union established a college for the training of students for the ministry, with nine students enrolled at its beginning. Previously students had been trained at Presbyterian College. The present principal of the union's college is E. Roberts Thomson; 20 students are enrolled (1955).

The union founded Manurewa Children's Home in 1893, Homes for Elderly Women at

Auckland in 1953, and Christchurch in 1955. A missionary society was organized at Dunedin in 1885, with 12 ministers and 16 delegates from 20 churches present for the meeting. The original mission field was East Bengal; Tripura was added in 1937. At present the main centers of mission work are Brahmanbaria with 50 members, Chandpur with 37 members, and Tripura with 3,116 members. In 1954, 18 missionaries were serving, the mission among the Maoris was reopened, and 131 New Zealand Baptists were serving on other mission fields. N. R. WOOD

NEW ZEALAND BAPTIST MISSIONARY SOCIETY. Constituted by the Baptist Union of New Zealand, at the third annual assembly of the union in 1885, as a result of an invitation to New Zealand Baptists by Silas Mead, of Australia, to join with the South Australian Baptist Missionary Committee in taking up work in East Bengal. The field of activities of the New Zealand Baptist Missionary Society consists (1955) of Chandpur and Brahmanbaria in East Pakistan, and Tripura in India. In Brahmanbaria the mission operates a hostel for girls (50 inmates), a dispensary, a girl's middle English school (174 pupils), quarters for teachers and Bible women, and a number of outstations. The total Christian community is 112. In the Chandpur district educational, medical, and general philanthropic work is maintained, but during 60 years of missionary effort there has been no general response to the gospel in this predominantly Moslem area. The total Christian community in 1955 in Chandpur was 99. The Tripura district is the most fruitful part of the field of the New Zealand Baptist Missionary Society. In contrast with the disappointing work in East Pakistan, the response in Tripura has been remarkable. There are 6,000 Christians comprising 85 churches and fellowships. About 200 converts are baptized annually. The mission operates a middle English school, a boarding school (50 boarders), 55 village primary schools, 60 Sunday schools, 2 cottage hospitals, 2 dispensaries, and a Bible training school. In the history of the New Zealand Baptist Missionary Society, 60 persons have served on the foreign mission field. In 1955 there were 21 missionaries, 5 ministers, 1 woman physician, and 15 other women missionaries. The income of the New Zealand Baptist Missionary Society comes chiefly from the annual Self-Denial Offering. In 1954 the Self-Denial Offering amounted to £16,490 (over $49,000), two thirds of which was used for the foreign missions program and one third used for the budget of the New Zealand Baptist Union. H. R. PETERSON

NEWMAN, ALBERT HENRY (b. Edgefield County, S. C., Aug. 25, 1852; d. Austin, Tex., June 4, 1933). Teacher and church historian. Reared at Thomson, Ga., Newman was tutored so thoroughly by his pastor, E. A. Steed, that he was admitted to the junior class of Mercer University and graduated first in the class of 15, in 1871. After teaching a year, he enrolled in Rochester Baptist Theological Seminary, specialized in Hebrew, and graduated in 1875. Then followed a year under Crawford Howell Toy (*q.v.*) for Hebrew, and John Albert Broadus (*q.v.*) for New Testament Greek. A born linguist with a phenomenal memory of words and facts, Newman read some dozen languages. Switching interest to church history, he taught this and other subjects for more than 50 years, as follows: Rochester Seminary, 1877–81; McMaster University, Toronto, 1881–1901; Baylor University, 1901–07; Southwestern Baptist Theological Seminary, 1907–13; Baylor University, 1913–21; he was a visiting professor at University of Chicago, 1906 and 1926; at Vanderbilt University, 1917–18; at Mercer University, 1921–27; and at McMaster University, 1927–29.

Newman was a prolific writer. His chief works are as follows: *A History of the Baptist Churches in the United States,* 1894 (rev. 1915); *A History of Antipedobaptism,* 1897; *A Manual of Church History,* Vol. I, 1899; Vol. II, 1902 (rev. 1931); *A Century of Baptist Achievement* (editor and part author), 1901; section on church history in *The New Schaff-Herzog Encyclopedia of Religious Knowledge,* 1910. He contributed hundreds of articles to magazines and religious journals, and other scholarly treatments and translations to dictionaries and encyclopedias.

As lecturer, Newman participated in notable meetings such as the American Baptist Education Society; Baptist World Alliance, London, 1905; Continental Congress, 1908; Four-hundredth Anniversary of Believer's Baptism, Goshen, Ind., 1925. Reared in the South, theologically trained in both South and North, long associated with Canadian and British Baptists, acquainted with leaders on all continents, and having profound knowledge of the entire sweep of church history, Newman was one of the best informed authorities on Baptist doctrines and affairs in his day. He gave the scattered groups of Baptists a common consciousness of one another. Scholarly societies in which he held membership included the American Society of Church History, *Comeniusgesellschaft, Kirchenegeschictliche Gesellschaft.* In 1873 Newman married Mary Augusta Ware of Seale, Ala. Four children constituted the family.

BIBLIOGRAPHY: F. Eby, *Newman, The Church Historian* (1947). FREDERICK EBY

NEWS AND TRUTHS. A weekly publication edited by H. Boyce Taylor, Sr., in Murray, Ky., from 1904 till 1932. The little magazine's pages contained a variety of articles: Sunday school lessons and doctrinal treatises by the editor; extensive reports of projects he promoted, such as an annual Bible institute, the Amazon Valley Baptist Faith Mission, and the West Kentucky Bible School; selections from other religious periodicals; and polemics against modernism, unionism, Masonry, Campbellism, questionable social practices, denominational "bossism," etc. These attacks grew in force and frequency through the editor's latter years. After his death on May 31, 1932, *News and Truths* ceased publication with a memorial issue of June 29.

WILLIAM N. MCELRATH

NEWSPAPER, THE DENOMINATIONAL. A fivefold purpose stimulates and directs the publication of Christian newspapers and periodicals: information, instruction, inspiration, enlistment, and unification. One of the first steps taken by Luther Rice (*q.v.*) in building a denomination to promote and strengthen American Baptist enterprises and institutions and educate the ministry was the establishment in 1822 of a Baptist newspaper, the *Columbian Star.* The *Latter Day Luminary,* a missionary magazine, had been established in 1818. *Rippon's Register,* first published in England in 1790 and circulated in the American states, aroused and sustained interest in missions and other scriptural undertakings.

In 1803 the first American Baptist periodical appeared under the title of *Massachusetts Baptist Missionary Magazine.* It was adopted in 1814 by the Triennial Convention, and the name was changed to *American Baptist Magazine.* Later it was known as the *Baptist Missionary Magazine,* which has had a continuous existence; the name, in recent years, was changed to *Missions.* In 1819 the first Baptist newspaper, the *Christian Watchman,* appeared, which, after a series of consolidations, is now known as the *Watchman-Examiner.* The *Columbian Star* continues as the *Christian Index.* Other well-known Baptist weeklies established in the North in the early years were *The Standard,* Chicago (first the *Christian Times,* 1853; changed to *The Standard,* 1867; discontinued, 1920; succeeded the same year by *The Baptist,* owned by the denomination until 1930; merged with *Christian Century,* Dec., 1932); the *Journal and Messenger,* 1831 (discontinued); and *Zion's Advocate,* 1828.

The Southern Baptist newspapers in the respective states and in order of dates established are: *Christian Index,* Georgia (1822); *Western Recorder,* Kentucky (1825); *Religious Herald,* Virginia (1828); *Biblical Recorder,* North Carolina (1833); *Baptist and Reflector* (several predecessors including *Tennessee Baptist*), Tennessee (1834); *Alabama Baptist,* Alabama (founded 1834; merged with *Christian Index* 1865–72); *Baptist Courier,* South Carolina (1869); *Baptist Record,* Mississippi (1877); *Baptist Message,* Louisiana (*Baptist Chronicle,* 1886; purchased by Convention, 1919, and name changed to *Baptist Message*); *Baptist Witness,* Florida (1887); *Baptist Standard,* Texas (*Western Baptist,* 1888; *Baptist Standard,* 1892; first Baptist paper in Texas was *Texas Baptist,* 1855); *World and Way,* Missouri (1896; in 1912 purchased *Central Baptist,* combination of two papers started in 1866); *Arkansas Baptist,* Arkansas (1902); *Illinois Baptist,* Illinois (1905); *Baptist Messenger,* Oklahoma (1912); *Maryland Baptist,* Maryland (1912); *Baptist New Mexican,* New Mexico (1915); *Arizona Baptist Beacon,* Arizona (1939); *California Southern Baptist,* California (1941); and *Baptist Digest,* Kansas (1945).

Beginning in 1912, with the transfer to the Arkansas Baptist State Convention of the *Baptist Advance,* as the Arkansas Baptist state paper was then called, and the purchase in 1913 of the *Baptist Standard* by the Baptist General Convention of Texas, the era of convention (or general association) ownership and control of Baptist state papers began. This relationship applies now to all Baptist weekly state papers in the territory of the Southern Baptist Convention with the exception of the *Religious Herald* of Virginia published by the Religious Herald Association, to which the Baptist General Association of Virginia makes a substantial annual appropriation.

In reviewing the development of these Baptist weeklies it will be noted in most cases that several predecessors have contributed to the resultant journals. For example: among the papers woven into the *Baptist and Reflector* were *The Tennessee Baptist, The Baptist, The Baptist Gleaner, The Baptist Reflector, American Baptist,* and *The American Baptist Reflector.* Back of the *Western Recorder* were the *Baptist Banner* and the *Baptist and Western Pioneer.* The *Journal and Messenger,* Cincinnati, now no longer published, was preceded by the *Baptist Weekly Journal of the Mississippi Valley, The Cross, The Cross and Baptist Journal of the Mississippi,* and the *Western Christian Journal.* With several papers there were breaks in the continuity.

Every religious body has made use of newspapers. The oldest missionary magazine in the United States with unchanged name is the *Missionary Herald* which since 1820 has been continued by the Congregationalists (American Board of Commissioners for Foreign Missions) when Adoniram Judson (*q.v.*), Luther Rice (*q.v.*), and other missionaries were appointed. It was rooted in 1805 as the *Panoplist and Missionary Magazine.* According to W. W. Sweet in *Religion in Development of American Culture,* about half of the periodicals published in 1830 were denominational in character, designed to promote the interests of definite ecclesiastical bodies. Among the denominations the Presbyterians led in the number of periodicals begun. The Methodists early gained the largest circulation. The Presbyterian *Christian Observer* published first at Philadelphia, Pa., later at Richmond, Va., and finally at Louisville, Ky., dates to 1813. It was probably the first religious newspaper published in the United States and it is one of the most popular family Christian papers published.

In 1826 the *Christian Advocate and Journal* (Methodist) began publication in New York. Alexander Campbell was publishing the *Christian Baptist* which later became the *Millennial Harbinger* to promote the "reformation" led by him. The *Churchman* was begun by the Protestant Episcopal church in 1804. The *Christian*

Register of the Unitarians was begun in 1821. Roman Catholics stress the circulation of their newspapers and periodicals. One of the most widely known newspapers is *The Christian Science Monitor,* published every day except Sunday in three editions (Atlantic, Central, and Pacific). According to the latest *Ayers Newspaper Directory,* it has a circulation of 165,872. It is considered by specialists in the field of journalism to be one of the best edited publications in the world with comprehensive coverage by special correspondents. Its religious affiliation is revealed by its title and by one article in each issue frequently in some language other than English.

BIBLIOGRAPHY: *Ayers Directory of Newspapers and Periodicals* (1956). A. H. Newman, *A Century of Baptist Achievement* (1901). *Southern Baptist Handbook* (1945).

E. C. ROUTH

NEWTON COUNTY ACADEMY. Founded in 1920, at Parthenon, Ark. The Home Mission Board and the Arkansas Baptist State Mission Board operated it with income from tuition and appropriations. With two buildings the school had an average attendance of 130 until 1927, after which the local board operated it alone until it closed in 1930. H. D. MORTON

NICARAGUA BAPTIST CONVENTION, THE. Missionaries from the American Baptist Home Mission Society and the Woman's American Baptist Home Mission Society began work in Nicaragua in 1917. At present the Nicaragua Baptist Convention, financed by gifts of the Nicaraguan churches, is active in missionary work in a number of places in the country. Appropriations from American Baptist home mission societies assist in the work in churches, schools, a seminary, and a hospital.

For the building of a new edifice at the First Baptist Church of Managua, members have been giving one thousand cordobas ($200) weekly for a period of nearly four years. A Jeep station wagon owned by the church at Masatepe makes it possible for outstations to be visited more regularly. A new church has been organized at Bethel.

Colegio Bautista has been an influential force among young people who have attended. Many local churches finance weekday schools; one at Corinto has six grades and is considered the best in that port town.

Pastoral institutes prepare pastors for better service; a Department of Christian Education promotes better Sunday schools and fellowship groups.

In the Hospital Bautista at Managua local doctors, nurses of the Training School, and a local Bible woman work with the missionaries.

The 19 churches, served by national leadership, have 1,978 members in a constituency of 7,880, 52 missions and outstations, and 42 Sunday schools with an average attendance of 2,324. Primary and secondary school enrolment totals 675, and high school enrolment, 180.

MRS. MILO E. WENGER

NIGERIA, MISSION IN. Begun when Thomas Jefferson Bowen (*q.v.*) entered Nigeria in Aug., 1850. Baptist mission work has permeated the western and much of the eastern parts of Nigeria and is spreading through the north. In the first 40 years, 1850–1890, health conditions, slave trade, and tribal war combined to keep mission work at a standstill. During part of this period Baptists had no missionary in the land known as the "white man's graveyard." Few missionaries endured more than two terms; several died within the first year. In 1891 the mission reported 4 churches, 111 members, 31 baptisms, and 124 day school pupils.

Following 1890 there was slow, steady growth. By 1914 there were 31 churches, 2,880 members, 705 baptisms (for the year), and 792 day school pupils. The same year 53 church representatives and three missionaries met in Ibadan to draft a constitution and organize the Yoruba Baptist Association (named for the Yoruba tribe, dominant in southwestern Nigeria). Later known as the Nigerian Baptist Convention, it has met annually since 1914 and includes Baptist churches of Nigeria and Gold Coast. Reported in 1944 were 193 churches, 12,588 members, 1,552 baptisms, 183 pastors, 9,379 pupils in day schools, 161 Sunday schools, and 59 Training Unions.

Between 1944 and 1955 growth was rapid. Missionaries under appointment to Nigeria numbered 71 in 1945, increasing to 193 by 1955. In 1954 there were 280 churches, 397 preaching stations, 5,790 baptisms, 41,410 church members, 304 pastors, 419 Sunday schools, 174 Training Unions, 250 day schools, 40,467 day school pupils.

With the advent of free primary education in the western region of Nigeria, Jan., 1955, the government asked the Baptist convention to assume proprietorship of new primary schools, bringing the total under Baptist management to 460 (Dec., 1955) with an enrolment of 69,793. Primary education in Nigeria is financed chiefly by the government, with mission agencies providing necessary supervision in schools allocated to them.

The Baptist schools of higher rank, with current enrolments, are: Abeokuta High School (boys), 271; Agbor Girls' High School, 74; Iwo Boys' High School, 30; Oyo Boys' High School, 197; Lagos Academy (boys), 321; Port Harcourt High School (boys), 287; Reagan Memorial, Lagos (girls), 83; Iwo Baptist College (boys), 158; Baptist Women's Training College, Abeokuta, Grade II, 61; Baptist Women's Training College, Abeokuta, Grade III, 48; Baptist Elementary Training Center, Benin City (boys), 91; Baptist Elementary Training Center, Ede (boys), 90. These schools provide a standard academic curriculum with Bible and Christian leadership courses added. Baptist day schools include religious knowledge courses based on a series of textbooks published by the mission.

The Nigerian Baptist Theological Seminary, starting in the home of Charles Edwin Smith (*q.v.*) in Ogbomosho in 1897, is now housed in a three-wing, two-story structure (Ogbomosho) built in 1955 at a cost of $140,000. Enrolment for 1956 was 158, including 47 wives of students. Twelve missionaries and five nationals comprise the faculty; James Christopher Pool has been principal since 1938. Theological courses are arranged on levels to meet the needs of students with varying degrees of education. In 1947 the seminary began operating as an extension of Southern Baptist Theological Seminary, Louisville, Ky. Qualifying students in Nigeria are awarded degrees by the Louisville seminary. Dormitories and living allowances are provided for all students.

George Green (*q.v.*), pioneer medical doctor, arrived in Ogbomosho in 1907, working with inadequate facilities until 1923 when Baptist women of Virginia gave funds for a hospital building. Enlarged to 54 beds Ogbomosho Hospital maintains a training school for nurses; near by a maternity center, opened in 1955 under Daisy Hicks Jester, has 24 beds. Hospitals built since 1946 are located at Eku (52 beds), Joinkrama (32 beds), and Shaki (20 beds). Dispensaries are located at Igboho, Iwo, Okuta, and Oyo; a welfare center at Ire and a maternity center at Igede. Medical statistics for 1954 report 38,393 outpatients, 7,304 inpatients, 226 beds, 15 missionary doctors, 19 missionary nurses, 38 national nurses and midwives, 41 buildings. Two homes maintained at Ogbomosho and Egboama care for 45 motherless children, with the one at Egboama supported solely by the Nigerian Baptist Convention and the other a joint mission-convention project. Ruth May Kersey served as head of the Ogbomosho home from its beginning in 1935 until her retirement in 1955.

Formerly allied with Ogbomosho Hospital, the Leprosy Service separated in 1948 with a full-time doctor, Robert Frederick Goldie, in charge. Begun by Basil Lee Lockett (*q.v.*), appointed in 1910, the Leprosy Service had 10 isolation settlements with 1,580 patients in Dec., 1955, and 172 additional outpatients were under treatment. The service admitted 429 new cases in 1955, of which 112 were discharged as arrested cases. The largest settlement is near Ogbomosho (869 patients), where a leprosy hospital of 16 beds and a school for 67 children are provided.

Appointed in 1908, Ewart Gladstone MacLean began dental work, which has developed into a modern clinic in the Baptist Building, Ibadan, with two dentists, Howard Douglas McCamey and William Wayne Logan. One dentist holds traveling clinics periodically.

An evangelism department, with John Edwin Mills, chairman, directs the work of convention evangelists, promotes associational and city-wide simultaneous revivals, and publishes evangelistic literature. I. A. Adejunmobi, convention evangelist, reported 249 preaching services, 1,000 conversions, and 2,300 rededications in 1954.

In addition to promoting the regular phases of Sunday school work, the Sunday school department, Ethel Rebecca Harmon, secretary, sponsors Bible schools during school holidays. In 1954, 185 Bible schools were held, with 23,495 enrolled, 1,053 conversions, and a mission offering of $383.75 sent to the Baptist hospital in Gaza, Palestine.

William Neville Claxon, Training Union secretary, reported 206 Training Unions with 12,388 members (including college unions unaffiliated with churches) in 1954. Study courses numbered 65, with 3,086 qualifying for certificates.

Published by the Nigerian Baptist Convention since 1923, the *Nigerian Baptist* is a monthly periodical, in Yoruba and English, with a circulation of 2,400. George W. Sadler, now foreign mission secretary for Europe, Africa, Near East, was the first editor; Carrol Frederick Eaglesfield has edited the paper since 1947. A Nigerian was approved in 1955 for an overseas scholarship in religious journalism.

The Nigerian Baptist Woman's Missionary Union (directed by Neale C. Young since 1922), auxiliary to the Nigerian Baptist Convention, was organized in 1919 with Mrs. Mojola Agbebi, wife of a national pastor, as first president. There were 453 organizations, including Woman's Missionary Society, Young Woman's Auxiliary, Girl's Auxiliary, and Sunbeam units, reported in 1942; increased by 1955 to 1,480. W.M.U. headquarters are at Ede.

Opened in Ibadan in Dec., 1954, Baptist Building accommodates a dental clinic, library, book store (Homer Arbon Brown, Jr., manager), and offices of general secretary (Ira Newherne Patterson), education secretary (Lionel Raymon Brothers), Sunday school secretary (Ethel Harmon), Training Union secretary (W. N. Claxon), promotion secretary (V. Lovell Seats), evangelism chairman (J. E. Mills).

Built in Ibadan in 1950 under the direction of Eaglesfield, Baptist Press is equipped with modern machinery including mechanical typesetting. Books, tracts, departmental literature, school supplies, and periodicals are printed. In 1950, 7,600,000 printed pages were produced, the bulk for Woman's Missionary Union, Sunday school, and Training Union departments. Capital investment is $70,000.

The 1953 Nigerian convention adopted a resolution establishing the Nigerian Baptist Home and Foreign Mission Board. Headed by Seats, the board directs the work of five national missionaries, two among plateau people, two among Ibaribas, and one to the Hausas.

In 1950 a committee was formed by the mission to study methods of implementing a program to place nationals in positions of greater responsibility. Due in part to work of this committee and also to natural development in Nigeria along all lines, nationals now hold in the Nigerian Baptist Convention the key positions of president, vice-president, secretary, treasurer, auditor, associate education secretary, and associate editor of the *Nigerian Baptist*. Baptist day schools are staffed by nationals; offices of principal or vice-principal are held by nationals in all except two Baptist higher schools. Formerly called "supervisors," missionaries in station work are now "advisers."

The Nigerian convention rapidly developed financial responsibility in the decade prior to 1955. Twenty-three students received university scholarships, awarded worthy Baptist nationals in 1955, to study in Great Britain, United States, or African universities. The convention had a 1955 budget of $21,000 covering 37 items, major ones being theological seminary, Home and Foreign Mission Board, secondary school fund, vehicles for convention workers, evangelism, relief and annuity, orphanages, and clerical expenses for departmental secretaries. To finance this program, the convention requests each Baptist church to contribute 15 per cent of its income to the convention fund.

E. F. EAGLESFIELD

NIGERIAN BAPTIST CONVENTION. Organized in 1914 with 31 churches and 2,880 members, developing slowly until the close of World War II, when all phases of Nigerian Baptist work began to progress rapidly. In Jan., 1956, 200 Southern Baptist missionaries, whose work is integrated with the Nigerian Convention, were under appointment to Nigeria. The convention budget, totaling $22,400 in 1956, included Baptist World Alliance, relief and annuity, Nigerian Baptist Theological Seminary, two homes for children, leprosy service, field workers, evangelists, home and foreign missions, secondary schools, scholarships, tuberculosis project, and nursing and midwifery schools.

In the convention organization Nigerians hold key offices of president, vice-president, assistant education secretary, treasurer, auditor, associate editor of the *Nigerian Baptist,* and make up the staff of all schools except 10. No Nigerian medical doctors are working in Baptist hospitals, but two students have medical scholarships. In 1955 there were 21 Nigerian registered nurses, 20 midwives, and 58 student nurses. Five hospitals, three dispensaries, and two welfare centers reported 7,304 inpatients, 38,393 outpatients, 1,117 operations, and 1,661 deliveries. The Baptist Dental Clinic in Ibadan with one missionary dentist (and one on leave) gave 2,400 treatments during the year. Baptist Leprosy Service, with 1,135 inpatients, 235 outpatients in 1955, launched a tuberculosis treatment and detection program in 1956.

The Baptist Woman's Missionary Union of Nigeria supports 44 full-time national workers and has three missionary leaders. In 1955, 1,504 organizations (including auxiliaries) had a total enrolment of 35,987.

The well-equipped Baptist Press at Ibadan, managed by a missionary, does all printing for the convention. In 1955, 7,600,000 printed pages were produced, consisting chiefly of departmental literature.

Twelve Baptist secondary schools and teacher training colleges have a total enrolment of 1,711. Scholarships provided by the convention aided 23 students in 1955, in British, American, or African universities. The Nigerian Baptist Theological Seminary (Ogbomosho) has 158 students with a faculty of 12 missionaries and 5 Nigerians. The seminary offers a B.D. degree granted through affiliation with Southern Baptist Theological Seminary, Louisville, Ky.

Established in 1953, the Nigerian Home and Foreign Mission Board directs the work of six nationals in Nigeria, with work outside Nigeria slated to begin in 1957. A monthly paper, the *Nigerian Baptist* (circulation 2,900), is edited by a missionary while a national is in training, on scholarship, preparing to take over editorial responsibilities. Baptist Building, Ibadan, is headquarters for departmental offices, the dental clinic, and the Nigerian Baptist book store.

C. F. EAGLESFIELD

NIGERIAN BAPTIST THEOLOGICAL SEMINARY, OGBOMOSHO. See NIGERIA, MISSION IN.

NOEL, SILAS MERCER (b. Henrico County, Va., Aug. 13, 1783; d. Lexington, Ky., 1839). Pastor. He was educated by his father and privately studied classical languages and law. Later, he immigrated to Frankfort, Ky., where he practiced law.

Converted about 1810, Noel was baptized by William Hickman, pastor of the Forks of Elkhorn Baptist Church. Shortly thereafter, Noel was licensed to preach, and in 1813 he was ordained as pastor of Big Spring Baptist Church, Woodford County, Ky. In 1816 Noel was appointed circuit court judge and consequently left the ministry for several years. After this period of public service, he returned to be greatly effective as an evangelical pastor. His pastorates included Stamping Ground, Great Crossing, and Lexington, where he died in 1839. For several years Noel published the *Gospel Herald,* a monthly magazine. He was also active in founding Georgetown College.

BIBLIOGRAPHY: J. H. Spencer, *A History of Kentucky Baptists* (1886). W. THOMAS LANE

NONRESIDENT CHURCH MEMBERS. The tremendous loss to the individual, to the local Baptist church, and to the broad program of the Southern Baptist Convention due to the residence of a large percentage of Southern Baptists too far from their respective churches to function therein in the New Testament sense was assumed as a problem for solution by the Convention in its annual meeting in Richmond, Va., May, 1938. Existing for a long time, this problem became aggravated by shifts in population due largely to industrialization and to the prosecution and aftermath of war. Another strong contributing factor has been prevalence of the idea that one's church membership resided in his name's being inscribed on the roll of some local Baptist church. Purges and ill-advised revisions of church rolls only served to enlarge the problem. The first step taken by the Convention was based on a previous independent convention-wide survey, showing that about 28 per cent of the members of the churches investigated were nonresident. It was evident from the beginning that the solution of this problem, which affects adversely the whole program of the Convention, lay in the direction of winning back the lost nonresident members and in taking preventive measures dictated by Scripture and Baptist polity. A representative Convention committee, appointed in 1938, filed reports on the subject at the next four annual conventions. In 1942 it was estimated that a million and a half Southern Baptists were separated in nonresidency and that on a per capita basis this meant the loss of $2,900,000 of Convention income that year. At the 1942 Convention the committee's report and work were referred to the state secretaries. By 1952 the Executive Committee of the Southern Baptist Convention noted "the gravity of the nonresident member problem" and on Mar. 6 and May 12 held convention-wide meetings of representatives seeking a solution. This conference recommended to the 1952 Convention an 11-point attack upon the problem. A year later, the Convention approved its Executive Committee's recommendation "that the Home Mission Board, through its department of evangelism, lead the promotion of this effort." As a result Transfer Church Membership Week was inaugurated. This issued in 472,292 nonresident members' being won to the churches in their new communities in 1953. In 1954 nonresident Southern Baptists totaled 2,609,335 out of an aggregate church membership of 8,169,491, or 31.9 per cent. By 1955 total membership had reached 8,474,741 and nonresident members had declined to 2,489,159, or 29.4 per cent. Since assuming this task the department of evangelism of the board has used *Home Missions* extensively for articles on the subject. Likewise Baptist state papers have included numerous articles and editorials. Also special articles on the subject in a variety of Southern Baptist literature and periodicals indicated by 1956 that Southern Baptists were alert to the situation and were making progress in correcting it. CHARLES F. LEEK

NORDEN, ROBERT (b. England; d. Prince George County, Va., Dec. 1, 1725). The name Robert Norden appears in 1704 records, when he attended the general assembly of the General Baptists of England as an elder from Warbleton, Sussex. At this assembly he was urged to accept the position of messenger, which involved itinerant preaching and general supervision, a position of great influence to which none but the most trusted brethren were elected. This responsibility Norden was unwilling to accept. In consequence of letters from Baptist colonists in Virginia to the General Assembly in England, Norden was ordained in London, May, 1714, and soon sailed for Virginia with an associate, who died on the voyage. In Prince George County, 1714, Norden gathered together the first Baptist church in Virginia. The church met in the home of Matthew Marks, which was registered as a "publick meeting house" for Anabaptists on June 14, 1715, according to the Toleration Act of William and Mary (1689). Norden lived with the Marks family on the plantation, Martins Brandon Parish, holding meetings there and in other places until his death "in a good old age."

BIBLIOGRAPHY: I. Backus, *A Church History of New England* (1839). P. P. Deans, *The First Baptist Church in Virginia* (1920). G. Ryland, *The Baptists of Virginia, 1699–1926* (1955). R. B. Semple, *A History of the Rise and Progress of Baptists in Virginia* (1810). C. H. Urner, "Early Baptist Records in Prince George County, Virginia." *Virginia Magazine,* Vol. XLI (1933). W. T. Whitley, ed., *Minutes of the General Assembly of the General Baptist Churches in England* (1908). J. LEVERING EVANS

NORMAN COLLEGE. A coeducational junior college at Norman Park, Ga., owned and controlled by 16 district associations, and partially supported by the Baptist Convention of the State of Georgia. Founded as a result of an action taken at Zion Hope Baptist Church in Mell Association Oct. 13, 1897, the school opened as Norman Institute in Sept., 1900, after some delay caused by the Spanish-American War. There were three buildings: Killis Horne dormitory for men, Fender Hall for women, and an academic building. The school was named for J. B. Norman, Jr., the unlettered benefactor who gave time and money until his death in 1914, and who, with P. A. Jessup, was primarily responsible for the school's founding. The purpose of the school at that time was to provide Christian secondary education for "wiregrass Georgia."

The school was first owned and controlled by trustees elected by Norman Park Baptist Church and Mell Association. In Dec., 1907, Mercer, Mallory, and Tucker associations and the Georgia convention also became sponsors. In 1934 the convention returned the school, at its request, to trustees chosen by 16 supporting associations, but continued to approve trustees and make annual appropriations for the school's support.

In 1920 one year of college work was added to the curriculum; the second year, in 1924. Charter renewals changed the name to Norman Junior College Jan. 16, 1928, and to Norman College Dec. 15, 1931.

At the end of 1955 Norman College had an endowment of $284,021.83, including Colquitt Hotel site in Moultrie given by the founder, fixed assets were $753,813.96. Since its beginning, a total of approximately 5,329 students had attended the school. For the 1954–55 session 205 students were enrolled, and the operating budget was $132,584.12. The school is accredited by the Georgia State Department of Education, and was put on the approved list of the Southern Association of Schools and Colleges in 1956.

PRESIDENTS

1900–07	E. G. Hall
1907–10	O. A. Thaxton
1910–11	E. G. Hall
1911–15	W. H. McDaniel
1915–18	J. A. Scoggin
1918–28	L. H. Browning
1928–32	R. K. White
1932–44	Paul Carroll
1944–48	W. T. Bodenhamer
Oct., 1948–Apr., 1949	Garnie Brand (Acting)
1949–52	Allen S. Cutts
1952–	Guy N. Atkinson

FRANK CLARK

NORRIS, JOHN FRANKLYN (b. Dadeville, Ala., Sept. 18, 1877; d. Fort Worth, Tex., Aug. 20, 1952). Pastor, editor, controversialist. The son of James Warner and Mary (Davis) Norris, he attributed his conversion to the religious instruction of his mother and the Bible she gave him at the age of eight. The family moved in 1888 from Alabama to a farm near Hubbard City, Tex. Though he received little formal education in his early years, he read widely, hoping to become a lawyer, but in 1898 he entered Baylor University to prepare for the ministry. While there he married Lillian Gaddy (1902). A year later, upon receiving his A.B. degree, he resigned his pastorate of four years at Mount Calm and entered Southern Baptist Theological Seminary in Louisville, Ky., which in 1905 awarded him the Th.M. degree. He then served as pastor of McKinney Avenue Baptist Church, Dallas, Tex., until 1907, when he became business manager of the *Baptist Standard*. The next year he bought the paper, which he edited until 1909, then sold to Texas Baptists. At that time he accepted the pastorate of the First Baptist Church of Fort Worth, Tex. There he remained for the rest of his life. This church lost 1,000 members in 1911 after a division, and the following year lost its building and its pastor's home by fire. Though indicted for arson, Norris was acquitted after a month-long trial.

Very early in his ministry Norris developed an antagonistic spirit toward the program of work of his own denomination, and became an extremist in certain matters of doctrine, aligning himself with Fundamentalism. He led his church to oppose Texas Baptists' new program of missions in 1914, and later to sponsor an interdenominational Bible school. By 1919 he had become a leader of the World's Christian Fundamentals Conference, and four years later helped to form the Baptist Bible Union of America. This divisive body, based on an extreme millennial position which it attempted to make a test of fellowship, attracted only a few Southern Baptists, in spite of Norris' persistent efforts in its behalf. When the Convention launched the 75 Million Campaign in 1919, Norris accepted a quota for his church, then openly criticized the program. He led his church to discontinue the use of Southern Baptist literature in 1920, and a year later began to attack Baylor University, which he charged with teaching "evolution and infidelity." Because of his spirit, methods, acts of non-cooperation, and the unbaptistic practices of his church, the association in 1922 withdrew fellowship from the church. The Baptist General Convention of Texas censured Norris in 1922, refused to seat him in 1923, and, after he had increasingly directed his criticisms against Baptist leaders and institutions, permanently excluded him in 1924. The convention and the association amended their constitutions to prevent readmission, except by majority vote. The agitation and disturbance raised by Norris and a few others caused the Southern Baptist Convention to adopt a revised and enlarged statement of faith in 1925. A constitutional amendment, which would have refused a seat in the convention to anyone not in good standing with his local association and state convention, was submitted in 1926, but it was permanently tabled.

Norris continued his agitation, however, from without the Convention and a definite Norrisite Fundamentalist movement began to emerge. The slaying of a Fort Worth business man in the church office by Norris in 1926, which received wide publicity and for which he was charged with murder but was later acquitted, had little adverse effect on the success of his career. As his attacks against Baptist institutions, agencies, and leaders continued, it became evident that he and his followers were not, as they professed, defenders of the faith, but they were extremists, motivated by self-interest. Through his charges of "modernism, denominational bishops, institutionalism, and communism," which he made from the pulpit and in his newspaper, *The Searchlight* (later *The Fundamentalist*), Norris succeeded in alienating a few ministers and churches from the denomination, organizing new Fundamentalist churches, and unifying the movement in 1934 as the Premillennial Baptist Missionary Fellowship. In 1935 he took a second pastorate in addition to his Fort Worth church—the Temple Baptist Church in Detroit, Mich., thus enlarging his movement, which is now called the World Baptist Fellowship. The churches of the movement are supplied with a ministry trained in the fellowship's seminary in Fort Worth.

The ministry of this effective preacher ended with his death on Aug. 20, 1952, but only after it had done much damage, engendered bitterness, and hindered many Baptist causes.

WILBURN S. TAYLOR

NORTH ALABAMA BAPTIST COLLEGIATE INSTITUTE AND NORMAL COLLEGE. A high school and normal college located in

Trinity Village, Morgan County, Ala., it was founded by the Muscle Shoals Association sometime between 1890 and 1900. The school properties, including eight acres of land, were offered to the Alabama Baptist State Convention in 1903 for the continued operation of the school, but the convention was not in a position to assume the responsibility, and the school was closed. JAMES E. DAVIDSON

NORTH AMERICA, GENERAL COUNCIL OF CO-OPERATING BAPTIST MISSIONS OF. See MID-MISSIONS.

NORTH AMERICAN BAPTIST ASSOCIATION. A group organized May 25, 1950, in Little Rock, Ark., by messengers from churches which had been members of the American Baptist Association. A controversy regarding the qualifications of the messengers to the American Baptist Association precipitated the division. For years, the American Baptist Association in its annual sessions had seated some messengers who were not members of the churches which elected them. Strong objections arose from many of the churches against this procedure. The 1949 sessions of the American Baptist Association referred back to the churches a resolution which required all messengers to be members of the churches which elected them. Proponents of this resolution charged that the churches were never permitted to vote on the matter in the 1950 session of the American Baptist Association which met at Lakeland, Fla.

Immediately after the 1950 session of the American Baptist Association, Temple and Park Place Baptist churches in Little Rock, Ark., issued a call for all protesting churches to send messengers to Little Rock for the purpose of organizing a new national association. Four hundred and sixty-three churches, from 16 states, responded by sending 828 messengers who organized the new association and chose for an official name The North American Baptist Association. In 1955 there were 14 state and 91 district associations co-operating with the North American Baptist Association. In its fellowship were 1,855 churches with a total membership of 276,395, and 1,650 ordained ministers. There were 1,850 Sunday schools with 284,498 members. Total gifts were $10,005,499.

In theology, this group is Calvinistic. Many of its ministers hold premillennial views, and believe in the historical succession of the local church from the time of Christ to the present. In government, each church is autonomous. However, the group holds to the traditional Landmark idea that the association is composed of churches as units.

Mission activities in 1955 include establishing work in five foreign fields, and the support of a rapidly increasing number of district, state, and interstate missionaries. A number of schools and colleges are supported on a state and associational level, and plans are made to establish a seminary on a national level.

The Arkansas Baptist State Convention in 1953 made an official overture for fellowship with the North American Baptist Association. While no merger was effected, or even attempted, much stronger fraternal ties were established between the two groups.

Headquarters for the North American Baptist Association are at 824 Main Street, Little Rock, Ark. Dr. W. J. Burgess is missions secretary. DON HOOK

NORTH AMERICAN BAPTIST GENERAL CONFERENCE. Churches of the North American Baptist General Conference were first organized by German Baptist immigrants more than a century ago, with the oldest church among them organized in 1843 by Konrad Anton Fleischmann in Philadelphia, Pa. Bilingual in their ministry for many years, the 288 churches with 47,319 members in 1954 have made the transition to English with ever increasing spiritual strength and missionary outreach. Baptisms in 1954 numbered 2,044. In 1934 membership of the 270 churches totaled 36,078.

North American Baptist churches are located in 29 states of the United States and in five provinces of Canada. Since 1922 the conference headquarters have been located at Forest Park, Ill. Frank H. Woyke is executive secretary, and a general council of 43 representative members supervises the denominational program. Nine regional conferences meet annually, but the general conference meets only triennially. The conference is affiliated with the Baptist World Alliance.

Church contributions for local and missionary purposes in 1955 amounted to $4,165,687.68 or $88.03 per member. The denominational budget has risen to about $550,000 annually. A church extension fund of $250,000 has helped to establish 15 new churches in strategic areas. Funds have been used to help more than 8,000 European refugees find homes in the New World, especially in Canada.

Serving North American Baptist mission fields are 74 missionaries, 40 of them in the British Cameroons of Africa, 7 in Japan, 10 in Austria, 6 among the Indian Americans on the Bull, Montana, and Muscowpetung Reserves of Canada, and 6 among the Spanish-Americans of Colorado and Texas. Home mission churches number 60.

The North American Baptist Seminary with new buildings in Sioux Falls, S. Dak., and the Christian Training Institute in Edmonton, Alberta, Canada, represent the denomination's educational institutions. The Commissioned Baptist Youth Fellowship and the Sunday School Union carry on an aggressive ministry with their own secretaries. The Sunday school enrolment in 1954 was 40,379 as contrasted with 35,581 in 1934. The Roger Williams Press, in Cleveland, Ohio, publishes the *Baptist Herald, Der Sendbote,* and all literature of the conference. The Woman's Missionary Union and Baptist Men are effective in enlisting the services of their respective groups. The conference sponsors a children's home at St. Joseph, Mich., and five homes for the aged, four of which are in the United States and one in Canada. MARTIN L. LEUSCHNER

NORTH AMERICAN BAPTISTS (TO 1845). Organized Baptist work in North America began in the United States and then spread to Canada. Although Baptists first introduced the Protestant cause to Mexico, undertaking colportage work as early as 1827, the denomination made little impression there prior to 1845.

UNITED STATES. *Beginnings.*—The first Baptists in the American colonies came predominantly from the British Isles, bringing with them radical traditions of dissent, for they sought relief from religious intolerance, fought for freedom in local church organization, and opposed the idea of a state church. Their earliest churches appeared in the New England colony of Rhode Island, founded in 1638 with a guarantee of religious liberty and first settled by refugees from the persecutions of the Massachusetts authorities. The First Baptist Church of Providence (organized in 1639) and the First Baptist Church of Newport, constituted in the same period, apparently share the distinction of being the oldest Baptist churches in North America. In the other New England colonies the environment proved uncongenial for Baptists, who frequently suffered persecution because they insisted upon the baptism of believers only, refused to baptize their infants, and propagated their views about religious liberty; they endured arrest, imprisonment, fines, and beatings. Notwithstanding, new churches sprang up, the first in Massachusetts at Rehoboth in 1663 and one in Boston in 1665, while in Maine a small group formed a church at Kittery in 1682. By 1700 New England had only about 300 Baptists in 10 small churches, but by then toleration prevailed in spite of compulsory tax support for the established church.

In the Middle Colonies Baptists found cultural diversity, toleration, and the absence of a state church—conditions favorable for growth—and in the early years this area, particularly the vicinity of Philadelphia, provided the center for their activity. A group of Baptists from Rhode Island came to Pennsylvania in 1684 and established a church in Bucks County. In 1688 British immigrants organized Old Pennepack Church, located in Philadelphia County. Later called the Lower Dublin Baptist Church, it still exists. This church ministered to widely scattered residents of a large area, its entire membership gathering twice yearly, and in time contributed leadership and members for the organization of numerous churches in New Jersey and Pennsylvania, including the First Baptist Church of Philadelphia in 1698. After a series of annual meetings, initiated by several of the churches in 1688 for the purposes of inspiration, fellowship, and consultation on common problems, the Philadelphia Baptist Association, the first organization of American Baptists, was organized in 1707. Composed originally of messengers from five small churches, the association served as an advisory council with reference to ordination, the settlement of disputes, and points of doctrine and church practice. Although the power of decision remained with the churches, thus preserving the autonomy of the local church, the association reserved the right to exclude from fellowship any church which deviated from generally accepted doctrine or practice. In 1742 the association adopted, with some additions, the Particular Baptist London Confession (1689), thus identifying this influential early organization with Calvinistic theology. The membership of the association in 1757 represented churches in Pennsylvania, New Jersey, Connecticut, New York, Virginia, and Maryland, and in 1762 the combined membership of its 29 churches numbered 4,018.

Baptists grew slowly in the Southern Colonies prior to the Great Awakening. Guarantees of religious liberty encouraged the movement of Baptists to the Carolinas. Accordingly, in the late 17th century a congregation from Maine settled in South Carolina near Charleston, while two groups of English colonists arrived about the same time, subsequently organizing the Euhaw and Ashley River churches, and Welsh Baptists in 1738 developed extensive work along the Pedee River. In the late 1720's Baptists organized churches in North Carolina and in 1742 the first in Maryland, but not until 1772 did organized work develop in Georgia. In Virginia the establishment of Anglicanism proved ominous for dissenters, but English General Baptists founded a church at Burleigh, near Jamestown, in 1714; settlers from Maryland organized several Baptist churches in northern Virginia between 1743 and 1756; and about 1760 New England New Light or Separate Baptists, evolved from the Great Awakening, settled in the Virginia back country.

Revival and growth.—As the Great Awakening gained momentum about 1740, opinion divided over evangelistic techniques, and the Separate Baptists emerged as a distinct group known for favoring extreme revivalism. A general impetus to evangelism followed: By 1790 Massachusetts had 92 Baptist churches; Connecticut had about 60 by 1800; and throughout New England similar growth resulted. The Philadelphia Association sent out itinerant evangelists, influencing the growth of many churches, while Separate Baptists from New England largely brought the revival to the South, particularly to Virginia and the Carolinas. In North Carolina, from the nucleus of Sandy Creek Church alone, 42 churches issued within a period of 17 years. Both Regular and Separate Baptists came to Kentucky with the opening of the territory and by 1792 had established 55 churches. New associations developed rapidly in all parts of the country, following the pattern of the Philadelphia Association; but 30 of the 48 existing in 1800 were located in the

South, while six of those eight beyond the Alleghenies were in Kentucky.

Revolution and liberty.—Baptist individualism, which led to growth through revival, found further expression in almost unanimous endorsement of the American Revolution, resulting in added prestige for the denomination and facilitating the successful battle for religious liberty. Taxed to support the established church, their property frequently sold to pay these levies, New England Baptists in 1767 organized the Warren Association in Rhode Island chiefly to strengthen their fight for religious liberty. They submitted their grievances to the authorities through committees and joined forces with the Philadelphia Association in a common cause. Baptists viewed the Revolution as a fight for religious liberty; they equated the principles for which they suffered with those which gave sanction to the patriot cause. In Virginia, where Baptists faced legal inequities, unjust imprisonment, and even physical abuse, they led the fight culminating in disestablishment in 1787 and paved the way for the final triumph embodied in Federal guarantees and in the disestablishment which came in Massachusetts in 1833.

National organization and foreign missions.—By the opening of the 19th century, a rising sense of nationalism, together with the new interest in foreign missions, influenced the organization of Baptists in the United States on a national scale. Organized in Philadelphia in 1814, the General Missionary Convention of the Baptist Denomination in the United States for Foreign Missions, generally called the Triennial Convention, agreed initially to support work in Burma. Favorably received throughout the nation and endorsed by most of the 115 associations, the Convention added home missions to its program in 1817 and adopted *The American Baptist Magazine* as its official organ. Within a short time increased support made possible the opening of new work in India and, in co-operation with Negro Baptists, the sending of missionaries to Africa. By 1835 the Convention had expanded its missionary enterprises to numerous countries in Europe; it reported 25 missionaries, 21 native workers, and almost 600 church members in Burma, while in all fields there were 25 mission stations, 72 missionaries, 40 native workers, 18 churches, and 1,350 members. The following three years witnessed the establishment of 20 new native churches and the baptism of 1,100 converts. By 1838 books were being circulated in 15 languages, 50 schools had been established, and the number of missionaries had increased to 98. Between 1838 and 1841, although expenditures of $261,000 exceeded income, missionary interest continued, and 31 new missionaries were employed.

Home missions and expansion.—Accompanying the awakened interest in foreign missions and resulting in phenomenal growth, Baptists experienced a fresh outbreak of revival and an acceleration of domestic missions in the first half of the 19th century. Although Baptists numbered less than 10,000 before the Revolution, by 1795 their churches had grown to a total of about 1,152 in 16 states and territories; and by the close of the century, membership amounted to more than 100,000. Illustrating the rapid growth in New England and the middle states, Baptists in New York State increased from 12,000 in 1800 to 60,000 in 1832, while gains in the South proved even more spectacular. Meanwhile, Baptists moved westward with the folding back of the frontier; uniquely adapted to frontier conditions and accompanied by leaders, they crossed the Alleghenies into the Ohio and Mississippi River valleys and beyond, some churches traveling westward in a body and holding services along the way. The first Baptist church organized west of the thirteen colonies was the Severns Valley Church in Kentucky, constituted in 1781. The churches generally held to a mildly Calvinistic theology, maintained a rigid discipline, and conducted fiery revivals. In Kentucky the Elkhorn Association alone grew from 29 churches in 1799 to 48 churches in 1802, while in the entire state Baptists had 50 associations by 1840 and a total membership of 49,308. Between 1800 and 1830 Baptists throughout the nation increased from 100,000 to 313,138. Four associations functioned in Tennessee by 1809, one in Mississippi by 1806, and the first Baptist church was organized in Missouri in 1804.

To expedite Indian missions and expansion on the frontier, independent missionary societies developed, the first state organization of its kind in the denomination being the Massachusetts Baptist Missionary Society, founded in 1802. Forerunners of the state conventions, such bodies existed in 14 states by 1830. Since the Triennial Convention had restricted its operations exclusively to foreign missions, except for work among the Indians, the American Baptist Home Mission Society was organized in 1832, and eventually most of the state missionary societies and conventions sustained a loose auxiliary relationship to it. With the close of its first decade of service, the Society reported 11,000 baptisms, 400 churches organized, 142 ministers ordained, and the establishment of numerous benevolent societies, Sunday schools, and Bible classes. A Baptist missionary preached the first sermon at Chicago. The First Baptist Church there, established in 1833, a tribute to home missions and the first church of any kind in Chicago, became the mother of many churches. From the beginning Baptists ministered to the Indians, although with disappointing results prior to the initiation of a constructive plan for the establishment of Indian Territory, which was largely the work of a Baptist missionary, appointed agent of Indian affairs for the Government in 1830. Principally through the work of domestic missions and evangelism, the denomination achieved a membership of 720,046 by 1844.

Education.—Aware of the needs for religious

training and an educated ministry, Baptists in the early 18th century contributed leadership and financial support for the operation of both elementary and secondary schools or academies. The Philadelphia Association pioneered in the educational field, leading the movement which resulted in the chartering of Rhode Island College in 1764, and in 1812 established the Baptist Education Society of the Middle States, which in turn influenced the organization of numerous state education societies. Efforts to launch a national Baptist college by the Triennial Convention resulted in the chartering of Columbian College in Washington, D. C., in 1821. Within the next few years Baptists in various states, including the West and the South, founded a considerable number of colleges, although rivalry between sponsoring agencies tended to deplete resources and retard the co-ordination necessary to success.

Negro Baptists.—The first ordained Negro Baptist in America, having been freed, organized the first Negro Baptist church in Georgia about 1778 and later went to Jamaica, where apparently his foreign mission service was the first among Baptists. Fugitives from slavery organized in 1836 the first independent organization of Negro Baptist churches, the Providence Missionary Baptist District Association of Ohio, and in 1839 the Wood River Baptist Association of Illinois. The American Baptist Missionary Convention, a foreign mission agency, was organized in 1840.

Diversity.—By the beginning of the 19th century, the distinctions marking Regular, Separate, General, and Particular Baptists had largely disappeared, due chiefly to the revivals. Regular Baptists, moderately Calvinistic and subscribing to the Philadelphia or New Hampshire Confession of Faith, became predominant. A variety of differing minority bodies maintained a separate existence, however. These included a few congregations of Separate, General, and United Baptists, the latter resulting from the union of Separate and Regular bodies. Other Arminian groups included the General Six-Principle, Original Freewill, and the more numerous Freewill Baptists, who adopted a confession in 1834. Extreme Calvinists comprised such small groups as the Baptist Church of Christ, the Two-Seed-in-the-Spirit Predestinarian Baptists, and the Primitive or Antimission Baptists. Other bodies included the Seventh Day Baptists and German immersionists closely related to the Mennonites (differentiated from regular German Baptists), called the Church of the Brethren or Dunkers. Still another group became known as River Brethren or Brethren in Christ, while somewhat related were the Winebrennerians, also called the Church of God.

Controversies.—Baptist growth came in spite of a series of controversies which threatened and sometimes crippled the work. In the late 18th century both Unitarianism and Universalism proved disturbing, although the churches and associations acted decisively to curb inroads upon the denomination. A strong antimission sentiment developed in the first quarter of the 19th century, opposing missionary societies, Sunday schools, and an educated ministry. One wing of movement crystallized in Campbellism, which adopted the guise of ecumenicity but ultimately resulted in a new denomination, disrupting many churches and associations and taking a heavy toll among Baptists. In the second quarter of the century, rather widespread anti-Masonry excitement stirred many churches, while at the same time Millerism, a chiliastic movement, drew away many Baptists. Added to the divisive agitation of the slavery issue throughout the era, basic differences relative to ways of promoting missionary work contributed to the controversy which resulted in establishment of the Southern Baptist Convention in 1845.

CANADA. *Maritime Provinces.*—Colonists from New England established the first Baptist work in the Maritime Provinces, effecting a permanent organization at Horton, Nova Scotia, in 1778, and at Sackville, New Brunswick, in 1799. These churches and one at Newport, Nova Scotia, led in the early expansion of the denomination and in 1800 inspired the organization of the Nova Scotia Baptist Association, initially comprised of nine churches. The general practice of mixed membership and open communion came into disfavor with the association in 1809, when a strongly Calvinistic confession of faith was adopted. For a time the association granted licenses to preach and until 1827 ordained ministerial candidates independently. In 1821 the association divided to form separate organizations for Nova Scotia and New Brunswick. A marked development of interest in missions followed, and the denomination grew so that by 1827 New Brunswick had 28 churches with 1,347 members and Nova Scotia had 29 churches with 1,711 members. Immigrants from Scotland developed the first Baptist work on Prince Edward Island, organizing a church there in 1812. The Island had seven organized churches by 1833, the first of them—the church at Bedeque—affiliating with the Nova Scotia Association in 1827.

Maritime Baptists agitated for religious liberty, helping to secure in 1834 the right for dissenting clergymen to marry by license. In 1827 they launched a missionary publication, the *Baptist Missionary Magazine*, which was replaced a decade later by a more ambitious weekly, *The Christian Messenger*. Under auspices of the association, Nova Scotia Baptists founded their education society in 1828, through which they operated Horton Academy and later Acadia College. New Brunswick Baptists opened a co-educational seminary at Frederickton in 1836.

Reflecting the success of the home mission movement, New Brunswick Baptists added 43 churches to the association between 1828 and 1845, while Nova Scotia Baptists, directing efforts toward Cape Breton Island, the Negroes, and neglected eastern areas of the province, grew to a total of 66 churches and more than 5,000 members by 1838 and came close to doubling these figures within the following 12 years. Wise leadership by home missionaries from Nova Scotia established a closer relationship between the Baptists of the mainland and Baptist work on Prince Edward Island, where certain differences of practice existed, and where the work found new strength with the organization of a church in the strategic center of Charlottetown in 1836. Maritime Baptists united in sending a foreign missionary to Burma in 1845, after initiating a financial plan for a single denominational fund to be apportioned to the various agencies on a percentage basis. This plan achieved greater success with the organization of the Baptist Convention of Nova Scotia, New Brunswick, and Prince Edward Island in 1846.

Regular or Calvinistic Baptists predominated in the Maritime Provinces, although small groups of Free Will or Free Christian Baptists, transplanted from New England and having roots in the New Light revivalism of the Great Awakening, formed organizations in both Nova Scotia and New Brunswick in the 1830's.

Ontario and Quebec.—In the late 18th and early 19th centuries Baptists from the United States founded numerous churches in Ontario and Quebec, while settlers from Scotland organized work in the Ottawa Valley, instituting the First Baptist Church of Montreal in 1830. The Ottawa Baptist Association, organized in 1836, included churches in eastern Ontario and Quebec, where growth came slowly due to the French Catholic influence. Efforts toward co-operative work included the launching of the *Canada Baptist Magazine and Missionary Register* in 1838, the Baptist Theological College at Montreal in 1839, and the Baptist Missionary Convention of Upper Canada in 1833, followed by the Canada Baptist Union in 1843. These early efforts proved frustrating because of controversies over open and close communion.

CONTRIBUTIONS. In the period of beginnings and expansion, which ended in 1845, Baptists contributed significantly to the cultural and religious heritage of North America. From their first appearance in the colonies, continuously thereafter, and almost alone, Baptists proclaimed the doctrine of religious liberty so strongly that it eventually became an American tradition. Emphasizing the Bible and requiring personal commitment, they contributed an evangelistic warmth to the tone of one of America's major religious faiths, while at the same time helping to impress democracy upon the genius of American life through their distinctive church government. In exercising a rigid church discipline, Baptists helped to establish moral order on a raw, chaotic, and sometimes lawless frontier, and while preaching a simple gospel they awakened a responsible awareness of missionary needs at home and abroad.

BIBLIOGRAPHY: I. Backus, *A History of New England with Particular Reference to the Denomination of Christians Called Baptists* (reissued 1871). R. A. Baker, *Relations Between Northern and Southern Baptists* (1948). D. Benedict, *A General History of the Baptist Denomination in America and Other Parts of the World* (1848). G. E. Levy, *The Baptists of the Maritime Provinces, 1753–1946* (1946). W. J. McGlothlin, *Baptist Confessions of Faith* (1911). W. W. Sweet, ed., *Religion on the American Frontier: I, The Baptists, 1783–1830* (1931). R. G. Torbet, *A History of the Baptists* (1952). H. C. Vedder, *A Short History of the Baptists* (1907); *A Short History of Baptist Missions* (1927).

GLEN LEE GREENE

NORTH BRAZIL, MISSION IN. See BRAZIL, MISSION IN.

NORTH BRAZIL SEMINARY. See BRAZIL, MISSION IN.

NORTH CAROLINA, BAPTIST STATE CONVENTION OF.

I. Baptist Beginnings. *Baptists among the first settlers.*—The first permanent settlers in North Carolina arrived from Virginia about 1660 and settled along the northern shore of the Albemarle Sound. Morgan Edwards, the Baptist historian who traveled in the province in 1771–72, stated, on the basis of evidence he had gathered, that there were Baptists among the first settlers.

Although there is little specific information on the subject, scattered references to various groups of dissenters indicate that for the first half-century there were probably a few Baptists in the Albemarle settlements. For example, among the religious groups described in 1704 by John Blair, a minister of the Church of England, was "a third sort . . . something like Presbyterians, which sort is upheld by some idle fellows who have left their lawful employment, and preach and baptize through the country, without any manner of orders from any sect or pretended Church." Many authorities regard this as a reference to Baptists.

The earliest unquestionable record of the presence of Baptists in the colony is the letter written by John Urmstone, a minister of the Church of England, on June 12, 1714, in which he complained that two of his vestrymen in Chowan Precinct were "professed Anabaptists." There is, however, nothing in available contemporary records to indicate that churches existed this early.

The first churches.—The first Baptist minister in North Carolina of whom there is a known record was Paul Palmer, a native of Maryland, who is mentioned in the court records of Perquimans Precinct for Apr. 3, 1720, as a resident of the precinct. Prior to that time he had married Joanna Peterson, the widow of a North Carolina planter. By 1726 Palmer had launched an evangelistic career, which, according to a contemporary diarist, resulted in 1727 in the establishment of North Carolina's first Baptist church. On Sept. 27, 1729, John Comer, a young Baptist historian of Newport, R. I., made the following entry in his diary: "This day I received a letter from ye Baptist church in North

Carolina, settled about two years (in ye year 1727) since, by Mr. Paul Palmer. . . . This church consists of 32 members, it meets at Chowan." Palmer's church was located in the vicinity of the present town of Cisco, Chowan County, but it probably had no meetinghouse other than the homes of members. In any event, the congregation was soon scattered and is heard of no more.

The oldest surviving Baptist church in North Carolina and the second known to have been established was founded two years later in present Camden County and is now known as Shiloh. It has been called successively the Church in Pasquotank, Burges's Meeting House, the Church in Camden (Camden County was formed from Pasquotank in 1777), and Shiloh. The petition for its registration with the court of Pasquotank Precinct bears the date Sept. 5, 1729. Although William Burges was the first pastor, it is certain that Paul Palmer was the leader in the formation of the church.

Growth of the General Baptists.—Primarily an evangelist, Palmer preached and baptized from the Virginia line to Onslow County. Governor Richard Everard complained to the Bishop of London on Oct. 12, 1729, that Palmer was causing a great tide of religious enthusiasm to sweep over the province. But Palmer did not, as a rule, organize into churches those who came under his influence. Others led in the performance of this task. About 1730 Joseph Parker moved from Chowan County to the region west of the Chowan River, where he established Meherrin Church in present Hertford County. Ten years later, Meherrin Church organized an arm known first as Bertie, later as Sandy Run. Another early Baptist leader was William Sojourner, a Virginian who came to present Halifax County in 1742 and before the close of the year organized the celebrated Kehukee Church. Kehukee became the leading church west of the Roanoke River and the mother of numerous other churches.

Among all the early Baptist leaders in North Carolina, none, according to Professor G. W. Paschal, was more active or able than Josiah Hart, whose work began about 1740. Morgan Edwards credits him with founding the church at Pungo in Beaufort County, and he is known from other sources to have made his headquarters in Warren County, where he gathered the congregation known as Reedy Creek.

In 1740 several Baptists petitioned the court at Craven County for the registration of their church, but the request was denied. At least two other congregations were formed in this area about the same date. Through the labors of Palmer, Parker, Sojourner, Hart, and other itinerant ministers, eastern Carolina as far south as the Great Cohara River in Sampson County gradually became the home of numerous Baptist congregations. All of the early ministers were General Baptists, and the churches they established were known as General Baptist churches. Largely because they were the first ministers on the ground, they had their greatest success in the region southwest of the Roanoke. In 1756–57 a traveling Quaker visiting the Edgecombe County area found that the inhabitants were principally of the Baptist faith.

In 1754 the total number of General Baptist churches known to have been established in the province reached 17:

Date of Formation	*Church*	*Present Name of County*
1727	Chowan	Chowan
1729	Shiloh	Camden
1730	Meherrin	Hertford
1740	Sandy Run	Bertie
1742	Kehukee	Halifax
1742	Pungo	Beaufort
1742	Swift Creek	Craven
1744	Falls of Tar	Nash
1746	Fishing Creek	Halifax
1749	Great Cohara	Sampson
1750	Reedy Creek	Warren
1750	Toisnot	Wilson
1752	Bear Creek	Lenoir
1753	Tar River	Granville
1754	Grassy Creek	Granville
1754	Red Banks	Pitt
1754	Flat Swamp	Pitt

The Particular Baptists.—Before the close of the 1750's, most of the General Baptist churches, which were Arminian in their theological views, had been transformed into Particular Baptist churches with rigid Calvinistic theology. The General Baptists, according to the early Baptist historians Lemuel Burkitt (*q.v.*) and Jesse Read, did not require an experience of grace as a prerequisite for baptism but baptized all who asked for baptism at their hands. The leader in introducing the doctrine of a converted membership was Robert Williams, a native of Northampton County, who had gone to Welsh Neck in South Carolina and become a Calvinist. Returning about 1750 to his native state, he soon won over the pastor of the Kehukee Church.

In the middle fifties the Philadelphia Association, which was largely responsible for the transformation of North Carolina's General Baptist churches, sent John Gano (*q.v.*) of New Jersey on the first of his missionary journeys to the South. In 1754 he preached to a group of eastern North Carolina Baptist ministers so effectively that many began to question the wisdom of their willingness to baptize all who presented themselves, whether they were repentant or not. A year later, Benjamin Miller and Peter Peterson Vanhorn were sent by the Philadelphia Association to North Carolina to take up the work where Gano had left off. The Kehukee Church, in which the way had already been prepared, fell under their influence and became the first in the region to embrace the "doctrine of grace." Its example was quickly followed by most of the other General Baptist churches of North Carolina.

It is a matter of record, however, that only

a small percentage of the members of these churches remained in them after they were transformed. The Calvinistic minority was usually able to take over the church name and property because the ministers had been won over. The method of reorganization was, first, for the church in conference to disband the organization that had previously existed. Then, those who desired to come into the new order were required to come under an examination conducted by approved ministers of the Particular Baptist faith. Those who gave satisfactory evidence of conversion were allowed, after acceptance of a Calvinistic church covenant, to become members of the transformed church.

For the next several decades the Baptist churches of eastern North Carolina were characterized by rigid Calvinism. They set new standards of morality and righteousness, which profoundly modified the lives of the people who came under their influence. Although all the other General Baptist ministers appear to have gone over to the Particular Baptists, Joseph Parker, William Parker, and John Winfield remained in the old faith. From their churches have come, with slightly amended teachings, the present Free Will Baptists of North Carolina.

The Jersey Settlement.—Among the thousands of immigrants who about 1750 came from the North to settle in the Piedmont section of North Carolina was a colony from New Jersey which occupied lands near the Yadkin River in the present county of Davidson. These newcomers founded what was known as the Jersey Settlement, and the Baptists among them had by the summer of 1755 established worship along Particular Baptist lines. This organization, called the Jersey Church, was the earliest Baptist congregation known to have been gathered in the central part of North Carolina. The minister in 1755 was Benjamin Miller, the New Jersey pastor sent by the Philadelphia Association to North Carolina to aid in the transformation of the General Baptist churches.

Miller was followed as minister in the Jersey Settlement by John Gano, who also had preached in eastern North Carolina. Oliver Hart (*q.v.*) of the Charleston Association was one of those who helped persuade Gano to come to the Carolinas. Gano remained in the Jersey Settlement about two and one-half years before the Cherokee Indian uprising endangered the safety of his family and convinced him that he should return to New Jersey. The departure of Gano and several of the members caused the church to disband. In 1762, however, a portion of the former members joined with other Baptists in the constitution of Shallow Fords, a Separate Baptist church located on the borders of Forsyth and Davie counties. A second Jersey Church, which still survives, was constituted on Oct. 16, 1784.

The Separate Baptists.—The most significant event in North Carolina Baptist history in the 18th century was the founding of Sandy Creek Church by Shubal Stearns and the Separate Baptists. The terms "New-Lights" and "Separates" were applied about 1740 to the New Englanders who became followers of George Whitefield. The expression "New-Lights" came from their belief in the possibility of individual inspiration and enlightenment through the Holy Spirit. They were called "Separates" because of their desire to separate themselves from the Congregational Church and organize separate societies. Their religious views were characterized by an intense devotion to evangelism. Many of these reformers adopted Baptist practices and thus became known as "Separate Baptists." Shubal Stearns, a native of Boston who had fallen under the influence of Whitefield's evangelical zeal, soon emerged as their leader.

David Benedict wrote that Stearns believed himself called to move far to the western settlements of that day to undertake an extensive work. Accordingly, in 1754 he and a portion of his members moved to the western part of Virginia, where they joined forces with his brother-in-law, Daniel Marshall (*q.v.*). Stearns learned from friends in the Piedmont section of North Carolina that preaching was greatly desired, that for a hundred miles there was no meetinghouse of any kind. Thus motivated, Stearns and his party got underway once more and traveled to Sandy Creek in present Randolph County, arriving Nov. 14, 1755. Within a few weeks this closely knit group of eight families had completed a small meetinghouse, which they called Sandy Creek, and formed a Separate Baptist church of 16 members, with Stearns as pastor and Daniel Marshall and Joseph Breed as his assistants.

The inhabitants around this colony knew little of the principles of the Christian religion. The Separates brought strange things to their ears. They could not comprehend how it should be necessary to feel conviction and conversion, points which were strenuously advocated by the new ministers. But their manner of preaching was, if possible, more novel than their doctrines. The Separates in New England had developed a warm and emotional address, accompanied by strong gestures and a singular nasal tone of voice, the so-called "holy-tone." Being deeply affected themselves when preaching, they often induced in their hearers feelings expressed by tears, trembling, screams, and exclamations of grief and joy.

Morgan Edwards wrote under the heading "Sandy Creek":

> The neighborhood was alarmed and the Spirit of God listed to blow as a mighty rushing wind in so much that in three years time they had increased to three churches, consisting upwards of 900 communicants, viz.: Sandy Creek, Abot's [*sic.*] Creek, Deep River. The most remarkable events are these: (1) It is a mother church, nay a grand mother, and a great grand mother. All the separate baptists sprang hence: not only eastward towards the sea, but west-

ward toward the great river Mississippi, but northward to Virginia and southward to South Carolina and Georgia. The word went forth from this sion, and great was the company of them who published it, in so much that her converts were as the drops of morning dew.

In the 17 years between 1755 and the date Edwards wrote his account, 42 churches and 125 ministers had "sprung from the parent church," which was indeed the mother of all the Separate Baptists in the South.

Shortly after their arrival at Sandy Creek, Stearns and Marshall had begun to preach in the Abbott's Creek section, which was located some 30 miles west of Sandy Creek. Abbott's Creek, the second Separate Baptist church to be organized, was probably formed late in 1756. Marshall was the pastor but remained in this charge only until 1760, when he left with some of his members for Beaver Creek, S. C. The next pastor was a combination preacher and teacher named Stotsmann. Like those ministers who combined preaching and farming, Stotsmann had to find support for his family at some occupation other than the ministry. George Soelle, a contemporary Moravian minister, explained in his diary, "It is the custom and rule of the Baptists not to pay their preachers, and that they must support themselves by the work of their own hands, in spite of the fact that they must visit and serve the people committed to their hands. Some of the members do not approve of this."

Although the other early Separate Baptist ministers traveled widely and established headquarters elsewhere, Stearns remained at Sandy Creek. In 1758 he founded there North Carolina's first Baptist association, which was called Sandy Creek. Soon after the Separates had begun to grow in numbers, Stearns reached the conclusion that an association composed of delegates from the churches would tend to stimulate progress and encourage co-operation. Accordingly, "he visited each church and congregation, and explaining to them his contemplated plan, induced them all to send delegates to his meetinghouse in January, 1758, when an association was formed." Delegates from Sandy Creek, Abbott's Creek, and Deep River attended this meeting. Seven additional churches sent delegates to a meeting held in June, 1758. For 12 years all the Separate Baptist churches in Virginia and the Carolinas remained in this association. In 1770, largely as a matter of convenience, the Sandy Creek Association was divided into three distinct bodies—the General Association of Virginia, the Sandy Creek of North Carolina, and the Congaree of South Carolina.

Beginnings in western North Carolina.—In 1766 Samuel Harris (*q.v.*), the well-known Separate Baptist minister of Virginia, made a preaching tour through the area of the Moravian settlements. The *Records of the Moravians* point out that "at this time the Baptists are the only ones in the country who go far and wide preaching and caring for souls." Joseph Murphy, a follower of Stearns, appears to have been the first resident Baptist minister west of the Yadkin River, and his meetinghouse, called Shallow Fords by Morgan Edwards but known more generally as Timber Ridge (in present Davie County), was certainly the first church in this area. The Shallow Fords meetinghouse had been built by 1768.

Murphy's church soon expanded into three branches—Shallow Fords or Timber Ridge, Mulberry Fields, and Forks of the Yadkin. In 1773 Murphy moved from Timber Ridge to the upper part of Deep Creek, where in 1777 a church named Deep Creek was constituted, but he continued to preach from time to time at Timber Ridge. During the seventies George Soelle, Richard Utley, and Johann Christian Fritz, all Moravian missionaries, also preached at Timber Ridge, on one occasion to "two hundred or more English hearers." In 1814 Timber Ridge meetinghouse and its ground were sold to a Methodist congregation, which has maintained Bethlehem Church on this location since that time.

By 1771, according to Morgan Edwards, Forks of the Yadkin Church had a meetinghouse located in present Davie County near the point where the South Yadkin River joins the Yadkin. He also reported that the congregation organized at Mulberry Fields in present Wilkes County in 1769 had a house of worship by 1771. The Deep Creek section to which Murphy moved was near the stream of that name in present Yadkin County. Although many settlers had already come to this area, Murphy appears to have been the only resident English-speaking minister until after the Revolutionary War. He served as pastor of Deep Creek Church until his death in 1816. Benedict wrote regarding the Yadkin Association that "Joseph Murphy has been, in most respects, the most distinguished minister among the churches in this body."

Meantime, on Oct. 5, 1772, Dutchman's Creek Baptist Church had been organized under the leadership of William Cook, who became the first pastor. It was located on Dutchman's Creek, a tributary of the South Yadkin, and was succeeded by present Eaton's Baptist Church. Despite the fact that it was a Regular Baptist congregation, Dutchman's Creek early welcomed Separate Baptists to observances of the Lord's Supper. This is the last Baptist church known to have been founded in the region west of the Yadkin prior to the Revolution.

The struggle for supremacy.—During the period between the coming of the Separates and the American Revolution, there occurred in North Carolina a fierce struggle for supremacy between adherents of the Anglican Church and the Dissenters, the largest group of whom were Baptists. The settlers in the west, where the Dissenters were strongest, began to demand equality in matters of religion and to show resentment against those of the Church of England who taxed them for the support of a ministry of another denomination than their own. Governor William Tryon (1765–71), zealous to defend the interests of the Crown, entered upon a vigorous promotion of the Anglican Church by which he hoped to rout dissent from the colony.

The struggle for religious supremacy became involved with Tryon's suppression of the Regulators, whom he believed to be made up largely of Baptists and Quakers. Because of his hostile attitude toward them, no community in which Baptists were strong sent soldiers to Tryon's aid. After the failure of the Regulation, more Baptist groups than any other left the province, seeking elsewhere the freedom which they despaired of finding in North Carolina. Tryon wrote to the Society for the Propagation of the Gospel that a portion of the province "is full of quakers and anabaptists, the first no friend, the latter an avowed enemy to the mother church." Later in the letter he stated that "Presbyterians and Quakers are the only tolerated sectaries under any order or regulation, every other are enemies to society and a scandal to common sense."

Baptists, for example, were discriminated against in the marriage laws. By the Act of 1741, the right to officiate at marriages was confined to ministers of the Church of England, and in those parishes where no minister was settled, to justices of the peace. In practice Quaker and, for a time, Presbyterian ministers officiated at marriages without question. Freedom for ministers of all denominations to perform marriages came to North Carolina only after independence from Great Britain had been won.

The enmity between Tryon and the Baptists was so strong that, in the opinion of many writers on the subject, nearly all the Baptists between Wake County and the Yadkin River were Regulators. The 6,409 Regulators who took the oath of submission after the defeat at Alamance (May 16, 1771) must have represented a population of 50,000, which was the greater part of the white people in this area and certainly included many of the Baptists. The defeat of the Regulators had a far-reaching effect on the spread of the Baptist denomination, not only in North Carolina but throughout the South. According to Edwards, the entire congregations of Deep River and Abbott's Creek and all of the 606 members of Sandy Creek except 14 migrated after Alamance because "they despaired of seeing better times." "It is said," he continued, "that 1,500 families departed since the battle of Alamance; and, to my knowledge a great many more are only waiting to dispose of their plantations in order to follow them." Some of the former Regulators from the Sandy Creek Association found homes in the Watauga settlements, where by 1786 they had formed the Holston Association. Others formed churches and associations in South Carolina and Georgia.

The Kehukee Association.—During the 1750's the General Baptists of eastern Carolina had been transformed into Particular Baptists. After the coming of the Separates to North Carolina, the Particular Baptists, in order to emphasize the distinction between the two groups, began to call themselves Regular Baptists. This soon became their commonly used designation. The Charleston Association, formed in 1751 in South Carolina of Particular Baptist churches, expanded to include the Particular or Regular Baptist churches of North Carolina. But the distance of the North Carolina churches from Charleston inevitably prompted them to withdraw to form an association of their own. This was done Nov. 6, 1769, when delegates from five churches (Kehukee, Bertie, Falls of Tar River, Toisnot, and Pitt) met at Kehukee Church in Halifax County and formed the Kehukee Association, the second oldest in North Carolina. The delegates adopted the Philadelphia Confession of Faith and a plan of association. The latter stated the duties of messengers and defined an association as an advisory council.

The Kehukee Association grew rapidly, adding both Regular and Separate churches throughout eastern North Carolina and Virginia. In 1773 Lemuel Burkitt (*q.v.*), co-author with Jesse Read of *A Concise History of the Kehukee Association* and for a third of a century "the most influential man among the Baptists of North Carolina," was made clerk. In 1775 the association divided over the question whether the rule requiring faith as a prerequisite to baptism should apply to persons who were already members of the churches. The reformers, who were led by Burkitt and who insisted that the churches should be purged of all members who had been baptized in unbelief, had a slight majority. Two years later, the reformers organized a new association but continued to claim the old name of Kehukee. In 1779 six or seven churches of the old Kehukee were admitted to membership in the new association, and the name became "The United Baptist Association, formerly called the Kehukee Association." This remained the official name until the churches south of the Tar River were dismissed to form the Neuse Association, after which the name Kehukee Association was again used.

The Kehukee was thus the first association in which Separate and Regular Baptist churches were united and the distinction between the two disregarded. Within a few years after its formation, "all the Baptist churches of eastern North Carolina, with the exception of two or three of the Free Will order, were united in one Association. The General Baptists had been either supplanted by the Regular Baptists or incorporated in their churches, and all together now were united with the Separate Baptists, and all lines of division declared obliterated." Gradually, throughout the state the use of all distinguishing words to denote Baptists was abandoned. "They were Baptists and nothing more." The question of missionary or antimissionary did not arise until about 1820.

The Yadkin Association.—At the close of the Revolution, Baptist churches in the northwestern part of North Carolina belonged to the Strawberry Association, most of whose churches were in Virginia. In 1786 William Petty, pastor of Petty's Meeting House (later called Flat Rock), invited the churches west of the Yadkin to send delegates to his church to consider forming an association. Eleven churches accepted the invitation but continued for the years 1787–89 to meet as "a branch of the Virginia (Strawberry) Association." On Aug. 28, 1790, delegates from these and other churches met at Eaton's Meeting House in present Davie County as an independent association called Yadkin. The 14 member churches in 1790 were Beaver Creek, New River, North Fork, Brier Creek, South Fork of Roaring River, Mitchell River, Head of Yadkin, and Roaring River in Wilkes County; Timber Ridge and Jersey in Rowan; Grassy Knob in Iredell; Catawba River in Burke; Hunting Creek in Surry; and Rye Valley in Virginia. These churches were scattered over all that part of North Carolina north of Salisbury and west of Guilford County, an area now occupied by 15 counties. That the association was too large for effective work soon became apparent. Accordingly, it voted during the session of 1797 to divide, the churches west of the Blue Ridge forming the Mountain Association. Since that date 31 associations have been formed in the original territory of the Yadkin Association.

By 1800 the views of the Regular Baptists, who were Calvinistic, had become predominant throughout western North Carolina. Many churches had accepted the Philadelphia Confession of Faith as a common creed for all Baptists, *with the provision that any reluctance to accept it in all its implications would be overlooked.* By about 1830, according to Professor Paschal, "it had become the rule of faith and practice with many Baptist ministers and Baptist churches, for all their profession that the Bible is a sufficient rule of faith and practice." The item most insisted upon at that time, and destined to cause the most dissension later, read, "We believe in the doctrine of eternal particular election," and was interpreted to mean that the non-elect could not be saved, however repentant they might be.

West of the Catawba River.—About the year 1750 settlers in considerable numbers began to cross the Catawba River and occupy the territory in which old Tryon County was later erected. Among these were Baptists, who, under the leadership of Separate Baptist ministers, established several churches prior to the Revolution. The earliest included Long Creek, near the present town of Dallas; Sandy Run, near Mooresboro; and Buffalo, just south of the state line in the vicinity of York, S. C. Sandy Run was constituted in 1771; Buffalo, in 1772; and Long Creek, probably in 1772. These churches belonged to the Sandy Creek Association during the first years. In 1789, however, the Bethel Association was formed by several churches located on both sides of the state line and included these three. In 1800 the Bethel, now numbering 52 churches, dismissed its six North Carolina churches and seven of those in South Carolina for the formation of a new association, the Broad River. Most of the seven South Carolina churches were in the Fairforest group, which had been established by Philip Mulkey and Daniel Marshall, ministers from Sandy Creek. The North Carolina churches were scattered from the Catawba River to the Tennessee line, an area which was ultimately divided into 22 Baptist associations.

In the year of its organization, the Broad River adopted a series of documents establishing what was called its "System." There was an introduction stating the character and advantages of an association, a constitution or plan of representation of the churches, and an abstract of principles based on the Philadelphia Confession but omitting the words, "We believe in the doctrine of eternal particular election," and adding, "We believe in the doctrine of *Election* through sanctification of the Spirit and belief of the truth." This "System" was adopted by most of the associations formed from the original territory of the Broad River. The first churches to withdraw from the Broad River were French Broad, Cane Creek, and Caney River, which in 1807 joined with Little Ivy, New Found, and Locust Old Fields of the Holston Association to form the French Broad Association.

The dawn of a new era.—During the 75 years immediately following the founding of the first Baptist church in the province, North Carolina Baptists had established churches from the Atlantic Ocean to the Tennessee line and had organized these into associations for cooperative activities of different kinds. In 1812, according to David Benedict, there were 11 associations, about 200 churches, and about 13,000 Baptists in North Carolina.

Baptists living in North Carolina at the beginning of the 19th century had derived their doctrines and practices from the General, the Particular or Regular, and the Separate Baptists of the 18th century. The General Baptists contributed liberality and breadth of view, charity toward Christians of other names, and receptivity to new ideas. They stood for Christian culture and an educated ministry. Their weakness was in loosely organized churches which had little power to enforce a wholesome discipline.

The group first known as Particular, later as Regular, Baptists insisted upon a close church organization and a strict discipline. They received into their churches only those who, in the opinion of the ministers, had experienced conversion. The weakness of the Regular Baptists was that they clung too tenaciously to their confessions of faith and became devoted to a narrow hyper-Calvinism which later led many churches to refuse to co-operate in missions and education.

The Separates taught North Carolina Baptists to look to the Bible for a creed rather than to rely heavily on confessions of faith. They also emphasized the work of the Holy Spirit in directing the affairs of men, insisting that it was possible for a person to feel conviction. Above all, the Separates contributed the enthusiasm for evangelism which has characterized North Carolina Baptists since that time.

It was in the Chowan-Roanoke region that the type of Baptists uniting the characteristics of General, Regular, and Separate first arose. This was also the area that produced the denominational leaders of the first third of the 19th century. In 1790 there had been 61 churches in the Kehukee Association, which stretched from the James River to the South Carolina line. During the session of that year, the 19 Virginia churches received permission to form the Portsmouth Association. Three years later, a division along the Tar River was approved, the 23 churches to the south forming the Neuse Association. In 1805 the Kehukee churches northeast of the Roanoke formed the Chowan Association.

In 1803 Martin Ross (*q.v.*), the state's outstanding Baptist leader, introduced before the Kehukee Association a resolution calling for the active support of missions. After the required delay of one year, a vote was taken and the resolution adopted. From then until the late twenties the Kehukee was in friendly correspondence with other missionary associations and the Board of Managers of the Baptist Board of Foreign Missions. Under the leadership of Ross, delegates from neighboring associations met at Cashie Meeting House in 1805 and organized the Baptist Philanthropic Missionary Society, the first missionary organization among North Carolina Baptists. A period characterized by increased co-operative activity at the district and state levels had begun.

HENRY SMITH STROUPE

II. History of Convention. By the beginning of the 19th century, the practice of Baptist churches forming associations had become firmly established in North Carolina. But the associations of that period met almost exclusively for worship and fellowship, with little thought of the organized activities now associated with such bodies. The idea of associations joining with other associations in co-operative ventures was only in its infancy.

Baptist Philanthropic Missionary Society.—Although the formation of associations had strengthened denominational unity at the district level, prior to 1803 there was no movement in North Carolina designed to bring about co-operation at the state or national level. In that year, however, Martin Ross (*q.v.*) presented to Kehukee Association the following query: "Is not the Kehukee Association, with all her numerous and respectable friends, called on in Providence: in some way to step forward in support of that Missionary spirit which the great God is so wonderfully reviving amongst the different denominations of good men in various parts of the world?"

In 1804 Kehukee Association appointed a committee to meet with delegates from the Portsmouth (Va.) and Neuse associations at Cashie Meeting House, Bertie County, in June, 1805, "to devise ways and means to support the missionary cause." From the scant records available it is known that the meeting was held and the Baptist Philanthropic Missionary Society was formed.

The society held its second anniversary session at Black Creek Meeting House, Virginia, with eight members of the board of directors present. Letters from societies in other states were read, and the committee of correspondence was instructed to open correspondence with the New York Baptist Missionary Society. The society directed its treasurer to put what money "he may or shall have in hand, belonging to the Missionary institution, on interest."

In 1808 the society assembled at Parker's Meeting House, Hertford County, with 16 members present. The committee appointed to receive contributions reported $41.35 total receipts for the year. The committee appointed to prepare a circular address reviewed the history of local interest in missions. After a reference to the formation of missionary societies in Europe and the North, the committee wrote:

> Fired by the same divine spirit, and animated by their noble example, the Kehukee, Portsmouth, and Neuse Baptist Associations have been called to action. The missionary spirit first made its appearance in the Kehukee Association in October, 1803, and the following May it was introduced into the Portsmouth, in such a feeling manner, that not only the Conference, but many of the spectators were flooded in tears. . . . But hitherto we have been but just able to meet and concert measures, without either suitable persons or means to effect our philanthropic design.

The remainder of the address consisted of biblical passages and exhortations designed to "touch the secret springs of sensibility" to the plight of "those unhappy savages" in other lands.

North Carolina General Meeting of Correspondence.—The Baptist Philanthropic Missionary Society was essentially an interassociational committee of correspondence and did not have a general plan for the support of missions. A broader view was needed. Accordingly, in 1809 Ross proposed before Chowan Association the organization of a body to be called the North Carolina General Meeting of Correspondence. The Chowan agreed and invited the nine other associations in the state to become members. Upon receipt of the invitation, Kehukee decided that since the matter was "entirely new," it ought to lie over a year, at which time four delegates to the organizational meeting were named.

Sandy Creek Association, according to its minutes, received the circular letter in 1810 and appointed four delegates. Four other associations, probably Raleigh, Flat River, Neuse, and Cape Fear, joined Chowan, Kehukee, and Sandy Creek in a meeting held in June, 1811, at the falls of Tar River. There delegates chosen by the associations organized the general body described below and designated Raleigh as the next meeting place. A constitution proposed in 1811 was adopted a year later.

This document bore the title "Constitution of the North-Carolina General Meeting of Correspondence," but the introductory sentence referred to the organization as the "General Convention of the North-Carolina Baptists." The idea of a statewide organization was gradually developing. The constitution provided that members of the body were to be chosen by the associations of the state. Article 9 stated the basic purpose: "That the General Meeting of Correspondence may adopt measures to extend religious acquaintance; to encourage the preaching of the gospel, and to diffuse useful knowledge." It was stipulated, however, that the general meeting would be "considered only as an advisory council," final authority resting with the associations.

The address sent by the general meeting of 1812 to the associations opened with the observation that the conversion of sinners was a matter of interest to all Baptists and could best be achieved through such an organization as the General Meeting of Correspondence. The address concluded:

> You have seen the necessity of corresponding with other neighboring associations, then why not extend further? Let your correspondence . . . embrace the State. . . . Let all the brethren of the same common parent meet as often as possible and combine their wisdom, their energy and zeal in opposing the common enemy and promoting the common good of Zion.

The address attached to the minutes for 1813 refuted the arguments of those who objected to continuing the organization. For example, to the objection "that the design is to raise a fund for the education of young ministers," the authors of the address replied to the effect that there was at that time no such design, but they added that if it should be decided to create a fund, "What evils would arise from such a decision? Shall we be told that the present aged servants of the Lord will be outshone by these brilliant stars?" But the address closed on a kindly note, inviting the critics to attend meetings and see for themselves the advantages of a body which had for its support "Scripture, reason, and piety."

For the next seven years delegates continued to hold annual sessions. These were occupied primarily with preaching and the reading of letters to and from similar bodies in other states. During these years some associations withdrew from the general meeting, but others joined, leaving the average number in co-operation about six. Luther Rice attended the 1816 session, which convened at Tanner's Meeting House in Warren County, and preached on foreign missions. There, for the first time in the history of the general meeting, contributions for missions were received. These amounted to $126.56, of which $5.00 was "contributed by the Black People." The entire sum was deposited in the hands of Rice.

Chowan Association had proposed the general meeting and had sent delegates to every annual session. In 1821, however, Chowan, for reasons not given, decided not to send delegates that year. With no delegation from the sponsoring association, the general meeting came to an end and gave place to another organization already in existence. Interest had shifted from correspondence designed to broaden acquaintanceship to a desire to promote missions. The general meeting had to a considerable degree prepared the way for a new type of co-operation.

North Carolina Baptist Society for Foreign Missions.—The organization which supplanted the North Carolina Baptist General Meeting of Correspondence had been formed in 1814 under the title "The North-Carolina Baptist Society for Foreign Missions." On Mar. 19, 1814, two months before the formation of the Triennial Convention, several Baptist leaders met at Still Bank Meeting House, Edgecombe County, and formed the organization. Item 2 of the constitution declared, "The avowed and determined object of this Society is, to aid in sending forth and supporting Missionaries for the purpose of translating the Scripture, preaching the Gospel, and gathering Churches in Heathen and Idolatrous parts of the world."

Membership was opened to anyone who would pay into the treasury as much as two dollars annually. The item which instructed the board of directors to appoint delegates "to meet with delegates from other similar societies, for the purpose of forming a 'General Committee'. . . to elicit, combine and direct, the energies of the Baptists of the United States" indicated the desire for general co-operation. The constitution bore the names of William Lancaster, president; Jesse Read, vice-president; James Woodberry, corresponding secretary; Josiah Crudup, recording secretary; Jacob Battle, treasurer; Jeremiah Battle, auditor; and James A. Ranaldson (*q.v.*), Joel Battle, Abner W. Clopton (*q.v.*), Charles McAllister, Benjamin Davis, Philemon Bennett, and Robert T. Daniel, trustees. Several of these were also leaders in the general meeting.

The circular address sent out by the society called attention to the fact that missionary societies had already been formed in most of the states of the union and heartily endorsed the general meeting soon to be held in Philadelphia by delegates from these societies. The address pointed with pride to the fact that Adoniram Judson (*q.v.*) and Luther Rice (*q.v.*), two of the missionaries sent to India by the Congregationalists and Presbyterians of New

England, had become Baptists. The willingness of Rice to serve as a Baptist missionary was emphasized in an effort to persuade others to volunteer.

Whereas the general meeting consisted of delegates chosen by the associations, the society welcomed as members all persons interested in foreign missions. The minutes of the society indicate that there was considerable interest among North Carolina Baptists in its activities. In 1816, for instance, the treasurer's account showed $629.22 on hand; in 1817 the sum of $300.00 was placed in the hands of Rice for the general missionary fund. A year later, the collectors brought to the annual meeting such sums as $38.38 from the Female Baptist Missionary Society near Fayetteville, $27.50 from the Hyco Baptist Female Cent Society, and $37.35 from the Female Society for Foreign Missions near Pittsboro. Abner W. Clopton, a tutor at the University of North Carolina, collected $81.75, mostly from the students there. The total for the year reached $612.54, of which $100.00 was forwarded to the Baptist Board of Foreign and Domestic Missions in Philadelphia and the remainder "put out to interest."

In accord with its expanding operations, the name of the organization was changed in 1819 to "The North-Carolina Baptist Society for Foreign and Domestic Missions." The first meetings of the society had been attended by almost no one except 12 or 14 of the officers and trustees, and gifts during the year were reported from only 40 or 50 persons. By 1824, however, knowledge of the work of other state societies and the Triennial Convention had combined with the persistent efforts of leaders within North Carolina to stimulate the enlargement of the work of the society. The 1824 meeting convened at Haywood's Meeting House, Franklin County, with 33 members and official delegates from four associations in attendance. Letters from 24 auxiliary societies and three churches were "read with great pleasure and interest."

Robert T. Daniel was already serving as agent, and seven ministers were named as domestic missionaries. Their work was to consist largely in organizing local societies auxiliary to the state society. The auditor's report showed a previous balance of $704.58, which was increased during the 1824 session to $2,088.72. The names of about 300 contributing organizations and individuals are given in the printed minutes. Daniel had obtained contributions from 23 members of the state legislature.

These various figures indicate that interest in organized activity directed toward the support of missions was becoming general among North Carolina Baptists. The circular address from the society to the auxiliary societies revealed the enthusiasm: "It is with peculiar satisfaction and unspeakable delight that we send you this communication relative to the activity, the zeal, and the success, which have attended the unwearied exertions of our brethren."

Although a spirit of progress had developed among North Carolina Baptists, it soon became apparent that the multiplication of societies was not the best means of turning the enthusiasm into practical accomplishments. Again Chowan Association took the initiative in proposing a solution. In 1826 Martin Ross, the leading member of that body, introduced and secured the adoption of a resolution calling for the formation of a Baptist state convention. He was appointed chairman of a committee authorized to put the proposal into effect but died before this could be done.

Opposition.—Meantime, several Baptist leaders had decided to oppose missionary operations, which had become the order of the day. Their efforts were sufficiently strong to inaugurate a general reaction against the entire missionary movement. In 1826 Joshua Lawrence, leader of the opposition, presented to Kehukee Association a document called the "Declaration of the Reformed Baptists in North Carolina." The association referred the matter to the churches for their consideration. A year later, the majority of the 35 churches in Kehukee Association endorsed Lawrence's proposals and agreed to "discard all Missionary Societies, Bible Societies, and Theological Seminaries, and the practices heretofore resorted to for their support, in begging money from the public: . . . believing these societies and institutions to be the inventions of men and not warranted from the word of God." Agents of such societies were to be discountenanced and no longer invited into the pulpits of the churches.

In 1828 only 22 churches were represented at the annual session of Kehukee Association, for the churches friendly to missions had begun to withdraw. Strong feelings and bitter words characterized the relationships of missionary and antimissionary Baptists, not only in this association but in several others as well. In the midst of the confusion, uncertainty, and changing loyalties, the North-Carolina Baptist Society for Foreign and Domestic Missions perished.

The North-Carolina Baptist Benevolent Society.—In 1829 friends of Ross and of missions attempted to revive organized work among North Carolina Baptists. On Feb. 10 several leaders met in Greenville and formed the North-Carolina Baptist Benevolent Society. The constitution stated, "The exclusive object of this Society shall be to raise funds and appropriate them to the support of travelling ministers, for preaching the Gospel and administering its ordinances within the bounds of North-Carolina." Membership was opened to "every person" who would pay $5.00 and subscribe to the constitution.

The officers chosen at the organizational meeting were Patrick W. Dowd of Raleigh, president; William P. Biddle of Craven County, Thomas Meredith (*q.v.*) of Edenton, and W. H. Jordan of Granville County, vice-presidents; Peter P. Lawrence of Tarboro, corresponding secretary; Reading S. Blount of Greenville, recording secretary; and Henry Austin of

Tarboro, treasurer. In addition, a board of directors consisting of 37 men selected from over the state was named. The first anniversary session was set for Friday before the fourth Sunday in Mar., 1830, in Greenville. The circular address attached to the minutes before they were printed revealed the discouragement and despair of the founders of this latest venture into organized mission work.

Formation of the convention.—The members of the benevolent society who assembled in Greenville Mar. 26, 1830, realized that previous organizations of this type had failed largely because of the limited scope of their plans and that this one as then organized would likely meet the same fate. Accordingly, on Mar. 26 the following brief resolution was unanimously adopted: "That this Society be transformed into a State Convention." The society had convened at 11:30 o'clock in the Baptist Meeting House, where Samuel Wait (*q.v.*) preached, but the business session beginning at three o'clock that day was held at the Greenville Academy. The minutes do not specify the place where other sessions of the first meeting of the convention were held.

There were 14 men present, seven ministers and seven laymen. The ministers were Patrick W. Dowd of Raleigh; William P. Biddle of Craven County; Samuel Wait and John Armstrong (*q.v.*) of New Bern; Thomas Meredith of Edenton; James McDaniel of Cumberland County; and Thomas D. Mason of Greenville. The laymen were R. M. Guffee of Raleigh; Charles W. Skinner of Perquimans County; Henry Austin, Peter P. Lawrence, and R. S. Long of Tarboro; and George Stokes and Reading S. Blount of Greenville. Officers elected were Dowd, president; Biddle, Meredith, and Charles McAllister, vice-presidents; Armstrong, corresponding secretary; Blount, recording secretary; and Austin, treasurer. A board of directors of 18 men was established, and 12 men were named as agents.

It appears that the plan to form a convention had already been decided upon when the society met, for Meredith, who had been a close friend of Martin Ross, brought to Greenville a completely written draft of a constitution and the framework of a circular address. Meredith's constitution was read and adopted, article by article. Although considerably expanded in recent years, the structure provided by the original document has not been discarded. Article II stated the objects: "the education of young men called of God to the Ministry, and approved of by the churches to which they respectively belong; the employment of Missionaries within the limits of this State; and co-operation with the Baptist General Convention of the United States, in the promotion of Missions in general."

The convention combined the membership features of the Baptist Philanthropic Missionary Society, the North Carolina General Meeting of Correspondence, and the North-Carolina Baptist Society for Foreign and Domestic Missions by providing that "every Association, Church, Society, or individual, shall be entitled to send to the Convention, one Delegate, who shall be a member of the Baptist Church, for every Ten Dollars paid into the Treasury." Article VIII charged the board of directors with the responsibility of adopting "such measures as shall best tend to carry into effect the different objects of the Convention."

Meredith's circular.—At the request of the convention, Meredith composed a circular letter to the Baptists of North Carolina. It fills 16 pages in the published proceedings and contains much useful historical information. Meredith pointed out that the Baptists of North Carolina, torn by dissension and without proper organization, were "practising a system, in almost all respects calculated to limit our resources, to paralyze our energies, and to impede our advancement in the progress of literary and evangelical improvement." He was convinced that the newly formed convention promised more to the Baptists of North Carolina than "any human institution" previously proposed.

Well aware of the opposition, he pleaded for unity and harmony. To those who called the convention a "monied concern," he pointed out with references to the Bible that all institutions since ancient times had been of necessity involved with money. Many objected to trained ministers. To Meredith it was a "matter of wonder" that men should object to knowledge in the man who ministered at the altar when they deemed it "necessary in every other official station in life."

Turning to the matter of what support the convention might expect, Meredith stated that in North Carolina there were 14 Baptist associations, 272 churches, and "upwards of 15,360 members." He supposed that not more than one half of the churches would patronize the convention, the other half being averse to conventions, missions, education, and benevolent societies.

The rise of the Primitive Baptists.—Opposition was centered in Kehukee Association, where the energetic Joshua Lawrence exercised a powerful influence. Other antimissionary leaders included Joseph Biggs of Kehukee and James Osborne and John Stadler of Country Line Association. However, with a single exception, the associations adjacent to Kehukee did not follow its leadership. Adhering to the principles of Ross and Meredith, Chowan Association became an early and strong advocate of the convention. But the churches in the northern part of Neuse Association withdrew from that body and formed Contentnea Association on the basis of hostility to missions. Several churches withdrew from Raleigh because of its support of missions and formed Little River Association. Throughout the turbulent years the opponents of missions retained control of Kehukee Association but not of all its churches. Nine of those in the western part secured letters of dismission in order to form Tar River Association, a missionary organization. Philemon Bennett, moderator of Kehukee in 1827, was among those who went over to Tar River.

Representatives from Kehukee traveled westward preaching opposition to missions, an educated ministry, and Bible societies. They gained control of Country Line Association, which in 1832 declared non-fellowship with all the benevolent societies of the day. Stephen Pleasant led those members of Country Line who favored missions in the formation of Beulah Association, which soon became strong in its support of the objects of the convention.

Ministers from Kehukee also entered the newly formed Abbott's Creek Union Association, where they gained the support of a majority of the churches. The members and churches that preferred to continue the support of missions withdrew and organized Liberty Association. Thus in three of the existing associations, Kehukee, Country Line, and Abbott's Creek, the opponents of the convention gathered a majority. There was opposition in all of the other associations, but here the proponents of the convention were in the majority. After a long search for a suitable name, the opponents of the benevolent movement became known as Old School or Primitive Baptists.

The expansion of convention activities.—During the first stage of the development of interest in missions, North Carolina Baptists had been interested primarily in foreign missions. As they sought to promote this enterprise, they found that it rested on state missions. Then they realized that a college, a newspaper, and Sunday schools were indispensable to the successful pursuit of the other operations.

The first anniversary session of the convention convened in 1831 at Rogers' Cross Roads Meeting House, Wake County. Delegates from 36 churches and missionary societies located in 15 different counties reported that funds in the amount of $791.79 had been contributed during the year. Samuel Wait, the general agent, had preached 243 sermons and organized 31 missionary societies. These and other local missionary societies gradually went out of existence, and the convention came to be composed wholly of messengers from churches.

In 1832, when the convention met at Reeves' Meeting House, Chatham County, the number of delegates reached 61, and they came from 31 counties. Within two years the convention had become statewide in its operations, surpassing all the pre-convention organizations in the scope of its activities. Encouraged by the large attendance, the delegates launched an ambitious program of expansion. The qualifications of the leaders in these ventures may be indicated by the fact that there were present five alumni of the University of North Carolina, three graduates of Columbian College, and one graduate of the University of Pennsylvania.

Meredith's periodicals.—In his report as general agent, Samuel Wait brought before the convention the matter of a denominational periodical. He felt that his work had been handicapped by the lack of a medium of communication. The committee appointed to study the matter reported that "the interests of our denomination require some medium by which our peculiar views may be made known and vindicated and by which the various objects of the Convention may be promoted." When Thomas Meredith revealed his plan to launch a periodical, a resolution was adopted stating "that this convention highly approve of the undertaking, and earnestly recommend their brethren to give it a liberal patronage."

In Jan., 1833, Meredith issued at Edenton the first *North Carolina Baptist Interpreter,* a monthly "Devoted to Sacred Criticism, Moral and Religious Essays, Miscellaneous Selections and General Intelligence." He defined his special interest as furthering the "Prosperity of the Denomination and the important objects of the Convention." On July 5, 1834, the place of publication was transferred to New Bern. The convention of that year stated that the publication had met with "universal approbation, and . . . produced much good, in removing the unfounded prejudices of our well meaning but misguided brethren and diffusing correct information."

On Jan. 7, 1835, the *North Carolina Baptist Interpreter* was replaced by a weekly newspaper called the *Biblical Recorder*. The failure, during the depression of 1837, of many subscribers to pay the subscription price caused Meredith to threaten to move "to Tennessee, or some other rich country, where a common spike nail, if stuck in the ground, will soon become a crowbar." Instead, on Jan. 13, 1838, he moved the publication to Raleigh, hoping that the central location would enable his paper to survive. Except for short suspensions in 1842 and 1865, the *Biblical Recorder* has been published in Raleigh continuously since 1838. From that date until 1938 it was the property of various individuals and companies; since 1938 it has been owned by the convention.

Leaders of the convention have at all times depended on the *Biblical Recorder* to place their programs before the denomination. In 1866, for example, the convention recognized "the tremendous power and influence" of its organ and called it "the organizer of our work in the world." Two years later, the author of the convention report on the *Recorder* doubted "whether the Baptists of North Carolina have any other agency, which . . . has done more for their advancement and prosperity than this. It is a power in our midst, and a potent power without which it is difficult to conceive how we could make progress."

Wake Forest College.—In 1832 the convention took the first step toward the establishment of the educational institution called for in the constitution by adopting a report that it was "expedient and highly important to afford to our young ministers facilities for obtaining such an education as will qualify them to be able ministers of the New Testament." A committee was then appointed to purchase a farm on which a Baptist literary institution based on the manual labor principle could be established. The committee purchased for $2,000 Dr. Calvin Jones' plantation in the forest of Wake County, where on Feb. 3, 1834, the Wake Forest Manual Labour Institute was opened.

The fact that in less than four years the convention had become strong enough to launch an ambitious program was due to the experience gained through the pre-convention organizations in North Carolina and the contacts with organized work in other states. The convention now had confidence, enthusiasm, broad views, and definite aims.

The board of directors.—At first the board of directors, known later as board of managers and now as general board, had charge of all the work of the convention. It had no permanent location but met quarterly in different parts of the state, first at Milton, then at Raleigh, then at Wake Forest, then at Raleigh again. The experiment of three boards—one for foreign missions, one for state missions, and one for education—was tried for a time before the Civil War and then abandoned. The general aims of the board were to stimulate the ministers and churches in every part of the state to increased activity and liberality, to aid feeble churches at important points, and to occupy sections of the country which were without preaching.

Western Baptist Convention.—In the early years the work of the convention was greatly hindered by the large extent of its territory and the inadequate facilities for travel. Delegates from west of the Blue Ridge found it impracticable to attend sessions held east of the mountains, where most North Carolina Baptists were located. In 1844 the convention appointed a committee to consult with representatives of the western associations on the best means of co-operating with the convention. As a result, in Aug., 1845, representatives of the western churches met at Boiling Springs Camp Ground near Hendersonville and formed the Western Baptist Convention as an auxiliary to the Baptist State Convention of North Carolina. The latter body approved the formation of the new organization and appointed delegates to its next session.

In 1857, at Berea Church in Buncombe County, the Western Convention resolved itself into an independent body with objects similar to those of the state convention. At first its territory extended as far east as the Yadkin River, but after the Civil War its activities were confined principally to the 14 counties west of the Blue Ridge. The Western Convention used three boards—a Sunday school board located at Asheville, a mission board at Waynesville, and an education board at Hendersonville. Its leaders included James Blythe, Thomas Stradley, N. Bowen, W. A. G. Brown, and John Ammons. During most of its life the Western Convention maintained its own newspapers, among which were the *Carolina Baptist, Baptist Telescope, Cottage Visitor, Western North Carolina Baptist,* and *Asheville Baptist.* Judson College and Mars Hill College were its principal efforts toward the provision of institutions of higher learning.

With the completion of railroads in that region, the principal reason for the formation of the Western Convention disappeared. Accordingly, in the early 1890's the Mitchell, Yancey, and French Broad associations launched movements which resulted in their withdrawal from the Western Convention in order to unite with the state convention. In 1898 at Hendersonville the Western Convention voted overwhelmingly to dissolve, and the nine associations with 21,860 members joined the state convention. The nine associations were Buncombe County, Carolina, Haywood County, Liberty-Ducktown, New Found, Tennessee River, Transylvania, Tuckaseigee, and Western.

Southern Baptist Convention.—From 1830 until 1845, North Carolina Baptists co-operated with those of other states in the work of the Triennial Convention. By 1841, however, many North Carolinians had begun to regard the attacks made on slavery by Northern abolitionists as a threat to peaceful relations. A contributor to the *Biblical Recorder* declared that North Carolina delegates to the Triennial Convention

> were unwilling to sit in council with certain abolitionists; not on account of their *opinions,* but on account of their *doings.* The latter had virtually expelled southerners from their pulpits, their communion tables, and their fellowship; and they had done this with the avowed purpose of producing a rupture between the Northern and Southern portions of the denomination.

Four more years of agitation caused another contributor to write: "We have adhered to the Triennial Convention, until adherence is no longer a virtue. And we believe that the peace and prosperity of our churches . . . require that we should respond to the call for a Southern Convention, and proceed forthwith to the formation of a missionary organization."

A. J. Battle and R. McNabb represented North Carolina Baptists at the meeting which convened in Augusta, Ga., May 8, 1845, and organized the Southern Baptist Convention. Although Meredith and other leaders had preferred union if it could be had on "honorable terms," once the break had been made there was no doubt as to where they stood. On Oct. 18, 1845, the convention unanimously adopted the following resolution: "That this Convention cordially approve the formation of the 'Southern Baptist Convention,' and the appointment of a Foreign Mission Board in Richmond, Va., and a Home Mission Board at Marion, Ala., and that we recommend the churches to contribute liberally to their funds."

Growth in organization.—The basic organization of the convention as provided by Meredith's constitution has been changed but little. From time to time, auxiliary organizations have been added for more effective work, but the original framework remains virtually intact. The principal officers of the convention during the early years were general agent and corresponding secretary. The general agent, which position was first held by Samuel Wait, was a paid field representative who traveled through the state presenting the objects of the convention and soliciting contributions. The corresponding secretary, a position first held by John Armstrong, was a minister who did the correspondence and office work connected with missionary operations. In 1858 the two officers were combined under the title of corresponding secretary.

During the 1836 session of the convention, a committee was appointed to inquire into the expediency of forming a state Bible society, auxiliary to the American and Foreign Bible Society. An organization so named was promptly formed, with Meredith as president. Within a few years it was engaged in the promotion of Sunday schools as well as in the printing of the Bible.

The convention had already begun to endorse reports encouraging the churches to establish Sunday schools. The 1838 report stated that there had been some Sunday schools in North Carolina since about 1805, and that the number had by 1838 reached approximately 200, with 10,000 pupils. On Oct. 20, 1845, a group of Baptist leaders organized the North Carolina Baptist Sunday School and Publication Society, auxiliary to the American Baptist Publication and Sunday School Society.

With regard to the expanding program, the board of managers reported to the convention in 1846 that "too much labor devolves on a few individuals." The board not only directed its own departments of home missions, foreign missions, and education, but the same persons were on the boards of the Bible and publication societies. At the suggestion of the board of managers, the convention appointed three boards instead of one—a home mission board to attend to the "destitution" in North Carolina, a foreign mission board to work with the Foreign Mission Board of the Southern Baptist Convention, and an education board to supervise the education of young men preparing for the ministry.

Despite the enthusiasm with which the reorganization was effected, the plan of appointing three boards proved unsatisfactory for lack of a sufficient number of qualified persons to serve. Accordingly, in 1847 the three were consolidated as a board of managers.

In 1849 the North Carolina Baptist Sunday School and Publication Society became auxiliary to the recently established Southern Baptist Publication Society. Although no longer affiliated with it, the North Carolina body continued to buy Sunday school books from the American Baptist Publication and Sunday School Society until 1857. By that date the attitude of the American Society toward slavery had become "so obnoxious to Southern Christians" that further co-operation was judged impossible. Therefore the North Carolina Society tendered "the whole of its books and funds to the North Carolina State Convention, on the condition that the Convention so amend its Constitution as to make the objects of the Society, a part of the primary objects of the Convention, to be managed by its Board." The convention unanimously accepted the offer and thus became directly committed to the task of supplying Sunday schools with suitable publications.

The Civil War years.—Convention activities reached their peak for the ante-bellum period during the late fifties. For example, during the 1856 session of the convention, $25,125 was pledged for Wake Forest College; in 1857 three new high schools were announced; and in 1858 Matthew Tyson Yates (*q.v.*) stimulated considerable interest in missions. In 1859 the board of managers appointed James S. Purefoy as general superintendent of colportage, to handle 3,000 books which had been contributed by the North Carolina Bible and Publication Society. A year later 10 colporteurs were distributing Bibles and other books.

With the beginning of the war, this work was directed primarily toward North Carolina troops in the Confederate Army. Purefoy was replaced by Needham B. Cobb, under whose direction army colportage became the major activity of the convention. Between Nov. 1, 1863, and Nov. 1, 1864, Cobb received from individuals, churches, associations, and the convention $54,253 for this purpose. With the help of 36 colporteurs, he distributed during the year 25,000 Bibles, 17,000 hymnbooks, and many thousand tracts.

In 1862 came a second attempt to divide the work of the board of managers. This body was abolished in order that it might be replaced by a board of missions located at Goldsboro and a board of education located at Wake Forest. State mission work soon had to be abandoned, but an effort was made to provide education for the children of deceased soldiers. The convention indicated its general attitude toward the war by "heartily and cordially" endorsing the efforts of Confederate officials to prevent the South from being "reduced to abject vassalage and servitude," and by resolving that "we will continue our prayers and efforts until the last armed foe expires or is driven from our land."

State missions.—Immediately after the war the principal convention emphasis was placed on state missions. This was deemed necessary not only because of the destitution wrought by the war in many places but because "error in new forms" had begun to penetrate the South. The convention declared,

> The Methodists, Presbyterians, Episcopalians and Baptists have heretofore had almost exclusive control

SOUTHWESTERN BAPTIST THEOLOGICAL SEMINARY (*q.v.*), Fort Worth, Tex. Student body of more than 2000 in schools of theology, religious education, and music. A $10,000,000 expansion program is in progress.

NEW ORLEANS BAPTIST THEOLOGICAL SEMINARY (*q.v.*), New Orleans, La. Founded 1917, enrolled 972 for 1955–56 session. DeMent building, shown, is one of eighty-two on campus valued at over $5,000,000.

of the religious interests of the Southern States, but now, Unitarianism and indeed all the isms which years ago gained a strong foothold in the Northern States, are looking upon our section of the country as a field already white for the harvest.

By 1867 the number of state missionaries in employment had reached 17 and the funds contributed for that purpose, $3,000. But the monetary panic of 1873 forced the curtailment of mission work, and the mission reports for the remainder of the seventies revealed a debt at the beginning of each year.

Sunday schools.—At the close of the war, the colportage work which Cobb had been pursuing was merged with that of the Sunday School and Publication Board established by the convention in 1863. In an effort to get Sunday school work underway once more, a supply of books was ordered, but when they arrived, there were no funds with which to pay for them. During the 1868 session of the convention, the discouraged Sunday school board proposed that its work be surrendered to the Sunday school association which had been organized earlier that year. The board was abolished and its work taken over by the Baptist Sunday School Association of North Carolina upon condition that it make annual reports to the convention.

Receiving little support, the association was dissolved prior to the 1871 session of the convention, when the Sunday school problem again came up for settlement. That year the convention appointed a Sunday school board, located at Shelby, N. C., to co-operate with the Sunday School Board of the Southern Baptist Convention in multiplying the number of schools in North Carolina.

Under the leadership of John E. Ray, the Sunday school board made progress, reporting, for example, 650 schools in operation in North Carolina in 1880. Upon the resignation of Ray, the convention in 1887 consolidated the board of missions and the Sunday school board under the title Board of Missions and Sunday Schools.

During the secretaryship of Columbus Durham, this agency enjoyed success. As the volume of Sunday school activity steadily increased, the convention in 1895 authorized the Board of Missions and Sunday Schools to establish a subcommittee to handle Sunday school affairs, colportage, and the Sunday school supply store, and to elect a secretary. The committee elected Bernard Washington Spilman (*q.v.*) to be the first Sunday school secretary under the new arrangement. It was under his leadership that Sunday school work in North Carolina reached the position of importance in Baptist life that it holds today.

Board of education.—Of the three objects of the Baptist State Convention of North Carolina as stated in its original constitution, "the education of young men called of God to the Ministry" was listed first. Working through its committee on education, the convention in 1834 established Wake Forest Institute. Except for the year 1846–47, until 1862 the general supervision of all convention work was vested in the board of managers. That year, however, the board of managers was replaced by three boards, one of which was called the board of education.

During the war the board of education solicited funds for the education of the children of indigent, deceased, or disabled soldiers. At the close of the conflict, William B. Royall (*q.v.*) became secretary of the board, which position he held for half a century, until the board was reorganized in 1914. At that time Richard Tilman Vann (*q.v.*) was made corresponding secretary and given greatly enlarged duties. In Mar., 1924, Malloy A. Huggins became corresponding secretary of the board of education. Vann remained associated with him until the reorganization of the board in 1926, when he was made secretary of the Department of Benevolences, and Huggins succeeded him in the education department, as the education agency was now called.

Although Thomas Meredith had made an appeal to the convention of 1838 to establish at once a college for women, no action on this proposal occurred until 1888. In that year a committee was appointed to make plans for such a college. The establishment of the institution now known as Meredith College resulted from this action.

During the 1890's friction developed between the denominational colleges of North Carolina and the institutions of higher learning operated by the state. Charles E. Taylor (*q.v.*) stated the Baptist view in his pamphlet entitled "How Far Should a State Undertake to Educate?" He affirmed that the state should furnish primary education because such education was necessary to intelligent citizenship, but that it had no right to furnish higher education. He held that to tax all the citizens of the state for the support of state colleges was unjust and wrong in principle. For years the convention passed resolutions protesting the appropriation of sums of public money to state colleges. North Carolina Baptists insisted that there should be more state aid to education but that it should take the form of higher appropriations for public primary schools.

The care of orphans.—During the late 1870's the convention began to show interest in new fields of activity, among which were the care of orphans and the work of women's missionary societies. By that time John Haymes Mills (*q.v.*) had begun to care for orphans in an institution located at Oxford. The first convention action came in 1876 when that body recommended Mills's work to the denomination and requested pastors to take collections for its support.

Eight years later a contributor to the *Biblical Recorder* asked, "Is it not time that we as a denomination were making arrangements for a Baptist Orphans' Home?" Thomas Henderson Pritchard (*q.v.*) endorsed the idea in a later issue of the *Biblical Recorder,* suggesting that

J. H. Mills be placed in charge. Pritchard declared that Mills's work at Oxford would "honor his name forever," and that he should head the enterprise "with full authority to work it up according to his own judgment."

So many North Carolina Baptists opposed the orphanage movement that the leaders who favored it decided not to bring the matter before the convention for fear of a discouraging defeat. Instead, during the 1884 session of the convention, they formed the North Carolina Baptist Orphanage Association. It was made up of individual members of the convention, but there was no organic connection between the two bodies.

After the opening of the orphanage at Thomasville in 1885, opinion gradually came to favor stronger support for the undertaking. In 1892 the convention recommended that each Baptist church in the state hold a special service on Thanksgiving Day of each year and take a collection in cash and kind for the orphanage. In 1904 the convention appointed a committee to confer with the trustees of the Baptist orphanage "with a view of establishing and if possible to establish organic connection between the Orphanage and this Convention." By that time the orphanage had become the "pet of the denomination" and, after the adoption of the above resolution, presented reports of its work to the convention, as did Wake Forest College and Meredith College.

Woman's Missionary Union.—Since about 1800 the Baptist women of North Carolina had formed local societies for the encouragement and financial support of missionary ventures. But it was 1877 before an attempt was made to bring these local groups into a statewide organization. In April of that year 20 members of the Baptist churches in Raleigh organized themselves as the Central Committee of the Woman's Missionary Society. When in Nov., 1877, the committee made its first report to the convention, it had received funds from 17 local societies.

The question of whether the convention would recognize the organization precipitated a lively discussion on the floor. Thomas Henderson Pritchard proposed that the convention commend the enterprise and "cordially invite the Committee to report the work they may be able to accomplish to this Convention at its Annual Sessions." Fearful that the management of the local societies would not be controlled by the churches, the convention amended the motion so as to allow the "Committee to report the work the societies organized in the churches may be able to do."

Although this committee functioned for only a few years, in 1886 a new organization called the Woman's Central Committee of Missions was appointed by the state mission board. Fannie Exile Scudder Heck (*q.v.*) served as president from that date until 1915. Meantime, in 1887, J. D. Hufham (*q.v.*) moved, on the floor of the convention, that a committee "consider the expediency of admitting female delegates into this body." This motion failed to be adopted, but the convention did "receive with pleasure the report of the excellent work done by the Woman's Central Committee of Missions, and we cordially bid them continue the same, assuring them of our sympathy, co-operation and aid." The men were willing to applaud the work of the women in raising money for missions but quite unwilling to admit them as delegates to the convention.

In 1888 the committee reported the organization of the first Sunbeam societies. Three years later the North Carolina Woman's Missionary Union became a part of the recently formed Southern group. By 1906 the annual meeting of the North Carolina union had grown so large it could no longer be held in conjunction with the Baptist state convention, and the holding of separate meetings was inaugurated. In 1911 Blanche Barrus became the first paid corresponding secretary.

The 75 Million Campaign.—Prior to the 1920's each agency of the convention had to appeal directly to individuals, churches, associations, or the convention for funds. This arrangement sometimes produced friction and was always expensive and precarious. State missions, which depended on an offering each autumn, may be cited as an illustration. If crops were poor that year or if there was inclement weather on the Sunday designated for the offering, total gifts were small, and this meant debt for the state mission board.

In 1919–20 all objects, whether supported by the North Carolina convention or the Southern Baptist Convention, merged their appeals, worked together in the promotion of the Baptist program, and shared in the receipts. A movement was launched in 1919 in North Carolina to raise one million dollars for all purposes. This was merged into the Southern plan, which had seventy-five million dollars as its goal. In North Carolina more than five million dollars were collected over a period of five years, a sum greater than Baptists had given in the previous 90 years of convention work. Seeking to preserve the principle of co-operation which had been so profitable, North Carolina and other Southern Baptists launched the Unified Program, later known as the Cooperative Program.

Reorganization of 1926.—Conscious of the need for better co-ordination of its many activities, in 1926 the convention made constitutional changes providing for the general reorganization of its work. The existing boards were consolidated into a single body known as the general board. The revised constitution stated that the "General Board shall have charge and control, except when otherwise directed by the Convention, of all work of the Convention, including Missions, Education, Benevolences, and all other general activities, in the interim between the sessions of the Convention." The revised constitution also provided that the convention would elect a general secretary "who shall have administrative supervision of the work of Missions, Education, Benevolences, and all other general training activities of the Convention." Charles E. Maddry held the position of general secretary until 1932, when he was succeeded by Malloy A. Huggins.

Recent developments.—The period from 1932 to 1956 was characterized by numerical growth and the expansion of convention activities. During the first year of this period, there were in the convention 2,374 churches with 433,046 members, and gifts for all purposes totaled $2,525,380. By 1954 these figures had increased to 3,141 churches, 758,482 members, and $32,561,353 total gifts.

In 1932 depression had come over North Carolina, and the convention found itself about one million dollars in debt. The Debt Advisory Commission, which had been charged with the duty of "safeguarding the financial honor and integrity" of the convention, devised means of handling the financial crisis. In 1945, after much careful planning and generous giving, the last of this debt was paid.

The following developments illustrate the expansion and growth of convention activities. During the last two decades a new wing has been added to the Baptist Hospital, a nurses' home has been built, and the North Carolina Baptist Homes for the Aging have been established. The convention has founded the Fruitland Baptist Institute and established summer assemblies at Caswell and Fruitland. Since the early thirties the circulation of the *Biblical Recorder,* now the property of the convention, has increased from 8,000 to 62,284.

Striking developments have occurred in the field of education. In 1946 the convention voted to accept the offer made by the Z. Smith Reynolds Foundation to move Wake Forest College to Winston-Salem, N. C. Despite difficulties brought on by war in Korea, Wake Forest was able to begin operations on the new campus on June 18, 1956. During this period Gardner-Webb College was received into the convention as one of the North Carolina Baptist colleges, and Chowan College, which had been closed for some years, reopened its doors to begin a second century of operations. During the academic year 1955–56 the convention contributed to the seven North Carolina Baptist colleges $438,322 for operational expenses and $345,059 to help meet capital needs. The total student enrolment of these colleges was 5,717. The nine-year program launched in 1951 will continue to aid the denomination's colleges.

During the first third of the 19th century, North Carolina Baptists failed repeatedly in their efforts to establish and maintain a statewide organization to sponsor co-operative ventures. Out of these failures grew the Baptist State Convention of North Carolina, an organization which not only has survived for 126 years but also has successfully co-ordinated Baptist activities in many fields of endeavor.

HENRY SMITH STROUPE

III. Program of Work of North Carolina Baptists. *General Board.*—The administrative body of the Baptist State Convention of North Carolina is called the general board. It is composed of the president and the recording secretary of the convention ex-officio, one member from each co-operating Baptist association, and one additional member from each association for every 20,000 members or fraction thereof beyond the first 20,000. No association has more than three members serving on the board, and no church more than one member. One fourth of the members are elected annually by the state convention. Persons receiving remuneration from any institution or agency of the convention are ineligible. Board membership is limited to one term of four years. Persons become eligible for re-election after one year.

The convention grants to this board authority to supervise and control all business and work, including missions, education and beneficences, and all other general activities in the interim between annual sessions, except those activities committed specifically by charter to the boards of trustees of its institutions and agencies. Two regular meetings of the board are held annually. A majority of the members constitute a quorum. The board elects its president, vice-president, and secretary, and organizes itself into seven standing committees. The chairmen of these committees and two others elected from the membership of the board at large become the executive committee. The president of the convention and the president of the board are ex-officio members. This committee has authority to act for the general board in all matters in the interim between board meetings except in those matters which would modify, enlarge, diminish, or alter divisions of work, or incur obligations in excess of a fixed budget. The executive committee examines all prospective employees and makes recommendations to the board.

The standing committees and the membership of each committee are specified as follows: administration and promotion, 15 per cent; Christian education, 20 per cent; social service, 15 per cent; training activities, 15 per cent; general missions, 15 per cent; Baptist Student Union, 10 per cent; evangelism, 10 per cent. The Christian education committee, together with the president, dean, and chairman of the board of trustees of each of the seven colleges receiving funds from the convention, and with the president of the convention, the president of the general board, and the president of the Woman's Missionary Union as ex-officio members, composes the Council on Christian Education. In the interim between meetings of the general board, the council, with Claude F. Gaddy as executive secretary, has oversight of the program of education in the colleges of the convention.

The state convention elects the general secretary and treasurer, whose duties are to promote missions, education, and social service and to serve as adviser to all the institutions, agencies, and committees of the convention. He works under the direction of the general board and is subject to its authority. As treasurer, he receives all funds sent him for the objects of the convention, acknowledging them in a manner determined by the general board. He countersigns all checks issued by the bonded bookkeeper and makes annual reports of his receipts and disbursements, which are published in the minutes of the convention. Malloy A. Huggins has held this office since 1932.

Missions.—The department of state missions was set up in 1953, with Edward Lowell Spivey as secretary. The department promotes and supervises the work of general state missions and the training and educational activities in the churches. The general missions program includes aid to missionary pastors, a rural church program, work with silent people, pastors' schools, and work in correctional institutions and sanatoriums. In 1954, 120 churches received aid on pastors' salaries in the amount of $73,507.11. In co-operation with Wake Forest College, a rural church department was set up in 1949. In 1951 it became a full-time department of state missions.

On May 15, 1952, Jerry F. Potter became full-time missionary to the silent people of the state, organizing Bible classes, conducting worship services, promoting assemblies, and otherwise providing a ministry of evangelism and training for the deaf. Aid was extended in the purchase of 24 lots during the year 1954 for the purpose of establishing new churches or assisting churches to relocate. Work in a state tuberculosis sanatorium and in a correctional institution for girls is carried on by near-by pastors who make frequent visits to conduct services and hold individual conferences. The salaries of these pastors are supplemented by state mission funds to cover expenses of the added duties.

Pastors' schools are of two types. The Fruitland Baptist Bible Institute, Hendersonville, came into being in 1946 with J. C. Canipe as director. The school, designed for pastors with limited training, is operated for 18 weeks each year. A certificate of graduation is awarded to those who complete the three-year course. The 1954–55 enrolment totaled 143. Schools or conferences of one week's duration are conducted each year at Mars Hill College and Caswell Assembly.

Educational ministry.—Sunday school, Training Union, Woman's Missionary Union, evangelism, and radio and visual education have departmental status, with a secretary directing the promotion of each. A department of music was authorized by the convention in 1954. Joseph O. Stroud became secretary of the department of music on Apr. 1, 1956.

In 1954 the Sunday School Department, L. L. Morgan, secretary, reported gains of approximately 61,000 in net enrolment, with a total enrolment of 703,853 and 32,464 training awards. A total of 2,549 Vacation Bible schools was reported. The Training Union Department, James P. Morgan, secretary, reported a Training Union enrolment of 160,046, with 173 additional churches having new units of Training Union work. Approximately 5,000 people attended one of the four state assemblies promoted by the Training Union Department.

Woman's Missionary Union in 1954 reported 2,102 Woman's Missionary Societies and 5,116 Young People's organizations, with a combined enrolment of 138,630. Miriam Robinson became executive secretary of this department June 20, 1955. Baptist Student Union work, with Bruce E. Whitaker, secretary, reported 30 B.S.U. organizations on college campuses and 12 schools of nursing with active organizations. The department has one associate secretary and eight campus directors paid by the convention and three paid by the institutions where they work. The present Brotherhood secretary, Horace Eason, also serves as Baptist foundation secretary. He reported a gain of 104 new Brotherhoods in 1954, bringing the total number in the state to 872. The total Brotherhood enrolment is approximately 50,000.

The Department of Evangelism was organized on a part-time basis in 1946, with J. C. Canipe serving as secretary of evangelism and director of the Preachers' School at Fruitland. There were 35,702 baptisms in 1954, a gain of 4,409 over the previous year. In 1954 the general board voted to put the Department of Evangelism on a full-time basis by July 1, 1955. Julian S. Hopkins became the first full-time secretary of the Department of Evangelism on Feb. 1, 1956.

The Department of Radio and Visual Education, with L. J. Morriss, secretary, produces visual material in the form of filmstrips and sound color films for use in mission education. Films are distributed to the churches without charge. Radio and visual workshops are conducted in associations to prepare leaders to select the right materials and methods in these fields. As a part of the educational ministry, the convention operates two summer assemblies: Caswell Baptist Assembly, Southport, and Fruitland Baptist Assembly, Hendersonville. Approximately 10,000 people attend the conferences scheduled at these assemblies during the summer of 1954.

Institutions.—North Carolina Baptists support and operate seven colleges, one hospital, two orphanages, two homes for the aging, and a Baptist foundation. Each of these institutions, except the Baptist foundation, shares in Cooperative Program receipts and receives designated gifts from the churches. The seven colleges are as follows: Wake Forest, Winston-Salem, Harold W. Tribble, president; Meredith, Raleigh, Carlyle Campbell, president; Campbell, Buies Creek, Leslie H. Campbell, president; Chowan, Murfreesboro, F. Orion Mixon, late president; Gardner-Webb, Boiling Springs, Phil L. Elliott, president; Mars Hill, Hoyt Blackwell, president; Wingate, Budd E. Smith, president.

The North Carolina Baptist Homes, Inc., James M. Hayes, general superintendent, operates two homes for aging people. One home is located in Albemarle, and the other, known as Resthaven, is at Winston-Salem.

The Baptist Orphanage of North Carolina, Weston C. Reed, general superintendent, operates two homes for the care of children: Mills Home, Thomasville, and Kennedy Home, Kinston. These homes served a total of 728 dependent children during 1954 and helped to locate 214 children with relatives.

These institutions have boards of trustees elected by the convention and responsible to the convention. Trustees must be residents of the state of North Carolina and members of churches co-operating with the convention.

A foundation was organized in 1919 to solicit endowment funds for Baptist institutions and agencies and to supervise the investment of the funds contributed. The foundation is composed of 15 directors elected by the convention for five-year terms, with three elected each year. The report for 1954 revealed assets of $225,-285.29, with earnings of $7,200.05, or 3.3 per cent. The foundation does not handle endowment funds owned by the educational and social service institutions, whose funds are supervised by the boards of trustees of the respective institutions.

Promotional work.—The *Biblical Recorder* has served North Carolina Baptists as the state publication since its founding in 1833 by Thomas Meredith. It was purchased by the Baptist State Convention of North Carolina in 1938 and has been the official organ of the convention since that time. Levy L. Carpenter, editor, reported a circulation of 62,284 in 1956. All institutions and agencies of the convention and all departments of state missions have access to the paper's columns. The paper is supported by Cooperative Program receipts, subscriptions, and advertising. A board of directors of 16—one fourth elected each year for a four-year term—is elected by the convention to direct the operations of the paper.

General promotion and stewardship are handled jointly by the general secretary and the Department of Promotion. The Department of Promotion was inaugurated in Jan., 1953, with Earle L. Bradley, secretary. This department does not handle publicity for the convention but is concerned with the promotion of mission schools, stewardship revivals, and other efforts to increase interest in the Cooperative Program. Stewardship tracts and promotional materials are distributed by this department.

Co-operative work.—The state convention cooperates with American Bible Society by encouraging the churches to make annual contributions for its support. These contributions amounted to $7,964.08 for the year 1954. The Allied Church League is the statewide interdenominational organization for the abolition of beverage alcohol in North Carolina. The league promotes an active program of temperance education in the churches and public schools and encourages county elections in an effort to outlaw the sale of beverage alcohol. The Baptist state convention contributed $9,500 for the support of the league in 1954 and elected 71 members to the board of trustees. The convention supports the work of Protestants and Other Americans United for the Separation of Church and State with an annual allocation of $1,200. During 1954 the Baptist churches of the state also designated $435 to be used by this organization. Work with the Negro convention is currently done through a direct annual grant, which in 1954 amounted to $2,141.16. On Jan. 1, 1957, the two conventions jointly employed a director of Negro work.

The associational missions program in North Carolina is a joint undertaking of the convention and the associations. The promotion department represents the convention in directing and promoting this work. In 1954 there were 55 associations with one or more full-time workers. These associations received appropriations from Cooperative Program funds amounting to $60,900. G. W. BULLARD

BIBLIOGRAPHY: Baptist Philanthropic Missionary Society (N. C.), *Minutes* (1807–08). Baptist State Convention of North Carolina, *Proceedings* (1830–1955). W. W. Barnes, *The Southern Baptist Convention, 1845–1953* (1954). D. Benedict, *A General History of the Baptist Denomination in America and Other Parts of the World* (1848). *Biblical Recorder* (1835–1955). J. Biggs, *A Concise History of the Kehukee Baptist Association* (1834). L. Burkitt and J. Read, *A Concise History of the Kehukee Baptist Association* (1803). M. Edwards, "Materials towards a History of the Baptists in the Province of North-Carolina" (1772). A. L. Fries (ed.), *Records of the Moravians in North Carolina,* Vol. 2 (1925). C. S. Green, *B. W. Spilman, the Sunday School Man* (1953); *The Growth of One Hundred Years* (1930). M. A. Huggins, *North Carolina for Christ* (1948). L. Johnson, *History of the North Carolina Baptist State Convention* (1908). Kehukee Baptist Association *Minutes* (1769–1951). J. R. Logan, *Sketches, Historical and Biographical, of the Broad River and King's Mountain Baptist Associations from 1800 to 1882* (1887). *North Carolina Baptist Almanac* (1865, 1882–1900). North Carolina Baptist Benevolent Society, *Proceedings* (1829). North Carolina Baptist General Meeting of Correspondence, *Minutes* (1811–1821). *North Carolina Baptist Historical Papers,* 3 vols. (1896–99). *North Carolina Baptist Interpreter,* (1833–34). *North Carolina Baptist Society for Foreign Missions, Circular Address of* (n.d.). *North Carolina Baptist Society for Foreign Missions, Constitution of* (n.d.). North Carolina Baptist Society for Foreign Missions, *Minutes* (1817–18). North Carolina Baptist Society for Foreign and Domestic Missions, *Minutes* (1819, 1824). G. W. Paschal, *History of North Carolina Baptists,* 2 vols. (1955); *History of Wake Forest College,* 3 vols. (1935–43). G. W. Purefoy, *A History of the Sandy Creek Baptist Association* (1859). W. L. Saunders (ed.), *The Colonial Records of North Carolina,* 10 vols. (1886–90). R. B. Semple, *A History of the Rise and Progress of the Baptists in Virginia* (1810). H. Sheets, *A History of the Liberty Baptist*

IV. NORTH CAROLINA STATISTICAL SUMMARY

Year	Associa-tions	Churches	Church Member-ship	Baptisms	S. S. Enrol-ment	V.B.S. Enrol-ment	T. U. Enrol-ment	W.M.U. Enrol-ment	Brother-hood En-rolment	Mission Gifts	Total Gifts	Value Church Property	State Capital Worth
1830	14	272	15,360	986	6,000	....	....	....	....	$ 515	$ 3,000	....	(Explanation: This column includes total value of Schools, Children's Homes, Hospitals, Foundation, Buildings, etc.)
1840	18	643	23,832	2,671	12,000	....	....	....	....	1,000	4,000	....	
1850	20	800	40,886	1,500	20,000	....	....	....	....	3,441	5,000	....	
1860	23	900	60,532	1,000	30,000	....	....	....	....	5,177	25,000	....	
1870	25	1,000	67,565	1,050	40,000	....	....	....	....	8,050	100,000	....	
1880	35	1,200	92,922	900	50,000	....	....	....	....	22,500	185,256	....	
1890	43	1,400	152,335	988	70,408	....	....	....	....	55,501	155,501	$ 1,115,196	
1900	56	1,668	169,436	8,065	91,346	....	....	....	....	74,476	290,734	1,225,453	
1905	60	1,816	174,125	9,801	104,534	....	....	11,076	....	80,281	428,738	1,456,290	
1910	62	1,904	221,518	12,269	166,636	....	500	16,300	....	150,250	749,127	3,022,366	....
1915	64	2,136	268,088	17,903	214,972	....	12,000	22,500	....	208,195	1,070,648	4,730,223	....
1920	66	2,219	301,611	16,088	221,028	....	20,000	36,955	....	1,117,447	2,500,000	7,110,231	....
1925	64	2,338	363,388	21,303	312,840	2,641	58,958	41,731	....	843,395	4,035,136	14,997,030	....
1930	69	2,415	410,842	20,265	358,046	8,492	58,537	51,135	....	709,910	3,451,901	22,761,603	....
1931	69	2,397	422,622	20,245	365,942	9,650	54,848	44,016	....	629,664	2,936,924	23,270,471	....
1932	70	2,408	435,732	23,548	384,548	11,244	58,068	44,204	....	480,885	2,528,114	22,767,324	....
1933	70	2,419	443,333	20,165	382,872	12,291	55,430	46,222	....	399,702	2,255,461	22,179,997	....
1934	70	2,444	453,374	19,785	387,199	12,976	60,375	51,467	....	496,097	2,532,198	21,806,405	$ 8,523,318
1935	71	2,471	461,363	18,827	386,771	10,080	61,048	52,657	....	516,731	2,715,933	21,010,159	....
1936	72	2,486	468,471	18,935	393,583	20,178	57,983	53,955	....	568,055	2,913,144	21,461,705	....
1937	72	2,501	474,221	19,610	387,644	25,380	56,380	58,857	....	639,797	3,261,859	21,766,928	....
1938	72	2,525	492,415	25,156	415,058	37,381	59,536	63,644	....	676,368	3,484,512	21,953,224	....
1939	72	2,567	509,864	25,714	428,725	43,615	66,330	69,442	....	717,485	3,777,855	22,878,569	....
1940	72	2,597	519,938	21,644	432,789	54,601	72,027	74,828	....	792,464	4,024,176	23,413,018	....
1941	72	2,618	530,378	18,610	416,797	54,864	49,268	81,322	....	887,279	4,527,331	24,328,866	....
1942	71	2,645	541,574	19,683	407,450	55,164	52,410	83,689	....	1,118,521	5,495,171	25,201,747	....
1943	71	2,680	555,475	21,552	406,082	52,481	49,195	84,816	770	1,424,077	6,473,582	26,027,721	....
1944	70	2,696	565,060	18,370	394,025	43,212	45,227	87,375	950	1,940,967	7,775,442	27,294,402	10,418,146
1945	70	2,735	588,402	26,805	416,485	71,581	54,895	89,592	1,412	2,297,033	10,175,920	29,317,405	....
1946	70	2,780	601,688	24,299	441,745	106,565	61,362	90,479	2,518	2,811,351	11,820,577	32,153,820	....
1947	70	2,821	627,575	26,367	471,606	138,361	74,085	80,633	3,843	2,960,774	14,174,024	31,153,852	....
1948	71	2,849	641,763	26,177	492,495	124,377	80,980	82,804	5,129	3,275,035	15,988,590	47,340,582	....
1949	72	2,903	669,136	33,318	542,363	168,823	93,543	93,189	5,972	3,216,338	18,687,067	56,362,712	....
1950	73	2,954	692,419	32,545	572,716	184,231	108,665	123,521	5,400	3,538,912	21,153,886	66,178,324	....
1951	73	2,998	719,293	34,545	599,298	200,091	115,851	132,212	12,672	3,821,762	23,888,668	78,620,280	....
1952	73	3,055	737,211	30,554	619,399	210,665	127,115	136,413	19,872	4,468,874	24,787,034	92,458,425	....
1953	73	3,107	758,482	31,293	642,741	225,150	139,996	144,433	24,032	4,494,668	29,159,490	106,242,531	....
1954	73	3,141	781,777	35,702	703,853	233,743	160,046	155,052	29,232	4,805,016	32,561,353	130,265,053	39,749,224

L. L. MORGAN

Association (1907). H. S. Stroupe, *The Religious Press in the South Atlantic States, 1802–1865* (1956). T. J. Taylor, *A History of the Tar River Association* (n.d.). *Wake Forest Student* (1905–10). (Contains Vol. 4 of *North Carolina Baptist Historical Papers.*)

NORTH CAROLINA ASSOCIATIONS. About the middle of the 17th century Baptist churches in England initiated the practice of joining together in associations, with the chief purpose to maintain fellowship among scattered congregations. American Baptists adopted the practice, forming the Philadelphia Association in 1707, the Charleston in 1751, and the Sandy Creek in 1758. Sandy Creek, North Carolina's first association, was thus the third formed in America. Shubal Stearns (*q.v.*), Separate Baptist leader and founder of the Sandy Creek Association, had become convinced that an organization composed of delegates from the churches was needed to impart stability, regularity, and uniformity to the work of the churches.

Since 1758 most of the Baptist churches organized in North Carolina have either joined an association already in operation or formed a new one more conveniently located. By 1793 the Sandy Creek, which embraced the piedmont region of North Carolina, had been joined by the Kehukee (1769) in the northeastern part of the state, the Yadkin (1790) in the northwestern, and the Neuse (1793) in the southeastern. These and other associations had constitutional provisions to the effect that "a Baptist Association . . . arrogates no higher a title than that of an Advisory Council." Therefore they claimed no coercive power or authority over churches but did assume the right to determine which churches would be admitted to the association or when fellowship would be withdrawn.

The early associations held meetings almost exclusively for worship and fellowship, with sessions which continued for four or five days until most of the ministers present had preached one or more times. After the Civil War associational meetings gradually took on more of the characteristics of business sessions, with emphasis on devising ways and means for the extension of missions, education, temperance, and Sunday school work.

Leaders realized from the first that the original associations were too large in territorial extent for effective work. Accordingly, as soon as enough churches had been established in an appropriate geographical area, they secured letters of dismissal from the mother association and formed one of their own. During the last quarter of the 19th century a large number of divisions occurred, most of them along county lines. New associations usually adopted the articles of faith of the parent bodies, many of which were based on the Philadelphia Confession of Faith. However, a majority of the associations formed during the last half-century have not adopted articles of faith. With few exceptions, North Carolina Baptist associations have published the minutes of their annual sessions which constitute the principal source of information regarding their activities. Many associations, especially the older ones, have also published histories based on their minutes.

I. Extant. Alexander. Organized at Macedonia Church Oct. 1–2, 1887, when 15 churches, with preliminary plans for the formation of a county association, secured dismissal from the Brushy Mountain and Brier Creek associations. In 1954, 21 churches reported 177 baptisms, 4,840 members, $142,170 total gifts, $17,459 mission gifts, $573,500 property value, and $29,157 church debt.

Alleghany and Grayson. Organized Nov. 5, 1897, at Sparta, N. C., by nine churches in the North Carolina county Alleghany and the Virginia county Grayson. It was organized as a result of the division at the county line of Ashe and Alleghany Association in 1897. In 1899 it adopted and printed the abstract of principles. Immediately after the 1908 session the Virginia churches withdrew, and the remaining churches formed the Alleghany in 1909. In 1954, 12 churches reported 62 baptisms, 919 members, $12,262 total gifts, $1,148 mission gifts, $54,104 property value, and $42 church debt.

Anson II. Organized Oct. 18, 1910, at the Cedar Grove Baptist Church as a result of Pee Dee's dismissal of 12 churches in Anson to form a county association, Oct. 23, 1909. The property of the Pee Dee Institute, which had flourished earlier, was sold and the money divided between the two associations. In 1954, 25 churches reported 240 baptisms, 4,951 members, $158,268 total gifts, $26,869 mission gifts, $646,285 property value, and $15,915 church debt.

Ashe. Formed Sept. 27, 1898, at Friendship Church after the Ashe and Alleghany had divided. The Ashe reaffirmed the articles of faith of the parent body and continued its numbering of the annual sessions. It launched an active mission program in an effort to overcome the destitution within the county. In 1954, 61 churches reported 220 baptisms, 6,130 members, $66,866 total gifts, $8,876 mission gifts, $398,900 property value, and $16,744 church debt.

Atlantic II. Organized Nov. 19, 1929, after the Neuse-Atlantic voted to divide because of its size. Delegates from 24 churches in Carteret, Craven, Pamlico, Jones, and Onslow counties met in First Baptist Church, New Bern, organized the association, and adopted the Philadelphia Confession of Faith. In 1954, 37 churches, from the five counties above, reported 650 baptisms, 8,162 members, $394,083 total gifts, $63,327 mission gifts, $1,047,789 property value, and $99,763 church debt.

Avery. Organized by delegates from 10 churches Sept. 20–22, 1912, at Aaron Church after the Roan-Grandfather Mountain, in order to divide the association into more workable units, granted dismissal on Sept. 12, 1912, to 15 churches interested in forming a county grouping. The association adopted articles of faith Sept. 22, 1914. In 1954, 29 churches reported

173 baptisms, 3,857 members, $49,749 total gifts, $4,849 mission gifts, $184,400 property value, and $10,580 church debt.

Beulah. Organized with three missionary churches in 1834 under the leadership of Stephen Pleasant. Pleasant, who opposed the Country Line Association's stand against missions and education in 1833, had been promptly excluded by his church, Ebenezer. Others joined the three churches which Pleasant organized located near Yanceyville, Caswell County, until in 1860 the association had 26 churches scattered over seven counties from Orange to Forsyth. J. D. Hufham (*q.v.*) said it was "easily the foremost body of its kind in the State." Beulah, among the first associations to form academies, organized several before the Civil War. In 1844 Elias Dodson began 11 years of service as associational missionary. The territory was gradually reduced by the formation of new associations to only Caswell and Person counties. In 1954, 33 churches reported 198 baptisms, 7,146 members, $185,050 total gifts, $30,520 mission gifts, $889,550 property value, and $35,796 church debt.

Bladen. Organized in 1892 when Bladen churches in Cape Fear Association received dismissal to form a county association. Delegates from most of the 24 member churches met at Mt. Pleasant Church Nov. 7, 1892, for the organization. In 1954, 32 churches reported 198 baptisms, 5,352 members, $190,918 total gifts, $31,594 mission gifts, $569,221 property value, and $22,075 church debt.

Blue Ridge. Organized in 1929 when the Green River divided for convenience, the McDowell County churches withdrawing to form the Blue Ridge. Delegates from 17 churches attended the first session, Oct. 1, 1929, at First Baptist Church, Marion, and adopted as the Blue Ridge articles of faith the "Associational Covenant" of Green River. In 1954, 41 churches reported 358 baptisms, 7,461 members, $321,759 total gifts, $34,552 mission gifts, $1,030,700 property value, and $73,280 church debt.

Brier Creek. Organized at Brier Creek Church Nov. 23, 1822, by delegates from nine Wilkes County churches which had withdrawn from the Yadkin because of its large territorial extent. During the fierce agitation of the 1830's the advocates of the objects of the convention maintained a majority. Missionary churches in Iredell, Yadkin, and Alexander counties joined the Brier Creek, giving it 25 churches by 1876. From 1894 until the 1920's Brier Creek followed The Gospel Method, which consisted in sending funds directly to missionaries on foreign fields. By 1954 withdrawals had reduced the Brier Creek to the southeastern corner of Wilkes County. In 1954, 34 churches reported 257 baptisms, 7,256 members, $70,242 total gifts, $9,729 mission gifts, $349,435 property value, and $10,200 church debt.

Brunswick. Organized when 10 Brunswick churches, immediately following the consolidation in 1898 of the Cape Fear and Columbus associations into a single large body, asked dismissal from it to form a county grouping. Letters were granted Nov. 18, 1899, and on Nov. 30 the first session of the Brunswick convened in Shallotte. In 1954, 28 churches reported 199 baptisms, 3,579 members, $91,695 total gifts, $13,119 mission gifts, $368,208 property value, and no church debt.

Brushy Mountain. Formed Nov. 24–25, 1871, at Three Forks Church by combining portions of the United Baptist and Lewis Fork associations. The 21 original members were joined by others until the association embraced churches in Wilkes, Alexander, Ashe, and Caldwell counties. The association adopted the abstract of principles Sept. 30, 1876. Reduced in size by the formation of Caldwell, Alexander, and Ashe associations and other withdrawals, it included in 1954 only the central and southern portions of Wilkes County. In 1954, 37 churches reported 342 baptisms, 7,833 members, $164,079 total gifts, $22,449 mission gifts, $759,500 property value, and $18,210 church debt.

Buncombe. Organized after a convention at Bethel Church, Buncombe County, in 1882 planned to organize a county association in a portion of the territories of the French Broad, New Found, and Salem associations. Although launched the next year at Flat Creek, the Buncombe had enrolled only half of the fifty Baptist churches in the county 25 years later. The association adopted the doctrinal views in the abstract of faith in Hiscox's *Star Book* in 1883. In 1954, 84 churches reported 1,101 baptisms, 24,600 members, $899,722 total gifts, $149,504 mission gifts, $3,987,556 property value, and $639,579 church debt.

Burnt Swamp. Organized by three churches Jan. 27, 1881, at Burnt Swamp, Robeson County, as "Burnt Swamp Missionary Baptist Association of the Mixed Race." Later the last two words in the name were changed to "Croatan Indians," and still later to "Cherokee Indians of Robeson County." Located near the center of Robeson, this association of Indian Baptists co-operates with the Baptist state convention. In 1954, 31 churches reported 163 baptisms, 3,814 members, $64,523 total gifts, $6,750 mission gifts, $211,450 property value, and no church debt.

Cabarrus. Organized Oct. 8, 1935, at Concord First, after the Mecklenburg-Cabarrus Association granted dismissal to the churches in Cabarrus to form a county association in Sept., 1935. In 1954, 45 churches reported 726 baptisms, 13,491 members, $655,683 total gifts, $113,516 mission gifts, $2,583,835 property value, and $201,867 church debt.

Caldwell. Organized after a convention met at Lower Creek Church June 5, 1885, and voted to form a county association in a portion of the territories of the Brushy Mountain, Three Forks, and Catawba River associations. Delegates from 16 churches met at Rocky Spring Oct. 22, 1885, organized Caldwell, and adopted an abstract of principles. In 1886 Union, a newly constituted Negro church, was admitted, but it later withdrew. In 1954, 64 churches reported 789 baptisms, 15,720 members, $614,265 total gifts, $101,281 mission gifts, $2,715,006 property value, and $245,755 church debt.

CAROLINA. Organized Oct. 19, 1877, at Double Springs Church, Henderson County, in territory of the Salem and Transylvania associations. The Carolina opened Judson College at Hendersonville Jan. 27, 1879, but the building had to be sold Mar. 7, 1892, because of indebtedness. On Nov. 5, 1886, Carolina absorbed Henderson Association; and the next year when South Carolina members withdrew, the boundaries of Carolina were about the same as those of Henderson County. In 1954, 60 churches reported 465 baptisms, 13,037 members, $387,082 total gifts, $57,537 mission gifts, $1,606,200 property value, and $39,336 church debt.

CATAWBA RIVER. Organized Nov. 16, 1827, at Head of the Yadkin Church in Caldwell County after the Yadkin dismissed five churches and the Broad River eight to form the association. Although there was considerable antimission sentiment in this area, Catawba River supported missions and education from its beginning. In 1878 the association divided, the western part retaining the name and the eastern part joining in the formation of South Fork. Further divisions left Catawba River only the western two-thirds of Burke County. In 1954, 47 churches reported 599 baptisms, 10,532 members, $469,534 total gifts, $65,512 mission gifts, $2,142,100 property value, and $264,198 church debt.

CHEROKEE. Formed in 1881 in Swain County as the "Cherokee Baptist Association." In 1936 the name was changed to "Cherokee Baptist Association of the Eastern Band of the Cherokee Indians." In 1954, 15 churches reported 83 baptisms, 1,227 members, $15,326 total gifts, $1,184 mission gifts, $45,217 property value, and no church debt.

CHOWAN. Organized May 16, 1806, at Salem Meeting House in Pasquotank by 18 churches released from the Kehukee in 1805, located east of the Roanoke River in Camden, Chowan, Currituck, Gates, Hertford, Pasquotank, and Perquimans counties. Chowan adopted the Kehukee abstract of principles and remained friendly with the mother association until 1827, when the latter severed relations on the ground that Chowan had "embraced Arminian doctrines." Under the leadership of Martin Ross, the Chowan invited other associations to attend the Baptist General Convention of North Carolina, which first met in 1812. The Chowan actively supported Wake Forest College and opened an associational school, Chowan Baptist Female Institute, at Murfreesboro in 1848, adding the Reynoldson Male Institute, Gates County, in 1855. By 1954 Chowan included all counties east of the Chowan River from Virginia to the Pamlico Sound. In 1954, 56 churches reported 511 baptisms, 15,236 members, $487,915 total gifts, $93,024 mission gifts, $1,696,298 property value, and $66,372 church debt.

COLUMBUS. Organized Dec. 26, 1888, by five churches in Columbus County, a former territory of the Cape Fear. Unable to become a strong body by enrolling all the churches in the county, the Columbus agreed in 1898 to unite with Cape Fear as the Cape Fear-Columbus. After 1900 the churches outside Columbus County withdrew to join county units, whereupon, the Cape Fear-Columbus voted Oct. 22, 1936, to drop "Cape Fear" from its name. In 1954, 43 churches reported 418 baptisms, 10,320 members, $320,328 total gifts, $57,816 mission gifts, $1,349,368 property value, and $54,713 church debt.

DAN VALLEY. Organized after Pilot Mountain dismissed 12 churches, Oct. 21, 1947, to form an association in Rockingham County and its environs. When the first annual session of the new association convened at Draper, Oct. 14, 1948, six additional churches joined. In 1954, 25 churches reported 277 baptisms, 6,371 members, $256,806 total gifts, $32,329 mission gifts, $1,089,000 property value, and $100,984 church debt.

DOCK. Organized in 1916 by Poly Bride, Palmira, Seven Creek, Magnolia, and New Life churches in southern Columbus County. In 1954, 15 churches reported 46 baptisms, 1,662 members, $43,564 total gifts, $3,385 mission gifts, $173,500 property value, and $8,000 church debt.

EASTERN. Organized in Oct., 1827, when Cape Fear dismissed 17 churches in Sampson, Duplin, Onslow, and New Hanover counties to form the Goshen. The Goshen and Neuse (located northeast of the counties named) combined in 1845 under the name Union. "In 1865 at Moore's Creek in deference to the sentiment of the Confederate soldiers the name of the Association was changed from Union to Eastern." The Atlantic was formed in 1884 by churches from the northern part of the Eastern, and the Wilmington in 1901 by several in the south. By 1954 Eastern occupied all of Duplin and most of Sampson counties. In 1954, 39 churches reported 445 baptisms, 9,210 members, $288,507 total gifts, $54,023 mission gifts, $1,073,292 property value, and $31,638 church debt.

ELKIN. Organized in 1879 in Wilkes and Surry counties largely from churches of the old "Primitive Association." Although Elkin cooperated with the state convention, there was considerable antimission sentiment in the area, and Elkin early adopted the principle that "The benevolent institutions of the day shall be no bar or test of fellowship, but all shall be free to sustain or not sustain, as they may choose." The association adopted articles of faith prior to 1944. In 1954, 21 churches, in the northeastern corner of Wilkes County, reported 203 baptisms, 5,337 members, $181,499 total gifts, $17,787 mission gifts, $867,320 property value, and $142,057 church debt.

FLAT RIVER. Formed by 10 churches in the

North Carolina counties of Granville, Warren, Franklin, Wake, and Orange when the Roanoke Association, which embraced 36 churches in the piedmont sections of Virginia and North Carolina, divided along the state line in 1794. The first session convened at Gardner's Meeting House, Warren County, with Grassy Creek, Tabb's Creek, Shearman's, Tanner's, Eno, Camp Creek, Lock's, Cedar Creek, and Neuse as original member churches. Beginning in 1806, the Country Line, Beulah, Central, Mt. Zion, and Tar River have been formed in whole or part from Flat River. In 1954, 32 churches, principally in Granville County, reported 357 baptisms, 10,374 members, $224,366 total gifts, $48,951 mission gifts, $428,700 property value, and $73,549 church debt.

French Broad. Formed in 1807 by three churches (Little Ivy, Locust Old Fields, and New Found) from Holston Association and three (French Broad, Cane Creek, and Caney River) from Broad River. During the 1820's several churches, rejecting the French Broad belief in the doctrine of election, formed the Big Ivy. In 1849, however, French Broad accepted the Big Ivy view, and the two reunited as French Broad. By the mid-century the Tuckaseigee, Salem, Valley, Roan Mountain, New Found, and Three Forks had been formed by peaceful divisions of the French Broad. County associations later took additional territory until by 1954 only a part of Madison County remained. In 1954, 45 churches reported 257 baptisms, 8,364 members, $150,958 total gifts, $17,872 mission gifts, $744,100 property value, and $176,454 church debt.

Gaston. Organized Nov. 4, 1919, at the First Baptist Church, Gastonia, by 26 churches in Gaston County. Twenty of these had been dismissed by South Fork to form a smaller association, four by King's Mountain, and two were new churches. In 1954, 65 churches reported 1,577 baptisms, 26,339 members, $1,271,055 total gifts, $227,144 mission gifts, $5,618,250 property value, and $519,843 church debt.

Green River. Organized in Nov., 1841, at Montford's Cove Church by five churches in the present counties of Polk and Rutherford which had obtained dismissal from the Broad River in Aug., and eight of the more southerly churches of the Catawba River. Articles of faith were adopted Oct. 4, 1856. The Sandy Run (1890) and Blue Ridge (1929) were formed from the Green River. In 1954, 39 churches reported 339 baptisms, 8,607 members, $311,117 total gifts, $39,897 mission gifts, $1,319,850 property value, and $129,120 church debt.

Haywood. Formed in 1886 as a county association by 14 former members of the Tuckaseigee. Haywood supported the western convention, Judson College, and the *Western North Carolina Baptist*. In 1954, 53 churches reported 525 baptisms, 11,252 members, $344,070 total gifts, $47,934 mission gifts, $1,898,717 property value, and $87,478 church debt.

Johnston. Organized as a county association in Selma Nov. 27, 1903, by 29 churches, most of them in Johnston County, which had obtained dismissal from the Raleigh. The Johnston churches left Raleigh because of the "great number of churches" (57) and the "vastness of territory" in the mother association. In 1954, 48 churches reported 476 baptisms, 12,044 members, $346,527 total gifts, $61,105 mission gifts, $1,618,300 property value, and $118,635 church debt.

King's Mountain. Formed in 1851 when the Broad River divided approximately along the state line, dismissing 12 churches, 10 in North Carolina and two in South Carolina, for this purpose. Delegates from these churches met at Double Springs Meeting House, Cleveland County, Nov. 7, 1851, formed King's Mountain, and adopted an abstract of principles. During the 1859 session the association resolved not to hold fellowship with any church having members who bought, drank, or sold liquor. This action produced a division of the body into "Regular" and "Constitutional" churches, the latter withdrawing on ground that the action was unconstitutional. In 1866 the resolution was rescinded, and the association reunited in harmony. In 1954, 64 churches in Cleveland County reported 976 baptisms, 21,933 members, $1,141,100 total gifts, $173,343 mission gifts, $4,458,493 property value, and $348,198 church debt.

Liberty. Organized during the 1832 session of Abbott's Creek Union Association at Mt. Tabor Meeting House, Randolph County. Lick Creek Church presented two letters, one missionary and one antimissionary; and the moderator, with the approval of the majority, asked all delegates favorable to the Baptist state convention to withdraw. While the parent body proceeded with business, the delegates who had been excluded met Sept. 24, 1832, in a tent on the grounds and organized the Liberty Association. Although these delegates represented only seven churches or parts of churches, they launched a program which kept a missionary in the field until the Civil War. In 1954, 37 churches reported 629 baptisms, 11,372 members, $516,527 total gifts, $76,024 mission gifts, $2,188,772 property value, and $289,523 church debt.

Little River. Organized by delegates from nine churches at Lillington Nov. 2–5, 1876, in territory formerly belonging to the Raleigh, Cedar Creek, and other associations. Reports show that the association supported Buie's Creek Academy, now Campbell College. In 1954, 31 churches reported 388 baptisms, 9,614 members, $297,955 total gifts, $54,559 mission gifts, $1,241,200 property value, and $83,200 church debt.

Macon. Organized Sept. 1, 1904, at Franklin Church, by delegates from 24 Tuckaseigee churches, adopting the articles of faith of the mother association. Macon co-operated with the Baptist state convention and maintained Macon County High School. In 1954, 42 churches reported 291 baptisms, 7,186 members, $124,887 total gifts, $16,942 mission gifts, $536,694 property value, and $85,000 church debt.

MECKLENBURG. A continuation of the Mecklenburg and Cabarrus. In 1954 this association consisted of the populous county of Mecklenburg and 54 churches reported 1,546 baptisms, 26,203 members, $1,845,632 total gifts, $260,539 mission gifts, $7,808,885 property value, and $1,-541,308 church debt.

MITCHELL. Organized as the Roan Mountain which changed its name to Mitchell in 1884. On Sept. 1, 1893, the Mitchell asked the western Baptist convention for dismissal in order to affiliate with the Baptist state convention, launching a movement which resulted in 1898 in the dissolution of the western convention. On Sept. 15, 1911, Mitchell changed its name to Roan-Grandfather Mountain, but the next year, when 15 churches were released to form the Avery, the name became Roan Mountain. The New Hampshire Confession of Faith was adopted Sept. 14, 1916, in order to have a basis for determining which of two factions composed the true Mine Creek Church. The name again became Mitchell in 1917. In 1954, 36 churches reported 324 baptisms, 7,380 members, $176,102 total gifts, $16,240 mission gifts, $629,512 property value, and $22,325 church debt.

MONTGOMERY. Organized Oct. 17, 1889, by Montgomery churches when Pee Dee Association in session at Bethel Church, Montgomery County, voted to dissolve. At its organization there were 15 churches, 960 members. In 1954, 30 churches reported 236 baptisms, 4,484 members, $149,028.00 total gifts, $16,178.00 mission gifts, $528,655.00 property value, and $25,-313.24 church debt.

MOUNT ZION. Organized at Moriah Church, Orange County, Sept. 23, 1870, by delegates from 13 churches in Sandy Creek, Beulah, and Raleigh associations favorable to the views of George W. Purefoy. Purefoy was the leader of a group in the Sandy Creek Association after the Civil War that did not want meetings of the association to include the sabbath, to continue so long, or to devote so much time to preaching. This group preferred "to make them more of a business session, to devise ways and means for the extension of missions. . . ." The new association included churches in Orange, Chatham, Alamance, and Wake. In 1954, 45 churches reported 516 baptisms, 12,974 members, $634,-585 total gifts, $112,684 mission gifts, $2,606,170 property value, and $225,816 church debt.

NEUSE III. Organized at Goldsboro in 1929 by delegates from 15 churches in Wayne, Lenoir, Pitt, and Greene when the Neuse-Atlantic voted to divide for convenience. In 1954, 29 churches reported 368 baptisms, 5,894 members, $334,807 total gifts, $71,784 mission gifts, $1,135,000 property value, and $67,506 church debt.

NEW FOUND. Organized Oct. 19, 1855, by delegates from 10 churches, seven formerly in the French Broad, which met at New Found Church in Buncombe County. Its territory included parts of Buncombe, Madison, Haywood, and Yancey counties. Articles of faith, adopted before 1879, repudiated the doctrine of unconditional election. County associations took over the territory of the New Found until by 1954 it occupied only that part of Madison southwest of the French Broad River. In 1954, 34 churches reported 157 baptisms, 4,217 members, $38,198 total gifts, $2,939 mission gifts, $130,196 property value, and $4,065 church debt.

NEW SOUTH RIVER. Formed Mar. 24, 1924, at Autryville by combining Cumberland and South River associations. The first regular session, attended by delegates from 50 churches located in Cumberland County and the western part of Sampson, met Oct. 15–17 of that year. In 1954, 66 churches reported 950 baptisms, 15,184 members, $641,488 total gifts, $89,173 mission gifts, $2,169,966 property value, and $279,821 church debt.

PEE DEE II. Formed by a union of Anson and Richmond associations, with the first regular session Oct. 19, 1893. Although a new association in 1893, the Pee Dee voted in 1930 to number the session for that year 115 instead of 38. On Oct. 23, 1909, letters were granted to Anson County churches, which formed Anson Association the next year. In 1954, 26 churches in Richmond and Scotland counties reported 391 baptisms, 7,657 members, $372,128 total gifts, $57,-668 mission gifts, $1,025,700 property value, and $117,023 church debt.

PIEDMONT. Organized Oct. 17, 1894, at the West Washington Street Church, Greensboro, by five churches located between Randolph County and the Virginia line, former territory of the Sandy Creek, Liberty, and Beulah associations. By 1934, when the Randolph churches withdrew to form a county association, the Piedmont had increased to 53 churches. Those in Rockingham were later dismissed to join in forming Dan Valley. In 1954, 76 churches reported 1,878 baptisms, 29,792 members, $1,641,-900 total gifts, $304,106 mission gifts, $5,884,960 property value, and $741,941 church debt.

PILOT MOUNTAIN. Organized Oct. 17, 1885, at Red Bank Church, Forsyth County, by 20 churches released for that purpose by Beulah and Yadkin associations. Rockingham County churches withdrew from Pilot Mountain in 1947 to join in forming Dan Valley. In 1954, 71 churches in Forsyth and Stokes counties reported 1,300 baptisms, 6,781 members, $1,266,-878 total gifts, $277,760 mission gifts, $5,867,900 property value, and $660,602 church debt.

RALEIGH. Formed in 1805 from the Neuse by four churches: Wake Union, Wake Cross Roads, Holly Springs, and Haywood's Meeting House. In 1830 there were 16 churches scattered over the area bounded by Wayne, Sampson, Orange, and Person counties. At mid-century Raleigh was supporting Matthew Tyson Yates (*q.v.*) in China and an associational school at Holly Springs. Since 1830 Raleigh has released churches to join in forming Tar River (1830), Central (1860), Mt. Zion (1869), Little River

(1876), and Johnston (1903). On Oct. 26, 1944, a proposal made the year before by Central that its churches be allowed to combine with Raleigh was effected, and by 1954 Raleigh included Wake and a small number of churches in adjacent counties. In 1954, 79 churches reported 1,110 baptisms, 30,564 members, $1,170,645 total gifts, $204,252 mission gifts, $4,988,977 property value, and $790,117 church debt.

RANDOLPH. Organized along county lines Oct. 25, 1934, when the 24 Randolph churches withdrew from Piedmont, Sandy Creek, Liberty, and Montgomery associations in the belief that more enthusiastic associational work would result from a county organization. In 1954, 45 churches reported 482 baptisms, 7,449 members, $370,880 total gifts, $54,610 mission gifts, $1,319,377 property value, and $117,092 church debt.

ROBESON. Organized Nov. 1, 1883, at Raft Swamp Church, Robeson County. The 26 churches were located in Robeson and its environs, former territory of Cape Fear and Cedar Creek associations. In 1954, 62 churches reported 662 baptisms, 16,177 members, $671,875 total gifts, $141,842 mission gifts, $2,504,150 property value, and $118,875 church debt.

ROWAN. Organized as a county association after the South Yadkin released Rowan County churches Sept. 1, 1927. Delegates from 20 of these met in Stallings Memorial Church, Salisbury, on Oct. 6 to form the association. In 1954, 32 churches reported 496 baptisms, 10,066 members, $407,893 total gifts, $60,025 mission gifts, $2,082,362 property value, and $89,569 church debt.

SANDY CREEK. North Carolina's first Baptist association. Soon after the founding of the Sandy Creek Church in 1755 by the Separate Baptists, Shubal Stearns (*q.v.*) visited neighboring churches and explained his contemplated plan of forming an association. Delegates from Sandy Creek, Deep River, and Abbott's Creek churches probably first met at Sandy Creek in Jan., 1758, with a larger gathering in July. To the latter also came delegates from Little River, Dan River, Grassy Creek, New River, Black River, Pittsylvania City, Va., and Lunenburg City, Va., to complete the formation of Sandy Creek Association. Within a few years it extended from the Potomac River to Georgia, and despite the early leanings of the Separates toward Arminianism, the Calvinistic Philadelphia Confession of Faith began to prevail. In 1770 the Virginia churches withdrew, leaving nine churches and 10 arms in Sandy Creek. Morgan Edwards reported in 1772 that 1,500 families, many of them Sandy Creek Baptists, had departed from North Carolina since the Battle of Almance the year before. Among the churches organized by these emigrants were five in Tennessee which for several years belonged to Sandy Creek but afterward formed the Holston. In 1805, when minutes were printed for the first time, there were 18 churches in North Carolina counties Montgomery, Anson, Rowan, Orange, Moore, Chatham, Randolph, Guilford, and Richmond. Luther Rice visited the association in 1816; in 1830 it "heard with pleasure" of the organization of the Baptist state convention of North Carolina.

In 1869 seven churches were released to join in forming Mt. Zion Association. South Sandy Creek, the last of several other divisions of Sandy Creek, was formed in 1949, leaving Chatham and Lee counties in the old association. In 1954, 33 churches reported 291 baptisms, 7,642 members, $303,383 total gifts, $46,460 mission gifts, $1,015,550 property value, and $14,403 church debt.

SANDY RUN. Organized Nov. 27, 1890, at Bethel Church, Ellenboro, by 19 churches dismissed for that purpose by Green River and King's Mountain associations. The abstract of principles of the latter was adopted that day. After the loss of some territory in the meantime, Sandy Run by 1954 included Polk and southern Rutherford counties. In 1954, 60 churches reported 637 baptisms, 18,554 members, $583,477 total gifts, $106,555 mission gifts, $2,388,763 property value, and $133,470 church debt.

SOUTH FORK. Organized when the Catawba River Association, which extended for 100 miles along the river for which it was named, divided in 1878, the western part retaining the name. The 10 eastern churches sent delegates to Kid's Chapel, Lincoln County, Nov. 22, 1878, to organize South Fork. In 1891 an associational newspaper, the *Baptist Worker*, was established, and on Sept. 2, 1903, the association opened South Fork Institute in Maiden. The Gaston County churches withdrew in 1919, leaving Catawba and Lincoln counties. In 1954, 63 churches reported 788 baptisms, 16,182 members, $802,856 total gifts, $140,727 mission gifts, $3,381,630 property value, and $422,768 church debt.

SOUTH MOUNTAIN. Organized Nov. 2–4, 1911, at Mt. Vernon Church by 16 churches in Cleveland, Burke, and Catawba counties, nine of them formerly in Catawba River Association. In 1954, 30 churches reported 233 baptisms, 4,712 members, $132,350 total gifts, $9,671 mission gifts, $532,386 property value, and $54,289 church debt.

SOUTH SANDY CREEK. Organized Oct. 24, 1949, at the First Baptist Church of Carthage by 19 churches, 17 of which had requested dismissal from Sandy Creek because it comprised "a large and scattered territory." The new organization was essentially a county association for Moore. In 1954, 22 churches reported 171 baptisms, 3,880 members, $134,648 total gifts, $16,096 mission gifts, $542,877 property value, and $30,462 church debt.

SOUTH YADKIN. Formed Oct. 17, 1873, at New Hope, Iredell County, by 12 churches in Iredell, Davie, Rowan, and Mecklenburg counties, former territory of Yadkin. Mecklenburg and Rowan churches later formed county associations, leaving those in Iredell and Davie to comprise South Yadkin. In 1954, 36 churches reported 603 baptisms, 10,429 members, $443,521 total gifts, $70,891 mission gifts, $2,072,932 property value, and $298,654 church debt.

STANLY. Organized Dec. 5, 1885, at Silver Springs Church by eight Stanly County churches which had requested dismissal from Pee Dee and Rocky River associations to form a compact county unit. In 1954, 45 churches reported 449 baptisms, 10,588 members, $412,-521 total gifts, $53,828 mission gifts, $2,074,750 property value, and $212,600 church debt.

STONE MOUNTAIN. Formed Nov. 19, 1897, at New Covenant Church, Dockery, by eight churches, five formerly in Elkin Association. Although located in an area of strong Primitive Baptist influences, Stone Mountain co-operated with the Baptist state convention from the first and adopted articles of faith Nov. 19, 1897. This body was one of five associations located in Wilkes County by 1954. In 1954, 27 churches reported 129 baptisms, 4,340 members, $55,681 total gifts, $5,695 mission gifts, $239,050 property value, and $11,878 church debt.

STONY FORK. Organized at Stony Fork, Watauga County, Nov. 9, 1860, by delegates from Buffalo Cove, Cool Spring, Elk, Stony Fork, and Yellow Hill churches. An abstract of principles was adopted Nov. 10. Although including churches in Wilkes, Watauga, and Caldwell counties in the early years, by 1954 Stony Fork was confined to the western part of Wilkes. In 1954, 20 churches reported 131 baptisms, 2,112 members, $13,811 total gifts, $1,461 mission gifts, $70,700 property value, and $3,179 church debt.

SURRY. Formed along county lines Aug. 13, 1903, at Richmond Church by 19 churches in former Yadkin territory. Convenience in travel was the reason given for wanting a compact group. The association adopted articles of faith the first day. In 1954, 65 churches reported 529 baptisms, 11,477 members, $296,461 total gifts, $34,684 mission gifts, $1,073,340 property value, and $84,548 church debt.

TAR RIVER. Organized in 1830, with the first regular session at Sandy Creek, Franklin County, in Oct., 1831. The churches of Quankey, Rocky Swamp, Fishing Creek, Mearn's Chapel, Sappony, Peach Tree, Red Bud, Sandy Creek, and Maple Spring had withdrawn from the Kehukee because of its action in 1827 declaring non-fellowship with churches engaged in missionary operations. They combined with Haywood's, Flat Rock, Shiloh, and Sandy Grove of Raleigh Association to form the Tar River, with territory including Franklin, Nash, and Halifax counties. On Oct. 3, 1874, articles of faith adopted prior to that time were ordered printed in the minutes. In 1907, with churches numbering nearly 100, Tar River divided at the Atlantic Coast Line Railroad, and the 49 churches east of that line formed the Roanoke. In 1954, 62 churches in Franklin, Vance, and Warren counties reported 587 baptisms, 16,630 members, $375,502 total gifts, $71,206 mission gifts, $1,956,-368 property value, and $126,917 church debt.

TENNESSEE RIVER. Formed in 1862 from the Tuckaseigee. By 1884 the association had adopted articles of faith, had 24 churches, an associational missionary, and a high school called Valley River. In 1954, 45 churches in Graham and western Swain counties reported 222 baptisms, 7,162 members, $79,842 total gifts, $9,423 mission gifts, $338,300 property value, and $60,000 church debt.

THREE FORKS. Organized Nov. 5, 1841, when ten churches dismissed by Mountain Association in Sept., 1841, met by delegates at Three Forks of the South Fork Church, Ashe County. A Calvinistic abstract of principles was adopted the next day. Later there were churches in Ashe, Watauga, Caldwell, and Johnson (Tennessee) counties, much the same territory as that covered by Stony Fork, whose members sympathized with the North. In 1879 Three Forks declined to combine with Stony Fork but agreed to "live together in christian love." In 1954, 45 churches in Watauga County reported 313 baptisms, 8,496 members, $159,119 total gifts, $17,996 mission gifts, $776,600 property value, and $45,286 church debt.

TRANSYLVANIA. Organized in 1863 at Little River by Henderson and Transylvania county churches which had come out of Salem Association. In 1877 six Henderson churches withdrew to join in forming Carolina Association. Five years later the parent body reorganized as Transylvania County Baptist Association. In 1954, 30 churches reported 217 baptisms, 5,355 members, $143,417 total gifts, $36,136 mission gifts, $338,600 property value, and $23,268 church debt.

TUCKASEIGEE. Organized Nov. 6, 1829, at Cullowhee Meeting House by delegates from Locust Old Field, Waynesville, Cullowhee, Mt. Zion, Cowee, Franklin, and Head of Tennessee churches, the territory extending from Madison County to Rabun County, Georgia. Articles of faith were adopted the next day. In 1859 the association formed the Tuckaseigee United Baptist Book Society to supply the local need for Bibles. Four years later it established Tuckaseigee Baptist High School, Holly Springs, Macon County, to train ministers. Churches withdrew to form county associations such as Haywood (1886) and Macon (1903), until in 1954 only Jackson County churches remained. In 1954, 47 churches reported 339 baptisms, 8,212 members, $134,023 total gifts, $11,512 mission gifts, $566,-600 property value, and $43,631 church debt.

UNION III. Organized out of Brown Creek, Oct. 18, 1884, which changed its name to Union County Baptist Association, after Anson County churches had withdrawn to form a county association. In 1895 the association authorized establishment of Wingate School, which began operations the next year. In 1954, 52 churches reported 464 baptisms, 12,015 members, $354,-263 total gifts, $47,727 mission gifts, $1,142,250 property value, and $44,890 church debt.

WEST CHOWAN. Organized July 27, 1883, at Winton by 33 churches which had withdrawn from the Chowan. The West Chowan annually adopted strong resolutions in support of Chowan Baptist Female Institute and Wake Forest College. Since 1883 West Chowan has embraced the three-county area between the Chowan and Roanoke Rivers. In 1954, 60 churches reported 467 baptisms, 16,906 members, $512,697 total gifts, $123,098 mission gifts, $2,164,700 property value, and $46,155 church debt.

West Liberty. Organized by North Carolina members of Liberty and Ducktown Association after a period between 1899 and 1920 when Georgia and Tennessee churches had withdrawn from it. The reorganized body continued to use the founding date (1850) of the parent body. In 1954, 29 churches in west Cherokee County reported 175 baptisms, 3,568 members, $26,874 total gifts, $3,275 mission gifts, $56,200 property value, and $90 church debt.

Western North Carolina. Organized in 1885 in territory once belonging to Broad River and later to French Broad associations. Articles of faith adopted previously were printed in 1891. In 1954, 45 churches reported 260 baptisms, 7,389 members, $109,084 total gifts, $23,893 mission gifts, $492,184 property value, and $943 church debt.

Wilmington. Organized by 19 churches which secured dismissal from the Eastern in Oct., 1901, in the belief that it had become too large for effective work. The new smaller association was organized Nov. 14, 1901, at Burgaw. In 1954, 50 churches in Pender and New Hanover counties reported 879 baptisms, 15,237 members, $633,275 total gifts, $97,247 mission gifts, $2,868,175 property value, and $333,711 church debt.

Yadkin. Organized as a branch of the Strawberry Association of Virginia with the churches in the Yadkin River country first meeting in an associational capacity in 1786. During the 1788 session the terms of union agreed upon the year before by Regular and Separate Baptists at Dover Church, Virginia, were presented and adopted. The first meeting as an independent association occurred Aug. 28–30, 1790, at Eaton's Meeting House, Rowan (now Davie) County, with local missionaries appointed. The 14 churches represented were scattered from the Yadkin River westward to the Tennessee line, and from the Virginia line southward to the Catawba River. Realizing that the area was too large, Yadkin divided in 1797 by setting off the western portion as Mountain Association, which later became antimissionary. Since 1797, 31 associations have been formed from the Yadkin territory. Articles of faith based on the Philadelphia Confession were adopted in 1793 and printed at various times thereafter. In 1954, 31 churches, all in Yadkin County, reported 293 baptisms, 7,948 members, $167,737 total gifts, $26,933 mission gifts, $668,750 property value, and $37,601 church debt.

Yancey. Formed when Black Mountain changed its name to Yancey during the session of Sept. 6–8, 1888. Although agreeing at first to co-operate with the western Baptist convention, Yancey nevertheless instructed its delegates to that body to seek union of the western with the Baptist state convention. In 1893 Yancey withdrew from the western and announced co-operation with the state convention. In 1954, 33 churches reported 264 baptisms, 3,788 members, $72,384 total gifts, $10,524 mission gifts, $330,400 property value, and no church debt.

Yates. Organized Nov. 7, 1948, at the First Baptist Church of Durham by 34 churches which had secured dismissal from Mt. Zion Association. It was named for Matthew Tyson Yates (*q.v.*), one-time member of the association's Mt. Pisgah Church, Chatham County. Twenty-nine of the churches were located in Durham County. In 1954, 41 churches reported 695 baptisms, 20,184 members, $861,997 total gifts, $173,146 mission gifts, $3,896,850 property value, and $188,249 church debt.

II. Extinct. Abbott's Creek Union. Organized Nov. 12, 1825, at Liberty Meeting House, Davidson County, of churches formerly in Sandy Creek and Pee Dee associations. In 1829 "utmost harmony" prevailed among the 11 churches and 536 members. During the next three years, however, the antimissionary group captured the association and, on Sept. 24, 1832, denied seats to all delegates who favored objectives of the Baptist state convention. The excluded minority organized the Liberty Association; the majority continued to function as a Primitive Baptist association.

Alleghany. See Alleghany and Grayson.

Anson I. Formed on Dec. 8, 1882, when 12 Anson County churches which had recently obtained dismissal from the Pee Dee and Brown Creek associations met in convention in Wadesboro. In Oct., 1893, it combined with the Richmond Association to form the Pee Dee.

Ashe and Alleghany. Organized Sept. 24–25, 1886, by nine small churches in convention at Buffalo Church, Ashe County, at which time they adopted the abstract of principles. These churches had belonged to the New River Association, whose territory extended into Virginia, until John E. Ray, secretary of the Baptist state mission board, persuaded them to form a new association in co-operation with the Baptist State Convention of North Carolina. Because of the "great area occupied," the association voted in 1897 to divide at the county line. The Ashe and the Alleghany and Grayson associations were established.

Atlantic I. Organized Oct. 29, 1884, when delegates from 20 churches which had obtained dismissal from Eastern Association met at La Grange; they adopted the New Hampshire Confession of Faith. The Atlantic embraced the territory from Wayne County to the ocean and from Pamlico River to New River. In 1899 it divided into eastern and western portions, the latter forming Neuse Association. In 1907 the Neuse and Atlantic combined as Neuse-Atlantic.

Bethel. Formed in 1789 from the Congaree,

including churches in the Rutherford County area of North Carolina and in adjoining South Carolina districts. The Broad River of North and South Carolina and other associations were later formed from the Bethel.

Big Ivy. Organized after the division, in the 1820's, of the French Broad Association on the doctrine of election. Stephen Morgan, an ardent Calvinist and leader of the United Baptists, succeeded in excluding Garrett Deweese, who opposed belief in election. The Deweese group, calling themselves Separate Baptists and accepting the evangelical teachings of Shubal Stearns, organized the Big Ivy Oct. 6, 1829, at Union Meeting House. Articles of faith were adopted that day. By 1841 there were 14 churches scattered over the triangle formed by Yancey and Macon counties and Spartanburg District, South Carolina. In 1848 the French Broad agreed to adopt the Big Ivy articles of faith which repudiated the doctrine of election, and the next year the two associations consolidated under the name French Broad, with the evangelical program of the Big Ivy.

Black Mountain. Organized at Zion Church, Yancey County, in Oct., 1870, after the Roan Mountain voted in Sept. to divide along the line formed by the turnpike from Marion to Tennessee. The Black Mountain, organized by churches south of the line, was superseded in 1888 by the Yancey.

Broad River. Organized in Nov., 1800, when delegates from nine North Carolina and seven South Carolina churches convened at Sandy Run Meeting House, now Cleveland County. The Bethel had dismissed 14 of these churches for that purpose. Broad River Association extended from the Catawba River to Tennessee, a region now occupied by 22 associations. The withdrawal in 1851 of the King's Mountain Association virtually ended the union in this area of churches of the two states. The Broad River abstract of principles modified the Calvinism of the Philadelphia Confession. It was widely copied in that area and by emigrants moving west and southwest.

Brown Creek. Organized at the Monroe Church by delegates from five former members of the Moriah (South Carolina) and Pee Dee associations Oct. 20, 1855, although a preliminary meeting had been held the year before. A declaration of principles was adopted that day. In 1882 six of the Anson churches withdrew to form a county association, whereupon, the name of the parent body, limited largely to Union County, was changed to Union Baptist Association.

Cape Fear. Organized in Oct., 1805, at Saddletree Meeting House (later called Union), Robeson County, after a division of the Neuse. In 1806 member churches were in Bladen, Brunswick, Cumberland, Duplin, New Hanover, Onslow, Robeson, and Sampson counties. The Cape Fear continued to use the Philadelphia Confession of Faith in the form previously adopted by the Neuse. In 1825 the Cape Fear "calmly agreed" to allow the churches east of the Black and Coharie rivers to form the Goshen, even though the Cape Fear was left "reduced and prostrated." Immediately following the session of Oct. 20–23, 1898, the Cape Fear, with 24 churches in Brunswick, Bladen, Columbus, and Horry (South Carolina) counties, united with Columbus as the Cape Fear–Columbus.

Cape Fear–Columbus. Organized in 1898 by the union of the Cape Fear, 24 churches, and the Columbus, 18 churches. The first session of the united body convened at Bogue Chapel, Columbus County, Nov. 16, 1899. By 1936 most of the churches outside Columbus County had withdrawn to join county associations, whereupon the name of the parent body was changed to Columbus on Oct. 22.

Cedar Creek. Organized Nov. 26–28, 1858, at Cedar Creek Church, Cumberland County, by 10 churches in Cumberland, Sampson, and Robeson counties—largely territory of the Cape Fear. As late as 1869 one fourth of the 2,876 members were Negroes. After several churches had withdrawn to join the South River, Robeson, and other associations, the Cedar Creek changed its name to Cumberland in 1908.

Central. Organized in the newly formed Forestville Church Oct. 25, 1860, by delegates from six churches holding letters of dismissal from the Tar River, Raleigh, and Flat River associations. A committee was appointed the next day to prepare an abstract of principles but its report did not appear in the minutes. The Central embraced parts of Wake, Granville, Franklin, and Vance counties; and in 1944, with 35 churches, it united with Raleigh, 34 churches, under the name of the latter.

Charleston. Organized in 1751 in South Carolina, the first Baptist association in the South. Ten of the 19 churches in the Charleston in its first decade were located in North Carolina. In fact, nearly all North Carolina's Regular Baptist churches were members until they began to form their own associations.

Country Line. Formed in May, 1806, when Flat River Association agreed to divide on a north-south line through Person County, with the 10 churches west of this line in Person, Caswell, Rockingham, and Orange counties organizing the Country Line. For the next 25 years Country Line was a missionary body, but in 1832, through the influence of James Osbourn and John Stadler, "this association declared non-fellowship with all the benevolent societies of the day."

Cumberland. Organized at the beginning of the present century as the Cedar Creek Association by churches in Cumberland County and adjacent areas. Most of the churches outside Cumberland having withdrawn to join county units, the parent body abandoned the old name in 1908 and on Oct. 13–15, 1909, reorganized as the Cumberland. On Mar. 24, 1924, the Cumberland consolidated with South River as the New South River.

GOSHEN. Organized Oct. 26, 1827, after the Cape Fear divided at Big Coharie River, Sampson County, in 1826. Delegates of the 20 churches east of the line met at Beulah Church, Sampson, to form the association. Since the "Neuse had become very weak and was fast disintegrating," Goshen proposed in 1843 to unite all churches between Wilmington, New Bern, and Goldsboro into "one strong body." This was done in 1844 under the name Union.

HENDERSON. Organized Oct. 19, 1882, as a county association by 11 churches in the same territory as that covered by the Carolina. On Nov. 5, 1886, at Refuge Church Henderson and Carolina associations united under the name of the latter.

HIWASSEE. Organized in 1849. At its fifth annual session, Sept. 23–26, 1853, Hiwassee had 16 churches in North Carolina, 16 in Georgia, and two in Tennessee. Representatives from Tuckaseigee, Mountain, and other associations attended this session, but correspondence with Union, which had repudiated the doctrine of election, was refused.

HOLSTON. Formed in 1786 by seven Separate Baptist churches which had been organized by followers of Shubal Stearns (*q.v.*). The Philadelphia Confession of Faith was adopted, and the distinction between Separates and Regulars soon abandoned. Located along what became the North Carolina–Tennessee line, the Holston in 1807 dismissed three churches to join in the formation of the French Broad.

JEFFERSON. Organized at Liberty Chapel, Ashe County, Oct. 27–30, 1848, by six transmontane churches which had secured dismissal from Brier Creek. It adopted articles of faith Oct. 30. In 1869 Jefferson invited the United Baptist and Lebanon associations to join in "a larger and stronger Association, upon Missionary principles." Accordingly, delegates from the three met at Baptist Chapel, Ashe County, on June 10, 1870, and agreed to form the New River, with mission sentiment not to be a test of fellowship.

KEHUKEE. Organized out of the Charleston Association, formed by three South Carolina churches in 1751. Sixteen other churches, 10 of them in North Carolina, joined Charleston within a decade, but the distance of the North Carolina churches from Charleston prompted their withdrawal to form an association of their own. The organizational meeting of Kehukee convened Nov. 6, 1769, at Kehukee Church in Halifax County, with five churches, all Regular Baptist, represented at the initial meeting: Kehukee, Bertie (Sandy Run), Falls of Tar River, Toisnot, and Pitt (Red Banks). The Philadelphia Confession of Faith was adopted during the first session.

The association grew rapidly, adding churches, some Regular, others Separate, in North Carolina and Virginia, but in 1775 the Kehukee divided over the question as to whether the rule requiring faith as a prerequisite to baptism should apply to persons already members of the churches. The reformers, led by Lemuel Burkitt (*q.v.*), with a slight majority, insisted that the churches be purged of all members baptized in unbelief. With both sides claiming the name Kehukee, two organizations existed until 1779, when some of the nonreforming churches joined the new body, and the name became the United Baptist Association, formerly called the Kehukee Association. A decade later the last of the nonreforming churches came in and Kehukee became once more the official name.

By 1790 there were 61 churches in the Kehukee, which stretched from the James River to the South Carolina line and as far west as Wake County. In that year the 19 Virginia churches received permission to form Portsmouth Association. Three years later a division along the Tar River was approved, with the 23 churches to the south forming the Neuse. In 1805 the churches northeast of the Roanoke River formed the Chowan.

Until the late 1820's Kehukee remained in friendly correspondence with other missionary associations and the board of managers of the Baptist Board of Foreign Missions. But in 1827 "it was agreed that we discard all Missionary Societies, Bible Societies, and Theological Seminaries, and the practices heretofore resorted to for their support, in begging money from the public." The next year only 22 of the 35 churches represented in 1827 sent delegates indicating the withdrawal of missionary churches had begun. After the Civil War the parent body adopted the name Kehukee Primitive Baptist Association.

LEWIS FORK. Formed Sept. 30–Oct. 2, 1836, at Lewis Fork Church, Wilkes County, by seven former members of Yadkin, Brier Creek, and Catawba River associations. An abstract of principles was adopted during the first session. On Nov. 12, 1859, Lewis Fork combined with Lower Creek and Taylorsville, temperance associations, to form the United Baptist. Some of the churches in the new body became dissatisfied and reorganized the Lewis Fork in 1863, operating separately for nine years. In 1872 United Baptist and Lewis Fork merged to form the Brushy Mountain.

LIBERTY AND DUCKTOWN. Organized in 1850. At the 41st session, Sept. 29, 1892, the association numbered 25 churches in North Carolina, Tennessee, and Georgia. Tennessee and Georgia churches later withdrew. The 1955 West Liberty Association, dated from 1850, continued the old organization.

LOWER CREEK. Organized Mar. 18, 1854, at Liberty Church, Caldwell County, by delegates from 13 churches, 11 of them released by Lewis Fork. An abstract of principles was adopted at this time. In 1859 Lower Creek united with Taylorsville and Lewis Fork to form a strong missionary and temperance association known as the United Baptist.

MECKLENBURG AND CABARRUS. Organized in 1885 at Clear Creek Church by seven churches in former territory of the Rocky River, Brown Creek, and South Yadkin associations. Four additional churches joined during the first annual session, Oct. 14–16, 1886. When the Cabarrus churches withdrew to form a county association in 1935, the parent body changed its name to Mecklenburg.

MOUNTAIN. Organized in Oct., 1797, when Yadkin dismissed Lewis Fork, Beaver Creek, Head of the Yadkin, Globe, and six other churches west of these four to form it. Most of the churches lay west of the Blue Ridge in the present Ashe, Alleghany, and Watauga counties. In 1836 the Mountain declared itself antimissionary and discontinued correspondence with associations which refused to adopt this view.

MOUNTAIN UNION. Formed in 1867 by about 20 churches in Ashe and Alleghany counties in North Carolina, and Grayson County, Va. These churches had withdrawn from Mountain Association to demonstrate their sympathy with the cause of the Union Government. Individual members wore the red string emblem of the Union League and were called "Redstring Baptists." Indefinite in its stand on missions, the association recommended the *Biblical Recorder,* offered membership to "any regular Baptist church," and adhered to a constitutional provision that "the benevolent institutions of the day shall be no bar nor test to fellowship." Articles of faith adopted previously were printed in 1896.

NEUSE I. Organized in 1793 when the Kehukee divided on a line along the Tar River, the 23 churches south of the line forming the Neuse. Six years later there were 29 churches in an area bounded by Beaufort, Wake, Cumberland, and Brunswick counties. Neuse held that a "Baptist Association . . . arrogates no higher a title than that of an Advisory Council." On Oct. 19, 1805, all churches south of the White Oak River and some of those between the White Oak and the Neuse were released to form Cape Fear Association. Active in support of cooperative ventures, the Neuse contributed to the Baptist Philanthropic Missionary Society and sent delegates to the General Meeting for Correspondence which convened at the Falls of Tar River. In 1830 the Neuse divided on the question of missions, the majority remaining missionary and retaining the name. Doctrinal views, which had always been based on the Philadelphia Confession, were clarified in a new statement drawn up in 1832. In 1844 the Neuse combined with the Goshen to form the Union Association.

NEUSE II. Organized at La Grange, Oct. 26, 1899, by 22 churches which the Atlantic had dismissed on Oct. 12. These churches were located in Wayne, Greene, Lenoir, Pitt, Jones, and Craven counties, but the Neuse did not include all Baptist churches in those counties. It adopted the New Hampshire Confession of Faith. In Nov., 1907, in order to have "meetings of greater power," the Neuse and Atlantic reunited as the Neuse-Atlantic.

NEUSE-ATLANTIC. Formed Nov. 5, 1907, at Middle Street Church, New Bern, by combining the Neuse and Atlantic associations. It divided in 1929 into two associations named Neuse and Atlantic.

NEW RIVER. Organized in Oct., 1870, at Mt. Pleasant Church, Ashe County, by about 13 churches formerly belonging to Jefferson, United Baptist, Mountain Union, and Lebanon (Virginia) associations. Believing they should affiliate with their own state organization, the North Carolina churches withdrew in 1886 and formed the Ashe and Alleghany Association.

PAMLICO I. Organized Nov. 28, 1851, at Parker's Chapel, Pitt County, by delegates from 17 churches, six formerly belonging to Union Association. Articles of faith were adopted the next day. The territory embraced 10 counties between Wayne and the Albemarle Sound. Except for army colportage carried on by N. B. Cobb, associational work dropped to a low point during the war. The clerk reported in 1870 that the "destitution . . . within the limits of our borders is absolutely appalling." Pamlico dissolved in 1872.

PAMLICO II. Formed Oct. 12, 1932, by 12 churches released by the Chowan and Roanoke associations. The churches gave poor roads as the reason for wanting a smaller association; when the roads had been improved, Pamlico dissolved, Sept. 24, 1941, the churches returning to the parent associations.

PEE DEE I. Organized at Richland Creek Meeting House, Montgomery County, Oct. 19–21, 1816, after the Sandy Creek divided along a line formed by the Deep River, Oct. 28, 1815. Delegates from the approximately eight churches southwest of the line met to organize. Several churches withdrew in 1825 to join in the formation of Abbott's Creek. Four county associations superseded the Pee Dee during the 1880's: Anson, 1882; Stanly, 1885; Richmond, 1888; and Montgomery, 1889. Thus at the 74th session action occurred "dissolving the Pee Dee Association."

PROVIDENCE. Organized Nov. 3, 1871, by Cross Roads Church, Union County, the sole member, after the Brown Creek Association, in 1870, for reasons not given, declined to seat J. W. Davis, pastor of the Cross Roads Church. Providence adopted the confession of faith of the Welsh Neck Association, South Carolina; Brown Creek then excluded Cross Roads Church, and the subsequent history of the association is obscure.

RICHMOND. Organized in 1889 at Spring Hill Church by Richmond County churches which the Pee Dee dismissed Oct. 19, 1888. Although joined by some Scotland churches, Richmond numbered only seven congregations in 1892 and voted to combine with Anson. Accordingly, the two bodies united as the Pee Dee.

ROAN MOUNTAIN. Organized Oct. 5, 1849, after the French Broad released 11 churches, which joined others in forming the new association and adopted the Big Ivy articles of faith. In 1870 Roan Mountain divided along the turnpike from Marion to Tennessee. The churches north of that line retained the name; those to the south formed the Black Mountain. In 1884 Roan Mountain changed its name to Mitchell.

ROANOKE I. Organized Oct., 1788, adopting the Philadelphia Confession of Faith. During the 1790's several North Carolina churches in Granville, Person, Caswell, and Rockingham counties belonged to the Roanoke, primarily an association of Virginia churches.

ROANOKE II. Organized after the Tar River, numbering 93 churches, Oct. 7, 1907, voted to divide along the line formed by the Atlantic Coast Line Railroad, with the churches to the west retaining the name. Those to the east met at Rocky Mount on Oct. 13, 1908, to form the Roanoke, which embraced the territory from the railroad to the Roanoke River, a total of seven counties. In 1954, 94 churches reported 1,353 baptisms, 28,884 members, $1,008,033 total gifts, $218,155 mission gifts, $4,116,162 property value, and $276,228 church debt. On Oct. 17, 1955, at Scotland Neck Baptist Church the Roanoke held its final session, dividing into two new associations, North Roanoke and South Roanoke.

ROCKY RIVER. Organized Nov. 2, 1867, at Pleasant Grove by 11 churches in Mecklenburg, Cabarrus, Stanly, Rowan, and Union counties. After other county groups had withdrawn to form more compact bodies, the Rocky River dissolved in 1885 into two associations, churches northeast of the Rocky River forming the Stanly, those to the southwest, the Mecklenburg-Cabarrus.

SALEM. Organized in 1838 by nine churches released by the French Broad in Buncombe, Henderson, and Transylvania counties. On Aug. 13, 1848, after a period of disagreement, eight churches not accepting the doctrine of election withdrew to join in forming Union Association. In 1863 Salem churches formed Transylvania Association. The Salem dissolved at Hominy Church, Buncombe County, in 1882, the Buncombe and Henderson being formed from its territory.

SOUTH ATLANTIC. Formed, probably in 1887 (the second session was held Nov. 1–2, 1888, at Long Branch Church, Brunswick County), in the Cape Fear territory. It was absorbed by the Cape Fear in 1895.

SOUTH RIVER. Formed Nov. 30, 1877, at Bethel Church, Sampson County, by nine churches from Cedar Creek and one from Eastern. In 10 years there were 28 churches in Cumberland, Harnett, Johnston, and Sampson counties. On Oct. 24, 1923, committees from South River and Cumberland united the two associations as the New South River.

STRAWBERRY. Organized about 1776 with Virginia and North Carolina churches. The latter group withdrew to form Yadkin in 1790.

TAYLORSVILLE. Organized after two members of Little River Church, Alexander County, were excluded for joining the Sons of Temperance in 1851. These two and those who supported them formed the Taylorsville Church, which the next year united with eight other like-minded churches to form the association. Not a territorial grouping but a temperance association, it enrolled churches in Alexander, Wilkes, Ashe, Iredell, and Caldwell counties. In 1859 Taylorsville combined with the neighboring Lewis Fork and Lower Creek associations to form the United Baptist.

UNION I. Organized after Goshen Association proposed, in 1843, to unite all Baptist churches between Wilmington, New Bern, and Goldsboro into one strong body. The Neuse, a weak association located in this area, accepted the proposal. Accordingly, delegates met at Kenansville Church Oct. 4–7, 1844, and formed Union Association. By the beginning of the war there were 54 churches, 3,206 white and 1,772 Negro members. "In 1865 at Moore's Creek in deference to the sentiment of the Confederate soldiers the name of the Association was changed from Union to the Eastern."

UNION II. Organized Oct. 31, 1848, in a convention held at Boiling Springs Camp Ground, Henderson County, by seceders from Salem, Big Ivy, and Green River associations. The constitution of this body specifically repudiated the doctrine of election. After nine years Union accepted the doctrine of election and united with Salem.

UNITED BAPTIST. Formed Nov. 11–12, 1859, as a missionary and temperance body by combining the 26 churches of Lewis Fork, Taylorsville, and Lower Creek associations. An abstract of principles was adopted Nov. 12. Although some Baptists in this area were in sympathy with the North, the United Baptist in 1861 adopted a resolution favoring the formation of a Baptist company to serve in the Confederate Army. In 1862 Lewis Fork churches reorganized their association; later the other areas formed county units.

WACCAMAW. Organized in 1875, with churches in Columbus and Brunswick counties and South Carolina counties Horry and Marion. It endorsed the Baptist colleges and newspapers of both the Carolinas. By the turn of the century the North Carolina churches had formed county associations.

WEST BUNCOMBE. Organized Jan. 3, 1909, by seven churches in the territory of the French Broad, New Found, and Buncombe associations. In 1922 West Buncombe disbanded, the 10 churches joining neighboring associations.

HENRY SMITH STROUPE

NORTH CAROLINA BAPTIST. Established by T. B. Newberry of Fayetteville, owner and managing editor, with W. B. Oliver, pastor of the First Baptist Church, Fayetteville, chief contributing editor, it was first issued Jan. 28, 1891. The stockholders organized in 1891. A year later John A. Oates became managing editor, purchased the paper's property, and continued as editor until the *North Carolina Baptist* was sold to and consolidated with the *Biblical Recorder,* official organ of the state convention, in Feb., 1908.

North Carolina Baptist was published during the period when the Gospel Mission Movement was rife in the state, and many contributions to the paper criticized the organized work of the convention. When Oates gained control, however, he was loyal to the denomination's work and used the editorial columns of the paper in a constructive way. An earnest advocate of prohibition, he influenced citizens to vote for prohibition in North Carolina.

Prior to 1907 a resolution had been introduced at a meeting of the state convention asking that a joint stock company be organized to publish *Biblical Recorder* and, if felt wise, to buy *North Carolina Baptist* and consolidate it with the *Recorder*. After satisfactory arrangements were made with Oates, the Recorder Company purchased *North Carolina Baptist*.

L. L. CARPENTER

NORTH CAROLINA BAPTIST FOUNDATION. Established as the result of a recommendation made to the Baptist state convention in 1919 that the president name a committee of five Baptists whose duty it shall be: "(1) to direct the application and distribution of any funds made available before the next session of the Convention; and (2) to take under consideration the whole matter of promoting gifts by deed or will or otherwise to Baptist causes and report with recommendations to the next session of the Baptist State Convention." The committee's report to the 1920 session of the convention, containing a proposed charter and by-laws, recommended

(1) that the Convention name five to become the incorporators, (2) that it authorize the incorporators to adopt the by-laws suggested in this report, and (3) that it authorize the holding of a State-wide conference or a series of conferences still further to acquaint the Baptists, particularly the ministers, lawyers and business men, with the objects and aims of the Foundation.

In 1922 the directors of the North Carolina Baptist Foundation made their third annual report to the state convention, and have continued to make yearly reports since that time. Assets totaled $225,285.29 on June 30, 1954.

M. A. HUGGINS

NORTH CAROLINA BAPTIST HISTORICAL COMMISSION. Attention was called to the need for such a commission by Charles E. Maddry, secretary of the North Carolina Baptist convention, in his report in 1921, which said, "Baptists have, through all the ages, been great makers of history, but have always been reluctant to record and preserve what they have done. It is high time that something official was done to gather and organize the wealth of historical data and information that may now be found throughout the State." Following this report and a recommendation, the convention created the historical commission, composed of five members.

The new commission, instructed to locate its headquarters at Wake Forest College, deposited collected material in the college library. An appropriation of "as much as three hundred dollars" was made to enable the commission to function, and in 1922 it became a regular department of the state board. In its report to the convention that year the commission called attention to the urgent need to produce and publish prior to the convention's centennial in 1930 a "complete history of the Convention." By 1929 the manuscript of "Our Baptist History by G. W. Paschal (*q.v.*) was about completed," and the general board was instructed to proceed with publication to have it ready for the centennial meeting of the convention the following year. Paschal's second volume of *A History of North Carolina Baptists* was published in 1955.

In its attempt to locate historical materials, the commission, to its surprise, found the convention minutes of 1862 and 1864 in the library of Colgate University after all efforts to discover them in the state had failed.

M. A. HUGGINS

NORTH CAROLINA BAPTIST HOSPITALS, INC. Located in Winston-Salem, N. C., the hospital itself was planned and constructed under direction of a hospital commission authorized by the Baptist state convention and was opened to patients May 28, 1923. An agency of the convention, the hospital operates under a convention-elected board of trustees. Through 1954 inpatient admissions totaled 174,340 and outpatient visits, 425,610. Total patient income was $12,270,109.79, denominational income, $3,735,108.22, and other designated gifts, $4,371,392.87. The hospital consists of three buildings: the original hospital building with three major additions, the original nurses' home with one major addition, and a laundry building. Adjoined by the Bowman Gray School of Medicine of Wake Forest College, it rents two apartment buildings and two other buildings for housing nurses and house staff. With present properties valued at $4,754,595.09, the hospital has an indebtedness of $596,789.31, which is secured by pledges. A 418-bed hospital in 1954, it reported 175 nursing students, 13,375 inpatient admissions, and 54,378 outpatient visits. It is fully accredited and approved for internships. The hospital does not receive Negro inpatients; one of the largest all-Negro hospitals in the United States is located in Winston-Salem and operates well below capacity. In 1954 income from patients totaled $1,516,964.00; from the Cooperative Program, $69,528.58; and from other designated gifts, $358,047.31. The value of charity work was $500,494.33, plus free professional services for all service patients.

WILLIAM K. MCGEE

NORTH GEORGIA, GENERAL MISSIONARY BAPTIST ASSOCIATION OF. A regional association organized July 25, 1878, at Hopewell Church in Hall County. The organization meeting was held at the request of the Chattahoochee Association. Messengers were present from 42 churches of the Chattahoochee, Lawrenceville, Hightower, Clarkesville, Sarepta, and Tugalo associations.

The immediate impetus behind the new venture was the cause of missions. A letter of William C. Wilkes tells of the discussions in the Chattahoochee Association, in which it was pointed out that the body was "doing almost *nothing* to send the Gospel to those who have it not; and, for the last twenty-five years or longer, it has done little." The accomplishments of the general association appear to have been quite modest, as revealed in the following report on its projects:

It has given comfort to two aged, worn-out soldiers of the cross. It is sustaining a native Chinese preacher in a city of 700,000 inhabitants in a province of the empire of "the Anglo-Saxons of the East." It has an Indian preacher, O-las-se Chub-be, laboring successfully among the red men of the West. It assists in the education of young brother Pruitt, a student in the Southern Baptist Theological Seminary.

C. W. Pruitt was from the Concord Church in Forsyth County. His going as a missionary from the General Missionary Association was adjudged by Ragsdale as perhaps the most significant event in the history of the association. One other significant event in the history of the organization was the operating of Hiawassee High School, which was established in 1885.

Relations between Georgia Baptist convention and the General Missionary Baptist Association of North Georgia appear to have been cordial. Correspondents from the General Association were exchanged with the Georgia Baptist convention. Indicative of the cordial relationship is the fact that Fernando Coello McConnell (*q.v.*) served for a number of years as assistant secretary of Georgia Baptist convention while he was pastor of the church at Gainesville which was through the Chattahoochee Association connected with the General Missionary Association.

The last meeting of the General Missionary Association appears to have been the annual meeting of 1894 at Lawrenceville.

EDWIN JOHNSTON

NORTH GEORGIA BAPTIST COLLEGE. Opened in the old Fannin County Court House at Morganton, Ga., in 1900, a member of the Mercer system in the 1920's. The Home Mission Board, first interested in the school in 1906, built a girls' dormitory in 1915, but transferred the "Institute" to Fannin County school authorities in 1925. ARTHUR JACKSON

NORTH GREENVILLE JUNIOR COLLEGE. Located at Tigerville, S. C., at the foothills of the Blue Ridge, 20 miles northwest of Greenville, S. C., the school opened for the first session Jan. 16, 1893. It was first mentioned at a union meeting of the North Greenville Baptist Association Sept. 30, 1891, when the time allotted for missions was devoted to the discussion of a school, and a committee was appointed to report at the annual associational meeting Oct. 14, 1891. At this meeting articles for the organization of North Greenville High School provided for a board of trustees responsible for the school, which was to be directly under control of the association. A committee appointed to choose a location selected Tigerville, some of whose citizens donated 10 acres and $2,500 for the school. Benjamin Franklin Neves, a local businessman, contributed the 10 acres and $500, and his final contribution was made after his death when Neves' family offered his 525-acre farm to the school at appraisal value.

In Feb., 1892, a contract for the first building, a threeroom frame structure, was secured, and on the following Aug. 19 the building committee reported completion of the building and collection of $2,005, an amount which nearly matched the total spent for all causes by the association in 1891.

With Hugh Lafayette Brock as the first principal, the school enrolled approximately 80 students from primary to high school for the 1893 session. Subsequent principals since Brock include John Silas Miles Finch, 1896–98; Oscar J. Peterson, 1899–1901; S. Frank Boyles, 1902–03; William Fletcher Scott, 1904–05; Leslie Augustus Jones, 1906–10; John Dean Crain (*q.v.*), 1911–12; Leonard K. Simpson, 1913–18; Henry Clayton Hester, 1919–27; and Murphree Claude Donnan, 1928– .

In 1905 the Home Mission Board accepted North Greenville as a mountain mission school with no change in the relation of the association to the school. North Greenville was affiliated with the Home Mission Board and the general board of the state Baptist convention from 1919 to 1924, when it aligned itself with the Home Mission Board only; and in 1925 the association designated 20 per cent of its total receipts for the school. The amount was raised to 25 per cent of receipts in 1926, with 20 per cent of that amount applied to the debt of the school and 5 per cent used for current operating expenses. In 1928 the amount contributed by the association was raised to 50 per cent. Thus North Greenville operated until 1929, when it went under control of the general board of the state convention for operating expenses. In Nov., 1949, the association turned North Greenville over to the state convention, which has since that time provided for both operating expenses and capital needs. The budget for 1955 amounted to $185,694.68. North Greenville was chartered as a state high school in 1904, a Baptist academy in 1915, and a junior college in 1936.

Murphree Claude Donnan (b. near Pelham, S. C., Jan. 11, 1892), a Furman University and Southern Baptist Seminary graduate, served as the last principal of the academy and first president of the junior college. College work started in 1934 with 22 students, and approximately 1,000 students have graduated since 1936. The college offers work leading to the A.B. and B.S. degrees and a terminal course in commerce. Although the school is not accredited by the Southern Association, graduates have been accepted by all senior colleges where admission was desired. Total enrolment for 1955 was 362. Buildings, equipment, endowment, and 650 acres of land are valued at present at $650,633.

BIBLIOGRAPHY: J. K. Coleman, *State Administration in South Carolina* (1935). J. D. Crain, *A Mountain Boy's Life Story* (1914). E. C. Magruder, *A Historical Study of the Educational Agencies of the Southern Baptist Convention 1845–1945* (1951). Y. Snowden, ed., *History of South Carolina* (1920). J. A. Stoddard, "Backgrounds of Secondary Education in South Carolina," *Bulletin of the University of South Carolina* (1924). JEAN MARTIN FLYNN

NORTH MISSISSIPPI, BAPTIST GENERAL ASSOCIATION OF. Constituted at Oxford, Nov. 4, 1859, under the leadership of William Carey Crane (*q.v.*), then president of Semple-Broaddus College. Membership, not determined on a money basis, consisted of one delegate from churches and associations for every 100 members. After Crane left the state in 1860, the annual session that year at Grenada, headquarters for the association, evidenced marked frustration. Poor attendance and languid interest characterized the next session held at Okolora, which was the association's last meeting. J. L. BOYD

NORTH ROCKY MOUNT CHURCH, THE CASE OF. The subject of local church autonomy among Baptists was thrown into focus and given nation-wide notice through events involving the efforts of Samuel H. W. Johnston, pastor of North Rocky Mount Missionary Baptist Church, Rocky Mount, N. C., to lead his congregation to sever co-operative relations with all agencies and institutions connected with the Southern Baptist Convention. Decisions made in this case by the Nash County North Carolina Superior Court and later by the state Supreme Court raised the question as to whether the courts had erred and gone beyond the bounds of their proper jurisdiction, and infringed upon the realm of local church autonomy, held sacred by Baptists, in their decisions rendered in the case.

Organized in 1894, the North Rocky Mount Church constructed a building upon land which had been conveyed to its trustees by deed from W. C. Trevathan and his wife. Deed to the property was given "upon this special trust—that the trustees shall hold and possess said land for the especial use and behoof and benefit of the Missionary Baptist Church (white) of Rocky Mount and none other." Soon after organization the church affiliated with the district association in which it was located (the Tar River, later the Roanoke) and with the state and Southern Baptist conventions, connections which it maintained until Aug. 9, 1953. In Feb., 1952, the church called Johnston as pastor. He was formerly pastor of the Woodlawn Baptist Church in Pawtucket, R. I., a church affiliated with the Northern Baptist Convention. After a short pastorate he differed with the doctrines, customs, and practices of this church and instituted a movement to have the church withdraw its affiliation from the Northern Baptist Convention. Unsuccessful, Johnston resigned, and with 43 members of the church he established Emanuel Baptist Church of Pawtucket, which affiliated with the General Association of Regular Baptist Churches. He subsequently served as pastor of Park Avenue Baptist Church in Binghampton, N. Y., a church affiliated with the general association, and also served as instructor in a seminary supported by the association. When Johnston accepted the call to the North Rocky Mount Church, he told the church he would not attempt to change its denominational ties but would himself try to become a good Southern Baptist.

Soon after becoming pastor, Johnston began attacking the Southern Baptist Convention, charging that its agencies and institutions were heretical and apostate. By Apr., 1953, he disclosed his plan to ask the church to sever all connections with the district association and with the state and Southern Baptist conventions. On Sunday, Aug. 9, 1953, Johnston read to the church a resolution setting forth his charges against the Southern Baptist Convention and calling for immediate severance of all denominational ties. The resolution concluded with the statement, "Be it further resolved that after withdrawal the North Rocky Mount Baptist Church continue its ministry in this community as an Independent Missionary Baptist Church." Of the congregation present, 241 voted for the resolution and 144 against it; about 200 abstained from voting. Subsequently Johnston put out of office all members of the church who opposed his resolution.

G. C. Reed, W. H. Pittman, and Frank Taylor, trustees of the church, and A. J. Silberhorn, a deacon, brought suit against Johnston and those associated with him for recovery of the church property. The case was tried in Dec., 1953, in a special term of civil court, Nash County, N. C., with Malcolm Paul acting as judge and juror by agreement of both parties. Paul ruled

> that the individual defendents have ceased to be a part of the true congregation of the North Rocky Mount Missionary Baptist Church and are not entitled to share in the use and possession of the church property. That the plaintiffs and all other members of said church who adhere and submit to the regular order of the church, local and general, are the true congregation and entitled to the use and possession of the church property.

Defendants appealed, assigning errors, and the decision of the trial judge was reviewed by the North Carolina Supreme Court. Its decision, written by Justice R. Hunt Parker, stated,

While it is true the membership of the North Rocky Mount Missionary Baptist Church is a self-governing unit a majority of its membership is supreme and entitled to control its church property only so long as the majority remains true to the fundamental faith, usages, customs and practices of this particular church as accepted by both factions before the dispute arose.

A majority of the membership of the North Rocky Mount Missionary Baptist Church may not, as against a faithful minority divert the property of that church to another denomination or to the support of doctrines, usages, customs and practices of that particular church recognized and accepted by both factions before the dissension, for in such an event the real identity of the church is no longer lodged with the majority group but resides with the minority adhering to its fundamental faith, usages, customs and practices before the dissension who though small in numbers are entitled to hold and control the entire property of the church.

The court further stated that the lower court had decreed: "That the plaintiffs and all other members of said church who adhere and submit to the regular order of the church, local and general, are the true congregation." The supreme court then ruled:

That part of the judgment will be modified to read as follows: That the true congregation of the North Rocky Mount Missionary Baptist Church consists of the plaintiffs and all other members of the true congregation who adhere and submit to the characteristic doctrines, usages, customs and practices of this particular church recognized and accepted by both factions of the congregation before the dissension arose.

DOUGLAS M. BRANCH

NORTH TEXAS BAPTIST. A paper published for a brief tenure in Decatur, Tex. Its subscription list was transferred to the *Baptist Standard.* E. C. ROUTH

NORTH TEXAS BAPTIST COLLEGE. A school at Jacksboro, Tex., promoted by an "Educational Conference" in which Jack County, Macedonia, Wise County, Parker County, Montague County associations were represented. The school was opened in 1891 and was maintained until 1897, when it was sold for payments of debts. It once had 350 pupils.

BIBLIOGRAPHY: C. B. Wilson, "A History of Baptist Educational Efforts in Texas," 1829–1900 (1934).

RUPERT N. RICHARDSON

NORTH TEXAS BAPTIST ENCAMPMENT. Organized in 1921 and located at Woodlake, Tex., halfway between Denison and Sherman. Grayson County Association made arrangements with the Interurban Railroad to use its recreation property, grounds, and lake for the camp. J. E. ROTH

NORTH TEXAS BAPTIST MISSIONARY CONVENTION. A Texas general body organized at Allen, Tex., Oct. 19, 1879, by a group of Baptists who were dissatisfied by failure of the Baptist General Association of Texas to accept certain proposed changes in procedure. This convention hoped to align all the churches of north Texas but was unable to achieve its purpose. At its peak it claimed but 22 churches and its total contributions were nominal. With the 1883 session at Bells, Tex., its last, it recommended that its co-operating churches send messengers to the Baptist State Convention of Texas, which indicated that its chief grievance was the general association in the heart of whose territory it operated.

J. M. DAWSON

NORTH WILKESBORO INSTITUTE. A Baptist school at Wilkesboro, N. C., "owned, controlled, and taught by Baptists" at the turn of the 20th century. D. L. SMILEY

NORTHEN, WILLIAM JONATHAN (b. Jones County, Ga., July 9, 1835; d. Atlanta, Ga., Mar. 25, 1913). Governor of Georgia and denominational officer. Of Scotch-Irish ancestry, his parents were Peter and Louisa Northen. He was reared in Penfield, Ga., where Mercer University, which his father served as steward, was then located and from which he was graduated in 1853 at the age of 18. The LL.D. honorary degree was conferred upon him by Mercer in 1892, by Richmond College, Virginia, in 1894, and by Baylor College, Texas, in 1900. He married Martha Neel of Mt. Zion, Ga., on Dec. 19, 1860. They had two children.

Northen was a teacher in Mt. Zion Academy from 1854 to 1861. Then for four years (1861–65), he served as private in the Confederate Army, in a company of which his father was captain. After the war he returned to the Mt. Zion school and taught from 1865 to 1874. During the major portion of those 16 years of service at Mt. Zion, he was a school principal. From 1874 to 1890, he resided on his farm in Hancock County, because impaired health had compelled him to leave the classroom.

Successful at farming, he entered politics and was elected to the house of representatives in the Georgia legislature, (1877–78). A second term followed (1880–81). He introduced the local option prohibition bill. Then came a term in the state senate (1884–85), and a term in the presidency of the Georgia Agricultural Society (1886–88). He was elected to the governorship of Georgia for two terms (1890–94) and in the first election was unopposed. He was elected president of the Georgia Educational Society, 1894. From 1869 until his death in 1913, Northen was a member of the board of trustees of Mercer University. For 14 years (1896–1910) he was president of the Georgia Baptist Convention and concurrently (1899–1902) held the office of president of the Southern Baptist Convention. At the conclusion of his second term as governor (1894), he became manager of the Georgia Immigration and Investment Bureau. He edited *Men of Mark in Georgia* (1906–12, 6 Vols.). He was a charter member of Ponce de Leon Baptist Church,

Atlanta, chairman of the board of deacons, and teacher of an adult Bible class.

EDWIN S. DAVIS

NORTHERN BAPTIST CONVENTION. See AMERICAN BAPTIST CONVENTION.

NORTHERN KENTUCKY, BAPTIST HOME OF. A home for the aged, located in Newport, Ky., begun in June, 1951, when the Baptist churches of Campbell County and North Bend associations agreed to sponsor jointly such a project and purchased the property of the Campbell County Protestant Orphans Home for $75,000. The board of directors appointed by the associations secured the support of the churches in remodeling one of the two commodious buildings on the five-acre property. The home opened in July, 1952, with W. N. Carnes as superintendent of building and grounds and Mrs. Carnes as matron. During the first year it was filled to capacity with residents and convalescent patients. Because of the pressing need for nursing care, the directors floated a $100,000 bond issue in 1953, paid the current indebtedness on the property, and remodeled the other building on the grounds as a convalescent annex. Equipped with modern hospital furniture, this fireproof structure accommodates 21 patients, while the other provides a place for 16 permanent residents. With every room filled, the home maintains a long waiting list. Members of churches participating in the Northern Kentucky Baptist Unified Program of Campbell County and North Bend associations have preference although other applicants may be considered. The former must pay an entrance fee of $750 as permanent residents, the latter, $1,500. Residents thereafter pay a monthly fee for room, board, laundry, and nursing care. Daily rates are charged for patients in the convalescent annex. As of Mar. 31, 1956, the home had assets of $178,533.56, and plans were under way for the addition of a third building at the cost of approximately $60,000.

LEO DRAKE

NORTHWESTERN BAPTIST. A small biweekly paper published at Chicago, Ill., from 1842 to 1845 and edited by C. B. Smith, pastor of the Chicago Baptist Church.

LYNN E. MAY, JR.

NORTHWESTERN BAPTIST ASSEMBLY. Founded by Northwestern Baptist Association at Crystal Beach Park, Woodward, Okla., Aug. 22–26, 1938. Sessions in 1939–52 were held at Boiling Springs State Park, five miles northeast of Woodward. Several churches from Panhandle and Salt Fork associations participated in the assembly for several years. In 1954 it moved to a 40-acre tract of land two and one half miles northeast of Vici, Okla., given by Mr. and Mrs. Chester Smith. In 1955 registration was 94, and property value was $10,000. It is owned and operated by the Northwestern Association, which finances it with a $500 supplement from the Baptist General Convention of Oklahoma.

J. M. GASKIN

NORTON BENEFACTIONS, SOUTHERN BAPTIST THEOLOGICAL SEMINARY. For several generations the Norton family of Louisville, Ky., has been closely related to the history of the Southern Baptist Theological Seminary. The head of the family, William Norton (b. 1781) was a Pennsylvania Quaker who, as a young man, migrated to Kentucky, and later became a Baptist. His first son, George Washington Norton, was born in 1814 in the country near Russellville, Ky. Leaving home at the age of 14 to begin work, George W. Norton obtained employment in a Russellville store, earning $25 for the first year and $50 the following year. After four years the young man started a store of his own, with his brother John as partner. The undertaking succeeded, and through his experiences Norton learned the basic principles of sound business and developed leadership ability. On Christmas Day, 1832, George Norton and his brother John were baptized into the Russellville Baptist Church. A successful merchant, trader, financier, and banker, George Norton, as president of his bank, steered it safely through the turmoil of the Civil War. In 1867 he, with his family, moved to Louisville, Ky., to begin larger operations in private banking as G. W. Norton and Company. Rising to distinctive leadership in this larger business community and to greater usefulness in his church and denomination, Norton recognized the responsibilities and privileges of trusteeship under God. Eventually he became the first treasurer of the Southern Baptist Convention. From time to time his brothers, William F. Norton and Eckstein Norton, participated with him in varying financial ventures and in many philanthropic gifts, including gifts to numerous Baptist institutions and churches. William F. was associated in G. W. Norton and Company until their mutual retirement in 1885 to manage their own holdings. Eckstein Norton became president of the Louisville and Nashville Railroad Company in 1887 and eventually retired and moved to New York.

The practical insight of these generous brothers early discovered in the young Southern Baptist Theological Seminary of Greenville, S. C., an objective worthy of their best thought and beneficence, and there are logical indications that their influence had its part in the removal of the seminary to Louisville in 1876. Their gifts of $156,500 provided the erection of its first main administration and classroom building, known as Norton Hall, on Broadway at 5th Street in Louisville. More than half of this amount was given by George W. Norton. Through the influence of his sound business leadership, the amended charter of the seminary of Mar. 31, 1880, provides wisely for a financial board of five capable men, all of them now being trustees, to have custody and management of all endowment funds and investments of the seminary, to protect them against any loss. This structure, later copied by some other institutions, has fulfilled its purpose for approximately 100 years. The original sum, still intact, has earned substantial profit and produces a steady income. Among the first elected members of this financial board were George W. Norton and William F. Norton, with George W. Norton as the board's first chairman. Their portraits are hung in the entrance of the present Norton Hall.

After the death of George W. Norton in 1889, his son, George W. Norton II, took his father's place in many important relationships. He also served as chairman of the seminary's financial board and became the second treasurer of the Southern Baptist Convention. He endowed the Norton Lectureship of the seminary, bringing great Christian scientific men to the seminary to reconcile the research of science with the study of spiritually inspired truth. George W. Norton II was chairman of the building committee when the seminary prepared to move from downtown Broadway to its larger Lexington Road site, and it was his genius that brought to the present seminary buildings their architectural beauty and the loveliness of its spacious campus landscaping. He and his then living sisters, Lucie U. Norton and Mattie A. Norton, gave $150,000 toward the assurance of the seminary's permanence. This and many other gifts were always voluntary and unsolicited. Like his father, George W. Norton II was a highly honored leader in his community, and a source of strength and wisdom in all the seminary's affairs. He died in 1924, at 58 years of age. George W. Norton III was still a university student at the time of his father's death. After completing his studies at Yale and at Harvard Law School, however, he was soon able to follow in his father's footsteps in various capacities. Through election he became the third treasurer of the Southern Baptist Convention. For some years he served on the seminary's financial board, and is now a member of the executive committee of the seminary.

Mrs. Margaret M. Norton, the wife of George W. Norton II, encouraged her husband's loyalty and generosity in many forms to the seminary. After her death in 1950 her home and grounds were given to the seminary, as her will directed, in memory of her husband, George W. Norton II. In value this is the greatest single gift ever made to the seminary. The total value of the Norton gifts exceeds a million dollars.

F. A. SAMPSON

NORTON LECTURES. A series of lectures on "Science and Philosophy in Their Relations to Religion" delivered at Southern Baptist Theological Seminary, Louisville, Ky. The lectureship was established in 1910 by a gift of $5,000 from George W. Norton II (1865–1924); and an additional bequest from the will of his widow, Margaret McDonald (Muldoon) Norton (1883–1950), in 1950 increased the endowment to more than $15,000, from which the income provides lectures almost every year. The first lectures were delivered by Sir William M. Ramsay (1851–1939) of Aberdeen, Scotland, in 1910. The lecturer for the 1954–55 session was Harold Henry Rowley, professor of Old Testament, University of Manchester, England; for 1955–56, William Foxwell Albright, professor of Semitic languages, Johns Hopkins University, Baltimore, Md. The lectures generally consist of a series of four addresses on a common topic delivered in the seminary chapel during a designated week. Manuscripts of all lectures since 1915 are on deposit in the seminary library, and some of the lectures have been published.

H. C. GOERNER

NORWAY, BAPTISTS IN. The first Baptist church in Norway was organized in Skien in Apr., 1860, with eight members. Pioneers among the early Baptists were Frederick L. Rymker (Dane), Gotfred Hübert (Norwegian), and O. B. Hansson (Swede). In 1956 the Baptist Union comprised 65 churches and 115 preaching stations, with a total membership of about 8,000. The co-operative work is organized in five district associations. A general conference is held annually. There are about 85 Sunday schools, 400 teachers, over 5,000 members.

The Norwegian Baptist Woman's Missionary Union, organized in 1915, has about 150 societies; contributes especially to foreign mission work in Belgian Congo. The Youth Association, organized in 1922, comprising 30 societies and 115 Primary and Junior groups, publishes its own paper, *Ungdomsbanneret.* Scout work was organized in 1947.

The Home Mission Society promotes evangelistic work in co-operation with the district associations, supplements the salary of mission pastors, and sponsors the ministers' retirement pension fund. The Foreign Mission Society began work in the Belgian Congo (Uélé) in 1918 and now supports about 35 Norwegian missionaries and several hundred national workers serving in four mission centers, three dispensaries, one mission school, one teachers' academy, and about 150 grade schools. The churches connected with the mission now have about 6,000 baptized members.

In co-operation with Swedish and Danish Baptists, the Norwegian Union organized the Scandinavian Seamen's Mission in 1946 and opened the Seamen's Home in San Francisco. In 1951 a boat was acquired for mission work among the people on the islands along the Norwegian coast. Three thousand of these islands have a population of 300,000. The Fishermen's Home in Hammerfest was destroyed in the war but has now been rebuilt. Also in northern Norway the Baptists maintain a home for aged at Kasfjord and a youth center at Skjaerstad. The Baptist Union owns and operates an assembly ground and summer hotel at Langesund in southern Norway. A theological seminary was established in Oslo in 1910 and is the only free-church seminary in Norway. Plans are ready for an adequate campus near Oslo, where the seminary will be co-ordinated with a folk high school. The ministers' society, *Adelfia,* is composed of all recognized Baptist preachers in Norway. The publication society, *Norsk Literaturselskap A.S.,* publishes the weekly Baptist paper *Banneret,* a Sunday school paper, and many books. The Baptist headquarters' office is in Oslo (Hausmannsgaten 22).

BIBLIOGRAPHY: I. Barnes, *Truth Is Immortal* (1955). *Det Norske Baptistsamfunds Aarbok* (1953). J. D. Franks, *European Baptists Today* (1952).

JOSEF NORDENHAUG

NORWEGIAN BAPTIST CONFERENCE OF AMERICA, THE. Organized in Fargo, N. Dak., Nov. 17–20, 1910, to promote co-operation between Norwegian churches and to supervise publication of literature, theological training, and the opening of new fields. Peder Stiansen was elected president; H. M. Anderson, vice-president; and E. P. Johnson, secretary. An official organ for the conference, *Missionaeren,* was published in 1911, with Stiansen as editor. Two years later the Norwegian Divinity House of the University of Chicago was organized, which became affiliated with Northern Baptist Theological Seminary in 1921. New work has since been opened in Montana, Washington, the Eastern states, and Canada; about 90 Norwegian churches have been organized. The conference, an associated organization of the American Baptist Convention since 1928, has accomplished its purpose with its churches now belonging to American associations; the conference will soon be dissolved. PEDER STIANSEN

NORWEGIAN BAPTIST FOREIGN MISSION SOCIETY (KONGOMISJONEN). Foreign mission agency of Baptists of Norway founded in 1915. The first missionary, Bernhard Aalbu, was sent to the Belgian Congo in 1919. The first permanent station was established in 1922 at Bondo, on the Welle River in the Uele district. Work has been expanded to include four main stations and 267 outstations. Educational and medical work has been developed, as well as the evangelistic program. In 1955 the mission had 107 schools for children, 54 Sunday schools, one seminary, and a teachers' academy. Six missionaries were assigned to educational work. At three polyclinics six nurses gave treatments numbering 149,361 during the year, and 400 lepers were under the care of the mission. Twenty missionaries were on the field, and three appointees were in preparation for service. There were 271 churches with a total membership of 9,246, 241 native evangelists in the district, and 3,352 persons applied for baptism during the year. The budget for 1955 amounted to 418,935 Norwegian kroner. Hans Asak Kristiansen is director of the mission at the home base, with headquarters at Hausmannsgt. 22, Oslo, Norway. The missionary publication is called *Banneret.* EGIL A. BAEKKELIE

NOVATIANS. A sect begun by Novatian, theologian and presbyter of the Roman Church, upon his failure to secure the bishopric of Rome in 251. He developed the strict policy of refusing to readmit into the church those who denied the faith during the Decian persecution. Though excommunicated *c.* 257, he and his followers claimed to be the "true church" and compelled all who came from the Catholic Church to be rebaptized. They refused to recognize as valid the ministry and sacraments of their opponents, but maintained their own episcopacy and sacraments, retaining the Catholic doctrine of baptismal regeneration. The Novatian idea of the church as a community of saints distinguished them from Catholicism at large. Their churches became widespread in the Roman Empire. The movement persisted to the seventh century. LYNN E. MAY, JR.

NUNNERY MOVEMENT, OKLAHOMA. Landmark in nature and the only distinct movement of its kind in Oklahoma Baptist history, this movement was the result of a controversy in Oklahoma Baptist life. It was led by Alonzo Nunnery (b. Camden, Tenn., Sept. 8, 1861; d. Chickasha, Okla., Sept. 25, 1939), pastor of Baptist churches in southwestern Oklahoma, 1907–39, and editor of the *Baptist Worker.* Causes of the controversy were personal and policy disagreements between Nunnery and Franz Marshall McConnell (*q.v.*), corresponding secretary-treasurer of the Baptist General Convention of Oklahoma, 1916–22; convention purchase, 1919, of the *Baptist Messenger,* a rival publication of the *Baptist Worker;* Nunnery's opposition to convention policies in promotion of the 75 Million Campaign; Falls Creek Assembly; operational policies in the Oklahoma Baptist Orphans' Home; and the indisposition of convention leaders to deal with the John L. Hardin Hawkins case. The latter incident involved a series of violent attacks by Nunnery, orally and in print through the columns of the *Worker* and *A History of the Hawkins Matter,* in which serious moral charges were brought against Hawkins, an Oklahoma pastor, ranging all the way from intimations of indiscretion to flagrant charges of gross immorality, including adultery. Hawkins was repeatedly vindicated, aided measurably by McConnell, which intensified the tension between Nunnery and the convention, resulting in his being denied a seat in the 1918 and 1919 convention sessions. This led Nunnery to organize the Baptist Convention of Oklahoma at Chickasha, Oct. 5–6, 1920, with 101 messengers from 48 churches and 165 visitors present. The following year 38 churches reported 2,509 members, and the 1925 report shows 54 churches with 3,938 members. On Dec. 29, 1925, this body merged with the Baptist Missionary Association of Oklahoma (Landmark) when 18 men from 13 of its churches met with 32 men from 20 Baptist Missionary Association churches at Chickasha and formed the Baptist General Assembly of Oklahoma. The new body adopted a typical Landmark constitution of nine articles.

In 1926, 95 churches reported 6,174 members and $97,008 property value. That year the assembly assumed ownership of the orphanage which Nunnery had founded in 1921 at Chickasha and which had been operated by the Oklahoma Baptist Convention. Nunnery continued as superintendent. By 1927 he was the target of criticism by many Baptist Missionary Association preachers, and announced his intentions of ultimately resigning from the orphanage. But as friction mounted between him and Ben M. Bogard, Little Rock, Ark., Landmark leader, Nunnery led in the reorganization of the Oklahoma Baptist Convention when representatives from 21 churches met at Chickasha Dec. 27, 1927. The Landmarks filed suit for possession of the orphanage and, after a three-year court battle, won, ousting Nunnery and ending his prominence as a leader. Nevertheless, he continued as editor of the *Baptist Worker* until his death. From the first his movement was limited to rural and small town churches, and no published minutes exist after 1925.

BIBLIOGRAPHY: R. D. Hebard, "A. Nunnery Movement in Oklahoma" (Unpublished thesis).

ROGER D. HEBARD

NURTURE, CHRISTIAN. The process through which professed Christians are led toward the highest possible level of spiritual maturity. Baptists assume that an individual is not by nature a Christian, and that salvation must be an individual experience based upon a voluntary acceptance of Christ as Saviour through personal faith. Christian nurture, therefore, must follow the initial experience of faith with which the Christian life begins. Then, capitalizing upon man's innate capacity for growth, which is present at all age levels, training in Christlikeness may be effective.

The basis of this training is the Bible, which Baptists believe is the Word of truth as inspired by the Holy Spirit. Training based on the Word has been a vital part of religious education at least since Moses, who exhorted the children of Israel: "And these words . . . thou shalt teach . . . diligently unto thy children" (Deut. 6:6–7). Paul wrote to the Ephesians: "Bring them up in the nurture . . . of the Lord" (Eph. 6:4). The Bible opens to the Christian his most reliable way for direct contact with the expressed will of God and serves as the rule and guide by which the Christian can direct his way.

Religious education endeavors to set the individual in a progressive motion toward Christlikeness. Religious teaching seeks to instill the knowledge necessary to make right choices and an awareness of the consequences of wrong choices. It includes guidance in those experiences which will provide atmosphere, example, and satisfaction in Christian living. This program is realized best through the work of the individual church, under church supervision and control. Pupils are grouped according to common interests and needs, usually on the basis of age and sex. This grouping serves as a means of enlisting others of corresponding age, and facilitates the provision of activities for those of common interests. Activities include regular worship experiences which are suited to each age level and which allow participation by the pupil, small groups assembled in a classroom under the guidance of a qualified teacher for Bible study and discussion, an organized plan of study and expression of the basic fundamentals of New Testament Christianity, and a regular church worship experience under pastoral leadership.

JOE DAVIS HEACOCK

O

OAK HILL ACADEMY. A Baptist school at Oak Hill, Va., operated during World War I by the Alleghany Association, N. C. under J. C. Cox.

D. L. SMILEY

OAKLAND ACADEMY. Opened at Milltown, Ga., in 1906, sponsored by Valdosta Association, with L. R. Christie, founder. The school existed until 1911.

ARTHUR JACKSON

OFFICERS OF THE CONVENTION. The officers elected directly by the Convention are a president, a first vice-president, a second vice-president, two recording secretaries, and a treasurer. The officers are elected annually, but the president cannot serve more than two terms successively. The treasurer of the Executive Committee is also the treasurer of the Convention, but is elected by the Convention. In case of the death or disability of the president, the vice-presidents succeed in order of their election. The Convention elected four vice-presidents until 1931, when the constitution was amended to provide for the election of two vice-presidents.

PORTER ROUTH

OGBOMOSHO BAPTIST HOSPITAL. See Nigeria, Mission in.

OHIO, STATE CONVENTION OF BAPTISTS IN.—Southern Baptist work in Ohio began as a spontaneous movement brought about by the influx of Southern people into the state. Groups of these people in communities located in the southern area of the state, just across the river from Kentucky, began to feel the need of the type of church they had left in the South. As a result they organized several small Baptist congregations made up of people who were largely of Southern Baptist background. These churches soon came to desire a closer co-operative relationship. On Tuesday, Nov. 1, 1940, five of them organized the White Water Association of Southern Baptists. This body gained recognition by Kentucky Baptists as a district association affiliated with their general association. V. B. Castleberry served the Ohio association as missionary for nine years. When he resigned in 1952 to work with a group of churches in Indiana, the body consisted of 19 churches and 6 missions, with a combined membership of approximately 4,000.

This group, feeling the need for a statewide program of missions and evangelism that would establish the work in other areas of the state, began to pray and plan for a state convention. With this goal in mind and the encouragement of Kentucky Baptists and the Home Mission Board, the White Water Association called Ray E. Roberts as missionary in the summer of 1952. The body secured a home for Roberts in Dayton and set up temporary headquarters in Westwood Baptist Church. Through the co-operation of this church and their pastor, John Kurtz, who allowed the use of their basement building and a part-time secretary, the Southern Baptists of Ohio launched out into a statewide program of work. Within two years their work had grown to such an extent that they were able to organize a state convention.

Organization.—On Jan. 8, 1954, 160 messengers, representing 39 Southern Baptist churches in Ohio, assembled at the Westside Baptist Church of Hamilton and organized the State Convention of Baptists in Ohio. Eleven alternates and 247 visitors also attended the historic meeting. All but 5 of the 39 churches which became co-operating members of the new convention had been affiliated with the White Water Association, which dissolved and surrendered its name in order to co-operate on an equal basis with the other associations of the new state body. The messengers, after being duly recognized and seated, adopted the proposed constitution with some amendments. Southern Baptist leaders—Porter Routh, J. P. Edmunds, Samuel F. Dowis, Will Cook Boone, Eugene Siler, Lewis W. Martin, Eldred M. Taylor, and Courts Redford—appeared on the program and helped guide the organization of the convention. The body elected as officers John Kurtz, moderator; Orden Rice, first vice-moderator; E. A. Petroff, second vice-moderator; Bunyan Wallace, recording secretary; Omar T. Roberts, assistant recording secretary; Gerald K. Ford, historical secretary; and Ray E. Roberts, executive secretary-treasurer. The Ohio convention became the 23rd state convention to come into co-operative relationship with the Southern Baptist Convention.

District associations.—Upon the recommendation of the Committee on Boundaries of Associations, the convention voted to divide its territory into three district associations: the Southern, which would include Cincinnati and the surrounding area; Central, the area surrounding Dayton; Northern, Akron, Wadsworth, Cleveland, and surrounding areas. On Feb. 25, 1954, messengers from 14 churches met in Dayton at the North Dayton Baptist Church and organized the Central Association. The 20 co-operating churches in the southern part of the state organized the Greater Cincinnati Association at a meeting held in the Blue Ash Baptist Church, Mar. 16, 1954. Those in the north met four days later at the Main Street Baptist Church, Wadsworth, and formed the Erie Association with eight co-operating churches and missions. During the following year churches in the state constituted three other associations. Eight churches and seven missions organized the Scioto Valley Association at the Emmanuel Baptist Church, Jackson, on Jan. 28, 1955. Greater Miami Valley Association was organized on Mar. 11, 1955, at the Westside Baptist Church of Hamilton, with 13 churches. On Aug. 13, 1955, five churches and one mission formed the Maumee Valley Association at Faith Baptist Church, Toledo.

Departments and women's auxiliary.—The state convention, with headquarters in Columbus, has two departments. The Religious Education Department grew out of the religious education work begun by George W. Fletcher on June 1, 1953, as an employee of the original White Water Association. When the Southern Baptists of Ohio organized their convention, they continued this work and made Fletcher the head of the department. The Brotherhood Department originated when the executive board in Oct., 1955, approved John H. Ashcraft as state Brotherhood secretary on a part-time basis. Ashcraft began his work on Jan. 1, 1956. The women of the churches organized the Woman's Missionary Union of Ohio, Auxiliary to the State Convention of Baptists in Ohio, on Feb. 23, 1954. The organization established headquarters at Wadsworth. Near the end of 1954, this auxiliary reported 36 societies with an enrolment of 635, and 62 young people's organizations with 633 enrolled.

Institutions.—The executive board of the state convention on Oct. 12, 1954, voted to buy a 152-acre tract of land near Seneca Lake. The convention secured the property and has begun the development of Seneca Lake Baptist Assembly. Ashcraft has served as camp manager on a part-time basis. In 1955 the executive board set up a fund for the construction of a children's home. The churches make an annual Thanksgiving offering to this fund.

Missions and promotion.—The state convention has employed four missionaries to establish new missions and churches and to promote all phases of Southern Baptist work. George R. Gaddie, Darty Stowe, Paul Nevels, and Garvey Brand served in this capacity in 1956 in four areas of the state. The Home Mission Board has assisted the work in the state through supplementing the salaries of pastors of missions and new churches. Over 14 received such aid in 1954. The *Ohio Baptist Messenger,* the official paper of the convention, began publication in July, 1953, through the work of Roberts, while he was a missionary of the White Water Association. The *Messenger,* which later came under the control of the educational secretary of the convention, has grown from a 4-page to a 12-page publication. Edited by Miss Pat Shelton since 1955, the paper on Apr. 1, 1956, had a mailing list of 2,942 subscribers. This organ has been a valuable means of promoting the state program.

Vital statistics and future planning.—As of 1955, the Southern Baptists of Ohio reported 75 churches, 27 missions, 6 associations, and a total membership of 12,957. The churches baptized a total of 1,779, contributed to all causes $792,932.52, and gave $63,848.20 to the Cooperative Program. The convention adopted a budget of $131,175 for 1956. This body in 1955 adopted a five-year program with the following goals: for 1956 a membership of 18,000, 7 associations, and 100 churches; for 1957 a membership of 22,000, 8 associations, and 125 churches; for 1958 a membership of 26,000 and 150 churches; for 1959 a membership of 30,000, 9 associations, and 175 churches; for 1960 a membership of 34,000, 10 associations, and 200 churches.

NOBEL THOMAS COTTRELL

OHIO ASSOCIATIONS. CENTRAL. Organized Feb. 25, 1954, with 14 churches and included the central third of the state. It now includes only the west central area. In 1955, 16 churches reported 640 baptisms, 4,367 members, $254,962 total gifts, $23,346 mission gifts, $893,000 property value, and $259,169 church debt.

ERIE. Organized Mar. 20, 1954, with eight churches. It includes the northeastern area of the state. In 1955, 14 churches reported 174 baptisms, 862 members, $71,422 total gifts, $5,213 mission gifts, $144,750 property value, and $14,000 church debt.

GREATER CINCINNATI. Organized Mar. 16, 1954, with 20 churches, and included the southern third of the state. It now includes the extreme southwestern area of the state. Two new associations have gone out from it. In 1955, 15 churches reported 383 baptisms, 2,891 members, $185,104 total gifts, $16,802 mission gifts, $748,850 property value, and $322,058 church debt.

GREATER MIAMI VALLEY. Organized Mar. 11, 1955, with 13 churches, 11 of which were previously affiliated with Greater Cincinnati Association and two of which were previously affiliated with Central Association. It includes an area in the southwestern area of the state with Hamilton as the center of the work. In 1955, 15 churches reported 385 baptisms, 3,037 members, $135,752 total gifts, $13,038 mission gifts, and $621,000 property value.

MAUMEE VALLEY. Organized Aug. 13, 1955, with five churches, previously affiliated with the Erie Association. It includes the northwestern area of the state. In 1955 five churches reported 89 baptisms, 517 members, $27,562 total gifts, $1,979 mission gifts, $96,200 property value, and $10,785 church debt.

SCIOTO VALLEY. Organized Jan. 28, 1955, with eight churches previously affiliated with Greater Cincinnati Association. It includes the southeastern area of the state. In 1955, 10 churches reported 241 baptisms, 1,283 members, $118,130 total gifts, $13,471 mission gifts, $147,000 property value, and $36,925 church debt.

NOBEL THOMAS COTTRELL

OHIO VALLEY BAPTIST COLLEGE. An academy and institute, first called the Sturgis Baptist Academy, located at Sturgis, Ky., from 1895 to 1913. It was opened in the Sturgis City Hall on Sept. 10, 1895, following five years of agitation and planning, under the sponsorship of the Ohio Valley Baptist Association, with I. M. Wise as its president. The name was changed to the Ohio Valley Baptist College in 1898, and the following year a debt of $6,000 was reported to its sponsor, the Ohio Valley Baptist Association. The enrolment was 131 in 1901, and its debt had been reduced to $4,000, which was underwritten by 25 men. A new dormitory was planned in 1907. Payment of $3,000 of indebtedness on the college was guaranteed if the association would raise $6,000 for the dormitory. So enthusiastic was the response that $6,500 was raised in cash and $1,000 in pledges, and the college was briefly out of debt. Wise resigned in 1908, and J. C. Midgett was president for the next two years. The new dormitory was completed, and named the McGill Home. The president's wife became matron. H. A. Watkins was made president in 1910. By 1912 the indebtedness reached $8,000 and the association voted to close the school. In 1914 the trustees of the college reported that the property was being disposed of for its indebtedness, then $11,000, to the Sturgis Baptist Church.

GEORGE RALEIGH JEWELL

OKLAHOMA, BAPTIST GENERAL CONVENTION OF.

I. Baptist Beginnings. *General summary.*—The history of Oklahoma Baptists prior to the organization of the general convention in 1906 can be roughly divided into two periods: the period of early settlement and the period of growth in organization. During the first period (1820–60) the population of the land which was to become Oklahoma consisted almost entirely of Indians and their few Negro slaves. A few Negro and Indian churches were constituted, and some mission work was carried on, but the growth of Christianity was hampered by a strong tide of anti-white sentiment which the Indian tribal leadership felt because of their ill treatment at the hands of the Government and people of the United States. The second period (1865–1906) saw the organization of more churches and the growth of organized mission work, but during this time the work was hampered by controversies over alignment with the Northern and Southern home mission organizations, and rival conventions sprang up.

With the great "runs" of the homesteaders beginning in 1889, which settled lands that the Government had previously ceded to the Indians, a white population became an important factor in Oklahoma affairs. Because of these white settlers, the region was divided in 1890 by the Organic Act of Congress into two halves: Indian Territory and Oklahoma Territory. Gradually the various Baptist groups of the region, white and Indian, came more closely together, until in 1906 a single comprehensive convention was formed to represent all of Oklahoma.

Early religious life.—In the beginning Oklahoma was not appreciably populated, and in 1830 the Federal Government appropriated the land for the colonization of the Indians who were unwanted elsewhere. The Indians came to Oklahoma in successive waves of migration, sometimes voluntarily, sometimes by force. Through the years many tribes were settled there, but the bulk of the population consisted of the five civilized tribes (Cherokee, Choctaw, Chickasaw, Creek, and Seminole) whose original domains had covered large sections of the middle and lower South. These migrations were often extremely difficult, even when voluntary. Whole nations were gathered and escorted to Oklahoma by the United States Army, and there were so many casualties along the way, from sickness and exposure, that the routes became known generally as the "Trail of Tears."

Although a group of Cherokees from Arkansas (the Missouri Territory) came to Oklahoma in 1831, bringing their missionary, Duncan O'Bryant, with them, the first Baptist church on Oklahoma soil was organized among a group of Georgia Creeks who had begun migrating to the Indian Territory a few years earlier. This church was organized by Isaac McCoy (*q.v.*) Sept. 9, 1832, at Ebenezer Station in the Creek (Muskogee) Nation, with six charter members, three of whom were Negroes (slaves to Creeks). There were two white people and one Creek. At the same time McCoy prepared, at the request of the church, a license to preach, for John Davis, one of the six who had been converted under the ministry of Lee Compere (*q.v.*) and had assisted him in mission work in Georgia. Already Davis had been doing mission work in Oklahoma for two years and had also been associated with a mission school. He later (Oct. 20, 1833) became the first Baptist preacher to be ordained in Oklahoma. He was the only Indian in the charter membership of the Ebenezer church.

The organization of the first Cherokee church followed closely, on Nov. 19, 1832. It was organized by Duncan O'Bryant, about 70 miles northwest of Fort Smith, Ark., on the Illinois River. This was actually the re-establishment of a church which had existed in Georgia since Dec., 1825, and which had moved intact to the West. Two other Cherokee churches, Amohee and Valley Towns, both from Georgia, likewise moved in organized capacity in the final removal in 1838–39. Their exact locations in the Cherokee Nation are unknown. The first Choctaw church was organized in Kiamichi County (southeastern Oklahoma) in 1836. A church was organized in the Chickasaw Nation in Panola County in 1858, and J. S. Murrow (*q.v.*) organized Ash Creek Church, near the present town of Sasakwa, in the Seminole Nation in 1860.

During this period there was almost no denominational or institutional organization. Often missionaries were appointed by various mission societies to administer and teach in the schools provided for the Indians by the tribal governments and by the United States. However, religious life as a whole centered more about the preaching ministries of the few churches and was largely led by the white missionaries who, in co-operation with native preachers, traveled about the country holding vigorous protracted meetings and establishing churches wherever possible. The natural antipathy of the Indians for all the institutions of their white persecutors greatly hampered the progress of Baptist work. The Creeks expelled all missionaries about 1836 and four years later passed an ordinance forbidding any Indian or Negro to preach, on penalty of whipping, and making it necessary for white ministers to secure special permission for their services. The Seminoles, who had been forced out of Florida only after years of bitter and bloody war, were perhaps the most hostile to white influence. It was largely on account of this bitterness that the Seminoles were the last major tribe in which a church was organized.

It was among the Cherokees that Christianity made its greatest progress. Jesse Bushyhead (*q.v.*), who was one of their greatest civil leaders, was also a Baptist minister. John B. Jones, son of Evan Jones, served them as a translator and publisher of the Bible, *Pilgrim's Progress,* sermons, and hymns. Evan Jones and Bushyhead began in Aug., 1844, the publication of the *Cherokee Messenger,* a Baptist newspaper, the first newspaper of any kind in Oklahoma, on a press donated by the Baptist Mission Society in Boston, Mass.

The establishment of schools began with the first influx of population. In some cases these were founded by the missionaries and supported by the mission boards they served. In other cases they received subsidies from the Federal Government and/or tribal funds. Basically, they were typical elementary schools, although commonly called academies and seminaries. Missions among the Choctaws began when Charles E. Wilson and Sampson Burch opened a school at the Choctaw Agency on the Arkansas River west of Fort Smith in 1832. Joseph Smedley (*q.v.*) came as a missionary teacher to the same tribe in 1835. Ramsey Potts came as a teacher the same year and settled near the present town of Fort Towson, Okla. A short time later Alanson Allen and Eben Tucker, missionary teachers, came under Government appointment. Armstrong Academy was established near Fort Towson under the direction of P. P. Brown and his wife, H. W. Jones, and a Miss Chenoweth.

Toward the end of this first period, early pioneer associations came into existence. The first known association in Indian Territory was the General Association of United Baptists of the Southern Part of Indian Territory, organized at Armstrong Academy in Oct., 1848, by messengers from 13 churches with 854 members. Next was the Creek Association, which came into existence in 1851 but did not meet during the Civil War. The Cherokee and Ramsey associations were both organized in 1860, but the Ramsey Association did not survive the Civil War.

Reconstruction and the home missions controversy.—After the Civil War organized life among the Indians was almost totally disrupted. The Indians were Southerners and slaveholders but were bound to the Federal Government by treaty obligations of various sorts, and out of these conflicting loyalties came many divisions. Regiments were sent to both armies, and the Indian Territory itself was subjected to pillage and destruction. Homes and churches were destroyed, schools interrupted, and the precarious civilization of the frontier torn down. Reconstruction days brought the Indian soldiers back with new hopes, only to find that the war had marked an end for their new home in the West, which McCoy had termed "a territory for the Indians, within, and yet never to be a part of, the United States." For the Indians returned to face a growing tide of white immigration.

Since reconstruction found the entire South destitute, it was a struggle for the Southern Baptist Home Mission Board to finance the work which it was trying to do in Indian Territory. Once again, as during the Civil War, the Indians found themselves involved in a conflict of loyalties. In 1875 there came from the Choctaw-Chickasaw association a request to the Home Mission Society (North) for help. After many similar requests the society entered the field the next year. That same year, a general Baptist body aligned with the Southern Baptist Convention was formed. It purported to embrace Indian Territory, though there was not a single messenger from Indian Territory present in the organizational meeting of the Baptist General Association of Western Arkansas and Indian Territory at Charleston, Ark., Nov. 24, 1876. The general association never gained any great following in Indian Territory, even after it greatly increased its gifts to the Indian Territory work in 1888.

The work of the Home Mission Society grew, however, and on June 1, 1883, messengers from the Cherokee, Muskogee, and Choctaw-Chickasaw associations met at Tahlequah to organize the Missionary and Educational Convention of Indian Territory, which co-operated with the Northern society. This action caused the Home Mission Board (South) to request its missionary to the Indians, Joseph Samuel Murrow (*q.v.*), to organize a new convention to co-operate with the South. Murrow refused, feeling that a new convention would breed controversy in the territorial work and hurt the cause of Indian missions. Intense strife developed between Murrow and Isaac Taylor Tichenor (*q.v.*), then secretary of the Home Mission Board, and in 1891 Murrow resigned his commission. The controversy which grew out of this conflict led to long and bitter strife among several leaders in the territory, the most prominent of whom were Murrow, E. L. Compere (*q.v.*), and H. F. Buckner (*q.v.*). The strife went so far as to involve the three men in a long series of conflicts charged with heated debates waged both through the press and in private correspondence. It destroyed the great friendship which had existed for many years between Murrow and Buckner after they had become associated in the Indian work in 1857.

Added to this controversy was the complication of ever-increasing white immigration, leading to large-scale homesteading after 1889, when the territory was officially opened for settlement. The Organic Act of 1890 which divided the land into Oklahoma and Indian territories was soon followed by a corresponding division in Baptist organization. The Oklahoma Baptist State Convention, the first such sectional body to be formed, was created by being "lettered" out of the General Association of Western Arkansas and Indian Territory. It was organized on Nov. 13, 1895, at Lexington, Oklahoma Territory. The Association continued in the Indian Territory, and both co-operated with the Home Mission Board (South). The Missionary and Educational Convention met in Oklahoma City, Dec. 1, 1898, and "mutually agreed" to divide and form two conventions, one for each territory co-operating with the Home Mission Society. The convention in Oklahoma Territory was named the Oklahoma Baptist Convention, and the one in Indian Territory was named the Baptist Convention of Indian Territory.

Expansion of organization and work.—In spite of the controversy over missionary alignment, which was not finally settled until single alignment was adopted by a united convention in 1914, the organizational and institutional development of the denomination continued. The Choctaw-Chickasaw Association was organized from 16 churches on July 5, 1872, and met with a Sunday school convention which had organized at the same time with J. S. Murrow as president. During the first session of this association, held with Rehoboth (now Atoka) Church, both the ordinances (baptism and Lord's Supper) were observed, and a minister and a deacon were ordained. Short Mountain, the first white association, was organized Oct. 24–25, 1884, meeting in a private home because the house of Short Mountain Church could not be finished in time. Enon Association held two organizational meetings, Aug. 29 and Oct. 16–17, 1885, with the Wilson and New Hope churches, respectively. During the next 20 years, 24 other associations were organized.

Organized women's work began also during this period, during a meeting of the Choctaw-Chickasaw Association in 1876 at Nunny-Cha-ha (High Hill) near the present city of McAlester. A Mrs. Blackall, who had come to the meeting from Chicago, gathered the women together one day and spoke to them about the work of the American Baptist Foreign Mission Society. The spirit generated in that meeting resulted in the organization of the Annual Choctaw and Chickasaw Missionary Society with Sallie Holston as president. The Women's Baptist Home Mission Society of the West was organized by Mrs. Blackall on Feb. 1 of the next year.

It was during this period, also, that various Baptist newspapers were founded, following the leadership of the *Cherokee Messenger* of 40 years before. The *Indian Missionary,* the first Baptist newspaper with a general circulation, was founded in 1884 and adopted in 1886 by the Missionary and Educational Convention as "the newspaper of this convention." After 1891 the name of the *Indian Missionary* was changed to the *Baptist Watchman,* which went out of existence in 1894. The *Baptist Beacon* was published for a brief time at Muskogee prior to 1900. The 1896 session of the Missionary and Educational Convention commended both the *Beacon* and another paper called the *Territory Baptist* when it resolved that "we bid them God speed." Other attempts at publishing Baptist papers resulted in *The Baptist Oklahoman* and *The Signal.* Much of the time during these early years, the territories were also served by the *Baptist Standard* of Texas and the *Word and Way* of Missouri.

Unification of the several conventions.—Aided by multiplying organizations, by these newspapers which served as channels of information, by the founding of Bacone College at Muskogee, the first Oklahoma Baptist institution of higher learning, and by a lessening of the heat of controversy, the Baptist denomination in Oklahoma gained more and more in maturity. Rival conventions began to come more closely together. The year 1900 marked the beginning of the process which led to the final unification of 1906. On Mar. 7 of that year, representatives from the general association and from the Baptist Convention of Indian Territory (both Indian Territory organizations) held a joint conference at South McAlester and recommended that the two bodies merge into one convention. The result was a meeting of both bodies on Sept. 10 at Durant, where they transacted their separate business, then dissolved and united to form the Baptist General Convention of Indian Territory. This convention adopted a dual alignment policy, providing for co-operation with both the Home Mission Board and the Home Mission Society. Each of the two boards gave four dollars for every dollar raised by the general convention for work in the territory, and each board appropriated $1,000 for new church buildings.

The two conventions in Oklahoma Territory met at Blackwell, Oct. 5, 1900, transacted their separate business, and then united by adopting recommendations from a joint committee representing the Home Mission Board and the Home Mission Society. Terms of dual alignment were adopted similar to those in Indian Territory.

The convention in each territory enjoyed a steady growth for the next six years. Other institutions were founded. Oklahoma Baptist College was established at Blackwell, Oklahoma Territory, in 1900. The Murrow Orphans' Home at Unchuka, near Atoka, was founded in 1902 by J. S. Murrow and in 1910 was moved to the campus of Bacone College, Muskogee, where it is today. J. A. Scott (*q.v.*) founded the Oklahoma Baptist Orphans' Home in 1903.

Prior to 1906 seven different conventions existed at some time or simultaneously in what is now Oklahoma. These, with the dates of their organization, were the Baptist General Association of Western Arkansas and Indian Territory, 1876; the Baptist Missionary and Educational Convention of Oklahoma and Indian Territories, 1883; the Oklahoma Baptist State Convention, 1895; the Oklahoma Baptist Convention, 1898; the Baptist Convention of Indian Territory, 1898; the Baptist General Convention of Indian Territory, 1900; and the Oklahoma Baptist State Convention, 1900. From 1898 to 1900, there were four conventions at the same time, two each in Oklahoma and Indian territories. In 1900 the two bodies in each territory united into single conventions and adopted a denominational policy of dual alignment. This arrangement continued for six years until leaders in both conventions could formulate plans for final unification.

In 1906 the Baptists of Oklahoma came to the point of final unification. On Nov. 8 of that year, both conventions met at Shawnee, the Territorial convention at the First Baptist Church and the Oklahoma convention at the First Methodist Church. On Nov. 9, after closing their work, each convention adjourned *sine die* at 10:00 A.M. According to previous arrangement the 400 messengers from the two conventions formed a line in front of the Methodist church and marched "two and two" to the opera house, where the Baptist General Convention of Oklahoma was organized. This event is known in history as the "combination." The following officers were elected: James Allen Scott, president; E. D. Cameron and Albert G. Washburn, vice-presidents; W. P. Blake, treasurer and recording secretary; Luther Whitfield Marks, historical secretary, and Joseph Cole Stalcup, corresponding secretary. J. M. GASKIN

II. History of General Convention. After organization, the new convention immediately assumed control of institutions owned or supported by the territorial conventions. Members of the former conventions mingled and joined together in the common work in such a way as soon to wipe out the line between Oklahoma and Indian territories and begin the making of a great Baptist state. There was a combined membership of 29,669 in the churches.

History of the executive committee and state mission board.—In 1906 the constitution provided for an executive board of 20 elected members plus the president, recording secretary, and treasurer. This number was changed in 1934 to 32 members and the president and recording secretary, and in 1952 the number of elected members was increased to 48. In addition to the president and recording secretary, officers of the convention are two vice-presidents, an assistant recording secretary, a corresponding secretary (who from the first has acted as secretary of missions and now serves also as treasurer), and a historical secretary. The duties of these officers are "those usually required in similar organizations."

The new convention in 1906 decided that no one employed by the convention would be appointed to serve on the executive board or hold any office under its authority. Members of the board are elected for maximum terms of four years and must be off the board one year to be eligible for re-election. Between convention meetings the board is the controlling organization of all agencies, departments, and institutions. However, Oklahoma Baptist University has a separate board elected by the convention.

The office of corresponding secretary gradually developed from a rather insignificant "superintendent of missions" to the position of executive secretary-treasurer of all departments, agencies, institutions, and other work of the convention. In a sense, he is the administrator of every Baptist institution in Oklahoma, except Oklahoma Baptist University, whose president is responsible solely to that institution's board of trustees.

One of the first problems confronting the new convention in 1906 was the alignment controversy, which was settled on a dual alignment basis such as the parent conventions had practiced. A period of profitable co-operation was carried on with the mission boards of both the Northern and Southern Baptist conventions until 1914, at which time single alignment with the Southern Baptist Convention was voted. Since then, the work of Northern Baptists in Oklahoma has been confined to the support of Bacone College and of some Indian mission work, primarily in southwestern Oklahoma.

State missions.—Broadly speaking, state missions refers to all the work of the convention, including institutions and agencies. J. L. H. Hawkins said in a report to the 1913 convention: "State Missions is a fundamental work and our whole structure will be enfeebled if we are wrong here." In 1921 state missions was called "the only recognized and efficient agency for promoting Baptist education, hospitals, orphans' home, and general Sunday School, B.Y.P.U. and the women's organizations within the limits of our commonwealth." In addition to the things mentioned, state missions in 1930 included work with Indians, the Baptist Book Store, the assembly, the *Baptist Messenger,* supplements to associational missions, and supplements to 56 pastors. As institutions, agencies, departments, personnel, and new work were added, they, too, were state missions. State mission offerings went for all the work or for any part to which they were designated. The chief work at first was Indian missions. Even in the early history there were three full-time men on the field. In 1927 a change in organization eliminated the position of secretary for Indian missions and added the responsibility for that work to the duties of the corresponding secretary. The Indian associations (five in 1927) and churches were to be considered as definitely a part of the convention as other churches and associations. It was agreed in 1934 "that all Indian Mission work be turned over to the Home Mission Board of the Southern Baptist Convention." The secretary of Indian work, who has been a part of the Oklahoma organization since 1954, is paid by the Home Mission Board. In 1954 there were 144 Indian churches with 7,793 members and five associations.

The state mission program has been promoted through the associations and through the churches. Early in the history of the convention, the program was promoted through a mission committee of each church and each association. Associations were repeatedly encouraged to employ missionaries to direct all the work of the association. This plan, however, was not completely successful, and, as associational missions declined, the district missionary came into prominence. At the height of this program, there were 10 men on the field. The association, however, was always considered the best organization through which to romote the work because it knew its constituency best, had the closest contact with the co-operating churches, and was most directly under church control. This last is true because most churches are represented by messengers in the annual sessions and have elected board members who sit in the monthly or quarterly associational board meetings for the transaction of business.

From the formation of the state convention in 1906 until 1926, state missions were supported by special offerings, usually taken in September, October, and November. Now the

GOLDEN GATE BAPTIST THEOLOGICAL SEMINARY (q.v.), Berkeley, Calif. Founded 1944, enrolled 331 for 1955–56 term. New campus, shown, to cost $9,000,000.

SOUTHEASTERN BAPTIST THEOLOGICAL SEMINARY (*q.v.*), Wake Forest, N. C. Founded in 1951. Scenes on the $3,000,000 campus where 1955–56 enrolment totaled 459.

only special offering annually taken for this cause is sponsored in September each year by Woman's Missionary Union, and the over-all state mission program is financed through the Cooperative Program. Since 1947 a supplement of $900 per year has been given each superintendent of missions in the district associations of the state. Prior to that time state mission work was promoted largely through the district plan, by which a missionary served a combined area of two or more associations. This plan of work began in 1921, and C. M. Curb was one of the first men to hold the title of district missionary. This type of mission work as a convention program was discontinued by vote of the state board Nov. 26, 1929, but was resumed in 1933, when Andrew Potter, state secretary, led Oklahoma County Association to set a precedent in this type of work by underwriting the salary of a district missionary, and Curb was elected to serve in this capacity. The state board asked Potter to contact other districts in the state and propose the adoption of this plan, and he complied with this request. This program continued through the depression years when some associations found it financially impossible to maintain a missionary alone. With the coming of more prosperous times, this plan of work was gradually replaced by the associational mission plan, by which most associations have their own missionaries. On Jan. 1, 1944, Sam W. Scantlan became superintendent of rural missions for the convention, and upon his recommendation the board voted to divide the state into eight districts. Once more this plan of district mission work was followed until Dec. 31, 1947, when it was dropped in favor of the state supplement to the salary of the associational missionary in each association.

On Mar. 25, 1954, the state board united with the boards of LeFlore and Frisco associations in a joint program of mountain missions. J. Spurgeon Richardson, a returned Southern Baptist missionary to Africa, was put on the field, to serve in the Kiamichi mountain area of southeastern Oklahoma. His work terminated Oct. 1, 1954.

Origin and development of departments and agencies.—The Sunday school and Training Union were at first loosely attached to the church, and the convention regarded their promotion as auxiliary to its work. By 1914 these two fields were recognized as of great importance. The first state B.Y.P.U. assembly at Falls Creek was held in 1917. By 1924 both the Sunday school and the B.Y.P.U. were asking for department status with a corps of workers, even though not many churches were including B.Y.P.U. work in their budgets. In 1933 the Sunday school and Training Union departments were merged into one department, and in 1945 this was named the Department of Religious Education. In 1954 there were 268,935 enrolled in Sunday schools and 100,947 enrolled in Training Unions in the state.

There was some concern for student work as early as 1915, and a report was made to the 1919 convention contemplating some definite program and equipment. The Baptist Student Union was added to the department of Sunday school and Training Union work in 1937. By 1939 there were 20 B.S.U.'s trying to minister to 9,000 Baptist students. In 1954 there were 11,000 Baptist students in 23 schools, with three full-time and six part-time student secretaries. The student work and music programs were combined in 1945 as a single department under one secretary. The two B.S.U. buildings at Norman and Stillwater were completed in 1953 and are in use.

In 1945 Ira C. Prosser became secretary of the Department of Baptist Student Union and Church Music. He served eight years and was succeeded by Gene Bartlett, Jan. 1, 1954. In 1946 there was one full-time minister of music in the state. In 1955 there were 20, with a total of 750 part-time, paid, and volunteer workers. *The Tuning Fork,* a monthly publication, was begun in 1950. The first music festival for high school students was held at Oklahoma Baptist University in 1953, with 27 churches represented. GENE BARTLETT

The Woman's Missionary Union since 1906 has been auxiliary to the convention but is also treated as a department. At first this organization co-operated with both Southern and Northern Baptists but later joined the Oklahoma convention in single alignment. In the early days the main purpose was considered to teach about missions rather than to raise funds. The women did, however, and still do, take part in all denominational drives for money, especially for mission causes. As early as 1922, the W.M.U. was "growing each year into a more efficient church and denominational agency." The W.M.U. has helped in a special way in building dormitories at Oklahoma Baptist University. Berta Keys Spooner (1874–1956) led in this phase of the work during her administration as executive secretary-treasurer of Woman's Missionary Union of Oklahoma, 1921–46. Mrs. Spooner, a native of Decatur, Ala., came to Hollis, Okla., in 1905. After the death of her husband in 1910, she continued to operate their hardware business for six years, then entered Southwestern Baptist Theological Seminary (1916–20), and worked as business secretary and visitor of the Baptist Student Missionary Movement before she became secretary of the Oklahoma W.M.U. in 1921.

The convention voted in 1910 to endorse laymen's work in the churches, and the corresponding secretary was requested to promote it through associational representatives. In 1923 a statewide Brotherhood organization was set up by the convention to promote study classes in stewardship and missions. Brotherhood work alone has not been given full department status. In 1940 the leader was called enlistment secretary. In 1943 the head of this work was called the secretary of Brotherhood and institutions. For a short time (1946–48) T. P. Haskins served as Brotherhood secretary. In 1948 J. A. Pennington became secretary of the Department of Brotherhood and Evangelism.

The establishment of a department of evangelism was considered in 1927, but no organization was effected until 1932. Since that time evangelism has been vigorously promoted over the entire state. Some meetings were held in 1935 in a somewhat simultaneous fashion. The department at first emphasized the summer campaigns. All institutions and agencies were led to participate in the program of evangelism.

In Aug., 1927, at Erick, C. E. Matthews conducted a revival which resulted in 371 additions. Preceding this there had been a religious census and a mission revival in which there were 51 additions. In 1939 Carlton Weaver, a Baptist layman of Wilburton, initiated a movement known as the "log fire revival" in eastern Oklahoma. Men and boys conducted services outdoors, usually in a wooded area, where huge log fires were built to furnish light and warmth in the winter. Early evening hours were given to singing, praying, preaching, and testimonies. These services continued intermittently for a number of years and were marked by attendance ranging to 500; as many as 75 conversions were reported in one service.

The first real simultaneous crusade was in 1948, on an associational basis, and resulted in 18,258 baptisms. The simultaneous effort has continued to date, including the big campaign in 1950 for all churches west of the Mississippi River, and in Apr., 1955, for all churches in certain zones of the state. There were 22,490 baptisms reported in 1954 and 28,771 additions to churches by letter and statement.

The Baptist Foundation was established in 1946 and has received money and property valued at $2,572,717.

The convention established a rural missions department Jan. 1, 1944, with Sam W. Scantlan as superintendent. On Dec. 2, 1947, the name of this department was changed to Rural and City Missions, and Scantlan continued as superintendent in a statewide program of missions in the rural and urban areas.

On June 1, 1953, the Department of Public Relations was created with Arthur S. Davenport as director, to correlate and co-ordinate the convention's public relations and activities.

Finance.—A committee on systematic benevolence made a schedule in 1907 for promoting the various objects and taking collections. This committee preceded the Cooperative Program and unified budget and was the forerunner of the present elaborate calendar of activities. In 1911, for the first time, the board made suggestions as to what amounts the churches ought to give for various causes. The idea of giving all home and foreign missions funds through the state office was meeting with increasing approval.

Borrowing began as early as 1907 and continued to be a regular policy even beyond the time of the 75 Million Campaign. This campaign was launched in 1919, and by vote for a "Carry-on Program," it continued to 1925. Oklahoma's quota was $2,500,000; by 1922, $3,197,106 had been pledged, but only $1,578,131 was paid by the close of 1925. All institutions, boards, and agencies had begun expansion programs based on anticipated receipts, and when these were not forthcoming, the convention was plunged into debt. One of the most tragic results was the withholding of funds from the home and foreign mission boards. Debt-paying began with paying the credit balances on the books of the mission boards. Various schemes, programs, and methods were used to collect funds with which to pay this out-of-state debt. By extending the campaign to 1926, the last $27,000 was put on the table at the convention, making what was called "the most jubilant hour ever experienced by Oklahoma Baptists in Convention assembled."

For 12 years prior to the time when all Baptist causes were supported through the Cooperative Program, the convention sought such a plan. The convention regretted the custom, into which churches had drifted, of sending all state mission money to the state treasurer at the close of the year. This compelled the board to borrow money and pay interest. The churches were constantly flooded with requests for offerings for denominational causes, and some phases of the work were undersupported while others received more than their share. The convention, in 1924, anticipated the launching of the Cooperative Program and voted to divide all general funds, 60 per cent to state causes, 35 per cent to Southern Baptist causes, and 5 per cent for debt payments.

Numerous special offerings were still taken. Less than one out of six Oklahoma churches adopted the Cooperative Program during its first five years of operation. In 1930, when 40 per cent of the Cooperative Program was pledged to the Southern Baptist Convention, an agreement was made whereby certain administration and promotion expenses were to be taken out before the funds were divided, thus charging promotion expenses to the whole program rather than the state only. With the beginning of the depression in 1930, the churches' Cooperative Program gifts dropped, but the state continued its 60–40 division. A goal of 75 per cent of the churches giving something annually through the Cooperative Program was set in 1931. Cooperative Program gifts received in the Oklahoma City office have been as follows:

1926	$116,368	1936	$ 91,924	1946	$ 591,878
1927	136,000	1937	133,271	1947	683,380
1928	138,841	1938	136,537	1948	756,997
1929	145,869	1939	140,852	1949	780,136
1930	143,545	1940	145,045	1950	881,256
1931	127,464	1941	180,655	1951	1,004,187
1932	93,733	1942	218,291	1952	1,304,393
1933	87,537	1943	317,377	1953	1,500,369
1934	74,197	1944	380,493	1954	1,622,279
1935	81,484	1945	477,919		

Per capita gifts through the Cooperative Program began at 87 cents in 1926, but dropped to 40 cents in 1934. From 1934 both per capita and total Cooperative Program gifts climbed steadily upward. Per capita Cooperative Program gifts for 1954 were $4.06. The number of churches giving through the Cooperative Program increased from 350 in 1926 to 1,175 in 1954. The percentage plan for church contributions of undesignated receipts through the Cooperative Program became popular during the 1940's, and in 1950 the convention began sending to each church a wall plaque indicating that church's percentage. In 1951 the convention began promoting an annual increase in the percentage of the church's undesignated receipts going to missions through the Cooperative Program. After the deduction of certain administrative and promotional expenses, which are shared with the Southern Baptist Convention, Oklahoma divides all Cooperative Program money 50–50 between the state and the Southern Baptist Convention. T. B. LACKEY

The genesis and growth of the Cooperative Program was closely related to a number of background and parallel factors. The 1926 state missions report included these words: "The Cooperative Program . . . is the outgrowth of many years of effort and earnest search after Divine leadership." The unified budget was developed as an Oklahoma adjustment of receipts to a co-operative plan of giving and included the Cooperative Program as a preferred item. In spite of better plans and promotion in finances, the debt kept growing and was measurably increased by the depression years. In 1933 Andrew Potter (*q.v.*) was elected secretary and began a vigorous campaign to pay debts. The convention soon absolutely forbade institutions, departments, or agencies to make more debts and required that something be paid every year on the debts. This work was promoted through and by a debt-paying committee, and after seven years of effort, the last of the debt, which had amounted to nearly half a million dollars, was paid at the convention meeting in Tulsa in 1940. The beginning of this campaign coincided with the beginning of the Hundred Thousand Club campaign, which continued until 1943. The period of expansion began immediately upon completion of debt liquidation. In fact, the enthusiasm for expansion, but without debt, was a powerful influence in liquidation of debts.

The future plans and policies committee, suggested by Potter in 1938, made its first report in 1939. The first project was to be the construction of the boys' dormitory at Oklahoma Baptist University. The purpose of this committee was to promote expansion but to direct it along sane lines, keeping it directly under convention control, and to correlate the expansion of all institutions, departments, and agencies. The committee continued to guide in finances until 1949, but shared part of its responsibility with the committee on enlargement, which began in 1941, and which was charged with all the problems of expansion; whereas the future plans and policies committee had dealt mostly with financial matters. This new committee promoted centennial programs in 1944–45, including a thank offering of $400,000. The total cash contributions for the year 1944–45 were $993,442. There were enough gifts other than cash to make this the first million-dollar year in the history of the convention. This committee also promoted the program of raising funds for the student buildings at Norman and Stillwater.

Stewardship was promoted in the local church, particularly after 1924. Apportionments were made as well as percentage suggestions; but the autonomy and absolute independence of the local church were always recognized, and no attempt was ever made to coerce any local church with regard to its finances. The Tither's Test Movement came in 1935. In 1938 Potter advocated the policy of developing the financial program from the local church to the association and then to the convention. In 1955 the convention was taking church and associational goals as the basis for the Cooperative Program goal. Oklahoma co-operated in the Convention-wide tither's crusade.

Several times in the convention's history, its work was hampered by financial crises. Oklahoma Baptist University, founded at Shawnee in 1910, closed its doors the next year for lack of funds, and in 1913 Southwest Baptist College closed for the same reason. The university reopened in 1915; in 1922 it had to borrow $85,000 to survive, and the convention at the same time was $144,845 in debt to convention-wide causes alone. The same year Oklahoma State Baptist Hospital, Oklahoma City, was ordered sold because it was more than $65,000 behind on operating expenses. Money matters grew worse until 1926, when a $300,000 debt-paying campaign was successfully concluded. In the depression years of the early thirties, the convention again fell behind with finances and faced a $450,056 debt. Under the new leadership of Andrew Potter, who became secretary Sept. 1, 1933, all debts were liquidated in six years, except the bonded indebtedness on Oklahoma Baptist Hospital, Muskogee, which was paid in full in 1943.

Baptist papers.—The present status of the *Baptist Messenger* in Oklahoma was the result of a long evolution of opinion in the state. Previous to convention ownership of a paper, several Baptist papers had been commended, such as the *Baptist Oklahoman* and the *Baptist Worker*. In earlier years there was much disfavor to convention ownership of a paper, but at the 1918 meeting a growing feeling among many brethren that the convention should have its own paper led to a unanimous vote for convention ownership. A committee recommended that the *Baptist Messenger* be purchased for $5,000 from C. P. Stealey and that Stealey be made editor and manager. The recommendation was accepted. This action precipitated the Nunnery Movement. Alonzo

Nunnery, owner and editor of the *Baptist Worker,* made editorial attacks on convention leaders, especially F. M. McConnell (*q.v.*), corresponding secretary. Nunnery was unseated at the 1919 convention, and he formed a separate organization which later joined the Landmark Baptist group. In 1955 the *Messenger* circulation reached 75,000.

The convention and institutions.—Schools, papers, and the orphanage began before the present convention. The immediate problem of schools was turned over to the education commission, which had been constituted at the first session of the convention to "carefully and impartially investigate existing conditions with reference to educational matters." In 1907 the commission reported the following schools in Oklahoma: (1) Bacone College at Muskogee, which was established by the American Baptist Home Mission Society, and (2) Cherokee Baptist Academy, also a home mission project. These two were to be perpetuated as Indian schools. (3) Oklahoma Baptist State College at Blackwell, the only one under the state convention. (4) Southwest Baptist Academy at Hastings. It was free of debt and offered to the convention.

The college at Blackwell was not selected to be the Baptist school of the state. After several bids had been considered, and after school had been carried on near Oklahoma City for a few weeks as a result of the tentative acceptance of an offer from I. M. Putnam, the Shawnee location was finally decided upon, and Oklahoma Baptist University was founded there in 1910. Attempts were made to combine several schools with Oklahoma Baptist University, but only one was actually brought into this plan. That was the school at Hastings called the Southwest Baptist Academy, which moved to Mangum in 1910 and changed its name to Southwest Baptist College. Because of financial reverses and disfavor from the education commission, the college at Blackwell was sold. The 1913 minutes reported: "The four successive years of drouth and the confusion which arose in our educational work a few years ago created barriers too great to be overcome by human effort." The education commission recommended in 1912 "the establishment of one, and only one . . . school of college grade and that any effort to establish any other college or university be discouraged." The commission was dissolved in 1913 and its work turned over to the board of directors of the convention. To this date there is only one Baptist school in the state, and it is owned and controlled by the convention. All rights to operate its own affairs are given by action of the convention. Oklahoma Baptist University became a large school; 1,193 students were enrolled the fall semester of 1954, and that year the property and resources were valued at $4,316,514.

The Baptist Orphans' Home actually began in Oklahoma City in the home of the James Allen Scotts (*q.v.*). It was accepted by the two conventions before the combination and continued to be the orphans' home for the Baptist General Convention of Oklahoma. However, the property title was not transferred to the convention until Dec. 20, 1915. Legal steps were taken in 1916 to dissolve the Indian Territory Baptist Orphans' Home, leaving none to compete with the Oklahoma Baptist Orphans' Home. In 1954 the home with room for 200 children was valued at $1,000,000.

The Boys' Ranch Town was started in 1953 as a result of a cash and property gift by Mr. and Mrs. James M. Johnson, valued at $537,787. M. Judson Cook became the first superintendent of the ranch Nov. 1, 1953. The first building was dedicated Nov. 9, 1954. Samuel W. Scantlan became superintendent in Feb., 1956.

Hospitals had no organic connection with the convention in the early years of its history, but two hospital associations (Oklahoma Baptist Hospital Association and the Baptist Memorial Association) were endorsed by the convention. A desire for properly located Baptist hospitals was often expressed, as reflected in these words: "If these institutions can be located in great centers of population where they will receive professional, financial and moral support they should be encouraged." The Oklahoma Baptist Hospital, Muskogee, was built in 1909 by the Oklahoma Baptist Hospital Association of that city. In 1915 its property value was $20,000. It was governed by its own board of trustees until May 3, 1916, when the board voted to deed it to the convention. Convention management began the next month. The Miami Hospital was built by Baptists and others of Miami and deeded to the convention in 1917. In 1919 the hospital committee reported that 20 hospitals were needed with 900 beds and that "the Catholics are far wiser in this line of effort than we Baptists are." At this time there were two other Baptist hospitals in the state, a small one at Cushing and the State Baptist Hospital in Oklahoma City. In 1928 the Enid Baptist Hospital was endorsed. Although the hospital in Oklahoma City had a good start, was well located, and enjoyed some prosperity, financial difficulties soon developed, and it was disposed of by the convention's board of directors in 1922. By 1932 the financial condition of the two hospitals remaining under convention ownership and control was deplorable, and some leaders favored their sale. Andrew Potter, then pastor of First Baptist Church, Enid, was put in direct charge of the seemingly hopeless Muskogee hospital, and the situation gradually improved. Eventually, both hospitals were saved. All Baptist hospitals are now directly under control of the convention. Since 1945 the convention has been deluged with offers of hospitals from communities all over the state. In 1949 Mangum citizens gave the convention $90,000 cash and a hospital valued at $250,000. The hospitals at Perry, Stillwater, Bristow, and Pryor were added on lease bases in the respective years of 1951,

1952, 1953, and 1954. The Enid hospital, valued at over $1,000,000, plus $100,000 cash, was given to the convention in 1953. In 1955 a site was purchased in Oklahoma City for the construction of a hospital in that city, and a fund-raising campaign was waged to match funds allocated in the Cooperative Program for that purpose.

On Nov. 12, 1953, at its annual session the convention accepted a recommendation from the board of directors favoring the establishment of a home for aging people, to be called "The Golden Age Home," and voted its erection when resources justified construction. The home was included in the 1955 budget for $10,000.

Controversies, special difficulties, and reactions.—The Nunnery Movement in 1919 was precipitated when the convention bought the *Baptist Messenger,* owned and edited by C. P. Stealey, instead of the *Baptist Worker,* owned and edited by A. Nunnery. The Stealey controversy was settled by convention action in 1927, relieving C. P. Stealey of the editorship of the paper. He claimed he was removed because of his criticism of Baptist leaders. No other serious controversies arose after 1927. However, there was considerable debate when the Minister's Retirement Plan was presented to the 1938 convention, but it was finally approved.

At the 1949 convention much debate was precipitated by the Ramay proposal to revise the constitution so that churches practicing open communion, alien immersion, and affiliation with any world or national council of churches would not be eligible for representation in the convention. The convention adopted a substitute motion which left the constitution as it was but made it the official policy of the convention to consider churches with the abovementioned practices as unsound in faith and practice. The resolution was so worded as to mean that the messengers of such churches would not be seated in the convention.

The convention expressed itself in relation to attempts of some to persuade Baptists to enter union movements. For example, in 1909 the convention authorized Joseph Cole Stalcup (*q.v.*) to inform a group that "we have our evangelistic work so arranged that it will not be at all practicable for us to enter into co-operation with an interdenominational evangelistic movement in our state." All through their history, this independence has been characteristic of Oklahoma Baptists.

Social, political, and educational problems.—In 1916 the convention expressed approval and hope that the President of the United States, Woodrow Wilson, would continue his policy of no liquor at the White House and refrain from having an inaugural ball. Also, the convention passed a strong resolution denouncing the position of Major General Frederick W. Funston, commanding officer of United States troops along the Mexican border, who reportedly consented to have religious services conducted among the soldiers only on the condition that the men would not be told they were lost, that revivals would not be held, and that nothing would be done to arouse the soldiers' emotions. From the very first (1906) actions were taken opposing the sale and consumption of beverage alcohol. Modernism and evolution were opposed vigorously. The action of the 1926 convention is a fair summary of the attitude of Oklahoma Baptists toward public school textbooks containing objectionable or antibiblical material. In that year they approved a resolution memorializing the Southern Baptist Convention in its 1927 session, to appoint a textbook commission with authority to secure competent scientists to write college textbooks which would in no sense do violence to the "Orthodox Baptist's conventional interpretation of the Book Divine." Alleged modernism in the college classroom, especially on the subject of evolution, was the prime object of this action. Rector introduced a resolution at the 1927 convention, reaffirming the textbook memorial, which had been referred to the Executive Committee of the Southern Baptist Convention, and this, too, was approved. After this date the social service committee continued to bring to the convention periodic recommendations concerned with beverage alcohol, religious persecution, dancing, and the character of public school curriculum, and for a number of years secured convention approval. However, as the list of social ills increased, and as the committee began to recommend expanding programs for direct action on the part of the churches, the feeling grew in the convention that the social service committee was acting beyond its authority and purpose. For this reason much of the 1949 report was rejected by the convention.

Buildings.—The convention owns two buildings in addition to those owned in connection with institutions and agencies. A three-story structure at 223 N. W. First Street, Oklahoma City, was purchased in 1924 for $27,000 and was used until 1950 as the convention's headquarters building, housing offices, the *Baptist Messenger,* the Messenger Book House, and later the Baptist Book Store. Nov. 5, 1945, a special committee appointed to study prospects for a new Baptist building reported favorably to the board, and a building site at 11th and Robinson in Oklahoma City was purchased for $20,000. In March of the following year, convention offices were moved to a new five-story Bedford limestone structure at that location, valued at $897,751. On June 29, 1950, dedication ceremonies were held for the new building, which houses all convention offices, the Baptist Book Store, and rental offices. Rental income from this and the old building provides a maintenance fund adequate for operation of both buildings, without use of mission funds for that purpose.

After the death of Andrew Potter Aug. 29,

1951, Thomas B. Lackey, assistant executive secretary-treasurer of the convention since 1946, was elected to succeed him in a called meeting of the board Sept. 4, 1951, and assumed office at once. Annual Cooperative Program receipts increased from $1,004,187 in 1951 to $1,828,703 in 1955, and baptisms increased from 21,739 in 1951 to 22,270 in 1955.

CHARLES H. BLACK and J. M. GASKIN

THOMAS BERT LACKEY, MARION EDGAR RAMAY, SAMUEL WILLIAM SCANTLAN, EUGENE MONROE BARTLETT, JR., ARTHUR STUART DAVENPORT, THOMAS PAUL HASKINS

III. Program of Work of Oklahoma Baptists. *Board of directors.*—The board of directors consists of 48 members plus the convention president and recording secretary. Regular members are elected to four-year terms, and 12 retire each year. These are ineligible for re-election for a period of one year. The president and recording secretary of the convention serve in the same capacities for the board. They are elected for one-year terms. The executive secretary, elected annually by the convention, may be replaced by the board in case of a vacancy. He is the official superintendent of all of the board's work and prepares an annual printed report to the convention regarding all work committed to the board. He also may serve as treasurer. Thomas B. Lackey has been secretary since 1951, and W. E. Grindstaff, assistant since 1952. The board elects all denominational workers whose salaries are paid by the convention, except those elected by the convention itself, and may approve those whose salaries are paid in part by the convention. It fixes all salaries and determines fields of work of denominational workers elected by the board. Annual meetings of the convention are fixed by the convention itself, but time and place of meeting may be changed by the board for any good cause. The directors hold semiannual meetings at Oklahoma City in December and July, plus any special meetings which the president may call. Sixteen members constitute a quorum. An executive committee of the board is appointed annually by the president, who serves as chairman. This committee performs such duties as the board may refer to it and makes regular reports of its activities to the board. The board has the power to appoint such legal counsel as it may deem necessary in executing its work, to form committees, and to provide for auxiliary corporations and associations, so long as such procedures are in harmony with the convention and subject to the control of the board. No agency or institution of the convention may incur indebtedness or launch a new enterprise calling for the expenditure of funds without the knowledge or consent of the convention or the board of directors.

Departments.—All convention departments maintain offices in the Baptist Building, 1141 N. Robinson, Oklahoma City, Okla. Sunday school and Training Union work is promoted through the Department of Religious Education, with E. W. Westmoreland as secretary since 1942. In 1954 enrolment statistics for the state showed 296,448 in Sunday school, 112,847 in Training Union, and 115,552 in 970 Vacation Bible schools held. The same year, 48,125 Sunday school training course awards and 46,777 Training Union study course awards were earned. Attendance at the December "M" Night meetings in 1954 totaled 19,070. In 1955, 1,515 standard Sunday school units were reported in the state. Two major conventions are sponsored annually. A Sunday school convention is held the second week in March, and since 1954 a Training Union convention has been held on Thanksgiving Day and the day following. Training classes are held at Falls Creek Assembly where 6,000 awards were issued in 70 classes in 1955. As its 1956 operation budget, the Department of Religious Education received an allocation of $51,000 from the Cooperative Program receipts of the state convention.

The work of Brotherhood and evangelism is promoted through one department with J. A. Pennington as secretary. All 39 white associations and three of the six Indian associations were organized for Brotherhood work in 1955, and 777 churches reported local organizations. In January of each year, the Brotherhood sponsors in the associations conferences for men and boys, to promote denominational work, and 8,226 men and boys attended these meetings in 1955. Simultaneous revivals are promoted, in which 1,028 churches participated in 1955, resulting in 9,260 additions by baptism and 4,110 by letter or statement. T. P. Haskins has served in this department as state evangelist since Sept. 1, 1951. This phase of the work was apportioned $26,483 of the 1956 Cooperative Program funds and had a total budget of $29,483.

The Department of Rural and City Missions is headed by Sam W. Scantlan. In 1955 this department reported 141 missions under the sponsorship of 1,299 churches; 12 associational schools of missions; 39 superintendents of missions in the associations; 12 summer student workers who served in nine different associations; and an enrolment of 91 at a summer school for preachers at Oklahoma Baptist University. For the year ending Aug. 31, 1955, this department showed the following statistics reported by the superintendents of missions: 262 revivals, 2,080 professions of faith, 1,075 baptisms, 1,031 other additions, 6,004 church and mission visits, 6,170 sermons preached, 177,341 copies of Scriptures and tracts given, 192 study courses held, 182 church fields surveyed, 5 dead churches reconstituted, 36 new churches constituted, 30 new missions started, 48 church houses built, and 128 church houses improved. Its 1956 budget of $54,000 was received as follows: $49,000 from the Cooperative Program and $5,000 from the Home Mission Board.

The public relations office, of which Arthur S. Davenport is director, serves the convention in formulating programs to meet the public interest through radio, television, the press, and special printed materials. The first regular convention-sponsored TV program, "Questions and Quotations," began in Jan., 1955, over Station KVOO-TV, Tulsa. This office also handles the convention's photographic work. In 1955 it produced a 16 mm. motion picture, *The Baptist Story,* to be used in 1956 in connection with the convention's Golden Jubilee observance. In 1956 the public relations office was appropriated $20,000 from the Cooperative Program and had a total budget of $20,350.

Baptist Student Union work and church music are promoted through one department, with Gene Bartlett as secretary. In 1955 the music program touched 37 associations, with awards for music studies in 170 churches. State youth and Junior choir festivals were held at Oklahoma Baptist University, with a total attendance of over 1,800. In 1955 B.S.U. had 21 organizations serving 8,000 Baptist students and 3,000 Baptist-preference students in the state schools. A state B.S.U. convention is held annually. A B.S.U. spring retreat is held at Falls Creek, where 350 were present in 1955. The B.S.U. department was appropriated $37,000 of Cooperative Program funds for its $52,809 operating budget in 1956.

Woman's Missionary Union, with Margaret Hutchison as secretary, functions as a department, although it exists as an auxiliary to the state convention; it holds its annual meetings at the same time the Brotherhood convention meets, just prior to the annual sessions of the state convention, and has its own executive board. This board is composed of the elected officers, chairmen, and representatives, and the associational W.M.U. presidents. Three board meetings are held each year. The executive secretary-treasurer handles all funds, serves as the medium of contact between all convention and local work, supervises all of the departments of W.M.U., and makes regular reports to the board concerning her work. In 1955 the state W.M.U. reported 874 societies with 27,091 members. Bob Banks was given full-time status as Royal Ambassador secretary, effective Jan. 1, 1956, under the joint sponsorship of the W.M.U. and the Brotherhood. In 1956 W.M.U. received an appropriation of $32,880 from the state Cooperative Program.

Institutions and agencies.—The work of all institutions and agencies of the convention is under the convention's board of directors, except Oklahoma Baptist University and the Oklahoma Baptist Foundation, which have their own boards elected by the convention. In 1956 the university was appropriated $300,000 from the convention's $2,000,000 Cooperative Program budget. The foundation, Auguie Henry, secretary, was allocated $45,500. Tom E. Carter is co-ordinator for the eight convention-operated hospitals, each of which has its own administrator. These hospitals in the 1955 convention year cared for 24,683 patients, gave 95,363 patient-days of care, attended the birth of 2,370 babies, served 498,091 meals, took 14,135 X rays, and made 78,867 laboratory examinations. Hospital work was given $71,000 in the 1956 convention budget. Carter also is business manager of the Baptist Building and Falls Creek Assembly. In 1956 the assembly had a $13,000 allocation from the Cooperative Program and a total budget of $88,000. The superintendents of the orphans' home and Boys' Ranch Town rank as department heads. The orphans' home, H. Truman Maxey, superintendent, had a 1956 budget of $258,500, of which all but $15,000 from the Cooperative Program was raised by special offerings and endowments. Boys' Ranch Town, Samuel W. Scantlan, superintendent, had a 1956 budget of $53,000, with $13,000 to come from the Cooperative Program and the balance from special gifts and trust funds. The *Baptist Messenger,* Jack L. Gritz, editor, is the convention's chief promotional agency. It is convention-owned and is controlled by the board. Its weekly circulation in 1955 reached 75,000, with 795 churches subscribing on the budget plan. The editor has the status of a department head. The *Messenger* had a 1956 budget of $150,000, of which $22,000 came from the Cooperative Program and the balance from subscriptions, advertising, and special editions. The Historical Commission, J. M. Gaskin, secretary, functions primarily in the interest of collecting and preserving Oklahoma Baptist history. The commission, created in 1952, has nine members, elected on a rotating basis for three-year terms. These members may succeed themselves.

Missions.—The state missions program includes a $900 annual supplement to each of 39 white Baptist associations to maintain a superintendent of missions; special assistance in operating Negro and Indian centers; and maintenance of summer workers, fieldworkers, and schools. Rural and city mission work is co-ordinated through the rural and city missions department, and Indian missions is directed by Bailey Sewell, who has headed this work since 1954 under the joint support of the convention and the Home Mission Board. Albert Lowther heads the city mission work in Oklahoma City and Leo M. Perry in Tulsa. Missionary education is conducted through Falls Creek and the other assemblies, schools of missions on the associational level, and Woman's Missionary Union organizations and weekday programs. A rural church building fund aids small churches in rural areas to construct houses of worship.

Promotion and finance.—The *Baptist Messenger* is the convention's organ of publicity, and all departments have access to its columns. General promotion for the convention is directed by W. E. Grindstaff, assistant executive secretary. Stewardship promotion objectives adopted in 1955 include continued emphasis on "Every Baptist a Tither," a goal of 50 per cent or more of the resident members of every church tithing, and the promotion of church giving through the Cooperative Program on a per-

IV. OKLAHOMA STATISTICAL SUMMARY

Year	Associa-tions	Churches	Church Member-ship	Baptisms	S. S. Enrol-ment	V.B.S. Enrol-ment	T. U. Enrol-ment	W.M.U. Enrol-ment	Brother-hood En-rolment	Mission Gifts	Total Gifts	Value Church Property	State Capital Worth
1830	..	....	....	....	....	....	....	....	....	....	....	....	(Explanation: This column includes total value of Schools, Children's Homes, Hospitals, Foundation, Buildings, etc.)
1840	..	....	....	125	....	....	....	....	....	....	....	....	
1850	..	....	....	....	....	....	....	....	....	....	....	....	
1860	..	....	....	400	....	....	....	....	....	....	....	....	
1870	..	....	....	....	....	....	....	....	....	....	....	....	
1880	..	....	....	141	....	....	....	....	....	....	....	....	
1890	..	....	....	487	....	....	....	....	....	....	....	....	
1900	..	....	....	....	....	....	....	....	....	....	....	....	
1906	40	855	44,971	5,187	21,904	....	....	....	....	$ 34,126	$ 265,410	$ 703,799	
1910	42	1,103	63,494	3,627	34,663	....	....	....	....	53,694	324,675	1,095,077	
1915	50	1,136	82,412	7,056	50,557	....	....	....	....	83,501	493,884	1,714,064	....
1920	49	1,181	94,488	6,395	60,533	....	....	6,273	....	222,073	860,336	2,530,298	....
1925	45	1,033	115,788	10,245	104,473	....	35,135	....	....	251,176	1,416,036	5,211,255	....
1930	41	1,083	150,324	10,586	130,947	....	32,526	....	....	386,170	2,232,444	9,634,683	....
1931	39	979	160,900	13,011	134,417	11,240	40,745	....	....	244,262	1,822,645	9,769,675	....
1932	40	983	165,884	14,180	139,811	7,517	37,628	....	....	187,529	1,371,612	9,044,916	....
1933	39	994	176,498	13,974	147,401	....	45,133	....	....	147,079	1,120,627	8,503,591	....
1934	39	1,032	186,314	14,496	152,007	....	41,059	....	....	184,019	1,226,884	8,365,065	$1,060,832
1935	39	1,073	199,039	13,578	160,846	....	46,426	....	....	208,514	1,422,592	8,359,348	....
1936	38	1,051	204,777	11,919	160,663	16,000	47,793	....	....	253,832	1,583,655	8,582,593	....
1937	38	1,061	211,978	12,956	161,008	23,000	50,130	....	....	265,878	1,739,807	8,987,622	....
1938	38	1,058	219,881	15,290	166,473	....	46,448	....	....	274,312	1,926,665	9,132,445	....
1939	39	1,072	234,676	17,883	179,873	....	68,373	....	....	293,353	1,978,466	9,263,416	....
1940	39	1,095	243,972	15,183	183,322	....	70,133	28,842	....	309,016	2,071,678	9,629,387	....
1941	39	1,117	253,062	13,588	180,407	39,236	68,271	....	....	380,755	2,348,360	10,253,385	....
1942	39	1,094	256,813	11,128	166,241	32,030	52,395	36,815	....	408,951	2,431,101	10,351,391	....
1943	39	1,048	256,342	10,555	156,652	31,212	50,204	35,683	2,197	553,123	2,986,184	10,843,869	....
1944	38	1,034	277,642	12,422	155,762	39,120	50,978	....	1,522	890,530	3,865,009	11,556,738	2,481,110
1945	38	1,050	280,304	15,147	167,150	40,484	41,707	....	2,308	1,148,340	5,002,404	12,643,108	....
1946	34	1,038	287,644	14,578	180,205	52,953	46,960	35,446	4,257	1,256,837	5,787,827	14,136,557	....
1947	38	1,038	298,739	16,470	196,316	62,561	54,289	31,780	6,905	1,257,109	6,625,648	16,787,172	....
1948	40	1,044	313,103	18,463	207,606	66,496	63,943	37,044	7,736	1,395,809	7,685,192	20,798,504	....
1949	38	1,072	323,839	17,537	219,708	64,358	69,288	38,566	9,603	1,445,090	8,881,744	25,356,302	....
1950	39	1,112	340,660	20,051	238,062	77,059	78,256	41,939	11,441	1,574,126	10,174,725	30,466,916	....
1951	38	1,140	398,184	21,739	320,639	113,101	94,565	92,451	8,486	2,422,262	10,600,291	35,504,700	....
1952	43	1,162	365,717	19,259	258,269	92,551	91,361	43,946	13,707	2,347,937	12,179,887	40,791,291	....
1953	43	1,213	379,861	19,954	268,935	97,552	100,947	46,965	15,339	2,402,907	13,702,275	48,409,787	....
1954	43	1,246	399,258	22,490	296,448	115,552	112,847	51,113	16,028	2,644,040	14,473,966	53,296,519	8,895,276

J. M. GASKIN

centage basis, with a minimum of 6 per cent of undesignated gifts marked for this cause. The 1956 convention budget included $29,650 for promotion.

The convention had a $2,000,000 Cooperative Program goal for 1956. In addition to department allocations, special items which shared in this budget included administration, $111,505; retirement, $96,000; O.B.U. operation, $75,000; beneficiary tuition, $25,000; building, $100,000; endowment, $100,000; Oklahoma City Hospital, $150,000; school of nursing and hospital help, $25,000; and Glorieta, $10,000. J. M. GASKIN

BIBLIOGRAPHY: C. H. Black, "One Hundred Twenty Years of Baptist Missionary Administration in Oklahoma" (1950). W. A. Carleton, *Not Yours But You* (1954). L. W. Marks, "The Story of Oklahoma Baptists" (n.d.). E. C. Routh, *The Story of Oklahoma Baptists* (1932). S. W. Scantlan, *Andrew Potter, Baptist Builder* (1955). L. W. Stigler, "A History of the Institutions of the Baptist General Convention of Oklahoma" (1945). J. B. Thoburn, *A Standard History of Oklahoma* (1916).

OKLAHOMA AND INDIAN TERRITORIES, BAPTIST MISSIONARY AND EDUCATIONAL CONVENTION OF. This body, commonly known as the Missionary and Educational Convention, was organized at Tahlequah, Indian Territory, June 2, 1883, pursuant to a call issued in the 1882 session of the Cherokee Association, for the purpose of uniting the Baptists of both territories into one general body. Joseph Samuel Murrow (*q.v.*) was chosen moderator and Daniel Rogers (*q.v.*), secretary *pro tem,* when the body convened on June 1. Almon Clematus Bacone (*q.v.*) was one of those appointed to draft a constitution. On June 2 the committee on the constitution reported favorably, and the convention was organized. Its object was "to unite all the Baptist churches of whatever tribe or nation of the Territories in a common effort for the spread of Christianity." The membership consisted of one person from each church and five from each association, plus one additional delegate from each church giving $5 and each association giving $10 into the convention treasury before the convention met in its annual session.

The convention sent William Conner as a missionary to the Plains Indians in 1884, but for lack of funds he served only a short time. In 1885 the *Indian Missionary,* a private publication, was endorsed, and in 1886 it was adopted as a convention paper. After 10 months, however, convention sponsorship of the paper was suspended. The body voted in 1897 to co-operate with the American Baptist Home Mission Society.

On June 16, 1898, the name was changed by striking out the words "Missionary and Educational." On Dec. 1, 1898, at a called meeting in Oklahoma City, it was mutually agreed to form two separate conventions for Oklahoma and Indian territories. The Indian Territory body adopted the name Baptist General Convention of Indian Territory, and the other body was named the Oklahoma Baptist Convention. J. M. GASKIN

OKLAHOMA ASSOCIATIONS.

I. Extant. ARBUCKLE. Organized out of Banner Association at Wynnewood, Okla., Oct. 14, 1949, by messengers from 16 churches in and adjacent to Murray and Garvin counties. A missionary is employed, and property consists of a missionary's home at Wynnewood valued at $7,000. By constitutional provision, trustees are moderator, vice-moderator, and clerk. In 1954, 21 churches reported 488 baptisms, 8,767 members, $292,692 total gifts, $52,188 mission gifts, $1,010,598 property value, and $140,286 church debt. J. M. GASKIN

ATOKA. Located in southeastern Oklahoma; organized 1911 with 20 churches, 16 of which came out of Bethel County Association upon its dissolution Sept. 8–9, 1911. In 1954, 20 churches reported 177 baptisms, 3,797 members, $83,843.36 total gifts, $15,137.43 mission gifts, $178,000.00 property value, and $8,036.10 church debt. ROGER D. HEBARD

BANNER. Organized in 1890 by churches in what are now Murray and Garvin counties. Articles of faith were adopted. In 1926 churches in Pontotoc Association merged with Banner. On Oct. 14, 1949, the churches in Murray and Garvin counties withdrew to form Arbuckle Association, leaving Pontotoc County churches as Banner Association. A superintendent of missions is employed. In 1954, 20 churches reported 379 baptisms, 8,872 members, $272,384 total gifts, $74,105 mission gifts, $978,550 property value, and $112,173 church debt.

BECKHAM. Organized at Sayre, Okla., Nov. 7, 1907, by messengers from 13 churches in Beckham County. In 1954, 14 churches and 4 missions reported 275 baptisms, 4,801 members, $150,306 total gifts, $35,694 mission gifts, $751,237 property value, and $25,758 church debt. A superintendent of missions is employed. J. M. GASKIN

BRYAN. Organized in 1911 by 12 churches in southeastern Oklahoma, bordered on the south by Red River and on the east by Frisco Association. In 1954, 37 churches and 2 missions reported 502 baptisms, 8,141 members, $219,136 total gifts, $30,322 mission gifts, $827,000 property value, and $73,475 church debt.

CADDO. Organized Aug. 30, 1904, at Hinton by 35 delegates from 13 churches in west central Oklahoma. Membership in the constituting churches totaled 361 and Sunday school enrolment was 702. Total gifts the first year were $4,127. Articles of faith were adopted. In 1954, 24 churches and 1 mission reported 495 baptisms, 6,565 members, $205,591 total gifts, $43,-451 mission gifts, $701,750 property value, and $51,000 church debt. A superintendent of missions is employed. ROGER D. HEBARD

CENTRAL. Organized in 1902, by churches in Blain, Kingfisher, Logan, Canadian, and Oklahoma counties. In 1907, 22 churches reported 374 baptisms, 2,520 members, $50,326 total gifts,

$199,300 property value. Articles of faith prepared by J. Newton Brown were adopted. In 1926, Oklahoma County Association was organized, leaving Central with 15 churches. In 1954, 23 churches reported 413 baptisms, 7,986 members, $271,546 total gifts, $56,956 mission gifts, $1,029,363 property value, and $59,523 church debt. A superintendent of missions is employed and lives in a home owned by the association. J. W. HODGES

CHEROKEE INDIAN. Organized Sept., 1860, in the Masonic Hall at Tahlequah, Indian Territory, with six churches. In 1879, 11 churches reported 40 baptisms and 1,069 members. In 1885, 22 churches reported 159 baptisms and 1,554 members. In 1943, they built a stone tabernacle on their assembly grounds six miles east of Tahlequah, which is their regular meeting place. Other buildings have since been added. In 1954, 34 churches reported 142 baptisms, 3,467 members, $12,186 total gifts, and $2,430 mission gifts. Since 1939, a general missionary has been provided by the Home Mission Board. BAILEY SEWELL

CHICKASAW. Organized *c.* 1894. Delegates met in special session Aug. 16, 1930, to consider uniting with Union Association since depression conditions had made it financially impossible to carry on a worthy mission program. This merger, formed Sept. 16, 1930, at Lindsay, was dissolved at Purcell Feb. 7, 1939, and Chickasaw was reorganized at Chickasha, Mar. 20, 1939. In 1954, 17 churches reported 395 baptisms, 7,013 members, $192,225 total gifts, $43,275 mission gifts, $487,950 property value, and $14,950 church debt. It is served by a superintendent of missions. J. M. GASKIN

CHI-KA-SHA INDIAN. Organized by eight churches Oct. 7, 1910, at High Hill Baptist Church No. 2. These churches came out of the Choctaw-Chickasaw Baptist Association and thought of their territory as being "within the bounds of the Chickasaw Nation." In 1954, 11 churches reported 43 baptisms, 493 members, $5,242 total gifts, and $852 mission gifts. Since 1950 the Home Mission Board has provided a missionary couple. BAILEY SEWELL

CHOCTAW-CHICKASAW INDIANS. Organized at Rehoboth Church (now Atoka), July 5, 1872, by 46 messengers from 16 churches with 724 members in the Choctaw and Chickasaw nations of Indian Territory. It included Indians, Negroes, and white people. Articles of faith were adopted at the first session. The associational Woman's Missionary Union organized in 1876 at Nunny-Cha-Ha (High Hill), with 46 charter members, was the first in Indian or Oklahoma territories. On Oct. 7, 1910, the Chickasaw churches organized the Chi-Ka-Sha Association, and the Choctaw churches continued as the original body, known as either the Choctaw, or Choctaw-Chickasaw Association. In 1954, 23 churches reported 72 baptisms, 458 members, and $1,984 mission gifts. HERBERT M. PIERCE

CIMARRON. Organized Oct. 11, 1951, by 34 churches in Creek, Pawnee, and Payne counties from the Pawnee-Creek and Pawnee-Payne associations. Articles of faith were adopted, expressly repudiating alien immersion. In 1954, 39 churches reported 829 baptisms, 16,552 members, $531,139.40 total gifts, $89,651.66 mission gifts, $1,792,400.00 property value, and $324,572.38 church debt. A missionary is employed. J. W. HODGES

COMANCHE-COTTON. Organized as Comanche County Association on June 17, 1902, by five churches with 150 members. In the 1903 session at Lawton, 12 new churches were admitted by petitionary letters, and articles of faith were adopted. It consisted primarily of churches in Comanche and Cotton counties and was renamed Comanche-Cotton *c.* 1919. In 1954, 30 churches reported 735 baptisms, 32,857 members, $495,107 total gifts, $114,798 mission gifts, $1,390,589 property value, and $115,361 church debt. A superintendent of missions is employed. J. M. GASKIN

CONCORD-KIOWA. Organized Aug. 31, 1927, by merger of two associations bearing those names, including 26 churches in Custer, Washita, and Kiowa counties. Kiowa was organized in 1902 at Hobard, by 10 churches with 286 members. Concord (Custer and Washita counties) was organized in 1914. The present body dates itself to 1927 because the merger at that time climaxed an invitation from Concord to churches of Kiowa County to unite in one body. In 1954, 26 churches and 3 missions reported 551 baptisms, 10,556 members, $322,182 total gifts, $81,786 mission gifts, $1,317,798 property value, including a $7,000 home for superintendent of missions employed by the association, and $37,883 church debt. R. L. MCCLUNG

CRAIG-MAYES. Organized Oct. 5, 1950, at Pryor, Okla., out of Northeastern Association by 97 messengers from 19 churches in Craig and Mayes counties representing 5,421 members. The New Hampshire Confession was adopted as its statement of faith. In 1954, 25 churches reported 382 baptisms, 6,078 members, $117,626 total gifts, $26,882 mission gifts, $612,700 property value, and $59,120 church debt. A superintendent of missions is employed. J. M. GASKIN

DELAWARE-OSAGE. Organized Sept. 13, 1932, by 25 churches in Osage, Washington, and Nowata counties in northeastern Oklahoma. The parent body was Delaware Association. Articles of faith were adopted. In 1954, 32 churches and 9 missions reported 780 baptisms, 12,572 members, $522,788 total gifts, $104,320 mission gifts, $1,903,500 property value, and $339,511 church debt. A missionary is employed.

ROGER D. HEBARD

EAST CENTRAL. Organized July 7, 1955, out of Muskogee Association with 27 churches and three missions in Adair, Cherokee, and Sequoyah counties. In 1954, 27 churches and 3 missions reported 546 baptisms, 5,156 members, $112,188 total gifts, $17,150 mission gifts, $334,600 property value, and $26,981 church debt. A superintendent of missions is employed. J. M. GASKIN

ENON. Oklahoma's oldest white Baptist association with a continuous history under the same name, held two organizational meetings, with the Wilson Creek and New Hope churches Aug. 29 and Oct. 16–17, 1885, respectively, in the southern part of Indian Territory. Enon adopted the articles of faith and constitution of Shiloh Association, presumably the one in North Texas, except for changing the name. It has been the parent body of four associations: Salem, 1891; Mullins, 1895; Philadelphia, 1910, and Johnston-Marshall, 1947. Enon has been served by an associational missionary most of the time since 1892. In 1954, 39 churches and 5 missions reported 769 baptisms, 10,050 members, $380,905 total gifts, $64,211 mission gifts, $1,106,284 property value, and $138,200 church debt. It owns the missionary's residence. MAX STANFIELD

FRISCO. Organized in 1894 by 11 churches with 253 members. It now includes churches in Choctaw, McCurtain, and Pushmataha counties. In 1954, 42 churches and 5 missions reported 629 baptisms, 8,576 members, $181,991 total gifts, $37,775 mission gifts, $502,971 property value, and $13,577 church debt. A superintendent of missions is employed. J. C. SEGLER

GREAT PLAINS INDIAN. Organized at the Indian mission, Colony, Okla., July 28, 1955, to serve Indian settlements of western Oklahoma. Four missions were represented, reporting 31 baptisms and 97 members. BAILEY SEWELL

HARMON. Organized Oct. 4, 1911, out of Greer County Association, by nine churches, at Hollis, in Harmon County. There were 16 churches represented in the third session in 1914. In 1954, 9 churches reported 63 baptisms, 2,143 members, $71,563.77 total gifts, $16,304.41 mission gifts, $158,500.00 property value, and $17,130.00 church debt.

HASKELL. Organized in 1912 in Haskell County by 17 churches from LeFlore County. In 1954, 17 churches and 1 mission reported 130 baptisms, 1,950 members, $52,192.18 total gifts, $8,232.45 mission gifts, $203,500.00 property value, and $18,787.00 church debt. It employs a superintendent of missions.

JACKSON-GREER. Organized Sept. 20, 1927, by messengers from 23 churches with 4,752 members in Jackson and Greer counties. Parent bodies were Greer County Association organized in 1889, and Jackson County Association organized out of Greer County in 1907. These two united to form the present association. In 1954, 25 churches reported 399 baptisms, 7,949 members, $346,171.00 total gifts, $56,815.78 mission gifts, $748,250.00 property value, and $26,996.00 church debt. The association owns a home for the superintendent of missions. Southwest Baptist Hospital, which is owned by the state convention, is located at Mangum, in Greer County. R. L. MCCLUNG

JOHNSTON-MARSHALL. Organized at Madill, Sept. 29, 1947, by 80 representatives from 13 churches in Enon and Bryan associations. In 1954, 27 churches in Johnston and Marshall counties reported 191 baptisms, 2,512 members, $126,474 total gifts, $18,635 mission gifts, $467,580 property value, and $15,399 church debt. A superintendent of missions is employed. J. C. SEGLER

KAY. Organized at Ponca City, Kay County, Okla., from Perry Association, Oct. 3, 1947, by messengers from 17 churches representing 5,085 members. Articles of faith were adopted. In 1954, 21 churches and 3 missions reported 334 baptisms, 7,482 members, $297,478 total gifts, $52,669 mission gifts, $1,251,750 property value, and $127,500 church debt. A superintendent of missions is employed. J. M. GASKIN

LATIMER. Organized at Wilburton, Oct. 23, 1935, by 35 messengers from 14 churches in Latimer County. Constitution and rules of decorum were adopted from the parent LeFlore-Latimer Association. The original membership was 1,530; $8,040 total gifts, $955 gifts to missions. A B.S.U. was established at Eastern A & M College, Wilburton, in 1937, and an $8,000 student center purchased by Latimer and adjacent associations in 1953. Kiamichi Assembly is located in its area. In 1954, 14 churches reported 110 baptisms, 1,905 members, $48,417 total gifts, $7,355 mission gifts, $115,000 property value, and $8,655 church debt. HERBERT M. PIERCE

LEFLORE. Organized as Short Mountain Association Oct. 24–25, 1884, in the home of A. F. Cowling in northern part of present LeFlore County with 12 messengers from eight churches. Articles of faith were adopted. At a meeting in Heavener in Oct., 1912, the name was changed to LeFlore-Latimer County Association. After meeting at the same place in Oct., 1935, Latimer County churches withdrew to organize the Latimer Association, and the original body continued as the LeFlore Association. In 1954, 45 churches reported 418 baptisms, 8,943 members, $224,756 total gifts, $37,549 mission gifts, $606,900 property value, and $23,739 church debt. This association owns a missionary's home, also a cabin at Kiamichi Assembly. A superintendent of missions is employed. J. M. GASKIN

MILLS. Organized in 1899 by churches in Mills County. Twelve churches reported at the second annual session. In 1954, 11 churches reported 158 baptisms, 1,304 members, $46,522 total gifts, $9,868 mission gifts, $157,725 property value, and $901 church debt. It is served by a superintendent of missions. J. C SEGLER

MULLINS. Organized in Oct., 1895, by messengers from 24 churches in western part of Enon Association. Articles of faith were adopted, and name assumed in honor of Daniel David Mullins (*q.v.*). Its boundaries were Red River on the south, Rush Creek on the north, Healdton on the east, and "the setting sun marked its western limits." Present area is Stephens and Jefferson counties. In 1954, 25 churches and 5 missions reported 617 baptisms, 10,639 members, $465,068 total gifts, $86,249 mission gifts, $1,453,500 property value, and $296,754 church debt. A superintendent of missions is employed. JESS KIRKLEY

MUSKOGEE. Organized in 1913 by 18 churches in Muskogee, Wagoner, and Okmulgee counties.

In 1954, it included Muskogee, Wagoner, Sequoyah, Cherokee, Adair, and part of McIntosh counties. On July 7, 1955, East Central Association was organized out of it, leaving it with 38 churches in Muskogee, Wagoner, and McIntosh counties. In 1954, these 38 churches reported 804 baptisms, 6,984 members, $417,212 total gifts, $63,315 mission gifts, $1,307,600 property value, and $131,619 church debt. In 1955 it adopted the New Hampshire Confession of Faith. A superintendent of missions is employed. ROGER D. HEBARD

MUSKOGEE, SEMINOLE, AND WICHITA INDIAN. Organized at old North Fork Town, Creek Nation, Sept., 1851. There are no known written accounts of the early history of this association, and no meetings were held from 1860–74. It was reorganized as Muskoke Baptist Association in 1874 and since has had a continuous history. The present name was adopted in 1885. That year reports showed 71 baptisms and 964 members. In 1954, 25 churches reported 98 baptisms, 1,978 members, $15,367 total gifts, and $4,425 mission gifts. Since 1948 the association has had the services of a general missionary of the Home Mission Board. BAILEY SEWELL

NORTH CANADIAN. Organized in 1895 by churches located in the present area of Hughes, Seminole, and Okfuskee counties. In 1911, 27 churches reported 202 baptisms and 1,409 members. Churches in Okmulgee County were added in 1935. The association adopted 13 articles of faith. On Sept. 17, 1948, it voted to divide, effective Jan. 1, 1949, with churches in Okmulgee and Okfuskee counties continuing as North Canadian Association and churches in Seminole and Hughes counties forming South Canadian Association. In 1954, 24 churches and 4 missions reported 477 baptisms, 9,349 members, $299,631 total gifts, $63,299 mission gifts, $814,600 property value, and $25,825 church debt. A superintendent of missions is employed. J. C. SEGLER

NORTHEASTERN. Organized Aug. 26–28, 1913, at Vinita, Okla., by messengers from churches in Craig and Ottawa counties. Dual alignment with Southern and Northern Baptist Conventions was adopted. Later 18 articles of faith were adopted, together with a single alignment policy. The area now served includes Ottawa and Delaware counties. In 1954, 38 churches reported 420 baptisms, 9,454 members, $286,665 total gifts, $54,542 mission gifts, $853,100 property value, and $86,155 church debt. An associational missionary is employed. J. M. GASKIN

NORTHWESTERN. Organized in June, 1902, by six churches in Northwestern Oklahoma Territory. Eight churches were added in 1904. The 1905 minutes state: "We recommend the adoption of the articles of faith as prepared by John Newton Brown and published in Pendleton's Manual." In 1908 six churches in Harper County formed Harper County Association, and the parent body became known as Woodward County (later Woodward-Ellis) Association. In 1923 these bodies merged and resumed the name Northwestern Association.

In 1954, 16 churches reported 155 baptisms, 3,239 members, $141,740 total gifts, $30,505 mission gifts, $661,000 property value, and $63,820 church debt. Since 1902, with the exception of four years, it has been served by an associational missions superintendent. HORACE L. JANES

OKLAHOMA COUNTY. Organized in a special meeting Sept. 13, 1926, at First Baptist Church, Oklahoma City, Okla., by messengers from 19 churches in Oklahoma County. Its first annual session was held at Immanuel Church, Oklahoma City, Sept. 20–21, 1927, when 23 churches reported 871 baptisms and 10,707 members. The parent body was Central Association. In 1944, in co-operation with the Home Mission Board, it began mission work among the Negroes. In 1954 the association purchased a $15,000 Negro center and a year later was helping to support work at the center and a Negro missionary.

Work among the Mexicans was begun in 1943 and among Indians and deaf people in 1944, all in co-operation with the Home Mission Board. The association pioneered in simultaneous and interracial revivals and has conducted them annually since 1944. It is incorporated and owns the following property: a missionary's home, value $15,000; a Mexican church, value $25,000; a Mexican pastor's home, value $10,000; a Negro center, value $15,000; lots for future mission or church buildings, value $51,000. In 1954, 94 churches and 14 missions reported 3,848 baptisms, 63,578 members, $3,011,122 total gifts, $496,424 mission gifts, $12,568,065 property value, and $2,851,000 church debt. In 1954, a total of 53,519 baptisms had been reported since organization. The association employs an executive secretary-treasurer, a position known in most associations as superintendent of missions. It has adopted the New Hampshire Confession of Faith. J. M. GASKIN

OKLAHOMA INDIAN. Organized Nov. 12, 1897, at Immanuel Chapel (now Rainy Mountain), with four churches. Oklahoma Territory was the area to be served. At the first anniversary meeting, held with the First Cheyenne Baptist Church near Kingfisher, June 10–12, 1898, five churches, including Second Cheyenne which had been added, reported 36 baptisms and 298 members. In 1917, the association divided over "the alignment issue." Eleven churches started the Western Oklahoma Indian Baptist Association, which affiliates with the American (then Northern) Baptist Convention. The Oklahoma Indian Baptist Association affiliates with the Southern Baptist Convention. In 1919 five churches reported 75 baptisms and a total membership of 515. In 1954, 7 churches reported 37 baptisms, 807 members, $6,080.82 total gifts, $1,248.42 mission gifts, and $26,500.00 property value. BAILEY SEWELL

PANHANDLE. Organized at Goodwell, Aug. 30, 1922, by a merger of Beaver County and Texas-Cimarron associations, comprising Beaver, Texas, and Cimarron counties, an area known as the Oklahoma Panhandle and formerly called "No Man's Land." The initial organization was formed by 45 messengers from 16 churches with 1,358 members; nine other churches in the area did not report. In 1954, 19 churches reported 229 baptisms, 4,076 members, $205,188 total gifts, $48,946 mission gifts, $926,250 property value, and $7,708 church debt. This association supports Gibson Assembly and employs a superintendent of missions.

PERRY. Organized Sept. 4, 1894, by messengers from 12 churches in the Cherokee Strip; assumed the name of its parent church. Until the organization of Kay Association in 1947, it included Noble, Garfield, and Kay counties. Since that time the original name has been retained by the body comprising Noble and Garfield counties. In 1954, 20 churches reported 285 baptisms, 7,134 members, $264,517 total gifts, $43,058 mission gifts, $1,072,684 property value, and $24,047 church debt. A superintendent of missions is employed; youth camp is held annually at Camp Wentz, Ponca City; and a B.S.U. program is maintained at the school of nursing, Enid General Hospital, with the superintendent of missions as director. J. M. GASKIN

PITTSBURG. Organized out of Zion Association in Oct., 1910, by 15 churches in Pittsburg County. In 1927 it merged with McIntosh County Association to form the Canadian Valley Association, which dissolved in 1931, and Pittsburg County took its original name again. On Oct. 1, 1936, churches of the recently dissolved McIntosh Association were invited to join Pittsburg; three responded with petitionary letters, and the next year the constitution was revised and the name changed by deleting the word "county." In 1954, 34 churches and 1 mission reported 535 baptisms, 9,096 members, $259,311 total gifts, $45,677 mission gifts, $671,400 property value, and $60,896 church debt. Since 1940 it has been served by a missionary, and it owns his residence. MAX STANFIELD

POTTAWATOMIE-LINCOLN. Organized at Meeker, Aug. 25–26, 1931, by a merger of Pottawatomie and Lincoln County associations, with 26 churches reporting 6,215 members. In 1954, 50 churches reported 743 baptisms, 16,691 members, $586,186 total gifts, $102,623 mission gifts, $2,105,970 property value, and $312,241 church debt. A superintendent of missions is employed. J. M. GASKIN

SALT FORK. Organized as Salt Fork Valley at Hawley, Oklahoma Territory, Oct. 2–4, 1896, by six churches in Grant and Woods counties. Many moderators and clerks served long periods, and four of the present churches, Alva, Medford, Bethel Hawley, and Mt. Zion, have celebrated their 60th anniversary. In 1954, 16 churches reported 172 baptisms, 2,790 members, $145,982 total gifts, $24,870 mission gifts, $465,000 property value, and $64,515 church debt. It has a superintendent of missions. HORACE L. JANES

SOUTH CANADIAN. Organized by 27 churches in Seminole and Hughes counties, Oct. 26, 1948, pursuant to resolutions adopted by the parent North Canadian Association, Sept. 17, 1948, which provided for a division effective Jan. 1, 1949. Its first annual session was held Sept. 23, 1949. In 1954, 29 churches reported 455 baptisms, 4,640 members, $430,949 total gifts, $75,062 mission gifts, $1,317,600 property value, and $65,844 church debt. A superintendent of missions is employed. J. W. HODGES

TILLMAN. Organized Jan. 25, 1907, at Frederick, Okla., by churches in Tillman County. At the sixth session in 1912, 18 churches reported 114 baptisms, 1,525 members and $11,927 total gifts. In 1954, 21 churches reported 235 baptisms, 4,544 members, $243,449 total gifts, $48,042 mission gifts, $767,200 property value, and $89,423 church debt. It is served by a superintendent of missions. J. C. SEGLER

TULSA-ROGERS. Organized in Oct., 1931, by churches in Tulsa and Rogers counties from Delaware Association. At the first annual session in 1932, 28 churches reported 9,307 members, 25 Sunday schools with 8,300 enrolled, and 19 Training Unions. A city mission program was adopted in 1943. In 1954, 79 churches reported 2,387 baptisms, 35,851 members, $1,925,519 total gifts, $293,219 mission gifts, $7,785,562 property value, and $1,597,500 church debt. A superintendent of missions, office secretary, and B.S.U. secretary are employed. In 1956 it owned property valued at $63,000 consisting of a home for superintendent of missions, value $18,000; home for minister of students, value $10,000; student center, value $10,000; and recreation park and equipment, value $25,000. Debt on these totaled $21,000. DAVID C. HALL

UNION. Organized 1921 by 16 churches in McClain County. Parent associations were Little River and McClain County. From 1930 through 1938, Union Association was united with the Chickasaw Association. In 1954, 26 churches reported 575 baptisms, 8,655 members, $227,353 total gifts, $59,059 mission gifts, $307,820 property value, and $143,077 church debt. Since 1922 it has been served by a superintendent of missions. H. L. JANES

II. Extinct. ARKANSAS VALLEY. Organized in 1891. At the second session 13 churches reported 418 members in Muskogee and Sequoyah counties. HERBERT M. PIERCE

BARON FORK. Organized before 1909 by churches in Adair, Sequoyah, and Cherokee counties.

BEAVER COUNTY. Organized at Tyrone, Sept. 16, 1904, by messengers from six of the seven churches in Beaver County, which then included all of Oklahoma Panhandle, a strip 168 miles long and 33 miles wide, bordered by Kansas, Colorado, New Mexico, and Texas. After Texas-Cimarron Association was formed in 1908, Beaver County continued until it merged with Texas-Cimarron in 1922 to form Panhandle Association. J. M. GASKIN

BETHEL. Organized at Durant Oct. 7, 1893, (probably in the Liberty Church, later called the First Baptist Church) by 11 churches at least half of which were affiliated with the Choctaw-Chickasaw Baptist Association. Part of the minutes were written in Choctaw. Six years later, because of "unsound doctrine," the association "unanimously declined to correspond" with the Choctaw-Chickasaw Association. The confession of faith was Calvinistic.

CANADIAN RIVER. Organized by five churches at Whitefield July 23, 1891. The first general session was held at Enterprise, Haskell County, Sept. 5, 1891. A Sunday school convention was organized while the association was in session with the Cowlington Church, Apr. 16, 1899.

HERBERT M. PIERCE

CANADIAN VALLEY. Organized Oct. 4, 1927, at Eufaula, by a merger of Pittsburg and McIntosh associations. The new body included 23 churches, with 4,035 members. The next year 35 churches reported 5,032 members. On Oct. 9, 1931, at Quinton this body dissolved to form two separate associations, Pittsburg and McIntosh.

J. M. GASKIN

CENTRAL DISTRICT. Also called Oklahoma District, organized in 1890 by six churches with a total membership of 158, in the First Baptist Church, Oklahoma City, serving Canadian, McClain, Blain, Logan, Kingfisher, and Oklahoma counties. Oklahoma County Association organized from it Sept. 26, 1926.

CHICKASAW. Organized in 1892 by Chickasaw Indian and Negro Baptists, to serve the Chickasaw Nation. It had in its fellowship 25 churches in 1902.

CHICKASAW. Organized Oct. 27, 1893, in Salt Creek Church by six churches in Pontotoc County. Joseph Samuel Murrow (*q.v.*) was moderator of the organizational meeting.

COLLATE MISSIONARY (Cherokee Indian). Organized in 1886 in the northeastern part of Indian Territory. It also fellowshiped Negro and white messengers, and sponsored both Sunday school and W.M.U. conventions. J. R. White (Negro) was sent as missionary to the Negroes among the Five Civilized Tribes.

DELAWARE. Organized Sept. 16–18, 1892, at Alluwe, Indian Territory, by 20 "delegates" from seven churches in northeastern Oklahoma. Its statement of faith was the one "published by the American Baptist Publication Society." From this parent body the following associations have been formed, in all or in part: Northeastern, Haskell, Creek County, Osage County, Tulsa-Rogers, and Muskogee.

FREEDMANS. First known Negro associatión in Indian or Oklahoma territories, organized Nov. 22, 1878, at the Freedmans Baptist Church, Creek Nation, with Munday Durant, moderator, and D. Perryman, clerk, with four churches represented. Messengers who disobeyed the moderator's commands while the association was in session were fined 10 cents for each offense.

FRIENDSHIP. Organized in 1893 serving the present Pottawatomie, Seminole, and Oklahoma counties. In 1897 there were 34 churches with a membership of 1,941. The Pottawatomie County Association came out of Friendship in 1893.

GRAND RIVER. Organized in 1897 by churches in the Vinita and Miami areas of Northeastern Oklahoma. Albert G. Washburn (*q.v.*) was moderator of the fifth session which took into its fellowship 505 members representing 10 churches.

HERBERT M. PIERCE

GRANT COUNTY. Organized Aug. 22, 1919, at Nash, out of Salt Fork Association in its 24th annual session. In the 1920 session at Pond Creek six churches with 32 delegates present reported six Sunday schools with 616 enrolled; $19,267 gifts, $5,628 mission gifts, and $36,100 property value.

J. M. GASKIN

ILLINOIS RIVER. Organized from the Cherokee Indian Association Nov. 14, 1896, at the Shiloh Church, Tahlequah District, Cherokee Nation, by three churches together with three other English-speaking churches. The confession of faith was Calvinistic.

INDIAN TERRITORY, GENERAL ASSOCIATION OF UNITED BAPTISTS IN THE SOUTHERN PART OF. Organized at Armstrong Academy (six miles east of Durant, Okla.) on the third Sunday in Oct., 1848, by 13 churches representing 863 members. Ramsey Potts was the first moderator and Americus L. Hay, clerk. The association was supported by the American Indian Mission Association; it was composed of Choctaw and Creek Indians and a few white people.

INTERNATIONAL BAPTIST. Probably Negro; organized in 1891, called a convention rather than an association. Its churches were scattered from Tahlequah to Atoka (150 miles apart) in Cherokee and Choctaw nations. Reporting to the second session were eight churches, one of which was the Ebenezer (Fountain) Negro church organized in 1832 seven miles north of Muskogee. They voted to do mission work among the Five Civilized Tribes in Indian Territory.

INTERNATIONAL BAPTIST SUNDAY SCHOOL CONVENTION. Organized in 1878, sponsored by the interdenominational American Sunday School Union. Baptists, Daniel Rogers (*q.v.*) and Aaron Frank Ross (*q.v.*) were president and secretary in 1883.

HERBERT M. PIERCE

LINCOLN COUNTY. Organized *c.* 1894, by churches in Lincoln County. Articles of faith were adopted. In 1931 the association merged with Pottawatomie County to form Pottawatomie-Lincoln Association.

J. M. GASKIN

LITTLE RIVER. Organized in 1891 serving convention churches in Cleveland County in and around Norman.

LONGTOWN. Organized in Oct., 1895, at the Longtown Church by 14 churches. It served churches in Pittsburg, Haskell, and McIntosh counties. The confession of faith was Calvinistic.

HERBERT M. PIERCE

MCCURTAIN COUNTY. Organized at Idabel, Oct. 4, 1921, with 14 co-operating churches listing 1,367 members. It adopted 19 articles of faith. Later the association dissolved to become part of Frisco Association.

MCINTOSH COUNTY. Organized 1914, by churches in McIntosh County. In 1927 it dissolved to unite with Canadian Valley Association, then when this body dissolved in 1931,

McIntosh was reorganized on Sept. 25 of that year. This body permanently dissolved in 1936, the churches joining Pittsburg and Muskogee associations. J. M. GASKIN

MT. ZION. Organized on Oct. 7, 1894, from the Choctaw-Chickasaw Association at the Pleasant Valley Church, Atoka County, by four churches. By 1897 it embraced widely scattered churches in Pontotoc, Pittsburg, and Payne counties. The confession of faith was Calvinistic.

OKLAHOMA. Organized before 1893. It was possibly the same as Central District Association or Oklahoma District Association.

OKLAHOMA DISTRICT. Organized before 1900 and probably before 1893. It was possibly the same as Central District or Oklahoma Association.

PAWNEE COUNTY. Organized in 1898 by six churches with a total membership of 146. Calvinistic in its confession of faith, it merged Oct. 14, 1925, with Creek County churches to form Pawnee-Creek Association.

HERBERT M. PIERCE

PAWNEE-CREEK. Organized Oct. 14, 1925, at Bristow, Okla., by messengers from 18 churches in Creek County, formerly in the Delaware Association, and churches of Pawnee County, formerly Pawnee County Association. The articles of faith adopted specifically repudiated alien immersion. On Oct. 15, 1946, at Yale, Okla., this body dissolved to form Creek County and Pawnee-Payne associations.

PHILADELPHIA. Organized 1910 at Madill. Participating churches had 699 members. Adopted 15 Calvinistic articles of faith bearing signs of Landmarkism.

PONTOTOC. Organized in 1910 by churches in Pontotoc County. In 1926 it merged with Banner Association.

POTTAWATOMIE COUNTY. Organized *c.* 1893, as Friendship Association, renamed Pottawatomie County at New Hope Church, southwest of Shawnee, Sept. 1, 1911. It merged with Lincoln County Association in 1931, to form Pottawatomie-Lincoln. J. M. GASKIN

RAMSEY. Organized in 1860 by Robert Jasper Hogue (*q.v.*) at Philadelphia Baptist Church, eight miles east of Durant with five widely spread Choctaw and Chickasaw Indian churches from San Bois and Blue counties. Willis Burns was the first moderator. Named in honor of the veteran missionary to the Choctaws, Ramsey D. Potts.

SALIM. Organized Oct. 9, 1891, at Duncan Prairie Church, Pickens County, by 19 churches in Love and other counties representing 674 members who had withdrawn with Christian harmony from Enon Association. The Sante Fe Railroad served as the dividing line.

SALT FORK VALLEY. Organized in 1896 at Hawley Church. The association served churches around Alva and Pond Creek.

HERBERT M. PIERCE

SEQUOYAH. Organized in 1909 out of Baron Fork, included Adair, Cherokee, and Sequoyah counties. J. M. GASKIN

SHORT MOUNTAIN. Organized Oct. 24, 1884, in the residence of A. F. Cowling, Cowlington, Indian Territory, by messengers from eight white churches, some of which continued to affiliate with the Choctaw-Chickasaw Association. Presumed to be the first white association in Indian and Oklahoma territories, it served churches from the Arkansas line, westward beyond Hartshorne, Indian Territory.

SOUTH CANADIAN. Organized in 1890 at Wynnwood, Garvin County, Okla. It adopted articles of faith as set forth in James Madison Pendleton's *Church Manual,* but professedly Landmark.

SOUTHEASTERN. Predominantly Negro, organized Sept. 25, 1891, at the Richland Church (Kully Inla) in Red River County (now McCurtain) in the extreme southeast corner of the Choctaw Nation. George W. Dallas, the first moderator, was superintendent of a Negro academy at Richland which burned in 1886 but was rebuilt, reporting teachers and 120 pupils in 1891.

SPRING VALLEY. Organized before 1886, reporting at that time three churches with a total membership of 175.

SUNDAY SCHOOL AND COLPORTAGE. Organized in 1897 and affiliated with the Oklahoma Sunday School and Colportage Convention. Partial toward the Southern Baptist Convention, it endorsed with some financial help 13 colporteurs between Mar. 12 and Oct. 1, 1898. The salary of the corresponding secretary of the association was paid by the Southern Baptist Home Mission Board. HERBERT M. PIERCE

TEXAS-CIMARRON. Organized out of Beaver County Association in 1908 by churches in Texas and Cimarron counties. It merged with Beaver County Association in 1922 to form Panhandle Association.

WASHITA. Organized Aug. 27, 1891, at Lone Star Church, Bitter Creek, Pontotoc County, Indian Territory, by messengers from seven churches. Adopted 16 Calvinistic articles of faith.

J. M. GASKIN

WASHITA AND CADDO. Organized in 1892 by eight churches in south central counties of Love, Garvin, and Carter (Ardmore), Oklahoma Territory, and possibly other counties.

WAYLAND MISSIONARY (Negro). Organized Sept. 6, 1883, in the Rehoboth Church at Atoka, Choctaw Nation, with Samuel Perry, first moderator, and J. E. Minton, clerk. Eleven churches were represented, eight of which reported a total of 108 members. HERBERT M. PIERCE

OKLAHOMA BAPTIST. A monthly paper established at Guthrie, Okla., in 1890, edited by J. S. Nasmith. It had four pages, 13 x 20 inches, and the price was 50 cents a year. The paper no longer exists. J. M. GASKIN

OKLAHOMA BAPTIST BULLETIN. A monthly, begun in Oklahoma City, Okla., in 1903. In Apr., 1904, the paper was moved to Norman, Oklahoma Territory, with Number 13 of Volume I distributed in May of that year.

C. W. Brewer edited the *Bulletin,* which had four pages originally 9 x 12 inches in size. In Feb., 1906, its size was changed to 10½ x 13 inches, with four columns to the page, and in Nov., 1906, to 9 x 12 inches, with three columns to the page; subscription price was 25 cents per year. Joseph Cole Stalcup (*q.v.*) replaced Brewer as editor in Dec., 1906. The paper is now extinct.

J. M. GASKIN

OKLAHOMA BAPTIST CONVENTION. Organized at Oklahoma City, Dec. 1, 1898, when by mutual agreement the Baptist Missionary and Educational Convention of Oklahoma and Indian Territories divided to form separate bodies in Oklahoma and Indian Territories. The Oklahoma Convention, serving Oklahoma Territory, effected a temporary organization with Luman Lucius Smith (*q.v.*) as chairman of a committee, which met Jan. 30, 1899, drafted a proposed constitution, and called a permanent organizational meeting at Enid, June 21, 1899. At the Enid meeting the committee's report was adopted, and officers were elected. This body co-operated with the Home Mission Society. At Blackwell, Oct. 12, 1900, it merged with the Oklahoma Baptist State Convention to continue as a united convention for Oklahoma Territory under the name of that body. Luman Lucius Smith was influential in bringing unification in 1900.

J. M. GASKIN

OKLAHOMA BAPTIST FOUNDATION. Created by the Baptist General Convention of Oklahoma in 1946 as an incorporated trust agency of the convention and for all institutions and agencies owned and operated by the convention. It was made responsible for procuring and properly servicing trust funds, according to the designation of the donors, including capital and endowment funds. It was chartered by the state of Oklahoma Oct. 31, 1946. Offices were opened in suite 308, Kerr-McGee Building, Robinson and N.W. Second Streets, Oklahoma City, Apr. 7, 1947. On Mar. 10, 1950, offices were moved to the new Baptist Building, 1141 North Robinson, Oklahoma City.

Andrew Potter was the first executive secretary-treasurer. Auguie Henry, pastor of the First Baptist Church, McAlester, Okla., succeeded Potter as executive secretary on Sept. 15, 1949, and as treasurer on Dec. 6, 1951.

An aggressive program has been inaugurated to procure capital and endowment funds by cash, "living trusts," wills, and annuities. The service of the foundation includes assistance in the planning of estates, in writing wills, and in acting as executor and administrator of estates and as trustee and guardian for minors and others. It also serves as trustee of trust funds for churches, associations, and other Baptist organizations.

Endowment.—The convention had no endowment program prior to 1934. Institutions and agencies promoted their own endowment programs.

At the 1934 convention, the endowment commission was established with five members consisting of "four men of wide and successful business or professional experience and the treasurer of this convention." This commission was charged with the responsibility of investing endowment funds. From July 2, 1943, to 1946 Elmer Ridgeway served as Brotherhood and institutional secretary. His major emphasis was to be upon capital needs, but the procurement of endowment funds for institutions and agencies was also one of his duties. Upon the establishment of the foundation, the endowment commission ceased to exist. The total amount of all trust funds transferred from the convention to the foundation on Apr. 7, 1947, was $76,776.29. From 1946 to 1955 it was necessary for most of the foundation's procurement efforts to be centered on capital needs, as a number of institutional and agency buildings were constructed during that time. However, as of May 31, 1955, endowment funds had increased to $1,069,145.91.

Church building loan fund.—The church building loan agency was established by the foundation, June 22, 1953, as an express trust of the foundation, and is known as the Church Building Loan Trust Fund. This trust fund provides a way for contributions to be made for the endowment of Baptist agencies and institutions. When building loans are made to Baptist churches, the interest is paid annually to the institutions and agencies as directed by the original donor.

This fund is controlled and administered by the Church Building Loan Trust Fund committee, composed of five members of the board of directors of the foundation. From Feb. 26, 1954, when the first loan was approved by this committee, until May 12, 1955, total funds committed amounted to $350,400.

Status and goal.—In 1954 an operating budget of $40,042.50 for the foundation was supplied by the convention from Cooperative Program funds. The 1954 income from investments totaled $69,964.30; receipts for capital assets, $93,025.23. During the first eight and one-half years of operation the foundation's receipts amounted to $2,904,151.17. Total assets as of Dec. 31, 1954, were $1,266,292.66. The assets as of Oct. 31, 1955, were $1,413,549.56. All but $154,929.80 of the total assets were raised or received by the foundation.

At the 1954 annual convention, the foundation launched a promotional program known as the Baptist Tour with a Forward Look, which was the first united institutional program in Oklahoma and the first major emphasis on endowment. The foundation's endowment goal by 1965 is a minimum of $10,000,000.

AUGUIE HENRY and HORACE L. JANES

OKLAHOMA BAPTIST HISTORICAL COMMISSION. Established by the Baptist General Convention of Oklahoma Nov. 12, 1952, the Oklahoma Baptist Historical Commission consists of nine members elected to staggered three-year terms. The convention's historical secretary serves as chairman. Publications issued in the Golden Jubilee observance of the Baptist General Convention of Oklahoma were *Trail Blazers of Sooner Baptists* by J. M. Gaskin, *Not Yours But You* by W. A. Carleton, *Andrew Potter, Baptist Builder* by Sam W. Scantlan, *A Question, Once Asked* by Argye M. Briggs, *And Now, the Chapel* by Helen Thames Raley, and *Annals of OBU* by James N. Owens. In 1954 the Oklahoma Baptist Historical Commission began to sponsor history writing contests on the local church and association level. The Oklahoma Baptist University library is the depository for the state historical collection. LEE B. SPENCER

OKLAHOMA BAPTIST HOSPITAL (Muskogee, Okla.). The hospital ministry of Baptist General Convention of Oklahoma began with the organization of the Oklahoma Baptist Hospital Association July 15, 1907. Mrs. Bertha L. Butte made the first gift toward the hospital. It was opened Aug. 8, 1909, with a capacity of 20 beds. On May 30, 1916, the board of trustees voted to deed the hospital to the Baptist General Convention of Oklahoma. It was accepted by the convention in Dec., 1916. In 1917 plans were started for an addition which opened June 1, 1919. A second addition was added and put into service Feb. 3, 1927. At the Sept. 8, 1932, meeting of the convention's board of directors, the hospital was taken from the local boards and placed under the direct supervision of the executive committee. This 88-bed institution has cared for over 100,000 patients and trained more than 300 nurses. The plant is valued at $465,079, with physical assets of $541,805 and a total indebtedness in 1954 of $33,871.

During the Chickasha Convention in Nov., 1909, $1,700 was pledged on a nurses' home for the Oklahoma Baptist Hospital. This was the nucleus for the Nurses Training School which has been operated since the opening of the hospital in 1909. TOM E. CARTER

OKLAHOMA BAPTIST ORPHANS' HOME. A motion "to consider the propriety of founding and locating a Baptist Orphans' Home for Oklahoma" was made by James Allen Scott (*q.v.*), first pastor of Washington Avenue Baptist Church, Oklahoma City, Oct. 10, 1902, in the annual session of the Oklahoma Baptist State Convention, meeting in Norman, Oklahoma Territory. The motion carried. The Baptist General Convention of Indian Territory was also invited to join in the establishment of the home. This invitation was accepted in its 1903 meeting.

J. A. Scott was elected superintendent and manager with power to open a home and employ help. He reported to the 1903 convention: "The Home was opened Mar. 5, 1903, and three little girls welcomed to its shelter, $570 received and $530 paid out, 15 children now in the Home, a rented house at 230 Pottawatomie St." (Oklahoma City). Articles of incorporation were filed Sept. 15, 1903. Miss Winnie Mitchell was the first matron and was later elected superintendent. In 1906 the present location at 63rd and Pennsylvania, N.W., Oklahoma City, was selected and 40 acres were purchased. Superintendent Elias Daniel Jeter solicited funds and began construction on a new $14,000 building. Under Superintendent William Alonzo McKinney the building was completed.

The home was operated by trustees as a private institution until 1915. Heavy indebtedness forced the trustees to seek the aid of the Baptist General Convention of Oklahoma in putting its financial strength back of the home, and this resulted in the convention's assuming ownership of the institution in 1915. Since 1903 the home has had 10 superintendents. They have been James Allen Scott (*q.v.*) (1903); Miss Winnie Mitchell (1903–06); Elias Daniel Jeter (1906–07); William Alonzo McKinney (1907–15); Joseph Cole Stalcup (*q.v.*) (1915–17); Franz Marshall McConnell (*q.v.*) (1917–22); James Burley Rounds (*q.v.*) (1922–24); Edward Allnut Howard (1924–35); Andrew Potter (*q.v.*) (1935–49); Henry Truman Maxey (1949–).

Gradually, needed buildings have been added, and in 1954 there were 16 fireproof buildings on the campus with cottage style residences for 200 children. In May, 1954, there were 187 children in the home. A dairy and beef farm of 800 acres was located five miles north of the campus. Total evaluation of all land and properties was $949,316. In 1954 the operating budget was $200,000. Per capita cost is $1,000 per year. One month's operation comes from Cooperative Program allotment and the remainder from special offerings such as birthday, personal gifts, food, Thanksgiving "One Day's Pay," and eggs and other commodities.

The children attend public school. They regularly attend four downtown Baptist churches. College and professional training is given. A homecoming is observed every even year on July 4.

Children received may be orphans, half orphans, or from broken homes; need is the deciding factor. Children other than Baptist are accepted. A limited amount of foster home placement and adoption is done. Since the home was founded, until Sept., 1955, 1,720 children had been cared for. H. TRUMAN MAXEY

OKLAHOMA BAPTIST STATE COLLEGE. An institution which lasted 14 years, established by the Oklahoma (Territory) Baptist Convention in 1899. The convention-appointed board of trustees met for organization Oct. 7, 1899; on Dec. 2 they voted to locate the school at Blackwell; on Dec. 4 appointed a building committee; and on Oct. 13, 1900, laid the cornerstone for the administration building. James A. Beauchamp was elected president Feb. 21, 1901, and on Sept. 4 of that year the college opened its first session. President Beauchamp resigned after two years, whereupon M. P. Hurst directed the school as chairman of the faculty for one year. Aychmonde Perrin Stone became president on Aug. 2, 1904, and served until Sept. 28, 1908. After a brief interim, J. R. Jester became president, but he resigned Sept. 28, 1909, and on Nov. 1, 1909, John Henry Moore was inaugurated his successor.

In the fall of 1910, a brick dormitory with capacity for 50 women students was completed. In May, 1911, President Moore resigned; he was succeeded on June 7 by Anderson E. Baten. That summer the faculty divided into three groups, one going to Mangum to join the faculty of Western Oklahoma Baptist College, another going to Oklahoma City to assist in the opening of the short-lived Carey College, and the third remaining with the school in Blackwell. Student enrolment at Blackwell, as reported to the convention in 1909, was 120, including 30 students for the ministry and 10 young women missionary volunteers. In the spring of 1911 the enrolment reached 208. President Baten resigned July 31, 1913, a few days before the main building was sold at sheriff's sale (Aug. 11) to satisfy an indebtedness of $22,000. On Aug. 12 the board of trustees met and declared the college closed. Bankruptcy proceedings followed soon thereafter, and all assets of the school passed into other hands. B. A. Loving, secretary of the board of trustees, stated a few days later that after all remaining property of the school had been assigned to the courts, "We had not at our disposal sufficient funds to satisfy the claims of our teachers and the other creditors who had no security."

BIBLIOGRAPHY: *Baptist Messenger* (1912–1914). Baptist General Convention of Oklahoma, *Minutes* (1906–1914). J. W. HODGES

OKLAHOMA BAPTIST STATE CONVENTION, THE. First organized at Lexington, O. T., Nov. 13, 1895, out of the Baptist General Association of Western Arkansas and Indian Territory. It co-operated with the Home Mission Board, and served Oklahoma Territory, the name designating the western half of Oklahoma, for 17 years before statehood in 1907. On Oct. 5, 1900, this body merged with the Oklahoma Baptist Convention at Blackwell to form a united convention in Oklahoma Territory, which continued under this convention's name until final unification of Oklahoma Baptists in 1906. In 1900, the Oklahoma Baptist State Convention adopted a dual alignment policy of co-operating with the Home Mission Board and the Home Mission Society. In 1906 the state convention merged with the Baptist General Convention of Indian Territory to form the present Baptist General Convention of Oklahoma. J. M. GASKIN

OKLAHOMA BAPTIST UNIVERSITY. A four-year liberal arts college owned and operated by the Baptist General Convention of Oklahoma. Located in Shawnee, Oklahoma Baptist University is a member of the North Central Association of Colleges and Secondary Schools, the Association of American Colleges, the American Association of Colleges for Teacher Education, and a constituent member of the Oklahoma State System of Higher Education. It is the only educational institution now supported by the Oklahoma Baptist convention. Early attempts at denominational education, largely on the secondary level, were made at Blackwell (Oklahoma Baptist College, 1901–13), Hastings (Hastings Baptist College, 1907–10), Mangum (Southwest Baptist College, 1910–13), and Oklahoma City (Carey College, 1911). Support of these one-building campuses was local and inadequate. An Indian University was opened at Muskogee in the spring of 1883 by the American Baptist Home Mission Society. This institution, known as Bacone College since 1896, is still a mission object of Northern Baptists.

Soon after the formation of the Baptist general convention, nine Oklahoma communities sought to secure the future university. Shawnee was finally chosen because of its neutral location, on the border between the Twin Territories, and because of the firmness of the civic development committee's offer: $100,000 cash and 60 acres with the highest elevation in Pottawatomie County. The central figure in the Shawnee effort was George E. McKinnis (born 1870). The decision of Oklahoma Baptists to support a single school was confirmed in the charter of Feb. 7, 1910. The site chosen for the first building was marked with the scriptural 12 stones. Founders' Day is celebrated on Feb. 22, anniversary of the Masonic cornerstone-laying of 1911. Classes were conducted in the First Baptist Church and in the Shawnee Convention Hall during the 1911–12 term. To pay teachers' salaries, President James Milton Carroll (*q.v.*) sold his bird collection to the University of Oklahoma and suspended classes until the completion of Shawnee Hall in Sept., 1915.

Since 1915 the operation of the institution has been continuous. Until 1924 more students were enrolled in the preparatory school (including the junior fine arts department) than in the college. The demand of mature students for pre-college instruction kept the "academy" alive, with dwindling enrolments, until 1935, when it was abandoned altogether. Enrolments in the university have increased steadily with the growth of the physical plant and the upgrading of standards. Some fluctuation may be accounted for by the effects of war and depression on Oklahoma's agricultural economy. (Until 1935 about 85 per cent of the students came from the non-urban areas. In 1955 the urban-rural division was even.) September registrations at five-year intervals have been:

1915....143	1930....583	1945..... 722
1920....496	1935....612	1950....1,347
1925....763	1940....729	1955....1,329

The cumulative enrolment for 1955 was 1,632.

The first president was James Milton Carroll, who served the one year the school occupied borrowed quarters (1911–12). During the years 1915–34 the school had six presidents, supplemented by vice-presidents, deans, and acting presidents in the frequent interims. During the administration of Frank Meriro Masters (1915–19), the academic program was enlarged, a World War I reserve unit trained, the second building occupied, and the third begun. A strongly evangelical emphasis is evident not only in the reminiscence of the students, but also in the minutes of the trustees and faculty of the period. The first faculty meeting was a prayer service in Masters' home. Seven professors, in addition to the president, comprised that first faculty in 1915: John Willian Jent (*q.v.*), history and sociology; William Durant Moorer (*q.v.*), Bible and Christianity; William Thomas Short, mathematics; W. P. Powell, English; John L. Guthrie, philosophy; Oral Lee Gulledge, piano and voice; and Josh Lee (later United States senator), public speaking. The absence of the laboratory sciences was conspicuous. Biology, chemistry, and physics were added within three years, along with ancient and modern languages.

Judson Allen Tolman was the first Ph.D. and the first layman to head Oklahoma Baptist University. He served from 1919 to 1922, and saw completion of the first men's dormitory and gymnasium. John Benjamin Lawrence, who went in 1921 to the pastorate of the First Baptist Church in Shawnee, later served in the dual capacity of pastor and university president (1922–26). Rapid growth came in student registration, which reached a new cumulative total of 1,207 in 1926.

Warren Waverly Phelan, the last layman elected president of O.B.U. (1926–30), served at a time when the Oklahoma denomination was rent by schismatic movements and the university was no sanctuary from the demands of the extremists. This was the era of the "evolution" controversy, and the fear of scholarship was real enough to prevent regular financial support needed to stabilize a college enterprise. During the brief presidency of William Cooke Boone, unity was restored within the state convention, but the great depression that began in 1929 made it impossible for the school to attain any degree of security. A new dormitory for women, erected by the state W.M.U. the previous year, helped to attract students during the difficult years of declining enrolment, flagging support, and mounting deficits. Mrs. Berta Keys Spooner (*q.v.*), state W.M.U. secretary, and Miss Annie Juliet Earle, dean of women (1924–38), were credited with the success of the dormitory project, which was paid for in the lean years. Hale Virginius Davis was the only O.B.U. alumnus elevated to the presidency. The times called for stringent economy, and the gloom of financial inadequacy continued the two years of his presidency (1932–34).

The present head, John Wesley Raley, has served as president longer than all his predecessors combined. Faculty building, accreditation, campus expansion, and the erection of 14 major buildings are fruits of his administration. When young President Raley was inaugurated in 1934, the university was $240,000 in debt, and he faced a discouraged faculty, a deteriorating plant, and virtually no endowment. By 1936 the state convention had placed the university in its budget for a regular subsidy of $34,000 a year. This was raised regularly until, in 1955, the university was receiving $100,000 for current operations, $100,000 for buildings, and $100,000 for endowment. Celebration of Raley's 20th anniversary in 1954 was climaxed by the completion of the $575,000 Thurmond Science-Administration building. This, like all recent structures, is neo-Georgian colonial style.

The Baptist Foundation of Oklahoma began, in 1954, a 10-year campaign to realize $10,000,000 for O.B.U. endowment. The permanent endowment rose from $88,130 that year to $789,783 in 1955. The original 60 acres has grown to 130 with the acquisitions of the Raley administration.

In academic affairs the institution enjoys a fine reputation for the quality of its graduates in the liberal arts, as measured by their records in professional schools of medicine, law, education, engineering, and theology. Because of the interest of Oklahoma Baptists in hospital work, the university began a program in hospital administration in 1947, and a collegiate degree in nursing in 1952. As the first dean of fine arts, the Italian-born concert organist, Paolo Conte, brought recognition to the university music program from its inception until 1936. Under the second dean, Warren Mathewson Angell, the music curriculum reached into every area of literature and performance.

In 1955 there were 2,936 living alumni and more than 12,000 former students on record with the Bison Association, O.B.U.'s alumni organization. The budget for 1955–56 was $1,012,939. JAMES RALPH SCALES and JAMES WATTS

OKLAHOMA EVANGELIST. Published at Watonga, Okla., by T. O. Reese in 1903. Issued for 50 cents a year, it had four pages of four columns each, 11 x 16 inches in size. It is now extinct. J. M. GASKIN

OKLAHOMA SCHOOL OF RELIGION. Founded in 1936 by the Oklahoma Baptist State Convention (Negro), adjacent to Langston University, Langston, Okla. The building site was purchased in 1936 and the cornerstone laid in Apr., 1937. Ezell Willie Perry, president of the convention since 1919, conducted an inter-faith institute for all Negro preachers in Oklahoma at Langston in 1937 which was attended by Noble Y. Beall of the Southern Baptist Home Misson Board. Beall was impressed with the prospects of the Negro school and promised the salary of a teacher-missionary upon its formal opening which took place the following year with J. N. Hughley as dean. Owned and operated by the Negro convention, the school has the convention's board of directors as trustees. From 1946 to 1951 the Woman's Missionary Union of Oklahoma (white) gave $10,000 to remodel the school's facilities and in 1939 gave $1,500 for equipment. The Baptist General Convention of Oklahoma contributes $2,000 annually to the school's support. Present property value is $250,000. The school's annual budget is $40,000, raised by student fees, contributions, and the Negro convention. Eight faculty members and 35 students were enrolled in 1955–56. J. M. GASKIN

OKOLONA FEMALE COLLEGE. Chartered in 1856 at Okolona, Miss. Although it was a private institution, it was supported and recommended by Baptists. It reached its peak during the presidency of J. G. Dupree, 1878–82, but closed in 1886. J. L. BOYD

OLD BAPTIST BANNER, THE. An antimission newspaper begun in May, 1838, by Washington Lowe, who edited and published the paper in Nashville, Tenn., for one year. When the church of which Lowe was pastor expelled him in 1839 on a charge of gross immorality, his paper fell into the hands of a physician, John M. Watson, who moved it to Murfreesboro. Watson published the paper under the title *The Correspondent* from May, 1839, until the lack of patronage caused its suspension a year or two later. Robert Boyté Crawford Howell (*q.v.*), who saw the effects of the paper firsthand, wrote in 1863 that the spirit of the paper "was excessively acrimonious, and the language harsh, denunciatory, and vituperative. . . . Its power of mischief was immense, nor did it fail to accomplish its mission."

LYNN E. MAY, JR.

OLD TESTAMENT LITERATURE. *The Law.*—The books of the Hebrew Old Testament are divided into three groups: Law, Prophets, and Writings. The first group, consisting of five books, is called the *Torah*, or Law, because it contains practically all of the legal system of the Jews. These five books probably were one originally but were divided at a very early time. Early rabbis spoke of these books as the "five fifths" of the Law, while the Greeks referred to them as the "Pentateuch," meaning "five rolls." The term Pentateuch is first found in the work of Origen. The division into five parts came about probably because of the difference in subject matter of the various sections and because of the practical necessity of having smaller scrolls from which to read. The name of the books in Hebrew is simply that of their first words. The names in the English Bible came through the Latin version of Jerome from the Greek translation, the Septuagint, and are meant to be descriptive of the contents.

The Pentateuch contains two main types of literature: narrative, or history, and law. There are some other kinds of literature, such as poems and songs, but these are neither lengthy nor numerous. Genesis is practically all historical, and Leviticus is almost entirely legal. The other three books, Exodus, Numbers, and Deuteronomy, contain both legal and historical sections. The Pentateuch contains the history of the world and of the Chosen People from creation until the death of Moses. Although more space is given to the historical, it is from the legal sections that these books get their name, Law. There are five main bodies of laws in the Pentateuch: the decalogue (Exod. 20; Deut. 5); the book of the covenant (Exod. 21:1 to 23:19); the code of Deuteronomy (Deut. 12:1 to 26:15); the holiness code (Lev. 17:1 to 26:46); and the priestly code (mainly Lev. 1:1 to 16:34).

The book of Genesis is a book of beginnings. Arranged in ten parts, each beginning with the phrase, "These are the generations of . . . ," the whole book can be divided into two main parts: the beginning of all things (Gen. 1–11), and the patriarchs—Abraham, Isaac, Jacob, and Joseph (Gen. 12–50). Exodus tells of the oppression of the Hebrews in Egypt and how God miraculously delivered them by Moses. The Ten Commandments were given at Mount Sinai, and a covenant was sealed between God and the people. The tabernacle was constructed as a temporary place of worship. Leviticus consists chiefly of laws of a ceremonial and priestly nature. Numbers describes the numbering of the people and the journey from Sinai to the Jordan River. This journey took 40 years and resulted in the loss of many lives because of the people's disobedience. Deuteronomy gets its name from a mistranslation of three Hebrew words (Deut. 17:18). The Hebrew reads "a copy of this law," but the Septuagint translators rendered it "a repetition of the law." This book is primarily one of oratory. It contains a series of addresses delivered by Moses in the plains of Moab. The first address (1:1 to 4:43) contains a rehearsal of the history from Mount Sinai to the Jordan. The second (4:44 to 26:19) sets forth the laws which were to be obeyed when the people entered the land of Canaan. The third (27:1 to 30:20) is an exhortation to keep these laws. The book ends with a section (31:1 to 34:12) on the closing days of Moses. Most Jews regard the Law with a sanctity above all of the other books of the Old Testament. Jesus had great respect for the Law, especially the book of Deuteronomy. RALPH L. SMITH

Prophecy.—The religion of Israel was in nature and history prophetic. Prior to the developed office of prophet, Abraham so witnessed disclosures of God that he was known as a prophet (Gen. 20:7; Psalm 105:15). Moses' leadership in founding the nation was based primarily upon authoritative pronouncements which resulted from intimate communion with God (Exod. 20:19; Deut. 18:18). During the era of the judges, Deborah spoke and acted under the compelling word of God and was called a prophetess (Judg. 4:4). Samuel, as theocratic judge and spiritual counselor, was remembered as the greatest of seers and a prophet (I Sam. 9:9). Elijah and Elisha stood in a procession of spokesmen for God during the growth of the kingdom (I, II Kings). There were times when prophetic vision and voice were lacking (I Sam. 3:1), but such periods were probably brief.

Prophecy reached its highest level in the literary prophets, whose works are preserved in the Old Testament, particularly in Amos, Hosea, Isaiah, Micah, Jeremiah, and Ezekiel. The oral ministries of these men, sometimes directed to individuals and sometimes to groups (Amos 3:1; 7:14), exhibited a discriminating choice of time and place (Isa. 7:1 ff.; Jer. 26:2), utilized frequently a combination of bold word and symbolic act (Jer. 13:1 ff.; Ezek. 24:15 ff.), and ranged in mood from glorious promises and dialectic propositions to emotion-charged preachments (Micah 4:1–5; Mal. 1:6 to 2:17; Hos. 4:1 ff.). Following a practice which possibly began with Obadiah and Joel prior to 800 B.C. and continued with others to about 400 B.C., the prophets or their disciples committed to writing these utterances, in part or in whole (Jer. 36:1–8; Isa. 8:16). Thus the messages of the prophets were intensified and projected toward the future.

The prophets were pre-eminently the spokesmen of and for God. Isaiah was overwhelmed by a sense of divine call (Isa. 6:1 ff.), and Amos and Jeremiah spoke under absolute religious compulsion (Amos 3:8; 7:14–16; Jer. 1:4 ff.; 20:9). This basic experience was apparently representative of men who linked profound moral and spiritual truth with a "thus saith the Lord." Micah made the distinction between truth and falsehood on the prophet's lips dependent upon the speaker's relation to God (Micah 3:7–8). Thus, while the diversity of literary and thought forms in prophetic writings testifies that individuality was not violated, the same literature consistently affirms that God spoke to and through these men and makes that basic inspiration the explanation of their genius.

Prophetic writings are in the main elevated both in thought and language. They exhibit literary forms as widely different as the peculiar dramatic narrative of Jonah and the poetic "servant songs" of Isaiah (e.g., Isa. 52:13 to 53:12), the practical preaching of Haggai and the visions of Zechariah. However, rhythmical prose, or poetry without rigid meter, usually prevails. Sermonic qualities remain evident in the general tone of exhortation, the numerous rhetorical periods, and the occasional finished sermon (Isa. 2:1 to 4:6).

The messages themselves are charged with that moral passion which was inherent in the prophets' supreme loyalty to the holy God and are burdened with deep solicitude for the fulfilment of Israel's divinely appointed mission in history. Thus, the spiritual subtleties of idolatry and superficial worship of the Lord are exposed (Isa. 44:9–20; Amos 5:21–24), and the personal and social wrongs of political corruption and economic tyranny are denounced (Amos 5:10–12; Micah 3:1–12). Although the predictive element is present (Jer. 28:16; Ezek. 12:8 ff.), especially in expression of messianic hope (e.g., Isa. 9:6–7), the direct word of instruction or warning concerning immediate national and international problems and current moral issues is more frequent. This pointed relevancy, with its presupposition that the God of moral perfection and universal compassion acts in the everyday situation, has given these prophetic utterances vitality and meaning for the past and for today. J. HARDEE KENNEDY

Poetry and Writings.—The third division of the Hebrew Old Testament, the "Writings," contained 11 books: three "poetical," Psalms, Proverbs, Job; the five "Rolls," i.e., Song of Songs (Canticles), Ruth, Lamentations, Ecclesiastes, Esther; and three "books," Daniel, Ezra-Nehemiah, and Chronicles.

The first book in this collection, in the ordinary Hebrew Bible, is the Psalter. The book itself furnishes no title for the collection of psalms, nor is such title found anywhere in the Old Testament (the nearest approach occurs in Psalm 72:20). In the Septuagint or Greek version of the Old Testament, the book is called the Psalms or Psalter. The Massoretic texts (Hebrew Bible) title it Book of Praises, which came to be the hymnbook of the ancient Jewish service.

In the English Bible there are 150 psalms; they are divided into five books corresponding to the five books of Moses (the Pentateuch). In some versions there are only 147 or 149 psalms, as some of them are merged. Psalm 1 is the introduction to the Psalter; Psalm 150, the conclusion. The first four books end in doxologies, and Psalm 150 serves as the doxology to the fifth book and also to the entire Psalter.

The book of Job is the greatest dramatic treatise in the Old Testament. It wrestles with the question which came to the forefront during Exilic and post-Exilic Israel: Why do the righteous suffer and the wicked prosper? The literary form of the book is primarily poetry. However, the prologue (chaps. 1–2, which record the consultation of God and Satan and Job's subsequent loss of his property, children, and health) is in prose. The epilogue (42:7–17) also is in prose. Throughout the drama God vindicates his servant Job because of Job's faith, and as a result of his experiences, Job's faith becomes more personal (Job 42:5).

The book of Proverbs is a collection of Hebrew and Jewish proverbial literature. It consists of a compilation of 31 chapters of pithy or pointed statements in the nature of fables, parables, proverbs, riddles, moral or political maxims, satires, and philosophical or speculative sentences. Five different classes of proverbs are found in the book. The book consists of eight parts of unequal length, each part having a general heading. Proverbs is a manual of human conduct, dealing with the problem of making the most out of life.

The five Rolls are so called because they were written upon rolls to be read at certain Jewish festivals. The Song of Songs was recited at the Passover; Ruth, at the Feast of Weeks (Pentecost); Ecclesiastes, at the Feast of Tabernacles; Esther, at Purim; and Lamentations, on the anniversary of the destruction of Jerusalem.

Ezra, Nehemiah, and the Chronicles formed originally a continuous history from creation to the middle of the Persian Period *c.* 430 B.C. Ezra and Nehemiah appear as one book called Ezra in the Hebrew manuscripts. Likewise the Septuagint also regards them as one book called Second Esdras, i.e., the second book of Ezra; but in the Vulgate they appear as two books, called First Esdras and Second Esdras, corresponding to the present division in the English Bible. The books of Ezra and Nehemiah cover a period of more than a century, from the decree of Cyrus in 537 B.C. to the second visit of Nehemiah in 432 B.C. D. W. DEERE

BIBLIOGRAPHY: W. J. Beecher, *The Prophets and the Promise* (1905). S. L. Caiger, *Lives of the Prophets* (1936). A. B. Davidson, *Old Testament Prophecy* (1903). F. C. Eiselen, *Prophecy and the Prophets* (1909); *The Book of the Pentateuch* (1916). W. A. Faus, *The Genius of the Prophets* (1946). C. T. Francisco, *Introducing the Old Testament* (1950). A. R. Gordon, *Prophets of the Old Testament* (1916). A. C. Knudson, *The Beacon Lights of Prophecy* (1914). R. H. Pfeiffer, *Introduction to the Old Testament* (1941). R. B. Y. Scott, *The Relevance of the Prophets* (1944). E. J. Young, *An Introduction to the Old Testament* (1950); *My Servants the Prophets* (1952).

ONCKEN, JOHANN GERHARD (b. Varel, Germany, Jan. 26, 1800; d. Zurich, Switzerland, Jan. 2, 1884). "Father of the German Baptists." Oncken was reared by his grandmother in an unimpressive Lutheran environment. In 1813 a Scottish merchant saw promise in the boy and apprenticed him. From Scotland he traveled much and was impressed by the warm religion and the Sunday schools of Presbyterians, Independents, and Methodists. His conversion came in a London Methodist chapel. He obtained appointment from the Continental Society to do mission work in Germany and settled in Hamburg, which remained the center for his work. His vigorous preaching in homes and on street corners aroused persecution, which continued irregularly until 1857.

By 1826 Oncken showed Baptist leanings resulting from New Testament studies. He wrote Baptists in Britain, and they advised either self-baptism or that he come to England for it. He did neither but awaited an opportunity, which came when Barnas Sears of Hamilton, N. Y., arranged to baptize him and six others in the Elbe on the night of Apr. 22, 1834. The next day, Sears organized the first Baptist church on German soil in modern times with Oncken as pastor. Oncken soon found two strong helpers: Julius Köbner (1806–84), the Danish Jew whom he baptized in 1836; and Gottfried Wilhelm Lehmann of Berlin (1799–1882), baptized by Oncken in 1837. These three formed the famous "clover leaf." Baptist work in Germany and elsewhere abounded under the motto, "Every Baptist a missionary." Oncken visited America in 1853. He organized the German Baptist Union in 1849, the J. G. Oncken Press (1838), and the seminary in Hamburg in 1880.

BIBLIOGRAPHY: J. H. Rushbrooke, *The Baptist Movement in the Continent of Europe* (1923). *Schaff-Herzog Encyclopedia of Religious Knowledge* (1910). H. C. Vedder, *A Short History of the Baptists* (1923).
S. L. STEALEY

O'NEALL, JOHN BELTON (b. Newberry District, S. C., Apr. 10, 1793; d. Dec. 27, 1863). Lawyer, educator, temperance leader. Son of Irish Quaker storekeepers, Hugh and Anne (Kelly) O'Neall, he attended Newberry Academy, 1808–10, and South Carolina College, 1811–12, graduating second honor man.

After being admitted to the bar in 1814, O'Neall represented Newberry District in the house of representatives, 1816–17 and 1822–27, and served as speaker of the house, 1824–27. Elected associate circuit judge in 1828, he remained on the bench the rest of his life and became chief justice in 1859, despite his opposition to nullification and secession.

After becoming a Baptist, Jan. 26, 1833, O'Neall was active in his local church and statewide Baptist affairs, serving as president of the South Carolina Baptist Convention, 1858–63, and president of the Bible board of the convention, 1852–63. He became president of the State Temperance Society in 1841, Grand Worthy Patriarch (president) of the Sons of Temperance of South Carolina in 1854, and Most Worthy Patriarch (president) of the Sons of Temperance of North America, 1852–54.

A trustee of South Carolina College, 1817–21 and 1822–63, O'Neall was a member of the board of agents supervising Furman Institution, 1833–35, a trustee of both Furman Theological Institution, 1835–52, and Furman University from 1850, when it was chartered, until 1863. He provided legal aid, able counsel, and inspired leadership to both the convention and the college, and was influential in the convention's founding of Greenville Baptist Female College in 1854.

O'Neall's published works include *The Negro Law of South Carolina* (1848); *The Annals of Newberry, Historical, Biographical, and Anecdotal* (1859); and *The Biographical Sketches of the Bench and Bar of South Carolina* (2 vols., 1859).

BIBLIOGRAPHY: J. P. Boyce and C. J. Elford, "Hon. J. B. O'Neall," *Minutes of the 43rd* (1863) *and 44th* (1864) *Anniversaries of the State Convention of the Baptist Denomination in S. C.* (1864). U. R. Brooks, *South Carolina Bench and Bar* (1908). R. N. Daniel, *Furman University, History* (1951). E. L. Green, *A*

History of the University of South Carolina (1916). D. W. Hollis, *University of South Carolina* (1951). M. King, "John Belton O'Neall," *The Biographical Sketches of the Bench and Bar of South Carolina* (2 vols., 1859). M. La Borde, *History of the South Carolina College* (1859). J. W. Patton, "John Belton O'Neall," *Dictionary of American Biography* (1928–36). B. F. Perry, *Reminiscences of Public Men* (1883).

ALBERT NEELY SANDERS

ONEIDA CAMP. Founded in 1948 at Oneida, Ky., supported and promoted by Oneida Baptist Institute. The institute's property provides facilities for six weeks of camp held annually for boys and girls. Camps are of a general nature with emphasis on Royal Ambassador and Girls' Auxiliary work. One week of family camp is held each year. The purpose is to provide Christian fellowship, inspiration, and information with a strong missionary emphasis.

ELDRED M. TAYLOR

ONEIDA INSTITUTE. A standard four-year high school and eighth grade, at Oneida, Clay County, Ky., in the Cumberland Mountains. The school was founded in 1899 by James A. Burns (Burns-of-the-Mountains), who saw in Christian education a way to help change the primitive and sometimes savage culture of the feuding mountain people. The enrolment the first year was five; in the fall of 1956 there were 180 students. The school is accredited by the Kentucky Department of Education and is supported by the General Association of Baptists in Kentucky, student fees, endowment income, and special gifts. Between 1899 and 1955, 680 students had graduated. In 1955–56 endowment amounted to $148,797, and property was worth $467,033. In the summer the buildings are used for camps, which attract large numbers.

ERWIN L. MCDONALD

ONTARIO AND QUEBEC, BAPTIST CONVENTION OF. The earliest appearance of a convention-type organization was in 1851, when delegates from the churches of "Canada West" (or Western Ontario) called a conference at Hamilton, out of which emerged the Regular Baptist Missionary Convention of Canada West. Seven years later the churches east of Kingston, Ontario, formed the Canadian Baptist Missionary Convention, East. In 1889 the two bodies were merged into the present Baptist Convention of Ontario and Quebec, with D. E. Thompson, K. C., LL.D., as the first president. The earliest presidents of larger Baptist bodies in Ontario were laymen, testifying to the historic principle of the priesthood of all believers. In 1835, largely through the leadership of John Gilmour, the Canada Baptist College was founded at Montreal. The Canadian Literary Institute, the forbear of the present McMaster University, was opened by R. A. Fyfe in 1860. Moulton Ladies' College, Toronto, and Feller College, near Montreal, have been strong preparatory schools under Baptist auspices through the years. Feller College, serving the cause of education among French Canadians, was founded by Madame Feller of Switzerland in 1835; its enrolment today is well over 150. *The Canadian Baptist* was founded in 1854. Serving the Baptist Union of Western Canada as well as the Ontario and Quebec Convention, the paper has a circulation of over 12,000. The Women's Missionary Society publishes a monthly, *The Link and Visitor,* which has a circulation of almost 10,000.

In 1934 there were 498 churches in the convention, and in 1954 there were but 421. This decrease is largely due to the closing of many small rural churches, founded in horse-and-buggy days three or four miles from other Baptist churches and in an age when rural populations were much larger than today. The membership of the convention churches in 1934 was 56,026, and in 1954 it was 51,551. This decrease was partly due to the rigorous revising of church membership rolls in the past few years. Frequently erasures have exceeded the total number of additions in a given year. Baptisms in 1934 numbered 1,819, and in 1954 the number reached 1,952. In 1955 there were 1,911 baptisms. Offerings for all purposes totaled $1,067,677 in 1934, and in 1954 they reached $3,360,000.

Foreign mission work has been strongly promoted and maintained. The first Canadian evangelical missionary ever to go to the Orient was a Baptist, Richard Burpee, in 1845. In 1954 Canadian Baptists supported 74 missionaries in India and 27 in Bolivia. Since that year a further mission has been opened in Portuguese West Africa. Canadian Baptists annually give about $65 per capita to the local church and the convention. There are 18 associations in the convention, holding annual sessions and, in most cases, an additional annual rally. The convention itself meets annually, with work being maintained month by month by the convention executive and 10 boards entrusted with various phases of denominational responsibility at home and overseas. Church extension has been strongly promoted in recent years, and many new churches have been established or are in the process of organization. The Ontario-Quebec Convention, with two other Canadian conventions, is a member body of the Baptist Federation of Canada, through which it is also affiliated with the Canadian Council of Churches and the Baptist World Alliance.

T. B. MCDORMAND

OPDYKE FUND. The Dorothea Van Deusen Opdyke Fund is a bequest left to the Southern Baptist Convention by Mrs. Ida Reed Opdyke, of Jamestown, N. Y., in 1927, as a memorial to her daughter, the income from which was to be used for the education of "mountain people." The Convention received from this bequest $114,267.08.

The Executive Committee of the Southern Baptist Convention handles this fund and makes all the scholarship awards through its

Opdyke Scholarships Committee. The scholarships are in the amount of $150 per session to senior college students; $100 per session to junior college students; $50 per session to academy students. Applications must be made through the school where the person plans to attend. The corpus of the fund on Jan. 1, 1956, was $239,446.68. Scholarships totaling $147,540.00 were paid between 1927 and 1956.

PORTER ROUTH

OPEN WINDOWS. A devotional magazine published by the Sunday School Board of the Southern Baptist Convention. *Open Windows* was first issued in Apr., 1937, as a monthly publication. At the beginning of 1941 it became a quarterly. At that same time the daily Scripture selections and devotional comments began to be based on the Home Daily Bible Readings related to the International Sunday School Lessons. In 1948 a further change related the selections and comments to the Training Union Bible Readers' Course. The circulation in 1956 was 339,449. DONALD F. ACKLAND

ORANGE GROVE SCHOOL. A school at Hillsboro, N. C. Established in 1897 under W. D. Bostic, the school was endorsed and supported by Mt. Zion Association. After 1906 it was no longer under Baptist control.

D. L. SMILEY

ORDINANCES. See BAPTISM and LORD'S SUPPER.

ORDINATION.

DEACONS. The office of deacon "is usually supposed to have originated in the election of the Seven, as helpers to the Apostles, as recorded in Acts 6:1–6." In the original Greek the word "deacon" meant simply servant. Deacons are the only permanent church officers, other than pastors, specifically authorized by the Scriptures. Their function is to assist pastors by counsel and work, in order to advance the general interests of the church, "both temporal and spiritual."

Because of the scriptural basis of their office, deacons are generally expected to fulfil the qualifications recorded in Acts 6:3 and I Timothy 3:8–13 and are chosen by means of a particularly careful procedure.

Scriptural precedent and long established tradition would indicate the following steps in the choice of deacons: (1) earnest prayer for guidance; (2) clear exposition of basic requirements and duties; (3) determination of the number of deacons needed (not necessarily seven); (4) nomination by a competent committee of certain men who seem to be qualified and who are available, usually more than the number to be elected so as to permit a choice; (5) other nominations by any members who so desire; (6) ballots cast by members to determine their choice; (7) election declared [of each who received a majority of the votes cast]; (8) ordination and induction into office.

The actual ceremony of ordination varies in different churches but generally follows, in intent if not in actual detail, the following outline:

Reading of minutes, showing the action of the church in election of the deacon or deacons.

Prayer of thanksgiving and for guidance.

Scripture reading: Acts 6:1–7; I Timothy 3:1–13.

Inquiry (led by pastor or other appointed minister): . . . deacon or deacons to be ordained may tell of their conversion experience, their activities in the church, . . . their conception of the office of deacon. . . .

Charge to the deacons: Brief address of exposition and exhortation directed to those being ordained by someone appointed for this service.

Charge to the church: . . . explanation of the significance of what the church is doing, the church's responsibility . . . , and how together they may aid the pastor, promote the church's well-being, and carry out Christ's commission.

Ordaining prayer: For divine approval, blessing, guidance, protection, that those thus set apart may be worthy of the honor and fruitful in lines of Christian service.

Laying on of hands: Ministers and deacons who themselves have been ordained will pass by the kneeling men, placing their hands on their heads, reverently and affectionately breathing a benediction.

Hand of fellowship: Extended by all present in token of fellowship, appreciation, co-operation, while "Blest Be the Tie" is sung.

In any case the deacons remain under the authority of the congregation which elected them. Deacons "sometimes arrogate to themselves more authority than is justified by the Scriptures," but the church, by proper action, can correct any abuse of the office. In an increasing number of churches a limitation is placed on the tenure of a deacon's office, which provides that, after a stated number of years, a deacon may not succeed himself but must be inactive for at least a year. This plan has gained wide acceptance because it prevents the formation of a ruling oligarchy, gives the church an opportunity to replace undesirable men, and tends to promote efficiency and democracy.

The duties of deacons are summarized in two statements: (1) to fulfil the directions given them in the Scriptures and (2) to render the services appointed them by their church.

JOHN E. BARNES, JR.

MINISTERS. The ceremony whereby those who have a vocation and have given some evidence of ability for the ministerial office are set apart for the work of their calling. It is based upon scriptural practice. The word "ordain" in the technical sense is not found in our English versions, its nearest resemblance being seen in such passages as John 15:16; Acts 14:23; I Timothy 2:7; and Titus 1:5. In none of the original Greek words in these references is the ecclesiastical idea of ordination present. But the practice of ordination does have a scriptural basis in the activity of the early church (Acts 6:6; 13:3; I Tim. 4:14; II Tim. 1:6). The last three of these references deal with ordination to the ministry. In Acts 13:3 the account is that of the setting apart by the church of Barnabas and Saul, separating them for a definite work to which they had been called by the Holy Spirit. The remaining references have to do with the setting apart of Timothy by a presbytery of which Paul was probably a member.

Baptists do not hold to the ecclesiastical tradition which leads some to consider ordination the channel through which the ordained receives special ministerial grace or powers not afforded to others. The silence of the New Testament as to the form and meaning of the rite of ordination tends to indicate that it was nothing more than a setting apart or approval of the ordained for the work of the ministry. Legally, the ordained person is empowered to perform marriages, to serve as a chaplain, and the like. Otherwise, the ordained minister possesses no peculiar powers denied to any Christian who is thoroughly consecrated to the will and purpose of God; he exerts no authority beyond that earned by the influence of character and ability.

Historically, Baptists have insisted on the ordination of their ministers but have not always followed exactly the same pattern. At one time associations ordained preachers. In England and in most Baptist bodies, other than the Southern Baptist Convention, ordination is the responsibility of a standing ordaining council. In the American Baptist Convention the state conventions vary in their practice. Generally, however, they maintain state or associational ordaining committees which, upon the request of the local church, will examine a given candidate. Upon this committee's recommendation the local church calls a local council which, following its approval of the candidate, may recommend that the local church proceed with ordination.

In Southern Baptist practice the local church is the ordaining body. Associations and conventions which are composed only of messengers from co-operating local churches are generally considered to have no authority in this regard.

While no binding rule covers the procedure in ordination, most Baptist churches follow a similar procedure. Whenever a man feels that he is called to the gospel ministry, he may request the church of which he is a member to license him for the ministry. If the church chooses to do so, it has simply approved him as a candidate for the ministry. While, according to the discretion of the local church, ordination may come earlier, a man is customarily ordained upon being called to become the pastor of a church. At that time the candidate or the church may request his ordination. The ordaining church in turn calls an ordaining presbytery, composed of ordained ministers (sometimes including deacons) from sister churches, which proceeds to examine the candidate as to his Christian experience, call to the ministry, doctrinal beliefs, and proposed conduct as a minister of the gospel. After the presbytery has approved the candidate, he is recommended to the church for ordination.

Care should be exercised by churches to heed the exhortation to "lay hands suddenly on no man" (I Tim. 5:22). The candidate should have proved himself as a licentiate. His examination for ordination should be thorough. It should be conducted prior to any announcement of an ordination service. Thus the candidate can be instructed, when necessary, and proved prior to the ordination. Caution at this point avoids problems later on.

Having approved the recommendation, the church holds a public ordination service, which generally includes a report of the presbytery, presentation of a Bible, a charge to the candidate (and sometimes to his prospective church), and a sermon. Following the sermon or at some other appropriate place in the service, the ordaining presbytery kneels about the candidate for the ordaining prayer. After the prayer the presbytery lays the hands of ordination upon the head of the candidate. The ordained man may then receive the hand of fellowship from the congregation. It is appropriate for the one ordained to pronounce the benediction. The ordained minister is then presented with a certificate of ordination which is signed, on behalf of the church, by the church clerk and by the ordaining presbytery.

The pastoral relationship is established whenever a given local church by vote of the congregation extends a call to a given minister, who in turn accepts the call thus extended.

In the event it seems necessary, because of heretical beliefs and practices or personal misconduct, at any future time to revoke the ordination, this may be done by vote of the church of which the minister is a member.

See also DEACON and MINISTER, THE SOUTHERN BAPTIST. H. H. HOBBS

ORDINATION, REVOCATION OF. Most Baptists believe that there are two church officers who are to be subjects of ordination—the deacon and the pastor. Since the basic principles in the ordination of each are quite similar, in the discussion of the revocation of ordination, more attention will be devoted to ministerial ordination and its revocation. The application to the diaconate can easily be made.

Problems in ministerial revocation.—Baptists have been lax in the revoking of ordination. One reason for this laxity is that Baptists have no official judicature or manual of standards for overseeing and judging the conduct of Baptist ministers. Ofttimes one church will ordain a minister; he will move his church letter to another church, not necessarily to act as pastor. The first church and the temporary council that aided in ordination then lose sight of him. The church holding his membership (which alone has disciplinary powers over him) does not know his history and background and in many cases is not sure of its authority.

Perhaps the principal problem in revocation of ministerial ordination stems from the dual nature of ministerial service. On the one hand, the minister is set forth for ordination by a single Baptist church, whose independence and authority have been jealously guarded through the centuries; at the same time, this minister will serve not simply that one church but many similar churches in his lifetime without an opportunity for subsequent churches to consider his call and fitness for the ministerial office. As a result, Baptists have wavered in their interpretations of the basic source of authority in ordination, which, of course, would fix the principles for revoking that ordination. Practically all Baptists have recognized that only an independent Baptist church is authorized to call for the ordination of a minister, basing that call upon a conviction by the candidate and the church that God has already extended a prior call to service. From this point on, however, there have been four general emphases as to the proper authority in the ordination of a minister. These several views greatly overlap and are never exclusive.

(1) The authority of an independent Baptist church. Many Baptists have insisted that each church has the only authority in ordination. This ordination, they insist, may take place with or without ministers. The choice of the people in a church and the acceptance of the office by the candidate are the only elements necessary in ordination. It would be expected that James Robinson Graves (*q.v.*) would hold this general position. James Madison Pendleton (*q.v.*), Graves' disciple before the Civil War, maintained this view in his church manual and in other writings. Augustus Hopkins Strong (*q.v.*) asserted that no other church or union of churches can take precedence over local independence, even in ordination. In general, E. T. Hiscox reflected this view in his ministerial manual, and the paper on ordination prepared jointly by the faculties of the seminaries of the Southern Baptist Convention appears to place some emphasis here. The most important confession of early English Particular Baptists belongs in this category.

(2) The authority of the ordained ministry. Although recognizing that a Baptist church must issue the call for ordination and form the channel for ordination procedures, many Baptists have felt that authority for ordination rests in the ministry itself. This view was often reflected in the course of newspaper controversies. The minutes of many ordinations seem to make the actual act of ordination the prerogative of the ministry. In some cases this implication could be based on a careless use of language. The early General Baptists of England explicitly asserted the authority of the bishop or messenger to ordain the pastors chosen by particular congregations, and even permitted the bishop or messenger to limit the field where such an ordained pastor may serve.

(3) The authority of a council. This view is similar in many respects to the one immediately preceding, but differs in that it insists that a council called by a Baptist church for ordination must consist of both ministers and laymen, in effect eliminating ministerial authority as the sole base for ordaining. A. H. Strong vigorously denied that only ministers are authorized to ordain at the call of a church; the whole body of believers (through a council) must have a part. W. H. Allison gives numerous examples in which the authority to ordain is ascribed to councils. Francis Wayland demanded that "the whole church" (through a representative council of lay and ministerial members) must have a voice in the action, and decried the ordination of ministers at associational meetings.

(4) The authority of a denominational body. By far the most common point of view for many years in American Baptist life was that denominational bodies (associations, state bodies, and even general organizations) should take the responsibility of ordaining those candidates certified to them by a church. J. R. Graves wrote in 1881 that fifty years before that time, it was the regular practice for churches to send their licentiates to the associations where a presbytery was selected for the ordination.

Principles involved in revocation.—At the present time a combination of these several views is practiced. Most Baptists recognize that only the independent church can issue the call for ordination; a council is called, with an emphasis among English, Canadian, and Northern Baptists (The American Baptist Convention) upon denominational supervision and registration; the ordination itself is generally undertaken by the church upon the recommendation of this council (although city or associational denominational ordination is not unknown in the North); and recognition is given either by the publication of the ordination minutes in the denominational newspapers (the regular practice in the South), or with this, the inclusion of the minister's name on the officially approved register of ministers of the Convention or Union, together with certification for denominational benefits (practiced in England, Canada, and in the North).

The revocation of ordination, it is clear, must follow the general principles involved in the ordination itself. There are not enough examples of revocation nor sufficient uniformity in the thinking of the various bodies of Baptists in the matter of ordination to speak with finality with regard to these principles. It would seem that the following procedures would be basic. (1) The revocation should be initiated by the church of which the minister is a member. No other body has disciplinary authority over him. Even if his accusers are denominational servants or ministerial brethren from other Baptist churches, the initial step toward revocation should be taken by the church of the accused. (2) To avoid local prejudice and insure disinterested judgment and general approval of the action, the church should call a large and representative council in every instance to furnish information and advice. (3) Although distasteful, the same media of publicity and registration given to ordination should be utilized to inform the community of the revocation of ordination.

The hurt inflicted in the case of one individual may serve as a warning and prove salutary to many. In the whole transaction the spirit should be one of righteous and sympathetic love.

BIBLIOGRAPHY: W. H. Allison, *Baptist Councils in America* (1906). Faculties of Seminaries of the Southern Baptist Convention, *The Ordination of Baptist Ministers* (n.d.). A. H. Strong, *Philosophy and Religion* (1888). R. G. Torbet, *The Baptist Ministry: Then and Now* (1953). ROBERT A. BAKER

ÖREBRO MISSIONARY SOCIETY (SWEDEN). Named after a city in Sweden, founded in 1892 for the purpose of sending out missionaries in connection with the Baptist Union of Sweden. A training school for mission workers was started in 1908 in Örebro under the leadership of John Ongman.

Doctrinal differences developed between leaders of the society and the union, which resulted in 1936 in a separation. Membership in the churches working in connection with the Örebro society numbered about 20,000 in 1956. The organization carries on widespread work in Sweden as well as abroad. In 1956 a total of about 170 missionaries were serving in Brazil, French Congo, India, and Japan. The annual budget for foreign missions was 1,500,000 Swedish crowns ($300,000).

The general secretary is John Magnusson, Örebro. The official publication is *Missionbaneret* (weekly). ERIC STRUTZ

OREGON-WASHINGTON, BAPTIST GENERAL CONVENTION OF.

I. Baptist Beginnings. The history of Baptists in the territory of Oregon-Washington (also including parts of Idaho and Montana, with affiliated churches in northern California and western Canada), prior to the organization of the state convention in 1948, can be roughly divided into two periods: the period of co-operation and progress (1844–84) and the period of expansion, frustration, and division (1884–1948).

Co-operation and progress (1844–84).—In spite of differences over such matters as the question of slavery, the Baptists of Oregon and Washington grew in co-operative relationship and formed several associations and a general body that enhanced their work during the years 1844–84. A small group of Baptists in Washington County, Ore., on May 25, 1844, organized West Union Baptist Church, the first Baptist body west of the Rocky Mountains. Vincent Snelling, who migrated from Kentucky in 1844, not only served this church as pastor but also helped to organize many of the early Baptist churches on the Pacific Coast prior to his death in 1856. Upon the invitation of the West Union Church, several churches on June 23, 1856, united to form the Willamette Association, the first to be formed in the territory. This body at first covered the whole of Oregon, but later other associations arose in various areas: Corvallis on Sept. 12, 1856; Central on Sept. 4, 1857; and Umpqua on Oct. 10, 1863. A majority of these Baptists came from the South. Although no association seems to have made the slavery issue a point of fellowship, the Willamette and Umpqua associations developed a strong antislavery sentiment, while the others were largely sympathetic toward slavery. The first Baptist newspaper in Oregon, *The Religious Expositor,* was antislavery in sentiment but made no issue of it. Started by C. H. Matoon in Polk County on May 6, 1856, this paper ceased publication after only 26 issues. The first lasting general body to be organized by the Baptists of Oregon and the territory of Washington resulted from a call extended by the Willamette Association for the formation of a larger co-operative relationship among the churches. Messengers from many churches thus met at Brownsville, Ore., July 4, 1868, and organized the General Baptist Association in Oregon. This body changed its name in 1870 to the Oregon Baptist State Convention and in 1871 to the Baptist Convention of Oregon and Washington Territory. On June 25, 1877, its constituents reorganized it as the Baptist Missionary and Educational Society of Oregon, Washington, Idaho, and British Columbia. Two years later it became the Baptist Convention of the North Pacific Coast.

One of the most significant accomplishments during this period was the founding and support of McMinnville Baptist College by Central Association, 1857–71. The 1866 report of the institution showed that the college was free of debt, had adequate buildings, and had an enrolment of 116. Though it had no endowment and depended on the association, which had only 750 members, for its support, the institution within 10 years "sent forth a class of students whose after course furnished a member of Congress, a circuit judge, a college president, a score or more of lawyers, physicians and clergymen, who became prominent." In order to promote harmony with the denomination, the association turned the college over to the Oregon Baptist State Convention in 1871, with the stipulation that 8 of the 14 trustees be from Central Association.

Strong and courageous leadership made possible the advance of these early years. Many Baptists, like Snelling, migrated from the South to Oregon and Washington, where they became pioneers in establishing the Baptist cause. James M. Fulkerson of Virginia and Missouri, who came to Oregon in 1847, helped many weak and struggling churches to become firmly established, assisted in the organization of the first association, and served for many years as one of the incorporators and trustees of McMinnville College. R. C. Hill, physician and minister, who came in 1851 from Kentucky and Tennessee, organized churches at Corvallis and Albany, served as moderator of Central Association for 12 years, and was a successful agent for McMinnville College. One of the best known of these early Baptist leaders was Joab Powell of Tennessee and Missouri, who arrived in Oregon in 1852. He became a copastor of Providence Church (for many years the largest in Central Association) and was so successful as an evangelist that he baptized 3,000 converts. Another successful evangelist, C. C. Riley, came from East Tennessee in 1853 and organized and strengthened numerous churches. As an extreme Landmarket, he proclaimed his views from the pulpit, circulated the *Tennessee Baptist,* and is largely responsible for the strong Landmark sentiment that appeared in the Central and Corvallis associations.

Expansion, frustration, and division (1884–1948).—During the second period a series of controversies with the American Baptist Home Mission Society and later the Northern Baptist Convention led to internal conflict and open division, but Oregon-Washington Baptists continued to grow. Disagreement regarding the missionary supervision exercised by the society (1884–88), which supplemented the salaries of many pastors, resulted in a threefold division of the North Pacific Coast Convention into the Oregon Baptist State Convention (1886), the Northwest Baptist Convention (western Washington and British Columbia, 1888), and the Baptist Convention of Eastern Washington and Northern Idaho (1884–86). A second controversy (1892–1915) arose over the alleged pressure of Home Mission Society employees against ministers and churches who held Landmark views with reference to the ordinances. A contemporary of this period, C. H. Mattoon, defined these views as rejecting "alien immersion and open communion." The churches were about equally divided on these issues from the beginning.

On Aug. 5, 1892, eight churches from the Middle Oregon and six from the Grande Ronde associations formed the East Oregon Baptist Convention. Later the Western Association of Oregon and several churches from Washington united with this convention. The body in 1893 changed its name to the Baptist Convention of the North Pacific Coast. These Baptists unsuccessfully sought recognition by the Southern Baptist Convention (1893–1900). They contended that representatives of the Home Mission Society brought pressure to bear upon pastors and churches over the ordinance issue. For example, one pastor, S. E. Milam, alleged that he lost his mission supplement from the Home Mission Society because he refused to accept alien immersion at Cottage Grove, Ore., in 1892. The ordinance issue occasioned a threat in 1915 to foreclose a Home Mission Society loan on the property of the First Baptist Church, Klamath Falls. The controversy over the ordinances ultimately became more of a North-South issue. Some churches, strongly Landmark in their views, arranged to deed their property to the Southern Baptist Convention if an opposition party ever gained control of them. After the Landmark element withdrew from the Southern Baptist Convention in 1905, the Middle Oregon Association (1907) and the Eastern Oregon–Northern California Association (1912) broke with the Oregon Baptist State Convention. These associations thereafter came more and more under "gospel mission" influence.

The third period of controversy (1915–48) involved alleged modernism and the support of the Federal Council of Churches in the program of the Northern Baptist Convention. In Washington some churches began looking toward co-operation with the General Association of Regular Baptists as early as 1934. Many churches have since withdrawn from the Washington State Baptist Convention. By 1955 the General Association of Regular Baptists reported 32 co-operating churches in the state with a combined membership of 5,000. The Washington State Baptist Convention, affiliated with the American Baptist Convention, had 154 churches and 31,296 members in 1955. In the state of Oregon, the Conservative Baptist Fellowship grew out of a division in the Oregon Baptist State Convention on Nov. 10, 1948. By 1955 the Conservative Baptist Association had 114 churches and 25,954 members, thus far outnumbering the Oregon Baptist Convention, which are affiliated with the American Baptist Convention and had only 45 churches and 15,336 members.

The series of events from 1941 to 1948 included the disintegration of the Eastern Oregon–Northern California Association in 1941–43, the division of the Middle Oregon Association and organization of the Interstate Baptist Mission in 1942, the dissolution of the Interstate Mission and the organization of the Northwest Baptist Association (affiliated with California Southern Baptists) in 1947, and the organization of the Baptist General Convention of Oregon-Washington (first called the Baptist General Convention of Oregon) in 1948. All this left even the leading participants a little dazed and puzzled.

In 1942 R. L. Powell, L. B. Sigle, F. C. Reusser, C. C. Brown, J. C. Moore, and W. I. Hargis organized the Interstate Mission out of the desire for a progressive program. At its dissolution in 1947, this body had seven co-operating churches in Washington, four in Oregon, and four in California. Internal difficulties and the pressure of Southern Baptist growth in California caused its untimely death. The Baptist general convention was organized one year after the organization of the Northwest Association, because of difficulty growing out of great distances.

II. History of General Convention. The brief history of this body (1948–56) will be discussed under the following topics: ties with the past, organizational development, the development of district associations, the development of institutional life, and the statistical summary.

Ties with the past.—When the Baptists who desired a co-operative relationship with the Southern Baptist Convention organized the Baptist General Convention of Oregon-Washington on Apr. 13, 1948, at the Antioch Baptist Church, Portland, Ore., at least two factors out of their past helped to cement them together. The first of these related to the previous relationships of member churches. Two of the 15 churches represented had Southern roots of long standing. One of these, the First Baptist Church, Klamath Falls, Ore., organized by J. B. Griffith of Georgia and Texas in 1884, was a member of the Eastern Baptist Association of California and Oregon. It broke with the Oregon Baptist State Convention and the American Baptist Home Mission Society over the church ordinances in 1915. This church called a Southern pastor, Leonard B. Sigle, in 1930. The other was the Antioch Baptist Church, Portland, Ore., organized in 1924 with the help of the Middle Oregon Baptist Association by J. T. Moore, who came to Oregon in 1886 from Missouri. Moore helped to organize the Baptist Convention of the North Pacific Coast in 1892, which in 1893 made application to the Southern Baptist Convention. All of the 15 original churches of the general convention had previously belonged to the Northwest Baptist Association, eight to the Interstate Baptist Mission, and five to the Eastern Baptist Association of California and Oregon and to the Middle Oregon Association. These churches in 1948 had a combined membership of about 2,000. Several of the officers elected by the new convention were related to the Southern men, S. E. Milam and J. T. Moore, who pioneered in the organized work of Oregon-Washington Baptists. Ten of the 11 convention officers had served with the Interstate Mission and the Northwest Association.

The official newspaper of the general convention, the *Pacific Coast Baptist,* also connected with this body's past, likewise helped to unify the new organization. This publication, incorporated by Leonard B. Sigle at Klamath Falls in 1931, has served in turn the Eastern Association of California and Oregon, the Middle Oregon Association, the Interstate Mission, the Northwest Association, and now the convention. Its editors have been L. B. Sigle (1931–35), J. T. Moore (1935–38), C. C. Brown (1939–43), R. L. Powell (1943–45), C. E. Boyle (1945–47), Bob Hite (1947–50), and C. E. Boyle (1951–). In 1955 the paper was the property of the convention.

Organizational development.—The development of an effective program of work has greatly enhanced Baptist progress in the two-state area of the convention. Constitutional provision, strong leadership, and the assistance of Southern Baptist agencies have helped to insure the convention's success. The object of the body has been to advance the work of the kingdom through promoting missions, colportage work, and Christian education, and by developing institutions of learning and benevolence. Out of a concern for doctrinal purity and uniformity, the convention in its constitution requires of its constituent churches assent to the following doctrinal statement:

> We as Baptists believe in: A verbally inspired Bible; the Blessed Trinity; the Deity, Virgin Birth, Vicarious Death, Bodily Resurrection, Second Coming of Jesus Christ; the Fall of man and Eternal Judgment for sin; Salvation by Grace through Faith unto Justification, Regeneration and Preservation; Immersion upon the authority of a New Testament Baptist church, of those who profess faith in Christ, and as a prerequisite to fellowship in the church, and to the Lord's Supper; Separation of Church and State; Resurrection and Eternal Bliss of the Saints.

Through 1955 five men had served the body as president: J. M. Cooper, H. C. Price, E. R. Jacks, E. M. Causey, and James Frost. R. E. Milam, who previously served as president of the Interstate Mission and moderator of the Northwest Association, has been executive secretary-treasurer since the formation of the convention. In addition to its official news organ, *Pacific Coast Baptist,* the convention had four departments in 1955, as follows: Woman's Missionary Union, organized in 1950 by Mrs. Roland P. Hood, executive secretary; Religious Education which John T. Sisemore, director, organized in 1950; Evangelism (1951) and Brotherhood (1952), formed by Paul A. McCasland, superintendent and secretary; Missions, set up in 1952 by Roland P. Hood, who had served the convention (1948–52) as its first missionary. The departments conduct annual conventions and conferences and promote their work through the convention, the churches, and the associations.

In 1949 the Southern Baptist Convention recognized the Baptist General Convention of Oregon-Washington as a co-operating constituency. Since that time the Home Mission Board has furnished general missionaries, summer student workers, mission pastor supplements, church loans, and supplements for the departments of Woman's Missionary Union and evangelism. The Sunday School Board maintains a Baptist Book Store and gives much assistance to the Department of Religious Education. The Relief and Annuity Board made retirement plans available in 1950. The Radio Commission has given direct aid with the *Baptist Hour.* The Texas convention has given assistance through a building loan fund. Many Southern Baptist churches have helped finance mission churches and sent their pastors for revival meetings. Many individuals have also given aid.

The development of district associations.—When the messengers of 15 churches convened in 1948 to form the general convention, they also organized two associations: Oregon Baptist Association, with eight churches, J. Richard DeLap, moderator; and Washington Baptist Association, with seven churches, J. M. Cooper, moderator. The latter body dissolved in Oct., 1950, and formed three new associations: the Evergreen Baptist Association in the Seattle-Bremerton area, organized Oct. 20, 1950, B. L. Millard, moderator; Columbia Basin Baptist

IV. OREGON–WASHINGTON STATISTICAL SUMMARY

Year	Associa-tions	Churches	Church Member-ship	Baptisms	S. S. Enrol-ment	V.B.S. Enrol-ment	T. U. Enrol-ment	W.M.U. Enrol-ment	Brother-hood En-rolment	Mission Gifts	Total Gifts	Value Church Property	State Capital Worth
1830													(Explanation: This column includes total value of Schools, Children's Homes, Hospitals, Foundation, Buildings, etc.)
1840													
1850													
1860													
1870													
1880													
1890													
1900													
1905													
1910													
1915													
1920													
1925													
1930													
1931													
1932													
1933													
1934													
1935													
1936													
1937													
1938													
1939													
1940													
1941													
1942													
1943													
1944													
1945													
1946													
1947	1	10	1,704	171	1,374	891	687	249	39	$ 8,208	$ 63,311	$ 176,500	. . . .
1948	1	21	2,506	268	2,825	. . . .	998	536	97	11,443	84,064	366,964	. . . .
1949	2	23	3,115	352	3,113	1,366	1,061	625	118	15,483	152,154	395,339	. . . .
1950	2	29	4,141	486	4,373	2,356	1,626	1,018	121	21,493	189,919	537,388	. . . .
1951	8	41	5,492	717	6,158	4,181	2,059	1,161	187	37,820	280,707	735,843	. . . .
1952	9	53	6,087	616	7,784	4,617	2,839	1,452	274	45,891	343,357	1,057,661	. . . .
1953	10	68	7,732	1,095	9,918	6,002	3,990	1,386	350	59,158	462,553	1,428,930	. . . .
1954	11	98	10,243	1,342	14,351	6,366	5,382	2,081	582	69,301	665,925	2,309,280	$63,875
1955	12	108	13,345	1,843	17,748	9,557	7,421	1,987	827	101,752	806,870	2,871,137	. . . .

R. E. MILAM

Association in the Richland-Yakima area, organized on the same day, E. D. Giddens, moderator; and Southwest Washington Baptist Association in the Longview-Vancouver area, organized Oct. 23, 1950, J. M. Cooper, moderator. On Oct. 7, 1951, several churches in northwestern Washington organized Mount Baker Baptist Association, with M. C. Wyatt as moderator. Evergreen Association divided Mar. 18, 1953, and added Olympic Baptist Association, which elected Ray Riddle moderator. Some of the churches of Columbia Basin Association withdrew Oct. 11, 1954, to form inland Empire Baptist Association in northeastern Washington and elected Gilbert Skaar moderator. Churches out of this association that were located in the north central part of the state on Sept. 16, 1955, organized Coulee Baptist Association and elected Cecil Sims moderator. Mount Baker Association also divided, Oct. 9, 1955, resulting in the organization of Capilano Southern Baptist Association in the province of British Columbia, which elected W. H. Ross MacPherson moderator. This made a total of seven associations in Washington and one in Canada.

During 1951 the Oregon Baptist Association dissolved and formed four associations: Klamath Baptist Association, organized in southeastern Oregon on Feb. 11, 1951, E. R. Jacks, moderator; Siskiyou Baptist Association, in southwestern Oregon on Apr. 29, 1951, J. A. Myers, moderator; Multnomah Baptist Association in northern Oregon on May 30, 1951, W. H. Travis, moderator; and Upper Willamette Valley Baptist Association, in west central Oregon, May 30, 1951, C. R. Barrow, moderator. Churches in the southern coastal area organized the Southwest Oregon Baptist Association on May 21, 1952, with Wayne Eurich, moderator. This association, later named Myrtlewood, divided on Sept. 17, 1955, to add the Coast Baptist Association in the central coastal area, Thomas Balch, moderator. On Apr. 4, 1955, Central Baptist Association in the Sweet Home-Salem area, Wayne Eurich, moderator, and Cascade Baptist Association in the Eugene-Roseburg area, John Canning, moderator, were organized out of the former Upper Willamette Association, thus resulting in a total of seven associations in Oregon.

On June 15, 1956, the 15 associations of the general convention had the following number of churches: Capilano, 4; Mount Baker, 6; Coulee, 3; Inland Empire, 12; Columbia Basin, 12; Evergreen, 11; Olympic, 12; Southwest Washington, 8; Multnomah, 18; Central, 6; Cascade, 4; Coast, 3; Myrtlewood, 4; Siskiyou, 7; Klamath, 5.

Institutional development.—A Bible Center was established in 1952, after the convention had bought for $100,000 a church building located two blocks off the campus of the University of Washington at Seattle for Bible Chair and Baptist Student Union purposes. Russell W. Wallis became the first Bible teacher. The first Baptist Student Union secretary, Janice Aiken, began work in Sept., 1954. By June 15, 1956, the convention reported Baptist Student Union chapters at the University of Washington, the University of British Columbia, and Portland State University. Student retreats were held at Mount Baker Assembly on Oct. 22, 1955, and at the First Southern Baptist Church of Portland, Ore., on Mar. 23–24, 1956, with 54 students attending who represented six college campuses.

Mount Baker Baptist Assembly, owned and operated by the convention, began with that body's Nov. 23, 1952, authorization of the purchase of 120 acres and improvements for an assembly at Maple Falls, Wash. The property in 1955 was valued at $26,525, not including private investments. E. R. Jacks, assembly manager, reported an attendance of 435 in 1955.

The general convention approved the articles of incorporation of the Northwest Baptist Foundation in its 1955 session. This corporation administers the property and trust funds committed to it by the convention. The foundation trustees elected J. Carey Moore president and R. E. Milam executive secretary at their first meeting, Jan. 5, 1956. The convention on May 15, 1956, purchased for $26,000 a headquarters property located at Northwest 20th and Johnson streets in Portland, Ore. The Sunday School Board opened a Baptist Book Store in Portland in Mar., 1951 (formal opening June 6, 1951), with Mildred I. Baker as manager. The store serves the northwestern states and western provinces of Canada. R. E. MILAM

OREGON-WASHINGTON ASSOCIATIONS. See OREGON-WASHINGTON, BAPTIST GENERAL CONVENTION OF, HISTORY OF.

ORGANIZED CLASS MOVEMENT, BAPTIST. This movement, which over a period of years brought millions of young people and adults into Sunday school classes for Bible study, grew out of the Worldwide Baraca-Philathea Union. An organized widespread effort to reach men for the Sunday school began with the Baraca Class in the First Baptist Church, Syracuse, N. Y., in 1890. The Philathea Class movement for women was begun in 1895. By 1909 there had developed an organized movement with international scope and with departments of promotion in many states.

An increasing number of Southern Baptist churches found themselves with large, aggressive Bible classes having loyalties and programs prescribed by sources outside the churches and outside the denomination. This led to Southern Baptist Convention action in May, 1912, calling for a Convention Adult Bible Class Department under denominational auspices. The Convention's Sunday School Board carried out this directive by assigning oversight of this work to its Educational Department. By the end of a year, 287 classes had registered with the board.

Interest developed rapidly, calling for specific promotion of Adult Bible class work. Upon further instruction by the Convention in May, 1916, the board created the Organized Class Department and in July elected Harry Lee Strickland (*q.v.*), Birmingham, Ala., as the secretary of Adult Sunday school work. He took up his work Sept. 1, 1916. In his first report Strickland set out two definite objectives—to enrol unenlisted church members in the Sunday school and to evangelize unenrolled men and women. The Organized Class Department, including in its scope classes in the Intermediate, Senior (now Young People), and Adult departments, adopted as its motto "For the Bible and the Church." By May 1, 1918, a total of 2,722 Senior and Adult classes, with a membership of 70,552, and 93 Intermediate classes with an enrolment of 1,076, had been registered.

The Organized Class Magazine, begun in 1915, provided a channel for effective guidance and promotion of organized classes in the churches of the Convention. Two textbooks were published, *The Intermediate Department of the Sunday School* by Landrum Pinson Leavell (*q.v.*) and *Building the Bible Class* by Harry L. Strickland and William Joseph McGlothlin (*q.v.*), which gave much impetus to the work. A strong factor in the success of this new work was the Southwide Organized Class Conferences inaugurated by Strickland. The first one, held in Mobile, Ala., Feb. 7–9, 1922, was so successful that others were planned in succeeding years—Hot Springs, Ark., Jan. 16–18, 1923; Atlanta, Ga., Jan. 15–17, 1924; Shreveport, La., Jan. 13–15, 1925; and Birmingham, Ala., Jan. 18–21, 1926.

Mary Virginia Lee came to the board in Jan., 1922, as assistant to Strickland, to give special emphasis to Intermediate work. In 1924 she was made secretary of the Intermediate Department. Upon the death of Strickland (Nov. 4, 1924), the board elected William Presley Phillips, of Texas, as Strickland's successor. Phillips assumed his duties in Nov., 1925. With the trend toward a departmental organization for young people and adults in the Sunday schools, emphasis began to be placed on the department rather than class. Thus the board, in 1925, changed the name of the Organized Class Department to the Sunday School Young People's—Adult Department (later the Department of Young People's and Adult Sunday School Work) with responsibility for promoting Young People's, Adult, and Extension departments. *The Organized Class Magazine* was changed to *Sunday School Young People and Adults,* and the textbook *Building a Bible Class* was replaced by *Young People's and Adult Department.* A new era of Sunday school work began, which was destined to see the enlistment of young people and adults grow to unprecedented proportions. A. V. WASHBURN

ORIENT, MISSIONS IN. See CHINA, MISSION IN; FORMOSA, MISSION IN; HAWAII, MISSION IN; HONG KONG–MACAO, MISSION IN; INDONESIA, MISSION IN; JAPAN, MISSION IN; KOREA, MISSION IN; MALAYA, MISSION IN; MANCHURIA, MISSION IN; PHILIPPINES, MISSION IN; and THAILAND, MISSION IN.

ORIGINAL SIN. See SIN, ORIGINAL.

ORPHANAGES IN MISSIONS. Several Southern Baptist missionaries serve on the staffs of orphanages on their respective fields. Most of these institutions are supported and operated by national Baptists. Six orphanages in four countries ministered to 361 children—199 boys and 162 girls—during 1954. On the staffs of these institutions were five Southern Baptist missionaries and 54 national workers.

In Latin America a number of orphanages are supported by national or state Baptist conventions. National Baptists support the George Boardman Taylor (*q.v.*) Orphanage for Boys and Girls in Rome, Italy. This institution, named in honor of Southern Baptists' first missionary to Italy, cares for approximately 90 children. A Baptist church in the vicinity helps minister to the children spiritually. The George Washington Truett (*q.v.*) Orphanage with about 20 children, begun in Nazareth, Israel, in 1945, has been moved to a small farm near the town of Petach Tikva (meaning "door of hope"). Southern Baptist missionaries think that the farm may well become the inspirational center of Baptist work in Israel. In Nigeria the Kersey Children's Home (formerly the Home for Motherless Children) is located on a hill two miles west of Ogbomosho. This orphanage, founded by Ruth Kersey (active missionary 1920–55, now emeritus) and named in her honor, serves approximately 50 children. Orphanages in Korea care for many children made homeless by the recent war. Relief funds sent by Southern Baptists have helped support these institutions, which are maintained by Korean Baptists. IONE GRAY

ORTHODOX MOVEMENT, OKLAHOMA. Fundamentalist in nature, this schism, with the possible exception of the Stealey controversy, represents the only outward break of its kind with the Baptist General Convention of Oklahoma. Leader in the movement was W. Lee Rector, former instructor at Oklahoma Baptist University and outspoken critic of Baptist life and institutions on the grounds of alleged modernism in their ranks. His prolific and sharp utterances resulted in difficulties in the membership of the First Missionary Baptist Church, Ardmore, where he was pastor; and he resigned Sept. 27, 1931. The same day he and more than 300 other members of the church withdrew to organize the First Orthodox Baptist Church, Ardmore, Okla., and Rector became pastor. The following excerpt from the church's minutes is typical of its emphasis on orthodoxy:

> The new body approved the church covenant and Articles of Faith as found in Pendleton's Manual,

CARVER SCHOOL OF MISSIONS AND SOCIAL WORK (*q.v.*), Louisville, Ky. Founded in 1907 as Woman's Missionary Union Training School for Christian Workers. Moved to present site in 1941. Enrolment 1955–56 term 152. Property including three buildings valued at $823,250.

AMERICAN BAPTIST THEOLOGICAL SEMINARY (q.v.), Nashville, Tenn. Jointly owned by Southern Baptist and National Baptist, Inc., conventions. It serves Negro theological students in 13 buildings including administration building, library, dormitories, and apartments.

but since such articles of faith do not positionize the church on modernistic tendencies and practices, the new body adopted as its Articles of Faith, those previously drawn and approved by the First Missionary Baptist Church of Ardmore.

These articles, fundamental and premillennial in spirit, are still in force. The church continued its affiliation with Enon Association and the Baptist general convention until 1935. The progression of pastor and church toward a completely independent status is seen in a resolution adopted Feb. 15, 1933, stating its right and intention to designate contributions instead of contributing through the Cooperative Program. In June of that year a letter was sent to Enon Association, defending the church's right to refrain from support of the associational missionary and still be in fellowship. On July 17, 1933, a resolution was adopted discontinuing the use of Southern Baptist Sunday school literature because of alleged modernism and a refusal by the Sunday School Board to recognize as standard a Sunday school that used only the Bible for literature. In 1944 this church organized the Orthodox Bible Institute for the instruction of ministers and religious workers in the English Bible. By 1954 it claimed 52 graduates, with 25 enrolled at that time.

The Orthodox church disclaims any nonmissionary and/or antimissionary tendencies, although it is entirely independent of all denominational connections. In Oct., 1954, its records for the previous 12 months show missions gifts at $5,504, most of which was sent direct to missionaries and institutions in Arizona, Maine, Colorado, Fort Worth and San Antonio, Tex., and India and Palestine. Besides these objects, the church supports radio work and gives about $10,000 per year to support the Orthodox Bible Institute. Since Rector's death in 1945, his successors have continued the church and its program essentially as he left it. A monthly publication, *The Orthodox Baptist,* was founded in 1931. MAX STANFIELD

OUACHITA BAPTIST COLLEGE. A coeducational senior college owned and operated by the Arkansas Baptist State Convention, and located originally and continuously on the banks of the Ouachita River in Arkadelphia, Ark., which opened for the first session Sept. 6, 1886. For many years prior to this date Arkansas Baptists had shown sporadic interest in education. Caleb Lindsey, a Baptist preacher from Kentucky, was operating a private school in what is now Randolph County in 1816. In 1857 the convention appointed a committee "to establish a college in Arkansas." In 1858 this committee recommended raising an endowment fund, and the following year pledges were secured amounting to $42,000. By 1860 the endowment reached $75,000 in pledges, but the Civil War wiped these out.

Following the Civil War, interest in a Baptist college in Arkansas revived. Several small Baptist schools were founded, among them the Arkadelphia Baptist High School, J. F. Shaw president, in 1875. This school was located on the site of the State Blind Institute, bought by the Red River Baptist Association for the establishment of a school. This was later to become the campus of Ouachita Baptist College.

The convention of 1882 reviewed the educational picture of the state, commending four schools then operating; but its committee on education added that "the advantages of concentration are incalculable." The committee on education reported to the convention of 1883 that a Baptist state college "was a necessity," and a commission was appointed to agitate the issue. In 1885 the commission reported that many associations had passed resolutions urging the convention to build and had pledged their support; so a board of trustees was appointed to locate and begin building the college. The board met in Little Rock Apr. 8, 1886, to consider bids from eight towns for the location of the school. On the 72nd ballot Arkadelphia was selected.

The Red River Baptist Academy (formerly Arkadelphia Baptist High School) was repaired at a cost of $600 to house the college, and assets of approximately $10,000 came to the school as a bonus for locating at Arkadelphia. On June 22, 1886, Professor John Walter Conger (*q.v.*), of Prescott, Ark., was elected president and instructed to organize the school, which was named Ouachita (pronounced Wash'i-taw) Baptist College after the Indian name for the river that formed the eastern boundary of the Caddo subtribe.

Enrolment reached 235 the first session. There were three departments—primary, preparatory, and collegiate—with music, art, and bookkeeping in addition. The institution opened in one building.

During President Conger's administration (1886–1907) a number of buildings were constructed, including Old Main in 1888, a girls' dormitory (later called North Dorm) in 1891, the conservatory building (later called Wallis Hall) in 1898, the president's home in 1898, the Mary Forbes Industrial Home for Girls (later the Home Management House) in 1906, and the chemical laboratory in 1905. The faculty expanded from 6 to 26, the enrolment grew from 235 to 476, and the graduating class increased from 3 in 1888 to 25 in 1907.

From early days the college faced the difficulty of trying to pay off indebtedness while attempting to expand. During the presidencies of Henry Simms Hartzog (1907–11) and Samuel Young Jameson (*q.v.*) (1913–16), several campaigns were waged to pay the debt; and Dec. 18, 1914, all existing mortgages were paid.

During the administration of Charles Ernest Dicken (1916–26) the endowment was raised from $51,000 to $532,466. The college was first put in the state convention budget in 1925. The gymnasium, to be converted into the Little Theater in 1938, and the dining hall were both built in 1920. In 1923 Cone-Bottoms Hall for young ladies was completed.

While Arthur B. Hill was president (1926–29), a bond issue by the state convention cleared the debt of $126,209 in 1926. Ouachita was admitted to membership in the North Central Association of Colleges and Secondary Schools on Mar. 18, 1927. Property value reached $428,000.

During his term as president (1929–33), Charles D. Johnson fought a constant battle against depression. Enrolment dropped, convention financial support was nonexistent, other income was negligible, and to keep the doors of the school open was a major struggle.

Upon Johnson's resignation, James Richard Grant was made vice-president and acting administrator until 1934, when he became president. During Grant's term the college experienced significant growth. A new gymnasium was finished in 1939, the Flenniken Memorial Student Center was built in 1941, Mitchell Hall (auditorium) was finished in 1942, and Ernest Bailey Hall, Terral-Moore Hall, and G. E. Cannon Infirmary were dedicated in 1949 as a result of a million-dollar campaign and gifts from the individuals for whom the buildings were named. After World War II. an all-time high enrolment of 1,123 students was reached in 1947, and the curriculum was greatly expanded. James Richard Grant Memorial Building, erected in 1953 to replace Old Main which was destroyed by fire in 1949, was named in appreciation of Grant's many contributions.

While Seaford William Eubanks was president (1949–51), Hamilton Moses Science Hall and Riley Library were built. Gifts through the Cooperative Program reached $100,000 for the operating budget and $50,000 for indebtedness in 1951.

Harold A. Haswell was made president in Jan., 1952, and served until Sept., 1953, when he resigned. During this period the curriculum was revamped, accreditation was regained, Conger and Grant halls were constructed, and convention support was increased.

During the administration of Ralph Arloe Phelps, Jr., (1953–) the curriculum was revised and expanded, W. S. Johnson Hall was completed, the faculty was increased to the total of 51, a comprehensive landscaping program was executed, a faculty housing project was developed, athletic fields were expanded, student apartments rebuilt, a new men's dormitory to house 100 erected, and a new president's home constructed.

Ouachita since her founding has conferred 3,175 degrees and is a four-year liberal arts college, offering the following degrees: bachelor of arts, bachelor of science, bachelor of music, and bachelor of music education. Enrolment for the 1955–56 school year was 802. On May 31, 1955, endowment totaled $636,466.77. Physical properties were valued at $1,847,082.23 and included 19 permanent buildings and 200 acres of land. Budget for 1956 was $680,113.

The college is owned and operated by the Arkansas Baptist State Convention, which elects all trustees and currently provides approximately one third of the total budget of the school. RALPH A. PHELPS, JR.

OUACHITA-BENTONVILLE ACADEMY. Established in 1901 at Bentonville, Ark., by Benton County Baptist Association. Operated in a three-story building, formerly the property of Bentonville College, the school's income came from tuition and voluntary contributions. It closed in 1930. H. D. MORTON

OUACHITA-JUDSON ACADEMY. A school at Fordyce, Ark., affiliated with Ouachita College. Its date of foundation unknown, the school was in operation in 1907 and closed in 1910. H. D. MORTON

OUACHITA-MAGAZINE ACADEMY. Established by citizens of Magazine in 1901, with 75 enrolled the first year and 203 the second. The two buildings, financed locally, were deeded to Arkansas Baptist State Convention, and the school was operated six years on income from tuition and voluntary contributions. H. D. MORTON

OVOCA ASSEMBLY. A Tennessee Baptist assembly from 1924 to 1936. After pioneer encampment programs at Estill Springs, beginning in 1907 and continuing several years thereafter, Tennessee Baptists, under the leadership of W. D. Hudgins of the Sunday School Department of their convention, began in 1924 to hold encampments, conferences, and conventions at Ovoca, three miles from Tullahoma, Tenn. Ovoca was owned by the Knights of Pythias and was leased from them for a nominal annual sum set aside in the convention's education department budget for this cause. Its facilities included a large assembly hall and comfortable cottages.

Among the various summer programs held at Ovoca were the encampment, Sunday school superintendents' conference, Baptist Young People's Union convention, and laymen's conference. It has been estimated by those who attended several of the meetings that during the lifetime of the activities at this camp site, some 4,000 attended the various meetings during the years 1924–36. Some of the featured speakers at Ovoca were the foremost leaders of the times—Bernard Washington Spilman (*q.v.*), John Richard Sampey (*q.v.*), Prince Emmanuel Burroughs (*q.v.*), and Arthur Flake (*q.v.*). The programs were noted for fellowship, inspiration, wholesome recreation, and a strong, personal appeal to higher Christian living.

HERBERT C. GABHART

OWEN, WILLIAM ALEXANDER (b. Tipton County, Tenn., Mar. 4, 1869; d. Jackson, Tenn., Feb. 3, 1933; buried Munford Cemetery, Covington). Lawyer, judge, Tennessee Baptist leader. After receiving a law degree from Vanderbilt University in 1890, Owen practiced law at Covington, Tenn. (1890–1917). Elected a judge of the West Tennessee Court of Appeals, he served with distinction from 1917 until his death in 1933. For 42 years he served as a deacon in the Covington Baptist Church and for 25 years as Sunday school superintendent. He was chairman of the building committee for the church's new edifice. For three terms (1921–23) he was president of the Tennessee Baptist Convention; he also served as a trustee of Union University and Baptist Memorial Hospital. He wrote a history of the Big Hatchie Association for its centennial gathering, and he wrote a history of Tipton County for the local paper. On Apr. 28, 1892, Owen married Claudia McFadden, granddaughter of the founder and first pastor of the Covington Baptist Church. Their three sons have been active in church and denominational life: Laurie, lawyer and deacon; Richard N., pastor and editor of the *Baptist and Reflector* since 1950; Hays E., businessman and deacon, and a former president of the executive committee of Baptist Memorial Hospital. R. H. WARD

OXFORD FEMALE SEMINARY. One of the oldest Baptist schools in North Carolina, located at Oxford, N. C. Its first session was held in 1850, with Samuel Wait as president. The school did not close during the Civil War, but suffered during that chaotic era, along with other educational institutions in the South. War was not the only problem, however. On Jan. 18, 1904, the school building was completely destroyed by fire, and in the same year a corporation was formed to rebuild the school. A majority of the stockholders were Baptists. Under President F. P. Hobgood, who took office in 1880, the school grew into a college, with a preparatory department in addition. It exerted strong influence upon the women of the state in its years of service. After World War I the Junior College was chartered by the state legislature. The school closed during the depression of the 1930's. D. L. SMILEY

OXNER-ALEXANDER MEMORIAL HOSPITAL, PINGTU. See CHINA, MISSION IN.

P

PACIFIC RECORDER. A Baptist paper launched in July, 1854, by Edward J. Willis, a native Virginian and former Sacramento County judge. Willis, recently ordained to the ministry, published the paper simultaneously in Sacramento and San Francisco twice a month. This was the first known "unofficial" Southern Baptist paper in California although Willis as a layman had joined O. F. Wheeler, pioneer Northern Baptist Convention missionary, in the publication of the *Pacific Banner,* a venture which lasted only one year before financial difficulties prevailed.

Pacific Recorder was edited as a weekly in 1856 by John Lewis Shuck (*q.v.*), a returned China missionary, working among the Chinese in Sacramento and San Francisco. Shuck served intermittently as editor until 1857 when the paper was discontinued because of financial difficulties. In May of that year the San Francisco Baptist Association urged members to patronize denominational journals published in the East and South in the absence of a California Baptist paper. W. BURMAN TIMBERLAKE

PACIFISM. War has been one of the most persistent and perplexing problems faced by Christians through the centuries. There have been and are at least three more or less clearly defined positions concerning the Christian's relation to war: (1) Participation in war is a phase of the Christian's citizenship responsibility—when his nation commands, he is to obey. (2) Participation in war is frequently the choice of the lesser of two evils. (3) War violates the Christian spirit and its love ethic; hence, participation in war is wrong for the Christian. The last position is usually labeled "pacifism."

In the years immediately following the New Testament era, Christians, for various reasons, maintained in the main the third position. "The evidence for the existence of a single Christian soldier between 60 and about 165 A.D. is exceedingly slight." On the other hand, as the church made its peace with the state and with the world, military service for Christians was not only approved but glorified. Periodically, however, the Christian conscience has been disturbed by war. The contemporary period seems to be one of unusual concern.

Southern Baptists, who are not "in any way committed to the pacifist position," have shared in this concern. As the United States approached World War II, the Social Service Commission (now the Christian Life Commission), in its report to the Southern Baptist Convention, said that the most vital question for Christians at such times was "whether a Christian may ever at any time and under any condition give his approval to war or take part in war."

It was also stated that "Baptists have always believed in liberty of conscience and have honored men who were willing to brave adverse public opinion for the sake of conscientious scruples."

The Convention itself went on record as recognizing the right of conscientious objection and instructed the executive committee of the Convention to provide facilities for the registration of conscientious objectors with the denomination, that they in turn might be accurately certified to the Government. The committee, which provided a registration card, reported to the Convention the next year that 125 conscientious objectors, representing 19 states, had been registered. The number later increased to 152. Twenty-three of these were in conscientious objector camps by 1944, and a total of 45 by the end of the war. Southern Baptists would not have been true to their belief in the right and authority of the individual conscience if they had not defended, at least to a degree, these conscientious objectors.

Later, the executive committee was also authorized by the Convention to receive and to transmit funds to the National Service Board for the support of Baptist young men who "had the moral courage to follow the dictates of their Christian consciences and to take the consequences." Most of the support came from the peace churches. The total cost during World War II for the maintenance of Southern Baptist men in conscientious objector camps was $20,956.84, with contributions totaling $3,248.67, leaving a balance as of Aug. 13, 1946, of $17,708.17. The Public Relations Committee, reporting to the Executive Committee, claimed that the Southern Baptist Convention had no official or legal obligation for the support of Southern Baptist conscientious objectors who served in the Civilian Public Service, and that the Executive Committee had no authority to appropriate any funds on hand to reimburse the peace churches. The Convention defended the right of conscience but did not provide, in any adequate way, for the financial support of the men who were placed in conscientious objector camps.

BIBLIOGRAPHY: C. J. Cadoux, *Christian Pacifism Re-examined* (1940); *The Early Christian Attitude to War* (1919). R. Jones (ed.), *The Church, the Gospel, and War* (1948). U. Lee, *The Historic Church and Modern Pacifism* (1942). G. H. C. MacGregor, *The New Testament Basis of Pacifism* (1953). R. Niebuhr, *Christianity and Power Politics* (1940). C. Raven, *The Theological Basis of Christian Pacifism* (1951). C. G. Rutenber, *The Dagger and the Cross* (1950). L. D. Weatherhead, *Thinking Aloud in War-Time* (1943). T. B. MASTON

PALACIOS BAPTIST ACADEMY. A coeducational school at Palacios, Tex. It came under control of the Baptist General Convention of Texas about 1910 and was maintained until 1917. RUPERT N. RICHARDSON

PALACIOS BAPTIST ENCAMPMENT. The second Baptist encampment organized in Texas, growing out of a resolution at the Baptist Young People's Union Convention at Bonham in 1901, which called for a committee to report plans for an encampment in the summer of 1902 to the executive committee of the Baptist General Convention. Held originally at La Porte, June 18–25, 1902, the encampment was moved to Palacios in 1906 with the B.Y.P.U. convention meeting in conjunction with it until 1923. For many years Palacios was owned by the Baptist General Convention of Texas and served primarily as a state B.Y.P.U. encampment. Located in District 4 and still one of the best encampments in Texas, Palacios was organized and promoted on the Texas coast by George Washington Truett (*q.v.*), Robert H. Coleman (*q.v.*), and Sam L. Smith. J. E. ROTH

PALESTINE-SYRIA. See ISRAEL, MISSION IN and LEBANON, MISSION IN.

PALMER, PAUL (fl. 1730–40). A native of Maryland, he was baptized at Welch Tract, Del., by Owen Thomas, and was ordained in Connecticut. He sojourned in New Jersey, then moved into Maryland, where he baptized nine persons, who formed Chestnut Ridge Baptist Church, the first in that colony. Before Apr., 1720, he settled in North Carolina and married Johanna (Laker) Peterson, widow of Thomas Peterson (d. 1714), a church warden of Chowan Precinct. Their children were Martha and Samuel. In 1727 he organized the first Baptist church in North Carolina, in upper Chowan County, and in 1729 he constituted the second, Shiloh, in Camden County. Churches in Onslow, Craven, Beaufort, Hyde, Lenoir, and Pitt counties were directly or indirectly the outgrowth of his labors. In 1730 he visited churches in New England and New Jersey. He was preaching in North Carolina in 1738. Morgan Edwards (*q.v.*) declared him "the father of the General Baptists in North Carolina." Apparently he died before 1754, but the exact date and place are unknown. J. A. EASLEY

PALMERVILLE SCHOOL. A school under Baptist control, located at Palmerville, N. C., founded by E. F. Eddins in 1887. Eddins operated the school for 48 consecutive years until his death in 1935. In 1902 Eddins offered the property to Stanly Association if it would improve the building, and the association voted to adopt it. In 1920 Palmerville became a public school, under public control. D. L. SMILEY

PALUXY COLLEGE. A coeducational school near Glen Rose, Tex. It was taken over by Paluxy Baptist Association in 1878 and was maintained for about two years. RUPERT N. RICHARDSON

PANAMA AND CANAL ZONE, BAPTISTS IN. The beginning of Baptist work on the Isthmus of Panama reaches back into southern United States. One of the very first churches among Negroes in the United States dates from the 1780's. George Leile (or Sharp) was a slave, born in Virginia about 1750. He belonged to a Baptist deacon, Henry Sharp of Burk County, Ga. He was baptized by a white pastor, Matthew Moore, and united with his church. The church, impressed by Leile's gifts and zeal, licensed him to preach and later ordained him. Leile baptized Andrew Bryan and his wife Hannah, Kate (Cate) Hogg, and Hagar Bryan. These four were gathered into the First African Baptist Church of Savannah after Leile left America.

Henry Sharp made legal provision for Leile's freedom to follow his master's death. When the British soldiers were leaving Georgia for Jamaica, late 1781 or early 1782, Leile went with them and began to preach to Jamaican Negroes. He organized the first Baptist church among them in 1784. In the early 1800's the Baptist Missionary Society (London) began work in Jamaica. The work prospered; ultimately, Jamaican Baptists became self-supporting and were themselves active in missions. About 100 years after Leile came there, the Jamaican Baptist Union began work among Negroes in Panama. In 1900 the Union sent S. M. Loveridge, an Englishman, as the first missionary to the West Indians in Panama. These had gone from Jamaica and other islands to work on the French project for a Panama Canal. When the United States Government took over the project, the number greatly increased.

In 1905 the Home Mission Board appointed J. L. Wise as a missionary to the Canal Zone. Wise reported that the Jamaican Baptist Union had been carrying on work for several years. In 1908 the Union transferred its work to the Home Mission Board. There were between 30,000 and 40,000 West Indians in the Canal Zone. The work under the Home Mission Board proceeded somewhat slowly; work was carried on among Americans employed in the project of digging the canal as well as among West Indian Negroes.

Two main difficulties confronted Wise and his fellow laborers. Many Baptist church members from the United States had come down to work in the canal project. "Church members came here, seemingly having said good-bye to mother, home, country and God." Such indifferent church members presented a problem to the mission work. The second difficulty was the effort on the part of some private individual Christians, chaplains in government service, and Y.M.C.A. secretaries to unionize all Christians into a church with no denominational connection and interest.

Another problem was faced in the fact that thousands were there temporarily during the digging of the canal; some were constantly returning to the United States. As the work on the canal was nearing completion, and especially when the Gatun Dam was completed, the lake forced the removal of some towns, which tended to disrupt the mission progress.

This temporary situation was faced during the first 10 years. By 1915 the canal was finished, and there came to be a more nearly settled population. It is true that there was a constant coming in from the United States and returning to the States, but the turnover was not so great as during the years of work on the canal.

During another 10-year period the Balboa Heights Church (white) became self-supporting and carried on in several different phases of work. The church now serves the Americans employed in the operation of the canal; assists in the work of the West Indian churches (Negro); indirectly influences citizens of the Republic of Panama; ministers to the spiritual welfare of soldiers and sailors in the United States forces; ministers to tourists from every part of the world. During this second 10-year period the West Indian churches continued to grow, and an entrance was made among Panamanians.

In the period following 1929, the financial condition of the Home Mission Board forced a reduction in appropriations, but the work continued. By the beginning of the 1940's, the board was enabled to increase its appropriations, and the work began to make better progress. Evangelical work overflowed into the republics of Panama, Costa Rica, Honduras, and Guatemala. In 1950 the work in all these republics, except that in Panama and the Canal Zone, was transferred to the Foreign Mission Board. With the material progress in the civil life of Panama, the mission work under the Home Board had to be stepped up.

The developing public schools of Panama are conducted in Spanish, although the West Indians have preserved their English speech. It, therefore, became necessary for the Baptist missionary work to provide a measure of education for children of West Indians who were hindered by the language barrier from attending public schools.

The oldest surviving Baptist church among the Spanish-speaking Panamanians is the First Baptist Church of Panama, organized as the Church of the Redeemer under the leadership of Paul Bell, Sr. (1886–1952), Sept. 1, 1943. The Ailigandi Baptist Church among the San Blas Indians was organized under the leadership of R. G. Van Royen, the Home Mission Board's superintendent for Panama and the Canal Zone, on Feb. 10, 1955.

In 1956 there were 19 Southern Baptist churches and 26 missions in Panama. The Home Mission Board had on the field 55 missionaries, of whom 4 were general, 14 were working with the West Indians, 12 with the Spanish-speaking Panamanians, 21 with the San Blas Indians, and 4 with the North Americans.

The West Indian congregations are organized into two associations: The Central Panama Baptist Association includes the First Isthmian Baptist Church in Cristobal; Calvary, Panama City;

First Baptist, Paraiso, formerly Red Tank; Bethany, Rainbow City; and Immanuel, Pueblo Nuevo. The Bocas del Toro Association is composed of Zion Baptist Church, Bocas City; Almirante Baptist Church, Guabito, just across the border from Costa Rica; Base Line Baptist Church; and Dos Canas.

The Spanish-speaking and the San Blas Indian congregations are organized into *La Convención Bautista de Panama,* which performs the functions of an association. It is made up of First Baptist Church of Panama and the churches of La Chorrera, Montero, Las Tablas, Vique, the San Blas Church of Ailigandi, and approximately 18 mission stations affiliated with these churches.

The Canal Zone Baptist Association is made up of three North American churches: First Baptist Church, Balboa Heights; Cocoli; and Margarita.

In 1954 the Baptists of Panama organized the Bible Institute for the training of their own pastors and leaders, housing it in temporary quarters at La Chorrera.

The value of properties owned by the Home Mission Board and the churches of Panama exceeds $600,000.

BIBLIOGRAPHY: E. K. Love, *History of the First African Baptist Church, Savannah* (1888). J. B. Myers, *Centenary Celebration of the Baptist Mission Society* (1893). LOYD CORDER

PAN-BAPTIST CONFERENCE. This term seems first to have been used about 1895 when William Warren Landrum (*q.v.*), learning that a Pan-Presbyterian gathering might be held, suggested to Robert Healy Pitt (*q.v.*), editor of the *Religious Herald,* that a Pan-Baptist Conference be considered. Though Pitt wrote briefly advocating such an assembly, the time was not right and nothing came of it.

The most important leadership in the development of the idea of a Pan-Baptist Conference was taken by the *Baptist Argus* of Louisville, Ky., through its editor, J. N. Prestridge, and through Archibald Thomas Robertson (*q.v.*), Southern Baptist Seminary professor, who was a regular contributor to the editorial columns of the *Argus.* The annual Baptist "outlook" number of the *Argus,* which had been suggested by Robertson, soon generated favorable opinion for a Pan-Baptist Conference, both in the United States and abroad. In 1904 Robertson suggested that the time was right to send representatives to London to confer about calling such a meeting.

The response to the suggestion of the *Argus* was immediate and favorable. Prestridge consequently introduced a resolution which was passed by the Southern Baptist Convention and which expressed the desire to hold a Pan-Baptist Conference "for the purpose of discussing matters of vital interest to the denomination." The Convention appointed a committee to work with other Baptists to bring such a conference to pass. This committee reported to the Convention in 1905 that a Baptist World Congress was assured. This congress meeting in London, July 11–19, 1905, brought the Baptist World Alliance into being and the idea of a Pan-Baptist Conference to fruition.

POPE A. DUNCAN

PAN-FORK BAPTIST ENCAMPMENT. One of four Texas encampments organized in 1946, located near Wellington, Tex., in District 10. In 1956 Therman Upshaw was director of this camp. J. E. ROTH

PANKEY, BENJAMIN FRANKLIN (b. Harrisburg, Ill., Aug. 10, 1861; d. Santa Fe, N. Mex., May 31, 1929). Cattleman, politician, Southern Baptist Convention vice-president. Son of William H. and Sarah Ann (Bickers) Pankey, he was educated at Ewing College, Ill.; he studied law but never practiced it. Pankey married Flora W. Harris in Jan., 1880, by whom he had one son and five daughters. He became interested in the cattle business and moved to Sante Fe, N. Mex., in 1907, where he bought large tracts of land, and at one time was the largest individual cattle shipper in the state. A member of the constitutional convention in 1909, he was elected senator from the 10th district in 1911, became a member of the first senate, 1912–17, lieutenant governor, 1919–21, and state land commissioner, 1926–29.

Pankey, a charter member of First Baptist Church, Santa Fe, was a member of the State Mission Board from 1919 to 1924, vice-president of the Southern Baptist Convention in 1921, and president of the board of trustees, Montezuma College, 1922–24, after which he was a member of the board, 1925–27.

HENRY CLAY REAVIS

PANTHEISM. The idea that reality is one simple being of which all things are modes, moments, members, appearances, or projections is known as pantheism (from Greek *pan,* all; and *theos,* God). A distinction is sometimes made between pantheism (all is God) and theopanism (God is all). Panentheism (God is in all) is often used to indicate God's presence in all things, good and evil, personal and impersonal, without making God dependent on them for his existence. Some views of the immanence of God approach pantheism, but the two generally differ where immanence rejects the identification of the Creator and the creature. Philosophical monism and idealism are often associated with both tendencies. Pantheistic personalism reduces all things to one Personality which exists neither before nor apart from the creation of persons.

See also GOD. DALE MOODY

PARACLETE, THE. The English word "paraclete" is a transliteration of a Greek word meaning "one called alongside." It is used five times in the New Testament: four times in the Fourth Gospel, referring to the Holy Spirit, and one time in the First Epistle of John, referring to Christ. There is actually no one word in English covering all the meanings which the Greek and the contexts require. "Comforter" will suffice for John 14:16 (cf. the Septuagint use of a cognate form in Job 16:2); "counselor" is more appropriate in John 14:26; "witness" in John 15:26; "prosecuting attorney" in John 16:7; and if John 16:12–15 be identified with "paraclete," a proper translation would be "revealer." In the single reference to Christ, I John 2:1, the translation "advocate" is correct; Jesus, by virtue of his atoning death, is cast in the role of a "defending attorney."

See also HOLY SPIRIT. JOSEPH R. ESTES

PARAGUAY, MISSION IN. Organized in Aug., 1952. Before that time it was a part of the three-country River Plate Mission. Baptist work in Paraguay was begun by Argentine Baptists, and the First Baptist Church of Asunción was organized in 1920. Sydney Langston and Frances (McCaw) Goldfinch, first Southern Baptist missionaries to Paraguay, arrived in 1945 after serving one term in Uruguay. By 1955 there were five organized churches in Paraguay: three in Asunción, with nine outstations; one in San Juan; and one in Encarnación. In 1948 Walter Eugene and Hazel (Thomson) Craighead, former missionaries in Europe, began working among Slavic-speaking people in Paraguay and Argentina, making Encarnación their headquarters.

Kindergartens (preschool and first grade) opened in Villa Morra Church and Barrio Chacarita, Asunción, in 1955. In Oct., 1955, the mission voted to begin a Bible institute in Asunción in 1956. Camps for church young people are held each summer at a camp site bought in Nov., 1953, in Itacurubi. Sadie Miriam Willis, missionary nurse, opened medical work in a slum area of Asunción in 1947. In 1953 Franklin Thomas Fowler, son of pioneer missionaries to Argentina, became director of a new 50-bed Baptist hospital. During its first three years it served 7,200 people through its inpatient and outpatient departments. On Dec. 31, 1955, the nursing school of the hospital was recognized by the Paraguayan University Medical School. FRANCES E. ROBERTS

PARDON. See FORGIVENESS.

PARKER, DANIEL (b. Culpeper County, Va., Apr. 6, 1781; d. Elkhart, Tex., Dec. 3, 1844). Antimission leader and founder of Two-Seed-in-the-Spirit-Predestinarian Baptists. Reared in Georgia in extreme poverty and without formal education, upon his conversion in 1802 he united with the Nails Creek Church of Franklin, Ga., which soon licensed him to preach. The following year he moved to Dixon County, Tenn., where the Trumbull Church ordained him on May 20, 1806. After serving as pastor in Tennessee until 1817, then in Illinois, he organized the Pilgrim Predestinarian Regular Baptist Church in the latter state in 1833 and moved it to Texas to circumvent the law of Mexico prohibiting the organizing of non-Catholic churches in Texas. Active in state affairs, Parker served as senator in Illinois (1826–27) and assisted in Texas' movement for independence (1834–36).

Best known as a controversial figure and leader of antimissionism, Parker was a man of astonishing ability and untiring industry. Though diminutive in size, uncouth in manner, slovenly in dress, and almost wholly without education, he was shrewd in debate, possessed considerable eloquence, and was a forceful speaker. This man, whose intense zeal approached insanity, appealed most effectively to the less educated class of frontier people. His bitter denunciation of all religious newspapers, tracts, and books (except his own) as attempts to supersede the Bible and his intense opposition to missions may at least in part be accounted for by the fact that his ambition to be a writer was suppressed when the editors of the *Columbian Star* (now *The Christian Index* of Georgia) rejected the articles that he submitted for publication. He first openly condemned missions, theological seminaries, and all benevolent and Bible societies in 1815 while he served as moderator of the Concord Association of Tennessee. In 1820 he published a 38-page pamphlet in which he viciously attacked such enterprises. By 1826 he had developed an elaborate theological basis for his opposition to missions in the form of the "two-seed" doctrine, which he borrowed from a preacher in Tennessee. That same year he set forth this doctrine, based on Genesis 3:15, in two books, *Views of the Two Seeds* and *The Second Dose of Doctrine on the Two Seeds.* According to this extreme theory of predestination, God created all things, but the devil begat a part of mankind. Since these are bona fide children of Satan, they can only go to him; and to send them missionaries or to present them Bibles is folly. On the other hand, the elect belong to God and have no need of help from mission societies to be saved.

Parker used innumerable measures to win Baptists to his views and to turn them against missions. For two years (1829–31) he published a monthly paper, the *Church Advocate,* which he devoted to opposing missions and to expounding his peculiar doctrine. He traveled widely, visiting churches and associations, always speaking against missions and sowing discord. By mixing his doctrines with genuine Baptist doctrines, he deceived many people and soon won them to his cause. As the arch-enemy of missions on the frontier, he extended his work through North Carolina, Tennessee, Kentucky, Illinois, Indiana, and Texas. Parker thus gave great impetus to the antimission movement among Baptists, and to the end of his life lost no opportunity of opposing the cause of missions.

A. B. RUTLEDGE and W. FRED KENDALL

PARLIAMENTARY AUTHORITY AND RULES OF ORDER. The first meeting of the Southern Baptist Convention, held in Augusta, Ga., May 8–12, 1845, adopted a "Rules of Order" consisting of six points. These constituted the sole parliamentary authority until 1868, when Mell's *Manual of Parliamentary Practice* was adopted. Patrick Hues Mell (*q.v.*), author of the manual, served as president of the Convention for 17 years, 1861–71 and 1879–87, longer than any other man. Barnes says:

> He [Mell] was one of the greatest of parliamentarians. Later, commenting on the Southern Baptist Convention which met in Waco, 1883, a Texas newspaper said: "Southern Baptists can never cease to admire the genius of Dr. Mell as a presiding officer. He rules with the inflexible rigor of a tyrant, and yet with a spirit so genial and sympathetic that no reasonable man can ever be embarrassed by his presence."

Mell continued as the Convention's sole parliamentary authority until 1913, when Franklin Howard Kerfoot's (*q.v.*) *Parliamentary Law* was added. The Convention bylaws provided that in cases of conflict between the two, the president would decide which authority would rule, subject to appeal to the Convention. In 1946 the Convention in a complete revision of its *Constitution and By-Laws* made Kerfoot's *Parliamentary Law* its only authority. However, state conventions, associations, and churches use either Kerfoot or Mell or Roberts as their authority. J. D. GREY

PARLOR VISITOR, THE. A monthly Baptist newspaper founded and edited in Nashville, Tenn., by a physician, William P. Jones, from 1852 to 1857, except the year 1856, when W. H. Bayless, pastor of the First Baptist Church of Nashville, edited the publication. The paper was moved to Murfreesboro, Tenn., in 1857, where Mrs. E. M. Eaton edited it as *The Aurora* until the Civil War forced its suspension. LYNN E. MAY, JR.

PAROUSIA. The Greek word meaning "being beside," used for the Second Advent of Christ. The meaning "presence" is clear in II Corinthians 10:10, "his bodily presence is weak." The further meaning, "arrival," found in the Koine Greek, is seen in II Corinthians 7:6, "by the coming of Titus." Both meanings are present in every occurrence, and the context must decide which is dominant.

Josephus used the word *parousia* to refer to God's "entry" into the "presence" in the tabernacle. In the Koine Greek it becomes a technical term to describe the "visit" of a king to his subject peoples, who, in preparation for this event, raised extra taxes, made feverish preparations, and gave him a special crown.

Because of such harsh experience, the New Testament writers use the word sparingly of the more welcome and permanent Advent of Christ. Matthew, alone of the Gospels, writing chiefly to Jews, uses it in only one chapter. This reference is not to be confused with the coming of Christ in judgment on Israel at the fall in A.D. 70 (cf. Matt. 24:32–35 with 36–44). Paul had difficulty with it at Thessalonica and used it again in speaking to Gentiles only in I Corinthians 15:23.

The parousia is seen to be a historical event whose purpose is final judgment and full redemption, the consummation of the messianic kingdom. Its glorious result for believers is permanent dwelling in Christ's revealed presence.

See also ADVENT. C. BROWNLOW HASTINGS

PARTICULAR BAPTISTS. From the beginning English Baptists were of two kinds. Those called the General Baptists held to a *general* redemption and the Arminian theology of John Smyth (d. 1612), Separatist preacher and Se-baptist, and others. Those called Particular Baptists followed the doctrine of *particular* election and predestination, along with most of the Puritans and Separatists of that day. It is misleading, however, to identify either group too closely with their respective schools of theology, as either strict Calvinists or Arminians.

Calvinism among these early Baptists was in large measure an influence of the Puritans and Separatists, out of which they had themselves directly sprung. The beginnings of the Particular Baptists in England may be traced from the formation of the now famed Jacob's Church, established in Southwark, London, in 1616. The church had a succession of noble pastors, who between 1616 and 1645 saw numerous groups dismissed to form Baptist fellowships; Jacob's Church itself became a Baptist church by the latter date. In 1633 a group under Samuel Eaton (1596?–1665), previously an Independent divine, was amicably dismissed because they thought the parish churches were completely false and unacceptable, especially with regard to parish baptisms, sacraments, and other gospel rites. Jacob's Church was not a Separatist group; their members should better be termed Independent Puritans. The dismission in 1633, then, was simply a further move in the direction of separation from the Church of England. Any concern for baptism at this point was probably limited to their doubt concerning the validity of a baptism administered at the hands of a parish priest and most likely not in the least related to the suitability of infant baptism, Thomas Crosby (*q.v.*) to the contrary notwithstanding. Sometime between 1633 and 1638, the first Particular Baptist Church (not then immersionist) in England was formed among these same Puritan Christians. In 1638 the records show that several of them, being "convinced that Baptism was not for Infants, but professed Believers [sic]," joined themselves to the church (presumedly already formed) of John Spilsbury (1593–*c.* 1668), an astute Calvinist, likewise being "of ye same Iudgment wth Sam. Eaton . . ."

The problem the critic has faced since then is the relationship between the 1633 group of Eaton, the 1633–38 group of Spilsbury, and the "Antipedobaptists" of 1638. Of the various solutions adopted, the most likely is as follows: (1) The Eaton group probably never completely severed relations with the original church; (2) several from both churches arrived at antipedobaptist positions together; and (3) under the leadership of Spilsbury, they formed a communion of baptized believers in Christ, yet still maintained some type of relationship to the old main line church under Henry Jessey (1601–63), pastor, Jacob's Church.

Although the General Baptists arose and were practicing believer's baptism a generation before the Particular Baptists, it was among the Particular Baptists that the mode of dipping arose. Around 1640 certain of the dissenters, in the congregations of Spilsbury and perhaps Jessey, after long deliberation in "prayer and conference [sic]," were persuaded that baptism, whether administered to infants or believers, ought not to be by sprinkling or pouring but rather after the apostolic custom of "diping ye Body into ye Water, resembling Burial & riseing again [sic]." Unable to find any on the island who practiced this mode, and hearing of the Rynsburgers or Collegiants (Mennonites) who did, they dispatched Richard Blunt (who spoke Dutch) sometime in 1641 to consult with those on the Continent.

It is now uncertain whether Blunt simply conferred with these Anabaptists or actually submitted himself to their baptism. At any rate, he returned to England in the same year and baptized a certain man named Blacklock, who may have then baptized Blunt, and the two of them in turn baptized 41 in all. By 1644 the confession of that year, which represented the thinking of the seven London churches, stated that "the way and manner of the dispensing of this Ordinance the Scripture holds out to be dipping or plunging the whole body under water. . . ."

Other significant Particular Baptists of this period include William Kiffin (1616–1701), pastor at the Devonshire Square Church, 1690–1716, wealthy merchant, lay preacher, and benefactor of the crown on several occasions; Jessey himself, who became a Baptist along with most of the original church in 1645; Hanserd Knollys (1599?–1691), Particular Baptist divine, great linguist and Baptist protagonist, and lifelong (died at 93) pastor of the famed Cripplegate Church; Benjamin Keach (1640–1704), Baptist minister, who was originally of the General Baptist connexion but became a Particular Baptist in London under the influence of Knollys and Kiffin, established the Horsley Down Church in Southwark, London, and was quite enthusiastic in his advocacy of congregational hymn-singing, laying of hands on the baptized, and paying the ministry.

BIBLIOGRAPHY: C. Burrage, *The Early English Dissenters* (1912). T. Crosby, *The History of English Baptists* (1738–40). A. C. Underwood, *A History of the English Baptists* (1947). EUGENE STOCKSTILL

PASCHAL, GEORGE WASHINGTON (b. Chatham County, N. C., July 7, 1869; d. Wake Forest, N. C., June 13, 1956). Author, historian. Son of Richard Bray and Matilda (Schmidt) Paschal, he received the A.B. degree from Wake Forest College in 1892 and the Ph.D. degree from the University of Chicago in 1900. He was connected with Wake Forest College for more than 60 years: as professor of Latin and Greek, 1896–1940; as professor emeritus, 1940–56; examiner and registrar, 1916–26; and curator of the college library, 1901–19. He wrote extensively, being the author of: *A Study of Quintus of Smyrna* (1904), *History of North Carolina Baptists,* Vol. I (1930) Vol. II (1955), *A History of Wake Forest College,* Vol. I (1935) Vols. II and III (1943), *A History of Printing in North Carolina* (1946), "A History of the Foreign Mission Board of the Southern Baptist Convention" (unpublished). He was co-editor of *A Young Man's Visions—An Old Man's Dreams* (1956). He was editorial writer of the *Biblical Recorder,* 1931–40. Paschal married Laura Allen, Dec. 21, 1905, and to them were born 10 children. EUGENE OLIVE

PASTOR. See MINISTER, SOUTHERN BAPTIST and ORDINATION.

PASTORAL CARE. Gregory the Great called pastoral care "the art of arts." Before him, Peter in his first epistle exhorted the elders, "Tend the flock of God that is in [your] charge." The apostle Paul, as a great pastor himself, comforted those in any affliction with the comfort wherewith he himself had been comforted of God. In a very real way, the ministry to individuals, families, and small groups in times of crisis and intense personal need is the responsibility of every Christian. The church itself is a prayerful fellowship of concern, a community of pastoral care and considerateness of the personal needs of others. The deacons in a Baptist church, in the tradition of those appointed to care for the needs of neglected widows, are responsible mediators of pastoral care to people today. The deaconship is more than an honorary position or that of managing the finances of the church. The Sunday school teacher, also, is responsible for "tending" to the spiritual needs of his or her class members.

Educational and music directors have many small groups of persons to whom they minister. They are responsible to a great extent for the pastoral care of the individual members and the leaders of groups with whom they work. Among Southern Baptists the importance of the small, closely related, face-to-face groups in the Sunday school, Training Union, Brotherhood, and Woman's Missionary Union cannot be overestimated. The extension of the fellowship through these groups results in rapid growth. The caring concern of these groups is a vital force in the total pastoral care of the church. Consequently, the educational workers are in a vital way involved in pastoral care.

The heaviest load of the care of the flock, however, falls both symbolically and literally upon the shoulders of the pastor. Symbolically, he is "the man of God" to his people; literally, he is the one most often expected to render these ministries. This fact is particularly true in the church which does not have other workers such as educational director, music director, etc. The minister wears the spiritual mantle of all the great pastors of the Christian heritage. He meets his people as individuals, families, and small groups with similar needs in times of joy and sorrow. In these crises individuals, families, and the whole church undergo testing, temptation, conflict, and spiritual reshaping through decision and suffering. The birth of a baby into the home, the choice of a life work, the marriage of a man and a woman, tragic accidents, illnesses, bereavements, family conflicts, and death are just a few of the crises in which a minister is expected to practice his "art of arts," pastoral care.

The pastor and his co-workers communicate the compassion of Christ to people at these times of need in many different ways. They visit in the home. They take initiative in the name of Christ. They may wait for people to call for them, to visit them in their studies. They may decide to invite a person to come to them for a private interview. The minister and his co-workers, furthermore, may suggest that the person "follow through" with a series of conferences over a period of time in a counseling relationship. The use of more time in such instances has several purposes: The person can gradually achieve insight into himself from interview to interview. He can grow through a process of spiritual self-encounter. He can think out his decisions under the guiding skill of the pastor as a counselor and thus avoid impulsive action.

The pastor and his co-workers may suggest that the person seek additional specialized assistance from professions such as medical doctors, social workers, etc. For instance, the couple who want to adopt a child need the help of a children's agency. Before that they need expert medical advice to make certain that they cannot have children of their own. In the midst of the many professional counselors who help the individual today, the pastor and his co-workers function as trained "team members." Faithful workers of every profession—public schoolteachers, college and university professors, religious counselors, medical doctors, lawyers, and business people—join with the pastor and other trained religious workers in an enlarged community of helping concern.

However, the work of the pastor and religious worker is different and even unique in several respects. It is not just "social service" in a humanitarian sense. First, last, and always, the pastor represents the church and religion in the eyes of his counselee. The church supports the pastor and makes his services available to the individual as an expression of the whole community's love for him. Most of the problems people present to a pastor, furthermore, have religious overtones, even if they are not explicitly expressed in so many words. Whether or not the counselee is aware of the religious element inherent in his problem, the pastor certainly recognizes it as such. He must deal with the problem in the light of his obligation to God, as well as to the person he is trying to help. Even a seemingly worldly problem, such as a quarrel with a neighbor, is attached to some larger questions as to the person's spiritual destiny under God.

In the eyes of the persons to whom he gives pastoral care, the pastor is the leader of the spiritual community of the church. On the one hand, this gives him the privilege of taking the initiative toward people in times of need. They expect him to visit. On the other hand, it may prevent a clearly defined situation in which he is formally accepted as a counselor. The people may be waiting for him to take initiative but may resent it if he does. The reason for this attitude is that the pastor must also function as preacher, teacher, administrator, and pastoral visitor in turn. In his own eyes, however, the pastor sees himself always in his larger context as a representative of God, of the Christ, of the Holy Spirit, of the church. He functions always as a pastoral counselor, not simply as a counselor. His work is distinguished always by the spiritual setting in which it is done. Both he and his counselee attach religious objectives, resources, and patterns of meaning to the counseling process. This is true whether or not the pastor and his counselee choose religious terms with which to understand and communicate with each other. Pastoral care is inseparable from the pastor's or religious worker's relationship to the total church fellowship. The church itself is the minister. The pastor and his associates are its servants. They direct the church in the pastoral care of those who are in "any affliction." This pastoral care is actually the fulfilment of the law of Christ in the body of Christ, because it is a practical means for the bearing of one another's burdens.

Pastoral care has a complementary relationship to preaching, religious education, and administration. It assists the individuals or families concerned to relate themselves satisfyingly to the church as a community. The redemptive power of the corporate fellowship, without specific aid of individual attention, often effects deep personal changes in lives touched by the church. Needless to say, in times of need the spiritual resources of the church are channeled to individuals and families through pastoral care.

In actual practice it is a fact that general pastoral care among Southern Baptists has not yet come up to the above standard. As one pastor puts it, "Zeal outweighs knowledge at this point. In many instances, even zeal is reduced to an ineffective wistfulness." In too many cases, leaders in the various ministries are more concerned about what the people do for them or the church rather than about caring for the people themselves. The education of ministers and other church workers toward greater realism and effectiveness is redoubled in importance by this confession of shortcoming. Meeting the personal needs of the tremendously expanding memberships of our churches in the increasingly urbanized and industrialized South, therefore, calls for the wisdom of the serpents and the harmlessness of the doves. Southern Baptists, for instance, are no longer a "one-class" rural people. Every social class is apparent in strength and must be dealt with helpfully.

Southern Baptist leaders in the field see some major needs at this time, both in the training for and the practice of pastoral care among Southern Baptists. Ministers and others who have finished their education and are actively engaged in the work of the churches need more information and guidance in order to minister effectively to their people in this field of pastoral care. Also, there is a need to provide laboratory experiences for young workers within the context of local church situations. One approach is through the placement of inexperienced graduates of seminaries in "internships" under older and more experienced pastors and staff members. However, the lack of an organization which can provide systematic supervision of the instruction between the pastor and the interns causes much to be desired in this program. The "associate pastor" relationship, furthermore, can be a "residence" relationship of learning. Here a young minister with experience can concentrate upon pastoral care. He can, for instance, give intensive attention to the needs of people for formal counseling in domestic difficulties.

In all of their work in the area of pastoral care, religious workers draw upon the resources of their religious heritage based upon the traditional function of shepherd, which has always been a part of the responsibility of the minister. But at the present, ministers and other religious workers are adding to their effectiveness by bringing their religious heritage into a more powerful co-operative relationship with the newer sciences of education, psychology, and medicine. They bring things both old and new out of their treasure in the pastoral care of their congregations. This co-operative fellowship with educators, psychologists, and medical doctors opens new channels of communication of the gospel, both to individual church members in need and to people of other professions. Ministers and religious workers are being trained today to do more than bring a shallow cheer to people in trouble. One of the best ways to understand their increasingly effective work in pastoral care is to see how the pastors, directors of religious education, and missionaries are being taught in our Southern Baptist seminaries and hospitals.

The intent and purpose of this training is perhaps nowhere better presented than in a statement written in 1945 by the late Ellis A. Fuller, president of the Southern Baptist Theological Seminary. In it he said the following:

> The need and value of clinical training in pastoral care for Southern Baptist students is impressed upon us in many ways. We are coming into an era in which people generally will seek hospitalization in sickness of all kinds. The denominations are building hospitals, communities are building hospitals and the Federal Government is in the business of building hospitals. Plans for insurance for individuals and groups which will provide hospital care for great numbers make certain greatly increased admissions to hospitals. There is a wide-spread interest in better health for all people. The place of religion in the prevention and cure of sickness is being recognized widely by men of science as well as by Christian ministers.
>
> Communities and churches are becoming more aware of the importance of institutions for the mentally ill, for delinquents and criminals, and for the promotion of social welfare through specialized agencies. Ministers and churches have a large part in the development of these means for the conservation of human life. Obviously the churches have a very great stake in this matter.
>
> Southern Baptists are not even remotely interested in training workers for a ministry which ignores or makes incidental the Christian gospel. But we are convinced that ministers need the resources which come from a better understanding of human nature and conduct, from an acquaintance with the techniques which psychiatrists and psychologists have developed for dealing with human problems and needs in sickness and in health, and from familiarity with the workings of hospitals and other institutions in which they will have opportunities to minister to those who need their Christian message and service. For these reasons, we feel it is wise to pursue our venture in giving to our student body such training in this area as may be possible under our limitations.
>
> Every minister would clearly profit from some training in this field. Through the years a certain amount of work has been offered as a feature of other courses. We recognize that such study can now well be expanded. To this end courses are being added, by vote of the faculty, for students who want further specialization in this field. In addition, it now seems timely for some students, called of God to be ministers of the gospel, to fit themselves for specialized services in eleemosynary institutions, where they will have peculiar opportunities for the specialized ministry usually referred to as the chaplaincy. There is a growing demand for this type of ministry, and the need is felt for specialized clinical training of certain students who will be fully equipped to furnish leadership in this field of pastoral care.

Seminary Training. *Southern Baptist Theological Seminary.*—Here the teaching of pastoral care is based upon the foundation of a clear understanding of the psychology of religious experience. A required course in the theory and practice of pastoral care covers the responsibilities of the pastor for the shepherding care of individuals and groups in the crises of life mentioned previously. Marriage and family counseling aims to equip the pastor for dealing with unhappy situations within families, as well as for increasing the happiness of what has been called "the happy family."

Smaller classes are taught in clinical pastoral training. Students are expected to spend considerable time working under supervision in general medical and surgical, psychiatric, delinquency, and family counseling agencies in the city of Louisville. The student can spend a fourth year and work toward the master's degree in theology in this kind of work. Persons who expect to teach in the field of pastoral care and psychology of religion are advised to take their doctorate in the field of Christian ethics and to write their thesis in the field of the psychology of religion. Clinical pastoral training is prerequisite to writing such a thesis. This training includes specific courses in the care of the mentally ill and in the care of patients in general medical and surgical hospitals, with some supervised experience in marriage counseling.

A selected number of qualified students are placed in institutional chaplaincies, teaching programs within the context of orphanages, social work with some of the local social agencies, and probationary work with the local courts. One of the local hospitals, the Norton Psychiatric Clinic, provides facilities for a supervised psychiatric-aide training program in which students are enabled to earn their expenses at the seminary while they work in the clinic and receive specific training in psychiatric information for the care of the mentally ill. This work is considered field work, and is correlated with courses at the seminary which give the student a theological and pastoral context for assimilating what he learns.

Southwestern Baptist Theological Seminary. Here, also, pastoral care is considered a necessary part of training qualified pastoral ministers. The care of souls is considered to be the essential ministry of all Christian leadership. Training in this area is provided by the departments of pastoral ministry, psychology of religion, and Christian ethics. Courses offered in the schools of theology and religious education may be taken for credit toward theology and religious education degrees. The method of training includes classwork in pastoral theology, principles of psychology, practical supervised field work, and clinical pastoral training. The psychology of Christian personality, pastoral guidance in individual and group counseling, the church's crisis ministry in the community, and group dynamics in the church are all dealt with.

Clinical training in the ministry to the physically and mentally ill is offered through several hospital training programs. Southwestern co-operates with the Institute of Religion of the Texas Medical Center at Houston. A thorough program of academic study, clinical training in patient care, and clinical research in pastoral psychology and spiritual therapy is conducted here. Students are prepared for the hospital chaplaincy and for the teaching of pastoral care, as well as for the regular work of the pastoral ministry in a local church. The medical center provides such training through a number of hospitals. Among those comprising the center are a crippled children's clinic, a children's hospital, a city-county hospital, a tumor institute, a tubercular hospital, several denominational general hospitals, a college of nursing, a hospital for the mentally ill, and several colleges of medicine, dentistry, and public health. Working scholarships for seminary students are being provided by various hospitals at the medical center and elsewhere in the city of Houston.

In addition to the work at the Institute of Religion, Southwestern conducts clinical programs at the Austin State Hospital, Rusk State Hospital, San Antonio State Hospital, and Terrell State Hospital of Texas. A special course is also available in the field of marriage and family counseling in conjunction with the Menninger Foundation in Topeka, Kans. In 1955 a two-month clinical program was arranged with Buckner Orphans Home, Dallas, for work with either elementary or adolescent groups. Beginning in 1956, the clinically approved State Hospital at Norman, Okla., also received Southwestern Seminary's students.

In the city of Fort Worth, the United States Public Health Service operates one of its two hospitals specializing in the treatment of drug addicts. Short-term clinical programs and class clinics are held here. Similar training is given in the Baylor Hospital, Dallas, and the Baptist Memorial Hospital of Houston. Field work is also done at a children's home in Fort Worth.

The School of Religious Education at Southwestern Seminary provides courses in psychology and counseling, not only for the minister but also for the missionary, minister of education, teacher, elementary director, youth director, student secretary, and dean of students. Eighteen courses are offered in the department of religious psychology and counseling of the School of Religious Education under three division headings: psychology of religion, counseling, and applied psychology.

New Orleans Baptist Theological Seminary. Through the department of Christian psychology and counseling in the School of Religious Education, this seminary seeks to prepare men and women for the personal ministry of pastoral care. Basic courses are taught in personality development, mature Christian personality standards, problems of abnormality, the psychology of religion, the place of religion in mental health, and the techniques of personal, group, and marriage counseling.

Supervised field work is done in several hospitals in the city by service groups interested in counseling. During the school year of 1952–53, a clinical education program was begun at the seminary in co-operation with the Southern Baptist Hospital. A joint program of supervision exists between the chaplains and the seminary faculty, integrating the clinical work with lectures in pastoral counseling. The students meet once a week in small groups for the purpose of discussing verbatim write-ups of counseling interviews. Many of these written accounts are the results of visits and interviews in the hospitals. Advanced students in counseling with the sick spend two afternoons a week in the hospital. The students' experiences in visitation and their write-ups are discussed thoroughly. Graduate students take seminars offered in the department of Christian psychology and counseling. They meet at the hospital, visit patients, write up their interviews, and share these in group study. Speakers and discussion leaders in medicine, surgery, psychiatry, and related fields are heard. Through these seminars clinical research projects are developed. This kind of instruction is intensified during the summers in an eight-week course in clinical pastoral education.

The department of principles and philosophy of religious education at New Orleans seeks to apply current educational psychology to the work the pastor does in caring for the needs of individual church members. Such studies as educational philosophy, curriculum building, and teaching and group dynamics seek to point the way for the personal and small group ministries of the churches. Actual supervised field projects in churches served by the students are conducted. The special care of small children is taught by the department of childhood education, utilizing the science of mental hygiene especially in its emphasis on normal child development. Theory and practice are brought together in the nursery-kindergarten and the day-care center on the seminary campus. Better parent-child relationships and pupil-teacher understanding result from this kindergarten atmosphere. Also, several programs are provided for campus Intermediates and Young People by the students, supervised by the professor of youth education. These efforts seek to prevent behavior problems and aid personal growth. Again, the department of religious social work assimilates all the resources of the science of social work. This integration in the clinical work is done in several Southern Baptist good will centers. Other religious social service centers, such as the Good Samaritan Home and the home for unwed mothers, provide clinical social work opportunities for students.

Golden Gate Baptist Theological Seminary. This seminary emphasizes the achievement of spiritual community in the life of the church through pastoral care. The pastoral ministry is conceived in terms of the total development of the church. In every course the question is raised as to how the insights, concepts, and techniques of the branches of psychology apply to pastoral care.

A more recent development at Golden Gate has been the emphasis upon family counseling and family life education. The main concern is to prevent rather than merely to cure the personal and socially shattered lives of people. The work at Golden Gate also emphasizes group counseling, because the character of the life of Christian fellowship as a meaningful group containing smaller and more intimate groups demands it. By being an effective group leader, the busy pastor can extend his ministry to more people by capitalizing upon the powerful quality of fellowship.

Golden Gate participates in a teaching program in local hospitals. In one hospital a resident in administration supervises the program so far as it touches the hospital generally. Ward supervision is carried out by a trained chaplain. The actual theological teaching is done by the professors from co-operating schools, of which Golden Gate is one. The seminary also participates in clinical training programs in several mental hospitals and in one state prison. Other clinical opportunities are being developed in the areas of juvenile delinquency, unwed motherhood, and alcoholism. The goal of the seminary is to provide eligible and interested students with opportunities for the clinical experience necessary for their future ministry, whether in a church as a pastor, in an institution as a chaplain, or in a school as a teacher.

Southeastern Baptist Theological Seminary. This seminary works with the North Carolina Baptist Hospital and the Bowman Gray School of Medicine, Winston-Salem, in teaching pastoral care to its students. The director of the department of pastoral care of the North Carolina Baptist Hospital also serves part-time as associate professor of pastoral care at the seminary. A survey course called "Introduction to Pastoral Care" is required of all seminary students and is prerequisite to intensive clinical training provided in an elective course for a selected number of students who go to Winston-Salem to the Baptist hospital. Only 10 students are allowed in each of these classes. Four classes are operated simultaneously throughout the summer months. In addition to the work at North Carolina Baptist Hospital, a course is offered in conjunction with the State Mental Hospital at Raleigh. In this course a student spends one afternoon a week throughout the semester at the mental hospital working under the supervision of the hospital chaplain.

The lecture course at the seminary, as well as the clinical work offered, is presented in such a way as to focus the student's attention upon the practical application of the gospel message to the needs of specific individuals.

Hospitals. *North Carolina Baptist Hospital.* The department of pastoral care offers different kinds of training in pastoral care of the sick and in pastoral counseling. Each winter, for instance, two six-week courses are offered that are designed to meet the needs of active pastors who did not have opportunity to get clinical training during their seminary education. The same curriculum content and methods of teaching are followed as in the summer courses. Furthermore, eight-week courses are offered for theological students.

The course consists of lectures each morning

by members of the department of pastoral care or of the medical staff. Then each student is assigned varied types of patients throughout the hospital and writes reports on his visitation. He is supervised in systematic reading. In addition, the students spend an hour and a half daily in a closely supervised group seminar.

Intern training is also provided. Five one-year internships are offered annually, three of which are filled by May 1 and two by Sept. 1. The training consists of active participation in psychiatric clinics, scheduled staff conferences, and pastoral care of hospitalized patients. The work involves active co-operation with all members of the healing team: doctors, ministers, nurses, and social workers. In the afternoons each intern engages in formal office counseling on an out-patient basis. This intensive office counseling is provided for persons who are referred to the department of pastoral care by ministers and doctors throughout the state.

Finally, residencies in hospital chaplaincy are offered yearly. A year of internship is prerequisite to a year of residency training. The resident is actively engaged in research in pastoral care and also serves as an assistant clinical supervisor.

Southern Baptist Hospital.—A program of clinical pastoral education is conducted in co-operation with the New Orleans Baptist Theological Seminary. Clinical education consists of hospital orientation, contact with hospital personnel, and visits with patients, all closely supervised by the hospital chaplains. This training is offered for individuals and small groups in the beginning phases of counseling studies. A minimum of eight hours a week for eight weeks is spent in counseling with the sick in the hospital by advanced students taking studies in the seminary. Specialized, full-time, eight-week courses for seminary doctoral students are offered four months each year. To do the work adequately, the students spend four to five hours daily in study, hospital visitation, preparation of verbatim write-ups, and group participation. Papers on some phase of clinical training are prepared by the individual student, who then leads a discussion of this paper in a group meeting. Members of the hospital staff are invited to speak to the group. The student is encouraged to build an appropriate bibliography and to spend some time each week with the chaplain supervisor to discuss his individual progress.

Shorter Term Types of Pastoral Care Education. The Louisiana Baptist Hospital, under the supervision of its chaplain, has offered clinical pastoral training for local ministers from time to time. Also, at the Memorial Hospital, Houston, Tex., an institute for pastors was held in 1953. Plans were under way in 1956 to integrate this program with the work of the Texas Medical Center Institute of Religion. In turn this will be related to the work of the Southwestern Baptist Theological Seminary. The Birmingham Baptist Hospital, in the spring of 1955, conducted a one-day institute on pastoral care. The Georgia Baptist Hospital sponsored a series of visiting speakers each Monday throughout the fall of 1954. The Southwide Baptist Chaplains Association, in 1952, held a two-week clinic on a workshop basis at the North Carolina Baptist Hospital with 18 chaplains present. The group was divided into several committees for the study of specific projects and then reassembled to hear and discuss all reports. A similar one-week clinic was held in 1954 at the Midstate Baptist Hospital in Nashville, Tenn. The Chaplains Association has now voted to sponsor such a clinic every two years.

In Jan., 1953, and Jan., 1955, the department of pastoral care of the North Carolina Baptist Hospital offered a three-day institute on pastoral care for pastors, religious workers, and other interested professional people. The registration for each of these institutes exceeded 350. The program consisted of lectures by leaders in the field of pastoral care, followed by discussion periods.

The Southern Baptist Hospital Administrators Association, through its executive officers, has appointed a committee consisting of pastors, seminary professors, and chaplains to study its work in the field of pastoral care. The purpose of this committee is to develop a regional program of educationally dependable pastoral-care training in the context of the local Southern Baptist hospitals throughout the South. One-day institutes in six of the hospitals were conducted in 1956.

Work also is done by Southern Baptists in the pastoral care of inmates of tax-supported institutions. The Central State Hospital at Lakeland, Ky., since 1945 has conducted intensive clinical pastoral education for students at the Southern Baptist Theological Seminary. The North Carolina State Mental Hospital at Raleigh, N. C., co-operates with the Southeastern Baptist Theological Seminary in providing clinical pastoral education for students enrolled there. The Napa State Hospital in the Bay Area of San Francisco and Berkeley provides clinical pastoral training for students at the Golden Gate Baptist Theological Seminary, and students care for the spiritual needs of patients here, also. The Louisville General Hospital and the Medical School of the University of Louisville provide a clinical training program for theological students at the Louisville Presbyterian Theological Seminary and the Southern Baptist Theological Seminary in conjunction with their Protestant chaplaincy program. The Mississippi State Hospital at Whitfield, Miss., is offering intensive training for small groups of theological students and one-year internships for one or two students each year. Although the program is not restricted to Baptists, the population in the area is predominantly Baptist and the training points in that direction. The Texas Medical Center's Institute of Religion, as has already been noted, is related to the Southwestern Baptist Theological Seminary, providing a one-year residency program in pastoral care, with clinical pastoral training for ministers beyond the B.D. degree. Credit is given toward both the Master's and Doctor's degrees.

To achieve practical ends, Southern Baptists have related themselves to these agencies in co-operation but not union with other denominational groups. Human suffering provides an undisputed ground of comradeship for members of all denominations who are seeking to learn more about its mysteries. Sickness, bereavement, death, and the shattering of personality are no respecter of persons.

Southern Baptists have added substantially to the literature of pastoral care, as is apparent from the following bibliography of books by Southern Baptist Ministers: R. Lofton Hudson, *The Religion of a Sound Mind* (1949); *The Religion of a Mature Person* (1952); *Growing a Christian Personality* (1955). Wayne E. Oates, *The Christian Pastor* (1953); *The Bible in Pastoral Care* (1953); *Religious Factors in Mental Illness* (1955); *Pre-Marital Pastoral Counseling* (1954); *Anxiety in Christian Experience* (1955); *Where to Go for Help* (1957). Samuel Southard, *The Family and Mental Illness* (1957); *Counseling for Church Vocations* (1957); Richard K. Young, *The Pastor's Hospital Ministry* (1954).

The following list is a selected general bibliography of some of the important sources in the fields of pastoral care, the psychology of religion, and religious education. It is intended as a guide to further study in this area.

BIBLIOGRAPHY: *Religious education references.*—F. B. Edge, *Teaching for Results* (1955). W. Fallaw, *Toward Spiritual Security* (1952). G. Highet, *The Art of Teaching* (1950). L. J. Sherrill, *The Struggle of the Soul* (1951); *The Gift of Power* (1955). S. R. Slavson, *Creative Group Education* (1940).

Homiletical references.—H. E. Fosdick, *On Being a Real Person* (1953). E. Mandrell, *The Relevance of Dynamic Psychology for Christian Preaching* (1953). W. E. Oates, "Mature Relationships," *Pastoral Psychology* (Dec., 1954); "The Daily Providences of God," *Pastoral Psychology* (Feb., 1955); "The Defense Rests," *Pastoral Psychology* (Sept., 1955); "The Second Touch of the Master," *Pastoral Psychology* (Feb., 1954). J. Pike, *Beyond Anxiety* (1953). D. Roberts, *The Grandeur and Misery of Man* (1955). P. Tillich, *The Shaking of the Foundations* (1948); *The New Being* (1955). L. Webb, *Conquering the Seven Deadly Sins* (1955).

Theological references.—E. Brunner, *Man in Revolt* (1947). M. Buber, *I and Thou* (1950). V. Frankl, *The Doctor and the Soul* (1955). A. R. Johnson, *The Vitality of the Individual in the Thought of Ancient Israel* (1949). A. Outler, *Psychotherapy and the Christian Message* (1951). D. Roberts, *Psychotherapy and the Christian View of Man* (1951). H. W. Robinson, *The Christian Doctrine of Man* (1926). P. Tillich, *Systematic Theology* (1951); *The Courage to Be* (1953).

Personality references.—G. Allport, *Becoming* (1955). A. Angyal, *Foundations for a Science of Personality* (1941). G. Murphy, *Personality: A Bio-Social Approach to Origins and Structure* (1947).

Psychology of religious experience.—G. Allport, *The Individual and His Religion* (1951). A. Boisen, *The Exploration of the Inner World* (1952). W. James, *The Varieties of Religious Experiences* (1902).

Counseling references.—A. H. Brayfield, *Readings in Modern Methods of Counseling* (1950). S. Hiltner, *Pastoral Counseling* (1949); *The Counselor in Counseling* (1952). C. Rogers, *Client-centered Therapy* (1951). H. S. Sullivan, *The Psychiatric Interview* (1954). C. A. Wise, *Pastoral Counseling: Its Theory and Practice* (1951).

Mental illness.—O. S. English and S. M. Finch, *Introduction to Psychiatry* (1954). H. S. Sullivan, *The Interpersonal Theory of Psychiatry* (1952). E. A. Streckner, *Basic Psychiatry* (1952). American Psychiatric Association, *Diagnostic and Statistical Manual-Mental Disorders* (1952).

Psychophysiological illness.—H. F. Dunbar, *Emotions and Bodily Changes: A Survey of Literature on Psychosomatic Interrelationships* (1954). L. Hinsie, *The Person in the Body: An Introduction to Psychosomatic Medicine* (1954). E. Weiss and O. S. English, *Psychosomatic Medicine: The Clinical Application of Psychopathology to General Medical Problems* (1943).

Historical references.—J. T. McNeill, *A History of the Cure of Souls* (1951). G. Murphy, *An Introduction to the History of Modern Psychology* (1932). G. Zilboorg, *A History of Medical Psychology* (1941).

WAYNE E. OATES—*Chairman*
A. DONALD BELL, JAMES LYNN ELDER, JOHN PRICE, JR., FRANKLIN SEGLER, RICHARD K. YOUNG

PATTERSON, LINSEY F. (b. Walker County, Ga., 1846; d. Mar. 2, 1924). Pioneer missionary in Indian Territory. Baptized into the Friendship Church, Lawrence County, Mo., in 1864, Patterson gave 54 years to missionary work in Indian Territory. During the first seven years of this work he received no salary, supporting himself and his family by farming. He was endowed with a powerful physique, a winning personality, and native wit which saved him from several perils. Once while in the vicinity of what is now Oklahoma City he was captured by Indians. Amusing them with his funny stories, he seized a gun and escaped. Patterson held several pastorates, served as moderator of three associations—Short Mountain of Indian Territory and Buckner and Concord in Arkansas—and greatly influenced Oklahoma and Arkansas by his missionary activities. He baptized 2,000 people. He is buried at Winfield, Ark.

HERBERT M. PIERCE

PAULICIANS. An oriental group of obscure origin, but with quite primitive elements in their thought and life. They were once thought to be principally a neo-Manichaean derivative, but this is questioned by Newman on the basis of the contents of their *The Key of Truth* (made available to the Western world in 1898). Newman sees them as an offshoot of an early form of Christianity in Armenia, having an adoptionist (heretical) Christology which claimed that Jesus became the adopted son of God in his baptism by John. They practiced believers' baptism, and for various reasons tended to reject the Old Testament. The question of whether there is a line of influence from the Paulicians, through medieval dissenting parties, to the radical evangelicals of the 16th century (including many called Anabaptists) is debated. The question, so far as the evangelical, non-violent Anabaptists were concerned, is probably to be answered in the negative.

BIBLIOGRAPHY: F. C. Conybeare, ed., *The Key of Truth* (1898). *Dictionary of Christian Biography* (1877). *New Schaff-Herzog Encyclopedia of Religious Knowledge,* VIII (1950). T. D. PRICE

PAXTON, WILLIAM EDWARDS (b. Little Rock, Ark., June 23, 1823; d. Fort Smith, Ark., Jan. 7, 1883). Author, preacher, teacher. Educated at Georgetown College, where he received the A.B. degree in 1847 and the A.M. degree in 1849, Paxton for a time taught school and read law in Kentucky. From 1853 to 1877, he practiced law, taught school, wrote articles for various papers, served as an officer in the Confederate army, and served as pastor of churches in Louisiana. He was also connected with educational institutions in Mt. Lebanon, Shreveport, and Minden. A prolific writer, Paxton served as associate editor or correspondent for papers in Louisiana, Mississippi, Tennessee, Kentucky, and Texas. He also wrote many pamphlets and several books; his most important books are *A History of the Baptists of Louisiana* and *The Apostolic Church*. In 1882 Keatchie College conferred upon him the D.D. degree. In 1878 he became pastor of the church and head of a school at Warren, Ark., and in 1883 he became pastor in Fort Smith, Ark., where he died. T. W. GAYER

PEACE AND SOUTHERN BAPTISTS. Between World Wars I and II, Southern Baptists manifested deep interest in world peace. As the horrors of war increased, they named a special committee on May 18, 1944, with J. M. Dawson as chairman, to study the problem of securing permanent peace. In addition to other literature published, the committee printed and distributed by May, 1945, 50,000 copies of a brochure that proclaimed six desired demands:

1. No isolation—recognizing that all nations are members one of another. 2. Democracy, or the right of all nations, both great and small, to self-government. 3. International organization for peace, implemented with necessary police power and an international court of justice. 4. The worth of every individual respected, toward the elimination of race prejudice and hatreds which undermine respect for the individual. 5. Economic opportunity for all peoples, toward elimination of disastrous trade barriers and enforced poverty. 6. Religious liberty, not alone tolerated worship but the right to conduct missions, to hold property dedicated to religious uses, to establish schools and printing presses, and to exercise civil rights without discrimination on grounds of religious faith.

The chairman of this special committee upheld these demands before national groups convened by Secretary of State Cordell Hull in Washington, D. C., in Oct., 1944, and also presented them at the National Conference of the Churches for a Just and Durable Peace, meeting in Cleveland in Jan., 1945, at which the Dumbarton Oaks proposals were considered with a view to revision. The chairman attended the organizational meeting of the United Nations held in San Francisco in the spring of 1945, and presented to the secretary of this international body certification of approximately 100,000 petitions for religious liberty, largely from Southern Baptist churches, asking that guarantees of such liberty be incorporated in the charter of the new organization. In 1946 the Baptist Committee on World Peace was discontinued and its work entrusted to the Baptist Joint Committee on Public Affairs and the Christian Life Commission of the Southern Baptist Convention. The denomination has shown abiding interest in the international organization, giving its moral support and supporting it with prayers. At all times admitting defects in the organization, and always holding that final world peace depends chiefly upon the spiritual transformation of the race, Southern Baptists believe the United Nations offers the best organizational hope for the peoples of the earth to achieve peace. JOSEPH MARTIN DAWSON

PECK, JOHN MASON (b. near Litchfield, Conn., Oct. 31, 1789; d. Rock Spring, Ill., Mar. 14, 1858). Pioneer missionary in the West, educator, journalist. Reared on a farm, Peck received little formal education; nevertheless, in 1807 he began to teach. In Dec., 1807, he was converted in a revival in the Litchfield Congregation Church. There he met Sally Paine, a New Yorker living in Litchfield, and they married on May 8, 1809. When their son was born, Sally came to question infant baptism. In seeking to answer her questions, Peck also developed doubts which the later renowned Lyman Beecher, then pastor at Litchfield, could not help him to resolve.

Early in 1811 the Pecks moved to Greene County, New York, near Sally's home. Having come to the Baptist position concerning believer's baptism, they presented themselves to the New Durham Church in August and were baptized in Oct., 1811. A month later Peck declared that God was calling him to preach; the church immediately gave him liberty to exercise and improve his gift within their bounds. He later served two New York churches (Catskill, 1812–13; Amenia, 1814–16) as pastor, teaching school to supplement his income. Shortly after his ordination in June, 1813, Peck, inspired by foreign mission reports, recognized that "there is an abundant field for missionary labor" in the United States and prayed for God to "open a door for my usefulness and labors in this way." Two years later Luther Rice (*q.v.*) visited Warwick Association (New York), and Peck invited Rice to his home. At Rice's request, Peck successfully visited several associations in behalf of foreign missions, thereby further exciting his mission interest and winning a valuable friend in Rice. By early 1816 Peck, encouraged by Rice, proposed to offer himself to the Triennial Convention's board as a domestic missionary in the West.

Peck went to Philadelphia in May, 1816, to study under William Staughton while awaiting appointment. There he met James E. Welch, also seeking domestic appointment. The board, however, postponed action on home missions, and they remained in Philadelphia until their appointment in May, 1817, "as missionaries to the Missouri Territory." Late in 1817 the Pecks and Welches arrived in St. Louis. Peck and Welch preached, taught school, and organized churches, Sunday schools, and female "mite" societies around St. Louis, in Missouri and Illinois. The first missionary society in the West, United Society for the Spread of the Gospel, was organized in 1818 under Peck's leadership.

In July, 1820, the board discontinued home mission efforts because of inadequate funds, expecting ministerial migration to be adequate for frontier needs, and because of opposition from the West. Peck was instructed to go to northeast Indiana to work with Isaac McCoy (*q.v.*) among Indians, but convinced that St. Louis was God's place for him, Peck refused to leave. He independently conducted missions in the St. Louis area until Mar., 1822, when the Massachusetts Baptist Missionary Society employed him at a salary of $5 a week (when engaged in mission activities). In Apr., 1822, he moved to a farm at Rock Spring, Ill., which thereafter was his official residence. Antimissioners were most vocal during the 1820's, but Peck successfully defended missions, noticing that the root of opposition lay in the ignorance, bigotry, and selfishness of preachers, such as Daniel Parker (*q.v.*), who feared the loss of their influence. Peck's slowly developed strategy included organization of Bible and Sunday school societies, systematic itineration, theological education, and journalism—in the order cited.

In Nov., 1823, Peck began to devote his efforts to organizing Bible societies, reasoning that antimissioners would harm themselves by opposing the distribution of Bibles. Within two years numerous societies were organized; on one tour in 1824 Peck organized eight, and on another, five. In Apr., 1824, he began to organize Sunday school societies, believing that they, in training laymen, would "silently undermine the prejudices against missions." Realizing that societies would die without periodic visitation, Peck conceived a system of regular, circuit itineration by a missionary. In 1826 he proposed this to the Massachusetts society, but no action was taken. In response to Peck's insistence, Jonathan Going was sent in 1831 "to explore the conditions of Baptists in the West," and for three months Peck guided Going through the valley of the Mississippi and its tributaries. Before parting, they agreed upon a new society, which was organized in 1832 as the American Baptist Home Mission Society, with Going as secretary.

Peck had theological education in mind as early as 1817, but after 1825 it became an obsession. Peck realized that Baptists could not rise above their preachers. In the East in 1826 he raised over $500, and early in 1827 he began to build Rock Springs Seminary on his farm. His first attempt to secure a charter failed when an antimission preacher-legislator cast the deciding vote. In 1832 the school was moved to Upper Alton. To prevent its closing, Peck went East in 1835 to raise funds. Benjamin Shurtleff, M.D., of Boston, donated $10,000, and in 1836 the school was renamed Shurtleff College. In 1836 the Illinois Baptist Education Society was formed, with Peck as secretary.

In Apr., 1829, with the appearance of *The Pioneer,* which he printed on his farm, Peck entered the field of religious journalism. As antimissioners were using the press to spread their "antimeans" view, Peck decided to use it to promote mission causes. Unfortunately, the paper was a financial failure. In 1836 *The Pioneer* was moved to Upper Alton, and in 1839 it was merged with the *Baptist Banner* in Kentucky.

After 1830 Peck's efforts were spent, not in field work, but in leadership roles where they counted most. In 1837 he became an emergency solicitor in raising funds to support American Baptist Home Mission Society missionaries whose livelihood was jeopardized by the eastern depression. In 1838 he explored northern Missouri and Iowa for American Baptist Home Mission Society, and from 1837 to 1839 he served as general agent (therefore supervisor of American Baptist Home Mission Society agents in Illinois) of the Illinois Baptist Convention. In 1840 Western Baptists organized into a convention. Many desired an independent publication society, but due to Peck's strong insistence and leadership (general agent, 1841–43) the Western Baptist Publication Society maintained co-operation with the American Baptist Publication Society in Philadelphia. Peck's extensive travels and thorough knowledge of the West convinced him that the West could not sustain its own literature. Therefore, in Feb., 1843, he accepted the secretaryship and general agency of American Baptist Publication Society, hoping to unite all Baptists behind one society; this objective was largely realized before his retirement in Dec., 1845. Peck encouraged efforts to preserve Baptist history; in 1840 he became the first secretary of the Western Baptist Historical Society, and in 1853 he urged the creation of the American Baptist Historical Society, an adjunct of the American Baptist Publication Society.

Peck's contributions to social and political life were numerous and varied. During the mid-1820's he vigorously contested the attempt to alter Illinois' constitution to permit slavery; he was an abolitionist, but he came to fear extremists, such as William Lloyd Garrison. Peck sponsored a temperance society and advocated public schools in Illinois. In the 1830's he encouraged immigration, believing the West's future depended on a higher quality of immigrants; through *Guide to Emigrants* (1831; revised 1836) and *Gazateer of Illinois* (1836), he greatly stimulated Eastern emigration. During his last 20 years he lectured and wrote on Illinois history. A near fatal accident in 1846 caused him to petition Congress to clear the Mississippi River of snags; in response, Congress passed its first river clearance bill.

Peck was a prolific writer. His diary of 53 volumes, containing accounts of activities and digests of correspondence, was mistakenly destroyed after 1860, but Rufus Babcock had fortunately utilized these accounts in preparing Peck's memoirs. Peck wrote biographies of Daniel Boone (1845) and "Father" John Clark (1855) and numerous magazine articles on frontier religious life. In 1840 he revised Dupuy's hymnbook, excising denunciatory doggerel which detracts from worship.

Peck's last 12 years were less active, but his reputation, both among and beyond Baptists as a pioneer statesman grew. In 1837 he accepted the quarter-time pastorate at Rock Springs, but it was only after 1846 that he gave much time to churches; most were located near Rock Springs, but he served briefly in St. Louis and Covington, Ky. In 1852 Harvard conferred on him an honorary degree. Also in 1852 he lost several thousand volumes and irreplaceable files on frontier life in a fire at Rock Spring. After his burial at Rock Spring, Peck's body was removed to Bellefontaine Cemetery, St. Louis.

BIBLIOGRAPHY: R. Babcock, *Memoirs of John Mason Peck* (1864). L. C. Barnes and A. K. DeBlois, *John Mason Peck and One Hundred Years of Home Missions 1817–1917* (1917). C. Hayne, *Vanguard of the Caravans,* A Life Story of John Mason Peck (1931).

HUGE WAMBLE

PEE DEE ACADEMY. Established by the South Carolina Baptist state convention in 1921 as the result of a movement initiated in 1920 by the Waccamaw Baptist Association. The academy was designed to serve the Pee Dee section in accordance with a general plan for promoting academies in different parts of the state. An offer by the Wannamaker community in Horry County of grounds and funds for the buildings was accepted in 1921, after which trustees were elected and authorized to begin operations. John Hampton Mitchell was elected principal, and the school opened with 40 students Oct. 3, 1921, in unused portions of the public school building. A principal's home was erected in 1921, and bricks were purchased for a school building. After two years Mitchell resigned and was succeeded by Wilbur Franklin Hagan. A brick school building was begun in 1924 but was never entirely completed. Because the academy suffered from the development and encroachment of the public school system of the state, the trustees were authorized in 1926 to sell the property and liquidate obligations.

W. C. ALLEN

PEE DEE INSTITUTE. A school operated by Pee Dee and Anson associations, located at Wadesboro, N. C. Established in 1897, the school was opened in September of the following year, under W. J. Ferrell. In 1900 the school received a gift of $1,000 from A. J. Battle of Wadesboro. The Wadesboro church and the silk mill also contributed to the school, but despite their efforts, the school's debts increased. In 1907, the trustees sold the property to the Wadesboro Graded School.

D. L. SMILEY

PENDLETON, JAMES MADISON (b. Spotsylvania County, Va., Nov. 20, 1811; d. Bowling Green, Ky., Mar. 5, 1891). Son of John and Frances J. (Thompson) Pendleton, who were married in 1806. When Pendleton (named for President Madison) was a year old, the family moved to a farm near Pembroke, Ky. On Apr. 14, 1829, he was baptized and in Feb., 1831, was ordained to the ministry. Educated in the Christian seminary at Hopkinsville, he enjoyed a fruitful ministry as pastor at Bethel, Hopkinsville, and Bowling Green, Ky.; Murfreesboro, Tenn.; Hamilton, Ohio; and Upland, Pa. He was the first man in southern Kentucky who abjured avocations, giving himself wholly to the ministry.

Pendleton married Catherine S. Garnett on Mar. 13, 1838, at Glasgow, Ky. They made their first home in Bowling Green, Ky., where their first child, Letitia, was born on Jan. 8, 1839. Their second child, John Malcolm, born May 5, 1840, later joined the Confederate army and was killed during the Civil War. Although he and his father, who advocated abolition, were thus on opposite sides of the question that convulsed the nation, this had made no difference in their relationship. Fannie, born Mar. 11, 1844, in 1867 married Leslie Waggener, who became president of Bethel College in Russellville, Ky., which Pendleton had helped to establish in 1849. A third daughter, Lila, was born on Aug. 25, 1850, while he was pastor at Russellville. He later returned as pastor to Bowling Green, where the birth of their last child, Garnett, occurred on May 24, 1855.

Upon the invitation of Pendleton, James Robinson Graves (*q.v.*) of Nashville, Tenn., came to Bowling Green in 1852 and conducted a successful revival, during which he also won the local pastor's acceptance of certain strict views regarding alien immersion and nonpulpit affiliation. At Graves's insistence he wrote a tract in which he expounded these views. Graves then published it as *An Old Landmark Re-set,* the magnum opus of Landmarkism. Thus began a close association between Graves and Pendleton, who became known as the theologian of the Landmark movement. On Jan. 1, 1857, Pendleton left Bowling Green and removed to Murfreesboro, Tenn., where he became a professor at Union University (of which Joseph H. Eaton was president). Teaching during the week, he filled the pastorate at Murfreesboro and preached every Sunday. In 1858 he became a joint editor (along with Amos Cooper Dayton [*q.v.*]) of the *Tennessee Baptist,* of which Graves had long been editor. When Union forces captured Murfreesboro in 1862, however, Pendleton, whose sympathies lay with the North, went to Hamilton, Ohio, where he served as pastor for a short duration.

Pendleton's last pastorate was the Upland Baptist Church in Pennsylvania. While there he helped to establish Crozer Theological Seminary. Because of his old age he resigned his church in June, 1883, and went to Nashville, Tenn. While there Mrs. Pendleton became blind because of cataracts on both eyes. They spent the winter of 1884–85 in Austin, Tex., where he wrote *The Atonement of Christ.* He was in the excursion to Monterrey to attend the dedication of the Baptist meetinghouse in that city, which was the first house of worship erected by Baptists in the Republic of Mexico. Early in May, 1885, he and his wife left Austin to return to Murfreesboro, Tenn., and on to Bowling Green, Ky., where he wrote the book, *Notes on Sermons.*

The remainder of his days were divided among his four children. He began writing *Reminiscences of a Long Life* on his 79th birthday in 1890, and finished it in two months. Other books written by him are: *Thoughts on Christian Duty* (1851); *Three Reasons Why I Am a Baptist* (1853); *An Old Landmark Re-set* (1856); *Church Manual* (1867); *Christian Doctrines: A Compendium of Theology* (1878); *Christianity Susceptible of Legal Proof* (1876); co-author with George W. Clark of *Brief Notes on the New Testament* (1883); *The Atonement of Christ* (1884–85). T. T. Eaton of Louisville conducted Pendleton's funeral service in the Baptist church at Bowling Green, and the burial was in Fairview Cemetery in that city.

LEO T. CRISMON and HAROLD STEPHENS

PENELOPE ACADEMY. A school operated under Baptist control in South Fork Association, located at Penelope, Catawba County, N. C. It was established in 1887 by C. M. Murchison, moderator of the association, but in 1902 the association founded a school at Maiden, a more central location. This action of the association forced the school at Penelope to close.

D. L. SMILEY

PENFIELD, JOSIAH (b. Fairfield, Conn., June 6, 1785; d. Rye, N. Y., Sept. 12, 1828). Philanthropist. Penfield was a successful jeweler and silversmith in Savannah, Ga., and a member of the First Baptist Church of Savannah during the pastorate of Henry Holcombe. His bequest of $2,500 to the Georgia Baptist convention to "create a fund for the education of pious young men for the gospel ministry" challenged Georgia Baptists to begin the school which has become Mercer University.

SPRIGHT DOWELL

PENFIELD CEMETERY. Located in Penfield, Ga., near the first campus of Mercer University, and named for Josiah Penfield (*q.v.*). In this cemetery are buried the bodies of Jesse Mercer (*q.v.*), Billington McCarty Sanders (*q.v.*) and wife, and other early leaders of Baptists in Georgia.

After Mercer University moved to Macon the cemetery was given little care until 1933, the year of Mercer's centennial, when its importance was recognized. The cemetery was then restored, and it is now under perpetual maintenance provided by endowment as a memorial to the founders of Mercer University. SPRIGHT DOWELL

PENFIELD FEMALE SEMINARY. The first Baptist school in Georgia providing education for women, established in Feb., 1838, in a building on land adjacent to the campus of Mercer Institute. The seminary never attracted more than local patronage, and in 1854 the Mercer trustees transferred it to the local board of trustees, who made it the village academy.

ARTHUR JACKSON

PENFIELD HIGH SCHOOL. Established in 1871 at Penfield, Ga., the year after Mercer University moved from Penfield to Macon. The trustees, who were to pay $2,000 each year to support it, defaulted in 1876. In 1879 the title to the property was transferred to Georgia Association, which in the mid-1890's transferred the chapel building to Baptists of Penfield for a church, retained the cemetery, and gave the remainder of the property to the village for a public school. ARTHUR JACKSON

PENICK, ISAAC NEWTON (b. Buena Vista, Carroll County, Tenn., Oct. 9, 1859; d. Jackson, Tenn., Sept. 8, 1942). Pastor, college professor, editor. Having studied medicine and law for a time at the University of Tennessee, Penick in 1896 received the A.B. degree from Southwestern Baptist University, Jackson, and in 1922 the Th.M. degree from Southwestern Seminary. From 1896 to 1918 he served as pastor of the First Baptist Church, Martin, Tenn., and from 1918 to 1937 he taught at Union University, serving also as dean a part of this time. For 16 years he was editor of the *Baptist Builder.* Penick was a member of the American Research Association and Southern Sociological Commission. He led in the building of Hall-Moody Institute at Martin and served as president of the Board of Trustees more than 20 years. He also served as a trustee of Southern and Southwestern seminaries. Penick held more than 400 revivals and participated in over 50 religious debates.

W. L. STIGLER

PENICK, WILLIAM SIDNOR (b. Halifax County, Va., May 12, 1836; d. Shreveport, La., June 30, 1907). Pastor, missionary, editor. Reared on a Virginia plantation, Penick received his early education under selected tutors. From Richmond College he received the A.B., A.M., and D.D. degrees. He married Bettye Tarpley Martin of Chatham, Va., where he held his first pastorate. In 1861 he entered the Confederate army as captain of the David Logan Guards. Penick served as missionary of the West Virginia State Board from 1868 to 1872, and afterward served seven years as pastor of the First Baptist Church of Alexandria, Va., and four years at the High Street Church, Baltimore, Md. In 1886 he accepted the call to the First Baptist Church of Shreveport, La., where he spent the next thirteen years. In addition, he served one year as the editor-owner of the *Baptist Chronicle,* and for a short time as associate editor of the *Baptist Record.* Following a three-year absence from the state due to ill health, Penick returned to the First Church, Shreveport, for a second pastorate of three years' duration. He then founded the Ardis Memorial Church (now the First Baptist Church) of Bossier City, La., and served for two years as its pastor. He led in establishing Parkview Baptist Church, Shreveport, and founded Genevieve Orphanage.

The following tribute appeared in the Louisiana Baptist *Annual,* 1907: "He [Penick] was also the first president of the Executive Board of our state under our present plan of work and did much to lay broad and deep foundations upon which [Louisiana Baptists] have builded."

W. A. BROWN

PENN, WILLIAM EVANDER (b. Tenn., Aug. 11, 1832; d. Eureka Springs, Ark., Apr. 27, 1895). Baptist evangelist. Converted at 15 and admitted to the bar at 20, Penn was a Confederate major and Federal prisoner of war and was removed to Jefferson, Tex., in 1866. He abandoned law practice in 1875 to become a lay evangelist and was ordained in 1880. The first Baptist lay evangelist and first full-time Baptist evangelist, Penn was also first to have a full-time singer. He held revivals in other states besides Texas and in England and Scotland. Preaching distinctive Baptist doctrines, using reason and persuasion without denunciation, and using simple methods without sensationalism were characteristic of his effective ministry. Penn relied upon the power of the Holy Spirit and prayer, and often the results of his preaching were phenomenal. Known as the "flaming evangel," he collaborated with H. N. Lincoln in composing and publishing a series of hymnals called "Harvest Bells." His best-known hymn is "The Sheltering Rock."

A. B. CULBERTSON

PENNINGTON COLLEGE. A coeducational school at Pennington, Tex., taken over by Neches River Association in 1874. Lack of patronage necessitated its being closed in 1882.

RUPERT N. RICHARDSON

PENSACOLA BAPTIST HOSPITAL. Admitting its first patient Oct. 17, 1951, the hospital opened after 10 years of work toward its establishment by Baptists in northwest Florida. On Oct. 6, 1941, the deacons of the First Baptist Church, Pensacola, appointed a committee to study the feasibility of establishing a Baptist hospital in that area. Earl R. Gaston, chairman of the committee, has served as president of the hospital's board of directors since the date of charter, Feb. 15, 1943.

Through Aug. 31, 1955, the hospital had treated 57,201 patients, including 29,295 inpatients. Total patient income since opening totaled $3,386,154, and denominational support for charity service, $11,934. Patient income during 1954 was $938,423; income from other sources, $27,442; and free service was valued at $31,193, of which $19,959 was charity. The hospital received designated gifts of $4,031. During Aug., 1955, the average census was 137.7, a 49 per cent increase over the first year, which ended in 1952. Over 50 doctors have established practice in Pensacola since construction started Dec. 27, 1949, and have made the city a medical center for northwest Florida and south Alabama. Since 1952 the number of nonresident patients has more than doubled.

The hospital is fully accredited by the Joint Commission on Accreditation of Hospitals and is approved by the American Medical Association for the training of resident physicians. All teaching programs are approved by the proper accrediting agencies. Property value of the 150-bed building and 14-acre site is estimated at $1,493,766, of which $132,941 represents a mortgaged indebtedness.

PAT N. GRONER

PERFECTION. The term which has been used in Christian theology to describe the human achievement of complete moral purity or sinlessness. For the most part, it has been treated as an eschatological hope of the Christian, not as a present attainment. In biblical language it is applied in the strictest sense to God alone, but it is held before the believer as the ultimate goal of his life in Christ—"Be ye therefore perfect, even as your Father which is in heaven is perfect" (Matt. 5:48).

Because the Greek word signifies "coming to maturity or completeness," the term has sometimes been weakened to the idea of a relative attainment of moral perfection, in order that it might be applied more realistically to the Christian life. Under the influence of Greek, Neo-Platonist mysticism, the doctrine of perfection viewed as mystical union with God, appeared in second- and third-century Gnostics and in such theologians as Clement and Origen of Alexandria in the main line of Christian thought. This teaching had a strong ascetic bent, consistent with the Greek dualism of flesh and spirit, and it issued in the monastical tradition which has been so persistent in the history of Christendom. During the Reformation period certain 16th-century sects, especially the Anabaptists and Spiritualists, opposed the Reformers' doctrine of justification of the sinner by their teaching of Christian perfection as a present ethical attainment. This teaching centered in their interpretation of the Sermon on the Mount as a noneschatological ethic, which is intended to serve as a pattern for Christian conduct and an attainable standard of Christian purity. This tradition persists in their direct descendants, the present-day Mennonites, and in their indirect heirs, the Quakers and other perfectionist sects.

From John Wesley's strong emphasis upon the doctrine has come the considerable influence of the doctrine of perfection through Methodism to the many Holiness sects in America today. This is basically a misinterpretation of Wesley, who, even in his admittedly ambiguous statements on the subject, never claimed that he had attained moral perfection but always emphasized the "perfection of love," which is the fulness of God's love being made manifest in the Christian. Too many of his followers have emphasized the non-Wesleyan, Gnostic concept of perfection as a negative withdrawal from the world and abstention from specific "sins of the flesh."

WAYNE E. WARD

PERQUISITES, MINISTERIAL. Early English Baptists favored the support of their ministers; however, they did not want them to receive the high salaries of the parish priests. The ministers themselves did not want to appear to lack faith in God's provision or to be dependent upon men. Consequently, most early Baptist pastors seem to have supported themselves. The Somerset Confession of 1656 approved "a comfortable subsistence" for ministers but argued "that it is commendable in cases of necessity, for them, for examples sake . . . to labor and work with their hands." The most complete defense of ministerial support appears in the Particular Baptist Confession of 1677, known in America as the Philadelphia and Charleston Confession: "It is incumbent on the churches . . . , not only to give them [ministers] all due respect, but also to communicate of all their good things, according to their ability, so as they may have a comfortable supply, without being themselves entangled in secular affairs." In 1689 Benjamin Keach published *The Gospel Minister's Maintenance Vindicated,* in which he argues that a minister should not leave a church which cannot support him, but that a prosperous congregation should provide more than bare necessities.

Early American Baptists held essentially these same views. Separate Baptists who came out of the Great Awakening took a negative view of ministerial maintenance, and this attitude was transferred to the frontier. Yet, as Separates grew more like the Regular Baptists, their attitude shifted back to the early Baptist position, though antisupport groups have remained. During the last century Baptist congregations have usually given their ministers at least a "bare maintenance." Often, especially in rural communities, congregations have given goods, food, clothing, etc., in addition to or instead of money. In some areas this method was the principal means of support.

Gradually, the idea of ministerial support has been enlarged. In addition to stated salaries, ministers now receive fees for marriages, gifts for funerals, honoraria for special occasions, and gifts of appreciation for pastoral service. Some ministers receive not only necessary but luxurious maintenance, especially in homes provided by congregations. V. L. STANFIELD

PERRY MEMORIAL HOSPITAL (Perry, Okla.). This new hospital was accepted from the city of Perry on a 25-year lease at $25 per year and opened Apr. 8, 1951. The building and equipment are the property of the city, and the hospital is operated by the Oklahoma convention. It has 30 beds and is valued at $337,024 plus $12,234 in convention assets.

TOM E. CARTER

PERRY-RAINEY INSTITUTE. Established at Auburn, Ga., in Mulberry Association in 1892. It became the property of the Disciples in 1914.

ARTHUR JACKSON

PERSECUTION, LOUISIANA. Religious persecution in Louisiana has occurred in various forms, the stage being set by the "Black Code" issued by Bienville in 1724. Enacted under Louis XIV with various provisions for Negroes in St. Domingo, its article 3 permitted "the exercise of the Roman Catholic creed only." Applied to Louisiana, it made illegal the practice of non-Catholic religion. In 1770 at Natchitoches, the Spanish de Mezieres demanded of two English Protestants that they either leave the province or join the Catholic Church. Religious discrimination may be illustrated by the case of a sailor from Philadelphia who, while in prison in New Orleans, was left to die when the attending surgeon learned that he was not a Catholic. An attempt by the Spanish Capuchin priest, Antonio de Sedella, to introduce the Inquisition in New Orleans was defeated by the governor, Don Estevin Miro (1785–91), who deported the priest and made protest to Madrid.

Persecution came to Bailey E. Chaney (*q.v.*), probably the first Baptist preacher to enter what is now Louisiana, who went there from Mississippi about 1798 or 1799. In 1798 Gayoso de Lemas, governor of Louisiana, required that children of non-Catholic immigrants become Catholic and prohibited the entrance into the province of non-Catholic preachers. Chaney was arrested near Baton Rouge and then released on promise that he would preach no more. Subsequent to the Louisiana Purchase (1803), no law prohibiting any religion has obtained, although attempts contrary to law have been made to persecute. A Catholic attempt to imprison Ezra Courtney when, sometime after 1802, he preached for Baptists about nine miles from Baton Rouge was frustrated by the alcalde. Up to the present, there have been numerous local incidents of discrimination, opposition, and annoyance in various forms and degrees. Public and private services have been disturbed, threats have been made, some actual violence has occurred, and non-Catholics have been refused burial in Catholic cemeteries. FRANK STAGG

PERSECUTION, OKLAHOMA. Religious persecution in Oklahoma centered in the Creek Nation of Indian Territory before 1860. It stemmed first from factional differences between the Upper and Lower Creeks. These factions existed at least 100 years before their removal to the West, which began in 1826. Baptist mission work started among the Western Creeks in 1829, but missionaries were not affected until the arrival of the Upper Creeks in 1835. Leaders who held to primitive tribal customs made capital of the strife engendered by the arrival of the Upper Creeks and charged the missionaries with meddling in Indian removal affairs. This led Major Armstrong, superintendent of Indian affairs in Indian Territory, to request all missionaries to withdraw from the Creek Nation. In a short time this tension abated, but by 1843 the same leaders fomented new strife, gained control of the Creek Council, and passed a law forbidding white men to preach in the Nation, and prescribing severe punishment for any Indian or Negro caught preaching or praying. Punishment was usually fixed at "fifty lashes on the bare back." Missionary Henry Frieland Buckner (*q.v.*) came to the Creeks in 1847, and as he slowly and patiently won the confidence of the Indians, his influence was effective in causing persecution gradually to diminish.

BIBLIOGRAPHY: J. B. Thoburn and M. H. Wright, *Oklahoma, A History of the State and Its People* (1929). J. B. Thoburn, *A Standard History of Oklahoma* (1916). J. M. Gaskin, *Trail Blazers of Sooner Baptists* (1953). E. C. Routh, *The Story of Oklahoma Baptists* (1932). GLENWOOD BUZBEE

PERSECUTION, VIRGINIA. "There is a Virginia Baptist temper," said Robert Healy Pitt (*q.v.*), and the beliefs, habits, and outlook of a people can best be understood in light of that people's history and tradition. The Baptists of Virginia are sensitive to the subject of religious freedom.

From the beginning of life in the colonies until 1786, the struggle for religious liberty was bitter and bloody. Foremost among the groups who challenged and defied both civil and religious authorities were the Baptists. Often illiterate, impoverished, and without prestige, the General, Regular, and Separate Baptists, though divided internally, united in one grand affirmation of faith: that in this new land absolute religious freedom must be granted to every church, denomination, and sect, and that every person must be given the unlimited right to worship and serve God according to the dictates of his own conscience. Concerning the exercise of "soul liberty" they held there was to be accounting to no other power than God himself. The government did not exist to prevent the subject from the enjoyment of this privilege but to protect him in it.

Two statements, written deep in American tradition, now guarantee freedom in the manner conceived by these forefathers. The first, Jefferson's Act for Establishing Religious Freedom in Virginia, 1786, reads,

> Be it enacted by the General Assembly, That no man shall be compelled to frequent or support any religious worship, place of ministry whatsoever; nor shall he be enforced, restrained or molested or burthened in his body or goods; nor shall otherwise suffer on account of his religious opinions or belief; but that all men shall be free to profess and by argument maintain their opinions in matters of religion, and that the same shall in no wise diminish, enlarge or affect their civil capacities.

Jefferson's Act provided the basis for the second important statement, the First Amendment to the Constitution of the United States. Adopted in 1789, it states that "Congress shall make no law respecting an establishment of religion or prohibiting the free exercise of same; or abridging the freedom of speech, or of the press; or the right of the people peaceably to assemble and to petition the Government for a redress of grievances." James Madison, pondering Jefferson's Act for Establishing Religious Freedom, declared it to be ". . . the greatest contribution of America to the sum of Western Civilization."

Garnett Ryland's *The Baptists of Virginia* reveals the story of Baptist persecution in early Virginia, as well as the unique role Baptists played in the accomplishment of religious freedom. Drawing heavily upon the *History of the Rise and Progress of the Baptists in Virginia* by Robert Baylor Semple (*q.v.*), Ryland sketches the activities of persons who will always be associated with the struggle for religious liberty. In 1768 John Waller (*q.v.*), James Chiles, James Read, and William Marsh defied authorities in Spotsylvania County by preaching the gospel according to the call of God. In Orange, 1768, these men were joined by Allen Wyley, John Corbley, Elijah Craig (*q.v.*), and Thomas Chambers, who preached through prison bars. James Ireland (*q.v.*), former Scotch Presbyterian, fearless leader in the Baptist struggle, pastor for more than 30 years of the Old Buck Marsh Church, Berryville, Va., was imprisoned in Culpeper from Nov., 1769, to Apr., 1770, suffering indecencies, indignities, and actual torture. In Chesterfield in 1770, William Webber (*q.v.*) and Joseph Anthony were arrested for preaching without a government license and were treated as criminals and imprisoned. William Burrus in Middlesex, 1769; John Pickett, Fauquier, 1770; John Young, John Burrus, and Lewis Craig, Caroline, 1771; Jeremiah Moore, Fairfax, 1773; Robert Ware and Ivison Lewis, Essex, 1774, and many others helped make religious freedom possible through their faith and suffering.

In the earliest days of the colonies, mandatory attendance at divine worship in the Established Church was decreed. According to Semple, the first act of 1623 provided that in every plantation or settlement there should be a house or room set apart for worship, but it soon appeared that this worship was to be according only to canons of the Church of England. A person absent from divine worship on Sunday without reasonable excuse forfeited a pound of tobacco; if absent a month, he forfeited fifty pounds. An enactment was passed in 1643 that "all ministers should be conformable to the orders and constitutions of the church of England and that no others be permitted to teach or preach, publicly or privately."

Compulsory baptism of children was a serious grievance to the nonconformists, according to Foote's *Sketches of Virginia* and Hening's *Statutes at Large,* Vol. II. In 1661–62 since many "schismatical persons, out of the new-fangled conceits of their own heretical inventions," refused to have their children baptized, it was enacted that "all persons that, in contempt of the divine sacrament of baptism, shall refuse, when they may carry their children to a lawful minister in that county to have them baptized, shall be amerced two thousand pounds of tobacco, half to the informer and half to the public."

Following the Act of Toleration, passed by the British Parliament in 1689 but not effective in the colonies until approximately 10 years later, several of the more flagrant restrictions binding the dissenters were lifted. The Act of Toleration granted limited religious freedom to the colonists by recognizing their right to worship and serve God outside the Established Church. This relaxation on the part of the government was greeted with joy by most nonconformist groups, including the Quakers, but all branches of Baptists continued to press for *absolute* freedom in religious expression. The Act of Toleration granted permission to nonconformist ministers to preach, provided they applied for and received a government license, which determined the place or places where the minister might preach and also specified the duration of the privilege. Men such as John Waller, John Corbley, Elijah Craig, and James Ireland were imprisoned for not conforming to the government's restrictions, but they continued to preach behind prison bars.

From the Act of Toleration in 1689 to Jefferson's Act of Religious Freedom in 1786, approximately 100 years later, Baptist dissenters risked life, limb, and reputation in their defiance of a law which required a minister's having a government license in order to exercise his religious convictions. During this period, although "government license" was the main point of controversy, three additional grievances were intolerable to persons seeking absolute freedom in religious expression. The first concerned *matrimony.* The clergy of the Established Church retained the exclusive right to perform legal marriage ceremonies until 1784, the date from which ministers of all denominations have had this privilege.

In the second grievance concerning *general assessment,* Patrick Henry was in the forefront in the effort to grant unlimited permission to all ministers to preach the gospel. Henry lined up with the clergy of the Established Church and the ministers of nonconformist groups such as the Presbyterians. The plan of general assessment provided for the incorporation of all the leading denominations, including Baptists, for their support by taxation. According to James, "It was a most subtle and plausible scheme, as it was thoroughly impartial and allowed every tax payer the privilege of designating the denomination which should receive his tax. And, it had the advantage of being fathered by Patrick Henry." On this issue Baptists virtually stood alone among all religious groups in open protests. Political opposition to the bill, which eventually was defeated, was led by James Madison, whose paper, "A Memorial and Remonstrance," still stands as a classic statement of the relation of the state to religion.

Another grievance of this period concerned the *glebes,* the homes and farms for the residences and support of ministers of the Established Church. They had been acquired in each parish by general taxation and had been given to the Episcopal Church by action of the legislature in 1784. Once again the persistent agitation of Baptists finally led to the conversion of glebes into public property. Both the Methodist Conference and the Hanover Presbytery refused an invitation from the Baptists to join in a memorial of protest in 1790, but the glebes issue was finally settled by an act of the legislature in 1794. At that point in Virginia's history, Jefferson's Act for Establishing Religious Freedom became law in all matters pertaining to the exercise of religious faith.

Bibliography: W. W. Henry, *Life, Correspondence and Speeches of Patrick Henry* (1891). G. Hunt, ed., *The Writings of James Madison* (1900). C. F. James, *The Struggle for Religious Liberty in Virginia* (1900). J. P. Kennedy and H. R. McIlwaine, ed., *Journals of House of Burgesses of Virginia, 1619–1775.* L. P. Little, *Imprisoned Preachers and Religious Liberty in Virginia* (1938). G. Ryland, *The Baptists of Virginia, 1699–1926* (1955). R. B. Semple, *A History of the Rise and Progress of the Baptists in Virginia* (1810).

W. WESLEY SHRADER

PERSEVERANCE. The perseverance of the Christian is based primarily on the fact that God takes the initiative in perfecting the believer's salvation: he who has begun a good work will perform it unto the end (Phil. 1:6; *cf.* I John 3:6–9; 4:4); God keeps his own (John 10:28–29; I Peter 1:5); nothing can separate the believer from the love of God (Rom. 8:38–39); Christ continues to intercede for the Christian (Luke 22:31–32; John 17:11–15; Rom. 8:34; Heb. 7:25); the Holy Spirit seals the believer unto the day of redemption (II Cor. 1:22; 5:5; Eph. 1:13–14; 4:30). Thus the biblical stress is more on the perseverance of the Saviour than on the perseverance of the saints. The mere initiation of a process without its consummation, therefore, should not be called salvation (Mark 4:16–17; II Peter 2:20; I John 2:19); there is no salvation apart from endurance (Mark 13:13; I Cor. 15:2; Rev. 2:7). Yet it is possible for believers to retard God's work (John 15:4–6; I Cor. 3:1–3, 15; Heb. 5:12 to 6:8), because of which there are repeated warnings to Christians (I Cor. 8:10–11; Heb. 4:1). Instead of interpreting passages such as Hebrews 6:4–6 and 10:26–27 as teaching falling from grace, it is better to understand them as suggesting a hypothetical possibility only or as referring to those never genuinely converted.

BIBLIOGRAPHY: W. T. Conner, *The Gospel of Redemption* (1945). W. BOYD HUNT

PERSONALISM. A type of philosophy which teaches that the nature of ultimate reality, the God of the universe, is found in the conscious unity, identity, and free activity of personality. It is a recent development in philosophy but is closely associated with ancient systems of thought. Greek idealists taught that reality is basically spiritual (non-material). Christianity has always emphasized the idea of a personal God and the personal immortality of man. These two sources have been combined in the development of personalism. Borden Parker Bowne (1847–1910) gave personalism its fullest initial statement.

BIBLIOGRAPHY: A. C. Knudson, *The Philosophy of Personalism* (1927). S. A. NEWMAN

PERU, MISSION IN. The first Southern Baptist missionaries to Peru, Marion Davis Oates and his wife, went to Lima Sept. 13, 1950. Aided by Antonio Gamarra of Argentina, they began services in the Miraflores section of Lima in Mar., 1951. The Miraflores Baptist Church, organized Aug. 19 of that year, started a primary school the next spring. The church entered a new church building, provided through mission funds, on June 20, 1954, and Luis Aguero of Cuba became pastor the following February.

Missionaries Robert Lawson and Mary Lillian (Culpepper) Harris, arriving Oct. 31, 1951, directed the Lince mission of the Miraflores Church, with a church organized there May 3, 1953. Alejandro Tuesta, a Peruvian, became pastor.

Services began in the center of Lima Apr. 10, 1952, and Gamarra became pastor of the church organized as a result on Nov. 16 of that year.

Lima pastors direct mission Sunday schools and a weekly radio program. In 1955 small churches were organized in Arequipa and Trujillo. ROBERT HARRIS

PETROBRUSIANS. A sect named after its founder, Peter of Bruys, who preached in Southern France from 1106 to 1126, when he was burned as a heretic. His adherents persisted until they disappeared among the Henricians in the middle of the century. They rejected the Eucharist, sacramentalism, prayers for the dead, and infant baptism; condemned the veneration of the crucifix and other such emphases on the cross; and repudiated ceremonies and church buildings. The Petrobrusians required a literal interpretation and application of the Gospels, but ascribed only a derivative authority to the Epistles. They practiced believer's baptism and sought a regenerate church membership. LYNN E. MAY, JR.

PETTUS, RICHARD EMMETT (b. Limestone County, Ala., Nov. 18, 1854; d. Huntsville, Ala., Apr. 5, 1929). Newspaper man, Baptist layman, United States senator. Pettus received the B.S. and M.A. degrees from the University of Alabama, where he also taught for a short time (1876–77). As a layman, he served as president of the Alabama Baptist convention (1910–11), moderator of the Madison-Liberty Association, and deacon and Sunday school superintendent in the First Baptist Church, Huntsville. One of his chief interests was the collection of documents of interest to Alabama Baptists; this collection he contributed to the historical association. Owner and publisher of the *Huntsville Daily Independent,* he served as United States senator from Alabama.

JOHN BOB RIDDLE

PHELPS, GENERAL LEE (b. Osage County, Mo., Jan. 1, 1864; d. Wetumka, Okla., Oct. 19, 1938). Missionary seven years for Dixon Baptist Association, Mo., before he went as missionary to Creek Indians at Okmulgee, Okla., Mar. 7, 1902. On Jan. 1, 1909, he was appointed by the American Baptist Home Mission Society to work with Cheyennes and Arapahoes, and in 1912 went to work with Sac and Fox. He became general missionary to the Indians in 1917, under the Baptist General Convention of Oklahoma, and until his death he continued to serve in this work after it was taken over by the Southern Baptist Home Mission Board in 1934.

BIBLIOGRAPHY: G. L. Phelps, *Tepee Trails* (1937).

DAVID C. HALL

PHILADELPHIA BIBLE INSTITUTE, RIVOLI. See ITALY, MISSION IN.

PHILIPPINE BAPTIST CONVENTION, THE. Organized in 1935 as the administrative body of churches related to the American Baptist foreign mission societies. The women's committee of the convention was organized in 1937. The convention co-operates with the Philippine Federation of Evangelical Churches and has rural evangelism as a major emphasis in Antique Province, on the adjoining island of Negros, and at Romblon on Mindoro Island.

Baptist work on Panay Island, where the major work is carried on, was opened in 1900 by Eric Lund (b. 1852; d. 1933), Swedish missionary under appointment in Spain by the American Baptist Missionary Union. An early convert, Braulio Manikan, a Filipino student from Capiz, Panay, taught Lund the Visayan language. The mission in Spain was abandoned at the time of the Spanish-American War, and both Lund and Manikan were designated to

Panay. Their major work was translation of the Bible into Visayan, completed in 1912. The Panay population is predominantly Roman Catholic with Spanish influence, giving strong opposition to "evangelicals," or Protestants.

Signatures of some 13,000 peasants on Panay petitioning for teachers impelled the American Baptist Union in 1905 to open Jaro Industrial School at Jaro, a suburb of Iloilo City. The school became a coeducational college in 1922 and a university in 1953, enrolling more than 2,500 students in its 10 component colleges. A college of agriculture and a five-year course in the college of nursing are the most recent additions. The college of theology trains men and women with equal status. A student center at Jaro ministers to students in large government schools near by. The U. S. Government provided public schools during its occupation, making a mission educational program unnecessary. Home School, now Filamer Christian Institute, opened at Capiz (Roxas City), meets local needs. Two hospitals, which developed the first nurses' training on the islands, are located at Roxas City and Iloilo.

During World War II most of the missionaries were interned. Eleven missionaries and a young son of one of them who had fled from their stations to the hills were beheaded by the Japanese military Dec. 21, 1943. Present staff is largely composed of missionaries in their first or second term or missionaries transferred from the China fields and restricted frontier areas of Assam. Extensive property damage in the war entailed a heavy burden in reconstruction.

DATA

	1934	*1954*
Baptisms	748	2,380
Churches	147	242
Church members	10,412	15,497
Missionaries	32	35
Filipino workers	259	310
Students	2,739	3,534
Schools	93	11
Patients	5,259	15,337
Hospital & dispensaries	3	4
Field contributions	$ 9,581	$73,323

ADA STEARNS

PHILIPPINE BAPTIST THEOLOGICAL SEMINARY, BAGUIO. See PHILIPPINES, MISSION IN.

PHILIPPINE HOSPITAL, MATI. See PHILIPPINES, MISSION IN.

PHILIPPINES, MISSION IN. Organized after Dec., 1948, when China missionaries moved to Baguio, Philippines, to continue language study, because of Communist advance in China. Evangelism beginning early in 1949 produced the Baguio Chinese Baptist Church, organized in May, 1950. A mission was established formally Aug. 30, 1950, with 23 missionaries. Work with the Chinese minority was extended to Dagupan and Manila in 1950, to San Fernando and Davao City in 1951, and to Tarlac in 1953.

Formal work among Filipinos began at Dagupan in 1951, and shortly afterward at Davao City. During 1952 an independent church at Cotabato affiliated with the mission. In succeeding years several churches on Mindanao (composed of migrants from an area where other Baptist missions have work) affiliated with Southern Baptists. Work with Filipinos was undertaken also at Baguio and Mati in 1953 and at Manila in 1954. Filipino churches on Mindanao organized associations in the Davao and Cotabato provinces in Oct., 1954.

The Philippine Baptist Theological Seminary (opened at Baguio in July, 1952) has both Chinese and English language divisions. A Bible school branch of the seminary opened at Davao City, Mindanao, in 1955. Beginning in 1953 missionaries were definitely assigned to an expanding work of literature publication and promotion. The Mati Baptist Hospital, on the east coast of Mindanao, opened in Mar., 1954.

By May, 1955, there were four Chinese churches and 13 Filipino churches connected with the Philippine mission, reporting 1,247 members. The first new missionaries appointed specifically for Filipino work arrived Mar., 1953. Many of the former China staff now work primarily with Filipinos. At the end of 1955, missionaries had increased to 40, assigned to three cities on Luzon and four on Mindanao.

JAMES WINSTON CRAWLEY

PHILLIPS, JOHN WALTER (b. Milton, Kent County, England, Nov. 1, 1855; d. Mobile, Ala., Sept. 2, 1938). Author, lecturer, philanthropist, denominational leader, and pastor. The son of Luke and Maria (Stephens) Phillips, he married Jane Graffety, Oswego, N. Y. Their children were Ethel, Bertha, Howard, Norma, Walter, and Sidney. Phillips received a Th.M. degree from Colgate Theological Seminary and a Ph.D. degree from London University. He came to America when 15 years of age, surrendered for the ministry at 18, and accepted his first church, Evans Mills, N. Y., 1878. After successive pastorates on four other New York fields, he served the First Church, Binghamton, N. Y., 1896–1911. He left there for 20 years of pastoral service at First Church, Mobile, Ala., 1911–31. His book of sermons, *Kept by the Power of God,* was edited and published after his death by his son, Sidney Phillips. Other sermons were published in pamphlet form, and he wrote for denominational periodicals. He served as president of the Alabama Baptist State Convention, 1928. He preached the annual sermon at the Southern Baptist Convention, Birmingham, Ala., May 13, 1931. Small churches, underprivileged groups, and hospitals were beneficiaries of his labors; the Broome County Tuberculosis Hospital, near Binghamton, N. Y., is a monument to such service.

BIBLIOGRAPHY: W. P. Wilks, *Biographical Dictionary of Alabama Baptists 1920–1947* (1947).

COLLIS CUNNINGHAM

PHILOSOPHY. Literally, "love of wisdom." As a discipline, philosophy is the attempt to formulate a rational explanation of the whole of life and existence. Since the universe consists basically of persons and material things, the fundamental task of the philosopher is to understand the nature of persons and things and the relationships between them. His attempt to understand their being is *ontology,* and his attempt to understand the knowledge of being or being of knowledge is *epistemology.* Other branches of philosophy are *logic, aesthetics, ethics,* and *axiology.* Further refinement of the philosophic quest will include such disciplines as the philosophies of history, science, nature, education, politics, religion, and many others.

See also THEOLOGY.

BIBLIOGRAPHY: E. S. Brightman, *An Introduction to Philosophy* (1925). D. J. Bronstein, Y. H. Krikorian, and P. P. Wiener, *Basic Problems of Philosophy* (1947). G. H. Clark, *A Christian View of Men and Things* (1952). TED R. CLARK

PIEDMONT INSTITUTE. Opened at Waycross, Ga., in 1904, sponsored by Piedmont, Consolation, New Sunbury, and Smyner associations. A member of the Mercer system, it existed until 1928. ARTHUR JACKSON

PILCHER, JOHN MASON (b. Richmond, Va., July 16, 1841; d. Petersburg, Va., Oct. 18, 1924). Pastor, church organizer. Son of John Alsop and Elizabeth Ann (Parsons) Pilcher, he attended the English and Classical School, Richmond, Va., and Richmond College, where his college career was interrupted by the Civil War. Following the war, Pilcher entered a coal business with his brother-in-law, Benjamin Cottrell, and for a long time resisted the call to preach, but was ordained by the Sidney Baptist Church (now Grove Avenue), Richmond, in 1870. Pilcher later began a nine-year pastorate at Covington and Healing Springs, Va., where he organized six churches and built seven meeting houses. In 1880 the Sunday School and Bible Board of the Baptist General Association of Virginia moved its office from Staunton to Petersburg and elected Pilcher secretary. He held this position until the board merged with the State Mission Board in 1908.

President of the Baptist General Association of Virginia and the Virginia Baptist Historical Society, Pilcher was at one time vice-president of the Southern Baptist Convention, moderator of the Portsmouth and Petersburg Baptist Association, and trustee of the University of Richmond. He married Mary Lucy DuVal, daughter of Edwin J. and Rhoda T. DuVal, by whom he had 12 children. CARRINGTON PAULETTE

PILGRIM, THOMAS J. (b. Middlesex County, Conn., Dec. 19, 1805; d. Gonzales, Tex., Oct. 29, 1877). Sunday school organizer. Converted early, Pilgrim joined a Baptist church, which requested he be licensed to preach. He attended Madison University, New York, and at 23 became Stephen F. Austin's official Spanish interpreter soon after joining his colony near San Felipe, Tex. Later as minister-schoolteacher, Pilgrim declared his conviction for "the necessity of moral . . . religious . . . intellectual culture and resolved . . . to found a Sunday school." The next Sunday (1829) he organized the first Sunday school in Texas in a black-jack, post-oak grove near the center of Felipe de Austin in a rude, dirt-floored, unhewn-log cabin about 18′ x 22′, with a superintendent, half a dozen teachers, and 32 children. This organization violated a Catholic order that no colonists should hold Protestant services. Pilgrim moved to Gonzales in 1840, engaged in banking, farming, and teaching, and served more than 30 years as superintendent of the Gonzales Union Sunday School, which later formed Baptist and Presbyterian Sunday schools. ANDREW ALLEN

PINE CREST CHILDREN'S HOME. For years Kentucky Baptists had considered establishing a third children's home to serve eastern Kentucky. At the meeting of the general association in Murray in 1950, it was voted to establish such a home to be operated as an arm of Spring Meadows. Careful study of various suggested locations was made. In July, 1953, a beautiful tract of approximately 125 acres, located two miles north of Morehead on Kentucky state highway 32, was purchased as the site of the new home. In Sept., 1954, construction was started on an administration building with central kitchen and dining room, 15-bed infirmary, and two cottage units, each housing 24 children and two house mothers. The buildings were erected at a cost of slightly more than $300,000. The city of Morehead extended a six-inch water main to the property. The home, given the appropriate name Pine Crest, opened in the fall of 1956 with a capacity of 50 children. The Kentucky Baptist Board of Child Care, which is the governing body for all Baptist homes in Kentucky, serves as the trustees of the home. Sam Ed Bradley, superintendent of Spring Meadows, serves also as the superintendent of Pine Crest. Mrs. Virginia R. Fields is the director. SAM ED BRADLEY

PINEYWOODS BAPTIST ENCAMPMENT. A Texas encampment organized in 1945 near Woodlake, Tex., in District 2. One of the leaders in its organization, V. G. Garrett, was manager and treasurer in 1956. J. E. ROTH

PIONEER. A semimonthly newspaper begun by John Mason Peck (*q.v.*), Apr. 25, 1829, at Rock Spring, Ill. Peck moved his paper to Upper Alton, Ill., in 1836, where he continued to publish it under the title *Western Pioneer and Baptist Standard* until 1839, when it was merged with the *Baptist Banner* of Louisville, Ky. LYNN E. MAY, JR.

PIONEER LEADERS, SOUTHERN BAPTIST. Although early Southern Baptist leaders were not solely the product of their environment, the times in which they lived and the circumstances under which they labored afforded a background which brought forth sterling qualities of character. These leaders were in a real sense pioneers. Not only did they face hardships and persecutions, but they confronted many handicaps due to the lack of materials, equipment, educational and religious institutions, and denominational organization and unity except for a few district associations. Their meager church buildings were simple, designed mainly for preaching and informal worship. For the most part, the ministers came from a poor class of people who had no developed sense of stewardship. Two main factors hindered unity of thinking and acting: first, the difficulty of communication; and second, the varying emphases in doctrine, ecclesiology, and church polity. The lack of an over-all denominational program and perspective challenged Baptist leaders to venture forth in soliciting and co-ordinating the interests and efforts of their people. Their concern for foreign missions, largely created by Luther Rice, brought the Triennial Convention into being in 1814.

A large proportion of the small Baptist constituency was comparatively illiterate. Though often untutored, in most instances the ministers were men of keen intellect, deep insight, and wide perception. However, they were usually despised and opposed by the biblical scholars of the world. Men of vision, early Baptist leaders recognized the imperative of establishing educational institutions, especially for the training of ministers and missionaries. At the second meeting of the Triennial Convention in 1817, president Richard Furman delivered an address of far-reaching significance on education. So potent was its effect that the convention went on record as favoring a classical and theological seminary as soon as funds could be received for the purpose. In 1822 Columbian College was established in Washington, D. C., under the leadership of Luther Rice. Shortly afterward, Furman University, Mercer University, Georgetown College, Richmond College, and Wake Forest College were established. A great segment of Baptist people in the South and West, however, were prejudiced against an educated ministry and against missionary work of any kind.

Passionately evangelistic, Baptist leaders preached a simple gospel message, calling people to repentance and faith and warning them of impending judgment. Personal witness based upon their own Christian experience and the use of the Scriptures was notable in their work. The prosecuting attorney at Spotsylvania Courthouse in Virginia said to the court concerning John Waller (*q.v.*), Lewis Craig (*q.v.*), James Chiles, James Reid, and William Marsh: "These men are great disturbers of the peace, they cannot meet a man upon the road, but they must ram a text of Scripture down his throat."

Among the outstanding qualities of the Baptist pioneers was their undaunted courage. Rugged individualists, they faced persecution, prejudice, and ridicule, the background of which was a union of church and state. Feared because of their radical democratic views in religion and in the state, they were often scorned and sometimes imprisoned. From 1766 to 1778, 83 Baptist preachers in Virginia suffered violent persecution in some form; 43 were placed in jail. Prison bars, however, did not stop them. Elijah Craig (*q.v.*), for instance, "was in gaol at Orange for a considerable time in 1768, preaching through the bars to the people, who resorted to the prison till he was confined to the inner dungeon where there was no opening save in a hole in the door through which he received his bread and water."

Early Baptist leaders believed in religious freedom. Any usurpation of religious authority by the state or any favoritism extended to any one denomination brought forth their serious protest. Their spirit and wholehearted support given to the cause of independence made a profound impression upon political leaders, particularly Patrick Henry, Thomas Jefferson, George Washington, and James Madison. By 1791 they had written their dream into the First Amendment to the Constitution of the United States. Their love of freedom contributed much to the rapid Baptist growth following the Revolutionary War.

Along with their courage, Baptist leaders demonstrated a vital, personal faith which not only gave impact to their views but caused them to launch forth in a vigorous program of education, missions, and evangelism. Their emphasis upon the simplicity of faith gave religion a personal flavor.

Another remarkable trait was their moral judgment, expressed by a rigid sense of discipline. The low moral conditions of people demanded rather stern measures of discipline. The prevalence of drinking, gambling, brawling, profanity, and immorality caused many new converts to fall back into old habits. Church meetings for discipline and business were usually held on Saturday before the preaching Sunday. Drastic moral sanctions were employed against offenders.

BIBLIOGRAPHY: T. Armitage, *History of the Baptists* (1887). W. W. Barnes, *The Southern Baptist Convention, 1845–1953* (1954). H. T. Cook, *Education in South Carolina under Baptist Control* (1912); *The Life of James Clement Furman* (1926). N. W. Cox, *Dreams, Dungeons, Diadems* (1954). R. N. Daniel, *Furman University* (1951). W. J. McGlothlin, *Baptist Beginnings in Education* (1926); *The Course of Christian History* (1919). A. H. Newman, *A Manual of Church History* (1903). G. Ryland, *The Baptists of Virginia* (1955). R. B. Semple, *History of the Rise and Progress of the Baptists in Virginia* (1810). H. Woodson, *Giant in the Land* (1950).

GARIS T. LONG

PIONEER MISSION PROGRAM, ILLINOIS. A program based upon establishment of new church organizations and planned to extend the area of Illinois Baptist work into unchurched areas.

Prior to 1945 the churches of the Illinois Baptist State Association were located primarily in the southern third of the state. Some interest in the northern area was expressed by a gift (1937) to complete a Decatur church building and by an appropriation in the 1941 state association budget of $2,000 for work in the northern territory. An editorial statement in the official paper said: "We must change our methods by shifting the emphasis further north." The state association board of directors "instructed the Missions Committee to . . . survey . . . the northern part of the state and bring . . . recommendations. . . ." Budget considerations were made by the state association. Fred Propst became state director of missions in the north and central sections for purposes of evangelizing and starting new churches. Associations developed. Great Lakes Association (1943) was organized with six churches. Other associations organized in northern Illinois were Illinois Valley, 1950; Sangamon Valley, 1950; East Central, 1955; Lake Michigan, Ind., 1955; Capitol City, 1956; Minnesota-Wisconsin, 1956. In 1945, as a result of a survey which revealed 391 towns in Illinois above 500 population with no Baptist church, the Southern Baptist Home Mission Board changed "the status of Illinois" and classified it "along with New Mexico, Arizona and California as a general mission field." The state association meeting in 1946 was challenged to start 40 new churches the next five years and evangelize the entire state. Regional and pioneer missionaries were employed after 1948. In 1951 the Southern Baptist Convention gave its Home Mission Board permission to do work anywhere invited. This deepened the interests of the Home Mission Board in Illinois.

New churches and associations reflected the accomplishments of the Pioneer Mission Program. The Missions Department secretary reported 26 new churches for 1954; 33 for 1955; 43 for 1956. E. HARMON MOORE

PIONEER MISSIONS. This term has meant varied things to Southern Baptists in the past and had a twofold meaning for the Home Mission Board and the state mission boards during the 1945–55 period of mission work.

The first is that of missions in new areas east of the Western mission field. To date it consists of mission work in the states of Minnesota, Iowa, Wisconsin, Michigan, Illinois, Indiana, Ohio, and West Virginia, and includes some work in Pennsylvania and New York through the Ohio state convention, with which churches from these states are affiliated. All this work is done through the state conventions of Missouri, Arkansas, Illinois, Kentucky, Virginia, and Ohio.

The other meaning of pioneer missions is applied to certain neglected but needy fields for mission work in older state conventions. The areas are not concerned enough to have a missionary but need one more than other fields. Here the Home Mission Board and state boards jointly employ a missionary for the work, and he is known as a pioneer missionary. This pioneer work has developed since 1947 when the Home Mission Board began pioneer work with the Missouri state convention in southwestern Missouri. Since that time requests have come from other states. The work of the pioneer missionary is a means to the better end, an associational missionary. He has done his best job when he has worked himself out of a job.

The new or expansion work of pioneer missions began in Illinois in 1949 when the Home Mission Board agreed to aid that state in extending its work in the area north of Springfield. Illinois extended her arms with the aid of the Home Mission Board to Wisconsin, Indiana, and Minnesota. Kentucky for many years had been sponsoring work in Indiana through the Long Run Association. Virginia and Kentucky have both sponsored work in West Virginia. Maryland has some work in Delaware and Pennsylvania. Arkansas has promoted work in Michigan, since the churches there are affiliated with the Arkansas Baptist Convention. In 1955 there were in these pioneer fields a total of 12 missionaries and 30 mission pastors supported by the Home Mission Board and state mission boards. S. F. DOWIS

PITT, ROBERT HEALY (b. Middlesex County, Va., June 26, 1853; d. Feb. 15, 1937). Editor, educator, pastor. Son of Douglas Pitt, a physician, Pitt was baptized into the fellowship of Harmony Grove Baptist Church in Sept., 1869. At the age of 20, Sept., 1873, Pitt entered Richmond College and was licensed to preach Jan. 3, 1875. His first pastorate was at Walnut Grove, where he was ordained in 1877, and other pastorates were at Venable Street, Richmond, Va. (twice); Martinsburg, W. Va.; Barton Heights, Richmond; and Ashland, Va. During his pastorate at Venable Street, Pitt began contributing articles for the *Religious Herald,* and Alfred Elijah Dickinson (*q.v.*), then editor, asked him to become his associate in 1888. Later, after Pitt acquired complete ownership and control of the paper, his clear, concise, and vigorous editorials attracted attention throughout Virginia and in many parts of the South and North and were frequently reproduced in religious journals of other denominations and in secular papers.

A vigorous proponent of temperance, missions, education, the consolidation of some schools, and the expansion of others, Pitt, while president of the Education Commission, made an effort to co-ordinate the schools under Baptist control, assist in paying debts, and plan for a central college "for the highest education of women."

Pitt was the first to urge a world organization, a Pan-Baptist Union, in Apr., 1895, and 10 years later the first Baptist World Alliance was held in London. When the Virginia General Assembly was about to authorize employment of a chaplain for the state penitentiary to be paid out of tax funds, Pitt opposed it successfully by pen and in voice before the legislature. Pitt and George White McDaniel (*q.v.*), pastor of the First Baptist Church, Richmond, led in opposing legislation that would have compelled daily Bible reading in the public schools. Pitt is regarded as father of the Religious Work Foundation, Inc., now supported by a number of Christian denominations. L. M. RITTER

PLACE OF MEETING, SOUTHERN BAPTIST CONVENTION. The place of meeting of the Southern Baptist Convention is recommended to the Convention by the committee on time, place, and preacher in accordance with authorized procedures and is adopted by Convention vote. The committee on Convention arrangements of the Executive Committee is charged with investigating possible invitations for the Convention's annual meeting and bringing its findings and recommendations to the committee on time, place, and preacher. The Executive Committee of the Convention has control of all exhibit space. The Convention pays for all essential costs of the annual meeting. PORTER ROUTH

PLAINS BAPTIST. A paper published in 1928 in Plainview, Tex. Isaac Edgar Gates and A. F. Aulick served as editors. E. C. ROUTH

PLAINS BAPTIST ASSEMBLY. One of two Texas encampments organized in 1948. It is located near Floydada, Tex., in District 9. J. E. ROTH

POINDEXTER, ABRAM MAER (b. Bertie County, N. C., Sept. 22, 1809; d. Gordonsville, Va., May 7, 1872). Pastor, foreign missions leader. Baptized in July, 1831, Poindexter was licensed to preach the following February and ordained in 1834. He preached frequently, although he had no pastorate at first nor any college training. However, in Feb., 1833, Poindexter entered Columbian College, Washington, D. C., preaching often at Washington churches. Ill health hampered his college work, and he left Columbian after a year to return to North Carolina. In 1843 Columbian conferred on him an honorary D.D. degree. Poindexter's first pastorate was in Halifax County, Va., where he associated with Luther Rice (*q.v.*), who considered Poindexter the most promising young preacher he knew. Poindexter married Eliza J. Craddock, May 25, 1837. He devoted time to agency work for the Baptist denomination, especially for Columbian College, Richmond College, and the Foreign Mission Board, and had a part in establishing Southern Baptist Theological Seminary at Greenville, S. C.

From 1853 to the early days of the Civil War, Poindexter served as associate secretary of the Foreign Mission Board, and during 1857–61 editorship of the *Commission* rested largely on him. Poindexter's wife died Sept. 14, 1867, and on June 27, 1871, he married Marcia P. Scott. He wrote articles for the *Religious Herald* and was author of several hymns, seven of which are included in the *Baptist Psalmody* (Charleston, 1850). In the memorial address at the 1886 session of the General Association of Virginia, John A. Broadus (*q.v.*) said, "Poindexter was a Boanerges, a son of thunder, earnest, impetuous, resolute, resistless. . . . His utterances, always weighty and powerful, were at times absolutely terrific and overwhelming."

BIBLIOGRAPHY: W. Cathcart, *Baptist Encyclopedia* (1883) revised. A. T. Robertson, *Life and Letters of John A. Broadus* (1910). G. B. Taylor, *Virginia Baptist Ministers,* Third Series (1912). E. C. ROUTH

POLAND, BAPTISTS IN. In the area which between the world wars was called Poland there were a variety of peoples. Sixty per cent of the people were Polish Roman Catholics. There were also some Germans, some Czechs who were nearly all Protestant, and some Russian-speaking people, who were Orthodox Catholic. Baptists tended to group themselves similarly, along national lines. Between the wars the German-speaking Baptists in Poland had a union with about 8,000 members. The Slavic Baptists (Poles, Russians, Czechs, and Ukrainians) also had a union of about the same size. Lodz, a city in which were located a large German-speaking Baptist church, a publishing house, and a hospital, was a center of Baptist work. W. O. LEWIS

POLISH BAPTIST CONFERENCE IN U. S. A. AND CANADA. Originally a part of the General Slavic Baptist Union organized in Chicago, Ill., July 1, 1909, when Polish, Czech, Slovak, and Serbian Baptists "united to mutually consider spiritual welfare of fraternal Slavic peoples belonging to our denomination." At a convention of the Slavic Union July 1, 1912, in Pound, Wis., the Polish delegates met in a separate session to further the interests and discuss objectives of Baptist missionary work among Poles and to plan future meeting of an independent Polish conference. Active in the groundwork of the Polish Conference were ministers previously elected as acting officers: Karol W. Strzelec, president; Henry Schilke, secretary; A. Bendżula, treasurer; Louis Adamus; and Gustaw Alf. The first Polish Baptist Conference met as an independent body the following year, May 15–19, 1913, at the First Polish Baptist Church in Buffalo, N. Y. Eleven churches and missions were represented.

Without established headquarters the conference has been meeting annually in its member churches in cities of the Middle East Atlantic states and in Toronto, Canada, since 1951 when Polish Baptists of Canada joined the conference.

The Polish Baptist missionary movement in the U. S. A. began in 1888 when a large number of Polish Baptist immigrants from Europe settled on farms of Pound, Wis., with L. Heine as pastor. In 1895 the first Polish Baptist church in the U. S. A. was organized in Buffalo, N. Y., with Joseph Antoszewski as pastor. Ministers were originally trained in Slavic Baptist Training School (1918–1921) in Chicago. Relocated in 1921 in East Orange, N. J., the school became known as International Baptist Seminary under sponsorship of the American Baptist Home Mission Society. Louis Adamus became head and instructor of the Polish department.

By 1934 there were 24 churches and missions with 2,000 members and nearly 1,000 pupils in Sunday schools. In 1954, 6 churches remained in the conference, reporting 24 baptisms and a membership of 430. Of the original 24 the oldest and largest congregations became entirely English speaking, those without pastors were absorbed by American Baptist churches, while the remaining churches in the conference are either bilingual or Polish.

Wolny Chrześcijanin (*The Free Christian*), founded in 1944 and edited since then by John Gilewicz, is the only existing Polish Baptist monthly in the world; it represents the work of the conference. JOHN GILEWICZ

POLITY, BAPTIST CHURCH. Church polity is deeply ingrained in Baptists' convictions and history. Innumerable statements of the Baptist views have been made. They agree as to a general pattern of the principal points, although varieties of emphasis and terminology and even some minor disagreements occur, due to three factors: (1) Baptist confessions or declarations of faith are voluntary expressions of individuals or independent bodies, rather than official creeds or dogmas. (2) There is no general council, synod, or other superior authority to require uniformity. (3) The dispersal, in time and place, of Baptist groups in different environments contributes to varieties of emphasis within the general pattern.

Definition.—Polity is the "form or constitution of the government of a state . . . or of any institution or organization . . . : the general or fundamental system or organization of a government as determined by the theory on which it is based, as to the object it aims to accomplish, its relation to the people, their political and civil rights, etc.: by extension, . . . especially in a religious denomination."

The Baptist definition of church polity may be viewed as a quadrilateral of essential concepts: (1) the "organization of a government," the local church (Matt. 18:17; Acts 20:17, 28; Rom. 16:1; Phil. 1:1); (2) a "theory [historical fact and principle] on which it is based," the sole authority of Jesus Christ (Matt. 28:18; Acts 2:36; Eph. 5:23–24); (3) an "object it aims to accomplish," setting men free from the bondage of sin into fellowship with Christ as Saviour and Lord (Rom. 6:6–14; 8:1–2), wherein they can grow in the knowledge of God's Word (John 8:32; I Peter 2:2), so as to become Christ's witnesses to a lost world (Acts 1:8; 2:32; 8:4); (4) to defend and contend for the religious, "political, and civil rights" of the individual against usurpation by state or church (Acts 24:10–16; 25:7–12)—in short, the complete freedom of every man, uncoerced by any human being or institution, to respond to the authority of the Lord Jesus Christ in all matters about which his conscience speaks (Matt. 23:8; Rom. 14:4; Acts 5:28–29).

History.—The historical development of the Baptist conceptions of church polity exhibits an essential unity in the quadrilateral with minor variations from the general pattern. Both the basic pattern and the variations can be fully understood only by understanding the civil and religious environment in which a particular confession was formed. While such an exploration is impossible in a brief review, the following summary of polity statements in the major confessions will emphasize the four basic principles as well as suggest some historical trends in polity development.

1. English Baptists. The early English Baptist confessions document Baptist struggles for religious liberty and self-expression in the 17th century. Seven of them are outstanding, four from the General or Arminian Baptists and three from the Particular or Calvinistic Baptists. The first, in 1611, was drawn by an individual, Thomas Helwys, and was Arminian. The other six were issued by representatives of groups of churches, from 1644 to 1689. These confessions set the pattern on matters of polity for subsequent confessions by both Arminian and Calvinistic groups, whether in England, the continents, or America.

(1) The authority of Christ. The first and third Arminian confessions, 1611 and 1660, imply that Christ is the only authority over the church; the 1651 and 1678 confessions expressly state that he is the only lawgiver and head of the church. The three Calvinistic confessions—1644, 1656, 1689—positively assert that Jesus Christ is the "King" or "head" of the church, and he alone.

(2) The individual believer. The first three Arminian confessions—1611, 1651, 1660—make no distinctive statement regarding the individual, but his liberty of conscience under Christ can be inferred from their other statements of polity. The confession of 1678, much longer and more explicit than the previous ones, insists on soul liberty for the individual and declares that "any usurpation, tyranny or command" contrary to "his [Christ's] revealed will in his word" is a betrayal of true liberty of conscience.

Of the three Calvinistic confessions, the first, 1644, gives priority to its statement that only the Word of God has authority over the Christian. The second, 1656, which is quite in harmony with its predecessor, leaves the concept to be inferred. The third, 1689, which is long and detailed, gives liberty of conscience free from interference by all men as its first statement of polity, bases this in a regenerated church membership, and makes each member equal in the "suffrage" of the local church.

(3) The local church. All seven of the English confessions expressly assert the authority of the local church to choose its own pastors and deacons. As to control of membership, the first and second Calvinistic confessions declare the local church's authority, while the third implies it. The four Arminian confessions make no direct declaration, but their assertions of the rights of the churches in other matters would imply their agreement with the Calvinistic statements. That the officers of the churches have authority to receive or dismiss members is never remotely suggested. Only two kinds of offices are recognized in these confessions: spiritual, served by bishops, elders, or pastors; and temporal, served by deacons. No grades of authority in the spiritual ministry nor any external authority over the churches is recognized in these confessions.

(4) Ecclesiastical authority. One exception occurs in the fourth Arminian confession of 1678. It provides for three groups of "officers": (1) "Bishops, or Messengers," who "have the government of those churches, that had suffrage in their election, and no other ordinarily"; (2) "Elders, or Pastors," who are to serve only in the church that chose them, and who are not in "anyway to infringe the liberty, or due power, or office of the bishop"; (3) the "deacons," who are to serve the benevolent office "in their particular congregations." In keeping with the elevation of "bishops" to a rank higher than pastors, this confession also provides (article 39) that "General councils, or assemblies, consisting of Bishops, Elders, and Brethren, of the several churches (Buckinghamshire, Oxfordshire and adjacent counties, west of London) . . . have lawful right . . . to preserve unity, to prevent heresy . . . in any congregation whatsoever within its own limits, or jurisdiction; . . . to such . . . assembly, appeals ought to be made . . . and such general assemblies have lawful power to hear, and determine, as also to excommunicate." These concessions as to "bishops" and "general assemblies" were not only a limited compromise with the established, authoritarian state-church system but were in conflict with the logic of article 29, which says that Christ is "the only head" of the church.

Against this twofold variation from the general pattern, the third Calvinistic confession, officially adopted in 1689 but privately prepared in 1677, took a strong stand. It explicitly asserts that Jesus Christ is the head of the church, that bishops and pastors denote the same office, that general assemblies "are not entrusted with any Church-power . . . or any jurisdiction over the Churches themselves" and may not "impose their determination on the Churches or officers."

2. American Baptists. These Baptists have produced many confessions or articles of faith —some by organized groups, more by individuals. None have any official or binding authority but are only declarations of the views of their authors. Some of these confessions have had considerable influence, two in a marked degree —the Philadelphia in 1742 and the New Hampshire in 1833.

The Philadelphia Association was organized in 1707. Calvinism was strong in this area. Among these churches the English Calvinistic Baptist confession of 1689 came naturally into general favor. References to it are scattered through the records, and in 1742 the Philadelphia Association adopted it, with two additional articles, and ordered it printed, the first so done in America. It widely diffused among the young American churches the quadrilateral pattern established by the English confessions, especially the Calvinistic.

The Baptist Convention of New Hampshire appointed a committee in 1830 to prepare a "Declaration of Faith and Practice." It was finally adopted by the five-member board of the convention and published in 1833. It sustains, although in condensed language, the four points of the Philadelphia Confession. It is explicit on the authority of Christ, the privileges of the members, the singularity of the ministerial office, and the autonomy of the church in relation to civil government.

In the latter part of the 18th century, Arminian theology took root among New England Baptists. Arminian or Free Will Baptist churches began to multiply after 1780, and in 1827 they organized a general conference. In 1834 it published "A Treatise on the Faith of the Freewill Baptists . . ." The section on the church is the most extended but has little explicit statement on principles of polity, the emphasis being on the qualifications and duties of members, pastors, and deacons. However, the phrases "believe in Christ," "agreeably to his word," "the regenerate, who obey the gospel." "[bishops, elders, evangelists, pastors, teachers] do not appear to be distinct officers, [their authority is spiritual] to instruct and rule them by the word," "adhere closely to the doctrine of Christ," all indicate the harmony of the Free Will polity with the prevailing Baptist convictions.

3. European Baptists. The English Baptist confessions belong to the 17th century. The struggles for the recognition of American Baptist polity are found in the 18th century, although Roger Williams belongs to the 17th century. The three leading European Baptist confessions were set forth in the 19th century.

The German Baptist confession took shape from 1837 to 1847. The Swedish Baptist confession appeared in 1861, and the French statement, in 1879. Others were made by Danish, Hungarian, and Russian Baptists. All are mildly Calvinistic. The German, Swedish, and French strongly maintain the quadrilateral of Baptist polity.

4. The 20th century. While no major body of Baptists has issued a confession of faith in the manner of the great English confessions of the 17th century, there has been a succession of discussions and declarations affirming contem-

porary adherence to the general pattern of historic Baptist polity.

There have been some able presentations by prominent individuals. A. H. Strong, president of Rochester (N. Y.) Theological Seminary, gave an extended discussion in his *Systematic Theology* in 1909. The year before saw the appearance of *The Axioms of Religion* by Edgar Young Mullins (*q.v.*), president of the Southern Baptist Theological Seminary, Louisville, Ky. In 1920, from the steps of the national Capitol, George W. Truett (*q.v.*), pastor of First Baptist Church, Dallas, Tex., delivered an address to nearly 15,000 people on the Baptist advocacy of religious liberty and related subjects. The views of these three men were given worldwide dissemination among Baptists and others because of their prominence in the Baptist World Alliance. Strong delivered the congress sermon at the initial meeting, and Mullins and Truett were elected president of the Alliance in 1923 and 1934, respectively.

In 1919 the Southern Baptist Convention, led by the president, James Bruton Gambrell (*q.v.*), took two important actions relative to church polity. The first was a strong condemnation of the policy of the War Department to break down all denominational lines in spiritual ministries in the army training camps and overseas during World War I. The second action was a refusal to enter the Interchurch World Movement, believing that a decision to enter would compromise their convictions. Again in 1951, for the same reason, they declined invitations to "enter into organic connection with the National Council of Churches, or the World Council of Churches," or any other body by which action they "would compromise Baptist principles . . . revealed in the inspired Word of God."

A rather full statement of belief was made by the Convention in 1925, the only one in its history. Of the 25 articles, two—"The Church" and "Religious Liberty"—are on polity. The right of all men to answer to God alone for their souls, the separation of church and state, the rule of the local church solely by the will of Christ revealed in the Scriptures, and the identity of bishops and elders as one office are affirmed.

The British Baptists have taken a similar stand. In 1926 they adopted and published a reply to the *Lambeth Appeal* of the Anglican bishops, declining the coalition the bishops desired and giving their convictions on matters of polity as part of the reason for their refusal.

The British and the two American Baptist bodies have incorporated in their organic instruments affirmations of the independence of the co-operating local churches. The American Baptist Convention has adopted a special *Statement by American Baptists Concerning Freedom,* in which they stress liberty of conscience, separation of church and state, and the principle of the democratic process and give a pledge to preserve the Baptist witness on these positions.

Through its half century of existence, 1905–55, the Baptist World Alliance has given prominence to Baptist polity convictions. In the papers presented at the successive congresses and through personal representations by its elected officers to officials of governments, it has maintained a continuing witness to these convictions. The activities of the Alliance representatives in behalf of persecuted Baptist minorities, as a practical expression of Baptist beliefs on religious liberty, has been described by Fred Townley Lord, pastor, Bloomsbury Central Baptist Church, London, former editor of the *Baptist Times,* London, and president of the Baptist World Alliance, 1950–55.

5. The future. At the heart of the quadrilateral is the question of authority. Civil government was ordained by God (Rom. 13:1–7), but he never gave it authority over the consciences and the faith of men (Luke 22:25–26). Men lust for power over their fellow men and from ancient times have either made religion the servant of the state or have become the police power of an authoritarian church (John 18:12–14).

Judging the future by the past, Baptists believe the struggle for religious liberty must continue on two fronts, the external and the internal. Involved are the two principles of autonomy and democracy for the local church. Autonomy means freedom from all human laws and authorities that would inhibit freedom to obey all the laws of Christ (John 14:21, 23). That this freedom is challenged and/or usurped on every continent today is common knowledge. The internal front concerns democracy within the local church. The New Testament locates authority for deciding all affairs of a church in the majority decisions of the assembled members (Acts 6:5; II Cor. 2:6, "many," the majority; I Peter 5:3; III John 9–10). "It is because men have an equal right to direct access to God that they are entitled to equal privileges in the church." Any decisions about the affairs of the church made by a bishop, elder, pastor, deacons, or committee is a usurpation of Christ's authority bestowed on the church. A British Baptist executive has expressed his concern at this point, as have some American Baptists.

In principle, of course, there is little choice between the violation of Christian liberty and equality by an oligarchy within the church or by a dictator without. Here lies the relevance of a regenerated membership. Only those who have been born anew will love Christ and keep his commands regarding his church. In opposition are the state church and infant baptism, leading to an unconverted church membership. In the future, as in the past, Christ's people must put on the whole armor of God and stand fast in the liberty wherewith Christ has made them free (Eph. 6:13; Gal. 5:1).

See also Independency and Co-operation, Baptist and Discipline.

NASHVILLE BUILDINGS

FROST BUILDING, 161 Eighth Ave., N., was the first of the present buildings constructed by the Board. Completed in 1914 debt-free, it now houses the Baptist Book Store and offices for various departments.

ADMINISTRATION BUILDING, 127 Ninth Ave., N., was begun with three floors in 1941; the other nine were finished in 1953. It includes a chapel, a cafeteria for employees, the Dargan-Carver Library, and offices for the Executive Committee and some agencies of the Convention, in addition to administrative offices for the Sunday School Board.

PRINTING BUILDING, located about 5 miles from downtown Nashville, was built in 1952, consisting of 125,000 sq. ft. of floor space on a 27-acre lot. Although owned by the Board, it is leased to the contract printers who manufacture most of the Board's periodicals.

RIDGECREST BAPTIST ASSEMBLY

PRITCHELL HALL, main hotel and administrative building, was opened in 1914 and remodeled in 1926. Comprising 1,900 acres and 170 buildings 18 miles east of Asheville, N. C., the assembly can entertain 3,000 guests per week through the summer season.

SPILMAN AUDITORIUM was built in 1938; expanded in 1953, it now seats 3,500 in addition to eleven classrooms.

DINING HALL, completed in 1948, will seat 1,800 guests with space for 600 more in adjoining Rhododendron Hall.

GLORIETA BAPTIST ASSEMBLY

GLORIETA BAPTIST ASSEMBLY comprises 1,238 acres 7,500 feet above sea level and 19 miles east of Santa Fe, N. Mex. It was opened in 1952. In 1956 there were 42 buildings, enough to care for approximately 1,000 guests per week.

TEXAS HALL, hotel building to accommodate 150–175 people, was largely financed by Texas Baptists. Some other buildings were provided in a similar manner.

NEW MEXICO HALL, administrative building, was named for the state whose Baptist people gave half the land for the assembly.

BAPTIST BOOK STORES

Typical Exterior View

Typical Interior View

FIFTY of these stores are operated by the Sunday School Board from Maryland to Oregon as service centers to Southern Baptist churches. Their merchandise includes Bibles, books, and church supplies; special help is offered in visual-aids and for church libraries.

BIBLIOGRAPHY: W. H. Allison, *Baptist Councils in America* (1906). American Baptist Convention, *Year Book* (1954). Baptist Union of Great Britain and Ireland, *The Baptist Handbook* (1955). Baptist World Alliance, *Eighth Baptist World Congress* (1950). Baptist World Alliance, Executive Committee, *Minutes* (Aug., 1952). W. W. Barnes, *The Southern Baptist Convention, A Study in the Development of Ecclesiology* (1934). W. R. Boggs, *The Baptists, Who Are They And What Do They Believe?* (1898). H. Cook, *What Baptists Stand For* (1947, 1953). H. E. Dana, *A Manual of Ecclesiology* (1941). E. C. Dargan, *Ecclesiology* (1905). J. M. Dawson, *Baptists and the American Republic* (1956). G. S. Dobbins, *Building Better Churches* (1947); *The Churchbook* (1951). J. B. Gambrell, *Baptists and Their Business* (1919). L. L. Gwaltney, *Heralds of Freedom* (1939). G. E. Horr, *The Baptist Heritage* (1923). P. L. Jones, *A Restatement of Baptist Principles* (1909). T. G. Jones, *The Baptists: Their Origin, Continuity, Principles, Spirit, Polity, Position, and Influence, A Vindication* (n.d.). F. T. Lord, *Baptist World Fellowship* (1955). G. W. McDaniel, *The People Called Baptists* (1919). W. J. McGlothlin, *Baptist Confessions of Faith* (1911); *A Guide to the Study of Church History* (1914). W. R. McNutt, *Polity and Practice in Baptist Churches* (1935). V. I. Masters, ed., *Re-thinking Baptist Doctrines* (1937). F. S. Mead, *The Baptists* (1954). E. Y. Mullins, *The Axioms of Religion* (1908). W. D. Nowlin, *What Baptists Stand For* (1918). E. A. Payne, *The Fellowship of Believers, Baptist Thought and Practice Yesterday and Today* (1944). J. M. Pendleton, *Distinctive Principles of Baptists* (1882). J. W. Porter, *The World's Debt to the Baptists* (1914). H. W. Robinson, *The Life and Faith of the Baptists* (1946). E. C. Routh, *The Life Story of Dr. J. B. Gambrell* (1929). H. K. Rowe and R. G. Torbet, *The Baptist Witness* (1951). J. H. Rushbrooke and others, *The Faith of the Baptists* (1926). P. Schaff, *The Creeds of Christendom* (1877). Southern Baptist Convention, *Annals* (1918–19, 1955). H. H. Straton, *Baptists: Their Message and Mission* (1941). A. H. Strong, *Systematic Theology* (1907–09). H. W. Tribble, *Our Doctrines* (1936). J. C. Turner, *Our Baptist Heritage* (1945). W. R. White, *Baptist Distinctives* (1946).

L. R. ELLIOTT

POLLARD, JOHN GARLAND (b. King and Queen County, Va., Aug. 4, 1871; d. Washington, D. C., Apr. 28, 1937). Lawyer, educator, statesman, and Baptist layman. Pollard attended Richmond College, earned his law degree at Columbian University, and was admitted to the Richmond bar at 21, where he practiced law 25 years. Rising rapidly as a lawyer, Pollard was elected to the Virginia Constitutional Convention in 1901 and to the electoral college in 1904. He published a *Supplement to the Code of Virginia* and *Annotated Code of 1904*. From 1913 to 1917 Pollard was attorney general of Virginia and member of the state board of education. During World War I, in 1918–19, he did welfare work in France and Germany. He was a member of the Federal Trade Commission, 1920–21; dean of the Marshall-Wythe School of Government and Citizenship, College of William and Mary, 1922–29; and governor of Virginia, 1930–34.

Pollard served for 20 years as president of the Children's Home Society of Virginia and was also president of the Virginia Museum of Fine Arts and chairman of the Board of Veteran's Appeals. He served Baptists as trustee of Woman's College, Richmond, and as president of Richmond College alumni. He drafted a memorial leading to the defeat of a legislative effort to pass a compulsory Bible reading law for public schools in Virginia. A Sunday school superintendent and teacher, Pollard was a pioneer in Baptist Young People's Union work.

BEN LYNES

POLLOCK, PINCKNEY DANIEL (b. Houston County, Ga., Nov. 22, 1860; d. Monroe, Ga., July 24, 1905). Educator. A student at Mercer 1879–80; he studied English and law at the University of Georgia, receiving the B.L. degree in 1884; then studied English, French, and German for one year in Paris and one year in Berlin. After teaching at Senoia and Newnan, Ga., he was in 1893 elected professor of English at Mercer University; in 1896, made chairman of the faculty; and in 1897, made president. In 1895 he married Eva Selman of Monroe, Ga., and had one son. As president he was counted by the trustees at that time to show "the most remarkable executive ability that has ever controlled the affairs of the institution"; under his "leadership the institution has had its greatest prosperity." But his success extended beyond practical business affairs. He also developed a "Mercer spirit," counted then to be unique both in quality and power. Student pranks ceased; and instead of the athletic loyalty then becoming common, students accepted the higher purpose of the college as a sacred trust and felt a deep and pervasive interest in matters of thought and outlook. John Temple Graves, after a visit to the college at this time, said: "I never saw such devotion in a student body to its *alma mater* . . . or such hearty sympathy between students and professors. . . . There is an atmosphere of mental vitality, a keenness of intellectual life, a spirit of philosophy, a purposefulness, an ambition, . . . which is simply thrilling with promise to the future."

Deteriorating health, however, brought an early end to President Pollock's most promising career. W. H. KILPATRICK

POND MEMORIAL CAMP. Owned and operated by the Woman's Missionary Union of Tate's Creek Baptist Association at Mallory Springs (Madison County), Ky. Opened in 1942, the camp is used one week annually for Royal Ambassadors and Girl's Auxiliary.

ELDRED M. TAYLOR

POOI CHING BOYS' SCHOOL, HONG KONG. See CHINA, MISSION IN.

POOI TO GIRLS' SCHOOL, HONG KONG. See CHINA, MISSION IN.

POPE, OWEN CLINTON (b. Washington County, Ga., Feb. 15, 1842; d. Abilene, Tex.,

Nov. 18, 1901). Editor, mission secretary, college president. Son of Owen Clinton and Sarah P. Pope, he graduated from Mercer University with the B.D. degree in 1860 and was ordained to the ministry in 1861. After serving as a volunteer in the Confederate army, Pope resumed his work of teaching and preaching and became principal of Jefferson High School at Stellaville, Ga. Moving to Tennessee in 1875, he served as pastor at Morristown and for two years edited the *Baptist Reflector* at Morristown. Pope moved to Texas in 1878 and became associated with John Bodkin Link (*q.v.*) in editing the *Texas Baptist Herald.* In 1881 he became superintendent of Texas missions and general missionary for the American Baptist Home Mission Society. Churches in Abilene, El Paso, and other communities were organized under his guidance.

In 1885 Pope moved to New York City to serve as superintendent and general solicitor for the church edifice work of the American Baptist Home Mission Society and continued to serve in that capacity for 11 years. Instrumental in interesting James B. Simmons in Simmons College, Pope became president of the college in 1898 and served until June, 1901, when he retired as president emeritus and died in November of that year. He willed his estate to his wife, who died June 7, 1930, willing the estate, valued at $50,000, to Simmons University.

BIBLIOGRAPHY: "History of the Baptist Denomination in Georgia," compiled for the *Christian Index* (1881). R. C. Crane, "O. C. Pope, Foundation Builder," *West Texas Baptist* (Oct. 28, 1937). The Pope Papers, Hardin-Simmons University Library.

RUPERT N. RICHARDSON

PORTER, DAVID TINSLEY, CHAIR OF CHURCH HISTORY. In 1903 Southern Baptist Theological Seminary announced in *The Baptist Argus* and to the Southern Baptist Convention that Mrs. Rebecca Porter Bartlett (1836?–1903) of Memphis, Tenn., had given $60,000 to the seminary to establish a chair or professorship to perpetuate the name of her brother, David Tinsley Porter (1827–98), a merchant, banker, and for a time mayor of Memphis. The seminary was to determine "the particular branch of education which shall be taught by the professor occupying said chair." On May 3, 1904, the executive committee of the seminary named the chair the David Tinsley Porter Chair of Church History and agreed that the first occupant should be William Joseph McGlothlin (*q.v.*), who held it from 1904 to 1919. Occupants since McGlothlin have been Frank Marion Powell, 1920–40, and Theron Douglas Price, since 1954. LEO T. CRISMON

PORTER, JOHN WILLIAM (b. Calloway, Fayette County, Tenn., Aug. 8, 1863; d. Lexington, Ky., Sept. 7, 1937). Attorney, pastor, author. Son of John Freeman and Martha Carolyn (Tharpe) Porter, he was educated at Cumberland University, receiving the LL.B. degree in 1882, and at Southern Baptist Theological Seminary, where he received the Th.G. degree in 1893. Porter married Lillian E. Thomas in July, 1891, by whom he had five children, three girls and two boys.

After practicing law, 1882–85, Porter was ordained to the Baptist ministry in 1890 and held pastorates at the Newdale Church in Canada, Germantown and Colliersville Baptist churches in Tennessee, Olive Branch Church in Mississippi, Pewee Valley Church and First Baptist, Maysville, in Kentucky, and First Baptist Church, Newport News, Va., after which he returned to Kentucky as pastor of the First Baptist Church of Lexington for 14 years. He was pastor for about three years of the Third Avenue Baptist Church, Louisville, and for 14 years, of the Immanuel Baptist Church, Lexington.

Porter was a trustee of Southeastern Kentucky Baptist School, Hall-Moody Institute, and Georgetown College. For 12 years he was a member of the Foreign Mission Board, preached the annual sermon at the Southern Baptist Convention in 1915, and was moderator of the General Association of Baptists in Kentucky, 1913–14. He served as editor of the *Western Recorder,* 1905–19, and president of the Baptist Book Concern, Louisville.

At one time president of the Anti-Saloon League of America, Porter was author of a number of books, including *Christian Science, Neither Scientific nor Christian; Assurance of Faith; The World's Debt to Baptists; The Baptists' Debt to the World; Feminism; Evolution Menace;* and *Alien Immersion.*

GEORGE RALEIGH JEWELL

PORTUGAL, BAPTIST UNION OF. In Portugal in 1956 there were 31 Baptist churches with a membership of 1,644. Fifteen of these were affiliated with the Portuguese Baptist Convention. Also related to the convention were eight churches in the colonies of Mosambique and Angola. An important factor in Portuguese Baptist work is the Foreign Mission Board of the Brazilian convention. In addition to sending missionaries to Portugal, the Brazilian organization has rendered aid in the purchase of property and the support of pastors. Brazil's two repersentatives at work in Portugal are Pastor Helcio da Silva Lessa and his wife. Under the leadership of this couple, unprecedented co-operation has been achieved. It is expected that other churches not now connected with the larger Baptist body will relate themselves to it. A Bible conference for Baptist youth was held two years ago. Eighty young persons from many of the churches were inspired by Bible study, singing, and fellowship. Another important innovation is an evangelistic season for young people. The young people themselves play principal parts in the programs, emphasizing winning the lost and the development of spiritual life. Retreats for pastors, conducted during the past three years, have cultivated fellowship and understanding and have led to over-all planning and a deepening of devotion. Study courses for lay workers have been inaugurated by the missionaries from Brazil. These studies are designed to bring laymen into the stream of acitvity of the churches. Woman's missionary work is not neglected. Portuguese Baptists are looking to their more experienced Brazilian W.M.U. friends for material aid and suggested plans. The only institution of welfare type in Portugal is what is called the Evangelical Home, established and presided over by the pastor of the Third Baptist Church of Porto. In this home there are 28 children and 11 old persons. The Portuguese Baptist Convention is now helping to support this work. GEORGE W. SADLER

POSEY, HUMPHREY (b. Henry County, Va., Jan. 12, 1780; d. Newnan, Ga., Dec. 28, 1846). He was ordained in Buncombe County, N. C., in 1805 and served Baptist churches in that area until 1817, when he was appointed missionary to the Cherokee Indians of western North Carolina and northwestern Georgia by the Triennial Convention. In 1824 he relinquished the appointment and moved to Georgia. He was present at the formation of the Georgia Baptist Convention in 1822 and afterward maintained a close identification with its work. In addition to serving churches in Carnesville, LaGrange, and Walker County, he was also, for a time, agent for both the Hearn Academy and Mercer University. His first wife, and mother of his 10 children, Lettice Jolly of Union District, S. C., died June 22, 1842, after 42 years of marriage. Two years later, he married Mrs. Jane Stokes of Newnan, Ga., and made his home in Newnan until his death. He was buried seven miles east of Newnan.

HAROLD L. MCMANUS

POSTWAR PROGRAM. A movement begun early in World War II, making preparation to meet the "tremendous need and great opportunity" of the postwar period. Immediate objectives were increased funds and missionary personnel, spiritual revival, and liquidation of debts.

In 1943 the committee in charge of planning further recommended that the Home Mission Board launch a Convention-wide revival effort and that Jan. 1, 1944, be set as the deadline for retirement of all debts. The next year, in cooperation with the Convention's Executive Committee, plans were recommended for a Centennial Crusade, a program for world redemption, to be conducted during 1945, the centennial of the Southern Baptist Convention. Two objectives were stated: the winning of one million souls and the giving of 20 million dollars through the Cooperative Program.

A serious decline in the ratio of baptisms to church membership was cited as a pressing reason for the evangelistic emphasis, which had fallen from a ratio of one baptism for 16.2 church members in 1925 to one baptism for 25.1 members in 1944.

The crusade resulted in a gain of 100,000 baptisms over 1944, for a total of 256,144 for 1945. The ratio of baptisms for 1945 showed one for 22.8 members compared with one for 25.1 in 1944, and in subsequent years more improvement was made.

The fund-raising phase of the crusade resulted in an increase in gifts to Convention-wide agencies through the Convention's Executive Committee of $1,458,067.53 in 1945 over 1944, for a total of $5,735,559.83. Centennial Thank Offering receipts through the Executive Committee were $234,942.71. Cooperative Program funds retained in the states were not tabulated. ROBERT J. HASTINGS

POTEAT, EDWIN McNEILL, JR. (b. New Haven, Conn., Nov. 20, 1892; d. Raleigh, N. C., Dec. 17, 1955). Minister, missionary, teacher, author. Son of Edwin McNeill and Harriet Haley (Gordon) Poteat. A brilliant scholar, Poteat studied at Furman University, where he received the A.B. (1912) and A.M. (1913) degrees; he received the Th.M. degree at Southern Baptist Theological Seminary (1916). He was awarded the D.D. degree by Wake Forest College (1934), Duke University (1936), and Hillsdale College (1940). After serving for a time as traveling secretary of the Student Volunteer Movement, New York (1916–17), Poteat served as a Southern Baptist missionary in Kaifeng, Honan, China (1917–26), and as associate professor of philosophy and ethics at the University of Shanghai, China (1926–29). Returning to the United States, he served as minister of the Pullen Memorial Baptist Church, Raleigh, N. C. (1929–37, 1948–55), and as minister of the Euclid Avenue Baptist Church, Cleveland, Ohio (1937–44). From 1944 to 1948, he was president of Colgate-Rochester Divinity School.

Active in many areas of public life, Poteat was a member of North Carolina State Board of Charities and Public Welfare (1930–37), president of the Committee on Interacial Cooperation (Atlanta, Ga., 1933–37), a member of the Committee on Worship, etc., of the National Council of Churches of Christ in America (1941–55), and a national president of Protestants and Other Americans United for Separation of Church and State.

A well-known author of books dealing with the impact of religion on life, touching the various fields of theology, economics, science, and other areas, Poteat wrote *Coming to Terms with the Universe* (1931); *Jesus and the Liberal Mind* (1934); *Rev. John Doe* (1935); *Thunder over Sinai* (1936); *The Social Manifesto of Jesus* (1937); *Centurion,* a narrative poem (1939); *These Shared His Passion* (1940); *These Shared His Cross* (1941); *Four Freedoms and God* (1943); *Over the Sea, the Sky,* poetry (1945); *Last Reprieve?* (1946); *Parables of Crisis* (1950); *God Makes the Difference* (1951); *Mandate to Humanity* (1953); *Jesus' Belief in Man* (1956); and a manuscript planned for publication by Harper and Brothers for Lent, 1957. Poteat also wrote an unpublished novel, short stories, verses published in smaller magazines, and a weekly column, "The Times in Rhymes," for an English language newspaper in Tientsin, China; he was also a composer of hymns and anthems. In 1940 he delivered the Lyman Beecher Lectures on Preaching at Yale University. He married Hilda Hardman, of Commerce, Ga. Their three children were William Hardman, Elizabeth McNeill, and Haley Gordon. EUGENE I. OLIVE

POTEAT, EDWIN McNEILL, SR. (b. near Yanceyville, Caswell County, N. C., Feb. 6, 1861; d. Durham, N. C., June 25, 1937). Pastor, professor, university president. Son of James and Julia (McNeill) Poteat, Edwin was the youngest of three children of a second marriage. His older brother was William Louis Poteat (*q.v.*). Edwin Poteat received the B.A. degree from Wake Forest College in 1881 and graduated from Southern Baptist Theological Seminary in 1885. After his ordination in 1884, he became pastor of the Baptist church in Chapel Hill but resigned in 1886 to become assistant professor of ancient languages at Wake Forest College. Poteat went to Johns Hopkins University for graduate study in psychology and philosophy from 1886 to 1888, and while a student in Baltimore, he served as acting pastor of Lee Street Baptist Church. After spending the summer of 1888 at the University of Berlin in graduate study, Poteat was called to Calvary Baptist Church of New Haven, Conn. On Oct. 24, 1889, he married Harriet Hale Gordon, daughter of the widely known Adoniram Judson Gordon (*q.v.*), pastor of Clarendon Street Church of Boston. Poteat remained as pastor of Calvary Church, New Haven, until 1898, during which time he was enrolled in Yale University as a special student. In 1898 he became pastor of Memorial Baptist Church in Philadelphia and served until 1903, when he became president of Furman University in Greenville, S. C. After a 15-year presidency at Furman, Poteat resigned in 1918 to become one of the promoters of the Laymen's Missionary Movement and the Interchurch World Movement, 1918–19. He was departmental executive secretary of the General Board of Promotion of the Northern Baptist Convention, 1919–21, and it was during this period that his wife died. In June, 1921, Poteat went to China to visit his two eldest sons, Gordon and Edwin McNeill, Jr. (*q.v.*), who were then missionaries under the Southern Baptist Foreign Mission Board. The University of Shanghai invited him to become professor in the department of philosophy and ethics, a post he held for six years. Poteat married Harriet Brittingham, a missionary of the Northern Baptist Convention, in 1925.

After his return to the United States in 1927 and a stay at the Mayo Clinic, Poteat became interim pastor of First Baptist Church, Richmond, Va., for two years. He then went to Atlanta, first as interim pastor of Second Baptist Church and then as permanent pastor from 1929 to 1931. When Second and Ponce de Leon churches in Atlanta merged, Poteat went to Mercer University, where he taught ethics and comparative religion, 1931–34.

He returned to Furman as a professor in 1934 and remained there until his death in 1937. His funeral service was arranged in every detail by himself with the intention, as he put it, that "there should be no paganism connected with the service." He instructed his son Edwin McNeill, Jr., who conducted the service, to speak on the text, "And Jesus said: he that followeth after me shall not walk in darkness but shall have the light of life." "Tell the people," he said, "that the reason I have had such a happy life is that I have been companioned by the light."

Poteat's published works include *The Religion of the Lord's Prayer; The Scandal of the Cross;* and *The Withered Fig Tree,* the last of which was translated and published in Chinese.

BIBLIOGRAPHY: *Who Was Who in America, 1897–1942.* Furman University *Catalogue* (1903–04, 1936–37). *Baptist Courier* (July 1, 1937). E. M. Poteat Memorial Number of *Furman Bulletin* (Nov., 1937).
EDWIN MCNEILL POTEAT, JR.

POTEAT, WILLIAM LOUIS (b. Caswell County, N. C., Oct. 20, 1856; d. Wake Forest, N. C., Mar. 12, 1938). Educator, graduated from Wake Forest College with the A.B. degree in 1877, and received the A.M. degree in 1889. He received LL.D. degrees from Baylor, North Carolina, Brown, Duke; and the Litt.D. degree from Mercer. He engaged in postgraduate studies at Marine Biology Laboratory and University of Berlin. He married Emma J. Purefoy of Wake Forest, June 24, 1881. Their children were Hubert McNeill, Louie (Mrs. Wheeler Martin, Jr.), and Helen Purefoy (Mrs. Lawrence Stallings).

Poteat played a prominent role in the development of Wake Forest College, serving on the faculty from 1878 until 1905, and as president from 1905 until 1927—longer than any other president in Wake Forest's history. He was active in the affairs of North Carolina Baptists and Southern Baptists. He was popular as a lecturer on religion, science, temperance, and education. He was a member of North Carolina Conference for Social Service (president), North Carolina Anti-Saloon League (president), Southern Baptist Education Association (president three terms), Council of Church Schools of the South (president), North Carolina Reconstruction Commission, North Carolina Academy of Sciences (president), and many other movements of his day. His books include *Laboratory and Pulpit* (1901), *The New Peace* (1915), *Can a Man Be a Christian Today?* (1925), *The Way of Victory* (1929), and *Stop Light* (1935). G. A. HENDRICKS

POTTER, ANDREW (b. Paris, Tenn., Jan. 4, 1886; d. Oklahoma City, Okla., Aug. 29, 1951).

Oklahoma Baptist denominational leader, son of Sam and Hasseltine Potter. Born on a Tennessee farm, he was educated in the public schools at Paris, Tenn., and at Hall-Moody College and Union University. He entered the ministry in 1907. After one year (1911–12) at Southern Baptist Theological Seminary, his doctor advised a drier climate, and he went west for his health.

He married Dathal Carroll of Bardwell, Ky., Apr. 5, 1911. In 1913 he moved to Collinsville, Okla., where he became pastor and later served as missionary for Delaware Baptist Association. After a year as pastor at Waurika, in 1917, he became pastor of the First Baptist Church, Enid, and remained there 17 years except for a brief time as "Y" chaplain to the expeditionary forces in France after Nov. 11, 1918. While at Enid, he became involved in a bitter controversy with C. P. Stealey, editor of the *Baptist Messenger,* over the matter of evolution. At the height of the dispute, Potter was voted off the Baptist State Executive Board. His attitude was so temperate that he was restored to that position and gradually became the strongest leader in his convention.

On Sept. 1, 1933, he began his work as executive secretary of the Baptist General Convention of Oklahoma. In that position he rallied Baptists to pay their debts and led them to increase their efforts in evangelism, to start building churches and institutions, and to increase their gifts to missions. When the debts were paid, he led the convention to erect new buildings at Oklahoma Baptist University in Shawnee, rebuild the Baptist Orphans' Home at Oklahoma City, build and increase hospital facilities, and enlarge the facilities of Falls Creek Baptist Assembly. His last achievement was the erection of a five-story Baptist building at Eleventh and North Robinson in Oklahoma City, at a cost of $800,000. He died at Oklahoma City and is buried there. His famous slogan was "Death to Deficit and Down with Debt."

BIBLIOGRAPHY: S. W. Scantlan, *Andrew Potter, Baptist Builder* (1955). SAM W. SCANTLAN

POWELL, JOHN (b. Nottaway County, Va., Jan. 13, 1825; d. Grenada, Miss., Mar. 22, 1893). Layman, benefactor of Baptist causes. Educated at Grenada, Miss., Powell entered business there in 1855 and became sheriff of Yalobusha County in 1860. He volunteered for service in the Confederate Army and returned home in June, 1864, severely wounded. After the Civil War, Powell was employed as a traveling agent for a leading commission house in New Orleans. He was elected treasurer of the Mississippi Central (Illinois Central) Railroad but had to resign because of ill health. An active member of First Baptist Church, Grenada, Powell contributed a lot for the church and half the cost of the building. He was also a generous supporter of First Baptist Church, Jackson, and insisted that the church be built on Capitol Street. Powell served as a member of the board of trustees of Mississippi College, 1881–93, and of the board of missions, 1875–93.

C. B. HAMLET III

POWELL, WILLIAM DAVID (b. Madison County, Miss., July 1, 1854; d. Opelika, Ala., May 15, 1934). Home and foreign missionary. Educated at Union University and Southern Baptist Theological Seminary, Powell was secretary, Sunday School and Colportage Convention, Texas, 1877–82, and missionary to Mexico, Southern Baptist Foreign Mission Board, 1882–98. While serving in Mexico, Powell won the friendship of Governor Madero, Coahuila, who offered him valuable property for school purposes with which Powell established Madero Institute at Saltillo. In 1883 he organized the first Baptist church in Saltillo and led in the organization of the Mexican Baptist Convention the next year. From 1899 to 1907, Powell served in Cuba under the Home Mission Board, in the pastoral ministry with the Home Mission Society (N. Y.), and as financial agent for Union University. He was corresponding secretary, General Association of Kentucky Baptists, 1907–17, and field secretary, Southern Baptist Foreign Mission Board, 1917–33. Known as "Guillermo," the Spanish equivalent of William, while in Mexico, Powell was author of *The Primacy of State Missions,* published in 1912. He married Mary Florence Mayberry (1859–1934) in 1876.

BIBLIOGRAPHY: J. M. Carroll, *History of Texas Baptists* (1923). W. P. Wilks, *Western Recorder* (May 24, 1934). A. Trevino, *Historia de los Trabajos Bautistas en Mexico* (1939). E. C. ROUTH

POWERS, WALTER ELLIS (b. Shelby County, Ky., June 24, 1824; d. Nov. 26, 1916). Minister. Son of Clement and Nancy (Ellis) Powers, he attended classes taught by Thomas Rice and P. D. Porter. At 16 he was converted at Dover Church in Shelby County under the preaching of John Dale and E. G. Berry, and was baptized by Berry Oct. 17, 1839. Powers married Mary Jane Hurstman Sept. 11, 1845. To them were born six boys and five girls. He was ordained by the Long Run Church in 1859 and was for more than 57 years a faithful and useful minister. For more than 30 years he was moderator of Long Run Association.

In 1860 Powers accepted the appointment as missionary of the Long Run Association. His successful advocacy of the cause of temperance attracted attention and favorable comment. He chose to work in destitute territories where there were no churches. He first served sections of Jefferson and Bullitt counties where there were only a few isolated Baptists and no regularly organized Baptist churches.

Although the Civil War interrupted missionary operations in the Long Run Association, Powers continued to preach once a month to Beechland and Knob Creek churches. In 1861 he resigned Knob Creek and took charge of Mount Washington Church in Bullitt County. At this time he was also pastor of Jeffersontown Church and began to supply for Long Run. At the end of 1867, he resigned Mount Washington and Jeffersontown churches to give an additional Sunday to Beechland and take charge of Sligo Church in Henry County. He remained at Beechland for 22 years, when he resigned to become pastor of King's Church. He was a contemporary of Alexander Campbell and probably did as much as any other preacher of his day to stem the tide of Campbellism. LEO T. CRISMON

PRAYER. Prayer, in its widest Christian meaning, is communion with God. Some form of prayer is found in the various world religions, and the study of the history of religions has focused much attention on primitive prayer. Yet Christian prayer is unique both in meaning and in manner. The root of the principal Hebrew verb "to pray" has been variously interpreted as "to cut, decide" and "to level, arbitrate." The Greek New Testament words used almost synonymously for prayer, *deēsis, proseuché,* and *enteuxis,* connote needful petition, devout entreaty to God, and confiding access, respectively. The English word "pray" is derived from the Latin *precari,* "to entreat."

Prayer is characterized by various moods such as adoration, thanksgiving, confession, petition, and intercession, no one of which can rightfully be regarded as the totality of prayer. Prayer may be either oral or silent, explicit or implicit, private or corporate.

Prayer in the Old Testament presupposed that God is personal, both transcendent and active. Motivated chiefly by human needs, prayer in Israel consisted of invocation, praise, confession, petition, intercession, thanksgiving, propitiation, benediction, and even imprecation. Significant prayers recorded in the Old Testament include those of Abraham, Moses, Hannah, Samuel, David, Solomon, Elijah, Isaiah, Hezekiah, Job, Daniel, and the Psalms. Frequently prayer was led by a national leader and was evoked by particular need, but with Jeremiah individual prayer attained great importance.

The Apocrypha, although containing some noteworthy prayers, reveals little development in prayer. Liturgical prayers in pre-Christian Judaism can be noted in the Talmud and Prayer Book.

Jesus, both by example and by teaching, emphasized the urgency of prayer. For him prayer was both daily communion with the Father and his special habit preceding the crises of his life. His prayers, as those uttered while on the cross demonstrate, were largely intercessory and not solely petitionary. The Lord's Prayer, probably designed for personal usage although containing social elements, proceeds from adoration to petition, from "Thy" to "us." Jesus stressed as essential elements in prayer sincerity without ostentation (Matt. 6:5 f.), simplicity without verbosity (Matt. 6:7 f.), humility (Luke 18:9–14), importunity (Luke 11:5–10; 18:1–8), forgiveness (Matt. 6:14 f.), faith (Matt. 17:20; Mark 11:22–24), and a vital relation with himself (John 15:7). His teaching on secret prayer, designed as a corrective for Pharisaism, was in no sense intended to discourage genuine public prayer. Prayer "in my name" involves the willing submission of the one praying to be Christ's agent.

The early Christians for a time simultaneously participated in Jewish worship and themselves engaged in communal prayer. Prayer characterized the leadership of the apostles. Directed to Jesus, it effected the work of the Holy Spirit, preceded providential deliverance, and issued in missionary expansion. According to Paul, prayer is to be in and by the Holy Spirit. The means of conquering anxiety, it is to be strongly intercessory and unceasing. Paul's prayer for removal of his "thorn in the flesh" (II Cor. 12:8 f.) is a classic illustration of the truth that, although a petition may not be granted, the prayer is answered. Hebrews stressed the new approach to God's throne of grace through Jesus' continuous work of intercession. James mentioned prayer in faith for wisdom and for healing, God's availability and prayer's efficacy, and neglected and misdirected praying. According to Peter, prayer should be offered seriously to the God who hears. Peter also pointed out that prayer can be hindered by domestic trouble. Boldness to ask according to God's will characterized John; "the prayers of the saints" and prayer for Christ's coming are found in Revelation.

The history of Christian prayer is largely the record, as Hughes asserts, of the struggle between two conceptions, the "prophetic" and the "mystical," the one leading to communion and the other to absorptive union with God. In the ancient era the formulation and usage of liturgies was marked by the decline of spontaneity in prayer. Prayer was offered for persecutors, for heretics, as propitiation, and commonly, by the fourth century, for the dead. Tertullian's *de Oratione* (A.D. 204) is the oldest extant commentary on the Lord's Prayer. Monasticism served to discourage petitions for temporal things and to make prayer the special continual task of its ascetical adherents. In the East mystical prayer soon prevailed in the mysterious complex of ritual and sacrament; later in the West prayer to Mary and the saints increasingly prevailed. Augustine, according to Heiler, effected a synthesis of the contemplative and the mystical in prayer. This synthesis Thomas Aquinas sought to preserve, but mystics such as Hugo of St. Victor gave the contemplative the pre-eminence—a trend followed by John of the Cross and Francis de Sales. The Fénelon-Bousset controversy centered in the proper motive of prayer, whether man's disinterested love of God or the love for God that pertains to human salvation. The Reformation brought about a renewal of prophetic prayer. For Luther and Calvin prayer was through Christ's intercession the privilege and duty of all Christians amid their vocations. Such a prophetic type of prayer prevailed among most of the Anabaptists, the Puritans, and the Pietists, but the Quakers extended the mystical tradition. Kant anticipated the modern denial of prayer's reality. Intercessory prayer was the matrix from which the modern Protestant missionary movement was born. The Social Gospel directed prayer toward social reform.

In the contemporary period prayer has been the object of a twofold assault. Philosophical naturalism under the guise of "natural law" and "scientific necessity" has argued the impossibility of prayer, especially petitionary prayer. From psychology have come the defective propositions that prayer is autosuggestion and that it is projection, rationalization, or wishful thinking. Modern man, to deny prayer, must nullify personality, even his own, or give assent to a solipsism which he never practices. Christian prayer cannot be adequately defined solely as a means of personality adjustment.

Practical difficulties regarding prayer often beset the Christian, viz., unanswered petitions, prayer in relation to God's will, petitions for physical healing, etc. Prayer interpreted as communion means that there can be petitions not immediately granted but not genuine prayer without "answer." Praying according to God's will may alter particular intentions or executive volitions of God but not the ultimate purpose of God for man and the world. Not all petitions for physical healing are necessarily to be granted.

Prayer is imperative for the Christian, for prayerlessness is the taproot of the Christian's sins and failures, and praying brings the believer into God's presence. It is at once privilege and duty, at once from God and by man. Prayer necessitates, as Hallesby contends, a veritable wrestling with God. Forsyth has affirmed that "it is truer to say that we live the Christian life in order to pray than that we pray in order to live the Christian life."

BIBLIOGRAPHY: K. Barth, *Prayer According to the Catechisms of the Reformation* (1952). G. A. Buttrick, *Prayer* (1942). J. M. Campbell, *The Place of Prayer in the Christian Religion* (1915). W. O. Carver, *If Two Agree* (1942). P. T. Forsyth, *The Soul of Prayer* (1916). O. Hallesby, *Prayer* (1931). G. Harkness, *Prayer and the Common Life* (1948). J. Hastings, *The Christian Doctrine of Prayer* (1915). F. Heiler, *Prayer* (1932). H. T. Hughes, *Prophetic Prayer* (1947). JAMES LEO GARRETT

PREACHING, CHRISTIAN. The definition of preaching by Phillips Brooks has been considered the great classic definition: "Preaching is the communication of truth . . . through personality." H. S. Coffin added to this definition by defining preaching as "truth through personality to constrain conscience at once." Etymologically, Christian preaching is the proclamation of the "good news." A more complete definition is this: Christian preaching is the proclamation of God's message as fully revealed in Jesus Christ by a chosen personality to meet the needs of men. This last definition has several focal points.

The first distinctive is God's message as revealed in Christ. The preacher does not have to invent his basic message; indeed, he cannot and be a true herald. The message is given; it is the preacher's task to interpret, explain, illustrate, and apply the message to the people who listen. Without this message there would be no need for a messenger, and the needs of men, however great, could not be met. Another element of this message is the chosen personality. The preacher is a herald of God's message because God has called him to speak in His stead. Like Paul, the preacher feels a sense of divine compulsion: "Woe is unto me, if I preach not the gospel!" (I Cor. 9:16). Moreover, preaching is purposive. It is to meet the basic needs of men. Some need to be saved, some instructed, some comforted, some inspired. The Christian preacher tries to relate God's message to man's need. V. L. STANFIELD

PREACHING, HISTORY OF. A means of presenting the gospel which is basic to Christianity. Preaching has strongly influenced the spread of Christianity and the depth of its impact upon human life.

Jesus made preaching a large part of his own ministry. In his inaugural sermon at Nazareth, Jesus conceived of much of his task in terms of preaching. Jesus also sent his disciples out to preach during his earthly ministry. Among Christ's last commands to all his followers was the injunction to preach. The apostles took this command of their Lord seriously and went out to be heralds of the good news. A divine compulsion urged them to declare what God had done in Christ and what Christ had done in them. In view of the rapid expansion of the Christian faith, all of the apostles must have been effective preachers, but Peter and Paul are the best representatives because excerpts of their sermons are preserved in the New Testament.

Though Paul gives evidence of knowledge of rhetorical principles, most of the New Testament preaching was simple in form, employing the homily (a running comment on Scripture) or a simple announcement of the good news (*kerugma*). Since there were no church buildings or large congregations, preaching during the first century was informal and conversational, though on a high level. The New Testament period is considered the first climactic age of Christian preaching.

During the first half of the second century, preaching was effective, but some of the glow and enthusiasm of the first century was gone. The preachers of the period came to be called "apostolic fathers" because they were believed to be the disciples of the apostles. The outstanding men of the period were Polycarp, Clement of Rome, Ignatius, Barnabas, and Hermas. These men were faithful to the *kerugma*, and there was a rapid expansion of the Christian faith. Christianity was still largely a lay movement, and the preaching method followed the simple, direct, personal, conversational style of the New Testament period.

The last half of the second century and the third century witnessed essential changes in the form, method, and context of Christian preaching. During this time church buildings were constructed and set liturgies for worship services developed. Various orders were evolving in the ministerial office, and distinctions were made between laity and clergy. Much of the spontaneity and enthusiasm of the early periods disappeared. In fact the preachers of this period were more defenders of the faith than heralds of the good news. Christianity was under attack by the government, by pagan philosophers, and by secular critics. Men like Justin Martyr (100–165), Clement of Alexandria (d. 215), Tertullian (150–225), Origen (185–254), and Cyprian (200–258) were the most effective preachers and the great defenders of the faith and the church. By the very nature of the approach, preaching was on a lower level.

The fourth century witnessed an upsurge of interest in preaching. Actually, the fourth century was another climactic period and produced some of the greatest preachers in the history of the church. Several factors account for the renewal of interest in preaching. In 313 Christianity became the recognized religion of the Roman Empire. Thus persecution ceased, the church had a new social standing, and it became popular and fashionable to attend church services. The study of rhetoric had a chief place in education; consequently, the preachers were trained rhetoricians, and some of them were teachers of rhetoric. Sermons were no longer simple homilies but elaborate discourses. After the Council of Nicea in 325, doctrine was more fixed, and the canon of Scripture was in the process of being closed. This gave a better basis for preaching. Church buildings lost their simplicity and became ornate structures. Worship services were more dignified and ritualistic. Some of the great liturgies of the church had their main development during this period. All of these factors made preaching more pleasing to the populace.

Some of the noted preachers of the fourth and fifth centuries were Basil and John of Antioch (Chrysostom) in the East and Ambrose and Augustine in the West.

Basil (330–379), born of a wealthy family, received the best education which the universities offered. Inspired by ascetic ideals, he renounced his wealth, dedicated his life to the church, and greatly expanded the monastic communities. After being ordained a presbyter in 364, he became Bishop of Caesarea in 370. His preaching centered primarily in ethical topics, and he was a preacher of unusual charm and effectiveness.

John of Antioch (347–407) had prepared himself for law or for government service. Libanius, the most famous rhetorician of the day, was his teacher. However, corruption in government and his mother's Christian example led John to adopt the monastic ideal. First at home and then in the monastery, he gave himself to Bible study, prayer, and the most rigorous ascetic habits. His ability and character soon being recognized, he was forced into ordination and then led to begin preaching. Because of his famous *Homilies on the Statues* and other sermons, he was hailed as the most eloquent preacher in the Eastern church. Taken by deception to Constantinople in 397, he was made Patriarch of that area. Though he interpreted this move to be the will of God, his ideals were so high and his reforms so far-reaching that he was soon banished. About a hundred years after his death, he was given the designation Chrysostom (golden-mouthed), a tribute to his unusual skill in preaching.

In the West, Ambrose (340–397) was a popular, influential preacher. While a government official, Ambrose was elected Bishop of Milan by popular acclaim. Already a skilled administrator and public speaker, he was baptized, was ordained, and gave himself to his new task with unusual diligence. He was a defender of Nicene doctrine and a friend of the poor. He contributed much to church music and worship.

So effective was Ambrose that a young teacher of rhetoric, Augustine (354–430), came to observe his technique. Many factors, including the preaching of Ambrose and the prayers of his own mother, led to Augustine's conversion. After his baptism Augustine began immediately to write and to preach. He had all the qualities of a great preacher. "He had zeal, enthusiasm, imagination, more than a touch of dogmatism, scholarship, a passionate devotion to his Lord, which was born out of a great experience." However, Augustine is probably best remembered as a great theologian and writer. His *Confessions* is a devotional classic; his *On Christian Instruction* is the first real work on interpretation and homiletics; and his works on the Trinity, freedom of the will, necessity of grace, predestination, the sacraments, and reconciliation are great theological treatises.

By the time of Augustine's death in 430, preaching had already begun to decline. The Roman Empire was disintegrating and being overrun by barbarian tribes. Formal liturgies and the centrality of the Mass led to less and less actual preaching. The *kerugma* was largely forgotten, and sermons centered on church duties, special observances, and relics. Christianity was no longer a lay movement with an enthusiastic witness, but a priestly movement, with many of the priests being immoral and unlearned. Moreover, there were no successors to the great preachers of the fourth century. In fact, during this period preaching reached the lowest ebb of any point in its history.

The only rays of light in this period of darkness were the missionary preachers. Some were motivated by a desire to make a spiritual pilgrimage, some to completely fulfil ascetic ideals by leaving the comforts of home or monastery, but many went to other lands to share the good news of Jesus Christ. The central message of these men was that their God was the true God and that men should worship him rather than the heathen idols. Their appeal was essentially that of destruction for those who would not turn to God and blessing for those who would. Beginning primarily in the British Isles, there was an expansion of Christianity on the continent of Europe.

There were a number of outstanding missionary preachers. Columba (521–597) was born in Ireland and trained in the monasteries of Moville and Leinster. In 563 he established a monastery on the Isle of Iona with 12 companions. For centuries this was the famous center of Scottish Christianity and of missionary activity. Augustine of Canterbury (566–607), a slave who was sent back to England by Gregory, was especially effective in winning others to Christ and establishing the policy of the Roman Church. Columban (540–615) was trained in the Irish monastery of Bangor. At the age of 45, he took 12 companions into the Frankish kingdom to spread the missionary message. Boniface (675–754) was not only a missionary to Germany but also an ecclesiastical statesman. He resigned the Archbishopric of Mainz in his last years in order to preach to the heathen, but on one of his first journeys, he was slain by the people he had come to help. Ansgar (801–865) has been called the Apostle to the North. Educated at the monastery of Corbie in France, he volunteered to carry the Gospel to Denmark and Sweden. In a time when preaching had almost ceased, these missionaries felt an inner call to share the *kerugma.*

After the year 1000, new hope came into many areas of life, including religious life. Predictions had been made that this year would bring the end of the world. When this dread prophecy was not fulfilled, men began to live and labor with a new optimism. During the next three centuries, preaching centered largely in the monasteries or in what were essentially monastic movements. By this time the monastic ideal had come to be accepted as the highest expression of the Christian life, and the monastic movement had developed into an affiliation of communities with strong influence on both religious and political life. However, the monastic ideal, though lofty and noble in theory, was unworkable in practice. A group of monks would go out to practice "poverty, chastity, and obedience." Labor brought riches and attracted new people, a town developed outside the monastery, rules were forgotten, worldliness and immorality became dominant. A new group would begin a reform, but the cycle would be repeated.

The outstanding representative of monastic preaching was Bernard of Clairvaux (1090–1153). Born of noble parents, he desired to become a knight but surrendered to a call to the monastic life. So persuasive was he that he took 30 companions with him into the Monastery of Citeaux in 1112. In 1115 Bernard led a group to establish a new monastery at Clairvaux. Largely through his efforts, the Cistercian order was greatly expanded. Bernard became an important man of affairs, the power behind emperor and pope, and the most effective preacher of his century. He was a mystic, giving himself to meditation and prayer; he was sensitive to the needs of others; he gave time to mastering the techniques of sermon preparation. Consequently, when he preached, both the monks in the monasteries and huge crowds in the cities thronged to hear him.

In the 13th and 14th centuries, two essentially preaching movements arose, the "Preaching Brothers" of Dominic and the "Brothers of the Poor" of Francis. Dominic's order was established in 1216, its chief purpose being to convert the heretics by preaching truth. Francis' order was established in 1210, a reform movement which opposed the wealth, luxury, and impurity of the existing monasteries. Dominic (1170–1221) was a preacher of unusual force and fervor, while Francis (1182–1226) was a quiet, conversational preacher, preaching more by example than by word.

The Franciscans and Dominicans made significant contributions to preaching. They were preaching orders when little preaching was being done; they added to the development of the art of preaching; and, along with their founders, other men in the orders were preachers of note. Among these were Anthony of Padua (1195–1231), Berthold of Regensburg (1200–72), Bonaventura (1221–74), and Thomas Aquinas (1225–74).

During the 14th and 15th centuries, preaching was again in a period of decline, with the forces of decay and the forces of reform struggling side by side. In the monasteries and in the regular clergy, there was little preaching. Sermons were usually in Latin and on some religious theme or relic. At the same time the church councils were calling for reform, and a few men were preaching reform. These men were called "morning stars of the Reformation."

Perhaps the most important prereformer was John Wyclif (1320–84). Trained at Oxford, he was a loyal Englishman who opposed interference by the papacy; gradually, he came to feel that many Roman doctrines, including indulgences, purgatory, and transubstantiation, were false. Wyclif's translation of the Bible into English and the sending out of the Lollards, lay preachers, were his greatest works. English Puritanism may have its roots in this background.

John Huss (1373–1415) was trained in the University of Prague, later taught there, and twice served as its rector. He saw many errors in Roman doctrine and was strongly influenced by Wyclif's writings. Huss preached to the Bohemian people in their native language, attacking Roman practices and doctrines. This led to his excommunication in 1412, his condemnation by the Council of Constance, and his burning at the stake July 6, 1415.

The ideas of Wyclif as they were preached by Huss were to influence Luther a century later. Thus the prereformers contributed to the main stream of the Reformation.

Many voices had clamored for reformation within the Church, saying that it should be reformed in "head and members." The 16th century was to witness this reformation. There was a rapid reorientation of religious faith and ideas. Though accused of promoting schism and heresy, the reformers felt that they were recovering the faith of the New Testament and the early church.

The Reformation saw an unusual revival in preaching. Whereas the Mass had been central in worship, the sermon was now restored to its place of importance. The pulpit, instead of the altar, symbolized the major emphasis in churches in Germany, France, Switzerland, Scotland, and other areas touched by the reformers. Preaching was in the language of the people and was bound to the Scriptures both in form and substance. The preaching of the word was recognized as the primary task of the ministry. The purpose of preaching was to lay bare, to expose, to interpret the word of God in the Scriptures. With this revival of biblical preaching, the 16th century has been designated as the third historic culmination of interest in preaching.

The originator and one of the key preachers of the Reformation was Martin Luther (1483–1546). Through a study of the Bible for his teaching at the University of Wittenberg and through an experience of grace which came to him by believing "the just shall live by faith," Luther was prepared to break with Rome. Disturbed by the selling of indulgences and the preaching of their merit, on Oct. 31, 1517, Luther posted his 95 theses, to precipitate debate on the issue. A furor resulted, and during the Leipzig debate (1519) and the Diet of Worms (1521), Luther was forced to deny the authority of the pope, the Church, and even of councils, and to assert the authority of the Scripture. The break was complete, and Luther began to defend his position in writing and to translate the Bible into German. The last years of Luther's life were given to preaching, organizing the new church, and developing a pattern of worship. As did many of the reformers, Luther returned to the use of the homily and gave more attention to the context of the message than to the form of the message.

Another man who began an independent reform work in Switzerland was Zwingli (1484–1531). His study of the Scriptures and the church fathers led him to revolt against the tyranny of Rome. His exposition of books of the Bible to teach true Christian ideas gave him great influence among his countrymen and caused him to be ranked as a gifted preacher and theologian.

Later in date, but perhaps greater in continuing influence, was John Calvin (1509–64). A Frenchman by birth, Calvin did his greatest work in Geneva. His Institutes of the Christian Religion established him as the leading theologian of the Reformation. His leadership, his system of discipline, and his faithful preaching of the word made Geneva a theocracy. As was true of the other reformers, exposition was central in Calvin's preaching. "His commentaries were the fruit of his preaching and lecturing, and his sermons were his commentaries extended and applied." Calvin also gave attention to the worship of the church, and the liturgy which he developed in Strasburg and Geneva was a pattern for others, especially John Knox in Scotland.

Though there were other reformers in England, Hugh Latimer (1490–1555) was the popular preacher. Latimer was witty and preached in a racy, familiar style, making use of the topical method of preaching as well as exposition.

John Knox (1513?–72) was the leader of the Reformation in Scotland. Under the most difficult circumstances Knox was able to effect reform by the sheer force of his character and strength of his preaching. Knox was a forceful, even vehement, preacher who employed invective and sarcasm as he castigated the Catholics for their unscriptural practices. In his pastoral preaching Knox was a faithful expositor. The Scottish pulpit has long followed his example of consecutive exposition.

Other reform preachers of importance were Henry Bullinger (1504–75), who succeeded Zwingli at Zurich and enjoyed unusual popularity; William Farel (1489–1565), who persuaded Calvin to work at Geneva; and Balthasar Hubmaier (*q.v.*) (1480–1528), the Anabaptist, a preacher of great force and eloquence. The reformers gave preaching a place it had not had since the first century.

In the 17th century preaching could not maintain the same high level it reached in the 16th. Nevertheless, the 17th century was called the "classic age of preaching," especially in France and England.

French preaching undoubtedly reached its highest peak during this period. Several factors account for this: (1) It was a period of great national prosperity and growing national spirit and strength. (2) It was a period of unusual intellectual activity in every area. (3) Louis XIV loved preaching and made it popular and fashionable. (4) The Edict of Nantes (1598) gave religious toleration and powerfully stimulated preaching.

Some of the most effective pulpit orators were Roman Catholics, though much of their preaching was art for art's sake. Men like Jacques Bossuet (1627–1704), Louis Bourdaloue (1632–1704), and Francois Fenelon (1651–1710) were masters of every oratorical technique, and their sermons were characterized by sheer beauty of language. Protestant preaching lacked some of the artistry of the Catholic preaching. However, Jean Claude (1619–87), Jacques Saurin (1677–1730), and some others preached sermons of great clearness and force. The scriptural content of Protestant preaching far excelled that of the Catholic. In fact each group served as a stimulus to the other. The Reformed preachers stirred the Catholics to a better content; the Catholics spurred the Reformed preachers to use a better method.

In 17th-century England factors were at work which contributed to preaching. The English people were interested in religious topics, which the King James Version of 1611 greatly stimulated. This century was a period of unusual literary development, and the language was a ready instrument of expression. The morals of the people were in a deplorable state, and this condition generated concern on the part of the ministry. Moreover, there was a struggle for religious freedom and toleration. The church was still dominated by the state, and one of the real struggles was for freedom and the separation of church and state. The preaching of the period by the Anglicans, the Puritans, and the Independents was characterized by a loyalty to the Scriptures. In form the sermons lost some of the naturalness of the previous century and were often long and analytical, having many minute divisions. Some of the leading preachers were Lancelot Andrewes (1555–1624), John Donne (1573–1631), Jeremy Taylor (1613–67), Richard Baxter (1615–91), and John Bunyan (*q.v.*) (1628–88).

In America preaching followed much the same pattern. The American preachers of the period had been trained in the English universities, especially Cambridge; therefore, American preaching was similar in form and content. However, there was much greater freedom, and the Colonial preachers had unusual influence because their preaching dealt with every relevant topic, political and social as well as religious. Some representative American preachers are John Cotton (1585–1652), Thomas Hooker (1586–1647), Roger Williams (1600–84), and Cotton Mather (1663–1728).

The 18th century witnessed a decline in preaching and vitality of church life in both England and America, especially during the early and latter parts of the century. In England the moral tone of the country reached its lowest stage. Drinking, gambling, profanity—every common vice—characterized the land. Because of the influence of deism and skepticism, there was little enthusiasm or desire on the part of the clergy to preach reform. In America only about 5 per cent of the people belonged to the churches, and many of the same moral conditions prevailed. However, a period of revival was to come in both nations—the Evangelical Revival in England and the Great Awakening in America.

Though the Great Awakening has often been termed an outgrowth of the Evangelical Revival, it actually began in the Colonies years before under the preaching of Theodore Frelinghuysen (1691–1751), a Dutch Reformed minister. The revival was continued by Gilbert Tennent (1703–64) and the other "log college evangelists" in New England, then in the middle colonies. In 1734 Jonathan Edwards (1703–58) led in an unusual awakening in his church at Northampton. Edwards possessed extraordinary ability as a thinker, writer, and preacher. He became the exponent and defender of the revival. In 1738 George Whitefield (*q.v.*) made his first of seven visits to America and added fuel to the revival fires. Due to Whitefield's travels and Edwards' writing, news of the revival spread over the colonies, and awakenings began in other areas. The revival moved into the southern colonies under the leadership of such men as Samuel Davies (1724–61), Shubael Stearns (*q.v.*) (1706–71), Daniel Marshall (*q.v.*) (1706–84), and John Gano (*q.v.*) (1727–1804).

The great preachers of the revival in England were George Whitefield (1714–70) and John Wesley (1703–91). Whitefield was a popular pulpit orator. He had a superb voice, a winsome personality, a lively imagination, a dramatic delivery, and intensity of purpose. He charmed audiences in both England and America by the wizardry of his oratory. Though Whitefield's power was chiefly on the platform, thousands believed in Christ because of his preaching, and educational and humanitarian institutions developed from his interests. Perhaps Whitefield's chief claim to fame is that he led John Wesley to begin field preaching. After ordination and after serving as a missionary to the colony of Georgia, Wesley felt his heart "strangely warmed" and came to trust "Christ alone for salvation" (1738). This transforming experience changed Wesley from a cold cleric to a flaming evangel. He began his field preaching in 1739 and rode, wrote, organized, preached, and taught for the next 52 years.

The Evangelical Revival completely changed the religious and social life in the British Isles. This revival saved the country from the moral degeneracy which befell France.

In the 19th century England came to her highest point of greatness in every realm. Naturally, the preaching was influenced by the times, and the 19th-century pulpit occupies an exalted place in the history of preaching. Judged by intellectual power and depth, tested by practical fruits, and viewed in the light of literary criticism, the preaching of this period is marked by maturity. In form and content the sermons have unusual variety. Though there is an increase in the use of topical sermons, there is still much expository preaching. The sermons are shorter and have less formality in organization. Preaching reaches a high level in 19th-century England—perhaps another historic culmination.

Leading British preachers of the century include: Edward Irving (1792–1834), who attracted the greatest crowds since Whitefield; Thomas Chalmers (1780–1847), who led in the formation of the Free Kirk of Scotland; Christmas Evans (*q.v.*) (1766–1838), the leading preacher in Wales; Robert Hall (*q.v.*) (1764–1831), a great metaphysical thinker; John Henry Newman (1801–90), leader in the Tractarian Movement and the leading 19th-century convert to Roman Catholicism; Frederick W. Robertson (1816–53), who skilfully related the Scriptures to personal and social needs; Charles Haddon Spurgeon (*q.v.*) (1834–92), a pastoral evangelist who won thousands to faith in Christ; Joseph Parker (1830–1902), whose popular exposition resulted in the *People's Bible;* and Alexander Maclaren (*q.v.*) (1826–1910), outstanding in his biblical scholarship and exegesis, seen in his *Expositions of Holy Scripture.*

After the Revolutionary War a decline came in religious life in America, except, perhaps, in the southern colonies. However, shortly after the beginning of the 19th century, revivals came in various sections of America. Timothy Dwight (1752–1817) led in an unusual revival among the students at Yale. Charles G. Finney (1792–1875), the leading evangelist during his lifetime, led highly successful evangelistic crusades. At this time revivals were going on in many frontier sections. The two decades before the Civil War (1840–60) witnessed an especially high point in American preaching. Some of the representative men of this era were William Ellery Channing (1780–1842), who crystallized liberal thought into the Unitarian faith; Lyman Beecher (1775–1863), a defender of orthodox faith and a man of evangelical and social passion; and Horace Bushnell (1802–76), who combined intellectual and spiritual power.

After the Civil War the United States changed rapidly from an agricultural to an industrial nation. This change brought both advantages and problems, but the industrial expansion was accompanied by expansion in education and the democratic process. The preachers of the era were shaped by the new movements and in turn influenced them. Preaching enjoyed almost absolute freedom and discussed every idea, political, social, and religious. Among the leading preachers were Henry Ward Beecher (1813–87), a gifted pulpit orator, ranked by some as the greatest in Christian history; Phillips Brooks (1839–93), whose sermons were of the highest literary merit; John A. Broadus (*q.v.*) (1827–05), who was both scholar and preacher; Thomas DeWitt Talmadge (1832–1902), an effective, gifted preacher to the common man; and Dwight L. Moody (1837–99), the leading mass evangelist of the last part of the century.

At the end of the 19th century and at the beginning of the 20th century, a new emphasis came into American preaching. An effort was made to apply the spirit and teaching of Jesus to the social order. The real prophet of the social implications of the gospel was Walter Rauschenbusch (*q.v.*) (1861–1918).

Since World War I American preaching has had many facets, representing different groups and views. When time enough has elapsed to evaluate the preachers, some of these names will probably be listed as the great preachers: George W. Truett (*q.v.*) (1867–1944), Henry Emerson Fosdick (b. 1878), Earnest Fremont Tittle (1885–1945), and Billy Graham (b. 1918).

BIBLIOGRAPHY: J. T. Addison, *The Medieval Missionary* (1936). J. A. Broadus, *Lectures on the History of Preaching* (1899). Y. Brilioth, *Predikans Historia* (1945). E. C. Dargan, *A History of Preaching,* 2 vols. (1954); "A History of Preaching in the United States" (MS); *The Art of Preaching in the Light of Its History* (1922). A. E. Garvie, *The Christian Preacher* (1928). C. S. Horne, *The Romance of Preaching* (1914). J. Ker, *Lectures on the History of Preaching* (1889). H. T. Kerr, *Preaching in the Early Church* (1942). T. W. Pattison, *The History of Christian Preaching* (1903). H. B. Workman, *The Evolution of the Monastic Ideal* (1927). V. L. STANFIELD

PREACHING, SOUTHERN BAPTIST. The activity of a ministry conceived to be divinely appointed, in proclaiming what is believed to be the message of God and in calling on members of a congregation or audience to make active decisions with regard to salvation or personal dedication. With this definition as a basis, Southern Baptist concepts of preaching are based on three implicit and fundamental ideas: that the minister, the one who preaches, is called of God to his work; that the message, that which is preached, is from God, inspired by his Word and his Spirit; and that the hearers, those to whom the message is preached, are intended to be moved to action, to dedication, and to service.

Traditionally, preaching has occupied a large place in the church activity of Baptists. Early Baptist congregations, in reaction against the sacramental ritualism of state churches and in the midst of a time when preaching was extraordinarily good, effective, and influential, gave it large emphasis. Their services usually included from one to several sermons in succession and little else except for prayers, which in length and content partook something of the nature of sermons. Gradually, after Benjamin Keach's time, congregational singing and other activities were included in the service of worship, but the sermon continued to be the focal point of the service and at present it generally occupies about half the total time given to the service of worship.

The relative importance of preaching in the church's program of activity has been affected to some extent by the rise of emphasis on religious education and upon programs of enlistment and instruction which are based more upon educational processes than upon preaching. But it is true that preaching maintains its theoretical importance, reinforced by a theology which gives large place to "preaching the Word," to the notion of the minister as prophet and spokesman of God, and to mass evangelism.

Baptists' belief in the necessity of a divine call for ministers and their conviction that preaching is the message of God delivered through God's appointed messenger have had a great effect on the character of Southern Baptist preaching.

In the first place, the idea of a divine call has clothed the minister and his message with a significant measure of authority. This authority is, of course, not nearly so great as the authority attributed to clerics who are keepers of sacraments—Baptists always reserve large room for the operation of individual judgment. But there is a difference, noticeable in the attitude of the minister and in the attitude of his hearers, between opinions and judgments expressed in preaching and the ordinary statements of man. Baptists are almost always willing to assume, until they have positive evidence to the contrary, that sincere and orthodox preaching, from whatever source, can be used of God to communicate his message.

In the second place, the idea of a divinely called ministry has in large measure kept Baptists from setting up any educational standards or requirements for their ministers. The primary requirement is a satisfactory testimony regarding Christian experience and divine calling. Convinced that God is able to use any talent, however unprepossessing, Baptists have given ordination to all sorts and conditions of men, particularly refusing to require any minimum of education prior to, or as a condition of, ordination. It is true, on the other hand, that churches do not call ministers whose educational level is deficient, measured in relation to their own. Thus the rising level of education among people generally has tended to encourage an increasing amount of preparation for the ministry.

The Baptist conviction that preachers are the messengers of God affects the content of sermons. Baptists have tended to major on fundamentals, on basic appeals to the lost, and on firm and positive affirmations of primary gospel truths and expositions of biblical ideas that are calculated to instruct their hearers and to aid them in their quest for growth in grace. The reality of sin, the goodness of grace, the motivation and necessity of good works, the love of God—these subjects have a large place in Baptist preaching, clothed in many topical forms.

Moreover, Baptists believe that the Holy Spirit is active in preaching. In the past some few ministers have, on the basis of this principle, denied the need for any preparation at all and have depended wholly upon the Spirit to "put words in their mouths" when the time came to preach. This attitude, however, was limited and extreme. In spite of the press of many other duties, the average Southern Baptist preacher considers preparation for preaching of serious importance. Some of them have acquired both depth of scholarship and spiritual maturity, and produce sermons of high excellence. However, many depend not so much on personal creativity but on published sermonic material for much of the content of their preaching.

Belief in the presence of the Spirit, which is generally accepted, lends a measure of authority to the message. In addition, it has led congregations to prefer sermons of a certain type. Baptist sermons are almost never read but are usually more or less extemporaneous in expression, even though studied in content. Occasionally they may be delivered from memory. They are almost always oral rather than literary in style. They contain strong emotional qualities. Since they are Spirit-inspired, they must be spiritually affective; they must strike at the heart. It is for this reason that Baptist sermons are frequently not logical discourses. They are usually more doctrinal than theological, more affirmative than explanatory. Congregations generally prefer preaching that seems to be the overflow of a full heart—spontaneous and fervent. This, they feel, is more spiritual—more in keeping with what they believe about the source and inspiration of the message.

The most determinative characteristic of preaching, as far as Southern Baptists are concerned, is the effect which it is intended to have upon those who hear it. Baptist preaching is preaching for decision, and much else is subordinated to this primary purpose. Preaching is intended to lead to many kinds of decisions. Congregations are asked to support the organizations of their church or its financial program. They are often asked to oppose, more or less actively, some besetting community sin. Individuals are asked to serve in various places of leadership and responsibility in the program of the church and at times are asked to commit themselves to enter definitely Christian vocations. But the most important decision for which preaching calls is the decision which leads to salvation—acceptance of the grace of God through Christ as a personal Saviour. Preaching, for Southern Baptists, is above all evangelistic.

This evangelistic intent has had powerful influence on the character of preaching. In order to be successful in evangelism, sermons must be hortatory. The preacher must be persuasive; the tenor of the sermon must be in harmony with the request for definite action which concludes it. The sermon which serves the ends of evangelism tends to produce an emotional climax. It operates more in the area of spiritual than logical decision, and upon people more easily moved through their feelings than by argument. The object of the sermon is to create the mood most helpful in the decision time at the end of the service.

In addition to these basic essentials, other features are characteristic of Baptist preaching. Baptist sermons of all types have generally been avowedly based on biblical content, but the Bible and preaching have been related in a variety of ways. Traditionally and predominantly, Baptist sermons have been largely either textual or topical. Therefore, ministers frequently have texts as the basis for the presentation of some truth in which they are particularly interested.

Not many give themselves to detailed explanations of texts themselves. The Bible has been interpreted in a variety of ways and with increasing reliability as the educational level of the ministry has gradually been raised. But regardless of vagaries of interpretation, the content of the Bible has been much present in Baptist preaching. Biblical terminology has become the language of doctrine; biblical metaphor, the means of expressiveness; biblical issues, the subject matter of preaching. The rhythms of King James English have had a powerful effect on Baptist rhetoric.

With the increase of formal training, some characteristics of the preaching of many Baptist ministers are changing. Their increasing biblical knowledge has given them greater confidence and ability in expository and didactic preaching. Speech training changes the style of their delivery. Study in related fields has made them aware of problems about which they and their churches had not been concerned. There has, therefore, been an increase in preaching which deals with personal problems, social responsibilities, and community relationships. But to a remarkable degree Baptist preaching has not been basically changed. The fundamental emphases—on the Word of God, on the call of the minister, and on the evangelical purpose of the preaching—have remained.

JUDSON BOYCE ALLEN

PREACHING IN WORSHIP. As in synagogue worship, in the earliest Christian services preaching was a central element. The reading of Scripture and comment upon it were vital parts of synagogue worship, and although a new content and emphasis were given to preaching, the pattern remained much the same throughout the first two centuries of the church's existence. Gradually the Lord's Supper was developed into the mass, and centrality was given to it. Preaching was relegated to an insignificant place and almost ceased. However, the Reformation—giving a new and prominent place to the Bible—again established the centrality of preaching.

In Baptist worship, preaching has always been the primary element in the worship service. Indeed, this has often been carried to such an extreme that the other elements in the service have been considered "preliminaries," or preparation for the main element, preaching. However, by means of the sermon, ideally conceived, God speaks through his called minister. The preacher stands in God's stead, delivering his message. The sermon, then, is the high point in the worship service. This fact does not depreciate the other elements of worship, i.e., praise, prayer, Scripture reading, and offering, but the sermon remains the central act of worship.

V. L. STANFIELD

PREDESTINARIAN BAPTIST. A short-lived newspaper started by R. N. Newport at Charleston, Ill., in 1842.

LYNN E. MAY, JR.

PREDESTINATION. The New Testament term is *proorizō*, "to mark out or determine beforehand." This verb appears in reference to the crucifixion (Acts 4:28), to God's wisdom (I Cor. 2:7), and to the redeemed (Eph. 1:5, 11; Rom. 8:28). Beginning with Augustine and his emphasis on irresistible grace, and continuing through Gottschalk's ninth century emphasis on predestination to reprobation, the doctrine of double predestination was fully developed by Calvin (*Institutes,* III, 21). God's sovereignty, his foreknowledge, divine initiative, his desire for the salvation of all, and human freedom must be considered in determining the biblical view. Baptists usually consider predestination as the act of God in predetermining a plan of redemption and through divine initiative seeking the salvation of all.

See also DETERMINISM.

BIBLIOGRAPHY: L. Boettner, *The Reformed Doctrine of Predestination* (1954).

R. E. GLAZE, JR.

PRE-EXISTENCE. Term referring to existence before the creation of the world. Plato taught that souls pre-existed before their habitation in a body, and was followed by the early Christian theologian Origen. Most Christian theologians have rejected this doctrine.

However, Christian theologians have held that the New Testament teaches the pre-existence of Christ (e.g., John 1:1–14), which is his existence with God the Father in the form of God (Phil. 2:6) from all eternity prior to his birth at Bethlehem in historical time.

See also JESUS CHRIST.

BERNARD RAMM

PREMILLENNIAL BAPTIST GROUPS. In practically every general body of Baptists in America today there are many premillennial Baptists. When division has occurred in Baptist ranks, premillennial views alone have not caused the separation; rather, the question of the millennium has usually been a part of a larger context. However, in practically every case where a schism has taken place in a Baptist general body in protest against theological liberalism, the separating group has held premillennial views. Undoubtedly a part of the great popularity of the premillennial position is that it has been used as a shibboleth against modernism. The usual premillennial view emphasizes the sudden supernatural intervention of Christ in a failing human order, while the usual postmillennial position places great stress on the gradual improvement of the temporal order through the slow working of the leaven of the gospel. Thus, the premillennialist has identified himself with a reliance upon supernaturalism and has related postmillennialism to faith in a social gospel. It is no accident that a strong resurgence of premillennialism occurred when theological liberalism and disastrous world conflict, which undercut the theory that great strides had been taken through human efforts toward a universal peace in the world, had galvanized traditional supernaturalists into revolt. The Baptist groups who separated on the basis of alleged theological liberalism assumed a strong premillennial position generally. This position in a sense was an indication of their basic faith in supernaturalism as the hope of the world rather than in the emphasis which theological liberals placed upon ethics and social elevation.

The General Association of Regular Baptist Churches.—In 1932 a group protesting against theological liberalism separated from the Northern Baptist Convention and formed the General Association of Regular Baptist Churches. The literature of this association makes it plain that the basis of fellowship includes a premillennial interpretation of the last article of the New Hampshire Confession of Faith. The independent agencies through which this association does its benevolent work are unequivocally sympathetic with this point of view. The Los Angeles Baptist Theological Seminary, for example, one of the association's approved schools, has as an article of faith an assertion of belief in "the personal, premillennial, and imminent return of our Lord Jesus Christ."

The Conservative movements.—The foreign and home mission societies bearing the name "Conservative" and the Conservative Baptist Association do not make as clear a statement concerning premillennialism as does the General Association of Regular Baptist Churches. Their constitution simply affirms belief in Christ's "bodily resurrection, His ascension and visible return to the world according to His promise." However, the Conservative groups have had a close relationship with the General Association and have quoted approvingly from the publication of the Southern Baptist Premillennial Fellowship. It is quite likely that the membership of all Conservative bodies favor the premillennial point of view.

Southern fundamentalism.—Premillennialism has been a basic tenet of the movement begun by J. Frank Norris (*q.v.*), Fort Worth, Tex., though the confession of faith by his church simply refers to Christ's "personal, visible return, according to His promise; . . . and the full and final establishment of His Kingdom upon the earth." Almost every issue of Norris' paper (begun in 1917 as *The Searchlight* and renamed *The Fundamentalist* in 1927) has had some reference to the importance of the premillennial point of view.

Southern Baptist Premillennial Fellowship.—On Aug. 5, 1946, John Farrell, Harold Harsh, and Henry Spencer met in Jacksonville, Ill., and launched the Southern Baptist Premillennial Fellowship. By 1953 most of the states in the South had their own Baptist premillennial fellowships, and membership in the larger body totaled over 10,000.

Other premillennial movements.—Various groups holding strongly to premillennial views are legion in Baptist life. Some of these are within the regular Convention territory, North and South; others are outside. There are many independent Baptist churches who are strong adherents of the premillennial doctrine. The American Baptist Association, a part of the Landmark group which separated from the Southern Baptist Convention in 1905, inserts in its doctrinal statement that the second coming of Christ will be premillennial. The group seceding from their ranks in May, 1950, which took the name North American Baptist Association, has the same doctrinal point of view. It reported 1,688 churches and 251,062 members in 1956. New figures showing the strength of the American Baptist Association since this division are not available.

The Northern Baptist Theological Seminary, Chicago, Ill., is generally looked upon as being strongly premillennial. The National Association of Evangelicals is also regarded as being strongly premillennial on an interdenominational basis, although their statement of faith is not specific.

A new organization, the Southern Baptist Fellowship, has a strong premillennial article in its statement of faith. On Mar. 20, 1956, about 100 ministers from the Southern Baptist Convention, the World Baptist Association, the Conservative Baptist group, and independent Baptist churches met at Chattanooga, Tenn., and organized this fellowship. The leader of the group was Lee Roberson, pastor of Highland Park Baptist Church of Chattanooga. The purpose of this body is to "offer fellowship to like-minded Baptists who subscribe to the articles of faith." In the statement of faith is included belief "in the premillennial second coming of the Lord." Along with the organization of this fellowship came the announcement of the withdrawal of Roberson and his church from co-operation with the Southern Baptist Convention.

See also REGULAR BAPTIST CHURCHES, GENERAL ASSOCIATION OF; FUNDAMENTALISM; and RECENT MINOR BAPTIST MOVEMENTS.

BIBLIOGRAPHY: W. H. Rutgers, *Premillennialism in America* (1930). C. E. Tulga, *The Foreign Missions Controversy in the Northern Baptist Convention* (1950). ROBERT A. BAKER

PRESBYTERIAN CHURCH. This denomination grew out of the Reformed tradition in Protestantism, of which John Calvin (1509–64), church reformer and theologian, was the chief architect. Reformed Protestantism spread from Geneva into France, Holland, Great Britain, and, to a less extent, throughout the world. Calvinism was vastly optimistic concerning God and deeply confident that human history could be molded to conform in a large measure to the divine law. This theological perspective gave to Reformed Protestantism a concern for culture and a thrust which issued in its widespread geographic distribution.

All of the churches which make up Reformed Protestantism are governed by presbyterian polity but are not all known as Presbyterian churches. In Scotland, for example, the Reformed faith is expressed in the Church of

Scotland, and in Holland, by the Dutch Reformed Church. The Westminster Confession of Faith, adopted in London in 1646 when the Presbyterians were temporarily in power in England, is the most significant creedal statement of Presbyterianism. Calvin's monumental *Institutes of the Christian Religion, The Westminster Confession,* and *The Canons of Dort* have dominated the theology of the Presbyterian church and have exerted a decisive influence upon the theological outlook of Protestantism.

The term "presbyterian" comes from the Greek *presbuteros,* meaning presbyter or elder. Presbyterianism is thus the name for the belief that the church should be governed by presbyters. The session, the court of the local church, is made up of the pastor, a "teaching elder," and laymen called "ruling elders" elected by the congregation. Presbyteries, synods, and the General Assembly are the other courts of the church. In America the presbytery is the actual center of the government of the church, though the final authority with reference to ecclesiastical or theological matters rests with the General Assembly.

James Moffatt defines the "constitutive principles" of the Presbyterian church as "(a) the parity of presbyters; (b) the right of the people, through their representatives or lay elders, to take part in the government of the Church; and (c) the unity of the Church, not simply in faith and order, but in a graduated series of Church Courts which express and exercise the common authority of the church as a divine society."

Records in early Colonial America indicate the presence of Presbyterian ministers and people in the middle colonies before 1650. The first Presbyterian church organized in the New World was probably at Jamaica, Long Island, N. Y., on June 3, 1672. Francis Makemie, the leading Presbyterian minister in America in the 17th century, was instrumental in the formation of a church at Snow Hill, Md., in 1684. The first presbytery organized in the American colonies, and the first Presbyterian organization in America beyond the level of the local churches, was organized in Philadelphia, Pa., in Mar., 1706.

According to J. C. Beckett in an exhaustive study of Protestant dissent in Ireland, the flow of Scotch-Irish Presbyterians to America began in 1717. Thus, individual Presbyterian churches and the first presbytery antedated the coming of the Scotch-Irish to the colonies. The Presbyterians who preceded the Scotch-Irish in America were English Puritans. There are, therefore, two major sources for the American Presbyterian church, English Puritanism and Scotch-Irish Presbyterianism. It is impossible to understand Presbyterian history in America apart from this twofold origin. English Puritanism afforded a source for American Presbyterianism which has been largely overlooked because the history of the Presbyterian church in America has been written as if it were primarily a projection of Scotch-Irish Presbyterianism into the New World. The co-mingling of these two major sources, plus subsidiary ones, accounts for the uniqueness of American Presbyterianism.

The Philadelphia Synod, the first in the colonies, was organized in 1716. Controversy concerning subscription to the Westminster Confession of Faith and revivalism split the synod in 1741, but the breach was healed in 1759, when the New York Synod, which had been formed in 1745, fused with the Philadelphia Synod. The moderator of the General Assembly, formed in 1788, was President John Witherspoon of the College of New Jersey, who was also the only clergyman to sign the Declaration of Independence.

The Plan of Union of 1801 was an agreement by which the Presbyterian and Congregational churches pooled their missionary resources on the American frontier by forming churches made up of Presbyterians and Congregationalists who might call a minister of either denomination. The Scotch-Irish element in the Presbyterian church became increasingly suspicious of this arrangement and ended it in 1837, forming the Old School Presbyterian Church. Princeton Theological Seminary was the theological center of Old School Presbyterianism, and Charles Hodge (1797–1878), the celebrated Princeton theologian, was its chief apologist. In 1838 the New School Church was organized. The two churches continued separately until 1869, when they united to form the Presbyterian Church in the United States of America—the Northern church. The Presbyterian Church of the Confederate States of America was organized in 1861 and, after the Civil War, became the Presbyterian Church in the United States—the Southern church. Despite recent efforts to unite them, the two groups still persist. The United Presbyterian Church of North America, organized in 1858, is the third largest Presbyterian body in America, with a membership of 217,644 in 1953. At that time the Presbyterian Church U.S.A. numbered 2,482,248 adherents and the Presbyterian Church U.S. had 718,761 members.

BIBLIOGRAPHY: M. W. Armstrong, *et al.*, eds., *The Presbyterian Enterprise: Sources of American Presbyterian History* (1955). J. C. Beckett, *Protestant Dissent in Ireland, 1687–1780* (1946). J. Moffatt, *The Presbyterian Churches* (1928). P. St. Amant, "The Rise and Early Development of the Princeton School of Theology" (1952). L. J. Trinterud, *The Forming of an American Tradition: A Re-examination of Colonial Presbyterianism* (1949). PENROSE ST. AMANT

PRESERVATION. The action of God directed to the sustaining of the world which he has created. God's sustaining relationship to the world and to all rational and irrational creatures therein is direct and immediate. The doctrine, therefore, avoids the deistic view that God is shut out of the world by a system of natural laws. It avoids, also, the pantheistic view that every part of the universe is a pulsation of the divine Being. God's preserving activity uses natural law and conserves human freedom, in accordance with his sovereign and redeeming purpose.

J. E. TULL

PRIEST. The term refers to a person consecrated to the service of deity and considered the medium between the deity and his worshiper. In Old Testament usage a priest was primarily one dedicated to the service of the sanctuary, particularly of the altar, and from the tribe of Levi (Num. 3:5ff.). Considered by many to be leaders of a legal, institutional type of religion which was completely opposed to the prophetic type, priests were conspicuous among those finally responsible for the condemnation and crucifixion of Christ. The term "priest" is also descriptive of Israel's mission to the world (Exod. 19:6) and of the mediatorial-intercessory work of the Messiah-Christ (Psalm 110; Heb. 5–7). In later nonbiblical usage a priest was one authorized or ordained to perform sacerdotal functions.

BIBLIOGRAPHY: W. Baudissin, "Priests and Levites," *A Dictionary of the Bible,* ed., J. Hastings, IV (1905). A. C. Hall, "Priests, Priesthood," *The New Schaff-Herzog Encyclopedia of Religious Knowledge,* ed., S. M. Jackson, IX (1950). W. G. Moorehead, "Priests," *The International Standard Bible Encyclopedia,* ed., J. Orr, IV (1952). A. C. Welch, *Prophet and Priest in Old Israel* (1953).

THOMAS MILES BENNETT

PRIESTHOOD OF BELIEVERS. The teaching that every Christian has direct access to God through the mediatorship of Christ without the necessity of earthly priests (I Tim. 2:5) is frequently called the priesthood of the believer. Each person is his own priest, and approach to God is a priestly function. Because of the holiness of God and the sinfulness of man, there must be a "go-between," a mediator, a priest. Thus Christ is the great high priest, the one and only mediator; and Christians have freedom of access to him by "a new and living way," that is, by their own priestly function (Eph. 2:18; 3:12; Heb. 10:19–22).

The universal priesthood of believers, clearly taught in the Bible, is a concept fundamental to an understanding of the religion of Christ. God's promise to Moses that Israel would be "a kingdom of priests, and an holy nation" (Exod. 19:6) was fulfilled in the New Testament by the ideal Israel, the people of God, the church. Christians are called "an holy priesthood, to offer up spiritual sacrifices" (I Peter 2:5, 9; Rev. 1:6; 5:10; 20:6). There is no priestly class in Christ's religion, for all Christians are on the same level. They are "brethren," and no disciple or group of disciples is above any other (Matt. 23:1–11). The test of acceptance with God is "whosoever shall do the will of my Father" (Matt. 12:46–50).

The priesthood of believers is an essential doctrine because of (1) creation, (2) God's commandments, (3) nature of salvation, and (4) individual responsibility. (1) In creation man was made by God "in our image, after our likeness" (Gen. 1:26–27), a statement which means that man was created with a spiritual nature akin to God. As a spiritual creature he has capacity for fellowship with his Creator. No priest is necessary to make this possible. Man is inherently capable of dealing with God for himself. (2) God's commandments to men, such as the Ten Commandments, are obeyed by individuals, rather than by nations or peoples or priests. (3) Salvation is a personal experience which no priest can produce for another and is a personal response to a personal God. People are saved individually as each of them approaches God for himself on the basis of the blood of Christ and through Christ as high priest (Heb. 10:19–21). (4) Individual responsibility means not only that every person must "give account of himself" (Rom. 14:12), but also that no priest, minister, church, or ordinance can enable a person to render his account to God. Each person is his own priest.

The activities of God's people are described in the New Testament as priestly functions. Access to God is available only to priests, but believers have free access to him; hence they are their own priests (Eph. 2:17–18; 3:12; Heb. 4:16). Coming to God and purification are both priestly functions and are ascribed to believers (I Peter 1:22; 2:4). Activities of God's people are "spiritual" sacrifices, in contrast to the material sacrifices of Old Testament priests (I Peter 2:5). Praise, doing good, and sharing are called "sacrifices" (Heb. 13:15–16). Paul's efforts to minister to the Gentiles is a "priestly service of the gospel of God" (Rom. 15:16 RSV); Paul is glad to be offered as a sacrifice (Phil. 2:17). Missionary gifts are priestly offerings (Phil. 4:18), and the gifts of the churches for the poor saints at Jerusalem are also called "offerings" (Acts 24:17). The priestly function of believers is evident in Paul's exhortation to Christians to present themselves "a living sacrifice, holy, acceptable unto God, which is your reasonable [or spiritual] service [or act of priestly worship]" (Rom. 12:1). God met his priests in the temple, and Christians are called "the temple of God" (I Cor. 3:16; 6:19; II Cor. 6:16; Eph. 2:20–22). Scripturally then, any act or service in the kingdom of God is a priestly act. Singing, praying, giving, worshiping, extending the gospel, and holy living are all activities of the kingdom of priests which God has made of Christians.

Not only are believers to act as priests for themselves, but they have a priestly function in relation to others. They are to make intercession for all men (I Tim. 2:1). Paul calls upon the Corinthian believer-priests for help through their prayers (I Cor. 1:11). Priests are to bring God to the people as well as the people to God. Hence, teaching, preaching, evangelism, and missions may be considered as extensions of the priestly function of believers.

There were no distinctions between clergy and laity in the early Christian fellowship. The concept of a priesthood gradually came into being and developed into the Roman Catholic hierarchy. The dominance of the priestly class and the subjugation of the people led to oppression, hardship, and suffering through the Christian centuries. Periodically, minor groups arose to protest against this dominance, but not until the Protestant Reformation was the yoke of bondage thrown off.

Martin Luther and other reformers used the doctrine of the priesthood of believers in their efforts to overthrow the doctrine of the priesthood of Rome. Later the Anabaptists, forerunners of modern Baptists, pressed the doctrine of universal priesthood into every realm of ecclesiastical life. Today Baptists are the chief exponents of the priesthood of believer's doctrine and its attendant implications.

Implications of the doctrine.—Because of their convictions about the priesthood of believers, Baptists preach (1) justification by faith, (2) believer's baptism, (3) regenerate church membership, (4) the church as a fellowship of believers in a spiritual democracy, (5) private interpretation of Scriptures, (6) freedom of thought, (7) religious liberty, (8) separation of church and state, (9) divine calling for every Christian's occupation, and (10) responsibility for the extension of the kingdom of God on the part of every Christian. Corruptions which Baptists oppose as violating the priesthood of believer's doctrine are (1) infant baptism, (2) baptismal regeneration, (3) forms of church government (such as presbyterian and episcopal) which violate the rights of the people, (4) distinctions between the clergy and laity, (5) an established or state church, (6) persecution, and (7) totalitarianism in any form.

BIBLIOGRAPHY: B. H. Carroll, *Baptists and Their Doctrines* (1910). T. F. Curtis, *The Progress of Baptist Principles* (1856). E. Y. Mullins, *The Axioms of Religion* (1908). W. BARRY GARRETT

PRIMITIVE BAPTISTS. Around the beginning of the 19th century there arose among Baptists much dissension over money-based mission boards, Sunday schools, Bible and tract societies, seminaries, etc. The dissension resulted in a general division, and churches opposing these types of work came to be known as Old School or Primitive Baptists. The first official action, taken in 1827 by the Kehukee Association, North Carolina, was a resolution which read in part: "It was agreed that we discard all Missionary Societies, Bible Societies and Theological Seminaries, and the practices heretofore resorted to for their support, in begging money from the public." Many other associations adopted similar positions.

In doctrine Primitive Baptists are strongly Calvinistic. They "believe and rejoice in the absolute sovereignty of God, their heavenly Father; in the entire dependence of all His creatures upon Him, both in nature and in grace; a doctrine that leads its adherents to abandon all creature power, and to exercise a living and loving trust in the Most High." Their ministers emphasize the doctrines of salvation by grace, election, predestination, effectual calling, and final perseverance of the saints. Since the division of 1832, there have been several subdivisions and factional disputes over points of doctrine and practice, such as predestination, the spiritual birth, resurrection, foot-washing, instrumental music, etc. In the great central doctrine of salvation by grace alone, through the electing love of God the Father, they are agreed. The church ordinances are baptism and the Lord's Supper. Baptism is by immersion only, to believers making a public profession of faith. Many of the churches in the South practice foot-washing; some churches make it a test of fellowship, while others do not.

In church polity Primitive Baptists are congregational, holding that each church should govern itself according to the laws of Christ and that no minister, association, or convention has any authority over the local church. Candidates for the ministry are first recognized by the church and, after being proved, are ordained by examination and laying on of hands by the presbytery. No required course of training is set forth, for they believe the same God who calls his ministers also qualifies them. Although not opposed to education in its normal channels for each individual, Primitive Baptists contend that human institutions were never authorized to prepare people for the gospel ministry.

Officers of the church include elders and deacons. A pastor is chosen by suffrage of the local body to serve for life or from year to year. He receives no set salary but is aided by free-will offerings. Primitive Baptist ministers rarely give full time to the ministry but have some additional means of livelihood. Most Primitive Baptist churches are affiliated in some local association or union, but they have no denominational or organizational headquarters. Their chief medium of communication is through visitation of messengers, church communion, and general correspondence.

Opposed to any auxiliaries to the church, Primitive Baptists, of course, maintain no Sunday schools, seminaries, Bible colleges, or missions. They publish about 15 religious periodicals. Individuals through the years have published various church histories, biographies, and doctrinal discussions. Most of the churches hold meetings once each month, on both Saturday and Sunday. This practice has been followed, no doubt, because churches are scattered in rural sections and pastors usually serve more than one church. The meetinghouses are of simple construction. Services are simple in form, consisting of singing of hymns by the congregation, followed by prayer and preaching, and concluding with a hymn and benediction. Sinners are not exhorted to "accept Christ" or join the church, but opportunity is given for all who feel burdened to make a public profession of Christ and be baptized.

Primitive Baptists do not favor their members' belonging to secret orders or any organization that would compromise Christian principles or alienate them from the church. They are strong defenders of ancient Baptist principles of religious and civil liberty, freedom of conscience, loyal and peaceful citizenship, and honesty and fairness to their fellow men.

Although in their present divided condition it is difficult to determine the exact number of Primitive Baptist churches, there are today approximately 300 associations, 3,000 churches, and over 100,000 members. These bodies are scattered mostly in rural sections through the Eastern, Southern, and Midwestern states.

W. J. BERRY

PRIMITIVE MISSIONARY. A paper begun in 1899 at Winchester, Ill., and edited by B. E. Anthrobus and J. O. Raines, promoting missionaries supported by the Baptist (Gospel) Missionary Convention (organized in same city, 1904) in Syria, Persia, and Galilee. The paper merged with the *Illinois Baptist* in 1905, and Raines became associate editor. The mission work was taken over by the Foreign Mission Board in 1919.

B. J. MURRIE

PRITCHARD, THOMAS HENDERSON (b. Charlotte, N. C., Feb. 8, 1832; d. Charlotte, N. C., May 23, 1896). The son of a Baptist preacher, he attended the academy at Mocksville, N. C., received the A. B. degree from Wake Forest College, 1845; and the D.D. degree from the University of North Carolina, 1868. He read theology with John Albert Broadus (*q.v.*), Charlottesville, Va., 1858, and studied at the University of Virginia, 1858–60. In 1854 he was agent of Wake Forest College. After ordination in 1855, he served as pastor of Hertford Church, N. C., 1855–58, as supply pastor in Fredericksburg, Va., 1859, and as pastor of Franklin Street Church, Baltimore, Md., 1860–63. In 1863 he was imprisoned for refusing to take the oath of allegiance to the United States; when banished to the South, he preached to the Confederate Army. He was supply pastor, First Baptist Church, Raleigh, N. C., 1863–65; pastor, 1868–79; and pastor, First Baptist Church, Petersburg, Va., 1865–68; then president and professor of moral philosophy, Wake Forest College, 1879–82; and pastor of Broadway Baptist Church, Louisville, Ky., 1882; First Baptist Church, Wilmington, N. C., 1883–92; and Tryon Street Baptist Church, Charlotte, N. C., 1892–96. He served as trustee of Wake Forest College, of the University of North Carolina, and of Southern Baptist Theological Seminary; he was one of the committee of seven to recommend removal of the seminary from Greenville, S. C., to Louisville, Ky., in 1872. After 1875 he served as associate editor of the *Biblical Recorder;* wrote one small book, *Infant Baptism,* 1871; and prepared biographical sketches for North Carolina Baptists in Cathcart's *Baptist Encyclopedia.* He was an advocate of common-school education for all. While pastor in Raleigh, he helped establish a college for agriculture and mechanics, now North Carolina State College. He married Frances Guglielma Brinson of New Bern, N. C., Nov., 1858. There were five children: Claudia (Mrs. Aaron Dallas Jenkins), William Broadus, Lauriston Levering, Thomas William, and Frances (Mrs. William Walter Holladay).

BIBLIOGRAPHY: G. W. Paschal, *History of Wake Forest College,* Vol. I (1935). *The National Cyclopaedia of American Biography,* Vol. XXIX (1941). W. Cathcart, *Baptist Encyclopedia.*

G. A. HENDRICKS

PROFESSION OF FAITH. See CONFESSION and REPENTANCE.

PROGRESSIVE REVELATION. The idea of progressive revelation was introduced among Southern Baptists by Edgar Young Mullins (*q.v.*) and followed by Walter Thomas Conner (*q.v.*). According to Mullins, "At each stage there was a communication of life and truth needed for that stage; the revelation contained in itself the principle for development to the next higher stage; the advanced stage in turn conserved the principle of the preceding stage and contained the germ which should expand into the next higher; the lines of development all converged toward fulfilment in Jesus Christ, the crowning revelation." With this underlying principle of progress, a solution is sought not only for the problem of the delayed revelation of God in Christ but also for certain ethical problems presented by the Old Testament. Some regard progressive revelation as in effect an unnecessary concession to the scientific idea of evolution and the philosophical idea of progress and prefer the term "historical revelation" to describe the view of revelation found in Hebrews 1:1–4, Galatians 4:4, and other scriptural references.

DALE MOODY

PROHIBITION. In common usage this term refers to the abolition of the manufacture and sale of alcoholic liquors by legislative enactments for moral reasons. From ancient times alcoholic beverages have been subjected to legal, customary, or religious regulation in nearly all societies, but the predominant association of the word prohibition with this method of dealing with the alcohol problem is a development of the late 19th and early 20th centuries.

National prohibition in the United States was preceded by wide experimentation with restrictions on the sale of intoxicants and with prohibition in local areas. During the first half of the 19th century, public opinion gradually came to favor a more stringent regulation of the sale of intoxicants. This growth in public opinion led to a well-organized temperance movement. Local agitation led to state temperance organizations in Connecticut and Massachusetts as early as 1813. Thirteen years later the first national temperance society was formed, which in 1833 became the American Temperance Union. Through temperance campaigns, education, and the dissemination of literature, the union led the nation to the verge of national prohibition by statewide enactment. But in 1855 there began a retrogression in the temperance movement. For the next 25 years not one additional state enacted a prohibitory law, and many of the states that had enacted such laws repudiated them.

It was at the end of this period, in 1880, that the temperance movement in the United States began to revive. The National Temperance Society had been inaugurated in 1856 to strengthen the temperance movement which had been weakened by the declining influence of the American Temperance Union and by the conditions leading up to the Civil War.

In Aug., 1865, at the Fifth National Temperance Convention meeting at Saratoga Springs, N. Y., with 325 delegates from 25 states, the American Temperance Union was merged with the National Temperance Society and Publication House, through which merger the temperance forces of the nation were united. The strong promotional and educational program of this society was augmented in 1874 by the organization of the Woman's Christian Temperance Union and, in 1893, by the Anti-Saloon League. From platform and printed page, through school and church, the temperance forces of America, working with the aid of an increasing number of state temperance groups, led in the adoption of the prohibition amendment to the national Constitution.

The first official action taken by the Southern Baptist Convention against the liquor traffic was in the annual Convention of 1886, 30 years after the organization of the National Temperance Society and 14 years after the organization of the Woman's Christian Temperance Union. In 1888 the president of the Convention ruled out of order a temperance resolution on the grounds that such an action was not in keeping with the purpose of the Convention. Every year since that time, with few exceptions, the Convention has approved statements opposing the traffic in beverage alcohol.

In 1908 the Convention appointed a standing committee on temperance, which was merged in 1915 with the Social Service Commission, and through which the Convention continued to carry forward its opposition to the liquor traffic.

The Convention has repeatedly declared its position on beverage alcohol to be "total abstinence for the individual and total riddance of its manufacture and sale by the state." In its annual session of 1955 the Convention adopted a program for alcohol education to be promoted by the educational facilities of the Sunday School Board, by seminars for leadership training, by wide distribution of effective literature, and by co-operation with the state and national leagues for necessary political action.

See also CHRISTIAN LIFE COMMISSION and NATIONAL TEMPERANCE SOCIETY and PUBLICATION HOUSE.

A. C. MILLER

PROMOTION, SOUTHERN BAPTIST METHODS OF. Those methods which Southern Baptist agencies employ to acquaint their constituencies with their program and needs and to secure adequate support for their work. Early emphasis was on special offerings for designated causes. Later, methods developed toward efforts to enlist all church members in the regular proportional support of a unified program for the local church and all denominational causes.

Prior to the Baptist 75 Million Campaign, projected in 1919, each agency of the Southern Baptist Convention and the state conventions conducted its own promotional programs in its own way without reference to what similar agencies were doing.

The Convention from its organization sought to elicit, combine, and direct the energies of the denomination for the propagation of the gospel. Much was done from the beginning. Its efforts were not completely successful, as indicated by the report of the Home Mission Board after its removal to Atlanta:

> What we need is some system of contribution in all our churches by which every member will be reached, and the mites of the poor as well as the munificent offering of the rich flow into the treasury of the Lord. That system, whatever it may cost . . . we must have. . . . The grandest duty of the hour . . . is to devise and make effective some plan.

Its report in 1900 asked the Convention whether, instead of giving its full time to "a Survey of the work on the mission fields," it might not use its brain-power and heart-power to find a way to reach the people and induce them to have part in the support of missions lest the denomination continue "simply to play at missions and our God-given Baptist church polity . . . be discounted among men for its inefficiency."

There was one vice-president of the Convention from each state. He was considered a promotional agent for the Convention in his state and was expected to do what he could and make a report of his efforts to the next Convention. In 1900 a committee on co-operation was named to seek a way of "securing the active and regular cooperation of every church . . . in the work of each of our Boards, and as far as possible personal contribution from every member of every church."

The Foreign and Home Mission boards, the Sunday School Board, and the seminaries made annual reports to the Convention, sent their representatives to address the state conventions, and provided news reports of their semiannual meetings and occasional display ads to the Baptist state papers. The mission boards and seminaries maintained representatives who visited the churches, presented the work of the agency, and took offerings. Most pastors preached special sermons on foreign and home missions in advance of the Convention, and on state missions shortly before the annual meetings of the state conventions in the fall. Following each sermon a public cash collection was taken for the cause presented. For financing their work the agencies relied upon the work of the field representatives and the special offerings taken by them and by the pastors. A special offering of cash, groceries, and clothing was usually taken for the orphanages around Thanksgiving. Every state agency was given a hearing at the sessions of the district associations. Many of the colleges and orphanages employed field representatives who traveled over the states, soliciting pupils and cash, while representatives of the seminaries visited the campuses of the larger colleges in the spring to confer with senior young men and women who were planning to enter the ministry and mission work.

The Foreign Mission Board projected its own mission magazine, *The Commission,* in 1849, which was published until 1851 and then resumed for five years, 1856–61. The board later published the *Foreign Mission Journal,* 1874–1916. The Home Mission Board published *Home Fields.* The Convention meeting in Asheville, N. C., in 1916 instructed the consolidation of these two publications. The first issue of the combined journal, *Home and Foreign Fields,* published by the Sunday School Board, appeared in November. This periodical was discontinued in 1937 when the Foreign Mission Board resumed the publication of *The Commission,* and the Home Mission Board established *Southern Baptist Home Missions.* Valuable work was done each year in behalf of both the general mission boards and state missions, as well as by the Woman's Missionary Union through its study courses and annual weeks of prayer and special offerings in behalf of each of these causes.

Limitations to the plan of relying upon the work of field agents were obvious. The number of churches which could be reached was severely limited, and the cost was high. Offerings received were often dependent on weather or other local conditions or upon the personality, speaking voice, and approach of the representative more than upon the needs and the merits of the cause. The total received by an agency during the year was determined, not by the need of the agency in comparison with that of other Convention agencies or the ability of Baptists to give, but by these other factors. Income was intermittent and seasonal and tended to come in larger amounts immediately preceding the meeting of the Convention. The Foreign Mission Board reported in 1899, "During the last 24 hours of the conventional year $20,000 came into the treasury—more than was received in May, June, and July." Sometimes the seasonal nature of receipts was even more striking. This led to keeping the books open to the last possible minute, which did little to improve habits of giving. Still worse, it compelled the agencies to borrow sometimes for nine to eleven months of the year in hope of paying with the last few months' offerings. Some part of the blame for the burden of debts in subsequent years was doubtless rooted in this pattern and practice. In 1909 in a report of the committee on systematic beneficence, Edwin Charles Dargan (*q.v.*), chairman, deplored this situation and sought a better way.

The 75 Million Campaign changed and improved this picture by seeking regular gifts each week throughout the year for each cause. Each pastor became in effect a field representative of each of the causes. Following the increased offerings for all denominational objects that attended the 75 Million Campaign, both the Convention and the various state conventions decided to follow up that movement with some combined educational and promotional program in behalf of all the general interest of the denomination, both Convention-wide and statewide.

Accordingly, the Convention at Washington in May, 1920, appointed a large Conservation Commission charged with conserving all the financial and spiritual aspects of the 75 Million Campaign by providing the needed information through printed matter and inspirational addresses. This commission was also asked to enlist the co-operation of all the state secretaries in promoting a unified support for all the general work of the denomination.

A new feature was added to the promotional program for the spring of 1921: a six weeks' intensive Convention-wide effort was projected by the Conservation Commission when the churches were asked to enlist their members in making monthly and weekly payments on their 75 Million Campaign pledges.

When the Convention met at Jacksonville, Fla., in May, 1922, a committee was named to bring a special report on stewardship. This report urged that all denominational officials and churches co-operate in an intensive teaching of the Bible doctrine of stewardship with all its implications and the duty of every Christian to give of his means, both proportionately and systematically.

At the same session the Conservation Commission recommended that the churches seek to enlist all new members in making pledges to the 75 Million Campaign, co-operate in a simultaneous every-member canvass in behalf of all denominational causes, and give consideration to the need of setting up permanent financial plans.

Again, in May, 1923, the Conservation Commission called the attention of the Convention to the need of continued emphasis upon systematic, proportionate, and regular giving to all general denomination causes, as well as local church support, until every member of every church had been enlisted in such a program. At this same session the Convention adopted a resolution calling upon its seminaries and training schools to place in their curricula a thorough, comprehensive course in church finance calculated to help pastors and their staffs organize the churches for using systematic and scriptural methods of finance. Baptist colleges were likewise urged to provide similar courses, while the International Lesson Committee was requested to provide in the Uniform Sunday School Lessons at least two lessons a year on stewardship.

At the Convention in Atlanta, Ga., in May, 1924, the Conservation Commission reported that Oscar Eugene Bryan (*q.v.*) had been engaged as budget director to encourage the churches in adopting annual financial budgets; that the state conventions had named budget workers; and that the message of systematizing kingdom finances had been carried through the district associations out to the individual churches.

At the same meeting the Convention named a Future Program Commission, which made a tentative report to the sessions. In its first annual report in 1925 to the Convention meeting in Memphis, Tenn., it was reported that about 500,000 Southern Baptists had been enlisted as regular givers and that approximately 28 per cent of the churches had adopted a well-defined system of finance.

Field agents continued to be used for a time, however. The Commission on the Cooperative Program, in its 1926 report, estimated that in the states and Convention "not fewer than 100 special paid agents have been employed at an estimated cost of more than $300,000." But it reported encouragement in the many large and influential churches committed to the budget plan of giving, resulting in "development of this steady and quiet stream of benevolence."

In 1927 the promotion work previously done by the Commission on the Cooperative Program was committed to the new Executive Committee and to a promotion committee, composed of the Executive Committee, executive heads of Convention boards and agencies, state secretaries, and state editors. In 1933 the entire work of promotion was committed to the Executive Committee, which was to plan all promotion programs in conference with executive heads of Convention boards and agencies and seek to mobilize, co-ordinate, and utilize the promotional possibilities in the agencies.

In 1933 the Baptist Hundred Thousand Club was formed to raise funds for the payment of Convention debts. Frank Tripp was named general leader. In 1936 the Convention authorized a director of promotion to promote the Cooperative Program, the Hundred Thousand Club, and stewardship. James Edgar Dillard (*q.v.*) served in that post 1936–48.

The objectives of the department of promotion were described thus in 1940:

> To inform all our people concerning all of the cooperative work of the denomination; to promote unity and cooperation among the agencies and institutions of the denomination; to promote without discrimination all the cooperative causes of the denomination; to enlist our people in the intelligent, cheerful, systematic and liberal support of all our work; to cultivate an intelligent cooperative constituency that will provide a permanent and stabilized income for the adequate support of our work; to pay all our debts before 1945 without crippling or curtailing any of our work.

Four primary elements in the promotion program were indicated: major on the Cooperative Program; promote the special days and seasons set out in the denominational calendar; stress the Hundred Thousand Club; promote the continuous systematic study, teaching, and practice of Christian stewardship with the tithe as the minimum standard of Christian giving.

The Convention by its bylaws instructs the Executive Committee "To conduct the general work of promotion and the general work of publicity for the Convention in cooperation with other agencies and institutions of the Convention." Thus the executive secretary, currently Porter Wroe Routh, has the primary responsibility, which in turn by the committee's bylaws is committed to its promotion committee.

In the office and staff organization the Convention's responsibility in promotion is shared by two divisions within the Executive Committee: promotion and publications. The division of promotion leads in long-range and immediate planning of the promotion programs in full conference with Convention and state promotion leaders in a semiannual promotion conference; maintains contact throughout the year with Convention and state promotion leadership on matters relating to the promotion programs; co-operates with all other Convention agencies and departments and all state agencies in programs related to promotion; writes tracts, articles, and booklets as needed; fills limited field engagements in promotion meetings in states, assemblies, meetings of leadership groups; participates in a limited number of state conventions annually; presents a promotion program to the Convention annually; studies current and prospective programs of enlistment in stewardship and related matters as used successfully in church, denominational, and business fields. It led in the development of the new church finance program of Southern Baptists, introduced in 1956. Merrill D. Moore has served as director of promotion and associate secretary since Jan., 1948.

The division of publications produces the literature and materials for implementing the promotion programs. The tract service edits and produces tracts and distributes them through state convention offices; the *Baptist Program*, a leadership magazine begun in 1919 as (75 Million) *Campaign Talking Points*, goes without charge to every Convention pastor; the weekly bulletin service is edited by the division and sold to the churches by the Sunday School Board; *Baptist Press*, a news service, goes to all Baptist state papers and certain other outlets. Southern Baptist Convention Stewardship Services distributes materials relating to the new church finance program of

Southern Baptists. Albert McClellan has served as director of publications and associate secretary since 1949. Predecessors who have served as publicity directors were Frank Burkhalter, 1919–30, Walter Murchison Gilmore (*q.v.*), 1930–46, and Cyril E. Bryant, 1946–49.

Promotion in most states is considered a function of the state executive secretary. In most states an associate to the secretary carries specific responsibilities in stewardship promotion. In a few, separate stewardship departments are set up. Georgia in about 1930 inaugurated an annual series of regional promotional meetings throughout the state in the spring. Now many states have regional meetings; others have a meeting in each association each year to promote the current stewardship and Cooperative Program emphases.

The church finance program of Southern Baptists introduced in 1956 has a specific, detailed, uniform, and complete program to offer all churches, whether rural, town, or city. The states are offering this plan in these promotion meetings and in state and associational clinics. MERRILL D. MOORE

PROMOTION CONFERENCE. A semiannual meeting of the promotion leadership of the Southern Baptist Convention to make advance plans for promoting the Cooperative Program and stewardship throughout the Convention and to consider promotion matters. Formerly called the Promotion Joint Conference, the conference is composed of members of the promotion committee of the Executive Committee, the executive secretaries of the state conventions and their promotion associates, editors of state papers, and executive heads of Convention boards and agencies and certain of their associates.

The pattern for the promotion conference was found in the action of the Convention in 1927 and 1928 when it named a promotion committee, composed of the Executive Committee, heads of Convention boards and agencies, secretaries of the state boards, and editors of state Baptist papers. In 1933 the promotion responsibility was committed entirely to the Executive Committee, which was to "plan the details of all . . . promotional programs" in conference with executive heads of Convention boards and agencies. The first promotion conference as such, however, met in Aug., 1949, at Ridgecrest, N. C., and the second in June, 1950, in Nashville, Tenn. It now meets one to three days in advance of the June and December meetings of the Executive Committee. Special conferences were held in May, 1951, at Edgewater Park, Miss., and in Mar., 1952, in Oklahoma City, Okla.

Promotion plans for each year are made in detail, and plans are projected several years in advance. A future program committee makes special studies and recommendations relating to programs for future years. The conference makes recommendations to the promotion committee, a subcommittee of the Executive Committee. The conference proposed graded Schools of Stewardship for 1953, which were reported by 10,000 churches. When Cooperative Program receipts reached approximately $19,000,000, it proposed a 1955 goal of $34,000,000. This goal was exceeded. The promotion conference originally proposed the Third Jubilee Program for Baptists and the $52,000,000 Cooperative Program goal for 1958. Through this conference were developed the plans for the new forward program of church finance of Southern Baptists.

The chairman of the promotion committee serves as chairman of the conference. Those who have served include C. C. Warren, J. Norris Palmer, and R. Archie Ellis.

MERRILL D. MOORE

PROMOTION IN RELIGIOUS EDUCATION, DENOMINATIONAL PROGRAM OF. Illustrative of early efforts to promote religious education in the states were: (1) the Virginia Baptist Sunday School Association, organized in 1838 and functioning under various names for more than 50 years before it was absorbed into the Virginia Baptist General Association; (2) a state Sunday School Association formed in Georgia in 1853 with a paid agent; and (3) the employment of full-time Sunday school agents in Kentucky in 1866, in Alabama in 1872, and in Georgia in 1874. The Sunday School Board, organized in 1891, gave great impetus to the promotion of Sunday school work in the states by contributing Bibles, books, periodicals, money, and the assistance of field secretaries. In 1906 the board enlarged its policy of co-operation to include cash contributions to the six state boards (Georgia, Kentucky, Mississippi, North Carolina, Oklahoma, and South Carolina) which had their own Sunday school secretaries. This policy, which continues in operation, has resulted in the establishment of Sunday school departments in all the states affiliated with the Southern Baptist Convention. The policy was extended to Training Union (B.Y.P.U.) work in 1915, student work in 1929, and church music promotion in 1944. In 1956 there were 16 state Sunday school departments, 16 state Training Union departments, 16 state student departments, and 11 state church music departments. Seven state conventions (California, Colorado, Kansas, Ohio, Oklahoma, Oregon-Washington, and District of Columbia) had departments of religious education in which two or more phases of the work were combined. In 1956 there were 312 workers employed in these departments. Each department has a secretary (sometimes called superintendent or director) elected by the state board. Many departments have additional workers specializing in the age groups, Vacation Bible school, and associational work. These departments are under the direction of the state boards but are financed jointly by the state boards and the Sunday School Board. Both state conventions and the Southern Baptist Convention maintain summer assemblies which are also means for educational promotion.

The Baptist district association offers another effective medium for promoting educational work. A completely organized Sunday school association has a superintendent, associate superintendents in charge of evangelism and training, group superintendents, and nine department superintendents. It meets monthly or quarterly. The Training Union association should have a director, an associate director, group directors, and seven department directors. The recommended schedule calls for executive committee, officers and leaders' council, and mass meetings each quarter. Both Sunday school and Training Union associations sponsor enlargement campaigns, training schools, clinics, and other improvement projects. The suggested associational organization for promoting church music consists of a director of music education and other officers recommended by the departments of music of the state and the Sunday School Board. The moderator and associational missionary work with all associational organizations. J. M. CROWE

PROPHECY. Through the prophets divine revelation was given during the Old Testament preparation for the coming of Christ.

The prophet and the shrine.—There seems much evidence that the prophets formed a large class in early Israel. The variety of Hebrew names given to them, although all were later embraced within the category "prophets," indicates the diversity of ways in which their message was given, from divination through dreams to ecstatic utterance. Their various means of prophecy constitute a similarity with the Near Eastern background. Some prophets banded themselves together in schools; others were solitaries. There are indications that the prophets were officers in the local high places and worked alongside the priests, being responsible for the oracular side of worship. From their ranks arose false prophets who prophesied smooth things. Undoubtedly, however, many were true servants of God, associated with the distinctive line of prophets which carried the burden of the divine revelation. In post-Exilic times the prophets' ministry was continued in the guilds of Temple singers and preserved in the book of Psalms.

The nature of prophecy.—Upon a psychological basis the prophets had features in common with phenomena in the religions of the ancient Near East; the prophets were distinguished not so much by their methods as by the content of what they said. Hence the predominant issue became that of differentiating between a true prophet who had the word of God and a false prophet who uttered lies and prophesied smooth things (Deut. 13:1–3; I Kings 22; Jer. 14:13–16; 23:9–32; 27:8–11; 28). The differentiating marks appeared, not in the way the message was delivered, but in its content and in the expression of that content in the prophet's own life. The essential word of God through the message of a true prophet had a self-authenticating quality; the true prophet could fall back upon his own inner assurance of God's truth, whereas the false prophet could not. Again, the true word of God was morally and spiritually consistent with what God had already shown himself to be also, the prophet's moral and spiritual life bore testimony to the authenticity of his message. Finally, what God had said through the prophet would be fulfilled through history and proved true by events.

Revelation through the prophets was marked by God's taking hold of the psychological makeup, moral consciousness, and religious capacities of a man so that he became God's mouthpiece, an extension of God's personality, thinking God's thoughts and revealing God's message. There was a unique *pathos* in the heart of the true prophet whereby he was enabled to enter sympathetically into God's counsels, share in the divine thoughts, and have insight into the eternal purpose.

The line of prophets.—Moses, according to the testimony of Deuteronomy (18:15), illustrates the true prophetic task in interpreting current events in the light of God's purpose for Israel. Thus Moses promised deliverance from the oppression of Egypt in the light of God's purpose for his chosen people, interpreted the crossing of the Red Sea in terms of that same purpose, and declared the conditions which God laid upon his people in the Decalogue given on Sinai. God's present action has to be interpreted in terms of God's ultimate intention. The prophet further declares that the underlying principles of God's historical activity are essentially moral. God is the Lord of history who requires obedience of his people; he will visit upon them and upon all nations their iniquity. Thus prophetic revelation speaks to the contemporary situation in the light of God's certain and moral purpose which is moving to fulfilment through the events of human history. God fulfils his moral purpose through and reveals it in human history; the long line of prophets draws out the deep significance of this revelation. Following Samuel, Nathan, Elijah, and Elisha is a succession of literary prophets whose messages are preserved in the books of Isaiah, Jeremiah, Ezekiel, and the twelve minor prophets, of whom Amos, Micah, and Hosea are the most significant.

The call of the prophets.—The unique quality of the prophets is seen in their sense of divine election for their task. Each began his ministry with an authentic experience in which God laid hold of him and gave him that insight into his purpose which was to constitute his message (Amos 7:14–15; Isa. 6:1–13; Jer. 1:1–19; Ezek. 1–3). The prophets stood uniquely within God's plan as men whom he had called.

The message of the prophets.—The prophets spoke to the present in the light of the future, condemning present sin in the light of the judgment which was soon to come and promising the hope of deliverance if Israel would repent. There were four elements in the prophets' message:

1. The Sovereignty of God. The prophets were certain that history is overruled by God in judgment and in mercy. They saw that God's sovereign power and purpose were behind the movements of nations and decisions of men. God used Assyria and Sennacherib as the scourge of judgment on sinful Judah; he employed Persia and Cyrus, who did not know him, as agents to deliver his people from exile (Amos 1–2; Isa. 10:5–19; Isa. 45:1–6).

2. The Day of the Lord. The present activity of God in history is clear only to faith; it is hidden by man's sin. Hence the prophet looked for final vindication to that day which would be filled with a revelation of God's sovereignty. The day of the Lord is the ultimate consummation of history in which God's glory will be disclosed in judgment and in mercy, and his purpose fulfilled (Zeph. 1–3).

3. The Remnant. The day of the Lord will be judgment on Israel, but it will be a purging judgment. The dross will be consumed, but a remnant will survive in whom God's promise to Abraham will be fulfilled (Isa. 1:25–27; 7:3). This remnant of the Chosen People will truly be God's people, fulfilling his will. Zion will be restored and become the center of the remnant's life and worship. Nature and the wild beasts will be renewed to provide a fitting environment for the restored community (Isa. 11:6; 65; 25). Jeremiah declared that all these things were possible for the remnant because God would make a new and inner covenant with his people and write his law on their hearts (Jer. 31:31). Ezekiel perceived that the day of the Lord would come when God created in man a right spirit and a new heart (Ezek. 11:19). The prophet of the Exile knew that such a new covenant could only come when the Suffering Servant of God would hear the sins of Israel and of all nations so that men might draw near to God through his sacrifice (Isa. 53).

4. The Messiah. The restored Israel would be ruled over by a Messiah appointed by God as his representative and springing from the seed of David (Jer. 23:5). The Messiah would rule with righteousness and judge with equity; the Spirit of God would rest upon him (Isa. 9:2–7; 11:1–5). God would bring him to his kingdom, riding on an ass (Zech. 9:9); the Messiah would spring from Bethlehem, the ancestral home of David (Mic. 5:2). It seems clear that the prophet of the Exile identified the Suffering Servant ultimately with the Messiah, although he seems also to have had Israel and the remnant in mind. The Servant would be the representative of the true Israel; through his suffering the promise to Abraham would come true. Thus the Messiah would also be Israel's Saviour. This concept of the Messiah is echoed in Psalm 22 and Jonah. The Messiah of the day of the Lord would be an eschatological Saviour who would establish a new covenant in the hearts of men.

Prophecy and the New Testament.—The preaching of the early church was filled with the conviction that the day of the Lord had dawned and the hopes of the prophets had been fulfilled. Careful examination of Christ's preaching makes it clear that he himself believed the day of the Lord had dawned with his coming, and the time had been filled full of God's kingly rule in judgment and grace. Christ identified himself with both the Messiah of David's line and the Suffering Servant; he believed that through his death a new Israel would be established, a new covenant would be made in the inner hearts of men, and the forgiveness of God to sinners would become a reality. The New Testament writers all affirm this, each in his own distinctive way. Christ is the Messiah, the Servant through whose suffering all men are brought near to God, the maker of a new covenant through his sacrificial death. The church is the new Israel, the true remnant of God. The believer can enter God's kingdom by faith and receive the Holy Spirit as an earnest of his future inheritance. Yet the hope still remains, and the promise to Abraham still awaits final consummation, when the return of the Lord will finally unveil his glory, and the humiliated Servant will be revealed as the glorious King in the midst of his people.

BIBLIOGRAPHY: T. H. Robinson, *Prophecy and the Prophets in Ancient Israel* (1953). R. B. Y. Scott, *The Relevance of the Prophets* (1952). A. Welch, *Prophet and Priest in Old Israel* (1953). E. C. RUST

PROPITIATION. The means of restoring fellowship between God and man. Paul said of this term, "Whom [Christ] God hath set forth to be a propitiation through faith in his blood" (Rom. 3:25). The original meaning of propitiation was to cause a hostile person to become favorable; this definition led men to think that God needed to be rendered favorable to man. According to the Christian view, God provided propitiation because he loved man and desired to remove the barrier of sin in order to reveal that love. And God was pleased, not by the death of Christ, but by the reconciliation which it accomplished (Heb. 2:17; I John 2:2).

See also ATONEMENT and EXPIATION.

BIBLIOGRAPHY: W. T. Conner, *The Gospel of Redemption* (1945). A. Ritschl, *The Christian Doctrine of Justification and Reconciliation* (Trans. by H. R. Mackintosh) (1902). CHARLES A. TRENTHAM

PROTECTION PLAN, BAPTIST EMPLOYEES. Designed to meet the basic retirement needs of ordained ministers and lay workers employed by the 56 boards and agencies cooperating in the Baptist board group. (The absence of the word "boards" indicates new board plans inaugurated Jan. 1, 1955, when the old Baptist Boards Employees Retirement Plan was closed to new members.) Dues are 5 per cent for employee and 11 per cent for employer, increasing ½ per cent at age 50 and another ½ per cent at age 60. If member works beyond age 65, dues increase another ½ per cent. The plan, designed for male employees, carries widow protection. The basic retirement annuity is based on number of years in the plan and salary on which dues are paid (limited to $4,000 per year). Credit of 1½ per cent is given for each year of participation in plan. For example: A member participates from age 25 to age 65 at an average salary of $4,000 per year. His annuity would be 60 per cent of this, or $2,400 per year. The widow annuity, after member has been in plan six years, is 40 per cent of his potential annuity. In the example given, widow annuity would be $960 per year. For total and permanent disability, an annuity up to $900 per year is payable, based on years of participation and salary. Early retirement after age 60 is available on a commuted annuity. If member leaves denominational service, 60 per cent of amount he has paid, plus interest, is returnable. RETTA O'BANNON

PROTESTANT EPISCOPAL CHURCH. Episcopalianism is the American version of Anglicanism. Its history, government, doctrine, and worship are properly understood only in the light of this fact. In the Colonial period no distinction was made between the Church in England and the Colonies, and no separate organization was formed. It was the established church of six Colonies. The Revolution brought great loss, and reorganization along national lines and provision for a native Episcopate became necessary. The General Convention of 1789 adopted a constitution and Prayer Book which set forth the name and general outline of the government and worship of the Protestant Episcopal Church in the United States of America. By this time, too, Samuel Seabury (1729–96), William White (1748–1836), and Samuel Provoost (1743–1815) had secured consecration as bishops from overseas.

The early 19th century was a difficult time for Episcopalianism. Gradually a new leadership and an aggressive program of expansion brought the church by 1840 into the relative position of strength that it holds today. There arose in these years two distinct parties, the High Church and the Evangelical, the latter absorbing the older Low Church party. The crest of Evangelicalism had passed by 1850, but the High Church party, as Anglo-Catholicism, continues to exert a powerful influence. Division of the church was prevented by men like William A. Muhlenburg (1796–1877) who regarded themselves as Evangelical Catholics. A permanent split over the slavery controversy and resulting war was also avoided, though a Protestant Episcopal Church in the Confederate States existed during the hostilities. A liberal spirit akin to that which characterized the Anglican Broad Church movement arose in the mid-19th century. It has maintained sufficient influence to make the Episcopal Church one of the most flexible and comprehensive in the United States.

Though the spiritual functions of the church are in the hands of the clergy, the priest is assisted in the local administration by the vestry, and the bishop in the diocese by conventions of clergymen and laymen. The highest authority, the General Convention, is composed of a House of Bishops and a House of Deputies consisting of an equal number of clergymen and laymen. The National Council, with its Presiding Bishop, is elected by the General Convention to act for it between its triennial sessions.

Episcopalianism holds that the Bible is the Word of God and that its principal teachings are clearly expressed in the Apostle's Creed and the Nicene Creed, which compose a sufficient statement of doctrine. The Thirty-Nine Articles, though important for information, are not essential statements. The words of the Prayer Book are, for practical purposes, a source of doctrinal expression, but even these are subject to change. There is, therefore, great possible latitude, room for independent thinking, and, hence, great variety in the doctrinal position of Episcopalians.

The principal source of unity appears to lie in the usage by all of the Book of Common Prayer, which outlines and gives content to a way of worship. The services of the Prayer Book are required usages, though deviations are tolerated. The resulting worship is primarily liturgical, with much emphasis upon the sacraments.

BIBLIOGRAPHY: J. T. Addison, *The Episcopal Church in the United States, 1789–1931* (1951). *Book of Common Prayer and Administration of the Sacraments.* E. C. Chorley, *Men and Movements in the American Episcopal Church* (1950). G. Hodges, *The Episcopal Church* (1935). *The Living Church Annual.* W. W. Manross, *A History of the American Episcopal Church* (1950). J. A. Pike and W. N. Pittenger, *The Faith of the Church* (1951). E. A. White, ed., *Annotated Constitution and Canons for the Government of the Protestant Episcopal Church in the United States of America* (1954).

POPE A. DUNCAN

PROVIDENCE. The biblical idea of providence is that the universe, which was created by an act of the will of God (Gen. 1:3), is so sustained and governed by God as to realize the all-embracing purpose of God for his creation. This purpose is related to all men, with Israel as the instrument of its revelation.

God's sovereignty is exercised in moral and ideal methods rather than mechanical and fatalistic ones. He designs to create and bring to maturity free and responsible persons. That his purpose involves real risk is evidenced by the fact of sin, the contradiction and rejection of much that is known to be the will of God.

That God does not control all of his creation is demonstrated by every appearance of evil. But taking into account the ethical nature of his purpose and limitations he has imposed on himself by the creation of moral personalities, God does govern the universe. He governs by means consonant with his character and purpose.

Bibliography: G. C. Berkouwer, *The Providence of God* (1952). S. A. NEWMAN

PROVIDENCE HIGH SCHOOL. An academy founded in 1889, sponsored by Clarksville Association and located in Habersham County, Ga. The school existed until 1897.

ARTHUR JACKSON

PROVINE, JOHN WILLIAM (b. Cole's Creek, Calhoun County, Miss., June 19, 1866; d. Clinton, Miss., Nov. 3, 1949). J. W. Provine, son of Civil War Captain Robert Neely Provine, received his bachelor's degree from the University of Mississippi in 1888, winning the chemistry fellowship in his senior year; he received the master's degree in chemistry in 1890; he spent three years in Germany at Munich and Goettingen and received the Ph.D. degree in chemistry from Goettingen in 1893. He began his long career of service at Mississippi College when he was elected to the chair of natural science on July 22, 1893; he was made chairman of the faculty on May 28, 1895. He was elected president of the college on June 1, 1897, and resigned as president on June 6, 1898. Provine was requested to act as president by W. T. Lowrey (*q.v.*) for the session 1905–06 and was elected president again on May 9, 1911, serving until 1932. He continued on the faculty as instructor in chemistry and German until 1941. Through his determined efforts, the college was admitted to the Southern Association of Secondary Schools and Colleges. In 1918 he led in the organization into one battery of many of the students of the college in World War I. He was a man of great energy and ability and held many important positions: mayor of Clinton, Miss.; commissioner and on the building committee of the state mental hospital at Whitfield, Miss.; member of the American Chemistry Society and *Deutsche Chemische Gesellschaft;* president of the Southern Intercollegiate Athletic Association for 25 years; president of Association of Mississippi Colleges, 1922–23; president of Mississippi Teachers' Association, 1922–29; and active in his church as a deacon and Sunday school superintendent. He championed amateur athletics and was always most popular among the students, being affectionately called "Dutchie." Mississippi College conferred on him the LL.D. degree in 1911 and the science building was named "Provine Hall." C. B. HAMLET III

PUBLIC AFFAIRS COMMITTEE, BAPTIST JOINT. The Committee on Public Affairs is a standing committee of the Southern Baptist Convention, affiliated with similar committees from the American Baptist Convention, National Baptist Convention, U.S.A., Incorporated, the National Baptist Convention of America, the North American Baptist General Conference, and the Baptist General Conference of America to form the Baptist Joint Committee on Public Affairs with offices in Washington, D. C.

The purpose of the Baptist Joint Committee is to act in the field of public affairs whenever the interests or rights of the co-operating conventions call for conference or negotiation with the Government of the United States or with any other governments, whenever Baptist principles are involved in governmental action, or when any of the co-operating conventions may refer to it any matter of common interest. The committee is empowered to enunciate, commend, and defend the historic Baptist principle of religious freedom, with particular application to the separation of church and state as embodied in the Constitution of the United States; to communicate and commend to the President, Congress, courts, and departments of the Federal Government or state governments such declarations as Baptists officially adopt concerning public matters; to make such contacts with departments of government as may be desirable in the transaction of business with Baptist agencies; and to inform Baptist constituencies of governmental movements affecting principles held essential to true relations between church and state and the application of Christianity to the life of the nation.

In 1936 the Southern Baptist Convention changed the name of its special Committee on Chaplains of Army and Navy to the Committee on Public Relations and enlarged the function of the committee with the provision that

> . . . the present work of the Committee shall be continued and that, as situations arise, in which agencies of this Convention are compelled to confer, to negotiate, to demand just rights that are threatened or to have other inescapable dealings with the American or other Governments, this Committee shall function, when so requested by any existing board or agency of this body, as a representative of Southern Baptists and shall report in detail to the Southern Baptist Convention the results of such conferences and negotiations.

The report of the Committee on Chaplains of Army and Navy which recommended this action was written by the chairman of the committee, Rufus Washington Weaver (*q.v.*), who thus became the founder of the Committee on Public Relations and the interpreter in his time of the Baptist position on religious liberty and the principle of separation of church and state.

In 1939 the Committee on Public Relations became a standing committee by action of the Convention, and was instructed to act as a joint committee with the Committee on Public Relations of the Northern Baptist Convention, with the provision that

> . . . the functions thus conferred are not to be construed as giving any authority to the committee which may lead to its merger with other agencies resulting in the loss of its identity as a committee of

the Southern Baptist Convention. This identity shall in all respects be maintained with the reservation of full powers on the part of the Committee to act independently of such agencies.

In 1950 the Convention changed the name of the Committee on Public Relations to that of Committee on Public Affairs. The joint committee, composed of similar committees from six national Baptist bodies, changed its name from Public Relations to Public Affairs.

Joseph Martin Dawson served as the first executive director of the joint committee from 1946 until his retirement in 1953. During this period he wrote several books interpreting the Baptist position on religious liberty. He was also a prime mover in the organization of "Protestants and Other Americans United for Separation of Church and State."

In 1954 C. Emanuel Carlson succeeded Dawson as executive director. Under his leadership the Baptist joint committee is functioning with a new constitution officially approved by the six co-operating Baptist bodies.

WALTER POPE BINNS

PUBLIC SCHOOLS AND RELIGIOUS INSTRUCTION. See EDUCATION, SOUTHERN BAPTIST and WEEKDAY RELIGIOUS EDUCATION.

PUBLICATION WORK IN FOREIGN MISSIONS. This kind of publication work achieved prominence in the Baptist modern mission movement when William Carey (*q.v.*) was reinforced by William Ward, a printer, and Joshua Marshman, "a literary man," in 1798. It continues to be an effective missionary agency.

The purpose of this phase of mission work is to prepare, publish, and distribute literature in the language of the people for Christian indoctrination, establishment of churches, cultivation of national leadership, and stimulation to indigenous mission work.

The printed page prepares the way for the coming of the missionary, serves as an efficient tool when fields are opened to him, and remains to give direction to the work in case he should be removed from the field. Mission literature unifies the thinking, harmonizes the method, and solidifies the fellowship of the language group that uses it.

Many problems experienced by publication agencies in the homeland are accentuated abroad, such as sectional and cultural differences. The emergence of millions from illiteracy in recent years has demanded a new and simple literature for those who can barely read. Some problems are peculiar to the foreign fields. Translation, when necessary, must be adapted to the needs of another race, the natural vernacular of the people must be approximated and foreign peculiarities avoided. The poverty prevalant on most mission fields makes subvention of publications a necessity.

Earliest publication work was begun by individual missionaries. George Boardman Taylor (*q.v.*), pioneer missionary to Italy, founded a Baptist paper, *Il Seminatore,* in 1876. In 1882 William Buck Bagby (*q.v.*) wrote from Brazil of translations and tracts he had prepared, and the following year appealed for "a publishing fund." Solomon L. Ginsburg made constant use of a printing press in Bahia in the 1890's. David Alexander Wilson, after publishing Bible study leaflets for a short time, launched the first Sunday school quarterly in Spanish at Guadalajara, Mexico, in 1890. That quarterly, *El Expositor Bíblico,* continues with a present circulation of 50,000.

Emergence of publication societies, committees, and boards on foreign fields correlated publication work within the framework of the missions and afforded closer co-operation with national Baptist bodies. The first such body was the China Baptist Publication Society, organized in 1899, followed by similar organizations in Brazil, 1900; Japan, 1903; Mexico, 1903; Argentina, 1908; etc.

The Foreign Mission Board of the Southern Baptist Convention has six major publishing houses which prepare and publish foreign language literature. They are, in order of their establishment:

The Baptist Press, publishing in Chinese, was established in Canton by the Chinese Baptist Publication Society in 1899, moved to Shanghai in 1926, and after the Japanese invasion located in Hong Kong in 1950.

The Carroll Memorial Baptist Publishing House of Rio de Janeiro, Brazil, was founded in 1900. Largest of the publishing houses, it produces, in addition to quarterlies, religious books, tracts, and more than 100,000 Portuguese Bibles annually.

The Jordan Press, begun by Ernest Nathan Walne as a book store in Nagasaki in 1903, is now located in Tokyo where it provides literature in Japanese for all church departments, including Sunday school, Training Union, and missionary organizations.

The Baptist Spanish Publishing House, founded by Jones Edgar Davis (*q.v.*) in Mexico in 1905, from its present site in El Paso, Tex., supplies quarterlies, tracts, and books to Spanish-speaking groups throughout the world. Other Spanish publication centers include Buenos Aires, where the Argentine Baptist Publication Board maintains a book store and editorial offices; Santiago, Chile, headquarters for the editorial office and five book stores of the Chilean Mission, and for Woman's Missionary Union literature; and Barcelona, Spain, where limited but excellent materials are published by the Spanish Baptist Publication Board.

The Baptist Press of Ibadan, Nigeria, founded in 1950, is making rapid progress. Prior to that time Baptist publication work for Nigeria was printed by other evangelical publishing houses or private concerns.

The Italian Baptist Publishing House was established in 1952, though Baptist periodicals and books had been printed by secular concerns for more than seven decades.

Publication committees of newer missions combine the use of duplicating machines and contract printing to provide their minimum literature needs.

In 1954 publication work of varied amounts, engaging 44 missionaries and 278 nationals, was done in 22 Southern Baptist foreign mission fields. Total production included 496,624 copies of 137 foreign language books; plus 121,600 Bibles; 2,312,200 copies of 108 magazines; and 7,158,605 copies of 312 tracts in nine languages. FRANK W. PATTERSON

PUBLICITY, CHURCH. *History.*—The first recorded use of publicity for religious purposes is described in Psalm 19:1, "The heavens declare the glory of God; and the firmament sheweth his handiwork." In the Old Testament the judges and kings sent messengers throughout the land to advertise religious services.

Word of mouth was the chief means of publicity for thousands of years, but there is in existence ancient written publicity: 19th-century B.C. papyri advertisements offering rewards for runaway slaves. Word of mouth was the publicity method used to bring together the multitudes to whom Christ spoke. Paul used publicity extensively, often in the form of letters.

Except for word of mouth, the form of church publicity in longest continuous use is the church bell. The first recorded installation by a church was in Italy in A.D. 585. Bells were being used in England less than 100 years later. Progress continues as miniature bells and electronic amplifiers are replacing the huge cast bells. Even before bells, trumpets were used to announce the arrival of important events and personages.

As century after century has softened the once traditional blunt lines of steeples, churches have come to use them so consistently that even the ultramodern, needle-like shaft of stainless steel is publicity that a building is a church.

A book published in 1913 (*Church Publicity* by Reisner) reveals that practically every church publicity technique used at the middle of the 20th century was being employed at the beginning of the century. A few of the more sensational methods have been dropped, but radio and television seem to be the only new tools employed during the past two generations. Gaining attention for a church service by exploding bombs, firing skyrockets, and burning red flares on street corners would no longer be approved, but today a few religious publicity promoters still expect an editor to compromise the freedom of the press by permitting a church's advertising funds to influence the content of editorial columns.

Printing.—The printing press makes possible much of the church publicity activity today. Gutenberg's European invention of movable type in 1437 did not leave some churches far behind. Perhaps the first printed advertisement of any kind was a small poster issued in 1480 to advertise a church service book, *The Pyes of Salisbury Use*. In the Orient, missionaries have made extensive use of printed publicity, at times even finding that the plan of salvation printed in paid newspaper advertising space resulted in numerous conversions.

Modern advertising in America developed rapidly after the United States postal system was improved in 1840 and was made economical for the distribution of periodicals. American churches soon started using journalistic publicity even before the beginning of journalism teaching or the first school of journalism, which was established at the University of Missouri in 1908.

Present activity.—Today the Baptist church publicity outside the congregation is generally in the form of newspaper stories prepared for the local editor by the pastor, educational director, or a church member who is also on the staff of the newspaper. The publicity committee is becoming a standard part of well-organized churches. Others use temporary publicity committees for revivals, Vacation Bible schools, and other efforts to go beyond "business as usual."

Revival and Vacation Bible school posters furnished at near cost by the Sunday School Board require little preparation and are used extensively. For city or associational simultaneous revivals, the Baptist Book Stores supply publicity items ranging from a huge poster for a 25-foot outdoor billboard to a small lapel button. Many books on publicity are available, including *Practical Church Publicity* (1953) by Brown.

Eight Southern Baptist colleges offered the B.A. degree with a major in journalism in 1956.

Baptist institutions whose major support comes from beyond their local communities are the most active users of publicity. The colleges have their news bureaus, often staffed chiefly by especially capable upperclassmen. In addition to the flow of news releases, these schools are showing a growing interest in producing motion pictures which will show the denomination what their institution is accomplishing and what it needs—multiple-purpose films which will attract the most promising students. Television's demand for enormous quantities of visual material is being utilized by a few colleges who film newsworthy events or musical performances and supply the "clips" free to co-operating stations. All Southern Baptist agencies diligently avoid Hollywood-type promotion (posters, special advertising) for showings of their motion pictures. They want to prepare the audience for learning rather than for entertainment.

The Foreign Mission Board is the major Baptist producer of motion pictures which publicize an organization's work. The Home Mission Board, which has been using still slides of the work of its missionaries, is increasingly depending on motion pictures. Other agencies and some state conventions are trying this medium. Even individual churches are using home movie equipment to film annual events for publicity use in preparing for similar events in succeeding years.

The Southern Baptist Convention meeting each year is the one event which receives the most publicity. For the annual meeting of the Convention, the Executive Committee provides choice floor space and a press room for 45 to 50 correspondents, prepares a press folio of background matter and printed speeches, and organizes press conferences. The Convention's Radio and Television Commission arranges for local radio and television coverage of parts of the proceedings.

Today church publicity includes public announcements, telephoned messages, church newspapers, newspaper editorial and advertising matter, radio and television programs and spot announcements, sound amplifiers, billboards, taxi and bus posters, signs, chimes, handbills, public directories, menu notes, blotters, mailing pieces, parades, motion pictures, and any other available publicity media.

See also BAPTIST PRESS. RICHMOND O. BROWN

PUERTO RICO BAPTIST CONVENTION. Organized in 1902, the Puerto Rico Baptist Convention celebrated its 50th anniversary in Mar., 1952. Puerto Rican Baptists observed the 50th anniversary of the coming of the missionaries under the boards of the American Baptists Home Mission Society and the Woman's American Baptist Home Mission Society in Mar., 1949. For more than 25 years no missionary from outside has served as pastor of a Baptist church in Puerto Rico, and for several years the only missionaries from the continent have been the English teacher in the Barranquitas Baptist Academy and the general missionary and his wife.

Total membership of the 48 churches and 277 missions and outstations is 6,493 in a Baptist constituency of 56,000. There has been an upsurge in stewardship with tithing much more widely practiced.

Churches are developing self support, but the financing of new buildings is still a major concern. Loans made through the American Baptist Home Mission societies are helping Baptists take advantage of opportunities for growth in the churches and for the establishment of churches in new housing areas. Puerto Rico faces a shortage of pastors with many leaving for the United States; the exodus of members is also affecting resources.

In Christian education, work in leadership training is being undertaken. The effectiveness of junior high, senior high, and young peoples' retreats has increased greatly, and the young people have asked for admission to the Baptist Youth Fellowship of the American Baptist Convention.

The woman's organization in the convention, through financial aid, assists young women in attending missionary training schools in the United States; it shares in the payment of salaries for these women missionaries after their appointment by the American Baptist Home Mission Societies.

Baptists have co-operated in the work of the Evangelical Seminary since it was established in 1919. The Baptist Academy in Barranquitas is serving more children than ever, with special religious emphasis through Bible study, chapel services, Sunday school classes, and prayer meetings.

The convention is a member of the Evangelical Council of Puerto Rico. Evangelistic efforts extend into public hospitals, prisons, jails, and reformatories. MRS. MILO E. WENGER

PUNISHMENT. See HELL.

PURITANISM, NATURE AND INFLUENCE OF. The origins of English Puritanism are obscure, lost in the labyrinthine literature of 16th- and 17th-century English religious life. Likely, William Haller is correct in feeling it rather fruitless to speculate about who "was the first Puritan and who may prove to be the last." Even the term "Puritan" is somewhat difficult to isolate in meaning but may generally be used in reference to those zealots in the Tudor-Stuart era who sought "a farther reformation" of the English church in several various ways. Leonard J. Trinterud in a recent article has again challenged the traditional account of the rise of Puritanism almost exclusively out of the influence of the "Marian Exiles" by demonstrating the "indigenous" rather than "exotic" character of the movement. Daniel Neal's (1678–1743) definition is suggestive: "A Puritan, therefore, was a man of severe morals, a Calvinist in doctrine, and a Nonconformist to the ceremonies and discipline of the church, though they [*sic*] did not totally separate from it."

Puritanism, it may be said with warrant, began in criticism of the compromise church-state of Elizabeth I (1558–1603). The controversy centered in three chief issues: the moral, the ecclesiastical, and the doctrinal. Of these, doubtless, the moral issues moved the Puritans at the deepest level. The Puritan was obsessed with the desire to eradicate sin in himself, in his church, and in his society. The evangelical ideas of repentance, conversion, and regeneration are traceable to the modern influence of Puritanism in some measure. Theology was manifestly secondary, though not unimportant, for the Puritan. However, it must be said that Puritanism comprised the ablest exponents of the Calvinistic scheme of doctrine in the 17th century. Puritan theology was in no sense unadulterated Calvinism, the principal admixture being the covenant idea. The Puritans, almost to a man, rejected episcopacy in favor of either Presbyterianism or Congregationalism.

The influence of Puritanism has been profound in the history of the church both in this country and Britain, although as a distinct movement it concluded with the settlement in religion effected under William and Mary (1688–1702). The Puritan influence has been felt in America chiefly in the Congregational, Presbyterian, and Baptist denominations, but in reality the whole tenor of American life has evidenced the Puritan spirit. Puritanism has remained in British Christianity in the Presbyterian and Congregational churches and in "low church" Anglicanism. Max Weber (1864–1919) attributes much of modern-day capitalism to the influence of the Puritan ethical emphasis.

BIBLIOGRAPHY: W. Haller, *Liberty and Reformation in the Puritan Revolution* (1955); *The Rise of Puritanism* (1938). M. M. Knappen, *Tudor Puritanism* (1939). P. Miller, *Orthodoxy in Massachusetts 1630–1650* (1933). *The Puritans* (1938). D. Neal, *The History of the Puritans* (various editions). P. Schaff, *The Creeds of Christendom* (1877).

EUGENE H. STOCKSTILL

PURSER, DAVID INGRAM (b. Copiah County, Miss., Dec. 27, 1842; d. New Orleans, La., Oct. 22, 1897). Pastor and denominational leader. He was baptized at the age of 11 into Damascus Baptist Church near Hazlehurst, Miss. His schooling was limited because of his father's ill health and because he volunteered at 17 for the Confederate Army. On Oct. 8, 1864, he married Dicy Jane Bass; his home church ordained him on Dec. 4, 1870. After serving as pastor of several churches, he did missionary work in western Mississippi from 1871 to 1884. He and his younger brother, John F., an evangelistic singer, worked for a while as an evangelistic team. His wife having died in 1879, he married Sallie Anna Moody, wealthy daughter of Judge Washington Moody of Tuscaloosa, Ala., June 28, 1883, and became pastor of the First Baptist Church, Birmingham, in 1884; became financial agent for Howard College and obtained the initial $400,000 subscription for their building program in moving from Marion to East Lake. In 1892 he went as Home Mission Board missionary to New Orleans as pastor of Valence Street Baptist Church. His younger brother, John F., went also in 1892 to New Orleans as pastor of the First Baptist Church. While there the two established the Pastors' Theological Institute, which was held in the First Church building, and which was somewhat a forerunner of the New Orleans Baptist Theological Seminary. D. I. Purser was also president of the Louisiana Baptist Convention for five years and vice-president of the Southern Baptist Convention for one year. When the yellow fever scourge hit New Orleans in 1879, D. I. Purser was on vacation seeking to regain his health. Despite the fact that he had resigned his church and the First Baptist Church of Opelika, Ala., had called him, he returned to minister to his New Orleans congregation. He contracted the fever and died Oct. 22, 1897. He was buried in New Orleans, but his body was moved in 1899 to Tuscaloosa, Ala.

BIBLIOGRAPHY: J. L. Boyd, *A Popular History of the Baptists in Mississippi* (1930). R. L. Bolton, "Kingdom Builders in New Orleans—the Pursers," *The Christian Index* (Aug. 6, 1931).

C. B. HAMLET III and T. W. GAYER

PURYEAR, GEORGE WASHINGTON (b. Jonesboro, Ark., 1858; d. Jonesboro, Ark., Aug. 27, 1954). Businessman, philanthropist, and churchman. He joined the First Baptist Church in Jonesboro in 1887 and was a trustee and deacon there 43 years. He married Flora Belle Carson, daughter of Judge James Carson, on Oct. 1, 1883, and had by her four children: Fred, Edgar, Neil, and Mary. After her death in 1927, he married Alice R. Witherspoon on June 10, 1929. He was a member of the Arkansas Baptist state executive board for 25 years and president of the Arkansas Baptist State Convention, 1923–25. He was a member of the board of trustees, Baptist Memorial Hospital, Memphis, Tenn., beginning on Feb. 13, 1914. He worked in the 75 Million Campaign, 1919, and assisted in raising money to settle a million-dollar Baptist state convention debt. In 1936 he became a member and honorary deacon at Bellevue Baptist Church, Memphis, Tenn., where he served until his death. He was buried in Jonesboro, Ark.

MRS. G. W. PURYEAR

Q

QUARTERLY REVIEW, THE. A quarterly publication of the Sunday School Board of the Southern Baptist Convention. The first issue was published Jan., 1941. It seeks to reach the pastoral and denominational leadership of Southern Baptists with vital statistical and general information. It features regularly historical information and seeks to interpret Southern Baptist progress and program. Circulation in 1956 was 10,715.

J. P. EDMUNDS

R

RACE QUESTION AND MISSIONS, THE. Of the estimated world population of 2,400,000,000, approximately one half belong to the Mongoloid race and an additional one tenth are Negroid. These colored peoples, along with the underprivileged masses of the world, are restless. They are searching for food, freedom, respect, and a sense of purpose. This march of the masses, which has been called "the basic factor of modern history," is inevitable and irresistible. Much of the mission work of Baptists and other major Christian groups is done among these colored masses.

The missionary's message that man is made in the image of God, the God is no respecter of persons, and that Christ died for all men has contributed to the movement of the masses. On the other hand, one of the missionary's greatest handicaps is the contrast between the message he preaches and the practice of those at home who support him. It is difficult for the peoples of the world to understand why Christians will send missionaries to proclaim Christian brotherhood and yet many of them will not practice that brotherhood in their churches and communities. The race question has become not only "an American dilemma" and "American Christianity's test case," it is also the dilemma for freedom-loving peoples of the world and the test case for world Christianity. T. B. MASTON

RACE RELATIONS. The proper relation of races, which is one of the most challenging and perplexing of problems, is, as Soper and Walter have suggested, worldwide in its scope. It is most acute in the Orient, in Africa, and in the United States. In the United States the most serious problem exists between the white majority and the Negro minority although every minority group is involved to some degree. The churches are involved in the conflict, which is not only a social and political problem but also a moral and spiritual one.

In the area of race relations certain behavior patterns tend to develop. In the realm of Negro-white relations the pattern has been characterized by discrimination against and segregation of the Negro. This discrimination-segregation pattern tends to enter into every phase of Negro-white relations, and to harden into a caste system, which has become particularly pronounced in the South. The caste system was supported by the courts until the 1930's when the Supreme Court in particular began to give preferential treatment to civil rights rather than property rights. The climax of legal action striking at the caste system was the Supreme Court decision, handed down on May 17, 1954, declaring segregation in public schools solely on the basis of race unconstitutional.

The pattern of race relations has not only changed in general; it has also changed for Christian groups including Southern Baptists. It may be that the church in the South has been "a silent but powerful accessory to the segregation pattern," and there may be some truth to Kelsey's charge that "caste stands in a position of priority to Christ" and that "the racial ethic of Southern Baptists is fundamentally the ethic of southern caste culture," but this is not the total picture and certainly it is not the contemporary picture.

In slavery days the slaves were usually accepted as members in the same churches as the white people. The Circular Church of Charleston, S. C., had 400 Negro members by 1804, and the First Baptist Church of Montgomery, Ala., reported 600 Negro and 300 white members at the end of the Civil War. By 1863, however, separate churches and meetinghouses were springing up everywhere, a trend that was "approved by the brethren" as it promised to increase the efficiency of the Negro churches.

With the separation Southern Baptists did not lose their interest in and sense of responsibility for the Negro, which they had expressed in their organizing convention in 1845. Their approach, however, continued to be paternalistic and was made within the segregation-caste pattern. At the same time there was a growing conviction that basic Christian principles were relevant to race relations but that they were not being applied consistently. This conviction found ultimate expression in a report of a special committee to the Southern Baptist Convention at St. Louis in 1947.

The report stated that "the time is upon us when we must consult our faith and bring ourselves to lay fresh hold upon those principles that are embedded in our Baptist faith and polity, and make them the basis of Christian action." Some of those principles outlined by the committee were a belief in the Lordship of Christ, in the Holy Spirit, in the Bible as the word of God, in the dignity and worth of the individual, in the fellowship of believers, and in the principle of democracy.

Based on those principles or doctrines the committee suggested the following principles of conduct:

1. We shall think of the Negro as a person and treat him accordingly.

WOMAN'S MISSIONARY UNION (*q.v.*) HEADQUARTERS BUILDING, Birmingham, Ala. The building houses executive and editorial offices, library, auditorium, and other facilities. Italian marble and growing plants in wrought iron urns are high lights of spacious lobby. Acquired in 1951, it is valued at $500,000.

FOREIGN MISSION BOARD (*q.v.*), HEADQUARTERS BUILDING, Richmond, Va. Built in 1957, this is the eighth location of the Board. The building contains about 50,000 square feet of floor space. It provides for offices and facilities for the administrative, promotional, and publication work of the Board, for its visual education ministry, and includes a chapel with organ and complete projection and sound facilities, a paneled parlor for social activities serviced by a kitchen, five conference rooms, and shipping and storage space.

2. We shall continually strive as individuals to conquer all prejudice and eliminate from our speech terms of contempt and from our conduct actions of ill-will.

3. We shall teach our children that prejudice is un-Christian and that good-will and helpful deeds are the duty of every Christian toward all men of all races.

4. We shall protest against injustice and indignities against Negroes, as we do in the case of people of our own race, whenever and wherever we meet them.

5. We shall be willing for the Negro to enjoy the rights granted to him under the constitution of the United States, including the right to vote, to serve on juries, to receive justice in the courts, to be free from mob violence, to receive a just share of the benefits or [*sic*] educational and other funds, and to receive equal service for equal payment on public carriers and conveniences.

6. We shall be just in our dealing with the Negro as an individual. Whenever he is in our employ, we shall pay him an adequate wage and provide for him healthful working conditions.

7. We shall strive to promote community good-will between the races in every way possible.

8. We shall actively co-operate with Negro Baptists in the building up of their churches, the education of their ministers, and the promotion of their missions and evangelistic programs.

The "with Negro Baptists" in the preceding represents the new approach of Southern Baptists to the Negro. They recognize, in the contemporary period, that their work must be *with* him and not *for* him. He must be accepted as a full partner. Progress is being made in this direction in some churches, associations, conventions, and institutions supported by Southern Baptists.

The Supreme Court decision declaring unconstitutional segregation in public schools solely on the basis of race has created a new racial situation in the South. The Southern Baptist Convention approved the report of its Christian Life Commission which declared that the decision by the Court was "in harmony with the constitutional guarantee of equal freedom to all citizens, and with the Christian principles of equal justice and love for all men." The report also urged "Christian statesmen and leaders . . . to use their leadership in positive thought and planning to the end that this crisis in our national history shall not be made the occasion for new and bitter prejudice, but a movement toward a united nation embodying and proclaiming a democracy that will commend freedom to all people."

BIBLIOGRAPHY: H. S. Ashmore, *The Negro and the Schools* (1954). M. Berger, *Equality by Statute* (1950). S. G. Cole and M. W. Cole, *Minorities and the American Promise* (1954). B. W. Doyle, *The Etiquette of Race Relations* (1937). E. D. Dvorin, *Racial Separation in South Africa* (1952). G. Myrdal, *An American Dilemma* (1944). W. S. Nelson, ed., *The Christian Way in Race Relations* (1948). E. D. Soper, *Racism: A World Issue* (1947). P. A. F. Walter, Jr., *Race and Culture Relations* (1952).

T. B. MASTON

RADIO, CHRISTIAN USE OF. Christian groups have made use of radio from the inception of broadcasting. The first religious program to be broadcast was a Sunday morning worship service from the Calvary Episcopal Church of Pittsburgh, on Jan. 2, 1921. From that beginning the Christian use of radio has increased until the average metropolitan radio station today is carrying some 160 minutes per week of religious material. Smaller stations in rural areas carry an even larger percentage of such programming.

There are many types of religious broadcasts. Categories include the local worship service, panel discussions, religious drama, and religious news.

A study of the use of radio by Baptist state conventions and local churches reveals that approximately 50 per cent of Southern Baptist pastors are making some use of radio in communicating the gospel. Many Baptist ministers believe that Baptist progress has been accelerated by broadcasts.

Because of the size of its audience, radio has an impressive potential for Christian use. For instance, Radio Ceylon, most powerful commercial station in the African and Asian continents, beams to an estimated 72 million people who understand English.

In 1951 the Federal Communications Commission reported that 2,284 standard broadcast stations and 651 FM stations were on the air. Since that time the number has increased. It has been estimated that fully 95 per cent of the family units in the United States own at least one radio set. These facts indicate the potential influence of the use of radio, and Christian forces are recognizing that "the new revolution in communications technology is just as fundamental and far more widespread in influence than was the printing press."

Even though the influence of radio has been altered to some degree by the growth of television, radio continues to offer a major audience potential. One author has estimated that "a hundred million of our countrymen have their radios turned on for an average of four hours each day." The survey work, *The Television-Radio Audience and Religion,* based on the test city of New Haven, Conn., proves that even in an area of maximum television viewing, a well-produced religious radio program which touches human need for a great many people can still have a large, appreciative audience.

The ability of radio to furnish an adjunct for all denominations in reaching unsaved individuals has prompted the use of this mass communications medium. Nonchurch members who listen to religious radio programs constitute an audience ratio of approximately one to 11. An inclusive statement made by leaders of the Presbyterian Church, U.S.A., recognizes the value of radio for the following Christian purposes: "to win converts, to restore the careless, to instruct in Christian living, to help both shut-ins and shut-outs meet problems, to create a better understanding of the Church and its ministry, to help different religious groups understand one another, to strengthen the Christian community and encourage it to accept its local and world task and to co-operate with broadcasters in their efforts to present the best of our cultural and religious heritage."

For Southern Baptists, as well as other denominations, the increasing use of the media of mass communication presents specific problems: the need for extended preparation and advanced curriculum for training ministers in radio methods, the need for enlisting more churches in support of the radio ministry, and the need for determining the denomination's aim and evaluating the current use of radio in relation to this aim.

BIBLIOGRAPHY: J. Alicoate, *1956 Radio Annual* (1956). H. L. Eubank and S. P. Lawton, *Broadcasting: Radio and Television* (1952). C. T. Griswold and C. H. Schmitz, *Broadcasting Religion* (1952). J. E. Lantz, *Speaking in the Church* (1954). E. C. Parker and others, *The Television-Radio Audience and Religion* (1955). GORDON CLINARD

RADIO AND TELEVISION COMMISSION, THE. Had its beginning at the Southern Baptist Convention held in Richmond, Va., in 1938. Samuel Franklin Lowe (*q.v.*) of Georgia petitioned the Convention to explore the field of radio broadcasting as a possible medium for projecting the Baptist message. The Convention appointed Lowe chairman of a seven-member committee to conduct the investigation. Other members of the committee appointed at the 1938 Convention were Adiel Jarrett Moncrief, Jr., Florida; James Douglas Carroll, Louisiana; Norfleet Gardner, North Carolina; E. P. Baker, Tennessee; Jesse Burton Weatherspoon, North Carolina; and Carr Pritchett Collins, Texas.

At its June meeting that year the Executive Committee allocated $200 to be used by the committee for essential expenses in making its survey. The Executive Committee expressed itself as favoring the committee's plans for some experimental broadcasts, provided the expense of such broadcasts be met through donations from individuals in a way that would not interfere "with the regular program of the local churches or the denomination."

Nine new members were added to the committee at the 1939 Convention meeting in Oklahoma City, bringing the total membership to 16. This committee was granted an expense fund of $1,200, and was authorized to promote Baptist broadcasts "over a territory-wide hookup and over a single powerful station."

At the 1940 Convention in Baltimore, Md., the committee reported that the quality of Baptist broadcasts had become a matter of concern, stating that "management in the radio world is now looking for religious programs of such character as to be demanded by the public." As a means of meeting the more rigid requirements, the committee reported that it had appointed a subcommittee to confer with the presidents of Southern Baptist seminaries,

> looking towards the training of . . . young preachers in the seminaries in the important field of building effective radio messages and programs, and also looking towards having tracts and booklets printed and conferences held and messages delivered which will help all . . . who have practical radio opportunity in the matter of giving and delivering more effective radio messages and programs.

The work of the subcommittee resulted later in the radio and television workshops which the commission conducts annually at Ridgecrest and Glorieta assemblies, and in areas where ministerial associations and other groups request them.

Acting on the authority granted it by the Convention, the committee scheduled a 13-week series of half-hour evangelistic programs on an independent network of 17 stations, beginning Jan. 5, 1941. This series, called the *Baptist Hour*, was scheduled on a public service basis by the co-operating stations. Eleven states were included in the network coverage. The total cost for this series of broadcasts, which originated in Atlanta, Ga., was $5,750. Fifteen stations were added to the original network for the first quarter series in 1942.

The 1942 Convention, meeting in San Antonio, Tex., granted the committee authority to employ a full-time director. The position was given to Lowe, who while a pastor had served as chairman of the committee during the four years of its existence.

Two other committee requests were granted at the 1942 meeting. The Convention voted to allot the committee $30,000 as an operating fund, with $25,000 to be allocated from undivided Cooperative Program receipts, and the other $5,000 to be granted by the Sunday School Board. Difficulties over the proposed allocation arose later in the year when the Convention, scheduled to be held in Memphis, Tenn., was canceled because of conditions growing out of World War II. The Executive Committee discovered that the action of the Convention in granting the committee money from Cooperative Program receipts contravened the constitution. The committee then appealed to the executive secretaries of the several states in the Convention to make up the amount.

In its 1943 report, filed with the Executive Committee, the committee revealed that $3,000 had been set aside for special transcription service. This service included a Bible study series by Harold Wayland Tribble, and a series of half-hour programs on the Christian home by Theodore Floyd Adams. The transcription project represented the first major expansion of services by the committee.

Year by year the committee continued to add to its services. By 1946 a substantial transcription library was available to churches and radio stations. Still another phase of the work was the committee's co-operation with the Home Mission Board.

The first radio program of the Home Mission Board was started in 1945 by Fred Eastham, superintendent of evangelism for the board. Time for a half-hour evangelistic broadcast each

Sunday evening over KWBU, Corpus Christi, Tex., a 50,000-watt station, was bought by the board.

On the recommendation of its executive secretary, John Benjamin Lawrence, the board voted to establish a radio program on an independent network of stations. The *Good News Hour* was inaugurated in Jan., 1946.

The Home Mission Board provided the funds and the program. The Radio Committee, which had become the Radio Commission and a recognized agency of the Convention at the 1946 meeting in Miami, transcribed and mailed the programs to the radio stations. The *Good News Hour,* with Lawrence as the speaker, was scheduled on a network of stations numbering from 40 to 65 in the United States, Alaska, Cuba, and the Canal Zone. Music on the programs was provided by the *Baptist Hour* choir.

All station contracts for the *Good News Hour* were terminated effective May 1, 1954, following the resignation of Lawrence in Dec., 1953. From Jan. 1 to May 1 the *Good News Hour* was replaced on all stations by the *Baptist Hour.* A few stations continued the *Baptist Hour* on a sustaining basis after the contracts expired.

The Home Mission Board, in co-operation with the commission, has also produced and transcribed other evangelistic programs.

Following the death of Lowe on Oct. 4, 1952, Dupree Jordan, associate director of the commission, was made acting director and served in that capacity until Aug. 26, 1953, when Paul Morris Stevens was elected director.

Stevens recommended to the Convention meeting in St. Louis, Mo., that the agency be known as the Radio and Television Commission, and the recommendation was approved.

The commission had already produced numerous television programs. For more than a year *Bible Story Time* was a regular feature over WSB-TV in Atlanta, Ga.

The pilot film for a proposed Southern Baptist television series, named *This My Son,* was released for rental through Baptist book stores in Oct., 1954. Based on the parable of the prodigal son, the half-hour dramatic film presented its message in modern setting, as did other parable-based films in the series, which began on television stations throughout the Convention's territory on Apr. 1, 1956. Several films broadcast during the first 13-week period were adaptations of films produced by the Sunday School Board.

Cost of producing *This My Son* was $27,500. Other films in the series cost approximately $25,000 each. In 1955 the commission received $200,000 from Cooperative Program receipts. Approximately $120,000 was received through the mails from persons interested in the work of the commission. Such "fan mail," as it is called, has furnished an important part of the support of the *Baptist Hour* through the years.

On the basis of $25,000 a film, a full-time television ministry would cost the commission $1,300,000 a year, exclusive of handling and extra film prints. But that was the goal the commission had set for itself late in 1955.

The Radio and Television Commission also serves as the public relations and production agency when Southern Baptist personalities are featured on network radio or television.

THEODORE LOTT

RADIO IN MISSIONS. Principles and motives which underlie the use of radio in Baptist missions are identical with those which underlie other Christian mission enterprises, the propagation of the Christian gospel. In South America religious radio programs are widely used in Ecuador, Bolivia, Chile, and Brazil, with Southern Baptists promoting broadcasting in Chile and Brazil. In Brazil there are 81 Baptist radio programs of all categories totaling 23 radio hours per week. In 1948 the Foreign Mission Board equipped Brazil's Atlas News Service with an adequate recording studio in Rio de Janeiro through which daily Baptist broadcasts have been furnished to all Brazil. Included in the broadcasts are the official programs of Brazilian Baptists' radio commission, *Batistas em Marcha,* initiated in Apr., 1955. Radio penetrates impervious homes, prison walls, and traverses deserts, reaching 35 per cent of all Brazilians. Southern Baptists, increasing their use of radio in proportion to their increasing knowledge of its advantages, are building it into their mission structure as a channel for the projection of their distinctive ideals. With air accessible at comparatively economical prices, Baptist radio programs put the gospel within reach of 20,000 Brazilians at a total estimated cost of $375 a week.

WILLIAM H. BERRY

RAGSDALE, BARTOW DAVIS (b. Dekalb County, Ga., Feb. 7, 1861; d. Atlanta, Ga., July 19, 1944). Educator, denominational official. Ragsdale was 16 years of age when his father died, leaving him little but a Primitive Baptist heritage. He graduated with highest honors from Mercer in 1886, received his M.A. degree there in 1892, and the honorary D.D. degree in 1895. Further education was received at the Southern Baptist Theological Seminary and the University of Chicago. He served a number of churches in Georgia, including ones at Albany, Quitman, Cairo, and Decatur. He occupied the chair of Bible at Mercer from 1896 to 1905, during the presidency of Pinckney Daniel Pollock (*q.v.*). During his administration of the office of treasurer and business manager of Mercer (1914–28) he participated in the 75 Million Campaign and was influential in increasing Mercer's endowment by $200,000. For nearly half a century he was recording secretary of the Georgia Baptist Convention (1896–1944). His contributions to Georgia Baptist bibliography consist of *The Story of Georgia Baptists,* 3 vols. (1932–38), *Memoir of P. D. Pollock* (1942), and articles and poems in the *Christian Index* and in brochure. In 1889 he married Lois Cloud, daughter of A. E. Cloud, pastor of the Jonesboro Church for 30 years. The parents are survived by their two children, Cary and Eunice (Mrs. A. E. Wolfe). Ragsdale was known by his students as "Pam" (Epaminondas). His burial place is "Rose Hill," Macon, Ga. JAMES L. CLEGG

RAINES, JOSEPH O. (b. Patterson, Ill., June 7, 1867; d. Chicago, Ill., July 1, 1941). Minister, editor, denominational organizer. He worked as a telegraph operator for the M. K. and T. Railroad, the Santa Fe and the Chicago railroads. He was also engaged in the real estate and mercantile business. Following his conversion, Raines joined Oak Grove Baptist Church in Whitehall, Ill., in 1887 and was ordained to the ministry by that church on July 30, 1899.

Raines led in the organization of the Baptist Missionary Convention at Patterson, Ill., in 1904 for the support of Baptist mission work in Syria, Persia, and Galilee. He served as financial secretary of this work until the Foreign Mission Board took it over.

Raines was a member of the committee which drew up plans for organization of the Illinois Baptist State Association in 1907. He was coeditor, with B. E. Antrobus, of *The Primitive Baptist Messenger* until it merged in 1906 with *The Illinois Baptist,* of which he was associate editor. He later published *The Orient,* a monthly publication. An ardent prohibitionist, which led him to seek election to the state legislature, Raines was in constant demand as a lecturer on temperance and Baptist history. He held more than 200 revivals resulting in over 2,000 professions of faith. ARCHIE E. BROWN

RALEIGH ASSOCIATIONAL ACADEMY. A Baptist school at Holly Springs, Wake County, N. C., operated from 1853 to 1861. D. L. SMILEY

RALEIGH BAPTIST. A newspaper started in Raleigh, Smith County, Miss., in 1927 by a Baptist minister, E. C. Crawford. This small eight-page paper of local circulation suspended publication after one year. A. L. GOODRICH

RANALDSON, JAMES A. (b. Scotland, *c.* 1788; d. near Port Hudson, La., June 17, 1849). Pioneer missionary and denominational promoter, initial promoter of the Alabama state convention. He was the only delegate from North Carolina to the organizational meeting of the Triennial Convention in 1814. He served as general missionary in New Orleans in 1817; he labored in Mississippi from 1818 to 1821. Later he moved to southern Alabama where he made a lasting contribution in launching the state convention. About 20 delegates accepted his invitation to meet in Oct., 1823, at Salem Church near Greensboro, Ala. He was chosen the recording secretary of the convention, and was re-elected at the second session in Marion, Ala., in 1824. Ranaldson's period of service in Alabama was brief. Early in his career he withdrew from public life.

BIBLIOGRAPHY: H. Holcombe, *History of the Rise and Progress of Baptists in Alabama* (1840). Z. T. Leavell and T. J. Bailey, *History of Mississippi Baptists* (1904). B. F. Riley, *History of Baptists of Alabama* (1895); *Memorial History of the Baptists of Alabama* (1923). J. E. BERKSTRESSER

RANKIN, MILLEDGE THERON (b. Newberry, S. C., July 28, 1894; d. Richmond, Va., June 27, 1953). Missionary and foreign mission leader. A Baptist minister's son, Rankin attended Furman University and graduated from Wake Forest College and Southern Baptist Theological Seminary. He earned the Ph.D. degree from Southern Seminary while on furlough from the foreign field. Appointed a missionary to China in 1921, Rankin was teacher and later president at Graves Theological Seminary, Canton. In 1935 the Foreign Mission Board of the Southern Baptist Convention elected him secretary for the Orient to supervise Southern Baptist mission work in China and Japan. Rankin represented Chinese Baptists at the International Missionary Council, Madras, India, in 1938. When the United States entered World War II, he was captured by the Japanese and imprisoned for nine months at Stanley Internment Camp, Hong Kong. On June 6, 1944 (D-Day), Rankin was elected executive secretary of the board, succeeding Charles Edward Maddry, and he served in this capacity from Jan. 1, 1945, until his death in June, 1953. When he became executive secretary, Rankin discovered that a limited number of mission volunteers and a meager overseas budget had frozen the number of Southern Baptist missionaries at about 500. Rankin initiated the Advance Program of Southern Baptists, working with his associates during the first three days of 1948 to plan a program of advance, station by station, country by country. This plan was presented to the board and later was unanimously adopted by the Southern Baptist Convention in May, 1948. Although missionaries had increased to 913 in 32 countries at Rankin's death, his dream was for 1,750 missionaries. Rankin was often characterized as a "man with a world inside his heart." He married Valleria Greene, a daughter of Southern Baptist missionaries to China, in 1922, and they had two daughters, Page (Mrs. J. J. McMillan) and Mary Lee (Mrs. T. E. McCollough). IONE GRAY

RAPTURE. This term designated by modern millenarians represents the belief that living Christians will be caught up from the earth to meet Jesus Christ at his second coming. Derived from the Latin translation of I Thessalonians 4:17 (*rapiemur,* caught up), the concept of rapture has become controversial since the publication of the second edition of the *Scofield Reference Bible* in 1917.

The relation of the rapture to the tribulation is so hotly debated that at least four theories have developed: (1) Pre-tribulationism, holding that the rapture takes place before the 70th week of Daniel (Dan. 9:27), locates the translation of the saints in the summons of Revelation 4:1. (2) Mid-tribulationism teaches that the rapture takes place in the middle of Daniel's 70th week and identifies the last trump of I Corinthians 15:52 with the seventh trumpet of Revelation 11:15. (3) Post-tribulationism, calling attention to the fact that the first resurrection is not mentioned until Revelation 20:4–5, postpones the rapture until the resurrection. (4) Partial-rapturism, introducing the idea that there are both spiritual and carnal Christians, argues that only the spiritual are translated before the tribulation, while the carnal are left to be tested.

Most Southern Baptists, although rather conservative and literal in eschatology, are bewildered by what appears to be undue speculation over highly symbolic teachings.

BIBLIOGRAPHY: E. S. English, *Re-Thinking the Rapture* (1954). G. E. Ladd, *The Blessed Hope* (1953).

DALE MOODY

RAUSCHENBUSCH, WALTER (b. Rochester, N. Y., Oct. 4, 1861; d. Rochester, N. Y., July 25, 1918). Baptist pastor, professor, author, and leader of the Christian social movement in America. Son of August Rauschenbusch, professor of church history at Rochester Theological Seminary, Rochester, N. Y. Rauschenbusch was educated in the University of Berlin, Germany, and in the University of Rochester and Rochester Theological Seminary. After graduation from the seminary in June, 1886, he became pastor of a small German Baptist church in New York City, bordering on Hell's Kitchen. In 1897, after a pastorate of 11 years, he succeeded his father in the chair of church history at Rochester Theological Seminary, a position which he held until his death in 1918.

A prolific writer, he was editor of the *Jugend-Herold* (1892–96); he wrote 11 books, four in German and seven in English. His works in English are: *Christianity and Social Crisis* (1907); *For God and the People: Prayers of the Social Awakening* (1910); *Christianizing the Social Order* (1912); *Dare We Be Christian?* (1914); *Social Principles of Jesus* (1916); and *A Theology for the Social Gospel* (1917). Some of these books have been translated into nine different languages.

Dominant ideas of Rauschenbusch were as follows: (1) the value of human personality; (2) the solidarity of the race; (3) love as the law of life; (4) the kingdom of God on earth written in evolutionary terms; and (5) the regeneration of the individual and of society. His optimism with reference to the kingdom of God in history is reflected in the fact that he believed that society had already been partially "Christianized." He held the economic order to be the "unsaved" institution of the social order. Steps in the Christianization of this unregenerate area of society involved social justice and economic democracy.

Rauschenbusch had his limitations and illusions. For one thing he was overly optimistic concerning the possibilities of the kingdom of God in history. But unlike many of his contemporaries and especially some of his followers, Rauschenbusch had a realistic view of sin and society. Consequently, he did not hold that progress is absolutely inevitable. The kingdom of God, he contended, could be retarded by the church's indifference to social issues.

Rauschenbusch's contributions to the social movement in American Protestantism may be summed up as follows: (1) He was a pioneer in American social Christianity and its most brilliant interpreter. (2) He made significant contributions to the study of Christian ethics in that he grounded social justice in theology and used the social sciences in his analysis of social issues. (3) He succeeded in arousing the social consciousness of American Protestantism as no other man; his influence is seen in the Social Creed of the Churches, in the Federal Council of Churches of Christ in America, of which he was a founder, and in theological seminaries where his works were sometimes required reading. (4) He helped to mold the political and economic movements of his day. (5) He contributed to a better understanding of the kingdom of God, which he conceived to be "a God filled humanity living in a righteous social order."

The Rauschenbusch Foundation was established in Mar., 1929, at Colgate-Rochester Divinity School in his memory.

BIBLIOGRAPHY: C. H. Hopkins, *The Rise of the Social Gospel in American Protestantism, 1865–1915* (1940). D. R. Sharpe, *Walter Rauschenbusch* (1942).

H. H. BARNETTE

RAY, JEFFERSON DAVIS (b. Mission Valley, Tex., Nov. 24, 1860; d. Fort Worth, Tex., June 18, 1951). Pastor, seminary professor. Son of William L. Ray, who was killed in the Civil War soon after the boy's birth, and Avarilla (Dollahite) Ray. Ray attended several elementary schools in Lockhart, Tex., conducted mainly in the four churches there. As a boy he served as printer's devil on the Lockhart *News Echo;* this work developed in him a love for journalism. After attending a private school he taught for a time in Caldwell County, Tex. In 1879 he attended the National School of Elocution and Oratory in Philadelphia, Pa. In 1880 he entered Baylor University, where he was greatly influenced by Benajah Harvey Carroll (*q.v.*), in whose home he lived. Ray's early pastorates were in the First Baptist Church, Huntsville, Tex. (1882–85, 1889–95), and the First Baptist Church, Georgetown, Tex. (1885–86). He also served for a time as superintendent of the Texas Sunday school and colportage work. From 1895 to 1897, Ray attended Southern Baptist Theological Seminary, Louisville, Ky., and served as pastor of the Fox Run Baptist Church, Eminence, Ky. Later pastorates included First Baptist Church, Caldwell, Tex. (1897–1901); First Baptist Church, Corsicana, Tex. (1901–03); and Seventh and James Baptist Church, Waco, Tex. (1903–07). He was professor of homiletics in Southwestern Baptist Theological Seminary, Fort Worth, Tex., from 1907 until his retirement in 1944. His career as teacher was briefly interrupted twice. During World War I he served as camp pastor at Camp Bowie, Fort Worth. Later he preached for a brief period at First Baptist Church, El Paso, Tex., where his wife was hospitalized.

Following his retirement in 1944, Ray worked actively as a newspaper writer and magazine correspondent, continuing his column, begun in 1935, for the *Fort Worth Star Telegram*. He also contributed to *Home Life* and other Southern Baptist periodicals. He was author of the following books: *The Highest Office* (1923); *The Country Preacher* (1925); *B. H. Carroll* (1927); *Trouble* (1929); *Expository Preaching* (1939); *Meant for Men* (1939); *The Scarlet Sin* (1942).

BIBLIOGRAPHY: J. M. Carroll, *A History of Texas Baptists* (1923). L. R. Elliott, ed., *Centennial Story of Texas Baptists* (1936). G. M. Ray, *The Jeff Ray I Knew* (1952). L. R. Scarborough, *A Modern School of the Prophets* (1939). JESSE J. NORTHCUTT

RAY, T. BRONSON (b. Buckeye, Garrard County, Ky., Aug. 14, 1868; d. Richmond, Va., Jan. 15, 1934). Editor of mission study materials, foreign mission leader. Son of William Ray, a physician who was a Baptist deacon for 40 years, Ray was educated at Georgetown College and Southern Baptist Theological Seminary, and was ordained by the Georgetown Baptist Church in May, 1893. While in the seminary he was pastor of the Clear Creek Baptist Church near Versailles, Ky. Ray served as pastor of Immanuel Baptist Church, Nashville, Tenn., 1898–1906, during which time he was a member of the Southern Baptist Sunday School Board and the Tennessee Baptist Board of Missions. President of the Tennessee Baptist Young People's Union for three terms, Ray was primarily responsible for publication of the union's quarterly. About 1901 he conceived the idea of organizing Southern Baptists for mission study, and in Nov., 1906, the Foreign Mission Board elected him to the newly created position of educational secretary. Ray edited and compiled mission study books, among them *The Highway of Mission Thought* and *Southern Baptist Foreign Missions,* and by May 1, 1907, he reported the organization of 84 mission study classes which increased to 517 by the following year. In 1912 he was chosen leader of the Judson Centennial Movement which, in four years, reached its goal of $1,250,000, one of the most significant achievements in the development of the Southern Baptist foreign missionary enterprise. In 1914 Ray became foreign secretary of the Foreign Mission Board, serving until 1927 when he became associate secretary. From 1930 to 1932 he was executive secretary of the Foreign Mission Board, and at his retirement in 1933, he was made secretary emeritus. During his service with the board, Ray visited mission fields in Europe, Brazil, Argentina, Chile, Mexico, Japan, and China. Editor of the *Foreign Mission Journal,* Ray's books include *Only a Missionary, Brazilian Sketches,* and *Southern Baptists in the Great Adventure.*

BIBLIOGRAPHY: B. J. W. Graham, *Baptist Biography* (1920). G. B. Taylor, *Virginia Baptist Ministers,* 6th series (1935). E. C. ROUTH

READ, HIRAM WALTER (b. Jewett City, Conn., July 17, 1819; d. El Paso, Tex., Feb. 6, 1895). Chaplain, evangelistic missionary, and pastor. The son of Caleb and Mary (Leffingwell) Read, he was educated at Oswego Academy, Hamilton College, and Madison University. Baptized into the Baptist church at Oswego, N. Y., Mar. 11, 1838, Read was later ordained to the ministry and began pastoral work at Whitewater, Wis., in 1844; he served as chaplain to the Wisconsin state senate.

On July 12, 1849, under direction of the Baptist Home Mission Society, Read, accompanied by his wife, arrived in Sante Fe, N. Mex. They were so impressed with the region that they decided against going farther west and became the first evangelical missionaries in the New Mexico territory. Read was appointed chaplain at Ft. Marcy, near Santa Fe, July 16, 1849, and served until Mar. 15, 1852. He established the first school in Santa Fe to teach English; he learned Spanish, distributed Bibles and tracts, and preached the gospel. At one time Read was captured by Indians and threatened with death by fire. He preached on the Sante Fe plaza immediately after his arrival in 1849 and within a matter of days launched a program of house-to-house visitation in an effort to win the people of the new field. He surveyed the area and helped to assign workers, visited most of the Indian pueblos and distributed Bibles when possible, and organized the first Sunday school. Read, who once traveled 950 miles on horseback from Santa Fe to El Paso and back, organized Albuquerque Baptist Church Oct. 10, 1853, and became its first pastor. In 1855 he went to Arizona, holding important positions there. He joined the Northern army, was captured, and was exchanged in 1862. Read settled in El Paso in 1885, where he remained until his death.

MRS. RICHARD THOMAS BAKER, SR.

RECEPTION OF MEMBERS, INDUCTION, TRAINING. *Congregational authority for reception of members.*—Although the Scriptures give no details regarding the organization and administration of the local church as we now know it, a study of the New Testament discloses that the churches were local, independent, democratic, and self-governing. Churches exercised authority over their membership, rebuked sin, and had the power to exclude. The Jerusalem church decided on Saul's petition to become identified with them (Acts 9:26). Paul instructed the church at Rome to "receive" certain believers (Rom. 14:1). In writing to the Corinthian church Paul definitely instructed them as to the course of action to be taken by the church against those who walk unworthy of the name of Christ (I Cor. 5).

Believers in Christ are led by the indwelling Holy Spirit. Although voting on the reception of new members is not specifically stated, it is implied and certainly not denied. In early churches, members were subject to the action of the body.

Since the Scriptures do not definitely state any specified time when such control should begin, the logical conclusion is that control begins at the very earliest inception of the relationship. The early church was made up of people who were familiar with democratic procedure and the use of the vote, and because of the democratic character of the church, there is every reason to believe the churches of the New Testament employed this method of expressing their desires.

Orientation of new church members.—True evangelism is defined by Christ in his command to go, preach, baptize, and teach. Teaching the young Christian and new church member is a vital part of New Testament evangelism. Most spiritual ills are rooted in ignorance. Inactivity and indifference are the result of lack of nurture. Spiritual growth and maturity for the "babe in Christ" is the direct and inescapable responsibility of the church which has led him to faith in Christ.

The proper orientation of the young Christian and new church member requires special attention of the church apart from the normal pattern of church activity. The task of giving this instruction normally falls upon the pastor because of the relationship already established. Experiments have justified the formation of a "pastor's class," where all who unite with the church (not only those who come on profession of faith) are taught by the pastor. This class meets during the Training Union hour. A series of lessons includes discussions of the experience of salvation, the meaning of baptism and church membership, aids to spiritual growth, Baptist principles and beliefs, the task of the church, and the place and responsibility of the new member in the work of the kingdom. Emphasis is placed upon stewardship and missions. (Due to age differences, there may be more than one class. Ideally, instruction should be given on the department level.)

Following this study the new member is enlisted in the organizations and work of the church. In order to discover aptitudes, abilities, and desires for service, the new church member is interviewed by a church-elected superintendent of enlistment. All organizations within the church keep this superintendent advised as to their need for workers, and he aids in determining where the new member can serve most effectively. Since the new member may have more than one ability or desire for service, a permanent record should be made of all his interests and capabilities. This indexed catalogue of experienced personnel is an invaluable source of information to the church, enabling it to utilize a majority of its membership without burdening a few.

Program of training for new church members.—Continuous training of new members is mandatory if spiritual maturity is to be attained. Such training is made available through the religious education organizations of the church.

H. B. KUHNLE

RECONCILIATION. The word itself means a change from one state or condition into another, resulting in harmony. Thus Paul uses the word, when understood in light of its context, to mean a change from the state of enmity to one of peace and fellowship. It is a reunion, an adjustment, a restoration.

The Old Testament usage of "reconciliation" does not help to elucidate the New Testament terms, since it is so interwoven with other phases of the redemptive work of God. In the New Testament *katallagē* is used only one time outside Paul's writings (Matt. 5:24), and then not in a doctrinal sense. Paul uses the term in its various forms in five different passages in four epistles (Rom. 5:8–11; 11:15; II Cor. 5:18–20; Eph. 2:12–16; Col. 1:19–22).

A study of II Corinthians 5:18–20 reveals the total New Testament scope of the doctrine of reconciliation. The passage presents (1) the subject of reconciliation, God; (2) the object of reconciliation, man and the world; (3) the means of reconciliation, Christ and his total redemptive work; and (4) the ministry of reconciliation, the Word committed to the Christian believer.

Paul always uses the word "reconciliation" to mean the change to the proper relationship between God and man or God and the world. Always, God takes the initiative, man is the object, sin is the cause, the atoning work of Christ is the means, and the Word committed unto believers is the ministry.

BIBLIOGRAPHY: E. H. Walker, "The Doctrine of Reconciliation in the Pauline Epistles" (1949).

ELBERT H. WALKER

RECORD, THE. Published as a result of the request for a religious weekly made by the Missouri Baptist state convention in Sept., 1865, at St. Louis, with Adin A. Kendrick, editor, and Chauncy R. Barnes, publisher. In Aug., 1868, *The Record* and the *Missouri Baptist Journal* were consolidated under the name *Central Baptist* in an effort to remove friction which developed between the two Baptist elements in Missouri as a result of the Civil War.

J. R. BLACK

RECREATION, CHURCH. Constructive, creative, leisure-time activities centered in the church as an integral part of its educational program are called church recreation. The specific activities of the program will vary according to such factors as the size of the congregation, facilities of the buildings and grounds, availability of leadership, the interests of the people, and the geographical location of the church.

Church recreation may be said to be of four types. It involves four general types of activity. They are social, physical, cultural, and creative. The social type is perhaps most widely used and, in the long run, is probably the most valuable to the life of the church. It includes parties, banquets, fellowship groups, and other gatherings of the members for the purpose of sharing in playing games, group singing, and eating. The physical type of church recreation includes playground activities, athletics, camping, and sports of all kinds. The cultural type refers to dramatics, glee clubs, choral speech groups, reading clubs, and other activities of general cultural value. Creative recreation includes activities which are the expression of the desire to create: crafts such as leather, copper, jewelry making, ceramics, basketry, and so on; also certain activities which have a service objective.

There is no arbitrary line of separation in these types of recreation. The cultural may also be creative and vice versa. The social and cultural may be the same, and it may be difficult to distinguish the physical from the social.

Church recreation is for all ages. It is far more than a youth program. Much emphasis is currently placed on recreation for the aging. Also, churches are providing constructive play programs for children. A program of church recreation—well planned, properly balanced, and skilfully directed—is designed to enrich the lives of the members, expand their interests, and help them use even their leisure hours to the glory of God. Its purpose, therefore, is more significant than a remedial measure for delinquency. Its object is to make a contribution to the development of personality in keeping with the Christian concept of wholesome and harmonious living. The values of a church recreation program are observable in the deepening spiritual interests of individuals, their improved skills of social adjustment, and the enriched attitudes of Christian joy and love.

AGNES DURANT PYLANT

REDEMPTION. Liberation from sin, provided by God himself and embracing the gift of eternal life and a new nature, and the reconstruction of life based on right relationship with God (I Cor. 1:30). At the consummation of God's redemptive purpose, there will also be complete deliverance from suffering, sin, and death (Eph. 1:14; Rom. 8:23).

In the Old Testament redemption is closely associated with money or property (Lev. 25:24 ff.); it is a release secured by payment of a price or ransom (Lev. 27:9–34). In the later Old Testament record there appears the higher concept of a divine deliverance from sin.

The New Testament teaches that God works in Christ for love's sake to emancipate his people from bondage, guilt, and sin. God gives a blood sacrifice as a means of life—that of his only Son. Thus redemption becomes a Christ-deliverance or the act of setting free (Rom. 3:24–25).

The idea of redemption finds its fruition in the atoning death of Christ (Eph. 1:7). At great cost Christ voluntarily died in man's place (I Pet. 1:18–19). This sacrificial death of Christ, when accepted by personal faith, becomes the means of forgiveness and reconciliation. It validates previous symbols and brings about the forgiveness of those who were called both before and after the cross (Heb. 9:15).

See also ATONEMENT; RIGHTEOUSNESS; RECONCILIATION.

BIBLIOGRAPHY: H. W. Robinson, *Redemption and Revelation* (1942). G. F. White, "The Meaning and Use of *Apolutrosis* and Its Cognates in the New Testament" (1947). GLENN F. WHITE

REEDER, EDGAR WILEY (b. Benton, Ky., Mar. 1, 1881; d. Jacksonville, Fla., Nov. 28, 1947). Pastor, missionary, Illinois Baptist leader. After receiving his elementary school education in Benton, Ky., Reeder moved to Ewing, Ill., in 1906, where he attended Ewing College. Ordained in the First Baptist Church at Ewing on Apr. 30, 1908, while attending college, Reeder served as pastor in Tamaroa, Coulterville, Willisville, and Brubaker.

In 1910 he was graduated from the Creal Springs College with the degree of Bachelor of Philosophy, and soon thereafter became pastor of the First Baptist Church in Dupo, Ill. Later that year he became pastor of the Winstanley Baptist Church in East St. Louis, Ill., where he served until 1917. Becoming superintendent of city missions in East St. Louis, Reeder helped to organize Franklin Park, Unity, 17th Street Belleville, Oak Park, Edgemont, and Granite City Second churches. He later led in organizing a missionary Baptist church in Carbondale, now known as Walnut Street Baptist Church.

In Nov., 1922, Reeder became executive secretary of Illinois Baptist State Association and served in this office until his retirement on Mar. 1, 1946. During these years he traveled more than a million miles. The number of churches increased from 471 to 566. Church membership increased from 58,373 to 89,631 and mission offerings increased from $69,088 to $301,709. Reeder led churches of Illinois to adopt a systematic financial plan, urging 25 per cent for missions. Under his leadership the state debt of $60,000 was paid in full. An evangelist at heart, Reeder preached in numerous revivals and won many to Christ. ARCHIE E. BROWN

REGENERATION. The means by which a human being is recreated into the image of Jesus Christ. The literal meaning of the word is "born again," designating the radical transformation of human life from self-centeredness to God-centeredness. Man may live in one of two orders of life: the "natural" or the "spiritual." Man lives in the "natural" order by being a human being; he comes to live in the "spiritual" order by God's action in Jesus Christ. Though the word itself is rarely used in the New Testament, the idea is found constantly. When Jesus tells men to become as little children (Matt. 18:1–4), he states the need for regeneration; Paul has the same meaning in mind when he speaks of "adoption" into God's family (Gal. 4:1–7). Regeneration is therefore a word taken from family life to designate incorporation into God's family. In John 3:3 the actual word is "born from above" and calls for a new birth from God. Regeneration may therefore be defined as the change of heart accomplished by Jesus Christ, "the firstborn among many brethren," through the effective power of the Holy Spirit whereby new life is given to men, renewing man's whole nature so as to give him a new relation to God, to other men, and to all things.

See also CONVERSION. W. C. STRICKLAND

REGULAR BAPTIST CHURCHES, GENERAL ASSOCIATION OF. A fellowship organized in May, 1932, in Chicago, Ill., by a group of churches that had withdrawn from the Northern (now American) Baptist Convention because of doctrinal differences. This body requires all of its churches to subscribe to the New Hampshire Confession of Faith with a premillennial interpretation of the final article of the confession. Members maintain that the Bible is the infallible Word of God; that Satan is a person and the author of all evil; and that man is a creation of God, yet is born in sin. They teach a bodily resurrection of the saints and the premillennial return of Christ to reign during the millennium. Church polity is strictly congregational. Baptism by immersion and the Lord's Supper are the two approved ordinances. The churches conduct educational and missionary work through independent schools and mission agencies approved by the association. This body, which in 1956 had 726 churches with a combined membership of 124,039, has its headquarters in Chicago, Ill. There it publishes a monthly periodical called *Baptist Bulletin*. LYNN E. MAY, JR.

REGULAR BAPTISTS. The name given to the Calvinistic Baptists who looked to Philadelphia as their center in the 18th century. They were the oldest and most prominent group of Baptists in the middle colonies of America. Before 1752 they were strongest in the general vicinity of Philadelphia, although after this date they spread rapidly through Virginia and eastern North Carolina, where the name Regular was especially useful after 1755 in distinguishing its bearers from the revivalistic Separate Baptists.

The evangelical Calvinistic theology of the Philadelphia Baptists, whose associational life began in 1707, prompted the sending out of pastors as itinerant preachers into neglected areas and in response to calls from weak, strife-torn, and pastorless churches. Among these early evangelists were Benjamin Miller, John Thomas, and John Gano (*q.v.*). In 1755 Gano made a prolonged tour of the Carolinas. By 1765 churches of the Philadelphia Association were found as far south as Charleston, S. C. Daniel Marshall (*q.v.*), converted under the preaching of Whitefield in New England and later a lay missionary to the Indians of western Pennsylvania, came into the northwest area of Virginia in 1754. He and his wife were baptized into the Opekon (or Mill Creek) Church, and here he was licensed to preach. His zealous preaching generated much enthusiasm, which startled the more conservative members but helped add many members to the church. Shubal Stearns (*q.v.*) and his party from Connecticut also settled in the vicinity of Opekon for several months of 1754 before going on to North Carolina, where he organized the Separate Baptist movement. In 1765, with permission from the Philadelphia Association, the four Regular Baptist churches in Virginia formed the Ketocton Association.

Philadelphia Association preachers who were sent forth to North Carolina attempted with remarkable success to change the theological views of General Baptists in the eastern part of that state. Benjamin Miller of Scotch Plains, N. J., and Peter Peterson Van Horn of Pennepak, N. J., were sent there in 1755 and reorganized many of the churches as Regular. These churches formed the Kehukee Association in 1769.

Regular Baptists accepted the Philadelphia Confession of Faith as their doctrinal symbol and often used it as a basis for intercongregational association. In accordance with that confession, they practiced hymn singing and imposition of hands upon baptized believers. They were greatly stimulated by the rise of the Separate Baptist movement in Virginia and the Carolinas.

As early as 1769, the Ketocton Association of Regular Baptists sent fraternal messengers to the General Association of Separate Baptists to propose a union. This proposal the general association rejected without explanation. In 1772 the Kehukee Regular Association sent deputies to establish contact with the Separate churches. The Separates refused the overture on the grounds that the Kehukee churches did not strictly require candidates for church membership to relate their conversion experiences before baptism, and that the Kehukee people were guilty of "superfluity of apparel." Several Kehukee churches soon sought to conform to Separate usage and in 1777 joined with four Separate churches in forming a new association. The Regulars and the Separates were brought together generally in Virginia through their common involvement in the struggle for separation of church and state and for complete religious liberty. In Oct., 1784, delegates from four associations, including the Ketocton, met to organize a general committee to guard the rights of Virginia Baptists against remaining religious discriminations. The committee met annually and made contributions to the cause of religious liberty in Virginia and the nation. The result of this co-operation between the two groups was a recommendation by the committee to district associations that they send delegates to its meeting in 1787 to form a permanent union of Separate and Regular Baptists. The union was consummated on the basis of the Philadelphia Confession.

Meanwhile, following the Revolution, both

Separate and Regular Baptists had moved westward into Kentucky, and they organized associations of both kinds. The first Regular Baptist association was the Elkhorn, organized in 1785; the first Separate association was the South Kentucky, organized in 1787. At length the Frontier Awakening of 1801–03 brought the Separates and the Regulars together, and they were united in 1801. After 1787 the names Regular and Separates were quickly dropped in Virginia, being replaced for a few years by the name United Baptists; in Kentucky the party distinctions continued for some years before fading out.

In isolated communities of the early Southern frontier of America, a few people retained the name Regular Baptists. They continued to exist independently of other Baptist groups and are today gathered in about 22 associations. They have no general organization. Total membership in 1951 numbered approximately 17,000.

Bibliography: L. Burkitt and J. Read, *A Concise History of the Kehukee Baptist Association* (1803). A. D. Gillette, ed., *Minutes of the Philadelphia Baptist Association* (1851). F. S. Mead, *Handbook of Denominations in the United States* (1955). G. Ryland, *The Baptists of Virginia, 1699–1926* (1955). R. B. Semple, *A History of the Rise and Progress of the Baptists in Virginia* (1810). J. H. Spencer, *A History of Kentucky Baptists* (1886). R. G. Torbet, *A History of the Baptists* (1950).

WILLIAM L. LUMPKIN

REGULAR BAPTISTS, CURRENT. Centering in North Carolina and Kentucky, Regular Baptists claim to be the modern representatives of the original English Baptists prior to division into Particular and General Baptists. Their doctrinal position is generally Arminian, although some lean toward Calvinism. Strict in holding to closed communion and foot-washing, they form associations for fellowship only, with little or no general organization. Each association has its own declaration of faith. In 1932 Regular Baptists reported 23,091 members; in 1956 there were only 17,186. These figures indicate decline and disintegration. At one time this group published in Kensington, Md., a magazine called the *Regular Baptist Magazine.* ALBERT MCCLELLAN

RELATIONS BETWEEN NORTHERN AND SOUTHERN BAPTISTS. Although Baptists in the northern and southern sections of the United States originally sprang from the same general stock, wide variations in cultural background have brought separate organizational bodies, and subsequent rivalry in geographical extension has resulted in strained relations. For well over a century after the first Baptist churches were constituted in the two areas, there was no sectional tension, probably because of the completely autonomous nature of the churches and associations. Although doctrinal differences produced several varieties of Baptists (General, Particular, Six-Principle, Seventh Day, etc.), the tensions generated were not primarily geographical.

The first distinctly sectional tension between Baptists in the North and the South arose after the organization of the three national benevolent societies for co-operative work: the foreign mission society in 1814, the tract society in 1824, and the home mission society in 1832. The basic source of this tension was the radically different cultures of the two sections: climate, geography, economy, and inheritance molded distinctive points of view. In particular, the institution of Negro slavery, which had been introduced and firmly established under English colonial policy during the infancy of the southern settlements in America, marked the southern area with an overwhelming uniqueness. The influence of geography and climate brought practically all of the slaves from northern ports into the South, where large, one-crop plantations in the midst of a warm climate and a "long year" made them useful. On the other hand, with diversified crops, small farms, and a rigorous climate, the North had little use for the slave as a laborer. Consequently, although economically unprofitable and morally wrong, Negro slavery was clung to by a minority and defended by the majority in the South as the cultural and economic inheritance from previous generations.

In the first half of the 19th century the strength of the system was deteriorating rather rapidly, and many Southerners were praying and predicting that it would be eliminated. However, the attacks of the Northern abolitionists, accentuated by the sharp rise of sectional sensitiveness, caused many Southerners who actually despised slavery to defend it against the "foreign" tirades. The clash between the cultures of the North and the South, each the product of the adaptation of previous generations to historic, geographic, and climatic factors, wrenched Northern and Southern Baptists apart in 1845.

The second major period of tension between Northern and Southern Baptists has been focused in geography. After the close of the Civil War in 1865, Baptists in the North determined to evangelize and teach the emancipated slaves of the South. This aim was soon broadened to include the evangelization and enlistment of all of the South, and from 1865 to 1887, Baptist missionaries from the North ministered throughout the Southern states. As a whole, Southern Baptists resented this program because they felt that it would destroy their own Southern Baptist Convention. Their attachment to this Southern Baptist Convention was grounded not only in sectional loyalty but in their conviction concerning the nature of the body. Purposely designed to be a true denominational body embracing all of the benevolent interests of Baptists in the South, the Southern Baptist Convention was meant to be different in character from the decentralized society plan of organization used by Northern Baptists for their benevolent work. Resentment against the extensive missionary activity in the South by the Northern society, the development of a centralized denominational program among Southern Baptists, gave to the constituents of the Southern Baptist Convention a strong sense of uniqueness and solidarity. This self-consciousness has contributed greatly to the present period of tension between Northern and Southern Baptists.

During the last half-century a number of factors have combined to shift the Baptist population from the South to all parts of the nation. New frontiers in the West, dislocations of a wartime economy, increasing mobility of Southern populations, and similar developments have settled Southern Baptists in every state. Because of their extensive training in the kind of denominational program and "Bible-belt" doctrines fostered by the Southern Baptist Convention, these Southern immigrants were not assimilated into the Baptist churches in Western and Northern areas.

Coincident with this self-consciousness on the part of the Southern Baptist immigrants was a widespread internal conflict within Northern Baptist ranks. A large segment in the Northern body vigorously charged their denominational leaders with doctrinal looseness and demanded the adoption of confessional standards of orthodoxy. Consequently, when Southern Baptists moved into Northern areas, conscious of this criticism and noting differences to which they were unaccustomed, many of them looked askance at all Northern Baptist churches. Therefore, for reasons partly doctrinal, partly cultural, and partly sectional, many Baptists from the South held aloof from fellowship with Baptist churches in the areas to which they had moved. Subsequently there followed the formation of Baptist churches, associations, and finally state conventions which sought and secured affiliation with the Southern Baptist Convention. This pattern has brought considerable tension in Northern and Western states since 1906. It is now being followed in Utah, Nevada, Idaho, Colorado, Wyoming, Montana, North Dakota, South Dakota, Wisconsin, Indiana, Michigan, and Ohio.

The Southern Baptist Convention did not inaugurate the movement that has brought this tension. Upon their own initiative Southern immigrants have organized Baptist churches in the new areas, have formed their own associations and state bodies, and then have applied for recognition to the Southern Baptist Convention. They have been recognized under the constitutional provisions of the Southern Baptist Convention as old as the Convention itself: the original article of 1845 described the geographical extent of the Southern Baptist Convention as the United States and its Territories. The official policy of the Home Mission Board of the Southern Baptist Convention states that they "discourage on the part of already established churches affiliation with our Convention work," and that they "grant no aid or assistance in establishing new work in any area that already has a Baptist church affiliated with any of the other conventions."

The two conventions have endeavored to maintain fraternal relations. In 1894 the Southern Baptist Convention refused to give favorable consideration to applications for assistance and affiliation from Baptists in New Mexico and Oregon. In that year at Fortress Monroe, Va., committees from each convention agreed on plans to co-operate in work with the Negroes and on policies aimed at avoiding antagonism in mission work. The formula adopted, however, was too indefinite to be useful and was repudiated by a joint committee in 1909.

The principles of comity that now form the permanent basis of agreement between Northern and Southern Baptists were formulated by committees from each convention in 1911–12. Meeting at Old Point Comfort, Va., and Hot Springs, Ark., the joint committee asserted the complete independence of a Baptist church and the advisory nature of all denominational organizations; at the same time the committee pointed to the moral interdependence of Baptists and the need for co-operation by all Baptist churches. It further agreed that the giving of financial aid by a denominational body does not impair the autonomy of a church; that denominational bodies should carefully regard the rights of sister organizations and of the churches, in order to promote unity and mutual liberty; and that Baptist bodies should never in any way injure the work of other Baptist groups. In recent years both Northern and Southern Baptists have reaffirmed these principles as constituting the basic points of agreement on comity.

BIBLIOGRAPHY: R. A. Baker, *Relations Between Northern and Southern Baptists* (1954). W. W. Barnes, *The Southern Baptist Convention 1845–1953* (1954). A. T. Foss and E. Matthews, *Facts for Baptist Churches* (1850). A. H. Newman, *A History of the Baptist Churches in the United States* (1898). R. G. Torbet, *A History of the Baptists* (1950). A. L. Vail, *Morning Hour of American Baptist Missions* (1907); *Baptists Mobilized for Missions* (1911).

ROBERT A. BAKER

RELIEF, MINISTERIAL. Prior to the organization of the Relief and Annuity Board in 1918, relief for Southern Baptist ministers and the widows of ministers had been carried on by the various state conventions. Eleven states were promoting such relief, mostly through endowment funds. The desire to provide more adequately for the more than 1,000 needy ministers in the Convention was the impetus that launched the Relief and Annuity Board.

After 1918 many of the state conventions transferred their endowment funds to the board. However, it was a year or more after the board's organization before it secured the co-operation of most of the states in channeling their relief funds through the board instead of through their own state societies. By 1925 all except one state were in full co-operation, and that state began co-operating in later years.

To strengthen the Relief Department, the board in 1929 secured the Convention's approval of its decision to place all Cooperative Program receipts not otherwise designated in the Relief Fund; previously, these receipts had been divided with the Annuity Fund. This was made possible by a $500,000 gift to the Annuity Fund by John D. Rockefeller. Since 1939 Cooperative Program receipts coming to the Relief and Annuity Board have been divided between relief and the (Old) Annuity Fund.

Income for the Relief Fund is provided from three sources: Cooperative Program, designated gifts by individuals or endowment, and special offerings by churches. The first year, only $1,397 was distributed in relief; by 1920 this had grown to $52,218, and in 1942 it was $102,929. By the end of 1954, the board had distributed a total of $321,059.91 in relief benefits.

The Relief Department has never been able to meet all of the need at any time during its existence, and even with the inclusion of more and more ministers in the various retirement plans of the board, the Relief Fund will still be needed. In 1954 there were 1,530 receiving aid.

Robert S. Jones, associate secretary, wrote,

> It will be necessary to have the Relief Department for many, many years, as numbers of our country pastors feel that they cannot afford to pay the 5 per cent of the small salaries they receive. Every year ministers are retiring who have never been enrolled in any retirement plan, and who have no source of income after retirement.

WALKER L. KNIGHT

RELIEF AND ANNUITY BOARD. Established in 1918, it was the culmination of efforts on the part of many Baptist leaders to make provision for the economic security of the pastor in old age.

As early as 1893, William Crane (*q.v.*) and J. H. Deems of Maryland organized the Widows and Superannuated Ministers Fund. In Virginia the Board of Ministerial Relief was organized in 1872, with Charles L. Cocke as the first president. An endowment fund of $69,886 was reported by the Virginia board in 1942. The Board of Ministerial Relief in South Carolina was first organized in 1813, disappeared in the '80's, and was revived again in 1890 under C. C. Brown (*q.v.*), pastor of the First Baptist Church, Sumter, S. C., who served as secretary. It eventually raised an endowment of $50,000.

William Huff led the creation of the Board of Ministerial Relief in Tennessee a few years after the close of the Civil War. The Tennessee board succeeded in raising an endowment of $10,000. T. E. Glass was secretary and treasurer of the board for many years. In Missouri C. H. Hardin and J. A. Guthrie led in this movement, gaining an endowment of $100,000. Texas organized its Board of Relief for disabled ministers in 1887, with H. M. Burroughs as executive secretary. For a number of years, a home for aged and disabled ministers was operated in Texas.

Green Clay Smith sponsored the movement in Kentucky. The Baptist Ministers Aid Society was organized in 1884, under J. S. Felix of Owensboro, creating an endowment of $65,000. In Georgia J. H. DeVotie (*q.v.*), for many years state mission secretary, stirred interest in the care of dependent ministers, eventually building an endowment of $45,000.

When the Convention-wide movement for ministerial relief and annuities was initiated, already nine other denominations in the United States, including Northern Baptists, were undertaking to raise endowment funds amounting to $65 million for ministerial relief and annuities, some $35 million already having been subscribed. Southern Baptists became the 10th.

The movement was initiated at a Nashville Baptist pastors' conference in 1916. At this meeting, William Lunsford (*q.v.*), pastor of Edgefield Baptist Church, Nashville, Tenn., addressed the group on the subject of ministerial relief. "Dr. Lunsford spoke with great feeling and stirred the hearts of those present." When he had finished, several short speeches were made by pastors present, endorsing his comments.

Several members of the Nashville pastors' conference, among them Lunsford, were members of the Sunday School Board. The matter was mentioned informally at the next board meeting. I. J. Van Ness (*q.v.*), acting corresponding secretary of the Sunday School Board, at the Jan., 1917, meeting recommended that the board set apart $75,000 to start a fund for the purpose of ministerial relief, and that the sum be reported to the Convention.

On the motion of Allen Fort (*q.v.*), pastor of the First Baptist Church, Nashville, Tenn., the amount was raised to $100,000, and the recommendation was passed unanimously, the board voting to request the Southern Baptist Convention, at its coming session, to consider the appointment of a commission to examine the various plans now being operated for ministerial relief in the various states.

The committee appointed by the Convention to study the recommendations of the Sunday School Board was as follows: William Lunsford, M. D. Jeffries, E. W. Stephens (*q.v.*), W. H. Morgan, H. F. Vermillion, W. N. Jones, and D. Y. Bagby. The committee recommended that the Convention adopt the report of the Sunday School Board in setting apart the $100,000 for this cause.

The report also recommended that

> . . . a committee of nine members or more be appointed by the president of the convention to work out a just and equitable pension plan during the ensuing year whereby the funds shall be protected from diminution or loss, and so safeguarded that only the meritorius can secure the benefits of them; that the members of the Commission reside in easy access of Nashville, Tenn., so as to be in close touch with the Sunday School Board, that the Sunday School Board shall be the custodian of this fund until otherwise directed by the Southern Baptist Convention, holding such money subject to such conditions and restrictions as the Commission of nine or more shall direct.

The report having been adopted, President James Bruton Gambrell (*q.v.*) appointed 12 members to the commission: Allen Fort, J. F. Brownlow, O. C. Barton, Howard E. Frost, W. W. Landrum (*q.v.*), William Lunsford, I. J.

Van Ness, Austin Crouch, A. C. Cree (*q.v.*), T. B. Ray (*q.v.*), A. B. Hill, and E. W. Stephens (*q.v.*).

The commission met in Nashville June 11, 1917, electing Allen Fort chairman and William Lunsford secretary. Responsibility for collecting facts and materials toward formulating an actual relief program was delegated to Lunsford. Work and study of the commission resulted in the comprehensive report which was made to the Convention at Hot Springs, Ark., in 1918, recommending: That "a Board of Ministerial Relief and Annuities be established"; that the board be located in Birmingham, Ala.; that the plan for ministerial relief and annuities as submitted by the commission be adopted.

The plan called for a relief department, to be financed from contributions from the churches, from endowment, and from an apportionment of the denominational budget. Ministers, missionaries, widows of ministers and missionaries, and minor children were to be included in its beneficences.

The annuity fund was to be built from contributions from members in the form of premiums based on member's age at entry, and contributions from churches and individuals. The Annuity Fund, now known as the (Old) Annuity Fund, proposed to pay a member annuity at the age of 68 not in excess of $500 per year, a widow annuity not to exceed $300 per year, and a minor children annuity, if no widow is left, of not more than $300 per year. The annuities were to be based on years of service. Disability benefits were also included. The minister would pay one fifth of the cost, and the denomination would pay four fifths.

Both divisions were to be endowed by a total of $3 million, to be divided two to one, i.e., $2 million for relief and $1 million for annuity fund. The commission stated that the plan submitted "provides for a system of relief never attempted before by Southern Baptists, that is, for ministers of all ages and their widows and orphans."

The commission felt it would take a year for the board to organize its work and "get it going," setting as its goal 300 members for the annuity fund. Expenses for thus beginning the work were to be taken from the $100,000 in trust with the Sunday School Board.

The report of the Commission on Ministerial Relief was adopted by the Convention May 20, 1918, with one change: The location of the board was to be Dallas, Tex., rather than Birmingham, Ala.

The committee on nominations appointed to the new board 18 state members and 18 local members. State members were: H. B. Foster, Alabama; G. W. Puryear (*q.v.*), Arkansas; J. J. Darlington, District of Columbia; N. A. Blitch, Florida; J. E. Sammons (*q.v.*), Georgia; D. C. Jones, Illinois; F. L. Hardy, Kentucky; G. M. Harrell, Louisiana; J. H. Strong, Maryland; A. H. Longino, Mississippi; J. J. Brown, Missouri; J. J. Hurt, North Carolina; W. Royal, New Mexico; A. N. Hall, Oklahoma; C. C. Brown (*q.v.*), South Carolina; William Lunsford, Tennessee; G. W. McDaniel (*q.v.*), Virginia; R. T. Hanks, Texas. Local members were: M. H. Wolfe, J. Dabney Day, L. R. Scarborough (*q.v.*), R. H. Coleman (*q.v.*), C. D. Fine, Cullen F. Thomas, O. C. Payne, J. L. Gross, Wallace Bassett, E. C. Routh, Hal White, D. Y. Bagby, George W. Truett (*q.v.*), O. S. Lattimore (*q.v.*), S. P. Brooks (*q.v.*), J. H. Moore, Rice Maxey, Sam H. Campbell.

The committee on nominations recommended that the election of the corresponding secretary be referred to the new board just created by the Convention. When the board held its first meeting July 10, 1918, in Dallas, William Lunsford was chosen to fill the position of corresponding secretary. Other officers were: S. P. Brooks, president; R. H. Coleman, recording secretary; Rice Maxey, vice-president; and J. Dabney Day, treasurer.

The charter was obtained July 1, 1918, under the Texas statutes, and later amended Sept. 17, 1920, when the corporate name of the board was changed from The Board of Ministerial Relief and Annuities of the Southern Baptist Convention to the Relief and Annuity Board of the Southern Baptist Convention.

Following the original thinking of the commission, the new board began immediately to set in motion the machinery of its two departments of work. By the end of the first year, Secretary Lunsford reported that Texas, Tennessee, Georgia, Mississippi, Louisiana, Florida, Alabama, Oklahoma, North Carolina, Kentucky, Arkansas, and New Mexico had endorsed the relief plan, with "matters of adjustment still to be made." Actually, it was 1925 before every state had turned over its relief work to the board. Immediate goal of the relief department was to give an allowance of $200 per year to every beneficiary that the states had turned over to the board.

The Annuity Department enlisted 133 members during its first year, but was unable to issue membership certificates until 300 members were secured. The first certificate in the Annuity Fund was issued July 1, 1919, to Allen Fort.

A period of concerted effort by Lunsford to achieve an endowment fund followed, resulting in the Rockefeller gifts, which in the end totaled a million dollars.

By 1923 assets of the board totaled $1,490,193.59, and benefits of $116,375.65 had been paid. Before the close of 1924, however, it became apparent that the (Old) Annuity Fund was inadequate to meet the growing needs of the Convention. The period of promotion and expansion of the board began in earnest. Not only was the annuity plan revised, but new retirement plans to meet the retirement needs of employees of Southern Baptist boards, hospitals, schools, and orphanages were inaugurated. Between 1925 and 1943, 11 new retirement plans were initiated.

It was at the beginning of this period that the

board lost its first secretary. After a long illness, William Lunsford died May 24, 1927. He was succeeded by Thomas J. Watts (*q.v.*), who held the post of executive secretary for a period of 18 years.

The Special Annuity or lump sum annuity was begun in 1929. This form of certificate met the requirements of those who desired to make lump sum payments from $1,000 to $5,000 or more and receive specified annuities beginning at once or at any deferred date. The plan is still open to membership.

The Savings Annuity Plan, inaugurated in 1930, was designed to aid ministers, missionaries, or other salaried denominational employees to conserve their savings, with an addition of interest paid by the board. The plan is still available.

The (Old) Annuity Fund was closed to new members Sept. 30, 1930, supplanted by the Service Annuity Plan, Jan. 1, 1932. The Service Plan, a contributory one, was never accepted wholeheartedly by the preachers and churches of the Convention, and was closed to new members Jan. 1, 1938.

The Foreign Mission Board Pension Plan was inaugurated Jan. 1, 1934. Dues were $2.50 per month and were remitted to the board by the Foreign Mission Board. The Foreign Mission Board contributed the same amount in behalf of each missionary. Guarantor of the plan was the Foreign Mission Board. Guarantor of the invested funds was the Relief and Annuity Board. Under this plan the missionary would receive $500 per year at retirement. Missionary couples would receive $1,000. In July, 1950, the Foreign Mission Board took over the administration of its own retirement plan.

On Jan. 1, 1936, the Institutional Employees Retirement Plan for orphanages was inaugurated. The plan was based on dues paid by the employer equivalent to 3 per cent of the member's monthly salary, and 3 per cent contributed by the member. Minimum benefit after 25 years' service is $500 per year. Dues are now increased to 5 per cent for employer in this plan.

The Age Security Plan was inaugurated Jan. 1, 1935. The plan provided that the pastor contribute 3 per cent to the plan and the church contribute 3 per cent. Later revised (1940), the plan now operates primarily for church employees who are not eligible for the minister's plans, although ministers may take out Age Security in addition to their own retirement plan. The plan is open to every employee who serves a church on a regular salary basis. In 1953 dues were increased as the plan was liberalized. Members may now participate on a 3 per cent member—3 per cent church, 4 per cent member—4 per cent church, or 3 per cent member—5 per cent church basis.

The Baptist Boards Employees Retirement Plan was the next retirement plan inaugurated by the Board during its period of expansion. Originated July 1, 1937, the plan provided for employee retirement benefits for employees of state boards, colleges, hospitals, or seminaries which participate in the plan. The board plan was closed to new groups Oct. 1, 1946. It was closed to new members Jan. 1, 1955, when the new plans, the Baptist Employees Retirement and Baptist Employees Protection plans, were inaugurated.

Also originated July 1, 1937, was the Institutional Employees Retirement Plan for colleges and seminaries. The plan was developed after full conference discussion at Birmingham, Ala., between the board's actuary, George M. Huggins of Philadelphia, Pa., Executive Secretary Watts, and a representative group of college presidents. The plan is not a general group plan. College heads at the Birmingham conference preferred an individual plan. Each group that enters into contract with the Relief and Annuity Board makes its own stipulations regarding maximum salary basis, amount of dues, etc.

Special Deferred Annuity Plan, inaugurated in 1935, is operated on a regular reserve basis. Units of $100 may be purchased in yearly, monthly, quarterly, or semiyearly premiums. Limit is five units. The plan has loan privileges and cash surrender values.

The 10th retirement plan inaugurated during this period of expansion was the Ministers Retirement Plan. First inaugurated in South Carolina July 1, 1938, the plan was gradually accepted by all states. Texas accepted the plan Jan. 1, 1939; Florida, Georgia, Louisiana, Missouri, Oklahoma, and Virginia, July 1, 1939. Alabama, Arkansas, Kentucky, and North Carolina (N. C. plan differs somewhat from plan in other states) inaugurated the plan Jan. 1, 1940; Illinois, Apr. 1, 1940. Tennessee and Mississippi, July 1, 1940; and Maryland, Sept. 1, 1940. On Jan. 1, 1941, Arizona and New Mexico joined the plan; Jan. 1, 1942, District of Columbia; July 1, 1942, California; with the final states, Kansas and Oregon-Washington joining in 1950.

The plan was established on the basis of the minister paying 3 per cent of his salary (up to $4,000 per annum), the church paying 3 per cent, and the Convention paying 2 per cent. The plan gives 2 per cent credit for the last 25 years before retirement, and an annuity is paid at retirement (maximum annuity $2,000 per year). The plan was closed to membership July 1, 1954.

After a period of a few years, however, it was seen that the Ministers Retirement Plan did not provide sufficient coverage for the widow of the minister. All she could receive, if he died in active service, was the amount of his dues, plus interest. A new supplement for those in the Ministers Plan was inaugurated July 1, 1945, in South Carolina—the Widows Supplemental Annuity Plan.

Other states, Oklahoma, Missouri, Illinois, Kentucky, and Virginia, initiated the plan July 1, 1946. Texas, Arizona, New Mexico, California, North Carolina, Louisiana, and Georgia began the plan Jan. 1, 1947; Alabama, July 1, 1947. Arkansas adopted the plan Jan. 1, 1948; Mississippi, July 1, 1948; Maryland, District of

Columbia, Florida, and Kansas, July 1, 1949; and Oregon-Washington and Tennessee, Jan. 1, 1951.

The plan provided for a widow annuity to be paid in the amount of 10 per cent of member's salary while in the plan, up to 20 per cent. Percentage due the widow increases each year until the sixth, when the maximum of 20 per cent is reached. The plan was also made available to those in board and institutional plans.

It was during this period of promotion of the Widows Supplemental Annuity Plan, in 1947, that Walter R. Alexander became executive secretary of the board, succeeding Watts, who retired at the age of 73.

Under Alexander the period of liberalization of the major retirement plans began. Assets of the board increased from $12,838,438.22 in 1947 to $35,091,515.37 in 1954. Ministers who transferred to churches in the American Baptist Convention territory could do so without loss of credits, according to an agreement signed with the American Baptist Convention, Jan. 1, 1953.

Ministers Security Plan, supplement to the Ministers Retirement Plan and Widows Supplemental Annuity Plan, was inaugurated July 1, 1954.

Southern Baptist Protection Plan, newest retirement plan for ministers was opened July 1, 1954, when the Ministers Retirement Plan was closed to new members. The member pays 5 per cent of his salary, the church pays 5 per cent, and the state convention pays 5 per cent. The member receives 1½ per cent credit for each year he is in the retirement plan. Salary participation is limited to $4,000 per year.

Work was begun on liberalization of the Baptist Boards Employees Retirement Plan, which was to be promoted Jan. 1, 1955. During this time Alexander died after a brief illness. His death in Dec., 1954, marked the second death in one year of an officer of the board. Orville Groner (*q.v.*), treasurer of the Relief and Annuity Board for 30 years, had died in January of the same year. R. Alton Reed succeeded Alexander as fourth executive secretary of the board. He was elected in Mar., 1955.

Reed completed the promotion of the Baptist Boards Security Plan, which was a supplement to the Baptist Boards and Widows plans. Two new plans, the Baptist employees Retirement Plan and the Baptist Employees Protection Plan, were inaugurated Jan. 1, 1955, when the old board plan was closed to new members.

Organization and personnel of the Board.—As authorized by the charter and bylaws, general officers of the Relief and Annuity Board consist of a president and two or more vice-presidents. The executive and administrative officers are: executive secretary, who directs the work of all departments, authorizes cash withdrawals and issuance of certificates, makes a report of the work of the board annually, and is an advisory member of all committees; the associate secretary-director of public relations, assistant to the executive secretary, who directs the publicity and distribution of literature for the board; the associate secretary-director of gift annuities, endowments, and relief, who is in charge of all relief matters, of enlisting endowments and legacies, and of the board's service of funding gift annuities for Baptist boards and agencies; the associate secretary-director of investments and the assistant director of investments, who are in charge of investing all funds of the board (this director is custodian of all securities, mortgage loans papers, and other investment records, and is authorized to attest deeds, releases, transfers, assignments, and other legal instruments, and to affix the seal to such papers); the treasurer, in charge of all funds, who directs the depositing and disbursing of monies (he is in charge of matters pertaining to actuarial studies, all accounts of members, churches and conventions, and the work of the annuity department; he is aided by an assistant treasurer); and the recording secretary-registrar, who keeps a full record of all proceedings of the board and executive committee, is custodian of the legal contracts pertaining to the various plans, and is in charge of the issuance of certificates of participation in the various plans.

The advisory counsels are: the general counsel, who renders legal advice, prepares and approves all legal instruments required by the board, and represents the board in all legal matters; the actuarial counsel, who advises with the board, through the executive secretary, concerning all matters that regard the actuarial element of the retirement plan; the auditor, who performs the audit twice yearly, June 30 and Dec. 31; and the medical director, who advises with the board through the executive secretary concerning applications for disability benefits in the various retirement plans.

Such other officers as are deemed necessary for the efficient conduct of the board's business may be employed with the approval of the board.

All officers of the board are elected annually. The annual meeting of the board is held the third Wednesday in March each year. The executive committee, made up of 18 local board members, acts with full authority for the board on all matters of business between sessions of the full board. The committee meets quarterly on the fourth Wednesday in January, April, July, and October.

Board members are appointed by the Southern Baptist Convention. Charter and bylaws operate under the state laws of Texas.

Standing committees of the board are: administrative, finance, and relief. The administrative committee studies the methods of management, advises with the executive secretary on such matters as have not been specifically delegated to standing committees, and recommends to the executive committee the budget of the board year by year. Matters concerning eligibility for membership in the several annuity plans may also be referred to this committee. The finance committee directs, authorizes, and supervises the purchase of all stocks, bonds, and mortgage loans, real estate and other investments, authorizes and supervises other financial transactions which have been delegated by the board. The relief committee approves or disapproves all applications for benefits and makes emergency grants.

The board is under a ruling passed by the Southern Baptist Convention limiting agencies and boards that have trust funds from "investing in the securities of any other denominational body or agency."

Financial structure.—Since the board was first organized to "provide for the relief and support of aged and disabled ministers and needy widows and orphans of deceased ministers of Baptist churches and missionaries of accredited mission boards within the bounds of the Southern Baptist Convention," the financial policies of the board have changed very little.

As foreseen by the original Commission on Ministerial Relief, money for ministerial relief and annuities is received from dues of members in the retirement plan, from contributions from the churches, from endowments, from Cooperative Program, and from investment earnings.

According to the report of the Relief and Annuity Board as of Dec. 31, 1955, investment earnings have been $13,083,347.08. For 30 years the investments department was under direction of Orville Groner. He joined the board as bookkeeper in 1923, was advanced to treasurer of the relief fund in 1924, and general treasurer in 1933, a position he held until his death in 1954.

The board's principal investments consist of first mortgage loans, real estate loans, real estate under liquidating lease, and bonds and stocks. Since Jan. 1, 1950, the board has retained the United States Trust Company of New York as its investments advisor in stocks and bonds. Four times each year the complete list is reviewed by that organization, enabling the board to secure information concerning the economic situation.

Investment objectives as adopted by the finance committee are: mortgage loans, 25 per cent; liquidating leases, 25 per cent; bonds, 25 per cent; common stocks, 15 per cent; and preferred stocks, 10 per cent.

By far the largest amount of money received each year comes from retirement dues from members, state conventions, churches, boards, and agencies. The board (as of 1956) operates 10 annuity plans and one savings plan currently open to membership: Southern Baptist Protection Plan, Baptist Employees Retirement Plan, Baptist Employees Protection Plan, Institutional Employees Retirement Plan (orphanages); Institutional Employees Retirement Plan (colleges and seminaries), Baptist Agencies Retirement Plan, Age Security, Special Deferred Annuity Plan, Life Annuities, Gift Annuities, and Savings Annuity Plan.

The supplemental plans, Widows Supplemental Annuity Plan (A) and Ministers Security Plan, are open to members of the Ministers Retirement Plan, Jan. 1 or July 1 of any year. The Baptist Boards Widow Plan and the Baptist Boards Employees Security Plan are open to members of the basic board plan on Jan. 1 or July 1 of any year.

Amount of benefits paid to relief beneficiaries and annuitants of retirement plans as of Dec. 31, 1955, was $22,494,443.98. All retirement plans are established on an actuarial reserve basis. Reserve for retirement plans in 1955 was $36,581,067.45. Relief reserve was $672,507.53, most of which was endowment, on which only interest could be spent. After interest has been credited to retirement plans each year, amount left is credited to Contingency Reserve. All Cooperative Program money received by the board is used for relief, for funding the (Old) Annuity Fund, and for capital funds, which is an additional safeguard on retirement reserves. Administrative expense is made up from Contingency Reserve and from small fees, which vary according to contract agreement, deducted from employer dues.

Relationship to the Southern Baptist Convention.—The Relief and Annuity Board is one

RELIEF AND ANNUITY BENEFITS BY YEARS

	Relief Benefits	*Annuity Benefits*	*Totals*
1919	$ 1,397.00	$	$ 1,397.00
1920	52,217.61	15.00	52,232.61
1921	118,988.82	450.00	119,438.82
1922	128,966.88	1,240.00	130,206.88
1923	113,322.15	3,053.50	116,375.65
1924	125,449.50	6,071.74	131,521.24
1925	127,021.35	10,145.24	137,166.59
1926	125,933.23	15,894.08	141,827.31
1927	133,551.12	22,964.58	156,515.70
1928	118,520.47	31,274.21	149,794.68
1929	121,884.51	40,821.35	162,705.86
1930 (Apr. 30)	126,193.44	55,101.70	181,295.14
1930 (Dec. 31)	85,205.39	45,491.66	130,697.05
1931	132,356.41	78,969.74	211,326.15
1932	108,070.57	95,066.84	203,137.41
1933	67,082.30	113,561.63	180,643.93
1934	68,037.43	144,446.13	212,483.56
1935	73,485.87	165,899.73	239,385.60
1936	84,942.16	193,071.98	278,014.14
1937	85,725.87	214,274.36	300,000.23
1938	90,776.28	233,748.38	324,524.66
1939	97,958.02	253,794.94	351,752.96
1940	100,205.77	314,895.00	415,100.77
1941	101,850.60	433,834.07	535,684.67
1942	102,969.38	526,195.53	629,164.91
1943	137,242.38	589,628.27	726,870.65
1944	142,215.36	631,927.63	774,142.99
1945	179,094.20	683,178.21	862,272.41
1946	192,508.63	809,229.28	1,001,737.91
1947	220,956.87	962,719.32	1,183,676.19
1948	237,252.09	1,055,089.75	1,292,341.84
1949	243,066.37	1,132,142.88	1,375,209.25
1950	253,776.53	1,160,109.29	1,413,885.82
1951	268,204.37	1,191,234.32	1,459,438.69
1952	298,558.14	1,337,430.79	1,635,988.93
1953	316,261.55	1,337,066.15	1,653,327.70
1954	321,059.91	1,442,406.91	1,763,466.82
1955	319,820.87	1,539,870.39	1,859,691.26
	$5,622,129.40	$16,872,314.58	$22,494,443.98

TOTAL ASSETS AND INVESTMENT EARNINGS BY YEARS

	Total Assets	Investment Earnings
1919	$ 106,428.53	2,685.00
1920	251,583.98	5,097.59
1921	914,897.70	24,186.89
1922	1,149,088.52	60,170.82
1923	1,490,193.59	73,240.23
1924	1,740,444.17	85,159.36
1925	1,964,672.06	117,046.92
1926	2,242,325.04	127,377.11
1927	2,470,486.83	150,982.66
1928	2,744,974.07	162,731.37
1929	3,028,504.93	175,956.72
1930 (Apr. 30)	....	193,792.40
1930 (Dec. 31)	3,698,554.74	125,858.74
1931	3,844,667.20	204,874.15
1932	3,921,314.89	210,980.76
1933	4,016,652.63	212,773.12
1934	4,212,678.89	224,161.30
1935	4,326,491.05	233,533.22
1936	4,473,901.00	234,646.05
1937	4,540,549.38	230,970.71
1938	4,604,498.08	220,453.76
1939	4,774,475.26	209,593.73
1940	5,149,663.24	215,916.73
1941	5,470,277.87	238,809.01
1942	6,031,213.84	269,588.34
1943	6,771,184.31	278,671.60
1944	7,907,136.76	289,541.18
1945	9,449,256.09	315,926.86
1946	10,909,740.27	359,005.99
1947	12,838,438.22	410,051.46
1948	15,094,093.60	487,832.04
1949	17,613,434.86	590,168.45
1950	20,518,200.12	714,064.76
1951	23,333,014.10	840,311.77
1952	26,478,390.96	923,894.06
1953	30,202,595.49	1,086,874.78
1954	35,091,515.37	1,268,512.89
1955	42,031,744.01	1,507,904.55
		$13,083,347.08

FRED W. NOE

of the four boards established by the Convention. Its purpose is to undergird the work of the Convention by providing financial security for aged ministers, widows of ministers, and for other lay employees through retirement plans and through the ministerial relief grants.

Altogether a service organization dedicated to the Convention, the board is also authorized to fund gift annuity contracts for Baptist boards, agencies, and schools. In funding gift annuity contracts, the board holds the annuity reserves, and the contracting agency receives the gift portion. The rates are actuarially computed.

Present rate basis is that which was adopted at the Gift Annuities Conference held in New York, Oct., 1955, and subsequently adopted as the legal rates for gift annuities written by the Relief and Annuity Board as of July 1, 1956.

The Relief Department of the board makes grants to needy Southern Baptist aged ministers and widows of ministers. Grants are disbursed from Cooperative Program funds and from gifts made directly to relief from churches and from individuals. Applications endorsed by applicant's pastor and state executive secretary are passed by the Relief Committee of the board, and a grant subsequently made each quarter. Relief grants may not exceed $500 per year.

RETTA O'BANNON

RELIGION. Religion may be defined as man's adoration and service of God. In history religion always has both internal and external characteristics. Its internal, spiritual qualities consist in its ideas and beliefs. Its external, visible characteristics are recognized as the forms and ceremonies it employs to express its beliefs. Religion engages that quality of human nature which lives always under the necessity of having to do with the divine.

S. A. NEWMAN

RELIGIOUS EDUCATION. The teaching of religion and the development of methods and curricula for the improvement of such teaching. Religious education, as the term is now used, should be distinguished from Christian education, which is simply general education as presented in church-related schools and colleges, and which deals with all areas of knowledge from the point of view of a firm basic commitment to Christian truth. Religious education became a distinct operation as a result of the Reformation and the subsequent separation of church and state. A system of education developed which made religion optional, and the churches either withdrew patronage from the public schools to form their own parochial schools, as did the Roman Catholics; or they patronized the public schools and established complementary schools for religious teaching.

Specifically, religious education includes the discipline of Bible teaching, the cultivation of Christian experience, and the teaching of doctrine; it is concerned with cultivating in student personalities Christian attitudes, leading to right actions, in all areas of life. Religious education would therefore include any type of training planned to result in a personal attachment to religion or to be instrumental in propagating religion. Any instruction aimed at deepening the religious life of an individual, or any informational work of any institution or agency for religious promotion, would qualify as religious education.

Biblical precedents.—Teaching has precedents in the Old Testament, the New Testament, biblical theology, and biblical ethics. These underlie any study of religious education practices in modern times. *The Old Testament* centers its message in the Shema. The Shema (Deut. 6:4–9) commands the teaching of the Torah (Law), which was God's voice to men. Thus the Shema served to build the homes, to establish moral standards, and to unify the people. The prophets, the priests, and the wise men were teachers to instruct in duties to God, to the nation, and to fellow men. *The New Testament* centers its message in the Great Commission (Matt. 28:18–20), which also enjoins teaching. The New Testament vocabulary stresses three words, "doctrine" (teaching), "doctor" (one competent to teach), and "disciple" (a learner). Followers of the Christian way were known as "learners." Through the centuries the New Testament church has followed the method of didactic preaching and evangelism through teaching in the homes, schools, colleges, and seminaries. The evangelist, the teacher, the lives of professing Christians (Heb. 5:12), and the Christian ordinances have conveyed lessons to the contemporary world. *Biblical theology* makes redemption through Christ (Rom. 5:10) the crucial point in religious education. Man must learn to commune with God, and he must learn to live with his fellow man. Interpretations of the biblical records of man's learning of God, and of man's need of God in human relations, make up the teaching content of religious education. Educational thinking in religion must stem from biblical theology. Psychology, sociology, and history provide assistance in the processing of belief. *Biblical ethics* is a study usually divided into judgments of value and judgments of obligation. The former relate to the goodness or badness of certain ends or experiences. The latter relate to rightness or wrongness of courses of action and are concerned with the "ought" or "must" of conduct. One must know what ends are good before he can know what he ought to do. The will of God as the source of duty implies, also, the goodness of God as the norm of life. The teachings of Jesus on human relations must constitute a major emphasis in the curriculum of the church school if the kingdom of God on earth is to be realized, and if the church is to survive.

Historical background.—Medieval learning (centered in the cathedral school and within monastic settlements) was controlled by a religious conception of the aims of life. The same educational process prepared the youth for both sacred and secular functions. Education was the prerogative and responsibility of the church. When the Reformation set in motion forces which dissolved the theocratic state into a free church and a free state, the secular state became responsible for fixing the content of nonreligious instruction. The churches supplied religious instruction. The French Revolution intensified the separation. A transplanted Protestantism eventually supported the American public schools, supplemented by separate schools of religion. The infiltration of Robert Raikes' Sunday school movement into wide areas of the newly born United States contributed further to produce the religious education movement of the 19th century. If general education had remained a function of the church, religion would have remained as the main purpose of educational efforts.

Protestant religious education.—Supplying the religious deficiencies of state education depends upon the attitude of the churches toward moral training in a state which is not opposed to religion, yet is free from religious control. The answer must be co-operative religious education or a parallel educational system. Education develops the individual toward better human relations, economic efficiency, civic responsibility, and self-realization. Religious education adopted for a period the technique of interpreting values in terms of general religious values which did not affect changes in personality. Christian religious education centers its teaching content and objective in the message of Christ and in the need for personal acceptance of Christ in faith, in life, and in social obligations. This approach makes God central, men secondary, in eternal need for right relations to God through Christ. It thus includes biblical instruction, presentation of the plan of salvation, and the encouragement of dedication of life and its relations to God through Christ.

Baptist religious education.—Interest of the churches in religious education arose with their acceptance of responsibility for that segment of education removed from the state by the separation of church and state. In this commitment Baptists hold much in common with other denominations, but in practice they subscribe to more or less distinctive approaches.

Characteristics of Baptist work.—All matters relating to religious education among Baptists are determined in the local church. No association, convention, or board has any authority over the local church. No Training Union or Sunday school association has any voice beyond the local church as the operational unit. Likewise, Southern Baptists cannot affiliate with any educational or promotional organization that functions in violation of the autonomy of the local church.

1. Baptists have no bishop or secretary with authority to impose any plan or directive on even the smallest church. Larger bodies of Baptists can function only as they inform the local church and exercise the power of appeal and persuasion for the support of a doctrine or practice. This logic is so pervasive that it becomes protective. Boards, departments, secretaries, committees, conventions, clinics, colleges, and seminaries operate under the same law and are accorded the same protections.

2. Christian nurture among Baptists becomes documented in their church covenant, which states, "We also engage to maintain family and secret devotions, to religiously educate our children." The Hebrew Shema (Deut. 6:4–9) antedates and implements the obligation. Religious education thus seeks to create "an environment . . . [for] the child which will predispose it to Christ and the church." A consciousness of wrong, of sin, is essential to moral and spiritual character. Baptists have intensified their efforts to this end through their Sunday schools and home training programs.

3. Baptists stress the determinative influence of God-awareness in the character of a person. Education with religion left out cultivates secularism and naturalism. Since the contemporary school system of the United States is not allowed to give instruction in religion, the implication for children is that religion is optional. Southern

Baptists have not only accepted responsibility for providing parallel instruction in religion but have sought to equal or to excel in quality the state's instruction. To this end constantly maturing provisions are fostered by the Sunday School Board of the Southern Baptist Convention in improving the curriculum, the teacher-training system, and technical equipment for instruction. All plans for religious education of American youth rest on parallel instruction and institutional co-operation.

History of religious education among Baptists.—This work had its beginning in theology or biblical doctrine. The doctrines setting forth the nature of God and the nature of man provided the content of religious education and determined its fundamentally evangelistic purpose. Preaching remained the sole method for generations, but, like other religious bodies, Baptists began to be concerned with formal measures for the religious instruction of their constituencies early in the 20th century.

1. Training young ministers marks the beginning of modern religious education among Baptists. Academies and manual labor schools led the way to the opening of Baptist colleges in and after 1820. Other young men and young women were later admitted for higher education to serve as lay leaders of the churches upon graduation. The theological seminary among Southern Baptists came into being in 1859 solely for the training of young ministers.

2. Evangelism has received intensive emphasis in Baptist religious education. A consciousness of sin is essential to both moral and spiritual character. Through the mediation of teachers and preachers, the child's impressions are being formed toward Christ, but Baptists hold that conscious choice must be made in becoming a Christian. Baptism follows the choice. Stemming from this doctrinal background, churches in all this educational work have labored to lead individuals to become Christians. This process is called evangelism. All missionary boards and agencies foster religious education as an invitation to discipleship on the basis of faith in Christ.

3. Training in church membership completes Baptist religious education. Among Baptists, who disclaim any formal creed, individuals are accepted for baptism upon a profession of their voluntary acceptance of Christ as Saviour. After their acceptance into the fellowship of the church, instruction begins in Christian doctrine and the discipline of Christian living. To baptize the individual and then neglect him at this point is a major failure. Lacking this culminating work of instruction, evangelical religion loses its power.

Teaching church members in the content and practices of the Baptist faith is achieved through the media of the doctrines, the ordinances, church discipline, and worship. To provide instruction, Baptists have developed Sunday schools since 1820, Baptist Training Unions (originally B.Y.P.U.) since 1891, Woman's Missionary societies since 1888, Baptist Brotherhood (Laymen's Missionary Movement) since 1907, and teacher-training classes since 1900. The Sunday school gives Bible-centered teaching about God, the meaning of life, and the hope of the Christian faith. The Training Union instructs in the duties of church membership and cultivates the skills necessary for active service within and without the church. The missionary society emphasizes missions and stewardship; the Brotherhood seeks to enlist men in increasingly active support of the total church program. Teacher-training classes prepare prospective and active leaders in the content and methods of religious education.

Principles of Baptist religious education.—Functionally, religious education among Southern Baptists subscribes to perhaps eight major principles:

1. The core of the curriculum literature of religious education is the Bible, which contains the experiences of spiritual men speaking the revelation of God. Baptists accept no creeds, no authoritative church, no liturgy, no human agencies as ultimately valid in the determination of faith.

2. Teaching is the major method for the propagation of the gospel. The Great Commission (Matt. 28:18–20) obligates every Christian to make disciples. Preaching is teaching men God's messages, expecting a reply.

3. Life situations constitute the application of Baptist religious education. Sin, sorrow, suffering, sacrifice, and human depravity find little satisfaction in merely "searching the scriptures," where Christ is not found (John 5:35–36). Wisdom comes from spiritual experience.

4. Religious education teaches for a verdict. The products sought are conversion, or the change from self-control to God-control; integration of character; social cohesion; compassion for human ills; realization of the reign of God among men; the assurance of redeemed immortality. Herein Baptists express their faith in the purpose of teaching.

5. Every Baptist church retains the right of freedom in the exercise of its educational duty to man and to God. Instruction of the local church is the key to denominational co-operation.

6. Religious education begins with adults, parents, neighbors, groups who understand the theology of faith and conduct. Experience communicated through parents and friends to children and youth leads to regeneration and growth in Christian character.

7. As universal missions, religious education extends Baptist responsibility to every human problem, recognizing no ecclesiastical or geographical monopoly in teaching the truths of God.

8. A church system of religious education is obligated to maintain the highest possible efficiency in teaching spiritual truth, even as is the public school system in teaching intellectual truth.

Growth of Church Membership, Sunday School, and Training Union, S.B.C., 1948–1955

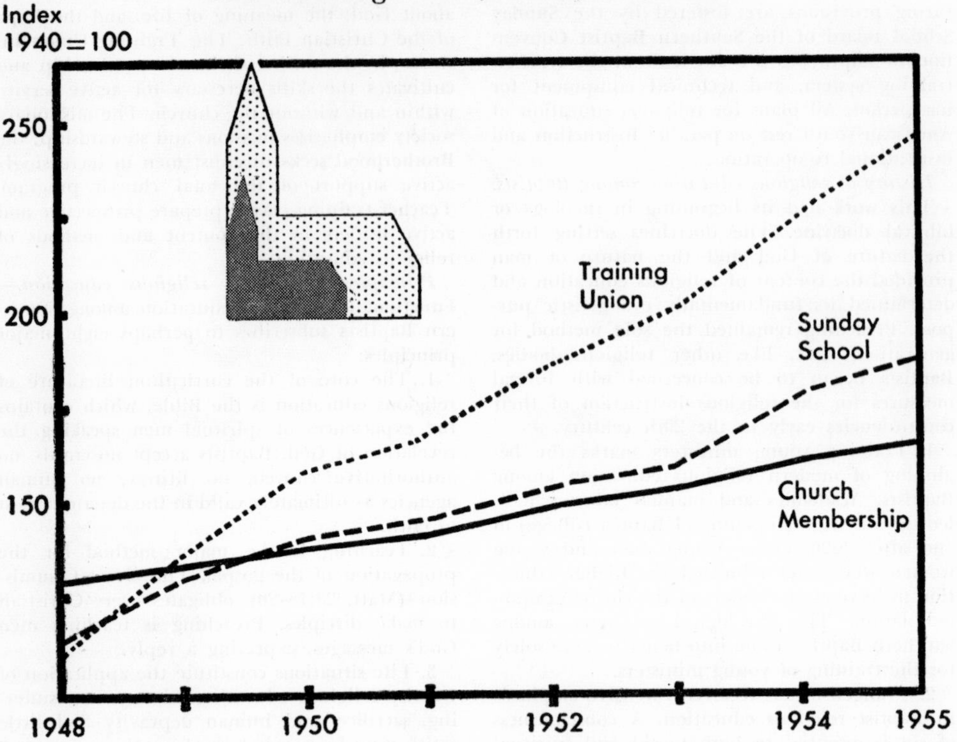

BIBLIOGRAPHY: W. W. Barnes, *The Southern Baptist Convention, 1845–1953* (1954). C. H. Brewer, *History of Religious Education in the Episcopal Church to 1835* (1924). R. C. Miller, *Education for Christian Living* (1956). E. Y. Mullins, *The Axioms of Religion* (1908). J. M. Price, L. L. Carpenter, and J. H. Chapman, *Introduction to Religious Education* (1932). L. J. Sherrill, *The Rise of Christian Education* (1944). JAMES HORTON CHAPMAN

RELIGIOUS EDUCATION, A CHURCH PROGRAM OF. *Functions.*—A church program of religious education seeks to prepare individuals for an understanding acceptance of Jesus Christ as Saviour and Lord, and through study and planned experiences, to help each individual to become a mature Christian, to find the Christian solutions to his needs, and to find and follow God's will. A well-developed program confronts Christians with their obligations as Christian citizens and helps equip them to achieve their divinely assigned tasks. Such a program prepares effective Christian witnesses and develops channels of communication to win an ever-widening circle of individuals to faith in Christ and fellowship in the church.

The church program of religious education is designed to meet the spiritual needs of the people it serves. It recognizes the need for worship, Bible study, Christian training, missionary education, church music, and recreation. The church seeks to develop an effective, correlated ministry in each of these areas to the various age groups in the church.

Organizations and meetings.—The purposes and functions of a church program of religious education are achieved through a variety of organizations. The need for worship is met through congregational worship services conducted on Sunday morning and Sunday evening, in mid-week prayer meetings, and in revival services. Additional worship experiences are provided in connection with the educational organizations.

The churches perform their Bible teaching ministry through the Sunday school, which usually meets for an hour or more preceding the Sunday morning worship service. In this organization the typical program includes an opening assembly, or worship period, of 15 or 20 minutes and a longer teaching period. Volunteer teachers, trained by the church, teach the Sunday school lessons to small classes, which are graded according to age and sex. Pupils are promoted annually on the basis of chronological age. In many churches Sunday school teachers and officers meet weekly to plan for more effective teaching and greater efficiency in the Sunday school ministry. Teachers, class officers, and departmental workers conduct a program of visitation designed to meet special spiritual needs of individual members and to enlist others in the Bible study program.

The central objective of the Baptist Training Union is training in church membership. The objective of its program for Nursery, Beginner, and Primary children is to prepare the children for an understanding acceptance of Jesus Christ and a love for him and his work. The Training Union usually meets for an hour or more preceding the Sunday evening worship service. Departments and unions are graded on the age basis. The program includes a brief opening worship period, review of the daily Bible readings, and discussion of a suggested topic. The principle of individual participation is emphasized. Discussion materials are provided in quarterlies prepared for each age group, from Juniors through Adults. Leadership materials are provided for workers with Nursery, Beginner, and Primary children.

Missionary education in the churches is conducted by the Woman's Missionary Society and several auxiliary organizations: Sunbeam bands for children through eight years of age, Girls' Auxiliaries for Junior and Intermediate girls, and the Young Woman's Auxiliary. The Royal Ambassadors, for Junior and Intermediate boys, are sponsored by the Baptist Brotherhood. Curriculum materials are being provided by Southern Baptist Woman's Missionary Union and Brotherhood offices. The Woman's Missionary societies, composed of adult women of the churches, hold general meetings once or twice each month. In larger churches, the membership is divided into circles, which meet at least once each month. Programs of these various missionary organizations are given largely to a study of missions and to prayer.

In many Southern Baptist churches there is now a graded music program, with choirs for each major age group. The music program is directed by a full-time minister of music or by a volunteer leader, according to the interests and financial abilities of the church.

Many social activities are provided in connection with the church organizations. In addition several churches conduct a church recreational program with planned activities for the various age groups.

To correlate the program, leadership, and space provision for the various organizations and meetings, churches may have a church council, composed of the head of each organization. This group meets with the pastor and church staff to work out a co-ordinated program, which seeks to provide for each individual in the church an opportunity for a complete and well-rounded Christian experience.

The pastor and church council will plan, at least one year in advance, a correlated leadership program for all church organizations. Usually the Sunday school teachers and officers, prospective workers, and other church members will meet for a week of intensive study at least once each year, giving careful attention to methods, teaching techniques, or Bible study. Similarly, the Training Union members engage in such weeks of training, studying methods and other subjects of interest to the growing Christian. More than 150 different books are provided in the graded courses of study for Sunday school and Training Union. W.M.U. and Brotherhood offices of the Southern Baptist Convention provide a series of leadership courses for workers in these organizations. Through the Missionary Education Council, a graded mission study series is produced and promoted for use in the churches.

The church leadership will plan each year a calendar which includes the total program of activities planned by the church for the year. Each year the Southern Baptist Convention adopts a proposed calendar as a suggested guide for co-ordinated denominational activities and emphases. The state Baptist organizations, and frequently associational groups, also formulate proposed calendars. With these suggestions and the particular needs of the local church in mind, the pastor and his church leadership plan the activities of the church, providing for evangelism, leadership training, Christian growth, missions, stewardship, recreation, and other phases of a complete church program.

Equipment.—A specialized building is essential for effective operation of the program of religious education conducted by Southern Baptists. In addition to a place of worship, there are needed several smaller rooms designed especially for the religious education of each age group. To aid in effective teaching the church will provide pictures, books, interest center equipment, and other materials. Basic curriculum materials will be provided for both pupil and teacher or leader. Books and magazines will be provided by the church-elected visual aids director, who will keep the church leaders informed of available materials and provide equipment and operators as needed. ALLEN W. GRAVES

RELIGIOUS EDUCATION, PROFESSIONAL ASSOCIATIONS. Organizations of teachers and vocational workers in the field of religious education, which seek to promote interest in the vocation of religious education, encourage young people to enter the field, and provide for mutual support and interchange of ideas among those actively working in the vocation. Regional and Convention-wide organizations have been established, which are as follows:

SOUTHWESTERN BAPTIST RELIGIOUS EDUCATION ASSOCIATION. The beginning was at Southwestern Baptist Seminary where the training of vocational religious educational workers started among Baptists. The first session was held Apr. 15–17, 1921, the meeting being called and the program prepared by J. M. Price, director of the School of Religious Education. It was intended to help those already working and to enlist new recruits. Representatives from 4 states, 16 colleges, and 64 churches attended. The various phases of Sunday school, Training Union, and B.S.U. work were discussed as related to the local church, the school, the field, and foreign lands. Out of this meeting came the Texas Religious Education Workers' Conference. In 1927 the name was changed to the Texas Baptist Religious Education Association, and two years later to the Southwestern Baptist Religious Education Association.

The organization has dealt with almost every phase and problem of religious education and has majored on free, informal group discussion. The association meets regularly in J. M. Price Hall at the seminary, and 301 were registered at the 35th annual meeting in 1955. Mrs. Ellis Province and Gracie Knowlton have served as secretary-treasurer most of the time.

SOUTHEASTERN BAPTIST RELIGIOUS EDUCATION ASSOCIATION. This was the second regional organization for vocational Baptist workers in religious education. It was initiated by W. Perry Crouch and the first session was held at Mars Hill College in Sept., 1941. There were no regular meetings during the war years of 1942–45, but there were meetings at Howard College in 1947–48. Since then the association has met regularly at Ridgecrest. Its constitution, membership, and programs are similar to those of the Southwestern association. More than 200 attended the 1955 session.

WESTERN RELIGIOUS EDUCATION ASSOCIATION. During the meeting of the Southern Baptist General Convention of California in 1951, R. F. Royal, professor of religious education at Golden Gate Baptist Theological Seminary, called the vocational religious education workers together for a luncheon, and the organization was formed. The first regular meeting was held in connection with the California Baptist Sunday School Convention, Apr. 1–2, 1952. It has met annually since at the Golden Gate Seminary and has followed the general policies of the other two associations.

In 1956 these three regional organizations held a joint meeting in Kansas City and the interest was so good it was decided to continue it. The idea was proposed by the Southeastern association in July, 1955, endorsed by the Southwestern association the next month, and the Western association later. W. L. Howse served as chairman of the joint organization and prepared the program; the first session was held in Kansas City on Monday night and Tuesday (May 28–29, 1956) before the meeting of the Southern Baptist Convention. Approximately 200 attended; splendid discussion was given, and a permanent organization was set up. J. M. Price served as chairman for 1956–57, and the meeting was held in Chicago.

COLLEGE ASSOCIATION OF BAPTIST TEACHERS OF RELIGION. This body was organized Feb. 2, 1928, at the St. Charles Hotel in New Orleans, La., during a session of the Southern Baptist Education Association, and was then called the Association of Southern Baptist Teachers of Bible and Religious Education. The name was changed to the above on Aug. 22, 1950. Its purpose has been fellowship, a study of problems, and the formation of ideals. It has helped to improve instruction, plan pre-seminary training for religious workers, and raise the standing of departments offering work in religion in the colleges. J. M. PRICE, SR.

RELIGIOUS EDUCATION, PROFESSIONAL TRAINING FOR. Professional training in religious education was not available to the first Southern Baptist vocational workers in this field. Many of them had enough knowledge of Baptist principles and methods and sufficient practical experience to succeed in spite of their lack of formal training.

Their need for specialized training soon became apparent. The new vocation called for knowledge and skill. Since it involved educational leadership, the workers needed to be familiar with such subjects as psychology, principles of religious education, history of religious education, and with materials and methods for the various age groups. Studies in the Bible, theology, Baptist history and missions, the philosophy of religion, and other subjects were necessary if the workers were to be trained adequately for their tasks. It was important to understand the organizations with which they worked. Information regarding religious publication, writing and editing, religious drama and recreation, and craft activities was needed.

It was felt that the place to receive such training was in the theological seminary. Here the worker in religious education could receive his training with those who were to serve as pastors and other staff members in the churches. In the theological seminary many courses which were needed were already being taught. The other courses could be added. In time, courses in religious education began to appear in the catalogs of the theological seminaries. These courses were taken not only by those specializing in religious education but by students majoring in theology as well.

With the growth of churches came an increasing demand for workers, and the departments of religious education in three of the seminaries grew into schools of religious education. The department of religious education at Southwestern Baptist Theological Seminary, Fort Worth, Tex., founded in 1915, became a School of Religious Education in 1921. J. M. Price became the first director of the school and continued in this position until his retirement in 1956. The department of religious education of New Orleans Baptist Theological Seminary, New Orleans, La., became a school in 1952. John M. Price, Jr., is director. The trustees of the Southern Baptist Theological Seminary, Louisville, Ky., on Mar. 10–11, 1953, authorized the establishing of a School of Religious Education there. Gaines S. Dobbins, who began teaching religious education and church administration at Southern Seminary in 1920, was elected the first dean of this school and served in this capacity until his retirement in 1956. These three schools have been accredited by the American Association of Schools of Religious Education.

Courses in religious education are offered in Golden Gate Baptist Theological Seminary, Berkeley, Calif., and Southeastern Baptist Theological Seminary, Wake Forest, N. C. These studies were incorporated in the curriculum of these institutions soon after their beginnings. Both seminaries offer degrees in religious education.

In general the seminaries have followed the plan of offering diplomas and degrees in religious education upon the completion of prescribed curricula. The diploma in religious education is granted upon the completion of a two-year course based upon a high school diploma. The Bachelor of Religious Education degree is conferred upon the completion of a two-year curricula with junior college training as prerequisite. The Master of Religious Education degree is a two-year course based upon a senior college degree. The Doctor of Religious Education degree is conferred after two years of residence work, an oral examination, and dissertation. The Master of Religious Education degree or its equivalent is prerequisite to the Doctor of Religious Education degree. The Southeastern Seminary offers a three-year course leading to the Bachelor of Divinity degree in religious education.

Many Baptist colleges now are offering religious education courses as a part of the total curriculum in their Departments of Bible or Religion. In general these courses are considered pre-seminary rather than terminal. W. L. HOWSE

RELIGIOUS EDUCATION, WEEKDAY. See WEEKDAY RELIGIOUS EDUCATION.

RELIGIOUS EDUCATION IN MISSIONS. That activity dedicated principally to evangelism and to the development of the Christian life of believers as carried on in and through the organizations of the churches on the mission field.

The aims of missions include not only the winning of people to acceptance of Christ as Saviour but also the teaching of these Christians to observe all things which Jesus has commanded. This teaching can be done through various means; but experience has shown that the Sunday school, Training Union, and missionary organizations of a local Baptist church, united in a program of religious education, can provide the effective means. Wherever Christ has been made known, the study of the Bible, the guide for the Christian, is of course imperative. The Bible is the source of the knowledge of God, of Jesus, of salvation, of the meaning of the Christian life. It presents the basis for the continuation of the divine cause on earth. The most effective means of Bible study is through the organized Sunday school, in which the Bible is taught to all age groups. Unbelievers are brought to take part in this study and are thereby led to become Christians. Evangelism in its fullest sense, however, includes indoctrination, growth in the knowledge of the Bible and in depth of Christian experience. The Sunday school is, in the fullest sense, an evangelistic agency. Individual Christians filled with the desire to see others receive the same blessing of salvation then take the Bible to others, encourage them in its study, bring them to their Sunday school. Or, according to the circumstances, perhaps a mission Sunday school is begun in a home. Within a short time this effort has led to the organization of another local church composed of those who have been won and baptized. These then repeat this cycle in the constant and ever-increasing expansion of the gospel.

The provision of means for training Christians is a necessity that arises as a natural result of the growth of the churches. Teachers and leaders are needed to direct and carry on the work. The Training Union meets this need. As a fully graded Sunday school provides opportunity for all to study the Bible, so the Training Union provides the means whereby all the members of the church may be trained in activities that not only develop their talents and enlarge their knowledge but also make it possible for them to apply their Christian principles to all phases of life.

The nature of the gospel demands co-operative effort on the part of the churches in their attempts to fulfil their mission. This in turn leads to denominational organization, for which informed and active church members are necessary. The Training Union meets a great need in that it teaches the individual Christian how to find his place in the program of his denomination. In addition to studying the Bible, he learns what his denomination is doing, how its work is done, and discovers what he himself can do. He studies methods of evangelism and practices winning people to Christ. He studies world need and his own part in meeting this need. He discovers his own talents and applies them. He learns of his financial responsibility and privilege and practices stewardship of his possessions. The Training Union is indispensable to the churches on the mission fields.

The missionary organizations—missionary societies for women and young women, Girl's Auxiliaries, and Royal Ambassadors—also fill a special need. In some countries national conventions promote home missions through their own boards, and in a few fields foreign missions also. The missionary organizations of the church serve the members by informing them of what is being done, of the needs, and of how they can help to meet these needs. World missions are presented, and Christians in the churches come to realize that they are a part of a world program of evangelization, with responsibility toward those who have not yet heard of Christ.

Vacation Bible schools provide an admirable means for winning children to Christ. Through these schools it is possible to gain entrance to homes that would otherwise be inaccessible.

Human nature is basically the same, regardless of color or race or nationality; and children anywhere love to sing, hear stories, do handwork, and play. When materials are provided and instruction given, the Sunday school workers and officers of the church can promote these Vacation Bible schools. The results often exceed all expectations. Children are won to Christ, and then the parents follow.

Experience through the years has demonstrated that the basic principles of organizational life as taught and promoted through the Southern Baptist Sunday School Board are not only fundamental but universal. On the mission fields methods are adapted to meet the specific needs and opportunities that are found, but the fundamental principles are the same. In some instances the organizational structure and functions can be adapted in churches on the mission fields with more ease than in some churches in the United States. In many cases the zeal and simple faith of national Christians, combined with a genuine and deep experience of salvation, more than compensate for the lack of formal training and preparation. It is true that in many churches there is a great need for trained workers to teach, to organize, to promote, and to lead in the program of religious education; but where work is being done in accordance with the basic principles laid down for Sunday school and Training Union, for the missionary societies and auxiliaries, and for other activities promoted by all of these, souls are being won for Christ, churches are being organized, co-operative enterprises appear, and the cause of Christ goes forward. EDGAR F. HALLOCK

RELIGIOUS FORUM. A 16-page monthly journal owned and edited by H. R. Bernard at Atlanta, Ga. Bernard began his publication in 1905, but discontinued it several years later.

JOHN J. HURT, JR.

RELIGIOUS HERALD, THE. A paper first published in Richmond, Va., Jan. 11, 1828. The previous year Henry Keeling, Jr., editor of the *Evangelical Inquirer,* a monthly magazine, had announced, in the *Inquirer's* final issue, plans for a weekly magazine which he expected to introduce in Dec., 1827. Since its first issue, the *Religious Herald* has had continuous publication in Richmond; it is the oldest such religious magazine in the United States. Keeling, who had financial assistance from William Crane, a layman in the Second Baptist Church, Richmond, and professional help from William Sands (*q.v.*), a printer, resigned as editor in June, 1831, and Eli Ball succeeded him. Ball became joint publisher with Sands, who in turn became co-editor in Jan., 1832. When Ball resigned in May, 1833, Sands became publisher and editor, and in Jan., 1834, he organized the Virginia Baptist Book and Tract Society to publish the *Religious Herald* and to distribute books and tracts. The society lasted only eight months until Sept., 1834, when Sands again became sole publisher and editor. During his editorship the *Religious Herald* played an important part in guiding Virginia Baptists through the controversy over Campbellism and later through the period of division within the Triennial Convention. The paper was the medium used by the Virginia Baptist Foreign Mission Society to call at Augusta, Ga., in 1845, the meeting at which the Southern Baptist Convention was organized. The *Religious Herald* first announced the meeting held at Greenville, S. C., in 1854 in the interest of founding a theological seminary.

In 1857 David Shaver left the pastorate of Hampton Baptist Church to become associated with Sands as part owner and associate editor of the paper. They organized Sands, Shaver and Company with A. M. Bailey, who had superintended printing and mailing of the *Religious Herald* since 1835, as partner. The paper continued publication with few omissions during the Civil War, although it was reduced from four to two pages in 1864. On Apr. 3, 1865, the Federal Army entered Richmond amid the conflagration set by retiring Confederates, and although fire destroyed all files and equipment of the *Religious Herald,* the paper continued publication.

In the fall of 1865, Jeremiah Bell Jeter (*q.v.*) and Alfred Elijah Dickinson (*q.v.*) purchased the *Religious Herald* from Sands, Shaver and Company, and the first number under the new publishers appeared Oct. 17, 1865. Prominent Baptists in other states who accepted appointment on the staff as associate editors included Richard Fuller (*q.v.*), of Maryland; Richard Furman (*q.v.*), of South Carolina; John Albert Broadus (*q.v.*), of Kentucky; and W. A. Montgomery (*q.v.*), of Tennessee. When Jeter, the senior editor, died in Feb., 1880, his wife retained interest in the paper and edited pages for the home circle and for children. She engaged Henry Herbert Harris (*q.v.*) to be associate editor with Dickinson and to care for her interest in the paper. Harris served from Apr., 1880, until Mar., 1882, succeeded by William Eldridge Hatcher (*q.v.*), who served until 1885.

After the death of Mrs. Jeter her interest in the *Religious Herald* was sold at public auction in 1888. The new owners, including J. Taylor Ellyson and J. T. Dickinson, obtained a charter of incorporation, and A. E. Dickinson continued as editor. The corporation, which engaged Robert Healy Pitt (*q.v.*) as associate editor and business manager Sept. 27, 1888, continued until 1919 when Pitt secured all stock and relinquished the charter. In 1898 the *Religious Herald* was changed from 4 to 16 pages and reduced in size to 10½ by 15 inches. Pitt continued as editor and publisher until his death in Feb., 1937.

In Sept., 1937, Reuben E. Alley purchased the *Religious Herald* from the Pitt estate. A new charter of incorporation was obtained that month with 10 stockholders, electing Alley as editor. In 1938 the paper introduced a club plan for subscriptions, and in 1950 a charter was issued to the Religious Herald Publishing Association, a nonprofit corporation. The charter provided for the nomination of trustees by the Baptist General Association of Virginia, which approved the charter and accepted the relationship in Nov., 1950, thereby making the *Religious Herald* an institution of the denomination.

The *Religious Herald* is owned by the Religious Herald Publishing Association, Incorporated, an agency of the Baptist General Association of Virginia. Circulation at the end of 1954 was 23,600. The general association nominates annually three of the 24 trustees of the corporation, and the trustees elect the editor. The general association paid $15,000 for publicity in 1954. A complete file of the *Religious Herald* is in possession of the Virginia Baptist Historical Society, and the file has been partially microfilmed. REUBEN ALLEY, SR.

RELIGIOUS LIBERTY. A term denoting the right of every man to worship God as his conscience dictates. It means equality before the law, not only of all forms of the Christian faith, but also of other religions. It has been a basic tenet of the position of Baptists throughout their history, and in the early days of the movement was insisted upon, in spite of persecution, to the point of imprisonment and even death. In England among the early Baptists, both Thomas Helwys and John Murton advocated full religious liberty and paid for their stand in imprisonment and probably death. Helwys published in 1612 his *A Short Declaration of the Mistery of Iniquity,* in which he upheld universal religious liberty, freedom of conscience for all, and declared that whether men be heretics, Turks, Jews, or whatever, the earthly power had no power to punish them for their views or to be intolerant of them. In the United States, Roger Williams took a similar stand and founded Rhode Island Colony with religious liberty as a basic principle in its charter.

Such a doctrine demands complete freedom of church from state and is opposed to any interference of the state in matters of religious faith. This is now the position of the United States and has become to a considerable degree the position of Great Britain, despite the presence of the established Church of England. Actually, in history three attitudes toward this principle may be noted. The first has been that of *territorialism,* in which various sections of a country have been granted a monopoly on one type of faith, and citizens have been allowed to migrate from one section to another according to their religious views. This regional division of religious faiths was tried initially in both Germany and the United States, when various states and colonies were at first allowed to retain their own established churches. The second attitude, *comprehension,* consists in having a state church so broad in its views that all can find a home within it. This was initially the situation tried in Great Britain. The third is that of full *religious freedom,* in which all faiths are equal before the law, and in which no preference is given to any one faith. The public educational system is thus set free from any specific religious directive. Only too often, unfortunately, this has meant no religion at all in the schools and a resulting secularism in the state. This arrangement is now the settled one in the United States and also to some extent in England, where the Established Church is no longer permitted to hold a monopoly. Religion still has a place in education, however.

In Russia and in the Moslem countries, communism and Islam respectively permit little or no religious liberty, and, despite its more liberal pronouncements, the Roman Catholic Church is likewise intolerant in countries where it can exercise such power—Spain and parts of Latin America.

See also FREEDOM. ERIC C. RUST

RELIGIOUS SOCIETY, THE. Established in Apr., 1755, in a meeting of the Charleston, S. C., Association when "a few serious, and well disposed persons . . . formed themselves into a Society with a sincere view to promote the interest of vital Religion in their own souls, and, as far as their influence might extend, amongst their fellow creatures in general." A "society" mentioned by Oliver Hart (*q.v.*) in 1754 was probably the antecedent of the Religious Society. Hart often spoke to a group so designated on Sunday evenings and several evenings during the week.

In 1756 messengers to the association pledged their churches to raise funds for ministerial education, a work soon assumed by the Religious Society. Constitutional rules were drawn up in 1768 and incorporation secured "to collect a library and to discuss theology weekly, but chiefly to further ministerial education." After 1779 this latter work passed to the general committee of the association. Three early and prominent beneficiaries of the society's funds were Evan Pugh (1729–1802), Samuel Stillman (1737–1807), and Edmund Botsford (1745–1819). To the Religious Society "is reckoned the honor of being the first religious partnership among Baptists in America in the interest of ministerial education." It ceased to function about 1780 and dissolved about 1815.

BIBLIOGRAPHY: W. Furman, *A History of the Charleston Association of Baptist Churches in the State of South Carolina* (1811). L. Townsend, *South Carolina Baptists, 1670–1805* (1935). JOE M. KING

REMNANT. See ESCHATOLOGY.

REPENTANCE. The biblical meaning of the term is the turning of a sinner toward God for forgiveness. The unfortunate emphasis of this Latin derivative, under the influence of the doctrine of "penance," has been upon a morbid grief and remorse for one's sin. The central biblical idea is a radical change of mind or will (*metanoeo*), away from sin and toward God.

John the Baptist demanded repentance as a condition of entrance into the kingdom (Matt. 3:2). Christ proclaimed it as the prerequisite to "believing the gospel" of the kingdom. The preaching of the gospel by the early church (Acts 2:38) required it as the necessary response if men would be saved. Another New Testament word, *metamelomai,* "to regret," is also translated "to repent"; it preserves the Old Testament idea of *naham,* "to groan," translated about 40 times "to repent," and almost always used of God. *Naham* signifies God's deep grief over man's sin; it does not indicate that God is like sinful man, "that he should repent" (I Sam. 15:29; Job 42:6; Jer. 8:6). The most commonly used and most emphatic Old Testament word for repentance is *shuv,* which means simply "to turn." The prophets pleaded with Israel, "Turn, O backsliding children" (Jer. 3:14), and with the wicked man to "return unto the Lord" (Isa. 55:7). This same radical reorientation of one's life toward God, embodied in the New Testament word *epistrepho,* was evident at Lydda, where all "turned to the Lord" (Acts 9:35), and at Antioch, where "a great number believed and turned unto the Lord" (Acts 11:21). Repentance undergirded the preaching of the gospel through the prophets, Christ, and the apostles with the absolute divine command of unconditional surrender of the human heart and mind to the will of God, renouncing sin to commit one's way to the Lord. As such, repentance is the initial act in faith which results in the total commitment of one's life to God in Christ.

See also CONVERSION. WAYNE E. WARD

REPRESENTATION, SOUTHERN BAPTIST CONVENTION BASIS OF. The purpose of the Southern Baptist Convention, as expressed in the organization in 1845, was for "carrying into effect the benevolent intentions of our constituents by organizing a plan for eliciting, combining, and directing the energies of the whole denomination in one sacred effort for the propagation of the gospel." This expressed purpose is the foundation stone of an adequate basis of representation in the Southern Baptist Convention. While the principle has remained unchanged, the details of organization have been changed from time to time as circumstances required. Crises and changes in the development of the Southern Baptist Convention called for amendments to Article III on the basis of representation. Factors involved in this process of evolution were: Transition from Society to Denominational plan, frequency of meetings, relation of Convention to churches and associations, growth of Convention, financial bases, admission of women to Convention, more effective enlistment, and closer co-operation. The amendments of Article III, as indicated in the following paragraphs, reflect the development, year by year, of a growing Baptist fellowship in line with the principle of voluntary co-operation. Each amendment remained in force until other changes were made.

1845.

A Triennial [meeting every three years, after the pattern of the General Convention] Convention shall consist of members who contribute funds, or are delegated by religious bodies contributing funds and the system of representation, and terms of membership shall be as follows, viz: An annual contribution of one hundred dollars for three years next preceding the meeting, or the contribution of three hundred dollars any time within said three years, shall entitle the contributor to one representative; an annual contribution of two hundred dollars, as aforesaid, shall entitle the contributor to two representatives; and so, for each additional one hundred dollars an additional representative shall be allowed. Provided, however, that when application shall be made for the first time by bodies or individuals to be admitted into the Convention, one delegate shall be allowed for each one hundred dollars. And provided, also, in cases of great collateral societies, composed of representatives, receiving contributions from different parts of the country, the ratio of representation shall be one delegate for every thousand dollars annually contributed for three years as aforesaid; but the number of representatives shall never exceed five.

1849.—Effective with the change from triennial to biennial meetings, the financial basis was changed from $300 to $200; and three years, to two years. This amendment became effective in 1851.

1866.—Effective in 1867, with the change from biennial to annual meetings, the financial basis was set at one hundred dollars.

1878.—Named in the amended Article III were co-operating state or sectional conventions or general associations in Maryland, Virginia, West Virginia, North Carolina, Western North Carolina, South Carolina, Georgia, Florida, Alabama, Mississippi, Southeast Mississippi, Louisiana, Texas, Eastern Texas, Arkansas, Western Arkansas and Indian Territory, Kentucky, Missouri, and Southwest Missouri. The financial basis was one representative for each five hundred dollars expended by such state or sectional bodies "for objects similar to those in the prosecution of which this Convention may be actually engaged, which objects are at present, Foreign Missions, Home Missions, Indian Missions, and Sunday School work." Representatives from these bodies were to be duly certified to the Southern Baptist Convention.

1885.—Article III was changed to read, "The Convention shall consist of brethren who contribute funds or are delegated by religious bodies contributing funds on the basis of one delegate for every one hundred dollars contributed to our funds at any time within the twelve months preceding the meeting of this body." The word "brethren" was used instead of "members," as theretofore, to eliminate the possibility of having women members of the Convention. Three years later, in 1888, the women organized a separate body, auxiliary to the Southern Baptist Convention. This auxiliary later became known as Woman's Missionary Union.

1886.—Article III was amended by adding, after the words "contributed to our funds" the words, "and received by the treasurer of the boards on or before the last day of April in the current year." (Later the statement was changed to "paid into the *treasuries* of the boards.")

1888.—"One hundred dollars" in Article III was changed to "two hundred and fifty dollars." Two new classifications were added: (1) One representative from each of the district associations which co-operate with the Convention, provided that such representative be elected by his district association, and his election certified to the secretary of the Convention, either in writing or by a copy of the printed minutes. (2) One representative for every $500 collected and expended conjointly with the boards of the Convention, by any state convention or general association, ending the 30th day of April next preceding the meeting of the Convention. (This $500 classification was deleted from Article III in 1894.)

1918.—In Article III, the word "messengers" is used for the first time in 1918, in admitting women to the Convention, instead of "members" (1845), or "brethren" (1885, when women were explicitly barred from the Convention). It is significant, too, that in the same amendment, in 1918, the word "delegated" which had been used from the organization in 1845, was changed to "elected."

1931.—Article III was amended to read:

> The Convention shall consist of messengers who are members of missionary Baptist churches which co-operate with the Southern Baptist Convention on the basis of one messenger for every church contributing to the work of the Convention, and one additional messenger for every $250 actually paid to the work of the Convention during the calendar year preceding the annual meeting of the Convention, such messengers to be appointed to the Convention by the churches and certified by the churches to the Convention, provided no church shall be entitled to more than three messengers.

The 1931 amendment eliminated associational representation and required that all messengers be appointed and certified by churches, rather than by "Baptist bodies" which included associational or state boards.

1933.—The maximum number of messengers from a church was increased from three to ten.

1946.—Article III was amended to provide "one additional messenger for every 250 members or for each $250." The maximum number of messengers remained the same.

1948.—The principle of voluntary co-operation in carrying out the purposes of the Convention was made more explicit by an amended section in Article III: "One messenger from each regular Baptist church which is in friendly co-operation with this Convention and sympathetic with its purposes and work, and has during the fiscal year preceding been a bona fide contributor to the Convention's work." E. C. ROUTH

RESCUE MISSIONS. The Seaman's Institute in Jacksonville, Fla., was established July 27, 1915, incorporated rescue mission work in 1934, and received support from the Home Mission Board until 1941.

The Baptist Rescue Mission at 740 Esplanade Avenue, New Orleans, La., began under the leadership of J. W. Newbrough (1859–1948) in 1927. A home to provide temporary lodging for transient women was begun on Oct., 1933. This home began caring for unwed mothers in 1937 and ceased to serve transient women in 1944. Babies born in the home were surrendered to public welfare agencies until the home received in 1948 legal authorization to place its own babies for adoption. On the average, 70 mothers are served in this home and 50 babies are placed for adoption each year. The property at 2010 Penniston Street was purchased in 1944. In 1956 the baby building was completed and the name of the home changed to Sellers Baptist Home and Adoption Center.

The Good Samaritan Home for transient women was established co-operatively by the Home Mission Board and the New Orleans Baptist Association in 1953. That same year, the board, together with the East St. Louis Association, established the Baptist Rescue Mission in East St. Louis, Ill. In 1955 the board, together with local forces in Memphis, Tenn., began the Baptist Center, which does both rescue mission work and good will center work.

Local Baptist forces operate rescue missions in the following cities: Little Rock, Ark.; Nashville, Tenn.; Tampa, Fla.; Houston, Tex.; Fort Worth, Tex.; Knoxville, Tenn. LOYD CORDER

RESPONSIBILITY. A term here meaning moral accountability. The significance and scope of this accountability, however, do not become plain until one knows to whom and for what he is responsible.

Man's primary responsibility is to God the Creator (cf. Rom. 14:12). As the moral ruler of the universe, he has predetermined the principles of righteousness by which every person is to be judged. These principles are revealed not only in the Ten Commandments but also in the teachings of Jesus and the gospel of redemption (cf. Rom. 2:16).

Man is responsible to Jesus Christ as the perfect revealer of God, to whom all judgment has been committed (John 5:22, 27). "We must all appear before the judgment seat of Christ; that every one may receive the things done in his body, according to that he hath done, whether it be good or bad" (II Cor. 5:10).

But this is a social world. Each man has relationships to his fellow men, and is responsible to them. Significantly, the first question recorded in the Bible implies man's responsibility to God (Gen. 3:9), and the second implies man's responsibility to and for his fellow man (Gen. 4:9). Social responsibility is also plainly marked in the second table of the Ten Commandments.

According to Jesus the one comprehensive word to describe man's responsibility is love. Jesus taught (Matt. 22:37–39; cf. Rom. 13:8–10)

that man's first duty is to love God supremely, and that the next in order is equal love to self and neighbor, one's neighbor being defined as any person anywhere whom one is in position to help (Luke 10:30–37).

Obviously man is responsible for his deeds (II Cor. 5:10) and omissions, but Jesus teaches that man is responsible also for his words (Matt. 12:36–37) and his attitudes (Matt. 5:21–22, 27–28).

In the last analysis there can be no real conflict of duties. Because the authority of God is always superior to the authority of man and human desire, one's obedience must be given to God above all (cf. Acts 5:29). In the final reckoning it will doubtless be shown that to be true to God is always to be true to the highest interests of mankind.

See also AGE OF ACCOUNTABILITY.

HOWARD P. COLSON

RESTHAVEN, BAPTIST HOME FOR THE AGING. Located at Winston-Salem, N. C., its establishment was authorized by the state convention in 1950, and it began operation on Mar. 6, 1951. The building was soon filled to capacity with 20 residents, and the demand so far exceeded facilities that the convention-elected board of trustees soon planned for enlargement. The purchase of a 34-acre tract of land provided space for new buildings to accommodate, ultimately, 250 residents. Construction of the first unit—administration and residential, capacity for 40 residents—was begun in Jan., 1956. Applicants for admission to the home must be at least 65 years of age, able to dress and come to meals; they must be church members. If they have no funds, the cost of their keep is met out of receipts from a special day offering and an allotment from the Cooperative Program.

JAMES M. HAYES

RESURRECTION. See JESUS CHRIST.

RETIREMENT, MINISTERIAL. The concept of ministerial retirement has fundamentally changed in the last 40 years. To earlier generations retirement was practically unknown. The call from God was construed for life, and the minister was expected to continue in active service until disability or death. Since in most instances salaries were very meager, ministers generally were unable to make provision for old age or disability. Therefore, when a minister was unable to continue in active service, he soon became an object of charity.

The first steps toward material provision for indigent ministers were made by Presbyterians as early as 1717 and by Methodists in the time of Francis Asbury. In time it became apparent that relief funds alone would not meet the long-range need. The Presbyterian Church, U. S. A., in 1907 organized the first annuity fund for ministers in America, known as the Ministers Sustentation Fund. This was followed in 1908 by the Conference Claimants Plan of the Methodist Episcopal Church. Other religious bodies soon organized similar plans, with benefits based on service rather than on need.

Southern Baptist efforts date from 1839, when Baptists of Maryland organized the Widows and Super-Annuated Ministers Fund. Virginia, South Carolina, Tennessee, Kentucky, Missouri, and Texas followed with similar efforts during the years 1872 to 1887. Not until 1917, however, did the Southern Baptist Convention as a body take action in this field. A commission was appointed to study the need and means of meeting it, and from this study came a recommendation leading to the organization of the Relief and Annuity Board in 1918.

In previous generations there was little demand for retirement plans for two reasons: first, the older minister had greater demand for his service because of his mature experience; second, the average income was so small that it precluded the possibility of contribution by the minister. Today the reverse is true: with expanded activity in the church the demand is for younger men who are able to bear the burden of the ministerial function; also the salary average is materially increased so that the minister is able to make provision. In spite of greater need and increased ability to provide, however, there are thousands of ministers today who have little or no security and who will finally reach the relief rolls of the denomination unless the situation is changed. This conclusion is based on two facts: first, relief rolls now stand at an all-time high; second, only about 35 per cent of the active Southern Baptist ministers participate in one of the denominational plans. The need for retirement planning by the minister is by no means limited to economic considerations. Many other factors, such as health, housing, leisure time, and spiritual activities, also are to be considered. Since retirement is the product of all habits and responses of the years gone by, a minister can come to security and happiness in retirement only by a lifetime of planning and cultivation.

First of all, a minister must cultivate an attitude favorable to retirement. Walter Pitkin says, "A retiring disposition is, in one way, like greatness: some are born with it, some achieve it, and some have it thrust upon them." Fortunately for the minister, he lives in a realm where he cultivates the philosophic virtues of learning, reflection, and meditation. These will carry over into retirement to give psychological insurance for older years.

The financial aspect of retirement planning begins with the denominational retirement plan, which provides for every life situation—old age, disability, and death. Primary provision is for old age, but substantial benefit is also made in these other areas. Although the denominational plan is basic, with it should be integrated life insurance and personal savings so as to afford maximum financial security in every situation.

The provision of a home for retirement must not be overlooked. The retiring minister will no longer have a pastorium provided, and few ministers will have sufficient retirement income to justify the payment of rent. The need for a home can be anticipated in advance and provided for either by early purchase as rental property to liquidate itself, or by accumulation of savings for the purchase at retirement time.

Temperance in habits during active years to preserve health will contribute greatly to one's well-being in old age. Regular vacations, periodic enjoyment of relaxation, and cultivation of subsidiary interests will contribute to maintenance of health and to one's ability to retire without emotional shock.

Edward J. Stieglitz, in *The Second Forty Years*, says, "Success or failure in the second forty years, measured in terms of happiness, is determined more by how we use or abuse our leisure than by any other factor." Many ministers give little attention to planning retirement activity. Adjustment is extremely difficult for the minister who has never learned to play during his active days. In preparation for this adjustment, ministers need to develop, during the active period, interests and hobbies that will carry over into years of retirement. One should give careful thought to the selection of these avocations. In the first place, one should develop several hobbies, or at least one that is very broad, so that he will not tire quickly and lose interest. Second, hobbies should be suited to physical limitations of old age and should include both active and sedentary pursuits. Again, creative hobbies are beneficial, since they will give the greatest sense of accomplishment. Hobbies that bring real satisfaction are those developed over a lifetime of familiarity. Few people can deliberately choose a hobby after age 60, for hobbies are born of curiosity, interest, and cultivation.

Above all in retirement a minister wants purposeful activity. The compensations that have come during active days have been largely emotional and spiritual—a sense of belonging, knowledge of being needed, expressions of love and appreciation, and the satisfaction of lasting achievement. To be happy in retirement the minister must still have these compensations, although probably in a lesser degree.

Success in retirement for a minister must include continued spiritual activity. Of course, he will preach as often as he is able and has opportunity. In addition, rewarding opportunities for volunteer services may be found in worth-while community activities, such as good will centers, hospitals, jails, etc. The seeker will not lack opportunities for service; the finder will not lack happiness.

Retirement, then, is but another phase of life. It is not a goal to be sought or a condition to be avoided. Rightly viewed, properly planned, and adequately lived, it is a full and rewarding experience. No longer does the minister need to face old age in want as an object of charity. Today he plans for this period. He joins with his church and his denomination in providing for this time. Then he enters joyfully into the experience of benediction upon a life well spent.

BIBLIOGRAPHY: J. C. Buckley, *The Retirement Handbook* (1953). G. Lawton, *Aging Successfully* (1946); *New Goals for Old Age* (1947). W. B. Pitkin, *The Best Years* (1946). E. J. Stieglitz, *The Second Forty Years* (1946). BAYNARD F. FOX

RETIREMENT PLAN, BAPTIST BOARDS EMPLOYEES. Inaugurated July 1, 1937, for employees of state boards and staff workers in colleges, seminaries, and hospitals. Fifty-six groups participate in this plan. It was closed to new groups Oct. 1, 1946, and closed to new members Jan. 1, 1955, when it was supplanted by the Baptist Employees Retirement Plan and the Baptist Employees Protection Plan. (Absence of the word "boards" from name indicates new plans now open to membership.) Annuity is paid when employee retires from all denominational service. Minimum retirement age for women is 60, and for men, 65. Automatic retirement age, generally 68, varies according to agreement with individual boards. Two per cent credit is given for each year of participation in the plan, up to 50 per cent of average salary on which dues have been paid. Maximum participation salary is limited to $4,000 annually. For example: If a member participates at an average salary of $3,600 per year for 20 years, his annuity would be $1,440 per year. Minimum annuity after 25 years' service is $600 per year. In case of total and permanent disability, annuity up to $500 yearly is paid, based on years in plan and the previous year's salary. Cost is 3 per cent of salary for member, deducted each payday. Employer dues are 5 per cent. Should a member die before retirement, the amount he has paid, plus interest, is returned to beneficiary, unless member holds a certificate in the Widows Supplemental Annuity Plan (B), in which case, amount is used to fund widow annuity. RETTA O'BANNON

RETIREMENT PLAN, BAPTIST EMPLOYEES. One of two retirement plans inaugurated Jan. 1, 1955, when Baptist Boards Employees' Retirement Plan was closed to new members. (Note: Absence of the word "Boards" from name of plan indicates plan is new one now open to membership.) This plan provides principally for female employees. Annuity is based on number of years in the plan and amount on which dues are paid. Maximum salary participation is limited to $4,000 yearly. A credit of 1½ per cent is given for each year of participation; the longer the member participates, the larger his annuity. For example: A member joins the plan at age 30, works until age 65, and averages $3,600 per year. Annuity will be 52½ per cent of $3,600 or $1,890 per year. Annuity paid for total and permanent disability is based on years in plan and salary. Maximum disability annuity is $900 per year. Early retirement after age 60 on an annuity reduced for each month of early retirement is included in the plan.

Member dues are 3 per cent of salary, and employer's dues are 5 per cent. In case a member leaves the service of the denomination, the amount he has paid, plus interest, is returnable. If he has been in the plan 10 years or more, he may leave his money with the Relief and Annuity Board and an annuity will be paid to him upon his retirement. RETTA O'BANNON

RETIREMENT PLAN, INSTITUTIONAL EMPLOYEES *Educational.* All participating schools, colleges, and seminaries work out provisions of their own contract with the Relief and Annuity Board as regards salary basis, dues, retirement age, withdrawal privileges, or prior service credits. Annuities are based on total accumulations of member and employer dues, plus interest, that have accrued to credit of member at retirement. One fourth of 1 per cent of employees' salary is assessed by the Relief and Annuity Board for administrative expenses.

MABLE MCCARTNEY

Orphanages. Inaugurated Jan. 1, 1936, for employees of orphanages that have a retirement agreement with the board. Credit is 2 per cent of salary for each year of participation up to 50 per cent of average salary during years of service. Up to Jan., 1953, maximum salary for participants was limited to $2,400 annually. Thereafter, it was raised to $4,000 per year. Minimum annuity after 25 years' service is $500 per year. This plan provides for disability annuity, based on years in the plan and last year's salary, up to $500 per year. Dues are 3 per cent for member unless he makes less than $1,000 per year, in which case dues are $2.50 per month. Employer dues are 5 per cent.

MABLE MCCARTNEY

RETIREMENT PLAN, MINISTERS'. State unit retirement plan operating in all states of the Southern Baptist Convention. This plan was closed to new members July 1, 1954, when the Southern Baptist Protection Plan was inaugurated. The member, church, and state convention each pay 3 per cent of member's salary. Maximum participation salary is $4,000 per year. Member's retirement annuity is two per cent per year times average salary while in the plan, if he has participated less than 25 years. If member has participated more than 25 years, his annuity is limited to 50 per cent of his average salary during last 25 years prior to retirement. Pastors who joined the plan before July 1, 1942, were allowed sufficient years of prior service credit to complete 25 years at retirement. If member did not enter plan when he was eligible, his annuity is reduced for years of unpaid dues. In event of total and permanent disability, member receives 30 per cent of his previous year's salary up to a maximum of $500 per year, provided he has five years' service in the Southern Baptist Convention, and one year in the retirement plan. If he has more than five years' service, he is allowed 1 per cent for each additional year, not to exceed 40 per cent or $500 in all. If member dies before retirement, his payments, plus interest, are returned to beneficiary unless member holds a certificate in the Widows Supplemental Annuity Plan, in which case payments are used to provide the widow annuity. MABLE MCCARTNEY

REVELATION. In Christian thought revelation means divine self-disclosure. God, because he is love and also the Creator, is everywhere related to the created order and discloses himself through and to his creatures. The beauty, order, and regularity of nature reveal God's faithfulness; the human conscience manifests his moral claims. Thus man can nowhere escape God, who may be known through the things that are made (Rom. 1; Acts 13, 17). Man's sin, however, blinds his eyes, and because his foolish mind is darkened, the general revelation of God through his created order brings no saving message. Man could know God, but he chooses not to know him. His religious consciousness keeps alive the need to worship, but he makes gods of his own who will not disturb his self-centered world. Even mysticism seeks a god within and unity with that being. The truth in all religions comes from the disclosure of God through and to his creatures, but the truth is overlaid by sinful perversion and is misconstrued.

Christians hold to a special revelation in which God breaks through man's sinful bondage and opens his blinded eyes. God's preparation for this act lies in the election of Israel, the deliverance at the Exodus, the covenant on Sinai, and the words through the prophets. The demands of God, declared through the prophets and codified in the law, were made that man might realize his own sinful inadequacy. Man could not save himself by works, for even his obedience was contaminated by pride. He needed to be remade from within. Thus, in the fulness of time God sent his Son, and disclosed himself in a saving act which was both revelation and redemption. In the life, death, and resurrection of Christ, man's sinful bondage is broken, and his blinded eyes are opened to the wonders of God's grace. Only then does God's revelation through the whole created order become plain. The man who is saved through Christ finds God revealed everywhere.

See also INSPIRATION OF THE SCRIPTURES and KNOWLEDGE OF GOD.

BIBLIOGRAPHY: J. Baillie, *Our Knowledge of God* (1939); *The Idea of Revelation* (1956). H. Kraemer, *Religion and the Christian Faith* (1956).

E. C. RUST

REVIEW AND EXPOSITOR. A quarterly theological journal published by the faculty of Southern Baptist Theological Seminary, Louisville, Ky. Founded in Apr., 1904, it was successor to *The Seminary Magazine,* which had been published monthly by students of the seminary since Feb., 1888. It took over the subscription list of *The Southwestern Theological Review,* Waco, Tex., two of whose editors became associate editors of the new quarterly. With a stated editorial policy to avoid partisan and sectional bias and to be "representative of American Baptists," the quarterly was called *Baptist Review and Expositor* until Oct., 1906, when its present name was assumed. For many years it had associate editors at Southwestern and New Orleans Baptist Theological Seminaries, but since 1952 the *Review and Expositor* has been edited solely by the Southern Seminary faculty. Since Edgar Young Mullins (*q.v.*) served as first editor-in-chief while president of the seminary, all subsequent seminary presidents have served as the quarterly's editors-in-chief. The position of managing editor was created in 1912, with William Joseph McGlothlin (*q.v.*) serving in that capacity. Other managing editors have been William Owen Carver (*q.v.*), 1930–42; Jesse Burton Weatherspoon, 1943–51; and Henry Cornell Goerner, 1952– .

Paid circulation in 1956 was approximately 1,800, primarily among alumni of Southern Seminary, with limited circulation among Baptists around the world and other denominations. The *Review and Expositor* is included in the *Index to Religious Periodical Literature* (from 1949) of the American Theological Library Association. H. C. GOERNER

REVIEWS, BAPTIST. The earliest British Baptist review dates from 1790, while the first American Baptist reviews began to appear early in the 19th century. In other countries Baptist reviews belong only to the 20th century.

Baptist journalism may be said to have had its beginning with the publication in 1790 of the *Baptist Annual Register* in London. This periodical, devoted to the spread of Baptist principles, was established by John Rippon, pastor of the church at Horsleydown, London. It published contributions from American as well as British writers and for a time served the needs of American Baptists. It continued in publication until 1802. It was replaced in 1809 by the *Baptist Magazine* of London which was continued until 1904. In 1844 *The Baptist Reporter* began its career of service as a review for both General and Particular Baptists of Great Britain. It continued until 1865.

In America the first Baptist periodical seems to have been *The Georgia Analytical Repository,* published by Henry Holcombe (*q.v.*) at Savannah, Ga., from 1802. This bimonthly of 48 pages contained biographical sketches, accounts of conversions and of religious movements, sketches of churches, reflections, and devotional and practical materials, but "no advertisements."

Next, in Sept., 1803, appeared the first number of the *Massachusetts Baptist Missionary Magazine,* under auspices of the Massachusetts Baptist Missionary Society, organized in May, 1802, in Boston. In 1826 the Triennial Convention adopted the magazine as its official organ, changing the name to *The American Baptist Magazine.* It was devoted to general denominational interests including missions news and essays on theological and practical topics. In 1835, due to the increase of Baptist newspapers, it became entirely a missionary publication and its name was changed in 1836 to *The Baptist Missionary Magazine.* It has continued until the present, and is currently published under the title *Missions.*

The Kentucky Missionary and Theological Magazine was first published in May, 1812, at Frankfort, under Stark Dupuy, but the war with Great Britain caused its suspension after one year. Likewise, the monthly *Gospel Herald* of Frankfort, begun by Silas Mercer Noel (*q.v.*) in 1813, was shortly suspended.

Of great significance was the beginning of *The Christian Review* in 1836. This first Baptist quarterly magazine had as its first editor, James D. Knowles of Newton Theological Institution, Newton Centre, Mass. From its beginning each issue of the magazine contained 150 or more pages, and leading Baptist and non-Baptist scholars contributed to it. Prominent editors of the quarterly in addition to Knowles included Barnas Sears, Samuel F. Smith, E. G. Sears, S. S. Cutting, George Boardman Taylor (*q.v.*), R. Turnbull, and J. N. Murdock. In 1863 the review suspended its distinct issues and merged with *Bibliotheca Sacra,* with Barnas Sears as one of the editors. In 1867 the review was revived by the American Baptist Publication Society as *The Baptist Quarterly,* with L. E. Smith as editor. At the end of the second volume, in 1869, Henry G. Weston assumed editorial control and continued to conduct the publication until it was discontinued at the end of 1877.

The Triennial Convention, sensing the need for a popular publication, began to publish *The Macedonian and Record* in 1842. An edition was issued at Cincinnati and one at Boston in 1845. The Missionary Union purchased the publication in 1851 and published it regularly until Jan., 1877.

The Baptist Memorial was commenced in New York in 1842 by R. Babcock. After nine years it was issued for a short time at Richmond, Va., then for six years, under the name *The Baptist Family Magazine,* in Philadelphia.

John Lightfoot Waller (*q.v.*) began publication of *The Western Baptist Review* in Louisville in 1845. The life of the review was interrupted in 1850, but the publication reappeared in 1852 as *The Christian Repository,* with Waller and Charles D. Kirk as editors. S. H. Ford became associated with Waller in 1853; and upon Waller's death in the next year, he became sole proprietor. The publication was interrupted again for a short period, but Ford re-established the *Repository* in St. Louis in 1871. Its life continued to 1904.

The *Southern Baptist Review* was published in Nashville from 1855 to 1861, under joint editorship of James Robinson Graves (*q.v.*), James Madison Pendleton (*q.v.*), and Amos Cooper Dayton (*q.v.*).

A quarterly called *The Baptist Review* was started at Cincinnati in 1879 by J. R.

Baumes; but in July, 1885, it was moved to New York. R. S. MacArthur and H. C. Vedder become joint editors, and Vedder was sole editor from 1889 to 1892, when the publication ceased.

In Feb., 1888, students of the Southern Baptist Theological Seminary, with faculty co-operation, began to publish a monthly called *The Seminary Magazine*. It became the *Review and Expositor* in Apr., 1904, and continues to the present as the only theological review of Southern Baptists. Other similar reviews in American Baptist Convention seminaries include *The Crozer Quarterly* of Crozer Seminary (began in 1924), *The Record* (*Colgate Rochester Bulletin* after 1929) of Colgate Rochester (begun in 1928), and *The Christian Review* of Eastern Seminary (1932–41). The American Baptist Historical Society issued *The Chronicle* in 1938, and it is still published today.

The British Baptist Historical Society began publishing its *Transactions* in 1908. Since 1922 the magazine has been known as *The Baptist Quarterly*.

Latin American Baptist reviews include *Revista Evangelica,* published at El Paso since 1940, and *Revista Theologica,* organ of the Baptist Theological Seminary of South Brazil, at Sao Paulo (since 1950). German Baptists have a quarterly, *Wort und Tat* (formerly *Hilsbote*), published at Hamburg. W. L. LUMPKIN

REVIVAL OF 1800, TENNESSEE. The religious revival of 1800 had a profound effect upon most of the evangelical groups in Tennessee. Baptists were no exception. In 1792 there were only 21 Baptist churches in Tennessee with a total membership of 900; but by 1812, after the revival had spread over the frontier, there were 156 churches with a membership of 11,325.

Moral and spiritual conditions in Tennessee were at a very low ebb following the Revolutionary War. "During the years following the War little attention was paid to the training of children or family devotions. During these same years the introduction and wide use of alcoholic beverages in the home and the formation of infidel clubs brought the morals of the people to the lowest ebb ever." There was a great shortage of ministers. Among the Baptists most ministers were untrained. Preaching was lengthy, dull, and inaccurate.

It was into this unlikely environment that the Holy Spirit introduced a most unusual revival. In July, 1800, James McGready, a Presbyterian minister, held the first camp meeting at Gasper River. From here the revival spread rapidly over Tennessee. Among the Baptist ministers who were active were Ambrose Dudley, J. Taylor, Moses Bledsoe, William Hickman (*q.v.*), and Louis and Elijah Craig (*q.v.*). It swept to the south and west under the preaching of men like these and "reached middle Tennessee where it spread its benign blessings upon hamlet, village and every community."

Emotional excesses appeared in many of the meetings, especially in East Tennessee. "In Middle Tennessee the strange exercises did not prevail among the Baptists." Generally speaking, the results of the revival of 1800 among Baptists in Tennessee were deep and powerful. It brought about great changes in ideals and effort among the churches. A great enlargement of territory and membership took place. All of this led to a new spirit of consecration and courage.

HAROLD J. PURDY

REVIVAL OF 1827 (GEORGIA). A period of nearly two years characterized by a great increase in baptisms reported by the churches and an accelerated interest and participation in missions, benevolences, educational work, temperance, and Bible and Sunday school societies, since referred to by Georgia Baptists as the Great Revival of 1827. The revival began at Eatonton, when Adiel Sherwood (*q.v.*) became pastor and teacher in the fall of 1826. The following July, under the leadership and preaching of its new and vigorous pastor, the Eatonton church experienced a revival of unusual intensity, resulting in the conversion and baptism of nearly 100 persons within a few weeks. In September of that year when Sherwood preached, by invitation, at a session of the neighboring Ocmulgee Association held "in a large grove, in the open air," many hundreds of people came forward for prayer at the conclusion of the sermon. Some years later Sherwood recalled the number of those who responded as "probably four thousand," and added that he and others spent two hours "praying for sinners in different parts of the congregation."

From the Ocmulgee the revival spread, with but one or two exceptions, to the remaining 15 associations which comprised the organized Baptist life of Georgia at that time. An increase of itineracy among the ministers and a contagious enthusiasm for evangelism among the church membership helped to account for the spread. In 1828 alone, Adiel Sherwood traveled on horseback over 3,000 miles and preached 333 times in addition to his regular labors. As for evangelical enthusiasm among the laity, what happened in the Flint River Association was probably typical. Upon returning home, the messengers representing that association at the Ocmulgee gathering so inflamed their fellows by reports of the meeting that in a short while the entire association was "ablaze with religious fervor." Referring to the revival then in progress in many quarters of the state, the Georgia Baptist convention at its 1828 session noted that the state of religion in Georgia was "more flattering than it ever was before" and blessed God that "the glorious light of Zion is spreading far and wide."

The numerical increase in church membership was probably the most noteworthy feature of the revival. It is claimed that from 1827 to 1831 the additions to the churches averaged at least 5,000 annually. In 1828 the Ocmulgee Association reported 1,772 baptisms during the

STATE BAPTIST HEADQUARTERS BUILDING, Albuquerque. A drawing of new $275,000 structure now in use.

NEW MEXICO BUILDINGS

SPANISH BAPTIST CENTER, Santa Fe

CHAMA VALLEY MEDICAL CENTER (*q.v.*), Park View

INDIAN MISSION BUILDING, Santa Clara Pueblo

INLOW YOUTH CAMP (*q.v.*), the Administration building, one of the twelve buildings at the camp.

NEW MEXICO BAPTIST CHILDREN'S HOME (*q.v.*), Portales. One of the six buildings at the Home.

ALABAMA BAPTIST CONVENTION (q.v.) BUILDING, Montgomery. Headquarters for 11 state departments. Acquired in 1946, now valued at $250,000.

CENTREVILLE BAPTIST CHURCH, Centreville, Ala. Formed in 1890, educational unit for 440 and auditorium of classical style seating 275 erected in 1922. Membership 1956 approximately 375.

previous 12 months and 810 the following year. The Georgia Association reported 1,761 baptisms in 1828 (as compared with 432 the previous year) and 708 in 1829. The Flint River Association outdistanced all others, reporting 1,900 baptisms in 1828. While the figures ran higher in these associations, most of the other associations reported considerable increases. In his private memoranda, Adiel Sherwood stated, probably with little exaggeration, that at least 16,000 persons were added to the churches of the state as a direct result of the revival, which was nearly a 100 per cent increase.

By 1829 the Great Revival was declining for various reasons. Many of the churches and associations experienced difficulty in assimilating the gains made during the revival and also failed very largely in maintaining a spirit of co-operation with one another and with their new convention in objects of mutual interest. At bottom, perhaps, the difficulty lay in a ministry which was almost wholly uneducated and, accordingly, inefficient.

BIBLIOGRAPHY: Georgia Baptist Convention, *Minutes,* (1827–31). [S. Boykin], *History of the Baptist Denomination in Georgia with Biographical Compendium* (1881). J. Mercer, *A History of the Georgia Baptist Association* (1838). B. D. Ragsdale, *Story of Georgia Baptists,* III (1938). Georgia Association, *Minutes* (1827–30). J. L. Sherwood, *Memoir of Adiel Sherwood, D.D.* (1884). HAROLD L. MCMANUS

REVIVALISM, BAPTISTS AND. Revivalism as a method for propagating the Christian faith is peculiarly suited to Baptist doctrine, polity, and organization. No other denominational group has profited more by the great revival movements in the past; yet many of these movements began without Baptist support and sometimes in the face of Baptist opposition.

When the Wesleyan revival swept across England in the 18th century, Baptist groups were either indifferent or openly antagonistic. The General Baptists, although in agreement with Wesley's Arminian theology, were repelled by his use of the term Anabaptist when referring to Baptists. Another cause of the opposition was a strong Socinian sentiment, denying such doctrines as the atonement, regeneration, and justification by faith alone, which had developed among the General Baptists. However, this group reaped benefits from the revival for, by 1760, five societies organized by David Taylor, a product of the revival, had become Baptist churches. Apparently these churches at first had no knowledge of other groups holding the same views, but after Dan Taylor, the leader of a new Baptist movement, visited them, they became affiliated with a Baptist general body. The latter Taylor, for a time associated with the Methodist movement, came to accept Baptist views, and applied to several Particular Baptist ministers for baptism. Being refused baptism by the Particular Baptists, he led in the organization of the New Connexion of General Baptists, who emphasized the general atonement and used the revival methods which were proving so successful.

The Particular Baptists, even less friendly to the evangelical revival than the General Baptists, accepted the viewpoint of extreme Calvinism, which largely nullified the sense of responsibility to win others to Christ. The effect of the revival on them was more gradual than among the General Baptists and cannot be identified with any one individual. However, among this group also, a shift of doctrinal emphasis took place and an evangelistic fervor was awakened. The revival enthusiasm resulted in missionary endeavors, in stronger associational life, and in increased interest in ministerial education. The Baptist cause in England, which had been on the decline since the closing years of the 17th century, was quickened in all of its phases. The revival, which they had opposed, saved the General Baptists from the drift to Socinianism and the Particular Baptists from hyper-Calvinism.

The story of revivalism among American Baptists is much like that of Baptists in England. Although most of the effective evangelists, from Jonathan Edwards to Billy Sunday, have been Presbyterians or Congregationalists, Baptists have reaped more abundantly from their labors than have their own church groups. When the Great Awakening began in New England, nearly all of the Baptist churches in that area were Arminian in their theology and the Calvinistic emphasis given to the movement by its Congregational promoters antagonized them. Their resentment of the Congregational state-church arrangement furthered this antagonism. Yet their gains as a result of the revival surpassed those of most other denominations. Although many of the converts won during the Great Awakening came to accept Baptist beliefs, they found the older Baptist churches reluctant to receive them. Therefore, they formed their own organizations and became known as Separate Baptists. They were zealous in their use of the revivalistic methods and some of their enthusiasm was imparted to the Regular Baptists even before the union of the two groups. Following this fusion, the spirit of revivalism continued as the dominant factor in the main stream of American Baptist life.

The great revival movement which came after the Revolutionary War, found Baptists represented throughout the western frontier and ready to share the benefits of the new spiritual impetus. Within a period of three years, Baptist churches of Kentucky received more than 10,000 new members, and there was a similar ingathering throughout the entire western region.

The revivals, by greatly multiplying their membership, made Baptists influential in political affairs, as was evidenced in the successful campaign against any form of state-church relationship. The effect of the revivals on the establishment of educational institutions was equally significant. Contrary to the widespread belief that revivalism goes with ignorance and superstition, in America it has served to promote the cause of education. By 1830 the Baptists had established four colleges and by 1861 they reported 25 colleges and universities.

Although most of the larger denominations have come to use revivalistic methods very sparingly, or not at all, the Southern Baptist Convention is a conspicuous exception. In Southern Baptist churches the revival as a method for evangelistic endeavor continues to prove very effective.

BIBLIOGRAPHY: W. M. Gewehr, *The Great Awakening in Virginia* (1930). A. H. Newman, *A History of the Baptist Churches in the United States* (1915). R. B. Semple, *A History of the Rise and Progress of the Baptists in Virginia* (1894). W. W. Sweet, *Religion in the Development of American Culture* (1952); *Religion on the American Frontier—The Baptists* (1931); *Revivalism in America* (1945); *The Story of Religion in America* (1950). R. G. Torbet, *A History of the Baptists* (1950). A. C. Underwood, *A History of the English Baptists* (1947). H. C. Vedder, *Short History of the Baptists* (1952). W. T. Whitley, *A History of British Baptists* (1932).

WILLIAM A. CARLETON

REVIVALS IN KENTUCKY. Kentucky Baptists experienced several occasional and spontaneous revivals between 1785 and 1840. In 1785 a revival broke out in the Bluegrass region under the preaching of John Taylor, later to become an antimissioner. Thirty persons were dismissed from the South Elkhorn church to form the Clear Creek church in Woodford County, which increased to 150 members in 1788. A more extensive revival broke out in 1789, lasting three years. Salem Association reported 34 baptisms in 1789 and 112 in 1790, and Elkhorn Association reported 288 in 1789. Baptists increased from nearly 400 in 1785 to over 3,100 in 1792. Except for the Mason County revival of 1797, resulting in around 300 baptisms, there was little revivalism between 1792 and 1800, for Kentuckians were more concerned with politics, agriculture, and commerce than with religion.

The greatest revival in Kentucky history was the Great Frontier Revival, 1800–03. Infidelity, crude immorality, and religious negligence produced a situation in which revivalism flourishes. The revival began in Logan County under the "sin-and-hellfire" preaching of James McGready, a Presbyterian. Initially, Baptists refused to participate, fearing a compromise of their doctrines of believer's baptism and the disciplined church. After a few months, however, revivalism spontaneously broke out among them, and they actually profited more from it than any other group. Camp meetings and spiritual exercises first appeared during this revival. The largest camp meeting, begun at Cane Ridge, near Paris, on Aug. 6, 1801, was attended by 20,000 persons; preaching services were held simultaneously on the ridge. Around 3,000 persons, seemingly involuntarily adopting such weird and ecstatic exercises as falling, jerking, rolling, running, dancing, laughing, barking, etc., gave physical evidence of conversion. A strong sense of guilt preceded these exercises, which were interpreted as struggles of the soul; spiritual calm, viewed as the sign of victory, followed enthusiasm. Initially, Baptists repudiated these excesses, but they soon recognized their validity. Baptist membership tripled from 5,119 in 1800 to 15,495 in 1803, and under the revival stimulus it increased to 22,694 in 1812. Several churches had phenomenal results from the revival: Great Crossing, numbering 107 in 1800, baptized 353 in 1801, and Forks of the Elkhorn reported 216 baptisms. Moreover, Separates and Regulars, who had stubbornly remained apart, united on "The Terms of General Union" in 1801, thereby ushering in the "golden age" of United Baptists. Other salutary results included the moral improvement of society and the decline of heresies.

In 1810 a revival broke out in the Long Run Association, resulting in 956 baptisms, and spread to other parts, especially eastward from Louisville, lasting two years. Another revival exercise, the "shakes," appeared, influenced by the earthquakes in the western region in 1811. The revival of 1817–20, stimulated by foreign mission interest, was unfortunately frustrated by the antimission controversy. A contagious revival, growing out of Alexander Campbell's agitation over ecclesiology, broke out in 1827. Statistically, around 15,000 baptisms were reported, mostly by associations to the east of Louisville. Actually, however, this revival was a mixed blessing, for most converts had been won to Campbellite views. Between 1830 and 1832 almost 10,000 Baptists united with Campbell, splitting congregations, taking over property, and engendering hostile attitudes.

The paralysis caused by antimissionism and Campbellism was not overcome until 1837 when the advocates of missions, after an initial failure, organized the Kentucky general association. Immediately a revival broke out, starting in the Louisville church where the general association was formed and spreading to missionary churches throughout the state during the next three years. Between 1837 and 1840 almost 18,000 persons were baptized, representing a 45 per cent increase over the membership of 1835. Of more consequence, however, was the introduction of "protracted meetings," which transformed revivalism from occasional to perennial and from spontaneous to planned efforts. Revivalism became thereafter the chief method of Baptist enlistment.

HUGH WAMBLE

REVIVALS IN VIRGINIA. Three great movements of religious revival in Virginia stand out above all others: the Great Awakening, 1740–76; the Great Revival, 1785–90; and the Revival of the Confederate Army of Northern Virginia, 1862–65.

The Great Awakening had already stirred New England and several of the Middle Colonies before it reached Virginia, where there were three phases of the movement with Presbyterian, Baptist, and Methodist groups assuming leadership successively. The Presbyterian revival began spontaneously in 1740 among some laymen, chief of whom was Samuel Morris, in Hanover County. Then in 1742 the New Brunswick Presbytery of New Jersey sent William Robinson to visit scattered groups of Presbyterians in Virginia and North Carolina. Robinson stirred a revival spirit wherever he went as he boldly attacked decadent conditions in the Established Church and ministered to the spiritual hunger of the masses. He returned to the North, but in 1748 sent young Samuel Davies, who firmly established Presbyterianism in eastern Virginia. Leading New Side (revivalistic) Presbyterian preachers, including Gilbert and William Tennent, Samuel Finley, and Samuel Blair, were evangelizing in Virginia. Two revivalists, Brown and Alexander Craighead, settled in Augusta County and started an awakening among the Scotch-Irish of the Shenandoah Valley. Davies worked in five counties, and in addition to establishing churches, he initiated a pioneer effort in evangelizing Negroes. Scarcity of ministers prevented noticeably large results.

The Baptist phase of the Awakening began with the preaching of the newly arrived Separate Baptists, a by-product of the New England Awakening. Shubael Stearns (*q.v.*) and Daniel Marshall (*q.v.*) came from New England in 1754 and moved into central North Carolina in 1755. From their center at Sandy Creek, the Separates moved into Virginia in 1760 and afterward, where their preaching, marked by strong emotional appeal, captivated plain audiences, unaccustomed to such preaching. After 1770 the growth of the Separate Baptist movement was phenomenal; in 1774, in spite of severe persecution, there were over 4,000 Separates in Virginia. After 1774, however, the Baptist phase of the revival declined, due to preoccupation with political and doctrinal matters and the appearance of another strong evangelical group, the Methodists, who assumed leadership of the revival by 1775. Not yet separated from the Episcopal Church, their revival represents a counter-awakening in the Established Church. Devereux Jarratt, an Anglican clergyman of Dinwiddie County, prepared the way for and worked with the Methodist itinerants after 1773. He introduced into Virginia the practice of holding testimony and prayer meetings in private homes. The revival reached its culmination in 1776 when the number of Methodists increased to 2,456, half the Methodist membership in the colonies. After 1776 the Revolution gradually brought an end to the movement, which has been called the greatest awakening in the history of American Methodism.

Following the Revolution in 1785, a new awakening began in different regions of Virginia, simultaneously affecting Methodist, Baptist, and Presbyterian denominations, reaching its climax in 1787–88. Among the Methodists the revival centered in the southern counties and was attended by physical and emotional outbreaks. The Baptist revival began in the upper James River region and reached its climax in 1787–89, although it continued until 1792. In the midst of this great revival, a union of Separate and Regular Baptists was consummated in 1787, and nearly all of eastern Virginia was swept by Baptists and Methodists during this period. The Presbyterian awakening began at Hampden-Sydney College in 1787, spread to near-by counties, and moved westward in 1789 to its chief centers in Bedford and Rockbridge counties. The emotional outbursts associated with the Methodist and Baptist revivals were not present in the Presbyterian meetings, due to the education of the Presbyterian preachers. William Graham, rector of Liberty Hall Academy (which became Washington and Lee University), visited Hampden-Sydney in 1789, and upon his return home, Lexington became the center of a revival in the Valley of Virginia. This movement spread to the frontier country of Kentucky and Tennessee, and Presbyterians thus became the principal representatives of the revival in the Valley and the southwestern counties. The earlier Baptist dominance in southeastern Virginia had given way to the Methodists during the revival period, which ended by 1790, but north of the James River, Baptists were the predominant group. The Established Church seemed to have fallen before a more vigorous and evangelical form of Christianity. Both of the 18th century religious awakenings made important contributions to American democracy, education, and social progress.

The revival in the Confederate Army of Northern Virginia began in the fall of 1862 and continued in the army until Apr., 1865. Beyond the army it extended to churches in many parts of the state in 1865–66. Estimates of the number of conversions in the army alone run from 15,000 to 50,000. The revival was particularly helpful in sustaining the people of Virginia during the Reconstruction era.

Numerous local or area revivals have occurred, including, notably, the Presbyterian revival of 1828–32 in central Virginia, led by Asabel Nettleton and Jesse Armistead; the Lexington revival of 1856; and the Baptist revival of 1811–12 in Essex, King and Queen, and neighboring counties. WILLIAM L. LUMPKIN

REWARD. Reward is prominent in the teachings of Jesus and in the New Testament. This prominence, however, has been a source of criticism because reward has been interpreted by some as a sanction for righteousness. The view of pure philosophical ethicists, from Kant until today, has been that the prominence of reward in Christian teaching makes the Christian way of life egocentric, happiness-seeking, and basically selfish.

Rightly interpreted, reward in the New Testament is conditioned by three other primary concepts: that of the nature of God; that of value; and, finally, that of universal order, which is the expression of the command of God. Reward is the frame which the New Testament utilizes to express the consequential results to men of God's goodness, the values that accrue from doing his will, and the lasting consequences of right action in a universal order. The New Testament speaks of things as they are, and, therefore, inevitably it speaks much of reward, not in terms of man's perspective or of sanction for ethical action, but as consequential results of ethical action.

BIBLIOGRAPHY: W. C. Dobbs, *The Concept of Reward in the Teachings of Jesus* (1954). P. S. Minear, *And Great Shall Be Your Reward* (1941).

W. C. DOBBS

REYNOLDS, ISHAM EMMANUEL (b. Shades Valley, near Birmingham, Ala., Sept. 27, 1879; d. Fort Worth, Tex., May 10, 1949). Church musician, educator, composer, and conductor. He was the son of Winfield Pickney and Mary (Eastis) Reynolds. His education included study at Mississippi College, Clinton, Miss., 1905–06; Moody Bible Institute, 1907–08; voice, theory, and composition under private tutors; Chicago Musical College, 1920; a Bachelor of Music from the Siegel-Myers University Correspondence School of Music, Chicago, 1918; and an honorary Doctor of Music degree, Southern School of Fine Arts, Houston, Tex., 1942.

He married Velma Burns, July 18, 1900, who, with an infant daughter, died in 1906. On July 17, 1912, he married Lura Mae Hawk of Oklahoma City, Okla. One daughter, Lurames, (Mrs. LeMoyne Michels) was born of this union.

Converted at the age of nine years, he joined the Cumberland Presbyterian Church. In 1904 he joined the North Highlands Baptist Church, Birmingham, Ala., and began work as an evangelistic singer. From 1906 to 1915, he served under the Mississippi Baptist State Mission Board and the Southern Baptist Home Mission Board.

In 1915 he accepted a teaching position at Southwestern Baptist Theological Seminary, Fort Worth, Tex., as head of the Department of Gospel Music, which became the School of Sacred Music, 1921. He retired on account of illness in May, 1945.

During this time he conducted schools of music in many states, associations, and local churches. He lectured and taught at Ridgecrest Baptist Assembly, pioneering the present-day church music leadership conferences. His influence throughout the Southern Baptist Convention had a telling effect upon the organizational activities at the state and convention levels. Besides five textbooks, he composed two sacred music dramas, four cantatas, miscellaneous anthems, hymns, and gospel songs, and he is the author of *A Manual of Practical Church Music* (1925), *Ministry of Music in Religion* (1928), *Church Music* (1935), *The Choir in the Non-Liturgical Church* (1938), and *Music and the Scriptures* (1942). SARAH THOMPSON

REYNOLDS, Z. SMITH, FOUNDATION. Established in 1936 by Richard J. Reynolds, Mrs. Mary Reynolds Babcock, and Mrs. Nancy Reynolds Bagley, for charitable, civic, and eleemosynary purposes within the state of North Carolina, by a grant of all the property which they received from the estate of their late brother, Zachary Smith Reynolds of Winston-Salem, N. C. At the death of W. N. Reynolds, uncle of the founders, on Sept. 10, 1951, the principal of the foundation was increased by a bequest in his will of approximately $14,000,000.

For a number of years after its organization the foundation made annual grants to the North Carolina State Health Department for the inauguration and maintenance of a campaign for the control of venereal disease in the state. But since July 1, 1947, a major part of the foundation's income has been contributed to Wake Forest College for a program of enlargement and relocation near Winston-Salem. The total amount contributed to the college for this purpose as of Oct. 31, 1955, was $4,700,426.05. By terms of agreements between trustees of the foundation and trustees of Wake Forest College, the school will receive in perpetuity for operating purposes up to $500,000 annually from the earnings of the foundation.

The market value of foundation assets on Oct. 31, 1955, was approximately $28,000,000; the total amount expended in grants, $7,949,-623.18; and for administrative expenses, $35,-255.77. The foundation, which is to be enlarged up to $50,000,000 by the addition to its principal of 20 per cent of its annual earnings, has as trustees Richard J. Reynolds, president; Charles H. Babcock, vice-president and treasurer; Stratton Coyner, secretary; Mrs. Nancy Reynolds Bagley, Thomas B. Butler, L. D. Long, and W. N. Lybrook. EUGENE OLIVE

REYNOLDSON ACADEMY. A school also known as Chowan-Reynoldson Seminary in Gates County, N. C. Founded in 1855 by James A. Delke, the school was operated, until the Civil War, by Chowan Association. D. L. SMILEY

RICE, LUTHER (b. Northborough, Mass., Mar. 25, 1783; d. Edgefield District, S. C., Sept. 25, 1836). Father of American Baptist foreign missions and denominational statesman. He joined a Congregationalist church Mar. 14, 1802, entered Leicester Academy, 1804, and Williams College as a sophomore in Oct., 1807. There he joined a society of inquiry on foreign missions with Samuel J. Mills, Jr., James Richards, Gordon Hall, Francis Robbins, Samuel Loomis, and Byram Cree. These conducted the Haystack Prayer Meeting at Williamstown. In 1810 Rice, Mills, Richards, Samuel Newell, Samuel Nott, Jr., and Adoniram Judson (*q.v.*) requested appointment as foreign missionaries by the general association of all evangelical ministers in Massachusetts. The result was the organization of the American Board of Commissioners for Foreign Missions. The board appointed Judson, Nott, Hall, and Newell. Rice was appointed on provision he raise the necessary money. On Feb. 6, 1812, the five were ordained at Tabernacle Church, Salem, Mass. Hall, Nott, and Rice sailed from Philadelphia Feb. 18 and arrived at Calcutta Aug. 10. Following a study on shipboard which continued after his arrival in India, Rice accepted the Baptist position on baptism and was immersed Nov. 1, 1812. This was two months after Judson and his wife had taken the same step.

Due to the opposition of the East India Company to mission activities and due to the need of establishing support of the Judsons and himself by the Baptists, Rice returned to America, arriving Sept. 7, 1813. The Congregationalist board in Boston rudely dissolved relations with Rice, and he then approached the Baptists. He determined to make a journey to acquaint the Baptists with their mission opportunities. His first travels took him from Boston through New York, Philadelphia, Baltimore, Washington, Richmond, Charleston, and Savannah. Riding in the stage between Richmond and Petersburg, he conceived the plan of a general mission society made up of representatives from smaller bodies. Thus, in Philadelphia on May 18, 1814, was formed the General Convention of the Baptist Denomination in the United States for Foreign Missions, popularly called the Triennial Convention.

Urged by Rice, in 1822 the new convention opened Columbian College in Washington. Rice was appointed agent. He started publication of *The Columbian Star* at Washington about the same time. It was the first weekly family newspaper published by Baptists. The Baptist General Tract Society was organized Feb. 25, 1824, with Rice as its treasurer. Twenty years later, the American Baptist Publication Society grew from this society.

As for Rice himself, his enthusiastic impulsive ness led him into impossible projects and deprived him of personal success. By 1826 Columbian College was swamped in debt, and Rice was forced to bring his visions closer to reality. He resigned as agent of the school and as treasurer of the tract society but continued his solicitations for missions and Christian education. He traveled especially in the South, where he was much loved. There he died and was buried in Pine Pleasant Church cemetery between Newberry and Saluda, S. C. In spite of disappointments, his enthusiasm was a challenge which Baptists could not forget. "He changed the scattered Baptist churches into a Baptist denomination."

BIBLIOGRAPHY: W. Cathcart, *The Baptist Encyclopedia* (1883). E. B. Pollard and D. G. Stevens, *Luther Rice* (1928). J. B. Taylor, *Memoir of Rev. Luther Rice* (1841). LOULIE LATIMER OWENS

RICHMOND FEMALE INSTITUTE AND WOMAN'S COLLEGE OF RICHMOND. For some years prior to 1853, Baptist leaders of Richmond had felt the need for a school for girls. As the result of a meeting called by J. B. Taylor, a charter for Richmond Female Institute was applied for and granted by the General Assembly of Virginia on Mar. 2, 1853. Land was obtained and a building erected on 10th Street, and Basil Manly, Jr., was elected president. The school opened for its first session on Oct. 2, 1854. From 250 to 300 young women were enrolled annually in the years before the Civil War.

It was the desire of the founders, who had secured the necessary money by forming a joint stock company, to develop a school in which women would have the same educational opportunities as men. Considerable progress toward this goal was achieved by 1861. In Oct., 1862, the school building became a Confederate hospital, and classes were suspended until Oct., 1865.

Manly resigned as president in 1859, being succeeded by Charles H. Winston. He was followed by John Hart, 1874–77. Sally Hamner was president, 1877–90, followed by James Nelson, who served until the school closed in 1916.

While the school had prospered and developed educationally, it had not been established on a strong financial foundation. Affairs developed into a crisis in 1894; in February of that year, a group of Richmond Baptists obtained a charter for the Woman's College of Richmond and purchased the property of the Richmond Female Institute. It seems there was little more change than that of the name, for Nelson was retained as president of the new school.

In 1903 the Baptist General Association of Virginia began to concern itself about the establishment of a standard liberal arts college for women. When the Education Commission of the association appealed to the General Education Board for funds, it was told that the board would be interested only if the proposed college were to be a part of the already established Richmond College. For some years there had been a growing desire on the part of the officials of the Woman's College to move the school to a more convenient and attractive part of the city and to have a closer co-operation with Richmond College. As a result of these factors, the property and franchise of the Woman's College were conveyed to the trustees of Richmond College in Sept., 1914, when Westhampton College, the co-ordinate woman's college, was opened. The Woman's College of Richmond was operated by the trustees of Richmond College through the session of 1915–16, after which the school was merged with Westhampton College. The alumnae of the Woman's College have transferred their loyalty and co-operation to the advancement of Westhampton College. RALPH MCDANEL

RIDDLE, JOE DUKE (b. near Canton, Van Zandt County, Tex., July 18, 1895; d. Abilene, Tex., Aug. 28, 1954). Church musician and educator. After graduating from Eustace (Tex.) High School, Riddle received a diploma of sacred music from Southwestern Baptist Theological Seminary in 1923; and the B.A. degree from Montezuma Baptist College, Las Vegas,

N. Mex., in 1925. He was awarded the doctor of music degree by Howard Payne College, Brownwood, Tex., in 1952. Riddle became superintendent of schools in Vaughn, Tex., and later head of the voice department and director of choral work in Montezuma College. He served as education-music director for the First Baptist churches of Mangum, Okla.; Amarillo, Abilene, and Lubbock, Tex. While at Lubbock, he collaborated with Robert Clifford Campbell (*q.v.*) in writing the stewardship book *God's Plan*. When the Texas general convention established a church music department in Dec., 1944, Riddle was elected secretary, a position which he began Jan. 1, 1945, and held until his death. He promoted music education in the churches through use of graded choirs, established a competitive church music festival program, and conducted choir schools and summer music camps.

V. F. FORDERHASE

RIDGECREST BAPTIST ASSEMBLY. A summer encampment near Asheville, N. C., owned and operated by the Southern Baptist Sunday School Board for all Southern Baptists, which presents each year programs dealing with every phase of the denominational program and ranging from the inspirational to the intensely practical.

The idea of a summer assembly for Southern Baptists was first conceived by Bernard Washington Spilman when he was beginning his work as Sunday school secretary in North Carolina in 1896. In June, 1901, he became the first field secretary of the Baptist Sunday School Board and pursued the idea further, investigating without success several locations in East Tennessee and Western North Carolina. At the Baptist state convention in Raleigh, N. C., Dec., 1905, Spilman requested a committee of five to consider the establishment of an assembly and report to the next convention.

The committee reported a suitable location 18 miles east of Asheville and an option on 940 acres of land. They recommended "that the Convention without assuming any financial responsibility give its endorsement to the establishment of these grounds" and also "that the Baptists of the South be invited to join in the movement." The assembly was chartered Mar. 8, 1907.

The following year (May 21, 1908) a group of stockholders met on the assembly grounds by the old stagecoach house (still standing) and the corporation was organized and plans made for beginning construction. No funds were available but on the personal endorsement of J. H. Tucker, chairman of the assembly committee, a loan of $8,000 was secured from the Battery Park Bank in Asheville. The grounds were surveyed and lots laid out. One hundred and forty lots were sold making available $14,000 which was used for the construction of the first buildings.

In May, 1907, the Southern Baptist Convention in Richmond, Va., endorsed the assembly, but "without assuming any financial responsibility." Thus began the first Southern Baptist assembly.

The record of early Ridgecrest was one continuous story of struggle against odds. A general panic paralyzed business. Changes in assembly management, a lawsuit for a portion of the land purchased, the destruction of the first auditorium by a hurricane, and the loss of the first hotel units (Blue Mont Inn and Sunset Cottage) by fire all greatly hindered the progress in those early days.

Many men served as manager in the early days. Spilman served from Sept., 1907, to Sept., 1909; E. L. Hon and Charles Edward Brewer, 1910; E. F. Mumford, 1911–12; Jesse Daniel Moore, 1913–15; O. L. Stringfield and H. B. Craven, 1915–19; Livingston Mays, 1919–22. The Education Board of the Southern Baptist Convention, with William Carey James, John Walter Cammack, and Rufus Washington Weaver (*q.v.*) as executive secretaries and Albert Richmond Bond as secretary of the assembly, administered the affairs of Ridgecrest 1921–28. Pritchell Hall, a hotel unit, a combination auditorium and dining hall, and five cottages were constructed during this period. Raymond F. Staples was elected manager in Jan., 1925, serving through Dec., 1935.

When the Education Board was dissolved and its work transferred to the Executive Committee of the Southern Baptist Convention, this committee requested the Baptist Sunday School Board to assume responsibility for the program and maintenance of the buildings and grounds for a period of three years beginning in 1928. This arrangement continued until 1944. The Southern Baptist Convention transferred to the Sunday School Board title to all its property at Ridgecrest, and provided that the Board would assume "all obligations implicit in this ownership," so that the assembly would be a trust of the Sunday School Board for Southern Baptists.

Because of limited funds, the programs at Ridgecrest in the early days were on a small scale. Attendance was likewise small. A school of religious education was opened with six present on Monday, June 11, 1910. Gradually attendance increased and the scope of the program was enlarged to take in all phases of Southern Baptist denominational life. In co-operation with other agencies and organizations, conference programs are provided for training and leadership for the Sunday school, Training Union, Woman's Missionary Union, Baptist student work, missions at home and abroad, and every phase of denominational life. From small beginnings the assembly has grown to a total attendance in 1955 of 27,660.

On Jan. 1, 1936, Perry Morgan, formerly of the Sunday school department of North Carolina, was elected general manager. Under his leadership there was great expansion and development with funds supplied by the Sunday School Board. In Dec., 1937, the Sunday School Board authorized its Ridgecrest committee to build a new auditorium at a cost of $50,000. Before another 10 years had elapsed it was necessary to double the capacity of the auditorium and build additional units with classrooms and other facilities. Because of ill health, Mr. Morgan gave up his duties as business manager and was given a new assignment as manager of the Ridgecrest Boys' Camp. From 1946 through Oct., 1950, Robert Guy served as manager.

Since Nov. 1, 1950, under the administration of Willard K. Weeks, many needed additional buildings and other facilities have been added to the assembly. In 1947 construction was started on a new dining hall with a seating capacity of more than 2,500. It was completed in 1952. Additional housing units have been built so that Ridgecrest can now accommodate approximately 3,000 guests each week.

Under assembly supervision, Camp Ridgecrest for Boys has been in operation since July 1, 1930. Charles W. Burts was the first director. Camp Crestridge for Girls was opened June 1, 1955, with Arvine Bell as director.

R. L. MIDDLETON

RIDGEDALE ACADEMY. A school proposed when the South Carolina state convention of 1920 authorized the election of a board of trustees who would have authority to negotiate with owners of a school at Speigner, S. C., to purchase the property for the convention. The purchase was not consummated, and the board of trustees was dissolved by the convention of 1922.

CHARLES W. BURTS

RIGGAN, GEORGE WASHINGTON (b. Isle of Wight County, Va., Feb. 22, 1855; d. Louisville, Ky., Apr. 18, 1885). Minister and theological professor. Educated in public and private schools of Virginia, at Richmond College, where he received his M.A. degree in 1878, and at Southern Baptist Theological Seminary from 1878 to 1881, Riggan was ordained at Leigh St. Baptist Church, Richmond, in Oct., 1875. While in college he preached in churches near Richmond and during his years at the seminary held a pastorate at Carlisle, Ky., and later at Forks of Elkhorn, Woodford County, 1880–85. Elected assistant instructor of Hebrew, Greek, and homiletics in Southern Seminary in 1881, he became assistant professor in 1883 and held that position until his death. Riggan married Sallie O. Garland June 1, 1882, and their son G. Garland Riggan became a professor at Kansas City Baptist Theological Seminary.

LEO T. CRISMON

RIGHTEOUSNESS. This term represents the state of being in right relation to God, who is righteous in himself and whose being defines the content of righteousness as it is seen in the person and work of Christ. Like most biblical words the emphasis in "righteousness" is upon an *active* ordering of one's life in obedience to the expressed will of God, rather than upon a passive moral state. By the absolute standard of the law of God written on tables of stone (Exod. 34:1), or the inward law written in the heart (Rom. 2:15), there is none righteous, "no not one" (Psalm 14:1, 3; Rom. 3:10). Only Christ, who in full obedience to the Father has become the revelation of God's righteousness, escapes this sweeping condemnation; this righteousness, manifested apart from the law but witnessed to by law and prophets, is appropriated by man through faith in Christ (Rom. 3:21 ff.).

In the whole history of Israel, the absolute demand for righteousness had a paralyzing effect. Paul recognized this effect (Rom. 7) left one in despair: the law issued the command but was powerless to justify (*dikaioō*), to "make one right" with God. Paul seized the brilliant, saving insight of Isaiah that the righteousness of God alone could become man's salvation (Isa. 42:6), for God speaks "in righteousness, mighty to save" (Isa. 63:1). On that theme of "the righteousness of God" as revealed in "the gospel of Christ" (Rom. 1:16–17), Paul built his whole argument in Romans. Saving righteousness becomes man's by faith, both beginning and ending in faith (Rom. 1:17). The attempt of theologians to make the appropriation of righteousness *only* a formal pronouncement has all but obscured the tremendous biblical truth that righteousness is no hollow shell, but rather the transforming act of God's grace in Christ, wrought in the repenting sinner through the Holy Spirit. By this transforming act guilty man is forgiven; his whole life is brought into *right* relation to God, and he lives in right relation with God and his fellow man.

See also GOD. WAYNE E. WARD

ROBB, CZARINA FOLSOM (b. Mar. 5, 1833; d. Atoka, Okla., Oct. 7, 1906). Daughter of Israel and Sophie Folsom (half Choctaw), educated at Wheelock Academy and baptized by R. J. Hogue (*q.v.*) into Philadelphia church, 1862. She married T. J. Bond, M.D., who died in 1876. In 1878 she married D. N. Robb, a white man of Atoka, Indian Territory. Active in mission work for 30 years, she served as Choctaw interpreter for Joseph Samuel Murrow (*q.v.*), also for Mrs. C. R. Blackall in the organization of the Choctaw-Chickasaw Woman's Missionary Society at High Hill in 1876. She was elected first corresponding secretary of this society and thus became the first woman elected to such a position in the United States.

BIBLIOGRAPHY: J. M. Gaskin, *Trail Blazers of Sooner Baptists* (1953).

J. M. GASKIN

ROBERTS, COLUMBUS (b. Lee County, Ala., Sept. 23, 1870; d. Columbus, Ga., Aug. 26, 1950). Son of a self-educated hill farmer and schoolteacher, and the eldest of 11 children. After four sketchy years of schooling, he became a tenant farmer to help supplement the family income. Eight successive failing years persuaded him to go to Atlanta, where he worked for railway express. When he was 20, his father died, leaving him responsible for the large family. He moved to Columbus, Ga., soon quit his work with the railway express, and, after brief ventures into wholesale and retail grocery businesses, he began a business in bottling operations. After the impetus given by World War I, the extraordinary growth of the Coca-Cola interests brought him a substantial fortune.

As leader of the Columbus Association in the 75 Million Campaign, which he conducted successfully, he found that the participation of the individual church in the Cooperative Program of the denomination was consistently more favorable in a church with an educated minister. He came to the deliberate conclusion that the best service he could render as a Christian steward would be to give his support to Christian education, especially to ministerial education and to Mercer University. As a deacon in the First Baptist Church of Columbus, moderator of the Columbus Association, chairman of the Georgia Baptist Holding Commission, and president of the Georgia Baptist Convention, he kept this objective in mind and implemented it by giving a total of more than one and a quarter million dollars to Mercer University, Bessie Tift College, Shorter College, Norman College, Brewton-Parker Junior College, Truett-McConnell Junior College, the Georgia Baptist Children's Home, and the Georgia Baptist Hospital.

As state commissioner of agriculture from Jan. 1, 1937, to Dec. 31, 1940, he greatly advanced the farming interests in Georgia, organized and financed the dairy farmers of the state for a period of years, and gave strong support to the paving of main highways and provision of good roads in rural sections. His major interest, however, was in philanthropy, and his gift of nearly one million dollars to Mercer made possible the establishment of the Columbus Roberts School of Christianity, a memorial to the man who gave more to the causes sponsored by the Georgia Baptist Convention than did any other man in its history of 130 years.

BIBLIOGRAPHY: S. Dowell, *Columbus Roberts, Christian Steward Extraordinary* (1950). SPRIGHT DOWELL

ROBERTS ACADEMY. A seminary-type school operated for several years immediately after 1800 by John Mitchell Roberts (1775–1822) near Stateburg, S. C. The "first educational institution under Baptist auspices in South Carolina," the academy is considered the forerunner of Furman Academy and Theological Institution and Furman University.

Roberts, one of the first native South Carolina Baptist preachers to attend college, returned from Rhode Island College in 1799 to the pastorate of High Hills church. His education had been fostered by the Charleston Association through its general committee, established to aid ministerial students. Later, Roberts served for several years as secretary for this general committee, with its president, Richard Furman (*q.v.*).

Latin and Greek were the principal subjects taught at the academy, and students sponsored by the general committee were exempt from tuition. The school apparently closed before 1810, and the Charleston Association donated the library which it had contributed to the school to the new Furman Academy and Theological Institution.

BIBLIOGRAPHY: R. N. Daniel, *A History of Furman University* (1951). W. J. McGlothlin, *A History of Furman University, Baptist Beginnings in Education* (1926). L. Townsend, *South Carolina Baptists, 1670–1805* (1935). J. M. KING

ROBERTSON, ARCHIBALD THOMAS (b. near Chatham, Pittsylvania County, Va., Nov. 6, 1863; d. Louisville, Ky., Sept. 24, 1934). World-famous Greek scholar, teacher, author. In 1875, when Robertson was 12, his family moved to Cool Spring, Iredel County, N. C., and he attended Boone Preparatory School, Statesville, N. C., until he was almost 16. From 1879 to 1885, Robertson attended Wake Forest College, combining some high school subjects with the standard college course, and earned the M.A. degree. When Robertson entered Wake Forest, he had little money and had a serious impediment in his speech. He spent many hours alone, reading aloud and reciting choice selections of literature, which he memorized for that purpose; and he later joined and participated in the Euzelian Literary Society to improve his reasoning and speaking abilities. Robertson's professors at Wake Forest included William Louis Poteat (*q.v.*), languages; William Bailey Royall (*q.v.*), Greek; and Charles Elisha Taylor (*q.v.*), Latin. Making grades of 95 per cent to 100 per cent in every course, he won medals in French and Latin and placed second in Greek. Robertson was co-editor of the college paper, *The Wake Forest Student*.

After becoming a Christian at 13, he united with the Statesville Baptist Church in Mar., 1876, and three years later he was licensed to preach. Before Robertson was 17, he preached his first sermon to a Negro congregation in North Carolina.

While attending Southern Baptist Theological Seminary from 1885 to 1888, Robertson studied Old Testament under Basil Manly, Jr. (*q.v.*), New Testament and homiletics under John Albert Broadus (*q.v.*), theology under James Petigru Boyce (*q.v.*), and church history under William Heth Whitsitt (*q.v.*). According to John Richard Sampey (*q.v.*), Robertson "was easily the foremost student of his period in the Seminary." He received the Th.M. degree in May, 1888, became Broadus' assistant the following October, and was made associate professor in 1890. Later he succeeded Broadus as professor of New Testament interpretation and continued in that position until his death. On Nov. 27, 1894, Robertson married Ella Broadus, daughter of John A. Broadus. They had three sons, John Albert, Cary, and Archibald Thomas, and two daughters, Eleanor and Charlotte.

Robertson, who twice delivered the Stone Lectures at Princeton University, was Bible interpreter repeatedly at Northfield and Winona Lake assemblies and was in great demand for Baptist summer assemblies, conferences, training schools, and young people's meetings. He especially enjoyed working with country preachers who lacked college or seminary training. A contributor to denominational papers and magazines and scholarly reference works, Robertson wrote the article in the *Baptist Argus*, "Why Not a Baptist World Congress?" which was a factor in the organization of the Baptist World Alliance.

At the seminary Robertson taught more than 6,000 students. He knew his subject and demanded honest, thorough effort on the part of his students. Employing original and effective methods and techniques, Robertson was a genius in detecting and exposing conceit, complacency, and insincerity. His accurate knowledge and historical imagination made biblical characters and events live again. According to Henry W. Tiffany, "Dr. Robertson began to write books at the age of 38 and ended at 70, during which time were published his 'Big Grammar' and 44 other books—4 grammars, 14 Commentaries and Studies, 6 Word Pictures of the New Testament, 11 histories and 10 Character Studies." WILLIAM W. ADAMS

ROBERTSON, NORVELL, JR. (b. Warren County, Ga., Nov. 14, 1796; d. Silver Creek, Miss., June 1, 1878). Minister, Mississippi Baptist leader. Elected vice-president of the Mississippi state convention for 10 consecutive years beginning in 1836, Robertson served for 44 years as pastor of Bethany church, Lawrence County. He was the author of *Church-Members' Hand-Book of Theology*.

BIBLIOGRAPHY: J. L. Boyd, *A Popular History of Baptists in Mississippi* (1930). W. Cathcart, *The Baptist Encyclopedia* (1883). L. S. Foster, *Mississippi Baptist Preachers* (1895). C. B. HAMLET III

ROBESON INSTITUTE. A Baptist school at Lumberton, Robeson County, N. C., founded in 1893 under T. F. Toon. In 1892 it received assistance from the Baptist state convention, and a new building was constructed. In 1900 the school was flourishing as a fully accredited high school. It closed, however, in 1907.

D. L. SMILEY

ROCK, CLIFTON MOORE (b. Norfolk, Va., Apr. 14, 1876; d. Phoenix, Ariz., July 9, 1936). Minister, Baptist leader in New Mexico and Arizona. Converted in his early years, Rock began preaching when he was 17. He attended Windsor and Richmond colleges in Virginia and graduated from each with high honors. Ordained to the ministry by Grove Avenue Baptist Church, Richmond, in 1901, Rock served for two years as state missionary in mountain areas of Virginia. He received seminary training in Crozier Theological Seminary, Pennsylvania, after which he held several pastorates in North Carolina. He was called to the pastorate of Calvary Baptist Church, Phoenix, Ariz., an affiliate of the Northern Baptist Convention, in 1917, and served for three successful years.

Then, called in 1921 as first pastor of the First Southern Baptist Church in Phoenix, and the first church of its kind in Arizona, Rock served the church until his death. In 1925 he led in organization of Gambrell Memorial Association, affiliated with the New Mexico Baptist convention. He was president of the New Mexico convention in 1926–27. In the annual meeting of Gambrell Memorial Association in 1928, Rock led in organization of the Baptist General Convention of Arizona. He was one of five messengers to the Southern Baptist Convention meeting in 1929 when the Baptist General Convention of Arizona was received into the Southern Baptist Convention. Member of Arizona's state executive committee for seven years, he was also a member of the Southern Baptist Convention executive committee from 1929 to 1936. MRS. W. C. HENDERSON

ROCK REST HIGH SCHOOL. Located near Monroe, N. C. It was opened in 1886 and was endorsed by Union Association, but in 1897 was overshadowed by the Wingate School, Union's associational school. D. L. SMILEY

ROCKFORD MALE AND FEMALE SEMINARY. A school at Rockford, N. C., founded in Oct., 1849. Until shortly after the Civil War, the school was operated in Yadkin Association by Abram Weaver. D. L. SMILEY

ROCKY MOUNT CASE. See NORTH ROCKY MOUNT CHURCH, THE CASE OF.

RODMAN, BENJAMIN FRANKLIN (b. Madisonville, Ky., Aug. 3, 1850; d. Pinckneyville, Ill., Nov. 13, 1932). Evangelist, missionary, Illinois Baptist leader. Prior to organization of the Illinois Baptist State Association, Rodman, who had moved to Illinois when he was six, was in the general work of the state convention for 25 years. He was the first general secretary of the state association and served in that position for 20 years. Associational missionary in Franklin Association and then district missionary of the general association for southern Illinois, Rodman helped to organize 25 churches and dedicated 50 houses of worship.

ARCHIE E. BROWN

ROGERS, DANIEL (b. Pittsfield, N. H., Apr. 13, 1844; d. Granville, Ohio, Jan. 30, 1933). Baptist preacher, pioneer missionary to Cherokee Indians. Rogers was a graduate of Colgate University, Hamilton, N. Y., and in 1876 was appointed by the American Baptist Home Mission Society to succeed John B. Jones (*q.v.*) in the Cherokee work at Tahlequah, Indian Territory. He helped establish Bacone College and helped organize the Baptist Missionary and Educational Convention, of which he was president 1884–87. In 1900 he retired from the Indian work to Granville, Ohio, where he was pastor of several churches. He is buried at Granville. J. M. GASKIN

ROGERS, STUART BEGGS (b. near Macon, Ga., Sept. 18, 1866; d. Atlanta, Ga., Aug. 16, 1926). Denominational leader. He attended local schools and studied at Mercer University and at the University of Chicago. In 1896 he married Daisy Walker and moved to the pastorate of the Baptist church in Marianna, Fla. After successful pastorates at Marianna, Chipley, and Gainesville, Fla., he was elected president of the Florida Baptist convention in 1904; on Apr. 29, 1909, following the death of L. D. Geiger (*q.v.*), he was elected corresponding secretary and treasurer of the Florida Baptist State Board of Missions. In Feb., 1921, he was elected a trustee of John B. Stetson University.

Because Rogers was an able administrator, the work of the state board of missions was expanded. The convention built a headquarters building in Jacksonville and named it the Rogers Building in his honor. He faced the difficult period of World War I, the collapse of Columbia College in 1918, and debt which was finally liquidated. In 1925 Rogers published a brief history of Florida Baptists, for the centennial celebration of the establishment of the first Baptist church in Florida. H. C. GARWOOD

ROMAN CATHOLIC CHURCH. That Christian denomination numbering about 380,000,000 members which gives its allegiance to the bishop of Rome, known as the pope. According to Romanists, the pope possesses "the supreme authority to teach the universal Church," an authority allegedly granted by Christ to the apostle Peter and transmitted by him through "apostolic succession" in unbroken line. The power derived from Christ through Peter includes the authority to administer the sacraments, which are channels of saving and sanctifying grace. This august authority is held only by those ordained by a bishop who stands in apostolic succession.

Beginning.—The Roman Catholic Church is the result of a historical development which started in the first century, expressed itself in the postapostolic Catholic movement, emerged into the Old Catholic Church around A.D. 200, and reached its specifically Roman form in, perhaps, the seventh century, following the Mohammedan conquests. The precise date for the appearance of Romanism is problematical because it is impossible to determine exactly the identity of the first bishop of Rome who was also regarded as the supreme bishop in the Church. Some have suggested Innocent I, who occupied the Roman See from 401 to 417, though this date is probably too early. The decision is a matter of judgment involving many complex issues and much elusive data, but it seems unlikely that the supreme authority of the bishop of Rome was achieved completely until the expansion of Islam neutralized all the eastern bishoprics except Constantinople, which was threatened, and left the Roman bishop alone in his supremacy. The bishop of Rome, who had been *primus inter pares*—first among equals—became *primus*. The date when this occurred is debatable, but the fact of it is not. It is the consequence of a historical development in which primitive Christianity was first structured in the Old Catholic Church and issued eventually in Roman Catholicism.

The medieval church.—The rise of the Roman Catholic Church was roughly contemporary with the collapse of the Roman Empire and the rise of the Middle Ages, though Roman Catholicism, strictly speaking, was still in its formative stage at this time. The decline and fall of the empire and the consequent lack of a political and social structure in the West presented the Catholic Church with an opportunity to provide precisely the order that was disappearing and, in the process, to project itself into the substance of the emerging medieval society. Thus an ecclesiastical civilization was born, and the medieval synthesis was forged. The political framework for this fusion was established in the fourth century when Constantine gave Christianity equal status with the other religions of the empire, and Theodosius made it the official religion of the state.

The administrative structure of the Roman Empire was arranged in graduated fashion, with the emperor holding supreme authority, at least theoretically. The rising Roman Catholic hierarchy fitted nicely into this arrangement, which helped to solidify the idea of the papacy with its great powers and a series of ecclesiastical officials under papal jurisdiction holding various ranks, beginning with the College of Cardinals and descending in honor and authority through the archbishops and bishops to the abbots, monks, and secular clergy.

With the flowering of the Frankish Kingdom into the Holy Roman Empire at the beginning of the ninth century, there appears a society which may be called a *corpus Christianum*. Christianity, which began as a voluntary association in response to the divine initiative seeking to establish a redeemed community, thus became a compulsory organization. This was the inevitable culmination of the idea of a state church. Charlemagne envisaged a Christian civilization whose unity was grounded in "one Lord, one faith, and one baptism." The vision faded and was followed by a period of chaotic confusion during the rise of feudalism. Within three centuries it was revived under the leadership of Hildebrand, and feudalism was absorbed into the new synthesis. Church and empire became two organs of a single "Christian" society. Kenneth Scott Latourette describes how the community as a whole embraced Christianity: "Sometimes this step was taken because of the example set by the leaders. In other instances the leaders coerced the subject majority into following them to the baptismal font."

It should also be said that feudalism, with its stratified patterns of superior and inferior honor and authority, was decisive in the ecclesiological development of medieval Roman Catholicism. The relationship of the lord to his vassals implies a social arrangement and a moral code. Feudalism was thus the basic social and moral pattern of the late Middle Ages and, as a consequence, heavily influenced the scholastic theological formulations of this time. The most celebrated theologian of the Roman Catholic Church, Thomas Aquinas (1225–74), composed the monumental *Summa Theologica,* a major landmark in medieval philosophical and theological history, in which Aristotelian philosophy and Catholic theology were fused. Two methods of approach were used, concerning which M. Deanesly says that "philosophy examined the natural order by the light of reason and theology the supernatural order as revealed by the Word of God." With minor qualifications the theological system persists powerfully in contemporary Roman Catholic thought. Leo XIII (1878–1903) declared the theology of Aquinas as the standard of Roman Catholic instruction.

The sacramental system.—The crux of the medieval theological outlook was the sacramental system. The seven sacraments as defined by Aquinas and reaffirmed by the Council of Trent (1545–63) persist today largely unaltered. A sacrament is more than a visible sign of an invisible grace; it is a rite, sometimes involving elements like water or wine and bread, which are the intrinsic bearers of divine grace. The water in baptism cleanses from sin *ex opere operato,* and the bread and wine in the Holy Eucharist are bearers of the substance of Christ's body and blood. The laying of hands on the ordainee by the bishop transmits to the new priest the authority held through apostolic succession, including the authority to dispense the sacraments. James J. Graham, a Catholic theologian, says that a sacrament is "an outward sign, instituted by Christ, to give grace." Concerning the sacraments, Karl Adam indicates that "the relation . . . of the individual soul to Christ is determined by a system of sacred ordinances of fixed and indissoluble form and of unalterable interconnection."

Two of the sacraments are for the spiritually dead, and five for the living. Baptism and penance are for those in a state of sin. Baptism cleanses the soul of sin, restores the supernatural virtues lost in the fall of man, and is the rite of initiation into the Church. The souls of unbaptized infants go to "limbo," not heaven, and never enter into the ultimate bliss. Penance provides absolution for sins committed after baptism through confession to a priest, who supplies satisfactions or penances which, if followed, will counterbalance the temporal penalties of sin that remain after absolution. Penance thus offers absolution for the guilt of sin and remission of all eternal penalties, but penalties in this life and purgatory remain unless they are removed through the observance of satisfactions assigned by the priest (or by indulgences).

The sacraments for those in a state of grace —the living—are confirmation, Holy Eucharist, extreme unction, marriage, and ordination. Confirmation is a rite administered in the Roman Church by the bishop's laying his hands on the young, who are thus prepared for the first communion. *Confirmatio* means "to strengthen," and confirmation provides a spiritual strengthening for those about to face the strains of maturity.

Holy Eucharist is the communion aspect of the Mass, of which the other facet is sacrifice. The term "transubstantiation" describes what allegedly transpires with the bread and wine in the miracle of the Mass. The accidents (*accidentia*), the physical properties of the elements, undergo no change; but the substance (*substantia*), the reality of the elements which makes them what they are, is changed into the substance of the body and blood of Christ. There is thus a communion, a communication, of the substance of Christ's body and blood to the participant. The sacrificial aspect of this sacrament is displayed each time the rite is observed, when an "unbloody" repetition of Christ's sacrifice is supposed to transpire.

Extreme unction, meaning "last anointing," is the application of "holy oil" to a person who presumably is dying, to prepare his soul for the next life by remitting the penalty of temporal punishment "proportionately to the disposition of the recipient." This sacrament can also be an instrument of therapy, physical and spiritual, for one who is seriously ill.

Marriage is a sacrament which, by the outward sign of a contract, was instituted by Christ to provide grace to enable two participants properly to fulfil the duties and purposes of the married life. Marriage between a Roman Catholic and a member of another denomination or of no religion at all is forbidden but, nevertheless, can be celebrated if a dispensation permitting the rite is secured from the Church. Canon law is relaxed to allow such a marriage only when the non-Catholic partner agrees by signing a prenuptial contract that the marriage will be carried on according to the Catholic understanding of this relationship. One who signs this contract agrees that "all the children" who may be born of the union into which he enters "shall be baptized and educated solely in the faith of the Roman Catholic Church" and that "the teachings of the Catholic Church regarding birth control" will be rigidly followed.

The sacrament of holy orders—or ordination —is a rite which, through the outward sign of the imposition of the bishop's hands, was instituted by Christ to confer "power and grace" upon the ordainee, enabling him to perform his sacred duties.

Except for baptism, which can be administered under certain circumstances by any seriously intending person, the sacraments are in the sole custody of those who have been ordained.

Modern Roman Catholicism.—The Reformation shattered the medieval unity, divided Christendom, and ushered in the modern age. Protestantism forced the Catholic Church to increasingly refined theological definitions. The Council of Trent, which reaffirmed the medieval outlook of the Church, the Society of Jesus, formed by Ignatius Loyola and authorized by Paul III in 1540, and the reorganization of the Inquisition provided spearheads for the Roman revival called the Counter-Reformation.

The Roman Catholic Church in the modern period has had a fluctuating history. The reawakening which followed the Reformation was succeeded by a time of retrogression due to the decline of Spain as a world power in the 17th century and the disrepute into which the Jesuits fell in the 18th. Northern Europe and Great Britain, almost entirely lost in the Reformation, were not won back into the Catholic fold but settled into the Lutheran, Reformed, and Anglican faiths, with sectarianism asserting itself here and there. America was settled largely by Protestant powers. Thus, what became the United States, with its incredible resources, was lost as a potential Catholic country.

The political and cultural leadership of Europe shifted from Spain to France in the 17th century. Spain, which had served as the spearhead of the Roman revival following the Reformation, was thus supplanted by France as the center of the Roman Catholic sphere. It was evident that the supremacy of the papacy could not again be restored to the pinnacle of power and prestige it reached in the Middle Ages, even in the restricted region in which it was recognized. Ultramontanism, a movement stressing papal supremacy, was held in check by the collective body of bishops, the Catholic princes, and lingering concepts of authority by decree of council. This critique of papal power, called Gallicanism in France, persisted until the 19th century, by which time the growing secularization of the West and the solidity of Protestant and humanistic opposition to the claims of the Roman Catholic Church had created a climate of opinion in which the resurgence of papal authority in ultramontanism affected Western culture much less than was the case in earlier periods of Roman supremacy.

The persecution of Protestants by Louis XIV, epitomized by the revocation of the Edict of Nantes in 1685, and the rise of Jansenism, which precipitated a doctrinal controversy that issued in the Jansenist Catholic Church in the 18th century, were preludes to a growing religious toleration that finally appeared in the French Revolution. The Jesuits bore the brunt of responsibility for both the power and the growing narrowness of Catholicism in France in the period prior to the Revolution. In the end, it was Jesuit bigotry that precipitated the downfall of the Church and produced a growing religious toleration. The society was suppressed in 1773 by Pope Clement XIV, but it was too late to stop the drift of anti-Catholic sentiment on the part of both the intellectuals and the masses. Consequently, the revolt against the crown was also a revolt against the Church, a revolt which has woven its way permanently into the French national character, especially among intellectuals.

The opposition of the Church to emerging democratic tendencies was not confined to France. The Roman Catholic Church found it impossible to assimilate political liberalism anywhere. This negative reaction to liberalism produced a growing administrative and theological rigidity symbolized in general by ultramontanism and specifically by several doctrinal declarations. The doctrine of the Immaculate Conception in 1854 declared that "the Virgin Mary was, in the first instant of her conception, preserved untouched by any taint of original guilt." Thus the immaculate conception of Mary became a dogma and heightened the growing Mariolatry of Romanism, a movement which was further strengthened by the dogma of the Assumption of Mary (her bodily ascension into heaven), declared in 1950. *The Syllabus of Errors* issued in 1864 condemned some things opposed by most Christians but also attacked democratic tendencies, specifically the doctrine of the separation of church and state. The climax of ultramontanism was reached in 1870 in the decree by which the pope is said to be endowed with "infallibility" when "he defines a doctrine concerning faith or morals to be held by the Universal Church." In 1894 Leo XIII declared that Anglican orders were invalid, and in 1907 Pius X issued an encyclical against "modernism."

The increasing isolation of the Catholic Church is displayed in the above declarations and most strikingly in the papal encyclical of Aug. 21, 1950. This carefully worded document enjoins a strict Thomism and puts Augustinianism beyond the pale of orthodoxy. Thus faith is not so much the presupposition of reason as the corrective of reason. The thought of Christian existentialists, such as Gabriel Marcel, is condemned, and biblical studies are severely restricted. Perhaps the most serious consequence of the encyclical is the declaration that all encyclicals are binding. Concerning this encyclical, Reinhold Niebuhr says, "Thus Papal absolutism takes one further step and the ossification of dogma is furthered to one more degree."

BIBLIOGRAPHY: K. Adam, *The Spirit of Catholicism,* D. J. McCann (1935). H. Bettenson, ed., *Documents of the Christian Church* (1947). M. Deanesly, *A History of the Medieval Church, 590–1500* (1954). J. J. Graham, *Faith for Life* (1939). P. Hughes, *A History of the Church* (1935). T. G. Jallard, *The Church and the Papacy* (1944). F. E. Mayer, *To Sign or Not to Sign* (1946). L. J. May, *Father Tyrrell and the Modernist Movement* (1932). R. Niebuhr, "The Increasing Isolation of the Catholic Church," *Christianity and Crisis,* Vol. IX, No. 15 (Sept. 18, 1950).

PENROSE ST. AMANT

ROMANCE OF A CENTURY. A 42-minute, black and white, 16mm, sound motion picture presenting the 1st century of Southern Baptist work with introductory sequences showing early Baptist work in America. It was authorized by the Executive Committee of the Southern Baptist Convention, Dec., 1944, for use on the 1945 Centennial Convention program and for showings later in the churches as a part of the Centennial Crusade. It was produced by Filmcraft Productions, New York, N. Y., with denominational supervision by a committee consisting of J. W. Marshall, James Edgar Dillard (*q.v.*), Louie DeVotie Newton, and Thomas Luther Holcomb. The script was based on an original film treatment by Dillard. The film was financed and distributed to the churches by the Sunday School Board of the Southern Baptist Convention. EARL WALDRUP

ROMANIA, MISSION IN. By agreement at the London Conference of 1920, Southern Baptists assumed responsibility for assisting the newly formed Baptist Union of Romania. As European representative, Everett Gill, Sr., gave assistance through counsel, financial aid, publication work, general evangelization, training leaders, and building "prayer houses." The Baptist Theological Seminary of Bucharest was established in 1922, and James Memorial Training School for young women in 1930. The missionaries who served in Romania were Walter Eugene and Hazel (Thomson) Craighead, who worked among Russian Baptists of Bessarabia; Dan T. and Ida (Flake) Hurley, instructors in seminary and girls' school; Earl Hester (Trutza), directress, James Memorial Training School; Ruby Daniel (Udvarnoki), instructor and directress of training school; Roy Franklin Starmer, seminary director and mission treasurer; Lillie Mae Hylton Starmer, seminary instructor; Everett and Emma (Williams) Gill, instructors in both schools, and he also served as mission treasurer.

EARL HESTER TRUTZA

ROMANIAN BAPTIST ASSOCIATION OF AMERICA. Organized in Cincinnati, Ohio, Sept. 1, 1913, under the leadership of L. A. Gredys, C. R. Igrisan, and T. Selegean, with nine churches and a religious publication *The Christian,* presently *The Illuminator.* Within its framework three other organizations were formed for missionary purposes: The Monument of the Gospel, Romanian Baptist Women's Association, and Romanian Baptist Youth Fellowship. The association printed, in Romanian, Bibles and Testaments, hymnbooks, *History of the Romanian Baptists in America,* and various religious tracts. It supports one missionary in California, four native missionaries in Yugoslavia, and partially supports one in France, Burma, Thailand, and Africa. Its membership is primarily in Michigan, Ohio, Illinois, and Indiana. In 1933, 16 churches reported 774 members, 1,090 in Sunday school, and $7,882.26 total gifts. By 1954 the association had 11 churches reporting 970 members, 664 in Sunday school, 40 baptisms, and $74,012.89 total gifts, or $76.31 per capita. V. W. JONES

ROSICRUCIANS. A worldwide fraternal organization which expounds an ancient heritage of esoteric knowledge dispensed primarily to initiates, although numbers of its publications are offered to the public. The order proposes to elucidate such subjects as memorization, foods and health, understanding psychic self, cosmic consciousness, "secret doctrines of Jesus," mystery of numbers, and reincarnation. Rosicrucians deny affiliation with any religious or political organization. Their name is derived from the name Ancient Mystical Order Rosae Crucis; their symbol is the cross and a single red rose. The American council maintains headquarters in San Jose, Calif. GEORGE JENKINS

ROSS, AARON FRANK (b. Neshoba County, Miss., Jan. 21, 1851; d. Durant, Okla., Aug. 6, 1908). Baptist preacher, missionary teacher, Masonic leader. Son of Abraham J. and Martha (Moore) Ross, he was educated at Baylor University, then located at Independence, Tex., and at Southern Baptist Theological Seminary, then at Greenville, S. C. After uniting with the Baptist church in Leon County, Miss., in 1866, he was there ordained to the ministry in 1868. In 1874 he went to Indian Territory as a missionary to the Choctaw Indians. Stationed near Fort Smith, Ark., he engaged in teaching and preaching. Later, as an educator, he served as an examiner of teachers over the Choctaw Nation. In Sept., 1884, he assisted William P. Blake in establishing *The Indian Missionary.* He also founded *The Fraternal Record,* a now extinct publication devoted to combining religion and the good influences of the Masonic and Odd Fellows fraternities. In 1893 Ross was elected Grand Patron of the grand chapter, Order of the Eastern Star. He was elected a member of the first legislature in Oklahoma as a representative from Bryan County. Re-elected in 1908, he died a few days thereafter and was buried in Highland Cemetery, Durant, Okla.

BIBLIOGRAPHY: C. T. Foreman, *Oklahoma Imprints, 1835–1907* (1936). D. C. Gideon, *History of the Indian Territory* (1901). LOREN J. BELT

ROSS, MARTIN (b. Martin County, N. C., Nov. 27, 1762; d. 1827). Son of William Ross, he served a period in the army of the Revolution. In 1783 he was married to Deborah Clayton Moore (d. 1796). His second wife was Mary Harvey (d. 1825). In Jan., 1784, he was baptized by John Page, who, with Lemuel Burkitt (*q.v.*), ordained him in 1787. His pastorates were Sewarky (Martin County), 1787–96; Yeopim (Chowan County), 1796–1806; Bethel (Perquimans County), 1806–27. He founded numerous churches, preached widely through northeastern North Carolina, and was a vigorous and highly respected leader, first in the Kehukee Association and then in the Chowan. He was a staunch advocate of training for ministers and co-operation among the churches. He was prime mover in organizing the General Meeting of Correspondence (1811–21), the forerunner of the North Carolina Baptist State Convention, and was advocating the organization of the convention at the time of his death.

BIBLIOGRAPHY: T. Meredith, "Memoir of Elder Martin Ross," Chowan Association (N. C.) *Minutes,* 1828. L. Burkitt and J. Read, *A Concise History of the Kehukee Baptist Association* (1803). G. W. Paschal, *History of North Carolina Baptists* (1930).

J. A. EASLEY

ROSS, REUBEN (b. near Williamston, N. C., May 9, 1776; d. Kentucky, Jan. 28, 1860). Tennessee Baptist preacher. Son of William and Mary (Griffin) Ross, Reuben Ross was the brother of Martin Ross (*q.v.*) and James Ross, Carolina Baptist ministers. His education was limited, consisting of only nine months in school during his whole life, "and that not consecutive" but over a seven-year period. Converted and baptized into the fellowship of Skewarky Church, North Carolina, in 1802, Ross was ordained to the ministry by that church May 6, 1807. Soon after his ordination he and his family moved to Tennessee, where he served as pastor of churches in Montgomery, Robertson, and Stewart counties. He also served churches in Todd and Christian counties, Ky. Ross stood firmly against hyper-Calvinism, an issue which caused a peaceful division of Red River Association, and resulted in the organization of the Bethel Association in 1817. The "father" of the Bethel Association, Ross served as moderator from 1825 to 1851. His longest pastorates were Bethel Church in Bethel Association (1835–52) and Little West Fork Church in Montgomery County (1818–60). A contemporary of Peter Cartwright and Alexander Campbell, Ross professed personal admiration for Campbell, but opposed his views on baptismal regeneration. Under Ross's leadership Bethel Association, in the path of the so-called "reformation," grew from 8 churches with 700 members to 62 churches with more than 7,000 members. When he died, he was buried at his home, Cedar Hill, in Montgomery County, Tenn.

BIBLIOGRAPHY: J. Ross, *The Life and Times of Elder Reuben Ross* (n.d.).

HAROLD D. GREGORY

ROUND HILL ACADEMY. School of Green River Association, at Union Mills, N. C. Established by J. D. Hunt in 1899, the school opened in October of that year with 60 pupils. On Oct. 6, 1900, the school was donated to Green River Association. A member of the state Baptist system of academies, soon after its opening it began to receive financial assistance from the Home Mission Board's program of aid to mountain schools. By 1925 it had received over $44,500, including nearly $30,000 for capital improvements.

With this financial help the school served its area well. "For a quarter of a century it flourished and, at a time when an institution of its nature was sorely needed, provided educational opportunities to the youth of the county which were not otherwise available."

In 1924 the academy became the Alexander School for Motherless Children.

D. L. SMILEY

ROWE, ABNER VERNON (b. Lexington, Miss., Apr. 28, 1848; d. Marshall, Tex., July 25, 1926). Minister, state convention secretary. After graduating from Mississippi College in 1872, Rowe entered Southern Baptist Theological Seminary, but left the seminary in 1874 for missionary work in Yazoo Association. He helped organize the church at Goodman, held several pastorates, and served for one year as professor of Latin in Mississippi College. In 1887 Rowe went to Winona as pastor, where he made his home until 1926. Upon the resignation of John Tyler Christian (*q.v.*) Mar. 10, 1893, Rowe was immediately elected corresponding secretary of the state convention board. Formerly connected with the old state mission board at Oxford and a member of the convention board when it was created in 1885, Rowe was well qualified for this position in which he served for 21 years. In 1905 he was sent by the state convention as a messenger to the first meeting of the Baptist World Alliance in London.

BIBLIOGRAPHY: J. L. Boyd, *A Popular History of the Baptists in Mississippi* (1930). L. S. Foster, *Mississippi Baptist Preachers* (1895). P. I. Lipsey, "Dr. A. V. Rowe," *The Baptist Record* (Aug. 5, 1926).

C. B. HAMLET III

ROYAL AMBASSADORS. A missionary organization for boys nine to 17 years of age, which includes a program of athletics, campcraft, and hobby activities along with an emphasis on missions. As early as 1853, the Young Men's Mission Society of Mercer University had grown enough to be entitled to a representative at the Southern Baptist Convention. Records show that by 1883 several groups of boys were organized to study missions. One of the first was a group 12–14 years of age in Owensboro, Ky., led by the pastor. In 1898 "The King's Sons" of Parker Memorial Church in Anniston, Ala., contributed to missions, and a Boys' Mission Band existed in Dalton, Ga., before July, 1907.

In May, 1908, in response to the need for an over-all organization to bind together the groups already existing in the churches and to reach a larger number of boys, Woman's Missionary Union voted to promote the Order of Royal Ambassadors. The first chapter organized after adoption of the name and plans for the order in 1908 was the Carey Newton Chapter of Goldsboro, N. C. It was organized by Mrs. W. M. Petway, who was so interested in the idea that she left the Woman's Missionary Union meeting early and hurried home so that the boys in her church could start the first Royal Ambassador chapter in the Southern Baptist Convention. Men volunteered to lead chapters, counseled with the women about plans for the program, and helped plan the Royal Ambassador ranking system and the first guide for counselors. In 1943 Woman's Missionary Union employed the first full-time Royal Ambassador secretary, J. Ivyloy Bishop. Built around knight errantry and the ambassador idea, the organization has as its motto, "We Are Ambassadors for Christ" (II Cor. 5:20).

An initiation service for Royal Ambassadors, written by G. L. Boles of Lonoke, Ark., after he began office as state leader in 1917, is in use today, and a ranking system, a plan of individual progress which co-ordinates and makes attractive missionary information and activities, was introduced in 1924. The four ranks for boys nine through 12 are Page, Squire, Knight, and Ambassador. Boys 13 years of age and up may work on two higher ranks—Ambassador Extraordinary and Ambassador Plenipotentiary, for which the requirements are taken from some 50 projects representing fields such as handicraft, sports, scientific research, missionary facts and biography, Bible knowledge, and actual visits to mission fields.

The local units within churches, called chapters, have boys as officers, with adult counselors. A church may have from one to 10 or more chapters, depending upon the number of boys enlisted; and the chapters are usually graded according to age. Current mission information, outlines for weekly meetings, and promotional materials are published in *Ambassador Life,* a monthly magazine for boys and counselors. Manuals for the boys and a guide for counselors furnish basic directions and helps.

Organized Royal Ambassador camps on the state, district, or associational level are held each summer. Virginia Royal Ambassadors held the first such camp in 1917 at Virginia Beach. The Young Men's Mission Conference for older Royal Ambassadors and boys with definite mission interest was started at Ridgecrest, N. C., in 1944. Conclaves, gatherings of chapter members in a city, an association, or a district, were started in Apr., 1915, when South Carolina's first associational conclave was held at North Greenville Academy. The first state conclave was held at Ouachita Baptist College in Arkansas in Oct., 1924. Now state congresses, convention type meetings with boys as officers, are held annually, bringing together as many as 4,000 boys in some states. The first national Royal Ambassador Congress was held in Atlanta, Ga., in Aug., 1953, with approximately 5,000 boys present.

Woman's Missionary Union recommendations in 1939 asked for more co-operation from Brotherhood organizations in local churches with Royal Ambassador work. Co-operation and interest of the Brotherhood grew, and more men became counselors. As a result the Southern Baptist Convention adopted the proposal of Woman's Missionary Union in 1953 to transfer sponsorship of the Royal Ambassador movement from Woman's Missionary Union to the Baptist Brotherhood Commission, effecting the transfer gradually over a three-year period with a joint committee directing the Royal Ambassador program during that time.

In 1954 there were 127,262 boys enrolled in 13,977 chapters in Southern Baptist churches. In addition to these, there were chapters in American and Negro Baptist churches, and in 28 countries where Southern Baptists have mission work.

J. IVYLOY BISHOP

ROYAL SERVICE. Official publication of Woman's Missionary Union. It began in July, 1906, as a quarterly named *Our Mission Fields,* with one copy distributed free to each missionary society, and subscriptions available at 15 cents, single copies at 5 cents. Since it was difficult to proceed on a half-free and half-paid-for basis, *Our Mission Fields* became a subscription publication only in 1912, with the understanding that it would become a self-supporting monthly in 1914 if subscriptions warranted the change.

The name *Royal Service,* adopted in Oct., 1914, was taken from *In Royal Service,* the history of the first 25 years of Woman's Missionary Union, published for the Jubilate in 1913. First editor of *Our Mission Fields* was Fannie E. S. Heck (*q.v.*), followed by a succession of editors from 1906 to 1920. For several months no editor was named, but the work was done by the Woman's Missionary Union literature committee or literature department. Kathleen Moore Mallory (*q.v.*), who carried the burden of the editorship after Woman's Missionary Union headquarters moved from Baltimore in 1921, served officially as editor from Nov., 1925, until 1948, when Juliette Mather succeeded her. The first monthly subscription rate was 25 cents per year which has gradually increased to $1.50, due to increased costs of production. A proposal was made in 1916 that *Our Home Fields* of the Home Mission Board, *The Foreign Mission Journal* of the Foreign Mission Board, and *Royal Service* all combine as one missions magazine. After consideration of the merger, the two mission boards, the Sunday School Board, and Woman's Missionary Union agreed that the union should continue the publication of *Royal Service,* since it was distinctive in purpose and plan, and should also contribute a Woman's Missionary Union department in the combined publication, which would be called *Home and Foreign Fields.*

Royal Service contains program material on the monthly missionary topic, and suggestions for circle programs. It carries mission stories, features of denominational interest, picture stories from mission fields, letters from missionaries, current events, hints on methods of Woman's Missionary Society chairmen and leaders of young people's organizations, and book reviews. The prayer calendar, incorporated in *Royal Service* in 1918, includes the names of all Southern Baptist missionaries, now listed on their birthdays. In the second issue of *Our Mission Fields,* Sunbeam Band programs and suggestions "For

Young Ladies" appeared, and in 1908 programs for boys were included. Later, in May, 1920, it was voted to enlarge *Royal Service* to provide more space for program material for young people. But even this was not adequate, and young people's magazines gradually developed out of *Royal Service—World Comrades, The Window of YWA, Ambassador Life, Tell: A Missions Magazine for Girls,* and *Sunbeam Activities.* Free subscriptions to *Royal Service* and the young people's publications are sent to all Southern Baptist home and foreign missionaries. Subscriptions to *Royal Service* at the end of 1954 totaled over 260,000. JULIETTE MATHER

ROYALL, WILLIAM BAILEY (b. Mt. Pleasant, S. C., Sept. 2, 1844; d. Wake Forest, N. C., Jan. 27, 1928). Pastor and teacher. The son of a Baptist minister, Royall at the age of eight began the study of Greek under his father. At the age of 12, he entered Furman University, and at 17 he received the B.A. degree from Wake Forest College. In 1866 he received the M.A. degree from Wake Forest. In addition, he received two honorary degrees: D.D., conferred by Judson College (1887), and LL.D. from Furman University (1907). Ordained to the ministry in 1869, Royall served as pastor of Baptist churches in Forestville, Youngsville, and Rolesville, N. C. After serving for a time in the Confederate army, he became a tutor at Wake Forest College and later professor of Greek there for more than 62 years. When Wake Forest was without a president (1882–83), he carried full administrative responsibilities as chairman of the faculty. He was one of the early members of the Board of Education of the North Carolina Baptist State Convention, serving for 50 years as secretary of that board. In this position he helped to raise the education standards for Baptist ministers. Royall also served for a time as professor at Furman University and was president of Baylor Female College. One of his pupils was Archibald Thomas Robertson (*q.v.*).

GARLAND A. HENDRICKS

RUHAMA ACADEMY. Began as a grammar school under the name of Bakers Academy in the Ruhama settlement of Jefferson County, Ala., in 1859, with Jacob H. Baker as first principal. The school is reported to have grown rapidly and was known for its discipline and academics throughout the South. It came under the auspices of the Canaan Association, later known as Birmingham Association, in 1872. The name was changed to Ruhama Academy, with A. J. Waldrop, principal. The properties of the school were given to Howard College upon its removal from Marion to Birmingham in 1887.

JAMES E. DAVIDSON

RURAL CHURCH COMMISSION, VIRGINIA. Authorized by the Baptist General Association in Richmond in Nov., 1949, and recommended by the Rural Church Committee, it was composed of 14 rural pastors who realized the Rural Church Committee could not meet rural church needs. The commission now has seven members, elected for an indefinite period, serving without honorarium but with an expense account. The purpose of the commission is to constitute a study group over a period of years, to work with the Board of Missions and Education, and to serve as an "eye and voice" for rural churches. Its ideal is "every Baptist church in Virginia full-time." Olin T. Binkley, professor of Christian ethics and rural sociology, Southeastern Baptist Theological Seminary, suggested the first subjects studied and often advises with the commission, which holds one meeting each year. Findings are read, studied, and discussed before they are approved, and no findings can be quoted in the name of the commission before they are approved. Approved findings become the property of Virginia Baptists. Subjects on which findings have been approved are: what Southern Baptists are doing for rural churches, what other denominational groups are doing, what Virginia Baptists have done during the last 25 years, and what colleges and seminaries have done. The commission has studied practical values in consolidating weak churches and has noted outstanding churches and methods they employ. Through continuing practical studies, the commission will publish its findings and assist all churches asking for help. D. S. DEMPSEY

RURAL MISSIONS. The present rural mission, or rural church, program was initiated Jan., 1944, by the Home Mission Board under Courts Redford, who came to the board as assistant to the executive secretary in June, 1943. The work was to be done in co-operation with the state mission boards, and direction was given by the state boards. In Jan., 1944, the program as outlined by Redford was authorized by the Home Mission Board and approved by the state mission boards as they were ready to begin the work. The first state to adopt the rural program was Oklahoma, and the Home Mission Board began co-operation with that state Feb. 3, 1944.

The first literature was a pamphlet by Redford entitled "The Rural Mission Program," published by the Home Mission Board in 1947. The same year, the Convention-wide promotion of rural missions was placed in the Department of Co-operative Missions, S. F. Dowis, secretary.

John D. Freeman, former editor of the *Western Recorder,* Louisville, Ky., had been employed by the Home Mission Board in Feb., 1946, to present the challenge of the rural church and community to the students in the schools and colleges and to promote the Eight-Day Revival Program, which he had developed in the rural churches. His book, *Buried . . . Living,* was effective in interesting young people in rural life.

The next step in rural missions was the organization of rural church departments in the state conventions with a state superintendent paid jointly by the state board and Home Mission Board. The second piece of literature, prepared jointly by Redford and Dowis, entitled "The Rural Church Program of Southern Baptists," was published by the board in 1952.

Southwestern Baptist Theological Seminary promoted annual rural church conferences on its campus from 1947 to 1953. Southern Baptist Theological Seminary promoted similar conferences from 1950 to 1953. The Home Mission Board joined the seminaries in promotion of these conferences from 1949 to 1953, when they were both merged with the Convention-wide conference held with the First Baptist Church, Decatur, Ga., May 11–14, 1954.

Upon the recommendation of the state superintendents of missions and state secretaries in their annual meeting at Ridgecrest, N. C., Aug., 1952, the Home Mission Board in its semiannual meeting in Aug., 1952, adopted a Long-Range Rural Church Program for Southern Baptists. All agencies of Southern Baptists were asked to join the Home Mission Board in the promotion of the program. A committee consisting of Chester Quarles, T. B. Maston, J. T. Gillespie, Sam Scantlan, Eldred Taylor, Merrill Moore, and Dowis was appointed to work out details of the program and report in 1953.

This committee made eight preliminary surveys and recommended to the state superintendents conference and to the Home Mission Board, in its semiannual meeting in Aug., 1953, a 25-year long-range rural church program. Seven special goals for the 25 years were set up and the period broken down into five periods of five years each; goals were set up for the first five-year period, 1954–58. All these plans were approved and goals adopted at the first annual Convention-wide rural church conference in Decatur, Ga., in May, 1954.

An executive committee of 30 members, representing all the boards, agencies, commissions, rural pastors, and missionaries, was set up for the promotion of the Long-Range Rural Church Program of Southern Baptists. The program, literature, goals, and plans for the program are found in the booklet entitled "Long-Range Rural Church Program of Southern Baptists" by S. F. Dowis, published Oct., 1955.

At the semiannual meeting of the Home Mission Board at Glorieta, N. Mex., on Aug. 16, 1955, Gillespie, who had formerly been with the Home Mission Board as a successor to Freeman in the rural church work, was elected director of the Rural Church Program, under the Department of Co-operative Missions. He began his work in the department Oct. 1, 1955.

S. F. DOWIS

RUSSELL CREEK BAPTIST ACADEMY. See CAMPBELLSVILLE COLLEGE.

RUSSIA, BAPTISTS OF. See ALL-SOVIET COUNCIL OF EVANGELICAL CHRISTIANS AND BAPTISTS.

RUSSIANS, HOME MISSIONS TO: It is estimated that there are 200,000 Russians and many other related Slavic people within the territory of the Southern Baptist Convention. A very large portion of these have come as refugees since World War II.

Home Mission Board missionary H. J. Mikhalchuk ministered to the Russians and other Slavic peoples of East St. Louis, Ill., from Jan., 1941, to May, 1949. Also, the Board operated the Gough St. Mission in Baltimore, Md., for the Poles, Russians, and other Slavic peoples from Mar., 1946, to May, 1953.

Rev. and Mrs. Paul Rogosin were appointed to serve in Hollywood, Calif., on Apr. 3, 1952. The Slavic Baptist Church of Hollywood was organized May 18, 1952, and property for the church was purchased Nov. 26, 1952. Rogosin's field of service was extended to include San Francisco, Calif., on June 15, 1955. Property was bought Dec. 16, 1955, and the Slavic Baptist Church of San Francisco was constituted on Mar. 3, 1956. Rodion Beresov served as assistant to Rogosin from Mar., 1955, to Aug. 31, 1956.

John Sylvester was appointed by the board to serve as pastor of the Slavic Baptist Church, Miami, Fla., to begin Apr. 1, 1956. There is also a self-supporting Russian Southern Baptist church in Bryte, Calif., made up mainly of people who were Baptists in Russia, and who migrated to this country by way of China.

The Home Mission Board properties used in Russian mission work are worth $76,000.

LOYD CORDER

RUSSIAN-UKRAINIAN BAPTIST UNION. Organized Apr. 5–6, 1919, in Philadelphia, Pa. After organization the founders called together representatives of the small Russian-Ukrainian Baptist churches and groups in New England, New York, New Jersey, and Pennsylvania at the Fourth Baptist Church, Philadelphia, for inspirational and business meetings. They elected the executive committee and decided to meet annually for strengthening the spiritual life and evangelism among their countrymen who came to live in the United States. One of the founders, John P. Daviduk of Hartford, Conn., served for a long time as the union's president. In the years following its organization new Russian-Ukrainian Baptist churches of other states joined this body, resulting in its influence and work reaching as far as Florida and California. Numerically the union has about 1,500 members. In 1954–55 the union received for missions, etc., $44,062.66. It supports missionary work mainly among the Slavic people in West Germany, Belgium, Australia, and Argentina. There were 32 baptisms in America in 1954 and almost twice that many on mission fields abroad. *The Sower of the Truth,* the union's monthly magazine, is published in both the Russian and Ukrainian languages, with Daviduk and Ivan Kmeta editors. The young people publish their *Herald* in English bimonthly. Conference grounds near Hartford, Conn., are the site for annual conferences and other summer activities.

IVAN KMETA

RUST, JACOB WARD (b. Logan County, Ky., Feb. 14, 1819; d. Hopkinsville, Ky., June 8, 1890). Educator. Although Rust's educational opportunities were limited, he became a scholar of considerable reputation. At first a teacher, he later became principal of Mount Carmel Academy, Springfield Academy, Clarksville Female Academy, and Lafayette Female Institute. In 1864 he was elected president of Bethel College, Russellville, Ky. Through his efforts this institution prospered. Because of illness, he resigned in 1868. Later, he with a Professor Dudley took over control of *The Western Recorder.* In 1871, having sold his interest in the paper, he became financial agent for the orphans' home in Louisville. A year later, he was elected principal of Bethel Female College, Hopkinsville, Ky., which position he held until his death, June 8, 1890. LEO T. CRISMON

RYALS HIGH SCHOOL. Established in 1891 at Sugar Valley, Ga., sponsored by the Middle-Cherokee Association. It existed until 1898.

ARTHUR JACKSON

RYLAND, CHARLES HILL (b. King and Queen County, Va., Jan. 22, 1836; d. Richmond, Va., Aug. 1, 1914). Son of Samuel Gaines and Catharine (Hill) Ryland. From Fleetwood Academy he entered Richmond College in 1854 and in 1859 was a member of the first class to enter the Southern Baptist Theological Seminary in Greenville, S. C. During the Civil War he served with the army in Virginia as colporteur and later as the depositary and treasurer of the Army Colportage Board. In 1863 he was ordained at Bruington, and in 1865 he became pastor of Carmel in Caroline County. In 1866 he was appointed general superintendent of Sunday schools in Virginia and reorganized them from the wreckage of war. He became pastor of the church in Alexandria in 1869 and in 1874 was elected by the trustees of Richmond College as its financial secretary; the next year, as its secretary-treasurer. This office he held until he retired in 1911. In addition to his success in gathering and investing the endowment of the college, Ryland was actively interested in all that pertained to Baptists in Virginia and their organized work. He obtained from the legislature in 1876 a charter incorporating the Virginia Baptist Historical Society, which he organized and served as secretary. In this position he was largely responsible for the assembling of the society's collection, now the largest such collection in the United States. A tablet on Charles Hill Ryland Hall at the University of Richmond commemorates his services as secretary, treasurer, and librarian.

BIBLIOGRAPHY: G. B. Taylor, *Virginia Baptist Ministers, Fifth Series* (1915). *Minutes of the Baptist General Association of Virginia* (1914). W. Cathcart, *The Baptist Encyclopedia* (1881). C. H. Ryland, *Southern Baptist Theological Seminary, Recollections of the First Year* (1911). GARNETT RYLAND

RYLAND, ROBERT (b. King and Queen County, Va., Mar. 14, 1805; d. Lexington, Ky., Apr. 23, 1899). He was the son of Josiah and Catharine (Peachey) Ryland and the grandson of Joseph Ryland, who came from England to Essex County. He was prepared by Thomas Nelson at "Humanity Hall" academy to enter Columbian College, from which he graduated in 1826. He was ordained at Bruington in 1827 and became the pastor of the Second (now First) Baptist Church in Lynchburg, which had 19 members worshiping in a borrowed hall. When he resigned five years later to take charge of the Virginia Baptist Seminary, the church had 120 members and a house of worship. The seminary was the child of the Virginia Baptist Education Society, organized two years earlier. It opened with ten students and one instructor, Robert Ryland. The next year there were 26 students and two instructors in addition to Ryland, who continued as principal except for one year when he served as chaplain of the University of Virginia. In 1840 the seminary was chartered as Richmond College, and Robert Ryland was elected its president. Under his vigorous administration, by 1860 the endowment had reached $100,000, the students numbered 114, there were six professors, adequate buildings, a library and a collection of apparatus for scientific demonstrations. In 1841, when the First African Baptist Church of Richmond was formed, Robert Ryland was asked to be its pastor in addition to performing his duties at the college. This arrangement proved so successful that it was continued until Ryland resigned in 1865. In 1866 he resigned the presidency of Richmond College and in 1868 moved to Kentucky where he engaged in educational and pastoral work to an advanced age. His grave in Hollywood Cemetery in Richmond is marked by a monument erected by the trustees of Richmond College.

BIBLIOGRAPHY: J. L. Burrows, ed., *American Baptist Memorial XIV* (1855). C. McCarthy, *First Century of the First Baptist Church,* Richmond, Virginia (1880). R. Ryland, *A Scriptural Catechism for the instruction of children and servants* (1848). R. Ryland, *The Virginia Baptist Education Society, The Society, The Seminary, The College* (1891). G. B. Taylor, *Virginia Baptist Ministers, Fourth Series* (1913).

GARNETT RYLAND

S

SABBATH. A word derived from the Hebrew *shabbath,* meaning to desist, cease, rest. Genesis 2:2–3 states that after six days of creative activity, God rested on the seventh day, blessing and sanctifying the day. In the creation account there is no mention of man's obligation to observe the day. Nor is there any mention of sabbath observance on the part of man prior to Moses' day. To attempt to prove that the sabbath was contemporary with the finishing of creation, one must go to sources other than the Bible. It is impossible to determine with accuracy whether there was any keeping of the sabbath in the pre-Mosaic period, though a septenary division of time was recognized (Gen. 7:4, 10; 8:10, 12; 29:27 ff.).

Due to the silence of the Scriptures on this point, various theories on the origin of the sabbath have been advanced. Perhaps the most widely recognized theory is that of the Babylonian origin; but the Babylonian day of pacification of deity, determined by the divisions of the moon, is not comparable to a recurring seventh day sabbath, which was a day of joy, delight, and rest. The seven-day weekly cycle seems to have been peculiar to Hebrew history.

Brief history of the sabbath.—The first biblical reference to sabbath observance is in connection with the giving of the manna in Exodus 16:1 ff. A double portion was given on the sixth day to make possible complete rest on the seventh day. It seemed necessary for Moses to explain carefully the provision, as if it were new and strange to Israel.

The weekly sabbath was a part of a larger sabbatical system given through Moses. In the original giving of the law pertaining to the sabbath (Exod. 20:8–11), the reason assigned for its observance was that Jehovah rested on that day. In the Deuteronomy account (5:12–15) the sabbath is said to be a sign of Israel's deliverance from Egyptian bondage. The sabbath is made a sign of the covenant between Jehovah and his people in Exodus 31:13–17.

In the Mosaic period and on to the Exile the sabbath was observed in simple fashion, primarily as a day of rest. It was unencumbered with the meticulous regulations which characterized the sabbath in New Testament times.

Following the Exile the sabbath received much attention. Israel's misfortunes were interpreted as being due to neglect of the Law. A better day was promised if attention were given to sabbath observance (Isa. 58:13–14). Rigorous attention to the sabbath had to be given in post-Exilic days (Neh. 13:15–18). The work begun by Ezra was continued and expanded by his followers. For a time the Jews were unwilling to fight a defensive war on the sabbath (I Macc. 2:37). The book of Jubilees, which is representative of the Midrashic tendency, claims that the sabbath is observed in heaven (Jubilees 2:18) and that eternal death is the penalty for sabbath violation (Jubilees 2:27).

There are two tractates of the Mishna dealing with the sabbath—*shabbath* and *erubin.* The Mishna represents Jewish thought current in the first century A.D., and during that time the growth of rabbinical exactions was rapid and almost without end.

In Jesus' day, not only was the seventh day to be observed but the sixth day, the preparation day, had to be filled with elaborate preparation for worthy sabbath observance. Thirty-nine classes of work were prohibited, and these were divided into further classifications and discussed as to their scope and meaning. Fasting was forbidden, and each Israelite was under obligation to eat three meals on the sabbath. One authority said that a person who observed the practice of three meals on the sabbath would be saved from three evils: the travails of the Messiah, the retribution of Gehinnom, and the wars of Gog and Magog.

Jesus and the Jewish sabbath.—The Gospels tell that Jesus encountered bitter hostility from the Jewish rulers over the sabbath question. However, Jesus never violated the original intent or purpose of the sabbath. This hostility, therefore, was more the result of his sabbath teaching than of sabbath violation. Jesus claimed to be the Son of God (John 5:1 ff.). He claimed that what was made available through his ministry was greater than the Temple (Mark 3:1–6; Matt. 12:9–14; Luke 6:6–11). He claimed to be Lord of the sabbath (Mark 2:27–28). The rulers were set on ridding themselves of one who dared to make such claims.

Paul interpreted the significance of Jesus' ministry in relation to the sabbath. Paul seemed to think of the sabbath as a positive ordinance of Judaism, one which was fulfilled in the work of Christ. In Galatians he mentions the Jewish system as being incomplete and undeveloped. It was a system which found reality in Jesus. In Galatians 4:10 the recipients of the Law are accused of yielding to the minute and scrupulous observance of days, months, times, and years. Paul condemns such actions as returning to the "weak and beggarly elements" that tend toward bondage, a bondage from which Christ had set them free (Gal. 4:9). Lightfoot thinks that the sabbath is clearly meant. Paul's clearest statement is found in Colossians 2:16–17. The Judaizers had been attempting to impose the ceremonial laws and positive commands of the Mosaic system upon Paul's readers. Paul felt that to conform to this system would be to revert to "shadows" of which Christ was the reality.

The author of Hebrews also interprets Jesus' ministry in relation to the sabbath. The writer of this book makes Christianity the fulfilment of Judaism. Christianity is presented as the "absolute revelation of God," bringing satisfaction to man's needs. The rest of the Jewish sabbath is held to be a symbol of the rest that the believer receives in Christian redemption (Heb. 4:3, 9–10). In Hebrews 4:9 the author uses *sabbatismos* and not *katapausis* in order to identify the rest of redemption with the sabbath. The believer enters into the rest of a continuous sabbath life. Israel's failure to enter the Promised Land because of their unbelief is a warning to those who through unbelief would neglect the real rest which God is seeking to give in Christ (Heb. 3:8–11). This rest, found in Jesus, is the fulfilment of the ancient sabbath (Matt. 11:28–30).

The sabbath, therefore, is inoperative in the Christian economy. It is not binding on the Christian conscience. The Christian's Lord's Day is of separate origin, and there is no connection between the Jewish sabbath and the Christian's Lord's Day. The obligation to observe the Lord's Day and the manner of its observance are matters of great concern to Christians, but are based on the writings of the New Testament.

EUGENE T. PRATT

SABINE BAPTIST COLLEGE. A school at Milam, Sabine County, Tex., opened in 1858 under the direction of Central Baptist Association. Closed during the Civil War, it was reopened and maintained from 1868 to 1870.

RUPERT N. RICHARDSON

SABINE VALLEY UNIVERSITY. A school at Hemphill, Tex., maintained by Mount Zion Baptist Association, 1876–81.

RUPERT N. RICHARDSON

SACRAMENTALISM. The religious emphasis and doctrine most often found among liturgical groups in Christianity. The word derives from the Latin *sacramentum* with its acquired meaning of oath or pledge. Sacramentalism is a method of stimulating the mind toward seeking and finding God in which much use is made of ceremony and sacred objects as symbols of spiritual truth.

Sacramentalism within Christianity has undergone much change. To Augustine of Hippo, "all holy usages and rites of the church" were sacraments. Peter Lombard and Thomas Aquinas fixed the sacraments at seven—baptism, the Eucharist, confirmation, penance, extreme unction, holy orders, and matrimony.

Among Protestants the term has varied significance. Episcopal communions tend more to preserve and reverence the emphasis. Baptism and the Lord's Supper are recognized as means of grace among most Protestant groups but not always as mechanically operative sacraments. As defined by one writer, sacramentals are "those signs and actions, less than the recognized and ecclesiastically prescribed rites, which are yet in the same general category in that they are outward and visible signs of inward and spiritual realities." To the true mystic, life itself is a sacrament.

Christians who place little emphasis on the sacramental fear that the symbol will be taken for that which is symbolized, hence idolatry. Sacramentarians maintain that "the significant truth is that the real reverence is paid to God, the divine object suggested by and worshipped through the natural object." "Through the symbol man lays hold, though doubtfully, on the fringes of Reality itself."

BIBLIOGRAPHY: T. Aquinas, *Summa Theologica,* Part III. J. Calvin, *Institutes,* Book IV. J. S. Candlish, *The Christian Sacraments* (1881). P. Lombard, *Sententiae,* Book IV. J. C. Lambert, *The Sacraments in the New Testament* (1903). F. R. Webber, *Church Symbolism* (1938).

JOE KING

SACRAMENTS. See MASS AND TRANSUBSTANTIATION.

SAINT. The Old Testament translates as saint two Hebrew words, *hasid* (I Sam. 2:9) and *qadosh* (Psalm 89:5), which denote mortals of high spiritual worth. *Hasid* carries the connotations of kind, godly, or pious; *qadosh* derives from the root meaning holy, in the sense of separateness, that is, of persons and things in peculiar relationship to deity as set apart for God's exclusive and special use. Hence, the *hasidim* (plural) and the *qadoshim* were called "holy ones" or "saints."

The New Testament use of *hagios* for *qadosh,* signifying both holiness and separateness, makes *hagios* its term for saint. The justification for speaking of a person or thing as holy derives from a relationship to God, who is holy. A saint, as one separated from things profane and dedicated in love and service to God, is one in whom the very character of the holy God becomes discernible. Man, made originally in the image of the holy God, is meant to be holy as he is holy. "Ye shall be holy: for I the Lord your God am holy" (Lev. 19:2). Applied first to ancient Israel, this commandment was later addressed to all Christians (I Peter 2:9). In the Old Testament all Israelites are called saints (Psalm 30:4; Deut. 33:3), and in the New Testament all believers in Christ are so designated (Eph. 2:19). This was Paul's favorite term for Christians: ". . . to all the saints in Christ Jesus" (Phil. 1:1); "thy saints at Jerusalem" (Acts 9:13); "called to be saints" (I Cor. 1:2). Peter's admonition describes both the purpose of God and the manner of its achievement when he says, "Sanctify the Lord God in your hearts" (I Peter 3:15).

To reserve sainthood only for those who supposedly have deposited with the church, as the divinely appointed treasure house, the extra merit (beyond their own needs) which they have achieved from deeds of supererogation (extra good works), such merit to be dispensed to ordinary Christians through sacraments so that they will receive grace otherwise unattainable from God, is an attitude totally foreign to the biblical teaching about saints. In popular usage, however, the term is still applied only to those persons characterized by distinctive charity, patience, and self-denial and is a state in some sense universally attainable only after death.

See also SANCTIFICATION.

BIBLIOGRAPHY: W. T. Connor, *What Is a Saint?* (1948). A. R. Richardson, ed., *A Theological Word Book of the Bible* (1951). W. E. Sangster, *The Pure in Heart* (1954). JOHN M. LEWIS

SALEM ACADEMY. A private school opened by Silas Mercer in the 1790's in Wilkes County, Ga., about nine miles from Washington. Mercer's son, Jesse Mercer (*q.v.*), for whom Mercer University was named, was a pupil at Salem; and when Mercer died in 1796, Jesse, with his brother Daniel, operated the school for a short time. Although not actually a Baptist school, Salem was a forerunner of the Baptist school movement in Georgia which began in the 19th century. ARTHUR JACKSON

SALLEE, WILLIAM EUGENE (b. Middleburg, Ky., Mar. 24, 1878; d. Raleigh, N. C., June 15, 1931). Missionary to China. Educated at Georgetown College and Rochester Theological Seminary, Sallee was appointed missionary to China in 1903, where he served until 1930. He married Annie Jenkins, Sept. 18, 1906, and they moved to Kaifeng two years later where they began building Kaifeng Baptist College in 1915. Sallee worked to improve agricultural conditions in China. Elected home secretary of the Foreign Mission Board in 1930, "he probably did more than any other man could have done in stemming the tide of reaction in interest against the foreign mission movement among Southern Baptists," according to William Owen Carver (*q.v.*).

BIBLIOGRAPHY: A. J. Sallee, *William Eugene Sallee; Christ's Ambassador* (1933). E. C. ROUTH

SALVADOREAN BAPTIST CONVENTION, THE. The American Baptist Home Mission Society sent the first missionaries to El Salvador in 1911. Since then the society and the Woman's American Baptist Home Mission Society have sent others to assist in the churches, establish schools, and train Christian leadership.

Twenty-three churches and 79 missions and outstations have a total membership of 1,692 in a Baptist constituency of 8,000. Baptist students number 739. In many of the churches, lay and pastoral leadership evidence the fact that schools under direction of missionaries and national teachers working together are good training ground. Vacation Bible schools are conducted in many of the churches, all of which are served by national leadership.

Three new chapels were dedicated in 1955. One of them was a house rebuilt into a chapel by means of a loan from the convention; when repaid, a parsonage and a larger church building will be erected. Dedication of another chapel took place where a former one had been destroyed by the 1951 earthquake. The convention's loan fund is making the erection of other church buildings possible.

The Colegio Bautista at Santa Ana exerts a strong Christian influence on its students. An alumna of the school attended a university in Puerto Rico on a Point Four scholarship.

The president of the convention, Don Esteban Rodriguez, is principal of Colegio Bautista, Santa Ana, serving with the missionary from the United States. MRS. MILO E. WENGER

SALVATION. As described in the Bible, has both a special and a general sense. The word in its Hebrew form means "to be wide" or "roomy," "to develop without hindrance." From this basic meaning came the general usage of the word: deliverance of a person from peril, danger, illness, starvation, and death. Any person who became the agent for such action was known as a savior. It was early recognized that God himself had raised up the savior, and so he was looked upon as Saviour. The word, therefore, came to be used to describe God's mighty work of redemption. God saved men from illness, starvation, and the like; but he also saved men from sin. Salvation took on a special, particular significance: The fundamental need of man is redemption from sin, and God acts on his behalf as Saviour. Man is made to trust, obey, and love God, but man rebels and becomes the sinner. In Jesus Christ, God acts redemptively for man. Salvation means the adoption of transformed sinners into God's family, which action is wrought solely by the power of God accepted by men through total surrender (faith) to Jesus Christ. Salvation is man made right with God.

See also CONVERSION. W. C. STRICKLAND

SAMMONS, JAMES ELLIS (b. Putnam County, Ga., May 9, 1876; d. Macon, Ga., Nov. 20, 1954; buried Riverside Cemetery, Macon). Pastor and denominational leader. The son of Charles Columbus and Alice (Hamilton) Sammons, he married Martha Walton, Reynolds, Ga., July 16, 1902; and two children were born of this union, Charles Everett and Martha (Mrs. William A. Snow, Jr.). Sammons joined Antioch Baptist Church, Morgan County, in 1885, and he was ordained there in Apr., 1900. After graduating with the A.B. degree from Mercer University in 1900, he attended Southern Baptist Theological Seminary, 1901–02. In 1920 Mercer University conferred upon him the D.D. degree.

At 18 he became principal of Godfrey School, 1894–96; he taught school in Reynolds, Ga., 1900–01, and was president of North Georgia Baptist College (later changed to Morganton Institute), Morganton, Ga., 1902–04.

He served the following Georgia pastorates: Decatur, 1904–06; Brunswick, 1906–11; Griffin, 1911–21; Rome, 1921–28; and Vineville Baptist Church, Macon, 1928–45. The Sammons Memorial Educational Building was dedicated in his honor by the Vineville Baptist Church in June, 1953. After retirement from his long and happy Vineville pastorate, he organized the Ingleside Baptist Church in Macon (constituted Dec. 23, 1951) and served as its first pastor. He also served as chaplain and director of the Memorial Chapel Funeral Home.

Sammons held many responsible denominational positions. He was president of the Georgia Baptist convention, 1931–33; a member of the board of directors, *Christian Index,* 1933 until his death in 1954; a trustee of Southern Baptist Theological Seminary, 1923–53; first vice-president of the seminary board, 1934–36; trustee, Mercer University, 1927–35; a member of the Home Mission Board, 1912–17; and a member of the executive committee of Georgia Baptist convention, 1919–21; 1924–27; 1936–46.

HANSFORD D. JOHNSON

SAMPEY, JOHN RICHARD (b. Fort Deposit, Ala., Sept. 27, 1863; d. Louisville, Ky., Aug. 18, 1946). Seminary professor and president, leader of International Sunday School Lesson Committee. Son of James L. and Louisa (Cochran) Sampey, he was converted at 14 and two years later was licensed to preach. At 16 he entered Howard College, Birmingham, Ala., and graduated with the A.B. degree. He attended Southern Baptist Theological Seminary, beginning in 1882, where he studied under James Petigru Boyce (*q.v.*), John Albert Broadus (*q.v.*), Basil Manly, Jr. (*q.v.*), and William Heth Whitsitt (*q.v.*). Although committed to foreign mission service, Sampey was persuaded by President Broadus to become a member of the seminary faculty upon graduation in 1885.

His first teaching assignment was as assistant to Broadus in New Testament and homiletics, along with the class in junior Hebrew. In addition to teaching, Sampey was called to the pastorate of the Forks of Elkhorn Church, of which Broadus himself had been pastor. Sampey was strongly influenced by his summer study under W. R. Harper, later president of Chicago University, whose new "inductive method" aroused an enthusiasm for Hebrew which characterized Sampey throughout his life. In Sampey's class in Greek was a brilliant student, Archibald Thomas Robertson (*q.v.*), who upon graduation was invited to become a member of the teaching staff of the seminary. Sampey voluntarily withdrew from the teaching of New Testament and Greek in favor of his young colleague and devoted himself thereafter to Old Testament and Hebrew. Four years of intense concentration on the study of the Old Testament followed, which laid solid foundations for a long and distinguished career as teacher and scholar in this field.

In 1895 Sampey succeeded Broadus as member of the International Sunday School Lesson Committee, became chairman in 1921, and served continuously on the committee for 46 years. Influential in the organization of the Baptist World Alliance, Sampey was increasingly in demand for lectures, sermons, and evangelistic meetings. Along with these multiplied responsibilities, he continued to serve as pastor of his country church, and also as seminary librarian from 1894 to 1928.

Sampey's original commitment to foreign mission service found partial fulfilment in his missionary journeys to Brazil in 1925, 1926, and 1928. While Sampey and his wife were in Brazil, Edgar Young Mullins (*q.v.*), president of the seminary, suffered a break in health which resulted in his death a few months later. During Mullins' illness, and often before in his absences, Sampey served as chairman of the faculty, and following Mullins' death, Sampey served as acting president until the annual meeting of the board of trustees in May, 1929, when he was unanimously elected to the presidency.

Sampey came into office in the year of the financial crash, which was followed by the great depression. Pledges made to the building fund became worthless, and Sampey thus inherited a building debt of $992,000, which he proceeded to reduce by payment of all accumulated cash, including a sum intended for the building of a chapel. The remaining debt was refinanced and foreclosure avoided. Sampey, along with the treasurer, Gaines Stanley Dobbins, practiced utmost economy while at the same time seeking additional funds, so that no salary payment was missed (although reductions were made) during the decade of the depression years; and before Sampey's death the entire indebtedness was liquidated.

Although 66 years of age when he became president of the seminary, Sampey continued vigorous service for 13 years. The seminary began an unprecedented era of expansion in 1934, when attendance was 353, to 1941–42, the last year of Sampey's active presidency, when attendance was 496. After Sampey's voluntary retirement, he was succeeded by Ellis Adams Fuller (*q.v.*).

On the anniversary of Sampey's 40th year of service as member and chairman of the International Lesson Committee, the appointed speaker said, "To be a member for forty years, and for many years chairman of the Interdenominational Committee which has produced the outlines of a series of lessons used by millions of people, is an achievement which, so far as I know, is without parallel in history."

In 1935 Sampey was elected president of the Southern Baptist Convention, and was re-elected for two succeeding years. The following year, accompanied by his wife and a group of friends, he made a missionary journey to Japan and China, where he preached in many centers. In 1937 Sampey was appointed Southern Baptist representative to the Conference on Life and Work in Oxford and the Conference on Faith and Order in Edinburgh; and in 1939 when the Baptist World Congress met in Atlanta, Ga., Sampey delivered a notable address on "The New Testament Doctrine of the Church." He continued to teach, preach, write, and administer affairs of the seminary until 1942, when he tendered his resignation after 57 years of continuous service. In addition to his *Memoirs,* written after his retirement, Sampey's other books include *The First Thirty Years of Southern Baptist Theological Seminary* (1890); *The Ethical Teachings of Jesus* (1909); *The International Lesson System* (1911); *The Heart of the Old Testament* (1922); *Syllabus for Old Testament Study* (1925).

Sampey's first wife, Annie Renfroe, died after a long illness Jan. 21, 1925, and the following year Sampey married Ellen Wood of Birmingham, Ala., of whom he wrote, "I do not know how I could get along with the details of my administration without her help."

GAINES S. DOBBINS

SAMPEY, JOHN R., CHAIR OF OLD TESTAMENT INTERPRETATION. In 1931 Gaines Stanley Dobbins (b. 1886), treasurer of Southern Baptist Theological Seminary, in an effort to perpetuate the memory of President John Richard Sampey (*q.v.*) (1863–1946), proposed that the seminary alumni raise $100,000 to endow the Chair of Old Testament Interpretation in his honor. The alumni committee which was appointed began to function enthusiastically, and by 1934 the fund had grown to $14,557. The idea was then conceived of a recorded message from Sampey to be used as part of a program in every church where one of his former students was pastor. This novel appeal brought immediate generous response, and a total of $70,000 was soon raised. A gift of $10,000 from James Hughes Anderson (*q.v.*) of Knoxville, Tenn., stirred the alumni to fresh effort, and as a result the full $100,000 was reported raised and the chair endowed at the seminary alumni meeting in Richmond, Va., in May, 1938. Additional sums continued to be received, and the final total to the credit of the chair was $105,000. Sampey, himself, was the first occupant of the chair from 1938 to 1943, followed by James Leo Green (b. 1912), 1943–48, and Clyde Taylor Francisco (b. 1916), since 1951.

CLYDE T. FRANCISCO

SAN MARCOS ACADEMY. A coeducational boarding school for grades 1–12, located on a ridge of hills in San Marcos, Tex., "founded for the primary purpose of giving students not only the highest type of academic but also Christian training." Its charter was enacted July 20, 1907. At a meeting in Lockhart, T. J. Dodson moved that the Baptists of southwest Texas build a school, but bids from four towns were rejected at a later meeting in 1906; it was agreed, however, that an academy should be built. James H. Carroll, who suggested that San Marcos raise its bid to $25,000 to be matched by the denomination, was elected president of the proposed school and leader of the forces to raise the money. The first board of trustees was elected Sept. 19, 1906. The cornerstone of Carroll Hall, a $107,000 brick structure, was laid Dec. 18, 1907, and San Marcos Baptist Academy had its formal opening Sept. 24, 1908, with an enrolment of 200 for grades 6–12. During Carroll's administration Talbot Hall, a $30,000 boys' dormitory, was erected. Grades 4 and 5 were added in 1917 and the first three grades in 1918.

In 1910 the academy was taken over by the Baptist General Convention of Texas, which annually elects a board of trustees to administer the affairs of the school. Although the school is non-sectarian in operation, a majority of the 13 trustees must be Baptists.

The academy is affiliated with the Texas Education Agency and is a member of the Southern Association of Colleges and Secondary Schools, offering 39½ affiliated high school units for college entrance. Private instruction in the fine arts is offered in all grades, and a unit in Bible must be included in the 16 units required for graduation. The military program for all boys is set up under the R.O.T.C.-55C National Defense Act. High school students may earn one and a half units in a 10-week summer school, while elementary students follow a camp program with two hours daily classroom instruction.

The 1955 enrolment of 387 included students from 10 states and 16 foreign countries. With the opening of Elizabeth Kokernot Hall, a $536,000 structure to house 200 girls, in Sept., 1955, the academy has facilities to house 475 boarding students. The cadets live in three brick dormitories, two of which have been built since 1949. There are 17 buildings and extensive recreation facilities on the 64-acre campus.

Robert B. Reed, a former student, assumed office as president July 17, 1947. Property value is currently estimated at $1,848,889.41; the $250,000 indebtedness is owed on Elizabeth Kokernot Hall. With permanent endowment at $58,723.68, the school operated on a budget of $424,787 in 1955–56. Through 1955 San Marcos Baptist Academy had 2,325 graduates.

BIBLIOGRAPHY: J. L. Childs, "The History of San Marcos Baptist Academy" (1938). H. P. Smith, "San Marcos Baptist Academy" (1954).

LUCY LAURENE LIGHTHOUSE

SANCTIFICATION. The consecration or dedication to God which makes one holy. Holiness means wholeness, or what God originally intended life to be. Sanctification or holiness is made possible through faith in Christ, which releases the energy of the Holy Spirit to transform and lift life to what God intends it to be. The Holy Spirit is the instrument of sanctification (II Thess. 2:13–14; I Peter 1:2; Rom. 8:1–17, 26–27). In the Old Testament the terms "sanctify" and "holy" are used to refer to the Temple, the altar, etc. In the New Testament these terms apply primarily to persons.

Traditional theology has thought of justification as the beginning of the Christian life and sanctification as the process by which the righteousness of Christ is actually infused into the Christian's life. Sanctification is thus the perfecting of the Christian life or the progressive cleansing of the soul (I Cor. 3:1; I Thess. 5:23; Heb. 12:14). In a sense, the Christian is sanctified at the beginning of the Christian life, for according to the New Testament, all Christians are "saints" or "sanctified ones" (Acts 9:13; Rom. 1:7; I Cor. 1:2; II Cor. 1:1; Eph. 1:1; Phil. 1:1; Col. 1:2). Thus in principle the Christian life is "holy" or "sanctified" from the beginning, and the New Testament recognizes no such thing as carnal Christianity. The only Christian life is a sanctified life.

See also SAINT.

BIBLIOGRAPHY: W. T. Conner, *The Gospel of Redemption* (1945). W. E. Sangster, *The Path to Perfection* (1934).
CHARLES A. TRENTHAM

SANDEFER, JEFFERSON DAVIS (b. Sharp County, Ark., Mar. 13, 1868; d. Abilene, Tex., Mar. 22, 1940). Educator, college president. Son of Samuel Butner and Mary Lucretia (Leverton) Sandefer, he was educated at Parker Institute, Whitt, Tex., and the University of Chicago. He married Lucile Gilbert in 1893. President of Strawn College from 1894 to 1900, and superintendent of schools in Granbury, Tex., 1900–01, Sandefer became professor of Latin and history at John Tarleton College, 1902–07, and its president, 1908–09. For 31 years he served as president of Simmons College, July, 1909, until his death Mar. 22, 1940. Sandefer, founder and trustee of Hendrick Memorial Hospital, was president of the Baptist General Convention of Texas, 1920–23; and vice-president of the Southern Baptist Convention, 1923–24. He was widely known as an effective, popular speaker, a champion of temperance, and an aggressive opponent of liquor traffic.

BIBLIOGRAPHY: I. W. Sandefer, "Jefferson Davis Sandefer," *Christian Educator* (1940). *Who Was Who in America,* Vol. 1, 1897–1942 (1942).
RUPERT N. RICHARDSON

SANDERS, BILLINGTON McCARTY (b. Columbia County, Ga., Dec. 2, 1789; d. Mar. 12, 1852). First president of Mercer University. A son of Ephraim and Nancy Sanders, he was left an orphan at the age of 10 and was reared in the home of Ambrose Jones. He attended Kiokee Seminary and the University of Georgia and then transferred to South Carolina College (later the University of South Carolina), from which he graduated in Dec., 1809.

Returning to Columbia County, he taught in Appling Academy for two years, then for the next 20 years was a successful farmer and preacher. He was baptized by Abraham Marshall in Jan., 1810, into membership in Kiokee Church. A little later he moved his membership to Union Church in Warren County, was licensed to preach in 1823, and was ordained in 1825 by a presbytery headed by Jesse Mercer (*q.v.*), in order to accept a call to the pastorate of Williams Creek Baptist Church. In 1812 he married Martha Lamar of Applington and had by her nine children. She died in 1822, and on Feb. 25, 1824, he married Cynthia Holliday of Lincoln County; he had by her 13 children.

He served for one term as a representative in the state legislature, but his experiences in politics were so distasteful that he never again consented to become a candidate. In 1831 he was invited to take charge of the classical and theological seminary which Georgia Baptists had decided to establish. The school began operations in Jan., 1833, in two double log cabins, each with a garret, and used for dwelling, dining, and study for teachers and students. Thirty-nine students, seven of whom were preparing for the ministry, were in attendance. During the time while Mercer was a manual labor school, Sanders had only one assistant besides his wife, and he served as superintendent, teacher, steward, and farmer. His time was absorbed in planning, teaching, clearing, fencing, cultivating, erecting buildings, soliciting financial support, administering discipline, and preaching regularly, with not more than five or six hours of sleep daily. As a result of his work, attendance increased, popular approval and support grew, and when the institution was advanced to Mercer University, he was unanimously elected as its first president. He accepted on condition that the trustees would secure a successor at their earliest convenience. He resigned in 1839 after conducting the institution during the first nine years of its memorable history.

Though no longer president, his interest was undiminished. As treasurer, member of the board of trustees, and secretary up to the time of his death, he did more than any other man to lay the foundations for the future growth of the institution. Sanders' stature is further revealed in his remarkable work in the Georgia Association as clerk for many years and moderator for nine years, and in the Georgia Baptist convention as a member and chairman of the executive committee for many years, as president for six years, and for a time as editor of the *Christian Index*.

His body rests fittingly entombed in the Penfield cemetery by the side of his beloved wife, Cynthia Holliday Sanders, his major partner and helpmeet in giving life and strength to Mercer University and in providing for a continuing stream of leadership for Georgia Baptists.

BIBLIOGRAPHY: C. D. Mallary, *Living and Dying unto the Lord* (1854). SPRIGHT DOWELL

SANDS, WILLIAM (b. Ulverstone, Lancaster, England, *c.* 1793; d. Richmond, Va., Aug. 30, 1868). Immigrant in 1818, Sands rose to the position of pioneer religious editor, respected Christian scholar, and active layman. After working in Washington and Baltimore, he moved to Richmond in 1827. From 1828 to 1833, he was publisher and associate editor of the *Religious Herald*. From 1834 to 1856 he was sole editor and publisher. He took David Shaver as associate in 1857, and they published the *Religious Herald* until 1865, when Richmond was burned.

Reared in an English Baptist home, having read many Baptist books by the age of 12, Sands "was sound and earnest, but not a bigoted and intolerant Baptist." In Richmond, he was an active member of the Second Baptist Church for 40 years, faithful in Sunday school associations, in missions, and in education and temperance movements. He was director of the Virginia Baptist Seminary, leader in organizing the Y.M.C.A. in Richmond, and moderator of the Dover Association during the last year of his life. He helped organize two African Baptist churches, and was a constant friend and adviser of the Negro community. BEN LYNES

SANDY CREEK BAPTIST INSTITUTE. Located at Mt. Vernon Springs, Chatham County, N. C. The school opened in Jan., 1856, closed during the Civil War, but reopened in 1881 as the "Mt. Vernon Springs School." In 1897 its name was changed to the Sandy Creek Baptist Institute. It closed in 1908. D. L. SMILEY

SANDY CREEK CHURCH. Founded in 1755 with a membership of 16 in Randolph County, N. C., near Liberty. A member of Randolph Association with a membership of about 50 in 1955, it was the first Separate Baptist church in North Carolina. Morgan Edwards indicated its extending influence in his *Notebook,* 1772.

> It is a mother church, nay a grand mother, and a great grand mother. All the separate baptists sprang hence: not only eastward towards the sea, but westward towards the great river Mississippi, but northward to Virginia and southward to South Carolina and Georgia.

Shubal Stearns (*q.v.*), founder of the church, hearing of the religious destitution in North Carolina, became a Baptist in 1751 in Connecticut. Stearns moved from Virginia to Sandy Creek in 1755, joined by his wife, Daniel Marshall, and a dozen others. The group immediately formed a church with Stearns as pastor and Marshall and Joseph Breed as assistants. They built a small house of worship which they abandoned in 1762 for a larger one. The preaching of Stearns and his assistants resulted in the establishment of a station at Abbott's Creek, 30 miles away, in less than a year. It soon became an independent church with Marshall as pastor, probably in 1756. In three years, when a station at Deep Creek became independent, the total membership of the three churches was 900. In 17 years 42 churches had been formed and 125 ministers, many of them ordained, had joined the movement. Among them were Dutton Lane, who became pastor of the first Separate church in Virginia, and Samuel Harris (*q.v.*). Marshall moved southward in 1760, first to South Carolina and then to Georgia, where he helped lay the foundation of Separate work. Breed, Philip Mulkey, and other followers of Marshall had by 1770 established seven churches, some with branches, in South Carolina.

Under the leadership of Stearns the churches at Sandy Creek, Abbott's Creek, and Deep River formed the Sandy Creek Association in 1758, which later included churches in North Carolina, South Carolina, and Virginia, formed as a result of the evangelistic impulse from Sandy Creek Church.

Stearns died Nov. 20, 1771, a few months after Tryon had repulsed the Regulators at Alamance and had marched through the Sandy Creek area. Writing in 1772, Morgan Edwards explained the waning of the Sandy Creek Church:

> It [the Sandy Creek Church] is reduced from 606 to 14 souls. The cause of this dispersion was the abuse of power which too much prevailed in the province. . . . They despaired of seeing better times, and therefore quitted the province. It is said 1,500 families departed since the battle of Almance [sic], and, to my knowledge, a great many more are only waiting to dispose of their plantations, in order to follow them.

The church never again exerted the influence it did for the first 17 years of its existence, although emigrants spread the Separate Baptist doctrine in many parts of the pioneer territory. G. W. PASCHAL

SANFORD, SHELTON PALMER (b. June 25, 1816, Greensboro, Ga.; d. Macon, Ga., Aug. 9, 1896). Teacher. He received the A.B. degree from the University of Georgia, 1838, sharing first honor, and the LL.D. degree from Mercer University, 1878. Elected tutor in mathematics at Mercer three weeks before graduation, he began teaching one week after graduation, advanced to assistant professor in 1839, and became professor of mathematics and astronomy in 1840. This position he held until he resigned in 1891.

In 1840 he was married to Maria F. Dickerman, and had one son, Charles V. Sanford (father of Chancellor Steadman V. Sanford, University of Georgia System), and one daughter, Mrs. Anna M. Cheves.

Beginning in 1870 Sanford published a series of "analytic" arithmetics and an algebra. The term "analytic" was derived from the Pestalozzian emphasis upon pupils' understanding their school work. In this the series marked a distinct advance over previous arithmetics. The series sold widely, at times 70,000 a year. An 1871 preface says: "The author believes the habitudes of thought engendered by the study of the analytic system will prove of inestimable value." In Sanford's own teaching his aim was, in his own phrase, to make each point "as clear as a sunbeam." W. H. KILPATRICK

SANYATI BAPTIST HOSPITAL. See SOUTHERN RHODESIA, MISSION IN.

SATAN. See DEVIL.

SAVAGE, GEORGE MARTIN (b. near Rienzi, Tishomingo County, Miss., Feb. 2, 1849; d. Jackson, Tenn., June 26, 1938). Educator. He was a son of Hamilton Giles and Eleanor Shields Savage and was one of ten children. One of his brothers was Giles Christopher Savage, M.D. (*q.v.*), a Nashville, Tenn., eye specialist. George Martin Savage received his higher education at Southwestern Baptist University (now Union) at Jackson, Tenn. He received the A.B. degree in 1871 and the LL.D. degree in 1891.

He was ordained in 1870. In 1871 he married Fannie F. Williams of Eagleville, Tenn. He taught at Henderson-Masonic and Female Institute, Henderson, Tenn. (1871–77, 1880–84) and served as principal of Eagleville High School (1884–90). With the exception of one year at Hall-Moody (1908–09), the majority of his years were given to leading and teaching at Union University, which he served at various times as president and as professor of English, French, philosophy, and Bible. An annual of Union describes him as "an ideal teacher, a cultured person." He was the author of *Greece and Bible Lands.* He traveled extensively in Europe and Asia and is reported to have read the Greek New Testament through 55 times. He served as president of the Tennessee Baptist Convention, 1924–26. G. ALLEN WEST

SAVAGE, GILES CHRISTOPHER (b. near Rienzi, Miss., Jan. 15, 1854; d. Apr. 8, 1930; buried Mt. Olivet Cemetery, Nashville, Tenn.). Doctor, professor, denominational leader, science and religious writer. The son of a minister, he was a brilliant student and a well-educated man. He earned his M.D. degree at Jefferson Medical College, Philadelphia, Pa., 1878. He did postgraduate work at Jefferson, in London, and in Vienna; he received the LL.D. degree from Union University in 1919. He married Lessie A. Jones, Oct. 4, 1881. Three sons and three daughters were born to this union. He practiced in Jackson, Tenn., 1878–86, and in Nashville, Tenn., 1886–1930. He was professor of ophthalmology at Vanderbilt University, Nashville, from 1886 until 1911, when he retired from teaching to give his entire time to private practice and to writing. Savage was the author of many scientific and religious works, including *Cycles of Time and Seasons* and *Harmony of the Gospels.* He founded the *Ophthalmic Record* in 1891. Savage served his denomination and profession faithfully. He was a member of the Baptist Sunday School Board, the Tennessee state mission board, and the Tennessee Anti-Saloon League. He received many honors: president, Tennessee Baptist Convention, 1909–11; president, Nashville Academy of Medicine, 1891–92; president, Tennessee Medical Association, 1896; Southern Medical Association, 1919; and first vice-president of American Medical Association, 1904–05. The Southern Medical Association was instituted on Oct. 3, 1906, in Chattanooga, as a result of Savage's efforts. W. LEONARD STIGLER

SCARBOROUGH, JOHN CATRE (b. Wake County, N. C., Sept. 22, 1841; d. Murfreesboro, N. C., Dec. 26, 1917). Educator. Son of Daniel and Cynthia (Horton) Scarborough, he was graduated from Wake Forest College in 1869, serving as tutor two years. He established Selma Academy, where he taught five years. He was state superintendent of public instruction, 1876–80; taught at Thomasville Female College, 1885–86; was appointed commissioner of labor and printing in 1886; and in 1892 began his third two-year term as state superintendent of public instruction. In 1897 he became president of Chowan College, and continued in this capacity until 1909. In 1911 he became superintendent of schools of Hertford County, retiring in 1915. In the Civil War he distinguished himself with Capt. William Henry Harrison's "Raleigh Rifles," later Company K, Fourth North Carolina Volunteer Regiment. As tutor and trustee, he served Wake Forest College more than 50 years. On Jan. 12, 1876, he married Julia Vass Moore, and to them were born six children. C. SYLVESTER GREEN

SCARBOROUGH, LEE RUTLAND (b. Colfax, La., July 4, 1870; d. Amarillo, Tex., Apr. 10, 1945). Pastor, evangelist, seminary president, denominational leader, and writer. His parents were George W. and Mary Elizabeth (Rutland) Scarborough, who were reared in Mississippi and Tennessee, respectively. His father was a faithful Baptist minister, and his mother a devout Christian. The family altar was a regular part of their home life. To them were born nine children, of whom Lee Rutland was the eighth.

In 1874 the family moved to Texas on a farm near Waco; later they settled in Jones County. In 1896 the family moved to the pioneer section of West Texas where Lee grew up on a farm ranch. In this area his father held many revival meetings in dugouts, brush arbors, log schoolhouses, and under trees. Lee's youth was spent in hard labor and with limited material resources, which was the accustomed lot of the cowboys of the West.

His education included the A.B. degree from Baylor University, Waco, Tex., in 1892; and the A.B. degree in 1896 from Yale, where he was a Phi Beta Kappa student. He received the honorary D.D. degree from Baylor, 1908, and an LL.D. degree from Union University, Jackson, Tenn., in 1927. He attended Southern Baptist Theological Seminary, Louisville, Ky., 1899–1900.

He was married in 1900 to Neppie Warren. To them were born six children: Warren, Emma Lee, Lawrence, Neppie, Ada Beth, and Byron.

Ordained to the gospel ministry in 1896, he served as pastor of the First Baptist Church, Cameron, Tex., from 1896 to 1901. He served as pastor of First Baptist Church, Abilene, Tex., from 1901 to 1908. He was in constant demand as a pastor-evangelist.

As a denominational leader he served in the following positions: member of Board of Missions and Education; director of the 75 Million Campaign, 1919; president of the Southern Baptist Convention, 1939–40; leader in securing funds for buildings at Hardin-Simmons University, Abilene, Tex.; member of the executive board of the Baptist General Convention of Texas; president of the Baptist General Convention of Texas; teacher in the first chair of evangelism at Southwestern Baptist Theological Seminary, 1908; and president of Southwestern Seminary, Fort Worth, Tex., 1914–45. He led in a program of evangelism for the Southern Baptist Convention and the Baptist World Alliance, and made an evangelistic tour of South America for the Foreign Mission Board in 1936. He had an intense spirit of co-operation in denominational work.

His published works include books on evangelism, travels, and sermons as follows: *Recruits for World Conquest; With Christ After the Lost* (revised in 1952 by E. D. Head); *Endued to Win; How Jesus Won Men; Tears of Jesus; Prepare to Meet God; Marvels of Divine Leadership; Christ's Militant Kingdom; Holy Places and Precious Promises; A Search for Souls; Ten Spiritual Ships; Products of Pentecost; My Conception of the Gospel Ministry; A Blaze of Evangelism Across the Equator; A Modern School of the Prophets.* He is buried at Fort Worth, Tex.

FRANKLIN M. SEGLER

SCHAFER MEMORIAL BAPTIST CAMP. Opened in 1951 at Floral (Hancock County), Ky., owned and operated by the Daviess-McLean Baptist Association, although facilities are made available to churches and associations of the western region. The main support is from the owning body, but others in the western region help in the support. All church organizations use the facilities with emphasis on Royal Ambassador and Girl's Auxiliary work. Nine weeks of camp are held annually.

ELDRED M. TAYLOR

SCOTLAND, BAPTIST UNION OF. The first union of Baptists in Scotland was originated by the Scots Baptists in 1765, who organized the Scots Baptist Connexion, a fellowship whose purpose was to stimulate mutual encouragement and inspiration. This connexion was short-lived and was succeeded in 1835 by the Scottish Baptist Association, later changed to the Baptist Union of Scotland (1843). Unfortunately, because of differences in doctrine and outlook the new association failed to attract the larger churches; and it was not until 1869, following a further Baptist association in 1856, that the union as it exists today was constituted. The formal constitution took place in Hope Street Church, Glasgow, on Oct. 21, 1869, with Jonathan Watson of Edinburgh elected president. The union consisted of 51 churches with 3,500 members.

After existing separately for over 50 years, the Baptist Home Missionary Society for Scotland, with primary influence in the remote areas of the Scottish highlands and islands, became an integral part of the union in 1931; this coalescing of forces and resources has given added efficiency to Baptist work. Names revered in the annals of the society include the brothers Robert and James Alexander Haldane; Sir William Sinclair, the founder and first pastor of the church at Keiss, the oldest of the Scottish churches (1750); and Sinclair Thomson, beloved "Apostle of Shetland." In 1925 the union, jointly with the Baptist Theological College of Scotland, acquired the historic Church House in Glasgow. It provides a headquarters ideally situated, with facilities for fellowship and witness, and a center for denominational life.

Since 1869 expansion has been slow but steady; the postwar years created difficulties. New churches have been established, especially in the cities and larger centers of population, and a scheme of church extension is in operation at present. To assist in the maintenance of the ministry, capital funds amounting in aggregate to about $280,000 have been raised; provision has also been made for a retired ministers' fund and a loan fund for churches.

Ministerial training is the prerogative of the Baptist Theological College of Scotland, formed in 1894; while independent, it works in close collaboration with the union. Keen missionary interest is evidenced by loyalty given to the Baptist Missionary Society. Forty missionaries serve under the society, and annual gifts for missions average about $40,600. Contemporary issues such as evangelism and social service are supervised by committees appointed for the purpose. A women's auxiliary is vigorous and flourishing. Denominational publications are the *Scottish Baptist Magazine,* issued monthly, and the *Scottish Baptist Year Book.*

DATA

	1934	*1954*
Number of churches	152	154
Number of associations	12	13
Baptisms	863	517
Members	23,189	19,263
Sunday school scholars	18,413	14,475

G. M. HARDIE

SCOTT, JAMES ALLEN (b. near Freedom, Barren County, Ky., July 4, 1864; d. Dec. 19, 1937). Lawyer, minister, and denominational leader. He received his early education in Flippin High School, taught three years, and then was admitted to the bar and practiced law 13 years. He was an alumnus of Southern Baptist Theological Seminary and received an honorary D.D. degree from Oklahoma Baptist College. Churches pastored include Washington Avenue, Oklahoma City; Calvary Baptist, Pomona, Calif.; and one in Glasgow, Ky. He was president of the Oklahoma Baptist Convention (1903–05) and the first president of the Baptist General Convention of Oklahoma (1906–07). Other denominational services include nine years as state evangelist and 20 years as Home Mission Board evangelist. In the 1902 meeting of the Oklahoma convention, Scott made the motion that led to the founding of the Oklahoma Baptist Orphans' Home, and as superintendent he opened the home on Mar. 5, 1903. He is buried in Mountain View Cemetery, Pasadena, Calif. H. TRUMAN MAXEY

SCOTTSBORO BAPTIST INSTITUTE (1901–08). A high school for boys and girls founded by the Tennessee River Association and the Alabama Baptist State Convention at Scottsboro, in Jackson County, Ala., John C. Dawson, president. The school was made a part of the mountain school system of the Home Mission Board in 1905. The properties were sold in 1908 because a "State District School had been located at Scottsboro." JAMES E. DAVIDSON

SCREVEN, WILLIAM (b. Somerton, Somersetshire, England, *c.* 1629; d. near Georgetown, S. C., Oct. 10, 1713). Pioneer Baptist in South Carolina. Screven came from England to Massachusetts about 1668 and on Nov. 15, 1673, bought land at Kittery, Me. In 1674 he married Bridget Cutt (Cutts), daughter of a prominent shipbuilding family, and they had 11 children.

On July 6, 1675, Screven was brought into court "for not frequenting the publique meeting according to Law . . . ," and in 1679 he joined other residents in appealing to the Crown to establish direct rule over Maine on the ground that Massachusetts was suppressing religious liberty.

Screven and his wife were baptized into First Baptist Church, Boston, Mass., in 1681, and on Jan. 11, 1682, the Boston church licensed Screven to preach. After helping to organize a church at Kittery, Screven was ordained Sept. 25, 1682, and that same year, after being jailed and fined for opposing infant baptism, Screven promised to leave Maine. However, on Oct. 9, 1683, he was brought to court for not departing and was ordered to appear again the following June, but there is no record that he did so. From 1685 to 1695, there are several references to one "William Screven" in Maine court records buying land, witnessing a will, serving as deputy to the Massachusetts General Court, and witnessing a mortgage, but it is not certain that this was the same William Screven. A warrant for 1,000 acres of land in South Carolina was issued to Screven on Dec. 7, 1696. A second warrant for 500 acres was issued, and by purchase in 1698 and grant in 1700, over 1,100 acres were added to the original 1,000, 40 miles from Charleston. There at Sumerton, Screven and those with him settled and were "probably the nucleus of the church which emigrated from Maine to South Carolina." This church, the first Baptist church in the South, seems to have moved to Charleston by 1693, where Screven served intermittently as pastor until his death Oct. 10, 1713, near present Georgetown, S. C. Screven has been characterized as a man who, in the face of intolerance and persecution, had "great ardor and energy in spreading and maintaining Baptist principles."

BIBLIOGRAPHY: H. S. Burrage, *History of the Baptists of Maine* (1904). M. Edwards, "Materials Toward a History of the Baptists in the Province of South Carolina" (1772). *Maine Province and Court Records,* Vol. II. A. S. Salley, Jr., ed., *Warrants for Land in South Carolina* (1915). R. G. Torbet, *A History of the Baptists* (1950). L. Townsend, *South Carolina Baptists, 1670–1805* (1935). M. L. Webber, "Historical Notes: The Burial Place of Reverend William Screven," *South Carolina Historical and Genealogical Magazine* (1915). JOE MADISON KING

SEARCY, JAMES BRYANT (b. Eufaula, Ala., July 18, 1838; d. Little Rock, Ark., Sept. 14, 1920). Minister, educator, editor. Son of Reuben and Isabella Searcy, he came to Bradley County, Ark., in 1857 and was ordained in 1860. For nine years he was secretary of the Arkansas Baptist State Convention, and in 1873 became state missionary. He held pastorates at Warren, Monticello, Dardanelle, Hope, and Malvern, Ark.; Monroe, La.; and Corinth and Biloxi, Miss. Among other services, he assisted in founding Ouachita College and making it coeducational and served as its financial secretary in 1887; he was the first editor and co-owner of the *Arkansas Evangel;* he was Arkansas editor of *The Baptist* (Memphis, Tenn.), 1880: for seven years he was vice-president of the Foreign Mission Board of the Southern Baptist Convention; and he was editor of *The Baptist* (Mississippi), 1898–99. Union University conferred upon him a D.D. degree. He was married first to Mary Killum of Mississippi, who died young; second to Mrs. M. F. Adkins of Drew County, Ark.; and third to Mrs. Lynwood Woodell of Little Rock in 1917. He was prominent in Baptist affairs in the state of Arkansas for more than half a century. L. C. TEDFORD

SECOND BIRTH. See REGENERATION and CONVERSION.

SECOND COMING. See PAROUSIA.

SECURITY PLAN, BAPTIST BOARDS EMPLOYEES'. Supplemental protection available to members of the Baptist Boards Employees Retirement Plan and the Widows Supplemental Annuity Plan (B). Under this supplement option on commuted annuity after age 60 is widow protection continues after member retires. Under the widows plan widow protection ceased when member retired. Early retirement option on commuted annuity after age 60 is available. Such annuity is reduced 0.6 per cent for each month of early retirement. Security plan increases the maximum disability annuity under the Baptist boards plan from $500 to $900 per year. Cost of this plan: up to age 49—Baptists boards 3 per cent, widows 1½ per cent, security ½ per cent for member; age 50 to 59—Baptist boards 3 per cent, widows 2 per cent, security ½ per cent; age 60 and thereafter—Baptist boards 3 per cent, widows 2½ per cent, security ½ per cent. Cost for the employer for full unit is 11½ per cent till member is age 50, 12 per cent from age 50 to 60, and 12½ per cent after age 60. RETTA O'BANNON

SECURITY PLAN, MINISTERS'. Inaugurated July 1, 1954, supplemental to the Ministers Retirement Plan and the Widows Supplemental Annuity Plan (A). Under this supplement, widow protection continues after member retires. Under the widows plan such protection ceased when member retired. Retirement after age 60 on a commuted annuity reduced 0.6 per cent for each month of early retirement is included. Security plan also increases the maximum disability annuity under the retirement plan from $500 to $900 per year. The cost of the complete program is: Ministers retirement 3 per cent, widows plan 1½ per cent, security plan ½ per cent for member until he reaches age 60. Then the cost increases under the widow plan to 2 per cent, and again at age 65 to 2½ per cent. The state convention contributes the same amount as the member, and the church pays 5 per cent. This plan is now open only to members of the Ministers Retirement Plan Jan. 1 or July 1 of any year. MABLE MC CARTNEY

SEINAN GAKUIN, FUKUOKA. See JAPAN, MISSION IN.

SEINAN JO GAKUIN, KOKURA. See JAPAN, MISSION IN.

SELF-SUPPORT ON MISSION FIELDS. A church is self-supporting when, from its tithes and offerings, it pays local expenses, including pastor's salary, and contributes to denominational causes.

In churches on mission fields self-support is encouraged by teaching converts church responsibility even before baptism, by holding study courses on church membership and doctrines, by frequent sermons on stewardship, and by stewardship literature such as Sundary school lessons, tracts, and denominational papers.

A major factor contributing to self-support is organization of a national Baptist convention to make possible co-operative financing of institutions and agencies. With the organization of the Brazilian Baptist Convention in 1907, for example, 84 member churches with 5,016 members evidenced greater stewardship and evangelistic concern, and in five years grew to 154 churches, 10,844 members. Of the 1,121 churches reported in 1955 by the three Brazilian missions, 928 were self-supporting.

Seminary training of pastors contributes to growing self-support through the encouragement better leadership provides. Church loan boards, which receive deposits from churches and, at reasonable interest, lend up to a certain percentage for purchase of property (60 per cent in Brazil), encourage self-support. In 36 years of the *Junta Patrimonial* (loan board in South Brazil), none of the more than a thousand churches it has served has defaulted. And through erecting their own buildings, churches learn their giving potentialities. J. J. COWSERT

SELLERS, ERNEST ORLANDO (b. Lansing, Mich., Oct. 29, 1869; d. Eola, La., Oct. 19, 1952). Evangelistic singer, Y.M.C.A. secretary, professor, composer. Son of William and Kate (Armstrong) Sellers, he attended public schools in Lansing, Mich., and served six years as city engineer for his home town, where a bridge was named in his honor. Sellers' training in music was under private teachers in Lansing and at Moody Bible Institute in 1895, where he studied under Homer Hammontree and D. B. Towner. Converted as a young man in the Lansing Y.M.C.A., Sellers entered evangelistic singing in 1896 as an associate of Fred B. Smith and was ordained as a minister about 1917 for work in army camps. He served as Y.M.C.A. executive secretary in Macon, Ga.; Washington, D. C.; and Wilmington, Del., (1901–05); and as director of men's work and assistant pastor in Euclid Avenue Baptist Church, Cleveland, Ohio, 1905–07. Sellers became assistant director of the music department and professor of Sunday school pedagogy at Moody Bible Institute, serving from 1908 to 1919, and was an associate in great evangelistic campaigns with J. Wilbur Chapman, Amzi Clarence Dixon (*q.v.*), Gypsy Smith, Sr., Dwight L. Moody, Billy Sunday, and others. He served on the staff of Sherwood Eddy, camp religious work director, Camp Grant, Rockford, Ill., in 1917; was a member of the Y.M.C.A. Speakers Bureau in France and Germany in 1918–19; and was director of the music department at Baptist Bible Institute, New Orleans, La., 1919–45.

Sellers' published works include *The Adult Bible Class, Personal Evangelism* (1923), *How to Improve Church Music* (1928), *Elements of Music Notation and Conducting* (1938), and *Worship, Why and How* (1941). He wrote the words and music for many hymns, including "Wonderful, Wonderful Jesus," "Thy Word Is a Lamp to My Feet," and "School of Providence"; and he served as a member of the committee which compiled the *New Baptist Hymnal* (1926). The school of sacred music in the New Orleans Baptist Theological Seminary was named for Sellers after his death.

J. WASH WATTS

SEMINARY, THE DENOMINATIONAL. See THEOLOGICAL EDUCATION.

SEMINARY EXTENSION COURSES. A department created to offer on-the-job training to preachers and other church leaders unable to attend an institution. Two types of studies are offered: correspondence and extension classes. The Inter-Seminary Conference, composed of representatives of the Southern Baptist seminaries, created the Seminary Extension Department in Dec., 1950, selecting two members of the faculty of each co-operating seminary to serve as a commission. The commission selected R. Lee Gallman, Th.D., as director.

On June 15, 1951, offices were opened in the Baptist Building, Jackson, Miss. At first only correspondence work was projected, and by June, 1952, 600 were enrolled. Extension centers were begun in Murphy, N. C., North Wilkesboro, N. C., Winston-Salem, N. C., San Antonio, Tex., and Jacksonville, Fla. By Mar., 1956, 106 centers had been established, enrolling 3,358 in 16 states. During the fall and spring sessions of 1955–56, 76 centers operated.

Two associates have been added to the staff, Ray K. Hodge, B.D., and W. A. Whitten, B.D. The correspondence instructors are Eugene Fleming, B.D., Herbert Batson, M.R.E., and Grady Smith, A.B.

Operation of the program.—Correspondence studies, consisting of appropriate texts and syllabi, are organized by various seminary teachers. Students enrol and carry on their studies at leisure and send lessons to the department to be evaluated. At the completion of 16 selected studies in Bible, religious education, and pastoral theology, the student receives a certificate.

Extension centers operate on the same basis as a university extension center, using the methodology and techniques of adult education. Classes meet in a church or associational headquarters under the guidance of qualified teachers (M.A., B.D., M.R.E. degrees are minimum requirements) once a week for 18 weeks per semester. The administration of the extension center is carried on as a project of one or more local associations. Usually the executive committee appoints an advisory committee to operate the center. A local director, registrar, and treasurer are needed. Many superintendents of missions serve as local directors.

Two series are offered by the department: Series A is designed for pastoral leadership, and Series B is planned for religious education leadership. The enrolment in June, 1956, totaled 5,082 with 1,735 studying by correspondence and 3,347 enrolled in extension centers.

The program receives $5,000 annually from each of the five Southern Baptist seminaries. The cost to the student for each course by correspondence is $5 plus the cost of the text, for each course in an extension center, $8 plus the cost of the text. R. LEE GALLMAN

SEMPLE, ROBERT BAYLOR (b. Rosemont, Va., Jan. 20, 1769; d. Fredericksburg, Va., Dec. 25, 1831. Son of a Scotch emigrant John and Elizabeth (Walker) Semple. When Peter Nelson established an academy at the Forks of Hanover, Semple was given free board and tuition. At 16 years of age Semple was chosen assistant teacher in the school. He then combined teaching in a private family with the study of law. Converted soon thereafter, Semple joined Upper King and Queen Church by baptism in Dec., 1789. Turning to the ministry, he was ordained Sept. 26, 1790, and the same year was called to be the first pastor of Bruington Baptist Church, where he served until his death. On Mar. 1, 1793, he married Ann Loury of Caroline County. Several years later the couple settled on a farm called Nordington, their home for the greater part of their lives. Here he conducted a school for a number of years. His missionary spirit was strong and his activities wide. As early as 1813 he had a general missionary society in the Bruington Church. He was president of the Baptist Convention of Virginia in 1813, trustee of Columbian College in 1821, moderator of General Meeting of Correspondence, 1807, and first president of the Baptist General Association of Virginia in 1823. In 1820 he was made president of the Triennial Convention, serving till his death.

In 1814 Semple received the D.D. degree from Brown University, Rhode Island, and the honorary A.M. degree from the same institution in 1815. Semple's main literary works were *The Faithful Servant of God Exemplified in the Life and Death of Samuel L. Straughan,* and the invaluable *History of the Rise and Progress of the Baptists in Virginia* (published in 1810). Of his 12 children only four survived him. He was buried in the cemetery of Bruington Baptist Church. J. L. ROSSER

SEMPLE-BROADDUS COLLEGE. Established in 1857 at Centre Hill DeSoto County, Miss., with William Carey Crane (*q.v.*) president, who had lofty ambitions for the school and named it DeSoto University. Backed by Baptists of North Mississippi, East Arkansas, and West Tennessee, it was chartered in 1858. The school collapsed, however, in 1860 when Crane moved to Louisiana. J. L. BOYD

SENTINEL. See SUNDAY SCHOOL BOARD.

SEPARATE BAPTISTS. The name is associated with the Edwards-Whitefield revival of the 1740's in New England, though as a movement, the Separate Baptists came into largest expression in Virginia and North Carolina through the evangelistic labors (after 1755) of Shubal Stearns (*q.v.*), his companions, and his successors.

The Great Awakening found spiritual life at a low ebb in the state churches (Congregational) in New England. It is not surprising, then, that the revival excitement had no appeal for the unawakened and formal church members of the region, nor that the revival folk felt uncomfortable in their cold, even hostile churches. The result was that many who favored the revival withdrew to form small groups, admission to which was on the basis of a vital personal faith. These seceders were called Separates or New Lights. For many of them it was but a short step, and a logical one, to require personal faith prior to baptism. These became known as Separate Baptists. The turning of these Separates to Baptist views was in considerable numbers: Between 1740 and 1768 Baptist churches in New England increased, in spite of persecution, from 23 to 69. After 1768 their growth was even more rapid. Baptists have been called the "true heirs" of the Great Awakening.

Shubal Stearns, pastor of a Separate Congregational church at Tolland, Conn., becoming a Baptist, left his pastorate in Aug., 1754, to begin a ministry on the western frontier. He and his party first moved to join his brother-in-law, Daniel Marshall (*q.v.*), at Mill Creek, Va. Then they lived for a few months in Hampshire County, Va. His preaching did not meet with expected success there, and he was ready to move on when a letter came from friends in North Carolina telling of the great spiritual needs of that area. Thus, in the summer of 1755, Stearns and a small company of followers traveled across Virginia and settled on Sandy Creek in Guilford (now Randolph) County, N. C. A church of 16 members, including Daniel Marshall, was quickly organized. The community was indeed receptive to the Baptist message, and within a few years the membership of the church reached 600. This and other churches were formed into Sandy Creek Association. Preachers went from the area into South Carolina, Georgia, and Virginia, where the first church was formed in 1760. The preaching of the Separates was novel in content as well as in delivery, and spread rapidly in Virginia. The Separate Baptists "emphasized the depravity of man, the atonement through Christ, consciousness of a 'new birth' and the baptism of believers as an outward sign of a previous inward change." They used strong gestures and a singular tone of voice. By 1774 there were 55 Separate Baptist churches in Virginia.

The Sandy Creek Association divided in 1770 into three associations, one in each of the Carolinas and one in Virginia. The South Carolina association was called the Congaree, while the Virginia body was called the General Association of the Separate Baptists of Virginia. The rise of the Separates to prominence in Virginia during the Revolutionary period contributed to raising the issue of religious liberty in that state. By their objections to, and repeated refusals of, taking licenses of the state in order to preach as dissenters, they brought the question into sharp focus. After severe persecution they were successful in securing, with the help of some liberal statesmen, the desired liberty for all; and, in the course of their striving for that liberty, they discovered unity with the Regular Baptists. The union of Regular and Separate Baptists occurred in Virginia in 1787 and in Kentucky in 1801. Differences which had delayed the union concerned the use of confessions of faith, theology, and disciplinary practices. Once united, the two groups soon dropped party labels.

In Kentucky and Indiana isolated groups of Separate Baptists continued to exist under the name of the oldest Separate association of the former state, the South Kentucky. Several other associations developed in the next century, and in 1912 the district associations were bound together in the General Association of Separate Baptists in Christ. The general body is made up of six associations having a combined membership of above 7,000 members. The theology of the group tends to be Arminian.

BIBLIOGRAPHY: *Minutes of the General Association of Separate Baptists in Christ* (1954). A. H. Newman, *A History of the Baptist Churches in the United States* (1898). G. Ryland, *The Baptists of Virginia, 1699–1926* (1955). W. W. Sweet, *The Story of Religion in America* (1950). R. G. Torbet, *A History of the Baptists* (1950). WILLIAM L. LUMPKIN

SEPARATE BAPTISTS, CURRENT. A Baptist group traceable to the evangelical Separate Baptists who began and multiplied during the Great Awakening in the middle of the 18th century in America. The present denomination of Separate Baptists is descended from the early churches and associations which did not join in the various unions between Regular and Separate Baptists that were effected toward the end of the 18th century and at the beginning of the 19th. The Separate Baptists, as presently constituted, hold to a generally fundamentalist doctrine and believe in three ordinances—the Lord's Supper, foot washing, and baptism by immersion only. Their main strength is in Tennessee, Kentucky, Indiana, and Illinois. They have no central headquarters, no definite periodicals, and no colleges or seminaries, because they hold to "the point of their ministers being called, endued, and taught by the Holy Ghost to preach the Gospel." The group is organized into six district associations which convene annually. The membership reported in 1956 was 7,065 in 87 churches.

JUDSON BOYCE ALLEN

SEPARATION OF CHURCH AND STATE, BAPTIST CONCEPT. *Meaning.*—The phrase "separation of church and state" has been part of Baptist vocabulary throughout the history of its movement. In 17th-century England where the government and the church were both under the authority of the sovereign, and all the people belonged to both the church and the state, the goals of the *separatists* were simple and clear. They were both responsible and responsive to God and wanted churches in which they could pray as the Spirit led them, and in which they could worship according to the dictates of their own consciences rather than as authorized by Parliament and the king in the Book of Common Prayer. It was for these simple desires that many were persecuted.

In other parts of the world where the union of the church with the state has made the former into an agency concerned primarily with social control of the people, the meanings of "separation" have been similar to those in 17th-

and 18th-century England. In most of these areas Baptists have been in the advance guard of the "free-church movement."

Fundamentally, however, "separation of church and state" has referred to a set of presuppositions and to a distinctive type of spiritual experience rather than to a social or political pattern. Fundamentally it means a personal commitment to God of such nature that the legislative and administrative functions of political agencies are crowded out from the soul's relationship to his Creator and Saviour. The specific political goals sought by Baptists with reference to separation have, of course, varied with the particular political situation and the particular time and place.

The basic need for separation.—The necessity for "separation of church and state" arises in Baptist thought out of their concepts of the church and of the state. Taking the New Testament fellowship of believers as the essence of church experience rather than the Old Testament idea of a chosen nation, Baptists have consistently rejected the idea of a church which automatically includes all the people. This means that the church involves a population which, although it overlaps with the state's population, is not coterminous with it. The church consists of and deals with those who have personally responded to God in Christ. While the church seeks to reach all if possible, the state must consist of all citizens and must administer the law with equity to all residents.

Furthermore, the state must be under the authority of a government. Rulers are chosen by a wide variety of techniques, including succession by inheritance, by election, by force, and by economic power. An objective study of the history of governments and of the spiritual waywardness of many persons of great political power makes the subjection of the church to the authority of the state into a spiritual compromise. In contrast, Baptists have looked unto Christ as the church's only authorized authority.

Separation is also necessitated by the difference in the methods of influence which are appropriate to the two institutions. The state operates by authority. It functions by means of the police and military powers, by taxation and coercion. Such methods work where law and order, social control, and social structure are the end results desired. These methods, however, are powerless to produce love, inner moral rectitude, faith, or hope. They are completely useless in an effort to bring the experience of forgiveness of sin, a fellowship with God, and a life under the guidance of the Holy Spirit. On the other hand the teaching and preaching of the message, the winsome act of love and concern, the humble and kindly admonition, and the lifting of the soul in worship and praise are the time honored methods of the church.

Finally, when the church and the state combine, the church tends to surrender its prophetic function and usually ceases to express the judgments of God upon the principles and practices of the human beings who make up the state. The church then becomes an instrument of the *status quo,* a steward of the moral and spiritual values as seen in a particular society. The church becomes a conserver, or a preserver, rather than a dynamic force in the experiences of the people. Such dethroning of the Lord of the church leaves people unable to discern the right or true course of life in the unfolding drama of history, and accordingly produces social disorganization and stagnation.

The continuing application.—Since "separation of church and state" is rooted in the deeper realities of human and spiritual relationships, each generation in each nation must continually strive toward the discernment and the interpretation of those principles in life. The principle is not a simple legal code which if once enacted lasts as a permanent achievement. If the spiritual roots die, the trunk cannot long stand. Neither does it consist of a set political platform which requires certain patterns of organization, certain forms of government, or certain administrative procedures. All forms of government can provide for separation of church and state. Conversely, modern techniques for education and for public opinion control can vitiate the freedom of the church even where there is provision for it in the instruments of government.

Among Baptists in America, certain principles have been quite generally held as serving the spiritual objectives described. First among these has been the guarding of the freedom of the church by keeping it financially independent of the state. This rests on the conviction that the church loses more than it gains by accepting funds from governments, and that as long as the church rests on the stewardship of the people of God it can proclaim the will and the message of God, but no longer.

Similarly, there has been awareness that the church must have an educational program of its own by means of which to convey Christian truth and by which to cultivate the insights and commitments which are embryonic in the new birth. While it is not necessary that the church monopolize the education of a person, nor indeed that the church take a great fraction of the child's educational experience, the educational program of the church must be vitally a part of the church and under its own control and support. Baptists have been prominent in the support of public education as the means of common learning.

The practice of separation also will require the church to maintain an aloofness from participation in economic interests of special groups and from partisan political efforts. This aloofness, however, will not stand in the way of nurturing people into adequate knowledge, interests, and social skills so that Christians become distinctively effective as citizens. Separation does not mean withdrawal from participation in group life; nor does it mean an acquiescence in the sins which have become so entrenched as to become part of the group at-

MARYLAND STATE CONVENTION (*q.v.*) HEADQUARTERS, Baltimore. Houses all departments of work. Purchased in 1952, now valued at $80,000.

LOUISIANA BAPTIST BUILDING, Alexandria. Headquarters since 1948 for eight departments of work. Present value, $100,000.

MISSISSIPPI BAPTIST CONVENTION (*q.v.*) BUILDING, Jackson. Since 1942 it has housed all departments, including *Baptist Record.* Replacement value $250,000.

KENTUCKY BAPTIST BUILDING, Middletown, near Louisville. Built for $425,000 in 1957. Home of the *Western Recorder* and 14 departments.

titudes or standards. Rather, separation means leaving the people so free in their spiritual seeking, their acts of worship, and their expressions of faith that the mind of Christ might be known through the people who are "in the world but not of it." C. EMANUEL CARLSON

SEPARATISM. A belief held by those people, the extremists of the English Reformation, who appeared about the middle of the 16th century as a variety of sects, or "gathered" churches. Their meetings, called conventicles and prohibited by law, their great diversity of doctrine, and their occasional and unfortunate tendency toward agitation involved them in controversy with the authorities and sometimes with each other. Differentiated from the Puritans, some of whom nonetheless wished to worship separately by "purified" forms, Separatist adherents probably originally used the term "Puritan" to indicate the thoroughness of their reformation. Often linked with the Separatists, the Independents opposed hierarchism and agitated for legal congregational independence and local church autonomy. As early as 1608, the term "Separatist" designated those Independents who sought separation from the established church, freedom from control of secular government and loss of its financial support, and a status equivalent to the modern free church. Separatism, in a renewal of activity, revolted against the Church of England under the Elizabethan settlement and, as a result of the Vestiarian Controversy, by 1593 was considered a serious menace. About 1594 a group of English Separatists formed in Holland the first English Anabaptist congregation of which there is certain knowledge. In 1607–08 Separatist congregations from Gainsborough and Scrooby reached Amsterdam, Holland. Here the Scrooby group joined with the exiled Ancient church and subsequently moved to Leyden; finally, part of them, the "Pilgrim Fathers," crossing the Atlantic on the *Mayflower,* planted Congregationalism in the New World. The Gainsborough group began a separate existence in Amsterdam and in 1611 or 1612 furnished a nucleus for the beginning of General Baptists in England. English Particular Baptists, originating about 1638, likewise had Separatist antecedents. Separatism, through the trials of persecution and exile, its fortunes varying with the changes in political rule, finally shared in the Protestant triumph of the right to dissent and to nonconformity, and made a profound impact upon the social, political, and religious life of England and the world.

BIBLIOGRAPHY: E. Arber, ed., *The Story of the Pilgrim Fathers, 1606–1623 A.D.; as Told by Themselves, Their Friends, and Their Enemies* (1897). C. Burrage, *The Early English Dissenters in the Light of Recent Research, 1550–1641,* 2 vols. (1912). H. W. Clark, *History of English Nonconformity from Wyclif to the Close of the Nineteenth Century,* 2 vols. (1911, 1913). H. Gee and W. J. Hardy, *Documents Illustrative of English Church History Compiled from Original Sources* (1896). M. M. Knappen, *Tudor Puritanism, A Chapter in the History of Idealism* (1939). K. S. Latourette, *A History of Christianity* (1953). W. J. McGlothlin, *Baptist Confessions of Faith* (1911). R. G. Torbet, *A History of the Baptists* (1952).

GLEN LEE GREENE

SERMON ON THE MOUNT. See JESUS CHRIST.

SERMON PREPARATION. The science of the preparation of a discourse based upon Scripture. Homiletics is the "sacred rhetoric" which has developed in relation to Christian preaching. This science evolved from two antecedents—Hebrew preaching and ancient rhetoric. From the Hebrew tradition came the idea of delivering to others a message which had come from God. The prophets were the grandest representatives of Hebrew preaching; they delivered God's message as it welled up in them and had to be shared. The successors of the prophets—the scribes—interpreted the message which had been written down. From them came the idea of the homily—a talk or running comment based on Scripture. The earliest Christian preaching followed this form or pattern. As the Christian message went out to the Gentile world, and as trained rhetoricians became Christian converts, the more formal rules of Greek and Latin rhetoric were applied to Christian sermons. These rules dealt with composition, arrangement, style, delivery, and memory. Thus the best rules of secular speech were applied to the Christian message, and sermons became less simple talks and more formal discourses. The union of Hebrew preaching and Greek rhetoric produced a new science—homiletics, the art of preparing and delivering messages based on Scripture. V. L. STANFIELD

SERMONS, BAPTIST. *Seventeenth-century sermons.*—Baptists were few in number, and most of the influences of society beset them, but among them, even in this early day, were some preachers of power. John Bunyan's (*q.v.*) published sermons, at first disappointing, were in the popular tradition of Bunyan's attractiveness and power. His vivid dramatic touch and imagination are clearly shown in such sermons as the "Barren Fig-tree" in Fish's collection. Benjamin Keach (1650–1704) was the most widely read Baptist of his day, publishing many devotional works in addition to *A Gold Mine Opened,* a volume of 40 sermons. He showed fine insight into Scripture, clear and convincing argumentation, and a simple, forceful style. Sermons of this period were few and, aside from Bunyan and Keach, scarcely read.

Eighteenth-century sermons.—Among English Baptists of this century, three names stand out: Robert Robinson (1735–90), Andrew Fuller (*q.v.*) (1754–1815), and William Carey (*q.v.*) (1761–1834). Robinson and Carey published few sermons. Fuller's sermons were widely read and wielded influence in both England and America. His method was expository and his thought solid. The sermons were unadorned, orderly, and logical. They contained no oratory but deep thought.

There was little publication among American Baptists until near the end of the century. The sermons of Isaac Backus (*q.v.*) (1724–1826) were full of solid sense, decided conviction, and strong appeal. His chief concern was religious freedom. The learned Samuel Stillman's sermons on the Stamp Act (1776) and on the French Revolution (1792) were masterpieces. Richard Furman (*q.v.*) (1755–1825), better known for his work in education and organization, nevertheless circulated many sermons in tract form, such as "America's Deliverance and Duty" and "A Sermon Occasioned by the Death of Honorable Major General Alexander Hamilton." Thomas Baldwin (1753–1826) published 30 sermons, most of which were preached on particular occasions. Dargan states that they are remarkable sometimes for acute and original argument and sometimes for tender and overflowing feeling and sincerity. His greatest sermon was his General Election sermon (before the Massachusetts legislature) which went through three editions. The sermons of Jonathan Maxcy (*q.v.*) (1768–1820) read well but were delivered brilliantly. They were clear and strong in thought, following Jonathan Edwards. They showed fine imagination and noble style but little emotional appeal. Most of the published sermons of this period were of a polemic cast; they defended Baptist principles, replied to attacks of pedobaptists and the challenge of debate, or gave reasons assigned by ministers from other denominations for becoming Baptists. This was a transition period. At the beginning the battle cry of soul freedom was heard; at the close the strains of the anthem of victory were heard.

Nineteenth-century sermons.—1. English Baptists. To the early part of this century belong two giant Baptist preachers, Christmas Evans (*q.v.*) (1766–1838) and Robert Hall (*q.v.*) (1764–1831). Evans, the Welshman, preached in his native tongue, but translations are available. These sermons exhibit a marvelous faculty of description which appeals to warmhearted people. They are extremely fanciful but have peculiar power.

Most of Hall's published sermons are topical, although he usually gave at least one exposition each Sunday. Hall presented a fine combination of philosophic thought and biblical truth. His sermons were thoughtful, accurate, and logical, with depth of feeling. The only real criticism of Hall's style is "its too uniform stateliness." Two of Hall's most famous sermons are "Modern Infidelity," a classic of clarity, insight, and feeling, and "The Death of Princess Charlotte," one of the great funeral orations of all time. John Foster declared him to be "unquestionably the greatest preacher in the world." Dugald Stewart says that Robert Hall continued in his writings the beauty of Johnson, Addison, and Burke without their imperfections. Mackintosh says that "whoever wished to see the English language in its perfection must read the writings of that great divine, Robert Hall."

The mid-19th century belongs to the justly famous Charles Haddon Spurgeon (*q.v.*) (1834–92), who had published nearly 2,500 sermons with an average sale of over 25,000 copies of each. (They are still being reprinted.) These sermons have been translated into German, Danish, Swedish, French, Italian, and Welsh. In doctrine Spurgeon was an evangelical Calvinist. In his early ministry he showed great theological power, although it was his later work that found its place in popular reading over all the world. Seafarers took his sermons to sea and soldiers to their barracks. Many were converted in reading them.

The latter part of the 19th century belongs peculiarly to Alexander Maclaren (1826–1910). This last of these great preachers was a profound and instructive Bible scholar. His published sermons are many—more than 20 volumes—almost all being expository. The Anglican Bishop of Manchester said of them, "In an age which has been charmed and inspired by the sermons of Newman and Robertson of Brighton, there were no published discourses which, for profundity of thought, logical arrangement, eloquence of appeal, and power over the human heart, exceeded in merit those of Dr. Maclaren." His sermons are thoughtfully evangelical with thorough and accurate exegesis. Robertson Nicoll once said that a man who read one of Maclaren's sermons must either take his outline or take another text. Maclaren's sermons, next to Spurgeon's, have been the most widely read of all time and are as well known in America as in England. "Logic on fire" is used aptly to describe them.

2. American Baptists. Adoniram Judson's (*q.v.*) sermon assigning the reasons for his change of belief about baptism was published and given wide circulation in 1817. During this period great numbers of sermons were published—in pamphlets, in the *National Preacher,* in the *Baptist Preacher,* in the *Southern Baptist Preacher,* in minutes of associations and conventions, and in magazines and newspapers. Daniel Sharp of Charles Street Church in Boston published more than 20 sermons, the most famous of which is his funeral sermon for Governor Eustie in 1824. Francis Wayland (1796–1865) published more than 20 sermons. Solidarity, rather than grace and nicety, was characteristic, as shown by his sermon on "The Moral Dignity of the Missionary Enterprise" and his expository gem, "A Day in the Life of Jesus of Nazareth." Richard Fuller (*q.v.*) (1804–76) was a preacher of the grand type, influenced by Robert Hall. He was at his best on state occasions. His two finest sermons are probably "The Cross," preached at the Baptist convention in Baltimore, Md., in 1841, and "The Desire of All Nations," preached at Richmond, Va., in 1846. Jeremiah Bell Jeter (*q.v.*) left no sermons, but many of his writings are expanded sermons. Sermons of Andrew Broaddus I (*q.v.*), Jesse Mercer (*q.v.*), and James Clement Furman (*q.v.*) are available in historical collections.

Sermons of roughly the first half of this century were scriptural, Calvinist, and non-creedal. Books of sermons were published by William Parkinson (two volumes), George Leonard (one volume), William T. Brantly, Sr. (*q.v.*) (one volume), Francis Wayland (three volumes), Rufus Criswold (one volume), C. W. Hodges (one volume), and Richard Fuller (one volume).

The latter part of the 19th century was marked by many American Baptist published sermons. George C. Lorimer (1838–1904) was particularly appealing to young people, his best-known book of sermons being "Messages of To-day for Men of Tomorrow." One of the preachers in greatest demand was Adoniram Judson Gordon (*q.v.*) (1836–95), whose best-known work was entitled *Grace and Glory*. There are those who consider him the most-read sermonizer of the 19th century. Better known as a teacher of preaching than as a publisher of sermons was John Albert Broadus (*q.v.*) (1827–95); however, his *Sermons and Addresses* still repay the thoughtful reader. James Robinson Graves (*q.v.*) (1820–93), father of Landmarkism, noted mostly for debate and argumentation, has a widely read book of sermons full of logic and imagination, entitled *Satan Dethroned and Other Sermons*. This century cannot be left without mention of the great Negro preacher of Richmond, Va., John Jasper (*q.v.*) (1812–1902), whose sermon on "The Sun Do Move" is known all over the Southland. His other sermons are preserved in William Eldridge Hatcher's (*q.v.*) biography. Two collections deserve note—Louthan's *The American Baptist Pulpit* and Love's *The Southern Baptist Pulpit*, both containing a wide selection of representative sermons.

Twentieth-century sermons.—F. B. Meyer (*q.v.*), Benajah Harvey Carroll (*q.v.*), Edgar Young Mullins (*q.v.*), and George Washington Truett (*q.v.*) began their work in the last century but belong primarily to the 20th century. The devotional works of Meyer, a great teacher, continue to bless countless numbers. Many of Carroll's sermons were published posthumously. Dargan observes that these sermons were often beyond the range of the hearers, with excessively long introductions. However, the intellectual height, depth, and breadth of Carroll's preaching were remarkable. Mullins' sermons were for the most part occasional sermons but given with clarity and stateliness. Truett's personality and voice made him great. His many published sermons, including radio sermons in leaflets, were simple, plain, reiterative, and liberally spiced with homely illustrations. There is intense emotional surge in his written sermons. Truett was not a controversialist but a preacher of the simple gospel. He exercised tremendous influence by both spoken and written word.

The great radio preacher of the first half of the 20th century was Harry Emerson Fosdick, a brilliant and controversial figure. He published as many as nine books of sermons in addition to leaflet radio sermons every Sunday for a quarter of a century. Few agree completely with Fosdick, but his written sermons have been the most influential since Maclaren. That influence sometimes convinced his readers—sometimes antagonized them. It is difficult to read Fosdick and remain neutral. He is the best example of the modern trend to life-situation preaching. By use of apt illustration, he marches with logic, paragraph by paragraph, to lead the way to some new truth, some fresh solution. Space allows only a mention of Walter Rauschenbusch (*q.v.*), prophet of a social awakening, of Cornelius Woelfkin, of Charles W. Gilkey, and their contemporaries, as well as the countless books of sermons coming from the press today whose merits are as yet untested by time.

BIBLIOGRAPHY: J. A. Broadus, *Sermons and Addresses* (1886). W. Cathcart, ed., *The Baptist Encyclopedia* (1880). W. Collier, ed., *The Baptist Preacher: Consisting of Monthly Sermons from Living Ministers* (Oct. 1827–Aug. 1830). E. C. Dargan, *A History of Preaching* (1905–12). A. Fuller, *The Complete Works of the Reverend Andrew Fuller* (1832). R. Fuller, *Sermons by Richard Fuller Preached During His Ministry with the Seventh and Eutaw Place Baptist Churches, Baltimore, 1874–1876* (1877). R. Hall, *Complete Works* (1828). A. Judson, *Christian Baptism; a Sermon Preached in the Lal Bazar Chapel, Calcutta, Sept. 27, 1812* (1812). H. Keeling, ed., *The Baptist Preacher. Original-Monthly* (1842–59). W. T. Louthan, *The American Baptist Pulpit at the Beginning of the Twentieth Century* (1903). J. F. Love, *The Southern Baptist Pulpit* (1895). J. Maxcy, *A Sermon Preached on the Lord's Day, Oct. 1, 1812* (1812). *The Missionary Jubilee: An Account of the Fiftieth Anniversary of the American Baptist Missionary Union* (1865). A. H. Newman, ed., *A Century of Baptist Achievement* (1901). *Southern Baptist Preacher* (1839–41). C. Woelfkin, *Religion, Thirteen Sermons* (1928).

DOTSON M. NELSON, JR.

SEVENTH DAY BAPTISTS. A group which sprang from the Baptists in the English Reformation, differing from them only in their observance of the seventh day (Saturday) as the sabbath. The first known Seventh Day Baptist church in England was organized before 1650; the first in America was organized at Newport, R. I., in 1671. For administrative purposes the Seventh Day Baptist General Conference was organized in 1801, and for closer fellowship churches are organized into nine associations. Denominational work is carried out through the Seventh Day Baptist Missionary Society, American Sabbath Tract Society, Women's Society, Seventh Day Baptist Board of Christian Education, Seventh Day Baptist Historical Society, and Seventh Day Baptist Memorial Fund. The colleges founded by this group are located in Alfred, N. Y.; Milton, Wis.; and Salem, W. Va. The School of Theology is a part of Alfred University. The Denominational Building and Publishing House are located in Plainfield, N. J. The *Sabbath Recorder*, a denominational paper, is the leading publication. Seventh Day Baptist churches include 62 American and 67 foreign, with a total membership of 8,812. Sabbath school membership in 1955 was 2,983; churches reported 102 baptisms; and gifts per capita were $43.56. EVALOIS ST. JOHN

SEVENTY-FIVE MILLION CAMPAIGN. A five-year program, 1919–24, which provided greatly increased support for all Baptist missionary, educational, and benevolent work in the states and Southern Baptist Convention and set a new pattern for Baptist co-operation.

While the campaign was formally projected by the Southern Baptist Convention meeting in Atlanta, Ga., May 14–18, 1919, need of a marked advance in support of missions, Christian education, and benevolences was obvious to numerous individuals in advance of that action. Several factors helped prepare the way for such an advance. The general prosperity of the people, marked unity of Southern Baptists, experience in giving large sums of money in war bond drives and campaigns for support of the war work of the Y.M.C.A. and Salvation Army, and the contacts of Baptist men in the armed services with citizens of foreign countries—all these showed the need and possibility of a more aggressive Southern Baptist mission program.

James Bruton Gambrell (*q.v.*), in his president's address in 1919, challenged Baptists to "adopt a program of work commensurate with the reasonable demands upon us." A committee of 29, including state secretaries, was named with George Hays of Kentucky, chairman, "to consider financial aspects of our denominational program."

This committee met immediately to survey its task. The short time before Convention adjournment was insufficient for planning the work in detail and setting up an organization which would raise the needed funds. It did recommend, "in view of the need of the world and this hour and . . . the numbers and ability of Baptists," that the Convention adopt a financial goal of $75,000,000, this sum to be subscribed at once and paid over a period of five years. Another recommendation was that the Executive Committee of the Convention, in conference with the executive secretaries of the general boards of the Convention and the state boards, be requested to distribute the total sum sought among the several objects due to participate in the campaign, and that the $75,000,000 objectives be apportioned among the various states of the Convention.

On motion of Lee Rutland Scarborough (*q.v.*), the following substitute motion on the personnel and procedure for the conduct of the campaign was adopted:

> We recommend that a committee of one member from each state be appointed by this Convention to plan, in co-operation with the state agencies and the organized agencies of this Convention, for a simultaneous drive to be taken each year in cash for a proportionate part of the $75,000,000, the campaign being so arranged that the part to be raised each year shall be larger than that of the year before, and thus secure the largest part in the last year of the five.
>
> We further recommend that this committee, in conference with the general boards and the state boards, be requested to distribute the amounts among the different objects fostered by the Conventions and state boards, outside of local church support, and apportion the amounts to the various states.

The group in charge of the campaign held its first session in Atlanta, Ga., June 4–5, 1919, in conference with the Executive Committee of the Southern Baptist Convention and the executive secretaries of the general and state boards. Here the general outline of the campaign for funds was agreed upon; Nashville, Tenn., was chosen as campaign headquarters, and the Baptist Sunday School Board was requested to provide the needed quarters for the campaign staff. Quotas for the various objects to be included in the campaign were fixed; the co-operating states were asked to assume certain proportions of the total financial objective; Scarborough, president of the Southwestern Baptist Theological Seminary, Fort Worth, Tex., was named general director of the campaign, and Isaac Jacobus Van Ness (*q.v.*), corresponding secretary-treasurer of the Baptist Sunday School Board, Nashville, was made treasurer.

The commission at this time allocated to the several causes embraced in the campaign the following sums: Christian education, $20,000,000; foreign missions, $20,000,000; home missions, $12,000,000; state missions, $11,000,000; ministerial relief, $5,000,000; orphanages, $4,700,000; hospitals, $2,125,000; National Memorial Baptist Church, Washington, D. C., $175,000.

States co-operating in the work of the Convention were asked by the Executive Committee to assume responsibility for raising the following quotas: Alabama, $4,000,000; Arkansas, $3,200,000; District of Columbia, $400,000; Florida, $1,000,000; Georgia, $7,500,000; Illinois, $1,200,000; Kentucky, $6,500,000; Louisiana, $3,325,000; Maryland, $750,000; Mississippi, $3,500,000; Missouri, $2,925,000; New Mexico, $250,000; North Carolina, $5,500,000; Oklahoma, $2,250,000; South Carolina, $5,500,000; Tennessee, $4,000,000; Texas, $16,000,000; and Virginia, $7,500,000.

Later, Benjamin Cabell Hening, North Carolina, was designated assistant director; Mrs. W. J. Neel (*q.v.*), Georgia, W.M.U. director; Mrs. Janie Cree Bose, Kentucky, W.M.U. organizer; Thomas Bronson Ray (*q.v.*), Virginia, survey director; Hight C Moore, Tennessee, director of religious publicity; and Frank E. Burkhalter, Texas, director of secular publicity. The various state executive secretaries were asked to serve as state directors, set up their state organizations, suggest to the district associations a proper proportion of the state financial goal, and ask the associations to suggest quotas to the individual churches. Executive secretaries of the general boards of the Convention were asked to assist in every way possible the promotion of the campaign objectives.

The executive secretaries of the general boards

were: James Franklin Love (*q.v.*), Foreign Mission Board; Baron DeKalb Gray (*q.v.*), Home Mission Board, Isaac Jacobus Van Ness, Sunday School Board, and William Lunsford (*q.v.*), Relief and Annuity Board.

Each of the remaining seven months of 1919 was designated for a special phase of promoting the campaign as follows: July, preparation; August, information; September, intercession; October, enlistment; and November, stewardship. It was planned that the campaign would reach its goal during the days of Nov. 30 to Dec. 7, and this period was designated Victory Week.

An intensive and extensive program of information, inspiration, and enlistment was set up by the campaign headquarters with a view to reaching as many churches and individual Baptists as possible with the whole message and aim of the forward movement. To carry this message to the people, both the Baptist and the secular newspapers were employed, along with millions of tracts, letters, posters, pamphlets, and charts. In addition, denominational leaders, pastors, laymen, and women went everywhere addressing conventions, associations, rallies, and churches in an effort to arouse and enlist all Southern Baptists in attaining the goals that had been set. Many churches on the foreign mission fields assumed a share in this undertaking.

Although unfavorable weather prevailed in much of the South as Victory Week approached, many of the churches exceeded their goals. As a result, the campaign director was able to report to the Washington convention in May, 1920, that a total of $92,630,923 had been subscribed to the campaign, and that $12,237,827 had been paid in.

Large spiritual, as well as financial, results characterized the campaign. The promoters had asked the pastors and presidents of Baptist colleges and seminaries to use the last week end in October to call upon their young people and students to publicly dedicate themselves to whatever types of full-time Christian service to which they felt Christ was calling them. From 600 pastors and numerous school presidents the general director received the names of more than 4,000 volunteers. In numerous churches and schools the response of the young people was followed by revivals.

While not all the pledges reported were redeemed in cash, the money that did come in represented a marked advance over what Southern Baptists had been giving to denominational causes during the years immediately preceding the campaign. In his final report upon the campaign to the Memphis, Tenn., session of the Convention in May, 1925, Scarborough reported the total cash received was $58,591,713.69.

Expenses of the general headquarters in Nashville for the inauguration and the conduct of the campaign for five and one-half years was $427,878, or less than three fourths of 1 per cent of the amount collected. Total expenses of general headquarters and the 17 state offices in the projection and conduct of the entire campaign amounted to less than 4 per cent of the total cash collected.

It was largely as the result of a widespread financial depression that the total receipts were $17,000,000 less than the original goal and $34,000,000 less than pledged. This financial crisis left state and Convention causes heavily in debt, since programs had been projected in anticipation of reaching the objective. These debts on state and Convention causes continued to grow, following the close of the campaign, until at one time they amounted to approximately $18,000,000.

It should be remembered that the campaign did raise $58,000,000 in cash for Baptist missionary, educational, and benevolent causes. This was several times what the same people were giving previous to the campaign. In five years state and associational missions received $9,900,785 from the campaign. Home missions received $6,622,725, as compared with only $8,188,730 in the preceding 74 years of its history. Foreign missions received $11,615,327, as compared with about $12,500,000 in the preceding 74 years. Seminaries, schools, and colleges received $16,087,942, or nearly as much as in all their years preceding.

Raising this amount introduced a new era in Baptist giving and missionary work. It lifted the sights of Baptists individually and as a denomination to a new realization of their potential in giving and missionary work. For the first time "laymen, women, young and old" "by the thousands" were brought into active, aggressive service to enlist Baptist people in giving to their churches and mission causes. For the first time an active effort was made to reach every Southern Baptist in a program of giving. Probably for the first time the average member of the average Baptist church was called upon to make a really significant missionary gift.

Results of the campaign listed in the report of the campaign commission to the Convention meeting in Washington, D. C., in May, 1920, would apply also at the close of the campaign five years later:

> It is confidently believed by your Commission that the denomination has come out of this year's struggles, labors, and achievements with an enormously increased profit account. The denominational assets have been greatly multiplied and strengthened. This large sum of money, when collected and appropriated to the various causes, will mean much to the glory of God and the extension of Christ's kingdom; but the money is not all the gain of the campaign. There are many other phases of denominational and spiritual enrichment coming out of this South-wide and world-wide victory.

A few of the other victories listed in the report were a greater unification of Southern Baptists, an enlarged vision, a more effective organization for promoting their denominational work, an increased liberality, a deeper spiritual life, and a stronger indoctrination of the people in the Bible faith. The financial goal of the campaign was not reached, but the contribution of the campaign to Baptist life can hardly be overestimated. FRANK E. BURKHALTER

SHACKLEFORD, JOHN (b. Caroline County, Va., 1750; d. Fayette County, Ky., 1829). Patriot and pioneer preacher in Virginia and Kentucky. At the age of 22, he was converted and called to preach but delayed ordination until 1778, after undertaking the care of Tuckahoe Church in Caroline County, Va. For being a Baptist preacher and being present at the constitution of Piscataway Church on Mar. 13, 1774, he was imprisoned with others in Essex County for a week and released on bond. In 1788 Tuckahoe Church experienced a great revival under his care. Because of lack of support for his family, he migrated to Kentucky in 1792. Arriving there at the time his early colaborer, Lewis Craig (1741–1824), was retiring from the pastorate of the South Elkhorn Church in Fayette County, Shackleford was called at once to the pastorate of that church, which he served for about 37 years. His pastorate was marked, on the one hand, by revival and success, and on the other, by strife and dissension due to the Elijah Craig (1743?–1808)—Jacob Creath, Jr. (1777–1854) dispute, Licking Association disturbances, and Campbellism. From Jan., 1808, to Dec., 1809, Shackleford was pastor of the Forks of Elkhorn Church, preaching one Sunday each month.
LEO T. CRISMON

SHACKLEFORD, JOSEPHUS (b. Portsmouth, Va., Feb. 6, 1830; d. Tuskegee, Ala., May 5, 1915). Baptist preacher, teacher, soldier, member of the Alabama legislature, and editor. A graduate of Mercer University, he married Ann Cordelia Stow on June 18, 1855. They had eight children. His pastorates included churches at Moulton, Ala., Tuscumbia, Ala., and Forest City, Ark. His school career started at Moulton where he was president of the Baptist Female Institute. He also held positions with schools in Forest City, Ark., and Morgan County, Ala., and was president of North Alabama Baptist Collegiate Institute and Normal School at Leighton, Ala. During the Civil War he served as captain of a cavalry unit, and later he became a regimental chaplain in the Southern army. *The Christian Herald,* a Baptist paper, started by Shackleford at Moulton, was moved to Tuscumbia at the beginning of his pastorate there in 1867. Five years later, this paper was moved to Nashville, Tenn., and he started *The Tuscumbia Times.* Although the paper was absorbed shortly into *The North Alabamian,* he continued as owner and editor until he sold out in 1875. He served as a member of the state legislature in 1882–83, while he was with the Morgan County School. He served as associate editor of *The Alabama Baptist* in 1886.

BIBLIOGRAPHY: T. M. Owens, *History of Alabama and Dictionary of Alabama Biography* (1921).
G. NELSON DUKE

SHAKI BAPTIST HOSPITAL. See NIGERIA, MISSION IN.

SHANGHAI, UNIVERSITY OF. See CHINA, MISSION IN.

SHAPE NOTE MUSIC. A perversion of the Guidonian gamut (notes of the musical scale) which developed in America at the beginning of the 19th century. It grew out of the efforts of singing schoolteachers to apply solfeggio in their classes. The manuals of the early American singing schools were notated in systems of four shape notes whose solmization was fa, sol, la, and mi. These popular fasola books contained the first combination of both hymns and tunes of the camp meeting songs. Their singing master compilers were the first to record the unwritten Baptist folk tunes. They, also, used the standard hymn tunes and earlier American fuguing tunes, adding to them many tunes of their own composition. Adopting the fuguing tune form, they changed the Baptist folk tunes into this form when they were given notation. Single tunes now appeared in three and four parts. The singing remained unaccompanied.

Although fasola singing was not denominationally orientated, many Baptists from the early 19th century sang from shape note hymnbooks; and individual Baptists had important places of leadership in the movement. Thousands of Southerners, many of them Baptists, still use a later edition of B. F. White's *The Sacred Harp,* first published in Philadelphia in 1844.

Among the shape note singers, a change from the four syllable and four shape note system to a seven syllable and seven shape note system gradually took place. Some years after the Civil War, with the establishment of a universally accepted seven shape note system and with the resultant autonomy in shape note circles, musical development became more separated between rural and urban music, between established denominations such as the Southern Baptists and the little rural denominations such as the Primitive Baptists whose hymn tunes were, as late as 1933, still primarily fasola tunes.

The publishers of shape note books became commercially important. They eventually became under almost complete domination of the gospel song type, after which their music degenerated to its present (1956) low musical and textual level. FLOYD PATTERSON

SHELBY COUNTY BAPTIST CAMP. Given to the Shelby County Baptist Association in 1943 and opened for use in 1948 near Chestnut Grove (Shelby County), Ky. Royal Ambassador and Girls' Auxiliary camps have been held annually by the associational Woman's Missionary Union since 1934 with the use of facilities of Camp Kavanaugh. Operated eight weeks annually, the camp provides for all church organizations with emphasis upon youth. Facilities are rented to Sulphur Fork Baptist Association and churches outside Shelby County Association.
ELDRED M. TAYLOR

SHELBY FEMALE COLLEGE. Located at Shelby, N. C., and operated by King's Mountain Association. The school was founded in 1874, and in the years which followed was alternately a coeducational and a girls' school. In 1877 the school was chartered by the state legislature and was given some land by C. C. Durham of Shelby. Although called a college, the school did not add a collegiate department until 1883. In that year the boys' and girls' departments were separated, and the girls' section, under R. D. Mallary and his wife, became Shelby Female College. In 1885 King's Mountain Association adopted the school and pledged itself to remove the institution's debt. In 1887 Mallary left the school because of ill health, and a few years later the college was closed. D. L. SMILEY

SHEPARD, JOHN WATSON (b. Gladeville, Tenn., Jan. 28, 1878; d. Atlanta, Ga., Aug. 12, 1954). Missionary, educator, pastor, and author. He was ordained to the gospel ministry at Gladeville, Tenn., Dec. 11, 1900. His academic study included a year at Bethel College, Hopkinsville, Ky., followed by four years in Richmond University, Virginia, where he received the A.B. and M.A. degrees (1900). In four years he graduated from the Southern Baptist Theological Seminary with Th.M. and Th.D. degrees (1906). In 1918 he earned the M.A. degree in education from Chicago University, and in 1926 he completed one year of residential credits toward the Ph.D. degree in George Peabody School for Teachers, Nashville. His pastoral ministries included student pastorates while in the seminary, interim pastor of First Baptist Church, Rio de Janeiro, Brazil; and pastor, First Baptist Church, Morgan City, La., 1930. He was appointed missionary to Brazil by the Foreign Mission Board on Apr. 4, 1906; he served until 1930. After language study in Recife, 1906, he was selected by the Brazilian Baptist Convention in Bahia to found a college and seminary in Rio. Foundation work in 1907 led to the creation of Rio Baptist College and Seminary of Rio de Janeiro. An elementary school opened in Mar., 1908, with 12 pupils. Five years later a high school was opened. The furlough year of 1912–13 was devoted to raising funds for the campus in Rio, thus enabling the college to open. The school is now known as the John W. Shepard Memorial College. In 1913 the Girls' School and Normal School were founded. By 1918 the Rio Seminary included 10 professors and about 75 students, and the college included 70 teachers with 835 students. Shepard served as president for 24 years. Joining the faculty of Baptist Bible Institute, New Orleans, he was professor of missions and religious activities, 1930–35; professor of New Testament interpretation and missions, 1936–37; and professor of New Testament interpretation and Greek, 1937–47, serving as head of the department. From 1930 to 1943, he was director of religious activities, during which time more than a dozen churches were organized. As an author, he wrote extensively in Portuguese and English. In Portuguese were published *Os Actos dos Apostoles, O Preador, O Epistola de Thiago,* and numerous leaflets and small books. Major English works were *The Christ of the Gospels* (1939) and *The Life and Letters of the Apostle Paul* (1950). Unpublished manuscripts include "Education on a Christian Basis" and "How Jesus Trains His Workers." He married Rena Groover on June 6, 1906, and to them were born six children: Ida (Shepard) MacRae, Alice (Shepard) Kimbrough, Mary Gertrude Shepard, Evelyn Rena Shepard, Samuel Groover Shepard, and John Watson Shepard, Jr. FRANK STAGG

SHERWOOD, ADIEL (b. Fort Edward, N. Y., Oct. 3, 1791; d. St. Louis, Mo., Aug. 19, 1879). Minister and educator. His father, Adiel Sherwood, colonel in the Revolutionary army and intimate friend of George Washington, once financially well-to-do, lost most of his wealth, and Adiel Sherwood had to work to earn his living while in school. He attended, with interruptions, Granville Academy, 1810–12; Middlebury College, Vermont, 1813–15; and Union College, Schenectady, 1816–17, where he graduated. During this period he also taught school in Kingsbury and Queensbury (N. Y.). He spent one year in Andover Theological Seminary, 1817–18. While in Boston he met and became a devoted admirer of Luther Rice, under whose influence he became a part-time city missionary and field representative for the Massachusetts Baptist Missionary Society. Late in 1818, because of the threat of tuberculosis, he went to Georgia for his health.

He carried with him helpful letters of recommendation to the Baptist leaders of the state, and quickly rose to a position of active and successful leadership in many phases of Baptist life. For the next 40 years he made substantial contributions to every phase of his denomination's progress.

He was ordained as minister by Bethesda Church, Greene County, Ga., Mar., 1820. He was effective as an active itinerant preacher, evangelist, and pastor of churches. By him churches were organized, Bible and mission societies were promoted, and Sunday schools were founded. In 1827 an extraordinary revival began in the four churches he served; and, according to Sherwood, "before the gracious influences had ceased more than sixteen thousand persons were baptized." During 1828 he rode on horseback more than 3,000 miles to preach 333 sermons in 40 counties.

His educational services were remarkable. He taught school in Savannah, Waynesboro, Eatonton, and Penfield, and in Oglethorpe and Greene counties. On the collegiate level he taught in Columbian College, 1836–38, during which time he raised sufficient money to retire a large debt that had distressed the school for a decade; and in Mercer University, where he organized the theology department, 1839–41. In 1820 he wrote the resolution which resulted in the organization of the Georgia Baptist Convention in 1822, of which he was treasurer and clerk 1822–33. He offered in 1831 the resolution which resulted in the founding in 1833 of Mercer Institute (later Mercer University). He was president of Shurtleff College, Alton, Ill., 1841–45. In 1846 he became secretary for a short time of the American Baptist Indian Missionary Society, with headquarters in Louisville, Ky. Then he became president of Masonic College, Lexington, Mo., 1848–49, and Marshall College, Griffin, Ga., 1857–61.

His crowded life included much travel. He was adept in winning friends. During his lifetime he saw every President of the United States except Washington and personally knew an unusual number of United States senators, judges, congressmen, and state governors. The Baptist leaders of America were his associates.

For 50 years, beginning in 1819, he regularly wrote articles that were published in Baptist periodicals. In addition to pamphlets his books were: *A Gazetteer of the State of Georgia* (1827), 4 editions; *Jewish and Christian Churches* (1850), 2 editions; and *Notes on the New Testament* (1856), 7 editions.

In 1856 his physician advised him to move to a warmer climate. He went back to Georgia where he lived until 1865. He then moved to St. Louis, Mo., where he lived until his death in his 88th year. He was married twice: first to Mrs. Anne Adams Early, May 17, 1821, who died in Nov., 1822; then to Emma C. Heriot, May 6, 1824, Charleston, S. C. She died Feb. 13, 1883. HANSFORD D. JOHNSON

SHILOH CHURCH. The oldest Baptist church in North Carolina, continuously active, authentic records show, since Sept. 5, 1729. (Baptists came to North Carolina as early as 1663.) The *Diary of John Comer,* Sept. 27, 1729, refers to a church founded earlier than Shiloh. Comer says:

> This day I received a letter from ye Baptist church in North Carolina, settled about two years (in ye year 1727) since, by Mr. Paul Palmer, signed by John Parker, John Jordan, Benjamin Evans, John Parker, John Brinkley, Michael Brinkley, Thomas Darker, James Copland, John Welch, Joseph Parke, William Copland, Joseph Parker.
>
> This church consists of 32 members, it meets at Chowan.

Formerly accepted as a reference to the Shiloh church, Comer's reference to a church in Chowan has been verified by other sources; it was not the church in Pasquotank which in 1812 became known as Shiloh. Joseph Parker, pastor of the Chowan church, moved to Bertie County about 1730, where he became pastor of the Meherrin church. According to tradition the Meherrin membership was composed of followers of Parker who moved from Chowan to Bertie to resume worship in his church.

The Shiloh Church, like Chowan owing its beginnings to Paul Palmer (*q.v.*), was first called the Church in Pasquotank, then the Church in Camden when Camden County was established. Originally meeting at the home of Pastor William Burgess, the church erected a small building in 1736 which was replaced in 1757. A General Baptist church at organization, reconstitution about 1757 made it a Particular church. Pastors led in evangelistic extensions in northeastern North Carolina and into Virginia. By 1800 Shiloh had established arms at Pungo, in Princess Anne County, Va., Cowenjock, Sawyer's Creek, Knobscrook, Flatty Creek, and Yoppim, with churches developing as a result at Black Water and London Bridge. William Burgess, John Burgess, and Davis Briggs were among the early pastors at Shiloh. G. W. PASCHAL

SHORTER, ALFRED (b. Wilkes County, Ga., Nov. 23, 1803; d. Rome, Ga., July 18, 1882). Philanthropist. He was the only son of Jacob Shorter of Washington, Wilkes County, Ga., and Delphia Bankston, widow of Lawrence Bankston, III. Alfred Shorter lost his mother in infancy, and before he reached young manhood was made an orphan by the death of his father. At 16 he went to Monticello, Ga., and worked as a clerk in a relative's store. He invested his savings in real estate in Alabama, Mississippi, and Georgia, and thus laid the foundation of his large fortune. During the Civil War he held large quantities of cotton and used his wealth to help support the Confederacy. In 1834 he married a wealthy widow, Mrs. John Baldwin, nee Martha Harper. They had no children but reared a niece and nephew of his wife, Martha Harper and Charles M. Harper. He moved from Monticello to Floyd County in 1837 and in 1847 to Rome, where, for the remainder of his life, he was active in church and civic affairs. Though he did not have a college education, he was not lacking in culture and was greatly interested in education. During the administration of Governor Colquitt (1877), he purchased the building of Cherokee Female College (chartered in 1873), founded Shorter College, and presented it as "a gift to our daughters." His wife died Mar. 22, 1877. They are buried in Myrtle Hill Cemetery at Rome. CECIL F. LEA

SHORTER COLLEGE. A coeducational liberal arts college located at Rome, Ga., founded in 1873 as a school for girls, and under the control of the Georgia Baptist convention since 1902. The school was organized by a group of Rome businessmen, including Alfred Shorter (*q.v.*), as a private stock company. Property known as Shelton Hill, located in the center of town, was bought and equipped. A charter was granted Sept. 20, 1873, to a board of trustees headed by Alfred Shorter. When the first president, A. B. Townes, resigned after one year, Luther Rice Gwaltney, who first conceived the project, assumed the presidency and remained until his call in 1876 to the presidency of Judson Institute in Marion, Ala.

In 1876 R. D. Mallory became president. The next year, because of debt obligations and threat of suit, the entire property was transferred to Alfred Shorter, who changed the name to Shorter Female College as a memorial to his wife. The college opened that September with a strong faculty, a large student body, and the nucleus of an endowment. For 33 years the college occupied buildings provided by Shorter.

In effect, Shorter College has been Baptist since its beginning, for Alfred Shorter stipulated that its trustees should always be members in good standing of some Baptist church. In 1902 it became a part of the Georgia Baptist Mercer system, and the Georgia Baptist convention was empowered to elect its trustees.

In 1910 Azor W. Van Hoose was called from Brenau College to be president of Shorter, and under his leadership a movement was launched by the trustees to move the college to a new and larger site. J. L. Bass, of Rome, gave his home, Maplehurst, and 20 acres one and a half miles west of Rome for the new campus. An adjoining tract of 135 acres was purchased and, with the citizens of Rome contributing $300,000, the new buildings, built in 1911, were placed on the crest of the hill overlooking the city.

In 1923 the college was admitted to membership in Southern Association of Colleges and Secondary Schools, being recognized as a standard four-year college of liberal arts and sciences. In 1924 it was admitted to the Association of American Colleges, in 1925 to American Council of Education, in 1929 to the American Association of University Women, and in 1931 was placed on the approved list, Association of American Universities. The Georgia Board of Education grants to qualified Shorter College graduates professional teaching certificates for elementary and high schools. The college holds membership in the Southern Association of Baptist Colleges and Schools of the Southern Baptist Convention and is affiliated with the Georgia Baptist convention.

Paul M. Cousins served as president, 1933–48. In 1937 the college was admitted to membership in the National Association of Schools of Music, and in 1947 a new gymnasium and a faculty apartment house were built. Two new faculty apartments and a new president's home were built during the presidency of Charles W. Burts, 1948–53. George A. Christenberry became the 12th president in July, 1953.

In 1949 the college became coeducational and in 1955 began a long-range development program to produce funds for the renovation of old buildings and the building of a new library-administration building and a men's dormitory. Enrolment in 1955 totaled 404. Total number of graduates since founding was 1,850. Total endowment for 1955 was $478,128, and the property value was $609,363. Total budget for 1955–56 was $312,810.

PRESIDENTS OF THE COLLEGE

A. S. Townes, 1873–75
Luther Rice Gwaltney (acting), 1875–76
Rollin D. Mallory, 1876–82
Luther Rice Gwaltney, 1882–90
A. J. Battle, 1890–98
T. J. Simmons, 1898–1910
Azor W. Van Hoose, 1910–21
W. D. Furry (acting), 1921–22
D. J. Blocker, 1922–25
W. D. Furry, 1925–33
Paul Mercer Cousins (acting), Mar.–April., 1933
C. R. Wilcox, Apr.–June, 1933
Paul Mercer Cousins, 1933–48
Charles W. Burts, 1948–53
George A. Christenberry, 1953–

CECIL LEA

SHUCK, HENRIETTA HALL (b. Kilmarnock, Va., Oct. 28, 1817; d. Hong Kong, Nov. 27, 1844). First American evangelical woman missionary to go to China and the second woman missionary to open a school in Macao for Chinese children. Her father, Addison Hall, was pastor of the Morattice and Wicomico churches for nearly 35 years. In a revival with James Barnett Taylor (*q.v.*) preaching, Henrietta, not quite 14 years of age, made a public profession of faith and was baptized by her pastor, Jeremiah Bell Jeter (*q.v.*). In May, 1834, John Lewis Shuck (*q.v.*) proposed to her that she go to China as his wife. She had been led to consider missionary service by reading the story of Ann Hasseltine Judson (*q.v.*). Two days after their marriage, Sept. 8, 1835, they were set apart as missionaries of the Triennial Baptist Convention, and they sailed Sept. 22. They arrived in Singapore, Mar. 31, where they spent five months studying the Chinese language. They arrived in Macao, a Portuguese settlement off the coast of China, in the middle of Sept., 1836. More than a year after leaving America they received their first letters from home. In Mar., 1842, the Shucks settled on the island of Hong Kong just after it had been ceded to Great Britain, and in May they constituted the first evangelical church in China. At the age of 27 years Henrietta Hall Shuck died in the birth of her fifth child and was buried in Hong Kong.

BIBLIOGRAPHY: T. S. Dunaway, *Pioneering for Jesus* (1930). F. S. Heck, *In Royal Service* (1913). E. C. Routh, *Evening and Morning in China* (1950).

E. C. ROUTH

SHUCK, JOHN LEWIS (b. Alexandria, Va., Sept. 4, 1814; d. Barnwell Courthouse, S. C., Aug. 20, 1863). First Baptist missionary to China. He was educated at Virginia Baptist Seminary, now University of Richmond. He was appointed missionary to China in 1835 by the Triennial Convention. Arriving at Macao in 1836, he baptized the first Chinese convert in 1837. With Dean, Roberts, and others, Shuck organized the first Baptist church in China at Hong Kong in 1843. He returned to the United States in 1845 and was appointed missionary to Canton in 1846 by the Foreign Mission Board of the Southern Baptist Convention. He was transferred to Shanghai, and with Matthew Tyson Yates (*q.v.*) and others he organized the first Baptist church in Shanghai in 1847, and became the first pastor. Following the death of his second wife in 1851, he returned to the United States and resigned from the Foreign Mission Board in 1853. Serving under the Domestic Board (Home Mission Board of the Southern Baptist Convention), he worked among the Chinese in California, 1854–61, and he organized the first Chinese Baptist church in America. J. B. HIPPS

SHUKQUALAK FEMALE COLLEGE. Established in 1880 at Shukqualak, Miss., with L. M. Stone principal. The school, which had an enrolment of 91 in 1885, moved to Meridian in 1893, then back to Shukqualak where it enrolled 142 students in 1897. On June 11 of that year the school's buildings were destroyed by fire.

J. L. BOYD

SIMMONS, EZEKIAS Z. (b. Tishomingo County, Miss., Mar. 1, 1846; d. San Francisco, Calif., Aug. 8, 1912). Missionary to China. A Confederate soldier as a very young boy, Simmons was baptized by Mark Perrin Lowrey (*q.v.*), a Confederate general, at Kossuth, Miss., in 1861. After studying at Georgetown and Bethel colleges in Kentucky, Simmons was appointed a missionary to Canton, China, in Oct., 1870, and on Nov. 23 he married Maggie McClamrock. They served as missionaries to China from 1870 to 1912. Later, home in the United States for a while because of the health of his wife, Simmons worked with the Chinese in California under the American Baptist Home Mission Society. He was among the first to suggest establishment of the Woman's Missionary Union Training School in Louisville, Ky., and helped found the great Chinese Baptist Publishing Society at Canton.

BIBLIOGRAPHY: J. L. Boyd, *A Popular History of the Baptists in Mississippi* (1930). L. S. Foster, *Mississippi Baptist Preachers* (1895). H. A. Tupper, *The Foreign Missions of the Southern Baptist Convention* (1880). C. B. HAMLET III

SIN. The fundamental description of actual human existence. It is described by various words in the Bible, covering various shades of meaning, such as, missing the mark, deviating from the right path, guilt before God, open rebellion, and unfaithfulness to the divine covenant. Thus sin is an act of the will, a result of the moral freedom with which the Creator has endowed man. Man the creature has chosen to rebel against his Maker, deviate from the divine will, and follow his own devices and desires. Because of sin man stands guilty before God.

Original sin.—The record of Adam in Genesis reflects the pilgrimage of every human soul. Man, like Adam, has acted as though he were the sole determiner of his destiny. He has chosen to be like God and thus has made the primal choice which lies behind all of man's other choices. In the depths of man's being lies the mysterious decision whereby he has rejected God and enthroned self. Man's original sin is the sin of Adam, the will to be like God. It is a sin strangely compounded of pride and anxiety; pride, which makes man want to be the center of his life, and anxiety, which makes him fear that God cannot manage his life as well as he can manage it himself. The mystery of the original sinful act of rebellion is that it must go on repeating itself. Once man has chosen to rebel against God, every subsequent act and decision is colored by this decision. The barred gate and the angel with the flaming sword which shut Adam and Eve out of paradise indicate the continuing coloration of sin. Once man has made the original sinful choice, his remaining existence is determined as sinful. Man is in bondage; every choice he makes, good though it may be, is colored by his sin.

The bondage of sin and the divine image of man.—Man is not what he ought to be. He was made to live in God's image, but, by his primal act of sin, he has denied his true destiny and chosen its opposite. He who was made to live in fellowship with God and to walk with him in the garden in the cool of the evening, has chosen to live for himself. He is thus a being in contradiction, although he still retains his sense of right and wrong. Man is a sinner; but he knows that he is a sinner and what he ought to be. The demands of God, originally gracious expressions of the Father's will, have become the binding cords of obligatory law. Man knows that truth, beauty, and righteousness are real, and he even sets up his standards for them, but every attempt to realize his goals is twisted by pride. Indeed, at this point man comes nearest to a failure to recognize his own sin. When he boasts of his ability to do good and know truth, he desires to set himself right with his Creator and becomes blind to his sinful condition. Man's effort to put himself right with God by his own efforts is the last stranglehold of sin upon him. Salvation by works is man's effort to retain his pride and burst open the gate into paradise. He does not want, as an humble and penitent supplicant, to kneel and await the gracious opening by God. Nowhere is the bondage of sin so apparent as in this instance. The very moral law, which expresses God's will, tempts man to believe he can put himself right with God by his own effort; in this way the law becomes man's bondage.

Sin is a disease which has affected man's spiritual constitution. The capacity to reason and think logically, the ability to investigate the secrets of nature and employ them for personal ends, moral conscience and the sense of obligation, religious consciousness and the sense of the holy which is evident in the multiplicity of man's religions—all these are reminders of what God intended man to be. But none of them can lead man back to God. The form of the divine image remains, but its content of fellowship with God is lost, and none of man's capacities is sufficient to enable him to regain it. Man's spiritual constitution is not lost, but perverted. His religions, philosophies, moral systems, and scientific investigations fail at the point where they are most needed. Man knows that he is self-centered but cannot save himself from it. Education and psychology cannot deliver man from sin and pride and produce a perfect society. On the one hand, man carries within him the vestiges of original righteousness, the signs of what God intended him to be. On the other hand, every God-given capacity man has is so contaminated by his primal sinful choice that none of his capacities can function as they ought unless God in his mercy makes man anew.

Acts of sin.—Paul's letters and the writings of John are full of ethical injunctions. Sin as a primal choice and as a disease results in continued acts of sin, colored by the original act which determined man's existence against the will and plan of God. Man's continuing acts of sin are colored, therefore, by the strange mixture of pride in his own powers and anxiety about his own existence which are the characteristics of sin. Man's sins range from the level of sensuality to the level of his intellectual and spiritual life (Gal. 5:19–21). Even in Christians sinful acts are not absent, but their decision of faith replaces the primal act of sin, and their existence is radically transformed by God's grace into existence in fellowship with God. The old Adam continues in man, as he remains in the flesh, even though by God's grace he does not live according to the flesh. Man deceives himself if he says he has no sin, for temptation is always present; but the redeemed man has chosen Christ over against the rejection of God which originally put man outside the garden. God sustains man's existence in his fellowship, and man no longer sins with Adam's sin of rebellious pride and anxious care. His acts of sin are deviations from the choice that directed his whole existence on God, which is faith. Because of faith, solely dependent upon God's grace, man can dare to affirm the final perseverance of the saints. The redeemed man does not fall into any cult of holiness or perfectionism, for he is conscious of his frailty and weakness; but he dares to believe that He who has begun his good work in him will carry it through to its end (Phil. 1:6).

See also Depravity; Fall of Man; Sin, Original; and Traducianism.

Bibliography: E. La B. Cherbonnier, *Hardness of Heart* (1955). R. Niebuhr, *Nature and Destiny of Man* (1941).

E. C. RUST

SIN, ORIGINAL. Refers to Adam's sin and its relationship to his posterity. Paul traced sin back to Adam (Rom. 5:12–21) without discussing inherited guilt, stating simply that death came upon all "for that all have sinned" (Rom. 5:12). Augustine (*c.* 400), viewing all as seminally present in Adam, and Cocceius, developing the federal theory that Adam was the representative of the race, taught inherited guilt as well as disability. Baptists, though they agree that all are sinners by nature and are unable to save themselves, differ in their view of inherited guilt. For example, Boyce followed the federal theory; Conner denied inherited guilt.

See also Depravity and Sin.

Bibliography: R. Neibuhr, *The Nature and Destiny of Man* (1942). J. Orr, *God's Image in Man and Its Defacement in the Light of Modern Denials* (1905).

R. E. GLAZE, JR.

SINGING SCHOOLS. Present-day Baptist schools of church music had their root in what is commonly known as the "singing school" which was first conducted in New England in the late 17th and early 18th centuries, particularly in the Massachusetts Bay Colony.

Owing largely to a scarcity of hymnbooks, congregational singing had become poor, slow, and at times unbearable. The more progressive church leaders began to demand better psalm-singing. The solution to the situation lay in a program of music education through the formation of singing schools to give instruction in music notation and note reading. Among leaders in the movement were three ministers, Thomas Symmes, John Tufts, and Thomas Walter, nobly supported by Cotton Mather and Nathaniel Chauncey.

Material for the new training program was provided by Tufts in several pamphlets from 1712 to 1721. In these he utilized his own adaptations of a system of solmization known today as the *fa-sol-la* (Sacred Harp) system.

The singing schools created a desire for further study and practice, which, in turn, resulted in the formation of many church choirs even though opposition to such organizations caused serious dissention in many churches.

The main path of the singing school movement appears to have been from New England to Pennsylvania, thence southward and westward. Since these latter areas were fast becoming Baptist strongholds, the singing school teachers and songbook compilers found Baptist churches to be fertile ground for their activities.

Toward the middle of the 19th century, William (Singin' Billy) Walker (*q.v.*) and the Sacred Harp movement, which he championed, gained in popularity and dominated the singing school field for many years. Walker's *Southern Harmony*, first published in 1835, sold more than 600,000 copies. He, in about 1866, wavered from his original concepts of note reading and came to accept the seven-shape *do-re-mi* system which seemed to be aligned with progress. The shape-note plan now began to dominate the singing schools which were finding their way increasingly into Baptist churches.

There were many indications of varied opinions among Baptist leaders about 1900 as to the wisdom of a denomination-sponsored program of music training. However, there was a growing interest in the possibility of not only singing schools, but a comprehensive music education program under denominational leadership which resulted in an action of the Southern Baptist Convention in 1944 instructing the Sunday School Board through its Church Music Department to lead in "a constructive, educational program of church music."

One phase of the work planned and promoted as a result of this action is schools of church music. Not only theory and note reading are taught, as was done in the original singing school, but many other aspects of church music are taught, thus making these schools more comprehensive than their predecessors.

See also MUSIC EDUCATION, BAPTIST.

CLIFFORD A. HOLCOMB

SINLESSNESS OF JESUS. The belief that Jesus Christ was free from the nature, acts, and possibility of sin is the widest statement of his sinlessness. Some modern thought has challenged this historic doctrine, either in part or as a whole, on the grounds that it undermines the humanity of Christ. Hans Windisch, although holding that Jesus did not sin, has rejected the idea that it was impossible for Jesus to sin because of his likeness to men in temptation (Heb. 4:15). Christology based on belief in the incarnation of the Son of God in flesh has found this view unsatisfactory because of the implications that the Son can be alienated from the Father. In an effort to defend himself against the charge of docetism, Karl Barth has declared himself in favor of the view that Jesus possessed a fallen human nature. Although this has previously been suggested on the basis of Romans 8:3, it seems contrary to Paul's cardinal teaching on Jesus as the Last Adam and head of a new humanity (I Cor. 15:22–45). One of the most radical rejections of the sinlessness of Jesus is that of Nels F. S. Ferre, who strongly insists that rebellion is a necessity for true freedom and that Jesus too shared in this rebellion. His effort to prove this from II Corinthians 5:21 is superficial exegesis, and the idea that freedom is gained through rebellion seems the very opposite to the truth. Freedom is found in obedience and lost in disobedience. Jesus lived in perfect freedom because of his perfect obedience to the Father's will. The sinlessness of the Son of God is the standard by which all human sin is measured.

See also CHRISTOLOGY.

BIBLIOGRAPHY: G. C. Berkouwer, *The Person of Christ* (1954). DALE MOODY

SIX MILE BAPTIST ACADEMY. Organized in the summer of 1910 at Six Mile, S. C., with V. E. Rector as principal. One of the Home Mission Board mountain schools, the academy was supported by Piedmont, Pickens, and Twelve Mile River Baptist associations. The site was donated by the heirs of James E. Hagood, of Pickens, and promoters of the school had as their purpose "to give the bright mountain boys and girls an opportunity to get an education near their home." Enrolment in 1919 reached 186, but by 1928 Six Mile Academy had ceased to operate as a Baptist school. ALBERT E. TIBBS

SIX-PRINCIPLE BAPTISTS, GENERAL. A group, originating in England in the 17th century, which emphasizes the "six principles" listed in Hebrews 6:1–2: Repentance, faith, baptism, laying on of hands, the resurrection of the dead, and eternal life. The fourth principle is the only one truly distinctive of the group. They refuse to fellowship any Baptist who does not believe in the laying on of hands after conversion as a token of a special impartation of the Holy Spirit. In England Six-Principle Baptists first appeared around the middle of the 17th century. They were strict communion in practice and Arminian in theology. Even though an association was organized in 1690, there were never more than 11 churches. In America they began to appear in 1639, and in 1653 a congregation was formed in Rhode Island, with some of the members coming from the original First Baptist Church at Providence. They gradually drifted to Arminianism. Their fellowship steadily increased until the period of the Revolution. At one time they led in 13 of the 36 towns of Rhode Island. Following the Revolution they declined because of neglect of education, literature, and the loss of an aggressive spirit. In 1944 they reported three churches with 280 members living mostly in Rhode Island and Pennsylvania. In 1949 they reported three Sunday schools with 284 enrolled.

ALBERT MCCLELLAN

SKEPTICISM. The word is derived from the Greek *skeptein,* meaning to reflect or consider. It is the philosophical belief that certain knowledge is impossible because the senses are often untrustworthy; reasoning, often fallacious; and evidence, often incomplete. Skepticism is Immanuel Kant's view that man can know only objects with which he has experience (the phenomenal world); he cannot know the world in itself (the noumenal world). Skepticism represents the concept of Descartes that to arrive at certainty one must be thoroughgoing with doubt. "The only thing that can't be doubted," said Descartes, "is that I am a doubter." As a concept of Herbert Spencer skepticism means that God and immortality belong to the "unknowable."

BIBLIOGRAPHY: W. E. Hocking, *Types of Philosophy* (1939); W. E. H. Lecky, *History of the Rise and Influence of the Spirit of Rationalism in Europe* (1910).

CHARLES A. TRENTHAM

SLAUGHTER, CHRISTOPHER C. (b. Sabine County, Tex., Feb. 9, 1837; d. Dallas, Tex., Jan. 25, 1919). Cattleman and philanthropist. At 18 years of age, Slaughter began ranching in Palo Pinto County, Tex., and accumulated a fortune from which he gave over $1,000,000 to Texas Baptist causes. Included in his contributions were $50,000 toward correlating Texas Baptist colleges, $60,000 to the endowment of Baylor University, and $500,000 to Baylor Hospital.

Slaughter paid all mortgages on the *Baptist Standard* and bought half-interest in it; he helped erase debt on the First Baptist Church, Dallas, where he later served as a deacon. Slaughter, who from young manhood had prayed, "Master, give me a hand to get and a heart to give," served on the executive board of the Baptist General Convention of Texas and was its president, 1898–1901. He was vice-president of the Baptist General Convention of Texas and of the Southern Baptist Convention. Charter director of Baylor Hospital, he was a member of the first board of trustees of Southwestern Baptist Theological Seminary and treasurer of the Texas Baptist Education Commission, which he helped organize in 1897.

BIBLIOGRAPHY: *Baptist Standard* (Jan. 30, 1919). J. M. Carroll, *A History of Texas Baptists* (1923). *Who Was Who in America,* 1897–1942.

FRANK E. BURKHALTER

SLEDD, BENJAMIN (b. Bedford County, Va., Aug. 27, 1864; d. Wake Forest, N. C., Jan. 4, 1940). Author, educator. Sledd received from Washington and Lee University the M.A. degree in 1886 and the Litt.D. degree in 1907. He was a special student at Johns Hopkins University, 1886–87, and traveling fellow, Albert Kahn Foundation, 1914–15. As professor of modern languages, 1888–94, professor of English, 1894–1938, professor emeritus of English, 1938–40, he was a favorite of Wake Forest College students for his love of poetry and keen sense of humor. Sledd was editor of *La Princesse de Cleves,* 1892, and author of *From Cliff to Scaur* (1897), *The Watchers of the Hearth* (1901), *The Fire from Heaven* (a play) (1930). He wrote numerous poems, including "At Lexington," "A Memorial Poem" (1913), "A Virginian in Surrey" (1914), "To England," "Afterthought" (1919), "The Dead Grammarian" (1924), "The Modernist and the Megatherium" (1927). Sledd married Neda Purefoy, June 11, 1889, and they had three children.

BIBLIOGRAPHY: *A Dictionary of North American Authors* (1951). *North Carolina Authors, A Selective Handbook* (1952). G. W. Paschal, *History of Wake Forest College* (1943). *Who Was Who in America* (1943).

G. A. HENDRICKS

SMEDLEY, JOSEPH (b. Westmoreland County, England, Dec. 5, 1792; d. Aug. 27, 1877). Employed by United States Government in 1835 as teacher and missionary to the Indians, and in 1844 by the Indian Mission Association as general missionary. He worked among the Choctaws, Creeks, and Cherokees in an area ranging some 80 miles west of Fort Smith along the Arkansas and Canadian rivers. He organized the first Negro Baptist church in Fort Smith in 1856. His wife, the former Mary Radcliff, whom he married Dec. 26, 1820, in Mansfield, England, died July 6, 1836, leaving seven children. The Civil War interrupted all his missionary work except occasional visits to his churches. He was buried at Shiloh near Mansfield, Ark.

DAVID C. HALL

SMITH, ARNOLD SHANK (b. Mill Town, Chambers County, Ala., May 18, 1864; d. Alexander City, Ala., Apr. 16, 1930). Pastor and denominational leader. He secured his early education in Shiloh, Mill Town, and Lafayette. He entered Howard College in 1887, and graduated as president of his class in 1891.

In 1884 he was licensed to preach, being ordained the following year. In 1892–93 he was a student in the Southern Baptist Theological Seminary, Louisville, Ky. He married Mamie Lou Watt in LaGrange, Ga., on June 6, 1894. Following her death, he was united in marriage on Dec. 21, 1898, to her sister Anne Blanche Watt at Forest Home, Ala. Children by his first marriage were Mary Mildred and Ely Watt, and by his second marriage, Manly Arnold, Kathleen Roberta, and Charles William.

He was pastor of several churches. Among them were First, Roanoke; First, Phenix City; Elyton; Columbia; and Dadeville. His last pastorate of 30 years duration was at Alexander City. He was awarded the D.D. degree in 1912. He was a member of the Baptist state executive board, 1917–26, of Howard College board, 1917–30, and he was vice-president of the state convention in 1920.

BIBLIOGRAPHY: Alabama Baptist State Convention, *Annual* (1930). T. M. Owen, *History of Alabama and Dictionary of Alabama Biography* (1921).

J. E. BERKSTRESSER

SMITH, CHARLES EDWIN (b. Conway, Mass., July 1, 1852; retired July 15, 1909; d. date unknown). Missionary to Africa. Converted at 15 years of age, Smith moved to Judsonia, Ark., in 1872, and was educated in Marshalltown, Iowa; Judsonia, Ark.; and Southern Baptist Theological Seminary. Appointed as a missionary to Africa Mar. 20, 1884, Smith served first at Lagos, then 16 years at Ogbomosho, and after 20 years of service retired due to ill health. His distinctive work was founding a theological seminary in 1901, the outgrowth of teaching the Bible to a class of adults. Smith kept before the African churches and schools the ideal of self-support.

BIBLIOGRAPHY: C. E. Maddry, *Day Dawn in Yoruba Land* (1939). G. W. Sadler, *A Century in Nigeria* (1952).

E. C. ROUTH

SMITH, LUMAN LUCIUS (b. Adams County, Ohio, Dec. 28, 1863; d. Oklahoma City, Oklahoma Territory, Nov. 23, 1903). Frontier Baptist missionary and denominational statesman. Educated in Kansas colleges, he married Carolyn Van Aken in 1893, served Kansas and Oklahoma pastorates, and was missionary for the American Baptist Publication Society in 1899. In an effort to combat dissension, disunity, and duplication characteristic of frontier mission work, he began in 1899 a movement which resulted in the unification of the Oklahoma Baptist Convention and the Oklahoma Baptist State Convention in 1900. Elected missionary to the southern half of the state, by extensive travel, wise Christian diplomacy, and friendly sympathy, he won confidence, disarmed opposition, and welded factions in the convention's fellowship. In 1901 he was unanimously elected as first corresponding secretary of the Oklahoma Baptist State Convention. Tireless service under adverse circumstances were considered contributing factors to his untimely death at the age of 39. R. L. MCCLUNG

SMITH, SARAH JULIA GUTHRIE (b. Louisville, Ky., Mar. 4, 1827; d. Louisville, Ky., July 24, 1901). Benefactor of Baptist institutions. Daughter of James Guthrie (1792–1869), Kentucky statesman and financier and secretary of the treasury under President Franklin Pierce, she married John Lawrence Smith, American scientist and teacher, June 24, 1852. In 1869 Mrs. Smith gave a lot 200 feet square at First and St. Catherine streets in Louisville and $5,000 for the Louisville Baptist Orphans Home (now Spring Meadows). Later, in 1888, she announced to John Albert Broadus (*q.v.*) that she planned to give $50,000 to Southern Baptist Theological Seminary for the erection of a library building as a memorial to her two nieces, Sarah Julia and Mary Elizabeth Caperton, daughters of her sister, Mrs. John Caperton, and her two nephews, William Beverly and Lawrence Smith Caldwell, sons of her sister, Mrs. William B. Caldwell. The building was completed and dedicated in May, 1891. When the seminary moved to 2825 Lexington Road in 1926, the library wing of Norton Hall was designated Memorial Library in recognition of Mrs. Smith's gift. Baptized into Walnut Street Baptist Church, Louisville, on June 7, 1851, Mrs. Smith remained a member there until her death. LEO T. CRISMON

SMOKY MOUNTAIN ACADEMY. The pioneer high school in upper Sevier County, Tenn., established by the Sevier Association of Baptists under the leadership of James Franklin Hale in 1915. The school was at first called Sevier County Baptist High School. After the school came under the supervision of the Home Mission Board of the Southern Baptist Convention about 1918, the name was changed to Smoky Mountain Academy. After the withdrawal of Home Mission Board support, the school was made a project of the Woman's Missionary Union of Knox County. It has also been generously aided by Sevier Association, alumni, and interested friends. Hundreds from every hill and cove of Sevier County attended the school, have gone to college, and are now in many professions. A large percentage of the graduates have become teachers. Emphasis has been given to thorough academic work and Christian training. Smoky Mountain Academy is one of the few Baptist mountain schools to survive. In 1955 the total enrolment was 56. The academy graduated eight from the grammar grades and five from high school. HARLEY FITE

SMYTH, EARL BROOKS (b. Mart, Tex., Aug. 27, 1890; d. Dallas, Tex., May 12, 1943). Business executive, benefactor to Baptist causes. Educated at Baylor University, Smyth was president of First National Bank of Mart and Fidelity Union Life Insurance Company of Dallas, and vice-president of Central Texas Oil Company of Mart. Chairman of the executive committee of Baylor University's board of trustees and a member of the executive board of the Baptist General Convention of Texas, Smyth, with his wife, Rosalind (Kyser) Smyth, set up endowment for Baylor University and the Foreign Mission Board now amounting to $285,000, and $10,000 for the benevolent fund of First Baptist Church, Dallas. A. B. CULBERTSON

SOCIAL CHANGE IN THE SOUTH. The South is in the midst of a major transition that is affecting every phase of the social, economic, and political life of the region. This fact has significance for the churches of the South and for church-related agencies and institutions. The South to which they will minister in the future will be noticeably different from the area they have served in the past.

No one factor contributes more to change in the South than rapid industrialization. Prior to 1860 whatever business and industrial life there was in the area was merely a supplement of the prevailing "plantation economy." While the South has not yet caught up with the national norm, beginning about 1910 its share of the nation's manufacturing began to increase and the trend has continued.

Most of the industrial expansion in the South, in the first half of the 20th century, has been financed and directed from outside the region. In 1939 in seven states of the Southeast 27.2 per cent of manufacturing establishments were branch plants, producing approximately 70.5 per cent of the region's total value of products; in contrast to national percentages of 18.5 per cent and 65.0 per cent respectively.

It seemed for a while that the Southern region might develop, in the main, only one type of industry, which would be closely related to the one crop cotton system which had characterized Southern agriculture. There has been a recent trend, however, toward industrial diversification, including the establishment of assembly or manufacturing plants by some of the high-wage industries dealing in automobiles, airplanes, agricultural implements, chemicals, and rubber tires. These industries help to raise per capita income and to move the general living standards of the South toward the national level.

Along with industrialization there has come a stimulus to all kinds of business in the South. From 1950 to 1954 the 11 Southeastern states had a net gain of 79,200 business firms and the 4 Southwestern states an increase of 36,100, which surpassed those of any of the other regions of the nation. One Southern state, Texas, had more new establishments than any of the other states except two—New York and California; while Florida was exceeded only by the

Population Shifts and Their Effect upon Southern Baptist Convention —Comparison of Total Population and Church Membership

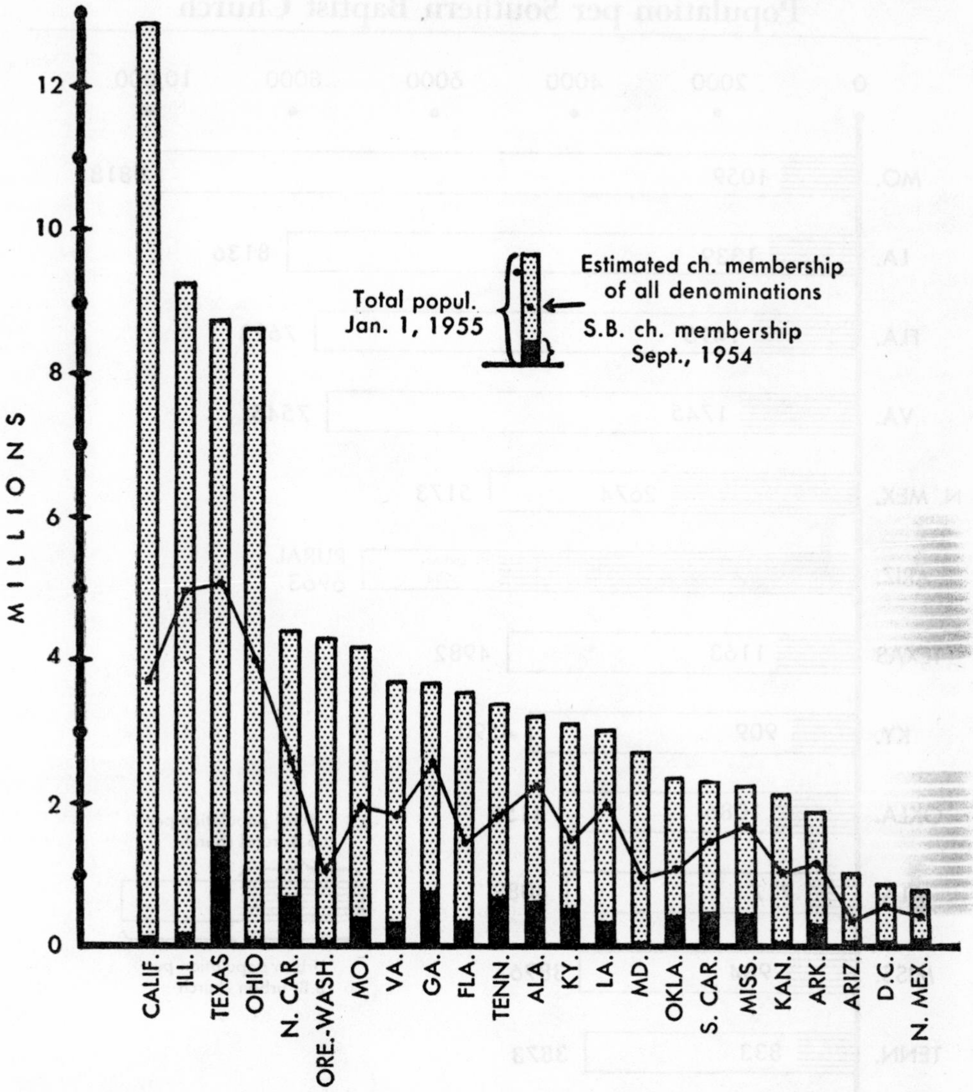

more highly industrialized and urbanized states of Illinois, Pennsylvania, Ohio, and Michigan.

This industrialization of the South, with its accompanying business development, has begun to change in many ways the general pattern of Southern life. One of the measurable changes is the growing urbanization of the area. The urban increase in the South from 1930 to 1940 was beyond the national level, a trend which continued through the 1950 census. For example, the urban population of the West South Central states (Arkansas, Louisiana, Oklahoma, and Texas) increased from 39.8 per cent of the total in 1940 to 55.6 per cent in 1950, or an increase of 15.8 per cent. This was the largest increase in any section, followed by a 12.2 per cent for the Mountain states, 10.3 for the South Atlantic, followed by the other regions with the increase for the New England states being only 0.1 per cent.

The development of the urban centers of the South has doubtless been a factor in slowing down the migration from the South to the industrial centers of the North and East. Over a 60 year period following 1870 the Southeastern states alone experienced a net loss of three and a third million native white people. From 1930 to 1940, however, the migration of native white people decreased to a mere trickle of less than 1,000. At the same time there was a sharp increase in the population of the urban centers of the South.

Population Shifts and Their Effect upon the Southern Baptist Convention—Population per Southern Baptist Church

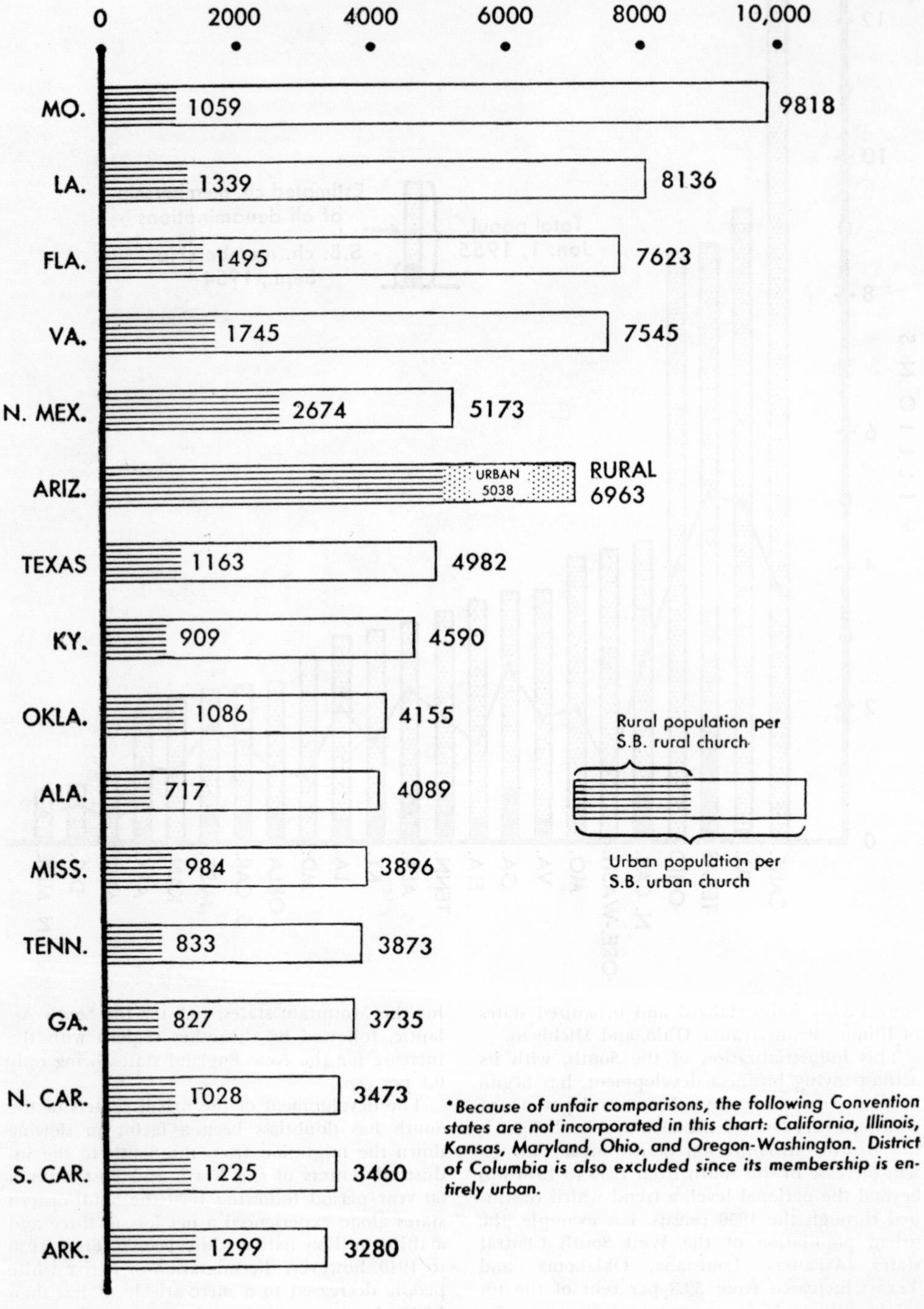

**Because of unfair comparisons, the following Convention states are not incorporated in this chart: California, Illinois, Kansas, Maryland, Ohio, and Oregon-Washington. District of Columbia is also excluded since its membership is entirely urban.*

Change in Number of Southern Baptist Churches, 1950–1955

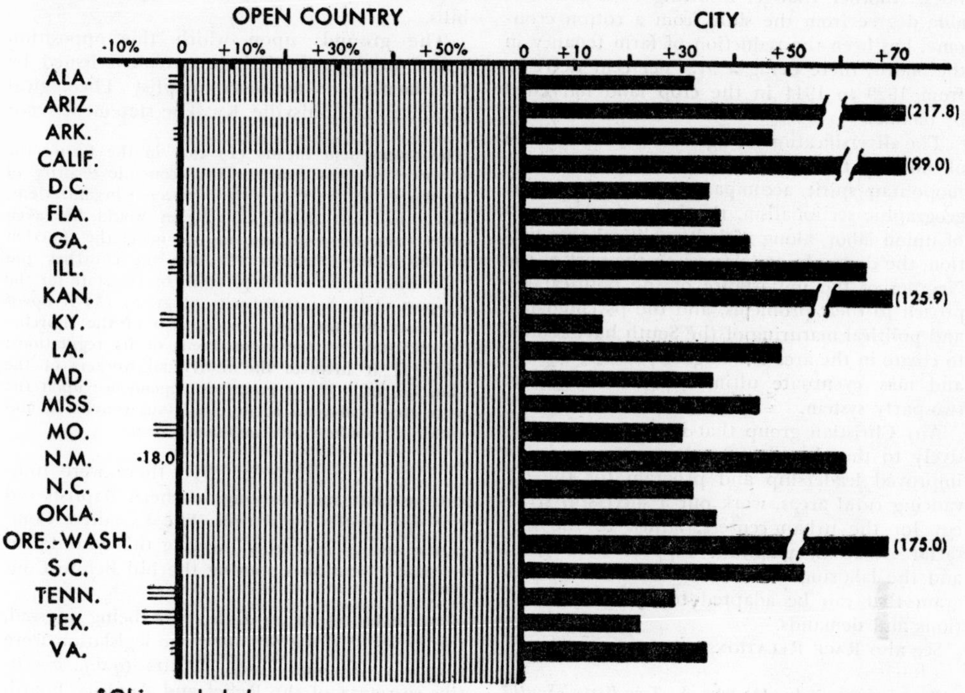

*Ohio excluded

These centers continued to grow rather rapidly from 1940 to 1950, more rapidly than those of any other region except the Far West. The percentage increase in population during the decade for some typical Southern urban areas was as follows: Atlanta, 29.7; Birmingham, 21.5; Dallas, 54.3; Houston, 52.5; Jacksonville, 44.7; Memphis, 34.7; Miami, 84.9; Mobile, 62.8; and New Orleans, 24.1. These percentages contrast with an average of 22.1 per cent for 172 urban areas of the nation, and with the following percentage increases of certain urban areas of the North and East: Boston, 8.8; Buffalo, 13.6; Chicago, 13.9; Cleveland, 15.6; Detroit, 26.9; Indianapolis, 19.7; New York, 10.7; Philadelphia, 14.7; Pittsburg, 6.3; and Providence, 8.9.

The effects of the industrialization and urbanization of the South on the migration of Negroes to the North and East is not entirely clear. It is known that most of the migration from the South in the 1930–40 decade was from among the Negroes with the Southeastern states having a net migration of 424,924 Negroes as compared to only 868 white people. The decline in the percentage of the total population that was Negro from 1940 to 1950, which was typical of the Southern states, would suggest that the migration of Negroes has continued. There also has been a noticeable decrease in the number of counties, most of which are predominantly rural and located in the so-called black belt, with more than 50 per cent of their population Negro. The number of such counties had decreased from 284 in 1900 to 221 in 1920 and to 180 in 1940, with 103 of these in three states—Georgia (46), Mississippi (35), and South Carolina (22). If the trend toward a decreasing percentage of the population that is Negro continues, it ultimately could change considerably the population picture for the South and the nation.

Closely related to and, to some degree, resulting from the industrialization and urbanization of the region, there are in process some other basic changes. Described a few years ago as the nation's number one economic problem, the South is progressively closing the gap between its income and wealth and the national norm. Although as late as 1953 every Southern state fell below the national average income per capita, yet the percentage increase from 1929 to 1953 was greater in the Southeast (337 per cent) and the Southwest (311 per cent) than in the other regions of the nation.

The changes in the rural South are also of considerable significance. Farms are being mechanized rapidly, with an increase of 83.7 per cent from 1940 to 1945 in the number of tractors on Southern farms as compared to a 49 per cent increase for farms in the non-South. During the same period there was a considerable decrease (25.8 per cent) in the Southern farm population. From 1929 to 1948 there was also a sharp decline in cotton acreage (52.7 per cent) accompanied by a marked increase of 76.6 per cent during 1930–47 in the number of beef cattle, 33.7 per cent of milk cows, 32.2 per cent of sheep, and 49.4 per cent of hogs. All of these increases were far ahead of the non-South, which actually had a decrease in the number of sheep and hogs. Another change, resulting to a considerable degree from the shift from a cotton economy, has been the reduction of farm tenancy in the South, there being a 31.3 per cent decrease from 1929 to 1944 in the crop land harvested by tenants.

The diversification of agriculture, the growth of industry, the rise of cities with a growing cosmopolitan spirit accompanied by a decreasing geographic sectionalism, the increasing strength of union labor, along with its political organization, the deepening awareness on the part of the Negroes of the importance of the political approach to their problems, and the psychological and political maturing of the South have tended to create in the area a changing political climate and may eventuate ultimately in an effective two-party system.

Any Christian group that is to minister effectively to the changing South must provide an improved leadership and program for the advancing rural areas, work out a successful strategy for the urban centers, adjust to the new racial situation, maintain rapport with labor and the laboring man, and sustain a vital program that can be adapted to changing conditions and demands.

See also RACE RELATIONS.

BIBLIOGRAPHY: A. Heard, *A Two-Party South?* (1952). C. B. Hoover and B. U. Ratchford, *Economic Resources and Policies of the South* (1951). V. O. Key, Jr., *Southern Politics* (1949). G. E. McLaughlin and S. Robock, *Why Industry Moves South* (1949). H. W. Odum, *The Way of the South* (1947). R. B. Vance, *All These People* (1946). R. B. Vance, J. E. Ivey, Jr., and M. N. Bond, *Exploring the South* (1949).

T. B. MASTON

SOCIAL SECURITY FOR ORDAINED MINISTERS. The Social Security Act of 1935 was opposed by religious groups during its drafting on the ground that the taxing of the churches would be a violation of the principle of the separation of church and state. Consequently, all nonprofit organizations and numerous other groups which had protested on other grounds were excluded.

Amendments in 1939 enlarged the protection against loss of family support due to old age and death. Attempts were made at this time and during the years following to extend the coverage. Previous to the passage of the 1939 amendments, the Executive Committee of the Southern Baptist Convention, through a subcommittee, studied the proposed coverage of religious workers. This was opposed and no amendment concerning religious workers was considered. In the years following, other bills sought to include lay workers employed by educational, charitable, and religious organizations.

Southern Baptists and many other denominations opposed these bills with a great show of unanimity. The Convention went on record in 1940 at Baltimore, Md., as opposed to Social Security for religious workers. Nearly every state convention passed resolutions opposing various bills.

The grounds upon which this opposition rested were set forth in a statement issued by the faculty of Southern Baptist Theological Seminary at Louisville, Ky. The statement read:

> The amendment means (1) that in the future the function of providing for the economic security of employees of churches, denominational organizations, and other institutions of religion would be taken away from these groups, and be made the function of the state; it means (2) that the churches and their institutions would be taxed by the state for the support of its Social Security program; (3) it opens the door for the punitive coercion of the churches by the state in the enforcement of its regulations; and (4) it involves the individual workers of the churches in a direct economic dependence upon the state that will tend to dull religious conviction and stifle independent conscientious action.

However, as early as 1941, there were indications that some among Southern Baptists did not oppose the legislation. The Executive Committee at its December meeting that year failed to pass a motion opposing the bill before Congress.

By 1944, as other bills were being pressed, the ranks of those opposing the legislation were thinning. Thomas Joseph Watts (*q.v.*), executive secretary of the Relief and Annuity Board, wrote on May 23, 1944: "Some of our Northern brethren have written me that they do not regard the taxation of churches for lay workers as a violation of the principle of church and state."

In 1949 House Bill 6000 was introduced, which provided compulsory coverage for the lay worker. Walter Richardson Alexander (*q.v.*), successor to Watts, testified before the Senate finance committee Feb. 20, 1950, setting forth Southern Baptists' position in opposing Social Security for lay workers. Alexander was the first to oppose the legislation, and his opposition came in the face of agitation by many denominations for the coverage. However, the stand of Southern Baptists rallied others; and though the lay workers were included, the opposition gained a voluntary provision instead of a compulsory one.

The new law provided that if both the organization and two thirds or more of the employees wished to come under the law, they could do so; otherwise they were excluded. However, the option lay only with the initial group. After that, all employees were covered without choice.

The Executive Committee on Dec. 14, 1950, passed a resolution expressing their opinion that participation of groups in Social Security did not violate the principle of separation of church and state. Consequently, many organizations entered the plan, but few of the churches did.

No sooner were lay workers covered than bills were introduced to include ministers. The 1953 Convention instructed the Executive Committee to appoint a committee to study Social

Security. The sentiment among Southern Baptists was no longer unanimous opposition. A college president said: "The whole argument against inclusion of church employees has come from denominational insurance agencies that are afraid of competition with their own plans."

In 1952 Virginia Baptists referred to a special committee a resolution asking Congress to cover ordained ministers under Social Security.

An editorial in the *Christian Index* asked that ministers be included and called for debate at the 1954 Convention on the matter. Five protestant denominations were already on record favoring the inclusion of ministers.

The Social Security committee appointed by the Executive Committee recommended education on the matter; representation at public hearings; a place on the 1954 Convention; and Southern Baptist's remembering that the Relief and Annuity Board is the denominational agency in the field.

By the time the Convention met in St. Louis in 1954, Southern Baptists found themselves faced with almost certain passage of Social Security legislation covering ministers. The Convention took little time in passing a resolution which asked for a "Social Security contract between the Federal Government and the individual without in any sense involving the churches." The Convention also asked that the coverage be voluntary.

At the Senate finance committee hearings in June, Executive Secretary Porter Routh and Herschel H. Hobbs, chairman of the Social Security committee, presented Southern Baptists' viewpoint. The idea of a voluntary participation, with ministers covered on a self-employed basis that did not involve the churches, had been presented in one of the bills before Congress. This was pushed by Southern Baptists.

The bill was passed (HR 9366), effective Jan. 1, 1955, and included everything for which Southern Baptists had asked. A minister is exempt from paying the Social Security tax, but may waive his exemption, and is given two years from the date of his ordination to decide. If the minister had been ordained before the new Social Security ruling took place, he, too, had two years to decide. However, once entering the plan, he must remain in it the rest of his employed life. The church is in no way involved, since the minister is placed in the self-employed classification; therefore, the principle of separation of church and state is not violated. WALKER L. KNIGHT

SOCIAL SERVICE COMMISSION. See CHRISTIAN LIFE COMMISSION.

SOCIAL SERVICE COMMISSION, ALABAMA. The first record of the appointment of a social service commission by the Alabama Baptist State Convention was in 1919. Previous to that time there was a functioning committee on temperance. In 1924 the two committees were combined and sometimes called the Committee on Social Conditions and Service. The name was changed in 1955 to Christian Life Commission. The purpose of the commission was expressed in 1947 as "to voice the Christian convictions and moral concern of our Convention and our people concerning the social and moral issues of contemporary society."

Some of the functional activities of the commission have been: to make annual report to the convention; to urge passage of Sabbath laws; to commend the work of the Anti-Saloon League and the W.C.T.U.; to study the temperance and civic conditions and appear before the temperance committee of the state legislature; to cooperate with the Alabama Temperance Alliance; to recommend a special offering in the churches to support said alliance; to urge a referendum of the Alabama Beverage Control Law; to urge Christian leaders of both white and Negro groups to practice and teach respect, sympathy, and good will in race relations; to urge Christian men and women to vote and to seek public office; and to urge the abolition of the Alabama Beverage Control Board.

The commission expressed moral concern and suggested areas such as the following about which churches should be concerned: the health system in the state; the teaching of good morals in the public schools and in the homes; the prevalence of major evils that imperil national and social life such as liquor traffic, divorce, mob violence, sexual sins, the conflict between labor and capital; undesirable picture shows; liberalism; the decadent condition of social life; the advertising of alcoholic beverages; gambling; racial prejudice; and the sale of narcotics.

The commission has expressed convictions about many subjects, such as the sending of an ambassador to the Vatican; the principle of church and state; the often emotionalized race question; communism as a constant threat to the free world; and the need for prayer and turning to God for the solution of social problems.
DAVIS COOPER

SOCIETY, THE BAPTIST. Baptists have followed two organizational methods for carrying on benevolent work—the society plan and the associational (also called the convention) plan. The society plan consists of a voluntary association by those interested in a common benevolence for the purpose of providing funds and management for the particular enterprise in which they are interested. Membership is based on financial contributions. A separate society is organized for each benevolent interest. That is, if a group is interested in foreign missions, it may organize a society for foreign missions, offering membership to all with a like interest on the basis of a specified gift for foreign missions each year. This society would consider only foreign missions. If some are interested in home missions, they may organize another society for home missions, completely separate from the foreign mission society, also basing membership on the giving of a certain sum to home missions each year. Other benevolent interests, such as publications, education, or Bible distribution, may be carried on through the organization of a separate society for each.

The society plan of organization for benevolent work has many advantages. For one thing, a comparatively small group of those vitally interested in a benevolence may organize a society without waiting to indoctrinate an existing organization in behalf of the benevolence. A society is completely separate from churches, associations, state conventions, and similar bodies, so it does not need their sanction or permission to organize. This was true in England in 1792 when William Carey (*q.v.*) appealed to the Northampton Association to consider sending foreign missionaries; when the association took no action, he and his friends organized a foreign mission society. Within five years a home mission society was also formed. Another advantage of the society plan is that this complete disconnection with the churches has recommended it to those who feared that if associations or conventions came to have supervision over the numerous and important benevolent activities involving the churches, the associations or conventions might become so powerful that they would "lord it over God's heritage"—usurp the autonomy of the churches. This was strikingly illustrated in the decade following 1802 (when the first American Baptist society for missions was organized). American Baptists had been doing mission work through the associations since 1755, but many were fearful lest the associations should acquire more and more control over the work of the churches; consequently, with the introduction of the society plan in American Baptist life in 1802, American Baptists flocked to this method of doing benevolent work. In 1814 they organized a society for foreign missions (although the name convention was attached to it); in 1824 a similar body was organized for publication work; in 1832 a home mission society was formed.

However, this very independence from church connection—the strength and genius of the society plan—was also its weakness, for it hindered denominational unity and development. A Baptist society is benevolence-centered, ignoring or in some cases combating other societies of the same denomination fostering different benevolences. Such a lack of unity and even the appearance of rivalry was a deterrent to denominational unification and strength. In 1845, when Baptists in the South formed a separate organization, they followed the associational or convention plan. In 1907–08 Baptists now forming the American Baptist Convention adopted a new organizational pattern which in most respects has moved away from the society idea. Other Baptists in America and in the world follow principally the convention method, although some Baptist bodies still cling to the society plan either wholly or in modified form.

BIBLIOGRAPHY: R. A. Baker, *Relations Between Northern and Southern Baptists* (1954). W. W. Barnes, *The Southern Baptist Convention 1845–1953* (1954). S. P. Carey, *William Carey* (1925). R. G. Torbet, *A History of the Baptists* (1950).

ROBERT A. BAKER

SOLDIER'S FRIEND. A weekly edited by A. S. Worrell at Atlanta, Ga., from Jan. 10, 1863, to Mar., 1864, or perhaps later. It was free to Confederate troops.

SPENCER B. KING, JR.

SOLITUDE BAPTIST INSTITUTE. Also known as Solitude Academy, located at Solitude, N. C. At the turn of the century the school was operated by L. M. Farthing in Ashe Association.

D. L. SMILEY

SON OF GOD. This title, applied to Christ approximately 45 times in the New Testament, signifies his pre-existent relationship to God from all eternity and his filial obedience to God in his messianic mission. Mark's Gospel is called in some Greek manuscripts "the gospel of Jesus Christ the Son of God." Although earlier manuscripts did not contain the phrase "Son of God" at that point, the entire Gospel is a commentary on the theme: Twice the voice from heaven pronounces his divine sonship, at the baptism (Mark 1:11) and at the transfiguration (9:7); twice the demons recognize his divine sonship (3:11; 5:7); twice Christ clearly implies it, in the parable of the wicked husbandmen (12:6) and in the saying about the end of the age (13:32); Christ, before the high priest, specifically admits that he is the "Son of the Blessed" (14:61). In the moment of Christ's death on the cross, the Roman centurion acclaimed him as "Son of God."

Later philosophical questions raised about the meaning of divine sonship in the creedal statements of the early church were overly influenced by the Greek idea of procreation and paternity in the Father-Son relationship. To the Hebrew mind the Son was distinguished by his unique, intimate relation to the Father and by his unquestioning obedience to the Father's will. This concept is certainly in the forefront of New Testament teaching of the sonship of Christ. He is distinguished from all other human beings: They are God's creatures, but he is God's Son, sharing the divine nature (Heb. 1:3), having equality with God by right (Phil. 2:6), and having the fulness of the Godhead bodily dwelling in him (Col. 2:9). Yet Christ demonstrates his unique relationship by perfect filial obedience: In Gethsemane he prays that the Father's will be done (Matt. 26:39), even calling on him by the familiar Aramaic title, "Abba, Father" (Mark 14:36); and in Hebrews (5:8) it is said, "Though he were a Son, yet learned he obedience by the things which he suffered." Even the familiar phrase "only begotten Son" (John 1:14; 3:16) carries primary emphasis upon Christ's unique filial relationship to the Father, rather than upon paternal generation of the Son. It signifies both his full deity and his perfect obedience.

WAYNE E. WARD

SON OF MAN. This term was used consistently by Christ to describe his own personal mission as a heavenly figure who would arrive at exaltation in his kingdom by the pathway of humiliation and the cross. Occurring 82 times in the Gospels, the term is always used by Christ as a self-designation except in one instance, John 12:34. In this passage the Jews asked Jesus what he meant by the title, how the Son of man could be a suffering Messiah. Elsewhere, Son of man is used only three times: once by Stephen (Acts 7:56) and twice in Revelation (1:13; 14:14) in a heavenly vision of the exalted Lord. Although sometimes used as an indirect substitute for the personal pronoun "I," Son of man is usually connected with references to the suffering and death of Christ (Mark 8:31; 9:12, 31; 10:33, 45; 14:21, 41) or to his triumphant "coming on the clouds of heaven" (Mark 8:38; 13:26; 14:62). The ordinary interpretation has been to find in the term a reference to the humanity of Christ, as contrasted with the phrase "Son of God," which emphasizes his deity. But the history of the term in Old Testament and interbiblical literature, together with its unique use by Christ in application to his messianic mission, gives it a significant technical meaning. Used in Psalm 8:4 as a synonym for "man" in parallel lines of poetry, in Psalm 80:17 as an equivalent for "the man of thy right hand" who will deliver Israel, and occurring 90 times in Ezekiel to designate the prophet himself as he responds to the divine message (cf. Dan. 8:17), Son of man in Daniel 7:13 has finally the significance of a heavenly figure who, as representative of the "saints of the Most High," comes on clouds of glory to receive the kingdom. This symbolic vision is reinforced in Jewish eschatology by many references to Son of man in the book of Enoch (*c.* 100 B.C.), where the heavenly figure presented in the section called the Similitudes (xxxvii–lxxi) bears a striking resemblance to the one portrayed in some sayings of Christ. Whether or not this writing exerted a direct influence upon him, Christ certainly assumed a similar context of ideas in telling of the triumphant victory of the Son of man. The central meaning of the term, as used by Christ, is the astounding revelation that the Son of man will come to his heavenly triumph by the pathway of suffering and death. This connection of the Suffering Servant motif of Isaiah (52:13 to 53:12) with the heavenly Son of man (Dan. 7:13) was the original, revelatory insight of Christ into his own messianic consciousness. WAYNE E. WARD

SONSHIP. Two words in the Greek New Testament designate men as sons of God. Paul uses *huios* to emphasize the dignity, privilege, and legal standing of mature sons as related to the Father by adoption. John prefers *teknon* to describe sons as derived from God by spiritual generation. As such, they have received his life and nature and exhibit a resulting likeness.

Either by divine adoption or by divine begetting, believer's sonship originates in God's grace and initiative rather than in any natural or inherited right or ability of men (Rom. 8:9, 14–17; John 1:13).

Since all persons are created in God's image, they are capable of becoming God's children. But because of human sin, God gives "the power to become" his sons only to those who, receiving Christ, are regenerated by the Holy Spirit (John 1:12–13; 3:3–5).

The indispensable human condition of spiritual birth is personal, penitent faith in Christ, the unique Son of God. To "believe" means to receive into a contrite heart him "who takes away the sin of the world" (John 1:12, 29).

The phrase "son of God" refers to a believer, therefore, as one who possesses and shows Godlike qualities in life and action resulting from the vital child-relationship which he has to God, his spiritual Father.

Christian sonship, then, is first of all kinship to God. As originally created, men have the capacity for sonship. They possess the image of God, now marred by sin, in three distinctive characteristics: self-determination, self-consciousness, and self-communication. By the new birth God imparts his own nature to men so that they are, not only potentially, but actually, the sons of God (I John 3:1). Through faith in Christ, human nature is reborn in divine likeness and quality. Therefore, kinship to the Father resides in new nature in the form of freedom, truth, and love.

Christian sonship is also fellowship with God. This oneness has three aspects. In disposition the Christian is inspired to filial obedience; in deeds he is motivated by sacrificial love; in destiny he is already fitted for eternal fellowship with the Father.

Kinship with God in nature is the principal essence of sonship; fellowship with God in life is its practical expression. The means and pattern of this relationship are found in Christ, the incarnate Son of God. The children of God manifest their life of kinship and fellowship with God by faith, love, righteousness, and heart-purifying hope—all centered in Christ. (See I John.)

BIBLIOGRAPHY: F. G. Schlafer, "The Johannine Doctrine of Sonship" (1949). F. G. SCHLAFER

SOUL. In biblical thought the word translated "soul" stands generally for man's inner nature, the combination of intellectual pursuits, moral aspirations, emotional colorings, esthetic visions, and religious faith which, at various levels, constitute him as he is. In this sense, the word translated "soul" is perhaps best rendered "mind," provided its meaning is not limited to mere rational thought. In biblical thought also the soul is the animating principle of the body, but it usually stands for more than this. Man as a living "soul" describes man *in his totality* as a worshiping, thinking, willing, and feeling creature. The soul then is the core of his distinctive personality, the inner principle that makes him what he is, that which most completely carries the marks of the divine image. Hence, man is "soul"; but he possesses a "spirit" and a "heart," because "spirit" and "heart" are synonyms for the highest aspects of "soul."

There is no thought in the Bible of the body as a prison house of the soul. Man is a compact unity of body and soul, of the outer and inner man. The body is the outward expression and instrument of the human personality which can be described in its inner life as "soul." Hence, the Bible does not speak of the immortality of the soul but of the resurrection of the body. Beyond death God provides the inner principle of personality, the soul, with a more adequate instrument for its expression, a body of glory, in which man will more perfectly reflect God's glory.

It is significant that modern psychology is increasingly recognizing the psychosomatic wholeness of man and emphasizing the intimate interrelationship of the physiological organism with the psychic aspects of man's personality. Man can no longer speak of the soul as if it were an alien agency in his body. It is the integrating, directing principle of the physical organism, present everywhere within it, being expressed through it, and yet transcending its limitations in moments of intellectual thought, esthetic vision, and religious faith. Chiefly because of the soul's transcendent capacity for religious faith, man becomes more than body; the soul which directs and integrates his body is the inner principle which, in its highest reaches, brings him near to God.

BIBLIOGRAPHY: E. C. Rust, *Nature and Man in Biblical Thought* (1953). H. W. Robinson, *The Christian Doctrine of Man* (1926).

E. C. RUST

SOUL COMPETENCE. See PRIESTHOOD OF BELIEVERS.

SOULE COLLEGE. A female school established at Murfreesboro, Tenn., in 1889. Zuinglius Calvin Graves was president of the institution during its brief life of three years. Courses were offered in philosophy, mathematics, ancient languages, modern languages, English, natural science, music, and art. In 1890 the school had a faculty of 10 and student body of 150.

LYNN EDWARD MAY, JR.

SOUTH AFRICA, BAPTIST UNION OF. The origin of Baptists in South Africa can be traced to the coming of British settlers to Cape Colony in 1820. Since growth was slow in the early years, it was not until 1877 that the Baptist Union was constituted at Grahamstown with seven member churches.

Fifteen years later the South African Baptist Missionary Society was organized at King William's Town, and since that time considerable progress has been made. Baptist work has reached beyond the Union of South Africa into the two Rhodesias to the border of the Congo. The main European membership is in the coastal areas around Cape Town, Port Elizabeth, East London, and Durban, and inland at Pietermaritzburg, Bloemfontein, Kimberley, Johannesburg and the Reef, and Pretoria.

The Baptist Union's membership embraces European (Afrikaans, English, and German), Negro, Chinese, Indian, and Bantu. Two magazines, *The South African Baptist* and *Die Goeie Tyding,* are published monthly.

The Baptist Theological College of Southern Africa was established at Johannesburg in 1950, with J. Charles Stern principal. The general doctrinal position is conservative.

	1934	*1954*
Number of Churches:		
European	49	87
Negro	14	17
Indian	2	2
Bantu	15	499 churches and preaching places.
Number of Members:		
European	6,616	10,408
Negro	364	817
Indian	536	1,076
Bantu	5,266	16,260
Sunday School Membership:		
European	4,622	8,376
Negro	1,465	2,755
Indian	460	591
Bantu	1,339	8,344
Number of Associations	9	
Income from all sources:		
B.U. and B.M.S.	£4,985	£18,210

Missionary work, confined to the Union of South Africa and Northern Rhodesia, covers the areas Ciskei, Transkei, Pondoland, Natal, Transvaal, Orange Free State, and Lambaland (N. Rhodesia). These fields are supervised by 23 missionaries. Practically all Baptist European churches have at least one member working under other missionary societies.

W. H. DOKE

SOUTH BRAZIL, MISSION IN. See BRAZIL, MISSION IN.

SOUTH BRAZIL SEMINARY. See BRAZIL, MISSION IN.

SOUTH CAROLINA, STATE CONVENTION OF THE BAPTIST DENOMINATION IN.

I. Baptist Beginnings. GENERAL SUMMARY. The Baptists in South Carolina have grown out of four distinct streams representing at least four separate cultures. The first work in the state and in the South, centering around Charleston, developed with the flavor of the low or tidewater country. Later, Welsh Baptists brought another culture to the northeastern area along the Pee Dee River, Dunkers and Seventh-Day Baptists propagated their views extensively in the heart of the state. Finally, Separate Baptists fanned out from North Carolina through the Piedmont down into the central section. After the Revolutionary War a composite Baptist culture emerged from these four streams.

Prior to 1700 there was only one Baptist

church in South Carolina. In 1704, at the time of the first act establishing the Anglican Church, dissenters in the province were "notoriously known to be above two-thirds of the people, and the richest and soberest among them." Yet Anglicans were more influential and monopolized public offices. In 1710 Baptists (called Anabaptists) constituted about one tenth of the white population. Of 30,000 to 40,000 white inhabitants in 1763, about 3,000 to 4,000 were Baptists. By 1800 there were 96 organized churches, 63 ministers, and 5,583 white and Negro communicants "in a connection of about 27,000." In 1800 the membership of 54 back country churches was 2,978; of 14 Pee Dee churches, 714; and of 6 low country churches, 515. After a brief period of intense revival, "the Baptists of South Carolina had 115 organized churches, approximately 76 ordained ministers, . . . numerous licentiates and exhorters, and about 10,000 whites and blacks in their communion at the close of 1803, a gain of eighty per cent in three years."

"Only one accusation of actual persecution has been brought by the Baptists against South Carolina provincial authorities—that of Joseph Cates, a Baptist itinerant, taken up and whipped for preaching near Cheraw Hill sometime before 1772. The community so frowned upon this action that it was justified on the ground of Cate's [*sic*] immorality." Of 1,500 Baptists known to be of military age, about 600 served in the American army or furnished supplies to the state during the Revolution.

In the early years education, ministerial and general, was supported by the Charleston Association in the low country and Pee Dee areas. Back country Baptists largely believed education to be hostile to religion. Roberts Academy at Stateburgh was the chief antecedent of Baptist educational institutions in South Carolina. Indicative of the Charleston Association's wider interest in education was its appointment of Oliver Hart (*q.v.*), Francis Pelot, and John Gano (*q.v.*) in 1773 as a committee to communicate with other American associations to raise funds for Baptist higher education. Rhode Island College (later Brown University) was the beneficiary of their efforts.

CHURCHES OF THE LOW COUNTRY. The traditional date for the beginning of Baptist work in South Carolina is 1683, when William Screven (or Scriven) is supposed to have emigrated from Kittery, Me., to the region near Charleston. Screven and those who came with him had organized a Baptist church in Kittery Sept. 25, 1682. Because of persecution, they allegedly came to the Charleston area and established a church at Somerton. To the present time it has been impossible, apart from tradition, to substantiate 1683 as the date of Screven's arrival in South Carolina.

Repeated references in Maine records attest to the presence of one "William Screven" in that colony until 1693. The first known record of Screven's presence in South Carolina is in connection with a warrant for 1,000 acres of land dated Dec. 7, 1696. Screven had been ordered to leave Maine in 1682. It is possible that he took a group to South Carolina and returned to Maine until 1696. Efforts to discover that he had been married prior to 1647, and thus to substantiate that the "William Screven" of the later Maine records was an older son of the first marriage, have thus far been unsuccessful.

It has been suggested that probably for three reasons Screven selected South Carolina for his settlement:

> . . . that toleration existed there; that the family of his wife, Bridget Cutt (or Cutts), had lived for sometime in Barbados, and may have received first-hand reports of the advantages of the settlement of 1670 on the Ashley River and coming himself from Somersetshire, Mr. Screven may have been in communication with the party brought over by Blake.

In the 1670's Joseph Blake had brought a group of dissenters to South Carolina, and in 1684 Lord Cardross brought others, among whom, it is claimed, were Baptists.

By 1693 there were many Baptists in Charleston, and by 1699 a congregation is clearly evident. For a time services were held in a temporary building or in the home of William Chapman. William Elliott, on July 18, 1699, gave to the congregation lot No. 62 on Church Street, where a meetinghouse was erected by Jan., 1701. Screven led the church to adopt the London, or Philadelphia, Confession of Faith "omitting the requirements of laying on of hands and ruling elders." Apparently, the majority of the members were Particular Baptists, as evidenced by the adoption of this strongly Calvinistic confession. In 1708 Screven listed the Charleston members as 90. He continued to serve the church intermittently during the early 1700's, though a Mr. White from England had been secured to preach. At White's death Screven again served the church regularly, declining to accept a call to become pastor of the Baptist church in Boston, Mass. Failing health and the urgent call from Charleston were factors in his decision. Death soon ended his labors on Oct. 10, 1713, at the age of 84.

Screven was assisted in his last years as pastor by a Mr. Sanford, who continued as pastor in Charleston until death. William Peart, from England, "a good preacher and a man of real piety," succeeded Sanford and served for about 11 years. During the pastorate of his successor, Thomas Simmons, who assumed the care of the church Mar. 20, 1725, new church buildings "were erected near Ashley River, on Edisto Island, and near the Stono" River, 16 miles from Charleston.

In the early 1730's William Elliott, Jr., led a group of those with Arminian beliefs out of the congregation. This group organized separately about 1735, "sent to England for one Mr. Ingram a minister holding the same tenets," and were afterward called General Baptists to distinguish them from the original Particular Baptists. The new group held meetings in the building at Stono.

The original church also experienced a division around the person of Simmons. The majority favored ousting him, and when a split resulted, the problem of possession of the church property emerged. In petitions to the Colonial Assembly, the General Baptists supported the Simmons minority against the ultra-Particular majority. The matter was settled with both groups sharing the property, though the ultra-Particulars built a second meetinghouse in 1745.

The coming of George Whitefield (*q.v.*) in 1740 further disturbed the Charleston Baptist scene.

> Charleston was the place of his greatest success and of the greatest opposition. . . . The factions seem clearly indicated—the Particular group led by Rev. Isaac Chanler, of Ashley River, warmly advocating Whitefield's course and doctrines, the Moderate group led by Rev. Thomas Simmons less enthusiastic, and the General Baptists openly opposed to Whitefield.

The nearly extinct Particular group in the old Charleston church experienced revival and growth. After Simmons' death in 1747, those of his faction were restored to communion with the Particulars. Isaac Chanler, from Ashley River, supplied interim pastoral services until a permanent minister could be secured.

Chanler died in 1749; and, with the coming of his successor, great strides were made by Charleston Baptists. Oliver Hart began his "Pastoral Charge of the Baptist Church in Chas: Town Feb. ye 16th, 1749–50." On Sundays Hart preached morning and afternoon and lectured in the evening to the "society." He also spoke several other times during the week. Hart also preached on James Island, which activity soon resulted in the collection of a congregation and the erection of a building. In 1751, through his efforts, several churches united in the formation of the Charleston Baptist Association, the first such association in the South. During Hart's pastorate, John Gano was also secured from the Philadelphia Association to go as a missionary to North Carolina and the back country of South Carolina.

Hart's ministry encouraged more cordial relations on the part of the Baptists with other denominations. On one occasion he conducted the burial service of a child in the place of his Anglican rector friend, who was ill. Again, Joseph Pilmoor, one of the first two Methodist missionaries sent to America, was much impressed by the cordial reception given him by the Baptists. He wrote: ". . . Tuesday I . . . went to dine with Mr. Patrick, where I met the Rev. Mr. Hart, the Baptist Minister, who is not only *sensible,* but truly evangelical, and very devout."

On Oct. 9, 1778, the act of incorporation of "The Baptist Church in Charlestown" was passed.

> The corporation consists indiscriminately of church members and pew-holders, and manages the secular concerns. Its officers are a President, Treasurer, Secretary, and two Wardens, chosen annually on the 3d Wednesday in Sept. It is governed by a system of Bye-Laws enacted in 1791. The spiritual concerns are managed by those who are strictly members.

Prior to the Revolution, Hart and the Baptists were honored in his being selected to journey with a committee in an effort to win the back country for the American cause. Later, the congregation seems to have been scattered, and Hart fled with his family to Euhaw. Five years later, Feb. 11, 1780, he was driven from Charleston by the British advance and never returned.

Religious activity in Charleston was greatly restricted during British occupation. From May, 1780, to Dec., 1782, there was no meeting of the Charleston Association, "and church life was at a low ebb among South Carolina dissenters." Both meetinghouses of Charleston Baptists were taken over by the British; beef was stored in one and forage in the other. In 1785, when organized Methodism was brought to Charleston by Francis Asbury, the Methodists "obtained the use of an old meeting-house belonging to the General Baptists, in which they had ceased to preach." In 1786 and 1787 the Particular Baptists petitioned the legislature for full possession of lot No. 62, as "there is no Society of the General Baptists now existing in Charleston." Though a counter-petition was presented by some General Baptists, the courts in 1787 granted full possession of the property to the Particular Baptists.

The Charleston church took another great stride forward under the leadership of Richard Furman (*q.v.*), who was called as pastor in 1787 from the High Hills of Santee. A man of "fine presence" and "natural dignity," Furman continued the work begun by Hart. Through his congregation of about 240 members, many of whom were Negroes, emphasis on ministerial education and missions was projected into the Charleston Association and wider Baptist circles. Furman was greatly respected by other denominations in Charleston and was much in demand as a speaker on public occasions. "With music and fine oratory and influential leadership . . . the First Church of Charleston entered the new century."

Ashley River was the first immediate branch of the Charleston church. On Nov. 22, 1725, a lot was donated "for the congregation of Antipedo Baptists" 14 miles from Charleston, and in 1727 a meetinghouse was built. The church was constituted as separate from Charleston May 24, 1736. Pastors at Ashley River were Isaac Chanler and John Stephens. During the Revolutionary War, it is said, the church became extinct.

The Euhaw church, "located at the head of the estuary from Port Royal Sound called Broad River," claims to have originated from the preaching of William Screven on Edisto Island about 1700. The predominant Presbyterians took over the first meetinghouse, leaving the Baptists to meet in private houses. In 1726 Baptists built their own place of worship. The church separated from Charleston May 5, 1746, and was finally incorporated in 1787. Early ministers at Euhaw included Francis Pelot, William Elbert, William Tilly, Joseph Cook, Henry Holcombe, Joseph B. Cook, and Aaron Tison. The Baptist church in Beaufort was constituted out of the Euhaw church Jan. 27, 1804, and entered the new Savannah Association. George Whitefield and Oliver Hart both ministered temporarily at Euhaw.

In 1759 the Coosawhatchie church was constituted largely by Baptists from the Pee Dee and Lynches Creek areas. Hart and Pelot aided in the organization of the church, of which James Smart became minister. The same year Coosawhatchie entered the Charleston Association. In 1769 the first building was erected, and in 1802 the church was dismissed from the Charleston Association to the new Savannah Association.

There was preaching at Pipe Creek as early as 1763, and the church there was constituted in Mar., 1775, as Savannah River Church. In 1786, under Henry Holcombe as pastor, it asked to be known as Pipe Creek church. In 1802 it also entered the Savannah Association.

Black Swamp church was originally a branch of Pipe Creek. However, in Feb., 1786, it was constituted as separate. The first meetinghouse was built "about 1781 on a lot . . . situated about three miles north of Robertville on tributary waters of Black Swamp." In the summer of 1794, seven churches, five from South Carolina and two from Georgia, met here to consider the formation of a new association. An alternate plan offered by the Charleston Association, to have a meeting every spring among the southern churches, prevented the break and formation of a new association at this time.

Wassamassaw seems to have originated from Lynches Creek church "soon after the peace of 1783." It entered the Charleston Association in 1801, being situated about 30 miles northwest of Charleston. Apparently, it had little connection with other low country churches.

The church at Stono was originally a branch of the Charleston Particular Baptists. After the schism, about 1735, a church of General Baptists was organized at Stono the following year. Robert Ingram served as minister, being succeeded, on his death in 1738, by Henry Heywood. Heywood led in the heated struggle with the Charleston Particular Baptists for lot No. 62 as the "Society of General Baptists" gradually dwindled. "The Society was officially recorded as extinct about January, 1791."

The Georgetown church likely grew out of the influence of William Screven. Elisha, his son, laid out the site of Georgetown and reserved one acre for a meetinghouse and place of burial of the "Antipedo Baptists." After the baptism of William Cuttino by Oliver Hart in 1767, the church gradually developed. Richard Furman, after several visits, was effective in bringing Georgetown to the point of constitution and admission to the Charleston Association in 1794. Edmund Botsford entered upon a lengthy pastorate in 1797, and a "handsome and commodious wooden meeting-house" was built in 1804. The Methodist Bishop Asbury wrote in his *Journal,* after passing through Georgetown in Jan., 1804: "The Baptists have built an elegant church, planned for a steeple and organ; they take the rich and the commonality and the slaves fall to us."

Churches of the Pee Dee Section. The second center of Baptist growth in South Carolina was along the Pee Dee River in the northeast area. Lured by encouraging colonizing conditions, many Welsh settlers began arriving in 1736 from the Welsh Tract of Delaware, then a part of Pennsylvania. David Lewis, Samuel Wild, and Daniel James presented the petition which initiated the colony. The early settlement was in the bend of the Great Pee Dee River opposite the present village of Society Hill. Soon the surrounding section was called the Welsh Neck.

In Jan., 1738, a Baptist church named Pee Dee was formed by 30 of the Welsh settlers. Later the name was changed to Welsh Neck. The group had organized its religious life in 1701 before leaving Wales. A church was established in Pennsylvania, and the Pee Dee church was actually an extension of that group. However, the "brothron [*sic*] and sisters" were carefully dismissed before they left for South Carolina.

A wealthy leader among the Welsh was James James, whose name has descended to some present-day Baptists in the state. In this early period an Anglican missionary wrote of "an ignorant set of Anabaptists" which he found in the Cheraws settlement, doubtless referring to Welsh Neck Baptists.

According to extant records, there was only one ordination into the ministry in the early years—that of Philip James on Apr. 4, 1743. Pastors from Ashley River and Charleston, Chanler and Simmons, were in charge of this service. In 1744 the first meetinghouse was built. From 1750 to 1796, the following men served as pastors at Welsh Neck: John Brown, Joshua Edwards, Robert Williams, Nicholas Bedgegood, Evan Pugh, Elhanan Winchester, and Edmund Botsford. Amid many fluctuations the church apparently experienced an unstable growth in the time of Winchester, with hundreds of converts. Under Botsford it seemed to experience a time of genuine revival. Its most difficult years were during and after the Revolution, 1779–93, when membership dropped from 220 to 48 white people.

In 1803 the meetinghouse was moved to Society Hill. The Welsh Neck church came to be known as one having a broad and tolerant spirit. It possessed a library and also supported the benevolent work of the Charleston Association's general committee with commendable zeal. After 1800 particularly, it appears to have been given to much charity. In a dispute concerning laying on of hands in ordination, a majority of the church voted that "ordination consists in the people's choice of a member to office, and his acceptance of the same; and needeth not the imposition of hands to make it valid." For a while, in 1761, the church admitted to membership those who had been baptized by sprinkling if they could relate a satisfactory experience of conversion. Close communion was not practiced for some time but was resumed July 4, 1761. "The facts support the tradition still extant in the Pee Dee that the Welsh Neck Church in its earlier days was more Arminian than Calvinistic in its beliefs and practices."

Welsh Neck had many direct and indirect church descendants in the Pee Dee section. Because several became extinct soon after being constituted and others descended irregularly, it is often difficult to trace lines of connection.

Catfish Church, located east of the Great Pee Dee at the first site of Welsh settlement in South Carolina, was the oldest branch of Welsh Neck, being constituted Oct. 3, 1752. After 1789, following a period of difficulty due to strong Arminian influence, the church disappeared from Charleston Association records. Beauty Spot, "a direct outgrowth of Catfish," was organized June 15, 1768, and entered the Charleston Association in 1782. The church was known as one that "had neither ruling elders nor laying on of hands," and also one that apparently supported an erring pastor, "to the scandal of other churches," until he had been openly acquitted. "More from proximity or occasional interchange of ministers than from any established connection, Dog Bluff, Terrell's Bay, Gapway, Buck Swamp, and Little Pee Dee churches are grouped with Catfish." In several of these churches, Thomas Blount, an Arminian preacher from North Carolina, apparently caused considerable difficulty.

The church at Cashaway Neck was constituted Sept. 28, 1756. During the perilous times of the Revolution, it was held together by pastor Evan Pugh. In 1791 a new building was erected at a new location, and the name was changed to Mount Pleasant. The old Cashaway–Mt. Pleasant church was dissolved in 1799. Cashaway did not have ruling elders or laying on of hands. The church attempted to legislate rather strictly in matters of morals. Of 33 disciplinary cases from 1759 to 1771, 16 were for excessive drinking.

Muddy Creek was constituted from Cashaway Aug. 15, 1789, as was Black Creek, Aug. 11, 1798. In the latter church a practice is noted that was likely common among its neighbors—one member was appointed to purchase wine for the Lord's Supper, and other members would pay him their proportionate share. "Meetings were opened and closed with singing and prayer, two discourses were often delivered on church business days and on the Sabbath, a door was opened for experience and baptism followed on that day or the next, after which the members returned to the church singing, and closed the service with the Lord's Supper." In 1803 a new Mt. Pleasant branch of Black Creek was established.

First Church on Lynches Creek was constituted Sept. 1, 1755, out of Welsh Neck and entered the Charleston Association the same year. An attempted "purge" by the minister, Henry Ledbetter from North Carolina, formerly a General Baptist, "together with danger from Indians, caused the membership to dwindle." Three branches of the church were formed from 1770 to 1772. "Though one hundred and fifty families were in the connection, and probably twice that number attended the four meeting houses, because of their lack of ministers there were then only twenty-four baptized members." The association reported the church extinct in 1777.

Second Church on Lynches Creek was situated about 50 miles from Georgetown and seems to have originated from High Hills of Santee. It joined the Charleston Association in 1778, but by 1803 it was dormant and near extinction. "The meeting about ten miles below the main meeting house in the fork of Lynches Creek, called variously Fork of Lynches Creek, Upper Fork of Lynches Creek, Upper Church on Lynches Creek, and Flat Creek Church, apparently absorbed its progenitor. . . ."

On Jan. 5, 1782, Welsh Neck agreed for "those members residing at and near the Cheraw Hill to be constituted into a distinct Church." One week later, Cheraw Hill was organized and the same year entered the Charleston Association. Three Creek Church was constituted by Cheraw Hill Oct. 12, 1793, and admitted to the Charleston Association in 1800.

Ebenezer, Jeffreys Creek, sustained no apparent connection with Welsh Neck, though it was situated only about 25 miles south of the older church. It grew out of what Evan Pugh referred to as "Spivey's meeting." Pugh, assisted by Richard Furman, organized the church Jan. 13, 1778. At first it was named Jeffer's Creek Church but was later incorporated as "Ebenezer, Jeffries's Creek." It has been claimed that this church was a branch of High Hills of Santee.

Other Pee Dee churches constituted as contemporaries of those cited and the dates of their organization were: Deep Creek, *c.* 1779; Lower Fork of Lynches Creek, 1789; and Lane's Creek, *c.* 1793.

The Charleston Association. On Oct. 21, 1751, the Charleston, Ashley River, and Welsh Neck churches met to plan an organization which was destined to become the second Baptist association in America. Oliver Hart, who had recently come from Philadelphia, was the moving force behind the constitution of this association. In 1752 delegates from Euhaw joined those of the other three. The association purposed to promote progress and fellowship in an advisory capacity without violating the autonomy of constituent churches. Ministers who favored the union and signed the articles were Francis Pelot, John Stephens, John Brown, Joshua Edwards, and Hart; the laymen were James Fowler, William Screven, Richard Bedon, Charles Barker, Benjamin Parmenter, Thomas Harrison, Philip Douglass, and John Mikell.

In 1767 the association adopted the Philadelphia Confession. Also, a system of discipline was worked out by Hart, Pelot, Morgan Edwards, and David Williams. Meetings were usually held annually, so often in Charleston in the early years as to take that name. Efforts were made to accommodate North Carolina churches by having spring conferences in the Pee Dee section, and also to accommodate the Savannah River region by having one of two annual sessions in that area. After 1795 the association agreed that it could serve all churches best by having annual meetings alternately among northern and southern churches.

A standing committee was first appointed in 1779 to transact emergency business between sessions and "to treat with government on behalf of the Churches; . . . to detect imposters, and recommend travelling Ministers of good character." In 1789–90, under the leadership of Richard Furman, the general committee received a definite status as the General Committee for the Charleston Baptist Association Fund. Its principal objects were supervision of mission activities among the churches and the fostering of ministerial education and aid. The Religious Society had been the committee's immediate antecedent in the latter interest.

Beginning about 1762, the Charleston Association carried on an extensive correspondence with other Baptist associations in the United States and England. John Gano was supported by the association in his work in the Yadkin country of North Carolina, and John Rooker was sent by the association in 1802 to preach to the Catawba Indians. In 1803 the churches at Charleston, Euhaw, High Hills, Wassamassaw, Welsh Neck, Ebenezer, and Wateree Creek were listed as contributing to the ministerial education fund, while the other Pee Dee churches, aside from Welsh Neck and Ebenezer, contributed to the missionary fund only. Of the 28 churches then in the association, only 12 gave to either fund.

It is readily apparent that the Charleston Association was the earliest unifying force and group effort among South Carolina Baptists. This association laid down a pattern which was followed by countless similar bodies throughout the South.

Early Back Country Churches. Immigration inland from the coast and overland from Pennsylvania, Virginia, and North Carolina provided settlers for the growing back country area of South Carolina after 1750. "The new settlers were largely German, Scotch-Irish, and dissenting English, and it was with these groups that new sects were introduced." Among the multiplicity of sects were German and English Seventh-Day Baptists, German Baptists or Brethren (generally called Dunkers, Tunkers, or Tumblers, according to their mode of baptism), and other pietistic sects, such as the Moravians.

The great majority of Baptists who came into the back country were first known as Separates. These had originated among the New Lights who had separated from Old Light Congregational churches following the first Great Awakening in New England. Many of the Separates had moved south and to the Baptist position on the subject of baptism. Separate Baptists stood for a vital expression of religious faith and in many practices were different from Regular, or Particular, Baptists. "They claimed to find in the New Testament and they zealously carried out in their religious exercises: Baptism, the Lord's Supper, love feasts, laying on of hands, washing feet, anointing the sick, right hand of fellowship, kiss of charity, and devoting children." Ruling elders, elderesses, and deaconesses were also allowed.

Civil authorities and Regular Baptist churches alike looked upon the Separates with suspicion. On one occasion the minister of the Welsh Neck church "sternly refused" to aid the Separate leader Shubal Stearns in the ordination of another Separate minister, Daniel Marshall (*q.v.*). The Welsh Neck minister, probably Nicholas Bedgegood, declared "that he held no fellowship with Stearns' party: that he believed them to be a disorderly set: suffering women to pray in public, and permitting every ignorant man to preach that chose, and that they encouraged noise and confusion in their meetings." However, as intercourse became more frequent between Regulars and Separates, they compromised their differences, and a growing Baptist co-operation emerged. One of the most influential of all Separate preachers of the back country in South Carolina was Philip Mulkey, who became a Baptist in 1756 and was ordained in Oct., 1757.

Fairforest Church, near the present Union, S. C., was first incorporated about 1759 or 1760 at Broad River before being moved in 1762 to Fairforest. Mulkey was the leader of the original group of 13 in their exodus from Deep River in North Carolina. The principles of this group spread rapidly, the church later being considered Particular Baptist and having communication with the Philadelphia and Charleston associations after 1772. It was first a member of the Sandy Creek Association, retaining certain Separate features. In 1771 it became a member of the Congaree Association; and in 1789, of the Bethel Association. The principal significance of Fairforest is in its being the oldest Baptist church of the back country. Among its many branches are the following churches: Boiling Springs, Goshen (Goucher Creek), Enoree, Tyger River (Friendship), Little River of Broad, Little River of Saluda, Buffalo (near Blacksburg), and Sandy River. All of these were constituted before 1790.

Another of the back country parent churches was Congaree, originally situated 12 miles below Columbia and later moved to a point 10 miles farther south. Constituted Nov. 30, 1766, the church was an outgrowth of Mulkey's preaching. At first it was a member of the Sandy Creek Separate Association; then in 1771 it entered Congaree. During the Revolution there were many skirmishes in the Congaree area, causing religious life to become disorganized. Throughout this period the church was guided by an able and respected pastor, Joseph Reese. Following Reese's death in 1795, he having been "averse to joining an Association," Congaree entered the Charleston Association in 1798. This church in central South Carolina was the parent of at least the following other churches in the region: Wateree Creek near Winnsboro, Twenty-five Mile Creek, Mine Creek, Red Bank, Amelia, Four Holes, and High Hills of Santee.

High Hills of Santee, situated about three miles north of Stateburgh, ranks high among the significant Baptist churches of South Carolina. In 1769 Reese preached in the "wicked" and "wild" High Hills section. A revival followed, and among Reese's converts were Joseph Howard, Thomas Neal, Lewis Collins, and Richard Furman. The congregation that was soon formed remained a branch of the Congaree church until Jan. 4, 1772, when it was constituted as separate. In Apr., 1772, Furman, at 18 years of age, was called to preach regularly. He was ordained May 10, 1774, and was "invested with the pastoral charge." In Apr., 1776, High Hills, as a place of marked religious activity and central location, was chosen as the meeting place of the churches in the province "to choose delegates to attend the Continental Association . . . in order to obtain our liberties, and freedom from religious tyranny and ecclesiastical oppressions." High Hills entered the Charleston Association in 1778. Following Richard Furman's move to Charleston in 1787, the church was weakened by experience with two pastors but continued as a place of influence. Among the traceable branches of High Hills are the following: Ebenezer (Jeffreys Creek), Second Lynches Creek, and Upper Fork of Lynches Creek (Flat Creek), all of the Pee Dee section and noted previously; also, Bethel (Black River) and Swift Creek.

Other Separate Baptist Churches. Daniel Marshall was one of the outstanding missionaries among the Separate Baptists in the back country of Virginia, North Carolina, South Carolina, and Georgia. In 1762 he moved from Beaver Creek near Broad River in South Carolina to Stevens Creek, where he began a church about 10 miles from Augusta, Ga. This Stephens Creek church, constituted in 1766, was first a member of the Sandy Creek Separate Association and later of Congaree Association. Its petition of 1785 to join the Charleston Association was approved, but the church apparently never sent messengers. By 1788 it had entered the Georgia Association, and in 1802, known as Big Stephens Creek, it entered Bethel Association.

Horns Creek was constituted about 1768, five miles south of Edgefield. It was probably a branch of the Stephens Creek church and later became large and very active. Horns Creek was a member of the Georgia Association before joining Bethel in 1802.

Bush River Church, between the Broad and Saluda rivers, was constituted in June, 1771, by Marshall and Mulkey. Strongly influenced at first by Sandy Creek Association, it entered Congaree in 1771 and Bethel in 1791. Raeburn's Creek, near the lower Reedy River, was organized in Sept., 1771, but it was never strong and apparently disintegrated soon after 1794.

Dunkers and Seventh-Day Baptists. The Dunkers and Seventh-Day Baptists "seem to have mingled and exchanged ministers to such an extent as to make any sharp division unnecessary, if not impossible." A group of Dunkers came from Pennsylvania and settled in the Beaver Creek neighborhood about 1748. John Pearson and David Martin were leaders among them. Of several churches claiming this group as progenitor, the Rocky Creek (Broad River) church is perhaps best known. It was constituted about 1789. In 1768 Martin preached among English Dunkers and Seventh-Day Baptists between the Edisto and Saluda rivers. Clouds Creek Church emerged as a result, constituted in 1790 or 1791.

In 1770 Martin began working along the Edisto River among English Dunkers and some Seventh-Day Baptists who had migrated from Virginia by way of Georgia. A Regular Baptist church named Edisto was constituted there in 1777. In 1787, while Nathaniel Walker was pastor, it entered the Charleston Association. Because of inactivity, in 1799 it was considered out of union with the association. Though its history is obscure, Edisto probably came to be known later as the Healing Springs church.

Other Seventh-Day Baptists moved into the Broad River area between 1745 and 1757. Thomas Owen and Victor Naley were leaders of the group. Later, some of the members were scattered as far east as the Wateree River and as far west as the Saluda. "Like other Tunker and Seventh-Day churches in South Carolina, it probably broke up during the Revolution, or turned toward the Regular position."

Congaree Association. The Congaree Association in South Carolina was an outgrowth of the Sandy Creek Association in North Carolina. Because the Charleston Association was the home of Regular Baptists of the low country and Welsh Tract, Congaree Association was the brief home of churches of Separate Baptist influence. When Sandy Creek Association dismissed the South Carolina congregations and the Congaree Association was formed Dec. 26, 1771, the following were constituent churches: Fairforest, Stephens Creek, Congaree, Bush River, Little River of Broad, Little River of Saluda, Mine Creek (or Little Saluda). Later, High Hills of Santee was a member for a time. The association's name was taken from Congaree Church, its first meeting place. Correspondence was begun with the Philadelphia and Charleston associations, and in 1775 Philip Mulkey, of Congaree, proposed to the Charleston Association to unite "the several Associations in this Province into one." As the Separates had been "tenacious of their peculiarities" before, nothing came of Mulkey's new offer. With the coming of the Revolution, and seemingly an undue interference of the association with the affairs of the churches, trouble arose, ending in the dissolution of the Congaree Association.

LATER CHURCHES. There is a dearth of information available on the activities of South Carolina Baptist churches during the troublous days of the Revolution. Oliver Hart, William Henry Drayton, and William Tennent were very active in the back country areas in 1775 in an effort to enlist more support for the American cause. There was often civil war in the back country between Revolutionists and Loyalists. Religious matters apparently were of secondary interest during this period, but for the Baptists the designations "Separate" and "Regular" began to disappear as they became more aware of similarities than differences.

One of the strong churches organized during the Revolutionary era was Turkey Creek (of Saluda), which was constituted Jan. 29, 1785, by Joseph Redding. It entered the Charleston Association the next year. From its beginning this church was accounted as "Regular," the Philadelphia Confession of Faith having been adopted as its standard. Frequent days of fasting and prayer were designated "on account of the Coldness of religion, that the Lord would revive his work and that truth and Love may abound." Turkey Creek was determined to do its "Church business Regular," and strict financial oversight was kept of its members. In 1792 it was dismissed to join the Bethel Association. Turkey Creek aided many neighboring churches and had at least two branches that later became churches: Little River (near Due West), constituted in 1791, and Poplar Spring (formerly Durham) in Laurens District, constituted in 1794.

Of the scores of churches organized throughout the state in the years following the Revolution, only ones with particular points of interest may be noted, because after 1800 the stream of churches constituted became a veritable flood. By 1790 a church named Shockley Ferry had been organized on the Savannah River in the Pendleton District. Early affiliated with the Georgia Association, and with the Bethel from 1794, it is of significance because of a wide influence and several branches which it established. Antioch Church, southeast of Edgefield, entered the Bethel Association in 1804; its date of origin is unknown. The church still worships in the building erected in 1804, and "this is the oldest Baptist church building in the State." The Head of Enoree church, three and one-half miles above Traveler's Rest in Greenville County, had wide influence in the area. It was constituted about 1789, and within 10 years had organized several branches. Shoal Creek church, originally in Georgia and later moved and named Chauga, was responsible for much Baptist growth in the extreme northwest section of the state. Several churches in later Oconee County trace their origin to Shoal Creek.

Cedar Spring is one of many noteworthy churches in the thriving Spartanburg area. Constituted in 1786, it was soon widely influential and "probably the mother church for Bethlehem, Holly Springs, Philadelphia, and others." In 1799 Cedar Spring referred to the association the question "wether [*sic*] or not it is agreeable to the gospel to hold Negroes in Slavery." No evidence is given of the association's action on the question. "The largest and probably the most influential Baptist church of the back country in the quarter century following the Revolution was located on the ridge between Enoree and Tyger Rivers and was known officially as Jameys Creek Church until 1798, when the Bethel Association agreed, upon request, that it 'be hereafter called Bethel' Church." It was organized about 1787 and for many years was the meeting place of the Bethel Association. Sugar Creek Church, constituted in 1792, was situated in Catawba Indian territory between the Catawba River and the North Carolina line. It is notable for work among the Indians and a strong co-operative effort with neighboring churches.

NEGRO BAPTISTS. In most of the Baptist churches of South Carolina, slaves were members along with whites. Laws were passed which restricted all but necessary work on Sunday. In 1800 a stringent law was enacted which forbade slaves meeting together before sunrise or after sunset, even in the company of white persons for religious purposes. The Charleston Association petitioned against this law in 1801 and 1802, and in 1803 it was modified "to the extent that religious assemblages with a majority of whites would not be disturbed by officers." In mixed congregations a gallery or some other portion of the meetinghouse was reserved for Negroes.

By 1779 so many Negroes had come into the Welsh Neck church through revival efforts that the blacks were constituted into a "Church by themselves." However, because of much excommunication and lack of a pastor, after 1782 they were gradually received back into the white congregation. For some time about one half of the total membership was Negro. In the low country Charleston in 1800 had about 63 Negro members. Euhaw likely had over 100 Negroes, which was only a fraction of the blacks that attended its services. Ordinarily, Negroes and whites were baptized together.

The number of Negroes in the back country was comparatively small; therefore, dealings of these churches with their black members were more personal. "Serious thought prompted Buffalo Church's two queries to the Bethel Association in 1793: May a negro member remarry if forced to leave his wife and brought to a great distance, and may a master beat a negro church member? The association answered both in the affirmative, the first with many qualifications." Bush River Church, in Oct., 1794, after due consideration, forbade a Negro, Moses Gift, to preach and exhort, thinking it best for him to keep silent. Upon refusing to submit, he was excluded from the church. A like situation arose at Cedar Spring, where one Titus was suspended in Nov., 1804, for preaching contrary to the orders of the church. At Turkey Creek a white woman was excluded for abusing her servant.

A rare exception among South Carolina Baptists in the early years was the Silver Bluff Regular Baptist Church, constituted in 1781 with a Negro pastor named Jesse Galphin (or Jesse Peter) and composed entirely of Negroes. Located on the Savannah River below Augusta in the Edgefield District, in 1792 it had 210 members. Another minister, Abraham Marshall, said of Jesse Galphin in 1793: "His countenance is grave, his voice charming, his delivery good, nor is he a novice in the mysteries of the kingdom." Galphin became pastor of a Negro church in Augusta in 1793, and Silver Bluff Church either disappeared or became a branch of his Augusta church.

LATER ASSOCIATIONS. The progress of Bethel Association is largely an index to back country post-Revolutionary Baptist growth. Its churches were in the northwest section of the state and the neighboring parts of North Carolina. The precise influences giving rise to Bethel Association are unknown, but its organization began in 1789 at a meeting at Cedar Spring Church. It seems that there were 16 constituent members, namely: White Oak, Bills Creek, Sandy Run, and Mountain Creek, all in North Carolina; Buffalo, Tyger River, Reedy Fork, Buck Creek, Head of Enoree, Fairforest, Padgetts Creek, Big Creek, Genestie, Horse Creek (Fork Shoal), Cedar Spring, and Upper Duncans Creek in South Carolina. It is uncertain whether Dirty Creek and Durbin Creek were constituent members. The association agreed to meet in August, and in the first year communication was begun with the Charleston Association. Charleston proposed an immediate effort to unite the two associations, but Bethel hesitated, desiring only "friendly correspondence" at the time. Bethel did go so far as to vote a day of "thanksgiving," Jan. 1, 1792, "for the blessings of peace, harmony and concord, enjoyed among ourselves, and for the union and good correspondence subsisting between us and the Charleston Association." Though Bethel did not early adopt the Philadelphia Confession of Faith, it was from the beginning Calvinistic in sentiment.

The procedure adopted by Bethel soon after organization seems to have been largely typical of that followed by other associations of the area. It

> . . . included the delivery of the introductory discourse at the beginning of business, receipt of letters and enrollment of messengers or delegates from member churches, choice of moderator and clerk; receipt of letters, messengers, or minutes of other associations; admission of new churches after inquiry into their faith and order through their delegates; dispatch of general committee business; consideration of queries from the member churches; appointment of committees, delegates to corresponding associations, supplies to vacant churches, writer of circular letter.

In 1794 Bethel adopted a resolution to the effect of attempting to engender interest among the corresponding associations in behalf of a general committee of associations in the Southern states similar to one in Virgina, but nothing came of this.

"In its relations with its member churches, Bethel observed great firmness and forbearance." As a part of its activity, the association appointed pulpit supplies for pastorless churches, settled difficulties among the churches upon request, and served as a warning agency against excommunicated preachers. Also, consistent with the policy and advice of the association, ordination practice gradually became standardized.

Answering a query of Fairforest in 1793 concerning the acceptance of immersed pedobaptists, the association "finally disagreed with the report of the committee advising the churches to admit such members without rebaptism." In answer to Brush Creek Church in 1795, the association deemed communing with other denominations disorderly. In 1790 Bethel declared nonfellowship "with members holding universal salvation." In 1803 the association gave little support to a tentative proposal for the creation of a ministerial education fund.

Agitation began in 1795 for the division of Bethel Association. In 1800, 14 churches secured dismissal to form Broad River Association: Greens Creek, Sandy Run, Green River, French Broad, Mountain Creek, Long Creek, and Bills Creek in North Carolina; in South Carolina, Tyger River (Concord), Boiling Springs, Goucher Creek (Goshen), Cedar Spring, State Line, Buck Creek, and Buffalo. In 1802 nine others were dismissed from Bethel to form the Saluda Association near the mountains in northwestern South Carolina. Those nine were Big Creek, Fork Shoal, Brushy Creek, Cross Road, Secona, Keowee, Oolenoy, Middle Fork Saluda, and Shoal Creek. From 52 churches in 1800, Bethel's membership dropped to 33 in 1803; however, membership within the constituent churches had grown steadily.

Sixteen churches on the south side of Saluda River were granted permission in 1807 to withdraw from Bethel and form a new association. These churches—Cloud's Creek, Cambridge, Little Stephens Creek, Providence, Salem, Siloam, Horns Creek, Big Stephens Creek, Goodhope, Antioch, Dry Creek, Calliham's Mill, Plumb Branch, Mountain Creek, John's Creek, and Sardis—met at Little Stephens Creek in Oct., 1808, to organize the Beulah Association. The next year its name was changed to Edgefield.

Moriah was the last association organized in South Carolina before the state convention was constituted. In 1815 Beaver Creek, Flat Rock, Upper Fork of Lynches Creek, Fork Hill, Richardson's Creek, Lane's Creek, Gourd Vine, Meadow Branch, and Rocky River met to constitute this newest association. Some of the churches were in Anson County, N. C., and some in Lancaster District, S. C.

THE TRIENNIAL CONVENTION. The contribution made by South Carolina Baptists to the Triennial Convention constitutes one of the truly significant chapters in their history. Luther Rice (*q.v.*) first visited South Carolina in 1813, organizing mission societies throughout the various associations. At the meeting of the Savannah Association William B. Johnson, then pastor in Savannah, agreed with Rice as to the desirability of a meeting of all American Baptists in behalf of missions. Rice contacted other associations, and the outgrowth was the organization of the "General Missionary Convention of the Baptist Denomination in the United States for Foreign Missions" at Philadelphia in May, 1814. Meeting thereafter every three years, it was designated the Triennial Convention. Richard Furman, of Charleston, served as the Convention's first president. In later years William Bullein Johnson (*q.v.*) was elected to this post.

TOWARD A STATE CONVENTION. At its annual meeting in 1819, the High Hills of Santee church queried the Charleston Association as follows: "Would not the formation of a General Association, composed of delegates from the several Baptist Associations in South-Carolina, be desirable, and advantageous to the interest of the Baptist denomination, and the advancement of the Redeemer's kingdom in general?" The answer being unanimously affirmative, the association began to search out ways and means.

JOE MADISON KING

II. History of Convention. ORIGIN. Because of jealousy for their freedom, some Baptists opposed in 1818 a proposal to the Charleston Association for a general association of Baptists; but in 1821 six delegates from the Charleston, two from the Edgefield, and one from the Savannah River associations met in Columbia to form a state convention. Richard Furman was elected president and Abner Blocker, secretary. In 1821 South Carolina Baptists comprised seven associations: Charleston, organized in 1751; Bethel, 1789; Broad River, 1800; Savannah River, 1802; Saluda, 1803; Edgefield, 1808; and Moriah, 1815.

PURPOSE. The purpose of the convention was to form a "bond of union, a center of intelligence, and a means of vigorous, united exertion in the cause of God, for the promotion of truth and righteousness."

> The grand objects of the Convention shall be, the increase of Evangelical and useful knowledge, and of vital, practical religion: The promotion of religious Education, and particularly that of indigent, pious young men, designed for the Gospel Ministry; . . . Missionary service . . . Sunday Schools . . . religious education in families . . . promote the true interest of the churches of Christ at large. . . .

In its earliest days the convention recognized the need for the organization and support of a seminary of learning in the state, not only for ministerial students but for other youths who were not ministerial students. In no case was the liberty of the churches to be infringed upon. This was guaranteed in the constitution and was strengthened by an 1840 amendment which read that the convention "will claim to itself no power to lord it over God's heritage."

ORGANIZATION. The convention recognized in its first meeting the need for a body to control and carry out the work of the convention ad interim. Thus, it anticipated what was to become the general board. In addition to the president and secretary, there were a vice-president, a treasurer, and a board of agents. There were originally 10 members of the board, whose business it was to transact the business of the convention when it recessed. The treasurer was to have charge of monies at the order of the convention or the board, and it was necessary for him to be bonded. The checks were to be signed by the presiding officer. The time for convening was at the discretion of the convention—once a year, once in two years, twice a year, or as called by the president, at the instance of the board.

The early work of the convention was often carried on through societies and various independent Baptist groups, each with its own budget and method of raising money. Associational agents raised money for convention causes. It was not until 1851 that the convention recommended that the state education and Bible societies dissolve and become absorbed in the greater convention. The reason given for lack of general interest in the work was that of preoccupation in Christian education. In 1825 a request, made to the state legislature to incorporate the convention, was granted.

ORGANIZATIONAL EVOLUTION. To carry on the work of the convention ad interim in 1822, a board of agents was suggested. Not until 1828 was it suggested that a full-time general agent be employed "for one year," at $1,000 per year. The title Executive Committee was being used as early as 1828, but this is not to be confused with the executive committee of the general board of 1954.

In 1827 the board of agents had a president, a vice-president, and a secretary and treasurer. Apparently, it was customary for the president of the convention to serve as president of the board.

In 1865 the boards of the convention were listed as: Education, Bible and Mission, Sunday School and Colportage, and the Board of Agents; but the following year, the "Executive Board" took the place, in the Rules of Order, of the "Boards of the Convention." The officers of the executive board by this time included a president, a vice-president, an auditor, and a general agent. J. O. B. Dargan was termed "General Agent" and "General Superintendent of Missions of the Baptist Convention of the State of South Carolina."

Thomas Herbert Pope served as general agent in 1860; John F. Morrall, 1870–71; Abner Whateley Lamar, 1872–76, on a full-time basis, and 1877–79, on a part-time scale. William Henry Strickland was elected general agent in 1880 and called corresponding secretary-treasurer. He served through 1882. Richard H. Griffith was corresponding secretary and treasurer, 1883–84. Thomas M. Bailey served in this capacity, 1885–

1909; William Thomas Derieux (*q.v.*), 1910–18. The suggestion had been made in 1879 that the state board become the General Mission Board. In 1919 when Charles Elford Burts (*q.v.*) became general secretary-treasurer, the board had become the general board. Charles Alfred Jones (*q.v.*) served as general secretary-treasurer, 1924–41; William Seldon Brooks (*q.v.*), 1942–48; and Charles Furman Sims, 1949– .

The decision was made in 1912 to move the mission headquarters from Greenville to Columbia. The general board was formed in 1919. A department of efficiency had been organized; a constitutional change was effected; and the board was composed of a president, a vice-president, a corresponding secretary and treasurer, and 22 other members. The board was subject to the convention and represented the convention ad interim.

By 1919 the convention had set up, not only the State Mission Board, but the Board of Ministerial Education, the Aged Ministers' Relief Board, the board of trustees of Connie Maxwell Orphanage, the board of trustees of Furman University, the board of trustees of the South Carolina Baptist Hospital, the board of trustees of the Greenville Woman's College, the board of trustees of Anderson College, and a general Board of Education. The convention officers included a president, two vice-presidents, a recording and statistical secretary, an assistant secretary, a treasurer, and an auditor. By 1954 the auditor was no longer listed as an officer, and the boards had grown to include North Greenville Junior College, the Baptist Foundation, the *Baptist Courier,* and the Bethea Home for the Aged. There had been added certain commissions and committees: Christian Life Commission, Evangelistic Committee, Radio Committee, and Baptist Historical Society. Departments at Baptist state headquarters had grown to four: Brotherhood, Training Union, Sunday School, and Student.

INSTITUTIONS. Schools, colleges, and academies that have been in some way connected with the convention are Furman University, chartered in 1850; Greenville Female (later Woman's) College, organized in 1854; Limestone College, 1845; Orangeburg Collegiate Institute, 1894; North Greenville High School (later Academy), 1893; Spartan High School (later Academy), 1906; Coker College, 1908; and Anderson College, 1912. Academies included a private school, Roberts Academy at High Hills of Santee; Spartan Academy, which began at Landrum; North Greenville Academy (later North Greenville Junior College), at Tigerville; Long Creek Academy, in Oconee County; Six Mile Academy, near Central; Edisto Academy, at Seivern. Some of these schools no longer exist, and some are no longer affiliated with the convention.

Papers which Baptists have owned, or which have had a bearing on their convention, are: the *Southern Baptist and General Intelligencer,* 1834; the *Carolina Baptist,* published monthly in 1846; the *Southern Baptist,* published only briefly; the *Confederate Baptist,* published during the Civil War; the *South Carolina Baptist,* published briefly after the war; and the *Working Christian,* which began in 1869, later to become the *Baptist Courier,* a private paper until 1920, when the convention bought it. Samuel Hovey Jones is the present editor.

Connie Maxwell Orphanage opened in 1892, with James Leland Vass as the first superintendent. Altha Thomas Jamison became superintendent in 1900, following Vass's resignation. Sam Mayer Smith followed as superintendent in 1946, at which time the name of the orphanage was changed to Children's Home. The Baptist Hospital opened in 1914, with John Joseph Gentry as the first superintendent, followed by Louis J. Bristow. The Six Mile Hospital was taken over by Baptists in 1943 to be developed into a rest-cure home for the aged, convalescents, and incurables. In 1946 plans for the Baptist Foundation were made, and by 1954 the convention had voted to open the Bethea Home for the Aged.

AUXILIARY. The Woman's Missionary Union is a recognized auxiliary of the convention, having played a significant role in its work. As early as 1913, W.M.U. women were presented to the convention. Actually, a connection was made between the two in 1876, and in 1897 the central committee of the W.M.U. was made a board of the convention. The W.M.U. included several departments and divisions: Youth, Royal Ambassadors, Fundamentals, Prayer, Stewardship, Mission Study, Community Missions, and the Margaret Fund.

EVOLUTION OF PURPOSE. Although in its early beginnings the convention had anticipated in its stated constitution the broad fields of associated work, structural and dynamic changes were inevitable. Aged Ministers' Relief was suggested in 1890. By 1913 the abstract principle of Christian education for children, in both the home and the church, had grown into a conception of a Sunday school department whose purpose included teacher training, denominational emphasis, enlargement, and evangelism. By 1914 there was an effort to co-ordinate the Sunday school, Baptist Young People's Union, and colportage under a field secretary; and the first summer assembly for Baptists was discussed. This field of educational endeavor extended to Negroes in the form of assistance to Morris Brown College, Sumter, S. C. It was suggested in 1917 that the department of evangelism be used as a means of implementing the over-all goal of all convention work. This work was later divided or increased. Secretaries in 1954 included Jesse Lynn Corzine, Sunday School; John B. Lane, Training Union; John Farmer, Brotherhood; Harold Cole, Baptist Student Union; and James A. Howard, Evangelism. A rural and city missions program was enlarged in 1950. A book store was set up in Columbia in 1926.

CONVENTION AUTHORITY. In its beginning the convention recognized that its stated purpose of union, intelligence, truth, love, and kingdom promotion would be hindered if there were any fear that the convention proposed to lord it over any other body of Baptists. The constitution, clear in the beginning, was later amended to strengthen the idea of the autonomy of Baptist bodies. However, there appeared certain logical inconsistencies: The word "delegate" was assigned those who represented any Baptist group in the convention, and it was not until 1949 that this designation was changed to "messenger." As the state convention recognized itself as having no authority over associated bodies within it, so did the Southern Baptist Convention, with whom the state associated. Such a respect for autonomy had its logical consequences when messengers finally were allowed only from co-operating Baptist churches rather than from societies, associations, etc.

The convention, however, does reserve to itself control over its institutions. "Each Board of Trustees elected by this Convention shall manage the affairs of the institution or agency entrusted to it, subject to direction by the Convention." The charters of some of the institutions belonging to the convention have maintained that the convention had power to elect trustees, "provide . . . for the terms of office," and remove "any member . . . at any time for any cause" that the convention deemed sufficient. An effort to make the article on removal of trustees applicable to all South Carolina Baptist institutions failed in 1950. Thus the convention controls its boards, and the boards are expected to manage the affairs of the various institutions according to Baptist principles and charters.

The principle of convention ownership and control of its institutions is of long standing and has rarely been questioned. In the rules for governing the new Furman Academy and Theological Institution, Article 2 states that "it [Furman] shall be under the general direction of the State Convention, of the Baptist denomination of South Carolina, who alone shall have power to alter or amend these rules." Article 3 leaves the "immediate management" to the board of agents. As applied to Greenville Female College in 1913, the words "Baptist control" were recognized as being of 60 years' standing. All Baptist educational institutions were considered under the "control" of the convention.

To insure convention control of its institutions, the convention in 1932 and 1951 voted "that hereafter all charters or amendments to charters of institutions of this Convention be submitted to the Convention itself before being put into effect." Through 1954 no change in the above policy had been made by the convention. The convention recognizes its responsibility, however, as is manifested in the fact that all designated monies were to be applied sacredly as designated.

Controversies. The convention has had its moments of unrest: slavery; heresy, the occasion when the theology of a professor at Furman was brought into question; such simple matters as the organization of the general board; denominational machinery versus simplicity; the technique of electing convention employees, whether annually or indefinitely; and, although the problems of Landmarkism, ecclesiology, freedom of the local church, and Calvinism versus Arminianism were Southern Baptist Convention problems more directly, they did affect the state convention.

Beyond the State Convention. South Carolina played a significant part in the organization of the Southern Baptist Convention, sending delegates to that body and receiving representatives from the Convention. It was the leader in organizing the first Southern Baptist theological seminary, supporting the larger work just as it had done when it raised money for Columbian College, Washington, D. C., and just as it was to do later in its support of Convention-wide Cooperative Program funds. Furthermore, in its early days the convention manifested a spirit of brotherly love toward Christians of other denominations. In 1896 the convention endeavored to raise $12,000 for foreign missions. In 1911 an effort was made, in co-operation with the Baptist World Alliance, to raise $8,000 for a Baptist college to be located in Europe. Work among Negroes, foreigners, in mountain schools, and among the Indians was stressed, and in 1919 the convention was hearty in its approval of the 75 Million Campaign.

Social Service. The convention has long fought for temperance, prohibition, total abstinence, and local option. It has been against gambling, passing resolutions against horse racing. In 1948 and 1954 the convention went on record on the race issue as favoring equality, justice, dignity, and all rights guaranteed under the Constitution. It also opposed all forms of prejudice. The convention has rather consistently expressed itself on Christian citizenship, the use and misuse of the Lord's Day, general lawlessness, the principle of separation of church and state, economic justice, home, and community life. In earlier days the matter of segregation itself was not considered a primary injustice. Actually, forced segregation in the South, or in Southern Baptist churches, was not practiced before 1866. Even then, segregation was begun in the churches "where the colored members become restiff [*sic*] from the continuance of such relations"—that is, when the Negroes began to feel that segregation was better for them.

Other Features. The Lord's Supper was observed at convention meetings at least as late as 1851. A wave of evangelism covered the state in 1832. In 1913 temperance was given an hour in the convention program. In 1857 no funds were received by the convention for colportage. In 1861, 1,000 Negro Sunday school pupils were listed with 7,000 whites. In 1863 the convention had 17 chaplains in the field. In 1866 efforts and plans were made to give the gospel to the ex-slaves. In 1871, for the first time in 50 years, a missionary addressed the convention. In 1879 there were 25 missionaries working in the state. In 1880 one person of seven in the state was a Baptist. Citadel Square, Charleston, reported gifts of $38 per member, whereas the average in the state was $2. In 1884 the convention asked the legislature for prohibition. In 1888 interest was manifested in Negro ministerial education. In 1919 universal military training was opposed.

Statistical Growth. Of the white population in the state prior to 1710, one in 10 was said to be Anabaptist. In 1950 the population of South Carolina included 823,622 non-whites and 1,293,405 whites, and there were 379,403 white Baptists. In 1824 three associations reported 842 baptisms, 97 churches, 10,212 members, 66 ministers, $631 for education, $74 for foreign missions, $323 for domestic missions, and $192 for general purposes. In 1908 money contributed through the convention amounted to $114,286.88; 19 new churches were organized, and 10 ministers ordained. There were 53,146 members of 731 Sunday schools, 443 W.M.U.'s with 7,032 members, and 37 associations, 410 ministers, 1,003 churches, 6,316 additions by baptism, 4,174 by letter, 122,471 church members, and church property valued at $2,024,486.

Cooperative Program money for the state increased from $1,201,076.91 in 1949 to $2,140,963.83 in 1953. In 1954 the convention comprised 1,385 churches, with 432,535 church members, and 18,094 baptisms during the year. There were 1,375 Sunday schools, 380,047 Sunday school members, 108,725 W.M.U. members, and 141,858 enrolled in Vacation Bible schools. The value of all church property was $70,361,000; pastors' salaries, $3,730,815; Cooperative Program gifts, $2,312,226; designated convention gifts, $1,469,582; and a total contribution from the churches for all purposes of $19,249,455. The 1955 budget goal was $2,500,000, of which $290,000 for general expense (state and Southern Baptist Convention) was to be deducted on a monthly basis before distribution. The causes included administration, promotion, foundation, W.M.U., convention expenses, retirement plan, *Baptist Courier,* and reserve. For current expenses $1,197,524 was to be divided equally between the Southern and state conventions. Of $1,012,475 (or excess), the state's capital needs program was to receive 60 per cent, and Southern Baptist causes 40 per cent. Ministerial students received $14,150 from the convention in 1954; missions and weak churches received $22,425 to apply to pastors' salaries; other churches and missions received $63,000 assistance on buildings.

In 1911 the convention enrolment was 319, whereas in 1954 there were 1,078 messengers and 465 visitors.

Constitution and By-law Change. In 1949 certain major changes were made in the constitution: "The work of colportage" was changed to "the distribution of God's word and approved Christian literature." "The maintenance of a children's home" was substituted for "an orphanage." The words "messengers or messenger" took the place of "delegates or delegate." Where the term "annually" was applied to the declaring of the general board treasurer as treasurer of the convention, the term was deleted. The election of the general secretary-treasurer was changed from annually to an indefinite period, with mandatory retirement at 68. An assistant secretary-treasurer to be responsible for "stimulating interest in missions" was provided, constitutionally, along with other department heads, with provision for termination of office with 30 days' notice by either party. All were to be elected for indefinite terms. Other changes simply brought up to date various boards of trustees and gave the purpose of the Baptist foundation, with "laymen's work" for "brotherhood" and consistency provided throughout. C. EARL COOPER

III. Program of Work of South Carolina Baptists. The General Board. The agency for carrying out the plans and purposes of the convention is officially named the General Board of the State Convention of the Baptist Denomination in South Carolina. The board acts for the convention and promotes all its interests (except as otherwise specified by the convention), such as missions, education, and benevolence. The board is the convention ad interim. Matters requiring special study are generally referred to the board for investigation and action. Special grant of authority has been extended by the convention to interpret (subject to approval by the convention) one article in the constitution which reads as follows: "No funds, gifts, or allowances that infringe upon the historic principle of the separation of Church and State shall be accepted by the Convention, the General Board, or any Institutions or agencies of the Convention."

Board membership is composed of "the President, Vice Presidents, Secretaries, and the Treasurer of the Convention, ex officio, one member from each of the Associations of the Convention and ten members from the State at large, all elected by the Convention, but no member shall be eligible to succeed himself until one year has elapsed." "The General Board shall have its headquarters in Columbia, S. C." The board owns the building which houses its offices and an adjacent structure, which it leases to the Baptist Sunday School Board to house a Baptist Book Store.

An executive committee of nine members and such officers as are needed are elected by the board annually. "The members from the Association [*sic*] and from the state at large shall be divided into six groups, as nearly equal as possible, and the terms of office of one-fifth of the members to expire annually." These groups are responsible for examining and reporting on reports from the special objects of the convention (missions, Sunday school, Training Union, etc.).

The board is required to have at least two meetings each year. In addition to its work for the convention, the board serves directly for all the denominational agencies of the Southern Baptist Convention. The board employs an auditor for all the institutions and agencies of the convention, assuring consistency in all financial reports.

A general secretary-treasurer is nominated by the board and elected by the convention to serve for an indefinite term with compulsory retirement at the age of 68. The constitution specifies: "He shall be the executive officer of the Board and it shall be his duty to unify and harmonize our work, to enlist and educate our people throughout the State to elicit, combine, and direct their energies and rèsources in support of the objects fostered by the Convention." He is an ex officio member of the board; and as treasurer of the board, he is treasurer of the convention.

The board elects an assistant general secretary-treasurer "who shall give his time to stimulating interest in missions." This he does through preaching appointments, associational meetings, distribution of promotional literature, and encouragement of mission study in all church groups.

The board elects directors for its departments—Sunday school, Training Union, Student Union, Brotherhood—and a superintendent of evangelism and associational missions program to work in the Missions Department, headed by the general secretary-treasurer. The 1954 convention authorized the election of a director of the Church Music Department. These officers are elected for an indefinite term. The term of office of any may be ended by either party with 30 days' notice.

The general board, through its general secretary-treasurer, renders a comprehensive report of all business and administrative proposals in the departments at the annual meeting of the convention. This accounting also includes reports on the work of the other boards and committees of the convention.

The interests of the convention to be promoted by the board are classified as missions, education, and benevolence; but the constitution carries the article: "Among the special objects of the Convention, the support of Institutions of Learning in this State shall be considered as primary."

Other boards of the convention are those for Connie Maxwell Children's Home, the Baptist Hospital, the *Baptist Courier,* the Baptist Foundation of South Carolina, and the Bethea Baptist Home.

The Christian Life Commission serves the convention directly and reports each year. Its functions are defined in these words: "It shall be the purpose of the Commission to serve the Baptist Denomination of South Carolina in a serious effort to offer to the people of the State wise and progressive leadership in a constructive attack upon the pressing social problems of the day." Its work is informative and advisory.

State Missions Department. This work centers in the office of the general secretary-treasurer, and its program is formulated and reported by the board's missions committee. The convention's co-operation in Southern Baptist missions is primarily through the Cooperative Program. After the expense of administering the Cooperative Program funds is deducted, the monies were divided (in 1954) on a 50–50 basis up to a given amount. When that amount is reached, the remaining receipts are divided 60 per cent for the capital needs of South Carolina institutions and 40 per cent for Convention-wide causes. A place is made on the program of each meeting of the convention for presentation of Southern Baptist missionary, educational, and benevolent causes.

The missions committee arranges the program for promoting evangelism in the state, determines the nature of the co-operative work for associational missions, and provides assistance for two Negro schools—Benedict College and Morris College—and for the Jenkins Orphanage (Negro). Mountain mission work and district work, as well as city and rural work, are supported through associational missions.

A superintendent of evangelism and associational missions serves in the Missions Department. Twenty associations had missionaries in 1954, their salaries being paid jointly by the board and the respective associations. The Home Mission Board of the Southern Baptist Convention contributes to this work. An annual state evangelistic conference is well attended by ministers and others. The board co-operates closely with all Convention-wide evangelistic programs. These efforts are directed by the superintendent. This department also administers a fund designated as "Aid to Ministerial Students," reflecting a very old assistance practice, maintained since 1752. It also administers the funds for supplementing the salaries of pastor missionaries and for helping weaker churches finance building projects.

Sunday School Department.—This phase of state missions is staffed by a director, an associate director in charge of Vacation Bible schools and teacher-officer training, an associate in charge of associational promotion, an associate in charge of children's work, including guidance of weekday church kindergartens, and an office secretary and two assistants. A complete staff of departmental workers is engaged on a part-time basis to promote the programs of the various departments. This department works closely with the Sunday School Department of the Baptist Sunday School Board, which makes annual contributions to the budget of this department.

The objectives of the department are to perfect the organization, advance the teaching procedures, improve the equipment, and increase the enrolment in all the Sunday schools of the convention. It also gives some assistance to

Negro churches in promoting teacher training and Vacation Bible school work. The department uses a weekly page in the *Baptist Courier* to promote its work and furnish Sunday school news from churches and associations.

Counting mission schools, there are more Sunday schools than churches in the convention's territory. There are, however, a few churches (10 in 1954) without Sunday schools. The Sunday school enrolment approaches equality with the total church membership. Vacation Bible schools are held annually in almost all the churches.

The department gives guidance to churches in their building programs. Many churches have buildings which provide for departmentalized Sunday schools. The department pioneered in the use of visual aids, the laboratory approach to teacher training, the weekday church kindergarten, and departmental Sunday school organization for small Sunday schools. All associations are organized for participation in the program of this department.

Training Union Department.—The board has a Training Union committee which officially observes and reports on the work of this department. The staff for the program includes a director, two associate directors, an office secretary, and an office assistant. The department closely co-operates with the Training Union Department of the Baptist Sunday School Board. Its budget is provided by funds from the Cooperative Program, supplemented by the Baptist Sunday School Board.

This work is promoted through associational rallies, associational officers' clinics, regional conventions, a state convention, and a series of conferences at Ridgecrest, N. C., when Training Union plans are discussed. A page in the *Baptist Courier* carries weekly announcements and elaboration of state program plans, as well as news items from the churches. Regular activities include an annual Sword Drill and speakers' tournament, each conducted on a progressive elimination plan, culminating in the selection of a person for each of these activities to participate in a final tournament at Ridgecrest. An annual hymn festival is a part of the state program. Once included in the state convention program, its growth in popularity now demands a special time and place for a separate hymn festival. An annual Youth Week, in which young people take over the functions of all church officers for a period of time, is successfully promoted. A military service plan, projected to help young people in the armed forces keep contact with their home churches and to help them utilize military service as an opportunity for Christian growth, is provided.

Woman's Missionary Union.—This work is carried on in close co-ordination with the program of the general board. Regular contributions from members are channeled through the board's offices. Special offerings for Convention-wide causes go to the Executive Committee of the Southern Baptist Convention. Special gifts for state work go to the treasurers of the appropriate agencies. The current operations are cared for by an appropriation from the general board in ways similar to those provided for its various departments. The organization makes annual reports directly to the convention, and its work is discussed without being referred to a committee such as examines and reports on convention agencies. The Woman's Missionary Union work is auxiliary to, not incorporated in, the program of the board.

Institutes for education of ministers.—Furman University provides extension classes for the education of ministers and refresher courses for pastors. Anderson College co-operates with the extension work of the Southern Baptist Theological Seminary in the education of ministers.

Assemblies.—From 1914 to 1941, the Sunday School and B.Y.P.U. departments conducted an assembly in which the W.M.U. participated. The program included a pastors' school of which the general secretary-treasurer of the board was dean. Sessions were held in Furman University and Coker College. The final session included a school of religious education which featured laboratories in Sunday school administration and teaching. A seashore assembly was conducted from 1924 to 1929 at Myrtle Beach.

The W.M.U. began its own assembly in 1942 at Camp Rawls near Wagener and has continued it successfully. In 1954 this group established a second camp at Long Creek Academy. Both camps offer programs for all age groups. The W.M.U. co-operates with the Christian Youth Assembly held in Benedict College at Columbia.

The various departments of the board have co-operated with the Southern Baptist assembly program at Ridgecrest. During the summer several thousand South Carolina Baptists participate in the various weeks. Various departments of the board participate in assemblies conducted by local leaders in Beaverdam, Pickens, and North Greenville associations.

Vacation Bible schools.—The board promotes its Vacation Bible school work through the Sunday School Department. Schools are conducted in almost all the churches each summer. Encouragement and direct assistance have been given Negro churches. Through the associational Sunday school organization, the department has helped finance assistance to churches unable to conduct their own schools. In the proportion of churches conducting Vacation Bible schools each summer, South Carolina is outstanding in the South. All Vacation Bible school offerings are channeled into the Cooperative Program.

Student Union Department.—The Baptist Student Union work is reported on by a committee of the board and guided by a staff including a state director, directors on the various campuses (or a city-wide director, where more than one union may be involved), and an office associate. A state executive council composed of representatives from the various local student union councils plans the implementation of the program. There are local Baptist Student Unions on 25 campuses, including every accredited college (state or denominational) in South Carolina, and in six schools of nursing. There are also three Baptist Student Unions on campuses of Negro colleges.

The program of work is synchronized with that of the Student Union Department of the Baptist Sunday School Board. Its main purposes are to keep students in touch with a local college church during their college years, to help them relate their learning to their Christian convictions, and to make them effective witnesses for Christ among their college associates.

The work is promoted through the *Signal*—a paper issued by the state office periodically throughout the school year; retreats clinically conducted on the local and state levels; associational rallies; planning conferences; and a state convention. The *Baptist Courier, Baptist Student,* and many local campus papers are additional outlets for information and promotion. Distinctive successes in South Carolina Baptist Student Union work include the participation of a large proportion of all South Carolina educational institutions, the large proportion of unions attaining First Magnitude recognition and the wide distribution and use of the *Baptist Student.*

Brotherhood Department.—Until the 1946 meeting of the state convention, a special committee reported annually on Brotherhood work. At that time a committee was appointed to find a director for this endeavor. Since then, the work has been reported on by an appropriate committee of the board and by the Brotherhood Department.

This department is conducted by a director and an office secretary and financed by appropriations from the state board. When the convention committee made its last report, there were 40 Brotherhoods with an aggregate membership of 1,463. Seven years later, there were 500 Brotherhoods with a total membership of 17,500. All associations were then organized to carry on this program. The major objectives of the Brotherhood are to develop in Baptist men greater loyalty to Christ, the church, and the denomination, and to encourage participation in the full Baptist program with special emphasis on evangelism, stewardship enlistment, and fellowship. The work with boys formerly carried on by the Woman's Missionary Union was transferred to the Brotherhood Department. The work is carried on in close co-operation with the Southern Baptist Convention's Brotherhood Commission. Free exchange of programs and plans for the work is made with similar departments throughout the convention. A state Brotherhood encampment is sponsored at North Greenville Junior College, and a state Brotherhood convention is held in January of each year.

Radio Committee.—The convention called for a radio committee in its 1939 session. The committee was set up and has since reported directly to the convention each year. For a time it carried on a state Baptist radio hour but abandoned this to support fully the Baptist Hour arranged by the Radio Commission of the Southern Baptist Convention. The committee has encouraged the use of recording machines at church and denominational meetings and has produced by transcription a series of programs under the general theme "Adventures in Christian Living," for use by pastors and radio stations on a weekly or daily basis. It informs the convention of radio and television advancement.

Church Music Department.—The convention in its 1954 session instructed the board to employ a director of music for South Carolina as soon as possible.

Historical Society.—The South Carolina Baptist Historical Society, composed of a volunteer membership, was organized in the fall of 1948 and made its first report to the convention in 1949. Its stated purpose is "promoting interest in Baptist history, collecting and preserving such books, pamphlets, periodicals, manuscripts, pictures, autographs, records, and other matter which will aid in the preservation of the history of the Baptists in general and of South Carolina Baptists in particular." The convention makes annual appropriations to the work of this society.

Since 1920 the library of Furman University has been the depository for South Carolina Baptist historical materials. The society has requested and received from the convention the necessary amount to classify and arrange all material in this collection. It has microfilmed the collection of association minutes and church record books and other primary source material. Copies of these films have been deposited with the Historical Commission of the Southern Baptist Convention. This group has sponsored history-writing contests among the churches of the state and is currently lending support to the convention's effort to have a history of South Carolina Baptists written.

INSTITUTIONS. *Furman University.*—"Furman University, the South's oldest Baptist college, had its beginning at Edgefield, S. C., in 1826. It is the mother of the Southern Baptist Theological Seminary, the latter having been an outgrowth of the Theological department of Furman in 1859." It has been located in Greenville, S. C., since 1851. Established primarily as a ministerial training school, it has been operated through most of its history as a men's college. In 1933, however, Greenville Woman's College was merged with it to make a coeducational institution. According to plans, a new campus five miles north of the Greenville district will be ready in 1957.

A Reserve Officers' Training Corps has existed on the campus since 1950. The department of religion is given major emphasis. Concessions on tuition rates are made to sons and daughters of ministers and missionaries and to families when two or more students are registered for the same period. Much of the convention ministerial student aid allotments goes to students at Furman.

Anderson College.—Established in 1912 as a senior college for young women, Anderson College, Anderson, S. C., has been owned and controlled by the convention throughout its history. In 1930 the institution was changed to a junior college, and young men of the community were admitted as day students. Anderson now offers courses for the 11th and 12th years of high school, as well as the first two years of college. Of the 46 men enrolled in 1953, 23 were ministerial students. Most of the men are enrolled on a part-time basis and would not be able to secure college training elsewhere. Courses offered are of both the terminal and transfer-of-credit type. Emphasis on the liberal arts is distinctive, but a wide variety of preparatory professional courses is included.

North Greenville Junior College.—Beginning as a high school in 1892 and supported by the North Greenville Baptist Association and the Southern Baptist Home Mission Board as a part of the mountain school program, the school became a junior college in 1934. It has been controlled by the state convention since 1940. It is located at Tigerville, S. C. An associate in arts diploma is offered.

Children's home.—Founded in 1891 as Connie Maxwell Orphanage (Greenwood, S. C.). The name became by action of the convention in 1946 Connie Maxwell Children's Home, because most of the children were from broken homes or had one living parent. In order to help underprivileged children who could not be housed at the home, a foster home and mother's aid service has been provided since 1925. The home seeks to provide for children in their care a distinctive program of Christian training, to make the service family-centered rather than institution- or child-centered, and to seek larger financial support to minister to larger numbers of underprivileged children. The home has social workers who in various ways minister to children not in the institution. The home pioneered in the cottage type of orphanage.

Financial support comes through the Cooperative Program, the Duke Endowment, and general endowment funds, and, in larger proportions for current operation, through monthly offerings from Baptist Sunday schools of the state. A Thanksgiving offering brings large amounts of food products from the churches and associations of the state. The production department of the home includes a truck farm, the Maxwell farm (stock raising), a poultry farm, and a print shop.

Hospitals.—The South Carolina Baptist Hospital, in operation since Oct., 1914, has acquired valuable property well adapted to its use in the heart of Columbia. The hospital has its own college for nurses and seeks to qualify to award the B.S. degree in nursing education. Its financial support comes largely from current operations funds, but it participates in the Cooperative Program distributions of the board and makes an appeal to churches on each Mother's Day. In 1950 a modern nurses' home was erected, the W.M.U. of South Carolina having raised approximately $170,000 for this purpose.

A branch hospital was established at Six Mile, S. C., in 1945. It has been operated since (at an annual loss) largely for the accommodation of indigent patients. A nominal monthly charge is made for this service. A hospital under construction at Easley is to be turned over to the board as soon as completed, according to agreement. The hospital does much charitable service, with assistance from the Duke Endowment of Durham, N. C.

Ministerial relief.—Ministerial relief and old age provisions have long been concerns of South Carolina Baptists. Money for this use was available from 1894, through what was called the Aged Ministers' Relief Board. A report of this board in 1905 shows that 40 ministers and widows of ministers received aid from the fund. It was thereafter used continuously for relief work among South Carolina Baptist ministers and was finally used to purchase the building in which the South Carolina Baptist Book Store is located. Rents coming from this source are now used as part of the normal payment of the board on the annuities contract with the Southern Baptist Convention's Relief and Annuity Board. No adequate arrangement was made, however, until the Relief and Annuity Board entered this field. The South Carolina general board made a contract with the Southern board to provide annuities for its employees in 1936. The widow's supplementary annuity was later provided. In 1954 the board asked the convention to place its employees under Social Security. The same year, a liberalized annuity plan, providing more adequate coverage, was set up. The new plan affected both the ministers' and board employees' contracts. "South Carolina has led all states in enlisting the larger proportion of eligible pastors," reports the director of this work.

Baptist Foundation.—The convention has set up what it calls the Baptist Foundation of South Carolina, Inc. This institution has its board of directors and reports annually to the convention through the general board. Its purpose is to collect, preserve, and invest funds donated by interested persons for perpetual use by the convention. Income from the funds collected goes to causes designated by donors, with returns from undesignated funds distributed to the Cooperative Program.

Bethea Baptist Home for the Aged.—A home for the aged was approved by the convention on recommendation by the board in 1952. The board's interest in the matter had been encouraged by a gift of land and money from Dr. and Mrs. Perry S. Bethea of Darlington, S. C. A constitution and by-laws were adopted

IV. SOUTH CAROLINA STATISTICAL SUMMARY

Year	Associations	Churches	Church Membership	Baptisms	S. S. Enrolment	V.B.S. Enrolment	T. U. Enrolment	W.M.U. Enrolment	Brotherhood Enrolment No. B.H. Enroll	Mission Gifts	Total Gifts	Value Church Property	State Capital Worth
1830	..	NOT AVAILABLE											(Explanation: This column includes total value of Schools, Children's Homes, Hospitals, Foundation, Buildings, etc.)
1840	11	NOT AVAILABLE											
1850	11	NOT AVAILABLE								$ 492.72	....	....	
1860	16	468	53,644	....	....	....	....	....	....	....	$ 13,739.05	....	
*1869 & 1870	18	443	42,746	3,088	7,308	....	....	....	....	2,761.78	....	....	
1880	26	639	55,183	4,298	21,549	....	....	....	....	14,568.00	117,641.00	....	
1890	30	819	80,197	4,563	40,335	....	....	....	....	55,663.15	227,498.16	$ 918,850	
1900	35	909	97,033	3,928	44,388	....	....	3,984	....	37,767.68	199,584.09	1,141,270	
1905	37	975	110,029	5,718	55,424	....	....	5,536	....	77,546.24	349,750.14	1,524,436	
1910	36	1,066	130,190	6,558	67,149	....	....	....	....	142,391.58	618,093.17	2,297,230	
1915	38	1,138	153,745	9,833	99,447	....	....	....	....	175,253.53	720,347.33	3,655,152	....
1920	39	1,148	176,394	8,751	110,020	....	5,745	....	....	1,255,203.10	2,654,744.17	6,919,110	....
1925	39	1,195	214,072	12,603	163,923	....	40,540	....	....	592,605.23	2,322,594.60	9,687,239	....
1930	38	1,162	226,748	9,113	177,636	....	23,716	....	....	368,249.47	1,856,134.86	12,348,413	....
1931	38	1,166	229,938	9,498	186,221	....	24,201	42,132	....	346,430.85	1,728,070.64	11,796,078	....
1932	38	1,180	238,048	10,737	195,013	....	27,475	39,067	....	296,324.51	1,386,533.26	11,640,810	....
1933	38	1,158	242,567	11,030	194,391	....	26,305	48,233	....	241,155.27	1,312,573.84	11,225,228	....
1934	38	1,189	245,090	11,058	198,198	....	34,506	43,003	....	278,244.90	1,455,577.89	11,464,828	$3,500,714.79
1935	38	1,204	257,391	11,654	203,264	....	27,400	49,661	....	201,681.06	1,497,146.93	11,011,026	....
1936	38	1,192	264,477	10,841	205,642	18,864	34,563	49,319	....	315,145.88	1,685,945.94	13,735,576	....
1937	38	1,192	271,329	10,750	207,303	17,446	37,480	53,151	....	371,050.00	1,993,826.96	11,874,112	....
1938	38	1,194	281,518	13,751	219,897	22,088	42,560	58,163	....	370,546.09	2,078,128.11	12,410,104	....
1939	38	1,215	285,590	11,898	223,163	1,772	37,749	60,490	....	414,526.30	2,205,444.41	12,511,012	....
1940	38	1,219	292,658	10,851	221,718	24,508	38,004	60,968	....	419,307.76	2,326,385.03	13,198,699	....
1941	38	1,202	295,206	9,359	217,208	28,151	35,679	58,678	....	489,434.19	2,573,212.05	13,635,882	....
1942	38	1,212	299,718	8,899	209,898	30,439	32,238	55,985	....	615,126.85	3,210,328.26	14,582,559	....
1943	38	1,215	304,979	10,419	206,224	33,043	31,960	55,251	....	811,189.53	3,684,561.98	14,962,343	....
1944	38	1,225	312,757	10,861	207,171	34,206	33,301	52,647	....	970,897.35	4,245,723.14	16,079,710	....
1945	38	1,229	322,377	12,846	215,659	44,143	38,065	57,159	....	1,251,236.54	5,784,037.52	16,955,690	3,793,949.43
1946	38	1,242	331,593	12,786	225,276	54,274	41,581	58,181	40 1,463	1,685,576.85	6,501,220.41	18,465,267	....
1947	38	1,249	341,603	13,707	242,217	73,904	47,762	61,366	64 2,112	1,707,832.92	7,779,264.84	21,437,960	....
1948	38	1,267	352,063	15,892	256,121	86,503	58,357	69,251	113 3,616	1,879,583.	9,414,019.	26,948,700	....
1949	38	1,273	365,048	17,357	281,343	102,816	70,804	79,398	163 5,216	2,165,107.	11,676,756.	32,823,150	....
1950	38	1,293	379,403	19,912	302,519	116,066	85,461	88,004	230 7,360	2,071,944.	14,050,073.	40,277,525	....
1951	39	1,319	398,724	21,699	322,572	124,518	95,131	94,637	316 10,112	2,693,091.	15,512,007.	49,340,350	....
1952	39	1,341	409,093	16,111	332,030	135,371	101,931	90,135	378 12,096	3,014,245.48	15,395,305.63	66,755,170	....
1953	39	1,361	418,067	16,934	344,281	138,363	111,152	105,857	440 14,520	3,391,144.	17,097,669.	62,954,750	....
1954	39	1,385	432,535	18,094	380,047	155,392	121,886	108,725	506 17,710	3,781,808.	19,249,455.	70,361,000	8,223,556.68

* The only statistics available for this year cover the two years 1869 & 1870.

IDA MARGARET JACKSON THOMAS

for this agency, and a board of directors was elected in 1953. This board later elected a superintendent-treasurer, who established an office in the general board's building and began an effort to secure the funds necessary for the initial capital needs. The home is to be located at Darlington.

PROMOTIONAL WORK. *The Baptist Courier.*—The primary promotional agency of the convention is the *Baptist Courier,* with offices in Greenville, S. C. Once privately owned, this paper has been the property of the convention since 1921. Its circulation is extended largely by the budget plan, through which a church subscribes for it in behalf of all the families in its membership, and the club plan, whereby a specified minimum number of families receive the paper. Its circulation in 1954 approximated 90,000. The convention subsidizes the publication when necessary, and the board has free use of its pages in promoting all phases of its work. The *Baptist Courier* makes annual reports to the convention through the general board, though it has its own board of directors selected by the convention.

Direct promotional work.—Each of the departments of the board carries on vigorous promotional work. Literature furnished each by its corresponding Convention-wide agency is supplemented by leaflets, bulletins, and other literature created to meet special needs in the state. All departments have associational organizations which advance their programs. Stewardship promotional work is headed by the assistant general secretary-treasurer, with all departments supporting. Each department has its associational, regional, and state convention on a somewhat different pattern. There is also an annual evangelism conference, the responsibility for which lies with the superintendent of evangelism and associational missions. The convention has a special standing committee on evangelism which makes no reports but consults with the superintendent of evangelism in the Missions Department.

Stewardship promotion.—Annually, the convention president appoints a committee on stewardship. This group studies the field for a year and makes a report carrying suggestions to the convention on plans and programs. It may also consult and advise the associate general secretary, who is charged by the board with responsibility for promoting this emphasis. The annual program carried out by the assistant general secretary includes an annual stewardship week in the churches, a church and denominational life day recommended for all, a mid-winter conference in each association, with a stewardship committee responsible for continuing this promotion, and summer and fall conferences in advance of the annual associations, at which time goals are proposed, and literature and films for use in promoting stewardship are made available.

Two meetings of the associations are held each year—a spring meeting, which is largely informational and inspirational, and a fall meeting for the official business of these denominational groups. The assistant general secretary is present or represented in each, primarily to present the stewardship emphasis.

Several new leaflets on stewardship originate annually in the general secretary-treasurer's office. Each of the educational departments gives an appropriate emphasis to this subject, and the W.M.U. carries on a continual appeal for faithfulness to Bible teaching about stewardship.

CO-OPERATIVE ACTIVITIES. *American Bible Society.*—The board co-operates with the American Bible Society in its efforts to distribute the Bible, both in English and in translations, to a multitude of peoples around the earth. A special Sunday for contributions to this work is designated each year. The Sunday School Department supports the effort; the general board receives and transmits the offering for the society; and the convention receives and prints in its *Annual* a report on the achievement of the Bible Society.

Temperance and social service.—The convention has a Social Service Commission which studies the problem of social applications of Christian teaching and makes an annual report direct to the convention. The commission also serves as the liaison agency between the convention and the South Carolina Christian Action Council, which advocates temperance measures and social improvement by the state legislature and before the public in general. The general board makes regular contributions to the council. J. L. CORZINE

BIBLIOGRAPHY: W. W. Barnes, *The Southern Baptist Convention* (1954). D. Benedict, *A General History of the Baptist Denomination in America and Other Parts of the World* (1813). H. S. Burrage, *History of the Baptists of Maine* (1904). Charleston Baptist Association, *Minutes* (1775–1955). H. T. Cook, *A Biography of Richard Furman* (1913). R. N. Daniel, *Furman University, a History* (1951). M. Edwards, "Materials Toward a History of the Baptists in the Province of South Carolina" (1772). J. C. Furman, "Historical Discourse" (1852). W. Furman, *A History of the Charleston Association of Baptist Churches in the State of South Carolina* (1811). C. M. Griffin, *The Story of South Carolina Baptists* (1934). W. B. Hesseltine, *A History of the South* (1941). R. A. Ivey, *A History of the Baptist Courier* (1955). W. J. McGlothlin, *Baptist Beginnings in Education* (1926); *Baptist Confessions of Faith* (1911). A. H. Newman, *A History of the Baptist Churches in the United States* (1894). South Carolina Baptist State Convention, *Minutes* (1821–1954). G. B. Taylor, *The Life and Times of James B. Taylor* (1872). R. G. Torbet, *A History of the Baptists* (1950). L. Townsend, *South Carolina Baptists, 1670–1805* (1935). H. A. Tupper, ed., *Two Centuries of the First Baptist Church of South Carolina, 1683–1883* (1889). H. Woodson, *Giant in the Land* (1950).

SOUTH CAROLINA ASSOCIATIONS.

I. Extant. ABBEVILLE. Organized in 1869 with 12 churches from Edgefield Association in the western part of the state on the Savannah River. The association adopted articles of faith in 1870.

It employs a missionary. In 1954, 35 churches reported 500 baptisms, 12,743 members, $674,-083 total gifts, $156,872 mission gifts, and $1,917,-600 property value, and $125,306 church debt.

AIKEN. Organized in 1891 with 21 churches from Edisto Association in the southwestern part of the state on the Savannah River. It adopted articles of faith in 1891. In 1954, 48 churches reported 878 baptisms, 13,929 members, $857,147 total gifts, $110,828 mission gifts, and $2,116,500 property value, and $318,379 church debt.

BARNWELL. Organized in 1856 with 14 churches partly out of Savannah River Association. It is in the southwestern part of the state on the Savannah River and employs a missionary. In 1954, 38 churches reported 519 baptisms, 9,399 members, $423,487 total gifts, $78,308 mission gifts, and $1,302,500 property value, and $33,610 church debt.

BEAVERDAM. Organized in 1887 with 29 churches from Fork and New Bethel associations. Located in the northwestern corner of the state, the association had adopted articles of faith by 1891. In 1954, 57 churches reported 539 baptisms, 12,314 members, $404,095 total gifts, $48,083 mission gifts, and $1,121,700 property value, and $27,407 church debt.

BROAD RIVER. Organized in 1800 with churches from Bethel Association. Located on the northern border of the state, it adopted articles of faith in 1905. In 1954, 50 churches reported 605 baptisms, 15,768 members, $692,957 total gifts, $133,848 mission gifts, and $2,238,000 property value, and $115,124 church debt.

CAROLINA. Organized in 1911 partly from Waccamaw Association. It is located on the extreme eastern tip of the state. It adopted articles of faith in 1947 and employs a missionary jointly with Waccamaw. In 1954, 41 churches reported 191 baptisms, 5,640 members, $78,469 total gifts, $13,383 mission gifts, and $393,800 property value.

CHARLESTON. Organized Oct. 21, 1751, the first Baptist association in the South and the second in America. Its four constituting churches were Charles Town (1683), Ashley River (1736), Welsh Neck (1738), and Euhaw (1746). Although present boundaries approximate those of Charleston County, the association once extended south into Georgia, north into North Carolina, and 100 miles into the center of South Carolina. The association was organized and nurtured by Oliver Hart (*q.v.*), and at the first session "the object of the union was declared to be the promotion of the Redeemer's kingdom, by the maintenance of love and fellowship, and by mutual consultations for the peace and welfare of the churches. The independency of the churches was asserted, and the powers of the Association restricted to those of a Council of Advice." The early activities of this association set a pattern which Southern Baptists have followed.

"Baptist education in South Carolina is the child of the Charleston Association." As early as 1754 the Religious Society, sponsored by the association, was active and had as its chief aim the collection of funds for training ministerial students. "To it is reckoned the honor of being the first religious partnership in America in the interest of ministerial education." Among those aided by it were Jesse Mercer (*q.v.*), Edmund Botsford, and probably Hezekiah Smith. Between 1800 and 1810 a private academy at High Hills gave free tuition to ministerial students, and the association purchased a library for its use in 1802, which was transferred to the Furman Academy and Theological Institution in 1826. Furman University was the direct outgrowth of the association's concern for ministerial education.

The association's loyalty to missions paralleled its zeal for education. John Gano (*q.v.*) was secured in 1755 as a missionary to the back country, and in 1802 the association employed John Rooker as missionary to the near-by Catawba Indians. Rooker founded a school which the association supported for several years.

Charleston Association promoted fellowship among pioneer Baptists and emphasized the oneness of their beliefs. It corresponded with other associations which were formed and as early as 1794 proposed a union of associations. Organization of the South Carolina Baptist convention in 1821 was due to its influence. The association had a stabilizing effect on morals and doctrines, dealing with erring churches and preachers alike. It helped to unify several branches of Baptists into one strong body and in 1767 adopted the Philadelphia Confession.

In 1954, 28 churches reported 940 baptisms, 18,603 members, $176,986 mission gifts, $946,418 total gifts, $2,964,000 property value, and $291,-190 church debt. It employs an associational missionary.

BIBLIOGRAPHY: W. Furman, *A History of the Charleston Association of Baptist Churches* (1811). W. J. McGlothlin, *Baptist Beginnings in Education* (1926). L. Townsend, *South Carolina Baptists, 1670–1805* (1935). O. Hart, "A memorandum containing some of the most remarkable concurrencies on providence relative to or noticed by an unworthy traveler towards the New Jerusalem, who desires ever to esteem himself a stranger and sojourner in this dreary wilderness" (Parts of a diary in the Furman University Library).

CHESTER. Organized in 1878 with 12 churches mostly from Bethel Association and located in the north central part of the state. In 1954, 18 churches reported 214 baptisms, 5,517 members, $231,174 total gifts, $38,917 mission gifts, and $774,000 property value, and $52,036 church debt.

CHESTERFIELD. Organized in 1891 with nine churches mostly from Moriah Association. Located on the northern border of the state, the association employs a missionary. In 1954, 51 churches reported 291 baptisms, 8,811 members, $180,324 total gifts, $40,172 mission gifts, and $847,300 property value, and $15,495 church debt.

COLLETON. Organized in 1863 partly from Savannah River Association and is located in the southern part of the state on the Atlantic coast. It had adopted articles of faith by 1879. In 1954, 29 churches reported 330 baptisms, 6,275 members, $277,163 total gifts, $48,158 mission gifts, and $1,021,000 property value, and $125,358 church debt.

EDGEFIELD. Organized in 1807 in western South Carolina on the Savannah River. It helped support Edisto Academy and by 1824 had adopted articles of faith. In 1954, 21 churches reported 96 baptisms, 3,746 members, $106,095 total gifts, $25,405 mission gifts, and $527,000 property value, and $3,550 church debt.

EDISTO. Organized in 1834 with 15 churches in the west central part of the state. With the help of several other associations, it maintained Edisto Academy. By 1853 it had adopted articles of faith. In 1954, 17 churches reported 64 baptisms, 3,260 members, $86,040 total gifts, $12,982 mission gifts, and $310,000 property value, and $3,571 church debt.

FAIRFIELD. Organized in 1863 in the central part of the state with 22 churches from Columbia and Salem associations. At its first annual session John A. Broadus (*q.v.*) spoke and took an offering, amounting to $300, for the newly organized Sunday School Board at Greenville. Fairfield employs a missionary. In 1954, 49 churches reported 1,227 baptisms, 24,363 members, $1,260,296 total gifts, $334,206 mission gifts, and $5,232,000 property value, and $1,035,000 church debt.

FLORENCE. Organized in 1890 in the northeastern part of the state with 12 churches from Welsh Neck Association. The association helped to maintain Welsh Neck High School, now Coker College. In 1954, 22 churches reported 491 baptisms, 9,235 members, $456,250 total gifts, $79,132 mission gifts, and $1,990,000 property value, and $185,596 church debt.

GREENVILLE. Organized in 1860 in the northwestern part of the state with 12 churches from Enoree Association. Moderator William Bullein Johnson (*q.v.*) made the first speech before the association. An agriculture society, active 1860–1866, met as a part of the association and raised money for missions and the Confederacy. Greenville employs a missionary jointly with North Greenville Association. In 1954, 74 churches reported 1,325 baptisms, 37,963 members, $1,773,752 total gifts, $447,890 mission gifts, and $6,429,000 property value, and $457,384 church debt.

KERSHAW. Organized in 1900 in the northeastern part of the state from Moriah Association. The association employs a missionary. In 1954, 35 churches reported 272 baptisms, 7,720 members, $335,763 total gifts, $48,109 mission gifts, and $1,353,700 property value, and $163,895 church debt.

LAURENS. Organized in 1896 out of Reedy River Association with 21 constituting churches. It is located in the northwestern part of the state. In 1954, 36 churches reported 351 baptisms, 9,447 members, $358,130 total gifts, $77,878 mission gifts, and $1,801,000 property value with no church debt.

LEXINGTON. Organized in 1877 in the central part of the state. It employs a missionary. In 1954, 37 churches reported 506 baptisms, 8,527 members, $355,916 total gifts, $59,709 mission gifts, and $1,513,500 property value, and $320,279 church debt.

MARION. Organized in the eastern part of the state in 1924 with 12 churches out of Pee Dee Association. In 1954, 13 churches reported 102 baptisms, 4,033 members, $86,305 total gifts, $26,683 mission gifts, and $339,000 property value, and $500 church debt.

MORIAH. Organized in 1815 on the northern border of the state. Articles of faith were adopted. In 1954, 40 churches reported 522 baptisms, 12,546 members, $871,651 total gifts, $117,242 mission gifts, and $2,531,500 property value, and $293,423 church debt.

NORTH GREENVILLE. Organized in 1887 with 22 churches mostly from Greenville Association. Located on the northwestern border of the state, the association helped support Spartan Academy and established North Greenville Academy, which became North Greenville Junior College. Jointly with the Greenville Association it supports a missionary. In 1954, 53 churches reported 710 baptisms, 17,071 members, $813,086 total gifts, $148,784 mission gifts, and $3,098,000 property value, and $169,914 church debt.

NORTH SPARTANBURG. Organized in 1912 with the 26 churches on the north side of Southern Railway's main line through the area of old Spartanburg Association. Located on the northwestern border of the state, the association helped support Spartan Academy. With the Spartan Association it employs a missionary. In 1954, 48 churches reported 695 baptisms, 20,026 members, $834,785 total gifts, $155,787 mission gifts, and $2,972,000 property value, and $182,927 church debt.

ORANGEBURG. Organized in 1870 from Charleston and Edisto associations with seven churches and located in the south central part of the state. It adopted articles of faith in 1870. In 1954, 32 churches reported 269 baptisms, 8,598 members, $298,605 total gifts, $83,480 mission gifts, and $1,235,000 property value.

PEE DEE. Organized in 1877 on the northeastern border of the state with 20 churches from Welsh Neck Association. In 1878 the association employed a missionary; also it helped to support Welsh Neck High School, now Coker College. In 1954, 29 churches reported 341 baptisms, 7,207 members, $254,812 total gifts, $43,667 mission gifts, and $1,020,400 property value, and $61,392 church debt.

PICKENS. Organized in 1903 with 10 churches from Twelve Mile River Association. Located on the northwestern border of the state, the association adopted articles of faith in 1903. Jointly with Twelve Mile River Association it employs a missionary. In 1954, 15 churches reported 139 baptisms, 3,830 members, $96,810 total gifts,

$21,885 mission gifts, and $415,500 property value, and $3,476 church debt.

PIEDMONT. Organized in 1878 with 11 churches from Twelve Mile River Association. Located in the northwestern part of the state, the association adopted articles of faith in 1883. Jointly with Saluda Association it employs a missionary. In 1954, 41 churches reported 401 baptisms, 11,562 members, $425,855 total gifts, $73,515 mission gifts, and $1,722,600 property value, and $87,662 church debt.

REEDY RIVER. Organized in 1826 with 11 churches from Saluda Association. Located in the northwest central part of the state, the association adopted articles of faith in 1830. In 1954, 16 churches reported 175 baptisms, 3,483 members, $169,659 total gifts, $34,174 mission gifts, and $659,000 property value, and $75,105 church debt.

RIDGE. Organized in 1886 with 18 churches from Edgefield Association. Located in the west central part of the state, the association adopted articles of faith in 1886. It helped to support Edisto Academy. In 1954, 19 churches reported 171 baptisms, 5,537 members, $206,229 total gifts, $44,017 mission gifts, and $738,500 property value, and $42,586 church debt.

SALUDA. Organized in 1802 with about 20 churches located in the western part of the state on the Savannah River. It adopted articles of faith in 1832 and adopted Johnson Female Seminary as associational high school in 1849. Jointly with the Piedmont Association it employs a missionary. In 1954, 62 churches reported 800 baptisms, 26,706 members, $1,020,234 total gifts, $204,118 mission gifts, and $4,375,000 property value, and $220,008 church debt.

SANTEE. Organized in 1877 with 13 churches, most of them from Charleston Association. Located in the central eastern part of the state, Santee helped to support Welsh Neck High School, now Coker College. In 1954, 28 churches reported 518 baptisms, 8,833 members, $365,752 total gifts, $62,009 mission gifts, and $1,195,500 property value.

SAVANNAH RIVER. Organized in 1802 at the southern tip of the state. In its early days it covered a large portion of the back country of the state. In 1954, 41 churches reported 436 baptisms, 9,232 members, $282,085 total gifts, $55,609 mission gifts, and $1,156,000 property value, and $82,225 church debt.

SCREVEN. Organized in 1950 on the eastern coast of the state with 32 churches, most of them from Charleston and Orangeburg associations. In 1954, 33 churches reported 248 baptisms, 6,189 members, $375,202 total gifts, $42,604 mission gifts, and $1,263,000 property value, and $206,674 church debt.

SOUTHEAST. Organized in 1886 on the eastern coast of the state. It helped to support Welsh Neck High School, now Coker College, and it now employs a missionary. In 1954, 34 churches reported 477 baptisms, 7,378 members, $336,020 total gifts, $43,558 mission gifts, and $1,308,200 property value.

SPARTAN. Organized in 1912 with the 28 churches on the south side of Southern Railway's main line through the area of old Spartanburg Association. Located in the northwestern part of the state, the association adopted articles of faith in 1912 and helped support Spartan Academy. Jointly with North Spartanburg Association it employs a missionary. In 1954, 49 churches reported 825 baptisms, 23,326 members, $1,157,269 total gifts, $322,562 mission gifts, and $4,458,500 property value, and $292,546 church debt.

TWELVE MILE RIVER. Organized in 1829 on the northwestern border of the state. By 1851 it had adopted articles of faith. Jointly with Pickens Association Twelve Mile River employs a missionary. In 1954, 25 churches reported 144 baptisms, 3,510 members, $50,300 total gifts, $6,442 mission gifts, and $281,000 property value.

UNION COUNTY. Organized in 1876 with 13 churches from Broad River and Bethel associations. Located in the north central part of the state, the association adopted articles of faith in 1876. It helped to support Spartan Academy. In 1954, 25 churches reported 315 baptisms, 8,320 members, $711,151 total gifts, $90,490 mission gifts, and $1,992,000 property value, and $113,385 church debt.

WACCAMAW. Organized in 1875 on the northwestern border of the state with a mixture of North and South Carolina churches. Jointly with Carolina Association it supports a missionary. In 1954, 39 churches reported 471 baptisms, 9,691 members, $389,373 total gifts, $58,700 mission gifts, and $1,313,200 property value, and $174,449 church debt.

WELSH NECK. Organized in 1832 with 19 churches from Charleston Association. Located in the northeastern part of the state, the association adopted articles of faith in 1832. It helped to support Welsh Neck High School and adopted an associational camp for missionary education in 1950. Welsh Neck has been the mother of several associations. In 1954, 30 churches reported 380 baptisms, 11,192 members, $467,279 total gifts, $95,068 mission gifts, and $2,300,500 property value, and $124,585 church debt.

YORK. Organized in 1868 on the northern border of the state with six churches from Broad River and Moriah associations. York employs a missionary. In 1954, 27 churches reported 616 baptisms, 11,005 members, $539,434 total gifts, $119,620 mission gifts, and $2,234,000 property value, and $91,148 church debt.

II. Extinct. BETHEL. Organized in 1788 in old Union and Chester districts with about 25 churches. In 1876 several churches went into the new Union County Association, and in 1878 the rest went into the new Chester Association.

BLACK RIVER. Organized in 1904 with six churches located near Greelyville and Manning in Clarendon and Williamsburg counties. In 1910 it dissolved, with most of its churches entering Santee Association.

COLUMBIA. Organized in 1858 with about eight churches located in the central part of the state near Columbia. In 1863 it combined with Salem to form Fairfield Association.

DORCHESTER. Organized in 1887 near Summerville in Dorchester County. Two of its four churches joined Charleston Association in 1926. The other two churches were very weak and probably disbanded.

ENOREE. Organized Oct. 4, 1850, with six churches located in old Greenville district. It dissolved in 1860 to form Greenville Association.

FORK. Organized about 1851, located near Walhalla, Seneca, and Westminster in Oconee County. In 1886 most of its churches combined with New Bethel to form Beaverdam Association.

LAKE SWAMP. Organized in 1890 in the extreme eastern tip of the state, mostly in Horry County. It dissolved in 1902 when most of its churches joined Waccamaw Association.

NEW BETHEL. Organized probably in 1880 with five churches. It was located in the northwestern tip of the state, in Anderson and Oconee counties. In 1886 New Bethel united with Fork to form Beaverdam Association.

SALEM. Organized in 1845 with nine churches located in the central part of the state just north of Columbia. In 1863 most of its churches combined with Columbia to form Fairfield Association.

SAULDAM. Organized in 1917 with four churches, near Summerville and Ridgeville in Dorchester County. It dissolved about 1929, and its three churches joined other associations.

SPARTANBURG. Organized in 1876 with 28 churches located in the Spartanburg district. In 1912 the 26 churches north of Southern Railway's main line became North Spartanburg Association, and the 28 south of the line became Spartan Association.

TYGER RIVER. Organized in 1833 with 12 churches, located in Greenville and Spartanburg districts. In 1875 its remaining churches became a part of Spartanburg Association.

LOULIE LATIMER OWENS

SOUTH CAROLINA BAPTIST. A weekly paper started through the efforts of W. E. Walters, editor, and first distributed in Apr., 1866. "Devoted to the dissemination of Christian truth and general news," this four-page paper was published in Anderson, S. C., every Friday. James Alfred Hoyt (*q.v.*) and Walters were the proprietors. The subscription price, first set at $2 per year, was later changed to $2.50, and the last known issue of the paper was dated Dec. 25, 1868.

ROBERT A. IVEY

SOUTH CAROLINA BAPTIST FOUNDATION. Created Nov. 16, 1948, by the Baptist state convention and chartered Mar. 15, 1949.

The principal object of the foundation is to acquire and administer funds, investing them to produce income for the benefit of Baptist educational and benevolent institutions, agencies, and causes in South Carolina. Only the net income realized from the funds and properties after the payment of necessary expenses may be used by trustees for current needs, and it may not be used for any other purpose. J. E. Rawlinson, Arthur L. Gross, and R. Frank Kolb have served as the foundation's executive secretaries, Kolb since Jan. 11, 1955. The foundation's total assets on Dec. 31, 1954, were $13,721.70, and income from investments for the year totaled $580.63. The operating budget for the foundation, supplied by the Baptist state convention from Cooperative Program receipts, was $12,500 in 1954.

R. FRANK KOLB

SOUTH CAROLINA BAPTIST HISTORICAL SOCIETY. Organized in 1948 "as a part of" the South Carolina Baptist state convention program, continues the effort begun by the abortive Baptist Historical Society of 1890–93 "to gather and to preserve as much as possible of the past records of the Baptists and of their work in the State." The early society stimulated the writing of a number of historical articles and helped Harvey Toliver Cook (1848–1943), Furman University professor, collect materials which eventually grew into the Baptist historical collection of Furman University Library, the official "custodian of material r[e]lating to Baptist History in this State" since 1920. Sporadic interest in denominational history, centered around the celebration of the hundredth anniversary of the state convention in 1921, was maintained by a small number of people, largely ministers; and various convention committees on history were appointed, but they accomplished little.

The present society was organized "to collect, record, preserve, and disseminate data on South Carolina Baptist achievements past and present." The convention created a standing committee to report annually on the work of the society, which was directed to "cooperate closely with the work of the Southern Baptist Historical Society." The convention has made an annual appropriation for the society's work since 1951. Membership is open to anyone interested in the work of the society, which elects its own officers. Regular meetings are held in the fall at the time of the annual meeting of the state convention and in the spring at the time of the statewide evangelistic conference.

The society has engaged in the following major activities: (1) placing markers at sites important in South Carolina Baptist history, (2) augmenting the Baptist historical collection of Furman University, (3) microfilming major records consisting of state and associational minutes, the *Baptist Courier* (*q.v.*), and many church minute books.

ROBERT C. TUCKER

SOUTH CAROLINA BAPTIST HOSPITAL. Located in Columbia and chartered Feb. 19, 1913, by the state of South Carolina, the hospital is owned by the Baptist state convention and operated by a board of trustees elected by the convention. With the conviction "that God's Word clearly teaches care of the sick," the original trustees set out to "project a hospital on a great and worthy scale."

The first effort in the hospital field by any Baptist group in South Carolina was begun by the Green Street Baptist Church of Spartanburg, and its success evidently prompted Louis Judson Bristow to offer a resolution Dec. 6, 1911, to the convention in session at Greenwood that a committee be appointed to consider the advisability of establishing a sanitarium. At Abbeville Dec. 12, 1912, the committee recommended that the work be undertaken and a committee be appointed to take it in hand. The recommendation was adopted when amended to the effect that the hospital would be free of any cost to the convention. Hospitals already in existence at Greenwood and Chester, a site at Shivar Spring, and $30,000 in cash from the city of Columbia were offered. The Columbia offer was accepted and reported to the convention Dec. 11, 1913.

The trustees bought the Colonia Hotel block in Columbia; but in July, 1914, when A. B. Knowlton died, the Knowlton Hospital in Columbia was offered for sale. It was bought and the Baptist Hospital was opened Sept. 1, 1914, one year earlier than had been expected. During its 40 years' history the hospital has had only three superintendents: John Joseph Gentry, Oct., 1914—Aug., 1915; Bristow, Aug., 1915—Dec., 1918; and William Marion Whiteside, since Dec. 18, 1918.

The convention was petitioned by the Twelve Mile River Association in 1943 to accept the Peak Hospital located at Six Mile, S. C., which it did, making this 35-bed hospital a unit of the South Carolina Baptist Hospital. During the next five years of operation it became evident that a general hospital could not be operated in a remote community; thus the Six Mile Hospital has come to be operated as a home for aged and chronically ill people. In 1948 the people of Easley, S. C., offered the convention $300,000 and six acres of land to build and equip a 50-bed hospital in Easley. Construction on the building was well under way in 1956.

A total of 155,701 patients have been served since the Baptist Hospital first opened. Income from the denomination totals $800,437.98. Free service totaling $2,274,466.26 has been given. Hospital assets include 10 buildings valued at $2,151,953.09, with 225 beds and 33 bassinets. The College for Nurses has graduated 743 nurses and now has a student body of approximately 200. In 1954, 9,399 patients and 1,251 infants were served, with a total of $223,223.98 given in free service. WILLIAM BOYCE

SOUTH FLORIDA BAPTIST HOSPITAL, Plant City. On Sept. 1, 1943, a Plant City civic council, the Presidents' Round Table, appointed a hospital committee to study methods by which a new hospital could be established in the city. Members of Baptist churches in Plant City took a leading part in this movement, and as a result, on Jan. 17, 1945, South Florida Baptist Hospital was chartered as a private Baptist nonprofit corporation with all trustees members of churches associated with the Florida Baptist State Convention. Following the leadership of Baptist churches, Plant City and surrounding communities contributed generously in raising funds to build the hospital. On June 17, 1945, the board of directors accepted the five-acre plot on which the hospital now stands as a gift from Mrs. S. E. Mays. Construction began Dec. 18, 1947, and the hospital opened to receive its first patient Dec. 29, 1953. Through July 31, 1955, the hospital admitted 5,472 inpatients. During this period patient income totaled $578,616, and denominational income, $11,000, exclusive of designated gifts. Prior to opening of the hospital, designated gifts of $147,963 were received, and $44,655 after opening. Free service rendered to charity patients totaled $26,835. Building, grounds, and equipment are valued at $1,662,977, with a mortgaged indebtedness of $510,529 as of July 31, 1955. In 1954 the hospital received $320,049 from 3,270 inpatients. Donations of $34,037 were made through designated gifts. South Florida Baptist Hospital serves patients of all races and creeds. Application for accreditation by the Joint Commission on Accreditation of Hospitals has been made. PAT N. GRONER

SOUTH FORK INSTITUTE. School of South Fork Association, located at Maiden, Catawba County, N. C. Founded in 1901, the school opened in 1903 on a site donated by Union Cotton Mills, with B. W. Allen as the first principal. In 1910 Catawba River Association adopted the school, and in 1911 Caldwell Association endorsed it. Despite assistance of these associations, financial problems increased. In 1917, when the town of Maiden made plans to open a public school, trustees were authorized to sell the South Fork property. The following year the buildings were sold, and the money was used to endow scholarships for South Fork students at wake Forest and Meredith colleges. D. L. SIMLEY

SOUTH GEORGIA BAPTIST CONVENTION. A regional association organized on Nov. 14, 1890, by a group of 27 messengers from 10 associations to meet the religious needs of the area within a 60-mile radius of Eastman and McRae, Ga. The purpose expressed by the body was "to effect a permanent organization for the more successful co-operation among ourselves and the better aiding of the Georgia Baptist Convention and its Mission Board to meet the wants of this section of the State."

At the organizational meeting plans were begun for the holding of a Bible institute for ministers, and a committee was appointed to consider the establishment of a Baptist school, the New Ebenezer School at Cochran having been established three years before. The man most responsible for the new movement was Philip

Andrew Jessup, pastor of the Eastman church, a man of wide influence in a number of South Georgia ventures, and the founder of the New Ebenezer College at Cochran, the Freddie Shipp College at Cordele, and Norman Institute.

The organization met at Abbeville in 1891, at Statesboro in 1893, at Cordele in 1894, and at Abbeville in 1897. One of the undertakings of the South Georgia group was the establishment of Freddie Shipp College at Cordele. The school opened in the fall of 1893 but lasted little more than a year. A more successful venture was the Bible institute held at Eastman for two months in the winter of 1896–97 under the leadership of pastor J. C. Brewton.

Sentiment for discontinuing the South Georgia Convention became strong in 1898. An appraisal of the South Georgia body was made for the *Index*. Replying to the question of the future of the body, Jessup wrote:

> My answer is, "It has none." Having helped to bring a needy field and needy people in touch with the needed help and encouragement, together with its own people becoming able to stand alone, what was known as the South Georgia Convention can afford to retire, giving place to stronger and better things.

The convention met at Ailey in 1898, and the suggestion of Jessup that the body be dissolved was rejected. Apparently, however, the opinion of Jessup prevailed, and the body soon disbanded. EDWIN D. JOHNSTON

SOUTH GEORGIA MESSENGER. A 12-page monthly newspaper published at Cochran, Ga., by B. J. W. Graham in 1897. When Graham became editor of *The* (Ga.) *Index* in 1899, he discontinued the *Messenger,* which at that time claimed 1,000 subscribers at 50 cents each. JOHN J. HURT, JR.

SOUTH RIVER BAPTIST INSTITUTE. School of South River Association, located at Autryville, Sampson County, N. C. By agreement with James L. Autry, donor of the property, the school opened Aug. 3, 1891, with John A. Oates as the principal. It was supervised by a board of trustees elected by the association which owned it. In 1898 Cedar Creek Association contributed to the support of the school, but despite this assistance it closed shortly thereafter. D. L. SMILEY

SOUTH TEXAS BAPTIST. Published originally as *Missionary Visitor* in 1903, then as *Baptist Visitor* in 1907, and as *South Texas Baptist* in 1909. The paper was edited by Eugene Coke Routh; it merged with the *Baptist Standard* in Feb., 1912. E. C. ROUTH

SOUTH TEXAS BAPTIST, THE. A paper published in 1892 in Navasota, Tex., with J. F. Dobbs, editor. E. C. ROUTH

SOUTH TEXAS BAPTIST COLLEGE. A school which opened at Waller, Tex., in 1898, promoted by the South Texas Educational Conference. After two years it was closed for lack of patronage.

BIBLIOGRAPHY: C. B. Wilson, "A History of Baptist Educational Efforts in Texas, 1829–1900" (1934).
RUPERT N. RICHARDSON

SOUTH TEXAS CHILDREN'S HOME. Located 18 miles northwest of Beeville, Tex., on a section of land given by Laura Boothe as a memorial to her husband, William Riley Boothe. She asked her pastor, J. M. Lunsford, to lead in founding the home, and he resigned his pastorate of the First Baptist Church in Beeville May 1, 1952, to start the project. The home opened Aug. 24, 1952, and was accepted by the Baptist General Convention of Texas in December of that year. It is operated by a board of 24 trustees, elected by the convention.

Operating on the cottage plan, the home has 10 to 12 children and the house parents in each unit. Meals are prepared and served in each cottage. Cottage life includes all normal home functions. Each child has light duties to perform in the cottages and on the farm and ranch. The children are given personal care and supervision, and each day is closed with a devotional period. As far as possible a natural home atmosphere is maintained.

Property consists of five cottages with present licensed capacity for 60 children, administrator's home, ranch supervisor's home, four farm buildings, food and clothing commissary. A church edifice is near by. Beef, pork, poultry, and dairy needs are produced on the ranch. The children attend public schools at Pettus, six miles away, and church at Mineral, three miles from the home. No child is separated from the home until he is situated in life, either in college, married, or with a job or trade. Since no foster home or adoption service is maintained at present, no case worker is employed.

The home is supported by gifts from churches and individuals. It does not share in the Cooperative Program. With property valued at $369,000, the home operated in 1955 on a budget of $100,000, and the actual child care cost per capita was $600 for the year. Total income during the first 36 months of the home's existence totaled $352,000; designated cash gifts, $250,000; and gifts in merchandise, cattle for the ranch and dairy, building materials, and other gifts in kind, $75,000. J. LOWELL PONDER

SOUTHWESTERN BAPTIST. See ALABAMA BAPTIST.

SOUTHEAST ACADEMY. This school, never actually established, was proposed when the citizens of Scranton, S. C., offered the South Carolina state convention 50 acres of land and $23,000, provided an academy be located in Scranton. The 1920 convention voted to accept the offer and elected a board of trustees who served through 1923. In 1925 the convention voted to re-elect the 1923 board of trustees for the purpose of returning the property to the donors, since plans to establish an academy did not materialize. CHARLES W. BURTS

SOUTHEAST MISSISSIPPI, BAPTIST GENERAL ASSOCIATION OF. Constituted in Nov., 1855, at Bethel Church in Newton County, with its primary aim domestic missions in Southeast Mississippi. Secondary aims were Indian missions among the Choctaws and, later, foreign mission work in Mexico, particularly through missionary James Garvin Chastain (*q.v.*). Nathan Lytle Clarke (*q.v.*) led in the organization of the association and served continuously as its president for 51 years until his death. The association, responsible for the founding of East Mississippi College and Clarke Memorial College, established two periodicals, *The Southern Baptist* and *The Mississippi Baptist*. Churches of the association also supported the Mississippi Baptist Orphanage. Although the association is still in existence, most of the Southeast Mississippi churches and associations have become affiliated with the Mississippi Baptist Convention. J. L. BOYD

SOUTHEAST MISSOURI STATE COLLEGE CHAIR OF BIBLE, Cape Girardeau. Incorporated as Southeast Missouri Baptist Foundation, the institution began its first term of work Sept. 11, 1939, with S. D. Aubuchon as instructor. During 1948–49 a $150,000 building was erected. On Nov. 10, 1950, the board of control offered this chair of bible to the Missouri Baptist General Association. The offer was accepted, together with $45,000 indebtedness, and the name of the building was changed to Baptist Student Center. On Feb. 15, 1952, Thomas S. Messer succeeded Aubuchon as professor of Bible. CLIFFORD INGLE

SOUTHEAST TEXAS, BAPTIST HOSPITAL OF (BEAUMONT). Established after a committee was appointed to study possibilities of a hospital Apr. 21, 1945, at a called meeting of the executive board of District Three, Baptist General Convention of Texas. Impetus for creation of the hospital began earlier when L. E. Stagg, Sr., a quiet but energetic Christian layman, deposited $10,000 to the account of "Baptist Hospital," which at the time was only a dream.

With the hospital's charter approved Nov. 24, 1945, a 10-acre tract of land was donated by Charles D. Smith and his wife, of Beaumont, and funds for construction were provided through a fund-raising campaign in which business, industry, and people of all faiths participated, supplemented by an appropriation from the Baptist General Convention of Texas. Construction began Sept. 14, 1947, and the completed 125-bed hospital opened for service to patients of all races Oct. 15, 1949. The balance of construction and equipment indebtedness was assumed by Baptist churches of District Three, aided by a semiannual appropriation from the convention.

Baptist Hospital of Southeast Texas had hardly admitted its first patients when the influx of new business and industries to the area and the corresponding increase in population made the need for additional hospital facilities urgent. Trained nursing personnel and housing facilities for prospective nursing students, which were also needed, were made possible by a gift of $250,000 from Mrs. Harry C. Wiess of Houston which provided for a nurses' home; and the school of nursing enrolled its first class in July, 1954. In 1956 contracts were let for construction of two additional five-story wings to the present building, with plans to enlarge existing auxiliary departments and increase bed capacity to 236.

Although aided by the Baptist General Convention of Texas, the hospital is owned and operated by Baptists of District Three. Approved by the Joint Commission on Accreditation of Hospitals, it is a member of the American Hospital Association, the Texas Hospital Association, the American Protestant Hospital Association, and the Southwide Baptist Hospital Association. The school of nursing is affiliated with Lamar State College of Technology and is accredited by Texas State Board of Nurse Examiners.

From Oct., 1949, through Sept., 1955, a total of 30,665 patients were admitted, and 4,764 babies were born. The net operating income from patients during this period was $4,666,175.61, denominational income $235,308.45, designated gifts $1,087,498.88, and a total of $88,311.81 expended in charity service.

The physical plant, consisting at present of three buildings, is valued at $1,602,647.26 with a mortgaged indebtedness of $236,250.00. Total assets are $2,669,167.52. GUY DALRIMPLE

SOUTHEASTERN BAPTIST RELIGIOUS EDUCATION ASSOCIATION. See RELIGIOUS EDUCATION, PROFESSIONAL ASSOCIATIONS.

SOUTHEASTERN BAPTIST THEOLOGICAL SEMINARY. Opened officially for enrolment of students Sept. 10, 1951, in the Music-Religion Building of Wake Forest College, Wake Forest, N. C. Previously, the Southern Baptist Convention, meeting in Chicago in May, 1950, had adopted a recommendation that the seminary be organized and had at that time named the first board of trustees.

Southern Baptists in 1859 had opened their first seminary, Southern Baptist Theological Seminary, in Greenville, S. C., at the center of Baptists' numerical strength. After the Civil War it became necessary to relocate the seminary in Louisville, Ky. Thus, from 1877 to 1951, there was no seminary in the populous southeastern area of the Southern Baptist Convention. As late as 1953, 33 per cent of all the churches in the Southern Baptist Convention were located in the seaboard states from Maryland to Florida. Though the majority of ministers in this area attended Southern Baptist seminaries, many found it more convenient to attend schools in the North or found it impossible to attend any seminary. The need for a seminary in this region became more obvious and acute with overcrowding enrolments in the three existing Southern Baptist seminaries in the middle 1940's. Southern Baptist growth was at an unprecedented rate, and Baptists were increasingly demanding an educated ministry.

In Dec., 1945, a memorial was presented from the Buncombe Baptist Pastors' Conference of North Carolina to the Executive Committee of the Southern Baptist Convention, requesting consideration of Ridgecrest, N. C., as a possible location for an eastern seminary. The Executive Committee appointed a committee of three to study the need of such a seminary. This committee's report in June, 1945, that there was rather widespread sentiment for such a seminary in the eastern part of the Convention, led to further discussion; and in May, 1947, the Executive Committee recommended to the Southern Baptist Convention, meeting in St. Louis, "that a committee of nine be appointed to study the whole question of theological education in the light of suggestions concerning the establishment of a new theological seminary." Such a committee was appointed and was given the additional responsibility of studying the Golden Gate Seminary in California.

The committee, through its chairman, John H. Buchanan, made a progress report to the Convention meeting in Memphis in 1948 and requested that the committee be continued for another year. After a thorough study of theological education among Southern Baptists, this committee reported to the Convention in Oklahoma City in 1949 and recommended "that two new seminaries, one in the west and one in the east, be established as soon as suitable sites can be had and adequate plans can be made for financing the same without injury or impairment to our existing seminaries." In addition to this recommendation, a further one was adopted setting up a committee on theological education with a member from each state, "authorized to recommend sites, enlist financial support, draw up charters and perform other necessary duties pertaining to the carrying out of the . . . recommendations." In 1950, at the meeting of the Southern Baptist Convention in Chicago, J. W. Storer brought the report of the committee on theological education, which, in addition to recommending the location of a western seminary at the site of the Golden Gate Seminary in Berkeley, Calif., recommended the location in Wake Forest, N. C., of "The Southeastern Baptist Theological Seminary, Inc." The Convention also agreed to accept the offer by the Wake Forest College trustees of the campus and buildings of the college in return for a payment of a sum of $1,600,000. At the same session articles of incorporation were adopted, and a board of trustees was elected for the new seminary.

The board of trustees of the new seminary met in its first regular meeting in Wake Forest, N. C., June 20, 1950. Previously, a group of the trustees had met briefly on the Convention platform after their election in Chicago and had elected Casper C. Warren of North Carolina as temporary moderator. Permanent officers were elected as follows: C. C. Warren, chairman; Leo Green, vice-chairman; John W. Kincheloe, Jr., secretary; and William L. Wyatt, treasurer.

One of the first tasks confronting the board of trustees was the selection of a president. W. Perry Crouch of North Carolina was named chairman of a committee to nominate the seminary president. The committee nominated Olin Trivette Binkley, who was then a professor at Southern Seminary. He was unanimously elected, but he declined to serve. Consequently, in its meeting in Feb., 1951, the board of trustees, on the recommendation of Crouch's committee, elected Sydnor Lorenzo Stealey, another professor at Southern Seminary. Stealey accepted the position and, soon after his election, recommended that the "Abstract of Principles," which has been used throughout the existence of the Southern Baptist Theological Seminary, be adopted as the abstract for Southeastern Seminary. This was done, and each faculty member affixes his signature to the "Abstract of Principles" before he becomes a full member of the faculty.

The first member of the seminary staff named by the president was Joseph R. Robinson, who was employed as comptroller. The first faculty members then elected, on Stealey's recommendation, were Leo Green, professor of Old Testament; J. B. Hipps, professor of missions; and William C. Strickland, tutor in New Testament. Marc H. Lovelace was elected visiting professor, 1951–52.

Though Wake Forest College would still occupy the campus, it was agreed to begin operation of the seminary in one building in the fall of 1951. In the first semester of the seminary's existence, 85 students were enrolled, and the total enrolment for 1951–52 reached 102. Thirty-three colleges and 14 states were represented in the student body.

Before the beginning of the second year of operation, the faculty was strengthened by the addition of six more full-time men, and the board of trustees elected a new chairman, Warren having resigned from the board. Edward Allison McDowell, Jr., professor of New Testament; Olin T. Binkley, professor of sociology and ethics; Stewart A. Newman, professor of theology and philosophy; Robert T. Daniel, professor of Old Testament; Marc H. Lovelace, associate professor of archeology; and M. Ray McKay, professor of homiletics, were elected to the faculty at the meeting of the board of trustees in Feb., 1952. At the same meeting Crouch was elected chairman; Emery B. Denny, vice-chairman; J. Glenn Blackburn, secretary; and Wyatt, treasurer.

During the second year of operation, the seminary enrolled a total of 230 students, representing 16 states and 49 colleges. Applications or inquiries from prospective students far outnumbered the available space.

The library grew steadily in the early years, and by the end of the second year, there were approximately 9,000 volumes on hand. The first large gift to the library came in the form of the William Hersey Davis (*q.v.*) collection of New Testament books. Edwin C. Osburn was secured in 1952 as catalogue librarian. Additional faculty members were added at the beginning of the session 1953–54: Pope A. Duncan, associate professor of church history; Richard K. Young, associate professor of pastoral care; and Garland A. Hendricks, associate professor of church community development and director of field work. In the early part of 1954, John T. Wayland, professor of religious education, and Ben C. Fisher, assistant professor of religious education, joined the faculty. In addition to his teaching responsibilities, Fisher serves as administrative assistant and director of public relations.

From the very beginning of the seminary's history, it was evident that, with the removal of Wake Forest College, a significant renovation program would be necessary on the campus. In Sept., 1952, the executive committee of the board of trustees recommended the establishment of a trustee-faculty committee to study, with the president, the long-range program and development of the seminary. The burden of the planning fell largely on the shoulders of the president and this committee. In Feb., 1954, Six Associates, Inc., of Asheville, N. C., was retained as architect for the renovation program.

During the third year of the seminary's existence, 343 students were enrolled, representing 17 states and 49 colleges. Two hundred of these men had regular church work, and many more supported themselves and their families by secular employment. At the end of the third year of work, the seminary graduated its first class. The first man to receive a diploma was William Franklin Askins. Sixty-three men received their Bachelor of Divinity degrees, and an alumni association was formed. J. W. Storer, president of the Southern Baptist Convention, and President Stealey were the first commencement speakers in 1954.

During the fourth year of operation, 392 students enrolled in the seminary. Many who desired to come could not be admitted because of lack of space. The curriculum was enlarged to care for Southeastern's first graduate students who enrolled for the course leading to the Th.M. degree, which was added in the fall of 1954. The faculty, too, was increased with the election of Denton R. Coker as assistant professor of religious education. Paul S. Robinson, professor of music in Wake Forest College, became part-time instructor in music, and L. J. Morriss became part-time instructor in religious education. From the beginning of the seminary's existence, student graders had assisted the professors. With the enrolment of graduate students in 1954–55, some graduate fellowships were offered, and these men assisted the faculty in many ways. The first class of Th.M. students was graduated in Apr., 1955.

In the session 1955–56, 459 students were enrolled. The seminary had 14 full-time and 4 part-time faculty members. The library had grown until it contained more than 20,000 catalogued volumes. The seminary began its session without the services of Robinson, who had died June 3, 1955. Gordon M. Funk was elected business officer, and Fred Sandusky assumed the responsibilities of the registrar. Though he continued to teach for the convenience of the seminary, Hipps became the first faculty member to be officially retired by reason of age. Lovelace was in Jerusalem, Jordan, serving as a fellow in the American School of Oriental Research during the session, thus becoming the first faculty member to be granted a sabbatical leave of absence. New faculty members continued to be added to the teaching staff: James E. Tull, special instructor in theology, and Julius Carroll Trotter, Jr., assistant professor of homiletics and speech. B. Elmo Scoggin served as visiting professor of missions.

Wake Forest College moved to its new campus in Winston-Salem, N. C., during June of 1956, and the seminary came into full possession of its campus July 1. Immediately, a program of building, repairing, remodeling, and renovating was begun. It was estimated that this program would cost in excess of $1,000,000. President Stealey; the long-range planning committee, Harold W. Seever, chairman; architect Henry I. Gaines; and Frank M. Swett, superintendent of buildings and grounds, carried principal responsibility in the program of building and renovation. The property consists of 449 acres of land; 29 buildings, 10 of which are residences; an athletic field; tennis courts; a golf course; and a stadium seating 15,000. The campus proper, which was originally built around a clump of oak trees which existed at the time Wake Forest College was founded in 1834, is a 25-acre plot situated within a rock wall.

It was anticipated that with the increased physical facilities of the seminary, enrolment would rapidly increase. At least 600 students were expected to enroll in the fall of 1956. To care for the larger student body, five men were added to the teaching staff: Scoggin, associate professor of Old Testament interpretation; John E. Steely, assistant professor of historical theology; E. Luther Copeland, assistant professor of sociology; and Ben S. Johnson, instructor in music.

From the beginning the primary purpose of Southeastern Seminary has been to prepare men and women for Christian leadership in the pastoral, educational, and missionary ministries. The seminary has expressed in its curriculum the conviction that all these areas of service demand an understanding of the origins, content, and history of the Christian faith and its special relevance to the needs of the modern world. All qualified students are required to undertake a series of courses which are considered basic for the preparation for any of these Christian ministries. Specialized work is given, in addition, for each ministry—pastoral, educational, and missionary. The Bachelor of Divinity degree is the basic degree given to all students, regardless of their specialization, and requires three years beyond college for completion. The only other degree offered by the seminary is Master of Theology. This degree requires one year beyond the B.D. degree for completion, and the student may major in any one of the four areas into which the seminary curriculum is divided: interpretation of the Bible, historical interpretation of Christianity, Christian interpretation of life and thought, and Christianity at work. The seminary presents a Certificate in Theology to students who complete satisfactorily two years of study but who do not have a standard college degree.

Under the leadership of Richard K. Young, Southeastern has pioneered in developing a counseling program which is related through Young to the North Carolina Baptist Hospital and the Bowman-Gray Medical School.

In addition to initiating a unique counseling program, Southeastern Seminary has inaugurated a new approach in meeting its responsibility to the rural ministry. This concept includes a working relationship with the heads of 10 departments of North Carolina State College, who participate on the seminary campus in a course designed to orient theological students to life and work in the agricultural community. This approach also includes the work of men on the seminary staff in the field of church-community development. Garland A. Hendricks, associate professor of church-community development and director of field work, is primarily responsible for this program.

Stealey and the board of trustees have put great emphasis upon gathering and developing a strong faculty. They have endeavored to add faculty members at a rate sufficient to keep the student-faculty ratio in proper bounds. In the first faculty meeting the President stated his ideal, to which he has faithfully adhered, that the president and the faculty constitute "a co-operative society."

There has always been a strong missionary emphasis at Southeastern Seminary. In addition to the regular curriculum in the field of Christian missions, several days have been set aside each year for special missionary emphasis, and prominent missionary leaders have been brought to the campus on those days to speak to the seminary family. Milledge Theron Rankin (*q.v.*), executive secretary of the Southern Baptist Foreign Mission Board, delivered one of the first public addresses in connection with the opening of Southeastern Seminary. A mission volunteer band has been one of the principal campus student organizations. Cecil Earl Carder was the first Southeastern student to receive appointment by a foreign mission agency (in his case, the American Baptist Foreign Mission Society), and Louis Edmond McCall was the first student to be appointed by the Foreign Mission Board of the Southern Baptist Convention. Missionaries on furlough have been present from time to time in the student body. In addition, several students from abroad have studied at Southeastern Seminary, including a vice-president of the Baptist World Alliance, Honorio Espinoza of Chile. One of the first sizable scholarship funds was the $26,000 J. F. Tompkins Missionary Scholarship Fund. The North Carolina Woman's Missionary Union supplied sufficient funds to furnish several residences on the campus for missionaries on furlough who wish to study at the seminary.

The principal financial support for the seminary comes through the Cooperative Program of the Southern Baptist Convention. Small student fees (no tuition is charged), designated gifts from individuals and churches, and the returns from some income-bearing property add to the seminary income. The purchase of the present campus, its renovation, and the addition of immediately essential buildings, have been provided for through the capital needs program of Southern Baptists. The first individual gift to the seminary came from John R. Crawford of Goldsboro, N. C. The first legacy, amounting to about $17,000, was received by the seminary from the estate of Ruby Reid of Wake Forest. The small endowment funds currently held by the seminary are being increased gradually. The first large gift to these funds was $100,000 made by Mr. and Mrs. P. A. Bethea of Darlington, S. C.

Southeastern Seminary, already an associate member of the American Association of Theological Schools, has applied for full membership. The seminary is approved by the United States Department of Justice for the training of non-immigrant students and is also one of the supporting members of the Corporation of the American Schools of Oriental Research.

See also STUDENT ACTIVITIES, SOUTHEASTERN BAPTIST THEOLOGICAL SEMINARY.

POPE A. DUNCAN

SOUTHEASTERN KENTUCKY BAPTIST INSTITUTE. See BARBOURVILLE BAPTIST INSTITUTE.

SOUTHERN ADVANCE. A monthly newspaper concerned with "method in church and denominational work," launched by H. R. Bernard in Jan., 1902, at Gainsville, Ga. Bernard suspended the *Advance* in Jan., 1905, and began publishing the *Religious Forum*.

JOHN J. HURT, JR.

SOUTHERN ASSOCIATION OF BAPTIST COLLEGES AND SCHOOLS, THE. Organized Nov. 29, 1948, and chartered Dec. 18, 1952, under the laws of Tennessee, this organization of administrators of Southern Baptist educational institutions is successor to a series of similar organizations dating back more than 60 years. First of these was the Southern Baptist Educational Conference, which met as early as May 7, 1892, with representatives of 30 colleges and schools in attendance.

Ceasing to function after a few years, the educational conference was reconstituted about 1910 as the Southern Baptist Education Association, which held annual meetings fairly consistently for about 20 years, and which served as an effective means of communication and coordination of interests of the institutions. Its activities declined in the early years of the depression of the 1930's, in part because of the preoccupation of the educators with the pressing financial problems of their individual institutions, and in part because the original purposes of the organization were being fulfilled to a large extent by the annual Christian Education Conference sponsored by the Education Commission beginning in 1929.

The education association was revived temporarily as a separate organization in 1937 when a meeting was called in Memphis, Tenn., for Feb. 11 and 12. Its activities during the next decade, however, continued to be limited almost entirely to participation in the annual Christian Education Conference and occasional conferences held in connection with the meetings of the Southern Association of Colleges and Secondary Schools.

The Christian Education Conference was held at Ridgecrest, N. C., each August from 1929 through 1948, with the single exception of 1945, bringing together the administrators of the Baptist colleges and schools, the members of the Education Commission, and usually the members of the College Association of Baptist Teachers of Religion. It was continued after 1948 as a joint annual meeting of the Southern Association of Baptist Colleges and Schools, organized Nov. 29, 1948, with the Education Commission. Since 1951 the joint annual meeting has been held at Nashville, Tenn., instead of Ridgecrest, the date varying from the middle of June to the latter part of July.

First president of the Southern Association of Baptist Colleges and Schools was Walter Pope Binns, elected at the initial meeting. The constitution of the new organization, published in Mar., 1949, and adopted that same year, identifies as its purpose "to provide and maintain an organization through which Baptist educational institutions in the territory of the Southern Baptist Convention may cooperate in promoting the interests of Christian Education." The charter identifies the same purpose, in the same words, and further specifies the receipt and making of gifts, donations, and benefactions, in the interests of the institutions, as proper activities of the organization.

The association works closely with the Education Commission and is served by the same executive secretary. It participates in the support of certain phases of the work of the commission, and joins with it in sponsorship of workshops and conferences, such as the College Business Management Workshop held in Nashville, June 18–20, 1956. Currently the president of the association is George Boyce Connell, president of Mercer University. H. I. Hester has served as recording secretary-treasurer continuously since the first meeting.

The association meets regularly twice each year, in the summer jointly with the Education Commission, and in the winter in connection with the annual meeting of the Southern Association of Colleges and Secondary Schools.

R. ORIN CORNETT

SOUTHERN BAPTIST. A newspaper started in Meridian, Miss., in July, 1875, to promote the interests of the General Association of Southeast Mississippi with A. Gressett as editor. The paper had a circulation of 2,400 when it was consolidated with the *Mississippi Baptist Record* in 1887.

A. L. GOODRICH

SOUTHERN BAPTIST (Florida). A newspaper started by the Stetson family at Jacksonville, Fla., in Apr., 1903. The editor, J. B. Holley, was a native of North Carolina and pastor at Gainsville, Fla. Through the efforts of W. A. Hobson and the generosity of John B. Stetson the paper merged with the *Florida Baptist Witness* on June 1, 1904. The consolidated paper was called the *Southern Baptist Witness* in 1904, *The Southern Witness* from 1905 to 1908, when it was changed back to the *Florida Baptist Witness.*

W. G. STRACENER

SOUTHERN BAPTIST, THE. A weekly first published as *The Carolina Baptist* in Charleston, Apr. 1, 1846, and sold at a subscription rate of $2 per year. On Jan. 2, 1847, the paper adopted for its motto "I Am Set for the Defense of the Gospel of Christ"; on May 1 of that year the subtitle "A Family Religious Newspaper" was added. The name of the paper was changed to *The Southern Baptist* June 5, 1847, although no change in editor, publisher, or heading was made at that time. By Oct. 20, 1847, however, the paper had been sold and was "published by a company and edited by a committee of brethren, of the Baptist churches in Charleston." The committee secured James Petigru Boyce (*q.v.*), who served as editor from Nov. 22, 1848, until May 2, 1849, after which members of the committee edited the paper at intervals for most of the remaining period of the paper's existence. Due to financial difficulties publication ceased Dec. 15, 1860.

ROBERT A. IVEY

SOUTHERN BAPTIST, THE. A paper published in San Antonio, Tex., edited by R. F. Stokes. In 1906 the paper was sold to *Baptist Tribune* of Dallas, owned by James Britton Cranfill (*q.v.*).

E. C. ROUTH

SOUTHERN BAPTIST ASSOCIATION OF TEACHERS OF BIBLE AND RELIGIOUS EDUCATION. See RELIGIOUS EDUCATION, PROFESSIONAL ASSOCIATIONS.

SOUTHERN BAPTIST CAMPUS DIRECTORY. Published at four-year intervals by the

Education Commission of the Southern Baptist Convention and distributed by the commission at a nominal price, this directory of Southern Baptist seminaries, colleges, academies, and Bible schools first appeared in Mar., 1954 (176 pp., 10,000 copies). It features two pages of information on the history, locale, curriculum, accreditation, student activities, religious life, costs of attending, and student aid program of each of the 70 educational institutions maintained by Southern Baptists in the Convention area. Other sections summarize the history of Christian education among Southern Baptists, identify the objectives and purposes of each of the several types of institutions, and list the Baptist Student Union directors on Baptist and other college campuses. R. ORIN CORNETT

SOUTHERN BAPTIST CAREER NEWS. A vocational guidance periodical for Southern Baptist teen-age youth, published monthly October–May, bimonthly June–September, by the Education Commission of the Southern Baptist Convention. Initiated in Oct., 1956, with a mailing of 3,500, this publication has four principal objectives: to provide up-to-date, authentic occupational information, also listing additional sources; to establish Christian standards for evaluation of vocational opportunities and responsibilities; to develop attitudes and attributes essential to maximum service through vocation; and to furnish educational guidance in which the values of Christian higher education are emphasized. Distributed by subscription only, *Southern Baptist Career News* is available at $1 per year, or at 75 cents per subscription in groups of 10 or more. R. ORIN CORNETT

SOUTHERN BAPTIST COLLEGE. A liberal arts college and theological seminary at Walnut Ridge, Ark., owned and operated by an independent board of trustees representing the local Baptist constituency. It was established to take the place of Jonesboro, Mountain Home, and Will Mayfield colleges, which had closed. The efforts of H. E. Watters to reopen Jonesboro Baptist College in 1936–37 had failed. When H. W. Williams, pastor at Pocahontas, Ark., and Golden Neely, pastor at Corning, Ark., visited a large number of pastors and laymen in the interest of a new college, they found an immediate and widespread response, much of it reflecting Watters' earlier efforts.

A mass meeting of some 200 supporters met in Pocahontas on June 10, 1941, in a large stone building offered by the city for the beginning of the institution. Interest in the new college was so intense that it was opened on Sept. 7, 1941. In July, 1941, Hubert Ethridge Williams was elected to serve as the president of the institution.

The institution planned special courses for rural ministers along with traditional liberal arts college courses. Later a department of rural ministerial training was established and in 1952 was reorganized into a full rural theological seminary course offering the Th.B. degree.

Enrolment has included about 5,950 students, about one-fourth of whom were training for Christian work. Mission work has resulted in thousands of additions to the churches in the area. Permanent buildings were being erected in 1955 to replace structures secured in 1947 at the Walnut Ridge Airfield. The Arkansas Baptist State Convention, though not organically related to the school, has given to it substantial appropriations every year since 1949. For the year ending Dec. 31, 1955, this appropriation amounted to $40,000; the amount allocated for 1956 was $30,000. HUBERT ETHRIDGE WILLIAMS

SOUTHERN BAPTIST CONVENTION, THE. The Southern Baptist Convention met for organization May 8–12, 1845, in Augusta, Ga., pursuant to a call by the board of managers of the Virginia Foreign Mission Society. "A large number of delegates assembled in the meeting-house of the Baptist Church in Augusta," to quote from the "proceedings." How many "delegates" (the nomenclature of the founding fathers) were present, and from what states? "The undersigned has found it difficult to arrange the list of delegates, and is still uncertain as to the entire correctness of the names of churches and individuals" (James C. Crane, one of the secretaries). According to the historical tables there were 236 "delegates" registered from 165 churches, nine associations, one ministerial conference (District of Columbia), the board of a state convention (Alabama), the executive committee of a state convention (Georgia), the executive committee of the Georgia Association, the Pennfield Young Men's Missionary Society (Georgia), Mercer University, and Furman Institute. The states represented in the above list were Maryland, Virginia, North Carolina, South Carolina, Georgia, Alabama, Louisiana, Kentucky, and the District of Columbia. There was only one "delegate" from Kentucky, but he was Isaac McCoy, the great missionary to the Indians.

It was no obsessional exclusiveness which prompted the organization of the Southern Baptist Convention, though that has been alleged and, in some quarters, is still insisted upon as a fitting description of Southern Baptists. "The formation of the Southern Baptist Convention," says William Wright Barnes in his *History of the Southern Baptist Convention,* "grew out of the division in the Home Mission Society and in the General Convention . . . over the question of slavery." But, though fully conceding the basic correctness of Barnes's statement, we must recognize there were other issues as great. William Owen Carver, one of the great Baptist historians and long-time professor at Southern Baptist Theological Seminary, once stated that "the Baptist denomination was a direct product of the missionary interest. Until 1814 there was in the United States a Baptist people but no denomination with unity of consciousness, with corporate fellowship, with organic life and implementation for common responsibility for the Gospel."

In a small booklet published by the Executive Committee of the Southern Baptist Convention, in speaking of the history of Southern Baptists and the essential elements which go to make up its rise and growth, attention is called to the impact made upon Baptists by Luther Rice, a returned missionary from India. In 1813 there were about 175,000 Baptists in the United States, and half of them lived in five Southern states: Virginia, the Carolinas, Georgia, and Kentucky. The first unit of fellowship among Baptists, aside from that found in each church, is the association of churches within a given locality. The oldest of these was the Philadelphia, organized in 1707. Altogether, in 1813 there were only 115 associations in North American Baptist life, and few of them were concerned with any form of mission work. Such a thing as joining in a co-operative mission endeavor was an unthought-of possibility. When the associations came together in annual session or in monthly meetings, they were given to introvert inspection and doctrinal discussions.

In 1813 the Baptists of the United States had no conventions and no denomination—"rugged individualists" best describes them. But individualism, if it is indeed rugged, sooner or later becomes aware of others. So it was that one day in the autumn of 1813, Luther Rice, while riding between Richmond and Petersburg on his way from Boston to Charleston, had a dream of a general convention of state conventions, associations, and churches to join in a movement to promote missions. He went to Savannah and conferred with W. B. Johnson, who about 30 years later was to lead in the formation of the Southern Baptist Convention and to be its first president. Largely as a result of this consultation, there was organized in May, 1814, "The General Missionary Convention of the Baptist Denomination in the United States of America for Foreign Missions."

The preamble to the constitution of the general convention above referred to reads:

> We, the delegates of the Missionary Societies, Churches, and other religious bodies of the Baptist Denomination, in various parts of the United States, met in Convention, . . . for the purpose of carrying into effect the benevolent intentions of our constituents, for organizing a plan for eliciting, combining and directing the energies of the whole denomination in one sacred effort, for the propagation of the Gospel, agree to the following rules, or fundamental principles. . . .

Thus was brought into use and accepted place the word "denomination." It is also worthy of note that the preambles to both the Triennial Convention (as the general convention, meeting every three years, was called) and of the Southern Baptist Convention were written by Johnson, and in each the words "elicit, combine, and direct" appear.

The organization of the general convention was the beginning of a new day for American Baptists. Leaders such as Rice, Johnson, Thomas Baldwin, John Gano, and Richard Furman, were men who wasted no time on small issues. Rice led in making Baptists conscious of their need for training missionaries and missionary-minded pastors.

Within 30 years of the organization of the general convention, at least three divisive issues began to emerge, all of them tending to bring a cleavage between Northern and Southern Baptists.

1. The general convention had been organized to promote foreign missions. In 1817 the scope of its interest had been widened to include home missions. To quote from *We Southern Baptists,*

> That brought into the picture J. M. Peck (who like Judson and Rice had been a Congregationalist before joining the Baptists), James E. Welch, Isaac McCoy, Jonathan Going and other home missionaries. But there was dissatisfaction over this plan, and the General Convention resumed its especial interest in foreign missions.
>
> After the division and organization of the Southern Baptist Convention the name of the old Triennial Convention was changed to the "American Baptist Missionary Union" with foreign missions as its chief interest. In 1824, the Baptist General Tract Society (name later changed to American Baptist Publication Society) was organized; in 1832, the Home Mission Society.
>
> The process of decentralization was accelerated with a separate organization for each phase of work. . . . Baptists of the North, who did not organize the "Northern (now American) Convention" until 1907, still have separate Societies.

2. There were growing complaints from the points in the South where home mission work was being done that such was neglected.

3. "It is a question admitting no debate, that the Triennial Convention was formed on the principle of a perfect equality of members, from the North and South." In this statement from the report of the committee to prepare a preamble and resolution for the action of the consultative convention in Augusta, 1845, there begins to emerge the basic cause for the organization of the Southern Baptist Convention. That resolution went on to elaborate:

> And what is all important, the very qualifications of missionaries are prescribed by the original constitution of that Convention,—the fifth article providing that "such persons as are in full communion with some regular church of our denomination, and who furnish satisfactory evidence of genuine piety, good talents and fervent zeal for the Redeemer's cause, are to be employed as missionaries." Besides this, too, the declaration of the Board, that if "any one should offer himself as a missionary, having slaves, and should insist on retaining them as his property, we could not appoint him," is an innovation and a departure from the course hitherto pursued by the Triennial Convention, (such persons having been appointed). And lastly, the decision of the Board is an infraction of the resolution passed the last spring, in Philadelphia; and the General Board at their late meeting in Providence, have failed to reverse this decision. Amidst such circumstances, your Committee esteem it absolutely necessary that the friends of the

Constitution of the Triennial Convention, and the lovers of the Bible, shall at once take their stand, and assert the great catholic principles of that Constitution, and of the Word of God.

Actually, the inability of some of the wisest statesmen the nation has ever produced to arrive at a solution which would stop the extremists in both North and South from exacting a verdict written in brothers' blood, had much to do with the breaking of old ties and the formation of the Southern Baptist Convention. Those statesmen followed many paths but mired down in all of them; they ignored the possible in order to insist on the impossible, only to finally pour the new wine of peace back into the old wineskin of conflict. Thus the Southern Baptist Convention was formed, while throughout the land men's minds were subjected to the explosive force of inconsiderate phrases uttered by gifted orators.

On Friday morning, May 9, 1845, the committee, appointed the day before to report a preamble and resolutions for the action of the convention, completed its work and submitted the following resolution, which was unanimously adopted:

Resolved, That for peace and harmony, and in order to accomplish the greatest amount of good, and for the maintenance of those scriptural principles on which the General Missionary Convention of the Baptist denomination of the United States, was originally formed, it is proper that this Convention at once proceed to organize a Society for the propagation of the Gospel.

The next day, May 10, a resolution was adopted that: "Br'n W. B. Johnson, T. Curtis, R. Fuller, and C. D. Mallary be a Committee to prepare an address to the public, setting forth the reasons which have led to the formation of the Southern Baptist Convention, and giving an exposition of its principles and objects. . . ." That address, given by Johnson, the president of the new Convention, is a remarkably restrained, cogent, and brilliant document. It is too long to print here but is worthy of studious reading by every Southern Baptist. The preamble, indeed, is both explicit and explanatory:

THE SOUTHERN BAPTIST CONVENTION,

To the Brethren in the United States; to the congregations connected with the respective Churches; and to all candid men.

A painful division has taken place in the missionary operation of the American Baptists. We would explain the origin, the principles and the objects of that division, or the peculiar circumstances in which the organization of the Southern Baptist Convention became necessary.

Let not the extent of this disunion be exaggerated. At the present time it involves only the Foreign and Domestic Missions of the denomination. Northern and Southern Baptists are still brethren. They differ in no article of the faith. They are guided by the same principles of gospel order. Fanatical attempts have indeed been made, in some quarters, to exclude us of the South from Christian fellowship. We do not retort these attempts; and believe their extent to be comparatively limited. Our Christian fellowship is not, as we feel, a matter to be obtruded on any one. We abide by that of our God, his dear Son, and all his baptized followers. The few ultra Northern brethren to whom we allude, must take what course they please. *Their* conduct has not influenced us in this movement. We do not regard the rupture as extending to foundation principles, nor can we think that the great body of our Northern brethren will so regard it. Disunion has proceeded, however, deplorably far. The first part of our duty is to show that its entire *origin* is with others. This is its history.

The men who formed the Southern Baptist Convention were moved by a spirit of conquest; they founded a society of co-operating believers who organized, to quote again from the preamble to the constitution of the Convention, "a plan for eliciting, combining, and directing the energies of the whole denomination in one sacred effort, for the propagation of the Gospel. . . ." The glory of the Southern Baptist Convention is that the design of its organization was to preach the gospel in its entirety to the entire world, motivated by the belief that He who has saved to the uttermost has called for the conquest of the uttermost.

(When next the Convention met in Augusta, 18 years later, a terrible war was being fought, and the territory of the Convention lay in economic ruins; as one embittered old veteran put it, "We are starving to death on a mattress stuffed with Confederate bills.")

A charter for the new Convention was secured in accordance with the laws of Georgia, Dec. 27, 1845. Actually, the numbering of the sessions began in 1846, since the Augusta Convention was consultative and organizational in character.

How was the new Convention received in the North? Doubtless this quotation from the *New York Baptist Memorial and Record,* July, 1845, as found in Barnes's history, will help answer that question:

A more intelligent or dignified body have rarely been assembled. The ministers of the gospel are not specified by any designation, so that we only recognise [*sic*] such as were before known to us in this relation; of whom there were a goodly number, probably one half of the whole. Besides these, there were found governors, judges, congressmen, and other functionaries of highest dignity—all moved by a common spirit, and apparently obeying the highest impulse of their natures. Such men may be mistaken; they may sometimes do wrong; but it is impossible not to respect them, and do homage to the sincere, manly ingenuousness, and the Christian forbearance which they evinced.

Aeschines, in an oration against Ctesiphone, exclaimed, "Our lives have transcended the limits of humanity, we are born to serve as a theme of incredible tales to posterity." That is a fitting portraiture of those great men, the founding fathers of the Southern Baptist Convention.

In these days of rapid communication between the most isolated parts of the Convention and its centers of activity, it is hard to realize the truth of such a statement as found in the *Religious Herald* of Aug. 12, 1847:

The Baptists of Virginia have always had much more of intercourse with the North than the South. Not twice a year can we send a package of books hence to Charleston, without sending it by way of Baltimore. And the South western states have had more intercourse with the North than they have had with Virginia. To carry a bookcase from Tuscaloosa, in Alabama, to Pennfield, in Georgia, you must first send it to Mobile, thence to New York, thence to Savannah, and thence via Augusta or Atlanta. . . . We mention these facts to show that it is not wonderful; if Virginia had more difficulty in severing the ties that attached her to the North, than Georgia or Alabama has had.

It is not without interest that one faces the question as to what might have been the verdict had it been possible for the delegates to assemble at Augusta in large numbers and speedily.

In his *Recollections of a Long Life,* Jeremiah Bell Jeter describes the trip of the Virginia delegates to Augusta—by rail to Wilmington, N. C., then by steamship down Cape Fear River and the Atlantic coast to Charleston, S. C., thence overland to Augusta. Referring to a terrific storm during the sea voyage, Jeter wrote, "The destruction of that living cargo would have been a great calamity to the Baptists of Virginia." What it would have meant to the Southern Baptist Convention is hazardous to envision.

"The new Convention, arising out of friction in mission work, was formed primarily for missions. There were many difficulties. . . . The task of enlisting the Southern churches in a program of missions at home and abroad was tremendous." There were many Baptists who were so extremely Calvinistic in their theology that they would not enter into missionary activity. There were many who stressed the local church idea to such an extent that they were afraid of the new Convention with its possibility, as they thought, of centralized authority. The student of Southern Baptist formation and development will find in those century-old discussions many things that sound familiar to modern ears. Challenging people's intelligence has never been a happy theological or Convention technique. If there ever was a successful experiment in self-persuasion and a recovery by suggestion, the founding fathers brought it to pass in Augusta. Their experience teaches that persistence can achieve a vast accomplishment.

The fifth article of the constitution adopted at Augusta indicates that the meeting of minds did not spend its time overmuch in elevated denunciation, but rather with the program of performance. The fifth article made provision for comprehensive achievement. "The Convention shall elect . . . as many Boards of Managers, as in its judgment will be necessary for carrying out the benevolent objects it may determine to promote. . . ." At first only two boards were formed: the Foreign Mission Board at Richmond, Va., and the Board of Domestic Missions (now Home Mission Board) at Marion, Ala.

Foreign Mission Board.—The history of the Southern Baptist Convention is the story of an ever-expanding mission motif. Frederic W. Maitland has a classic expression concerning the origins of English law which bears heavily on any attempt to record the growth of the movement which began with a handful of dedicated and determined men at Augusta in 1845. Said Maitland, "Such is the unity of all history that anyone who endeavors to tell a piece of it must feel that his first sentence tears a seamless web. The web must be rent, but as we rend it, we may watch the whence and whither of a few of the unraveling threads." The unraveling of these threads will give great light, not only on the origins of the Southern Baptist Convention, but also on the unfolding purposes of its development.

A committee was formed at Augusta to arrange with the board of the general convention an equitable division of funds, forces, and fields. The committee reported at the meeting of the Convention in Richmond, Va. (1846), that the Northern board declined to transfer to the new Convention any of the funds or mission fields. The final agreement was that the Northern organization should retain the corporate name and all the property and assume the debts.

The missionaries, of course, were left free to choose the board under which they would labor. John Lewis Shuck, who had been working in China for eight years under the old board, chose service under the new Convention, as did others. At the Richmond Convention the Foreign Mission Board announced the appointment during the preceding year of S. C. Clopton and George Pearcy as missionaries to China, which thus became the first foreign mission field of the Southern Baptist Convention. James B. Taylor, pastor of the Second Baptist Church in Richmond, became the first corresponding secretary of the Foreign Mission Board and for 25 terribly trying years led it through war and reconstruction, giving it stability in an unstable world and lending correctional direction to its work.

Significant are the words from the opening paragraph of the 1940 Southern Baptist Convention *Annual,* meeting in Baltimore—also "a year of foreboding and uncertainty," with the fall of Paris imminent and the lights going out one by one all over Europe.

Nine and one-half decades have come and gone since our Baptist forefathers met in Augusta, Georgia, and launched the Foreign Mission Board of the Southern Baptist Convention. It was a time of foreboding and uncertainty. Within fifteen years from the date of this first meeting of the Convention, the whole structure of the Federal Union was to be shaken to its very foundations. The South was to emerge from that bitter and wasting conflict prostrate and helpless, and it was fifty years after the Augusta Convention before the Baptist churches of the South came to the support of the Foreign Mission Board in any worthy or adequate way.

Through wars, depressions, denominational strife, in perils often within the very house of its friends, the Foreign Mission Board has come to be one of the mightiest evangelizing agencies not only of the day and denomination but of all the forces impacting the world for good. In its 110th annual report to the Convention, meeting in Miami, is found a section well worth pondering, "Only a small portion of the story can be told. The remainder will have to be visualized by the reader in terms of love, devotion, and sacrifice making possible what has been done." When wars forced evacuation of the first and greatest mission field, China, the missionaries were relocated in such portions of the world as were open for witnessing, a repetition of an earlier necessity: "They that were scattered abroad went every where preaching the word."

The Foreign Mission Board has been domiciled continuously in Richmond and consists of state members (31) from each state forming the constituency of the Convention and local members (18) residing in or near Richmond. It has an executive secretary and three regional secretaries. It publishes its own informational and promotional organ, *The Commission.* It maintains a constant recruiting service, with a secretary in charge who meets with college and seminary students throughout the South and on a selective basis brings volunteers to Richmond to be commissioned to the various mission fields.

Home Mission Board.—The beginnings of the Domestic Board (now the Home Mission Board) were not so propitious as were the beginnings of the Foreign Mission Board. Its first secretary was elected in Aug., 1845, but declined. Another was elected but resigned in November, and a third was elected in December—the great difficulty being, as one secretary said when he resigned, "I have learned by visiting many, and by an extensive correspondence, that our brethren prefer carrying on their domestic missionary operations through their Associations and State Conventions." Nevertheless, the Domestic Mission Board had missionaries at work sooner than did the Foreign Mission Board.

There had been much criticism of the American Baptist Home Mission Society for their neglect of the Southern states. Now that the Domestic Mission Board undertook to remedy that situation, many of the associations and some of the state conventions, having established mission work of their own, declared there was no place for the Domestic Board—an attitude that has taken vocal prominence from time to time since. In its first report to the Convention, the Domestic Mission Board outlined its responsibility for 14 states with a population of 8,000,000. The Indian Mission Association had been organized in 1842, and in 1855 it was incorporated with the Domestic Mission Board, with a resultant change in name, i.e. "The Domestic and Indian Mission Board."

But upon all these plans for the furtherance of the gospel, the blight of civil strife cut down the bright growth until only the strong and sturdy roots were left. Every phase of the Domestic Mission Board's work was either destroyed or seriously impaired, and even the local churches were vitally affected because of the control exerted over them by the federal military. By an order of Secretary of War Stanton, Jan. 14, 1864, addressed "to the Generals Commanding the Military Division of the Mississippi, and the Department of the Gulf, of the South, and of Virginia and North Carolina, and all the Generals and Officers commanding Armies, Detachments and Posts, and all officers in the service of the United States, in the above mentioned departments," they were "to place at the disposal of the American Baptist Home Mission Society all houses of worship belonging to the Baptist Churches South, in which a loyal minister . . . does not officiate." The Home Mission Society appointed J. W. Parker of Boston as its agent for fulfilment of this order. He could take possession of any Baptist church property in any territory held in the South by federal military power and appoint pastors for the same.

It is only fair to state that the excuse for all this was, on the surface, valid. To quote a portion of the minutes of the American Baptist Home Mission Society for 1864, "In all this the Board have to do only with meeting houses, or Baptist Church property . . . and their whole object will be accomplished if, by thus occupying the property, they can save it from being destroyed, or passing into other than Baptist hands, and preserve it as an inheritance for future Baptists who may live to own and occupy it." Benevolent as was the avowed purpose, in most cases malevolent was its execution—becoming a part of that heritage of ill will known as "reconstruction." The Southern Baptist Convention did not meet in 1865, but did meet in 1866, at Russellville, Ky. (From this date on, the sessions have been annual, save for 1943 and 1945 when World War II interfered.)

To the credit of the delegates, the 1866 Convention made no pronouncement on political matters but did feel constrained to make a strong statement on religious liberty. Reconstruction, as it was called, had for its object the elimination of the old South and, as a beginning, divided the fallen Confederate states into military districts, each under the control of a federal general. This period lasted from 1865 to 1879.

The Southern Baptist Convention met in Atlanta, Ga., in 1879, and action was taken which definitely set it on the path it has steadfastly pursued since in its relation to the Northern Baptist—now the American Baptist—Convention. Isaac Taylor Tichenor, who was, as Barnes correctly declares, one of the greatest Christian statesmen the Convention has ever had, introduced a resolution requesting:

> . . . that five brethren be appointed by this Convention to bear our Baptist brethren of the Northern States, at their approaching anniversaries, expressions of our fraternal regard and assurances of our fraternal goodwill, and assurances of our readiness to co-operate cordially with them in promoting the

cause of Christ in our own and all foreign lands; that we respectfully suggest to them the propriety of holding, at some convenient time and place, a meeting of representative men from all sections of our common country, to devise and propose such plans of co-operation between this Convention and other Baptist bodies of the United States as may best contribute to the more efficient working of the Baptist brotherhood, to the good of all men, and to the glory of our Redeemer.

Tichenor's proposals were subjected to long debate. Finally, the proposal of John A. Broadus was adopted. It read:

Resolved, That five brethren be appointed by this Convention to bear to our Baptist Brethren of the Northern States at their approaching anniversaries, expressions of fraternal regard, and assurances that, while firmly holding to the wisdom and policy of preserving our separate organizations, we are ready, as in the past, to co-operate cordially with them in promoting the cause of Christ in our own and foreign lands.

One of the messengers sent by the Southern Baptist Convention to the Northern anniversaries in 1879 was Henry H. Tucker of Georgia. In answer to the question as to why there should not be a union of the Southern Baptist Convention and the Northern brethren in order to promote the mission enterprises, he gave the reply which was true then and equally so at the present time. Said he, "I can answer this question satisfactorily and in a word—it is because we can accomplish more for the cause of Christ when left to ourselves. If united the body would be too large, too unwieldy, few cities in the North and none in the South could accommodate it. . . ." Factual and prophetic were these words, as the rapid growth of the Southern Baptist Convention was to evidence.

In 1882 Tichenor became secretary of the Home Mission Board, and it was moved to Atlanta. With the coming of Tichenor, a new day dawned with such success that in the Southern Baptist Convention *Annual* for 1892 are found these words:

Ten years ago the Convention then in session in Greenville, S. C., resolved to move the Board from Marion, Ala., to Atlanta, [Ga.]. The condition of the Board at that time excited the gravest apprehensions. Its total receipts for the year were about $28,000. It had but forty missionaries. Except for those in the Indian Territory it had few west of the Mississippi River. The Baptist Convention in Arkansas was in co-operation with the Home Mission Society of New York. Nothing had been attempted in Missouri for years, and that State seemed lost to the Board forever. Texas was divided into five missionary organizations, four of which were receiving aid from the Home Mission Society, and the fifth was paralyzed by its own dissensions. Thus the entire territory west of the Mississippi River had passed out of the hands of the Home Board.

East of the river, Mississippi was in alliance with the Publication Society [North]. . . . The state Boards [of the South] had grown vigorously, and from several of the states the Home Mission Board was excluded by action of their State Conventions. . . . When it was decided to remove it to Atlanta, and the present Board was put in charge of its affairs, the outlook was by no means reassuring. A survey of the field indicated a great defeat and a lost cause.

Impressed with the conviction that the existence of this Convention depended on the resuscitation of its fortunes, the new Board threw itself into the arduous work before it with the determination to use every proper effort to reclaim its lost territory and make itself a support to the Convention. . . . Such were the earnestness of its efforts, and the happy results of its policy that in five years there was not a missionary to the white people of the South who did not bear a commission from either the Home Mission Board of the Southern Baptist Convention, or one of our State Boards in alliance with it. Its territory had been reclaimed. Texas had been united in one great Convention in hearty sympathy and co-operation with the Board. So was Arkansas, so was Louisiana. A new spirit had possessed Missouri, and our cause had risen there until that state is among the strongest supporters of the Board, and of the Convention.

Significant indeed is the paragraph which Tichenor, in his report to the Convention in 1893, quoted from J. B. Gambrell:

Multitudes of people speaking strange tongues will flow into this Southland. At first the Northern man with American ideas will come, but he will be followed by men from every nation under heaven. To prepare for, meet and Christianize these millions is the work of the Home Board. Along the mountain fastnesses . . . and [in] the great coming cities of the South the battles are to be fought within a generation which will decide the spiritual destiny of this country for a thousand years. . . .

In his Centennial report to the Convention in 1946, the then secretary of the Home Mission Board, J. B. Lawrence, with pertinent prophecy said:

Aristotle, over two thousand years ago, made a survey of the whole field of knowledge of his day. If he were here now he would be perfectly at home with our statesmen in discussing government and politics. In those fields there has been very little change in the fundamental principles, but if he were to meet with a group of present-day scientists he would be completely lost. He would not know what they were talking about because science has gone so far beyond anything every dreamed of in the day of Aristotle. . . .

The world we live in today is the world science has given us. . . .

Our mission work cannot escape the changes in the new age. The foundation principles on which our present social order is based will be re-arranged, and human relationships will be re-adjusted so that individual, national, and international life will be given a new pattern. . . .

The new day now dawning will shed its light to all our institutions and will reveal needs and tasks unknown to former periods. Our denominational work of every sort and kind, yea, the churches themselves cannot escape the demand of this coming day. . . .

Every generation begins its march of progress from its own campground. The churches . . . travel from where they are. . . . Nothing should be done because it has been done through all the years. . . .

Then Lawrence went on to speak of the function of the Home Mission Board, which he said was unique in many respects.

It is a missionary board, a board of survey, a unifying agency for Southern Baptists, and a connectional board through which the impact of the entire denomination can be brought to bear upon the missionary tasks which are southwide in their nature. In its cooperation with the state mission boards it can give, and does give, Southern Baptists a unity in effort in undertakings which are common to all the states.

The state conventions and organizations are not an integral part of the Southern Baptist Convention and never can be if we maintain our Baptist polity. But they are an important part of our denominational life and should have some means by which and through which they could, as organizations, cooperate in those mission tasks which are southwide in their nature. The Home Mission Board is an agency of all the churches in all the states, and in cooperation with the State Mission Boards can and does furnish the means by which each and every state convention can have a part in the unified mission program covering the entire territory of the Southern Baptist Convention.

The Home Mission Board furnishes the nexus between the state mission boards which our Baptist polity cannot otherwise provide, and give to Southern Baptists a solidarity in our mission work in the homeland, on a cooperative basis, which other denominations secure by ecclesiastical overhead direction.

What Lawrence said in this trenchant apothegm has become a guiding light for Southern Baptist thought in appraising the place, the power, and the program of the Home Mission Board in the last decade.

Its board members are elected, as is true of all Convention boards, agencies, and commissions, by the Convention. There are 31 state members and 18 local members (the latter residing in or near Atlanta, Ga.).

Sunday School Board.—During the period 1879–99, the expansion program of the Foreign Mission Board was one of the greatest unifying influences actively at work in the Convention. The South (and to a very real degree, the mission boards) had successfully passed through a collective cleansing ritual. The Southern Baptist Convention was never to forget its inherited treasure store of great memories nor permit too big a gap between the Great Commission and its achievement because of any self-contained stagnation. To that end men of vision had recognized that the printed page was all-important. The early disciples had their ministry of publication—the handwritten Gospels; the letters of Paul, Peter, James, and John were circulated among the churches. As Prince Burroughs well said, "The teaching and publication departments of these first century believers, undergirded and stabilized the Christian movement, and under God saved it from dissipation and dissolution."

Southern Baptists, in setting their hands to the organizational plow in 1845, pitched their plans on a basis broad enough to support a complete program, and they determined to set that program in motion. In 1847 there was launched by leaders of the Convention, but acting independently of the Convention, what they called the Southern Baptist Publication Society, located at Charleston, S. C. It fell victim to the economic and political disasters of the period. Another attempt to inaugurate "an efficient plan for the circulation of the Scriptures" resulted in the Southern Baptist Convention's creating "The Bible Board of the Southern Baptist Convention" at its 1851 session and locating it in Nashville, Tenn. When the Convention met in Augusta, Ga., in 1863, Nashville was in the hands of the federal army, the executive secretary of the board and its president were confined in federal military prisons; not a representative of the board could pass through the lines to Augusta, and the work was suspended. It had served well for 12 years and then had become a casualty of fratricidal battles.

To many the mere task of getting enough to eat was more engrossing than maintaining any denominational board. But there were great hearts who did not despair, and at this same Southern Baptist Convention a haggard handful (182 representatives from eight states: Tennessee, Mississippi, and Florida had but one each) led by Basil Manly, Jr. (*q.v.*), and John A. Broadus (both teachers in the Southern Baptist Theological Seminary in Greenville, S. C.) voted to establish "The Board of Sunday Schools of the Southern Baptist Convention" and locate it in Greenville, S. C.

The end of the war brought even more difficult times, and when the Southern Baptist Convention convened at Baltimore, Md., in 1868, the extreme suffering, poverty, and distress caused the Convention to order the Board of Sunday Schools to be moved to Memphis, Tenn. But reconstruction was just getting into its personal and venomous stride. Coupled with the national and international depression which climaxed in 1873, the Convention which met in May of that year at Mobile, Ala., turned over the work of the heroically dying board to the Domestic and Indian Mission Board. Students of the history of the Southern Baptist Convention have agreed that this period (1873–91) was the most trying test of the Convention; it was said that the lionhearted Hatcher, looking at the staggering wrecks of institutions born of high hopes, now one by one dropping along this trail of tears, exclaimed: " 'Tis as familiar as an old mistake, and as futile as regret."

The year 1890 may be said to mark a distinct epoch in the life of the Southern Baptist Convention. It was 45 years since the organization of the Convention—it was but 25 years since the surrender of Robert E. Lee at Appomattox. The economic life of the South was rising, Phoenix-like, from the fiery furnace of the war and its aftermath; the smogs of hate and bitterness were beginning to drift away. In 1890 the Sunday School Board was just around the corner; born from the matrix of necessity, its birth was to be accompanied by such travail as the Convention had never known nor has known since. It was in 1890 at the session of the Southern Baptist Convention in Fort Worth, Tex., that the committee was appointed, after giants in debate had given their best to every facet of the question, to report to the next annual session at Birmingham, Ala.

At this Convention in 1891, a subcommittee was appointed to formulate a report. This Committee consisted of two, James Marion Frost (*q.v.*) of Virginia and James Bruton Gambrell (*q.v.*) of Mississippi. The story of their memorable day-long discussion and prayer and mutual "give and take" does not belong to this monograph. Suffice it to say that out of the beaten oil of Christian diplomacy came a report which was adopted. It provided for a Sunday School Board, co-ordinate with the other boards of the Convention, and directed that the new board should be located in Nashville, Tenn. No sooner had the report been adopted than Gambrell and Joshua Levering presented the name of Frost as corresponding secretary. The Convention acquiesced, and thus did the hour, the cause, and the man meet, to give to Southern Baptists what was to become its mightiest implementing force for the propagation of the gospel.

In summation, the Sunday School Board is a vast and living organization—an organism. It lives to serve, and right nobly does it serve. To quote Prince Emmanuel Burroughs (*q.v.*), "The story of its development and expansion is a story of life and growth. Strong hands guided, loving hearts guarded, a great people sponsored, and the Sunday School Board grew, 'after its kind,' in accordance with its own genius." Today its consolidated balance sheet reads like that of a great bank; its employees number several times more than the number of messengers to the Southern Baptist Convention in 1891, which saw its birth; its service extends beyond Jerusalem to the uttermost parts of the world.

Relief and Annuity Board.—This board was founded in 1918, but that does not mean that prior to that year Southern Baptists had been wholly unmindful of their obligation to provide sustenance for their aged and disabled ministers and for the widows and orphans of their deceased ministers. It is a fact that from the beginning of the revitalization of the Convention following the Civil War and the reconstruction period, there was promoted in some measure, by most of the states in the Convention, the cause of ministerial relief. It can be said that actually the years between 1845 and 1918 constituted a period of preparation for the truly large work upon which Southern Baptists entered in 1918. Prior to that time state organizations or committees for the promotion of ministerial relief came into being in many of the states. Maryland was the first, where William Crane suggested the organization of the Widows and Superannuated Ministers Fund, dating from 1839.

The actual beginning of the present Relief and Annuity Board began in a meeting of the Nashville pastors conference on a Monday morning in the autumn of 1916. "At that time," so Allen Fort, pastor of the First Baptist Church in Nashville, wrote,

> The business having been concluded, a motion to adjourn was about to be made, when Dr. William Lunsford, pastor of the Edgefield Baptist Church, Nashville, asked if he might speak a word of general interest. . . . [He] spoke with great feeling and greatly stirred the hearts of those present. . . . Several members of the Nashville Pastors' Conference, along with Lunsford, were members of the Sunday School Board. . . . The matter was mentioned informally at the next board meeting. . . . At the January meeting the board voted to request the Southern Baptist Convention, at its coming session, to consider the appointment of a commission to consider the various plans now being operated for ministerial relief in the various states, and pending . . . the report of such a commission if appointed, the board set aside the sum of $100,000 to be held intact as a contribution to such a fund when established. . . . The entire $100,000 for this fund is now in hand and is included in the invested funds of the board. It will be held subject to the decision of the Convention. . . . The report was adopted [by the Convention] and President Gambrell . . . appointed twelve members on this commission . . . [which] met in Nashville on the 11th day of June, 1917, and organized by electing Allen Fort chairman and William Lunsford secretary. . . . The leadership of the secretary, Doctor Lunsford, and the co-operation of the members of the commission resulted in the comprehensive report of the Commission which was made to the Convention at Hot Springs, in 1918. Perhaps the most important phase of this report, so far as the future of the work was concerned, was the recommendation that a BOARD OF MINISTERIAL RELIEF AND ANNUITIES BE ESTABLISHED. This recommendation was suggested by Dr. I. J. Van Ness [*q.v.*] [secretary of the Sunday School Board]. He realized the limitations of a commission and felt that a board should be organized to continue the work permanently.

The report of the Commission on Ministerial Relief and Annuities having been adopted by the Convention, the committee on boards appointed the members, and that committee chose William Lunsford as its first executive secretary. It has been domiciled continuously in Dallas, Tex., and is chartered under the laws of that state. The charter was amended on Sept. 17, 1920, whereby the name was changed from The Board of Ministerial Relief and Annuities of the Southern Baptist Convention to Relief and Annuity Board of the Southern Baptist Convention.

Without the first gift of $100,000 by the Sunday School Board, the organization of the Relief and Annuity Board would not have been effected in 1918. In addition, John D. Rockefeller had given to the board, before the end of 1925, an aggregate of $400,000. The growth, both financially and in the confidence of and service to those participating, is ample evidence of the soundness of the plan upon which the board functions.

This board operates along two main lines, as expressed in its corporate title:

> 1. It extends financial aid to aged ministers, missionaries and other denominational servants, and their dependent families; and

2. It builds retirement annuities, through individual participation and denominational co-operation, that will prevent dependency in old age. This coverage is offered every denominational servant, regardless of age, sex, race, or type of service rendered.

J. B. Gambrell, speaking two decades ago, wrote concerning the Relief and Annuity Board, "Our new Board is like a tree. It is now small, but if it is cultivated and watered, some day it will be a giant tree. It will bear fruit to gladden the hearts of men and women who have put their all into the work of the kingdom." Time has shown the truth of that prophecy.

Executive Committee.—The Executive Committee of the Southern Baptist Convention, as presently constituted, was established in 1927. For 72 years, since the birth of the Convention in 1845, there had been no central committee of any type. The Executive Committee is domiciled in Nashville, Tenn., and its duties and functions are in the main:

1. To act for the Convention ad interim in matters not otherwise provided for in its plan of work.
2. To hold title to all property, real and personal, belonging to the Convention, and to do all things necessary thereto.
3. To have oversight of arrangements for meetings of the Convention, with authority if necessary to change the time and place of meeting.
4. To represent the Convention in all negotiations with State Conventions, State Boards, and other cooperating bodies in matters of common interest.
5. To present to the Conventions a consolidated financial statement of all agencies of the Convention.
6. To recommend to the Convention an operating budget, including all of its agencies.
7. To conduct the promotion work of the Convention.
8. To perform all tasks assigned to it from time to time by the Convention.
9. To have no authority to control or direct the several Boards, Agencies, or Institutions of the Convention.

Southern Baptist Theological Seminary.—The moving figures in organizing the Southern Baptist Convention were keenly aware of the necessity for a seminary-trained, prepared, and wide-visioned ministry. Their awareness was not matched by that of a majority of the constituency, particularly if it were to be *a* seminary sustained by and responsible to the Convention. So, although at Augusta in 1845, the necessity and possibility of a Southern Baptist Convention theological seminary was talked about, nothing was done other than keeping the idea alive through discussion, much of which contained more lightning than light. Finally, the Southern Baptist Theological Seminary, as it is now called, opened in Greenville, S. C., in the fall of 1859, with 26 students and a faculty of four, James P. Boyce (*q.v.*), John A. Broadus, Basil Manly, Jr., and William Williams (*q.v.*). In June, 1862, because of the war, the work of the seminary was suspended. When work was resumed in Oct., 1865, there were but seven students to listen to the four teachers. Because of conditions in South Carolina, prostrate following the war, the Southern Baptist Convention, at its session in 1877, gave its consent to the removal of the seminary to Louisville, Ky., where it has weathered many storms, within and without, until today it has the respect, love, and devotion of literally all who call it "Alma Mater" and the multiplied hosts of Baptists who have been blessed by its living and teaching testimony to the grace of Jesus Christ.

Southwestern Baptist Theological Seminary.—With the expanding areas of the Southern Baptist Convention activities and the unparalleled growth of the people, it became necessary to add other seminaries to provide carefully trained ministers and leaders. The second of the seminaries, Southwestern Baptist Theological Seminary, grew out of the theological department of Baylor University, Waco, Tex. In 1908 a charter was granted by the state of Texas, creating the new seminary. It was moved from Waco to Fort Worth, Tex., in 1910. When the Convention met in Atlanta in 1924, the offer to transfer to the Southern Baptist Convention the ownership and control of the Southwestern Seminary was accepted. It is the largest of the seminaries and has been peculiarly gifted in leadership in furnishing missionary candidates for the foreign field and in emphasizing the evangelistic call at home and abroad.

New Orleans Baptist Theological Seminary.—The third in chronological order of the Southern Baptist Convention seminaries, located in New Orleans, began as a Bible institute. One of the early Baptists of New Orleans, Cornelius Paulding, expressed to Basil Manly, Sr. (*q.v.*), a desire to "do something noble for the cause of religion and the Baptists." This was in 1849, and Manly wrote a letter to his son Basil, suggesting a Baptist seminary in New Orleans, giving cogent reasons which were later advocated when the 1917 Southern Baptist Convention met in New Orleans. A memorial was presented recommending the establishment of a training school and was adopted. The Baptist Bible Institute opened in Sept., 1918. In 1946 the Southern Baptist Convention approved an amendment to the charter whereby the name was changed to New Orleans Baptist Theological Seminary. The old location, on what was formerly the Sophie Newcomb College, which had been purchased by the institute, was sold, and 75 acres on Gentilly Boulevard was purchased. The magnificent new plant was opened and formally dedicated in 1953. Its ministry has completely changed the situation in New Orleans from what it was before the seminary was located there, and it is a potent force for kingdom extension at home and abroad. There are many, qualified to judge, who think the Gentilly campus to be the most beautiful in the nation.

Golden Gate Baptist Theological Seminary.—The three seminaries became so crowded that in response to necessity, at the Chicago Southern Baptist Convention in 1950, the report of the committee on theological education, appointed in 1947, which had given much time

Ratio of Baptisms to Church Membership, 1955

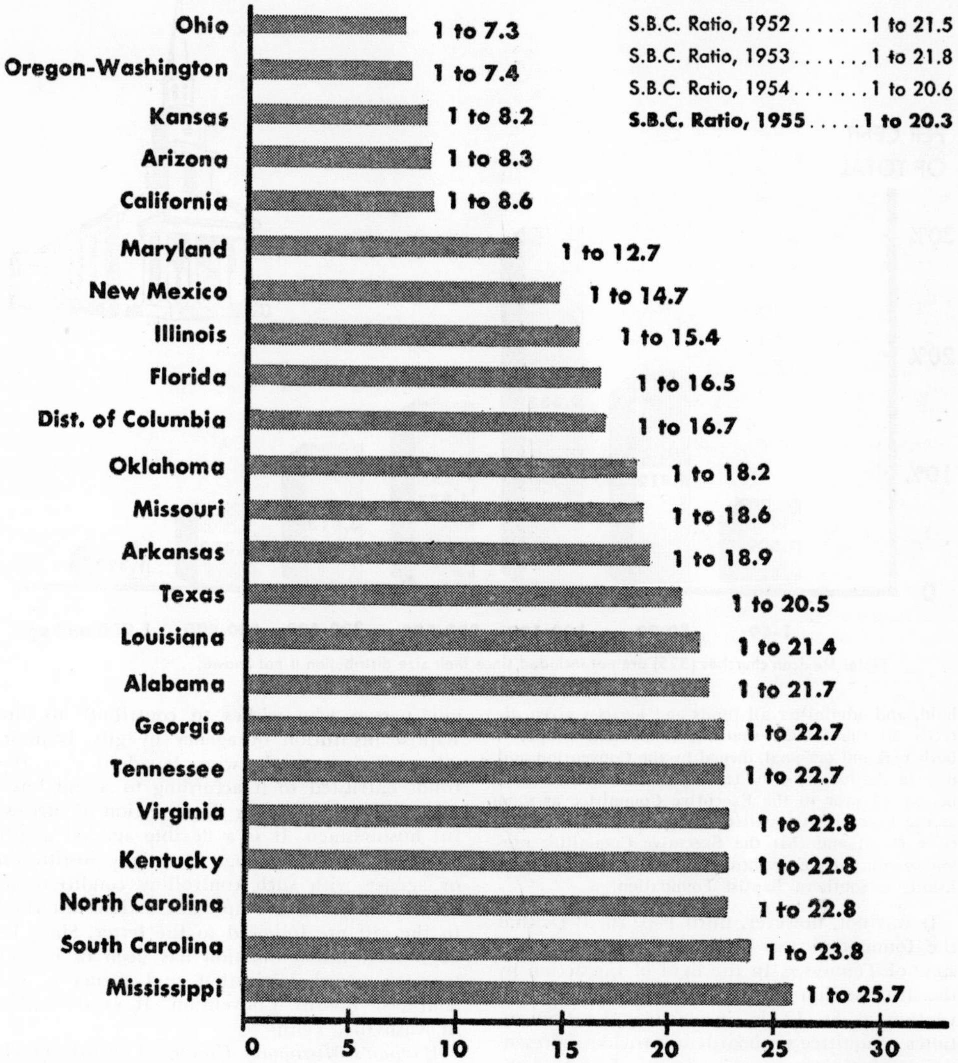

to the instructions of the Convention that it study the whole question of theological education, was adopted. This recommendation was that there be two new seminaries, one in the West at Berkeley, Calif., the other in the East, at Wake Forest, N. C. By this action the Convention took over what was an existing regional Baptist seminary, retaining its name, Golden Gate Baptist Theological Seminary. Its location was changed to a beautiful 126-acre tract of land on Strawberry Point in Marin County, overlooking San Francisco Bay, with nearly a mile of shore line. Work on the new campus was begun in 1954.

Southeastern Baptist Theological Seminary.—Wake Forest College was moving to its new campus at Winston-Salem, N. C., and for the site of the new seminary in the East, the Southern Baptist Convention authorized the purchase, for $1,600,000, of the old location—a century-old campus in Wake Forest, N. C. It was given the name Southeastern Baptist Theological Seminary.

Thus the Southern Baptist Convention now has five theological seminaries, and the 1956 Convention adopted a recommendation of its theological committee that a sixth seminary be founded when "a suitable site can be found and adequate plans can be made for financing the same without injury or impairment to other existing institutions."

Southern Baptist Foundation.—On page 30 of the 1928 Southern Baptist Convention *Annual* is this paragraph:

We recommend that the Executive Committee be the Fiduciary Agency of the S.B.C.; that it receive,

Distribution of S.B.C. Churches by Size of Membership, 1955

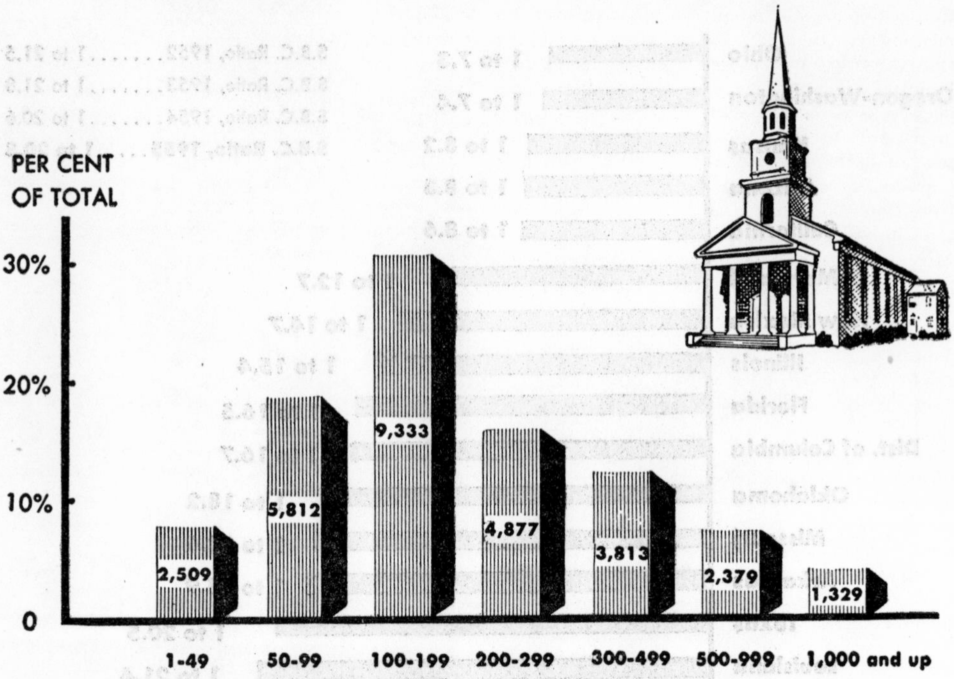

Note: Mexican churches (325) are not included since their size distribution is not known.

hold, and administer all funds and legacies given directly to the S.B.C.; that all funds and property, both real and personal, owned by the Convention and now in the hands of the treasurer of the Convention, be turned over to the Executive Committee as soon as the Executive Committee is legally qualified to receive them; and that the Executive Committee present to the next Convention detailed plans for establishing a Southern Baptist Foundation.

It was not, however, until Feb. 26, 1947, that the foundation was granted a charter by the state of Tennessee. In the light of the action by the 1947 session of the Southern Baptist Convention at St. Louis, instructing the Convention's committee on boards to provide representation of various agencies on the board of directors of the foundation, there was adopted at the next annual meeting of the directors, as an amendment to its bylaws:

The Board of Directors shall be constituted as follows: The President of the Convention ex-officio member. Nine Baptist laymen of business experience, five of whom shall live in Nashville. The other members of the Board of Directors shall be: one member from the Executive Committee, one member from each of the four general boards, one member of the boards of the five Southwide institutions, a member from the Executive Committee of the Baptist Brotherhood, a member from the Woman's Missionary Union, and a member from the boards of such other agencies as the Southern Baptist Convention may hereafter create and designate as entitled to representation for membership on this Board.

The Southern Baptist Foundation is a permanent trust, established and chartered to serve any person who wishes to contribute to any Baptist institution or agency by gift, bequest, gift annuity, or otherwise. It administers the funds entrusted to it according to sound business practice and under the direction of successful businessmen. It is a flexible agency; a gift may be directed through it to any institution or agency with such controlling conditions as may be desired, and any instructions attached to the gift are followed to the letter. Since its beginning, the foundation has been of benefit to every board, institution, and agency of the Southern Baptist Convention. It is domiciled in Nashville, Tenn.

Woman's Missionary Union.—The present efficiently working organization known as Woman's Missionary Union, Auxiliary to the Southern Baptist Convention, is the result of the development which began with local societies of women, the purpose of which was to raise funds for home and foreign missions. A missionary society of women was formed in Richmond, Va., in 1813. While there were no representatives of women's societies at Augusta in 1845, the constitution did provide for representation from mission societies that sent funds for missions. In 1868 was held the first general meeting of Southern Baptist women. The Southern Baptist Convention was meeting in Baltimore, and the meeting of the women was called to hear a report of mission work in China. In 1875 the Southern Baptist Convention, in session at Charleston, S. C., took official recognition of the work of the women's societies and the next year adopted a report on women's work, commending it. It was not until 1888, at the meeting of the Convention in Richmond, Va., that the women, meeting in the old Broad Street Methodist Church, voted to organize Woman's Missionary Union. Its growth has been marvelous and has been marvelously blessed of God, stimulating larger gifts to the Cooperative Program on the part of both men and women, and training in a graded missionary educational system all ages, from four years to adults. It is no exaggeration that, during the dark days of 1929–33, Woman's Missionary Union saved the mission causes from disaster. Its headquarters are in Birmingham, Ala.

Southern Baptist Hospital.—In 1920 the Southern Baptist Convention, in Washington, D. C., took the first step in constructing a Southern Baptist hospital in New Orleans; and in 1923 at Kansas City, Mo., the Convention created a hospital commission to which was committed the responsibility of constructing and administering it. The Southern Baptist Hospital, as the original commission is now known, is domiciled in New Orleans, La.

Education Commission.—The Education Commission, as it is now called, passed through a metamorphosis of terminology, beginning as Education Commission in 1916, changed to Education Board in 1919, and back to Education Commission in 1928. According to its charter, issued in 1951 under the laws of Tennessee and approved by the Southern Baptist Convention in 1952, it was established to "serve the educational interests of the Southern Baptist Convention and any and all agencies now or at any time hereafter created by, controlled by, fostered by, or officially sanctioned by the Southern Baptist Convention." Its domicile is in Nashville, Tenn.

Christian Life Commission.—The Christian Life Commission has been charged by the Southern Baptist Convention with the task of moral education through research, analysis, and the implementation of social action. Its official residence is in Nashville, Tenn.

Radio and Television Commission.—What is now called the Radio and Television Commission (being given that name by Convention action in 1946) grew out of a Convention radio committee. It is financed partly from Cooperative Program funds and partly from voluntary contributions. It is domiciled in Fort Worth, Tex.

Historical Commission.—For years the Convention had a committee on preservation of Baptist history, created by Convention action in 1936. Eleven years later, the Convention gave the committee the status of a commission. The Historical Commission is duly recognized as the agency of the Southern Baptist Convention to serve in all phases of the field of its history. It is domiciled in Nashville, Tenn.

Brotherhood Commission.—The Brotherhood Commission was founded in 1907. Its purpose is to enlist, develop, and utilize all men of the Southern Baptist churches in promoting the work of the churches and of the Convention. The offices of the Brotherhood Commission are located in Memphis, Tenn.

Commission on the American Baptist Seminary.—In 1894 there was founded what is now the Commission on the American Baptist Seminary. This commission, in conjunction with the National Baptist Convention, Inc. (Negro), combines in the operation of a training school for Negro ministers, located in Nashville, Tenn.

The Cooperative Program.—Perhaps no more startling metamorphosis has ever taken place in the thinking of the denomination than that which had to do with its finances. For many years the support of its mission causes, as well as that of the churches from whence comes its membership, was pitched on an emotional chord. Well within the memories of those now considered as its leaders, official representatives of the various boards and agencies made, either in person or through appointed individuals, visits to the churches appealing for funds. The one who could tell the most tearful story got the most money. Often the visitors trod on each other's heels (more frequently on each other's toes), and the interval between collections left little time for the financial blood bank to become replenished. The result was that for each dollar of increase to Convention-wide causes, there were very many irritated individuals. Both pastors and church members were complaining, and it was rapidly becoming a field of gold on which the contesting knights reaped only dribs of silver.

So it was that at the meeting of the Convention in Memphis, Tenn., 1925, there was set in motion what is now called the Cooperative Program of the Southern Baptist Convention. As with anything which is a departure from the accustomed, the Cooperative Program at first met with vociferous objections from Baptists who (at least some of them) honestly felt that it was a violation of their dearly bought freedom of choice. These objectors and their objections have now come to be an almost negligible quantity by virtue of measures taken to safeguard their freedom of choice and by the undeniable success of the Cooperative Program.

What is meant by this term? It is self-explainatory—a method whereby the Convention-wide receipts are augmented in a united and cooperative effort, and whereby they are disbursed to all the boards and agencies, the distribution being made upon an agreed percentage. These percentages are arrived at in a simple way, but one which involves much hard work and frequently great self-denial by the participating boards and agencies.

The finance committee of the Executive Committee, after a careful analysis of the past year's receipts and the next year's expectancy, sets up an operating budget and a capital needs budget, of, by way of illustration, $8,000,000 and $3,000,000, respectively. When these budgets are agreed upon by the entire committee, at the December

SOUTHERN BAPTIST REPORTS—1845–1956

Year	Membership	Baptisms	S.S. Enrolment	V.B.S. Enrolment	T.U. Enrolment	W.M.U. Enrolment	Brotherhood Enrolment	Church Property	Mission Gifts	Total All Gifts	Churches
1845	351,951	23,222									4,126
1846	367,017	24,062									4,411
1847	376,851	25,629									4,501
1848	385,803	27,412									4,695
1849	404,600	33,497									4,874
1850											
1851	423,507	33,831									5,113
1852	467,334	37,611									5,817
1853	495,945	41,863									6,209
1854	519,210	43,423									6,394
1855	542,396	43,722									6,590
1856	568,973	43,065									6,777
1857	580,296	43,122									7,062
1858	617,723	51,007									7,338
1859	639,240	49,127									7,701
1860	649,518	51,342									
1861–71 No data available											
1872	956,067	68,017	287,658								
1873	1,098,808	50,532									
1874	1,200,106	67,498									
1875	1,249,073	62,679									
1876	1,342,432	69,448									
1877	1,418,296	63,680									
1878	1,483,660	70,568									
1879	1,516,351	53,760									
1880	1,672,631	78,243	377,214								13,455
1881	961,435	47,575	396,359								13,527
1882	915,140	47,886	458,917								13,438
1883	934,817	53,908	502,105								13,513
1884	975,153	62,424	556,715								14,102
1885	1,013,160	65,197	326,003					$ 4,700,893	$ 202,170	$1,513,640	14,488
1886	1,071,823	90,877	372,929					6,840,281	209,116	1,603,934	14,346
1887	1,125,892	83,158	448,365					9,180,634	219,282	1,876,260	14,874
1888	1,165,812	73,052	539,083					11,515,881	295,394	2,203,700	15,343
1889	1,194,654	77,507	549,127					13,282,024	306,493	2,287,930	15,894
1890	1,235,908	81,806	577,230					13,382,359	398,916	2,876,927	16,091
1891	1,282,220	84,076	494,845					14,703,308		3,252,716	16,654
1892	1,321,540	82,478						15,600,061		3,045,689	17,710
1893	1,363,351	93,842						17,361,794		3,218,789	17,346
1894	1,431,041	105,190	414,379					17,913,444		2,927,162	17,803
1895	1,468,991	90,877	576,711					19,551,268		2,970,429	18,143
1896	1,529,191	97,557	611,528					18,351,855	425,871	2,547,347	18,678
1897	1,568,906	98,984	611,612					18,681,227	667,190	2,895,080	18,922
1898	1,586,709	77,243	628,002					19,207,537	613,946	2,857,071	18,873
1899	1,608,413	73,635	636,944					19,437,323	701,323	3,069,507	18,963
1900	1,657,996	80,465	670,569					20,025,344	881,219	3,456,014	19,558
1901	1,683,039	95,610	712,012					20,637,619	971,984	4,016,394	19,653
1902	1,737,446	108,517	745,474					21,513,888	1,086,308	4,571,325	19,911
1903	1,805,889	103,241	761,059					22,828,672	1,127,794	5,038,253	20,431
1904	1,832,638	103,021	776,248					23,824,590	1,210,134	5,379,081	20,402

SOUTHERN BAPTIST REPORTS—1845–1956— (Continued)

Year	Membership	Baptisms	S.S. Enrolment	V.B.S. Enrolment	T.U. Enrolment	W.M.U. Enrolment	Brotherhood Enrolment	Church Property	Mission Gifts	Total All Gifts	Churches
1905	1,899,427	105,905	844,040					$ 25,471,209	$ 1,476,330	$ 6,083,860	21,802
1906	1,946,948	124,911	876,682					27,917,149	1,704,130	7,108,934	20,776
1907	2,015,080	129,152	959,795					30,861,438	1,817,556	7,863,416	21,266
1908	2,139,080	146,717	1,055,721					34,637,020	1,997,634	8,522,652	21,887
1909	2,218,911	140,980	1,131,981					37,203,522	2,264,198	9,474,777	22,438
1910	2,332,464	134,440	1,248,116					43,393,899	2,480,207	10,424,486	23,248
1911	2,421,203	132,396	1,288,014		60,700			46,843,897	2,522,161	10,926,406	23,676
1912	2,446,296	123,471	1,329,720		76,665			48,634,360	2,631,976	10,883,092	23,982
1913	2,522,633	137,396	1,491,426		117,695			53,392,795	2,811,515	12,158,587	24,171
1914	2,588,633	151,441	1,705,871		159,932			56,861,492	3,038,044	13,073,940	24,338
1915	2,685,552	168,235	1,760,802		153,071			58,319,638	2,977,667	12,541,890	24,451
1916	2,744,098	160,497	1,784,992		175,540			61,159,186	3,233,011	13,415,884	24,602
1917	2,844,301	148,699	1,835,811					64,772,860	3,560,963	15,346,158	24,883
1918	2,887,428	113,833	1,759,208		230,540			69,974,092	4,911,105	17,852,929	24,851
1919	2,961,348	123,069	1,835,936		301,873			74,273,728	7,331,266	21,327,446	25,303
1920	3,149,346	173,595	1,926,610		322,011			97,732,990	14,038,661	34,882,082	27,444
1921	3,220,383	233,571	2,147,654		384,215			102,404,038	10,962,725	33,432,746	27,634
1922	3,366,211	224,844	2,220,035		483,166			115,346,960	9,849,857	32,167,978	27,919
1923	3,494,189	195,864	2,381,717		495,149	148,108		127,121,096	9,393,618	34,439,436	27,611
1924	3,574,531	209,676	2,536,953		546,193	269,906		141,737,127	9,863,154	37,359,615	27,517
1925*	3,649,330	224,191	2,691,828	28,167	531,415			165,909,278	8,255,435	39,027,009	24,341
1926*	3,616,964	193,279	2,683,331	38,077	498,426			195,005,216	8,161,411	39,855,829	24,774
1927*	3,673,712	197,155	2,780,043		480,190	440,009		205,705,944	7,843,652	39,787,237	24,274
1928*	3,705,876	183,020	2,797,129	44,230	500,564	523,736		207,614,545	7,402,788	39,927,910	25,705
1929	3,770,645	175,631	2,776,665	51,079	501,405	531,394		213,327,088	7,641,330	39,337,149	24,010
1930	3,850,278	198,579	2,839,183	57,983	533,976	624,659		217,979,116	6,763,837	37,489,021	23,731
1931	3,944,566	211,253	2,952,910	68,786	546,948	651,690		217,066,775	5,819,375	32,618,128	23,806
1932	4,066,140	226,855	3,051,469	71,568	583,842	563,830		209,719,089	4,951,011	27,341,488	24,035
1933	4,173,928	211,393	3,069,484	83,600	618,283	581,442		204,376,293	3,880,774	23,289,361	24,270
1934	4,277,052	209,364	3,104,411	100,902	649,773	571,702		202,095,794	4,251,668	24,653,276	24,360
1935	4,389,417	202,047	3,157,458	140,878	662,004	593,766		202,101,914	4,624,515	26,888,567	24,537
1936	4,482,315	191,993	3,173,356	198,153	693,186	595,852		203,469,481	4,986,885	29,188,687	24,671
1937	4,595,602	204,567	3,211,707	264,247	742,201	612,075		206,668,413	5,702,150	32,265,687	24,844
1938	4,770,185	256,814	3,368,851	375,455	805,945	715,402		210,466,838	5,798,529	35,265,340	24,932
1939	4,949,174	269,155	3,523,853	421,377	874,791	747,845		214,724,695	6,267,263	37,136,531	25,018
1940	5,104,327	245,500	3,590,374	541,206	919,689	758,151		221,974,479	6,787,627	40,359,038	25,259
1941	5,238,132	209,593	3,553,467	617,404	954,179	768,976		232,944,315	7,822,340	44,857,607	25,603
1942	5,367,129	209,127	3,430,929	590,114	801,567	748,465	54,868	240,131,184	9,681,772	52,247,622	25,737
1943	5,493,027	202,301	3,332,978	548,707	777,732	715,433	33,009	248,168,495	13,455,640	63,067,085	25,790
1944	5,667,926	218,223	3,372,909	635,947	759,885	719,186	34,750	259,534,009	17,300,389	76,588,615	25,965
1945	5,865,554	256,699	3,525,310	801,218	703,332	739,360	38,538	276,089,771	22,490,751	98,458,425	26,191
1946	6,079,305	253,361	3,738,924	1,055,678	802,859	767,521	71,412	313,053,779	27,240,704	115,226,949	26,401
1947	6,270,819	285,152	4,004,705	1,328,790	927,908	761,907	97,146	366,830,652	28,472,014	132,162,846	26,764
1948	6,489,221	310,226	4,301,490	1,268,171	1,079,024	856,332	119,230	450,489,517	30,605,598	155,574,504	26,822
1949	6,761,265	334,892	4,643,650	1,443,072	1,235,438	943,135	142,412	548,261,564	31,316,818	178,337,307	27,285
1950	7,079,889	376,085	5,024,553	1,642,772	1,440,895	1,033,479	167,744	645,271,741	33,402,224	197,242,154	27,788
1951	7,373,498	375,525	5,253,695	1,770,418	1,554,660	1,087,427	185,587	761,510,838	37,268,172	222,838,109	28,289
1952	7,634,493	354,384	5,491,056	2,059,163	1,677,293	1,143,993	214,486	890,697,339	45,822,830	248,004,289	28,865
1953	7,886,016	361,835	5,759,128	2,108,370	1,849,544	1,188,080	242,918	1,020,504,214	48,427,760	278,851,129	29,496
1954	8,169,491	396,857	6,356,489	2,570,290	2,062,952	1,302,060	273,406	1,162,761,138	52,926,157	305,573,654	29,899
1955	8,474,741	416,867	6,641,715	2,652,788	2,223,502	1,245,358	404,281	1,323,453,534	58,360,247	334,836,283	30,377
1956	8,708,823	384,627	6,823,713	2,733,990	2,316,354	1,267,850	445,630	1,491,385,336	64,954,516	372,136,675	30,834

*B.M.A.'s dropped from list.

HISTORICAL TABLE

Of the Southern Baptist Convention Since Its Organization

Date	Place of Meeting	Registration	Presidents	Secretaries	Preachers
1845	Augusta, Georgia	236	William B. Johnson, S. C.	Jesse Hartwell, Ala.; James C. Crane, Va.	
1846	Richmond, Virginia	162	William B. Johnson, S. C.	Jesse Hartwell, Ala.; James C. Crane, Va.	Richard Fuller, Md.
1849	Charleston, South Carolina	103	William B. Johnson, S. C.	James C. Crane, Va.; Basil Manley, Jr., Ala.	W. B. Johnson, S. C.
1851	Nashville, Tennessee	124	R. B. C. Howell, Va.	James C. Crane, Va.; William Carey Crane, Miss.	J. B. Jeter, Va.; J. L. Reynolds, S. C.
1853	Baltimore, Maryland	154	R. B. C. Howell, Va.	H. K. Ellyson, Va.; William Carey Crane, Miss.	R. B. C. Howell, Va.; S. Baker, Ky.
1855	Montgomery, Alabama	235	R. B. C. Howell, Va.	William Carey Crane, Miss.; James M. Watts, Ala.	A. D. Sears, Ky.
1857	Louisville, Kentucky	184	R. B. C. Howell, Va.	William Carey Crane, Miss.; George B. Taylor, Md.	William Carey Crane, Miss.
1859	Richmond, Virginia	580	Richard Fuller, Md.	William Carey Crane, Miss.; George B. Taylor, Md.	Duncan R. Campbell, Ky.
1861	Savannah, Georgia	177	Richard Fuller, Md.	William Carey Crane, Miss.; George B. Taylor, Va.	William H. McIntosh, Ala.
1863	Augusta, Georgia	181	P. H. Mell, Ga.	George B. Taylor, Va.; Sylvanus Landrum, Ga.	J. L. Burrows, Va.
1866	Russellville, Kentucky	244	P. H. Mell, Ga.	George B. Taylor, Va.; W. Pope Yeamann, Ky.	Richard Fuller, Md.
1867	Memphis, Tennessee	250	P. H. Mell, Ga.	A. Fuller Crane, Md.; A. P. Abell, Va.	W. T. Brantley, Md.
1868	Baltimore, Maryland	327	P. H. Mell, Ga.	A. P. Abell, Va.; A. F. Crane, Md.	T. E. Skinner, Tenn.
1869	Macon, Georgia	266	P. H. Mell, Ga.	A. P. Abell, Va.; A. F. Crane, Md.	E. T. Winkler, S. C.
1870	Louisville, Kentucky	399	P. H. Mell, Ga.	J. Russell Hawkins, Ky.; E. C. Williams, Md.	J. L. Burrows, Va.
1871	St. Louis, Missouri	360	P. H. Mell, Ga.	E. Calvin Williams, Md.; Truman S. Sumner, Ala.	William Williams, S. C.
1872	Raleigh, North Carolina	304	James P. Boyce, S. C.	E. Calvin Williams, Md.; Truman S. Sumner, Ala.	J. W. M. Williams, Md.
1873	Mobile, Alabama	259	James P. Boyce, S. C.	M. B. Wharton, Ky.; W. O. Tuggle, Ga.	T. G. Jones, Tenn.
1874	Jefferson, Texas	222	James P. Boyce, Ky.	G. R. McCall, Ga.; W. O. Tuggle, Ga.	E. G. Taylor, La.
1875	Charleston, South Carolina	302	James P. Boyce, Ky.	W. O. Tuggle, Ga.; G. R. McCall, Ga.	T. H. Pritchard, N. C.
1876	Richmond, Virginia	289	James P. Boyce, Ky.	C. C. Bitting, Va.; E. Calvin Williams, Md.	George C. Lorimer, Mass.
1877	New Orleans, Louisiana	164	James P. Boyce, Ky.	O. F. Gregory, Ala.; W. E. Tanner, Va.	Henry McDonald, Ky.
1878	Nashville, Tennessee	253	James P. Boyce, Ky.	C. E. W. Dobbs, Ky.; W. E. Tanner, Va.	B. H. Carroll, Texas
1879	Atlanta, Georgia	313	James P. Boyce, Ky.	C. E. W. Dobbs, Ky.; W. E. Tanner, Va.	J. C. Furman, S. C.
1880	Lexington, Kentucky	360	P. H. Mell, Ga.	C. E. W. Dobbs, Ky.; O. F. Gregory, S. C.	P. H. Mell, Ga.
1881	Columbus, Mississippi	270	P. H. Mell, Ga.	C. E. W. Dobbs, Ky.; Lansing Burrows, Ky.	Sylvanus Landrum, Ga.
1882	Greenville, South Carolina	335	P. H. Mell, Ga.	Lansing Burrows, Ky.; O. F. Gregory, N. C.	T. T. Eaton, Ky.
1883	Waco, Texas	612	P. H. Mell, Ga.	Lansing Burrows, Ky.; O. F. Gregory, N. C.	John A. Broadus, Ky.
1884	Baltimore, Maryland	637	P. H. Mell, Ga.	Lansing Burrows, Ga.; O. F. Gregory, N. C.	Lansing Burrows, Ga.
1885	Augusta, Georgia	528	P. H. Mell, Ga.	Lansing Burrows, Ga.; O. F. Gregory, La.	J. L. M. Curry, Va.; J. L. Burrows
1886	Montgomery, Alabama	488	P. H. Mell, Ga.	Lansing Burrows, Ga.; O. F. Gregory, Md.	J. B. Hawthorne, Ga.
1887	Louisville, Kentucky	689	P. H. Mell, Ga.	Lansing Burrows, Ga.; O. F. Gregory, Md.	George Cooper, Va.
1888	Richmond, Virginia	835	James P. Boyce, Ky.	Lansing Burrows, Ga.; O. F. Gregory, Md.	Francis M. Ellis, Md.
1889	Memphis, Tennessee	706	Jonathan Haralson, Ala.	Lansing Burrows, Ga.; O. F. Gregory, Md.	J. P. Greene, Mo.
1890	Fort Worth, Texas	801	Jonathan Haralson, Ala.	Lansing Burrows, Ga.; O. F. Gregory, Md.	J. W. Carter, N. C.
1891	Birmingham, Alabama	915	Jonathan Haralson, Ala.	Lansing Burrows, Ga.; O. F. Gregory, Md.	Carter H. Jones, Tenn.
1892	Atlanta, Georgia	978	Jonathan Haralson, Ala.	Lansing Burrows, Ga.; O. F. Gregory, Md.	J. B. Gambrell, Miss.
1893	Nashville, Tennessee	818	Jonathan Haralson, Ala.	Lansing Burrows, Ga.; O. F. Gregory, Md.	W. E. Hatcher, Va.
1894	Dallas, Texas	772	Jonathan Haralson, Ala.	Lansing Burrows, Ga.; O. F. Gregory, Md.	F. H. Kerfoot, Ky.
1895	Washington, District of Columbia	870	Jonathan Haralson, Ala.	Lansing Burrows, Ga.; O. F. Gregory, Md.	Geo. B. Eager, Ala.; W. H. Whitsitt, Ky.
1896	Chattanooga, Tennessee	819	Jonathan Haralson, Ala.	Lansing Burrows, Ga.; O. F. Gregory, Md.	Chas. A. Stakely, D. C.
1897	Wilmington, North Carolina	724	Jonathan Haralson, Ala.	Lansing Burrows, Ga.; O. F. Gregory, Md.	R. A. Venable, Miss.
1898	Norfolk, Virginia	857	Jonathan Haralson, Ala.	Lansing Burrows, Ga.; O. F. Gregory, Md.	B. L. Whitman, D. C.
1899	Louisville, Kentucky	869	W. J. Northen, Ga.	Lansing Burrows, Ga.; O. F. Gregory, Md.	Geo. W. Truett, Texas
1900	Hot Springs, Arkansas	646	W. J. Northen, Ga.	Lansing Burrows, Tenn.; O. F. Gregory, Md.	J. J. Taylor, Va.
1901	New Orleans, Louisiana	787	W. J. Northen, Ga.	Lansing Burrows, Tenn.; O. F. Gregory, Md.	E. Y. Mullins, Ky.
1902	Asheville, North Carolina	1,093	James P. Eagle, Ark.	Lansing Burrows, Tenn.; O. F. Gregory, Md.	F. C. McConnell, Ga.
1903	Savannah, Georgia	1,136	James P. Eagle, Ark.	Lansing Burrows, Tenn.; O. F. Gregory, Ala.	W. J. Williamson, Mo.
1904	Nashville, Tennessee	1,095	James P. Eagle, Ark.	Lansing Burrows, Tenn.; O. F. Gregory, Ala.	W. W. Landrum, Ga.
1905	Kansas City, Missouri	816	E. W. Stephens, Mo.	Lansing Burrows, Tenn.; O. F. Gregory, Ala.	W. H. Felix, Ky.
1906	Chattanooga, Tennessee	1,451	E. W. Stephens, Mo.	Lansing Burrows, Tenn.; O. F. Gregory, Va.	W. R. L. Smith, Va.
1907	Richmond, Virginia	1,411	E. W. Stephens, Mo.	Lansing Burrows, Tenn.; O. F. Gregory, Va.	A. J. Dickinson, Ala.
1908	Hot Springs, Arkansas	1,258	Joshua Levering, Md.	Lansing Burrows, Tenn.; O. F. Gregory, Va.	Henry W. Battle, N. C.

HISTORICAL TABLE—(Continued)

Date	Place of Meeting	Registration	Presidents	Secretaries	Preachers
1909	Louisville, Kentucky	1,547	Joshua Levering, Md.	Lansing Burrows, Ga.; O. F. Gregory, Va.	Edwin C. Dargan, Ga.
1910	Baltimore, Maryland	1,641	Joshua Levering, Md.	Lansing Burrows, Ga.; O. F. Gregory, Va.	W. L. Pickard, Ga.
1911	Jacksonville, Florida	1,558	Edwin C. Dargan, Ga.	Lansing Burrows, Ga.; O. F. Gregory, Va.	C. S. Gardner, Ky.
1912	Oklahoma City, Oklahoma	1,228	Edwin C. Dargan, Ga.	Lansing Burrows, Ga.; O. F. Gregory, Va.	Z. T. Cody, S. C.
1913	Saint Louis, Missouri	1,403	Edwin C. Dargan, Ga.	Lansing Burrows, Ga.; O. F. Gregory, Md.	T. W. O'Kelley, N. C.
1914	Nashville, Tennessee	1,930	Lansing Burrows, Ga.	O. F. Gregory, Md.; Hight C Moore, N. C.	Geo. W. McDaniel, Va.
1915	Houston, Texas	1,408	Lansing Burrows, Ga.	O. F. Gregory, Md.; Hight C Moore, N. C.	J. W. Porter, Ky.
1916	Asheville, North Carolina	2,125	Lansing Burrows, Ga.	O. F. Gregory, Md.; Hight C Moore, N. C.	Chas. W. Daniel, Ga.
1917	New Orleans, Louisiana	1,683	J. B. Gambrell, Texas	O. F. Gregory, Md.; Hight C Moore, N. C.	C. W. Duke, Fla.
1918	Hot Springs, Arkansas	2,043	J. B. Gambrell, Texas	O. F. Gregory, Md.; Hight C Moore, Tenn.	W. H. Geistweit, Mo.
1919	Atlanta, Georgia	4,224	J. B. Gambrell, Texas	Hight C Moore, Tenn.; J. Henry Burnett, Ga.	M. E. Dodd, La.
1920	Washington, District of Columbia	8,359	J. B. Gambrell, Texas	Hight C Moore, Tenn.; J. Henry Burnett, Ga.	Jno. E. White, S. C.
1921	Chattanooga, Tennessee	5,313	E. Y. Mullins, Ky.	Hight C Moore, Tenn.; J. Henry Burnett, Ga.	H. L. Winburn, Ark.
1922	Jacksonville, Florida	4,272	E. Y. Mullins, Ky.	Hight C Moore, Tenn.; J. Henry Burnett, Ga.	S. J. Porter, Okla.
1923	Kansas City, Missouri	4,193	E. Y. Mullins, Ky.	Hight C Moore, Tenn.; J. Henry Burnett, Tenn.	R. G. Bowers, Texas
1924	Atlanta, Georgia	5,622	Geo. W. McDaniel, Va.	Hight C Moore, Tenn.; J. Henry Burnett, Tenn.	F. F. Gibson, Ky.
1925	Memphis, Tennessee	5,600	Geo. W. McDaniel, Va.	Hight C Moore, Tenn.; J. Henry Burnett, Tenn.	Len. G. Broughton, Fla.
1926	Houston, Texas	4,268	Geo. W. McDaniel, Va.	Hight C Moore, Tenn.; J. Henry Burnett, Tenn.	F. F. Brown, Tenn.
1927	Louisville, Kentucky	4,424	Geo. W. Truett, Texas	Hight C Moore, Tenn.; J. Henry Burnett, Tenn.	Wallace Bassett, Texas
1928	Chattanooga, Tennessee	3,810	Geo. W. Truett, Texas	Hight C Moore, Tenn.; J. Henry Burnett, Tenn.	J. R. Hobbs, Ala.
1929	Memphis, Tennessee	3,999	Geo. W. Truett, Texas	Hight C Moore, Tenn.; J. Henry Burnett, Ga.	W. L. Ball, S. C.
1930	New Orleans, Louisiana	3,342	W. J. McGlothlin, S. C.	Hight C Moore, Tenn.; J. Henry Burnett, Ga.	Robt. G. Lee, Tenn.
1931	Birmingham, Alabama	3,195	W. J. McGlothlin, S. C.	Hight C Moore, Tenn.; J. Henry Burnett, Ga.	John W. Phillips, Ala.
1932	St. Petersburg, Florida	2,178	W. J. McGlothlin, S. C.	Hight C Moore, Tenn.; J. Henry Burnett, Ga.	W. Marshall Craig, Texas
1933	Washington, District of Columbia	2,765	F. F. Brown, Tenn.	Hight C Moore, Tenn.; J. Henry Burnett, Ga.	J. L. White, Fla.
1934	Fort Worth, Texas	4,435	M. E. Dodd, La.	Hight C Moore, Tenn.; J. Henry Burnett, Ga.	T. L. Holcomb, Okla.
1935	Memphis, Tennessee	4,268	M. E. Dodd, La.	Hight C Moore, Tenn.; J. Henry Burnett, Ga.	J. B. Weatherspoon, Ky.
1936	Saint Louis, Missouri	3,702	John R. Sampey, Ky.	Hight C Moore, Tenn.; J. Henry Burnett, Ga.	John A. Huff, La.
1937	New Orleans, Louisiana	4,507	John R. Sampey, Ky.	Hight C Moore, Tenn.; J. Henry Burnett, Ga.	Solon B. Cousins, Va.
1938	Richmond, Virginia	5,785	John R. Sampey, Ky.	Hight C Moore, Tenn.; J. Henry Burnett, Ga.	E. P. J. Garrott, Ark.
1939	Oklahoma City, Oklahoma	4,598	L. R. Scarborough, Texas	Hight C Moore, Tenn.; J. Henry Burnett, N. C.	Perry F. Webb, Texas
1940	Baltimore, Maryland	3,776	L. R. Scarborough, Texas	Hight C Moore, Tenn.; J. Henry Burnett, N. C.	W. R. White, Oklahoma
1941	Birmingham, Alabama	5,884	W. W. Hamilton, La.	Hight C Moore, Tenn.; J. Henry Burnett, N. C.	J. Clyde Turner, N. C.
1942	San Antonio, Texas	4,774	W. W. Hamilton, La.	Hight C Moore, Tenn.; J. Henry Burnett, N. C.	Ellis A. Fuller, Ga.
1944	Atlanta, Georgia	4,301	Pat M. Neff, Texas	Hight C Moore, N. C.; J. Henry Burnett, N. C.	John H. Buchanan, Ala.
1946	Miami, Florida	7,973	Pat M. Neff, Texas	Hight C Moore, N. C.; J. Henry Burnett, N. C.	J. W. Storer, Okla.
1947	St. Louis, Missouri	8,508	Louie D. Newton, Georgia	Porter Routh, Tenn.; Joe W. Burton, Tenn.	W. A. Criswell, Texas
1948	Memphis, Tennessee	9,843	Louie D. Newton, Georgia	Porter Routh, Tenn.; Joe W. Burton, Tenn.	W. R. Pettigrew, Kentucky
1949	Oklahoma City, Oklahoma	9,393	Robert G. Lee, Tennessee	Porter Routh, Tenn.; Joe W. Burton, Tenn.	Norman W. Cox, Mississippi
1950	Chicago, Illinois	8,151	Robert G. Lee, Tennessee	Porter Routh, Tenn.; Joe W. Burton, Tenn.	R. C. Campbell, North Carolina
1951	San Francisco, California	6,493	Robert G. Lee, Tennessee	Porter Routh, Tenn.; Joe W. Burton, Tenn.	C. Roy Angell, Florida
1952	Miami, Florida	10,960	J. D. Grey, La.	Porter Routh, Tenn.; Joe W. Burton, Tenn.	Ramsey Pollard, Tenn.
1953	Houston, Texas	12,976	J. D. Grey, La.	George B. Fraser, Wash.; D. C.; Joe W. Burton, Tenn.	J. H. Landes, Texas
1954	St. Louis, Missouri	10,962	J. W. Storer, Okla.	Joe W. Burton, Tenn.	Slater A. Murphy, Tenn.
1955	Miami, Florida	10,837	J. W. Storer, Oklahoma	James W. Merritt, Ga.; Joe W. Burton, Tenn.	Monroe F. Swilley, Ga.
1956	Kansas City, Mo.	12,254	Casper C. Warren, N. C.	James W. Merritt, Ga.; Joe W. Burton, Tenn.	Harry P. Stagg, N. M.

NUMBER OF CHURCHES REPORTING MAJOR ITEMS, 1955

S.B.C.	NUMBER REPORTING:											
	Total No. Ch's	Pastor	Bap-tisms	Addi-tions by Letter	Sunday School Enrol.	V.B.S.	T.U.	W.M.U.	Broth-erhood	Church Prop-erty	Mis-sion Gifts	Total Gifts
S.B.C.	30,377	27,226	25,578	24,960	29,498	21,849	21,217	19,382	11,142	28,373	28,471	29,781
Open Country	14,779	13,105	11,477	10,770	14,305	8,946	8,236	6,794	3,021	13,750	13,500	14,563
Village	4,863	4,306	4,046	4,049	4,789	3,630	3,349	3,124	1,365	4,639	4,726	4,837
Town	3,925	3,560	3,622	3,678	3,830	3,373	3,376	3,469	2,054	3,659	3,782	3,827
City	6,810	6,255	6,433	6,463	6,574	5,900	6,256	5,995	4,702	6,325	6,480	6,554
Alabama	2,707	2,438	2,174	2,080	2,646	2,057	1,914	1,587	704	2,565	2,567	2,703
Open Country	1,646	1,465	1,220	1,123	1,594	1,128	987	713	232	1,541	1,520	1,644
Village	418	365	340	338	409	336	311	280	77	398	409	417
Town	267	250	245	251	267	244	248	245	124	261	264	267
City	376	358	369	368	376	349	368	349	271	365	374	375
Alaska	20	19	20	20	20	17	18	18	13	19	20	20
Open Country	1	1	1	1	1	1	1	1	1	1	1	1
Village	......	......	......	......	......	......	......	......	......	......	......	......
Town	2	2	2	2	2	2	......	1	......	2	2	2
City	17	16	17	17	17	14	17	16	12	16	17	17
Arizona	209	189	194	199	209	176	196	172	118	181	207	208
Open Country	5	5	4	5	5	4	4	3	2	5	5	5
Village	24	19	20	21	24	23	18	17	8	23	24	24
Town	37	34	33	33	37	31	35	30	10	33	37	37
City	143	131	137	140	143	118	139	122	98	120	141	142
Arkansas	1,146	959	959	962	1,132	710	941	626	358	1,076	1,107	1,139
Open Country	511	391	386	380	500	237	358	164	84	464	482	505
Village	253	205	200	207	250	147	207	108	46	237	247	253
Town	163	149	155	158	163	134	157	149	81	163	162	163
City	219	214	218	217	219	192	219	205	147	212	216	218
California	516	477	488	506	515	410	483	433	301	439	507	510
Open Country	19	18	18	19	19	11	17	12	7	14	19	19
Village	25	22	20	22	25	20	21	14	9	20	25	25
Town	90	83	89	89	90	71	77	69	36	80	88	88
City	382	354	361	376	381	308	368	338	249	325	375	378
Dist. of Columbia	49	47	46	47	49	41	48	46	29	48	49	49
Open Country	......	......	......	......	......	......	......	......	......	......	......	......
Village	......	......	......	......	......	......	......	......	......	......	......	......
Town	......	......	......	......	......	......	......	......	......	......	......	......
City	49	47	46	47	49	41	48	46	29	48	49	49
Florida	1,067	981	955	976	1,052	792	916	770	512	1,037	1,050	1,065
Open Country	354	314	280	292	344	200	261	165	94	339	344	353
Village	173	154	143	154	169	120	137	106	53	166	169	173
Town	182	173	178	177	182	156	172	167	103	180	181	182
City	358	340	354	353	357	316	346	332	262	352	356	357
Georgia	2,763	2,526	2,340	2,233	2,677	1,702	1,860	1,664	965	2,705	2,525	2,740
Open Country	1,576	1,418	1,251	1,163	1,502	759	889	694	339	1,541	1,388	1,560
Village	334	295	272	257	323	211	215	225	82	328	319	331
Town	344	321	317	321	343	282	296	303	169	339	330	343
City	509	492	500	492	509	450	460	442	375	497	488	506
Hawaii	17	17	16	16	17	16	16	16	12	13	17	17
Open Country	......	......	......	......	......	......	......	......	......	......	......	......
Village	......	......	......	......	......	......	......	......	......	......	......	......
Town	3	3	3	3	3	3	3	3	2	2	3	3
City	14	14	13	13	14	13	13	13	10	11	14	14
Illinois	716	620	594	559	709	481	435	381	235	663	672	711
Open Country	257	216	183	164	253	123	91	80	31	237	244	255
Village	136	114	109	93	136	90	78	60	29	131	134	136
Town	126	109	110	108	124	101	91	83	56	121	120	124
City	197	181	192	194	196	167	175	158	119	174	194	196
Kansas	111	97	104	107	111	88	102	95	60	100	109	109
Open Country	9	6	8	7	9	6	7	6	3	8	8	8
Village	10	9	8	8	10	7	8	5	1	8	9	9
Town	31	28	28	31	31	24	29	28	14	28	31	31
City	61	54	60	61	61	51	58	56	42	56	61	61
Kentucky	2,247	2,048	1,824	1,692	2,109	1,500	1,109	1,067	456	2,114	1,967	2,175
Open Country	1,288	1,171	976	843	1,163	713	452	388	113	1,190	1,044	1,226
Village	428	390	346	341	418	332	231	230	70	411	409	423
Town	255	226	235	241	255	213	188	212	104	250	250	255
City	276	261	267	267	273	242	238	237	169	263	264	271
Louisiana	1,163	1,056	1,020	1,050	1,159	793	1,025	831	629	1,141	1,109	1,158
Open Country	612	539	504	511	609	337	505	344	263	601	565	609
Village	161	148	135	151	160	118	141	128	90	157	159	161
Town	152	140	146	150	152	132	145	141	101	150	150	151
City	238	229	235	238	238	206	234	218	175	233	235	237
Maryland	133	126	123	119	129	116	108	117	73	124	129	131
Open Country	24	23	20	21	24	20	14	17	9	22	24	24
Village	16	16	15	12	12	16	11	14	7	15	15	16
Town	27	24	24	23	27	22	22	23	13	23	26	27
City	66	63	64	63	66	58	61	63	44	64	64	64

NUMBER OF CHURCHES REPORTING MAJOR ITEMS, 1955—(Continued)

S.B.C.	NUMBER REPORTING:											
	Total No. Ch's	Pastor	Bap-tisms	Addi-tions by Letter	Sunday School Enrol.	V.B.S.	T.U.	W.M.U.	Broth-erhood	Church Prop-erty	Mis-sion Gifts	Total Gifts
Mexican	325	......	......	......	......	......	......	......	......	......	......	......
Open Country	1	......	......	......	......	......	......	......	......	......	......	......
Village	7	......	......	......	......	......	......	......	......	......	......	......
Town	90	......	......	......	......	......	......	......	......	......	......	......
City	227	......	......	......	......	......	......	......	......	......	......	......
Mississippi	1,734	1,589	1,433	1,415	1,681	1,249	1,342	1,006	536	1,667	1,673	1,727
Open Country	1,066	962	813	800	1,018	672	744	445	207	1,015	1,009	1,059
Village	293	260	255	246	288	229	236	200	85	282	290	293
Town	181	177	174	178	181	168	171	172	91	178	181	181
City	194	190	191	191	194	180	191	189	153	192	193	194
Missouri	1,711	1,501	1,404	1,360	1,690	1,329	1,129	1,189	710	1,499	1,674	1,702
Open Country	771	644	553	516	754	521	388	391	179	693	743	766
Village	405	346	331	319	401	310	246	285	140	379	398	403
Town	254	237	243	247	254	234	220	245	164	153	254	254
City	281	274	277	278	281	264	275	268	227	274	279	279
New Mexico	221	195	201	204	220	189	187	157	133	207	219	219
Open Country	41	32	32	35	41	31	27	16	11	34	41	41
Village	48	41	42	42	47	36	37	25	17	45	47	47
Town	43	38	38	39	43	37	36	33	24	41	42	42
City	89	84	89	88	89	85	87	83	81	87	89	89
North Carolina	3,179	2,965	2,726	2,576	3,166	2,459	1,867	2,124	974	2,991	3,071	3,171
Open Country	1,964	1,823	1,600	1,437	1,953	1,351	907	1,064	386	1,805	1,872	1,957
Village	425	395	359	362	423	369	266	324	116	407	412	424
Town	327	306	311	318	327	305	272	305	180	320	325	327
City	463	441	456	459	463	434	422	431	292	459	462	463
Ohio	74	70	67	71	74	48	54	36	14	50	71	73
Open Country	5	5	5	5	5	4	4	4	2	4	5	5
Village	8	8	8	8	8	4	3	4	0	5	8	8
Town	10	9	9	10	10	4	7	3	2	8	8	10
City	51	48	45	48	51	36	40	25	10	33	50	50
Oklahoma	1,263	1,131	1,118	1,095	1,252	895	1,024	850	555	1,149	1,221	1,230
Open Country	440	372	345	314	430	206	271	186	85	348	404	409
Village	285	252	247	253	284	190	226	159	89	273	282	284
Town	211	197	204	206	211	193	204	200	127	210	211	211
City	327	310	322	322	327	306	323	305	254	318	324	326
Oregon-Washington	105	98	100	103	104	90	98	80	40	91	100	105
Open Country	1	1	1	1	1	....	1	1	1	1	1	1
Village	1	1	1	1	1	1	1	1	......	1	1	1
Town	26	25	24	26	26	21	23	19	6	22	23	26
City	77	71	74	75	76	68	73	59	33	67	75	77
South Carolina	1,404	1,326	1,231	1,238	1,390	1,174	1,119	1,185	626	1,351	1,378	1,401
Open Country	826	777	691	687	814	643	601	638	286	786	805	823
Village	148	140	127	132	147	130	113	132	55	140	144	148
Town	169	157	158	161	168	154	150	160	89	167	168	169
City	261	252	255	258	261	247	255	255	196	258	261	261
Tennessee	2,558	2,277	2,129	1,975	2,499	1,657	1,492	1,253	673	2,405	2,173	2,490
Open Country	1,587	1,385	1,224	1,092	1,530	839	713	503	223	1,452	1,251	1,524
Village	336	301	290	267	335	255	209	200	77	324	309	332
Town	223	198	213	214	223	206	200	196	99	221	219	223
City	412	393	402	402	411	357	370	354	274	408	394	411
Texas	3,641	3,283	3,206	3,358	3,605	2,860	2,999	2,609	2,019	3,473	3,588	3,632
Open Country	1,097	924	828	908	1,072	661	714	457	308	992	1,070	1,092
Village	730	647	611	666	721	543	540	451	259	694	723	730
Town	551	520	534	546	550	502	517	527	393	549	548	550
City	1,263	1,192	1,233	1,238	1,262	1,154	1,228	1,174	1,059	1,238	1,247	1,260
Virginia	1,298	1,191	1,106	999	1,283	1,000	735	1,070	397	1,265	1,268	1,296
Open Country	678	613	534	446	664	479	280	502	155	657	655	677
Village	199	178	167	149	198	143	94	156	55	195	196	199
Town	161	154	149	146	161	134	113	155	66	158	159	161
City	260	246	256	258	260	244	248	257	121	255	258	259

meeting each participant presents its individual budget requirement, which has been prepared by its own finance committee. Frequently, that total will be greatly in excess of a reasonable income. Then very carefully, and in mutual willingness to consider each other, individual budgets are brought within the anticipated income and are divided percentage-wise. Then the Executive Committee, the report having been adopted, will recommend to the Convention in its next annual session on this wise: "We recommend that a full $11,000,000 of Cooperative funds be distributed for current operating expenses and capital funds in (blank) year, as shown by the following schedule"; then follows the names of the participating agencies and, opposite each, the sum produced by the quoted percentage.

Upon adoption of the budget by the Convention, the boards and agencies project their work on an assured basis. The Cooperative Program does not distribute percentage-wise any sum, large or small, which has been given and designated for a particular cause or causes. This is the provision which gives security to those who wish their money to go, by way of example, to foreign missions solely.

The Cooperative Program is the greatest forward step ever taken by Southern Baptists in securing and disbursing funds for its mission causes. By it the members of the churches give through the central distributing office in Nashville in a fair and equitable manner to the propagating of the gospel at home and around the world. Confusion and competition of appeals are avoided, and each of the boards and agencies speaks for the other. Through it they have a united voice for the whole cause—all for one and one for all.

Debts paid, honor saved.—When what has been called "the great depression" came upon the denominational life of Southern Baptists, it found them peculiarly vulnerable because of a rapid financial expansion based on the seeming success of what was known as the 75 Million Campaign. This was a movement adopted by the 1919 session of the Convention in Atlanta, Ga., whereby $75,000,000 was to be raised for mission causes over a five-year period. It was received by the constituency of the Convention with enthusiasm and, headed by Lee Scarborough, succeeded in a large degree, $92,630,923 being pledged. It proved to be a great stimulus to an enlarged mission and educational work at home and abroad. Work was projected on anticipated receipts, so much so that large indebtedness was incurred.

Then something which Southern Baptists refer to as "the dark ages" took place; only $58,591,713.69 was ever collected. In the meantime the boards and agencies had spent the money which had been allotted them on the basis of the pledged sums, and by the end of 1926, there was an accumulated debt of some $6,500,000. Money was borrowed at a high rate of interest, and creditors clamored for payment even to the point of threatening legal proceedings. What was true of Convention causes was also true of state conventions, churches, and individuals. Baptists (nor were they alone) became despondent and discouraged; morale was almost at the point of no return.

But to its everlasting credit the Convention took seriously the fact that, though there were legal loopholes through which an escape was possible, a debt was a debt, and honor made necessary the payment of that debt. The meeting of the Convention's Executive Committee, Apr. 12–13, 1933, was largely concerned with plans for payment of the debt. Out of this meeting grew the movement known as the Baptist One Hundred Thousand Club, the essence of which was that the members were to pay one dollar a month over and above their regular subscriptions to their church budgets. This was the first of several movements among Southern Baptists to pay their debts. And, through hard and strenuous work, often through discouragement from the home constituency, by the close of 1943, every Convention agency was out of debt, and there was a balance in the debt-paying fund of over $38,000.

When all the records of the Southern Baptist Convention shall have been written, it will be recorded of the debt-paying determination and sacrificial giving of Southern Baptists that "out of darkness came forth light—this was their finest hour."

Authority and function.—Having looked at the reasons for the formation of the Southern Baptist Convention and having sketched the rise and growth of its functioning boards, agencies, and commissions as the growth of Southern Baptists gave necessity for such in order to implement these reasons for existence, it may be asked, What authority does this Convention have over either individuals or churches? The answer is, absolutely none. It may exert pressure through suggestion, but it does not issue a single command, nor can it compel any church or individual to carry out its proposals.

Its mission work is financed through the Cooperative Program, but on the basis of voluntary co-operation, not compulsion. In its unity there is diversity, and in its diversity there is unity. In the eyes of the world, the Southern Baptist Convention is the most illogical of all Christian groups. Love is never logical; and that which binds the Southern Baptist Convention into one great body is love—love for Christ, who loved us and gave himself for us.

To articulate its work, to relate the labors of these varied boards, agencies, and commissions to each other and to the churches, is a monumental task and must be done with due regard for each component part. Unity of action without centralization of power is the Convention's problem, and it can only be solved by the Holy Spirit's guidance. In the development of the organization, stages are reached when a higher principle of life reacts upon the accumulated results of previous processes, thereby lifting it to a higher plane whence may be unfolded new potentialities. This is the constant story of the Southern Baptist Convention. J. W. STORER

SOUTHERN BAPTIST EDUCATIONAL CONFERENCE. See SOUTHERN ASSOCIATION OF BAPTIST COLLEGES AND SCHOOLS, THE.

SOUTHERN BAPTIST EDUCATOR, THE. Official journal of the Education Commission of the Southern Baptist Convention; published monthly, November through April, bimonthly, May through October. This periodical was initiated in 1936, with the title *Southern Baptist College News and Views,* and was given its present name in 1947. It is distributed to the trustees and faculty members of Southern Baptist educational institutions, to denominational leaders, and to others interested in Christian higher education. The subscription price is $1.25 per year; circulation in Oct., 1956, was 4,420. R. ORIN CORNETT

SOUTHERN BAPTIST FOUNDATION. An institution of the Southern Baptist Convention, chartered in the state of Tennessee Feb. 26, 1947. It is responsible for the custody, investment, and administration of permanent funds entrusted to it by the Convention "or any of its agencies, or any causes controlled, fostered, or officially sanctioned by it" and for the solicitation of gifts to be added to those funds.

Prior to the establishment of the foundation, the Convention dealt with occasionally received bequests and endowments in various ways, none of which were completely adequate. Until 1927 the trust funds owned by the Convention were the responsibility of the Convention's treasurer. This arrangement left much to be desired. The treasurer was never a full-time employee of the Convention, and possessed no authority to act without a specific Convention action, even on so small a matter as the disbursement of an unexpected stock dividend. From time to time, committees were required to study problems arising out of various bequests and trusts, which the Convention received at infrequent intervals after 1870. Clearly some more efficient financial arrangement was necessary; therefore, in 1927, the Convention's new executive committee was made the "Fiduciary Agency" of the Convention. All funds and property in the hands of the Convention treasurer were ordered turned over to the Executive Committee, and all future funds and legacies "given directly" to the Convention were to be its responsibility. The committee was also instructed to present to the next Convention "detailed plans for establishing a Southern Baptist Foundation."

By "Foundation," however, the Convention meant only a trust fund, or a collection of such funds, rather than an administrative investment agency. This foundation was duly established in 1928 with the Executive Committee in charge.

Gradually the need for a separate agency responsible for the administration of trusts became more obvious. On May 9, 1944, the Executive Committee secured a separate charter in the names of its members for a Southern Baptist Foundation, to be under "the direct supervision" of the Executive Committee. Two years later another charter was approved by the Convention, which gave to the foundation a separate board of directors, constituted as follows: "The President of the Southern Baptist Convention and the President of the Executive Committee of the Southern Baptist Convention, ex officio members; nine Baptist laymen of business experience, five of whom shall live in Nashville; the other members shall be the Presidents of the four General Boards, the Presidents of the Boards of the five Southwide institutions, the Chairman of the Executive Committee of the Baptist Brotherhood, and the President of the Woman's Missionary Union." In addition the recommended charter provided that the directors of the foundation elect an investment committee, "the members of which may or may not be members of the Board of Directors." This arrangement was unique, and was expressly prohibited by the by-laws of the Convention, which provided that no person should serve "on more than one of the boards or commissions or standing committees of the Convention." This problem was solved by an amendment to the by-laws, passed in 1948.

Once securely established, the new foundation began to develop an increasingly valuable program. "An initial gift of $10,000 by the Sunday School Board . . . enabled it to begin to function"; and a trust fund of $25,000, also from the Sunday School Board, designated for the support of Bible distribution, was its first responsibility. In Jan., 1948, securities worth $252,-185.92, the total accumulation of the Southern Baptist Convention in a period of almost 80 years, were turned over to the foundation. Other funds came in gradually, and by the end of 1948 the foundation's corpus amounted to $290,676.99. During these first two years the foundation was operated from the office of the Convention's Executive Committee. The hiring of a full-time executive for the foundation had been authorized by Oct., 1947, but it took much time for operating funds to be secured and the right man found. On Feb. 23, 1949, Charles Houston Bolton was elected executive secretary of the foundation. He began his work the following May, and served until Jan. 1, 1953. On his resignation, the foundation elected as executive secretary Thomas Luther Holcomb, who was then nearing retirement as executive secretary of the Sunday School Board. Holcomb served from June, 1953, to June, 1956 and was succeeded by J. W. Storer.

Under the leadership of these two men, the responsibilities of the foundation were increased and its program of promotion developed. In 1950 the Executive Committee of the Convention began to accumulate a reserve fund, which was placed with the foundation. The various agencies of the Convention were requested to "deposit some investment with the Foundation," in order to hasten the "creation of confidence" in its work. Gradually the money did come—$25,000 from the Foreign Mission Board and $100,000 from the Relief and Annuity Board in Jan., 1951; a bequest worth $52,000 from the Executive Committee in June, 1952; $200,000 from the Home Mission Board and $100,000 from the Sunday School Board in June, 1952; and other donations in the following years. A large part of this money, however, was accompanied by specific instructions as to its investment, and was often subject to recall whenever the needs of the donors demanded.

In addition to receiving deposits from agencies, the foundation set about to solicit funds on its own. After some initial hesitation over possible competition with the Relief and Annuity Board, the foundation began aggressively to promote the donation of gift annuities. At the suggestion of the 1950 Convention, a ministerial aid trust was established to help men "called to the ministry . . . who must have financial assistance in their efforts to secure an education." Bequests, gifts, and trusts of all sorts were solicited, and wills were prepared for interested individuals. The mailing list of the Brotherhood was utilized in direct mail advertising. The foundation was given a place in the emphases of the Southern Baptist denominational calendar. A promotional organization with representation in all the district associations of the Convention was projected, with significant success. A convention-wide conference on "The Ministry of Foundations in our Baptist Life" was held in co-operation with state foundation organizations.

The investment policy of the foundation has not been changed since the beginning, except for the addition of a single phrase allowing the purchase, by unanimous approval, of stocks not listed on the New York exchange and is as follows:

(1) That not less than 70 per cent be invested in prime first mortgages, preferred stocks and bonds not below *A* grade according to Moody's rating; and not more than 30 per cent invested in equities. (2) That being an instrument of the Southern Baptist Convention we deem it inadvisable to make loans on church property or church-related institutions. (3) That neither preferred nor common stocks are to be purchased except those listed on the New York stock exchange unless unanimously approved.

Within the framework of this basic policy, however, there has been a considerable development of practice, which has been reflected in steadily increasing efficiency and rate of earnings. In 1948 the foundation's executive committee agreed that "the major emphasis of the Foundation . . . should be placed on security of the corpus rather than earnings at this time." For that reason the foundation decided that major investment should be in "high grade bonds, with immediate preference running to the investment in Series G government bonds." By the end of 1952 the practice of the foundation had changed to the point that 21.48 per cent of its funds were invested in common stock, and only 21.59 per cent in bonds. By the end of 1955 the percentage of common stocks had climbed to 28.77, very close to the 30 per cent maximum, and the percentage of bonds had declined to 5.67. This development was reflected in the foundation's earning power. For the year 1949 the percentage rate of returns was 4.35. By the end of 1956 the rate had risen significantly to 4.79 per cent. For the same period, the rate of return on funds held but not controlled by the foundation, which were largely invested in bonds and subject to call, averaged about 2.50 per cent.

From 1949 through 1955 the foundation had written 47 annuities amounting to $128,819.16, prepared 29 trusts coming from 10 different states totaling $82,908.99, and written 18 wills. At the end of 1955 the foundation held reserve funds from various Southern Baptist agencies and institutions amounting to $1,384,968.79, and was administering a total corpus of $1,838,168.66. Total assets amounted to $1,873,069.22.

JUDSON BOYCE ALLEN

SOUTHERN BAPTIST HISTORICAL SOCIETY. Organized in Richmond, Va., on May 13, 1938, under the leadership of William Owen Carver (*q.v.*) and others to promote interest in Baptist history by enlisting in membership as many Southern Baptists as possible. Its officers and directors were the members of the Southern Baptist Convention's standing Committee on the Preservation of Baptist History, which made annual reports to the Convention. Its headquarters from 1938 to 1952 were in the Southern Baptist Theological Seminary. During these years it promoted the history interests of Southern Baptists; stimulated the work of state historical organizations; and gathered a substantial collection of excellent basic and secondary materials which was processed by its curator, Leo T. Crismon, the seminary librarian. Led by Carver and his associates, it grew in importance and was recognized in 1947 as the official historical agency of the Southern Baptist Convention, with the status of a commission. Its offices and collection were moved to Nashville in 1952, into space furnished by the Sunday School Board. The Convention's constitution and bylaws, however, required a different type of organization, and a Historical Commission conforming to Convention requirements was chartered in Tennessee in 1951. The society was rechartered in Tennessee in 1952 as an auxiliary to the commission. Since that time it has continued, through varied ministries, to promote the history interests of Southern Baptists.

See also Historical Commission, Southern Baptist Convention. JUDSON BOYCE ALLEN

SOUTHERN BAPTIST HOSPITAL. A corporation, chartered Sept. 5, 1924, by the state of Louisiana, established by the Hospital Commission of the Southern Baptist Convention, located in New Orleans.

So far as can be determined, the first suggestion that a hospital be established in the city of New Orleans was made by Mrs. C. M. Kelly, a former Catholic and member of a Baptist church for only seven years, in a talk to the B.Y.P.U. of the Central Baptist Church in New Orleans *c.* Aug., 1919. The matter was taken up by the Orleans Baptist Association and later by the Louisiana Baptist Association and presented to the Executive Committee of the Southern Baptist Convention on Feb. 19, 1920. The Committee recommended the construction of such a hospital and referred it to the Home Mission Board, which reported to the Convention at Chattanooga in 1921 that it had studied the question, had conferred with representatives of New Orleans, and had agreed to establish a hospital there. A site had been selected and was given the board by the Association of Commerce of New Orleans on Dec. 24, 1922.

In 1923 the Convention created a special hos-

BAPTIST BUILDING, Dallas, Tex. Owned jointly by Relief and Annuity Board (q.v.) and Baptist General Convention of Texas (q.v.), it was completed in 1952 at a cost of $1,086,-000, equipped.

OKLAHOMA BAPTIST BUILDING, Oklahoma City. Erected in 1950, valued at more than $1,000,000. Houses 12 convention departments.

SOUTH CAROLINA BAPTIST HOUSE, Columbia. Home of seven departments of state convention. Acquired in 1924, now worth $200,000.

VIRGINIA STATE CONVENTION (*q.v.*) BUILDING, Richmond. Since 1944 the home of eight departments of work. Present value, $115,000.

pital commission to supervise erection and administration of the proposed New Orleans hospital. The Home Mission Board contributed $250,000 toward the enterprise; responsibility was then transferred from the board to the commission. The transfer of the site was made, and construction began on Thanksgiving Day, Nov. 27, 1924. Completed at a cost of over $2,000,000, the hospital was opened to receive patients on Mar. 8, 1926.

Southern Baptist Hospital is approved by the American College of Surgeons and the American Medical Association. It is approved for one-year rotating intern training and also for resident training in internal medicine, obstetrics and gynecology, pediatrics, pathology, surgery, and radiology. It is a member of the American Hospital Association and the Southwide Baptist Hospital Association. Through an affiliation with Tulane University of Louisiana, students in the hospital's school of nursing take their first nine months of training at the university.

From 1926 through 1954, a total of 509,178 patients had received service at Southern Baptist Hospital, 408,376 of whom were admitted as bed patients. There were 46,219 babies born in that period of time, and a total of 882 nurses were graduated from the Mather School of Nursing. Receipts from operating income amounted to $31,036,844.98, and from denominational income totalled $1,147,826.08. Designated gift income was $197,676.81, and a total of $1,636,344.80 was given in free service. Free service is given to any foreign missionary needing hospitalization while home on furlough.

At the end of 1954, the physical plant consisted of seven buildings valued at approximately $6,000,000. In 1956 the original buildings were in the process of being renovated and air-conditioned. There are 500 beds and 85 bassinets for newborn babies. FRANK TRIPP

SOUTHERN BAPTIST HOSPITAL COMMISSION. When the Southern Baptist Convention met in Atlanta, Ga., in May, 1919, the Committee on Committees was authorized to appoint a committee of one from each state in the Convention to report on hospitals and sanitariums. At the meeting of the Southern Baptist Convention in Kansas City in May, 1923, the Committee on Hospitals recommended "that a special hospital commission consisting of one member from each state be created by this Convention, and that the erection and administration of the proposed New Orleans Hospital be turned over to this Commission."

The first members of the newly formed Commission were Frank Shelby Groner (*q.v.*), Texas; Louis J. Bristow, Alabama; Barbour Vaughn Ferguson (*q.v.*), Arkansas; C. G. Johnson, District of Columbia; Bunyan Stephens, Florida; Archibald Cunningham Cree (*q.v.*), Georgia; B. J. Rodman, Illinois; Marion Palmer Hunt, Kentucky; E. D. Solomon, Louisiana; W. H. Baylor, Maryland; Plautus Iberus Lipsey (*q.v.*), Mississippi; S. E. Ewing, Missouri; A. L. Maddox, New Mexico; G. T. Lumpkin, North Carolina; G. M. London, Oklahoma; T. Claggett Skinner, South Carolina; Powhatan W. James, Virginia; A. E. Jennings, Tennessee; O. O. Benway, James H. Tharp, A. T. Terry, Cicero Ramsay, and R. F. Reynolds, New Orleans, La. Frank Shelby Groner was the first president, James H. Tharp, vice-president, and Louis J. Bristow, secretary-treasurer.

The Committee on Hospitals further recommended "that this hospital commission shall make a survey of the hospital situation in the south from a Baptist standpoint, with the view of bringing definite recommendations to this Convention one year hence in regard to a permanent hospital policy for the future."

The following policy was recommended by the Hospital Commission at the meeting of the Convention in Atlanta, Ga., in May, 1924, and adopted:

> First, That the general policy of this Convention be to observe denominational state ownership and control of Baptist hospitals;
>
> Second, That the Convention recognizes certain outstanding exceptions, such as the Tuberculosis Sanatorium at El Paso, Texas, and the General Hospital at New Orleans, for which the Convention stands committed;
>
> Third, That this Hospital Commission with five local members shall be incorporated and shall hold in trust and operate all hospitals of this Convention; and shall act in an advisory capacity with such other Baptist Hospitals within our territory as may desire same; it being understood that in this recommendation no elaborate or expensive organization is contemplated, but only an administrative commission adequate to successful business operation.

On Apr. 4, 1941, the charter was amended changing the name from "Hospital Commission of the Southern Baptist Convention" to "Southern Baptist Hospital Commission." The commission became a board of directors.

At the meeting of the Convention in May, 1953, at Houston, Tex., the charter was again amended to provide for a local board in Jacksonville, Fla., as well as at New Orleans, La. An executive committee, consisting of three members from New Orleans, three from Jacksonville, and the state member from Georgia, Alabama, and Mississippi, is elected by the board of directors and is vested with the authority to control and manage the affairs of the board in the interim between annual meetings. The meetings were changed from semiannual to annual, to be held the last Thursday in January. The officers, elected to serve one year, consist of a president, vice-president, and recording secretary. The executive secretary is elected by the board and is the executive officer who exercises general supervision over the work of the board, particularly the supervision of its hospitals. Louis J. Bristow, who had served as executive secretary from the time it was organized, was retired on May 1, 1947, at his own request. His many years of experience in hospital organization and administration were invaluable in planning the first buildings of the Southern Baptist Hospital at

New Orleans and in the organization of the staff. The hospital's present sound financial structure and position of influence and prestige in the city of New Orleans is very largely due to his wise leadership and administrative ability. Frank Tripp succeeded Bristow as executive secretary of the board on May 1, 1947, and led in the establishment of the Baptist Memorial Hospital, San Antonio, Tex., the Baptist Memorial Hospital, Jacksonville, Fla., and the $3,500,000 expansion program at New Orleans, La.

There are two administrative committees, one consisting of nine members from New Orleans and one consisting of nine members from Jacksonville, Fla. Each committee performs such duties in the management of its respective hospital as may be designated by the board or its executive committee. FRANK TRIPP

SOUTHERN BAPTIST MISSIONARY JOURNAL. See MISSIONARY JOURNALS, EXTINCT.

SOUTHERN BAPTIST PREACHER, OR, SERMONS BY LIVING BAPTIST MINISTERS IN THE SOUTH. A monthly, edited by William H. Stokes at Washington, Ga., Nov., 1839, to July, 1840, and at Penfield, Ga., Jan.–Nov., 1841. SPENCER B. KING, JR.

SOUTHERN BAPTIST PRESS ASSOCIATION. An organization of Southern Baptist state paper editors and editors of the publications of the Executive Committee, the Sunday the Executive Committee, the Baptist Sunday School Board, the Foreign Mission Board, and the Home Mission Board. In the case of the Southern Convention institutions, membership is limited to the principal editors and their assistants. For many years the group was loosely organized with a president and secretary, but in 1950 at Tampa, Fla., a constitution was adopted that outlined the scope of the organization and provided a full corps of officers. The group officially meets twice a year, in February for a three-day workshop, and in connection with the sessions of the Southern Baptist Convention for fellowship. ALBERT MCCLELLAN

SOUTHERN BAPTIST PROTECTION PLAN. Inaugurated July 1, 1954, when Ministers Retirement Plan was closed to new members. It combines retirement, widow, and disability benefits into one plan. The cost of the plan is 5 per cent of member's salary (limit $4,000 per year) payable in monthly dues from member, church, and state convention. When member reaches age of 60, dues increase ½ per cent on the part of member and ½ per cent on the part of convention. There is another increase of ½ per cent at age 65. Church dues remain 5 per cent.

Annuity is based on 1½ per cent credit for each year of participation in plan times average salary during participation. For example: A member joins the plan at age 25, retires at age 65, and has an average salary of $4,000. His annuity is 60 per cent of $4,000, or $2,400 per year.

Widow annuity is based on percentage of member's potential annuity: 20 per cent the first year of participation, 24 per cent the second year, 28 per cent the third year, 32 per cent the fourth year, 36 per cent the fifth year, and 40 per cent the sixth year and thereafter. For instance, in example cited above, widow annuity after a member participates in the plan six years is $960 per year for the rest of her life or until her remarriage. If no widow survives, a lump sum death benefit of twice the potential annuity is payable to the beneficiary. For example: A member's potential annuity is $2,400. The lump sum death benefit if no widow survives is $4,800 payable to estate or beneficiary.

Disability benefits, based on years of participation and average salary, not to exceed $900 per year or 90 per cent of member's potential annuity, are payable in event of total and permanent disability. Early retirement option after age 60 is also available. Annuity is reduced 0.6 per cent for each month of early retirement.

In event that a member transfers into secular work or out of the Southern Baptist Convention territory (except where agreement that members may transfer into American Baptist Convention territory without loss of credits applies) 60 per cent of dues he has paid, plus interest, is returnable. WALKER L. KNIGHT

SOUTHERN BAPTIST PUBLICATION SOCIETY (Charleston, S. C., 1847–63). A publication agency serving Southern Baptists, but having no organic connection with the Southern Baptist Convention. When the Southern Baptist Convention at its first regular session at Richmond, June, 1846, resolved not "to embarrass itself with any enterprise for the publication and sale of books," some of those who disagreed met at Savannah, Ga., May 13, 1847, at the session of the Georgia Baptist convention, to consider the matter of a publication society. Those present from Alabama, Georgia, South Carolina, and Virginia decided to engage at once in the work of circulating religious publications and take the initial steps in forming the Southern Baptist Publication Society. They adopted a constitution and selected Charleston, S. C., for the headquarters, Charleston then being the foremost publication center in the South.

The society was to be composed of life managers, and life and annual members. Its object was "to publish and distribute such books as are needed by the Baptist denomination in the South." Its bylaws provided for a system of agencies; a depository in Charleston; the publication of books by contract as funds were available; the establishment of auxiliary societies; and the winning of the co-operation of conventions, general and district associations, churches, Bible and tract societies, and churches as auxiliaries. A charter from the South Carolina legislature was obtained Dec. 17, 1847; and the depository began operations Feb. 20, 1848.

Richard Furman, Jr., was corresponding

secretary the first year. Abram Maer Poindexter (*q.v.*) then served four years. James Ryland Kendrick served a year, and Edwin Theodore Winkler (*q.v.*) served three years. Then J. P. Tustin, from Virginia, served from 1855 until June, 1858.

The various Southern organizations that had been auxiliary to the American Baptist Publication Society became auxiliary to the Southern Baptist Publication Society. The former society, having been organized by Southern men and largely supported until 1845 by the South, and not being a party to the controversy that forced the formation of the Southern Baptist Convention, wished to continue as the publication society for the South. However, without passion or prejudice, Southerners decided that they should have their own organization. The American Baptist Publication Society, therefore, kept out of the South from 1847 until the Civil War.

The Southern Baptist Publication Society, conservatively operated, had a slow but steady growth. It issued its first booklet in 1848, reproducing Charles Dutton Mallary's (*q.v.*) sermon, "The Advancement of Sabbath School Instruction," and its first book in 1849, *The Way of Salvation* by Robert Boyté Crawford Howell (*q.v.*). In 1850 it employed two colporteurs. It lightened the work of its corresponding secretary in 1856 by employing a financial secretary.

Edmund King, of Alabama, endowed the society in 1857 by a liberal gift. The society then became an independent publishing concern, with its own plant. Its depository agents expanded the business of book selling. That same year the society stated that a special vocation had been assigned to it in preparing works suitable to the Sunday schools of the South, and of works adapted to the oral instruction of the colored population. It was planned to print Sunday school books as fast as means would permit.

It was at this time that the Southern Baptist Sunday School Union and Graves, Marks & Co. entered the field of Sunday school publications and became competitors of the society.

The society had annual meetings for its membership, usually at the place and time of either state conventions or the Southern Baptist Convention. The latter approved its purpose, often adjourned so that its messengers could attend the society's meeting, gave it the privilege of making reports to the Convention, and co-operated with it in various ways.

In 1858 the society voted in favor of becoming a part of the Convention, but a minority of its membership objected. The question of consolidation continued to arise. At the Convention in 1861 a committee was appointed to confer with the society concerning consolidation with the Bible Board of the Southern Baptist Convention, and report in 1863; but when the Convention met at Savannah that year, the Bible Board had ceased operation because of the capture of Nashville by the Union army in Feb., 1862.

When the society met at Hampton, Va., in 1858, it faced serious problems. Secretary J. P. Tustin resigned, but became a member of the society's board of managers. This proved to be a mistake because a short time thereafter he received ordination as an Episcopal priest. Overexpansion of the society's depository and its failure to collect large amounts due it, made it necessary to move to less expensive quarters, greatly reduce the scope of the depository's work, and concentrate on publishing. Bad management and the conditions brought about by the Civil War forced the society to advertise Jan. 6, 1864, that it had engaged a firm to make collections. Sometime during late 1863 or 1864 it ceased operation. During its existence it received gifts of more than $100,000 for its work. It printed more than 80 different books and booklets, and sold in excess of 230,000 copies. It did much to develop Southern Baptist authors, and made a lasting contribution to Southern Baptist life.

See also Bible Board, Southern Baptist Convention and Graves (James Robinson) Publication Organizations. HOMER L. GRICE

SOUTHERN BAPTIST PUBLICATION SOCIETY (Graves-Memphis). See Graves (James Robinson) Publication Organizations.

SOUTHERN BAPTIST REVIEW. A newspaper published for a brief time in 1847 at Penfield, Ga., by J. S. Baker, editor of *The Christian Index*. J. L. Reynolds, professor of biblical literature at Mercer University, edited the *Review*. JOHN J. HURT, JR.

SOUTHERN BAPTIST STAMINA. A four-page monthly started by G. Dallas Faulkner in Nov., 1941, and adopted as the official organ of the Southern Baptist General Convention of California on Nov. 27. Dissatisfaction arose, however, and in May, 1942, the convention's board of directors voted to terminate Faulkner's services as editor. Faulkner contended that the convention did not own the paper and therefore refused to surrender the masthead. He continued to publish the paper intermittently for two or three years as a private venture before it was discontinued. W. BURMAN TIMBERLAKE

SOUTHERN BAPTIST SUNDAY SCHOOL UNION. A body, located at Nashville, Tenn., which was temporarily organized Oct. 23, 1857, by Amos Cooper Dayton (*q.v.*) and James Robinson Graves (*q.v.*), and permanently organized at Memphis, Nov. 12, 1858. It ceased operation in Feb., 1862, when the Union army captured Nashville. Under Landmark control from its beginning, it was both divisive and sectional, and had no support from anti-Landmark Baptists.

The union resulted from a call of the Concord Association, Tennessee, for a Southern Baptist Sunday school convention in Nashville to meet a day prior to the annual session of the Baptist General Association of Tennessee. Eighty people attended. Nine were from Kentucky, Mississippi, Alabama, Georgia, and Virginia, at least three of whom were on business. The rest were from Tennessee, largely Middle Tennessee. When the convention met, Dayton at once presented a constitution for the Southern Baptist Sunday School Union. A stormy session followed. The constitution was approved by a large majority, and a temporary organization was set up. Robert Boyté Crawford Howell (*q.v.*), who had just returned to Nashville for his second pastorate at the First Baptist Church, led the opposition. The majority were ardent followers of Graves, whose Landmarkism was then dominant in Tennessee. The Graves-Howell controversy began in this meeting and precipitated a Southern Baptist crisis for some two or three years.

The union resolved to meet for permanent organization at Americus, Ga., Apr., 1858, prior to the annual session of the Georgia Baptist convention. The controversy became so heated that the Americus church asked that no meeting be held. (The *Tennessee Baptist,* Graves's paper, was the only Southern Baptist paper that favored the union's organization.)

Several hundred met at Memphis, Nov. 12, 1858, and effected the union's permanent organization, locating its headquarters at Nashville, where operations began in Mar., 1859. At this meeting none were present from Maryland, Virginia, North Carolina, Florida, Missouri, and Texas. One was reported present from South Carolina, 4 from Kentucky, 17 from Arkansas, 24 from Georgia, 59 from Alabama, and about 300 from Mississippi and Tennessee.

Dayton, elected the president, became also corresponding secretary in Feb., 1859, and served until Feb., 1862, when the union ceased work. The union began publication of the *Children's Friend,* May, 1859, but it was not self-supporting. It also published in 1859 more than 40 volumes for its Sunday school library, Graves, Marks & Co. being its contract printers. By December it owed $1,308, most of it to the printers. Its financial difficulties were due to its failure to collect the pledges made at Memphis. Of these pledges, 16 per cent were fully paid; 26 per cent partially paid; and 58 per cent unpaid.

Dayton had an editorial in his Sunday school column in the *Tennessee Baptist,* Dec. 15, 1860, entitled, "Must the Work Cease?" In another editorial, May 4, 1861, he wrote, "We have not suspended." The following Oct. 5, he said, "We are absolutely paralyzed." Work had evidently ceased, for he asked if it were not possible to resume work on a limited scale, implying that offerings would enable it to do this. A month later, Nov. 9, he stated that the union's debts were due to unpaid pledges, but that it could not afford to sell its stereotyped plates, lose its copyrights, throw out its subscription list, and lose its paper.

At its first annual session, Canton, Miss., Nov. 22, 1859, the union changed "Sunday" in its title to "Sabbath." This was a well-attended, enthusiastic convention. Only a few attended the next meeting at Louisville, Ky., Oct. 26, 1860. The meeting scheduled for Helena, Ark., Nov., 1861, was not held. When the next meeting was held at Paducah, Ky., Nov. 23, 1867, only 14 attended. This group ratified the proceedings at a called meeting of the union just before the Southern Baptist Convention meeting at Memphis the preceding May, when Charles Carroll Bitting, the corresponding secretary of the first Sunday School Board, was elected to be its secretary also, and *Kind Words,* published by the board, was made its paper for children.

The union had only a nominal existence after the war. Graves tried hard to revive it, but his adherents now favored its being consolidated with the first Sunday School Board of the Southern Baptist Convention. The union had been conceived and born in strife, and was dedicated to Landmark principles. Most Southern Baptist leaders opposed it, not only because they regarded it as a competitor of the Southern Baptist Publication Society, but also because its most ardent and devoted champion, J. R. Graves, determined to abolish the Bible Board of the Southern Baptist Convention and take from the Foreign Mission Board its authority to select, appoint, direct, and pay its missionaries.

These Southern Baptist Convention leaders were overwhelmingly responsive to two requests the union made at its called meeting in May, 1867: (1) to move the Sunday School Board from Greenville, S. C., to Memphis, and (2) take over the work of the union. The Sunday School Board was moved to Memphis in 1868, and it accepted the plates of the Sunday School Union. However, in spite of the desire of all Southern Baptists to work together in their Sunday school efforts, the Sunday School Board could not, under conditions then existing, get the necessary funds for operation. It lost its identity in 1873, when it was consolidated with the Convention's Domestic and Indian Mission Board. This also brought to an end the vestiges of the Sunday School Union and the denominational strife its creation had engendered.

The successive failures of the Southern Baptist Publication Society of 1847–63, the Sunday School Union, and the Sunday School Board of 1863–73 developed a defeatist attitude which prevailed among Southern Baptists for many years and which discouraged organized Sunday school and publication work. The American Baptist Publication Society entered the vacant field and became so entrenched that Southern Baptists did not again authorize a Sunday School Board until May, 1891. Even then they provided no funds for their venture and until 1910 forbade it to publish books. They did, however, support it increasingly by purchasing its lesson helps and periodicals, and thereby enabling it to survive the long-continued and determined efforts of the publication society to keep it from becoming established.

See also Graves-Howell Controversy, Graves (James Robinson) Publication Organizations, Sunday School Board of the Southern Baptist Convention (1863–73). HOMER L. GRICE

SOUTHERN BAPTIST THEOLOGICAL SEMINARY. Located in Louisville, Ky., an agency of the Southern Baptist Convention, existing for the training of ministers and other religious workers. Controlled by a board of trustees nominated by the Convention, it receives its support from the Cooperative Program of the Southern Baptist Convention, from endowment, and from private contributions. It is a fully accredited member of the American Association of Theological Schools and of the American Association of Schools of Religious Education.

Greenville, S. C.—Founded in 1859, the result of action taken at the organization of the Southern Baptist Convention in 1845, the seminary was first located in Greenville, S. C. This site was selected because South Carolina Baptists offered to turn over to the trustees of the new seminary the theological funds of Furman University and to increase these funds to $100,000, provided other states would raise an equal amount.

The organization and policies of the seminary were so formed as to make it a *Southwide* institution. In his report to the Southern Baptist Convention in 1954, President Duke K. McCall stated: "This Seminary has a unique place among Southern Baptist agencies. It grew up alongside the Convention rather than inside it. Its roots are in Baptist individualism rather than Baptist organization. . . . The leaders of the Seminary drew it as close to the Convention as they could and bound it with unbreakable ties to the denomination."

At Greenville the seminary first rented and later purchased the abandoned house of worship of the First Baptist Church. The theological portion of the Furman University library became the seminary library. By the close of the second session, a valuable collection of theological books was contributed by the trustees of Columbian College, Washington, D. C. In 1867 a former hotel, the Goodlet House, was purchased, repaired, and furnished as a dormitory and a dining hall for the students. These two buildings were the extent of property owned by the seminary in Greenville. The first faculty was composed of James Petigru Boyce (*q.v.*), chairman; John Albert Broadus (*q.v.*); Basil Manly, Jr. (*q.v.*); and William Williams (*q.v.*).

The subscribed endowment, theoretically $200,000, agreed upon at the time of organization, proved to be practically worthless at the close of the Civil War, although more than $130,000 had been fully subscribed. In the wake of the war, which had virtually wiped out possible financial resources, the future of the seminary was uncertain. Early in the summer of 1865, Boyce conferred with the other professors.

> The end of the Seminary seemed at hand. When they all came together, Broadus said: "Suppose we quietly agree that the Seminary may die, but we'll die first. . . ." When the Seminary did reopen on Nov. 1st, it was with only seven students. In homiletics Doctor Broadus had only one student, and he was blind. But it was like Doctor Broadus to give this one blind student the best he had. The careful preparation of full lectures for the blind brother led to the writing of "Preparation and Delivery of Sermons."

During the years at Greenville, the faculty members increased to five. Crawford Howell Toy (*q.v.*) and William Heth Whitsitt (*q.v.*) were added, but Manly resigned in 1871 to become president of Georgetown College in Kentucky.

The curriculum was divided into eight departments or schools. Students, either college graduates or men with only grade school education, took the courses they chose and received a diploma for each course. Those who satisfactorily completed all the courses received the General Diploma of the seminary. The number of students increased from 26 during the first session to 36 in 1860–61, but decreased to 20 the following term. Due to the Civil War there were no sessions from 1862 to 1865. When the school reopened in Nov., 1865, seven students enrolled. The number slowly increased to 65 for 1876–77, the last session at Greenville. Financial difficulties in South Carolina and in other Southern states necessitated the removal of the seminary from Greenville to another area, preferably farther north.

Louisville, Ky., Fourth Street.—During the summer of 1872, the decision was made to move the seminary to Louisville, Ky. James P. Boyce moved to Louisville in Oct., 1872, but difficulty in raising necessary funds delayed the seminary's move until the fall of 1877. The plan was to raise for endowment $300,000 in Kentucky and $200,000 in other Southern states. The first session of the seminary in Louisville opened on Sept. 1, 1877, "in the Lecture Room of Walnut Street Baptist Church. The Elliott House at the Southwest corner of Second and Jefferson, and a portion of the National Hotel, at the Southeast corner of Fourth and Main Streets, were used for dormitories."

Williams had died during the last session of the seminary in Greenville, and Toy resigned from the faculty at the close of the 1878–79 session, because of his views of "the evolutionary reconstruction of Old Testament history and literature." Later he joined the Harvard University faculty. Manly returned to the faculty for the session 1879–80. George Washington Riggan (*q.v.*) taught as an instructor and assistant professor from 1881 until his death in 1885. John Richard Sampey (*q.v.*) began teaching as an assistant instructor in 1885 and was elected to the faculty in 1887. Eighty-nine students were enrolled during the first session of the seminary on Fourth Street in Louisville. The number increased to 157 in 1887–88.

No property was purchased during the early years in Louisville. Lecture rooms and a library room were rented on the third and fourth floors of the Public Library Hall (later the Polytechnic Building, now the Kaufman-Strauss Building). In July, 1880, "The Waverly Hotel, on the north side of Walnut Street, between Sixth and

Seventh Streets, was rented as a Boarding Hall for the students."

In Feb., 1880, former Governor Joseph Emerson Brown (1821–92), of Georgia, gave $50,000 toward the endowment of the seminary. This large gift inspired others to give so that in May, 1883, at the meeting of the General Association of Baptists in Kentucky, Boyce reported that the $300,000 endowment promised by Kentucky Baptists had been obtained. The $200,000 to be contributed from other states was pledged at that time. However, the endowment did not actually reach $400,000 until about 1891.

Louisville, Ky., Broadway.—In June–July, 1884, "property was purchased on the southeast corner of Fifth and Broadway for the purpose of erecting permanent buildings for the Seminary." New York Hall was erected by Mar., 1888, largely with funds ($60,000) contributed by friends of the seminary in New York. It was reported that this building "furnishes dormitories for about two hundred students (two in a room), with a beautiful dining-room and an ample culinary department, and also professors' offices and lecture rooms, so arranged that they could in future be converted into dormitories whenever other buildings should be erected. There is also an admirable gymnasium." Since New York Hall was not completed until Mar., 1888, students lived in the Standiford Hotel during the first part of the 1887–88 session.

In 1887 Franklin Howard Kerfoot (*q.v.*) began teaching as co-professor of theology, becoming full professor in May, 1889. Archibald Thomas Robertson (*q.v.*) began teaching in 1888 and became professor in 1890. Boyce died on Dec. 28, 1888, leaving a faculty of six. In May, 1888, only seven months before his death, Boyce was named president of the seminary, having served until that time as chairman of the faculty, since the office of president had not been created. Under Boyce's administration the enrolment of the seminary reached 164 in the session of 1888–89. In 1887 Broadus stated, "Here is our Seminary that has grown after years of struggle to be the largest Baptist Seminary in the land, and it bids fair to outstrip all those of other denominations."

In May, 1889, Broadus was elected president. During his administration additional endowment was obtained and the Memorial Library, a gift of Mrs. John Lawrence Smith (*q.v.*), of Louisville, was built. It was formally opened in May, 1891. Norton Hall, the classroom and administration building, was completed in the fall of 1893 at a cost of $60,000. It was formally dedicated Nov. 1, 1893. The enrolment increased from 164 during the session 1889–90 to 267 during the session 1894–95, the year of Broadus' death. Manly died on Jan. 31, 1892. Edwin Charles Dargan (*q.v.*) was added to the faculty in 1892, and in May, 1894, William Joseph McGlothlin (*q.v.*) became an instructor, making a teaching staff of six during the last session of Broadus' administration.

The first Doctor of Theology degrees were conferred in May, 1894. Broadus established the first lectureship of the seminary, the Gay Lectures, through a gift of $5,000 in 1893–94 from William David Gay, of Montgomery, Ala., in honor of his father, Julius Brown Gay. The initial course of lectures was delivered in Mar., 1895, by Henry Herbert Harris (*q.v.*) and published in *Three Lectures on Missions.*

In 1895 Whitsitt became president. The student body had increased to 316 during 1895–96. The catalogue for this session carried the following statement: "The remarkable increase in the number of students, larger this session than at any other theological seminary in America, occasions a great need of increased endowment." A similar statement in regard to the number of students remains in the catalogues through 1916–17. Enrolment declined to 262 in 1898–99, the last year of Whitsitt's administration. Henry Herbert Harris and William Owen Carver (*q.v.*) were added to the teaching staff in 1895, but Harris died in Feb., 1897, leaving the teaching staff at seven. A gymnasium was erected during the 1896–97 session at a cost of $10,000, a gift of Joshua Levering (*q.v.*), president of the board of trustees. The endowment of the seminary in the form of the Broadus Memorial Library Endowment was increased by about $8,000 in 1895–96.

Whitsitt's administration (1895–99) was marked by controversy. The evident issue was the origin of Baptists and of immersion as a mode of baptism, but personal matters also were involved. In May, 1899, Whitsitt was forced to resign as president "because he could neither deny what he believed to be an historical fact nor bear to blight the Seminary because of his personal opponents. The important legacy from the Whitsitt controversy to the Seminary was the action of the trustees. While accepting his resignation, they expressly reaffirmed their adherence to the principle of freedom of research and refused to set up any new standards of orthodoxy."

Edgar Young Mullins (*q.v.*) was elected president a few weeks after the resignation of Whitsitt. The enrolment again rose to more than 300. As early as 1913, Mullins wrote that the seminary had "grown to be perhaps the largest protestant theological seminary in the world." The enrolment passed 400 during the 1921–22 session and reached 423 in 1927–28, the last year of Mullins' administration.

In 1907 the Woman's Missionary Union Training School opened in Louisville. Located near the seminary, it was designed for single women and wives of students. Previously student wives had audited classes at the seminary, without receiving credit.

The seminary faculty increased from 7 in 1899 to 12 in 1928. Because of the increasingly large number of students in classes, "fellows" were added to the teaching staff in 1916 to assist the professors in teaching and grading papers.

During the session 1909–10 the Jubilee Celebration of the seminary was held. A project was launched to increase the endowment of the seminary by $600,000. Within three years $670,000 was raised. Under President Mullins' leadership the endowment was increased to $1,336,000 in 1919 and to $1,803,000 in 1928.

During Mullins' administration a series of Sunday School Lectures was founded by the Sunday School Board, Southern Baptist Convention, 1901–02, and a series of Lectures in Evangelism, supported by funds provided by the Home Mission Board of the Southern Baptist Convention, was begun during the 1906–07 session. The former series was continued through the 1911–12 session, and the latter through the session 1910–11. The Norton Lectures, established by a $5,000 endowment donated by George Washington Norton of Louisville, were begun during the 1910–11 session. The observance of Founders' Day on Jan. 11, the birthday of James P. Boyce, began in 1907. In 1904 *The Review and Expositor,* the only Baptist theological quarterly published in the South, was first published and edited by the faculty of the seminary.

Louisville, Ky., Lexington Road.—Because of the increase in the number of students and the impossibility of adequately expanding the plant on Broadway, a 45-acre lot, located on the north side of Brownsboro Road, was purchased in 1911. It was sold in 1921, and 53 acres designated "The Beeches," on Lexington Road were purchased on Aug. 21. Ground-breaking for the new Norton Hall took place on Nov. 29, 1923, and the cornerstone was laid on Nov. 5, 1924. Mullins Hall, the new men's dormitory, was begun in the spring of 1925. In Mar., 1926, after the completion of the two buildings, the seminary moved from Broadway to "The Beeches."

During the summer and fall of 1926, Rice Hall and Judson Hall were built for married students. Two years later a new Levering Gymnasium was completed. The total cost of all the buildings erected on the new site during Mullins' presidency was $2,000,000. Largely because of his many interests and activities, the seminary became known around the world. He and Mrs. Mullins gave $13,000 to establish the Mullins Lectures on Preaching, which were first delivered in 1942.

John R. Sampey was elected president of the seminary in May, 1929, having served as acting president since Mullins' death in Nov., 1928. The financial program of the seminary as worked out by President Mullins was considered sound for normal times, but with the financial crash and depression many persons were unable to pay their obligations to the seminary. There was an indebtedness of $992,000 on the seminary soon after Sampey became president. All available funds were used to pay on the indebtedness, and it was reduced to about $750,000 in a few months. By a gradual plan of repayment, the principal was reduced to $180,000 by the time President Sampey retired. This reduction of debt in the midst of the depression (1935–38) was largely due to the leadership of Gaines Stanley Dobbins, assistant financial agent and treasurer. Also as a result of his efforts, the John R. Sampey Chair of Old Testament Interpretation was endowed in the amount of more than $105,000. By 1941–42 the student body numbered 520. Faculty members had increased to 13, and the number of teaching fellows to 18. About this time the Woman's Missionary Union Training School sold its property on Broadway and erected a building adjoining the seminary campus. The cornerstone was laid Oct. 2, 1940, and the building was dedicated Oct. 2, 1941. After that time the women attended many of the seminary classes.

Sampey retired from the presidency in May, 1942, but continued as a teacher of Hebrew Old Testament during the 1942–43 session. During 1944–45 he wrote his *Memoirs,* which were published in 1947, after his death in Aug., 1946.

Ellis Adams Fuller (*q.v.*) came to the presidency in May, 1942. Building needs became the primary concern during his administration, as the student enrolment increased from 538 in 1942–43 to 1,009 in 1950–51. The buildings at "The Beeches" had been designed originally to accommodate only 500. More student housing, more classrooms, a larger chapel, more library space and books, and more office space for additional faculty were needed.

In the fall of 1943, the School of Church Music began its first session in Cooke Hall, which had been donated to the seminary earlier by Mr. and Mrs. V. V. Cooke of Louisville. Barnard Hall, given to the seminary in 1945, was first used as a dormitory for single women. The classroom wing of Norton Hall was completed in 1947. Another gift, Foster Hall, a 12-apartment building, came to the seminary in 1947. The Faculty Center (guest house) was obtained and its renovation completed in early 1949. The Alumni Memorial Chapel was completed in Mar., 1950. In the fall of 1951, Fuller Hall, with apartments for 97 student families, was occupied. After the death of Mrs. George W. Norton II, in Jan., 1950, the seminary received the 22-acre estate from the Norton family, who had already given much to the seminary. The Norton home was given to be used as a president's home, and Fuller moved into it a few months before his death in Oct., 1950.

During the administration of Fuller, the faculty increased from 13 (in 1942) to 20 (in 1950). In addition, in 1950 there were 31 fellows, 4 teaching assistants, and 1 visiting lecturer. The last indebtedness of the seminary had been paid in Nov., 1943, and the endowment was increased to more than $2,400,000 in 1950.

Dobbins served as acting president for 10 months after the death of President Fuller. During this time the old chapel in Norton Hall was converted into a reserve reading room for the library. Duke Kimbrough McCall became the seventh president of the seminary on Sept. 15, 1951. In the spring of 1953, Green Tree Manor, a 26-building, 265-apartment housing project located a mile northeast of the main campus, was purchased and the name changed to Seminary Village. This purchase greatly eased the acute housing problem. Important installations at the heating plant of the seminary were made in 1951–52, and the Maintenance Building was erected.

In 1953 the seminary was organized into three schools: the School of Theology, with President McCall as dean; the School of Church Music, with Forrest Henry Heeren as dean; and the School of Religious Education, with Gaines S. Dobbins as dean. The School of Church Music had been an auxiliary of the seminary since 1943. The School of Religious Education was an outgrowth of the seminary's Department of Religious Education, which had been in existence for many years.

For the session 1955–56 the School of Theology faculty included 23 faculty members, 1 visiting professor, 9 instructors, and 30 fellows; the School of Church Music faculty numbered 10 faculty members, 10 resident artists, 1 fellow, and 3 student assistants; and the School of Religious Education faculty was composed of 7 faculty members, 3 instructors, and 4 fellows. During that session the student enrolment was as follows: School of Theology, 1,073; School of Church Music, 94; School of Religious Education, 129; with a total of 1,775, including special students during the session.

Those who have served on the faculty of the seminary, named in the order of their election by the board of trustees, are as follows:

Boyce, James Petigru (1827–88), 1859–88
Broadus, John Albert (1827–95), 1859–95
Manly, Basil, Jr. (1825–92), 1859–71; 1879–92
Williams, William (1821–77), 1859–77
Toy, Crawford Howell (1836–1919), 1869–79
Whitsitt, William Heth (1841–1911), 1872–99
Riggan, George Washington (1855–85), 1883–85
Sampey, John Richard (1863–1946), 1887–1942
Kerfoot, Franklin Howard (1847–1901), 1887–99
Robertson, Archibald Thomas (1863–1934), 1890–1934
Dargan, Edwin Charles (1852–1930), 1892–1907
Harris, Henry Herbert (1837–97), 1896–97
McGlothlin, William Joseph (1867–1933), 1896–1919
Carver, William Owen (1868–1954), 1898–1943
Mullins, Edgar Young (1860–1928), 1899–1928
Eager, George Boardman (1847–1929), 1900–20
DeMent, Byron Hoover (1863–1933), 1906–14
Gardner, Charles Spurgeon (1859–1948), 1907–29
Wayman, Harry Clifford (1881–), 1915–23
Leavell, Landrum Pinson (1874–1929), 1915–20
Powell, Frank Marion (1886–), 1918–41
Dobbins, Gaines Stanley (1886–), 1920–56
Davis, William Hersey (1887–1950), 1920–50
Adams, James McKee (1886–1945), 1921–45
Yates, Kyle Monroe (1895–), 1922–42
Tribble, Harold Wayland (1899–), 1925–47
Weatherspoon, Jesse Burton (1886–), 1929–
McDowell, Edward Allison, Jr. (1898–), 1937–52
Johnson, Robert Inman (1895–), 1938–
Goerner, Henry Cornell (1908–), 1938–57
Green, James Leo (1912–), 1941–48
Stealey, Sydnor Lorenzo (1897–), 1942–51
Fuller, Ellis Adams (1891–1950), 1942–50
Peterson, Hugh Raymond (1903–), 1943–
Binkley, Olin Trivette (1908–), 1944–52
McGlon, Charles Addis (1910–), 1944–
Almand, Claude Marion (1915–), 1944–53
Winters, Frances Weaver (1908–), 1944–52
Cook, W. Lawrence (?), 1944–47
Walker, Helen Smith (?), 1946–47
Winters, Donald (1910–), 1946–52
Francisco, Clyde Taylor (1916–), 1947–
Edge, Findley Bartow (1916–), 1947–
Nossaman, Audrey M. (1923–), 1947–54
Packard, Donald Wheeler (1914–), 1947–57
Pool, Frank Kenneth (1925–), 1947–54
Owens, John Joseph (1918–), 1948–
Moody, Dale (1915–), 1948–
Morton, William Hardy (1915–), 1948–
Oates, Wayne Edward (1917–), 1948–
Mueller, William Arthur (1902–), 1948–
Price, Theron Douglas (1916–), 1948–
Turlington, Henry Eugene (1918–), 1949–
Stanfield, Vernon Latrelle (1920–), 1949–
Frenz, Mary Lou (1927–), 1949–51
McElrath, Hugh Thomas (1921–), 1949–
Smith, Taylor Clarence (1915–), 1950–
Barnette, Henlee Hulix (1911–), 1951–
Jones, John Estill (1921–), 1951–
McCall, Duke Kimbrough (1914–), 1951–
Eddleman, Henry Leo (1911–), 1952–54
Ranson, Guy Harvey (1916–), 1952–
Coker, Denton Reuben (1920–), 1952–54
Heeren, Forrest Henry (1915–), 1952–
Ward, Wayne Eugene (1921–), 1953–
Landry, Sabin Paul (1917–), 1953–
Dahlin, Walter O. (1921–), 1953–
Stephens, Farrold (1919–), 1953–
Loessner, Ernest Joseph (1907–), 1953–
Rust, Eric Charles (1910–), 1953–
Adams, William Walter (1892–), 1954–
Hargis, Pauline (1916–), 1954–
Lumpkin, William Latane (1916–), 1954–
Jackson, Herbert Cross (1917–), 1954–
Jenkins, Paul Rogers (1929–), 1954–56
Wood, James Henry (1921–), 1954–
Ashcraft, Jesse Morris (1922–), 1955–
Proctor, Robert Allen (1920–), 1955–
Graves, Allen Willis (1915–), 1955–
Elliott, Ralph Harrison (1925–), 1956–
Lewis, John Moore (1921–), 1956–
McClanahan, John Howard (1929–), 1956–
Peacock, Heber Fletcher (1918–), 1956–
Wamble, Gaston Hugh (1923–), 1956–
Warkentin, Mabel (1926–), 1956–
Crismon, Leo Taylor (1906–), 1956–
Hall, Thomas Oscar, Jr. (1923–), 1956–
Stiles, Joseph (1903–), 1956–

See also STUDENT ACTIVITIES, SOUTHERN BAPTIST THEOLOGICAL SEMINARY.

BIBLIOGRAPHY—BOOKS: W. W. Barnes, *The Southern Baptist Convention, 1845–1953* (1954). J. P. Boyce, "The Two Objections to the Seminary," *The Baptist* (Apr. 18, 25; May 2, 23; July 18, 1874). J. A. Broadus, *Memoir of James Petigru Boyce* (1893).

Memorial Volume . . . General Association of Baptists in Kentucky (1887). P. Monroe, *A Cyclopedia of Education,* 5 vols. (1913). Isla May Mullins, *Edgar Young Mullins; an intimate biography* (1929). A. T. Robertson, *Life and Letters of John Albert Broadus* (1901). J. R. Sampey, *Memoirs of John R. Sampey* (1947); *Southern Baptist Theological Seminary, The First Thirty Years, 1859–1889* (1889). PERIODICALS: Southern Baptist Convention, *Annual.* Southern Baptist Convention, *Book of Reports* (1954). "Chronology of the Southern Baptist Theological Seminary," *The Lyceum* (May, 1887). J. S. Dill, "Our Seminary, the Transition from Greenville to Louisville," *The Review and Expositor* (Apr., 1931). D. K. McCall, "Southern Seminary and the Denomination: Inaugural Address," *The Review and Expositor* (July, 1952). B. Manly, Jr., "The Beginnings of the History of the Seminary," *The Seminary Magazine,* Vol. 5 (1891), Vol. 5 (1892); "The Session of '87 and '88," *The Seminary Magazine* (May, 1888). *Southern Baptist Theological Seminary Catalogs.* "The Theological Seminary," *Western Recorder* (Oct. 6, 1887). *The Tie.*

LEO T. CRISMON

SOUTHERN FEMALE COLLEGE. Established on the former site of Cox College at LaGrange, Ga., in 1895. The school ceased to exist about 1917 largely because of debts, and the remaining buildings were converted into apartment houses. ARTHUR JACKSON

SOUTHERN ILLINOIS COLLEGE OF THE BIBLE. Began to emerge as a plan Oct. 1, 1937, when Saline Association, in session at Bankston Forks Church, took an offering for establishing a chair of Bible at Carbondale. The Illinois Baptist State Association endorsed the project at its annual session in Nov., 1937, and I. E. Miller and H. C. Croslin were elected field representatives to promote it. The organization became known as the Baptist Foundation, and in 1938 the first classes were held in the home of Mrs. J. M. Etherton. George L. Johnson was elected dean and later became the first president. A gift of $10,000 from C. M. Wasson gave the Foundation a good beginning. In Dec., 1938, 61 students were enrolled in the first night classes. In 1939 a $50,000 campaign was launched, and by May property for a permanent site had been purchased. The cornerstone of the first building was laid in Apr., 1941, and the building was completed in June at a cost of $30,546.

The college is owned, financed, and operated by the Illinois State Association. In 1955 the plant included, in addition to the original unit, Doyle Dormitory for men, Johnson Hall Dormitory for women, and a chapel.

In 1954–55, 266 students enrolled in three departments: Bible and Greek, religious education, and sacred music. The faculty consisted of George L. Johnson, Eugene F. Quinn, and Harral Hall. Twenty-six courses were offered, some of which were accepted for full credit at near-by Southern Illinois University. In Apr., 1955, the name was changed from Baptist Foundation to Southern Illinois College of the Bible.

S. C. MARTIN

SOUTHERN LIGHT. A monthly periodical first published in Edgefield, S. C., in Jan., 1856. This independent, religious, and literary journal, edited by E. L. Whatley, had two mottos: "Set for the Defense of Truth and Devoted to the Diffusion of Knowledge" and "Prove All Things, Hold Fast That Which Is Good." Subscriptions for the 40-page *Southern Light* sold for $2 per year. At least four issues were published, but there is no record of when the periodical ceased to exist. ROBERT A. IVEY

SOUTHERN MESSENGER. A semimonthly paper started in 1876 in New Orleans by J. L. Furman but soon discontinued for lack of support. T. W. GAYER

SOUTHERN MISSIONARY NEWS BUREAU. Organized Sept. 15, 1913, in Nashville, Tenn., to act as clearinghouse for foreign mission boards with constituency in the South and desiring to transmit news of foreign mission activities to 2,000 secular weekly and daily newspapers. The Southern Baptist Foreign Mission Board participated until 1916 when the Convention instructed them to discontinue the appropriation. In the three years the board was associated with the bureau they paid out $4,450 for its support. ALBERT MCCLELLAN

SOUTHERN MISSISSIPPI AND EASTERN LOUISIANA, GENERAL BAPTIST ASSOCIATION OF. Organized at Summit, Miss., Oct. 7, 1871, with headquarters at Liberty. The association sponsored the establishment of Lea Female College at Summit and voted to co-operate with the Mississippi Baptist State Mission Board in 1873. The following year, in response to a bid from the state convention, the association agreed to dissolve and become a part of the Mississippi Baptist Convention. J. L. BOYD

SOUTHERN RELIGIOUS INTELLIGENCER AND BAPTIST REPOSITORY (1836?). According to a prospectus in the *Alabama Intelligencer and States Rights Expositor,* Nov., 1835, John G. Davenport planned to publish the *Repository* in Tuscaloosa.

RAY M. ATCHISON

SOUTHERN RHODESIA, MISSION IN. Southern Baptists assumed responsibility for Baptist work among Africans in Southern Rhodesia in Sept., 1950, when Clyde J. and Hattie (Thigpen) Dotson, independent Baptist missionaries in the area, were appointed by the Southern Baptist Foreign Mission Board. Ralph Treece and Betty Jean (Thedford) Bowlin were appointed the following December for work in Southern Rhodesia. Both families were stationed at Gatooma and held the first services under trees.

European Baptists living in Southern Rhodesia had established four Baptist churches between 1917 and 1950 but had not organized Baptist work among the African population. O. Connally, a Christian of Bulawayo, gave the mission a thousand acres of land.

A major mission station, opened in May, 1952, at Sanyati Reserve, has a hospital (1953), an elementary school (1952), and five *kraal* schools. A seminary was opened in 1955 at Gwelo.

In 1955, 11 churches and 40 outstations, served by six national pastors, reported a membership of 682. At the end of 1955, 24 missionaries were serving in six stations: Gatooma (1950), Sanyati (1952), Bulawayo (1952), Gwelo (1954), Salisbury (1954), and Umtali (1955). The mission was officially organized in Apr., 1953. CLYDE DOTSON

SOUTHERN RHODESIA SEMINARY, GWELO. See SOUTHERN RHODESIA, MISSION IN.

SOUTHERN WATCHMAN AND GENERAL INTELLIGENCER. Originally called *The Southern Baptist and General Intelligencer,* it was first published in Charleston, S. C., Jan. 3, 1835. William Henry Brisbane was the first editor and James S. Burges, publisher. A 16-page weekly, the paper was first distributed on Saturday afternoons at a subscription rate of $3 per year. Between Sept. 23, 1836, and Feb. 3, 1837, *Southern Watchman and General Intelligencer* became the name of the journal, after which Basil Manly, Sr., (*q.v.*) became editor, using for the paper's motto "Speaking the Truth in Love." In 1838 William Theophilus Brantly, Sr., (*q.v.*) became editor of the paper, serving only until March, when the *Watchman* was bought by owners of *The Biblical Recorder,* Baptist paper of North Carolina. The joint publication, *The Biblical Recorder and The Southern Watchman and General Intelligencer,* was published throughout 1838 in Charleston and Raleigh and then completely incorporated into *The Biblical Recorder.* ROBERT A. IVEY

SOUTHWEST BAPTIST. A New Mexico paper. It was edited by George H. Brewer from 1901 to 1904 at Alamogordo, then, after a three-year interim, was resumed at Roswell with Perry Wilson Longfellow (*q.v.*) and J. W. Johnson as co-editors. Publication ceased in 1908.
MRS. RICHARD THOMAS BAKER, SR.

SOUTHWEST BAPTIST ASSEMBLY. A regional assembly in southwest Oklahoma serving Caddo, Norman, Jackson-Greer, and Beckham associations. Founded in 1945 on a 17-acre tract of leased land seven miles south of Lone Wolf, Okla., near Lake Lugert, a $350 fee is paid annually for use of the land. The assembly is governed by a board of directors of six to 12 members, who with the president, vice-president, secretary, business manager, and assistant business manager are elected annually during assembly sessions. The constitution provides for 50-year lease tenures on lots by churches. Property value in 1956 was $15,000. Enrolment at the first session was 81, and in 1955, 231. J. M. GASKIN

SOUTHWEST BAPTIST COLLEGE. Chartered Mar. 19, 1878, by the Southwest Missouri Baptist Convention, opened Sept. 17, 1878, to 69 students. After a year at Lebanon, the college was moved to Bolivar, where the cornerstone of the first building was laid Apr. 18, 1879. James Roger Maupin and Abner Smith Ingman were the founders of the school.

From the first, Polk County Baptist Association endorsed the college and contributed to its support; and from 1881 Southwest Baptist College was included in the "Report of Schools and Colleges in Missouri" to the Missouri Baptist General Association. In the year 1924 the school was included in the Unified Budget, and since 1928 it has been owned and controlled by the general association through the election of the trustees and through the annual appropriation from the Cooperative Program funds.

The first building, containing classrooms and chapel, was erected in 1879; to it in 1902 was annexed a dormitory for women. The building burned in 1910, and the present Administration Building was erected in 1913. There are now 15 buildings on the campus, including four dormitories for women and two for men. The newest buildings are the Library and Science Building (1953), and Maupin Hall and Ingman Hall (1954).

J. R. Maupin served as president from 1879 until 1885. In addition to the task of securing students and donations for the school, he worked to erect dwellings for the faculty and students and to secure a railroad for Bolivar. When he resigned in 1885, he recommended as his successor the cofounder, A. S. Ingman. The trustees elected Ingman, but ill health forced him to resign during the first year.

The enrolment during the first six years was estimated as 791; during the first 32 years it was approximately 2,973. There have been 2,704 graduates (1955).

Alternating periods of difficulties and triumphs mark the history of Southwest Baptist College. In 1883 a typhoid epidemic almost devastated the school; in 1906 the mortgaged property went to the receivers; in 1910 the building burned. Then in 1912 the rebuilding campaign was begun under the leadership of Francis L. Stufflebam, a trustee; and in 1913 the college was opened again. President John Calvin Pike led the struggle for survival and growth from 1916 to 1927. In 1918 the Southern Baptist Convention adopted the college as a mountain school and made an annual contribution to its support. In 1921 the University of Missouri granted academic accreditation to the junior college department.

The school was under the direction of Courts Redford from 1931 to 1943; on June 6, 1941, it became debt free, and Pike Auditorium was dedicated. Under the presidencies of Samuel Hovey Jones (1943–48) and John W. Dowdy (1948–), the college has expanded its physical plant and equipment, its assets, and its academic standing. It is now serving about 650 students annually and receives stated support from the Cooperative Program funds. During fiscal 1955 the total income was $295,824.54, and the assets are listed as $875,383.18. The annual budget is $320,000. The work is accredited by the state Department of Education and the University of Missouri.

BIBLIOGRAPHY: J. W. Haines, *History of Polk County Baptist Association* (1897). Southwest Baptist College catalogues, 1884–89, 1902, 1914–16, 1928 ff. *The Bolivar Herald* (1897–1955). *The Central Baptist* (1879–97). *The Word and Way* (1898–1955).

MAYME L. HAMLETT

SOUTHWEST BAPTIST COLLEGE. An Oklahoma institution, owned by the Oklahoma Baptist convention for six years, purchased by the Baptists at Hastings, Okla., in 1907, and tendered to Comanche and Mullins County associations at their respective sessions of that year. The school was discontinued in 1915. It was founded as an academy in 1903 by the Southwestern Association of Congregational Churches, and in 1907 it was sold by order of the court to satisfy the claims of creditors. After the school became the property of the Comanche and Mullins County associations, the name was changed to Southwest Baptist College. School opened Oct. 28, 1907, under the auspices of the Hastings Baptist Church, with the pastor of the church, C. R. Hairfield, as president. The enrolment the first day was 29, but by the close of the session 115 had matriculated.

In 1910 its trustees offered the school to the Baptist General Convention of Oklahoma, and the convention immediately assumed its ownership with subsequent action by the Education Commission correlating it with Oklahoma Baptist University. This gave the school statewide recognition with the status of an academy. Financial difficulties soon arose, and in 1912 the school was moved to Mangum, Okla., and occupied the newly completed First Baptist Church building as temporary facilities while the property at Hastings was sold at auction to foreclose a mortgage and current bills were paid in part with $3,300 raised by the Mangum Baptist Church. It reopened at Mangum on junior college level. Convention action in 1912 to establish "one and only one thoroughly equipped co-educational college" resulted in immediate termination of convention relationship and the final closing of the school in 1915. While operated by Baptists it gave instruction to over 600 students at a cost of about $100,000.

O. O. MORGAN

SOUTHWEST BAPTIST HOSPITAL (MANGUM, OKLA.). In 1948 citizens of Mangum petitioned the Oklahoma convention board of directors to establish a hospital in their city. Building and grounds valued at $250,000 were offered. These citizens later raised $100,000 to remodel and equip the building. It was opened June 5, 1949. This 50-bed hospital is valued at $188,747.42. Total assets are $225,394.01 with a total indebtedness of $6,390.40. TOM E. CARTER

SOUTHWEST MISSOURI STATE COLLEGE CHAIR OF BIBLE, Springfield. In 1950 Greene County Baptist Association purchased property for a student center with the understanding that the Missouri Baptist General Association would establish a chair of Bible. This was done, and Clifford Ingle was secured as professor. The Bible courses were accredited through William Jewell College. In 1954, the property was deeded to the Missouri Baptist General Association, and in 1956 construction was begun on a new $150,000 building. CLIFFORD INGLE

SOUTHWESTERN BAPTIST CHRONICLE. Published by W. C. Duncan at New Orleans, La., from Mar. 13, 1847, until 1850, when Duncan contracted yellow fever and was forced to discontinue his paper. It was the first Baptist paper in Louisiana. F. W. TINNIN, SR.

SOUTHWESTERN BAPTIST PIONEER (1834–36?). The earliest experiment in Alabama Baptist journalism, established at Jacksonville in 1834 by William Wood. Though short-lived for lack of support, it created some interest, for at the state convention in 1835, the first serious efforts were made to establish a denominational paper. RAY M. ATCHISON

SOUTHWESTERN BAPTIST RELIGIOUS EDUCATION ASSOCIATION. See RELIGIOUS EDUCATION, PROFESSIONAL ASSOCIATIONS.

SOUTHWESTERN BAPTIST THEOLOGICAL SEMINARY. The story of the seminary may be divided into three well-defined periods:

I. The Formative Period (1841–1908).
   1. Beginnings and Preparation (1841–1901).
   2. The Baylor Period (1901–08).
      a. The Theological Department (1901–05).
      b. The Theological Seminary (1905–08).
II. The Texas Convention Period (1908–25).
III. The Southern Convention Period (1925–).

THE FORMATIVE PERIOD (1841–1908). *Beginnings and preparation* (*1841–1901*).—The foreign mission movement that arose out of the conversion of Luther Rice and Adoniram Judson to Baptist principles emphasized the need of more and better-trained ministers for the home and foreign fields and called attention to the need for more systematic and comprehensive methods. Out of that situation arose, from the second decade of the 19th century onward, a number of Baptist colleges, many of which are still carrying on with enlarging scope and increasing efficiency. These colleges were established primarily for training ministers, but other students were also admitted. The course of study was largely literary or classical rather than theological. During the decade preceding and the one following the formation of the Southern Baptist Convention (1845–46), it was advocated in the South that the colleges should offer the general literary preparation, and that special theological schools should be established to give ministers their necessary technical training. It was in that period that Baptist life in Texas began to be established and organized.

Baptists entered the province of Texas as early as the 1820's; the first church appeared in 1833. Texas declared its independence from Mexico in 1836. Immigrants by the thousands began to pour into the new republic. Among them were many Baptists, some of whom were preachers. Some of these preachers were college trained; some were not. They recognized the need for more and better-trained pastors and the necessity for Texas Baptists to begin to meet that need.

The church at Washington, Tex., sent a Macedonian call (1837) to each of the mission societies in the United States—the board of the Triennial Convention (foreign missions), located in Boston, and the board of the American Baptist Home Mission Society, located in New York. The copy of the appeal to the board of foreign missions was sent through S. G. Jenkins of Mississippi (brother of one of the members of the committee of the Washington church) to Jesse Mercer (*q.v.*), editor of the *Christian Index* and president of the foreign board. He published the appeal and sent it to the board, expressing the hope that the call would be heeded.

But the republic of Texas was a part of the field allotted to the Home Mission Society—*North America for Christ*. The appeal to that board was sent by Robert Alexander, a Methodist missionary in Texas and formerly a pastor in Natchez, Miss. He delivered it to Ashley Vaughn, Baptist pastor in Natchez and editor of the monthly, *Southwestern Religious Luminary*. Vaughn published the appeal in his paper and forwarded it to the board of the society, urgently requesting that a missionary be sent.

It was two years before a missionary was found. James Huckins (*q.v.*) of Vermont, agent of the society in South Carolina and Georgia, landed in Galveston in Jan., 1840. He and others decided that Texas Baptists must train leaders. About 1841 the Texas Baptist Education Society was formed. In 1845 this society established Baylor University at Independence. The school existed primarily for the training of ministers, but was not limited thereto. The curriculum stressed general culture rather than special theological training. Beginning in 1867, a special course was outlined for ministers in addition to the general cultural curriculum. Such a program was offered until the death of William Carey Crane (*q.v.*) (1885). Effort was made to continue the school, but there was no special program for ministerial training.

A classical academy was conducted at Waco under the patronage, first of the Trinity River Association (1856), and then of the Waco Association (1861). President Rufus Columbus Burleson (*q.v.*) of Baylor University, with most of the faculty and the senior class, left Baylor and went to Waco in 1861. The enlarged school was called Waco University. The course offered was cultural, but the main objective was still ministerial training. In 1871 Benajah Harvey Carroll (*q.v.*) became pastor of the Waco Baptist Church. The next year Waco University offered a special curriculum for ministerial students. President Burleson was the principal teacher; Pastor Carroll was assistant.

By the time of the death of President Crane (1885) the progress of settlement was bypassing Independence. The railroads were making Waco a center of traffic, business, and population. The Waco Association was increasing in number of churches and in Baptist population. President Burleson led in chartering a new school (Aug. 6, 1886), Baylor University at Waco. Baylor University (at Independence) suspended operation, but in 1895 the charter was renewed for another 50 years. President Burleson continued the course of study for ministerial students, Pastor Carroll continuing as assistant. In the 1890's, as the number of students for the ministry increased, John Stevenson Tanner, professor of philosophy, assisted in conducting classes in English Bible.

By the end of the 19th century, Baptist leaders in Texas had projected a larger educational program. Baptist schools were functioning with limited equipment and laboring under heavy indebtedness. In 1899 Carroll resigned the pastorate of the First Church, Waco, and became secretary of the newly created Education Commission, set up by the Baptist General Convention of Texas for the purpose of clearing the debts on Baptist schools and enlarging their equipment and efficiency. Under his leadership the campaign was successful. Not only were needed funds secured, but also the number of students enrolled in the schools was increased. It was decided to enlarge the sphere of ministerial training of Baylor University at Waco.

The Baylor period (*1901–08*).

1. In 1901 Carroll became head of the new theological department. Two new professors were secured for the enlarging program: Albert Henry Newman (*q.v.*) of McMaster University, Toronto, and Robert N. Barrett, pastor of the First Church, Waxahachie, Tex. The brethren on the Atlantic seaboard, perhaps because of distance, had a better perspective of what was being done than did those who were leading in Texas. The keen-minded young editor of the *Biblical Recorder* (N. C.), later United States senator from North Carolina, Josiah William Bailey, wrote (July 10, 1901):

> It is understood that the removal of Rev. Dr. A. H. Newman from McMaster College, Toronto, Canada, to Baylor University, Texas, has regard to the establishment of a theological school in connection with that University. With such a host of Baptists as Texas counts, it is not unreasonable that it be made the home of a theological school which shall hold the young men thus educated to their own section of the country. Heretofore it has been difficult to get them back again when once they get as far away as Louisville.

From Texas came prompt denial of the implication in Bailey's editorial. But in the *Baptist Standard,* Aug. 29, 1901, Robert N. Barrett, speaking for President Oscar Henry Cooper (*q.v.*) of Baylor, wrote:

> For some time there has been a demand and expectation that a full department be announced, but as the Education Commission does not make a final report till November, it is not yet known whether all debts will be paid, so that endowment can be claimed. For that reason the trustees prudently refrain from promising too much, but have authorized what is here outlined as the first year's work in a course leading to the degree of Bachelor of Theology. But next year it is confidently expected that there will be a large endowment, which will enable the institution to employ the best instructors, who will proceed with the full curriculum of a well-organized theological Seminary.

The development during the next two years brought forth another comment from Bailey and an answer from Carroll:

> The *Christian Index* of March 12 quotes a paragraph from the *Recorder* that I must have overlooked in your columns. The paragraph quoted says: "Baylor University has been bidding for a place as rival of the Louisville Seminary with the Whitsitt controversy as a basis."
>
> This however unintentionally, does great injustice to Baylor University in two particulars: (1) The Institution here has not been bidding as a rival of the Louisville Seminary. (2) The Whitsitt controversy is not a basis of any thing done here.
>
> Whenever I regard Baylor University's theological department as a rival of the Seminary, then I will resign as Seminary trustee and quit influencing Texas preachers to attend the Seminary. The Seminary sustains a peculiar relation to the whole Southern Baptist Convention which, as far as I know, no theological department in any Southern Baptist college or University seeks to share.

In the lengthy article Carroll emphasized the loyalty in Texas to the Louisville seminary, due to the work its alumni were doing and to the assistance the seminary professors rendered in Texas. He decried the tendency to engender a hostile sentiment between the seminary and Southern colleges and universities. Notwithstanding Carroll's disclaimer, however, seminary sentiment increased in Texas, and the theological curriculum in Baylor University was being expanded.

2. In 1905 the department was enlarged into the Baylor Theological Seminary.

> The Baptists of Texas have entered upon the work of enlarging the theological department of Baylor University. At the recent opening of the University Dr. B. H. Carroll, Dean of the Theological Department, outlined the plans in a great address.

The brilliant editor of the *Biblical Recorder* could not refrain from an "I told you so": "Once upon a time we pointed out that another theological Seminary was rising in Baylor University, Texas; and promptly did we receive most weighty denials from the men in charge."

In the opening address of the new seminary, Dean Carroll set out his ideals of a theological school, his plans therefor, the methods by which the objective could be reached, and the basis of his assurance of success. On the last point he spoke as follows:

> Here I was, writing no articles, making no pulpit or platform allusions to my work; but seeking to accomplish the desired object by private visitation and face to face conference with a hundred select friends, to whom it was supposed this work was dear, and whose prayers would likely accompany their contributions. And ever recurred the burning question: Will they see this as I do? Will they count it an honor to share this burden with me? Suddenly, and in a most startling and realistic manner, I recalled John's vision of the Lord in the Island of Patmos, and a quickened memory repeated His words with such emphasis that they seemed almost audible and personal to me: "Fear not: I am the first and the last, and the Living One; and I become dead, and behold I am alive forever more, and I have the keys of death and of the Spirit-world . . . and am He that hath the key of David, that openeth and none shall shut and that shutteth and none openeth."
>
> Instantly peace and rest poured like a river into my heart, expelling all anxiety and perplexity. My heart leaped and my soul exalted. I kept repeating: "Jesus is alive! Jesus is alive!"
>
> In a moment my faith saw a wonderful sight, even the Throne of Grace, and read its inscription: "Let us therefore draw near with boldness unto the Throne of Grace, that we may receive mercy, and find grace to help us in time of need."
>
> And instantly memory and heart repeated the benediction of Revelation: "Unto Him that loveth us, and looses us from our sins by His blood; and He hath made us to be a kingdom, to be priests unto His God and Father; to Him be the glory and the dominion for ever and ever. Amen. Behold He cometh with clouds."
>
> It was a most gracious experience whose blessings linger yet. The lesson was well learned, and of surpassing value.

The sentiment for a full-fledged seminary had become so strong by the end of the school year, June, 1905, that the trustees of Baylor authorized the enlarged program with the understanding that the enlargement would not be chargeable to Baylor's budget. Carroll assumed the financial responsibility. He proposed to raise $30,000 to finance the seminary for three years in order to show the need of it. He argued that people would not give money to endow an institution that did not exist; but if they saw an institution proving its place in the life of Texas Baptists, the money would be contributed for its endowment. He spent the summer of 1905 in securing about three fourths of the $30,000. The balance was secured later. President Samuel Palmer Brooks (*q.v.*) of Baylor University was in Europe that summer.

The success of the three-year experiment brought forth a conviction on the part of many that the theological seminary should be separated from the university. That conviction and the arguments therefor were set forth in a long article by W. K. Penrod, pastor of the First Baptist Church, Cleburne, Tex., in the *Baptist Standard,* Oct. 17, 1907. It is remarkable how the subsequent history of the seminary has followed the pattern of Penrod's argument. He even named the institution and showed why it should be so called.

In addition to the growing conviction of the need of a separate theological institution, a local condition in Baylor University created a situation which called for settlement. Carroll was president of the board of trustees of Baylor University during his last years as pastor. When he became a member of the Baylor faculty and head of the theological department, later dean of the theological seminary of the university, he remained president of the board. As dean of the seminary, he was technically under the authority of President Brooks of the university; as president of the board of trustees, he was technically above the president of the university. Brooks was in Europe when Carroll led the board to create the theological seminary of the university. The personal relations between the two were never marred, but there existed a situation that might produce more or less serious friction in the official relations of the seminary and the university. As a consequence there was much discussion concerning the relation of the university as a whole to the seminary as one of its constituent schools. Brooks at first strongly opposed separation and removal. However, in a long article in the *Baptist Standard*, Jan. 23, 1908, he indicated his complete about-face and presented the reasons therefor.

The first definite step toward separation from Baylor University and removal from Waco came in a letter from Brooks to Carroll, Sept. 19, 1907:

Before the meeting of the Committee to which was referred the consideration of the question of the Baylor Theological Seminary and the University I submit to you the following suggestions: In view of the facts (a) that you do not think that the Seminary can reach its highest usefulness as now situated, and (b) that it is your "profound conviction that a Theological Seminary west of the Mississippi River, to attain its full legitimate life, must *ultimately* be placed on its own distinct habitat and under a distinct charter and management, separate from any other institution,"

(1) I believe now that the Seminary should be (a) under a distinct charter, (b) located in a different city (preferably Fort Worth), (c) with a temporary home in the Baylor buildings, at least for a year or two, pending a legitimate effort at establishing the new location.

(2) I believe if you the Dean, and I the President, backed by a request from the trustees, will go before the State Convention, a practically unanimous vote can be had to the above suggestion.

(3) If the Theological ideals are so radically different from those of the college ideals as set forth by you to the trustees, then our differences are not personal but professional. For either of us to yield what we believe to be fundamental to get temporary relief from friction is not settling the matter wisely since our successors in office would meet the same difficulties. Then surely the friction should be permanently removed at once.

(4) If I understand the public mind at all it is no secret that the Seminary may move. This fact has grown since the Convention at Dallas, 1905. It is true that people do not agree as to whether it should remain in Waco or go elsewhere. It is also true that very many who primarily like myself believe that the Seminary ought to have grown up as a part of the University, now in the light of circumstances think it ought to be set up elsewhere. There are very many who do not believe it ought to have been enlarged two years ago, but now that it is enlarged, believe it ought not to be neglected, but can grow best under its own habitat and management.

(5) You do not believe it should remain as now. Your paper submitted to the Trustees practically separates and remains in Waco. Bro. Ray's suggestions mean actual separation and yet location in Waco. I do not believe it should separate and remain in Baylor or in Waco. I believe it would mean endless conflict of student bodies and of the faculties, that the very fraternity that should exist, and that you and I want so much to develop, would fail utterly.

In very fact you and I believe in absolute and complete separation. Let us work together to attain it. But to guard against mistakes let us . . . officially invite at once a group of denominational leaders, pastors and laymen, to come to Waco or elsewhere in a short time, to consider the Seminary and the University, to advise with us and help us to arrive at what is right and most far-reaching for Christian Education in Texas, preacher and layman alike, all for the glory of God.

If such a group of men, and we, agree, then there is no probability of the coming convention being hurt by hasty or unwise resolutions from anybody. I believe that such a body of men would meet with us. They would have no power, or right to force us, and though our judgment might remain the same after the conference as it is now, surely no harm but only good would come of it.

I write this letter with the prayer that the Seminary and the University may come to live in harmony here in Baylor or to live in harmony apart, each helping the other.

Fraternally,
S. P. Brooks

An unofficial group such as suggested by President Brooks met and submitted to the board of trustees of Baylor University the question of separation and removal of the seminary. The board made recommendation to the Baptist General Convention of Texas. The convention adopted the following:

1. That the Convention grant the request of the Board of Trustees of Baylor University for separation as desired.

2. That a committee of five be appointed by the chair to nominate a Board of Trustees for the Seminary, who shall be charged with the duty of securing a charter and as soon as practicable a habitat for said Seminary; and to do such other things as shall be necessary, permanently to establish said institution.

3. That a provision be made in said charter for other advisory boards, large enough to conserve the highest ideals of sound orthodoxy and solid business management.

The Texas Convention Period (1908–25). The Baptist General Convention of Texas (1907) adopted the resolutions authorizing the separation and removal of the seminary. A board of trustees was appointed by the convention. A charter was granted by the secretary of state of Texas, Mar. 14, 1908. The 10th article of the charter read:

The primary right of appointing Trustees of said Seminary as hereinbefore vested in the Baptist General Convention of Texas shall so remain exclusively, unless in the judgment of said Convention it shall become advantageous to said Seminary to have trustees from other States, then the same may be so appointed, by similar Baptist bodies of other States which may desire to cooperate in maintaining said institution, in such proportion and on such terms as may be satisfactory to the Texas Convention on the recommendation of the Seminary Board of Trustees.

Ten state conventions (or general associations)—Arkansas, Florida, Illinois, Kentucky, Louisiana, Mississippi, Missouri, New Mexico, Oklahoma, Tennessee—accepted the invitation and began to appoint members to the board of trustees during this period.

Carroll published five articles in the *Baptist Standard*—Mar. 12, 26, Apr. 2, 16, 1908, and Jan. 13, 1910—setting forth the ideals, standards, and safeguards of the seminary. The second article (Mar. 26, 1908) contains the charter with comments thereon. The second section of the charter reads: "The purpose of said corporation is hereby declared to be for the promotion of theological education, but to include the instruction of Women's Training School for special Christian service and such other instruction as is needful to equip preachers for their life work." At first glance that last clause, "and such other instruction as is needful to equip preachers for their life work," is puzzling. Carroll's comments on the charter clarify that statement. It was his thought that a large number of Baptist preachers in Texas, particularly those of mature years, would not attend college. A seminary therefore ought to give such students not only a distinctly theological course, but also a measure of training in some of the more important features of a literary curriculum. In fact he favored for all preachers, older and younger, a training on one campus that combined the literary and theological. He says:

The only ultimate solution is for the Seminary to go back to the Bible model of the School of the Prophets, and which was also for quite a while the historical model in post-Biblical times, namely, that the Seminary teach the preacher on all lines of his education. I say we must ultimately come to that. And when we do, one part of the preacher's education will not forever war with another part.

At the first meeting of the board of trustees of the seminary (Dallas, May 8, 1908), it was reported:

Good brethren in Texas had come to have apprehension as to the possible scope of the work which it was intended that the Seminary should do, questioning whether or not it was the purpose of the Board to establish an institution that would in any sense duplicate the work already being done by Baylor University and other schools and colleges. This apprehension, as we were advised, was based on the last clause of Section 2 [quoted above]. Possibly the apprehension of the brethren had been strengthened also by some personal views held and expressed by the president as to the type of institution best suited to the training of young ministers. To allay this apprehension the Board passed unanimously the following resolution: "Resolved that there is nothing in the charter that allows the establishment of a literary college, and that the Board has no purpose to establish such an institution."

Southwestern Seminary continued the work of Baylor Seminary and remained on the Baylor University campus until a permanent location could be secured. A committee on location was named by the board. The offers of several towns and cities, including several locations adjacent to Fort Worth, were considered. A committee of the board of trustees—composed of George Washington Truett (*q.v.*), Prince Emmanuel Burroughs (*q.v.*), Arthur James Barton (*q.v.*), D. I. Smyth, and W. K. Penrod—met in Fort Worth, Sept. 12, 1909, and submitted in writing what was necessary to secure the seminary, namely, $100,000 in cash and a site. A local committee of 100 Baptists from all the churches of Fort Worth unanimously and joyously accepted the conditions. In a special meeting of the board in Fort Worth (Nov. 2, 1909), the site recommended by the committee on location was accepted. Known as Seminary Hill, it was then located two miles south of the city, but now is within the city limits.

The first building.—A campaign was begun immediately to raise the bonus of $100,000. The first building, Fort Worth Hall, was to be ready by Oct. 1, 1910, for the opening of the seminary in its new and permanent home. The campaign faced difficulties, which were summarized by J. Frank Norris in the *Baptist Standard,* Nov. 11, 1909:

Other interests, too, were crowding for appeal. There was the raising of the $150,000 to secure certain manufacturing enterprises, $125,000—interurban proposition, $75,000 for the Polytechnic College, and the raising of $120,000 to rebuild burned churches; all these things in the face of the most distressing drought for a generation. The cattlemen, and there are a large number of them here, have lost heavily this year with prospects of losing still more. Yet heroically and religiously one and all said, "The Seminary can be landed," and landed it was. . . .

It was Seminary morning, noon and evening. Seminary for prayer-meeting. Seminary for Ladies' Aid Society. Seminary for B.Y.P.U., Seminary for Sunday School, Seminary for saloon talk, so much so that a bartender said, "We will have preachers to burn." It is reported, how true I dare not say, that one hotel had a Seminary menu card. . . .

The Lawgiver Moses was forty days in the mountain receiving the Law; the Prophet Jonah preached the forty days repentance to Nineveh; the Saviour was forty days in the wilderness preparing for his ministry; and the Prophet Scarborough was forty days in Fort Worth loosening the purse-strings of the brethren to the amount of $200,000, or more. With deepest reverence, and true to fact, it can be said the fourth forty day instance was as successful as the others. And it might be said to be even greater when considered in the light of Jesus' words, "Greater work than these shall ye do." Just forty years old, standing full fledged in the prime of his strong young manhood, Christly in his motive, world-wide in his vision, Pauline in his faith and doctrine, richly endowed with many natural gifts, abundantly endued with supernatural power, Scarborough stands forth among his fellows like Saul among the brethren—a born leader of men.

The seminary opened on schedule, Oct. 3, 1910. Unavoidable delays prevented the completion of Fort Worth Hall by the contract date. The building was so far advanced that the first floor furnished accommodation for the first months, while the construction was being completed.

From the beginning of the development that led to Southwestern Seminary, B. H. Carroll was responsible for financing the growing concern. It was specifically stated in the action of the trustees of Baylor University in 1905 that the expense of the enlarged program should not fall on the university. Carroll's assurance to that effect was the condition upon which the trustees created Baylor Theological Seminary. A casual journey through Carroll's correspondence brings stirrings of heart to see the pleas, pathetic pleas, that he made to individuals and to churches for funds. Now and then the strain is relieved by flashes of his humor. He must have found relief in the expression thereof, and at the same time he set forth his underlying philosophy of life. Soon after the seminary came to Fort Worth, he sent an appeal to many pastors: "I am up a tree. Can't you and your fine men help me?" Frank Shelby Groner (*q.v.*), pastor of the First Church, Stamford, Tex., replied: "I am in a hole. I must call my fine men together to raise $14,000.00 to pay on a pressing debt on our building. How can a man in a hole help a man up a tree?" Carroll replied: "When you come up the tree to help me down, you will be out of your hole." These constant appeals not only secured funds, however inadequate, but also made Texas Baptists seminary-conscious and aided in creating interest in the growing institution.

THE SOUTHERN CONVENTION PERIOD (from 1925). From 1908 to 1925, the seminary was largely a Texas institution. It began in Texas, was located in Texas, and was largely controlled and supported in Texas. During those years, however, other state conventions, under the 10th section of the charter, were invited to appoint trustees and thus to share in the conduct of the school. These began to develop sentiment that the Southwestern Seminary should become Southwide in its outlook and control. Such sentiment had become so evident by 1917 that President Scarborough raised in faculty meeting the question of offering the Southwestern Seminary to the Southern Baptist Convention. The point was made by a member of the faculty that it would be better to wait until the sentiment grew to the point that the proposal would come from the Convention rather than from the seminary. That point of view was accepted. The question was precipitated earlier than was anticipated by the professor. Following the successful canvass for subscriptions in the 75 Million Campaign (1919) of the Southern Baptist Convention, Southern Baptist leaders expressed the opinion that all institutions and agencies receiving funds through the campaign ought to be under the control of the Southern Convention. The seminary authorities readily agreed to the transfer. The legal technicalities involved were worked out by 1925. In the annual meeting of that year, the Convention accepted the offer of ownership and control of the seminary presented by the Baptist General Convention of Texas and the conventions and general associations of the states that had hitherto participated in control. Since 1925 the Southern Baptist Convention has elected the members of the board of trustees under the provisions of the amended charter.

Administration.—B. H. Carroll served as dean of the Baylor Theological Seminary from its origin in 1905. He became president of Southwestern Seminary under its charter (1908) and served until his death, Nov. 11, 1914. For the year and a half during which he was ill, Lee Rutland Scarborough (*q.v.*), professor of evangelism since 1908, served as acting president. He was elected president Feb. 9, 1915. He retired from the presidency July 31, 1942, and was succeeded by Eldred Douglas Head, pastor of the First Baptist Church of Houston, Tex. Head retired July 31, 1953, and John Howard Williams, executive secretary of the Baptist General Convention of Texas, became president Aug. 1, 1953.

Internal organization.—By the end of the second decade of its history, the seminary had begun to increase in numbers (in faculty, in students, and in number and complexity of courses of study) to such an extent that it seemed wise for efficiency both in training and in administration to organize the seminary into schools with separate faculties and separate curricula, offering separate degrees. This development in complexity resulted from the objectives in the life and work of the seminary expressed even from its beginnings at Baylor. This program of adjustment to current conditions and needs has become more evident as the seminary has grown with the years. New departments of study have been added to the curriculum as the needs of each decade have demanded, and new degrees have been offered accordingly.

In the last years of the 19th century and the first years of the 20th, women began to push forward into business, the professions, public life, and every phase of human activity. Their place in church life—local and denominational—was becoming a prominent topic of discussion. Mission boards, foreign and domestic, were calling for trained women workers. Special training schools were opening in different areas of the United States. Baptist women of the South were forming societies (of different names) in the churches; these were gravitating into state groups, all moving toward a Convention-wide organization, auxiliary to the Southern Baptist Convention. Young women from Southern churches were going to training schools in other areas. Forward-looking leaders among Southern

Baptist women saw the need of a school to train young women for work at home and abroad. As a private venture, local women began a woman's training school in Louisville, Ky., in 1904. Three years later, the year the Baptist General Convention of Texas voted to establish Southwestern Seminary, the Woman's Missionary Union of the South assumed control and direction of the school in Louisville.

About the same time a group of pastors and women, led by Robert Cooke Buckner (*q.v.*), began a private training school for women in Dallas, Tex. When Southwestern Seminary moved to Fort Worth (1910), Buckner and his co-workers released this work to the seminary. This institution was coeducational from the beginning, and women, married and single, were admitted as regular students.

About the beginning of American national life, Sunday schools (for children) began to be formed. Toward the end of the 19th century, the work of reaching more adults through the teaching function of the church and the work of training church members for a larger and more efficient program of activity gained rapidly in momentum. Courses in Sunday school work were being offered in several schools in the United States. While the work of Southwestern Seminary was conducted in Waco, a course in religious education, offered by Frederick Eby, professor of education at Baylor University, was included in the seminary curriculum. When the seminary moved to Fort Worth, a similar course was listed in the schedule and was conducted for three years in relays by members of the faculty and visiting teachers. Beginning with the school year 1913–14, two courses in Sunday school pedagogy were conducted for two years by William Wright Barnes, professor of church history.

In the spring of 1915, the administration decided to establish a full department of religious education. John Milburn Price was elected to the professorship, beginning his work with the school year 1915–16. Additional courses were added, covering the work in religious education being done generally at the time. Beginning with the school year 1919–20, there were several distinct enlargements—courses in the study of age groups, the first such studies in Southern Baptist educational work, were begun. The curriculum was enlarged as a basis for the degree of Bachelor of Religious Education, which was then offered for the first time. Advanced courses were instituted, offering a major in religious education to graduate students in the seminary working for a doctorate in theology. The added courses of study necessitated increase in the number of teachers. With the next school year a three-year curriculum was instituted, leading to the degree of Master of Religious Education. The prerequisite for this degree was an academic bachelor's degree. Beginning with the school year 1921–22, for more effective work in administration and in teaching, the School of Religious Education, a constituent unit in the seminary's program, was instituted. By 1925 the school was departmentalized. In that year the first doctorate in religious education was conferred by the seminary.

In 1951 the School of Religious Education was accredited by the American Association of Schools of Religious Education. This school was a charter member of the national organization. J. M. Price, director, served four terms as president of the national body.

The School of Religious Education has pioneered in several directions: vocational training in religious education, a major in religious education for the doctor's degree, the requirement of collegiate prerequisites for degrees in religious education, Baptist Student Union work, visual aids, religious counseling, and several other distinct phases in the present Southern Baptist program in religious education.

In the sphere of church music, Southwestern Seminary has responded to current developments. The programs of music in public schools and colleges, the higher standard of music teaching in the conservatories, the greater extension of music appreciation through radio and other channels—all these created a demand for a higher level of music in church life. Early in its history, Southwestern Seminary took the lead in responding to this need for development of programs of church music and for the training of leadership. The program of musical training was begun in a small way and enlarged year by year. In 1911 Mrs. Herbert Haywood, wife of a senior student in the seminary, was employed to teach choral music and voice culture. In 1913 Joseph Rosenfelt, who conducted a private studio in Fort Worth, was employed on a part-time basis. In 1914 R. H. Cornelius was elected instructor in music (full-time).

With the beginning of the school year 1915–16, Isham Emmanuel Reynolds (*q.v.*) became head of the department of gospel music. Professor Reynolds came from the staff of the evangelism department of the Home Mission Board of the Southern Baptist Convention. He was already widely known and began to build on the foundations already laid. As the number of students enrolled in the department of music increased, the number of courses was increased and the teaching staff was enlarged. As previously indicated, the department was enlarged in 1921 into the School of Gospel Music. The title was changed in 1926 to the School of Sacred Music. The degrees Bachelor of Sacred Music and Master of Sacred Music were offered, based on curricula indicating the various departments into which the school had been divided. The year the new title for the school was taken, the new building was occupied for the first time.

The enlarging program, intended to train leaders demanded in the several phases of church life and activity, brought problems of administration and internal articulation in the seminary. Many problems of types of work to be done concerned immediately only a part of the faculty or of the student body. By 1921 the decision was made to meet the problems of external growth and internal development by grouping the seminary life and activity into schools, each with its own faculty, caring for the tasks and activities incident to each respective group. (The School of Theology was definitely identified later.) A faculty council, composed at first of representatives from each school, but later composed of the entire teaching force, constituted the unifying, comprehensive body. The schools of theology, of religious education, and of gospel music were already fairly well identified and differentiated. The Woman's Missionary Training School did not have a distinct corporate identity. The courses of study leading to the degrees offered in missionary training were selected from the other three disciplines, most of them taught by the faculty of theology; therefore there was no faculty of the missionary training school. The superintendent of that school, in the new organizational plan, was a member of the faculty of the school of theology, and that faculty had responsibility for the affairs of the training school. Within a few years, since the women, wives of students and unmarried, were enrolling for degrees in theology, in religious education, or in sacred music, the concept of a missionary training school was dropped. The superintendent of the training school became the dean of women.

The organization of the schools of religious education and of gospel music began to function in the following scholastic year, 1921–22. They had already developed a measure of identity in that they had been considered as adjuncts to the time-honored pattern of a theological seminary. A seminary taught and trained men for the pastoral and preaching ministry. These new fields were opening mainly to laymen and women. (It has become recognized on Seminary Hill that any and all courses of study in any of the schools are open to ministers, laymen, and women.) Hence, there was not the developing concept of a distinct school of theology; the seminary as a whole was so considered in the first years. The disciplines of missionary training, of religious education, and of gospel music were considered additions to a theological school. In all the discussions that led to the creation of the seminary as one of the schools of Baylor University and in the further development that led to the separate identity of Southwestern Seminary, the special objective held forth was the training of a more efficient preaching and pastoral ministry. The degrees first offered were those in the field of theology.

However, laymen and women were enrolled as students. The question of their receiving theological degrees did not arise until several years after the beginning of the seminary. In 1914 the wife of a ministerial student applied for permission to enrol with her husband in the course leading to a degree in theology. Reference to the charter indicated that the corporation had authority "to confer upon any pupil of said Seminary—or upon any other person any of the degrees usually conferred by theological seminaries, or other degrees arising from its curriculum." Since it is a fair inference that a woman may be included in the category, "pupil . . . or any other person," it was decided that any student enrolled in the seminary might take any of the degrees offered then or later.

When the enlarging work of the departments of music, education, and missionary training resulted in the creation of the three distinct schools, each offering degrees in their respective disciplines, the seminary continued to be considered as *par excellence* a school for training preachers. There was not needed a separate school of theology, since the seminary had been such from the beginning. But after two years of the functioning of the schools of music, education, and missionary training, it was realized that the original purpose of the seminary—training preachers—needed re-emphasizing. Accordingly, the school of theology was created (1923). The heads of the schools of sacred music and of religious education had been designated directors from the beginning; the head of the school of theology was called chairman of the faculty until 1949, when the title was changed to director.

The new plan was an experiment; detailed specifications were adopted by the entire faculty, so that the new system might function to the best interests of the seminary as a whole. It was agreed that

> . . . the President of the Seminary is president of each of these faculties and the director of each of the Schools will act as chairman of the faculty of that School in the absence of or on the request of the President. The Theological Faculty shall elect each year a chairman who will preside over that Faculty in the absence of the President.

Equipment.—Nov. 2, 1909, the board of trustees accepted the gift of Joe K. Winston, deacon in College Avenue Baptist Church, Fort Worth, of 50 acres of land for the campus and half interest in 250 homesites adjacent thereto for endowment. In 1954 the seminary bought from the city of Fort Worth 32 acres situated half a block north of the campus. This area will be used for the construction of 900 apartments for living quarters for married students. The seminary owns less than 100 apartments on and adjacent to the campus already being occupied by student families.

When the seminary opened in Fort Worth, 1910, and for five years thereafter, Fort Worth Hall, financed by the bonus contributed as a part of the inducement to move to Fort Worth, was the only building. The first and second floors housed every phase of activity—administration, library, classrooms, dormitory, chapel, etc.—for four years. In the summer of 1914 the third floor was completed. On the opening day of the school year 1914–15, ground was broken for the building to house the Woman's Missionary Training School. The women of the churches of Texas contributed $110,000 toward its cost.

In the fall of 1915, the building was occupied. Some years later it was enlarged, doubling its capacity. That addition has since been changed into apartments for married students. In 1954 the building was named Barnard Hall in honor of Floy Barnard, D.R.E., the first dean of women.

The growth of the seminary demanded larger accommodations. In the spring of 1921, a temporary chapel and classroom building was constructed just east of Fort Worth Hall. This was used through the summer of 1926. It was sold to the Seminary Hill Church (now Gambrell Street Church) and moved to the corner of Gambrell and James Streets.

In 1925 Mrs. George Edgar Cowden of Fort Worth gave $150,000 toward the construction of a home for the School of Gospel Music (since 1926 the School of Sacred Music). The building —first in the country dedicated to church music —contains recital hall, classrooms, studios, offices for members of the music faculty, library, and every facility for a school of music. It was occupied in the fall of 1926 and named the George Edgar Cowden Music Building, in memory of the donor's husband, long-time friend of President Scarborough and of the seminary.

In 1945, following the deaths of President Scarborough of the seminary and President G. W. Truett of the board of trustees, alumni and friends of the seminary began a campaign for the construction of a long-needed administration building, at a cost of $1,400,000. The south wing bears the name Truett Chapel, in memory of the great preacher of Dallas, long-time friend of the seminary; the west wing (administration and school of theology), Scarborough Hall, honors the memory of President Scarborough, who served from 1915 to 1942; the east wing houses the Fleming Library, so named in gratitude to William Fleming of Fort Worth, for many years an active trustee and friend of the seminary, who gave largely toward financing the cost of the building. The frieze above the portico bears the likenesses of 21 ministers prominent in Southern Baptist history. Memorial Hall occupies the center of the campus; its dome may be seen from afar from any direction.

This hall, occupied at the beginning of the school year 1949–50, became overcrowded within five years. In 1954 construction was begun on an addition to the east wing, thereby more than doubling the floor space of Fleming Library. At the same time an addition to the west wing was constructed to relieve the congestion in the School of Theology and in the administration offices. The enlarged Scarborough Hall provides accommodation for the president's suite, offices for the members of the faculty of theology, much-needed classrooms, and other provision for the work of the School of Theology. These additions were occupied in the summer of 1956.

Also, in 1945 plans were begun looking toward the construction of a home for the School of Religious Education. It was completed in 1949 and named John Milburn Price Hall in honor of the director of the School of Religious Education, 1921–56. The building contains faculty offices, classrooms, chapel, kindergarten, and every needed equipment. Price led in raising funds among the alumni of the school and friends.

The library.—The beginning of the library is lost in the mist of an obscurity caused by the lack of full documentation. While the seminary was located in Waco, it used the library of Baylor University. The first record of its own library is implied by the announcement of a librarian and by a reference to the "nucleus already secured." This was in 1910, the year of moving to Fort Worth.

The next reference to the library is the recorded entry of the first book, the *Standard Dictionary of the English Language* (1897), dated Feb. 13, 1911. The book was a "Gift," donor not named. The next 3,510 books were given by unidentified donors.

Whence came this "nucleus" and these earliest "gifts"? Possibly, some of them were books which had belonged to the Adelphian Theological Society, which moved with the seminary to Fort Worth. This society was in existence as early as 1888 and had a "Library." The first named donors are James Franklin Love (*q.v.*) and James Marion Frost (*q.v.*), who gave a bound set of the annuals of the Southern Baptist Convention. But this was three years after the seminary began work on its own campus in Fort Worth.

The first known effort to buy books for the library occurred in May, 1912, when "a subscription fund . . . was started and $275.00 was subscribed to be supplemented to the amount of $500 from the Emergency fund if possible." A year later the faculty appropriated $700 for books; in 1914, $500; in 1916, another $500; after this date book appropriations became actions of the president rather than the faculty.

The library grew from one to 6,050 books between Feb. 13, 1911, and July 18, 1919. This was the period when the seminary was small and three professors, Charles Bray Williams (*q.v.*), William Wright Barnes, and Walter Thomas Conner (*q.v.*), successively acted as librarians. At the end of 1955, the total number of accessions was well over 100,000. In 1955 the circulation record was 292,741. The library staff has grown from one part-time librarian with one student assistant to five full-time librarians and more than 500 hours a week of student assistance.

The first librarian who was not also a professor was Leonidas Marcellus Sipes, from June, 1919, to Feb., 1922. He also served half-time as pastor of the Seminary Hill Baptist Church. Leslie Robinson Elliott, who had been student assistant under Sipes, served as acting librarian for the remainder of the session. On June 1, 1922, he became the seminary's first full-time librarian.

During the whole existence of the library, there has been a faculty library committee. During the earlier years this committee functioned with the librarian in book selection and in administrative regulations. After the coming of a full-time librarian, the committee served as an advisory body in the formulation of library policy. The librarian is solely responsible to the president for the administration of the library.

In keeping with many American institutions of higher education, the library's academic position is recognized as educational rather than administrative. The trustees formally approved this definition in 1947 by giving the librarian and his professional associates full faculty status.

The library, after occupying space in Fort Worth Hall and then Barnard Hall, was moved into its own building in 1949. Named Fleming Library Building after its donor, it has 20,880 square feet of space on three floors and provides room for 300 students, 15 librarians, and 125,000 volumes. The addition, which was completed in 1956, increased the capacity to 700 students and 250,000 volumes, besides 20 faculty study rooms. In Cowden Hall there is a branch music library with more than 3,000 volumes and a large collection of records and sheet music.

The library's service to the students is extensive, since a large proportion of the class work—62 per cent in the school of theology, not counting Hebrew and Greek—depends on library materials rather than textbooks. An expanding research service for the faculty and graduate students is a library feature which is used to capacity.

In 1938 the library pioneered in studies in the use of microfilm for theological library service and has contributed through this medium to theological education and historical research in America. During the session of 1946–47, the library was the base of a movement which led to the organization of the American Theological Library Association. The library has the largest theological collection west of the Mississippi River and is the 10th largest in the United States. Numerous personal contacts with American centers of theological education and two trips overseas by the librarian, Leslie Robinson Elliott, have given Fleming Library valuable connections at home and abroad. It is fully accredited by the American Association of Theological Seminaries. The library is the depository of the records of many churches, associations, and conventions, especially in Texas. The families of many denominational leaders have deposited their correspondence and literary remains here. The large collection of Baptist records is growing year by year.

Through nearly a half-century the Southwestern Seminary has enrolled 16,959 students, ministers, laymen, and women, from 46 states and 35 foreign countries. They have returned as pastors and church workers to nearly all the states and to the lands of every continent. They have come from Baptist groups outside the Southern Convention, and from at least 10 denominations other than Baptist. All races have come, studied, enjoyed an equal share of Christian fellowship, and returned to their own people to extend and expand the Christian message in obedience to the Great Commission.

The schools of the seminary have their respective affiliations. The School of Theology is a member of and accredited by the American Association of Theological Schools; the School of Religious Education is a member of and accredited by the American Association of Schools of Religious Education; the School of Sacred Music is a member of the Texas Association of Music Schools. Members of the faculties are members of their respective professional societies. The librarian, Elliott, who has served since 1922, led in organizing the American Theological Library Association and has been its president from the beginning.

From the beginning evangelical zeal and missionary fervor have dominated the campus. Of the seminary's alumni 986 have gone into mission fields at home and abroad, entering every phase of church and school activity.

See also STUDENT ACTIVITIES, SOUTHWESTERN BAPTIST THEOLOGICAL SEMINARY.

BIBLIOGRAPHY: Annual Catalogs of the Seminary. *Baptist Courier,* Sept. 21, 1905. *Baptist Standard, passim. Biblical Recorder, passim. Christian Index,* Feb. 22, 1838. *Columbian Star,* Dec. 5, 1825. *Southern Baptist,* Mar. 13, 1835. *Southwestern Religious Luminary,* Jan., 1839. *Southwestern Reporter,* Vol. 26. Records of the Baptist Congress, 1887. Records of the Baptist General Convention of Texas, 1907, 1923. Records of the Southern Baptist Convention, 1923–25. Records of the Faculty of the Seminary. Records of the Board of Trustees of the Seminary. W. W. Ledlow, "History of Protestant Education . . . in Texas" (1926). W. W. Barnes, *History of the Southern Baptist Convention, 1845–1953.* J. M. Carroll, *History of Texas Baptists.* W. W. BARNES

SOUTHWESTERN JOURNAL OF THEOLOGY, THE. A quarterly magazine published by the faculty of Southwestern Baptist Theological Seminary beginning in Apr., 1917. The journal was published to provide an official voice for the school, to magnify the peculiar emphases of the seminary, to promote the interests of Christ's kingdom, and to encourage writers. The faculty provided most of the scholarly articles. The first editor-in-chief was Lee Rutland Scarborough (*q.v.*), the president of the seminary. The managing editors successively were Charles Bray Williams (*q.v.*), Walter Thomas Conner (*q.v.*), and Harvey Eugene Dana (*q.v.*). The journal was published quarterly until July, 1924, when it was announced that a new type of publication would be issued. Beginning in Oct., 1924, the successor to this journal was a popular and promotional monthly magazine, *The Southwestern Evangel.* This was published until June, 1931, under the editorship of H. E. Dana and Lewis A. Myers, successively, when it succumbed to the financial depression. ROBERT A. BAKER

SOUTHWESTERN PUBLISHING HOUSE. See GRAVES (JAMES ROBINSON) PUBLICATION ORGANIZATIONS.

SOUTHWESTERN REGION WOMAN'S MISSIONARY UNION CAMP. Founded in 1939 in co-operation with the Woman's Missionary Union of the western region. Camps were held for Royal Ambassadors, Girls' Auxiliary, and Young Woman's Auxiliary with facilities of Camp Kuttawa, a nonreligious camp at Kuttawa, Ky., rented each year through 1952. In 1951 the western region began using the Schafer Memorial Camp, and southwestern region held camp at Bethel College, Hopkinsville, Ky., in 1953 and 1954. Since 1955 the new Western Kentucky Baptist Camp facilities have been used.

ELDRED M. TAYLOR

SOUTHWESTERN RELIGIOUS LUMINARY. A monthly Baptist newspaper, now extinct, which began publication in Natchez, Miss., in 1836 with Ashley Vaughn as editor. The Mississippi Baptist Convention purchased it that year and sponsored the paper, which had a circulation of 1,000, as a denominational organ. The convention sold it after 28 months to the *Mobile Monitor,* which consolidated the two as the *Southern Monitor and Religious Luminary.*

A. L. GOODRICH

SOVEREIGNTY, LOCAL CHURCH. *General backgrounds.*—The principle of local church sovereignty has belonged to Baptists since the early days of Baptist life in England. In fact, it was not until 1653, when the first Baptist association was formed, that there arose any conflict between church and denominational sovereignty. The question which has remained with Baptists is how to maintain local church sovereignty and yet co-operate with other churches most effectively in carrying out the Great Commission.

Although the prevailing opinion among Baptists has been to the effect that the local church is sovereign, there have been some Baptists who have disagreed on the definition of the term. Although there had been many divergent views, the preponderance of debate was not on local church sovereignty, but on whether such sovereignty could be maintained within the framework of associations and conventions. An essay presented to the Philadelphia Baptist Association in 1749, and approved by that body, stated:

> Such churches there must be, agreeing in doctrine and practice, and independent in their authority and church power, before they can enter into a confederation, as aforesaid, and choose delegates or representatives to associate together; and thus the several independent churches being the constituents, the association, council, or assembly of their delegates, when assembled, is not to be deemed a superior judicature, or having a superintendency over the churches, but subservient to the churches, in what may concern all the churches in general, or any one church in particular.

History may show that *some* Baptists have not believed in local church sovereignty, but the prevailing opinion is that held by typical and effective groups of Baptists in the present, e.g., conventions, associations, and churches.

Position of the Southern Baptist Convention.—The Southern Baptist Convention states in its constitution: "While independent and sovereign in its own sphere, the Convention does not claim and will never attempt to exercise any authority over any other Baptist body, whether church, auxiliary organizations, associations, or conventions." This position is further clarified in a statement adopted by that Convention on the subject, "Relation of Southern Baptist Convention to Other Baptist Bodies," in which the Convention declared that "each church is autonomous or self-determining in all matters pertaining to its own life and activities. . . . All Baptist general bodies are voluntary organizations . . . cooperating . . . without surrendering in any way or degree their right of self determination."

Position of state convention and associations.—The South Carolina Baptist Convention in its constitutional principles, in 1821, stated: "The Convention shall recognize the independence and liberty of the churches of Christ, and consequently shall not in any case arbitrarily interfere in their secular interests. But, when requested, will be considered as under obligation to afford them any assistance which may be in their power."

The Charleston, S. C., Baptist Association, the oldest in the South, stated in 1850, not long after the Southern Baptist Convention was organized: "The Association shall regard the Churches as independent bodies, in all their internal affairs, and exercise no ecclesiastical jurisdiction, or claim any legislative or judicial prerogative over them."

Other states and associations co-operating with the Southern Baptist Convention wrote the same general concept of local church sovereignty into their constitutions in various ways:

Alabama stated, "This Convention disclaims all right of exercising authority over any church, association, or any other Baptist body, recognizing the complete independence of the churches and the autonomy of all Baptist bodies."

Illinois was equally as explicit, declaring:

> This Association is, and shall ever remain, only and solely a medium through which Baptist Churches may work harmoniously in cooperation with each other, promoting the work and objects set forth in this Constitution and By-Laws. It has not, to any degree and shall never presume to have, any ecclesiastical authority. It shall not have and shall never attempt to exercise authority over any church, or the Messengers of the churches in such wise as to limit the sovereignty of the local churches.

Georgia was almost identical with Alabama.

Missouri had a slightly different emphasis: "The General Association shall never exercise any authority over the churches nor do anything that would in any way interfere with their complete autonomy and independence as New Testament churches nor to limit the exercise of their freedom."

Mississippi said, "This Convention shall always recognize and observe the equal rights and independence of the churches; it shall not possess nor attempt to exercise power or authority over any church or association of Churches. This Convention is hereby irrevocably committed to the principle of the complete sovereignty of local Churches."

Louisiana had perhaps a stronger statement of its position: "This Convention shall have no ecclesiastical jurisdiction over the churches, nor act as advisory council in any case of differences between the churches, nor shall interfere with the constitution of any church or association."

Oklahoma added still another point:

> This Convention shall have no ecclesiastical authority or power whatever and shall never assume to write creeds or to exercise judicial or legislative control of the churches. . . . This Convention is a purely co-operative body and its purpose shall be to furnish a means by which the churches of Christ in their sovereign capacity can work together.

Texas added the line that the convention would exercise no control over even "the messengers of the churches in such wise as to limit the sovereignty of the churches, but shall recognize the sovereignty of the churches under the one Sovereign, Jesus Christ our Lord."

Florida emphasized the independent sovereignty of all Baptist bodies.

Kentucky was similar.

North Carolina, Tennessee, Arkansas, Virginia, and California maintained completely the idea of church sovereignty in their constitutions.

Kansas added still another note on church sovereignty, recognizing "the right of any co-operating church to withdraw from its affiliation with the Convention."

In the exercise of this sovereignty, churches and associations have withdrawn, or threatened to withdraw, fellowship from the larger bodies.

Responsibility in association.—Although a local church is recognized as sovereign, capable of self-determination, the churches themselves, in convention, have understood that an association or convention may withdraw fellowship from a church. The first Separate Baptist Association, held at Craig's Meeting House, Orange County, Va., in 1771, adopted the following article in its constitution: "We believe we have a right to withdraw ourselves from any church unsound in doctrine or irregular in practice."

The comments by John Lightfoot Waller (*q.v.*), of Kentucky, are somewhat typical of a widespread viewpoint:

> When a church violates the compact upon which she agreed to meet in association with her sister churches, she forfeits her rights under that compact, and may, and ought to be denied the privileges of the association. But so long as she adheres to the terms of compact, she has a right to be regarded as a member. She can commit no offense over which the association can exercise jurisdiction, except a plain and obvious violation of the terms of compact; and when dropped from correspondence and association, she is still as much a church as she ever was.

But what is traditional among Baptists is not sufficient. As Waller has said:

> But we beg leave to premise that we have given very little study to that code of discipline, held in high esteem by some brethren, called "Baptist custom," or "Baptist usage,"—a kind of ecclesiastical common law, found in tradition touching the practices of the churches in Virginia, the Carolinas, or New England; or else of the churches fifty years ago. We hope the brethren will avoid the yoke of "custom" and "usage" as much as possible. For ourselves, we have no more respect for Baptist than for Papistical "usage," unless it is sustained by the Bible, or supported by sound Christian expediency.

The matter of church sovereignty has meant more to Baptists than merely an exercise of freedom. It is a means of most practicably carrying out the Great Commission. It is founded in a basic ecclesiology, of which, according to Hiscox, there are three kinds, Prelatical, Presbyterian, and Independent, Independent being that form in which "the governing power resides entirely in the body of the members of each single and separate church, or congregation."

A Baptist church may thus choose to affiliate with other like-minded churches. It may unite with churches which maintain many minor differences. It may maintain the affiliation or withdraw it. It can direct its own internal affairs by any form it chooses, whether democracy, by boards, or by constitution.

Knowing the security of its sovereignty, a Baptist church can freely co-operate, under Christ, with other Baptist churches. Co-operation in the larger work is a cardinal principle intensified in the knowledge that it is freely given.

BIBLIOGRAPHY: Alabama Baptist State Convention *Annual* (1955). Arkansas Baptist State Convention *Annual* (1950). W. W. Barnes, "Churches and Associations Among Baptists," *Review and Expositor,* LII, No. 2 (Apr., 1955); *The Southern Baptist Convention, 1845–1953* (1954). J. M. Bulman, "The 1956 Southern Baptist Convention and the Issue of Local Church Autonomy," *Southern Baptist Free Press* (July, 1956). The Southern Baptist General Convention of California *Annual* (1955). J. C. Carlile, *The Story of English Baptists* (1905). J. T. Christian, *A History of the Baptists* (1922). V. Fern, ed., *The American Church of Protestant Heritage* (1953). Florida Baptist State Convention *Annual* (1955). Baptist Convention of the State of Georgia *Annual* (1955). E. T. Hiscox, *The Baptist Short Method* (1868). Illinois Baptist State Association *Annual* (1954). Kansas Convention of Southern Baptists *Annual* (1954). General Convention of Baptists in Kentucky *Annual* (1955). M. M. Lappin, *Baptists in the Protestant Tradition* (1947). Louisiana Baptist Convention *Annual* (1955). W. J. McGlothlin, *Baptist Confessions of Faith* (1911). Mississippi Baptist Convention *Annual* (1955). Missouri Baptist General Association *Annual* (1955). Baptist General Convention of Oklahoma *Annual* (1955). Baptist State Convention of North Carolina *Annual* (1955). State Convention of the Baptist Denomination in South Carolina *Annual* (1821, 1850). *A Short Confession of Faith,* signed by J. Smyth and 41 others. Southern Baptist Convention *Annuals* (1928, 1946). Tennessee Baptist Convention *Annual* (1949). Baptist General

Convention of Texas *Annual* (1955). "The Philadelphia Confession," *The Baptist Encyclopedia,* ed. W. Cathcart (1881). Baptist General Association of Virginia *Annual* (1950). H. Woodson, *Giant in the Land* (1950).

C. EARL COOPER

SOWELL, SIDNEY McFARLAND (b. Hardware, Va., Dec. 18, 1871; d. Buenos Aires, Argentina, Mar. 2, 1954). Missionary to Argentina. Sowell received the M.A. degree from Richmond College and Th.M. and Th.D. degrees (*magna cum laude*) from Southern Baptist Theological Seminary. When 17 years old, Sowell dedicated his life "in a letter to God, deposited in a hollow stump." Appointed May 5, 1903, he was the first Southern Baptist missionary to Argentina and first editor of the Argentine Baptist paper, *El Expositor Bautista.* Sowell served as pastor of the Once (on-say) and Chacarita churches, Buenos Aires, and of the North District Church, Rosario; he was president of the River Plate Seminary, 1918–42, and of the River Plate Baptist Convention in 1912 and 1917; he was treasurer of the convention in 1925 and preached the convention sermon in 1908 and 1922. Sowell also served the River Plate Mission at various times as chairman, secretary, treasurer, vice-president, and president. He married in 1906 Ermine Bagby (1881–1939), daughter of the first Southern Baptist missionaries to Brazil. Sowell wrote *Caminatas por Palestina, Parábolas de Jesús, Caracteres Bíblicas* (unpublished manuscript), and commentaries of Sunday school lessons for *El Expositor Bautista,* 1943–49. The Sowells had four children: Benjamin, Anne (Mrs. Herbert George Margrett, missionary to Argentina), Maurice, and John.

MINNIE D. MCILLROY

SPAIN, MISSION IN. William Knapp organized a Baptist church in Madrid in Aug., 1870, and soon after was employed by the American Baptist Missionary Union. A few years after he left Spain in 1876, the Baptist groups he had started in Madrid, Alicante, and elsewhere disappeared. Erik Lund of Sweden, who became a missionary of the American Baptist Missionary Union, established a new Baptist center in the region of Barcelona. Swedish Baptists, represented by Charles Haglund, John Uhr, and Nils John Bengtson, concentrated their efforts in the region of Valencia, where a church was organized in 1888. Swedish Baptists of America began work in Alicante and Madrid. After the London Conference of 1920, Southern Baptists assumed responsibility for Baptist missions in Spain. With their assistance, Spanish Baptists increased from about 600 in 1920 to 2,245 in 1955. Despite restrictions upon freedom, progress under the Franco regime has been steady.

BIBLIOGRAPHY: J. D. Franks, ed., *European Baptists Today* (1952). E. Gill, *Europe and the Gospel* (1931). J. D. Hughey, Jr., *Religious Freedom in Spain: Its Ebb and Flow* (1956). J. H. Rushbrooke, *The Baptist Movement on the Continent of Europe* (1923). N. F. Weeks, ed., *Europe—Whither Bound?* (1951).

J. D. HUGHEY, JR.

SPALDING SEMINARY. First school established by Georgia Baptists after the Civil War, founded in 1868 at Montezuma, Ga. The school was a family project, with William Clay Wilkes, who had served as the first elected president of Monroe Female College (see Tift College), the founder and only president. Some boys attended, but the school was primarily for girls. It closed in 1873.

ARTHUR JACKSON

SPANISH BAPTIST EVANGELICAL UNION. Organized, with Julio Nogal as president, in a meeting of Baptist leaders in Valencia, Aug. 21–31, 1928. A meeting was held in Barcelona, Aug. 19–21, 1929, with 61 delegates attending. Young people's and women's societies were regarded as entities which functioned within the framework of Spanish Baptist churches. Sixteen churches were members of the convention, with a total membership of 895.

The convention meeting in Sabadell, Aug. 27–29, 1953, changed the name from Spanish Baptist Convention to Spanish Baptist Evangelical Union, and agreed to meet every two years when political conditions permitted. The Union has an executive board, board of publications, and legal, missions, woman's missionary, young people's, educational, and benevolence committees.

In 1955 the union included 38 churches and 31 missions with 2,245 church members, 33 Sunday schools, and one theological seminary located in Barcelona. The union sponsors three magazines: a general Baptist monthly, *El Eco de la Verdad;* a W.M.U. monthly, *Nuestra Labor;* and a young people's quarterly, *La Voz Juvenil.*

Unofficial regional conferences are held annually in Catalonia, the Valencia area, and south central Spain. The constitution of the union recognizes a fraternal relation to the Southern Baptist Convention. With limited freedom, growth under the present regime has been constant.

CHARLES W. WHITTEN

SPANISH BAPTIST PUBLISHING HOUSE. An agency of the Foreign Mission Board of the Southern Baptist Convention located in El Paso, Tex. It prepares, publishes, and distributes literature to 35 countries.

Missionary Jones Edgar Davis (*q.v.*), founder of the publishing house, printed tracts in his home in Toluca, Mexico, for nearly a year before establishing The Mexican Baptist Printery, in León, Mexico, in Jan., 1906. The first year it published two Sunday school quarterlies, *El Expositor Biblico* and *Nuestros Niños,* a large number of tracts, and began publication of its first book, a translation of *Immersion, the Act of Christian Baptism,* by John Tyler Christian (*q.v.*), completed May 6, 1907. Continued revolution in Mexico caused the removal of the publishing house to El Paso in 1916, where it became an international institution, with additional modern equipment. Aquisition of the Southern Baptist Sanatorium property from the

Home Mission Board in 1937 made possible continued expansion. Building, equipment, and stock were valued in 1955 at more than half a million dollars. Part of the Mexican Mission for 43 years, the publishing house was declared a separate mission in 1949.

Eight Sunday school quarterlies, five Training Union quarterlies, a religious education magazine, and a monthly Baptist magazine are published in Spanish. Copies totaled 677,650 in 1955. Tracts totaled 2,534,000 in 1955, and 100,500 copies of 38 book titles were published. Approximately 300 book titles published to date (1955) include a New Testament, hymnals, commentaries, textbooks, manuals, study course books, religious novels, etc. Correspondence courses reach many countries. In the present staff of 47 persons, eight are missionaries.

FRANK W. PATTERSON

SPANISH MISSIONS, ARIZONA. Two Spanish missions were organized in Tucson in 1944 and 1953, under the leadership of I. B. Williams and his wife. A kindergarten started in one of the missions in 1946 with 19 enrolled, reported 108 in 1954. Property value of the two missions totals $19,270.01. In Casa Grande a mission, established in 1945, has property valued at $4,108. It assisted in the opening of work in Chandler. Williams and his wife organized a mission in Miami in 1946, and a kindergarten opened there in 1951 with 28 enrolled. The mission's property was later purchased by the Home Mission Board for $17,000. In Phoenix three missions have been organized under the leadership of three Baptist churches there. North Phoenix Baptist Church purchased property in Aug., 1953, for a mission, in which Joe D. Hardcastle and wife directed the work. First Southern Baptist Church sponsored the opening of a mission in South Phoenix under direction of Mr. and Mrs. Abel Tamez. Central Baptist Church organized a mission in Phoenix in 1955. Missions at Ashfork, Williams, and Flagstaff were established in 1954–55, under the leadership of the Williamses. Work was organized at Willcox in 1953.

MRS. CHARLES M. GRIFFIN

SPANISH MISSIONS, NEW MEXICO. Although the Spanish were not omitted in the work of Hiram Read (*q.v.*), James Milton Shaw and his wife, serving under American Baptist Home Mission Society, were the first Baptist missionaries to work specifically with the Spanish-speaking people of New Mexico. Working first in Albuquerque and later in Santa Fe, often under persecution, the Shaws established their work permanently at Socorro and organized a Baptist church there in 1857. They had operated a school at Santa Fe for a while, although it is not certain whether it was exclusively for Spanish students. The Home Mission Society was forced to withdraw support in 1868, primarily due to oppressive Catholic domination, and did not reopen work until 1880. During the period of withdrawal, most of the work which had been established disappeared. With the return of workers in 1880, Spanish schools and missions were again established, notably at Velarde, with both a school and a mission, at Alamogordo, and at Roswell. The leading native worker was the first known Baptist convert in the territory, Blas Chavez.

When the New Mexico work came under Southern affiliation in 1911, the Southern Baptist Home Mission Board was not prepared to assume a large Spanish mission responsibility. Much of the work, therefore, was temporarily discontinued, and it was not until 1920 that Spanish missionaries were increased and activities extended. In the process of development, a Spanish convention came into existence, and a building valuation of $400,000 was created. Spanish churches have been established at Alamogordo, Albuquerque, Clovis, and two at Roswell, and organized work is in progress at several other points. When there are no mission or church buildings, converts are baptized into near-by Anglo churches where fellowship is welcomed and full rights are granted. The Anglo orphanage admits Spanish children.

There are no schools, only one paper, *The Missionary Bautista,* and no hospitals, although a new medical center has been established at Parkview. A co-ordinator directs the over-all program of Spanish work under the Baptist Home Mission Board in full co-operation with the Baptist Convention of New Mexico. An annual summer camp is promoted where doctrines, church polity, administration, Bible study, and recreation are offered for study and enjoyment.

CALOWA WILLIAM STUMPH

SPANISH-SPEAKING PEOPLE, MISSIONS TO. The Spanish were the first explorers of most of the southern and western areas of the United States. Descendants of the original Spanish colonists still form a considerable portion of the populations of New Mexico, Colorado, and Arizona; together with their Spanish-speaking cousins from Spain, Puerto Rico, Cuba, and especially Mexico, they now make up a total Spanish-speaking population of approximately 3,500,000 within the territory of the Southern Baptist Convention. These are found in all the states, but more especially in Texas, California, New Mexico, Arizona, Colorado, and Florida. Most of them have immigrated to this country within the past 50 years. Besides those who live here, thousands come each year on contract to work in the fields for a few months and then return to Mexico.

In 1822, among the first Anglo-American colonists in Texas, New Mexico, Arizona, and California, about 1,850 were Baptists, who began to witness to the Spanish-speaking people. Organized Baptist mission work among them began in Texas in 1851, in New Mexico about 1860, in Florida in 1884. The present work began in Arizona in 1944 and in California in 1948.

Texas has approximately 325 Spanish-speaking Southern Baptist churches and missions. New Mexico has 45; Arizona, 12; California, 21; Colorado, 3; Oklahoma, 3; Missouri, 2; Michigan, 1; Louisiana, 1; Mississippi, 1; and Florida, 11. Seasonal mission work is being carried on among Mexican national migrant laborers in all these states and in Arkansas, Tennessee, Georgia, and Virginia.

In Texas the Home Mission Board has 86 Spanish-speaking missionaries (including wives); in New Mexico, 44; Arizona, 12; California, 32; Colorado, 2; Oklahoma, 2; and Florida, 8. The Baptist General Convention of Texas supports 258 missionaries. Most of the work is also supported in part by local associations or individual Anglo-American churches. Six Spanish-speaking churches are fully self-supporting in reference to current operational expenses, including pastor's salary, maintenance of property, etc. The evaluation of properties used in Spanish-speaking mission work under all Southern Baptist auspices is approximately $2,500,000. It is estimated that there are now about 25,000 Spanish-speaking Southern Baptists.

Many Spanish-speaking mission volunteers have not had the background for college and seminary or could not attend because of other circumstances. Since shortly after 1900, there have been regular preachers' institutes to help those in service to further their preparation. In 1945 there was begun also in San Antonio, Tex., a school of two weeks' duration each year known as *"La Escuela de Profetas"* to which all of the Spanish-speaking workers of the Southern Baptist Convention were invited. This has become limited practically to the workers from Texas.

From 1926 to 1941, the Paul Bell Institute in Bastrop, Tex., gave formal training to many who could not go to college or seminary. From 1936 to 1938 in San Antonio, Tex., and from 1938 to 1946 in El Paso, the Foreign Mission Board's Mexican Baptist Seminary, with the cooperation of the Home Mission Board, trained many workers who are now serving in the United States. In 1947 the Lower Rio Grande Valley Baptist Association, with the help of the Baptist General Convention of Texas and the Home Mission Board, began the Valley Baptist Academy in Brownsville, Tex., for the purpose of giving secondary academic instruction and certain practical seminary work to Spanish-speaking mission volunteers who could not yet enter college or seminary. This school recently (1956) moved to Harlingen, Tex., with an enrolment of 78. In 1947 the San Antonio Association, with the help of the Baptist General Convention of Texas, began the Mexican Baptist Bible Institute for the purpose of giving practical instruction to Spanish-speaking mission volunteers who would not be able to attend college or seminary. This school had 47 enrolled in 1956. In 1951, with the help of some of the professors of Golden Gate Seminary, there was begun in San Pablo, Calif., an institute for the training of Spanish-speaking workers. This school continued under Southern Baptist auspices through 1954. Spanish-speaking students have always been welcomed in Southern Baptist colleges and seminaries. More and more, the leadership for their mission work is coming from these institutions. Since 1941, out of the March Week of Prayer offerings, the Home Mission Board has made 590 individual annual scholarship grants to them. These have also received such ministerial scholarship assistance as is given to other ministerial students by the state conventions and the schools.

Beginning with the Mexican Baptist Convention of Texas in 1910 and continuing with the Spanish-American Baptist Convention of New Mexico in 1923 and the Association of Mexican Southern Baptists in California in 1950, the Spanish-speaking brethren have had their own separate denominational units. Of these the Mexican Baptist Convention of Texas in particular has been a strong, fully organized, and aggressive organization. However, almost all of the Spanish-speaking congregations are also affiliated with the English-speaking Southern Baptist convention of their state and are participating more and more in the full Southern Baptist program as promoted through those conventions.

In its beginning the Paul Bell Institute was also an orphanage. This service was discontinued, and there was no Baptist orphanage for Mexican children until 1944, when the Mexican Baptist Orphans Home of Texas in San Antonio was organized under the joint auspices of the Baptist General Convention of Texas and the Mexican Baptist Convention of Texas. This home now cares for 120 Mexican children and has property and assets valued at $500,000. For many years the Spanish-American Baptist Convention of New Mexico has worked toward having a Baptist orphanage in New Mexico for Spanish-speaking children. This aspiration became a reality in 1955 by the admission of Spanish-American children to the New Mexico Baptist Children's Home at Portales.

Sunday school and Training Union literature and all general Spanish literature is provided by the Foreign Mission Board's Baptist Publishing House in El Paso, Tex. The Home Mission Board provides literature in Spanish for the W.M.U. organizations of the United States, Cuba, and Panama. Brotherhood programs are provided through the Mexican Baptist Convention of Texas' publication, *El Bautista Mexicano.* The Spanish-American Baptist Convention of New Mexico publishes *El Misionero Bautista,* and the association of Mexican Southern Baptists in California publishes occasionally a paper known as *La Antorcha.*

Because there is a "captive audience" which can listen to radio without incurring resentments and social pressures from nonevangelical relatives and friends, great use is made of Spanish-speaking evangelistic radio programs. The most outstanding of these is *Hora Bautista* daily over station KLVL, Houston, Tex., under the direction of James L. Navarro, having a regular listening audience of approximately 75,000. LOYD CORDER

SPARTAN ACADEMY. Familiarly known as "S. A.," the school was founded by the Spartanburg (S. C.) Baptist Association in 1906 as a high school to train for Christian service. It was later fostered and owned by Spartan, North Spartanburg, Broad River, and Union County Baptist associations. The Home Mission Board "endorsed and helped" the academy, which was supervised and supported by the Education Commission of the Baptist convention of South Carolina.

The purpose of the founders and owners of "S. A." is achieved in the character and careers of approximately 1,500 of its students, of whom three are presidents of Baptist colleges; several, foreign missionaries; a number, pastors of Baptist churches; and many of its alumni and alumnae, serving as leaders in church and civic affairs. Known first as Spartan High School (1906–1912), then as Spartan Academy (1912–1922), it became Spartan Academy—"a fitting school of Furman University" (1922–1923). Before the girls' dormitory burned in 1922, "S. A." had become a boys' fitting school for college entrance and had ceased to be coeducational. Spartan Academy was located at Landrum, S. C., until 1915, when it moved to Groce (Lyman), S. C., on a site donated by A. B. Groce. This site and the buildings were sold in 1923 for $42,500 of which $35,000 was distributed to its owners, after debts had been paid.

BIBLIOGRAPHY: J. M. Flynn, *History of North Greenville Junior College,* (1908–1909). *The Journal and Carolina* (*Spartanburg Herald*), June 12, 1922; July 6, 1922; Dec. 11, 1922. R. F. TERRELL

SPENCER, JOHN HENDERSON (b. Allen County, Ky., Sept. 9, 1826; d. Eminence, Ky., Dec. 21, 1897). Pastor, missionary, evangelist, teacher, author, historian. The son of William and Sally Caldwell (Richey) Spencer, he was converted Jan. 19, 1849, at a "protracted meeting" at Hopewell Baptist Church and joined the church the next day. He was licensed to preach in 1853 and ordained May 6, 1854. After his ordination he entered Bethel College at Russellville, Ky., only to leave in his junior year because of illness.

He was employed as missionary of Bays Fork Association and became pastor at Cloverport, Ky., in 1857. In 1859 he decided that he was better qualified as a missionary or evangelist than as a pastor. He then served as an evangelist, either independently or as a missionary, for Nelson Association (1861), Long Run Association (1864), or the Kentucky general association (1870), organizing new churches, reviving dead churches, strengthening weak ones, helping pastors in revivals in Kentucky, Indiana, Tennessee, Illinois, and Missouri.

In 1861 Spencer married Alice Lavelia Everhart, daughter of G. W. Everhart, a steamboat captain. Mrs. Spencer died Aug. 19, 1872. Three years later, on May 11, 1875, he married Burilla Burton Waller.

"As a writer, he was strong, clear, and vigorous." In 1863 he published a pamphlet on the "Action of Baptism." He published the life of Thomas Jefferson Fisher (1812–66) in 1866. He was a principal contributor to Cathcart's *Baptist Encyclopedia.* As early as 1865, Spencer was appointed to serve on a committee of the general association to make plans for writing a history of Baptists in Kentucky. When the committee failed to procure facts or to obtain a historian, the whole matter was transferred to Spencer in 1876. After laboring nine years on this work, he submitted it to the publishers in Apr., 1885. This work was in two volumes containing over 1,400 pages.

Spencer died Dec. 21, 1897. He is buried in Bell Cemetery across from Greenwood School. LEO T. CRISMON

SPIGHT, WILLIAM REYNOLDS (b. near Salem, Miss., Oct. 11, 1863; d. Decatur, Ala., Sept. 2, 1936). Christian businessman, faithful deacon, Sunday school teacher, humanitarian, and Baptist benefactor. He was educated in Mississippi public schools and graduated from Southwestern Baptist University, Jackson, Tenn. He received the LL.D. degree from Howard College. Converted while at the university, he joined the Baptist church. Spight spent a number of years as post office inspector. He moved to Decatur in 1896 where he and John L. Brock organized a wholesale grocery business which became extremely profitable and successful. Spight also organized and owned the Home Oil Mills Company and built the Cornelian Hotel in Decatur. He amassed a large fortune. A gifted speaker, he frequently supplied pulpits in the Decatur area. He was largely instrumental in building the Benevolent Society Hospital in Decatur and served as its business director. He served on the board of trustees for Howard and Judson colleges; he gave strong financial support to the building of a new Central Baptist Church in Decatur. Greatly interested in foreign missions, he supported a missionary for many years. Spight left an estate worth more than one million dollars and directed 50 per cent of it to the Foreign Mission Board with the balance to other mission causes and ministerial education. He is interred at Decatur.

BIBLIOGRAPHY: M. B. Owen, *The Story of Alabama* (1949). *The Alabama Baptist* (Jan. 18, 1945). W. P. Wilks, *Biographical Dictionary of Alabama Baptists 1920–1947* (1947). Alabama State Convention *Annual* (1936). LESLIE S. WRIGHT

SPILMAN, BERNARD WASHINGTON (b. Weldon, N. C., Jan. 22, 1871; d. Kinston, N. C., Mar. 26, 1950). Pioneer Sunday school fieldworker. He was a graduate of Wake Forest College (B.S., 1891) and attended Southern Baptist Theological Seminary, 1892–94. After brief pastorates in Smyrna and Kinston, N. C., he was elected in 1896 as the first Sunday school missionary for North Carolina Baptists. In 1901 he became the first field secretary of the Sunday School Board of the Southern Baptist Convention and served until retirement in 1940. His *Normal Studies for Sunday School Workers,* published in 1902, initiated the first teacher training course in the denomination. As chairman of a committee seeking a site for a denominational assembly, he founded the Ridgecrest Baptist Assembly in 1907 and served successively as manager, general secretary, and president until 1933. In 1908 the Sunday School Board gave him a special assignment to visit Southern colleges and universities to encourage the teaching of religion and to enlist students in local churches. He received D.D. degrees from Stetson University, 1911; Baylor University, 1920; Wake Forest College, 1921. Besides serving as lesson writer for Sunday School Board periodicals, 1907–14 and 1920–38, Spilman wrote a number of pamphlets and the following books: *A Study in Religious Pedagogy* (1920); *The Sunday School Manual* (1924); *The Mills Home —A History of Baptist Orphanage Movement in North Carolina* (1932). After he wrote his *Normal Studies for Sunday School Workers* (1902), he led in the planning and development of the Sunday school methods books which grew out of this early work. The first such book, *The Convention Normal Manual* (1909), was a combination of Spilman's *Normal Studies for Sunday School Workers* with two others, written by Hight C Moore and Landrum Pinson Leavell (*q.v.*). Subsequent revisions were *The New Normal Manual* (1913) and *The New Convention Normal Manual* (1918). He served from 1918 to 1924 as president of the Baptist State Convention of North Carolina. Spilman was well known as a humorist, especially as a teller of Uncle Remus stories; his stature (weight, 290 pounds; height, 5 feet 6 inches) contributed to his reputation of joviality. WILLIAM J. FALLIS

SPIRIT. The word "spirit" defies complete analysis. It may mean in its Hebrew and Greek forms "wind," "breath," and "spirit." As "spirit," it is a synonym for "soul" and "heart" as the emotional, intellectual, and volitional aspects of human life (Psalm 51:10; Matt. 15:19; 16:23; Eph. 2:3). Therefore, "spirit" is used to designate the inner self of a human being (cf. Mark 2:8; John 11:33). Spirit may be contrasted with flesh (Rom. 7:14; Gal. 5:19–23), not as describing different parts of the human anatomy, but as the means of stating possible human responses to God's demands.

See also HOLY SPIRIT. W. C. STRICKLAND

SPIRITUALISM. A popular term for what is more correctly called spiritism. Spiritism may be defined as the belief that it is possible to communicate with the "spirits" of the dead so as to receive from them intelligent messages and proofs of their identity.

The whole phenomenon of spiritism is based on the presupposition that during sleep the soul or "spirit" is detached from the body and capable of wandering about while the body sleeps. Being thus independent of the body during life, the spirit survives death and is constantly seeking to return to bodily existence. The owner of a body capable of receptivity to a wandering "spirit" is technically called a medium. The theory of mediumship and the idea of using a code of signals for spelling out communications are the two foci of modern spiritualism.

Its historical emergence is associated with John D. Fox and his three daughters of Hydesville, N. Y., in 1848. One of the daughters suggested a code: three raps for yes, one for no, two for doubtful. With this code communication was established with what was claimed to be a "spirit." The three sisters became the first mediums, and the practice of sitting in circles (holding séances) for the purpose of communicating with "spirits" who answered by raps, tilts of the table, or other signals, rapidly spread over the whole world. L. E. SMITH

SPOONER, BERTA KEYS (b. Decatur, Ala., July 16, 1874; d. San Angelo, Tex., May 14, 1956). Executive secretary-treasurer of Woman's Missionary Union of Oklahoma, 1921–46. She came to Hollis, Okla., in 1905, where her husband was a successful hardware merchant. Widowed in 1910, she ran the business for six years and then went to Southwestern Baptist Theological Seminary at Fort Worth, Tex., 1916–20. She was business secretary and college visitor of the Baptist Student Missionary Movement. She received a LL.D. degree from Oklahoma Baptist University, 1939. Under her leadership pioneer work was done by the Woman's Missionary Union in fields of Indian and Negro work, the Oklahoma School of Religion building was furnished at Langston University, and Women's Memorial Dormitory at Oklahoma Baptist University was erected in 1928 at a cost of $200,000. ARGYE M. BRIGGS

SPRING MEADOWS CHILDREN'S HOME. Established as the Louisville Baptist Orphan's Home, June 30, 1869, in a rented house at 828 West Walnut Street, Louisville, Ky. George C. Lorimer, pastor of the Walnut Street Baptist Church, was one of the leaders in its founding. The charter was granted on Jan. 29, 1870, by the Kentucky legislature. It is the oldest Baptist children's home in the South under continuous operation. In Dec., 1870, the home moved to a large three-story building erected for its use at the corner of First and St. Catherine streets. In Oct., 1892, another three-story building was completed, adjoining the first structure. The charter was amended in 1947, with the home taking the new name Spring Meadows. In Jan., 1950, Spring Meadows moved to a new location at Middletown, Ky., 12 miles east of Louisville. Seven cottages and an administration building had been erected at a cost of $800,000 on an 82-acre campus. In 1953 two additional cottages were completed.

Spring Meadows is supported through a small percentage of the Cooperative Program, an annual Thanksgiving Offering, designated gifts, bequests in wills, etc. In 1953, 252 children were cared for by the home. All children attend public schools, and the children and staff attend six of the Baptist churches within reach of the home. Sam Ed Bradley serves as superintendent of the home. In 1953 the General Association of Baptists in Kentucky set up a "Board of Child Care" which became the governing body for all the Baptist children's homes in Kentucky. SAM ED BRADLEY

SPURGEON, CHARLES HADDON (b. in Kelveden, Essex, England, June 19, 1834; d. Mentone, France, Jan. 31, 1892). English Baptist preacher, author, and evangelist. He was the first child of John and Eliza Spurgeon. When Spurgeon was 10 months old his parents moved to Colchester where his father was a businessman and a successful preacher at the Independent Church at Tollesbury.

When he was 18 months old, he went to live with his grandparents because of unfavorable circumstances at home, and he lived there for six years. His grandfather, James Spurgeon, a pastor at Stambourne for 54 years, was a preacher of unusual ability.

Spurgeon never attended college, but his educational advantages were above those of many in the sphere of life in which his parents moved. He went first to Mr. Walker's school at Colchester, and afterward spent four years in the same town in the school conducted by Henry Lewis. He was also, for 12 months, at an agricultural college at Madistone, and in 1849 he went to Newmarket to be an assistant in the school of Mr. Swindell.

Spurgeon was converted on Jan. 6, 1850, at the Artillery Street Methodist Church. After his conversion he visited the poor and talked to classmates about their lives. He read the Bible night and day and became convinced that he should be baptized. On May 3, 1850, he was baptized in the Lark River by a returned Baptist missionary. He moved to Cambridge in Aug., 1850, to be an usher in a school. At Cambridge he immediately united with the St. Andrews Baptist Chapel. Before the end of 1850 he was sent out with a fellow student to the village of Taversham where he preached his first sermon on I Peter 2:7.

From Jan., 1852, to May, 1854, Spurgeon was pastor of a Baptist church at Waterbeach, five miles from Cambridge. In a short time the little thatch-roofed chapel was filled. On Apr. 19, 1854, he was called as permanent pastor by the New Park Street Baptist Church in London. Almost overnight he became London's most popular preacher.

He was married on Jan. 8, 1856, to Susannah Thompson, a member of his congregation. They had twin sons. In 1868, at the age of 33, Spurgeon's wife became a helpless invalid, but this experience really brightened the spiritual atmosphere of their home because of the extra care and consideration which she needed.

Spurgeon's church completed a new building in 1861, and its name was changed to the Metropolitan Tabernacle. For 31 years the average attendance for the morning and evening services was 5,000. During his ministry at this church a total of 14,700 members was added: 10,800 by baptism, 2,923 by letter, and 1,000 by statement and restoration. At Spurgeon's death the membership of the church was 5,307.

Besides his work as a pastor and preacher, Spurgeon engaged in many other activities. He began the Pastor's College with two students. In 1856 it had eight students, and it grew rapidly thereafter. The primary aim of the college was to provide elementary education for those who were called to preach but who lacked education. It continues at South Norwood to provide thorough training for an evangelical ministry.

The Stockwell Orphanage was started by Spurgeon and his church in 1866. A monthly paper, *The Sword and Trowel,* was begun in 1865. It was designed primarily to solicit financial aid for Spurgeon's enterprises. Day, one of Spurgeon's biographers, points out that Spurgeon was the author of 135 books, with 28 others which he edited, making, with albums and pamphlets, the unbelievable total of more than 200.

He compiled and published *Our Own Hymn Book* (1866), to which he contributed 14 psalms and 10 original hymns. The hymn by Spurgeon which he himself liked best and which has become best known is "The Holy Ghost Is Here."

Spurgeon preached his last sermon at the Metropolitan Tabernacle on Sunday morning, June 7, 1891. On Jan. 31, 1892, he died at the Hotel Beau Rivage, Mentone, France. He was buried at Norwood Cemetery. A simple monument was erected at his grave on which were inscribed these words: "Here lies the body of Charles Haddon Spurgeon Waiting for the Appearing of His Lord and Savior Jesus Christ."

BIBLIOGRAPHY: E. F. Adcock, *Charles H. Spurgeon: Prince of Preachers* (1925). R. E. Day, *The Shadow of The Broad Brim* (1934). R. Shindler, *The Life and Labors of Charles Haddon Spurgeon* (1892).

HUDSON BAGGETT

STAGG, ADOLPHE (b. near Opelousas, St. Landry Parish, La., Dec. 16, 1834; d. near Eunice, La., Apr. 17, 1914). Pioneer missionary to the French and defender of the faith. His father was a country merchant with 16 children; his mother was a Roman Catholic. His education was limited; he and his brother Etienne attended a private school taught by Thomas Rand, a Baptist minister from New England. Later both brothers became Baptists. Before his conversion in 1870 he married Ultima Carrintine, and spent four years in the Confederate army.

In 1870 he and his wife united with Mt. Olivet Baptist Church. In 1872 he was ordained and became pastor of his home church. In 1873 he was employed by the Louisiana Baptist Convention as first missionary to the French. For four years he was parish assessor; while serving as a member of the state legislature, he helped to outlaw the notorious lottery business in Louisiana. He spoke both French and English but was more fluent in French. The 1885 minutes of the Louisiana Association say, "We have only two ministers, Adolphe Stagg and J. F. Shaw, who can preach in French." For 11 years he was moderator of this association and was an outstanding leader. Always ready to defend the Baptist faith, he often debated with Catholic priests. He was buried at Pilgrim's Rest Church in Acadia Parish. T. W. GAYER

STAKELY, CHARLES AVERETT (b. Madisonville, Monroe County, Tenn., Mar. 3, 1859; d. Montgomery, Ala., May 22, 1937). Pastor, builder of churches, and denominational leader. His father was a Confederate soldier, Captain Samuel Smith Stakely (the name in German was Stöckl), and his mother was the former Susan Frances Fonville (French, de Fontvieille). Stakely married Sarah Jessie Davis on Feb. 15, 1882. His children were Davis Fonville, Anne Kilpatrick (Mrs. Henry F. Martin), Frances Sloan (Mrs. James D. Willcox), Flora McIver (Mrs. Aurelian H. Coolidge), and Charles A., Jr.

During the Civil War Stakely's mother moved with her children to Lowndes (later Crenshaw) County, Ala. After the war the family settled in Montgomery. Here Charles was baptized by D. W. Gwin "at age of about 13." His father died in 1872, and the family moved to LaGrange, Ga. There he attended high school and studied law in the law firm of Tuggle and Cox. He was admitted to the bar at 18, the first solicitor appointed under the county court system in Georgia. He practiced law till he was 22.

Stakely was ordained to the ministry in 1880. He left the law practice and accepted pastorates at Elberton and Hartwell, Ga. Other pastorates were at Augusta, Ga. (very brief); Citadel Square Baptist Church, Charleston, S. C. (1884–87); First Baptist Church, Washington, D. C. (1887–1900); First Baptist Church, Montgomery, Ala. (1900 to retirement in 1929). He received several honorary degrees: A.M. from Mercer University, 1884; D.D. from Richmond University; LL.D., from Furman University; and another from the University of Alabama.

His training as a lawyer made him a forceful speaker. His sermons were brief and to the point, often lasting only 15 minutes. His ability and Christian spirit kept him in constant demand. He served his denomination well and in high places. He was trustee of Southern Baptist Theological Seminary for 36 years; twice moderator of Columbia Association of Baptist Churches (Washington, D. C.); trustee for 13 years of Columbian College or University (now George Washington University); trustee of Wayland University (Negro—later to become Union Theological College, Richmond, Va.); member of a committee of the American Baptist Publication Society; and trustee of Alabama State Teachers College (Negro), Montgomery, Ala.

His progressiveness was evident from many angles. He was founder of Charleston Ministerial Association (interdenominational) and helped found the Washington Ministers Club (interdenominational). He moved his last two churches and built imposing houses of worship. He served on the state mission board from 1900 to 1929. He was elected pastor emeritus for life, upon retirement from First Baptist Church, Montgomery. He was a Mason.

He wrote many articles for magazines and compiled and helped to write *The History of the First Baptist Church of Montgomery.*

BIBLIOGRAPHY: J. W. Abercrombie, *Dr. Charles Averett Stakely—His Services to Education* (1936). Alabama Baptist State Convention, *Annuals* (1874–1942). *Alabama Blue Book and Social Register* (1929). W. B. Crumpton, *A Book of Memories 1842–1920* (1921); *Our Baptist Centennials* (1923). T. M. Owen, *History of Alabama and Dictionary of Alabama Biography,* Vol. 4 (1921). B. F. Riley, *A Memorial History of the Baptists of Alabama* (1923). H. W. Samson, "The Rev. Charles Averett Stakely, D.D. LL.D." (MS, 1936). P. H. Smyth, "Charles Averett Stakely" (MS, 1936). C. A. Stakely, *The History of the First Baptist Church of Montgomery* (1930). W. P. Wilks, *Biographical Dictionary of Alabama Baptists 1920–1947* (1947).

GARNETT EATON PUCKETT

STALCUP, JOSEPH COLE (b. Athens, Tenn., Feb. 20, 1851; d. McAlester, Okla., May 26, 1938). School teacher, court clerk, businessman, and denominational leader. He served the Baptist General Convention of Indian Territory as president 1900–1903 and as corresponding secretary 1903–06. In 1906 he led in the organization of the Baptist General Convention of Oklahoma and served as its corresponding secretary 1906–16 and as president 1916–20. He led the convention to adopt single alignment in 1914, helped to found Oklahoma Baptist University, and was superintendent of Baptist hospitals at Miami, Okla., in 1919 and Muskogee in 1920.

BIBLIOGRAPHY: L. V. Stalcup, *Life and Labors of J. C. Stalcup* (1937). HARRY M. ROARK

STANDARD. A weekly paper, originally started as a semimonthly in Chicago, Ill., by C. B. Smith on Sept. 20, 1842, under the name of *Northwestern Baptist.* It was the first periodical published in that city, and was the official organ of the Northwestern Baptist Convention. Neutrality on the slavery issue caused suspension early in 1845 after the First Baptist Church split over slavery and Smith, the pastor, left the city. In Feb., 1845, *The Western Star,* a weekly started Jan. 7, 1845, and published at Jacksonville, Ill., by Alvin Bailey, under the sponsorship of the Baptist General Association of Illinois, took over the subscription list. On Aug. 10, 1847, Luther Stone (Sept. 26, 1815—July 9, 1890) purchased it, removed it to Chicago, and edited it under the name *Watchman of the Prairies.* He sold the paper, and the name was changed to *Christian Times* on Aug. 31, 1853; it was "edited by an association of clergymen," J. C. Burroughs, pastor of First Baptist Church, chief, A. J. Josyln, and H. G. Weston. In Apr., 1858, the first *Illinois Baptist* was consolidated with the paper. The Indiana *Witness* of Indianapolis, started by M. G. Clarke, consolidated on Aug. 31, 1865, with the *Times* and was called the *Christian Times and Witness* until Dec. 19, 1867, when another consolidation took place with the *Michigan Christian Herald* (started 1842), edited by G. W. Harris. The paper was renamed the *Standard* in 1867. J. A. Smith and Leroy Church served as editors. Church sold his interest in the paper in 1875 to J. C. Dickerson. Dickerson died Mar. 21, 1876, and his interest was taken over by his oldest son, J. S. Dickerson, who served on the editorial staff until 1903. The *Ensign,* a Baptist paper of Minneapolis, Minn., was purchased and combined with the paper Aug. 10, 1893. Smith died Feb. 4, 1896, after serving 42 years as editor-in-chief.

On Mar. 16, 1896, John R. Slater became one of the editors. In June, 1901, R. N. Van Doren joined the editorial staff and served until 1912. In Sept., 1901, the *Outlook,* Indianapolis, Ind., was purchased and merged with the paper. In June, 1920, the paper was discontinued and was succeeded by *The Baptist,* which was discontinued in 1932 and its subscription list merged with *Christian Century.*

BENJAMIN JACKSON MURRIE

STANDARDS OF EXCELLENCE. A term denoting statements which embody the accepted standards of procedure and achievement for certain church organizations. They are designed to set forth a program of work and to measure efficiency in doing the work undertaken.

Training Union Standards of Excellence.—The first Standard of Excellence for a B.Y.P.U. appeared in *The B.Y.P.U. Manual* by Landrum Pinson Leavell (*q.v.*), published by the Sunday School Board in 1907. It was stated as follows:

Section I

Organization

1. Attendance. An average attendance of at least one half the enrolment.
2. Officers. Have at least the following: President, Vice-President, Secretary, Treasurer.
3. Committees. Have at least the following: Membership, Devotional, and Social.
4. Reports. At least once per quarter each officer and each committee will read to the union a written report of work done.

Section II

Educational Work

1. Bible Reader's Course. At least one half the enroled membership keeping up with the Daily Readings.
2. Monthly Missionary Meetings. One missionary meeting per month, based upon topic outlined in "The B.Y.P.U. Quarterly."
3. Study Course. Each year at least one study or thirteen weeks as recommended by the Educational Committee of the B.Y.P.U. of the South.
4. Developing the Individual. At least once per quarter, each active member takes part in the open meeting, apart from singing.

This standard was intended to be a fair average for B.Y.P.U.'s to attain. Its aim was to indicate the difference between a young people's prayer meeting and a real B.Y.P.U.

By 1914 the Standard of Excellence for a B.Y.P.U. had been recast and stated in three divisions (organization, meetings, and educational work) of three statements each. As stated then, the purpose of the Standard was to "set forth clearly and briefly the essential elements in an efficient B.Y.P.U." A Standard of Excellence for a Junior B.Y.P.U. (ages 13–16) similar to the Standard for a B.Y.P.U. appeared in 1914 also.

The state B.Y.P.U. secretaries in their annual conference at the Sunday School Board, Jan. 1, 1925, officially adopted the Standard of Excellence for a General B.Y.P.U. Organization. Any Baptist church with at least one each of the Junior, Intermediate, and Senior unions was encouraged to set up the general organization and reach and maintain this standard. In 1931 the Standard of Excellence adopted in 1925 was completely revised to take care of the rapidly developing organization. This revision went into effect in 1932. It presented a program of training—"an outline of essential things to be done in training young Christians in church membership." The values of the Standard of Excellence became so apparent that Standards were developed for all departments and unions as well as the general and the associational Training Union organizations. These are constantly revised as changing conditions demand restudy.

Sunday school Standards of Excellence.—The first Standard of Excellence for Baptist Sunday schools was adopted by the Sunday School Field Workers Association of the Southern Baptist Convention May 13, 1908. Harvey Beauchamp (*q.v.*), field secretary of the Baptist Sunday School Board, led in planning and presenting it. It recognized three classes of schools, "A," "B," and "C," and three grades in each class. The requirements of any class or grade included all in the grades below. The nine grades listed were as follows:

Class A. The School Graded

Grade 1.—The school graded and using our Supplemental Lessons (or others equal to them). Graded on the following plan: Primary 0–8 (Cradle Roll 0–3, Beginners 4–5, Main Primary 6–8); Junior 9–12; Intermediate 13–15; Senior 16–20; Adult 20–up. Adults may be included in the senior in a small school. A Teacher-Training (or Normal) Class, and at least one Organized Class for men and one for women.

Departments Separated

Grade 2.—Primary and Junior Departments organized and occupying their own quarters, separated from the rest of the school by walls or movable partitions (or at least curtains). Classrooms or curtained space for at least 50 per cent of the remaining classes.

Church Members Enroled

Grade 3.—Seventy-five per cent of the church members to which the school belongs enroled in the Sunday school, including the Home Department; and the average attendance in the main school, 75 per cent of its enrolment.

Class B. Normal Course

Grade 1.—Our Normal Course Diploma, held by at least 50 per cent of the officers and teachers, or the Reading Course certificate by at least 75 per cent of the officers and teachers.

Regular Teachers' Meetings

Grade 2.—Regular teachers' meetings, attended by at least 50 per cent of the officers and teachers.

Bible Used in School

Grade 3.—Bibles used in the school session by scholars, instead of quarterlies. The use of both Bibles and quarterlies discouraged when the teacher is testing the scholar's lesson study.

Class C. School Under Church Control

Grade 1.—School under control of the church—making stated reports to the church—church electing officers and teachers—school contributing annually to at least two general causes fostered by the church.

Baptist Literature

Grade 2.—Use of only Baptist literature by scholars recommended by the school.

A Perennial School

Grade 3.—A session of the school every month in the year.

The Sunday School Standard of Excellence as revised in 1913 was, in the main, the same Standard as that stated by the Sunday School Field Workers Association of the Southern Baptist Convention in 1908. The differences were: (1) The three classes of schools, formerly established as Class "A," Class "B," and Class "C," with three grades "1," "2," "3" within each class, were abolished and one Standard of Excellence for Baptist Sunday schools was established. (2) The more compact Standard of 1913 contained all of the same features as the Standard of 1908, but added a section on evangelism—"making special appeals to the unconverted to accept Christ."

By 1918 an Advanced Standard or AA-1 had been placed in service. Beauchamp also played the major role in its development. A report to the Southern Baptist Convention that year stated: "Our field workers and our Sunday school forces generally declare that the A-1 Standard for Sunday schools has brought unmeasured blessings. This standard has been carefully revised, and yet a higher Standard (AA-1) has been erected. Attention has also been given to special class and department standards. These are involved in the general Sunday school standards mentioned above, but are also issued and applied separately to classes and departments." By 1919 standards had been developed for the following areas: Intermediate, Senior, and Adult classes and departments. An increasing number of classes reported having reached many of the requirements and having received stimulation for all class activities.

By 1920 the following Sunday school Standards had been developed and were in use in the churches of the Convention: (1) A-1 Standard; (2) AA-1 Standard; (3) Department Standards; (4) Class Standards.

The first Standard of Excellence for Vacation Bible schools appeared in the *Daily Vacation Bible School Guide* in 1926. It was developed on the point basis. Each of the eight sections had an assigned point value. The total possible points was 1,000. In 1956 the Standard had two divisions, A and B. Division A related to achievements possible in every school. The total point value remained at 1,000 with 10 sections with assigned point values. Division B covered 19 items not included in Division A. Many of these could be achieved by any school. The points made could be several hundred depending upon what each school was able to do. If the points made in Division B totaled 300 or more on 10 or more of the 19 sections of Division B, the school was given a final rating doubling the grade achieved under the requirements of Division A. Thus a grade "A" school would become "AA"; a grade "B" school, "BB"; etc.

The Vacation Bible school Standard is considered primarily a measuring instrument. The principal may use it before the school to determine if the faculty is ready. He may use it during the school to determine what is and what is not being done. After the school he may use it to see how effective the school was.

Church music Standards of Excellence.—The Church Music Department of the Sunday School Board fosters three Standards of Excellence in the promotion of better church music. They are the Standard and the Advanced Standard for the music program of a Baptist church, also one for an associational music organization. Requirements of the first Standards were worked out in 1954 by a committee of state music secretaries with representatives of the Church Music Department of the board. The Standards became effective on Oct. 1, 1954. These Standards were revised in 1956 and the revisions went into use in October of that year.

The Standard of Excellence for a church music program has 10 sections. The Advanced Standard has additional requirements beyond the first Standard and is organized under five general sections. There are eight divisions within the associational Standard of Excellence. Standard requirements must be met for one quarter and the leaders must be satisfied Standard work is being done before the award is issued.

W. L. HOWSE

STARKVILLE FEMALE INSTITUTE. Established about 1868 in Starkville, Miss., with T. G. Sellers president. Considered Baptist although it was a private institution, it had its peak attendance of 186 in 1885. The institute was sold to the city in 1892. J. L. BOYD

STATE MISSIONS. One of the three general divisions of the Southern Baptist program of missions. The other divisions are home missions and foreign missions. These divisions are based on the territory or field of work covered by each of three mission agencies, and not on differences of functions.

The field of work covered by state missions is limited to the area of a given state, or a state convention which may include the area of more than one state like that of Oregon and Washington. That of home missions covers all the states within the bounds of the Southern Baptist Convention, and includes some border states and Alaska, Panama, and Cuba. The foreign mission field of work includes all the nations of the world outside the United States where Southern Baptists may find missionary opportunities.

The churches affiliated with each of the state conventions foster a program of state missions. The Southern Baptist Convention program of home missions and foreign missions is fostered by all the churches in the various states of the Convention. Each state convention elects an executive board which is commonly known as a state mission board. This board is charged with the responsibility of promoting a program of missions in the area covered by the convention. The Southern Baptist Convention elects a home mission board and a foreign mission board to promote the work of home missions and foreign missions respectively. Southern Baptists have one home mission board, one foreign mission board, and 23 state mission boards, one for each state convention. Each of these mission boards has an executive secretary, who is elected by the board and has general supervision over its work.

The program of state missions varies in the several states according to the needs in each particular state. The needs differ in the territory covered by each of the state conventions, and the state mission program is organized to meet these needs. The work is organized into several departments such as evangelism, rural missions, city missions, Sunday school, Training Union, Baptist Student Union, Baptist Brotherhood, music, mission pastors, Negro work, Indian missions, aid in church building, and others. Perhaps no state board will find a need for all of these departments of work in a given state. Also in some states two or more departments may be combined. A departmental secretary, who is elected by the state board, is placed in charge of each department or combined departments. Associated with him is a staff of workers, the number being determined by the needs of each particular department in a given state. The departmental secretaries and associates work under the general supervision of the state executive secretary.

Even though the several state mission boards, the Home Mission Board, and the Foreign Mission Board are each independent of the others, there is a close co-operation between all of these boards in a united missionary effort. The work of state missions does not stop with the boundaries of a given state. It is the home base for all missions and it promotes all missions. It seeks to lead the individual Baptists and the churches in the state to have a concern for all missions, and to share in the support of the program of world missions as carried on by both the state conventions and the Southern Baptist Convention.

The territory of the Home Mission Board overlaps that of the several state boards. The Home Mission Board co-operates in a special way with the state boards by extending financial assistance and other aid according to the needs. Also the Sunday School Board of the Southern Baptist Convention co-operates with the various state boards by granting financial assistance, and by furnishing literature and the help of its workers in several departments of state missions especially in the educational phases.

The promotion of all the causes fostered by both the state conventions and the Southern Baptist Convention is channeled in the main through the state boards. Also almost all of the funds contributed by the churches for the support of both state convention causes and Southern Baptist Convention causes are channeled through the state boards. The state boards through their executive secretaries, who are usually the boards' treasurers, are charged with the responsibility of receiving all Cooperative Program or designated funds for denominational causes, and of disbursing them to state and Southern Baptist Convention causes as instructed by the several state conventions or the contributing churches or individuals.

A. HAMILTON REID

STATISTICS AND RECORDS. At a meeting of the Southern Baptist Convention on May 10, 1882, at Greenville, S. C., Lansing Burrows (*q.v.*), one of the secretaries of the Convention, presented the first statistical report. It was referred to a special committee. In a later session of the Convention, Gustavus Alonzo Nunnally, chairman of the committee, said, "We regard the report as perhaps the most valuable contribution which has been made to the history of Southern Baptists in many years. . . . We recommend that it be published in the Minutes of this Convention . . . and that he [Burrows] be requested to continue in the good work." Burrows served as the statistician of the Convention from this date until his death in 1919.

In 1918 the Convention transferred the responsibility of gathering statistics to the Sunday School Board; and upon the death of Burrows, the work was temporarily assigned to Hight C Moore. In 1921 Eugene Perry Alldredge (*q.v.*) came to the board as secretary of the Department of Survey, Statistics, and Information. In stating the purpose of the new department, Isaac Jacobus Van Ness (*q.v.*) said in his report to the 1921 Convention: "We propose to do something more than number our people. . . . We need to know ourselves, and to know ourselves

ARIZONA BAPTIST BUILDING, Phoenix. Acquired 1956, costing $180,000. Houses all departments of state work.

FLORIDA BAPTIST CONVENTION (*q.v.*) BUILDING, Jacksonville. Purchased in 1924, now valued at $300,000. Home of all state departments, *Baptist Witness*, and book store.

ILLINOIS STATE CONVENTION BUILDING (q.v.), Carbondale. Completed in 1954, now valued at $500,-000. Headquarters for nine departments.

MISSOURI BAPTIST BUILDING, Jefferson City. State headquarters since 1949. The $260,000 home of 12 branches of work.

with accuracy. We must study unflinchingly for the facts. In addition, we propose to study and inform ourselves about religious conditions in the South, in the nation, and in the world."

Alldredge compiled in 1921 the first issue of the *Southern Baptist Handbook,* an annual publication of vital statistics. In 1941 *The Quarterly Review,* a new informational publication dealing with statistics, history, and analysis of trends in Southern Baptist life, was published. Alldredge, upon retirement in 1945, was succeeded by Porter Routh, during whose administration the board installed IBM calculating machines, making possible a more detailed study of the characteristics of the Baptist population and achievements. Routh served the department until he became executive secretary of the Executive Committee of the Southern Baptist Convention in 1951. He was succeeded by Jacob Pinckney Edmunds, at that time associate secretary of the Sunday School Department of the Sunday School Board.

Church clerks, associational clerks, state statistical secretaries, and others co-operate with the Department of Survey, Statistics, and Information in getting vital statistics from every church on all phases of Southern Baptist life. In addition, the department on its own initiative and upon request, makes special studies and surveys each year in all areas of Baptist life. The results of its annual compilations and special surveys are shared with the Baptist constituency through the *Southern Baptist Handbook, The Quarterly Review,* and the weekly news release called the *Survey Bulletin,* the three publications of the department. J. P. EDMUNDS

STAUGHTON, WILLIAM (b. Coventry, Warwickshire, England, Jan. 4, 1770; d. Washington, D. C., Dec. 12, 1829). Minister and educator. The son of Sutton and Keziah Staughton, he was educated at Bristol Baptist College. As a student he attended the meeting in Kettering, England, on Oct. 2, 1792, at which the Particular Baptist Society for Propagating the Gospel amongst the Heathen was organized. He signed as "a Friend" the historic original document that set forth the objective of this pioneer mission society, and considered the half a guinea he contributed "the best achievement of his life." In 1793 he removed to America and, at the request of Richard Furman (*q.v.*), became a pastor at Georgetown, S. C. Eighteen months later he went to New Jersey, established seminaries, and preached at Bordentown and Burlington. He was ordained at Bordentown June 17, 1797, and received the D.D. degree from Princeton in 1798. His long-time ministry was in Philadelphia, at the First Baptist Church and at Sansom Street Baptist Church, which was organized in 1811 as an outgrowth of the First Church. While at Sansom Street, he gave instruction for a year to John Mason Peck (*q.v.*) and to seven other young men who lived in his home and were given lectures on the "doctrines and duties of the Christian religion, on the ministerial office and the composition of sermons . . . Latin, Greek, and Hebrew."

From 1822 to 1827 he served as the first president of Columbian College (later George Washington University). In 1829 he died while on the way to Kentucky to assume the presidency of Georgetown College. He held important denominational offices: recording secretary of the Philadelphia Bible Society, a founder of the Baptist Education Society of the Middle States, corresponding secretary and president of the Board of Governors of the General Convention of the Baptist Denomination in the United States for Foreign Missions (the Triennial Convention).

He married first Maria Hanson (died 1823), by whom he had four children, and second Anna Claypoole Peale, whom he married shortly before his death. For years he was the outstanding preacher in Philadelphia, where he preached four sermons each Sunday, taught daily, and exerted a significant influence on missions and education.

BIBLIOGRAPHY: W. A. Allison, "William Staughton," *Dictionary of American Biography* (1935). W. Cathcart, ed., *The Baptist Encyclopaedia* (1883). *Daily National Intelligencer* (Washington, D. C., Dec. 14, 1829). S. W. Lynd, *Memoir of the Rev. William Staughton, D.D.* (1834). WINSTON C. BABB

STEALEY, CLARENCE PERRY (b. Shinnston, W. Va., Apr. 15, 1868; d. Oklahoma City, Okla., Feb. 11, 1937). Baptist minister, editor, denominational leader, and controversialist. At the age of 18 he moved to Lincoln, Neb., as Y.M.C.A. secretary. He held pastorates at First Baptist Church, Martinsburg, W. Va. (1896–1901); Broadus Memorial Church, Richmond, Va. (1901–05); and West Washington Baptist Church, Washington, D. C. (1905–09). He moved to Oklahoma and in 1912 founded the *Baptist Messenger;* he was editor of the *Messenger* until 1928. He became pastor of the Hudson Avenue Baptist Church, Oklahoma City, Apr. 11, 1929, and remained there until his death. An outspoken fundamentalist, he opposed the teaching of evolution and caused much controversy in the 1920's. He is buried at Oklahoma City.

J. M. GASKIN

STEALEY CONTROVERSY, OKLAHOMA. Centered mainly in fundamentalist agitation led by Clarence Perry Stealey (*q.v.*), editor, *Baptist Messenger,* 1912–27, against alleged modernism and evolutionary teachings in Southern Baptist educational institutions. He sought unsuccessfully to get anti-evolution resolutions passed by the Southern Baptist Convention in 1924, but he succeeded in 1925. His support of the (Southern Baptist Convention) McDaniel statement and the (Oklahoma) Morris resolution (withholding state financial support from such schools where administration and faculty failed to sign creedal statements rejecting evolutionary theories of man's origin) eventuated in his removal from editorship Dec. 13, 1927, by a vote of 13 to 7 by the board of directors of the Baptist General Convention of Oklahoma. The opposition was led by J. W. Bruner and Andrew Potter (*q.v.*). Stealey immediately established *The Baptist Trumpet,* Jan., 1928, through which the controversy was continued with diminishing bitterness until publication of the *Trumpet* was suspended Apr. 22, 1938. By that time it had become merely the official organ of the Hudson Avenue Baptist Church, Oklahoma City, where Stealey was pastor. ROGER D. HEBARD

STEARNS, SHUBAL (b. Boston, Mass., Jan. 28, 1706; d. Sandy Creek, N. C., Nov. 20, 1771). Preacher. Son of Shubal and Rebecca (Larriford) Stearns, Stearns received little formal education, but he read extensively. About 1745, influenced by "Whitefield's evangelical zeal," he joined the New Lights, and after preaching among them until *c.* 1751, he joined the Baptists at Tolland, Conn. Baptized by Wait Palmer, he was a short while later ordained to the ministry by Palmer and Joshua Moss (or Morse).

Moving to Opeckon Creek, Berkeley County, Va., in 1754, he joined his brother-in-law, Daniel Marshall (*q.v.*). The two preached for a time in Hampshire County, but were disappointed with the response. Learning of a strong desire for the gospel among the fast-growing population of Piedmont, N. C., Stearns set out with a company of eight families for that region. They arrived at Sandy Creek in present Randolph County, Nov. 14, 1755; within a short time they built a small meetinghouse and formed a Separate Baptist Church (Sandy Creek), with 16 members. Stearns served as pastor, and Daniel Marshall and Joseph Breed were his assistants.

The response to the work of this church was immediate. Within three years it had increased to three churches—Sandy Creek, Abbott's Creek, and Deep River—with more than 900 members. Morgan Edwards asserts,

> All the separate baptists [*sic*] sprang hence: not only eastward towards the sea, but westward towards the great river Mississippi, but northward to Virginia and southward to South Carolina and Georgia. The word went forth from this sion, and great was the company of them who published it, in so much that her converts were as the drops of morning dew.

In 17 years 42 churches and 125 ministers had sprung from this church.

In 1758 Stearns led in organizing the Sandy Creek Baptist Association. Messengers from Sandy Creek, Abbott's Creek, and Deep River churches attended a preliminary meeting in January, and a larger gathering, including messengers from Little River, Neuse River, Black River, Dan River, Grassy Creek churches in North Carolina, and Pittsylvania City and Lunenburg City churches in Virginia, was held in June. After 12 years, as a matter of convenience, the association was divided into three distinct bodies—the General Association of Virginia, the Sandy Creek Association in North Carolina, and the Congaree Association in South Carolina.

A preacher of unusual power, Stearns was small in stature but forceful in personality. He was the recognized leader of the Separate Baptists in the southeastern colonies. A prime influence in their rapid spread, he helped to stamp them firmly with both a modified Calvinistic doctrine and an evangelistic zeal.

J. ALLEN EASLEY

STEPHENS, EDWIN WILLIAM (b. Columbia, Mo., Jan. 21, 1849; d. Columbia, Mo., May 22, 1931). Journalist and denominational leader, who had the unique distinction of serving as an executive officer for three Baptist conventions. He was educated at the University of Missouri (A.B., 1867; A.M., 1870), received the LL.D. degree from the University of Missouri and from William Jewell College, and was an honorary member of Phi Beta Kappa. In 1870 he bought an interest in the *Boone County Journal,* soon gained complete control, and until 1905 edited and published the paper, which he renamed the *Columbia Herald.* Good writing and good printing made the paper "America's Model Weekly." He also established flourishing printing companies in Jefferson City and Columbia.

Stephens served in the following positions: moderator of Missouri Baptist General Association (20 years, except one year while on world tour); president of Southern Baptist Convention; vice-president of Northern Baptist Convention; first president of General Convention of Baptists of North America; vice-president and American treasurer of Baptist World Alliance university in Russia; treasurer of Roger Williams Memorial Church Fund, Washington, D. C.; president of Missouri Home and Foreign Mission Board; president of Missouri Baptist Hospital; president of board of curators of Stephens College (40 years); president of Missouri University curators; building chairman of National Baptist Memorial Church, Washington, D. C.; deacon and deacon emeritus of the First Baptist Church, Columbia, Mo., until the time of his death; and chairman of commission which erected Missouri State Capitol Building.

H. H. MCGINTY

STETSON UNIVERSITY. Located at De Land, Fla., Stetson is the product of a merger of De Land Academy, founded in 1883 by Henry A. De Land, a Baptist from Fairport, N. Y., with Florida Baptists' plan to establish "a female academy." The resulting "De Land College" came into being as "a Christian school for both sexes" in 1886, and the following year it obtained from the state legislature a permanent charter for its existence as "De Land University." Because of "the generous gifts" to the university of John B. Stetson, Philadelphia hat manufacturer, also a Baptist, the trustees changed the school's name to John B. Stetson University in 1889. Since 1951 the shortened form of the title has been used for all except legal purposes.

The university charter, framed by the founder, Henry A. De Land, with the advice of the first president of the school, John F. Forbes, conformed generally to the charters of independent Christian universities of that period; it was modeled after the charter of the University of Rochester. Stetson's charter provides for an independent, self-perpetuating board of 24 trustees, three fourths of whom "shall be members of the Baptist denomination in good standing in their several churches." Contrary to the practice in some Southern states, De Land thus created an independent Baptist university with "absolutely no organic relation of any kind with the Florida Baptist Convention and no control of any kind except that . . . provided for in the charter." As though "to the denomination," De Land deeded the entire property of De Land Academy to the board of trustees and added $10,000 for endowment, to be matched by "the denomination in the State at large." When fund-raising proved almost impossibly difficult and only $4,000 of the $10,000 promised by the constituency was paid, the secretary of the Florida Baptist Convention repudiated the note on the grounds it had been made "by individuals and not by the State Board of Missions. . . ." Misunderstanding of the contractual nature of the charter and of the founders' insistence that the university rest upon a legislative charter not subject to amendment as the condition of their gifts, led the convention in 1907 to an unsuccessful attempt to change the charter so as to give full ownership and direct control to the convention. Failing in this effort, the state body established a new school, Columbia College, and withdrew all support from the university.

Stetson found itself, therefore, almost entirely dependent upon its original benefactor and others whom he interested. John Stetson, in a variety of personal benefactions and others through members of his family, gave the university almost a half-million dollars during its first 20 years and thus provided it with the main outline of its present campus and buildings. Other large benefactors of that period included C. T. Sampson, whose interest created the library, which early became the first United States Government Document Depositary in Florida; Henry M. Flagler, who anonymously gave funds for the erection of Flagler Science Hall; Andrew Carnegie, who donated $40,000 toward the library building; John D. Rockefeller, who added $150,000 to the endowment through the General Education Board; and the American Baptist Education Society.

Convinced that there was "a demand in this State for a Christian school that would offer to both young men and young women a collegiate training equal in breadth and thoroughness to the best given in our country," the founders chose a strong faculty which soon established a tradition of high scholarship. The College of Liberal Arts required from its beginning 16 Carnegie units for admission and four years work for the bachelor's degree. Since many other schools of the region were content with a three-year program, Stetson was one of the first colleges in the South to establish more rigorous requirements. It also had an unusual reciprocal agreement for the exchange of students with the University of Chicago. Curricula in music, art, business, and teacher training were added before 1900, and in October of that year, the first law curriculum in Florida was inaugurated.

When Columbia College collapsed in 1919, harmonious relations between the Florida Baptist Convention and the university were resumed. In that year the two agreed that a majority of the members of the university board of trustees should be Florida Baptists approved by the convention. In return, the convention resolved to "throw its whole influence, moral, religious and financial," to the support of the university. Since that occasion, relations between the two have become increasingly close, reaching the highest level of co-operation in the entire history of both during the 1940's and '50's, when the convention contributed capital gifts of nearly one and one-half million dollars to the university. It began making annual appropriations for the school's operating expenses in 1931.

During the presidency of Lincoln B. Hulley (1904–34), while the size of the university grew to an average student body of 500, accreditation was obtained from the regional association; the College of Law was recognized by the American Bar Association; the first summer session in Florida was held; and the Stover Little Theatre pioneered in dramatics. Curricular expansion and fresh upgrading of standards characterized the administration of William Sims Allen (1934–47). The department of music became a co-ordinate college of the university and obtained accreditation in 1936. Four years later the School of Business also became a co-ordinate college.

During the administration of J. Ollie Edmunds (1948–), general education and American studies programs were initiated, and Stetson was invited to participate in the Washington Semester of the American University. Approval of the American Association of University Women was won; a chapter of Omicron Delta Kappa was installed; the financial base of the university was broadened; and an alumni and development program was established. The Florida Baptist Convention erected Allen Hall, a religious center in memory of President Allen. New dormitories, housing 250 men and 120 women, were completed in 1954–55, and a combined commons and student union building was erected. In 1954 the College of Law was moved to St. Petersburg.

During the academic year 1955–56 enrolment of regular students totaled 1,325, and the faculty numbered 110 on the De Land campus, which comprised 50 acres with 30 buildings, valued at $5,000,000. Nine faculty members and 138 students were located at St. Petersburg. The educational budget for the year was $1,305,000, and the productive endowment approximately $1,-700,000. Plans for the Diamond Jubilee projected a new library, fine arts center, recreational facilities, and a science center.

C. HOWARD HOPKINS

STEWARDSHIP. A Bible doctrine relating to the use of all of life and property, which involves partnership with God and is fundamentally concerned, not with material property, but with spiritual surrender. Because stewardship is in essence simply the practice of the Christian religion in all areas of life, it is not so much man's plan for raising money as God's pattern for Christian growth. The principles of stewardship, which emphasize personal responsibility for one's own life and for the proper administration of one's endowments, talents, and property, are basic to Christianity. With the coming of state-supported churches after the establishment of the Roman Church, members lost their sense of personal responsibility, and the active practice of stewardship largely disappeared, to be rediscovered centuries later by missionary Christians and by free church congregations. Baptists have grown in strength as they have grown in the practice of stewardship, in spite of the fact that they have never come very close to the practice of the biblical ideal.

Stewardship in the Bible.—Jesus and the writers of the Bible had more to say about the right use of property than about any other single theme. The Bible teachings may be summarized in these statements: (1) Nothing belongs to man; all is God's, who made all things and is sovereign over them—"In the beginning God created the heaven and the earth" (Gen. 1:1; Psalm 24:1; Hag. 2:8). (2) All one's life, talents, opportunities, and income are without exception held as a trust from God, to be used to accomplish his purpose—"For of him, and through him, and to him, are all things: . . . I beseech you therefore, . . . present your bodies a living sacrifice . . . unto God" (Rom. 11:36 to 12:1; Matt. 25:15–21). (3) Everyone must give an account to God for his use of everything—"Every one of us shall give account of himself to God" (Rom. 14:12; Luke 16:2; I Cor. 4:2). (4) The tithe is the Lord's, and to return it to him is right, beneficial to the Christian, and the beginning point for larger Christian liberality—"Will a man rob God? . . . Bring ye all the tithes into the storehouse" (Mal. 3:8–10; Lev. 27:30; Matt. 23:23). (5) The Christian gives more, not less, than the law requires, because he has cause for greater gratitude—"Unto whomsoever much is given, of him shall much be required" (Luke 12:48). (6) Through faithful stewardship one conquers covetousness and lays up treasures for eternity—"Take heed, and beware of covetousness." (Luke 12:15; Col. 3:5). "Lay not up . . . treasures upon earth . . . but . . . in heaven" (Matt. 6:19–20). (7) The Christian is to give with liberality—"Freely ye have

Number of Southern Baptist Churches Giving Specified Size Mission Gifts, 1955

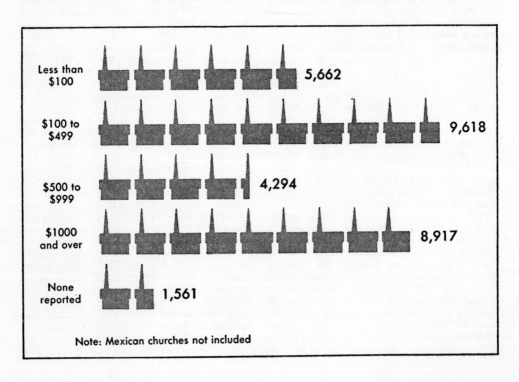

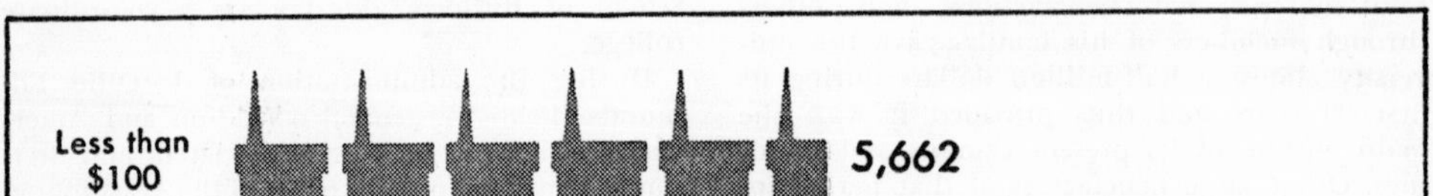

received, freely give" (Matt. 10:8); "the churches of Macedonia . . . in a great trial of affliction the abundance of their joy and their deep poverty abounded unto the riches of their liberality" (II Cor. 8:1–2); sacrificially—"For to their power . . . and beyond their power they were willing of themselves" (II Cor. 8:3; Acts 4:31–37); and cheerfully—"Every man according as he purposeth in his heart, so let him give: not grudgingly, or of necessity: for God loveth a cheerful giver" (II Cor. 9:7). (8) Each one is to give regularly—"Upon the first day of the

Growth of Per Capita Total Gifts 1947–1955

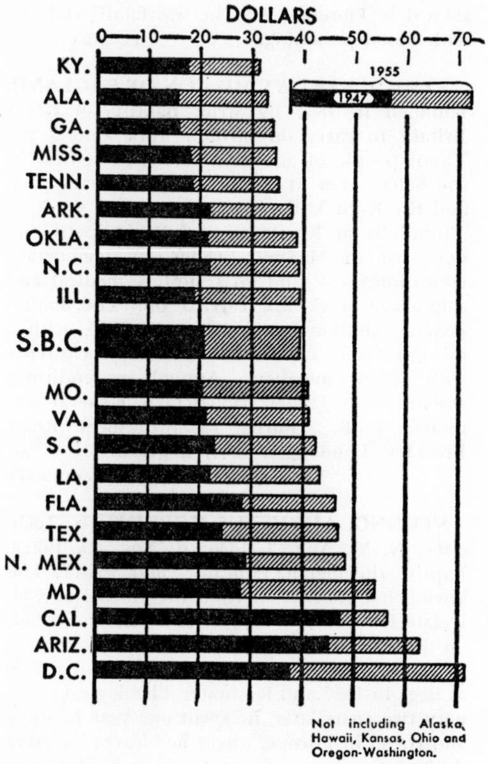

week let every one of you lay by him in store, as God hath prospered him" (I Cor. 16:2). (9) There are rewards for the faithful steward which sometimes but not always include material blessings—"Well done, thou good and faithful servant: . . . enter thou into the joy of thy Lord" (Matt. 25:21). "I will . . . open you the windows of heaven, and pour you out a blessing" (Mal. 3:10). (10) One is to give the Lord's money where it will bring glory to the Lord rather than praise to himself—"They glorify God for the obedience of your confession unto the gospel of Christ, and for the liberality of your contribution" (II Cor. 9:13 ASV); "Bring ye all the tithes into the storehouse" (Mal. 3:10). (11) Christian motivation to giving is not exhibition but worship, not bargaining but surrender, not legalism but love—"Bring an offering, and come into his courts" (Psalm 96:8); "riches of their liberality . . . beyond their power . . . first [they] gave their own selves to the Lord" (II Cor. 8:2–5); "The love of Christ constraineth us" (II Cor. 5:14; John 14:15).

Stewardship in Baptist faith and life.—Stewardship as a Bible doctrine permeates the Scriptures. In theology it stands alongside the doctrines of God, sin, salvation, sanctification, evangelism, missions, etc. In life it is the expression of the total content of the Christian faith.

Stewardship includes all of life in every relationship at all times: body, mind, abilities, time, influence, and possessions and estate.

Stewardship, once neglected, is being recovered. The medieval church departed from the teachings of the Scriptures on the tithe as in many other things. Abuses followed, continuing for several centuries in serious form. The Protestant Reformation in the 16th century was a reaction against these serious abuses in the realm of stewardship as well as error in other areas. The Baptist pioneers did not favor the tithe because the "tithe" they knew was a caricature of biblical stewardship, a government tax, collected by force for the support of an oppressive state church. Protestant churches in European countries continued the state-church relationship, deriving their support from the governments. There was no mission task to call to the practice of Bible stewardship until late in the 18th century when William Carey aroused Christians to send missionaries to evangelize the world and give their tithes to supply needed funds. The call to missions stimulated study of the Bible, leading to a rediscovery of God's plan of stewardship.

In America Luther Rice (*q.v.*) led American Baptists to support Adoniram Judson (*q.v.*). In 1814 the Triennial Convention was organized. New publications were begun to tell of missionary need and to call Baptists to liberal giving. The sacrifices of Judson and other missionaries stimulated many Christians to make sacrificial gifts, but the practice of stewardship was not yet general. Ministers largely labored for their own support. There was little systematic development of individual Christians in stewardship until the 20th century.

A growing vision of the world, its needs, and the Christian's missionary obligation stimulated the development of programs of church finance for enlistment of Christians in missionary giving and church support. Church budgets, the Cooperative Program, the every-member canvass, teaching of stewardship and missions in missionary societies, Brotherhoods, Training Union, and Sunday school, sermons on stewardship, schools of missions, and the church finance program of Southern Baptists have made their contribution to Southern Baptist growth in stewardship. MERRILL D. MOORE

STILLWATER MUNICIPAL HOSPITAL (STILLWATER, OKLA.). Accepted on a 25-

year lease at $25 per year from the city of Stillwater, Okla., on May 1, 1952, this 104-bed hospital is valued at $546,111 plus Oklahoma convention assets of $7,069. TOM E. CARTER

STOCKS, THOMAS (b. Washington County, Ga., Feb. 1, 1789; d. Greene County, Ga., Oct., 6, 1876). Judge and trustee of Mercer University. He was already a prominent figure in Georgia political life when he became a professing Christian in 1828 at the age of 42. In political life Stocks was judge of the Inferior Court of Greene County for more than 20 years, beginning in 1813. For eight years he served as president of the state senate. As a Baptist leader in Georgia, Stocks was instrumental in the founding of Mercer University in 1833. He was a member of its board of trustees from 1838 until his death, succeeding Jesse Mercer as president of the board, and gave liberally of his means toward its support. In 1837 and again in 1844, he served as clerk of the Georgia Baptist Convention and was its president from 1847 to 1856. For more than 40 years he was a member of the convention's executive committee. Stocks married twice but had no children. HAROLD L. MCMANUS

STOCTONS VALLEY INSTITUTE. A coeducational school founded in 1909 at Helena, Tenn., by Christopher Columbus Choate and William Lewis Reagan. It grew steadily, and at the close of the third year had 101 students. In July, 1911, the school came under the supervision of the Home Mission Board of the Southern Baptist Convention. The Tennessee Mission Board assisted the local Baptist church in completing in 1912 a church building near the campus and the Home Mission Board assisted the board of trustees in building a dormitory containing 25 rooms the same year. The influence of the institute for good in this mountain area is inestimable. It closed about 1930. The property was deeded to the Fentress County Board of Education July 21, 1941. HARLEY FITE

STORYTIME. See SUNDAY SCHOOL BOARD.

STOUT MEMORIAL HOSPITAL, WUCHOW. See CHINA, MISSION IN.

STRICKLAND, HARRY LEE (b. Collierville, Tenn., Sept. 26, 1876; d. Nashville, Tenn., Nov. 4, 1924). Originator of the Southern Baptist Organized Class Movement. He was one of a family of nine children and the son of a public school teacher and principal, under whom he received most of his schooling. He was converted in Grand Rapids, Mich., in 1893 and joined a Baptist church. Later he entered business in Memphis, Tenn., and became active in church work. He married Laura Scott, Germantown, Tenn., Oct. 13, 1897. His first major responsibility as a Sunday school worker came as state Sunday school secretary of the Alabama Baptist State Convention. In July, 1916, he was elected a field secretary of the Southern Baptist Sunday School Board and, the following year, became the head of the Organized Class Department. Under his leadership the board promoted the Organized Class Movement as distinctive from the interdenominational Baracca-Philathea Movement. In this connection he initiated Convention-wide organized class conferences and helped to popularize the concept that classes should be an integral part of the local church, under its control and sharing its objectives and activities. His vigorous leadership helped to lay the foundation for a rapidly developing program of Sunday school work for both young people and adults. Through his initiative *The Organized Class Magazine* was begun, but the first issue, Jan., 1925, came from the press after his death. While conducting a revival in Florence, Ala., he was fatally stricken with blood poisoning. FLORIDA WAITE

STRICT BAPTIST MISSION OF ENGLAND. Founded in 1861 by Strict Baptists of Great Britain to carry on mission work among the Tamil people of South India. Work centers in the Salem area at Namakkal, Sendamangalam, and the Kolli Hills, but has extended south to Tinnevelly at Kovilpatti and Paniadipatti and northeast to Madras. Evangelism, elementary education, boys' and girls' hostels, medical and colportage work are carried on. The Ladies Zenana Auxiliary co-operates. In 1955, with a mission staff of 21, there were 67 Tamil churches with 2,204 members. Annual expenditures amounted to £21,097 ($59,071.60). General secretary: J. K. Thorpe, 61 Breakspear Road, Brockley, London, S. E. 4, England.

H. C. GOERNER

STRONG, AUGUSTUS HOPKINS (b. Rochester, N. Y., Aug. 3, 1836; d. Nov. 29, 1921). Baptist theologian, educator, and writer. Following his graduation from the Rochester Collegiate Institute, he served for a year and a half on the staff of the *Rochester Daily Democrat,* of which his father was publisher. Finishing Yale College in 1857 and Rochester Theological Seminary two years later, he spent one year in study and travel in Europe, where he "learned a great deal of German and got together a library of German books" but experienced a dulling of his "Christian feeling."

Strong was ordained to the Baptist ministry Aug. 3, 1861, and was married to Harriet Louise Savage Nov. 6, 1861. He served as pastor of the First Baptist Church of Haverhill, Mass., until 1865. For the next seven years he was minister of the First Baptist Church, Cleveland, Ohio, where one of the members was John Davison Rockefeller, whose daughter married Strong's eldest son. Perhaps Strong introduced to Rockefeller the idea of establishing a great Baptist university, which eventually became the University of Chicago.

In 1872 he became president and professor of theology at Rochester Theological Seminary, serving in both positions until his retirement in 1912. During these years he shared the theological leadership of American Baptists with William Newton Clarke, Alvah Hovey, and George W. Northrup. His gifts as a teacher, preacher, and Christian statesman were equally significant. He has been described as "vigorous minded, affable, yet somewhat awe-inspiring."

Strong described his "theological development" during the forty years he spent in the seminary in an address given on Jan. 13, 1913, entitled "Theology and Experience." In the final edition of his *Systematic Theology* and in a little book completed the day before his death, entitled *What Shall I Believe?* he set forth a faith which to him was basically biblical. This must be understood in estimating Carl F. H. Henry's belief that Strong's theology was marked by "halfness and hesitancy" due to an unresolved tension in it between "the idealistic tradition" and "the Christian revelation."

In 1916–17 Strong and his second wife, Marguerite Geraldine Jones, a widow whom he married Jan. 1, 1916, following the death of his first wife, toured the mission fields. His observations and conclusions concerning the trip were recorded in *A Tour of the Missions* (1918). His life and thought were imbued with the missionary imperative.

BIBLIOGRAPHY: W. H. Allison, "Augustus Hopkins Strong," *Dictionary of American Biography*, ed., D. Malone (1936). C. F. H. Henry, *Personal Idealism and Strong's Theology* (1951). A. H. Strong, *Chapel Talks and Autobiographical Addresses* (1913); *Christ in Creation and Ethical Monism* (1899); *Philosophy and Religion* (1888); *Systematic Theology* (1907); *What Shall I Believe?* (1922). PENROSE ST. AMANT

STUBBLEFIELD, CORTEZ (b. McMinnville, Tenn., Jan. 12, 1848; d. Miami, Okla., Nov. 6, 1930). Pioneer pastor and denominational statesman. When he was three, the family moved in a covered wagon to Texas, and at 17 he began the nomadic life of a cowboy on the "Texas Trail" across Indian Territory to Baxter Springs, Kans. He was ordained to the ministry Aug. 30, 1889. Soon thereafter he moved to Oklahoma and served pastorates at Ardmore, Duncan, Durant, Ada, and Miami. He was corresponding secretary of the Baptist General Convention of Indian Territory, 1899–1901, and president of the Baptist General Convention of Oklahoma, 1912–15. In the transition to statehood in Oklahoma (1907), Stubblefield worked to heal sectional strife, led in unifying northern and southern factions in the Indian Territory convention in 1900, and led in final unification in the present convention in 1906. He was the first field secretary for Oklahoma Baptist University, and Mrs. Stubblefield was the first dormitory matron. He was married twice, first to Sally Miller, who died in 1885, and then to Jessie Huff, who survived him. He is buried in the Grand Army of the Republic cemetery at Miami, Okla.

BIBLIOGRAPHY: W. A. Carleton, *Not Yours but You* (1954). J. M. Gaskin, *Trail Blazers of Sooner Baptists* (1953). E. C. Routh, *The Story of Oklahoma Baptists* (1932). JAMES RALPH SCALES

STUDENT ACTIVITIES, GOLDEN GATE BAPTIST THEOLOGICAL SEMINARY. In order to furnish the students with service opportunities and to meet the needs of its California constituency, the seminary has a program of practical activities. Students not holding paid church positions are offered many opportunities of service. They conduct services in rescue missions and rest homes, serve with the Home Mission Board in ministries to foreign students and minority groups, and work with the Baptist Student Union. The program is flexible; it can be greatly expanded during the fall when there are many students without church work and can be decreased as spring approaches. In addition, a more concrete program for helping students start new missions and churches is being initiated. Opportunities for service during the summer are almost unlimited. Demands for workers in the churches, in the state mission program, and with the Home Mission Board exceed the supply.

The location of Golden Gate Baptist Theological Seminary makes practical work on the part of the students and faculty a necessity. Since three fourths of the 3,000,000 people who reside within a 40-mile radius of the seminary have no religious affiliation, an active gospel witness is necessary for two reasons: (1) that students may have a place of service, and (2) that the seminary may justify its existence.

From the time the seminary was started in 1944 until 1956, approximately three fourths of the students have held church jobs. They serve as pastors, mission pastors, church secretaries, and educational and music directors. The salaries received have seldom been sufficient to support the students. In many cases the students have organized the churches they serve. With help from the G.I. Bill, working wives, parents, friends, established churches in the East, or by working a 40-hours-per-week "swing-shift," they have supplemented their incomes sufficiently to live while building churches and attending school.

The students have followed the accepted procedure of having their missions sponsored by organized Baptist churches, but the act of voting to sponsor a mission has often been the only support given by the sponsoring church, since in many instances it has been too small to do anything more. In one case, a church with a membership of 65 (with a student pastor) sponsored 10 missions at one time, eight of which have become self-supporting churches. The student has often located the area needing a church, found and rented a building (usually paying the rent himself), used other students to take a census, enlisted other students to teach and sing, borrowed pianos, seats, and hymnals, gathered a small group of interested people, and organized a church. In a few cases the growth has been phenomenal, but usually, it has been painfully slow. The major handicap in the initial stages has been the lack of suitable meeting places.

The situation has not changed materially during the period from 1950 to 1956. The number of churches has more than doubled, and twice as many students now hold paid church positions, but the percentages have not changed. The fact that some churches no longer use student pastors plus the increase in the student body exerts a continuing pressure on the students to find their own preaching places. The growth of the churches has multiplied the opportunities in the fields of religious education and sacred music and promises to multiply even more in the years ahead. The demand exceeds the supply, especially in the field of music leadership.

The students continue to prove their resourcefulness. At the beginning of the school year, 1955–56, there were 135 students who did not have church work. By the end of the school year, 76 per cent of these held paid church positions. A survey of the beginnings of Southern Baptist churches in California reveals some of the results of their missionary efforts. Of the first 533 Southern Baptist churches organized in California, 142 were organized by Golden Gate students while they were still in school. Former students organized an additional 60 churches, and students or ex-students had some part (such as being the pastor of the sponsoring church) in organizing 91 more. Of these 293 churches 287 have survived. Other missions have been organized which did not grow into churches. Thirty of the 32 associations affiliated with the Southern Baptist Convention of California have churches which were organized by students or ex-students of Golden Gate; and in 12 of the associations, over half of the churches were organized by students attending the seminary.

Four "Mission Day" services are held during each school year, at which time outstanding missionary leaders present the needs of a world without Christ. An annual "Seminary Conference" is held each February. Noted speakers are brought to the campus for one week, and the services are open to the public. Among those who have been featured in recent years are W. W. Barnes, Clyde T. Francisco, Ralph Herring, McCloud Bryan, and J. W. Storer.

In 1956 among other former students were 11 chaplains serving with the armed forces, 30 foreign missionaries, 41 home missionaries, 297 pastors, 22 educational directors, 16 general denominational workers, 32 other full-time religious workers, and 28 teachers. J. W. MANNING

STUDENT ACTIVITIES, NEW ORLEANS BAPTIST THEOLOGICAL SEMINARY. One of the distinctive features of New Orleans Baptist Theological Seminary since its founding has been its provision for each student "to secure training for service through service." The first president wrote in 1925: "From the very first week of our existence, assignments to practical work have been made. . . ." The catalogue of 1918–19 stated:

All students of the Institute are expected to spend part of their time in practical work. This work is done under the oversight and supervision of the Director of Practical Activities and includes church work, such as preaching, Sunday School teaching, visitation, etc., and also other forms of Christian activity, such as mission work, hospital visitation, personal work with individuals, etc. It is expected at an early date to add to the present activities jail work, street and other open air preaching, gospel wagon work, weekly shop meetings, etc.

Each week the students report on the work of the week, and at the weekly report hour these reports of the students are discussed, with suggestions and criticism. In this way each student gets the benefit of the work and experience of all and all together learn to do the work in the most effective way.

No student can graduate from the Institute who has not done satisfactory work along this line.

This phase of our work means that our students not only learn the theory of Christian work in the most thorough way, but also learn to put the theory into practice, and so go from our school fully prepared to undertake the work which will face them in the pastorate or other spheres into which they will enter, thus exemplifying our motto "Training for Service by Training through Service."

Professor Ernest Orlando Sellers (*q.v.*) was the first director of practical work and was succeeded in 1922 by George Harvey Crutcher (*q.v.*). R. P. Mahon assumed leadership in 1927. However, the greatest contribution in this department was made by John Watson Shepard (*q.v.*) former missionary to Brazil, who began its direction in 1931. The work prior to 1931 had been largely in the city of New Orleans. As the student body grew, the number of preaching points increased. New open-air services were held in various locations within the city. Interest was great, and the work of the students so effective that it was reported that through their work 25,000 persons had professed faith in Christ during the first seven years of the institute's existence.

When Baptist Bible Institute was launched, there were only six white Baptist churches in New Orleans. The institute aided these churches and helped to organize others. The school paper, quoting *The Baptist Program,* noted in 1927:

From fourth place among the evangelical denominations of New Orleans ten years ago, Baptists have come to occupy first place in point of both numbers and aggressiveness. Much of the credit for this achievement, as well as for the viewpoint that has come to the Baptist people of that strategic city is given to the Baptist Bible Institute.

The work of the Practical Activities Department by 1927 included "work in jails, hospitals, street meetings, Chinese meetings, service among the Jews, Good-Will centers, boys' work, docks," and regular church work. At one street meeting sermons were preached in three languages—Italian, French, and English. By November of 1927, students from the institute were preaching in the French Market every Tuesday, Thursday, and Friday evening. In 1928 R. P. Mahon estimated that the work done by Baptist Bible Institute students in New Orleans would cost the

Baptists at least $40,000 per year as a missionary project, though the students received no remuneration for it.

No provision is made in the budget for the equipment used in practical work. The equipment has been purchased with money contributed by students, faculty, and interested friends. In 1929 the equipment consisted of five portable organs and one old Ford bus. The school had an opportunity to purchase at great saving two busses which were ideal for mission work. The matter was brought to the attention of the student body, and the students enthusiastically welcomed the opportunity. "Expressions were heard indicating that they were willing to give and to solicit gifts from their friends and churches. . . . They asked in unanimous vote that the deal be closed. Each student indicated the amount which he expected to give or raise."

The additional equipment enabled the department to expand its work, and in 1930 the students established 40 preaching points in the city and surrounding area; 1,284 people made professions of faith during that school year.

When Shepard assumed the direction of practical work in 1931, the work was expanded to reach the vast mission field of south Louisiana. In 1937 the ministry of the department was extended to Negro ministers through the Union Theological Seminary in New Orleans. Qualified students of New Orleans Baptist Theological Seminary were employed to teach at Union, and this work is still being carried on.

The expansion of mission work was rapid in the French country in south Louisiana, and by 1939 about 10 new towns and country places had been entered. Work was begun in Morgan City in 1933 with a group of four active Baptists; the work in Jeanerette was begun in 1936, and one of the students at Baptist Bible Institute took over in 1938 with 17 Baptists living there, but no church. A church was organized and in little more than a year listed 194 members. The students of the institute opened work in Shell Beach in St. Bernard Parish, at Pointe a la Hache in the heart of Plaquemines Parish, and in Patterson in St. Mary's Parish. In Nov., 1939, services were held in Raceland and Donaldsonville, which were both highly successful. Shepard wrote: ". . . Recently a new Baptist Association—the Evangeline Association—has been organized in the Sugar Bowl region, composed mainly of churches which are manned by Institute students, many of which churches have sprung up as a result of work done by Institute teachers and students."

In Jan., 1940, a public address system was purchased, and this greatly increased the effectiveness of outdoor services. Trips were made to Whitecastle, Napoleonville, L'Abbi D'ville, and Luland, and also to Thibodeaux and Luling. In Nov., 1940, new mission stations were opened in Paradis, Des Allemands, Lockport, and Larose. Shepard and J. W. Watts were active along with the students in promoting this work. Many of the preaching points in the French country became missions, then churches, at an average of about one a year, so that the Baptist denomination was greatly strengthened in south Louisiana because of the work of the department.

Fred Schatz succeeded Shepard as director of practical activities in 1944 and was in turn succeeded by E. N. Patterson in 1948. Patterson was granted a leave of absence for the 1954–55 session, and B. G. Allison was named acting director. The name of the department was changed in 1955 to Department of Field Mission Work, and Allison was named director.

In 1955 the physical equipment for field mission work consisted of four busses, three station wagons, and five portable organs. The work was carried on in the same manner as it had always been, but an attempt was made better to harmonize the theory of the classroom and the practical work on the field. All first-year students meet in a group once a week for a period of testimony about the mission work. Each second-year student is required to meet with a small group, under the direction of a faculty member, for reports, counseling, instruction, and prayer. During the 1954–55 session the students dealt personally with 41,812 people in need of Christ, and as a result of their work, 2,116 persons were baptized. There were 903 people who professed faith in Christ to students on field work assignments.

BIBLIOGRAPHY: P. H. Anderson, *New Orleans Baptist Theological Seminary, A Brief History* (1949). J. Caylor, *In Evangeline's Country* (1954). M. L. Jenkins, *Around the World in Louisiana* (1937). R. Q. Leavell, *President's Thirty-Eighth Annual Report to the Board of Trustees* (1956). H. E. Reynolds, *God's Dividends in Louisiana* (1950). *The Magnet* (1925–33, 1938–40). *Vision* (1946–56). B. G. ALLISON

STUDENT ACTIVITIES, SOUTHEASTERN BAPTIST THEOLOGICAL SEMINARY. Southeastern Seminary undertakes to achieve for the student a balance of academic study and practical usefulness in the churches. An effort is made to help the student learn skills which will enable him to think wisely and act properly when dealing with life situations in a church. Faculty members offer personal counsel to students who serve in churches, and a family-spirited relationship is maintained between students and faculty.

The seminary insists that a student who accepts church or secular work has a moral obligation to perform his duties there in a worthy manner. A student minister who works in a church every week is expected to carry a lighter class load at the seminary so that he may do both school and church work effectively.

Southeastern Seminary students engage in a varied ministry in the churches, serving as pastors, associate pastors, educational directors, music directors, youth directors, pianists, organists, revival preachers, summer workers, directors of recreation, and teachers of study courses. During the summers, students who do not have regular church work engage in ministries of mission boards, Baptist state conventions, assemblies, camps, and local churches.

A Student Coordinating Council serves in an advisory capacity in promoting the general welfare of all students, stimulating participation in campus and off-campus activities which are vital for the spiritual, social, mental, and physical well-being of every student. Nine student committees help with these activities: dramatics committee, sponsoring religious plays, skits, and other related activities; athletic committee, promoting forms of relaxation and exercise for the students' mental and physical development; campus ethics committee, promoting the best ethical relations among students, between students and faculty, and between students and other groups; devotional committee, strengthening the devotional life of students through chapel services, supervision of a room for prayer, and other activities; radio committee, using facilities available in the development of a devotional and co-operative spirit among the students; social committee, developing the social life of students and faculty and creating a spirit of fellowship among them; music committee, promoting music as an aid to worship; welfare committee, assisting with such problems as housing, employment, and financial difficulties of students; and religious off-campus committee, serving as intermediary between the students and the churches and institutions which afford opportunity for religious work.

GARLAND A. HENDRICKS

STUDENT ACTIVITIES, SOUTHERN BAPTIST THEOLOGICAL SEMINARY. Practical religious activities have always been a vital part of the training of the students of the Southern Baptist Theological Seminary. The first catalogue of Southern Seminary, published in 1860, carried the following announcement:

> The vacation of four months affords opportunity for students to engage in colportage and missionary work. Positions of usefulness in these labors may readily be obtained. Even during the Session, there are various opportunities for doing good in such labors. . . . Several prayer-meetings and Sunday schools have been established in the churches around Greenville [where the seminary was originally located] by the students during the present session. These opportunities will be constantly on the increase. As our students become known, their labors will be highly appreciated and earnestly sought after.

The prophecy of this early announcement was amply fulfilled with the passing of the years. In the 1920–21 session (the earliest date for which complete statistics are available), for example, the students of the seminary reported the following religious activities: sermons preached, 14,019; conversions, 3,789; baptisms, 2,746; pieces of literature distributed, 28,927; prayer meetings conducted, 1,811; Sunday school classes taught, 4,690.

The religious activities program of Southern Seminary was given impetus and direction from the beginning by the observance, one day each month, of a missionary day. While home and foreign missions have always been at the focal point in the missionary day exercises, more and more emphasis was given, from year to year, in these services, to reports and announcements concerning the voluntary religious activities of the students.

In 1920 Gaines S. Dobbins was elected to the faculty of the seminary as professor of church efficiency and Sunday school pedagogy. Under his energetic leadership the student religious activities program was organized in five "interest groups" as follows: the teaching and local church activities group; the evangelistic and street-preaching group; the institutional group; the missions and missionary group; and the pastoral group. Constant effort was made by the student chairmen, encouraged and directed by the faculty advisers, to expand the activities of each of the groups and to increase the scope and effectiveness of these ministries to include: regular services in many of the local hospitals and other similar institutions; weekly noonday preaching services in several of the larger shops and factories of Louisville; the teaching of Sunday school classes in local orphanages and other homes for children; weekly preaching services in the local jails; work in virtually all of the Baptist churches in the Louisville area; and missionary deputation work during the week ends. In 1943 a Negro work group, which later became designated as the Human Relations Group, was created. Under the direction of the student chairman of the group, and in co-operation with the Baptist Fellowship Center sponsored by the Long Run Association of Baptists, a number of students found opportunity for fruitful service in many of the Negro Baptist churches of the city.

In 1946 some 60 per cent of the students of the School of Theology were serving as student pastors, ministering to churches most of which were within a radius of 150 miles of the seminary, a few students, however, traveling as far as 400 miles or more each week end to churches in Tennessee, Mississippi, and Alabama. In several of the district associations close to the seminary, during some years as many as 90 per cent of the pastorates in an association have been held by seminary students. The growth of not a few of these churches from quarter-time and half-time churches to full-time churches with a full church program has clearly demonstrated that competent and dedicated student pastors are able to render effective pastoral leadership while pursuing their studies at the seminary. A goodly number of thriving churches in and around Louisville were begun as missions by seminary students working in co-operation with the parent churches or with the associational missionary.

In 1955 the School of Religious Education made field work a requirement for graduation. All of the first-year students of this school are required to do volunteer field work in the educational program of churches in the Louisville area, under the general direction of a professor of the School of Religious Education, and under the immediate direction of the pastors of the churches in which they work. In the second year of candidacy for the degree in Religious Education, each student is obliged to fulfil a field work requirement for which credit toward graduation is given. The required field work program was directed in 1956–57 by Ernest J. Loessner, associate professor of administration, with the assistance of Professors Landry and Hargis. Weekly seminars are held, at which time the students are given individual help and instruction in the work in which they are serving. Regular reports are received from the pastors of the churches. Every effort is made by the faculty of the School of Religious Education to make this practical experience a real part of the student's preparation for his future ministry in this vital area of the life of the churches.

Students in the School of Church Music have been required since its establishment in 1943 to participate in directed field work under the supervision of the faculty of the school. As a result the majority of the students of the School of Church Music are afforded an opportunity to serve, during their student years, as ministers of music, choir directors, church organists, church and departmental pianists, and revival song leaders.

In 1955 an hour was set apart each missionary day, at which time the several religious activities groups met under the sponsorship of faculty members to discuss their practical religious activities, to receive counsel, and to discuss ways and means of rendering better service in the work to which they have set their hands.

In 1956 Joseph Stiles, formerly pastor of the Park Place Baptist Church of Houston, Tex., was elected professor of church administration in the School of Religious Education and director of the field work program of the seminary.

In 1957 five semesters of field work were made a requirement for graduation from the School of Theology and an extended program of field work was inaugurated to include a monthly field work conference with the students meeting in groups of approximately 25 under the direction of a faculty member. Attention is given to problems that students face in their practical activities and instructions and suggestions are given in such matters as soul-winning, personal counseling, preparation for revivals, and so forth.

As a rule, one week each year is designated as the annual revival recess to enable the students to participate in revival meetings without interfering with their regular class work. This week is scheduled as far as possible to coincide with the period designated by the Convention or the state board as simultaneous revival week. The revival recess also enables a large number of the professors to participate in revival meetings.

It is the firm conviction of Southern Seminary that practical religious activities are a vital part of the training of the students of all three schools, the School of Theology, the School of Church Music, and the School of Religious Education. Practical work also affords an excellent opportunity for the students of the seminary to vitalize and enrich their spiritual lives while they are engaged in the academic process of preparing themselves to be good ministers of Christ in the years of service that lie ahead of them.

HUGH R. PETERSON

STUDENT ACTIVITIES, SOUTHWESTERN BAPTIST THEOLOGICAL SEMINARY. From the very beginning of Southwestern Baptist Theological Seminary, a strong emphasis has been placed on the practical religious activities of the students. While the seminary was meeting on the campus of Baylor University in Waco, Tex., a soul-winners band was organized under the direction of Lee Rutland Scarborough (*q.v.*), then the professor of evangelism, to encourage those students who desired "to do practical work in the city of Waco in winning lost men to Christ and engage in prayer for the power of the Holy Spirit for special service." In 1908 it was reported that "not less than seventy-five churches, accessible from Waco, have Seminary or University (Baylor) students for their pastors."

In 1910 the seminary was moved to its permanent location on Seminary Hill, Fort Worth, Tex. The 1909–10 issue of the seminary's catalogue stated that the president and members of the faculty would do everything possible and proper to help students secure supply and pastoral work. In addition to his duties in teaching the courses in evangelism, Scarborough was elected in 1913 to act together with the Tarrant County Baptist missionary in helping students to find places of service in mission stations and churches. At this time the practical religious activities of the students were on a voluntary basis. However, the students were all expected to engage in some form of religious service. There was some limitation on the services of music students. They were permitted to go out and sing in meetings under the direction of the head of the music department of the seminary.

In Oct., 1918, a report of the practical work of students for the preceding year revealed that 74 students (and some faculty members) had held 263 revivals, preached 9,376 sermons, delivered 1,136 other addresses, made 13,497 pastoral visits, reported 5,459 professions of faith in their services, baptized 3,205 candidates, reported 5,218 additions to their churches, and raised $216,279 in various offerings. This report did not indicate the various mission stations served by students.

In 1920 the Practical Work Department of the seminary was established. The regulation was made that "every student is required to take an active part in at least four religious services each month." W. A. Hancock was made the general superintendent of this department, and H. E. Waldrop was superintendent of the downtown mission and institutional work. The following opportunities were presented for the student religious activities: (1) street services, work in downtown missions, jail and hospital services; (2) settlement work among the underprivileged (recommended especially for the Training School girls); (3) work with the Russian and Mexican settlements in Fort Worth; (4) extension work by the Schools of Music and Religious Education and by the Department of Missions; (5) any work done on a local church field. According to the seminary's regulations, a student who failed to participate in the practical religious activities required by the seminary would not be graduated. The faculty ruled that a student must participate in at least 75 per cent of the assignments to religious services in order to meet this requirement for graduation. In 1928 this requirement was removed. However, it was emphasized that the failure of students to participate faithfully in religious services each week would "influence the character of any recommendations made on their behalf."

The religious activities of the seminary students have been extensive and varied. In local churches they have served, and are serving, as pastors, associate pastors, ministers of education and music, pianists or organists, church secretaries, youth directors, financial secretaries, recreation directors, nursery superintendents, and visitation directors. These have been employed positions. Seminary students serve in practically all of the places of voluntary leadership in the churches of Fort Worth where they hold membership. In addition to direct service in local services of the churches, seminary students serve in positions as Baptist Student Union workers, city mission superintendents, associational missionaries, Bible teachers in some of the high schools in Fort Worth, chaplains in orphanages and other such institutions, and directors of Good Will Centers.

For many years Southwestern Seminary students have engaged in city mission work in Fort Worth. Preachers are furnished for numerous mission stations in the city. Over a long period of time, seminary students did the preaching on the week ends at the Union Gospel Mission, an independent ministry to the indigent transients passing through the city. In more recent years the seminary has carried on a similar ministry through the Faith Baptist Mission. In the past six years students have conducted services at this mission each evening of the week and each Sunday morning. An average of 460 professions of faith each year were made. The report for the year 1954–55 indicates that 813 professions of faith were made.

Students conduct services on the streets of Fort Worth, at the city jail, in several hospitals, in convalescent homes, and in other institutions where the opportunity is offered. This city mission program has resulted in many individual professions of faith, in the establishing of several permanent mission stations, and in the organization of new churches in the city of Fort Worth.

In the spring of 1950, a special mission project was launched under the guidance of the missions department of the seminary. Professor Jack MacGorman led a team of students on a mission to the Bahama Islands to hold evangelistic services, conduct Vacation Bible schools, and teach Bible courses. The financial support of this mission was provided through freewill offerings of the students. The mission was conducted during the months of June, July, and August. Each summer since 1950 the mission band of the seminary has promoted the Bahama Mission Project. In the summer of 1953 the Bahama Bible Institute was organized as the direct result of this mission project. This Bible institute is carrying on a Bible teaching program for the natives of the Bahama Islands during the regular school term.

Southwestern Baptist Theological Seminary has made a profound spiritual impact upon the city of Fort Worth and the surrounding region through the ministry of its students. Many Baptist churches have been organized and many people enlisted through the activities of students. FELIX M. GRESHAM

STUDENT HOMES, CHIHUAHUA AND GUADALAJARA. Where the laws of a nation prohibit Christian schools, student homes meet a special need on mission fields. This is true in Mexico, the one country where Southern Baptists maintain student homes. There are few town schools in Mexico above the sixth grade, and not many cities have universities. Student homes provide Christian home training for students who must leave their families to attend city schools. A number of the students go out from the homes each year in various professions —law, medicine, engineering, and others. They may help convert business and professional classes to Christianity.

Orvil Wilson Reid, a missionary, began in his own home in Guadalajara in 1941 the first Southern Baptist student home in Mexico, a home for boys. In 1942 Reid founded a home for girls and bought a print shop to give employment to students. Other missionaries have worked in the two Guadalajara homes—Alma (Ervin) Reid, Ruth Miriam McCullough, Martha Mae Davis, and Wyatt Wain and Edrie E. (Morris) Lee.

Abel Perly and Coy L. (Childress) Pierson founded boys' and girls' student homes in Chihuahua in 1945 and 1946. Katherine Ruth Skinner directed the girls' home for a time; later Roberta Elizabeth Hampton took her place.

Buildings are under construction in Chihuahua to care for 70 boys and 50 girls. Land has been bought for buildings in Guadalajara. In 1956 William Milton and Lois (Nichols) Haverfield opened a student home in Mexico City, the location of a large university.

See also MEXICO, MISSION IN. ORVIL W. REID

STUDENT SUMMER MISSIONS. This discussion is limited to the work of students serving under the direction of the Home Mission Board of the Southern Baptist Convention. Many of the state conventions and district associations also have plans whereby students are employed for various phases of church and denominational activity during the summer months.

In 1942 W. W. Hamilton, president of the Baptist Bible Institute, New Orleans, La., requested that the Home Mission Board give financial assistance to certain students who served during the winter in the practical-work department of the institute but had no provision for employment during the summer months. In response to this request, the executive committee of the board, on Apr. 9, 1942, requested the executive committee and J. W. Beagle to "employ such of these students to do mission work among the French in South Louisiana during the summer months as, in their judgment, it seems advisable." Following these instructions, Beagle reported to the executive committee on May 7, 1942, that he had interviewed 11 ministerial students whom he was recommending for employment. These students were employed for four months to serve in southern Louisiana at a salary of $35 or $40 per month.

Thus the Student Summer Mission Program was started. The following year, $10,000 was appropriated by the executive committee of the board for such work, and 24 students were employed to serve in the mountains of Kentucky, in East St. Louis, Ill., in South Carolina, in city mission work, Houston, Tex., and in the French fields in southern Louisiana. Twelve were appointed from the Southern Baptist Theological Seminary at Louisville, Ky., and 12 from the Baptist Bible Institute of New Orleans, La. They served three months at salaries ranging from $20 to $75 per month, "the traveling expenses to be allowed as agreed upon by the Executive Secretary."

In 1944 the Convention-wide Woman's Missionary Union designated $3,000 of the Annie Armstrong Offering to be added to the board's appropriation of $10,000 for the "employment of young women from colleges and seminaries to work in co-operation with our missionaries during the summer months." The total amount made available for the summer mission work was later increased to $20,000, and 71 students worked during the months of June, July, and August. They represented 44 colleges and 4 seminaries and were recruited from 17 states.

The program continued to grow. On Feb. 7, 1946, definite regulations relative to qualifications, salary, and direction of the students were adopted.

In the report of the board in 1946, the purpose of the program was briefly stated as follows:

1. Help young missionary volunteers to find themselves by actual work on the mission field.
2. Help our Mission Boards to discover desirable missionaries.
3. Help get as much mission work done as possible during these important summer months.
4. Through the testimonies of these summer workers to give publicity to the work and the opportunities on our home mission fields.

In 1951 the Convention-wide Baptist Student Union agreed to send the workers supported by various Baptist Student Union groups and assigned to fields in the homeland through the Home Mission Board so that their work and activities might be directed in the same way as the students employed by the board. The number of students thus supported by the various Baptist Student Union groups has constantly increased until in 1955, 45 of the 388 students appointed were provided in this way.

The 1955 report of the board reveals the growth and scope of the Student Summer Mission Program. There were 388 students from 23 states and 10 foreign countries participating, from 106 colleges and 8 seminaries. No difference is made in the appointment of qualified students because of race or nationality. Those selected by the board are mission volunteers who have completed at least two years of college, university, or seminary training. They serve under the direction of the regular missionaries of the board or denominational leaders in mission areas.

During 10 weeks in the summer of 1955, the 388 students reported 4,849 sermons and addreses, 75,597 homes visited, 104,521 pupils taught in Vacation Bible schools, 4,061 professions of faith, 1,760 dedications for full-time service, and 64 new missions and churches started. COURTS REDFORD

STUDY COURSES. A term used to designate popular textbook courses for the training of church workers and the development of Christians in various areas of knowledge, faith, conduct, and service. These courses have been planned and promoted by the Sunday School Board of the Southern Baptist Convention. Through a half-century process they have evolved into three major courses: (1) Sunday School Training Course; (2) Graded Training Union Study Course; and (3) Church Music Training Course.

Sunday school.—The development of a training course for Sunday school workers began with the election of Bernard Washington Spilman (*q.v.*) of North Carolina as field secretary by the Sunday School Board in 1901. He began his duties June 1 of that year. In 1902 the board issued *Normal Studies I*. Written by Spilman, it was a discussion of Sunday school methods and teaching. Later in the same year *Normal Studies II* was published. It was written by Hight C Moore and bore the subtitle *Books of the Bible*. In 1909 these books, together with a discussion of the pupil by Landrum Pinson Leavell (*q.v.*), were combined under the title *The Convention Normal Manual*. The revision of this material in 1913 bore the title *The New Normal Manual.* The 1918 revision was entitled *The New Convention Normal Manual,* and the fourth revision in 1923 was issued as *The Sunday School Manual.* The purpose of these first textbooks was described as follows: "to help the average Sunday school worker to better do the work which he seeks to do."

Very early, agreement was reached that certain subjects should be included in any training course offered to Sunday school teachers. Among these were Bible, doctrines, evangelism, methods, pedagogy, and psychology. By 1931 the circulation of *The Sunday School Manual* was reported to have reached 529,163 copies. In the process of the development of this course it became known as the King's Teacher Course. A diploma was given for the completion of the manual. Seven other seals were added to the diploma—one for each additional book completed. When all eight books had been finished, a red seal was issued. In 1915 the board reported that it had begun its postgraduate course, which comprised a selection of five advanced books.

The Department of Sunday School Administration was established at the board in 1920, and Arthur Flake (*q.v.*) was elected to head the department. Soon after the department was established, a training course in administration was developed. It offered seven books with an appropriate diploma and seals granted for their completion.

The Vacation Bible School Department was created by the board in 1924. Homer Lamar Grice was elected secretary and opened the department on Sept. 1. He began immediately to develop a Daily Vacation Bible School Study Course "to assist in the training of teachers and workers." A diploma was awarded for the completion of *The Daily Vacation Bible School Guide.* Places on the diploma provided for the Sunday School Normal Course red and blue seals and seven additional seals. The seven seals were granted for the study of books dealing with such subjects as story-telling, dramatization, handwork, project teaching, and pictures or art.

In 1927 a Department of Church Administration was created by the board with Prince Emanuel Burroughs (*q.v.*) as secretary and Clay Irby Hudson as associate secretary. This department soon developed a course of study for pastors, deacons, and other church officers, known as the Church Administration Study Course. There were nine books in the course, eight of which were to be studied to complete the diploma.

In July, 1934, the Sunday School Administration Course, the Normal Course, and the Vacation Bible School Course were combined into a new Training Course for Sunday School Workers. In 1944 the name of the course was changed to Sunday School Training Course. It offers three diplomas, each of which requires 16 books to complete. These diplomas are: the Worker's, the Advanced, and the Master. In 1956 the Sunday School Department began issuing a Worker's Citation based upon the completion of 16 additional books.

Baptist Training Union.—The B.Y.P.U. Manual by Landrum Pinson Leavell was the first volume published in the B.Y.P.U. study course series. It appeared in 1907. It was revised in 1914, and the group plan of organization was included at that time. *Training in Church Membership* by Isaac Jacobus Van Ness (*q.v.*) was published in 1908. *Senior B.Y.P.U. Administration* by Arthur Flake appeared in 1926—published since 1940 under the title of *Baptist Young People's Union Administration.* Other titles were added to the Senior (now Young People's) course; from time to time some were dropped. Beginning in 1932 the Senior and Adult books were arranged in 10 sections with one or more books in each section. In 1935 the *Baptist Adult Union Manual* by Jerry Elmer Lambdin was published. That year a separate Adult Union Study Course was announced. Some of the textbooks which appeared first in the Church Administration Study Course were placed in the Adult course when the Church Administration Course was discontinued.

In 1949 the books for all departments were arranged under ten sections as follows: Principles and methods, the church, the Christian life, the Bible, doctrine, the home, missions, stewardship, soul-winning, and the denomination.

Courses have been developed for Juniors and Intermediates and for general officers and leaders. *The Junior B.Y.P.U. Manual* (for ages 13–16) by Ernest Eugene Lee was published in 1916. It was revised and reissued as *The Intermediate B.Y.P.U. Manual* in 1922. In 1942 it became *The Baptist Intermediate Union Manual. The New Junior B.Y.P.U. Manual* (for ages 9–12) by Lucy Sprecker was published in 1922. This was succeeded by *The New Junior B.Y.P.U. Manual* by Ina Smith Lambdin in 1928. In 1942 it was revised as *The New Baptist Junior Union Manual.*

A General B.Y.P.U. Organization by Jerry Elmer Lambdin was published in 1925. It was for general officers and leaders. Its title was changed to the *General B.Y.P.U. Manual* in the revised edition of 1933, and to *The Baptist Training Union Manual* in 1935. *The Junior and Intermediate B.Y.P.U. Leaders Manual* appeared in 1926. It was revised in 1932 and again in 1942 under the title of *Junior and Intermediate Leaders Manual. The Junior Leadership Manual* by Ina Smith Lambdin was published in 1943. *The Intermediate Leadership Manual* by Elaine Coleman Pearson was published in 1944. In that same year *The Story Hour Leadership Manual* by Thelma Arnote was published. In 1951 it was revised under the title of *The Nursery, Beginner, and Primary Leadership Manual. Building a Church Training Program* by Lambdin was published in 1946. It was written for those churches which do not have a department organization.

There is a system of awards for the accredited courses. These awards consist of diplomas for completing the books on principles and methods, then seals for the other books.

In 1956 the Training Union began issuing a certificate of merit to each person upon the completion of all work on the diploma.

Church music.—Prior to 1946 only two study course books had been prepared by Southern Baptist church musicians to serve as guides and source books for music leaders and directors in Southern Baptist churches. The books were: (1) *Church Music* by Isham Emmanuel Reynolds (*q.v.*), published by the Sunday School Board, 1935; and (2) *Let Us Sing* by Baylus Benjamin McKinney (*q.v.*) and Allen W. Graves, published by Broadman Press, 1942. *Church Music* was first prepared for the Training Union and was carried for some time in its study course.

The Church Music Training Course was envisioned and the basic planning for it was started in Jan., 1946. McKinney, then secretary of the Church Music Department, church music educators, and the secretaries of music from five states were present for the planning meeting. In this initial meeting and succeeding sessions a training course was planned and completed. It was developed around four main sections: music fundamentals, music appreciation, music ministry, and integrating courses. The latter included: *Building a Standard Sunday School, The Baptist Training Union Manual, What Baptists Believe,* and *Every Christian's Job.* A certificate was presented the individual upon the completion of each book. Upon completing the first book of each division, a church music diploma was awarded. A red seal could then be earned by completing four additional books; a blue seal required four books above the red seal; and a gold seal required four books above the blue seal. This applied to individuals 15 years of age and above. Boys and girls, ages 9–14, received a Certificate of Achievement. Children below nine were awarded a Certificate of Participation for rhythm band, rote singing, piano, and elementary theory. Any book other than those under music fundamentals could be taken by correspondence.

Basic planning for a revised church music course began in the Dec., 1953, meeting of the state music secretaries. The revision was completed and approved in the 1954 meeting. The recommendations from this meeting were approved by the curriculum committee of the Sunday School Board Feb. 28, 1955. Specific approval for the following titles and authors was made: *Christian Hymnody* by Edmond Dale Keith; *Music in the Bible* by Paul McCommon; *Graded Choir Handbook* and *Hymn Playing* by Loren Raymond Williams; *The Church Pianist* by Helen Midkiff; *The Church Orchestra, Church Music Manual,* and *Song Leading* by Walter Hines Sims; *Choir Directing* by DuPre Rhame. Other books were added subsequently.

All training and study courses require that ten 45-minute periods or the equivalent be offered for study and that class members must attend six of them to qualify for credit. No examination is required of those who have a perfect attendance record. All who receive credit must read the book being studied and, when an examination is required, must make a grade of 70 per cent. W. L. HOWSE

STURGIS BAPTIST ACADEMY, HIGH SCHOOL, OR INSTITUTE. See OHIO VALLEY BAPTIST COLLEGE.

SUCCESSION, CHURCH. The fundamental principle of the Protestant Reformation, justification by faith (however poorly applied), left a deposit in the thought of Europe that continued to influence men in church and state during the succeeding centuries. Worldly authorities in church and state became more difficult to justify, and men began to question the age-old theory, divine right of kings and priests. Justification of the individual by faith in the sight of God posits democracy in religious and civil life.

Such ideas resulted in the English Revolution —the downfall of the Stuarts and the theory of divine right; the American Revolution, a sequel to its English prototype; and the French Revolution, leading to the ultimate downfall of the Bourbons and theories of state associated with that dynasty.

Comparable trends and reactions are evident in the religious sphere as in the secular. So in the religious sphere there was a passionate search for ultimate authority. In the beginning of the English Baptist Movement (first half of the 17th century) the question of authority and its method of transmission were thoroughly discussed. Thomas Crosby sets forth the two methods of reviving believers' baptism. He first recounts the story of a congregation in London and its effort to secure valid baptism. One of the leaders, Richard Blunt, who knew the Dutch language, was sent to Holland (1640–41) to secure immersion from a congregation of immersing Anabaptists. Blunt returned to London, immersed Samuel Blacklock, and these two immersed 53 others. Crosby then continues as follows:

> But the greatest number of the *English Baptists,* and the more judicious, looked upon all this as needless trouble, and what proceeded from the old *Popish Doctrine of right to administer sacraments by an uninterrupted succession,* which neither the church of *Rome,* nor the church of *England,* much less the modern *Dissenters,* could prove to be with them. They affirmed therefore, and practised accordingly, that after a general corruption of *baptism,* an unbaptized person might warrantably baptize and so begin a reformation.

Crosby quotes John Spilsbury, one of the leading advocates of the latter theory, as saying that "where there is a beginning, some one must be first." The theory of succession as set forth in the embassy of 1641 to Holland seems to have played little part in English Baptist history thereafter.

In America, a new country with new conditions and new problems of civilization, in the effort to found a new nation which was not only new in being but new in character, the question of authority in religion was discussed by religious leaders in many denominational groups. The Romanists, of course, took their lead from Rome, recognizing the Bishop of Rome as the successor of Peter and therefore infallible. The high churchmen of the Protestant Episcopal Church, taking their cue from the Church of England, found the source of authority in the church, the body of Christ, speaking through all of the bishops.

Among Baptists there were several reactions to the search for authority. The Campbells, father and son, emphasized first, historicity (Thomas) and later, apostolicity (Alexander); Alexander Campbell "restored the ancient gospel." James Robinson Graves (*q.v.*) "reset the old landmark" and stressed both apostolicity and historicity. The Hardshell (antimission) Baptists calmly named themselves Primitive Baptists and pursued the even tenor of their way.

The Campbell reaction was no doubt much conditioned by the religious atmosphere of the times. The revival that swept over America just after the Revolution and extended into the 19th century placed emphasis upon the subjective, mystical element in religion. It was an over-emphasis upon emotional manifestations.

> There exists within every ecclesiastical organization, if not a High-church party and a Low-church party, at least a High-church tendency and a Low-church tendency: One of these lays stress upon the objective, the other upon the subjective in religion. . . . During and subsequent to the great religious awakening, . . . evils sprung up among the churches which "were seen, deplored, and opposed by all well-informed Christians." These consisted mainly in the somewhat extended prevalence of a tendency toward Mysticism. Too much attention was paid to the subjective, to the partial neglect of the objective. This state of things could not fail, sooner or later, to result in a reaction. It was only a question of time as to when it would occur.
>
> Most likely, if Mr. Campbell had not appeared on the scene it would not have taken the form of a rupture of ecclesiastical relations; the influence of the more discreet would have gradually restored the desired equilibrium. . . . By patience and wise counsel, and mutual confidence, a satisfactory arrangement could have been effected, for it is certain the opinions of Mr. Campbell were in a chaotic state at this time of life, the principal idea and instinct of the man being to set bounds, if possible, to subjectivety [*sic*].

Campbellism was *one* phase of the inevitable reaction against this manifestation. Alexander Campbell chained the Holy Spirit in his operation to the written Word to avoid extreme emotionalism. He emphasized the objective, formal element to the point of rupture of ecclesiastical relations.

Almost a generation after Campbell, there began *another* reaction against the subjective element in religion in the same geographical area. Just as the Southern Baptist Convention began its existence, the Landmark type of formal, High-church emphasis began to appear as a phenomenon. Within the Protestant Episcopal Church in the United States high-churchism put the emphasis upon the church (in the general use of the term) as the body of Christ. The Baptist counterpart began by putting the emphasis upon the church (in the local use of the term) as the apostolic institution on earth which had had a continuity of existence since the days of the apostles. Within 10 years after the Southern Baptist Convention was formed, the movement was in full swing.

Theories of succession.—The source of authority in religion and the external form of that authority involve some theory of historical succession. The Romanist theory located succession in *one* bishop; the Anglican finds it in *all* the bishops. Among Southern Baptists there have been four theories, or four emphases in the theory, of historical succession.

According to the theory of *church succession,* one congregation grows out of and is formed by the authority of another. A church in Arkansas traces its ancestry through Dyersburg, Tenn., then to a church in Virginia, thence to Welsh Tract Church, Delaware. The Welsh Tract Church emigrated from Wales. The Welsh received the gospel from Vienne in Gaul. Hither it came from a church in northern Italy. To Italy the gospel came from Antioch in Syria. This church sprang from the church in Jerusalem, which was the church organized by Jesus. This theory of succession requires congregational church government from the first century to the present and historical connection from one congregation to another. The congregations are independent ecclesiastical entities and are interlocked historically.

The theory of *apostolic succession* holds that continuity consists in a succession of validly ordained ministers from the apostles, who were ordained by Jesus, to the present. Under this theory, the validity of the "orders" (ordination), and not the form of church organization, furnishes the channel through which the stream of history flows and assures the apostolicity of the church. Only ordained ministers may be members of the presbytery to ordain a minister, and each ordaining presbytery must have at least three members.

According to the theory of *baptismal succession,* historical externality consists in valid baptism, that is, baptism performed by a validly baptized and authorized minister. The Broad River Association, South Carolina, in 1818, answered in a circular letter a query as to the acceptance of alien immersion:

> . . . that as certain priests anciently failed to show their genealogy among the lawful priests, and were rejected; in like manner should all administrators of the ordinance of baptism be rejected, who fail to show their own baptism according to the gospel, by a minister who has himself been baptized in a regular line from the Apostles down to the present day.

The theory of *spiritual succession* emphasizes that true historical continuity (Matt. 16:18) consists in a succession of genuine followers of the Lord Jesus, a succession of Christian experience.

What Baptists claim . . . is simply this: that along the whole tract of time there are traces of our principles and of adherents to our principles. . . . In the year 1615 appeared "Persecution for Religion, Judged and Condemned"—a work written by those who styled themselves "Christ's unworthy Witnesses, commonly (but most falsely) called Anabaptists." On the subject before us it says:

"Who shall then baptise after anti-Christ's exaltation? For answer to this, there are three ways professed in the world; one by the Papists, and their several successors, professing succession from the Pope and his ministers; another by the Familists and scattered flock, that none may intermeddle therewith lawfully, till their extra ordinary men come; another, we and others affirm that *any disciple of Christ, in what part of the world soever, coming to the Lord's way, he by the word and Spirit of God preaching that way to others and converting; he may and ought also to baptize them*. . . . An Israelite circumcised in heart, God stirring him up, to build the temple made without hands from the first stone to the last. . . ."

. . . It does not follow that what is rendered necessary at one conjuncture, by a "general corruption of baptism," must therefore be legitimate, when "the building of the church of Christ" has gone prosperously forward, and the (sufficient) plea of necessity avails no longer. The contrary is the obvious dictate of reason: the right of the church *to be*, is not a right to change the order her Head appoints for her! This was also the judgment of our fathers.

That is to say, regular baptism is necessary for the well being, but not the being of the church.

J. R. Graves, in his own theory of succession, endeavored to distinguish between the succession of the church and of the kingdom. Christ's kingdom shall never be destroyed. Since the kingdom is composed of the sum total of all the local churches, and the kingdom is external, therefore local churches, the constituent units of the kingdom, have existed from the time Jesus founded the first one.

Since I have used the terms church and Kingdom, it may be well to explain here what I understand by them and their relation to each other. They were used as synonymous terms by the evangelists so long as Christ had but *one* organized church for they were then one and the same body. So soon as "churches were multiplied," a distinction arose. The kingdom embraced the first church, and it now embraces all the churches. The churches of Christ constitute the kingdom of Christ, as the twelve tribes, each separate and independent of itself, constituted the kingdom of Israel; as the provinces of a Kingdom constitute the kingdom; as all the separate sovereign States of these United States constitute the Republic of America. Now, as no foreigner can become a citizen of this Republic without being naturalized as a citizen of some one of the States, so no one can enter the Kingdom of Christ without becoming a member of some one of his visible churches.

The organization he first set up . . . which Christ called his church, constituted that visible kingdom, and to-day all his *true* churches on earth constitute it; and, therefore, if his *kingdom* has stood unchanged, and will to the end, he must always have had true and uncorrupted churches, since his kingdom can not exist without true churches.

This is the Roman Catholic theory of church succession—identification of the Catholic Church with the kingdom. Graves had a catholicism of his own, often using, under the pseudonym *Fidus*, "Baptist Church" largely in the same sense as the Romanist uses "Catholic Church." His theory of succession was not really a distinct one, but was covered by the first and second theories.

These four theories of historical succession may yet be seen in Southern Baptist life. However, they have become practically two in vivid contrast—the external, mechanical; the inner, spiritual. The first three are logically related and historically associated. A valid church must validly authorize a minister in order that a baptism may be valid. These theories were not welded into one until there emerged about 1850 the high-church movement known as Landmarkism. Since the precipitation of the high-church elements into that rigid system, the two contrasting theories of succession—the external and the internal—stand out in more vivid contrast.

BIBLIOGRAPHY: W. W. Barnes, *The Southern Baptist Convention: 1845–1953* (1954). T. Crosby, *History of English Baptists* (1738). J. R. Graves, *Old Landmarkism: What Is It?* (1928). F. M. McConnell, *Manual for Baptist Churches* (1926).

WILLIAM W. BARNES

SUFFERING. Religion is concerned with suffering because of the observed relationship between man's well-being and the quality of his character and conduct.

The Bible closely associates suffering and sin. This is usually taken to mean that suffering is the result of sin. The Old Testament contains several examples of the theory that each person suffers for his own sin. The difficulties involved in this idea are considered by the book of Job. Others, like Augustine and Calvin, interpret the Bible as teaching (Rom. 5:12 ff.) that the penalty is suffered by the race as a whole.

There are many who believe suffering to be not so much a penalty for sin as a part of the structure of consciousness. These would insist that its chief function is protective and educative, a means whereby life's highest values are enjoined and conserved.

The biblical ideas are gathered up in the thought that suffering is closely related to the good as well as to evil. The highest qualities of suffering are identified with the character and experience of God himself, actualized in the crucifixion of Jesus Christ.

BIBLIOGRAPHY: H. W. Robinson, *Human and Divine* (1939).

S. A. NEWMAN

SULPHUR FORK BAPTIST ASSOCIATIONAL CAMP. Founded in 1951 in Shelby County, Ky. Facilities are rented from the Shelby County Baptist Camp for one or two weeks per year. The Sulphur Fork Association supports the camps, proposing to promote Royal Ambassador and Girls' Auxiliary camp work at low cost.

ELDRED M. TAYLOR

SULPHUR SPRING ACADEMY. A Baptist school in Alexander County, N. C., operated after 1876 by G. W. Greene in Yadkin Association. D. L. SMILEY

SUMMERS, LUTHER DAVIS (b. Paris, Tenn., Apr. 27, 1875; d. Hot Springs, Ark., June 15, 1953). Denominational leader. He married Clara Petty, May 20, 1899. They had four children. He was educated in Union University, Jackson, Tenn., moved to Arkansas in 1914, and was pastor of the First Baptist Church, Blytheville, 1914–20. He was financial secretary for the Baptist College, Jonesboro, Ark., 1920–24; assistant general secretary of the Arkansas Baptist Convention in 1924; and financial secretary for Central College, Conway, Ark., 1925–28. He was vice-president of the Arkansas Baptist Convention, 1922 and 1929. He served as pastor of Park Place Baptist Church, Hot Springs, 1928–35; First Church, Mena, 1935–43; First Church, Prescott, 1945; Emmanuel Church, Hot Springs, 1949–51. He organized Lake Hamilton Church, Hot Springs, 1932; Bethel Church, near Prescott, 1941; and Emmanuel Church, Hot Springs, 1949. He was moderator of seven associations in Arkansas. In 1942, while pastor at Mena, he set in operation legal procedure for ousting Commonwealth (Communist) College from that place. MRS. L. D. SUMMERS

SUNBEAM ACTIVITIES. A quarterly publication of Woman's Missionary Union containing plans for Sunbeam Band leaders, which first appeared in 1953. It was started because the age span reached through *World Comrades,* its predecessor, was too great for one magazine. "*World Comrades* must attempt an all but impossible service in appealing to Sunbeams from four to eight years of age as well as to Girls' Auxiliary members, nine to sixteen." Edited by Juliette Mather, secretary of the Woman's Missionary Union Department of Publications, *Sunbeam Activities* contains programs, stories, songs, pictures, and activities. Subscriptions transferred to *Sunbeam Activities* from *World Comrades* totaled 10,611, and circulation increased to 27,238 by 1955. MARY PATRICIA POWELL

SUNBEAM BAND. The oldest young people's organization of Woman's Missionary Union, for children under nine years of age, it began in 1886 before Woman's Missionary Union was organized. In 1955, 14,224 Sunbeam Bands had 228,289 members.

Children were led into missions as the result of the missionary awakening started by Mary Webb in 1800 in Boston. The idea of missions moved on to Virginia and other Southern states where there are early records of juvenile missionary societies and Children's Cent Societies. Organization of the first Sunbeam Band may be credited to George Braxton Taylor, who, as a young pastor, coupled his missionary earnestness with the zest of Mrs. Anna L. Elsom of his church at Fairmont, Va., and started the band to give children missionary intelligence. The children were enthusiastic about the meetings, which Mrs. Elson, "Mother of Sunbeams," helped to plan and conduct, and news of the organization spread until requests for Taylor's programs led to inclusion of material from "Cousin George" in the *Foreign Mission Journal.* Catechistic in nature, the material consisted of imaginary question-and-answer journeys and brief stories.

Three years after Sunbeam Band beginnings in 1886, Mississippi and North Carolina Woman's Missionary Union central committees endorsed the work. Virginia Sunbeams were supporting a missionary on the field, while Sunbeams in Mississippi, Alabama, and other states had contributed generously to the Italian Chapel Fund. By 1889 a total of 284 Sunbeam Bands reported 8,000 to 10,000 members. Correspondence between Taylor and the Woman's Missionary Union executive committee led to a plan of work for 1892 which urged the society of every church to appoint a bright, consecrated woman to organize children's bands, attend meetings, and impress upon children the importance of praying for people on mission fields. In 1889, at the request of Foreign and Home Mission Board secretaries, Woman's Missionary Union suggested that a specific sum be set up for the children's organizations for home missions, and another for foreign missions. Subsequently, Sunbeam schools and churches were built in Yintak and Canton, China, and in Cardenas, Cuba. Although the children gave generously, leaders agreed that "their education in missions is more important than the gifts they bring."

In 1896, at the Foreign Mission Board's request, Woman's Missionary Union assumed full responsibility for development of the Sunbeams. Sunbeam Band superintendents had already been appointed in some states, and with the women's added responsibility for promoting the work, all states were urged to appoint state leaders. More space was offered for the Sunbeams in the *Foreign Mission Journal* in 1892, and Fannie E. S. Heck (*q.v.*) agreed to supply the material. Programs were moved into *Our Mission Fields* in 1906, and into *World Comrades* in 1922, when more space for Sunbeam Band programs made possible the suggestion of special adaptations for younger children. By 1942 a separation of preschool and school-age Sunbeams was recommended in the plan of work. *Sunbeam Activities* appeared as a quarterly for leaders devoted entirely to Sunbeam work in 1953. It contained suggestions for preschool and school-age children and later used the terms Beginner and Primary Sunbeams. Mission storybooks have been published for Sunbeams, as have programs on stewardship and for the weeks of prayer. In 1955 Elsie Rives, a trained specialist in elementary education, became the first Convention-wide Sunbeam secretary.

JULIETTE MATHER

SUNDAY. Appreciation of the Lord's Day (Christian Sunday) involves understanding the

Jewish sabbath, its relation to the Lord's Day, and the ethical and religious values of both.

Though seven-day units of time were common in primitive societies, historians have been unable to find in them any trace of a sabbath.

The concept of rest was prominent when Moses introduced the sabbath in Exodus 16. This idea is uniformly traced back to the account of the creation. When the law was given on Sinai, God commanded, "Remember the sabbath day, to keep it holy" (Ex. 20:8 RSV). Here the sabbath became a religious institution. Sabbath observance early came to comprise rest, worship, and sacrifice; but by the time of the Babylonian captivity, the observance had deteriorated into ceremony and festivity. During the Exile the Jews re-evaluated the sabbath, and sabbath-keeping became the distinguishing mark of Judaism. The Ezra-Nehemiah reform movement stressed the Torah, and Scripture reading became an integral part of sabbath worship.

The Mosaic meaning of the sabbath had been lost in ritualism by the time Jesus came. First-century Jews were required to keep not only the law but the rabbis' numerous, extravagant, and often absurd interpretations, which overshadowed the sabbath's intrinsic meaning.

When Jesus came, he declared, "The sabbath was made for man, not man for the sabbath" (Mark 2:27 RSV). He thus left no doubt that the institution of the sabbath was to be sublimated to the good of mankind. Jesus did not teach that ceremonial law was intended to be absolute. The institution was always a means, never an end.

Precisely when or why the early Christians adopted the first, in preference to the last, day of the week as their day for worship is obscure. For some years Christians observed both sabbath and Lord's Day. It was not easy for Christian Jews to break completely with Judaism. The two days were, however, distinct and separate. Most references to the first day of the week in the New Testament derive their meaning from the resurrection of Jesus. Since the resurrection, the focal point of the Christian faith, occurred on the first day of the week, it was logical for that day to be adopted by the early Christians as their day of fellowship and worship, even though neither the acceptance of that day nor its use was commanded. Existing fragmentary evidence indicates the observance of the day involved various activities—singing, prayer, Scripture reading, preaching, breaking of bread, and fellowship.

The relationship of the Jewish sabbath to the Lord's Day is clarified by Paul in Colossians 2:16–17. According to him there are transient and permanent aspects of the sabbath. That which is Jewish is transient. Only the substance, that which belongs to Christ, is permanent. The sabbath principle is still in effect, even as it always has been, but the last day of the week is no longer a symbol. The Lord's Day "is the sign that the earthly work of God in Christ has been accomplished in Christ's death and resurrection."

God has created man for himself. Man can only fulfil his purpose as he comes to full maturity in Christ. The Lord's Day provides an opportunity for man to nurture his soul as he confronts the source and meaning of life.

After the time of Constantine the Christian church sought to fence the Lord's Day about with civil prohibitions, much as Judaism had done for the sabbath, but the value of the Lord's Day cannot be protected primarily by civil law. Keeping it is essentially a matter of choice. A legalistic approach to the day turns it into a day of tyranny and gloom and a contradiction of the spirit and intention of Jesus, whose ethic is not enforceable but inward.

BIBLIOGRAPHY: J. H. Breasted, *Ancient Times, A History of the Early World* (1916). W. H. Davis, "The Relation to the Jewish People Claimed by Jesus in His Sabbath Teaching," *The Review and Expositor* (Oct., 1933). F. J. Foakes-Jackson, *History of the Christian Church to A.D. 461* (1902). A. R. S. Kennedy, *Exodus* (1912). R. C. Lenski, *The Interpretation of St. Mark's Gospel* (1946). F. F. Moore, *Judaism* (1944). J. Orr, ed., *The International Standard Bible Encyclopedia* (1915). CLAYTON WADDELL

SUNDAY SCHOOL. The term "Sunday school" is of 18th-century origin, meaning, at first, a school which met on Sunday, and finally coming to mean the school of the church, meeting on Sunday, to serve the church in its teaching mission. The Sunday school movement has differed from the religious education of the Middle Ages and the Reformation in that it is (1) a laymen's movement, (2) a Sunday enterprise, and (3) an organized program.

Religious teaching was given prominence in both the Old Testament and the New Testament. As the number of nominal adherents to Christianity during the earlier centuries of the Christian era outstripped the provision of the churches for teaching them, ritualism and symbolism largely replaced the teaching ministry. The Protestant Reformation revived emphasis on teaching: Luther, Calvin, Zwingli, Knox, and others promoted Christian education. However, the teaching ministry of the Jesuits largely checked the Reformation in Europe.

Traditionally, Robert Raikes (1736–1811), printer and publisher of Gloucester, England, is considered the father of the modern Sunday school movement although a number of Sunday schools antedate the one he opened in Gloucester in July, 1780. Through his newspaper, the *Gloucester Journal,* Raikes did much to promote the movement. John Wesley (1703–91), founder of Methodism, gave it his full support. William Fox of Clapton, England (1736–1826), a layman in a Baptist church, was instrumental in leading to the organization of the first Sunday school society (in London, Sept. 7, 1785). James Marion Frost (*q.v.*) says: "That date . . . marked the real beginning of the modern Sunday school movement as an organized effort for the study of God's Word." The various Sunday school societies, unions, conventions, and associations—such as the London Sunday School Union (1803–); the American Sunday School Union (1824–); the National Sunday School Convention in America (1832, 1833, 1859, 1869); the International Sunday School Convention (1875–); the World Convention (1899–) —have been major forces in promoting, directing, and unifying the Sunday school movement.

There were Sunday schools in America prior to that of Raikes in England, although full information about them cannot be substantiated. Christ Church Parish, Savannah, Ga., claims a Sunday school in 1737. As early as 1740, a Seventh-Day German Baptist Church in Ephrata, Pa., had what was claimed as a Sunday school, meeting on the seventh day. Prior to 1780 New England had schools meeting on Sunday, using such materials as the *Hornbook;* John Cotton's catechism, "Milk for Babes" (1646); and *The New England Primer* (1690). At first the common schools of New England, the parochial schools of the Middle Atlantic states, and the private schools of the South all had the Bible or 1750 the content of the day-school curriculum so that there was little feeling of need for religious instruction on Sunday. Beginning about 1750 the content of the day-school curriculum gradually shifted from religious to secular materials, and the need for Sunday schools for religious education became more marked.

Some historians consider the Sunday school established in the home of William Elliott, in Accomac County, Va., in 1785 as the first true Sunday school in America.

The Sunday school movement and the United States of America were born together. The Methodist Conference meeting in Charlestown, S. C., 1790, gave official recognition to the Sunday school. Historians record Sunday schools in various sections of the country during the last decade of the 18th century and the first decade of the 19th, but they were not church schools as we use the term today. The Sunday school movement was largely "sustained by laymen, and upon a union basis; not opposed to, though not a part of, the organized work of the local church."

Prior to the formation of the Sunday and Adult School Union in 1817, there were probably not more than 100 Sunday schools in the United States. Practically none were in the South. Seven years later, more than 700 Sunday schools were listed as voting assent to the name, American Sunday School Union. The first known Baptist Sunday school in the South was organized by 1803 (possibly in 1797) in Second Baptist Church, Baltimore, Md. It is claimed that this school was distinctive in having religious instruction as its sole objective, and it may have been the first denominational Sunday school.

During the first part of the 19th century, there were local Sunday school unions in Philadelphia, New York, and elsewhere; and some denominations had unions. The American Sunday School Union, organized in 1824, absorbed most of the existing unions and gave Sunday school work a national scope. In 1830–32 the union promoted a Sunday school missionary enterprise in the Mississippi Valley (an area covering about 20 states). It is estimated that through this effort half of the 10,000 new settlements in that area were supplied with Sunday schools, many of which became churches. A similar undertaking proposed for the Southern states was questioned on the grounds of separation of church and state and was later suspended by the Civil War. Over a 50-year period, 1824–74, the union sold and donated literature valued at about $6,000,000 and organized over 60,000 schools with 2,500,000 pupils. Some of its active supporters were Francis Scott Key (1780–1843), Daniel Webster (1782–1858), Lyman Beecher (1775–1863), and Stephen H. Tyng (1810–85). Rice lists ten union missionaries who organized over 1,000 Sunday schools each. Steven Paxton (1808–81), in 20 years, reported 1,314 new Sunday schools which he had organized, with over 83,000 members.

The Sunday school movement developed slowly in the South, retarded by the vast distances, the poor transportation, the isolation and smallness of the churches, and the inadequate church buildings. The stratification of society, with the existence of an aristocracy, delayed the establishment of public schools until after the Civil War. Illiteracy was common; the ministry uneducated; teachers were hard to secure. War and post-war conditions reduced finances, produced a paper shortage, and made it difficult to secure literature and other supplies.

In the United States the Sunday school curriculum has passed through several stages, which may be designated, in general, as: (1) catechistical (1790–1815); (2) memory period, following the formation of the American Bible Society (1816); (3) the period of experimentation (about 1840–72) during which time various denominations created lesson committees; (4) development of Uniform Lessons (1872 ff.); and (5) development of graded Sunday schools and Graded Lesson series, in the 1890's. Today Southern Baptists are extensive users of the Uniform Lessons, but they use also Graded Lessons on the children's and youth levels. In both cases the lessons are prepared by denominational writers and editors.

Prior to 1850 Southern Baptist Sunday schools depended largely upon the International Sunday School Association and the American Baptist Publication Society for direction and for literature. The Southern Baptist Convention, organized in 1845, had no Sunday School Board until 1863; and not until May, 1891, was its present Sunday School Board established, although publication of *Kind Words,* which later grew into a series of Sunday school literature, had been carried on since 1866.

James Marion Frost, the first corresponding secretary of the Sunday School Board of the Southern Baptist Convention, and Bernard

Washington Spilman (*q.v.*), the first field secretary, during the first quarter of the 20th century, built on the Sunday school methods already in use by the International Sunday School Association. Even so, they developed a distinctive program of Sunday school work suited to Southern Baptist needs and doctrines. Field promotion was carried on in co-operation with the state Sunday school secretaries and financed through the earnings of the publication work of the board.

By the early 1900's there were many teacher-training courses extant, and teacher training was receiving active promotion. Spilman led Southern Baptists to launch a comprehensive training program geared to reach Sunday school workers and potential workers with only average schooling and designed to be taught by local church leaders. A popular historian from outside the denomination has called this training program "the Southern Baptist miracle," because of the number of workers it has reached and the effect it has had on the Sunday schools of the denomination.

Under the leadership of Spilman and later of Arthur Flake (*q.v.*), the first secretary in the Department of Sunday School Administration (1920), and other leaders, the board developed a science of Sunday school expansion based on well-defined laws of growth. Practices inherent in these laws are (1) close age grading, covering the entire life span of every individual; (2) use of adequate, pupil-centered records; (3) annual promotion; (4) small units; and (5) constant multiplication of units (classes, departments, new Sunday schools). Even during the general decline in Sunday school enrolment during the period between World War I and World War II, there were only three years (1918, 1926, 1929) in which Southern Baptist Sunday schools showed a loss of enrolment. Southern Baptists insist that the Sunday school is the church at work in its reaching and teaching ministry; also that the Bible is the center of the curriculum as to content, and that the pupil is the center as to approach, application, and teaching methods.

Today the Sunday school is proving an effective agent within the churches for evangelism; for the teaching of missions, stewardship, and doctrines; for enlistment in service; for developing denominational loyalty; and for cultivating Christian faith and character.

BIBLIOGRAPHY: A. A. Brown, *A History of Religious Education in Recent Times* (1923). P. E. Burroughs, *Fifty Fruitful Years* (1941). C. S. Green, *B. W. Spilman, the Sunday School Man* (1953). E. W. Rice, *The Sunday School Movement and the American Sunday School Union* (1917). J. N. BARNETTE

SUNDAY SCHOOL BOARD, THE. An agency of the Southern Baptist Convention, located at 127 Ninth Avenue, North, Nashville, Tenn., which was authorized by action of the Convention, May 11, 1891, and was organized by the elected trustees in a meeting at the First Baptist Church, Nashville, Tenn., May 26, 1891. In its present bylaws it is declared:

> The Board is responsible to the Convention, but is a servant of the churches. It serves the churches through the development of curricula for Bible study and Christian training, the preparation and distribution of literature and supplies, and the development and promotion of a methodology in harmony with the great doctrines of the Bible and the purposes of a church.

The board is incorporated under a charter granted by the state of Tennessee—the first one obtained in 1897; the second one, June 23, 1921, amended May 4, 1950.

In this monograph are presented the essential facts of the board's history, explanations of its major emphases and policies, and descriptions of its services. Other related subjects, such as Sunday school, Training Union, and other specific activities and enterprises, are treated separately.

I. Survey of History. PRIOR MOVEMENTS. The board was the fruition of various movements in Southern Baptist life. Religious tract societies had arisen in response to the need for religious literature. The Sunday school movement, growing in popularity, created a demand for teaching materials. Though the Convention in its first regular session (1846) decided against creating a publishing enterprise, some dissenting messengers a year later organized the Southern Baptist Publication Society. It operated until 1863. That year Basil Manly, Jr. (*q.v.*), and John Albert Broadus (*q.v.*) led the Convention to organize the first Sunday School Board (1863–73). This board rendered notable service through the publication of question books, catechisms, teachers' books, and hymnbooks. Most notably, it began the publication of *Kind Words* (Jan., 1866). Developing frictions, particularly with the doctrinal and publication interests of James Robinson Graves (*q.v.*), and economic problems arising out of the Civil War, made the survival of this board, which had been moved to Memphis in 1868, impossible. The Convention decided to consolidate it with the Domestic and Indian Mission Board (Home Mission Board) in 1873. A year later it was relieved of the responsibility for Sunday school work but was instructed to continue the publication of *Kind Words,* which in 1887 became the basis of a series of Sunday school lesson helps.

There were other factors, also, antedating the organization of the Sunday School Board. The South was destitute financially; hence the churches were in like condition. There was still much prejudice against Sunday schools. The American Baptist Publication Society of Philadelphia had a sizable business in the South. Many churches depended upon it for Sunday school lesson materials and supplies. The society vigorously developed its work by locating branch offices in Atlanta, Dallas, and St. Louis. Through influential Southern Baptist pastors and denominational leaders, most of whom were preparing material for the society's publications, the society sought to discourage and prevent, first, the publication of Sunday school lessons by the Home Mission Board, and second, any movement within the Convention to create a publishing house of its own. But a sense of denominational mission was growing, also a conviction that a denominational agency to produce literature for the churches was indispensable to unity and progress.

Dramatic Beginning. The effort to create a new Sunday School Board came to focus in the person of James Marion Frost (*q.v.*), then pastor of the Leigh Street Baptist Church in Richmond, Va. He published an article in *The Religious Herald*, Feb., 1890, proposing the idea. He later declared, "God touched me and I thought it." Both opposition and commendation followed. The Convention set up a Sunday School Committee instead of a board of publication. The new committee accomplished little but recommended to the Convention in 1891 the appointment of a Sunday School Board. The report was referred to a special committee, of which Frost and James Bruton Gambrell (*q.v.*) were members. They represented opposing views and were asked to formulate the committee's report. Finally they reached this agreement: Frost could write the report, provided Gambrell could write the last paragraph, provided further that Frost could add one sentence. This historic paragraph and the last sentence were

> In conclusion your committee, in its long and earnest consideration of this whole matter in all its environments, have been compelled to take account of the well known fact, that there are widely divergent views held among us by brethren equally earnest, consecrated and devoted to the best interest of the Master's Kingdom. It is therefore, recommended that the fullest freedom of choice be accorded to every one as to what literature he will use or support, and that no brother be disparaged in the slightest degree on account of what he may do in the exercise of his right as Christ's freeman.
>
> But we would earnestly urge all brethren to give to this Board a fair consideration, and in no case to obstruct it in the great work assigned it by this Convention.

Then the report calling for the creation of a board co-ordinate with the other two boards, with Nashville as its location, was presented to the Convention, acted on without debate through the plea and influence of Broadus, and adopted with only 13 dissenting votes. Primarily, the board was to be entrusted with the Convention's Sunday school series and the Sunday school interests in the Convention territory. It was not to engage in other publication work. Also, it was to bring out periodicals under a printing contract and to aid mission Sunday schools "through state organizations."

The members of the board met in Nashville, May 26, 1891, and elected Lansing Burrows (*q.v.*) corresponding secretary. When he declined, the board a month later elected Frost, who accepted the call and began his new task July 1. At the same meeting it elected Samuel Boykin (*q.v.*) "editor of all the *Kind Words* series," which was transferred by instruction of the Convention to the new agency. He was already the editor, in the employ of the Home Mission Board.

Early Years. The board had a corresponding secretary and an editor. It had no capital, no office, no facilities. But it had a mission, and friends were ready to be of assistance. For a few months Frost, with a small desk of his own brought from Richmond, occupied space without charge in the office of the *Baptist and Reflector*. After six months he moved to the Presbyterian Building, and two months later to offices offered free by the Methodist Publishing House, with which firm a printing contract had been made. Here the board's office remained until Feb. 27, 1897.

Frost borrowed personally a small amount of money to begin operations. Two short-time bank loans, endorsed by board members, took care of needs until there were receipts from the sale of literature. A year after the board's organization its financial condition was declared "exceedingly satisfactory." It could report to the Convention in 1892 a balance above liabilities of $4,081.63. The secretary also reported: The board "now promises to be a unifying element in our denominational life and enterprises." He emphasized its spiritual mission: "to awaken, develop, organize and strengthen our churches in the great work of teaching God's truth to young and old."

At the end of 1892, Frost resigned to accept the pastorate of the First Baptist Church in Nashville, sincerely believing that the new board could go on without peril and that he in his new position could reinforce his successor and serve the board almost as effectively as he had in an employed relationship. Theodore Percy Bell (*q.v.*), then assistant corresponding secretary of the Foreign Mission Board, was elected to succeed Frost. His tenure likewise was brief, for he resigned Jan. 30, 1896, because of having purchased *The Christian Index* of Atlanta. But the three-year period was significant. The circulation of literature showed a steady increase. Grants were made from financial receipts to the states for their Sunday school mission work. Initial steps were taken to encourage B.Y.P.U. work as indicated by the publication of *Young People's Leader* (1894), which was later (1900) to become *The B.Y.P.U. Quarterly*. Bell led the board to take charge of missionary day in the Sunday schools and to create a reserve fund for future developments. His service as corresponding secretary was chiefly that of stabilizing all that the board had undertaken.

The trustees unanimously turned to Frost again, who had been serving as president, and he was called back to the corresponding secretaryship. In his letter of acceptance he declared his conviction that the board "carries within itself . . . the very life of the Convention. . . . We are working at the very base of things" related to denominational progress and the bringing in of the kingdom of Christ.

The board faced the need for suitable property. The purchase of a building at 167 North Cherry Street (now Fourth Avenue) was approved Sept. 14, 1896. The board met in its assembly room Mar. 5, 1897, and by the end of the year paid the last note on the property. The American Baptist Publication Society had continued its efforts to hold the loyalties of Southern Baptists and to supply the literature needed by their churches. Through its corresponding secretary it made direct overtures to Frost, subtly disparaging the prospects of the new board, claiming the prior right to serve Southern Baptist churches, and offering to absorb the new board into its own life and work. The offer was courteously but firmly declined with pointed affirmation that the board had no thought of retiring from the field or betraying the trust committed to it by the Convention.

The board weathered the financial depression of the 1890's. Receipts increased each year except 1898, when there was a reduction in the price of periodicals. Growth marked each phase of its work—the circulation of periodicals; missionary day offerings, which were sent to the Home and Foreign Mission boards; proceeds from Children's Day offerings, which were used for Bible distribution; appropriations to the states for mission Sunday school work and for Bible and tract distribution; and accumulations in the reserve fund, started afresh in 1898 after former accumulations had been used in the purchase of property. The board began promoting (1897) a Home Department, providing materials to encourage Bible study in the home.

A major development came in 1897. The board published its first book, *The Story of Yates the Missionary* by Charles Elisha Taylor (*q.v.*). This action was contrary to the instructions of the Convention when the board was authorized in 1891. Frost reported in detail to the Convention in 1898, explaining how the board had set aside $500 as the Matthew T. Yates Publishing Fund to make the publication of this book possible. He reported that the book was already a financial success and appealed to the Convention to allow the board liberty in book publication on the basis of endowments which might be received for such purposes. The request was granted. But the board was admonished to be cautious, and much caution prevailed in the years that followed. From year to year, reports stressed book publication. The Eva Garvey Fund (Jan. 21, 1899) and the Constance Pollock Fund (Mar. 8, 1902) made possible a succession of volumes, among which were *Baptist Why and Why Not* by some 20 writers on various subjects, *Parliamentary Law* by Franklin Howard Kerfoot (*q.v.*), and *The Pastor and the Sunday School* by William Eldridge Hatcher (*q.v.*).

Boykin died Nov. 3, 1899. He had been editor of *Kind Words* for more than 30 years and was the one person whose service had formed a link with the first Sunday School Board (1863–73) on through the Home Mission Board to the second Sunday School Board in the publication of literature for the churches. Isaac Jacobus Van Ness (*q.v.*), then joint editor of *The Christian Index,* was elected to succeed Boykin. He began work with the board Jan. 1, 1900. His former experience as a pastor, his editorial experience, and his personal gifts qualified him well for the position which he was to fill with distinction for 17 years.

Pioneering Education Work. *Field secretaries.*—As the new century began, there were 9,711 Sunday schools but 9,000 churches without schools. The corresponding secretary felt keenly the need, even in the best schools, "for better equipment, better teaching, better methods, and better results." The board needed a field secretary, and it elected Bernard Washington Spilman (*q.v.*) to this position. He began his work in June, 1901, 10 years after the board was created. Of him Frost said: "He came to Nashville, looked into the little dingy office, . . . and decided to open his office on the field and set up his study in railroad trains along the wayside."

A new era of pioneering in the development of an educational program had begun. Field secretaries were employed as the board's resources made such possible. Covering a 10-year period, the following persons were employed, the years each one served being indicated: Spilman, 1901–40; Richard M. Inlow, 1903–06; Landrum Pinson Leavell (*q.v.*), 1903–29; Harvey Beauchamp (*q.v.*), 1905–38; W. E. Brittain, 1905–06; Hight C Moore, 1907–08; C. E. Crossland, 1909–10; Ernest Eugene Lee, 1909–46; Arthur Flake (*q.v.*), 1909–36; Annie Laurie Williams (*q.v.*), 1909–32; Prince Emmanuel Burroughs (*q.v.*), 1910–43; William Sherman Wiley (*q.v.*), 1910–35; Margaret A. Frost, 1910–41. This group of workers charted courses and laid foundations for Southern Baptist Sunday school and B.Y.P.U. work which made possible the growth and victories of future years. Along with these board workers, many of the states were employing Sunday school secretaries who were in reality associates in the denomination's program of Sunday school work.

Training leadership.—The board sought to develop "better methods in Sunday school teaching and equipment and management." Spilman's first efforts were directed chiefly toward the training of teachers. He wrote a booklet, *The Sunday School,* treating such subjects as history and methods, organization and management, and teachers and teaching. A companion booklet was *The Books of the Bible* by Hight C Moore. Both were published by the board in 1902, the beginning of the Normal Course for Sunday School Workers. Later they became *The Convention Normal Manual* (1909), which included a section by Leavell dealing with the pupil. The board had announced earlier in 1907 "The Teacher Training System," which included the lecture course, the reading course, and the normal course, each one requiring a prescribed amount of work. Spilman and the other field secretaries traveled over all parts of the Convention, visiting churches, attending conventions, holding institutes, speaking in assemblies and camps, going to colleges, always proclaiming the gospel of Sunday school improvement. Some of the strongest churches of the Convention were led to conduct training schools with able faculties—notably the First Baptist in Nashville (1906), in Fort Worth (1908), and in Dallas (1908). In a short time "the training class and the training school had become established institutions."

Other means of Sunday school improvement were given attention. Emphasis was placed on the grading of pupils in classes by age groups. In 1908 Beauchamp outlined the Standard of Excellence, which became a basic pattern of work and objective in Southern Baptist Sunday schools. Also, he wrote *The Graded Sunday School,* which was published by the board in 1911. The emphasis on Sunday school work, including improved organization and methods, created the demand for improved building facilities, so that the workers of the board sought continually to interpret and promote the educational significance of properly designed and adequate church buildings.

The corresponding secretary of the board was quick to realize the importance of helping pastors to be instructed about Sunday school work. In June, 1901, he recommended to the board that it furnish means for an annual lecture course at the Southern Baptist Theological Seminary to be related distinctively to Sunday school work. It elicited much interest on the part of pastors and provided helpful literature on Sunday school work. In 1906 the board agreed to pay half the salary to provide for a chair of Sunday school pedagogy at the seminary and set aside $6,000 to cover the five-year agreement. Byron Hoover DeMent (*q.v.*), pastor of the First Baptist Church, Waco, Tex., was elected to this position. In connection with the seminary's special effort to raise endowment funds in 1909, the board pledged $1,000 for every $2,000 raised by the Sunday schools for this purpose, up to an aggregate of $60,000, and requested that this sum be used to endow permanently the chair of pedagogy in honor of Basil Manly, Jr. The final payment of $30,000 was made in 1916. The money given for the lecture course and the chair of pedagogy was considered an investment in training pastoral and denominational leadership in the interest of Sunday school progress.

Improvement of literature.—Constant emphasis was given to improving the literature provided for the churches. The *Bible Class Quarterly* was added to the list with the beginning of 1902. *Baptist Boys and Girls* was started in 1904. A *Superintendent's Quarterly* was begun in 1905. With the beginning of 1909, a *Children's Quarterly* was added and the former *Primary Quarterly* was changed to the *Junior Quarterly*. The *Home Department Magazine* (1910) was published to encourage Bible study at home. The quality of paper, format of the pages, and size of the periodicals were matters of concern and areas of improvement.

Another emphasis in the board's pioneering educational program related to the B.Y.P.U. The *B.Y.P.U. Quarterly* was begun in 1900. It was published at the request of the B.Y.P.U. of the South. Interest in B.Y.P.U. work increased. The field secretaries of the board gave attention to B.Y.P.U. as well as Sunday school work. The board reported to the Convention in 1907 the plan of using distinctively Southern Baptist subjects rather than those of the B.Y.P.U. of America in the *B.Y.P.U. Quarterly*. It published the *B.Y.P.U. Manual* by L. P. Leavell, who was specifically assigned to the promotion of the B.Y.P.U. among the churches. In 1908 it announced plans to publish the *Junior B.Y.P.U. Quarterly,* which was really for the Intermediate age group. A year later a joint committee had been appointed by the board and the executive committee of the B.Y.P.U. of the South to prepare a course of study and direct B.Y.P.U. education for Juniors, Intermediates, and Seniors.

Graded Lessons were being widely discussed by interdenominational educators. The board began an experiment in 1907 by providing in the regular lesson quarterlies material for a "Graded Supplemental Course." It issued also an elective course, "Advanced Course of Study in the Ethical Teaching of Jesus" by John Richard Sampey (*q.v.*), in four pamphlets treating a total of 58 lessons. The Graded Supplemental Lessons were for the Beginner, Primary, Junior, and Intermediate (one year) departments. A strong protest to the International Sunday School Association relative to Graded Lessons strongly liberal in theological viewpoint resulted, with opposition in other circles, in such modification of the outlines that they later became the basis, with considerable adaptation, for the development of Graded Lessons by the board. By 1914 the board could report a "full graded course" for Beginners up through Intermediates, with consideration being given to a Senior course which did materialize beginning in 1915.

Book publishing.—The board's program of book publishing was carried forward timidly, the board reporting each year to the Convention on new projects. The books published were worthy but not pretentious; they were chiefly doctrinal or related to educational aspects of Sunday school work. The Convention in 1910 approved resolutions that "the board be authorized and urged to enter, at as early date as possible, on the work of supplying the brethren of our churches with books, tracts, hymn and songbooks, and indeed all supplies for churches, Sunday schools, missionary societies, Young People's Unions, such as are suitable and desirable." The board was thereafter under specific instruction to serve the denomination in a way commensurate with its needs in the book field. By 1911 the board reported that it had printed a total of 32 books with total copies of 292,251.

Denominational service and summary.—Other important developments in the board's life during this period were the following: Appropriations for mission work and the various causes of the Convention increased from year to year. In 1908 the board reported a gift of $20,500 to Woman's Missionary Union, the purchase price of a house in which to conduct the W.M.U. Training School. It published (1905) a hymnbook containing more than 500 hymns and songs, which became widely used. It served the Convention in the distribution of Bibles and for this one cause encouraged contributions to the board. It promoted the idea that the B.Y.P.U. supplements the Sunday school. Leavell and Flake gave much of their time to this object, and Lee all of his time. It organized the Adult Bible Class Department to encourage class organization and a close relationship of Adult Sunday school classes to the churches. It added in 1915 a postgraduate course of five books to the regular training course for teachers. The board's growth required the expansion of its plant and the improvement of its property. It bought the Cole property, 710 Church Street, in 1903 for $60,000. It later sold its Cherry Street property for more than $10,000. In 1912 it purchased property on Eighth Avenue for future building purposes, the amount involved being $60,000. The following year it erected a building at this location at a cost of $150,000 and sold its Church Street property for $200,000.

The death of Frost on Oct. 31, 1916, ended an administration of remarkable achievement. Almost four months later, Edgar Estes Folk (*q.v.*) died. He had served as president of the board from 1895 until his death and had been a wise counselor in the determination of board policy and in developing the board's program. Under Frost's leadership the board's financial resources had grown to more than $600,000. The annual receipts had grown to almost a half-million dollars. Its contributions to benevolence and missions had gone beyond $800,000. Much more important, the board had developed a program of teaching and training in the churches that was achieving inspiring results. A bronze plaque in the entrance of the building on Eighth Avenue, placed there in 1936, appropriately sums up Frost's relationship and contribution to the board, as follows: "Divinely Led/His Faith Conceived It/His Genius Planned It/His Courage Built It." By action of the board in June, 1955, the building on Eighth Avenue was named the Frost Building.

EXPANDING PROGRAM. *Under the new administration.*—Pending the next annual session of the Convention, a committee of the board appointed "to examine into all the work of the Board" recommended the election of Van Ness as acting corresponding secretary, which was done on Nov. 28, 1916. The committee decided that the "work has been well established, that it is today in the very best condition, with its funds intact and well invested." Certain organizational adjustments, likely growing out of the committee's exploration, were made in the following months. The business department was organized into three divisions: a bookkeeping and cashier's department, an order and mailing department, and a sales department. Van Ness's election received Convention approval in the 1917 session. The new executive had served as editorial secretary for 17½ years and was well qualified for administrative leadership. His plans and policies were cautiously conceived, and they were carefully administered in an expanding program related to every phase of the board's life and work.

Growing out of previous exploration, the board requested the Convention (1917) to explore plans for ministerial relief and reported that it had set aside $100,000 to be held intact for this purpose if the Convention were to authorize the creation of an agency for this function. The Convention did create the Board of Ministerial Relief; and in Sept., 1918, the board transferred to this agency the full amount plus some accumulated interest. Thereafter it was not contemplated that large appropriations would be made. It was decided that funds would be used (1) to maintain field work; (2) to co-operate with state boards in the expansion of their work; (3) to extend free tract distribution; (4) to carry forward Bible and colportage work, in co-operation with states and other agencies; (5) to help the Home and Foreign Mission boards in the areas related to the Sunday School Board's responsibility; and (6) to assist educational institutions (seminaries) insofar as they might become helpers in the work of Sunday school extension. The basic provisions of that policy guided the board in the decades which followed.

Other matters of import under the new administration were the following: The board elected (1917) Edwin Charles Dargan (*q.v.*), pastor of the First Baptist Church of Macon, Ga., and Hight C Moore, editor of *The Biblical Recorder* (North Carolina), as its chief editors. Dargan was to be editor of *The Teacher* and expository periodicals, and Moore was to be managing editor and editor of the weekly papers and *The Home Department Magazine.* The board thus had for its editorial leadership two men of mature scholarship, influential in the Convention's life. The first of that year (1917) Gaines Stanley Dobbins had joined the board's editorial staff and was assigned the editorship of *Home and Foreign Fields,* a missionary journal being undertaken for the two mission boards. In 1918 L. P. Leavell, who had been a field secretary since 1903, was asked to become the secretary of the newly established B.Y.P.U. Department and the editor of the B.Y.P.U. periodicals and the *Organized Class Magazine.* Upon instructions from the Convention, the board established the Organized Class Department and designated Harry Lee Strickland (*q.v.*) as the secretary. The Organized Class Movement, originating from the Baraca-Philathea Movement, had grown to a position of strong influence. The board's new department was designed to give guidance to this movement, tie it closely to the churches, and capture the potential for constructive denominational values. The department made provision also for the promotion and guidance of Intermediate classes. Also in 1917 the board created the Architectural Department, assigning the leadership responsibility to Burroughs with the understanding that he would divide his time between teacher training and guidance for the right kind of church buildings. He developed a book of plans, *Church and Sunday School Buildings,* and discovered rising interest in providing buildings for graded and departmental Sunday schools.

There was a developing interest among Southern Baptists in the board's book publishing program. In substance, the Convention in 1917 called for enlarging this service. Van Ness reported in 1918 the board's eagerness to carry out the instructions, the difficulties due to lack of any effective means of book distribution, and the purpose to try to work out the problem. The board was of course confronted by problems incident to World War I. A special publication for servicemen was issued, *On the March with the Master,* and tracts and New Testaments were generously supplied.

The board carried out Convention instructions (1917) to co-operate with the Home Mission Board and other bodies in starting the Baptist Bible Training School in New Orleans (later Baptist Bible Institute and subsequently New Orleans Baptist Theological Seminary). It gave $10,000 as the initial payment on the new property. It made an appropriation for the Department of Sunday School Education of Southwestern Baptist Theological Seminary in keeping with its policy of helping institutions of learning.

The venture in publishing a missionary journal, *Home and Foreign Fields,* which was begun by action of the 1916 Convention, was a financial liability from the beginning. The board's losses from year to year amounted to from $5,000 to $10,000—even more in some years.

Postwar expansion.—The postwar era confronted the board with expanding needs and opportunities. There were 75 regular employees. The board (1919) had eight departments with a responsible person over each one: Order, Accounting, Sales, Editorial, Architectural, Educational, Organized Class, and B.Y.P.U. Within a short time it created two more—Elementary (1919), under the leadership of Lilian Stevenson Forbes (*q.v.*), and Sunday School Administration (1920), of which Arthur Flake was elected secretary.

The Convention launched a movement in 1919 to raise $75,000,000 over a five-year period. The board furnished the headquarters for the campaign commission, acted as the fiscal agent, and made the campaign a major emphasis in its periodicals and field program. The growing denominational life demanded statistical information. Work in this area had been done almost singlehandedly by Lansing Burrows, but in 1918 the Convention transferred this responsibility to the board. The action of the Convention was implemented through the work of Hight C Moore, 1919–20, until the board created in 1921 a Department of Survey, Statistics, and General Information and elected Eugene Perry Alldredge (*q.v.*) as the secretary.

Another area of expansion was in B.Y.P.U. work. The B.Y.P.U. of the South disbanded in 1918. Its work was turned over to the board, which had promoted it through the years. The board now set up (1919) the B.Y.P.U. Department with L. P. Leavell as its secretary and editor, it being understood that he would continue teaching at the Southern Seminary four months each year in the chair of Sunday school pedagogy. By this time nine states had separate B.Y.P.U. secretaries. Representative persons were invited to join with Leavell in planning topics for the *B.Y.P.U. Quarterly* and working out a course of daily Bible readings.

The board all along had been concerned about the needs and development of rural churches. In 1918 it initiated more vigorous efforts to help them, offering to work with the states in a special program and give dollar for dollar to develop rural work. Annual reports recorded increasing appropriations—for example, in 1928 an expenditure of more than $81,000 for this purpose. While the board never had a department of rural work, its field program through the years addressed itself to the needs of rural churches and became, through the development of Sunday school and Training Union work, the foremost factor in the growth of country churches. In the years following World War I the board began conducting annual conferences with the field forces of the states, first with Sunday school workers and later with Training Union workers as well, through which unified plans of promotion and co-operation for all phases of work were developed.

Decade of growth.—In 1921 the board was 30 years old. It now had 115 employees. The first issue of the *Southern Baptist Handbook* appeared that year. The receipts of the preceding year passed $1,000,000, making a total for its 30 years of $7,768,069.17, with total appropriations, not including losses through *Home and Foreign Fields* and offerings on special days for Convention causes, of $1,526,307.92. The board's book publishing program had been carried on cautiously, handicapped chiefly by the problems of distribution. It worked out a co-operative relationship with the book stores operated by state boards for some centralized purchasing and handling of merchandise. A significant advance came in the election of John Leonard Hill, on the faculty of Georgetown College (Kentucky), as book editor and head of a new Book Editorial Department. He began work with the board in June, 1922. The board also entered into a publishing arrangement with George H. Doran Company of New York, seeking through this connection to obtain better manufacturing and to achieve wider distribution. George Waldo Card became the head of the Sales Promotion Department in 1924. The board offered in 1925 to go into partnership with the state book stores, and the following states entered into the arrangement: Virginia, South Carolina, Georgia, Texas, Arkansas, Louisiana, Florida, and Oklahoma. By 1927 there were 15 stores in the chain. A movement had begun which would have increasing bearing on the board's history, both as to ministry and influence.

In 1920 the board purchased property on Ninth Avenue, North. Later it bought property on Commerce Street. Two buildings were erected, the first one for merchandise and mailing purposes and the second one to be leased to the firm having the printing contract. They were occupied in 1923. A new charter was obtained by the board, June, 1921, to bring the board "under absolute control of the Convention."

The board's organization was expanding. By 1922 it had 11 departments. Within six years it added four more: Intermediate, Daily Vacation Bible School, Student, and Church Administration. The board issued, beginning in 1923, a new series of Graded Lessons under the editorial supervision of the new book editor, John L. Hill. They were for the Beginner, Primary, Junior, Intermediate, and Senior departments. The board decided to renew its printing contract with Marshall & Bruce Company—"on a cost-plus basis"—having the privilege of auditing the books of the printers. This contract ran until 1928, when it was renewed for five years on the same basis.

The following persons were called to join the board's staff, adding much strength to both the editorial and field force: Noble Van Ness, assistant managing editor, 1921; Harold Edward Ingraham, associate in the Department of Sunday School Administration, 1922; Mary Virginia Lee, an assistant in the Organized Class Department, to give special attention to Intermediates, 1922; Willie Jean Stewart, associate editor of Sunday school elementary materials, 1924; Homer Lamar Grice, secretary of the Vacation Bible School Department, 1924; Jerry Elmer Lambdin, field secretary for the B.Y.P.U. Department, 1925; William P. Phillips, to succeed Strickland, who had died, as the head of the Organized Class Department, later changed to Young People's-Adult Department, 1925; Robert Lee Middleton, head of the Accounting Department, 1925; William Asa Harrell, associate in the Young People's-Adult Department, 1926; Jasper Newton Barnette, associate in the Department of Sunday School Administration, to give special attention to rural Sunday school administration, 1927; Clay Irby Hudson, associate in the Department of Church Administration, 1927; Herman Franklin Burns, staff artist in the Editorial Department, 1928; Robbie Trent, editor of elementary Uniform Lessons, 1929. The board sustained three major losses: the death of Strickland in 1924, the retirement of Dargan after 10 years of notable service as editorial secretary in 1927, and the death of L. P. Leavell in 1929.

The board entered into a program of student work by action of the Convention in 1921. The Inter-Board Commission, composed of the executive heads of the Home Mission, Foreign Mission, and Sunday School boards and the Woman's Missionary Union, was made responsible for work in the interest of the religious life of students in the colleges. Frank Hartwell Leavell (*q.v.*) was elected secretary, and he began work with the commission, Jan. 1, 1922, with headquarters established in Memphis. The work of the Inter-Board Commission was transferred to the board and established as the Department of Student Work by action of the Convention in 1928. The board thereafter became the agency of student activities for the Convention. The office was transferred to Nashville, Oct. 1, 1928. William Hall Preston had become Leavell's associate in 1927.

An expansion of Bible teaching in the churches came through the Daily Vacation Bible school. The board sought first to promote it through the Department of Sunday School Administration (1922–24). Then it called Homer Lamar Grice from the pastorate of the First Baptist Church, Washington, Ga., to take charge of a newly created department. He began the work in Sept., 1924. His assignment called for the preparation of a curriculum, the development of plans and materials for promotion, and the field work necessary to arouse interest throughout the Convention and train leaders in the churches. He succeeded, with the assistance of writers, in developing a textbook course, according to a cycle plan, ready for use in 1925. Other materials for the school's leadership were added, also the literature for promotion. Progress was slow at first. But the foundation was laid and principles were conceived that, in subsequent years, made possible remarkable development in Vacation Bible school work.

B.Y.P.U. work during the period 1920–30 became solidly established as an organization for the training of all church members. As early as 1922, full grading of the B.Y.P.U. was promoted. Emphasis was placed on a director for the entire church B.Y.P.U. organization, like the Sunday school superintendent. In 1925 B.Y.P.U. began to be referred to as the General B.Y.P.U. Organization. The coming of Lambdin to the board's staff made possible the development of more promotional literature and another worker giving himself to field promotion. The publication of *The Monthly B.Y.P.U. Magazine* (July, 1926) was a significant factor in promotion. With the death of Leavell, Lambdin succeeded him as secretary and editor. The department began promoting the Baptist Adult Union. Program material was first provided through *The Monthly B.Y.P.U. Magazine,* beginning in Jan., 1929. A year later the new *B.A.U. Quarterly* was added. The enlistment of Adults meant that provision had to be made for children; hence the Story Hour for Beginners and Primaries became a new phase of B.Y.P.U. work.

As a means of effective promotion, the board promoted and conducted Southwide conferences and clinics. The Organized Class Conference met annually, 1922–26. It was succeeded by a general Sunday school conference for all departments and aspects of work. Five were held from 1927 to 1935. Sunday school clinics were conducted. In these a select group of workers were brought together for from one to three weeks of intensive training and laboratory experience in an enlargement campaign. These clinics helped to equip workers with a mastery of the fundamentals of building larger and better Sunday schools. An annual Southwide Student Retreat at Ridgecrest, beginning in 1926, and quadrennial student conferences helped to set forward the program of student work. Southwide Training Union conferences were conducted at intervals beginning with one in 1930.

In response to action by the Convention, the board created (June, 1927) the Department of Church Administration and combined with it its Architectural Department. Burroughs was asked to serve as its secretary, along with his responsibility for the Educational Department. The new department was designed especially for a ministry to pastors, deacons, and general church leaders—to deal with church organization, methods, finances, evangelism, missions, etc. A monthly magazine, *Church Administration*, was published and a study course was developed. Major attention was given to stewardship training and church architecture. There was some duplication in the department's work; also, there was difficulty in implementing its objectives for lack of a specific channel of organization in the church through which to work. Even so, it prepared materials and promoted a unified church ministry that proved valuable to the churches. Its functions were transferred to other departments in 1936, chiefly to the Educational and Training Union departments.

Progress during difficult years.—For the period 1929–35, the board shared the general difficulties of the times. It was called on to render assistance in various ways. It provided office space for the Convention's Executive Committee, which was reorganized by the 1927 Convention and established with headquarters in Nashville; also, it provided funds for the Convention's fixed expenses. It was called on for assistance to the Baptist World Alliance. It was requested by the Convention to take over the operation of the Ridgecrest Baptist Assembly (1929). The property was maintained in good condition and the summer program made a definite denominational asset. There was a drop in board receipts of $40,000 reported in 1929, but a slight gain the next year. Through rigid economies the board maintained an excellent financial condition. A decrease of more than $200,000 was reported in 1933, but contributions to denominational work decreased only $72,000. Prices of certain periodicals were reduced, and a 10 per cent reduction for cash was allowed. The board had to draw to some extent on its reserves in order not to let its denominational appropriations sag. There was fear that some of the book stores would have to be closed; most of them, however, were operated in co-operation with state boards. They were maintained as "service agencies" for the people.

In the meantime there was growing criticism of the board's operations. The board in its meeting, Mar., 1930, took note of certain criticism about the content of its periodicals and declared its purpose that its literature should be constructive and in full support of the "great fundamental principles of our denomination." A survey committee of five board members was appointed at the called meeting of the board Mar., 1931. Frank expression had been invited through previous notices sent to the state Baptist papers. Certain adjustments and improvements were authorized by the board. Later the board authorized a new executive officer to serve as business manager and elected one of its members, James Thomas McGlothlin (*q.v.*), to this office. He assumed his duties Aug. 1, 1932. When he died suddenly in June, 1934, the board elected Jerome Oscar Williams (*q.v.*), another of its members, and pastor of the First Baptist Church, Bowling Green, Ky., to succeed him. A new printing contract had been worked out with Marshall & Bruce Company to cover a five-year period with provision for an adjustment in the amount of $70,000 to the board for work during the past 10 years. The financial stability of the board was indicated by its ability to go through the depression without having to discharge personnel and with no real decrease in its appropriations and services to the denomination.

In spite of the depression, the board carried all phases of its work forward, the chief exception being a recession in book publishing. John L Hill, book editor, suggested "Broadman Press"—from the names of John A. Broadus and Basil Manly, Jr.—as the imprint for general book publishing, and it was officially adopted. Under the leadership of the editorial secretary, Hight C Moore, a writers' conference for writers and editors was instituted at Ridgecrest in Aug., 1931, a pioneer effort among denominations. *Home and Foreign Fields* continued to be published at a considerable annual loss. Dobbins, who had continued to serve as editor along with his professorship at the Southern Seminary, gave up the editorial responsibility in Sept., 1932. This responsibility was assigned to John L. Hill, the book editor. The promotion of Sunday school libraries became a new feature in the work of the Department of Sunday School Administration, Leona Lavender being made responsible for this emphasis. The B.Y.P.U. Department undertook to give some direction and promotion to church drama. A revision of the Graded Lessons had been started in 1929. The new course was completed with the publication of the fourth-year Intermediate lessons beginning in the fall of 1934.

Plans were instituted in 1934 for merging the three Sunday school training courses (Normal Course, Sunday School Administration Course, and Vacation Bible School Course) into a new Training Course for Sunday School Workers. There had been a growing demand throughout the Convention, especially vocal on the part of educational leaders, for correlation of the courses and for a different type of course. The termination of the former courses, the institution of credits only for the books in the new course, and efforts to lift the course to a higher educational level caused confusion and criticism. Even so, the new course was received with commendation by the denomination's leadership; and it grew in favor in the churches. Somewhat simultaneously, the B.Y.P.U. Study Course became fully graded to provide for a popular type study for all church members from Juniors through Adults. The board approved changing the name of the B.Y.P.U. to Baptist Training Union in June, 1934.

When the Convention (1933) approved the Hundred Thousand Club as a special debt-paying movement, the board offered to pay all expenses for the promotion of the movement so that every dollar given could be applied to debts. This assistance strengthened the appeal of the movement throughout the Convention. The expenses for the first year were $14,874.38.

At the board meeting in June, 1934, Secretary Van Ness asked that he might retire during June, 1935. By then he would complete 35 years of service—17½ as editorial secretary, 17½ as executive secretary. The board acceded to his request and on Mar. 13, 1935, elected Thomas Luther Holcomb, then pastor of the First Baptist Church of Oklahoma City, to succeed Van Ness. During the Van Ness administration the board's resources grew from $681,167.09 to $1,939,874.68. Sunday schools increased from 18,394 with an enrolment of 1,784,992 to 21,784 with an enrolment of 3,069,484. Receipts increased from $515,821.14 to $1,703,885.05. During the period the board contributed out of its earnings to denominational causes and to Sunday school and Training Union development $6,028,531.22. Net assets increased from $681,167.09 to $1,939,874.68.

Maturing Strength. *New secretary.*—When Holcomb became executive secretary in 1935, the board was 44 years old. In terms of resources, organization, personnel, program of work, and influence in the Convention, it had come to full stature. General economic recovery was taking place. Conditions were opportune for the board to assume vigorous initiative in its program of service to the churches and to the denomination. The new executive secretary had been born, reared, and educated in Mississippi, had received his theological training at Southern Seminary, but had spent more than a decade in Texas and Oklahoma in two pastorates at Sherman and Oklahoma City, with a period between them as executive secretary of the Baptist General Convention of Texas. By nature and experience, he possessed splendid promotional gifts. He was able to impart to the board staff and to the church educational forces throughout the denomination a new spirit of zeal. Known for a dual emphasis on evangelism and education in his pastorates, he elicited a new response throughout the Convention for the board's total program. The executive secretary was reinforced by the business manager, J. O. Williams. They both came from the pastorate to their positions at the board, and both were peculiarly sensitive to the church situation.

Five-Year Program.—Holcomb conceived a new strategy as indicated by a recommendation approved by the board, Nov. 26, 1935, namely, to recognize "the district association as the major unit of promoting every phase of Sunday school and Baptist Training Union work." The idea was presented to a joint meeting of board and state workers, chiefly Sunday school and Training Union secretaries, in Birmingham, Ala., on Dec. 30. The new approach was "unanimously approved." Plans were launched for two-day conferences in each state for a selected group of both Sunday school workers and Training Union workers (meeting at different times) in an effort to enlist and train 30,000 voluntary workers. The board appropriated funds to assist the states in bringing the workers to these conferences. J. N. Barnette and W. A. Harrell were asked to lead in this new associational emphasis for Sunday school and Training Union. Goals were set. New literature was developed. The Five-Year Program was projected to culminate with the 50th anniversary of the board in 1941. Under the leadership of board and state forces, conferences were held in all states each year, 1936–40, with a purpose to enlist and train volunteer associational workers. Reports given in 1941 indicate some results in part attributable to the special efforts of the Five-Year Program. Some reports about Sunday school work were: gain in Sunday school enrolment, 432,916; gain in number of Sunday schools, 1,839; number of Vacation Bible schools, 5,756; Vacation Bible school enrolment, 541,206; Sunday school training awards (for the five years), 756,251; Sunday school enlargement campaigns (for five years) in 7,525 churches. Some gains in Training Union work were: gain in Training Union enrolment, 250,459; increase in the number of churches having Training Union work, 2,174 (from 12,006 to 14,180); Training Union study course awards (for the five years), 1,160,858. Comparable gains were made in other phases of the board's ministry: the circulation of periodicals, the distribution of books, the development of student work, the circulation of general tracts, the improvement of efficiency as indicated by the increased number of Standard schools and Standard unions, the development of church libraries, and the increased attention given to improving church buildings.

Personnel additions.—An emphasis on church

music as a part of the board's service to the churches was one of Holcomb's first objectives. Baylus Benjamin McKinney (*q.v.*), a former professor in Southwestern Seminary's School of Sacred Music, was invited to become the board's music editor and to help to produce and promote through the periodicals the right kind of music for the churches. He began his work Dec. 1, 1935. His position on the board staff was an expression of the board's concern to improve the level of music in the churches. His creative contribution of music and song poems increased the board's resources in this area. His engagements with individual churches and his participation in the board's field program did much to foster an educational emphasis in the area of church music. He edited songbooks published by Broadman Press, notably *The Broadman Hymnal,* which was published in 1940. A music conference at Ridgecrest began the same year and became an annual event. On Aug. 20, 1941, the board authorized the establishment of a Department of Church Music with McKinney as secretary.

H. E. Ingraham succeeded Flake as secretary of the Department of Sunday School Administration (June, 1936), and Mattie C. Leatherwood succeeded Lilian S. Forbes as secretary of the Elementary Department at the same time. Other additions to the board's staff included Jacob Pinckney Edmunds, associate in the Department of Sunday School Administration (Mar., 1937); Clifton Judson Allen, associate editorial secretary (July, 1937); Ina Smith Lambdin, Junior-Intermediate Training Union editor (Oct., 1937); Sibley Charles Burnett, associate in the Vacation Bible School Department (May, 1938).

Publishing activity.—When the printing contract with Marshall & Bruce Company expired, the board made a new contract, on the basis of bids received, with Baird-Ward Printing Company of Nashville. The contract became effective July 1, 1939, and was to cover a 10-year period. The terms of the new contract provided for substantial economies in printing expense. Also, improvements were made in format and mechanical production.

A new periodical providing daily devotions—*Open Windows*—was begun with Apr., 1937. *The Story Hour Leader,* providing materials for Story Hour workers in the Training Union, was published beginning with Jan., 1937. Book publication increased—31 new titles in 1937, 36 new titles in 1938, and 58 new titles in 1939. An agreement was made, July, 1938, with the Foreign Mission Board to print all the books of that board to be used in the study of missions. A similar arrangement was made with Woman's Missionary Union. This indicated the board's desire to serve all the agencies of the Convention in the area of book publication.

In Dec., 1938, the board authorized a revision of the Primary and Junior Graded Lessons. This was to be under the editorial direction of Clifton J. Allen. A new course of lessons for the two departments was prepared, featured by full-color pictures in the pupil's and teacher's books, special attention to the type and format of the pupils' books, and units for each age year closely related to the experiences of the pupils to allow for the most effective use of Bible material. The new Primary course was published beginning with Oct., 1941, and the new Junior course was published beginning with Oct., 1943. As the work on revising the Primary and Junior Graded Lessons was carried forward, a decision was made to discontinue the Beginner Graded Lessons and issue a new course for Beginners related only loosely to the Bible content in the Uniform Lessons but graded closely to the needs of Beginner children. *Beginner Teacher* was much enlarged and *Beginner Bible Story* improved. This change took place in Oct., 1940. At the same time improvements were made in the Uniform Lessons for Intermediates with a new periodical, *The Intermediate Teacher,* being issued. A new course for three-year-olds was issued beginning with the fall quarter, 1943. Pictorial inserts appeared in Sunday school quarterlies for Young People and Adults until the paper shortage during World War II made necessary their elimination. A new Vacation Bible school textbook course was issued beginning in 1938.

Division organization.—A large-scope change was made in the board's organization in 1939. A committee on reorganization reported to the June meeting and also to the December meeting. Three divisions according to major functions were created as follows: Education and Promotion, Editorial Service, and Business Management. On the recommendation of the executive secretary, P. E. Burroughs, Hight C Moore, and J. O. Williams were elected to direct the respective divisions. The existing departments were placed in these divisions with a new Manufacturing (later designated Production) Department in the Business Division. Other new departments and adjustments came later. Further major personnel changes came in 1943. Burroughs and Moore retired from their positions in June. Burroughs had been with the board since 1910. He had been the chief builder and promoter of the board's Sunday school training program, also the leader in its church architectural ministry. Moore had served the board since 1917. As the editorial secretary he had guided its editorial ministry, had written the expositions for *Points for Emphasis* since 1918, had served as editor of *The Teacher* for 16 years, had contributed hundreds of articles to the board's periodicals, and had served on the International Sunday School Lesson Committee for 20 years. In addition to his board responsibilities, he was the recording secretary of the Convention, 1914–46. Williams was transferred to the Division of Education and Promotion to succeed Burroughs. H. E. Ingraham, secretary of the Department of Sunday School Administration, was elected business manager. William Richardson White, then president of

Hardin-Simmons University (Texas), was elected editorial secretary to succeed Moore, though Moore was requested to continue in the employ of the board for special work until the end of the year.

Fiftieth anniversary.—The board celebrated this anniversary in 1941. A history, *Fifty Fruitful Years,* by Burroughs was published. Its new building (then only three floors) on Ninth Avenue, designated as the Administration Building, had been completed and occupied. It reported to the Convention increased receipts, increased appropriations, and increases in its publishing and educational work. The Five-Year Promotional Program through the associations was concluded that year, and a Four-Year Program looking toward the Convention's centennial in 1945 was launched. Spilman, pioneer in teacher training, retired at the beginning of 1941. Mitchell Ewing Dunaway, who had been an employee of the board for 50 years, almost from its beginning, and for a period of years the head of the Order Department, retired at the end of 1941. Dunaway is reported to have wrapped the board's first package of literature. Keith Croswell Von Hagen was elected to succeed him. In 1942 the board began observing each June its anniversary with a program designed to keep alive its history and interpret its mission.

The assembly at Ridgecrest experienced steady growth under the board's management. Perry Morgan, who had served the North Carolina Baptist Convention as B.Y.P.U. secretary and then as Sunday school secretary, was elected manager of the assembly in 1936. He served until failing health required his relinquishing the responsibility in 1946, but continued to carry the management of the Boys Camp and other matters until retirement. Due to war conditions and regulations, the assembly program was cancelled in 1945. The board had operated the assembly in behalf of the Executive Committee of the Convention since 1929. Discussions continued through the years as to the disposition of the property. In 1944 the Convention authorized the Executive Committee to transfer the entire property by deed to the board "to be held in trust for the Convention . . . to assume all obligations implicit in this ownership."

World War II years.—During World War II the board's work prospered in spite of necessary difficulties. Staff workers were given leave for military duty. Responsibilities were reassigned when necessary. Paper rationing required reducing the number of pages in various periodicals. One quarter the lesson quarterlies had to be published without covers. Book publishing had to be reduced because of the paper shortage. Field promotion was carried on with adjustments made to fit conditions in the churches. Special materials were published to enable the churches to minister to persons in the armed services. These included special tracts (made available to chaplains), a Sunday school lesson quarterly (*On Duty for God and Country*), and *On to Victory,* a booklet containing apt Scripture selections.

Other significant developments during the war years were: (1) the merging of all the departments engaged in Sunday school work into the Sunday School Department, Nov., 1943, with J. N. Barnette as secretary; (2) simultaneously, the creation of Church Library Service as a separate unit with Florida Waite as secretary; (3) the creation of Visual Education Service, Jan., 1944, with Norman O'Neal as secretary. These units were in the Division of Education and Promotion. The Department of Student Work began promoting Religious Focus weeks on college and university campuses. The action of the Convention (1944) charging the board to develop and promote a church music educational program led to greater emphasis upon its music ministry. The board instituted (1942) a special effort to combat the influence of beverage alcohol by a special crusade led by John L. Hill. The crusade emphasis continued in a definite way for four or five years and then was integrated more definitely into the literature and educational program of the board. In co-operation with the Convention's effort to liquidate all the debt from its agencies by the end of 1943, the board made a special contribution of $25,000. The board offered to the Convention to provide space and an annual budget of $12,000 for administrative expense if the Convention should see fit to locate its radio service in connection with one of its boards. The Convention did not decide to locate this agency in Nashville. As a part of the Convention's centennial (1945), the board produced a film, *The Romance of a Century,* and promoted its use throughout the denomination.

Postwar era.—During this period the board experienced its most rapid development to date. Improved printing conditions made possible notable improvements in the periodicals, in size and format and number. *The Braille Baptist,* a monthly magazine for blind people, was published beginning with Oct., 1946. The board created a Department of Home Curriculum, Jan., 1946, calling Joe W. Burton, then secretary of the Education Department of the Southern Baptist Home Mission Board, to become the editor. *Home Life,* replacing *The Better Home* and *The Cradle Roll Home,* was begun, Jan., 1947, as a monthly Christian family magazine. The plan of circulation through the Sunday school and Training Union made possible a more rapid increase in circulation than was expected. The first issue had a circulation of 250,000. By 1956 it increased to 780,000. This magazine was expressive of the board's greatly expanded efforts through all departments to serve the cause of Christian home building. To implement the Convention's request for the development of a church music educational program, Walter Hines Sims was elected associate secretary in the Church Music Department to assist McKinney in this work. A Church Music Training Course including 13 books, for use in church music training schools, was announced in 1947. *The Church Musician,* a monthly magazine promoting the whole church music program and providing in each issue supplementary music selections, chiefly for choir purposes, was published (Oct., 1950). A new course of Graded Lessons for Intermediates, under the editorship of William Joseph Fallis and Annie Ward Byrd, was published beginning with the fourth quarter, 1948. A new course of lessons for two-year-olds, including a series of letters to the parents of the children, was published beginning with Oct., 1949. Beginning with 1947, all the regular periodicals of the board were copyrighted. The editorial staff was strengthened in Sept., 1949, by the addition of Howard Paul Colson, who later became editor in chief of Sunday school lesson courses, and Donald Frank Ackland as editor of general tracts and devotional materials.

Entering a new field, the board authorized (1945) the publication of children's books. Upon the retirement of John L. Hill, W. J. Fallis was elected to succeed him as book editor, assuming this responsibility June 1, 1949. Hill had served the board for 27 years, during which time it had published 571 general books, 267 study course books, and 14 songbooks, or a total of 852 titles, with an estimated publication of 23,739,916 volumes. In 1950 the board approved the launching of an expanded book publishing program.

To improve its Training Union materials, the board replaced *Story Hour Leader* with two periodicals beginning the first quarter of 1950: *The Nursery-Beginner Leader* and *The Primary Leader.* Two quarterlies rather than one were issued for the Intermediate Training Union beginning with Jan., 1952. Raymond May Rigdon, Apr., 1953, was appointed general editor of Training Union lesson courses. A new course of Sunday school materials for three-year-olds was issued beginning with the fall quarter of 1952.

Following the death of Frank H. Leavell, Dec., 1949, G. Kearnie Keegan was elected secretary of the Department of Student Work and assumed this responsibility May 1, 1950.

Following the war Sunday school teaching clinics, both Convention-wide and state, were promoted, largely under the leadership of Alphonso Victor Washburn, Jr., of the Sunday School Department, as a means to improving teaching. These matched clinics in the area of Sunday school administration. Christian Home Week, first promoted in 1940, was promoted jointly by the Sunday School and Training Union departments and became a period of specialized emphasis with materials prepared by the Department of Home Curriculum. The association continued to be a major medium of promotion for both Sunday school and Training Union work. The rapid increase in church building throughout the Convention called for expansion of the ministry and the activity of the board's Department of Church Architecture. During 1950 the department rendered service to 4,168 churches, representing 22 states in Convention territory and 15 states outside Convention territory. Assistance was given also to 12 foreign countries. By action of the Convention (May, 1950) the board was requested to set up production facilities in the field of audio-visual aids for Southern Baptist agencies and institutions. While the assistance intended by the Convention's action was not fully appropriated by other agencies, the board did serve other agencies in an increasing number of capacities.

The Convention in 1950 definitely approved plans for Glorieta Baptist Assembly at Glorieta, N. Mex., and instructed its executive committee to convey to the Sunday School Board the property which had been turned over to the committee by the Baptist Convention of New Mexico for a Southern Baptist assembly. The board, therefore, began immediately to develop the property and initiate plans for a building program. Edgar Allison Herron, at that time Sunday School secretary in Alabama, was elected by the board as manager. A "Pioneer Week" assembly was held in 1952, and full-length summer programs began in 1953. The development of the assembly called for large appropriations, which amounted to more than $2,000,000 through 1955.

Another significant development in denominational co-operation was the offer of the board (Mar. 28, 1946) to provide space and facilities for the collections of the Historical Commission of the Convention. Later by mutually acceptable plans, the office of the Historical Commission was established at the board, Feb., 1951. The historical collection was then integrated with the board's Dargan Library and became (June 17, 1953), by approval of both the Historical Commission and the board, the Dargan-Carver Library. Its function was to serve the staff of the board and to be a center for research in Baptist history. The board likewise provided offices for the Southern Baptist Foundation (May, 1949), the Education Commission (Feb., 1951), and the Christian Life Commission (Jan., 1953)—agencies of the Convention.

By 1950 the demand for additional building facilities for the board's operations required decisive action. The board decided to purchase an acreage outside the city limits on which to build a large one-floor printing plant. This action made additional office, warehouse, and shipping facilities available at the downtown plant. Board action also authorized the erection of a nine-floor addition to the Administration Building. The work was begun on this building in the late months of 1950 and completed, except the interior work on three floors, in the spring of 1953.

Concluding a period of 18 years of service, Holcomb retired as executive secretary-treasurer, May 31, 1953. His purpose, often expressed, was to serve every Southern Baptist church with the full program of the board. His leadership had contributed to a stronger evangelistic emphasis in the board's ministry, a new emphasis upon the association as a medium of promotion,

GEORGIA BAPTIST BUILDING (*q.v.*), Atlanta. Headquarters for 13 divisions of the Georgia Baptist Convention. Purchased in 1943, now valued at $625,000.

TENNESSEE BAPTIST CONVENTION (*q.v.*) HEADQUARTERS, Nashville. Houses 16 departments and agencies. Purchased in 1951, now valued at $800,000.

SOUTHERN BAPTIST HOSPITAL (q.v.), New Orleans, La. Established in 1926, 580 beds and bassinets, valued at $7,000,000. Left: Main entrance on Napoleon Avenue. Right: South wing where one of first blood banks was established.

the development of a church music educational ministry, the launching of a second Convention-wide assembly in the West, an emphasis upon adequate training for the board's personnel, the expansion of the board's book store interests to provide for the purchase of full ownership of all the stores in the various states, and the rounding out of the board's service program to include audio-visual aids and church recreation. During the 18-year period the number of board employees increased from 361 to 1,100, its volume of business from $1,703,885.05 to $12,696,-200.45, its denominational appropriations from $431,150.40 to $1,584,663.93, its number of book stores from 17 to 44, its property value from $866,857.22 to $5,782,684.67, its circulation of general tracts from 2,099,790 to 13,020,000.

Long-Range Planning. The board appointed a committee in Dec., 1952, to nominate a successor to Holcomb. In a called meeting Mar. 3, 1953, the board approved the committee's nomination of James Lenox Sullivan, then pastor of the First Baptist Church, Abilene, Tex. A native of Mississippi, trained at Mississippi College and the Southern Baptist Theological Seminary, he had served previously as pastor of churches in Kentucky, Tennessee, and Mississippi.

Prior to Holcomb's retirement some of the trustees had advocated organizational changes in the board's plan of administration. The matter received consideration after the new executive secretary took charge. The board, in its regular June meeting, appointed a plans and policies committee to consider with the secretary basic policies and adjustments. Also, it was decided to create the office of administrative assistant. In August John Marvin Crowe, educational director of the First Baptist Church, Abilene, Tex., was elected to this position. He began his work Sept. 7. In December the board approved a revision of the bylaws as recommended by the plans and policies committee. This committee was instructed to have a study made of the internal organizational structure. J. O. Williams had died in November, but a successor was not elected pending the completion of the organizational study. A firm of management consultants (Booz, Allen, and Hamilton of Chicago) was engaged to make the study desired. Its survey was completed in May, 1954. On the basis of its report and recommendations by the plans and policies committee, the board in a called meeting at the Convention session in St. Louis, June 1, 1954, created four divisions instead of three, involving a merger of certain departments and new alignment of others. It elected directors of these divisions as follows: Education Division—William Lewis Howse, Jr., professor of administration in the School of Religious Education of Southwestern Baptist Theological Seminary; Service Division—Harold E. Ingraham, transferred from the position of business manager of the business division; Merchandise and Sales Division—Keith C. Von Hagen, then in charge of the Merchandising Department; Business Division—Robert Lee Middleton, then in charge of the Accounting Department. Also, the board created four staff positions in the executive office and filled the positions as follows: editorial secretary—Clifton J. Allen; administrative assistant—J. M. Crowe; personnel manager—Leonard E. Wedel; contracts and investment counselor—Norris Gilliam (a member of the board and secretary of the Tennessee Baptist Foundation who was elected at the regular meeting of the board June 23). The action taken in the meeting in St. Louis was further implemented by the board, June 23, by a further revision of the bylaws and the approval of the personnel to be in charge of the various departments. Details of the reorganization were to be effected as soon as possible.

On the basis of the executive secretary's recommendation, the board, July 1, 1953, appointed a committee to re-examine the printing contract with the Baird-Ward Printing Company and confer about negotiation or cancellation. The board in December approved a recommendation of this committee that Baird-Ward be notified of the cancellation of the existing contract, which had been entered into Dec. 5, 1952, and which provided for termination on the basis of a two-year notice. A new contract was negotiated, which was approved by the board Dec. 22, 1954. At the same time a contract for the printing of study course books was signed with R. R. Donnelly & Sons of Chicago. A standing committee on printing was one of the provisions of the new bylaws. The new contracts contained provisions which would involve large savings on printing expense. During the following year other printing and paper contracts were negotiated that effected further economies.

In its Nov., 1953, meeting the board took note of the long period of service of Ethel Allen as secretary to the executive secretary. Plans were authorized for an appreciation service for her at the meeting on Dec. 15, anticipating her approaching retirement at the end of the year. She had served the board more than 45 years, having been employed Apr. 1, 1908, and having been secretary with four of the board's executive officers—Frost, Van Ness, Holcomb, and Sullivan. She had earned an enviable place in the confidence and affection of the entire board staff. Former Secretary Holcomb expressed appreciation and presented a gift to her in behalf of the board.

William Francis Powell, by virtue of the termination of his term on the board of trustees, May, 1954, retired as president of the board. He had served in this capacity for 33 years, with one year's interruption when he was not eligible for election to the board. W. A. Criswell was elected president, June 23. He served until June, 1956, when B. Locke Davis was elected.

A definite formula, aimed at better equity, was approved to guide the appropriations made to the states for assistance in their religious education programs. A second phase of the management study made by the plans and policies committee, with the aid of professional consultants, related to job description, job evaluation, and salary administration. The report was received in Sept., 1954, and the executive secretary was instructed to put the revised salary structure into effect. A management control survey was authorized by the board in Apr., 1955; its report was accepted in Oct., 1955. It recommended the reports needed at each organizational level and the steps necessary to initiate a system of cost accounting and budgetary control.

Plans had been laid by the Sunday School Department in co-operation with state forces for a campaign in 1954 to increase Sunday school enrolment by one million. "A Million More in '54" was the slogan for the campaign. Other agencies of the denomination gave sympathetic support. The campaign was promoted through state, associational, and church planning meetings. Special literature was produced. Many enlargement campaigns were conducted. A net increase of 597,361 in enrolment was reported. Reactions from this special campaign led to increase in Training Union enrolment, in the circulation of periodicals, in the requests for free literature, in the services of the architectural department for building undertakings, in training awards, in Vacation Bible schools, and in the evangelistic and missionary activity in the churches. The board authorized (June, 1954) the preparation of materials for weekday religious teaching and elected James Clinton Barry for the editorial responsibility in this area. The Training Union forces co-operated in the Convention-wide emphasis on evangelism with a series of study course textbooks on soul-winning in 1955 and another on church membership in 1956. The church music training course was enlarged to include 26 books.

In the area of publication, the board approved a reactivation of its children's book publishing program, Jan., 1954. A plan had been initiated in 1952 for the publication of a new hymnal. A committee co-operated with the responsible board workers in making the selections, choosing the tunes, and appraising editorial problems. *Baptist Hymnal* was published under the imprint of Convention Press in 1956. It contained 554 selections with complete indexes of authors, composers, tunes, meters, topics, first lines and titles, doxologies, responses, and benedictions, as well as 102 responsive readings accompanied by topical and scriptural indexes. The first edition of the hymnal was 500,000. Curriculum materials were improved by new periodicals for young Adults and married Young People, in both Sunday school and Training Union; new materials for the Nursery, Beginner, and Primary groups in the Training Union; and an additional quarterly for the Junior Training Union. The curriculum committee approved the launching of a crusade for Christian morality, and the various board publications put special emphasis on it throughout 1956. A new series of Vacation Bible school textbooks was authorized, with plans for publication in 1957.

The curriculum committee of the board began in late 1955 an over-all study of the objectives of Christian training and teaching. This study gave promise of becoming an instrument by which to evaluate the board's total educational program and all the materials prepared for use in the churches.

In recognition of its value to the employees, the board in Nov., 1954, approved the organization of a credit union. The participation of employees demonstrated the need for such, and the first two years gave promise of a successful operation. A new retirement program for the employees was put into effect in Jan., 1956, which provided for age annuity, a widow's supplementary annuity, and disability benefits.

Extensive building operations were carried on at the Glorieta Baptist Assembly to provide increased hotel facilities, conference rooms, and dining room facilities. A children's building, to be used chiefly for laboratory purposes during the conferences, was erected at Ridgecrest in time for use in 1956. Camp Crestridge, a camp for girls, was built at Ridgecrest, the first season being 1955. The three unfinished floors of the administration building were prepared for occupancy in 1955, and the executive office was moved to this building. In 1955 the board approved Convention Press as a new imprint for the publication of books prepared for curricular purposes and others of strictly denominational character designed for sale primarily through the board's book stores.

The work of the board, as carried on through all the divisions and departments, was marked by increasing growth. Development throughout the entire denomination was similar. The Convention in 1956 approved resolutions calling for a denomination-wide effort to undertake to double the number of preaching and teaching points by 1964, the 150th anniversary of the organization of Baptist work on a national level in the United States. This indicated that the board would face greater demands in terms of publication and educational promotion and larger opportunities to serve the churches. This fact brought to focus exploration already under way for a long-range projection of the board's future needs and work. The matter was brought to the attention of the trustees of the board by the executive secretary in successive sessions, and the administrative staff gave consideration to it. Consumating investigation which had been quietly pursued for more than a year, the board purchased two choice pieces of property adjacent to its buildings. This insured adequate space for additional buildings commensurate with needs which could be anticipated for some 50 years. Under the executive secretary's leadership, plans were in the process of formulation designed to give scientific guidance for the development of the physical plant and to give sound direction for developing the staff and program commensurate with the board's mission.

The board observed its 65th anniversary in

1956. Its foundation and structure were strong. Its future gave promise that it would continue to offer the materials and leadership needed for the cause of religious education in the churches.

II. Organizational Development. The board began with a mission but without an organization. The work of the board created an organization. The preparation of literature called for writers and editors. Publishing and selling called for warehousing, mailing, and accounting. The needs of the churches called for a staff of field secretaries and educational workers. For some 25 years the organization was chiefly a matter of individuals given specific assignments, with the clerical assistance needed. By the beginning of the Van Ness administration there was need for a departmental organization. With the approval of the trustees, departments were created and competent persons made responsible for their administration. The business department became three: Accounting, Order and Mailing, and Sales—later, Sales Promotion (1924). The Editorial and Educational departments continued, but their areas of work were more clearly defined. The following new departments came into being in order: Architectural (1917); Organized Class (1917); B.Y.P.U. (1919); Elementary (1919); Missionary Publications (1919); Sunday School Administration (1920); Survey, Statistics, and General Information (1921); Book Editorial (1922); Vacation Bible School (1924); Intermediate (1924); Church Administration and Buildings (1927); Student Work (1928).

The next major organizational development came in 1939. The conviction had been growing among board members that the growth in personnel and operations called for an increase in administrative organization and more efficient execution of the board's policies and work. Following a study made by a committee, the board created three divisions: Education and Promotion, Editorial Service, and Business Management. Each division was to be under the direction of an administrative officer and answerable to the executive secretary, and each division was to include the proper departments of work. As admitted by the committee, in some respects the lines of responsibility did not follow the type of organization created. But it was believed that the existing departments could be brought under the new general organization, and the administration was instructed to put it into effect as rapidly as practicable.

The Division of Business Management included the Accounting, Order and Purchasing, Sales and Advertising, Mailing and Shipping, Manufacturing, and Maintenance departments. The Division of Education and Promotion included all the separate departments related to Sunday school work (Educational, Sunday School Administration, Young People's and Adult Work, Intermediate Work, Elementary Work, and Vacation Bible School); also the Training Union, Student Work, Architectural (brought into being as a separate unit, Mar., 1940), and Survey, Statistics, and Information departments. In creating the Division of Editorial Service, the board anticipated that its work would be divided into two major departments, periodicals and books. The Book Editorial Department maintained its function and identity. The periodicals department did not become a reality as a separate unit due to problems and the dual responsibilities of various editors; it functioned chiefly in the Sunday school lesson field. The art service functioned as a part of the editorial division and was established as a regular department in Dec., 1943. The church music ministry was established as a department in the education and promotion division in Aug., 1941. The merging into one of all departments for Sunday school work (Nov., 1943) unified that area of work. Church Library Service and Visual Education Service became definite units in the education and promotion division in Nov., 1943, and Jan., 1944, respectively.

Within the structure of the three divisions, new departments and a more careful definition of functions marked the development from 1945 to 1953. The Department of Home Curriculum in the editorial division was established in Jan., 1946. Upon the recommendation of the editorial secretary, the board in its Dec., 1945, meeting approved assigning the work of the editorial division to the following departments: Book Editorial, Sunday School Curriculum, Training Union Curriculum, Home Curriculum, and Art. The Personnel Department was created by the board, Oct., 1951, and placed in the business division. In Oct., 1953, it was transferred to the executive office. In 1952 two departments of the business division—Order, Sales and Advertising—were reorganized into three: Book Store, Merchandising, and Advertising. The Convention in 1948 requested the board to establish the Church Recreation Service. Complex problems delayed carrying out the request. It was actually brought into being as a functioning unit in Feb., 1954. All along, the business operations of Ridgecrest Baptist Assembly and Glorieta Baptist Assembly (after it was established) were considered a part of the business division.

Another major organizational development took place in 1954. Under the leadership of the new executive secretary in 1953, a study of the board's organizational set-up was initiated. The board's expanding program of service to the churches, its developing book store ministry, its increase in personnel, its increase in responsibility in the light of Convention assignments, and its increasing volume of business led to the study. A firm of management consultants was engaged to make an organizational survey. On the basis of its report and recommendations of the plans and policies committee, the board at a called meeting on June 1, 1954, revised and enlarged its administrative organization, redefined its divisions, and realigned its departments. The new organization provided for four staff positions in the executive office: administrative assistant, editorial secretary, contracts and investment counselor, and personnel manager. It provided for four divisions: Business, Education, Merchandise and Sales, and Service. The objective in setting up the new organization was

> . . . to define responsibilities of divisions and departments, to prevent overlapping of functions and duplications of effort, to unify editorial and educational activities in purpose, direction, and administration, to provide adequate supervisory personnel with sufficient delegation of responsibility to insure a smooth flow of work, and to make use of the best business and merchandising procedures in order to provide an increasing support for educational and service activities.

The new organization was implemented in the months immediately following the board action. Further studies by management consultants gave assistance in putting into operation procedures which expedite communication and the execution of assignments. The organizational structure under which the board operates may be set forth by the following chart, with the responsible personnel in 1956:

III. Major Emphases. The emphasis in the board's program of work is twofold: biblical and denominational. The emphasis which controls its publication and educational program and guides its business operations is grounded upon the Bible and directed toward a ministry to the denomination. The editorial policy controlling its periodicals, tracts, and books is one of fidelity to the Scriptures in the context of traditional Baptist principles. This policy has been applied with emphasis upon the right of the individual to interpret the Bible for himself under the leadership of God and the responsibility of the individual to test his faith and practice by the New Testament. The publications of the board have always been checked carefully for biblical accuracy and doctrinal soundness but never with the thought of an authoritarian viewpoint. Sectarianism has been avoided. The major emphases in the board's publications and program of work may be stated as follows:

EVANGELISM. Emphasis on evangelism has per-

THE SUNDAY SCHOOL BOARD

OF THE SOUTHERN BAPTIST CONVENTION

Executive Secretary-Treasurer
James L. Sullivan

Contracts and Investment Counselor
Norris Gilliam*

Personnel Manager
Leonard E. Wedel

Administrative Assistant
J. M. Crowe

Editorial Secretary
Clifton J. Allen

Merchandise and Sales Division
Keith C. Von Hagen
Director

- *Merchandise Control Department*
H. S. Simpson
Manager
- *Merchandise Selection Department*
E. Odell Crowe
Manager
- *Sales Department*
J. O. Turner, Manager

Education Division
W. L. Howse, Director

- *Audio-Visual Aids Department*
Earl Waldrup, Secretary
- *Broadman Books Department*
W. J. Fallis, Secretary
- *Church Music Department*
W. Hines Sims
Secretary
- *Home Education Department*
Joe W. Burton
Secretary
- *Student Department*
G. Kearnie Keegan
Secretary
- *Sunday School Department*
J. N. Barnette
Secretary
- *Training Union Department*
J. E. Lambdin
Secretary

Service Division
H. E. Ingraham
Director

- *Advertising Department*
W. D. Kendall
Secretary
- *Art Department*
Herman F. Burns
Secretary
- *Church Architecture Department*
W. A. Harrell
Secretary
- *Church Library Service*
Florida Waite
Secretary
- *Church Recreation Service*
Agnes Durant Pylant
Secretary
- *Dargan-Carver Library*
Helen Conger
Librarian
- *Survey, Statistics, and Information Department*
J. P. Edmunds
Secretary

Business Division
R. L. Middleton
Director

- *Accounting and Control Department*
Ben R. Murphy
Manager
- *Contracts and Insurance Department*
John H. Williams
Manager
- *Glorieta Baptist Assembly*
E. A. Herron, Manager
- *Operations Department*
Noble Van Ness
Manager
- *Ridgecrest Baptist Assembly*
Willard K. Weeks
Manager

* Deceased 1957.

vaded the board's literature from the beginning. This has involved, first, clear and constant presentation of New Testament teaching about personal salvation; second, confronting readers with the claims of Christ as Saviour; third, confronting Christians with their obligations to win lost people to faith in Christ. Evangelism has been conceived to be a major objective of the Sunday school. Guidance has been given as to how the church can use its Sunday school in carrying out its evangelistic mission. This emphasis on evangelism has found expression in the board's lesson periodicals, its promotional magazines, its free literature, its general tracts, its study course books, its general books, its field program, its organizational standards, its co-operative work with other agencies, and its appropriations.

Missions. The action of the Convention in creating the board specified that it should aid mission Sunday schools. Its first appropriations were for this cause. In the secretary's first report to the Convention (1892) he said of the board, "It becomes a missionary power on home fields and foreign fields through its missionary literature." The board's literature has presented missionary information, has put major stress upon the missionary message of the Bible, has confronted young people with the call to missionary service, has sought to cultivate missionary interest in the churches, has emphasized Bible teaching relative to the support of missionary causes, and has fostered a ministry of intercession in behalf of missionary personnel and institutions. The publication of missionary books has been a large part of the board's book publishing program. Its field program and its appropriations have been Christian missions in action.

Doctrine. Doctrine, in the true concept of teaching, has been a characteristic emphasis and a central objective throughout the board's history. One reason for the board's establishment was that it might provide literature for the indoctrination of the churches. The treatment of Sunday school lessons interprets biblical doctrine. The curriculum for the Training Union, both in program materials and in study course books, has development in doctrine for a major objective. This includes the basic doctrines of the Christian faith as well as the distinctive doctrinal viewpoints of Baptists. The general tracts published by the board, distributed free year after year, are designed chiefly for doctrinal teaching in the comprehensive sense. The training program for Sunday school workers includes doctrinal books. Publications of Broadman Press present Christian doctrine. The board's field program is a channel for the same emphasis. The concept always controlling this emphasis is that understanding of and conviction about basic Christian teachings are the foundation for Christian conversion, Christian growth, and Christian service. Theological content is the first requirement for a sound educational program.

Stewardship. The stewardship emphasis in the board's publications and educational program has been consistently strong. This emphasis has also been inclusive—the stewardship of the total life. The emphasis on the stewardship of money has been presented in the larger concept of biblical teaching about stewardship. The stress on Christian giving has been grounded more upon its relation to Christian growth than upon the immediate ends of providing money for Christian causes. In the framework of this concept, however, there has been prevailing emphasis on the necessity for worthy financial support of the church's entire program and on the missionary and benevolent causes of the denomination calling for adequate financial support. Under the leadership of P. E. Burroughs, Arthur Flake, and others, the board conceived a plan whereby a church could use the Sunday school as the major means for enlisting its total membership in giving according to biblical teaching and for the support of the church's total program of work. This plan, which began to be widely advocated about 1928, came into increasing acceptance during the next 20 years. It has become the prevailing method in most well-organized churches for implementing the financial program. The board seeks to anchor the stewardship emphasis in the whole context of its educational program and to relate it to other Christian objectives.

Christian Conduct. Examination of the board's publications reveals that constant stress has been put on the biblical standards of conduct and the moral ideals of Christianity. This emphasis is set forth apart from a legalistic concept of Christian duty or an authoritarian concept of the church. The obligations of Christian conduct are related to biblical authority, the individual's right and competence in the realm of moral choices, and the Christian's commitment to Christ as Lord. Christian behavior from this viewpoint is stressed through all the board's media of instruction, training, and influence. A specific example of the emphasis was the "Crusade for Christian Morality," first conceived by the curriculum committee of the board and promoted co-operatively with other Southern Baptist agencies throughout 1956.

Social Issues. The approach to social issues has been more indirect than direct, more educational than immediately corrective. An emphasis on such matters as beverage alcohol, lawlessness and crime, labor-management relations, race relations, economic poverty, political freedom, and world peace has been given in connection with Bible study as the Bible truth related to these personal and corporate problems. The effort is made to develop a social conscience closely related to basic Christian principles. The board's emphasis reflects the denomination's conservative approach to social problems. These issues are treated with sensitiveness to the divergent views of the denomination's constituency. The problem of beverage alcohol has called forth a relatively strong emphasis throughout the board's history. Sunday school "temperance" lessons dealt with it. Training Union programs and activities confronted Christians of all age groups with information and duty related to beverage alcohol. Other social issues were not overlooked but were not made the basis of concrete objectives.

The Church. The program of the board has been church-centered. It has sought to propagate the concept that churches are essentially alike in nature and mission, irrespective of location or size of membership. The board's program possessed both strength and weakness in this respect: the needs of some churches were not adequately met, but a class consciousness with respect to churches was avoided and a strong degree of unity achieved. Also, there has been a strong emphasis in the curriculum on the nature and mission of the individual church, designed to help church members grow in understanding of New Testament teaching, learn better how to carry forward the total life and work of the church, and have a growing sense of loyalty to the church. The teaching about the church in its universal sense has received relatively little attention, in harmony with the climate of the denomination.

IV. Principles of Operation. Certain principles of operation are evident from a study of the board's history. These are set forth as they pertain to areas of major importance in policy and activity.

Printing Policy. The board does its printing by contract. The instruction of the Convention to this effect, when the board was authorized, likely was not meant to be permanently binding. But it determined the first course of action taken by the board, and the principle has since prevailed. Consideration was given to the matter by Frost and the trustees after the board became strong enough to do its own printing, but the former policy continued. Similar consideration was given under the leadership of Van Ness, Holcomb, and Sullivan, as each printing contract expired. Always the trustees of the board made the decision, in nearly every instance after special committees explored the matter. The board protects itself with provisions to do its own printing if conditions make such necessary or desirable. The policy followed rests on the belief that no significant economies would be effected through the board's doing its own printing and on the desire to conserve the energies of the administration for the spiritual objectives of the board.

Relations with the States. In the Convention's authorization of the board, there was the instruction that the board should work co-operatively with state organizations. It was thus decided from the first that its efforts for Sunday school assistance and promotion—and later for other phases of the church educational program—would be in co-operation with the forces of the state conventions. This principle led to the appropriation of earnings to the states for Sunday school, Training Union, church music, and student work. The staff of the board seeks to give guidance in developing the church educational program. Conferences are held annually with state workers for a joint consideration of the common task. Emphases, methods, and goals are worked out together. In large measure specific projects of promotion are planned by state forces, and board staff workers respond to invitations for assistance. Financial requirements are shared for such undertakings as conferences, clinics, campaigns, and training efforts of all kinds.

Relations with other Baptist Agencies. The board feels bound to all other units of Southern Baptist life by a common sense of responsibility to the Convention and to the churches. The leadership of the board has consistently cultivated understanding and co-operation. Relations with Woman's Missionary Union found concrete expression in a gift for the purchase of property for the Woman's Missionary Union Training School, the policy (prevailing until 1953) of this school to invite the executive secretary of the board to serve on its governing body in a counseling capacity, and an annual contribution by the board to the expenses of the Woman's Missionary Union from 1896 to 1953. The two institutions share a common concern for the cause of missionary education in the churches.

Relation with the mission boards was illustrated by the promotion of missionary day in the Sunday school and the cultivation of offerings for their work. The board publishes the Foreign Mission Board's series of mission study books and supplies much literature on a complimentary basis to the missionaries. Board workers have accepted invitations of the Foreign Mission Board for tours of mission fields in order to assist nationals and missionaries in developing the church educational program. The board shares with the Home Mission Board in concern for the establishment and development of churches in needy areas, but it renders its service through promoting mission Sunday schools fostered by established churches rather than through any assistance in personnel or appropriation other than supplying literature for the first quarter of the school's operation. The two boards have been mutually concerned to reinforce rural churches. There is much co-operation with the Department of Evangelism of the Home Mission Board through the preparation of supplies, the publication of books, and the promotion of the Sunday school and the Training Union as the church's best means of winning the lost and nurturing new converts.

The board emphasizes its relationship with the seminaries. Understanding its task to be that of serving the churches in their educational program, the board recognizes the correlation with the function of the seminaries in training the pastoral and church educational leadership. This principle led to the appropriations made to all the seminaries, chiefly in the interest of religious education. The board considers it a privilege to have the offices of the Executive Committee of the Convention, the Christian Life Commission, the Education Commission, the Historical Commission, and the Southern Baptist Foundation located in its buildings. Through its editorial and educational ministry, the board seeks to promote the total program of the Convention. The service of the book stores, the supplying of statistical information, and the facilities of the two assemblies are channels through which the fellowship with other agencies is implemented. The Inter-Agency Council is a major medium for co-operative discussion and planning with the agencies responsible for preparing materials for the educational program of the churches.

Interdenominational Relations. The board has followed the policy of maintaining fraternal relations with other Christian bodies and institutions in matters of common concern; but it has avoided organic connections which would have restricted its operations or been out of keeping with prevailing denominational policy. From its beginning it made use of outlines prepared by the International Sunday School Lesson Committee. Later on, it participated in the work of the committee through active membership on it. When this committee came to be sponsored by the International Council of Religious Education (and since 1951 by the Division of Christian Education of the National Council of the Churches of Christ in the United States of America), board workers continued to serve on the committee inasmuch as participation in it was not contingent upon the organic affiliation of the Southern Baptist Convention. This relationship has been helpful to the board and has been a channel through which it has made a significant contribution to the religious education program of other evangelical denominations. Employed staff members hold membership on an individual basis in the advisory sections of the Division of Christian Education. The board holds membership in the Religious Booksellers Association, the Protestant Church-Owned Publishers Association, and other similar groups through which values are obtained and co-operative study made without commitment to co-operative programs of work. The board co-operates freely with other Christian bodies in the exchange of materials and in efforts to promote Christian unity independent of organizational expression.

Employee Relations. The policy controlling the employment of persons is one which magnifies the board's concept of its work, namely, that it is definitely Christian in nature and purpose, that it is a part of Christ's program for world redemption. Persons are invited to accept employment with a sense of Christian mission. This has special force for those invited to assume the leadership for the administrative, editorial, and educational aspects of the board's life. In recent years the policy has prevailed of employing as regular workers only persons who are members of Baptist churches. No distinction is made in the employment of persons between lay folk and ordained ministers. The board's traditional policy as to wages and salaries is in conformity with the prevailing scale in Nashville for manual and clerical workers and a scale commensurate with denominational practice for administrative, editorial, and educational workers. In both areas the board's scale is perhaps slightly higher.

In 1934 the board inaugurated a retirement program for its employees. Employees participated voluntarily. The board co-operated with those who entered the plan to provide a fixed income upon retirement. Another plan was inaugurated in 1950—mandatory for all new employees—through a contract with the Relief and Annuity Board of the Southern Baptist Convention. In Jan., 1956, both plans were merged into a new contract with the Relief and Annuity Board, under which all employees are required to participate. The plan now in effect provides an annuity following retirement, a widow's supplementary annuity, and disability benefits. The board's plan provides co-operatively with the employees for a retirement income of at least 50 per cent of the salary at retirement for those whose period of service covers 25 years or longer, including the amount provided under Social Security. Through the Personnel Department of the board, a progressive program of services and training are maintained in behalf of the employees and as the expression of the board's concern to motivate a high level of work efficiency and employee advancement.

Appropriations. During the earlier years of the board's history, after its earnings made such possible, it made reasonably large contributions to other agencies and causes, notably $60,000 for a chair of Sunday school pedagogy at Southern Seminary and $100,000 for assistance to aged ministers in connection with the beginning of the Relief and Annuity Board. A change in policy announced in 1917 declared that thereafter available funds would be used primarily in the areas of work for which the board was responsible, namely, Sunday school and Training Union work, assistance to the states for work in these areas, Bible distribution, tract distribution, assistance to the seminaries for the training of workers in the field of religious education, and literature for mission situations. The board followed that general policy with the conviction that its earnings should be expended to serve the churches in the development of their educational program. Attention is called to the fact that the board never received any appropriation from denominational funds for the maintenance or expansion of its work. Southern Baptist progress in the field of religious education has been judged by many as evidence of the soundness of the board's policy to make its earnings the means of fostering a church-centered program of Bible teaching and training.

V. Property and Plant Development. The board was brought into being without provision for headquarters or the purchase of property. At first an office was provided by the *Baptist and Reflector* and then by the Methodist Publishing House, its contract printer. Its first property was a house at 167 North Cherry Street (now Fourth Avenue), purchased for $10,000 and occupied Feb. 27, 1897. The next location was at 710 Church Street, Oct., 1903, in a house costing $60,000. The third location was 161 Eighth Avenue, North, where a lot was bought in 1912 and a building erected in 1913 at a combined cost of $210,000. Two floors were added to the rear portion of this building in 1919. Two pieces of property, one on Ninth Avenue, North, opposite the Eighth Avenue building and one on Commerce Street diagonally opposite the Ninth Avenue lot, were bought and two buildings erected (1922–23), one for mailing and warehousing and one for printing. The buildings were occupied in 1923, the cost involved being $247,000 and $240,000, respectively. The remaining lots facing Ninth Avenue within this block were obtained as they came on the market. The first unit of the Administration Building, erected at a cost of $572,682.62, including the land, was completed in 1941. It provided a chapel, facilities for the business division, and offices for the Convention's Executive Committee.

The next major expansion of the board's plant came in 1950–53. A printing building was erected (completed in 1952) on Thompson Lane just outside the city, the combined cost of the lot and the building being $1,205,029.62. The administration building was completed with the erection of nine additional stories (the interior of three floors not being completed until 1955) at a cost of $1,333,836.47.

An analysis of the board's past operations led the administration in 1955 to seek to anticipate the property and plant needs of the institution for the next 25 years. Previously, small lots on Berryhill Street had been obtained for parking space. Exploration was initiated as to the availability of additional property adjacent to the present buildings. The investigation, pursued over nearly two years, brought fortunate results. The trustees authorized the purchase of three additional lots on Berryhill Street; property extending from Ninth Avenue to Tenth Avenue on Commerce Street, approximately 169 x 420 feet; and property on Tenth Avenue extending from Broadway to Church Street, 250 x 1,037 feet, including the freight depot formerly used by the railroads and air rights over certain additional railroad property. The cost of these combined pieces of property was $1,431,873.00. The board thus succeeded in obtaining adequate space for any conceivable expansion for an indefinite period. The new pieces of property acquired were so situated that future expansion and building could be projected into a long-range pattern and with a view to achieving maximum efficiency in the location of departments and in the use of automation in storing and shipping activities. As to current needs, part of the property on Commerce Street provided needed parking facilities. Existing buildings on part of the property relieved some urgent need for warehousing and other activities.

The board's policy, generally, is to lease property for the book stores. However, the property occupied by the stores in Kansas City (Mo.), Jackson (Miss.), Charlotte (N. C.), and Phoenix (Ariz.) is owned by the board.

The total property holdings of the board in 1956, including the four book stores and Ridgecrest and Glorieta assemblies, was $10,326,504.14.

VI. Financial Policy and Growth. The board began without capital. Its first operations required small loans, but within the first year its earnings placed it on a cash basis. It has always been dependent on its earnings for its operating expenses and its service program. The basic policies which control its financial operations may be stated as follows: (1) Obligations are paid promptly, and discounts are claimed when available. (2) Expenditures are kept within income. (3) Reserve funds are maintained for capital expansion (including buildings), printing contingencies, and emergency needs. (4) Prices for periodicals, books, and supplies are fixed with concern to make them available to churches with limited resources but at a level to make possible sound business operation. (5) Bequests are used according to the specifications of the donors. (6) Provision is made for the safe handling of reserve funds through consultation with an investment committee of the board and with the trust departments of designated banks. (7) Provision is made for the adequate bonding of the administrative officers. (8) An annual audit of all funds and the board's entire business operation is made, and an audit committee reports its findings to the board. (9) An adequate insurance program is maintained to cover property interests and liability requirements. (10) Expenditures are made according to a budget recommended to the board by a budget committee and approved by action of the board. (11) The earnings of the board are used, aside from maintaining necessary reserve funds and contributing to the operating expenses of the Convention, for a service program to the denomination and the promotion of the teaching and training ministry of the churches.

It is the policy of the board to sell and mail all periodical literature from headquarters in Nashville. Books and supplies are sold and distributed through the book stores.

The financial growth of the board developed steadily from the beginning. With exceptions during depression years, the income showed an annual gain. Competent administrative leadership, sound business policies, and responsible control by the board of trustees were factors in financial growth. Other important factors are the loyalty of the churches and the growth of the denomination. The chief explanation, in the conviction of the board's leaders, is the favor of God. The total assets of the board in 1956 were $19,369,810.58. A statistical table at the end of this monograph presents additional financial information.

VII. Areas of Service. An adequate understanding of the board's program of work and contribution to the Convention calls for a summary of the major areas of service.

PUBLICATION MINISTRY. There are three fields of publication. (1) Periodical literature: The board was created primarily for this purpose. It seeks to publish adequate materials for the church program of teaching and training. These include lesson helps for pupils and teachers, promotional and guidance magazines for church workers, training materials for all church members, materials for Christian family life, and papers and magazines for devotional enrichment, character building, and Christian growth. (2) Tracts: These are of two kinds—tracts for promotional purposes related to Sunday school, Training Union, and other educational work; tracts of doctrinal, evangelistic, and general nature. All such tracts are distributed free for use in the churches. (3) Books: The board publishes study course textbooks to serve the churches for leadership training and to nurture Christians in faith, doctrine, moral living, and Christian service. It publishes general books of religious nature designed for interpretation, guidance, and inspiration. Through Broadman Press the board offers to Christian authors the facilities for desirable publication.

List of periodicals, extinct and current, with dates indicated:

Adult Bible Class Quarterly (1910–35), formerly *Bible Class Quarterly,* changed to *Adult Quarterly. Adult Quarterly* (1935–49), formerly *Adult Bible Class Quarterly,* changed to *Sunday School Adults. The Adult Teacher* (1956–), monthly. *The Advanced Quarterly* (1887–1935), changed to *Senior-Advanced Quarterly* (1919) and *Senior Quarterly* (1920–26) and in 1935 to *Sunday School Young People's Quarterly. The Ambassador* (1932–41), weekly, formerly *The Intermediate Weekly,* became *Upward.*

Baptist Adult Union Quarterly (1940–56), changed to *Baptist Adults. Baptist Adults* (1956–), quarterly, formerly *Baptist Adult Union Quarterly. Baptist Boys and Girls* (1904–22), weekly, changed to *Boys' Weekly* and *Girls' Weekly. Baptist Intermediate Union Quarterly* (1940–51), formerly *Intermediate B.Y.P.U. Quarterly,* changed to *Baptist Intermediate Union Quarterly I* and *Baptist Intermediate Union Quarterly II. Baptist Intermediate Union Quarterly I* (1952–), formerly *Baptist Intermediate Union Quarterly. Baptist Intermediate Union Quarterly II* (1952–), formerly *Baptist Intermediate Union Quarterly. Baptist Junior Union Quarterly* (1940–55), formerly *The Junior B.Y.P.U. Quarterly,* changed to *Baptist Junior Union Quarterly I* and *Baptist Junior Union Quarterly II. Baptist Junior Union Quarterly I* (1955–), formerly *Baptist Junior Union Quarterly. Baptist Junior Union Quarterly II* (1955–), formerly *Baptist Junior Union Quarterly. Baptist Married Young People* (1956–), quarterly. *The Baptist Student* (1922–), monthly. *The Baptist Training Union Magazine* (1935–), monthly, formerly *The Monthly B.Y.P.U. Magazine. Baptist Young Adults* (1956–), quarterly. *Baptist Young People* (1956–), quarterly, formerly *Baptist Young People's Union Quarterly. Baptist Young People's Union Quarterly* (1940–55), formerly *Senior B.Y.P.U. Quarterly,* changed to *Baptist Young People. The B.A.U. Quarterly* (1930–39), changed to *Baptist Adult Union Quarterly. Beginner Bible Story* (1940–), quarterly, formerly *Beginner Picture Story. Beginner Picture Story* (1931–40), quarterly, formerly *Picture Lesson Card,* changed to *Beginner Bible Story. The Beginner Picture Story Teacher* (1931–35), quarterly, changed to *The Beginner Teacher. The Beginner Teacher* (1935–39), quarterly, formerly *The Beginner Picture Story Teacher. Beginner Teacher* (1940–), quarterly, formerly *The Beginner Teacher. The Better Home* (1935–46), quarterly, formerly *Home Department Magazine,* changed to *Home Life. Bible Class Quarterly* (1902–10), changed to *Adult Bible Class Quarterly. The Bible Reader's Guide* (1955–), quarterly. *The Boys' Weekly* (1922–29), weekly, formerly *Baptist Boys and Girls,* changed to *The Junior Boy. The Braille Baptist* (1946–), monthly. *B.Y.P.U. Quarterly* (1900–29), successor to *Young People's Leader,* changed to *Senior B.Y.P.U. Quarterly.*

The Challenge (1929–38), weekly, formerly *Kind Words,* changed to *Try. Children's Quarterly* (1909–35), changed to *Pupil's Primary Quarterly. Child's Gem* (1879–1929), weekly, changed to *Storytime. Church Administration* (1927–31), monthly. *The Church Musician* (1950–), monthly. *The Convention Teacher* (1892–1927), monthly, formerly *Kind Words Teacher,* changed to *The Teacher. The Cradle Roll Home* (1925–47), quarterly, absorbed in *Home Life.*

The Elementary Guide (1940–44), quarterly, formerly *The Elementary Messenger,* absorbed in *The Sunday School Builder. The Elementary Messenger* (1920–39), quarterly, changed to *The Elementary Guide. Every Day with Beginners* (1956–), quarterly. *Every Day with Nursery Children* (1956–), quarterly. *Every Day with Primaries* (1956–), quarterly.

Girls' Weekly (1922–29), weekly, formerly *Baptist Boys and Girls,* changed to *The Junior Girl. Graded Elementary Magazine* (1930–33), monthly, formerly *The Graded Lesson Helper. The Graded Lesson Helper* (1926–30), monthly, changed to *Graded Elementary Magazine.*

Graded Lessons. See the monograph on SUNDAY SCHOOL LESSONS, GRADED.

Home and Foreign Fields (1916–37), monthly. *Home Department Magazine* (1910–34), quarterly, changed to *The Better Home. Home Life* (1947–), monthly, formerly *The Better Home.*

Intermediate B.Y.P.U. Quarterly (1922–39), changed to *Baptist Intermediate Union Quarterly. Intermediate Counselor* (1922–44), quarterly, absorbed in *The Sunday School Builder. The Intermediate Leader* (1940–), quarterly, formerly *Intermediate Leader's B.Y.P.U. Quarterly. Intermediate Leader's B.Y.P.U. Quarterly* (1917–39), changed to *The Intermediate Leader. The Intermediate Quarterly* (1887–1949), changed to *Sunday School Intermediate Pupil. Intermediate Teacher* (1940–), monthly.

Junior B.Y.P.U. Quarterly (1922–39), changed to *Baptist Junior Union Quarterly. The Junior Boy* (1929–31), weekly, formerly *The Boy's Weekly,* changed to *Junior Weekly. The Junior Girl* (1929–31), weekly, formerly *The Girls' Weekly,* changed to *Junior Weekly. The Junior Leader* (1940–), quarterly, formerly *The Junior Leader's B.Y.P.U. Quarterly. The Junior Leader's B.Y.P.U. Quarterly* (1925–

39), changed to *The Junior Leader. Junior Quarterly* (1909–49), changed to *Sunday School Junior Pupil. The Junior Teacher* (1935–), quarterly, formerly *Junior Teacher's Quarterly. Junior Teacher's Quarterly* (1924–35), changed to *The Junior Teacher. Junior Weekly* (Apr., 1931–Dec., '31), formerly *The Junior Boy* and *The Junior Girl.*

Kind Words (1866–1929), monthly (1866–1901), also semi-monthly (1869–1901) and weekly (1871–1929) editions, changed to *The Challenge. Kind Words Teacher* (1887–91), monthly, changed to *The Convention Teacher.*

Lesson Cards (1892–96), quarterly, changed to *Picture Lesson Cards. Lesson Leaf* (1892–1940), weekly, changed to *Visitor's Lesson Leaflet.*

The Monthly B.Y.P.U. Magazine (1926–34), changed to *The Baptist Training Union Magazine.*

The Nursery-Beginner Leader (1950–), quarterly.

On Duty for God and Country (1942–46), quarterly. *On the March with the Master* (1918–19), quarterly. *On the Wing With the Word* (1922–), quarterly. *Open Windows* (1937–), monthly (1937–40), quarterly (1941–). *The Organized Class Magazine* (1915–26), quarterly 1915–19, monthly 1919–26, changed to *Sunday School Young People and Adults.*

A picture set for teaching purposes to accompany lesson materials for elementary age groups was published beginning in 1892. This eventually developed into separate sets of teaching pictures, one for each elementary department.

Picture Lesson Cards (1897–1931), quarterly, formerly *Lesson Cards,* changed to *Beginner Picture Story. The Primary Leader* (1950–), quarterly. *The Primary Leaf* (1897–1924), weekly. *Primary Quarterly* (1887–1909), changed to *Junior Quarterly. The Primary Teacher* (1935–), quarterly, formerly *The Primary Teacher's Quarterly. The Primary Teacher's Quarterly* (1924–35), changed to *The Primary Teacher. Pupil's Primary Quarterly* (1935–49), formerly *Children's Quarterly,* changed to *Sunday School Primary Pupil.*

The Quarterly Review (1941–), quarterly.

Senior-Advanced Quarterly (1919), formerly *Advanced Quarterly,* changed to *Senior Quarterly. Senior B.Y.P.U. Quarterly* (1929–39), formerly *B.Y.P.U. Quarterly,* changed to *Baptist Young People's Union Quarterly. Senior Quarterly* (1920–26), formerly *Senior-Advanced Quarterly. The Sentinel* (1932–), weekly, formerly *The Junior Weekly. The Story Hour Leader* (1937–49), quarterly, changed to *Nursery-Beginner Leader* and *Primary Leader. Storytime* (1929–), weekly, formerly *Child's Gem. Sunday School Adults* (1950–), quarterly, formerly *Adult Quarterly. The Sunday School Builder* (1920–), monthly, formerly *The Superintendent's Quarterly. Sunday School Intermediate Pupil* (1950–), quarterly, formerly *Intermediate Quarterly. Sunday School Junior Pupil* (1950–), quarterly, formerly *Junior Quarterly. Sunday School Married Young People* (1956–), quarterly. *Sunday School Primary Pupil* (1950–), quarterly, formerly *Pupil's Primary Quarterly. Sunday School Young Adults* (1956–), quarterly. *Sunday School Young People* (1950–), quarterly, formerly *Young People's Quarterly. Sunday School Young People and Adults* (1926–44), monthly, formerly *The Organized Class Magazine,* absorbed in *The Sunday School Builder. Sunday School Young People's Quarterly* (1935–49), formerly *The Advanced Quarterly. The Superintendent's Quarterly* (1905–20), changed to *The Sunday School Builder.*

The Teacher (1928–56), monthly, formerly *The Convention Teacher,* changed to *The Adult Teacher* and *The Young People's Teacher. Try* (1938–41), weekly, formerly *The Challenge,* changed to *Upward.*

Upward (1941–), weekly, formerly *Try* and *The Ambassador.*

Visitor's Lesson Leaflet (1940–), quarterly, formerly *Lesson Leaf.*

Young People's Leader (1894–1900), monthly (1894–96), weekly (1896–1900), succeeded by *B.Y.P.U. Quarterly. The Young People's Teacher* (1956–), monthly. *Youth's Kind Words* (1902–18), semi-monthly.

Development of an Educational Program. In recognition of the educational mission of the churches, the board seeks to give guidance to them in developing a program for effective teaching and training. This involved the development of educational concepts, organizational patterns, administrative procedures, learning goals, and sound methods of teaching and training. It called for the preparation of standards and records and curricular materials. In developing this program board workers receive the co-operative assistance of state forces. The educational program thus conceived is designed to be adaptable to churches of different sizes, to be implemented by volunteer workers in the churches, and to be educationally fruitful for persons of varying cultural and spiritual backgrounds and progress.

Field Promotion. The duties of a large number of board workers are chiefly in the area of field promotion. In co-operation with state workers, they direct enlargement campaigns, conduct workshops, assist in clinics, participate in conferences and conventions, and teach in training schools. The field promotion program of the board reaches into all the states of the Convention territory. It relates to all phases of the church program of education and service: Sunday school. Vacation Bible school, Training Union, student work, church music, church libraries, church recreation, church architecture, home education, audio-visual education, leadership training, stewardship, evangelism, and world missions.

Specialized Ministries. Through various departments the board engages in specialized activities that help the churches. (1) Leadership training: The Sunday school, Training Union, and church music study courses offer to the churches a fruitful means of developing workers for the responsibility of leadership. The field work program and the Ridgecrest and Glorieta assemblies are effective for the same objective. (2) Architectural guidance: The service of the architecture department is extended to churches to assist them in construction plans. This involves interpreting the spiritual values of properly designed buildings, evaluating building needs, relating building facilities to a sound educational program, advising about building materials and equipment, and evaluating preliminary and final architectural plans. (3) Music ministry: The purpose of this ministry is to assist churches to develop a graded choir program, train a music leadership, and develop the general appreciation and participation that will implement the values of music for Christian worship. (4) Audio-visual aids: The board through its responsible department provides guidance and production assistance to other agencies, produces materials under the imprint of Broadman Films, distributes films and equipment through the book stores, and promotes the educational values and proper use of audio-visual materials in the churches. (5) Church library service: This program of service interprets the values of church libraries, gives guidance as to methods of effective operation, offers help in training library workers, and supplies materials to assist in book selection and library efficiency. (6) Church recreation: The board offers to the churches guidance for developing a church-centered program of recreation based on sound concepts and designed to serve Christian objectives. Emphasis is placed on implementing the program through existing church organizations. (7) Student work: The purpose of this service is to cultivate and capture the Christian potential in the student life of the colleges and universities. Through the Baptist Student Union, students are encouraged to maintain an active church relationship, offered activities designed to cultivate a vital Christian life, given opportunities for positive Christian service, and confronted with values calling for Christian commitment.

STATISTICAL INFORMATION. A denomination's progress needs to be factually recorded. Its responsibility needs to be seen in factual perspective. The statistical department of the board is the channel for supplying to the denomination information that will interpret its opportunities and its achievements. Information is gathered from the churches and reduced to statistics so that facts in many fields are available to the agencies of the denomination and to statistical agencies outside the denomination.

ASSEMBLIES. The board owns and operates the two Convention-wide assemblies—one at Ridgecrest, N. C., and one at Glorieta, N. Mex. These assemblies provide a summer program of week-long conferences related to all phases of the church educational program and to general areas of denominational interest. Other boards and agencies are responsible for certain conferences. The instruction and inspiration gained by those attending the assemblies contribute significantly to personal growth, improved church work, and denominational unity and progress. The capital investment in the two assemblies in 1956 was $3,650,997.79.

DARGAN-CARVER LIBRARY. This unit of the board's work, which is a joint enterprise with the Convention's Historical Commission, provides a research center for students, writers, and denominational workers. Its facilities for research in Baptist history are unexcelled.

BOOK STORE MINISTRY. The board operates 50 book stores. These are distributed over the states in the Convention territory. The stores carry a full line of books, chiefly in the religious field, and supplies for the churches. The stores are considered as service centers for the churches and as forces for a Christian witness through the distribution of worthwhile books.

MISSION WORK. The board's service in this area is, first of all, the assistance given to the states for the development of religious education in the churches. Several hundred thousand dollars are expended annually for this service. A second aspect of this service is the distribution of Bibles and literature on a free basis. This assistance provides Bibles for underprivileged and handicapped persons, periodicals for mission situations, and free tracts and free promotional literature for use in all the churches. A third phase of this service is the assistance given to the cause of world missions. The curricular materials emphasize missionary education. The periodicals feature information about missionary agencies. The service ministries promote missionary causes. Specific assistance is given to mission work by supplying proofs of curricular publications to the publishing houses overseas to use in preparing materials for the churches.

DENOMINATIONAL ASSISTANCE. The board seeks to reinforce the denominational program and render assistance to Convention agencies. Office space is provided for the Convention's Executive Committee and certain commissions. A fixed amount of money is contributed annually for the operating expenses of the Convention. Through the statistical service, book store ministry, and assemblies, assistance is given to all areas of organized Baptist life. CLIFTON J. ALLEN

SUNDAY SCHOOL BOARD STATISTICAL SUMMARY, 1900–1955

	1900	*1920*	*1930*	*1940*	*1950*	*1955*
Sunday school enrolment	670,569	1,926,610	2,839,183	3,590,374	5,024,553	6,641,715
Training Union enrolment		322,011	533,976	919,689	1,440,895	2,223,502
Vacation Bible school enrolment			57,983	541,206	1,642,772	2,652,788
Vacation Bible schools			432	5,756	20,124	25,458
Sunday school training awards		21,351 *	90,162		365,895	681,194
Training Union study course awards			184,549	283,038	473,913	688,772
Periodical circulation (total copies during year)		2,440,300	23,775,945	38,400,000	42,816,297	65,855,363
Tract distribution				3,000,000	8,735,000	9,631,460
Net sales	$ 72,468	$ 862,732	$ 1,827,992	$ 2,322,329	$10,432,495	$19,520,365
Appropriations to denominational service	$ 19,478	$ 157,439	$ 495,853	$ 520,241	$ 1,134,303	$ 1,782,027
Book store units			17 **	21	34	48
Book store sales				$ 940,000	$ 4,968,546	$ 9,636,987
Total assets	$ 52,819	$ 759,752	$ 2,324,063	$ 2,440,219	$ 9,171,706	$18,938,434
Number employees		115	244	461	786	1,087

* A total of 84,000 Sunday school training awards had been issued prior to 1920.

** 1935 figure—16 stores jointly owned by Sunday School Board and state conventions.

SUNDAY SCHOOL BOARD OF THE SOUTHERN BAPTIST CONVENTION (1863–73). An agency authorized by the Southern Baptist Convention, May, 1863, when the Civil War was in its third year. No Southern denomination was printing Sunday school literature, or able to get it from the North. The board, located at Greenville, S. C., had for its object: "to promote the establishment, enlargement, and higher efficiency of Sunday schools throughout our land." It was instructed not to establish a printing house.

The first president was Basil Manly, Jr. (*q.v.*), the real founder of the board. After three months, his able associate in promoting its establishment, John Albert Broadus (*q.v.*), became part-time secretary with an annual salary of $300. The board could do but little before 1864. By then, much of the South was occupied by Union armies. For much of 1865 and the first half of 1866 the board was inactive on account of war conditions.

The board planned to put a general missionary in each state, but could not, because funds were not available, and even if they had been, workers could not have been procured. Manly and Broadus, aided by a few others, rapidly prepared question books, lesson books, catechisms, a classbook for teachers, a little hymnbook and a larger one, and the *Confederate Hymn Book.* It also published *The Sunday School Primer,* which began with the A B C's, and had simple reading and spelling lessons, and a few very short moral and Bible stories—all this because most of the children could not read.

The board began in Jan., 1866, to publish *Kind Words,* a "little paper for little children," but soon had no pictures, cuts, and paper, and no funds to purchase them. Secretary C. C. Bitting visited Philadelphia and sought help from Benjamin Griffith, corresponding secretary of the American Baptist Publication Society. This help was given in a noble way: Griffith made available cuts of pictures for 50 to 75 cents each that otherwise would have cost Bitting from $50 to $300; he procured paper for the Sunday School Board at the same price he was paying; he had his contract printer print the board's publications at the same price paid for his own; and he vouched for the board's integrity. (Obligations to the publisher were not liquidated until 1874–75.)

The board purchased 25,000 New Testaments from the American Bible Society through Richard Fuller (*q.v.*), Baltimore, who procured their passage through Union lines. They were for distribution among Confederate soldiers. At the war's end the board could not pay for them, but the Bible society, with much tact and a fine spirit, gave assurances that from the first the books had been considered a gift.

Prevailing conditions made it impossible for the board to remain at Greenville. There was a strong sentiment for moving it to Memphis when the Southern Baptist Convention met there in 1867, but action was postponed. At Baltimore, 1868, it relocated the board at Memphis by a vote of 140 to 40. A conviction had developed that the Convention should locate one of its boards in the West; and an almost unanimous feeling prevailed that the bitter strife which followed the establishment of the Southern Baptist Sunday School Union in Nashville, 1858, and the resulting Graves–Howell controversy, should be brought to an end and forgotten. The Sunday School Union was merged into the Sunday School Board, and a new era of good feeling began. However, the board was penniless, and the broken and poverty-stricken people did not respond to imploring pleas for help.

The new secretary, T. B. Kingsbury of Maryland, who had lost his property because of the war, went at once from Alabama to Maryland seeking funds for the board, but did not get enough money to pay the expenses of the trip. He had to resign and do something else to support his family.

T. C. Teasdale, a Mississippi pastor who was president of the Sunday School Union from 1860 to 1867 and was in favor with all parties, became corresponding secretary Sept. 15, 1869, and served exactly two years. His annual reports to the Convention were masterful statements of what the board ought to be and could do. He revitalized the work of the board, and might have made it permanent, but he became discouraged. Hard days followed. Seemingly unsolvable problems arose. Mass sentiment had not yet crystallized in favor of Sunday schools. Many leaders advocated discontinuance of the board in favor of the American Baptist Publication Society or private publishers.

Samuel Boykin (*q.v.*) became the board's editor. His *Child's Delight* was purchased and combined with *Kind Words.* After Teasdale resigned, he became the board's acting secretary and served until its abolishment in 1873. He edited *Kind Words* and other Sunday school publications of the Home Mission Board from 1873 until they were transferred to the second Sunday School Board in 1891. Thereafter he was the board's editor until his death Nov. 3, 1899. He thus became the connecting link between the two Sunday school boards. His some 30 years of continuously able service did much to develop unity among Southern Baptists in doing their own Sunday school work.

The increasingly difficult problems the board faced in Memphis led to a developing sentiment for its abolition. At Raleigh, N. C., 1872, the Southern Baptist Convention, after a vigorous discussion, voted 96 to 85 to continue the board. The next year at Mobile, Ala., it voted 140 to 21 to consolidate it with the Domestic and Indian Mission Board, which it renamed the Domestic and Indian, and Sunday School Board. A year later, 1875, it relieved the consolidated board from the responsibility for doing Sunday school work and deleted "Sunday School" from its name, but instructed it to continue *Kind Words* and liquidate the Sunday School Board's indebtedness.

The Sunday School Board, begun in 1863 because of dire necessities imposed by war, continued for 10 years in extreme poverty among a discouraged, bankrupt, and chastened people. It did much good in spite of its great handicaps. It did not live in vain, for it helped to create a desire among Southern Baptists for their own Sunday schools and Sunday school literature. This growing desire, which survived years of frustration and controversy, culminated in a determined purpose to have another Sunday School Board. The result was the authorization of the new and second board at Birmingham, Ala., May, 1891. HOMER L. GRICE

SUNDAY SCHOOL BUILDER, THE. A monthly magazine published by the Baptist Sunday School Board of the Southern Baptist Convention. It provides guidance materials for Sunday school workers and suggested assembly program materials. The first issue of the magazine was published in Oct., 1920. In 1944 three other magazines, *The Elementary Messenger, The Intermediate Counsellor,* and *Sunday School Young People and Adults,* were combined with *The Sunday School Builder,* thus making it serve the leadership of all age groups. Its contents treat the values and methods of successful Sunday school organization and work. In 1956 the circulation was 303,020. J. N. BARNETTE

SUNDAY SCHOOL LESSONS, GRADED. Graded lesson courses for the Sunday school are composed of units of Bible study which proceed step by step according to the particular interests, needs, and expanding capacities of boys and girls from early childhood to late adolescence. From the standpoint of content, Graded Lessons are thoroughly biblical; from the standpoint of educational approach, they are pupil-centered.

Whereas, in the case of Uniform Lessons, on any given Sunday all age groups study the same basic Bible passage or passages, in the case of Graded Lessons (as used in Southern Baptist churches) each age year has its own distinct lesson. To illustrate, there is a separate lesson for six-year-olds, a different one for seven-year-olds, still another for eight-year-olds, and so forth. Another difference is that whereas Uniform Lessons are rather like beads on a string, each one being more or less a separate unit, Graded Lessons are more like rungs of a ladder, each one being a part of what follows, and all making planned progress toward a well-defined goal.

Four series of Graded Lessons have been published by the Sunday School Board of the Southern Baptist Convention. The first, begun in 1911 and completed in 1916, was based on the Biblical Series of Graded Lessons planned by the International Lesson Committee (after a Southern Baptist Convention committee, appointed in 1910 at the request of the Sunday School Board, had made a strong protest against earlier extra-biblical outlines); it provided pupil and teacher material for each age year from the fourth through the nineteenth. The second series, a revision of the first, was begun in 1923 and included each age year from the 4th through the 20th. In 1928 *Nursery Class Stories* was added as a course for three-year-olds. The third series was based on outlines prepared by an interdenominational group composed of representatives of Northern and Southern Presbyterians, Northern and Southern Baptists, Disciples of Christ, the Reformed Church, and the United Church of Canada. It included each age year from the 4th through the 16th and was issued, a year's lessons for each department at a time, Oct., 1930, to Oct., 1934.

Plans were initiated in 1939, by the board working independently, to publish a fourth series of Graded Lessons. The lessons for four- and five-year-olds were merged with other lessons for this group, related to the Bible content of the Uniform Lessons. The new lessons, though appearing in the format of Uniform Lessons, actually constituted a single departmentally graded course for Beginners. A new course of Primary Graded Lessons was issued in 1941–42, a new Junior course in 1943–44, and a new Intermediate course in 1948–49. A new course for Nursery children, first for three-year-olds an later to provide for the two-year-olds, had been published in 1943 (revised in 1952) and 1949, respectively. Thus, the entire graded course, designed to serve churches with a sufficient number of pupils for close grading, covered the children's and youth levels up to age 16. HOWARD P. COLSON

SUNDAY SCHOOL LESSONS, UNIFORM. The Uniform Lessons promoted by the Sunday School Board and used in practically all Southern Baptist Sunday schools are so planned that on any given Sunday all age groups (Primary through Adult) which use them study the same general Bible material, with suitable adaptations being made for children's groups. Lesson outlines are planned with a view to giving a reasonably well-balanced coverage of the entire Bible during a six-year period. Effort is made to include each major type of Bible study. Some phase of the life of Christ is studied each year. Almost from the beginning of the Uniform Lesson Committee in 1872, Southern Baptists have played a leading part in its work of selecting the lessons.

Leaders in launching the Uniform Lesson system were J. H. Vincent, a Methodist preacher, and B. F. Jacobs, a Baptist layman, both of Chicago. Active on the lesson committee from 1878 to 1895 was John Albert Broadus (*q.v.*). He was succeeded by John Richard Sampey (*q.v.*) who served for nearly half a century and was chairman of the committee for 27 years. Other Southern Baptists who were leaders on the committee were Isaac Jacobus Van Ness (*q.v.*) and Hight C. Moore.

The present committee, known as the Committee on Uniform Series, in 1955 had a membership of 84 persons representing 33 denominations.

Southern Baptists are actively and influentially represented on this committee by the editorial secretary of the Sunday School Board and six additional editors representing age groups from the Primary through the Adult. Whereas the lesson committee selects the Bible material to be studied, it offers no interpretation of it. In fact, full freedom is allowed the co-operating denominations in the use of the committee's outlines so that they may be adapted to denominational needs and doctrinal distinctives. The lessons developed from the outlines are written and edited by persons chosen on the basis of qualifications to prepare lessons suited to the churches of the denomination. HOWARD P. COLSON

SUNDAY SCHOOL LITERATURE (1873–1891). See HOME MISSION BOARD, SUNDAY SCHOOL WORK.

SUNDAY SCHOOL MISSIONS. In the formative years of Southern Baptist life, hundreds, and likely thousands, of the churches in the different states from Virginia to Texas resulted from mission Sunday schools established by the American Sunday School Union from 1825 to 1865 or later.

In 1863, at the meeting of the Southern Baptist Convention in Augusta, Ga., when the first Sunday School Board was created, the following resolution was adopted: "That the Board be charged with the duty of taking all measures adapted to promote the establishment, enlargement . . . of Sunday schools throughout the land."

Thomas Boykin, brother of Samuel Boykin (*q.v.*), was elected Sunday school evangelist by the Alabama board in 1871. He had a genius for Sunday school organization. A record tells that in the first eight years of his work he organized 500 Sunday schools. In 27 years he organized 1,500 schools. In other states and places others were working at the same task. The Baptist state conventions as they were organized, and various Sunday school societies and conventions in the states, through colporteurs and missionaries, started Sunday schools in weak churches and also many Sunday school missions that later developed into churches. The present Sunday School Board of the Southern Baptist Convention, as soon as it could begin the work after its establishment in 1891, gave increasing attention to establishing mission Sunday schools from which new churches could and would develop. The action of the Convention that created this board instructed that "The Board in its work will aid mission Sunday schools by contribution of literature and money; doing this, however, through state organizations."

The Sunday School Board has vigorously promoted this program throughout its history. Constant emphasis has been placed on it through promotional literature and field work. The endeavor has been carried forward in co-operation with state conventions. These efforts account for much of the growth in Southern Baptist life. The importance of mission Sunday schools for evangelism is indicated by the appraisal (given in 1953) of the following Southern Baptist pastors: Casper C. Warren (First Church, Charlotte, N. C.) reported that the six mission schools of the church, with an enrolment of 850 and an average attendance of 400, were the source of 43 per cent of the additions to the church by baptism for a year. W. O. Vaught, Jr. (Immanuel Church, Little Rock, Ark.) stated that over a period of eight years 500 persons were baptized from the nine mission schools of the church. Herschel H. Hobbs (First Church, Oklahoma City, Okla.) wrote: "Every unchurched community is a potentially pagan cell in our nation. Only through the establishing of new Sunday schools or mission points can we hope to minister to the needs of the people in these communities."

Southern Baptists reported an average net gain of nine new churches for every week of 1955. Most of these churches developed from mission Sunday schools. The Southern Baptist Convention in the 1956 session took action, following a suggestion by Casper C. Warren, president, calling for an effort "to double the number of Southern Baptist preaching places by adding 5,000 new churches and 25,000 missions before the celebration of our third jubilee in 1964." This action expressed a denomination-wide view about the ways and means for church extension. CHARLES L. MCKAY

SUNNY CREST BAPTIST CHILDREN'S HOME. Now under construction at Bakersfield, Calif. Support for the home is derived from an annual Thanksgiving offering made by the churches, church budget designations, birthday offerings, and other special gifts.

At the first annual meeting of the San Joaquin Valley Missionary Baptist Association one year before the Southern Baptist General Convention of California was organized, a committee recommended that birthday offerings be taken in the churches and sent to children's homes located in New Mexico, Oklahoma, and Arkansas. A few months after the convention was organized Marvin Mouser, of Shafter, contributed $1 to start a fund to build a children's home. He later gave the home 40 acres of land which was sold for $12,000. At the 1951 meeting of the convention a committee reported that $18,000 was on hand and recommended that a board of trustees be appointed and machinery set in motion to get the home in operation. Two years later W. A. Herring of Arkansas was employed as superintendent; in 1953 a 23-acre site was purchased in Bakersfield, and it was agreed to refer to the home as Sunny Crest.

By Sept., 1955, two cottages and a superintendent's home were under construction, but no date had been set for a formal opening.

JAMES E. CARROLL

SUNSET GLOW (Home for the Aged). A Baptist boarding home for elderly people, located in Dade City, Fla., it opened to receive men and women on Apr. 15, 1952. The home was a venture of faith by Mrs. S. T. Stallings, a business woman and member of the First Baptist Church of Dade City, who disposed of her personal business and devoted her entire time to its planning and projection. During World War II the Pasco Packing Company of Dade City constructed a five-winged, one-story dormitory to house several hundred women employees. No longer needed when the war ended, the property was deeded to Pasco County on Sept. 30, 1949. Mrs. Stallings went to the Pasco Baptist Woman's Missionary Union, told the members of her desire to secure the unused dormitory and establish a home for elderly people, and requested the group to consider its sponsorship. The Woman's Missionary Union approved this suggestion and appointed a committee to appear before the board of county commissioners. On Feb. 12, 1952, the commissioners transferred the property to the Pasco Baptist Woman's Missionary Union, and the long-dreamed-of institution became a reality. Sunset Glow is not equipped as a nursing home, although those who become ill are given excellent care. Guests are encouraged to care for their own small but adequate rooms, and those physically able enjoy work among the flowers and vegetables. Sunset Glow is now self-sustaining.

ELBERT C. TYNER

SUPERNATURALISM. A school of thought in modern theology which arose out of the conflict between traditional and natural theology during the age of rationalism. The deists and especially Socinians attacked traditional theology at the point of its doctrine of revelation. They contended that God is known through reason, which they called the light of nature. Replying to the rationalistic attack, the supernaturalists insisted that while the central beliefs of Christianity are reasonable in the sense that they may be above reason but not against reason, they are nevertheless not apprehended by reason alone. The truth of Christianity comes through revelation corroborated by the fulfilment of prophecies and miracles. Pascal was the first to maintain clearly that the revelation of God comes through the Bible. While the rationalists contended for the essential oneness of all reality, the supernaturalists insisted that God transcends his created world and is essentially different from it. Supernaturalism entered a second phase with Kant's and Hegel's philosophies and Schleiermacher's theology, which created a new confidence in human reason. The critical study of the Bible began. The supernaturalists countered with the insistence of the absolute transcendence of God (Kierkegaard and Barth).

BIBLIOGRAPHY: J. Orr, *The Christian View of God and the World* (1947). A. K. Rogers, *A Student's History of Philosophy* (1935). CHARLES A. TRENTHAM

SWEDEN, BAPTISTS IN. The pioneer of the Baptist movement in Sweden was F. O. Nilsson, a sailor who had been converted in the Baptist Seamen's Church in New York. In 1847 he went to Hamburg, Germany, and was baptized by Johann Gerhard Oncken (*q.v.*). He returned to Sweden and organized the first Baptist church at Vallersvik south of Gothenburg on Sept. 21, 1848. Persecution began, and Nilsson was banished from Sweden in 1851. After working in Denmark and the United States, he returned to Sweden in 1860 when the king annulled his sentence of banishment. Andreas Wiberg, a well-educated minister of the Lutheran state church, undertook to prepare a book against "the Anabaptist errors." He became convinced that the Baptist view was in accord with the New Testament, and the book turned into a defense of Baptist views. Wiberg was baptized in Copenhagen by Nilsson in 1852. After three years in the United States, he returned to Sweden and became pastor of the church in Stockholm. The American Baptist Publication Society underwrote the support of Wiberg and four evangelists.

The Swedish General Conference was organized in 1857 with 19 delegates. The attendance the following year was about one hundred. In 1866 K. O. Broady was sent by the American Baptist Missionary Union to organize a seminary (Bethel) in Stockholm for the training of pastors and missionaries. The college opened the same year. C. Wingren was sent as their first missionary to China in 1890, and a few months later W. Sjöblom was sent to the Belgian Congo. In both fields flourishing missions developed. When China came under Communist rule, the work there had to be discontinued, and a mission in Japan was opened. Foreign mission work was begun in India in 1944. In 1956 the number of foreign missionaries was about 60, with approximately 500 national workers. The membership on the foreign field stood at 20,600.

Swedish Baptists had increased to about 40,000 in 1900. In 1907 the Pentecostal movement began and drew many members away from the Baptist union. One branch of Pentecostals remained within the union but started their own mission work and seminary in Orebro. Increasing internal tension led to a crisis in the late 1930's, and many churches left the Baptist union to affiliate with the Orebro movement. The Swedish Baptist membership was thereby reduced from 61,000 to about 35,000. In 1956 there were 530 Baptist churches with a membership of 36,000 served by about 400 pastors and 350 lay preachers. There were 885 Sunday schools with 40,000 members. The youth work comprised about 6,000 members in 200 societies.

The seminary in Stockholm (Betelseminariet) had 29 students enrolled in 1956, six of them women. The weekly paper *Vecko-Posten* has a circulation of 17,000. The young people publish their own periodical *Ungdomens Veckopost*. Several other publications deal with Sunday school work. Music and singing are well developed and about 1,800 Baptists belong to national associations for choirs and bands. In Christian education the Sjövik folk high school does significant work. Swedish Baptist women have been organized in a union since 1914. Trained nurses and deaconesses have worked together in an association since 1922. The pastors also have their national conference. Social institutions include a youth home in Stockholm and a home for boys in Kungsangen. A resort in Vallersvik serves as a conference center during the summer. Swedish Baptists participate with other Scandinavian Baptist unions in the Seamen's Mission in San Francisco.

The Baptist headquarters are located in Stockholm (Klarabergsgatan 50).

BIBLIOGRAPHY: I. Barnes, *Truth Is Immortal* (1955). J. D. Franks, ed., *European Baptists Today* (1952).

JOSEF NORDENHAUG

SWEDISH BAPTIST UNION MISSION BOARD. Directs home and foreign mission work of the Swedish Baptist Union. The board consists of 24 members with a general director, Erik Rudén, and a secretary, Eric Strutz. The weekly publication, *Veckoposten,* deals with the work at home and abroad. The board is located at Klarabergsgatan 50, Stockholm.

Swedish Baptists began foreign mission work in 1872, by collecting funds to support an evangelist in Burma under the American Baptist Missionary Union. In 1877 the first Swedish Baptist missionary, Erik Lund, was sent to Spain. Work in that country was carried on until 1921, when it was taken over by the Foreign Mission Board of the Southern Baptist Convention. In 1891 work was begun in Shantung, China, which continued until 1951. Late statistics show 15 churches with 5,000 members and 120 Chinese workers. In 1892 E. W. Sjoblom was sent to the Belgian Congo, where he served in co-operation with the American Baptist mission until his death in 1903. Work started anew in 1914 in Basakata, the country between the Kasai and Lukenie rivers. This developed as an independent Swedish Baptist field, later being enlarged. In 1952 there were 38 missionaries in the area. In 1956 there were 6 churches with 1,000 members. Since 1945 work has been done in South India in connection with the American Baptist Telugu mission. In 1956 six missionaries were stationed there. In 1951 missionaries formerly stationed in China were transferred to Japan, where they co-operate with the American Baptist Foreign Mission Society. Baptist work in Estonia and Finland has been supported for many years with money and missionaries. In 1956 a total of 70 missionaries were serving in the three foreign fields: Belgian Congo, India, and Japan. The 1956 budget was 800,000 Swedish crowns (approximately $160,000). ERIC STRUTZ

SWEETWATER SEMINARY. A female college at Sweetwater, Tenn., founded in 1886. It opened in 1886 with J. H. Richardson as president, a faculty of five, and an enrolment of 80. The curriculum included music, art, science, elocution, and business. The school reached its peak in 1893 with an enrolment of 130 and property valued at $40,000. The lack of adequate support and an indebtedness of $18,000 resulted in the school's closing in 1897.

LYNN EDWARD MAY, JR.

SYLVA COLLEGIATE INSTITUTE. Associational school at Sylva, Jackson County, N. C., operated by Tennessee River, Tuckaseige, and Macon County associations. It was one of the most important of the Baptist mountain schools. The school was established in 1899 by trustees chosen by Tennessee River and Tuckaseige associations, and the first session began Aug. 7, 1900, with Harry L. Sams as principal. The trustees leased a building which was used until the completion of the school building in 1903. Sylva was a member of the state system of Baptist academies, and from its first session received financial assistance from the Home Mission Board's program of aid to mountain schools. By 1931, when the program was discontinued, the school had received over $60,000, including $24,000 for capital improvements. In 1909 the Macon County Association adopted Sylva as its associational school.

Although the school was well-supported from the first session, in the 1920's it was at the height of its influence. In that decade the school was accredited by the state, enrolled over 200 pupils each year, and in 1924 owned property at an estimated value of $74,000. After the Home Mission Board withdraw support in 1931, the school suspended its operations with the intention of reopening later as a junior college, but this was never done. In 1934 the trustees reported that the school had closed "due to the indifference of the Baptists of Western North Carolina." In 1940 title to the property was vested in the Home Mission Board. The board rented the buildings to pay the upkeep.

D. L. SMILEY

T

TAIWAN BAPTIST CONVENTION. See FORMOSA, TAIWAN BAPTIST CONVENTION.

TALBOT, BENJAMIN (d. Nov. 10, 1834). Pioneer preacher. Presumably, Talbot (also spelled Tolbart) was from North Carolina, for he was the stepson of a North Carolinian who had immigrated to Kentucky. His conversion came while suffering from a flesh wound in the thigh, received either while fighting in the Revolutionary War or with Indians on the frontier. He was the founder of Hazel Creek Baptist Church (1797), the oldest church west of Elizabethtown, and continued as pastor until his death. During the same period he served several other churches, including Beaver Dam (1803–33); Sandy Creek (1805–34); Walton's Creek (1814–31); and Pond Run (1820–33). Having been one of the organizers of the Gasper River Association, he served as its moderator from 1824 to 1830. W. C. SMITH, JR.

TALBOT, MATTHEW (b. Amelia County, Va., 1729; d. Wilkes County, Ga., Oct. 12, 1812). Moved to the Watauga settlement in Tennessee from Bedford County, Va., where he had already achieved distinction in civil and military life as justice of the peace and as a captain in the Virginia militia. He moved to Watauga between 1770 and 1775, as the Watauga Fort was erected during the early years of the American Revolution on land that had once belonged to him. Thus he was the first Baptist preacher to become a regular settler in Tennessee; Jonathan Mulkey (*q.v.*) did not come until the autumn of 1775. Talbot married in 1753 and is reported to have become a Baptist soon afterward. He was baptized by William Murphy, who later moved to Tennessee. He became a large landowner, holding title at one time to nearly 1,500 acres of land. He served as one of the first justices of the peace in Washington County, was surveyor of roads, overseer of roads, foreman of the grand jury, etc. He combined the functions of minister and citizen. There are indications that he saw military service during the Revolutionary War. He moved to Georgia about 1784. Here he served as justice of the peace and was active in church and denominational life. He was affiliated with the Georgia Baptist Association in 1795, and perhaps earlier, as the records are not extant from 1788 to 1795. R. H. WARD

TALLADEGA BAPTIST MALE HIGH SCHOOL. A school for young men founded by local Baptists at Talladega, Ala., *c.* 1851. It was reported to be one of the flourishing Baptist schools in Alabama in 1858. The school properties were sold to satisfy a heavy mortgage in 1866. JAMES E. DAVIDSON

TAYLOR, ALFRED (b. Warren County, Ky., July 19, 1808; d. near Bowling Green, Ky., Oct. 9, 1865). The son of Joseph Taylor. He became the leading preacher of his generation in the Gasper River Association and the lower Green River country. A biography of 123 pages was written by his son, William Carey Taylor, Sr., in 1875, and published by the Gasper River body, which he served as treasurer for eight years, as moderator for 13 years, and as preacher of the introductory sermon nine times. He was converted in his 22nd year and was baptized into the fellowship of Sandy Creek Church, Butler County, Ky.

His educational advantages were very limited, but after entering the ministry in May, 1831, he studied under David Mansfield and William Warder, prominent Baptist ministers in Logan County, Ky., being ordained at Sandy Creek Church, Butler County, Ky., in May, 1834, by Joseph Taylor, David J. Kelley, and William Childress. He served churches in Butler, Warren, Muhlenberg, Ohio, and Daviess counties.

He held the first "protracted meeting" ever held in the Green River country at Walton's Creek Church, Ohio County, in Dec., 1837. Opposition to this "new fad" arose, but over 180 persons professed conversion. The revival spread all over the Green River country, and Alfred Taylor himself baptized between 600 and 800 persons in two years' time, with over 1,000 professions. "For twenty years after this gathering," it was reported, "his word was as good authority among Baptists, upon all questions, as Webster's dictionary is in determining the meaning of words." He strongly opposed the legalism of Campbellism and the antinomianism of antimissionism and saw their consequent decline in his area.

Alfred Taylor strongly preached Baptist doctrine and conducted four public debates. He baptized many from other denominations. He led in the organization of the Green River Bible Society in 1837 and consistently promoted the cause of missions in the Green River area. He also served as an associational missionary, revivalist, and general association missionary. He preached the annual sermon before the general association at Shelbyville in 1839, the third annual session. He led the first temperance reform movement ever inaugurated in Butler County.

He was married four times. Three of his sons by the first marriage became Baptist ministers—James Pendleton, William Carey, Sr., and Judson.

One of his staunchest lifelong friends was James Madison Pendleton (*q.v.*), who said of him: "Few ministers in his day spent more time in preaching, sacrificed more for the cause of Christ, and received smaller compensation for faithful work." He is buried in Slaty Creek Cemetery, Ohio County, Ky.

BIBLIOGRAPHY: W. H. Rone, *A History of the Daviess-McLean Baptist Association in Kentucky, 1844–1943* (1944). W. C. Taylor, Sr., *Biography of Alfred Taylor* (1875). WENDELL HOLMES RONE

TAYLOR, CHARLES ELISHA (b. Richmond, Va., Oct. 28, 1842; d. Wake Forest, N. C., Nov. 5, 1915). Educator. Charles was the son of James Barnett Taylor (*q.v.*), the first corresponding secretary of the Foreign Mission Board of the Southern Baptist Convention. At the age of 15, Taylor entered Richmond College. In 1861 he joined the Confederate army. He graduated from the University of Virginia with the degree of B.Litt. in 1870 and was ordained to the ministry in 1871 at Wake Forest. Later he was awarded these honorary degrees: D.D., Richmond College, 1884; LL.D., University of North Carolina, 1889; and LL.D., Mercer University, 1889. He accepted a position as professor of Latin and German at Wake Forest College in 1870 and served in that capacity until 1883. In 1884–85 he was professor of Latin and moral philosophy; from 1884 to 1905, president of the college; and from 1885 to 1915, professor of moral philosophy.

Beginning in 1875 Taylor led a movement to increase the endowment of Wake Forest College to $20,000; then to $100,000 in 1883. As president he kept a steady appeal before the Baptist people to help Wake Forest. The student body grew from 144 in 1883 to 328 in 1903. He erected three new buildings on the campus and installed adequate lighting, running water, and comfortable seats in all buildings. He increased the faculty from 6 professors and 2 tutors to 17 professors and 7 assistants; and the number of academic departments from 8 to 21. By the end of his administration he had multiplied the endowment fivefold. He was an outspoken proponent of public school education. Taylor married Mary Hinton Pritchard, daughter of J. L. Pritchard of Pasquotank County, N. C., on Sept. 11, 1873. There were seven children: Charles Elisha, Fanny (Mrs. J. Herndon Gorrell), Mary, Ethel (Mrs. Christopher C. Crittenden), Janie (Mrs. William D. Duke), Agnes (Mrs. Aubrey Hawkins), and Edith (Mrs. Elliott B. Earnshaw).

He wrote "Gilbert Stone," a poem (1891); *How Far Should a State Undertake to Educate?* (1894); and *The Story of Yates the Missionary* (1898).

BIBLIOGRAPHY: W. Cathcart, *The Baptist Encyclopaedia* (1883). G. W. Paschal, *History of Wake Forest College* (1943); "Charles Elisha Taylor," *The Wake Forest Student*. Vol. XXXV (1916). *The National Cyclopaedia of American Biography* (1935).

GARLAND A. HENDRICKS

TAYLOR, GEORGE BOARDMAN (b. Richmond, Va., Dec. 27, 1832; d. Rome, Italy, Sept. 28, 1907). Missionary to Italy. Son of James Barnett Taylor (*q.v.*), he was educated at Richmond College and University of Virginia. Taylor served pastorates at Franklin Square Church, Baltimore, and at Staunton, Va.; he was chaplain of the University of Virginia and Stonewall Jackson's Corps; he was recording secretary of the Southern Baptist Convention, 1857–66. Appointed missionary to Italy in 1873, Taylor led in establishing the Baptist theological school in Rome. Author of *Italy and the Italians, Life and Times of James B. Taylor,* and other volumes, Taylor also wrote frequently for Baptist periodicals and served on the commission for revision of the Italian New Testament. He married Susan Spotswood Braxton May 13, 1858.

BIBLIOGRAPHY: G. B. Taylor, *Life and Letters of George Boardman Taylor* (1908); *Virginia Baptist Ministers,* Fifth Series (1915). E. C. ROUTH

TAYLOR, HARVEY BOYCE, SR. (b. Ohio County, Ky., Sept. 29, 1870; d. Memphis, Tenn., May 31, 1932). Preacher, editor, educator, promoter of missions. A fourth-generation Baptist minister, Taylor was the eldest son of W. C. and Frances A. (Stevens) Taylor, Sr. His brother, W. C. Taylor, Jr., was a long-time missionary to Brazil.

Taylor received the A.B. degree (1890) and the M.A. degree (1896) from Bethel College. From the Southern Baptist Theological Seminary he received three diplomas, including the Th.M. (June 4, 1896) and two certificates for special work in Greek and Hebrew. He received the D.D. degree from Hall-Moody Institute, Martin, Tenn.

Taylor served as pastor in Cove Hill, Providence, and Murray, Ky., 1897–1932. During his pastorate the latter became noted as one of the greatest missionary churches in the denomination, receiving acclaim from J. F. Love of the Foreign Mission Board. An annual "Bible institute," wherein outstanding preachers spoke on missions, doctrines, and practical Christian living, continued for most of his ministry in Murray.

As early as 1900 the Murray church, through his leadership, adopted the budget plan of finances which was soon adopted by other churches. In 1914 he served as chairman of a committee which presented the plan to the General Association of Baptists in Kentucky, which appointed a committee of nine, with Taylor as chairman, to make a thorough study and report to the association at Jellico in 1915. The committee's report on the budget plan was adopted and was put into operation in the state on Jan. 1, 1916. This plan for unification, with some modifications, became the background of the Southern Baptist Convention's Cooperative Program, adopted in 1925. During his pastorate the Murray church gave over $180,000 to missions, with $37,268 being given in one year of the 75 Million Campaign.

Taylor served on the Kentucky state board of missions for a number of years. He served as clerk of Blood River Association and later as treasurer for 18 years. In 1917 he was moderator of the general association. Originator of the West Kentucky Baptist Assembly, Dawson Springs, he served for several years as manager of the assembly. In Jan., 1906, he began publication of a paper, *News and Truths,* which continued until shortly after his death. He was an ardent supporter of the missionary and colportage work of the denomination; he spoke to numerous associations each year in the interest of his paper and missions and was in constant demand for revival meetings. The founder of West Kentucky Bible School, Murray, Taylor was the organizer and moving spirit in the Amazon Valley Baptist Faith Mission from 1922 until his death. For about 10 years he served as the Kentucky member of the Sunday School Board of the Southern Baptist Convention. Taylor was the author of two books, *Bible Briefs Against Hurtful Heresies* and *Why Be a Baptist?* His defense of Baptist faith included over 50 public discussions with representative men of numerous denominations.

WENDELL HOLMES RONE

TAYLOR, JAMES BARNETT (b. Lincolnshire, England, Mar. 19, 1804; d. Richmond, Va., Dec. 22, 1871). Pastor and foreign mission leader. After coming to America with his parents in 1805, Taylor spent 12 years in New York. He persuaded his father, who had been inclined toward infidelity, to go into a church they were passing when they were attracted by the music. First his parents and then Taylor were converted and baptized into the fellowship of the First Baptist Church, New York. The family moved to Virginia in 1817. Licensed to preach in 1824, Taylor was ordained two years later and became pastor of the Second Baptist Church, Richmond. Although not a preacher of superior ability, he devoted a great deal of time to pastoral visitation.

On the basis of recommendations by a committee of which Taylor was a member, the Virginia Baptist Education Society was organized in 1830. The school, which opened in Oct., 1830, as a result of the previous action, evolved into the Virginia Baptist Seminary, with Taylor as one of the trustees. In 1839 he became chaplain of the University of Virginia but later returned to Richmond as pastor of the Third (later Grace Street) Baptist Church.

When the Foreign Mission Board of the Southern Baptist Convention was constituted, Taylor was urged to accept the secretaryship. He wrestled with the choice between the pastorate and the mission board and finally decided to remain with Grace Church, although he agreed to give two days a week to the service of the board and to make a tour of the South in behalf of foreign missions. Just before leaving on tour, Taylor met Adoniram Judson (*q.v.*), missionary home on furlough in Richmond. As Taylor traveled, the conviction deepened that he should give his life to the foreign mission enterprise, and as a result he served as secretary of the Foreign Mission Board for 26 years. Through the Civil War and reconstruction period when the Southern Baptist Convention did not meet every year, Taylor kept the organization intact. By private and public appeals, he secured money for immediate and for future needs. In 1855 Columbian College conferred on Taylor the honorary D.D. degree. Taylor was author of *Memoir of Luther Rice, Life of Lott Carey,* and *Lives of Virginia Baptist Ministers* (First and Second series).

BIBLIOGRAPHY: G. B. Taylor, *Virginia Baptist Ministers,* 3d series. *Southern Baptist Handbook* (1945). G. B. Taylor, *Life and Times of James B. Taylor* (1908).

E. C. ROUTH

TAYLOR, JOHN (b. Faquier County, Va., Oct. 27, 1752; d. Frankfort, Ky., Apr. 12, 1835). Preacher, farmer, author. Reared in the "backwoods of Virginia," Taylor "never heard a man preach" until he was 17 years old. In 1772 he was converted and was baptized by James Ireland (*q.v.*). He soon became a traveling preacher and was ordained in 1776 or 1777 by South River Church in the Shenandoah Valley. In 1783 he moved to Kentucky.

In Virginia he was a member of South River Church and of Lunies Creek Church, and in Kentucky he was a member or pastor of eight churches in succession: Gilbert's Creek, South Elkhorn, Clear Creek, Bullittsburg, Corn Creek, Big Spring, Frankfort, and Buck Run. These churches were the subjects of his book, *A History of Ten Baptist Churches, of which the author has been alternately a member* (published in 1823; second edition, 1827). A prosperous farmer, Taylor received little remuneration from churches he served. Present at the organization of Elkhorn Association, Oct. 1, 1785, he regularly attended the annual sessions of that and other associations.

Much of Taylor's activity was directed against Luther Rice and the missionary interests. In 1819, in opposition to missions, he wrote *Thoughts on Missions,* which he later seemed to regret. Although he wavered in aligning himself with the best-trained Baptist leaders of Kentucky in the missions controversy, when Campbellism arose in the late 1820's, he stood firm in his support of the Baptists from his very first meeting with Alexander Campbell. In 1830 he published *History of Clear Creek Church and Campbellism Exposed.* Although Taylor died before the organization of the General Association of Baptists in Kentucky, there is evidence that he was present at a meeting of its predecessor, the Kentucky Baptist Convention, Jan. 10–13, 1835.

BIBLIOGRAPHY: J. H. Spencer, *A History of Kentucky Baptists* (1886). W. B. Sprague, *Annals of the American Pulpit* (1856). J. B. Taylor, *Lives of Virginia Baptist Ministers* (1838). J. Taylor, *A History of Ten Baptist Churches* (1823); *History of Clear*

Creek Church and Campbellism Exposed (1830); *Thoughts on Missions* (1820). LEO T. CRISMON

TAYLOR, ZACHARY CLAY (b. near Jackson, Miss., Jan., 1851; d. Corpus Christi, Tex., Sept. 14, 1919). Missionary to Brazil. Converted at 17 years of age, he joined a Baptist church, and moved with his parents to Texas at the close of the Civil War. Taylor attended Waco and Baylor universities and was ordained at Independence, Tex., in 1879. His interest in foreign missions was stimulated by reading the *Texas Baptist Herald* and meeting Ezekias Z. Simmons (*q.v.*), missionary to China. He was impressed with South America as a mission field, and after a few months at Southern Baptist Theological Seminary, he married Kate Stevens Crawford Dec. 25, 1881, and they sailed Jan. 12, 1882, to Brazil. Serving with the William Buck Bagbys (*q.v.*) at Bahia in 1882, Taylor was publishing a monthly paper, *The Echo of Truth*, by 1884. He emphasized evangelism, distributed Christian literature, and stressed the importance of occupying strategic centers of influence. After Taylor's wife died in Bahia, Aug. 19, 1894, he married Laura Barton, who had spent one term of service in China, in Dec., 1895. Taylor returned to the United States in Sept., 1909, because of ill health, and he and his wife were drowned in a devastating hurricane.

BIBLIOGRAPHY: A. R. Crabtree, *Baptists in Brazil* (1953). W. S. Stewart, *Later Baptist Missionaries*, Vol. II (1929). E. C. ROUTH

TAYLORSVILLE CLASSICAL INSTITUTE. A Baptist school also known as United Baptist Institute, located at Taylorsville, Alexander County, N. C. It was founded on Jan. 8, 1856, by United Association. The school was closed for a short time during the Civil War. In 1874 it became the associational school of Brushy Mountain Association and in 1891 the school of Alexander Association. D. L. SMILEY

TEACHER, THE. For 70 years this publication was a widely circulated and influential Southern Baptist monthly containing helps for teachers of the Uniform Sunday School Lessons. First known as *Kind Words Teacher* (1887–91), later as *The Convention Teacher* (1892–1927), it finally was called simply *The Teacher* (1928–56). Authorized by vote of the Southern Baptist Convention and first published by the Home Mission Board, it was taken over by the Sunday School Board with the January issue of 1892. From 1888 through 1891, it was edited by Basil Manly, Jr., Samuel Boykin, and David Shaver. After 1891 its successive editors were James Marion Frost (*q.v.*) (1892–1900), Isaac Jacobus Van Ness (*q.v.*) (1900–17), Edwin Charles Dargan (*q.v.*) (1917–27), Hight C Moore (1927–43), Clifton Judson Allen (1943–53), and Howard Paul Colson (1953–56). Its final issue was in Sept., 1956, being succeeded by two publications, *The Young People's Teacher* and *The Adult Teacher*. The circulation for the last issue was 264,736. HOWARD P. COLSON

TELEVISION, CHRISTIAN USE OF. While television cannot and should not replace personal church attendance, it can and does offer supplementary inspirational and educational opportunities to the active church member, and at the same time serves to reach those who either cannot or will not attend church. The qualities which have contributed to the success of television as an advertising and entertainment medium are equally as effective when used in the presentation of the Christian message. Television incorporates the prime features of the printed page, theater, and radio into one continuous presentation in both picture and sound of events as they occur. Various portions of this presentation reach every member of the family, regardless of age or physical condition. More than just a combination of other media, television attains a unique person-to-person relationship with the viewer in the privacy of his own home without the actual presence of a second party which might inhibit the admission of his innermost needs and shortcomings. Television offers the unusual opportunity of making this personal presentation of the Christian message to an ever-increasing number of TV viewers simultaneously. Many who never venture into a church or permit any personal discussion of their spiritual life are reached through either televised religion or religious television.

Televised religion.—This type of program is produced by either placing television equipment at the scene of a religious service, or by presenting a regular sermon or devotional program from a TV studio. In either instance, television is used as a means of enlarging the audience, while the program itself is changed little if any from that originally planned for the church alone.

The remote telecast of a local church service is the most widely used form of televised religion. The TV station parks its mobile unit near the church and places cameras and microphones in the sanctuary, which has been lighted and wired to meet television requirements. Pictures of the service (video) are transmitted to the TV station via microwave, and sound (audio) travels over special telephone circuits. At the station both picture and sound are then broadcast over the station's regular TV channel.

The primary value of this use of television is its extension of the preaching ministry of the church. To some degree it brings the service to those who cannot attend, either temporarily or permanently. Many churches which televise their services regularly, once a month or oftener, find that the worth of this ministry to their members alone makes the added effort and expense worth while. Of course, many who are not members of the church are reached as well. These include those willing but unable to attend other churches, and the semi-indifferent who are not interested enough to attend a church but will watch a service on TV.

Another value of televising the church service is that the church becomes widely known throughout the telecast area. Naturally, this is of great help to the public relations program of the church. Families seeking a church home often visit and later join a church after seeing its televised services. Also, those who visit *for* the church find a quicker response from families already familiar with the church because of television.

Religious television.—This type of program utilizes the techniques and qualities unique to television in the presentation of the Christian message. While appreciated by the same audience attracted by a televised religious service, programs in the religious television category may also appeal to the larger audience which includes the nonreligious and even antireligious. Almost all standard TV types are used for effective religious presentations including drama, news, variety, music, interview, panel, quiz, and dominant personality programs. When the Christian theme is introduced in these various program types, it is not to disguise or sugar-coat the gospel but simply to claim for the cause of Christ the techniques which have proved so effective in promoting other messages.

While all program types are viewed by varying segments of the television audience, the one with the largest following and with the greatest potential for Christian use is the drama. For this reason Southern Baptists have concentrated on this form of presentation for national release. The Radio and Television Commission released its first series, "This Is the Answer," from its Fort Worth headquarters in Apr., 1956. The initial 13 color films in this series were dramatic presentations of scriptural episodes in present-day settings. Response from television stations and the general public led to the immediate preparation of additional films of a similar nature.

While recognized as the best vehicle for religious television, the drama is usually limited by production requirements to network and film presentations. However, all other program types are used quite effectively for local religious programs. Since most local programs are produced with a minimum of studio rehearsal due to limited space and budget, the informal technique is quite practical as well as popular. Although informal in presentation and limited in studio rehearsal, the better programs are those which are carefully planned and rehearsed before entering the production studio.

The complete program need not be one planned by or in behalf of a religious organization in order to qualify as religious television. A very effective use of the medium (both network and local) is the integration of Christian material into existing secular programs which already have a large established audience. Some Christian groups maintain representatives responsible for providing appropriate material to capitalize on all opportunities as they arise. These opportunities include the use of properties for which recognition is given on the air, the placing of personalities or groups on programs as guests or contestants, and sometimes the planning of an entire program or episode around a Christian theme at Christmas or Easter or on other special occasions.

Like other mass media, television becomes the instrument of those who use it most effectively. Southern Baptists, along with other leading Christian groups, propose to redeem every television opportunity as a God-given means to go "into all the world, and preach the gospel to every creature" (Mark 16:15).

LUTHER ADKINS

TELL, A MISSIONS MAGAZINE FOR GIRLS. A monthly publication of the Woman's Missionary Union for girls 9–16 years of age who are members of a Girls' Auxiliary. The editor is Juliette Mather, secretary of the Department of Publications of Woman's Missionary Union; associate editor is Dorothy Weeks. Programs for Girls' Auxiliaries first appeared in *Royal Service* in 1914, and later in *World Comrades,* published as a quarterly in 1922 and as a monthly after 1924. Celebrating the 40th anniversary of Girls' Auxiliary in 1953, *Tell, A Missions Magazine for Girls* was inaugurated. The name was chosen in a contest for Girls' Auxiliary members, won by 11-year-old Mary Agnes Sanders, of Seneca, S. C. The magazine began in May, 1953, with an initial subscription list of 70,423, transferred from *World Comrades.* By Dec., 1954, at a subscription rate of $1.50 per year, circulation had reached 94,000. *Tell* contains mission stories, the daily prayer calendar of missionaries (listed on their birthdays), and features to stimulate missionary interest among girls. Programs for Girls' Auxiliaries and ideas for organizational activities appear monthly. Creative suggestions, party ideas, and mission games are part of the editorial plan to make the magazine entertaining as well as informative. Major contributors are home and foreign missionaries, leaders in denominational life, and members of the Woman's Missionary Union and Girls' Auxiliary.

DOROTHY LOUISE WEEKS

TELUGU BAPTIST CONVENTION, SOUTH INDIA. Representing the largest one-language group of Baptists in the world except the English-speaking, this convention had its first meeting in 1897. The large convention meets for "fellowship and maintenance of essential unity," and a widely representative executive council cares for administrative matters. Five associations, based on geographical areas, are divisions of the body. The Telugu Baptist Women's Convention meets separately and supports convention and women's projects. Work in Telugu was begun when Samuel S. Day (1808–71) opened a mission in 1836. Church members have come largely from the outcastes since the pentecost of 1876–79, when John E. Clough (1836–1910) negotiated with the British Government for a contract on the Buckingham Canal to provide relief work for outcastes starving during a famine. In 1878, 9,606 were baptized at Ongole within six months. Smaller mass movements have occurred from time to time. In recent years caste members have been coming into the churches in larger numbers.

Due to poverty, substantial support has had to come from American Baptist foreign mission societies, providing medical care, a seminary and teacher training schools, and grade and high schools, several of which have classes in vocational training. Evangelism is conducted in thousands of villages in districts related to a central church, with a single district as large as Rhode Island supervised by an associational missionary and Telugu associates. Telugu workers number 3,000, working with associations and the convention and as heads of schools. Self-support is increasing in proportion to economic improvement of the area.

The Telugus won a separate state within the Republic of India in 1953, known as Andhra State, Andhra being the original name of the Telugus. The new state, formed on a linguistic basis, has a population of 20 million. Under the sponsorship of the Andhra Christian Council, a meeting of Christians was held in 1954 with 15,000 in attendance. A part of Hyderabad State is included in the mission and has its own Christian council.

Characteristic of the co-operative work are Vellore Christian Medical College aided by 40 American and British denominations and mission societies, Madras Woman's Christian College, St. Christopher's Training College at Madras, and Andhra Christian College at Guntur.

DATA

	1934	*1954*
Churches	346	461
Baptisms	3,497	4,754
Church members	111,307	131,341
Indian workers	2,692	2,995
Missionaries	89	66
Schools	1,303	827
Students	36,533	48,986
Hospitals	3	3
Dispensaries	9	11
Patients	52,412	33,093
Field contributions	$20,366	$26,697

ADA STEARNS

TEMPERANCE AND SOCIAL PROBLEMS, LOUISIANA. In the early years of the associations and the state convention, there were no reports on temperance; these social problems were handled by the churches through discipline. The first association to pass upon alcoholic beverages was Red River in 1854, when the use of alcohol was said to be "contrary to the genius of Christianity and injurious to the cause of Christ." The first report on temperance by the state convention was made in 1867, when it was said: "The use of ardent spirits as a beverage is one of the greatest, if not the greatest, evils of our age." After these Baptist bodies began to pass upon this problem, Baptists became the leading advocates of temperance. The 1889 convention condemned the Louisiana lottery evil in strong terms. The 1929 convention went on record as being opposed to the nomination to office of any man or woman who favored the repeal of the national prohibition law. The 1932 convention condemned "the illegal, unconstitutional methods" then being used to repeal or erase the state prohibition enforcement law in Louisiana. Baptists are now leading the Louisiana religious forces in temperance and social reform movements. They are the largest contributors to the Louisiana Moral and Civic Foundation, Inc. MARK A. LOWER

TEMPERANCE BANNER, THE. A Baptist newspaper begun in 1834 at Washington, Ga., under the direction of Jesse Mercer and W. H. Stokes. Mercer the year before had become editor and owner of *The Christian Index* with Stokes as his junior editor. *The Banner,* a semi-monthly, rode the wave of popularity for the temperance movement which was sweeping the state but operated at a loss to Mercer. He eventually suspended its publication.

JOHN J. HURT, JR.

TEMPTATION. In its most developed biblical sense, inducement to sin. In the Old Testament *nasah* and *bachan,* translated "to try, test, prove, tempt," may signify either God's testing or proving man, even by adversity (Gen. 22:1; Deut. 8:2; Job 7:18), or man's tempting or doubting God or rebelling against him (Deut. 6:16; Psalm 95:9). In the New Testament *pierazein* and its cognates may mean either to test (Matt. 22:35; John 6:6) or to induce to sin (Gal. 6:1; II Peter 2:9). Temptation to sin is due to Satan the tempter (Matt. 4:1; I Thess. 3:5) and to lust (Jas. 1:14). Christ experienced real temptations of a distinctly messianic import, and "was in all points tempted like as we are, yet without sin" (Heb. 4:15). His temptations enable him to succor men (Heb. 2:18). God is neither tempted nor able to be tempted (Jas. 1:13), but he provides for the tempted a way of escape (I Cor. 10:13).

BIBLIOGRAPHY: D. Bonhoeffer, *Temptation* (1955). C. S. Lewis, *The Screwtape Letters* (1943).

J. LEO GARRETT

TEMUCO COLEGIO BAUTISTA. See CHILE, MISSION IN.

TENNESSEE, BAPTIST GENERAL ASSOCIATION OF. Organized at Mill Creek Church, Davidson County, Oct. 21, 1842. It succeeded the Tennessee Baptist Convention (1833–42) and continued until 1874, when it merged into the new Tennessee Baptist Convention. In 1849 it became the Baptist General Association of Middle Tennessee and North Alabama. There were probably no annual sessions during 1862–66. By 1867 it was called the Baptist General Association of Middle Tennessee. (The churches in North Alabama organized into the

Baptist General Association of North Alabama.) In 1869 it was again the Baptist General Association of Middle Tennessee and North Alabama. In 1874, a railroad having been completed north and south through Alabama, the Baptists in North Alabama from Jefferson and Walker counties to the Tennessee line united with the Alabama Baptist Convention.

At the organization of the general association, four societies which had been auxiliary to the Tennessee Baptist Convention were merged into it, and five boards were established: the executive and publishing boards at Nashville, the Bible and education boards at Murfreesboro, and the foreign mission board at Shelbyville.

The purpose of the general association was somewhat broader than that of its predecessor: (1) to aid feeble and destitute churches in its bounds and supply destitute areas with missionaries; (2) to devise plans for giving the "unadulterated word of life" and preachers "to the destitute in our own and foreign lands"; and (3) to "supply our people and the community at large with such books as shall be approved by this body."

At its 1845 session, the general association approved the formation of the Southern Baptist Convention and related its activities to the Convention but continued its Bible work as auxiliary to the American and Foreign Bible Society until the establishment of the Southern Baptist Bible Board (1851). At this session, after addresses were made to a "vast concourse of people" on Sunday, two ministers administered the Lord's Supper, after which the right hand of fellowship was given during the singing of a hymn.

Robert Boyté Crawford Howell (*q.v.*) gave *The Baptist* to the general association in 1846. Its education board assumed charge and contracted with James Robinson Graves (*q.v.*) and Alex Shankland to publish it and have charge of the depository. The next year, under Graves's leadership, the general association created a new publication society, procured a charter for it, and made it responsible for the paper.

The general association established Union University at Murfreesboro. Howell did much to shape and guide the general association from its organization until he left the state in 1850, and was usually its moderator. Graves was the aggressive leader from 1850 until the Civil War and was usually moderator during this period.

The Graves-Howell controversy almost wrecked the general association, even though Graves and his party were almost wholly dominant (1858–61). Support of the Southern Baptist Convention and its boards almost ceased, and direct missionism advocated by Graves greatly weakened its own missionary activities as well. When Graves attended the annual session in 1868 (he was then residing in Memphis), he said that he had not attended a session since 1861 and stated that the Concord Association was the only one "that works solely through the general association, and all the others seem to prefer to do their own missionary work."

Controversy and dissension, the ravages of the Civil War, and the following Reconstruction era brought the general association to the verge of collapse, but it endured and began to improve. A growing conviction developed throughout the state that the three Baptist bodies should unite. They did so in 1874. The general association, at its 1873 session, appointed delegates to meet at Murfreesboro in Apr., 1874, with delegates from the West Tennessee Baptist Convention and the General Association of Baptists of East Tennessee to "effect the unification of Baptists of Tennessee." The general association held its final session at Nashville in Oct., 1874, and merged with the new Tennessee Baptist Convention.

HOMER L. GRICE

TENNESSEE ASSOCIATIONS.

I. Extant. BEECH RIVER. Organized about 1871 at Union Hill Church by eight churches with 480 members located in Henderson, Decatur, Perry, Chester, and Hardin counties, and coming from Southwestern District Association. In 1954, 50 churches reported 164 baptisms, 5,824 members, $94,164 total gifts, $8,801 mission gifts, $397,400 property value, and $12,079 church debt.

BEULAH. Organized about 1853 by nine churches from Central and Big Hatchie associations. Comprising the larger part of Obion and Lake counties, the association employs a superintendent of missions. In 1954, 44 churches reported 599 baptisms, 8,967 members, $262,035 total gifts, $41,917 mission gifts, $919,450 property value, and $60,274 church debt.

BIG EMORY. Organized at Big Emory Church, Roane County, in Sept., 1875, with 17 churches. It employs a superintendent of missions. In 1954, 50 churches reported 598 baptisms, 12,053 members, $366,664 total gifts, $50,939 mission gifts, $1,169,791 property value, and $164,096 church debt.

BIG HATCHIE. Organized about 1828 by messengers from 15 churches in Hardin, McNairy, Madison, Hardeman, Fayette, Haywood, Shelby, Tipton, and portions of Dyer, Gibson, and Henderson counties, at Big Black Creek Church near Denmark. The association employs a superintendent of missions. In 1954, 36 churches reported 467 baptisms, 9,407 members, $301,905 total gifts, $45,673 mission gifts, $1,145,776 property value, and $91,355 church debt.

BLEDSOE. Organized Dec. 4, 1915, at Gallatin. The New Hampshire Confession of Faith has been adopted. In 1954, 20 churches reported 191 baptisms, 3,958 members, $105,012 total gifts, $18,879 mission gifts, $428,750 property value, and $14,750 church debt.

BRADLEY COUNTY. Organized Oct. 14, 1949, at First Church, Cleveland, with 37 churches originally in Ocoee and McMinn associations. It employs a superintendent of missions. In 1954, 45 churches reported 438 baptisms, 8,933 members, $239,729 total gifts, $30,724 mission gifts, $669,000 property value, and $37,214 church debt.

CAMPBELL COUNTY. Organized in Nov., 1908, at Cedar Hill. It has adopted articles of faith and now employs a superintendent of missions. In 1954, 58 churches reported 395 baptisms, 11,169 members, $136,359 total gifts, $18,444 mission gifts, $656,280 property value, and $179,-800 church debt.

CARROLL-BENTON. Organized Jan. 12, 1930, at Huntingdon, with the first session held Oct. 22, 1930, with 17 churches from Southwestern District and Weakley County participating. At the 1940 session, the name was changed to Carroll-Benton. A superintendent of missions is employed. In 1954, 22 churches reported 283 baptisms, 5,267 members, $153,670 total gifts, $22,-752 mission gifts, $634,250 property value, and $39,846 church debt.

CHILHOWEE. Organized at Mount of Olives Church, Knox County, Oct. 16–17, 1885, with 29 churches. It has adopted articles of faith and now employs a superintendent of missions. In 1954, 62 churches reported 798 baptisms, 16,622 members, $620,554.00 total gifts, $95,827.00 mission gifts, $3,229,150.00 property value, and $324,849.98 church debt.

CLINTON. Organized in Sept., 1853, at Clinton Church in Anderson County, evidently a product of Tennessee Association. With 15 churches, 1,337 members, comprising the membership of the association at organization, articles of faith were adopted. In 1892 Anderson, Union, Campbell, Knox, and Roane counties were represented. The location of the atomic energy plant at Oak Ridge has greatly increased the strength of the association, which now employs a superintendent of missions. In 1954, 59 churches reported 802 baptisms, 16,707 members, $532,006 total gifts, $64,393 mission gifts, $1,598,300 property value, and $234,587 church debt.

CONCORD. Organized Sept. 25, 1810, at Hodges meetinghouse, Statesville, in Wilson County. It came out of Cumberland Association which was preceded by Mero District Association, organized about 1796. Dating from its predecessors, Concord, along with Cumberland, is the oldest association in middle Tennessee. The association has adopted articles of faith and now employs a superintendent of missions. In 1954, 33 churches reported 305 baptisms, 6,737 members, $205,906 total gifts, $30,498 mission gifts, $624,813 property value, and $57,729 church debt.

CROCKETT COUNTY. Organized Sept. 8, 1926, at Alamo, with 13 churches participating. A product of Friendship Association, Crockett County has adopted articles of faith. In 1954, 14 churches reported 79 baptisms, 3,561 members, $97,466 total gifts, $12,984 mission gifts, $434,335 property value, and $47,200 church debt.

CUMBERLAND. Organized about 1803 with 15 churches from Mero District Association which had been organized about 1796. Dating from Mero, Cumberland shares with Concord the rank of oldest association in middle Tennessee. However, either the original Cumberland Association disbanded or was temporarily absorbed by other associations, for the oldest minutes of Cumberland Association available are dated 1870, and current minutes refer to that year as the date of organization. A superintendent of missions is employed. In 1954, 27 churches reported 377 baptisms, 6,515 members, $274,743 total gifts, $28,607 mission gifts, and $1,188,050 property value. No church debt was reported.

CUMBERLAND COUNTY. Organized at First Baptist Church, Crossville, Sept. 16, 1953, by messengers from 15 churches in Cumberland County, from Big Emory and Riverside associations. Cumberland County employs a superintendent of missions. In 1954, 17 churches reported 149 baptisms, 2,205 members, $56,437 total gifts, $7,873 mission gifts, $215,500 property value, and $9,845 church debt.

CUMBERLAND GAP. Organized in Oct., 1884, at Cedar Grove. It employs a superintendent of missions. In 1954, 78 churches reported 342 baptisms, 11,291 members, $81,584 total gifts, $30,381 mission gifts, $521,850 property value, and $19,900 church debt.

DUCK RIVER. Organized about 1826, has adopted articles of faith, and now employs a superintendent of missions. At the 28th annual session, Sept. 11, 1854, held at New Hope Church in Bedford County, the association passed the resolution,

> Whereas this association believes that the religious sentiments of Rev. Alexander Campbell of Bethany, Virginia, as published by himself, are in their nature unscriptural and in their tendency soul-destroying; therefore, resolved unanimously, that we the members of Duck River Association assure Brother J. R. Graves [*q.v.*], Editor of the *Tennessee Baptist*, of our undivided sympathy and hearty cooperation with him in the manly and Christian course he is pursuing in his controversy with Mr. Campbell, in exposing the errors of the system of said Alexander Campbell, and that the clerk mail a few copies of our minutes to his clerk at Bethany, Virginia.

In 1954, 23 churches reported 323 baptisms, 5,145 members, $172,536 total gifts, $21,123 mission gifts, $900,731 property value, and $132,-387 church debt.

DYER COUNTY. Organized Sept. 7, 1926, at Mt. Vernon Church with 15 churches participating. A product of Friendship Association, which disbanded in 1925, Dyer County has churches located in Dyer, Lauderdale, and Haywood counties. It has adopted articles of faith and now employs a superintendent of missions. In 1954, 35 churches reported 578 baptisms, 9,134 members, $290,065 total gifts, $54,232 mission gifts, $1,136,049 property value, and $184,-746 church debt.

EAST TENNESSEE. Organized at Pleasant Grove with four churches, 169 members, Aug. 31, 1839. It has adopted articles of faith and now employs a superintendent of missions. Outstanding ministers working in this association for many years were Ephream Moore and Joseph Manning. In 1954, 35 churches reported 244 baptisms, 5,891 members, $146,132 total gifts, $12,647 mission gifts, $399,883 property value, and $50,357 church debt.

FAYETTE COUNTY. Organized by 10 churches, with its first session at the Moscow Baptist Church July 23, 1927. A superintendent of missions is employed. In 1954, 15 churches reported 108 baptisms, 2,159 members, $46,601 total gifts, $6,395 mission gifts, $179,000 property value, and $625 church debt.

GIBSON COUNTY. Organized by messengers from 37 churches from Central Association, Gibson County, at First Baptist Church, Humboldt, Sept. 10, 1924. A superintendent of missions is employed. In 1954, 43 churches reported 448 baptisms, 12,842 members, $466,654 total gifts, $70,589 mission gifts, $1,561,601 property value, and $123,160 church debt.

GILES COUNTY. Organized Sept. 7, 1922, at Pulaski, with its first meeting Sept. 19–20, 1923, at Union Valley. It has adopted articles of faith and now employs a superintendent of missions. In 1954, 18 churches reported 140 baptisms, 2,957 members, $103,942 total gifts, $8,126 mission gifts, $300,077 property value, and $36,560 church debt.

GRAINGER COUNTY. Organized Oct. 25, 1918, at Rutledge with 17 churches from Grainger County. It has adopted articles of faith and now employs a superintendent of missions. In 1954, 34 churches reported 255 baptisms, 6,760 members, $90,701.00 total gifts, $8,253.00 mission gifts, $296,275.00 property value, and $14,933.81 church debt.

HAMILTON COUNTY. Organized Oct. 12–13, 1950, at Eastdale Church in Chattanooga. A product of Ocoee Association, Hamilton County had 96 churches participating in its organization. It employs a superintendent of missions. In 1954, 108 churches reported 3,120 baptisms, 52,581 members, $2,365,908 total gifts, $549,668 mission gifts, $8,853,592 property value, and $793,769 church debt.

HARDEMAN COUNTY. Organized Oct. 20, 1923, at Bolivar with 13 churches from Unity Association participating. A result of the trend to county unit organization, Hardeman County now employs a superintendent of missions. In 1954, 29 churches reported 316 baptisms, 5,827 members, $100,013 total gifts, $16,516 mission gifts, $323,550 property value, and $5,995 church debt.

HIWASSEE. Organized about 1821, has adopted articles of faith, and now employs a superintendent of missions. In 1954, 17 churches reported 52 baptisms, 2,521 members, $22,486 total gifts, $3,305 mission gifts, and $70,800 property value.

HOLSTON. Organized by messengers from seven churches, at Cherokee Baptist Church, near Jonesboro, Oct. 30, 1786. The first association in Tennessee, Holston has furnished churches to form Tennessee, Nolachucky, and Watauga associations. It has adopted articles of faith and now employs a superintendent of missions. In 1954, 106 churches reported 1,491 baptisms, 30,818 members, $1,092,763 total gifts, $163,530 mission gifts, $4,444,055 property value, and $350,079 church debt.

HOLSTON VALLEY. Organized about 1884 by messengers from 15 churches, mostly from Holston Association, at Persia Baptist Church, Persia. Has adopted articles of faith. A superintendent of missions is employed. In 1954, 50 churches reported 199 baptisms, 7,866 members, $173,966 total gifts, $20,334 mission gifts, $690,450 property value, and $46,106 church debt.

INDIAN CREEK. Organized in 1846 at Good Hope, has adopted articles of faith, and now employs a superintendent of missions. In 1954, 25 churches reported 132 baptisms, 2,665 members, $66,665 total gifts, $6,368 mission gifts, $252,244 property value, and $17,123 church debt.

JEFFERSON COUNTY. Organized Sept. 20, 1919, at First Baptist Church, Jefferson City, with 15 churches represented. The first session was held Sept. 8–9, 1920, at Nances Grove. It has adopted articles of faith and now employs a superintendent of missions. In 1954, 25 churches reported 174 baptisms, 6,369 members, $166,839.00 total gifts, $31,672.00 mission gifts, $412,050.00 property value, and $16,635.50 church debt.

JUDSON. Organized about 1849. In 1954, 16 churches reported 75 baptisms, 1,139 members, $16,078 total gifts, $1,138 mission gifts, $39,850 property value, and $849 church debt.

KNOX COUNTY. Organized as the Tennessee Association of Baptists Dec. 25, 1802, by 12 churches from Holston Association at Beaver Creek meetinghouse. With its name changed to Knox in 1917, the association has adopted articles of faith and now employs a superintendent of missions. In 1954, 131 churches reported 2,459 baptisms, 64,391 members, $2,699,593.00 total gifts, $527,574.00 mission gifts, $11,605,380.00 property value, and $1,192,235.33 church debt.

LAWRENCE COUNTY. Organized by 18 churches, with its first annual session at Leoma Church Sept. 13, 1919, when it adopted articles of faith. It now employs a superintendent of missions. In 1954, 29 churches reported 219 baptisms, 4,866 members, $90,269 total gifts, $9,150 mission gifts, $326,500 property value, and $17,200 church debt.

LOUDON COUNTY. Organized as Providence Association Oct. 11, 1873, with six churches at New Providence. It now employs a superintendent of missions and became Loudon County Association in 1955. In 1954, 35 churches reported 392 baptisms, 7,393 members, $195,053 total gifts, $29,758 mission gifts, $600,123 property value, and $47,767 church debt.

MCMINN. Organized at First Baptist Church, Athens, Sept. 17, 1923, by messengers from 12 churches in McMinn County from Sweetwater and Eastanallee associations. A superintendent of missions is employed. In 1954, 64 churches reported 680 baptisms, 13,343 members, $394,949.00 total gifts, $51,026.00 mission gifts, $1,243,061.00 property value, and $90,872.30 church debt.

MCNAIRY. Organized Sept. 26, 1924, by messengers from 18 churches in McNairy County, at Chewalla. It employs a superintendent of missions. In 1954, 24 churches reported 132 baptisms, 3,895 members, $94,521 total gifts, $8,113 mission gifts, $336,160 property value, and $25,620 church debt.

MADISON-CHESTER. Organized at Pleasant Plains Church, six miles northeast of Jackson, Sept. 17, 1924, by messengers from 27 churches from Central, Friendship, and Unity associations. Articles of faith have been printed, and a superintendent of missions is employed. In 1954, 40 churches reported 806 baptisms, 14,072 members, $651,096 total gifts, $122,771 mission gifts, $2,266,800 property value, and $402,465 church debt.

MAURY COUNTY. Organized out of Ebenezer Association at Pulaski, Sept. 7, 1922, holding its first annual session at Knob Creek Sept. 5, 1923, with 18 churches participating. Has adopted articles of faith. A superintendent of missions is employed. In 1954, 24 churches reported 255 baptisms, 4,239 members, $176,514 total gifts, $20,269 mission gifts, $721,800 property value, and $73,586 church debt.

MIDLAND. Organized Nov. 29, 1894, with its first meeting at Fairview Church, Knox County. It has adopted articles of faith and now employs a superintendent of missions. In 1954, 29 churches reported 292 baptisms, 5,625 members, $81,686 total gifts, $2,397 mission gifts, and $254,900 property value.

MULBERRY GAP. Organized in Sept., 1836, at Blackwater. Articles of faith have been adopted. In 1954, 72 churches reported 420 baptisms, 11,941 members, $48,650 total gifts, $2,609 mission gifts, $178,000 property value, and $2,340 church debt.

NASHVILLE. Organized at Nashville in 1900 with 17 churches from Dickson, Wilson, Sumner, and Davidson counties. It adopted the New Hampshire Confession of Faith and now employs a superintendent of missions. In 1954, 79 churches reported 2,851 baptisms, 44,776 members, $2,177,952.00 total gifts, $401,827.00 mission gifts, $8,267,345.00 property value, and $1,184,537.35 church debt.

NEW DUCK RIVER. Organized from Duck River Association by messengers from 15 churches in Moore, Bedford, and Marshall counties, at First Baptist Church, Shelbyville, Oct. 8, 1945. It adopted articles of faith and now employs a superintendent of missions. In 1954, 24 churches reported 311 baptisms, 5,936 members, $172,701 total gifts, $23,574 mission gifts, $740,600 property value, and $77,295 church debt.

NEW RIVER. Organized at River Church, Scott County, Apr. 17, 1886, with 10 churches. It has adopted articles of faith and now employs a superintendent of missions. In 1954, 45 churches reported 291 baptisms, 5,540 members, $55,132 total gifts, $4,793 mission gifts, $243,100 property value, and $5,815 church debt.

NEW SALEM. Organized at Buena Vista Church, Grant (Smith County), Oct. 30, 1888, by messengers from 19 churches, largely from Salem Association. A superintendent of missions is employed. In 1954, 16 churches reported 103 baptisms, 2,860 members, $56,313 total gifts, $8,435 mission gifts, $220,400 property value, and $1,560 church debt.

NOLACHUCKY. Organized by messengers from 13 churches from Holston Association at Bent Creek Church, Hamblen, in Nov., 1828. It has adopted articles of faith and now employs a superintendent of missions. In 1954, 46 churches reported 458 baptisms, 9,945 members, $273,604 total gifts, $37,429 mission gifts, $890,321 property value, and $67,674 church debt.

NORTHERN. Organized about 1838. In 1954, 22 churches reported 124 baptisms, 3,428 members, $17,963 total gifts, $3,161 mission gifts, $130,400 property value, and $200 church debt.

POLK COUNTY. Organized Oct. 21, 1921, at Mine City Church, Ducktown, with messengers from 19 churches, primarily from Eastanallee Association. In 1954, 43 churches reported 240 baptisms, 7,142 members, $87,760.00 total gifts, $10,177.00 mission gifts, $241,900.00 property value, and $2,797.16 church debt.

RIVERSIDE. Organized about 1888 by a group of churches from Stockton Valley Association. The organization, effected at Union Church, was a protest against the "anti-board" spirit of Stockton Valley. The association did not meet from 1888 until 1894, but meetings have been held annually since that date. Riverside employs a superintendent of missions. In 1954, 24 churches reported 100 baptisms, 3,315 members, $39,495.00 total gifts, $4,557.00 mission gifts, $144,400.00 property value, and $690.60 church debt.

ROBERTSON. Organized by messengers from 16 churches from Cumberland Association, Robertson County, at First Baptist Church, Springfield, Nov. 9, 1915. A superintendent of missions is employed. In 1954, 23 churches reported 256 baptisms, 8,041 members, $235,832 total gifts, $46,556 mission gifts, $583,200 property value, and $141,265 church debt.

SALEM. Organized by messengers from 27 churches from Concord Association at Cedar Creek Church, Wilson County, in Oct., 1822. Salem has adopted articles of faith and now employs a superintendent of missions. In 1954, 30 churches reported 113 baptisms, 4,482 members, $81,329 total gifts, $8,232 mission gifts, $372,100 property value, and $21,135 church debt.

SEQUATCHIE VALLEY. Organized *c.* 1882. Articles of faith have been adopted. A superintendent of missions is employed. In 1954, 24 churches reported 197 baptisms, 3,475 members, $109,649 total gifts, $14,109 mission gifts, $252,500 property value, and $3,655 church debt.

SEVIER COUNTY. Organized Nov. 5–6, 1886, at Sevierville with 24 churches. It employs a superintendent of missions. In 1954, 53 churches reported 367 baptisms, 10,946 members, $182,259 total gifts, $18,859 mission gifts, $881,600 property value, and $2,000 church debt.

SHELBY. Organized in 1904, as a result of a meeting of Memphis Association at Moscow

Church in July, 1903, in which it was decided to dissolve and organize a new association. The first session of Shelby Association was held at Collierville in July, 1904. At the 1906 meeting H. P. Hurt presented the idea of starting a Baptist hospital in Memphis, and a committee was appointed to investigate possibilities. The association employs a superintendent of missions. In 1954, 83 churches reported 3,805 baptisms, 74,759 members, $3,663,787 total gifts, $663,053 mission gifts, $15,840,604 property value, and $3,481,727 church debt.

STEWART COUNTY. Organized Oct. 30–Nov. 1, 1901, at Model, Stewart County, with 11 churches. A continuation of Dover Furnace Association, which was organized about 1889, Stewart County has adopted articles of faith. In 1954, 16 churches reported 53 baptisms, 1,420 members, $24,049 total gifts, $3,579 mission gifts, $93,950 property value, and $1,500 church debt.

STONE. Organized about 1868 by Chorder Stone and his son Thomas, under the name Stone Association of Christian Baptists, with only Boiling Springs Church named among churches effecting the organization. The churches, either new or revived after the Civil War, were located in the Upper Cumberlands in Putnam and White counties. About 1900 a Free Will Baptist minister influenced the association's addition of "free will" to its name. Stone was accepted into the fellowship of the Tennessee Baptist Convention in 1919 upon adopting the New Hampshire Confession of Faith, agreeing to co-operate in supporting the program fostered by Southern Baptists, and changing its name to Stone Association. It now employs a superintendent of missions. In 1954, 29 churches reported 204 baptisms, 4,549 members, $119,772 total gifts, $16,781 mission gifts, $532,500 property value, and $46,317 church debt.

SWEETWATER. Organized in Nov., 1830, at Sweetwater with 18 churches represented. Articles of faith were adopted. A superintendent of missions is employed. In 1954, 72 churches reported 621 baptisms, 14,267 members, $232,587 total gifts, $25,038 mission gifts, $730,350 property value, and $14,928 church debt.

TENNESSEE VALLEY. Organized Aug. 13, 1896, at Mt. Vernon Baptist Church by 11 churches from Hiwassee and Rhea associations which united under the name of Tennessee Valley. The articles of faith have been adopted. A superintendent of missions is employed. In 1954, 31 churches reported 262 baptisms, 4,288 members, $110,153 total gifts, $13,073 mission gifts, $516,148 property value, and $11,701 church debt.

TRUETT. Organized Oct. 29, 1950, at Sylvia, with three churches from Judson Association. The first annual meeting was held at Sylvia Church, Aug. 3, 1951. Truett employs a superintendent of missions. In 1954 six churches reported 22 baptisms, 584 members, $14,739 total gifts, $1,110 mission gifts, and $57,450 property value.

UNION. Organized by 11 churches on Nov. 5, 1847, at Blue Spring meetinghouse in Warren County, Tenn., as a result of the efforts of a missionary from East Tennessee named Johnson. He constituted the churches and formed them into an association. A superintendent of missions is employed. In 1954, 19 churches reported 137 baptisms, 2,777 members, $61,529 total gifts, $4,257 mission gifts, $241,475 property value, and $22,960 church debt.

WATAUGA. Organized at Cobb's Creek Baptist Church Sept. 18–19, 1868, by 14 churches (one Negro) with a total membership of 1,233. At the first meeting A. J. F. Hyder was appointed "local missionary" to labor in destitute areas of the association, especially among the Negroes. Watauga employs a superintendent of missions. In 1954, 66 churches reported 567 baptisms, 16,017 members, $429,435 total gifts, $51,981 mission gifts, $1,929,446 property value, and $108,630 church debt.

WEAKLEY COUNTY. Organized at Pleasant Hill about 1887. It has adopted articles of faith and now employs a superintendent of missions. In 1954, 34 churches reported 162 baptisms, 6,169 members, $141,665 total gifts, $14,258 mission gifts, $416,885 property value, and $16,032 church debt.

WEST UNION. Organized in Nov., 1870, at Old Jellico Creek Church, Whitley County, Ky., with 13 churches, 655 members, participating. Articles of faith have been printed, and a superintendent of missions is employed. In 1954, 60 churches reported 416 baptisms, 8,506 members, $38,630 total gifts, $7,250 mission gifts, and $228,750 property value.

WESTERN DISTRICT. Organized at Spring Creek in July, 1823, the first association organized west of the Tennessee River. It comprised all the churches from the Tennessee to the Mississippi River and from Kentucky to Mississippi. With organization completed later at Bird's Creek, the association has adopted articles of faith and now employs a superintendent of missions. In 1954, 29 churches reported 201 baptisms, 5,401 members, $130,704 total gifts, $29,730 mission gifts, $506,150 property value, and $40,953 church debt.

WILLIAM CAREY. Organized Sept. 30–Oct. 2, 1892, at Oak Hill Church. It has adopted articles of faith and now employs a superintendent of missions. In 1954, 25 churches reported 259 baptisms, 5,373 members, $109,617 total gifts, $10,863 mission gifts, $457,865 property value, and $39,274 church debt.

WILSON COUNTY. Organized in Sept., 1921, at Shop Springs Church with 20 churches participating. A superintendent of missions is employed. In 1954, 26 churches reported 298 baptisms, 7,286 members, $193,531 total gifts, $31,369 mission gifts, $840,600 property value, and $80,581 church debt. E. E. DEUSNER

II. Extinct. CANEY FORK. Organized 1813 with churches from Stockton Valley Association and covering parts of Jackson, Smith, and present DeKalb, Putnam, White, and Warren counties.

In 1832, 22 churches reported 7 ministers and 716 members. It went out of existence *c.* 1850–60 due to influence of Parkerism.

CENTRAL. Organized in 1836 with five churches located in Madison and Gibson counties. It dissolved in Sept., 1923, to form Gibson and Madison associations.

CUMBERLAND PLATEAU. Organized in Sept., 1940, with nine churches in Cumberland County and adjacent area. This association is still in existence but not co-operating with Tennessee state convention, as it withdrew in 1953 due to internal dissension concerning convention policies and alleged endorsement of the Revised Standard Version of the Bible.

EASTANALLEE. Organized in 1870 at Zion Hill with 37 churches in Meigs, McMinn, and Polk counties. It dissolved to form Polk Association in 1921 and McMinn Association in 1924 with the latter designated as successor to Eastanallee.

EBENEZER. Organized in 1894 with 14 churches in Hickman, Maury, Lewis, Giles, and Lawrence counties. It dissolved in Sept., 1922, to form Maury and Giles associations.

ELK RIVER. Organized in 1808 with churches in Franklin, Lincoln, and Rutherford counties. Influenced by Campbellism by 1810, in 1826 half of the churches withdrew to form New Duck River. In 1833, 24 churches reported 10 ministers and 1,394 members.

ENON. Organized in May, 1850, with 16 churches located in Sumner, Trousdale, Smith, Macon, and Clay counties. It continues extant but was dropped for failure to report to state convention.

FORKED DEER. Organized in Oct., 1825, at Liberty meetinghouse, Madison County, with 15 churches. In 1830, 17 churches reported 8 ministers and 575 members. It dissolved in 1834 due to internal dissension over antimissions and Parkerism or Two Seed Doctrine.

FRIENDSHIP. Organized in Oct., 1884, at Friendship with 16 churches located in Gibson, Dyer, and Lauderdale counties. In Sept., 1925, it "disbanded to organize the county unit association."

HARMONY. Organized *c.* 1892 and in 1901 had eight churches. There has been no report since 1921.

JOHNSON. Organized in May, 1853, by churches from Salem Association east of Caney Fork River. It was named for Jesse Johnson.

LITTLE HATCHIE. Organized in West Tennessee in Oct., 1904, with 14 churches reporting. It dissolved in 1927.

MEMPHIS. Organized in Aug., 1891, with 22 churches in Shelby County area. It dissolved in July, 1903, to form Shelby County Association.

MERO. Organized in 1796 with five churches in Mero District. It dissolved in 1803 because of internal dissensions. The Cumberland formed the same year.

OCOEE. Organized *c.* 1841 with eight churches in Bradley, Meigs, Hamilton, and James counties. It dissolved in Oct., 1949, to form Hamilton and Bradley associations.

POWELL'S VALLEY. Organized in 1818 with 13 of the churches coming from Tennessee Association. In 1835 it had 25 churches in Claiborne and Grainger counties with 1,790 members.

PROVIDENCE. Organized in 1873 with six churches in Loudon County and adjacent area. It dissolved in 1955 to form the Loudon County Association.

RHEA. Organized with eight churches in Rhea County. Reported to convention in 1891, but is now extinct.

SOUTHWESTERN DISTRICT. Organized in July, 1846, with 14 churches in Carroll, Benton, Decatur, and Henderson counties. It was dropped from the list of associations because of failure to report to state convention.

STOCKTON VALLEY. Organized in 1805 with 14 churches, eight in Kentucky and six in Tennessee in the neighborhood of present Fentress County. The association is extant but has been dropped from published list because of failure to report to state convention.

TENNESSEE. Organized Dec. 25, 1802, by 19 churches at Beaver Creek meetinghouse and serving churches "in the neighborhood of Knoxville . . . on the Holston, Tennessee, and Clinch Rivers." It dissolved in Oct., 1917, to form Knox Association.

UNITY. Organized in Oct., 1858, with 24 churches within the boundaries of an area formed by lines from Van Buren to Bolivar to Jackson to Lexington to Perryville. It dissolved in Aug., 1923, to form Hardeman and McNairy associations.

WALNUT GROVE. Organized in 1878 in Meigs County. It appeared the first time in the records in 1952 but had not reported since 1927. The few churches joined McMinn Association.

WISEMAN. Organized in Nov., 1891, by 14 churches from Enon Association and by 1901 had 23 churches with 1,748 members located in Trousdale, Smith, Macon, and Sumner counties. It is still extant but has been dropped from published lists because of failure to report to state convention. CARL P. DAW

TENNESSEE BAPTIST CHILDREN'S HOMES, INC. Formerly Tennessee Baptist Orphans' Home, founded by a group of women representing the Baptist churches of Nashville, and meeting in the First Baptist Church of that city on May 5, 1891. The first officers elected were Mrs. Roger Eastman, president; Mrs. I. N. Phillips, vice-president; Lucille Cunningham, secretary; and Mrs. A. J. Harris, treasurer. An advisory board, "composed of one gentleman from each church," was also elected at this meeting. The first charter was secured in Oct., 1891, and the home was opened in the Hotel Delaware building, West Nashville, Nov. 16, 1891. The work was supported almost entirely by the Nashville churches and individual Baptists until 1894.

The program of care for homeless children, as sponsored by the Nashville group, was presented to the Tennessee Baptist Convention meeting in annual session at Clarksville in 1891 and was "commended" by that body. A report on orphanage work was made to the convention, meeting in Knoxville in 1892, and again the following year when the convention met in Jackson. The institution was accepted by the convention, meeting with the Edgefield Baptist Church in Nashville in 1894. The home was operated at the West Nashville location until June, 1912, when it was moved to the present location near Franklin, Tenn.

In 1954 four children's homes were operated by the Children's Homes Corporation under one general management. In addition to the original home, the second one was built at Memphis in 1949–50. Another was constructed at Chattanooga in 1953. Min-Tom, a home for Negro children, was accepted from the Hamilton County Baptist Association in 1954.

Property at the four locations consists of 941 acres of land, with 42 buildings. This property is valued at $1,750,000. The budget for 1954 was $244,756.92. The total income from the beginning through 1954 was $3,805,457.29, of which $3,626,939.13 came through denominational channels and $178,518.16 from other sources.

This work is supported through the Cooperative Program, an annual Thanksgiving Offering, special gifts from individuals, bequests, etc. One treasurer handles all funds, and all disbursements are made from the general office, where records are kept of the over-all operation, with separate records for each home and for designations.

High school training is provided for all children. The Franklin home has its own school through the tenth grade, sending children to public school for the last two years of high school. Children in the other three homes all attend public schools. Scholarships and other assistance are offered for college training. Courses in music, including piano, voice, and band, are provided for those who show interest and aptitude.

The program of the institution is that of child care and training. There is no foster home or adoption service, although a limited mother's aid service is available. Case work is being provided. The charter was amended in 1954 to clarify the program of service and to change the name of the institution. Amended bylaws also provide for changes in keeping with accepted methods of institutional and social service.

The corporation is an institution of the Tennessee Baptist Convention, which elects its board of managers. This board holds title to the property, formulates the policies of the institution, elects its own officers and its executive officer. A total of 1,777 children have been cared for in the homes, and in 1955 there were 335 children in residence. The annual per capita cost of care is approximately $728. W. C. CREASMAN

TENNESSEE BAPTIST CONVENTION.

I. Baptist Beginnings. Baptist witness began in Tennessee among the earliest permanent settlers and continued to grow in spite of the hardships of the frontier, competition by other groups of Christians, and internal differences regarding doctrines and practices until, at the time of the first organization of a state convention in 1834, there were approximately 30,000 Baptists in the state. Upper East Tennessee was the first scene of westward expansion by emigrants from Virginia and North Carolina, and in step with this westward progress moves the record of Baptist peoples and their churches. Historical documents relating to this early period are scarce and sometimes contradictory, but the important facts are sufficiently established.

The division of the state into three sections by the severe Cumberland Mountain range in the east and by the Tennessee River in the west effectively separated the life and history of the people so that their history must be given in distinct sections.

Early background.—The name "Tennessee" is derived from *Tanase,* the name of one of the lesser Cherokee Indian towns on the west bank of the Little Tennessee River. Tanase gave its name to the two rivers and to the state formed in 1796 from territory ceded to the United States by North Carolina.

The first Europeans known to explore this region were de Soto and his adventurers, who in 1540 came from Florida as far as the valleys of Hiwassee. Don Pardo followed in 1566, Marquette and Jolliet touched the western border on the Mississippi in 1673, and La Salle established a trading post and Fort Prud'homme at the site of Memphis in 1682. These groups included Roman Catholic missionaries, but no further Catholic mission to Tennessee is found until William Rohan came to East Tennessee in 1790.

The first English outpost, Fort Loudon, stood 30 miles south of the present site of Knoxville and near the Overhill Cherokee Indian towns, from 1756 to 1760, when the Indians destroyed it. Here, as early as 1757, two Presbyterian missionaries, John Martin and William Richardson, worked, but they met with little success and soon departed.

First Baptists.—Many Baptists were among those who made the first permanent white settlements in Tennessee, other than the purely military outposts of Fort Loudon and Long Island (1758). Two Baptist churches are said to have been started among these earliest settlers in 1765 and broken up during the Indian wars of 1774. No clear record of these churches is found. There is reason to believe that one of these churches was about three miles southwest of Bristol, near Major Bledsoe's fort. Old records speak of "Meeting House Branch" at Bledsoe's near Beaver Creek, where there was a community of about 25 families. A Chambers family had received an original grant adjoining Bledsoe's grant, and a James Chambers was one of the early pastors of Sinking Creek Church. In 1786 Bledsoe and an Alexander Chambers represented Beaver Creek Church at Holston

Association. This Beaver Creek Church may have been at this very early Bledsoe settlement, for we know of no other Beaver Creek Church among the first settlements. Another church was probably in the Watauga settlement, where there were many Baptists among the earliest settlers. Of 39 patentees who obtained land titles at the treaty of Sycamore Shoals (Mar., 1775), the names of nine are found on the roll of the Sinking Creek Church. These include Julius C. Dugger, the first settler to arrive in 1766; Michael Hyder; Peter Nave; Henry Lyle; Isaac Lincoln; David Pugh; William Pugh; Baptist McNabb, who built the first mill in Tennessee; and Matthew Talbott, the owner of a large tract of land on Gap Creek on which was built Fort Watauga and one of the first mills in the state.

The large number of Baptists among these first settlers, the religious zeal that characterized Separate Baptists, their continued emphasis on assembly for worship, and the fact that able ministers were among them make it almost certain that there was much Baptist work and witness then of which we have no record. A tradition handed down by Uncle Hampie Hyder, a pioneer preacher for more than 40 years, who came to the Sinking Creek Church in 1836, tells that during the winter of 1774–75 two preachers, John and Charles Chastain, held a revival at the home of Charles Robertson, which home was also the seat of the first court of justice in the state. The worship thus begun was continued under the leadership of Matthew Talbott, a preacher of the Separate order who had come from Virginia. After being disrupted by the Indian raids in 1776, the work was revived by Talbott, who served as pastor of the church until his removal to Georgia in 1783.

Many of the earliest Baptists came to Tennessee from Sandy Creek Association in central North Carolina. There the Separate Baptists had for 15 years enjoyed phenomenal growth, and revival fires had burned brightly under the powerful ministry of Shubal Stearns and his companions. But after the severe suppression of the Regulator movement (a popular rebellion against the tyrannies of Governor Tryon) in the Battle of Alamance in May, 1771, there was a wholesale exodus from central Carolina to the frontier. Some 1,500 families moved westward. The Sandy Creek Association had sternly disapproved any rebellion against legal authority and decreed excommunication for any who took part in it. The historian Morgan Edwards declared after careful examination that there had been only seven Baptists among the 4,000 Regulators. Yet Governor Tryon chose to place particular blame on the Baptists, and they, anticipating worse oppression, hastened westward. The flourishing Sandy Creek, mother church of the Separate Baptist fellowship in North Carolina and neighboring states, was reduced from 606 to 14 members. Many of the ones who left came to Holston and Watauga settlements. One group moved in something of a church capacity to the Boone's Creek country and in 1779, under the leadership of Tidence Lane (*q.v.*), built the Buffalo Ridge Church, which is often referred to as the first Baptist church in Tennessee. The Cherokee Church was organized four miles south of Jonesboro in 1783, under the leading of William Murphy, who served as its first pastor. Jonathan Mulkey (*q.v.*), a Separate Baptist preacher from Carolina, is named among the foremost of the pioneers in Carter's Valley in 1775. He accompanied the Indian campaign of Colonel William Christian, preached early in the Watauga settlement, and succeeded Lane in 1785 as pastor of Buffalo Ridge Church, where he served in an outstanding ministry until his death in 1826. Other able Baptist preachers known to have preached in this section about this time were Thomas Kelly, Isaac Barton, James Keel, John Chastain, and William Reno. There is scant record of their work, but the effective influence of their presence is seen in the number and size of the Baptist churches which soon appeared.

Other denominations.—Meanwhile the Presbyterian ministry was gaining a strong foothold under the leadership of several well-educated and vigorous preachers. Joseph Rhea was preaching in the country north of Holston as early as 1771. He was being assisted by 1773 by the able labors of Charles Cummings, and about 1777 by Samuel Doak, a Princeton graduate, who in that year founded Salem Church near Jonesboro and the adjacent school now long known as Washington College. It was the first institution of learning south of the Alleghenies. Presbyterian churches were founded at Concord, now Weaver's Store near Bristol; at Taylor's Meeting House, now Gunnings Cemetery; and at New Bethel. In 1777 Cummings held a revival in the Watauga settlement which resulted in the building of a meeting house on the land of Henry Massengill. Here Cummings and the Baptist preacher Jonathan Mulkey preached at intervals until the building was burned by a band of Tories while the settlers were absent in an Indian campaign led by General Ivan Shelby. Denominational divisions received small emphasis on a frontier where any house of worship was open to anyone who could preach the gospel. With its strong leadership Presbyterianism took the religious lead. In 1788, while the Baptists had only 18 small churches, the Presbyterians had 23 large congregations. Their advantageous position, however, was lost when internal dissension caused their work to decline. Then the Methodists, who had a later start in Tennessee, pressed into the lead under the influence of Bishop Asbury and their many itinerant preachers. For years their numbers increased over those of either Baptists or Presbyterians. But the frontier was a hard place for religious work. Widespread indifference to religion and low moral conditions caused Lorenzo Dow, the Methodist Savonarola, to call Tennessee "a Sink of Iniquity, a Black Pit of Irreligion."

Baptist upsurge.—Baptist fortunes began to

rise sharply about this time. At the beginning of the Revolutionary War, Baptists were in the main a minority of socially, economically, and educationally underprivileged people. But within 15 years a tremendous change had taken place. Baptists, almost without exception, had been hearty supporters of the cause of freedom. They had led in the struggle for complete religious liberty, which had been won so dramatically in Virginia and which had been written into the basic law of the land. A Baptist church is credited with providing the idea of democracy from which Thomas Jefferson derived the concept of a truly democratic nation. By 1790 many wealthy and influential people had joined the Baptists, and they were as much respected as any denomination. Members of John Sevier's family, if not the governor himself, were associated with Baptist worship. This influence reached into the formation of Tennessee's constitution, which provides that

> All men have a natural and indefeasible right to worship Almighty God according to the dictates of their own conscience; that no man can of right be compelled to attend, erect, or support any place of worship, or to maintain any minister against his consent; that no human authority can, in any case whatever, control or interfere with the rights of conscience; and that no preference shall ever be given, by law, to any religious establishment or mode of worship.

These safeguards, as well as those regarding religious tests for any officeholders, were included in every constitution adopted in Tennessee (1796; 1834; 1870). This emphasis on full religious liberty was peculiarly Baptist in those days, and theirs is the chief credit for its presence in these documents.

Holston Association.—In 1781 five or six churches, which had been formed mainly of Baptists coming from Sandy Creek Association of North Carolina, met in a fellowship which they chose to consider a branch of the Sandy Creek group. They met twice a year and submitted their reports to the Sandy Creek Association for approval. Because of the distance separating them, and with approval of the older group, they met at Cherokee Church on Aug. 31, 1786, to form a separate and independent body which they named Holston Association. There were seven churches in this organization: Kendrick's Creek, Bent Creek (now Whitesburg), Beaver Creek, Greasy Cove, Cherokee, North Fork of Holston, and Lower French Broad. Ministers on record then were Jonathan Mulkey, Isaac Barton, Tidence Lane, James Keel, William Murphy, John Frost, and Alexander Chambers. The Philadelphia Confession of Faith was adopted, and until 1795 the association met twice a year, usually in May and October.

Holston Association has had a continuous and prosperous history until the present, has been the parent of other East Tennessee associations and is still one of the strongest in the state or in the South. The record of its proceedings is practically complete. The original leather-bound ledger with its record in longhand of meetings from 1786 to 1865 is carefully guarded at the Central Church of Johnson City. Printed minutes began in 1806. Early records were brief, giving only a list of churches and messengers and a short record of proceedings. These usually consisted of a sermon or two and the discussion and answering of questions relating to doctrine and practice. For many years after 1792, there was a practice of having a preacher write a circular letter, usually a sermon of instruction and exhortation, which was passed among the churches.

For some years the association assumed many responsibilities of oversight and counsel with regard to the churches, although the constitution assured the basic independence of the churches. In 1788, at the request of Maiden Church, it ordained a man to the ministry; but in 1794 in answering a question it declared that "all ecclesiastical power is vested in the churches to carry on worship and discipline. The ordination of ministers must be by that power." In 1790 it appointed a committee to settle differences between two churches on Little Pigeon River. The Richland church was refused a seat in the association in 1793 because she had received a member who had "grieved" the association. In reply to several queries, the association in 1800 appointed "Brethren Jonathan Mulkey, William Randolph, and Joel Matthews to attend upon said [Sinking Creek] church to dissolve same on her discretion." In 1804 a committee was appointed to resolve differences at Mockason Church, and the same year the association nullified the ordination of a preacher. At times there was debate as to the propriety of the laying on of hands. This practice was in 1802 declared a gospel ordinance but was later declared a matter for the discretion of each church. In 1802 the association declared that the dedication of infants was not a gospel ordinance, and that "it is not according to gospel directions to commune with any one who have [sic] not been regularly baptized by immersion on profession of their [sic] faith."

These early Baptists were alert to social evils. Their church business meetings were often devoted to the correction of evils among the members, such as drunkenness, immorality, gambling, personal strife, or worldliness. In 1793 the association took notice of the evil of slavery and advised against the parting of Negro families whenever possible. In 1828 it approved a protest from the Cherokee church against the unlimited traffic in slaves. Negroes were accepted as members in the churches from the earliest days, and for years their numbers in each church were reported to the association.

Tennessee Association formed.—Holston Association, which in 1784 (when still a part of Sandy Creek) had only 6 churches and 400 members, in 1792 had 21 churches and 900 members and by 1802 included 36 churches and between 2,000 and 3,000 members. It was the center of Baptist fellowship throughout East Tennessee. Because the association included so many churches and such a widely scattered membership, the proposal was made in 1801 that it be divided. Out of reluctance to break ties of such long standing, the division was postponed until 1802. Then a rough line was drawn from Powell's River across Flat Gap of Clinch Mountain to English's Mountain, and all churches south and west of the line withdrew to form Tennessee Association.

Meeting at Beaver Creek Church in Knox County on Dec. 5, 1802, the new association organized with 12 churches located in Knox, Claiborne, Sevier, and Jefferson counties. William Johnson was elected moderator, and Francis Hamilton, clerk. Instead of the Philadelphia Confession of Faith, the association adopted, with some modifications, a statement of faith from John Asplund's *Register*. Churches multiplied in this association along the banks of the Tennessee, Holston, and Clinch rivers and to the Cumberland Mountain range, keeping pace with the advance of the frontier. The association's records show 23 churches by 1803 and 29 by 1805. In 1804, 243 baptisms were reported. Year by year fraternal messages were sent by some honored brother to Holston, Green River, and Stockton's Valley associations, and to the other Baptist associations as they were formed. A name appearing as a messenger from French Broad Church, now Dandridge, through many of those early years is that of Duke Kimbrough (1762–1849), whose position of high esteem is indicated by the number of times he preached to the body, was named to important committees, and was sent as fraternal messenger to other associations. One of his descendants is Duke Kimbrough McCall, president (1951–) of the Southern Baptist Theological Seminary.

Problems of doctrine and church polity were often put before it for advice, but the association disclaimed any authority over the churches, insisting that the church is the "highest tribunal on earth." Differences of teaching on the doctrine of the Trinity disturbed the fellowship for some years prior to 1808, when a clear statement of the orthodox position was approved. Luther Rice was welcomed in 1815 and in 1816 to present the cause of missions to the association, which voted to send him such information as he requested and appointed a committee to co-operate with Holston Association in helping Rice. A missionary society was organized among certain individuals, but it was specified that this did not involve the association in any way. Repeated queries to the association as to the parting of Negro slaves reveal a real concern for social righteousness; and an earnest appeal from several churches for a special day of prayer for revival testifies to the spiritual life among these churches.

Powell's Valley Association.—At the 1817 meeting of the Tennessee Association, 12 churches located north of Knoxville in Claiborne, Campbell, and Anderson counties withdrew from the association, in accordance with an agreement made the year before, to form the Powell's Valley Association. This association continued many years as a group of small churches, seldom over 75 in membership. They continued to send fraternal messengers to Holston and Tennessee associations but did not approve of benevolent and mission causes and were finally separated from the Tennessee Baptist fellowship. In 1824 their records show a total of 741 members in 16 churches.

Hiwassee Association.—Occupation by white men of the Indian lands in the Hiwassee district, in what is now the Sweetwater Valley, was not permitted until the year 1820 but by June of that year, a Baptist church was organized at the home of Daniel Duggan on Fork Creek and held services alternately at Duggan's and at John Fine's on Sweetwater Creek. This was the earliest church in this section and the parent of other churches. The number and prominence of its members made it the most influential church of any denomination in the valley. Jesse Dodson, who served 60 years in the Baptist ministry, had come to McMinn County in 1819. With seven others he established Estanalee Church. With Silas Witt he organized New Hopewell Church; with James Courtney, Hiwassee Church; with Howard Wilson, Salem Church; and with John Short, Friendship Church. Other churches developed, and in 1822, 10 of these churches withdrew from the Tennessee Association to meet in May, 1823, and form the Hiwassee Association.

Other associations in East Tennessee.—The growth and multiplication of Baptist churches continued to result in the organization of new associations. On the first Friday of Nov., 1828, 14 churches of Holston Association met at Bent Creek Church (now Whitesburg) in Jefferson County to form Nolichucky Association. Thomas Hill was made moderator, and Thomas Hale, the clerk. The next year 17 churches and 553 members were reported. This body became concerned in 1832 with assisting young men of promise to secure "a useful if not a liberal education." The next year it was decided that this worthy purpose was outside the control of the association, but recommendation was made that interested people promote the matter. This incident indicates the rising interest in the education of ministers which later resulted in the Tennessee Baptist schools.

Middle Tennessee.—In the year 1780 General James Robertson led a party of about 40 families, emigrants from Virginia and North Carolina, from East Tennessee, through a wilderness of 300 miles, across the Cumberland Mountains, to the French Lick, and there established Nashville, on the banks of the Cumberland River. It is probable that there were many Baptists in this group. Robertson had been closely associated with his cousin Charles Robertson, in whose home was held the first Baptist revival in the Watauga settlement. Also significant is the fact that the Baptist church on Sulphur

BAPTIST MEMORIAL HOSPITAL (q.v.), Jacksonville, Fla. Opened in 1955 with capacity of nearly 400 beds and bassinets. One of the features is Wolfson Memorial Children's Wing with 50-bed capacity.

OKLAHOMA HOSPITALS

STILLWATER MUNICIPAL HOSPITAL (*q.v.*), Stillwater, Okla. Erected in 1941, leased to Oklahoma Baptist Convention in 1952. Facilities include 85 beds and special polio ward.

SOUTHWEST BAPTIST HOSPITAL (*q.v.*), Mangum, Okla. Founded 1949, includes 35 beds and convalescent facilities.

PERRY MEMORIAL HOSPITAL (*q.v.*), Perry, Okla. Opened 1951, operated under lease by Oklahoma Baptist Convention, houses 30 beds.

OKLAHOMA BAPTIST HOSPITAL (*q.v.*), Muskogee. First Baptist hospital in Oklahoma, established 1909, accommodates 88 bed patients.

OKLAHOMA HOSPITALS

MIAMI BAPTIST HOSPITAL (q.v.), Miami, Okla. Established 1919, being expanded to include 100 beds.

GRAND VALLEY HOSPITAL (q.v.), Pryor, Okla. Opened in 1954, leased by Oklahoma Baptist General Convention, 40-bed capacity.

ENID GENERAL HOSPITAL (q.v.), Enid, Okla. Founded 1917, deeded to Baptist General Convention of Oklahoma in 1953, houses 110 beds, cost $1,200,000.

BRISTOW MEMORIAL HOSPITAL (q.v.), Bristow, Okla. Opened in 1954, leased by Baptist General Convention of Oklahoma, 30-bed capacity.

GEORGIA BAPTIST HOSPITAL (*q.v.*), Atlanta. Housing more than 500 beds and bassinets and costing over $8,700,000, the cancer clinic is among special services available.

Fork of Red River is the first church of any denomination of which we have any mention in the Cumberland country. This church was gathered in 1786 under the care of John Grammar, but his pastorate was brief, and after his departure the church dissolved. The number of Baptists settling in the section increased, and about the year 1790 several Baptist preachers were ministering there, including Daniel Brown, Joseph Dorris, Nathan Arnett, and Patrick Mooney. A year later, Ambrose Dudley and John Taylor came 200 miles through the wilderness from Elkhorn Association of Kentucky to help Elias Fort and others organize the church named Tennessee, which united with the Elkhorn Association. This was the only Baptist church within a radius of 100 miles until White's Creek Church was formed six miles north of Nashville in 1794. A church formed on the head of Sulphur Fork in 1794, which had moved as a body from North Carolina with Joseph Dorris as its pastor, was known as Dorris Church. A church was formed at Middle Sulphur Fork, and one at Station Camp in 1796. These churches, with another known as Head of Sulphur Fork, met in 1796 to form the first Baptist association in Middle Tennessee. It was called Mero District Association after the name of the civil district, which in turn was named for the Spanish governor of Louisiana. Three new churches were added the next year, including Richland Creek, the first located south of the Cumberland River. This church had as its first pastor John Dillahunty (*q.v.*), an emigrant from Neuse Association of North Carolina and an eminent Baptist leader for 55 years. A second church received in 1797 from the south side of the river was Mill Creek, which ordained James Whitsett of Virginia as its pastor on the day it was organized and enjoyed a prosperous growth under his esteemed ministry for many years. Robert C. Foster, a wealthy planter and state senator, was a member of this church.

Mero Association grew and prospered until in 1801 it had 18 churches, 16 ministers, and about 1,200 members. That year a breach of fellowship was declared by White's Creek Church against the popular Joseph Dorris on charges of "imprudent or criminal conduct with women," (Benedict—p. 221–23) and against his church for not correcting the alleged wrong. The association held a special investigation of the charges, but the examination was unsatisfactory to both sides. On this report to the association, White's Creek and Richland withdrew in 1802. A second examination was called for the following April. Again the association failed to reach a verdict. Dorris' following was strong enough to prevent his dismissal, but he was too much opposed to be retained in fellowship.

As a final means of resolving the difficulty, the association dissolved in 1803, and the churches other than the four attached to Dorris formed a new association which was called Cumberland. For some years the four Dorris churches continued to meet as the Mero Association, but they did not prosper and were not accepted into the fellowship of neighboring associations. The new Cumberland Association grew from 15 churches in 1803 to 39 churches and 1,900 members within three years. The mother of all Baptist associations in Middle Tennessee, it at one time included the older churches in all this territory and still exists as a small antimission body in Williamson County. Red River Association was formed in 1806 by churches withdrawing from Cumberland Association by agreement. It included many of the oldest churches in the northwest section along the Red River in Montgomery and Robinson counties; for many years it prospered and was quite influential.

Stockton's Valley Association was formed in 1805 by eight Kentucky churches and six Tennessee churches from the large Green River Association of Kentucky. Formed agreeably, the new association was soon disturbed by the "New Light" teachings of Barton Stone; and in 1808 it excluded some of its more prominent preachers, who held these views. But in spite of difficulties, it prospered so much that in 1813 a group of churches on its southern side, some as far south as Warren County, withdrew to form Caney Fork Association. Both of these associations were disturbed for some years by an antimission element and by followers of Alexander Campbell who pretended to be orthodox Baptist preachers.

Soon after the purchase of the Indian lands in the region of the Elk and Duck rivers in south-central Tennessee, immigrants pressed eagerly into the territory. Many were Baptists from Georgia. Soon several churches were formed, and in 1808 seven churches formed the Elk River Association. The next year, five more churches were added; in another year, 10. By 1813 there were 24 churches and about 2,000 members. These continued to prosper until upset and disturbed by the divisions and bitterness over the doctrines of Alexander Campbell.

Concord Association.—Twenty-one churches of the eastern part of Cumberland Association, located mainly in Davidson, Sumner, Wilson, and Rutherford counties, withdrew by agreement in 1809 and met the following year at Hodge's Meeting House at Statesville, now Smith's Fork Church, to form Concord Association. They elected Thomas Durham of Round Lick as moderator and R. C. Foster of Nashville as clerk, and adopted decidedly Calvinistic articles of faith. Among many noted leaders were James Whitsett, Moore Stevenson, Cantrel Bethel, William Flowers, John Wiseman, and Joshua Lester. Complete records of the meetings of Concord reveal some years of happy fellowship and growth. It is the oldest association in Middle Tennessee which has remained missionary. Early meetings were usually three-day sessions with organization on Saturday; worship, with three sermons, on Sunday; and business on Monday.

A successful revival marked the year 1812, during which 866 baptisms were reported; but the next year there were only 122. The excitement of the War of 1812 disturbed the churches so severely that many were left neglected. In 1814 the churches were divided over the proposed Tennessee Baptist Meeting of Correspondence, an early abortive effort at a state convention organization, and only 64 baptisms were reported. The next year, R. C. Foster was appointed to correspond with the Board of Foreign Missions; John Wiseman and Cantrel Bethel were appointed as missionaries; and Jeremiah Burns was appointed general agent to visit churches, explain the mission plan, and solicit offerings. There was opposition to both of these projects, and baptisms dropped to 31. In 1816 Daniel Parker, the brilliant and popular but quite uncultured pastor of New Hopewell Church, bluntly threatened to break the association unless the ties to the mission board were severed. To save the association, the brethren yielded. A visit by Luther Rice in 1817 resulted in an offering for missions but not in renewed correspondence.

Fortunately, Parker moved to Illinois that year, and the association met in peace again. In 1821 another revival resulted in 673 baptisms and a total membership of 3,345. It was decided in 1822 that 49 churches with 3,399 members in such a vast territory should divide. The next year, churches east of a line from the Kentucky border through Lebanon and Winchester withdrew to form Salem Association. The Concord Association met jointly with the Cumberland Association in 1824; a union of the two was proposed, discussed, and refused. By 1827 the Baptist churches throughout this section were in an uproar over the teachings of Alexander Campbell. His opposition to mission boards or conventions, because of his fear of centralized authority, agreed with the antimission attitude promoted by Daniel Parker and others. Campbell also denounced the clergy as hireling priests and seminaries as priest factories. Aided by the *Christian Baptist,* published from 1823 by Campbell, these ideas infected many Baptist preachers in Concord, particularly Elders Calvin Curlee, Peyton Smith, and Philip Fall.

The Nashville church, organized in 1820 by Elder R. Dabbs, had grown to more than 300. Philip Fall succeeded as pastor at Dabbs's death. The membership fell to 131, and Fall led all but five of these to follow the new sect after Campbell. These five, led by Peter Smith Gayle (*q.v.*) (1802–53), reorganized with 29 members, worshiped in homes after losing the church property to the larger faction, and rejoined the Concord Association in 1831. So began Nashville's First Baptist Church.

The Concord Association was reduced by the Campbellite division from 49 churches and 3,399 members to 11 churches and 805 members. These grew in peace and fellowship until in 1834 there were 2,028 members and 432 baptisms reported. In this year Robert Boyté Crawford Howell (*q.v.*) of Virginia began his great work as pastor of the Nashville church, and the Tennessee Baptist Convention was formed to assist ministers in preaching in neglected areas.

Salem and Duck River associations.—In Oct., 1822, by agreement 27 churches with 900 members withdrew from Concord and formed Salem Association. Situated in Wilson and Smith counties and under the guidance of strong pastors, these churches so prospered that for years their section was known as "the Baptist kingdom." The Campbell division and the antimission movement carried away only a few of its people.

A resurgence of Arminian teaching, agitated by the Campbell movement, increased in the Elk River Association until it led to a breach out of which grew the Duck River Association in 1826. William Keele of Liberty Church led the division and with his followers started what became known as the Separate Baptist Church. Some joined them from Salem Association, and these, with the more extreme element from Duck River, joined the Campbell sect. Duck River Association then resumed the Baptist position.

West Tennessee.—The first association west of the Tennessee River was Western District, which once included all the churches in that section. A majority of the people were Baptists. These churches were favorable to missions, benevolences, and education. Organized in 1822 of churches in Weakley and Henry counties, Western District was the origin of the other associations west of the Tennessee River. Forked Deer Association was organized in Oct., 1825, with 15 churches and over 400 members. S. Depew was the first moderator, and J. W. Fort was clerk. In 1828, 15 churches from Forked Deer Association formed a new association called Big Hatchie. All Tennessee churches south of a line from the mouth of Forked Deer River to Jackson and to the Tennessee River were for a time in this association.

Conclusion.—Not satisfied with this record of Baptist expansion, Peter Smith Gayle wrote in the January, 1835, issue of *The Baptist* concerning the now 30,000 Baptists in Tennessee: "The churches throughout our state are extremely unsettled. Conflicting and injurious systems of theology disturb, and oppositions to benevolent effort that prevail are agitating every part of Zion." But Baptists prosper. TRUETT COX

II. History of Convention. The development of a unified Baptist organization for the state of Tennessee was greatly hindered by geography and by religious controversy. The state, about 450 miles long and 100 miles wide, is divided into three sections by geographical barriers more distinct than those which separate many states. Difficulty of east-west communication caused the population to gravitate into three distinct groups, which have not been easily unified. In addition, every denominational program initiated by Tennessee Baptists has been tried by conflict and has had to overcome strong opposition in order to justify its claim to the support of the people.

The need for a comprehensive statewide organization was recognized long before any effort was made to organize a state convention. In 1812 the Cumberland Association approached the Concord Association with the suggestion that a joint meeting be held for correspondence purposes.

First state convention.—The first effort to organize a state convention in Tennessee was at Mill Creek Baptist Church, near Nashville, in Oct., 1833. James Whitsitt (1771–1849), pastor of Mill Creek Church, presided over the meeting; a constitution was adopted; and an executive committee of 30 members, 10 from each major division of the state, was appointed.

From 1833 to 1842, the original state convention struggled hard to weather the storms of criticism and opposition hurled against it; but the individual and combined attacks of Primitive Baptists, Gospel Mission Baptists, and the Disciples of Christ were too much for it. The dissenting Baptists looked upon the new convention with dire misgivings and regarded with suspicion anything which tended toward the centralization of authority or threatened the autonomy of their churches. The spearhead of the attack had been directed against the name "convention." Therefore, in 1842 the convention again met at its birthplace, Mill Creek Church, and decided to change its name to General Association of the Baptists of Tennessee. In his report of the convention during its short term of existence, Robert Boyté Crawford Howell stated: "The Convention was in existence nine years. During this time it placed on the field an average of 15 missionaries annually; they assisted in the ordination of about forty ministers, organized about 150 churches and baptized about 15,000 persons."

Period of three conventions.—From 1842 to 1874, there was in reality no comprehensive state convention. Instead, there were three sectional conventions: the Middle Tennessee Association of Baptists, the East Tennessee General Association of Baptists, and the West Tennessee Convention of Baptists. The next 32 years were the darkest in Tennessee Baptist history, a period of theological debate which left the churches torn and divided into various contending factions. Missionary Baptists, Gospel Mission Baptists, Primitive Baptists, and Campbellite Baptists were arrayed against one another in constant debate. The efforts of Alexander Campbell to unite all denominations into one merely resulted in adding another to those already in existence. The question of boards and conventions became a most divisive issue among Baptists. In addition, the region was involved in the political strife which resulted in the Civil War, 1861–65.

Through all this strife and contention, Tennessee Baptists were aware of the importance of Christian education, and various schools sprang up throughout the state. In 1846 Union University was chartered at Murfreesboro. In 1851 Mossy Creek Missionary Baptist Seminary was chartered and located at Mossy Creek, now Jefferson City. In 1882 Newman College for girls was established there, and in 1889 the two schools were merged into a coeducational school and given the name Carson-Newman. During this period some of the opposition to a state convention subsided; but the Civil War and the subsequent trying period of reconstruction hindered efforts at reorganization.

Present convention.—On Apr. 10, 1874, the present state convention of Tennessee Baptists was organized at Murfreesboro. Individual Baptist leaders from East, Middle, and West Tennessee met to form some kind of a statewide organization. The primary interest of the original convention was missions; the principal objective of the founders of the second convention was the promotion of Christian education. The first president of the new convention was W. P. Bond, and the first secretary was W. T. Russell. A constitution was adopted, which included nine articles, three of which we quote here:

> ARTICLE 2. This Convention shall be composed of delegates from Baptist Churches, Associations, Conventions and individual contributors.
>
> ARTICLE 3. Any Baptist Church, Association or Convention shall be entitled to one representative for every dollar contributed annually to the funds of the Convention, and any individual member of the Baptist Church in good standing contributing one dollar shall be entitled to membership: Provided, That no church shall have more than one delegate for every twenty-five members, but any church having less than twenty-five members shall still be entitled to one delegate.
>
> ARTICLE 5. This Convention shall promote the educational interests of the Baptists of Tennessee, as a special object, but may patronize other objects of benevolence, and may appoint commissioners to whose special charge such objects shall be submitted—said commissioners to report at its annual meetings.

This constitution remained practically unchanged until 1904, when the second article was made to prohibit convention representation and individual representation based on contributions. The article then read: "This Convention shall be composed of messengers from churches and associations, cooperating with and contributing annually to the objects of the Convention." This article, defining the nature of representation in the convention, remained unchanged for the next 36 years. In 1941 the constitution was amended to eliminate associational representation. In 1951 the constitution was again revised. It is in general not unusually distinctive but does reflect the peculiar geographical predicament of Tennessee Baptists:

> This Convention shall elect at each annual meeting an Executive Board of the Tennessee Baptist Convention to be composed of fifty-four members, of whom not fewer than seventeen shall reside in each grand division of the state, which Board shall have charge of all its missionary, educational, and benevolent enterprises.

On Apr. 10, 1875, the convention, meeting in Nashville, authorized the appointment of a statewide Sunday school superintendent whose duty would be to attempt to organize a Sunday school in every church in the state. This convention also approved the recommendation that the new university be called the Southwestern University, that it be located at Jackson, Tenn., and that Union University, then located at Murfreesboro, be merged with it.

The convention of 1876, meeting in Jackson, appointed its first state missionary, J. H. Cason, who was to receive a salary of $100 per month, "provided he could raise it on the field."

In 1877 the convention met with the First Baptist Church, Chattanooga. It was during this year that the state mission board elected William Allen Montgomery (1829–1905) as its first secretary and gave him the title of corresponding secretary. His first duty was to unify the Baptist work in the three sections of the state. In his first report Secretary Montgomery said that the task was difficult because "the State is really three instead of one."

At this session the report on Christian education mentioned the following Tennessee Baptist schools: Mary Sharp Female College, Brownsville Female College, Southwestern Baptist University, Baptist Normal Theological School (Negro), Mossy Creek College, and Bristol Female College. In 1881 Boyd's Creek Academy was established in the Sevier Association, and in 1887 it was renamed Chilhowee Academy. In 1931 it was approved by the state convention. The Baptist Orphans' Home was established in Nashville with Mrs. Roger Eastman as its first president. In June, 1912, it was moved to its present site near Franklin. In 1950 the second branch was added at Memphis, and in 1952 the third branch was established at Chattanooga.

The Woman's Missionary Union of Tennessee Baptists was organized on Oct. 18, 1888, at Columbia; and the convention meeting in Chattanooga in 1890 recognized it as an auxiliary of the convention.

The first Baptist Young People's Union convention was held in Chattanooga in 1896, and the state convention in 1916 made B.Y.P.U. work a responsibility of the convention and its promotion a part of the work of the Department of Education.

Development of departments.—In 1908 William Douglas Hudgins (1873–1934) was elected to head the comprehensive work of the education department. Hudgins continued as head of this department for the next 26 years. His work included the supervision and direction of these organizations: Sunday school, Baptist Young People's Union, Brotherhood, and Baptist Student Union.

When Hudgins died, his work was divided into two departments: one responsible for Sunday school and Brotherhood; the other, for Training Union and Student Union. In 1935 Andrew Q. Allen was elected head of the Department of Sunday School and Brotherhood, and Henry C. Rogers was elected head of the Department of Training Union and Student Work. Allen resigned in 1938, and Jesse Daniel was elected to become superintendent of Sunday school work. The department was again divided in 1940 when E. Kirby Wiley was elected the first secretary of the new Brotherhood Department. In 1942 Rogers resigned the Department of Training Union and Student Work, and Charles Norton was elected to succeed him. This department was divided, and Rogers Smith became the first secretary of the new Baptist Student Union Department.

In 1952 the Department of Music was established, and Genter Leroy Stephens was elected part-time secretary. In 1955 Frank Charton was elected the first full-time secretary of the music department. In 1955 the combined budgets of these five departments were $157,000.

Executive Board.—The executive agency of the Tennessee Baptist Convention. At the organization of the convention in 1874, an executive committee was appointed and charged with the responsibility of attending to all the convention's business between sessions. In 1876 the name of the committee was changed to Executive Board and in 1877 to State Mission Board. The board retained this title until 1918, when the name was changed to the Executive Board of the Tennessee Baptist Convention. Prior to 1918 the board was composed of 33 members. In 1955 there were 54 members, 17 elected from each of the three grand divisions of the state. The members are elected by the convention to serve for a term of three years. They serve without pay.

The duties of the board are purely executive. The board is subject to the convention, and matters of policy and principle are decided by the convention. However, the convention may refer any matters to the board for consideration and action. The board employs and determines the salaries of all paid employees of the convention. All employees except the executive secretary are employed indefinitely; and service may be terminated at will, by either the employee or employer. The executive secretary is elected annually at the first meeting of the board after the annual session of the convention. The board has numerous committees, among which are the administrative committee and the appropriation committee. The administrative committee is empowered to act for the executive board on matters of administration or on any matter referred to it by the board. The board directs all the educational work of the convention; it supervises, but does not direct, the work of the institutions.

Executive secretary-treasurer.—The executive board annually elects an executive secretary. It has been the custom to elect as secretary the man who was elected by the convention at its previous session to the office of treasurer, thus giving him the title of executive secretary-treasurer. The term means secretary of the board and treasurer of the convention. The secretary is paid a stipulated salary for his work as secretary of the board but receives no salary for the work of treasurer. The duties of the executive secretary are both administrative and promotional. He is charged with the responsibility of promoting and directing the work of the several departments of the convention throughout the state. He is also charged with certain supervisory duties in connection with the institutions and agencies of the convention. As treasurer, he is responsible for handling all funds collected for denominational purposes.

The first secretary elected was William Allen Montgomery, in 1877. His title was corresponding secretary-treasurer, a title which the office retained until 1929 when, during the administration of O. E. Bryan, the title was changed to executive secretary-treasurer. The following men have served in this capacity:

William Allen Montgomery	May, 1877, to Oct., 1878
Jonathan Fleming Bingham Mays	Dec., 1878, to Aug., 1879
John D. Anderson	Oct., 1879, to Nov., 1882
James Waters	Nov., 1882, to Nov., 1884
E. C. Gates	Mar., 1885, to Nov., 1885
Crockett Carter Brown	Nov., 1885, to July, 1887
J. H. Anderson	Oct., 1887, to Oct., 1893
Adoniram Judson Holt	Dec., 1893, to Sept., 1902
John Thompson Henderson	Elected but declined to serve
William Cornelius Golden	Nov., 1902, to Oct., 1910
John W. Gillon	Nov., 1910, to Nov., 1919
Lloyd T. Wilson	Dec., 1919, to Nov., 1924
Oscar E. Bryan	Nov., 1924, to July, 1933
John D. Freeman	July, 1933, to Nov., 1942
Charles Wesley Pope	Nov., 1942, to Nov., 1956
W. Fred Kendall	Nov., 1956—

Baptist and Reflector.—The official journal of the Tennessee Baptist Convention. The title resulted from the consolidation of *The Reflector* and *The Baptist* in 1889. The paper is owned and published by the Tennessee Baptist Convention. Edgar Estes Folk and Orren Lucio Hailey were coeditors of the original *Baptist and Reflector*. Among other editors were John D. Freeman and Oury Wilburn Taylor. Richard Newton Owen was the editor in 1955. That year the paper had a circulation of 60,000.

Cooperative Program.—The birth of the Cooperative Program in Tennessee grew out of the successes and failures of the 75 Million Campaign. In 1919 the Southern Baptist Convention authorized the launching of a five-year 75 Million Campaign. Pledges were secured from individuals aggregating 92 million dollars, to be paid over a period of five years. Economic reverses and a loss of interest during the five-year period prevented the collection of a large part of the pledges. However, the campaign movement taught Baptists the necessity of a co-operative system of finances which would give to all denominational causes a percentage of all denominational gifts, according to their relative needs. When Oscar E. Bryan, in 1924, was elected corresponding secretary of the executive board, he was committed to the idea of a permanent co-operative system of finances for the Tennessee Baptist Convention. At a meeting in Murfreesboro, Nov. 26, 1924, the executive board recommended that "we wind up the 75 Million Campaign by Dec. 31," and "that the convention endorse the 1925 program for Tennessee." The various percentages for statewide and Southwide causes appeared for the first time in the state convention minutes of 1924 as follows:

1. Southwide Objects		
1. Foreign Missions	23½%	$176,250.00
2. Home Missions	10 %	75,000.00
3. Christian Education	10 %	75,000.00
4. Ministerial Relief	5 %	37,500.00
5. New Orleans Hospital	1½%	11,250.00
Total Southwide	50 %	$375,000.00
2. Statewide Objects		
1. State Missions	18 %	$135,000.00
2. Christian Education	19 %	142,500.00
3. Orphanage	8 %	60,000.00
4. Hospital	5 %	37,500.00
Total Statewide	50 %	$375,000.00
TOTAL	100 %	$750,000.00

The amounts to Christian education were allocated as follows:

1. Southwide Education		
1. S.B. Theo. Seminary	5 %	$ 37,500.00
2. S.W.B. Theo. Seminary	2 %	15,000.00
3. Baptist Bible Institute	1½%	11,250.00
4. W.M.U. Training School	½%	3,750.00
5. S.W. Training School	¼%	1,875.00
6. Education Board	½%	3,750.00
7. Negro Seminary	¼%	1,875.00
Total Southwide	10 %	$ 75,000.00
2. Statewide Education		
1. Union University	5 %	$ 37,500.00
2. Carson and Newman	5 %	37,500.00
3. Tennessee College	5 %	37,500.00
4. Hall-Moody Normal	3 %	22,500.00
5. Min. Ed. in C. & N. and U. U.	1 %	7,500.00
Total Statewide	19 %	$142,500.00

The adoption of the Cooperative Program by the Tennessee convention did not mean its immediate acceptance. A long program of education was necessary before its merits became apparent to all Tennessee Baptist churches. Bryan devoted the remainder of his life to the promotion of the program. The receipts at the end of the first year were $329,695.35. In 1933, in the midst of the depression and nine years after the program was adopted, the receipts had reached their all-time low level, $184,352.34. Crushed with disappointment and in failing health, the founder of the Tennessee Baptist Cooperative Program resigned the same year. In July, 1933, John D. Freeman was elected executive secretary, and he gave nine years to the continued promotion of the Cooperative Program. When he resigned in 1942, the Cooperative Program receipts had reached a new high of $381,393.87. In 1942 Charles Wesley Pope was elected executive secretary in the midst of World War II. He continued the emphasis upon the Cooperative Program as a means of financing the denominational work. In 1943 receipts for the Cooperative Program were $499,662.32; in 1947, $1,144,585.37; and in 1955, $2,425,479.35.

In 1933 the Tennessee Baptist Convention reaffirmed its approval of four special offerings as a part of the Cooperative Program system: Christmas, Orphans' Home; March, Home and Foreign Missions; June, Christian Education; and October, State Missions.

The Tennessee Baptist Foundation.—An agency authorized by the convention, Nov. 16, 1938. John D. Freeman was the first secretary-treasurer. In 1954 Henry Jeremiah Huey was elected to this position. The foundation is a trust organization and on Dec. 31, 1954, had fund balances of $1,092,413.83. The foundation's board of 27 trustees is elected by the Tennessee Baptist Convention.

Hospitals.—The first effort of Tennessee Baptists to enter the field of service by healing resulted in the establishment of the Baptist Memorial Hospital at Memphis, Tenn. This hospital is owned and sponsored jointly by the state conventions of Mississippi, Arkansas, and Tennessee. It has 800 beds and is one of the largest hospitals owned and operated by Southern Baptists.

The East Tennessee Baptist Hospital was built by a group of private citizens and was offered to the Tennessee Baptist Convention in 1947. In 1948 it was opened for service. The hospital has assets of approximately $5,000,000 and has 300 beds.

In Apr., 1948, the trustees of the Protestant Hospital, Nashville, tendered their entire property, including lands, building, and equipment, to the Tennessee Baptist Convention. The lot covers a city block. A new charter was adopted, and the hospital was renamed Mid-State Baptist Hospital (later Baptist Hospital, Inc.). Additional buildings costing approximately $2,000,000 have been constructed. In 1955 the hospital had 325 beds.

Assemblies.—The convention owns and operates two camps for assembly purposes, Camp Linden at Linden and Camp Carson at Newport. These camps were authorized by the convention in 1946. Each camp has a capacity of approximately 275 persons.

Belmont College.—This college, located at Nashville, is the latest result of the efforts of the Tennessee executive secretary, Charles Wesley Pope, to provide an institutional basis for the growth of Baptists in Middle Tennessee. The eastern and western sections of the state have traditionally been the centers of Baptist strength. Of the 674,979 members of Tennessee Baptist Convention churches in 1955, more than half resided in East Tennessee. Approximately 200,000 of these church members resided in West Tennessee, and 122,000 in Middle Tennessee. It was felt that Baptist institutions, particularly the coeducational schools, were major factors in the development of Baptist strength in the eastern and western sections of the state, and that similar institutions were necessary to stimulate Baptist growth in Middle Tennessee. The missionary and pastoral work of ministerial students attending Baptist schools has contributed largely to the strength of Baptists in other areas. Therefore, in 1946 Tennessee College for Women at Murfreesboro and Cumberland University at Lebanon were merged and, until 1951, were operated under the auspices of the Tennessee Baptist Convention. In that year the convention acquired the properties of Ward-Belmont College for girls in Nashville, and the Baptist state headquarters were moved to that site. Failure to secure accreditation for Cumberland University in Lebanon, Tenn., caused Baptists to abandon that institution to its former owners, and on Mar. 13, 1951, Belmont College was founded as a coeducational institution, occupying the properties once owned by Ward-Belmont College. CHARLES WESLEY POPE

III. Program of Work of Tennessee Baptists. ADMINISTRATIVE ORGANIZATIONS OF THE CONVENTION. The Tennessee Baptist Convention, through the messengers of the 2,572 co-operating churches, elects annually one third of the trustees of agencies and institutions, commissions, and committees. The convention reserves the right to recall any and all of the various board and committee members and elect their successors at any session of the Convention. These institutions, agencies, commissions, and committees promote their phases of the state program.

The convention hears the reports from all institutions, agencies, commissions, and committees (departments). After discussions and changes, if any, it adopts them with the recommendations for program guidance. The convention elects annually a treasurer, without salary, who is bonded and whose books are audited by a company of certified public accountants.

Executive board.—The executive board, a corporation created by the convention, is authorized to work out all details of the state mission program, appropriate the funds, elect and dismiss the personnel, fix the manner and amount of remuneration, and through its elected executive secretary, who is also the convention treasurer, supervise the institutions. The executive board is the convention *ad interim* and "shall have all the powers of the Convention except as limited by this Convention, the by-laws of the Convention, and specific action taken by the Convention in session."

Executive secretary.—The duties of this officer are as follows:

The Executive Secretary shall be charged with the raising of all funds throughout the state for the various enterprises of the Board, and with the direction and presentation of our unified Baptist program to our constituency. In conference with the heads of the departments and agencies of the Convention as soon as possible after the annual meeting of the Board, he shall arrange for systematic visitation of the associations for the purpose of acquainting the people with this program and stirring up the churches to good works. He shall render written reports to the Board at their quarterly meeting, with whatever recommendations he may deem wise.

The Treasurer of the Board shall receive and disburse to their proper agencies all funds raised as directed by the Board. He shall give good and sufficient bond for the faithful discharge of his duties and for the proper accounting of all funds handled by him, the amount of this bond to be fixed by the Board. The bond shall be in a solvent surety company and the premium shall be paid by this Board.

Administrative committee.—This committee is defined by the convention's constitution as follows:

An Administrative Committee of seven shall be elected from the members of the Executive Board, two from East Tennessee, two from West Tennessee, and three from Middle Tennessee, five of whom shall constitute a quorum. This Administrative Committee shall have charge of the Board's business in the interim between meetings of the Board for its ratification.

Church loan program.—In 1952 the Tennessee Baptist Convention authorized the executive board to set up a church loan fund to assist small churches to secure funds for church building purposes. This fund was not designed to compete with commercial lending agencies, but to help churches finding it difficult to secure commercial loans. At its meeting on Dec. 9, 1952, the executive board adopted general principles to govern the administration of the church loan program and appointed a committee to complete details and to serve as a committee to consider applications.

The maximum amount which can be loaned to one church is $50,000. Loans must be paid monthly over a period of time not less than one year and not more than six years. The rate of interest is six per cent on the unpaid balance. The loan cannot exceed fifty per cent of the completed project. A first mortgage is required on the church building. Loans are consummated only when the building project is completed; however, pending the completion of the project the Church Loan program will give the church an irrevocable commitment which the church can use at the banks to borrow building funds. When the building is completed according to specifications the Church Loan program will take up the loan at the banks.

Church lot fund.—The Tennessee Baptist Church Lot Fund is designed to help purchase lots for mission stations and new churches. These grants are gifts to the churches and are financed from annual appropriations by the executive board. A prerequisite to this grant is that the property be deeded to the executive board, and the executive board then deeds the property to the new church. The deed form requires that the church shall co-operate with the Tennessee Baptist Convention and the Southern Baptist Convention, and that in the event of a controversy in the church, a minority group of co-operating members may retain the property.

State Missions. The Tennessee Baptist program is a term that designates the work of institutions, agencies, and state missions—the whole program. State missions proper confines its activities to the departments of Sunday school, Training Union, Woman's Missionary Union, Brotherhood, Student Union, church music, retirement, camps, promotion and evangelism, and missions. State missions is supported by special offerings and a percentage of the state's share of the Cooperative Program offerings. All the departments except missions will be treated briefly elsewhere in this monograph. The department of missions is subdivided into associational, city, general, special, and Negro missionary activities. In 1955 the superintendent was L. G. Frey, and the total budget amounted to $128,471.60.

Associational missionaries.—The state contains 64 co-operating associations, 53 of which have missionaries who live among the people and give their time to the program of strengthening the voluntarily co-operating churches. Approximately 800 pastor's and missionary's homes are owned, and others are in process of being built or bought. Many churches are encouraged to establish and support mission points in neglected areas and to furnish Sunday schools and preaching to the people until these groups mature sufficiently to become self-supporting churches. The associational missionary correlates all the work and encourages the other associational officers—Sunday school superintendent; Training Union director; Woman's Missionary Union president; and the chairmen in charge of church music, stewardship, and evangelism—to perform their duties. The records reveal that more baptisms were reported, more mission money raised, more pastor's homes built, and more churches strengthened where missionaries were employed than where they were not.

Special missionaries.—Special missionaries serve in associations too undeveloped to share their proportionate part of the cost. As the work grows, they become regular associational missionaries. The state board supplements the operating costs in these associations. The basic plan is for the association to pay about 75 per cent of the missionary's salary. The budgets for the two were $58,741.76 in 1955.

City missionaries.—Four of Tennessee's 64 associations are influenced by large cities to such an extent that special types of programs have been provided for their needs. City missionaries lead the churches to sponsor missions in neglected as well as rapidly growing areas. The latter soon become churches, although the former may continue indefinitely as missions. Good Will

Centers are outlets for special church service. Many churches furnish both men and women as counselors for boys and girls from the juvenile courts. Knox and Nashville associations have well-advanced programs; Shelby and Hamilton are setting them up. Nashville is having its first experience with an association-wide program of recreation designed for churches and directed by a trained leader. The remainder of the program resembles that carried on in less urban associations. These city-influenced programs are intended to be largely promotional and not institutional, in order to reduce the use of salaried personnel to a minimum and make maximum use of volunteer workers. From two to three per cent of the total offerings of the churches in these associations will suffice for operating budgets. The state board pays most of the salary of these four missionaries. The budget for 1955 was $20,190.

General missionaries.—The four women employed in 1955 as general missionaries devoted themselves largely to pioneer work planned to pave the way for regular missionaries. They worked largely in undeveloped communities with Vacation Bible schools, study courses, conferences, and surveys. They spent several weeks in the summer camps as counselors for boys and girls. Other weeks were devoted to speaking in schools of missions in the various associations. One worker is located in West Tennessee, the other three in Middle Tennessee. This work has produced a desire on the part of many associations for services of a regular missionary. These women are employed, paid, and directed by the missions department of the Tennessee board. The total budget for 1955 was $8,275.

Negro missionaries.—A limited amount of work was done in 1955 by Negroes employed, directed, and paid by the Department of Missions. The Home Mission Board shares equally with the state board in paying the salaries of two of these workers: a Student Union secretary in Nashville and one pastor at Oak Ridge. Two other pastors have their salaries supplemented while they are strengthening the churches at Winchester and Cookeville. Three women are regularly employed jointly by the state board and the two Negro Baptist conventions, but the workers are paid in full by the state board. These women have developed friendly relations among all three conventions. Churches of both Negro conventions open their doors for Vacation Bible schools, study courses, and personal evangelism. One woman has done special work among the Negro churches of Haywood and Lauderdale counties, where the Negro population exceeds the white. This was a joint venture, for the summer months only, between the state board and the Negro churches. The budget amounted to $4,680.

EDUCATIONAL MINISTRY. *Sunday School Department.*—The Sunday school is regarded by Tennessee Baptists as their most successful means of enlisting the unchurched and unsaved people within their territory. It is designed to reach people, teach the Scriptures, win the lost, enlist the saved, and train for service. Thorough Bible teaching is the foundation and largest part of the Sunday school program, which involves four primary emphases: (1) enlistment, based on the belief that Bible study as provided in the Sunday school is the best entrance into the full activities of church membership; (2) training and study courses, including the regular Sunday curriculum and special classes for more intensive work; (3) records and standards of excellence, used to measure and promote efficiency in methods and results; and (4) Vacation Bible school, providing special training for children and young people during the summer months. The Sunday School Department promotes all this work through the Tennessee associations, through regional meetings, in the state convention, and at the summer assemblies—Camp Carson and Camp Linden. In 1955 the department budget amounted to $42,461.21. Jesse Daniel was the secretary in charge.

Training Union Department.—The training program promoted by this department is more concerned with methods and with the practical development of leadership ability. It is designed specifically for church members and provides activities for all age groups. Members are taught to speak publicly and preside over meetings. They are instructed in the details of program planning and committee work. They are encouraged to follow a program of daily Bible reading and prayer and to become active in the work of enlistment and soul-winning. Editors of the Southern Baptist Training Union curriculum and state workers work out in conference the Training Union calendar and monthly themes. A state Training Union convention meets biannually and holds regional conventions every year. During June, regional Sword Drill and speakers' tournaments are held, with the state elimination coming the first part of July. At the state elimination one person is chosen to represent Tennessee at the assembly at Ridgecrest, N. C., in each of these events. The Training Union promotes one week at each of the Tennessee Baptist camps. In 1955, 60 associations reported Training Union organizations in 1,670 churches with a total enrolment of 159,913. Charles L. Norton was department secretary. The budget for 1955 was $42,085.88.

Baptist Student Union and student department.—The Baptist Student Union movement of Tennessee promotes a program of devotional, social, and church enlistment activities for all Baptist students in the state. It has organized work on the following 23 campuses: Austin Peay State College; Baptist Hospital, Nashville; Baptist Memorial Hospital, Memphis; Belmont College; Carson-Newman College; Draughon's, Nashville; Draughon's, Memphis; East Tennessee Baptist Hospital; East Tennessee State College; Erlanger Hospital, Chattanooga; Harrison-Chilhowee Academy; Memphis State College; Middle Tennessee State College; Nashville General Hospital; Vanderbilt-Peabody; Southwestern at Memphis; Tennessee Tech; Union University; University of Chattanooga; University of Tennessee, Knoxville; University of Tennessee, Martin; University of Tennessee Medical Units, Memphis; and Andrew Jackson Business University, Nashville.

An elected council of students serve as state B.S.U. officers and plan the work on a statewide basis. In 1955 the state B.S.U. held a convention, two spring retreats, and three evangelism clinics and participated in two weeks of missionary tours and in the two convention assemblies at Ridgecrest and Glorieta. In a summer service project the students raised $3,014.89, with which they sent 10 students to mission fields and brought Alexander Beerwish of Belgrade, Yugoslavia, to tour the campuses of Tennessee.

Baptist Student Center buildings are located adjacent to the campuses of Memphis State College, Vanderbilt University, the University of Chattanooga, and the University of Tennessee. In 1955 the budget of the department amounted to $38,883,76, and Charles M. Roselle was the secretary in charge.

Church Music Department.—Tennessee's first full-time secretary for church music, Frank Garner Charton, was elected on July 1, 1955. That year a few church music schools were conducted. Plans made for the following year provided for 18 associational schools of music, one state and eight regional music festivals, a youth music camp, a state leadership clinic, various associational hymn-sings, participation in the convention-wide music weeks at the assemblies at Ridgecrest and Glorieta, and a goal of 1,500 music awards from 150 churches in 35 associations. The department was made responsible for the music at three 1956 state conventions. Its budget for the year was $13,852.85.

Brotherhood Department.—The Brotherhood program in Tennessee in 1955 featured one convention at Camp Linden, work clinics in each of the eight Tennessee regions, and various associational clinics held in the fall. Paul R. Cates became Brotherhood secretary for Tennessee on July 1, 1955. The budget for the year was $20,474.56. Planning meetings for the coming year gave particular emphasis to the needs of the Royal Ambassadors, the boys' missionary organization transferred from Woman's Missionary Union to Brotherhood sponsorship in 1954.

Department of Promotion and Evangelism.—Stewardship in Tennessee in 1955 was promoted through every associational missionary. In addition the department conducted simultaneous stewardship revivals in Watauga and Cumberland Gap associations. By means of tracts, posters, and articles in the *Baptist and Reflector,* the department strives to keep the whole Tennessee Baptist constituency informed and contributing. This stewardship program emphasizes particularly the importance of the Cooperative Program and seeks to encourage churches to give regularly through it and to increase each year the percentage of their contributions given to missions. As many pastors and churches as possible were enlisted in the Southern Baptist Security (pension) Plan.

The 1955 program of evangelism in Tennessee gave major emphasis to participation in the Convention-wide Evangelistic Crusade. An evangelistic conference was held in January in preparation. Steering committees in each association were enlisted, guided, and kept informed. In conformity with the general plan for the whole crusade, the state was divided into two zones, and meetings were held for two weeks, first in the southern part of the state, and then in the northern part. The report for the crusade showed 10,121 baptisms, 5,490 other additions, and 249 dedications to religious vocations. Sixty-two associations and 1,800 churches participated in the crusade. In addition the department requested the churches to hold one other revival during the year. Baptisms reached a total of 31,772 by Dec. 31, 1955. The secretary of the department was Leonard Sanderson, and the budget was $25,437.55.

Summer camps.—The Tennessee Baptist camps at Linden and Carson Springs were used during 1955 by Sunday school, Training Union, Woman's Missionary Union, Brotherhood, and Student Union departments for instruction, inspiration, and recreation. The season lasted from June 13 through Aug. 28, 1955. Except for administrative costs, the camps were self-supporting. At the end of the season, the combined registered attendance at both camps totaled 5,301, and the total investment in property was $205,442.32.

Institutes for the education of ministers.—The 1955 Summer Preachers' Schools, held for one week during the month of June on the campuses of the three Tennessee Baptist colleges, offered refresher courses in Baptist doctrines, polity, and practice, and in stewardship, homiletics, and church history. The host schools, in collaboration with the state board's department of missions, arranged the courses of study and selected the faculty. Rooms were furnished rent free by the schools, and the state board purchased books, paid for meals, and provided traveling expenses and a small honorarium for the teachers.

INSTITUTIONS. *Colleges.*—The purpose of the three senior colleges, Belmont College, Carson-Newman College, and Union University, is to train young men and women in an environment which will develop both high scholarship and Christian character. These schools seek to stimulate the students in their quest for knowledge, to provide Christian guidance in this quest, to separate truth from error, and to develop skills in the technique of using this knowledge, to the end that the individuals may be intelligent, competent, well adjusted, and happy as they serve through whatever occupation they may choose. The churches and religious agencies of Tennessee Baptists make constant requests of these colleges for pastors, missionaries, educational directors, ministers of music, and other full-time Christian workers. Out of their total enrolment of 2,638 in 1955, 500 students were preparing for definite religious vocations. Total assets of these colleges in 1955 amounted to $7,392,051.18. Designated and Cooperative Program contributions to them amounted to $399,479.91. Christian education is inextricably bound up in the total mission program of Tennessee Baptists.

Harrison-Chilhowee Academy, Seymour.—From its beginning, through its period as a normal academy, as a part of the Home Mission Board Mountain School System and as an institution of Tennessee Baptists, Harrison-Chilhowee Academy has stood for the best in high school education from the Christian point of view. Since 1932 it has been an increasingly useful part of the educational program of the Tennessee Baptist Convention. In addition to the regular high school curriculum, Bible is required of all students for three years. In a particular way this school meets the needs of the man or woman entering the ministry or other Christian service late in life. Father and daughter have been graduated in the same class without embarrassment. In 1955, 40 ministerial students were enrolled, and the total convention gifts amounted to $71,099.34. Total assets were $712,119.44.

Junior High School, Franklin.—All children in the three Tennessee Baptist children's homes are given high school education, but at Franklin since 1942 an educational program covering the first 10 grades of school has been provided on the grounds. Manual training with modern equipment has been made available for the boys. This school is accredited with the State Department of Education. James R. Banton is the principal.

Hospitals.—Baptist Memorial Hospital at Memphis was born out of a deep sense of need and a conviction, emphasized by years of experience, that it is the Christian duty of Baptists to care for people in their afflictions. With the building of East Tennessee Baptist Hospital at Knoxville and the acquiring by outright gift of the Protestant Hospital at Nashville, Baptists in Tennessee came, except for emergencies, within reach of one of the three. And in addition to providing for the needs of Baptists, these institutions offer a unique opportunity to bring the influence of religion to all. In 1955, 472 nurses were in training, both men and women. Some of these graduates eventually became foreign missionaries. These hospitals operate at nearly full-bed capacity.

In 1955 contributions through the Cooperative Program to these hospitals amounted to $186,-878.59, and $709,900.54 worth of charity service was performed. The full-time chaplain on duty at each of these institutions reported many professions of faith.

Children's homes.—Four children's homes minister to destitute children and children from broken homes between the ages of 2 and 18. None of these children are eligible for adoption. They are furnished comfortable home conditions, taught personal responsibility, and given a high school education and special training for places in the business world. Assistance is given those desiring college training. At the Franklin home a modern and completely furnished hospital served by a volunteer staff renders valuable service. The children receive the very best of medical and surgical attention. There also a full church program of training on the grounds ministers to the spiritual life of the children. Superintendent John M. Wenger is pastor. Professions of faith and baptisms were reported. The Min-Tom Home, Chattanooga, for Negro children gives the same high type of service found in the other three homes. W. C. Creasman, Nashville, is general superintendent; J. E. Tanksley and V. Wayne Tarpley are superintendents of Memphis and Chattanooga homes, respectively.

Tennessee Baptist Foundation.—This agency is responsible for the administration and investment of the permanent funds of the Tennessee convention and for much of the endowments of Tennessee Baptist institutions. All special money-raising campaigns are channeled through this agency. In 1955 the foundation's executive secretary was Henry J. Huey; the year's budget was $20,537.08; and the total assets amounted to $1,148,110.61.

Ministerial Relief and Retirement Plans.—Liberalization of the Ministers Retirement Plan, by joint action of the Relief and Annuity Board and the Tennessee convention, gave pastors the Ministers Security Plan, which protects the widow before and after her husband's retirement age. This plan enables the pastor to retire on commuted annuity if disability occurs after age 60, early retirement on reduced annuity, maximum of disability benefits $900, and eligibility beginning at age 25, or date of first denominational position after age 25. Monthly dues on annual salary up to $4,000 on Security Plan are 5 per cent for pastor, 5 per cent for church, and 5 per cent for state board. Maximum retirement benefits on this plan are $2,000. The Southern Baptist Protection Plan carries the same provisions as the Ministers Security Plan and in addition offers 1½ per cent of the salary as retirement annuity for each year of actual participation in the plan. Ministers and their widows not in any retirement plan have drawn a small quarterly annuity from the relief fund. During the year ending Sept. 1, 1955, 56 ministers drew $9,591.50, and 80 widows, $10,500.98. The Baptist Board Employees Security Plan is similar to the Ministers Security Plan. When the fiscal year closed Oct. 31, 1955, 592 ministers and 828 churches were in the various plans. Total contributions to all plans amounted to: pastors, $73,646.34; convention and state board, $103,605.31; churches, $85,323.08; and employees, $9,057.95. Grand total contributions amounted to $271,632.68. Eighty-four pastors and widows received age and disability retirement benefits from the various plans.

Promotional Work. *Baptist and Reflector.*—This paper, owned and operated by the Tennessee Baptist Convention since 1921, promotes the

IV. TENNESSEE STATISTICAL SUMMARY

Year	Associ-ations	Churches	Church Member-ship	Baptisms	S. S. Enrol-ment	V.B.S. Enrol-ment	T. U. Enrol-ment	W.M.U. Enrol-ment	Brother-hood En-rolment	Mission Gifts	Total Gifts	Value Church Property	State Capital Worth
													(Explanation:
1832	20	413	20,472	805	....	....	....	....	....	....	....	....	This column
1836	30	514	27,245	1,240	....	....	....	....	....	....	....	....	includes
1840	44	666	29,483	938	....	....	....	....	....	....	....	....	total value
1851	18	455	36,009	3,263	....	....	....	....	....	....	....	....	of Schools,
1857	25	655	50,539	3,124	....	....	....	....	....	....	....	....	Children's
1876	51	1,162	101,241	3,825	....	....	....	....	....	....	....	....	Homes, Hos-
1880	35	699	57,090	2,814	....	....	....	....	....	$ 1,328	....	....	pitals,
1890	44	1,174	96,094	6,650	36,300	....	....	....	....	26,614	$ 132,808	$ 924,945	Foundation,
1900	51	1,518	133,630	6,008	34,267	....	....	....	....	28,167	198,578	....	Buildings,
1905	53	1,562	143,393	7,841	52,054	....	....	....	....	59,831	261,950	1,680,690	etc.)
1910	54	1,669	170,589	10,462	72,237	....	....	....	....	97,288	485,645	2,398,112	
1915	54	1,785	194,229	11,665	122,843	....	....	....	....	141,831	692,925	3,467,950	....
1920	54	1,796	210,788	8,178	129,406	....	....	....	....	238,351	1,072,213	3,997,394	....
1925	63	1,858	261,406	17,235	159,602	1,270	25,706	....	....	461,137	2,350,143	10,307,190	....
1930	65	1,855	284,481	17,333	186,980	1,230	27,244	28,959	....	522,862	2,547,315	12,827,162	....
1931	65	1,852	296,474	17,150	188,495	1,210	30,159	34,627	....	481,621	2,361,963	13,643,250	....
1932	64	1,873	301,377	22,780	211,736	1,988	34,892	39,731	....	370,116	1,930,804	14,817,868	....
1933	64	1,894	315,453	17,335	219,528	2,773	36,225	40,809	....	236,775	1,617,657	13,147,249	....
1934	64	1,938	328,011	17,377	212,902	4,300	37,821	36,285	....	277,214	1,698,063	12,923,461	....
1935	64	1,970	341,418	16,872	208,880	8,974	39,116	35,562	....	329,998	1,944,450	13,168,569	....
1936	65	2,038	354,879	15,757	224,602	25,688	40,055	34,383	....	335,463	2,061,713	12,391,727	....
1937	65	2,064	366,854	16,521	232,507	33,760	43,473	36,677	....	350,061	2,160,610	13,469,568	....
1938	64	2,077	378,643	19,380	242,183	48,909	49,707	49,872	....	369,063	2,345,954	13,830,737	....
1939	64	2,142	389,326	23,551	253,906	53,006	67,043	47,362	....	584,706	2,593,932	14,429,260	....
1940	64	2,152	397,184	19,576	262,955	63,256	70,016	46,882	....	450,020	2,959,930	14,019,195	....
1941	64	2,238	424,047	17,134	268,399	65,550	72,226	41,182	....	538,343	3,412,586	15,451,700	....
1942	65	2,260	427,323	16,862	240,729	61,843	61,670	40,707	....	687,665	4,136,920	14,687,553	....
1943	65	2,284	445,183	17,705	253,044	58,532	48,178	40,482	1,932	1,023,386	4,944,392	16,600,751	....
1944	65	2,292	453,365	19,217	254,578	66,888	49,288	40,256	2,012	1,249,587	5,599,880	17,874,935	....
1945	65	2,329	478,302	23,077	272,816	79,588	57,758	40,286	2,086	1,468,663	7,380,896	17,799,736	....
1946	66	2,345	497,164	21,548	292,325	99,875	46,926	33,874	1,691	1,861,346	8,560,826	21,371,881	....
1947	66	2,439	525,856	25,208	325,977	113,290	72,779	53,024	8,328	1,749,378	9,479,451	24,768,035	....
1948	66	2,443	549,692	29,703	350,419	128,217	86,309	60,503	6,590	2,083,773	11,275,703	31,738,682	* Baptist Memorial
1949	68	2,515	572,762	31,648	382,070	142,140	99,325	66,250	8,876	2,392,240	13,265,474	39,427,525	Hospital owned
1950	69	2,564	604,781	34,550	411,858	158,585	116,112	72,725	9,022	2,378,107	14,842,333	46,564,359	jointly by Tenn.,
1951	68	2,599	629,145	31,880	432,031	150,931	118,152	74,083	10,909	2,643,908	17,582,379	55,071,705	Miss., & Ark.
1952	68	2,652	677,192	29,859	438,428	156,103	128,323	78,325	11,903	2,773,267	17,783,493	65,743,712	Liabilities
1953	69	2,687	665,258	29,501	451,396	167,340	134,576	78,628	13,277	3,444,084	20,041,278	74,396,245	$4,515,538.
1954	64	2,572	675,979	31,715	499,076	189,747	137,084	86,724	15,889	3,710,328	26,042,101	85,585,665	Assets:
1955	64	2,644	687,393	30,143	510,682	190,706	160,113	82,441	25,015	4,066,468	23,676,997	87,432,035	$24,409,327.

L. G. FREY

whole Tennessee program and publishes news of the churches every week. Richard Newton Owen is editor. Its circulation, as of Dec. 31, 1955, was 60,266.

Hospital commission.—This commission was created to study any or all matters relating to successful hospital administration and operation and to suggest ways and means for improvements. The commission is a purely advisory body, with no legal power or authority over the hospitals. It consists of six members, two each from the three grand divisions of the state, one third of whom are elected annually by the convention, according to the by-laws of the Tennessee Baptist Convention.

Education commission.—This body, also advisory and without authority, was created to co-ordinate the program of promotion of the Tennessee convention for Baptist education in Tennessee. It is not allowed to assume or perform the duties of the boards of trustees of the schools and agencies nor of the Tennessee convention or its executive board. This commission consists of the presidents of the four Baptist schools supported by the convention and six additional members, two each from the three grand divisions of the state, one third of whom are elected annually. The Education Commission is a convention agency, subject to the direction of the state convention and its executive board.

Co-operative Work. *American Bible Society.*—The special offering for the work of the American Bible Society, approved in general by the convention but referred to the executive board for final action as to details, is presented to the churches each year for such consideration and action as they individually may deem proper to give it. American Bible Society work is presented each year at the convention, and a report is filed for information but is not adopted. Total gifts in 1955 from the churches amounted to $2,735.04.

Temperance and social service.—The Tennessee convention, concerned with the problem since the first report on temperance was adopted in 1885, maintains a committee which furnishes information on social issues and suggests and leads in programs of positive and negative action. The committee is concerned with family and home life, juvenile delinquency, obscene literature and amusements, gambling, narcotics, world peace, race relations, institutional relations, temperance, and other subjects. In the field of temperance, the convention co-operates, through this committee, with the United Temperance League Against Beverage Alcohol, a Tennessee organization which unites the efforts of interested groups in the state. L. G. FREY

Bibliography: R. Anderson, *The New Bethel Sesqui-Centennial, 1782–1932* (1932). J. Asplund, *The Annual Register of the Baptist Denominations in North America, 1790* (1791). D. Benedict, *A General History of the Baptist Denomination in America* (1813). J. Bond, *History of the Concord Association* (1860). W. Cathcart, *The Baptist Encyclopedia* (1883). J. T. Christian, *A History of the Baptists of the United States* (1926). R. B. Cook, *The Story of the Baptists in All Ages and Countries* (1886). D. Davidson, *The Tennessee* (1946). L. Edwards, "The Primitive Baptists" (1940); "The Baptists of Tennessee" (1940). J. H. Grime, "History of Middle Tennessee Baptists," *Baptist and Reflector* (1902). Historical Records Survey Project, *Inventory of the Church Archives of Tennessee* [*c.* 1939]. Holston Association, *Minutes* (1786–). R. B. C. Howell, "A Memorial of the First Baptist Church, Nashville, Tennessee" (1863). D. E. Johnston, *History of Middle New River Settlements* (1906). W. B. Lenoir, *History of Sweetwater Valley* (1916). I. P. Martin, *Methodism in Holston* (1945). F. Merritt, *Early History of Carter County* (1950). A. H. Newman, *A History of the Baptist Churches in the United States,* Vol. II (1894). W. D. Nowlin, *Kentucky Baptist History* (1922). G. W. Paschall, *History of North Carolina Baptists* (1930). J. Phelan, *History of Tennessee* (1888). J. W. Porter, *The World's Debt to the Baptists* (1914). J. G. M. Ramsey, *Annals of Tennessee* (1853). B. F. Riley, *A History of the Baptists in the Southern States* (1898). M. U. Rothrock, *The French Broad—Holston Country* (1946). G. Ryland, *The Baptists of Virginia* (1955). R. B. Semple, *History of the Rise and Progress of the Baptists in Virginia* (1809). W. W. Sweet, *Religion on the American Frontier: The Baptists, 1783–1830* (1931); Tennessee Baptist Association, *Minutes* (1802–). Tennessee Baptist Convention, *Minutes* (1875–). S. W. Tindell, *The Baptists of Tennessee* (1930). R. G. Torbet, *A History of the Baptists* (1950).

TENNESSEE BAPTIST CONVENTION, THE. Organized at Mill Creek Baptist Church, Davidson County, Oct. 25, 1833, following a preliminary meeting in 1832 and an unsuccessful effort at the session of the Cumberland Association in Sept., 1833. Its sole purpose, as stated in Article V of the constitution, was to "devise and execute plans for the dissemination of the gospel in the destitute sections of the state; and, as far as practicable, supply such churches as solicit aid."

Soon thereafter the Baptists in both East and West Tennessee formed auxiliary organizations (General Association of Baptists for East Tennessee, and West Tennessee Baptist Convention). The convention held three sessions yearly—a state meeting and adjourned meetings in both East Tennessee and West Tennessee. It established three executive committees with headquarters at Knoxville, Nashville, and Jackson.

The convention's first missionary in East Tennessee, Daniel Buckner (salary, $15 a month), was excluded by his church, Big Spring, for joining the convention and refusing to withdraw and for being charged as a "money grubber." Strong opposition rapidly developed against the convention. The split between missionaries and antimissionaries occurred, both in churches and associations. Following so soon after the destruction wrought by Daniel Parker (*q.v.*) in the state from about 1814 to 1817, and the inroads made by Alexander Campbell and his associates during the 1820's, antimissionism made it difficult for the convention to achieve its limited aims.

In 1835 the convention gave its approval to the American Baptist Home Mission Society and to Bible, tract, and missionary societies, but not to abolitionist societies. Jan. 1, 1835, Robert Boyté Crawford Howell (*q.v.*) aided the first year by the Home Mission Society, became pastor of the Nashville Baptist church. At once he began publishing *The Baptist,* a monthly paper, and through it and other means he did much to promote the convention and its work. He led in organizing three societies: (1) the Baptist Education Society for Ministerial Improvement, Oct. 8, 1836; (2) the Bible Association of the Baptists of Tennessee, Oct. 10, 1836; and (3) the Tennessee Baptist Publication and Sunday School Society, Oct., 1841, which immediately took over the depository the Nashville church had begun about 1831 and gave itself to printing, purchasing, and distributing tracts. In Oct., 1839, he revived the Tennessee Foreign Mission Society, established by Luther Rice (*q.v.*) in 1817. All these societies were auxiliary to the convention.

In 1838 general agent B. Kimbrough reported total receipts of $400.78¾—public offerings, $227.16¼, and private offerings, $175.62½. That year, after James Barnett Taylor (*q.v.*) of Virginia spoke to the convention, and offering of about $22 was made for foreign missions.

A conviction grew that "general association" would be a better name than "convention" for organized Baptist work. The convention held its last session in Oct., 1841, but continued its work until Oct., 1842, when the Baptist General Association of Tennessee was organized to succeed it, and its auxiliary societies were absorbed into the general association and boards established to take their place. Howell said that this reorganization led the auxiliary bodies in East and West Tennessee to cease their auxiliary relationships and become independent bodies.

HOMER L. GRICE

TENNESSEE BAPTIST FOUNDATION. The agency of the Tennessee Baptist Convention responsible for receiving, holding, and investing all kinds of properties for the promotion, maintenance, and extension of all Baptist causes. It was created by vote of the convention on Nov. 16, 1938, and was chartered as a trust corporation the following Dec. 9. The foundation idea in Tennessee was promoted by John D. Freeman during his term as executive secretary of the executive board of the Tennessee Baptist Convention. He served as the first executive secretary of the foundation, from 1938 to 1942. Other secretaries have been Charles Wesley Pope (Nov. 1, 1942—Dec. 31, 1945), Norris Gilliam (Jan. 1, 1946—Sept. 1, 1954), and Henry Jeremiah Huey (Nov. 1, 1954–). Leibert Garland Frey served as treasurer from 1942 to 1946. The foundation is owned and controlled by the Tennessee Baptist Convention; its trustees are elected and subject to recall by the convention. The foundation's operating budget, which in 1954 was $18,284.21, is supplied from Tennessee Cooperative Program receipts. As of Dec. 31, 1954, the assets of the foundation totaled $1,092,413.83. Of this amount $661,989.19 was deposited by institutions, and the rest was raised by the foundation itself. In 1954, $32,390.55 was received for capital assets, and income from investments amounted to $43,678.73.

HENRY JEREMIAH HUEY

TENNESSEE BAPTIST HISTORICAL SOCIETY. An organization that exists primarily in the occasional meetings of various successive committees of the Tennessee state board, charged with the responsibility for publishing a history of Tennessee Baptists. W. G. Inman's manuscript, "The Rise and Progress of the Baptist Cause in Tennessee," was submitted in 1910. Later Orren Luico Hailey (*q.v.*) was employed to write a history. His manuscript was accepted and filed in 1930. O. W. Taylor began work on a history, under the employment of the board, in 1951 after he had retired from the editorship of the *Baptist and Reflector.* The manuscript of the first volume was finished in 1956, and subsequent volumes were being planned. In addition, the society holds a collection of primary materials on Tennessee Baptist history that has been assembled during recent years. It includes Baptist papers, church and associational minutes, and manuscripts.

L. G. FREY

TENNESSEE COLLEGE FOR WOMEN. An institution of higher education for women in Tennessee, authorized by the state Baptist convention, and chartered on Dec. 18, 1905, by the state of Tennessee. The college was located at Murfreesboro on the campus of an early Baptist school called Union University, which had not been in operation for many years. When Tennessee College first opened in Sept., 1907, with George J. Burnett as president, it was housed in a new $60,000 brick building on the 15-acre campus in the heart of town. Its total value at that time was over $100,000. Tennessee College had a junior and a senior college department, and a preparatory section. The student enrolment the first year was 200 of which 132 were boarders. Its first course of study included Latin, Greek, French, German, English, English language and literature, philosophy, Bible, history, economics, and mathematics. In addition, there was a home department as well as departments of music and art and expression.

In the first *Announcement* of the opening of the college, issued in Dec., 1906, C. H. Byrn, president of the board of trustees, wrote: "Never was an institution launched under more favorable conditions." The succeeding years seemed to justify this statement. Within two years the student body had greatly increased and additional courses, including sciences, had been added. Emily H. Dutton came as academic dean. Frances Bohanon, who became instructor in piano, remained with the college throughout the remainder of its existence. In 1906 a $10,000 annex was built providing a gymnasium, several large classrooms, and practice rooms.

In the years that followed, Tennessee College strengthened both its curriculum and its faculty. The preparatory section was discontinued and the other departments developed. Both B.A. and B.S. degrees were offered. An outdoor swimming pool and tennis courts were installed. These, together with a large playing field back of the college, made possible a thorough sports program. Eventually courses in secretarial sciences were offered students who wished business training, and in 1943, in co-operation with the accelerated wartime program then in force, the college opened its first summer quarter. The student body, representing many states, remained comparatively small, and the college became known for the warm, personal attention and homelike, cultural atmosphere it provided.

Although Tennessee College never achieved membership in the Southern Association of Colleges, it did remain on the accredited list. Its graduates obtained higher degrees in such institutions as George Peabody College and Columbia and Harvard universities. Alumnae are represented in almost every area of professional life and denominational service.

In the depression years of the early 1930's, Tennessee College, never possessed of abundant financial resources, suffered a setback from which it could not recover. Changing times and the increasing trend toward coeducation lessened the need for a small college of this type. Enrolment dropped and financial support diminished. When Cumberland University in near-by Lebanon was taken over by the Tennessee Baptist Convention in 1946, Tennessee College had been operating at a deficit for a number of years. It was decided to discontinue the college. The property was sold and all records were transferred to Cumberland.

KATE ELLEN GRUVER

TENNESSEE NORMAL COLLEGE. A school at Fountain City, Tenn., founded c. 1900 as Holbrook Normal College. It was reported in 1901 to be "the only Baptist Normal College in the state, and indeed in the South, and bids fair to become a great Normal like those of the North." The curriculum of music, art, elocution, bookkeeping, shorthand, and telegraphy was taught by 16 teachers and President W. S. Bryan. The school closed about 1910 for lack of support. LYNN EDWARD MAY, JR.

TENNESSEE VALLEY INSTITUTE. A school at Evansville, Tenn., established as a "feeder" for Carson-Newman College *c.* 1897. The academy was the property of Tennessee Valley Association and was directed by a President Cheek.

LYNN EDWARD MAY, JR.

TERRILL COLLEGE. A school at Decherd, Tenn., established *c.* 1889. An enrolment of 200 and a faculty of 10 were reported in 1891. It became an academy in 1895 and ceased to exist soon afterward. LYNN EDWARD MAY, JR.

TEXAS, BAPTIST GENERAL ASSOCIATION OF. A Texas general body organized in 1868 at Chatfield, Navarro County, and having as one of its major purposes the support of Waco University against the rival claims of the older Baylor University at Independence for the support of all Texas Baptists. The general association grew out of an earlier organization which began at Larissa, Cherokee County, in 1853 as the Baptist General Association of Texas and which on May 24, 1855, became the Baptist Convention of Eastern Texas. This body, which covered a territory in east central Texas generally north and east of the territory of the Baptist State Convention of Texas, was founded to provide a more equitable distribution of mission activity than that of the state convention, which was primarily interested in the West. This frictional issue later turned into the conflict over rival educational institutions.

The general association began with four boards —missionary, Bible, colportage, and Sunday school—but eventually all were merged into a board of missions. Unlike the Texas state convention, the general association sought no outside financial aid. Throughout its 18 years of regular meetings, the general association generated an extraordinary interest in evangelism, as exemplified in William Evander Penn (*q.v.*), and was quite successful in winning the great numbers of settlers which came into north and central Texas during the period. In addition the general association assisted the Buckner Orphans' Home at Dallas, and paralleled the state convention in ardor for education and missions. It reported $15,175.18 total collections in 1885 as compared to $29,203.30 reported by the state convention the same year. The Southern Baptist Convention met in its territory in 1874 at Jefferson, Tex., and in 1883 at Waco, Tex. In 1886 it entered the merger which produced the Baptist General Convention of Texas. J. M. DAWSON

TEXAS, BAPTIST GENERAL CONVENTION OF.

I. Baptist Beginnings. Freeman Smalley, a native of Ohio or Pennsylvania, upon his arrival at Pecan Point on the Red River in 1822, is known to have preached a sermon in the home of William Newman. It is believed by many that this was the first Baptist sermon in Texas. Joseph Bays, born in North Carolina, a friend of Moses Austin, father of Stephen F. Austin, may have preached somewhat earlier. It is certain that he delivered the first Baptist sermon heard west of the Brazos, in the home of Moses Shipman, near San Felipe in 1823. Bays was attempting to start missionary effort but was interrupted by the Mexican authorities, who were determined to enforce the law against any but Roman Catholic worship. He then retired to Sabine Parish, La., where he had previously labored while waiting for Stephen Austin's colony to be admitted, and where he had frequently crossed the Texas border to the home of Joseph Hinds to conduct Baptist worship. In Hinds's home a Universalist preacher, Billie Cook, was converted and baptized. Bays and his son fought at San Jacinto, and afterward Sam Houston, president of the Texas Republic, appointed him commissioner to the Cherokee Indians.

Before the Texas revolution of 1836, other Baptists in the colonies asserted their faith. In 1829 Shipman again opened his home for a Baptist sermon, preached by Thomas Hanks, when James D. Allcorn, afterward a deacon in the Independence Church, made a profession and was later baptized. Mrs. Massie Millard, living north of Nacogdoches in 1832–33, conducted a prayer meeting in a thicket where her company sought safety from the Indians. Isaac Reed came out from Tennessee in 1834 and preached in East Texas till his death in the '50's. He opposed all missionary organization. Abner Smith, more definitely antimissionary, brought a church of so-called primitive character from Alabama in 1834, settling on the Colorado River near Bastrop. Probably the most publicized of the "bodily removed" churches into the Roman Catholic territory was that of Daniel Parker's Pilgrim Church from Crawford County, Ill., Jan. 20, 1834. Strongly predestinarian in creed, it proclaimed the "Two Seed Doctrine," a particularly rigid form of double predestination. Despite this church's opposition to missions, it organized nine new churches during its 34 years' meandering existence, at no time with a settled home, though continuously operating in East Texas. Parker participated in the consultation meetings of the colonists preceding the Texas revolution. He was elected to the congress of the Texas Republic in 1839 but was found ineligible to a seat under the state constitution, which forbade preachers to serve.

Thomas J. Pilgrim (*q.v.*), a young schoolteacher from New York, thought a Sunday school might escape prohibition by the Roman Catholic authorities. In 1829 at San Felipe, in a log room 18 x 22, he gathered 32 pupils. In the same year a similar school began at El Caney near Wharton in the home of an unbaptized Baptist believer, William Kincheloe, and one at Matagorda was functioning. But the Mexican National Church construed Sunday schools of the Pilgrim variety undesirable, and they were discontinued.

The rising revolutionary spirit in the period immediately preceding independence emboldened the Baptists throughout the colonies. Some of those outstanding in the war may be mentioned. Noah T. Byars (*q.v.*), of Washington-on-the-Brazos, in whose blacksmith shop the Texas declaration of independence was signed, armorer to General Houston, afterward ordained to the ministry; Wilson Simpson, of Fayette County, who escaped the massacre at Goliad to fight at San Jacinto; A. C. Horton, who also escaped Goliad, subsequently elected lieutenant governor of Texas; Thomas Anderson of Webberville, physician to the Indian victim, Josiah Wilbarger; Gail Borden, Jr. (*q.v.*) of Galveston, editor of the first Texas newspaper, *Texas Telegraph,* 1835 and onward, famed as manufacturer of condensed milk; the Bowles family, afterward charter members of First Church, Houston; Arthur Burns, first child born in Gonzales; Mrs. Goldsby Childress, mother of George C. Childress, author of the Texas declaration of independence; J. P. Coles and family, with Austin's first 300; William B. Dewees, author of *Letters from an Early Texas Settler;* Judge Richard Ellis, president of the Texas constitutional convention,. 1836; the J. L. Ellis family, ancestors of several preachers; David S. Kornegay, member of the La Grange Volunteers and a hero of San Jacinto; Samuel E. Pearce, preacher with descendants in the Baptist ministry; George Webb Slaughter, scout of General Houston, father of C. C. Slaughter (*q.v.*), preacher to ranchmen; Eli Mercer, who fought in the battle of San Jacinto, a cousin of Jesse Mercer (*q.v.*), the Georgia Baptist philanthropist; many others unidentified as Baptists because there were no churches for them to join, and many predisposed but uncommitted, who like General Houston later united with the Baptists.

Because of his extensive creative labors and his charming reminiscent book, *Flowers and Fruits,* Zacharius N. Morrell (*q.v.*), who came out from Tennessee in 1835 in search of health, stands as the most cherished of the Baptist pioneers. On his prospecting journey he visited Baptist acquaintances near the present city of Marlin and on Little River, scarcely suspecting that within a few weeks many of them would be slain by the Comanche Indians, especially the Parkers, who had barricaded themselves in a fort of their construction. Returning to Tennessee for his family, Morrell paused on Jan. 10, 1836, at Nacogdoches, where he felt impelled to preach to a hastily summoned crowd on a street corner from the text, "The wilderness and solitary place shall be glad for them, and the desert shall blossom as the rose."

First church organization.—Washington claimed the first regular missionary Baptist church in Texas, which was constituted by Morrell in 1837. Acting with him were J. R. Jenkins, N. T. Byars, A. Buffington and wife, and H. R. Cartmell. Soon afterward the church named Jenkins, Buffington, and Cartmell "to correspond with mission boards North and East and request that Texas be taken into consideration as a mission field." Among papers endorsing the appeal to the American Baptist Home Mission Society was the *Christian Index* of Georgia, the editor of which, Jesse Mercer (*q.v.*), was president of the board of the Triennial Convention (foreign missions) in Boston. James Huckins (*q.v.*), the first missionary of the Home Mission Society to Texas, landed in Galveston in Jan., 1840. Jesse Mercer (died Aug., 1841) bequeathed 25 shares in the Bank of Georgia (presumably $2,500) to the society for its missions in Texas. The will was contested by relatives. In 1846 the society, in the settlement, received $1,331.87.

Plum Grove Church in Bastrop County, under the leadership of Deacon William Scallorn, supported missions against strong antimissionism. Among the earliest ordained to the ministry were

Noah T. Byars, A. Buffington, and Richard Ellis (not to be confused with Judge Ellis).

On Aug. 31, 1839, Thomas Spraggins instituted Independence Church in Washington County, "cradle of Texas Baptists." Joining with him were John, Ivy, Mary, and Jeannette McNeese; J. J. and Biddy Davis; Thomas and Martha Tremmier. They were soon reinforced by a layman, O. H. P. Garrett, and two preachers, J. L. Davis and Jeremiah Vardeman (*q.v.*), with their families. Into this church were baptized James D. and Lydia Allcorn, converted under Hanks's sermon at Shipman's home back in 1829. Independence steadily forged to the forefront of all the churches in missionary, educational, and denominational leadership.

Upon taking up his duties as missionary of the Home Missionary Society, New York, James Huckins, a native of New Hampshire and graduate of Brown University, in 1840 organized First Baptist Church, Galveston. A little later he constituted First Baptist Church, Houston. He reported that immigrants were pouring in at the rate of 50,000 a year and clamoring for religious care. On tours through 15 years, he established many other churches before he moved to Charleston, S. C. William M. Tryon (*q.v.*), of New York state, came out as the second Home Mission Society representative in 1841. Upon advice of Huckins, he proceeded to Independence, where he became pastor and served as chaplain in the congress of the republic. Tryon's zeal and ability were much esteemed, and Baptist felt great loss when he died in 1847 of yellow fever while ministering to the stricken in his Houston church. He, more than any single individual, is credited with the founding of Baylor University and with naming it.

Associations.—In 1840, upon invitation of Independence Church, 25 messengers assembled with a view to inaugurating an association. Prolonged debate ensued over the proposed articles of faith and constitution. T. W. Cox, the pastor, refused to endorse them. On Oct. 8 of the same year, at Travis, however, messengers from Independence, Travis, and La Grange churches organized the Union or United Association, despite the fact that Cox was pastor of all three churches represented. The following year Clear Creek Church at La Grange, of which Cox was both a member and pastor, excluded him on grounds of advocating doctrines of Alexander Campbell and sustaining an unsavory reputation in Alabama. Z. N. Morrell presided at the conference. The action precipitated division in the churches at Independence and Travis, resulting in withdrawals and new churches which chose Cox for their pastor; but Tryon soon healed the breach in the older bodies. Such troubles had previously caused men like Morrell, in co-operation with conservatives in other denominations, to form a committee for the protection of their churches against inroads by imposters. Cox, though a man of talent, faded from the scene. Union Association, flourishing through the years, is today, though curtailed somewhat in territory, still one of the largest of Baptist district associations.

At the Clear Creek session of Union Association in 1841, Tryon induced the messengers to form an education society which became the mother of Baylor University, chartered by the Republic of Texas in 1845 at Independence. At the same meeting the zealous pioneers began the Texas Home Mission Society, auxiliary to the New York agency, and designated Morrell, Byars, and Buffington as their missionaries.

With the annexation of Texas in 1845 and the triumph of the United States in the war with Mexico, there began a great influx of ordained ministers from the other states, who supplied the multiplying Texas churches with pastors. J. W. D. Creath of Virginia went to Huntsville, P. B. Chandler of Georgia to La Grange, R. H. Taliaferro of Kentucky to Austin, William M. Pickett of Kentucky to Clarksville, Noah Hill of Georgia to Matagorda, Hosea Garrett to Chappell Hill, John Brice to Marshall, W. H. Ray to Tyler. Judge Robert Emmett Bledsoe Baylor (*q.v.*), on hand from Alabama and living at La Grange, held court by day and preached by night over an extended area. D. B. Morrill and J. H. Stribling, among the first graduates of Baylor, entered upon careers of unusual significance.

State convention.—In 1848 messengers from 35 churches in four associations, meeting at Anderson, organized the Baptist State Convention of Texas. Z. N. Morrell, in the introductory sermon, sounded the keynote. H. L. Graves, president of Baylor, was selected to head the new body. Rufus C. Burleson (*q.v.*), successor to Tryon in the Houston pastorate, accepted the responsible office of corresponding secretary, which involved long itineraries and onerous administrative tasks. He rendered this service with such distinction that in 1851 he was selected to undertake the direction of the sinking Baylor University, which he succeeded in reviving.

The state convention greatly stimulated activity. Its missionary, Noah T. Byars, founded First Baptist Church, Waco, and pushed on ultimately to constitute about 60 churches, among them churches at Belton and Brownwood. United States Senator Sam Houston (*q.v.*), baptized by Burleson at Independence in 1854, proposed missions to the Indians, but his recommendation caused only a futile attempt to establish the Brazos River Institute, a school for the Comanches. Due to clamant calls from the west, the convention concentrated on that section. Pastor G. G. Baggerly of Tyler vigorously attacked the western policy, and those sympathetic with him formed the Texas Baptist General Association in 1853 at Larissa in Cherokee County. Two years later it changed its name to the Baptist Convention of Eastern Texas and launched Tyler Baptist University. In 1867 it assumed the name of the Baptist General Association of Texas.

The growth of the period may be seen in the rapid organization of new associations. In addition to the four which participated in the first state convention—Union (1840), Colorado

(1847), Eastern Missionary (1847), and Trinity (1848)—others were organized, as follows: Red River (1848), Elm Fork (1849), Eastern Texas United (1849), Cherokee (1851), Bethlehem (1852), Sister Grove (1853), Judson (1853), West Fork (1855), Little River (1855), Rehoboth (1856), Austin (1857), Mt. Zion (1857), Richland (1857), Tryon (1858), Leon River (1858), Saline (1858), Brazos River (1858), San Antonio River (1858), San Marcos (1858), New Bethel (1860), and Waco (1860). Such expansion was based on the large immigration flowing into the state and illustrated the alertness of the Baptists in capturing and conserving the new recruits.

Awakening concern for Christian education, deepened by a sense of the state's failure to furnish worthy public schools, prompted several associations to start their own. In 1859 Sister Grove Association opened Ladonia Institute, which suspended in 1865 but reopened in 1867, owing much to its benefactor, W. B. Featherstone. A similar school, Concrete College at Cuero, proved useful in the same period. Pennington College in Trinity County likewise assisted in the education of boys and girls. Bosqueville Male and Female College, near Waco, was presided over by S. G. O'Bryan, a former teacher at Baylor University at Independence and later pastor of First Church, Waco. Such schools continued to originate throughout Texas after what might properly be called the era of beginnings.

Sunday schools.—In spite of the present lively interest of the Texas Baptists in Christian education and the fact that a Baptist deacon, William Fox of London, was one of the originators of the modern Sunday school, it is surprising that the churches showed such little interest in them during the first quarter century of organized endeavor. Sparse settlements, inadequate housing, and lack of literature may have explained this situation. In 1851 Thomas J. Pilgrim, who started Sunday schools in Texas, reported to the Colorado Association the existence of 5 Methodist and 24 Union Sunday schools in all Texas, but no Baptist ones. He strongly recommended co-operation with existing schools. The Baptists, always commending Sunday schools and continuing to explore the possibilities, seem not to have set themselves to providing such religious education until after the Civil War. In Aug., 1865, Union Association, R. E. B. Baylor presiding, put in motion a movement which resulted in the first Sunday School Convention at Independence in October of that year. To its instructional work was added colportage, and from that date onward enthusiasm prevailed.

Denominational papers.—At the organization of Union Association in 1840, the question of a Baptist newspaper arose, but the group decided it unwise to undertake one at that time. Meantime *The Baptist Banner and Western Pioneer* of Louisville and *The Southwestern Baptist Chronicle* of New Orleans received official approval. With the organization of the state convention in 1848, J. W. Barnes urged the institution of a paper, but the next year the convention still deemed the undertaking inadvisable. By 1852 the convention stood ready to commit itself to establishing a publication, and in 1853 it voted to launch *The Texas Baptist* at Independence, if a publisher could be found. In 1855, after repeated attempts to secure the necessary funds for printing, it gave assurances of co-operation to G. W. Baines and a private publisher at Anderson in projecting *The Texas Baptist* there, with J. B. Stiteler as assistant editor. Maintenance in succeeding years remained difficult, but the paper found favor. During the Civil War it was suspended. The next venture, *The Texas Baptist Herald*, J. B. Link, editor, issued from Houston, Dec. 13, 1865, and served more than any of several sporadic sheets which were somewhat local in nature as a general organ with wide acceptance, obtaining not only official endorsement but financial assistance from devoted individuals. The demand for a denominational newspaper stemmed from a profound realization of the need for a distinct Baptist witness in the printed word and of a need for a means of publicizing and supporting Baptist missions and Baylor University. To help supply general reading, Union Association established a depository of books at Independence, which was well patronized, and colporteurs sold books directly to homes.

Effects of Civil War.—At the outbreak of the Civil War, two general bodies and 24 associations covered most of the state, with the membership of the churches exceeding 50,000. Aside from work among the soldiers of the South, extension of religious effort practically ceased. The Baptist Governor Houston, a strong Unionist, suffered impeachment because of his resistance to Texas' joining the Confederacy and died before his time, July 26, 1863, from weariness and heartache. While Baptists with virtual unanimity supported the Confederacy, they suffered serious division among themselves over Baylor University, when President Burleson and his faculty left Independence in 1861 to take over Waco University. Amid the reigning desolation toward the end of the war, the bare survival of the churches was a significant achievement.

First Negro church.—Prior to the end of the war, the Negroes had joined white churches and worshiped with the regular congregation, seated in assigned sections of the meetinghouse. Not a half dozen Negro preachers could be counted in the state. From the beginning of Baptist mission work in Texas, concern for the spiritual welfare of the Negroes had often been the subject of committee report and the occasion of solicitude in the associations and conventions. In the main throughout the war, the relation between the white people and the slaves in the churches had been almost normal, with many instances of beautiful devotion on the part of the servants toward their masters. After the war separation of the races in the churches seemed desirable, first, to the Negroes, who wished to express their independence; and, next, to the whites, who thought it better for the Negroes to control and direct their own religious affairs, though always assured of sympathy and aid from their white brethren. The first Negro church in Texas was organized by I. S. Campbell, a Negro Baptist minister sent by the Ohio convention. This was the Avenue L Church in Galveston, constituted as a freedman's church in 1865. The Negroes subsequently organized associations and conventions along the lines of white Baptists and fared no better in respect to preserving ideal unity. They patronized Bishop College at Marshall, the gift of a New York Baptist in 1870 as a result of an appeal mainly from Burleson.

II. History of General Convention. *Origin.*—In varied, far-spreading Texas, almost 50 years intervened between organization of the first Baptist church at Washington-on-the-Brazos in 1837 and achievement of general organizational unity in 1886. Diverse interests, however, could not prevent the desired end. Formal unity came at length in the consolidation of the Baptist State Convention, organized at Anderson in 1848, and the Baptist General Association of Texas, originally constituted at Larissa in 1853, under the fused name of the Baptist General Convention of Texas in 1886 at Waco. The merger enabled Texas Baptists thereafter to demonstrate over a thousand-mile area, east and west, north and south, the power of principles and policies more or less unitedly supported, resulting in the largest success, measured in number of churches and ministers and amount of financial contributions, reached by any state or provincial Baptist general body in the world.

The pastor of First Church, Waco, B. H. Carroll (*q.v.*), took the initial step toward this union by inducing the general association in its session at Cleburne, July 23, 1883, to propose that each of the five general bodies of Baptists in Texas be requested to appoint a committee of five to confer on the expediency of uniting. His resolution deplored the fact that overlapping organizations caused confusion in councils, tended to factionalism, and developed sectionalism. Perhaps for prudential reasons he omitted mention of the major conflict which had arisen in the existing situation, namely: whether the state convention's Baylor University at Independence or the general association's Waco University should be recognized as the one educational institution supported by the majority throughout Texas. The view that Baptists should undertake only one university, commonly held in most states, at the time when Texas was establishing a state university and other public schools, received unusual favor out of fear that tax-supported schools might eliminate all church schools, if more than one were attempted.

Carroll's proposal aroused profound interest among the churches. Almost immediately the North Texas Convention dissolved, permitting its adherents to go where they wished, and East Texas Convention two years later formally joined the state convention. Strangely, the latter at first practically ignored the approach to unity. Ardently pursuing the matter, however, the general association in its meeting at Ennis, July, 1885, adopted extended resolutions offered by S. A. Hayden, urging the combining of both schools and general organizations. The association went further and appointed its president, L. L. Foster, together with S. L. Morris and Henry Furman, to visit the forthcoming state convention at Lampasas in October and present the appeal.

The state convention, meeting as scheduled, on motion of G. W. Smith, enthusiastically voted to appoint a committee of five "to confer with any like committee that may have been, or may hereafter be appointed by other bodies, and report some suitable expression from this body on this subject of consolidation of our missionary bodies in the state." Aware of the prevailing anxiety about conserving the interests of both existing schools, the general association, on resolution by Hayden, assured the friends of Waco University that there was no design to injure that institution; and the state convention adopted a report on the expected removal of Baylor University, assuring that all endowment and property funds would be faithfully preserved as Baylor's own.

Terms of merger.—The long-gathering sentiment for unification then began to crystallize into quick action. Within a few weeks after the 1885 sessions of the two bodies, their respective committees assembled in Temple on Dec. 9 to work out details of the consolidation which all now took for granted. Somewhat hurriedly the executive board of the state convention and the board of trustees of Baylor University and Baylor Female College had convened at Brenham in late October and acquiesced in the expressions of the Lampasas meeting. Apparently all misgivings over past failures of joint committees to agree, as in the serious effort at Bremond in 1875, frequently referred to as "the light that failed," were brushed aside, and the state convention stood convinced. For the Temple conference it sent 25 of its most trusted leaders. The general association sent 31.

Addressing itself first to the basic school question, the Temple joint committee, upon recommendation of a subcommittee of ten, voted:

1. That Waco and Baylor University be consolidated.

2. That the name of the school shall be Baylor University.

3. That Baylor University be located at Waco, and we further agree that the female department be continued there as it now exists.

Provided, that Waco gives as a bonus: (1) The old buildings and grounds of Waco University; (2) The $60,000 already secured for an endowment; (3) Forty-five thousand dollars additional building fund; and (4) Twenty acres of ground suitable for a new site for the University. Provided, further, that at the expiration of ten years the continuance of the system of co-education at Waco be determined by a majority of the consolidated general body, to which the institution, with its funds and property shall belong.

4. That, as very many Baptists oppose co-education, Baylor Female College be located at some central point, the place where located to give as a bonus at

least suitable grounds and buildings. And that Baylor Female College, thus located, be also the property of the consolidated general body.

5. That the endowment of the present Baylor University go to Waco with the new Baylor University, according to the terms agreed upon by the State Convention, and published in their minutes.

By special resolution it was added that "the alumnae and alumni of both Baylor and Waco University be made and reported in the catalogue and the new consolidated University, as alumnae and alumni of it." The new school, Baylor University at Waco, was chartered Aug. 6, 1886. The charter of Baylor University (1845–95) was renewed for another 50 years, Jan. 25, 1895. The name of *Baylor University at Waco* was changed July 16, 1936, to *Baylor University*.

The school question being settled, the whole committee next adopted the recommendation offered by the committee of five from each of the general bodies, as follows:

1. That the Baptist General Association be consolidated with the Baptist State Convention of Texas.

2. That the name of the consolidated body shall be "The Baptist General Convention of Texas."

3. That the basis of representation in the first meeting of the consolidated body shall be the same as heretofore (i.e., as in each of the former bodies).

The first meeting was set for Waco on Tuesday before the first Sunday in July, 1886. On motion of Hayden, the joint conference committee voted that the phraseology used in the name of the new convention was "an accommodation to the legal status of affairs and not in any sense to be construed as an invasion of the equality of the two bodies entering into the consolidation."

The convention in Waco, June 29, 1886, ratified the actions of the joint committee in Temple. In deference to the former older body, the new convention elected A. T. Spalding, pastor, First Church, Galveston, president; but, respecting the former younger body, the convention chose its A. J. Holt as superintendent of missions and corresponding secretary.

Constitution.—For the formulation of its fundamental law, the convention appointed B. H. Carroll, F. M. Law, R. T. Hanks, W. H. Dodson, and E. Z. F. Golden. The salient features of the constitution, as adopted, were patterned closely after the constitution of the Baptist State Convention of 1848, and are as follows:

Article I, Section 2. The objects of this Convention shall be Missionary and Educational, the promotion of harmony of feeling and concert of action among Baptists, and a system of operative measures for the promotion of the interest of the Redeemer's Kingdom; but no individual enterprise shall be formally entertained or acted upon by this body.

Article II, Section 1. This body shall be composed of messengers from regular Baptist Churches, and Associations of Baptist Churches, and Baptist Missionary Societies, co-operating with the Convention.

Section 2. Each church shall be entitled to two Messengers, and one additional Messenger for each $25 contributed to the funds of the Convention, and in no case shall any one Church be entitled to more than eight Messengers. [Similar provisions applied to associations and missionary societies, but the money condition was subsequently eliminated.]

Article III, Section 2. The Convention does not have, and shall never attempt to exercise, a single attribute of power or authority over any Church, but it cheerfully recognizes the absolute sovereignty of the Churches.

At this first session the last clause of Section 2 of Article I of the constitution was put to the test. In the spirit of unification prevailing, all hoped that the two rival newspapers might be combined. Editor J. B. Link accordingly volunteered to sell his *Texas Baptist Herald* to Editor S. A. Hayden of *The Texas Baptist,* but the convention did not presume to pass upon the transaction, although, at the request of Hayden, it did voice its opinion by a narrow majority that the publication should issue from Dallas, even if convention headquarters were established in Waco.

An alleged extraconstitutional matter, but construed as a proper interest of the group, came to the fore when James Britton Cranfill (*q.v.*), in connection with the report on temperance, asked endorsement of the declaration, "The old slogan, 'Moral Suasion,' has ceased to be potent . . . no man can be in favor of moral suasion unless he is also in favor of legal suasion." The convention approved, and this action initiated the memorable campaign of 1887 for state prohibition in which Carroll led the citizen voters very near to success.

Under specific provisions of the constitution, the convention launched its program with a board of directors consisting of 30 members, a board of trustees for the convention, two college boards, and a ministers' relief board. To insure adequate attention to mission interests, it appointed R. R. White to act as agent for the Southern Baptist Home Mission Board and James Milton Carroll (*q.v.*) as agent for the Southern Baptist Foreign Mission Board. At the same time it elected J. B. Cranfill to promote state missions and H. M. Burroughs to foster ministerial relief. It also recognized special agents for the two Baylors and the Southern Baptist Theological Seminary.

Confident outlook.—With harmony and co-operation established, the first year of the convention set a new pace of progress. Waco fulfilled its pledges to Baylor University. Belton, on promise of ample grounds and a fine stone building, claimed the Baylor Female College, with John Hill Luther as president. Probably the total membership in the churches at the beginning approximated 100,000. The two Sunday school conventions coalesced and aided greatly in recruiting the ranks. The Woman's Missionary Union, auxiliary to the state convention (1880), and the Ladies General Aid Society in Northeast Texas united in 1886 to form the Baptist Women Mission Workers and reinforced the full program. In 1919 the name was changed to Woman's

Missionary Union, auxiliary to the Baptist General Convention of Texas. Secretary Holt reported 3,015 converts, 128 new churches organized, and 124 new Sunday schools. The board of directors employed 120 missionaries, with several allotted to the Negroes, who had an estimated 50,000 members in their churches; also some were assigned to work among Germans and Mexicans. The convention steadily improved along these lines for a decade.

Meanwhile the policy of maintaining only one college underwent radical revision. Between 1890 and 1891 several new colleges were originated —Simmons at Abilene, Howard Payne at Brownwood, one at Jacksboro, another at Decatur— and talk spread of yet others to be founded at Greenville and Rusk. Coincidentally Baylor University staggered under alarming debt occasioned by drought, diminished attendance, and deepening financial depression. Only the most heroic efforts of Carroll, chairman of the trustees, assisted by an eloquent young newcomer from North Carolina, George Washington Truett (*q.v.*), availed to save foreclosure.

An evil omen on the horizon, too, appeared when R. T. Hanks, pastor of First Church, Dallas, and S. A. Hayden became involved in a newspaper controversy. Hanks, by purchasing the local *Baptist News* from Lewis Holland of Ladonia and moving it to Dallas, offered rebuttal of charges against him published by Hayden in *The Texas Baptist and Herald*. Gradually the nucleus of creative leaders of the convention, never hoping for uniformity but still confident that co-operative unity was possible, determined to fight for it. The Hayden-Hanks controversy grew more bitter, and secretary J. B. Cranfill announced his resignation and his purpose to work for peace. He bought out Hanks's paper, changed its name to *The Baptist Standard*, and removed it to Waco. He started his crusade for reconciliation by associating with himself the peaceful M. V. Smith. He also persuaded B. H. Carroll, cherished by both sides as the ablest religious statesman in the denomination, to supply a weekly sermon along constructive lines.

Trouble with Hayden.—To the grief of the leaders of the peace movement, Hayden attacked Cranfill's secretarial administration and then turned on J. M. Carroll, his successor in office. Fearing he might complicate the work of his brother by personal relationship, B. H. Carroll resigned as president of the convention's board of directors. The board submitted answers to the charges published by Hayden. When it became evident that the board meant to stand by its servants, Hayden put forth a theory of "church sovereignty" as opposed to what he termed "the rule of boards." The convention at Belton in 1895 countered with a definite statement in amplification of its constitution: "The Convention is composed of persons chosen by churches, associations and missionary societies as their messengers, and that when said persons are convened they, and not the churches, are the Convention."

These measures in no way mollified Hayden. At Houston in 1896, he all but monopolized the annual session by pressing his charges. Feeling that patience had ceased to be a virtue, the board, through its president, W. H. Jenkins, and its secretary, George W. Truett, presented what was intended to be a devastating answer to every charge brought by Hayden. Five members of the board—indicative of the real minority character of the opposition—protested the answer. After five days of stormy debate, the convention adjourned in something akin to frustration.

Pronounced opposition to Hayden's strategy asserted itself in San Antonio the next year. Both Cranfill and Carroll had resigned from office because of persistent attack, and the later secretary, M. D. Early, sick in body and spirit, had stepped down. When Hayden arrived at the convention, the credentials committee informed him that his seat had been challenged. He demanded that he be heard. He was granted 45 minutes, and W. H. Jenkins took 35 minutes for reply. The vote stood 582 to 102 for expulsion. Still unconvinced, he sought admittance at Waco in 1898 and again at Dallas in 1899, only to be denied by a larger majority each time. Then he instituted suit for $100,000 damages, naming key leaders, including millionaire C. C. Slaughter; but after four years of legal battle, he failed to gain any financial advantage, although the suit was settled by Cranfill, Apr. 28, 1905, "without the knowledge, consent or cooperation, fraternally, financially or otherwise, of any of the defendants. . . ."

The end of the century.—The positive element received powerful reinforcement in the person of James Bruton Gambrell (*q.v.*), who had resigned, in June, 1896, the presidency of Mercer University. On Dec. 1, 1896, he became superintendent of missions. One of his many gifts was a talent for pungent writing. As editor of the *Missionary Worker*, organ of the board, and in other capacities from this date onward until his death in 1921, he was one of the convention's most influential servants. The troubled period came to a close by 1900, and it appeared that afflictions of the Baptists called forth surprising spiritual blessings. The convention at long last had cleared the way of obstructionists to its growing program. By the severest of tests, it had demonstrated its indestructibility and vindicated its desire for harmony and co-operation. Paradoxically, throughout the ordeal its institutions had prospered, evangelism continued; giving, too, increased greatly, and the membership advanced to 200,000, exclusive of Negroes in their own conventions.

Further progress.—With the beginning of the new century, the convention strengthened its policy of unification. As early as 1892, it had placed all its missions—state, home, foreign— under the direction of a single secretary. In 1893 the ministerial relief board yielded to the control of the board of directors. In 1900 the Sunday school convention consented to the same management, as did also the Baptist Young People's

Union, organized in Fort Worth in 1891. Buckner Orphans' Home had not as yet offered itself to the convention, but it enjoyed the general and generous support of the co-operating churches.

The multiplying number of Baptist schools constituted the convention's most acute problem. To those already named were added Canadian Academy, Goodnight Academy, Bryan Woman's College, Palacios Academy, Wayland College at Plainview, San Marcos Academy, the College of Marshall, and a school starting at Jacksonville. To cope with total debts against them, amounting to $212,000, and to guard against potential disunity, J. M. Carroll proposed the establishment of the Education Commission. C. C. Slaughter approved and challenged with a gift of $25,000, conditioned on a statewide campaign for debt liquidation. John D. Rockefeller in New York contributed $35,000. B. H. Carroll resigned his Waco pastorate, which he had held for 28 years, to help save the schools. The needed sum was raised, and the schools entered into a correlated system, with Baylor University at the head. This device worked fairly well while it lasted.

Seeing the necessity for endowment, the convention in 1905 elected J. M. Carroll as secretary of the Education Commission to seek it. He associated with himself two young Baylor graduates, I. E. Gates and J. M. Dawson, and the enterprise met favor. Upon J. M. Carroll's retirement Samuel Palmer Brooks (*q.v.*), president of Baylor University, undertook the task. During Brooks's 29-year tenure as president (1902–31), he advanced the institution from the status of a small college to that of a strong university. In 1902 F. L. Carroll of Waco and his son, George W. Carroll of Beaumont (no relation to the Carroll brothers, B. H. and J. M.), presented Baylor with a library building and a science hall, recognized as the largest donations yet made to education in Texas. No doubt this university, which has largely supplied Texas Baptists with their ministerial and missionary force and furnished the state with leaders in all fields, helped to account for Texas Baptists' strong position in their state.

Southwestern Baptist Theological Seminary.—In 1907 B. H. Carroll asked the convention to separate the Baylor Theological Seminary from Baylor University in order to launch the Southwestern Baptist Theological Seminary. He had taught the Bible to students in the university during his Waco pastorate and in 1905 had led in establishing the Baylor Theological Seminary. The convention endorsed his plea for a larger, independent institution for supplying the demand for trained pastors. In 1910 the seminary was moved from Waco to Fort Worth. Before Carroll's death in 1914, he built the new seminary into the promise of what it has since become, the largest evangelical seminary in the world. Under his successor, Lee Rutland Scarborough (*q.v.*), the Southern Baptist Convention in 1925 acquired ownership and control.

Hospitals added.—In 1907 the convention added hospitals to its program—Memorial of Houston, started by D. R. Peveto; and Memorial of Dallas, for a time called Baylor University Hospital, now Baylor Hospital, begun by R. C. Buckner, J. B. Cranfill, J. B. Gambrell, and George W. Truett in 1909. Similar institutions at Waco, Abilene, Harlingen, and Beaumont were later accepted. All received encouraging individual donations and substantial support from the churches. Texas Baptists thereafter preached that healing completed the New Testament scope of Christian service expressed in missions, education, and benevolence, as exemplified by Jesus in his ministry described in Matthew 4:23.

Second test of unity.—During World War I and for some years after, the convention again encountered peril of disunity.

The friction in the convention arose over an anti-heresy movement led by J. Frank Norris (*q.v.*), pastor of First Church, Fort Worth. Using his weekly publication, *The Searchlight,* and his radio station, together with his pulpit and extensive speaking itineraries, Norris alleged the convention's schools were teaching evolution and salvation by culture. This caused distress and, in some cases, dismissal of teachers. He also criticized prominent pastors, particularly Texas officials of the Southern Baptist Convention 75 Million Campaign, then in progress. He had previously owned and edited *The Baptist Standard,* but since he was not fully co-operative, the convention bought the paper and appointed its own editors. Eventually on much the same grounds as in the case of Hayden, the convention expelled Norris.

In spite of this burden of controversy, the convention maintained a large program and was quite successful in its work with soldiers. The constituency stood unitedly behind J. B. Gambrell in his winning contention with General Funston of the War Department that the principle of freedom of religion necessarily implied opportunity for Baptists as such to conduct their own religious work among the servicemen. In Texas, where numerous camps held hundreds of thousands of trainees from all states, Baptist chapels multiplied, and their ministers worked with gratifying results. George W. Truett and others answered the call of President Wilson to go overseas and preach to the fighters.

The 75 Million Campaign and aftermath.—With secretary F. S. Groner as chairman, T. V. Neal as state organizer, and J. M. Dawson as publicity director, Texas Baptists pledged $15,000,000 to the 75 Million Campaign during 1919–20. They emerged into a brief period of unprecedented good will and progress. The campaign immediately produced enormous growth. Membership to nearly three quarters of a million in over 3,000 churches, and property values rose markedly. President Scarborough's "calling-out-the-called" canvass brought the seminaries and the colleges more candidates for all kinds of ministry than they could house. Increased enrolment in churches and schools overtaxed limited facilities so that many new buildings had to be erected.

Suddenly with postwar inflation, followed by contracting credits and shrinking collections, enthusiasm cooled into a sobering awareness of the imprudence of overexpansion. Reaction threatened to destroy what had been accomplished. The convention and its institutions owed more than $6,000,000, and local churches, caught in the prevailing excess-building error, staggered under the load of almost hopeless debt. In 1926 at its San Antonio session, the convention, after all-night prayer, resolved upon a conservation campaign. H. L. Kokernot, a benevolent ranchman, set forth with 100 dedicated committeemen, intent upon retiring the debts and stabilizing operations. The identical leaders of the former 75 Million Campaign conducted the effort. Missing was J. B. Gambrell, who had died in 1921; but T. L. Holcomb of Sherman, W. R. White of Lubbock, and J. Howard Williams of Corsicana shouldered responsibilities, as had F. S. Groner upon Gambrell's retirement from the office. Beginning as an up-hill pull against seemingly insuperable odds, the Conservation Campaign gradually gained momentum.

Mr. and Mrs. John G. Hardin.—To the inspiration of the responding churches, an oilman and his wife, Mr. and Mrs. John G. Hardin of Burkburnett, stepped out in the van of large givers. These two gave to Baylor University and its medical college, to Baylor College for Women, to Simmons University, to Howard Payne College, and to the Buckner Orphans' Home a total of $5,000,000, besides leaving a large trust to be administered for convention interests.

To achieve such a large objective as that undertaken in 1926 required years under conditions then existing. Not all the convention's debts were finally retired until 1942. In 1936 the convention joined with all Texas in celebrating the Texas Centennial and put forth a commemorative volume summarizing statistics of a healthy denomination. Fear of disaster had vanished, giving place to a stable sense of assurance. A pleasing evidence of growing unity at this time was an overture from the Baptist Missionary Association, organized at Jack's Creek in 1900 in token of loyalty to Hayden's ideas. Harmony and co-operation existed as never before.

Attitude toward interdenominationalism.—With regard to union with Christians of other denominations, the convention affirmed hearty fraternal relations for all who acknowledged Jesus Christ as Saviour and Lord but declined to assume official connection in organization. During World War II, however, in line with many patriotic gestures offered jointly by the different Christian bodies, Texas Baptists united with others in supporting basic freedoms; they no longer insisted on a strictly Baptist type of ministry to the military forces but emphasized the regular chaplains in the recognized channels: Protestant, Jewish, and Roman Catholic.

Balanced program.—More recently the convention has developed a number of new agencies and has sought through departments to avoid neglect of any interest or overlapping. In its promotion of unity and co-operation, it has centered more and more control and direction in its executive board and its finance, budget, and executive committees. In its endeavor to function for "Enlightenment, Enlistment and Enlargement," as enunciated by George W. McDaniel (*q.v.*) while pastor at Temple in 1901, it has since steadily given attention to measures judged essential to these three ends. To facilitate the execution of the slogan, it approves a missionary for each of the 17 districts, each composed of several associations. Once a quarter the state executive secretary publishes a list of all gifts from the churches by districts. This information appears in *The Baptist Standard,* which, under the editorship of David Gardner, attained a circulation of over 300,000 and continues to advance with E. S. James as editor.

The convention constantly aims at giving to outside interests as much as to state enterprises, especially emphasizing home and foreign missions. The Southern Baptist Relief and Annuity Board, established in 1918 with headquarters in Dallas, in charge of William Lunsford (*q.v.*), former pastor of First Church, Waco, has from the first enjoyed powerful aid from local business personnel as well as funds from the churches. The Southern Baptist Sunday School Board has won loyal support from the convention for its liberal assistance to Texas missions. In 1949, after some years of co-operative proprietorship, the Sunday School Board acquired its first retail book store in Dallas and has since added stores at Fort Worth, Austin, Lubbock, San Antonio, and Houston.

In Texas several phases of Baptist activities adopted generally have first been noted. The Department of Student Work, under the name Baptist Student Union, came into being in 1920, with J. P. Boone as state secretary, two years prior to its formal launching by the Southern Baptist Sunday School Board under Frank H. Leavell (*q.v.*), Convention-wide secretary. The Baptist Foundation of Texas, a corporation, was created by the convention in 1930 to handle endowment trust funds. Preceded by North Carolina and Virginia, it has enlisted the capabilities of outstanding laymen in a manner to encourage other states and the Southern Baptist Convention to follow suit. Its first secretary was George J. Mason.

In 1945 the convention instituted a department of music; in 1946 it established a department of evangelism; in 1950, the Christian Life Commission; in 1952, an organization dealing with church loans; and in 1952, work in public relations, outfitted with a secretary, staff, and extensive equipment for press releases and for radio broadcasts. In 1938 the convention inaugurated an endowment agency with J. W. Bruner in charge, having as its purpose the securing of funds through wills, trusts, and gifts. By 1954 this agency reported endowment for institutions had increased to $23,000,000 and property values to more than $60,000,000. While a policy of undesignated contributions through a unified budget in each local church is strongly advocated, the convention gives ample opportunity for individual, specified donations, and some large ones have resulted. Each department of work has produced an extensive literature descriptive of its work, notably the endowment agency.

To implement its oft-asserted conviction that missions must ever be central in its concerns, the convention in 1950 founded the Department of Direct Missions for the purpose of cultivating urban and rural areas and all elements in the population, irrespective of race. It supplements the salaries of 17 district and 30 associational missionaries, sustains superintendents in cities exceeding 100,000, and aids on the average of 125 mission churches each year. The department assists churches to buy sites and devise suitable building plans. The Spanish staff maintains headquarters in San Antonio near the Mexican Bible Institute and the Mexican Orphanage, in easy access to the Valley Academy at Brownsville and the institute for training at El Paso.

While the convention usually accords prime rank to its executive secretary, the president comes next in order. The first president (1886–89), Albert T. Spalding, was pastor of First Church, Galveston. L. L. Foster, a lawyer, served from 1890 to 1891. R. C. Burleson, president of Baylor University, took over in 1892. In that year the convention turned to R. C. Buckner, honored for his work with orphans, and continued him for 20 years until he resigned with the exhortation that no man should be perpetuated as president. President S. P. Brooks of Baylor University served from 1914 to 1916. Then in succession the following have held the office: M. H. Wolfe, 1917–19; J. D. Sandefer, 1920–22; O. S. Lattimore, 1923–25; Pat M. Neff, 1926–28; Lee R. Scarborough, 1929–31; J. C. Hardy, 1932–34; J. B. Tidwell, 1935–37; J. Howard Williams, 1938–39; A. D. Foreman, Sr., 1940–42; W. R. White, 1943; E. D. Head, 1944–46; Wallace Bassett, 1947–48; William Fleming, 1949–50; F. C. Feezor, 1951–52; James N. Morgan, 1953–54.

Comparison of population growth and Baptist growth in Texas.—(The figures for 1940 and 1950 are taken from the decennial census reports of the United States Bureau of Census. The 1945 and 1954 estimates are from the United States Bureau of Census. The Baptist statistics are only for the members of the churches affiliated with the Baptist General Convention of Texas.) J. M. DAWSON

Date	*Population*	*Members of churches in the Baptist General Convention of Texas*	*Per cent of population*
1940	6,414,824	756,784	11.79
1945	6,786,740	873,153	12.86
1950	7,711,194	1,163,241	14.47
1954	8,468,000	1,363,685	16.10
Rate of increase	32.02%	80.19%	

III. Program of Work of Texas Baptists. EXECUTIVE BOARD. The executive board of the Baptist General Convention of Texas is made up of 191 directors, as authorized in the convention's constitution. Sixty members are elected each year for a term of three years, making a total of 180 elective members. The 11 ex officio members are the convention president, two vice-presidents, two recording secretaries, the secretary of the corporation, the president of Woman's Missionary Union, the president of the Brotherhood, the president of the Sunday school convention, the president of the Training Union convention, and the president of the Baptist Student Union convention.

The constitution prescribes certain regulations governing selection of board members. No direct beneficiary of convention funds and no one employed by any institution belonging to the convention is eligible for election to membership on the board. No district may have fewer than five or more than 20 board members. One third of the elective members must be lay workers. No person is eligible to serve more than two successive elective terms of three years each, but he may be re-elected after the lapse of one year.

The executive board exercises delegated authority in several areas of work. It has charge of the work of the convention between sessions of the convention. It elects an executive secretary and such assistants as deemed necessary, fixes salaries and transacts business and financial affairs, and makes a complete report annually to the convention.

The board, by choice and custom, normally meets four times each year, in December, March, June, and September, plus any necessary called meetings. The body elects its chairman, vice-chairman, and secretary at its annual meeting in December. Each year shortly after this meeting, the chairman names two major committees of the board, the Plans and Policies Committee and the Appropriations Committee. The latter serves in the area of studying needs and recommending specific appropriations for the general work of state missions, including the 12 departments and all phases of direct mission work. In this responsibility the committee is limited only by the total allocations for state mission causes already recommended by the Finance Committee and approved by both the board and convention.

The Plans and Policies Committee serves from the time of appointment through the current year and makes its major report to the annual board meeting in December. It nominates for re-election the executive secretary, his associates, and department heads upon the secretary's recommendation, and also recommends the salaries of these persons for board approval.

This committee has full freedom to commend and evaluate phases of the board's work for the year and to recommend such methods in policy and procedure as it finds necessary to carry on the work of the board. The other major responsibility of this committee is at the point of nominating to the board an executive committee to act for it if needed between sessions and also to place in nomination all standing committees, advisory committees, and commissions of the board.

The executive secretary is responsible for giving guidance and direction to all of the administrative and promotional phases of the board's work. Forrest C. Feezor, executive secretary since Sept., 1953, is assisted in his administrative office by the associate secretary and the treasurer. J. Woodrow Fuller, the associate executive secretary, handles many details of administration and engagements too numerous for the chief executive. He joins in committee and executive conferences at the executive secretary's invitation and automatically in his absence.

The position of treasurer is a separate office from that of executive secretary, and is thus unlike the combined office used in many states. R. A. Springer works in this administrative relationship in close harmony with the executive secretary. He serves as recording secretary of the board, the executive committee, and the finance committee and usually sits in on other administrative committee meetings, particularly those dealing with financial transactions and appropriations. The treasurer works with department heads and others to see that they keep their spending within the budget allocations, and he administers all budget items to the state and Southern conventions. Each month he sends a report of gifts of all the churches by associations to the stewardship chairman in each association and to the district missions secretary, and once a quarter he publishes a report of the mission gifts of every church in Texas in the *Baptist Standard*. The treasurer's books are audited annually by a competent firm of auditors. Their report, which gives a breakdown of receipts and disbursements and a complete record of the financial affairs of the executive board, is published in the convention's *Annual*. All employees of the board who handle money in any way are bonded; all checks drawn on convention funds must carry the signature of both the treasurer and the executive secretary.

Departments of Work. There are 12. The executive secretary has the general responsibility of all. The head of the state missions ministry has the responsibility for the administration of this division of the work. Each department is under the immediate direction of its own head or secretary. Six of these departments are generally classified as church-related because they find their basic tie and expression in the life of a local church. The others, while just as definitely missionary and vital, function in the larger areas of Baptist life and have as their peculiar ministry a special group or phase of the Christian life.

Department of Evangelism.—This work is directed by C. Wade Freeman, who is assisted by an associate secretary and five staff members. These men lead in the organization of the entire state through district and association leadership for the purpose of marshalling all the local church forces to seek the lost and unchurched. One staff member ministers to the Latin American churches and missions. Another devotes much of his time to prison evangelism. Each year this department sponsors a state evangelistic conference in addition to planning conferences in each of the 17 districts and 122 associations. The department promotes district simultaneous evangelistic crusades on alternating years. This plan was popular in its reception but difficult to maintain in the light of periodic Convention- and nation-wide crusades. Extensive tracts and literature are distributed in the state by this department, having been produced both in Texas and in Southern Baptist Convention agencies. Churches affiliating with the state convention in 1955 baptized 70,000 converts. Between 1948 and 1955 they reported a total of 500,000 baptisms.

Sunday School Department.—Composed of a general director, an associate general fieldworker, an associate in charge of Vacation Bible schools, and four full-time office helpers. One of the major functions of the department is to promote better teaching and the enlistment of larger numbers in regular Sunday morning Bible study by working through superintendents of local Sunday schools in over 3,600 co-operating churches, which in 1955 reported an enrolment of 1,054,822. Approximately 140,000 training awards are issued each year for the completion of training course books designed to improve teaching methods and organization procedures. The Vacation Bible school program, sponsored by this department, annually enrols an average of one-third million boys and girls in approximately 3,300 schools, which report from 6,000 to 10,000 conversions. Many of these schools are held in mission areas, including those for Negroes, Mexicans, and other groups. The department promotes an annual state Sunday school convention and state clinics, organized as a workshop-type activity, which offer direction for Sunday school work in the churches. As a service channel, the department answers from 15,000 to 20,000 requests annually, and distributes more than a million free tracts dealing with the duties of Sunday school teachers and officers. Service, promotion, Bible education, stewardship, and missions form the pattern for the work of this department.

Andrew Q. Allen, secretary of this department, has given attention to better buildings for expanding department organization, more classes, better training, and state clinics. He originated the first tour of educational workers to South American churches in 1952 and personally led another to the same area in 1954 in the interest of a wider use of the Sunday school in growing churches.

Baptist Training Union Department.—This department has given much emphasis to a fully graded course of Christian life study. Study books are taught during church training schools, Training Union revivals, encampments, and assemblies. The purpose of the course is to deepen spiritual lives, increase Bible and doctrinal knowledge, and intensify devotion in Christian service. In 1955 Training Union members in Texas earned 174,715 study course awards. Texas has pioneered in almost every phase of the development of this Christian training agency in Southern Baptist life and developed many distinctive patterns which became an integral part of its work. Much of this department's success can be attributed to the leadership of Thurman C. Gardner, who was secretary of this department from 1916 to his retirement in 1956. During his last year of active service, the executive board and the convention emphasized 1956 as a year of Training Union advance.

Brotherhood Department.—Employs a staff of three workers. L. H. Tapscott has served as secretary since 1945. The annual operating budget includes a part of the expenses of the Royal Ambassador work, but this work became the department's full responsibility after 1957.

The statewide organization of pastors and laymen, the Texas Baptist Brotherhood convention, has three elected convention officers, a president, first vice-president, and a recording secretary; and advisory committee of two pastors and three laymen; and 17 district Brotherhood presidents. It conducts annual sessions during the two days prior to the general convention's meeting. Each district, comprising several associations, holds one annual meeting. The state advisory committee meets semiannually. Each of the 122 associations has its own Brotherhood organization, which meets each quarter. As of 1955, 1,868 churches had local Bortherhood organizations with a total enrolment above 70,000.

Woman's Missionary Union of Texas.—This organization is an auxiliary to the Baptist General Convention of Texas. For all practical purposes it operates as a department and is a regular member of the state board family. Eula Mae Henderson is the secretary. The W.M.U.'s objectives, to distribute missionary information, stimulate missionary effort, and secure the earnest co-operation of women and young people in giving to missions, are reached through these four fundamentals: prayer, mission study, tithes and offerings, and community missions.

This organization promotes special weeks of prayer with mission study and giving. During the week of prayer for foreign missions, a study is made of Southern Baptist foreign mission fields in a suggested daily program with emphasis on prayer and participation in a special foreign mission offering. This offering in Texas has become a churchwide offering sponsored by the W.M.U. and frequently led by the pastor. This full church participation perhaps accounts for the large sum of $1,428,000 given in 1954. A similar week of prayer is conducted for home missions and another for state missions, with a special offering for each. These weeks provide not only increased mission gifts but also increased interest in mission needs here at home and around the world. This organization in recent years has given increasing emphasis to the Cooperative Program. The increased percentage in many church budgets to missions through the Cooperative Program can be attributed in part to this emphasis among missionary-minded women.

Church Music Department.—Established in 1944, this department has followed the pattern established by the Convention-wide Church Music Department. The present secretary, V. F. Forderhase, in 1954 succeeded J. D. Riddle, the first secretary of the department. A secretary, an associate secretary, a graded choir worker, and an office secretary compose the present staff. The purpose of the department is to raise the standard of music in our churches, to increase participation in worship through singing, to lead Texas Baptist churches to feel the responsibility for promoting music education in the local church, and to help establish a fully graded choir program in every church. To accomplish these objectives, the department promotes church schools of music, association-wide schools, district festivals, statewide conference festivals, and graded choir camps. Church schools of music are conducted on the same basis as the training schools of other state departments. Awards are given to all above Intermediate age, and certificates are presented to those under the Intermediate age group. The purpose of the district festival is to inspire and challenge church musicians to make a greater contribution to their churches through better stewardship of talents that are trained and used for the Lord, to encourage participation in the music program of all churches, and to help the people recognize the contribution of fine church music to services of worship. The statewide conference festival is designed to inspire young people to dedicate their talents, and to lift the level of music used in most churches. The graded choir program is a major factor in enlisting every member of the family in music education and participation. Graded choir camps, held in every section of the state, help in training directors for children's choirs and in building a challenging and useful repertoire for every choir.

Most churches throughout the state are using the *Church Musician* and other literature published and recommended by the Baptist Sunday School Board. The state department distributes 26 different sets of pamphlets dealing with every phase of the music education program, wall charts on the standard of excellence, and many other materials. "Texas Baptist Music Notes" is the promotional bulletin published by the department, and some 10,000 copies are mailed to pastors and ministers of music every quarter.

Department of Student Work.—Organized at the local level and promoted co-operatively by the state convention and the college area churches, the Baptist Student Union undertakes the full enlistment of the student in the local church as its basic objective. Trained directors of student work promote a program that includes Bible study, fellowship, evangelism, missions, and other opportunities for Christian growth. Texas Baptists also provide for their program 18 chairs of Bible, which offer courses whereby a student may earn up to 12 semester hours of degree credit. The Baptist Student Union on Baptist campuses functions within the framework of regular college life and serves as the co-ordinating agent for all campus-centered religious activities, in addition to being a link between the student and his church.

Through a state department staff of six under the direction of W. F. Howard, secretary, approximately 25 full-time student directors, and 19 student centers, Texas Baptists minister to the needs of the 35,000 Baptist and Baptist-preference students on nearly 100 campuses in the state.

Endowment Department.—This department is unique in Texas in its relationship both to the state board and also to the Baptist Foundation. The general state pattern has been for the foundation to operate in the fields of both procurement and investment of trust and endowment funds, but in Texas this responsibility is divided. The endowment work is a regular department of the state board under the direction of the executive secretary.

The endowment secretary, George Shearin, gives his time and attention to study of tax structures and benefits, promotes will making, and endeavors to create a consciousness of a larger and continuing stewardship among the Baptists of the state. He is impartial as to institutions and causes in Baptist life and seeks only to show the prospective donor how he can make his estate do what he would like to do both in life and after death. The secretary of this department works in close relationship with the Baptist Foundation.

Christian Life Commission.—Established in 1950 for the purpose of emphasizing the practical nature of the Christian faith. It challenges Texas Baptists not to minimize their faithful emphasis on the necessity of the new birth but to proclaim with proportionate emphasis the moral responsibilities of the new life in Christ. The commission is committed to the concept that man's spiritual relationship to God imposes on him a moral responsibility for his fellow man. It is dedicated to the task of helping Texas Baptists to carry into every area of life the whole gospel of Christ. Composing the Christian Life Commission at present are eight pastors, one medical doctor, one lawyer, and two educators. The heads of the various departments in the state mission program also serve as members. Although the help of part-time workers is sometimes secured, the only full-time employees of the commission are its director and his office secretary. Foy Valentine, the present director, succeeded A. C. Miller in 1953.

The Christian Life Commission has divided its responsibilities into five general areas. Under the division of family life, it deals with the subjects of courtship and marriage, the Christian home, divorce, and juvenile delinquency. Under the division of race relations, it works among the minority groups in Texas and seeks to give assistance to pastors, churches, and interested individuals who want help with problems pertaining to race relations. Under the division of moral issues, it deals with gambling, alcohol, narcotics, salacious literature, and crime, seeking to keep Texas Baptists informed and active in the improvement of this state's moral standards. Under the division of economic life, it seeks to interpret, in the spirit and mind of Christ, the issues involved between employees and employers and strives to point up God's concern with man's relationship to material things. Under the division of Christian citizenship, it deals with such problems as war and peace, the Christian ballot, church and state, and religious freedom.

The commission has prepared and printed for free distribution a series of pamphlets under the general heading, "The Bible Speaks," on the subjects of the Christian life, family, race, Christian citizenship, economics, moral issues, sex, divorce, and war and peace. Other literature is available from the commission on the separation of church and state, crime comics, smoking, and the general application of Christian principles to life. The production and distribution of this type of literature is one of the commission's primary responsibilities and means of giving information or assistance with community or church problems in the realm of social ethics. In co-operation with Southwestern Baptist Theological Seminary, the commission sponsors and promotes 29 seminary extension classes for Negro preachers, which currently enrol 500 students.

Church Loan Department.—Established Jan. 21, 1952, for the purpose of making money available to churches to assist them in their building needs when commercial loans cannot be obtained. An executive vice-president and a board of directors administer the business affairs of the department. The department does its work through two legal corporations, the Church Loan Association of the Baptist General Convention of Texas and the Baptist Church Loan Corporation. The executive board elects the board of directors, three fourths of whom are successful businessmen and the other one fourth capable and interested pastors. Though it functions as a business enterprise, the department is motivated only by a desire to serve the churches, doing for them what no other financing agency can or will do. It is vitally related to every phase of our denominational mission cause and makes possible the establishment of new churches in areas where they are desperately needed. A. B. White, head of this department since its establishment, has conducted his work in close co-operation with the executive secretary and the executive board.

Christian Education Commission.—This agency consists of nine commissioners, who serve overlapping terms of three years each. Two of the commissioners are businessmen, two are professional individuals, three serve public educational institutions, and two are ministers. All are active members of Baptist churches in Texas. The commission is the liaison between the general convention and its nine educational institutions, Baylor University and its affiliated colleges of dentistry and medicine, the University of Corpus Christi, Decatur Baptist College, East Texas Baptist College, Hardin-Simmons University, Howard Payne College, Mary Hardin–Baylor College, Wayland Baptist College, and San Marcos Baptist Academy. These schools work together in a voluntary organization known as the Texas Baptist School Administrators Association.

The executive board has delegated certain specific responsibilities to the new agency. It is the duty of the commission to recommend annually to the Finance Committee a basis for division of the convention's Christian education appropriation. The commission also has limited authority to control the curricula for the several institutions, especially where expansion of the curriculum would entail additional expenditures on the part of the convention, or where offerings were judged to be unnecessary duplications of some existing program within the system. It also is to "study the needs and the problems of the schools and to seek means of supplying the same" without usurping the prerogatives of local boards of trustees. Authorized to employ an executive co-ordinator and define his duties, the commission secured Harold A. Haswell, who has since continued to serve in this capacity.

The commission serves the convention in many ways. It makes recommendations regarding educational policies and programs, compiles and tabulates helpful educational data, gives constant direction to a statewide publicity program benefiting all of the schools, recommends the allocation of the convention's educational appropriations, and provides convention leadership for a long-range program of educational development. The basic purpose of the commission is to work with all of the schools in such a way as best to serve their common interests. Thus it co-ordinates any joint project which might benefit the member schools. It makes available consultative services through the Dallas office, strives to interpret the schools' total program to the convention, works with individual schools on problems peculiar to a single given campus, and co-operates with other convention agencies in an effort to secure additional funds to be used by the schools for operation, for capital needs, and for endowment.

The executive co-ordinator of the commission also serves as the secretary of the School Administrators Association, thus facilitating communication between the two organizations, which hold separate meetings in close proximity each quarter. Opinions and recommendations agreed upon by the school administrators are referred to the commission for its consideration. Serious problems affecting the over-all program of Christian education in Texas are usually settled only after the commission has conducted a hearing on the matter. Persons interested in a particular problem are invited to appear before the commission to present factual information bearing upon the problem under consideration. The commission has also made effective use of fact-finding studies and surveys wherever such data enabled it to act with greater intelligence. Most of the detailed work of the commission is carried out by the executive co-ordinator.

Public Relations Department.—This department is responsible for providing information and publicity material to Texas Baptists and the general public. A small staff of information specialists conducts the department's activities, which include news releases, feature stories, promotional literature, posters, advertising layouts, radio and television programming, photography, promotional movies, and visual aids. Through public relations facilities the department works with other promotional departments in the state convention, with educational and benevolent institutions operated and owned by the convention, and spreads information about the Southern Baptist program in the state. At all times the department prepares material to benefit directly the program of each Texas Baptist church. Mats and promotional pieces for specific emphases, which can be adapted for church programs, are made available to churches on a production cost or, at times, a no-cost basis. Each year an average of three 16 mm. color sound movies are written and produced for specific projects, for general mission areas, or some phase of the work of Texas Baptist institutions. Current color slide series on Texas Baptist life are also made available. A biweekly public relations newsletter is sent to all pastors in the state as a personal source of information which can be reproduced in church publications. Sixty-eight radio stations broadcast one of three weekly public service programs, and a weekly television program is produced over a Dallas station. A weekly state missions promotion page is published in the *Baptist Standard,* and all convention activities which are not covered by the *Baptist Standard* staff are reported by the department.

The department works through an advisory committee of Texas Baptist laymen who have successful careers in the public relations media of newspaper, radio, television, advertising, and community interest promotion. A pastor and an educational director with public relations experience are also members of this 10-member committee. The department staff consists of director, secretary, two staff artists, press relations representative, photographer-radio technician combination, part-time secretary, and part-time radio technician. Leonard Holloway, the present director, succeeded R. Alton Reed in 1953. All members of the staff work in two or more related fields in order properly to carry on a public relations program for the Baptist General Convention of Texas.

Department of Direct Missions and Stewardship Promotion.—Established in 1951, it is under the direction of the associate executive secretary, in order to keep its various functions as close to the executive secretary's office as possible. Texas has led the way for Southern Baptists in several phases of stewardship emphasis. R. C. Campbell, while secretary, did much to popularize tithing in the best sense. J. Howard Williams blazed new trails by taking the best stewardship methods and ideas out to the church leaders in district and associational conferences. Many of these principles and techniques are used today in the progressive promotional program. The promotion conference of the Southern Baptist Convention committee furnishes the basic pattern for all stewardship advance. Much of the material used in the churches of the state is created and produced by the Executive Committee offices in Nashville.

L. B. Cobb has served as associate in this department since 1953, devoting his full time to stewardship emphasis. He has given attention to improved record forms and procedures in handling tithes and offerings. The department has promoted numerous treasures' clinics in associations across the state to demonstrate better procedures. It has given great emphasis to budget percentage giving to missions through the Cooperative Program, with some increase in the percentage each successive year. Attention has also been given to selection and training of a limited number of "approved workers" for the conducting of both budget and building fund campaigns. This emphasis is yet in its infancy but shows great potential. In spite of all their mission responsibility in the state, Texas Baptists are showing an increased awareness of their responsibilities for Southern Baptist work in the homeland of America and in 36 countries beyond. They gave 33.6 per cent of the operating budget dollar and 40 per cent of the overplus mission dollar to causes beyond the state in 1954, and a year later raised this to 35 per cent of the operating and 45 per cent of the overplus section.

The work of direct missions in Texas is both comprehensive and intensive. The state board shares in the work of each of the 17 districts in the state by jointly employing a district missions secretary, who is responsible for co-ordination and promotion of every related phase of denominational program. The board shares with the district one half of the salary and expenses of this man plus some limited assistance on office help. The executive secretary and his associates hold regular staff meetings with these men for purposes of planning and sharing for improvement of the mission program. To a lesser degree the board also supplements the salary of an average of 35 associational missionaries and 8 superintendents of city missions. For many years the board has also granted salary supplements to mission pastors in new or exceedingly difficult areas. All such applications are considered only after approval by the church, the executive board of the association, and a letter of evaluation by the district missions secretary or some other missionary or associational leader having first-hand knowledge of the situation.

The work of promoting mission stations and growing new churches in both city and rural areas is a part of the program of direct missions. At present R. Elmer Dunham, an associate in the department, directs this phase of the work. The program involves securing both building fund loans and gifts from state board funds for the beginning of new churches. Since 1953 an increased emphasis has been placed on rural leadership and churches through developing pilot point areas of demonstration pattern and, in conjunction with Southwestern Seminary, through providing a teacher for courses in rural church needs and program. This work is done by Carl Clark on a half-time teaching schedule, which permits him to spend the rest of his available time on the field in rural church clinics, surveys, and counseling work.

The third large area of direct mission work, the evangelistic and missionary ministry to the Mexican or Latin American people in Texas, receives the largest annual appropriation for direct mission work in the state. L. D. Wood, the associate with direct responsibility for this work, serves as co-ordinator to administer the work of both the home and state mission boards. To facilitate economy and effectiveness, his office is located in San Antonio near the greatest concentration of Mexican population. Increasingly the Mexican Baptist Convention, organized under Home Mission Board leadership, is becoming a fellowship meeting, and the Mexican churches and missions are seeking fellowship in associations co-operating with the Baptist General Convention of Texas. Under this emerging pattern the Mexican churches and missions are participating in the state program and increasing their gifts to missions through the Cooperative Program.

In addition to salary supplements, which constitute its largest item, the Latin American budget also provides substantial aid to the Valley Baptist Academy in the lower Rio Grande Valley and the Mexican Bible Institute in San Antonio. These institutions are helping train area leadership by offering basic elementary courses for those who did not finish grade or high school.

The executive board in 1954 provided an additional service to churches through securing J. W. Caldwell as architectural consultant for all types of missions and church congregations contemplating building programs. This service was at first a joint responsibility of the Church Loan Department and the executive board through the direct missions department, but in 1955 it became the sole responsibility of the latter department.

The *Baptist Standard* and the Baptist Founda-

IV. TEXAS STATISTICAL SUMMARY

Year	Associa-tions	Churches	Church Member-ship	Baptisms	S. S. Enrol-ment	V.B.S. Enrol-ment	T. U. Enrol-ment	W.M.U. Enrol-ment	Brother-hood En-rolment	Mission Gifts	Total Gifts	Value Church Property	State Capital Worth
1830													(Explanation: This column includes total value of Schools, Children's Homes, Hospitals, Foundation, Buildings, etc.)
1840													
1850	...	43	1,897	213	....	....	....	....	....	....	....	....	
1860	...	450	18,259	1,880	....	....	....	....	....	....	....	....	
1870	...	712	33,095	3,763	10,000	....	....	....	....	....	....	....	
1880	...	1,910	107,578	5,649	15,256	....	....	....	....	....	....	....	
1890	...	3,202	201,283	12,851	22,627	....	215	....	....	....	$ 183,082	....	
1900	...	2,740	190,098	10,479	57,353	....	2,851	....	....	....	347,556	....	
1905	...	2,905	224,623	12,893	74,356	....	4,500	....	....	....	781,501	....	
1910	...	3,433	299,718	23,165	151,564	....	11,985	....	....	....	1,812,230	....	
1915	...	3,623	352,409	24,623	214,687	....	16,841	....	....	....	2,021,676	....	
1920	126	3,274	377,251	24,279	242,078	....	64,121	....	....	....	5,672,987	....	....
1925	120	3,249	468,065	34,651	368,171	1,770	108,172	....	....	$ 1,416,166	6,773,751	$ 23,584,925	....
1930	108	2,973	521,462	31,850	419,615	10,098	122,774	52,904	....	1,157,753	6,708,643	32,945,560	....
1931	108	2,992	537,388	34,390	429,899	11,370	128,605	70,412	....	1,070,083	5,741,040	32,586,768	....
1932	109	3,104	563,078	31,462	441,544	8,322	131,789	63,827	....	836,781	4,629,129	32,254,425	....
1933	108	3,153	576,945	32,492	441,682	9,915	132,959	67,186	....	578,392	3,860,515	31,846,620	....
1934	108	3,125	599,793	35,900	457,347	10,707	145,605	65,021	....	659,399	4,282,609	31,140,796	$13,010,212
1935	108	3,123	615,596	32,582	471,064	21,461	158,535	64,018	....	690,653	4,523,154	31,535,046	....
1936	108	3,151	630,756	31,748	481,006	23,286	166,039	73,375	....	766,722	5,027,503	32,006,403	....
1937	108	3,214	659,186	36,939	496,836	29,284	167,751	71,859	....	899,968	5,675,168	32,599,639	....
1938	109	3,235	696,014	41,816	523,522	41,877	169,372	74,389	....	948,406	6,608,019	33,445,491	....
1939	110	3,204	730,637	44,224	551,616	55,312	183,906	87,317	....	1,043,357	6,878,509	34,395,182	....
1940	112	3,221	756,784	40,895	566,112	72,661	201,186	102,262	....	1,166,024	7,696,958	36,022,585	....
1941	113	3,298	781,249	36,335	570,272	92,376	211,611	101,549	....	1,290,992	8,077,607	37,536,459	....
1942	114	3,312	805,612	35,873	541,106	89,621	217,263	110,549	....	1,588,575	9,195,638	38,935,476	....
1943	115	3,281	834,922	33,919	532,933	78,158	217,009	108,415	13,461	2,384,255	11,784,537	40,484,545	....
1944	114	3,301	873,153	39,596	549,192	104,636	196,703	100,129	14,168	2,927,449	14,556,004	42,462,860	25,995,330
1945	114	3,262	920,952	41,534	573,522	109,797	173,544	97,143	15,805	3,688,383	18,619,999	45,939,493	....
1946	114	3,300	970,970	44,419	619,202	168,606	183,607	115,243	27,834	5,169,576	22,396,278	55,132,701	....
1947	114	3,310	1,022,783	49,792	665,479	203,849	193,709	98,157	32,550	5,388,618	25,161,203	66,815,386	....
1948	114	3,377	1,053,979	49,339	712,780	202,411	203,499	110,807	36,501	4,536,605	31,225,465	85,110,909	....
1949	115	3,445	1,106,686	51,006	753,329	227,348	242,894	119,821	40,624	6,094,733	35,001,708	104,246,690	....
1950	116	3,519	1,163,241	57,156	804,363	240,000	274,105	131,140	45,900	6,570,413	39,264,882	126,028,502	....
1951	118	3,598	1,220,272	63,102	848,112	283,804	298,412	142,531	49,813	7,699,832	44,013,408	147,154,309	....
1952	119	3,411	1,262,451	61,715	886,296	314,689	326,158	148,637	56,274	9,631,965	49,545,049	171,033,609	....
1953	121	3,503	1,318,942	62,593	929,909	339,539	358,719	155,071	60,420	10,401,921	55,506,986	200,253,276	....
1954	122	3,569	1,363,685	66,634	1,009,385	404,290	395,197	172,745	64,690	10,956,358	61,203,915	227,629,399	86,772,623

R. A. SPRINGER

tion of Texas are treated in separate monographs because they were not created by the executive board but by the Baptist General Convention of Texas. The convention, according to charter provisions, annually elects directors for these agencies, which co-operate closely with the executive secretary's office and are considered a normal part of the total Baptist family, though not responsible to the executive board. The educational and benevolent institutions of the convention are also treated in separate monographs.

BAPTIST GENERAL CONVENTION OF TEXAS
EXPENDITURES FOR STATE MISSIONS, CHRISTIAN EDUCATION, AND HEALING
YEAR ENDED OCT. 31, 1955

State Missions	
Administrative	$ 96,488.45
Promotion	30,472.93
Net General	498,718.57
Direct Missions and Promotion:	
Department	52,349.34
Associational Missionaries	25,014.14
District Missionaries	32,247.17
District Missionaries' Secretaries	8,158.39
Missionary Pastors	72,004.75
Spanish Missions	152,829.60
City Missions	15,239.59
Rural Missions	20,246.93
Jewish Missions	900.00
Baptist Standard Publishing Co.	11,000.00
Retirement Plans	265,528.67
Christian Life Commission	35,200.00
Evangelism	57,518.21
City Extension	100,000.00
Miscellaneous and Emergency	127,262.12
Reserve	75,000.00
New Baptist Building	50,000.00
State Missions Unclassified:	
Annuitants	300.00
Annuities Paid on Contract	1,221.00
Convention Expense	17,988.52
Other	32,963.99
Retirement Plans	31,461.50
Training Union	50,706.71
Sunday School	56,875.63
Vacation Bible School	11,000.00
Baptist Student Union:	
Department Expense	42,900.90
Bible Teachers	16,291.92
Student Directors—Who Teach Bible	58,424.03
Student Directors—Who Do Not Teach Bible	16,567.15
Student Directors—Who Do Not Teach Bible, Paid in Part by State Board	15,496.26
Woman's Missionary Union	63,229.26
Less Mary Hill Davis Offering Refund	57,500.00
Endowment	29,234.63
Brotherhood	39,696.55
Church Music	31,987.94
Historical Committee	300.00
Public Relations	55,005.06
Contingent	19,842.60
Christian Education and Healing	
Student Centers	100,000.00
Endowment for Institutions	100,000.00
Appropriations to Institutions	1,487,500.00
Ministerial Tuition	200,000.00
Christian Education Commission	49,486.19
Less Mary Hill Davis Offering Refund	24,272.01
GRAND TOTAL	$4,172,886.69

BAPTIST BUILDING. Located at 703 North Ervay at San Jacinto in Dallas, Tex., this building is owned jointly and equally by the Relief and Annuity Board of the Southern Baptist Convention and the Baptist General Convention of Texas. Dedicated June 3, 1952, it is a four-story building with full basement. It fronts 75 feet on Ervay, is a block long or 169 feet lengthwise on the San Jacinto side. It contains 50,400 square feet of floor space. The cost was $1,086,646.20.

J. WOODROW FULLER

BIBLIOGRAPHY: J. P. Boone, *It Came to Pass* (1953). J. M. Carroll, *A History of Texas Baptists* (1923); *Texas Baptist Statistics* (1895). J. B. Cranfill, *From Memory* (1937); *Dr. J. B. Cranfill's Chronicle* (1916). J. M. Dawson, *A Century with Texas Baptists* (1947). L. R. Elliott, ed., *Centennial Story of Texas Baptists* (1936). B. F. Fuller, *History of Texas Baptists* (1900). J. B. Gambrell, *Ten Years in Texas* (1907). P. W. James, *George W. Truett, A Biography* (1945). C. D. Mallory, *Memoirs of Elder Jesse Mercer* (1844). Z. N. Morrell, *Flowers and Fruits from the Wilderness* (1872). Mrs. R. T. Patterson, *Candle by Night* (1955). B. F. Riley, *A History of Texas Baptists* (1907). E. C. Routh, *The Life Story of Dr. J. B. Gambrell* (1929). Mrs. W. J. J. Smith, *A Centennial History of the Baptist Women of Texas* (1933).

TEXAS, BAPTIST STATE CONVENTION OF. A Texas general body organized by a group of messengers from 23 churches in Union, Eastern Missionary, Colorado, and Trinity River associations, who met with Antioch Church at Anderson in Grimes County, Sept. 8–12, 1848. This convention, the oldest Baptist general body in the state, was primarily supported by churches in the region around Independence and Houston, where the Baptists first achieved strength. The churches represented were: Independence, Washington, Dove (Caldwell), Providence (in Washington County), Providence (in Burleson County), Houston, Galveston, Austin, Gonzales, Rocky Creek, Antioch, Cuero, Post Oak Grove, Bedias, Mount Giliad, Wharton, La Grange, Plum Grove, Bethany, Concord, Hamilton, Matagorda, and New Year's Creek. After all the other ministers present demurred at preaching the introductory sermon, Zachariah N. Morrell (*q.v.*) responded with a message from Isaiah 9:7: "Of the increase of his government and peace there shall be no end." Hosea Garrett led the opening prayer. Officers chosen were president, H. L. Graves, president of Baylor University; vice-presidents, J. W. D. Creath, Hosea Garrett, and James Huckins (*q.v.*); corresponding secretary, Rufus Columbus Burleson (*q.v.*), pastor, First Baptist Church, Houston; recording secretary, J. G. Thomas; treasurer, J. W. Barnes.

The president appointed committees on worship, constitution, education, home missions, foreign missions, temperance, Bible distribution, Negro population, printing, finance, and nominations. During 38 succeeding sessions the body regularly appointed these committees and from time to time added others. The initial statement of purpose was perpetuated almost word for word in the constitution later adopted by the Baptist General Convention of Texas (the present Texas convention) under which the state convention entered into consolidation with the Texas Baptist General Association in 1886. The state convention named a board of directors with power to appoint all agents and missionaries. The constitution stipulated that the absolute sovereignty of the churches should forever be acknowledged by the convention. In harmony with its purely deliberative character, the convention never sought to impose any creedal declarations on the churches, but it was always attentive to their demand for sound doctrine. Any church, association, or mission society could be represented in the convention upon payment of five dollars as evidence of co-operation.

Throughout its existence the convention's primary state interest was Baylor University and after 1866 the university's affiliate, Baylor Female College, but its contributions to all missions and several distinct forms of benevolence were notable for pioneer times. In 1886 it entered the merger which produced the Baptist General Convention of Texas. J. M. DAWSON

TEXAS ASSOCIATIONS. Since 1840 there have been 209 associations organized in Texas which have co-operated with the Baptist work now known as the Baptist General Convention. In 1955 there were 122 active associations, 3,655 churches, 70,110 baptisms, 1,419,802 members, $65,877,755 total gifts, $8,890,421 mission gifts. The remainder of the associations have become extinct in the following ways: disbanded, changed name, or united with other associations.

In 1933 under the direction of J. Howard Williams, state executive secretary, the associations were grouped into 17 districts. In each was placed a district missionary. (In 1955 name changed to secretary.) The purpose of the district organization is to develop fellowship, promote all phases of the work of the state convention, gather statistical data, attempt to keep the organization intact and functioning, as well as render aid in the churches and in the associations, and give direction to concerted effort.

I. Extant. AMARILLO. Organized Sept. 22, 1953, with 18 churches out of Palo Duro Association. In 1954, 23 churches reported 1,052 baptisms, 18,127 members, $1,021,061 total gifts, $147,614 mission gifts, $4,011,252 property value, and $600,608 church debt.

ATASCOSA. Organized Sept. 20, 1941, with 16 churches. Willis J. Ray was the district missionary leading in the organization. A committee composed of moderators of associations in District 6 recommended the boundaries of the association and the churches to be contained in it. In 1954, 14 churches reported 112 baptisms, 2,346 members, $90,382 total gifts, $12,925 mission gifts, $384,770 property value, and $70,687 church debt.

AUSTIN. Organized July 24, 1857, with 13 churches, six of them out of Colorado Association. Zacharius N. Morrell (*q.v.*) was present. Articles of faith were adopted. In 1954, 52 churches reported 969 baptisms, 23,461 members, $960,475 total gifts, $146,401 mission gifts, $4,362,206 property value, and $1,254,475 church debt.

BAYLOR-KNOX. Organized in 1892 under the name of Little Wichita Association. The name was changed to Baylor County Association in 1907 and to Baylor-Knox in 1930. In 1954, 9 churches reported 110 baptisms, 2,680 members, $72,619 total gifts, $21,037 mission gifts, $344,300 property value, and $9,632 church debt.

BELL. Organized at Salado as the Salado Association in the fall of 1874 by messengers from 20 churches from Bell, Milam, and Williamson counties, all previously affiliated with Leon River Association. Articles of faith were adopted. Mary-Hardin Baylor College is located in this association. In the 1923 session, with 31 churches representing a membership of 3,100, it voted to change the name to Bell County Association. In 1954, 37 churches reported 531 baptisms, 13,595 members, $504,425 total gifts, $72,922 mission gifts, $1,784,263 property value, and $199,579 church debt.

BIG BEND. Organized Feb. 13, 1940, with nine churches. In 1954, 13 churches reported 96 baptisms, 3,062 members, $123,278 total gifts, $20,448 mission gifts, $533,000 property value, and $36,347 church debt.

BIG SPRINGS. Organized Sept. 23, 1909, with 28 churches. In 1954, 24 churches reported 354 baptisms, 8,723 members, $369,494 total gifts, $80,224 mission gifts, $1,154,209 property value, and $106,735 church debt.

BLANCO. Organized at Refugio, Oct. 4, 1873, with nine churches represented. Articles of faith were adopted. In 1954, 45 churches reported 636 baptisms, 10,479 members, $523,567 total gifts, $80,574 mission gifts, $1,594,756 property value, and $152,549 church debt.

BRADY. Organized Sept. 7, 1906, at Brady with 20 churches. In 1954, 22 churches reported 238 baptisms, 4,544 members, $124,196 total gifts, $17,188 mission gifts, $519,871 property value, and $44,702 church debt.

BROWN COUNTY. Organized Aug. 14, 1907, when the Pecan Valley Association, meeting in its 32nd annual session, voted to change its name to Brown County Baptist Association. This association is the home of Howard Payne College. In 1954, 33 churches reported 379 baptisms, 10,547 members, $303,307 total gifts, $53,022 mission gifts, $1,358,517 property value, and $102,057 church debt.

BROWNFIELD. Organized in 1906. The first minutes available are from the sixth session which met in 1912 at Lubbock First Church. Nineteen churches were represented. In 1954, 25 churches reported 327 baptisms, 7,326 members, $296,397 total gifts, $53,828 mission gifts, $964,000 property value, and $32,296 church debt.

BURNET-LLANO. Organized Aug. 29, 1913, at First Church, Llano, with 17 churches out of Llano River Association. This association is the home of San Marcos Academy. In 1954, 12 churches reported 188 baptisms, 2,623 members, $79,902 total gifts, $12,693 mission gifts, $163,000 property value, and $16,026 church debt.

CALLAHAN. Organized Sept. 29, 1889, at New Hope Church in Callahan County with seven churches from Cisco and Sweetwater associations. Two other churches were received during the first session. In 1954, 14 churches reported 139 baptisms, 2,987 members, $69,331 total gifts, $11,-967 mission gifts, $192,700 property value, and $11,300 church debt.

CANADIAN. Organized Sept. 6, 1895, at First Church, Amarillo, with eight churches. In 1954, 10 churches reported 181 baptisms, 3,192 members, $195,571 total gifts, $34,091 mission gifts, $981,996 property value, and $63,585 church debt.

CASTLE GAP. Organized Oct., 1954, at the First Church, Crane, with 16 churches out of Pecos Valley Association. In 1954, 14 churches reported 281 baptisms, 4,419 members, $202,534 total gifts, $32,480 mission gifts, $748,396 property value, and $60,321 church debt.

CHEROKEE. Organized Dec., 1851, with three churches, Harris Creek and Mt. Zion, of Smith County, and Sharon of Rusk County, meeting at Mt. Zion Church. Out of this association came the Baptist Missionary Association (Landmark), which was organized on July 6, 1900, at Troup, and which was called the East Texas Baptist Convention until Dec. 8 of that year. In 1954, 18 churches reported 201 baptisms, 4,336 members, $187,969 total gifts, $31,435 mission gifts, $703,974 property value, and $36,242 church debt.

CISCO. Organized as the Battle Creek Association in 1883 by the churches of Callahan and Eastland counties, and four or five churches of Shackelford and Stephens counties at Battle Creek Church, Stephens County. The total membership of the churches was 250. At the second annual session held with Zion Hill Church of Callahan County the name was changed to Cisco Association. In 1954, 35 churches reported 461 baptisms, 11,618 members, $343,353 total gifts, $80,871 mission gifts, $1,294,400 property value, and $57,223 church debt.

CLAY COUNTY. Organized Oct. 1, 1896, at Blue Grove Church, with 16 churches, 12 of them from Clay County with letters of dismissal from Montague County Association with which they had been co-operating. Articles of faith were adopted. In 1954, 15 churches reported 114 baptisms, 2,653 members, $88,967 total gifts, $18,878 mission gifts, $331,559 property value, and $24,-641 church debt.

COASTAL BEND. Organized Oct. 12, 1953, out of Corpus Christi Association. The Laredo Association disbanded at the close of 1954 session, and eight churches of that body and three new ones aligned themselves with Coastal Bend. In 1954, 22 churches reported 443 baptisms, 8,882 members, $440,026 total gifts, $79,355 mission gifts, $1,476,700 property value, and $189,888 church debt.

COLEMAN. Organized Aug., 1906, with 20 churches reporting 1,524 members. In 1954, 26 churches reported 100 baptisms, 4,713 members, $113,305 total gifts, $21,716 mission gifts, $461,-051 property value, and $13,478 total church debt.

COLLIN COUNTY. Organized Oct. 29, 1886, at First Church, McKinney, with 29 churches and 2,500 members. In 1954, 54 churches reported 518 baptisms, 15,227 members, $478,983 total gifts, $92,333 mission gifts, $1,254,609 property value, and $86,417 church debt.

COLORADO. Organized Nov. 18, 1847, at Rocky Creek Church in Lavaca County with nine churches from six neighboring counties, five of these from Union Association. The second session met at First Church, Austin, in 1848. In 1954, 28 churches reported 546 baptisms, 8,124 members, $409,491 total gifts, $67,554 mission gifts, $1,408,143 property value, and $180,032 church debt.

COMANCHE. Organized Oct. 1, 1875, at Zion Hill Church of Comanche County with eight churches from Bosque Association having 388 members. At the first session three other churches were admitted. In 1954, 32 churches reported 204 baptisms, 5,357 members, $112,388 total gifts, $23,211 mission gifts, $358,500 property value, and $6,500 church debt.

CONCHO VALLEY. Organized Aug. 28, 1891, at First Church, San Angelo, with eight churches, 247 members, from San Saba Association. In 1954, 26 churches reported 704 baptisms, 13,067 members, $569,953 total gifts, $71,177 mission gifts, $2,545,500 property value, and $487,009 church debt.

COOKE COUNTY. Organized as Shiloh Association on Oct. 18, 1862, at Friendship Church, Denton County, with five churches. J. T. Harris was elected moderator. In Aug., 1902, five churches out of Shiloh Association met at Bloomington Church and organized Cooke County Association. The 1903 session reported 11 churches. In 1954, 21 churches reported 201 baptisms, 5,784 members, $177,308 total gifts, $35,186 mission gifts, $724,800 property value, and $84,904 church debt.

CORPUS CHRISTI. Organized Sept., 1911, at Sandia Church with 14 churches represented. In 1953 this association released 12 churches to help organize Coastal Bend Association. In 1954, 23 churches reported 937 baptisms, 15,474 members, $953,334 total gifts, $157,838 mission gifts, $3,195,000 property value, and $848,073 church debt.

CORSICANA. Organized Sept., 1910, with 12 churches. In 1954, 23 churches reported 355 baptisms, 10,570 members, $317,000 total gifts, $66,-969 mission gifts, $1,165,500 property value, and $66,365 church debt.

CORYELL. Organized as the Leon River Association on Sept. 24, 1858, at the Belton Church with 11 churches. In 1945 at the 88th session the name was changed to Coryell County Association. In 1954, 24 churches reported 137 baptisms, 4,901 members, $111,068 total gifts, $16,-

MISSOURI BAPTIST HOSPITAL (*q.v.*), St. Louis. Baptists' oldest hospital, established 1884, houses 525 beds. Special services include school of nursing; an additional building program in progress.

BAPTIST MEMORIAL HOSPITAL (*q.v.*), Houston, Tex. Has 545-bed capacity. Expanded facilities include seven-story nurses' home and fifteen-story medical building.

285 mission gifts, $488,600 property value, and $7,816 church debt.

CREATH-BRAZOS. Organized Oct. 25, 1901, with 21 churches out of Grimes and Walker County associations, meeting at the Union Grove Church. At the 27th annual session of the Creath Association with 24 churches represented and at the fifth annual session of the Brazos County Association with 14 churches represented, the two bodies voted to unite and form Creath-Brazos Association on Oct. 25, 1927. In 1954, 40 churches reported 487 baptisms, 12,953 members, $530,244 total gifts, $109,528 mission gifts, $2,187,893 property value, and $508,248 church debt.

DALLAS. Organized in 1886 at the 38th annual session of Elm Fork Association of United Baptists, held at Antioch Church in Dallas County, when the name was changed to Dallas County Association. In 1954, representing the largest association in Texas and one of the largest in the South, 171 churches reported 6,553 baptisms, 123,057 members, $7,088,559 total gifts, $1,183,014 mission gifts, $27,633,734 property value, and $5,558,094 church debt.

DEL-RIO-UVALDE. Organized in 1902. The first minutes available are from the 21st session, held in 1923. In 1954, 19 churches reported 187 baptisms, 5,217 members, $213,893 total gifts, $44,249 mission gifts, $806,700 property value, and $81,589 church debt.

DENTON COUNTY. Organized as the Shiloh Association, Oct., 1862, with two churches from Denton County. The churches of this area continued to co-operate with Shiloh, West Fork, and Sister Grove associations until May 29, 1886, when at the First Church, Denton, 18 churches formed the Denton County Association. The association adopted articles of faith found in Pendleton's *Manual*. In 1954, 33 churches reported 354 baptisms, 10,655 members, $344,666 total gifts, $69,246 mission gifts, $1,201,950 property value, and $115,467 church debt.

DICKENS COUNTY. Organized in 1910 in Dickens County. The first minutes available are from the ninth session when the association met at Friendship Church, Sept. 11–14, 1919, with 18 churches. In 1954, 11 churches reported 28 baptisms, 1,764 members, $47,845 total gifts, $8,985 mission gifts, $160,100 property value, and $4,200 church debt.

ELLIS COUNTY. Organized as the Waxahachie Association, Oct. 11, 1873, at Liberty Church, Ellis County, with 12 churches, 354 members. The 12 churches from Ellis, part of Dallas, Hill, Johnson, Tarrant, and Navarro counties adopted articles of faith from *Encyclopedia of Religious Knowledge*. In 1954, 14 churches reported 275 baptisms, 7,169 members, $287,701 total gifts, $72,381 mission gifts, $745,676 property value, and $74,667 church debt. Name changed to Ellis County in 1893.

EL PASO. Organized Oct. 24, 1902, with 10 churches. Articles of faith were adopted. In 1954, 23 churches reported 723 baptisms, 12,034 members, $615,818 total gifts, $120,867 mission gifts, $2,478,165 property value, and $301,815 church debt.

ENON. Organized Oct., 1873, with 16 churches. Articles of faith were adopted. In 1954, 45 churches reported 399 baptisms, 8,820 members, $256,439 total gifts, $31,292 mission gifts, $935,540 property value, and $45,447 church debt.

ERATH. Organized Oct. 21, 1887, at Stephensville, by 14 churches with 656 members. Thirty churches met at the next annual session at Oak Dale, Sept. 14–17, 1888. Articles of faith were adopted. Early churches in the area first belonged to Brazos River Association. In 1954, 30 churches reported 199 baptisms, 5,887 members, $169,301 total gifts, $31,958 mission gifts, $799,250 property value, and $41,517 church debt.

FALLS COUNTY. Organized Nov. 14, 1891, at Reagan Church with eight churches, 586 members, out of Waco and Little Brazos associations. In 1954, 21 churches reported 113 baptisms, 4,625 members, $107,188 total gifts, $18,486 mission gifts, $592,200 property value, and $20,865 church debt.

FANNIN COUNTY. Organized Aug. 5, 1887, at High Prairie Church, now Bonham, with 35 churches, 30 of them out of Sister Grove and Honey Grove associations. In 1954, 39 churches reported 389 baptisms, 8,964 members, $274,914 total gifts, $40,702 mission gifts, $805,600 property value, and $12,265 church debt.

FISHER. Organized Sept. 11, 1909, at Roby, with 17 churches out of Stonewall Association. In 1954, 18 churches reported 124 baptisms, 3,730 members, $87,065 total gifts, $14,208 mission gifts, $261,625 property value, and $895 church debt.

FLOYD COUNTY. Organized in 1917, composed of churches from Floyd, Crosby, Motley, and Briscoe counties. The first minutes available are from 1921 when 21 churches reported. In 1954, 29 churches reported 358 baptisms, 7,858 members, $342,317 total gifts, $74,467 mission gifts, $974,860 property value, and $35,619 church debt.

FREESTONE-LEON MISSIONARY. Organized Oct. 6, 1916, in the First Church of Teague, with 13 churches. In 1954, 11 churches reported 103 baptisms, 2,862 members, $92,542 total gifts, $13,914 mission gifts, $409,663 property value, and $18,190 church debt.

G.A.Y. Organized Sept. 21, 1943, at First Church, Seminole, with 12 churches, several of which came out of Lamesa Association. In 1954, 17 churches reported 345 baptisms, 5,527 members, $265,277 total gifts, $46,092 mission gifts, $810,912 property value, and $147,601 church debt.

GALVESTON. Organized Oct. 20, 1949, at Dickinson with 12 churches out of Union Association. C. O. Overstreet was elected moderator; M. Y. Rucker, clerk. In 1954, 19 churches reported 651 baptisms, 8,687 members, $454,011 total gifts, $60,212 mission gifts, $1,453,816 property value, and $242,554 church debt.

GAMBRELL. Organized in 1922 with 19 churches. In 1954, 19 churches reported 141 baptisms,

3,730 members, $154,305 total gifts, $29,471 mission gifts, $515,200 property value, and $25,251 church debt.

GONZALES. Organized Sept. 28, 1877, with 15 churches at North Grove Church, Lavaca County, under the name of Lavaca River Association. Articles of faith were adopted. The name was changed to Gonzales Association in 1924 when W. K. Penrod was elected moderator; C. E. Saxon, clerk. In 1954, 21 churches reported 196 baptisms, 3,674 members, $159,129 total gifts, $30,301 mission gifts, $670,664 property value, and $40,848 church debt.

GRAYSON COUNTY. Organized Oct. 20, 1886, at Sherman with 24 churches out of Sister Grove and Honey Grove associations when these two bodies disbanded in favor of a county association. Articles of faith were adopted. In opposition to the Grayson County Association, there was organized Sept. 28, 1900, The Missionary Baptist Association of Grayson County, Texas, which was a group of 27 churches which refused to work with the state convention and aligned themselves with the Baptist Missionary Association (Landmark). By 1950 six of them returned to Grayson County Association, several ceased to exist, and others continued to work with the Baptist Missionary Association. In 1954, 42 churches reported 888 baptisms, 20,145 members, $684,371 total gifts, $102,328 mission gifts, $2,354,253 property value, and $241,374 church debt.

GUADALUPE. Organized in 1919 with 19 churches. In 1954, 32 churches reported 516 baptisms, 8,869 members, $450,806 total gifts, $63,436 mission gifts, $1,575,006 property value, and $353,073 church debt.

GULF COAST. Organized Oct., 1946, with 17 churches out of Union and Colorado associations. In 1954, 21 churches reported 580 baptisms, 11,451 members, $553,412 total gifts, $100,445 mission gifts, $2,093,700 property value, and $507,432 church debt.

HAMILTON COUNTY. Organized July 4, 1877, at Cottonwood Springs, near Evant, with nine churches, four from Leon River Association and five not connected with any association. In 1954, 19 churches reported 100 baptisms, 3,245 members, $84,818 total gifts, $13,028 mission gifts, $263,300 property value, and $8,758 total church debt.

HARMONY. Organized Sept. 15, 1865, out of Rehoboth Association with four churches. In 1870 at Quitman, in Wood County, the association evidently reorganized with seven churches and began counting annual sessions from this date. An "Abstract of Principles" was adopted. In 1954, 19 churches reported 172 baptisms, 4,136 members, $186,118 total gifts, $38,300 mission gifts, $709,598 property value, and $53,827 church debt.

HASKELL-KNOX. Organized Oct. 27, 1906, in Prairie Dale Church at Pinkerton with 13 churches out of Stonewall Association. Little Wichita Association disintegrated and churches went into Haskell-Knox and Baylor County associations in 1906 and 1907. In 1954, 20 churches reported 220 baptisms, 6,276 members, $199,716 total gifts, $47,269 mission gifts, $630,442 property value, and $52,900 church debt.

HENDERSON. Organized Oct. 30, 1902, at First Church, Athens, with 12 churches from Saline Association. Articles of faith were adopted. In 1954, 21 churches reported 195 baptisms, 4,738 members, $162,863 total gifts, $24,149 mission gifts, $457,700 property value, and $15,950 church debt.

HILL COUNTY. Organized Mar. 26, 1881, at Brandon Church with seven churches represented. At a joint session Aug. 16, 1886, with Osceola Church in Hill County, the group voted to unite with Towash Association. The consolidated body was called Hillsboro Association. Hubbard City Association meeting at Parr's Chapel, Oct. 6, 1906, voted to disband, join the Hillsboro Association, and recreate the Hill County Association. In 1954, 25 churches reported 190 baptisms, 6,151 members, $202,930 total gifts, $25,524 mission gifts, $846,000 property value, and $60,503 church debt.

HOCKLEY-COCHRAN. Organized Sept. 4, 1941, with 13 churches out of Lubbock Association. In 1954, 15 churches reported 377 baptisms, 7,274 members, $263,356 total gifts, $63,009 mission gifts, $893,000 property value, and $88,970 church debt.

HUNT COUNTY. Organized Oct. 12, 1886, with nine churches. The history of the association, written in 1935, refers to a ministerial relief movement started in the 1919 session at Greenville. D. Y. Bagby was the originator of the movement. In 1954, 45 churches reported 457 baptisms, 13,090 members, $372,397 total gifts, $73,690 mission gifts, $1,124,930 property value, and $112,876 church debt.

INDEPENDENCE. Organized in 1948 at the 26th session of the Burleson-Lee Association when the name was changed to Independence. In 1954, 21 churches reported 97 baptisms, 3,148 members, $144,937 total gifts, $21,316 mission gifts, $508,342 property value, and $64,039 church debt.

JACK COUNTY. Organized Sept. 15, 1876, as Jacksboro Association. The name was changed to Jack County Association in 1903 because of a split in the Jacksboro Church. Under Harlan J. Matthews, pastor of the First Baptist Church of Mineral Wells, Palo Pinto and Jack counties united on Oct. 6, 1927, as the Palo Pinto–Jack County Baptist Association. The Jack County churches became dissatisfied and withdrew Oct. 29, 1931, reorganizing the Jack County Association. In 1954, 15 churches reported 101 baptisms, 2,520 members, $90,902 total gifts, $22,741 mission gifts, $229,550 property value, and $12,089 church debt.

JOHNSON COUNTY. Organized as the Alvarado Association in 1864. The name was changed to Johnson County Association, Sept. 13, 1900, with 42 churches representing 3,000 members. It adopted the New Hampshire Confession of Faith. In 1954, 31 churches reported 432 baptisms, 10,944 members, $319,359 total gifts, $73,586 mission gifts, $1,244,900 property value, and $131,189 church debt.

JONES. Organized Oct. 20, 1906, at First Baptist Church, Anson, in Jones County, with 16 churches out of Stonewall Association. In 1954, 23 churches reported 253 baptisms, 7,211 members, $271,092 total gifts, $53,491 mission gifts, $781,000 property value, and $35,544 church debt.

KAUFMAN. Organized Oct. 4, 1904, at Grove Church, with nine churches out of East Fork Association. In 1923 the name was changed to Kaufman-Rockwall Association. At the ninth session of this body the name was changed again to Kaufman Missionary Association. Several of the churches went into R. C. Burleson Association at its first meeting in 1930; some co-operated with Burleson-Lee Association, helping organize Independence Association in 1948. In 1954, 18 churches reported 231 baptisms, 5,609 members, $176,194 total gifts, $33,046 mission gifts, $506,700 property value, and $23,759 church debt.

LAMAR COUNTY. Organized Feb., 1887, at Paris, with 18 churches from Lamar County, Red River, and North Sulphur associations. In 1954, 30 churches reported 693 baptisms, 8,381 members, $233,829 total gifts, $38,937 mission gifts, $516,485 property value, and $48,425 church debt.

LAMESA. Organized in 1924 with 13 churches out of Dawson and Gaines counties. In 1954, 18 churches reported 297 baptisms, 5,114 members, $212,009 total gifts, $31,724 mission gifts, $741,222 property value, and $127,135 church debt.

LAMPASAS. Organized Sept. 16, 1896, at Lampasas, with 12 churches. Articles of faith were adopted. In 1954, 15 churches reported 220 baptisms, 3,241 members, $97,845 total gifts, $17,484 mission gifts, $361,450 property value, and $11,160 church debt.

LIMESTONE COUNTY. Organized Nov. 12, 1892, at First Church, Grosbeck, with 17 churches, 1,406 members. In 1954, 27 churches reported 220 baptisms, 6,300 members, $164,733 total gifts, $26,970 mission gifts, $653,000 property value, and $43,818 church debt.

LOWER RIO GRANDE. Organized as the Cameron-Hidalgo Association March 25, 1912, at San Benito with eight churches. Due to enlargement of territory the name was changed to Lower Rio Grande Baptist Association at Mercedes in 1921. In 1954, 41 churches reported 1,050 baptisms, 17,767 members, $818,997 total gifts, $189,772 mission gifts, $3,604,150 property value, and $508,200 church debt.

LUBBOCK. Organized Nov. 3, 1924, at First Church, Lubbock, with 10 churches from Lubbock, Hockley, and Cochran counties. In 1925 the Garza Association disbanded, and the churches came into Lubbock Association. In 1954, 42 churches reported 1,038 baptisms, 23,242 members, $1,101,781 total gifts, $213,609 mission gifts, $4,550,395 property value, and $503,736 church debt.

MEDINA RIVER. Organized Oct. 27, 1888, at Medina Church in Bandara County with 12 churches, 11 of them from Perdinales Association, with 342 members. In 1954, 18 churches reported 238 baptisms, 4,389 members, $213,277 total gifts, $25,403 mission gifts, $883,377 property value, and $104,208 church debt.

MERIDIAN. Organized June 27, 1884, at Meridian Church, with 13 churches of Bosque County. Articles of faith were adopted. In 1954, 7 churches reported 117 baptisms, 3,558 members, $90,460 total gifts, $14,859 mission gifts, $417,500 property value, and $23,029 church debt.

MILAM. Organized in 1854 in Cameron Church as the Little River Association. At a meeting of the association, Oct. 11, 1918, a resolution was passed that the Little River Association would no longer exist, but would be replaced by Milam County and Burleson County associations upon their organization. In 1954, 24 churches reported 78 baptisms, 3,938 members, $140,307 total gifts, $20,427 mission gifts, $346,510 property value, and $8,145 church debt.

MILLS COUNTY. Organized Jan., 1889, at Bennett Creek Church, with seven churches. Articles of faith were adopted. At the first annual meeting eight churches reported 364 members. In 1954, 9 churches reported 64 baptisms, 1,606 members, $47,390 total gifts, $9,291 mission gifts, $201,820 property value, and $1,174 church debt.

MITCHELL-SCURRY. Organized Oct. 14, 1924, with 18 churches from Scurry, Mitchell, Borden, Nolan, and Coke counties meeting at the First Baptist Church of Snyder. In 1954, 29 churches reported 354 baptisms, 8,145 members, $326,090 total gifts, $71,511 mission gifts, $1,076,522 property value, and $82,874 church debt.

MONTAGUE. Organized Sept. 20, 1878, in Montague Church, Montague County, with six churches represented. In 1954, 17 churches reported 228 baptisms, 4,229 members, $154,509 total gifts, $33,588 mission gifts, $496,700 property value, and $26,369 church debt.

NECHES RIVER. Organized in 1866, but earliest minutes available are from the eighth annual session, Oct. 25, 1873, meeting at Liberty Church in Houston County. At this time two new churches were added making a total of 23 churches reporting. In 1954, 31 churches reported 241 baptisms, 5,397 members, $197,712 total gifts, $36,133 mission gifts, $916,700 property value, and $90,575 church debt.

NEW BETHEL. Organized in 1860, at Woodville, Tyler County, where Bethlehem Association had been formed seven years before. New Bethel was composed of 15 churches from Bethlehem and Tryon associations. Articles of faith were adopted. In 1954, 33 churches reported 220 baptisms, 4,587 members, $139,467 total gifts, $25,720 mission gifts, $462,140 property value, and $195,597 church debt.

NORTHFORK. Organized in 1913. The first minutes available are from the 12th session at Shamrock in 1925 with 29 churches represented. In 1954, 24 churches reported 239 baptisms, 6,627 members, $176,734 total gifts, $34,829 mission gifts, $782,466 property value, and no church debt.

ORANGE. Organized Oct., 1950, by representatives from 21 churches in the Orange area. In 1954, 26 churches reported 720 baptisms, 12,751 members, $451,400 total gifts, $56,464 mission gifts, $1,804,426 property value, and $331,639 church debt.

PALO DURO. Organized Sept. 19, 1891, at Claude with eight churches from the Panhandle section not previously connected with an association. At the first annual session at First Church, Amarillo, six new churches were received, and the total membership was 327. In 1954, 21 churches reported 781 baptisms, 15,151 members, $620,256 total gifts, $105,161 mission gifts, $2,167,500 property value, and $106,521 church debt.

PALO PINTO. Organized Oct. 3, 1879, at Bethel Church in Palo Pinto County, near Santo, with six churches, 213 members, from Comanche and Brazos River associations. In 1954, 23 churches reported 220 baptisms, 5,654 members, $193,005 total gifts, $26,995 mission gifts, $644,000 property value, and $66,234 church debt.

PALUXY. Organized Sept. 3, 1880, at Hopewell Church on Squaw Creek, with nine churches from Bosque River and Brazos associations. Articles of faith were adopted. In 1954, 17 churches reported 171 baptisms, 2,704 members, $71,071 total gifts, $14,540 mission gifts, $213,700 property value, and $35,650 church debt.

PANHANDLE. Organized Jan. 28, 1905, at Memphis, with 11 churches out of Red Fork Association and the southeast part of Palo Duro Association. In 1954, 14 churches reported 191 baptisms, 4,651 members, $100,695 total gifts, $23,640 mission gifts, $353,750 property value, and $2,921 church debt.

PARKER COUNTY. Organized Oct. 30, 1886, at Weatherford in Parker County with 13 churches. In 1954, 31 churches reported 285 baptisms, 6,172 members, $186,239 total gifts, $34,526 mission gifts, $621,500 property value, and $18,095 church debt.

PECOS VALLEY. Organized in 1909. In 1940 after division the Pecos Valley Association had 18 churches, and the Big Bend Association had nine. In 1954, 13 churches reported 404 baptisms, 6,942 members, $375,475 total gifts, $57,480 mission gifts, $1,130,222 property value, and $158,304 church debt.

PERMIAN BASIN. Organized Sept. 13, 1950, at Midland with 18 churches from Big Spring Association. In 1954, 29 churches reported 1,186 baptisms, 20,566 members, $1,172,067 total gifts, $155,135 mission gifts, $3,664,083 property value, and $963,876 church debt.

PITTSBURG. Organized in 1911 with 12 churches from the eastern border of Rehoboth Association. In 1954, 44 churches reported 527 baptisms, 11,373 members, $446,618 total gifts, $79,473 mission gifts, $1,453,100 property value, and $212,757 church debt.

RED FORK. Organized Oct. 20, 1877, by delegates from four churches. In 1954, 25 churches reported 261 baptisms, 7,616 members, $196,556 total gifts, $44,359 mission gifts, $867,742 property value, and $43,162 church debt.

RED RIVER–TEXARKANA. Organized at DeKalb Oct. 8, 1929, when executive boards of Red River and Texarkana associations met in joint session and voted to consolidate as Red River–Texarkana Association. In 1954, 58 churches reported 878 baptisms, 17,252 members, $662,729 total gifts, $105,653 mission gifts, $2,589,058 property value, and $288,508 church debt.

REHOBOTH. Organized Oct. 31, 1856, at Liberty Church, now Mt. Vernon, with 18 churches representing 637 members. Articles of faith were adopted. In 1904 Hopkins and Wood associations, organized out of Rehoboth, joined the Baptist Missionary Association organized at Troup, June, 1900. Delta County united with Rehoboth in 1932. In 1954, 52 churches reported 343 baptisms, 10,685 members, $319,022 total gifts, $52,080 mission gifts, $1,277,000 property value, and $35,648 church debt.

ROBERTSON. Organized Nov. 20, 1897, at Franklin Church with 13 churches represented. In 1923 the association reorganized with 15 churches and began renumbering their minutes. In 1954, 19 churches reported 162 baptisms, 3,970 members, $133,851 total gifts, $19,580 mission gifts, $579,500 property value, and $64,938 church debt.

RUNNELS COUNTY. Organized Sept. 27, 1889, as the Content Association. In 1908 the name was changed to Runnels County Association. In 1954, 25 churches reported 302 baptisms, 6,070 members, $226,604 total gifts, $45,130 mission gifts, $803,799 property value, and $17,883 church debt.

RUSK-PANOLA. Organized Oct., 1926, with 21 churches. In 1954, 38 churches reported 441 baptisms, 11,556 members, $632,024 total gifts, $108,974 mission gifts, $1,656,730 property value, and $168,449 church debt.

SALINE. Organized in 1858 in a territory including Wood, Van Zandt, Anderson, and Henderson counties. In 1954, 22 churches reported 178 baptisms, 6,318 members, $230,936 total gifts, $42,855 mission gifts, $885,600 property value, and $64,842 church debt.

SAN ANTONIO. Organized Nov. 5, 1858, at New Salem Church in De Witt County with seven churches, probably from Colorado Association. Articles of faith were adopted. In 1954, 54 churches reported 2,286 baptisms, 37,588 members, $1,735,622 total gifts, $370,760 mission gifts, $7,251,221 property value, and $1,072,636 church debt.

SAN FELIPE. Organized Oct. 21, 1948, at Katy under J. Lowell Ponder, with 11 churches from Union Association. In 1954, 16 churches reported 283 baptisms, 4,037 members, $284,819 total gifts, $27,792 mission gifts, $1,060,200 property value, and $255,818 church debt.

SAN JACINTO. Organized Oct. 21, 1947, at Goose Creek (now Central, Baytown) under District Missionary J. Lowell Ponder, with 16 churches. Fifteen of these were from Union Association, Harris County; Hoffman came from Tryon-Evergreen Association. The San Jacinto Battleground and a commemorative monument located in the area provided the name. A. L. Jordan was elected moderator; Bert Mattingly, clerk. In 1954, 22 churches reported 760 baptisms, 13,174 members, $683,339 total gifts, $114,805 mission gifts, $2,202,037 property value, and $357,761 church debt.

SAN MARCOS. Organized Nov. 12, 1858, at Elm Grove Church, Gonzales County, with 10 churches from Colorado Association. At the second session seven more churches were received, and the 17 churches reported 718 members of whom 142 were Negroes. Articles of faith were adopted. The association owned and operated Kyle Seminary at Kyle, Tex., suspended Apr., 1891, for lack of funds. In 1954, 24 churches reported 301 baptisms, 7,154 members, $246,265 total gifts, $43,725 mission gifts, $914,126 property value, and $36,826 church debt.

SAN SABA. Organized Sept. 23, 1876, with seven churches. At the second session, Sept. 21, 1877, at Lynch's Creek, 13 churches, 368 members, were represented. In 1954, 13 churches reported 70 baptisms, 2,118 members, $58,510 total gifts, $11,705 mission gifts, $198,250 property value, and $2,200 church debt.

SHELBY-DOCHES. Organized Oct. 8, 1925, when Nacogdoches and Saline River associations met at Martinville, with 18 churches combining to form Shelby-Doches Association. In 1954, 30 churches reported 249 baptisms, 9,020 members, $336,429 total gifts, $67,278 mission gifts, $1,255,100 property value, and $57,755 church debt.

SMITH. Organized Dec. 6, 1898, at Dean Church in Burlingame Community with four churches from Smith County. The churches, Dean, Noonday, Tyler First, and North Tyler, had withdrawn from Cherokee Association. Articles of faith were adopted. In 1954, 53 churches reported 842 baptisms, 17,817 members, $793,017 total gifts, $139,749 mission gifts, $3,566,745 property value, and $467,528 church debt.

SODA LAKE. Organized Sept., 1848, at the second session of Eastern Missionary Association, which had been organized out of Sabine Association Dec. 3, 1847. The association changed its name to Soda Lake, adopting articles of faith from *Encyclopedia of Religious Knowledge*. In 1954, 56 churches reported 1,293 members, $1,268,970 total gifts, $184,630 mission gifts. A division of the association was approved at the 105th annual session in 1955, Soda Lake retaining churches in Harrison County, and Gregg County Association to be organized from the remaining churches in Soda Lake Association.

SOUTH EAST TEXAS. Organized Feb. 11, 1888, in the First Church, Beaumont, with four churches. In 1954, 53 churches reported 1,998 baptisms, 39,349 members, $2,037,582 total gifts, $372,602 mission gifts, $7,356,788 property value, and $1,192,933 church debt.

STAKED PLAINS. Organized Aug. 18, 1891, as the Llano Estacado Association at Plainview with 11 churches and 163 members from Floyd, Hale, and Swisher counties. In 1900 its name was changed to Staked Plains Baptist Association. In 1954, 25 churches reported 491 baptisms, 9,834 members, $626,699 total gifts, $178,680 mission gifts, $1,959,807 property value, and $153,070 church debt.

STONEWALL. Organized Aug. 22, 1890, at Plum Creek Church in Jones County with 11 churches and 329 members out of Sweetwater Association. In 1954, eight churches reported 102 baptisms, 1,734 members, $60,000 total gifts, $8,060 mission gifts, $134,500 property value, and $4,250 church debt.

SWEETWATER. Organized Aug., 1885, with 12 churches out of Red Gap, now Cisco Association. In 1954, 39 churches reported 767 baptisms, 18,894 members, $980,949 total gifts, $188,134 mission gifts, $3,989,866 property value, and $647,249 church debt.

TARRANT. Organized as the West Fork Association in the Birdville Church on Oct. 12, 1855, with 12 churches from seven counties. In the annual session Aug. 12–13, 1886, it was recommended that a county association be organized, as a result of which representatives from 12 churches met at First Church, Fort Worth, Oct. 14, 1886, and organized Tarrant County Association. The New Hampshire Confession of Faith was adopted. In 1954, 129 churches reported 4,145 baptisms, 82,469 members, $4,137,740 total gifts, $788,172 mission gifts, $15,129,258 property value, and $2,915,311 church debt.

THROCKMORTON-YOUNG. Organized in 1927 when the Throckmorton and Young associations united to form Throckmorton-Young Association. In 1954, 22 churches reported 228 baptisms, 6,528 members, $222,713 total gifts, $47,884 mission gifts, $767,300 property value, and $16,861 church debt.

TIERRA BLANCA. Organized Aug. 15, 1905, at Canyon City with seven churches out of the southern part of Palo Duro Association. In 1954, 21 churches reported 486 baptisms, 8,455 members, $474,921 total gifts, $127,635 mission gifts, $1,810,275 property value, and $65,981 church debt.

TRANS-CANADIAN. Organized 1908. The first minutes available are from the 1913 meeting at Hartley when 12 churches reported. In 1954, 11 churches reported 251 baptisms, 4,831 members, $235,580 total gifts, $64,751 mission gifts, $868,300 property value, and $30,000 church debt.

TRINITY RIVER. Organized July, 1848, at Providence Church with six churches from Union Association. Having co-operated with the Baptist Missionary Association in the early 1900's the group, reorganized in 1944, adopted articles of faith and began counting sessions from that date. In 1954, 32 churches reported 445 baptisms, 8,263 members, $424,085 total gifts, $72,720 mission gifts, $1,460,780 property value, and $246,308 church debt.

TRYON-EVERGREEN. Organized in 1902 from the union of Evergreen and Tryon Associations. In 1954, 51 churches reported 610 baptisms, 12,-

480 total members, $475,700 total gifts, $66,896 mission gifts, $1,867,000 property value, and $105,331 church debt.

UNION. Organized on Oct. 8–9, 1840, when three churches: Independence, 17 members; La Grange, 15 members; and Travis, 13 members, sent 10 messengers to convene at Travis Church 10 miles south of Brenham. The resulting Union Association was the first Baptist association in Texas. An earlier effort in June, 1840, at Independence, Washington County, of 25 Baptists to organize an association was fruitless because of confusion between missionary and antimissionary attitudes.

After adopting articles of faith and a constitution, Union Association adopted at the first session a "bill of inalienable rights" which provided that "each church is forever free and independent," that each member has the full right to exercise his or her discretion. Union Association, composed of churches from nine counties in the Houston-Galveston area for many years, was organized in 1937 by District Missionary J. D. Brannon into five "Regional Workers Conference" groups, four of which, from 1946 to 1950, grew into Galveston, San Felipe, Gulf Coast, and San Jacinto associations. In 1954, 133 churches reported 7,341 baptisms, 121,561 members, $6,100,194 total gifts, $1,100,244 mission gifts, $24,003,081 property value, and $6,059,089 church debt.

UNITY. Organized in 1908. On April 12, 1928, Angelina and Unity associations combined as the Unity Association. A. F. Peters was elected moderator; A. E. Ellis, clerk. In 1954, 35 churches reported 437 baptisms, 10,801 members, $839,892 total gifts, $75,176 mission gifts, $1,353,966 property value, and $246,368 church debt.

VAN ZANDT COUNTY. Organized Nov. 11, 1853, as the Baptist General Association of the State of Texas, with eight churches, James Colthorp being the only member listed from Van Zandt County. Three of the churches became associated with Saline Association in 1858 and New Bethlehem Association in 1881. In 1905 the name was changed to Van Zandt County Association because of co-operation with Baptist Missionary Association. It was reorganized Oct. 8, 1935, at Turner Church, and the name became Van Zandt County Missionary Baptist Association. At this time it began co-operating with the general convention. In 1954, 21 churches reported 209 baptisms, 5,050 members, $165,828 total gifts, $32,638 mission gifts, $485,600 property value, and $1,578 church debt.

WACO. Organized Nov., 1860, at First Church, Waco, with nine churches, 541 members. Waco Classical School, later Waco University, and Baylor University since 1886, was under "patronage" of this body. In 1954, 61 churches reported 1,272 baptisms, 33,796 members, $1,587,919 total gifts, $317,473 mission gifts, $6,800,068 property value, and $1,335,209 church debt.

WEST PLAINS. Organized in 1927 with J. W. Hembree and C. M. McSpadden as early leaders. In 1954, 23 churches reported 338 baptisms, 7,492 members, $351,624 total gifts, $64,539 mission gifts, $1,221,659 property value, and $33,792 church debt.

WICHITA-ARCHER. Organized in 1910 as the Wichita County Association. It united with Archer Association in 1927 to form Wichita-Archer Association, and articles of faith were adopted. In 1954, 31 churches reported 912 baptisms, 21,267 members, $933,144 total gifts, $168,656 mission gifts, $2,981,721 property value, and $541,216 church debt.

WILBARGER FOARD. Organized Sept. 16, 1913, as the Wilbarger Association in the Oklaunion Church with 17 churches. In 1923 the name was changed to the Wilbarger-Foard Association. In 1954, 19 churches reported 258 baptisms, 7,134 members, $264,060 total gifts, $59,875 mission gifts, $1,371,700 property value, and $66,790 church debt.

WILLIAMSON COUNTY. Organized Sept. 26, 1917, at the First Church of Georgetown in Williamson County with 21 churches. Articles of faith were adopted. In 1954, 20 churches reported 174 baptisms, 4,548 members, $140,253 total gifts, $25,583 mission gifts, $430,500 property value, and $37,878 church debt.

WINTER GARDEN. Organized in 1880 as the Rio Grande Association. The name was changed to Winter Garden in 1938. In 1954, 20 churches reported 228 baptisms, 5,172 members, $200,448 total gifts, $30,511 mission gifts, $986,945 property value, and $84,973 church debt.

WISE. Organized Sept. 11, 1886, at Pleasant Grove Church with 38 churches. Articles of faith were adopted. In 1954, 30 churches reported 151 baptisms, 4,967 members, $163,071 total gifts, $38,567 mission gifts, $422,500 property value, and $11,988 church debt.

II. Extinct. ALVARADO. Organized in 1864, with no minutes being printed; reorganized in 1866 at Alvarado with seven churches. J. J. Sledge was elected moderator; W. S. Jackson, clerk. At the fourth session 17 churches from Hood, Johnson, Ellis, Hill, and Bosque counties reported. In 1869 emphasis was placed on religious care of Negroes. Cleburne Institute, a high school owned by the association, was begun in 1886, with J. R. Clarke, principal. On Sept. 13, 1900, with 42 churches represented, 40 of them from Johnson County, the name was changed to Johnson County Association. New Hampshire Articles of Faith were adopted. In 36 years it had grown from 200 to 3,000 members.

ANDERSON COUNTY. Organized Nov. 9, 1890, at Friendship Church in Anderson County with nine churches from Neches River Association and five new ones, representing a total membership of 394. Articles of faith were adopted. At the fourth session 16 churches reported. In 1911 or 1912 it became Landmark Missionary Baptist Association of Anderson County. At 28th annual session in 1918, with 14 churches, the name changed back to Anderson County Association.

ANGELINA. Organized Nov. 6, 1875, at O'Quin

with ten churches from Bethlehem and Central associations. In its first year the churches baptized 15, excluded 17 of whom four were restored. It dissolved to join Unity Association in 1927.

ARCHER. Organized in 1891 out of the Little Wichita Association. The first minutes available are from the 1911 session at Rice Church in Archer County, with 14 churches represented. On Sept. 8, 1927, it united with Wichita Association to form Wichita-Archer Association.

BATTLE CREEK. Organized in 1883 at Battle Creek Church, Stephens County, by the churches of Callahan and Eastland counties, and four or five churches of Shackelford and Stephens counties. The total membership of the churches was 250. At the second annual session held with Zion Hill Church of Callahan County the name was changed to Cisco Association.

BAYLOR COUNTY. Organized in 1892, as the Little Wichita Association. In 1907 the name was changed to Baylor County Association, which it retained until 1930 when it became the Baylor-Knox Association.

BETHLEHEM. Organized Oct., 1853, at Woodville in Tyler County with five churches representing a membership of 88. The New Hampshire Confession was adopted in 1858. Bethlehem is now extinct.

BOSQUE RIVER. Organized at Paluxy Nov. 10, 1869, with seven churches from five counties in an area thickly populated by hostile Indians. After adopting articles of faith, because of Indian raids, it dissolved Oct. 21, 1887, and the churches joined Erath and Meridian associations.

BRAZOS RIVER. Organized in Oct., 1858, at Providence Church in Parker County, with 12 churches from four counties having a membership of 411, 40 per cent of whom were baptized the previous year. Noah T. Byars (*q.v.*), in whose blacksmith shop the Texas Declaration of Independence was signed, was the first moderator. Articles of faith from *Encyclopedia of Religious Knowledge* were adopted. Indian raids hindered the work, and many of the churches disbanded. The home of the Brazos River Institute 1858–1862, at Palo Pinto (Golconda), closed during the war as a result of defective buildings. The association dissolved Aug., 1887. Many churches joined Erath Association.

BRYAN. Organized Nov. 15, 1888, at Shiloh Church, Robinson County with nine churches out of Navasota River Association. Sixteen churches, representing 1,073 members, were present at the Aug. 24, 1889, session. During the first year the association baptized 90 and excluded 36. It adopted articles of faith and is now extinct.

BURLESON COUNTY. Organized in 1918 at Summerville with 10 churches, three from the Little River Association. These churches joined Burleson-Lee County Association in 1921 at Lexington. They later joined Kaufman and Independence associations.

CAMERON-HIDALGO. Organized Mar. 25, 1912, with eight churches at San Benito. Due to enlarged territory the name was changed later to Lower Rio Grande Association.

CENTRAL. Organized in 1852 at fourth annual session of Eastern Texas Association of United Baptists. Articles of faith were adopted.

CLARKSVILLE. Organized Oct., 1881, at Macedonia Church with 14 churches from the Red River Association, which withdrew because a majority vote refused to seat certain churches. In 1887 these churches began to join the Montague and Clay associations, and Clarksville soon became extinct.

COKE COUNTY. Organized Sept., 1910, with three churches. At the second session six more churches were received. The churches of this association joined the Runnels Association in 1919 and 1920.

COLLINGWORTH-CHILDRESS. Organized Oct. 1, 1915, at Dodson Valley Church with 10 churches from the Panhandle Association which had unanimously voted to divide. Articles of faith were adopted. In 1921 it disbanded; the churches joined Red Fork Association.

CONTENT. Organized Sept. 27, 1889, with 15 churches, having 658 members. The New Hampshire Confession of Faith was adopted. The name was changed to Runnels County Association in 1908.

COTTLE-KING. Organized in Cottle and King counties out of Leon River Association. The only minutes available are from 1925 with 11 churches reporting, 1926 with eight churches reporting, 1927 with only five reporting pastors. This body became extinct.

DELTA COUNTY. Organized Sept., 1886, with five churches. In the 1932 session with 14 churches represented, eleven without pastors, Delta voted to unite with Rehoboth Association at the latter's invitation.

EASTERN MISSIONARY. Organized Dec. 3, 1847, with four churches: Macedonia of Panola County, Henderson of Rusk County, and Border and Eight Mile of Harrison County. These churches withdrew from Sabine Association after a disagreement and met at Borden Church (Jonesville) to form Eastern Missionary Association, adopting articles of faith from *Encyclopedia of Religious Knowledge*. At the Sept., 1848, session at Macedonia Church the name changed to Soda Lake Association.

EASTERN TEXAS. Organized Nov., 1849, with 12 churches at Old Union Church four miles from Nacogdoches where Sabine Association was organized six years earlier. At the fourth session in 1852 the name changed to Central Baptist Association.

EAST FORK. Organized Nov., 1870, with 12 churches out of Sister Grove and Elm Fork associations, at Mt. Pleasant Church in Collin County. Articles of faith were adopted. The 1902 minutes record an offering for the Baptist Missionary Association, which East Fork joined soon after. The 1905 minutes are the last available.

ELM FORK. Organized Oct., 1849, at Union

Church with Lonesome Dove and Wilson Creek (now Rowlett) represented. The three churches had a membership of 131. At the annual session held Nov. 4, 1849, at Lonesome Dove Church in Navarro County (now Tarrant) near Grapevine, Bethel Church with eight members was admitted. At the 38th annual session meeting with Antioch Church in Dallas County in 1886 the name was changed to Dallas County Association.

EVERGREEN. Organized Dec. 2, 1881, at Union Grove Church in Grimes County with nine churches out of Union Association. Articles of faith from *Encyclopedia of Religious Knowledge* were adopted. It united with Tryon Association in 1902 to form Tryon-Evergreen Association.

GARZA. Organized in 1920 with seven churches in the area of Lubbock. It disbanded in 1925 and united with Lubbock Association.

GREER COUNTY. Organized Sept. 11, 1890, at Fairview Church, Martha, Texas (now Oklahoma), with six churches, 141 members, from Red Fork Association. Articles of faith were adopted. This body is now extinct.

GREGG COUNTY. Organized in 1955 when the 105th annual session of the Soda Lake Association voted to divide, the churches in Harrison County remaining with Soda Lake and others organizing Gregg County Association.

HILLSBORO. Organized Aug. 16, 1886, at Osceola Church when 33 churches from Towash and Hill County associations consolidated to form Hillsboro Association. It disbanded in 1906 and joined with Hubbard City Association to reorganize Hill County Association.

HONEY GROVE. Organized July 30, 1880, in Fannin County when 17 churches withdrew from Sister Grove Association because of internal dissension. It dissolved in 1886 when the churches joined Grayson and Fannin County associations.

HOPEWELL I. Organized in Parker County, with date unknown. In 1875 or 1876 it dissolved to join Jacksboro Association. Two of the churches went into the Jacksboro Association at the time of its organization, the others later.

HOPEWELL II. Organized Oct. 21, 1880, by representatives of 10 churches at Damascus Church, Titus County, from the Salem and Rehoboth associations. It is now affiliated with the Baptist Missionary Association.

HUBBARD CITY. Organized Sept. 6, 1889, at Mt. Antioch Church in Limestone County with nine churches reporting 440 members from Hillsboro, Prairie Grove, Richland, and Waco associations. At the Oct. 6, 1906, session at Parr's Chapel, east of Hillsboro, the association voted to disband to unite with the Hillsboro Association in recreating the Hill County Association.

JACKSBORO. Organized Sept. 15, 1876, at Dry Creek Church in Wise County with 16 churches, 431 members, from Clay, Montague, Jack, Wise, Parker, and Palo Pinto counties. One church was from West Fork Association, two from New Hope I, and 13 not connected with any association. Four were from Jack County. The following year 18 new churches were admitted, making a total of 34 churches with 1,110 members. The name changed to Jack County Association in 1903 because of a split in the Jacksboro Church.

JUDSON. Organized at Larissa, Cherokee County, Nov., 1853, with 17 churches reporting 800 members. In 1857 the territory embraced Anderson, Henderson, Cherokee, Houston, Nacogdoches, Rusk, and Trinity counties, having 36 churches and 1,400 members. The association passed out of existence. Its churches were absorbed in Neches River, Anderson County, Cherokee associations, and other bodies.

LAKE CREEK UNION. Organized Sept. 17, 1892, at New Hope Church in Knox County with eight churches and 190 members. Four churches came from Providence Association, three from Red Fork, and the church at Benjamin. At the 10th session in 1901 according to the last minutes printed, the number of churches had dwindled to four. The churches are now in Haskell-Knox Association.

LAREDO. Organized Oct. 18, 1938, at the First Church, Hebbronville, with 11 churches out of Winter Garden and Rio Grande associations. This body voted to dissolve at the 1954 session. Eight churches went into Coastal Bend Association; the others were undecided as to an affiliation.

LAVACA RIVER. Organized Sept. 28, 1877, at North Grove Church in Lavaca County with 15 churches, 12 of them reporting 702 members, from Colorado, San Marcos, and Union associations. Zacharius N. Morrell (*q.v.*) preached and presided until the moderator was elected. In 1924 the name was changed to Gonzales Association.

LEON RIVER. Organized Sept. 24, 1858, at Belton Church on Nolan Creek, six miles west of Belton, with 11 churches. Zacharius N. Morrell (*q.v.*) was present and took part in the organization; articles of faith were adopted. The name was changed to Coryell County Association at the 88th annual session in 1945 and it still exists under this name.

LIBERTY. Organized in 1882 with 17 churches out of Gregg, Upshur, Camp, and Wood counties. It began co-operating with the Baptist Missionary Association in 1901.

LITTLE BRAZOS. Organized Sept., 1875, at New Hope Church in Falls County. The churches went into Robertson County Association in 1897, reorganized in 1923, and began counting sessions at that date.

LITTLE RIVER. Organized Nov. 9, 1855, with 11 churches and 565 members from Cameron and Milam counties. Articles of faith were adopted. In 1918 the churches went into Milam and Burleson associations.

LITTLE WICHITA. Organized July 29, 1892, at Archer City with 11 churches and 215 members. After working with Baylor County Association

1907–1930, the name was changed to Baylor-Knox Association in 1930.

LLANO ESTACADO. Organized Aug. 18, 1891, at Plainview with 11 churches and 163 members from Floyd, Hale, and Swisher counties. The boundaries of the association were thus defined: "On the east by the Red Fork Association, on the south by the Texas and Pacific Railway, on the north and west by the providences of God." In 1900 the name was changed to Staked Plains Baptist Association.

LLANO RIVER. Organized in 1881 at Bethel Church, Squaw Creek, with the first session on Sept. 8, 1882. There were nine churches with 297 members. The association united with Burnett-Llano Association in 1913.

MACEDONIA. Organized Sept. 28, 1888, at Graham with 13 churches from Red Fork Association. In 1911 the Macedonia Association dissolved and the churches joined Young and Throckmorton County associations.

MCGREGOR. Organized Oct. 30, 1885, at Moody, in McLennan County, with 10 churches. Articles of faith were adopted. In 1890 it dissolved and joined Waco Association.

MONTAGUE-WISE. Organized Sept. 11, 1928, at Alvord when Montague and Wise associations merged. The union continued until 1935 when two county-wide associations were organized in its place.

MOUNT ZION. Organized Oct. 30, 1857, at Mt. Zion Church in Rusk County with 13 churches having 530 members, most of them from Soda Lake Association. Articles of faith were adopted. The last minutes available, 1908, indicate that the churches had begun to join Neches River and Rusk-Panola associations.

NACOGDOCHES. Organized Friday before the fifth Sunday in Oct., 1887, at Antioch Church, Nacogdoches County, with 20 churches from Angelina, Mt. Zion, and Central associations. Union Church, the oldest church in Texas, organized in 1838 with seven members, was a member of this association. On Oct. 8, 1925, this group joined Saline River Association to form Shelby-Doches Association.

NAVARRO COUNTY. Organized in 1858 with churches out of Richland Association. It joined the Baptist Missionary Association in 1900.

NAVASOTA RIVER. Organized Oct. 21, 1874, at the Shiloh Church in Grimes County with 19 churches from the Trinity River Association. Articles of faith were adopted. In 1888 the association divided, the churches on the west side of Navasota River forming Bryan Association. From 1927 to 1936 the remaining churches joined Creath-Brazos Association.

NEW BETHLEHEM. Organized Sept., 1881, at Snyder Springs Church in Van Zandt County. It was composed of 13 churches from Old Landmark and Saline associations. It began co-operating with the Baptist Missionary Association in 1904; later, many of the churches came back into the co-operating associations in that area.

NEW UNION. Organized Oct. 29, 1892, at Concord Church, Angelina County, with three churches having 90 members. Articles of faith were adopted. In 1897 the "gospel mission plan" of mission work was adopted.

NORTH COLORADO. Organized in 1891, with the first session on Aug. 26, 1892, when five churches were represented and three others received; the eight reported 162 members. The last minutes available are for 1922 after which the association soon disintegrated. Some of the churches may have joined the Baptist Missionary Association.

NORTH SULPHUR. Organized in 1871, holding its first session at Post Oak Grove Church, 1872, with nine churches, 606 members. It dissolved in 1886, and the churches united with the associations in Lamar, Fannin, Delta, and Hunt counties.

OLD LANDMARK. Organized July, 1879, with six churches which had withdrawn from Saline Association due to doctrinal differences. In Sept., 1881, it united with other churches from Saline Association to form New Bethlehem Association.

PECAN VALLEY. Organized Sept. 9, 1876, with five churches. Several associations came out of this body, one of the largest associations in central Texas. On Aug. 17, 1907, the name was changed to "Brown County Baptist Association, the Legal Successor to the Pecan Valley Baptist Association" which was retained until 1916 after which it became known as Brown County Association. The legal action was taken to protect the charter rights of Howard Payne College which had been vested in the Pecan Valley Association, when the college was instituted at a called meeting of the association June 29–30, 1889. Paint Creek Association was organized from four churches out of this body and co-operated with Baptist Missionary Association. In 1904 it had six churches; by 1910 all had returned to Brown County Association.

PENTACOST. Organized July 23, 1903, at Little Bluff Creek Church in Mason County. A very small group, it disintegrated about 1906. The 1905 minutes are the last ones available.

PERDINALES. Organized in 1874 at Dripping Springs Church in Hayes County with 10 churches, most of them from Austin Association in Kerr and Blanco counties. Articles of faith were adopted. In 1888, 11 of the churches joined in the organization of Medina River Association, and Perdinales became extinct.

PLEASANT GROVE. Organized in 1881 at Pleasant Grove Church in Shelby County, with the first session, Sept. 16, 1882, at Mt. Zion Church in Rusk County. The association was composed of 11 churches, 10 of them from Mt. Zion Association. At the eighth session, Oct., 1888, an amendment was proposed to change the name to Shelby County Missionary Baptist Association, which was passed at ninth session Oct., 1889.

PRAIRIE GROVE. Organized Oct. 30, 1881, with 14 churches from Richland and Trinity River associations, at Prairie Grove Church, Limestone County. In 1892 at Prairie Grove Church,

10 churches were granted letters to join Limestone Association.

PROVIDENCE. Organized the fifth Sunday in Dec., 1888. The first session was held Aug., 1889, at Miller Creek Church in Throckmorton County. In 1892 the body dissolved, three of the churches joining Stonewall, and four joining Lake Creek Association.

RAINS COUNTY. Organized July 30, 1904, at Emory Church with 14 churches "in sympathy with Baptist General Convention of Texas and Southern Baptist Convention." In 1909 the name was changed to Harmony Baptist Association.

RED GAP. Organized in 1878 or 1879 with the first annual session held in 1879. In the third annual session six churches were represented and five new churches were added. In 1883 the churches joined Battle Creek (now Cisco) Association.

RED RIVER. Organized Oct. 30, 1848, at Honey Grove Church, with eight churches represented. About 1907 Red River began co-operating with the Baptist Missionary Association. On Oct. 8, 1929, at DeKalb, the executive boards of Red River and Texarkana associations met in joint session, voted to consolidate and form Red River–Texarkana Association.

RED RIVER MISSIONARY BAPTIST. Organized in 1904 with four churches from Red River Association. In 1914 it joined the Red River County Association which became the Red River–Texarkana Association in 1929.

REGULAR PREDESTINATION BAPTIST. Organized Nov. 8, 1844, at Antioch Church near Jasper, with one church from Louisiana and four from southeast Texas. Levi A. Durham was elected moderator. This body was opposed to missions, Sunday schools, Bible and tract societies, and conventions. After six years it had only six churches and 73 members and finally disintegrated.

RICHLAND. Organized in 1857 with nine churches out of Falls, Freestone, Limestone, Navarro, Hill, Johnson, Ellis, and part of Tarrant counties. In 1867 the association split and disintegrated over the doctrine of total depravity. Some churches went into Navarro County Association.

RIO GRANDE. Organized in 1880. At the second annual session, July 15, 1882, at Carrizo Springs, Dimmitt County, nine churches with 281 members were represented. The name was changed to Winter Garden Association in 1938.

ROUND GROVE. Organized Dec. 4, 1897, at Live Oak Church with eight churches reporting 725 members from Erath and Hamilton counties. At the 29th session held at Saint Joe Church on Sept. 9–10, 1925, the association dissolved.

SABINE VALLEY. Organized Nov., 1843, at Union Church, Nacogdoches County, the second association organized in Texas. It was composed of Bethel Church of Harrison County, Bethel of Sabine County, and Mt. Zion and Union of Nacogdoches County. Strong antimissionary feeling led to three parties in the association—missionary, antimissionary, and free will. At the 1847 session the missionary group formed the Eastern Missionary Baptist Association, and the other groups went into other bodies.

SALADO. Organized in the fall of 1874 when messengers of 20 churches from Bell, Milam, and Williamson counties previously affiliated with Leon River Association met at Salado. Articles of faith were adopted. In the 1923 session with 31 churches represented, it voted to change the name to Bell County Association.

SALEM. Organized in 1862 with churches out of Titus, Marion, Lafayette, and Caddo counties. Some of these churches began co-operating with Pittsburg Association in 1927, and Salem soon became extinct.

SALOME. Organized in 1880. The only minutes available are from the fifth session, meeting Oct. 10–12, 1885, at Cedar Creek Church in Hopkins County, with 10 churches represented. This body is now extinct.

SCURRY COUNTY. Organized in 1907, and on Oct. 14, 1924, joined with churches from Mitchell, Borden, Nolan, and Coke counties to organize Mitchell-Scurry Association.

SHELBY COUNTY MISSIONARY. Organized in 1880. The first minutes available are for 1892 when 32 churches reported. Some of the churches went into Shelby-Doches Association from 1925–1935. This body is now extinct.

SHILOH. Organized Oct. 18, 1862, at Friendship Church, south of Pilot Point, with five churches: Clear Creek, Indian Creek from Cooke County; Friendship, Pilot Point from Denton County; Whitesboro from Grayson County; all from Sister Grove Association except Friendship from West Fork. Shiloh joined Denton County Association at its organization, May 29, 1886.

SISTER GROVE. Organized June 25, 1853, near Kentuckytown in Grayson County with three churches—New Hope, Pleasant Hill, and Salem. On Oct. 6, 1886, this association dissolved and the churches went into Fannin and Grayson associations.

SMYRNA. Organized Nov. 21, 1885, by churches which had withdrawn from Rehoboth Association due to dissatisfaction. The second session had five churches. The body ceased to exist sometime after 1903; some churches returned to Rehoboth, and some went into Wood County Association, Baptist Missionary Association.

STEPHENS COUNTY. Organized Oct. 5, 1894, in the First Church, Breckinridge, with 15 churches. The association adopted articles of faith used by Macedonia Association. In 1920 churches began joining Cisco Association.

TEXARKANA. Organized in 1874 with nine churches, electing John R. Alexander moderator; J. M. Renfro, clerk. At the second session, at Sand Hill Church in Bowie County, three new churches were added. On Oct. 8, 1929, at DeKalb, the executive boards of Red River and Texarkana associations met jointly and voted to consolidate as Red River–Texarkana Association.

THROCKMORTON. Organized in 1911 when Macedonia Association dissolved, and the churches went into Throckmorton and Young associations. In 1927 the two groups formed Throckmorton-Young Association.

TOWASH. Organized in 1873 at Prairie Valley Church near Whitney with churches from Bosque and Hill counties. In 1882 a committee reported exonerating Mt. Zion Church on charges of disorder. At the last annual session July 18, 1886, Towash united with Hill County, organizing Hillsboro Association on Aug. 16–17 at Osceola. Hillsboro Association disbanded in 1906 to re-create Hill County Association.

TRYON. Organized Feb. 14, 1858, at Laurel Hill (Cold Springs) Church with eight churches from Union Association. Named for William Melton Tryon (*q.v.*), an early pastor of Independence Church, it adopted articles of faith from the *Encyclopedia of Religious Knowledge.* The Lord's Supper was observed at the first session, a customary practice in associations until James Robinson Graves' (*q.v.*) teachings permeated this area in the late 1800's. Tryon joined with Evergreen Association in 1902 as Tryon-Evergreen Association.

WAXAHACHIE. Organized in 1873. In 1893 the name was changed to Ellis County Baptist Association.

WELLINGTON. Organized Sept. 6–8, 1895, at Buck Creek Church, with six churches from Childress County. This body is now extinct.

WEST FORK. Organized Oct. 12, 1855, at Fossil Creek Church (now Birdville) with 12 churches from seven counties, 38 messengers representing 300 members. The counties were Tarrant (Lonesome Dove, Bear Creek, now Euless, Mt. Gilead, Fossil Creek churches), Dallas, Denton, Ellis, Johnson, Parker, and Wise. In the last annual session, Aug. 12–13, 1886, representatives from 12 churches met at First Church, Fort Worth, and organized Tarrant County Association. The New Hampshire Confession of Faith was adopted.

WESTERN BRANCH. Organized Oct. 8, 1881, at Giddings, in Lee County, with five churches from Little River Association. This association joined Burleson County Association (Burleson-Lee) in 1930 and became Independence Association in 1948.

YOUNG. Organized Sept., 1888, at Graham as Macedonia Association. In 1911 Macedonia voted to dissolve, forming Throckmorton and Young associations. In 1927 these two united as Throckmorton-Young Association.

BIBLIOGRAPHY: A. D. Brooks, *History of Ellis County Baptist Association* (1907). Associational Committee, *History and Doctrine of the Hunt County Missionary Baptist Association* (1937). J. M. Carroll, *Texas Baptist Statistics, 1895* (1895). L. Cole, *Historical Survey of Baptist Work in El Paso* (1936). J. C. Daniel, *A History of the Baptists of Hill County, Texas* (1907). W. M. Ethridge, "The Story of Tryon-Evergreen Association" (1950). Inman, *Centennial History of Colorado Baptist Association* (1947). R. L. Johnson, *The Story of Rehoboth—History of Rehoboth Baptist Association 1856–1938* (1938). R. L. Johnson, *The Baptists of Tierra Blanca* (1945). K. Moore, "History of Johnson County Baptists" (1924). Z. N. Morrell, *Flowers and Fruits in the Wilderness* (1886). S. A. Newman, "Missionary Baptist Work in Jack County" (1939). W. E. Norman, "A History of Baptists in Van Zandt County, Texas" (1951). D. R. Pevoto, *The Union Baptist Association, Centennial History 1840–1940* (1940). D. A. Porter, *History of San Marcos Baptist Association, 1858–1903* (1904). B. Ramsey, "History of Grayson County Missionary Baptist Association, 1900–1950" (1955). J. N. Razor, *History of Denton County Baptist Association* (1936). D. D. Tidwell, *History of the Baptists in Erath County* (1937); "History of West Fork Baptist Association" (1940). W. A. Todd, "A History of Pecan Valley Baptist Association and Its Successor Brown County Baptist Association" (1940). W. T. Updike, *The Beginnings in Limestone Baptist Association 1892–1910* (1940). W. Shamburger, "History of Tarrant County Baptist Association, 1886–1922" (1953). J. L. Walker and C. P. Lumpkin, *History of Waco Baptist Association of Texas* (1897).

J. D. BRANNON

TEXAS BAPTIST. First published as *Religious Messenger,* Jan. 3, 1874, 12 years after the suspension of the first *Texas Baptist.* Robert Cooke Buckner (*q.v.*), editor, published the first issue at Paris, Tex., but moved the paper to Dallas the next year. In Jan., 1876, the name of the paper was changed to *Texas Baptist,* Buckner continuing as editor. In Aug., 1877, the name of Benajah Harvey Carroll (*q.v.*) appeared as associate editor. S. A. Hayden purchased the *Texas Baptist* in 1883. E. C. ROUTH

TEXAS BAPTIST, THE. First published at Anderson, Tex., in Jan., 1855, with George W. Baines, Sr. (*q.v.*), as editor and J. B. Stiteler, assistant editor. Publication of a Baptist paper in Texas was discussed when the state convention was organized in 1848; it had formerly been discussed in the organization of Union Association in 1840. *The Texas Baptist* was suspended in 1861; due to war conditions, it was impossible to obtain paper. E. C. ROUTH

TEXAS BAPTIST AND HERALD. A consolidated paper, resulting from the merging of *Texas Baptist* and *The Texas Baptist Herald* in 1886. Adoniram Judson Holt (*q.v.*) bought half interest in the *Texas Baptist and Herald,* but resold his interest to S. A. Hayden, who had purchased both the merging papers, *Texas Baptist* in 1883 and *The Texas Baptist Herald* in 1886. The last issue of the *Texas Baptist and Herald* was published in Dec., 1908. E. C. ROUTH

TEXAS BAPTIST CHILDREN'S HOME. Located at Round Rock, Tex., and dedicated Sept. 5, 1950, the home is built on the cottage plan, with each cottage having a capacity for 20 children. There is no central dining hall since each cottage is a separate unit. The original three cottages, superintendent's home, and office were a gift of Louis Henna and his wife of Round Rock. Owned by the Baptist General Convention of Texas, the home, with 10 cottages, now has capacity for 200 children. A chapel on the campus helps in the spiritual development of the children who attend public school and Round Rock Baptist Church. The home is operated for the benefit of dependent and neglected children. It seeks to develop three phases of their lives—physical, mental, and spiritual. All buildings on the campus are made of Austin stone, and the home is maintained by gifts of churches and interested individuals.

JARED I. CARTLIDGE

TEXAS BAPTIST COLLEGE. Opened in 1861 at Tyler, Tex., under the direction of the East Texas Baptist Convention. Male and female departments were reported "doing well" in 1863. The school was closed near the end of the Civil War.

BIBLIOGRAPHY: C. B. Wilson, "A History of Baptist Educational Efforts in Texas, 1829–1900" (1934).

RUPERT N. RICHARDSON

TEXAS BAPTIST FOUNDATION. A religious and benevolent corporation created by The Baptist General Convention of Texas in 1930 and chartered by the state of Texas in Feb., 1931. With no capital stock or assets of its own, the foundation is a trust agency with the sole purpose of investing and handling trust funds which have been left for the benefit of Baptist institutions and agencies under control of the general convention and the Southern Baptist Convention and to return the income to the respective institutions. The foundation has no control or voice in deciding who shall receive the income, nor does it have any control over the institutions it serves. Nine directors, elected by the general convention (three elected each year for a period of three years) to manage and govern the work of the foundation, are selected from capable businessmen in Texas who donate their services for the management of the foundation.

Each investment of foundation funds is carefully studied and passed upon by a trained office staff, after which it is presented to an outside committee of able and qualified businessmen in the field of finance who make the final determination. The committee not only makes certain that the investment is sound from a business angle but that it fits into a diversified investment pattern so as to protect the total fund of the foundation against the pressures of both inflation and deflation. Each investment is also screened from a moral standpoint, and no investments are made in the liquor or tobacco industries or in any business or industry which will reflect upon the Christian purpose served by the foundation.

During 25 years of operation the foundation has paid out to the institutions which it serves a total of $9,354,247.07. In the next 25 years, at the present rate of growth, the foundation will pay out approximately $45,000,000. Foundation assets Aug. 31, 1955, were $24,123,520.96.

The first executive secretary of the foundation was George Mason, succeeded in 1951 by Ambrose Brazier Culbertson. James Clifton Cantrell became the third executive secretary in 1954.

JAMES CLIFTON CANTRELL

TEXAS BAPTIST HERALD, THE. First published Dec. 13, 1865, in Houston, Tex., with John Bodkin Link (*q.v.*), editor. It absorbed the small subscription list of the projected *Christian Herald,* appeared intermittently until July, and then continued regularly until 1867 when it was suspended because of the yellow fever epidemic. In Jan., 1869, *The Texas Baptist Herald* resumed regular publication with enlarged format. Jonas Johnston bought half interest in the paper in 1877, and Owen Clinton Pope (*q.v.*) became joint editor in 1878. When Johnston died in 1881, Link again became sole proprietor. The paper was moved to Austin in 1883 and to Waco in 1886. As part of the Texas Baptist consolidation program in 1886, *The Texas Baptist Herald* was purchased by S. A. Hayden and merged with *Texas Baptist,* which Hayden had bought in 1883. The consolidated paper was called *Texas Baptist and Herald.*

E. C. ROUTH

TEXAS BAPTIST WORKER. Published in San Antonio, Tex., in 1889 as an organ of the Baptist Women's Mission Workers. Fannie Breedlove Davis served as editor, and the paper moved to Dallas in 1895.

E. C. ROUTH

TEXAS DISTRICT 8 ENCAMPMENT. Organized near Big Spring, Tex., in 1940, one of 10 encampments owned by Texas districts. In 1956 the district missions secretary J. William Arnett was manager of the camp.

J. E. ROTH

TEXAS DISTRICT 11 ENCAMPMENT. Organized near Vernon, Tex., in 1932, one of 10 encampments owned by Texas districts. In 1956 the district mission secretary S. F. Martin was director of the camp.

J. E. ROTH

TEXAS HISTORICAL AND BIOGRAPHICAL MAGAZINE. Published in two volumes in 1891–92 at Austin, Tex., with John Bodkin Link (*q.v.*) as editor. It contained biographical sketches of prominent Texas Baptists, histories of several churches and associations, and accounts of regional organizations.

E. C. ROUTH

TEXTBOOK COMMISSION. Suggested to the Convention May 6, 1927, in a memorial from the Baptist General Convention of Oklahoma, which called for an organization "to secure competent scientists to write college textbooks which do no violence to orthodox Baptists' conventional interpretation of the Book Divine." Both the memorial and an amendment offered by W. E. Hunter, of Kentucky, were referred to the Executive Committee, with power to act. The Executive Committee directed its executive secretary to write to the presidents of the Southern Baptist colleges and universities for suggestions regarding the need for and practicability of appointment of such a commission; on the basis of the replies and its own deliberation, the Committee reported to the Convention on May 16, 1928, that it was impracticable to appoint "at this time" a Textbook Commission. Among the reasons cited for this decision were the range of subjects covered, the heavy cost, and the lack of assurance that the textbooks would be adopted if published. The committee suggested the selection of teachers in accord with Christian and Baptist principles and doctrines, who would seek satisfactory textbooks, and who would counteract offensive ideas in the textbooks by effective presentation of a Christian interpretation. R. ORIN CORNETT

THAILAND, AMERICAN BAPTIST MISSION IN. Work in Thailand was begun by American Baptist missionaries from Burma, John Taylor Jones (1802–51) and wife, who left Moulmein in 1833 to open work among the Buddhist Siamese. William Dean (1807–95) arrived in Bangkok July 18, 1835, to work among Tie Chiu Chinese, who speak the Swatow dialect. In 1836 he formally organized the first Protestant church in all Asia composed of Chinese members. Following the treaty of 1842 opening China to the West, missionaries moved to Hong Kong pending permanent assignment to the mainland. Although the American Baptist Missionary Union voted in 1872 to abandon Siam for China, missionaries continued there until 1909. Dean served 25 years, during which time he translated the Bible and other literature into the Tie Chiu dialect. Jones died before completing his translation of the Bible into Siamese. In 1872 C. H. Carpenter (1835–87) and wife, missionaries from Burma, arrived in Siam with 12 Karen Christians, thus beginning the co-operation between Karens in the two missions.

In 1932 Siam adopted the name Thailand, land of the free. The church founded by Dean in Bangkok continued under Chinese pastors and in 1954 had 400 members. The American Baptist Foreign Mission Society took official action to reopen the Thailand mission in 1952, and a missionary family was transferred to Thailand from south China. Earlier, in 1949, the society assigned its first missionary couple to the Karens.

DATA

	1954
Churches	20
Baptisms	33
Church members	1,212
Missionaries	14
National workers	46
Students	784
Schools	2
Field contributions	$13,048

ADA STEARNS

THAILAND, SOUTHERN BAPTIST MISSION IN. Four former China missionaries, transferred in 1949, opened Thailand as a new Southern Baptist mission field. The mission was formally organized in Bangkok in 1950, and the Hai Tien Lou Chapel for Cantonese (later Swatow) Chinese was begun. Grace Baptist Church (Mandarin), organized Sept. 16, 1951, with 15 charter members, was the source of two other churches, Immanuel (Thai) in 1953, and New Hope (Chinese) in 1954.

Led by Missionary John Glenn Morris, a Baptist theological center opened in Bangkok Oct. 1, 1952, to train preachers and other Christian workers, both Chinese and Thai. Christian literature went on sale at a Baptist book room in 1953, and the publication of literature in the Thai language was initiated in 1954. The Baptist Student Center, an English-teaching approach to the Thai students of Bangkok, was opened in connection with Immanuel Church in 1953.

Three centers of work outside of Bangkok have been inaugurated: Ayuthia, ancient capital of Thailand, 1952; Nondaburi, provincial center 16 miles from Bangkok, 1953; Cholburi, provincial center south of Bangkok, 1954.

In 1955 a total of 25 missionaries and 182 baptized communicants constituted the mission in Thailand. FRANCES HUDGINS

THAILAND SEMINARY, BANGKOK. See Thailand, Southern Baptist Mission in.

THARP, VINCENT ALLEN (b. Va., Nov. 18, 1760; d. Twiggs County, Ga., Sept. 24, 1825). Tharp left Virginia prior to the American Revolution but took part in the fighting while living in the Carolinas. He was twice married; first to a Miss Rogers, by whom he had two children; then to Sarah Pierson, by whom he had eight children. After moving to Georgia in 1784, the Tharp family settled in what was then Warren County. It was while there at the age of 40 that Vincent united with Briar Creek Baptist Church and was subsequently ordained a minister. In 1811 he settled in Twiggs County, where he engaged in farming and preaching. Just a few months after his arrival in Twiggs, he became pastor of the community church, Stone Creek, where he remained until his death. At that time Stone Creek was one of the most flourishing churches in Middle Georgia and the parent church to several churches in that area. For several years he was moderator of Ebenezer Association and served as pastor to many of the surrounding churches, including Richland Creek and Antioch. Tharp was a sound and earnest preacher and his ministerial influence is still felt in Middle Georgia. Before his death in 1825 he baptized most of his family into the fellowship of Stone Creek Church.

In almost each succeeding generation there has been a Tharp minister: Charnick, Benjamin, Simeon, Washington, George, Ralph Hubert, and Edgar. Charnick Tharp, a son, served as moderator of the Ebenezer Association for 22 years, supported missions and education at a time when anti-missionary sentiment was most prevalent, and helped to constitute several churches, among which was the First Baptist Church of Macon. Benjamin F. Tharp, a grandson, was a member of the first graduating class of Mercer University, and later a trustee of that institution. BILLY WALKER JONES

THEISM. The belief in the existence of a god or gods, the opposite of which is atheism. Agnosticism, deism, pantheism, henotheism, and polytheism are all forms of theism denoting the various interpretations of the relations of a god or gods to the universe and men. In a more limited sense, theism is usually associated with the biblical conception of God. Whereas agnosticism denies the knowledge of God, biblical theism maintains that God is known to men through revelation; whereas deism stresses the transcendence of God, biblical theism holds that God is truly transcendent yet immanent; whereas pantheism identifies God and universe, biblical theism acknowledges the active presence of God in the universe without making him one with it; whereas henotheism and polytheism assume the existence of many gods, biblical theism teaches that God is the one and only God, the absolute and eternal Person.

The biblical theist believes that the absolute living Person, God the Father, has entered human history and life, first, through the human persons of the Old Testament period, and last, uniquely and supremely in Jesus the Christ for the salvation of all who will come to him in faith. Biblical theism stresses the personal encounter between men and God, making faith, prayer, and worship real and abiding elements in the life of men.

See also AGNOSTICISM, DEISM, KNOWLEDGE OF GOD, TRANSCENDENCE, PANTHEISM.

BIBLIOGRAPHY: H. H. Farmer, *God and Men* (1948). W. M. Horton, *Theism and the Modern Mood* (1930). A. C. Knudson, *The Doctrine of God* (1930).

TED R. CLARK

THEOLOGIANS, BAPTIST. If 1641 is set as the date for the full elaboration of Baptist principles in a self-conscious denominational movement, neither in England nor in America were there any "theologians," in the strictest sense of the word, during the 17th century. Roger Williams (1599–1683), contrary to the secular characterizations often offered, was basically a religious thinker, and cannot be labeled a "theologian" or a Baptist. John Smyth (? –1612) likewise was "pre-Baptist" and, like Williams, showed, in his later life, some characteristics of the "seeker."

John Gill (*q.v.*)—Gill (1697–1771), the stern Calvinist and successor to Benjamin Stinton in the Goat Street Church, London, was likely the first articulate "theologian" of English or American Baptists. Gill was a learned man, especially skilled in Hebrew and rabbinical studies, as his Biblical commentaries reveal, and acquainted also with the history of philosophical thought, particularly in the classical period, as his chief theological work *Complete Body of Practical and Doctrinal Divinity* clearly manifests. Gill's doctrine of scriptural authority and inspiration were high in the extreme. He held that "the very words" and not just "the matter of scriptures" were "of God." His Calvinistic orthodoxy carried him to the extremes of double-edged, unconditional predestination and particular redemption and close to supralapsarianism. Atonement was construed in terms of strict satisfaction. Gill's unilateral Calvinism vitiates his efforts to espouse a covenant theology. The practical effect of his rigid orthodoxy can be seen in his refusal to address himself to the unconverted, to "apply" the gospel in an indefinite fashion, or to give the invitation of the gospel, reckoning these practices presumptuous toward God.

Andrew Fuller (*q.v.*)—John Collett Ryland (1723–92) and Fuller (1754–1815) represent a more evangelical reaction against this stereotyped orthodoxy in what was widely and popularly known as "Fullerism." Ryland pleaded plenary inspiration of the Scriptures, the satisfaction theory of atonement, the five general points of Calvinism, and faith and repentance as divinely bestowed means. On the other hand, he defended vigorously the theological soundness of foreign missions and sought to hold together the doctrine of limited atonement and the universality of the gospel. Ryland suggested that his comrade Fuller write a system of theology to express their common point of view, which Fuller commenced in 1814 but only partially completed. He equalled his contemporaries in orthodoxy but in a more openly evangelical manner. In *The Gospel Worthy of All Acceptation* he does not allow any inconsistency between discriminate decrees, including limited atonement, and the universality of the gospel call. Fuller was a worthy apologist of convention against the secular skepticism of Thomas Paine and others and the universalism of religious liberalism. Concerning "Christian evidences" Fuller was extremely subjective, believing that the Scriptures and Christianity in all its parts were self-validating. The 18th century produced no significant Baptist theologian in America.

John Leadley Dagg (*q.v.*).—Though handicapped for most of his life by physical disabilities, Dagg (1794–1884) was the first American Baptist thinker to complete a comprehensive and thorough systematic theology. When he was forced by a throat ailment to stop preaching, he turned to education, and spent the rest of his life in teaching, administration, and writing. His health was perennially bad, and for many years he was crippled and nearly blind, but his writing was so able that his *Manuel of Theology* (1857) remained in print for many years after his death.

In his views Dagg was representative of the majority of Baptists in the ante-bellum South. Though a Calvinist, he was a strong proponent of missions. His doctrines of God, the Bible, sin, and salvation were widely approved. "His defense of slavery from the economic, political, and racial standpoints, was typical. At the single point of the Church Universal, Dagg differed from his fellows—and this was in degree, not in kind. Almost all except the Landmarkers adopted such a concept, but Dagg alone made extensive use of it." He devoted a large section in his "Treaties on Church Order" to a refutation of the Landmark views expressed on the apologetic novel, *Theodosia Ernest,* by Amos Cooper Dayton (*q.v.*), and to a careful presentation of the church universal as a visible, though non-institutional body.

Alvah Hovey.—Hovey (1820–1903), an American Baptist theologian who served as teacher and administrator at Newton Theological Institution for fifty-four years, was in his day most influential. In his firm conservatism was united with candor, and he achieved an authority in American Baptist thought far greater than he would have sought. Even in controversial matters, his word was depended on as the basis of unity and agreement. A manual called *Outlines of Christian Theology* (1861), published for the use of his students, contains his basic contribution. In addition he wrote other books on a variety of religious and historical subjects, and was general editor of *An American Commentary on the New Testament.*

George Washington Northrup.—Northrup (1826–1900), an American Baptist theologian who is primarily remembered as a teacher, served at Rochester Theological Seminary (1857–67), at the University of Chicago (1867–69), and as president and professor of theology at the Baptist Union Theological Seminary (1867–92). Cathcart valued him for his conservative attitude toward the claims of science and philosophy with regard to the doctrines of the Christian faith.

Augustus Hopkins Strong (*q.v.*).—Strong (1836–1921), long-time president and professor of theology at Rochester Theological Seminary, was the center of a whole movement of Baptist conservatism. The twin doctrines of theological orthodoxy—Scripture inspiration and authority and the atonement of satisfaction—are sounded throughout Strong's writings. He held to a mild or modified Calvinism, but his doctrine of man was much less Calvinistic than his doctrine of God. He rejected the "New Theology" on many scores but most especially on the basis of the rejection of biblical authority in favor of "moral experience." However, he recognized the values in the German critical method and was socially conscientious; he was deeply disturbed about the graft surrounding President Garfield's death.

Shailer Mathews.—Mathews (1863–1941) was, together with Walter Rauschenbusch (*q.v.*) (1861–1918), a pioneer in the "social gospel." Mathews felt that the transition in his thought from the older, more conservative theology to the modern liberalism was representative of many in his time. Actually, he attempted to harmonize the old conservatism with the new social approach and remained in the official affairs of his denomination until his death. Rauschenbusch made great inroads into the popular mind with his strong advocacy of practical social readjustment and equity. He thought of his "theology" not in contradiction to the old order of evangelicalism but as being supplementary. His low view of Scriptural authority is typical of his school.

Edgar Young Mullins (*q.v.*).—Mullins (1860–1928), president and professor of theology in the Southern Baptist Theological Seminary, followed the Calvinistic line of James Petigru Boyce (*q.v.*) at first, but in the process of his teaching he changed the center of gravity in his theological thought. William Owen Carver (*q.v.*) said that Mullins came under "the influence of Schleiermacher and was a great admirer of Charles Hugh Foster. In this way his theology became more centered in experience and much more vitally religious rather than stiffly philosophical and dogmatic." He did not formulate a system of theology. His *Christian Religion in Its Doctrinal Expression* was an effort to blend a mild Calvinism and a theological empiricism.

Henry Wheeler Robinson.—Robinson (1872–1945), British theologian, chairman of the Oxford Board of Theology, president of Oxford Society of Historical Theology, was for 22 years principal of Regent's Park College. He held to a modified Calvinism, though he deviated far from Calvin in his doctrine of man. His thought was characterized by a "pragmatic" rather than an "acadamic" approach to the great themes of theology. The conviction that "Psychology, philosophy, and history each make an essential contribution to theology . . ." led him to assimulate them into his evangelical thought. His last major work, *Redemption and Revelation in the Actuality of History,* which E. A. Payne said contained "some of his most mature and profound thinking," illustrates this assimulation. Edwin Bevan's work, *Symbolism and Belief,* influenced Robinson's thought perhaps more than any other.

Walter Thomas Conner (*q.v.*).—Conner (1877–1952), professor of theology at Southwestern Baptist Theological Seminary, was influenced by his teachers Strong and Mullins and also by the challenge of major twentieth-century theological movements. Although fully committed to the evangelical tradition of Baptists, he worked toward a constructive synthesis of the best insights of his day. He advocated recognition of the dynamic nature of biblical inspiration and the human factor in the writing of Scripture, Christ's victory over sin as the central meaning of the atonement, and amillennialism. Of the fifteen books that he wrote, *Revelation and God* (1936) and *The Gospel of Redemption* (1945) together serve as the most systematic summary of his positions.

BIBLIOGRAPHY: A. G. Fuller, ed., *The Complete Works of the Rev. Andrew Fuller* (n.d.). R. G. Gardner, "John Leadley Dagg," *Review and Exposition* (Apr., 1957). J. Gill, *An Exposition of the New*

Testament (1774–76); *Complete Body of Practical and Doctrinal Divinity* (1769). S. Mathews, *New Faith for Old* (1936). E. Y. Mullins, *The Christian Religion in Its Doctrinal Expression* (1917). W. Rauschenbusch, *A Theology for the Social Gospel* (1918); *Christianity and the Social Crisis* (1912). A. H. Strong, *Philosophy and Religion* (1888); *Systematic Theology* (1907). EUGENE H. STOCKSTILL

THEOLOGICAL EDUCATION. To assure a trained ministry suited to the development of their cause in every situation, Baptists have had to found and maintain their own theological schools. Schools supported by other interests were either closed to the Baptists, unfriendly to them, or failed to give them adequate training.

Bristol Baptist College of England is the oldest of the theological seminaries of the denomination. "Many of the eminent men who founded the early Baptist Churches in England and Wales had been educated at the Universities of Oxford and Cambridge." But after the restoration of Charles II in 1662, these universities were closed to Baptists and other nonconformists by law. Consequently, "to provide for the continuance of an educated ministry," in 1675 the Baptist pastors of London led in a movement which developed into Bristol Baptist College, training candidates for the ministry as early as 1689. The more permanent organization of the school came in 1770. Some early men who were graduated from the school and who became prominent in English Baptist affairs were John Ryland, Sr. (1753–1825), John Rippon (1751–1836), and Robert Hall, Jr. (*q.v.*) (1764–1831). Two of those who came to America and were influential here were Morgan Edwards (1722–95) and William Staughton (*q.v.*) (1770–1829).

The earliest colleges in America were founded for the preparation of ministers. Harvard was founded (1638) in order not "to leave an illiterate ministry to the churches, when our present ministers shall lie in the dust."

Isaac Eaton (1725–72) of Hopewell, N. J., is considered "the first teacher among American Baptists who opened a school for the education of young men for the ministry." This was immediately after the Philadelphia Association, Oct. 5, 1756, took action "toward the encouragement of a Latin grammar school." Among the early students of this school was James Manning, the first president of Brown University (then Rhode Island College).

Brown University, the seventh American college in order of date, was founded in 1764 by the Baptists in order "to secure for their churches an educated ministry, without the restrictions of denominational influences and sectarian tests." At that time the Baptists were at variance with religious opinions which prevailed in the American colonies, and the "dislike to the Baptists as a denomination, or rather to their principles, was very naturally shared by the higher institutions of learning then in existence."

The earliest method of ministerial training in the South is stated by William Joseph McGlothlin (*q.v.*) (1867–1933):

> Up to 1800 the young ministers who were receiving assistance were placed with some capable minister who took them into his home, gave them instruction and admitted them to the use of his books. Dr. Richard Furman and others served the denomination in this way at considerable sacrifice to themselves, since they received no compensation for this work.

Richard Furman (*q.v.*) (1755–1825) learned to read the English Bible before he could hold the large family Bible. He acquired a fair knowledge of Greek and Hebrew seemingly before he was 19 years of age when he assumed his first pastorate. So it is evident that along with a great admiration for the English Bible in his teaching there was also a basic knowledge of Greek and Hebrew.

Education among Baptists in the South owes a greater debt to Richard Furman than to any other person. The impulse started by him resulted in the organization of Hamilton Literary and Theological Institution in New York state in 1818, of Columbian College in Washington, D. C., in 1822, and of Furman Institution in 1825, as well as indirectly in the organization of other schools in the South and of some in the North.

"The original purpose of Baptist colleges in the South was to educate men for the ministry." They either began as theological institutions and afterward grew into colleges, or they began as colleges with a theological department, some of them retaining the theological department, others dropping it. In regard to Furman University, Colyer Meriwether stated in 1889:

> The title "University" was an unfortunate one, since the school, owing to circumstances, has been forced to confine itself to academic training only. But the intention at the start was to have an academic, a collegiate, a theological, and a law department; the last, indeed, was on the point of being established when the War came on.

Luther Rice (*q.v.*) (1783–1836) put great effort into Columbian College.

> This was to be, first of all in its purpose, a theological school for the Baptists of the whole country. . . . His plan was premature, for the college must come before the seminary. Rice knew before he died that he had failed in his immediate purpose. And yet . . . he had been building better than he knew. . . . Largely, perhaps mainly, as a result of conditions created by the work of Rice, there sprung into life during the early thirties, ten Baptist institutions of learning, six of them in Southern States.

Furman Institution began in South Carolina in 1825 for the purpose of training ministerial students, and it developed into Furman University in 1852. Mississippi College had its origin in Hampstead College in 1826, becoming Mississippi Academy in 1827 and taking its present name in 1830. Georgetown College in Kentucky began in 1829. The University of Richmond had its beginning in Virginia Baptist Seminary in 1832 which became Richmond College in 1840. In Georgia, Mercer Institue began in 1833 and became Mercer University in 1837. These schools were followed by Howard College

(Alabama, 1842), Union University (Tennessee, 1845, located at Murfreesboro and not related to the present school at Jackson). Baylor University (Texas, 1846), William Jewell College (Missouri, 1849), Carson-Newman College (Tennessee, 1851), and Wake Forest College (North Carolina, 1853).

Baptists did not develop fully expanded universities in all areas of learning, although some colleges expanded their theological departments, for there were no great Baptist universities with schools of theology. The trend among them was to develop separate theological schools for training beyond the college level. The first such efforts were in the North and students from the South had access to them. Hamilton Seminary at Hamilton, N. Y., was founded in 1818. Henry Allen Tupper (*q.v.*) (1828–95), of South Carolina and Virginia, graduated from Hamilton in 1850. Newton Theological Seminary, at Newton Centre, Mass., was founded in 1825. Basil Manly, Jr. (*q.v.*) (1825–92), of Alabama, and John Wilson Montgomery Williams (1820–94), of Virginia, were students there during the session 1844–45; Edwin Theodore Winkler (1823–83), of Georgia and Alabama, and Samuel Cornelius Clopton (*q.v.*) (1816–47), of Virginia, were students for two sessions, 1843–45. Rochester Theological Seminary was founded in 1850. An early alumnus of Rochester (1858) was Alexander Cotton Caperton (*q.v.*) (1831–1901), of Alabama, Mississippi, and Kentucky.

Baptist ministerial students from the South also attended seminaries of other denominations in the North. Basil Manly, Jr., states,

> When the disruption of 1845 occurred between Northern and Southern Baptists . . . it led to the withdrawal from Newton of the four Southern students who were there. . . . The other three went directly into ministerial work, while I determined, as I was younger, to prosecute further preparatory study, and went . . . to Princeton Theological Seminary [1845–47].

James Petigru Boyce (*q.v.*) (1827–88), after having graduated from Brown University (1847), went to Princeton Theological Seminary (1849–51).

In regard to curriculum, it has been pointed out that "the seminary programs of this period (up to 1850) like those of other institutions had little form of measurement. They consisted of brief lists of titles to be given with time and extent left largely to the discretion of the lecturers. The subjects were not usually listed by hours or terms. No clear-cut quantitative idea is discernible."

In 1837–38 Newton Theological Seminary offered courses in Biblical literature and interpretation (consisting of Hebrew and Chaldee languages, biblical geography, Canon of the Bible, the Greek New Testament), biblical theology (consisting of evidences of Christianity and Christian doctrine), ecclesiastical history and sacred rhetoric, and pastoral duties.

In 1845–46 Hamilton Theological Seminary had an Academic Department, a Collegiate Department, and a Theological Department with separate curricula. The latter of these departments offered the following:

I. Biblical literature and interpretation (consisting of general introduction to Old Testament, Hebrew, antiquity of the Jews, sacred geography, Chaldee, Syriac, introduction to New Testament, Greek language, and interpretation).

II. Ecclesiastical history (first year: history of Jewish church, Christian fathers, Middle Ages; second year, Reformation and subsequent periods).

III. Theology (consisting of evidences of Christianity, biblical and systematic Theology, composition of sermons, church government, and pastoral duties).

Basil Manly, Jr., states, "There was not at this period (1845) an institution at the South, where anything like a full theological course could be enjoyed. It was felt that that state of things ought not to remain so." There was, however, in existence at that time the Western Baptist Theological Institute at Covington, Ky., a co-operative effort of both Northern and Southern Baptists, for three sessions, 1845–48. Because there were on the faculty men who were suspected as being abolitionists, although they were well prepared as teachers in theological and biblical studies, most Southerners considered it an unsuitable institution for their young men to attend and they refused to send them to it. Rufus Columbus Burleson (*q.v.*) (1823–1901), of Alabama, an outstanding leader in later years, was a student at the institute for two sessions, 1845–47, and expressed satisfaction in the school. Kentucky interests seized the school in 1848 and held it until 1853 when a legal division of property was made, and the southern or Kentucky portion of the school was related to Georgetown College.

From 1845 until 1859, Southern Baptist ministerial education continued in the colleges, but there was a growing interest in developing one central Southern Baptist theological seminary. Basil Manly, Jr., pointed out in 1849 at the Southern Baptist Convention that "there were then seven theological professors, in as many Southern Baptist institutions, having in all about thirty students." He pointed out that there was "not one really good library." John Albert Broadus (*q.v.*) (1827–95) pointed out that "several of these professors were among the most earnest advocates of the establishment of a common seminary, though each naturally wished that the institution with which he was connected might become the nucleus for such a new organization." South Carolina leaders put forward Furman Theological Institution "as the nucleus of a common seminary." The trustees of Mercer University took action about the same time (1849), favoring the idea of a concentration upon that institution.

John Albert Broadus wrote that in 1856, "it soon became evident, as B. Manly, Jr., had held seven years before, that the existing theological departments in several states could not be combined into one institution; and the only hope lay in the establishment of an entirely new theological seminary, or of a seminary incorporating into itself some one of the existing theological departments." By this time there were "twenty-four colleges and ten departments or institutions for theological instruction" belonging to Baptist in the United States.

In some areas there was ". . . the fear of the colleges that the building of a seminary would dry up their resources and kill off their Bible Departments." Assurance was given by advocates of the new seminary that "the scheme will interfere with no existing institution. It does not propose to curtail the labors or influence of any of our state colleges."

In the organization of the Southern Baptist Theological Seminary at Greenville, S. C., in 1859, there came the culmination of all these efforts and the relationships involved. Furman Theological Institution became the nucleus, also providing James Petigru Boyce as a professor and furnishing a beginning at building up a library, as well as some necessary funds. Mercer University provided William Williams (*q.v.*) (1821–77) who had been on its faculty as professor of theology. Richmond, Va., provided Basil Manly, Jr., who had founded Richmond Female Institute there, as a professor of the new seminary. John Albert Broadus, active in the effort to establish the new seminary, had been at the University of Virginia. Columbian College at Washington, D. C., donated a valuable collection of theology books during the first sessions of the new seminary (1859–60).

In regard to curriculum of the Southern Baptist Theological Seminary in its first session (1859–60) it is stated:

The Institution shall comprise eight distinct departments of Instruction or Schools, viz.:

I. Biblical Introduction—Canon, Inspiration, Biblical Antiquities, Geography, and History.
II. Interpretation of the Old Testament—In English, Hebrew, Chaldee, Arabic, and Syriac.
III. Interpretation of the New Testament—In English, Greek, and Greek Exegesis.
IV. Systematic Theology—General Course—Latin Theology.
V. Pauline Theology and Apologetics.
VI. Preparation and Delivery of Sermons.
VII. Church History.
VIII. Church Government and Pastoral Duties.

In *The Education of American Ministers* it is pointed out that the old curriculum of the 19th century consisted of four divisions:

Exegetical Theology (Hebrew, Greek, English Interpretation of the Scriptures)
Historical Theology (church history with emphasis on the denomination involved)
Systematic Theology (called the center of the curriculum, doctrinal position of the church or denomination involved; natural theology; revealed theology)
Practical Theology (in liturgical churches, the liturgy and prayer books; in the non-liturgical churches, the preparation and delivery of sermons).

Important changes are (1) enlargement in the subject matter to be taught, (2) increased provision in electives, (3) meeting of vocational needs, (4) inclusion of cultural and educational experiences beyond the course of study.

The trend over a period of years has been to add more courses in the curriculum and to decrease the amount of time given to any one particular subject. In recent years more elective courses have been added, making it possible for students to vary their studies. In the area of music and religious education, separate schools have been organized in some of the seminaries which give greatly expanded curriculum in those areas. Although "Missionary Instruction" appears in a Princeton Theological Seminary catalogue for the session 1841–42, departments of missions in most seminaries did not appear until the 1890's or later. Psychology of Religion and Pastoral Counseling are perhaps the areas in which there has been the most recent expansion in the curriculum. In earlier years the curriculum was designed for pastors primarily, but in recent years provision has been made for training men and women for other ministries in the churches and for denominational leadership in other areas.

Figures are not available for the proportion of college and seminary trained pastors and denominational leaders among Southern Baptists in the early 1800's or in 1859. In 1899, according to Rufus Washington Weaver (*q.v.*) (1870–1947), using *The Ministerial Directory of the Baptist Churches* of George William Lasher (1831–1920), there were only 5.4 per cent of the Southern Baptist preachers who were college graduates and who took a degree in the Southern Baptist Theological Seminary or in some other theological seminary. The "Theological Education Survey" of Southern Baptists in 1949 reveals that less than one third of our ministers had both college and seminary training at that time.

From 1859 to 1908 Southern Baptists had only one theological seminary. In the latter year Southwestern Baptist Theological Seminary, at Fort Worth, Tex., was established. The Baptist Bible Institute of New Orleans, La., was established in 1917, and it became the New Orleans Baptist Theological Seminary in 1946. These were followed by Golden Gate Baptist Theological Seminary at Berkeley, Calif., in 1944 and by the Southeastern Baptist Theological Seminary in 1951.

These seminaries are all the more valuable to the Southern Baptist Convention because of the relationship they sustain to the denomination. Unlike seminaries serving most other Baptist groups, Southern Baptist theological seminaries are owned, controlled, and supported by the Southern Baptist Convention. Their trustees are elected by the Convention and are rotated after limited terms of service. A large portion of their support comes from a percentage allocation from the Convention's Cooperative Program. They do not have large endowments, and no other dependable sources of independent income. Thus they are and remain closely related to the churches from which their support comes. As a result, Southern Baptists have great confidence in them and in their graduates. Most Southern Baptist pastors who have seminary training received it from one of the Southern Baptist-owned institutions. This has contributed to the unity in doctrine and fidelity to a co-operative attitude which is generally characteristic of their pastors.

See also EDUCATION, SOUTHERN BAPTIST.

LEO T. CRISMON

THEOLOGICAL EDUCATION IN MISSIONS. The Southern Baptist Foreign Mission Board appointed its first Bible teacher, Francis C. Johnson, in 1847, two years after its organization. The first annual report of the board records recognition of the need for theological education: "The importance of securing a competent individual to give biblical instruction to native Chinese preachers, has been brought before the attention of the Board. . . . It is manifest, that if the millions of China are to be evangelized, it must be mainly by the instrumentality of natives. . . ."

Three general levels of theological training are recognized: that primarily for lay workers, that for pastors, generally, and that for advanced students—"the first-aid worker, the general practitioner, and the specialist."

Most leadership training with which Southern Baptist missionaries are associated is institutional. A number of the schools are extremely small. The fact that they are maintained at all indicates the importance attached to theological education. Training, especially for women, may not be strictly for a church ministry; it may combine elements such as teacher training (in Nigeria) or kindergarten work (in Japan). Training for women may be with or separate from men; sometimes special provision is made for wives of ministerial students, such as teaching illiterates in Africa to read. Various levels of training are provided; many institutions admit students with lower scholastic rating than ordinarily required for theological education, giving them a different course of study or a different type of recognition upon completion. Non-institutional training includes informal courses for brief periods, often night classes; in China short-term Bible schools used effectively were aimed sometimes at laymen, sometimes at untrained pastors. Correspondence or extension courses are provided by seminaries in Brazil and Japan.

The function of theological education is regarded as more important than the institution. Records show schools disappearing and reappearing, changing in form and number. Chinese schools moved about from place to place before Japanese invaders. The Mexican seminary moved to Texas and back again. The Recife (North Brazil) seminary came to a standstill for a year because of a conflict between trustees and church constituency. The Japan seminary twice united with other Baptists and separated again, and ceased to exist during two other periods.

The proportion of missionary personnel on theological faculties tends to be high. This indicates either lack of mature leadership among the nationals or paternalism on the part of the missionaries. It also indicates that theological education is one of the largest and longest-continuing places of service for the missionary. Cases in which missionaries are in a minority (e.g. Canton in 1934, when the seminary was formally turned over to the Chinese association, or Tokyo in 1940) indicate an able national constituency as well as a dearth of missionaries.

The proportion of foreign money also tends to be high in theological education, indicating that the Foreign Mission Board has chosen to support education rather than force a lower quality of work through self-supporting institutions.

Problems of scope and constituency are met in different ways. The international seminaries in Zurich (Switzerland), Buenos Aires (Argentina), and Cali (Colombia) aim successfully at constituencies crossing several national boundaries. The Zurich seminary draws most of its students from countries of Europe and the Near East, Buenos Aires from southern South America, and Cali from northern South America. (Many of the countries thus served by advanced theological education also have Bible schools or seminaries for the rank and file of pastors and lay workers.) In the Cali and Buenos Aires seminaries, which minister to Spanish-speaking constituencies, the language of instruction is Spanish; at the Zurich seminary, whose students have no common language, instruction is in English. A different type of problem is presented at Baguio (Philippines), where parallel courses are taught in English and in Chinese. In Brazil several seminaries are maintained within the one nation for transportational and functional convenience. The same was true in China where, in addition, there was the problem of varying dialects; but there was also a central theological school for advanced students set up first at the University of Shanghai and later as an independent institution at Kaifeng.

Curriculums of the theological schools are generally patterned after those of American seminaries. Since the students have generally a briefer Christian background than American students, there is often greater emphasis on Bible courses. In higher theological education much emphasis is placed on the knowledge of one or more modern languages, especially English, through which world theological literature becomes available.

Systems of accreditation and degrees vary. Hong Kong seminary offers a Bachelor of Divinity degree for a three-year course after university, or a Bachelor of Theology or Bachelor of Religious Education degree for three years after high school plus two years of pre-theological work. Japan offers a government-authorized degree (Th.B.) for a four-year university course specializing in theology, and continues with a fifth year. Zurich seminary offers a degree (B.D.) for a four-year course after completion of pre-university work, and sponsors work for the doctorate in the University of Zurich. The Nigerian seminary is affiliated with the Southern Baptist Theological Seminary, Louisville, which grants a degree (Th.B.) for work done at Ogbomosho.

The matter of effectiveness with regard to long-term fundamental aims is more difficult to evaluate than more external matters. An important step in the direction of self-criticism and corporate planning was taken in the Orient in 1955 when the first conference of representatives of all Southern Baptist related theological institutions in the area was held.

Statistics given in the 1955 report of the Foreign Mission Board list 23 theological seminaries in 21 countries. Other countries are served by the international seminaries, and Hawaii uses those on the mainland. Student bodies range from 133 (Nigeria) to three (Italy), with an average of 43. The 10 training schools in 5 countries have an average enrolment of 66.

W. MAXFIELD GARROTT

THEOLOGICAL INSTITUTE, GEORGETOWN COLLEGE. See GEORGETOWN COLLEGE.

THEOLOGY. "The science of God and of the relations between God and the universe." Theology is founded upon a revelation of the divine Being and upon the apprehension in the human consciousness of that revelation. Christian theology is the study of that body of knowledge which is based upon the Christian revelation. This knowledge arises from the faith of the Christian community, and its study is the task of the church. The aim of Christian theology is not to determine what the Church ought to believe, but to find out what the Church does believe and to expound with consistency and clarity the declarations and judgments of the Christian faith.

See also PHILOSOPHY. J. E. TULL

THEOLOGY, HISTORY OF BAPTIST. Baptists, whose historical origin as such occurred early in the 17th century, have in common with various pre-Reformation bodies certain cherished principles. Likewise, Baptists share with the majority of the 16th-century Anabaptists the tenet of believers' baptism, the ideal of churches composed solely of the regenerate who are walking in fellowship, and a belief in the separation of church and state. Other Anabaptist teachings—such as an anti-Augustinian theology; a negative attitude toward civil office, oaths, and warfare; and violent chiliasm, such as that practiced at Munster—have not been generally accepted by Baptists.

Baptist theology, like Baptist churches, had a twofold origin in England. General Baptists arose out of English Separatism when John Smyth's congregation, exiled in Holland, rejected infant baptism and began (1609) *de novo* believers' baptism by affusion. General Baptist theology, however, was essentially Arminian on election, free will, and universal atonement. Smyth and Thomas Helwys were pioneer protagonists of religious liberty, contending for it on Christological and theological grounds. After division between Smyth and Helwys, Smyth's congregation was absorbed by the Waterlander Mennonites, and Helwys' congregation returned to England to become the mother church of General Baptists. Helwys rejected historical succession and free will. Contact with the Mennonites caused the General Baptists to face the problem of Hoffmannite Christology.

Particular Baptists, so designated because of their doctrine of limited atonement, retained the basic Calvinistic theology of the Separatists, which they regarded as scriptural. A peaceful defection from a London Separatist church on the issue of believers' baptism resulted in the first Particular Baptist congregation. Richard Blunt obtained immersion (1641) from the Dutch Collegiants, but John Spilsbury insisted that "baptizedness is not essential to the administrator." The First London Confession (1644), moderately Calvinistic, was distinctive in prescribing single immersion as baptism. The General Baptists also adopted immersion.

Because of the oppressive measures of the Restoration era, English Dissenters were led to consider beliefs held in common. The Orthodox Creed of General Baptists (1678) mediated between Calvinism and Arminianism. Thomas Grantham defended the General Baptist practice of laying on of hands and the office of messenger. The Particulars adapted (1677) the Westminster Confession with modifications concerning baptism and church polity, yet retaining its strong Calvinism, even in regard to the Lord's Supper. The controversy between John Bunyan (*q.v.*), an open communionist, and William Kiffin, who held to immersion as prerequisite, opened a recurring and divisive issue among Baptists.

In the 18th century General Baptists suffered from deadening Socinianism, while Particular Baptists became hyper-Calvinistic, developing the "non-invitation, non-application" scheme of John Gill (*q.v.*) and others. The Evangelical Revival attracted neither the Particulars, who objected to John Wesley's Arminianism, nor the Generals, who refuted him on baptism. Yet the new evangelicalism did produce the Leicestershire movement, which became immersionist. The resulting New Connexion of General Baptists, formed (1770) under Dan Taylor, taught both universal atonement and universal invitation, while the General Assembly of General Baptists became increasingly unitarian. Particular Baptist hyper-Calvinism was modified under Andrew Fuller (*q.v.*), who, opposing Socinianism and Arminianism, combined limited atonement with universal invitation. William Carey (*q.v.*) and the missionary movement issued from Fuller's theology, while William Gadsby's Strict and Particular Baptists refused to accept it. Calvinistic-Arminian differences diminished so that Particulars and Generals were fused by 1891.

The earliest Baptist churches in America were principally Calvinistic, but Arminian teaching soon increased. The Philadelphia Confession (1742) was the Second London Confession (1677) with two articles added. The Separate Baptists, a product of the Great Awakening, added a conversion-centered evangelistic fervor to the Baptist stream. Benjamin Randall's Free Will Baptist movement was Arminian and practiced a connectional polity and open communion. American hyper-Calvinism resulted in the Primitive Baptists, who resisted efforts initiated by Luther Rice (*q.v.*) to organize Baptists for educational and missionary purposes. In Daniel Parker's teaching hyper-Calvinism was joined with dualism. The main body of American Baptists, incorporating the Calvinistic, the General, and the Separate sources, became moderately Calvinistic, as may be noted in the New Hampshire Confession (1833).

Alexander Campbell's identification with the Baptists (1813–30) was marked by increasing tension. Campbell's Sandemanian and Arminian idea of faith, doctrine of baptism for the remission of sins, and criticism of Baptist ministers, denominational bodies, and confessions of faith, produced the inevitable separation.

In the 1850's there arose in the South a Baptist "high church" movement called Landmarkism, led by James Robinson Graves (*q.v.*), James Madison Pendleton (*q.v.*), and Amos Cooper Dayton (*q.v.*). The kingdom of God was said to be visibly composed of the true churches of Christ, identified as local Baptist organizations whose unbroken existence from the Jerusalem church was deduced from the perpetuity of the kingdom and demonstrated as historical. Landmarkers, denying any nonlocal meaning of *ecclesia,* opposed preaching by pedobaptists in Baptist pulpits, rejected "alien" immersion, and advocated local church communion. The Landmarkers' unsuccessful insistence on a local church basis of representation in the Southern Baptist Convention led to their defection (1905). The Convention later adopted this principle.

Baptists were not unaffected by liberal theological trends. The English Downgrade controversy found scientifically trained John Clifford, advocate of biblical criticism, theological reconstruction, and social reform, pitted against Charles Haddon Spurgeon (*q.v.*), the defender of Puritan supernaturalism. Augustus Hopkins Strong's (*q.v.*) early conservative theology was modified by personal idealism, while William Newton Clarke reflected idealism and Ritschlianism. Walter Rauschenbusch (*q.v.*) articulated the theology of the social gospel; Shailer Mathews expounded and Harry Emerson Fosdick popularized modernism; and George Burman Foster denied the absoluteness of Christianity. The Northern Baptist convention declined (1922) to adopt any confession of faith. Fundamentalism, taking its name from *The Fundamentals* (1910), elicited Baptist support, especially in William Bell Riley, T. T. Shields, and John Franklyn Norris. The challenge of evolution and other issues led the Southern Baptist Convention to modify (1925) the New Hampshire Confession and add eight new articles. Edgar Young Mullins (*q.v.*), leading apologist and champion of Baptist "soul competency," interpreted conservative theology on the basis of religious experience. Defections from the Northern Convention produced two new bodies, the General Association of Regular Baptists (1933) and the Conservative Baptist Association of America (1947), both of which are premillennial.

The relation of Baptists to Protestantism became a more acute issue with the rise of the ecumenical movement. Although British Baptists declined to accept the Lambeth Appeal (1926), yet from the time of John Howard Shakespeare, they co-operated with the free churches. Henry Wheeler Robinson's teaching made the term "sacrament" more acceptable. In the North open communion and open membership increased. The Northern Baptist Convention, a charter member of the Federal Council of Churches (1908), participated in its program of social action. But the Southern Baptist Convention, influenced by Landmark teachings, fearful of a highly organized world Protestantism, and seeking to safeguard its conservative theology and freedom of missionary activity, refused to participate in the faith and order conferences, the Federal Council, and the World Council of Churches. British, Northern, and certain other Baptists joined the World Council (1948).

From its origin (1905) the Baptist World Alliance has been a forum for the enunciation of Baptist distinctives in the context of world Christianity. After heated debate led by Henry Cook and Monroe Elmon Dodd (*q.v.*), the alliance voted (1947) not to affiliate with the World Council.

Efforts have been made to delineate a central Baptist principle such as would imply the other basic Baptist emphases. Among the principles advocated have been the authority of the New Testament, the competency of the individual under God, the doctrine of the church, and the lordship of Christ.

Bibliography: W. W. Barnes, *The Southern Baptist Convention, 1845–1953* (1954). S. G. Cole, *The History of Fundamentalism* (1931). J. R. Graves, *Old Landmarkism: What Is It?* (1880). F. H. Littell, *The Anabaptist View of the Church* (1952). W. J. McGlothlin, *Baptist Confessions of Faith* (1911). E. Y. Mullins, *The Axioms of Religion* (1908). A. H. Newman, *A History of Anti-Pedobaptism* (1896). E. A. Payne, *The Fellowship of Believers* (1952). E. Roberts-Thomson, *Baptists and Disciples of Christ* (n.d.). R. G. Torbet, *A History of the Baptists* (1950). A. C. Underwood, *A History of the English Baptists* (1947).

James Leo Garrett

THEOLOGY AND PHILOSOPHY, BAPTIST. The theology and philosophy of Baptists should be viewed both from the standpoint of what they have written and from the observation of their point of view as that has become articulate in their history. It is easy to analyze and classify their writings; it is not always easy to interpret their actions, many of which seem to be guided more by an attitude than by a doctrinal formula. In their conduct, however, there is an implicit philosophy.

On the formal side their ideas have been deduced from the traditional teachings of Christianity. On the practical side their ideals have been induced from their life experience, from a work which they have felt they must do as well as a doctrine to which they could subscribe. These two elements, the formal and the practical, are paradoxically related to each other, and the genius of Baptists can be understood only by taking into account both factors of the paradox.

For example, on the one hand Baptists have subscribed to an authoritarian revelation of God, thought of as standing creatively above the human situation and as being embodied in the Bible, the Word of God. On the other hand their chief claim to distinction among evangelical Christians has been their advocacy of the principle of "the competency of the individual soul, under God, in all matters pertaining to religion." Motivated by this concept, Baptists, in their ecclesiology, have always emphasized the human element in religion.

However, the theology which Baptists have written has been rather consistently Calvinistic in content. But along with its central theme of the absolute sovereignty of God, Baptist theology has also set forth a semi-mystical definition of religious experience, which makes the internal condition of the individual believer a primary concern and Christian experience the touchstone of all other definitions of the faith.

Just as paradoxical has been the ratio of Baptists' involvement in the theory and the practice of their religion. Although rejecting the authority of formal creeds, they have usually been diligent in the formulation of specific statements of their belief, which they have frequently made tests of fellowship in their church life. These statements have constituted a body of doctrine, rigid and traditionally supernaturalistic. But Baptists have also been known for their practical social consciousness, for their social gospel movement as well as for their fervent espousal, by the majority of their group, of causes called "civic righteousness."

The formal literature which has been produced by Baptists has been characterized by its scarcity and its conservatism. Relatively few Baptists have made any considerable contribution to theological literature. This fact has been due, in part, to Baptists' disposition toward activism rather than to more scholarly pursuits. It may also have been due to the fact that their life as a distinct group has been spent largely under circumstances which are hardly conducive to creative writing. They have flourished principally among the English-speaking people, especially in the New World during its pioneer era. The conservative complexion of the literature is due, no doubt, to its identity with the Calvinistic tradition, with its anchorage in the teachings of the Bible.

The implicit humanism of Baptists has been expressed in a variety of ways. In religious vocation it has been embodied in the enthusiasm with which Baptists have evangelized the frontiers of the New World geography and the Old World culture. It has been expressed in the modern missionary movement, which was chiefly inspired by William Carey and his kind.

Baptists have shared their inheritance of the best traditions of Puritan individualism and separatism generously with those who forged the institutional democracy of North America. With tongue and pen Baptists have affirmed their faith in the freedom of conscience and the inherent worth of the human spirit, in the autonomy of religion and the separation of church and state. These are elemental ingredients of the public philosophy and of a new way of life. STEWART A. NEWMAN

THOMAS, ANDREW JACKSON SPEARS (b. Marlboro County, near Bennettsville, S. C., Dec. 14, 1852; d. Greenville, S. C., Apr. 1, 1911). Minister, editor, South Carolina Baptist leader. Son of Mary Spears and J. A. W. Thomas, a Baptist minister, he was educated at Furman University (1872–75) and Southern Baptist Theological Seminary (1876–79). Ordained to the ministry June 24, 1877, Thomas married Isabelle Roempke of Charleston, S. C., the following August. His early pastorates were Batesburg, 1880–83; First Baptist Church, Charleston, 1883–87; and Orangeburg, 1887–91. In 1891 Thomas purchased the financial interests in the estate of James Alfred Hoyt (*q.v.*) in the *Baptist Courier* and on June 1 became editor of the paper. In that position he dealt with controversial issues in a spirit of moderation, but in "matters of civic righteousness his words were as clear and true as the ring of a steel hammer." Thomas, secretary of the State Baptist convention from 1885 to 1894, served as moderator in 1908 and 1909. He served on the state board of missions and as trustee of Southern Baptist Theological Seminary and of Benedict College.

BIBLIOGRAPHY: J. C. Hemphill, ed., *Men of Mark in South Carolina* (1908). L. E. SMITH

THOMAS, DAVID (b. London Tract, Penn., Aug. 16, 1732; d. Jessamine County, Ky., *c.* 1801). Pioneer Virginia Baptist minister. After studying under the famous Isaac Eaton at Hopewell, N. J., Thomas attended Rhode Island College (Brown University), receiving the M.A. degree. According to Robert Baylor Semple (*q.v.*), "Besides the endowments of his mind, he had a melodius and piercing voice, pathetic address, expressive action, and . . . a heart filled with the love of God and sympathy for his fellowmen."

In 1759 Thomas married a widow, Mrs. William Shreve, and the following year he came from Pennsylvania to Mill Creek, Berkley County, Va. (now W. Va.), on a ministerial visit. He evidently felt called as a "self appointed missionary to Virginia."

Later, Thomas accepted the invitation of Peter Cornwell to preach at Broad Run, Fauquier County, which led to the organization of Broad Run Church in 1762 with Thomas as pastor. Under his leadership Broad Run became a center of evangelism and the mother of other churches in Virginia, including Chappawamsic in Stafford County, constituted with 55 members from Broad Run in 1766; Mountain Run in Orange County, an "arm" of Broad Run, constituted as a church in 1768; Little River in Louden, also constituted in 1768, with 15 members from Broad Run; and Birch Creek Church in Halifax County, constituted in 1769.

Thomas assisted in the organization of the Ketocton Baptist Association, Aug. 17, 1766, the first association of Regular Baptists in Virginia. He exerted even wider influence in early Virginia Baptist history through his book, *The Virginian Baptist,* published in 1774. The first printed presentation of Baptist faith and order distributed in Virginia, Thomas' book contained three parts, "a true and faithful account (I) Of their Principles, (II) Of their Order as a Church, (III) Of the Principal Objections made against them, especially in this colony, with a serious answer to each of them."

Other pastorates besides Broad Run were Occoquan and Mill Creek in Virginia. Thomas left Mill Creek in 1796 as a result of a doctrinal dispute and became pastor of Washington Church in Kentucky. A champion of religious freedom and a friend of both Thomas Jefferson and Patrick Henry, Thomas wrote a stirring poem on religious liberty entitled *Freedom.*

CLAYTON PITTS

THOMAS, WOODLIFF (b. Williamson County, Tenn., Oct. 5, 1828; buried Cotulla, Tex., May 12, 1888). Pioneer preacher and educator. He was also listed as "William" and as "W." by reports of the Board of Domestic Missions. Thomas graduated from Union University, 1856. He was missionary pastor of a Baptist church, Delaware City, Kans., 1857–58; first moderator of *East Kansas Association of Baptists,* Oct. 1, 1858; pastor, First Baptist Church, Austin, Tex., 1859–61, closely associated with Baptist governor, Sam Houston; and chaplain in the Confederate army, Darnell's regiment, Texas Mounted Volunteers, Apr. 17, 1862 to July 28, 1864. He married Janie Covey, Oct. 25, 1865, and to them were born seven children. Thomas was vice-president and professor of mathematics, Concrete College, Concrete, Tex., 1865–80. He was elected to Texas legislature, 1879, from DeWitt County.

N J WESTMORELAND

THOMASVILLE FEMALE COLLEGE. A Baptist school at Thomasville, Davidson County, N. C. Established in 1849 as the Sylva Grove Female Seminary, the school was moved to Thomasville some years later. In 1874 the school property was purchased by H. W. Reinhart, a Baptist. He operated the seminary as a private school with Baptist support. The school was a four-year college with a course equal to any in the state at the time. In the years when good schools for girls were scarce, Thomasville served its area commendably. In Aug., 1884, another Baptist, J. N. Stallings, leased the property and operated the school. In 1889 it was moved to High Point.

D. L. SMILEY

THOMPSON, CALVIN MILES, SR. (b. Muskingum County, Ohio, Nov. 19, 1866; d. Philadelphia, Pa., July 17, 1944). Pastor and Kentucky Baptist leader. While he was a boy, his father and mother, Charles and Sarah Thompson, moved to Louisville, Ky., where Thompson attended Louisville Male High School. The Walnut Street Church licensed him to preach Feb. 4, 1885, and ordained him June 24, 1888. As assistant pastor to Thomas Treadwell Eaton at Walnut Street Church, beginning in 1885, Thompson led in the establishment of the "B" Street Mission, which soon became Third Avenue Baptist Church. While assistant to Eaton, he attended Southern Baptist Theological Seminary, receiving the Th.B. and Th.M. degrees, the latter in 1898.

Thompson held short pastorates in Clayton, N. Y., and Clarksburg, W. Va., after which he became pastor of Portland Avenue Baptist Church, Louisville, in 1895, and of Baptist Tabernacle, Louisville, the following year.

After serving for two years as editor of the *Western Recorder* and president of the Baptist Book Concern, 1907–09, Thompson became pastor of First Baptist Church, Hopkinsville, Ky., where he remained eight years. During his later two-year pastorate at First Baptist Church, Winchester, Ky., he was elected corresponding secretary of Kentucky Baptists, serving 1921–38. Thompson was moderator of the General Association of Baptists in Kentucky, 1911–13, and chairman of the board of trustees of Bethel Woman's College while in the pastorate at Hopkinsville.

He married Clara Belle Morrison, Dec. 27, 1888, and they had six children, one of whom, Calvin Miles Thompson, Jr., is a Baptist minister.

GEORGE RALEIGH JEWELL

THREE FORKS BAPTIST HIGH SCHOOL. Located at Boone, Watauga County, N. C., established by Three Forks Association, in 1883. Because of lack of patronage the school operated for only one term. The building was given to the Boone Baptist Church for use as a school.

D. L. SMILEY

THROGMORTON, WILLIAM PINCKNEY (b. Henry County, Tenn., Sept. 19, 1849; d.

Marion, Ill., Dec. 22, 1929). Minister, editor, denominational organizer. After moving to Illinois at the age of 14, he spent most of the rest of his life in the southern part of the state. Converted in a meeting at Pleasant Hill Baptist Church in Williamson County, Ill., in 1870, Throgmorton was ordained to the ministry the following year. After teaching school for two years he became pastor of Hopewell Baptist Church, and later held a number of other pastorates in Illinois.

In 1877 Throgmorton became editor of *The Baptist Banner* in Benton, Ill., and in 1895, of its successor, *The Baptist News.* His last and most outstanding editorship was as editor of *The Illinois Baptist,* which first appeared on Thanksgiving Day, 1905. Throgmorton led in the organization of the Illinois Baptist State Association, and served as chairman of the state board of directors for 16 years. Leader of the movement for admission of the Illinois Baptist State Association into the Southern Baptist Convention, he introduced the motion which defined a Baptist church and resulted in establishment of the state body on Jan. 31, 1907. Credited with organizing 25 churches, Throgmorton is said to have preached 2,175 sermons and delivered 2,466 addresses. ARCHIE E. BROWN

TICHENOR, ISAAC TAYLOR (b. Spencer County, Ky., Nov. 11, 1825; d. Atlanta, Ga., Dec. 2, 1902). Pastor, educator, home mission secretary. The son of James and Margaret (Bennett) Tichenor, he was a descendant of Martin Tichenor, said to have been of French extraction, who took the oath of allegiance at New Haven, Conn., in 1644 and was later one of the settlers of Newark, N. J. Martin's great-grandson Daniel, grandfather of Isaac, moved from New Jersey to Kentucky in 1790. At the age of 15 Isaac entered Taylorsville Academy, where he was under two able teachers, Moses and David Burbank, graduates of Waterville College, a Baptist school in Maine, and there received good training. An attack of measles, however, ended his schooling and left him with infirmities which troubled him for a long time. When he was sufficiently recovered, he engaged in teaching in a neighborhood school and was for three years connected with the Taylorsville Academy, as principal the last year.

In the meantime, at the insistence of local Baptists, he had begun to preach (licensed Dec. 19, 1846, at Taylorsville, Ky.), and his effectiveness soon won for him the title "boy orator of Kentucky." In 1847 he accepted an appointment as agent for the American Indian Mission Association, and while traveling about in its interest he was called as pastor of the Baptist church in Columbus, Miss., where in 1848 he was ordained. He served there until 1850, then preached in revivals in Texas, was in charge of the church at Henderson, Ky., for a little over a year, and on Jan. 1, 1852, began a 15-year pastorate at the First Baptist Church, Montgomery, Ala. There he joined in the movement to establish a Southwide seminary in Greenville, S. C., and in 1860 preached its first commencement sermon. For a year during the Civil War he served as chaplain of the 17th Alabama Regiment—not confining himself strictly to his prescribed duties, for he acquired reputation as a sharpshooter and at the Battle of Shiloh went to the front of his regiment and rallied the wavering lines. Briefly in 1862 he was with Bragg's army as a missionary of the Domestic Board, and the next year took part in creating the Greenville Sunday School Board. In 1863 he became one of the owners of the Montevallo Coal Mining Company in Shelby County, Ala. As its president, in 1867 he began to make geological surveys of what later became the Birmingham mineral region, prophesying the coming greatness of that section of the state. He was one of the first in Alabama to mine coal scientifically with the use of steam machinery. In 1868 he resigned his church in order to devote himself to these material interests, feeling that such a move was in the best interest of the state. The death of his wife, however, caused him to change his plans and return to the active ministry. He accepted a call to the First Baptist Church, Memphis, Tenn., in 1871, but the next year returned to Alabama to be the first president of the State Agricultural and Mechanical College, located at Auburn.

During the 10 years that he served as head of this institution, he laid a broad and firm foundation for its subsequent development. He studied the agricultural, mineral, and manufacturing resources of the state, and in his many addresses awakened its people to a greater appreciation of them. He foresaw the industrial development which has since taken place and labored to prepare the way for it. Throughout this period he continued to maintain a position of leadership among the Baptists of the South, and in June, 1882, he resigned his collegiate position and became secretary of the Home Mission Board of the Southern Baptist Convention, the headquarters of which had recently been moved to Atlanta, Ga.

For 17 years he carried on the work of that office with a statesmanship that resulted in great constructive achievements. His leadership virtually saved the Southern Baptist Convention; he stemmed the current that was turning Southern Baptists toward the Northern society (the American Baptist Home Mission Society of New York) and turned it back, strong and bold, toward the Convention; inaugurated extensive work west of the Mississippi; spent about $100,000 on Texas and held the state to the Southern Baptist Convention; developed a definite plan of co-operative support of home mission work through regular giving; established a church building department; originated and sustained Sunday school literature until it was ready to go ahead on its own power under the Sunday School Board organized in 1891—in the face of opposition from the more aggressive and better equipped American Baptist Publication Society of Philadelphia; and made the South a base for world missions. He inaugurated work on the island of Cuba, enlarged the program for Negro education, initiated educational projects in the mountain regions, dealt with problems created by growing industrial centers, and encouraged women's work and Indian missions. In July, 1899, he retired from the chief responsibility of the home mission work and was made secretary emeritus. His health soon began to fail, and, after prolonged suffering, he died at Atlanta.

He was four times married: first, Dec. 16, 1852, to Monimia C. Cook, who died Feb. 13, 1860; second, in Apr., 1861, to Emily Catherine Boykin, who died Sept. 7, 1864; third, in Nov. 1865, to Lulah Boykin, who died in Sept., 1869; and fourth, in Feb., 1876, to Mrs. Eppie Reynolds McGraw, who died Mar. 6, 1878. He had children by each, four of whom survived him.

KIMBALL JOHNSON

TIDWELL, JOSIAH BLAKE (b. Cleveland, Ala., Oct. 8, 1870; d. Waco, Tex., Mar. 17, 1946). Bible professor, author of books on the Bible. Converted and called to preach when 21 years old, Tidwell, with an invalid wife and three small children, constantly harassed by poverty, worked his way through Howard College, Birmingham, Ala., graduating in 1898. He later received the M.A. degree from Baylor University. From 1899 to 1907 Tidwell taught Greek and Latin at Decatur Baptist College, Decatur, Tex., after which he served for two years as president. He became endowment secretary of Baylor University, Waco, Tex., in 1909, and was elected head of the Baylor Bible department in 1910, serving in that position until his death in 1946.

Tidwell wrote more than a dozen books, principally for use in his classes at Baylor. The most popular ones have been *The Bible Book by Book* (1914), *The Bible Period by Period* (1923), *Christ in the Pentateuch* (1940), and *John and His Five Books* (1940). For over 20 years he wrote a weekly exposition of the Sunday school lesson for the (Texas) *Baptist Standard,* and has prepared articles for practically every Southern Baptist publication. Tidwell served from 1935 to 1938 as president of the Baptist General Convention of Texas, and ministered in scores of Texas churches as supply pastor, evangelist, and teacher of Bible and doctrines. Perhaps the best-known teacher of Bible in Texas Baptists' summer encampments, Tidwell helped found the Baylor Religious Hour and worked extensively with Baylor's Baptist Student Union and Ministerial Alliance. Baylor named the Tidwell Bible Library and the magnificent Tidwell Bible Building in his honor.

BIBLIOGRAPHY: R. A. Baker, *J. B. Tidwell Plus God* (1946). J. S. Ramond, *Among Southern Baptists* (1936). J. C. Schwarz, *Religious Leaders of America,* Vol. II, p. 1054. *Who Was Who in America* (1950).

ROBERT A. BAKER

TIFT COLLEGE. Earlier known as Monroe College and Bessie Tift College. It is a four-year liberal arts college for women, located at Forsyth, Ga. Since 1898 the property of the Baptist convention of the state of Georgia, it was chartered on Dec. 21, 1849, as Forsyth Female Collegiate Institute.

A private school which for several years prior to 1849 was conducted by a local minister E. C. J. B. Thomas, became the nucleus of this institution, and the teacher became its first principal. Under the first elected president, William Clay Wilkes, 1850–67, who was the real founder, the institute took its place among the schools pioneering in the education of women. Locally projected, organized, and controlled, it had on its first board of trustees three Baptists, three Methodists, and one Presbyterian. Plans were made to accommodate 70 to 80 students, but increased attendance during the next two years demanded expansion. The Southern Botanico Medical College building was purchased and completed for $10,000, the president contributing one third and Forsyth citizens the remainder.

After 1856, paying $3,500 to the Methodists for their interest, the Baptists of Forsyth assumed complete control of the institute. School records, made shortly thereafter, show the name Monroe Female University; after 1873, the name Monroe Female College was used.

In 1864–65 the Civil War disrupted the academic program for one year, and the college building and grove served as a hospital for wounded brought from the battles of Atlanta and Stone Mountain. The school reopened in 1866 faced with serious debt and a building in disrepair, and those responsible for it displayed sacrificial courage amounting to heroism. Only seven years after the war, Forsyth floated bonds and raised another $10,000 for Monroe College. In 1879 fire completely destroyed the college, causing another suspension of school activities pending the erection of a new building. This hall, with the support of Forsyth citizens, was opened in 1883 and in 1956 still served as the academic building.

While the institution was known as Monroe Female College, distinct contributions were made by three outstanding presidents who were also teachers: William Clay Wilkes, Shaler Granby Hillyer, and Richard Thomas Asbury. In reality these were the founders. Asbury, sometimes teacher, sometimes president, and sometimes both, from 1856 to 1891, excepting the period following the fire, holds one of the longest records of service in the school's history.

In 1898, 25 years after Hillyer first attempted to interest the Georgia Baptist Convention in supporting a girls' school, the convention assumed control of Monroe Female College, operating it for a few years on a normal and industrial basis, but it soon reverted to a liberal arts college.

On May 11, 1907, the name of the institution legally became Bessie Tift College, thus honoring a devoted alumna, Mrs. Bessie Willingham Tift, class of 1878, whose husband, Henry H. Tift of Tifton, Ga., was in 1905 and thereafter its generous benefactor. The name was abbreviated to Tift in 1956.

From 1907 to 1955 the college progressed under seven presidents, until the physical plant comprised 10 buildings on a 250-acre campus; the endowment reached $806,322; and full accreditation had been accorded by the Southern Association of Colleges and Secondary Schools.

Older buildings on the campus include Bessie Tift dormitory, which bore Mrs. Tift's name before the college did, and Addie Upshaw dormitory, honoring the mother of William David Upshaw, so designated in recognition of his service as financial agent. Recently constructed, the president's home and the Hardin Library reflect the gifts and financial assistance of Hugh H. Hardin; the Fannie Cobb Roberts Memorial Chapel, the gift of the Columbus Roberts family; and the organ housed therein, that of Mr. and Mrs. Charles O. Smith.

Intangible resources include the influence of several long-term trustees, 12 having acted for 25 years and six for more than a generation. Oliver Hazzard Bartlow Bloodworth, John James Cater, Hugh H. Hardin, Thomas Romalgus Talmadge, Augustus George Cabaniss, in point of service, head a list which includes many eminent ministers, jurists, and businessmen who have contributed to the advancement of the school in this capacity.

The first graduating class, 1854, numbered six, the degree conferred being M.A. (Mistress of Arts). Through 1955 the college has granted 2,329 degrees, and presently offers the A.B. and B.S. degrees in elementary education and in home economics. Enrolment in 1954–55 was 273, endowment was $779,023, and property value was $771,421. The school is supported by appropriations from the Georgia convention, by gifts and grants, by tuition and fees, and by income from endowment, with no category predominating. In 1954–55, operating income was $224,598.74.

PRESIDENTS OF THE COLLEGE

1850–67	William Clay Wilkes
1867–72; 1880–81	Shaler Granby Hillyer, D.D.
1872–79; 1884–90	Richard Thomas Asbury
1883–84	Moses N. McCall
1890–95	James E. Powell
1895–97	Marshall H. Lane
1897–98	Mrs. Carrie D. Crawley
1898–99	Samuel Clinton Hood
1899–1900	Alexis Abraham Marshall, D.D.
1899–14	Charles Haddon Spurgeon Jackson, M.A., LL.D.
1915–22	Joshua Hill Foster, D.D.
1922–38	Aquila Chamlee, D.D.
1938–47	Claudius Lamar McGinty, D.D.
1947–52	William Frederick Gunn, LL.D.
1952–	Carey Truett Vinzant, D.D.

BIBLIOGRAPHY: E. Amos, "Historical Sketch of Monroe College," *Monroe College Monthly* (1906). R. T. Asbury, *Reminiscences of Monroe Female College* (Tift College library). J. H. Foster, "History of Bessie Tift College," *The Christian Index* (Dec. 25, 1920). C. L. McGinty, *A Survey of the History of Bessie Tift College* 1847–1947 (1947). B. D. Ragsdale, *Story of Georgia Baptists,* Vol. II (1935). T. E. Smith, *History of Education in Monroe County* (1934).

EUGENIA W. STONE

TITHE, THE. In religious usage, a tenth of one's personal income, which is devoted to the support of the church, or through the church to specifically Christian ministries. Historically some form of proportionate giving has been an integral part of nearly all systems of religious practice. The tenth, the basic proportion in Hebrew-Christian religion, is also basic in quite a number of other traditions. As Christians understand it, the tithe as instituted by God and as rightly practiced in all ages is not religious legalism. Tithing is not, except derivatively, a plan for raising money. It is rather a ritual act through which man testifies to, and at the same time cultivates in himself, the spiritual dedication of which the overt giving of money or goods is but the adequate and impressive symbol.

Tithing existed as a widespread practice even before it formally became a part of the law of the ancient Hebrews. The presentation of the tithe was a part of religious observance long before the time of Moses, as is seen archetypically in the offering of firstfruits by Cain and Abel, and quite definitely in Abram's gift to Melchizedek in Genesis 14:18–20: "And Melchizedek king of Salem brought forth bread and wine: and he was the priest of the most high God . . . and he [Abram] gave him tithes of all." This early observance of the tithe, coming as it did before the law was formally given, was not based on any requirement, but is evidence of the fact that the giving of tithes is a part of the basic moral nature of men who genuinely worship God. The incorporation of the tithe into the Scriptures recognizes it as a part of the enduring moral law of God, which applies to all those who would do the will of God in every century of time. Therefore it is a part of the religious duty of all Christians.

In the Scriptures, after the time of Abraham, the tithe was observed, then written into Hebrew law. Later, neglect brought condemnation from the prophets, and Pharisaical corruptions led Jesus to reinterpret the tithe as a spiritual privilege instead of a material duty. The following examples illustrate this scriptural development. To Jacob, the tithe was involved in a covenant made with God. Awakening from his vision at Bethel and overcome with the realization that God was present, he made a vow—"If God will be with me, and will keep me in this way that I go, and will give me bread to eat, and raiment to put on, so that I come again to my father's house in peace; then shall the Lord be my God: . . . and of all that thou shalt give me I will surely give the tenth unto thee" (Gen. 28:20–22). When Jacob failed to keep his promise, God reminded him of it (Gen. 31:13). Later Moses declared to Israel in the wilderness: "All the tithe . . . is the Lord's: it is holy unto the Lord" (Lev. 27:30). When sin corrupted the lives of the Jews and they failed to keep the laws of God, the prophets denounced their waywardness and graphically reminded them of their obligations. The prophet Malachi said: "Will a man rob God? Yet ye have robbed me. But ye say, Wherein have we robbed thee? In tithes and offerings" (Mal. 3:8). But this rebuke was accompanied by a promise, one of the great invitations in the Scriptures: "Bring ye all the tithes into the storehouse, that there may be meat in mine house, and prove me now herewith, saith the Lord of hosts, if I will not open you the windows of heaven, and pour you out a blessing, that there shall not be room enough to receive it" (Mal. 3:10). Jesus also supported the tithe, for it was a vital part of the law. He clearly stated, "Think not that I am come to destroy the law, or the prophets: I am not come to destroy, but to fulfil" (Matt. 5:17). It was motive that concerned Jesus. Prompted by love for God and fellow man, Jesus' followers would surely obey the law; but their standards should be beyond the minimum legal requirement. To a strict, law-abiding Pharisee he said one day, "Woe unto you, Pharisees! for ye tithe mint and rue and all manner of herbs, and pass over judgment and the love of God: these ought ye to have done, and not to leave the other undone" (Luke 11:42).

Significantly, mention of the tithe is not limited to the Scriptures alone. Throughout ancient secular history there are accounts that tell of the dedication of a tenth of one's possessions. The Assyrian ruler Tiglath Pilesar presented a tenth of the pillage of war to his gods Asshur and Ramman after a victory north of the Tigris River. Other accounts tell of Ahmosis, an Egyptian military leader, giving a tenth of his slaves, cattle, and precious metals to be used in enlarging the temple of his cult. Records also show that this custom was prevalent among the Phoenicians, Greeks, and Romans. Seemingly, this belief in dedicating a tenth to religious purposes is basic in the nature of man.

The Christian church has had various attitudes toward the tithe. The Scriptures record that the early Christians simply shared their possessions as needs arose (Acts 2:44–45). Later, but still early in the Christian era, ministers began to devote all their time to preaching and therefore were in need of financial support. Gradually, therefore, the early church began to re-emphasize the old tithing law. Christian preachers were compared by the church fathers to the Jewish priests and Levites of the Old Testament, and many church fathers gave their support to reinstituting, among Christians, the Jewish practice of tithing. Clement and Cyprian were especially outspoken. The church continued to face difficult tasks as Christians withheld their tithes. In A.D. 585, at the council of Macon, Lyon, France, the payment of tithes was declared divine rule, and those who did not pay were excommunicated. Similar action was taken by other councils. Not until A.D. 778, however, was payment of the tithe legally enforced by Charlemagne (Charles the Great). Legal enforcement did not change hearts, and the custom was a long time in gaining support. Pope Hadrian in A.D. 785 imposed tithe payment on the Anglo-Saxon church. Payment was not legally enforced, however, until A.D. 967 during the reign of King Edgar, son of Edmund. After this time the practice continued.

As clerical corruption and abuses became apparent, people felt that the money was being misused; for this reason as well as selfish ones, they began to chafe under the legal obligation to pay tithes. Wycliffe openly complained to King Richard II that the clergy put tithes to wicked use. Many people claimed that the clergy used church income for their own pleasure or gave it to laymen as a reward for favors. Another complaint was that the tithes were being sent out of the country to the treasury in Rome.

The colonists who emigrated to America brought harsh memories of enforced tithes that were collected by the state church. Soon, however, several colonies resorted to the same expedient, and required all residents to pay a tax for the support of preachers of the state church. This tax was especially unpopular with Baptists and other groups who had their own ministers, and it was opposed with great determination but little success until about the time of the American Revolution, when the established colonial churches began to lose their special privileges.

During all this time Baptists and other extralegal sectaries paid little attention to voluntary tithing, doubtless because they were so much occupied with opposition to religious taxation. In the middle of the 18th century, all other concerns were engulfed in a vast and quite successful period of revival, which added great numbers to the churches, but which laid much greater emphasis on evangelical fervor than on systematic benevolence. Many churches, in fact, were definitely opposed to what they considered a "hireling ministry," and paid their preachers (when they had them) nothing. Preachers who were supported at all usually received food or farm products, such as tobacco or, occasionally, whiskey, which could be exchanged for money. At least until the beginning of the 19th century, most Baptist ministers worked at secular jobs in addition to preaching. The attitude of John Courtney, for 40 years (1784–1824) pastor of the First Baptist Church of Richmond, Va., was characteristic of many other Baptist ministers of his day.

Working as a carpenter, he accepted no regular salary—only a "hat collection" each Sunday. In his sermons Courtney often quoted a couplet that characterized his beliefs on ministerial support. "No foot of land do I possess, / Nor cottage in the wilderness." In 1809, after living many years in a rented house, he was given a deed to this house by the church at the morning service. That night, in preaching, he began to quote his beloved lines—but stopped! The next day he relinquished his property, saying, "I'd rather have my lines than the land."

With the advent of the mission movements, tithing gained more prominent support. Missions and tithing have always strengthened each other. The New York Missionary Society, formed in 1796, sent missionaries to the Indians in the South. The Triennial Convention, formed in 1814, was a distinctive Baptist mission movement. Its need for stronger financial support helped to foster among Baptists a new attitude toward giving and greater willingness to support all phases of religious work. In the 1890's the Layman's Movement, started by Thomas Kane, swept the country with its major emphasis on tithing for support of missions.

Southern Baptists about this time were also concerned about tithing and systematic giving, and adopted a recommendation at the Southern Baptist Convention in 1894, "that the Special Committee of seven . . . be appointed to consider the subject of urging church members to give at least one-tenth of their income to the cause of Christ." The committee reported the next year that "full relief need not be hoped for until our church members individually and voluntarily adopt the Scriptural systematic plan of paying God at least one-tenth of his [*sic*] income." This the church members did not do. Little real progress was made until the time of World War I, which was a period of financial drives. Tithing was emphasized with strong fervor, and soon various promotional movements were launched. Disciples had the Men and Millions Movement; Presbyterians, the New Era Movement; Southern Baptists, the 75 Million Campaign; and Methodists, the Centenary Celebration which had for a slogan "A Million Tithers in Methodism."

Tithing was emphasized strongly throughout the Southern Baptist Convention and in 1921 a campaign was set to enrol a half-million tithers among members of the denomination. It was recommended that the Layman's Missionary Movement, the Woman's Missionary Union, and all the agencies of the general boards and of the state boards unite in this effort. There was great achievement for several years; then during the depression of 1930–33, the churches were severely handicapped because of the low income of their members, and because of their debts from overexpansion during the previous era. Three plans for increased giving found popular support. Two, the Lord's Acre Plan for rural areas and the Lord's Hour Plan for city dwellers, stressed general stewardship. The Belmont Plan, started by Belmont Presbyterian Church, Roanoke, Va., projected a three-month adventure in tithing. As the region's economy gained strength and prosperity came with war, Southern Baptists launched a series of stewardship campaigns. In 1947 a crusade was inaugurated to enlist a million Southern Baptist tithers for Christ. The tithers' enlistment visitation plan was presented in 1950 and subsequent years. Later, a school of stewardship in every church was promoted as a part of the Southern Baptist advance in stewardship, and stewardship study course books stressing tithing were being taught extensively. Stewardship revivals were promoted in 1954, and every church was encouraged to have a one-night stewardship conference in 1955. In 1955 there were 1,013,973 tithers reported in the Southern Baptist Convention. World Missions Week, encouraging churches to contribute to world missions through the Cooperative Program, was the plan for 1956. This was to be followed with emphasis on a forward program of church finance, stressing the promotion of tithing and benevolence through detailed and effective methods.

These various programs of promotion have helped greatly to raise the standard of giving among Southern Baptists. Though tithing is far from universally practiced, there does exist a significant and growing awareness on the part of church members of their financial responsibilities both to their own local churches and to the wider interests of the whole denomination. In principle at least, the tithe is accepted as the ideal minimum standard; many avoid it, but there is no opposition based on religious reasoning.

For those who do tithe, some questions remain. Many wonder where the tithe should be given, reasoning that since various charitable works now carried on by civic agencies were once functions of the church, they may properly share in Christian tithes. For most Southern Baptist churches at least, the admonition of Malachi, "Bring ye all the tithes into the storehouse," is clear indication that only the church can be properly considered the recipient of tithes.

Another pressing question, on which there is real and honest difference of opinion, concerns the computation of the tithe. Many Southern Baptists insist that the tithe is one tenth of a person's gross income, before taxes. Others, feeling that money deducted as taxes from a person's salary, over which he has no real control, is not to be considered a part of his tithable income, compute the tithe on the basis of gross income after the deduction of such taxes. On this point there is no specific guidance in Scripture. Both methods are widely used, and each person's decision must be determined by his own conscience. It is true, however, that the deductibility of religious contributions from taxable income has encouraged some to increase the level of their giving. HOWARD FOSHEE

TITHERS' ENLISTMENT VISITATION. A program developed by the Executive Committee of the Southern Baptist Convention for the enlistment of tithers through personal visitation, using as the basic tool a turnover chart with

22 pages, 10 x 13 inches in size. Two trained visitors who are tithers visit in the homes of the membership. With the aid of the turnover chart they explain what tithing is, what the Bible teaches concerning it, why one should tithe, and what happens when one does tithe. They share their own experiences as tithers and invite these persons to join them in Christian stewardship through tithing.

This program provides, in addition to the turnover chart, a pastor and leader's guide, a visitor's handbook, and training sessions for the visitors. The plan has been used successfully in many Southern Baptist churches, where it has resulted in many new commitments to tithe after other methods had failed. Typical reports show that in the churches that have used this program the number of tithers greatly increased, the spiritual life of the people deepened, the financial receipts of the congregation multiplied, in some cases several times over, and the spirit of evangelism increased.

The turnover chart, professionally produced in two colors with display art work, incorporated the best experience in the business world and in church budget promotion in the preparation and plan for use. This tool for teaching, promotion, and enlistment was the first of this type known to be used in whole or in part to present the message of tithing. MERRILL D. MOORE

TITHES, VIRGINIA. From the founding of the colony until 1776 the tithe-tax was levied for support of the Established Church. The earliest record of the tithe in Virginia is 1624, when ministers were allowed "ten pounds of tobacco and a bushel of corn per poll, provided the whole allowance did not exceed fifteen hundred pounds of tobacco, and sixteen barrels of corn."

Opposition to the tithe by dissenters, who contended that "their property had been wrested from them and given to those from whom they received no equivalent," came to a head with the Revolution. The first Virginia legislature, meeting in Williamsburg, Oct., 1776, was flooded with petitions, some persons asking to be relieved of the tax to support the Established clergy, others holding that its repeal would deprive them of their just livelihood. A great struggle ensued from 1776 to 1779, during which time the issue was hotly contended in every session of the legislature. James Madison, Thomas Jefferson, and George Mason led the fight for abolition of the tithe. Final revocation of the tithe-tax was accomplished in 1779, although a determined effort was made in 1784 to pass a law assessing every citizen for the support of his chosen church, but it was abandoned the following year. L. D. JOHNSON

TODD, ANDREW LEE (b. Rutherford County, Tenn., July 27, 1872; d. Rutherford County, Tenn., Mar. 24, 1945). Educator. He was the son of Aaron and Elizabeth Todd and was educated in the schools of Rutherford County and at Union University, Jackson, Tenn. He later studied law at the University of the South at Sewanee and at Cumberland University in Lebanon. He was a great believer in public education and served in many capacities in that field—as teacher at Union University for three years; as principal at Wartrace, Tenn.; as superintendent of schools for Rutherford County; and as assistant state superintendent of education. He was a member of the board of trustees for Tennessee College for Women from its founding until his death. In addition, he served as president of the Tennessee Baptist Convention (1926–29) and was a long-time member of the State Mission Board. For a number of years he served his church as a deacon and as chairman of deacons. He married Miniola Wilson, and to this union were born a daughter and two sons, one of whom became mayor of Murfreesboro. G. ALLEN WEST

TOLERATION, VIRGINIA ACT OF. Rigid conformity to Anglican principles, expected in Colonial Virginia, was not immediately changed by the Act of Toleration of 1689, which exempted dissenters from attendance at Anglican services, but not from tithes, if they attended their own services conducted by an ordained minister in a registered meetinghouse. The English Act of Toleration was not extended to the colony until 1699, and then only in a general way by the House of Burgesses. Dissenting ministers were not mentioned.

In 1739 Governor Gooch granted "liberty of conscience and of worshipping God" to Presbyterians providing Act of Toleration rules were fulfilled and ministers "behaved peaceably towards the government." Evidently this policy was not continued, for a decade later Samuel Davies was fighting for rights of dissenters, at which time Attorney General Randolph said the act did not extend to the colony. When the law was passed no mention was made of the dominions.

Davies won toleration, but Baptists, formerly beneath the notice of authorities, soon faced persecution. "Men in power strained every penal law in the Virginia code to obtain ways and means to put down these disturbers of the peace, as they were now called." They were imprisoned as vagrants because they preached without licenses for themselves or their meetinghouses, and when Baptist ministers offered to conform to the spirit of the Toleration Act, licenses were refused by examining Anglican clergymen.

Beginning in 1770 petitions for relief were sent to the General Assembly, but by 1775 "toleration" was forgotten when demands were being made for full liberty and the separation of church and state. WESLEY LAING

TOMKIES, CHARLES WILLIAM (b. Hanover County, Va., Oct. 18, 1847; d. Dallas, Tex., Aug. 28, 1902). Administrator, educator, pastor. Educated at Randolph-Macon College, he moved to Louisiana in 1869. He taught in Helm College and Shreveport University, united with Salem Baptist Church in DeSoto Parish in 1878, and was pastor of Summer Grove and other churches near Shreveport. In 1885, as a member of a committee, he led in organizing the Louisiana executive board. He was chosen its first secretary, served for four years, and laid the foundation of the present work of that board. He resigned this position to become president of Keachie College where he did much for the education of Louisiana. In 1899 he became pastor of Valence Street Church, New Orleans, succeeding David Ingram Purser (*q.v.*). His last pastorate was at Cameron, Tex.; his last service was as field secretary of Baylor University. T. W. GAYER

TONGUES, GIFT OF. Technically called glossolalia, this phenomenon, as presented in the New Testament, finds its origin, not in the Greek mystery cults of Asia Minor, but in the spiritistic quality of ancient Hebrew prophecy. A classic example is the gift of prophecy which came to Saul when he met a company of prophets at Gibeah (I Sam. 10:9 ff.), and to those with Samuel at Ramah (I Sam. 19:18–24). Prior to the conquest, the 70 elders (Num. 11:24–29) had a similar experience. Specific reference to glossalalia is found in II Kings 9:11; and in Micah 2:6, Amos 7:16, and Jeremiah 29:26 we see that such speech makes the *neb'im* the objects of scorn (cf. Isa. 28:10 ff.).

Paul's treatment of the matter in I Corinthians 12–14 is the earliest written record on the subject in the New Testament. Paul warned against disorderly behavior (14:39–40) and carefully distinguished between intelligible prophecy and tongue-speech (14:2–3). He ranked the "gift of tongues" below other "gifts of the Spirit" (12:27 ff.; 14:12, 18–19). It is certain that the tongue-speech of which Paul spoke was unintelligible to the average person because he spoke of the need for an interpreter (14:6–11, 27–28). He indicated that "tongues" were a sign to the unbeliever (14:21–24) and suggested that too much reliance on tongue-speech indicated immaturity (14:20).

Luke's account of Pentecost has been held by some to be contradictory to Paul's discussion, because Luke apparently indicated that the apostles spoke foreign languages (Acts 2:4, 8). However, it is most likely that there was a mass enthusiasm in which the entire assembly shared, so that, as William Michaelis says, "the people understood the speaking with tongues though it was genuinely unintelligible—they understood because they too had been filled with the Spirit and had received the gift of understanding." This is the Christian reversal of the confusion of tongues at the tower of Babel. Two other occurrences of the gift of tongues are recorded in Acts: at the home of Cornelius (10:44–46) and at Ephesus (19:1–7). Apparently this gift was considered an immediate sign of receiving the Holy Spirit, and probably this explains Paul's injunction in I Thess. 5:19–20.

BIBLIOGRAPHY: M. Barnett, *The Living Flame* (1953). G. B. Cutten, *Speaking with Tongues* (1927).
JOSEPH R. ESTES

TORREON MEXICAN BAPTIST THEOLOGICAL SEMINARY. See MEXICO, MISSION IN.

TOTAL DEPRAVITY. See DEPRAVITY and SIN.

TOWNES, JOHN CHARLES (b. Ala., Jan. 30, 1852; d. Austin, Tex., Dec. 18, 1923). Lawyer, law professor, influential layman. Educated at Baylor University, where he received the LL.B. degree, Townes was twice district judge but gave up his law practice to become professor of law at the University of Texas. He later became dean of the university's Law School, where he served until his death. Author of several textbooks, including *Civil Government, Texas Pleading and Practice, Torts, Elementary Law,* and *Law Books and How to Use Them,* Townes was president of the Association of American Law Schools, vice-president of the Baptist General Convention of Texas, and member of the Education Commission. Through his logical mind, exact knowledge, strength of character, and beaming, mellow personality, Townes exercised moral power over a generation of lawyers who referred to him as "God Almighty's gentleman." A. B. CULBERTSON

TOWNES, JOHN LEIGH (b. Amelia County, Va., Nov. 15, 1774; d. Tuscumbia, Ala., July 28, 1846). Planter, lawyer, soldier, legislator, and pastor in Tennessee Valley. He was educated at Hampden-Sidney College, Virginia. On Dec. 24, 1806, he married Polly Segar Eggleston of Virginia. During that year he began the practice of law. At the outbreak of the War of 1812, he enlisted in the army and served as captain of a volunteer company. In 1815 he was elected to the Virginia legislature and served two years.

He moved to Alabama in 1817 and settled in Madison County. Two years later, when Alabama became a state, he was elected a member of the constitutional convention. In 1820 he moved to Town Creek, Lawrence County.

At the age of 50, he answered the call to preach and was ordained in Mt. Carmel church. For nine years he was clerk of the Muscle Shoals Association; and for two years, the moderator. He was pastor of churches at Courtland, Russell Valley, Bethel, and Mt. Pleasant among others. His last residence was Tuscumbia.

BIBLIOGRAPHY: T. M. Owen, *History of Alabama and Dictionary of Alabama Biography* (1921). B. F. Riley, *History of Baptists of Alabama* (1923).
J. E. BERKSTRESSER

TOWNSEND, MRS. ELLI MOORE (b. Fayette County, Tex., Sept. 21, 1861; d. Belton, Tex., Dec. 10, 1953). Women's college educator. After studying at Baylor College, Independence, Tex., 1876–79, she served as a member of the Baylor College (now Mary Hardin–Baylor) faculty or administration from 1881 to 1944. She married E. G. Townsend in 1899. An influential member of Texas Woman's Missionary Union for 60 years, Mrs. Townsend established and promoted a loan fund for deserving students and a special fund for helping those preparing to be missionaries. She was author and publisher of *Our Baylor* and *Know Your Bible Better,* and compiler of *After Seventy-five Years.* Mrs. Townsend originated Baylor's Cottage Home, a self-help plan for students.

ELIZABETH ALEXANDER

TOY, CRAWFORD HOWELL (b. Norfolk, Va., Mar. 23, 1836; d. May 12, 1919). Professor, language and Bible scholar, writer. Son of Thomas Dallam and Amelia Anne (Rogers) Toy, members of notable Virginia families, Toy graduated from the University of Virginia in 1856 and taught three years at Albemarle Female Institute in Charlottesville before entering Southern Baptist Theological Seminary in Greenville, S. C. Committed to mission service in Japan while in the seminary, Toy, at the outbreak of the Civil War, enlisted in the Confederate Army, first as private and then as chaplain. After the war he joined the faculty of the University of Virginia, where he taught Greek for a year, and then spent two years in Germany studying theology and the Semitic languages. Elected professor of Old Testament interpretation at Southern Baptist Theological Seminary in 1869, Toy resigned 10 years later because of advanced views of biblical criticism which had become unacceptable. During the following year he served as literary editor of the New York *Independent,* and in 1880 went to Harvard University as Hancock Professor of Hebrew and other Oriental languages. At Harvard he achieved distinction as teacher, scholar, and author, writing *Quotations in the New Testament* (1884); *Judaism and Christianity* (1890); *A Critical and Exegetical Commentary on the Book of Proverbs* (1899); and *Introduction to the History of Religions* (1913). He contributed two volumes to the Polychrome Bible Series and articles for the *Encyclopaedia Biblica, Encyclopaedia Britannica,* and *The Jewish Encyclopedia.* GAINES S. DOBBINS

TRACT SOCIETIES AND SOUTHERN BAPTISTS. The first Baptist tract society in the United States was organized in Washington, D. C., Feb. 25, 1824—the Baptist General Tract Society. For some years it was almost wholly supported by Southern Baptists, who gave $877 of the $1,038 received in its first year, and furnished 21 of its 26 life members. In 1826 it recognized the importance of Sunday schools for getting its tracts read, both by the children and their parents. Tract and publication societies soon set up Sunday school libraries. Tracts were bound together and sold as books for these libraries. The Southern Baptist Publication Society, Charleston, S. C., for example, in 1857 printed nine tracts in a book called *Tracts on Important Subjects,* and two years later 19 additional tracts were listed.

The Southern Baptist Sunday School Union (1857–68) launched its Sunday school library by printing more than 40 books in 1859. They were booklets, not much more than tracts, for the whole library was sold for about $8. The American Tract Society and the American Sunday School Union also circulated their tracts among Southern Baptists. Some of the states, through their depositories, their Sunday school, Bible, and colportage societies, and their local societies, gave a wide distribution to tracts. Colporteurs and missionaries gave them away in large numbers where they could not be sold. These tracts, widely read by children, young people, and adults, created a growing desire for books.

The American Baptist Publication Society, which succeeded the Baptist General Tract Society in 1840, began publishing books for its Sunday school library in 1842. It bound some of its tracts into volumes. Through its colportage work (it also called its colporteurs traveling agents), North and South, it gave wide distribution to its tracts while selling books and Bibles to the people. Inactive in the South from 1846 until 1865, it resumed its work there in 1866 and continued until about 1910.

The Sunday School Board of the Southern Baptist Convention, established in 1891, has printed millions of general, doctrinal, evangelistic, missionary, and promotional tracts for the church educational organizations and has made them available without cost to pastors, churches, missionaries, and other denominational workers. Tracts have become less essential to the people than formerly, but they are still widely used by the boards and other agencies of the Southern Baptist Convention, and by the several state Baptist conventions and their various departments of work. HOMER L. GRICE

TRADITION, FORCE AND EFFECT OF. Customs and beliefs which have become established through usage over a period of years are considered traditions. These may, or may not, be profitable. Tradition may represent a philosophy or procedure so deeply intrenched in channels of prejudice or conviction that only with great difficulty can its course be changed. For example, the elders, chief priests, and scribes of Christ's day were fettered by lifeless legalism, inert tradition. The apostle Peter was enslaved by the tradition of ages that the Gentiles could not become heirs of the grace of God; he broke through the barriers of Judaism only when he was enlightened by the Spirit of God and visited the home of Cornelius. Traditions may signify life or death. Paul referred to traditions either to be treasured (I Cor. 11:2; II Thess. 2:15) or to be discarded (Col. 2:8).

The history of Baptists is linked with tradition. Although established over a long period of years, many of these traditions have not remained in effect to the present. In 1860 David Benedict, well-known Baptist historian, wrote a book entitled *Fifty Years Among the Baptists.* He noted changes—ecclesiastical, social, cultural, financial, missionary, and evangelistic—which he had observed during the preceding half-century. At least 50 years is required as a measuring stick for the determination of the nature and value of tradition.

A similar study by S. L. Morgan appeared in *The Chronicle,* American Baptist Historical Quarterly, Oct., 1948. The writer noted the following changes in American Baptist life: acceptance of women as men's equals, lowering of standards in church membership, less rigid church discipline, decreased interest in distinctive Baptist doctrines, gradual growth in ecclesiasticism, and increasing study of the social application and implications of the gospel. In the same issue of *The Chronicle* was a similar article by O. C. S. Wallace, who referred to the place of women in the churches, changed views concerning the Lord's Supper, tendency toward liturgical church order, complex activities of churches, and multiplied denominational programs and organizations.

Among distinctive changes which have occurred within the past 70 years are the following:

(1) Women are recognized in churches and general Baptist bodies. In some churches, in the early days, modesty forbade men and women to be seated on the same side of the meetinghouse. Women were not admitted to the Southern Baptist Convention as messengers until 1918, 73 years after the Convention was organized. In some associations women were not permitted to read the reports of their work.

(2) Southern Baptist laymen waited 25 years after Southern Baptist women were organized in 1888, before organized Baptist laymen's work was reported to the Southern Baptist Convention. Activities and addresses had been left largely to ordained preachers.

(3) Not until the beginning of the 20th century did churches begin to give places of leadership to young people. In some cases preachers charged that young people's societies were the work of Satan. Only within the last 40 years has any provision been made for organized work among Baptist students in state schools.

(4) Southern Baptists waited more than 70 years after the 1845 Convention before definite worth-while steps were taken to share the burdens of aged and disabled preachers. Tradition, linked with the antimissionary spirit, held that preachers should not expect a living from their ministry. Churches had not learned the scriptural teaching, "that they which preach the gospel should live of the gospel" (I Cor. 9:11, 14; II Cor. 12:13).

(5) Baptist polity in various expressions was slow to change. For years Baptist churches did not consider baptized believers as members of Baptist churches until either the hands of blessing were placed on their heads or the hand of fellowship was given them after baptism. Tradition formerly called for the observance of the Lord's Supper at associational meetings, and it did not invite members of other churches of "like faith and order" to participate in the observance. Other traditions in force in early years were postures in prayer (kneeling or standing), length of associational meetings (at least three days), use of terms "brother" and "sister," number of deacons and terms of their service, discipline for failure to attend church regularly, etc.

(6) Subservience to tradition was seen in the insistence that every Baptist should subscribe, word for word, to statements of faith written by fallible men. Barely a quarter of a century ago, a Baptist state convention spent hours in debate over the demand of one man that the convention adopt, literally, a statement of orthodoxy which he had written. The autonomy of Baptist churches is still being threatened by efforts to impose on churches creedal statements adopted by general Baptist bodies. E. C. ROUTH

TRADUCIANISM. This term applies to the theory of the origin of the soul first propounded by the Latin father, Tertullian. Traducianism holds that the soul of the child is not a fresh creation but is derived from or generated by the souls of its parents. The opposing theory, labeled creationism, holds that the soul of each child is created by a direct act of God. Fitting in with many of the findings of modern biology and psychology, traducianism explains the issues raised by heredity—the similarity of a child to its ancestors in spirit and inner personality, as well as in bodily form or structure. According to this theory, man is one with his physical progenitors in body and personality. Traducianism does not argue against God's creative activity, since God's will can control the generation of the new personality as much as it could produce it completely new, which is the view of creationism. Traducianism further sustains the solidarity of the human race in Adam and in this sense is more in keeping with scriptural revelation. Actually, the biblical viewpoint does not help one to decide between traducianism and creationism. Both theories preserve elements of truth and, being matters of speculation, do not fundamentally affect the relation of each individual soul to the Creator.

See also SIN.

BIBLIOGRAPHY: H. W. Robinson, *The Christian Doctrine of Man* (1926). E. C. RUST

TRANSCENDENCE. Emphasizes God's superiority to the created universe; God is active in the universe, but he is not limited to it. Deism so far stresses and exaggerates God's transcendence as to remove him entirely from the realm of human knowledge and experience; pantheism, urging God's omnipresence and neglecting to state that God is distinct from creation, concludes that the totality of the universe *is* God.

Either extreme presents logical problems that the church has traditionally avoided by maintaining that even though God is "other" and

BATON ROUGE GENERAL HOSPITAL (*q.v.*), Louisiana. Founded 1950, valued at $3,500,000. Includes 250 beds, general service departments, and special services including polio unit.

NORTH CAROLINA BAPTIST HOSPITAL (*q.v.*), and Bowman Gray School of Medicine (*q.v.*), Winston-Salem. Established 1923. Present $9,000,000 plant houses 450 beds and cobalt teletherapy unit.

above the created world he can make himself known to man through it.

See also DEISM, GOD, and PANTHEISM.

BIBLIOGRAPHY: K. Barth, *The Epistle to the Romans* (1950). R. Otto, *The Idea of the Holy* (1952).

A. ELLISON JENKINS

TRANSFIGURATION. See JESUS CHRIST.

TRANSLATIONS AND VERSIONS, THE BIBLE. Throughout the centuries men have, by a long series of translations, expressed their need for copies of the Bible in their own language, a need best realized since the Reformation. This process extends from the third century B.C. until the present and may conveniently be divided between the Old Versions in foreign languages and the English Translations.

The Septuagint was the first major version of biblical material; it was translated from the Hebrew into the Greek during the reign of Ptolemy Philadelphus and his successors of the third and second century B.C. This work was a result of the need of the Jews of Alexandria for the Hebrew Scriptures in the vernacular. However, the early Christians used it so extensively that the Jews were forced to make other Greek versions. Aquila, an anti-Christian Jew, made a very literal translation of the Hebrew Scriptures about A.D. 150. Other Greek versions by Theodotian and Symmachus followed during the next 50 years. These primary versions were gathered together by Origen and placed in his *Hexapla* or "sixfold" version of the Old Testament along with the Hebrew text and his personal translation. During this same period, the second and third centuries A.D., several versions appeared in the Syriac or Aramaic language and in the Coptic tongue of Egypt. Likewise, an old Latin version was available for Latin-speaking Christians by the beginning of the third century A.D., existing in European and African editions.

The period from the fourth to fifteenth centuries was dominated by the Latin version, translated by Jerome and called the Latin Vulgate. This translation was begun by Jerome about 382 at the request of Pope Damasus and completed about 404. This text became the standard source for biblical instruction during the Middle Ages. Translations were made into other languages, but the source was always the Latin Bible. However, it was 1546 when the Council of Trent officially adopted it as the Latin Bible of all Roman Catholic bodies. The invention of the printing press about 1450, the Soncino Hebrew Old Testament in 1488, and the Greek Testament of Erasmus in 1516 opened a new era in Bible translation. The Latin version of Pagninus (1528) was of further help to Hebrew and Greek students because of the literal nature of its translation. Luther was likewise indebted to the original tongues in his German version (1522–34).

Interwoven with the ascendency of the Latin Vulgate was the beginning of English translation efforts. During the Middle Ages Latin remained the official and religious language of the Anglo-Saxons and the Vulgate was the principal source of religious instruction. The paraphrases of Caedmon, the translation of John by Bede, the selected passages of Alfred the Great, and the interlinear Gospels of Aelfric were all important attempts to provide the Scriptures in the vernacular during the eighth, ninth, and tenth centuries. It was John Wycliffe and his followers who actually provided the complete Bible in the English language. Completed about 1582, Wycliffe's version was a translation of the Latin Vulgate. After Wycliffe's death his followers made a revision which rapidly supplanted the original version.

The century and a half which followed Wycliffe's labors saw many changes, such as: the invention of the printing press, the rebirth of language study, and the beginning of the Reformation. With new tools available translations began to appear rapidly. William Tyndale, armed with Greek and Hebrew manuscripts and knowledge of seven languages, published his translations between 1525 and 1535. He was not able to complete the Old Testament, but his work was the ancestor of the major versions since his time. In 1535 Miles Coverdale published the first complete Bible to be printed in the English language and the first to be circulated without hindrance. Another revision appeared in 1535 as John Rogers, a disciple of Tyndale, published the version called Matthew's Bible. This was a completion of Tyndale's version with selections from the work of Coverdale and was further revised by Taverner in 1539.

Previously some versions had been licensed, but the Great Bible, published in 1539, was directly authorized by Henry VIII to be placed in the churches and commissioned by Cromwell. In spite of its large size, it was used for family study and promoted new interest in the Scriptures. The Geneva Bible followed in 1560 and soon became the version of the Puritans. The bishops of the Church of England published yet another version in 1568 which found much use in the worship services. While the Roman Catholic Church did not desire English translations, popular demand made it necessary to publish the Rheims-Douai Bible between 1582 and 1610.

The King James or Authorized Version of 1611 ushered in a stability that was sorely needed. Although not fully accepted at first, it soon became the most popular English version, standing as one of the great monuments of English literature. While minor changes were made through the years, a thorough revision was not attempted until 1885 when the Revised Version was published. This was followed by the American edition of this same work in 1901, The American Standard Version.

The Revised Standard Version followed next, a complete revision of the American Standard Version, appearing in New Testament form in 1946 and the complete work in 1952. These later English translations have proceeded from common sources but have benefited much from the 19th-century discoveries of Hebrew and Greek texts and the 20th-century discoveries of papyrus and Dead Sea manuscripts. Mention should also be made of the Confraternity Bible begun in 1941 by Roman Catholic scholars as well as the Improved Edition of 1912, sometimes called The Baptist Bible.

In addition to the more standard versions, many modern translations have appeared during the 20th century. Such works as Weymouth's New Testament (1902), The Centenary New Testament (1924), Moffatt's Bible (1924), Smith-Goodspeed Bible (1927), and William's New Testament (1936), aided many in Bible understanding and helped pave the way for a recognition of the need for the Revised Standard Version.

BIBLIOGRAPHY: J. M. Adams, *Our Bible* (1937). J. Baikie, *The English Bible and Its Story* (1928). C. C. Butterworth, *The Literary Lineage of the King James Bible* (1941). J. Eadie, *The English Bible* (1876). E. J. Goodspeed, *The Making of the English New Testament* (1946). W. J. Heaton, *Our Own English Bible* (1913). H. G. G. Herklots, *How Our Bible Came to Us* (1954). F. Kenyon, *Our Bible and the Ancient Manuscripts* (1939); *The Story of the Bible* (1936). H. G. May, *The English Bible in the Making* (1952). H. Pope, *English Versions of the Bible* (1952). I. M. Price, *The Ancestry of Our English Bible* (1949). B. J. Roberts, *The Old Testament Text and Versions* (1951). H. W. Robinson, ed., *The Bible in Its Ancient and English Versions* (1940). S. Rypins, *The Book of Thirty Centuries* (1951). J. P. Smyth, *Our Bible in the Making* (1914). L. A. Weigle, *The English New Testament from Tyndale to the Revised Standard Version* (1949). B. F. Westcott, *A General View of the History of the English Bible* (1927).

KYLE M. YATES, JR.

TRAVIS, ALEXANDER (b. Edgefield District, S. C., Aug. 23, 1790; d. near Evergreen, Ala., 1852). Pioneer minister. Travis was converted at the age of 19, and baptized into the fellowship of the Addiel Church in South Carolina in 1809. A year later (1810) he was licensed to preach. In 1813 he was ordained to the full work of a Baptist minister and was pastor of several churches. It was in 1817 that he moved to Alabama territory and located near what is now Evergreen in Conecuh County. The early settlers responding to the ministry of this pioneer preacher constituted under his leading the Beulah Church in 1818. Travis was pastor of Beulah Church for 35 years. He was elected a domestic missionary in 1823 at the first meeting of the Baptist state convention in Alabama, and was later elected a trustee of Howard College, a place which he held for six years. For 20 consecutive years he was moderator of the Bethlehem Association, one of the oldest associations in the state, which was constituted as the Beckbee Association in 1816. In 1835 he was invited to Montgomery to assist in solving a difficulty that had arisen in the young church there. He visited the members and held reconciliation prayer meetings, healing the rupture. Travis died in 1852 after a full life of pioneer missionary service to his denomination. Hosea Holcombe in 1840 said of him, "[He was] one of the oldest and most indefatigable ministers in Alabama."

DAVIS WOOLLEY

TRIBBLE, ANDREW (b. Caroline County, Va., Mar., 1741; d. Dec. 22, 1822). Son of George Tribble, he was among the first converts to the Baptist faith in Virginia. He became a member of Thompson's (Goldmine) Church, in Louisa County. He began preaching soon after his conversion about the same time that Waller, Childs, the Craigs, and others began their meetings in Elijah Craig's (*q.v.*) tobacco barn. He was probably baptized by James Read. In 1777 he became pastor of a church in Albemarle County, near the residence of Thomas Jefferson. Many Virginians, especially the able and learned Robert Boyté Crawford Howell (*q.v.*), claim that Thomas Jefferson conceived the idea of a popular government while observing the business transactions of the little Baptist church, of which Tribble was pastor.

In 1783 Tribble moved to Kentucky and settled on Dix River. In Jan., 1786, he united with Howard's Creek (now Providence) Church, of which Robert Elkin was pastor. During this year Tribble gathered Tate's Creek Church and became its pastor. About three years later, a personal difficulty arose between him and his pastor at Howard's Creek, which resulted in a nearly equal division of the church. Tribble's party was constituted a new church, called Unity. The Elkin party, at Howard's Creek, according to the terms of adjustment, retained the old constitution and the church property but changed its name to Providence.

Tribble was accepted as a member and chosen pastor of Unity Church. He soon became entangled in a lawsuit with one of the members, named Haggard, which was settled by Tribble's making satisfactory acknowledgments. This seems to have resulted in severing his pastoral relations to that church. He continued to serve Tate's Creek, however, till the infirmities of old age made it necessary for him to retire. He died in 1822.

He was a zealous and able preacher. In Virginia he endured a term in a Virginia jail for preaching the gospel contrary to law. He married Sally Burrus in early life, by whom he raised a large family. His son Peter became a Baptist preacher. LEO T. CRISMON

TRIBULATION. Tribulation or affliction is a frequent biblical theme (Hebrew *oni*, "affliction," *tsar*, "straitness"; Greek *thlipsis*, "pressure"). Closely related are the concepts of persecution (*diogmos*) and distress (*stenochoria*). Tribulation has a general and a particular eschatological usage in the New Testament.

While tribulation sometimes is a punitive consequence of sin (Rom. 2:9; II Thess. 1:6; Rev. 2:22), the term is more often used of the

Christian life. Tribulation for the Christian calls for and produces steadfastness or patience (Rom. 5:3; 12:12), may involve the loss of material possessions (Rev. 2:9), can be met with joy and confidence (John 16:33; II Cor. 7:4), makes desirable comfort, both divine and human (II Cor. 1:4), cannot separate from Christ's love (Rom. 8:35), and completes Christ's sufferings (Col. 1:24).

Jesus in his eschatological discourse spoke about a "great tribulation" preceding the end of the age (Matt. 24:21, 29). Pretribulational premillennialism teaches that a distinct period of such tribulation will be preceded by the "rapture of the church" so that Christians will not experience it, and interprets the period as constituting all or the latter half of the seventieth week of Daniel 9:24–27.

See also ESCHATOLOGY.

BIBLIOGRAPHY: G. E. Ladd, *The Blessed Hope* (1956). H. W. Robinson, *Suffering Human and Divine* (1939).

JAMES LEO GARRETT

TRIENNIAL CONVENTION. "The General Missionary Convention of the Baptist Denomination in the United States of America for Foreign Missions," meeting triennially and hence called the "Triennial Convention," was organized on May 18, 1814, with 33 delegates from 11 states and the District of Columbia. The convention was to consist of delegates, not to exceed two in number, from each missionary society and other religious bodies of Baptists contributing at least $100 a year to the work of the convention. The first president was Richard Furman (*q.v.*) (1755–1825) of South Carolina, and the first secretary was Thomas Baldwin (1753–1826) of Massachusetts.

This organization climaxed a series of Baptist efforts in the direction of co-operation. In 1707 the first association, the Philadelphia Baptist Association, was organized, and it was soon followed by others. For an interval the association met the need for co-operation; then the need for wider co-operation was felt, and calls were sounded for a national organization. In 1767 the moderator of the Philadelphia Association mentioned the need for co-operation; in 1770 Morgan Edwards, a prominent Baptist, suggested a plan for national organization; in 1776, Virginia Baptists called for a "continental association," and in 1799 the Philadelphia Association urged a national meeting.

It remained, however, for an emergency in the growing foreign mission enterprise of American Christianity to provide the occasion for such an organization. In Feb., 1812, Luther Rice (*q.v.*) (1783–1836) and Adoniram Judson (*q.v.*) (1788–1850) were sent out to India by the "American Board of Commissioners for Foreign Missions," a Congregational body. En route they became convinced of the authenticity of believers' immersion as held by Baptists and, having embraced it, felt compelled to resign as Congregational missionaries. Since they were left without financial support, they decided that Judson should remain in India, while Rice should return to America to rally the Baptists to Judson's support. Rice made extensive tours and labored valiantly, and it was largely due to his efforts that the meeting out of which grew the first national Baptist organization was convened.

To implement the missionary work for which the Triennial Convention was organized, and to transact business ad interim, a board of 21 members, with headquarters in Philadelphia, Pa., was elected, denominated the Baptist Board of Foreign Missions for the United States, with Baldwin as president. Rice was chosen by the board to continue his work of mission promotion in the states, while Judson was appointed as the first foreign missionary of the new organization.

The meeting of the convention in 1817 was again held in Philadelphia. Furman was reelected president. At this meeting the work of the convention was expanded to take in both home missions and education. The board was instructed by an amendment to the constitution to devote a part of the funds collected to home mission purposes. This it did by appointing James Welch (1789–1876) and John Mason Peck (*q.v.*) (1789–1874) to establish mission stations in Missouri.

A second amendment directed the board to establish a "classical and theological seminary" for the training of young preachers, but specifically stated that money for it was to be raised apart and kept separate from mission funds. In response William Staughton (1770–1829) began a school in Philadelphia in 1818. In 1822, after Columbian College was chartered in Washington, D. C., the school in Philadelphia was transferred to Washington and became the theological department of the embryonic institution.

The *Minutes* for 1817 reveal the growth of interest in the convention, by recording 51 delegates and proxies, representing 40 societies, with 187 societies supporting the work.

The convention met again in Apr., 1820, at Philadelphia, with Robert B. Semple (*q.v.*) (1769–1831) of Virginia chosen as president. Here the words "and other important objects relating to the Redeemer's kingdom" were added to the name of the convention. Also, the mission stations for the settlers in Missouri were closed, with increased emphasis on work among the Indians. The work of the convention was given increasing support, as evidenced by attendance and contributions.

In 1823 the meeting of the convention produced some significant changes in scope of work. Upon recommendation of the committee on domestic missions, all home mission work except that among the Indians was curtailed by the convention and left to state and home mission societies.

This regression toward the single purpose which was promoted by the first convention was continued in 1826. The amended constitution specified the appropriation of money to "Foreign and Indian Missions," omitting home missions. However, the convention heartily urged the formation of a home mission society. In addition, the convention nullified its right to elect the trustees of the debt-ridden Columbian College, thus disassociating itself from direct educational endeavor. Also, the location of the board was changed from Philadelphia, Pa., to Boston, Mass.

In the following years more and more missionaries were sent out by the convention, and many new mission stations were opened. Missionary work increased, and as a concomitant to the convention's work in foreign missions, the American Baptist Home Mission Society was formed during a recess of the 1832 meeting of the convention, with the approval of that body.

The work progressed so well that by 1838 the convention had employed 98 missionaries and had 38 active native churches. It continued to prosper until growing tensions between North and South resulted in the organization of the Southern Baptist Convention in 1845. In the same year the Triennial Convention changed its name to the American Baptist Missionary Union, which in 1910 became the American Baptist Foreign Mission Society.

The process of expansion and recession in the work of the convention from 1814 until 1826, when it reverted to the single purpose of foreign missions, is reflective of the difference in ecclesiastical ideology between Baptists of the North and South. The South preferred one denominational organization promoting every phase of endeavor, which preference was achieved in the Southern Baptist Convention, and the North preferred a separate society for each facet of the work, a policy which prevails until today in the American Baptist Convention.

BIBLIOGRAPHY: W. W. Barnes, *The Southern Baptist Convention, 1845–1953* (1954). A H. Newman, *A History of the Baptist Churches in the United States* (1898). *Proceedings of the Baptist Convention for Missionary Purposes, 1814. Proceedings of the Fifth Triennial Meeting of Baptist General Convention, 1826. The First Annual Report of the Baptist Board of Foreign Missions for the United States* (1815). *The Latter Day Luminary,* 6 vols. (1818–26). R. G. Torbet, *A History of the Baptists* (1950). A. L. Vail, *The Morning Hour of American Baptist Missions* (1907).

RAYMOND A. PARKER

TRINIDAD AND TOBAGO BAPTISTS. Baptist work in Trinidad began in 1843 when a British Baptist, George Cowen, then an agent in the island of the Mico Charity, was recognized as a missionary by the Baptist Missionary Society, London. He was located at Port of Spain where he hired a room for services, and also preached in the open air. The first church was formed by him together with several members of Baptist churches in America and one from Sierra Leone. In 1844 premises were purchased from the Mico Charity to serve as headquarters of the mission. The work extended to other centers in the North and developed in the South and in Tobago. At present there are 5 missionaries of the Baptist Missionary Society (Great Britain); 17 churches with 488 communicant members; 6 Sunday schools with 300 scholars and 12 teachers; and 2 day schools with 471 scholars and 11 teachers. The churches are linked together in the Baptist Church in Trinidad, which acts through a church council representative of the North District Union, the South District Union, and the Tobago District Union. The establishing of strong, vigorous churches has been hampered chiefly by two factors: the economic plight of the people, and their emotional instability which has expressed itself from time to time in various ecstatic sects. Recently there has been increased evangelistic activity in Port of Spain; Baptists have co-operated with other Christians in large organized campaigns. J. B. MIDDLEBROOK

TRINITY. The fact that baptism is administered in the threefold name of Father, Son, and Holy Spirit (Matt. 28:19) constitutes the most crucial point for understanding the relation between the biblical revelation and the historical formulations of the doctrine of the Trinity. There is only one name but three persons.

The root of the doctrine of the Trinity is found in the revelation of the "name" of God in the Old Testament. This does not mean that the doctrine of the Trinity is explicit in the Old Testament. The doctrine is implicit, however, in the fact that God reveals himself. If God did not reveal himself, nothing at all could be said of him, but the confession that he has spoken is at once a declaration of self-communication and self-relatedness in God. Communication is revealed in the fact that God speaks, and relation is indicated by the fact that he speaks to another.

God's name is manifested in the Old Testament by certain forms and powers that amount to extensions of God's personal being. The forms are the angel of the Lord, the face of God, and the glory of God. The relation between the angel of the Lord and the Lord is clearly indicated in the fact that Exodus 13:21 speaks of the Lord as going before Israel, while Exodus 14:19 identifies the one going before as the angel of the Lord. The face of God as a manifestation of God's name is indicated in meeting God himself (Gen. 32:30). The glory of the Lord is God's personal presence (Exod. 24:15–18). The Spirit of the Lord (Psalm 139:7–12), the word of God (Isa. 55:10–11), and the wisdom of God (Prov. 8), all powers of God, are also personal manifestations of his presence. These manifestations of God represent the Old Testament preparation for the doctrine of the Trinity.

In the New Testament the relation between the Father and the Son is clarified in the Synoptic Gospels and Acts, but an unmistakable Trinitarian pattern emerges in Paul and John. Paul not only declares the deity of the Holy Spirit (II Cor. 3:18) along with the Father and the Son, but he forms a number of Trinitarian patterns (I Cor. 12:4–6; II Cor. 13:14; Eph. 1:3–4; 2:18–21; 3:14–21; 4:4–6; 5:18–20). The deity of the Father, Son, and Spirit are most explicit in the five statements regarding the Spirit in

John's Gospel (14:15–17, 25–26; 15:26–27; 16:5–11, 12–15).

Confusion about the doctrine of the Trinity arises largely in the transition from the concrete language of biblical revelation to the abstract language of historical formulations. Abstract thought moves away from an organic to a mathematical unity. The formula of Greek Christianity, discussed most fully in Cappadocia in the fourth century, became one essence in three persons (*mia ousia kata treis hypostaseis*). The classic statement of this view in the *Exposition of the Orthodox Faith* (Bk. I. chap. 4–8) by John of Damascus (*c.* 676–770) represents God as one abstract being in three individuals or persons, not as one personal being in three relations. Consequently, the threat of the East has been more in the direction of tritheism than unitarianism.

The formula of Latin Christianity, originated by Tertullian (160?–230?), became one substance in three persons (*una substantia in tribus personis*). Tertullian's major contribution is the argument that the immanent Trinity, i.e., God as he is in himself, is revealed in the economic Trinity, i.e., God as he appears in history (*Against Praxeas,* 8). The most important treatise on the Trinity in Latin Christianity is the *De trinitate* by Augustine (354–430). Augustine made no further claim than that the Trinity could be *illustrated,* but those who built on his foundation soon attempted to prove it could be *demonstrated.* Instead of speaking of the three persons as three men, as was done by the Cappadocian fathers, Augustine compared them to memory, understanding, and love (Bk. IX), or to memory, understanding, and will (Bk. X).

Thomas Aquinas (1225?–1274?) systematized and supplemented the psychological analogy of Augustine, but the outgrowth of unitarianism in the West proves the weakness of this type of argument. Richard of St. Victor (d. 1173), building also on Augustine, anticipated the modern social analogy with a Trinity of lover, beloved, and mutual love (*De trinitate,* III, 1–25); in contemporary theology this idea of God as a community of persons has been most thoroughly developed by Leonard Hodgson.

Recent discussions on the Trinity in relation to historical revelation have raised the question as to whether the Trinity is the *arche* or the *apex* of Christian faith. Karl Barth (*Church Dogmatics,* I/1:339–560) has defended the Trinity as the very arche of theology, but he has met resistance in Emil Brunner (*Dogmatics,* I:205–240), who argues the Trinity is a defensive doctrine (*Schutzlehre*) to protect the gospel. Barth's view seems valid in reference to the being of God, but Brunner has a good argument in relation to the historical formulations of the Trinity.

See also God.

Bibliography: L. Hodgson, *The Doctrine of the Trinity* (1943). C. Welch, *In This Name* (1952).

DALE MOODY

TRINITY BAPTIST CHURCH ACADEMY. A school located 11 miles west of Yanceyville, Caswell County, N. C., founded in Nov., 1845. A female department was added in 1846, but the school was discontinued soon after 1849.

D. L. SMILEY

TRINITY RIVER HIGH SCHOOL. A school for boys, later called Waco Classical School, opened by Trinity River Association at Waco, Tex., in 1856. It became Waco University in 1861. RUPERT N. RICHARDSON

TRI-STATE COLLEGE. A school established in 1901 at Texarkana, Tex. It was maintained for one year only by Red River, Enon, and Southwest Arkansas associations.

RUPERT N. RICHARDSON

TRI-STATE HOSPITAL. See Memorial Hospital, Baptist (Memphis, Tenn.).

TROY NORMAL SCHOOL. Established about 1880 in Troy, Miss., and regarded as Baptist. It had a peak attendance of 200 students in 1885. It is now extinct. J. L. BOYD

TRUE LIGHT AND BAPTIST MONTHLY VISITOR, THE. A monthly newspaper, now extinct, published in Jonesboro, Tenn., by Rees Bayless in 1836–37. LYNN E. MAY, JR.

TRUETT, GEORGE WASHINGTON (b. Hayesville, Clay County, N. C., May 6, 1867; d. Dallas, Tex., July 7, 1944). Pastor, Southern and world Baptist leader. The seventh child of Charles L. and Mary R. (Kimsey) Truett, he graduated from Hayesville Academy in 1885; he was converted and joined Hayesville Baptist Church in 1886. Truett, founder and principal of Hiawassee Academy, Towns County, Ga., 1887–89, followed his parents when they moved to Whitewright, Grayson County, Tex., in 1889, where the Whitewright Baptist Church ordained him to the ministry in 1890. As financial secretary of Baylor University, Waco, Truett raised $92,000 in 23 months (1891–93) to wipe out Baylor's indebtedness. Following this he entered Baylor as a freshman in Sept., 1893, and graduated with the A.B. degree in June, 1897. Truett married Josephine Jenkins of Waco in 1894 and served as student-pastor of East Waco Baptist Church while at Baylor.

He became pastor of the First Baptist Church, Dallas, in Sept., 1897, and remained there until his death in July, 1944. During his 47-year pastorate, membership increased from 715 to 7,804; a total of 19,531 new members were received, and total contributions were $6,027,741.52. President of the Southern Baptist Convention, 1927–29, and of the Baptist World Alliance, 1934–39, Truett was a trustee of Baylor University; Southwestern Baptist Theological Seminary, Fort Worth; and Baylor Hospital, Dallas. Constantly in demand for evangelistic, academic, and denominational sermons and addresses, Truett, in addition to his pastorate, was for 37 summers preacher to the "Cowboy Camp Meetings" in west Texas; he preached to Allied Forces for six months in World War I, by appointment of President Woodrow Wilson; he made an address on *Baptists and Religious Liberty,* on the Capitol steps, Washington, D. C., May 16, 1920; he went on a preaching tour in South America during the summer of 1930; he was the sole American speaker on the program of the Spurgeon Centenary, London, England, in Apr., 1934; he toured world mission fields as president of the Baptist World Alliance in 1935–36.

Since Truett's death, religious, educational, and healing institutional buildings erected or designated as memorials to him are the seven-story educational building of First Baptist Church, Dallas; Truett Auditorium, Southwestern Baptist Theological Seminary; Memorial Chapel, Dallas; three Truett memorial churches located in Denver, Colo.; Hayesville, N. C.; and Los Angeles, Calif.; Truett-McConnell Junior College, Cleveland, Ga.; Baptist Orphanage, Nazareth, Israel; and the Truett Building of Baylor Hospital erected at a cost of $5,500,000.

His published works, compiled and edited by others, include 10 volumes of his sermons, two volumes of addresses, and two volumes of his annual Christmas messages which originally appeared as personal letters to a large list of friends. His authorized biography, entitled *George W. Truett—A Biography,* by Powhatan W. James has appeared in six issues, five by the Macmillan Co., New York (1939–45) and the sixth, "Memorial Edition," by Broadman Press, Nashville (1953). POWHATAN W. JAMES

TRUETT, GEORGE W., HOME AND MEMORIAL. An effort to secure the home place of George Washington Truett (*q.v.*) was begun at Ridgecrest, N. C., in the summer of 1936, and many of Truett's friends made donations for that purpose. After the matter was presented to the state convention in 1936, general secretary Malloy Alton Huggins was instructed to "take such additional steps as were necessary that title to the property be perfected in the Convention." Following this action the property was acquired by deed, Jan. 26, 1937, at a purchase price of $2,500. Arrangements were later made for the pastor of a near-by church to use the home as a residence, and the property has been used as a camp ground for churches of region 10 in Western North Carolina. M. A. HUGGINS

TRUETT-McCONNELL JUNIOR COLLEGE. A two-year, coeducational institution located in Cleveland, Ga., and designed to meet the needs of mountain youth of the area. It perpetuates the memory of George Washington Truett (*q.v.*) and of his cousin, Fernando Coello McConnell (*q.v.*), who in 1887 had established at Hiwassee a school which closed two years later.

The only Baptist college in the state established directly by the Baptist Convention of the State of Georgia, Truett-McConnell was founded on July 23, 1946, and formally opened on Sept. 15, 1947, with 54 students. The first president was L. Clinton Cutts.

In 1955 the school, administered by 24 trustees elected for four-year terms by the Georgia convention, had a campus of 410 acres, with six temporary buildings completed and one permanent classroom and administration building under construction. The total physical valuation was $596,033.64, and total endowment was $151,000. For the 1954–55 session enrolment was 244, including 56 ministerial students. The operating budget for 1955–56 was $124,900.00. Joe Hardy Miller had been president since 1951. The staff numbered 16, of whom 10 comprised the teaching faculty. Of the faculty, one held the doctor's degree, six the master's, and three the bachelor's. The school was accredited by the state of Georgia. JOE HARDY MILLER

TRUSTEES OF AGENCIES AND INSTITUTIONS, ELECTION AND TENURE OF. The term "board" had its origin in the Anglo-Saxon "bord" which at first meant a flat piece of structural timber. Later it was applied to articles made of boards. So a table became a board. Finally, since any group of people who met to consider business matters usually sat about a table, the name was applied to them. An official or a representative committee to whom has been assigned some task by a larger body is very generally designated as a board.

For many years a Baptist board was merely a special committee. With the growth of the denomination, however, and especially with the rising of a need to care for bequests and trusts, Baptists found it wise and expedient to incorporate such groups. "Board" being a familiar name for such a legal entity, it was generally adopted, usually with a modifying word added, as board of managers, board of trustees.

In Oct., 1792, as a result of appeals from William Carey (*q.v.*), a group of Baptists met in Kettering, England, to "consider a way to send the Gospel to heathen lands." The conference set up The Particular Society for the Propagation of the Gospel among the Heathen. Twelve of its members were named to constitute a board of directors. Prior to this, Virginia Baptists, aroused by the need for protection against the Colonial government, called a conference to consider steps for self-defense against persecutions. It set up a special committee to "consider all political grievances of the whole Baptist society."

In 1802 a commission was called to meet in Boston, Mass., to consider the challenge of foreign missions. This body set up a Foreign Mission Society which immediately assumed the duties of a board. In 1821 a movement was started in Pennsylvania and adjoining states to provide a supply of religious literature for needy fields at home and abroad. They met in Columbian College, Washington, D. C., and out of it came the American Tract Society. A board of directors was to be elected annually.

With the growth of associations and the organization of larger Baptist bodies, the importance of the special committee increased. As a rule the association committees had few if any legal obligations; hence they were not incorporated. But as the denomination grew in numbers and the work of its agencies and institutions expanded, the need for giving managers legal standing increased, and the major Baptist bodies secured charters for the special committees to which they entrusted the management of their affairs during the interims between regular meetings.

When the Southern Baptist Convention was organized in 1845, one of its first tasks was to provide for the continuance of the work it had been carrying on in connection with the other Baptists of the nation. The constitution which it adopted provided for "as many boards of managers as will be necessary for carrying out the benevolent objects it may determine to promote." Such managers were to be chosen annually by the parent body, distributed among the various co-operating states. The Baptist Sunday School Board was chartered in 1891, following several years of discussion as to the wisdom of interfering with the efficient work of the American Baptist Publication Society. The Convention set the number of members of the board as a vice-president from each co-operating state and 18 members chosen from the area contiguous to the headquarters city. The members were to be elected annually. Not infrequently they continued uninterrupted service for a long period of years.

In 1946 the Convention modified its constitution so as to limit the tenure of its board members to two continuous terms of three years each, with the requirement that a year must pass before a member can be re-elected after his second term. With a few exceptions, the members of agency and institutional boards are elected for a term of three years, each board being divided into three groups so that only one third of the members are elected each year. In the Southern Baptist Convention, board members are elected by the assembled Convention. Nominations are made by a regularly appointed special committee. Other nominations may be made from the floor, but usually the committee's choices are accepted. JOHN D. FREEMAN

TRYON, WILLIAM MILTON (b. New York City, N. Y., Mar. 10, 1809; d. Houston, Tex., Nov. 16, 1847). Minister, Texas Baptist leader, organizer. Son of William and Jane Eliza (Phillips) Tryon, he experienced a difficult childhood following the death of his father when he was only nine years old. He also suffered ill health. At 17, Tryon was converted and baptized; and two years later, he went to Savannah, Ga., where he was licensed to preach in 1832. He entered Mercer University in 1833 and, during his three-year stay there, served as student instructor. In 1837 Tryon was ordained to the ministry, with Jesse Mercer (*q.v.*) serving as one of the presbytery. After serving the Georgia convention, he moved to Wetumpka, Ala., in 1839, where he was pastor of churches there and in near-by Bethlehem. He was appointed missionary to Texas by the American Baptist Home Mission Society in 1841, and moving to Texas, he replaced Zacharias N. Morrell (*q.v.*) as pastor at Washington-on-the-Brazos.

Tryon served twice as chaplain of the Texas Congress, organized the famous church at Independence, revived the church at Galveston, and in 1845 organized a new church at Houston. He was active in and wielded the deciding influence in organization of the Texas Baptist convention; he was also one of the organizers of Clear Creek Association, which became the Texas Baptist Education Society. Persistently urging the founding of a Baptist college for Texas, in 1845, with Robert Emmett Bledsoe Baylor (*q.v.*) and James Huckins (*q.v.*), he drafted the charter for Baylor University and secured its approval by the government of the Republic of Texas on Feb. 1, 1845. Returning from the United States, where he had been sent to solicit funds for the advancement of his work, Tryon died of yellow fever in Houston, Tex., in 1847.

BIBLIOGRAPHY: Mrs. G. J. Burleson, *Life and Writings of Rufus C. Burleson* (1901). J. M. Carroll, *A History of Texas Baptists* (1923). J. B. Link, *Texas Historical and Biographical Magazine* (1891). Z. N. Morrell, *Flowers and Fruits in the Wilderness* (1872). Mrs. L. M. Russell, "Life of William Milton Tryon" (1955). Texas State Historical Association, *Handbook of Texas* (1952). W. M. Tryon Papers, MS, Baylor University, Texas Collection. GUY B. HARRISON, JR.

TUBERCULOSIS SANATORIUM, SOUTHERN BAPTIST. Operated under the direction of the Home Mission Board of the Southern Baptist Convention in El Paso, Tex., with H. F. Vermillion as superintendent from 1920 to 1937. Plans for the establishment of the sanatorium were begun in 1916 when the Southern Baptist Convention adopted a resolution by Vermillion authorizing appointment of a committee to consider the advisability of a sanatorium in the Southwest for the care and treatment of tubercular patients. Such an institution to be located at El Paso was approved by the 1917 Convention. In 1920 the sanatorium was reported in operation. The building and equipment cost almost $500,000. Financial difficulties soon developed, and in 1924 bonds were issued by the Home Mission Board. In Oct., 1937, the sanatorium was closed. In 1938 the Home and Foreign Mission boards exchanged their properties in El Paso. The former sanatorium building now houses the Baptist Spanish Publishing House for the Foreign Mission Board.

E. C. ROUTH

TUCKER, HENRY HOLCOMB (b. Warren County, Ga., May 10, 1819; d. Atlanta, Ga., Sept. 9, 1891). Minister, editor, educator. Tucker was the son of wealth and culture and had unusual educational opportunities. Moving to Philadelphia as a child, he entered the University of Pennsylvania in 1834, and transferred in the middle of his senior year to Columbian College in Washington, D. C., where he was graduated in 1838. While there he spent much time listening to the Senate debates of Clay, Calhoun, and Webster. In 1846 he was admitted to practice of law in Forsyth, Ga., and in 1848 entered Mercer University to prepare for the ministry. A change of plans carried him into educational work as teacher in Southern Female College, LaGrange, Ga., and afterward in the Richmond Female Institute, Richmond, Va. While at LaGrange he was ordained in 1851. Declining the presidency of Wake Forest College in 1853, he became pastor of the Baptist church in Alexandria, Va., on Jan. 1, 1854. In 1856 he was elected professor of belles-lettres and metaphysics in Mercer University and remained until 1862. On July 1, 1886, after a brief tenure as editor of *The Christian Index,* he assumed the presidency of Mercer. It was during his administration and under his leadership that the university was moved from Penfield to Macon. Resigning in 1871, he spent a year traveling in Europe with his family, where he preached often in Rome and Paris. He assisted in the formation of a Baptist church in Rome. In 1874 he was elected chancellor of the University of Georgia, and remained four years. In 1878 he again became editor of *The Christian Index.* His sermon on baptism, preached in 1879, was published by the American Baptist Publication Society. Other writings of note were a series of letters on religious liberty, addressed to Alexander H. Stephens, a small volume entitled *The Gospel in Enoch* (1868), and *The Old Theology Re-Stated in Sermons* (Philadelphia, 1884).

During his stay in Forsyth he married Mary Catherine West, who died less than a year later. While in Alexandria, Va., Tucker married Sara O. Stevens. The degree of D.D. was conferred on him by Columbian College, Washington, in 1860, and the degree of LL.D. by Mercer University in 1876. As a preacher he was bold, original, and eloquent; his general aim was to convict the mind while effectively reaching the heart. As a teacher, he had no superior in the state of Georgia, due to his originality, wit, boldness, independence, and humor. He was recognized as a scholar of unusual training and development. HENRY J. STOKES, JR.

TUGALO INSTITUTE. Opened Oct. 1, 1900, at Carnsville, Ga., existing about two years.

ARTHUR JACKSON

TULAKOGEE BAPTIST ASSEMBLY. Owned and operated jointly by the Tulsa-Rogers and Muskogee associations, located 10 miles northeast of Wagoner, Okla., on 186 acres of land fronting Fort Gibson Lake, leased from the United States Government on a 25-year renewal basis. The initial meeting of 21 pastors on the building site Sept. 8, 1947, resulted in subsequent actions in both associations leading to development of the site in 1954. On Aug. 17, 1954, lots were selected and leased by 33 churches. Development of church cabin sites began in Oct., 1955. These are leased for $100 for 25 years, with $500 charged each church for installation of utilities, development of sites, and professional architectural and engineering services. It is incorporated, governed by a board of 12 members, 6 elected by each co-operating association. Leo M. Perry is president, and Jewell M. Green is secretary-treasurer. The first meeting on the grounds was a Men's Rally, June 25, 1954. The first group to meet after construction of the initial building, a pavilion-type structure, was a Y.W.A. camp, June 22–23, 1956. J. M. GASKIN

TUPPER, HENRY ALLEN (b. Charleston, S. C., Feb. 29, 1828; d. Richmond, Va., Mar. 27, 1902). Pastor, foreign missions leader, educator. He was the son of a railroad builder and president, who was especially interested in the business training of his son. His mother, educated in Philadelphia, a beautiful and intelligent woman, was interested in the intellectual religious education of her children. Tupper attended Madison University, later Colgate. Baptized by Richard Fuller (*q.v.*), Apr. 17, 1846, and licensed to preach Nov. 14, 1847, he married Nancy Johnstone Boyce Nov. 1, 1849. Following a pastorate at Graniteville, S. C., he served as pastor at Washington, Ga., from 1853 to 1872 and was chairman of the executive committee on missions formed by the Georgia Association.

In Jan., 1872, Tupper was elected corresponding secretary of the Board of Foreign Missions of the Southern Baptist Convention. During his administration as secretary, fields of mission work were expanded, with work begun in Mexico, 1880; Brazil, 1881; and Japan, 1889. Tupper made a trip to Mexico in 1884, and under the leadership of William David Powell (*q.v.*), plans were worked out for acquirement of Madero Institute.

During Tupper's tenure at the board, the interest of Southern Baptist women in missions was stimulated and directed in channels of practical work. The first report on women's activity was given in the meetings of the Southern Baptist Convention in 1872. "Central" committees were organized in 1876 and developed in succeeding years, resulting eventually in the Woman's Missionary Union, Auxiliary to Southern Baptist Convention. The first foreign mission offering sponsored by the women, to be known years later as the Lottie Moon Offering, was made in Dec., 1888.

After retirement from the secretaryship in June, 1893, Tupper became instructor of Bible at Richmond College, president of the trustees of Woman's College, Richmond, and member of the Richmond College Board. He was author of two significant volumes, presenting the early history of the Foreign Mission Board, *The Foreign Missions of the Southern Baptist Convention* and *A Decade of Foreign Missions.*

Bibliography: J. A. Broadus, *Memoir of James P. Boyce* (1927). W. Cathcart, *The Baptist Encyclopedia* (1881). "100 years of Foreign Missions," *Southern Baptist Handbook* (1945). G. B. Taylor, *Virginia Baptist Ministers* (1915).
E. C. ROUTH

TWO GRAY HILLS DAY SCHOOL. A school given to New Mexico Baptists by the Woman's National Indian Association, Sept. 17, 1901. Navajo Indians were the beneficiaries of the school's ministry. In 1912, after 11 years of operation, the school passed into the hands of the Christian Reform group.

HERBERT E. BERGSTROM

TWO-SEED-IN-THE-SPIRIT PREDESTINARIAN BAPTISTS. A group Baptist originating in the second half of the 18th century as a result of the protests of Daniel Parker (*q.v.*) against missions and Sunday schools, and his opposition to the Arminian doctrine of the Methodists, and following his Two-Seed doctrine, the conviction that two seeds entered the life stream of humanity in the garden of Eden, a good seed planted by God and an evil seed planted by the devil. Every child is predestined, born with one seed or the other, and nothing can be done to change his destiny. Thus missions is useless; moreover, it "usurps the privileges of God." The seed is not in the flesh but in the spirit. In addition to this cardinal point in their theology, members of this group emphasize salvation by grace alone. The churches practice foot washing, follow congregational polity, and voluntarily form associations for fellowship only. They have no paid ministry, and for many years they have decreased in membership. According to the last available report (1945), they had 16 churches with a total membership of 201.

LYNN E. MAY, JR.

TYLER UNIVERSITY. Established in 1852 at Tyler, Tex., by the Cherokee Baptist Association. The male department was closed in 1857; the female department, called Tyler Female Seminary, was continued until 1867.

RUPERT N. RICHARDSON

U

UNAKA ACADEMY. A school at Erwin, Tenn., chartered on Nov. 11, 1907. It first was sponsored by the "Missionary Baptist Churches in Unicoi County," but in 1912 the sponsorship was taken over by the Holston Association of Baptists. The curriculum eventually included music, art, and two classes per week in Bible, in addition to regular work. A. R. Brown was president of the board of trustees; S. W. Tindell and H. T. Bradford served as principal. The Home Mission Board of the Southern Baptist Convention gave some assistance to the school until it was sold for $10,000 to Unicoi County for high school purposes in 1916. After all debts were paid and $6,000 appropriated to the Home Mission Board of the Southern Baptist Convention, the remainder of the proceeds were given to Carson-Newman College for scholarships, the beneficiaries to be named by the Holston Association or its executive board.

HARLEY FITE

UNION ACADEMY. A school under Baptist control in 1877, located at Farmington, Davie County, N. C. Moses Baldwin, a Baptist minister, directed the academy, and Yadkin Association endorsed it.

D. L. SMILEY

UNION ACADEMY. A school at Clinton, Tenn., sustaining some connection with Baptists, whose history, including various interims, extended from 1806 to sometime after 1887. "In 1806 Arthur Crozier, B. C. Parker, J. Roysden, Hugh Barton, and Samuel Frost were appointed trustees of Union Academy. . . . At what time the Academy was put into operation is not known, but it was probably late in the twenties." About 1845 the Baptists, led by John Jarnigan, erected a brick building near the first academy and established a school, which was maintained until the Civil War, when it was destroyed by fire. After the war a new lot was purchased and a substantial frame building was erected upon it. In 1887 the school was under the control of a board of trustees composed of some of the leading citizens of the town. The date of the school's closing is undetermined.

D. HARLEY FITE

UNION BAPTIST BIBLE INSTITUTE. Chartered in Montgomery County, Ga., in 1904. It became Brewton-Parker in 1914.

ARTHUR JACKSON

UNION UNIVERSITY. A co-educational liberal arts college operated by Tennessee Baptists at Jackson, Tenn., since 1874. The school was a continuation of an earlier institution, West Tennessee College, also located at Jackson, which had grown out of a Jackson Male Academy founded in 1825.

Baptist sponsorship of the school grew out of a proposal to unite all of the Baptists in the state into one organization, which was made in a pastors' conference in Nashville in 1872. Education proved to be the core of the plan for unification. Committees were appointed from the three general organizations of Baptists which then existed in the state. These committees, meeting jointly at Humbolt, Tenn., Mar. 15, 1873, issued a resolution favoring "the establishment of a first class college." They called for an educational convention in Murfreesboro on Apr. 10, 1874, the purpose of which was to "promote the educational interests of Baptists of Tennessee."

At this meeting the Tennessee Baptist Convention was organized. The report of the joint committee on education was accepted, and the convention appointed a committee on location with instructions to recommend a suitable site and ways and means of endowing and establishing a university. The committee on location met in Nashville, July 2, 1874, and after considering several offers decided to recommend that the university be located in Jackson, Tenn. The Baptists were to receive the buildings, grounds, and endowment funds of Jackson's West Tennessee College, on the condition that an endowment of $300,000 for the school be raised in 10 years.

At a meeting in Trezevant on Aug. 12, 1875, the convention accepted the recommendation of the committee on location, elected trustees for the new university, and named it Southwestern Baptist University. The new school opened Sept. 14, 1874, with only the preparatory department, which consisted of a primary school and grammar school. The charter was secured from the state June 25, 1875, and the college opened for classes in Aug., 1875. The collegiate department of the university was organized with two departments: the department of literature and science and the department of law. Four degrees were to be conferred: three regular degrees (M.A., A.B., Ph.B.) and one professional degree (LL.B.). Two auxiliary schools were to be established—one at Mossy Creek and one at Murfreesboro. Their objective was to prepare students for admission to the university. This plan, however, did not materialize.

The new school was soon very popular and enrolment increased rapidly. However, successive efforts at raising funds for endowment and additional buildings met with little success and the school found itself struggling to survive. Since the university had not been able to raise the necessary endowment named in the contract of 1874, the trustees of West Tennessee College declared the contract null and void. Finally, however, an agreement was reached which provided that the contract would remain in force if the University could raise $100,000 in six years. Two successive campaigns and a gift of $5,000 from the American Baptist Education Society brought the endowment to the stipulated figure, and on Aug. 5, 1890, the campus and buildings of West Tennessee College were formally deeded to Southwestern Baptist University.

In 1891 the American Baptist Education Society promised the university $12,700, provided the university would raise an additional $40,000. This condition was met within the allotted time. Beginning in 1879 and continuing for some 10 years, a medical college was operated in Memphis under the charter of the university. In 1897 the university first offered courses for teachers. By 1913 these courses had grown into a department of education.

The name was changed from Southwestern Baptist University to Union University Sept. 17, 1907.

The first dormitory for men was made possible in 1895 through the liberality of W. Thomas Adams of Corinth, Miss. The first dormitory for women was built in 1897 and named Lovelace Hall. A new chapel was built in 1899 and named Powell Chapel in honor of William David Powell. The administration building and Powell Chapel were destroyed by fire Jan. 12, 1912. These buildings were replaced with a single building in 1913.

A Students' Army Training Corps was located on the campus during World War I.

During the time since 1907 the university had nine presidents and one acting president: John William Conger, 1907–09; Isaac Burton Tigrett, 1909–11; Robert Alexander Kimbrough, 1911–13; Richard Moorehead Inlow, June–Sept., 1913; Albert Tennyson Barrett, 1913–15; George Martin Savage, 1915–18; Henry Eugene Watters, 1918–31; Arthur Warren Prince, acting president, 1931–32; John Jeter Hurt, Sr., 1932–45; and Warren Francis Jones, Sr., 1945– . The first part of this period can be characterized as a time of enlargement, the second as a debt-paying phase, and the last as a time of internal strengthening, accreditation, and gradual expansion.

In 1922 the citizens of Jackson contributed $25,000 to an enlargement fund. Following the campaign three buildings were erected: a dining hall, a gymnasium, and a dormitory for women, at a total cost of $60,000. A debt-paying campaign was launched, 1927–30. The campaign resulted in approximately $220,000 in cash and pledges. Approximately $100,000 of the pledges were not paid, however, because of economic conditions. After 1928, debts continued to mount from year to year. By 1939 the indebtedness of the university reached a total of $256,929.47. The board of trustees and friends of the institution launched a campaign in 1940 to relieve the school of all indebtedness. This goal was reached by July, 1944, as a result of this campaign and with the help of an allotment from the Cooperative Program and a debt-paying campaign authorized by the Tennessee Baptist Convention in 1942 and executed in 1943 for the purpose of liquidating the indebtedness of all of its institutions. From bequests and other sources the endowment of the university was increased, and by 1945 had reached more than $300,000. The university secured a new charter Oct. 20, 1925, which gave the Tennessee Baptist Convention the right to select the board of trustees.

Hall-Moody Junior College was consolidated with Union University at the close of the school year 1926–27. The summer school was organized in 1918. The university was admitted to full membership in the Southern Association of Colleges and Secondary Schools in Dec., 1948.

In 1946 a successful campaign was launched to raise funds for needed buildings. It provided for the Emma Watters Summar Library, opened in 1947; for the Student Union Building, housing the cafeteria, (David Alvin) Ellis Chapel, music studios, and home economics laboratories, which was opened for use in 1948; and for the purchase of the College Street Elementary School building, which in 1950 was remodeled and converted into a science building. From Nov., 1954, to Apr., 1955, the United Campaign for Tennessee Baptist Schools was conducted. Union's quota was $600,000. As a result in 1955 a gymnasium was completed and opened for use and the Warren Francis Jones Hall for girls was under construction.

In 1946 a guidance program was begun, and a reading clinic was instituted. An extension center was opened in Memphis in 1952. This work grew in strength and numbers, until in 1955 there were two centers with an enrolment of 155 students, taught by men of superior training and doing work comparable to that on the campus.

For the fall of 1955 the university had a campus enrolment of 517 students, a plant valued at $1,864,992.85, endowment of $526,210.97, and an operating budget for the school year 1955–56 of $404,300.00.

For 130 years Union University and its ancestral institutions have sent out thousands of men and women, approximately 3,640 of whom have received degrees. For 80 years of this period, this institution has operated as a Christian college under Baptist auspices. Its graduates have made contributions in all areas of life, in both secular and Christian enterprises.

WARREN F. JONES and HARLEY FITE

UNION UNIVERSITY. A college operated at Murfreesboro by Tennessee Baptists from Sept., 1848, until the autumn of 1861. The school was projected by the Tennessee Baptist Education Society for Ministerial Improvement, which had been organized under the leadership of Robert Boyté Crawford Howell (*q.v.*) and others on Oct. 8, 1836. Howell's resolutions authorizing the organization of the school were as follows:

1. *Resolved.* That an institution be forthwith originated and established for the purpose of educating young ministers of the Gospel.

2. *Resolved.* That a suitable agent be immediately appointed to collect the necessary funds to carry this design into execution.

These resolutions, together with others calling on all Baptists throughout the state to co-operate in the enterprise, were adopted unanimously and with "great spirit," on the evening of Oct. 13, 1839. As agent-president, charged with the responsibility for securing funds and organizing the institution, the society's executive board chose B. F. Farnsworth, formerly the president of Georgetown College in Kentucky. Farnsworth went to work to secure a charter, and announced later that the college had been located in Murfreesboro, Tenn., in the buildings of the Bradley Academy there, and had commenced its first session on Monday, May 2, 1841. The faculty included Joseph Haywood Eaton as professor of Latin, C. Smith as professor of Greek, and William Williams (possibly the same man who later became one of the first professors of the Southern Baptist Theological Seminary) as tutor. But Farnsworth had been too busy with other matters to raise any money, and those who tried to help him had also failed. It is therefore quite likely that his elaborate announcement meant very little, for at that time the major asset of the school was a charter, which had been secured in 1842.

On May 18, 1845, the society resolved to start over. Bradley Kimbrough was appointed agent. Under his leadership an endowment of $60,000 in cash, bonds, and pledges was raised, and in Jan., 1848, Union University was "organized, officered, and commenced its career as a chartered Institution." The president was Joseph Haywood Eaton. An 18-acre campus at Murfreesboro was secured, and a building begun. One hundred students were enrolled. The new college building was opened in the fall of 1850.

Under Eaton the college prospered. Enrolment reached 300. But the usual financial difficulties were present, and the death of the president on Jan. 12, 1859, left the school too weak to cope with the problems of war. Union's professor of theology, James Madison Pendleton (*q.v.*), an associate of James Robinson Graves (*q.v.*) in his promotion of Landmark theories, succeeded Eaton as acting president and served until the school closed before the threat of war in the fall of 1861. Efforts to revive the school after the war finally failed in 1873. JUDSON BOYCE ALLEN

UNITED BAPTISTS. A group first known in North Carolina in 1786, resulting from the union of Regular and Separate Baptists, with the first advances toward union made by Kehukee Association of Regulars and Sandy Creek Association of Separates in 1772. The union was evident in Virginia in 1787, and in Kentucky in 1801. In Virginia the movement was initiated by the General Committee of Separates and the Ketockton Association of Regulars, and in Kentucky by Elkhorn (Regular) and South Kentucky (Separate) associations. Regular and Separate Baptists in the three states had only minor differences, and upon the reconciliation of them, both former names were dropped and the name United Baptists adopted. Southern Baptists largely came from this union, dropping the word "united" in their name. However, a small group of United Baptists perpetuates the name.

Ben M. Bogard, beginning his ministry among United Baptists, had much to do with the organization of the American Baptist Association in 1924, an organization which provides Sunday school literature widely used by United Baptists. Mission activities are maintained almost entirely on the local church level, making total figures difficult to obtain. However, in 1954, 564 churches in 28 associations had a total membership of 60,525 and a Sunday school enrolment of 14,983. The churches maintain Eastern Baptist Institute in Somerset, Ky.

See also American Baptist Association.

I. K. CROSS

UNITED BAPTISTS, KENTUCKY. See Co-operation, Terms of General Union in Kentucky, 1801.

UNITED BAPTISTS OF TENNESSEE. A group which has existed in the state since about 1800. Stockton Valley, the oldest United Baptist association in the state, was organized in 1805 and was still in existence in 1957. Before 1846 at least 12 United Baptist associations had been organized in the state. A few others were organized later. Some probably dropped "United" and co-operated with the Tennessee Baptist Convention or one of its predecessors. Others disintegrated. A few remained; there were at least four as late as 1945: Hiwassee, New River, Stockton Valley, and West Union. The Stockton Valley and the West Union have co-operated partially with the Tennessee Baptist Convention. All these associations were in eastern Tennessee, for the most part in the general area south of Cumberland Falls in Kentucky. The minutes of some of these associations, and probably all, carried no reports on education, benevolence, and missions. Their activities were largely restricted to preaching the gospel in their own territory and to Sunday schools.

HOMER L. GRICE

UNITED FREE WILL BAPTISTS, THE. A body of Negro Baptists who trace their history back to the same original 18th-century sources from which came the white Free Will Baptists, though they formed their organization in 1870 and have been independent of the parent organization since 1901. Arminian in doctrine, they teach that Christ died for all men and that all can be saved. They practice foot washing and anoint the sick with oil. Even though these Baptists are in general agreement with the congregational polity of other Baptist bodies, their system of general conferences, which may even exclude members from fellowship, limits the autonomy of the local church. Members of this body are located largely in North Carolina, Florida, Georgia, Mississippi, Louisiana, and Texas. In 1952 they reported 836 churches with a total membership of 100,000, and 915 ordained ministers. The organization publishes a semi-monthly periodical, *The Free Will Baptist Advocate,* at Kinston, N. C., where it also operates an educational institution, Kinston College.

LYNN E. MAY, JR.

UNIVERSAL MILITARY TRAINING. In resolutions and reports from the Social Service Commission, the Southern Baptist Convention urges United States citizens to concern themselves with economic, social, political, and moral counter-measures against the threat of war rather than to concentrate on military measures to assure peace; to strive continually for the multilateral reduction and control of armaments through the United Nations; and to prevent policy-making power from passing predominantly into the hands of those who think primarily in military terms. The necessity of preparation for national defense is recognized, but any effort of the military to establish a continuing policy of universal requirement of military service is opposed, since Baptists believe that the fruits of universal military training would further weaken the principle of freedom and increase the danger of development into a military civilization.

ADIEL J. MONCRIEF, JR.

UNIVERSITY HIGH SCHOOL. An academy founded in 1883 at Macon, Ga., in connection with Mercer University. It existed until 1900.

ARTHUR JACKSON

UNIVERSITY OF CORPUS CHRISTI. Established Apr. 1, 1947, and formally opened Sept. 15, 1947, the university is located on a 233-acre campus at the southern tip of the city of Corpus Christi, Tex., overlooking Corpus Christi Bay. It was founded by the Executive Board of the Baptist General Convention of Texas, acting on the recommendation of a survey committee appointed at the urging of Aubria A. Sanders, then pastor of the First Baptist Church, Beeville, Tex. Originally located at Beeville and chartered as Arts and Technological College, the university moved to Corpus Christi before its first classes met, with its name changed to the University of Corpus Christi.

Permanent brick buildings on the campus include Gazzie Warren Hall for women and an administration building completed in Sept., 1956. Approximately 30 frame structures, remaining from a radar school formerly operated on the site by the United States Navy, are used by the university.

Enrolment since the first session of the university has increased from 233 to 525 in 1955–56. Founding of the school was the climax of efforts made since about 1900 to establish a Baptist educational institution in South Texas. The university has served a total of 5,442 students who have come from a 100,000-square-mile area covering Texas and northern Mexico. Enrolment in 1956 included students from seven countries, 11 states, the District of Columbia, and 78 Texas counties.

A senior, coeducational, liberal arts college, the University of Corpus Christi also offers work in the technological fields of agriculture and petroleum engineering. It is the only Texas Baptist college offering a degree in petroleum engineering. Other degrees offered include bachelor of arts, science, business administration, music education, and bachelor of science in chemistry.

Work done at the university is accredited by the Texas Association of Colleges and the Texas Association of Music Schools. The university holds full membership in both of these groups, is approved by the Veterans' Administration, and is recognized by the Texas Education Agency. Equipment of the university includes 32 major buildings, a campus of 233 acres, and an experimental farm of 100 acres. Total value of land and property in 1956 was listed at $1,-091,776, and endowment at $125,185.

A. R. HOWARD

UNIVERSITY OF ILLINOIS CHAIR OF BIBLE. A professorship attached to the University of Illinois and supported by Missouri Baptists through their Baptist Student Union organization. Continuously, and particularly in its beginning it has been linked with the Baptist Student Union work at the university. The Baptist Student Union was organized on Sept. 20, 1949, upon recommendation of the education committee of the Illinois Baptist State Association. The first office was in the living room of the director's apartment at 304 W. Clark St., Champaign, Ill. Daily campus prayer meetings were begun Dec. 19, 1949, in one of the university buildings. V. W. Entrekin was the first director and teacher, beginning his work in Sept., 1949. Fourteen students enrolled the first semester, and by 1955 enrolment had reached 102. Two credit courses in Bible were offered each semester. The University of Illinois accepted up to 10 semester hours credit for courses offered. In addition to Baptist Student Union and chair of Bible activities, the student union promoted a seminary extension program. The staff consisted of a director, office secretary, part-time Bible teacher, dormitory manager, and janitor. There was no endowment. Property had been purchased for a building site. The 1956 state mission offering was devoted to the erection of a building on this property. C. M. MARTIN

UNIVERSITY OF RICHMOND. Although as early as 1788 some Virginia Baptist leaders had championed better educational facilities, very little was done about the matter until 1830. On June 8 of that year, at five o'clock in the morning, the Virginia Baptist Education Society was organized by a group of Baptist leaders who were in Richmond for the meeting of the Baptist General Association of Virginia.

At least three factors contributed to the sense of urgency that prompted these Baptists to meet before sunrise to discuss the limited educational facilities available to their people and to decide what could be done to remedy the situation. First, Columbian College in Washington, D. C., was in financial difficulties. When this school was established by Luther Rice in 1819, many Virginia Baptists felt it would be better to support the Washington school than to start one of their own, but they had come to doubt the wisdom of continuing this policy. Further, the formation of the general association in 1823 brought Virginia Baptists closer together and served to consolidate their belief that better educational facilities were needed. Third, the *Religious Herald*, established in 1828, had taken a leading role in awakening the denomination to its educational needs.

The organization of the Virginia Baptist Education Society marked the dawn of a new era in education for Virginia Baptists, who agreed to take immediate steps to obtain funds. While the campaign was in progress, the society asked two of the state's better-educated ministers to take a few students into their homes for instruction. Elder Edward Baptist took nine young men at his plantation in Powhatan County and Elder Eli Ball took four in his home. The arrangement with Elder Baptist was continued for a second year, but in 1832 the education society decided to establish a seminary nearer Richmond. A tract of 220 acres north of Richmond was purchased, and the Virginia Baptist Seminary was opened July 1, 1832, with Robert Ryland of Lynchburg as president. The 14 students enrolled for the first year were required to work on the farm for three hours a day to pay for their board and lodging, but this manual labor experiment proved unsuccessful. Therefore, the education society disposed of the farm and in 1834 purchased a smaller tract of land, known as the Haxall estate, west of Richmond. There the institution remained until 1914, when it moved to the western outskirts of Richmond.

Although the seminary prospered in the new location, it became increasingly clear that the real need was for pre-theological education and for a chartered institution which could acquire and hold property and receive bequests. Since the Virginia general assembly would not charter a theological institution, the education society applied for a charter for a liberal arts school to be known as Richmond College. The charter was granted Mar. 4, 1840, and in Jan., 1843, seminary property was turned over to the trustees of Richmond College. For its first session the college had 68 students and three teachers; only two years of college work was offered. The junior year was added in 1845 and the senior year in 1848. The first degrees were conferred in 1849.

During the 12 years from 1849 to 1861, the enrolment reached a maximum of 161, and 68 degrees were conferred. At the outbreak of the Civil War in 1861 the college was closed. The endowment was invested in Confederate bonds, and the buildings were used first as a Confederate hospital and then as a barracks for Federal troops. In June, 1866, the Baptist general association agreed to reopen the college, and class work began on Oct. 1, 1866. The prospects were bleak. Buildings had deteriorated, books and equipment had been destroyed or carried away, faculty and students were scattered, the endowment was worthless. Tiberius Gracchus Jones was elected president, a faculty of four was appointed, and 90 students were enrolled. A campaign to raise $75,000 was partially successful, and in 1873 a campaign for $300,000 was launched in connection with the 50th anniversary celebration of the general association. In an impoverished South it was remarkable that a third of the amount was raised in cash and pledges. The panic of 1873 cut down payments on the pledges, but the college managed to survive and added to its physical plant during the following two decades.

After President Jones resigned in 1868, the trustees decided to adopt a system similar to that in use at the University of Virginia, with the institution being directed by a faculty chairman instead of a president. In 1870 a law school was established with Roger Gregory as the first professor. After a quarter of a century of administration of the college by a faculty chairman, the trustees decided, in Dec., 1894, to return to the earlier system of administration by a president. The trustees were not unanimous in their action, however. For president the trustees chose 26-year-old Frederic William Boatwright (*q.v.*), professor of modern languages and youngest member of the faculty. There was opposition from faculty, students, and alumni, both to the change in the system of administration and to the youth of the new president. Boatwright accepted the appointment in Jan., 1895, and in June began an administration of 51 years.

In the first session of Boatwright's administration there was a faculty of nine with 183 students, less than $500,000 in endowment, and a total income of less than $30,000. When he resigned as president in 1946, there was a faculty of 112, a student body of 2,174, an endowment of almost $3,000,000, and an income of $648,729. This growth and development was largely due to the energy, ability, and complete dedication of the president, who organized and conducted campaigns to raise money for buildings and endowment. He and the school's treasurer, Charles H. Ryland (*q.v.*), finally succeeded in collecting $25,000 from the Federal Government for the damage done to the college by Union troops in 1865.

In June, 1898, the trustees agreed to admit women students under certain restrictions, requiring that they reside with parents or relatives or in a home approved by the president, since the college had no dormitory facilities for women. Although the number of women attending Richmond College showed a consistent and steady increase from the four who entered in the session of 1898–99, Virginia Baptists grew in their conviction that they should have a collegiate institution for women with "scholastic standards in keeping with the best colleges in the land." The general association at its meeting in 1903 urged its Education Commission to submit plans for such an institution. There were many difficulties, chiefly financial problems, and an appeal was made to the general education board. In the meantime the need for a more spacious campus for Richmond College became more definite. When representatives of the Education Commission and the college met with the president of the general education board, the board expressed interest in helping them only if they would unify their efforts. The two groups agreed in 1906 to unite their efforts, and a campaign was started to raise $500,000 to build and equip a woman's college.

The decision to move Richmond College to a location west of the city was made in Feb., 1910. Through gifts and purchase, a site of 293 acres was acquired at a total cost of $17,500. In recent years additional purchases have enlarged the holdings to 350 acres. Construction was begun on the new site at Westhampton, and the college moved in Sept., 1914. The new buildings included a co-ordinate college for women named Westhampton College. In July, 1914, the Woman's College of Richmond transferred its property and franchise to Richmond College and, after being operated for two years under the direction of the trustees of Richmond College, was merged with Westhampton. Because of World War I, it was impossible to dispose of the property in the city of Richmond, and some financial stringency resulted until the close of the war. During the session of 1918–19, the property at Westhampton was turned over to the United States Army as an evacuation hospital, and the colleges moved back to the old campus. Richmond and Westhampton colleges returned to the Westhampton site in Sept., 1919, but the law school remained at the old Columbia building until 1954.

The existence of three "colleges" under a charter granted to Richmond College posed some difficulties of nomenclature and led the trustees to change the corporate name to University of Richmond in 1920. The university includes: Richmond College (1840), T. C. Williams School of Law (1870), Westhampton College (1914), the Summer School (1920), the Graduate School (1921), and the School of Business (evening division, 1924; morning division, 1949). In addition, the university's School of Christian Education conducts off-campus classes in several areas. During World War II the university operated a Navy V-12 unit, training approximately 1,000 college men in preparation for commissions as naval officers, and conducted classes for air cadets and for the Engineering, Science, and Management War Training Program.

Upon the resignation of Boatwright as president in 1946, the trustees elected him chancellor of the university and selected as president George M. Modlin, who for eight years had been professor of economics and dean of the Evening School of Business Administration. During his administration the university has made notable advances. Physical facilities include the completion of a new dormitory and dining hall for Westhampton College; a social center building for Richmond College made possible by alumni gifts; the Boatwright Memorial Library, a gift of the Baptists of Virginia through a campaign launched in 1944; the law school building; and Wood Memorial Hall, a dormitory for men, a substantial portion of the cost of which came from the Endowment Fund of the First Baptist Church of Richmond. Notable additions to the financial resources of the university have been the A. D. Williams bequest of trust funds in the amount of $2,700,000 and the Ford Foundation grant of approximately $450,000. The university endowment is $3,564,967, with a current budget of $1,621,780. Denominational contributions during the year ending Apr. 30, 1956, were $142,754 for current purposes and $75,000 for capital improvements, both amounts coming from the Cooperative Program of Virginia Baptists. Total assets, including physical property, endowment, reserves, trust funds, etc., are $12,107,678.

The total enrolment in all branches of the university reached a peak of 4,794 in 1948–49 because of returning veterans. For the session of 1955–56 enrolment was 4,160. Through the session 1954–55 there have been 8,582 graduates from the various schools of the university. The university is fully accredited and holds membership in the Southern Association of Colleges and Secondary Schools, the Southern University Conference, the Association of American Colleges, the Association of American Universities, and the American Council on Education. The law school is a member of the Association of American Law Schools and is on the approved list of the American Bar Association. The university (then Richmond College) was the first Baptist school to meet the membership requirements of the Southern Association of Colleges and Secondary Schools, which it joined in 1910. In 1955 it was reported that the university had the highest percentage, 52.6, of faculty members holding earned doctor's degrees in the Southern Baptist senior colleges. RALPH MCDANEL

UPWARD. See SUNDAY SCHOOL BOARD.

URUGUAY, MISSION IN. Organized Feb. 19, 1954. From 1911, when James C. Quarles (*q.v.*) and Helen Taylor Quarles moved from Argentina to Montevideo, until 1954, Uruguayan Baptist work was part of the Argentine Mission. An Argentine minister, Antonio Gonzalez, Quarles, his brother Lemuel Cleveland Quarles, and wife Jennie (Saunders) Quarles went to Uruguay in 1912 and manned three centers. The first church was organized Aug. 13, 1911, in Montevideo, with six members.

The Quarles families returned to Argentina, J. C. in 1918 and L. C. in 1929, leaving Bailis William and Vera (Humphries) Orrick, who arrived in 1921, the only Southern Baptist missionaries in Uruguay. Sydney Langston and Frances (McCaw) Goldfinch joined them in 1939 and opened work that led to organization of a church in Salto before their transfer to Paraguay in 1945. Robert Lee Carlisle, Jr., and Ruth (Newport) Carlisle reached Uruguay in 1940 and helped to organize the Paso Molino Church. He became director of the Bible institute opened in 1956 in Montevideo.

Jesse Daniel and Mary Jo (Henry) McMurray went to Uruguay in 1946 and worked in Paysandú. Ray Ellis and Mary (McKee) Shelton, arriving in 1950, opened work in San Carlos and Pan de Azucar. In 1954 James Willard, Jr., and Peggy Jean (Place) Bartley, and Matthew Anderson and Dora Jean (McDonald) Sanderford increased the mission staff to 12.

M. A. SANDERFORD

URUGUAY BAPTIST CONVENTION. Organized June 16, 1948, in a meeting called for that purpose in the First Baptist Church of Montevideo. Fifty-seven delegates from 11 churches were present. Two of the four officers elected were nationals, R. Alvarez Blanco, president, and Enrique Francia, secretary; two were missionaries, Bailis William Orrick, vice-president, and Robert Lee Carlisle, Jr., treasurer. Boards of directors, evangelization, and Christian education were established.

Seven churches have been admitted into the convention since its organization, making a total of 18 with 867 members. These churches maintain 16 mission points, 23 Sunday schools, and 10 young people's unions.

The convention publishes a monthly paper called *El Fanal* and also pamphlets and booklets for distribution. It conducts encampments, missionary enterprises, simultaneous revivals, and has voted the establishment of an old-age pension plan.

Women of the convention are organized in a federation composed of 16 societies and 16 auxiliary groups. The federation publishes a monthly bulletin called *Nuestra Siembra,* engages in regular missionary activities within the country, and sponsors annual camps for the Girl's Auxiliary and Royal Ambassadors.

MRS. MARY JO MCMURRAY

UTICA FEMALE INSTITUTE. A school in Utica, Miss., which began operation in 1848, with William H. Taylor president. It was strongly recommended by Central Baptist Association in 1851, but is now extinct. J. L. BOYD

V

VACATION BIBLE SCHOOL. As presently promoted among Southern Baptists, a school conducted under church auspices during the vacation period for two weeks for ages 3 to 16. The program includes Bible and practical instruction, worship, recreation, handwork and crafts, and often refreshments. Mrs. Walker Aylett Hawes, of the Epiphany Baptist Church in New York City, a native of Charlottesville, Va., conducted a school in July, 1898, from which the movement developed. She called it an Everyday Bible School. It was an effort to care for the spiritual needs of neglected immigrant children who played in the streets of the city's East Side. The school was so successful that another was planned in 1899 and a third in 1900. In 1901, Robert G. Boville, the newly elected secretary of the New York City Baptist Mission Society, promoted five vacation schools in the society's mission churches on the East Side. He was no doubt inspired by the success of Mrs. Hawes. His own schools were so successful that 10 were held the next year, 17 in 1903, and 16 in 1904. College and seminary students were employed to conduct these schools. The program sought to use "idle students" and "idle churches" to teach "idle children" the Word of God.

In 1916, when the movement had spread into Canada, Boville organized the International Association of Daily Vacation Bible Schools. In 1922 he organized the World Association of Vacation Bible Schools through which he promoted the schools in many foreign lands and on mission fields. The Presbyterian Church in the U.S.A. was the first denomination to utilize Vacation Bible schools as a part of its denominational mission program. In 1910 it assigned the promotion of the schools to the Department of City and Immigrant Work of the Board of Home Missions. The Northern Baptist Convention was the second denomination to promote Vacation Bible schools. Under the guidance of Charles H. Sears, the promotion of the schools became the responsibility of the American Baptist Publication Society. Many other denominations quickly followed the Presbyterians and Northern (American) Baptists in becoming vitally interested in Vacation Bible schools and in promoting them among their churches.

Southern Baptists have also done a major work in the area of the Vacation Bible school. Active promotion of this work began Sept. 1, 1924, when Homer Lamar Grice was elected by the Sunday School Board as secretary of its new Daily Vacation Bible School Department. He faced the responsibility for developing a course of study, establishing the plan of operation, formulating methods of procedure, prescribing principles of administration, devising means for training a church and denominational leadership, and developing a program of promotion. With vision, insight, and zeal, he directed the board's program of field promotion and prepared the materials for study and training. The outstanding record of progress in Vacation Bible school work among Southern Baptists was a testimony to Grice's leadership.

For the first 10 years growth was slow. The number of schools grew from 300 in 1925 to 1,044 in 1935. In 1934 the word "Daily" was dropped from the title, and the Vacation Bible School Department was made a section of the Sunday School Department for promotional purposes. In 1936 the board made the district association the unit through which Vacation Bible schools in the churches was to be promoted. That year there were 1,810 vacation schools. The first series of textbooks began in 1925 and was completed in 1928—for the Beginner, Primary, Junior, and Intermediate departments. The second series of textbooks was produced 1938–41, except the fourth Intermediate book, which was published in 1945. A book for three-year-olds was added to the course in 1952.

In 1938 Sibley Curtis Burnett was elected as associate in the Vacation Bible school section to aid in promotion of schools and in the training of workers over the Convention. From 1940 through 1955, Southern Baptist Vacation Bible schools grew in number from 5,756 to 25,458, or an average increase of 1,231 schools each year. By 1945 there were over 10,000 schools, and in 1946 the enrolment exceeded 1,000,000 pupils and workers for the first time. The second million in enrolment was reached by 1952, when there were more than 21,000 schools. By 1955, with 75.4 per cent of Southern Baptist churches having a school, the enrolment reached 2,652,788. Almost 48,000 professions of faith were reported, and over $400,000 given in the mission offering, of which $285,000 was given through the Cooperative Program to all causes supported by the denomination.

In 1952 Charles Franklin Treadway became an associate in the Vacation Bible school section of the Sunday School Department. On Jan. 1, 1953, he succeeded Grice as editor of Vacation Bible school materials, and Burnett became the secretary of Vacation Bible school promotion. Plans were begun for a new series of textbooks, providing for a standard school of two weeks, with 10 three-hour daily programs. The first of these materials was scheduled for use in the schools of 1957.

The program and curriculum of Southern Baptist Vacation Bible schools include various elements. Bible material is presented through stories for the younger age groups and through directed study for older pupils. Memorization of Bible passages is encouraged. Stories based on present-day situations apply the truths of the Bible material. Workbooks for pupils facilitate learning and allow for creative expression. Recreation and refreshments serve to increase interest on the part of pupils and to provide wholesome experiences in social relations. Handwork and crafts activities encourage attendance and cultivate valuable skills. An opening worship service—which includes such elements as marching to music, singing, pledges to flags, group recitations and responses, guided by a carefully planned procedure—cultivates reverence and good order in the church sanctuary and enriches the spiritual experience of those in attendance.

CHARLES F. TREADWAY

VALLEY BAPTIST HOSPITAL (HARLINGEN). Owned by the Baptist General Convention of Texas, established in Jan., 1925, by groups of Christians, primarily Baptists. Owned and operated by the Lower Rio Grande Baptist Association until 1945, it was then accepted by the Baptist General Convention of Texas, meeting at Fort Worth.

Plagued by problems, chiefly financial, the hospital struggled in its growth from a 35- to a 65-bed capacity, and by 1943 to 135 beds and 20 bassinets. In June, 1950, the hospital opened a polio center for the Lower Rio Grande Valley and South Texas.

Serving all races, including many charity patients, the hospital has three main objectives: rendering the best possible hospital care, assisting and educating the medically indigent, and providing an effective spiritual ministry for its patients.

The school of nursing, established in 1947, was abandoned in Sept., 1950, due to financial limitations. The hospital, a fully accredited institution, is not approved for internship. With two buildings in 1954, the value of land, buildings, equipment, and other assets was $356,987.62, with an indebtedness of $158,963.07. The annual income in 1954 from patients was $728,433.59, from the Cooperative Program, $40,000, and designated gifts, $16,063.44. Charity service in 1954 amounted to $48,263.28.

An intensive building campaign culminated in the occupancy June 10, 1956, of the new $2,225,000 Valley Baptist Hospital and Sams Memorial Children's Center. Of this amount, approximately $500,000 was provided by the Sams Foundation as a memorial to Earl Corder Sams (1884–1950, chairman of the board, J. C. Penney Co.). The new plant, consisting of three buildings with 153-bed capacity, had upon occupancy an indebtedness of $720,833.35.

T. H. MORRISON, JR.

VAN HOOSE, AZOR WARNER (b. Griffin, Ga., Oct. 31, 1860; d. Rome, Ga., Dec. 11, 1921). Educator. Son of Azor Warner and Missouri (Daniels) Van Hoose, he was educated in the public schools of Georgia and Tennessee; received the A.B. degree as first honor graduate from the University of Georgia in 1882; and was awarded the LL.D. degree from Mercer University in 1911. He married Lucy Rucker on Aug. 1, 1887. He taught at the following colleges: South Georgia Agricultural College, Thomasville; University of Georgia, Athens; and Howard College, Marion, Ala. From 1887 to 1909, he was president of Brenau College, Gainsville, Ga.; and from 1910 to 1921, he was president of Shorter College, Rome, Ga. He completely revitalized the latter institution, enlarging the campus, erecting modern buildings, increasing the assets by more than $600,000, and laying the foundation for membership in the Southern Association of Colleges and Secondary Schools and other accrediting agencies. Through his influence Shorter College reached a place of distinction among colleges for women in the South and in the nation.

PAUL M. COUSINS

VAN NESS, ISAAC JACOBUS (b. East Orange, N. J., July 15, 1860; d. Nashville, Tenn., Feb. 13, 1947). Baptist minister, editor, executive. He was baptized at age 17 by Edward Judson. He was graduated from the Southern Baptist Theological Seminary in 1890. Mercer University conferred the D.D. degree upon him in 1897 and Baylor University the LL.D. degree in 1920. He married Frances V. Tabb, June 24, 1891. Their five children were: Stephen Austin, Allan Edward, Noble, Lucy Tabb (Hagan), and Edwin Bell.

He was ordained in 1890 by the First Baptist Church, Nashville, Tenn., and served as pastor of the Immanuel Baptist Church, Nashville, 1890–96. While pastor in Nashville, he was a member of the Sunday School Board, 1893–95; also, he edited the *Young People's Leader,* the first publication of the board for the B.Y.P.U. He resigned his pastorate in 1896 to become joint editor of *The Christian Index* with Theodore Percy Bell (*q.v.*), who had just purchased the paper and who had been corresponding secretary of the Sunday School Board. Van Ness's ability as an editor, together with his former acquaintance, led to his election as general editor of the board following the death of Samuel Boykin (*q.v.*). He served the board as editorial secretary, 1900–17. After James Marion Frost (*q.v.*) died, Van Ness was elected corresponding secretary, which position he filled until his retirement, June 6, 1935. In both of these positions he led the board in significant achievements. He kept the literature related in a vital way to the needs and mission of the churches. He possessed a sense of balance as to doctrine and methodology. His pastoral, editorial, and denominational experience gave him a comprehensive view of the board's mission, related to both the publication of literature and the development of a field program. Under his leadership the board created many new departments and entered new areas of work. Van Ness was successful in enlisting strongly qualified persons to direct new phases of work, and he gave them much freedom in developing the work committed to them. During his administration the board expanded its plant by erecting two commodious buildings, one for warehouse and shipping purposes and one for lease to the firm having the printing contract.

Van Ness was a member of, and held office in, the International Lesson Committee (Improved Uniform Series), the Sunday School Editorial Association of the United States and Canada, the Sunday School Council of Evangelical Denominations, the Editors Section of the International Council of Religious Education, and the Executive Committee of the World Sunday School Association. He served as trustee of the Southern Baptist Theological Seminary and of Baptist Bible Institute, New Orleans, La. In addition to a great amount of writing for the periodicals of the board and for other religious journals, he was author of *Training in Church Membership* and *Training in the Baptist Spirit.*

J. M. CROWE

VANN, RICHARD TILMAN (b. Hertford County, N. C., Nov. 24, 1851; d. Raleigh, N. C., July 25, 1941). Denominational leader. Vann was the son of Albert and Harriet (Gatling) Vann. In spite of a severe physical handicap, the loss of both arms when he was 12 years old, he was graduated from Wake Forest College in 1873 at the head of his class. After studying for two years at the Southern Baptist Theological Seminary, he served as pastor in Murfreesboro, in Wake Forest, in Edenton, and at two different times in Scotland Neck, N. C. In 1900 Vann was elected president of the Baptist Female University, now Meredith College, where he served until 1915. Later he served as executive secretary of the education board of the North Carolina Baptist State Convention (1915–26) and as secretary of benevolence (1926–45). He was for many years a trustee of Wake Forest College and of the Southern Baptist Theological Seminary. A volume of his sermons, *The Things Unseen,* was published in 1931.

BIBLIOGRAPHY: Meredith College, *Catalogue* (1900–15). R. T. Vann, *The Things Unseen* (1931). W. H. Vann, "Richard Tilman Vann," *News and Observer* (Sept. 7, 1941). MARY LYNCH JOHNSON

VARDEMAN, JEREMIAH (b. Wythe County, Va., July 8, 1775; d. Elk Lick Springs, Mo., May 28, 1842). Clergyman. Even as a child, Vardeman was aware of much conflict between the white man and Indians in Kentucky, and he and his brothers at times were actually engaged in conflict with Indians. As a result of these experiences he became a great outdoorsman. Although he made a profession of faith at the age of 17, for several years he was inactive in Christian work. After an experience of rededication, as a result of the ministry of a blind, uneducated preacher, Thomas Hansford, Vardeman shortly thereafter became a preacher whose evangelistic fervor was greatly rewarded; his total ministry, though characterized by humility, is said to have resulted in 8,000 conversions. His preaching has been compared with that of Jonathan Edwards: as he would ask those of the congregation who were not Christians, "How can ye dwell in devouring flames?" many would "cry out in agony of soul and rush forward begging the preacher to plead for them at the throne of grace." He has been compared with Whitefield in his emotions and power of eliciting sympathy. Some believe that he was the originator of the invitation to penitents to come forward for prayer and inquiry.

A great opponent of Campbellism in Kentucky, Vardeman preached at Lexington, Louisville, and Bardstown, Ky., and at Nashville, Tenn. In each of these places Baptist churches were established, and 400 people were converted as a result of his preaching. In 1830 he and his family moved to Ralls County, Mo. He became the first moderator of the Central Society, now the Missouri Baptist General Association, in the year it was organized (1834). W. C. LINK, JR.

VAUGHN, ASHLEY (b. 1808?; d. Natchez, Miss., Mar. 29, 1839). Pastor, Mississippi Baptist leader. Because of ill health Vaughn moved in 1833 to the Natchez country, where he served as a home missionary of the American Baptist Home Mission Society. On Dec. 12, 1835, he became pastor of the Clear Creek Baptist Church of Washington. In Sept., 1836, he began publishing the first Baptist paper of the state, *The South-Western Religious Luminary,* for the purpose of crystallizing sentiment among Baptists of the state for a convention. On Dec. 24, 1836, a group met in the Clear Creek Church for the purpose of reorganizing the Mississippi Baptist Convention, with Vaughn offering the resolution to organize. He was elected president, made chairman of the committee to draft the constitution, and named chairman of the committee to prepare "an address for ministers and members of churches to commend the new convention to them." Called the "father of the Mississippi Baptist Convention," he served as president of the convention and board of directors, and a member of the board of directors of Judson Institute until his death. He died at the age of 31, after serving among Mississippi Baptists fewer than five years.

BIBLIOGRAPHY: J. L. Boyd, *A Popular History of the Baptists in Mississippi* (1930). L. S. Foster, *Mississippi Baptist Preachers* (1895). Mississippi Baptist Historical Collection, "Reverend Ashley Vaughn."

C. B. HAMLET III

VAUGHN, WILLIAM (b. Westmoreland County, Pa., Feb. 22, 1785; d. 1877). Pioneer preacher. Vaughn immigrated with his family to Scott County, Ky., in 1788. When 18 years old, he married Lydia Wing Allen and soon afterward became a tailor in Winchester. He was greatly influenced by current rationalism and joined an infidels' club. In 1810, though an avowed deist, he was turned by the death of a friend to the Bible and a personal faith in Christ. He "related his experience" to Friendship Church and was baptized in Oct., 1810.

In 1811 Vaughn was licensed to preach and began a thorough study to educate himself. The following year he was ordained at Lulbegrud Church, Montgomery County, by Jeremiah Vardeman (*q.v.*) and David Chenault. Vaughn served as pastor of churches at Sycamore, Lees Creek, Augusta, Falmouth, Carlisle, Bethel, Bloomfield, and Lawrenceburg, Ky. In 1845 he was called to the Little Union Church, Spencer County, and until retirement divided his duties between Little Union and Bloomfield. His activities included moderator of Bracken Association, Kentucky agent of the American and Foreign Bible Society, and North Kentucky agent for American Sunday School Union.

BIBLIOGRAPHY: J. H. Spencer, *A History of Kentucky Baptists* (1886). W. THOMAS LANE

VELARDE DAY SCHOOL. Established by New Mexico Baptists at Rinconada, N. Mex., in Dec., 1894. The school enlisted 167 Spanish students, ranging in age from five to 28. A Spanish Baptist church was organized at Velarde to which the school was moved in 1896. Teaching continued until the dissolution of the Northern Baptist Convention in the state in 1912. HERBERT E. BERGSTROM

VENABLE, ROBERT ABRAM (b. Madison County, Ga., Sept. 2, 1849; d. Meridian, Miss., July 27, 1933). Pastor, college professor and president, author. Although reared a Methodist, Venable became a Baptist while in his teens. Eager to secure a college education, he, having only 75 cents, rode muleback from Camden, Ark., to Clinton, Miss., to enter Mississippi College, from which he was graduated with highest honors in 1876. Sept. 19, 1877, he married Fannie Webb, daughter of W. S. Webb, president of Mississippi College. As pastor of the First Baptist Church, Memphis, Tenn. (1879–91), Venable helped to vitalize that church after the yellow fever epidemic of 1878–79. During his pastorate the membership of the church greatly increased, the building was remodeled, and an educational building was added. He served as president of Mississippi College and also as instructor from 1891 to 1894. From 1894 to 1907, he was pastor of the First Baptist Church of Meridian. Later he served as president of Clarke Memorial College, also teaching Greek and theology. A denominational leader, Venable in 1897 preached the annual sermon before the Southern Baptist Convention. He was active in the organization of the first B.Y.P.U. in Lauderdale County at Poplar Springs in 1906. He was a teaching preacher and a careful expositor. In his last years he served as pastor of rural churches in Mississippi and did mission work among the Negroes. He was author of *The Origin of Sprinkling for Baptism* (1882) and *The Baptist Layman's Hand-Book* (1894).

BIBLIOGRAPHY: L. S. Foster, *Mississippi Baptist Preachers* (1895). C. B. HAMLET III

VENEZUELA, MISSION IN. Organized Nov. 29, 1953, in Maracaibo. Before that time the missionaries belonged to the Colombian Mission, which initiated Baptist work in Venezuela Oct. 14, 1945, through Julio Moros, a pastor in Caracas. Thomas Lawton and Carolyn (Switzer) Neely transferred from Colombia to Caracas Apr. 16, 1949, and James Ulman and Ruth (Jordan) Moss transferred to Barquisimeto in Apr., 1950. Charles Barton and Shirley (Risk) Clark went to Maracaibo Nov. 21, 1952; Clyde Eugene and Betty Lou (Young) Clark went to Barquisimeto in Oct., 1953. In Feb., 1953, the Neelys left the field and did not return.

The mission aids six of the 11 Venezuelan Baptist churches, two outstations, a primary school, and the convention paper, and operates the Baptist book store in Barquisimeto. Missionaries serve as fieldworkers, helping in evangelistic efforts, study courses, new centers, and general co-ordination of Baptist work.

CHARLES B. CLARK

VENEZUELAN BAPTIST CONVENTION. Organized in Acarigua Aug. 8, 1951, with six churches. The Colombian mission initiated Baptist work in Venezuela in 1945. The Central Baptist Church of Caracas, organized May 2, 1946, and four other Venezuelan churches affiliated with the Colombian-Venezuelan Baptist Convention between Feb., 1949, and Jan., 1951. Member churches besides Central Baptist were located in Acarigua, Guanare, San Nicolás, and Barquisimeto, the latter formerly connected with the Association of Baptist Churches for World Evangelism from which it withdrew because of financial difficulties. The First Baptist Church of Maracaibo was organized July 23, 1950, and the *Luminar Bautista,* monthly publication of the convention, began in Oct., 1951. Two independent churches, Valle de la Pascua and La Mensura, were received into the convention in Aug., 1952, and a national Woman's Missionary Union and Young People's Union were founded. The First Baptist Church of Valencia, organized Apr. 18, 1953, was admitted into the convention in Aug., 1953, along with the Mene Grade Baptist Church, an independent church which had declared itself Baptist. The Pueblo Nuevo Baptist Church, organized Apr. 17, 1954, became a member of the convention in Aug., 1954. There are now 11 churches, 12 pastors, and 484 members. The churches, three of which are self-supporting, give 10 per cent of their income to the convention, which distributes its funds among boards for evangelism, education, benevolence, finance, judicial service, publications, and home missions. The convention aids one church in supporting a full-time pastor. CHARLES B. CLARK

VIRGIN BIRTH. This phrase refers to the scriptural teaching that Christ was "conceived of the Holy Spirit, born of the Virgin Mary." According to the New Testament, Mary was a *virgo intacta* at the time of Christ's birth. Recent discussion has centered around three areas of investigation.

Biblical criticism has disclosed certain critical problems concerning the belief. Secure on the basis of sound biblical criticism, the teaching appropriately maintains its place in the New Testament. The problems which are present are not, in themselves, determinative. Objection to the teaching on the basis of biblical criticism alone is unwarranted. In the nature of the case the evidence is as abundant as one might rightly expect it to be.

A second inquiry seeks to determine the probable origin of belief in the virgin birth. Matthew's and Luke's gospels evidence that they accepted the historical accuracy of the nativity narratives. But the question remains as to whether the narratives were originally founded upon historical fact or myth. The origin of belief in the virgin birth is best accounted for on the basis of the actuality of the event. Although history does not offer absolute proof for this basis, the assumption that the belief is based upon error rather than upon historical fact raises more problems than it solves.

The crucial issue concerning the doctrine lies in the field of Christian theology. The idea of virgin birth possesses significance and plausibility only because of the person of Christ. The supreme miracle of Christianity is the incarnation of God in Christ. Being God-man, Christ is true God and true man. He came into history from outside the historical process and therefore constituted a new force in history. His very coming was miraculous. Logically, therefore, the miracle of the incarnation postulates a miracle in the birth of Christ unless a form of adoptionism is accepted. Virgin birth cannot be predicated as the one indispensable mode of the incarnation. God alone determines the way in which his wonders are accomplished. With belief in a true incarnation, it is difficult to comprehend that any particular mode of birth should be considered incongruous. Unless there is adequate scriptural and theological justification for rejecting virgin birth, the reasonable course is to accept it.

Theologically, virgin birth is significant and appropriate. It is a positive witness to the unity of deity and humanity in the person of the one man, Christ. The doctrine of virgin birth teaches without compromise that Christ is by nature God; it asserts the presence of Emmanuel, God with us. The miracle of Christmas points to the mystery of incarnation. Virgin birth is, therefore, a steadfast repudiation of all toned-down Christologies, and the individual who professes belief in it commits himself to far more. He aligns himself wholly with the supernaturalistic view of Christ.

See also MIRACULOUS CONCEPTION.

BIBLIOGRAPHY: J. G. Machen, *The Virgin Birth of Christ* (1932). CHARLES R. TUCKER

VIRGINIA, BAPTIST GENERAL ASSOCIATION OF.

I. Baptist Beginnings. Although it lacks supporting evidence, the first record of Baptists in Virginia is found in the journal of Thomas Storey, a Quaker, who refers to a meeting in York County in Jan., 1699, in the "house of one Thomas Bonger, a Preacher among the General Baptists." As far as the historical record is concerned, the Baptists of Virginia have their origin in three separate groups: (1) General Baptists, emigrants from England who arrived about 1714; (2) a group generally known as the Regular Baptists, who arrived from Maryland in 1743; (3) the strongest and most important group, the Separate Baptists, who, coming originally from New England, first settled in North Carolina and spread from there into Virginia.

The General Baptists.—In 1714 the General Assembly of the General Baptists of England appointed Robert Norden and Thomas White to "go to Virginia to propagate the Gospel of truth." White died en route, but on June 14, 1715, Norden appeared in the court of King George County to take the oaths and subscribe to the declarations prescribed by the Toleration Act of 1689. He was thereupon licensed to preach. On the same date the house of Matthew Marks was licensed as a public meeting house "for those persons called Anabaptists." Norden was pastor of the church thus established until his death in 1725. It is possible that he organized a church in Surrey County and another in Isle of Wight from which families migrated to tidewater North Carolina and established churches. These churches were Arminian in theology. They grew weak and possibly disappeared sometime after 1756, when several members of the Isle of Wight Church addressed a letter to the Philadelphia Association asking for aid in their confusion over theological questions.

Regular Baptists.—The first of these churches in Virginia was organized in 1743 at Mill Creek, a tributary of the Opequon River, in Frederick County (now Berkeley County, W. Va.) by a group of General Baptists from Maryland. Their minister having proved unworthy of his office and having been excluded from the church, the group applied to the Philadelphia Association for advice. The association sent certain members to examine the situation at Mill Creek (frequently referred to as Opekon) and also at Ketocton in Loudon County, which had been established in 1751 by John Thomas. The Philadelphia delegation, finding Mill Creek not "regular," reorganized the church according to the principles of the Philadelphia Association. Samuel Heaton became the first pastor of the reconstituted church and was succeeded in 1754 by John Garrard, who remained pastor until his death in 1787. In Oct., 1754, the Philadelphia Association "concluded to receive the church of Ketocton, and the church of Opekon, in Virginia, into fellowship." As a result of dangers from Indians after Braddock's defeat in 1755, the Mill Creek congregation was forced to retreat to the eastern side of the Blue Ridge Mountains, where they remained for two years, returning to Mill Creek in 1757. During this period Mill Creek and Ketocton joined forces with Garrard as pastor. John Marks, a Pennsylvanian, served Ketocton from 1757 until his death in 1788.

Another group in Virginia to be admitted to the Philadelphia Association was Smith's Creek in what is now Shenandoah County. Organized in 1756 by 11 Pennsylvanians who had settled in that region, the church immediately faced difficulty similar to that suffered by Mill Creek as a result of Braddock's defeat. John Alderson, pastor from its organization until 1777, was sent to Philadelphia in 1762 and gained admission for the church to the Philadelphia Association.

As a result of the enthusiasm of Peter Cornwall, whose "manner of life procured to him the name Saint Peter," Broad Run Church in Fauquier County was constituted in 1762 with the assistance of John Marks and David Thomas (*q.v.*), who was visiting from Pennsylvania. Thomas became pastor of the congregation and soon gained recognition throughout northern Virginia as a preacher of great power and ability. Together with Garrard, he made numerous preaching tours which resulted in many conversions and in the establishment of several new churches.

Beginning in 1756, Mill Creek, Ketocton, and Smith's Creek held annual meetings for communion and fellowship. On Aug. 19, 1766, delegates from the three churches met at Ketocton meetinghouse with delegates from Broad Run and organized the Ketocton Association. The total membership of the four churches was 142. The association held two meetings each year—one in June, which was devoted to preaching, and one in August, when church letters and correspondence with other groups were read and matters of doctrine and discipline were discussed. By 1772, the date of the oldest known minutes, the association had grown to 13 churches with a membership of 1,121. Only one church was without an ordained pastor.

Baptist churches of that day devoted much time to discipline and frequently suspended or excluded members who were guilty of excessive drinking, brawling, gambling, or other immorality. Generally, individuals thus excluded were restored on evidence of sincere repentance. In addition to deacons, the churches for a short while selected ruling elders, but the office soon disappeared. They also practiced the laying on of hands after baptism, and most of them engaged in "devoting children," which was satirically referred to by some as "dry christening." The churches generally accepted the theology of the London Confession of 1689 as adopted with revisions by the Philadelphia Association in 1742.

Immediately after expansion began, it met with opposition of all sorts. The Established Church was strong in colonial Virginia, and the royal governors, almost without exception, held to an exceedingly narrow interpretation of the Act of Toleration. Thus, even the Baptist ministers who were willing to apply for licenses to preach found it difficult to obtain them, and congregations found it equally difficult to acquire licenses for meetinghouses. In addition to the legal barriers put in their way by the governors and the general court, Baptists were subjected to harassment in the form of mob violence. David Thomas was frequently prevented by mobs from preaching. Often meetings ended in general fights as the rougher element of a community attempted to break up a service, and the congregation responded by ejecting the ruffians. Many of the higher social classes showed less violent opposition by refusing to let their wives and children hear the Baptist preachers. The clergy of the Established Church attacked Baptists from the pulpit and attributed to them a great variety of heresies and strange practices. It appears, however, that the Regular Baptists suffered less from persecution than other Baptist groups because they complied with the law in applying for licenses. Also, "the Regulars were not thought so enthusiastic as the Separates; and having Mr. Thomas, a learned man, in their society, they appeared much more respectable in the eyes of the enemies of truth."

Separate Baptists.—Separate Baptists in Virginia had their beginnings in Sandy Creek Church established in Randolph County, N. C., in 1755 by Shubal Stearns (*q.v.*). Stearns was among those who had "separated" from the Established Church in New England and later became a Baptist. Members of the group were called "Separate Baptists." Stearns's work in North Carolina prospered so that by 1758 several congregations had organized into the Sandy Creek Association. Among them was Abbott's Creek, of which Daniel Marshall (*q.v.*) was pastor. These North Carolina congregations soon spread their efforts into adjacent regions of Virginia. In Aug., 1760, Marshall and Phillip Mulkey established Dan River Church in Halifax (now Pittsylvania) County. This was the first Separate Baptist church in Virginia and consisted originally of 63 white and 11 Negro members. Among them was Samuel Harris (*q.v.*), a leading citizen of the community who had been burgess of the county, sheriff, justice of the county court, and colonel of militia. Harris was baptized by Marshall in 1758 and immediately relinquished public office to become a leader in the establishment of Baptist churches in Virginia, confining his labors first to Halifax and adjacent counties.

In Jan., 1765, Allen Wyley, who had been baptized by David Thomas, traveled to Halifax and persuaded Harris to return with him to

Culpeper, where local opposition had previously prevented Thomas from preaching. Harris, also meeting with opposition, soon went into Orange County to continue his labors. The Separate and Regular Baptists first met in Culpeper. After Harris' departure the people of the town requested Thomas to return. A well-educated man, he expressed disapproval of the preaching of some of the Separates who were poorly educated and untrained. Resenting this, Elijah Craig (*q.v.*), a leader of the Culpeper group, and two others returned to Halifax to procure the services of Harris again. Harris had not been ordained, but he persuaded James Read to accompany him, and the two returned to Culpeper, where Read preached to a large crowd gathered at the home of Craig. Thomas and John Garrard, both Regular Baptist ministers, were present at the meeting. Although the leaders of both groups appeared desirous of combining their efforts, the people were not so inclined, the majority, apparently, favoring the Separates. On the following day both groups held meetings and administered baptism. These activities widened the breach between the two groups.

Harris and Read continued to preach, going through parts of Caroline, Hanover, Goochland, and Spotsylvania counties. On Nov. 20, 1767, with the assistance from Dutton Lane, they constituted the first Separate Baptist church north of the James River. This was called Upper Spotsylvania and consisted of 25 members representing all the Separate Baptists north of the James River. It became the mother of many churches in that section. Read and Harris continued their work for three more years, resulting in the organization of Lower Spotsylvania Church on Dec. 2, 1769, with 154 members, and Blue Run Church two days later. In the following year three men, Lewis and Elijah Craig and John Waller (*q.v.*), who had been preaching with zeal for several years, received ordination and took over the pastorates of Upper Spotsylvania, Blue Run, and Lower Spotsylvania, respectively.

During this time several efforts were made by leaders to effect a union of the Separate and Regular Baptists. The Regulars seemed to favor union, provided the Separates would accept the Philadelphia Confession. The Separates were afraid of being too much bound by a confession, and they believed that the Regulars were not sufficiently particular in certain matters, such as dress. In 1769 Ketocton Association sent a delegation to Sandy Creek Association with a letter proposing union. After lengthy debate the proposal was rejected by a small majority.

The year 1769 marked the beginning of a rapid spread of the Separate Baptists in Virginia. Jeremiah Walker and Harris established Amelia Church that year. Harris was ordained by Sandy Creek Association in 1769. James Ireland (*q.v.*) attended the meeting and returned home with Harris. Later, Ireland accepted baptism and received credentials as an itinerant preacher. In Nov., 1769, Ireland and Harris established Carter's Run in Fauquier County, the first Separate church in northern Virginia. Other churches were organized in rapid succession so that by May, 1771, there were 16 Separate Baptist churches in Virginia, with total membership in excess of 1,400.

In 1770 the Sandy Creek Association agreed to split into three groups. All except two of the churches in Virginia thus became constituting members of the "General Association of the Separate Baptists in Virginia" when it was organized in Orange in May, 1771. The establishment of the association was followed by still more rapid growth, which in turn evoked rising opposition by the authorities. Mob violence of various sorts took place even before legal persecution began. Harris, Walker, and others were frequently the victims of fightings, beatings, and whippings, often instigated by the clergy of the Established Church. Frequently, there were general fights between supporters and hecklers of Baptist preachers.

Legal persecution.—These acts of violence soon gave place to "legal persecution." It "seems by no means certain that any law in force in Virginia authorized the imprisonment of any person for preaching"; however, those in authority made use of the laws for what they termed preservation of the peace. It was on such a peace warrant that they first seized and imprisoned preachers in Virginia. On June 4, 1768, in Spotsylvania County, Waller, Lewis Craig, James Childs, and others were carried before three magistrates, who bound them over to appear in court two days later on a charge of disturbing the peace. After hearing their defense, the court offered to release them on the promise that they would preach no more in the county for a year and a day. Refusing to make this promise, they were jailed. A month later, the court allowed Craig and Waller to go to Williamsburg to plead their case before John Blair, the acting governor. A letter from Blair, in which he urged moderation in dealing with the Baptists, effectively silenced the local attorney but gave no relief to the imprisoned preachers. After remaining in jail for 43 days, the prisoners received unconditional release. Persecution spread to other counties. In Dec., 1770, two young ministers were jailed in Chesterfield County. In this case, as in many others, the prisoners continued preaching from the jail.

> Many people attended their ministry. . . . This was the beginning of God's work in the county of Chesterfield; no county ever extended its opposition and persecution to the Baptists, farther than this; and yet, in few counties, have Baptist principles prevailed more extensively, than in Chesterfield.

Baptist preachers were imprisoned in other counties of Virginia. Sometimes they gained freedom after short terms, upon giving bond to keep the peace. Others stayed in jail for long periods before they had opportunity to give bond not to preach. Then they uniformly refused to accept freedom on these terms.

Baptists continued to plead that their imprisonment was illegal, on the ground that they were entitled to the same privileges enjoyed by dissenters in England. In the spirit of the Act of Toleration, some Baptists sought licenses to preach and to gather in meetinghouses. However, these were more difficult to obtain, since the power to grant licenses, which had originally resided in the county courts, was now reserved to the general court, consisting of the governor and his council, which met in Williamsburg only twice a year. Members of the council, selected mainly from the aristocracy of the colony, were more narrow in their views than either the governor or the local courts. At the time of the Revolution, it had become difficult indeed to obtain licenses. Faced with greater oppression, Baptists found a champion in Patrick Henry, who continually supported them in their attempts to obtain freedom to preach.

In spite of the persecution, Baptist churches continued to flourish in the colony. At its organization, the Separate General Association enrolled delegates from 12 churches with 1,335 members. In 1773 the association divided into two districts, one north and one south of the James River. In May, 1774, the northern district had 24 churches with 1,921 members, while the southern district had 27 churches with 2,033 members. Ketocton Association of Regular Baptists also continued to grow, so that in 1775 the association reported 23 churches with 1,349 members.

The Kehukee Association was formed in 1769 in eastern North Carolina. The churches of this association were originally organized by the General Baptists and reorganized as Regular in 1755 by representatives from Philadelphia. Representatives of Kehukee attended the Virginia General Association in 1772 to discuss union of the two groups. The principal reason for failure lay in the fact that Kehukee churches had members who had been baptized by the General Baptists before they had been converted. The Kehukee Association continued to expand and in the next two years founded several churches in Virginia, some of which soon withdrew over the same issue of baptism and joined the Separates.

Religious liberty gained.—In 1770 Baptists sent a petition to the House of Burgesses seeking relief from various religious disabilities to which they were subjected. Having obtained no relief, they repeated their petition in 1772 and in 1774. In 1775 they joined in a petition from "Baptists and other Protestant dissenters." This petition had support from the Hanover Presbytery. However, revolution was in the air, and Baptists with their allies soon began to press for freedom rather than for toleration.

In Aug., 1775, at a joint meeting of the northern and southern district associations, Baptists took the first organized action in Virginia for religious freedom by addressing a petition to the Virginia convention (called by the House of Burgesses to replace the Colonial government) for the abolition of the Established Church. Baptists continued to gather and present petitions to the General Assembly (which replaced the House of Burgesses as the governing body in Virginia). In 1776 an act established freedom of religious opinion and worship, suspended payments to the clergy of the Church of England, and relieved dissenters from contributing to the support of the Established Church.

For years a plan to legalize a form of an established church continued to receive support by Methodists and German Lutherans as well as Episcopalians. Even the successful conclusion of the Revolution did not solve the problem. A bill which would have compelled every person to contribute for the support of some form of religious teaching passed the House of Delegates in 1784, but the assembly postponed final action by a narrow vote on the third reading. This delay gave opponents an opportunity to make effective protests which included memorials from various religious societies and the historic "Memorial and Remonstrance" by James Madison. An act for "Incorporating the Protestant Episcopal Church" was passed in 1784 but was repealed two years later. In 1786 the assembly enacted laws to secure properties to various religious bodies; to authorize appointment of trustees for holding the properties; and to repeal legislation which prevented religious bodies from regulating their own discipline.

The Established Church, however, continued to find support among many leaders in the General Assembly. In 1788 a law gave to the trustees of the Episcopal Church power to act as successors to the vestries in administering the glebes, the houses and lands which the Established Church acquired with tax funds which the colony authorized for the support of ministers of the Church of England. Baptists sent memorials to the General Assembly protesting the action. Finally, in 1794 the General Assembly repealed every prior act which had to do with religion except the Act for Religious Freedom. Thus the ownership of the glebes reverted to the commonwealth.

Growth and consolidation.—During the Revolution Baptists faced difficult times both because of external turmoil and because of internal dissension. Nevertheless, they continued to expand by establishing churches throughout eastern Virginia, including the Eastern Shore. In the west and northwest both Regular and Separate ministers crossed the mountains and organized churches in Kentucky, Pennsylvania, and what is now West Virginia.

As the number of Separate churches increased, they faced the problem of gathering from greater distances for regular meetings. After attempting numerous subdivisions, the association decided in 1783 to divide into four districts which were designated as upper and lower on each side of the James River. To take the place of the general association, a general committee was constituted to meet annually and to consist of not more than four delegates from each district association. It was thought that such a group could meet promptly and, with few local matters to consider, could devote attention to questions of general concern.

The general committee.—The general committee met first on Oct. 9, 1784. The first business was the preparation of a memorial to the general assembly concerning the incorporation of the Episcopal Church. Year after year, the general committee continued the fight for religious liberty and separation of church and state. Due to the efforts by the committee, the final act of 1794 was passed.

Delegates of the Ketocton Association of Regular Baptists attended the meeting of the general committee on Aug. 5, 1786. At that session the committee adopted the following recommendation: "It is recommended to the different associations to appoint delegates to attend the next General Committee for the purpose of forming an union with the Regular Baptists." Accordingly, on Aug. 10, 1787, the representatives of the district associations, then six in number, met in Goochland County. After considerable discussion in which the main issue seemed to be an objection that "the Separates were not sufficiently explicit in their principles, having never published or sanctioned any confession of faith," the two groups agreed upon union on the basis of the Philadelphia Confession, which the general association had adopted upon its dissolution in 1783. In order to avoid future misunderstandings concerning the status of the confession, the representatives adopted the following statement:

> To prevent the confession from usurping a tyrannical power over the conscience of any, we do not mean, that every person is bound to the strict observance of every thing therein contained; yet that it holds forth the essential truth of the Gospel, and that the doctrine of salvation by Christ and free unmerited grace alone, ought to be believed by every Christian, and maintained by every minister of the Gospel. Upon these terms we are united and desire hereafter that the names Regular and Separate, be buried in oblivion; and that, from henceforth, we shall be known by the name of the *United Baptist Churches of Christ, in Virginia.*

The years of the Revolution had been a period of difficulty for the Baptists in Virginia; yet they continued to expand both in number and in area. In 1785 a great revival of spiritual awakening spread throughout the commonwealth. Thousands were converted and baptized. Though other denominations received blessings from the revival, Baptists were its chief promoters and beneficiaries. As a result of this awakening, which lasted for about six years, the membership of the Baptist churches changed until it represented more nearly a cross-section of the community population. Baptist churches became larger than those of other denominations, and Baptists began to have greater influence in the state, particularly east of the Blue Ridge Mountains.

Apart from its interest in legislation to guarantee religious liberty and the complete separation of church and state, the general committee engaged in various other endeavors. It entered into correspondence with other Baptist groups in the United States and sent copies of its minutes and those of the district associations to Rippon's *Baptist Annual Register* in London. As early as 1787, the committee considered writing a history of Virginia Baptists and in 1788 appointed a committee to gather materials for the preparation of such a history. Many changes in the committee by death or removal to other parts of the country slowed the progress of this work, but collection of material continued.

In 1788 the general committee received a communication from James Manning, president of Providence College in Rhode Island, "recommending and encouraging the Baptists of Virginia to erect a seminary of learning." The committee discussed the matter and appointed a committee to "forward the business respecting a seminary of learning." This appears to be the first recorded action of a Virginia Baptist body with regard to support for higher education. The committee continued from year to year until 1793, when John Williams and Thomas Read proposed that the general committee appoint 14 Baptists as trustees, that they in turn select 7 additional members of other denominations, and that these 21 members undertake the organization of a seminary. The plan got as far as the selection of trustees. After a few meetings lack of funds and other discouragements led to abandonment of the project.

At its meeting in 1789, the general committee adopted a resolution introduced by John Leland (*q.v.*) with regard to slavery. It said, in part, that "slavery is a violent deprivation of the rights of nature, and inconsistent with a republican government, and therefore recommend it to our brethren, to make use of every legal measure to extirpate this horrid evil from the land." In the years that followed, some district associations considered the matter with various results. Frequently, actions were in response to queries submitted by member churches. While some associations adopted strong antislavery statements, others refused to consider the matter. For example, Ketocton, in 1796, considered it "an improper subject of investigation in a Baptist Association, whose only business is to give advice to the churches respecting religious matters; and considering the subject . . . to be the business of government and a proper subject of legislation." In its next session, however, the same body stated that hereditary slavery was "a transgression of the Divine Law." Many individuals, clergy and laymen, spoke out strongly against the institution of slavery, and several either freed their slaves outright or provided in their wills for their gradual emancipation.

It was the custom in Baptist churches, from their beginning in Virginia, to admit Negroes to membership and to allow them to "exercise their gifts" as preachers. On occasion a church would send a Negro as one of its representatives to an association meeting. The Portsmouth Association, upon being queried, replied that there was nothing to prevent a church from sending any male member it chose. As might be expected, many churches in Virginia had more Negro than white members, and some congregations were preached to more or less regularly by Negroes.

The meeting of the general committee in Goochland County in May, 1791, had significant consequences. The original constitution had provided that the committee should "consider all the political grievances of the whole Baptist society in Virginia, and all references from the district associations, respecting matters which concern the Baptist society at large." However, the meeting of 1791, after long debate, decided that its original purpose had been to consider only political matters. It voted, therefore, to strike out the phrase "and all references from the district associations, respecting matters which concern the Baptist society at large." At the next meeting in 1792, the general committee essentially reversed its action, and this reversal raised the question whether the constitution of the general committee could properly be altered by other than the member associations. This uncertainty was followed by expressions of concern by individuals and associations that the general committee might exercise too much power. "This, added to some other causes, produced a gradual declension in the attendance of members as well as nerveless languor [*sic*], in the transaction of business. The remonstrances respecting glebes, etc., was the only business which excited no jealousies and that was the only matter which was ever completed after the year 1792." In 1799 the general committee met at Waller's meetinghouse in Spotsylvania County and agreed to dissolve. Its final action was to recommend to the associations the setting up of some form of regular meetings "to promote and preserve union and harmony among the churches."

General meeting of correspondence.—In May, 1800, delegates from several of the Baptist associations in Virginia gathered at Lyle's meetinghouse to form a convention and to revise the Philadelphia Confession of Faith, which had been adopted with certain qualifying conditions by the general association in 1783 and by the general committee in 1787. After several years' work a revision was prepared, but only four of the Virginia associations adopted it. Ketocton and Culpeper associations jointly published the revised confession in 1806. This was the last attempt toward the adoption of a confession of faith by Virginia Baptists.

The same convention undertook to draw up a constitution for an association or general meeting which would serve as the general committee had done in promoting fellowship and co-operation among the various district associations. However, in an effort to avoid the difficulties which had caused the dissolution of the general committee, the convention gave the new body virtually nothing to do. For this reason the general meeting of correspondence was poorly attended, and only three of the associations adopted the constitution. Finally, in 1807 delegates from Dover, Goshen, Albemarle, and Appomattox associations, along with a messenger from the Roanoke who had come as an observer, drew up a new constitution "such as they in their judgements, believed to be for the good of the cause, and not merely with a view to adapting it to the suspicious minds of a few leading characters, who were perhaps actuated from upright, though mistaken motives." The constitution provided for the consideration of any matter previously decided upon by any district association.

During the following 18 months, six associations adopted the new constitution, namely, Dover, Goshen, Albemarle, Appomattox, Roanoke, and Meherrin. In Oct., 1808, these sent delegates to Bethel meetinghouse in Chesterfield County, where Robert B. Semple (*q.v.*) was chosen moderator and Reuben Ford, clerk. The body unanimously decided to send an "address" to Thomas Jefferson, who was completing his second term as President of the United States. The meeting resolved to publish a circular letter to rebut the statements in various publications to the effect that Baptists held that "human learning is of no use."

The year 1810 marked the publication of Semple's *History of the Rise and Progress of the Baptists in Virginia.* In addition to histories of the Regular, General, and Separate Baptists, the volume includes accounts of 19 of the 20 district associations which existed in 1810, histories of 287 churches, and biographies of 22 distinguished Baptist preachers. This work is the most important source of information about Baptists in Virginia prior to 1800. At the time the history was published, there were 31,052 Baptists in Virginia.

Baptists multiplied rapidly in Virginia during the first two decades of the 19th century. Five new associations were constituted between 1800 and 1810. Three additional associations were organized by 1820.

Missions.—Although the district associations engaged in little co-operative activity during the first two decades of the 19th century, the Baptists of Virginia were stirred by a widespread interest in missions. Portsmouth was the first district association to undertake organized mission work by sharing in the formation of the Baptist Philanthropic Missionary Society for work among the Creek Indians.

American Baptists had a remarkable introduction to foreign missions through the unusual experiences of Ann and Adoniram Judson and Luther Rice, who found themselves in India as Baptist missionaries without denominational support. Rice returned to the United States to enlist support for a Baptist mission in India and Burma. Even before Rice's arrival Massachusetts Baptists organized the Boston Baptist Foreign Missionary Society to support the Judsons. Rice traveled extensively along the eastern seaboard organizing local mission societies and encouraging them to form state groups which, in turn, would send delegates to a national society. On Oct. 28, 1813, under the direction of Rice, the Richmond Mission Society, the first in Virginia, was organized. Baptists in other communities soon followed the example, and the women in particular organized societies for foreign missions.

In 1814 R. B. Semple and Jacob Grigg represented the Richmond Mission Society at the formation, in Philadelphia, of a body which came to be known as the Triennial Convention. Several of the Virginia societies sent representatives to the first triennial meeting in 1817. All the women's societies were represented by men. To the meeting in 1820, Virginia sent more representatives than any other state. That session elected Semple president, an office which he held for four terms. REUBEN E. ALLEY, JR.

II. History of the General Association. *Organization and early years.*—Under the revised constitution few matters of importance engaged the attention of the general meeting of correspondence. Although it continued to meet annually, both interest and attendance constantly diminished until 1821, when only three delegates and no officers attended the meeting. Two of these delegates, Edward Baptist (*q.v.*) and James Fife, consulted about conditions and agreed upon the need for a "new organization for the definite purpose of inquiring into the spiritual destitution in Virginia and devising means of relieving it." In June, 1822, only five associations were represented at the final session of the general meeting of correspondence. The only business transacted was the approval of a constitution for a new organization which it recommended to the district associations, in the following words:

> Whereas the General Meeting of Correspondence for Virginia, having in our opinion failed to produce the enlarged benefits hoped for by its friends, we, the members of the meeting, desirous of uniting the efforts of all the Baptists in Virginia for the spread of the Gospel, and for the advancement of vital piety throughout the state . . . do adopt and recommend to the several Associations for their approbation the following Constitution.

Article I of the constitution stated the name selected for the new group: "This meeting shall be called the General Association of Baptists of Virginia."

Minutes of the meeting and the constitution were sent to the association, with a circular letter appealing for their support of the next meeting, to be held in Richmond on the first Saturday in June of the following year. On June 7, 1823, the first meeting of the general association was held at the Second Baptist Church of Richmond with representatives of seven district associations present. Robert Baylor Semple, Baptist historian and scholar, was elected moderator, and under his able leadership the meeting was continued. A board of managers consisting of 21 members was set up to execute the objectives of the new organization and to have full authority during the period between sessions.

The object of the general association, as stated in Article II of the constitution, was "to propagate the Gospel and advance the Redeemer's Kingdom throughout the State, by supplying vacant churches with the preached word, and by sending preachers into destitute regions within the limits of the State." This brief, seven-article constitution, drafted by Edward Baptist, was careful to assure the Baptists of Virginia that "their representatives, when convened, shall in no case interfere with the internal regulations of the churches or Associations, nor shall they pursue any other object than that specified in the second article."

In order to survey religious conditions in the "destitute regions" of the state, the board of managers selected Jeremiah Bell Jeter (*q.v.*) and Daniel Witt, two young Bedford County preachers, to make a two-month tour of churches and areas not affiliated with the general association. They were cordially received and were asked to establish churches, or mission stations, in many areas. This apparent interest did not extend to the meetings of the general association; attendance declined until it was obvious that something should be done. Hoping to broaden interest and increase financial support, members of the group revised the constitution in 1829 to eliminate membership by associations and to provide that "any person contributing ten dollars annually to the funds of this Association shall be a member and shall have the privilege of appointing a representative to the body." Persons contributing $30 or more would become life members, and every "Association, Church or Missionary Society" contributing $10 was entitled to one representative. At the next meeting in Richmond, "the number in attendance not only increased but all who came were interested, for it was the money they and their churches had contributed which they were required to distribute."

The 1829 changes in the constitution also specified that no person should be entitled to a seat in the general association who was not a Baptist in good standing. This was necessitated by internal dissensions stirred up by the Campbellite movement, which was having disturbing success in Virginia at that time. Some of the constituent associations and churches within them were split over the issues raised by Alexander Campbell, and some withdrew their allegiance from the Baptist cause altogether. There was much confusion, and the conflict retarded the progress of the Baptist program in the state as well as that of the new general association.

In spite of controversies and the loss of several churches to the Campbellite movement and to antimissionary associations, the number of district associations and churches within the associations increased. During the 1830's there was increasing interest in the general association and in the possibilities of better co-operation. At the meeting in 1831, 52 delegates were present, representing "five district associations, twelve churches, twenty-two missionary societies, four life members, four individuals and one group." Minutes of the meeting listed the names and addresses of 200 ordained ministers and 17 licentiates living in Virginia. The following 10 district associations were represented by delegates: Albemarle, Appomattox, Columbia, Dover, Goshen, Greenbrier, Ketocton, Middle District, Portsmouth, and Strawberry. A summary of the "state of religion" in these associations closed with the statement: "Where religious papers have been read, and where prayer meetings have been kept up, there has the church increased, there have sinners been converted. Ministers, who promoted among their people the great plans of Christian benevolence, increase their usefulness in the ministry."

Missions.—In 1835 the Baptist Union of England sent two fraternal representatives to the Baptists in the United States and Canada, and they attended the sessions of the general association in Richmond. They summarized their impressions as follows:

The churches of Virginia are numerous, opulent and prosperous. . . . It is to be regretted that the proportion of ministers to churches is small. Some have to officiate in two, three, and sometimes four places; but they are aware of the evil and will gradually remedy it. The ministry as a whole is deficient in education . . , and the advocates of education and of missions are multiplying every day, while their opponents, with their pseudo-Calvinism, are rapidly diminishing. Some of the churches have been affected with an anti-effort spirit, and with the anti-missionary and anti-union views of the Campbellite Baptists, but the denomination is advancing in intelligence and exertion. . . . The operations of the General Association are extensive, and the aid afforded to home and itinerant efforts is cordial and generous.

Missionary interest noted by the English brethren was present from the beginning and so stated in the constitution. (It must be clearly understood, however, that the general association, at its inception, was concerned primarily with what is termed today "home missions." Foreign missions was a responsibility of numerous missionary societies formed earlier for that explicit purpose. In the 10th chapter of his book, *The Baptists of Virginia,* Ryland tells the story of these societies. Not until 1855 did the general association itself begin to assume direct responsibility for foreign missions.) Jeter's and Witt's exploratory tours had emphasized the need for state missions, and they and other young ministers were engaged for four-month periods to extend the ministry of the association, at a salary of $25 per month. Four years later, the board of managers confessed that their missionaries had not been successful and "attributed the lack of the success expected from the work of its missionaries to the distances from their homes to their fields and to the facts that the territory assigned them was so extensive and their stay in any locality was so short that few deep impressions could be made and that the period of months or weeks of their employment was too brief." The board recommended that the missionaries live on their fields of labor, and that their employment be on a yearly basis.

By 1831 there appeared increasing interest in missions within the state. A full-time "general agent" was appointed, at an annual salary of $500, to carry out the plans for evangelizing the state. Ten years later, the board had in its employ 12 missionaries east of the Blue Ridge, two in the Valley, and 10 in western Virginia. In his report Eli Ball, who had succeeded the first general agent, Valentine Mason, told of 500 Baptist churches with 60,000 members in 30 associations. Nineteen of these associations, with 390 churches and 53,850 members, were favorable toward the general association. "The remainder, either from the want of light or from some other cause, do not cooperate with us in our plans of benevolences."

Reports in subsequent years continued to show an interest in missionary activities within the state and therefore an increase in the number of churches and adherents to the Baptist faith. By 1857 the number of Missionary Baptists in Virginia had increased to more than 100,000 with over 600 churches and 300 ordained ministers. Additions by baptism, that year alone, were almost 7,000.

This work of evangelizing the "destitute areas" was given form and systematized by the organization of the State Mission Board in 1855. Help was received from the Home Mission Board of the Southern Baptist Convention in the early stages, but later the state assumed full responsibility. Since 1921 the work of state missions has been under the supervision of the Virginia Baptist Board of Missions and Education. This ministry reached every area of the state under the State Mission Board and continues to do so under the Board of Missions and Education. In order to extend and stimulate this important work, the Department of Enlistment and Evangelism was organized in 1944.

City mission work was begun in Richmond as early as 1880. A Baptist missionary society was formed by laymen who paid monthly dues into the organization for the dissemination of the gospel throughout the city. Later, similar programs were set up in Norfolk, Petersburg, Roanoke, Newport News, Lynchburg, Danville, Arlington, and Alexandria. Full-time city missionaries are employed at the present time in Richmond and Norfolk.

Virginia Baptists, interested in missionary activities early in their history, formed "societies" to spread the gospel, even to foreign lands. One of these was the Richmond Baptist Mission Society for propagating the Gospel in India and other Heathen Countries. The name was changed in 1826 to the Baptist Mission Society in Virginia.

Luther Rice was a frequent visitor to the state, and considerable money was raised by his efforts. By 1835 Virginia was sending her young men and women, as well as money, to serve on foreign fields. In that year three young couples, including John Lewis Shuck (*q.v.*) and his wife Henrietta Hall Shuck (*q.v.*), the first woman missionary to China, were sent out under the auspices of the Triennial Convention. This body, however, was soon torn by controversy over slavery. Abolitionists agitated the subject with such determination that an impasse was reached at the triennial meeting in Apr., 1844, at Philadelphia. The delegates to this meeting had declared neutrality, but individual members of the board indicated they would not vote to appoint a slaveholder as a missionary. This led the Alabama convention, in Nov., 1844, to ask the acting board of the convention whether a slaveholder would be appointed. The answer was no. Following this action the Virginia Baptist Foreign Missionary Society took the lead and issued a call for a convention to decide on the best means to promote the work of missions.

Thirty-one delegates from Virginia met at Augusta, Ga., on May 8, 1845, with delegates from seven other states, and organized the Southern Baptist Convention. Instead of the usual societies for missions, a system of boards was inaugurated through which the new Convention would carry on its activities. This meant that both domestic and foreign missions would be the concern of the same general body. Later, other activities of the denomination would come under its supervision. The Foreign Mission Board was set up at Richmond with Jeremiah Bell Jeter as president and James Barnett Taylor (*q.v.*) as corresponding secretary. From this time forward, Virginia served the rest of the world through the South.

At the Charlottesville meeting of the general association in 1855, a significant change was inaugurated. Work of the denomination had been carried on through organizations allied with the association and meeting at the same time and place. They held their sessions in succession in what were called the June meetings. These various societies, the Virginia Baptist Foreign Mission Board, the Education Board, the Sunday School and Publication Board, the Bible Board, and the Domestic Mission Board, were consolidated with the association. Their work was henceforth carried on through boards appointed by the general association. The treasurer of the association received all the funds and distributed them to the treasurers of the several boards according to the designations of the donors. After the action of 1855, both home and foreign missions were the concern of the general association.

In 1857 the association authorized the Sunday School and Publication Board to employ a general superintendent of colportage and Sunday schools at an annual salary of $1,000. The number of colporteurs increased, and, the year before hostilities between the North and South broke out, gifts to the Sunday School and Publication Board were nearly $11,000. When the Civil War began in 1861, the missions boards and the educations boards were unable to carry on their work, but the colportage work continued, confining its activities to serving the men in the Confederate Army. The cause was well supported; in 1863 collections for the work amounted to about $60,000, which was used to finance 80 colporteurs and evangelists and to publish tracts and distribute the Scriptures. There resulted a notable revival in the Army of Northern Virginia in 1863–64. It was reported that not less than 15,000 soldiers were baptized.

Activity immediately after the Civil War.—At the 1865 meeting of the general association, Virginia Baptists realistically approached the work of religious reconstruction. The assembled delegates adopted a resolution stating:

> That whatsoever may be our past views, aims or efforts regarding the issues which have divided the Northern and Southern States, we deem it our duty as patriots and Christians to accept the order of Providence, yield unreserved and faithful obedience to the "powers that be" and to cultivate such a spirit and to preserve such a course of conduct as shall best promote the peace and prosperity of the country; and we earnestly recommend to our brethren throughout the State to prove themselves to be loyal citizens of the United States; and enter with zeal and activity upon the discharge of the responsibilities devolved on them by their new social and civic relations.
>
> That recent events have neither destroyed nor diminished our obligation as Christians to prosecute the work of instructing and evangelizing the colored people among us, in which we have been for so many years and with such gratifying success engaged.

In the past, Baptist church membership had been extended to slaves, who, like their masters, were baptized on personal confession of faith, were gathered around the table of the Lord, and were looked after by the pastor. Their religious training was somewhat haphazard because of legal restrictions; nevertheless, there were sporadic efforts to systematize religious instruction for slaves on a planned basis.

The few African churches which had been organized prior to 1865 were received into the fellowship of the general association through district associations. In 1868 several Negro churches organized themselves into the Virginia Baptist State Convention and withdrew from the general association. Some attempts were made from time to time to secure co-operation between the two organizations, but the extent of this co-operation involved no more than friendly regard, sympathy in the work, and a willingness to co-operate as far as circumstances would permit. In recent years the general association has conducted studies on interracial relations and, further, has helped in a financial way to support a Negro orphanage near Petersburg, Va.

In 1868 district associations within the state of West Virginia left the general association of Virginia and united to form the West Virginia General Association, taking with them 249 churches with nearly 15,000 members. There remained with the general association 19 district associations, 545 churches, 361 ordained ministers, nearly 66,000 white members, and 10,000 colored members.

Again in 1868 the general association adopted a plan for recommending that contributions be made to missionary purposes at least once a month and, when practical, on the first day of every week instead of just once a year, as had been customary. Also, a resolution was enacted authorizing the appointment of a "Corresponding Secretary of the General Association to whom should be committed all the interests of the General Association." He was not to collect money but to arrange plans to help each church to make regular contributions to each board designated.

State missions received a renewed impetus in the early 1870's. The matter of evangelizing the state took on new interest, and as a result contributions for that purpose were increased. There was likewise an effort made to help the aged and destitute ministers and their widows and orphans by incorporating the Baptist Ministers' Relief Fund of Virginia, which had been chartered in 1866. This organization was largely absorbed by a statewide board at a later time, and today only a small fund remains, which is used for emergencies and exceptional cases.

Education.—The Semicentennial of the general association was celebrated in Richmond in 1873 with exercises centering largely around Richmond College, which was in need of revamping. A stimulating address was made by Jabez Lamar Monroe Curry (*q.v.*). The funds contributed to the endowment of the college as an outcome of this celebration amounted to $150,000. This sum of money put the institution on a sound footing for advancement.

The first record of any interest in education by Virginia Baptists was in 1788 at a gathering of the general committee at DuPuy's Meeting House in Powhatan County. At this session a letter was read from the president of what was later Brown University, the country's oldest Baptist college, in which he encouraged Virginia Baptists to erect a seminary of learning. As a result, a committee of 10 persons, 5 from the north side of the James River and 5 from the south side, was appointed "to consider and forward the matter of a college." Apparently, this committee did not make its report until five years later, in 1793, at a meeting held at Muddy Creek Church in Powhatan County. At that time a board of 21 trustees was appointed to plan a college and arrange for its establishment. It is interesting to note that one third of these trustees were non-Baptists, an indication that from the beginning Virginia Baptists have recognized the wider Christian service of their institutions. Unfortunately, this early plan failed to materialize, probably because of lack of revenues, the unsettled conditions of the times, and the continued migration of persons, including some of the trustees, to the developing West.

As the years passed, however, the growing need for an institution of learning became more and more evident. At a meeting of the general committee of correspondence held at Bethel Church in Chesterfield County in 1808, Elder John Kerr, pastor of the First Baptist Church of Richmond, was authorized to write a circular letter in defense of education. The letter declares, among other things, that "learning is held in high estimation" among Baptists, that many of them "are willing to educate their children," that Baptists in England and America have accomplished much in the field of higher education, and that fully nine tenths of Virginia Baptists "value human learning as among the most precious of mere earthly things."

Finally, in June, 1830, seven years after the founding of the Virginia Baptist General Association, there was organized at the Second Baptist Church in Richmond an education society for the improvement of the ministry. The moving spirits in this undertaking were Kerr, Jeremiah Bell Jeter, William F. Broaddus (*q.v.*), James Barnett Taylor, and Edward Baptist.

Baptist was elected first vice-president of the newly established society and accepted for instruction a dozen or more ministerial students on his farm at Dunlora, an estate of 900 acres five or six miles northwest of Powhatan Courthouse.

Baptist conducted Dunlora Academy for the sessions of 1830–31 and 1831–32, when because of failing health he retired and shortly thereafter moved to Alabama. Robert Ryland (*q.v.*) was elected president, and the school, renamed the Virginia Baptist Seminary, was removed to Spring Farm in Henrico County near Richmond. The seminary remained there until 1835, then moved to a new site in Richmond, where in Mar., 1840, it was chartered as Richmond College. In 1914 the college was moved to its present campus and in 1920 was chartered as the University of Richmond.

Within a few years after the establishment of this institution for men, Virginia Baptists began to look toward the education of their young women. In June, 1838, there was held in Richmond a meeting of a group of Baptists who appointed a committee to consider the feasibility of organizing a female seminary in Fredericksburg. Although the committee reported that the founding of such an institution was expedient, and a leading Baptist elder was appointed to organize it, the school was not established.

In 1845 the Virginia Baptist Education Society looked with approval upon the purchase by a group of men, mostly Baptists, of the Botetourt Springs to be converted into a school. It was named Valley Union Seminary, and Charles L. Cocke, a former member of the faculty of the Virginia Baptist Seminary in Richmond, was elected president in 1846. When it received a gift of $5,000 from John and Ann Hollins, of Lynchburg, the school was chartered as Hollins Institute in 1855, later becoming Hollins College. Although most of its students have been Baptists, it has never been owned by the denomination.

In 1853 the Richmond Female Institute was chartered and opened by Basil Manly, Jr. (*q.v.*), who was its first president until 1859. Later, in 1894 its name was changed to the Woman's College of Richmond, and in 1916 it was absorbed into Westhampton College of the University of Richmond.

The Chesapeake Female College was organized in Hampton in 1854 by Martin Foley. It continued in operation until the Civil War, when its property was sold and later made into a soldiers' home.

The Albemarle Female Institute was organized in Charlottesville in 1856 and was incorporated in 1857 with John Hart as president. It survived the Civil War and was operated until the first decade of the 20th century, when the school was closed and the property sold to the Episcopal Church for a girls' school.

In 1859 the Union Female College of Danville was founded, and a few years later the name was changed to the Roanoke Female College. It later was known as the Roanoke College for Women and then as Roanoke Institute. In 1917 the name became Averett College in honor of S. W. and J. T. Averett, who rendered outstanding services to the college during the years 1872–92. The first president was W. H. Tyree.

Since the Civil War a number of colleges, academies, and mission schools have been organized in Virginia under Baptist auspices. In 1884 the Southwest Virginia Institute for young women was established in Glade Spring. In 1891 the school was moved to Bristol, and soon thereafter its name was changed to Virginia Institute. Again, in 1912 the name was changed to Virginia Intermont College, which it has since remained.

Among the academies that have been organized by Baptists are the Richmond Academy for Boys, which was operated in close co-operation with Richmond College from 1901 until it was closed in 1916; Glade Spring Academy for Boys, which existed from about 1887 to 1894; Jeter Female Institute in Bedford, which operated during the 1890's; Southside Virginia Institute for girls and the Southside Academy for boys, both in Chase City; and Allegheny Institute for boys in Roanoke. In a number of instances, these academies were sponsored by Baptist district associations.

In 1898 William Eldridge Hatcher (*q.v.*) established an academy for boys at Fork Union. Chatham Training School for boys was organized in 1909, and later, because of the benefactions of J. Hunt Hargrave, the name was changed to Hargrave Academy. Bluefield College, the youngest junior college, was established in 1922 under the leadership of President R. A. Lansdell. It is today an important part of the Baptist system of schools in Virginia.

Several mission schools have been established through the years, usually by district associations. Among these are Buchanan School, which was begun in 1911 and discontinued in 1932; Blue Ridge School, which operated in Patrick County from 1916 to 1941; Piedmont School, which began operation in Nelson County in 1921 and closed a few years later; and Oak Hill Academy, which has continued its service from 1880 until the present.

Since the organization of the Baptist General Association of Virginia, the colleges and schools have received varying degrees of support and supervision from Virginia Baptists. In the early years the Virginia Baptist Education Society, which existed from 1830 to 1855, was instrumental in organizing educational institutions. In 1855 the society was absorbed by the general association, and its functions were continued by the education board of the association. In 1901 an education commission was created to stimulate interest in the schools and strengthen them. It was not until 1922, when both the education board and the education commission were terminated and their functions assumed by the Board of Missions and Education, that the general association began to exercise full control over the schools.

Growth and activities since 1875.—The state of Virginia in 1876 granted a charter to the Virginia Baptist Historical Society, which was designed to gather materials and preserve Baptist history. The depository for such materials has always been at Richmond College and its successor, the University of Richmond. This society, to all intents and purposes, is subsidiary to the general association, which co-operates with it and which has always appreciated the service it has rendered and is still rendering to the cause of Baptist history.

The 1880's proved to be a most constructive decade for the general association. The leadership was directed largely by Henry Keeling Ellyson (*q.v.*), who was a sound organizer and the general agent of the organization, serving without pay. There were problems, however. State missions needed to be stimulated constantly. Churches being served by missionaries were not making adequate effort toward self-support. Therefore a committee of five on co-operation was set up to contact the executive committee of the district associations and individual churches with a view to strengthening the support of missions. This committee worked effectively and helped to work out more definite and businesslike policies for state mission work.

Legal aspects of organization, particularly with regard to the holding of money or property, were discussed at several meetings, and it was finally decided that the general association as such need not become incorporated, but that all boards of the association holding property should secure proper sanction from the state of Virginia.

In 1890 William Ellyson became the executive officer of the general association upon the death of his father, Henry K. Ellyson. Since 1848 H. K. Ellyson, as secretary of the board of managers of the general association and later of the state mission board, had directed Baptist missionary activities in Virginia. His was one of the most remarkable contributions to Baptist work in Virginia.

The turn of the century found 952 churches with 122,455 members co-operating with the general association. There were 584 ministers serving as pastors of churches, and 870 Sunday schools reporting 67,193 members. Contributions to local purposes amounted to $374,405.59, and to the causes fostered by the general association, $84,822.21.

In 1918 the general association received an appeal from the Southern Baptist Convention to co-operate in a campaign to raise $75,000,000 for missions, benevolences, and education during a five-year period. The distribution of the receipts so collected was to be apportioned on a predetermined percentage basis among the agencies representing foreign missions, Christian education, home missions, state missions, orphanage, ministers' relief, and hospital. The appeal was accepted as a challenge, and, at the conclusion of the campaign, it was found that Virginia had raised $6,339,466.01.

The Virginia Baptist Foundation was authorized in 1919 and chartered in 1923. This branch of the general association was designed to receive legacies as memorials or otherwise to the denomination and to administer the income as the donors might desire. Since its beginning several large estates have been turned over to this board, which is increasing in its service.

As the work of Virginia Baptists expanded, it became apparent that reorganization was necessary in order better to carry out the functions of a large organization. There was a great deal of decentralization, and it seemed to some of the brethren that a more centralized organization would facilitate the cause of the kingdom. A committee was appointed to study the problems involved and to suggest possible changes.

In 1921 this committee on reorganization reported to the general meeting and recommended, "after looking extensively into the organizations that are in other states," that certain specific changes be made. The Virginia Baptist Board of Missions and Education, as presently constituted, is the result of their recommendation. The general association assigned to the board responsibilities previously committed to the Board of Education, the State Mission Board, and the Education Commission. The state, foreign, and home mission boards were discontinued. The work of Virginia Baptists came under the direction of one single unified executive board.

At Roanoke in 1950, the general association took under its management the *Religious Herald,* which had reflected for years the will of Virginia Baptists concerning matters pertaining to the welfare of the general association.

The executive secretaries, holding office from 1928 to 1956, have been George T. Waite (*q.v.*), Frank T. Crump (*q.v.*), James R. Bryant, and Lucius M. Polhill. During the administration of these leaders, considerable progress has been made. New departments, Training Union—supplanting the former Baptist Young People's Union—Evangelism and Enlistment, and Baptist Student Union, have been formed. In May, 1956, a Brotherhood secretary began his work. The Sunday School Department has been a vital part of Baptist life in Virginia for many years. The areas of education and missionary activity have been emphasized, and improvement in the functional operation of the boards and departments have been noticeable. Capable and well-trained personnel have been employed for special services. The range of interest has included problems of a moral and social nature as they are applicable to Christianity.

In 1954 there were co-operating with the general association 36 district associations with some 1,300 churches, the membership of which was over 400,000. Their contributions to missions amounted to over $2,500,000. There were over 100 mission pastors serving 200 churches.

DAVID N. DAVIDSON and WESLEY N. LAING

III. Program of Work of Virginia Baptists. *Board of Missions and Education.*—The board is elected by the general association and it consists of the president of the association, one member from each association in the state, and 15 members at large. Each district association may nominate to the general association, through the nominations committee, a representative on the board. Each member of the board is elected for a term of three years, and no member may serve more than two successive terms. No person, except the president, may serve on the board if he is a member of a board or an employee of any agency or institution of the general association, or if he is a member of any church participating in the revenues of the general association.

The board acts in the interim for the general association on such matters as the officers of the association may determine to be emergencies.

The board divides itself equally into the following three committees: administration, education, and missions. Each of these committees nominates five of its members to serve on the executive committee of the board. These 15 and the president comprise the executive committee of the board.

The board has the responsibility for all matters committed to it by the general association. The executive secretary and the treasurer, elected by the general association upon nomination by the board, make reports to the board and its executive committee. Lucius M. Polhill is executive secretary and Kenneth E. Burke is treasurer. The board promotes a program of missions and education in the local churches through the following departments: Sunday School, Training Union, Student Work, Evangelism and Enlistment, Brotherhood, and Summer Assemblies. The board employs, upon nomination by the executive secretary, persons to serve as secretaries of these departments. The board recommends to the general association a financial budget which includes allocations and operating expenses for the general association and operating and capital needs expenses for all agencies of the general association. The executive committee meets monthly except during July and August. The committee acts for the board during the interim. All acts of the committee are reported for review to the board.

The committee on administration considers and makes recommendations upon matters of policy and works with the executive secretary in defining and promoting the work of the departments. The committee reviews the budgets of the departments. The committee consults with administrators and trustees relative to the program and finances of benevolent institutions. The committee studies and recommends to the board through its budget committee any allocations for these institutions.

The committee on education formulates and presents to the board general policies for the adequate support and operation of Virginia Baptist schools and colleges. The committee proposes to the board, for recommendation to the general association, an annual allocation for schools and colleges and recommends to the board the annual distribution of these funds. The committee consults with the administration and trustees of the educational institutions upon matters deserving attention or approval by the board or the general association.

The committee on missions works with the churches and the district associations in studying needy areas and establishing new churches. The committee receives applications from the churches and district associations to supplement salaries of pastors in mission fields and encourages these churches to become self-supporting. The committee recommends to the budget committee allocations for mission projects. The committee consults with the extension board of the general association relative to requests for assistance by the extension board.

The Board of Missions and Education nominates three persons to fill each vacancy on the board of trustees of the University of Richmond. It maintains complete authority over the three committees, administrative, educational, and missions, which have fixed responsibilities to but no independence from the board. The actions of the executive committee, which acts ad interim for the board, are reported for review to the board. The division into three committees results in efficiency in the work, a grasp of denominational endeavor, and a measure of responsibility for all the members of the Board of Missions and Education.

Missions in Virginia.—The main emphasis is upon the organization, building, and development of churches. Relying upon recommendations from executive committees of district associations concerning locations for new work and continued support of established work in needy areas, the general association carried in the state mission budget for 1955 an item of $154,865.15 for supplemental aid for pastors' salaries. Aid was given to 134 mission pastors serving 200 churches. It is the policy, recently renewed, of the Board of Missions and Education to encourage local churches and district associations to establish and sustain, as much as possible, local mission stations. Such a program, it is believed, will foster a renewed missionary concern in the churches. While the board looks with great favor upon the initiative of local churches in suggesting building sites, describing acuteness of need, and pointing out probabilities of growth, it reserves the right to withhold financial aid if, upon thorough investigation, it has reservations about the feasibility of the work. It is the policy of the board to aid newly established work for five years only. In very rare cases continuing mission stations will be assisted 10 years or longer, at the discretion of the board.

In addition to funds allocated for salaries for mission pastors, allocations were made in 1955, among others, to interracial work ($1,300), work in prisons ($3,600), Virginia Negro Baptist Children's Home ($5,000), and Blacksburg Baptist Church Building Fund ($5,000). The Board of Missions and Education has on occasion given financial aid to churches in three towns where state colleges are located and in certain other strategic areas. Since 1950 this assistance has been limited to loans made through the Baptist extension board at a low rate of interest. The total allocations to the Missions Department in 1955 was $173,861.17.

Associational missions.—The program of associational missions is in the process of reorganization. Associational leadership is encouraged and developed by conferences on missions, stewardship, evangelism, and related subjects. The work of the various state board departments is promoted largely through committees in the 36 associations. In 1956 four associations had full-time missionaries. In Apr., 1956, it became the policy of the Board of Missions and Education to allot as much as $100 monthly as supplementary financial aid to any associational missionary approved by the board. Present plans call for increasing the number of missionaries,

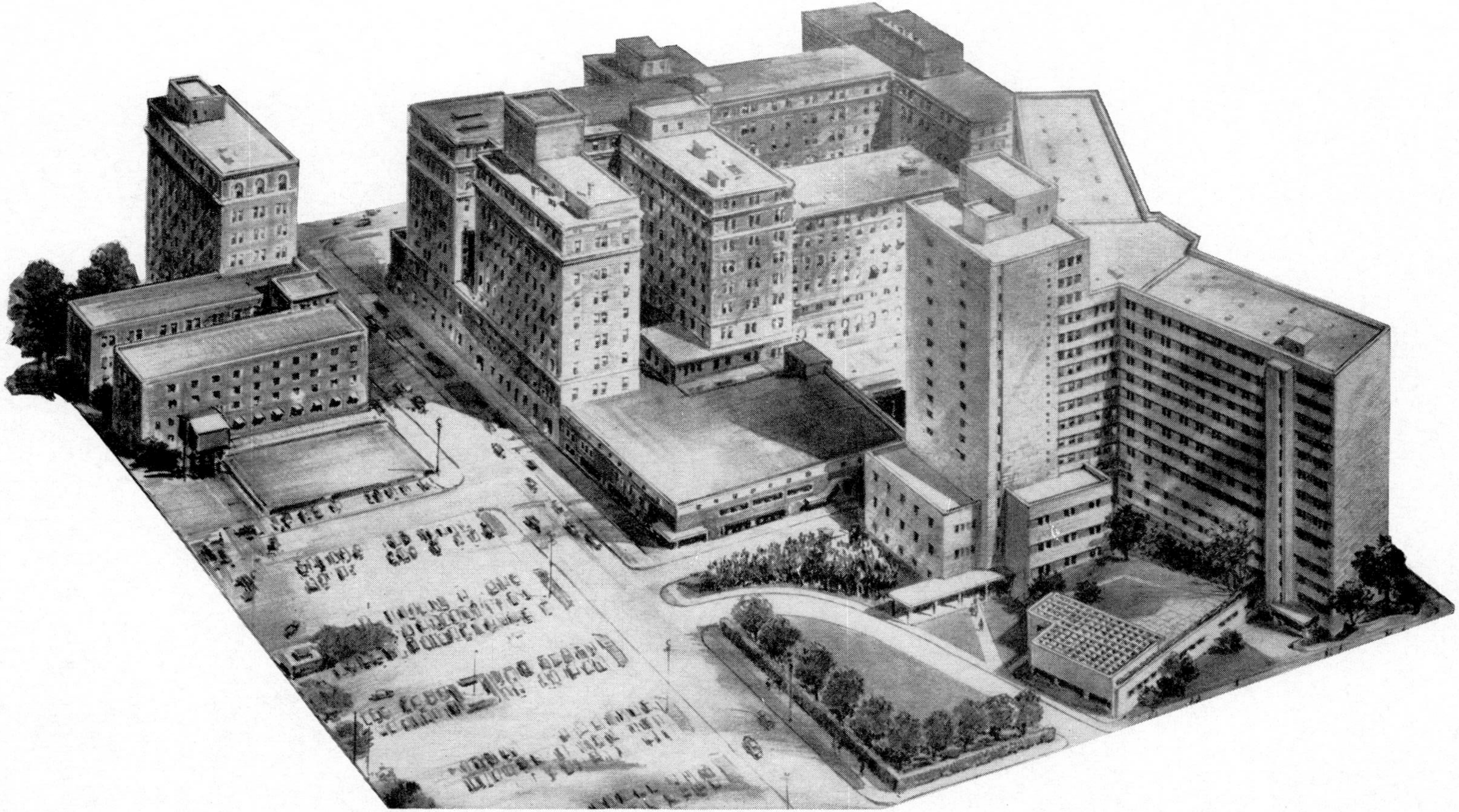

BAPTIST MEMORIAL HOSPITAL (*q.v.*), Memphis, Tenn. Established 1912, owned by Arkansas, Mississippi, and Tennessee Baptists. Valued at $20,000,000, it includes over 800 beds and bassinets and special psychiatric unit.

BAYLOR UNIVERSITY HOSPITAL (q.v.), Dallas, Tex. Occupying entire block, large center building is Truett Memorial unit. Other buildings include medical library, dentistry college, and research institute.

IV. VIRGINIA STATISTICAL SUMMARY

Year	Associ-ations	Churches	Church Member-ship	Baptisms	S. S. Enrol-ment	V.B.S. Enrol-ment	T. U. Enrol-ment	W.M.U. Enrol-ment	Brother-hood En-rolment	Mission Gifts	Total Gifts	Value Church Property	State Capital Worth
1824	8	....	....	....	....	....	....	....	....	$ 359.92	....	....	(Explanation: This column includes total value of Schools, Children's Homes, Hospitals, Foundation, Buildings, etc.)
1836	25	484	59,470	3,483	....	....	....	....	....	3,289.35	....	....	
1845	35	312	84,258	4,622	4,211	....	....	....	....	13,366.36	....	....	
1850	24	612	89,805	5,269	5,438	....	....	....	....	8,898.07	....	....	
1860	....	....	108,888	7,736	5,018	....	....	....	....	15,607.52	....	....	
1870	19	620	60,015	5,113	....	....	....	....	....	12,351.20	....	....	
1880	22	683	69,702	3,889	47,904	....	....	....	....	22,870.69			
1890	23	785	89,359	5,435	51,088	....	....	....	....	60,644.00	$ 340,462.00	$ 952,056.00	
1900	24	952	122,455	5,220	76,137	....	....	....	....	84,852.00	374,405.00	2,262,916.00	
1905	27	1,011	131,874	6,479	89,845	....	....	....	....	135,356.16	655,254.95	2,953,149.00	
1910	29	1,060	149,480	6,837	102,951	....	....	....	....	177,480.00	958,064.17	3,656,801.00	
1915	29	1,107	162,189	7,799	114,175	....	....	....	....	289,085.00	1,200,562.00	4,947,755.00	
1920	29	1,143	193,376	10,502	137,237	....	....	....	....	1,191,555.00	2,526,578.00	7,323,833.00	
1925	29	1,175	219,166	10,669	187,302	1,338	35,320	....	....	834,783.00	3,215,405.14	12,379,363.15	
1930	30	1,152	231,408	9,432	202,541	2,149	35,451	55,600	....	584,892.00	3,310,534.00	16,445,206.00	
1931	30	1,153	232,201	9,392	210,093	2,693	31,742	60,433	....	533,175.00	2,995,890.94	19,605,753.00	
1932	30	1,159	234,514	9,329	212,183	3,053	28,009	62,328	....	632,744.00	2,761,088.77	19,235,711.00	
1933	30	1,158	233,695	9,769	216,438	4,562	32,930	63,752	....	420,094.00	2,399,471.46	18,638,666.00	
1934	30	1,158	241,380	9,435	212,754	4,327	34,759	64,504	....	445,616.00	2,204,877.76	18,513,976.00	$ 9,022,810.04
1935	30	1,154	243,512	7,745	211,637	7,140	31,820	64,264	....	474,485.00	2,357,223.65	18,446,352.00	
1936	30	1,153	241,330	7,768	210,455	11,285	32,007	70,877	....	504,588.00	2,368,582.05	18,322,038.00	
1937	30	1,163	249,961	9,999	214,818	14,016	32,428	72,277	....	521,881.00	2,554,208.49	18,495,275.00	
1938	30	1,153	257,874	10,362	216,882	24,636	30,908	76,478	....	586,040.00	2,725,191.92	18,760,655.00	
1939	30	1,162	266,371	11,813	216,777	29,263	34,321	81,435	....	573,627.00	2,805,973.82	18,805,118.00	
1940	30	1,162	269,998	12,442	222,100	31,680	35,620	81,235	....	632,145.00	2,979,229.00	18,675,260.00	
1941	30	1,170	276,767	9,225	218,922	41,577	38,960	79,451	....	716,019.00	3,334,345.77	20,917,682.00	
1942	30	1,173	284,239	9,528	220,182	37,210	32,780	78,439	....	865,757.00	3,584,032.00	20,680,635.00	
1943	30	1,185	288,507	8,970	215,247	27,391	31,415	78,785	....	1,035,181.00	3,879,186.75	21,328,967.00	
1944	30	1,187	308,374	9,071	211,380	33,416	28,477	77,291	161	1,208,868.00	4,493,830.34	21,516,556.00	11,557,013.43
1945	30	1,195	306,265	10,108	211,781	39,667	21,929	79,002	187	1,511,823.00	5,100,997.00	21,968,665.00	
1946	30	1,211	301,462	11,813	217,000	48,275	25,038	81,809	997	1,781,377.00	6,054,637.00	23,089,000.00	
1947	30	1,212	319,413	11,322	224,359	62,716	25,952	72,672	1,254	1,681,140.00	6,782,271.00	24,411,206.00	
1948	30	1,228	324,520	12,150	239,575	62,135	29,304	75,869	1,307	1,773,347.00	7,781,651.00	27,616,900.00	
1949	30	1,244	336,881	14,699	253,753	70,880	35,414	86,322	1,852	1,807,027.00	8,947,304.00	33,625,334.00	
1950	30	1,249	351,359	15,470	284,834	71,331	38,991	96,343	2,020	1,894,261.00	10,093,701.00	42,235,795.00	
1951	31	1,262	356,599	14,040	284,510	85,882	42,061	90,702	2,426	2,100,676.00	10,780,854.00	46,033,903.00	
1952	31	1,282	373,834	14,496	297,854	88,208	44,806	97,689	3,890	2,352,193.00	11,944,337.00	52,420,374.00	
1953	34	1,304	386,927	16,106	309,328	95,744	50,079	99,382	4,465	2,535,759.00	13,205,956.00	57,792,759.00	
1954	36	1,310	400,661	17,403	353,958	115,369	60,653	114,719	5,024	3,165,503.00	17,953,494.00	77,692,202.00	20,541,699.60

KENNETH E. BURKE

in co-operation with the Department of Missions, which is being organized.

City missions.—City mission work began in Virginia as early as 1880, when the first minute book of the Baptist Council of Richmond reported the formation of the Baptist City Missionary Society in the Second Baptist Church. In 1956 two city missionaries were employed, one in Richmond and the other in Norfolk. Both missionaries were employed by the Richmond and Norfolk district associations, which are composed largely of churches located within the cities or their suburbs. The Board of Missions and Education has no program providing for the employment of city missionaries. The Home Mission Board of the Southern Baptist Convention grants $1,000 yearly to the Richmond Baptist Association, thus maintaining a close relationship with the City Missions Department of the Home Mission Board.

Work with minority groups.—Virginia Baptists manifest their interest in the Negro people by co-operating with two state Negro conventions in the support of the Negro Baptist Children's Home near Petersburg, Va. The Baptist general association nominates annually five trustees who are elected by the board of the Negro orphanage for terms of one year. The Richmond and Norfolk associations promote and sustain work among the Chinese.

Enlistment and evangelism.—In 1944 the Department of Enlistment and Evangelism was organized. Under the direction of the late Robert L. Randolph, who became secretary of the department in 1946 and served until Apr., 1956, Virginia Baptists have manifested a wholesome interest in stewardship and evangelism. Regional conferences on stewardship have been held annually, directed by competent leaders. In the annual conference on evangelism, men from varying backgrounds and with various experiences have made contributions to the cause of evangelism in the state.

In 1954 the per capita giving of Virginia Baptists to missions was $6.81, and the total number of baptisms was 17,403. Both these figures were the highest in history. Total membership in 1,310 Baptist churches at the end of 1954 reached 400,651. Expenditures of this department in 1955 amounted to $11,566.39.

Sunday school.—This department promotes new Sunday school organization, teacher and officer training, proper planning for educational and church buildings, summer assemblies, regional Sunday school conventions, Vacation Bible schools, and improvement of existing Sunday schools. The department staff, consisting of the Sunday school secretary, his associate, a fieldworker, and a director of children's work, have regular planning meetings with associational Sunday school officers to promote and plan the Sunday school program in the local association. In September of each year, several district Sunday school conventions are held to present the Southern Baptist Sunday school plans for the ensuing year. In 1954 the number of Sunday schools reached 1,289 with 330,135 members enrolled. In 1955 the number of members increased to 352,272, a growth of 6.7 per cent. In 1954 there were 946 Vacation Bible schools reported, with an enrolment of 111,722. In 1955 there were 1,043 Vacation Bible schools held in Virginia with an enrolment of 127,455. From these schools 2,083 children made professions of faith. Each year, a state Vacation Bible school clinic is held to train associational Vacation Bible school leaders. A representative of the Sunday School Department also assists in the various associational Vacation Bible school clinics. College students and other workers are employed in the summer in a mission Vacation Bible school program. Expenditures of this department in 1955 amounted to $43,577.53.

Training Union.—By 1955 Training Union membership in Virginia reached 60,594. This figure represents an increase of more than 100 per cent since 1948. In addition to the Sunday evening meetings, the Virginia Training Union program includes a summer assembly, leadership convention, Young People's convention, Young People's state tour of Baptist work, and the following personal interest projects: Junior sword drill and scrapbook display, Intermediate sword drill and speaker's tournament, Young People's speaker's and essay tournaments, Adult essay and scripture reading tournament, hymn festival, poster exhibit, and drama tournament. Expenditures in this department in 1955 amounted to $42,293.81.

Institutes for the education of ministers.—The Pastors' School in Virginia began with the School of Religion for Preachers and Their Wives conducted at the University of Richmond from June 24 through July 3, 1929. Since 1947 there have been two schools each year, one at Bluefield College and the other at the University of Richmond. The program consists of lectures, inspirational addresses, sermons, classes, and discussions. The schools are in session from four to five days and in 1955 had a total registration in excess of 200, with many visitors in attendance.

Assemblies.—Eagle Eyrie, an estate of 200 acres near Lynchburg, Va., was purchased in Nov., 1950. Plans call for auditorium, classroom, and departmental buildings, dining hall, five or six hotel units, 48 cottages, and recreational facilities to care for 1,500 persons per week. Building is on a pay-as-you-go basis. In May, 1956, the roads, water tanks, water and sewer lines, disposal plant, and pumping station had been completed. The dining hall, to be used temporarily as a combination auditorium–dining hall–classroom building was completed. Two weeks of daily introductory programs were planned for July, 1956. Plans call for facilities by July, 1957, to start regular assemblies on a limited basis. As funds are available, additional buildings will be erected year by year until over-all plans have been attained.

Baptist Student Union.—Resolutions to the general association from student groups were

PARTICULARS	COOPERATIVE PROGRAM ALLOCATIONS	DESIGNATIONS		TOTAL
		W. M. U. SPECIALS	OTHER	
Southwide:				
Southern Baptist Convention Budget Fund	$ 5,548 30	$ 1 22	$ 1 27	$ 5,550 79
Foreign Missions	294,861 51	300,506 23	93,086 06	688,453 80
Home Missions	97,812 96	114,866 54	7,731 18	220,410 68
Relief and Annuity Board	43,959 57	112 90	4,265 62	48,338 09
Southern Baptist Seminary	30,683 76	6 77	207 01	30,897 54
Southwestern Baptist Seminary	33,464 37	7 38	107 64	33,579 39
New Orleans Baptist Seminary	32,559 05	7 18	7 43	32,573 66
Golden Gate Seminary	22,438 91	4 95	5 12	22,448 98
Southeastern Seminary	43,636 24	9 63	9 96	43,655 83
Radio Commission	11,769 11	12 60	262 65	12,044 36
American Baptist Seminary Commission	5,664 69	1 25	1 29	5,667 23
Carver School of Missions and Social Work	3,388 47	75	77	3,389 99
Southern Baptist Hospital	8,878 57	1 96	2 03	8,882 56
Baptist Brotherhood Commission	3,938 13	87	90	3,939 90
Public Affairs Committee	834 18	18	19	834 55
Baptist World Alliance	1,661 90	36	32 51	1,694 77
Southern Baptist Foundation	1,390 31	31	32	1,390 94
Education Commission	1,778 30	39	41	1,779 10
Historical Commission	1,442 04	32	33	1,442 69
Christian Life Commission	944 12	21	22	944 55
American Bible Society		473 74	2,372 90	2,846 64
Braille Evangel		60 00	122 15	182 15
Missionaries' Library Fund		1,020 01		1,020 01
White Cross		6,852 41		6,852 41
Protestants and Other Americans United			50 00	50 00
Spanish Mission, Santa Fe, New Mexico			4,000 00	4,000 00
Las Tablos and Chorrora Churches, Canal Zone			50 00	50 00
Totals	$ 646,654 49	$423,948 16	$112,317 96	$1,182,920 61
Virginia:				
Virginia Baptist Board of Missions and Education	$ 336,486 55	$ 309 89	$ 7,370 76	$ 344,167 20
Eagle Eyrie	52,356 58	596 84	35,061 80	88,015 22
Oak Hill Academy	36,867 32	342 00	708 56	37,917 88
Virginia Baptist Children's Home	49,001 53	1,276 70	101,247 08	151,525 31
Baptist Extension Board	49,386 81			49,386 81
Virginia Baptist Hospital	18,939 93	332 36	35,893 37	55,165 66
Ministerial Education	13,664 46	11 00	1,093 87	14,769 33
Virginia Baptist Home	39,223 47	2,465 59	97,914 97	139,604 03
University of Richmond	227,230 57	267 78	2,141 78	229,640 13
Averett College	66,933 77		28 16	66,961 93
Bluefield College	107,109 14		694 17	107,803 31
Hargrave Military Academy	69,502 45		817 59	70,320 04
Fork Union Military Academy	16,379 72		3 61	16,383 33
Virginia Intermont College	60,175 82		20 27	60,196 09
Virginia Advance Program	10,429 27			10,429 27
W. M. U. Camps		110 35		110 35
Educational Fund, Virginia Indians		433 31		433 31
Benedict Good Will Center		62 50		62 50
George Braxton Taylor Good Will Center		37 50	25 21	62 71
First Baptist Good Will Center		612 79		612 79
Petersburg Good Will Center		594 42		594 42
Roanoke Good Will Center		2,640 66		2,640 66
Educational Fund		16 06		16 06
August Christmas Tree		15 00		15 00
State Mission Thank Offering:				
Benedict Good Will Center		4,435 09		4,435 09
George Braxton Taylor Good Will Center		6,452 83		6,452 83
Norton Area		1,125 00		1,125 00
Schools Committee		11,531 64		11,531 64
Blue Ridge Missionary		2,625 00		2,625 00
Clinch Valley Missionary		3,343 97		3,343 97
Lebanon and New Lebanon Missionary		1,968 75		1,968 75
New River Associational Missionary		2,031 98		2,031 98
Valley Associational Missionary		2,625 00		2,625 00
Camp Fund		20,358 90		20,358 90
Interracial		7,500 00		7,500 00
Oak Hill Academy		5,765 00		5,765 00
Baptist Historical Society		3,541 63		3,541 63
Carver School of Missions and Social Work		650 00		650 00
Educational Fund		750 00		750 00
Indian Scholarships		380 00		380 00
Interdenominational Religious Work Foundation		2,500 00		2,500 00
Virginia Church Temperance Council		2,000 00		2,000 00
Keokee Work		1,200 00		1,200 00
Shenandoah Project		300 00		300 00
Vacation Bible Schools and Summer Workers		2,300 00		2,300 00
Young People's Fund		2,000 00		2,000 00
State Mission Thank Offering:				
Promotion		270 00		270 00
Missionary Pastors and New Work		10,000 00		10,000 00
Station Wagon		1,200 00		1,200 00
Swimming Pool		5,000 00		5,000 00
Ministerial Education—Beazley Fund			4,150 00	4,150 00
Salary of Missionary Pastors			5,900 04	5,900 04
Virginia Negro Baptist Children's Home			135 45	135 45
Vacation Bible Schools			87 96	87 96
Indian View Baptist Church			100 00	100 00
Totals	$1,800,341 88	$535,927 70	$405,712 61	$2,741,982 19

largely responsible for beginning organized student work. Arthur Stovall became first state secretary in 1925 with headquarters at Charlottesville. Woman's Missionary Union began a student program in 1941, financing some local directors and student centers. This work was later transferred to the state board. In 1955 nine local directors served on major state college campuses. Two Baptist schools employed three others, with financial support for two being furnished by the Woman's Missionary Union. The Virginia board owns student centers at Radford and Harrisonburg; rents property at Farmville; uses church-owned property at Fredericksburg and Charlottesville and a section of the church building at Blacksburg and Williamsburg. Fall convention attendance in 1955 was over 400, spring retreat, 200. There are 18 local Baptist Student Unions, three of which have been First Magnitude for several years. Students have served as summer missionaries throughout Southern Baptist Convention territory and in Alaska, Hawaii, and Jamaica. Expenditures in 1955 amounted to $40,369.80.

Brotherhood.—The first state Brotherhood committee was appointed in 1950, and in 1954 it recommended to the Virginia general association that a state department of Brotherhood work be established with a full-time secretary. This recommendation was accepted enthusiastically, and the department was set up May 1, 1956, with George Euting as secretary. Statistics for 1955 record a Brotherhood enrolment of 5,255 in 125 churches. This movement in Virginia has been largely spontaneous. Where effective Brotherhoods have been organized, the churches have been vitalized.

Radio and television.—The general association does not sponsor a denominational program in the field of radio and television. However, individual churches and pastors, from the earliest days of radio, have been broadcasting religious services; more recently, a few of them have projected regular television programs successfully. The general association looks with favor upon radio and television services. A committee reports annually on the progress of such work, and the churches are encouraged to support the missionary and evangelistic activities of the Home Mission Board and the Radio and Television Commission of the Southern Baptist Convention in this field.

Church music.—At the request of a group of church musicians, the Board of Missions and Education appointed a committee in Apr., 1951, to study the advisability of establishing a Department of Music. The Board voted in Nov., 1951, to assign responsibility for the promotion of church music to the Training Union Department, and to add a full-time fieldworker to the staff of this department for that purpose. Since Mar., 1952, an annual statewide church music conference has been conducted.

Other work.—For a number of years, the general association has endorsed the American Bible Society in its work of Bible distribution. Designations by individuals and churches are encouraged. In 1955 the sum of $2,846.64 was given to the society. The association co-operates with the Virginia Temperance Council in promoting temperance and moral education through the churches and the schools. An annual appropriation is made to this work by the state board; in 1955 this amounted to $9,200. The interest of Virginia Baptists in safeguarding religious liberty is shown by the annual appropriation to Protestants and Other Americans United. In 1955 this sum was $1,000. The budget of the board makes provision for prison and institutional ministry through the Interdenominational Religious Work Foundation. For this work $3,600 was appropriated in 1955.

Financial program for 1955.— A statement of the financial program for the year ending Dec. 31, 1955, and including contributions made through the W.M.U. appears on page 1459.

LUCIUS POLHILL

VIRGINIA ASSOCIATIONS.

I. Extant. ACCOMACK. Organized at Pungoteague, Aug., 1809, with seven churches from the Salisbury Association which included churches in both Virginia and Maryland. The seven churches were located in Accomack and Northampton counties, Virginia, and had a total membership of 891. The Accomack Association was the last association in Virginia that arose from the labors of the Separate Baptist ministers. In 1954, 25 churches reported 192 baptisms, 4,948 members, $40,246.98 total gifts, $30,345.02 mission gifts, and $940,000.00 property value.

ALBEMARLE. Organized Oct. 13, 1791, by nine churches in Albemarle, Amherst, and Fluvanna counties. In 1792 this association reported 526 members. The Albemarle was one of the three groups into which the Orange Association was divided in 1791. In 1841 this body declared that traffic in ardent spirits was not consistent with Christian character. Hardware, the home church of Lottie Moon, is in this association. In 1954, 28 churches reported 285 baptisms, 8,480 members, $267,390.13 total gifts, $66,728.72 mission gifts, $1,582,650.00 property value, and $55,665.00 church debt.

APPOMATTOX. Organized Oct., 1804, at Walker's Church in Prince Edward County, with about 13 churches from the Middle District Association, located in Campbell, Charlotte, Buckingham, Prince Edward, and Amelia counties. By their original constitution no person could be moderator more than two years in succession, and their moderator could not speak on any subject. This body took the first formal action in Virginia against Campbellism. In 1954, 41 churches reported 347 baptisms, 9,220 members, $52,932.26 mission gifts and $928,647.00 property value.

AUGUSTA. Organized Oct. 24, 1876, at Goshen Bridge, Rockbridge County, by 24 churches from the Albemarle and Valley associations located in Rockingham, Augusta, Bath, Alleghany, and Rockbridge counties. At the 1954 meeting of the general association, 20 churches withdrew from the Augusta to form the Natural Bridge Association. In 1954, 43 churches reported 556 baptisms, 11,475 members, $68,365.17 total gifts, $72,590.45 mission gifts, $2,243,800.00 property value, and $171,764.00 church debt.

Blackwater. Organized Sept., 1906, at the Second Baptist Church in Petersburg by 26 churches which had constituted the Middle District of the Portsmouth Association. These churches were located in Isle of Wight, Southampton, Surry, and Nansemond counties. This association reported 5,438 members at its first meeting in 1907. In 1954, 32 churches reported 258 baptisms, 10,294 members, $103,309.07 mission gifts, and $2,185,367.00 property value.

Blue Ridge. Organized at Mayo meetinghouse in Henry County, Oct. 24, 1858, by nine churches, seven of which were from the Strawberry Association and two were newly constituted. These churches had a total of 466 members and were located in Floyd, Franklin, Henry, and Patrick counties. In 1954, 65 churches reported 652 baptisms, 11,394 members, $65,940.24 mission gifts, and $2,171,050.00 property value.

Clinch Valley. Organized Aug., 1856, by four churches from the Lebanon Association and other churches in Lee, Scott, and Washington counties. In its first report to the general association in 1857, the Clinch Valley reported 17 churches in Lee, Scott, Russell, and Wise counties with 45 baptisms and 745 members. This is the smallest association in Virginia at the present time. In 1954, 16 churches reported 61 baptisms, 1,432 members, $2,529.53 mission gifts and $223,300.00 property value.

Concord. Organized July 24, 1833 at James Square Church in Brunswick County by eight churches, located in Brunswick, Charlotte, Dinwiddie, and Mecklenburg counties. Five of these churches were from the Meherrin Association, two from the Portsmouth, and one newly organized. The Concord was formed by missionary minded churches, wishing to separate from antimission elements and Campbellism. In 1954, 41 churches reported 341 baptisms, 10,138 members, $52,878.48 mission gifts and $1,112,600.00 property value.

Dan River. Organized at County Line Church, Sept. 28, 1839, by 12 churches from the Roanoke Association, located in Halifax County, with a total membership of 1,065. This is the second association of that name in Virginia—the first, formed in 1791, also from the Roanoke, lasted only two years. In 1954, 32 churches reported 289 baptisms, 9,227 members, $50,518.16 mission gifts and $902,700.00 property value.

Dover. Organized in 1783 as the Lower District with at least 21 scattered churches in southeast Virginia. It was named Dover, Oct. 3, 1788. For a time it was the largest district association of Baptist churches in the United States. In 1843, 74 churches reported 26,134 members. From it came the Rappahannock and Peninsula associations and most of Hermon and Richmond. It recommended a catechism for children in 1809. In the Dover Association Robert B. Semple (*q.v.*) and Andrew Broaddus (*q.v.*) were born and labored. This association sent Henrietta Shuck (*q.v.*) to China. In 1925 it led the movement which prevented passage of a bill for compulsory reading of the Bible in the Virginia public schools. It has had an executive secretary since Jan. 1, 1955. In 1954, 44 churches reported 437 baptisms, 11,045 members, $74,247.57 mission gifts, and $1,834,400.00 property value.

East River. Organized Oct. 19, 1954, at College Avenue Baptist Church, Bluefield, W. Va., by 24 churches from the New Lebanon Association and one from the Valley. Over half of these churches were in West Virginia; the others were in Bland and Tazewell counties, Va. The churches of the East River Association are included in the 1954 reports of the New Lebanon and Valley, there being no report of the East River until 1955.

Goshen. Organized Oct. 17, 1792 by 15 churches from the Orange Association, located in Spotsylvania, Louisa, and adjacent counties. Samuel Harris and John Waller were instrumental in planting 13 of these churches. The total membership of the Goshen Association for 1792 was reported as 2,203. From 1844 until the Civil War it supported missionaries in parts of Virginia, California, Indian Territory, Africa, and China. The home church of William Webber and the birthplaces of H. H. Harris and A. E. Dickinson are in this association. In 1954, 45 churches reported 380 baptisms, 13,442 members, $73,698.58 mission gifts, $1,506,700.00 property value, and $94,232.00 church debt.

Hermon. Organized Oct. 7, 1902, at Mt. Hermon Church, Caroline County, by 13 churches from the Dover, Goshen, and Rappahannock associations located in Caroline and adjacent counties. It erected in 1922 the first memorial in Virginia to imprisoned Baptist preachers. Four of its churches were forced to close when the A. P. Hill Military Reservation was established. In 1954, 19 churches reported 115 baptisms, 4,458 members, $126,807.79 total gifts, $23,523.62 mission gifts, $626,000.00 property value, and $32,095.00 church debt.

James River. Organized Oct. 6, 1832, at Buckingham Church, Buckingham County, by nine churches mostly from the Appomattox Association located in Buckingham, Cumberland, Fluvanna, and Amelia counties. In 1841 the James River declared that traffic in ardent spirits was not consistent with Christian character. In 1954, 29 churches reported 116 baptisms, 4,434 members, $73,000.29 total gifts, $15,422.62 mission gifts, $394,672.00 property value, and $13,345.00 church debt.

Lebanon. Organized May 8, 1846, at Castle's Woods meetinghouse, Russell County, by 11 churches in Russell, Scott, Smyth, and Washington counties. These were the missionary-minded churches from the Washington Association. The Lebanon constitution forbade making a test of fellowship on either missionary or antimissionary sentiments. In 1954, 58 churches reported 859 baptisms, 11,904 members, $402,029.00 total gifts, $59,878.43 mission gifts, $1,480,804.00 property value, and $127,626.00 church debt.

MIDDLE DISTRICT. Organized in 1784 to contain all churches below the James River between the Kehukee Association (east) and Henry District (west). There were at least 35 churches in this territory, located in 12 counties. The Roanoke, Meherrin, and Appomattox were formed from the Middle District. In 1834 it refused to receive two prominent Campbellite messengers from the Meherrin. Edward Baptist was born and labored in this association. It was served by a missionary from 1857 to 1861 and from 1874 to 1875. In 1954, 33 churches reported 327 baptisms, 6,693 members, $256,262.54 total gifts, $39,270.00 mission gifts, $1,018,400.00 property value, and $135,714.00 church debt.

MOUNT VERNON. Organized Aug. 28, 1952, at Columbia Baptist Church, Falls Church, Va., by 25 churches from the Potomac Association, located in Arlington and Fairfax counties. In 1954, 32 churches reported 795 baptisms, 15,087 members, $978,441.58 total gifts, $159,850.58 mission gifts, $4,601,000.00 property value, and $1,382,704.00 church debt.

NATURAL BRIDGE. Organized tentatively Sept. 28, 1954, at Kerr's Creek Church, Rockbridge County. It began to function as a separate body Jan. 1, 1955. It was formed by 20 churches from the Augusta Association, located in Alleghany, Bath, and Rockbridge counties. These churches are included in the Augusta statistics of 1954, as the Natural Bridge did not report until 1955.

NEW LEBANON. Organized Oct. 8, 1875, at Sulphur Spring Church, Russell County, by 13 churches from the Lebanon Association, located north of Clinch Mountain in Russell and adjacent counties. In 1954, 58 churches reported 462 baptisms, 10,366 members, $380,017.97 total gifts, $55,721.22 mission gifts, and $1,399,400.00 property value.

NEW RIVER. The second of that name in Virginia, was organized Aug. 11, 1871, at Baptist Union Church, Grayson County, by 11 churches from the Jefferson, Mountain Union, Lebanon, and United associations, located in Grayson County, Va., and adjacent parts of North Carolina. It employed associational missionaries. It owned and operated for many years Oak Hill Academy. In 1954, 42 churches reported 331 baptisms, 4,737 members, $92,244.64 total gifts, $18,049.93 mission gifts, $534,200.00 property value, and $93,579.00 church debt.

NORFOLK. Organized at the Larchmont Church, Jan. 1, 1953, from the Portsmouth Association. Thirty-nine churches in Norfolk, South Norfolk, Virginia Beach, Princess Anne, and Norfolk counties reported at the first annual session. It has had a superintendent of missions since 1954. In 1954, 42 churches reported 1,178 baptisms, 23,287 members, $1,172,050.00 total gifts, $188,154.03 mission gifts, $3,719,500.00 property value, and $524,670.00 church debt.

PENINSULA. Organized Aug. 23, 1904, at Liberty Church, New Kent County, by 20 churches, 17 from the Dover, two from the Accomack, and one new church. These churches were between the James and York rivers in southeastern Virginia. The Peninsula oversubscribed its quota to the 75 Million Campaign by $75,000. It employed an associational worker in 1925. In 1954, 34 churches reported 1,933 baptisms, 22,119 members, $801,432.72 total gifts, $218,900.40 mission gifts, $4,594,500.00 property value, and $585,960.00 church debt.

PETERSBURG. Organized Sept. 26, 1906, at the Second Church, Petersburg, by 22 churches from the Upper District of the Portsmouth Association located in Chesterfield, Greenville, Prince George, Southampton, and Sussex counties. In Prince George County in this association, Robert Norden gathered the first Baptist church in Virginia. In 1954, 40 churches reported 524 baptisms, 12,840 members, $513,511.33 total gifts, $88,318.16 mission gifts, $2,464,000.00 property value, and $218,075.00 church debt.

PIEDMONT. Organized Aug. 18, 1903, at Jonesboro Church, Nelson County, by 26 churches from the Albemarle Association, located in Amherst and Nelson counties. The Piedmont Mission School was located in this Association. In 1954, 31 churches reported 172 baptisms, 6,165 members, $120,758.65 total gifts, $28,887.03 mission gifts, $526,000.00 property value, and $1,564.00 church debt.

PITTSYLVANIA (ROANOKE). Organized Oct. 16, 1788, at Watkins meetinghouse as the Roanoke Association with 21 churches from the Middle District, in Charlotte, Halifax, Mecklenburg, and Pittsylvania counties. Several churches in North Carolina joined this association. Its first moderator was Samuel Harris (*q.v.*), who lived and labored in Roanoke territory. In 1790 it adopted an abstract of principles. Dan River, the first Separate Baptist church in Virginia, was gathered in Roanoke territory. The name was changed to Pittsylvania in 1923, and from it the Dan River Association was formed. Seven of its churches withdrew in 1841 to organize the Staunton River Antimission Association. It has had an associational missionary (now secretary of missions) since 1947. In 1954, 44 churches reported 425 baptisms, 12,461 members, $509,190.06 total gifts, $83,132.28 mission gifts, $2,143,200.00 property value, and $146,280.00 church debt.

PORTSMOUTH. Organized May 21, 1791, at Portsmouth, by the Virginia churches of the Kehukee Association, as the Virginia Portsmouth Association. Seventeen churches, located in Dinwiddie, Isle of Wight, Nansemond, Norfolk, Princess Anne, Prince George, Southampton, and Sussex counties sent delegates to the first meeting. It adopted the Kehukee abstract of principles. It was the first Virginia association to promote a missionary society. From it the Blackwater, Petersburg, and Norfolk associations were formed. In 1954, 21 churches reported 575 baptisms, 14,006 members, $598,-955.00 total gifts, $130,104.75 mission gifts, and $2,945,800.00 property value.

POTOMAC. Organized Aug. 6, 1856, at Pleasant Vale Church, Fauquier County, by the union of Columbia and Salem Union associations. There were 41 constituent churches, with a combined membership of 3,925, located in Berkeley, Clarke, Culpeper, Fairfax, Fauquier, Frederick, Hampshire, Jefferson, Loudoun, Page, Stafford, and Warren counties, and Washington, D. C. From it the Shenandoah and Mount Vernon associations were formed. It employed an associational worker from 1925 to 1936. In 1954, 39 churches reported 90 baptisms, 6,582 members, $72,377.74 total gifts, $29,243.36 mission gifts, $844,750.00 property value, and $45,116.00 church debt.

POWELL RIVER. Organized Oct. 4, 1894, at Thompson's Settlement Church as Powell's River by 19 churches in Lee County. It reported in 1895 an associational membership of 1,029. Generally it was called Powell River by 1920. This association founded Lee Baptist Institute at Pennington Gap, Va., in 1904. In 1954, 28 churches reported 143 baptisms, 4,279 members, $62,770.92 total gifts, $8,425.37 mission gifts, $364,500.00 property value, and $15,299.00 church debt.

RAPPAHANNOCK. Organized Aug. 5, 1843, at Coan meetinghouse, Northumberland County, by 33 churches from the Dover Association, in Caroline, Essex, Gloucester, King George, King and Queen, Lancaster, Matthews, Middlesex, Northumberland, Richmond, and Westmoreland counties. In 1811 a far-reaching revival began in Essex and King and Queen counties. George William Beale (*q.v.*), Robert Healy Pitt (*q.v.*), and Henrietta Shuck (*q.v.*) were born in Rappahannock territory. In 1954, 65 churches reported 527 baptisms, 14,984 members, $456,-794.27 total gifts, $93,701.11 mission gifts, $2,-033,929.00 property value, and $87,300.00 church debt.

RICHMOND. Organized June 1, 1950, at First Baptist Church, Richmond, by 18 churches from Dover and six from Middle District. This is the territory where Frederic William Boatwright (*q.v.*), Henry Keeling Ellyson (*q.v.*), Robert Ryland (*q.v.*), James Barnett Taylor (*q.v.*), and George White McDaniel (*q.v.*) lived and labored, and the territory which sent Lott Carey (*q.v.*) to Africa. It has had an executive secretary since its organization. In 1954 it owned property valued at $120,996.76, and operated four Good Will Centers and a camp for children. Seven churches have been organized since 1950. In 1954, 49 churches reported 1,322 baptisms, 38,110 members, $2,097,972.14 total gifts, $361,134.01 mission gifts, $8,993,826.00 property value, and $1,087,588.00 church debt.

SHENANDOAH. Organized Sept. 13, 1882, at Berryville Church by 13 churches, 12 from the Potomac Association and one from the Shiloh Association, in Clarke, Frederick, Page, and Warren counties in Virginia, and Berkeley, Hampshire, Hardy, and Jefferson counties in West Virginia. It still contains churches in Berkeley and Jefferson counties, W. Va. Mill Creek Church, which exerted the first permanent Baptist influence in Virginia, was in Shenandoah territory. In 1954, 21 churches reported 127 baptisms, 5,962 members, $102,198.21 total gifts, $35,026.98 mission gifts, and $1,170,-450.00 property value.

SHILOH. The northern division of the Orange, was organized at the meeting commencing Oct. 26, 1792, at Smith's Creek meetinghouse, Shenandoah County, as the Culpeper Association. In 1793 it contained 12 churches in Culpeper, Hardy, Madison, Orange, and Shenandoah counties with a total membership of 1,173. The name was changed to Shiloh in 1812. From it the Rappahannock Old School and Ebenezer associations were formed. Within its bounds John A. Broadus (*q.v.*), William F. Broaddus (*q.v.*) and Henry M. Wharton (*q.v.*) were born. In 1954, 39 churches reported 177 baptisms, 6,557 members, $30,743 mission gifts, and $544,700 property value.

STAUNTON RIVER. Organized Oct. 5, 1951, at Central Baptist Church, Altavista, Campbell County, by 19 churches from the Appomattox, Pittsylvania, and Strawberry associations in Campbell and Pittsylvania counties, with a total membership of 4,991. In 1954, 22 churches reported 158 baptisms, 5,043 members, $27,297 mission gifts, and $702,000 property value.

STRAWBERRY. Organized 1776 at Strawberry Church, Pittsylvania County, as Upper District. At least seven churches in Bedford, Botetourt, Franklin, Henry, Patrick, and Pittsylvania counties were admitted in 1776. It was also called Henry District and in 1791 it adopted the name Strawberry. It admitted churches in North Carolina. It adopted a confession of faith. From it Blue Ridge, Mayo, New River (first), Pig River, and Valley associations were formed. Jeremiah B. Jeter (*q.v.*), William E. Hatcher (*q.v.*) and Daniel Witt were born in Strawberry. In 1954, 58 churches reported 566 baptisms, 16,736 members, $122,389 mission gifts, and $2,624,752 property value.

VALLEY. Organized Aug. 7, 1841, at Zion's Hill Church, Botetourt County, by 13 churches from the Strawberry and Albemarle associations and 4 new churches, with 1,077 members, in Alleghany, Botetourt, Giles, Roanoke, and Rockbridge counties. It contributed churches to the Augusta Association. Valley is the largest association in Virginia. Here George Braxton Taylor lived and labored. In 1954, 79 churches reported 1,169 baptisms, 35,245 members, $232,-333 mission gifts, and $6,996,910 property value.

WISE. Organized Aug. 18, 1927, by the Wise County churches, dismissed from Clinch Valley at East Stone Gap Church, Wise County. At its first annual meeting 13 churches reported 1,487 members. It was called Wise County until 1945. In 1954, 20 churches reported 217 baptisms, 3,779 members, $17,237 mission gifts, and $707,000 property value.

WOODFORD BROADUS HACKLEY

II. Extinct. CHAPPAWAMSICK. Organized in 1789 by 11 churches from the lower district of the Ketocton. It adopted a confession of faith. It dissolved in 1792, and the churches reunited with the Ketocton Association.

COLUMBIA. Organized in Sept., 1820, at Grove meetinghouse, Fauquier County, by 16 churches from the Ketocton and Baltimore associations, located in Maryland; in Fauquier, Stafford, Fairfax, and Loudoun counties, Va.; in Alexandria; and in Washington. In 1836 five churches left the association because of antimission tendencies. In 1856 the Columbia united with the Salem Union to form the Potomac Association.

EBENEZER. Organized in 1828 by 10 churches from the Shiloh Association, mostly in Shenandoah and Rockingham counties. It became antimission. In 1890 some of its churches joined the Ketocton Association of Regular Baptists.

HEBRON. Organized in 1857 by five churches from the Rappahannock and Goshen associations. It adopted articles of faith that positively forbade use of intoxicating liquors. This "test" association dissolved 10 years later, and its churches returned to mother associations.

HOLSTON. Organized in 1786 by seven churches in southwest Virginia and Tennessee. It adopted a confession of faith. In 1807 it comprised 15 churches in Tennessee and 10 in Virginia with 1,619 members. In 1810 this body contained 10 churches in Washington, Russell, and Lee counties, Va., with 591 members. In 1811 eight Virginia churches were dismissed to form the Washington Association. The Holston Association continued in Tennessee.

JEFFERSON. Organized Oct. 30, 1848, at Rockford Church, Surry County, N. C., by six churches from Briar Creek Association, in Ashe County, N. C., and Grayson and Smyth counties, Va. It dissolved when most of its churches joined the New River Association in 1871.

KEHUKEE. Organized about 1765 at Kehukee, Halifax County, N. C., as a Regular Baptist association. Beginning in 1772, it admitted southeastern Virginia churches, both Regular and Separate. It adopted an abstract of principles. In 1790 the 19 Virginia churches withdrew to form the Virginia-Portsmouth Association.

KETOCTON. The first Baptist association formed in Virginia was organized Aug. 19, 1766, at Ketocton Meeting House, Loudoun County, by Regular Baptists—three churches from the Philadelphia Association and one unattached church in northern Virginia, with a total of 142 members. It adopted articles of faith. It expanded to include churches throughout northern Virginia, in Maryland, west of the Alleghanies, and in North Carolina. From it Columbia, Salem Union, Red Stone, and Patterson's Creek associations were formed. David Thomas, William Fristoe, James Ireland, and Jeremiah Moore labored in Ketocton. In 1806 it published *The Baptist Declaration of Faith, Revised and Adapted by Several District Associations of the United Baptists in Virginia.* It was reduced to 12 churches during the antimission movement; it became a Primitive Baptist association. After more vicissitudes three of its churches joined others in 1890 to reorganize the Ketocton Association of Regular Baptists. The present Ketocton associations both adhere to the articles of faith of the original Ketocton, and both claim 1766 as their organizational date.

MAYO. Organized in Oct., 1798, apparently by nine churches from the Strawberry Association, mostly in Henry and Patrick counties, Va., and North Carolina. It became antimission in 1831.

MEHERRIN. Organized in Oct., 1804, at Ebenezer meetinghouse, Mecklenburg County, by 12 churches located in Brunswick, Charlotte, Dinwiddie, Lunenburg, and Mecklenburg counties. In 1805 it adopted in principle a confession of faith. In 1826 in this association the first Temperance Society in Virginia was formed at Ash Camp. The Meherrin Association was wrecked by the antimission element and Campbellism. Upon its dissolution in 1836, the missionary churches joined the Concord Association.

MOUNTAIN. Organized in Aug., 1799, by three churches in Grayson County, Va., and others in North Carolina and Tennessee from the Yadkin Association. It became antimission. Grayson County missionary churches now belong to New River Association.

NEW RIVER. Organized in Oct., 1794, by seven or eight churches in the Strawberry Association west of the Blue Ridge located in Montgomery and adjacent counties. From it the Greenbrier Association was formed in 1801. It became a Primitive Baptist association.

ORANGE. Organized May 8, 1789, at Crooked Run Church, Culpeper County, by 22 churches in northern Virginia, being the "Upper District." John Leland (*q.v.*) and Elijah Craig (*q.v.*) labored in Orange territory. In 1791 it divided into the Goshen, Albemarle, and Culpeper associations.

PIG RIVER. Organized in 1825 by 12 churches from the Strawberry Association in Henry, Patrick, and Franklin counties. By Oct., 1833, it had become antimission.

RAPIDANN. Organized in May, 1771, at Blue Run meetinghouse, Orange County, by 12 churches with 1,335 members, two new churches, and 10 from Sandy Creek Association, located in 11 counties in central Virginia, ranging from Pittsylvania to Shenandoah. It was the first Separate Baptist association in Virginia. It adopted the Philadelphia Confession. From it the Strawberry Association was formed in 1776. It dissolved in 1783 upon division into districts and became the Dover, the Middle District, and the Orange associations.

SALEM UNION. Organized Sept. 21, 1833, at Long Branch Church, Fauquier County, by six churches in northern Virginia—one from Ketocton, one from Columbia, and four new ones. In 1856 it united with the Columbia Association to form the Potomac Association.

SALISBURY. Organized in 1784 by the churches

on the eastern shore of Virginia, Maryland, and Delaware. In 1809 its seven Virginia churches withdrew to form the Accomack Association.

SANDY CREEK. Organized in Jan., 1758, at Sandy Creek meetinghouse, North Carolina, by nine churches. All the early Separate Baptist churches in Virginia joined this association. In 1770 it divided and the Virginia churches withdrew to form the Rapidann Association.

WASHINGTON. Organized in 1811 by eight churches from the Holston Association, located in Washington, Russell, and Lee counties. In 1845 the missionary churches of this association formed the Lebanon Association, and the Washington continued as a Primitive Baptist association.

WESTERN VIRGINIA. Organized Sept. 25, 1843, at Lewisburg, Greenbrier County, by seven Virginia district associations and 11 churches, as an auxiliary to the Virginia general association. It was a missionary association to promote missionary work by the churches west of the Blue Ridge. At its last meeting in 1860, it reported 20 missionaries working in its territory. The Civil War caused its dissolution.

III. West Virginia. Associations formed prior to 1863 in that part of Virginia which became West Virginia: BROAD RUN, 1835, from Union; GREENBRIER, 1801, from New River; JUDSON, 1847, from Broad Run; MT. PISGAH, 1854, from Broad Run; NORTHWESTERN VIRGINIA, 1850—a missionary association, composed of Broad Run, Judson, Parkersburg, and Union district associations; PARKERSBURG, 1812, from Union; PATTERSON'S CREEK, 1827, from Ketocton; RED STONE, 1776, from Ketocton, included churches in Pennsylvania; TEAY'S VALLEY, 1812, from Greenbrier; UNION, 1804, from Red Stone; ZION, 1848, from Paint Union Association of United Baptists, Kentucky. WOODFORD BROADUS HACKLEY

VIRGINIA BAPTIST CHILDREN'S HOME. The Baptist General Association of Virginia voted to establish a Baptist orphanage at its meeting in 1889 and appointed a board of trustees with instructions to seek incorporation. After a charter was granted in Feb., 1890, the board, at its first meeting, elected William Eldridge Hatcher (*q.v.*) president and arranged for visits to proffered sites. In Nov., 1890, Salem, Va., was chosen as the home's location, and George J. Hobday was elected superintendent. The first orphans were received in July, 1892, when one building had been completed. A charter amendment, approved in 1953, changed the name of the corporation to the Virginia Baptist Home for Children, effective Jan. 1, 1954. The home had, in 1956, 12 dormitories, each accommodating about 20 children and a house mother, seven other buildings, and homes for certain employees. Land holdings total 700 acres, with 350 of them constituting the farm, gardens, and pasture for the beef and dairy herds, while the remainder of the land is a mountainous watershed area.

Boys of suitable age work on the farm in season, operate the dairy, and care for the stock, under a farm manager; the girls have assignments in the dining room, kitchen, laundry, and cannery. Both boys and girls work in the print shop. All these services, with provision for diversions, promote health and happiness, reduce costs, and aid in adjustment to life outside. The children attend Sunday school and other services at Salem Baptist Church, and the pastor conducts a weekly service at the home. Children of school age attend public schools of Salem, and the home provides a kindergarten for younger ones. High school graduates who wish to attend college and have high academic records are assisted by the home, generous friends, and work assignments in the college chosen.

The trustees, elected for four-year terms by the board from nominations approved by the general association, elect a superintendent for an indefinite term. He is responsible for all divisions and for the efficient service of all hired employees. Providing three types of care, the home has about 250 children in the home itself, 90 under the mother's aid plan, and 25 in foster homes. Since its founding, the home has cared for 3,600 children.

Land, buildings, and equipment are valued at about $1,500,000; trust funds amount to $500,-000; and invested funds of $500,000 form a reserve in case of urgent need. Operating on an annual budget of $250,000, the home is supported by the state Cooperative Program monthly collections in Sunday Schools, contributions by churches and individuals, and income from investments and legacies. Ray F. Hough has been superintendent of the home since June, 1928.

R. E. LOVING

VIRGINIA BAPTIST FOUNDATION. Incorporated in Mar., 1923, with its principal office in Petersburg, Va. In addition to the power to encourage the making of gifts by deed, will, or otherwise, the foundation has full and complete authority to receive, administer, and distribute all kinds and classes of property. Its chief function, however, is the creation and administration of trust funds, large or small, from which the income is to be used for any denominational agency, institution, or church. It also has power to act as executor of a decedent's estate and has general corporate powers in the establishment and maintenance of Baptist causes, local or statewide.

The foundation has seven trustees, elected by the Baptist General Association of Virginia, with terms of office for seven years, one expiring annually. In 1955 the office of executive secretary was created with James R. Bryant as the first to hold that position. The office was made possible by an appropriation of the general association at its annual meeting in Norfolk in Nov., 1954.

It has never been the foundation's policy to persuade prospective donors to prefer one Baptist agency over any other; it has simply acquainted them with needs and circumstances, according to which they decide how to designate their gifts. The estimated total value of all estates handled is $334,248.41. JAMES R. BRYANT

VIRGINIA BAPTIST HISTORICAL SOCIETY. Interested in the history of Virginia Baptists and impressed with the importance of gathering and preserving materials relating to the Baptist churches of the state, Charles Hill Ryland (*q.v.*) of Richmond appeared before the General Assembly in Mar., 1876, requesting a charter for the organization of the Virginia Baptist Historical Society. The request was granted, and the society was incorporated by an act set forth in Senate Bill Number 232. The society was not organized, however, until June, 1876, when the organizational meeting was held in conjunction with the annual Baptist general associational meeting in Culpeper Baptist Church, which at that time stood on the site of the colonial jail where Baptist ministers had been imprisoned for preaching the gospel. Jeremiah Bell Jeter (*q.v.*) was elected president; R. L. T. Beale, vice-president; and Henry Herbert Harris (*q.v.*), secretary-treasurer. Presidents of the society following Jeter have included George William Beale (*q.v.*), James Barnett Taylor (*q.v.*), William Heth Whitsitt (*q.v.*), John Mason Pilcher (*q.v.*), and George Braxton Taylor (*q.v.*).

Three major objectives of the society have been the preservation of historical material relating not only to Virginia Baptists but also to Baptists in general, the encouragement of research in Baptist history and publication of the findings, and the placing of monuments and tablets to commemorate Baptist forebears and to mark the sites of early Baptist churches.

The University of Richmond has always supplied storage quarters for the historical data, which has been assembled largely through the efforts of the secretaries. In 1955, when the Boatwright Memorial Library was dedicated, one wing of the building was set apart for the exclusive use of the society, provided as a result of the foresight and generosity of the Woman's Missionary Union of Virginia, under the leadership of Blanche Sydnor White. In this wing of the library the name of the society is engraved above the main door and inside is found an inscribed plaque bearing these words:

> In grateful memory of the Baptist fathers through whose persistent efforts religious liberty was won, this wing of the Boatwright Memorial Library is given by the Woman's Missionary Union of Virginia to house the collection of the Virginia Baptist Historical Society.

In 1951, 254 churches and other Baptist organizations had deposited original manuscript records with the society for safekeeping. These deposits totaled 630 volumes, of which 133 dated back 100 years, and 32 for more than 150 years. Other manuscripts in the society's collection include the original warrants for the arrest and imprisonment in Middlesex County of Calvin Bernard Waller (*q.v.*), Edwin Oswald Ware (*q.v.*), James Greenwood, and William Webber (*q.v.*) for preaching in 1771; copies of similar indictments in other counties; and photostats of all unpublished documents in the Library of Congress and in the Virginia State Library that have to do with Virginia Baptists and their activities in the complete separation of church and state. The society has Luther Rice's (*q.v.*) journal of a journey through Virginia in 1819 and Henrietta Hall Shuck's (*q.v.*) letters from China; it is custodian of Foreign Mission Board correspondence from its beginning in 1845. The society's 6,420 volumes of religious history include 1,700 volumes by or about Virginia Baptists and their organizations, files of general association and district association minutes, and files of the *Religious Herald,* all from their beginnings. E. T. CLARK

VIRGINIA BAPTIST HOME. Established by unanimous vote of the Baptist General Association of Virginia in 1945 as the Virginia Baptist Home for Aged, Inc. A charter of incorporation was secured in 1946, and the home began operations Aug. 2, 1948, managed by a board of trustees nominated by the general association.

In addition to the main buildings, the home owns 306 acres of land and has total assets valued at $1,500,000. In 1954 Virginia Baptist Home, Inc., was adopted as the official name. All applicants for admission to the home, which is approved by the State Department of Welfare and Institutions, "must be members of a Baptist church co-operating with the Baptist General Association of Virginia for the past five years and in good standing with the church." JAMES T. EDWARDS

VIRGINIA BAPTIST HOSPITAL. The first positive action toward erection of a Baptist hospital in Virginia was taken by the general association in 1919, when 15 men were named as trustees, and the Woman's Missionary Union of Virginia was asked to name 10 women. Lynchburg was chosen as the site because of its healthful climate, central location, excellent rail and highway facilities, property availability, and citizen interest. The first building, with a 54-bed capacity, was opened in July, 1924, with the "open staff" policy. Mary F. Cowling, superintendent, continued to serve for 30 years. The hospital now has four buildings, joined by heated corridors, 96 beds in addition to a maternity department, and accommodations for 65 nurses. A building under construction in 1954 will increase capacity to 150 beds and add to laboratory and obstetrical facilities. In 1954, 4,100 patients were admitted, and 1,054 babies were born.

The nonsectarian patronage is restricted to whites. The nursing school, fully accredited, has affiliation with the Children's Hospital of Philadelphia for pediatrics, and with the Delaware

State Hospital for nervous and mental diseases. The hospital is not yet certified for internships. Value of the land, buildings, and equipment in 1954 was $1,500,000. Income from the $800,000 Trust Fund is used for needy patients, mainly children. The state co-operative plan, Mother's Day collections in churches and Sunday schools, patient income, and designated gifts provide approximately $500,000 annually for support of the hospital. Trustees are elected for five-year terms, from lists approved by the general association.

R. E. LOVING

VIRGINIA EXTENSION BOARD, INC. Inaugurated by the Virginia Baptist Board of Missions and Education Nov. 13, 1939, and incorporated June 11, 1940, the board was empowered to acquire gifts, legacies, and bequests; to assist missionary Baptist churches in Virginia in securing sites; to erect and maintain suitable buildings; to make loans at a low rate of interest; to purchase, receive, and hold property; to invest, sell, and reinvest. It is a lending agency and does not and cannot make gifts.

W. H. Baylor served as chairman of the committee which secured the board's charter, and James R. Bryant and Lucius Polhill have served as executive secretaries. In 1954 assets totaled $279,893.35; interest on loans, $3,293.74; and receipts for capital assets, $34,048.18. Operating expenses taken from interest received totaled $1,094.00 in 1954.

J. P. GULLEY

VIRGINIA INTERMONT COLLEGE. The incentive for the founding of this institution came from Hollins College, which had been visited by J. R. Harrison and M. M. Morris of Glade Springs, Va. Both these men were convinced of the need for a college for women in southwestern Virginia and, by their observation of the successful operation of Hollins, were encouraged to believe that a similar institution could be established at Glade Springs.

After the voters of the small town got rid of the six saloons within the town limits and Harrison had been able to interest others in his plans, property was purchased, and Southwest Virginia Female Institute was opened in 1884. For the first session there were three teachers, 13 boarding students, and others who came as day students. Allison Hutton was selected as the first president, and in 1886 the school was chartered as Southwest Virginia Institute.

Within five years the school had outgrown the facilities available in Glade Springs and in 1891 moved to its present location in Bristol. For the next seven years there was steady growth and development, but after the resignation of President D. D. Jones in 1898, the financial position of the school deteriorated to such an extent that it was sold to a group consisting of the pastor and some members of the First Baptist Church of Bristol. The name was changed to Virginia Institute, and J. T. Henderson of Carson-Newman College became president in 1903. Under his leadership the curriculum was reorganized in 1910 to make the institute a college; in 1912 the name was again changed, this time to Virginia Intermont College.

H. G. Noffsinger began his 31-year presidency in 1914. When he retired in 1945, he left a school enlarged in enrolment, expanded physically, stabilized financially, and greatly improved academically. Changing the school from a senior to a junior college was the most significant academic innovation. As such, the school has been accredited by the Southern Association of Colleges and Secondary Schools and is a member of Southern and national associations of junior colleges. Rabun L. Brantley gave 10 years of distinguished service to the school until his resignation in 1956. In his place the trustees elected Floyd V. Turner of Belmont College, Nashville, Tenn.

Since the founding of the school, there have been approximately 4,000 graduates. The total enrolment for the session 1955–56 was 420. The co-operative funds of Virginia Baptists contributed $59,634 of the capital and operating budgets. The endowment is $572,772, and total assets are $2,072,772.

RALPH MC DANEL

VIRTUE, CHRISTIAN. A study of Christian virtue is an intrinsic part of the field of Christian ethics. It calls for an understanding of the meaning of the term, the historical development, an exploration of the source of virtue, and an analysis of those traits of character practiced by Jesus, recommended in the New Testament, and observable today in the life of one committed to the Christian faith.

Meaning.—The English word "virtue" is derived from the Latin *virtus,* meaning generally "manliness" or "manhood," i.e., "the sum of all the corporeal or mental excellences of man"; more particularly the thought is that of "moral perfection." In classical Greek thought the idea was "goodness" or "excellence," as seen in the word *aretė,* a word which appears but four times in the Greek New Testament. Although the word was seldom used, the idea contained within it was not ignored. Virtue involves a disposition of mind or a trait of character, and its consequent effect upon moral conduct.

Historical development.—Much stress had been placed upon virtue in the ethical thought of Greek philosophy, especially in the teachings of Socrates, Plato, Aristotle, the Stoics, and the Epicureans. In the New Testament, areas of moral conduct entirely unknown to the earlier Greek philosophers are revealed. Christian virtues are set in a Godward direction, with the ultimate standard for moral conduct being seen in the person of Christ.

Source.—A Christian interpretation of virtue recognizes that it is through faith that the soul is converted and brought into a world of new values. In the thought of Jesus, goodness is dependent upon a right disposition or the condition of the heart. For him there could be no perfect morality so long as the desire to do evil was alive in the heart.

One should not conclude, however, that virtue is automatic, once the commitment has been made. Paul, like Jesus, taught that the "inward man" must be changed before right action can be expected (Rom. 8:7–9), but this new sphere of life into which the believer has been translated is one which calls for moral effort and strenuous self-discipline (cf. I Thess. 5:8; Eph. 6:10–17; II Cor. 10:3–6; Phil. 3:14; Gal. 2:2; II Tim. 4:7). After the new life in Christ is begun, virtue is further realized through moral instruction and the repeated practice of virtuous conduct. John Wick Bowman observes that Christian personality can be *developed* through various stages until it arrives at maturity, but the beginning point must be right.

A final factor in the origin and development of virtue is the role of the Holy Spirit and the strength of the fellowship within the church in providing guidance and in empowering the Christian for moral and virtuous living according to the ethical teaching recorded in the New Testament.

Analysis.—Several passages of Scripture can be said to contain catalogues of virtues, the most significant of which are Matthew 5:3–12; Galatians 5:22–23; Colossians 3:12–14; I Corinthians 13:13. The personal virtues mentioned in these passages were exemplified in the life of Jesus and, to a lesser extent, in the lives of his followers. They are recommended in his teaching and emphasized in the writings of Paul. Brief mention is herein made of twelve virtues. To avoid duplication, other qualities which might be included are discussed in relation to one or another of the twelve.

Philosophical ethics placed stress upon four qualities which in historical ethics have been designated as the "cardinal virtues": wisdom, justice, temperance, and courage. These cardinal virtues found a place in Christian ethics, although Christian writers sought to interpret them in the light of the Christian revelation. This attempt is most prominent in the works of Ambrose (d. 397), of Augustine (d. 430), and of Thomas Aquinas (d. 1274) in his synthesis of Christian theology and Aristotelian philosophy.

Both Jesus and Paul emphasize the value inherent in the cardinal virtues, but the meaning attached to each is different in some respects. *Wisdom,* for them, consists of the knowledge of God's will or the understanding of his purpose which will enable one to walk in the way of God and do his will on earth. *Justice* has a twofold meaning. The word itself, *dikaiosunē,* in the broad sense is best translated "righteousness" and describes "the state of him who is such as he ought to be . . . ; the condition acceptable to God." In the more narrow sense the word is best translated "justice" and so designates "the virtue which gives each one his due." The Christian idea of justice places emphasis upon the inner motive as well as the deed. Justice, as a Christian virtue, never stands alone. It is never cold and formal; never merely legal. If one is to deal rightly with others, he must exercise not only justice but love. *Temperance,* or *self-control,* is the restraint of natural appetites in accordance with the will of God. Jesus never expects a man to engage in asceticism as an end within itself, but in order to hold himself in subjection that his witness may not be nullified. Jesus does not suggest discipline as such in the moral life, but submission to a higher will. In a more specific way Paul warns against sensuality, seeing that the physical nature must be disciplined and properly related to the whole of life. *Courage* is associated with patient endurance (*hupomonē*). The thought of Jesus is that one should exercise courage which is rooted in faith in God and which, regardless of circumstance or consequence, compels the Christian to strive to do the will of God. Consider his frequent admonition to "fear not."

Thomas Aquinas designated faith, hope, and love as the "theological virtues." As a virtue, *faith* denotes both one's attitude toward God and ". . . the character of one who can be relied on." Many Scripture references place stress upon this attitude of trust in God and fidelity both to him and to one's fellow man. In the New Testament *hope* means the expectation of good, an attitude which is derived from man's relation to God and which is itself the source of Christian endurance in the face of trial and persecution. *Love,* by far the most important virtue and, indeed, the unifying principle among all virtues, suggests an attitude of mind not governed by emotions alone. It is a disposition which reveals, as C. A. Anderson Scott says, three elements: recognition, consideration, and care. This love is best designated by the Greek word *agapē.* Such love does not crave but gives. God exercises this love toward man; and when man responds in faith to God's love, such love is implanted in man. The supreme commandment of Christianity is "Thou shalt love," and this love is to know no boundaries and permit no barriers. Actually, Christian love in its full sense creates and strengthens other virtues, binding all together into one disposition, as described by Paul in I Corinthians 13.

There are still other virtues which are distinctively Christian and which receive appropriate stress in the New Testament. *Benevolence* is a virtue of positive helpfulness toward others and is seen in kindred dispositions such as mercy, kindness, graciousness, compassion, and goodness. Jesus taught that every person who has received mercy from God ought to exercise this attitude of benevolence toward others. *Chastity* is an important part of purity. In the Beatitude, "Blessed are the pure in heart," Jesus used the word *katharos,* which when used in an ethical sense means "free from corrupt desire, . . . from every admixture of what is false." He regarded purity and chastity as internal qualities. Both Jesus and Paul condemned sexual vice and indicated that chastity and purity are necessary for fellowship with God. It should be remembered, however, that

Jesus was considerate of those who had violated the ideal and was ready to forgive them and to assist them in personal adjustments toward righteousness. *Honesty* is expected by Jesus on the part of his followers. He wants their lives to manifest a vital union of inward sincerity and outward truthfulness. *Patience,* closely connected with the Christian view of courage, springs from belief in divine goodness. It suggests a temper of mind which does not easily succumb under suffering, and a certain self-restraint which does not hastily retaliate a wrong. In the New Testament, patience is associated with long-suffering, forbearance, and forgiveness. *Humility,* an almost exclusive Christian virtue, and a primary one, is associated with meekness. The person who is meek and humble has an awareness of his limitations and need; he exhibits good will toward man and reverent obedience toward God. Humility and meekness do not imply self-depreciation and spiritlessness but do stand opposed to a false pride. The strongest rebukes which Jesus uttered were directed toward the Pharisees in denunciation of their pride and self-righteousness.

Christian virtues are not limited to the individual, for there is a vital relationship between personal virtue and social virtue. The moral virtues analyzed above have a direct bearing upon Christian social ethics.

BIBLIOGRAPHY: T. Aquinas, *Summa Theologica.* Augustine, *City of God; On the Morals of the Catholic Church.* G. W. Bennett, "A Comparative Study of the Cardinal Virtues in Philosophical Ethics and the Personal Virtues in the Teaching of Jesus and Paul" (1954). N. Hartmann, *Ethics* (1932). S. Kierkegaard, *Works of Love* (1946). A. C. Knudson, *The Principles of Christian Ethics* (1943). L. H. Marshall, *The Challenge of New Testament Ethics* (1948). A. Nygren, *Agape and Eros* (1953). P. Ramsey, *Basic Christian Ethics* (1950). E. F. Scott, *The Ethical Teaching of Jesus* (1949). H. Sidgwick, *Outlines of the History of Ethics* (1949). H. R. Williamson, *The Seven Christian Virtues* (1949). G. WILLIS BENNETT

VISITATION. In Southern Baptist churches, the systematic solicitation of prospects for the purpose of enlisting them in the educational organizations of the local church and, ultimately, in the church itself. The work of the pastor and other Christians in calling on church members and others who because of illness or for other reasons need religious help and counsel should be distinguished from visitation, which in Southern Baptist usage is an enlistment method. The emphasis which Southern Baptists have placed on visitation is an evidence of their conviction that evangelism can be efficiently carried on in an educational context, and, consequently, that the most dependable way of adding to church membership is through the work of the church's various organizations. Success in visitation depends on two factors: the availability of information on prospects and the willingness of church members generally to participate in the work.

Information on prospects is obtained in many ways. The church roll itself contains the names of many persons who are totally or relatively inactive, and who are potential members of the organizations. Each organization has the names of some persons who are not members of others and who are prospects for enlistment. In many cases the name of one member can lead the church to his unenlisted family. Members can supply the names of their friends and acquaintances. Outside the context of its own membership, the church discovers prospects through a general census of all the people living in a given area; through information supplied by various agencies, such as the local Chamber of Commerce, civic welcoming committees, or college registrars, on new arrivals; and through information secured from visitors in church services. In addition, there are other more informal sources of information.

Given information on prospects, the church succeeds in its program of visitation to the extent that it can enlist church members generally in the work. This is best done systematically. Information on each prospect is given to that organization or class working with his particular age group, and the members of that class or organization are encouraged to persist in contacting the prospect until he is enlisted. Various competitive schemes are used to build interest and effort. In addition, many churches promote a specific time, usually one weekday evening, to be devoted especially to visitation. Often there is a fellowship supper held at the church, during which prospects are assigned to those who will do the visiting.

The goal of the visitation program is to enlist every possible potential member in all of the church organizations for which he is eligible, and through them, by personal faith in Christ, in the church itself. To this end all who visit are asked to consider themselves as primarily representatives of the church, and then of their particular organizations. If this program is carried on effectively, the pastor and other vocational church workers are relieved of the major responsibility for this work and can concentrate on difficult cases, or can give themselves to more explicitly spiritual ministries, such as counseling and the visiting of the ill and troubled.

JUDSON BOYCE ALLEN

VOCATION. From *vocare,* "to call,"—and defined as "the special gift of those who, in the church of God, follow with a pure intention the ecclesiastical profession or the evangelical counsels." Another source defines vocation as (1) "The action on the part of God of calling a person to exercise some special function, especially of a spiritual nature, . . . divine influence or guidance towards a definite (esp. religious) career"; (2) "The action on the part of God (or Christ) of calling persons or mankind to a state of salvation or union with Himself"; (3) "One's ordinary occupation, business, or profession."

Within the Christian community there have been two major concepts of vocation. There are those who feel that vocation (or calling) is only for those who are in the direct service of the church.

The monk had a divine call, . . . it was a "conversion," a "second" or "new baptism," and particularly a summons to a special mode of life, which henceforth came to be known in a distinctive sense as a "calling" or "vocation." People engaged in manual or other forms of secular work might be regarded as rendering a divinely appointed service, but they had no "calling" or "vocation" in the proper sense of the term.

"To say that the call to preach is no different than [*sic*] the call to be a Christian lawyer, doctor, teacher, business or professional man is to cheapen the work of God."

There are others who place the emphasis of vocation on a full life and obedience to God in all areas of life. Whatever contributes to human welfare is a sacred calling. Vocation for the Christian is defined, not in terms of titles, ecclesiastical offices, words, or social changes, but in terms of a vital personal relationship to God. Man is created for the glory of God (Isa. 43:7), and all work of any vocation should be done for God's glory (I Cor. 6:20; 10:31). God is at work in history (John 5:17), and each Christian has been assigned his work by God (Gen. 3:23; Mark 13:34). To give God the glory due him, a Christian must interpret his vocation in terms of salvation, discipleship, and witnessing.

Vocation as salvation.—Until man accepts Christ as Saviour, there can be no vocation for him (Rom. 8:9). Salvation is for all (John 3:16; II Peter 3:9), and God, in Christ, is the only source (Acts 4:12; Matt. 26:28). Not only is Christ the source; he seeks man to save him (Luke 19:10). This great salvation (Heb. 2:3) is offered freely as a gift to man (Rom. 6:18–23), who responds in faith (Eph. 2:8), repentance (Acts 2:38), and confession (Rom. 10:10). God not only has power to save (Rom. 1:16) but to keep that which is saved, both in life and throughout eternity (John 10:28–29; 17:12; Rom. 8:35–39).

Vocation as discipleship.—Vocation begins for all Christians in salvation and continues to develop in discipleship. Jesus called disciples to himself early in his ministry (Matt. 4:18; Mark 1:16). This group continued to grow until there were 12 (Matt. 10:1), then 120 (Acts 1:15), and later a multitude (Acts 6:2). Jesus gave the 12 disciples special training concerning his kingdom (Matt. 5–7), his death (Matt. 16:21), and later the making of disciples (evangelization of all nations, Matt. 28:19).

Later in New Testament history we find others called disciples (Acts 9:10, 25–26). Finally at Antioch disciples were called Christians (Acts 11:26). The epistle of Ephesians points to "the glory of the Christian movement in the Christian Church viewed as the progressive life of God in Christ reconciling the world unto himself."

Jesus invited all to come under his yoke and learn of him (Matt. 11:28–29). Those who took the yoke of preaching, teaching, prophesying, and evangelizing had no more vocation than those who performed other tasks.

The New Testament concept of vocation as discipleship for all men has received new emphasis in recent times. "The difference between clergy and laity is one of function, arrangement, and mutual relations, not a difference of fundamental opposites." All Christians today are called to be priests, and there is no division of occupations into secular and sacred. Robert Calhoun emphasizes the Protestant Reformers' protest against the monastic life. The point the Protestant reformers were trying to make was that total faith and obedience may be expressed in whatever place a person may have been called to fill.

God's call to men does not come in one loud shout, to be heard once and heeded or rejected; . . . it comes in a constant process. It bids men be lawyers and doctors, not less than ministers and professors. It demands the construction of homes and the rearing of children. It summons men to the slums of America and the dusty village of India. To catch it in its varied implications, men must be continually responsive.

Vocation as witnessing.—Just as God gives every Christian a vocation in salvation and teaches him through discipleship, he expects him to fulfil his vocation in witnessing. This witness is to be everywhere (Acts 1:8) and to all men (Acts 22:15). It is not confined to those who have an ecclesiastical office, but all Christians are to be witnesses (Acts 8:4). The place or time of witnessing is not important (Acts 16:25; Deut. 6:7); neither are the forms of witnessing. Teaching, preaching, healing, singing, and all other forms of work are witnesses if they are done in the Father's name (John 10:25). One of the most heartening signs of this day is the growing awareness of the New Testament and Protestant idea of the meaning of vocation. The teaching that "all things work together for good to them that love God, to them who are the called [*vocati*—Vulgate] according to his purpose" (Rom. 8:28) is beginning to strengthen the Christian sense of divine vocation in daily work.

BIBLIOGRAPHY: R. L. Calhoun, *God and the Day's Work* (1943). W. O. Carver, *The Glory of God in the Christian Calling* (1949). F. S. Hickman, *Christian Vocation* (1930). E. Trueblood, *Your Other Vocation* (1952); *The Common Ventures of Life* (1949).

VICTOR T. GLASS

VOICE OF TRUTH, THE. A monthly Baptist newspaper, now extinct, published and edited by Alvin Bailey at Winchester, Ill., from July, 1842, to the middle of 1843.

LYNN E. MAY, JR.

W

WACO UNIVERSITY. A coeducational school from its founding, in 1861, at Waco, Tex. It received the patronage of the Baptist General Association and was under the control of Waco Association. In 1881 and again in 1882 proposals were considered by both bodies to transfer the control from the smaller to the larger body. There is no evidence in the records of either body that this transfer was ever legally or officially executed. This matter was pending when Waco University became Baylor University at Waco in 1886, and came under the control of the Baptist General Convention. During its 26 years, Waco University conferred 199 degrees.
RUPERT N. RICHARDSON

WAIT, SAMUEL (b. Washington County, N. Y., Dec. 19, 1789; d. Wake Forest, N. C., July 28, 1867). Educator, denominational leader. Son of Joseph and Martha (Smith) Wait, he was baptized at Middletown, Vt., 1809. From 1816 to 1822, he served as pastor of the Baptist church at Sharon, Mass., where he was ordained in 1818. Wait was student and tutor, Columbian College (now George Washington University, Washington, D. C.), 1822–26, and he received the A.M. degree from Waterville College, Me., 1825. As pastor of First Baptist Church, New Bern, N. C., 1827–30, he proved a key figure in organizing the Baptist State Convention of North Carolina, 1830; and served as its first agent, 1830–32, touring the state in a covered wagon with wife and child at a salary of $1 per day. Wait helped secure the site for a school for ministers and, while still agent for the convention, assisted in getting a charter for an institute at Wake Forest, 1833. On May 10, 1833, he was elected principal of Wake Forest Institute, which began operating in 1834. When the institute was changed to Wake Forest College, he served as its president, 1838–45. He later was pastor of Yanceyville and Trinity churches, Caswell County, N. C., 1846–51; president of Oxford Female Academy, 1851–56; president of board of trustees, Wake Forest College, 1845–66; and helped establish the *Biblical Recorder*. He married Sarah Merriam, June 17, 1818. To them were born two children.

BIBLIOGRAPHY: *Dictionary of American Biography*, Vol. XIX (1936). G. W. Paschal, *History of Wake Forest College* (1935). *The Baptist Encyclopaedia*, Vol. II (1881). *The National Cyclopaedia of American Biography*, Vol. XXI (1931).
GARLAND A. HENDRICKS

WAITE, GEORGE THOMAS (b. Caroline County, Va., Sept. 22, 1883; d. Richmond, Va., May 13, 1936). He was educated at Richmond College, where he was known as an able athlete and a high-minded young man, and at Southern Baptist Theological Seminary. He was married to Evelyn Gardner and after her death to Mildred Davis, who bore him two children. He held pastorates at Herndon, Va., Marion, Ala., and Barton Heights Baptist Church in Richmond, Va., before being elected executive secretary of the Virginia Baptist Board of Missions and Education in 1928.

A man of deep convictions, intense enthusiasm, and far-seeing judgment, he was conspicuous in his leadership of Virginia Baptists in a trying period of financial depression. JACK MANLEY

WAKE FOREST COLLEGE. Established in 1834 at Wake Forest, N. C., and moved to Winston-Salem in 1956, the college, coeducational since 1942, is owned by the Baptist State Convention of North Carolina and governed by a board of trustees elected by the convention. The 36 board members serve four-year terms, with nine chosen each year at the annual convention meeting.

Initial interest in establishment of a Baptist educational institution in North Carolina began in the late 1820's when Samuel Wait (*q.v.*), a Baptist minister who had taught at Columbian College, now George Washington University, came to the state and met Thomas Meredith (*q.v.*), a graduate of the University of Pennsylvania, and John Armstrong (*q.v.*), a graduate of Columbian College at the time Meredith was teaching there. Under the leadership of these men the Baptist state convention was organized in 1830 with one of its primary purposes to provide some means within the state for "the education of young men called of God to the ministry." After two years of campaigning by Wait, who acted as the convention's general agent, the 615-acre farm of Calvin Jones in Wake County was purchased for $2,000 as a school site.

In 1833, following a bitter fight in the state legislature, a charter, limited to 20 years, was granted to provide for "A Literary and Manual Labor Institution in the County of Wake," officially designated as Wake Forest Institute. With Wait elected principal, the school opened in Feb., 1834, and 16 students registered the first day. Within the first few weeks enrolment increased to 48 and before the end of the year to 72. Of this number only four were preachers, and only 18 professed any religion. During the first year when the college was housed in the mansion and other dwellings of the Jones farm together with temporary structures erected at small expense with the help of student labor, plans for the erection of a four-story brick building of Georgian architecture, to house 100 students and take care of other school needs, were approved, and $13,000 in cash and subscriptions was raised for that purpose. Completed in 1837, it was perhaps the best college building in North Carolina, and two brick faculty residences of similar architectural design were built the following year.

When the institute was rechartered as Wake Forest College in 1838, Wait's title changed to president, in which position he served until 1845. Largely because of debt incurred in building costs, however, the college underwent a period of financial difficulties. Subscription pledges went unpaid, patronage decreased, and accumulated debt finally amounted to $20,000. Closing the college appeared imminent, although Wait spent much of his time trying to collect funds. William Hooper, who succeeded Wait as president, resigned in discouragement. During the administration of John Brown White (*q.v.*) from 1848 to 1853, however, conditions began to improve, and student enrolment reached the 100 mark for the first time. In 1850, when subscriptions were large enough to cover the college debt, the trustees began an endowment campaign, which was so successful that over $56,000 was invested in Confederate bonds during the Civil War. However, at the end of the war, from the $53,500 in other bonds which remained, only $13,000 was salvaged. Much of the credit for raising funds was due to the efforts of Washington Manley Wingate (*q.v.*), president from 1854 to 1879, who served as agent for the college for two years preceding his administration.

Under Wingate, Wake Forest began to fulfil its founders' dreams, but at the beginning of the Civil War almost all of the students volunteered for the army, and only 30 enrolled in the fall of 1861. In 1862 the college suspended operation, and the property was later turned over for use as a Confederate hospital. Led by the venerable Wait, the trustees authorized the reopening of the college on Jan. 15, 1866, and the only compensation they could offer a faculty member was the amount derived from student fees plus the almost negligible income from the little endowment. Two former professors, William Royall and W. G. Simmons, agreed to undertake the task of reopening the school on these terms. Royall's son, William Bailey Royall (*q.v.*), joined them, as did Wingate a little later after completing arrangements to leave several pastorates. Another faculty member whom they invited to return decided the situation was too hopeless and declined.

In the session which began in Jan., 1866, 51 students registered, 17 of whom were collegiate and 34 preparatory. No one who seriously wanted an education was turned away. Despite dire poverty and hardships of reconstruction days, Wingate succeeded in increasing endowment to $40,000 before the end of his presidency and in constructing one, and projecting another, new building.

Three characteristics, identified with Wake Forest more than others perhaps, were evident during the postwar period of Wingate's administration. One, the power of the college to attract scholarly teachers who have devoted their entire lives to Wake Forest, has made possible a continuity of policy, tradition, standards, and atmosphere due to remarkably little faculty turnover. A second characteristic was the large percentage of sons of alumni who enrolled, an indication of the loyalty of former students, and this has been as important as faculty loyalty in the building of the college. Composition of the student body after the war indicated a third characteristic, when predominant enrolment, which had formerly come from counties where slaves had been numerous, shifted to counties primarily composed of an independent middle class, the class which has been the mainstay of the college ever since. This fact has apparently accounted for the democratic atmosphere on the campus, recognized even by visitors and newcomers.

The classical, liberal arts curriculum of the college changed little before the administration of Charles Elisha Taylor (*q.v.*) from 1884 to 1905. Taylor expanded the usefulness of the college by organizing and increasing the academic departments, enlarging the curriculum, and establishing professional schools, the first of which was the school of law in 1894, followed by the school of medicine in 1902, now named the Bowman Gray School of Medicine of Wake Forest College. Taylor also doubled the number of college buildings, beautified the campus, raised endowment to $200,000, and increased the teaching staff from six to 17 members, two of whom were Benjamin F. Sledd (*q.v.*) and George Washington Paschal (*q.v.*). One of the friends of the college added by Taylor was Jabez A. Bostwick of New York City, who made generous contributions to the college. By the terms of Bostwick's will, endowment was increased in 1923 by stocks valued at about $1,500,000. During Taylor's administration enrolment increased from 145 to 313, and Taylor's successor, William Louis Poteat (*q.v.*), president from 1905 to 1927, continued a program of development and progress. New buildings and facilities were acquired, endowment was increased, student enrolment enlarged, and the curriculum strengthened. Wake Forest's distinction during this administration, however, was due to Poteat's defense of academic freedom to teach the knowledge acquired as a result of sound scholarship. With the finest scientific training afforded in America and Germany, Poteat was also a true Christian and at the time of his death was president of the Baptist state convention.

As Poteat's successor, the trustees elected Francis Pendleton Gaines of Furman University, the first nonalumnus president since 1854. An influential Baptist denominational leader, a literary scholar, and a popular speaker, Gaines entered upon his work with youthful enthusiasm. But the years of his administration, 1927–30, were difficult ones for the college, with a drop in student enrolment and a reduction in faculty staff. Although Gaines took drastic steps to solve these problems, in 1930 he accepted the presidency of Washington and Lee University.

Thurman Delna Kitchin, dean of the medical school and an alumnus of the college, followed Gaines as president in 1930 and served until 1950. Kitchin entered office under adverse conditions, aggravated in one of the early years of his administration by a series of mysterious fires on the campus which resulted in damage to some buildings and the complete loss of two of them: the administration building and the chapel. Under these unpropitious circumstances, Kitchin adopted a bold policy in launching a rebuilding and enlargement program which resulted in the construction of eight new buildings and an athletic stadium, student enrolment at a peak of 2,026 in 1949, and the addition of the schools of Religion (1946) and Business Administration (1949). The Bowman Gray Foundation of Winston-Salem was offered to the college in 1939 on condition that the two-year medical school located at Wake Forest move to Winston-Salem and operate as a four-year school in conjunction with the Baptist hospital there. When this offer was accepted by the trustees, the Bowman Gray School of Medicine began functioning in Winston-Salem in 1941.

More revolutionary than the removal of the medical school to Winston-Salem in Kitchin's administration was the decision to move the entire college there. In 1946 the Z. Smith Reynolds Foundation of Winston-Salem offered an annual grant in perpetuity from the foundation income of $350,000 (increased to $500,000 in 1955) to Wake Forest on condition that the college move to Winston-Salem. As a site for the new campus and a further inducement to move, Charles H. Babcock and his wife proposed to give the college part of the Reynolds estate. The trustees of the college accepted the foundation's offer, and the Baptist state convention, meeting in special session at Greensboro, approved the acceptance. Following the decision to move, the campus and other properties owned by the college at Wake Forest were sold to the Southern Baptist Convention for the establishment of a seminary, which opened its first session at Wake Forest in Sept., 1951, as Southeastern Baptist Theological Seminary. Before his resignation, Kitchin saw a campaign launched to raise building funds for the new college, Jens F. Larsen employed as architect to design the buildings, and a master plan for the campus adopted.

Actual building of the new college at Winston-Salem began under Kitchin's successor, Harold Wayland Tribble, who came to Wake Forest in 1950 from the presidency of Andover Newton Theological School. On Oct. 19, 1951, with an address delivered by the President of the United States, Harry S. Truman, ground was broken for the construction of the first building, the college chapel. During ground-breaking ceremonies, Babcock presented Hubert E. Olive, chairman of the board of trustees, a deed to the property to be occupied by the college. Construction work proceeded rapidly after the groundbreaking, and when the move was completed in 1956, 24 of the proposed buildings had been built at a cost of over $19,000,000.

The course of study at Wake Forest is designed to provide substantial mastery of some one field in the liberal arts or sciences, along with an intelligent acquaintance with allied subjects, while the professional schools, medicine, law, business, and religion, provided for concentration in their respective fields.

Among distinguished alumni of the college are poet John Charles McNeill, Shakespearian scholar Joseph Quincy, Greek scholar and lexicographer Archibald Thomas Robertson (*q.v.*). missionary Matthew Tyson Yates (*q.v.*), bibliophile, publisher, and college president Charles Lee Smith, congressional leader Claude Kitchin, ministers Amzi Clarence Dixon (*q.v.*) and J. D. Hufham (*q.v.*), editor and author Gerald White Johnson, author and college dean Roger Philip McCutcheon, United States senators Josiah William Bailey (*q.v.*) and Joseph Melville Broughton (*q.v.*), federal judges Isaac Melson Meekins, Johnson Jay Hayes, and Edwin Yates Webb, and Latin scholar Hubert McNeill Poteat.

Among the 134,926 books (1955) in the Wake Forest College libraries are several collections, of which the Baptist collection of books, manuscripts, unpublished minutes, periodicals, and newspapers, and the Charles Lee Smith Collection of rare works and first editions, are the most significant.

Wake Forest College is a member of the Southern Association of Colleges and Secondary Schools, the Association of American Colleges, and the Atlantic Coast Conference. The School of Law is a member of the Association of American Law Schools and is on the approved list of the Council on Legal Education of the American Bar Association. The Bowman Gray School of Medicine is a member of the Association of American Medical Colleges, and is on the approved list of the Council on Medical Education of the American Medical Association. The School of Business Administration is a provisional associate member of the American Association of Collegiate Schools of Business. The college has chapters of the principal national social and professional fraternities.

College endowment in 1956 was $3,420,491 (book value); funds invested in buildings totaled $19,500,000, and equipment value, $403,-332. The school operated on a budget of $2,250,-000 in 1956, when its enrolment was 2,500. A total of 27,199 students have attended Wake Forest. Sources of income include the Baptist state convention, endowment, student fees, gifts, and auxiliary enterprises.

BIBLIOGRAPHY: G. W. Paschal, *History of Wake Forest College,* 3 vols. (1935–1943).

FORREST W. CLONTS

WALDENSES. A movement, possibly representing the coalescence of earlier protesting groups, which is apparently named for Peter Waldo (died before A.D. 1218). The group stressed apostolic poverty. They ran afoul of the papacy, not for heresy but for refusing to obey the pope's ban against their lay preaching. Entry into the early movement seems to have been by renunciation of one's property and worldly vocation, and after the dissolution of marriage ties which would hinder one's life of "perfect" gospel obedience. The movement changed greatly in the course of time as it was blended with other movements. Brief characterization of its doctrine is therefore impossible. While there is continuity between medieval and contemporary Waldensianism, the movement was altered in its whole character by the Reformation. Since the 16th century it has been clearly an evangelical and not merely an anti-Roman group.

BIBLIOGRAPHY: E. Comba, *The Waldenses of Italy* (1889). E. Davison, *Forerunners of St. Francis* (1927). *New Schaff-Herzog Encyclopedia of Religious Knowledge,* XII (1950).

T. D. PRICE

WALES, BAPTISTS IN. *The beginnings.*—In Wales the Baptists were of differing types and commenced as follows: (1) About 1633 a bilingual church was formed at Olchon, where the English County of Hereford and the Welsh counties of Brecknock and Monmouth meet. (2) Mixed Communion Particular Baptists, with their pastor William Thomas, worshiped with Congregationalists at Llanfaches, South Monmouthshire, for a period after 1639. (3) Strict General Baptist churches were formed in 1646, in Radnorshire, Montgomeryshire, and Brecknockshire, by Hugh Evans. (4) Open Communion Particular Baptists, followers of Vavasor Powell, later appeared in the same counties. (5) A strong Particular Baptist church was founded, Oct., 1649, at Ilston, near Swansea, by John Miles. About 1663 Miles, with some of his followers, fled to America and formed the old church of Rehoboth. (6) Another community of Baptists, members of Nantwich Church, Cheshire, England, settled at Nantybelan, North Wales, about 1655.

Associations.—All communities of Baptists, with a few exceptions, in time joined the Particular Baptist Section. John Miles established in 1650 an association which was suppressed during the persecution period (1660–88). Resuscitated after the "Glorious Revolution" of 1688, this association was attached for 10 years to an English association. The Welsh Baptists formed a separate association in 1700. In 1791 it was divided into three associations and in 1832 into 10. Later three English associations were formed.

Religious equality.—Welsh Baptists emphasized religious equality, with Morgan John Rhys being the foremost advocate. Rhys, who fled to America in 1794, denounced oppression of every kind in his *Welsh Magazine* (1793–94) and in the *Western Sky,* the periodical of the Cambria Colony which he founded in 1796.

Colleges.—Four Baptist theological colleges were founded in Wales. Trosnant Pontypool was established in 1732; Abergavenny was begun in 1807, moved to Pontypool in 1836, and moved to Cardiff in 1893; Haverfordwest, begun in 1839, moved to Aberystwyth in 1894; Llangollen, established in 1862, moved to Bangor in 1892. Aberystwyth College was closed in 1899, and its endowments and students were divided between Cardiff and Bangor colleges.

Several Welsh Baptists became presidents of English Baptist theological colleges. Some founded schools in England and in the United States. Others served as educators in India, the Congo, and Jamaica.

Missionaries.—Many Welsh Baptists have volunteered for missionary work in foreign lands, and there are some 17 on the mission field today. The Baptist Missionary Society is supported by both Welsh and English Baptists.

Literature.—John Jenkins wrote the first *Commentary on the Bible* in the Welsh language (three volumes); John Jones and others published a *Bible Dictionary* (three volumes). Others wrote historical works of a high standard.

Periodicals published by Welsh Baptists are as follows: *Seren Cymru* (weekly), *Seren Gomer* (quarterly), *The Crusader* (monthly), *Y Seren Fach* (monthly), *Y Trafodion* (yearly historical transactions), *Llawlyfr Undeb Bedyddwyr Cymru* (a history of the churches in the locality where the union holds its annual meeting), *Y Dyddiadur* (a diary, published annually, containing statistics with reference to the churches, associations, union meetings, etc.).

Other achievements.—Several Welsh Baptists have achieved the distinction of having been crowned or chaired bards at the annual Eisteddfod (Welsh National Competitive Festival). Others have gained prizes for singing, elocution, literature, drama, choral conducting, etc.

Preachers famed for their eloquence have been numerous from the eras of Vavasor Powell and Christmas Evans. Many Welsh Baptists have been members of Parliament, and several are today members of the House of Commons. David Lloyd George, M.P. (afterward Earl Lloyd George), became Prime Minister.

Doctrinal Disputations.—During the 18th and part of the 19th centuries, the denomination was perturbed and rent by disputations concerning Calvinism, Arianism, Sabellianism, Unitarianism, Arminianism, Sandemanianism, etc. Today no disputations exist, and Welsh Baptists are in general open-minded, evangelical Calvinists.

Organizations and funds.—Organizations and funds, with the date of beginning, are as follows: Building Fund (1862); The Welsh Baptist Union (1866); Annuity Fund (1871); Temperance Society (1870); Sunday School Union (1887);

Assurance (1888); Century Fund (1901); Historical Society (1901); Young Baptists Union (1905); Welsh Zenana Auxiliary (1905–06); Ilston Press and Bookshop (1912); Morning Star Order (1929); Women's League (1933); Relief and Reconstruction Funds (1936, 1944). Many of the associations conducted home missions as early as 1832, but since 1921 this work has been continued by the Sustentation Organisation.

STATISTICS

Associations	13
Churches, 1934	949
Churches, 1954	951
Communicants, 1934	123,136
Communicants, 1954	100,195
Sunday school scholars, 1934	123,033
Sunday school scholars, 1954	72,737
Baptisms, 1954	1,985

The decline in the number of members, scholars, and baptisms is attributed to the materialistic outlook following World War II.

WILLIAM JOSEPH RHYS

WALKER, WILLIAM (b. near Cross Keys, Union County, S. C., May 6, 1809; d. Spartanburg, S. C., 1875). Singing-school teacher and author. His father emigrated from Wales in the 18th century. Through his mother's family he was related to the general, T. J. (Stonewall) Jackson. His family moved to Spartanburg, S. C., when he was 18 years of age. As a lad he joined the local Baptist church and at an early age manifested an extraordinary interest in music. Known as "Singing Billy" Walker, he traveled throughout several Southern states holding singing schools. He compiled and published the *Southern Harmony* (1835), *Southern and Western Harmonist* (1845), *Christian Harmony* (1866), and *Fruits and Flowers* (1869). The *Southern Harmony* was widely used by *fa-sol-la* singers throughout the Southern states. Later editions appeared in 1847, 1849, and 1854, and it was second only to the *Sacred Harp* in its popularity and influence. Like the *Sacred Harp*, the major portion of this material was composed of folk hymns, religious ballads, revival spirituals, and fuguing pieces.

WILLIAM J. REYNOLDS

WALLACE, OATES CHARLES SYMONDS (b. Canaan, Nova Scotia, Nov. 28, 1856; d. Baltimore, Md., Aug. 29, 1947). Teacher, preacher, writer, denominational leader. Son of William John and Rachel (Witter) Wallace, he was baptized at the age of 16 at Greenwich, Nova Scotia, where he was teaching. Entering Christian work on a student mission field, Wallace at 18 became pastor of the Baptist church at Chelmsford Center, Mass., where he served for two and one-half years. He was educated at Worcester Academy, Acadia University, and Newton Theological Seminary, and was given degrees by Acadia University, McMaster University, and Queens University, all Canadian institutions, and by Mercer University in Macon, Ga.

Ordained at First Church, Lawrence, Mass., in 1885, Wallace served as pastor there until Jan., 1891, when he began his pastorate at Bloor Street Church, Toronto. In 1895 he became chancellor of McMaster University, Toronto, and served in this position for 10 years as professor, counselor, and administrator.

Re-entering the pastorate, Wallace served in the First Baptist Church, Lowell, Mass., First Baptist Church, Baltimore, Md., and Westmount Church, Montreal, Canada. At the age of 65 he became pastor of Eutaw Place Church, Baltimore, and remained for 15 years until his retirement as pastor emeritus in Jan., 1936. Blind in the latter years of his life, he made his last public appearance in 1940, when he gave an address of welcome to the Southern Baptist Convention meeting in Baltimore. He died in Baltimore, and his body was returned to Canada for interment in Mt. Pleasant Cemetery, Toronto.

Wallace was the author of several books, including *What Baptists Believe* and *Pastor and People.*

BIBLIOGRAPHY: C. J. Cameron, *The Life Story of Oates Charles Symonds Wallace* (n.d.). *The Maryland Baptist* (Sept. 1947). W. H. BRANNOCK

WALLACE, WILLIAM LINDSEY (b. Knoxville, Tenn., Jan. 17, 1908; d. Wuchow, China, Feb. 10, 1951). Medical missionary to China. Wallace received his M.D. degree from the University of Tennessee Medical College. He was appointed to China in 1935 to serve as surgeon at the Stout Memorial Hospital, Wuchow, where he continued to work during World War II and the Communist invasion. In Dec., 1950, a gun was planted in his room by Communists, and he was subsequently arrested. He died the following February and was buried in an old Christian cemetery near Wuchow. IONE GRAY

WALLACE MEMORIAL HOSPITAL, PUSAN. See KOREA, MISSION IN.

WALLBURG ACADEMY. See LIBERTY PIEDMONT INSTITUTE.

WALLER, CALVIN BERNARD (b. Jeraldstown, Tenn., July 30, 1874; d. Little Rock, Ark., Dec. 6, 1944). He was the son of William A. and Sarah C. (Wilcox) Waller. He was educated at Carson-Newman College, Jefferson City, Tenn., and was given the D.D. degree by Union University, Jackson, Tenn. He married Leila Mae Reed, June 21, 1898. They had three children, Anna, Grace, and Dorothy. He was ordained Jan. 6, 1896, and was a pastor in Elizabethton, Chattanooga, and Knoxville, Tenn.; Asheville, N. C.; Portland, Ore.; Winchester, Ky.; and Little Rock, Ark. (Second Baptist Church), where he was pastor emeritus when he died. He is the author of *The Blessed Life.* He held many denominational and civic positions, including these: president of the Arkansas Baptist State Convention and of its executive board, chairman of the debt-paying committee in 1936, member of the centennial commission of Arkansas, and chairman of the state clergymen's committee of the Arkansas centennial commission. Waller preached with power and pathos, and was an ardent premillennialist. MRS. A. B. HILL

WALLER, JOHN (b. Spotsylvania County, Va., Dec. 23, 1741; d. near Greenwood, S. C., July 4, 1802). Converted opponent of Baptists, pastor, evangelist. Educated for law, Waller manifested great talent for satirical wit and later became a notorious and profane gambler. A particularly zealous opponent of the Baptists, he was a member of the grand jury which indicted the first Baptist preacher imprisoned for preaching in Virginia and was regarded by Baptists as the ringleader of the confusion and opposition which befell them. Following a dramatic conversion experience, he was baptized in 1767 and ordained to become pastor of Lower Spotsylvania Church—later known as Waller's Church—in Spotsylvania County, Va., on June 20, 1770. He was elected clerk of the first association of Separate Baptists in Virginia in 1771 and later held pastorates in South Carolina, moving there from Virginia in 1793.

A man of strong will and one who never dodged controversy, Waller was recognized in his later years as an exemplary preacher and, ironically, became one of the most severely persecuted of the early Baptist preachers in Virginia. He was stoned, publicly whipped, maligned, and imprisoned four times for a total of 113 days. As a result of a controversy occasioned by his Arminian views, he declared himself as an independent Baptist and withdrew from his local association about 1776, taking his church with him. In 1787, however, he returned to the association, and that same year a widespread revival broke out under his preaching. During a ministry of 35 years, Waller baptized more than 2,000 persons and assisted in ordaining 27 ministers and constituting 18 churches.

In his last sermon he spoke until he was completely exhausted and had to be carried home. He died a short time later, at 62 years of age, and is buried in a family plot near Greenwood, S. C. JACK MANLEY

WALLER, JOHN LIGHTFOOT (b. Woodford County, Ky., Nov. 23, 1809; d. Louisville, Ky., Oct. 10, 1854). Pastor, editor, denominational leader, Christian statesman. Born into a family of Baptist preachers, Waller was the son of Edmund Waller (1775–1842), who served churches in Kentucky, a nephew of George Waller (1777–1860), who was the first moderator of the General Association of Baptists in Kentucky, and a grandson of William Edmund Waller, who came from Virginia and served churches in Kentucky. Waller was educated at home by his older brothers, at the Nicholasville Academy, and by private study of the textbooks used at Transylvania University. In 1852 Madison University (New York) conferred on him the LL.D. degree.

Waller was among those who supported the Kentucky Baptist Convention (1832–37), the first effort of Kentucky Baptists to co-operate on a statewide basis. He took an active part in the organization of the General Association of Baptists in Kentucky, serving as clerk of the convention which formed it and as the first corresponding secretary (1837–39). He was general agent of the general association for two years (1841–43) and moderator for one year (1852). Waller was for several years editor of the *Baptist Banner* (1835–41; 1850–51); he was founder and editor of the *Western Baptist Review* 1845–51); he was editor of the *Western Recorder* (1851–54); and he was founder and editor of the *Christian Repository* (1852–54). Leader of the movement to organize the Bible Revision Association, he was elected president when the association was constituted in 1852 and served until his death. In 1849 he was elected a member of the Kentucky constitutional convention as a delegate from Woodford County. Two pamphlets were published by him: *The Reformation, or Protestant Societies not Christian Churches, and Baptists not Protestants* (1855) and *Letters to a Reformer, Alias Campbellite* (1835). He was also author of one book, *Open Communion shown to be Unscriptural and Deleterious . . . to which is added a History of Infant Baptism* (1859). He contributed the section, "Historical Sketch of the Baptist Church," in Lewis Collins' *Historical Sketches of Kentucky* (1847).

LEO T. CRISMON

WALNE, THOMAS JEFFERSON (b. Halifax County, Va., Oct. 3, 1838; d. Dallas, Tex., July 2, 1905). Pastor of the church in Vicksburg, Miss., for 10 years, Walne was also unsalaried Sunday school missionary. While serving as first corresponding secretary of the Mississippi state mission board, 1874–83, Walne chose as the board's motto, "A Baptist Church and a Baptist Sunday School in every city, town, village and neighborhood within the territory of this Convention." Walne continued his effort to advance the denominational program in all areas until, because of broken health, he was forced to resign his secretaryship in 1883.

BIBLIOGRAPHY: J. L. Boyd, *A Popular History of Baptists in Mississippi* (1930). L. S. Foster, *Mississippi Baptist Preachers* (1895). J. A. Hackett, "A Memorial," *The Baptist* (Aug. 31, 1905).

C. B. HAMLET III

WALNUT CREEK SCHOOL. Located at Walnut Creek, N. C., under Baptist control in 1873. J. White directed the school, and French Broad Association endorsed it. D. L. SMILEY

WAR AND PEACE. While historic attitudes of professing Christians toward war and peace have ranged all the way from absolute pacifism to the idea of "the holy war" and the propagation of Christianity by the sword, the general point of view of Southern Baptists, as reflected in their Convention resolutions, beginning with 1861, may be said to be a mediating position, varying to some extent with the current national and international situation. Always Southern Baptists have condemned war in principle and have held up peace as a Christian ideal, but during periods of national crisis, they have reluctantly admitted defensive warfare as a last resort of practical necessity.

Previous to the Civil War, the Southern Baptist Convention records contain practically no references to the subject of war and peace. But with the coming of the conflict of 1861–65, we find the Convention expressing itself on the matter.

In the 1863 meeting a resolution declared that "the events of the past two years have only confirmed the conviction . . . that the war which has been forced upon us is, on our part, just and necessary." But there was also a statement calling for "penitence, humiliation and a hearty turning to God" since "our sins have deserved the terrible calamities that God has sent upon us."

In 1861, just after the beginning of the conflict, the Convention had said, "God forbid that we should so far forget the spirit of Jesus, as to suffer malice and vindictiveness to insinuate themselves into our hearts."

In 1895 a resolution was adopted "petitioning the governments of the world to resort to arbitration instead of war for the settlement of all disputes." This resolution also favored the establishment of a world court. The Convention in 1911 commended President Taft for proposing to England an agreement to arbitrate questions of disagreement rather than go to war.

In July, 1914, World War I began. The following May the Convention commended President Wilson for his "firm stand . . . for the ideals of peace." But on Apr. 6, 1917, the United States entered the war. Just a little over a month later, a Convention resolution said:

> It is of special significance to Baptists that the issues involved in the great war concern fundamental human rights and liberties. The cause of democracy is at stake. . . . Deeply as we deplore war, ardently as we longed and labored to avert or avoid it, we may be cheered and heartened in remembering that we are moved in entering it, neither by lust nor hate, but by the love of humanity.

During the years between the two world wars, a time which might be called the great era of pacifism, many sessions of the Convention passed resolutions condemning war, supporting disarmament, favoring arbitration of all international disputes, approving the World Court, and urging the entrance of the United States into it. From 1925 to 1939, almost no meeting of the Convention failed to pass some resolution or report condemning war and the war spirit.

However, by the time of the 1940 meeting, the dark shadows of World War II were casting their menacing shadows over the world. Reports and resolutions that year condemned the imperialistic purposes of Japan, Germany, and Russia and, with reference to the nations defending themselves against aggression, stated "That while we acknowledge the right of self-defense, our utter abhorrence of war and its attendant evils compels us to voice the conviction that even a defensive war should be waged only as a last resort." The right of conscientious objection was recognized, and churches were urged not to become agents of war propaganda. Resolutions of the Convention in 1941 again declared abhorrence of war but went on to say that "some things . . . are worth defending even unto death," and significantly urged our government "to quicken rather than slacken all measures needed to strengthen the defenses of the Western Hemisphere against all kinds of aggression." That was in May, 1941. In December of that year, the Japanese made their attack on Pearl Harbor, and the United States was shortly in all-out war.

The 1942 Convention declared that "while we did not seek the war, there seems to be no honorable way out of it except to fight it through to a conclusion. All we hold dear as a Christian people is at stake." But it also recognized that back of the war was sin, and individuals and nations were alike called to deep searching of heart and penitence.

In 1945 a Convention committee on world peace issued a statement listing six attitudes and principles "which it is believed make for a righteous and lasting peace": (1) no isolation, (2) a democratic world, (3) a world organized for peace, (4) Christian race relations, (5) equal economic opportunity, and (6) religious liberty. These principles were given wide publicity.

In 1946, the war having ended, the Convention approved the idea of the United Nations Organization and went on record as opposing universal and compulsory military training. More recent resolutions have reiterated and re-emphasized the Convention's stand on these points.

The report of the Social Service Commission in 1952 listed six Positive Steps Toward Peace in Our Time: (1) Redouble our efforts to reconcile men with God. (2) Do not tolerate any complacency about war. (3) Combat a mood of hysteria or blind hatred. (4) Reject fatalism about war. (5) Oppose primary reliance on military strategy to meet Communist aggression. (6) Press for positive programs which have immediate possibilities for peace and justice. In its 1955 report the Christian Life Commission gave as the primary factor in the final attainment of world peace the preaching of the gospel among all people. HOWARD P. COLSON

WARD, JESSE LAWRENCE (b. Deep Creek Community, Wise County, Tex., Sept. 24, 1866; d. Decatur, Tex., July 3, 1952). College president, Bible professor. Educated in public schools and at Baylor University, Ward was converted at 13 years of age and joined the Baptist church at Springtown when he was 21. In 1892 he retired from a prosperous mercantile business to become pastor of four rural churches and later served as pastor of the Baptist church of Itasca and First Baptist Church, Decatur, Tex. His pastoral ministry was characterized by evangelistic zeal, missionary enthusiasm, and special emphasis on the stewardship of money. Secretary of the Baptist State Education Commission from 1904 to 1909, Ward served as president and Bible teacher of Decatur Baptist College for 43 years. In 1897, in conjunction with James Milton Carroll (*q.v.*) and George Washington Truett (*q.v.*), Ward persuaded the Baptist state convention to purchase property of Northwest Texas Baptist College at Decatur, which had been sold for debt, and establish Decatur Baptist Junior College. In 1898 the college property consisted of eight acres of land and two buildings, a stone administration building and a wooden dormitory. During Ward's administration the campus was expanded to 100 acres, and by personal efforts he secured for the college an endowment of $223,000 before his retirement.

BIBLIOGRAPHY: J. M. Carroll, *History of Texas Baptists* (1923); *Texas Centennial History of Texas Baptists* (1936). R. E. BELL

WARDER, WALTER (b. Fauquier County, Va., 1787; d. Missouri, Apr., 1836). Evangelist, preacher. The fourth son of Joseph Warder, he came to Kentucky at the age of 20 where he immediately began teaching school, although his own education was limited. He and his brother William covenanted to seek earnestly for the salvation of their souls in the winter of 1806–07; and, upon William's return from Virginia, they were baptized into the fellowship of Dripping Springs Church in Apr., 1807. On Dec. 8, 1808, he married Mary Maddox. Ordained a Baptist minister in 1811, he became pastor of Dover Church, Barren County, for three years.

In 1814 he accepted a call to Mays Lick Church, Mason County, where his influence was felt throughout the whole of Bracken Association. In 1829 his church is said to have had over 800 members, probably the largest in Kentucky. In 1828 he alone baptized 485 into its fellowship. In 1830 Mays Lick reasserted the doctrines on which it was constituted by a vote of 189 to 100, losing by this action 383 members to the Campbell movement. The strife of the next few years was bitter, but Warder stood firm and labored on unfalteringly until his strength failed. In Mar., 1836, he went to Missouri to regain his health but died the following month. VICTOR MANTIPLY

WARE, EDWIN OSWALD (b. West Berea, Powell County, Ky., Oct. 29, 1853; d. Alexandria, La., Dec. 6, 1933). Pastor, administrator, educator, editor. Ware received his education in the Kentucky public schools, the University of Kentucky, and the Southern Baptist Theological Seminary, Louisville, from which he was graduated in 1887. Migrating to Louisiana in 1888, Ware became pastor of the Baptist church at Cheneyville and engaged in mission work in the Louisiana Association. In 1892 he became corresponding secretary of the state mission board, where he served for 14 years. After serving for one year as financial agent of Louisiana College at Pineville, he became that institution's first president. When it appeared as though the young senior college would have to close its doors for lack of funds, Ware mortgaged his own home to secure the needed resources.

In 1910 Ware was elected secretary of the state mission board, serving in that capacity until Nov., 1912. In 1913 he purchased the *Baptist Chronicle* and for six trying years was its owner-editor. He became general missionary under the state mission board in 1919 and served until his death in 1933. Ware served Louisiana Baptists in numerous other denominational activities. He was president of the Louisiana Baptist Convention in 1892, 1922, and 1923. In 1893 he offered to the convention a resolution which culminated a few years later in the establishment of Louisiana College. During his first term as state missions secretary, he established churches in north and central Louisiana, helped execute proposals for an orphanage near Monroe and a hospital in Alexandria, and suggested a plan of "systematic beneficence," which was the first co-operative plan of systematic giving in the state.

In an editorial tribute to Ware, the following lines were written by F. W. Tinnin, editor of the *Baptist Message,* Dec. 7, 1933:

> He was a pioneer of pioneers in the early days of our organized work in Louisiana. He gave Louisiana Baptists 45 years of his life. As pastor, secretary, editor, educator and missionary, the footsteps of E. O. Ware were left in every section of the state.

W. A. BROWN

WARREN, EBENEZER WILLIS (b. Conecuh County, Ala., May 16, 1820; d. Macon, Ga., Nov. 26, 1893). Minister. The son of Kittrell Warren, he was reared in Houston County, Ga. Warren studied under his father and later received a liberal education in English and Latin at Minerva Academy. He taught school one year near West Point, then studied law in Perry, Ga. Admitted to the bar in 1843, he practiced his profession for five years. He was baptized in 1845 and preached as a layman. He was licensed in 1848 and was ordained at a session of the Bethel Association, Nov., 1849, abandoning a lucrative law practice to enter the ministry. His chief pastorates were Cuthbert, 1853–55; Lumpkin, 1855–58; First Church, Macon, 1859–71, 1879–91; First Church, Atlanta, 1871–76; First Church, Richmond, Va., 1876–79; Tattnall Square, Macon, Ga., 1891–93.

Warren received the honorary D.D. degree from Mercer University in 1875. He was a trustee of the institution (1860–76; 1879–90) when the question of removal from Penfield was considered, and it was largely through his influence that Macon donated bonds and land to induce the Georgia Baptist convention to move the university to that city. EDWIN S. DAVIS

WARREN, JAMES THOMAS (b. Corinth, Miss., Dec. 5, 1884; d. Jan. 16, 1948). Baptist deacon, educator, and college president. He was married to Martha Vincent of Manchester, Tenn., Dec. 26, 1912. There were no children. In 1921 and 1926 he received the B.S. and M.A. degrees from George Peabody College, Nashville, Tenn., and in 1929 the LL.D. degree from Georgetown College, Georgetown, Ky. He attended Columbia University in 1912, the University of Tennessee in 1916, and taught at Peabody College in 1921 and 1926. He was president of Hall-Moody Junior College, 1917–26, and vice-president and teacher at Tennessee College for Women, 1926–27.

From 1927 until his death he was president of Carson-Newman College, Jefferson City, Tenn. Under his administration, Carson-Newman was admitted to membership in the Southern Association of Colleges in 1927 and in 1928 to the Association of American Colleges. Warren served his denomination and church in various capacities—as associational moderator, as president of the Tennessee Baptist Convention, as vice-president of the Southern Baptist Convention, and for several years as a member of the board of trustees of Southern Baptist Theological Seminary. He was a popular speaker and could be found almost any Sunday filling the pulpit of some church in East Tennessee. His last engagement was at Calvary Baptist Church, Knoxville, Tenn., on Jan. 4, 1948. JAMES F. BREWER

WARREN FEMALE INSTITUTE. Established at Oxford, Miss., about 1880 and chartered in 1882. With Mrs. C. A. Lancaster, a "rigid" disciplinarian, as principal, the school enrolled 96 in 1885, but declined in the 1890's. J. L. BOYD

WARREN MEMORIAL HOSPITAL, HWANGHSIEN. See CHINA, MISSION IN.

WARSAW HIGH SCHOOL. Located at Warsaw, Duplin County, N. C., under Baptist control. The school opened on Sept. 20, 1856, with Solomon J. Faison as principal. In 1861 the principal was Isham Royall. Eastern Association held the title to the school property.

During the Reconstruction era financial difficulties caused the association to lease the school to principals to make what they could of it. In 1885 the building was entirely destroyed by fire, but in 1887 a new building was constructed. The school closed for lack of support in 1896, but it was reopened in 1905. In 1906 the school was sold to the Warsaw Special Tax District for $100, a fraction of its value. Other properties belonging to the association were deeded to Dell School. D. L. SMILEY

WASHBURN, ALBERT G. (b. near Mobile, Ala., Mar. 14, 1845; d. McAlester, Okla., Oct. 18, 1918). Confederate soldier, lawyer, physician, pioneer Baptist preacher, missionary, and Masonic leader. Reared in Alabama, Washburn served under General Joseph Wheeler in the Confederate Army during the Civil War (1863–65). Soon after the war, he moved to Arkansas, took a medical course, and practiced medicine for a time. A few years later, however, he changed to law. In 1890 he was Grand Master of the Grand Lodge, A.F. and A.M., in Arkansas. About the same time he entered the Baptist ministry, and in 1893 settled in Indian Territory. Active for a few years as a pastor and denominational leader, he devoted most of his time to Indian mission work, serving under the Baptist General Convention of Indian Territory beginning in 1900. He led in the consolidation of the Baptist General Association and Baptist Convention of Indian Territory in 1900. After the organization of the Baptist General Convention of Oklahoma on Feb. 1, 1907, he was elected by that convention as superintendent of Indian Missions and served until June, 1917. On Nov. 6, 1913, he introduced in the convention the Washburn Resolution, which abolished the specially appointed education commission and placed education under control of the convention's board of directors. The resolution further provided for the appointment of an educational missionary to collect funds and remit them to the convention; these funds would be disbursed by the superintendent of missions, who would report to the convention. The resolution also provided for all Christian education campaigns to be controlled by the board, demanded strict adherence to previous convention action correlating all Baptist education in Oklahoma under one coeducational institution of senior college grade, and called for stringent restrictions on the encumbrance of any school property in sale or indebtedness without the board's approval. The board was to report annually to the convention on all Christian education proceedings. Following his resignation from the Indian work, Washburn served as enlistment secretary for the Baptist General Convention of Oklahoma until his death. J. M. GASKIN

WASHINGTON, D. C. See DISTRICT OF COLUMBIA.

WASHINGTON ASSOCIATION INSTITUTE. Opened at Linton (near Darien) Ga., early in 1858, with Carlos W. Stevens as principal. Due to declining patronage, the trustees leased the school to Thomas J. Adams and Ivey W. Duggan, but canceled the lease in 1875. Patronage continued to decline in the 1880's; some of the buildings were burned in 1895, and the school was deeded to Hancock County for a public school in 1897. ARTHUR JACKSON

WATAUGA ACADEMY. Located at Boone, Watauga County, N. C. Also known as Boone High School, it was operated 1899–1907 in Three Forks Association under D. D. and B. B. Daughtery. Watauga was a private school under Baptist control. D. L. SMILEY

WATAUGA ACADEMY. A school at Butler, Tenn., operated from 1902 to 1940 with Baptist support. The school was founded in 1886 by James H. Smith, who had come to Butler in 1882 to teach in Aenon Seminary, and was called Holly Springs College. Local citizens assisted in the erection of the two-story brick building, and a program including elementary, high school, and college courses leading to the B.A. degree was offered until 1902. In that year the Watauga Baptist Association purchased the school. In 1906 the name was changed to Watauga Academy, and the institution became a part of the mountain school system of the Southern Baptist Home Mission Board. In 1924 the academy reported an enrolment of 97 and property valued at $30,000. From 1931, when the Southern Baptist Convention withdrew its support, until 1940 the Watauga Baptist Association and the Johnson County Board of Education jointly operated the school. In 1940 the county purchased the property, and Watauga Academy became a public high school.

HARLEY FITE

WATCHMAN OF THE PRAIRIES. A Baptist newspaper, now extinct, published at Chicago, Ill., from Aug., 1847, to Feb., 1853. Luther Stone owned and edited the paper.

LYNN E. MAY, JR.

WATERTOWN SCHOOL. A preparatory school at Watertown, Tenn., founded in 1890 with F. M. Bowling as principal, four teachers, 127 pupils, and classes in elementary branches, Latin, Greek, and higher mathematics. It was auxiliary to Southwestern Baptist University, Jackson, Tenn. LYNN EDWARD MAY, JR.

WATTS, THOMAS JOSEPH (b. Raleigh, N. C., Mar. 19, 1874; d. Waco, Tex., Dec. 20, 1948). Pastor, executive secretary of the Relief and Annuity Board 1927–47. Watts was one of twins, Thomas Joseph and Joseph Thomas. They were sons of a devout Roman Catholic, Josiah Turner Watts, and an equally devout Baptist mother, Annie McIver Watts. The Watts brothers bear the same Christian names in opposite order because of a mistake made at their christening. The father intended that the boys be christened, one for Saint Thomas and one for Saint Joseph. However, the priest, during the ceremony, got the twins mixed and found it impossible to tell Thomas from Joseph. The Christian name is very sacred in the Catholic Church, being the name by which the Church recognizes him in life, death, and the beyond. To solve the problem, the priest added an extra name to each twin, calling one Thomas Joseph and one Joseph Thomas. That is the way in which the Watts brothers came to bear the same Christian names in opposite order. The boys were educated in the public and private schools of Raleigh.

The boys accepted Christ in an interdenominational meeting led by a Presbyterian minister and were ordained to the ministry in Baptist churches. Thomas Joseph was 25 years of age, had married Margaret Glenn Whitelaw five years before, and was about to enter upon a promising business enterprise when he felt called to enter the ministry. Within a few weeks after deciding to do so, he received a call to the church at Forsythe, Ga., where he remained for four years (1900–03).

Opportunity opened for him to enrol in Southern Baptist Theological Seminary while he was serving as pastor of Immanuel Church, Louisville, Ky. (1903–06). He became pastor at New Liberty, Ky., immediately after his graduation (1906–09). In 1909 he was appointed field representative of the seminary. After a period of similar service with the Baptist Educational Society of Kentucky, he served as Sunday School and Baptist Young People's Union secretary for Missouri (1912–14). In 1914 South Carolina called him for the same work, and he served there for more than 10 years. Furman University conferred on him the D.D. degree in 1923.

He became associate secretary of the Relief and Annuity Board in 1925 and, upon the death of William Lunsford (*q.v.*) in 1927, succeeded to the executive secretaryship, a position he held for 20 years.

He had twin daughters, Mary Emily and Emily Mary, by his first wife, who died in Aug., 1933. On Oct. 6, 1934, he married Sarah Jenkins Graves of Waco, Tex. In 1947, at the age of 73, he retired from the work of the Relief and Annuity Board. RETTA O'BANNON

WAYLAND COLLEGE. A coeducational, liberal arts institution located at Plainview, Tex., chartered by the state of Texas in Aug., 1908, under the name Wayland Literary and Technical Institution. Two years later the name was changed to Wayland Baptist College. First proposed in 1906 at the annual meeting of the Staked Plains Baptist Association, the establishment of the college was officially launched the following year when the association accepted from James Henry Wayland and his wife a gift of 25 acres of land and $10,000 with the provision that the cash commitments would be increased to $50,000 by the association and citizens of Plainview.

Construction of the administration building was begun in 1909, and facilities for boarding students and classrooms were provided in time for the beginning of the first session in Sept., 1910. Wayland, pioneer physician, and his wife, whose original gift was later increased, were the guiding spirits and major donors during the early struggles of the college.

The first president, I. E. Gates, was elected in Aug., 1909, and served until 1917. G. W. McDonald became president in 1923 and served until his retirement in 1947. J. W. Marshall, president 1947–53, was succeeded by A. Hope Owen. Financial worries have beset the college administrators from the beginning, but the records show a gradual, steady growth in student body, physical plant, and academic recognition.

For the first session in 1910, 225 students, ranging in classification from the primary grades through college, were enrolled. Except during the critical periods of World War I and the depression years, enrolment averaged about 200 until the end of World War II. Since then total annual enrolment has averaged more than 500. From 1910 to 1955, 6,567 college students have been admitted.

College catalogs from 1910 to 1913 outline a four-year college program, but from 1913 to 1947 only the first two years of college work were offered. In 1947 the college again offered a four-year course of study leading to a bachelor's degree. When the public school system had become well established, the elementary and preparatory courses were discontinued.

In 1926 Wayland became a member of the American Association of Junior Colleges. As a senior college, Wayland was approved by the Texas State Department of Education in 1948, and was admitted to full membership in the Association of Texas Colleges and the Southern Association of Colleges and Secondary Schools in 1956. Wayland is also a member of the Texas Association of Schools of Music and of the Southern Association of Baptist Colleges.

School properties, valued at $1,879,312, include 11 permanent buildings on the main campus and 15 other permanent housing units. Temporary buildings are being replaced by permanent structures as the over-all expansion and development program of the college progresses. Endowment totals more than $400,000.

The school was admitted as a member of the System of Correlated Schools of the Baptist General Convention of Texas in 1914, and today policies are determined by a board of trustees elected by the state body. An annual appropriation is received from the convention for regular operating expenses. Other sources of income are student fees and tuition, individual gifts and grants, gifts from churches, and income from endowment.

Wayland was the first privately operated college in the South to admit Negro students voluntarily on the same basis as other students. This decision in 1951 brought the most widespread publicity the college has ever had.

FLORRIE CONWAY

WEAVER, RUFUS WASHINGTON (b. Greensboro, N. C., June 3, 1870; d. Washington, D. C., Jan. 31, 1947). Denominational leader. He received his education at Wake Forest College and at the Southern Baptist Theological Seminary, and did graduate work at the University of Cincinnati and Johns Hopkins University. Bethel College in Kentucky conferred on him the D.D. degree; Baylor University gave him the LL.D. degree. After serving pastorates in High Point, N. C., Middletown, Ohio, Baltimore, Md., Cincinnati, Ohio, and Nashville, Tenn., he was president of Mercer University in Georgia from 1918 to 1927. Later, Weaver moved to Washington, D. C., where he served as pastor of the First Baptist Church for two years, resigning to assume the position of executive secretary of the District of Columbia Baptist Convention. It was during this time that Weaver was instrumental in organizing the Baptist Joint Committee on Public Affairs, an organization representing the major Baptist bodies in the United States, both white and negro. Interested in the cause of religious liberty, he warned of various encroachments upon this principle and labored constantly to arouse Baptists and others to defend their American heritage of freedom. He stimulated study of our Baptist history and did much to acquaint Baptists in the United States with the life and labors of Luther Rice. He was the author of several books, including such volumes as *History of the Doctrine of Inspiration, The Christian Conversationalist, The Reconstruction of Religion, Religious Development of the Child, The Revolt Against God,* and a book of sermons and addresses delivered while serving in Washington. A man of scholarly gifts and great energy, Weaver made a great impact upon his generation in the interest of America's basic religious inheritance. EDWARD HUGHES PRUDEN

WEBBER, WILLIAM (b. Goochland County, Va., Aug. 15, 1747; d. Goochland County, Va., Feb. 29, 1808). Early Virginia Baptist leader, minister. With only three years' schooling, although his parents had substantial means, Webber was a master housejoiner when converted at 23. Before his ordination, and by invitation, he preached with Joseph Anthony in Chesterfield County, Va. He and Anthony were imprisoned from Dec., 1770, until Mar., 1771, but they preached to large congregations through prison gates with powerful effect. Webber spent several weeks in 1771 in Middlesex County jail, enduring a serious prison illness.

The first pastor of Dover Baptist Church, Webber served it until his death. He was the first known moderator of Dover Association, elected in 1786. Participating in the formation of the General Association of Separate Baptists in 1771, Webber served as its moderator in 1778, and from 1781 to 1783. He was first moderator of the General Committee in 1784 and again in 1785, and of the General Committee of Correspondence from its beginning in 1800 until his incapacity by illness in 1807. BEN LYNES

WEEKDAY RELIGIOUS EDUCATION. A term applied to any organized effort to teach religion during the weekdays. It supplements the Sunday teaching program of churches. Also, it recognizes the importance of religious instruction for the moral and spiritual training of children and youth and the limitations of public schools to carry forward a formal program of religious teaching.

Weekday work began on the secondary level with the establishment of the "seminary" program in Salt Lake City, Utah, in 1912 under the auspices of the Church of Jesus Christ of Latter Day Saints. A more extensive pattern of weekday religious education was begun in Gary, Ind., in

1914. This was a co-operative effort on the part of the Protestant ministerial association and the public schools to promote religious education for the elementary grades on a "released time" basis. This latter pattern has been followed more extensively by local, state, and national councils of churches. A National Council of Churches bulletin, "Introducing the Weekday Church School," announced in 1956 that "almost three million boys and girls in approximately 3,000 communities" were enrolled in weekday classes.

Two United States Supreme Court decisions have aimed at clarifying the status of weekday released time classes. The McCollum Case of 1948 decided that released time classes in religious education could not be held in the public school classrooms in Champaign, Ill. The Zorach Case of 1952 established the legality of releasing pupils on the request of parents for classes in religion not conducted on public school property. There are various patterns of weekday religious teaching in relation to public schools, namely: (1) pupils released on request of parents to go to churches for class periods, in some cases with credit being given by the school; (2) school facilities rented by church groups for religious instruction periods; and (3) Bible courses offered as electives in the public school under teachers paid by church groups.

Another significant area of weekday work is represented by the growing number of nursery schools and kindergartens. These programs for children of four and five years of age run concurrently with the public school year, with daily sessions usually from nine to twelve each morning. In some communities nursery schools accept children from two and a half years up and offer all-day care in order to help working mothers. Nursery school and kindergarten activities are a part of the public educational program in most of the Northern states, while in the South a majority of these programs are under church auspices.

A growing concern of weekday workers is the precarious place of religion in public education. These leaders believe that religious neutrality is an impossible position and that a religion of some kind will be communicated in the public classrooms. This being true, it is felt that a public educational program which assumes the existence of God and the primacy of moral and spiritual values would be more in accord with the American way of life than would be a thoroughly secularized public school system.

For a period of years some Southern Baptist churches have maintained kindergartens. A very few churches have operated a Christian day school. In response to the needs of the churches, the Sunday School Board in 1954 elected James Clinton Barry as editor of materials for weekday religious teaching. A limited survey made that year of churches having educational directors disclosed 29 kindergartens and five nursery schools. The July–Sept., 1954, issue of *The Quarterly Review* was devoted to a "Survey of Weekday Religious Education in Southern Baptist Churches." A similar survey made two years later revealed 183 kindergartens. The board has accepted the responsibility for developing a program for weekday teaching and the materials needed for such by the churches.

See also EDUCATION, SOUTHERN BAPTIST.

JAMES CLINTON BARRY

WELFARE CENTER, IRE. See NIGERIA, MISSION IN.

WEST CHINA BAPTIST CONVENTION. Organized in 1928 with missionaries and Chinese enjoying equal status by 1931. When the convention area went behind the Bamboo Curtain in 1952, missionaries were evacuated, and church activities became controlled by Communist regulations. Work in Szechuan province began when W. M. Upcraft (b. 1860; d. 1915) and George Warner (b. 1858; d. 1937), missionaries of the American Baptist Missionary Union, opened a mission at Chengtu in 1889. Mountainous terrain, poor communications, and strong anti-foreign feeling retarded full development of the mission. In Jan., 1899, the first interdenominational West China Mission Conference, held in Chungking, drew up comity agreements, planned future conferences, and launched *West China Missionary News,* an English monthly for three western provinces.

The Boxer Rebellion in 1900 drove out all missionaries, but revival and expansion came upon their return. In 1906 the West China Educational Union developed a union high school, women's normal school, and West China Union University. The Woman's American Baptist Foreign Mission Society opened schools for women and girls and the first kindergarten in the entire province in 1904. The closing in 1913 of the Central China Mission (opened in 1893 at Hankow) strengthened finances and staff of the West China mission. In 1923 the West China convention ordained the first Chinese pastor and organized a home mission society. This society and the convention stabilized the churches during several intervals when western missionaries were forced out of the area.

In 1937 Szechuan province became the refuge of millions fleeing from coastal cities being occupied by Japanese forces, and the burden of human misery overtaxed all mission facilities and staff. Five refugee schools from the eastern

DATA

	1934	*1949**
Baptisms	217	—
Churches & outstations	42	14
Church members	2,880	2,842
Missionaries	46	3
Chinese workers	165	150
Students	2,679	4,135
Schools	30	14
Patients	37,992	55,159
Hospitals & dispensaries	7	4
Field contributions	$ 1,424	—

*Latest figures.

areas found temporary wartime homes on the Chengtu campus. E. H. Cressy (b. 1883), a Baptist and executive secretary of the Council of Higher Education of China, with headquarters at Chungking and later at Chengtu, co-ordinated the religious program of more than a dozen Christian colleges, 117 Christian high schools, and 53 nursing schools in Free China. Finally, when China fell to the Communists in 1952, the mission had to be evacuated.

ADA STEARNS

WEST KENTUCKY BAPTIST ASSEMBLY. Founded in 1910 at Dawson Springs, Ky., emphasizing recreation, edification, inspiration, and information, with study classes covering many phases of church and denominational life. This assembly was moved to the campus of Bethel College, Russellville, Ky., in 1915. An annual session was held for 15 consecutive years, with the last session in July, 1924. ELDRED M. TAYLOR

WEST KENTUCKY BAPTIST BIBLE INSTITUTE. A school for the training of ministers whose educational backgrounds are not adequate for admission to colleges or seminaries, established in the fall of 1945 by action of the West Kentucky Baptist Association. As the Preacher's Bible School, it first opened for classes on Jan. 10, 1949, in First Baptist Church, Clinton, Ky. Curry O. Simpson, moderator of the association, was named acting president. Members of the original faculty included O. C. Marcum, G. R. Abernathy, and L. W. Carlin. The present name of the institution was adopted in July, 1949. In the fall of 1945, West Union, Blood River, and Graves County associations joined the West Kentucky Association in the operation of the school. Approximately 260 students have attended the institute, of whom 27 are graduates of the three-year course. In 1956 enrolment was 38. W. A. Sloan, the first full-time president, has served since May, 1953. ERWIN L. MCDONALD

WEST TENNESSEE BAPTIST CONVENTION. A regional general body in Tennessee which existed prior to the time of the Tennessee Baptist Convention. Before 1845 this group had several titles. At Brownsville during its first annual session in July, 1835, the Baptist Convention of the Western District of Tennessee changed its name to the Baptist Convention for West Tennessee. It was auxiliary to The Tennessee Baptist Convention during the latter's 10-year existence (1833–42); but when the convention ceased in 1842 and was replaced by the Baptist General Association of Tennessee, the Baptist Convention for West Tennessee became an independent body. In 1845 it voted to call itself the West Tennessee Baptist Convention and operated under this title until 1874, when it voted to help form the Tennessee Baptist State Convention.

The West Tennessee Baptist Education Society was organized in 1834 to establish a literary institution and to educate young men for the ministry. Its life was short, its work being taken over by the education board of the convention. Brownsville Female Institute resulted from the work of the society and the convention.

The Bible Society of the Western District of Tennessee was organized in Nov., 1839. For a number of years it held its meetings simultaneously with the convention and was at one time auxiliary to the American and Foreign Bible Society.

The convention through the years employed a number of missionaries to cope with widespread spiritual destitution. It established the Baptist Male Institute in Madison County, and changed its name to Madison College in 1859. Although the Graves-Howell controversy of 1858–61 created considerable disturbance in the convention, the convention itself did not become involved.

In 1847 the four associations affiliating with the convention reported 121 churches, 89 ordained ministers, and 7,044 members. At the 1847 session a committee was appointed to report in 1848 on Sunday schools with a view to "exciting in the minds of the brethren a deep interest" with reference to Sunday schools. In 1865 and 1866 most of the churches in the convention had no Sunday school. In 1872 two of the seven associations had schools in more than half the churches, and the other five had fewer than half. Pastors and elderly church members were reported as being indifferent to and unable to do Sunday school work. Some churches could not even get a superintendent.

The corresponding secretaries of the Southern Baptist Domestic and Sunday School boards attended the convention session of 1868, as did President Boyce of the Southern Baptist Theological Seminary. The convention had a Sunday school missionary that year.

At its 1873 session the convention voted unanimously for one Baptist general organization in the state and appointed delegates to represent it at the meeting in Murfreesboro in Apr., 1874, to work out plans for the unification of the three Baptist bodies. At its 1874 session it voted to participate in the first annual session of the Tennessee Baptist Convention at Nashville in 1875, and also to have a final session in 1875 for concluding its affairs. HOMER L. GRICE

WEST TEXAS BAPTIST. First published in Oct., 1892, with G. W. Smith as editor and George S. Anderson as business manager. The paper was sold in 1905 to James Britton Cranfill (*q.v.*), who merged it with the *Baptist Tribune.*

E. C. ROUTH

WEST TEXAS UNION ENCAMPMENT. The first of 20 Baptist encampments to be organized in Texas. Members of Baptist Young People's Unions in Haskell, Albany, Anson, and Abilene in west Texas met in a grove on the Clear Fork of the Brazos River, July 12–14, 1898, and voted to establish the encampment permanently.

J. E. ROTH

WESTERN BAPTIST. Established in 1873 by T. B. Espy and T. P. Boone. The paper continued for two years with Boone as editor. Established at Searcy, it was moved to Little Rock in 1874, its last year of existence.

B. H. DUNCAN

WESTERN BAPTIST. Founded in South McAlester, Indian Territory (Okla.), 1903, and adopted that year as the organ of the Baptist General Convention of Indian Territory. When Number 13, Volume II appeared June 30, 1904, the paper had 16 pages, 8½ x 11 inches, divided into three columns each. The price was $1.50 per year. J. L. Walker was the first editor and manager; later, William P. Blake (*q.v.*) and J. L. Watson were associate editors. The paper, published in Chickasha, Oct. 4, 1905, had eight three-column pages and sold for $1 per year. In 1907 it returned to South McAlester and reported a circulation of 2,000. It is now extinct.

J. M. GASKIN

WESTERN BAPTIST. Published originally as *Baptist News,* its name was changed to *Western Baptist* in 1890 when Robert Taylor Hanks bought half interest in the paper from Lewis Holland. Early in 1892, Holland and Hanks sold the *Western Baptist* to M. V. Smith and James Britton Cranfill (*q.v.*), and the name of the paper was changed to *The Texas Baptist Standard.* From that point on, the *Baptist Standard* represented the constructive work of the Baptist General Convention of Texas.

E. C. ROUTH

WESTERN BAPTIST CONVENTION (1833–42). An early effort to promote the interests of Baptists west of the Appalachian Mountains. With the development of territory west of the Appalachian Mountains in the first third of the 19th century, the need for a gathering of Baptists in the West, whose problems differed from those in the East, was suggested by Ephraim Robins and promoted by *The Baptist Weekly Journal,* Cincinnati, Ohio, beginning in 1831. On Nov. 6, 1833, "A General Meeting for the Promotion of the Cause of Christ, as Connected with the Interests of the Baptist Denomination in the Western States" was held in Cincinnati. This meeting, held 12 years before the organization of the Southern Baptist Convention, was attended by 74 representatives from Cincinnati; 18 from Kentucky; 8 from Indiana; 1 from Illinois; and 7 from the East. At that time the rumblings of opposition to slavery were becoming vocal in the North, and an effort was made to keep the new enterprise aloof from involvements in the seaboard states. John Mason Peck (*q.v.*) said that the convention was "strictly and solely a Western one and that the ultraists North and South have no business with it."

According to William Carey James, "The Western Baptist Convention was short-lived. For six years it held annual sessions in Cincinnati. There was no meeting in 1839. The sessions of 1840–41 were held in Louisville. By this time the object which had called it into being was almost secured, and the convention accordingly dissolved." However, Baptists from various churches west of the Allegheny Mountains (but only one Baptist from west of the Mississippi River) assembled in the Ninth Street Baptist Church, Cincinnati, Ohio, Oct. 27–29, 1842, to organize a Western Baptist Convention for the promotion of Indian Missions. (Most of those present were from Ohio and Kentucky, but there were seven from Indiana, one each from Illinois, Missouri, and Tennessee.) This new organization was named the American Indian Mission Association, and headquarters were in Louisville, Ky. It lasted for approximately six years, issuing printed annuals of its meetings.

There were five results of the Western Baptist Convention, namely, (1) the Western Baptist Education Society; (2) the Western Baptist Theological Institute; (3) the American Indian Mission Association; (4) Linden Grove Cemetery, still in operation; and (5) Western Baptist Theological Institute Sub-Division, a real estate development in Covington, Ky.

GEORGE RALEIGH JEWELL

WESTERN BAPTIST EDUCATION SOCIETY. An organization of the Western Baptist Convention for the purpose of establishing a school of higher learning for the education of preachers.

In spite of opposition by some in Kentucky who feared that the organization of a new theological school might cripple the work of Georgetown College and opposition by those in Ohio who were afraid that Granville College (now Dennison University) might be hurt by another school, the Western Baptist Education Society was organized on Nov. 10, 1834, for the purpose of establishing a theological school at Covington, Ky. Although the society's president, secretary, and treasurer were all from Cincinnati, there was a vice-president from each of the following states: Ohio, Kentucky, Indiana, Illinois, Missouri, and Tennessee. The board of directors was composed of two each from Kentucky, Ohio, Illinois, Indiana, Missouri, Mississippi, and Tennessee, and one each from Michigan, Alabama, Virginia, Arkansas, and Pennsylvania. The executive committee, selected by this board, was composed of 12, with seven from Ohio, two from Kentucky, and one each from Tennessee, Indiana, and Missouri.

The Western Baptist Education Society spent years in preparing to open the school it was created to establish. Time was consumed in finding a financial agent to raise money, trying to decide where to locate it, floating loans, erecting buildings, selling lots, landscaping, and related matters. On Jan. 1, 1835, Ezra Going became part-time financial agent. The society agreed to place the school in Kentucky provided that Kentucky Baptists could raise $20,000 of the $40,000 needed. The remainder was to be solicited from other places. Kentuckians decided to raise $25,000.

Three tracts of land south of Covington, totaling 370 acres, were purchased for $33,250. A down payment was made, and annual payments were to be made thereafter. Jonathan Batcheller, a Baptist layman from Lynn, Mass., loaned the society $5,000 with which to purchase a small tract. They were to pay him 6 per cent on the loan, and in appreciation of his generosity they gave him one acre of the land. A citizen of Cincinnati purchased 90 acres for $22,500, with a down payment of $10,000, and five annual payments later. The society then spent three years renting out the land to farmers, without making any sales of property.

After unsuccessful efforts to raise money in the East, the society employed Ephraim Robins, one of the early prime movers in the cause and a member of the executive committee living in Cincinnati, to manage the property. In 1839 a public sale of lots brought $10,000, and the next year another block of lots was sold for $5,000. In 1841, $11,000 more was secured from sale of lots, and a private sale yielded $3,000. The society then had $29,000 and 198 acres to be sold, excluding the tract being held in reserve for the Western Baptist Theological Institute. Robins carried on ambitious landscaping—planting trees, bushes, shrubs, vines, and flowers—to make them more attractive to buyers and to increase the value of the grounds. During 1840–43 about 150 houses were erected by owners who had purchased the lots. W. C. James wrote:

> An interesting and useful appendage of the property and one which shows the completeness of the plans which the executive committee had for the little city, of which the seminary was to be the center, was the Linden Grove Cemetery, located at the extreme southwestern limit of the whole tract. At the entrance to the cemetery stood the gardner's lodge, a neat brick edifice, and near the center of the grounds was the receiving vault for the temporary deposit of bodies. The whole area of 22 acres was tastefully laid out and adorned with forest trees, shrubbery and evergreens. Adjoining it was another tract of 30 acres, mostly woodland, which, when necessary could be used for cemetery purposes. The owners of the property hoped to make it one of the most beautiful cemeteries in the West.

In the winter of 1839–40, the Society secured a charter from the Kentucky legislature for the Western Baptist Theological Institute of Covington, Ky. At that time the society reorganized itself into a board of trustees to operate the school and transferred the property of the education society to the trustees.

GEORGE RALEIGH JEWELL

WESTERN BAPTIST HOSPITAL. In Sept., 1945, George Phillips, moderator of the West Union Baptist Association, Kentucky, appointed a seven-man committee to study the need for a Baptist hospital in Paducah and the possibility of a hospital's being established by West Union Baptist Association and adjacent associations. The committee reported that a hospital project was feasible, and the first campaign for funds was started in Oct., 1945. The following February, Dr. A. Mack Parrish was employed as executive secretary. The first contract, to construct a basement, was awarded in Apr., 1948, and the ground-breaking ceremonies for the hospital were held on May 2, 1948. A second contract, for foundations, was awarded in Sept., 1948, and a third, for concrete structure, in May, 1949. Income for the entire project, however, was slow in accumulating.

After Dr. Parrish's death in Oct., 1949, Dr. S. E. Tull served as executive secretary for about 14 months, during which time the contract for external brick work was let. During this same year, Dr. Tull successfully presented the need for support from the entire General Association of Baptists in Kentucky. Finally, the formation of the Hospital Commission of Kentucky Baptists was implemented by the general association in Nov., 1951. A little more than $1,000,000 was borrowed against a mortgage of Kentucky Baptist Hospital in Louisville for the completion of Western Baptist Hospital. The final contracts were let in June, 1952. On July 21, 1952, Emmett R. Johnson was employed as administrator. When the hospital accepted its first patient on Oct. 21, 1953, the building, equipment, and inventories were valued at more than $1,500,000. Western Baptist has become one of the outstanding hospitals in western Kentucky and is fully accredited by the Joint Commission on Accreditation of Hospitals. It is operated under the philosophy that the hospital should "render the best possible care at the least possible cost in an atmosphere of Christian love and understanding." H. L. DOBBS

WESTERN BAPTIST MONITOR (proposed 1835?). The Canaan Association (Ala.) *Minutes,* 1835, recommended the patronage of the *Western Baptist Monitor,* a paper scheduled to appear in Jacksonville. RAY M. ATCHISON

WESTERN BAPTIST MONITOR, THE. A newspaper begun in Madisonville, Tenn., sometime in 1833 or 1834. According to Robert Boyté Crawford Howell (*q.v.*) in *The Baptist,* the *Monitor* published its last issue in Tennessee in Aug., 1835. A Mr. Wood then moved it to Jacksonville, Fla., where he published it as the *Jacksonville Register.* The paper is now extinct. LYNN E. MAY, JR.

WESTERN BAPTIST REVIEW, THE. A monthly which appeared regularly at Frankfort, Ky., from September, 1845, through August, 1849, in four complete volumes, and at Louisville in six issues of a fifth volume from June, 1850, through Nov., 1851. The principal editor for the periodical was John Lightfoot Waller (*q.v.*) (1809–54); Robert Rhodes Lillard (1826–49) was associated with him from 1846 until his death, June 7, 1849. This paper is called by William Cathcart (1820–1908) "at that time the ablest periodical in the West." Publication ceased when *The Christian Repository* was begun by Waller in Jan., 1852. LEO T. CRISMON

WESTERN BAPTIST THEOLOGICAL INSTITUTE. A theological school at Covington, Ky., which grew out of an earlier organization, the Western Baptist Convention. Chartered in 1840, the new theological school opened five years later. Its three buildings included the theological seminary building, the president's home, and the professors' residence. After the presidency had been declined by three men in the South and by Barnas Sears of Newton Theological Institution, R. E. Pattison became president and professor of Christian theology. Asa Drury was made professor of Greek, and Ebenezer Dodge became professor of Hebrew and church history. Dodge was succeeded by Ezekiel Gilman Robinson the second year, and no other change was made in the faculty for two years.

Later, S. W. Lynd' was made president and Duncan R. Campbell became a teacher. During the first semester of 1849 only one student enrolled. However, nine enrolled the next session (1849–50), and in 1850–51 there were also nine in the Literary Department, making a total of 18. In 1851–52 the number of students increased to 25, but the next year it dropped to 17.

Although the faculty members were able men, because of their backgrounds they were suspected of opposing slavery. The eight trustees from Northern states soon became eight trustees from Ohio, largely from Cincinnati. The seven trustees from Southern territory soon became seven trustees from Kentucky. Thus the strategy was narrowed to two states in their grapple for power. The Kentuckians claimed that the Ohioans, because of their majority, were controlling the policies of the school. With no support coming in from the South, the president turned to the North for students and for financial support and further threatened to move the seminary across the Ohio River. The rumor that the property was to be sold to another denomination also was circulated. Since the school was chartered in Kentucky, the Kentuckians proceeded to have the charter changed, giving themselves control and complete management of the institute at Covington.

After several legal battles, the two sides submitted the case to Justice McLean, of the United States Supreme Court, for arbitration. He decided that the property should be divided equally between the two groups. The library went to Granville College (now Dennison University) in Ohio. The Northern trustees took their part of the proceeds for Fairmount Theological Seminary, Cincinnati, which operated for about five years and then ceased to exist for lack of funds. The Southern trustees moved the Western Baptist Theological Institute to Georgetown College, where it was operated with nominal success some of the years which followed, with one or two teachers. For some of the years it had neither students nor teachers. It had some meager existence until 1879, when Basil Manly, Jr. (*q.v.*), resigned as president of Georgetown College to return to the faculty of Southern Baptist Theological Seminary, which two years before had moved to Louisville. All functions of the institute then seemed to stop. The Kentucky legislature of 1889–90 permitted the trustees of the institute to transfer its funds to the Kentucky Baptist Education Society, which operated Georgetown College. The charter was dissolved June 9, 1891.

The Covington property which was owned by the institute is today worth millions of dollars, which, on a business venture alone, could well underwrite a school of enormous proportions. But Baptists of the 19th century had not learned how to work together well in any form of co-operation and management. If this school had been successful, the Southern Baptist Theological Seminary might never have been moved to Louisville, for the institute at Covington would have supplied the need for trained preachers in the Ohio Valley. GEORGE RALEIGH JEWELL

WESTERN BAPTIST TRIBUNE. A weekly paper established in 1898. In 1907 circulation was 3,500. It is now extinct. J. M. GASKIN

WESTERN BAPTISTS AFFILIATED WITH ARIZONA. Baptists in Utah, Idaho, Nevada, Colorado, Wyoming, Montana, North Dakota, South Dakota, and Nebraska, co-operating with Southern Baptists through the Arizona Baptist Convention. In 1954 there were 459 American Baptist churches and 128 others, not including Southern Baptists. In the nine states 1,366 cities with populations of 250-up had no Baptist church. Many Southern Baptist families who moved into these communities were not content without a Baptist church. Even in cities where there was a Baptist church, some Southern Baptists were not satisfied with its program. Conditions thus led these Southern Baptists to establish their own churches, after which they requested fellowship with the Baptist General Convention of Arizona. Because churches in the affiliated states were so far removed from Arizona, general missionaries were elected to serve in the various states. At the time the work was begun, however, there were only 80 churches in the Baptist General Convention of Arizona. Therefore, help was sought from the Home Mission Board. which promised to provide: (1) salaries for general missionaries and $4,000 per year to apply on the salary of the superintendent of missions; and (2) money directed through the Baptist General Convention of Arizona to help supplement salaries of mission pastors.

DEVELOPMENT BY STATES. *Utah*.—In 1950 when Ira I. Marks went as a general missionary to Utah, there were four churches affiliated with the Arizona convention. Southern Baptist work in Utah began with layman Harold Dillman, a converted Mormon, and his family, who led the First Baptist Church of Carrizo Springs, Tex., to extend an arm to Roosevelt. The pastor from Carrizo Springs preached a revival at Roosevelt which resulted in establishment of a church in July, 1944. By Nov. 1, 1955, 10 other Southern Baptist churches had been established. The two Baptist associations in the state are Utah, organized Nov. 18, 1950, and Salt Lake, organized Sept. 23, 1955.

Idaho.—On Nov. 1, 1955, eight churches in Idaho, with a combined membership of 407, were affiliated with the Baptist General Convention of Arizona. Idaho's one association, Twin Buttes, was organized Oct. 5, 1953.

Colorado.—Baptist work in Colorado developed much faster than in other affiliated states. Denver Temple, the first Colorado church to affiliate with the Arizona convention, was constituted Aug. 19, 1951, with 61 members. First Southern, Colorado Springs, was constituted Dec. 31, 1952, with 14 members; and in the three and one half years that followed, 1,251 members were received and a $225,000 building was erected. By Nov. 1, 1955, 59 Southern Baptist churches had been established in Colorado, although 13 of these affiliated with the New Mexico convention. Five associations have been organized in the state; the Colorado Baptist General Convention was constituted Nov. 21, 1955.

Wyoming.—Work in Wyoming began when a group of Southern Baptists in Casper asked O. R. Delmar of Tollison, Ariz., to come and help them organize a church. As a result the First Southern Baptist Church, Cooper, was constituted with 18 members on July 18, 1951. Four years later it had property valued at $185,000 and a membership of 374. By 1955, 15 other Southern Baptist churches existed in Wyoming, and they with the Casper church reported a combined membership of 1,591 and property valued at $314,135. These churches together with churches in South Dakota composed Old Faithful Association which was organized Sept. 24, 1953.

Montana.—In Nov., 1955, nine Southern Baptist churches in Montana reported a combined membership of 545 and property valued at $128,000. These churches composed the Montana Association organized Sept. 24, 1953.

North Dakota.—A total of five Southern Baptist churches in North Dakota in 1955 reported a combined membership of 211 with property valued at $80,000. These five churches composed the North Dakota Association.

South Dakota.—As of Nov. 1, 1955, there were four Southern Baptist churches in South Dakota with combined membership of 304 and property valued at $71,000. Twenty-three people of Ellsworth Air Base, Rapid City, had formed the First Southern Baptist Church there with 43 members on Mar. 26, 1953.

Nevada.—The Baptist General Convention of Arizona led in establishment of five churches in southeast Nevada, organized in Lake Mead Association. On Nov. 1, 1955, these five churches had a combined membership of 255.

Nebraska.—Only one church in Nebraska, Trinity at Scottsbluff, was co-operating with the Arizona convention as of Nov. 15, 1955. Constituted Nov. 14, 1955, with 16 members, Trinity was a mission of the Trinity Church in Longmont, Colo.

WESTERN CANADA, BAPTIST UNION OF. Baptist work in Western Canada began in June, 1873, when the pioneer worker reached Winnipeg, Manitoba. The first Baptist church in Western Canada was organized in Winnipeg in 1875. Baptist headquarters, originally established in Winnipeg, were moved in 1929 to Edmonton, Alberta. The area of membership for the Baptist Union of Western Canada includes Manitoba, Saskatchewan, Alberta, British Columbia, and the Northwest Territories.

In 1869 Thomas C. Davidson, Aylmer, Ontario, and Thomas Baldwin, Ingersoll, Ontario, were appointed by the missionary convention's board to survey Western Canada as a possible field for Baptist work. Their favorable report led to the appointment of Alexander McDonald, Sparta, Ontario, who became the pioneer and principal founder of the present work.

Following the organization of the first church in Winnipeg, other Anglo-Saxon churches were organized throughout the four provinces. With the incoming of so-called non-English peoples, Baptist churches were first organized for the Germans in 1886, the Swedes in 1894, the Ukrainians in 1904, the Norwegians and Hungarians in 1911, and the Czechoslovakians in 1930. The first church for Negro Baptists was organized in Edmonton, Alberta, in 1910. In 1947 the first Baptist work was opened in Yellowknife, Northwest Territories.

Various organizational steps for united fellowship and action, taken gradually, led in 1909 to the Baptist Union of Western Canada as organized today. Now integrated in the union are the non-English churches with the exception of the German and Swedish groups which have their respective conferences. The Baptist union, an incorporated body for Baptist work in Canada's four western provinces and the Northwest Territories, is a union not only of churches but also of departments, including the Women's Missionary Auxiliary and the Baptist Young People's Union in its administrative structure.

For more local and intensive promotion each of the three Prairie provinces is organized into two associations. British Columbia's province-wide organization is a convention. Thus a total of seven area units make up the union.

The *Canadian Baptist,* incorporating the biweekly *Western Baptist,* serves Baptists of Ontario, Quebec, and western Canada.

The Baptist Leadership Training School located in Calgary, Alberta, trains lay leadership. Western Baptist students preparing for Christian vocations attend, for the most part, the divinity school at McMaster University, Hamilton, Ontario.

The Grande Ligne Mission, a Baptist mission to French Canadians with which the union co-operates, has 12 churches, Feller College, and a French language broadcast. The union co-operates in the work of the Canadian Baptist Foreign Mission Board, which has overseas fields in India, Bolivia, and Angola. In India churches affiliated with the work number 160 with 40,-

000 members; in Bolivia, 28 with 1,218 members; in Angola, 2 with 2,395 members. Missionaries include 75 in India with 21 from Western Canada; 37 in Bolivia with 11 from Western Canada; and 2 under appointment for Angola.

In Western Canada in 1954, 146 churches reported 640 baptisms, 17,181 members, $1,028,806.51 total gifts, and $46,076.78 mission gifts.

FLORENCE H. MCDONALD

WESTERN CHRISTIAN, THE. A Baptist newspaper founded in Elgin, Ill., in 1845 by a joint-stock company. Warham Walker edited the paper, which after five years was transferred to New York. LYNN E. MAY, JR.

WESTERN EVANGEL. First published in Abilene, Tex., in 1906, with Joseph Martin Dawson as editor. It was sold to the *Baptist Standard* in 1920. E. C. ROUTH

WESTERN KENTUCKY BAPTIST CAMP. Purchased in 1955 in the Johnathan area of Kentucky Lake, Marshall County, Ky., by the West Union Baptist Association. Emphasizing religious education and recreation, camps for various phases of Baptist work are held approximately six weeks each year. The camp is supported and used by Baptist associations and churches in the western part of Kentucky.

ELDRED M. TAYLOR

WESTERN KENTUCKY BIBLE SCHOOL. Established Nov. 7, 1921, in Murray, Ky. Although not its founder, H. Boyce Taylor, Sr., almost immediately took full responsibility for the school, which was coeducational but primarily intended for needy young preachers. Taylor conducted it as a nontuition faith venture, using the Bible as the sole textbook. In the first 10 years a total of 381 attended. Upon Taylor's death in 1932, the school was in decline, finally closing in 1935.

WILLIAM N. MCELRATH

WESTERN MISSIONS. This term applies to mission work of the Home Mission Board in 15 states west and north of Texas and Oklahoma. The dividing line runs north of Oklahoma between Kansas and Missouri, Nebraska and Iowa, and North and South Dakota and Minnesota. The term also applies to the work done in co-operation with state mission boards.

The first work in this area began with New Mexico in 1910 when the Southern Baptist Convention authorized the Home Mission Board to do work in that state. In 1911 the Baptist General Convention of New Mexico was organized, and the Home Mission Board has worked in co-operation with that convention ever since.

The first churches in Arizona were affiliated with the New Mexico Convention and remained with that body until the General Baptist Convention of Arizona was organized in 1928 with 10 churches. Little was done for Arizona until 1943, when the Home Mission Board began co-operative work with the convention.

The Southern Baptist Convention of California was organized with 13 churches, Sept. 13, 1940, and the Home Mission Board began work with the convention in 1944.

The Kansas Convention of Southern Baptists was organized on Mar. 19, 1946, with nine churches and was recognized as an affiliated, co-operative constituency of Southern Baptists in 1948. The Home Mission Board began its co-operation with Kansas in 1948.

The Baptist General Convention of Oregon-Washington was organized Apr. 13, 1948, with 15 churches from the two states. This convention was recognized by Southern Baptists in 1948, and the Home Mission Board began work with this convention in 1949.

In 1944 a Baptist church was started in Roosevelt, Utah, and became affiliated with the Arizona convention. Since that time other churches have developed and worked with Arizona. Since 1944 Arizona extended her arms, and through them the Home Mission Board, to the states of Utah, Idaho, Nevada, Colorado, Wyoming, Montana, North Dakota, South Dakota, and western Nebraska. The California convention aided in western Nevada; the Oregon convention in northern Idaho; and Kansas in Nebraska. At the end of 1955, there were Southern Baptist churches in each of the 15 Western states.

On Nov. 21, 1955, the Colorado Baptist General Convention was organized at Colorado Springs, Colo., with 96 churches and 11,000 members. Willis J. Ray was the first executive secretary. This convention consisted of churches from the states of Colorado, Wyoming, Montana, North Dakota, and western Nebraska.

On Jan. 1, 1955, the work in Alaska was transferred from direct missions to co-operative missions of the Home Mission Board. This placed Alaska under the direction of the Western Mission Program. S. F. DOWIS

WESTERN NORTH CAROLINA BAPTIST. A paper founded in 1884 by Joseph E. Carter, who became editor of the *Baptist Telescope* and changed its name to *Western North Carolina Baptist*. During early years it was published at Hendersonville; later Millard A. Jenkins, pastor of Waynesville Baptist Church, became editor of *Waynesville Courier* and changed the name to *Western North Carolina Baptist*. The paper retained this name until the dissolution of the Western convention in 1898, when it was suspended permanently. L. L. CARPENTER

WESTERN RECORDER. The official newspaper of the General Convention of Baptists in Kentucky, published by a variety of owners under its present name since 1851. It claims as its date of origin Dec. 15, 1825, through a chain of predecessor papers. The first of these was *The Baptist Register,* which was succeeded in 1830 by *The Baptist Chronicle & Georgetown Literary Register*. This paper succumbed to hard times in 1832 and was followed in 1834 by *The Baptist Banner,* published from Shelbyville and, after Nov. 29, 1836, from Louisville. John L. Waller, then editor, merged his paper with *The Baptist* of Nashville, Tenn., of which Robert Boyté Crawford Howell (*q.v.*) was editor, and with *The Western Pioneer* of Rock Spring (Alton), Ill., of which John Mason Peck (*q.v.*) was editor. The merged paper was continued at Louisville under the name *The Baptist Banner & Western Pioneer,* with both Peck and Howell as coeditors with Waller. In 1848 the name was once again *The Baptist Banner,* and three years later, in 1851, it became the *Western Recorder*. From that time on, the paper had a number of editors or corps of editors. Thomas Treadwell Eaton (*q.v.*), who became editor in 1887, used the paper to champion the views of those opposed to William Heth Whitsitt (*q.v.*), and was instrumental in forcing his resignation from the presidency of Southern Baptist Theological Seminary. Eaton died in 1907; after an interim, John William Porter (*q.v.*) was editor from 1909 to 1921.

The paper was purchased by the Kentucky general association in 1919, when, at the beginning of the 75 Million Campaign, there was a general trend to consolidation, unification, and reorganization in the interests of efficiency. The executive board of the General Association of Baptists in Kentucky bought three papers, *The Baptist World, The Kentucky Mission Monthly,* and the *Western Recorder,* merging them under the name of the latter. Victor Irvine Masters, Sr. (*q.v.*), became editor in 1921 and served for 21 years—until Oct. 10, 1942. John D. Freeman was editor from 1942 to 1945 and was succeeded in July, 1946, by Reuel Tipton Skinner.

Since its purchase in 1919, the paper has been the property of the Kentucky general association (now the General Convention of Baptists in Kentucky). It is managed by a board of directors of eight people elected by the general association and supported by subscription, gifts from Cooperative Program, and advertising. The budget for 1955 was $15,169.75, advertising; $80,503.24, subscriptions; $77,543.06, job printing; $10,000.00, Cooperative Program; and other items, $449.14, or a total of $183,665.19; and the weekly circulation was 65,000.

GEORGE RALEIGH JEWELL

WESTERN REGION WOMAN'S MISSIONARY UNION CAMP. Founded in 1939 in cooperation with the Woman's Missionary Union of the southwestern region for Royal Ambassador, Girls' Auxiliary, and Young Woman's Auxiliary camps. The facilities of Camp Kuttawa, a nonreligious camp at Kuttawa, Ky., were rented each year until 1951, when Western Region opened its own camp at Schafer Memorial, where camps promoting all phases of Baptist work are held annually. ELDRED M. TAYLOR

WESTERN RELIGIOUS EDUCATION ASSOCIATION. See RELIGIOUS EDUCATION, PROFESSIONAL ASSOCIATIONS.

WESTERN STAR. A Baptist newspaper started by Alvin Bailey at Jacksonville, Ill., in Feb., 1845. Two years later, Bailey sold the paper to Luther Stone, who moved to Chicago and published a paper entitled *Watchman of the Prairies.* LYNN E. MAY, JR.

WESTERN WATCHMAN. A Missouri Baptist paper established in May, 1848, when a contract was made for its publication. It was established as a result of reports made by committees on religious periodicals at the Missouri Baptist General Association meetings in 1845, 1846, 1847. Fire destroyed the newspaper's office before all issues of Vol. I had been published, and the paper was discontinued. In May, 1851, William Crowell, editor and proprietor, published the paper with 1,700 subscribers; but disfavor was incurred, and the paper was discontinued again in 1859. J. R. BLACK

WESTHAMPTON COLLEGE. See UNIVERSITY OF RICHMOND and RICHMOND FEMALE INSTITUTE AND WOMAN'S COLLEGE OF RICHMOND.

WESTMINSTER INSTITUTE. A school at Westminster, Tex., also called North Texas Baptist Academy. It came under the control of Baptists about 1901, was taken over by the Baptist General Convention about 1911, and was maintained until about 1917. RUPERT N. RICHARDSON

WESTRUP, JOHN O. (b. London, England, May 3, 1847; d. Progreso, Coahuila, Mexico, Dec. 21, 1880). Missionary. John Westrup served as agent of the American Bible Society and in 1871 was appointed missionary of the Baptist Home Mission Society of New York. Appointed missionary to Mexico in 1880 by the Texas Baptist state convention, he was accepted later by the Foreign Mission Board as its first missionary to Mexico; but on Dec. 21, 1880, he was murdered by Indians. His brother, Thomas Westrup, had been baptized Jan. 30, 1864, by James Hickey, who, the same day, organized the first evangelical church in Mexico.

BIBLIOGRAPHY: J. G. Chastain, *Thirty Years in Mexico* (1927). T. B. Ray, *Southern Baptists in the Great Adventure* (1934). A. Trevino, *Historia de los Trabajos en Mexico* (1930). E. C. ROUTH

WESTWARD EXPANSION, SOUTHERN BAPTIST. A territorial growth based on certain distinctive principles, which began in the middle of the 18th century during the American Great Awakening, and which has continued since. The expansion originally was westward, reflecting the pattern of growth of the country as a whole, and has at various times been pushed in other directions under the influence of special migration patterns brought by wars, economic cycles, and industrial development.

In general terms the history of Southern Baptist territorial expansion may be divided into three periods. During the first period Baptists were gradually diffused over vast areas of the United States as they followed the basic migration patterns of the country into new settlements in successive frontier regions. This period ended at the Civil War, by which time Southern Baptists had co-operating churches and active mission work throughout the South, the then-settled Southwest, and in the Californian Far West. During the second period, which lasted from the Civil War until 1910, a strong spirit of unity was created out of the struggle for regional and denominational survival. The Southern Baptist Convention developed a rigid sectional and territorial emphasis behind which could be built a united constituency. The third period began in 1910 with the admission of a Southern Baptist general body from the traditionally Northern state of Illinois to fellowship in the Southern Baptist Convention. During this last period the sectional emphasis was abandoned, and the territory actually served by co-operating Southern Baptist churches was enlarged into most of the states of the United States. It is true that Southern Baptist groups in many regions are small and often weak, but they are quite widely dispersed.

In the two periods of greatest expansion, the principles of growth are generally the same. To a large extent this expansion has been based on the inability of many Southern Baptists who have moved into new territories to adjust themselves to the prevailing religious practice in their new environment. Although few in number in any given place, they found strength in fellowship with each other and organized churches of their own. Often they were able to add to their group one of their own ministers who had also migrated in search of economic opportunity. After a church was organized, the evangelistic zeal of those who had constituted it brought in others.

This pattern was characteristic of pioneer days, when most Baptist ministers supported themselves by secular labor and were thus, for economic reasons, a natural part of every frontier movement. The same pattern is also characteristic of modern expansion. Not all ordained Baptist ministers can be supported by their churches but supplement their livings by secular pursuits. These men are often the ones who migrate to Northern industrial centers or to the Far West in search of opportunity. Thus they are naturally the ones called on to lead the small new churches of migrant Baptists in new territories.

In modern times these ministers are an important source of denominational unity. Familiar with the benefits of associational and state convention work in the areas from which they have come, they often seek to align their churches and newly organized associations with stronger centers of Southern Baptist work. Thus Ohio and Indiana associations were related to the Kentucky convention, Michigan associations to the Arkansas convention, and associations in many states throughout the West to a central Arizona or Colorado organization. Through these alignments the ministers and their people express the essential unity which they all feel with the denomination as a whole, in all its programs and activities.

Southern Baptist territorial expansion, therefore, is a phenomenon dependent upon three rather constant though dynamic factors. These are: migration of Baptists and their ministers, rigid sectarian preferences which cause these migrant Baptists to remain loyal to their own church practices and organize their own churches, and zealous evangelical activity. These three factors have significantly characterized the stages of Baptist territorial expansion. They have been created or manifested, however, in a variety of ways.

Migration of Baptists is sociologically and geographically determined. They did not go into new areas as missionaries, but rather moved in search of economic opportunity and carried with them unchanged their particular brand of church life. Their evangelical zeal, whether manifested polemically or beneficently, has been persistently present and has benefited from successive improvements in methodology and leadership. Their denominational loyalty which leads them to hold tenaciously to their own church practices is a crucial and distinctive factor. It has been created and conditioned by various factors within their own polity and fellowship, and its influence has varied in strength and character through the years.

Baptists of various sorts were present in America almost from the beginning. They gravitated to those areas which were most tolerant, but eventually managed to exist, albeit in weak and scattered congregations, throughout the colonies. In the wake of the Great Awakening after 1740, they miltiplied with almost explosive rapidity. A new kind of Baptists arose, called variously Separates, New-Lights, and disturbers of the peace. Many of these people had been state church Congregationalists who were converted in the Great Awakening and who got their Baptist convictions from later Bible study. In the beginning many were extreme enthusiasts. Their zeal in preaching at every opportunity to all and sundry, and their doctrinal instability, at first made them suspect, and they were opposed by their Regular Baptist brethren. In the South, where they were to grow most notably later, they were alternately harassed and endured by the condescending Anglican establishments. Persecution brought them imprisonment, beatings, and riots, but they won great numbers.

As they multiplied, they moved, joining the multitudes of their countrymen who were settling the advancing frontier. By the time of the Revolution, the territory between the Tidewater and the Appalachian Mountains was settled, and the population west of the mountains had grown from nothing to many thousands. Baptists, since they were in the social class from which most of the pioneers came, went in strength to all the new settlements, forming churches and constantly evangelizing. Their preachers, who made their own livings from secular labor, also went in numbers to the new lands. They moved for economic reasons, but they never forgot their religious calling. Thus the Baptists did not have to wait on salaried missionaries or trained and imported ministers to lead them. The ministers had come with the people. When more were needed, the churches ordained whatever men were available and willing. They, of course, demanded certain qualifications of their ministers, but these qualifications were usually more concerned with orthodoxy or eloquence than with ability or training, so it was easy to find suitable candidates. This progressive attitude toward ordination gave the Baptists an advantage of leadership through which they surpassed other denominations over much of the frontier.

At the same time Baptists were expanding over so much new territory, they were also growing toward a notable unity. Persecution and opposition forced Baptists to stand together, in spite of their suspicions of each other. Gradually, the radically evangelical Separate Baptists and the older and more conservative Regular Baptists discovered that their common cause was more important than their differences, and so they compromised. The formal union was achieved in Virginia in 1787, in North Carolina earlier, and in Kentucky in 1801. For a while distinctions were blotted out under the name "United Baptists."

The union came just in time for the Baptists to profit from another period of evangelical enthusiasm which swept the frontier at the beginning of the 19th century. This revival, more extreme in many of its manifestations than the Great Awakening, began with the Presbyterians, but it brought large benefits to the Baptists, who had the advantage of a quite obviously biblical doctrine. Large numbers of those who fell under the converting influence of the revival enthusiasm were brought into Baptist churches, which thus grew and multiplied. As the population followed the westward-moving frontier, Baptists enjoyed another era of rapid growth. As during the Great Awakening, churches were formed wherever Baptists went, and new areas of strength were built on these fundamental organizations. The zealous evangelicalism with which the Baptists built their churches was reinforced by the general religious excitement, and on the strength gained in this revival Baptists extended their territory during the next 50 years into Texas, Missouri, Kansas, Oklahoma, and California.

It was during this period that Luther Rice came, in 1814, to organize a society for the support of foreign missions. He found, in the beginning, a widespread and reasonably united Baptist constituency. This unity, however, did not last. Rice's society-type organization did not allow the churches any really active expression of deominational loyalty, and other issues arose which sowed division and discord for the next several decades. Thus, in spite of a greatly increased territory and perhaps a slight increase in total numbers, Southern Baptists were too crippled by controversy to grow significantly as a denomination. The only loyalties which were successfully cultivated during this period were factional, group loyalties.

In spite of the factional manifestation during the first half of the 18th century, group loyalties were a basic and potentially good principle in Baptist life. As a principle, group loyalty existed from the beginning. It was forged in persecution. There could be no such thing as halfhearted devotion when one was faced with paying for his Baptist convictions with his liberty, his property, or even his life. In order to survive at all, Baptists had to be dogmatic, rigid, exclusive—completely unwilling to compromise the principles which they knew to be true.

When the time of persecution was over, however, and the common enemy had been defeated, Baptists turned this rigid exclusiveness on each other and so were frustrated by a long period of violent factional strife. They believed that the basis for their unity should be doctrine, and they were slow in deciding what that doctrine was. Many of their arguments were semantic, and many of the ones based on a real difference were not of basic importance. Relative importance of issues, however, has never been able to temper controversial heat, and factions multiplied.

The three major evidences of unity among American Baptists prior to the Civil War really had very little to do with the doctrinal matters which Baptists then thought were the only bases of workable unity. The union of Regular and Separate Baptists was based on the practical unity of struggle against a common persecutor and resulted in a doctrinal compromise—the agreement each made to be tolerant of the other's convictions on Calvinism and Arminianism. The Triennial Convention was formed in support of foreign missions—more a method of doctrinal expression than a doctrine in itself. The Southern Baptist Convention was based solely on a disagreement over missionary administration, and the leaders in its organization specifically stated that there was no doctrinal difference involved.

Because overt conscious group loyalty among Southern Baptists in this era was largely a loyalty to a theological point of view, both theology and loyalty became divisive forces. Denominationalism degenerated past sectarianism into pure factionalism. Antimissionism, Campbellism, and Landmarkism brought bitter and crippling division, but at the same time forced Southern Baptists to answer their opposition by taking sides, by defining ever more clearly their distinctive position, and by strengthening more and more their loyalty to it. Southern Baptists thus forged in the heat of controversy the form of the rigid denominationalism which became, when it was later given an appropriate content, one of the chief causes of their continued growth and unity.

In spite of division, growth continued after the same essential pattern. In the new frontier areas from Texas to California, Baptists settled and organized churches, then evangelized their neighbors. After these individuals had on their own adventurous initiative begun religious work, they often appealed to the denomination for help. Home missionaries were sent to them to lead and reinforce their work. These missionaries generally did not initiate Baptist work in the territories into which they were sent; rather they helped to develop the work that was already there. They would preach to a circuit of weak churches and assist in constituting others as needed. They would help in the ordination of ministers and in the forming of associations. They would preach in revivals and lead the work of evangelism. Altogether they did great good. But they were not necessary either to the beginning or to the survival of Baptist work, as was proved when they were withdrawn during and after the Civil War.

This war and its aftermath were times of supreme crisis for Southern Baptists. Their Convention, which had been formed in 1845, was a truly denominational organization through which the churches could actively express their unity. However, it was not at first fully appreciated as such. At least until after the Civil War, the rank and file of Southern Baptists did not fully understand the radical distinctiveness of the organization which a few wise leaders had brought them to create. During reconstruction and the difficult years which followed, they gradually came to appreciate their Southern Baptist Convention as the organized expression, not only of their wish to do mission work, but of their total oneness as a denomination.

This understanding grew out of the travail of poverty and the struggle for survival. During this period Southern Baptists did not significantly expand. The country continued to grow, but Southerners in large numbers did not have the money or the inclination to leave home, and so for more than a generation were left behind. Instead of looking out for new worlds to conquer, the Southern Baptist Convention, under the leadership of Secretary Tichenor of the Home Mission Board, adopted a policy of rigid territorial sectionalism, giving up to the aggressive American Baptist Home Mission Society all outlying territories in order to preserve themselves at the center. With no money for active mission work, Tichenor relied on the same forces which in politics were creating the "solid South" to capture the loyalty of the constituency for the Southern Baptist Convention. This sectional loyalty was at first based more on opposition to invasion than on any positive affection for the Southern Baptist Convention, but it was enough. The Southern Baptist Convention was saved, and Baptists in the South became more rigidly sectarian than ever. They became increasingly devoted to their own distinctiveness, even though at this time many of them were not at all sure what their distinctives were. In essence they became accustomed to the pure activity of being loyal.

When the South began to recover from its economic prostration, Southern Baptists entered into another era of expansion. This time, however, their spirit of loyalty was not divisive but unifying and grew more and more so as their churches began to develop common ways of doing things. Increasingly the denomination was able to ignore radicals who tried to stir up destructive controversy over disputed points of polity or doctrine. Broad agreement on basic fundamentals coupled with a pointed and insistent tolerance of fringe differences made doctrine more of a foundation than an issue. The unity which has grown so strong that it might be termed compulsive was built on a different kind of content. This content was method.

In the 20th century the practices and procedures of Southern Baptist churches have grown more and more uniform. The work of the Southern Baptist Sunday School Board in providing published materials for church educational work, and in developing and promoting an ever more efficient and comprehensive methodology for the accomplishment of that work, has given to Southern Baptists a large part of their common pattern of church activity. The mission emphases of the Woman's Missionary Union, Auxiliary to the Southern Baptist Convention, have led to the development of elaborate programs and activities, which give to Baptist women and children an important measure of uniform and devotedly shared practice. The work of the Executive Committee of the Southern Baptist Convention, particularly through its Promotion Committee, has given to Southern Baptists various programs of stewardship, culminating in the Cooperative Program. In the area of church finance, effective methodologies have been created and promoted. Through it all Southern Baptists have achieved a large measure of uniformity in this major area of church life. In addition, co-operative planning and promotion by various state and regional workers with similar responsibilities has added still more uniformity. The net result is that a Southern Baptist, relatively speaking, can feel at home in almost any Southern Baptist church. There are, of course, cultural, economic, and social differences, but these are uniformly present and understood and are therefore much less important an influence on denominational unity than this overriding uniformity of church practice.

Thus a Southern Baptist tends to remain a Southern Baptist, whether he lives in Virginia, Georgia, California, Ohio, or Montana. He does not easily adjust to a church fellowship in which methods and practices are different from those to which he has been conditioned. Churches which are methodologically different are automatically suspect. If in addition these other Baptist churches are rumored to be different also in doctrine, then they are regarded by some as being untouchable and heretical.

Therefore, when the 20th century brought, through two wars and a depression, a great increase in the number of migrants, Southern Baptists were in a peculiar position to profit therefrom. The South, the area of their strength, did not receive much Baptist immigration. But Southerners did move out in vast numbers. They went to the Far West, to the great industrial centers of the North, to army camps throughout the whole country and beyond. The Baptists among them for the most part remained tenaciously Southern Baptist. The pattern first manifested in the great revivals of 1750 and 1800, reinforced by a denominational unity far stronger than it had been before, was repeated as Southern Baptists began their era of greatest expansion. In times when the whole country was disturbed, in transition, or on the move, Southern Baptist churches sprang up spontaneously wherever Southern Baptists went and found each other. Weak congregations rapidly grew strong by evangelizing their rootless neighbors. Their success is demonstrated by the organization and successful growth of associations and even state conventions in areas far outside territory traditionally considered Southern.

At first the Southern Baptist Convention, officially, was disposed to ignore these people. Still thinking in the sectional, territorial terms which had saved them from destruction at the hands of Northern mission advance, they hesitated to recognize these other Southern Baptists as a part of their fellowship. Gradually, however, opinion shifted and finally reversed. Southern Baptists became convinced that their field was all North America, and the Northern (now American) Baptist Convention, in self-defense, came more and more to the sectional, territorial position which they had before opposed from their position of previous strength.

In all their expansion Southern Baptists have demonstrated the power of a denominationalism properly defined. In their polity there is no unifying principle beyond voluntary co-operation. In doctrine there is basic agreement but a broad array of difference in interpretation. In their commonly shared church practices, on the other hand, there is a strength which does not compromise liberty. By working together in the same ways at the same tasks, Southern Baptists build a powerful emotional and spiritual unity which leaves the mind and heart free but channels action into one concerted and effective effort.

BIBLIOGRAPHY: R. Babcock, ed., *Forty Years of Pioneer Life, Memoir of John Mason Peck* (1864). R. A. Baker, *Relations Between Northern and Southern Baptists* (1948). W. A. Carleton, *Not Yours But You* (1954); "Westward, Southern Baptists Wend Their Way," *The Quarterly Review* (April, May, June, 1957). F. Looney, *History of California Southern Baptists* (1954). Z. N. Morrell, *Flowers and Fruits in the Wilderness* (1886). R. B. Semple, *A History of the Rise and Progress of the Baptists in Virginia* (1810). J. H. Spencer, *A History of Kentucky Baptists* (1886). J. W. Sherwood, *Memoir of Adiel Sherwood* (1884). W. W. Sweet, *Religion in Colonial America* (1942); *Religion in the Development of American Culture* (1952); *Religion on the American Frontier, the Baptists, 1783–1830* (1931).

JUDSON BOYCE ALLEN

WHARTON, HENRY MARVIN (b. Western View, Culpeper County, Va., Sept. 11, 1848; d. Baltimore, Md., June 23, 1928). Lawyer, clergyman, evangelist, publisher, and Chaplain General of the United Confederate Veterans. At the age of 16, Wharton enlisted in the Confederate army, serving first as a dispensary clerk in a hospital at Lynchburg, Va., and later in General Lee's army until its surrender at Appomattox Court House. A year later he entered Roanoke College, Salem, Va., where he studied law. For five years he practiced law at Amherst, Va. In 1874 he was baptized by his brother and later entered Southern Baptist Theological Seminary. After he was ordained to the ministry, he became pastor of First Baptist Church, Eufaula, Ala. Later he served as pastor at Luray and Fort Royal, Va. In Jan., 1881, he went to Lee Street Church, Baltimore, Md., but resigned in 1883 to engage in the publishing business in connection with the *Baltimore Baptist.* He was called in 1886 to the newly established Brantly Baptist Church, where he served as pastor until Jan. 1, 1900, when he resigned to engage in full-time evangelistic work in the United States and England. In May, 1909, he was recalled to the pastorate of Brantly, where he spent 33 of his 55 active years in the ministry. The D.D. degree was conferred on him by Howard College in 1890. MRS. LESLIE M. BOWLING

WHARTON, LUCY KIMBALL POLLARD (b. Baltimore, Md., Dec. 9, 1871; d. Weems, Va., July 30, 1948). Woman's Missionary Union secretary and first personal service chairman. Her father, James Pollard, a prominent Baltimore attorney, was active in the Eutaw Place Baptist Church and founder of its Chinese Sunday school for the Chinese immigrants of Baltimore; her mother, Susan (Tyler) Pollard, assisted him in this work for many years. "Lulie" said of her childhood, "I absorbed atmosphere rather than facts. One of my first memories was a gold-lettered mite box put out by 'Woman's Mission to Women' which stood on our dining table awaiting contributions." Woman's Missionary Union was of prime importance in the family, since Lulie's father helped frame its constitution and her mother was its first recording secretary. Original headquarters for the Woman's Missionary Union were in the office building of the *Baltimore Baptist,* a denominational weekly edited and published by Henry Marvin Wharton (*q.v.*), who invited the women to hold their meetings there. Wharton, whom Lulie later married on Oct. 31, 1893, baptized her when she was nine years old at Lee Street Baptist Church in Baltimore. After education in Baltimore public schools and musical studies at the Peabody Institute there, she attended Mary Baldwin College at Staunton, Va., 1889–90.

For a few years following her marriage, Mrs. Wharton's home was in Baltimore, where her husband was pastor of Brantly Baptist Church, which he had founded. Her first daughter was born in 1896, and the family later moved to Philadelphia, while Wharton engaged in extensive evangelistic work at home and abroad. A son was born in 1899 and another daughter, in 1907. Returning to Baltimore in 1910, Mrs. Wharton helped organize Woman's Missionary Union's personal service department, became its first chairman, and developed the various branches of its work until her resignation in 1924. From 1913 to 1938, she served first as assistant recording secretary and then as recording secretary of the union. In 1936 Mrs. Wharton wrote the booklet, "Ready Pens Proclaiming Missions," a history of the publication activities of Southern Baptist women from 1886 to 1936, which the Woman's Missionary Union literature department published in observance of its 50th anniversary. At the completion of 25 years of service in 1938, Mrs. Wharton resigned her secretaryship. A coworker recalls "her gracious platform presence, her beautiful voice reading the minutes of the session, her spiritual approach to every problem." She was an honorary member of the Woman's Missionary Union executive committee, 1938–48.

Although she was not regularly active as a public speaker, one of her addresses was published in the 1938 Woman's Missionary Union *Annual Report*—"As My Mother Knew Them," a story of the union's early struggles. She wrote *The Fruits of the Years* as the preparatory book for study prior to the 1938 Week of Prayer for Home Missions. Her last years were devoted to study, correspondence, and the preparation of missionary publications. "I could go to missionary meetings three times a day every day," she used to say. No one could know her, even casually, without realizing that Woman's Missionary Union was the central interest of her life.

JAMES WHARTON

WHITE, BENJAMIN FRANKLIN (b. near Spartanburg, S. C., Sept. 20, 1800; d. Atlanta, Ga., Dec. 5, 1879). Southern singing-school teacher and the author of *Sacred Harp.* The youngest of 14 children, White had little formal education and was self-taught in music. About 1840 he moved to Harris County, Ga., and there published the newspaper, *The Organ,* in which many of his sacred songs first appeared. Although he considered teaching in singing schools his life work, he never employed his musical talent for financial gain. He served at one time as clerk of the superior court in Harris County. He married Thurza Golightly in 1825, to which marriage were born 14 children. In 1844, with E. J. King as coeditor, he published the *Sacred Harp,* the foremost *fa-sol-la* book of the 19th century. Revised editions appeared in 1850, 1854, 1859, 1869, 1911, and 1936, giving this book the longest continuous history of any of the shape-note singing books. White became founder and president of the Southern Musical Convention, organized in 1847 in Upson County, Ga., for the purpose of promoting *fa-sol-la* singing. He was a member of a missionary Baptist church.

WILLIAM J. REYNOLDS

WHITE, JOHN ELLINGTON (b. Clayton, N. C., Dec. 19, 1868; d. Savannah, Ga., July 21, 1931). Minister, educator. Son of James McDaniel and Martha (Ellington) White, he received from Wake Forest the A.B. degree, 1890; D.D., 1905; and from Baylor, D.D., 1910. Ordained to the ministry in 1892, he served as pastor of First Baptist Church, Edenton, N. C., 1893–96; Second Baptist Church, Atlanta, Ga., 1901–16; First Baptist Church, Anderson, S. C., 1916–27 (while president of Anderson College); and First Baptist Church, Savannah, Ga., 1927–31. White was secretary of missions of the North Carolina Baptist convention, 1896–1901. He was founder of Baptist schools for mountaineers; president of Clifton Conference for Negro schools; president of Georgia Baptist Board of Education; president of Georgia Baptist convention, 1929–31; vice-president of Southern Baptist Convention, 1930–31; first vice-president of Southern Social Congress; stated preacher and lecturer, University of Chicago, 1914–16. His writings include *The Silent Southerners* (1906), *My Old Confederate* (1907), *The New Task and Opportunity of the South* (1908), *Southern Highlanders* (1913), *Thinking White in the South* (Phelps-Stokes lectures, U. of Va.) (1914), *A Yielded Pacifist* (1917). White married Effie L. Guess, Oct. 12, 1892.

BIBLIOGRAPHY: *Who Was Who in America,* Vol. 1, 1897–1942 (1943). "Tributes of Love to John E. White," *The Christian Index* (July 30, 1931).

S. L. MORGAN

WHITEFIELD, GEORGE (b. Gloucester, England, Dec. 16, 1714; d. Newburyport, Mass., Sept. 30, 1770). The evangelist most responsible for the Great Awakening in the American colonies beginning in 1740. He was the son of Thomas Whitefield, a descendant of a noted family of ministers, dating back to William Whytfeild, vicar in Sussex in 1605. Thomas, an innkeeper, died when George was two. At 12 the son was placed in St. Mary de Crypt School, where he studied for three years. Then he worked for a brief time in his mother's public house as a drawer in the tavern, where he became "proficient in the school of the devil." In Nov., 1732, he entered Oxford University, having secured a servitor's scholarship to Pembroke College. Outraged by the wickedness of students, he lived much to himself. Later, impressed by the asceticism and good works of the Holy Club which the Wesleys had founded, he became such an ardent disciple that he suffered a serious illness during which he had a miraculous conversion.

Ordained a deacon in Gloucester June 30, 1736, he preached his first sermon the following Sunday. A great crowd heard him, and 15 people were so affected that they were reported as mad. His fame immediately spread. He went to London, boldly proclaiming the necessity of the new birth; youths flocked to his services along with the nobility, some of whom were converted. Attractive pastorates were opened to him.

Then through the Wesleys came the call to America. On board ship he started a revival among the wicked seamen as well as passengers. He landed at Savannah, sought a location for an orphanage, and began preaching. He remained long enough to secure from the Georgia Colony a tract of 500 acres for the orphanage, then returned to England to raise funds. During his stay, London felt the power of his preaching. In Scotland violent emotions, jerks, and convulsions gripped some congregations.

He returned to America in 1739 with helpers. His orphanage was begun. Soon he was in New England, a region already much affected by the revival which Jonathan Edwards had launched in 1735. Throngs heard him in Philadelphia, including Benjamin Franklin, who wrote in his *Memoirs,* "It is wonderful to see the change so soon made in the manners of our inhabitants." After a few days in Philadelphia he went to New York and along the way preached to throngs of people who heard him with unashamed tears. The Church of England had closed its doors to him, so he turned to free church groups and to fields.

He began the year 1740 in Savannah, where calls for his services were incessant. In February he visited James Oglethorpe, founder of the colony, and remonstrated with him about restrictions which he had placed upon the settlers. He preached in Charleston, S. C., where great emotional outbursts resulted. In April he returned to Philadelphia, where, the parish church being denied him, he preached on Society Hill to some 15,000 people. On Apr. 29 he was back in New York City, where for nine days he preached from two to seven times daily.

June found him back in Savannah, where work on his orphanage was progressing. July was spent in and near Charleston. On Sept. 14 he was in Newport, R. I., where the legislature adjourned to hear him. In Bristol, Mass., the court invited him to speak at noon. In Boston he preached on the Commons to 4,000 one day, to 6,000 the next, and on the Lord's Day to 8,000. Five busy weeks were spent in New England, and he returned to Boston for a farewell message on the Commons, which was heard by some 30,000 people. He returned to Savannah that fall and renewed his evangelistic work there and in Charleston.

He was a powerful preacher, with a voice that could be heard for great distances. "He loved those who thunder out the Word". . . because . . . "nothing but a loud voice can awaken sinners." "His preaching was a triumph of impassioned oratory." The awakening which he inaugurated resulted in the multiplication of churches, a new spirit of fellowship among churches, a distinct and nobler evangelism, opening the way for the Sunday school movement, promoting Christian education and missions, and the unification of the colonies, making the way for the union of states. Following a strenuous campaign in New England, he died suddenly Sept. 30, 1770, in the home of the pastor of First Presbyterian Church, Newburyport, Mass., which congregation had developed out of his Calvinistic preaching. At his request his body was buried under the church pulpit.

BIBLIOGRAPHY: *Dictionary of American Biography* (1932). *Dictionary of National Biography* (1891). L. Tyerman, *The Life of the Rev. George Whitefield* (2 vols., 1876–77). JOHN D. FREEMAN

WHITEHEAD ACADEMY. A Baptist school at Whitehead, Allegheny County, N. C., operated in 1897–98 by E. Leff Wagoner. It was endorsed by Ashe and Allegheny, Ashe, and Allegheny and Grayson associations.

D. L. SMILEY

WHITINGTON, OTTO (b. Waldron, Scott County, Ark., July 4, 1880; d. Little Rock, Ark., Feb. 2, 1951). Minister, fund-raiser, and evangelist. He received his Th.M. degree from Southern Baptist Theological Seminary, May, 1908, and his D.D. degree from Ouachita College, Arkadelphia, Ark. He married Minnie Lou Hulsey, Apr. 20, 1904. To them were born five children: Harry, Martha, Mary, Otto, Jr., and Omar H. He was pastor of the following Arkansas Baptist churches: Midland; Hartford; Ohio St., Pine Bluff; First, Conway; Immanuel, Little Rock; and First, Springdale; and of the Fordsville church in Kentucky. He was president of the Arkansas Baptist Convention, 1929–30; state organizer of the 75 Million Campaign; director of the debt-paying campaign, 1936–37; evangelist for Southwestern Seminary, 1916–19; secretary of Arkansas evangelism, 1945–47; and leader of the Ouachita College million-dollar campaign, 1947–49. He was an enthusiastic evangelist and an able debater who made telling use of humorous stories and apt illustrations.

C. HAMILTON MOSES

WHITSITT, JAMES (b. Amherst County, Va., Jan. 31, 1771; d. Nashville, Tenn., Apr. 12, 1849). He was converted in a revival in 1789 under the preaching of Joseph Anthony and began preaching immediately. He married Jane Cardwell, 1792; they had 11 children. He was one of the leading organizers of Missionary Baptist work in Tennessee, including the Moro District—the first association formed in the Cumberland Valley. Originally this association included all the churches in Tennessee west of the mountains. Later, when the Cumberland Association was organized, his churches were transferred there. Then, because the Cumberland Association's territory was too large, the Concord Association was started. Whitsitt's churches were a part of Concord from the beginning. The history of Whitsitt's labors was substantially the history of the Baptist denomination in the Cumberland Valley from the time he became pastor at Mill Creek in 1794 until he had to retire because of old age. While at Mill Creek he was pastor of three other fourth-time churches: Concord in Williamson County, Rock Spring and Providence churches in Rutherford County. A few years later, the church at Antioch, on Mill Creek, was organized, and he became pastor of it and gave up Rock Spring. He labored with these churches about 30 or 40 years.

> [He was] a man of striking personal appearance and manners—frame tall, combining elegance and strength, hair black, eyes dark . . . manly and intellectual, uniting great benevolence and unyielding firmness. . . . [An] earnest friend of missions, [he] had a primary agency in originating and sustaining the missionary operations of our State. He left a broader mark upon his generation than almost any of his associates in the ministry.

W. LEONARD STIGLER

WHITSITT, WILLIAM HETH (b. near Nashville, Tenn., Nov. 25, 1841; d. Richmond, Va., Jan. 20, 1911). Seminary president, professor, author of books on Baptist history. Son of Rubin Ewing and Dicey (McFarland) Whitsitt; his grandfather, James Whitsitt, was pastor of Baptist churches in middle Tennessee. Whitsitt attended Mount Juliet Academy and graduated from Union University, Jackson, Tenn., in 1861. During the Civil War he served first as a scout and then as chaplain in the Confederate Army, after which he continued his education at the University of Virginia (1866), Southern Baptist Theological Seminary (1866–68), and spent two years of study in the universities of Leipzig and Berlin. In 1872, while serving as pastor in Albany, Ga., Whitsitt was elected to the Chair of Ecclesiastical History at Southern Seminary, then located in Greenville, S. C. At the death of President John Albert Broadus (*q.v.*) in 1895, Whitsitt was elected president of the seminary, which had been moved to Louisville, Ky., in 1877.

The "Whitsitt Controversy," which stirred Southern Baptists, grew out of an article by Whitsitt published in *Johnson's Universal Cyclopaedia* in 1886. Whitsitt reported in the article that according to extant evidence, "believer's baptism" by immersion was restored by English Baptists in 1641. This statement greatly disturbed persons who believed that an unbroken succession of Baptist churches could be traced from the apostolic era, and relentless warfare was waged on Whitsitt and the seminary by some Southern Baptist newspaper editors and correspondents. At length seminary trustees became convinced that harmony could be restored only by President Whitsitt's resignation, which was offered and accepted in 1899. Soon thereafter he was elected professor of philosophy in Richmond College, Richmond, Va., where he continued to teach until his death in 1911. Whitsitt's published works include *Position of the Baptists in the History of American Culture* (1872); *The History of the Rise of Infant Baptism* (1878); *The History of Communion Among Baptists* (1880); *A Question in Baptist History* (1896); *The Origin of the Disciples of Christ* (1888); *The Life and Times of Judge Caleb Wallace* (1888); and *A Genealogy of Jefferson Davis* (1908). GAINES S. DOBBINS

WIDOWS AND SUPERANNUATED MINISTERS' FUND (Maryland). This fund consists entirely of money bequeathed to the Maryland Baptist Union Association, the income only to be used. For many years, it was administered by a state associational committee which determined the amount to be paid each beneficiary. On Sept. 30, 1930, this committee was discontinued and its function assumed by the advisory committee of the state board. The income was paid to the Relief and Annuity Board. Since 1940, when the state was obligated to pay a percentage on ministers' salaries in the pension plan, the income has been used to pay part of the state expense.

MRS. FRANCIS A. DAVIS

WIDOWS SUPPLEMENTAL ANNUITY PLAN (A). Supplemental to Ministers Retirement Plan, calling for an additional 1½ per cent of salary, matched by state convention. After one year of participation, annuity for a widow in the amount of 10 per cent of salary is available (salary participation limited to $4,000 per year). The amount of annuity increases 2 per cent each year until the sixth year when the maximum of 20 per cent is reached. Dues increase ½ per cent at age 60 and another ½ per cent if member continues in active service after age 65. In case of total and permanent disability, the widow plan is kept in force free of charge to member. Protection under this plan ceases at time of member's retirement unless he holds a certificate in the Ministers Security Plan.

Widows Supplemental Annuity Plan (B), Supplement to the Baptist Boards Employees Retirement Plan. Benefits are the same as under the Widows Supplemental Annuity Plan (A) with exception that dues increase at age 50 and again at age 55. The Baptist Boards Employees Security Plan may be added to this supplement.

MABLE MCCARTNEY

WILBUR, WILLIAM ALLEN (b. Mystic, Conn., Aug. 15, 1864; d. Washington, D. C., Jan. 25, 1945). Teacher and educator. A graduate of Brown University with the A.B. and M.A. degrees, Wilbur taught in various New England institutions from 1890 to 1895, when he went to Washington, D. C. From 1895 to 1897, he was dean of Columbian College, which later became George Washington University. From 1897 to 1935, Wilbur served as head of the English department of that institution. After his death *The Evening Star* of Washington carried the following tribute: "Even after his retirement from the University in 1935 and his withdrawal from active Bible teaching . . . 'Dean Wilbur' was known to thousands of Washingtonians who had come under his wholesome and lasting classroom influence."

Active in denominational affairs, Wilbur was for a time a member of the First Baptist Church of Washington and of Calvary Baptist Church, Washington, where he taught the Wilbur Class for 30 years. From 1913 to 1916, he was moderator of the Columbia Association of Baptist Churches. He was the author of *Chronicles of Calvary Baptist in the City of Washington* (1913), *History of the Columbia Association of Baptist Churches* (1928), and *The Ministry of Samuel Harrison Greene* (1936). He also wrote an English rhetoric, which he used in his classes in the university. DOROTHY CLARK WINCHCOLE

WILEY, WILLIAM SHERMAN (b. Watson, Ill., Mar. 17, 1867; d. Muskogee, Okla., Mar. 30, 1935). Field secretary of the Sunday School Board of the Southern Baptist Convention from 1910 until his death. He was converted Sept. 21, 1881. In 1885 he married Nannie McDonald. To this marriage five children were born, two boys and three girls. Mrs. Wiley died in 1896. In 1900 he married Mrs. Susan Cowan. Wiley moved to Indian Territory in 1887 and taught in the schools for Indians. He organized a church and was called to be the first pastor. From 1896 to 1908, he served as field missionary for the American Baptist Publication Society. While field secretary for the Baptist Sunday School Board, his greatest contribution was the promotion of Sunday school work through study classes for training workers rather than through inspirational institutes and rallies. He gave particular impetus to Sunday school work for Intermediates.

BIBLIOGRAPHY: P. E. Burroughs, *Fifty Fruitful Years* (1941). J. M. Price, *Baptist Leaders in Religious Education* (1943). E. STANLEY WILLIAMSON

WILLET, JOSEPH EDGERTON (b. Macon, Ga., Nov. 17, 1826; d. Atlanta, Ga., Feb. 12, 1897). Teacher of science. He was the son of Joseph and Margaret (McKay) Willet and was of Welsh and Scottish descent. On Jan. 2, 1851, he married Emily Sanders, daughter of Billington McCarty Sanders (*q.v.*), first president of Mercer University, from which (June, 1846) young Willet graduated. The honorary LL.D. degree was conferred upon him by Howard College in 1884. He studied law in Macon, 1847. In that year, before his 21st birthday, he was elected professor of chemistry and natural philosophy at Mercer, which position he retained for 46 years, until June, 1893. In 1848 he entered Yale for postgraduate study and was one of the founders and first president of the Berzelius Society (Oct. 13, 1848), the objective of which was scientific research. His portrait hangs in the society's hall. He returned to his position at Mercer in 1849.

During the Civil War he was superintendent of the laboratory for the manufacture of ammunition in the Confederate arsenal, Atlanta. In 1869 he became a fellow of the American Association for the Advancement of Science, and wrote for the Baptist Publication Society an article entitled "Wonders of Insect Life," for which a prize of $500 was awarded. From Sept., 1871, to Oct., 1872, he suffered nervous prostration as a result of overwork. In 1873 his writings contributed to the defeat of a scheme to unify and to give state financial aid to denominational schools. He was a member of United States Commission (1878–79) to investigate the ravages of the cotton caterpillar on the staple. He continued for some years as a lecturer on science and as a writer of scientific articles for the *American Journal of Science*. Willet was a lover of music and was a member of a church choir directed by Mrs. John Joyner Brantley (*q.v.*).

The Mercer hall of science is a memorial to, and bears the name of, Joseph E. Willet. One of the Willet sons, Hugh M., became president of the Mercer board of trustees in 1927.

After serving as chairman of the faculty, 1893, Willet retired from Mercer and joined the teaching staff of the medical department of the University of Georgia at Augusta. EDWIN S. DAVIS

WILLETT, JAMES OLIVIER (b. Mo., Feb. 27, 1867; d. Phoenix, Ariz., Sept. 22, 1954). Indian mission pastor. After graduating from Southern Baptist Theological Seminary, Willett served pastorates in Carruthersville, Poplar Bluff, West Plains, and Joplin, Mo. He moved to Arizona because of his health in 1918 and operated Four Mile Trading Post, near Sacaton, Pima Indian Reservation. Willett was invited by a resident missionary of another denomination to teach in Sunday school, and his interpretation of New Testament doctrines of regeneration, the Lord's Supper, and baptism led to a request by Indians for a New Testament Baptist church. As a result Willett organized a mission of First Baptist Church, an affiliate of the National Baptist convention, in Tempe, Ariz., in 1921. Two years later Willett led the Indian mission to First Southern Baptist Church, Phoenix, and after a few months the mission was organized into First Pima Indian Baptist Church, Sacaton.

Willett, as the first pastor, served until 1932, when he resigned because of ill health. He was first president of the Baptist General Convention of Arizona from 1928 to 1930.

MRS. W. C. (CARRIE W.) HENDERSON

WILLIAM CAREY COLLEGE. A four-year liberal arts college in Hattiesburg, Miss., owned and operated by Mississippi Baptists and established in 1906. The school has operated under three names: South Mississippi College (1906–09), Mississippi Woman's College (1911–40; 1946–54), and William Carey College since 1954. W. I. Thames, a pioneer educator in South Mississippi, founded South Mississippi College in Hattiesburg in 1906, and the school operated successfully until 1909 when fire destroyed the administration building with all contents. Early in 1911, W. S. F. Tatum, a Methodist layman who had acquired the college property, offered it to Baptists as a gift, conditioned upon the successful operation of a Christian school for girls for five consecutive years, with an attendance of not less than 100 the first year. A corporation was organized under Mississippi state laws to own and control the college, and nine trustees were chosen from four Baptist churches of Hattiesburg: First, Columbia Street (now Main Street), Immanuel, and Fifth Avenue (now Temple). The nine trustees elected W. W. Rivers, president of Central College, Conway, Ark., to the presidency, and at the opening exercises in the Old Red Circle Auditorium in Sept., 1911, Rivers gave the new institution the name Mississippi Woman's College. The charter was granted Oct. 31, 1911.

When the school was offered free of debt to the convention in 1911, the convention formally accepted it, and John Lipscomb Johnson, Jr., was elected the first president under convention control. Following Johnson, who served until his death on Feb. 1, 1932, W. E. Holcomb assumed the presidency and continued through the session of 1939–40 when financial troubles and the college's loss of accreditation caused Holcomb and the entire board of trustees to resign. After operation was suspended, the plant was leased to the army as a housing project for the use of officers at Camp Shelby.

Trustees reopened the college Sept. 9, 1947, under I. E. Rouse, president and business manager.

In 1953, after three years of survey, the Mississippi Baptist Convention voted a coeducational status to Mississippi Woman's College and authorized a new name in keeping with this status. Trustees selected the name William Carey in honor of the "father of modern missions," and the Mississippi convention's board approved it in Apr., 1954.

The campus, comprising 40 acres within the Hattiesburg city limits, includes eight buildings: Tatum Court, the administration building; Ross and Johnson Halls, twin dormitories for girls; a boy's dormitory; a dining hall; Mary Ross Hospital; a science hall; and the president's home. Carey College is accredited by the Mississippi Accreditation Commission and is approved by the Department of Education of Mississippi for teacher training and by the University of Mississippi. With an enrolment of 402 in the 1954–55 session, it operated on a budget of $199,600.00. Property value totals $1,048,788.01, and endowment, as of Aug. 1, 1955, $457,276.95.

J. RALPH NOONKESTER

WILLIAM CAREY CRANE COLLEGE. A coeducational school, opened on a part of the old Baylor campus, at Independence, Tex., after the removal of Baylor University to Waco in 1886. Tryon Baptist Association sponsored the school. It ceased to operate after 1889.

RUPERT N. RICHARDSON

WILLIAM JEWELL COLLEGE. This college had its inception in 1843 when Dr. William Jewell, a prominent physician of Columbia, Mo., tendered to the Baptist General Association of Missouri $10,000 as a nucleus for the endowment of a college. In 1844 the general association declined this offer because it could not raise an additional contingent sum. However, in 1847 the association appointed a committee of Roland Hughes, William Carson, Wade M. Jackson, R. E. McDaniel, and David Perkins to originate an institution of learning for the Baptists of Missouri, upon a plan by which its endowment and perpetuity might be secured. This committee reported in 1848, and the charter for the college was granted by the state legislature of Missouri and approved by the governor, Feb. 27, 1849, a date which is celebrated as Founder's Day.

The charter of William Jewell College provides for a self-perpetuating board of trustees. Although it has legal authority to fill vacancies, the board co-operates with the Baptist General Association of Missouri in selecting trustees.

On Aug. 21, 1849, the trustees who had been appointed and named in the charter met at Boonville and selected Liberty, Mo., as the location for the new college which at that time had a total subscription of $59,432. Alexander W. Doniphan of Mexican War fame and James T. V. Thompson of Liberty presented the case for Liberty and submitted $7,000 which they had collected from the citizens of Clay County. At this time the college was named for the Columbia physician who had also been prominent in founding the University of Missouri and Hardin College.

Instruction began Jan. 1, 1850, in rented rooms with E. S. Dulin, principal and professor of ancient languages; T. F. Lockett, professor of mathematics; and William M. Hunsaker, principal of the preparatory department. In Sept., 1850, the college transferred to the basement of the Second Baptist Church and remained until it could occupy the building being constructed. Jewell Hall was erected in 1851 and 1852 under the supervision of Dr. William Jewell. He was unduly exposed to the heat of the summer of 1852, and died in Liberty, Aug. 7, 1852, at 64 years of age. In 1853 the financial condition of William Jewell College having become brighter, the trustees reorganized the faculty to consist of Robert S. Thomas as the first president and professor of moral philosophy; Thomas Bradley, professor of ancient languages; James Love, professor of mathematics and natural sciences; T. C. Harris, professor of English literature; L. M. Lawson, tutor; and William P. Lamb as principal of the preparatory department.

In 1855 William Jewell College graduated its first class of five members who received the A.B. degree. The first catalogue of the college was issued in 1854 reporting attendance of 110 in the preparatory department and 50 in the college classes. The college subjects at that time were Latin, Greek, algebra, geometry, trigonometry, analytic geometry, differential and integral calculus, natural philosophy, chemistry, geology, mineralogy, mental philosophy, logic, rhetoric, ethics, history, constitutional and international law, political economy, and the evidences of Christianity.

Because of financial difficulties, William Jewell College was closed from June, 1855, to Sept., 1857, when the endowment was $25,472, and the indebtedness was $10,000. The citizens of Clay County agreed to pay off this indebtedness, and an additional endowment of $50,000 was secured. William Thompson was elected the new president, May, 1857; he opened the college that fall with M. W. Robinson, John T. Davis, J. B. Bradley, E. S. Dulin, W. C. Garnett, and G. L. Black as members of the faculty. The session of 1857–58 had an enrolment of 91 students.

In 1853 the Philomathic Literary Society was organized, and the Excelsior Literary Society was organized in 1857. These two societies dominated the student body activities for the next 75 years. In 1857 a Board of Ministerial Education was formed which obtained an additional endowment of $40,000 in order that the college could afford to give reduced tuition, and in some cases full tuition, to students studying for the ministry.

William Jewell was flourishing and had the support of the entire state of Missouri when the Civil War broke out. But in Aug., 1861, the presidency and all the professorships were declared vacant by the trustees and so remained until the end of the war. At various times during the war, however, Thompson and three others taught from time to time and depended entirely upon the receipts from tuition. Federal troops on two different occasions in '61 and '62 occupied Jewell Hall.

It was not until June 24, 1867, that the trustees elected Thomas Rambaut to the presidency. He toured the states to raise an endowment of $250,000. The college reopened Sept. 28, 1868; with an attendance of 81 students and with R. B. Semple, professor of French and Latin; A. F. Fleet, professor of Greek and German; John F. Lanneau, professor of mathematics; and James R. Eaton, professor of natural sciences. Dr. Rambaut reorganized the college into eight schools following the plan of operation at the University of Virginia. Norman Fox was appointed to the chair of English and history in 1869. The total assets of the college then were $101,547, and in 1870 the amount was $200,502. During the school year 1871–72, there were 152 students of whom 46 had the ministry in view. Dr. Rambaut broke his health by his great activity in behalf of the college and resigned the presidency in 1874.

W. R. Rothwell, who had come on the faculty in 1871, became the chairman of the faculty; no president was elected until 1892. James G. Clark became professor of mathematics and French in the fall of 1873. It was this strong faculty of the 1870's and the 1880's without a president which enhanced the academic, spiritual, and cultural place which William Jewell began to fill in the Middle West. During these years, W. Pope Yeaman, Lewis B. Ely, and G. W. Hyde promoted the financial stability of the institution. In 1881 a brick three-story men's dormitory was erected and named Ely Hall; this building today is called Old Ely Hall.

In 1885 the Virginia plan of college education was abandoned; the course for the Bachelor of Arts degree was arranged in four classes, freshman, sophomore, junior, and senior, with certain elective subjects for the junior and senior years.

With the endowment having reached $215,000 in 1892, the trustees called to the presidency John Priest Greene, pastor of Third Baptist Church of St. Louis, and it was during his 30-year tenure that William Jewell developed into one of the outstanding institutions of the Middle West. The first faculty under Greene consisted of W. R. Rothwell, Robert B. Semple, J. R. Eaton, J. G. Clark, Charles Lee Smith, J. H. Simmons, Richard P. Rider, J. R. Gibbs, John O. Turnbaugh, Harry G. Parker, and R. I. Fulton.

During the presidency of Greene, William Jewell erected the first gymnasium building west of the Mississippi for a college or university (named for A. D. Brown of St. Louis), New Ely dormitory for men, Marston science hall, Wornall Hall (burned in 1913), the Carnegie library building, and the president's home. By 1898 the faculty had expanded to 13 members for the college, including John Phelps Fruit who later became famous as head of the department of English, and 10 instructors in the preparatory department. During the first year of Greene's presidency, there were 103 students in the college and 134 in the academy. In 1898 there were 170 students in the college and 159 in the academy. Of the 329 students, 118 were ministerial students.

In 1920 Greene resigned and became president emeritus; David J. Evans, who had been on the faculty for more than 10 years and who had been trained by Greene to become his successor, became the first William Jewell alumnus to be president of the college. After a year and a half as president, Evans resigned and Greene resumed the presidency until July 1, 1923, when Harry Clifford Wayman of the faculty of the Southern Baptist Theological Seminary became the president. During his presidency the Melrose dormitory for girls and the John Gano Memorial Chapel were erected. Wayman resigned in June, 1928.

John F. Herget, of Cincinnati, became the second alumnus president of the college in the summer of 1928. The old Brown Gymnasium having burned in 1927, the first project of Herget was the completion of a large modern gymnasium which was also named Brown Gymnasium. Herget resigned to become president emeritus in 1942, and Hubert Inman Hester, a member of the faculty and head of the department of religion since 1926, was chosen interim president for one year.

Walter Pope Binns, of Roanoke, Va., was elected by the board of trustees and became president, July 1, 1943. With Binns's incumbency, William Jewell College began its greatest period of advancement, development, and expansion. Jewell Hall, the historic center of the college, was renovated and made fireproof, retaining every detail of its classical-revival architecture which makes it one of the most beautiful buildings in the state of Missouri. The money for this was provided by William Deven Johnson, president of the board of trustees and a member since 1909.

Johnson also gave the money for the erection of an administration building as a memorial to John Priest Greene. A complete new heating plant with all extensions was built. Marston science hall was renovated and new equipment purchased at a cost of $130,000. In 1954 the Minetry Jones girls' dormitory was erected. In the summer of 1955 a football stadium was built at a cost of $91,000. In 1956–57 two additional buildings were erected at a combined cost of $950,000, one to be a student union building and the other a girls' dormitory to replace three resident houses owned off the campus.

Because such a large number of William Jewell alumni have been listed in *Who's Who in America* since its first edition, William Jewell College gradually acquired its now nationally known subtitle, the Campus of Achievement. Throughout these years the number listed in *Who's Who* in proportion to the size of its student body has been among the highest of the colleges and universities of the country.

Since the presidency of Greene, the student body has come from an increasing number of states, the average being approximately 30 states each year. Many foreign students are enrolled each year, most of them studying to become Christian workers in their home countries.

During most of the last 20 years, William Jewell graduates have been pastors of churches in all 48 states, and William Jewell alumni missionaries have been on foreign fields in most foreign countries since the 1870's. A William Jewell alumnus, Walter O. Lewis, for many years was the executive secretary of the Baptist World Alliance.

On June 30, 1956, the total assets of William Jewell College were $5,681,288.88. The endowment was $3,472,768.09; and the investment in plant and equipment was $2,208,520.79.

The financial budget of 1955–56 showed receipts of $773,079.90 and expenditures of $763,662.03. The sources of income were: student revenue, $280,655.67; endowment, $159,214.62; gifts, $136,625.88; auxiliary enterprises, $189,985.51; and non-educational miscellaneous, $6,598.22

Six of the departments have a special quarter-million-dollar endowment: the Robert Baylor Semple department of classics has been endowed by Dr. and Mrs. W. T. Semple; the James Andrew Yates department of chemistry endowed by Mr. and Mrs. W. F. Yates; the John Phelps Fruit department of English endowed by the alumni of the college and the Baptists of Missouri; the W. D. Johnson department of philosophy endowed by W. D. Johnson; the E. S. Pillsbury department of physics endowed by Mr. and Mrs. E. S. Pillsbury; and the W. D. Johnson department of religion endowed by W. D. Johnson.

It is the permanent policy of William Jewell College to maintain a small Christian liberal arts coeducational college affiliated with the Baptist denomination. The enrolment for the fall of 1956 was 785, of which 183 were students preparing for the ministry or full-time Christian service. The faculty and administration numbered 61.

Since its founding, William Jewell has granted 3,918 Bachelor of Arts degrees; and since the founding of the college, 16,548 students have enrolled. The campus of William Jewell occupies 106 acres in the eastern edge of Liberty, Mo., an historic pioneer Missouri town which was incorporated in 1822 and is located 14 miles from downtown Kansas City. P. CASPAR HARVEY

WILLIAMS, ALVIN PETER (b. St. Louis County, Mo., Mar. 13, 1813; d. Glasgow, Mo., Nov. 9, 1868). Clergyman. Williams was converted at 16 years of age and one year later was ordained to the ministry. During most of the years of his ministry he had to perform manual labor to earn a living. In his early days he is said to have made rails at 50 cents a hundred to support his family and to buy books. Much of the inspiration for his self-education came through the influence of John Mason Peck (*q.v.*). Despite his labors, Williams found time to study Greek, most of this study being done while riding horseback to preaching appointments. He had an extremely retentive mind and memorized much of the New Testament. Because of his original expositions of the Scriptures and the calm thoroughness with which he dealt with those from whom he differed, Williams was referred to as the "Andrew Fuller of America."

An itinerate worker in central and western Missouri, Williams held pastorates in Lexington, Richmond, St. Joseph, Liberty, and Pleasant Ridge (Platte County) and established Baptist churches at Richmond, Liberty, and Pleasant Ridge. In 1865 he was indicted for preaching the gospel without taking the controversial "test oath." For some reason his case never came to trial. (In 1867 the United States Supreme Court rendered the test oath unconstitutional.)

Williams served four times as moderator of the Missouri Baptist General Association, and four times he preached its annual sermon. A great evangelist, he baptized more than 3,000 persons during his ministry. One revival meeting he held in Cooper County resulted in the baptism of more than 400 converts. Williams' most widely read book, *Campbellism Exposed,* was written as the result of a controversy with Moses Lard, who had continually challenged the Baptist position. At the request of the Missouri Baptist General Association, he wrote *The Lord's Supper*. Williams was awarded the D.D. degree by Bethel College and by one or two other colleges. He died from injuries received in falling from a horse.

BIBLIOGRAPHY: W. Cathcart, *Baptist Encyclopedia* (1883). R. S. Douglass, *History of Missouri Baptists* (1934). R. S. Duncan, *History of the Baptists in Missouri* (1882). J. C. Maple and R. P. Rider, *Baptist Biography* (1914). J. C. Maple, *Missouri Baptist Centennial 1906* (1907). R. P. Rider and A. M. Tutt, *History of the Second Baptist Church, Liberty, Missouri* (1943). A. P. Williams, *The Lord's Supper* (1869). W. P. Yeaman, *A History of the Missouri Baptist General Association* (1899). W. C. LINK, JR.

WILLIAMS, ANNIE LAURIE (b. Montgomery, Ala., Dec. 13, 1861; d. Birmingham, Ala., Feb. 14, 1932). First elementary worker employed by the Baptist Sunday School Board (1909); author of first book in Southern Baptist training course to feature elementary departments (*Plans and Programs,* 1918). Daughter of a Baptist minister and successful businessman, she was educated in the best private schools of her day. Her love of art, music, and good books contributed much to her attractiveness. While superintendent of the Primary department at Southside Baptist Church, Birmingham, Miss Williams attracted attention to quality of work she was doing by adapting the room, equipment, and lesson materials to the needs of the children. As a fieldworker for the Sunday School Board (1909–32), she traveled extensively in the North as well as in the South, lecturing on the importance of providing the best for children. Her effectiveness as a lecturer and as a conference leader had much to do with moving elementary departments from church basements to more desirable locations and with setting up high standards for elementary church workers. In contrast to the repressed method of Bible teaching current in her day, Miss Williams introduced handwork, action stories, music, and other variations.

ANNIE WARD BYRD

WILLIAMS, CHARLES BRAY (b. near Shiloh, Camden County, N. C., Jan. 15, 1869; d. Lakeland, Fla., May 4, 1952). Preacher, author, and educator. Son of Simeon Walston and Mary (Bray) Williams, Charles was reared near Shiloh, N. C., and in 1890 was ordained to the ministry by the Baptist church there. He received the B.A. degree from Wake Forest College (1891); the B.D. degree from Crozer Theological Seminary (1901); the M.A. degree (1908) and the Ph.D. degree (1909) from University of Chicago; and an honorary D.D. degree from Baylor University (1917). He held pastorates at North Chester, Pa.; Olive Street Church, Texarkana, Tex.; First Church, Stephenville, Tex.; Brucetown, Tenn.; and Shiloh, N. C. From 1905 to 1919, he taught Greek in Southwestern Baptist Theological Seminary in Fort Worth, Tex.; from 1919 to 1921, he was president of Howard College, Birmingham, Ala.; from 1921 to 1925, he taught New Testament Interpretation at Mercer University, Macon, Ga.; and from 1925 to 1932, he taught Greek and Ethics at Union University, Jackson, Tenn. After his retirement in 1946, he assisted for one year at Baptist Bible Institute, Lakeland, Fla.

A well-known writer, Williams received wide acclaim for his *Translation of the New Testament,* in which he rendered the Greek verbs, in particular, with unusual accuracy and skill. He also wrote *The History of the Baptists in North Carolina* (1901), *The Participle in the Book of Acts* (1910), *The Function of Teaching in Christianity* (1913), *New Testament History and Literature* (1916), *Citizen of Two Worlds* (1919), and *Introduction to New Testament Literature* (1929). He was a member of a number of learned societies, both American and foreign.

BIBLIOGRAPHY: J. S. Ramond, *Among Southern Baptists* (1936). ROBERT A. BAKER

WILLIAMS, JEROME OSCAR (b. Clanton, Ala., Mar. 29, 1885; d. Nashville, Tenn., Nov. 26, 1953). The son of Joseph Lebingston and Lelia (Brown) Williams, his training was received at Howard College, Birmingham, Ala., A.B. degree, 1912; D.D. degree, 1924; Southern Baptist Theological Seminary, Louisville, Ky., Th.M. degree, 1915; graduate study, 1921–22. He married Kathleen Jeanette Akans, Nov. 16, 1915 (d. Apr. 14, 1922). Their two children were Jerome Otis and Margarette Jeanette. He married Ethel Hudson, June 29, 1927. He began preaching in 1909. After ordination by the Mulberry Baptist Church, Clanton, Ala., 1916, he served as pastor of the following churches: First Baptist, Sylacauga, Ala., 1916–17; First Baptist, Athens, Ala., 1919–23; First Baptist, Bessemer, Ala., 1923–26; Fourth Avenue Baptist, Louisville, Ky., 1926–32; First Baptist, Bowling Green, Ky., 1932–34. From 1918 to 1919, he was a chaplain in the American Expeditionary Force (remaining after the war with the American Army of Occupation).

Williams was a member of the Sunday School Board of the Southern Baptist Convention from 1932 to 1934. His acquaintance with the board's work, together with proved qualifications, led to his election July 3, 1934, as business manager of the board. In 1943 he was asked to accept the secretaryship of the board's Division of Education and Promotion, which position he filled until his death in 1953. In both positions he discharged heavy responsibilities with dedication and efficiency. Aside from his service with the board, he was in much demand as an evangelist and as a speaker in denominational meetings. He was author of the following books: *The Gospel of Christ* (1935), *Definite Decisions for New Church Members* (1936), *Pastor's Record of Weddings* (1937), *Pastor's Record of Funerals* (1938), *Sermons in Outline* (1943), *Seed for*

Sermons (1945), *Heart Sermons in Outline* (1949), *The Gospel Preacher and His Preaching* (1949), *Evangelistic Sermons in Outline* (1951), *Let Me Illustrate* (1953). NOBLE VAN NESS

WILLIAMS, JOHN (b. Hanover County, Va., 1747; d. Apr. 30, 1795). Soon after his birth his family moved to Lunenburg County, Va., where he grew up. In 1769 he was elected sheriff of that county. He was ordained in Dec., 1772, and soon earned a reputation as an eloquent, methodical, and warmly evangelistic preacher and an able expounder of Baptist doctrine. He was active in the affairs of the Association of Separate Baptists in Virginia, was elected its clerk in 1774, and made the motion which resulted in the adoption of the Philadelphia Confession by the Association in 1783. During a ministry of 23 years, his pastorates in Virginia included Meherrin Baptist Church in Lunenburg County, Sandy Creek Baptist Church in Charlotte County, and Bluestone Baptist Church in Mecklenburg County. A crippling fall in 1793 imposed severe limitations on his activities, but not before he had gained wide recognition as a champion of religious liberty, a patron of education, a meticulous Baptist historian, and an able opponent of infant baptism. JACK MANLEY

WILLIAMS, ROGER (b. London, England *c.* 1603; d. Providence, R. I., Mar., 1683). Statesman and advocate of religious liberty. The son of an influential merchant, he was educated through the patronage of Sir Edward Coke, the great English jurist. He attended the Charterhouse (1621–23) and Pembroke College, Cambridge (1623–29), entered Anglican orders, and became chaplain to Sir William Masham, where he was for a time safe in his puritan opinions. Soon, however, he had progressed beyond the point of safety to separatism. The rigid conformity which Charles I insisted upon, and which Bishop Laud enforced with fervor, led Williams to emigrate, and he arrived with his new wife in Boston, Mass., on Feb. 5, 1631. Reputed a "godly minister," he was made a teacher in the Boston church but soon repudiated his position because he dared not "officiate to an unseparated people." He moved to Salem, to Plymouth, and back to Salem. He attacked the Boston authorities for cheating the Indians out of their land, the ministers of the colony for holding meetings which "might grow in time to a presbytery . . . to the prejudice of the churches' liberties," and the civil government for its interference in religious affairs. Governmental pressure forced the Salem church to leave off protecting him, and he was sentenced to banishment. Narrowly escaping deportation to England, he left Massachusetts in January of 1636 and went into hiding in the towns of his Indian friends, with whom he had wisely made a previous verbal treaty. In the spring he began, after some additional difficulty with Massachusetts, the settlement at Providence which was the nucleus of the future state of Rhode Island, establishing finally a haven for persecuted peoples of every religious persuasion under a government claiming jurisdiction "only in civil things."

In the fall of 1636 Williams, the white man most trusted by the Indians, was able to prevent a general Indian alliance against the English and proved constantly useful as a negotiator during the war which followed. But in spite of his services, his settlement was under constant attack from the neighboring colonies, whose governments opposed his intrusion into their theocratic absolutism. Williams therefore went to England in June of 1643 to secure a charter which would give legal standing to his colony. The charter was awarded by the Parliamentary Commission on Plantations on Mar. 14, 1644, but the intrigues of William Coddington, one of the settlers in Rhode Island, made it necessary for the charter to be reconfirmed, and Williams returned to England, this time with John Clarke (*q.v.*). The two left Boston in Nov., 1651, and in 11 months had completed their mission. As an intimate of Sir Henry Vane, an acquaintance of Cromwell, and friend and tutor in Dutch to John Milton, Williams moved in the highest circles of government and society and remained until the summer of 1654.

The rest of his life was given to the leadership of his Rhode Island commonwealth. He helped to create a democratic unity of government in the colony. He arbitrated between his people and the Indians, and was active in King Philip's War. When the Quakers, persecuted in the rest of New England, took refuge in Rhode Island, he resisted all attempts to have them dislodged. At the same time, he published in defense of his own belief a vigorous polemic against their doctrine, called *George Fox digg'd out of his Burrowes* (1676). When he died he was buried with "all the solemnity that the colony could show," in a place on his own land which he had selected.

Although Williams entered Anglican orders about the time he left Cambridge, he was never an Episcopalian by conviction. Progressing beyond puritanism and separatism, he was baptized by Ezekiel Holliman in March of 1639 and organized a Baptist church. But shortly thereafter he withdrew from this fellowship because of his doubts regarding the authority of his baptism and became a Seeker, without relationship to any church.

Most of Williams' writings were controversial. *The Bloudy Tenent of Persecution* (1644) and *The Bloody Tenent Yet More Bloody* (1652) are the documents of his great controversy with John Cotton on the separation of church and state and his chief contribution to the theory of religious liberty. In addition, he wrote *A Key into the Language of America* (1643), a remarkable book on the vocabulary of the Indians, and one devotional book, *Experiments of Spiritual Life and Health* (1652). Contemporary opinions of him varied: Milton thought him "a noble confessor of religious liberty"; Bradford called him "godly and zealous, having many precious parts, but very unsettled in judgemente [*sic*]." It could justly be said of him that he was a person of great ability and strong opinions, although untempered by any reticence in expressing them.

BIBLIOGRAPHY: S. H. Brockunier, *Irrepressible Democrat, Roger Williams* (1940). J. Ernst, *Roger Williams* (1932). J. K. Hosmer, *Winthrop's Journal* (1908). JUDSON BOYCE ALLEN

WILLIAMS, WILLIAM (b. Eatonton, Putnam County, Ga., Mar. 15, 1821; d. Aiken, S. C., Feb. 20, 1877). Pastor and theological professor. Son of William and Rebecca Williams, he was converted and joined the Baptist church at Athens, Ga., in 1837. After graduating from the University of Georgia in 1840, he married Ruth Bell, Aug. 26, 1845. Williams attended the Law School of Harvard University and graduated in 1847, but four years later he decided to preach and held his first pastorate at Auburn, Ala. In 1856 he left a quiet and successful pastorate to become professor of theology at Mercer University, then at Penfield, Ga., and in the fall of 1859, when Southern Baptist Theological Seminary was established at Greenville, S. C., he became professor of ecclesiastical history and church government and pastoral duties. Due to James Petigru Boyce's (*q.v.*) continued absence from the Greenville campus, while raising money for the seminary, Williams was transferred to the Chair of Systematic Theology in 1872. Elected vice-president of the Southern Baptist Convention several times, Williams preached the annual sermon in St. Louis, Mo., in May, 1871. He suffered for a long time from consumption, which finally caused his death. He was buried in Greenville, S. C., where former students erected a monument to his memory. Williams' one published work was a small booklet, *Apostolical Church Polity*. However, a manuscript of notes on lectures which he delivered on systematic theology, taken by William Harrison Williams (1840–93) during the 1866–67 session, is preserved in the library at Southern Seminary. LEO T. CRISMON

WILLIAMSBURG BAPTIST INSTITUTE. See CUMBERLAND COLLEGE.

WILLINGHAM, ROBERT JOSIAH (b. Beaufort District, S. C., May 15, 1854; d. Richmond, Va., Dec. 20, 1914). Foreign mission leader and promoter. Baptized in Aug., 1867, Willingham entered the University of Georgia the next year and after graduation spent four years in teaching and business. One day a deacon asked him, "My young brother, has it ever occurred to you that God wants you in some other business than that in which you are now engaged?" When Willingham was born, his father had prayed that God, if it were his will, would make his son a minister. On Jan. 1, 1878, Willingham entered Southern Baptist Theological Seminary and was ordained by the First Church, Macon, Ga., June 2, 1878. Unable to return to the seminary after the second year, Willingham held pastorates first at Talbotton, and then at Barnesville, Ga. In 1887 he went to First Church, Chattanooga, Tenn., and in 1891 to First Church, Memphis, after which he became corresponding secretary of the Foreign Mission Board, Sept. 1, 1893, serving until his death in 1914. Under Willingham's leadership Southern Baptists' gifts to missions increased from $106,332 to $587,458. He and his wife visited Southern Baptist missions in Japan, China, and Italy and other mission fields in Burma and India, with their expenses provided without cost to the board.

During Willingham's tenure at the Foreign Mission Board, the oldest seminary on Southern Baptist mission fields was established, Graves Theological Seminary in Canton, China. Theological training was begun at Ogbomosho, Nigeria, and seminaries were located at Rome, Torreon, Pernambuco, Rio de Janeiro, Hwanghsien, Shanghai, Fukuoka, and Buenos Aires. Publishing houses were established at Shanghai, Rio de Janeiro, El Paso, and Shimonoseki. Hospitals, very simple in the beginning, were opened at Hwanghsien, Pingtu, Laichow-fu, Yangchow, Chengchow, Wuchow, Kweilin, and Ogbomosho.

Following a speech by Willingham at the Southern Baptist Convention, someone asked T. P. Bell (*q.v.*), "What is there in Willingham's speaking that produces such effect?" Bell replied: "He is the incarnation of a great cause, and that cause speaks out through him without blot or hindrance. It is not Willingham; it is foreign missions."

BIBLIOGRAPHY: E. W. Willingham, *Life of Robert Josiah Willingham* (1917). *Southern Baptist Handbook* (1945), pp. 10–25. G. B. Taylor, *Virginia Baptist Ministers* (1915), pp. 462–473. E. C. ROUTH

WILLIS, JOSEPH (b. Bladen County, N. C., 1758; d. Rapides Parish, La., Sept. 14, 1854). Pioneer Baptist preacher in Louisiana. Of English and Cherokee Indian ancestry, Willis was largely responsible for the early progress of the gospel in southwest Louisiana. In 1798 he settled in Mississippi, laboring with some success near Natchez. Migrating to Louisiana in 1804, he preached in what is now Lafayette and in Bayou Chicot. In 1812 he was ordained to the ministry and assisted in the organization of the Calvary Baptist Church near Opelousas, the first Baptist church west of the Mississippi in Louisiana. In 1818 the Louisiana Baptist Association, the first in the state, was organized with five churches, all of which Willis had founded.

After his death in 1854 "Father Willis," as he was often called, was paid the following tribute by the Louisiana Association:

> The gospel was proclaimed by him in these regions before the American flag was hoisted here. Before the church began to send out missionaries into destitute regions, he, at his own expense, and frequently at the risk of his life, came to these parts preaching the gospel of the Redeemer.

W. A. BROWN

WINBURN, HARDY LATHAN (b. Bells, Tenn., Apr. 16, 1877; d. Arkadelphia, Ark., Sept. 2, 1936). Pastor. Son of Hardy Lathan Winburn, merchant, and Susan Caroline (Sinclair) Winburn, he was ordained as a Baptist minister in 1897. He was graduated from Southwestern Baptist College (Tenn.) in 1899, and from Union University (Tenn.) in 1912. He received the D.D. degree from Ouachita College in 1912 and the LL.D. degree from Georgetown College in 1921. He married Lena Barnes of Tenn., July 11, 1899. There were seven children. He served as pastor in Tullahoma, Tenn. (1899–1900), Taylorville, Ill. (1900–03), First Baptist Church, Arkadelphia, Ark. (1903–14; 1918–36), and Walnut Street Baptist Church, Louisville, Ky. (1914–18). He was a member of the executive committee of the Southern Baptist Convention from its origin to his death. Winburn organized and was first president of the Arkansas B.Y.P.U. and pioneered the summer assembly. He served on the boards of the Southern Baptist Convention, Arkansas Baptist State Convention, and was an early supporter of the Baptist World Alliance. He was president of the Arkansas Baptist Convention, 1926–28. He was author of *A Man and His Money, First Christian Impulses,* and *Lead Hunters of the Ozarks.*

MRS. H. L. WINBURN

WINDOW OF Y.W.A., THE. A monthly magazine, published since 1929 by Woman's Missionary Union, for young women 16 through 24 years of age and members of Young Woman's Auxiliary. The first editor, Juliette Mather, secretary of Woman's Missionary Union's Department of Publications, served until 1955, when Ethalee Hamric became editor. Short suggestions as program helps "For the Young Ladies" appeared first in *Our Mission Fields,* begun in 1906, and fuller programs were continued in *Royal Service* from 1914 until Aug., 1929. A gift of $1,600 from the Woman's Missionary Union literature department made possible the publication of a magazine for Young Woman's Auxiliary beginning in Sept., 1929. *The Window of Y.W.A.* is designed to provide basic missionary programs and organizational helps for Young Woman's Auxiliary members, along with missionary information and inspiration, and suggested creative activity. The name of the magazine was chosen "that more light may come into our souls and that our vision may go out more clearly . . . letting the vision out and the light in." At a rate of $1.50 per year, subscriptions totaled 37,000 in 1955, or 53 per cent of the 70,312 members of Young Woman's Auxiliary.

ETHALEE HAMRIC

WINGATE, WASHINGTON MANLY (b. Darlington District, S. C., July 28, 1828; d. Wake Forest, N. C., Feb. 27, 1879). Awarded the A.B. degree by Wake Forest College in 1849 and received honorary D.D. degrees from Columbian College (now George Washington University), 1865, and University of North Carolina, 1871. He studied at Furman Theological Institution, 1849–51. He married Mary E. Webb of Bertie County, N. C. He was ordained Mar. 3, 1852, by Darlington Church, while pastor of Ebenezer Church and assistant pastor at Darlington. At the age of 24, in Oct., 1852, he became agent for raising $50,000 in endowment for Wake Forest College, a task completed when he was president in 1857. He was elected professor of moral and intellectual philosophy and rhetoric, and president of Wake Forest College, pro tempore, June, 1853; served as acting president, 1854–56; and as president, 1856–79. While president of the college, he was also pastor of Wake Forest Baptist Church. During the Civil War he preached as an evangelist in the Confederate Army; served as associate editor of the *Biblical Recorder;* and from 1862 through 1866, while the work of the college was suspended on account of the war, he served as pastor of the Baptist churches at Franklinton, Oxford, and Wake Forest. In 1865 the Wake Forest church paid him 12 barrels of corn for his services. He was considered one of the greatest Baptist preachers in North Carolina of his time.

BIBLIOGRAPHY: G. W. Paschal, *History of Wake Forest College* (1935, 1943). W. Cathcart, *The Baptist Encyclopedia* (1881), Vol. II.

G. A. HENDRICKS

WINGATE JUNIOR COLLEGE. Located 30 miles east of Charlotte, N. C., and originally known as Wingate School, it was organized after being authorized by Union Baptist Association in Oct., 1895, with its first school session beginning in Aug., 1896. Chartered the following year by the state of North Carolina, the institution was operated until 1917 as a preparatory school by Union and Mecklenburg-Cabarrus associations and by the public school system of Union County. Since 1917 ownership and control have been vested in Baptist organizations, and the college charter has been amended twice. Several Baptist associations have at various times controlled and operated the institution, which became a junior college in 1923, but for the most part it has been under direction of the state convention. The 24-member board of trustees, appointed by the convention, has complete power and control in the operation of the school.

A coeducational college with a ratio of two men to every woman, Wingate offers basic liberal arts courses, terminal work in secretarial science, and pre-engineering in co-operation with engineering schools. The college is fully accredited by the Southern Association of Colleges and Secondary Schools, the North Carolina State Board of Certification, the American Association of Junior Colleges, the Southern Association of Baptist Colleges, and is approved by the Department of the Interior for the training of foreign students. More than 25 per cent of the students are preparing for work as ministers, missionaries, or church youth directors. A total of 10,000 students have attended Wingate, 4,608 of whom have graduated. Located on a 35-acre campus, Wingate has endowment of $103,000 and property value, $511,000. The school operated on a budget of $218,000 in 1954–55, and increased from an enrolment of 200 in 1953 to an enrolment of 487 in 1955. BUDD E. SMITH

WINKLER, EDWIN THEODORE (b. Savannah, Ga., Nov. 13, 1823; d. Marion, Ala., Nov. 10, 1883). Pastor, editor, and writer. The son of Shadrach and Jane (Wetzer) Winkler, he prepared for college at Chatham Academy, was graduated from Brown University in 1843, and studied at Newton Theological Institution for two years. He returned to Georgia in 1845 where he became assistant editor of the *Christian Index* for one year. After his ordination in 1846, he served successively until 1852 as pastor of the Baptist churches at Columbus, Ga., Albany, Ga., and Gillisonville, S. C. He labored from 1852 to 1854 as corresponding secretary of the Southern Baptist Publication Society and also edited the *Southern Baptist* in 1853. The First Baptist Church of Charleston, S. C., called him as pastor in 1854. During the Civil War he left this pastorate and became a chaplain in the Confederate army. Returning to Charleston, he served the Citadel Square Baptist Church as pastor until 1872 when he accepted the call of the Baptist church in Marion, Ala. Two years later he became editor of the *Alabama Baptist*. By the end of his editorship in Apr., 1881, he had forged the paper into a strong denominational organ.

For 10 years Winkler served as president of the Home Mission Board of the Southern Baptist Convention. Twice he declined the offer of a professorship in the Southern Baptist Theological Seminary. Reared in the South and educated in the North, he became deeply interested in the moral and spiritual welfare of the Negroes and sought to promote good feeling between the white and Negro races. In 1857 he prepared a catechism, *Notes and Questions for Oral Instruction of Colored People,* which was widely accepted. Religious institutions and bodies called on him to address them upon important occasions, such as in 1872 when he delivered a sermon upon the education of the Negro ministry before the American Baptist Home Mission Society. He served on the staff of Baptist papers, North and South, as corresponding editor. His *Commentary on the Epistle of James* (1888) in the American Commentary Series exhibits scholarly accuracy and a clear and forcible style. The same is true of his other published works: *The Spirit of Missions* (1853); *The Sacred Lute* (1855), a collection of popular hymns; and *Rome, Past, Present and Future* (1877). Furman University conferred on him the D.D. degree in 1858. LYNN E. MAY, JR.

WINTERVILLE HIGH SCHOOL. Located at Winterville, N. C., founded by members of Neuse Association on land donated by A. G. and B. T. Cox. In 1900 the school was offered to the association if the Baptists would equip and operate it. The offer was accepted and 18 trustees were appointed. The school opened with G. E. Lineberry as the first principal. Winterville was an accredited high school with a full course for preparatory and primary work. In 1901 Atlantic Association endorsed the school, and in the following year two buildings were completed. Despite high enrolments (219 pupils in 1909), debts increased. In 1906 Tar River Association refused an offer of half ownership of the school because of its indebtedness, but in 1910 Roanoke Association accepted a similar offer. In 1909 the school's debt was $4,000, and in 1915 it had increased to $6,000. The buildings burned in 1916 and the school closed about 1920.

D. L. SMILEY

WISE, IVAN MONROE (b. Lisbon, Claiborne Parish, La., July 15, 1854; d. Duback, Union Parish, La., May 22, 1912). Pastor, educator, scholar, historian, and missionary. Wise was converted at Sharon church, Claiborne Parish, in 1866 and was ordained by that church in 1871. Studying at colleges in Mississippi, he earned the M.A. degree and later was awarded an honorary LL.D. degree. Wise served in pastorates in Missouri, Arkansas, Tennessee, and Kentucky. He raised money for Ohio Valley College, supervised the building of it, and served for a time as its president. Later he did home mission work in Kentucky and in the southern area of Louisiana. He spoke in Bible conferences, preachers' schools, and other meetings. He aided W. E. Paxton in collecting information for Paxton's history of Louisiana Baptists and later wrote his own history, *Footsteps of the Flock.* He died before completing the second volume.

CARL CONRAD

WOLFE, MANSON HORATIO (b. Fannin County, Tex., Dec. 10, 1866; d. Dallas, Tex., Oct. 14, 1942). Businessman, Texas Baptist leader. Son of Lemuel Pinckney and Penelope Katherine (Jackson) Wolfe, he became a cotton buyer at Wolfe City and president of Wolfe City National Bank. In 1905 Wolfe moved to Dallas, where he founded a cotton exporting firm, M. H. Wolfe and Co., and M. H. Wolfe Cotton Factors, Inc. General manager of Farmers' Marketing Association and director of Texas Power and Light Company, Wolfe served as vice-president of the Southern Baptist Convention, president of the Baptist General Convention of Texas, 1917–19, and chairman of its executive board for several years. Leader of a successful state prohibition campaign, he helped finance Carroll's *A History of Texas Baptists* and was a generous financial supporter of all denomination enterprises. A. B. CULBERTSON

WOMAN'S AMERICAN BAPTIST FOREIGN MISSION SOCIETY. Organized in the Clarendon Street Baptist Church, Boston, Mass., Apr. 3, 1871, having for its purpose "the elevation and Christianization of women and children in foreign lands." The Woman's Baptist Missionary Society of the West was organized May 9, 1871, in the First Baptist Church of

Chicago; and a similar society on the Pacific Coast was organized in Oct., 1875, with headquarters in San Francisco. These societies merged May 15, 1914, under the name Woman's American Baptist Foreign Mission Society, with Mrs. Helen Barrett Montgomery as the first president. Incorporated in Massachusetts, the society immediately became a co-operating agency of the Northern Baptist Convention. In May, 1955, the membership of its board of managers and that of the board of the American Baptist Foreign Mission Society became identical, although both societies continue as autonomous bodies. Mrs. Frank C. Wigginton, Carnegie, Pa., became the first chairman of the newly organized American Baptist Foreign Mission Boards, with headquarters in New York.

DATA

	1934	*1954*
Financial Assets	$2,388,538	$3,105,212
Annual Budget	328,624	596,798
Missionaries	178	102
National Workers	2,652	2,387

See also AMERICAN BAPTIST FOREIGN MISSION SOCIETY. IRENE A. JONES

WOMAN'S AMERICAN BAPTIST HOME MISSION SOCIETY. Founded in 1873, the Woman's Baptist Home Mission Society of Michigan had for its purpose the "evangelization of the freed men and other needy people of this country." Four years later, Feb. 1, 1877, the Women's Baptist Home Mission Society was organized with headquarters in Chicago, and on Nov. 14, 1877, the Woman's American Baptist Home Mission Society was organized in Boston for "the evangelization of women among the freed people, the Indians, the heathen immigrants and the new settlements of the West." These bodies worked independently until their union in 1909 as the Woman's American Baptist Home Mission Society. Later, when Free Baptists joined the American Baptist Convention, the Free Baptist Missionary Society, organized in 1873, merged with the combined body.

The society, whose motto is "Christ in Every Home," had 124 missionaries in 1954, many of them serving in co-operation with Baptist state conventions and city mission societies. Four children's homes in Alaska require the services of house fathers and mothers; a gospel boat, the *Evangel,* reaches men and women in fishing villages around the island of Kodiak. In Puerto Rico young women, trained at home and in the United States serve in local churches and day schools connected with them. Work in Cuba, Mexico, El Salvador, and Nicaragua is administered through teachers, evangelistic missionaries, trained leaders in Christian education, and a hospital with missionary nurses and doctors. In the United States work is done in Christian centers; on rural fields; in Negro educational centers, schools, and colleges; among the American Indian and other national groups; in trailer and migrant camps; with foreign students, overseas brides, and refugees; and in church extension.

The work of the society was integrated with that of The American Baptist Home Mission Society in May, 1955, after years of close co-operation. The two societies remain intact for legal purposes but function under identical officers. MARGARET NOFFSINGER WENGER

WOMAN'S CHRISTIAN TEMPERANCE UNION. Organized at Cleveland, Ohio, Nov. 17, 1874, to enlist an increasing number of individuals to abstain from the use of alcoholic beverages and to unite the efforts of Christian women for the extinction of the manufacture, sale, and use of intoxicating drinks and all other forms of narcotics. It seeks to achieve these goals by education, legislation, and religion. Its wide and varied educational program gains in effectiveness as church groups participate as members in the Woman's Christian Temperance Union and its affiliates, the Youth Temperance Council and the Loyal Temperance Union. These groups help to distribute and use the vast amount of literature produced by the Woman's Christian Temperance Union. Church-related colleges give valuable co-operation in the inter-collegiate original oration contest sponsored by the union. A full-time legislative director in residence in Washington, D. C., keeps Woman's Christian Temperance Union members and numerous other Christian citizens informed through continuous personal conferences with legislators. This representative also does effective service at the time of public hearings of congressional committees on the liquor problem. The national Woman's Christian Temperance Union publishes the *Union Signal,* a weekly magazine, which is one of the most prominent and widely circulated of temperance periodicals.

A. C. MILLER

WOMAN'S MISSIONARY UNION. Auxiliary to the Southern Baptist Convention, this missionary organization of Southern Baptist women, with a graded system of missionary education in 19,896 churches, in 1955 had a membership of 1,281,936. The union, organized in 1888, is distinctive among women's missionary endeavors in its auxiliary relationship to the Convention. Women of other denominations organized independently, collected money, appointed their own missionaries, and supported them; but Southern Baptist women, under the wise counsel of certain denominational leaders, chose to be auxiliary, "to stimulate the grace of giving" and "aid in collecting funds for missionary purposes to be disbursed by the Boards of the Southern Baptist Convention."

UNION BEGINNINGS. The union's voluntarily dependent relationship to the Convention was the result of many factors. During the 19th century, often referred to as the "woman's century," women began thinking in terms of voting, owning property, becoming profitably employed, and receiving educational privileges equal to men.

At the same time many groups of Baptist women were gathering in their churches, growing in world understanding, increasing their gifts to missions, and learning to do more effective witnessing.

Beginning of societies in local churches.—Before 1800 Pastor Richard Furman (*q.v.*) had enlisted the children of the Baptist church in Charleston, S. C., in a Juvenile Missionary and Education Society in behalf of missions to the Catawba Indians and the education of young ministers. He was instrumental in the organization of the Wadmalaw and Edisto Female Mite Society of South Carolina, which the 1812 minutes of the Charleston, S. C., Association listed as contributing $122.50 to missions. When Ann and Adoniram Judson (*q.v.*) and Luther Rice (*q.v.*) went out as missionaries in 1812, the general impetus of missionary giving increased. Later, after they became Baptists and Luther Rice returned to promote the Baptist missionary enterprise, female and mite societies sprang up more rapidly. "Indeed," Rice exclaimed, "the great numbers and rapid increase of these laudable Female Institutions cannot fail to create emotions the most lively and gratifying—hopes and anticipations of the most ardent and animating nature." The Wadmalaw and Edisto Female Mite Society, which made a gift of $44 to Luther Rice on Jan. 14, 1814, was the only Southern society mentioned in Rice's list of donors reported the following May at the organization of the General Missionary Convention of the Baptist Denomination of the United States of America for the Promotion of Foreign Missions, more commonly called the Triennial Convention. Although records are sketchy, it is known that missionary societies were formed in Richmond and Fredericksburg, Va., in 1813 and 1814; then in Georgia, North Carolina, and Kentucky. By 1817, 110 women's societies made reports at the second Triennial Convention.

When the Alabama Baptist Convention was organized in 1823, seven Alabama societies sent half of the 20 delegates, and asked pastors to represent their own missionary societies. More female mite societies were organized in South Carolina, while in Mississippi and other states women were meeting regularly to pray for and learn about missions.

Sewing societies provided additional opportunity for talking of and praying for the Judsons. One such society, organized in 1832 for home and foreign missions in Beulah, Va., aided John Lewis Shuck (*q.v.*) as a student in the University of Richmond. When he and his wife, Henrietta Hall Shuck (*q.v.*), sailed for China in 1835, the society outfitted him with clothes made from Virginia cloth. Boxes of clothing from female societies went to the Carey Station in India and to Indian settlements in North Carolina. The societies contributed money to the Judsons and their Burma missions, to the Baptist Tract Society, and to the American and Foreign Bible Society, and also aided the "education of pious young men" at Furman Academy and other schools. Interest in specific projects brought women together in societies to pray for and learn more about those to whom they sent their gifts.

Moving toward co-operative efforts.—By 1840 contributions of the women's societies received special commendation in the report of the Triennial Convention. A few missionaries were going out to China and Africa and to the states west of the Mississippi, and the women felt they must help support women missionaries especially with gifts and intelligent prayers. At the Southern Baptist Convention's triennial meeting in 1849, men delegates represented the Charleston, S. C., and Bruington and St. Stephen's Female Mission Society in Virginia. The Convention treasurer's report of that year listed gifts from individual women and from female missionary and education societies, a Needlework Society for Foreign Missions, and a Needlework Society for Domestic Missions. Each year, the Convention's register of delegates indicated that such societies as the Female Mission Society of First Baptist Church, Baltimore, or the Female Domestic Mission Society of First Baptist Church, Nashville, were represented by men. The constitution of the Convention permitted one delegate for $300 in gifts during three years, or $100 in each year.

In 1855 Mrs. L. G. Clark of South Carolina sent a gift of $100 enclosed in a letter from Richard Furman. Jeremiah Bell Jeter (*q.v.*), delegate of the Female Mission Society of Bruington and St. Stephen's, King and Queen County, made a resolution "that the thanks of the Convention be tendered sister Clark and that the $100 be appropriated in equal sums to the Boards." Other individual women and female missions societies continued contributions which sent pastors or deacons as delegates to the Southern Baptist Convention meetings and indicated their desire for far-reaching usefulness.

In 1855 when Rosewell Hobart Graves (*q.v.*) went to China as a missionary of Southern Baptists, his mother, Mrs. Ann Graves, became more zealous for missions. She called together women attending the Southern Baptist Convention in Baltimore in 1868 for a meeting in the basement of the church for prayer and conversation, passing on missionary information. This is considered the first general meeting of Southern Baptist women in the interest of missions. In 1870 an interdenominational society of women known as the Baltimore Auxiliary of the Woman's Missionary Society was organized, and Mrs. Graves became its secretary.

Baptist women of Baltimore started a federation of Baptist women's societies in Oct., 1871, known as Woman's Mission to Woman. A circular letter outlining its plan and purpose suggested:

> . . . the organization of branches in each state to attend to the business, and missionary circles in each church or neighboring churches united, to meet regularly for prayer and the dissemination of missionary intelligence. The co-operation of the different branches should be arranged in the simplest form of organization that each and all may be willing to unite

> with one heart and mind in carrying out the work to the glory of God and the extension of the knowledge of Christ, that through him all the families of the earth may be blessed.

This plan, with its "branches" and "co-operation" may have foreshadowed the present state and Southwide organizations.

Reporting to the Convention in 1872, the Foreign Mission Board included remarks on woman's work under the heading "Bible Women." It recognized "the hand of the Lord in moving the hearts of Christian women in England and America to organize among themselves missionary societies to support Bible readers to labor among the women of foreign lands." The report urged delegates present to take steps immediately to organize female missionary societies in their churches.

> . . . Select some active, pious woman who will assemble the sisters together and organize them for the purpose of cultivating missionary spirit and systematic contributions. We would commend the plan adopted by women of Baltimore, Richmond, and other places where each family as far as possible is supplied with a mission box (which costs five to ten cents) and every member of the household contributes two cents a week.

Later in the same meeting the board stated, "Women's societies are organized to support Bible women. God helping them, our sisters will do a good work. The sisterhood of our Southern Zion should be aroused to the grand mission of redeeming their sister-woman from the degrading and destroying thraldom of Paganism."

As news of Baltimore's mission rallies spread, the women responded. During the Civil War they had assumed new responsibilities and enlarged duties, and their latent talents of management were stirred to action. Women were not content with intellectual, physical, or charitable activity; they wanted to take part in the expansion of missions around the world. Questions concerning woman's new role were being raised: "Woman or man—which is the weaker?" "May women speak in the churches?" Discussion was based on "fine distinctions of words." "The injunction of silence" could not forbid the use of words in any form of utterance, for that would conflict with prayer and prophesying, which were the result of the Holy Spirit's presence. One preacher commented that "the hostility of some men to woman's active gospel work looks a little like envy and jealousy rather than stern regard for theories of inspiration and Scriptural prohibition."

Meanwhile, the spirit of missionary zeal spread news to South Carolina of Baltimore's Woman's Mission to Woman. There the United Women's Missionary Society of Newberry came into being in Oct., 1871, after correspondence between Mrs. Graves and the Newberry church pastor. Two years later, the Woman's Missionary Society of Richmond brought together societies to support Edmonia Harris Moon (*q.v.*) in China. The Foreign Mission Board undertook to supply mite boxes to societies and found that their offerings increased. New societies and more federations of societies were being formed.

In July, 1848, the Quakers had called the first Woman's Rights Convention in all history, and in 1869 the National Woman Suffrage Association brought together in New York representatives from 19 states. The Women's Christian Temperance Union was organized in 1874, the World's Christian Temperance Union, in 1883. With Federated Woman's Clubs established in 1890, organization of women was increasingly in the air. Women wanted to learn to think on their feet and to conduct affairs in correct parliamentary procedure. They wanted to have an appreciable share in the work of missions, yet desired "to emphasize the fact that our Woman's Mission work is church work, that we are co-laborers under the bonds of church membership."

State central committees develop.—With the Baltimore, Richmond, and Newberry societies working together well in their cities and environs, plans for co-operation between societies in other cities and sections were inevitable. Henry Allen Tupper (*q.v.*), secretary of the Foreign Mission Board, and many other leaders in the Southern Baptist Convention encouraged the women's organization. They sensed the change in conditions, saw clubs of a secular nature and organizations in other denominations affording development for women, and they wanted to use the best in devoted Baptist womanhood for missions. Some denominational leaders, however, feared the progress of the emancipation of women, feeling they must always be "cabined, cribbed, confined." Some were pleased by the development of the missionary spirit among women and children through mite societies, Dorcas Societies, The Reapers, Young Ladies' Societies, Female Missionary Societies—societies with a variety of names, but all with the missionary purpose of multiplying messengers of the gospel to fields around the world.

As early as 1874, the Richmond Woman's Missionary Society endeavored to promote missionary societies in the churches of Virginia for the support of foreign missions. By 1875 J. A. Chambliss, Charleston, S. C., member of the state executive committee of foreign missions, asked the Welsh Neck Missionary Society to consider a proposition regarding construction of a home for Lula Whilden and Mrs. N. B. Williams in China and furthermore asked that the society "act as the Central Committee of the state with Miss Martha McIntosh as chairman, to arouse an interest in the work among the women of the state and secure contributions. The propositions were assented to unanimously."

In a letter to Virginia's *Religious Herald* in Apr., 1875, "J. S. J." reported that the Welsh Neck Association Woman's Missionary Society had sent out a circular about the support of two missionaries in China, appealing to both duty and sympathy "in behalf of thousands of your sex who have never heard the precious Words of life." Would not "at least one sister in every congregation in our state take an active part in the matter? Send your address to Miss M. E. McIntosh, and she will send a circular containing instructions on how to obtain mite boxes and organize a society to assist."

That same year the Southern Baptist Convention adopted a report which stated that the committee on woman's work deemed it very desirable that the Convention recognize and commend the successful work of women's mission societies, co-operating with the Foreign Mission Board.

> . . . Enough is known of the results of the agencies adopted by our Christian sisters to attest the enlarged zeal and practical wisdom, in executing our Redeemer's Great Commission to preach the gospel to every creature. Too much commendation can scarcely be bestowed upon the noble achievements of these gentle and loving servants of Jesus. All our pastors are affectionately urged to "help those women" who are laboring and ready to labor with us in the gospel. . . . The native earnestness, the loving sympathy, and the ready intuitive tact of woman, most happily qualify her as a valuable auxiliary in this work.

Southern Baptist Convention reports in 1876 show that the committee on woman's work noted the growth of missionary societies:

> Perhaps the largest number is in South Carolina, 68 or 69. These have greatly increased missionary contributions, as in Maryland, Virginia, Georgia, Alabama, Kentucky, and other states. It is desirable that they should be established in all. Female Societies, co-operating in the general work of the Board, have from the beginning largely contributed to its revenues and successes. . . . We think it would be a good plan to establish a female society in every church which all ladies should be invited to join. A monthly meeting encouraged by the pastor, and an annual meeting, with a special service, would nourish its vitality.

The report pointed out the value of specific objectives for women's gifts and mentioned the building of the mission house at Tungchow. The mission house at Canton (China) had already aroused the zeal of women in South Carolina and Alabama. "In selecting other objects of Christian benevolence we recommend that the society correspond with Rev. Dr. Tupper. Not a few societies might each support a child in a mission school. . . . Others, individually, or by forming an alliance embracing the societies of a city or a district, might support a female missionary or a Bible reader." The Foreign Mission Board organized central committees for women's work in most of the Convention states by 1876.

The following year, the committee of woman's work of the Home Mission Board made an earnest appeal for women's help in home missions. The chairman was the same J. A. Chambliss who had asked the Welsh Neck Society to serve as central committee for South Carolina.

> . . . We rejoice to know that . . . in co-operating through various associations for the accomplishments of objects quite away from their own doors and looking to the general extension of the Lord's Kingdom in the world, the Christian women of our own day are doing more than . . . women have [ever] done for Christ. It is well known that within the last four years they have become well organized and devoted fellow-helpers of the truth in the work of Foreign Missions. Their sympathies have been deeply enlisted in behalf of their heathen sisters, they have manifested a charming eagerness to share with them the blessings which they enjoy under the gospel. But it is not within the knowledge of your Committee that the women of our Southern Baptist Churches are making any organized effort in the line of work pursued by our Home Mission Board. Yet surely the time has come when this department of christian service, as well as every other, should be blessed with the special prayers and gifts and labors of our Marys and Joannas, our Dorcases, Phoebes and Priscillas.

After pointing out "the vortex of shameful vice" in cities and conditions of frontier settlements, the report concluded with the resolution "That our sisters in all our churches be and hereby are invited and urged to co-operate with us in the work of home missions by such special methods of organization as they may judge wisest and most efficient." All opposition to women's organizations seemed to be breaking down by sheer force of the increase of gifts where societies were organized, especially where guided by state central committees.

The committee of woman's work of the Foreign Mission Board, in its report to the Convention in 1877, likewise held forth at length on the record of the eighth chapter of Luke, on "the fitness and efficiency of christian women for noble undertakings," with the reminder that "an *apostate church* has long employed them in stupendous and successful endeavors." Pleading the cause of women in missions, the report continued:

> Not only are they our most effective workers, because of their greater zeal, persistency and unselfish love, but there are *more of them* than of men. And besides all this, they are the most available and valuable power in a true pastor's hand, for securing the aid of the men.
>
> The result of their own special work in the past twelve years has been a universal surprise, as is also the recently announced fact that of the four hundred laborers for Jesus in the land of China, three hundred are christian women.
>
> We hail their coming to our help. We commend to our churches the employment of their hands, the encouragement of their hearts, in methods of their own devising, whereby the stream of christian beneficence shall move with a broader flow.

The reference to a central committee intimated a general Southwide central committee or may have referred to establishment of more state central committees; in either case Foreign and Home Mission Board reports both added their encouraging but veiled words regarding the value of "adopting some plan of combined effort."

Encouragement by Southern Baptist Convention committees on woman's work.—The report of the committee on woman's work in 1878 boldly recommended:

> 1. That the Boards . . . organize Central Committees of women in each State represented in that body.

2. It shall be the object of these Central Committees to organize Missionary Societies and by the circulation of periodicals and other means, to cultivate the missionary spirit.

3. Each society may decide in what direction its funds shall go—either to the Foreign or to the Home field, and to what objects to be appropriated.

4. These Societies should be auxiliary to the State Conventions, or to the Southern Baptist Convention.

5. They may select their own way to report to the Boards of this Convention, either through the Central Committee, or through their churches, or directly to the Boards.

6. We further recommend that the Boards strictly appropriate the funds these Societies may send to the objects mentioned by them. . . .

The boards reiterated their pleasure in these recommendations concerning women's societies, and the Foreign Mission Board expressed anticipation of "grand results from their pious and self-denying labors." The Home Mission Board earnestly appealed to Baptist women of the South for "more general co-operation in the work of Domestic and Indian Missions, by organized Church Societies"; it appealed to Convention delegates "to bring the matter before the female members of their Churches and urge their adoption of this, or some such plan, by which systematic and concentrated action may be secured." The boards did not want the strength of Southern Baptist women lost to the churches; nor did they want a separate independent organization.

By 1879 there were still delegates to the Southern Baptist Convention representing women's missionary societies and one representing the Georgia woman's central committees. The boards, therefore, had to reassure the brethren that they were not leading women away from proper femininity. The committee on woman's work reported:

In view of the vast power for good which rests with the women of our churches, and in view of the great needs of the work of Home and Foreign Missions, your Committee would urge the importance of enlisting as thoroughly as possible the energies of the Baptist women of the South in this great cause. While we do not approve of women's speaking before popular assemblies, or in any way usurping the duties which the New Testament imposes exclusively upon men, we yet recognize the fact that much can be accomplished for the work of our Boards through the agency of women. The two . . . contributions which . . . called forth the commendation of our Saviour, were both from women.

Then the committee made four recommendations:

1. That two Central Committees be appointed in each state, the one for Home and the other for Foreign Missions, and that these appointments be left to our two Boards to arrange as . . . deemed best.

2. That the women of all our churches be urged to form in each church a Missionary Society, which shall raise money and divide it between the Boards in such a manner and in such proportion as may seem . . . best.

3. That these societies report regularly to the two Central Committees . . . and that these Committees report to our Boards.

4. That the special object of these Central Committees shall be to awaken the missionary spirit among the women of our churches, as well as to direct their zeal, for the extension of Christ's kingdom in the world.

The Home Mission Board added in its report that it had endeavored to organize central committees and through them Woman's Missionary Societies. The board reported progress but realized that any new system required gradual growth. It found that some state central committees addressed themselves to one department of missionary effort, while others combined; and it was the board's opinion that unity, not division of counsel, would form a true policy in church work for missions, as in all things else.

The Foreign Mission Board report was more enthusiastic: "Their first fruits [of missionary societies] already cheer [the Board] with the prospect of abundant harvests." Then it allayed any fears by the comment: "So far as the Board are informed, the Central Committees and Societies are opposed to any other general organizations than their present State Associations and Conventions, and the Southern Baptist Convention." In 1880 the Home Mission Board committee on woman's work, stating that it had received aid from the women, hoped for a gradual enlargement of aid and wished to "acknowledge our indebtedness to the sisters who have diligently endeavored to carry out the wishes of the Convention and the Board."

By 1881, 350 societies had reported to H. A. Tupper, who thought that fact indicated at least 500 organizations in existence. The committee on woman's work repeated the recommendation for formation of central committees in states which did not have them and urged those already formed to enter into active correspondence with church societies, imparting missionary information and stimulating the women to work diligently and faithfully in the mission cause. A third recommendation suggested, "When the Foreign Mission Board deems wise they appoint some competent woman as superintendent whose duty would be to collect and disseminate information and in other ways stimulate and strengthen Woman's Work for Women. The said superintendent to act under the direction of the Board." The report further urged pastors to aid in the work and asked for quarterly reports of the societies to state central committees and, in turn, to the board at Richmond. Seventeen men joined in the discussion, after which the recommendations passed.

In its report to the Convention in 1884 the Foreign Mission Board included the statement, "No reader of the New Testament with mind directed to the subject can fail to be impressed with the prominence given women in the propagation of the gospel."

The board had furnished 28,520 mite boxes for the use of co-operating societies, and this expenditure ($733.40) had been repaid many times by gifts of $16,985.58. The board "congratulated our Southern sisters that the natural tendency to separate and independent organization is resisted by them, and that our respective works for the spread of the gospel in pagan and papal lands promise to go on. . . ."

Some pastors were not yet convinced of the value of woman's work. The first resolution of the Foreign Mission Board instructing "vice-presidents and agents of the Board and pastors to enlist more generally the women by forming Woman's Missionary Societies in all churches" carried the clause, "where such societies would be approved and fostered."

Meanwhile, women were gathering annually at Southern Baptist Conventions. In 1883 they met quietly in the Methodist church in Waco, Tex., while the Convention was in session. Sallie Rochester Ford of Missouri, author of *Grace Truman,* fictionized presentation of Baptist doctrine, presided, and the women, hearing Martha Foster Crawford, home from 32 years in China, were so touched that they immediately gave her $200.

The following year in the Westminster Presbyterian Church of Baltimore, Md., was held what is now considered the first regular meeting of Southern Baptist women, since state central committees were asked to send formal reports of their work to Lily Graves in preparation for the meeting. The women resolved "that the societies here represented make the Union meeting permanent; to meet annually during the session of the Southern Baptist Convention; the Central Committees of the state in which the Convention is held having charge of the meeting that year." Significantly, the word "Union" was used in this resolution.

The record book of the minutes of the Maryland Woman's Mission to Woman for May 8, 1884, includes the minutes of this convention meeting since previous minutes had included plans for it. When interesting gleanings from letters received by the corresponding secretary in reference to conditions of numerous mission societies of the South were read, the women decided unanimously that the report be printed in pamphlet form and distributed through churches of the South. The secretary read the report of 26 missionary societies organized since the mission society in Florida had been established three years earlier. The Florida society was organized as a result of the inspiration of letters received from Ann Graves, as was the case of many other women's organizations in the South.

The committee on woman's work at the Convention in 1885 in Augusta, Ga., reported steady increases in gifts and expressed the view that "the work is entitled to appropriate recognition from this body." Reassuringly, the committee observed "there is no dissatisfaction on the part of Baptist women with the plans and methods of our Boards." The committee recognized that it was important for women's central committees to be established and fostered by state conventions or associations with the co-operation of the boards. "Central Committees should be aided and encouraged by pastors in establishing local societies in churches. Money would be reported to churches as well as Boards and credited also to general state conventions and associations." This plan relieved the complications of two central committees—one for home and one for foreign missions.

At the 1885 Convention a resolution was presented which had been adopted at a woman's missionary meeting held simultaneously in St. John's Methodist Church.

Resolved,

1. That it is not the desire of the Baptist women of the South to have a separate and independent organization for the prosecution of Woman's Work.

2. That we desire to prosecute our work directly through the churches and to have representation in the Southern Baptist Convention through our respective State Conventions as heretofore.

The Foreign Mission Board urged aid to our "sisters in giving the general form to their work which would secure unity and efficiency as wise foresight, quickened by the experience in other parts of our country"—no doubt referring to the independent organizations of other denominations in which women handled their own money and appointed their own missionaries. The Foreign Mission Board wanted the work of the women's state central committees clearly and fully presented to the Convention, while the Home Mission Board believed that the women would contribute to all phases of Home Mission Board work. As the annual women's meetings became a custom, the board felt that the women could not take exclusive management of a large meeting without becoming public speakers, "which was regarded as contrary to Scriptural teaching, as all speaking should be done by brethren," although written reports might be "read by a lady." Another resolution relieved the situation by stating that the meetings "shall be for women only, the committee having the privilege of inviting speakers if so desired."

While the Southern Baptist Convention was in session in 1886 in Montgomery, Ala., the women, in their meeting, led devotional exercises, read reports and papers, and spoke as they desired. The Convention appointed a committee on the relation of woman's work to the Convention, which reported at a later session that there was cause to "rejoice in the Spirit of God graciously stirring the hearts of the women, and it would be for the best interest of the Convention to encourage these godly women in all suitable ways." The committee considered the central committees worthy of praise and suggested that encouragement, prayers, sympathy, and co-operation should be pledged to the woman's work.

With more courage the women gathered in the Broadway Methodist Church in Louisville, Ky., in 1887. Both Maggie Rice, an appointed missionary for Brazil, and Ann Luther Bagby (*q.v.*), home on furlough from Brazil, spoke at the meeting. Representing home missions, Annie

Armstrong (*q.v.*) told of mission work among Chinese and others in Baltimore. Many women had come anticipating that a Southwide organization in permanent form would be effected. However, the women realized that the Convention would sanction their organization more readily if the delegates voting to organize were elected by their respective state central committees. Therefore, they adopted three resolutions: First, because they were deeply impressed with the importance of having a thorough and efficient organization among women in the South, they desired the appointment of a committee to request each state central committee to send three women delegates to meet during the next Convention and decide on the advisability of a general committee; and if agreeable to "provide for the appointment, location, and duties thereof." The second resolution disclaimed any desire to interfere with the existing boards and emphasized the chief purpose of collecting more money and disseminating information. The third suggested appointment of a committee to confer with the Virginia Central Committee to arrange a program for the 1888 gathering.

Martha McIntosh, president of the South Carolina Central Committee, was appointed to carry out the first resolution. She had a folder containing the three resolutions printed and distributed so that every society would know the purpose of the meeting of delegated women in Richmond. Alice Armstrong of Baltimore, at the request of Alfred Elijah Dickinson (*q.v.*), wrote a series of articles on "General Organization for Woman's Missionary Societies of Southern Baptist Convention" for publication in the *Religious Herald,* under the pseudonym "Ruth Alleyn." According to her thesis, "the charitable world" had felt the force of the awakened energy of women, and woman had lost none of her womanliness in organized charities. Comparison with the gifts of Methodist women caused "mortifying discomfiture." "Would we be willing to admit that Baptist women in the South are inferior to their Methodist sisters in intelligence, energy, or ability? No answer is necessary. The methods of work are different; they work through general organization, which plans, suggests, consults together, and succeeds." Included in her 10 statements on "How May General Organizations Help Us?" two were especially significant:

8. A woman's organization is an institution specially adapted to reach the individual, the Bible unit of responsibility and service. She has time, patience, tact, ingenuity, consecration, and a sense of the value of littles peculiarly her own, fitting her for the work. The unused forces of the church may be thus developed, utilizing much that would otherwise be wasting.

9. Children's work is a prominent feature of woman's general organization effort. With mothers more interested, and children directed and encouraged by attractive methods of work and literature suited to their capacities, may we not hope to prevent such a return to the Foreign Mission treasury as that of 1887—an average of one and a half cents from Southern Baptist women and children toward evangelizing 600,000,000 heathen women?

State papers published articles and editorials pro and con. The Maryland Society of Woman's Mission to Woman in Foreign Lands, which was the central committee of Maryland, voted to approve organization in Richmond. Annie Armstrong's conclusive proof of the value of organization was the 1½ cents to foreign and ¾ cent to home missions average per capita gift of Southern Baptist women in general, as contrasted with 37 cents in Maryland where there had been organization since 1871. Delegates to the 1888 meeting knew there was talk of selecting Baltimore as headquarters of the proposed organization, although Maryland women were instructed to vote for a South Carolina location.

The organization meeting.—For a year the meeting in Richmond had been anticipated by both men and women. Tupper, feeling responsible for a hostess for the woman's meeting, at the suggestion of Mrs. W. E. Hatcher, president of the Virginia Central Committee, appointed Mrs. Theodore Whitfield, wife of a Richmond pastor, to preside. Thirty-two delegates from 12 states and other women from three more states attended the meeting in the basement of the Broad Street Methodist Church in Richmond on May 11, 1888. F. M. Ellis, who delivered the Convention sermon, led the religious exercises, advising the group that criticism would be determined by the character of the organization; therefore, if the women knew what to do, they would be wise to go ahead and do it, for taking more time was losing time. After he retired, Miss McIntosh announced that the meeting would proceed with the program arranged by the women of Virginia. Mrs. John Stout of South Carolina read a paper entitled "Shall the Baptist Women of the South Organize for Mission Work?" Then Annie Armstrong moved that the subject of organization be considered with informal and free interchange of views in order to decide what to do. As the roll of states was called, it became apparent that the majority would vote for organization. Miss Armstrong was opposed to further delay. Women would be judged in the Last Day for what they had done or not done; to put off for another day would not leave time to plan and consult, and the plans must be the plans of all, not simply of a committee. Many men of the Convention had already advised going forward, and the states had virtually decided to organize unless the women retracted what they had said. A motion carried to set aside the program and go into the work of organization immediately, and a committee of conference, with one member from each of the 12 states, was appointed to draft a constitution and report the following Monday.

On Monday, May 14, 1888, following religious exercises led by John Eager, missionary to Italy, and a paper read by Alice Armstrong, the committee on organization brought its report. The report was read as a whole, after which each state was asked to express itself for or against. Virginia requested leave to retire for consultation. As the roll call was read, 10 states heartily favored organization: Maryland, South Carolina, Missouri, Tennessee, Texas, Arkansas, Florida, Georgia, Louisiana, and Kentucky. Virginia and Mississippi preferred to delay action, and the women from West Virginia, North Carolina, and Alabama were not delegated representatives. The women selected Baltimore as the location of the executive committee of Woman's Mission Societies, auxiliary to Southern Baptist Convention.

Several factors distinguished the new organization from other denominational woman's organizations. It combined home, foreign, and state mission interests in one body. Through its auxiliary relation to the Southern Baptist Convention, it would not handle money and duplicate mission boards; its collected money would be disbursed by Convention boards; it would not independently appoint its own missionaries. The Convention was relieved. Later in Nashville, Tenn., Edgar Young Mullins (*q.v.*) called attention to the Convention's gratitude for this auxiliary and begged that more recognition be granted women on boards lest they not always wish to remain auxiliary.

The organization's constitution has held with only minor changes through the years. Its purpose was simple and clear:

We, the Women of the churches connected with the Southern Baptist Convention, desirous of stimulating the missionary spirit and the grace of giving, among women and children of the churches, and aiding in collecting funds for missionary purposes, to be disbursed by the Boards of the Southern Baptist Convention, and disclaiming all intention of independent action, organize and adopt the following:

CONSTITUTION

Article I—Name

This organization shall be known as the Executive Committee of the Woman's Mission Societies (Auxiliary to Southern Baptist Convention).

Article II—Object

The twofold object of this Executive Committee shall be:

1st. To distribute missionary information and stimulate effort, through the State Central Committees, where they exist; and where they do not, to encourage the organization of new societies.

2nd. To secure the earnest systematic co-operation of women and children in collecting and raising money for missions.

Other articles of organization followed. Officers included Martha McIntosh, president, 10 vice-presidents (one from each original state); Annie Armstrong, corresponding secretary; Mrs. J. T. Pullen, treasurer; and Mrs. James Pollard, recording secretary. The local committee consisted of nine residents of Baltimore.

Meanwhile, the Convention was uneasy, not knowing what action the women would take. The Foreign Mission Board's committee on woman's work again recommended encouraging the formation of woman's missionary circles and children's bands in all the churches and Sunday schools for the double purpose of exciting interest in mission work and raising funds for the spread of the gospel. It recommended the use of the established channels for giving money and annual reports by the societies. The committee commended the Bureau of Missionary Information in Baltimore, maintained by the Maryland Society of Woman's Mission to Woman, and the boards expressed a desire for more such mission rooms and willingness to print tracts for distribution through them. The Home Mission Board sent immediate requests to the new organization, asking specific aid of the women.

Reaction to the organization was vigorous. State denominational papers and state conventions had much to say. Some pastors, certain that the movement was of God and could not be stopped, foresaw immediate fruits in more comfortable houses of worship, better instruction in the Sunday schools, more reading of God's Word and religious literature, more money in God's treasury, and, in the future, a mission ministry in the pulpits and mission membership in church pews. Some recognized that "organization is the keynote and condition of success in this age." Others felt that there must be some restriction and limitation on woman's work in the churches. Women could sing, and they could teach in Sunday school; but they must not speak out in meetings, and they must be subject to husbands in voting. They must not take the reins of government, church, or state out of male hands. There was fear that if the conventions and churches did not give fostering care to the women's organization, their indifference or opposition might result in independence and perpetual separation of the missionary work of the women from the Convention.

The executive committee of Woman's Missionary Societies begins work.—The new executive committee undertook its duties without delay, meeting June 9, 1888, in Baltimore. It had been agreed in Richmond in May that Miss McIntosh and Miss Armstrong would confer with the two Convention mission boards about paying necessary expenses, thereby forming a close connection between the executive committee and the boards. Since the boards would receive all funds the women collected for missions, the women requested $100 from each to begin the work in a creditable manner.

The papers read at Richmond on "The Special Obligation of Women to Spread the Gospel" were printed as requested; and a "Sketch and Constitution" was printed for free distribution through state central committees. The executive committee agreed to purchase from the Maryland mission rooms prayer cards containing statistics and synopses of missionary reports for free distribution. "Go Forward," with Hebrews 10:24 as its selected motto, was to be stamped on all executive committee issues.

By the time of meeting in May, 1889, Mississippi had "wheeled into line," and Virginia had joined in. The new organization had agreed to have a plan of work, the first of all subsequent working bases for local societies, and quarterly report blanks to be filled out regarding progress. The two boards had sent recommendations regarding their wishes for special emphases in gifts and study. Another policy inaugurated for continued observance was the nomination of a vice-president from each state by each state delegation, elected by the whole body.

The new organization, after proving its worth in one year, was well launched in implementing its purpose of disseminating missionary information and stimulating missionary giving. The system of granting free literature to the states, prorated according to the number of societies reported, proved the foundation for subsequent distribution.

At the 1890 meeting in Fort Worth, Mrs. Stainback Wilson, president of the Georgia Central Committee, moved that the organization's name be changed to Woman's Missionary Union, auxiliary to Southern Baptist Convention. By Dec., 1890, all the states in the Southern Baptist Convention were included in the Woman's Missionary Union.

Frequent visits of Isaac Taylor Tichenor (*q.v.*) and Tupper and correspondence with them or their associates show the close relationship between Woman's Missionary Union and the work of the boards. For years the boards recommended to the delegates at annual meetings special projects for their gifts. Committees on woman's work were continued by the boards and the Convention; the committees received reports and presented them to the Convention in behalf of Woman's Missionary Union until 1913, when William Owen Carver (*q.v.*) championed the idea of a direct report from the union. The report was thereafter published in entirety, but with a resumé drawn up and presented by the committee on the union's work. A pastor served as chairman until 1938, when the last committee on Woman's Missionary Union work was made up of women. Since 1938 the union has arranged for the presentation of its own report without a committee's summary.

In 1889 the new organization cautioned loyalty to Southwide and state boards and urged that boards be consulted before adopting special objects for contributions. This loyalty continues today.

GROWTH AND DEVELOPMENT. *Presidents.*—The first president of Woman's Missionary Union, Martha E. McIntosh, served in the originating years of 1888–92 when early policies were being formed. Traveling frequently from South Carolina to Baltimore for monthly executive committee meetings, she established the unity of Woman's Missionary Union in the work of the societies and states, but she equally respected and wrought into the permanent policies of the W.M.U. the separate responsibility of each state for its own development.

Fannie Exile Scudder Heck (*q.v.*) led the W.M.U. in three separate terms—1892–94, 1895–99, and 1906–15. During her administration the centennial of foreign missions was observed, Missionary Day in Sunday school was begun, Sunbeam Bands became the responsibility of Woman's Missionary Union, and the Babies Branch was formed. Also while Miss Heck was in office, the Woman's Missionary Union Training School was established; *Our Mission Fields,* which became *Royal Service* in 1914, was inaugurated; and Miss Heck's own 25-year history of the union, *In Royal Service,* was written and published. Young Woman's Auxiliary was organized in 1907, the Order of Royal Ambassadors in 1908, and Girls' Auxiliary in 1913. The Jubilate, which significantly set forward union activities, was observed. Miss Heck began the plan of an annual letter from Woman's Missionary Union to women foreign missionaries, acquainting them with the union's work and requesting in return that they tell of their responsibilities and work. This practice was enlarged to include women home missionaries in 1899 and has been continued regularly by the executive secretary.

Between Miss Heck's first and second terms, 1894–95, Mrs. Abby Manley Gwathmey of Virginia, mother of nine children, served as president. During that year the week of self-denial for home missions was begun. Mrs. Charles Stakley of Alabama was president from 1899 to 1903, when the Sunbeam Band pin was designed and adopted. Her administration witnessed discussion of the necessity for a graded system of missionary education, initiation of the annuity plan for the boards and the Church Building Loan Fund, and promotion of the New Century Plans. Mrs. J. A. Barker, the only president who had served under appointment of the Foreign or Home Mission Board, was a missionary to Brazil who returned to the United States because of her health. She served as union president from 1903 to 1906, during which time the Margaret Home was established in Greenville, S. C.

Following the death of Miss Heck in 1915, Mrs. W. C. James was elected president and served until 1925. Progress was marked in her administration with the erection of a new Training School building, election of a young people's secretary, removal of headquarters from Baltimore to Birmingham, Ala., publication of *World Comrades,* initiation of a Young Woman's Auxiliary camp at Ridgecrest, and inauguration of union and Convention fieldworkers. Mrs. W. J. Cox of Tennessee became president in 1925 and served through the Ruby Anniversary and until 1933. She established the policy of having chairmen for the fundamentals, saw the need for an associate young people's secretary, wrote *Following in His Train,* the 50-year history of Woman's Missionary Union, in 1938, and contributed the inspiration of unusual devotion to the cause of Christ and rare ability in address. Following Mrs. Cox, Mrs. Frank W. Armstrong's (*q.v.*) administration as president, from 1933 until her death in 1945, witnessed the Golden

Jubilee and its attendant growth, projects of the new Training School building, and promotion of interracial activities.

Mrs. George R. Martin followed Mrs. Armstrong as president in 1946. She was a forceful leader, whose many contributions to missions include establishment of Woman's Missionary Union conferences at Ridgecrest and Glorieta and a Young Woman's Auxiliary conference at Glorieta, increased personnel at union headquarters, purchase of adequate headquarters building, marked changes in curriculum of the Training School, and the change of its name to Carver School of Missions and Social Work.

Corresponding and executive secretaries.—Annie Walker Armstrong (*q.v.*) of Baltimore, the pioneer corresponding secretary, was elected at the organization meeting May 14, 1888, and served without salary until her resignation in 1906. Following Miss Armstrong, Elizabeth Crane served as secretary from the fall of 1907 until Jan., 1912, when she resigned because of her health. Then for 36 years Kathleen Mallory (*q.v.*), elected in May, 1912, continued remarkable service until her retirement in 1948. Alma Hunt was elected her successor in May of that year, although Miss Mallory continued as acting executive secretary until Sept. 1. An exceptionally effective speaker, Miss Hunt contributed to conferences and public relations her brilliant gifts of leadership, which resulted immediately in the purchase of a headquarters building. Two assistant corresponding secretaries have served the union: Elizabeth Poulson, 1906–07; and Nancy Lee Swann, 1911–12, after which she left for China as a missionary of the Foreign Mission Board.

Fundamentals.—Through the administrations of all the presidents and secretaries, the program of Woman's Missionary Union has developed along the lines of four aims, or fundamentals, rooted in the life of the societies even before they were first listed as aims in the "Recommendations of the Executive Committee" from 1913–14 to 1917–18, or called fundamentals in the resolutions which became the Plan of Work as adopted annually after 1918–19. The promotion of mission study, stewardship, community missions, and prayer reaches into every woman's missionary society and young people's organization.

1. Promotion of mission study. In 1906 Mrs. J. A. Barker, then president of the Southwide union, advanced the idea that a program once a month was not sufficient for the study of mission needs and announced the initiation of study courses in the Young People's Missionary Movement. In May, 1906, Miss Heck, who had succeeded Mrs. Barker as president, represented Woman's Missionary Union at the annual interdenominational Mission Study Conference, after which she became even more enthusiastic about the necessity for promoting mission study.

The *Digest of State Reports* in 1907 indicated that systematic mission study was already being carried on in the societies. So, following the usual policy of building from the society activities into general union plans, the "Recommendations of the Executive Committee" of that year, addressed to all the societies, included a new section: "10. Study Courses—That the societies, as far as possible, at some time during the year take up the ten weeks' study course as arranged by the educational secretary of the Southern Baptist Convention." The section referred to the Forward Mission Study Courses under the special care of T. Bronson Ray (*q.v.*) of the Foreign Mission Board. Two years later, in 1909, the *Annual Report* of the union's corresponding secretary stated: "The mission study class is coming to be a well-recognized agency for increasing our active support of missions. The educational secretary, Dr. T. B. Ray of Richmond, with whose work along this line we co-operate, reports 315 classes formed among members of woman's and young woman's societies." When Miss Heck's book, *In Royal Service,* was published and financed by the Foreign Mission Board, Ray coupled the history of the development of Southern Baptist women in missions and the first 25 years of Woman's Missionary Union activity with heroic stories of national workers and used it as the distinctive mission study book of 1913–14 for Southern Baptists.

By 1918 the Home Mission Board had produced several books which it asked Woman's Missionary Union to study and promote, and over 2,900 societies in 15 states reported study courses. The *Manual of W.M.U. Methods,* prepared by Miss Mallory in the spring of 1917 and published by the Sunday School Board, was ready for sale in October. In 1918 Mrs. W. C. James, while president of the union, saw it was possible to supply a genuine course of mission study. With many books available, including *In Royal Service,* the *Manual of W.M.U. Methods, Stewardship and Missions,* W. O. Carver's *All the Word in All the World,* books on home and foreign missions, *Talks on Soul-winning,* and books on intercessory prayer, two basic certificate courses for Woman's Missionary Societies were arranged, with a certificate showing the home and foreign mission books studied; later, an advanced course was started. During the next year 2,115 seals were awarded in 15 states for the study of one of these mission books, while 38 women and two men earned the large Woman's Missionary Union official seal for the study of six books. Similar courses and certificates for Sunbeams, G.A.'s, and R.A.'s were provided, and reading stamp cards were supplied, with space for five stamps to indicate five mission books read. After a course for Y.W.A.'s had been offered for only one year, 158 official seals for completion of the course had been issued.

As encouragement to the women to become teachers of mission study classes, a special course and certificate were provided, with books for reading and study selected by the state Woman's Missionary Union from a list recommended by the Southwide body, thereby maintaining unity yet freedom among the states instead of static conformity. The union's Plan of Work in 1925 mentioned church schools of missions, which the union promised to assist in every way possible. Recognizing the value of books in giving impetus to the spread of the gospel, the union promoted missionary libraries in denominational schools and the building up of missionary libraries in churches. Women and Y.W.A.'s began to rally to a missionary or denominational secretary visiting an association or city to teach a large class made up of groups from adjacent churches; such co-operative study was promoted in the Plan of Work for 1928–29. Mission study institutes, added in 1929, helped teachers learn how to teach.

The article on mission study in the 1933 Plan of Work mentioned the value of associational Woman's Missionary Union libraries, so that books used by the society in one church could be lent to another and passed on throughout the association, overcoming the handicap raised when church organizations did not know the worth of such study and were not willing to spend money for books.

In 1934 a special effort was begun to reach women and young people who had never before engaged in mission study, and these classes later adopted the name "Pioneer Classes." Books written at the request of Woman's Missionary Union for study included *Following in His Train* by Ethlene Boone Cox and *Helping Others to Become Christians* by Roland Q. Leavell. The aim of mission study since its initiation has been "more women and young people in more classes studying more books that we may give more money to send more missionaries to more people who do not know the gospel."

In 1945 Missionary Round Tables were launched for wide reading of books on the background of missionary life and work in which 12 to 20 women each bought a book on a selected subject, passed the books around, and read and discussed their messages. The White Cross work, which grew out of a study of "A Crusade of Compassion" and resulted in sending money and boxes of supplies to overseas hospitals, is an example of the interrelationship of Woman's Missionary Union fundamentals. Some states have continued this project through the years. Following the pattern of leadership worked out in the states, Mrs. Irvin (Una Roberts) Lawrence was appointed mission study chariman in 1930 and continued until 1948. In Oct., 1931, Mrs. Cox appointed the mission study chairmen of the states as the mission study committee of Woman's Missionary Union to take over the work of the standing committee of the executive body and effect closer relationships with all the societies and states.

The awarding of certificates and seals was discontinued at the end of 1949, and since then only the number of mission study books taught in classes and the number of round tables and book clubs have been reported. Mrs. William McMurry, who became mission study director in 1951, introduced the achievement chart the following year as the new program of mission study. She planned the mission study council meeting, a workshop for state mission chairmen held at headquarters in 1951, which proved valuable in promoting mission study.

2. Promotion of community missions. Before the organization of Woman's Missionary Union, in Richmond the women missionary leaders recognized the charge to use their natural arts and training to study individual cases and lead them to Christ. Soul-winning and personal witnessing were woven into the warp and woof of Woman's Missionary Union plans.

At its beginning the young organization did not hesitate to score the liquor traffic as a hindrance to the progress of the gospel and to resolve that Woman's Missionary Union would "give all its influence and exert its power in the destruction of the traffic by all lawful means in accord with the spirit of our Lord Jesus Christ." Also from the first, the women were concerned about the Negro people and continually emphasized that without fail they must "gather our colored women and teach them by precept and example the way of the Lord." "Neighborwork" was the term used for Sunday schools held on Sunday afternoon, which proved valuable with Chinese people, especially, as one Chinese person met with a Chinese teacher, learning the English language by way of the Gospels as the two studied together Sunday after Sunday.

The women realized that gifts to missions were not an adequate expression of concern for a lost world; there must be the "unpaid personal missionary effort." Each woman was to give herself to the little span about her, using her own personal effort in soul-winning. She must visit the afflicted; she must make it possible for the poor to hear the gospel. Giving money was not sufficient; a woman must give herself to reach and lift her fellows.

Plans grew as the women provided Bibles for those who had none and persuaded foreigners and others to attend worship services. Dismayed by the growth of Mormonism, the women were spurred to more personal giving of themselves to work as missionaries.

By 1908 plans were crystallizing, and the "Recommendations of the Executive Committee" to the union included as the last article, "Study and Service." The "service" was to be the establishment of mothers' meetings, sewing schools, neighborhood prayer meetings, and similar undertakings "that in our own neighborhoods we may be factors in bringing all people of all nations to the feet of his Son."

The term "Personal Service" was the first used in the recommendations of 1909: "That we hold up before all our societies the need for personal service in our own needy communities, as expressing the Spirit of the Master." Recognizing the growing efforts and rising need for more definite planning, Woman's Missionary Union devoted a separate paragraph to personal service in the annual recommendations of 1910 and appointed Mrs. Henry Marvin Wharton (*q.v.*) chairman of a personal service department. The union sent out a circular letter to all state vice-presidents urging the fostering of the new department.

Recommendations in 1911 set forward a preliminary statement of society aims which included "spiritual deepening of life for all our societies by the practice of prayer, Bible study, and definite forms of personal service." Further emphasis was assured by adoption of a clause on personal service in the standard of excellence at the annual meeting in 1912 after the first report of the personal service department of Woman's Missionary Union had been presented. The report summarized the variety of activities so admirably that the union printed it in leaflet form for distribution in the states. The personal service committee recommended state surveys of conditions and needs to bring home to individual societies the facts closely related to them. A handbook, *The Homemaker,* was published in 1912 with valuable material for the conduct of mothers' meetings.

A five-pointed star, adopted as the symbol of "Personal Service to make Christ known as Redeemer and King," suggested that as Wise Men followed a star to Christ, wise women would follow a star which would lead others to him. Pray, study, enlist, use, and teach were the star's five points of personal service. To deal wisely with problems in the community required investigation, surveys, and study. Orphanges, hospitals, prisons, and county homes provided unlimited opportunities. Personal service activities grew in influence and participation, so that even through the 1919 influenza epidemic, reports were made of methodical, continuing ministry which constituted real assistance in that time of critical need.

After Mrs. Wharton resigned as chairman of the personal service department in 1924, a committee supervised the work, with Mrs. P. A. Eubank chairman, until 1930. The union decided that only personal service directed by a society's personal service committee should be reported, and that soul-winning should be reported only when known to be the direct result of personal service efforts. Personal service endeavored to avoid being merely neighborly deeds. The union's Plan of Work annually encouraged the study of state and federal laws relating to health, employment of women and children, general public welfare, and reporting to proper authorities infringement of labor laws. The union urged women to co-operate in interracial committees, to hold classes for adult illiterates, to establish Good Will Centers, hold Vacation Bible schools, start and maintain mission Sunday schools, and have neighborhood Bible classes, but urged them to remember that "personal service is Christlike living in one's own community."

As activities in this area increased, reports of visits, trays, flowers sent, and similar services became astronomical in number; thus in 1928 reporting was changed to the number of societies conducting various activities, rather than the number of visits, etc. Mrs. Una Roberts Lawrence, appointed personal service chairman in 1930, wrote the *Personal Service Guide,* which later, with revisions, became the *Community Missions Guide.* Her successor, Mrs. P. B. Lowrance, who served from 1932 to 1937, promoted Open Doors for Negroes, similar to Good Will Centers, and Friends of Israel for Jews. In 1941, when Mary Christian became personal service chairman, "personal service" was changed to "community missions," a term considered more definite of the activities comprehended. Plans for a full-time, salaried director of community missions (instead of the chairman who worked only part-time) were adopted in 1948, and the following year Edith Stokely became community missions director. She conducted Community Missions Council meetings for state leaders in 1952 and 1955 and led Woman's Missionary Union participation in the Southern Baptist Convention's simultaneous evangelistic campaigns. Soul-winning is the major emphasis of community missions, but work with Negroes, Vacation Bible schools, and Good Will Centers are important areas of the work.

Plans for working with Negroes grew through experience as the women realized how imperative the need was. At first mothers' meetings and sewing schools proved successful, and the societies which sponsored them agreed that "patriotism and religion cry aloud for this effort."

When leaders of the National Baptist Convention requested Woman's Missionary Union leaders to help prepare a constitution for their societies, the union was happy to assist, and in 1901 Miss Armstrong accepted an invitation to address the national convention in Cincinnati. Growing out of mutual interest in interracial work came an advisory committee on co-operation with the National Baptist Woman's Auxiliary which decided to foster regional institutes for training Negro Baptist women leaders, to assist in launching a quarterly for Negro Baptist societies, and to prepare two texts for their mission study. The interracial institutes were further promoted until 1948 by $10,000 from the Golden Jubilee offering, which aided in providing promotional and travel expenses in states desiring the meetings. Woman's Missionary Union participates through appointed representatives in Southern Baptists' advisory council for work with Negroes. Continually the union's Plan of Work sets forth a section on Christian standards in international and interracial justice.

Vacation Bible schools became a part of personal service in 1913, and Y.W.A.'s were especially urged to assume leadership in the schools. As they grew in number, the Sunday School Board announced in 1923 its readiness to help in carrying on daily Vacation Bible schools and later, to appoint a secretary to give special attention to the work. Woman's Missionary Union has continued to list Vacation Bible schools as a form of community missions, however, especially those conducted among unchurched groups, while the Sunday School Board has enlarged its program to supply materials and trained leadership for the schools.

The third branch of community missions grew out of the Good Will Center established in 1912 at the Woman's Missionary Union Training School to give students practical training. With an already vigorous promotion of clubs, classes, and recreation in mission centers, conducted for soul-winning and Christian development, it was not long before a recommendation was passed that settlements directed by Woman's Missionary Union workers be named Good Will Centers. Each state was urged to establish at least one fully-manned, well-equipped, up-to-date center located at a populous and needy point to contribute to this "social service upheld by grace." Subsequently, some of these and other Good Will Centers have become projects of the Home Mission Board, often supported by Annie Armstrong Offerings.

3. Stewardship. One of the real considerations which led to organization of Woman's Missionary Union was the comparison of gifts of Methodist women and Southern Baptist women made by Annie Armstrong in 1888. When Methodist women organized in 1878, they were giving $4,014; they reported $48,092 in 1887. Southern Baptist women, working independently and spasmodically with no central organization, were giving only $11,333 in 1887. With 710,114 Southern Baptist women and children, that was 1½ cents per capita. When organization came, the preamble to the constitution referred to the stimulation needed for "the grace of giving among women and children of the churches" and the purpose of "aiding in collecting funds for missionary purposes to be disbursed by the Boards." A primary object was "to secure earnest and systematic co-operation of women and children in collecting and raising money for missions." By Oct., 1888, a leaflet entitled "God's Tenth" became available, and the Plan of Work in 1890 warned of the necessity for discretion lest unwise zeal weaken the foundation of future action, since money was not the sole objective. No unchristian or questionable methods should be employed to procure contributions; rather, all methods should tend to permanent development and the maintenance of a spirit of benevolence, not undue excitement. The monthly envelope system worked well where the women pushed it. Believing that each church should have a system of giving, the women tried to create a sentiment for it. The report in 1890 advised that the best plan for raising money was putting aside a certain proportion of earnings and doing without some object of convenience or self-indulgence. Woman's Missionary Union resolved to train children to consider all money they receive as belonging to God, and for that purpose arranged a box of four sections, called the Young Banker's Friend, to separate money for dividing, saving, giving, spending.

By 1894 per capita gifts from the women, although they had increased to over six cents, seemed still a "deep discredit." Miss Armstrong urged women who actually could not give more to enlist other women to join in giving and thus raise the total amount. Immediately after the union's organization, the Foreign Mission Board asked support for all its women missionaries, apart from the specific objects in the Christmas offering. The Home Mission Board asked that boxes be sent to missionaries on the frontier, and that special gifts be designated for the work in Cuba. So, specific causes for regular contributions were named year after year. The boards asked the union to participate in the 1892 centennial of missions, and the women responded. From 1895 on, when any goal has been set, a committee serving with the treasurer has divided the amount on a pro rata basis to each state as an apportionment to be reached, and the usual goal has been a 10 per cent increase over the previous year. In 1900 the Southern Baptist Convention made the first formal request of its auxiliary, asking Woman's Missionary Union "to co-operate with the Committee on Observance of the year 1900 in effort to induce every church to take regular collections and every member to make regular contributions."

Tithing received emphasis through the years of publication of the *Baptist Basket* with its subtitle, "Ho, ye that be wise, Oh, bring to Him His tithes," an emphasis never permitted to be lost. In 1901 Miss Armstrong urged each Woman's Missionary Union worker to adopt a systematic and proportionate plan of giving, stating bluntly that unfaithfulness in paying the tithe was termed robbery by Malachi. Continually, year after year, tithing and faithful stewardship have been promoted through the aims and Plan of Work. In 1918 a stewardship covenant card was introduced, and with 1919 came the upswing of the 75 Million Campaign.

Woman's Missionary Union demonstrated its auxiliary position to the Southern Baptist Convention in shifting its financial plans to join wholeheartedly in the 75 Million Campaign. Before the plan was suggested, the union had arranged apportionments of about $5,000,000 on the customary basis of specific gifts to Sunday school and Home and Foreign Mission boards, Christian education and ministerial relief, Margaret Fund and Training School; then it changed the entire set-up to meet its $15,000,000 share of the 75 Million Campaign. From 1919 through 1924, *Royal Service* and the Year Book proclaimed the campaign from every angle, and gifts recorded from union members up to May 1, 1924, totaled $14,738,141.

In 1928 the Ruby Anniversary goal of $4,000,000 and its emphasis on sacrifice underscored again the necessity for faithful stewardship and tithing. Special tithing stories and stewardship declamation contests developing the stewardship education of young people, climaxed in a church night of stewardship. Names of churches with 100 per cent resident women members giving to missions were published from 1934 until 1947.

Beginning in 1929, a chairman appointed by the Southwide Woman's Missionary Union president centered her leadership planning on stewardship. First chairman was Mrs. George R. Martin, 1929–33, followed by Mrs. Carter Wright, promoter of a debtless denomination with the slogan, "Missions Wait on Stewardship, and Stewardship Waits on You." Mrs. C. D. Creasman, the first salaried stewardship director, served from 1949 until her retirement in 1954 following the first stewardship council meeting, which brought together state stewardship chairmen for discussion and planning.

With the birth of the Cooperative Program in 1925, Woman's Missionary Union immediately became a chief promoter with literature, programs, talks, and personal enthusiasm, all means for inspiring understanding of the plan. Some states made no effort to report accurately the actual gifts of union members through the Cooperative Program but counted one third of total gifts as from the women; others kept accurate reports. Since 1952 Woman's Missionary Union has made no attempt to report union gifts through the Cooperative Program but has given only the statement of mission offerings as reported by the boards. In the Southern Baptist Convention centennial celebration of 1945, Woman's Missionary Union agreed to set as its goal $6,666,666.66 in designated and undesignated gifts, one third of the financial goal of the Southern Baptist Convention centennial celebration; and in 1946 the union joined the Southern Baptist Convention effort to win a million tithers.

Fannie Heck once said, "Write over every mission board's deficit sheet 'robbed of God' and you write the truth." In 1895 Woman's Missionary Union raised $5,397.49 on the current debt of the Foreign Mission Board, only to find that the debt of the Home Mission Board was growing and the need very great. The union gave increased amounts which helped the Home Mission Board close the year with a balance.

By 1916 the Foreign Mission Board had accumulated a debt of $180,000 and Woman's Missionary Union resolved to wipe out $60,000 of it in 60 days and in a whirlwind campaign gave more than that amount. When other crises presented themselves, the union rallied, as in 1933 when, having voted to enter a Foreign Mission Board debt-paying campaign, the organization authorized the executive committee to swing the union full force into the Hundred Thousand Club plan formulated by the Convention. The Jubilate, the Ruby Anniversary, and the Golden Jubilee gave much emphasis to stewardship, but the regular teaching of stewardship and tithing continues vigorously year after year among women's and young people's organizations. The standards of excellence require at least 75 per cent of the members to be regular contributors through the Cooperative Program and at least 50 per cent of the membership to be tithers, in order to secure an A-1 rating.

4. Prayer. In June, 1884, according to a record concerning prayer, the fourth fundamental of Woman's Missionary Union, "Mrs. Graves read a letter from Mrs. Wilson of Georgia, requesting our society to remember in secret prayer home and foreign missions the first Sunday morning in each month. This plan of united prayer has been adopted in many missionary organizations." The Maryland Mission Rooms prepared prayer cards which named a different mission field for prayer each month, and many women bought them. In 1891 Woman's Missionary Union recommended the use of the prayer card in order that prayer for missionaries on the field, and for more consecrated workers at home, might be a part of daily private and family devotions. The noon hour was suggested as the best time for this concerted daily prayer for world evangelization.

The union resolved in 1889 "that the first Sunday of every month and first week of every year be observed as a special season of prayer for missions." To encourage united prayer, articles on intercessory prayer have been published from time to time, beginning with a request for such a leaflet in 1890. As summarized later, "underlying all else was the spirit of prayer. The Woman's Missionary Union was founded on prayer, its achievements are the results of prayer, and its hope for the future lies in prayer."

The centennial movement in 1892 called for earnest dedication to prayer; the first week in January was set apart for prayer for foreign missions and a week in early spring for home missions. In 1926 the week of prayer for foreign missions was changed to December. These weeks are high peaks of mission inspiration in which thousands of women and young people participate simultaneously. For many years books for study were prepared especially for use prior to and in preparation for the weeks.

A daily missionary prayer calendar, begun in 1905, was published annually until 1918, when it was included in *Royal Service*. In 1952 the Inter-Agency Council agreed that Training Union and Woman's Missionary Union publications would list the names of home and foreign missionaries on their birthdays. *Royal Service, The Window of YWA, Ambassador Life,* and *Tell,* all publish this birthday prayer calendar and also observe other emphases on the denominational calendar.

In 1921 the Plan of Work promoted the change of the hour for united prayer from noon to nine A.M. and also the suggestion that the prayer calendar be used in the family worship period which Woman's Missionary Union members are urged to establish and maintain. In anticipation of the Golden Jubilee of 1938, a special committee to stimulate the prayer life of Woman's Missionary Union prepared a brochure, "Prayer, the Golden Chain." A union-sponsored Intercessory Prayer League reminds shut-ins that they have a part in mission activities through their intelligent, understanding prayers for missions and missionaries.

Young people's organizations.—On the afternoon of the organization of Woman's Missionary Union, May 14, 1888, Mrs. Eva Brown, delegate from Tennessee, observed that the new organization must seek to train young people to see the whole scope of missions. Since Sunbeam Bands had already been started and other young people were becoming interested in missions, a graded system of missionary societies was soon outlined with Baby Bands, Sunbeam Bands for girls and boys, Young Ladies Societies, and Ladies Societies, to provide a program of progress in missionary information and zeal through infancy, childhood, youth, and mature life. The Foreign Mission Board at once asked that all the young people's organizations combine in the support of a missionary in Japan, in addition to other objects, and the Home Mission Board distributed Brick-Cards as a means of receiving gifts from young people for buying a church building in Havana.

"Our Duty to Our Young People," written by Alice Armstrong, and "Garnered Gleanings," a pamphlet of methods already successfully used by societies to interest young people, were published in 1889. The growing Woman's Missionary Union "recognized in woman's position as trainer of the young, a great opportunity for service to the cause of missions, urging special attention to forming of societies of young women, boys and girls, and appointment of Band superintendents in states where it was not already done." State central committees were urged to appoint or elect an able woman to take charge of young people's work in each state. But each society was responsible for the formation of mission bands and the special training of young people in the privileges and services of mission work. Programs for Sunbeam Bands and other young people's organizations were first outlined with suggested material in *Our Mission Fields* and later in *Royal Service*.

A series of conferences with Baptist Young People's Union leaders in 1915–16 resulted in recognition of the distinct functions of young people's missionary organizations, to prevent the danger of overlapping. Plans and purposes for midweek activities were different from Sunday school and young people's unions. More intensive mission study and training in missionary giving seemed needed than that provided on Sunday evening. Similar conferences held since 1916 include a Committee on Co-ordination and Correlation, which met for several years, beginning in 1937, and suggested organization of the Church Council, and the Committee on Church Organization, called in 1946. Discussion has always reached the same general result, committee members realized more after their study the value of distinctive midweek missionary education organizations.

Some states had appointed volunteer leaders for Sunbeam Bands even before they were turned over to Woman's Missionary Union for promotion in 1896, and for young women before their organization into Young Woman's Auxiliary in 1907. In 1908 the union recommended that Sunbeam Band state leaders assume direction of Royal Ambassadors, calling them "superintendents of young people's societies." Girls' Auxiliary leaders were frequently combined with Young Woman's Auxiliary state leaders after the two organizations were separated in 1914. By 1910 some states were employing salaried young people's leaders, and in 1916 Mary Faison Dixon became the first Southwide salaried young people's leader. Woman's Missionary Union has had a committee on young people's work to make general plans and to advise with the young people's secretary. When Miss Dixon resigned in 1919, Susan Bancroft Tyler, chairman of the young people's committee, virtually became young people's secretary until the election of Juliette Mather, who served from 1921 until she was elected editorial secretary in 1948. Margaret Bruce became young people's secretary at that time.

The idea of a young people's director as coordinator of the activities of the young people's missionary education organizations, reporting inclusively to the individual society when desired, was advanced through the 1924–25 Year Book and, proving successful, has been continued. Each church's young people's director serves as chairman of the committee on young people's work in her church, keeping the full program of activities before her church through focus week observances, family night, church night of stewardship, and promotion. If a Woman's Missionary Society has a Sunbeam Band and one other missionary education organization reaching the standard of excellence requirements, the society receives an A-1 rating. Since 1926 a list of churches with A-1 societies has been published in the Annual Report of Woman's Missionary Union and of the Southern Baptist Convention, giving the name of the pastor, the society president, and the young people's director.

To train counselors and leaders in missionary education, a correspondence course in leading each young people's organization was introduced in 1917, and, as adjusted later for conference use, the courses have continued to be of value.

According to a graded system of missionary education, Sunbeam Babies include the group from birth to 4; Sunbeam Bands, preschool, 4–6, school, 6–9; Girls' Auxiliary, Junior, 9–13, Intermediate, 13–16; Young Woman's Auxiliary, single young women, 16–25; Royal Ambassadors, Junior, 9–13, Intermediate, 13 and up. There are also special plans for Ann Hasseltine (college) and Grace McBride (nurses) Young Woman's Auxiliaries.

Magazines for programs and missionary inspiration have included *World Comrades*, 1922–53; *The Window of YWA*, 1929; *Ambassador*

Life, 1946; *Tell,* 1953; and *Sunbeam Activities* for Sunbeam Band leaders, 1953. Summer camps for Royal Ambassadors, Girls' Auxiliary, and Young Woman's Auxiliary members have developed into a program reaching approximately 78,925 young people in missionary education camps each year. Radio, first used in Southwide organization celebrations by Y.W.A.'s in 1932, and by R.A.'s in 1933; focus weeks started in 1936; state house parties for G.A.'s and Y.W.A.'s and conclaves for Royal Ambassadors; all provided additional means of increasing interest in missions. The values of Woman's Missionary Union programs and activities for young people are attested by Home and Foreign Mission boards, by individual pastors, church workers, denominational personalities, and missionaries.

Standard of excellence.—In 1911 uniform standards of excellence were adopted as measuring rods of achievement for societies and young people's organizations. These standards have not included the total activities but have gauged what has been accomplished in certain areas of effort as set forth in the over-all objectives adopted annually in the Plan of Work.

Publications.—When the executive committee of Woman's Mission Societies (auxiliary to Southern Baptist Convention) was organized, Maryland Baptist women already had a successful system of distributing available mission literature through their Maryland Mission Rooms to any societies applying for it. The Foreign Mission Board, however, had only five leaflets at that time—three on China, one on Italy, and one on South America; thus, leaflets were secured from boards of other denominations and, if deemed worthy of distribution, were stocked for sale.

More than one state central committee had a paper which it offered to the executive committee as an official organ, but the committee had not been instructed to enter upon such publication effort. Yet, with its first objective to disseminate missionary information, the committee felt it must distribute literature. It accepted the invitation of the Maryland Mission Rooms to occupy space as executive committee headquarters, and by May, 1889, Miss Armstrong reported 11,915 prayer cards, 52,141 leaflets and pamphlets, and 1,644 subscriptions to monthly leaflets, mailed out for use with monthly programs.

The first publications of the executive committee were a pamphlet, "Sketch and Constitution of Woman's Mission Societies and Fields and Work of Southern Baptist Convention," and the two prepared papers read at the organization meeting issued in tract form by request of the meeting. In 1899 a sample package of all mission literature issued by the Home Mission, Foreign Mission, and Sunday School boards was sent to all Southern Baptist pastors, financed by the boards. The women addressed the packages. Woman's Missionary Union used every opportunity to put "missionary intelligence" where it could be read by Southern Baptists. *Our Home Field* and *The Foreign Mission Journal* granted space for articles immediately, and in 1890 when *The Foreign Mission Journal* was enlarged, additional six pages were offered to the union. State papers asked for items regarding woman's work, and *Kind Words* offered a page for the union's use.

Leaflets were published as needed on different subjects, one to excite interest in missionary boxes, another, "A Lesson in Stewardship," and another, "Japan and Its People." Programs and appeals in behalf of financial progress were planned and published. "Chips from Many Workshops"—"a treasury of good things, extremely timely, most valuable hints to workers" —appeared by Oct., 1888, as the first methods material published for societies. "Garnered Gleanings," full of suggestions for young people's missionary meetings, followed later. Finally, on May 12, 1906, the executive committee voted to request the Maryland Baptist Union Association to give Woman's Missionary Union the fund in its possession to establish a literature department. This was done, and on July 1, the Woman's Missionary Union Literature Department opened rooms in the Wilson Building, Baltimore, with new stocks of mission leaflets and literature. The department was considered essential to the successful carrying out and enlargement of Woman's Missionary Union work. The $1,402.17 involved was to be returned to Maryland Baptist Union Association if the department was discontinued. Manuals, guides, and leaflets for directing missionary education organizations in print in 1955 totaled 104 separate pieces of literature, which are sent in bulk to state headquarters and given by states to local societies following the pattern established for distribution of free materials in 1888. Additional playlets, stories, accouterments of missionary education such as organization pins, seals, sweaters, awards, pennants, and similar objects are sold from the Birmingham headquarters.

Mrs. W. R. Nimmo, who wrote in some capacity or served as chairman or secretary of the literature department from 1892 to 1921, guided the editing of *Our Mission Fields* and *Royal Service* for 21 years. In 1928 a gift of $500 was made by the literature department to each of the mission boards for translation of literature to be used in other countries in memory of Mrs. Nimmo. Ethel Winfield, who became secretary of the department in 1923, developed and enlarged it so that it now does a $175,000 nonprofit business annually. Rachel Colvin, art editor since 1940, has contributed to the department's publications in making them more appealing and attractive and conducive to wider reading. In 1936, as a special feature of the union's 50th anniversary, the literature department joined the three magazines of Woman's Missionary Union (*Royal Service, World Comrades,* and *The Window of YWA*) in making a gift of $250 toward a similar literature department for the Woman's Convention, Auxiliary to the National Baptist Convention. The amount was given annually until the Home Mission Board included $500 for the department as an allocation of the Annie Armstrong Offering.

Relationships to boards and institutions.—The close relation of Woman's Missionary Union to the Home and Foreign Mission boards is indicated by the boards' support in the union's development and the union's promotion of annual weeks of prayer and offerings for each of the boards. Woman's Missionary Union received recommendations from each board regarding gifts and directions in general activities until 1914, after which time objectives were included in the Plan of Work until 1928. In subsequent years the 75 Million Campaign and the Cooperative Program have made special objectives unnecessary for the gifts of women and young people through the churches.

Immediately after the union's organization in 1888, Foreign Mission Board secretary Tupper and Miss Armstrong discussed the possibility of an offering to send at least one missionary to relieve Lottie Moon, who had been in China without furlough for 11 years. With daring faith the letters were written; $72.82 was spent for printing, and $2,833.49 was received. Named Lottie Moon Christmas Offering in 1918, this offering, begun for China, now encompasses all Southern Baptist foreign mission fields. Increasing annually, the amount in 1955 totaled $4,628,691.03. A committee, appointed each year by the union's president, makes plans for the week of prayer for foreign missions, which was observed in January until 1926, when it was changed to the first week in December.

In 1894, following a great effort to help remove Foreign Mission Board indebtedness, Woman's Missionary Union learned of a $25,000 debt on the Home Mission Board and thus proposed a week of self-denial to acquaint the people with the needs of the field and the Home Mission Board treasury. When Woman's Missionary Union gave more than the $5,000 requested of it, an annual offering for home missions was inaugurated, named the Annie Armstrong Offering for Home Missions in 1934. The Home Mission Board recommends the specific causes for use of the annual gift, as the Foreign Mission Board does in regard to the Lottie Moon Christmas Offering. In 1955 the Annie Armstrong Offering totaled $1,256,254.58.

Another project inaugurated by Woman's Missionary Union for the Home Mission Board, the Church Building and Loan Fund, was begun in 1899 by a gift of $1,000, increased to $3,500 from "a worker in Maryland," later revealed to be Mrs. Anna G. Schimp. The W.M.U. caught the idea of helping struggling new churches, developed the fund, and by 1908 had given $20,298.97 as the Tichenor Memorial Church Building and Loan Fund. In 1918 Mrs. George W. Bottoms of Arkansas gave $50,000 toward the $325,000 total promised by Woman's Missionary Union to the fund, and the union more than reached its goal with $337,239 given.

Woman's Missionary Union encouraged and co-operated with the Sunday School Board, which began sending recommendations to the union in 1894. A year earlier, the Foreign and Home Mission boards asked the union to arrange for the observance of Missionary Day in the Sunday schools in co-operation with the Sunday School Board, and the union supplied this program annually through 1905. For several years the board repeatedly asked Woman's Missionary Societies to aid in securing the patronage of the Sunday schools for its publications. Soon after Woman's Missionary Union's organization, the board began giving $100 each year toward union expenses, and by 1922 it had increased the amount to $800, paid annually until 1935. The Sunday School Board offered to pay the union's office rent in 1921, and contributed toward it until 1948.

From 1897 to 1930, the Sunday School Board offered to match Woman's Missionary Union gifts, in a Bible fund to supply Bibles for distribution by home and foreign missionaries, and by W.M.U. members to aliens receiving naturalization papers, to foreign-speaking people, prisoners, or needy people without Bibles. Woman's Missionary Union promoted the sending of boxes to Sunday school missionaries from 1897 to 1905, and 20 years later, the board offered $10,000 to be matched by the states for organizing missionary societies in rural churches. Beginning in 1891, Woman's Missionary Union provided pages for *Kind Words,* even before the Sunday School Board acquired this series of publications, and the union gave its corresponding secretary the responsibility of working out the Young People's Scripture Union, which later developed into Daily Bible Readings. In 1916 Miss Mallory was elected union representative on the executive committee of the Baptist Student Missionary Movement. Woman's Missionary Union supported the Southern Baptist Student Association, and later the Baptist Student Union when it became a department of the Sunday School Board. Until 1914 the board sent annual recommendations to the union; then in 1925 it joined other boards in an annual message until 1952.

At Woman's Missionary Union's executive committee meeting in May, 1919, the year after the Relief and Annuity Board was inaugurated, William A. Lunsford (*q.v.*) outlined the board's plans. Upon presentation at its annual meeting, the union agreed to undertake to raise one fifth of the amount to be proposed to the Convention. This plan was fitted into the 75 Million Campaign, but in 1923 Woman's Missionary Union included a section in the Plan of Work on gifts to the Relief and Annuity Board to be made through the campaign and gifts and boxes to be sent to aged ministers and their families. From 1923 to 1952, the Relief and Annuity Board joined other boards in sending an annual message to the union, which entered the board's plan in 1941, so that its employed personnel might benefit thereby.

WOMAN'S MISSIONARY UNION STATISTICAL SUMMARY

Year	No. of States	MEMBERSHIP IN: W.M.S.	Y.W.A.	G.A.	R.A.	Sunbeams	NO. ORGANIZATIONS W.M.S.	Y.W.A.	G.A.	R.A.	Sunbeams	Total
1888	11	....	....	....	....	....	1,560	....	....	....	....	1,560
1890	11	....	....	....	....	....	669	....	....	....	....	669
1895	7	....	....	....	....	....	1,557	....	....	....	109	1,666
1900	14	....	....	....	....	....	1,663	....	....	....	546	1,663
1905	2	....	....	....	....	....	752	....	....	....	54	806
1910	8	59,201	12,402	....	1,526	44,344	6,503	1,299	....	299	2,526	10,627
1915	18	....	....	....	....	....	8,203	1,739	531	566	3,624	14,663
1920	18	....	....	....	....	....	10,522	1,920	1,456	950	4,637	19,485
1925	18			Total W.M.U., 359,368 in 15 states			10,623	2,548	2,948	1,527	5,298	22,944
1926	18	197,598		all young people-150,907			10,739	2,740	3,428	1,706	5,295	23,908
1927	18						10,989	3,147	4,029	2,128	5,858	26,151
1928	18	311,255		all young people—212,481			11,628	3,814	5,296	2,931	6,746	30,415
1929	19	314,237		all young people—217,157			11,107	3,863	5,403	2,981	6,423	29,777
1930	19	338,598		all young people—212,086			10,940	3,883	5,692	3,217	6,288	30,020
1931	19	425,027		all young people—226,663			10,888	3,819	5,840	3,516	6,086	30,149
1932	19	284,045		all young people—212,086			10,459	4,343	6,525	3,829	6,393	31,549
1933	19	282,114	64,425	84,906	41,865	108,132	11,002	4,690	6,997	4,369	6,620	33,678
1934	19	282,505	62,259	85,877	....	....	11,053	4,593	6,904	4,206	6,107	32,863
1935	19	293,883	....	....	....	103,232	11,407	4,902	7,471	4,499	6,366	34,645
1936	19	297,594	64,269	82,237	42,644	109,108	11,360	4,794	7,385	4,355	6,334	34,228
1937	19	315,613	65,292	92,899	44,233	93,838	11,423	4,882	7,699	4,410	6,180	34,594
1938	19	361,159	77,423	109,416	47,745	109,656	12,326	5,381	8,703	5,316	6,871	38,597
1939	19	389,129	77,872	113,245	55,332	111,267	12,648	5,474	9,134	5,544	6,920	39,720
1940	19	399,003	78,839	109,416	56,332	109,656	12,722	5,643	9,465	5,711	7,073	40,614
1941	19	412,325	73,766	115,715	57,484	109,686	12,995	5,694	9,934	5,918	7,178	41,719
1942	19	404,144	65,260	113,686	57,827	107,548	12,845	5,169	9,687	5,879	6,892	40,472
1943	20	388,314	59,011	108,066	55,862	104,180	12,387	4,734	9,312	5,644	6,618	38,695
1944	20	381,655		all young people—337,531			12,651	4,563	9,744	5,985	6,724	39,667
1945	20	400,464	58,861	115,385	59,488	105,162	12,734	4,605	10,378	6,590	6,920	41,227
1946	20	420,592	52,003	116,361	63,416	115,149	13,326	4,460	10,944	6,954	7,397	43,081
1947	20	438,324	55,942	120,953	67,047	123,785	14,043	4,751	12,040	7,795	8,093	46,722
1948	21	482,476	52,084	133,426	75,939	131,373	14,812	5,078	12,937	8,231	8,555	49,613
1949	22	517,265	54,608	141,541	85,009	144,565	15,693	5,540	14,106	9,654	9,581	54,574
1950	22	548,532	55,300	151,637	87,586	153,069	16,451	5,429	15,161	9,864	9,969	56,874
1951	22	596,838	58,346	160,026	90,649	161,723	17,237	5,809	16,265	10,711	10,790	60,812
1952	22	613,822	....	....	105,834	....	18,219	6,123	17,550	11,492	11,741	65,125
1953	22	641,096	61,238	189,192	115,294	190,544	19,207	6,486	19,288	12,856	12,882	70,719
1954	23	667,527	70,312	206,709	127,262	210,126	19,896	6,927	20,613	13,977	14,224	75,637

JULIETTE MATHER

WOMAN'S MISSIONARY UNION STATISTICAL SUMMARY OF TOTAL CONTRIBUTIONS

Date	Foreign Missions	Home Missions	State Missions	Margaret Home	Training School	Church Bldg. Fund	Ministerial Relief	Christian Education	Orphanage	Hospitals
1888	$ 14,316.06	$ 6,723.10	$ 2,865.50	....	....	....	....	....	....	....
1890	21,222.91	10,014.85	7,956.67	....	....	....	....	....	....	....
1895	24,933.64	23,515.61	11,421.29	....	....	....	....	....	....	....
1900	31,757.65	18,114.13	....	....	....	....	....	....	....	....
1905	53,678.45	30,698.32	....	$10,500.00	....	....	....	....	....	....
1910	123,216.16	77,881.23	....	1,555.58	$11,965.94	....	....	....	....	....
1915	242,018.43	128,114.12	....	13.60[1]	32,785.09[2]	....	....	....	....	....
1920	636,178.09	308,631.54	288,723.18	3,458.71	50,847.75[2]	$78,238.50	....	....	....	....
1925	679,073.43	359,024.83	297,667.05	....	43,934.15[3]	....	....	....	....	....
1926	909,100.06	140,999.66	337,935.84	....	21,307.87[3]	....	....	....	....	....
1927	998,384.07	364,770.95	539,805.16	....	14,354.55	....	$ 56,449.22	$ 492,889.10	$ 97,811.31	$ 61,428.44
1928	804,102.94	365,152.43	458,292.73	....	30,066.20[4]	....	68,466.93	542,794.71	211,144.19	105,373.72
1929	1,000,233.08	543,913.13	504,850.43	....	....	....	52,131.24	479,238.44	144,979.68	66,782.66
1930	843,365.31	326,757.39	515,955.40	....	24,222.92	....	72,148.96	496,718.72	194,182.33	98,708.89
1931	800,312.31	363,494.77	536,384.28	....	17,309.98[4]	....	73,970.15	437,464.69	201,096.94	105,166.25
1932	704,070.05	359,902.28	469,927.84	28,878.33[5]	15,644.81[4]	....	76,438.61	727,202.97	312,962.61	144,565.83
1933	612,246.24	312,168.63	344,927.52	28,703.10[5]	11,498.91	....	67,210.67	535,304.22	182,903.62	98,913.16
1934	632,703.79	251,324.27	293,996.78	602.25[5]	....	....	51,547.29	509,244.37	143,782.96	98,627.91
1935	726,817.36	286,891.17	324,868.89	29,325.22[5]	8,997.59[4]	....	51,973.75	431,517.45	131,926.99	96,108.50
1936	785,037.72	306,317.62	334,179.59	28,854.02[5]	11,236.15[4]	....	39,461.78	312,339.70	131,622.94	90,757.67
1937	881,403.09	346,007.40	359,792.25	28,718.38[5]	10,737.59[4]	....	2,112.96	12,194.06	110,358.41	63,015.32
1938	863,028.89	384,500.39	368,600.57	29,776.90[5]	14,790.19[4]	....	35,345.20	275,295.38	116,247.08	69,449.55
1939	957,737.82	422,711.20	414,644.88	....	32,813.85[4]	....	36,401.01	235,387.12	146,018.39	76,108.37
1940	637,326.48	287,333.72	434,208.20	1,052.81	68,946.33[4]	....	37,986.78	284,010.72	157,074.99	79,522.77
1941	705,117.36	299,316.87	485,776.47	2,775.62	31,375.90[4]	....	40,332.53	322,168.55	189,613.52	89,707.46
1942	809,621.16	361,936.58	594,396.76	3,177.20	29,097.55[4]	....	51,695.02	354,415.98	154,202.75	102,267.18
1943	981,184.70	418,727.98	698,511.91	4,422.64	27,990.62[4]	....	60,513.44	358,715.77	152,456.86	95,858.61
1944	1,273,587.86	515,070.59	891,112.27	4,139.53	31,291.98[4]	....	64,293.40	354,812.94	160,604.16	102,785.01
1945	1,556,481.34	665,830.88	1,126,952.63	6,875.50	30,582.22[4]	....	71,098.59	425,786.73	213,959.79	118,039.57
1946	2,062,349.21	849,754.87	1,506,278.00	17,643.83	36,223.24	....	82,418.29	423,451.38	222,527.07	123,156.62
1947	2,136,647.40	907,223.27	1,415,431.30	11,202.53	41,722.07	....	105,214.19	571,980.76	299,190.47	133,350.23
1948	2,685,655.30	946,036.93	1,672,408.07	10,643.06	36,928.19	....	125,487.75	1,201,887.22	444,989.88	478,909.22
1949	3,019,315.11	1,068,016.27	1,935,248.52	10,919.67	35,062.72	....	184,046.46	1,143,907.17	374,624.80	276,080.77
1950	3,018,518.87	1,148,101.11	2,058,953.52	10,550.15	37,486.82	....	182,266.07	1,174,396.73	476,653.01	313,958.43
1951	3,192,109.69	1,130,193.40	2,143,014.59	10,928.38	35,705.38	....	309,479.57	1,403,993.03	512,869.43	246,282.57
1952	4,561,276.86	1,770,755.95	764,870.97	10,563.23	31,024.68	....	338,447.97	1,583,286.93	593,378.65	28,150.30
1953	3,331,766.33	1,018,173.43	1,094,969.42	12,056.71	35,895.28[6]	....	330,538.09	1,619,265.11	498,786.72	299,919.94
1954	3,602,554.86	1,119,864.60	734,281.00	11,084.14	39,081.57	....	346,558.72	1,735,257.62	546,973.44	272,811.89

[1] Margaret Home sold and Margaret Fund established.
[2] Current operating expenses, student and enlargement funds.
[3] Student fund and operating expenses.
[4] Current expense and scholarship fund.
[5] Margaret Fund and Training School.
[6] Name of school changed to Carver School of Missions and Social Work.

WOMAN'S MISSIONARY UNION STATISTICAL SUMMARY OF TOTAL CONTRIBUTIONS

Date	S.B. Theol. Seminary	W.M.U. Specials [7]	Undesignated Specials	S.S. Board	World Relief	Headquarters Bldg. Fund	S.B.C. Objects	100,000 Club	State Debt	Cooperative Program	Value W.M.U. Property [8]
1888	....	....	....	....	....	....	....	....	....	....	....
1890	....	....	....	....	....	....	....	....	....	....	....
1895	....	....	....	....	....	....	....	....	....	....	....
1900	....	....	....	$1,364.42	....	....	....	....	....	....	....
1905	....	....	....	417.55	....	....	....	....	....	....	....
1910	....	....	....	1,340.63	....	....	....	....	....	....	$ 31,659.47
1915	....	....	....	1,765.71	....	....	....	....	....	....	145,006.77
1920	....	....	$249,194.85	1,786.77	....	....	....	....	....	....	395,902.31
1925	$66,888.50	$31,673.62	525,842.12	....	....	....	....	....	....	....	515,060.24
1926	....	20,899.56	200,213.31	....	....	....	....	....	....	....	528,448.54
1927	....	35,434.96	298,929.26	....	....	....	....	....	....	....	539,054.74
1928	....	32,792.34	516,634.70	....	....	....	....	....	....	....	550,134.91
1929	....	34,447.66	367,245.30	....	....	....	....	....	....	....	555,816.42
1930	....	33,968.56	216,225.28	....	....	....	....	....	....	....	565,080.60
1931	....	31,769.47	252,900.25	....	....	....	....	....	....	....	562,599.82
1932	....	....	158,592.73	....	....	....	....	....	....	....	568,253.28
1933	....	....	204,128.75	....	....	....	....	....	....	....	568,306.01
1934	....	....	165,688.33	....	....	....	....	$ 373.47	....	....	576,212.29
1935	....	....	176,143.65	....	....	....	....	74,100.65	....	....	585,669.82
1936	....	....	283,999.66	....	....	....	....	70,039.41	....	....	595,069.82
1937	....	....	313,071.60	....	....	....	....	77,136.91	....	....	600,724.23
1938	....	....	353,230.00	....	....	....	....	120,959.63	....	....	626,768.33
1939	....	....	464,695.06	....	....	....	....	126,078.52	....	....	653,384.54
1940	....	....	363,087.73	....	....	....	....	124,995.39	....	....	760,230.63
1941	....	....	455,514.67	....	....	....	....	133,712.96	....	....	660,786.00
1942	....	....	329,387.71	....	....	....	....	211,967.85	$120,959.44	....	698,208.50
1943	....	....	300,376.80	....	....	....	....	290,545.93	222,863.77	....	724,708.00
1944	....	....	260,504.05	....	....	....	....	395,842.98	189,713.38	....	725,308.00
1945	....	....	756,477.42	....	....	....	....	....	....	$2,600,192.92	725,308.00
1946	....	....	736,989.00	....	....	....	....	....	....	3,469,588.65	739,971.00
1947	....	....	149,044.46	....	$1,009,229.60	....	....	....	....	3,660,000.68	814,873.00
1948	....	....	93,419.44	....	....	....	$87,373.41	....	....	4,562,799.90	876,503.00
1949	....	....	93,247.15	....	....	$ 6,730.65	42,862.59	....	....	4,888,511.03	895,903.00
1950	....	....	99,219.40	....	....	70,926.55	47,088.18	....	....	5,453,491.25	942,158.00
1951	....	....	143,649.61	....	....	32,881.54	47,273.89	....	....	5,570,806.00	961,180.00
1952	....	....	96,286.66	....	....	431,234.90	27,922.21	....	....	.00 [9]	1,477,680.00
1953	....	....	68,953.86	....	....	....	23,075.66	....	....	....	1,841,100.00
1954	....	....	....	....	....	....	....	....	....	....	2,227,350.00

[7] Includes gifts to Sunday School Board, current operations Training School, and Margaret Fund Scholarships.

[8] Includes value of Carber School (former Training School) property, Margaret Fund, Margaret Home, Union Headquarters Building, Birmingham, Ala., and Baltimore, Md., all Carver School, Training School, Margaret Fund and Union endowments, trust funds and reserves.

[9] Discontinued reporting amounts.

LA VENIA NEAL

The professor of missionary education methods of Woman's Missionary Union of each seminary of the Southern Baptist Convention is invited to the meetings for promotion during the winter session of the executive board and extended all privileges.

Close co-operation for the union was natural with Southern Baptist Theological Seminary, where young women of the Woman's Missionary Union Training School were studying under seminary professors. The union paid a stipulated sum to augment professors' salaries and on two occasions made gifts of considerable amount. In 1926 the union contributed a building fund of $107,058, in memory of the six former Woman's Missionary Union presidents. In 1945 it voted to give the seminary $50,000 for more classroom space.

New Orleans Baptist Theological Seminary, in its early days when it was Baptist Bible Institute, asked for an executive committee of seven women to be appointed by the Woman's Missionary Union president, to assist the advisory board of the women's department. This board grew until it included a member from each state, elected or appointed according to the state plan. The union, evidencing its continued interest in the seminary, contributed $25,000 for buildings and equipment in 1946. An advisory board relationship similar to that at New Orleans was maintained in the training school of Southwestern Seminary until 1951, and an equal gift of $25,000 was agreed upon by the union in 1946.

In 1911 Fannie Heck spoke to the woman's section of the Baptist World Alliance meeting in Philadelphia, and Miss Crane, Woman's Missionary Union executive secretary, was elected secretary of the women's committee. Since then, every president and every secretary has served on Alliance committees and has contributed to the women's activities. Mrs. G. R. Martin, who served as chairman of the revived women's committee and presided at women's sessions in Copenhagen, 1947, Cleveland, 1950, and London, 1955, was unique in organizing the Baptist women of other continents. The women's department of the Alliance now promotes a Day of Prayer Around the World on the first Friday of December.

Union symbols.—In its Jubilate year, 1913, Woman's Missionary Union adopted an official seal and pin, designed by Emma M. Whitfield of Richmond, Va., whose mother presided when the union was organized in 1888. Any member of a Woman's Missionary Union organization, from Sunbeams up, is entitled to wear the emblem, although each of the young people's organizations has its own pin. The shape of the emblem represents a double fishhead, taken from a custom in the early days of Christianity when persecuted followers adopted the practice of making the mark of a fishhead when they met a stranger. If the person were also a Christian, the sign was understood; if an enemy, it meant nothing. To the Christians its meaning was especially significant since the letters in the Greek word for fish are the first letters in each word of the expression "Jesus Christ, God's Son, Saviour." Around the border of the emblem is engraved "Women's Missionary Union, S.B.C., 1888." In the center appears the open Bible with the union watchword engraved on it; the Bible rests on a map of the world, and above the Bible is a flaming torch.

Each year Woman's Missionary Union selects a Scripture verse to serve as a slogan of strength or invigoration and couples it with a hymn of the year. The permanent watchword, "Laborers together with God," I Corinthians 3:9, was authorized on the emblem adopted in 1913, with the Woman's Hymn written by Miss Heck. Before 1913 the union considered this watchword, "inherited" from the Maryland Foreign Mission Society, and in 1910 Miss Heck referred to it as the motto which "the Union took long ago."

Current polity.—Many state central committees were busily engaged in mission activities before the executive committee of Woman's Mission Societies was organized in 1888. States have never been bound by Woman's Missionary Union actions but have chosen to work together. The Woman's Missionary Union of each co-operating state in the Southern Baptist Convention nominates as a vice-president for the Convention-wide W.M.U. its current state organization president. Vice-presidents, general Convention-wide officers, and resident members nominated by the nominating committee are elected at the annual session. These members and employed department heads compose the executive board. Within the states are divisions, districts, or regions, named according to each state's plan, and associations, many of which antedate 1888. After Woman's Missionary Union was organized, the value of associational superintendents became obvious, in order to spread plans quickly from the state office to associations and on to societies.

State Woman's Missionary Unions have representation in the annual session of the Convention-wide union according to membership. Delegates are not instructed by their state organizations but vote as individuals. In order to care for properties and investments, Woman's Missionary Union was first incorporated under the laws of Baltimore City (Oct. 19, 1906) and later under the laws of the state of Alabama (June 3, 1925). The policy of the executive board, first formulated by Miss Heck in 1907 and adopted annually by the executive board, supplements the constitution and bylaws, so that together they give direction to the board, committees, officers, and department and division heads. Since 1950, Oct. 1 has been considered the beginning of the promotional year, although financial accounts are kept according to the calendar year. Woman's Missionary Union brings out annually a year book slanted for local church societies, which presents emphases and plans for the year as well as the Plan of Work formulated by the executive board, state executive secretaries, and state youth secretaries in semiannual session in January, for adoption by the union in annual session in May.

Headquarters.—Because of the pre-organization leadership of the Maryland Society of Woman's Mission to Woman in Baltimore and the contribution of Ann Graves, Annie Armstrong, and others, it was natural for Baltimore to be chosen as the first headquarters. The Maryland Baptist State Mission Rooms at 10 East Fayette Street offered a central place for monthly committee meetings. When the Mission Rooms moved, the executive committee headquarters changed also.

In 1908 Woman's Missionary Union authorized investment of $8,500 of the Training School's endowment funds in property for headquarters. By Oct., 1909, a building was purchased, the upstairs rented, and the first floor and basement used by the union.

On Feb. 19, 1920, a committee of five was appointed to look into the advisability of moving headquarters to a central location which would make all sections of the Convention territory more accessible for trips of the corresponding secretary and for quicker postal and express facilities. The question was discussed at the 1920 annual meeting, but action was deferred until 1921, when the union decided, after much discussion, to move to Birmingham. Rooms were rented in the Jefferson County Bank Building, later the Comer Building. In Jan., 1951, the union purchased for $475,000 an excellent building on the corner of 20th Street and 6th Avenue in Birmingham's best downtown section. An amount totaling $100,000 was given in honor of Miss Mallory, and with continued gifts from the states, the remainder of the cost was paid by Jan., 1953.

Expenses.—Woman's Missionary Union has always been concerned with being as economical as possible without handicapping its mission efforts. Not collecting mission money for itself, the union has continued the plan begun by H. A. Tupper of the Foreign Mission Board and I. T. Tichenor of the Home Mission Board. The union would call back money needed for its expenses from the contributions made by women and young people to the boards through the churches. Beginning with $100 from each board, this recall of funds from Home and Foreign Mission boards increased slowly. Although expenses the first year were $353.04, which required $200 from each board, the union returned $4,400.22 more for foreign missions and $5,334.31 more for home missions than women's societies had given the previous year. By 1891 a refund of $600 was requested from each board, from the gifts contributed by Woman's Missionary Union through the churches. By the time the W.M.U. was 30 years old, its expenses were running about 3.5 per cent of its reported gifts to missions. In 1955 the two boards contributed approximately one tenth of the union's budget, supplementing approximately nine tenths received from magazine subscriptions and from literature and supply orders. The amount from the boards equaled only 1.6 per cent of the combined Annie Armstrong and Lottie Moon Christmas offerings. JULIETTE MATHER

WOMAN'S MISSIONARY UNION, Auxiliary to the Alabama Baptist Convention. Begun by the appointment of a state central committee for women's work in 1889. Missionary organizations of various kinds, however, had existed in the state since the early years of the 19th century. Pioneer organizations for women and youth sent nearly half of the delegates to the organizational meeting of the Alabama Baptist Convention in 1823. Seventeen were recorded by subscriptions to *The Luminary* and by contributions to Columbian College, both instituted by Luther Rice, and by gifts and messages. Records of gifts from children indicate early attention to their missionary education.

Thereafter references to women's organizations were occasional and records meager, and largely financial. Small groups were organized in increasing numbers for the study and support of missions.

During the Civil War Southern women discovered their talents and qualifications for leadership and co-operative effort. A missionary awakening followed, which brought pleas for women foreign missionaries and meetings of women at the Southern Baptist Convention. This resulted in the federation, Woman's Mission to Woman. In 1874 the Foreign Mission Board recommended the appointment of state central committees on woman's work. In 1881 the Alabama convention instructed its board to appoint such committees, which reported through 1886. There was no report in 1887. The committee's recommendation was rejected by the convention in 1888. Alabama was not represented at the organizational meeting of Southern W.M.U. In the 1889 convention state secretary Washington Byran Crumpton (*q.v.*) stated that Alabama societies had no central committee as had most other states. John W. Stewart moved "that a State Central Committee be appointed by this Convention, to co-operate with the Executive Committee, on Woman's Work, which is located in Baltimore." The motion carried, and the Woman's Missionary Union, Auxiliary to Alabama Baptist Convention, was established to give unity and direction to the scattered societies of the state. The officers were Mrs. T. A. Hamilton, president; Mrs. George B. Eager, vice-president; Mrs. I. C. Brown, secretary-treasurer. The committee and four pastors met Dec. 14, 1889. They made an application for membership in the Southern W.M.U., which was approved Apr. 11, 1890. Delegates to the 1890 annual meeting in Fort Worth, Tex., were Mrs. G. R. Farnham and Hermoine Brown (Mrs. D. M. Malone). Annie Grace Tartt (Mrs. H. L. Mellen) also attended. That year the Alabama union reported to the convention 29 associational vice-presidents, 112 societies, 28 Sunbeam Bands, and $5,963.50 in contributions.

The Alabama union regularly adopts the plan of work, policies, and objectives of the Southern Baptist W.M.U. Besides generous contributions through general denominational channels, observances of weeks of prayer and mission study have led to steady increases in Lottie Moon Christmas Offering from $87.97 to $170,935.00 in 1955, and in Annie Armstrong Offering from $500.00 to $75,836.90 in the same year. In participation in anniversaries, debt-paying campaigns, and extra Convention-wide and state endeavors, the union accepted and met its various organizational, membership, and financial quotas. The inspiration and attainments of the Ruby Anniversary became the criterion for future progress.

The Alabama union observed its first state season of prayer in 1906. The offering was designated for mission church buildings throughout Alabama. The 1909 goal was $5,000.00; the 1954 offering, $33,883.87. This offering, now called the Kathleen Mallory Mission Offering, has contributed to many causes. It has provided promotional workers for many activities, including Royal Ambassadors. For the Negroes it provides a full-time worker, scholarships for students, and annual youth camps, and gives support to Selma University and a Good Will Center in Mobile. For south Alabama mission work, the offering supplies workers, assembly buildings, scholarships, and various materials. At Howard College the offering built a nursery building and provides a staff. Scholarships are offered for wives of ministerial students. Assistance on various buildings was given to Shocco Springs Assembly.

In addition the Alabama union has provided funds for a dormitory at Judson College, the Kathleen Mallory Hospital in China, nurses' home in Japan, Willie Kelly Memorial. Scholarships have been given to many young women preparing for church work or missions. Quotas were met for the Woman's Missionary Union Training School (now Carver School of Missions and Social Work) and for the Southern W.M.U. headquarters building. Money was provided for a Hamilton chapel fund.

During its history the Alabama W.M.U. has grown in many ways. The number of societies increased from 17 to 1,701 with 49,861 members reported in 1955; of youth organizations, from 28 to 4,579 with 49,374 members. Contributions increased from "$20.00, two pairs of socks . . . a gold watch and chain, a $15.00 box of clothing" to $318,736.10, not including funds received for the Cooperative Program through local church budgets.

In 1955 the following persons were serving as officers and workers with the Alabama union: Mrs. Fred W. Kilgore, president; Mrs. James W. Wood, vice-president; Mrs. Travis H. Wood, treasurer; Mary Essie Stephens, executive secretary; Marjorie Stith, youth secretary; Lois Privett and Vanita Baldwin, field representatives; and Lee Ferrell, Royal Ambassador secretary. The office was located at 403 South Perry Street, Montgomery, Ala. FLORENCE THOMASSON

WOMAN'S MISSIONARY UNION, Auxiliary to the Baptist General Convention of Arizona. The history of Arizona Woman's Missionary Union runs parallel with the history of the Baptist General Convention of Arizona. When the First Southern Baptist Church, Phoenix, was organized, Mar. 27, 1921, a fully-graded W.M.U. was begun. When Gambrell Memorial Baptist Association was organized Nov. 26, 1925, an associational W.M.U. was started. When the Baptist General Convention of Arizona was organized Sept. 21, 1928, the state W.M.U. was organized. The first officers of Arizona W.M.U. included Mrs. G. H. Woodson (who later became Mrs. W. C. Henderson), president (1928–40), and Floy Hawkins, executive secretary (1928–29). Mrs. Cecil M. Stewart has served as president since 1954, and Mrs. Charles M. Griffin has served as executive secretary since 1950.

At the 1955 state convention the W.M.U. reported 169 Woman's Missionary Societies with 3,402 members, 112 Sunbeam Bands with 1,238 members, 154 Girls' Auxiliaries with 1,119 members, 77 Royal Ambassador chapters with 842 members, and 29 Young Woman's Auxiliaries with 165 members. The 1955 auditor's report of the Baptist General Convention of Arizona reported gifts totaling $9,600.49 for state missions, $7,509.41 for home missions (Annie Armstrong Offering), and $20,138.20 for foreign missions (Lottie Moon Offering). MRS. W. C. HENDERSON

WOMAN'S MISSIONARY UNION, Auxiliary to the Arkansas Baptist State Convention. Had its beginning in the hearts of pioneer women such as those in Lawrence County who, in 1828, wrote David Orr, missionary in Missouri, urging him to come to Arkansas; "Grandma Hale" who gave land and built a log house (completed 1842), the First Baptist Church in Hot Springs; George Ann Bledsoe, Tulip, Ark., who longed for the organization of a state convention to promote missions and at her death, 1847, left her piano to be sold for missions; and Mary Brantly, called the "Baptist bell" of Little Rock, who went from home to home to announce services.

The central committee, forerunner to the W.M.U., was formed at a meeting called by M. D. Early, vice-president of the Home Mission Board, Sept. 19, 1883, at the Baptist church in Russellville. Mrs. J. P. Eagle was elected president. This committee reported to the state convention each year. Mrs. Eagle and Mrs. Early attended the Southern Baptist Convention in Augusta, Ga., 1885, as duly accredited messengers of the convention, and created such agitation and alarm on the convention floor that the constitution was amended by striking out the word "members" and substituting the word "brethren."

Mrs. Eagle and Mrs. W. A. Forbes were at the 1887 planning meeting in Louisville, Ky.; and in 1888 in Richmond, Va., Mrs. J. K. Pace and Ella Miller were Arkansas delegates taking part in the Convention-wide organization. Thus Arkansas became one of the "ten heroic and historic states" voting for the organization.

Organization in Arkansas was accomplished

in Little Rock in 1888, in time to plan for the first annual meeting, 1889, at First Baptist Church, Little Rock. Twenty-nine societies sent 41 delegates. Mrs. Eagle became president. The union has met annually except in 1945.

At the convention in Richmond, Va., 1888, a young woman from Arkansas sat in the balcony and listened to the brethren's discussion of the "new women's movement." She was Ida M. (Blankenship) Bottoms (*q.v.*) who later gave gifts totaling hundreds of thousands of dollars to missions at home and abroad.

The first decade of the W.M.U. brought the first constitution, the first printed minutes, the first field work, and the first mission offerings. In the second decade young people's work was developed. Mayme Gardiner, Monticello, had organized the first Sunbeam Band in 1891, and a state leader, Mrs. O. E. Bryan, was secured in 1907. Mrs. W. I. Moody, Little Rock, became the first active state leader of Young Woman's Auxiliaries, 1908. These organizations raised funds to help support two missionaries, Perle Harrison (China) and Genevieve Voorheis (Brazil). In 1907, 180 societies reported.

The third decade saw permanent headquarters established, 1912, and the first full-time salaried secretary, Mrs. W. S. Farmer, succeeded by Mrs. J. G. Jackson, 1914–29. Other secretaries have been: Mrs. W. D. Pye, 1929–37; Mrs. C. H. Ray, 1938–48; Nancy Cooper, 1949– . Shortly after 1908 Mrs. Farmer became state Royal Ambassador leader. Mrs. A. L. Aulick in 1916 was elected state Girl's Auxiliary leader. The 1914 annual meeting was the first held separately from the convention.

In 1920 Una Roberts became first full-time young people's secretary. Conferences and camps for young people were promoted. Other young people's secretaries have been these: Mary Christian, 1927–29; Margaret Hutchison, 1929–46; LaVerne Ashby, 1947–48; Doris DeVault, 1949–55; Sara Ann Hobbs, 1956– .

May, 1930, brought near disaster. The convention was in debt and withdrew support. For seven months the W.M.U. operated on a loan, arranged through friends, with some help from the organizations. Curtailment of office and field-workers was necessary, but new growth took place in almost every branch of service.

In the years since the 50th anniversary celebration at Second Church, Little Rock, 1938, there has been steady growth. Changes have come, but the fundamental objectives remain the same. These have served as W.M.U. presidents: Mrs. J. P. Eagle, 1889–92, 1894–1902; Mrs. A. L. Crudup, 1893; Mrs. E. Longley, 1902–09; Mrs. H. C. Fox, 1910–11; Mrs. M. G. Thompson, 1912–13; Mrs. W. T. McCurry, 1914–15; Mrs. C. M. Roberts, 1916–18; Mrs. J. H. Crawford, 1919–22; Mrs. O. O. Florence, 1923; Mrs. W. D. Pye, 1924–29; Mrs. J. M. Flenniken, 1929–32; Mrs. C. H. Ray, 1932–38; Mrs. L. M. Sipes, 1938–41; Mrs. J. E. Short, 1942–48; Mrs. F. E. Goodbar, 1948–52; Mrs. J. R. Grant, 1953– .

The first Christmas offering, 1889, from nine societies was $32.45. The Lottie Moon Christmas Offering, 1955, from 638 societies and 2,113 young people's organizations was $138,448.99. The first Self-Denial Offering was in 1894, with no record of amount. The Annie Armstrong Offering, 1955, was $41,987.57. The Dixie Jackson Offering (state missions), 1955, was $25,374.65. Members of the Woman's Missionary Societies and youth members, respectively, 1955, totalled 20,919 and 19,922. MRS. J. R. GRANT

WOMAN'S MISSIONARY UNION, Auxiliary to the Southern Baptist General Convention of California. The first Southern Baptist Woman's Missionary Society organized in California was in the First Southern Baptist Church, Shafter, Apr. 6, 1938. Mrs. Sam Wilcoxon was the president; Mrs. Guy Mouser, secretary. When San Joaquin Valley Association was organized Apr. 13, 1939, Mrs. Edith Billingsley was elected Woman's Missionary Union president; Mrs. Averil Mouser, vice-president; and Mrs. Ora Ware, secretary-treasurer. When the association met for its first annual meeting four months later, Mrs. Billingsley gave a glowing report of the activities of Baptist women. In 1940 there were missionary societies in nine of the 13 churches which organized the Southern Baptist General Convention of California. Six months after the Southern Baptist General Convention of California was organized, its board of directors elected Mrs. J. O. Crow corresponding secretary of Woman's Missionary Union. There was no statewide organization of women except in San Joaquin Valley Association, which included churches scattered over the state.

At the first annual meeting of the convention, the women held a meeting and nominated the following officers who were elected by the convention: president, Mrs. Kate Colvard; corresponding secretary, Mrs. Katherine Looney.

The first paid W.M.U. worker was Naomi Readdy who came from Texas in Oct., 1943, as executive secretary of the organization. Others who have since held the post include Mrs. W. C. (Brooksie) Howell, Mrs. E. E. Steele, and Clara A. Lane. Marjorie Stephens became the first paid young people's secretary in June, 1947. Others who have since held the position are Mary Jo Lewis, Betty Noe, Charlene Wuest, and Dorris Stringer.

In 1942 the women began holding annual conventions and electing their own officers. All officers, including the executive secretary and the secretary of youth are elected annually. All paid workers are nominated by the W.M.U. executive committee and elected by the board of directors of the general convention. All salaries and other expenses of the organization are paid out of the convention's treasury the same as for other employees.

California Woman's Missionary Union promotes four special offerings preceded by a season of prayer, namely: Home missions, education, state missions, and foreign missions. It fosters missionary education among its own members and among young people and gives major emphasis to summer camps for youth.

In 1955 the women reported W.M.S. organizations in 445 of the 516 churches. Of the 7,418 women who were members of the various societies, 5,536 of them were tithers. There were 82 Young Woman's Auxiliary organizations with 486 enrolled, 345 Girls' Auxiliaries with a total membership of 2,501, 182 Sunbeam Bands with 2,111 members, and 208 Royal Ambassador chapters with 1,622 members. POLLY ANNA MCNABB

WOMAN'S MISSIONARY UNION, Auxiliary to the Florida Baptist State Convention. Officially organized in 1894, after the Florida Baptist State Convention had approved a petition by the women for permission to elect their own officers. As early as 1881, a "sister," Mrs. N. A. Bailey, had been appointed by the Florida convention to act as secretary of woman's work. To her was assigned the task of organizing Ladies' Mission Societies in the churches. She served for almost five years, in connection with the state board of missions. Her successor, Mrs. L. B. Telford, served eight years. Mrs. Telford and Mrs. W. D. Chipley of Pensacola were Florida's two delegates at the meeting in Richmond, Va., in 1888, at which the Woman's Missionary Union, Auxiliary to the Southern Baptist Convention, was organized.

After the Florida W.M.U. was organized in 1894, Jennie L. Spaulding became the first corresponding secretary. She served for 18 years, resigning in 1911. Mrs. H. C. Peelman, who succeeded her, served for 25 years, a longer term than anyone before or after her has filled. Under her leadership unusual growth and achievement took place. Work with youth was given a new impetus. Mrs. Peelman went to Cuba and organized the W.M.U. there. The circle plan, believed to have originated in Florida, was adopted by Southern W.M.U. in 1918. The 75 Million Campaign was launched enthusiastically, and though the Convention-wide goal was not met, Florida Baptists and Florida W.M.U. went well over their respective goals.

A young people's secretary was employed. Business women's circles were organized. The Co-operative Program came into being, and the W.M.U. channeled its gifts through this new medium.

In 1936 Louise Smith became secretary. Florida W.M.U. was the first to reach its apportionment in the effort to pay off the debts of the denomination.

Miss Smith visited the mission fields of South America and led the Florida W.M.U. to assume responsibility for building a much-needed Baptist church in Mendoza.

Under the leadership of Josephine Jones, who became secretary in 1944, the W.M.U. became concerned about Florida missionaries. A book, *God's Troubadours,* written by Elizabeth Provence, was studied by many groups in the state. A statewide program of camps for young people flourished.

In 1955 the Florida Woman's Missionary Union reported 3,595 organizations, with a total membership of 67,681 women and young people. The Annie Armstrong Offering amounted to $56,239.20; the Lottie Moon Christmas offering, to $137,443.83. Special clinics for officer training has been held in 11 locations over the state, with a total attendance of 2,185.

MRS. JOHN MAGUIRE

WOMAN'S MISSIONARY UNION, Auxiliary to the Baptist Convention of the State of Georgia. Organizations of women in Georgia for the promotion of interest in missions were among the first such groups to be formed. Soon after the visit of Luther Rice (*q.v.*) to Georgia in 1813, at which time he recounted the work of the Judsons in Burma, missionary societies were formed in Baptist churches. A committee appointed by the Triennial Convention in Philadelphia in 1814 to locate all Baptist women's missionary organizations reported 17 societies, eight of which were in the South, one being the Savannah Baptist Society for Missions. The Triennial Convention on June 23, 1817, recorded a gift of $101 by the Female Mite Society at Sunbury on the coast. The constitution of the Female Mite Society, Athens, is dated July 13, 1819. The organization began in the Trail Creek Church but was transferred to First Church, Athens.

In the years that followed, missionary societies were organized in many churches in Georgia, some being designated benevolent or prayer bands but giving to missions. Prior to the organization of a central committee in 1878, societies were reported in Georgia Association and in churches at Eatonton, Monroe, Cave Springs, Americus, LaGrange, Greensboro, Atlanta Second, Marietta, Barnesville, Cartersville, and Macon.

Organization.—The first recognition by the Georgia Baptist convention of women's work was acceptance of their gifts. Later some societies were allowed to be represented by men at the convention meetings. Under direction of Henry Allen Tupper (*q.v.*) of the Foreign Mission Board and with the co-operation of pastors Albert T. Spalding and David William Gwin, a central committee for Georgia was organized in Second Church, Atlanta, on Nov. 18, 1878, for the purpose of organizing mission societies, circulating missionary literature, and stimulating the spirit of giving to objects fostered by the convention. Officers chosen were: Mrs. Stainback Wilson, president; Mrs. M. A. Norcross and Mrs. M. A. Stanton, vice-presidents; Mrs. A. C. Kiddoo, corresponding secretary; Mrs. V. C. Norcross, recording secretary; and Mrs. R. E. Gardner, treasurer.

Presidents since Mrs. Wilson's administration have been Mrs. R. M. Seymour, elected in 1888; Mary E. Wright, 1900; Mrs. Edward George Willingham, 1906; Mrs. William J. Neel (*q.v.*), 1911; Mrs. Ben S. Thompson, 1932; Mrs. Frank Burney, 1937; Mrs. Peter Kittles, 1942; Mrs.

Paul Sharp Etheridge, 1947; and Mrs. John Inzor Alford, 1952.

There was much opposition from the brethren, and the first missionary society reports to the convention were not received. However, with the encouragement of such men as Gustavus Alonzo Nunnally and Robert Benjamin Headden, the central committee called for a meeting of delegates from all societies to be held in connection with the state convention at Second Church, Atlanta, in 1884. There were 75 delegates present, though many other women and men attended. Reports came from 66 societies with gifts of $4,665.24.

In 1889 a resolution that the organization be called the Woman's Baptist Missionary Union of Georgia was adopted. In 1919 the name was changed to Baptist Woman's Missionary Union of Georgia and was stated to be auxiliary to the Georgia Baptist convention. In 1901 the central committee, a self-perpetuating body, became an executive committee elected by a nominating committee at the annual meeting.

Headquarters.—A Sunday school room of Second Church, Atlanta, was first used as headquarters for the newly organized central committee. Frequent meetings for prayer and conferences were held there. Literature was provided by the Home and Foreign Mission boards. Service was voluntary. In 1890 Lucy Kicklighter was appointed field organizer at a salary. Emma Lenora Amos was the first employed corresponding secretary in 1906.

Later the Mission Rooms of the Baptist Woman's Missionary Union were with offices of the Georgia Baptist convention and have continued so. Executive secretaries following Miss Amos have been Evie Campbell, 1914; Susan Anderson, 1918; Kate Coleman Wakefield (Mrs. George Fiske), 1919; Maud Powell, 1921; Laura Lee Patrick (Mrs. Henry Weston Munger), 1922; Mrs. Andrew Farmer McMahon, 1924; Mary Christian, 1935; and Janice Singleton, 1939.

Magazine.—A monthly magazine, *Our Mission Helper,* was begun in 1893. Its name was changed in 1895 to *The Mission Messenger.* In 1921 it was discontinued in favor of pages in *The Christian Index.*

Children's bands.—As early as 1883, the central committee was urging mission societies to organize children's bands. Savannah reported two in 1885. In 1887 a Sunbeam Band was organized in Greensboro by Mrs. Thomas Jefferson Bowen, whose husband was the first Southern Baptist missionary in Africa. A state Band Superintendent was elected in 1894.

Foreign missions.—An appeal to Georgia missionary societies made possible the sending in 1901 of the first Southern Baptist medical missionary to China, Thomas Willburn Ayers, who served in Warren Memorial Hospital at Hwanghsien. In 1915 Georgia Woman's Missionary Union gave $20,000 toward the girls' school in Kokura, Japan, and $15,000 toward Georgia Hall in Shanghai, China.

State missions.—Achievements at home include the establishment and maintenance of Mary P. Willingham School for mountain girls at Blue Ridge, 1916–30; reopening of Georgia Baptist Orphans' Home in 1890 (now operated by Georgia Baptist convention); support of Herman Charles Buckholz as state evangelist, 1906–16; and a gift of $64,000 toward endowment of Bessie Tift College, 1928–35. In 1900 the first week of prayer for state missions was observed by the societies. In 1939 the state mission offering was named for Mrs. William J. Neel (*q.v.*), fifth Georgia W.M.U. president.

Work with Negroes.—In 1896 Mrs. James Bruton Gambrell, corresponding secretary, reported the organization of a Woman's Missionary Society in a Negro church. The first interracial meeting was held in the summer of 1940 at Tremont Temple Baptist Church in Macon. In 1955 a Negro worker, Mrs. Charlie Mae Pearson, was employed part-time. Three camps for Negro young people and an institute for women were held, with a total attendance of 488.

Young people's work.—In 1884 the central committee appointed a committee to organize young ladies' missionary societies. The first young people's leader, Pearl Todd (later a missionary to China), served from 1915 to 1917. From 1919 to 1955, one young people's secretary was responsible for the work; in 1955 separate secretaries were elected for Young Woman's Auxiliary and Sunbeam organizations.

House parties, conclaves, camps.—In 1922 camps for Girls' Auxiliaries and Young Woman's Auxiliaries were held in Mary P. Willingham School in connection with the Baptist assembly. In 1925 a girls' house party was held during the W.M.U. institute at Bessie Tift College. The first separate Y.W.A. and G.A. house party was held in 1926 at Bessie Tift. A Royal Ambassador conclave was held at Bessie Tift College in 1933.

Need for camping facilities was recognized, and in 1944 it was voted to accept offers for a site and set a goal of $40,000 for building a camp. Camp Pinnacle, Clayton, was opened in 1947. In 1951 it was voted to build another camp, located in South Georgia. A camp advisory board was set up at this time. In the summer of 1956, buildings were completed at Camp Glynn, Brunswick.

Royal Ambassadors.—When in 1908 this name was adopted by Southern Woman's Missionary Union, 20 Royal Ambassadors were presented on the state W.M.U. convention program. Young people's secretaries continued to work with the boys. In 1944 the need for a man's leadership was met in the election of Glendon McCullough as R.A. secretary. He served until 1955, at which time, following the precedent of the Southern W.M.U., R.A. work was transferred to the Georgia Baptist convention to be directed by the Brotherhood department. JANICE SINGLETON

WOMAN'S MISSIONARY UNION, Auxiliary to the Illinois Baptist State Association. Cooperating with Woman's Missionary Union, Auxiliary to the Southern Baptist Convention, the

Illinois Woman's Missionary Union seeks to promote missions among women and young people through the unit organizations of Sunbeam Bands, Girl's Auxiliaries, Young Woman's Auxiliaries, and Woman's Missionary Societies. During the period of early beginnings prior to 1907, there were scattered women's groups throughout Illinois. In 1895 "sisters everywhere" were "requested to send in news items concerning women's work." The missionary circles co-operated with the Woman's Baptist Foreign Missionary Society and the Woman's Baptist Home Missionary Society, and women's work became a part of the Illinois Baptist General Convention.

On Oct. 23, 1907, a group of women met at the first annual meeting of the Illinois Baptist State Association to draw up a proposed constitution for Woman's Auxiliary, to be voted upon the following year when the women of southern Illinois came together for their first meeting under the Southern plan. Although the women approved the constitution in 1908, it was revised two years later in order for Illinois women to work more harmoniously with the Convention-wide Woman's Missionary Union. That year, a group of Illinois women attended the annual Convention-wide meeting.

During the period of missionary expansion following 1915, full-time salaried workers were employed to do office and field work. In 1915 Mary Northington of Tennessee, after serving a short time as fieldworker, became the W.M.U.'s first executive secretary. In 1924 Pearl Baugher began serving as office secretary and young people's leader, the first such worker in the state. The name, Illinois Woman's Auxiliary, was changed in 1920 to Illinois Woman's Missionary Union.

> Through the years women have had a part in helping to pay the debts incurred by the Illinois Baptist State Association and the Southern Baptist Convention . . . and helping in Southwide causes through the Annie Armstrong Offering, Lottie Moon Christmas Offering, and the Co-operative Program.

Providing for the support of the work, the state association budget includes allocations for salaries, travel expenses, and promotional activities. Through the Illinois Special Woman's Missionary Union Fund, the women help support Carver School of Missions and Social Work, provide scholarships, contribute to Burney Gift Fund, and defray office and camp expenses of the department. Each Woman's Missionary Society is asked to contribute through this fund.

MRS. HELEN SINCLAIR

WOMAN'S MISSIONARY UNION, Auxiliary to the Kansas Convention of Southern Baptists. See KANSAS CONVENTION OF SOUTHERN BAPTISTS.

WOMAN'S MISSIONARY UNION, Auxiliary to the General Convention of Baptists in Kentucky. The first Woman's Missionary Societies in Kentucky were Indian Creek and Bethel Female Society, near Hopkinsville, both organized in 1882. Other early societies were organized at Frankfort in 1868 and at Russellville in 1874. The state central committee for women's societies in Kentucky was formed in 1878, with Leora B. Robinson as first president. Eliza S. Broadus, serving as president from 1887 until 1919, was a missionary society member for 53 years. Soon after the central committee was formed, there were seven societies in Kentucky, and when the first report was printed in 1880, there were 19 such organizations. The central committee published the first magazine for women's societies in the South, *The Heathen Helper,* in 1882, with Agnes Osborne as editor. *The Baptist Basket* succeeded *The Heathen Helper* in 1888.

In May, 1884, a woman's meeting was held during the general state association's sessions at Glasgow, and it was agreed to hold such a meeting annually, to which societies would send either a member or a letter. Kentucky women, represented by three delegates, participated in organizing the Woman's Missionary Union, Auxiliary to the Southern Baptist Convention, at the historic meeting in Richmond, Va., in 1888. The Woman's Missionary Union of Kentucky was organized for the first time on a state level on June 16, 1903, at First Baptist Church, Winchester. Seventy-four delegates were present for the meeting, at which 64 societies and bands presented reports.

In 1910 Nona Lee Dover was employed as the first paid secretary of the Kentucky Woman's Missionary Union, and offices were established in the building of the Baptist state board of missions. The plan of the W.M.U. work follows the pattern of the Convention-wide organization, which is based on fundamentals of prayer, study, stewardship of possessions, community missions, and missionary education of young people. Special emphases include the standard of excellence, circle plan, intercessory prayer league, and observance of weeks of prayer for foreign, home, and state missions.

The Woman's Missionary Union Training School was established by Louisville women in 1904, in response to a plea by Edgar Young Mullins (*q.v.*) for living quarters for young women studying at Southern Baptist Theological Seminary. Kentucky women later joined in support of the school, which was adopted by the Convention-wide Woman's Missionary Union in 1907. Aid to work among Negroes, which was begun in 1907, now includes a gift scholarship at National Woman's Missionary Training School, Negro leadership training conferences, and the provision of part salary for a Negro fieldworker. Other scholarship funds provided by the Kentucky Woman's Missionary Union include the Mary H. Wilson College Loan Fund, Mrs. George B. Eager Gift Scholarship, Carver School Loan Scholarship Fund, Fiftieth Anniversary Scholarship Fund, State Missionaries Scholarship Fund, Mrs. James H. Anderson Gift Scholarship, and, at intervals, a scholarship for a foreign student to study in the United States.

Since 1919 the Kentucky Woman's Missionary Union has had a weekly page in the state Baptist paper, *The Western Recorder*. In 1922 it began to help finance summer assemblies in Kentucky, first on Baptist college campuses and, beginning in 1923, at Clear Creek Springs. Each year a W.M.U. Day was observed in the assemblies. A Labor Day Week-end Camp for Business Women was begun at Clear Creek Springs in 1946 and moved to Cedarmore in 1952, where a week's Woman's Missionary Union leadership conference was begun the same year. The State Federation of Business Women's Circles was organized in 1949.

Several women from Kentucky have been chosen for Convention-wide leadership, among them Eliza Broadus, who served as vice-president of Woman's Missionary Union; Mrs. Eureka Whiteker, personal service chairman, 1937–40; and Janie Cree Bose, principal of the Training School, 1925–30.

Before 1815 only a few young people's societies had been organized in the state. Records indicate the existence of a Sunbeam Band at Russellville in 1880, and a Boy's Mission Band in Owensboro supported a girl in Lottie Moon's (*q.v.*) school in China in 1883. The first Young Ladies' Missionary Society was evidently organized at Frankfort in 1884. Youth work became a department of the Kentucky organization's over-all program under bylaws adopted in 1955.

Total membership in the Kentucky Woman's Missionary Union in 1955 was 78,921 in 4,312 church organizations, 75 associational organizations; receipts totalled $361,358.76.

MRS. GEORGE R. FERGUSON

WOMAN'S MISSIONARY UNION, Auxiliary to Louisiana Baptist Convention. Auxiliary to the Louisiana Baptist Convention; organized on July 14, 1899, as the Union of the Woman's Missionary Societies of the Baptist Churches of Louisiana, in the Alexandria Methodist Church. Twenty-one delegates were present. Formerly the work had been promoted by a central committee with headquarters in New Orleans. This committee functioned as an executive board until 1919, when it was voted to appoint an executive committee. In 1903 a pin was adopted, made of silver with a blue enamel border, and containing the seal of the state of Louisiana, a pelican feeding its young, and the letters W.M.U. above the seal. Work was done in the home of the president or corresponding secretary until 1920, when an office in the administration building of the Baptist Bible Institute was given to the union. This was used until 1943, when headquarters were moved to an office in the building with the other Baptist headquarters. In 1948 all headquarters moved to Alexandria. Annual meetings were held at the time and place of the Louisiana Baptist Convention through 1922. The first separate W.M.U. convention was held in Apr., 1923, in Monroe.

The first week of prayer for state missions was observed in 1907. The amount given to state missions that year was $13,203.38. The amount in 1954 was $52,235.16. In 1949 a graded series of state mission books was prepared to be used in connection with the annual observance. In 1944 a day of prayer for Christian education was observed for the first time. A goal of $5,000 was adopted for that year. The goal for 1955 was $15,000, including 50 scholarships.

Definite work with Negro women began in 1942 when a Negro woman was secured to work with her people under the direction of the union. The following year plans were promoted for an institute for Negro women in co-operation with the Southern W.M.U., which furnished the funds. An approporiation for these institutions has been included in the state mission offering.

Emphasis has been given to Girls' Auxiliary and Royal Ambassador camps as an important means of missionary training for members of these youth organizations. These camps have been held in various sections of the state. In 1954 some property was purchased near Alexandria for a W.M.U. camp.

Through White Cross work, cash and supplies have been sent to Baptist hospitals in the state and in Nigeria. In 1954 hospitals in Nigeria were the only recipients; 36 drums of supplies were shipped from New Orleans by the state chairman.

The 1955 W.M.U. Convention registered 583 messengers and 285 visitors. The report showed that $295,980.50 had been given through mission offerings. In 1899 the records showed 40 societies; in 1955 reports were received from 863 societies and 2,420 young people's organizations.

KATHRYN E. CARPENTER

WOMAN'S MISSIONARY UNION, Auxiliary to the Maryland Baptist Union Association. Woman's Missionary Union, auxiliary to the Maryland Baptist Union Association, had its beginning in scattered "female" societies, which prayed and worked for missions at home and abroad. However, as the need increased for a more united effort for missions, in 1868, when the Southern Baptist Convention met in Baltimore, Mrs. Ann J. Graves, mother of Rosewell Hobart Graves (*q.v.*), called the women attending the Convention to come together for prayer. In Oct., 1871, the women of Baltimore organized a federation known as "Woman's Mission to Woman." The organized work of Maryland and Southern Baptist women had its beginning in this organization. In 1893 this organization became the Woman's Foreign Missionary Society of Maryland. The Woman's Home Missionary Society of Maryland was organized in 1882, with Annie Walker Armstrong (*q.v.*) as president. In 1898 the Woman's Baptist State Mission Society was organized, and the Young Woman's Auxiliary of the state was organized in 1910.

In 1913 the Foreign and Home Missionary societies united to form Woman's Missionary Union of Maryland. Three years later the Woman's Baptist State Mission Society joined with the Missionary Union, "thus uniting the three sources of missionary influence." When Woman's Missionary Union, auxiliary to the Southern Baptist Convention, was organized in 1888, Maryland was one of the 10 states voting for the organization. Annie Armstrong of Maryland was elected corresponding secretary of the newly formed organization. While the headquarters were located in Baltimore (1888–1921), many Maryland women served as executive board members.

The literature work now carried on by the Maryland W.M.U. was begun in Oct., 1886, when the Maryland Baptist Union Association voted to establish a missionary library and reading rooms. Through the co-operative efforts of members of Woman's Baptist Home Missionary Society and Woman's Mission to Woman in Foreign Lands, the Maryland Baptist Mission Rooms opened in Mar., 1887. Annie W. Armstrong led the Baltimore women in making available magazines, leaflets, prayer cards, and programs. In June, 1906, the accumulated funds were transferred to Woman's Missionary Union, Southern Baptist Convention, for the establishment of the Literature Department.

Until 1944, when a full-time secretary of youth was employed, youth work was carried on by volunteer leaders. In 1956 Mrs. J. Winston Pearce was serving as president of Maryland W.M.U., Josephine Carroll Norwood as executive secretary, and Erleen Gaskin as secretary of youth. The number of organizations and total gifts for missions has shown a steady increase through the years. The bylaws have been revised to conform to new plans projected by the Southern Baptist Convention Woman's Missionary Union.

BIBLIOGRAPHY: E. B. Cox, *Following in His Train* (1938). J. T. Watts, *The Rise and Progress of Maryland Baptists* (c. 1951).

JOSEPHINE CARROLL NORWOOD

WOMAN'S MISSIONARY UNION, Auxiliary to the Mississippi Baptist Convention. Organization of Mississippi Baptist women for missions began in 1878 with appointment by the Foreign Mission Board of a central committee with headquarters in Oxford, Miss. Prior to 1878, women's mission work was carried on by scattered individuals and groups. A missionary, James A. Ranaldson (*q.v.*), sent by the Triennial Convention to the Mississippi territory, reported organization of the Ladies Charitable Mission Society in 1822. After organization of the Southwestern Home Mission Society in 1839, when the first missionary was sent to Texas, the Ladies Society in the Columbus, Miss., church agreed to pay half his salary. H. F. Sproles organized a Ladies Missionary Society at Carrollton, Miss., in 1870 and at least eight other societies in Baptist churches, all of which joined together in a union, pledging themselves to support a Bible woman for five years and to build a chapel in China. The Baptist state convention placed its seal of approval upon women's work in 1875, and four years later the first women's meeting was held at Grenada, with 15 local societies reporting membership of about 100.

With each move of the state Baptist headquarters, the central committee personnel changed. Presidents of the organization have included Julia Anna (Toy) Johnson (*q.v.*), Mrs. Adelia M. Hillman, Mrs. Mary Bailey Aven (*q.v.*), Mrs. George W. Riley, Mrs. Wilma B. Sledge, and Almarine Brown. In 1888 Mississippi's two delegates to the Convention-wide women's meeting in Richmond felt they should confer with the state convention board before becoming a part of the new Convention-wide Woman's Missionary Union; but when endorsement was given on July 18, 1888, Mississippi joined the W.M.U.

Women's work in Mississippi was led on a voluntary basis until 1912, when Margaret McRae Lackey was elected full-time corresponding secretary. Frances Traylor and Edwina Robinson have also served in this position. Mississippi Baptist women early manifested an interest in missionary education of children and established juvenile missionary societies and mission societies for young girls. Frances Traylor, the first young people's leader employed, 1915, has been followed by Frances Landrum, Edwina Robinson, and Nell Taylor. Interest in young people's work crystallized in an aggressive camp program launched in 1935, which the building of Camp Garaywa in 1947 greatly implemented. Mississippi was one of three states which jointly employed Ivyloy Bishop as the first Royal Ambassador secretary.

The State Mission Day of Prayer, inaugurated in 1903, was extended to a Week of Prayer in 1917. Woman's Missionary Union Special Day was begun in 1951 as a plan to include a program of information, prayer, and offering for definite objectives of the union. Work among Negro women and young people was greatly strengthened by the employment in 1945 of a full-time Negro fieldworker. Since institutes for Negro women were first begun in 1940, a camp program for Negro boys and girls was started in 1947. Camps for Choctaw Indian boys and girls have been held annually since 1950.

Since 1879, when 15 women's societies had about 100 members and made total gifts of $116.90, the W.M.U. had increased by 1955 to 1,092 societies, 31,733 members, reporting $351,603.65 total gifts for the Season of Prayer offering.

In 1889 there were 178 Sunbeam Bands, and in 1955, 986, with 11,339 members. Between 1907 and 1955, the number of Young Woman's Auxiliaries increased from 30 to 393, while Girls' Auxiliaries increased from 10 in 1914 to 1,356 in 1955. Between 1931 and 1955, the amount of the state mission offering increased from $6,163.95 to $50,473.37; the home mission offering, from $7,047.34 to $70,089.71; and the foreign mission offering, from $7,777.40 to $211,319.79.

The Diamond Jubilee of Mississippi Woman's

Missionary Union, 1953, was climaxed at the 1954 convention with the release of the printed history, *Hearts the Lord Opened.*

BIBLIOGRAPHY: J. L. Boyd, *A Popular History of the Baptists in Mississippi* (1930). Woman's Missionary Union of Mississippi, *Hearts the Lord Opened* (1954). Mrs. J. L. Johnson, Sr., *Organized Work of Baptist Women in Mississippi 1878–1888* (n.d.). *Latter Day Luminary* (1822). Mrs. A. J. Quinche, *Pioneer Work of Baptist Women in Mississippi* (1888). *The Religious Hearld* (1839).

EDWINA ROBINSON

WOMAN'S MISSIONARY UNION, Auxiliary to Missouri Baptist General Association. An outgrowth of female mite societies, the Missouri Baptist Woman's Foreign Missionary Society was organized Apr. 18, 1877, in Second Baptist Church, Liberty, Mo. The purpose of the organization, which was auxiliary to the Foreign Mission Board of the Southern Baptist Convention, was to enlist the active sympathy and co-operation of the women of the state in the work of foreign missions. In 1885 the word "foreign" was dropped from the name, and the field was broadened to include home, state, and district missions, as well as ministerial education and foreign missions. In 1923 the name and plans of Woman's Missionary Union were adopted.

The history of the Missouri Baptist women's work falls naturally into four periods: (1) For 24 years, 1877–1900, the women worked independently of the Missouri Baptist General Association in choosing their own officers and in sending the money they collected direct to the national mission boards. They never, however, projected and promoted a program other than that of the general association. (2) For 15 years, 1900–15, the general association appointed a central committee of women to have charge of the work of the women and to work under the direction of the general association. This committee in 1906 became a Woman's Board and was so organized until 1915. (3) For eight years, 1915–23, there was a Committee of Woman's Work of the general association, consisting of the 10 women members of the 30-member state executive board, entrusted with the promotion of the women's missionary work in the churches. (4) Since 1923 the organization has been known as Woman's Missionary Union of Missouri, auxiliary to Missouri Baptist General Association. This state body is a co-operating member of Southern Baptist Woman's Missionary Union in methods, programs, and departmental organization.

A unified budget adopted by the general association in 1917 put an end to sending apportionments to the societies. Women were urged to support missions through the local church budget; later they were urged to give through seasons of prayer offerings to state, home, and foreign missions, through the Cooperative Program, and through W.M.U. Specials Fund. The W.M.U. Specials Fund, later called Madge N. Truex Fund, includes interracial work; scholarships for girls to W.M.U. Training School (later called Carver School of Missions and Social Work), the seminaries, and nurses' training; Burney Gifts; magazine subscriptions to missionaries from Missouri; overseas student fund; and current expenses to Carver School of Missions and Social Work.

From 1887 to 1900 the women published *Missionary Interchange,* and since that time have been allotted space in the state Baptist paper, first *Central Baptist* and later *The Word and Way.* Beginning in 1917 *Missouri Baptist Bulletin* was published by the general association for promotion of all Missouri Baptist work and was later continued by the women until 1933.

In the 32 years of Woman's Missionary Union only six presidents served. The first president was Mrs. F. W. Armstrong (*q.v.*) (1923–34); in 1952 Mrs. O. R. Burnham was elected.

Young people's work was begun through the correlation of Sunday schools, B.Y.P.U.'s, and missionary organizations. This plan was followed until 1923, when as a result of closer co-operation with Southern Baptist Woman's Missionary Union the auxiliary plan of organization, program, and promotion was adopted.

BIBLIOGRAPHY: R. S. Duncan, *A History of the Baptists in Missouri* (1882). Mrs. G. A. McWilliams, *Women and Missions in Missouri* (1951).

HILDA BEGGS

WOMAN'S MISSIONARY UNION, Auxiliary to Baptist Convention of New Mexico. The first reference to the organization of a missionary society in New Mexico was in 1903 at Roswell, where the women elected officers and adopted a constitution. The term Ladies' Aid Society originated in 1905, and by 1909 the resulting societies were actively directed by the Woman's Auxiliary of the Northern Baptist Convention. On Dec. 4, 1909, a territorial union was organized, with 32 societies embracing five associational units participating. Reflective of the spirit of the times was a statement in one report: "Sisters of Central Association, organize here and send your messengers out—woman rocks the cradle, why not help Christianize the world." A set of missionary programs for an entire year was presented through the state paper.

Recognition of the organization by the general convention came Nov. 12, 1910, in the new constitution which stated, "The woman's work shall be given an appropriate place on the programs of the Convention." As a result of the convention's division between Northern and Southern sympathies, the women effected a new organization. Confusion, related to the division from the Northern affiliation, led gradually to the desire for a Southern alliance. Under the united organization which resulted, associational work was constantly emphasized; delegates came from afar. On one occasion a successful discussion was in progress in Pecos Valley Association when a train came in sight. The meeting adjourned abruptly, for trains were few, and departing messengers could not afford to miss one.

As late as 1911, the missionary union was still not well established, but nevertheless was recognized at the W.M.U. convention, Jacksonville, Fla., as an integral part of the whole. This recognition and the fact that a New Mexico woman spoke at the convention constituted the first printed W.M.U. report to reach the state paper *New Mexico Baptist.* At this time the editor was requested to grant space for a woman's page. Henceforth, secretaries of the Home and Foreign Mission societies (Northern) were dropped from printed notices, and New Mexico officers were listed instead.

The full transfer from the Northern to the Southern alliance was completed in June, 1912. After the dissolution of the two old groups, women massed to form the Woman's Missionary Union, Auxiliary to the Baptist Convention, with 11 messengers representing 13 societies and 187 members. A keynote of the hour was, "Woman has been denied the pulpit, but the missionary society is all her own." At this time (1912) the women were doing more than society work; some superintended Sunday schools and even conducted funerals.

The first society in New Mexico to make the Roll of Honor, the Ladies' Aid of Carrizozo, held the first Jubilate meeting in the state in 1913 and ranked first in total mission gifts. In all, a total of $1,015.87 was forwarded to the Home and Foreign Mission boards.

Too little had been done in enlisting children, as indicated by state junior superintendent Fannie E. Formby's report of only three Sunbeam Bands in the state. Special emphases of 1921 were personal service, intercessory prayer, Bible study, and systematic giving. The state board established an appropriation for woman's work in July, 1916.

The women assumed one-fifth of the New Mexico quota in the 75 Million Campaign, encouraged the convention in the founding of Montezuma College, and urged establishment of a youth camp, finally realized in a Y.W.A. and Intermediate camp in the Sacramentos.

The 1930's were a period of W.M.U. advance. Aid was given to students in Texas and Baylor universities; the W.M.U. reached all goals in the Golden Jubilee; the Inlow Youth Camp was inaugurated; a dormitory costing $7,600 was erected at the children's home with the assistance of the Brotherhood and under W.M.U. sponsorship; a new and more adequate Inlow site was located in 1940; house parties, councils, conclaves, and associational conferences were held.

In 1947 a determined effort was made to assist in Spanish and Indian work through the all-Spanish and all-Indian camps held in the summer. In 1948 the W.M.U. assumed responsibility for the education of a Filipino student, Abraham Paler, providing four years at Eastern New Mexico University, and three at Baylor University and Southwestern Seminary.

The first statewide Queen's Court was held in 1954, and Royal Ambassadors were brought to Albuquerque for the first congress. This was the banner year for the International, Interracial Camp, and the associational Federation of Business Woman's Circles. In 1954, 157 societies with 487 auxiliaries and 9,444 members reported $5,466.69 Annie Armstrong Offering and $24,831.46 Lottie Moon Offering.

EVA R. INLOW

WOMAN'S MISSIONARY UNION, Auxiliary to Baptist State Convention of North Carolina. Originated in female mite and children's cent societies, which were started as a result of the efforts of Luther Rice (*q.v.*) to arouse American Baptists to missionary activity. The first attempt to gather the scattered groups into a state organization was made in Apr., 1877, when the North Carolina Woman's Central Committee of Missions was formed, with Mrs. J. M. Heck as president. In December of that year the committee reported to the state convention 17 new societies organized and contributions to missions amounting to $342.16.

> Instead of the approval which they so fondly expected, a very storm of dissension between the brethren who favored encouraging the women in mission endeavor and those who opposed it, broke out, and rose to such height that the little bark, the unwitting cause of the storm, was crippled and soon sank out of sight.

"The Convention could kill a Woman's Central Committee of Missions, but no power on earth could destroy the God-given missionary fervor that burned in the hearts of women who had heard the command, 'Go—tell.' " On Jan. 8, 1886, the second Woman's Central Committee of Missions was organized, with Fannie Exile Scudder Heck (*q.v.*) as president and Sallie (Bailey) Jones (*q.v.*) corresponding secretary. Fourteen of the societies reported in 1877 were active; with these the work began. At the end of the year the report showed 75 new societies and contributions amounting to $1,000.

Fannie Heck was present when Woman's Missionary Union, auxiliary to the Southern Baptist Convention, was organized May 11, 1888, but because of the opposition of the men, North Carolina was not one of the 10 "heroic and historic" states entering into the organization. In 1891, with the sanction of the state board of missions, North Carolina W.M.U. made its first report to the Convention-wide W.M.U., of which it was then an integral part.

In Dec., 1891, the first annual meeting was held in Goldsboro; 14 societies sent delegates and missions offerings totaling $3,192.14 were taken. Except in 1893, when Miss Heck was ill, and in 1945, when travel was restricted by the Government, the W.M.U. has met annually. The first session separate from the Baptist state convention of North Carolina was held in Durham, Apr., 1908.

Until 1911, when Blanche Barrus was elected as full-time corresponding secretary at a monthly salary of $60, the work was done on a voluntary basis. Other corresponding (now executive) secretaries have been Bertha Carroll, Mrs. W. H. Reddish, Mary Warren, Mrs. Edna R. Harris, Mrs. W. D. Briggs, Mary Currin, Mrs. Foy J. Farmer (acting), Ruth Provence, and Miriam Robinson. From 1886 Elizabeth (Briggs) Pittman (Mrs. T. M.) was in charge of children's societies in North Carolina, and she became "band leader" in 1896 when responsibility for Sunbeam Bands was given into the hands of W.M.U.

Young people's organizations also were at first promoted by volunteer workers. In 1924 Dorothy Kellam was elected as full-time paid young people's secretary. Other young people's secretaries have been Alva Lawrence, Mary Currin, Kathryn Abee, Hilda Mayo, Marie Epley, and Janet Wilson.

A comparison of figures shows the growth of the W.M.U. (1) The smallest attendance at any annual meeting was in 1896, when eight delegates were enrolled, with about 20 or 30 Methodist and Presbyterian visitors. At that time some Baptist pastors had instructed the women of their churches to "have nothing to do with so undesirable an endeavor." The record attendance to date is 3,022 delegates and visitors in 1954. (2) In Jan., 1886, there were 14 organizations, but the number of members was not recorded. In Oct., 1954, there were 7,244 organizations, with 138,650 members. (3) In 1888 the first Christmas offering was $256.28. In 1954 the Christmas offering totaled $310,549.16. (4) In 1895 the first home mission offering was $79.28. In 1954 the home mission offering amounted to $116,134.57. (5) In 1891 the first state mission offering was $70.00. In 1954 the state mission offering reached $70,514.95. (6) In 1924 the Heck Memorial Offering was $714.14. In 1954 the Heck-Jones Offering amounted to $47,673.74.

The Heck Memorial Offering was established in 1924 as a special offering in memory of Miss Heck, to be allocated by the W.M.U. In 1947 the name of the offering was changed to Heck-Jones Memorial Offering. The amount given 1924–55 is $477,829.11.

Among other honor and memorial gifts made by the W.M.U. are the return of Mr. and Mrs. T. C. Britton to China in 1895 as a "living memorial" to Matthew T. Yates (*q.v.*) and his wife; a Good Will Center in Soochow, China; library and furnishings at W.M.U. Training School; $5,000 toward Jones Hall at Meredith College in honor of Mrs. Sallie Bailey Jones; furnishings for Elizabeth Briggs Nursery at North Carolina Baptist Hospital by the Sunbeams; the Heck Memorial Fountain at Meredith College; the Edna R. Harris Scholarship at Carver School of Missions and Social Work.

The organization of W.M.U. in North Carolina is simple and effective. The department of missionary fundamentals has four divisions: prayer, mission study, stewardship, and community missions. The department of youth has three divisions: Sunbeams, Girls' Auxiliary, and Young Woman's Auxiliary.

BIBLIOGRAPHY: E. B. Cox, *Following in His Train* (1938). F. J. Farmer, *Sallie Bailey Jones* (1949); *Hitherto* (1952). F. E. S. Heck, *In Royal Service* (1913). L. Johnson, *Christian Statesmanship* (1914).

FOY J. FARMER

WOMAN'S MISSIONARY UNION, Auxiliary to the State Convention of Baptists in Ohio. See OHIO, STATE CONVENTION OF BAPTISTS IN.

WOMAN'S MISSIONARY UNION, Auxiliary to Baptist General Convention of Oklahoma. The Women's Baptist Missionary Society, cooperating with the Baptist General Convention of Oklahoma, was organized at Shawnee, Nov. 7, 1906. Its object was "to cultivate a missionary spirit, especially among the women, young women and children throughout the state, and to aid in the spread of the gospel." The new organization was formed by a combination of the two territorial organizations then functioning, viz., the Women's Baptist Home Mission Society of Indian Territory, auxiliary to the Baptist General Convention of Indian Territory, and the Woman's Home and Foreign Missionary Society, auxiliary to the Oklahoma Baptist State Convention. There were 22 messengers from the Indian Territory and 46 from Oklahoma. This body followed a dual alignment policy in cooperation with the state convention until the end of the fiscal year, Mar. 31, 1915, when single alignment with the Southern Baptist Convention began. In 1923 the name was changed to Woman's Missionary Union. From the beginning, Oklahoma W.M.U. promoted mission study through the use of traveling libraries. A unit of 10 mission study books made a library. There were 12 of these reported in 1907, 22 in 1908, and 30 in 1910. These were discontinued in 1916. Through the years, official Southwide W.M.U. periodicals, study books, mission study institutes, and general promotional plans have been used in Oklahoma. Stewardship is promoted through the Cooperative Program and the usual home, foreign, and state mission offerings, and a practical program of evangelism and community missions is advocated on the local society level.

These missionary fundamentals are operative in youth work through these missionary organizations designed for specific age groups: Young Woman's Auxiliary, Girls' Auxiliary, Order of Royal Ambassadors, and Sunbeam Band. Impetus is given to the cultivation of spiritual growth and missionary spirit among youth through state and associational camps, house parties, and congresses. The first state camp reported was in 1931, and district and associational camps and house parties began as early as 1938.

Since 1939 the Oklahoma W.M.U. mission offering has been named for Mrs. Edna McMillan, state W.M.U. president 1927–37. This offering aids general Baptist work in the state and assists special W.M.U. causes, including Indian and Negro work and tuition for rural preachers' wives in the summer school for preachers at Oklahoma Baptist University. Christian education, orphan child care, and the hospital ministry are allied causes of W.M.U. Gift scholarships are given annually to young women who desire to train for full-time religious work. In 1954, $3,782 was given to provide 13 of these scholarships, eight to the Carver School of Missions and Social Work, one to the University of Arizona School of Pharmacy, and four to Oklahoma Baptist University. An allocation from the state apportionment is made annually to the Carver School of Missions and Social Work. This amounted to $3,050 in 1955–56. In 1928 the W.M.U. led in raising funds and constructing a W.M.U memorial dormitory for women at O.B.U. at a cost of $200,000 which was cleared of indebtedness in 1937. Seven different women have served as executive secretary-treasurer of the state W.M.U. They were Mrs. Gladys Dicken, 1906; Mrs. Josie Chase Porterfield, 1907; Miss Sue Howell, 1908–18; Miss Pearl Todd, 1919–20; Mrs. Berta Keys Spooner, 1921–44; Mrs. William Vernon Cardin, 1945–47; and Miss Margaret Hutchison, 1948– . The title of this office has varied, from corresponding secretary in 1906, corresponding secretary and treasurer in 1907, to executive secretary-treasurer in 1941.

The Oklahoma Baptist Orphans' Home has received help through the practice of societies "adopting" children to be clothed and through gifts of food, clothing, and cash. Societies assist the convention's hospitals through gifts of linens, other articles, and cash. In 1955, 28 young women received nurses' scholarships from local or associational W.M.U. organizations.

The 1955 statistics show 874 societies, 2,245 youth organizations, 3,119 total organizations; 27,091 W.M.S. members, 25,779 members of youth organizations, 52,870 total membership; 238 business woman's circles; 12 associational B.W.C. federations; 259 attending state B.W.C. federation, 16,637 tithers, 492 societies doing community missions with 14,328 women and 8,580 youth participating, and 9,400 women and 9,662 youth taking mission studies. Reports in 1955 on the weeks of prayer observed show these totals: foreign missions, 716 societies with $166,398 offering; home missions, 651 societies with $48,937 offering; Edna McMillan offering for state missions, $28,259 from 596 societies; and state apportionment offerings, $11,879. Records of young people's meetings held in 1955 show 1,026 attending six youth camps, 366 attending the Royal Ambassador congress, 405 in the G.A. house party, and 207 at the Y.W.A. house party. Fourteen district meetings were held in the state the same year, with 20 simultaneous conferences in each and a total attendance of 3,915. The W.M.U. shared in the operating budget of $32,880 appropriated from the state convention's 1956 Cooperative Program.

Bibliography: E. C. Routh, *The Story of Oklahoma Baptists* (1932). J. M. Gaskin, *Trail Blazers of Sooner Baptists* (1953). A. M. Briggs, *A Question, Once Asked* (1956). ARGYE M. BRIGGS

WOMAN'S MISSIONARY UNION, Auxiliary to State Convention of the Baptist Denomination in South Carolina. The Wadmalaw and Edisto Female Mite Society, organized by 1811 under the leadership of Hephzibah Townsend, was the first society of Baptist women in the South to report contributions to missions. Female mite societies were organized and were active until 1860. Following the Civil War missionary endeavor began again. The first Woman's Missionary Society, by that name, in South Carolina was organized in Newberry in Oct., 1871. By 1875 there were four societies, located at Newberry, Welsh Neck, Darlington, and Mt. Elon. On Jan. 10, 1875, the Welsh Neck Society accepted the appointment of the Foreign Mission Board as the central committee of Baptist woman's mission societies of South Carolina, "commissioned to enlist and interest the women of South Carolina in world-wide missions." Martha E. McIntosh, later first president of the southwide Woman's Missionary Union, was elected chairman. During the first 10 years the societies contributed to foreign missions only; then the work was enlarged to include home and state missions as well.

The first statewide meeting was held in Florence in 1889, and three years later representatives from associations met in Greenville and formally organized Woman's Missionary Union, Auxiliary to the South Carolina Baptist Convention, electing Mrs. James D. Chapman president. The central committee continued until 1904.

In two separate periods, 1902–07, 1913–30, Mrs. Chapman served 23 years as president of Woman's Missionary Union. Other presidents have been Mrs. I. W. Wingo, Mrs. A. L. Crutchfield, Mrs. J. B. (Inez) Boatwright, Mrs. Charles M. Griffin, Mrs. D. C. (Mildred) Bomar, and Mrs. James F. Burriss. Mrs. A. L. Crutchfield was elected corresponding secretary in 1904; Mrs. J. R. Fizer, in 1912. Her successor, Vonnie E. Lance, served for 32 years (1922–54) in this office, known as executive secretary since 1939.

With the election of Mrs. Joel E. Rice in 1912, South Carolina became the first state with a superintendent of mission study. After years of volunteer leadership, the union elected Clara Lane as mission study chairman and field secretary in 1939. Before 1800 Richard Furman (*q.v.*) had organized the Juvenile Missionary and Educational Society of Charleston. Other children's bands came into being, and in 1893 Eliza Hyde was selected to lead the band work in South Carolina. Promotional emphasis on missionary education of young women and girls began in 1903. In 1913 Mrs. George E. Davis became superintendent of Young Woman's Auxiliary and was also responsible for the newly organized Girls' Auxiliaries. Royal Ambassador chapters providing missionary education for boys were first organized in 1908 and were maintained under volunteer state leadership.

In 1930 Mary E. Lawton was elected as the first employed young people's secretary in the South Carolina organization. Sunbeam Bands were under the leadership of Mrs. Charles M.

Griffin until 1937. South Carolina was one of the first three states to employ masculine leadership for Royal Ambassadors. J. Ivyloy Bishop served South Carolina, Alabama, and Mississippi from 1941 to 1943. In 1955 South Carolina's Woman's Missionary Union entered into joint sponsorship of Royal Ambassadors with the Baptist Brotherhood.

A summer camping program for young people in connection with the Baptist summer assemblies was launched in 1922. In 1941, 50 acres of land near Wagener in Aiken County were donated by W. C. Rawls for a permanent camp. Opened in 1942 Camp Rawls was dedicated two years later, debt free, and now provides camp facilities for hundreds of boys and girls each summer.

Since 1953 the Baptist good will center in Charleston, previously a project of the State Federation of Business Woman's Circles, has been operated by Woman's Missionary Union in cooperation with the Charleston Baptist Association. The association owns the property, and Woman's Missionary Union provides the operating budget. The board of trustees consists of representatives from both organizations.

Ten regional Woman's Missionary Unions and 39 associational organizations strengthen the work of local church societies. Woman's Missionary Union is organized into two departments of work: Department of Youth with divisions of Sunbeam Band, Girls' Auxiliary, and Young Woman's Auxiliary; and Department of Missionary Fundamentals with divisions of prayer, mission study, community missions, and stewardship. The following table indicates growth and expansion since 1902:

	1901–02	*1954–55*
Woman's missionary societies	287	1,229 with 55,457 members
Young people's organizations	61	3,765 with 36,645 members
Christmas offering for foreign missions	$1,024.33	$215,098.65
Home mission offering	721.69	82,434.82
State mission offering	834.77	45,512.81
	(General Fund)	(Mrs. J. D. Chapman Offering)

Gifts from 1902 to 1955 totaled $10,605,979.01

Special financial projects of South Carolina Woman's Missionary Union have included gifts to the Hyde Memorial Chapel in Charleston, forerunner of Hampton Park Church; $1,487,674.74 during the 75 Million Campaign; funds for the church building at Connie Maxwell Orphanage; and $170,689.48 contributed toward the Lily Hardin Home for nurses at the Baptist Hospital, Columbia.

BIBLIOGRAPHY: F. E. S. Heck, *In Royal Service* (1913). E. Cox, *Following in His Train* (1938). L. Owens, *Banners in the Wind* (1950). J. Chapman, "The Development of the South Carolina Woman's Missionary Union as I Have Known It" (1916); "Brief Historical Background to the Golden Jubilee of Woman's Missionary Union, Auxiliary to Southern Baptist Convention." RUTH PROVENCE

WOMAN'S MISSIONARY UNION, Auxiliary to Tennessee Baptist Convention. Missionary-hearted women in 24 churches in Tennessee were meeting regularly before the organization of a Woman's Missionary Union. In 1882 the secretary of the Foreign Mission Board encouraged the women of Nashville to form a Central Committee. Although its work was interrupted, it was reorganized in 1887.

When the Woman's Missionary Union of the Southern Baptist Convention was organized in Richmond, Va., in 1888, Tennessee representatives favored the organization. That same year plans were made to organize the women of the state at the meeting of the Tennessee Baptist Convention in Columbia.

Mrs. George A. Loftin was elected the first president of Tennessee W.M.U.

Until 1909 there were no full-time paid workers and no headquarters building. The state mission board then offered a desk in their office for the fieldworker, Mary Northington, who served four years in this capacity.

The young people's work was emphasized from the first. Many served as volunteer leaders, for the Sunbeams first, Young Woman's Auxiliaries second, then Girls' Auxiliaries and Royal Ambassadors.

Tennessee has had only three full-time executive secretaries: Margaret Buchanan (1913–23); Mary Northington (1923–53); and Mary Mills (1953–). The W.M.U., with seven regular employees, now occupies eight rooms at Headquarters Building, Belcourt at 16th Avenue, South, Nashville. Mrs. Douglas J. Ginn served as office secretary from 1921 until 1957.

In Jan., 1957, 35,765 women and young people in 1,547 churches were enlisted in the Woman's Missionary Union in Tennessee. The Woman's Missionary Union started the movement for camps. For many years they rented camps for young people, but in 1946 the state convention voted to take the responsibility for financing the camps at Carson Springs and Linden. Women serve on the committee, and most of the time is given to the activities of the Woman's Missionary Union. Designations from the Golden State Mission Offering make possible the expansion of the buildings at both camps.

The schools for preachers' wives, held each summer in the colleges, are a project of the Woman's Missionary Union. All expenses are paid by the Golden State Mission Offering. Scholarships and loans are given each year to many young women who need financial assistance to attend a Baptist college or one of the seminaries or training schools.

The Tennessee Woman's Missionary Union does not designate its gifts to the Lottie Moon Christmas Offering or to the Annie Armstrong Home Mission Offering, but these gifts have increased steadily until in 1956 they amounted to $300,035.22.

Mission study, prayer, stewardship, and community missions are the four fundamentals of the work. Each one has a volunteer director who gives much time to the promotion of these fundamentals. MARY NORTHINGTON

WOMAN'S MISSIONARY UNION, Auxiliary to Baptist General Convention of Texas. Organized as an auxiliary to the Baptist General Convention of Texas in Oct., 1880, in the basement of the First Baptist Church of Austin, Tex. Individual mission societies for women date back to the 1830's with varying names such as Female Missionary Society of Baylor University, The Ladies Sewing Circle, Ladies Indian Education Society, and Ladies Aid Society.

At the organizational meeting representatives from 12 societies elected the first president, Fannie Breedlove Davis, and collected an offering of $35.45 for missions. At the same time as this meeting, held in the basement of the church, there was a meeting in the auditorium above where Annie Luther (Ann Luther Bagby, *q.v.*) was questioned concerning her qualifications for appointment as a missionary. Later she married William Buck Bagby (*q.v.*), and in Jan., 1881, they sailed for Brazil, where they served as missionaries for more than 50 years. Mrs. Davis and her co-workers encouraged the organization of Annie Luther societies, and within a year's time more than 345 Annie Luther societies had been formed, along with additional societies called by other names.

In 1886 the organization took the name Baptist Women Mission Workers, retaining it until 1919, when the state organization was again called Woman's Missionary Union, frequently referred to as W.M.U. The constitution adopted in 1886 included as objects:

(1) To organize societies;
(2) To win the cooperation of women and children in the systematic study of missions and in collecting money for missions;
(3) To spread missionary information;
(4) To assist, through our churches and their agencies, state denominational enterprises.

From the beginning the object was to distribute missionary information, stimulate missionary effort, and secure the earnest co-operation of women and young people in praying for and giving to missions.

Mrs. Davis served as the organization's president from 1880 to 1895, succeeded by Mrs. W. L. Williams, 1895–1906; Mary (Hill) Davis (*q.v.*), 1906–31; Mrs. B. A. Copass, 1931–46; Mrs. Earl B. Smyth, 1946–49; Mrs. R. L. Mathis, 1949–55; Mrs. Clem Hardy, 1955– .

Until 1889, when Mina Everett was elected full-time corresponding secretary, that work was on a voluntary basis. The full-time young people's secretary, Ann Hasseltine (Stallworth) Maxwell, was elected in 1937.

Three representatives from Texas, including Fannie Davis, were present in Richmond, Va., in 1888 for the organization of Woman's Missionary Union, Auxiliary to the Southern Baptist Convention, formed by representatives from 10 states.

Four fundamentals, prayer, study, tithes and offerings, and community missions, form the basis for the work of the Texas organization. During the week of prayer for foreign missions in December, study is made of Southern Baptist foreign mission fields in a suggested daily program with emphasis on prayer and the Lottie Moon Offering for missions. A similar week of prayer for home missions is held in March and one for state missions in September, along with emphasis on the Annie Armstrong and Mary Hill Davis offerings, respectively. These special weeks provide increased gifts to missions (more than $1,500,000 in 1955 for the Lottie Moon Offering), specific interest in mission needs, intercessory prayer, influence channeled to enlist others, and volunteers for mission service.

The state organization has helped to remedy important needs through such projects as building the Woman's Building at Southwestern Seminary, Fort Worth, and Memorial Dormitory at Baylor University, Waco; increasing its 1952 goal for the Mary Hill Davis Offering to aid in church building programs in the Western states; combining emphasis on state missions and Christian education in the 1955 Mary Hill Davis Offering.

Within the state organization are 17 district Woman's Missionary Unions, which include 122 associational unions. Each organization has its own officers and chairmen patterned after the state organization. The state body works through districts and associations to the local organizations. A system of reporting from the local organization to the association, to the district, to the state office unifies the work.

The state executive board, composed of district and associational presidents, district young people's directors, state chairmen and members at large, transacts business between annual sessions. At the close of the diamond jubilee year (75th anniversary) in 1955, there were 2,755 Woman's Missionary Societies; 784 Young Woman's Auxiliaries; 3,187 Girls' Auxiliaries; 1,893 Royal Ambassador chapters; 2,371 Sunbeam Bands.

BIBLIOGRAPHY: Baptist General Convention of Texas, *Centennial Story of Texas Baptists 1836–1936* (1936). J. M. Carroll, *A History of Texas Baptists* (1923). Ethelene Boone Cox, *Following in His Train* (1938). Mary Hill Davis, *Living Messages* (1935). J. M. Dawson, *A Century with Texas Baptists* (1947). Fannie E. S. Heck, *In Royal Service* (1913). *Minutes* Annual Meetings, Woman's Missionary Union of Texas (1898–1955). *Minutes* Woman's Missionary Union of Texas Executive Board (1904–55). R. T. Patterson, *Candle by Night* (1955). Mrs. W. J. J. Smith, *Baptist Women, 1830–1930* (1933).

EULA MAE HENDERSON

WOMAN'S MISSIONARY UNION, Auxiliary to Baptist General Association of Virginia. On Sept. 17, 1874, officers of the Woman's Missionary Society of Richmond took the initiative in launching the organization which, in 1932, became formally known as Woman's Missionary Union, Baptist General Association of Virginia.

The immediate objective of the Richmond women in organizing woman's work, statewide, was the collection of $1,500 to be used by the Foreign Mission Board in the erection of a combination home, schoolhouse, and dormitory for the use of Lottie and Edmonia Moon, missionaries in Tengchow, Shantung province, China, in the school which they wished to establish. Organized in 1872 for the support of Edmonia Moon in China, the Richmond society was the successor of the Richmond Female Missionary Society, pioneer society in Virginia, organized in 1813, and the Richmond Female Judson Society through which Richmond Baptist women made foreign mission contributions during 1823–45.

Prior to 1874, 104 missionary societies for women and young people had been organized in Virginia Baptist churches. In 1878 the Foreign Mission Board accepted as its Central Committee for Woman's Work in Virginia, the organization launched in 1874. Ten years later (1888), the Baptist General Association of Virginia, upon recommendation of the Foreign Mission Board, accepted the committee as its auxiliary agent. In 1899 an agreement was reached by which the women's committee, at that time known as Woman's Missionary Union, Auxiliary to the Baptist General Association of Virginia, could draw from the general treasury an expense account not to exceed 5 per cent of the total annual contributions received by the treasurer of the general association from organizations affiliated with Woman's Missionary Union. Since 1908 Woman's Missionary Union has elected as its treasurer the treasurer of the general body.

The Virginia Central Committee became a member of the Southwide organization for woman's work Apr. 1, 1889, and was reorganized Oct. 6, 1898, as Woman's Missionary Union, with provision for representation in annual meetings of local societies. In 1902 a Day of Prayer for State Missions was inaugurated, with a thank offering for that cause. In 1910 the state Woman's Missionary Union, in co-operation with the Home Mission Board and the Portsmouth organization, established Norfolk Settlement House. Reports to the general association were made through "friendly gentlemen" until 1914, when the women's corresponding secretary was permitted to report directly. Camps for young people were held at Virginia Beach beginning in 1917; medical work in Nigeria became the recipient of funds and supplies from the newly established White Cross Department in 1921. A Missionaries' Library Fund, provided through collections at state annual meetings, was started in 1922, and eight years later good will centers were established in Hopewell and Norton. The 1932 quarter-a-week offering for payment of Foreign Mission Board debts resulted in gifts equaling one third of all received by the board for this purpose from Southern Baptist churches. An interracial department was established in 1934 as a part of women's work, with a Negro woman as secretary, and in 1936 a good will center was opened in Lee County named for George Braxton Taylor (*q.v.*), founder of Sunbeam Bands. The first volunteer summer workers in Virginia went to destitute sections of the state to conduct evangelistic Vacation Bible schools in 1937; construction of a camp near Marion and establishment of a camp for Negro girls in Chesterfield County in 1940 extended the program for young people. A third camp opened in Albemarle County in 1951.

Early presidents of the state organization included Mrs. Jeremiah Bell Jeter, 1874–87; Mrs. William Eldridge Hatcher, 1887–92; Mrs. Abby Manly Gwathmey, 1893–97; and Mrs. George White McDaniel, 1907–09. Four full-time executive secretaries have been employed, Mrs. Julian P. Thomas, 1906–21; Lizzie Savage, 1921–24; Blanche Sydnor White, 1925–49; and Ellen Douglas Oliver, since 1950. In 1954, 5,137 societies for women and young people reported 110,780 members and $1,310,958.87 total contributions through the general association.

BLANCHE SYDNOR WHITE

WOMAN'S MISSIONARY UNION AND FOREIGN MISSIONS. Providing an organization with worldwide concern, Woman's Missionary Union has contributed greatly to the foreign mission enterprise. When the W.M.U. was organized in 1888, societies were almost exclusively devoted to foreign missions. The corresponding secretary of the Foreign Mission Board, Henry Allen Tupper (*q.v.*), helped guide their activities.

The new organization stated its purpose as "the stimulation of missionary spirit and the grace of giving among women and children." The funds it collected were to be disbursed by the boards. It determined not to interfere with the administration of the mission boards, either in the appointment of missionaries or in the direction of mission work, and it has continuously adhered to this basic purpose. In 1889 there were 1,600 societies; in 1954, 19,696. Approximately half of the programs planned for use by the societies are related to foreign missions. Woman's Missionary Union sponsors the Sunbeam Band and Young Woman's Auxiliary and Girls' Auxiliary organizations for youth.

Missionary education was emphasized at first by pamphlets and programs, monthly missionary columns for the state Baptist papers, and departments in the *Foreign Mission Journal.* Since 1906 the W.M.U. has had its own mission magazine with a present subscription of 465,000; it also has magazines for each of its youth organizations. Mission study classes, begun in 1907 in co-operation with the educational secretary of the Foreign Mission Board, were officially adopted in 1908. The women promote the Foreign Missions Graded Series of study books along with their own special literature for the December Week of Prayer. The Girls' Auxiliary has a "Forward Steps system which requires study of missions. Missionary reading is encouraged in all of the organizations. Since 1916

Woman's Missionary Union has made use of summer assemblies, camps, and conferences to spread missionary information.

Women were convinced that prayer was one of the greatest contributions they could make to the spread of the gospel. The first report of Woman's Missionary Union indicates that 11,915 monthly mission topic prayer cards were sent out. In 1892 when the denomination undertook to send out 100 missionaries and build 100 chapels, one for every year since Carey, Woman's Missionary Union set apart the first week of January as a Week of Prayer for worldwide missions. Such a week, changed in 1926 to early December, is observed annually. Since 1931 a Day of Prayer Around the World (Friday of the Week of Prayer) has linked Baptist women everywhere. In 1907 the W.M.U. began the use of a daily prayer calendar suggesting that members pray for missionaries on their birthdays.

The stated purpose of Woman's Missionary Union "to stimulate giving" has brought bountiful returns. Money raised by the women for foreign missions during their first year of organization totaled $17,882.58. After five years they were asked to support all female missionaries, which required $30,600 at the time and $100,000 by 1907. In 1913 they added the support of all schools under the care of female missionaries. The foundation of the annuity plan for the Foreign Mission Board was made possible by a gift of $2,000 in 1899. Again and again W.M.U. contributed to remove Foreign Mission Board debt. They paid more than their goal in the 75 Million Campaign, a large part of which went into foreign missions. After World War I they inaugurated the White Cross plan of furnishing supplies for Baptist hospitals overseas. They met appeals for relief with money and boxes of clothing for Europe in the 1920's. After World War II and for Korean relief, many societies participated in gathering and packing tons of clothing, milk powder, vitamins, and food parcels for destitute people abroad.

A Christmas offering, inaugurated for China the first year of Woman's Missionary Union, became permanent. In 1893 it was given for Japan. Since 1918 it has been a worldwide offering named for Lottie (Charlotte) Moon (*q.v.*), whose appeal began it. This offering saved the Foreign Mission Board from near defeat during the depression years, and now provides more than a third of its income. Through 1954 the offering totaled $30,339,641.49.

Woman's Missionary Union takes a personal interest in missionaries and their children. In 1897 the W.M.U. began writing annual letters of greeting to all female missionaries on foreign fields, and since 1918 it has sent them the W.M.U. yearbook, minutes of the annual meeting, and the monthly magazine, *Royal Service*. Their letters appear in the magazines, and any missionary woman may have a letter mimeographed and mailed out by sending an address list to W.M.U. headquarters. For sons and daughters of missionaries, the Margaret Fund has provided college scholarships and many personal remembrances. Woman's Missionary Union camps and assemblies always feature the missionaries and introduce them as "our own."

Since 1913, reports of woman's work in each mission field have been included in the annual report of the Southern Baptist Woman's Missionary Union. Since 1930 this work has been encouraged by a gift from the Lottie Moon Christmas Offering. Named the Mrs. W. J. Cox Fund in 1933, it helps develop woman's organizations by providing literature, travel, and Good Will Center expenses, and furnishing scholarships for training in work with women and young people.

To prepare young women to become missionaries, Woman's Missionary Union established a training school in Louisville, Ky., in 1907, which has contributed 397 foreign missionaries. It has also trained students from abroad. By providing young women with work or loan scholarships that need not be repaid if missionary appointment follows, W.M.U. helps to make foreign mission service possible. Christ's command, "Go ye into all the world," is at the heart of the Woman's Missionary Union's program and work.

MRS. B. J. CAUTHEN

WOMAN'S MISSIONARY UNION TRAINING SCHOOL. See CARVER SCHOOL OF MISSIONS AND SOCIAL WORK.

WOMAN'S MISSIONARY UNION TRAINING SCHOOL, RECIFE. See BRAZIL, MISSION IN.

WOMAN'S MISSIONARY UNION TRAINING SCHOOL, RIO DE JANEIRO. See BRAZIL, MISSION IN.

WOMEN, CONVENTION PRIVILEGES OF. The general emancipation of women in the United States was reflected in the unceasing activity of local missionary societies, which gave women a chance for development within the life of the church. The Foreign Mission Board, Home Mission Board, and Sunday School Board early realized that in the economy of life in the United States women would have time and desire for reading and study which the boards could use in promoting their distinctive phases of work. The early annuals of the Convention contain references to woman's ability to serve, teach in Sunday school, become "devoted fellow-helpers to the truth in the work of foreign missions." The Home Mission Board, deploring what it felt was a lack of interest in home missions, in 1877 urged the co-operation of "the sisters" by "such special methods of organization as they may judge wisest and most efficient."

Realizing that in other denominations women had organized as independent bodies, appointing their own missionaries, holding mission properties, and collecting money which they disbursed in their own way, the boards by 1875 were using the word "auxiliary" in referring to the Woman's Missionary Union, apparently hoping to insure that Southern Baptist women did not organize independently, own property on mission fields, appoint their own missionaries, and control the expenditures of money they inspired as gifts for missions. Although the boards wanted to increase the number of missionary societies and the efficiency of the state central committees, they carefully sought to avoid the women's "usurping any of the New Testament duties imposed exclusively upon men or by speaking before popular assemblies." In its 1884 report to the Southern Baptist Convention, the Foreign Mission Board ventured to say that the work of the women was quite in keeping with the New Testament, which gave prominence to women in the propagation of the gospel.

In 1877 and again in 1882 Mrs. Myra E. Graves from Brenham Baptist Church in Texas registered as a delegate to the Southern Baptist Convention. However, in 1885, when two women from Arkansas registered, the question of the eligibility of women to seats as delegates was raised, and the matter was referred to a committee of one from each state. As a result of the committee's report, the word "members" in the Convention's constitution was changed to the word "brethren." Yet at that same convention the committee on women's work recorded its gratitude for the "noble achievements of the gentle and self-sacrificing women of the South," noting with delight the "steady increase in gifts to the two Boards" and suggesting that this work was "entitled to appropriate recognition by the body." Thus the women's work was recognized, although the women who did the work were denied the privileges of recognition as members of the Convention. At an earlier convention (1877), however, the fact had been pointed out that "the blotting out of dividing lines in religion between station and station, between race and race, between sex and sex was a glory peculiar to the gospel." And "especially must it be remembered that with the rise of Christ's kingdom on earth began the elevation of women to a fair and equal share with man in all that constitutes the highest good and glory of human nature." In 1894 the Convention commended the women and congratulated the Home and Foreign Mission boards for "so much at so little cost for our missions."

In 1913 the Convention decided that "whatever fears and forebodings may have existed at the beginning were long ago overcome by the loyal wisdom which has guided and the undeniable tokens of divine favor on" women's work, and the Woman's Missionary Union was asked to make its report direct to the Convention, that "the Convention could express its sense of obligation to them as one of the chief constructive factors in our rapid growth in all lines of missionary endeavor." Therefore, that year Fannie Exile Scudder Heck (*q.v.*), president, prepared the report which was presented to the Convention and spoken to by William Owen Carver (*q.v.*). Yet it was not until 1919 that the reports to the boards were actually discontinued.

In 1917 the Convention went on record that "in a democracy so pure as a Baptist church, all the members were entitled to equal privileges yet the Convention prohibited representation of women who are so vital a part of the membership both as members and as workers." A motion to table a recommendation to alter the constitution was lost, and consideration of the matter was referred to a committee of five, which was to report at the next convention.

In 1918 the word "brethren" in the constitution was changed again, this time to "messengers." That same year, in connection with a stereopticon display in behalf of the new W.M.U. Training School building, Kathleen Mallory (*q.v.*), corresponding secretary of Woman's Missionary Union, and Mrs. Maude R. McLure, principal of the school, made some explanatory remarks which evoked much discussion about women speaking at the Convention. Yet several women had sung solos at the Convention, and single women missionaries had been presented publicly.

As early as 1928, a woman home missionary spoke on Sunday afternoon at the home mission program. This 1928 convention, with no adverse comment, recorded in connection with the report of the committee on the American Baptist Theological Seminary that Georgianna Union Parks, a Liberian girl being educated in this country, spoke and an offering of $402.10 was given at the conclusion of her talk. Also, in 1928, the report of the committee on the work of Woman's Missionary Union closed with a recommendation that Mrs. W. J. Cox, president, be invited to address the body in 1929 on the achievements of the Woman's Missionary Union Ruby Anniversary. After discussion the entire report was adopted. In 1929 a memorial from Kentucky in opposition to speaking by women was presented but not adopted, and "in compliance with the request of the Convention a year ago, the Convention was addressed by Mrs. W. J. Cox."

In 1928 Kathleen Mallory, Mrs. Carter Wright, and Mrs. Ella B. Walker, who were in Detroit at the time of the Northern Baptist Convention, en route to the Baptist World Alliance meeting in Toronto, were appointed by George Washington Truett (*q.v.*) as fraternal messengers. That was the only time women have been so appointed.

In 1930, at the request of John R. Sampey (*q.v.*), who was then presiding, the corresponding secretary spoke to the report of Woman's Missionary Union following its presentation by Louie D. Newton. Since then women have spoken to the W.M.U. report with some frequency, but usually the secretary of one of the boards or a missionary-minded pastor is invited by the Woman's Missionary Union to do this.

The Convention has frequently recognized with expression of thanks the readiness of the Woman's Missionary Union to delay urgent needs of its own organized life for the sake of the two great causes of Baptists. The W.M.U.

joined in the 75 Million Campaign instead of pursuing the plan voted in compliance with the Education Commission, which would have provided $300,000 endowment for the W.M.U. Training School. In 1928 Woman's Missionary Union changed its voted plan of paying the Foreign Mission Board debt first to join in the Hundred Thousand Club plan.

The reaction of some of the Convention to the idea of paying the corresponding secretary of the Woman's Missionary Union a salary seems strange. Annie Walker Armstrong (*q.v.*) worked for 18 years without salary, but when the Woman's Missionary Union felt it must provide at least a token salary for her tireless hours in keeping with the idea of remunerating the secretaries of Home and Foreign Mission boards and others, an uproar of "dimming the glory" arose. The same state paper which attacked the W.M.U. for "commercializing" its service in such a way commended an increase in professors' salaries at the seminary. "Equal salary for equal work" is not a rule in Southern Baptist circles. Salaries of female ministers of education, ministers of music, and of other denominationally employed women are lower than those of men, although the preparation and experience of women may be superior. Southern Baptist women do not preach and are not pastors.

The 1955 Southern Baptist Convention, meeting in Miami, Fla., seems to have heard more women than any other. Mrs. D. C. Bomar, president of South Carolina W.M.U., read from the Scriptures and led in prayer at the Wednesday night session. Primrose Funches brought greetings from the National Baptist Convention, and Mrs. Gordon Maddrey of North Carolina joined in presenting the recommendation from the promotion report of the Executive Committee. In the Home Mission report Mrs. Ernest Geer of Arizona spoke on "What a Church Means to My Family." Saturday morning Marjorie Jones read from the Scriptures and led in prayer, and Mary Christian read a memorial tribute to Kathleen Mallory.

Only five women have served as members of the Executive Committee of the Southern Baptist Convention. In 1927 Mrs. F. W. Armstrong (*q.v.*) became Missouri representative on the Executive Committee. She continued until her death in 1945, some years serving as a member "at large" and some years representing Missouri. Mrs. Eugene Levering of Maryland was elected on the Executive Committee in 1928, but the "Mrs." was omitted from the Southern Baptist Convention annual. She served until 1934. Mrs. Frank S. Burney served from 1946 until 1952, Mrs. George R. Martin became a member of the Executive Committee in 1946 after becoming W.M.U. president, and Mrs. Gordon Maddrey was elected in 1954.

On the Convention boards the records show Mrs. J. M. Dawson pioneering in 1923 as Texas member of the Relief and Annuity Board. Mrs. Frances Hays became a member of this board in 1946. Mrs. Raymond Moorman, Virginia, seems the only woman state representative ever on the Home Mission Board (1944–48). On the Foreign Mission Board four women have served as state representatives: Mrs. W. C. Henderson, Arizona (1935–37); Mrs. George McWilliams, Missouri (1944–47); Mrs. Foy J. Farmer, North Carolina (1954–); and Mrs. R. L. Mathis, Texas (1954–). A few women have been local members of the Home and Foreign Mission boards, and even fewer local members of the Sunday School Board.

In the field of denominational schools, one woman, Annie D. Denmark, has been president of a Baptist junior college, Anderson College, South Carolina, 1929–54.

Although large gifts have been stimulated by W.M.U. and allocated by the mission boards and a large number of women serve in leadership positions in local churches, progress in full recognition of the abilities of women for leadership in the denomination has been slow.

JULIETTE MATHER

WOMEN'S COMMITTEE, BAPTIST WORLD ALLIANCE. See BAPTIST WORLD ALLIANCE.

WOOD, MORGAN MARION (b. Huffman, Ala., Aug. 15, 1853; d. Birmingham, Ala., Sept. 4, 1939). Pastor and Alabama Baptist leader. Wood was educated at Howard College, from which he received the A.B. degree and the honorary D.D. degree. His pastorates, all in Alabama, included Brighton, Acipco, Vinesville, and 11th Street in Birmingham. For 35 years (1905–39) he served as recording secretary of the Alabama Baptist State Convention. He served as chaplain of the Old Folks' Home of Jefferson County and at Hillman Hospital, Birmingham.

JOHN BOB RIDDLE

WOODLAND BAPTIST COLLEGE. An academy at Jonesboro, Ark., founded in 1902. Mt. Zion Association operated it for eight or nine years with 60 to 110 students. H. D. MORTON

WOODLAND COLLEGE. A school at Jonesboro, Ark., owned and operated by the Mt. Zion Baptist Association from Sept., 1903, through the spring of 1912. Pulaski Clingman Barton (*q.v.*) and George W. Puryear (*q.v.*) were members of the first board of trustees.

Funds for the college were raised by offerings and bank loans. An administration building was erected, and a girls' dormitory, built by President Carpenter with his personal funds, was purchased. Woodland offered literary, normal, commercial, and music courses. The latter included piano, organ, violin, and voice.

Lack of funds prevented the opening of the college in the fall of 1912. Plans to affiliate Woodland with other colleges supported by the Arkansas Baptist State Convention did not mature. The association organized Woodland Realty Company with authority to sell the college property, and pay all accumulated debts. C. E.

Dicken was president 1910–12. In all, Woodland College served some 600 students.

DOLLIE E. HIETT

WOODLAND FEMALE SEMINARY. Opened in Cedartown, Ga., in 1851, first called Cedartown High School. Jesse M. Wood, pastor of the Cedartown Baptist Church, was owner and president. In 1854 the school was partially taken over by Coosa Association, and its name was changed to Woodland Female College. The Cherokee Baptist Convention, which had founded Cherokee Baptist College in 1853, assumed control in 1856. The school existed until about 1864.

ARTHUR JACKSON

WORD AND WAY. Weekly newspaper published by Missouri Baptists. Founded in 1896 as an independent, privately owned and edited religious paper, the *Word and Way* was purchased by the executive board of the Missouri Baptist General Association in 1945. Convinced that there should be "a little paper somewhere out in this middle-west standing up for the simplicity of New Testament church organization and work" and that it should be a free and independent journal, Sanford M. Brown (*q.v.*) founded the *Word and Way*, with R. K. Maiden as coeditor. The first issue was published in Kansas City, Mo., in July, 1896. The slogan carried in the masthead as long as the paper was under private editorial management indicated its program: "The Bible, The Home, The Church, The Faith, The Ordinances, The Life."

Prior to the founding of the paper, Brown had been for nearly five years secretary of missions in Missouri and for several years assistant editor of the *Central Baptist*, published in St. Louis, which, though privately owned, was regarded as the denominational organ for Missouri Baptists. In 1912 the Western Baptist Publishing Company, owner of the *Word and Way*, purchased the *Central Baptist* upon the recommendation of a committee of the Missouri Baptist General Association. Thus the *Word and Way* became the denominational paper in Missouri. For many years it furnished the executive board of Missouri Baptist General Association from one to four pages of the 16 pages of each issue for the promotion of Baptist causes fostered by the general association.

In 1928, with the failing health of Brown and Maiden, Brown's son, Joseph Everingham Brown, became associate editor; in 1929, upon Maiden's retirement, he became coeditor with his father. After the death of S. M. Brown in 1938, Joseph E. Brown became editor. Among the numerous movements supported by the *Word and Way* was that which, against considerable opposition, culminated in 1919 in aligning the Missouri Baptist General Association solely with the Southern Baptist Convention.

In June, 1944, in line with a definite trend toward denominational ownership of state Baptist papers, a committee of the executive board of Missouri Baptist General Association recommended that the executive board inaugurate negotiations for the purchase of the *Word and Way* at a reasonable price. While the board had been allotting to the paper the sum of $3,000 per year for the use of four pages each week for the promotion of its causes, rising costs of production were entailing a too heavy financial burden on the owners. A contract was therefore consummated early in 1945 for the purchase of the paper by the executive board, and the transfer took place at the end of the year 1945. Thomas W. Croxton, pastor of the First Baptist Church, Sedalia, Mo., served as interim editor. He was succeeded in Mar., 1946, by Lewis A. Myers, who served as editor until Oct., 1947, when H. H. McGinty, pastor of the First Baptist Church, Cape Girardeau, became editor.

Largely through the use of the church budget plan, the number of subscribers increased from 17,112 in Dec., 1945, to 51,525 as of Sept. 15, 1956. Since 1949 the *Word and Way* has been published at Jefferson City, Mo., where the executive board maintains its headquarters and owns and maintains a well-equipped printing plant. The *Word and Way* is owned by the Missouri Baptist General Association and is directly responsible to this body. Reports are made each quarter to the executive board of the general association. The paper has an advisory committee, but this group has no authority. There is no publication board or committee. The Missouri Baptist General Association annually allocates $15,000 of Cooperative Program funds to the *Word and Way*. The paper keeps all of its subscription accounts, but receipts are funneled into the general business office, which handles all banking. Checks are written and signed by the executive secretary and the treasurer of the general association. The staff consists of an editor, an editorial assistant, circulation assistant, and four mailing clerks. The editor, with the counsel of the executive secretary, also serves as business manager.

JOSEPH E. BROWN

WORD OF GOD. The spoken utterance of God, commanding the response of man, nature, or history. Although the Bible may be correctly regarded as the Word of God, the Bible itself uses the expression in a richer, more comprehensive way.

The word of God (Hebrew, *dabar*) is the authoritative divine message orally proclaimed by God's prophet (Exod. 4:10 ff.; Amos 7:15; Isa. 5:9; 22:14). There is also a written word of God, comprised of the Ten Commandments (Deut. 18; Psalm 119) and the messages of the prophets (Isa. 30:8; Jer. 36:1 ff.; 25:3). The word of God, whether living or written, is creative in the realm of history (Deut. 1:6 ff.; Psalm 119:81; Isa. 9:8; 55:10–11; Jer. 1:10). Furthermore, the word of God is the creative factor in the realm of nature. The universe is created and preserved by the word of God (Gen. 1–2; Deut. 8:3; Psalms 33:6, 9; 147:15–18; Isa. 44:26–28; II Peter 3:5, 7). These biblical concepts of the word are historically oriented, redemptive in purpose, and thoroughly moral. In the New Testament "the word" (Greek, *logos* or *rhema*) often refers to the content of the Christian message (Acts 4:29; 6:2; 14:3; I Cor. 1:18; II Cor. 6:7). The Gospel of John calls Christ "the Word" (John 1). This concept is rooted in the Old Testament (Heb. 1:1–2), although cast in Greek philosophical terminology. Christ is the supreme and final revelation of God.

BIBLIOGRAPHY: J. W. Cox, "The Doctrine of the Word of God in the Old Testament" (1953).

JAMES W. COX

WORLD. This word has many scriptural meanings which may be grouped in four classifications. It denotes (1) *land area,* such as tilled land, Palestine, the Roman Empire, or the entire earth; (2) *time* or *time periods,* which may be an age, or ages, or ages of the ages (cf. Isa. 64:4, I Cor. 8:13); (3) *humanity* or *the earth as populated* (John 3:16); (4) *a godless, sensuous, anti-Christian society.* Some of the Hebrew and Greek words translated "world" are used in more than one of these four classifications (e.g., *kosmos*). BERNARD RAMM

WORLD COMRADES. Began in Oct., 1922, as a quarterly magazine for young people, issued on a subscription basis by Woman's Missionary Union. From its beginning, Woman's Missionary Union realized the need for publishing literature, since workers, who used material in *The Foreign Mission Journal, Kind Words,* and other similar publications, required more helps. Suggestions headed "For Young Ladies" and programs for Sunbeam Bands appeared in the second number of *Our Mission Fields* in Oct., 1906. In addition, the *Junior Portfolio,* containing 12 monthly programs for the use of Sunbeams, with directions and suggestions for leaders, was "published in attractive form," and many narrative leaflets, exercises, and recitations for young people were added to the stock of the literature department and were "much called for." However, in an address to the annual meeting of Woman's Missionary Union in 1911, Fannie E. S. Heck (*q.v.*) stated, "I wish someone would endow a missionary magazine for Southern Baptist children. The editors of the department in *Our Mission Fields,* and other departments, are doing wonderfully well under the limitations forced upon them, but in this age of the child, these departments should not be 'tagged on' to anything."

The dream of early leaders was realized when the W.M.U. took action to issue a quarterly magazine containing weekly programs and other helps for the various young people's organizations. The W.M.U. bore the expense of the first issue itself, recording its sentiment toward the new publication in its annual report: "Genuinely proud is the Union of this, her youngest child, for whose initial issue she gladly contributed nearly $1,000, the 'layette,' shall we call it!" A 48-page magazine, with Juliette Mather, secretary of the Department of Publications, as editor and Ethel Winfield as associate, *World Comrades* had for its motto, "To Girdle the World with Friendliness." The new magazine proved so successful that it was changed to a monthly in Oct., 1924. When *Ambassador Life* began as a separate monthly magazine for boys, *World Comrades* supported it until its subscription list was established.

Circulation of *World Comrades* increased to 99,000, but as young people's work continued to expand, provision had to be made for more materials. *World Comrades* ceased publication in Apr., 1953, replaced by *Tell,* a magazine for members of Girl's Auxiliaries, and *Sunbeam Activities,* a quarterly publication with plans for Sunbeam Band leaders. MARY PATRICIA POWELL

WORLD EMERGENCY OFFERING. At the 1946 session of the Southern Baptist Convention, the Foreign Mission Board reported a crisis of world need, both in the area of direct relief and in rehabilitation, spawned by World War II. Although the board had already spent $1,127,000 for world relief during 1942–45, it warned that unless emergency funds were forthcoming, mission advance would be crippled by trying to meet relief needs.

Acting quickly, the Convention set May and June, 1946, for preparation for a world emergency offering of $3,500,000. Plans called for the offering to begin in July and continue until completion, but not beyond Sept. 30, 1946. Campaign expenses were to be paid out of receipts, and uniform promotional literature was to be prepared by the Southern Baptist Convention Executive Committee. The Executive Committee appointed a special campaign steering committee composed of members of the Executive Committee and the Foreign Mission Board, with Frank Tripp, chairman. The executive secretary of each state was asked to head the campaign in his state.

Loose offerings for the campaign were received at the 1946 and 1947 sessions of the Convention, at which $10,897.17 and $5,077.03, respectively, were collected. Exceeding the original goal, the total offering was $3,910,085, with $1,500,000 earmarked for relief and $2,000,000 for rehabilitation. ROBERT J. HASTINGS

WORLD EVANGELISM, ASSOCIATION OF BAPTISTS FOR. Independent faith mission loosely related to General Association of Regular Baptist Churches, founded at Watch Hill, R. I., Aug., 1927, by Mrs. George W. Doane, Mrs. Henry W. Peabody, and others. It is not affiliated with Southern Baptist Convention. Its first missionaries, Dr. and Mrs. R. C. Thomas and Miss Ellen Martien, had worked in the Philippines under the American Baptist Foreign Mission Society but resigned because of doctrinal differences. Fundamentalist and premillennial, this association has a doctrinal platform of 10 points, which every missionary and board member is required to sign annually. For 10 years its only field was the Philippine Islands.

In 1938 Ceylon was entered; in 1939, the Amazon Valley in Peru; in 1942, Brazil; and in 1945, South China. Unsuccessful attempts were made to enter Tibet and New Guinea in 1948. Japan and Chile were entered in 1954; India was entered in 1955. In Jan., 1956, there were 192 active missionaries assigned to eight fields: 76 in the Philippines (Luzon, Palawan, Mindanao, and Visayas); 8 in Hong Kong; 2 in India; 4 assigned to Pakistan; 12 in Japan; 33 in the Upper Amazon (Peru, Colombia, Brazil); 19 in Chile; and 38 in Brazil (Rio Grande do Norte and São Paulo). The headquarters of the association are at 1505 Race Street, Philadelphia 2, Pa.; the president is Harold T. Commons; the official publication is *The Message*.

H. C. GOERNER

WORLD MISSIONARY CONFERENCE. See EDINBURGH MISSIONARY CONFERENCE.

WORSHIP, CHRISTIAN. Christian worship is in essence the communion of the soul of man with God in Christ. It is man's response in faith to the transcendent God who makes himself known in Jesus Christ and who is eternally present in the Holy Spirit. Worship involves a sense of God's otherness and of human need, sublimated in the communion of the I-Thou relationship. Two acceptable definitions of worship are these: "Worship is an acknowledgment of Transcendence; that is to say, of a Reality independent of the worshipper, which is always more or less colored by mystery, and which is there first. As Von Hugel would say, 'It is rooted in ontology.'" "Worship may be defined as the acknowledgment by some formal act of mind or body, or both, of God's supreme dominion."

Worship and theology are inseparably bound together. Man worships according to what he believes. Faith can no more dispense with worship than sincere worship can dispense with faith. Worship is an intelligible experience. Man's highest idea comes to expression in the institution known as worship. Whatever be the intellectual elements of faith, it implies a volition, and that volition finds expression in individual acts. "The reasoned idea without the worship is cold, formal theology; the worship without any reasoned idea is superstition; but the two in wholesome and corporate union make a wholesome religion." In worship intellect, emotion, and will are united in a single act of personal experience. The whole man appears face to face with God to adore and to pray.

Psychologically a worship experience has both objective and subjective aspects. God is objective in his holiness and transcendence and absoluteness. He is not a part of man, nor is he dependent upon man for his being. In worship man's mind and heart must be directed upward toward God. "Worship is objective as people think primarily about God; it is subjective as they think primarily about themselves. A balance of the two is realized in genuine communion." Worship is more than a sentiment or an emotional outreach. It finds objective reality in God. Man's faith comes to rest in Christ. Worship is a creative encounter and a redemptive act. "Subjectiveness is an indispensable preliminary to a sense of guilt and need for purification." Objectiveness is an indispensable end to a sense of forgiveness and healing.

Public worship is both an individual and a corporate experience. It is only in the common utterances and acts of worship that faith can find social expression. "By that expression the individual faith verifies itself and educates itself." Individual worship is indispensable to the worship of the church. "Without it the church would lose its devotional character. The individual, on the other hand, is dependent upon the *koinonia,* the 'fellowship' of all the believers." As Sperry reminds us, an institution is history's protest against the futility and waste of vain individualism. "A church gives adequate expression to our experiences, which, as individuals we have believed and discovered to be universal."

As an activity worship consists of our words and actions, the outward expression of our homage and adoration when we are assembled in the presence of God. These words and actions are governed by two things: our knowledge of the God whom we worship and the human resources we are able to bring to the worship. Worship is an effort to express an inward attitude. Among the attitudes or moods of the human heart that seek expression are those of adoration, praise, confession, thanksgiving, supplication, and dedication. Worship is the act of expressing these inner longings. The primary means of expressing these moods in private and public worship are music, reading of the Scriptures, prayer, preaching, witnessing, bringing offerings, and personal dedication.

Free or evangelical worship is to be distinguished from liturgical worship. The liturgy is a fixed form adopted by a given institution, to be followed by the congregation as it meets for worship. Free worship consists of such planning and order as the leader and the congregation choose to utilize. It may make use of the best literature of history without the restrictions of an ecclesiastical liturgy. Based upon the responsibility and capacity of each soul, the priesthood of all believers, and the call to universal sanctity, it involves a direct personal and individual relationship to God. Free worship is characterized by a deep conviction of sin and a serious pursuit of personal holiness, a passion for sincerity, a high standard of self-discipline, a profound Christocentric devotion, and a genuine dedication of life to the will of God. It is a perpetuation of the spiritual realism of the New Testament. The ideal of free worship is to find the meeting place of spontaneity and order. Today many of the free churches are attempting to make use of available historical materials in developing a better order in worship. Many of the liturgical churches are seeking to bring more personal experience and spontaneity into their orders of worship. Genuine Christian worship results in purity of heart, strength of conviction, power for living, and zeal for service.

FRANKLIN SEGLER

WORSHIP SERVICES, BAPTIST. Services of corporate worship, for Baptists as well as for other groups, are and have traditionally been the focal point of church activity. These services existed before the development of subsidiary church organizations of various sorts and before the development of complex educational and promotional programs. Today, in spite of increasing educational emphasis among Southern Baptist churches, worship services have a major place in the church program. These periods serve to unify the membership, promote fellowship, and magnify such attitudes as awe, reverence, adoration, praise, gratitude, and other emotions usually associated with a worship experience.

Worship services described in the New Testament were simple in form and included singing, Scripture reading, prayers, and a sermon. The people met in homes, in the out-of-doors, and sometimes in the synagogues. By the second century trends were under way which eventually produced an elaborate ritual conducted in a ceremonial type of service. The preacher became a priest, a mediator between God and man, and a manipulator of a magical religious ceremony. The ritual became the all-important thing. The people were incidental to the performance and were spectators rather than participants. Among some groups in Christendom this type of service still prevails.

With the Reformation and the rise of denominations, some Christian groups attempted to recover the New Testament pattern and therefore reacted against formalism and ceremonialism. In a few instances groups went to an extreme and followed no particular form in their worship. Baptist worship has traditionally been free and informal. Wide variations exist in present practice, but there is evidence of an increasing emphasis on dignity and beauty as found in more formal orders of worship, which helps to avoid the confusion and irreverence that often accompany very informal services. It is probable that a typical Baptist order of service would include the following minimum elements: hymns, Scripture reading, prayers, offering, sermon, and a conclusion giving opportunity for individuals to make public decisions. Both large and small churches have services in which these elements prevail. Through these elements churches seek to attain in public worship the values and purposes which Baptists feel are important.

EXAMPLES OF BAPTIST PRACTICE. Contemporary denominations have varying types of worship services. Some use images; others use symbols. Some emphasize ritual; others magnify preaching. A few insist that silence should prevail during most of the service; others permit hysterical participation by the worshipers as they give vent to their emotions. Baptist procedure stresses free, democratic services, allowing participation by the people in music, prayers, and offerings. Preaching still occupies a third to a half of the time set apart for worship. Spiritual aids to worship are permitted, and the services are conducted in architectural settings of beauty and simplicity. The orders of service may be elementary or elaborate. Typical of the simplest orders of service as followed in many Baptist churches is the following:

MORNING SERVICE

Prelude
Doxology and Invocation
Choral Response
Hymn 19
Recognition of Visitors
Scripture and Prayer
Hymn 276
Tithes and Offerings
Offertory
Message in Song . . . . Choir
Sermon . . . . Pastor
Hymn of Invitation 197
Benediction
Postlude

An example of a much more elaborate order of service, which is representative of only the most formal Baptist churches, is the following:

THE MORNING WORSHIP
Eleven O'clock

I SAW THE LORD SITTING UPON A THRONE, HIGH AND LIFTED UP

THE PRELUDE

HOLY, HOLY, HOLY IS THE LORD OF HOSTS

THE BELL
THE CHORAL INTROIT: "Sanctus" Gounod
THE CALL TO WORSHIP

Minister:	Come ye, and let us walk in the light of the Lord.
People:	He will teach us of His ways, and we will walk in His paths.
Minister:	The hour cometh, and now is, when the true worshippers shall worship the Father in spirit and in truth:
People:	For the Father seeketh such to worship Him.

THE GLORIA PATRI
INVOCATION
THE DOXOLOGY
THE OLD TESTAMENT LESSON
THE PRAYER OF PRAISE AND THANKSGIVING—CHORAL AMEN
HYMN No. 309, "For the Beauty of the Earth" DIX

THEN SAID I WOE IS ME FOR I AM UNDONE

Psalm 51:1–3

THE PRAYER OF CONFESSION
CHORAL RESPONSE "Hear My Prayer" O'Conner

DRAW NIGH UNTO GOD AND HE WILL DRAW NIGH UNTO YOU

ANTHEM: "The Beatitudes" Evans
THE READING OF THE SCRIPTURES
THE CHORAL CALL TO PRAYER: "Hear Our Prayer, O Father" Bruner
THE MORNING PRAYER
HYMN NO. 202, "I Am Trusting Thee, Lord Jesus"

SUCH AS I HAVE GIVE I THEE
The Offertory Prayer of Dedication
The Offertory Solo: "Thy Mercy, O Lord Is In The Heavens" La Forge

AND HE SAID GO, TELL THIS PEOPLE
Sermon Pastor

I HEARD THE VOICE OF THE LORD SAYING, WHOM SHALL I SEND?
The Invitation to Christian Discipleship

MY PRESENCE WILL GO WITH THEE AND I WILL GIVE THEE REST
Benediction
Choral Response
The Postlude

These samples are not patterns which would fit every Baptist church. Each church's practice has distinctive features, and in any given church the same order of service will not be slavishly followed every Sunday.

Trends in Baptist worship services can be summarized as follows:

The Sunday morning service is more formal and more strictly planned. The evening worship hour is more likely to be informal, varying in plan from week to week. Sermons are growing shorter. The day of the 60-minute sermon has practically passed, and almost all ministers limit their sermons to 30 minutes or even 20 minutes.

The most significant recent trend is in church music. Large and small churches are adopting graded choir programs with a minister of music on the church staff or a group of volunteer choir leaders directing the activities. Choirs are graded by ages of members. The choirs do not all sing in a single service except in a special concert. In addition to the choirs, smaller choral groups, male choruses, women's ensembles, quartets, and instrumental groups are trained. Paid soloists and paid quartets have almost disappeared. The musical groups wear robes, frequently of a different color for each choir. This new emphasis upon music has brought more choral responses, musical interludes, and introits into the order of service. Some churches designate types of hymns in their order of service, using a hymn of worship, hymn of praise, hymn of dedication, hymn of consecration, and hymn of invitation. Hymn anthems are frequently used.

Another feature of Baptist worship services which is growing in prominence is the time of emphasis given to Sunday school and Training Union activities. This emphasis may take the form of an announcement or a report, or it may be a much more elaborate presentation. Generally presented by or under the direction of the superintendent or the director in charge, this feature is useful chiefly as a means of promoting interest in the educational organizations of the church.

A trend to magnify the two church ordinances in the worship services can be noted. While the Lord's Supper is still a "tacked on" feature in many churches, an increasing number give an entire service to it. Some have the ordinance near the center of the service with only a brief message by the pastor, either before or after the ordinance. Some eliminate the sermon entirely and use music and Scripture passages to precede the ordinance. Likewise, baptismal services may be held in the morning or in the evening, either at the beginning or at the close of the service. Both ordinances are frequently held in the same service.

The practice of using responsive readings, based on Scripture passages as printed in pew hymnals, is increasing.

Special Baptist Emphases. *Participation.*—A Baptist service of worship is presided over by the pastor. Very few Baptist pastors wear pulpit robes. They most frequently wear business suits of dark material. Some wear white in the summer. Other colors may be worn. The pastor usually carries the responsibility for the public prayers and the sermon, but may and often does call on members of the congregation for extemporaneous prayers, particularly in the evening. As indicated above, the choirs participate in many ways. The ushers, in greeting and seating the people, and the deacons, in receiving the offerings, are important participants. The number of churches that have a responsive Scripture reading is increasing.

Variety.—Most churches probably follow the same orders of morning and evening worship services every week. Variety is achieved by choral programs, by the observances of the ordinances, by the use of religious motion picture films, by religious dramas and plays. Most churches conduct two revivals a year, the Sunday services during these meetings being definitely evangelistic in nature. Budget loyalty days, anniversaries, dedications of buildings or various items of equipment provide further varied orders of service. Variety is also achieved by the pastor through altering the types of sermons he presents week by week.

Reverence.—Baptist churches recognize the difficulty of maintaining reverence in their free-style services, but seek to promote a spirit of reverence in many ways. Reminders may be printed at the beginning of the order of worship. Proper decorum in the choir aids in reverence. The physical surroundings in the auditorium, such as the pews, windows, hymnbooks, curtains, drapes, air ventilation, color schemes, baptistry, and pulpit furniture, all enter into the helpful creation of reverent atmosphere.

Beauty.—Within recent years many Baptist churches have remodeled, modernized, and beautified their buildings. Many churches have erected completely new structures, using Gothic, Romanesque, colonial, or contemporary designs. Interior decorative schemes that are pleasing to the eye have been selected. Floral arrangements are used. Robed choirs are much more attractive, in their uniformity, than choirs whose members wear whatever they choose.

Purpose.—Perhaps the chief distinctive of Baptist worship services is that they are designed to bring men and women in the congregation to spiritual decisions. These may be first decisions as the individuals become converts to Christ. They may be decisions of rededication. The purpose is not to present a parade, a pageant, or a performance. Rather the worship service is planned to meet such spiritual needs of the worshipers as forgiveness, assurance, conviction, and dedication. GAYE L. MCGLOTHLEN

WYER, HENRY OTIS (b. Beverly, Mass., Mar. 19, 1802; d. Alexandria, Va., May 9, 1857). Evangelist, denominational statesman. Educated at Waterville College (Colby), Maine, and at Columbian College, Washington, D. C., Wyer began to preach when he was about 18. In 1824 he served as a missionary in Savannah, Ga., under the direction of the Savannah Missionary Society. Two years later, in 1826, Wyer married Mary S. Hartstene, by whom he had two sons, one a physician and the other a minister.

In the fall of 1825, after Wyer had supplied in the pulpit of the Savannah Baptist Church, the congregation and pew holders extended him a call to become their pastor. He accepted and was ordained by the church Nov. 6, 1825. He served in this pastorate until the spring of 1834, when impaired health made it necessary for him to retire. In 1843 he was recalled as pastor, but ill health forced him to retire again about a year later. After serving as pastor of the Second Baptist Church for two years, 1847–49, Wyer supplied destitute churches whenever his health permitted.

While pastor at Savannah, Wyer preached three services every Sunday, twice to his congregation and once to Negroes, and several times during the week. Often he preached in revival meetings in other Georgia and South Carolina communities.

He organized the church's Sunday school, Apr. 29, 1827, one of the first in the state, and led the church, called First Baptist Church since 1847, in securing its present site on Chippewa Square, where he directed erection of the sanctuary. The church with its colonial design, though several times remodeled and enlarged, still bears the marks of architectural beauty given it by Wyer.

Wyer baptized several young men who became foremost preachers of their day. Among these were Richard Fuller (*q.v.*), a preacher of national renown, considered one of the greatest pulpit orators of the South; James Harvey DeVotie (*q.v.*), first secretary of the Georgia Baptist state mission board; David G. Daniells, who established the First Baptist Church in Atlanta; and Edward Lathrop, distinguished pastor in Boston.

Wyer was one of four ministers appointed by the Georgia Baptist Convention in 1829 to raise funds required to meet the conditions of a bequest from a member of his congregation, which resulted in the founding in 1833 of Mercer Institute, now Mercer University.

LEROY G. CLEVERDON

Y

YADKIN ASSOCIATION HIGH SCHOOL. Located at Boonville, Yadkin County, N. C., established in 1881 by Yadkin Association with L. N. Chappel as principal. In 1883 the school was closed, for the reason that it "seems to have been neglected by the Yadkin Association."

D. L. SMILEY

YALOBUSHA BAPTIST FEMALE INSTITUTE. Established in 1851 by Yalobusha Baptist Association at Grenada, Miss., with W. S. Webb principal. The school enrolled 125 students in 1858 and amended its charter in 1859 to allow Zion Association to become a partner in its operation. Although Confederate soldiers used the school as a hospital during the Civil War, Baptists reactivated it in 1867 with Mrs. Emma Holcombe as principal and operated it as Emma Mercer Baptist Institute until 1874. The school was then operated by a stock company as Grenada Female College until 1882, when it was sold to Methodists. J. L. BOYD

YANCEY COLLEGIATE INSTITUTE. The school of Yancey Association, located at Burnsville, N. C. The school was established in 1900, after 12 years of preliminary effort, on a site donated by Samuel Rennett. Albert Erskine Brown (*q.v.*) of Asheville, regarded as the father of Baptist mountain education, raised the funds. The school opened on Sept. 9, 1901, with Roswell E. Flack as the first principal. Beginning in 1905, Yancey received financial assistance from the Home Mission Board's program of aid to mountain schools. By 1926 it had received more than $84,000, including more than $60,000 for capital improvements. Despite this assistance difficulties arose. On Nov. 11, 1918, the administration building was completely destroyed by fire, but plans were immediately made for a larger one. In 1922 the new building burned. The same year Holston Association in Tennessee and Avery Association in North Carolina adopted the school. A new building was constructed, even finer than the other, but in 1924 the trustees deplored the lack of support. In 1925 the property—appraised at $105,000—was sold to the Board of Education of Yancey County for $65,000. D. L. SMILEY

YATES, MATTHEW TYSON (b. Wake County, N. C., Jan. 8, 1819; d. Shanghai, China, Mar. 17, 1888). Missionary to China. Converted in his 17th year, Yates, as he grew into manhood, resisted the call to preach. With a Christian family background, some assistance from Wake Forest College, and encouragement from James Barnett Taylor (*q.v.*), first secretary of the Southern Baptist Foreign Mission Board, Yates completed his course in Wake Forest. He and Eliza E. Moring (1821–1894) married Sept. 27, 1846, were appointed missionaries to China in 1846, and arrived in Shanghai Sept. 13, 1847. They served under difficult conditions due to the Taiping Rebellion, isolation from America during the conflicts of the 1860's in the United States, scourges of cholera in China, and Yates's illness. For approximately 20 years they served with no reinforcements, but David Wells and Maggie (Nutt) Herring and Robert Thomas and Lula (Freeland) Bryan arrived to help in 1886. In Feb., 1888, Yates suffered his second paralytic stroke.

BIBLIOGRAPHY: F. C. Bryan, *At the Gates* (1949). W. S. Stewart, *Early Baptist Missionaries and Pioneers* (1926). C. E. Taylor, *The Story of Yates the Missionary* (1898). E. C. ROUTH

YEAMAN, WILLIAM POPE (b. Hardin County, Ky., May 28, 1832; d. Columbia, Mo., Feb. 19, 1904). Clergyman. As a young man Yeaman practiced law in Kentucky until, at the age of 28, he surrendered to the call to preach. He held several pastorates in Kentucky and served for a time as pastor of the Third Baptist Church in St. Louis, beginning in 1870. As a pastor he manifested much insight into human nature and used great ingenuity in dealing with people.

He organized the Delmar (Avenue) Baptist Church, which was originally called the Garrison Avenue Church. Twice, in response to an appeal for his help, he became half-owner and coeditor of the *Central Baptist,* which was then the official organ of Missouri Baptists. In 1875 Yeaman served as chancellor of William Jewell College. For 20 years, beginning in 1827, he served as moderator of the Missouri Baptist General Association. He also served as president of Grand River College in Gallatin, Mo. (1893–97), president of the board of curators of Stephens College, and a member of the board of trustees of William Jewell College. He received the honorary D.D. degree from William Jewell College.

Yeaman served for several years on the Foreign Mission Board of the Southern Baptist Convention, and for one year as a vice-president of the Southern Baptist Convention. In 1886 he ran for the United States Congress and was defeated. As a result he advised preachers not to run for political office. He wrote a treatise on Christology, entitled *The God-Man,* and, at the request of the General Association of Missouri Baptists, *A History of the Missouri Baptist General Association.*

BIBLIOGRAPHY: W. Cathcart, *Baptist Encyclopedia* (1883). R. S. Duncan, *History of the Baptists in Missouri* (1882). J. C. Maple, *Memoirs of William Pope Yeaman* (1906); *Missouri Baptist Centennial 1906* (1907). J. C. Maple and R. P. Rider, *Baptist Biography,* Vol. I (1914). W. P. Yeaman, *A History of the Missouri Baptist General Association* (1899).

W. C. LINK, JR.

YOUNG WOMAN'S AUXILIARY. An organization for young women 16–24 years of age, part of the local, state, and Convention-wide organization of Woman's Missionary Union. It began on the local level, resulting from mission interest among young ladies years before W.M.U. was organized in 1888. Earlier than 1815, when Luther Rice (*q.v.*) visited the states on behalf of the Adoniram Judsons (*q.v.*) in Burma, there were young people's societies in Kentucky. Georgia had a Young Ladies' Cent Society at Sweet Hill School in 1817, and a mission organization, named for Ann Hasseltine Judson (*q.v.*), was formed in 1838 on the campus of Judson Female Institute in Marion, Ala. Issues of *The Heathen Helper* printed before 1888 carried numerous references to organizations for young people. The first interest of young women in missions grew from their desire to support and pray for young women in schools on home and foreign fields.

Early records of state women's mission groups indicate that the women recognized their responsibility to encourage mission endeavors of young women, and in May, 1888, at the organizational meeting, women from 10 states agreed that the Convention organization must especially be concerned with the training of young women.

The societies for young ladies spread until in 1907 Woman's Missionary Union, after a general poll, accepted the name already adopted by Alabama for the young ladies' mission groups—Young Woman's Auxiliary—and also adopted their pin and their watchword, Daniel 12:3. In 1909 there were 992 organizations, an increase of 50 per cent over the previous year. At first the ages for Young Woman's Auxiliary varied in different states, but in 1909 the committee on Young Woman's Auxiliary work recommended that girls 12–16 be organized into Junior Young Woman's Auxiliaries, and four years later, when Girls' Auxiliary was organized, it included those ages.

The early purpose of Y.W.A. was twofold—to develop a symmetrical Christian young womanhood and to bind together the young women of the church for worldwide service for Christ. *The Foreign Mission Journal, Our Home Fields,* and *The Baptist Young People's Union Quarterly* were the chief printed sources of missionary information for Y.W.A. before W.M.U. began publication of the quarterly *Our Mission Fields* in July, 1906. The second issue contained the first suggestions headed "For the Young Ladies." When *Our Mission Fields* became *Royal Service* in Oct., 1914, Young Woman's Auxiliary and Girl's Auxiliary programs were presented together, but separate programs for Y.W.A. appeared in July, 1915, and continued until Sept., 1929, when the first issue of *The Window of Y.W.A.*, a monthly magazine for Y.W.A., was published.

In addition to Young Woman's Auxiliaries in local churches, many were organized on college campuses and in hospitals. The Ann Hasseltine Young Woman's Auxiliary for young college women was organized in 1910, and the Grace McBride Young Woman's Auxiliary for nurses, in 1923.

The election of the first college correspondent, Susan Bancroft Tyler, in 1911 strengthened work in that area. She served with young people's workers in states so effectively that in 1913 she reported 800 college women in Y.W.A. in a single state. Mary Faison Dixon, who followed Miss Tyler as college correspondent in 1916, served only two years, and in 1921 Juliette Mather became college correspondent and young people's secretary. Under her leadership Y.W.A. work grew through the inauguration of a Convention-wide camp at Ridgecrest (1924), *The Window of Y.W.A.* (1929), Young Woman's Auxiliary Book Club (1946), and Citation (1947). Miss Mather served until 1948 when Margaret Bruce was elected young people's secretary. In 1954, 6,927 auxiliaries reported 70,312 members, and in 1955 Dorris DeVault became Convention-wide secretary.

See also Ann Hasseltine YWA and Grace McBride YWA.

ETHALEE HAMRIC

YUGOSLAVIA, BAPTIST UNION OF. Initiated in 1922 when Everett Gill, Sr. (*q.v.*), and James Henry Rushbrooke (English Baptist) held a conference in Zagreb with Baptist leaders of several language groups in the nation. The Yugoslav Baptist Union is composed of autonomous district conventions, each using its native language: German (ceased 1945), Slovak, Croatian, Serbian, Romanian, Hungarian, Slovenian.

Baptist work in areas now Yugoslav dates from 1875 when Heinrich Meyer, German preacher from Budapest, baptized five persons in Novi Sad and organized a church. One of the converts, Adolf Hempt, did evangelistic work in Sarajevo, where a few Baptists lived. Baptist beginnings among Serbs, Hungarians, and Slovaks may be traced to the 1890's. Work among Croats, Romanians, and Slovenes began just after the Yugoslav state came into being in 1918. The membership in 1923 was 810.

The union established an old people's home in Novi Sad in 1923, and published a denominational monthly in Croatian (*Glas Evandjelja*, Voice of the Gospel) 1923–40. *Evangeliumsbote* was the periodical of German-speaking Baptists. A seminary, established in Belgrade in 1940 and closed by war six months later, was reopened in 1954.

In 1955 there were 40 churches, 70 other congregations, 13 pastors, and a total membership of 3,176. Forty-six Sunday schools enrolled 726 children. There were eight women's groups and about 35 young people's societies.

JOHN ALLEN MOORE

YUGOSLAVIA, MISSION IN. In 1922 the Foreign Mission Board sent to Yugoslavia Vinko Vacek, Yugoslav national who had been in the United States for several years. Vacek led in organizing the Yugoslav Baptist Union, serving as its president until shortly before his death in 1939; edited a Baptist magazine; and did evangelistic work throughout Yugoslavia. Everett Gill, Sr., the board's representative in Europe, supervised the work of the mission, making occasional tours among the churches. In 1938 John Allen Moore was appointed first Southern Baptist missionary to Yugoslavia; he settled in Belgrade. In 1940 Moore married Pauline Willingham and together they opened a seminary. Due to war conditions they were expelled in 1941, but returned for extended visits beginning in 1948, and settled again in Yugoslavia in 1955, with a permit for at least eight months' residence. The board aids in the support of 13 pastors, contributes to the seminary budget, and helps finance church building.

JOHN ALLEN MOORE